ROCK
RECORD

ROCK RECORD

Terry Hounsome
and
Tim Chambre

Facts On File, Inc.
460 Park Avenue South
New York, N.Y. 10016

ROCK RECORD

Original limited edition (*Rockmaster,* 1978) and revised, expanded edition (*Rock Record,* 1979) published and produced in the United Kingdom by Terry Hounsome.

This edition published in the United Kingdom in 1981 by Blandford Books Ltd., as *New Rock Record.*

This edition published in the United States of America in 1981 by Facts On File, Inc.

Library of Congress Cataloging in Publication Data
Hounsome, Terry.
  Rock record.

  Includes index.
  1. Rock music—Discography. I. Chambre, Tim.
II. Title.
ML156.4.R6H68   016.7899'12454   81-12489
ISBN 0-87196-547-X   AACR2
ISBN 0-87196-548-8 (pbk.)

Printed in the United States of America

Contents

This book is dedicated to my wife
Chris

my children
Claire, Steven & Jon

and to all musicians everywhere.

Introduction

ROCK RECORD has taken five years to produce in its present form. It lists groups and artists together with their LP records and the musicians who have played with them. It includes an index to all the groups and musicians.

ROCK RECORD contains some 4,500 entries, 30,000 LP records and 25,000 different musicians. It takes in all forms of "rock" music, from its roots to the present day; it contains much information on pop, soul, reggae, jazz rock, blues, country and folk music as well as mainstream rock. Imports and reissues are listed, together with some EPs, but singles and bootlegs are beyond the scope of this book. Material up through early 1981 has been added to the book.

The aim of ROCK RECORD is to provide a useful, accurate and enlightening guide to rock music albums and the people who have made them. As a discography its main purpose is to aid identification: It does not set out to review the records or musicians; for this reason, apart from a few factual notes, no text has been added.

Details have been checked from more than one source whenever possible—but, unfortunately, different sources frequently provide conflicting information. This is particularly true in respect to musicians' names, and in such cases the most common spelling has generally been used.

The size of each entry is governed by the amount of information available, not by the relative importance of each group or artist.

In many entries musicians have been linked by symbols to the albums or dates on which they played; musicians are listed even if they have played only on one track of a particular LP. Many musicians play more than one instrument, and where space permits these have been listed. Instruments are listed in groups—e.g., "guitar" covers all types of guitars. Where string sections or orchestras appeared on a given record, individual musicians are not listed.

Record catalogue numbers are listed from the U.S.A., Britain, Europe and in some cases Japan.

Generally the entries run alphabetically, but some entries are not in strict alphabetical order. Also, some entries were originally allocated numbers but have been withdrawn as it was decided they were unsuitable for this edition. Some entries begin on one page and continue on the next page. These are noted at the top and bottom of the appropriate pages.

The editor is aware that some entries are incomplete and that there are some omissions. Anyone, musician or collector, who is able to supply further information or any other suggestions is invited to contact the editor by letter or telephone at the address given below. Correspondents seeking a reply are requested to enclose an international reply coupon.

Terry Hounsome
13, Stanton Road
Regents Park
Southampton
Hampshire
SOl 4HF
England

Telephone: 0703 771639

How To Use This Book

Each entry carries a code symbol consisting of its initial letter and running order number. Check in the index for the symbol of any particular group or artist. This will point you to the precise location of that entry.

* To save space, where the number of musicians in an entry exceeds the number of records, the listing of musicians continues in columns across the page.

** In many cases there has not been enough room to indicate all the instruments or the specific type of instrument played by musicians. This abbreviation should only be taken as a general indication.

*** Wherever possible the appearance of a musician on an album has been indicated by coding the album alphabetically or numerically and placing the code after the musicians name and instrument. As an alternative, where musicians have been known to belong to a group at a particular date, the date has been stated and coded. In cases where both dates and albums are listed, a mixture of alphabetical and numerical symbols have been used.

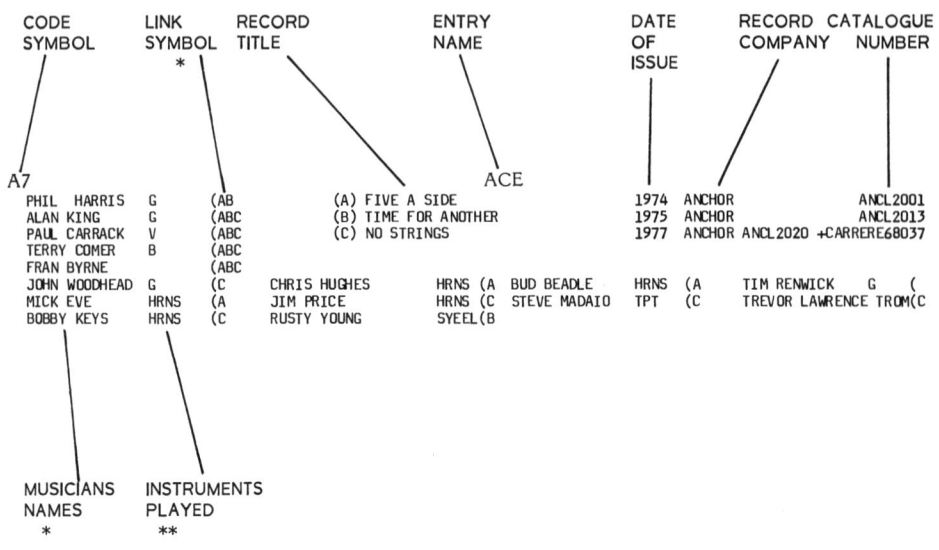

viii

Acknowledgements

DEVISED, COMPILED & EDITED
By Terry Hounsome

The editor would like to thank everyone who has helped produce this book.

CONSULTANT EDITOR & INDEX
By Tim Chambre

MAIN CONTRIBUTORS TO ROCK RECORD

Terry Hounsome	Bri Lockyear	Norbert Obermanns
Tim Chambre	Les Raphael	Ron Hockings
Dave Smith	Ted Pinch	Paul Cole
Alan Dawson	Malc Tipping	Eiji Sashida
Bernd Matheja	John Clare	Torben Nielsen

EDITORIAL ASSISTANCE

Chris Hounsome	Sarah Freeman	Sue Powell
Claire Hounsome	Jon Hounsome	Steven Hounsome

ADDITIONAL INFORMATION

GEOFF COX	ANDY READ	KURT GLASE	BERNARD LENNARD	J MATLATHRONAS
GUY HAMILTON	RICHARD SADLER	SPENCER LEIGH	PAUL WILLIAMS	A MAUNDER
JEFF LAMBERT	NEIL LITTMAN	OLAF OWRE	STEVEN HAMMOND	GEOFF ELDRIDGE
IAN WALKER	DEREK HENDERSON	ZBIGMEW NOWARA	PAUL SOPER	ALAN LORD
PAUL BARBER	B N BROOMFIELD	STEVE MORGAN	GARY MOBERLEY	FRANCIS M WARD
PHIL HAWOOD	ANDY NEAL	JOHN GRAVE	D GOODYEAR	D GREENHALGH
NEAL FARNSWORTH	PETE DREWSON	CAROL SHIPP	GERHARD TAVFER	FRANK PLOURIGHT
BRUNO HAAS	WOLFGANG HIESE	STEVE BLAMIRE	DAVID THOMPSON	BRIAN COPE
CLIFTON YORKS	C WOOD	M BRUSSELMAN	PAUL MANN	STUART HEATHER
JOHN HUGGINS	BOB PEARCE	LUDWIG WEBEL	DAVID TREITLEL	FUMIKOW ITO
HUGH MACLIAN	CHILLI CHARLES	GEOFF ELDRIDGE	R G ALLEN	ROGER JOYE
PHIL BROUGHTON	OLAF BENZINGER	TIM DEAL	HARRY SHAPIRO	BRIAN COPE
ADRIAN BOOTH	PETE YORK	ANDY DOBBS	J YOUNG	YVONNE COPE
ROSS JOHN ANGEL	STEVE YORK	MIKE TRESISE		NORMAN READ

REPLAYS Southampton
HENRYS Southampton
COB Porthmadog
GI Edinburgh
EZY RYDER Edinburgh
CRUISIN' Bath
OASIS London
SUMMIT London
WEST FOUR London
BEANOS Croydon
ARMADILLO Bournemouth
TUMBLEWEED CONNECTION London
SHADE RECORDS London
VINYL SOLUTION London

VIRGIN RECORDS London & Branches
W E A Records London
PYE Records London
E M I Records London
POLYDOR Records London
PHONOGRAM Records London
Decca Records London
LOGO Records London
RED LIGHTNIN' Records
LINE Records Hamburg Germany
UNITED ARTISTS London
CBS RECORDS London

Abbreviations

ACC	ACCORDION
A'HARP	AUTOHARP
B	BASS
BAN	BANJO
BAZ	BOUZOUKI
BOD	BODHRAN
BOMBA	BOMBARDE
CLAR	CLARINET
COMP	COMPILATION ALBUM
CONC	CONCERTINA
D	DRUMS
DBL	DOUBLE ALBUM SET
DOB	DOBRO GUITAR
DULC	DULCIMER
EURO	EUROPEAN
FDL	FIDDLE
FLT	FLUTE
FR	FRANCE
G	GUITAR
GERM	GERMANY
HCA	HARMONICA
HRNS	HORNS(TRUMPETS,TROMBONES, TUBA ETC)
IT	ITALY
JAP	JAPAN
K	KEYBOARDS(ALL TYPES)
MAND	MANDOLIN
MEL	MELODEON
NOR	NORWAY
ORG	ORGAN
PERC	PERCUSSION
PNO	PIANO
R I	RE ISSUE
SAX	SAXOPHONE
SIT	SITAR
STEEL	STEEL GUITAR /PEDAL STEEL GUITAR
STR	STRINGS(VIOLIN, CELLO, BASS VIOLA)
SYN	SYNTHESIZER
SWED	SWEDEN
TPT	TRUMPET
TROM	TROMBONE
UK	GREAT BRITAIN /UNITED KINGDOM
US	UNITED STATES OF AMERICA
V	VOCALS/ BACKING VOCALS
VLA	VIOLA
VLN	VIOLIN
WIND	SAXOPHONE,FLUTE, CLARINET ETC

Directory

A B SKHY
A1

```
JIM MADCOTTE      B    (AB                        (A) A B SKHY              1969 MGM              SE4628
DENNIS GEYER      G/V  (AB                        (B) RAMBLING ON          1970 MGM              SE4676
TERRY ANDERSEN    D/V  (A
HOWARD WALES      K    (A  RICK JAEGER  D    (B  CURLEY COOKE    G    (B  JIM LIBAN       HCA(A
OTIS HALE         FLT  (A  RUSSELL DaSHIELL  G   (A  LAROON HOLT  TPT  (A  MARVIN BROWN    TPT(A
BUD BRISBOIS      TPT  (A  PHILLIP PRUDEN   SAX  (A  JIM HORN     SAX  (A  DONALD WALDROP  TROM(A
DAVE ROBERTS      TROM (A
```

AC.DC
A2

```
ANGUS YOUNG       G    (ABCDEF     (A) HIGH VOLTAGE            1976 ATLANTIC   UK K50257 US SD36142
MALCOLM YOUNG     G    (  DE       (B) DIRTY DEEDS DONE CHEAP  1976 ATLANTIC   UK K50323
PHIL RUDD         D    (  DE       (C) LET THERE BE ROCK       1977 ATLANTIC   UK K50366 US SD36151
BRIAN JOHNSON     V    (F          (D) POWERAGE                1978 ATLANTIC   UK K50483 US SD19180
BON SCOTT         V    (ABCDE      (E) IF YOU WANT BLOOD       1978 ATLANTIC   UK K50532
CLIFF WILLIAMS    B    (DEF        (F) HIGHWAY TO HELL         1979 ATLANTIC   UK K50628
                                   (G) BACK IN BLACK           1980 ATLANTIC   UK K50735
```

AALON
A2A

```
AALON BUTLER                       (A) CREAM CITY             19   ARISTA     US           4127
```

AARDVARK
A3

```
FRANNK CLARK      D    (AB         (A) PRE LP LINE UP
DAVE SKILLIN      V    (AB         (B) AARDVARK
STAN ALDOUS       B    (AB                                    1970 NOVA                    SDN .17
PADDY COULTER     K    (A  STEVE MILLINER   K   (B
```

ABBA
A4

```
ANNA ULVAEUS      V    (123ABCDEFGHJKZ  (A) WATERLOO          1974 EPIC       UK         80179
BJORN ULVAEUS     V/G  (4ABCDEFGHJKZ    (A) WATERLOO          1974 ATLANTIC   US         18101
BENNY ANDERSSON   V/K  (4ABCDEFGHJKZ    (B) ABBA              1975 EPIC       UK         80835
ANNIFRID LYNGSTAD- V  (ABCDEFGHJKZ      (B) ABBA              1975 VOGUE      FR LDY 28039
     FREDRIKSSON                        (B) ABBA              1975 ATLANTIC   US         18146
WITH                                    (C) GREATEST HITS     1976 EPIC       UK         69218
MATS RONANDER     G    (Z              (C) GREATEST HITS     1976 VOGUE      FR LDY 28047
BRUNO GLENMARK    TPT  (B              (C) GREATEST HITS     1976 ATLANTIC   US         18189
AKE SUNKVIST      PERC (JZ             (D) ARRIVAL           1976 EPIC       UK         86018
JANNE SCHAFFER    G    (ABCDFHJ        (D) ARRIVAL           1976 VOGUE      FR LDA 20238
FINN SJOBERG      G    (B              (D) ARRIVAL           1976 ATLANTIC   US         18207
ANDERS EIJAS      K    (Z              (E) GOLDEN DOUBLE      1977 VOGUE      FR SLULX.685
ANDERS DAHL       STRG (D              (F) THE ALBUM          1977 EPIC       UK         86052
ANDERS GLENMARK   G    (D              (F) THE ALBUM          1977 ATLANTIC   US         19164
MALANDO GASSAMA   PERC (ADFH           (G) LES PLUS GRANDS SUCCES 19 RCA      FR XL13036
PER LINDVALL      D    (J              (H) VOULEZ LOUS        1979 EPIC       UK         86086
KAJREK WOJCIECHOWSKI SAX(JH            (J) SUPER TROUPER      1980 EPIC       UK         10022
JANNE KLING       WIND (J              (K) GREATEST HITS VOL 2 1980 EPIC      UK         10017
LASSE WELLANDER   G    (BDFJH
LARS CARLSSON     HRNS (DFJH           ABBA SOLO ALBUMS
ULF ANDERSSON     SAX  (B              (1) AGNETHA   (ANNA)
PER SAHLBERG      B    (A              (1) AGNETHA   (ANNA)  19   CUPOL      IMP CLPL.1002
CHRISTER EKLUND   SAX  (A              (2) AGNETHA VOL 2 (ANNA) 19 CUPOL      IMP CLPL.1003
RUTGER GUNNARSSON B    (ABDFHJ         (3) AGNETHA           1974 EMBASSY    UK         31094
MIKE WATSON       B    (BHJ            (4) LYCKA(BENNY & BJORN) 1970 POLAR    IMP POLS.226
OLA BRUNKERT      D    (ABDFHJ
ROGER PALM        D    (BDF  JOE GALDO    D    (H  ARNOLD PASEIRO  B (H  ISH LEDESMA  G   (H
GEORGE TERRY      G    (H    HALLDOR PALSSON  SAX  (H  JOHAN STENGARD  SAX (H  NILS LADGREN TROM (H
ROLF ALEX         D    (H    JAN RISBERG      OBOE (H
```

JOHN ABERCROMBIE
A4A

```
JOHN ABERCROMBIE  G    (ABCDE        (A) GATEWAY            19   ECM        FR   ECM1061
DAVE HOLLAND           (AE           (B) SARGASSO SEA       19   ECM        FR   ECM1080
JACK DeJOHNETTE        (ACDE         (C) TIMELESS           19   ECM        FR   ECM1047
RALPH TOWNER           (B            (D) PICTURES           19   ECM        FR   ECM1079
JAN HAMMER        K    (C            (E) GATEWAY 2          19   ECM        FR   ECM1105
JEFF WILLIAMS     G    (F            (F) FRIENDS            1972 OBLIVION   US         003
CLINT HOUSTON     B    (F
MARK COHEN        SAX  (F
```

MICK ABRAHAMS
A5

```
MICK ABRAHAMS     G/V  (ABC1         (A) MICK ABRAHAMS      1971 CHRYSALIS  ILPS 9147
BOB SARGEANT      G V K (AB          (B) AT LAST            1972 CHRYSALIS  CHR 1005
RITCHIE DHARMA    D    (AB           (C) LEARNING GUITAR WITH 1975 SRT      SRTM 73313
WALT MONGHAN      B    (AB           (1) AUG>SEPT 1978
JACK LANCASTER    WIND (B
TOM DOWNING       FDL G (1    DAVE BRISTOW   PNO   (1  PETE CLEMMINS      (B
```

ABSOLUTELY ELSEWHERE
A5A

```
PAUL FISHMAN      K    (A            (A) IN SEARCH OF ANCIENT GODS 19 WEA    FR?        56192
BILL BRUFORD      D    (A
PHILIP SAATCHI    G    (A    JON ASTROP        B      (A)
```

```
A6                              ABYSSINIANS
  BERNARD COLLINS      (            (A) FORWARD TO ZION        19    KLIK                      KLP9023
  DONALD MANNING       (            (B) ARISE                  197   FRONT LINE                FL1019
  UNFORD MANNING
  JAH JERRY        G   (AB  FRANKLYN WAUL   K   (AB  EARL SMITH    G   (AB  CARLTON MANNING  G    (A
  ROBBIE SHAKESPEARE B (AB  PABLO BLACK     K   (AB  SLY DUNBAR    D   (AB  MICHAEL COOPER   K    (AB
  DEVON RICHARDSON  D  (AB  RAS JAWBONE     D   (AB  LLOYD PARKS   B   (AB  BONGO HERMAN     PERC (AB
  WINSTON BOWEN     G  (AB  GLEN DE COSTA   SAX (A   CEDRIC BROOKS SAX (AB  BOBBY ELLIS      TPT  (AB
  HERMAN MARQUIS    SAX (AB  GEORGE FULLWOOD B   (AB  SANTA         D   (AB  TONY CHIN        G    (AB
  TOMMY McCOOK      WIND (AB  VIVIAN HALL    TPT (AB
A6A                             ACCOLADE
  GORDON GILTRAP    G   (A            (A) ACCOLADE              19    COLUMBIA        UK    SCX6405
  DON PARTRIDGE         (A
A7                                ACE
  PHIL HARRIS       G   (AB            (A) FIVE A SIDE          1974  ANCHOR                  ANCL2001
  ALAN KING         G   (ABC           (B) TIME FOR ANOTHER    1975  ANCHOR                  ANCL2013
  PAUL CARRACK      V   (ABC           (C) NO STRINGS          1977  ANCHOR ANCL2020 +CARRERE 68037
  TERRY COMER       B   (ABC
  FRAN BYRNE            (ABC
  JOHN WOODHEAD     G   (C    CHRIS HUGHES    HRNS (A   BUD BEADLE    HRNS (A   TIM RENWICK    G    (
  MICK EVE          HRNS (A   JIM PRICE       HRNS (C   STEVE MADAIO  TPT  (C   TREVOR LAWRENCE TROM(C
  BOBBY KEYS        HRNS (C   RUSTY YOUNG     STEEL (C
A8                                ACES
  LOUIS MYERS     G V HCA(ABC           (A) CHICAGO BEAT       1976  BLACK & BLUE            BB.33508
  DAVE MYERS        B   (ABC           (B) ACES & GUESTS       1977  MCM             FR      900293
  FRED BELOW        D   (C            (C) KINGS OF CHICAGO BLUES 19  VOGUE                   LDM 30174
  SAMMY LAWHORN     G   (C
  EDDIE TAYLOR      G   (C
A9                              DAVID ACKLES
  DAVID ACKLES      V   (ALL           (A) DAVID ACKLES        1968  ELEKTRA US EKS74022 UK RI K42020
  MICHAEL FONFARA   ORG  (A           (B) SUBWAY TO THE COUNTRY 1970 ELEKTRA US EKS74060 UK RI K42092
  DOUG HASTINGS     G    (A           (C) AMERICAN GOTHIC      1972  ELEKTRA US EKS75032 UK RI K42112
  JOHN KELIEH       ORPERC (A          (D) FIVE & DIME         1973  CBS        US 32466
  DAWN WEISS        PIC  (D
  GEORGIA MOHAMMER  FLT  (D   LOREN PICKFORD  WIND (D   EARLE DUMLER  WIND (D   JAMES KANTER   CLAR  (D
  GENE CIPRIANO     SAX  (D   TODD MILLAR     HRNS (D   ROBERT HENDERSON HRNS (D RUSSELL KIDD  TPT   (D
  ZIGMANT KANSTUL TPT (D    JOHN DALEY      TROM (D   EDMOND WELTER TUBA (D   COLIN BAILY    PERC  (D
  LOU ANNE NEILL    HARP (D   BRUCE LANG HORNE G  (D   JANICE GRAHAM G   (D   RED RHODES     STEEL (D
  DEAN TORRANCE     V    (D   DOUGLAS GRAHAM  V   (D   DANNY WEIS    G   (A   JERRY PENROD   B     (A
A10                          ADAM & THE ANTS
  ADAM ANT          V    (1AB          (1) NOVEMBER 1977
  JOHNNY BIVOUAC    G    (!           (A) DIRK WEARS WHITE SOX  1979  do it            RIDE    3
  ANDY WATSON       B    (1           (B) KINGS OF THE WILD FRONTIER 1980 CBS                 84549
  DAVE BARB         D    (1
  MATTHEW ASHMAN    G K  (A   ANDREW WARREN   B   (A
A11                            ARTHUR ADAMS
  ARTHUR ADAMS      G V  (ABC          (A) ITS PRIVATE TONIGHT  1972  BLUE THUMB          BT 543
  PHIL UPCHURCH     G    (A           (B) HOME BREW            19    FANTASY             9479
  WILTON FELDER     B    (A           (C) MIDNIGHT SERENADE    19    FANTASY             9523
  JOE SAMPLE        K    (A
  GENE ESTES        VIBES (A   ERNIE WATTS     HRS  (A   PAUL HUMPHREY  D    (A
  MIKE ALTSCHUL     HRS  (A   JACKIE KELSO    HRS  (A   PAUL HUBINON   HRS  (A
  BILL GREEN        HRS  (A   CHUCK FINDLEY   HRS  (A   BOBBYE HALL    PERC (A
  GEORGE BOHANON    HRS  (A   JAMES JAMERSON  B    (B   DENNIS COFFEY  G    (B
  EARL PALMER       D    (B   VANETTA FIELDS  V    (A   CLYDIE KING    V    (A
  SHIRLEY MATTHEWS  V    (A
A12                            JOHNNY ADAMS
  JOHNNY ADAMS           (ABC          (A) HEART & SOUL        19    SSS INT     US      SSS5
                                      (A) HEART & SOUL        19    CHARLY      UK    CR 30154
                                      (B) AFTER ALL THE GOOD IS GONE 19 ARIOLA  US    SW 50036
                                      (C) STAND BY ME          19    CHELSEA     US      S 25
A13                            ADVERTISING
  TOT TAYLOR        G K  (A           (A) JINGLES              1978  EMI         UK    EMC 3253
  PAUL BULTITUDE    D    (A
  DENNIS MSITH      B    (A   SIMON BOSWELL   G    (A
A14                              ADVERTS
  GAYE ADVERT       B    (A1B          (1) MARCH 1978 GIG
  T V SMITH         V    (A1B          (A) CROSSING THE RED SEA 1978 BRIGHT      UK    BRL 201
  LAURIE DRIVER     D    (A           (B) CAST OF THOUSANDS    1979  RCA         UK    PL25246
  HOWARD PICKUP     G    (A1B
  JOHN TOWE         D    (1    TIM GROSS       K    (C   ROD LATTER     D    (B
  RICHARD STRANGE   SYN  (B    TOM NEWMAN      SYN  (N
A14A                              AEC
                                      (A) FANFARE             19    WEA                 50305
A15                              AERIAL
  LAURIE CURRIE     D V  (A           (A) IN THE MIDDLE OF THE NIGHT 1978 CAPITOL GER IC 064 8590
  MALCOLM BUCHANAN  K    (A
  BRIAN MIESSNER    B V G (A   GARY O'CONNOR   G B V (A
A16                            AEROSMITH
  STEVE TYLER    HCA PERC K B V(ABCDEF (A) AEROSMITH          1974  CBS UK 65486  US      32006
  BRAD WHITFORD     G    ( BCD EF     (B) GET YOUR WINGS      1974  CBS UK 80015  US      32847
  JOEY KRAMER       D V  ( BCDEF      (C) TOYS IN THE ATTIC   1975  CBS UK 80773  US      33479
  SCOTT CUSHNIE     PNO  (  C         (D) ROCKS              1976  CBS UK 81379  US      34165
  JOE PERRY      V B G PERC (ABCDEF   (E) DRAW THE LINE      1977  CBS UK 82147  US      34865
  TOM HAMILTON      3 G  (BCDEF       (F) LIVE BOOTLEG       1979  CBS UK 88325  US      35564
  JAY MESSINA       PERC (C           (G) NIGHT IN THE RUTS  1979  CBS UK 83680
  PAUL PRESTOPINO   BANJ (D           (H) GREATEST HITS      1980  CBS UK 84704
```

AFFINITY   A17

LINDA HOYLE	V	(A	(A) AFFINITY	1970 VERTIGO	UK	6360004
MIKE JOPP	G	(A	(A) AFFINITY	1970 PARAMOUNT	US	PAS 5027
MO FOSTER	B	(A				
GRANT SERPELL	D	(A				

AFTER TEA   A18

(A) AFTER TEA   19   ACE OF CLUBS   UK   SCLR1251

AFTER THE FIRE   A19

PETER BANKS	K	(BC	(A) SIGNS OF CHANGE	1978 RAPID	UK	RR 001
IVOR TWIDELL	D	(B	(B) LASER LOVE	1979 CBS	UK	83795
ANDY PIERCY	V G B	(BC	(C) 80F	1980 EPIC	UK	84545
TIM HAYWELL	B	(				
NICK BATTLE	B	(				

JOHN RUSSELL   G   (BC   PETE KING   D   (C

AGITATION FREE   A19A

LUTZ ULBRICHT	G K	(ABC	(A) MALESCH	19 VERTIGO	UK	6360607
JORG SCHWENKE	G	(ABC	(B) 2nd ALBUM	19 VERTIGO	UK	6360615
MICHEL GUNTHER	B	(ABC	(C) LAST	19 BARCLAY	FR	80615
MICHAEL HOENIG	K	(ABC				
BURGHARD RAUSH	B V	(ABC				

ULI POP   PERC   (A

AGNES STRANGE   A20

JOHN WESTWOOD	G	(A	(A) STRANGE FLAVOUR	1975 BIRDSNEST	UK	BRL 9000
ALAN GREEN	B	(A				
DAVE RODWELL	D	(A				

DON AGRATI   A21

(A) HOME GROWN   1973   ELEKTRA UK K42141 US EKS 75057

DON AGRATI	V K B D	(A	RIC RICCIO	FLT	(A	KARLA PAYNE	B	(A
JAMES GANDUGLIA	PERC	(A	PHIL AYLING	HRS	(A	BOB CASSENS	B	(A
GIL ROGERS	G	(A	FRED LAWRENCE	HRS	(A	LIZA REY	HARP	(A
SKIP SHORTLEDGE	HRS	(A	JIM STOUDER	CLAR	(A			
MIKE FRANCIS	HRS	(A						
DAVE KAUFMAN	HRS	(A						

AIM   A21A

(A) AIM FOR THE HIGHEST   1973   BLUE THUMB   US   BTS 64

MICHAEL OVERLY	G V FLT	(A	ALAN ESTES	CONGA	(A	LOREN NEWKIRK	K	(A
WARREN PEMBERTON	D	(A						
DAVID M SHERR	OBOE	(A						
PATRICK O'CONNOR		(A						

CHARLIE AINLEY   A22

CHARLIE AINLEY	V G	(AB	(A) TOO MUCH IS NOT ENOUGH	1978 NEMPEROR	US	35080
HENRY SPINETTI	D	(A	(B) BANG YOUR DOOR	1978 EMI	UK	EMC 3285
ROB HENDRY	G	(1	(1) LIVE DATE NOV 1979			
CHARLIE HARRISON	B	(A				

RICHARD WORTHY	G	(AB	JOHN PORTER	G B	(A	PRESTON HEYMAN	PERC	(A
TOM WILDY	HCA	(A	MEL COLLINS	HRS	(A	KOKOMO	V	(A
JOE PARTRIDGE	G MAND	(A	MICK WEAVER	K	(A	PETE WINGFIELD	K	(A
MIKE STOREY	K	(A	DAVID HENTSCHEL	SYN	(A	STUART ELLIOTT	D PERC	(B
CHAS HODGES	B	(B	HOWIE CASEY	HRS	(B	TONY ASHTON	ORG	(B
MARTIN FRITH	HRNS	(B	ROBIN BIBI	G	(1	SAM HARLEY	B	(1
RON TELEMACQUE	D	(1						

JANE AIRE & BELVEDERES   A23

(A) JANE AIRE & THE BELVEDERES   1979   VIRGIN   UK   V2134

JANE AIRE	V	(A	EMILY RUTH	VLN V		FRANCOIS DE CHANCY	G K	
PIETRO NARDINI	G K	(A	LU EDMUNDS	G	(A	GAVIN POVEY	K	(A
GALEN STUDEBAKER	D		JOHN MOSS	D	(A	CHRIS JENKINS	G	(A
CHRIS BUTLER	B	(	MIKE DAVIS	TPT	(A	MALCOLM GRIFFITHS	TROM	(A
GLYN HAVARD	B	(A	RAY WARLEIGH	SAX	(A	JOAN ASHLEY	V	(A
MARTIN DROVER	TPT	(A	RACHEL SWEET	V	(A	DAVID ARNOLD	PERC	(A
GEOFF DALEY	SAX	(A						
KIRSTY MACCOLL	V	(A						
CHRIS PYNE	TROM	(A						

AIRTO   A24

AIRTO MOREIRA	PERC V D	(ALL	(A) SEEDS ON THE GROUND	19 POLYDOR	2310 040
WITH			(A) SEEDS ON THE GROUND	19 BUDDAH	5085
FLORA PURIM	V PERC	(BJH	(B) FINGERS	1973 CTI	CTL 18
DAVID AMARO	G	(B	(B) FINGERS	1973 CTI	CTI,6028
HUGO FATTORUSO	K V	(B	(C) VIRGIN LAND	1974 CTI	CTL 23
JORGE FATTORUSO	D V	(B	(C) VIRGIN LAND	1974 SALVATION	701
RINGO THIELMANN	B V	(B	(D) IN CONCERT	1974 CTI	CTL 21
SIRVUCA	G	(J	(F) FREE	19 CTI	CTI 6020
HERMETO	K FLT	(J	(G) IDENTITY	1976 ARISTA	ARTY,119
RON CARTER	B	(J	(G) IDENTITY	1976 PATHE	4068
DEODATO		(D	(H) PROMISES OF THE SUN	1976 ARISTA	AL 4116
KEITH JARRETT		(F	(H) PROMISES OF THE SUN	1976 PATHE	FR 98770
STANLEY CLARKE	B	(F	(I) I'M FINE	19 WEA	K 59420
JOE FARRELL		(F	(J) THE ESSENTIAL AIRTO	19 BUDDAH	BDS25668
CHICK COREA	K	(F	(J) THE ESSENTIAL AIRTO	19 BUDDAH	87 003 2

(GINGER BAKER'S)AIRFORCE   A25

GINGER BAKER	D	(AB	(A) AIRFORCE	1970 POLYDOR	UK 2662 001
STEVE WINWOOD	K V G	(A	(B) AIRFORCE 2	1970 POLYDOR	UK 2383 029
RICK GRECH	B	(AB			

CHRIS WOOD	SAX	(A	HAROLD McNAIR	SAX	(AB	PHIL SEAMAN	D	(A
DENNY LAINE	G V	(A	GRAHAM BOND	K SAX	(B	BUD BEADLE	HRNS	(A
DIANE STEWART	V	(B	REMI KABAKA	PERC	(A	KEN CRADDOCK	K	(B
ALIKI ASHMAN	V	(B	STEVE GREGORY	HRNS	(B	COLIN GIBSON	B	(B
NEEMOI ACQUAYE	PERC	(B	CATHERINE JAMES	V	(B	ROCKY DZIDZORNU	PERC	(B

AIRWAVES   A26

RAY MARTINEZ	V G K	(AB	(A) NEW DAY	1978 MERCURY	9109 613
OHN DAVID	V B K	(AB	(A) NEW DAY	1978 A&M	IMP
DAVE CHARLES	D	(AB	(B) NEXT STOP	1979 MERCURY	9109 625
PAUL COBBOLD	CELLO	(A			

A27   JAN AKKERMAN

Personnel	Inst		Album	Year	Label	Country	Cat.
JAN AKKERMAN	G	(ALL	(A) PROFILE	1972	HARVEST	UK	SHSP 4026
WITH			(A) PROFILE	1972	SIRE	US	SAS 7407
KAZ LUX	V	(D	(B) GUITAR FOR SALE	1973	BOVEMA	IMP	IC 048 51105
JOACHIM KUHN	B	(E	(C) TABERNAKEL	1974	ATLANTIC	UK	K 40522
CEES VAN DER LAARSE	B	(EG	(C) TABERNAKEL	1974	ATCO	US	7032
BRUNO CASTELUCCI	D	(EG	(D) ELI	1977	ATLANTIC	UK	K 50320
NEPPIE NOVA	PERC	(DEG	(D) ELI	1977	ATLANTIC	US	18210
RAY LUCAS	D	(C	(E) JAN AKKERMAN	1978	ATLANTIC	UK	K 50420
TIM BOGERT	B	(C	(E) JAN AKKERMAN	1978	ATLANTIC	US	SD 19159
CARMINE APPICE	D	(C	(F) ARANJUEZ	1978	CBS	UK	81843
GEORGE FLYNN	K	(C	(G) LIVE	1979	ATLANTIC	UK	K 50560
BERT RUITER	B	(A	(H) TALENT FOR SALE	19	M F P	HOLL	5036
PIERRE VAN DER LINDEN	D	(ADE					
DANIEL WAITZMAN	FLT	(C	FRANS SMIT	D	(A	FERRY MAAT	PNO	(A
JAAP VAN EYCK	B	(A	JASPER VAN'T HOF	K	(DG	TOM BARLAGE	SAX K	(G
WILLEM ENNES	K	(G	RICK VAN DER LINDEN	K	(D	WARWICK READING	B	(D
RICHARD DE BOIS	D	(D	MARGARET ESHUIS	V	(D	MAGGIE McNEAL	V	(D
PATRICIA PAAY	V	(D					

A28   ALABAMA STATE TROUPERS

Personnel	Inst		Album	Year	Label	Country	Cat.
DON NIX	G V	(A)	(A) ALABAMA STATE TROUPERS	1972	ELEKTRA	US	EKS75022
FURRY LEWIS	V G	(A)					
CLAYTON IVEY	PNO	(A)	TIPPY ARMSTRONG	G	(A)	FRED PROOTY	D	(A)
BOB WRAY	B	(A	KEN WOODLEY	K	(A)	CAROLYN WATKINS	V	(A)
JEAN GREENE	V	(A	BRENDA PATTERSON	V	(A	WAYNE PERKINS	G	(A)
MARIANNE WATKINS	V	(A	MARLINE GREENE	V	(A	MARY ANDERSON	V	(A)
TARP TARRANT	D	(A					

A29   ALBERTO Y LOS TRIOS PARANOIAS

Personnel	Inst		Album	Year	Label	Country	Cat.
CHRIS LEE	V G	(ABCD	(A) ALBERTO Y LOS TRIOS PARANOIAS	1976	TRANSATLANTIC		TRA 316
BOB HARDING	V G B	(ABCD	(B) ITALIANS FROM OUTER SPACE	1977	TRANSATLANTIC		TRA 349
BRUCE MITCHELL	PERC	(ABCD	(C) SNUFF ROCK (EP)	1977	STIFF		LAST 2
TONY BOWERS	G B	(ABCD	(D) SKITE	1978	LOGO		1009
SIMON WHITE	STEEL	(ABCD					
JIMMY HIBBERT	V B	(ABCD	LES PRYOR	V	(ABCD	CHAS JANKEL	K	(D
ROGER RUSKIN SPEAR	SAX	(D	ALBE DONNELLY	HRS	(A	GRAHAM ROBERTSON	HRS	(A
DAVE TOMLINSON	CLAR SYN	(A	ANTHONY MOORE	ORG	(A			

A30   THE ALBION BAND

Personnel	Inst	
ASHLEY HUTCHINGS	B V	(ALL
MARTIN CARTHY	V G	(EFMO
SUE HARRIS	V OBOE DULC	(EF
JOHN KIRKPATRICK	V CONC	(AEFO
MARTIN NICHOLLS	SACKBUTS	(F
SIMON NICOL	V G K DULC	(ABCDEFKLMN
ROGER SWALLOW	D	(EF
DAVE MATTACKS	D	(BCEFJKLM
JOHN IVESON	SACKBUTS	(F
COLIN SHEEN	SACKBUTS	(F
PAUL BEER	SACKBUTS	(F
STEVE ASHLEY	V G HCA	(B
ROYSTON WOOD	V CONC	(AB
SUE DRAHEIM	FDL BANJO	(ABC
ANDY FAIRWEATHER LOW	V	(M
RICHARD THOMPSON	G V	(ACDM
LINDA THOMPSON	V	(CDM
BILL CADDUN	V PERC	(O
SHIRLEY COLLINS	V	(DGHJKL
IAN HOLDER	ACC	(GHJ
PETER KNIGHT	FDL	(J
MADDY PRIOR	V	(N
MICHAEL GREGORY	D	(KLMO
RIC SANDERS	VLN	(M
KATE McGARRIGLE	V	(M
HOWARD EVANS	HRNS	(O
STEVE SAUNDERS	TROM	(O

THE ALBION COUNTRY BAND
(A) JAN 1972   (B) JAN OCT 1972   (C) OCT 1972
(D) DEC 1972   (E) 1973
(E) BATTLE OF THE FIELD   1976 ISLAND HELP 25

ETCHINGHAM STEAM BAND
(G) JAN 74 JULY 74   (H) SUMMER 1974   (J) APRIL 1975

ALBION DANCE BAND
(K) FORMED NOV 75
(L) THE PROSPECT BEFORE US   1977 HARVEST SHSP4059

ALBION DANCE BAND
(M) RISE UP LIKE THE SUN   1978 HARVEST SHSP4092
(M) RISE UP LIKE THE SUN   1978 SONOPRESSE FR 068 06612
(N) ALBION RIVER HYMN MARCH 1979
(O) LARK RISE TO CANDLEFORD   1980 CHARISMA CD 54020

Personnel	Inst			Personnel	Inst	
JOHN WATCHAM		(D		TERRY POTTER	HCA	(GJ
VIC GAMMON		(HJ		EDDIE UPTON	V HCA	(JKL
JOHN RODD	V CONC	(KL		WILL DUKE	CONC MEL	(K
JOHN SOTHCOTT	VIELLE	(KLN		PHIL PICKETT	WIND K	(LMN
PETE BULLOCK	K WIND	(MNO		JOHN TAMS	V MEL	(LMO
GRAWMW TAYLOR	G K	(LMO		DAVE BRISTOW	K	(M
JULIE COVINGTON	V	(M		PAT DONALDSON	V	(M
DAVE MORTER	G	(O		BRIAN PROTHEROE	K V	(O
MARTIN SIMPSON	BAN	(O				

A30A   ALCO

Personnel	Inst		Album	Year	Label	Cat.
TIM CAESAR	V	(A	(A) THREADS OF LIFE	1972	ALCO	ALC 530
JULIAN CAESAR	D V K	(A				
PAUL FIDLIN	B G V	(A	BEN BROOKE	G B V	(A	MARTIN KENNARD	V	(A
RICHARD WILLIAMS	V	(A	JONATHAN PALMER	V	(A	STEPHEN HARBACH	V	(A
NORMAN FRASER	V	(A	RAY DAVISON	V	(A	ITCHEN ORCHESTRA		(A

A31   ALESSI BROTHERS

Personnel	Inst		Album	Year	Label	Cat.
BOBBY ALESSI	V G	(ABC	(A) ALESSI	1977	A&M	AMLH64608
BILLY ALESSI	K V	(ABC	(B) ALL FOR A REASON	1978	A&M	AMLH68446
JAMES DIVISEK	D	(C	(C) DRIFTIN'	1978	A&M	AMLH64713
DENNIS BELFIELD	B	(C	(D) WORDS & MUSIC	1979	A&M	AMLH64776
JIM SEALS	SAX	(C				
LOUIE SHELTON	G	(C	BRIAN WHITCOMB	K	(C	STEVE PORCARO	SYN	(C
ALAN ESTES	PERC	(C	VINCE CHARLES	PERC	(C	ED GREENE	D	(C
DAVID HUNGATE	B	(C	LEE RITENOUR	G	(C	MELVIN WATSON	G	(C
GREG PHILLINGANES	K	(C	ABE LABORIEL	B	(C	RICHIE HAVENS	V	(C
MICHAEL BAIRD	D	(C	DASH CROFTS	V	(C	GREG MATHIESON	K	(C
DON MENZA	SAX	(C				

A32   WILLY ALEXANDER & THE BOOM BOOM BAND

Personnel	Inst		Album	Year	Label		Cat.		Cat.
WILLY ALEXANDER	V K	(AB	(A) WILLY ALEXANDER & BOOM BOOM BAND	1978	MCA	UK	MCF 2835	US	2323
BILLY LOOSIGIAN	G	(AB	(B) MEAN WHILE BACK IN THE STATES	1979	MCA	UK	MCF 2876	US	3052
SEVERIN GROSSMAN	B	(AB							
DAVID McLEAN	D PERC	(AB							

ALFALPHA

```
NICK LAIRD CLOWES V HCA G (A    (A) ALFALPHA                    1977   EMI              UK   EMC 3213
ANDY HARLEY       V G    (A
SAM HARLEY        B G    (A    STEVE CHAPMAN      D     (A    ADRIAN REA       D     (A
RAY COOPER        PERC   (A    JIM CUOMO          SAX K (A    BILL COLE        STEEL (A
JOHN MEALING      PNO    (A    DEL NEWMAN         K     (A    FRED SHUSTER     G     (A
ISAAC GUILLORY    G      (A
```

ALICE

```
DOUDON WEISS      D      (AB   (A) ALICE                       1970   METRONOME        FR   MLP15391
ALAN SUZAN        V B    (A    (A) ALICE                       19     BYG              FR   529016
PAUL SEMANA       G      (B    (B) ARRETEZ LA MONDE            19     POLYDOR          FR   2393 043
LUC BERTIN        K      (B
IAN JEFFS         G V    (B    BRUNO BESSE        G     (A    SYLVAIN DUPLANT  B V   (A
```

ALKATRAZ

```
WILL YOUATT       G      (A    (A) DOING A MOONLIGHT           1976   UA               UAS 30001
JAMES DAVIES      G      (A
JEFF SINGER       B      (A    STUART HALLIDAY    G     (A    JIMMY JEWEL      SAX   (A
CLIVE JOHN        K      (A    RAY MARTINEZ       G     (A
```

DAEVID ALLEN

```
DAEVID ALLEN      V G    (ALL  (A) OBSOLETE                    19     SHANDAR 83512    SR 10009
DASHIELL HEDAYAT         (A    (B) BANANA MOON                 1975   CAROLINE         C 1512
ROBERT WYATT      G D V  (B    (B) BANANA MOON                 1975   BYG              FR   529 345
ARCHIE LEGGET     B      (B    (B) BANANA MOON                 197    CHARLY           CR 30165
GARY WRIGHT       VLN    (B    (C) GOOD MORNING                1976   VIRGIN           UK   V 2054
GERRY FIELDS      VLN    (B    (D) NOW IS THE HAPPIEST TIME.........1977   AFFINITY    AFF 3
MAGGIE BELL       V      (B    (E) MAGICK BROTHER              1978   AFFINITY         AFF 4
SHAKTI YONI       V      (B    (E) MAGICK BROTHER              1978   BYG              FR   529 305
BARRY ST JOHN     V      (B    ( ) N'EXISTE PAS                1979   CHARLY           UK   CRL5015
PIP PYLE          D      (B
CHRISTIAN TRITSCH G      (B    NICK EVANS         TROM  (B
```

LUTHER ALLISON

```
LUTHER ALLISON    G V    (AB   (A) BLUES NEBULAE               19     DELMARK          IMP  DS 625
WITH                           (B) NIGHT LIFE                  1976   MOTOWN           G 974V1
RICHARD TEE       K      (B    (C) LUTHERS BLUES               19     GORDY            US   967
ROBIN KENYATTA    SAX    (B
GERRY BROWN       D      (B    STEVE KHAN         G     (B    JOHN LEE         B     (B
JEFFREY ALDRICH   B      (B    MICHAEL CARVIN     D     (B    LARRY BYRNE      K     (B
DR JOHN           K      (B    RAY ANDERSON       TROM  (B    JIM SOLBERG      G     (B
RALPH McDONALD    PERC   (B    RANDY BRECKER      TPT   (B    MICHAEL BRECKER  SAX   (B
LEW DEL GATTO     SAX    (B    RICHARD DRAKE      SAX   (B    BRUCE JOHNSTONE  SAX   (B
TASHA THOMAS      V      (B    MAERETHA STEWART   V     (B    HILDA HARRIS     V     (B
GAIL KANTOR       V      (B    DAVID NEWMAN       SAX   (B
```

DUANE ALLMAN

```
DUANE ALLMAN      G      (ALL  (A) ANTHOLOGY                   1972   CAPRICORN UK K 67502 US  0108
                               (A) ANTHOLOGY                   1974   CAPRICORN        UK   2659 035
                               (B) ANTHOLOGY VOL 2             1974   CAPRICORN UK 2659037 US  0139
                               (C) BEST OF DUANE ALLMAN        1979   CAPRICORN        UK   2429 187
```

GREGG ALLMAN

```
GREGG ALLMAN      K V    (ALL  (A) LAID BACK                   1973   CAPRICORN        UK   K 47508
WITH                           (A) LAID BACK                   1973   CAPRICORN        UK   2429 103
CHER              V      (D    (A) LAID BACK                   1973   CAPRICORN        US   CP 0116
NEIL LARSEN       K      (CD   (B) GREGG ALLMAN TOUR (DBL)     1974   CAPRICORN        UK   2659 038
STEVE BECKMAIER   G      (C    (B) GREGG ALLMAN TOUR (DBL)     1974   CAPRICORN        US   2C 0141
MAC REBENNACK     K      (C    (C) PLAYIN' UP A STORM          1977   CAPRICORN        UK   2473 131
BILL PAYNE        K      (C    (C) PLAYIN' UP A STORM          1977   CAPRICORN        US   CP 0181
DAVID LUELL       SAX    (C    (D) TWO THE HARD WAY            1977   W B              UK   K 56436
VICTOR FELDMAN    PERC   (C    (D) TWO THE HARD WAY            1977   W B              US   BSK 3120
BILL STEWART      D      (CD
JOHN HUG          G      (CD
WILLIE WEEKS      B      (CD   RICKY HIRSCH       G     (CD   FRED BECKMAIER   B     (C
MILT HOLLAND      PERC   (C    RED CALLENDER      B     (C    STEVE MADAIO     HRNS  (C
SHIRLEY MATTHEWS  V      (CD   PAT RIZZO          HRNS  (C    CLYDIE KING      V     (CD
RON EADES         SAX    (D    VANETTA FIELDS     V     (CD   JIM HORN         HRNS  (D
DOUG HAYWOOD      V      (D    HARRISON CALLOWAY  HRS   (D    PAT HENDERSON    V     (D
TIM SCHMIT        V      (D    DENNIS GOODE       TROM  (D    HARVEY THOMPSON  SAX   (D
SCOTT BOYER       G      (D    SID SHARP          STRINGS(D   BOBBYE HALL      PERC  (D
RANDALL BRAMBLETT SAX    (D    FRED TACKETT       G     (D    MICKEY RAPHAEL   HCA   (D
                               BEN CAULEY         TPT   (D    RUSSELL MORRIS   V     (D
```

ALLMAN BROTHERS BAND

```
GREGG ALLMAN      K V    (ALL        (A) THE ALLMAN BROTHERS BAND      1969   ATCO          US   SD33308
DUANE ALLMAN      G      (ABCDI      (A) THE ALLMAN BROTHERS BAND      1969   CAPRICORN     UK   228 033
BERRY OAKLEY      B      (ABCDE      (A) THE ALLMAN BROTHERS BAND      1969   CAPRICORN     US   0196
RICHARD BETTS     G V    (ABCDEFGHJ  (B) IDLEWILD SOUTH                1970   ATCO          US   SD 33342
JAI JOHANSON      PERC   (ABCDEFJ    (B) IDLEWILD SOUTH                1970   CAPRICORN     UK   2400 032
BUTCH TRUCKS      PERC   (ABCDEFJ    (B) IDLEWILD SOUTH                1970   CAPRICORN     US   0197
THOM DOUCETTE     HCA    (B          (C) LIVE AT FILLMORE EAST  (DBL)  1971   CAPRICORN     UK   K 60011
CHUCK LEAVELL SYN PNO V  (EF         (C) LIVE AT FILLMORE EAST  (DBL)  1971   CAPRICORN     US   2659 039
LAMAR WILLIAMS    B      (EF         (C) LIVE AT FILLMORE EAST  (DBL)  1971   CAPRICORN     US   2CX40131
LES DUDEK         G      (E          (C) LIVE AT FILLMORE EAST  (DBL)  1971   POLYDOR            2639 102
TOMMY TALTON      G      (G          (D) EAT A PEACH            (DBL)  1972   CAPRICORN     UK   K 67501
JOHNNY SANDLIN    G PERC (F          (D) EAT A PEACH            (DBL)  1972   CAPRICORN     UK   2659 034
BILL STEWART      PERC   (F          (D) EAT A PEACH            (DBL)  1972   CAPRICORN     US   2C4 0102
DAN TOLER         G      (J          (D) EAT A PEACH            (DBL)  1972   POLYDOR            2639 101
DAVID GOLDFLIES   B      (J          (E) BROTHERS & SISTERS            1973   CAPRICORN     US   CP 0111
                                     (E) BROTHERS & SISTERS            1971   CAPRICORN     UK   2429 102
                                     (E) BROTHERS & SISTERS            1974   CAPRICORN     UK   K 47507
                                     (F) WIN LOOSE OR DRAW             1975   CAPRICORN     UK   2476 116
                                     (F) WIN LOOSE OR DRAW             1975   CAPRICORN     US   CP 0156
```

(CONTINUED)

ALLMAN BROTHERS BAND

(G) THE ROAD GOES ON FOREVER (DBL)	1975	CAPRICORN	UK	2637 101
(G) THE ROAD GOES ON FOREVER (DBL)	1975	CAPRICORN	US	2CP 0164
(H) WIPE THE WINDOWS,....... (DBL)	1976	CAPRICORN	UK	2637 103
(H) WIPE THE WINDOWS,....... (DBL)	1976	CAPRICORN	US	CP 0177
(I) DUANE & GREGG	1973	POLYDOR		2310 235
(I) DUANE & GREGG	197	SPRINGBOARD	US	4046
(J) ENLIGHTENED ROGUES	1979	CAPRICORN	UK	POLD5016
(AB) BEGINNINGS (DBL)	1973	ATCO	US	SD 2 805
(AB) BEGINNINGS (DBL)	1974	CAPRICORN	UK	2569 040
(AB) BEGINNINGS (DBL)	1974	CAPRICORN	UK	K 60046
(AB) BEGINNINGS (DBL)	1974	CAPRICORN	US	2CX 0123
( ) THE ALLMAN BROTHERS (DBL)	19	ATLANTIC		K 60070
( ) ALL MENS BROTHERS (DBL)	19	ATCO	US	40424
( ) THE BEST OF	1980	CAPRICORN	UK	2429 198
(K) REACH FOR THE SKY	1980	ARISTA	UK	SPART 1146

A39   ALLMAN JOYS

GREGG ALLMAN	K V	(A		
DUANE ALLMAN	G V	(A	(A) ALLMANJOYS	1973	DIAL	US	DL 6005
RALPH BALINGER	D	(A	(A) ALLMANJOYS	197	MERCURY	UK	6398 005
RONNIE WILKINS	PNO	(A		
JACK JACKSON	G	(A	TOMMY AMATO	D	(A	BOBBY DENNIS	G	(A

A40   JOHNNY ALMOND

JOHNNY ALMOND	SAX K	(ALL
WITH		

(A) MUSIC MACHINE PATENT PENDING 1969 DERAM UK SML 1043
(B) MUSIC MACHINE HOLLYWOOD BLUES 1970 DERAM UK SML 1057

JEFF CONDON	HRNS	(A						
JIMMY CRAWFORD	G	(A	ROGER SUTTON	B	(A	JOHNNY WIGGINS	K	(A
STEVE HAMMOND	G	(A	ALAN WHITE	D	(A	CHARLES KYNARD	ORG	(B
JOE PASS	G	(B	RAY NEOPOLITAN	B	(B	EARL PALMER	B	(B
JOE HARRIS	HRS	(B	HADLEY CALIMAN	HRS	(B	CURTIS AMY	SAX	(B
PAUL WILLIAMS		(A	ZOOT MONEY		(A			

A41   ALPHA BAND

STEVE SOLES	V G	(ABC	(A) ALPHA BAND	1977	ARISTA	UK	ARTY 143
DAVID MANSFIELD	G	(ABC	(A) ALPHA BAND	1977	ARISTA	US	AB 4102
T BONE BURNETT	V G	(ABC	(B) SPARK IN THE DARK	1977	ARISTA	US	AB 4145
DAVID JACKSON	B	(A	(B) SPARK IN THE DARK	1977	PATHE	FR	06860066
MATT BETTON	D	(AB	(C) STATUE MAKERS OF HOLLYWOOD	1978	ARISTA	UK	SPART1039
BILLY MAXWELL		(BC	(C) STATUE MAKERS OF HOLLYWOOD	1978	ARISTA	US	AB 4279
DAVID MINER	B	(BC	(C) STATUE MAKERS OF HOLLYWOOD	1978	PATHE	FR	06860885
CINDY BULLENS	V	(BC					
EVERETT BRYSON	PERC	(C	LEE PASTORA		(C	K O THOMAS	K	(AB
ROSCOE WEST	V	(A	ROSANNA TAPLIN	V	(A	JOE CORRERO	D	(B
RINGO STARR	D	(B	MIKE UTLEY	K	(B	OSAU KITAJIMA	KOTO	(B
GEOFFREY HALES	D	(B					

A41A   ALPHA RALPHA

MICHAEL MARESKA	G	(A	(A) ALPHA RALPHA	19	WEA	K 56330
CHARLIE CHARRIROW	B	(A				
EMMANUEL LACORDAIRE	PERC	(A	CLAUDE ALVAREZ	PERC G (A	JEAN GARDET	K	(A

A42   ALQUIN

FERDINAND BAKKER	G K V	(ABC	(A) MARKS	1972	POLYDOR 2646 101	UK 2480 152
RONALD OTTENHOFF	HRS	(ABC	(B) MOUNTAIN QUEEN	1973	POLYDOR	UK	2480 179
DICK FRANSSEN	K	(ABC	(C) NOBODY CAN WAIT FOREVER	19	POLYDOR 2925 045	UK 2480 262
MICHAEL VAN DIJK	V	(C	(C) NOBODY CAN WAIT FOREVER	1975	RCA	US	APLI 1061
HEIN MARS	B	(A	(D) CRASH	19	POLYDOR		2646 101
PAUL WESTSTRATE	D	(A	(E) BEST KEPT SECRET	1976	POLYDOR		2925 045
JOB TARENSKEEN	WIND	(ABC	(F) ON TOUR	1976	POLYDOR		2441 067
JAN VISSEN		(					
THUNDERTHIGHS	V	(					

A43   ALTERNATIVE T V

MICKY SMITH	B	(1	(A) THE IMAGE HAS CRACKED	1978 DEPTFORD FUN CITY	DPL 01
ALEX FERGUSSON	G	(123D	(B) WHAT YOU SEE IS WHAT YOU ARE	1978 DEPTFORD FUN CITY	DLP 02
MARK PERRY	V G	(ABCD12345	(C) VIBING UP THE SENILE MAN	1979 DEPTFORD FUN CITY	DLP 03
JOHN TOWE	D	(12	(D) LIVE AT THE RAT CLUB 77	1979 CRYSTAL	CLP 001
TYRONE THOMAS	B	(A234D	(1) APRIL 1977 (2)MAY JULY 1977 (3) AUG OCT 1977
CHRIS BENNETT	D	(AD34	(4) OCT 1977 1978 (5) 1979 (B) WITH HERE & NOW
DENNIS BURNS	B	(ABC45		
MARK LINEHAM	G	(	DAVE GEORGE	D	(C5

A44   ALTHEA & DONNA

ALTHEA	V	(A	(A) UPTOWN TOP RANKING	1978	FRONT LINE	FL 1012
DONNA	V	(A				

A45   AMAZING RHYTHM ACES

BARRY BYRD BURTON	V G	(ABCD	(A) STACKED DECK	1975	ABC UK ABCL5152	US ABCD 913
BILLY EARHEART	K	(ABCD	(B) TOO STUFFED TOO JUMP	1976	ABC UK ABCL5160	US ABCD 940
JIM KERSHAW	G	(A	(B) TOO STUFFED TO JUMP	1976	CARRERE	FR	68024
BUTCH McDADE	V D	(ABCD	(C) TOUCAN DO IT TOO	1976	ABC UK ABCL5219	US AB 1005
			(C) TOUCAN DO IT TOO	1976	CARRERE	FR	1005
JEFF DAVIS	B	(ABCD	(D) BURNING THE BALLROOM DOWN	1978	ABC UK ABCL5244	US AA 1063
RUSSELL SMITH	V G	(ABCD	(D) BURNING THE BALLROOM DOWN	1978	CARRERE	FR	68057
JAMES HOOKER	K V	(ABCD	(E) AMAZING RHYTHM ACES	1979	ABC UK ABCL5267	

A46   AMAZORBLADES

BENNO MENDELSON	FDL	(
BOB KEYLOCH	G	
STEVE HAINS	D	RAY COOPER	B	ROBIN WATSON	SAX

A47   AMBERGRIS

LARRY HARLOW	K PERC	(A	(A) AMBERGRIS	1970	PARAMOUNT	PAS 5014
JERRY WEISS	B K	(A				
CHARLIE CAMILLARI	TPT	(A	HARRY MAX	B VLN TPT	(A	GIL FIELDS	D	(A
GLEN JOHN MILLER	TROM	(A	JIMMY MAELEN	V PERC	(A	LEWIS KAHN	TROM VLA	(A
BILLY SHAY	G HCA	(A				

AMBROSE SLADE A47A

JIM LEE	B VLN (A	(A) AMBROSE SLADE	1969	FONTANA	SRF67598
DON POWELL	D (				
NODDY HOLDER	G V (A	DAVE HILL	G (A		

AMBROSIA A48

CHRISTOPHER NORTH	K V (A	(A) AMBROSIA	1975	20th CENTURY		BT 434
DAVID PACK	G K V (A	(A) AMBROSIA	1975	DISCODIS	FR	199
JOE PUERTA	B G V (A	(B) SOMEWHERE I'VE NEVER TRAVELLED	1976	20th CENTURY		BTH 510
BURLEIGH DRUMMOND	D PERC V(A	(B) SOMEWHERE I'VE NEVER TRAVELLED	1976	DISCODIS	FR	224
IAN UNDERWOOD	SAX (A	(C) LIFE BEYOND L A	1978	W B	UK	K 56525
RUTH UNDERWOOD	MARIMBA(A					

AME SON A48A

MARK BLANC	D (	(A) AME SON	19	BYG	FR	529 325
BERNARD LAVIALLE	G (	(B) CATALYSE	19	METRONOME	FR	MLP 15 373
PATRICK FONTAINE	B (					
FRANCOIS GARREL	FLT (					

AMEN CORNER A49

ANDY FAIRWEATHER LOW	V G (ALL	(A) ROUND AMEN CORNER	1968	DERAM	UK	DML 1021
NEIL JONES	G (	(B) NATIONAL WELSH COAST LIVE	1979	IMMEDIATE	UK	IMSP 023
BLUE WEAVER	K (	(C) FAREWELL MAGNIFICENT SEVEN	1969	IMMEDIATE	UK	IMSP 028
ALAN JONES	SAX (	(D) WORLD OF AMEN CORNER	1969	DECCA	UK	SPA 13
MIKE SMITH	SAX (	(E) AMEN CORNER & SMALL FACES	1975	NEW WORLD		NW 6001
CLIVE TAYLOR	B (	(F) RETURN OF THE MAGNIFICENT SEVEN	1976	IMMEDIATE	UK	IML 1004
DENNIS BRYON	D (	(G) GREATEST HITS	1978	IMMEDIATE	UK	IML 2004

AMERICA A49

GARY BECKLEY	G V (ABCDEFGHJ	(A) AMERICA	1971	WB	UK	K 46093
DAN PEEK	G V (ABCDEFGHJ	(A) AMERICA	1971	WB	US	B 2576
DEWEY BUNNELL	D G V (ABCDEFGHJ	(B) HORSE WITH NO NAME	19	WB		K 46157
WITH		(C) HOMECOMING	1972	WB	UK	K 46180
HAL BLAINE	D (C	(C) HOMECOMING	1972	WB	US	B 2655
DAVE ATTWOOD	D (A	(D) HAT TRICK	1973	WB	UK	K 56016
DAVID LINDLEY	STEEL (A	(D) HAT TRICK	1973	WB	US	B 2728
RAY COOPER	PERC (A	(E) HOLIDAY	1974	WB	UK	K 56046
GARY MALLABER	D (C	(E) HOLIDAY	1974	WB	US	W4 2808
JOE OSBORN	B (C	(F) HEARTS	1975	WB	UK	K 56115
HENRY DILTZ	BANJO (C	(F) HEARTS	1975	WB	US	BS4 2852
DAVID DICKEY	B (FHJ	(G) HISTORY (GREATEST HITS)	1975	WB	UK	K 56169
TOM WALSH	PERC (J	(G) HISTORY (GREATEST HITS)	1975	WB	US	K 3110
GEORGE MARTIN	PNO (H	(H) HIDEAWAY	1976	WB	UK	K 56236
WILLIE LEACOX	D (HJ	(H) HIDEAWAY	1976	WB	US	BS 2932
JIMMY CALIRE	K SAX (J	(I) HARBOR	1976	WB	UK	K 56351
VANETTA FIELDS	V (F	(I) HARBOR	1976	WB	US	BK 3017
CLYDIE KING	V (F	(J) LIVE	1977	WB	UK	K 56434
JESSICA SMITH	V (F	(J) LIVE	1977	WB	US	K 3136

AMERICAN BLUES LEGENDS A50A

JOHNNY BARNES	CLAR (A	(A) AMERICAN BLUES LEGENDS	1972	POLYDOR		2460 186
EDDIE TAYLOR	G (A	(A) AMERICAN BLUES LEGENDS	1974	BIG BEAR	USBM150202 UK	BEAR 1
BIG JOHN WRENCHER	V HCA (A	( ) AMERICAN BLUES LEGENDS	1975	BIG BEAR		BEAR 8
DR ROSS	V G HCA(A					
COUSIN JOE	V PNO (A	G P JACKSON	V G (A	BOB HALL	PNO (A	
BOB BRUNNING	B (A	PETE YORK	D (A	ROGER HILL	G (A	
GRAHAM GALLERY	B (A	GEORGE CHISHOLM	TROM (A	COLIN SMITH	TPT (A	

AMERICAN BREED A51

GARY LOIZIO	V G (A	(A) AMERICAN BREED	1967	DOT DOLP0255 ATLANTIC		38002
CHUCK COLBERT	B (A	(B) BEND ME SHAPE ME	1968	DOT SLPD 502 ATLANTIC		38003
AL CINER	G (A	(C) PUMPKIN,POWDER,SCARLET & GREEN	1968	ATLANTIC		38006
LEE GRAZIANO	D (A	(D) LONELY SIDE OF THE CITY	1968	ATLANTIC		38008

AMERICAN FLYER A52

STEVE KATZ	(AB	(A) AMERICAN FLYER	1976	UA	US	UALA 650
ERIC KAZ	(AB	(A) AMERICAN FLYER	1976	UA	UK	UAS29991
DOUG YULE	(AB	(B) SPIRIT OF A WOMAN	1977	UAS	UK	UAS30078
CRAIG FULLER	(AB	(B) SPIRIT OF A WOMAN	1977	UA	US	UALA 720
J D SOUTHER	(B					
LINDA RONSTADT	V (B	SYLVIA TYSON	V (B	TRACY NELSON	V (B	
BEN MINK	(B	WHITEY GLAN	D (B	PRAKASH JOHN	B (B	
BOBBY KEYS	HRS (B	JERRY SCHEFF	(B	JOHN KAPEC	(B	
ALVIN TAYLOR	D (B	FRED BECKMAIER	B (A	LARRY CARLTON	G (A	
SCOTT EDWARDS	B (A	GARY COLEMAN	PERC (A	RUSTY YOUNG	STEEL (A	
JOE SAMPLE	K (A	LELAND SKLAR	B (A	ERNIE WATTS	SAX (A	
BYRON BERLINE	FDL (A	EARL DUMLER	HRN (A	VINCE DEROSA	HRNS (A	
HARRY BLUESTONE	STRINGS (A					

AMERICAN GYPSY A53

JOE SKEETE	B V K (A	(A) AMERICAN GYPSY	1975	CHESS		CH 60034
STEVE CLISBY	K HCA V (A	( ) AMERICAN GYPSY	1975	BTM		BTM 1001
MICHAEL HAMANE	G V (	( ) AMERICAN GYPSY	1975	CHESS		BTM 5003
DALE HARREL Jr	G V (A	( ) ANGEL EYES	19	PHILIPS		6410 066
RICHARD JAMES	PERC D(A					
LORENZO MILLS	PERC V(A					

AMERICAN GYPSY (2) A53A

JOE LALA	PERC (B	(A) GYPSY	1971	CBS		66270
WILLIE WEEKS	B (B	(B) IN THE GARDEN	1972	METROMEDIA		KMD1044
BILL LORDON	D (A	(C) UNLOCK THE DEAD GATES	19	RCA	IMP	APLI0093
JAMES WALSH	V K D (ABD	(D) ANTITHESIS	19	RCA		LSP 4775
ENRICO ROSENBAUM	PERC V G(ABD					
JAY EPSTEIN	D (A	JAMES JOHNSON	V G (ABD	DONI LARSON	B (A	

AMERICAN SPRING A54

DIANE POWELL	V (A	(A) AMERICAN SPRING	1974	UA		UAS29363
MARILYN POWELL	V (A					

[7]

A55   AMERICAN TEARS

MIKE MANGOLD	K V	(	(A) BRANDED BAD		1974	CBS	US	KC 33038
GLENN KITHCARL	D	(	(B) TEARGAS		1975	CBS	US	PC 33847
KIRK POWER	B V	(	(C) POWERHOUSE		1977	CBS	US	PC 34676
CRIAG EVAN BROOKS	G V	(						
GARY SONNY	B	(	TOMMY GUNN	D	(	GREG BAZE	B	(

A56   AMERICAN TRAIN

TOM HOWE	G					
CHRIS SCHINDLER	B	MIKE SKINNER	D	JOHN SULLIVAN	V	

A56A   AMM II

KEITH ROWE	G	(A	(A) IT HAS BEEN AN ORDINARY DAY	1980	JAPO		60031
EDDIE PROVOST	D	(A)					
LOU GARE	SAX	(A					

A57   AMON DUUL

RENATE KNAUP	V	(EFHJKLNO	(A) DISASTER		19	BASF		290 9
DANNY FISHELSCHER	D	(HJK	(A) DISASTER	(DBL)	19	BASF	GERM	2929 079
JOHN WEINZIERL	G	(EFGHJKLOPT	(B) PSYCHEDELIC		19	METRONOME		15332
CHRIS KARRER	G	(EFGHJKLNOP	(C) COLLAPSING		19	METRONOME		SMLP 012
FALK ROGNER	K	(EFGJKLNO	(D) PARADIES WARTZ		19	OHR		56068
LOTHAR MEID	B	(HKLN	II					
PETE LEOPOLD	D	(EFGHKL	(E) PHALLUS DEI		1969	LIBERTY		LBS83279
SHRAT	BONGO	(EF	(E) PHALLUS DEI		1972	SUNSET		SLS50257
DAVE ANDERSON	B	(EF	(F) YETI		1970	LIBERTY		LSP101/2
KALLE HAUSMAN	K	(GH	(F) YETI		1970			83359 60
OLAF KUBLER	SAX	(HJN	(G) DANCE OF THE LEMMINGS		1971	UA		UAD 60003 4
RAINER BAUER	G V	(R	(G) DANCE OF THE LEMMINGS		1971	LIBERTY		83473 74
ULLRICH LEOPOLD	B	(R	(H) CARNIVAL IN BABYLON		1972	UA		UAG29327
ELLA BAUER	V PERC	(R	(J) WOLF CITY		1972	UA		UAG29406
USCHI OBERMEIER	PERC	(R	(K) LIVE IN LONDON		1973	UA		USP 102
WOLFGANG KRISCHKE	PNO	(R	(K) LIVE IN LONDON		1973	UA		UAS29466
HELGA FILANDA	V PERC	(R	(L) VIVE LA TRANCE		197	UA		UAS29504
BOB HEIBL	B	(O	(M) LEMMINGMANIA		1973	UA		UAG29723
KLAUS EBART	B	(PTO	(N) HI JACK		1974	ATLANTIC		K 50136
STEFAN ZAUNER	K	(PTU	(N) HI JACK		1974	ATLANTIC		SD 36108
			(O) MADE IN GERMANY(DBL)		1975	NOVA		628350DX
			(O) MADE IN GERMANY		1975	ATCO	US	SD 36119
			(O) MADE IN GERMANY		1975	ATLANTIC		K 50182
			(P) PYRAGONY		197	NOVA		622890AS
			(Q) CLASSIC GERMAN ROCK SCENE		19	SONOPRESSE	FR	29770 71
			(R) MINNELIED		19	BRAIN	GER	0040 149
			(S) THIS IS		1973	METRONOME	GER	200 146
			(T) ALMOST LIVE		1977	NOVA	GER	623305A0
			(U) ONLY HUMAN		1978	STRAUD	GER	623561A0

A57A   ANARCHIC SYSTEM

(A) CHERIE SHA LA LA	19	DISCODIS	FR	85064/65
(B) GENERATION	19	DISCODIS	FR	7 00005
(C) SPECIAL CLUBS	19	DISCODIS	FR	700008/9

A58   ANCIENT GREASE

JOHN WEATHERS	D	(A	(A) WOMEN & CHILDREN FIRST	1970	MERCURY	UK	6338 033
GARY PICKFORD HOPKINS	V	(A					
PHIL RYAN	K	(A					

A59   ERIC ANDERSEN

ERIC ANDERSEN	HCA V G	(ALL	(A) TODAY IS THE HIGHWAY		1965	FONTANA	UK	TFL 6061
WITH			(A) TODAY IS THE HIGHWAY		1965	VANGUARD		VSD 79157
DEBBY GREENE	G	(A	(B) 'BOUT CHANGES & THINGS		1966	VANGUARD		VSD 79206
DEBORAH ANDERSEN	V	(K	(C) 'BOUT CHANGES & THINGS TAKE 2		1968	FONTANA	UK	STFL 6068
JOHN GUERIN	D	(K	(C) 'BOUT CHANGES & THINGS TAKE 2		1968	VANGUARD		VSD 79236
RUSS KUNKEL	D	(K	(D) MORE HITS FROM TIN CAN ALLEY		1968	VANGUARD		SVRL19003
SCOTT EDWARDS	B	(K	(D) MORE HITS FROM TIN CAN ALLEY		1968	VANGUARD		VSD 79271
DEAN PARKS	G	(K	(E) A COUNTRY DREAM		1968	VANGUARD		VSD 6540
TOM HENSLEY	PNO	(K	(F) AVALANCHE		1969	W B	US	WS 1748
HOWARD EMERSON	G	(K	(G) ERIC ANDERSEN		1970	W B	US	WS 1806
GARY COLEMAN	PERC	(K	(H) THE BEST OF ERIC ANDERSEN (DBL)		1971	VANGUARD		VSD 7/8
TOM SCOTT	SAX	(K	(J) BLUE RIVER		1973	CBS	UK	65145
TOM SELLERS	K	(K	(J) BLUE RIVER		1973	CBS	US	KC 31062
EMANUEL MOSS	VLN	(K	(K) BE TRUE TO YOU		1975	ARISTA	UK	ARTY 114
CHRIS BOND	G	(K	(K) BE TRUE TO YOU		1975	ARISTA	US	4033
RICHARD BENNETT	G	(K	(L) SWEET SUPRISE		19	ARISTA	US	4075
ERNIE WATTS	SAX	(K	(M) THE BEST SONGS		1977	ARISTA	US	4128
ANDY ROBINSON	V	(K	(M) THE BEST SONGS		1977	PATHE	FR	AL 4148
ALAN LINDGREN	K	(K	(N) STAGE		19	CBS	US	65571
DENNIS ST JOHN	D	(K						
EMORY GORDY	B	(K	JENNIFER WARREN	V	(K	MAXINE WILLARD	V	(K
GINGER BLAKE	V	(K	JULIA TILLMAN	V	(K	DOUG HAYWOOD	V	(K
JACKSON BROWNE	V	(K	HERB PEDERSEN	V	(K	MIKE CONDELLO	V	(K
JONI MITCHELL	V	(K	RAY BUCKWICH	V	(K	ORWIN MIDDLETON	V	(K
MARIA MULDAUR	V	(K	PAUL HARRIS	K	(C	HARVEY BROOKS	B	(C
HERBIE LOVELLE	D	(C	MARK SPORER	B	(K	JESSE EHRLICH	CELLO	(K

A60   IAN A ANDERSON

IAN A ANDERSON	V G	(ALL	(A) STEREO DEATH BREAKDOWN		19	LIBERTY		LBS 83242
WITH			(B) ROYAL YORK CRESENT		19	VILLAGE THING	UK	VTS 3
PICK WITHERS	D	(C	(C) A VULTURE IS NOT A BIRD YOU CAN...	1971	VILLAGE THING	UK	VTS 9
KIPPS BROWN	ORG	(C	(D) SINGER SLEEPS ON		197	VILLAGE THING	UK	VTS 18
JOHN TURNER	B	(C	(1) COUNTRY BLUES BAND 1968					
KEITH WARMINGTON	HCA	(C	(2) COUNTRY BLUES BAND 1968					
PAUL ROWAN	HCA	(1						
BOB ROWE	B	(12	CHRIS TURNER		(2	PAT MORAN	V	(D
PETE SIDDONS	BOUZ	(D	MIKE COOPER	G	(D	LES CALVERT	K B	(D
IAN FOSTER	D	(D	BILL BOAZMAN	G V	(D	MAGGIE HOLLAND	G	(D

JON ANDERSON

JON ANDERSON	ALL	(ABC	(A) OLIAS OF SUNHILLOW	1976 ATLANTIC UK K50261 US SD18180
VANGELIS	K	(B	(B) SHORT STORIES	1979 POLYDOR	POLD 5030
			(C) SONG OF SEVEN	1980 ATLANTIC UK K50756

MILLER ANDERSON

MILLER ANDERSON	G V	(A	(A) BRIGHT CITY	1971 DERAM UK SDL 3
WITH

PETER DINES	K	(A	GARY THAIN	B	(A
MICK WEAVER	K	(A	NEIL HUBBARD	G	(A	LYN DOBSON	FLT	(A
ERIC DILLON	D	(A	MADELINE BELL	V	(A	LIZA STRIKE	V	(A
HAROLD BECKETT	HRNS	(A
TRACY MILLER	V	(A

HARVEY ANDREWS

A62

HARVEY ANDREWS	V G	(ALL	(A) PLACES & FACES	1970 DECCA	SDN 9
WITH			(B) WRITER OF SONGS	1972 CUBE	HIFLY 10
MIKE MORAN	PNO	(C	(C) FRIENDS OF MINE	1977 ELECTRICAL	GNAT 2
GRAHAM COOPER	G	(CD	(C) FRIENDS OF MINE	1973 FLY	HIFLY 15
TERRY COX	D	(C	(D) FANTASIES FROM A CORNER SEAT	1975 TRANSATLANTIC	TRA 298
ROY BABBINGTON	B	(C	(E) SOMEDAY	1976 TRANSATLANTIC	TRA 329
CHRIS KARAN	D	(C	(F) BRAND NEW DAY	1980 POLYDOR	2383 595
GEOFF BODENHAM	G V	(F
PHIL KENZIE	SAX	(C	DAVE COXHILL	SAX	(C	JIMMY HELMS	TPT	(C
MIKE BAILEY	TPT	(C	BERNIE HOLLAND	G	(E	MARK WARNER	G	(E
BOB JONES	G	(E	PETE WILLSHER	STEEL	(E	PETE WINGFIELD	K	(DE
JIM TOOMEY	D	(E	MO FOSTER	B	(E	CHRIS MERCER	SAX	(E
RON CARTHY	TPT	(E	GRAHAM PRESKETT	MAN VLN	(C	PAUL KEOGH	G	(C
DAVE MATTACKS	D	(C	DAVE CARTWRIGHT	G HCA	(C	FRANCIS MONKMAN	K	(C
MIKE PAGE	SAX	(C	PAT DONALDSON	B	(D	RICHARD THOMPSON	G	(D
LINDA THOMPSON	V	(D

ANDROMEDA

A63

JOHN CANN	G V	(A	(A) ANDROMEDA	1969 RCA	SF 8031
MICK HAWKSWORTH	B V	(A
IAN McCLANE	D V	(A

ANGE

A64

JEAN MICHEL BREZOVAR	G V	(ABD	(A) LA CIMETIERE DES ARLEQUINS	19 PHILIPS	6325 037
CHRISTIAN DECAMPS	K V	(ABD	(A) LA CIMETIERE DES ARLEQUINS	19 PHILIPS	9101 022
FRANCIS DECAMPS	K V	(ABD	(B) CARICATURES	19 PHILIPS	6325 181
DANIEL HAAS	B G	(ABD	(B) CARICATURES	19 PHILIPS	6332 066
JEAN PIERRE COUCHARD	D	(	(C) AU DELA DU DELIRE	1975 PHILIPS	9101 044
GERALD JELSCH	D	(AB	(D) EMILE JACOTEY	1975 PHILIPS	9101 012
GUENOLE BIGER	G D	(D	(E) PAR LE FILS DU MANDARIN	1976 PHILIPS	9101 090
			(F) ANGE TOME (DBL)	1977 PHILIPS	6641 715
			(G) IN CONCERT	19 RCA	PL 37153
			(G) GUET APENS	1978 PHILIPS	9101 184

ANGEL

A65

BARRY BRANT	D	(CD	(A) ANGEL	1976 CASABLANCA	CBC 4007
FELIX ROBINSON	B	(D	(A) ANGEL	1976 CASABLANCA US	7021
PUNKY EDWIN MEADOWS	G	(CD	(B) HELLUVA BAND	1976 CASABLANCA	CBC 4010
GREGG GIUFFIA	K	(CD	(B) HELLUVA BAND	1976 CASABLANCA US	7028
FRANK DIMINO	V	(CD	(C) ON EARTH AS IT IS IN HEAVEN	1977 CASABLANCA	CAL 2002
MICKIE JONES	B	(C	(C) ON EARTH AS IT IS IN HEAVEN	1977 CASABLANCA US	7043
			(C) ON EARTH AS IT IS IN HEAVEN	1977 CASABLANCA FR	CBLA71007
			(D) WHITE HOT	1978 CASABLANCA	CSL 2023
			(D) WHITE HOT	1978 CASABLANCA US	NBLP 7085
			(E) SINFUL	1979 CASABLANCA US	NBLP 7127
			(F) LIVE WITHOUT A NET	1979 CASABLANCA	NBLP 2703

ANGEL CITY

A65A

	(A) FACE TO FACE	1978 EPIC	84253
	(B) DARKROOM	1980 EPIC	84502

ANGLETRAX

A66

JERRY MINGE	K	(	(A) ANGLETRAX	1979 ARIOLA	AHAL8009
MARTIN HEATH	B
RENE RENNO	G
WENDY HERMAN	V		DAN WHO	D

ANIMALS

A67

ALAN PRICE	K	(	(A) IN THE BEGINNING (EP)	1965 DECCA DFE8643	WAND 690
JOHN STEEL	D	(	(B) THE ANIMALS	1964 COLUMBIA UK	33SX1669
HILTON VALENTINE	G	(	(B) THE ANIMALS	1969 STARLINE UK	SRS 5006
CHAS CHANDLER	B	(	(C) THE ANIMALS	1964 M G M US	SE 4264
ERIC BURDON	V	(	(C) GET YOURSELF A COLLEGE GIRL	1965 M G M US	SE 4273
DAVE ROWEBERRY	K	(	(D) ANIMALS ON TOUR	1965 M G M US	SE 4281
JOHN WEIDER	B	(	(E) ANIMAL TRACKS	1965 COLUMBIA UK	33SX1708
VIC BRIGGS	G	(	(E) ANIMAL TRACKS	1965 M G M US	SE 4305
DANNY McCULLOCH	B	(	(F) BRITISH GO GO	1965 M G M US	SE 4306
BARRY JENKINS	D	(	(G) ANIMALISMS	1966 DECCA UK	LK 4797
ANDY SOMERS	G	(	(G) ANIMALISMS	1966 M G M US	SE 4414
ZOOT MONEY	K	(	(H) AMINALIZATION	1966 M G M US	SE 4384
			(I) MOST OF THE ANIMALS	1966 COLUMBIA UK	SX 6035
			(I) MOST OF THE ANIMALS	1973 M F P UK	MFP 5218
			(J) WIND OF CHANGE	1967 M G M US	CS 8052
			(J) WIND OF CHANGE	1971 M G M UK	2354 001
			(J) WIND OF CHANGE	1967 M G M US	SE 4484
			(K) ERIC IS HERE	1967 M G M US	SE 4433
			(L) EVERYONE OF US	1968 M G M US	SE 4553
			(M) TWAIN SHALL MEET	1968 M G M	CS 8074
			(M) TWAIN SHALL MEET	1968 M G M US	SE 4602
			(N) LOVE IS (DBL)	1969 VERVE	6651 09/10
			(N) LOVE IS	1969 M G M	CS 8105

(CONTINUED)

ANIMALS

(N) LOVE IS	1968	M G M	US	SE 4591
(N) LOVE IS	1971	M G M	UK	2619 002
(N) LOVE IS	1972	M G M	US	690
( ) BEST OF THE ANIMALS	1966	M G M	US	SE 4324
( ) BEST OF THE ANIMALS (DBL)	1973	ABCKO		AB 4226
( ) BEST OF THE ANIMALS	19	SPRINGBOARD	US	4025
( ) BEST OF THE ANIMALS	19	PATHE	FR	C062 91190
( ) BEST OF VOL2	1967	M G M	US	SE 4454
( ) GREATEST HITS	1969	M G M	US	SE 4602
( ) IN THE BEGINNING	1973	WAND		V6 5083
( ) ERIC BURDON & THE ANIMALS	1975	POLYDOR		2356 142
( ) NEWCASTLE 63	1976	D J M		DJSL 069
( ) NEWCASTLE 63	1977	CHARLY	UK	CR 30016
( ) LIVE IN NEWCASTLE	1976	D J M		DJB26069
( ) WITH SONNY BOY WILLIAMSON 63	1977	CHARLY	UK	CR 30018
( ) WILD ANIMALS	1966	DECCA	IMP	XLB 646028
( ) HITS OF THE ANIMALS	1969	COLUMBIA	IMP	SGHX 10048
( ) HOUSE OF THE RISING SUN	1970	EMI	IMP	048 50731
( ) STAR PORTRAIT	1971	M G M	IMP	665 102
( ) POP HISTORY	1971	M G M	IMP	2625 011
( ) MADMAN	1971	M G M	IMP	2674 044
( ) EARLY ANIMALS WITH ERIC BURDON	1973	PICKWICK	IMP	SPS 3330
( ) BEFORE WE WERE SO RUDELY INTERUPTED 77		BARN		2314 104
( ) BEFORE WE WERE SO RUDELY INTERUPTED 77		JET	US	JTLA790H
( ) NIGHTTIME IS THE RIGHT TIME	19	SPRINGBOARD	US	4065

A67A
ANNEXUS QUAM

(A) ANNEXUS QUAM	19	OHR	
(B) BEZIEHUNGER	19	OHR	OMN556028

A67B

PETER WATERHOUSE   G
ANDREW WATERHOUSE   B

ANSWER

STEVE ELLEY   K   CARL MATTHEWS

A67C

CLIVE GREGSON   G V   (A
NICK SIMPSON
MEL HARLEY   D   (A

ANY TROUBLE

(A) WHERE ARE ALL THE NICE GIRLS	1980	STIFF	SEEZ 25

PHIL BARNES   CHRIS PARKS   G V (A

A67D

BILLY JONES
JIM DONLINGER
JIM NYEHOLT

AORTA

(A) AORTA	19	CBS	CS 9785

BILLY HERMAN

A67E

VANGELIS PAPATHANASSIOU K B (ABC
DEMIS ROUSSOS   V B G   (ABC
LUCAS SIDERAS   D V   (ABC
WITH
SILVER KOULOURIS   G PERC AC
VANNIS TSAROUCHIS V   (C
IRENE PAPAS   V   (C
JOHN FROST   V   (C
ARRIS HALKITIS B SAX V PERC (C
MICHEL RIPOCHE   TROM SAX   (C

APHRODITES CHILD

(A) END OF THE WORLD RAIN & TEARS	19	VERTIGO		6333 008
(B) ITS FIVE O'CLOCK	19	VERTIGO		6333 009
(C) 666,APOCALYPSE OF JOHN	1972	VERTIGO		6673 001
(C) 666,APOCALYPSE OF JOHN	1972	VERTIGO		6641 581
(D) APHRODITES CHILD	1978	MERCURY		6886 650
(D) APHRODITES CHILD	19	MERCURY	US	VEL 2 500
(D) APHRODITES CHILD	1975	MERCURY		138 351
(E) BEST OF	1975	MERCURY		6333 002
(E) BEST OF	19	VERTIGO		6583 025
(F) RAIN & TEARS	19	VERTIGO		6483 035

A68

TERENCE BOYLAN   (

APPLETREE THEATRE

(A) PLAYBACK	19	POLYDOR	2353 051

A69

BRIAN GREEWAY   (L
JERRY MERCER   D V   (CDEL
STEVE LANG   B V   (EL
JIM CLENCH   B V   (C
MYLES GOODWYN   V G K (CDEL
GARY MOFFET   G V   (CDE

APRIL WINE

(A) APRIL WINE	197	BIG TREE	US	2012
(B) ELECTRIC JEWELS	1973	AQUARIUS	US	AQR 504
(C) LIVE	1974	AQUARIUS	US	AQR 505
(D) STAND BACK	197	BIG TREE US89506		AQUARIUS506
(E) WHOLE WORLDS GONE CRAZY	1976	LONDON	UK	SHU 8503
(E) WHOLE WORLDS GONE CRAZY	1976	LONDON	US	PS 675
(F) FOREVER FOR NOW	1976	AQUARIUS		AQR 511
(G) LIVE AT THE EL MOCAMBO	1977	LONDON	UK	SHU 8510
(G) LIVE AT THE EL MOCAMBO	1977	LONDON	US	PS 699
(H) FIRST GLANCE	1978	CAPITOL		11852
(J) HARDER ...FASTER	19	CAPITOL	US	12013
(K) ONRECORD	197			
(L) NATURE OF THE BEAST	1981	CAPITOL		12125

A70
AQUARIAN DREAM

(A) FANTASY	1978	ELEKTRA		K 52109
(B) NORMAN CONNORS PRESENTS A' DREAM	19	BUDDAH	US	5672

A71

RALPH DENYER   V G   (A
PHIL CHILDS   B K   (A
GEORGE LEE   WIND   (A

AQUILA

(A) AQUILA	1970	RCA	SF 8126

MARTIN WOODWARD   K   (A   JAMES SMITH   D   (A

A72

PAUL CAFFREY   V G   (AB
TONY DAVISON   B   (AB
ROGER ASKEW   G PNO (AB
BILL BISSET   D   (AB

ARBRE

(A) TIME & AGAIN	1976	DJM	DJF20480
(B) ARBRE	1978	DJM	DJF20527

PHIL CAFFREY   V G   (AB   PETER CAFFREY   G V   (AB

A73

MICK GALLAGHER   K G V (A
JOHN TURNBULL   G   (A
TOM DUFFY   B V   (A

ARC

(A) ARC AT THIS	1971	DECCA	SKLR5077

DAVID MONTGOMERY   D   (A

A73A
ARCADIUM

( ) ARCADIUM	1969	MIDDLE EAST	MDLS

NEIL ARDLEY

NEIL ARDLEY	K SYN (ABC	(A) SYMPHONY OF AMARANTHS
WITH		(B) KALEIDOSCOPE OF RAINBOWS
BOB BERTLES	WIND (B	(C) HARMONY OF SPHERES

(A) SYMPHONY OF AMARANTHS — 1972 REGAL ZONOPHONE SLRZ1028
(B) KALEIDOSCOPE OF RAINBOWS — 1976 GULL GULP1018
(C) HARMONY OF SPHERES — 1979 DECCA TXSR 133

BOB BERTLES	WIND (B				
PAUL BUCKMASTER	CELLO (B				
IAN CARR	HRNS (BC	GEOFF CASTLE	K (BC	TONY COE	WIND (BC
DAVE McCRAE	K (B	ROGER SELLERS	D (B	KEN SHAW	G (B
BRIAN SMITH	WIND (B	ROGER SUTTON	B (B	BARBARA THOMPSON	WIND (BC
TREVOR TOMKINS	PERC (BC	STAN SULZMANN	WIND (B	JOHN TAYLOR	K (B
JOHN MARTYN	G (C	BILLY KRISTIAN	B (C	RICHARD BURGESS	D (C
PEPI LEMER	V (C	NORMA WINSTONE	V (C		

AREA

DEMETRIO STATOS	V (A	(A) CRAC	19 BARCLAY	IT 940 512
ARES TAVOLAZZI	B (A			
PATRIZIO FARISELLI	K (A	GIAMPAOLO TOFANI	G (A	

AREA CODE 615

WELDON MYRICK	STEEL G (AB	(A) AREA CODE 615	1969	POLYDOR	UK	583572
BOBBY THOMPSON	BAN K (AB	(A) AREA CODE 615	1969	POLYDOR	US	24 4002
BUDDY SPICHER	FDL (AB	(B) A TRIP IN THE COUNTRY	1970	POLYDOR		2425 023
CHARLIE McCOY	HCA (AB	(B) A TRIP IN THE COUNTRY	1970	POLYDOR	US	24 4025
MAC GAYDEN	G (AB	(AB)AREA CODE/A TRIP	(DBL)	1974	POLYDOR	2683 040
WAYNE MOSS	B G (AB					
KENNY BUTTREY	D (AB	NORBERT PUTNAM	B (AB	KEN LAUBER	PNO (A
DAVID BRIGGS	PNO (B					

JOSE 'CHEPITO' AREAS

JOSE CHEPITO AREAS	PERC (A	(A) JOSE CHEPITO AREAS 1974 CBS US 33062 UK 80296

ARGENT

ROD ARGENT	K V (ABCDEFGH	(A) ARGENT 1970 CBS UK 63781
ROBERT HENRIT	D (ABCDEFGH	(A) ARGENT 1970 EPIC US 26525
JIM RODFORD	B (ABCDEFGH	(B) RING OF HANDS 1971 EPIC UK 64190
RUSS BALLARD	G V (ABCDEF	(B) RING OF HAND 1971 EPIC US E30128
JOHN VERiITY	V (GH	(C) ALL TOGETHER NOW 1972 CBS UK 64962
JOHN GRIMALDI	G (GH	(C) ALL TOGETHER NOW 1972 EPIC US 31556
PHIL COLLINS	PERC (H	(D) IN DEEP 1973 EPIC UK 65475
DEREK GRIFFITHS	G (D	(D) IN DEEP 1973 EPIC US 32195
		(E) NEXUS 1974 EPIC UK 65924
		(E) NEXUS 1974 EPIC US 32573
		(F) ENCORE (DBL) 1974 EPIC UK 88063
		(F) ENCORE (DBL) 1974 EPIC US 33079
		(G) CIRCUS 1975 EPIC UK 80691
		(G) CIRCUS 1975 EPIC US 33422
		(H) COUNTERPOINT 1975 RCA UK RS 1020
		(H) COUNTERPOINT 1975 U A US LA 560G
		( ) BEST OF ARGENT 1976 EPIC UK 81321
		( ) HOLD YOUR HEAD UP 197 EMBASSY UK 31640
		( ) ANTHOLOGY 197 EPIC US 33955

ROD ARGENT

ROD ARGENT	K V (A	(A) MOVING HOME 1978 MCA MCF 2854
WITH		
PHIL COLLINS	PERC (A	MORRIS PERT PERC (A ALPHONSO JOHNSON B (A
CLIVE CHAMAN	B (A	GARY MOORE G (A JACK LANCASTER WIND (A

ARIEL

MICHAEL RUDD	V G (B	(A) STRANGE FANTASTIC DREAM 1973 HARVEST SHSP4039
WILLIAM PUTT	B (B	(B) ROCK N ROLL SCARS 1974 HARVEST SHSP4039
HARVEY JAMES	G (B	
JOHN LEE	D (B	

ARIZONA

PETER KUCH	(B	(A) ARIZONA 1976 RCA SF 8465
DOUG HOLZWARTH	(B	(A) ARIZONA 1976 RCA US LPL1 5123
MARY DOBBINS	(B	(B) LOWDOWN 1977 RCA PL 25103
WILLIE KNOWLES	(B	
PAT MURPHY	(B	KEN ASHBY (B

ARMAGEDDON

KEITH RELF	V HCA (A	(A) ARMAGEDDON 1975 A&M US SP4513 UK AMLH 64513
LOUIS CENNAMO	B (A	
BOBBY CALDWELL	B PERC(A	MARTIN PUGH G (A

JOAN ARMATRADING

JOAN ARMATRADING	V G (ALL	(A) WHATEVERS FOR US 1974 CUBE 2338 023 UK HIFLY 12
RAY COOPER	PERC(A	(A) WHATEVERS FOR US 1974 A&M 4382
HENRY SPINETTI	D (ADE	(B) BACK TO THE NIGHT 1975 A&M US 4525 UK AMLH 68305
DAVEY JOHNSTONE	G (A	(C) JOAN ARMATRADING 1976 A&M US 4588 UK AMLH64588
KENNEY JONES	D (CD	(D) SHOW SOME EMOTION 1977 A&M US 4663 UK AMLH 68433
TONY CARR	D (C	(E) TO THE LIMIT 1978 A&M AMLH 64732
CHRIS KARAN	PERC(D	(F) STEPPING OUT 1979 A&M AMLH 64789
LON PRICE	WIND(F	(G) ME MYSELF I 1980 A&M AMLH 64809
DAVE BROOKS	SAX (B	(1) 1975 TOUR (2) 1975 TOUR (3) 1977 IN CONCERT TV SHOW
COLIN PINCOTT	G (B			
JEAN ROUSSEL	K (B	JOHN HALSEY	D (B	ANDY SOMERS	G (B	PETE GAGE	K G (B
BERNIE HOLLAND	G (B	SHAMSI SARUMI	PERC (B	PHIL CHEN	B (B	TONY NEWMAN	D (B
GASPAR LAWAL	PERC(B	JERRY DONAHUE	G (CD23	DAVE MATTACKS	D (C2	JIMMY JEWEL	SAX (C
B J COLE	STEEL(C	PAT DONALDSON	B (2	GERRY CONWAY	D (A	BRYAN GAROFALO	B (D3
DAVID KEMPER	D (D3	JOHN BUNDRICK	K (D	GEORGIE FAME	K (D	PETE CLARKE	V (D
JOE SCOTT	V (D	MEL COLLINS	SAX (D	TIM HINKLEY	K (D	GRAHAM LYLE	G (C
PETE WOOD	K (C	BRYN HAWORTH	G MAND(2	ALBERT LEE	G (2	QUITMAN DENNIS	SAX (E3
RED YOUNG	K (3E	PHILIP PALMER	G (E	THE MOVIES	(1	DICK SIMS	K (E
MARCUS MILLER	B (G	STEVE YORK	B HCA (B	WILL LEE	B (G	ANTON FIG	D (G
CHRIS SPEDDING	G (G	HIRAM BULLOCK	G (G	RICKY HIRSCH	G (FG	DANNY FEDERICI	K (G
PAUL SCHAEFFER	PNO (G	CLIFFORD CARTER	PNO (G	PHILLIP ST JOHN	PNO (G	CLARENCE CLEMONS	SAX (G
GEORGE KERR	V (G	SAMMY TURNER	K (F	RED YOUNG	K (F	RITCHIE HAYWARD	D (F
BILL BODINE	B (F	LARRY STEELE	B (A	DAVE MARKEE	B (CDE	RON MATHESON	B (B

A82A FRANKIE ARMSTRONG

FRANKIE ARMSTRONG	V	(AB	(A) LOVELY ON THE WATER	1972	TOPIC	12TS 216
JEFF LOWE	DULC WIND(A		(B) SONGS & BALLADS	1975	TOPIC	12TS 273
JACK WARSHAW	G BANJ(A					

A83 BILLY BOY ARNOLD

BILLY BOY ARNOLD	V HCA(ALL		(A)KING OF CHICAGO BLUES VOL 3	1975	VOGUE	30285
WITH			(B) BLOW THE BACK OFF IT	1975	RED LIGHTNIN	RL 0012
JOHNNY WALKER	PNO	(C	(C) SINNERS PRAYER	1976	RED LIGHTNIN	RL 0014
CHRIS MOSS	D	(C	(D) MORE BLUES ON THE SOUTH SIDE	19	BELLAPHON	BJS 40108
ODELL CAMPBELL	B	(BC	(E) CHECKIN' IT OUT	1979	RED LIGHTNIN	RL 0024
LOUIS MYERS	G	(C	(F) CRYING & PLEADING	1980	CHARLY	CRB 1016
SAMMY LAWHORN	G	(C				

BO DIDDLEY G (B OTIS SPANN PNO (B JEROME GREEN PERC (B FRED BELOW D (B
REYNOLDS HOWARD D (B JAMES BRADFORD B (B CLIFTON JAMES D (B HENRY GRAY PNO(B
JODY WILLIAMS G (B SUNNYLAND SLIM PNO (B MILTON RECTOR B (B EARL PHILIPS D (B
QUINN WILSON B (B SYLVESTER THOMPSON G (B MACK THOMSON G (B MIGHTY JOE YOUNG G (D
LAFAYETTE LEAKE PNO (D JEROME ARNOLD B (D JUNIOR BLACKMAN D (D TONY McPHEE G (E
WILGAR CAMPBELL D (E ALAN FISH (E

A84 P P ARNOLD

P P ARNOLD	V	(AB	(A) KAFUNTA	1968	IMMEDIATE	IMSP017
WITH			(B) GREATEST HITS	1977	IMMEDIATE	IML2006
KEITH EMERSON	K	(				
DAVY O LIST	G	(BRIAN DAVISON	D (LEE JACKSON	B	(	

A85 ARRIVAL

DYAN BIRCH	V	(ABC				
FRANK COLLINS	V	(ABC	(A) ARRIVAL	1970	DECCA	SKL5055
PADDY McHUGH	V	(ABC	(B) HEARTBREAK KID	1973	CBS	70125
TONY O'MALLEY	V	(ABC	(C) ARRIVAL	1972	CBS	64733
CARROLL CARTER	V	(ABC				

RAPHAEL PEREIRA G (C LEE SUTHERLAND B (C GLEN LEFLEUR D (C DON HUME B (A
LLOYD COURTENAY D (A RON CARTHY TPT (D ED REAY SMITH TROM (B ROY CARTER OBOE (D
PETE ZORN HRNS (D PHIL CHEN B (D

A86 ARS NOVA

JON PIERSON	TROM V(AB		(A) ARS NOVA	1968	ELEKTRA	US EKS74020
WYATT DAY	G K V (AB		(B) SUNSHINE & SHADOWS	1969	ATLANTIC	8221
WARREN BERNHARDT	K	(B	(B) SUNSHINE & SHADOWS	1969	ATLANTIC	588 196
MAURY BAKER	PERC K(A					

GIOVANNI PAPALIA G (A SAM BROWN G (B JIMMY OWENS TPT (B BILL FOLWELL TPT B V(A
ART KOENIG B (B JOE HUNT D (B JONATHAN RASKIN B V G (A

A87 ART

LUTHER GROSVENOR	G	(A	(A) SUPERNATURAL FAIRYTALES	1967	ISLAND	ILP 967
MIKE KELLIE	D	(A				
MIKE HARRISON	V K	(A	GREG RIDLEY	B	(A	

A87A ART & LANGUAGE

MAYO THOMPSON		(A	(A) CORRECTED SLOGANS	197	MUSIC LANGUAGE US	1848
JESSE CHAMBERLAIN		(				

A88 ART BEARS

FRED FRITH	G VLN K(A		(A) HOPES & FEARS	1978	RE	2188
CHRIS CUTLER	D PERC(A		(A) HOPES & FEARS	1978	RANDOM RADAR	RRR 004
DAGMAR KRAUSE	V	(A	(B) WINTER SONGS	1979	RECOMMENDED	RE 0618
GEORGE BORN	V	(A				

A89 ART ENSEMBLE OF CHICAGO

ROSCOE MITCHELL	SAX	(	(A) PHASE ONE	19	AMERICA	AM 6116
LESTER BOWIE	TPT	(	(A) PHASE ONE	19	PRESTIGE	US 10064
MALACHI FAVORS	B	(	(B) WITH FONTELLA BASS	19	AMERICA	AM 6117
JOESEPH JARMAN	WIND	(	(B) WITH FONTELLA BASS	19	PRESTIGE	PR 10049
DON MOYE	D	(	(C) SPIRITUAL	1974	POLYDOR	2383 098
FONTELLA BASS	V	(BJ	(C) SPIRITUAL	1974	FREEDOM	28 428
			(D) FANFARE FOR WARRIORS	1974	ATLANTIC	US SD 1651
			(D) FANFARE FOR WARRIORS	1977	ATLANTIC	UK K 50304
			(E) TUTAMKHAMUN	1975	FREEDOM	28 473
			(F) PEOPLE IN SORROW	19	PATHE	2C062 10523
			(F) PEOPLE IN SORROW	19	NESSA	US N3
			(G JACKS ONLY YOUR HOUSE	1978	AFFINITY	AFF 9
			(I) CHI CONGA	19	PAULA	US LPS 4001
			(J) LES STANCES A SOPHIE	19	NESSA	US N4
			(K) THE PARIS SESSION	19	FREEDOM	US AL 1903
			(K) THE PARIS SESSION (DBL)	197	FREEDOM	41106 /7
			(L) CERTAIN BLACKS	19	INNERCITY	US IC 1004
			(M) NICE GUYS	1979	ECM	ECM 1126
			(N) REESE & THE SMOOTH ONES	197	FREEDOM	AFF 22

A90 ARTFUL DODGER

STEVE BRIGADA	B PERC(		(A) ARTFUL DODGER	19	CBS	US PC 33811
STEVE COOPER	B	(	(B) HONOUR AMONG THIEVES	1976	CBS	US PC 34273
GARY COX	G V	(	(C) BABES ON BROADWAY	19	CBS	US PC 34846
GARY HERREWIG	G V	(				
BILL PALISELLI	V	(				

A91 ARTI & MESTIERI

ARTI			(A) TILT	19	BARCLAY	
MESTIERI			(B) GIRO DI VALZEPER	19	BARCLAY	940 518

A92 ARTWOODS

ART WOOD	V	(	(A) GALLERY	1964	DECCA	LK 4830
JON LORD	K	(	(A) ARTWOODS	1973	SPARK	SRLM2006
KEEF HARTLEY	D	(	(B) ART GALLERY	1974	ECLIPSE	ECS 2025
DEREK GRIFFITHS	G	(	(C) JAZZ IN JEANS (EP)	1966	DECCA	DFE 8654
MALCOLM POOL	B	(				

ASCEND
A93

AMIN MOHAMMED	SITAR B	(A	(A) CREATURES OF LIHGT & DARKNESS	1978		
CHRIS BISCOE	SAX	(A				
NICK JONES	G	(A	EDDY SAYER	D	(A	PETER LEMER	K	(A
GRAHAM SMITH	VLN	(A				

ASGARD
A94

(A) IN THE REALM OF   1972   THRESHOLD   THS 6

DOUG ASHDOWN
A95

DOUG ASHDOWN   G V   (A   (A) A WINTER IN AMERICA   1977   DECCA   TXSR 125

ASHFORD & SIMPSON
A96

NICKOLAS ASHFORD	V	(ABCDEFG	(A) GIMME SOMETHING REAL	1974	WB		K 46283
VALERIE SIMPSON	V K	(ABCDEFG	(A) GIMME SOMETHING REAL	1974	WB	US	BS 2739
WITH			(B) I WANNA BE SELFISH	1974	WB		K 56050
ERIC GALE	G	(CF	(B) I WANNA BE SELFISH	1974	WB	US	BS 2789
ELLIOTT RANDALL	G	(C	(C) COME AS YOU ARE	1976	WB		K 56159
HUGH McCRACKEN	G	(C	(C) COME AS YOU ARE	1976	WB	US	BS 2858
RICHARD TEE	K	(C	(D) SEND IT	1977	WB		K
STEVE GADD	D	(C	(D) SEND IT	1977	WB	US	BS 3088
FRANCISCO CENTENO	B	(CF	(E) SO SO SATISFIED	1977	WB	US	BS 2992
RALPH McDONALD	PERC	(CF	(F) IS IT STILL GOOD TO YOU	1978	WB		K 56547
RICK MAROTTA	D	(C	(G) KEEP IT COMING	197	TAMLA	US	T 7351
STEVE JORDAN	D	(F	(H) STAY FREE	1979	WB		K 56703
JOHN DAVID	HRNS	(F				
OHN SUSSEWELL	D	(F	JOSHIE ARMSTEAD	V	(C	JEFF MIRANOV	G	(C
RAY SIMPSON	V	(CF	DON GROLNICK	K	(C	GEORGE YOUNG	HRNS	(C
RAY CHEW	K	(F	PAUL RISER	STRINGS (F	YOLANDA McCULLOUGH	V	(F

ASHKAN
A97

STEVE BAILEY	V	(A	(A) IN FROM THE COLD	1974	NOVA	SRNR 1
RON BENDING	B V	(A				
TERRY SIMS	PERC	(A	BOB WESTON	G V	(A	

STEVE ASHLEY
A98

STEVE ASHLEY	HCA V G	(AB	(A) STROLL ON	1974	GULL	GULP1003
RICHARD BYERS	G	(B	(B) SPEEDY RETURN	1975	GULL	GULP1012
ROYSTON MITCHELL	K	(B				
MADDY PRIOR	SPOONS (B	DENNIS LOPEZ	PERC	(B	DAVE PEGG	B	(B
DAVE MATTACKS	D	(B	LYLE HARPER	B	(B	SIMON PHILLIPS	D	(B
BARRY DRANSFIELD		(A	ASHLEY HUTCHINGS	B	(A	LEA NICHOLSON		(B
SIMON NICOL	G	(A	B J COLE	STEEL	(A	CLAIRE DAWSON		(A
RAINER SCHUELEIN		(A	DANNY THOMPSON	B	(A	BRIAN DIPROVE		(A
SUE DRAHEIM		(A	REDD McREADY		(A	CHRISTOPHER TAYLOR		(A
ROYSTON WOOD		(A	THOM FRIEDLEIN		(A	CHRIS KARAN	PERC	(A
DARRYL RUNSWICK	B	(A	RICHARD TAYLOR		(A		

ASHMAN REYNOLDS
A98A

ALIKI ASHMAN	V	(A	(A) STOP OFF	1972	POLYDOR	2383 114
HARRY REYNOLDS	B G V	(A				
BOB WESTON	G	(A	MICKY KEEN	G	(A	ROD EDWARDS	K V G	(A
KEITH BOYCE	D	(A	TONY CLARKE	PERC	(A	MADELINE BELL	V	(A
LIZA STRIKE	V	(A	LADBROKE HORNS	HRNS	(A		

ASH RA
A99

MANUEL GOETTSCHING	G SYN (ALL	(A) ASH RA TEMPLE	19	OHR	OMM 556013
UDI ARNDT	G	(H	(B) SCHWINGUNGEN	19	OHR	OMM 556020
LUTZ ULBRICHT	G	(I	(C) SEVEN UP	19	KOMISCHE	KM 58001
KLAUS SCHULZE	K	(	(D) JOIN IN	19	OHR	OMM 556032
HARMUT ENKE	B G	(	(E) STARRING ROSIE	19	KOMISCHE	KM 58007
WOLFGANG MULLER	B	(	(F) INVENTIONS FOR ELECTRIC GUITAR	19	KOMISCHE	KM 58015
HARALD GROSSKOPF	D SYN (I	(F) INVENTIONS FOR ELECTRIC GUITAR	19	BARCLAY	840066
MATHIAS WEHLER	SAX	(	(G) NEW AGE OF EARTH	1977	VIRGIN	V 2080
			(G) NEW AGE OF EARTH	1977	RCA	9003
ULI POP	PERC	(	(H) BLACKOUTS	1977	VIRGIN	V 2091
			(H) BLACKOUTS	1977	POLYDOR	2373 740
			(I) CORRELATIONS	1979	VIRGIN	V 2117

MARK ASHTON
A99A

MARK ASHTON	G V	(A	(A) SOLO	1979	ARISTA	ARL 5023
WITH						
STEVE GOULD	G	(A	MICK FEAT	B	(A	PETER VAN HOOKE	D	(A
PHIL WAINMAN	D	(A	WINSTON DELANDRO	G	(A	DEREK AUSTIN	K	(A
TONY BRAUNAGEL	D	(A	TERRY WILSON	B	(A	BOB WESTON	G	(A
PETE WILLSHER	STEEL	(A	CHRIS FLETCHER	PERC	(A	MIGUEL BARRADOS	D	(A

ASHTON & LORD
A100

TONY ASHTON	K V	(A	(A) FIRST OF THE BIG BANDS	1974	PURPLE	TPS 3507
JON LORD		(A	(A) FIRST OF THE BIG BANDS	1974	PATHE	FR 2C064 95592

ASHTON GARDNER & DYKE
A101

TONY ASHTON	K V	(ABC	(A) ASHTON GARDNER & DYKE	1969	POLYDOR	583 081
KIM GARDNER	B	(ABC	(B) WHAT A BLOODY LONG DAY ITS BEEN	1972	CAPITOL	EAST 22862
ROY DYKE	D	(ABC	(C) THE WORST OF	1971	CAPITOL	EST 563
JOHN MUMSFORD	TPT	(B				
DAVE CASWELL	TPT	(B	LYLE JENKINS	WIND	(B	MICK LIBER	G	(B

ASLEEP AT THE WHEEL
A102

RAY BENSON	G V	(ABCDEFGHI	(A) COMIN' RIGHT AT YA	1973	UA		UALA 038
LUCKY OCEANS	D STEEL	(ABCDEFGHI	(A) COMIN' RIGHT AT YA	1973	UA	UK	UAS 29454
LEROY PRESTON	G D V	(ABCDEFGHI	(B) COMIN' RIGHT AT YA	1978	SUNSET	UK	SNS 50415
CHRIS O'CONNELL	V G	(ABCDEFGHI	(B) ASLEEP AT THE WHEEL	1974	EPIC	US	KE 33097
FLOYD DOMINO	PNO	(ABCDEFGHI	(C) TEXAS GOLD	1975	CAPITOL	UK	EST 11441
TONY GARNIER	B	(DFG	(D) WHEELIN 'N' DEALIN	1976	CAPITOL		EST 11546
DANNY LEVIN	MAN FDL	(CDFG(	(E) TEXAS COUNTRY (ONE SIDE)	1976	UA	US	UALA 574H2
ED VIZARD	SAX	(C	(F) THE WHEEL	1977	CAPITOL		EST 11620
SCOTT HENNIGE	D	(CD	(G) COLLISION COURSE	1978	CAPITOL		EST 11726
LINK DAVIS	FDL SAX	(DFG	(H) SERVED LIVE	1979	CAPITOL		ST 11945
JOHNNY GIMBLE	FDL	(ABCD	(I) FATHERS & SONS (DBL)1WHEEL 1 WILLS		EPIC	US	BG 33782
							(CONTINUED)

[13]

ASLEEP AT THE WHEEL

A102 (CONTINUED)

BILLY JOOR	TPT	(C
BILLY BRIGGS	SAX	(C
BOBBY WOMMACK	TPT	(C
BILL MABRY	FDL	(DFG
LINDA HARGROVE	G	(D
ELDON SHAMLIN	G	(D
GENE DOBKIN	B	(A
ANDREW STEIN	FDL	(AG
CHRIS YORK	D	(FG
PHILLIP BALLOU	V	(G

DAVID POE	SAX	(C
MIKE O'DOWD	WIND	(C
DENNIS SOLEE	SAX	(D
BUCKY MEADOWS	G	(D
JACO	WIND	(F
BUDDY SPICHER	FDL	(A
LEON RAUSCH	V	(F
DOLORES HALL	V	(G
BOB WILLS	FDL HRN	(I

TOMMY ALLSUP	B	(C
HURSHAL W WIGGINGTON	V	(C
JOEL SONNIER	ACC	(D
TINY MOORE	MAND	(D
ED FREEMAN	PNO	(
RICHARD CASONA	FDL	(A
PAT RYAN	WIND	(FG
BENNY DIGGS	V	(G
ARNETT COBB	SAX	(D

VERA & GARY ASPEY

A103

VERA ASPEY	V G	(AB
GARY ASPEY	V G	(AB
BERNARD WRIGLEY	V CONC	(A
WILF DARLINGTON	V MAND	(A

(A) FROM THE NORTH	1975	TOPIC	12TS 255
(B) A TASTE OF HOTPOT	1976	TOPIC	12TS 299

VERA ASPEY

A104

VERA ASPEY	V G	(A
DAVE GOTLIFFE	PNO	(A
JOHN LUCE	G	(A

(A) THE BLACKBIRD	1977	TOPIC	12TS 356

ASSAGAI

A105

UIS MOHOLO	D	(AB
DUDU PUKWANA	SAX	(AB
MONGEZI FEZA	TPT	(AB
BIZO MNGQIKANA	SAX	(AB
FRED COKER	G	(A
FRED FREDERICKS	SAX	(B
JON FIELD		(B

CHARLES ONONOGBO	B	(A
MARTHA MDENGE	V	(B
GLYN HAVARD		(B

TERRI QUAYE	CONGA	(B
TONY DUHIG		(B
SMILEY DE JONNES	PERC	(B

(A) ASSAGAI	1971	VERTIGO	6360 030
(B) ZIMBABWE	1972	PHILIPS	6308 079
( ) ASSAGAI	1975	CONTOUR	2879 394

ASSOCIATES

A105A

BILLY McKENZIE	(A) AFFECTIONATE PUNCH

(A) AFFECTIONATE PUNCH	1980	FICTION	UK FIX	005

ASSOCIATION

A106

RUSS GIGUERE	G V	(ABCDEFGH
JIM YESTER	SAX V G K	(ABCDEFGHIJ
TED BLUECHEL	D V	(ABCDEFGHIJ
BRIAN COLE	CLAR B V	(ABCDEFGHIJ
TERRY KIRKMAN	D V WIND	(ABCDEFGHIJ
GARY ALEXANDER	G V	(ABEGHIJ
LARRY RAMOS	SAX HCA G V	(CDEFGHIJ
RICHARD THOMPSON	G V	(IJ

(A) AND THEN...ALONG CAME ASSOCIATION	1966	VALIENT	US	VLS 25002
(A) AND THEN...ALONG CAME ASSOCIATION	1966	LONDON	UK	HAT 8305
(A) AND THEN...ALONG CAME ASSOCIATION	1966	W B	US	1702
(B) RENAISSANCE	1967	VALIENT	US	VLS 25004
(B) RENAISSANCE	1967	LONDON	UK	HAT 8313
(B) RENAISSANCE	1967	W B	US	WS 1704
(C) INSIGHT OUT	1967	LONDON	UK	MHAT 8342
(C) INSIGHT OUT	1967	WB	US	WS 1696
(D) BIRTHDAY	1968	WB	US	WS 1733
(E) GREATEST HITS	1969	WB	US	WS 1767
(F) GOODBYE COLUMBUS (SOUNDTRACK)	1969	WB	US	WS 1786
(G) ASSOCIATION	1969	WB	US	WS 1800
(H) LIVE (DBL)	1970	WB	US	2WS 1868
(I) STOP YOUR MOTOR	1971	WB	US	WS 1927
(J) WATERBEDS IN TRINIDAD	1972	CBS	UK	S 65009
(J) WATERBEDS IN TRINIDAD	1972	CBS	US	KC 31348

ASWAD

A107

BRINSLEY FORDE	PERC G V	(A
DON GRIFFITHS	PERC G V	(A
BUNNY McKENZIE	HCA	(A
COURTNEY HEMMINGS	PERC V K	(A
CANDY McKENZIE	V	(A
ADETOKUMBA ILLORIN	G	(A

GEORGE OBAN	PERC B	(A
TREVOR BOW	PERC	(A

ANGUS GAYE	D K	(A
DELROY WASHINGTON	V	(A

(A) ASWAD	1976	ISLAND	UK ILPS9399
(B) HULET	19	GROVE MUSIC	

ATACAMA

A108

(A) ATACAMA	1971	CHARISMA	UK	CAS 1039
(B) SUN BURNS UP ABOVE	1972	CHARISMA	UK	CAS 1060

PETE ATKIN

A109

PETE ATKIN	G V PNO	(ALL
STEVE COOK	B	(A
BRIAN ODGERS	B	(A
TONY MARSH	D	(A
HENRY MACKENZIE	CLAR	(A
RUSSELL DAVIES	HRNS	(A
ALBERT HALL	HRNS	(A
FRANK RICOTTI	PERC	(D
CHRIS SPEDDING	G	(BC
HERBIE FLOWERS	B	(BC
KENNY CLARE	D	(B
DENNIS CLIFT	TPT	
LEON CALVERT	HRNS	(B
DAI DAVIS	TROM	(B
ALAN PARKER	G	(B
TONY COE	WIND	(D
ALAN WAKEMAN	WIND	(BC
MIKE MORAN	K	(CD
RALPH IZEN	TPT	(C
DICK HART	TUBA	(C
RONNIE ROSS	SAX	(E

(A) BEWARE OF THE BEAUTIFUL STRANGER	1970	FONTANA	UK	6309 011
(A) BEWARE OF THE BEAUTIFUL STRANGER	1974	RCA		SF 8387
(B) DRIVING THROUGH MYTHICAL AMERICA	1971	PHILIPS		6308 070
(B) DRIVING THROUGH MYTHICAL AMERICA	1974	RCA		SF 8386
(C) A KING AT NIGHTFALL	1973	RCA		SF 8336
(D) THE ROAD OF SILK	1974	RCA		LPLI 5014
(E) SECRET DRINKER	1974	RCA		LPLI 5062
(F) LIVE LIBEL	1975	RCA		RS 1013
( ) MASTER OF REVELS (BEST OF)	1977	RCA		PL 25041
(G) RIDERS TO THE WORLDS END (CASS)	19	RCA		PK 11677

(NOTE (A) RECORDS HAVE ONE DIFFERENT TRACK)

JIM WORTLEY	TROM	(B
BARRY MORGAN	D	(BC
CLIVE BAKER	TPT	(BC
DON FAY	SAX	(B
RAY COOPER	PERC	(C
NAT PECK	TROM	(C
BOB SYDOR	WIND	(C
HOWARD BALL	STRINGS	(C

RICHARD IHNATON WIEZ	WIND	(B
DAVE BELL	B	(B
DARRYL RUNSWICK	B	(DE
BARRY DE SOUZA	D	(E
TERRY COX	D	(D
BILL GELDARD	TROM	(C
MIKE PAGE	WIND	(C
CLIVE JAMES	LYRICS	(

CHET ATKINS

A110

CHET ATKINS AT HOME	RCA	1958	LPM 1544	TEENSVILLE	RCA	1960	LPM	2161
SESSION WITH	RCA	1959	LPM 1090	TEENSVILLE	RCA UK	1960	RD	27168
STRINGING ALONG WITH	RCA	1959	LPM 1236	THE OTHER CHET ATKINS	RCA	1960	LPM	2175
IN THREE DIMENSIONS	RCA	1959	LPM 1197	WORKSHOP	RCA	1961	RD	27214
FINGER STYLE GUITAR	RCA	1959	LPM 1383	WORKSHOP	RCA	1961	LPM	2232
HI FI FOCUS	RCA	1959	LPM 1577	MOST POPULAR GUITAR	RCA	1961	LPM	2346
IN HOLLYWOOD	RCA	195	LPM 1993	& HIS GUITAR	CAMDEN	1961	CDN	160
HUM & STRUM ALONG	RCA	1959	LPM 2025	BACK HOME HYMNS	RCA	1962	LSA	2007
MISTER GUITAR	RCA	1960	LPM 2103	DOWN HOME	CAMDEN	1962	CDN	165

(CONTINUED)

[14]

DOWN HOME	RCA	1962	LSP	2450	COUNTRY PICKIN'	RCA	19		X9006
DOWN HOME	CAMDEN	1962	SND	5016	REMINISCING (HANK SNOW)	RCA	19	RD	7691
CARRIBBEAN GUITAR	RCA	1962			REMINISCING (HANK SNOW)	RCA	19	LSP	2952
CHRISTMAS WITH CHET	RCA	1962	LSP	2423	SOLID GOLD 68	RCA	1968	LSP	4061
THE POPS GOES COUNTRY	RCA	196	LSC	2870	HOMETOWN GUITAR	RCA	1968	LSP	4017
CHET PICKS ON THE POPS	RCA	196	LSC	3104	SOLID GOLD 69	RCA	1969	LSP	4244
RELAXIN' WITH CHET	RCA	19	INTS	1004	C B ATKINS & C E SNOW	RCA	1969	LSP	4254
TRAVELLIN' GUITAR	RCA	19	INTS	1141	THIS IS CHET ATKINS	MCA	19	VPS	6030
TRAVELLIN'	RCA	19	LSP	2678	BY SPECIAL REQUEST	RCA	1970	LSP	5254
THE EARLY YEARS	CAMDEN	19	CAS	659	SOLID GOLD 70	RCA	1970	LSP	4244
OUR MAN IN NASHVILLE	RCA	1963	LSP	2616	SOLID GOLD 70	RCA	1970	SF	8092
OUR MAN IN NASHVILLE	RCA	19	SE	7529	ME & JERRY	RCA	19	LSA	3033
GUITAR COUNTRY	RCA	1964	LSP2783BE		ME & JERRY	RCA	1971	LSP	4396
BEST OF	RCA	1964	LSP	2887	YESTERGROOVIN'	RCA	1970	LSP	4331
BEST OF	RCA	196	RD	7664	YESTERGROOVIN'	RCA	1970	SF	8130
& HIS OTHER GUITAR	RCA	19			ME & CHET	RCA	19	LSA	3091
PICKS ON THE POPS	RCA	19	LSC	3104	ME & CHET	RCA	1972	LSA	3091
IN CONCERT	CAMDEN	19	CPL2	1014	ME & CHET	RCA	1972	ANLI	2167
PICKIN' MY WAY	RCA	19	LSA	3051	FOR THE GOOD TIMES	RCA	1971	LSP	4464
PICKIN' MY WAY	RCA	1970	LSP	4585	NOW & THEN	RCA	1972	VPSX	6079
MY FAVOURITE GUITARS	RCA	1965	LSP	3316	NASHVILLE GOLD	RCA	1972	CAS	2551
MY FAVOURITE GUITARS	RCA	1965	RD	7710	FINGER PICKIN' GOOD	RCA	19	CAS	2600
MORE OF THAT GUITAR COUNTRY	RCA	1965	LSP	3429	PICKS THE HITS	RCA	1973	LSA	3121
TEENSCENE	RCA	19	ACLI	7005	STRUM ALONG GUITAR METHOD	RCA	1973	PRP	36932
AMERICAN SALUTE	RCA	19	LSC	3277	PICKS THE HITS	RCA	19	LSP	4754
GUITAR COUNTRY	RCA	1965			PICKS ON JERRY REED	RCA	1974	APLI	0545
PICKS ON THE BEATLES	RCA	1966	LSP	3531	SUPERPICKERS	RCA	1974	APLI	0329
BESY OF VOL 2	RCA	1965	LSP	3558	ALONE	RCA	19	APLI	0159
BEST OF VOL 2	CAMDEN	19	CAS	10261	GOES TO THE MOVIES	RCA	19	APLI	0845
PICKS ON THE BEATLES(REISSUE)	RCA	1977	ANLA	2002	THE NIGHT ATLANTA BURNED	RCA	1975	APLI	1233
BEST OF CHET ATKINS	RCA	1966			FAMOUS COUNTRY MUSIC MAKERS	RCA	1975	DPS	2063
MUSIC FROM NASHVILLE	CAMDEN	1966	CAM	981	LOVE LETTERS	CAMDEN	19	ACLI	7042
THE GUITAR GENIUS	CAMDEN	196	CDS	1067	CHET & BOOTS	CAMDEN	19	CAS	2523
THE GUITAR GENIUS	CAMDEN	19	CAS	753	THE BEST OF CHET & FRIENDS	RCA	1976	APLI	1985
FROM NASHVILLE WITH LOVE	RCA	1966			CHESTER & LESTER	RCA	1976	APLI	1167
GUITAR WORLD	RCA	1967	LSP	3728	CHESTER & LESTER	RCA	1977	LPS	3290
PICKS THE BEST	RCA	1967	LSP	3818	ME & MY GUITAR	RCA	1977	PL	12405
PICKS THE BEST	RCA	1967	ANLI	0981	CHET FLOYD & DANNY	RCA	1977	APLI	2311
MR ATKINS GUITAR PICKER	CAMDEN	196	CDS	1090	GUITAR MONSTERS (LES PAUL)	RCA	1978	PL	1286
MR ATKINS GUITAR PICKER	CAMDEN	196	CASX2464E		GUITAR MONSTERS (LES PAUL)	RCA	1978	APLI	2786
CLASS GUITAR	RCA	1967			LEGENDARY PERFORMER	RCA	1978	PL	12503
CHET	CAMDEN	1967	CDS	1014	FIRST NASHVILLE GUIT QUARTET	RCA	1979	AHLI	3302
SOLO FLIGHTS	RCA	1968	LSP	3922					
SOLO FLIGHTS	RCA	1968	RD	7934					

ATLANTA RHYTHM SECTION   A111

PAUL GODDARD	B G	(ABCDEFGHI	(A) ATLANTA RHYTHM SECTION		1972	MCA		MAPS 5594
BARRY BAILEY	G B	(ABCDEFGHI	(A) ATLANTA RYHTHM SECTION		1972	MCA	US	2 4114
J R COBB	G B	(ABCDEFGHI	(B) BACK UP AGAINST THE WALL		1974	MCA		MCF 2670
RONNIE HAMMOND	V	(BCDEFGHI	(B) BACK UP AGAINST THE WALL		1974	MCA	IMP	MAPS 6465
DEAN DAUGHTRY	K	(ABCDEFGHI	(C) THIRD ANNUAL PIPE DREAM		1975	POLYDOR	UK	2391 136
ROBERT NIX	D	(ABCDEFGHI	(C) THIRD ANNUAL PIPE DREAM		1975	POLYDOR	US	6027
RODNEY JUSTO	V	(A	(D) DOG DAYS		1976	POLYDOR	UK	2391 179
BILLY LEE RILEY	HCA	(B	(D) DOG DAYS		1976	POLYDOR	US	6041
MYLON LEFEVRE	V	(C	(E) RED TAPE		1976	POLYDOR	UK	2391 223
HUGH BABY JARRET	V	(C	(E) RED TAPE		1976	POLYDOR	US	PDI 6060
MIKE HUEY	CONGA	(C	(F) ROCK'N'ROLL ALTERNATIVE		1977	POLYDOR	UK	2391 255
JO JO BILLINGSLEY	V	(G	(F) ROCK'N'ROLL ALTERNATIVE		1977	POLYDOR	US	PDI 6080
PAUL DAVIS	V	(G	(G) CHAMPAGNE JAM		1978	POLYDOR	UK	2391 319
ARTIMUS PYLE	PERC	(G	(G) CHAMPAGNE JAM		1978	POLYDOR	US	PDI 6134
ROY YEAGER	D	(I	(H) ARE YOU READY	(DBL)	19	POLYDOR	UK	2672 050
			(H) ARE YOU READY	(DBL)	19	POLYDOR	US	PD2 6236
			(I) UNDERDOG		1979	POLYDOR	UK	2391 398
			(J) THE BOYS FROM DORAVILLE		1980	POLYDOR		2391 467

ATLANTIC BRIDGE   A112

(A) ATLANTIC BRIDGE		1971	DAWN		DNLS 3014
(B) I CANT LIE TO YOU (EP)		1971	DAWN		DNX 2507

ATLANTIS   A113

GASPAR LAWAL	PERC	(B	(A) ATLANTIS	1973	VERTIGO	UK	6360 609
INGA RUMPF	V PERC	(ABC	(B) ITS GETTING BETTER	1974	VERTIGO	UK	6360 614
JEAN JACQUES KRAVETZ	K	(ABC	(C) ATLANTIS	1974	POLYDOR	US	PD 6513
KARLHEINZ SCHOTT	B	(BC	(C) ATLANTIS	1974	POLYDOR	UK	2391 176
RINGO FUNK	D	(BC					
DIETER BORNSCHLEGEL	G	(B	REEBOP BAAH	PERC	(A	JEAN ROUSSEL	K	(A
LINDA FIELD	V	(C	JACKIE DIEZ	V	(A	FRANK DIEZ		(A
ADRIAN ASKEW	K G V	(C	ALEX CONTI	G V	(C	JASPER VANT'HOF	PNO	(C

ATOLL   A114

MICHEL TAILLEY	K	(AB	(A) L'ARAIGNEE MAL	1975	EURODISC	913	002
RICHARD AUBERT	VLN	(A	(B) TERTIOS	1978	ARIOLA	ARL	5008
CHRISTIAN BEYA	G	(AB					
ANDRE BALZER	PERC	(AB	ALAIN GOZZO	D	(AB	JEAN LUC THILLOT	B	(AB

A115 — ATOMIC ROOSTER

Member	Inst		Album		Year	Label		Country	Cat	
VINCENT CRANE	K	(ABCDEFGH	(A) ATOMIC ROOSTER		1970	B &C		UK	CAS	1010
CARL PALMER	D	(A	(B) DEATH WALKS BEHIND YOU		1970	B & C		UK	CAS	2026
NICK GRAHAM	B	(A	(B) DEATH WALKS BEHIND YOU		1970	ELEKTRA		US	EKS	74094
RICK PARNELL	D	(DE	(C) IN HEARING OF		1971	PEGASUS		UK	PEG	1
STEVE BOLTON	G	(D	(C) IN HEARING OF		1971	B&C		UK		
JOHN MANDELLA	G	(E	(D) MADE IN ENGLAND		1972	DAWN			DNLS3038	
CHRIS FARLOWE	V	(DE	( ) ATOMIC ROOSTER IV		19	ELEKTRA		US	EKS	75074
JOHN CANN	G	(BC	(E) NICE & GREASY		1973	DAWN		UK	DNLS	3049
PAUL HAMMOND	D	(BC	(F) ASSORTMENT		1974	B & C		UK	CS	9
DORIS TROY	V	(D	(G) HOME TO ROOST		1977	MOONCREST		UK	CDR	2
LIZA STRIKE	V	(D	(H) ATOMIC ROOSTER		1980	EMI		UK	EMC	3341
BILL SMITH	B	(D	(I) THIS IS ATOMIC ROOSTER		1977	BRAIN		GER	200	151
PETER FRENCH	V	(C								
PRESTON HEYMAN	D	(H								

A116 — ATTITUDES

Member	Inst		Album		Year	Label		Country	Cat	
DANNY KOOTCH	G	(AB	(A) ATTITUDES		1975	DARK HORSE			AMLH22008	
JIM KELTNER	D	(AB	(B) GOOD NEWS		1977	DARK HORSE		K	56385	
PAUL STALLWORTH	B V	(AB	(B) GOOD NEWS		1977	DARK HORSE		US	3021	
DAVID FOSTER	K	(AB								

WITH

			CARMEN TWILLIE	V	(A	KATHRYN COLLIER	V	(A		
VENETTE GLOUD	V	(A	CHUCK HIGGINS	V	(AB	PAT MURPHY	CONGA(AB			
COSMO DE AGUERO	CONGA	(A	JESSE ED DAVIS	G	(A	VINCE CHARLES	PERC	(Ab		
WADDY WACHTEL	G	B	TOWER OF POWER	HRNS	(B	DONNY GERRARD	V	(B		
MARVIN BRAXTON	HCA	(B	JAY LEWIS	G	(B	GEORGE BELL	FLT	(B		
JAY GRAYDON	G	(B	EMIL RICHARDS	PERC	(B	JORGE CALDERON	V	(B		
RINGO STARR	D	(B	BOOKER T JONES	K	(B	YVONNE RANKIN	V	(B		

A117 — AUBREY SMALL

Member	Inst		Album		Year	Label		Country	Cat	
PETER PINCKNEY	G V	(A	(A) AUBREY SMALL		1971	POLYDOR		UK	2383	048
ROD TAYLOR	K V	(A								
ALAN CHRISTMAS	G	(A	DAVID YEARLEY	B	(A	GRAHAM HUNT	D G V(A			

A118 — AUDIENCE

Member	Inst		Album		Year	Label		Country	Cat	
TONY CONNOR	D	(BCD	(A) AUDIENCE		1969	POLYDOR			583	065
HOWARD WERTH	V G	(BCD	(A) AUDIENCE		19	CHARISMA			CS	7
GUS DUDGEON	PERC	(C	(B) FRIENDS FRIENDS FRIENDS		1970	CHARISMA			CAS	1012
TREVOR WILLIAMS	B	(BCD	(C) HOUSE ON THE HILL		1971	CHARISMA			CAS	1032
KEITH GEMMELL	SAX	(BCD	(C) HOUSE ON THE HILL		1971	ELEKTRA		US	EKS	74100
JIM PRICE	HRNS	(D	(D) LUNCH		1972	CHARISMA		UK	CAS	1054
BOBBY KEYS	SAX	(D	(D) LUNCH		1972	ELEKTRA		US	EKS	75026
NICK JUDD	K	(D	(E) YOU CANT BEAT THEM		1973	CHARISMA				

A119 — MICK AUDSLEY

Member			Album		Year	Label			Cat	
MICK AUDSLEY			(A) DARK & DEVIL WATERS		1973	SONET			SNTF	641
			(B) STORYBOARD		1974	SONET			SNTF	659

A120 — BRIAN AUGER

Member	Inst		Album			Year	Label		Country	Cat	
BRIAN AUGER	K V	(ALL	(A) OPEN			1967	MARMALADE			607	002
WITH			(B) DEFINITELY WHAT			1968	MARMALADE			607	003
JIMMY PAGE	G	(M	(B) DEFINITELY WHAT			1968	ATCO		US	SD33	273
JULIE DRISCOLL(TIPPETTS)	V(ACORS		(C) STREETNOISE	(DBL)		1968	MARMALADE			608005/6	
RICK LAIRD	B	(	(C) STREETNOISE	(DBL)		1968	KARUSSELL		IMP	2674	014
PHIL KINORRA	D	(	(D) BEFOUR			1970	RCA		UK	SF	8101
JOHN McLAUGHLIN	G	(	(D) BEFOUR			1970	RCA		US	LSP	4372
GLEN HUGHES	SAX	(	(E) OBLIVION EXPRESS			1971	RCA			SF	8170
RICK BROWN	B	(MS	(E) OBLIVION EXPRESS			1971	RCA		US	AFLI	4462
MICK WALLER	D	(MS	(F) A BETTER LAND			1971	POLYDOR			2383	042
LONG JOHN BALDRY	V	(	(F) A BETTER LAND			1971	RCA		US	LSP	4540
ROD STEWART	V	(	(G) SECOND WIND			1972	POLYDOR			2383	104
VIC BRIGGS	G	(S	(G) SECOND WIND			1972	RCA		US	AFLI	4703
DAVE AMBROSE	B	(ABCDR	(H) CLOSER TO IT			1973	CBS				65625
GARY BOYLE	G	(DR	(H) CLOSER TO IT			1973	RCA		US	AFLI	0140
CLIVE THACKER	D	(ABCDRS	(J) STRAIGHT AHEAD			1974	CBS				80058
BARRY REEVES	D	(D	(J) STRAIGHT AHEAD			1974	RCA		US	AFLI	0454
COLIN ALLEN	D	(D	(K) LIVE OBLIVION	VOL 1		1974	RCA		US	ANLI	2481
JACK MILLS	G	(HJKLN	(L) LIVE OBLIVION	VOL 2	(DBL)	1974	RCA		US	CPL2	1230
STEVE FERRONE	D	(JKL	(M) JAM SESSION			1975	CHARLY		UK	CR	30011
ROGER SUTTON	B	(DS	(N) HAPPINESS HEARTACHES			1977	WB			K	56326
BARRY DEAN	G	(EFGHJKL	(N) HAPPINESS HEARTACHES			1977	WB		US	BS	2981
JIM MULLEN	G	(EFG	(O) ENCORE			1978	WB			K	56458
ROBBIE McINTOSH	D	(EFG	(O) ENCORE			1978	WB		US	BSK	3153
GODFREY MACLEAN	D	(H	(P) BEST OF BRIAN AUGER & TRINITY			1970	POLYDOR			2334	004
MIRZA AL SHARIF	PERC	(J	(Q) BRIAN AUGER & THE TRINITY			19	POLYDOR			2384	042
DAVE CRIGGER	D	(O	(R) GENESIS			1975	POLYDOR			2383	277
JESSICA SMITH	V	(O	(R) GENESIS			1975	POLYDOR		US	PDI	6505
CLEM CATTINI	D	(S	(S) LONDON 1964 67			1977	CHARLY			CR	300019
ALEX LIGERTWOOD	V	(GKLN	( ) THIS IS			1975	METRONOME		IMP	200149	
LENNOX LAINGTON		(HJN	( ) STAR PORTRAIT			19	POLYDOR			2625	008
DAVID McDANIELS	B	(O	( ) BRIAN AUGER			19	SPRINGBOARD		US	SPB	4044
GEORGE DOERING	G	(O	( ) THE BEST OF BRIAN AUGER			19	RCA		US	AFLI	2249
MAXINE WILLARD	V	(O	( ) REINFORCEMENTS			19	RCA			AFLI	1210
LENNY WHITE	D	(N									
CLIVE CHAMAN	B	(N	SONNY BOY WILLIAMSON (RICE MILLER) HCA (M			JOE HARRIOT	SAX	(M			
ALAN SKIDMORE	SAX	(M									

MIKE AULDRIDGE — A121

MIKE AULDRIDGE DOBRO V G (A
WITH
DAVID BROMBERG G (AB
BEN ELDRIDGE BAN G (AB
VASSAR CLEMENTS FDL (AB
CHARLIE WALLER G (A
BUCK GRAVES DOB (A
BILL EMERSON BANJO (A
JOHN DUFFY G MAND(AB
ED FERRIS B (A
JEFF NEWMAN (E
BOB LAWRENCE D (A
TOM GUIDERA G (B
PAUL CRAFT G (B

DOYLE LAWSON G (AB
STEVE BURGH B (A
JOHN STARLING G (B
GERRY MULE G (B
FAYSSOUX STARLING V (B

TOM GREY B (AB
BILL YATES B (A
RICK SCAGGS G (B
LOWELL GEORGE G (B
LINDA RONSTADT V (B

(A) DOBRO — 1974 SONET SNTF 657
(A) DOBRO — 197 TAKOMA US TAK 1033
(B) BLUES & BLUEGRASS — 1977 SONET UK SNTF 673
(B) BLUES & BLUEGRASS — 1974 TAKOMA US 1041
(C) MIKE AULDRIDGE — 19 FLYING FISH US FF029+FLY 0003
(D) OLD DOG — 19 FLYING FISH US FF054+FLY 0004
(E) SLIDIN' SMOKE — 1979 FLYING FISH US FF080

AURACLE — A122

BILL STAEBELL B (AB
RON WAGNER D (AB
RICHARD C BRAUN TPT (AB
STEPHEN KUJALA WIND (AB
BIFF HANNON PNO (B
DONNA DELORY V (B
STEVE JOHNSON HRNS (B
TIM MAY G (B

STEVEN REHBEIN PERC (AB
STACEY O'BRIEN V (B
LEE RITENOUR G (B
ROBERT PAYNE HRNS (B
AFREEKA TREES V (B

JOHN SERRY JNR K (A
GLORIA O'BRIEN V (B
JEFF TKAZYAK HRNS (B
STACEY CLINGER V (B
GLORIA GOLDSMITH V (B

(A) GLIDER — 1978 CHRYSALIS CHR 1172
(B) CITY SLICKER — 1979 CHRYSALIS CHR 1210

PATTI AUSTIN — A123

PATTI AUSTIN V (AB
WITH
DAVE GRUSIN PNO (B
ERIC GALE G (AB
WILL LEE B (B
MICHAEL BRECKER SAX (AB
ANTHONY JACKSON B (B
ALAN RUBIN TPT (B
GERRY NIEWOOD SAX (B
LANI GROVES V (B
KEN WILLIAMS V (B
RANDY BRECKER HRNS (A

STEVE KHAN G (AB
STEVE JORDAN D (B
RICHARD TEE K (AB
DAVE VALENTIN PERC (B
MARVIN STAMM TPT (B
LOU MARINI SAX (B
GWEN GUTHRIE V (B
JEFF BERLIN B (A
STRINGS (B

HUGH McCRACKEN G (B
RALPH McDONALD PERC (B
FRANCISCO CENTENO B (B
FRANK GRAVIS B (B
WAYNE ANDRE TROM (B
RONNIE CUBER SAX (B
YOLANDA McCULLOUGH V (B
STEVE GADD D (A
GLORIA AGOSTINI HARP (A

(A) END OF A RAINBOW — 1976 CTI CTI 5001
(B) HAVANA CANDY — 1977 CTI CTI 5006

SIL AUSTIN — A124

SIL AUSTIN SAX (

( ) HONEY SAX — 19 POLYDOR 583 758
( ) SLOW ROCK ROCK — 19 WING US MGW 12168
( ) EVERYTHINGS SHAKIN' — 19 MERCURY US MG 20320

AUTOGRAPHS — A125

RAGGY LEWIS G
CHRIS GENT SAX V
DAVE SPICER B

JIM WARD G (
PAUL TULLEY D

AUTOMATIC FINE TUNING — A126

PAT McDONNELL G (A
ROBERT CROSS G (A
DAVID BALL D (A

TREVOR DARKS B (A

(A) AUTOMATIC FINE TUNING — 1976 CHARISMA CAS 1122

AUTOMATIC MAN — A127

MICHAEL SHRIEVE D (A
PAT THRALL G V (AB
BAYETE K V (AB
DON HARVEY B (AB

JEROME RIMSON B (B
GLENN SYMMONDS D (B

(A) AUTOMATIC MAN — 1976 ISLAND ILPS 9397
(B) VISITORS — 1977 ISLAND ILPS 9429

AUTOMATICS — A128

RICKY ROCKET D K
DAVID PHILP V G
WALLY PIERCE V

BOBBY COLLINS B V

AUTOSALVAGE — A129

THOMAS DANAHER V G (A
DARIUS DAVENPORT V G K B (A
RICK TURNER DULC BANJO G(A

SKIP BOONE B PNO (A

(A) AUTOSALVAGE — 1968 RCA US LSP3940

AVENGERS — A130

PENELOPE HOUSTON V
GREG INGRAHAM G
JIMMY WILSEY B

DANNY F D

AVERAGE WHITE BAND — A131

ALAN GORRIE V G B (ALL
HAMISH STUART V G B (ALL
ROGER BALL K SAX (ALL
ONNIE McINTYRE V G (ALL
MALCOLM DUNCAN SAX (ALL
ROBBIE McINTOSH D (ABCD
STEVE FERRONE D (FGHJ
WITH
CORNELL DUPREE G (H
RANDY BRECKER HRNS (BEHJ
MICHAEL BRECKER HRNS (BEHJ
BEN E KING V (G
MARVIN STAMM TPT (BE
KEN BISCHEL K (B
AIRTO MOREIRA PERC (J
LEW DELGATTO SAX (HJ
MEL DAVIS TPT (B
DEBRA GRAY V (B
RALPH McDONALD PERC (B
LUIS DOS SANTOS (J
LUTHER VANDROSS V (J
BARRY ROGERS TROM (EH
DAVE BRIGATI V (E
NICHOLAS MARRERO PERC (G

RAY BARRETTO CONGA (CH
TOM MALONE TROM (H
JIM MULLEN G (E
EDDIE BRIGATI V (E
ZECA DA CUICA (J

GLENN FERRIS TROM (B
RONNIE CUBER SAX (E
CARLOS MARTIN PERC (E
RUBENS BASSINI PERC (H
ROBIN CLARK V (H

(A) SHOW YOUR HAND — 1973 MCA MUPS 486
(A) SHOW YOUR HAND — 1974 MCA MCF 2514
(B) AVERAGE WHITE BAND — 1974 ATLANTIC UK K 50058
(B) AVERAGE WHITE BAND — 1974 ATLANTIC US QD 7308
(C) CUT THE CAKE — 1975 ATLANTIC UK K 50146
(C) CUT THE CAKE — 1975 ATLANTIC US SD 18140
(D) PUT IT WHERE YOU WANT IT — 1975 MCA MCF 2705
(D) PUT IT WHERE YOU WANT IT — 1975 MCA US 475
(E) SOUL SEARCHIN' — 1976 ATLANTIC UK K 50272
(E) SOUL SEARCHIN' — 1976 ATLANTIC US SD 18179
(F) PERSON TO PERSON — 1976 ATLANTIC UK K 60127
(F) PERSON TO PERSON — 1976 ATLANTIC US 2 1002
(G) BENNY & US — 1977 ATLANTIC UK K 50384
(G) BENNY & US — 1977 ATLANTIC US SD 19105
(H) WARMER COMMUNICATIONS — 1978 RCA UK XL 13053
(H) WARMER COMMUNICATIONS — 1978 ATLANTIC US SD 19162
(J) FEEL NO FRET — 1979 RCA UK XL 13063
(NB) (D) IS A SLIGHTLY DIFFERENT REISSUE OF (A)

[17]

AVIARY

A131A

Musician	Instr.	
BRAD LOVE	K V	(A
PAUL MADDEN	K	(A
KEN STEINMONTS	B V	(A
TOBY BOWEN	G	(A

A131B

Musician	Instr.	
MICK ROGERS	G V	(AB
CLIVE BUNKER	D	(AB
JOHN G PERRY	B V	(AB
JACK LANCASTER	WIND	(A

A131C

Musician	Instr.	
MICHAEL TURPIN	B V	(AB
TEDDY MUELLER	D	(AB
BOBBY BARTH	G V	(AB
EDGAR RILEY JR.	K V	(AB
MICHAEL OSBORNE	G V	(AB

Album		Year	Label		Cat.	
(A) AVIARY		1979	EPIC	UK	EPC	83572
(A) AVIARY		1979	EPIC	US	JE	35716

RICHARD BRYANS   D V   (A

AVIATOR

Album		Year	Label		Cat.	
(A) AVIATOR		1979	HARVEST	UK	SHSP	4096
(B) TURBULENCE		1980	HARVEST	UK	SHSP	4107

AXE

Album		Year	Label		Cat.	
(A) AXE		1979	MCA	UK	MCF	3033
(B) LIVING ON THE EDGE		1980	MCA	UK	MCA	3224

DAVID AXELROD

A131D

Musician	Instr.	
DAVID AXELROD	V	(ALL
WITH		
NDUGU LEON CHANCLER	D	(C
MAILTO CORREA	PERC	(C
JIM HUGHART	B	(C
GARY COLEMAN	VIBES	(AC
BILLY FENDER	G	(C
EUGENE SNOOKYYOUNG	TPT	(C
JEROME RICHARDSON	SAX	(C
GENE CIPRIANO	WIND	(C
ARNOLD BELNICK		(A
ALVIN DINKIN		(B
FREDDIE HILL	TPT	(A
TONY TERRAN		(A
RICHARD LEITH	TROM	(A
OLLIE MITCHELL	TPT	(A
NATHAN ROSS		(A
HENRY SIGISMONTI	WIND	(A

Album		Year	Label		Cat.	
(A) SONGS OF INNOCENCE		1968	CAPITOL	UK	ST	2982
(A) SONGS OF INNOCENCE		1975	CAPITOL		ST	11362
(B) THE AUCTION		1974	MCA		MCF	2664
(C) SERIOUSLY DEEP		1975	POLYDOR	US	PD	6050
(C) SERIOULY DEEP		1975	POLYDOR	UK	2391	193

Musician	Instr.	
JOHN MORELL	G	(C
JIMMY CLEVELAND	TROM	(C
ERNIE WATTS	WIND	(C
JOE SAMPLE	K	(C
AL CASEY	G	(B
ALLEN DI RIENZO		(A
BILL HINSHAW		(A
PETE WYANT		(A
ARTHUR MANEBE	HRNS	(A
EARL PALMER	D	(A
MYRON SANDLER		(A
MARSHALL SOSSON		(A

Musician	Instr.	
STRINGS		(A
DICK HYDE	TROM	(C
JAY MIGLIORI	WIND	(C
BENJAMIN BARRETT		(A
VINCENT DE ROSA	HRNS	(A
GENE ESTES	PERC	(A
HARRY HYAMS		(A
CAROLE KAYE	B	(A
LEW McCREARY	HRNS	(A
HOWARD ROBERTS	G	(A
HAROLD SCHNEIER		(A

AXISPOINT

A131E

Musician	Instr.	
EDDIE HARDIN	K V	(AB
CHARLIE WITNEY	G	(AB
CHARLIE McCRACKEN	B V	(AB
ROB TOWNSEND	D	(AB
LES BINKS	D	(A

Album		Year	Label		Cat.	
(A) AXIS POINT		1979	RCA		PL	30039
(B) BOAST OF THE TOWN		1980	RCA		PL	25277

JOHN GUSTAFSON   B   (A
COLIN JENNINGS   PERC   (A

LOUIE AUSTIN   V   (A

HOYT AXTON

A132

Musician	Instr.	
HOYT AXTON	G V	(ALL
WITH		
MIKE BOTTS	D	(LJ
EMORY GORDY	B	(HL
DAVID JACKSON	PNO B	(JHL
GUSTAVO RAMOS	TPT	(L
FRANCISCO ARELLANO	TPT	(L
SAMMY CREASON	D	(HL
MIKE UTLEY	K	(HL
JAMES BURTON	G	(JHL
RED RHODES	STEEL	(HL
RENEE ARMAND	V	(LHJ
RALPH MOONEY	STEEL	(HL
JEFF PORCARO	D	(L
HANK DE VITO ,	STEEL	(L
ED KOLLIS	HCA	(L
BOB WILSON	K	(L
DANA BRADY	V	(HL
WILLIAM GRIFFIN	V	(L
WARREN MOORE	V	(L
RONEE BLAKLEY	V	(HL
MARK DAWSON	G V	(HJLM
JEFF BAXTER	G	(LMJ
ROGER JOHNSON	AUTOHARP	(LJ
BOB LIND	G	(H
MAX BENNETT	B	(L
JIM KELTNER	D	(HL
HOWARD KAYLAN	V	(HL
MIKE OMARTIAN	K	(L
MARC EDELSTEIN	V	(L
DONNA WEISS	V	(L
CATHY SMITH	V	(L
LINDA RONSTADT	V	(HL
DICK HYDE	TROM	(L
LEE SKLAR	B	(HL
MAC GAYDEN	G	(L
TERRY REID	G	(H
MILT HOLLAND	PERC	(H
MERRY CLAYTON	V	(H
DENNY BROOKS	V	(H
DONNA ROBERTS	K	(H
PETE GRANT	AUTOHARP	(M
JIM MESSINA	G	(M
PAUL LEWINSON	K	(J
JOHN GUERIN	D	(J
GEORGE CLINTON	PNO	(J
JOHN HARTFORD	FDL	(J
TOM SCOTT	WIND	(L

Album		Year	Label		Cat.	
(A) GREENBACK DOLLAR		1964	STATESIDE	UK	SL	10082
(A) GREENBACK DOLLAR		1964	HORIZON	US		1601
(B) THUNDER & LIGHTNIN'		1964	STATESIDE	UK	SL	10096
(B) THUNDER & LIGHTNIN'		196	HORIZON	US		1613
(C) EXPLODES		196	JOY		JOYS	119
(C) EXPLODES		196	VEE JAY	US	VJS	1098
(D) SINGS BETTY SMITH		196	EXODUS	US	EX	301
(E) JOY TO THE WORLD		196	CAPITOL	US	EST	788
(F) SATURDAYS CHILD		196	VEE JAY	US	VJS	1127
(G) COUNTRY ANTHEM		19	CAPITOL			SMAS850
(H) LIFE MACHINE		1974	A&M			AMLH63604
(H) LIFE MACHINE		1974	A&M	US		3604
(I) LESS THAN A SONG		1973	A&M			AMLH64376
(I) LESS THAN A SONG		197	A&M	US		4376
(J) SOUTHBOUND		1975	A&M			AMLH64510
(J) SOUTHBOUND		1975	A&M	US		5410
(K) FEARLESS		1976	A&M			AMLH64571
(K) FEARLESS		1976	A&M	US		4571
(L) ROADSONGS		1977	A&M			AMLH64669
(L) ROADSONGS		1977	A&M	US		4669
(M) SNOW BLIND FRIEND		1977	MCA		MCF	2803
(M) SNOW BLIND FRIEND		1977	MCA	US		2263
(N) MY GRIFFIN IS GONE		197	CBS	US		33103
(O) A RUSTY OLD HALO		1979	JEREMIAH	US	JH	5000
( ) FREE SAILIN'		1978	MCA	UK	MCF	2831

Musician	Instr.	
LOREN NEWKIRK	PNO	(LH
LARRY CARLTON	G	(L
JOE SAMPLE	K	(L
CLAUDIA LENNEAR	V	(L
ROBERT ROGERS	V	(L
LARRY MUHOBERAC	PNO	(L
JERRY SCHEFF	B	(JL
JOHN ROTELLA	CLAR	(L
TEDA BRACCI	V	(L
KARL HIMMEL	D	(L
DR ERIC HORD	G	(H
LEE MONTGOMERY	V	(HJ
SHIRLEY MATTHEWS	V	(H
MIMI FARINA	V	(M
JACK SKINNER	B	(M
GARY WATTMAN	D	(M
BYRON BERLINE	FDL MAN	(M
JOHNNY ROTELLA	WIND	(J
JOE LAMANO	B	(J
MARTY HOWARD	G	(J
FRANK REKARD	G	(J
ERNIE CARLSON	TROM	(L

Musician	Instr.	
MARK VOLMAN	V	(HL
BEN BENAY	G	(L
GARY COLEMAN	PERC	(L
DONNA WASHBURN	V	(L
RONALD WHITE	V	(L
NICOLETTE LARSON	V	(L
GEORGE CLINTON	PNO	(L
GAIL DAVIES	TAMB	(JL
RON CORNELIUS	G	(L
TIM DRUMMOND	B	(L
DOUG DILLARD	BANJ V	(HJ
CLYDIE KING	V	(H
SKITCHY WASHBURN	V	(H
KATHY WARD	V	(M
ALAN THORNHILL	G	(M
PIERRE LA PORTE	HCA	(M
VICTOR FELDMAN	PERC	(J
DICK HYDE	TROM	(J
MAX BENNETT	B	(J
DICK ROSMINI	G	(JL
JUDY ELLIOTT	V	(J

KEVIN AYERS

KEVIN AYERS	V G	(ALL	(A) JOY OF A TOY		1970	HARVEST	UK	SHVL 763
WITH			(B) SHOOTING AT THE MOON		1971	HARVEST	UK	SHSP 4005
TONY CARR	D	(CH	(AB)JOY OF A TOY/SHOOTING AT THE MOON	1975	HARVEST DBL	UK	SHDW 407
JOHN VAN DERRICK	VLN	(C	(AB)JOY OF A TOY/SHOOTING AT THE MOON	19	PATHE DBL	FR	C18452277/8
ROBERT WYATT	D V	(ABCDF	(C) WHATEVERSHEBRINGSWESING		1972	HARVEST	UK	SHVL 800
ROB TAIT	D	(A	(D) BANANAMOUR		1973	HARVEST	UK	SHVL 807
DIDIER MALHERBE	SAX	(C	(CD)WHATEVERSHEBRINGSWESING/BANANAMOUR		PATHE DBL	FR	C15052507/8
MIKE RATLEDGE	K	(ABDE	(E) CONFESSIONS OF DR DREAM	1974	ISLAND	UK	ILPS 9263
HUGH HOPPER	B	(A	(F) JUNE 1st 1974		1974	ISLAND	UK	ILPS 9291
DAVID BEDFORD	K	(ABCDH	(G) SWEET DECEIVER		1975	ISLAND	UK	ILPS 9322
LOL COXHILL	SAX	(BEH	(H) ODD DITTIES		1976	HARVEST	UK	SHSM 2005
MIKE OLDFIELD	G	(BCEHF	(J) YES WE HAVE NO MANANAS	1976	HARVEST	UK	SHSP 4057
WILLIAM MURRAY		(C	(J) YES WE HAVE NO MANANAS	1976	ABC	US	ABC 1021
RICHARD SINCLAIR	B	(BH	(K) RAINBOW TAKEAWAY		1978	HARVEST	UK	SHSP 4085
DAVE DUFORT	D	(CH						
GERRY FIELD	VLN	(C	HOWIE CASEY	G	(D	ROY SMITH—FIELD	PICC (H
ARCHIE LEGGET	B	(DFH	DAVE CASWELL	TPT	(D	MICK FINCHER	D (H
KEITH BATCHELOR	FLT	(H	LYLE JENKINS	SAX	(D	RICHARD COUGHLAN	D (H
ROB TOWNSEND	D	(JK	TRISTAM FRY	PERC	(D	DAVE SINCLAIR	K (H
BILLY LIVSEY	K	(JK	OLLIE HALSALL	B G	(EFGJK	B J COLE	STEEL(J
RICK WILLS	B	(J	MARK WARNER	G	(E	TONY NEWMAN	D (J
EDDIE SPARROW	PERC	(DHF	SAMMY MITCHELL	G	(E	ROGER POPE	D (J
RON PRICE	PNO	(DH	RUPERT HINE	K	(E	RAY COOPER	PERC (E
LIZA STRIKE	V	(DH	JOHN PERRY	B	(E	SEAN MILLIGAN	V (H
BARRY ST JOHN	V	(DH	MIKE GILES	D	(E	LADYBIRDS	V (H
DORIS TROY	V	(DEH	ROSETTA HIGHTOWER	V	(E	JOHN ALTMAN	CLAR (G
GEORGE ZOOT MONEY	K	(J	CHARLIE McCRACKEN	B G	(JK	DUNCAN BROWN	TPT (H
JACOB MAGNUSSON	V K	(G	CAL BATCHELOR	G	(E	CHARLIE ROSE	HRNS (G
BRIDGET ST JOHN	V	(BH	RONNIE EADES	HRNS	(G	HENRY CRALLAN	PNO (E
HARRISON CALLOWAY	HRNS	(G	JOANNE WILLIAMS	V	(E	STEVE NYE	ORG (E
STEVE HILLAGE	G	(D	HARRY SMITH		(H	MIKE MORAN	PNO (E
FRED SMITH	D	(G	ELTON JOHN	PNO	(G	NICO	V (E
BIAS BOSHELL	PNO	(G	CHILI CHARLES	D	(G	MICK FEAT	B (J
ANDY ROBERTS	G	(J	NICK ROWLEY	K	(J	FUZZY SAMUELS	B (G
TREVOR JONES	B	(E	JOHN GUSTAFSON	B	(E	HARVEY THOMPSON	HRNS (G
GRAHAM PRESKETT	VLN	(K	BARRY DE SOUZA	D	(K	ROGER SAUNDERS	G (J
ANTHONY MOORE		(K	DAEVID ALLEN		(B	HULLOO CHOIR	V (E
BRIAN ENO	V SYN	(F	JOHN CALE	VIOLA	(F	RABBIT BUNDRICK	K (F

ROY AYERS

ROY AYERS			( ) VIRGO VIBES		19	ATLANTIC	US	SD 1488
WAYNE HENDERSON		(*	( ) DADDY BUG & FRIEND		19	ATCO	US	SD 1692
			( ) UBIQUITY		1975	POLYDOR	US	PD 6046
			( ) TEARS TO A SMILE		19	POLYDOR	US	
			( ) MYSTIC VOYAGE		1975	POLYDOR	US	PD 6057
			( ) RED BLACK & GREEN		197	POLYDOR	US	PD 1-6078
			( ) VIBRATIONS		1976	POLYDOR	UK	2391 256
			( ) EVERYBODY LOVES THE SUNSHINE	1976	POLYDOR	US	PD 16070
			( ) LIFELINE		1977	POLYDOR	UK	2391 292
			( ) YOU SEND ME		1978	POLYDOR	UK	2391 365
			( ) LETS DO IT		1978	POLYDOR	US	2490 145
			(*) STEP INTO OUR LIFE		1978	POLYDOR	US	PD 16179
			(*) STEP INTO OUR LIFE		1978	POLYDOR	UK	2391 380
			(*) STEP INTO OUR LIFE		1978	POLYDOR	UK	POLS 1004
			( ) FEVER		1979	POLYDOR	UK	2391 396
			( ) THE BEST OF ROY AYERS		1979	POLYDOR	UK	2391 429

AYERS ROCK

(A) BIG RED ROCK	1975	A&M	AMLH64523

AZTEC TWO STEP

NEAL SHULMAN	V G	(ALL	(A) AZTEC TWO STEP		1972	ELEKTRA	UK	K 42118
REX FOWLER	G V	(ALL	(A) AZTEC TWO STEP		1972	ELEKTRA	US	EKS 75031
DAVID VAUGHT	B	(A	(B) SECOND STEP		1975	RCA	UK	RS 1034
JOHN SEITER	D	(A	(B) SECOND STEP		1975	RCA	US	AFLI 1161
SPANKY McFARLANE	V	(A	(C) TWOS COMPANY		197	RCA	US	AFLI 1497
PETER KLIEMES	BANJO	(A	(D) ADJOINING SUITES		197	RCA	US	AFLI 2453
BOBBY TORRES	CONGA	(A						
JERRY YESTER	BANJO V PNO	(A	RANDY BENSON	V	(A	DOUG DILLARD	BANJO (A
JOHN SEBASTIAN	HCA	(A	DENNIS WITCHER	V	(A	JOHN TROPEA	G (B
KEN ASCHER	K	(B	DON PAYNE	B	(B	ALLEN SCHWARZBERG	D (B
EMILE LATIMER	PERC	(B	DON ELLIOTT	VIBES	(B	FRANK SIMS	V (B
GEORGE SIMS	V	(B	DAVID KONDZIELA	V	(B		

AZTECA

BOB FERREIRA	WIND	(B	(A) AZTECA		197	CBS	65011
PAT O'HARA	TROM	(B	(B) PYRAMID OF THE SUN	1973	CBS	US KC 32451
TOM HARREL	HRNS	(B					
MEL MARTIN	WIND	(B	WENDY HAAS	V	(B	ERROL KNOWLES	V (B
PETE ESCOVEDO	PER V	(B	PAUL JACKSON	B	(B	BILL COURTIAL	G (B
GEORGE MURIBUS	K	(B	FLIP NUNEZ	ORG	(B	GEORGE DI QUATRO	K (B
COKE ESCOVEDO	PERC	(B	VICTOR PANTOJA	CONGA	(B	JOHN BRINCK	D (B
LENNY WHITE	D	(B	RICO REYES	V	(B	TOM RUTLEY	B (B
TONY JUNCALE	B	(B	MIKE NOCK	K	(B	NEAL SCHON	G (B

AZTECS

(A) LIVE AT SUNBURY	(DBL)	19	HAVOC	NZ	HST4003/4

B1

B BUMBLE & THE STINGERS
(A) PIANO STYLINGS OF B BUMBLE (EP) 19 STATESIDE UK SE 1001

B2
```
BRIAN GODDING  V PNO G K  (A
KEVIN WESTLAKE      D G   (A
BRIAN BELSHAW       B V   (A
BRIAN AUGER         K     (A
CHRIS KIMSEY        PNO   (A
```

B B BLUNDER
(A) WORKERS PLAYTIME 1971 U A UK UAG 29156

```
JULIE DRISCOLL   V     (A   BARRY JENKINS   D     (A
MARK CHARIG      TPT   (A   MICK TAYLOR     G     (A
NICK EVANS       TROM  (A   GRAHAM SMITH    PERC  (A
```

B2A
```
KEITH STRICKLAND
CINDY WILSON
RICKY WILSON
FRED SCHNEIDER
KATE PIERSON
```

B52s
(A) B52'S   1979 ISLAND UK ILPS 9580
(B) WILD PLANET 1980 ISLAND UK ILPS 9622

B3
```
JAMAL RASOOL      B V      (E
LESLIE MING       D        (E
RICHARD THOMPSON  G V      (E
KASHIF SALEEM     K V      (E
DENNIS ROWE       PERC V   (E
CARLOS WARD  WIND K V      (E
```

B T EXPRESS
```
(A) DO IT TILL YOURE SATISFIED  1975  PYE       UK  NSPL28207
(A) DO IT TILL YOURE SATISFIED  1975  ROADSHOW  US  SDS  5117
(B) NON STOP                    1976  EMI       UK  INA  1501
(B) NON STOP                    1976  ROADSHOW  US  RS  41001
(C) ENERGY TO BURN              1977  EMI       UK  INA  1502
(C) ENERGY TO BURN              1977  CBS       US  PC  34178
(D) FUNCTION AT THE JUNCTION    19    CBS       US     34702
(D) FUNCTION AT THE JUNCTION    1977  EMI       UK  INS  3009
(E) SHOUT                       19    CBS       US  JC  35078
(E) SHOUT                       1978  EMI       UK  INS  3016
```

B3A

B Z N
(A) MAKING A NAME 19 NEGRAM NN2

B4
```
REBOP KWAKU BAAH   PERC  (ABC
```

REBOP KWAKU BAAH
```
(A) REBOP                        1972  ISLAND   US    SW 9304
(B) ANTHONY REBOP KWAKU BAAH     1973  PHILIPS  SWED  6316 008
(C) TRANCE                       1977  ISLAND   UK    ILPS 9491
```

B5
```
DAVE PUNSHON     K      (A1
DICK POWELL      D      (AB1
ALAN SHACKLOCK   G      (123ABC
DAVE HEWITT      B      (A12345BC
JENNY HAAN       V      (ABC1234
ED SPEVOCK       D      (23456CDE
STEVE GURL       K      (3456CDE
BERNIE MARSDEN   G      (456E
ELLIE HOPE       V      (56E
GASPAR LAWAL     PERC   (AB
BRENT CARTER     SAX    (A
RAY KNOTT        B      (6
CHRIS HOLMES     K      (2
DUNCAN LAMONT    FLT    (B
KEITH CHRISTIE   TROM   (B
BRIAN WARREN     FLT    (B
NICK MOBBS       PERC   (B
DON AIREY        K SYN  (E
CHRIS KARAN      PERC   (E
```

BABE RUTH
```
(A) FIRST BASE      1972  HARVEST  US  SHSP 4022
(A) FIRST BASE      1972  HARVEST  US  SW 11151
(B) AMAR CABALLERO  1973  HARVEST  UK  SHVL 812
(C) BABE RUTH       1975  HARVEST  UK  SHSP 4038
(D) STEALIN HOME    1975  CAPITOL  UK  EST 11451
(E) KIDS STUFF      1976  CAPITOL  UK  EST 23739
(E) KIDS STUFF      1976  CAPITOL  US  ST 11515
(F) BEST OF         1977  HARVEST      SHSM 2019
```

```
(1) 1971    (2) 1973    (3) 1975
(4) 1975    (5) 1976    (6) 1976
```

```
JEFF ALLEN      D       (A   RAY HARRIS   HRNS  (B
STEVE GREGORY   SAX     (B   DAVE WHITE   FLT   (B
RAY PREMRU      TROM    (B   JACK ELLORY  FLT   (B
RON CARTHY      TPT     (B   BUD BEADLE   SAX   (B
ANGELITO PEREZ  V PERC  (B   NEIL MURRAY  B     (E
FRANK RICOTTI   VIBES   (E   TONY CARR    PERC  (E
HARRY MIER      OBOE    (A
```

B6
```
JOHNNY LEE SCHELL  V K G  (A
STEVE CRANE        B V    (A
WOODIE PUTMAN      D      (A
```

BABY
(A) WHERE DID ALL THE MONEY GO 1977 CHELSEA CHL 517

JOHN MARK CAMP G V (A TOM SCOTT HRNS (A

B7
```
DAVID KAGAN      V     (A
ROB HYMAN        K V   (A
ERIC BAZILIAN    G V   (A
RALPH SCHUCKETT  K     (A
MICHAEL BRECKER  HRNS  (A
```

BABY GRAND
(A) BABY GRAND 1978 ARISTA UK SPART1061
(A) BABY GRAND 1978 ARISTA US AB 4148

```
JOHN SIEGLER       B  (A   RICK CHERTOFF  PERC  (A
DAVID DARTH PRATER D  (A   RICK MAROTTA   D     (A
```

B8
```
JOHN WAITE     V B    (ABCDE
MIKE CORBY     G K    (ABC
WALT STOCKER   G      (ABCDE
TONY BROCK     V D    (ABCDE
MARTI McCALL   V      (C
JONATHAN CAIN  K V    (DE
DIANA LEE·     V      (C
ROB LAWRENCE   MAND   (C
PAT HENDERSON  V      (BC
KEVIN KELLY    PNO    (C
```

BABYS
```
(A) BABYS         1976  CHRYSALIS  CHR 1129
(B) BROKEN HEART  1977  CHRYSALIS  CHR 1150
(C) HEAD FIRST    1979  CHRYSALIS  CHR 1195
(D) UNION JACKS   1980  CHRYSALIS  CHR 1267
(E) ON THE EDGE   1980  CHRYSALIS  CHR 1305
```

```
MIKE JAPP        V     (C    JOHN SINCLAIR       SYN  (C
BOBBYE HALL      PERC  (C    LISA ROBERTS        V    (BC
MYRNA MATTHEWS   V     (BC   JACK CONRAD         B    (C
RICKY PHILLIPS   B     (CE   ANNE MARIE LECLERC  V    (DE
```

B8A
```
PETER KIMBERLEY  B K V  (AB
COLIN SWINBURNE  G V    (AB
BRIAN SMITH      D      (AB
KAREL BEER       K G    (AB
```

BACHDENKEL
(A) STALINGRAD 1977 INITIAL IRL 002
(B) LEMMINGS   1978 INITIAL IRL 001

IRVIN MOWREY V (A ANDY SCOTT K (A

B9
```
RANDY BACHMAN   G V B  (AB
WITH
BURTON CUMMINGS K      (A
JEFF PORCARO    D      (A
IAN GARDINER    D      (A
PATTY BROOKS    V      (A
```

RANDY BACHMAN
(A) SURVIVOR 1978 POLYDOR UK 2490 146
(A) SURVIVOR 1978 POLYDOR US PD1 6141
(B) AXE   19   RCA   US LSP 4349

```
TOM SCOTT      SAX  (A   BECKY LOPEZ   (A
PETSYE POWELL  V    (A
```

BACHMAN TURNER OVERDRIVE B10

RANDY BACHMAN	G V	(ALL	(A) BACHMAN TURNER OVERDRIVE	1973	MERCURY	UK	6499	509
ROBBIE BACHMAN	PERC D V	(ABCDGJ	(A) BACHMAN TURNER OVERDRIVE	1973	MERCURY	US	SRM 1 673	
TIM BACHMAN	V	(	(B) BACHMAN TURNER OVERDRIVE 2	1974	MERCURY	UK	6338	482
FRED TURNER	B V	(ALL	(B) BACHMAN TURNER OVERDRIVE 2	1974	MERCURY	US	SRM 1 696	
BLAIR THORNTON	G V B	(CDEFGHJ	(C) NOT FRAGILE	1974	MERCURY	UK	9100 007	
JIM CLENCH	D	(J	(C) NOT FRAGILE	1974	MERCURY	US	SRM 11004	
			(D) FOUR WHEEL DRIVE	1975	MERCURY	UK	9100 012	
			(D) FOUR WHEEL DRIVE	1975	MERCURY	GERM	6338 566	
			(D) FOUR WHEEL DRIVE	1975	MERCRUY	US	SRM 11027	
			(E) AS BRAVE FELT	1975	WB		K 54036	
			(E) AS BRAVE FELT	1975	WB	US	MS 2210	
			(F) HEAD ON	1976	MERCURY	UK	9100 020	
			(F) HEAD ON	1976	MERCURY	US	RMS 11067	
			(G) FREEWAYS	1977	MERCURY	UK	9100 035	
			(G) FREEWAYS	1977	MERCURY	US	SRM 13700	
			(H) STREET ACTION	1978	MERCURY	UK	9100 051	
			(H) STREET ACTION	1978	MERCURY	US	SRM 13713	
			( ) THE BEST OF	1976	MERCURY	UK	9100 026	
			( ) THE BEST OF	1976	MERCURY	US	SRM 11101	

BACK DOOR B11

COLIN HODGKINSON	B	(ALL	(A) BACK DOOR	1972	BLAKEY		BLP 5989	
FELIX PAPPALRDI	K	(C	(B) BACK DOOR	1973	WB		K 46231	
ADRIAN TILBROOK	D	(	(B) BACK DOOR	1973	WB	US	BS 2753	
RON ASPERY K FLT SAX		(ALL	(C) EIGHTH STREET NITES	1973	WB		K 46265	
TONY HICKS	D	(BC	(D) ANOTHER FINE MESS	1975	WB		K 56098	
			(E) ACTIVATE	1976	WB		K 56243	

BACK STREET CRAWLER B12

PAUL KOSSOFF	G	(AB	(A) THE BAND PLAYS ON	1975	ATLANTIC		K 50173	
TERRY WILSON-SLESSER V		(AB	(A) THE BAND PLAYS ON	1975	ATCO		36125	
MIKE MONTGOMERY	K	(AB	(B) SECOND STREET	1976	ATLANTIC		K 50267	
TONY BRAUNAGEL	D	(AB						
TERRY WILSON	B	(AB						
GEORGE LARNYOH	WIND	(A	GEOFF WHITEHORN	G	(B	PETE VANDER PUIJE	SAX	(A
			EDDIE QUANSAH	HRNS	(A			

BACKHAUSEN B12A

PETER BACKHAUSEN	V K G D	(A	(A) PLANET SHOW	1979	SKY		SKY 037	
KARL GILLAUT	G	(A						
STEFFI STEPHAN	B	(A	BERTRAM ENGEL	D	(A	SIDDARTHA GAUTAMA	D	(A
KARL SCHOTT	B	(A	GEOFF PEACEY	K	(A	GEORG FUNKE	B	(A
WILLY TJON AJONG	K	(A						

BACONFAT B13

GEORGE SMITH	V HCA	(B	(A) GREASE ONE FOR ME	1970	BLUE HORIZON		7 63858	
BUDDY REED	G V	(AB	(B) TOUGH DUDE	1971	BLUE HORIZON		2431 001	
DICK INNES Jr	D	(AB						
GREGG SCHAEFER	G HCA	(AB	JERRY SMITH	B	(AB	ROD GINGERMAN PIAZZA	V HCA	(AB
J D NICHOLSON	V PNO	(AB						

BAD COMPANY B14

PAUL RODGERS	PNO V G	(ALL	(A) BAD COMPANY	1974	ISLAND	UK	ILPS 9279	
SIMON KIRKE	D	(ALL	(A) BAD COMPANY	1974	SWANSONG	US	8501	
BOZ BURRELL	B	(ALL	(B) STRAIGHT SHOOTER	1975	ISLAND	UK	ILPS 9304	
MICK RALPHS	G K	(ALL	(B) STRAIGHT SHOOTER	1975	SWANSONG	US	8502	
MEL COLLINS	SAX	(A	(C) RUN WITH THE PACK	1976	ISLAND	UK	ILPS 9346	
SUE & SUNNY	V	(A	(C) RUN WITH THE PACK	1976	SWANSONG	US	8503	
			(D) BURNING SKY	1977	ISLAND	UK	ILPS 9441	
			(D) BURNING SKY	1977	SWANSONG	US	8500	
			(E) DESOLATION ANGELS	1979	SWANSONG	UK	SSK59408	

BADDO B15

	(A) BADDO	1974	CONYU		CY103
	(B) THE GOODO,THE BADDO ,THE UGLYO	1975	CONYU		AGAIN 104
	(C) NOT TOO GOOD	1975	KIDDY		JO123KE

BADFINGER B16

PETE HAM	V G	(ABCDEF	(A) MAGIC CHRISTIAN MUSIC	1970	APPLE		SAPCOR12	
MIKE GIBBINS	D	(ABCDEF	(A) MAGIC CHRISTIAN MUSIC	1970	APPLE	IMP	ST 3364	
TOM EVANS	V B	(ABCDEFG	(B) NO DICE	1970	APPLE		SAPCOR 16	
JOEY HOLLAND	G V	(ABCDEFG	(C) STRAIGHT UP	1972	APPLE		SAPCOR 19	
PETER CLARK		(G	(D) BADFINGER	1974	WB		K 56023	
DAVID MALLONY	V	(G	(E) ASS	1974	APPLE		SAPCOR 27	
JOE TANSIN	G	(G	(E) ASS	1974	APPLE	IMP	SW 3411	
DUANE HITCHINGS	SYN	(G	(F) WISH YOU WERE HERE	1975	WB		BS 2827	
ANDY NEWMARK	D	(G	(G) AIRWAVES	1979	ELEKTRA US 6E175 UK K52129			
STEVE FORMAN	PERC	(G						
KEN HARCK	D	(G	NICKY HOPKINS	K	(G			

BADGER B17

TONY KAYE	K	(AB	(A) ONE LIVE BADGER	1973	ATLANTIC		K 40473	
ROY DYKE	D	(AB	(B) WHITE LADY	1974	EPIC		80009	
DAVID FOSTER	B V	(A	(B) WHITE LADY	1974	EPIC	US	KE 32831	
BRIAN PARRISH	G V	(A						
JACKIE LOMAX	G V	(B	JOAN HARMON	V	(B	BRY HAWORTH	G	(B
PAUL PILNICK	G	(B	BARRY BAILEY	G	(B	JOHN LANGO	TROM	(B
KIM GARDNER	B	(B	LESTER CALISTE	TPT	(B	BOBBY MONTGOMERY	V	(B
TERESIPA HENRY	V	(B	CARL BLOUIN	WIND	(B	JESSIE SMITH	V	(B
JEFF BECK	G	(B	ALVIN THOMAS	SAX	(B	MERCEDES DAVIS	V	(B
ALLEN TOUSSAINT	K PERC	(B						

B17A

JOAN BAEZ	G V	(ALL	(A) JOAN BAEZ	1960	VANGUARD	VSD79073	VSD	2077
WITH			(A) JOAN BAEZ	1960	FONTANA		STFL	6002
HAL RUGG	G	(M	(B) JOAN BAEZ 2	1961	VANGUARD	VSD 79094	VSD	2097
JERRY REED	G	(M	(B) JOAN BAEZ 2	1961	FONTANA		STFL	6025
JERRY KENNEDY	G	(M	(C) IN CONCERT	1962	VANGUARD	VSD79112	VSD	2122
HAROLD BRADLEY	G	(M	(C) IN CONCERT	1962	FONTANA		STFL	6033
PETE WADE	G	(M	(D) IN CONCERT 2	1963	VANGUARD	VSD79113	VSD	2133
TOMMY JACKSON	FDL	(M	(D) IN CONCERT 2	1963	FONTANA		STFL	6035
BUDDY SPICHER	FDL	(M	(E) JOAN BAEZ 5	1964	VANGUARD		VSD79160	
JUNIOR HUSKY	B	(M	(E) JOAN BAEZ 5	1964	FONTANA		STFL	6043
NORBERT PUTNAM	B	(M	(F) FAREWELL ANGELINA	1965	VANGUARD	VSD79200	VSD	23006
HARGUS PIG ROBBINS	K	(M	(G) FAREWELL ANGELINA	1965	FONTANA		STFL	6058
KENNY BUTTREY	D	(M	(H) NOEL	1966	VANGUARD	VSD79230	VSD	23018
FRED CARTER	MAND	(M	(H) NOEL	1966	FONTANA		STFL	6078
BILL PURCELL	K	(M	(H) PORTRAIT	1966	VANGUARD		SVRL19025	
GRADY MARTIN	G	(M	(J) JOAN	1967	VANGUARD	VSD79240	VSD	23011
JIM GORDON	D	(	(J) JOAN	1967	FONTANA		STFL	6082
LARRY CARLTON	G	(X	(K) BAPTISM	1968	VANGUARD	SVRL19000	VSD	79225
DEAN PARKS	G	(1X	(L) ANY DAY NOW	1968	VANGUARD	VSD79306/7	55/66	
JOE SAMPLE	K	(X	(M) DAVIDS ALBUM	1969	VANGUARD	VSD79308	SVRL19050	
DAVID PAICH	K	(X	(N) ONE DAY AT A TIME	1970	VANGUARD	VSD79310	VSD	23010
LARRY KNECHTEL	K	(X	(O) FIRST TEN YEARS	1970	VANGUARD		VSD	6560
REINHOLD PRESS	B	(1X	(P) BLESSED ARE	1971	VANGUARD		VSD6570/1	
RED RHODES	STEEL	(X	(Q) CARRY IT ON	1972	VANGUARD	VSD79313	VSD	41/42
JIM HORN	SAX	(X	(R) COME FROM THE SHADOWS	1972	A&M		AMLH64339	
MALCOLM CECIL	SYN	(X1	(S) THE BALLAD BOOK	1972	VANGUARD		VSD 41/42	
HAMPTON HAWES	K	(X	(T) WHERE ARE YOU NOW MY SON	1973	A&M		AMLH64390	
TOM SCOTT	WIND	(X	(U) GRACIAS A LA VIDA (HERES TO LIFE)	1974	A&M		AMLH63614	
MAX BENNETT	B	(X	(V) CONTEMPORARY BALLAD BOOK	1974	VANGUARD		VSD	49
JOHN GUERIN	D	(X	(W) PROFILES	1974	IRL		IC054 95128	
RICK LOTEMPO	G	(X	(X) DIAMONDS & RUST	1975	A&M		AMLH64527	
OLLIE MITCHELL	TPT	(X	(Y) LIVE IN JAPAN	1975	VANGUARD		GP	315
DONALD DUNN	B	(1	(Z) LOVE SONG ALBUM	1976	VANGUARD		VSD	79
JONI MITCHELL	V	(X	( ) FROM EVERY STAGE	1976	A&M		AMLH64704	
BUCK MONARI	TPT	(X	( ) GULF WINDS	1976	A&M		AMLH64603	
BILL WOOD	V	(9	( ) BLOWING AWAY	1977	PORTRAIT	34697	PRT 82011	
TED ALEVIZOS	V	(9	( ) GOLDEN HOUR	1972	PYE		GH	843
TED DRAKE	STEEL	(M	( ) HITS THE GREATEST & OTHERS	1973	VANGUARD		VSD 79332	
			( ) GREATEST HITS	19	IRL		Ic062 93622	
			( ) BEST OF	1977	A&M		AMLH64665	
			( ) INTRODUCTION TO	1976	IRL		IC18892665/6	
			(9) THE BEST OF	1968	SAGA		EROS 8075	
			( ) GOLDEN HOUR VOL 2	19	PYE		GH	863
			( ) HOUSE OF THE RISING SUN	1978	MUSIDISC			1367
			( ) SUPER DISC OF JOAN BAEZ	19	A&M		GXM	9002
			( ) HONEST LULABY	1979	PORTRAIT		PRT 83474	
			( ) COUNTRY MUSIC	1979	VANGUARD		VSD	105

B18

DUCK BAKER

DUCK BAKER	G V	(ALL	(A) THERES SOMETHING FOR EVERYONE	19	KICKING MULE	SNKF	116
WITH			(B) WHEN YOU WORE A TULIP	19	KICKING MULE	SNKF	123
STEFAN GROSSMAN	G	(C	(C) KING OF THE BONGO BONG	1977	KICKING MULE	SNKF	137
MIKE PIGGOTT	VLN	(C	(D) FINGER STYLE JAZZ GUITAR	1979	KICKING MULE	SNKF	154

B19

GINGER BAKER

GINGER BAKER	D	(ALL	(A)STRATAVARIOUS	1972	POLYDOR		2383 133	
WITH			(B) AT HIS BEST	1973	POLYDOR		2659 023	
			(B) AT HIS BEST	1973	POLYDOR	US	PD	3504
HENRY THOMAS	B	(1	(C) POP HISTORY	19	POLYDOR		2668 002	
MIKE DAVIS	G	(1	(D) ELEVEN SIDES OF BAKER	19	MOUNTAIN		TOpC 5005	
JOHN MIZAROLLI	G	(1	(D) ELEVEN SIDES OF BAKER	19	SIRE	US	SA	7532
FELI RANSOME KUTI		(E	(D) ELEVEN SIDES OF BAKER	19	PHONOGRAM		6370 419	
			(E) KUTI & AFRICA	19	REGAL	UK	062043933	
			(1) 1980 LIVE BAND					

B20

BAKER GURVITZ ARMY

GINGER BAKER	D PERC	(ABC	(A) BAKER GURVITZ ARMY	1974	VERTIGO		9103 201
ADRIAN GURVITZ	G V	(ABC	(A) BAKER GURVITZ ARMY	1974	JANUS	US	7015
PAUL GURVITZ	B V	(ABC	(B) ELYSIAN ENCOUNTER	1975	MOUNTAIN		TOPS 101
SNIPS	V	(BC	(B) ELYSIAN ENCOUNTER	1975	ATCO	US	36123
PETER LEMER	K	(B	(C) HEARTS ON FIRE	1976	MOUNTAIN	UK	TOPS 111
JOHN NORMAN	B		(C) HEARTS ON FIRE	1976	PHONOGRAM		9103 206
NORMAN MITCHELL	K		(C) HEARTS ON FIRE	1976	ATCO	US	SD 36141

B21

MICKEY BAKER

MICKEY BAKER	G	(ALL	(A) TAKE A LOOK INSIDE ME	1975	BIG BEAR		BEAR 5
WILLY MABON	K HCA	(A	(B) THE BLUES IN ME	1975	BLACK & BLUE		33507
DAN ARMSTRONG	B	(A	(C) BLUES & JAZZ GUITAR OF M BAKER	197	KICKING MULE		SNKF 127
PETE MORGAN	B	(A	(D) JAZZ ROCK GUITAR	1978	KICKING MULE		SNKF 145
PETE YORK	B	(A					
KIERAN O'CONNOR	PNO	(A	KEN ELLIOTT	K	(A	DYAN BIRCH	V	(A
PADDY McHUGH	V	(A	FRANK COLLINS	V	(A			

B22

BAKERLOO

DAVE CLEMSON	G HCA K	(A	(A) BAKERLOO	1969	HARVEST	UK	SHVL 762
TERRY POOLE	B	(A					
KEITH BAKER	D	(A	JERRY SALISBURY	TPT	(A		

LONG JOHN BALDRY

B23

```
LONG JOHN BALDRY   V HCA (ALL
WITH
IAN ARMIT          K    (ABC     (A) LONG JOHNS BLUES            1964  U A                 ULP  1081
RICK BROWN         B    (B       (A) LONG JOHNS BLUES            1964  ASCOT       US      ALM 13022
RONNIE WOOD        G    (B       (B) IT AINT EASY                1971  WB                  K  46008
SAM MITCHELL       STEEL (BC     (B) IT AINT EASY                1971  WB          US      WS  1921
RAY JACKSON        MAND (B       (C) EVERYTHING STOPS FOR TEA    1973  WB                  K  46160
MAGGIE BELL        V    (B       (D) HEARTACHES (GOLDEN HOUR)    1974  PYE                 GH   572
ALAN SKIDMORE      SAX  (B       (E) LOOKING FOR LONG JOHN       1966  U A                 SULP 1146
JIMMY HOROWITZ     K    (C       (F) GOOD TO BE ALIVE           197   CASABLANCA   US          7012
JEFF BRADFORD      G HCA (A      (G) BALDRY'S OUT                1979  EMI                 AML 3002
ELTON JOHN         PNO  (BC
IAN DUCK           V HCA (B      CLIFF BARTON    B    (A      BILL LAW         D    (A
NIGEL OLSSON       D    (C       CALEB QUAYE     G    (B      DAVE GLOVER      B    (B
STEFAN DELFT       VLA  (C       ROGER POPE      D    (B      DAVEY JOHNSTONE  G    (C
BILL SMITH         B    (C       KLAUS VOORMANN  B    (C      RAY COOPER       PERC (C
DORIS TROY         V    (C       JAMES LITHERLAND G   (C      ROBERT WESTON    G    (C
JOHN PORTER        B    (C       JOHN DENTITH    D    (C      LIZA STRIKE      V    (C
MICKEY WALLER      PERC (C       BARRY ST JOHN   V    (C      TERRY STANNARD   D    (C
                                 ROD STEWART     BANJ (C      MADELINE BELL    V    (C
                                 ORCHESTRA            (C
```

HANK BALLARD

B24

```
HANK BALLARD       V    (ALL
WITH
LAWSON SMITH                     ( ) HANK BALLARD & THE MIDNIGHTERS   19   STARDAY        US   K5003X
NORMAN THRASHER                  ( ) HANK BALLARD & THE MIDNIGHTERS   19   POWERPAK       US   PO   276
BILLY DAVIS                      ( ) HANK BALLARD BIGGEST HITS        19
HENRY BOOTH                      ( ) THOSE LAZY LAZY DAYS             19
CHARLES SUTTON                   ( ) GLAD SONGS SAD SONGS             19
ARTHUR PORTER                    ( ) JUMPIN' HANK BALLARD             19   LONDON         HA   8101
SONNY WOODS                      ( ) GREATEST JUKE BOX HITS           19   KING           US    541
                                 ( ) HANGING WITH HANK                19   STANG          US   ST  1031
                                 ( ) SPOTLIGHT ON HANK BALLARD        19   STARDAY GUSTO  US   SK   740
```

RUSS BALLARD

B25

```
RUSS BALLARD  V D K B G HCA(ALL
WITH
NICK NEWELL        SAX  (AB      (A) RUSS BALLARD               1974  EPIC                EPC 80341
CHRIS MERCER       SAX  (AB      (B) WINNING                    1976  EPIC                EPC 69210
MICK EVE           SAX  (A       (B) WINNING                    1976  EPIC        US      PE  34093
STEVE GREGORY      SAX  (A       (C) AT THE THIRD STROKE        1978  EPIC                EPC 82629
DENNIS BELFIELD    B    (A       (C) AT THE THIRD STROKE        1978  EPIC        US      JE  35035
STEVE FREDIANI     HRNS (C
BOBBYE HALL        PERC (C       MIKE BAIRD      D    (C      CRAIG DOERGE     K    (C
DENNY HENSON       V    (C       TOM SCOTT       SAX  (C      DAVID HUNGATE    B    (C
MIKE PORCARO       B    (C       DAVID FOSTER    K    (C      FRED TACKETT     G    (C
TOM KELLY          V    (C       LEE SKLAR       B    (C      JEFF PORCARO     D    (C
CHRIS KARAN        PERC (B       KEITH OLSEN     PERC (C      DAVID PAICH      K    (C
TERRY STARR        TPT  (B       DAVE MATTACKS   D    (B      DAVE MARKEE      B    (B
SUNNY LESLIE       V    (B       GEOFF SKATES         (B      PETE ZORN        B    (B
RABBIT BUNDRICK    K    (B       PIP WILLIAMS         (B      MADELINE BELL    V    (B
                                 JOANNE WILLIAMS V    (B      LIZA STRIKE      V    (B
```

BALLS

B26

```
TREVOR BURTON      B    (ABCD    (A)1969                (B) 1969
DENNY LAINE        G V  (ABCD    (C) 1970 SUMMER        (D) 1970 WINTER
ALAN WHITE         D    (B
JACKIE LOMAX       G V  (C       STEVE GIBBONS   V G  (D      MIKE KELLIE      D    (CD
DAVE MORGAN        B    (A       KEITH SMART     D    (A      RICHARD TANDY    K    (A
```

BAMBOO

B27

```
DAVE RAY      HCA V G   (A
WILL DONIGHT    V B PNO (A       (A) BAMBOO                     1969  ELEKTRA     US   EKS 74048
DANIEL LEE HALL V K G   (A
PETER HODGSON      B    (A       SANFORD KONIKOFF D   (A      RED RHODES       STEEL (A
                                 BRENDAN HARKIN  PERC (A      KEN JENKINS      B    (A
```

BANCO

B28

```
PIER LUIGI CALDERONI D  (D       ( ) BANCO DEL MUTUO SOCCORSO   1972  ORIZZONTE   ITAL ORL  8041
FRANCESCO DI GIACOMO V  (D       ( ) DARWIN                     1972  ORIZZONTE   ITAL ORL  8094
RENALTO D'ANGELO   B G  (D       ( ) LO SONO NATO LIBERO        1973  ORIZZONTE   ITAL ORL  8202
GIANNA NOCENZI     K CLAR(D      (D) BANCO                      1975  MANTICORE   UK   K  53507
VITTORIO NOCENZI   K    (D       (D) BANCO                      1975  MANTICORE   US   MA6 50551
                                 ( ) GAROGANO ROSSO             1976  ORIZZONTE   ITAL ORL  8334
                                 ( ) DI TEARO                   19    DISCHI      ITAL SMRL 6226
                                 ( ) CANTO DI PRIMAVERA         19    DISCHI      ITAL SMRL 6247
                                 ( ) CAPOLINEA                  19    DISCHI      ITAL SMRL 6260
```

THE BAND

B29

```
ROBBIE ROBERTSON   G V K (ALL    (A) MUSIC FROM THE BIG PINK            1968  CAPITOL          ST   2955
RICK DANKO       B V VLN (ALL    (B) THE BAND                           1969  CAPITOL          ST    132
RICHARD MANUEL   D K V   (ALL    (AB)MILESTONES                        1973  EMI      IMP     5C18450195/6
LEVON HELM       V D G   (ALL    (C) STAGE FRIGHT                       1970  CAPITOL          EASW  425
GARTH HUDSON     K SAX   (ALL    (D) CAHOOTS                            1971  CAPITOL          EAST  651
WITH                             (E) ROCK OF AGES                       1972  CAPITOL          EASSP  11
TOM MALONE         HRNS  (HJ     (E) ROCK OF AGES                       1972  CAPITOL          5ABB11045
JIM GORDON         HRNS  (HJ     (F) MOONDOG MATINEE                    1973  CAPITOL          ESW 11214
JOHN SIMON         K HRNS (BEHJ  (G) NORTHERN LIGHTS SOUTHERN CROSS     1975  CAPITOL          EST 11440
LARRY PACKER       VLN   (HJ     (H) ISLANDS                            1977  CAPITOL          EST 11602
VAN MORRISON       V     (DJ     (J) THE LAST WALTZ          TRIPLE     1978  WB       UK      K  66076
ALLEN TOUSSAINT    K     (DJ     (J) THE LAST WALTZ          TRIPLE     1978  WB       US      3WS 3146
SNOOKY YOUNG       HRNS  (E      ( ) THE BEST OF THE BAND               1976  CAPITOL          EAST23927
HOWARD JOHNSON     HRNS  (EJ     ( ) THE BEST OF THE BAND               1976  CAPITOL  US      ST 11553
DOC POMUS          HRNS  (E      ( ) THE BEST OF THE BAND               1976  CAPITOL  UK      ST  3927
JOE FARRELL        HRNS  (E      ( ) MASTERS OF ROCK                    1975  EMI INT          IC 054 81735
EARL McINTYRE      TROM  (E      ( ) IN CONCERT                        1973  EMI      IMP     5C 054 81466
J D PARRON         WIND  (E      ( ) ANTHOLOGY                          1978  CAPITOL          ESTSP  19
BOBBY CHARLES      V     (EJ     ( ) ANTHOLOGY                          1978  CAPITOL  US      SKB011856
                                                                                          (CONTINUED)
```

```
B29  (CONTINUED)                    THE BAND
BOB DYLAN        V    (EJ
DrJOHN        K PERC(EJ   BILLY MUNDI        (F    BEN KEITH            (F
RICH COOPER   HRNS (J     JERRY HEY    HRNS (J    CHARLIE KEAGLE  HRNS (J
RONNIE HAWKINS V   (J     NEIL YOUNG   V G  (J    JONI MITCHELL   V G  (J
NEIL DIAMOND  V G  (J     DENNIS ST JOHN  D (J    PAUL BUTTERFIELD HCA V (J
MUDDY WATERS  G V  (J     BOB MARGOLIN    G (J    PINETOP PERKINS   K  (J
ERIC CLAPTON  G V  (J     RINGO STARR     D (J    RON WOOD          G  (J
EMMYLOU HARRIS V G (J     STAPLES SINGERS V (J
B30                              BAND OF JOY
ROBERT PLANT  V    (      (A) BAND OF JOY          1978  POLYDOR      2310 588
JOHN BONHAM   D    (
PAUL LOCKEY   G V  (      KEVIN HAMMOND   G V (    JOHN PASTERNAK B V (
MICHAEL CHETWOOD K (      FRANCESCO NIZZA   D (
B31                              BANDIT
JAMES LITHERLAND G (A     (A) BANDIT             1977  ARISTA    ARTY 148
JIM DIAMOND      V (A     (A) BANDIT             1977  ARISTA    US      4113
GRAHAM BROAD   D K (A     *(B) PARTNERS IN CRIME 1978  ARIOLA    UK  ARL 5010
DANNY McINTOSH G V (AB*
CLIFF WILLIAMS B V (A     THEODORE THUNDER D V (B  GERRY TREW      V  (B
TONY LESTER    B V (B     MICK GRABHAM    G V (B*
*TWO DIFFERENT COVERS GIVING DIFFERENT GUITARIST*
B32                              BANDOGGS
TONY ROSE          (      (A) BANDOGGS           1978  TRANSATLANTIC LTRA 504
NIC JONES          (
PETE COE           (      CHRIS COE
B33                        BANGOR FLYING CIRCUS
MICHAEL TEGZA    D PERC(A  (A) BANGOR FLYING CIRCUS 1969 STATESIDE   SSL 5022
DAVID WOLINSKI PERC K V B (A
ALAN DE CARLO    PERC G V (A
B33A                           DARRELL BANKS
DARRELL BANKS       (A    (A) DARRELL BANKS IS HERE 19  ATCO      US  SD 33216
B34                             PETER BANKS
PETER BANKS    G (ABC     (A) PETER BANKS & JAN AKKERMAN 19 SOVEREIGN  SVNA 7250
JAN AKKERMAN   G (A       (B) PETER BANKS         19   SOVEREIGN    SVNA 7256
                         (C) TWO SIDES OF PETER BANKS 19 CAPITOL   SMAS11217
B35                              BANNED
PETE FRESH    G
RICK MANSWORTH G V
JOHN THOMAS   B          PAUL SORDID    B V  TOMMY STEELE  B
B35A                             BANZAI
EVERT VERHEES G V K B (A  (A) HORANATA           19   DELTA         DG 10 001
PETER TORFS   K V (A
JOHN McO      G V (A      LUDWIG KERMAT VIBES PERC  (A  ERRY FOX   D PERC  (A
B36                              BAR KAYS
JIMMY KING        (*     ( ) SOUL FINGER          19   ATCO           228 030
RONNIE CALDWELL   (*     ( ) SOUL FINGER          19   ATCO        SD 33287
PHALIN JONES      (*     ( ) SOUL FINGER          19   ATLANTIC     K 40184
CARL CUNNINGHAM   (*     ( ) GOTTA GROOVE         1969 STAX        STATS1009
FRANK THOMPSON    (      ( ) GOTTA GROOVE         1969 VOLT            6004
JAMES ALEXANDER   (      ( ) BLACK ROCK           19   POLYDOR     2362 003
BEN CAULEY        (      ( ) DO YOU SEE           19   POLYDOR     2325 087
LLOYD SMITH       (      ( ) COLD BLOODED         1976 STAX        STX 1033
CHARLES ALLEN     (      ( ) TOO HOT TO STOP      1976 MERCURY     SRM 11099
MICHAEL BEARD     (      ( ) FLYING HIGH ON YOUR LOVE 1978 MERCURY UK 9100 048
WINSTON STEWART   (      ( ) FLYING HIGH ON YOUR LOVE 1978 MERCURY  SRM 1181
HARVEY HENDERSON  (      ( ) MONEY TALKS          1979 STAX        STX 3023
                        ( ) MONEY TALKS          1979 STAX            4106
                        ( ) AS ONE               1981 MERCURY     UK 6337 108
              (*) THE FOUR MEMBERS WHO DIED WITH OTIS REDDING(*)
B37                        BARCLAY JAMES HARVEST
JOHN LEES       G V (ALL  (A) BARCLAY JAMES HARVEST 1970 HARVEST    SHVL 770
STEWART WOLSTENHOLME K (ALL (B) ONCE AGAIN        1971 HARVEST     SHVL 788
MEL PRITCHARD   D (ALL    (C) OTHER SHORT STORIES 1971 HARVEST     SHVL 794
LES HOLROYD     B (ALL    (D) BABY JAMES HARVEST  1972 HARVEST     SHSP 4023
                         (E) EVERYONE IS EVERYBODY ELSE 1974 POLYDOR 2383 286
                         (F) LIVE                 1974 POLYDOR     2683 052
                         (G) TIME HONOURED GHOSTS 1975 POLYDOR     2383 361
                         (G) TIME HONOURED GHOSTS 1975 POLYDOR  US    6517
                         (H) OCTOBERON            1976 POLYDOR     2442 144
                         (H) OCTOBERON            1976 MCA      US    2234
                         (I) GONE TO EARTH        1978 POLYDOR     2442 148
                         (I) GONE TO EARTH        1978 MCA      US    2302
                         (J) LIVE TAPES           1978 POLYDOR     PODV 2001
                         (K) NUMBER 12            1978 POLYDOR     2442 153
                         (K) NUMBER 12            1978 POLYDOR     POLD 5006
                         ( ) BEST OF VOL 2        1979 HARVEST     SHSM 2023
                         (M) EYES OF THE UNIVERSE 1980 POLYDOR     POLD 5029
B38                            NICKEY BARCLAY
NICKEY BARCLAY    (       (A) DIAMOND IN A JUNKYARD 1976 ARIOLA      AAS 1503
WITH                     (A) DIAMOND IN A JUNKYARD 1976 ARIOLA   US ST 5006
WADDY WACHTEL  G (A
JEFF RICH      B (A       BUGS PEMBERTON    D  (A
```

PETER BARDENS
B39

PETER BARDENS	K V	(ALL	(A) THE ANSWER	1970	TRANSATLANTIC	UK	TRA	222
WITH			(A) THE ANSWER	1970	VERVE	US		3088
ANDY GEE	G	(A	(A) THE ANSWER	1970	METRONOME	IMP	MPL 15	389
BRUCE THOMAS	B	(A	(B) PETER BARDENS	1971	TRANSATLANTIC	UK	TRA	243
ALAN MARSHALL	V PERC	(A	(B) PETER BARDENS	1971	VERVE	US		3091
STEVE ELLIS	V	(A	(C) VINTAGE 69	1976	TRANSATLANTIC	UK	TRASAM36	
REG ISADOR	D	(A	(D) HEART TO HEART	1979	ARISTA		SPART1108	
ROCKY	PERC	(A						
DAVID WOOLEY	V	(A						

LINDA LEWIS   V   (A

BARDOT
B40

RAY McRINER   V G   (A

(A) ROCKIN IN RHYTHM   1978   RCA   PL 25121

CHRIS BRADFORD	V	(A				
LAURIE ANDREW	V	(A	PIP	G	(A	FRANK RICOTTI	D	(A
GEOFF WESTBY	K	(A	MIKE GILES	D	(A	DAVE MARKEE	B	(A
BOB YOUNG	HCA	(A				

BAREFOOT JERRY
B41

WAYNE MOSS G V K B PERC		(ALL	(A) SOUTHERN DELIGHT	1971	CAPITOL		EST	786
MAC GAYDEN G V K		(A	(B) BAREFOOT JERRY	1972	WB	US	BS	2641
JOHN HARRIS	K	(ABC	(B) BAREFOOT JERRY	1972	WB	UK	K	46268
KEN BUTTREY	D	(BC	(C) WATCHIN' TV	1974	MONUMENT		KZ	32926
RUSS HICKS STEEL G V HRS		(BCDEF	(C) WATCHIN' TV	1974	MONUMENT		MC	6631
KENNY MALONE	D	(BC	(D) YOU CANT GET OFF WITH YOUR SHOES ON 75		MONUMENT		MNT	80695
BUDDY SPICHER	FDL	(BC	(D) YOU CANT GET OFF WITH YOUR SHOES ON 75		MONUMENT		MC	6631
DAN FLICKENGER	K	(B	(D) YOU CANT GET OFF WITH YOUR SHOES ON 75		MONUMENT		KZ	33381
TOM KNOX	K	(B	(E) KEYS TO THE COUNTRY	1976	CBS			34252
BUDDY BLACKMON BANJ DOBRO		(F	(E) KEYS TO THE COUNTRY	1976	MONUMENT	US	MG	7605
DAVE DORAN	B V G	(C	(F) BAREFOOTIN'	1977	MONUMENT		MG	7610
FRED NEWELL V B BANJO		(CD	(F) BAREFOOTIN'	1977	MONUMENT		MNT	82413
BARRY CHANCE	K B G	(EF	(G) GROCERY BEST OF DBLE	1976	MONUMENT		KZ	33381
COSTO DAVIS	STRING	(E	(G) GROCERY BEST OF DBL	1976	MONUMENT			33909
CHARLIE McCOY HCA V FLT PNO		(DEF	(G) GROCERY BEST OF DBL	1976	MONUMENT		MP	8603
JIM COLVARD	G B	(DE						
BOBBY THOMPSON	B V G	(BCD	SI EDWARDS	PERC	(CDEF	STEVE DAVIS	K	(E
BUDDY SKIPPER HRNS V PERC		(CD	JOHN MOSS	HRNS	(EF	WARREN HARTMAN	K	(DE
JIM ISBELL		(D	TERRY DEARMORE	B G	(DE	BILLY SWAN	V	(D
MIKE McBRIDE B G PERC		(F						

PATRICK BARNES
B41A

PATRICK BARNES   G   (A

(A) GUITAR   1980   STIFF   SEEZ 22

BAROOGA BANDIT
B42

BRUCE MECHAN	G V	(A	(A) COME SOFTLY	1979	CAPITOL		EST 11924
DAN O'CONNELL	B V	(A					
MAT DE RAAD	K V	(A	FRANZ DE RAAD	D V	(A	DREW ABBOTT	G	(A
CHARLIE MARTIN	PERC V	(A	TOM NEME	G	(A	ALTO REED	WIND	(A
MICHAEL STOKES	PERC	(A					

BARRABAS
B43

JOAO A VIDAL	K	(ABCD	(A) POWER	1973	RCA	US	SPLI 2000	
JOSE LUIS TEJADA	V HCA	(ABCD	(B) BARRABAS	1975	ATLANTIC		K 50152	
ENRIQUE MORALES	G V	(ABCD	(B) BARRABAS	1975	ATLANTIC	US	913 092	
ERNESTO DUARTE WIND PERC V		(ABCD	(B) BARRABAS	1975	ATCO	US	36110	
MIGUEL MORALES	G B V	(ABCD	(C) RELEASE	1975	ATLANTIC		913 207	
DANIEL LOUIS	D	(D	(D) HEART OF THE CITY	1975	ATLANTIC		ATC 9590	
JOSE MARIA MOLL	D	(AB	(D) HEART OF THE CITY	1975	ATCO	US	36 118	
MAXINE WATERS	V	(B	(D) HEART OF THE CITY	1975	ATLANTIC		913 039	
PATTI WATERS	V	(B	(E) HI JACK	19	ATLANTIC		87912	
JULIA WATERS	V	(B	(F) WATCH OUT	19	ATCO	US	36 136	
HERNANOS MORALES	V	(B	(F) WATCH OUT	1976	ATLANTIC	UK	K50285	

BARRELHOUSE
B43A

JOHNNY LA PORTE	G	(ABC	(A) BARRELHOUSE	1974	MUNICH		BM 150205
TINEKE SCHOEMAKER	V	(ABC	(B) WHO'S MISSING	1975	MUNICH		BM 150213
BARRELHOUSE BAILEY	PNO	(A	(C) HARD TO COVER	1977	MUNICH		BM 150214
BOB DROS	D	(ABC					
JAY WALKER	B	(A	HAN VAN DAM	PNO	(BC	JAN WILLEM SLIGTING	B	(BC
GUS LA PORTE	G	(C					

SYD BARRETT
B44

SYD BARRETT	G V	(AB	(A) MADCAP LAUGHS	1970	HARVEST		SHVL	765
JERRY SHIRLEY	D	(B	(A) MADCAP LAUGHS	1970	HARVEST	US	SABB11314	
DAVID GILMOUR	B	(B	(B) BARRETT	1970	HARVEST		SHSP 4007	
RICHARD WRIGHT	K	(B	(AB) MADCAP/BARRETT (DBL)	1974	HARVEST		SHDW 404	
			(AB) MADCAP/BARRETT (DBL)	197	PATHE		FR C18450350/1	

RONNIE BARRON
B44A

RONNIE BARRON   (A

(A) REVEREND ETHER   1971   DECCA   US   DL 75303

BARRON KNIGHTS
B45

DUKE D'MOND	V	(ALL	( ) CALL UP THE GROUPS	1964	COLUMBIA	UK	335X 1648
BARRON ANTHONY	V	(ALL	( ) BARRON KNIGHTS	1966	COLUMBIA	UK	SX 6007
PEANUTS LANGFORD	G V	(ALL	( ) SCRIBED	1967	COLUMBIA	UK	SCX 6176
BUTCH BAKER	G V	(ALL	( ) KNIGHTS OF LAUGHTER	1975	PENNYFARTHING		PAGS 533
DAVE BALLINGER	D	(ALL	( ) ONE MANS MEAT	1973	PENNYFARTHING		PELS 536
			( ) LIVE IN TROUBLE	1977	EPIC		EPC 82451
			( ) NIGHT GALLERY	1978	EPIC		EPC 83221
			( ) KNIGHTS OF LAUGHTER	1979	PICKWICK		SHM 981
			( ) TEACH THE WORLD TO LAUGH	1979	CBS		83891

NEIL BASHAN
B45A

NEIL BASHAN		(AB	(A) YOU GOT THE POWER	1978	ARIOLA		ARL 5005
PETE VAN HOOKE	D	(AB	(B) HIGH ON A EASY FEELING	1979	ARIOLA		ARL 5026
ROY BABINGTON	B	(B					
PAUL WESTWOOD	B	(B	RAY RUSSELL	G	(B	LYNTON NAIFF	K	(B
VICKY BROWN	V	(B	HELEN CHAPELL	V	(B	LIZA STRIKE	V	(B
GARY OSBORNE	V	(B					

B46

MICHAEL BASS

| MICHAEL BASS | PERC K V TROM(A | (A) PARCHESI PIE | 1978 | RANDOM RADAR | RRR 3 14 |

WITH
DAVE NEWHOUSE WIND K V (A
GLENN WISER B G V (A

B47

BASTARD

CARLOS BASTARDOS V B (A
KEITH KOSSOFF G (A (A) BACK TO NATURE 1977 NOVA 6 23288
THEO TREMOLO G (A
TOTO PETTICOATO D (A

B47A

BATDORF & RODNEY

JOHN BATDORF G V K (A (A) BATDORF & RODNEY 1972 ASYLUM 5056
MARK RODNEY G V K (A (B) OFF THE SHELF 1972 WEA US SD 8298
RUSS KUNKEL V (C (C) LIFE IS YOU 1975 ARISTA US 4041 UK ARTY 112
SCOTT EDWARDS B (C
RICK CARLOS B (C DEAN PARKS G (C GARY COLEMAN PERC (C
TOM HENSLEY K (C GINGER BLAKE V (C MAXINE WILLARD V (C
JULIA TILLMAN V (C MARTY GWINN V (C JOE SIDORE V (C
TOM SELLERS K (C STRINGS (C

B47B

MIKE BATT

MIKE BATT (( ) SCHIZOPHONIA 1977 EPIC EPC 82001
FRANK RICOTTI PERC (C (B) TAROT SUITE 1979 EPIC EPC 86099
FRANK McDONALD B (C (C) WAVES 1980 EPIC EPC 84617
CLEM CATTINI D (B
CHRIS SPEDDING G (B RAY COOPER PERC (B TERRY COX D (B
RICK KEMP B (B ROGER CHAPMAN V (B RAY RUSSELL G (C
EDDIE COWARD CONG (C B J COLE STEEL (C MEL COLLINS SAX (C
TREVOR MORAIS D (C JIM CREGAN G (C NIGEL JENKINS G (C
AMSTERDAM CHAMBER ORCH (C

B47C

DAVID BATTEAU

DAVID BATTEAU V G (A (A) HAPPY IN HOLLYWOOD 1976 A&M AMLH64576
WITH
WILLIE WEEKS B (A KENNY ALTMAN B (A JEFF PORCARO D (A
MILT HOLLAND PERC (A DAVID PAICH K (A ROY DAVIES K (A
DAVID SPINOZZA G (A ROBERT AHWAI G (A STEVE GREGORY FLT (A
MICHAEL BAILEY TPT (A MARTIN DROVER TPT (A CHRIS MERCER SAX (A
DENIECE WILLIAMS V (A JULIA TILLMAN V (A MAXINE WILLARD V (A
JOAN SLIWIN V (A

B48

BATTI MAMZELLE

PETER DUPREY B V (A (A) I SEE THE LIGHT 1974 CUBE HI FLY 17 2326 037
WINSTON DELANDRO G K (A
RICHARD BAILEY D V (A MIGUEL BARRADAS PERC (A RALPH RICHARDSON PERC (A
RUSSELL VALDEZ PERC (A FRANK INCE CONGA (A JIMMY CHAMBERS CONGAS(A

B49

SKIP BATTIN

SKIP BATTIN B V (A (A) SKIP 1973 SIGNPOST UK SG4255 US SP 8408
CLARENCE WHITE G (A
BILLY MUNDI d (A JOHN GUERIN D (A ROGER McGUINN G V (A
SPANKY McFARLANE V (A

B50

LUCIO BATTISTI

LUCIO BATTISTI V (ALL (A) IL MIO CANTO LIBERO 1973 COLUMBIA SCX 6540
RAY PARKER G (D (B) IL NOSTRO CARO ANGELO 1975 VOGUE LDM 30254
DENNIS BUDIMIR G (D (C) ANIMA LATINA 1975 VOGUE LDM 30282
DANNY FERGUSON G (D (D) IMAGES 1978 RCA PL 31889
MIKE MELVOIN K (D
SCOTTY EDWARDS B (D JIM HUGHART B (D ED GREENE D (D
HAL BLAINE D (D MICHAEL BODDICKER K (D

B51

BATTLEFIELD BAND

PAT KILBRIDE MAND V(B (A) BATTLEFIELD BAND 1977 TOPIC 12TS 313
ALAN REID K V (b (B) AT THE FRONT 1978 TOPIC 12TS 381
BRIAN McNEILL FDL V (B (C) STAND EASY 1979 TOPIC 12TS 404
JAMIE McMENEMY G V (B

B52

PETER BAUMANN

PETER BAUMANN K (AB (A) ROMANCE 76 1977 VIRGIN V 2069
W THIERFELD D (B (B) TRANS HARMONIC NIGHTS 1979 VIRGIN V 2124
B JOBSKI HRNS (B

B53

CAROL BAYER SAGER

CAROL BAYER-SAGER V (AB (A) CAROL BAYER SAGER 1977 ELEKTRA K 52059
(B) TOO 1978 ELEKTRA US 6E 151 UK K 52093

B54

BE BOP DELUXE

BILL NELSON G V (ALL (A) AXE VICTIM 1974 HARVEST SHVL 813
WITH (B) FUTURAMA 1975 HARVEST SHSP 4045
ROBERT BRYAN B (AH (B) FUTURAMA 1975 HARVEST US ST 11432
NICHOLAS DEW D (AH (C) SUNBURST FINISH 1976 HARVEST SHSP 4053
IAN PARKIN G (AH (C) SUNBURST FINISH 1976 HARVEST US ST 11478
RICHARD BROWN K ((D) MODERN MUSIC 1976 HARVEST SHSP 4058
MILTON REAME JAMES K ((D) MODERN MUSIC 1976 HARVEST US ST 11575
PAUL JEFFREYS B ((E) HOT VALVES (EP) 1976 HARVEST HAR 5117
SIMON FOX D (BCDEFGH (F) LIVE IN THE AIR AGE DBL 1977 HARVEST SHVL 816
CHARLIE TUMAHAI B (BCDEFGH (F) LIVE IN THE AIR AGE DBL 1977 HARVEST US SKB 11666
ANDREW CLARK K (CDEFGH (G) DRASTIC PLASTIC 1978 HARVEST SHSP 4091
NICK CLARK G ((G) DRASTIC PLASTIC 1978 PATHE FR C066 06598
(H) THE BEST OF & THE REST DBL 1978 HARVEST SHDW 410

B56

BEACH BOYS

BRIAN WILSON (MIKE LOVE (AL JARDINE G (DENNIS WILSON (
BRUCE JOHNSTON (BLONDI CHAPMAN (CARL WILSON (RICK FATAAR D (
JAMES GUERCIO (DAVID MATTS (GLEN CAMPBELL (
TONI TENNILLE V (MARILYN WILSON V (STEVE DOUGLAS SAX (JACK NIMITZ SAX (
MIKE ALTSCHOL SAX (DENNIS DREITH SAX (JOHN J KELSON (SAX (JAY MIGLIORI SAX (
PLAS JOHNSON SAX (JULES JACOBS CLAR (CAROL LEE MILLER A'HARP(GENE ESTES PERC (
JULIUS WECHTER PERC (HAL BLAINE D (DENNIS DRAGON D (RON ALTBACH PNO (
ED CARTER G (BILLY HINSCHE G (BEN BENAY G (JERRY COLE G (
(CONTINUED)

[26]

TOMMY TEDESCO	G (	LYLE RITZ	B (	TIM DRUMMOND	B (	RAY POLMAN	B (
JAMES HUGHART	B (	BOBBY SHEW	TPT (	GARY GRIFFIN	K (	MIKE KOWALSKI	D (
CHRIS MIDAUGH	STEEL(	MICHAEL ANDREAS	HRNS (	CHARLES LLOYD	HRNS (	LANCE BUTLER	HRNS (
JOHN FOSS	HRNS (				

SURFIN SAFARI		1962	CAPITOL	T1808	SURFS UP	1971	STATESIDE	SSL10313
SURFIN SAFARI		1962	CAPITOL	SY 4572	BEACH BOYS	1971	STARLINE	SRS 5074
SURFIN U S A		1963	CAPITOL	ST 1890	LIVE IN LONDON	1972	CAPITOL	ST21715
SURFER GIRL		1963	CAPITOL	ST 1891	LIVE IN LONDON	197	M F P	50345
SURFER GIRL		19	PICKWICK	SPC3351	SO TOUGH	1972	REPRISE	K 44184
GREAT CONCERT		19	PICKWICK	SPC 3309	SO TOUGH	1972	REPRISE	2083
LITTLE DEUCE COUPE		1963	CAPITOL	ST 1998	HOLLAND	1973	REPRISE	K 54008
SHUT DOWN VOL 2		1964	CAPITOL	ST 2027	HOLLAND	1973	REPRISE	2118
ALL SUMMER LONG		1964	CAPITOL	ST 2110	SUNFLOWER/SURFS UP (DBL)	1973	EMI	5C184502156
ALL SUMMER LONG		19	MFP	50065	IN CONCERT	1973	REPRISE	84001
CHRISTMAS ALBUM		1964	CAPITOL	ST 2164	ENDLESS SUMMER	1974	CAPITOL	EAST11307
CHRISTMAS ALBUM		1977	CAPITOL	CAP1014	FRIENDS /SMILEY SMILE DBL	1974	REPRISE	2MS 2167
BEACH BOYS CONCERT		1964	CAPITOL	ST 2198	VERY BEST OF 63-69	1974	ELECTROLA	1C15281482
BEACH BOYS TODAY		1965	CAPITOL	ST 2269	STARS OF THE SIXTIES	1974	BOVEMA	5C05081596
SUMMER DAYS SUMMER NIGHTS		1965	CAPITOL	ST 2354	DO YOU WANNA DANCE	1975	EMI	140502545
SUMMER DAYS SUMMER NIGHTS		1965	CAPITOL	CAPS 1023	WILD HONEY/20 20 (DBL)	1975	REPRISE	2MS 2166
BEACH BOYS PARTY		1965	CAPITOL	ST 2398	WILD HONEY/FRIENDS	1975	CAPITOL	ESTSP 14
BEACH BOYS PARTY		1965	CAPITOL	MAS 2398	OLDIES	1975	EMI	048 0776
PET SOUNDS		1966	CAPITOL	ST 2458	GOOD VIBRATIONS BEST OF	19	REPRISE	K 2280
PET SOUNDS		1966	CAPITOL	MS 2197	GOOD VIBRATIONS	1975	REPRISE	K 52223
BEST OF THE BEACH BOYS		1966	CAPITOL	ST 2545	GOOD VIBRATIONS	1975	REPRISE	6484
BEST OF THE BEACH BOYS		1966	CAPITOL	ST20856	GOOD VIBRATIONS	1975	BROTHER	2223
SMILEY SMILE		1967	CAPITOL	ST 9001	GOOD VIBRATIONS	197	M F P	50234
SMILEY SMILE (GERM)		1967	CAPITOL	SMK 74330	GOOD VIBRATIONS	197	PICKWICK	SPC3769
SMILEY SMILE		19	BROTHER	9001	SPIRIT OF AMERICA DBL	1975	CAPITOL	SVBB11384
BEST OF VOL 2		1967	CAPITOL	ST 2706	SPIRIT OF AMERICA DBL	1975	REPRISE	VMP1007
BESY OF VOL 2		1967	CAPITOL	ST20956	15 BIG ONES	1976	REPRISE	2251
WILD HONEY		1967	CAPITOL	ST 2859	15 BIG ONES	1976	REPRISE	K 54079
FRIENDS		1968	CAPITOL	ST 2895	STACK O TRACKS	1976	CAPITOL	DKAD 289
FRIENDS (GERM)		1968	CAPITOL	SMK 74456	STACK O TRACKS	1977	CAPITOL	EST24009
BEST OF VOL 3		1968	CAPITOL	ST 2945	20 GOLDEN GREATS	1977	CAPITOL	EMTV1
BEST OF VOL 3		1968	CAPITOL	ST21142	LOVE YOU	1977	CAPITOL	K 54087
BEACH BOYS		1968	M F P	MFP 1382	LOVE YOU	1977	REPRISE	MSK 2258
20/20		1969	CAPITOL	EST 133	M I U	1978	REPRISE	MSK 2268
CLOSE UP		1969	CAPITOL	EST 253	M I U	1978	REPRISE	K 54102
BEACH BOYS 69		1969	CAPITOL	ST 11584	40 GREAT HITS (DBL)	19	CAPITOL	CAPITOL 1/2
SUNFLOWER		1970	REPRISE	6382	30 GREATEST HITS'TRIPLE)	19	CAPITOL	2813
SUNFLOWER		1970	STATESIDE	SSLA 8251	BEACH BOYS	19	PICKWICK	SPC3221
BUG IN		1970	STARLINE	SRS 5014	FUN FUN FUN (DBL)	19	CAPITOL	SF702/703
GREATEST HITS		1970	CAPITOL	ST21628	FUN FUN FUN (DBL)	19	CAPITOL	5TB 701
SURFS UP		1971	REPRISE	6453		

PAUL TARTACHNY	G V (AB	(A) EYES OF THE BEACON STREET UNION	1968	MGM	US SE 4517
WAYNE ULAKY	B V (AB	(B) CLOWN DIED IN MARVIN GARDENS	1968	MGM	US
JOHN WRIGHT	V PERC(AB		
RICHARD WEISBURG	D (AB	ROBERT RHODES	K WIND (AB	

RICHARD T BEAR   K (A   (A) RED HOT & BLUE   1979 RCA   PL 12927

WITH

ALLAN SCHWARZBERG	D PERC(A	LES DUDEK	G (A	ELLIOTT RANDALL	G (A
STEVE GELFAND	B (A	MIKE FINNIGAN	K (A	NEIL JASON	B (A
GEORGE GOMEZ	G (A	PAUL SCHAEFFER	K (A	GORDON GRODY	V (A
JOHN BARRANCO	V (A	BOB GURLAND	TPT (A	ANNIE SUTTON	V (A
DIVA GRAY	V (A	SHARON LEE WILLIAMS	V (A	ZULEMA CUSSEAUX	V (A
TRACY RICHARDSON	V (A	BILLY SQUIRE	G (A	KATHY INGRAHAM	V (A
CHRISTINE FAITH	V (A	DAVE WOODS	TPT (A	JACK ZAZA	ACC (A
RANDY BRECKER	HRNS (A	MICHAEL BRECKER	HRNS (A	GEORGE YOUNG	HRNS (A
RON CUBER	HRNS (A	TONY PRICE	HRNS (A	TOM MALONE	HRNS (A

GEORGE GIL	G
RON WEST	B
CALLY	D
KRIS KERSHAW	SAX

JOHN LENNON	G V K (ALL	EPs
PAUL McCARTNEY	B G K V(ALL	BEATLES HITS	1963 PARLOPHONE	GEP 8880
GEORGE HARRISON	G V (ALL	TWIST & SHOUT	1963 PARLOPHONE	GEP 8882
RINGO STARR	D V (ALL	BEATLES NO 1	1963 PARLOPHONE	GEP 8883
		ALL MY LOVIN'	1964 PARLOPHONE	GEP 8891
WITH		LONG TALL SALLY	1964 PARLOPHONE	GEP 8913
PETE BEST	D	HARD DAYS NIGHT	1964 PARLOPHONE	GEP 8920
STUART SUTCLIFFE	G	HARD DAYS NIGHT 2	1964 PARLOPHONE	GEP 8924
KLAUS VOORMANN	B	BEATLES FOR SALE	1965 PARLOPHONE	GEP 8931
ERIC CLAPTON	G	BEATLES FOR SALE 2	1965 PARLOPHONE	GEP 8938
GEORGE MARTIN	K	MILLION SELLERS	1965 PARLOPHONE	GEP 8946
		YESTERDAY	1965 PARLOPHONE	GEP 8948
		NOWHERE MAN	1966 PARLOPHONE	GEP 8952
		MAGICAL MYSTERY TOUR	1967 PARLOPHONE	SMMT 1

LPs

THE BEATLES & TONY SHERIDAN	1962	CONTOUR	CN 2007
THE EARLY YEARS	1962	CONTOUR	2870111
THE BEATLES FIRST	19	POLYDOR	24001
IN THE BEGINNING	19	POLYDOR	2664 107
THIS IS WHERE IT STARTED	19		

THE BEATLES

PLEASE PLEASE ME		MONO	1963	PARLOPHONE	UK	PMC 1202
PLEASE PLEASE ME		MONO	1963	PARLOPHONE	UK	PCS 3042
PLEASE PLEASE ME			1963	PATHE	FR	C06604219
PLEASE PLEASE ME			196	APPLE	JAP	AP8675
WITH THE BEATLES		MONO	1963	PARLOPHONE	UK	PMC 1206
WITH THE BEATLES		STEREO	1963	PARLOPHONE	UK	PCS 3045
WITH THE BEATLES			196	PATHE	FR	C06604181
WITH THE BEATLES			19	APPLE	JAP	AP 8678
INTRODUCING THE BEATLES			1964	VEE JAY	US	SR1062
THE BEATLES			1964	MGM	US	4215
MEET THE BEATLES			1964	CAPITOL	US	2047
MEET THE BEATLES		VOL1	19	APPLE	JAP	AP 80011
MEET THE BEATLES		VOL2	19	APPLE	JAP	AP 8026
BEATLES SECOND			1964	CAPITOL	US	2080
BEATLES SECOND		VOL1	19	APPLE	JAP	AP80012
BEATLES SECOND		VOL2	19	APPLE	JAP	AP8027
SOMETHING NEW			1964	CAPITOL	US	2108
SOMETHING NEW			19	PATHE	FR	C062 04600
SOMETHING NEW			19	APPLE	19	AP 80033
AINT SHE SWEET			1964		US	
BEATLES STORY			1964	CAPITOL	US	2222
HARD DAYS NIGHT		MONO	1964	PARLOPHONE	UK	PMC 1230
HARD DAYS NIGHT		STEREO	1964	PARLOPHONE	UK	PCS 3058
HARD DAYS NIGHT			1964	PATHE	FR	C06604145
HARD DAYS NIGHT			196	APPLE	JAP	AP8147
HARD DAYS NIGHT			1964	U A	US	3366 64
BEATLES FOR SALE		MONO	1964	PARLOPHONE	UK	PMC 1240
BEATLES FOR SALE		STEREO	1964	PARLOPHONE	UK	PCS 3062
BEATLES FOR SALE			1964	PATHE	FR	C06804200
BEATLES FOR SALE			1964	APPLE	JAP	AP8442
BEATLES 65			1965	CAPITOL	US	2228
BEATLES 65			1965	PATHE	FR	C07204201
EARLY BEATLES			1965	CAPITOL	US	2309
EARLY BEATLES			1965	APPLE	JAP	AP 80034
BEATLES VI			1965	CAPITOL	US	2358
BEATLES VI			1965	APPLE	JAP	AP 80035
HELP		MONO	1965	PARLOPHONE	UK	PMC 1255
HELP		STEREO	1965	PARLOPHONE	UK	PCS 3071
HELP			1965	PATHE	FR	C06604257
HELP			1965	APPLE	JAP	OSX 230
HELP VOL 1			19	APPLE	JAP	AP 50060
HELP VOL 2			196	APPLE	JAP	AP 8151
HELP			1965	CAPITOL	US	2386
HELP			1965	APPLE		SMAS 2386
RUBBER SOUL		MONO	1966	PARLOPHONE	UK	PMC 1267
RUBBER SOUL		STEREO	1966	PARLOPHONE	UK	PCS 3075
RUBBER SOUL			1966	CAPITOL	US	2442
RUBBER SOUL			1966	PATHE	FR	C06604115
RUBBER SOUL			1966	APPLE	JAP	AP 8156
YESTERDAY & TODAY			1966	CAPITOL	US	2553
YESTERDAY & TODAY			1965	APPLE	JAP	AP 80061
REVOLVER			1966	PARLOPHONE	UK	PCS 7009
REVOLVER			1966	CAPITOL	US	2576
REVOLVER			1966	PATHE	FR	C06604097
REVOLVER			1966	APPLE	JAP	AP8443
COLLECTION OF OLDIES			1967	PARLOPHONE	UK	PCS 7016
COLLECTION OF OLDIES			1967	APPLE	JAP	AP 8016
SGT PEPPER			1967	PARLOPHONE	UK	PCS 7027
SGT PEPPER			1967	CAPITOL	US	ST 2653
SGT PEPPER			1967	PATHE	FR	C06604177
SGT PEPPER			1967	APPLE	JAP	AP 5163
MAGICAL MYSTERY TOUR			1968	CAPITOL	US	ST 2835
MAGICAL MYSTERY TOUR			1976	EMI	UK	PCTC 255
THE BEATLES WHITE (DBL)			1968	PARLOPHONE	UK	PCS7067/8
THE BEATLES WHITE(DBL)			1968	APPLE	US	101
THE BEATLES WHITE (DBL)			1968		JAP	AP 5570/1
YELLOW SUBMARINE			1969	APPLE	UK	PCS 7070
YELLOW SUBMARINE			1969	APPLE	IMP	SMO 74585
YELLOW SUBMARINE			1969	PATHE	FR	C06604002
YELLOW SUBMARINE			1969		JAP	AP8610
YELLOW SUBMARINE			1969	CAPITOL	US	SW 153
ABBEY ROAD			1969	APPLE	UK	PCS 7088
ABBEY ROAD			1969	CAPITOL	US	SO 383
ABBEY ROAD			1969	PATHE	FR	C06604243
ABBEY ROAD			1969		JAP	AP8815
BEATLES AGAIN			19	PATHE	FR	C06604348
BEATLES AGAIN			19		JAP	AP8940
LET IT BE			1970	APPLE	UK	PCS 7096
LET IT BE			1970	APPLE	US	34001
LET IT BE		BOX SET	1970	APPLE		PXS1
LET IT BE			1970	PATHE	FR	C06604433
LET IT BE			1970	APPLE	JAP	AP 801891
HEY JUDE			1970	CAPITOL	US	SW 385
HEY JUDE			1970	APPLE		CPCS 106
1962 66		DBL	1973	PARLOPHONE	UK	PCSP 717
1962 66		DBL	1973	CAPITOL	US	SEBX11842
1962 66		DBL	1973	CAPITOL	US	3403
1962 66		DBL	1973	PATHE	FR	C16205307
1962 66		DBL	1973		JAP	EAP 9032

(CONTINUED)

THE BEATLES

1967 70	DBL		1973	PARLOPHONE	UK	PCSP	718
1967 70	DBL		1973	CAPITOL	US	SEBX11843	
1967 70	DBL		1973	CAPITOL	US		3404
1967 70	DBL		1973	PATHE	FR	C16205309/0	
1967 70	DBL		1973		JAP	EAP	9034
THE EARLY YEARS			1973	ELECTROLA	IMP	2870	111
RARITIES			19	PARLOPHONE	UK	PMC	1001
LIVE AT THE STAR CLUB HAMBURG			1977	BELLAPHON	GERM	BLS	5560
LIVE AT THE STAR CLUB HAMBURG			1977	ATLANTIC	US	SD2	7001
LIVE AT THE STAR CLUB HAMBURG			1977	RCA			7375
LIVE AT THE HOLLYWOOD BOWL			1977	EMI	UK	EMTV 4	
LIVE AT THE HOLLYWOOD BOWL			1977	PATHE	FR	C06806377	
LIVE AT THE HOLLYWOOD BOWL			1977	CAPITOL	US	SMAS11638	
ROCK'N'ROLL			197	PARLOPHONE	UK	PCSP	719
ROCK'N'ROLL			1976	CAPITOL	US	SKBO11537	
LOVE SONGS			1977	PARLOPHONE	UK	PCS	7211
LOVE SONGS			1977	CAPITOL	US	SKBL11231	
BEATLES BEAT			19	PATHE	FR	C07204363	
BEATLES GREATEST			19	PATHE	FR	C06204207	
BEATLES TAPES			1977	POLYDOR		2683	068
LIVE AT THE STAR CLUB			1977	LINGASONG			LNL1
BEATLES BALLADS			1980	PARLOPHONE		PCS	7214
HEAR THE BEATLES TELL ALL			1981	CHARLY		CRV	202

BEAU

C J T MIDGLEY(BEAU)	G V	(AB	(A) BEAU	1969	DANDELION		63751
JIM MILNE		(B	(B) CREATION	19	DANDELION		DAN 8006
STEVE CLAYTON		(B					

BEAU BRUMMELS

SAL VALENTINO	V	(ABCDEFGHJ	(A) INTRODUCING	19	AUTUMN		SLP 103
RON ELLIOTT	G	(ABCDEFGHJ	(B) BEAU BRUMMELS	19	AUTUMN		SLP 104
RON MEAGHER	G B	(ABDEF	(C) BEAU BRUMMELS	1966	PYE		NPL 28062
DECLAN MULLIGAN	B	(A	(D) BEAU BRUMMELS 66	1966	W B		WS 1644
JON PETERSON	D	(ABD	(E) TRIANGLE	1967	W B		WS 1692
VAN DYKE PARKS	K	(E	(F) BEST OF	1967	VAULT		LPS 114
JERRY REED	G	(H	(G) VOL 44	196	VAULT		LPS 121
NORBERT PUTMAN	R	(H	(H) BRADLEYS BARN	1968	W B		WS 1760
DAVID BRIGGS	K	(H	(J) THE BEAU BRUMMELS	19	W B		WS 2842
KENNY BUTTREY	D	(H	(K) GREATEST HITS	19	JAS		JAS 5000
DAN LEVITT	G	(					

BEAUREGARD

	(A) BEAUREGARD	19	SOUND PROD	

D BEAVER

D BEAVER	K V	(A	(A) COMBINATIONS	1973	TMI	BTLI 0118
PAUL ALLAN TAYLOR	G V	(A				
JIMMY JAMISON	V	(A	TOMMY CATHEY	B	(A	JOEL WILLIAMS	G D	(A
CARL MARSH	WIND	(A	J A SPELL	FDL	(A	STEVE SPEAR	B	(A
JIMMY TARBUTTON	G	(A	DAVID MAYO	V PNO	(A	RENI CROOK	V	(A
LEO LEBLANC	STEEL	(A	RUDY GARNER	CLAR	(A	JACKIE COOK	V	(A

BEAVER BROTHERS

	(A) VENTRILOQUISMS	197	AURA	AUL 701

BEAVER KRAUSE

PAUL BEAVER	K	(ALL	(A) RAGNAROK ELECTRONIC FUNK	19	LIMELIGHT	US	86069
BERNARD KRAUSE	K	(ALL	(B) IN A WILD SANCTUARY	19	W B		WS 1850
WITH			(C) GANDHARVA	1971	W B	US	WS 1909
MIKE BLOOMFIELD	G	(	(C) GANDHARVA	1971	W B	UK	K 46130
RAY BROWN	B	(	(D) ALL GOOD MEN	197	W B	UK	K 46184
RIK ELSWIT	G	(	(D) ALL GOOD MEN	197	W B	US	BS 2624
LEE CHARLTON	D	(	(E) GUIDE TO ELECTRONIC MUSIC	1975	NONSUCH	UK	K 73018
ROD ELLICOTT	B	(					
LAMONT JOHNSON	K	(					
GEORGE MARCH	D	(	MIKE LANG	K	(	GAIL LANGTON	HARP	(
HOWARD ROBERTS	G	(	RONNIE MONTROSE	G	(	GERRY MULLIGAN	SAX	(
CLYDIE KING	V	(	BUD SHANKS	SAX	(	PATRICE HOLLOWAY	V	(

JEFF BECK

JEFF BECK	G	(ALL	(1) PRE FIRST LP LINE UP	(2) PRE FIRST LP LINE UP			
WITH			(A) TRUTH	1968	COLUMBIA	UK	SCX 6293
JET HARRIS	B	(1	(A) TRUTH	1968	EPIC	US	PE 26413
VIV PRINCE	D	(1	(B) BECK OLA	1969	COLUMBIA	UK	SCX 6351
RAY COOK	D	(2	(B) BECK OLA	1973	PATHE	FE	2C062 90496
RON WOOD	G	(AB2	(B) BECK OLA	1975	EPIC	US	BN 26478
ROD STEWART	V	(AB2	(AB)TRUTH/ BECK OLA	19	EPIC	US	BG 33779
NICKY HOPKINS	K	(AB	(C) ROUGH & READY	1971	EPIC UK 64619	US	30973
TONY NEWMAN	D	(B	(D) THE JEFF BECK GROUP	1972	EPIC UK 64899	US	31331
MAX MIDDLETON	K	(CDEF	(CD) ROUGH & READY/JEFF BECK GROUP DB	19	EPIC	US	PE 30973
COZY POWELL	D	(CD	(E) BLOW BY BLOW	1975	EPIC UK 69117	US	33409
BOB TENCH	G V	(CD	(F) WIRED	1976	EPIC UK 86012	US	33849
PHIL CHEN	B	(E	(G) LIVE	1977	EPIC UK 86025	US	34433
WILBUR BASCOMB	B	(F	(H) THERE & BACK	1980	EPIC UK 83288		
FERNANDO SAUNDERS	B V G	(G	( ) MASTER OF ROCK	1974	EMI 054 92207 FR PATHE 06295122		
JOHN PAUL JONES	ORG	(A	( ) THE MOST OF JEFF BECK	1971	M F P	UK	MFP 5219
SIMON PHILLIPS	D	(H	( ) BEST OF JEFF BECK	19	CBS	HOLL	
TONY HYMAS	K	(H	( ) GOT THE FEELING & OTHERS (EP)	19	PLAYBACK		1026
MO FOSTER	B	(F					
STEVE KINDLER	VLN K	(G	TONY SMITH	D V	(G	JAN HAMMER	K	(FGH RICHARD BAILEY	D	(EF
NARADA MICHAEL WALDEN	D	(F	CLIVE CHAMAN	B	(CD	MICK WALLER	D	(A	AYNSLEY DUNBAR	D	(

BECK BOGERT & APPICE

B64A

JEFF BECK	G	(AB
CARMINE APPICE	D	(AB
TIM BOGERT	B	(AB
DANNY HUTTON	V	(A
DUANE HITCHINGS	K	(A
JIM GREENSPOON	PNO	(A

(A) BECK BOGERT & APPICE	1973	EPIC	UK	EPC 65455
(A) BECK BOGERT & APPICE	1973	EPIC	US	KE 32140
(B) LIVE IN JAPAN	1975	EPIC	JAP	EPCO 58
(C) LIVE IN JAPAN (DBL)	1977	cbs/SONY	JAP	ECPJ11/12
(D) ALIVE	1974	EPIC		22001

JOE BECK

B65

JOE BECK	G V	(ALL

(A) NATURE BOY	1969	VERVE	US	FTS 3081
(B) WATCH THE TIME	1977	POLYDOR		2391 257
(B) WATCH THE TIME	1977	POLYDOR	US	PD 6092
(C) BECK	1977	KUDU		KU 21
(C) BECK	1977	KUDU	US	KU 2151

BECKETT

B66

ROBERT BARTON	G V	(A
KENNY MOUNTAIN	G V	(A
TERRY WILSON-SLESSER	V	(A
IAN MURRAY	B	(A

(A) BECKETT	1974	RAFT	UK	RA 48502

KEITH FISHER	D	(A	FRANKIE GIBBONS	B	(
TIM HINKLEY	K	(A			

HARRY BECKETT

B67

HARRY BECKETT

(A) FLARE UP	1971	PHILIPS		6308 026
(B) WARM SMILES	1972	RCA		SF 8225
(C) THEME FOR FEGA	1973	RCA		SF 8264
(D) JOY UNLIMITED	1975	CADILLAC		SGC 1004
(E) MEMORIES OF BACARES	1976	OGUN		OG 800
(F) GOT IT MADE	1978	OGUN		OG 020

BECKIES

B68

MICHAEL BROWN	K	(A
MAYO JAMES McALLISTER		(A
GARY HODGDEN		(A

(A) THE BECKIES	1976	SIRE		SASD 7159

SCOTT TRUSTY	(A

DAVID BEDFORD

B69

DAVID BEDFORD	K	(ALL
WITH		
MICHAEL OLDFIELD	G B	(BC
CHRIS CUTLER	B	(B

(A) NURSES SONG WITH ELEPHANTS	1972	DANDELION		2310 165
(B) STARS END	1974	VIRGIN		V 2020
(C) ORCHESTRAL TUBULAR BELLS	1975	VIRGIN		V 2026
(D) RIME OF THE ANCIENT MARINER	1975	VIRGIN		V 2038
(E) ODYSSEY	1976	VIRGIN		V 2070
(E) ODYSSEY	1976	POLYDOR		2933 735
(F) INSTRUCTIONS FOR ANGELS	1977	VIRGIN		V 2090
(F) INSTRUCTIONS FOR ANGELS	1977	POLYDOR		2437 738

BEDLAM

B70

COZY POWELL	D	(A
FRANCESCO AIELLO	V	(A
DENNIS BALL	B	(A
DABE BALL	G	(A

(A) BEDLAM	1973	CHRYSALIS		CHR 1048

FELIX PAPPALARDI	K	(A	MAX MIDDLETON	K	(A

BEE GEES

B71

MAURICE GIBB	V	(ALL
BARRY GIBB	V	(ALL
ROBIN GIBB	V	(ALL
WITH		
COLIN PETERSEN	D	(
VINCE MELOUNEY	G	(
ALAN KENDALL	G B	(
VINCE BYRON	G	(

BEE GEES FIRST	1967	POLDOR	UK	583 012
BEE GEES FIRST	1967	ATCO	US	SD 33 223
HORIZONTAL	1968	POLYDOR	UK	583 020
HORIZONTAL	1968	ATCO	US	SD 33 233
RARE PRECIOUS & BEAUTIFUL	1968	POLYDOR	UK	236 221
RARE PRECIOUS & BEAUTIFUL	1968	ATCO	US	SD 33 264
RARE PRECIOUS & BEAUTIFUL VOL2	1968	POLYDOR	UK	236 513
IDEA	1968	POLYDOR	UK	583 036
IDEA	1968	ATCO	US	SD 33 253
RARE PRECIOUS & BEATIFUL VOL 3	1969	POLYDOR	UK	236 556
ODESSA	1969	POLYDOR	UK	582049/50
ODESSA	19	RSO	US	1 3007
ODESSA	1969	ATCO	US	SD 2702
ODESSA	19	POLYDOR		2674 012
THE BEST OF	1969	POLYDOR	UK	583 063
CUCUMBER CASTLE	1970	POLYDOR	UK	2383 010
SOUND OF LOVE	1970	POLYDOR	UK	2447 005
TWO YEARS ON	1970	POLYDOR	UK	2310 069
MARLEY PURT DRIVE	1970	POLYDOR	UK	2447 012
TRAFALGAR	1971	POLYDOR	UK	2383 052
TO WHOM IT MAY CONCERN	1972	POLYDOR	UK	2383 139
TO WHOM IT MAY CONCERN	1972	ATCO	US	SD 7012
LIFE IN A TIN CAN	1973	RSO		2394 102
THE BEST OF VOL 2	1973	RSO		2394 106
THE BEST OF VOL 2	1973	RSO	US	SO 875
GOTTA GET A MESSAGE TO YOU	1973	CONTOUR		2870 404
MrNATURAL	1974	RSO		2394 132
MAIN COURSE	1975	RSO		2394 150
MAIN COURSE	1975	RSO	US	1 3024
PORTRAIT	1975	POLYDOR		2482 092
S W A L K (SOUNDTRACK)	197	POLYDOR		2383 044
CHILDREN OF THE WORLD	1976	RSO	US	1 3003
GOLD	197	RSO	US	1 3006
HERE AT LAST.....LIVE	1977	RSO		2658 120
HERE AT LAST.....LIVE	1977	RSO	US	1 3901
SATURDAY NIGHT FEVER	1977	RSO		2658 123
SPIRITS HAVING FLOWN	1979	RSO	UK	RSBG 1
SPIRITS HAVING FLOWN	1979	RSO	US	1 3041
BEE GEES GREATEST	1979	RSO		RSDX 001
EARLY DAYS VOL 1	1978	PICKWICK		SHM 971
EARLY DAYS VOL 2	1978	PICKWICK		SHM 973
EARLY DAYS VOL 3	1978	PICKWICK		SHM 982
BONANZA	1978	PICKWICK		PDA 048

```
CAPTAIN BEEFHEART              (A) SAFE AS MILK              1967   BUDDAH         US   BDS   5001
(DON VAN VLIET)     G V HCA(ALL (A) SAFE AS MILK              1970   BUDDAH         US   BDS   5063
                                (A) SAFE AS MILK              1968   PYE INT        UK   NPL   28110
RY COODER           G    (A     (B) DROP OUT BOOGIE           1967   BUDDAH              2349  002
                                (C) STRICTLY PERSONAL         1968   LIBERTY LBR1006          83172
ANTENNAE JIM SEMENS)            (C) STRICTLY PERSONAL         19     UA UAS29540   SUNSET     50208
(JEFF COTTON)       G    (ACDEH (C) STRICTLY PERSONAL         1968   BLUE THUMB     US   BTS    1
                                (D) TROUT MASK REPLICA(DBL)   1969   STRAIGHT       US   STS   1053
ZOOT HORN ROLLO                 (D) TROUT MASK REPLICA(DBL)   1969   REPRISE             K   64026
(BILL HARKLEROAD)   G    (DEFGJ (D) TROUT MASK REPLICA(DBL)   1969   REPRISE        US   RS    2027
                                (E) LICK MY DECALS OFF        1970   STRAIGHT       US   STS   1063
ROCKETTE MORTON                 (E) LICK MY DECALS OFF        1970   REPRISE             K   44244
(MARK BOSTON)       B G  (DEFGJ (E) LICK MY DECALS OFF        1970   REPRISE        US   RS    6440
                                (E) LICK MY DECALS OFF        19     ELECTROLA      IC  062 92092
ED MARIMBA(ART TRIPP) K D (FGJ  (F) SPOTLIGHT KID             1971   REPRISE        UK   K   44162
                                (F) SPOTLIGHT KID             1971   REPRISE        US   RS    2050
OREJON (ROY ESTRADA)  B  (G     (G) CLEAR SPOT                1972   REPRISE        UK K54007
                                (G) CLEAR SPOT                1972   REPRISE        US   MS    2115
SNOUFFER(ALEX ST CLAIRE)G (ACHJ (H) MIRROR MAN               1971   BUDDAH              2365  022
                                (H) MIRROR MAN               1974   BUDDAH              BDLP  4004
DRUMBO ( JOHN FRENCH) D (ACDEFHL(H) MIRROR MAN               19     BUDDAH         US   BDS   5077
                                (J) UNCONDITIONALLY GUARANTEED 1974  VIRGIN         UK   V    2015
WINGED EEL FINGERLING           (K) BLUEJEANS & MOONBEAMS    1974   VIRGIN         UK   V    2123
  (ELLIOT INGBER)    G   (1FK   (K) SHINEY BEAST BAT CHAIN PULLER 1978 W B         US   BSK   3256
JEFF MORRIS TEPPER   G   (L     (L) CAPT BEEFHEART FILE      1977   PYE            UK   FILD  008
ERIC DREW FELDMAN   B K  (L     (M) DOC AT THE RADAR STATION 1980   VIRGIN         UK   V    2172
ROBERT WILLIAMS     D    (L     (1) LIVE TOUR BAND
BRUCE FOWLER        TROM (L
MASCARA SNAKE       CLAR (DE    JERRY HANDLEY       B    (ACDEH  MARC MARCELLINO    K   (CH
HERB BETMEN              (A     RUSS TITELMAN       G    (A      ANDY DI MARTINO    G   (J
DEL SIMMONS         WIND (J     RHYS CLARK          D    (F      JIMMY CARL BLACK   D   (1
GREG DAVIDSON       G    (1     DOUG MOON           G    (DE     TED CACTUS             (F
MILT HOLLAND        PERC (G     DEAN SMITH          G    (K      TY GRIMES          PERC (K
BOB WEST            B    (K     MICHAEL SMOTHERMAN  K V  (K      MARK GIBBONS       K   (K
GENE PELLO          D    (K     JIMMY CARAVAN       K    (K      GARY LUCAS         G   (L
```

BEES MAKE HONEY   B73

```
BARRY RICHARDSON  B SAX (ABCDE  (A) MUSIC EVERY NIGHT              1972  EMI        EMC   3013
RUAN O'LOCHLAINN  G K SAX (AB   (B) 1971/72    (C)  1973   (D) 1974   (E) 1974
MICK MOLLOY       G     (ABCD   ( ) BEES MAKE HONEY   (EP)        1977  CHARLY      CEP   117
DEKE O'BRIEN      G     (ABCD
BOB CEEMANBERG    D     (AB
FRAN BYRNE        D     (ABCD   CLIFF BILLETT    TPT   (A      GERRY HOGAN    STEEL(A
MALCOLM MORLEY    G     (C      ROD DEMICK       B     (DE     ED DEAN        G    (E
KEVIN McALEA      PNO   (E      WILLIE FINLAYSON G     (E      JEDD KELLY     D    (A
```

BEGGARS OPERA   B74

```
MARTIN GRIFFITHS   V    (ABC    (A) ACT ONE                  1970  VERTIGO              6360  018
ALAN PARK          K    (ABC    (A) ACT ONE                  197   VERVE         US           5080
RAYMOND WILSON     D    (ABC    (B) WATERS OF CHANGE         1971  VERTIGO        UK    6360  054
RICKY GARDINER    G V   (ABC    (C) PATHFINDER               1972  VERTIGO        UK    6360  073
MARSHALL ERSKINE  B FLT (AB     (D) GET YOUR DOG OFF ME      1973  VERTIGO        UK    6360  090
GORDON SELLAR     B G V (BC
VIRGINIA SCOTT          (B
```

GRAHAM BELL   B75

```
GRAHAM BELL       V G   (A      (A) GRAHAM BELL              1972  CHARISMA       UK    CAS   1061
MEL COLLINS       SAX   (A
RON CORNELIUS     G     (A      TIM DRUMMOND     B     (A     IAN WALLACE    D    (A
TIM HINKLEY       K     (A      BOB WILSON       K     (A     GASPAR LAWAL   PERC (A
DEREK QUINN       PERC  (A
```

MADELINE BELL   B76

```
MADELINE BELL     V    (ALL     BELLS A POPPIN'             1967  PHILIPS        SBL   7818
                                DOIN' THINGS               1969  PHILIPS        SBL   7865
                                MADELINE BELL              1971  PHILIPS        6308  053
                                16 STAR TRACKS BY MADELINE BELL 1971 PHILIPS     6308  066
                                COMIN' ATCHA               1974  RCA            SF    8393
                                THIS IS ONE GIRL           1976  PYE            NSPL18483
```

MAGGIE BELL   B77

```
MAGGIE BELL        V    (AB     (A) QUEEN OF THE NIGHT      1973  POLYDOR        2383  239
REGGIE YOUNG       G    (A      (B) SUICIDE SAL            1975  POLYDOR        2383  313
CORNELL DUPREE     G    (A      (B) SUICIDE SAL            1975  SWANSONG   US   SS    8412
JOHN HUGHEY        STEEL (A     (D) GREAT ROCK SENSATION   19    POLYDOR    IMP  2499  <07
MICKEY KEENE       G    (B
HUGH McCRACKEN     G    (A      RICHARD TEE      K    (A     ARTHUR JENKINS  K    (A
LEON PENDARVIS     K    (A      BARRY GOLDBERG   K    (A     CHUCK RAINEY    B    (A
BILL SALTER        B    (A      STEVE GADD       D    (A     RALPH McDONALD  PERC (A
SWEET INSPIRATION  V    (A      PAUL FRANCIS     D    (B     DELISLE HARPER  B    (B
PETE WINGFIELD     K    (B      ROY DAVIES       K    (B     BRIAN BREEZE    G V  (B
TERRY              G    (A      HUGH BURNS       G    (B     JIMMY PAGE      G    (B
RAY GLYNN          G    (B      JIMMY JEWELL     SAX  (B     CUDDLEY JUDD  BAGPIPES (B
BILLY LAWRIE       V    (B      MARK LONDON      V    (B
```

WILLIAM BELL   B78

```
B78
WILLIAM BELL       V    (ALL    PHASES OF REALITY          19    STAX           2362  027
SWEET INSPIRATION  V            BOUND TO HAPPEN            1974  STAX           2363  002
BOOKER T JONES                  COMIN BACK FOR MORE        1977  MERCURY        9100  038
                                COMIN BACK FOR MORE        19    MERCURY    US  SRM1  1146
                                ITS TIME YOU TOOK ANOTHER LISTEN 19 MERCURY  US  SRM1  1193
                                RELATING                   19    STAX           STX   1010
                                BOUND TO HAPPEN            19    STAX           STX   1050
```

B79

MICK GALLAGHER	K	(A
GRAHAM BELL	V G	(A
TOM DUFFY	B	(A
JOHN TURNBULL	G	(A
ROB TAIT	D	(A

BELL & ARC

(A) BELL & ARC				1971	CHARISMA	UK	CAS	1053
JOHN WOOD	PERC	(A	ALAN WHITE	PERC	(A
STEVE GREGORY	SAX	(A	BUD BEADLE	SAX	(A
JEFF CONDON	CORNET	(A	KEN CRADDOCK	G	(A

B80

BELLAMY BROTHERS

DAVID BELLAMY	V	(ALL	(A) LET YOUR LOVE FLOW	1976	W B US 2941	UK		K56242
HOWARD BELLAMY	V	(ALL	(B) PLAIN & FANCY	1977	W B US 3034	UK		K56357
RICHARD BENNETT	G	(AB	(C) BEAUTIFUL FRIENDS	1978	W B US 3176	UK		K56485
DOUG RHONE	G	(A	(D) TWO & ONLY	1979	W B 337			
DENNIS ST JOHN	D	(A	(E) YOU CAN GET CRAZY	1980	W B	UK		K56777
ALAN LINDGREN	K	(AB	(F) SONS OF THE SUN	1980	W B	UK		K56872
KING ERRISON	PERC	(AB						
EMORY GORDY	B	(AB	MIKE HUEY	D	(B	JOHN SELK	B	(B
ALAN ESTES	PERC	(E	BOBBY BRUCE	FDL	(E	DANNY JONES	STEEL	(E
CARL CHAMBERS	G	(E	JON LAFRANDE	K	(E	RODNEY PRICE	D	(E
JESSE CHAMBERS	B	(E	CARLOS VEGA	D	(E			

B81

DAVID BENDETH

DAVID BENDETH	G V	(A	(A) ADRENALIN		1979	SIDEWALK		SWK 2004
WITH								
JOHN CLEVELAND HUGHES	K	(A	MARCUS MILLER	B	(A	LENNY WHITE	D	(A
RANDY BRAMWELL	B	(A	DAVID SPAN	D	(A	MEMO ACEVEDO	PERC	(A
BOYER BROTHERS	V	(A	JOHN JOHNSON	SAX	(A	BILLY COBHAM	D	(A
DAVID DUNLOP	TPT	(A						

B81A

BRIAN BENNETT

BRIAN BENNETT	D	(ALL	(A) CHANGE OF DIRECTION	1968	COLUMBIA	UK	SCX	6144
			(B) THE ILLUSTRATED LONDON PRIDE	1969	STUDIO 2	UK	TWO	268
			(C) ROCK DREAMS	1977	DJM	UK	DJF	20499
			(D) VOYAGE	1978	DJM	UK	DJS	

B82

CLIFF BENNETT

CLIFF BENNETT	V	(ALL	(A)CLIFF BENNETT & THE REBEL ROUSERS	1964	PARLOPHONE	UK	PMC	1242
ROY YOUNG	K V	(	(B) DRIVING YOU WILD	196			REG	1035
MICK BURT	D	(	(B) DRIVING YOU WILD	1966	M F P	UK	MFP	1121
CHAS HODGES	G	(	(C) GOT TO GET YOU INTO MY LIFE	1968	PARLOPHONE	UK	PCS	7017
MOSS GROVES	SAX	(	(D) BRANCHES OUT	1968	PARLOPHONE	UK	PCS	7054
SID PHILLIPS	SAX	(	(E) REBELLION	1971	CBS	US		64487
JOHN GRAY	B	(E	(F) CLIFF BENNETT & THE REBEL ROUSERS	1978	EMI	UK	NUT	14
MAREK KLUCZYNSKI	FLT	(E						
DEREK WIER	PERC	(E	ROBERT SMITH	G	(E			

B83

DUSTER BENNETT

DUSTER BENNETT	V G HCA PERC	(ALL	(A) SMILING LIKE IM HAPPY	1968	BLUE HORIZON		7	63208
WITH			(B) BRIGHT LIGHTS	1969	BLUE HORIZON		7	63221
PETER GREEN	G	(A	(C) 12 DBs	1970	BLUE HORIZON		7	63868
JOHN McVIE	B	(A	(D) FINGERTIPS	1974	TOADSTOOL		L	35436
HAM RICHMOND	K	(A	(E) BENNETT	19	BLUE HORIZON	US		4812
STELLA SUTTON	V	(AB	(F) JUSTA	19	BLUE HORIZON	US		4804
MICK FLEETWOOD	D	(A						
TOP TOPHAM	G	(BC						
TONY MILLS	B	(BC	NICKY HOPKINS	K	(D	JOHN SIOMOS	D	(D
RICK WILLS	B	(D	HUGH BURNS	G	(D	MORRIS PERT	PERC	(D
PETER FRAMPTON	G	(D	TERRY STANNARD	D	(D	LIZA STRIKE	V	(D
ROB ROBERTSON	B	(D	PHIL WAINMAN	D	(D	PETE WINGFIELD	K	(D
PIP WILLIAMS	G	(D	BARRY ST JOHN	V	(D	LINDA KENDRICK	V	(D
ANN SIMMONDS	V	(D	BOZ BURRELL	B	(D	IAN WALLACE	D	(D
BILLY GRAHAM	HRNS	(D	HOWIE CASEY	HRNS	(D	DICK PARRY	HRNS	(D
REG BROOKS	HRNS	(D	CECIL MOSS	HRNS	(D	JOHNNY HUCKRIDGE	HRNS	(D
MIKE DAVIS	HRNS	(D	JOHN DONNELLY	HRNS	(D	PETER BLUE	B	(B

B84

MARC BENNO

MARC BENNO	G V K	(ALL	(A) MARC BENNO	1970	A&M	US	SP	4273
WITH			(B) MINNOWS	1971	A&M	UK	AMLS64303	
CLARENCE WHITE	G	(B	(B) MINNOWS	1971	A&M	US	SP	4303
JESSE ED DAVIS	G	(BC	(C) AMBUSH	1972	A&M	UK	AMLS64634	
BOBBY WOMACK	G	(B	(C) AMBUSH	1972	A&M	US	SP	4364
JERRY McGEE	G	(B	(D) LOST IN AUSTIN	1979	A&M	UK	AMLH64767	
CARL RADLE	B	(BCd						
JERRY SCHEFF	B	(B	CHUCK DOMANICO	B	(B	GARY ILLINGSWORTH	K	(B
JIM KELTNER	D	(BCD	NICK DE CARO	ACC	(B	RITA COOLIDGE	V	(B
CLYDIE KING	V	(B	VENETTA FIELDS	V	(B	MIKE UTLEY	K	(C
BOBBY KEYS	SAX	(C	BOOKER T JONES	HRNS G	(C	RAY BROWN	B	(C
BONNIE BRAMLETT	V	(C	ALBERT LEE	G	(D	ERIC CLAPTON	G V	(D
DICK SIMS	K	(D	DICK MORRISSEY	SAX	(D			

B85

GEORGE BENSON

GEORGE BENSON	G V	(ALL	(A) ITS UPTOWN	19	CBS	US	CS	9325
WITH			(B) GEORGE BENSON COOKBOOK	19	CBS	US	CS	9413
RON CUBER	SAX	(A	(C) BENSON BURNER (DBL)	19	CBS	US	CH	33569
JIMMY LOVELACE	D	(A	(D) WILLOW WEEP FOR ME	19	CBS			63533
LONNIE SMITH	K	(A	(E) BEYOND THE BLUE HORIZON	19	CTI	US	CTI	6009
PHIL UPCHURCH	G	(LP	(F) WHITE RABBIT	19	CTI	UK	CTI	6
RONNIE FOSTER	K	(LP	(F) WHITE RABBIT	19	CTI	US	CTI	6015
JORGE DALTO	K	(LP	(G) BODY TALK	1974	CTI	UK	CTI	20
STANLEY BANKS	B	(LP	(G) BODY TALK	1974	CTI	US	CTI	6033
HARVEY MASON	D	(LP	(H) BAD BENSON	197	CTI	US	CTI	6045
RALPH McDONALD	PERC	(LP	(I) GOOD KING BAD	1976	CTI	UK	CTI	6062
LEE RITENOUR	G	(U	(J) BENSON & FARRELL	1977	CTI	US	CTI	6069
GEORGE DUKE		(U	(K) IN CONCERT	1977	CTI	US	CTI	6072
HERBIE HANCOCK		(U	(L) BREEZIN'	1976	W B	UK	K	56199
JACK McDUFF		(R	(L) BREEZIN'	1976	W B	US	K	3111
JOE FARRELL	HRNS	(J	(M) SHAPE OF THINGS TO COME	1976	A&M	US	SP	3014
(CONTINUED)								

(CONTINUED)

GEORGE BENSON
B85

(N) TELL IT LIKE IT IS	197	A&M	US	SP	3020
(O) THE OTHER SIDE OF ABBEY ROAD	1976	A&M	US	SP	3028
(P) IN FLIGHT	1977	W B	UK	K	56327
(P) IN FLIGHT	1977	W B	US	BK	2983
(Q) SUMMERTIME	1977	EMBASSY	UK	EMB	31566
(R) BENSON & McDUFF	1977	PRESTIGE	UK	PR	2407
(S) WEEKEND IN L.A. (LIVE) DBL	1978	W B	UK	K	66074
(T) STORMY WEATHER	19	EMBASSY	UK	EMB	31689
(U) GIVE ME THE NIGHT	1980	QUEST	UK	K	56823

OSCAR BENTON BLUES BAND
B85A

(A) FEEL SO GOOD	1969	DECCA		NO 418
(B) BENTON 71	1971	DECCA		SLK 16724
(C) DRAGGIN' AROUND	197	IMPERIAL		IC054 24550

OSCAR BENTON   G V   (ALL
H J B HAWKINS   B   (A
BARRELHOUSE BAILEY   PNO   (ABC
LONESOME TANNY LANT   D   (AB
JAY WALKER   B D   (BC
RUUEL BRINK   SAX   (C

GUS LA PORTE   G B   (BC   JOHNNY LA PORTE   G   (C

CHUCK BERRY
B87

CHUCK BERRY   G V   (ALL
WITH
BO DIDDLEY   G   (
JOHNNY JOHNSON   PNO   (
WILLIE DIXON   B   (
JASPER THOMAS   D   (
JEROME GREEN   PERC (
OTIS SPANN   PNO   (
EDDIE HARDY   D   (
L C DAVIS   SAX   (
JIMMIE ROGERS   G   (
FRED BELOW   D   (
LAFAYETTE LEAKE   PNO   (
G SMITH   B   (
MATT MURPHY   G   (
ODIE PAYNE   D   (
PAUL WILLIAMS   PNO   (
THE FIVE DIMENSIONS(GB)   (
MARTHA BERRY   V   (
WAYNE GABRIEL   G   (
ADAM IPPOLITO   PNO   (
GARY VAN SCYOC   B   (
STAN BRONSTEIN   SAX   (
RICK FRANK   D   (
BILLY PEEK   G   (
RON NEED   G   (
GREY EDRICK   B   (
ELLIOTT RANDALL   G   (
WILBUR BASCOMB   B   (
ERNIE HAYES   PNO   (
INGRID BERRY   V   (

STEVE MILLER BAND   (
KENNY BUTTREY   D   (
JIM MARSALA   B   (
BOB WRAY   B   (

( ) AFTER SCHOOL SESSIONS	1958	CHESS	US	LP	1426
( ) ONE DOZEN BERRY'S	1958	CHESS	US	LP	1432
( ) CHUCK BERRY IS ON TOP	19	CHESS	US	LP	1435
( ) ROCKIN' AT THE HOPS	19	CHESS	US	LP	1448
( ) NEW JUKE BOX HITS	19	CHESS	US	LP	1456
( ) NEW JUKE BOX HITS	1960	PYE INT	UK	NPL	28019
( ) CHUCK BERRY	1960	PYE INT	UK	NPL	28024
( ) CHUCK BERRY	19	CHESS	US		60032
( ) CHUCK BERRY	1967	MARBLE ARCH	UK	MAL	611
( ) ON STAGE	1960	CHESS	US	LP	1480
( ) ON STAGE	1960	PYE INT	UK	NPL	28027
( ) MORE CHUCK BERRY	1960	CHESS	US	LP	1465
( ) MORE CHUCK BERRY	1960	PYE INT	UK	NPL	28028
( ) TWIST	1960	chess	US	LP	1466
( ) LATEST & GREATEST	196	PYE INT	UK	NPL	28031
( ) YOU NEVER CAN TELL	1964	PYE INT	UK	NPL	28039
( ) YOU NEVER CAN TELL	1967	MARBLE ARCH	UK	MAL	702
( ) GREATEST HITS	1964	CHESS	US	LP	321
( ) GREATEST HITS	1964	CHESS	US	LP	1485
( ) GREATEST HITS	1967	MARBLE ARCH	UK	MAL	660
( ) 2 GREAT GUITARS	1964	PYE INT	UK	NPL	28047
( ) CHUCK BERRY IN LONDON	1965	CHESS	UK		4005
( ) CHUCK BERRY IN LONDON	1965	CHESS	US	LP	1495
( ) FRESH BERRYS	1965	CHESS	UK		4506
( ) FRESH BERRYS	1965	CHESS	US	LP	1498
( ) ST LOUIS TO LIVERPOOL	196	CHESS	US	LP	1514
( ) BACK HOME	186	CHESS	US	LP	1550
( ) GOLDEN HITS	1967	MERCURY			61103
( ) FROM ST LOUIS TO FRISCO	19	MERCURY			6463 015
( ) AT THE FILLMORE	1967	MERCURY			6463 016
( ) AT THE FILLMORE	19	MERCURY			SMCL20110
( ) MEDLEY	1967	MERCURY			6851 002
( ) IN MEMPHIS	1967	MERCURY			6430 022
( ) IN MEMPHIS	19	MERCURY			SMCL20110
( ) CONCERTO IN B GOODE	1969	MERCURY			61233
( ) HOME AGAIN	1971	CHESS			6310 113
( )ST LOUIS TO FRISCO TO MEMPHIS DBL	1972	PHILIPS			6619 008
( ) THE LONDON SESSIONS	1972	CHESS	UK		6310 122
( ) THE LONDON SESSIONS	1972	CHESS	US		50001
( ) THE LONDON SESSIONS	19	CHESS	US		60020
( ) SAN FRANCISCO DUES	1972	CHESS	UK		6310 115
( ) SAN FRANCISCO DUES	1972	CHESS	US		50014
( ) BACK HOME	1972	CHESS	US		50024
( ) GOLDEN DECADE	1972	CHESS			6641 018
( ) GOLDEN DECADE VOL 2	1973	CHESS			6641 058
( ) GOLDEN DECADE VOL 2	1973	CHESS	US		60023
( ) BIO	1973	CHESS			50043
( ) BIO	1973	CHESS			6499 650
( ) BACK IN THE USA	1973	PHILIPS			6336 216
( ) ALLTIME GREATEST R'N'R PARTY HITS	1974	CHESS			6310 130
( ) ALLTIME GREATEST R'N'R PARTY HITS	1974	CHESS	US		ACB 00208
( ) GOLDEN DECADE VOL 3	1974	CHESS			6641 177
( ) GOLDEN DECADE VOL 3	1974	CHESS			50039
( ) GOLDEN DECADE VOL 3	1974	CHESS	US		60028
( ) I'M A ROCKER	1975	CONTOUR	UK		6870 638
( ) CHUCK BERRY 75	1975	CHESS	UK		9109 101
( ) CHUCK BERRY 75	1975	CHESS			50047
( ) MOTORVATIN'	1976	CHESS			
( ) ROCKIT	1979	ATLANTIC	UK	K	50648
( ) ROCKIT	1979	ATLANTIC	US		SD38118
( ) CHUCK BERRY	19	IMPACT	FR		6499671
( ) LOUISIANA	19	CHESS	US		26 130
( ) THE SECOND COMING	19	W B	US		0598
( ) WILD BERRY'S	19	PICKWICK	US	SPC	3392
( ) AMERICA'S HOTEST WAX	19	REELIN'	US		001
( ) FLASHBACK DBL	19	PICKWICK	US	PTP	2061
( ) THE BEST OF	19	STARDAY	US		
( ) CHUCK BERRY VOL I	19	IMPACT	FR		6886 403
( ) CHUCK BERRY VOL 2	19	IMPACT	FR		6886 407
( ) CHUCK BERRY	19	IMPACT	FR		6995 402
( ) CHUCK BERRY	1979	CONTOUR	UK	CN	2019

CHUCK BERRY

( ) 20 GOLDEN GREATS		1979	HAMMER	UK	HMR	9003
(EP) CHUCK & BO		196	PYE INT	UK	NEP	44009
(EP) CHUCK BERRY		196	PYE INT	UK	NEP	44011
(EP) CHUCK & BO 2		196	PYE INT	UK	NEP	44012
(EP) THIS IS CHUCK BERRY		196	PYE INT	UK	NEP	44013
(EP) CHUCK & BO 3		196	PYE INT	UK	NEP	44017
(EP) BEST OF		1964	PYE INT	UK	NEP	44018
(EP) HITS		1964	PYE INT	UK	NEP	44028
(EP) BLUE MOOD		1965	PYE INT	UK	NEP	44033
(EP) PROMISED LAND		1964	CHESS	UK	CRE	6002
(EP) COME ON		1965	CHESS	UK	CRE	6005

B88

DAVE BERRY

DAVE BERRY	V	(ALL	(A) DAVE BERRY	1964	DECCA	UK	LK	4653
			(B) A DOZEN BERRY'S	1966	ACE OF CLUBS	UK	SCL	1218
			(C) SPECIAL SOUND OF DAVE BERRY	1968	DECCA	UK	LK	4823
			(D) DAVE BERRY 68	1968	DECCA	UK	LK	4932
			(E) REMEMBERING	1976	DECCA	UK	REM	3

B89

MIKE BERRY

MIKE BERRY	V	(ALL	(A) DRIFT AWAY	1972	YORK	UK	FYK	409
MEL JONES	D	(B	(B) ROCKS IN MY HEAD	1976	POLYDOR	UK	2383	392
GERRY CONWAY	D	(B	(B) ROCKS IN MY HEAD	1976	SIRE	US		7524
KEN LUNDGREN	B	(B						
BILLY KUY	G	(B	GEOFF WHITEHORN	G	(B	CHAS HODGES	K	(B
ANDY PARKER	G	(B	TERRY BRITTON	G	(B	CLEM CATTINI	D	(B
GRAHAM TODD	K	(B	KEN FREEMAN	SYN	(B			

B90

BETHNAL

GEORGE CSAPO	V K VLN	(AB	(A) DANGEROUS TIMES	1978	VERTIGO	UK	9102	020
EVERTON WILLIAMS	B V	(AB	(B) CRASH LANDING	1978	VERTIGO	UK	9102	029
PETE DOWLING	D	(AB						
NICK MICHAELS	G	(AB						

B91

RICHARD BETTS

RICHARD(DICKIE)BETTS	G V	(ALL	(A) HIGHWAY CALL	1975	CAPRICORN	UK	2429	117
WITH			(A) HIGHWAY CALL	1975	CAPRICORN	US		0123
DAVE TOLER	D	(1	(B) DICKIE BETTS & GREAT SOUTHERN	1977	ARISTA	UK SPARTY	1005	
DAN TOLER	G V	(B	(B) DICKIE BETTS & GREAT SOUTHERN	1977	ARISTA	US		4123
KEN TIBBETTS	B	(B	(C) ATLANTA BURNING DOWN	1978	ARISTA	UK SPARTY	1046	
TOM BROOME	K V	(B	(C) ATLANTA BURNING DOWN	1978	ARISTA	US		4168
DONNIE SHARBONO	D	(1B	(1) 1978 UK TOURING BAND					
JERRY THOMPSON	PERC	(						
DAVID GOLDFLIES	B	(1	CHUCK LEAVELL	PNO	(A	DAVID WALSHAW	D PERC	(A
MICHAEL WORKMAN	K V	(1	JOHN HUGHEY	STEEL	(A	JOHNNY SANDLIN	B PERC	(A
DON JOHNSON	V	(1	TOMMY TALTON	G	(A	STRAY STRATON	B V	(A
TOPPER PRICE	HCA	(B	WALTER POINDEXTER	BAN V	(A	FRANK POINDEXTER	DOBRO V	(A
MICKEY THOMAS	V	(B	OSCAR UNDERWOOD	MAND	(A	LEON POINDEXTER	G V	(A
VASSAR CLEMENTS	FDL	(A	JEFF HANNA	G	(A	REESE WYNANS	HCA	(A
BUCK	V	(A	DOTTIE	V	(A	REBA	V	(A

B92

BIG BALLS & THE GREAT WHITE IDIOT

ATLI GRUND	G V	(A	(A) BIG BALLS & THE GREAT WHITE IDIOT	1977	NOVA		6 23280
ALFRED GRUND	B V	(A					
PETER GRUND	D V	(A	WOLFGANG LORENZ	G V	(A	BARON ADOLF KAISER	V	(A

B93

BIG BOPPER

BIG BOPPER(J P RICHARDSON	V		(A) CHANTILLY LACE	1958	.		
DIED 1959 IN PLANE CRASH WITH			(A) CHANTILLY LACE	1974	CONTOUR		6870 531
BUDDY HOLLY							

B93A

BIG BROTHER

CHRIS SHAKESPEARE	V							
NICK GUYLER	G							
ARNIE COTRELL	G V		RONNIE TAYLOR	SAX		JOSS JONES	B	(
SIMON TILLEY	D		BOB PETTIT	SAX		MARTIN WHITE	TROM	
CHRIS BROWN	G							

B94

BIG BROTHER & THE HOLDING COMPANY

JANIS JOPLIN	V	(AB	(A) BIG BROTHER & THE HOLDING COMPANY	1967	LONDON	UK	SHT	8377
SAM ANDREWS	G	(ABC	(A) BIG BROTHER & THE HOLDING COMPANY	1967	FONTANA		TL	5457
JAMES GURLEY	B	(ABC	(A) BIG BROTHER & THE HOLDING COMPANY	1967	MAINSTREAM	US		6099
DAVID GETZ	D PNO	(ABC	(A) BIG BROTHER & THE HOLDING COMPANY	1967	CBS	US	KC	30631
PETE ALBIN	B	(ABC	(B) CHEAP THRILLS	1968	CBS	UK		63392
NICK GRAVENITES	V	(C	(B) CHEAP THRILLS	1968	CBS	US	PC	9700
DAVID SCHALLOCK	G V	(C	(C) BE A BROTHER	1971	CBS	UK		64118
MIKE FINNIGAN	K V	(C	(C) BE A BROTHER	1971	CBS	US	KC	30222
KATHY McDONALD	V	(C	(D) HOW HARD IT IS	197	CBS	US	KC	30738
IRA KAMIN	K	(C						
TOWER OF POWER	HRNS	(C						

B95

BIG JOHNS ROCK'N'ROLL CIRCUS

BIG JOHN	(	(A) ACT 1	1974	DJM		DJLPS 438
		(B) ACT 2	1975	DJM		DJLPS 463
		(C) ON THE ROAD	1977	DJM		DJF 30511

B95A

BIG JOE

BIG JOE	V	(A	(A) KEEP ROCKING & SWINGING	197			LAP	001
SLY DUNBAR	D	(A	(B) AFRICAN PRINCESS	1978	TROJAN		TRLS	152
JOHNNIE CLARKE	PNO	(A						
CARLTON DAVIS	D	(A	ROBERT SHAKESPEARE	B	(A	LLOYD SPARKS	B	(A
EARL SMITH	G	(A	BOOFA	G	(A	TONY CHINN	G	(A
ANSEL COLLINS	ORG	(A	BERNARD HARVEY	ORG	(A	AUSSIE HEBERT	PNO	(A

B96

BIG SLEEP

JOHN WEATHERS	D	(A	(A) BLUEBELL WOOD	1971	PEGASUS	UK	PEG	4
PHIL RYAN	K	(A						
GARY PICKFORD HOPKINS	V G		RAY TAFF WILLIAMS	G	(A	RITCHIE FRANCIS	B PNO V	(A

BIG STAR   B97

ALEX CHILTON	V	(ABC	(A) RADIO CITY		1971	ARDENT	US	ADS
CHRIS BELL	G V	(	(B) BIG STAR		1972	ARDENT	US	ADS
ANDY HUMMELL	B	(	(AB) RADIO CITY/BIG STAR		1978	STAX		SXSP 302
JODY STEPHENSON	D	(	(C) THIRD ALBUM		1978	AURA		AUL 703

BIG THREE UK   B98

BRIAN GRIFFITHS	G	(B	(A) LIVE AT THE CAVERN	(EP)	196	DECCA	UK	DFE 8552
JOHN GUSTAFSON	B	(B	(B) RESURECTION		19	POLYDOR	UK	2383 199
JOHN HUTCHINSON	D	(						
PETER ROBINSON	PNO	(B	HENRY LOWTHER	HRN	(B	JOHN SMITH	TUBA (B
LES THATCHER	BANJO	(B	MICK GRAHAM	G	(B	NIGEL OLSSON	D (B

BIG THREE US   B99

CASS ELLIOTT	V
TIM ROSE	V
DENNY DOHERTY	V

BIG WHA KOO   B100

DAVID PALMER	V TAMB(AB	(A) BIG WHA KOO		1977	ABC	ABCL 5208
DANNY DOUMA	V G (AB	(B) BERKSHIRE		1978	ABC	ABCL 5238
DON FRANCISCO	PERC V(AB					
RICK VAN MAARTH	G V (AB	RICHARD KOSINSKI	VIBES V K(AB	ANDREW SYLVESTER	B G (A
CLAUDE PEPPER	D VIBES(AB	REINIE PRESS	B SAX (AB	LEE RITENOUR	G (A
PETER FREIBERGER	(B				

BIG YOUTH   B101

BIG YOUTH	PERC V(ALL	(A) SCREAMING TARGET	1973	TROJAN	.	TRLS 61
		(B) NATTY CULTURAL DREAD	1976	TROJAN		TRLS 123
		(C) HIT THE ROAD JACK	1976	TROJAN		TRLS 137
		(D) DREADLOCKS DREAD	1976	KLIK		KLP 9001
		(D) DREADLOCKS DREAD	1978	FRONT LINE		FL 1014
		(E) ISAIAH FIRST PROPHET OF OLD	1978	FRONT LINE		FL 1011
		(F) REGGAE GI DEM DUB	1979			
		(G) REGGAE PHENOMENON	1977	BIG YOUTH		BYD 1
		(H) EVERYDAY SKANK(BEST OF)	19	TROJAN		TRLS 189

BIJOU   B102

PALMER	G V (A	(A) DANSE AVEC MOI	1977	PHILIPS	9101 138
PHILIPPE DAUGA	B V (A	(B) OK CAROLE	197	PHILIPS	9101 178
DYNAMITE YAN	D (A				

BILLION DOLLAR BABIES   B103

MICHAEL BRUCE	G V (A	(A) BATTLE AXE	1977	POLYDOR	UK	2391 273
NEAL SMITH	D (A	(A) BATTLE AXE	1977	POLYDOR	US	1 6100
DENNIS DUNAWAY	B (A					
BOB DOLIN	K (A	MIKE MARCONI	G V (A			

TREVOR BILLMUSS   B104

TREVOR BILLMUSS	(A	(A) FAMILY APOLOGY	1970	CHARISMA	CAS 1017

BINTANGS   B104A

GUS PLEINES	V HCA (A	(A) GENUINE BULL	1975	RCA	HOLL YHPL10982
JAPIE CASTRICUM	G PNO (A				
JACK VAN SCHIE	G (A	FRANK KRAAIJEVELD	B V (A	HARRY SCHIERBEEK	D PERC (A
ALBERT	PERC (A	WILLEM	PERC (A	LEO	PERC (A
JIM CUOMO	WIND (A				

TONY BIRD   B105

TONY BIRD	V G (AB	(A) TONY BIRD		1976	CBS		81183
WITH		(B) BIRD OF PARADISE		1978	CBS		82498
EMMANUEL RENTZOS	K (A						
WINSTON DELANDRO	G (A	RICHARD BAILEY	D (A	ERNEST BAIDO	B (A
LUCKY RANKU	G (A	JAMES MENE	D (A	ERNEST MOTHLE	B (A
JOHN KIRKPATRICK CONC/ACC (A		GRAHAM SMITH	HCA (A	SETH SIBANDA	V (B
KWA ZULU SINGERS	V (A	T L BEDEAU	SAX (A	GEORGE LEE	SAX (A
STEVEN AMAZING	B (A	JEREMY TAYLOR	G (A	ARLEN ROTH	G BAN(B
JOEL REIFF	B (B	JOHN SIEGLER	B (B	STU WOODS	B (B
FRANK CENTENO	B (B	CHRISTOPHER PARKER	D (B	RICHARD CROOKS	D (B
BARRY LAZAROWITZ	PERC (B	CRUSHER BENNETT	PERC (B	FALUMI PRINCE	PERC (B
JOHN LISSAUER V K PERC (B		DOMINIC CORTESE	ACC (B	MORRIS GOLDBERG	WIND (B
DAVID SAMUELS	PERC (B	MAERETHA STEWART	V (B	DEBORAH MACDUFFIE	V (B
JOHN CROWDER	V (B	LINDA TSHABALALA	V (B	SELAELO DAN MAREDI	V (B
RON GETMAN	V (B	GORDON GRODY	V (B	THEMBI MISHALI	V (B
THEMBA NTINGA	V (B	FANA DAVID KEKANA	V (B		

BIRDS   B106

RON WOOD	G	(A) HARD UP HEROES (1TRACK)	1974	DECCA	DPA 3009/ 10
ALISTAIR McKENZIE	V				
KIM GARDNER	B	TONY MUNROE	G	PETE McDANIELS	D

BIRTH CONTROL   B107

BERND NOSKE	D PERC V (DFGHI	(A) BIRTH CONTROLL	1969	METRONOME	MLP15 336
DIRK STEFFENS	G V (D	(A) BIRTH CONTROL	1971	CHARISMA	CAS 1036
BRUNO FRENZEL	G V (DFGHI	(B) GOLD ROCK	1973	METRONOME	0040 019
PETER FEOLLER	B V (DFG	(C) HOODOO MAN	1974	CBS	65316
HORST STACHELHAUS	B (HI	(D) RE BIRTH	1974	CBS	65963
MANFRED VON BOHR	D (HI	(E) LIVE	1974	CBS	88088
ZEUS B HELD	V SAX K (DFGHI	(F) PLASTIC PEOPLE	1975	CBS	80921
		(G) BACKDOOR POSSIBILITIES	1976	BRAIN	0060 019
		(H) INCREASE	1977	BRAIN	0060 066
		(H) INCREASE	19	BRAIN RI	GERM 0040 122
		(I) TITANIC	1978	BRAIN	0060 149
		(J) LIVE 79	1979	BRAIN	0060 240

BIRTHA   B108

SHELE PINIZZOTTO	G V (AB	(A) BIRTHA	1972	PROBE	SPBA 6267
LIVER FAVELA	V PERC D (AB	(A) BIRTHA	1972	ABC DUNHILL	DSK 50127
SHERRY HAGLER	K (AB	(B) CANT STOP THE MADNESS	1973	PROBE	SPBA 6272
ROSEMARY BUTLER	B V (AB				

ELVIN BISHOP

ELVIN BISHOP	G V	(ALL	(A) ELVIN BISHOP		1969	FILLMORE			30001
WITH			(B) FEEL IT		1970	CBS			30239
STEVEN MILLER	PNO	(ABE	(B) FEEL IT		1970	EPIC			64180
JOHN CHAMBERS	D	(AB	(C) ROCK MY SOUL		19	EPIC			31563
APPLEJACK	HCA	(A	(C) APPLEJACK		19	EPIC			65295
ALBERT GIANQUINTO	PNO	(A	(D) BEST OF (CRABSHAW RISING)		1972	EPIC			33693
ART STAURO	B	(A	(E) LET IT FLOW		1974	CAPRICORN	UK	2429	116
JO BAKER	V PERC	(BEF	(E) LET IT FLOW		1974	CAPRICORN	US	CP	0134
KIP MAERCKLEIN	B	(B	(F) JUKE JOINT JUMP		1975	CAPRICORN	UK	2429	127
PERRY WALSH	V	(B	(F) JUKE POINT JUMP		1975	CAPRICORN	US	CP	0151
MIKE CARABELLO	PERC	(B	(G) STRUTTIN' MY STUFF		1976	CAPRICORN	UK	2429	136
CHEPITO AREAS	PERC	(B	(G) STRUTTIN' MY STUFF		1976	CAPRICORN	US	CP	0165
POINTER SISTERS	V	(B	(H) HOMETOWN BOY MAKES GOOD		1976	CAPRICORN	UK	2429	147
PHIL AABERG	K	(EFGHJ	(H) HOMETOWN BOY MAKES GOOD		1976	CAPRICORN	US	CP	0176
DON BALDWIN	D V	(EFGHIJ	(I) RAISIN' HELL		1977	CAPRICORN	UK	2637	104
JOHN VERNAZZA	G	(EFGHIJ	(I) RAISIN' HELL		1977	CAPRICORN	US	2CP	0185
MICK THOMAS	V	(EFGHIJ	(J) THE BEST OF		1979	CAPRICORN	UK	2429	189
TOY CALDWELL	STEEL	(E							
JOHN SANDLIN	G PERC	(EF	DICKIE BETTS	G	(EF	SLY STONE		K	(E
CHARLIE DANIELS V FDL	G	(E	ROSS MASON	B	(F	RICK KELLOGG		HCA	(F
STEPHEN STILLS	G V	(F	ROSS HAYASHIDA	V	(FH	BILL SLAIS		K	(GHIJ
MIKE KECK	K	(G	TERRY HANCK	SAX	(G	RENI SLAIS		V	(H
DEBBIE CATHEY	V	(EI	MELVIN SEALS	K	(IJ	CHUCK BROOKE		HRNS	(IJ
BOB CLAIRE	HRNS	(IJ	DAVE GROVER	HRNS	(IJ	BILL LAMB		HRNS	(IJ
MIC GILLETTE	HRNS	(HI	STEVE KRUPKA	HRNS	(HI	GREG ADAMS		HRNS	(HI
PAUL HORNSBY	K	(E	BILL MEEKER	D	(E	JEROME JOSEPH		CONGA	(E
DAVID WALSHAW	PERC	(E	RANDALL BRAMBLETT	SAX	(E	DAVID BROWN		SAX	(E
HAROLD WILLIAMS	SAX	(E	VASSAR CLEMENTS	STRINGS	(E	GIDEON DANIELS		V	(E
ANNIE SAMPSON	V	(E	TOWER OF POWER	HRNS	(H	JUNE POINTER		V	(F
MICHAEL BROOKS	B	(EFGHIJ							

STEPHEN BISHOP

STEPHEN BISHOP	TROM V G	(ALL	(A) CARELESS		1976	ABC			ABCL 5201
WITH			(A) CARELESS		1976	ABC	US		D954
ANDREW GOLD	G	(A	(B) BISH		1978	ABC	UK		ABCL 5252
RUSS KUNKEL	D	(A	(B) BISH		1978	ABC	US		1082
MAC CRIDLIN	B	(A	(C) RED CAB TO MANHATTAN		1980	WB	UK		K 56853
TOMMY VIG	PERC	(B							
MICHAEL STATON	V STEEL	(AB	VICTOR FELDMAN	PERC	(A	STEVE PORCARO		SYN	(B
STEVE PAIETTA	ACC	(A	LARRY BROWN	D	(A	LEE RITENOUR		G	(A
CRAIG DOERGE	K	(A	REINIE PRESS	B	(A	JIM GORDON		D	(A
CHAKA KHAN	V	(AB	ALAN LINGREN	SYN	(A	LARRY KNECHTEL		K	(A
ERIC CLAPTON	G	(A	RAY PIZZI	SAX	(A	MAX BENNETT		B	(A
JOHN GUERIN	D	(A	ART GARFUNKEL	V	(AB	TOMMY TEDESCO		MAND	(A
JEFFREY STATON	G V B	(AB	LEAH KUNKEL	V	(AB	ED SHAUGHNESSY		D	(B
RAY BROWN	B	(B	RICK SCHLOSSER	D	(B	DAVID FOSTER		K	(B
GREG PHILLINGANES	K	(B	MIKE McDONALD	V	(B	LEE SKLAR		B	(B
ABE LABORIEL	B	(B	DAVID HUNGATE	B	(B	JOHN JARVIS		K	(AB
TOM SCOTT	SAX	(B	RAY POUNDS	D	(B	NATHAN WATTS		B	(B
MICHAEL SEMBELLO	G	(B	RAY PARKER	G	(B	PAULINHO DA COSTA		PERC	(B
KEITH HOLLAR	B	(B	BILL PAYNE	K	(B	STEVE CROPPER		G	(B
NATALIE COLE	V	(B	HAL ATKINSON	D	(B	DAVID SHIELDS		B	(B
BOBBY CHADWICK	K	(B							

BILL BLACK COMBO

BILL BLACK	B	(	MEMPHIS TENNESSEE	19	HI	US		8004
			AWARD WINNERS	19	HI	US		6005
BOB TUCKER	G V	(*	BILL BLACK COMBO	19	ZODIAC	US		5006
RONNIE SCAIFE	G	(*	SAXY JAZZ	19	HI	US	SHL	32002
ROBERT GLADNEY	SAX V	(*	SOLID & RAUNCHY	1962	LONDON	UK	HAU	2310
GIL MICHAEL STEEL FDL		(*	SOLID & RAUNCHY	1962	HI	US	HL	12003
PHIL MUNSEY	B	(*	SOLID & RAUNCHY	1977	HI	US	SHL	32003
BILL COMPTON	D	(*	MOVIN'	1962	HI	US	HL	12005
BUTCH CARTER	K	(*	MOVIN'	196	LONDON	UK	HAU	2433
LARRY ROGERS	HCA	(*	LETS TWIST	196	LONDON UK HAU2427	SAHU	6222
DANNY HOGAN	V	(*	THE MEMPHIS SCENE	1967	MEGA	US	M31	1008
			LETS TWIST HER	19	HI	US	SHL	32006
			THE BEAT GOES ON	1968	LONDON	UK	SHU	8367
			TURN ON YOUR LOVE LIGHT	1969	LONDON	UK	SHU	8373
			UNTOUCHABLE SOUND	19	HI US SHL32009 LONDON UK 8080
			GREATEST HITS	19	LONDON UK HUA8113	SHL	32012
			PLAYS THE BLUES	19	HI	US	SHL	32015
			SOULIN' THE BLUES	1969	LONDON	UK	SHU	8389
			PLAYS CHUCK BERRY	19	HI	US	SHL	32017
			PLAYS CHUCK BERRY	19	LONDON	UK	HAU	8187
			GOES BIG BAND	19	HI	US	SHL	32020
			MORE SOLID & RAUNCHY	19	HI	US	SHL	32023
			JUKE BOX FAVOURITES	19	NASHVILLE	UK	NAB	2003
			ROCK'N'ROLL FOREVER	1973	NASHVILLE	UK	NAB	2005
			BILL BLACK IS BACK	1974	NASHVILLE	UK	NAB	2007
			BILL BLACK IS BACK	19	MEGA	US	MLPS	600
			GREATEST HITS VOL 2	19	HI	US	SHL	32078
			SOLID & COUNTRY	1975	HI	US	SHL	32088
			WORLDS GREATEST HONKY TONK BAND	1975	HI	US	SHL	32093
			(*) ITS HONKY TONK TIME	1977	LONDON	UK	ZGU	140
			(*) ITS HONKY TONK TIME	197	HI	US	SHL	32104
			BLACK WITH SUGAR	19	CBS			63672

PABLO BLACK

PAUL DIXON

( )Mr MUSIC ORIGINALLY	1978	STUDIO ONE	IMP		B111A

BLACK CAT BONES

SIMON KIRKE	D	(	
PAUL KOSSOFF	G	(	
STU BROOKS	B	(A	
TERRY SIMMS		(	
ROD PRICE	G V	(A	
ROBIN SYLVESTER	PNO	(A	

(A) BARBED WIRE SANDWICH	1970	NOVA	SDN	B112 15

DEREK BROOKS	G	(A	BOB WESTON	G	(	
PAUL TILLER		(	BRIAN SHORT	V	(A	
STEVE MILLINER	PNO	(A	PHIL LENOIR	D	(A	

BLACK HEAT

B113

( ) NO TIME TO BURN	1973	JAM		JAL	104
( ) NO TIME TO BURN	1974	ATLANTIC	US	SD	7294

BLACK MERDA

B113A

ANTHONY HAWKINS	G	(A	
CHARLES HAWKINS	G	(A	
TYRONE HITE	D	(A	
L VEASEY	B	(A	

(A) BLACK MERDA	19	CHESS	US	569517

BLACK OAK ARKANSAS

B114

JIM DANDY MANGRUM	V	(ALL	
RICKY REYNOLDS	G	(AC	
JIMMY HENDERSON	G	(	
STAN KNIGHT	G	(AC	
PAT DAUGHERTY	B	(AC	
TOM ALDRIDGE	D	(C	
A K A DORK JACKSON			
HARVEY JETT	G	(AC	
JACK HOLDER	SAX G K	(	
GREG REDING	G V K	(	
ANDY TANAS	V B	(	
JOEL WILLIAMS	D	(	
WAYNE EVANS	D	(A	

( ) THE KNOWBODY ELSE	1969	STAX	US		
(A) BLACK OAK ARKANSAS	1970	ATCO	US	SD	33354
(A) BLACK OAK ARKANSAS	1971	ATLANTIC	UK	2400	180
(A) BLACK OAK ARKANSAS	19	ATLANTIC	UK	K	40215
(B) KEEP THE FAITH	1972	ATCO	US	SD	33381
(C) IF AN ANGEL CAME TO SEE YOU	1972	ATCO	US	SD	7008
(D) HIGH ON A HOG	1974	ATLANTIC	UK	K	40538
(D) HIGH ON A HOG	1974	ATCO	US	SD	7035
(E) STREET PARTY	1974	ATLANTIC	UK	K	50057
(F) HOT & NASTY	1974	ATLANTIC	UK	K	20083
(G) RAUNCH & ROLL LIVE	1975	ATLANTIC	UK	K	40451
(G) RAUNCH & ROLL LIVE	1975	ATCO	US	SD	7019
(H) AINT LIFE GRAND	1975	ATLANTIC	UK	K	50150
(I) X RATED	1975	MCA	UK	MCF	2734
(I) X RATED	1975	MCA	US		2155
(J) BALLS OF FIRE	1976	MCA	UK	MCF	2762
(J) BALLS OF FIRE	1976	MCA	US		2199
(K) LIVE MUTHA	1976	ATLANTIC	UK	K	50220
(K) LIVE MUTHA	1976	ATCO	US	SD	36128
(L) 10 YEAR OVERNIGHT SUCCESS	1976	MCA	US		2224
(M) RACE WITH THE DEVIL	1977	CAPRICORN	UK	2429	156
(M) RACE WITH THE DEVIL	1977	CAPRICORN	US	CP	0191
(N) BEST OF	19	ATCO	US	SD	36150
(O) I'D RATHER BE SAILING	19	CAPRICORN	US	CP	0207
( ) EARLY TIMES	19	STAX	US	STS	5504

BLACK SABBATH

B115

TONY IOMMI	G	(ALL	
GEEZER BUTLER	B	(ALL	
BILL WARD	D V	(ALL	
OZZIE OSBOURNE	V HCA	(ABCDEFGH	
GERALD WOODRUFFE	K	(G	
RONNIE JAMES DIO	V	(I	
RICK WAKEMAN	K	(E	

(A) BLACK SABBATH	1970	VERTIGO	UK		V06
(A) BLACK SABBATH	1974	WWA		WWA	006
(A) BLACK SABBATH	1977	NEMS	UK	NEL	6002
(A) BLACK SABBATH	197	WB	US		1871
(A) BLACK SABBATH	197	WEA		913	193
(B) PARANOID	1970	VERTIGO	UK	6360	011
(B) PARANOID	1975	EMI		WS4	1887
(B) PARANOID	1977	NEMS	UK	NEL	6003
(B) PARANOID	19	WB	US	K	3104
(B) PARANOID	19	WEA		913	194
(C) MASTER OF REALITY	1971	VERTIGO	UK	6360	050
(C) MASTER OF REALITY	1974	WWA		WWA	008
(C) MASTER OF REALITY	1977	NEMS	UK	NEL	6004
(C) MASTER OF REALITY	197	WB	US	BS	2562
(C) MASTER OF REALITY	197	WEA		913	195
(D) BLACK SABBATH 4	1972	VERTIGO	UK	6360	071
(D) BLACK SABBATH 4	1974	WWA		WWA	009
(D) BLACK SABBATH 4	1977	NEMS	UK	NEL	6005
(D) BLACK SABBATH 4	197	WB	US	BS	2602
(D) BLACK SABBATH 4	197	WEA		913	196
(E) SABBATH BLOODY SABBATH	1973	VERTIGO	UK	6360	115
(E) SABBATH BLOODY SABBATH	1974	WWA		WWA	005
(E) SABBATH BLOODY SABBATH	197	WB	US	BS	2695
(F) SABOTAGE	1975	VERTIGO	UK	9119	001
(F) SABOTAGE	197	WB	US	BS	2822
(G) TECHNICAL ECSTACY	1976	VERTIGO	UK	9102	750
(G) TECHNICAL ECSTACY	1976	WB	US	BS	2969
(H) NEVER SAY DIE	1978	VERTIGO	UK	9102	751
(H) NEVER SAY DIE	197	WB	US	K	3186
(I) HEAVEN & HELL	1980	VERTIGO	UK	9102	752

COMPILATION ALBUMS

( ) ATTENTION (	1975	VERTIGO		6438	057
( ) ATTENTION (	19	WWA		WWA	101
( ) BLACK SABBATH VOL 2	1975	VERTIGO	UK	9199	133
( ) WE SOLD OUR SOULS FOR ROCK'N'ROLL	1976	VERTIGO	UK	6641	335
( ) WE SOLD OUR SOULS FOR ROCK'N'ROLL	1977	NEMS	UK	NALD	101
( ) WE SOLD OUR SOULS FOR ROCK'N'ROLL	19	WB	US	BS	2923
( ) GREATEST HITS	1977	NEMS	UK	NELS	6009
( ) GREATEST HITS	1977	WEA		913	192

BLACK SLATE

B116

DESMOND MAHONEY	D	(A	
KEITH DRUMMOND	V	(A	
CHRIS HANSON	G	(A	
ANTHONY BRIGHTLY	K	(A	
HERSCHEL HOLDER	TPT	(A	

(A) AMIGO	1980	TCD	TLDLP	1

ELROY BAILEY	B	(A	CLEDWYN ROGERS	G	(A	
NICKY RIDGUARD	TROM	(A	RUDY HOLMES	SAX	(A	
RAY CARNESS	SAX	(A				

B117
BLACK UHURU

BLACK UHURU

(A) LOVE CRISIS   1978   THIRD WORLD   TWS 925
(B) SHOWCASE   19   D ROY

B118
PETE MORRIS
CLINTON CREASEY
LYNTON STEEL
BRIAN CLARK

BLACK VELVET

(A) THIS IS BLACK VELVET   1971   BEACON   BENS 16
(B) PEOPLE OF THE WORLD   1972   PYE   NSPL18392
(C) CAN YOU FEEL IT   1973   SEVEN SUN   SUN LP1

B119
JIM GANNON   V G VIBES   (ABC
ZOOT TAYLOR   K   (ABC
KIP TREVER   V   (AB
CLIVE JONES   WIND   (ABC
BOB BOND   B   (A
ROMEO CHALLENGER   D   (C

BLACK WIDOW

(A) SACRIFICE   1970   CBS   63948
(B) BLACK WIDOW   1970   CBS   64133
(C) THREE   1972   CBS   64562

JOHN CULLEY   G V   (C   CLIVE BOX   D   (A
GEOFF GRIFFITHS   B V   (C

B120
DENNIS 'BLACKBEARD'BOVELL   B G K(AB
TONY ROBINSON   K   (B
ANGUS GAYE   D   (B
JOHN KPIAYE   G   (B
JAH BUNNY   D   (B

BLACKBEARD

(A) STRICTLY DUB WIZE   1978   TEMPUS   TEM 001
(B) I WAH DUB   1980   MORE CUT   RDC 2002

PATRICK TENYUE   K V   (JULIO FINN   HCA   (B
NICK BAILEY   SYN   (B

B121
BLACKBLOOD

BLACKBLOOD

( ) BLACKBLOOD   1976   BRADLEY   UK   BLAK 9001
( ) BLACKBLOOD   19   MAINSTREAM   US   416
( ) BLOOD BROTHER BLOOD SISTER   19   CHRYSALIS   US   1144

B122
KEVIN TONEY   K   (E
KEITH KILLGO   D   (E
JOE HALL   B   (E
ORVILLE SAUNDERS   G   (E
STEPHEN JOHNSON   SAX   (E

BLACKBYRDS

(A) BLACKBYRDS FIRST   1975   FANTASY   FT 9444
(B) FLYING START   197   FANTASY   FT 522
(B) FLYING START   197   FANTASY   US   FT 9472
(C) CITY LIFE   197   FANTASY   US   FT 9490
(D) UNFINISHED BUSINESS   197   FANTASY   US   FT 9518
(E) ACTION   1978   FANTASY   UK   FT 534
(E) ACTION   1978   FANTASY   US   FT 9535

B123
GREG WALKER   B   (
RICK MEDLOCKE   G V   (
JAKSON SPIRES   D V   (
CHARLIE HARGRETT   G   (
ROGER HAWKINS   (
LAURA STRUZICK   V   (

BLACKFOOT

(A) NO RESERVATIONS   1975   ISLAND   UK   ILPS 9326
(B) FLYIN' HIGH   1976   EPIC   US   PE 34378
(C) TOMCATTIN'   1980   ATCO   K 50702

BARRY BECKETT   (SUZI STORM   V   (
BARBARA WYRICK   (

B123A
J D BLACKFOOT   (

J D BLACKFOOT

(A) THE ULTIMATE PROPHECY   19   MERCURY   61288
(B) SONG OF CRAZY HORSE   1974
(C) SOUTHBOUND & GONE   1975

B124
TOM FARMER   (A
DAVE FARMERS   (A
EDDIE GALGA   (A
ALAN JONES   (A

BLACKFOOT SUE

(A) NOTHING TO HIDE   1973   JAM   JAL 104
(B) GUN RUNNING   1975   DJM   DJLPS 455
(C) STRANGERS   1977   1007

B124A
MICHAEL BOLOTIN   V   (A
BRUCE KULICK   G   (A
SANDY GENNARO   D   (A
JIMMY HASLIP   B   (A
TONY BATTAGLIA   V   (A

BLACKJACK

(A) BLACKJACK   1979   POLYDOR   US   PD1 6215
(A) BLACKJACK   1979   POLYDOR   UK   2391 411

JAN MULLANEY   K   (A   CHUCK KIRKPATRICK   V   (A

B125

BLACKWATER JUNCTION

( ) BLACKWATER JUNCTION   1973   MCA   MUPS 469
( ) BLACKWATER JUNCTION   1974   MCA   MCF 2663
(BLACKWATER JUNCTION   196   DJM   DJF 20465

B125A
TIM BLAKE   SYN   (ALL

TIM BLAKE

(A) CRYSTAL MACHINE   1977   EGG   900 545
(B) BLAKES NEW JERUSALEM   1978   EGG 90 288 +BARCLAY   7005

B126
RONEE BLAKLEY   V G K(ALL
WITH
ROGER HAWKINS   D   (B
BARRY BECKETT   K   (B
DAVID HOOD   B   (B
REGGIE YOUNG   G   (B
JOHNNY GIMBLE   FDL   (B
RANDY McCORMICK   V   (B

RONEE BLAKLEY

(A) RONEE BLAKLEY   1972   ELEKTRA   US   EKS 75027
(B) WELCOME   1975   WB   US   BS 2890
(B) WELCOME   1975   WB   UK   K 56174

PETE CARR   G   (B   JIMMY JOHNSON   G   (B
EDDIE HINTON   G   (B   MUSCLE SHOALS HRNS   HRNS   (B
JOHN HUGHEY   STEEL   (B   BUDDY EMMONS   STEEL(B
JERRY BRIDGES   V   (B   GERRY MASTERS   B   (B

B127
BOBBY BLAND   V   (ALL
WITH
MIKE OMARTIAN   K   (LMQN
BEN BENAY   G   (LMNQ
LARRY CARLTON   G   (LM
DEAN PARKS   G   (LMQ
ED GREENE   D   (LMQ
WILTON FELDER   B   (LMQ
PAUL HUBINON   HRNS   (MQ
JIM HORN   HRNS   (MQ
LEW McCREARY   HRNS   (M
SID SHARP   STRING(LMQ
MAXINE WILLARD   V   (LMQ
JOHN KELSO   HRNS   (LM
TONY TERRAN   HRNS   (M
ERNIE WATTS   HRNS   (LMQ

BOBBY BLAND

(A) BAREFOOT ROCK AND YOU GOT ME   196   DUKE   US   X72
(B) LIKE ER RED HOT   196   DUKE   US   X73
(C) TWO STEPS FROM THE BLUES   196   DUKE   US   X74
(C) TWO STEPS FROM THE BLUES   19   VOCALION   VAP160183
(D) HERES THE MAN   196   DUKE   US   X75
(D) HERES THE MAN   19   VOCALION   VAP 8041
(E) CALL ON ME   196   DUKE   US   X77
(E) CALL ON ME   19   VOCALION   VAP 8034
(F) AINT NOTHIN' YOU CAN DO   196   DUKE   US   X78
(F) AINT NOTHIN' YOU CAN DO   19   VOCALION   VAP 8027
(G) SOUL OF THE MAN   196   DUKE   US   X79
( ) BEST OF BOBBY BLAND   1973   DUKE   US   X84
( ) BEST OF VOL 2   19   DUKE   US   X86
(H) TOUCH OF THE BLUES   19   DUKE   US   X88
(H) TOUCH OF THE BLUES   1968   ISLAND   UK   ILP 974
(I) A PIECE OF GOLD   1969   ACTION   UK   ACLP 6006

(CONTINUED)

(CONTINUED)

BOBBY BLAND   B127

PETER CHRISTLIEB	HRNS (M	(J) SPOTLIGHTING THE MAN	19	DUKE	US	X89
JULIA TILLMAN	V (LMQ	(K) INTROSPECTIVE OF THE EARLY YEARS	19	DUKE	US	D92
GINGER BLAKE	V (LMQ	(K) INTROSPECTIVE OF THE EARLY YEARS	19	ABC		DLBD 92 2
JOE SCOTT	TPT (	(L) HIS CALIFORNIA ALBUM	1973	ABC	UK	ABCL 5044
WAYNE BENNETT	G (	(L) HIS CALIFORNIA ALBUM	1973	ABC DUNHILL	US	DSX 50163
PAT HARE	G (	(M) DREAMER	1974	ABC	UK	ABCL 5053
B B KING	G V (NO	(M) DREAMER	1974	ABC DUNHILL	US	DSX 50169
SCOTT EDWARDS	B (Q	(N) TOGETHER FOR THE FIRST TIME	1974	ABC	UK	ABCD 605
CHUCK RAINEY	B (Q	(N) TOGETHER FOR THE FIRST TIME	1974	ABC	US	DSY50190/2
JAY GRAYDON	G (Q	(N) TOGETHER FOR THE FIRST TIME	197	IMPULSE	US	
RAY PARKER	G (Q	(O) TOGETHER AGAIN...LIVE	1976	IMPULSE		AMPL 8027
LEE RITENOUR	G (Q	(P) GET ON DOWN	1975	ABC	UK	ABCL 5139
VICTOR FELDMAN	PERC (Q	(P) GET ON DOWN	19	ABC	US	895
STEVE BARRY	PERC (Q	(Q) REFLECTIONS IN BLUE	1977	ABC	UK	ABCD 5196
NINO TEMPO	HRNS (Q	(Q) REFLECTIONS IN BLUE	197	ABC	US	AB 1018
CHUCK FINDLEY	HRNS (LQ	(R) COME FLY WITH ME	1978	ABC	UK	ABCL 5249
STEVE MADAIO	HRNS (Q	(R) COME FLY WITH ME	1978	ABC	US	AB 1075
ORRIN WATERS	V (Q					
LUTHER WATERS	V (Q	MICHAEL PRICE	V (Q	DAN WALSH	V (Q	
DICK HYDE	HRNS (L	MEL BROWN	G (L	DAVID COHEN	G (L	
MAX BENNETT	B (L					
JUNIOR PARKER	(A	ALSO SEE B B KING FOR LINE UP OF (N)				

BLAST FURNACE   B129

BLAST FURNACE	G (A	(A) LIVE LINE UP 1978				
KEVIN ALLEN	B (A					
BLITZ KRIEG	G (A	JOHN MACKIE	D (A	SKID MARX	V HCA(A	

BLAZER BLAZER   B130

SIMON FOX	D
DEREK O'NEIL	G
STEVE BARNACLE	B JEB MILLION G V

CARLA BLEY   B131

CARLA BLEY	V K (ALL	(A) ESCALATOR OVER THE HILL	1972	JCOA		EOTH 3
ROSEWELL RUDD	TROM V(ADEFG	(A) ESCALATOR OVER THE HILL	1974	JCOA		JT 4001
PERRY ROBINSON	CLAR (A	(A) ESCALATOR OVER THE HILL	1974	BARCLAY		840050 1 2
GATO BARBIERI	SAX (AB	(A) ESCALATOR OVER THE HILL	1974	JCOA	US	1003 4 5
CHARLIE HADEN	B V (AF	(B) TROPIC APPETITES	1974	VIRGIN JCOA		WATT 1
MIKE MANTLER	TPT PNO(ABCDEFG	(C) 13/3/4	1975	VIRGIN		WATT 3
PAUL MOTIAN	, D PERC(AB	(D) DINNER MUSIC	1977	VIRGIN		WATT 6
BOB STEWART	V TUBA(ACDEF	(D) DINNER MUSIC	1977	ECM		2313 106
KAREN MANTLER	V GLOC(AF	(E) EUROPEAN TOUR	1977	VIRGIN		WATT 8
JULIE TIPPETTS	V (B	(E) EUROPEAN TOUR	1977	ECM		2313 108
HOWARD JOHNSON	WIND (B	(F) MUSIQUE MECANIQUE	1979	WATT		WATT 9
DAVID HOLLAND	CELLO (B	(F) MUSIQUE MECANIQUE	1979	ECM	·	2313 109.
TONY MARCUS	VLN (B	(G) EUROPEAN TOUR LINE UP 78				
CARLOS WARD	SAX (D					
RICHARD TEE	K (D	ERIC GALE	G (D	CORNELL DUPREE	G (D	
GORDON EDWARDS	B (D	STEVE GADD	D (D	ELTON DEAN	SAX (EG	
GARY WINDO	SAX (EF	JOHN CLARK	HRNS (EF	TERRY ADAMS	PNO (EF	
HUGH HOPPER	B (EG	ANDREW CYRILLE	D (EG	STEVE SWALLOW	B (F	
D. SHARPE	D (F	EUGENE SHADBOURNE	G (F	SAM BROWN	G (	
RON McCLURE	B (	DON CHERRY	TPT PERC (A	JACK BRUCE	V B (A	
DON PRESTON	SYN (A	JOHN McLAUGHLIN	G (A	LINDA RONSTADT	V (A	
PAUL JONES	V (A	ORCHESTRA & STRINGS	(AC			

BLIMPS   B132

GRAHAM HINE	G V
JIM PITTS	SAX
KEITH TRUSSELL	D

BLIND FAITH   B134

ERIC CLAPTON	G V	(A) BLIND FAITH	1969	POLYDOR	UK	583 059
STEVE WINWOOD	K V	(A) BLIND FAITH	1969	RSO	US	1 3016
RICK GRECH	B V					
GINGER BAKER	D					

RORY BLOCK   B135

RORY BLOCK	V G (ALL	(A) RORY BLOCK	1976	BLUE GOOSE	BG	2022
WITH		(B) AURORA BLOCK	197	RCA		
BILL PAYNE	K (C	(C) INTOXICATION	1977	CHRYSALIS	UK	CHR 1157
ROLAND JOHN HINES	B V (C	(D) YOU'RE THE ONE	1978	CHRYSALIS	US	CHR 1233
KEITH BENSON	D (D					
SAM CLAYTON	CONGA V(C	RICK SCHLOSSER	D (C	FRED TACKETT	G (C	
JACK ASHFORD	PERC (C	WILLIAM COLLETTE	FLT (C	WILLIAM SMITH	K (C	
JIM HORN	SAX (C	RITCHIE HAYWARD	D V (C	PAUL STALLWORTH	B (C	
JOE PORCARO	CONGA (C	REV JAMES CLEVELAND	CHOIR (C	CINDY BULLENS	V (C	
ARTIE TRAUM	G (A	ROLEY SALLEY	B (A	PAT MURRAY	CONGA(A	
ERIC VALDINA	D (A	ALAN SEIDLER	PNO (A	KEN KOSEK	FDL (A	
COTTON KENT	K (D	VINCE FAY	B (D	JAMES WILLIAMS	B (D	
LENNY PAKULA	K (D	DENNIS HARRIS	G (D	LARRY WASHINGTON	PERC (D	
RONNIE JAMES	G (D	T J TINDALL	G (D	JIMMY MAELEN	PERC (D	
GORDON TITCOMB	STEEL (D	BOBBY ELI	PERC G (D	GRANT MACAVOY	D (D	
BRUCE GRAY	K (D	DEXTER WANSEL	SYN (D	VINCE WARSAVAGE	PERC (D	
BARBARA INGRAM	V (D	EVETTE BENTON	V (D	CARLA BENSON	V (D	

BLODWYN PIG   B136

JACK LANCASTER	WIND (AB	(A) AHEAD RINGS OUT	1969	ISLAND	UK	ILPS 9101
MICK ABRAHAMS	G (AB	(A) AHEAD RINGS OUT	1969	A&M	US	AM 4210
ANDY PYLE	B (AB	(B) GETTING TO THIS	1970	CHRYSALIS	UK	ILPS 9122
RON BERG	D (AB					
GRAHAM WALLER	K (B	PETER BANKS	G (	CLIVE BUNKER	D (	

B137

				BLONDE ON BLONDE				
GRAHAM DAVIS BANJ V G B	(C	(A) CONTRASTS	1969	PYE	UK	NSPL18288
GARETH JOHNSON	G	(C	(B) REBIRTH	1970	EMBER	UK	NR 5049
DAVE THOMAS HCA B V G	(C	(C) REFLECTIONS ON A LIFE	1971	EMBER	UK	NR 5058
LES HICKS	PERC	(C	(D) BLONDE ON BLONDE	1972	EMBER	UK	
KIP	MELLA	(C					

B138

			(AMAZING)BLONDEL				
TERRY WINCOTT	V G	(ABCDEFGH	(A) AMAZING BLONDEL	1970	BELL	UK	SBLL 131
EDDIE BAIRD	V G K	(ABCDEFG	(B) EVENSONG	1970	ISLAND	UK	ILPS 9136
JOHN GLADWIN		(ABCD	(C) FANTASIA LINDUM	1971	ISLAND	UK	ILPS 9156
WILLIAM MURRAY	D	(FG	(D) ENGLAND 72	1972	ISLAND	UK	ILPS 9205
MICK FEAT	G	(FG	(E) BLONDEL	1973	ISLAND	UK	ILPS 9257
EDDIE JOBSON	K VLN	(F	(F) MULGRAVE STREET	1974	DJM DJF 20443 +		DJLPS 443
ALAN SPENNER	B	(F	(G) INSPIRATION	1975	DJM DJF 20446 +		DJLPS 446
PAUL KOSSOFF	G	(F	(H) BAD DREAMS	1976	DJM		DJLPS 472
SUE GLOVER	V	(EF	(H) BAD DREAMS	1976	DJM		DJF 20472
SUNNY LESLIE	V	(EF	(I) LIVE IN TOKYO	1977	DJM		48089
SIMON KIRKE	D	(EF	(I) LIVE IN TOKYO	1977	DJM		DJF 20503
JOHN RABBIT BUNDRICK K	(F	(FG) MULGRAVE/INSPIRATION	197	DJM	US	2239 701
STEVE WINWOOD	K	(E					

ADRIAN HOPKINS	K	(CE	BOZ BURRELL	B	(F	MICK RALPHS	G	(F
PAT DONALDSON	B	(F	PAUL RODGERS	V	(E	CHRIS KARAN	PERC	(B
ALAN SKEAPING	VLN	(B	DAVE SKINNER	PNO	(G	MEL COLLINS	SAX	(G

B139

			BLONDIE				
DEBBIE HARRY	V	(ALL	(A) BLONDIE	1976	PRIVATE STOCK		PS 2023
CHRIS STEIN	G	(ALL	(A) BLONDIE	1976	PRIVATE STOCK		PVLP 1017
CLEM BURKE	D	(ABC456789DE	(A) BLONDIE	1978	CHRYSALIS	UK	CHR 1165
JIMMY DESTRI	K	(ABCDE789	(A) BLONDIE	1978	PHONOGRAM	FR	6307 616
GARY VALENTINE	B	(A67	(B) PLASTIC LETTERS	1978	CHRYSALIS	UK	CHR 1166
FRANK INFANTE	B G	(BCDE89	(B) PLASTIC LETTERS	1978	PHONOGRAM	FR	6307 617
NIGEL HARRISON	B	(CDE9	(C) PARALLEL LINES	1978	CHRYSALIS	UK	CHR 1192
BILLY O'CONNOR	D	(123	(C) X OFFENDER	19	SONOPRESSE	FR	PS 69673
FRED SMITH	B	(1234	(D) EAT TO THE BEAT	1979	CHRYSALIS	UK	CDL 1225
JULIE	V	(1	(E) AUTO AMERICANS	1980	CHRYSALIS	UK	CDL 1290
JACKIE	V	(1	(1) AUTUMN 74 (2) OCT 74 JAN 75 (3) JAN 75 MAY 75 (4) MAY 75
IVAN KRAL	G	(2	(5) MAY 75 AUG 75 (6) AUT 75 (7) OCT 75 AUG 77 (8)AUG 77 (9) NOV 79
TISH	V	(2	
SNOOKIE	V	(2	

B139A

		BLONKER				
		DIE ZIET STEHT STILL	1979	BRAIN		0060 104

B140

		BLOOD				
		BLOOD	19	ENTERPRISE		ENTF 3002

B141

			BLOOD SWEAT & TEARS				
AL KOOPER	K V	(AM	(A) CHILD IS FATHER TO THE MAN	1968	CBS	UK	63296
BOBBY COLOMBY	D	(ABCDEFGHM	(A) CHILD IS FATHER TO THE MAN	1968	CBS	US	PC 9619
STEVE KATZ	V G	(ABCM	(A) THE FIRST ALBUM	1973	EMBASSY	UK	EMB 31028
JIM FIELDER	B	(ABCM	(A) THE FIRST ALBUM	1977	EMBASSY	UK	EMB 31492
RANDY BRECKER	TPT	(AM	(B) BLOOD SWEAT & TEARS	1969	CBS	UK	63504
JERRY WEISS	TPT	(AM	(B) BLOOD SWEAT & TEARS	1969	CBS	US	PC 9720
DICK HALLIGAN	TROM	(AMBC	(C) THREE	1970	CBS	UK	64024
FRED LIPSIUS	PNO SAX	(ABCM	(C) THREE	1970	CBS	US	KC 30090
DAVID CLAYTON THOMAS	V	(BCDHM	(D) FOUR	1971	CBS	UK	64355
CHUCK WINFIELD	TPT	(BCM	(D) FOUR	1971	CBS	US	KC 30590
LEW SOLOFF	TPT	(BCM	(E) NEW BLOOD	1972	CBS	UK	65252
BOBBY DOYLE	V	(	(E) NEW BLOOD	1972	CBS	US	KC 31780
JERRY FISCHER	V	(G	(F) NO SWEAT	1973	CBS	UK	65725
JERRY LA CROIX	V	(G	(F) NO SWEAT	1973	CBS	US	KC 32180
TONY KLATKA	SAX	(GH	(G) MIRROR IMAGE	1974	CBS	UK	80153
LARRY WILLIS	K	(GH	(G) MIRROR IMAGE	1974	CBS	US	KC 32929
GEORGE WADENIUS	G	(GH	(H) NEW CITY	1975	CBS	UK	80784
DAVE BARGERN	TROM	(GH	(H) NEW CITY	1975	CBS	US	PC 33484
RON McCLURE	B	(GH	(J) MORE THAN EVER	1976	CBS	UK	81465
BILL TILLMAN	SAX	(GH	(J) MORE THAN EVER	1976	CBS	US	PC 34233
JERRY HYMAN	TROM	(BM	(K) BRAND NEW DAY	1978	ABC	UK	ABCL 5234
ALAN RUBIN	TPT	(B	(K) BRAND NEW DAY	1978	ABC	US	1015
			(K) BRAND NEW DAY	1978	CARRERE	FR	68055
			(L) IN CONCERT (DBL)	19	CBS		22006
			(BC) BLOOD SWEAT & TEARS/THREE (DBL)	1976	CBS	U	22015
			( ) GREATEST HITS	1972	CBS	UK	64803
			( ) GREATEST HITS	1972	CBS	US	PC 31170
			( ) BLOOD SWEAT & TEARS	1978	HALLMARK		SHM 963
			(M) CLASSIC B S T	1980	CBS		31824
			(N) NUCLEAR BLUES	1980	MCA	UK	MCF 3061

B141A

			BLOODGROUP			
JOHN HAYWARD	V					
BARRY MOORE	G					
CLIVE ROUTLEDGE	D	BARBARA PAWULSKA	B	MATT GUNTRIP	G	

B142

				BLOODROCK				
STEVE HILL	K V	(C	(A) BLOODROCK	19	CAPITOL	US	ST 435
ED GRUNDY	B V	(C	(B) BLOODROCK TWO	19	CAPITOL	US	ST 491
WARREN HAM	V WIND	(C	(C) BLOODROCK THREE	19	CAPITOL	US	EST 765
RICK COBB	D PERC	(C	(D) LIVE	19	CAPITOL	US	SVBB11038
NICK TAYLOR	G V	(C	(E) U S A	19	CAPITOL	US	SM 645
JIM RUTLEDGE	V	(C	(F) PASSAGE	1973	CAPITOL	US	SW 11109
LEE PICKENS	G	(C	(G) WHIRLWIND TONGUES	1974	CAPITOL	US	EST 11259
			(H) BLOODROCK'N' ROLL	19	CAPITOL	US	SM 11417

BLOODSTONE B143

HARRY WILLIAMS	V PERC(ABCD	(A) BLOODSTONE	1972	DECCA	UK	TXS	110
CHARLES McCORMICK	B V (ABCD	(B) NATURAL HIGH	1973	DECCA	UK	SKL	5150
CHARLES LOVE	G V (ABCD	(B) NATURAL HIGH	1973	LONDON	US		620
WILLIS DRAFFEN	G (ABCD	(C) UNREAL	1974	DECCA	UK	SKL	5156
ROGER DURHAM	V PERC(ABC	(C) UNREAL	1974	LONDON	US		634
EDDIE SUMMERS	D (A	(D) I NEED TIME	1974	DECCA	UK	SKL	5185
HARRY WILKINS	G B (C	(D) I NEED TIME	1974	LONDON	US		647
DARRYL CLIFTON	D (C	(E) RIDDLE OF THE SPHINX	1975	DECCA	UK	SKL	5202
MARVIN WEBB		(E) RIDDLE OF THE SPHINX	1975	LONDON	US		654
		(F) LULLABY OF BROADWAY	1976	DECCA	UK	SKL	5238
		(G) TRAIN RIDE TO HOLLYWOOD	197	LONDON	US		665
		(H) DO YOU WANNA DO A THING	197	LONDON	US		671
		(J) DONT STOP	1979	TAMLA	UK	STML	12097

MIKE BLOOMFIELD B144

MIKE BLOOMFIELD	K G V (ALL	(A) SUPER SESSION	1968	CBS	UK		63396
MARK NAFTALIN	K (BC	(A) SUPER SESSION	1968	CBS	US	CS	9701
IRA KAMIN	K (BCH	(A) SUPER SESSION	1973	EMBASSY	UK	EMB	31029
JOHN KAHN	B (BCD	(B) ITS NOT KILLING ME	1969	CBS	UK		63652
BOB JONES	D V (BCJ	(C) LIVE AT BILL GRAHAMS FILLMORE WEST	1969	CBS	UK		63816
DINO ANDINO	CONGA (C	(C) LIVE AT BILL GRAHAMS FILLMORE WEST	1969	CBS	US	CS	9893
NOEL JEWKIS	SAX (C	(D) LIVE ADVENTURES	1969	CBS	UK		66216
JOHN WILMETH	TPT (C	(E) TRY IT BEFORE YOU BUY IT	1973	CBS	US	PC	33173
JESSE ED DAVIS	G (C	(F) TRIUMVIRATE	1973	CBS	UK		65659
TAJ MAHAL	V (C	(F) TRIUMVIRATE	1973	XBS	US	CS	32172
NICK GRAVENITES	V (BCHJ	(G) MILL VALLEY SESSION	1976	POLYDOR			
AL KOOPER	K V G (AD	(H) IF YOU LOVE THOSE BLUES	1977	GUITAR PLAYER	US		3002
STEPHEN STILLS	V G (A	(H) IF YOU LOVE THOSE BLUES	1977	SONET	UK	SNTF	726
CARLOS SANTANA	G (D	(J) ANALINE	1977	TAKOMA	US		1059
DOUG KILMER	B (H	(J) ANALINE	1977	SONET	UK	SNTF	749
DR. JOHN	PNO G (F	(J) ANALINE	1977	CBS	US	TRK	82516
CHRIS ETHRIDGE	B (D	(K) COUNT TALENT & THE ORIGINALS	1978	CLOUDS	US		
ERIC KRISS	K (H						

BENNIE PARKS	PERC (F	JAMES GORDON	HRNS (F	JESSIE SMITH	V (F				
ROY RUBY	K (B	RON STALLINGS	SAX (BD	MARCUS DOUBLEDAY	TPT (B				
DIANE TRIBUNO	V (B	SNOOKY FLOWERS	SAX (C	JOHN BOUDREAUX	PERC (F				
GEORGE BOHANON	TROM (F	ROBBIE MONTGOMERY	V (F	ROGER TROY	B (HJ				
JOHN HAMMOND	V G HCA (F	THOMAS JEFFERSON KAYE G V (F	RICHARD BLUE MITCHELL	HRNS (F				
JEROME JUMONVILLE	HRNS (F	LORRAINE REBENNACK	B (F	MICHAEL MELFORD MAND G V (B				
MARK TEEL	SAX (B	RICHARD SANTI	ACC (B	ANNA RIZZO	V (J				
FRED STAEHLE	D (F	FRED OLSEN	G (B	RED RHODES	STEEL(B				
GERALD OSHITA	SAX (B	ACE OF CUPS	V (B	MARCIA ANN TAYLOR	V (J				
SKIP PROKOP	D (D	ELVIN BISHOP	G (D	ROOSEVELT GOOK	K (D				
TOM DONLINGER	D (H	HART McNEE	SAX (H	DAVE NEDITCH	B (H				

STEVE BLOOMFIELD B145

STEVE BLOOMFIELD	G (	(A) ROCKABILLY ORIGINALS	1978	CHARLY		CR	30159

BLOSSOM TOES B146

BRIAN GODDING	G V K (AB	(A) WE ARE EVER SO CLEAN	1967	MARMALADE	UK		607001
BRIAN BELSHAW	B V (AB	(B) IF ONLY FOR A MOMENT	1969	MARMALADE	UK		608010
JIM CREGAN	G V (AB						
KEVIN WESTLAKE	D (A	BARRY REEVES	D PERC (B	POLI PALMER	D (B		
SEAN PHILLIPS	SITAR G(B						

BLOW FLY B147

( ) ZODIAC PARTY	1978	WEIRD WORLD			2031

BLUE B148

IAN MACMILLAN	B G V (ABCD	(A) BLUE	1973	RSO		SO	873
HUGH NICHOLSON	G V K (ABCD	(A) BLUE	1973	RSO	UK	2394	105
SMIGGY	G V (B	(B) LIFE IN THE NAVY	1974	RSO	UK	2394	133
TIMMY DONALD	D V (A	(C) ANOTHER NIGHT TIME FLIGHT	1977	ROCKET	UK	ROLL	7
BEN KEITH	STEEL (B	(D) FOOLS PARTY	1979	ROCKET	UK	TRAIN	4
RAY COOPER	PERC (C						
CHARLIE SMITH	D (CD	DAVID NICHOLSON B K (CD					

DAVID BLUE B149

DAVID BLUE(COHEN)	G (ALL	(A) SINGER SONGWRITER (3 TRACKS)	1965	ELEKTRA			
WITH		(B) DAVID BLUE	1966	ELEKTRA	US	EKS	74003
BOB RAFKIN	B G (E	(C) 23 DAYS IN SEPTEMBER	1968	REPRISE	US		6293
RUSS KUNKEL	D (E	(D) ME	1970	REPRISE	US	RS	6375
JAMES KARSTEIN	D (E	(E) STORIES	1972	ASYLUM		SYL	9001
		(E) STORIES	1972	ASYLUM			5052
JOHN BARBATA	D (E	(F) NICE BABY & THE ANGEL	1973	ASYLUM		SYL	9009
RY COODER	G (E	(G) COMIN' BACK FOR MORE	1975	ASYLUM		SYL	9025
MILT HOLLAND	PERC (E	(G) COMIN' BACK FOR MORE	1975	ASYLUM			1043
RALPH SCHUCKETT	K (E	(H) CUPIDS ARROW	197	ASYLUM		SYL	1077
PETE JOLLY	ACC (E						
CHRIS ETHRIDGE	B (E	RITA COOLIDGE V (E					

BLUE ASH B149A

(A) NO MORE NO LESS	19	MERCURY		SRM 1	666
(B) FRONT PAGE NEWS	1978	PLAYBOY			34918

BLUE CHEER B150

PAUL WHALEY	D (C	(A) VINCEBUS ERUPTUM	1968	PHILIPS			600 264
RANDY HOLDEN	G (C	(A) VINCEBUS ERUPTUM	1968	PHILIPS		SBL	7839
DICK PETERSON	B (C	(B) OUTSIDE INSIDE	1968	PHILIPS			600 278
GENE ESTES	PERC (C	(B) OUTSIDE INSIDE	1968	PHILIPS		SBL	7860
BRUCE STEPHENS	(C	(C) NEW IMPROVED	1969	PHILIPS			600 305
LEIGH STEPHENS	G (	(C) NEW IMPROVED	1974	PHILIPS		SBL	7896
BURNS KELLOGG	K (C	(D) BLUE CHEER	19	PHILIPS			600 333
		(E) ORIGINAL HUMAN BEINGS	1970	PHILIPS	6336 004		600 347
		(F) OH PLEASANT HOPE	19	PHILIPS			600 350

[41]

```
B151                          BLUE JAYS
   JOHN LODGE          B V   (    (A) THE BLUE JAYS              1975   THRESHOLD         UK    THS    1
   JUSTIN HAYWARD      G V   (    (B) NASCENCE                   19     MAPCITY           US           3014
   GRAHAM DEACON       D     (
   KIRK DUNCAN         PNO   (    JIM COCKNEY         VLN   (    TOM TOMPKINS       CELLO         (
B151A                         BLUE MAGIC
                                 (A) BLUE MAGIC                  19     ATCO US 7038      UK    K40532
                                 (B) MAGIC OF THE BLUE           19     ATCO US 36103     UK    K50112
                                 (C) 13 BLUE MAGIC LANE          19     ATCO US 36120     UK    K50181
                                 (D) MYSTIC DRAGONS              19     ATCO             US           36140
                                 (E) MESSAGE                     19     ATCO             US           38104
B152                          BLUE MINK
   MADELINE BELL       V     (F   (A) OUR WORLD                  11970  PHILIPS           UK    6308  024
   ROGER COOK          V     (F   (B) MELTING POT                1970   PHILIPS           UK    SBL   1029
   BARRY MORGAN        D     (F   (B) MELTING POT                1970   PHILIPS           UK    600   323
   HERBIE FLOWERS      B     (F   (C) LIVE AT THE TALK OF THE TOWN 1972 REGAL ZONOPHONE         SLRZ 1029
   ALAN PARKER         G     (F   (D) A TIME OF CHANGE           1972   REGAL ZONOPHONE         SRZA 8507
   ANN ODELL           K     (F   (E) REAL                       197    PHILIPS           US    600   339
   ROGER COULAM        K     (F   ( ) BEST OF BLUE MINK          1973   PHILIPS           UK    6382  077
   RAY COOPER          PERC  (F   (F) ONLY WHEN I LAUGH          1973   EMI               UK    EMA   756
                                  (G) FRUITY                     1974   EMI               UK    EMC   3021
                                  ( ) THE BEST OF BLUE MINK      1974   EMI               UK    EMC   3043
                                  ( ) HIT MAKING WORLD OF BLUE MINK 1975 DECCA            UK    SPA   437
                                  ( ) ATTENTION                  1975   PHONOGRAM               6434  064
B152A                         BLUE MOUNTAIN EAGLE
   DAVID PRICE         G     (    (A) BLUE MOUNTAIN EAGLE        197    ATCO             US           33324
   RANDY FULLER        B G V (    (B) SECOND                     197    ATCO             US
   BOB JONES           G V   (
   JOEY NEWMAN         G     (    DON PONCHER         D V   (
B153                          BLUE NOTES
                                  (A) BLUE NOTES FOR MONGEZI (DBL) 1977 OGUN                   OGD 001/2
                                  (B) BLUE NOTES IN CONCERT VOL1 1978  OGUN                    OG   220
B154                          BLUE OYSTER CULT
   ERIC BLOOM          G V   (ABCDEFGH (A) BLUE OYSTER CULT      1973   CBS               UK          64904
   ALLEN LANIER        K     (ABCDEFGH (A) BLUE OYSTER CULT      1973   CBS               US          31063
   ALBERT BOUCHARD     D     (ABCDEFGH (B) TYRANNY & MUTATION    1974   CBS               UK          65331
   JOE BOUCHARD        B V   (ABCDEFGH (B) TYRANNY & MUTATION    1974   CBS               US    KC    32107
   DONALD ROESER       G V   (ABCDEFGH (C) SECRET TREATIES       1974   CBS               UK          80103
   PATTI SMITH         V     (E       (C) SECRET TREATIES        1974   CBS               US    PC    32858
   RANDY BRECKER       HRNS  (E       (D) ON YOUR FEET OR ON YOUR KNEES 1975 CBS          UK          88116
   MICHAEL BRECKER     HRNS  (E       (D) ON YOUR FEET OR ON YOUR KNEES 1975 CBS          US    PG    33317
   MARK RIVERA         SAX   (J       (E) AGENTS OF FORTUNE      1976   CBS               UK          81385
                                      (E) AGENTS OF FORTUNE      1976   CBS               US    PC    34164
                                      (F) SPECTRES               1977   CBS               UK          86050
                                      (F) SPECTRES               1977   CBS               US    JC    35019
                                      (G) SOME ENCHANTED EVENING 1978   CBS               UK          86074
                                      (G) SOME ENCHANTED EVENING 1978   CBS               US    JC    35563
                                      (H) MIRRORS                1979   CBS               UK          86087
                                      (J) CULTOSAURUS ERECTUS    1980   CBS               UK          86120
B154A                         BLUE STEEL
   LEONARD ARNOLD      G     (A   (A) NO MORE LONELY NIGHTS      1979   INFINITY INF9018   +    INS2011
   RICHARD BOWDEN      G     (A
   HOWARD BURKE        G     (A   MARC DURAM          B     (A   MICKEY McGEE        D     (A
   MICHAEL HUEY        D     (A
B154A                         BLUES BAND
   PAUL JONES          V HCA (AB  (A) OFFICIAL BOOTLEG ALBUM     1980   ARISTA                  BBBP  101
   TOM McGUINNESS      G     (AB  (B) READY                      1980   ARISTA                  BB    2
   HUGHIE FLINT        D     (AB
   DAVE KELLY          G V   (AB  BOB HALL        PNO   (A  IAN STEWART   PNO (B  GARY FLETCHER  B (AB
   GERAINT WATKINS     PNO   (B   ROCKIN' DOPSIE  ACC   (B  CHESTER ZENO  PERC (B
B155                          BLUES BROTHERS
   JOLIET JAKE BLUES   V     (ABC (A) BRIEFCASE FULL OF BLUES    1978   ATLANTIC          UK    K 50556
   (JOHN BELUSHI)                 (B) BLUES BROTHERS(SOUNDTRACK) 1980   ATLANTIC US 16017 UK    K 50715
   ELWOOD BLUES        HCA V (ABC (C) MADE IN AMERICA            1980   ATLANTIC US 16025 UK    K 50768
   (DAN AKROYD)
   PAUL SHAFFER        K V   (AC  STEVE CROPPER    G     (ABC  MATT MURPHY    G     (ABC
   DONALD DUCK DUNN    B     (ABC STEVE JORDAN     D V   (ABC  LOU MARINI     SAX V(ABC
   ALAN RUBIN          TPT V (ABC TOM SCOTT        SAX V (AC   TOM MALONE     HRS  (ABC
   MURPHY DUNNE        K     (BC  JEFF MIRONOV     G     (C
B155A                         BLUES DIMENSIONS
   HELMIG VAN DER VEGT K     (A   (A) BLUES DIMENSION            1969   DECCA            GERM   ND254
   RUDY VAN DIJK       SAX   (A
   HERMAN DEINUM       B     (A   HANS LAFAILLE    D     (A   RIPKE                 (A
B156                          BLUES INCORPORATED
   CYRIL DAVIES        V HCA (    (A) BLUES INC/ALEXIS KORNER ALL STARS 19  TRANSATLANTIC       TRASAM  7
   ALEXIS KORNER       G V   (
   MICK JAGGER         V HCA (    CHARLIE WATTS    D     (    IAN ARMITT        K     (
   DICK HECKSTALL SMITH SAX  (    JOHN PARKER            (    RONNIE JONES            (
   JACK BRUCE          B     (    GRAHAM BOND      K SAX (    GINGER BAKER      D     (
B157                          BLUES MAGOOS
   PEPPY THIELHEIM     G V   (ABCDEF (A) BLUES MAGOOS            19     FONTANA                 STL   5402
   RALPH SCALA         V K   (BCD  (B) PSYCHEDELIC LOLLIPOP      1966   MERCURY
   RON GILBERT         B     (BCD  (C) ELECTRIC COMIC BOOK       1967   MERCURY
   GEOFF DAKING        D     (BCD  (D) BASIC BLUES MAGOOS        1968   MERCURY           US    ST  61167
   MIKE ESPOSITO       G     (BCD  (E) NEVER GOING BACK TO GEORGIA 1969 ABC               US    ABCS  697
   JOHN LIELLO   VIBES PERC  (EF   (F) GULF COAST BOUND          1970   ABC               US    ABCS  710
   ERIC KAZ       HCA V K    (EF   (F) GULF COAST BOUND          1972   PROBE             US    SPB  1024
   RICHIE DICKON       PERC  (EF
   ROGER EATON         B V   (E    HERB LOVELL      D     (E   DEAN EVANSON      FLT   (E
   TITO                CONGA (E    SOTO             SAX   (E   PEE WEE ELLIS     PERC  (F
   COOKER LOPRESTI     B     (F    JIM PAYNE   [42]  D     (F   DADDY YA YA       PERC  (F
```

BLUES PROJECT   B158

AL KOOPER	K	(AG	(A) LIVE AT THE CAFE AU GO GO	1966	VERVE		FT	3000
STEVE KATZ	G	(AG	(B) PROJECTIONS	1967	VERVE		FTS	3008
TOMMY FLANDERS	V	(AEF	(B) PROJECTIONS	1969	VERVE		SVLP	6009
DANNY KALB	G	(ABCEFG	(C) LIVE AT THE TOWN HALL	1967	VERVE		FTS	3025
ANDY KULBERG	B	(ABCDG	(D) PLANNED OBSOLESCENCE	1968	VERVE		FTS	3046
RAY BLUMENFIELD	D	(ABCDEFG	(E) LAZARUS	1971	CAPITOL		ST	872
RICHARD GREENE	VLN	(D	(F) BLUES PROJECT	1972	CAPITOL		EST	11017
DON KRETMAR	SAX	(DEF	(F) BLUES PROJECT	197	MGM		GAS	118
JOHN GREGORY	G V	(D	(G) REUNION IN CENTRAL PARK	1973	MCA			
DAVID COHEN	G K	(EF	( ) BEST OF	197	VERVE		FTS	3069
BILL LUSSENDEN	G	(F	( ) POP HISTORY	19	POLYDOR		2625	020

BLUESOLOGY   B159

ELTON JOHN	ORG					
MARC CHARIG	CLAR		ELTON DEAN	SAX		FRED GANDY	B
JOHN BALDRY	V		PETE GAVIN	D		NEIL HUBBARD	G

COLIN BLUNSTONE   B160

COLIN BLUNSTONE	V G	(ALL	(A) ONE YEAR	1971	EPIC	UK		64557
WITH			(A) ONE YEAR	1971	EPIC	US	E	30974
PETE WINGFIELD	K	(BC	(B) ENNISMORE	1973	EPIC	UK		65278
DEREK GRIFFITHS	G	(BC	(C) JOURNEY	1974	EPIC	UK		65805
TERRY POOLE	B	(BC	(C) JOURNEY	1974	EPIC	US	KE	32902
JIM TOOMEY	D	(BC	(D) PLANES	1976	EPIC	UK		81592
ROBERT HENRIT	D	(B	(E) NEVER EVEN THOUGHT	1978	EPIC	UK		82835
BYRON LYEFOOT	D	(B	(E) NEVER EVEN THOUGHT	1978	EPIC	US	BXL	12903
ROD ARGENT	K	(BC					
MIKE SNOW	K G	(B	PHIL DENNYS	K	(B	RUSS BALLARD	K G	(B
STEVE BINGHAM	B	(B	JIM RODFORD	B	(B	MIKE COTTON	HRNS	(C
NICK NEWELL	HRNS	(C	JOHN BEECHAM	HRNS	(C	DUNCAN BROWNE	G	(C
RICHARD KERR	PNO	(C	KINGS SINGERS	V	(C			

BO STREET RUNNERS   B161

MICK FLEETWOOD	D	(A	(A) READY STEADY WIN (1 TRACK)	196	DECCA	UK	LK	4634
TIM HINKLEY	K	(A	(1) 1963					
JOHN DOMINIC	V	(A1						
MIKE PATTO	V	(A	GARY THOMAS	G	(1	GLYN THOMAS	D	(1
DAVE CAMERON	B	(1	ROYSTON FRY	K	(1			

BOB & EARL   B162

BOB RELF	V	(ALL	(A) BOB & EARL	19	CRESTVIEW	US		3055
EARL NELSON	V	(ALL	(B) TOGETHER	19	JOY	U	JOYS	199
			(C) HARLEM SHUFFLE	19	JAYBOY	U	JSX	2004
			(D) BOB & EARL	1969	B&C	U	BCB	1

BOB & MARCIA   B163

| BOB ANDY | V | (| (A) YOUNG GIFTED & BLACK | 1976 | TROJAN | | TBL | 122 |
| MARCIA GRIFFITHS | V | (| | | | | | |

BOBBIDAZZLER   B164

GRANT GULLICKSON	V	(A	(A) BOBBIDAZZLER	1978	RCA		PL	12196
LANCE GULLICKSON	V	(A	(A) BOBBIDAZZLER	1977	RCA	US	APLI	2196
JAMES DIVISEK	D	(A						
GEORGE MARINELLI	G	(A	BRIAN WHITCOMB	K	(A	DENNIS BELFIELD	B	(A
FRED DIVISEK		(A	PETE HENDERSON		(A	JAY LEWIS	G	(A
TONY PELUSO		(A	STEVE PINKSTON		(A			

BODACIOUS   B165

MARTY BALIN	G V	(A	(A) BODACIOUS D F	1974	RCA	US	APLI02067
GREG DEWEY DAGREAZE	D	(A	(A) BODACIOUS D F	1974	RCA	UK	SF	8391
VIC SMITH	G	(A						
MARK RYAN	B	(A	CHARLIE HICKOX	K	(A			

CURT BOETCHER   B166

CURT BOETCHER	V K G	(A	(A) THERE'S AN INNOCENT FACE	1973	ELEKTRA	US	EKS 75037
WITH							
WEBB BURREL	V G K	(A	RED RHODES	STEEL	(A	SKIP KONTE	K	(A
RIC DE CONG	B	(A	WAYNE YENTIS	SYN	(A	LES THORNTON	TUBA	(A
TESSIE	PERC	(A	WILLIS MASONHEIMER	TUBA	(A			

BOGEY BOYS   B166A

| JIMMY SMYTH | G | (A | (A) FRIDAY NIGHT | 1979 | CHRYSALIS | UK | CHR | 1241 |
| PAUL MORAN | D | (AB | (B) JIMMY DID IT | 1980 | CHRYSALIS | UK | CHR | 1298 |

BOIZE   B167

RICK CORACIO	B					
BILLY CONNORS	G V					
JOHN KELLY	V		PAUL ROBINSON	D		DON RANDALL	HCA V

MARC BOLAN & T REX   B168

MARC BOLAN	G V	(ALL	(A) MY PEOPLE WERE FAIR	1968	REGAL ZONOPHONE	UK	SLRZ 1003
WITH			(B) PROPHET	1968	REGAL ZONOPHONE	UK	SLRZ 1005
STEVE TOOK D B PNO PERC		(ABC	(AB) MY PEOPLE/PROPHET	1972	CUBE/FLY	UK	TOOFA	3
MICKY FINN	D	(D	(C) UNICORN	1969	REGAL ZONOPHONE	UK	SLRZ 1007
TONY VISCONTI	PNO	(C	(C) UNICORN	19	BLUE THUMB	US	
JOHN PEEL	V	(C	(D) BEARD OF STARS	1970	REGAL ZONOPHONE	UK	SLRZ 1013
BILL LEGEND	D	(	(CD) UNICORN/BEARD OF STARS DBL	1972	CUBE	UK	TOOFA	9
STEVE TURNER	B	(	( ) T REX	1970	FLY	UK	HIFLY	2
STEVE CURRIE	B	(	( ) ELECTRIC WARRIOR	1971	FLY	UK	HIFLY	6
IAN McDONALD	D	(	( ) THE BEST OF T REX	1971	FLY	UK	TON	2
			( ) BOLAN BOOGIE	1972	FLY	UK	HIFLY	8
			( ) BOLAN BOOGIE	197	CUBE	UK	HIFLY	8
			( ) RIDE A WHITE SWAN	1972	MFP	UK	MFP	5274
			( ) HARD ON LOVE	1972	TRACK	UK	2406	101
			( ) THE SLIDER	1972	EMI	UK	BLN	5001
			( ) TANX	1972	EMI	UK	BLN	5002
(CONTINUED)			( ) GREAT HITS	1972	EMI	UK	BLN	5003

[43]

B168   (CONTINUED)

MARC BOLAN & T REX

( ) ZINC ALLOY	1974	EMI	UK	BLNA 7751
( ) BEGINNING OF DOVES	1974	TRACK	UK	2410 201
( ) LIGHT OF LOVE	1974	CASABLANCA		NBLP 7005
( ) ZIP GUN	1975	EMI	UK	BLN 7752
( ) GET IT ON	1975	MFP	UK	90059
( ) FUTURISTIC DRAGON	1976	EMI	UK	BLN 5004
( ) DANDY IN THE UNDERWORLD	1977	EMI	UK	BLN 5005
( ) WORDS & MUSIC	1978	CUBE	UK	HIFLD 1
( ) GREATEST HITS VOL 1	1978	PICKWICK	UK	SHM 953
( ) T REX COLLECTION (DBL)	1978	PICKWICK	UK	PDA 044
( ) SOLID GOLD	1979	EMI	UK	NUT 5

B169

TOMMY BOLIN	G V K	(AB
STANLEY SHELDON	K	(A
DAVID FOSTER	K	(A
JEFF PORCARO	D	(A
PRAIRIE PRINCE	D	(A
PHIL COLLINS	PERC	(A
SAMMY ZIGUERON	PERC	(A
BOB BERGE	D	(A

TOMMY BOLIN

(A) THE TEASER	1975	ATLANTIC	UK	K 50208
(A) THE TEASER	1975	NEMPEROR	US	436
(B) PRIVATE EYE	1976	CBS	UK	81612
(B) PRIVATE EYE	1976	CBS	US	C 34329

JAN HAMMER	K	(A	DAVID SANBORN	SAX	(A
NARADA MICHAEL WALDEN	D	(A	PAUL STALLWORTH	B	(A
RON FRANSEN	K	(A			

B169A

MICHAEL BOLOTIN	V G	(AB
WILBUR BASCOMB	B	(A
PATRICK HENDERSON	PNO	(B
JAN MULLANEY	ORG	(B
JAY MICHAELS	D	(B
SHARON LEE WILLIAMS	V	(B
DAVE SANBORN	SAX	(A

MICHAEL BOLOTIN

(A) MICHAEL BOLOTIN	1975	RCA UK SF 8451	US	APLI 1550
(B) EVERY DAY OF MY LIFE	1976	RCA	US	APLI 1550

BILLY ELWORTHY	G	(B	GARY FERRARO	B	(B
PAPA JOHN CREACH	FDL	(B	COLINA PHILLIPS	V	(B
RHONDA SILVER	V	(B	WAYNE PERKINS		(A

B170

BILL CUOMO	K V	(A
MICHAEL HOSSACK	D PERC V	(A
ROBERT LICHTIG	B HRNS V	(A
MILT HOLLAND	PERC	(A

BONAROO

(A) BONAROO	1974	WB	UK	K 56096

JERRY WEEMS	G V	(A	BOBBY WINKELMAN	G V	(A

B171

GRAHAM BOND	K SAX V	(ALL
DICK HECKSTALL SMITH	SAX	(ABCJ
GINGER BAKER	D	(ABCJ
JOHN McLAUGHLIN	G	(C
JACK BRUCE	B	(ABCJ
JON HISEMAN	D	(C
TERRY POOLE	G B	(E
DIANE STEWART	V	(DE1LK
HENRY WILLIAMS	G	(E
GASPAR LAWAL	PERC	(E
STEVE GREGORY	SAX	(E
JOHN WEATHERS	D	(E
VICTOR BROX	V	(D
ANNETTE BROX	V	(D
PETE BROWN		(H
RIC GRECH	B	(D
STEVE YORK	B	(D
JOHN GROSS	SAX	(D
ALIKI ASHMAN	V	(D
KEITH BAILEY		(1D
JOHN MOORSHEAD	G	(D
EDDIE HOH	D	(K
RAY RUSSELL	G	(

GRAHAM BOND

(A) THE SOUND OF 65	1965	COLUMBIA	UK	33SX 1711
(B) THERE'S A BOND A BETWEEN US	1966	COLUMBIA	UK	33SX 1750
(C) SOLID BOND	1970	WB	UK	K 66004
(C) SOLID BOND	1970	WB		3001
(D) HOLY MAGICK	1971	VERTIGO	UK	6360 021
(E) WE PUT OUR MAGICK ON YOU	1971	VERTIGO	UK	6360 040
(E) WE PUT OUR MAGICK ON YOU	1974	PHILIPS		SRMI 612
(F) BOND IN AMERICA	1971	PHILIPS		6499200/1
(F) BOND IN AMERICA	1971	MERCURY	UK	6499200/1
(G) THIS IS GRAHAM BOND	1972	PHILLIPS		6382 010
(H) 2 HEADS ARE BETTER THAN ONE	1972	CHAPTER 1	UK	CHSR 813
(H) 2 HEADS ARE BETTER THAN ONE	1972	PATHE	FR	C064 93869
(J) BEGINNING OF JAZZ ROCK	1977	CHARLY	CR	30017
(K) MIGHTY GRAHAM BOND	1968	PULSAR	AR	10606
(L) LOVE IS THE LAW	1968	PULSAR	AR	10604
(1) INITIATION 1969 NO RECORDS				

ALEX DMOCHOWSKI	B	(D	PETE BAILEY	PERC	(D
DAVE HOWARD	SAX	(1D	DAVE USHER		(1
KEVIN STACEY		(1D	GODFREY McLEAN	D	(D
JERRY SALISBURY	HRNS	(D	HAL BLAINE	D	(L
HARVEY MANDEL	G	(K	HARVEY BROOKS	K	(K

B172

GABRIEL BONDAGE

GABRIEL BONDAGE				
(A) ANOTHER TRIP TO EARTH	1978	DHARMA	IMP	D 808

B173

CASEY CUNNINGHAM	D	(A
JIMMY FARAGHER	SAX B V	(A
DANNY FARAGHER	HRS HCA K V	(A
GREG TORNQUIST	G V HCA	(A

BONES

(A) BONES	1972	SIGNPOST		SP 8402
(A) BONES	1972	SIGNPOST		SG 4251

B174

MARCIA BARRETT	V	(AB
BOBBY FARRELL	V	(AB
MAIZIE WILLIAMS	V	(AB
LIZ MITCHELL	V	(AB
WITH		
MATS BJORKLUND	G	(AB
FRANK FARIAN	V	(B
M CRETU	K	(B
LISA GRODANIER	SAX	(B
GEOFF STRADLING	TROM	(B
KARL BARTELMES	TPT	(B
GEORG DELAGALTE	TROM	(B

BONEY M

(A) NIGHT FLIGHT TO VENUS	1978	ATLANTIC		K 50498
(A) NIGHT FLIGHT TO VENUS	1978	SIRE	US	K6062
(B) OCEANS OF FANTASY	1979	ATLANTIC		K 50610

KEITH FORSEY	D	(AB	NICK WOODLAND	G	(AB
GARY UNWIN	B	(AB	CHICO DE LOS REYES		(A
PRECIOUS WILSON	V	(B	R BESSER	B	(B
JIM POLIVKA	TPT	(B	SCOT NEWTON	TPT	(B
BOBBY STERN	SAX	(B	LANCE BURTON	SAX	(B
ETIENNE CAP	TPT	(B	WALTER RAB	TPT	(B
BENNY GEBAVER	SAX	(B	DINO SOLERA	WIND	(B

B174A

JUKE BOY BONNER	HCA V G	(ALL

JUKE BOY BONNER

(A) I'M GOING BACK TO THE COUNTRY	1968	ARHOOLIE		F 1036
(B) THE STRUGGLE	19	ARHOOLIE		F 1045
(C) LEGACY OF THE BLUES	19	SONET		SNTF 634
(C) LEGACY OF THE BLUES	19	GNP CRESCENDO	US	GNP 10015
(D) LOUISIANA BLUES	19	STORYVILLE		SLP 177
(E) ONE MAN TRIO	1979	FLYRIGHT		FLY 548

```
GRAHAM BONNET      V       (A    (A) GRAHAM BONNET              1977   RING O RECORDS   UK   2320  103
MIKE GILES         D       (A
DAVE MARKEE        B       (A    CATHERINE HOWE      V     (A    MICK MOODY        G     (A
PIP WILLIAMS       G MAND  (A    JACQUIE SULLIVAN    V     (A    JOY YATES         V     (A
STEVIE LANGE       V       (A    FRANK RICOTII       PERC  (A    PETER ZORN        SAX   (A
TERRY POPPLE       D       (A    COLIN GIBSON        B     (A    KEN CRADDOCK      PNO   (A
GRAHAM PRESKETT    G       (A    TONY HYMAS          K     (A    BARDOT            V     (A
```

KARLA BONOFF   B175

```
KARLA BONOFF       V K G   (A    (A) KARLA BONOFF              1977   CBS US 34672     UK   82455
WITH                             (B) RESTLESS NIGHTS           1979   CBS              UK   83587
RUSS KUNKEL        D       (AB
LEE SKLAR          B       (A    MICHAEL BOTTS       D     (A    ANDREW GOLD       G K   (AB
LINDA RONSTADT     V       (A    JAI WINDING         PNO   (A    WADDY WACHTEL     G V   (A
GREG LADANYI       PERC    (A    KENNY EDWARDS G MAND B V (A    BROCK WALSH       V     (A
J D SOUTHER        V       (A    STEVE FORMAN        PERC  (AB   GLENN FREY        V     (A
DAN DUGMORE        STEEL   (A    WENDY WALDMAN       V     (A STRING SECTION         (B
DON HENLEY                 (B    GARTH HUDSON              (B    DANNY KORTCHMAR         (B
DAVID LINDLEY              (B
```

BONTEMPS ROULEZ   B176

```
TONY DOWNES        K       (1    (1) 1975 LINE UP
P C BAILEY         G V     (1
STEVE BONNETT      G V     (1    ANDREW BODNAR       B     (1    STEVE GOULDING    (D    (1
```

JACK BONUS   B177

```
JACK BONUS    V G SAX FLT K (A   (A) JACK BONUS                1972   GRUNT            FTR  1005
TOM COSTER         K       (A
BRUCE CONTE        G       (A    FREDDIE ROULETTE    G     (A    TONY SMITH        D     (A
ED BOGAS           VLN     (A    STRING SECTION            (A    JAMIE HOWELL      G     (A
ANDY LIFLAND       D       (A    JON DETHERAGE       PNO   (A    SKIP  OLSON       B     (A
LORIN ROWAN        G       (A    CHRIS ROWAN         G     (A    DAVID DIADEM    MAND K  (A
BILLY WOLF         B       (A    GLENN CRONKHITE     D     (A    EDDIE ADAMS       B     (A
STAN MONTEIRO      CLAR    (A    IVORY SMYLIE        CONGA (A    JACK DORSEY       D     (A
JACKIE KING        G       (A    BENNY VELARDE       PERC  (A    KEN BALZELL       TPT   (A
STEVE TURRE        TROM    (A
```

BONZO DOG DOO DAH BAND   B178

```
NEIL INNES      K B G V    (     (A) GORILLA                           1967   LIBERTY    UK   LBS 83056
VIVIAN STANSHALL   V TPT   (     (A) GORILLA                           1970   SUNSET     UK   SLS 50160
ROGER RUSKIN SPEAR SAX     (     (A) GORILLA                           19     IMPERIAL   US        12370
DAVE CLAGUE                (     (B) DOUGHNUT IN GRANNYS GREENHOUSE     1968   LIBERTY    UK   LBS 83158
BUBS WHITE         G       (     (B) DOUGHNUT IN GRANNYS GREENHOUSE     1971   SUNSET     UK   SLS 50210
RODNEY SLATER      SAX     (     (C) TADPOLES                          1969   LIBERTY    UK   LBS 83257
LEGS LARRY SMITH   D       (     (D) KEYNSHAM                          1969   LIBERTY    UK   LBS 83290
VERNON NOWELL              (     (D) KEYNSHAM                          1975   SUNSET     UK   SLS 50375
SAM SPOONS         PERC    (     (D) KEYNSHAM                          19     IMPERIAL   US        12457
DENNIS COUBIN      B V     (     (E) THE BEAST OF THE BONZOS  (COMP)   1970   LIBERTY    UK   LBS 83332
DICK PARRY         WIND    (     (E) THE BEAST OF THE BONZOS  (COMP)   19     UA         US         5517
ANDY ROBERTS       G       (     (F) LETS MAKE UP & BE FRIENDLY        1972   UA         UK   UAS 29288
DAVE RICHARD       B       (     (F) LETS MAKE UP & BE FRIENDLY        1978   SUNSET     UK   SLS 50418
HUGHIE FLINT       D       (     (G) URBAN SPACEMAN                    1973   SUNSET     UK   SLS 50350
                                 (G) URBAN SPACEMAN                    197    IMPERIAL   US        12432
                                 ( ) HISTORY OF THE BONZOS    (DBL)    1974   UA         UK   UAD60071/2
                                 ( ) HISTORY OF THE BONZOS    (DBL)    1974   UA         US   LA 321 H
```

JAMES BOOKER   B179

```
JAMES BOOKER       B             ( ) JUNCO PARTNERS                   1976   ISLAND     UK   HELP   26
B180
```

BOOKER T & THE MGs   B180

```
BOOKER T JONES     K G B   (ALL  GREEN ONIONS               1962   LONDON     UK   1640  354
WITH                             GREEN ONIONS               1966   ATLANTIC   UK    587  033
STEVE CROPPER      G       (     GREEN ONIONS               19     STAX       US   STAX  701
LOUIS STEINBERG    D       (     GREEN ONIONS               19     PICKWICK         SHM  3031
AL JACKSON         D       (     AND NOW                    1966   STAX       UK    589  002
DONALD DUCK DUNN   B       (     AND NOW                    1966   STAX       US   STAX  711
WILLIE HALL        D       (     IN THE XMAS SPIRIT         19     STAX       US   STAX  715
                                 HIP HUG HER                196    STAX       US   STAX  717
                                 BACK TO BACK(WITH MARKEYS) 196    STAX       US   STAX  720
DAVID T WALKER     G       (     DOING OUR THING            1968   ATLANTIC   UK   2464  011
JIM KELTNER        D       (     DOING OUR THING            1968   STAX       US        1040
SAMMY CREASON      D       (     DOING OUR THING            19     STAX       US   STAX  724
BOB GLAUB          B       (     BEST OF                    1968   ATLANTIC   UK    228  015
ALEXANDER SMITH    B       (     BEST OF                    19     STAX       UK   2325  018
BOBBYE HALL        PERC    (     BEST OF                    19     STAX       US        8202
                                 BEST OF                    197    ATLANTIC   UK    K 40072
                                 UPTIGHT                    1968   STAX       UK   SXATS1005
                                 UPTIGHT                    1968   STAX       US        2006
                                 SOUL LIMBO                 1968   STAX       UK   SXATS1001
                                 SOUL LIMBO                 1968   STAX       UK   2325  001
                                 McLEMORE AVENUE            1970   STAX       UK   2362  016
                                 McLEMORE AVENUE            1970   STAX       US        2027
                                 McLEMORE AVENUE            1970   STAX            SXATS1031
                                 BOOKER T SET               1970   STAX       UK   2362  012
                                 BOOKER T SET               1970   STAX       UK   SXATS1015
                                 BOOKER T SET               19     STAX       UK   2325  003
                                 BOOKER T SET               19     STAX       US   STAX 2009
                                 MELTING POT                1972   STAX       UK   2325  030
                                 MELTING POT                1972   STAX       UK   STAX 1054
                                 MELTING POT                197    STAX       US   STAX 2035
                                 STAR COLLECTION            1973   WB              MID 30042
                                 STAR COLLECTION            19     WB         UK   MID 20032
                                 GREATEST HITS              1974   STAX       UK   STX  1017
                                 GREATEST HITS              1974   STAX       UK   2362  002
                                                                              (CONTINUED)
```

BOOKER T & THE MGs

MEMPHIS SOUND	1975	STAX	UK	STX 1037
UNION EXTENDED	1976	STAX	UK	STXS 2041
UNION EXTENDED	1976	STAX	UK	STX 1045
POP HISTORY	19	POLYDOR		2625 013
POP HISTORY	19	POLYDOR		2612 016
UNIVERSAL LANGUAGE	19	ASYLUM	US	7E 1093
UNIVERSAL LANGUAGE	19	ASYLUM	UK	K 53057
GET READY	19	ATLANTIC	UK	228 004
TIME IS TIGHT (WITH MARKEYS)	1979	STAX	UK	STX 3007
SOUL DRESSING	19	STAX	US	STAX 705

B181

BOOMTOWN RATS

BOB GELDOF	V SAX (ALL	(A) THE BOOMTOWN RATS	1977	ENSIGN		ENVY1
JOHNNIE FINGERS	K V (ALL	(A) THE BOOMTOWN RATS	1977	MERCURY	US	SRM 1188
GERRY COTT	G (A	(A) THE BOOMTOWN RATS	1977	MERCURY		9102 800
PETE BRIQUETTE	B V (AB	(B) TONIC FOR THE TROOPS	1978	ENSIGN		ENVY3
GERRY ROBERTS	G V (AB	(B) TONIC FOR THE TROOPS	1978	CBS	US	35750
SIMON CROWE	D V (AB	(C) FINE ART OF SURFACING				
ALBE DONNELLY	SAX (A	(D) MONDO BONGO	1980	MERCURY	UK	6359 042

B182

KEN BOOTHE

KEN BOOTHE	V (ALL	(A) BLACK GOLD & GREEN	19	TROJAN	UK	TRLS 58
		(B) LETS GET IT ON	1974	TROJAN	UK	TRLS 83
		(C) EVERYTHING I OWN	1974	TROJAN	UK	TRLS 95
		(D) FREEDOM STREET	1975	TROJAN	UK	TRLS 120
		(E) LIVE GOOD	1978	U A		LA 801
		(F) 20 GREATEST REGGAE HITS	1979	CHARMERS		
		(G) BLOOD BROTHERS	1978	TROJAN	UK	TRLS 148
		(H) WHO GETS YOUR LOVE	1979	TROJAN	UK	TRLS 164

B182A

BOOTS

WERNER KRABBE	V HCA (A	(A) HERE ARE THE BOOTS	1966	TELEFUNKEN	GERM	SLE 14399
WILI GRUN	ORG (A					
BOB BRESSER	B (A	HEINZ HOFF D (A	JOERG SCHULTE	G (A		

B183

BOOTSY'S RUBBER BAND

WILLIAM BOOTSY COLLINS	GVB(ABC	(A) STRETCHIN OUT	1976	WB	UK	K56200
WITH		(A) STRETCHIN OUT	1976	WB	UK	B2920
PHELPS COLLINS	B G (ABC	(B) AAH...THE NAME IS BOOTSY BABY	1977	WB	UK	K 56302
GARY SHIDER	G (AB	(B) AAH...THE NAME IS BOOTSY BABY	1977	WB	US	2972
MIKE HAMPTON	G (AB	(C) PLAYER OF THE YEAR	1978	WB	UK	K56424
FRANKIE KASH WADDY	D (ABC	(C) PLAYER OF THE YEAR	1978	WB	US	K 3093
BOOGIE	D (A	(D) THIS BOOT IS MADE FOR FONK'N	1979	WB	UK	K 56615
GARY COOPER	D V (AB					
CASPER	B D G (ABC	FRED WESLEY	TROM (ABC	MACEO PARKER	SAX (ABC
RANDY BRECKER	SAX (AB	RICK GARDNER	TPT (ABC	MICHAEL BRECKER	TPT (A
BERNIE WORRELL	K (AB	SONNY TALBERT	K (A	FREDRICK ALLEN	K (A
LESLYN BAILEY	V (A	ROBERT JOHNSON	V (ABC	JOEL JOHNSON	K (BC
RICHARD GRIFFITHS	HRNS (BC	GLEN GOINS	G (B	JEROME BRAILEY	D (B

B184

BOSTON

BOBBY GOULDREAU	G (AB	(A) BOSTON	1976	EPIC	UK	EPC 81622
TOM SCHOLZ	G K (AB	(A) BOSTON	1976	EPIC	US	BL 34188
SIB HASHAIN	D (AB	(B) DONT LOOK BACK	1978	EPIC	UK	EPC 86057
BRADLEY DELP	V (AB	(B) DONT LOOK BACK	1978	EPIC	US	FE 35050
FRAN SHEEHAN	B (AB					
JIM MASDEA	D (A					

B185

BOTHY BAND

TRIONA O'DONNELL	K V (BCD	(A) BOTHY BAND	1976	POLYDOR	UK	2383 379
PADDY KEENAN	PIPES (BCD	(A) BOTHY BAND	1976	MULLIGAN	IR	LUN 002
TOMMY PEOPLES	FDL (	(B) OLD HAG YOU HAVE KILLED ME	1976	MULLIGAN	IR	LUN 007
MATT MOLLOY	WIND (BCD	(B) OLD HAG YOU HAVE KILLED ME	1976	POLYDOR	UK	2383 417
DONAL LUNNY	G K (BCD	(C) OUT OF THE WIND	1977	POLYDOR	UK	2383 456
MICHAEL O'DONNELL	G (BCD	(C) OUT OF THE WIND	1977	MULLIGAN	IR	LUN
KEVIN BURKE	FDL (BCD	(D) AFTER HOURS	1979	POLYDOR	UK	2383 530
		(D) AFTER HOURS	1979	MULLIGAN	IR	LUN 030

B185A

CHRISTIAN BOULE

CHRISTIAN BOULE		( ) PHOTO MUSIC	19	POLYDOR		2473 086

B186

DAVID BOWIE

DAVID BOWIE	V G SAX K (ALL	(A) DAVID BOWIE(LOVE YOU TILL TUESDAY)	1967	DERAM		SML 1007
		(A) DAVID BOWIE	196	DERAM		18003
WITH		(A) THE WORLD OF DAVID BOWIE	1967	DECCA	SPA	58
CARLOS ALOMAR	G (1LMOPRT	(B) MAN OF WORDS SPACE ODDITY	1969	PHILIPS		SBL 7912
DENNIS DAVIES	PERC (1LMOPR	(B) MAN OF WORDS SPACE ODDITY	1969	MERCURY	US	ST 61246
GEORGE MURRAY	B (1MOPR	(B) MAN OF WORDS SPACE ODDITY	1969	RCA		LPS 4813
BRIAN ENO	K (OPS	(C) MAN WHO SOLD THE WORLD	1970	RCA		LPS 4816
ROBERT FRIPP	G (PT	(C) MAN WHO SOLD THE WORLD	1970	PHILIPS		461 006
SIMON HOUSE	VLN (1RS	(C) MAN WHO SOLD THE WORLD	1971	MERCURY US 61325 UK	6338 041
ROGER POWELL	K (1R	(D) HUNKY DORY	1971	RCA		SF 8244
ADRIAN BELEW	G (1R	(D) HUNKY DORY	1971	RCA		AFLI 4623
MICK RONSON	G (CDEFG	(D) HUNKY DORY	197	RCA		443 041
STACEY HAYDEN	G (	(E) RISE & FALL OF ZIGGY STARDUST	1972	RCA		SF 8287
KEITH CHRISTMAS	G (B	(E) RISE & FALL OF ZIGGY STARDUST	1972	RCA		AFLI 4702
MICK WAYNE	G (B	(E) RISE & FALL OF ZIGGY STARDUST	1972	RCA		443 051
TIM RENWICK	G (BCP	(F) ALADDIN SANE	1973	RCA		RS 1001
TONY VISCONTI	B WIND (BCP	(E) ALADDIN SANE	1973	RCA		AFLI 4852
HERBIE FLOWERS	B (B	(F) ALADDIN SANE	1973	RCA		461 004
JOHN CAMBRIDGE	D (B	(G) PIN UPS	1973	RCA		RS 1003
TERRY COX	D (B	(G) PIN UPS	1973	RCA		AFLI 0291
PAUL BUCKMASTER	CELLO (B	(H) IMAGES 66 67	1973	LONDON		DPA3017/8
RICK WAKEMAN	K (BDE	(H) IMAGES 66 67	19	LONDON	US	BP 62819
BENNY MARSHALL	HCA (B	(J) DIAMOND DOGS	1974	RCA		APLI 0576
DIANE SUMLER	V (L	(K) LIVE	1974	RCA		APL2 0771
		(CONTINUED)				

(CONTINUED)

DAVID BOWIE
B186

LUTHER VANDROSS	V	(L	(L) YOUNG AMERICANS	1975	RCA		RS	1006
ANTONIA MAASS	V	(P	(L) YOUNG AMERICANS	1975	RCA	US	AFLI	0998
ROY YOUNG	PNO	(O	(M) STATION TO STATION	1976	RCA		APLI	1327
RICKY GARDINER	G	(O	(N) CHANGESONEBOWIE	1976	RCA		RS	1055
IGGY POP	V	(O	(N) CHANGESONEBOWIE	1976	RCA		AFLI	1732
ANDY NEWMARK	D	(L	(O) LOW	1977	RCA		PL	12030
JOHN LENNON	V G	(L	(P) HEROES	1977	RCA		PB	1121
DAVID SANBORN	SAX	(L	(P) HEROES	1977	RCA		AFLI	2522
LARRY WASHINGTON	PERC	(L	(P) HEROES	1977	RCA		PL	42373
AYNSLEY DUNBAR	D	(G	( ) STARTING POINT	1977	LONDON		LC	50007
KEN FORDHAM	WIND	(FG	(Q) PETER & THE WOLF	1978	RCA		RL	12743
JUANITA FRANKLIN	V	(F	(R) STAGE	1978	RCA		PL	02913
AVA CHERRY	V	(L	(S) LODGER	1979	RCA AZLI 3254		BOW	LP1
ANTHONY HINTON	V	(L	( ) GOLDEN DOUBLE	1979	RCA	JAP	SRA9503/4
ROY BITTAN	K	(M	( ) BEST OF	1980	K TEL		NE	1111
RALPH MACE	K	(C	( ) PROFILE	19	TELDEC	GERM	624009
ROBIN CLARK	V	(L	(T) SCARY MONSTERS	1980	RCA		BOW	K2
SEAN MAYES	K	(R	(T) SCARY MONSTERS	1980	RCA		PL	13647
MARY VISCONTI	V	(O						
WARREN PEACE	V	(ML						
EMIR KSASAN	B	(L	WILLY WEEKS	B	(L	EARL SLICK	G	(LM
RALPH McDONALD	PERC	(L	TREVOR BOLDER	B	(DEFG	MAC CORMACK	V	(FG
LINDA LEWIS	V	(F	JEAN FINEBERG	V	(L	JEAN MILLINGTON	V	(L
JOHN MAYER	K	(1	CHUCK HAMMER	G	(T	MICHAEL GARSON	K	(FGL
PABLO ROSARIO	PERC	(L	MICK WOODMANSEY	D	(CDEF			

BOWLES BROTHERS BAND
B187

BRIAN BOWLES	G V	(A	(A) ROGER BUYS A FRIDGE	1978	DECCA		TXS	127
RICHARD LEE	B	(A						
JULIAN SMEDLEY	G V VLN	(A	SUE JONES DAVIS	V	(A	RICHARD MARCANGELO	D	(A
CHARLES SEAWARD	FLT	(A	JONATHAN WADE	K	(A	COLIN FRECHTER	PNO	(A
CHRIS KARAN	PERC	(A	ROGER RETTIG	STEEL	(A			

ALAN BOWN SET
B188

ALAN BOWN	TPT	(ALL	(A) LONDON SWINGS	(½ LP)	1966	PYE		NPL 18121
WITH			(B) OUTWARD BOWN		1967	MGM	US	CUBLM 1
JOHN GOODSALL	G	(	(B) OUTWARD BOWN		1967	MUSIC FACTORY	UK	M F 1
JESS RODEN	V	(CD	(C) THE ALAN BOWN		1968	DECCA		SML 1049
ROBERT PALMER	V	(	(D) SECOND ALBUM		1968	DERAM		
DAVE GREEN	SAX	(	(D) SECOND ALBUM		1968	MGM	US	
STAN HALDANE	B V	(C	(E) LISTEN		1970	ISLAND		ILPS 9131
PETE BURGESS	G V	(	(F) STRETCHIN' OUT		1971	ISLAND		ILPS 9163
VIC SWEENEY	D	(C						
DAVE LAWSON	K	(	TERRY STANNARD	D	(	JOHN ANTHONY HELLIWELL	SAX	(C
GORDON NEVILLE	V	(F	ANDY BROWN	B V	(F	JEFF BANNISTER	K V	(CF
TONY CATCHPOLE	G	(CF	JOHN HEMMINGS	TROM	(C			

ANDY BOWN
B189

ANDY BOWN	G V	(ALL	(A) GONE TO MY HEAD	1972	MERCURY	UK	6310 002
WITH			(A) GONE TO MY HEAD	1972	MERCURY	IMP	SRM 1625
HAROLD FISHER	PERC	(D	(B) ANDY BOWN SWEET WILLIAM	1973	G M		GML 1001
FRANK RICOTTI	D	(D	(C) COME BACK ROMANCE	1976	EMI		EMC 3176
MO FOSTER	B	(D	(D) GOOD ADVICE	1978	EMI		EMC 3283
DAVE MARKEE	B	(D	(E) DROWNED IN TEXAS	19	SONOPRESSE	FR	06806605
GEOFF WESTLEY	G	(D						
PHIL PALMER	G	(D	CHRIS NEILL	V	(D	DOMINIC BUGATTI	V	(D
FRANK MUSKER	V	(D	SHARAN CAMPBELL	V	(D	NICO RAMSDEN	G	(B
BARRY DE SOUZA	D	(B	CHRIS BELSHAW	B	(B	B J COLE	STEEL	(B
GLEN LEFLEUR	PERC	(B	JIMMY HOROWITZ	CELESTE	(B	SKAILA KANGA	HARP	(B
CAROLINE ATTARD	V	(B	LESLEY DUNCAN	V	(B	SUE GLOVER	V	(B
SUNNY LESLIE	V	(B	STRINGS		(B			

BOX TOPS
B190

ALEX CHILTON	G V	(ALL	(A) THE LETTER NEON RAINBOW	1968 STATESIDE	UK	SSL 10218
GARY TALLEY	G	(123	(A) THE LETTER NEON RAINBOW	1968 BELL	US	6011
JOHN EVANS	G K	(1	(B) NON STOP	1968 BELL	US	6023
BILL CUNNINGHAM	K B	(12	(C) CRY LIKE A BABY	1968 STATESIDE	UK	SBLL 105
RICK ALLEN	B K	(2	( ) SUPERHITS	196 BELL	US	6025
DANNY SMYTHE	D	(1	( ) THE BEST OF THE BOX TOPS	1974 SOUNDS SUPERB	UK	SPR 90051
TOM BOGGS	D	(23				
SWAIN SCHARFER	K	(3	(1) 1967	(2) 1968	(3) 1969	
HAROLD CLOUD	B	(3				

B191

BOXER
B191

MIKE PATTO	V	(ABC	(A) BELOW THE BELT	1975 VIRGIN	UK	V2049
OLLIE HALSALL	G	(A	(A) BELOW THE BELT	1975 VIRGIN	US	PZ 34115
KEITH ELLIS	B	(A	(B) BLOODLETTING***	1976 VIRGIN	UK	V2073
TONY NEWMAN	D	(A	(C) ABSOLUTELY	1977 EPIC	UK	EPC 82151
CHRIS STAINTON	K	(C	(C) ABSOLUTELY	1977 EPIC	US	PE 34812
TIM BOGERT	B	(C				
ADRIAN FISHER	D	(C	EDDIE TUDURI	D	(C	(B)**NOT RELEASED

EDDIE BOY BAND
B192

JOSH LEO	G V	(A	(A) EDDIE BOY BAND	1975 MCA US 2153	UK	MAPS 8150
MARK GOLDENBERG	V G PNO	(A	(A) EDDIE BOY BAND	1975 MCA	UK	MCF 2735
TIM WALKOE	B V	(A				
JOHN PARUDO	K V	(A	DENNIS EBERT	D PERC	(A	MIKE LERNER	D PERC	(A
DAVID WOLINSKI	SYN	(A	JON CARSON	G	(A	DICK CAINE	G	(A

B193A

EDDIE BOYD

EDDIE BOYD	V PNO (ALL	(A) FIVE LONG YEARS	19	FONTANA		STJL	905
WITH		(B) EDDIE BOYD & HIS BLUES BAND	1967	DECCA	UK	SKL	4872
PETER GREEN	G (C	(C) 7936 SOUTH RHODES	1968	BLUE HORIZON	UK	7	63202
JOHN McVIE	B (C	(C) 7936 SOUTH RHODES	1968	EPIC	US	BN	26409
MICK FLEETWOOD	D (C	(D) EDDIE BOYD LIVE	1968	STORYVILLE		SLP	268
STOCKHOLM SLIM	V (E	(E) LEGACY OF THE BLUES VOL 10	1974	SONET	UK	SNTF	670
ED THIGPEN	D (E	(E) LEGACY OF THE BLUES VOL 10	1974	GNP	US	GNP	10020
ROLF ALM	B (E	(F) VACATION FROM THE BLUES	1976	JEFFERSON	SWED		601
CHRISTER ECKLUND	SAX (E						
PEPS PERSSON	G HCA V (E						
WILLIE COBBS	B HCA (F	SAM LANGHORN	G (F	RICO COLLINS	SAX (F
CHINK EVANS	D (F	BONES	D (F	EDDIE KING MILTON	G (F
PERCY WALKER	D (F	DAYLIGHTERS	V (F	ERNEST COTTON	SAX (F
ROBERT JUNIOR LOCKWOOD	G (F	JIMMY CONLEY	SAX (F	FRED BELOW	D (F
SONNY ALLEN	D (F	RONALD WILSON	SAX (F	BOB CARTER	B (F
L C McKINLEY	G (F	WILLIE JONES	B (F	CHRISTINE KITRELL	V (F
LESTER JONES	B (F	ALFRED ELKINS	B (F	LOUIS MYERS	G (F

B193A

BOYFRIENDS

STEVE BRAY	D (AB	(A) 1978 (B) 1978	
PAT COLLIER	V G (AB		
MARK HENRY	B V (AB		
		CHRIS SMITH	K V (A
		CHRIS SKORNIA	K (B

B194

TERENCE BOYLAN

TERENCE BOYLAN	G V (ABC	(A) ALIAS BOONA	1969	VERVE FORECAST	US	FTS	3070
WITH		(B) TERENCE BOYLAN	1977	ELEKTRA	US	7E	1091
WALTER BECKER	B G (A	(C) SUZY	1980	ELEKTRA	US	6E	201
DONALD FAGAN	K V (AB						
HERB LOVELLE	D (A	JIMMY JOHNSON	D (A	DARIUS DAVENPORT	D (A
JIM GORDON	D (BC	RUSSELL KUNKEL	D PERC (BC	JEFF PORCARO	D (B
CHUCK RAINEY	B (B	DAVID JACKSON	B (B	LELAND SKLAR	B (B
DEAN PARKS	G (B	VICTOR FELDMAN	PERC (BC	JAI WINDING	K (BC
TIM SCHMIT	V (BC	JOHN KLEMMER	SAX (B	GARY FOSTER	SAX (BC
WILTON FELDER	B (B	DON HENLEY	V (BC	BEN BENAY	G (BC
MICKEY McGEE	D (B	AL KOOPER	ORG (B	DON EVANS	G (B
DAVID PAICH	PNO (B	BOB GLAUB	B (B	STEVE LUKATHER	G (B
DODIE PETIT	V (B	JOHN GUERIN	D (B	MAX BENNETT	B (B
TOM KELLY	V (B	DENNIS WHITTED	D (C	WILL McFARLANE	G B (C
JOHN HOLBROOK	B (C	ED GREENE	D (C	MICHAEL PORCARO	B (C
MICHAEL OMARTIAN	PERC (C	JEFF BAXTER	G (C	LARRY CARLTON	G (C
PAUL HARRIS	PERC (C	JAY GRAYDON	G (C	DON FELDER	G (C
DAVID KEMPER	D (C	CHEVY CHASE	PERC (C	EMIL RICHARDS	PERC (C
MIRANDA McGRATH	V (C	ALMA BOYLAN	V (C	STRINGS	(C

B195

GARY BOYLE

GARY BOYLE	G (AB	(A) THE DANCER	1977	GULL	UK	GULP	1020
WITH		(B) ELECTRIC GLIDE	1978	GULL	UK	GULP	1028
ROBIN LUMLEY	K (A						
ROD ARGENT	K (A	DONI HARVEY	B (A	SIMON PHILLIPS	D (AB
ZOE KRONBERGER	K (A	DAVE McCRAE	K (A	STEVE SHONE	B (A
JEFF SEOPARDI	D (A	MAGGIE PERT	V (A	MORRIS PERT	PERC (A
ROBERT AHWAI	G (B	PETE JACOBSON	K (B	JOHN GIBLIN	B (B
SIMON MORTON	PERC (B	PHIL CHEN	B (B	RICHARD BAILEY	D (B
KENNY SHAW	G (B	GARY MOORE	G (B		

B196

THE BOYS

MATT DANGERFIELD	V G (ABCD	(A) THE BOYS	1977	NEMS	UK	NELS	6001
CASINO STEEL	PNO (AB	(B) ALTERNATIVE CHARTBUSTERS	1978	NEMS	UK	NELS	6015
KID REID	V B (ABD	(C) TO HELL WITH THE BOYS	1978	SAFARI	UK	1 2 BOYS	
JACK BLACK	D (ABB	(D) BOYS ONLY	1980	SAFARI	UK	BOYS	4
JOHN PLAIN	G (ABD						

B197

BOYZZ

MIKE TAFOYA	(	(A) TOO WILD TO TAME	1978	EPIC	UK	EPC 82995
DIRTY DAN BUCK						
GIL PINI		ANATOLE HALINKOVICH		KENT COOPER		
DAVID ANGEL						

B197A

BRAINBOX

JAN AKKERMAN	G (A	(A) BRAINBOX	19	CAPITOL	IMP	ST	596
PIERRE VAN DER LINDEN	(A						

B197B

BRAINS

(A) THE BRAINS	1980	MERCURY	6337	103

B198

BRAINSTORM

(A) STORMIN'	1977	RCA	UK	PL	12048
(A) STORMIN'	197	CBS	US		35327
(b) JOURNEY TO THE NIGHT	1978	TABU			
(b) JOURNEY TO THE NIGHT	19	CBS	US	JZ	2048
(C) FUNKY ENTERTAINMENT	1979	TABU	UK	TBU	83736

B199

BRAINTICKET

JANE FREE	V PERC (B	(A) CELESTIAL SEA	1974	RCA		SF 8389
JOEL VANDROOGENBROECK	K V (B	(B) PSYCHONAUT	19	BELLAPHON		BLPS19104
ROLF HUG	V G PERC (B					
MARTIN SACHER	B FLT (B	BARNEY PALM	D PERC (B	CAROLE MURIEL	V (B
PETER GOOD	VIBES (B					

B199A

BRAKES

JOE FADIL	G V (A	(A) FOR WHY YOU KICKA MY DONKEY	1979	MAGNET	MAGL 5029
KEITH WILSON	G V (A				
JOHN BROWN	D (A	BOB PENNY	B (A		

BONNIE BRAMLETT   B200

Personnel			Album	Year	Label	Country	Cat. No.
BONNIE BRAMLETT	V	(ALL	(A) SWEET BONNIE BRAMLETT	1973	CBS	UK	65001
WITH			(B) ITS TIME	1975	CAPRICORN	UK	2429 125
BARRY BECKETT	K	(C	(B) ITS TIME	1975	CAPRICORN	US	0148
DAVID HOOD	B	(C	(C) LADY'S CHOICE	1976	CAPRICORN	UK	2429 145
JOHNNY SANDLIN	G	(C	(C) LADY'S CHOICE	1976	CAPRICORN	US	0169
ROGER HAWKINS	D	(C	(D) MEMORIES	1978	CAPRICORN	UK	2429 162
TOMMY TALTON	G	(C	(D) MEMORIES	1978	CAPRICORN	US	0199
HARVEY THOMPSON	HRNS	(C					
RICHARD BETTS	G	(C	RANDALL BRAMBLETT	SAX	(C	ANITA BALL	(C
CHARLES ROSE	HRNS	(C	RON EADES	HRNS	(C	HARRISON CALLOWAY	HRNS (C
RICKY HIRSCH	G	(C	PAUL HORNSBY	K	(C	CHUCK LEAVELL	PNO (C
GREGG ALLMAN	ORG	(C	DIANNE DAVIDSON	V	(C		

DELANEY BRAMLETT   B201

Personnel			Album	Year	Label	Country	Cat. No.
DELANEY BRAMLETT	G V	(ALL	(A) MOBIUS STRIP	19	CBS	US	KC 32420
WITH			(B) SOMETHINGS COMING	1972	CBS	UK	65131
SPIDER TAYLOR	G	(D	(C) GIVING BIRTH TO A SONG	19	MGM	US	M3G 5011
RANDY SHARP	G	(D	(D) CLASS REUNION	1977	PRODIGAL	US	P7 10017
CHUCK RAINEY	B	(D	(D) CLASS REUNION	1977	PRODIGAL		PDL 2005
CHRIS ETHRIDGE	B	(D					

RICK SUTHERLAND	K	(CD	JIM HOBSON	K	(CD	STU PERRY	D	(CD
JIM KELTNER	D	(D	CHUCK FINDLEY	HRNS	(D	OLLIE MITCHELL	HRNS	(D
JACKIE KELSO	HRNS	(D	DICK HYDE	HRNS	(D	QUITMAN DENNIS	HRNS	(D
CLYDIE KING	V	(D	SHIRLEY MATTHEWS	V	(D	MONALISA YOUNG	V	(D
SUSIE ALLANSON	V	(D	PAT ERICKSON	V	(D	PATTI QUATRO	V	(D
STRINGS		(D	JIM McGREW	G	(C	VICTOR PANTOJA	PERC	(C
NICK VAN MAARTH	G	(C	FRED RIVERA	B	(C	COLE KESLER	HCA	(C

DELANEY & BONNIE BRAMLETT   B202

Personnel			Album	Year	Label	Country	Cat. No.
DELANEY BRAMLETT	G V	(ALL	(A) HOME	1969	STAX		
BONNIE BRAMLETT	V	(ALL	(A) HOME	1974	STAX		2362 001
WITH			(B) ACCEPT NO SUBSTITUTE	1969	ELEKTRA	US	EKS 74039
BOOKER T JONES	K	(A	(B) ACCEPT NO SUBSTITUTE	1969	APPLE	UK	SAPCOR 7
DONALD DUNN	B	(A	(B) ACCEPT NO SUBSTITUTE	1971	ELEKTRA	UK	K 42024
STEVE CROPPER	G	(A	(C) ON TOUR	1970	ATLANTIC	UK	2400 013
AL JACKSON	D	(A	(C) ON TOUR	1970	ATCO	US	33326
BEN BENAY	G	(D	(C) ON TOUR	1071	ATLANTIC	UK	K 30030
DUANE ALLMAN	G	(D	(D) TO BONNIE FROM DELANEY	1970	ATLANTIC	UK	2400 029
JERRY JUMONVILLE	SAX	(D	(D) TO BONNIE FROM DELANEY	1970	ATCO	US	33341
FRANK MAYES	SAX	(D	(D) TO BONNIE FROM DELANEY	1971	ATLANTIC	UK	K
DARRYL LEONARD	HRNS	(D	(E) MOTEL SHOT	1971	ATCO	US	33358
JIM GORDON	K	(D	(F) COUNTRY LIFE	197	ATCO	US	33383
KENNY GRADNEY	B	(D	(G) GENESIS	1971	LONDON	UK	ZGL 113
CHUCK MORGAN	D	(D	(G) GENESIS	1971	CRECSENDO	US	2054
KING CURTIS	SAX	(D	(H) TOGETHER	1972	CBS	UK	64959
CHARLIE FREEMAN	G	(D	(H) TOGETHER	1972	CBS	US	KC 31377
BOBBY WHITLOCK	K V	(BCD	(I) BEST OF	1973	ATLANTIC	UK	K 40429

TOM McCLURE	B	(D						
JERRY SCHEFF	B	(D	RITA COOLIDGE	V	(BC	TEX JOHNSON	CONGA	(C
RON TUTT	D	(D	SAMMY CREASON	D	(D	ANDREW LOVE	SAX	(D
ED LOGAN	SAX	(D	FLOYD NEWMAN	SAX	(D	WAYNE JACKSON	TPT	(D
JACK HALE	TROM	(D	SAM CLAYTON	CONGA	(D	ALAN ESTES	PERC	(D
LITTLE RICHARD	PNO	(D	MIKE UTLEY	PNO	(D	JIM DICKINSON	PNO	(D
SNEAKY PETE KLEINOW	STEEL	(D	ERIC CLAPTON	G	(C	DAVE MASON	G	(C
CARL RADLE	B	(BC	JIM GORDON	D	(C	JIM PRICE	HRNS	(BC
BOBBY KEYS	SAX	(BC	GEORGE HARRISON	G	(	LEON RUSSELL	G K	(B
JERRY McGEE	G	(B	JIM KELTNER	D	(B			

BRAND X   B203

Personnel			Album	Year	Label	Country	Cat. No.
PERCY JONES	B	(ABCDEF	(A) UNORTHODOX BEHAVIOUR	1976	CHARISMA	UK	CAS 1117
ROBIN LUMLEY	K	(ABCF	(B) MOROCCAN ROLL	1977	CHARISMA	UK	CAS 1126
JOHN GOODSALL	G	(ABCDF	(B) MOROCCAN ROLL	1977	PASSPORT	US	98022
PRESTON HEYMAN	D	(	(C) LIVE STOCK	1977	CHARISMA	UK	CLASS 5
PHIL COLLINS	PERC	(ABCF	(C) LIVE STOCK	1977	PASSPORT	US	9824
JOE BLOCKER	PERC	(	(D) MASQUES	1978	CHARISMA	UK	CAS 1138
MORRIS PERT	PERC	(BDF	(D) MASQUES	1978	PASSPORT	US	9829
KENWOOD DENNARD	D	(C	(E) PRODUCT	1979	CHARISMA	UK	CAS 1147
CHUCK BURGI	D	(D	(F) DO THEY HURT	1980	CHARISMA	UK	CAS 1151
PETER ROBINSON	K	(F	MIKE CLARKE	D	(F	JOHN GIBLIN	B	(F

BRASS CONSTRUCTION   B204

Personnel			Album	Year	Label	Country	Cat. No.
LARRY PAYTON	D	(	(A) BRASS CONSTRUCTION	1976	UA	UK	UAS 29913
SANDY BILLUPS	V PERC	(	(A) BRASS CONSTRUCTION	1976	UA	US	LA 545G
WAYNE PARRIS	TPT	(	(B) 2	1976	UA	UK	UAS 30016
WADE WILLIAMSON	B	(	(B) 2	1976	UA	US	LA 677G
MICHAEL GRUDGE	SAX	(	(C) 3	1978	UA	UK	UAS 30124
RANDY MILLER	V K	(	(C) 3	1978	UA	US	LA 775H
MORRIS PRICE	TPT	(	(D) 4	1978	UA	UK	UAS 30210
JESSE WARD	SAX	(	(D) 4	1978	UA	US	LA 916H
JOSEPH ARTHUR WONG	G	(					

BRATS   B204A

SCOTT SHEETS	G				
RICK RIVETS	G				
SPARKY DONOVAN	D	JOEY GUIDO	B V	KEITH WEST	V

RICHARD BRAUTIGAN   B205

Personnel	Album	Year	Label	Country	Cat. No.
RICHARD BRAUTIGAN	(A) LISTENING TO	19	STRAIGHT	ST	424

B206   BREAD

DAVID GATES	V	(
LARRY KNECHTEL		(
JAMES GRIFFIN		(
MIKE BOTTS		(
DEAN PARKS	G	(

Album	Year	Label	Country	Prefix	Number
(A) BREAD	1969	ELEKTRA	UK	K	42029
(A) BREAD	1969	ELEKTRA	US	EKS	74044
(B) ON THE WATER	1970	ELEKTRA	UK	K	42050
(B) ON THE WATER	1970	ELEKTRA	US	EKS	74076
(C) MANNA	1971	ELEKTRA	UK	K	52001
(C) MANNA	1971	ELEKTRA	US	EKS	74086
(C) MANNA	197	ELEKTRA	IMP	K	42081
(D) BABY IM A WANT YOU	1972	ELEKTRA	UK	K	42100
(D) BABY IM A WANT YOU	1972	ELEKTRA	US	EKS	75015
(E) GUITAR MAN	1972	ELEKTRA	UK	K	52004
(E) GUITAR MAN	1972	ELEKTRA	US	EKS	75047
(F) BEST OF BREAD	1974	ELEKTRA	UK	K	42115
(F) BEST OF BREAD	1974	ELEKTRA	US	EKS	75076
(F) BEST OF BREAD	1974	ELEKTRA		EQ	5056
(G) BEST OF VOL 2	1974	ELEKTRA	UK	K	42161
(G) BEST OF VOL 2	1974	ELEKTRA	US	7E	1005
(H) LOST WITHOUT YOUR LOVE	1976	ELEKTRA	UK	K	52044
(H) LOST WITHOUT YOUR LOVE	1976	ELEKTRA	US	7E	1094
(I) SOUND OF BREAD	1977	ELEKTRA	UK	K	52062

B207   BREAD LOVE & DREAMS

Album	Year	Label	Country	Prefix	Number
(A) BREAD LOVE & DREAMS	1969	DECCA	UK	SKL	5008
(B) STRANGE TALE OF CAPTAIN SHANNON	1970	DECCA	UK	SKL	5048
(C) AMARYLLIS	1971	DECCA	UK	SKL	5081

B208   THE BRECKER BROTHERS

RANDY BRECKER	HRNS	(ALL
MICHAEL BRECKER	HRNS	(ALL
DAVE SANBORN	SAX	(AB
DON GROLNICK	K	(AB
BOB MANN	G	(A
WILL LEE	B V	(AB
HARVEY MASON	D	(A
SAMMY FIGUEROA	PERC	(BD
RAFAEL CRUZ	PERC	(BD
BARRY FINNERTY	G	(D
KASH MONET	PERC	(D
PAUL SCHAEFFER	K	(D
STEVE KHAN	G	(B
LEW DELGATTO	SAX	(B
ROBIN CLARK	V	(B
TERRY BOZZIO	G	(D
RALPH MACDONALD	PERC	(AB
JEFF SCHOEN	V	(D
VICTORIA	TAMB	(D
CHRIS PARKER	D	(B
DAVE FRIEDMAN	PERC	(B
DIANE SUMLER	V	(B
NEIL JASON	B V	(D
ALLEE WILLIS	V	(B
ROY HERRING	V	(D
ALLEN SCHWARZBERG	D	(D
STEVE GADD	D	(B
LUTHER VANDROSS	V	(B
PATTI AUSTIN	V	(B

Album	Year	Label	Country	Prefix	Number
(A) THE BRECKER BROTHERS	1975	ARISTA	UK	ARTY	103
(A) THE BRECKER BROTHERS	1975	ARISTA	US	AL	4037
(B) BACK TO BACK	1976	ARISTA	UK	ARTY	128
(B) BACK TO BACK	1976	ARISTA	US	AL	4061
(C) DONT STOP THE MUSIC	1977	ARISTA	UK	SPARTY	1007
(D) HEAVY METAL BE-BOP	1978	ARISTA	UK	SPART1070	
(D) HEAVY METAL BE-BOP	1978	ARISTA	US	AL	4085

B209   PAUL BRETT

PAUL BRETT	G V	(ALL
WITH		
NICKY HIGGINBOTTOM	WIND	(H
DEREK AUSTIN	K	(A
BOB VOICE	B	(A
DICK DUFALL	B	(A
MEL COLLINS	SAX	(H
STEVE GREGORY	SAX	(H
DAVID GRIFFITHS	B	(H
DELISLE HARPER	B	(H
ROD COOMBES	D	(H
TOM NICHOL	D	(IJ
ROB YOUNG	K	(I
JOHNNY JOYCE	G	(I
DAVE WILLIAMS	B	(I
DAVE OLNEY	B	(I
CHRIS MERCER	SAX	(I
ALAN TODD	G	(IJ
RICHARD HARVEY	K	(J
GRAHAM JARVIS	D	(I
RAY WARLEIGH	SAX	(I
TOM NEWMAN	V	(I
PAUL TOWNSHEND	B	(J

Album	Year	Label	Country	Prefix	Number
(A) PAUL BRETT SAGE	1970	PYE		NSPL18347	
(B) JUBILATION FOUNDRY	1971	DAWN	UK	DNLS	3021
(C) SCHIZOPHRENIA	1972	DAWN	UK	DNLS	3032
(D) PAUL BRETT	1973	BRADLEY	UK	BRADL1001	
(E) CLOCKS	1974	BRADLEYS	UK	BRADL1004	
(F) PHOENIX FUTURE	1975	PHOENIX FUTURE	UK		
(G) EARTHBIRTH	1977	RCA	UK	PL	25080
(H) INTERLIFE	1978	RCA	UK	PL	25149
(I) ECLIPSE	1979	RCA	UK	PL	25219
(J) GUITAR TREK	1980	RCA	UK	PL	25283

B210   BREWER & SHIPLEY

MIKE BREWER	G V	(ALL
TOM SHIPLEY	B V	(ALL
WITH		
JERRY GARCIA	G	(
NICKY HOPKINS	K	(
MARK NAFTALIN		(E
RED RHODES	STEEL	(
BILLY MUNDI	D	(E
PRAIRIE PRINCE	D	(E
FRED BURTON	G	(E
JOHN KAHN	B	(E
LEON OAKLEY	CORNET	(E
BILL VITT	D	(E
TURK MURPHY	TROM	(E
PHIL HOWE	WIND	(E
MIKE LEECH	B	(G
REGGIE YOUNG	G	(G
WELDON MYRICK	G	(G
FARRELL MORRIS	PERC	(G
RONNIE EADES	KRNS	(G
MARY HOLLADAY	V	(G
JAMES MAIHACK	TUBA	(E
NORBERT PUTNAM	B	(G
CHRIS LEUZINGER	G	(G
KEN BUTTREY	D	(G
SHANE KEISTER	SYN	(G
HARVEY THOMPSON	HRNS	(G
GINGER HOLLADAY	V	(G
BUDDY CAGE	K	(E
DAVID BRIGGS	K	(G
PAUL FRANKLIN	STEEL	(G
CHARLIE McCOY	HCA	(G
CHARLES ROSE	HRNS	(G
HARRISON CALLOWAY	HRNS	(G

Album	Year	Label	Country	Prefix	Number
(A) DOWN IN L A	1968	A&M	US	SP	4154
(B) WEEDS	1969	KAMA SUTRA	UK	2361	005
(B) WEEDS	1969	KAMA SUTRA	US	BS	2016
(C) TARKIO	1970	KAMA SUTRA	UK	2316	001
(C) TARKIO	1970	KAMA SUTRA	US	BS	2024
(C) TARKIO	19	KAMA SUTRA		2319	004
(D) SHAKE OFF THE DEMON	1972	KAMA SUTRA	US	BS	2039
(E) RURAL SPACE	1973	KAMA SUTRA	UK	2319	028
(E) RURAL SPACE	1973	KAMA SUTRA	US	BS	2058
(F) BREWER & SHIPLEY	1974	CAPITOL	US	ST	11261
(G) WELCOME TO RIDDLE BRIDGE	1975	CAPITOL	UK	EST	11402
(H) NOT FAR FROM FREE	1978	MERCURY	US	9100	044
( ) BEST OF	19	KAMA SUTRA	US		2-2613

B211   BREWERS DROOP

RON WATTS	V PERC	(A
STEVE DARRINGTON	K HCA V	(A
JOHN McKAY	G V	(A
PETE DUNCAN	HRNS	(A
BOB WALKER	D PERC	(A
DAVE GELLY	SAX	(A
MALCOLM BARRETT	B VLN	(A
JOHN WILLIAMS	SAX	(A

Album	Year	Label	Country	Prefix	Number
(A) OPENING TIME	1972	RCA	UK	SF	8301

B212   BRICK

JIMMY BROWN	WIND V	(AB
RAY RANSOM	B V	(AB
REGI HARGIS	G V	(AB
EDDIE IRONS	K V	(AB

Album	Year	Label	Country	Prefix	Number
(A) GOOD HIGH	1976	BANG		SHOT	003
(B) BRICK	1978	BANG		SHOT	004

ALICIA BRIDGES

<pre>
ALICIA BRIDGES   V   (A   (A) ALICIA BRIDGES   1978   POLYDOR   UK   2391 364
RANDY McCORMICK   K   (A   B213
TOM ROBB   B   (A   ROY YEAGER   D   (A   KEN BELL   G   (A
STEVE BUCKINGHAM   G   (A   MICKEY BUCKINS   G PERC (A JOHN FRISTOE   G V   (A
ALAN FEINGOLD   ORG (A   STEVE McRAY   ORG (A   BERNADINE MITCHELL V   (A
VINNI O'NEAL   V   (A   KEITH'DOC'SAMUELS V   (A
</pre>

DEE DEE BRIDGEWATER
B214

<pre>
DEE DEE BRIDGEWATER V   (AB   (A) JUST FAMILY   1978   ELEKTRA   UK   K 52067
WITH   (A) JUST FAMILY   1978   ELEKTRA   US   6E 119
STANLEY CLARKE   B   (A   (B) DEE DEE BRIDGEWATER   19   ATLANTIC   US   18188
CHICK COREA   K   (A
GEORGE DUKE   K   (A   ALPHONSO JOHNSON   B   (A   RAY GOMEZ   G   (A
HARVEY MASON   D   (A   SCARLET RIVERA   VLN (A   DAVID T WALKER   D   (A
</pre>

B216
MARC BRIERLEY
B216

<pre>
MARC BRIERLEY   (A) HELLO   19   CBS   UK   63835
</pre>

BRIGHTWINTER
B217

<pre>
                               (A) A BAND FOR ALL SEASONS   1975   MYRR   MYR 1030
</pre>

BRINSLEY SCHWARZ
B218

<pre>
BRINSLEY SCHWARZ   G V (ALL (A) BRINSLEY SCHWARZ   1970   UA   UK   UAS 29111
NICK LOWE   B V (ALL (A) BRINSLEY SCHWARZ   1970   CAPITOL   US   SWBC11869
BARRY LANDER   K   ((B) DESPITE AT ALL   1970   LIBERTY   UK   LBG 83427
BOB ANDREWS   K   (ABCDE (C) SILVER PISTOL   1972   UA   UK   UAS 29217
IAN GOMM   G   (CDEF (D) NERVOUS ON THE ROAD   1972   UA   UK   UAS 29374
PETER WHALE   D   ((E) PLEASE DONT EVER CHANGE 1973   UA   UK   UAS 29489
BILLY RANKIN   D   (ABCDEF (F) NEW FAVOURITES   1974   UA   UK   UAS 29641
DAVE JACKSON   SAX (B   (G) ORIGINAL GOLDEN GREATS   1974   UA   UK   USP 101
JOHN WEIDER   FDL (B   (H) 15 THOUGHTS OF BRINSLEY SCHWARZ 1978 UA   UK   UAK 30177
B J COLE   STEEL (B
</pre>

BRITISH LIONS
B219

<pre>
JOHN FIDDLER   V   (A   (A) THE BRITISH LIONS   1978   VERTIGO   UK   9102 019
BUFFIN GRIFFIN   D   (A
OVEREND WATTS   B   (A   RAY MAJOR   G   (A   MORGAN FISHER   K   (A
</pre>

BROKEN GLASS
B220

<pre>
MILLER ANDERSON   G V (A   (A) BROKEN GLASS   1975   CAPITOL   UK   EST 11510
STAN WEBB   G V (A
ROBBIE BLUNT   G   (A   MAC POOLE   D   (A   ROB RAWLINSON   B   (A
TONY ASHTON   K   (A
</pre>

BROKEN HOME
B220A

<pre>
DICKEN   V G (A   (A) BROKEN HOME   1980   WB   UK   K 58148
PETE CROWTHER   B K G (A
RONY WILLSON   G V (A   PETE BARNACLE   D V (A   RORY WILLSON   (
</pre>

DAVID BROMBERG
B221

<pre>
DAVID BROMBERG   V G (A   (A) DAVID BROMBERG   1971   CBS   US   C 31104
WITH   (A) DAVID BROMBERG   1971   CBS   UK   64906
JODY STECHER   MAND V(A   (B) DEMON IN DISGUISE   1972   CBS   US   C 31753
STEVE BURGH   B V (AC   (C) WANTED DEAD OR ALIVE   1974   CBS   US   KC 32717
DAVID NICHTERN   K V (A   (D) MIDNIGHT ON THE WATER   1975   CBS   US   80885
STEVE MOSLEY   D V (ACE (D) MIDNIGHT ON THE WATER   1975   CBS   US   PC 33397
DAVID AMRAN   HRNS (A   (E) HOW LAT'LL YA PLAY TILL 1976   FANTASY   FTSP 53
RICHARD GRANDO   SAX (A   (E) HOW LAT'LL YA PLAY TILL 1976   FANTASY   US   79007
VASSAR CLEMENTS   FDL (AJK (F) RECKLESS ABANDON   1977   FANTASY   FT 536
TUT TAYLOR   MAND (A   (F) RECKLESS ABANDON   1977   FANTASY   US   9540
NORMAN BLAKE   G   (A   (F) RECKLESS ABANDON   1977   MUSIDISC   5960
RANDY SCRUGGS   B   (A   (G) BANDIT IN A BATHING SUIT 1978   FANTASY   FT 548
PETER ECKLUND   HRNS (CDFG (G) BANDIT IN A BATHING SUIT 1978   FANTASY   9555
JERRY GARCIA   G   (BC   (G) BANDIT IN A BATHING SUIT 1978   MUSIDISC   5966
PHIL LESH   B   (C   (H) MY OWN HOUSE   1978   FANTASY   F   9572
NEIL ROSSI   FDL (C   ( ) BEST OF OUT OF THE BLUES 19   CBS   US   C 34467
WILLOW SCARLET   HCA (A   (J) HILLBILLY JAZZ VOL 1   1977   SONET   UK   SNTF 721
ANDY STATMAN MAND SAX (C   (K) HILLBILLY JAZZ VOL 2   1977   SONET   UK   SNTF 722
WINNIE WINSTON   BANJO (C
TRACY NELSON   V   (C   JOE FERGUSON   SAX (C   HUNGRIA GARCIA   PERC (C
KEITH GODCHAUX   K   (C   JEFF GUTCHEON   K   (C   JOEY HARRISON SCARBURY V (G
TONY MARKELLIS   B   (C   JOHN PAYNE   WIND (C   JAY UNGAR   FDL   (CD
JACK LEE   V   (C   ANDY McMAHON   V   (C   SWEET INSPIRATION V   (C
EVAN STOVER   FDL (D   BILLY NOVICK   CLAR (D   PAUL FLEISHER   WIND (D
BRIAN AHERN   G   (D   HUGH McDONALD   B   (DEF JESSE ED DAVIS   G   (D
Dr JOHN   PNO (DE   JOE DARENSBOURG   CLAR (A   LYNDON UNGAR   V   (D
LINDA RONSTADT   V   (D   EMMYLOU HARRIS   V   (D   HAIM SHTRUM   V   (D
RICHARD FEGY   G FDL (DEFGH BUDDY CAGE   G   (D   ERNIE WATTS   SAX   (D
BERNIE LEADON   G   (DE   BONNIE RAITT   V   (D   JOHN HERALD   V   (D
BRANTLEY KEARNS   V   (DE   DOYLE LAWSON   V   (D   RICKY SKAGGS   V   (D
RED RHODES   STEEL (D   BILL KREUTZMANN   D   (BC   CURT LINBERG   TROM (EFG
JOHN FIRMIN   SAX (EFG GEORGE KINDLER   FDL (EFGH HANK DE VITO   STEEL (E
HERB PEDERSEN   V   (EG   JIM ROTHERMEL   WIND (E   JANE SHARP   V   (E
PHOEBE SNOW   V   (E   STEVE MADAIO   TPT (F   LANCE DICKERSON   D   (FG
STEVE FORMAN   PERC (F   DANIEL MOORE   V   (F   MATTHEW MOORE   V   (F
JIM PRICE   V   (F   DARRELL LEONARD   TPT (F   BILL KURASCH   V   (F
BUDDY COLLETTE   V   (F   PEGGY SANDVIG   PNO (F   DONNA GODCHAUX   V   (B
DAVID SCHALLOCK   B V (G   MARTH E WASH   V   (G   MARGARET REDMOND V   (G
MARILYN BRYAN
</pre>

BRONCO
B222

<pre>
KEVIN GAMMOND   G V (AB   (A) COUNTRY HOME   1970   ISLAND   UK   ILPS 9124
JESS RODEN   V   (AB   (B) ACE OF SUNLIGHT   1971   ISLAND   UK   ILPS 9161
ROBBIE BLUNT   G V (AB   (C) SMOKIN' MIXTURE   1973   POLYDOR   UK   2383 215
JOHN PASTERNAK   B   (AB
PETE ROBINSON   D   (AB   JEFF BANNISTER   PNO (A   CLIFFORD WARD   V   (A
IAN HUNTER   K   (B   PAUL BENNETT   V   (B   TREVOR LUCAS   V   (B
TERRY ALLEN   ORG (B   PAUL DAVENPORT   PNO (B   MICK RALPHS   K   (B
</pre>

B223
```
STANLEY BRONSTEIN      V SAX (AB
WITH
DANNY SAIRMAN          K      (B
DOROTHY TERRELL        V      (B
ARNOLD RAMSEY          D      (B
LARRY ROSEN            PERC   (B
CLAUDETTE WASHINGTON   V      (B
```
B224

STANLEY BRONSTEIN

```
(A) OUR ISLAND              19     MUSE         US    MR  5072
(B) LIVING ON THE AVENUE    1976   MUSE               MR  5113

STEVE TARSHIS     G    (B     VAL BURKE          B     (B
ANGEL JUSTINADO   PERC (B     DENNIS BELL        K     (B
TERRI BRONSTEIN   V    (B     SHERROIL JENNINGS  V     (B
```

BRONX CHEER

```
(A) BARREL HOUSE PLAYER    (EP)  1971   DAWN          DNX   2522
(B) GREATEST HITS                1972   DAWN          DNLS  3034
```

B224A

HERMAN BROOD

```
HERMAN BROOD       K V   (ALL   (A) THE FLASH & DANCE BAND        1975   UNIVERSE             HOT  1-08
HANS LAFAILLE      D     (A     (B) IN VITESSE                    1975   REPRISE              REPN54058
PAUL BAGMEIJER     B     (B     (C) STREET (WITH WILD ROMANCE)    1977   AVES INT  146506 ARIOLA  28711
ROB TEN BOKUM      G B V (B     (D) SHPRITSZ (WITH WILD ROMANCE)  1978   AVES INT             146   503
HERMAN VAN BOEYEN  D V   (B     (E) CHA CHA                       1978   AVES INT             146   507
MARGRIET HILDE     V     (B     (F) HERMAN BROOD & WILD ROMANCE   1979   ARIOLA               ARL   5029
ROB VAN DONSELAAR  K     (B     (G) GO NUTZ                       1980   AVES INT             146   527
BIG JOHN           HCA   (B     (H) SOUNDTRACK CHA CHA ( 5 TRACKS) 1980  CBS                        70183
FERDIE KARMELK   G HCA V (C     (I) WAIT A MINUTE                 19                   IMP
KIM FOWLEY               (I
GERRIT VEEN        B     (C     PETER WALRECHT     D    (C     ELLEN PIEBES       V     (C
RIA RUITER         V     (C     JAN AKKERMAN       G    (C     FREDDIE LAVALLI    B     (DE GH
ANI MEERMAN        D     (DEGH  DANNY LADEMACHER   G    (DEGH  BERTUS BORGERS     SAX   (DE
ROBERT JAN STIPS   K     (D     MONIKA TJEN AKWOEI V    (DE    JOSEE VAN LERSEL   V     (DE
LENNY MACALUSO     G     (H     ERIC NELSON        B    (H     ROGER GORDEN       D     (H
CRAIG KRAMPH       D     (H     STEPHEN HINES      K    (H     PAGE PORRAZZO      PERC  (H
D'ARNEL PERSHING   K     (H     RYAN VIYATE        PERC (H     RICK KELLIS        SAX   (H
```

B225

BROOKLYN DREAMS

```
JOE ESPOSITO     G V    (AB    (A) BROOKLYN DREAMS         1978   RCA          XL   13047
EDDIE HOKENSON   V PERC (AB    (B) SLEEPLESS NIGHTS        1979   RCA          XL   13071
BRUCE SUDANO     K V G  (AB
WITH
ANDRE FISCHER           (A     DENNIS BELFIELD    B     (A     VEYLER HILDERBRAND B     (A
AL CINER                (A     TONY D EISENBARGER       (A     RON STOCKERT       K     (A
SNUFFY WALDEN    G      (A     SKIP KONTE         K     (A     JOE LALA           PERC  (A
DONNA SUMMER     V      (A     TONY MAIDEN        G     (A     MARK OLSON         K     (A
ED GREENE        D      (B     MIKE BAIRD         D     (B     CHUCK RAINEY       B     (B
SCOTT EDWARDS    B      (B     DAVID HUNGATE      B     (B     JAY GRAYDON        G     (B
THOM ROTELLA     G      (B     BOB ESTY           PNO   (B     JAI WINDING        K     (B
VICTOR FELDMAN   PERC   (B     DAN WYMAN          SYN   (B     LEE RITENOUR       G     (B
JERRY JUMONVILLE SAX    (B     JERRY DOUCETTE     G     (B     GAIL LEVANT        HARP  (B
LEW SOLOFF       TPT    (B     BARRY ROGERS       TROM  (A     MICHAEL BRECKER    SAX   (B
LEW DEL GATTO    SAX    (B     JERRY HEY          TPT   (B     STEVE MADAIO       TPT   (B
CHUCK FINDLEY    TPT    (B     GARY HERBIG        SAX   (B     JOHN KIP           SAX   (B
DAVID LUELL      SAX    (B     DICK HYDE          TROM  (B     BILL REICHENBACH   TROM  (B
STRINGS                 (B     VOCAL BACKING            (B
```

B226

ELKIE BROOKS

```
ELKIE BROOKS     V     (ALL    (A) RICH MANS WOMAN    1975   A&M   UK   AMLH64554
STEVE BURGH      G     (A      (A) RICH MANS WOMAN    1975   A&M   US        4556
DAVID KEMPER     D     (A      (B) TWO DAYS AWAY      1977   A&M   UK   AMLH68409
DENNIS KOVARIK   B     (A      (B) TWO DAYS AWAY      1977   A&M   US        4631
NINO TEMPO       SAX   (A      (C) SHOOTING STAR      1978   A&M   UK   AMLH64695
JEAN ROUSSEL     K     (CD     (C) SHOOTING STAR      1978   A&M   US        4695
ELLIOTT RANDALL  G     (C      (D) LIVE & LEARN       1979   A&M   UK   AMLH68509
JERRY WHITMAN    V     (A
JERRY KNIGHT     B     (C      BEN BENAY        G     (AD    MAX BENNETT        B     (A
ANDY NEWMARK     D     (C      MIKE BODDIKER    SYN   (AD    ALAN ESTES         PERC  (A
PETE GAGE        G     (C      GENE ESTES       PERC  (A     JOHN GUERIN        D     (A
SIMON MORTON     PERC  (C      DAVID PAICH      K     (A     STAN FARBER        V     (A
JIM GILSTRAP     V     (AD     VENETTA FIELDS   V     (AD    GERRY GARRETT      V     (A
RON HICKLIN      V     (A      CLYDIE KING      V     (A     GENE MORFORD       V     (A
VERLENE ROGERS   V     (A      JOHN BARNES      K     (D     SCOTT EDWARDS      B     (D
JAMES GADSON     D     (D      HAL BLAINE       D     (D     MARLO HENDERSON    G     (D
TIM MAY          G     (D      SPENCER BEAN     G     (D     TOWER OF POWER     HRNS  (D
PAULINHO DA COSTA PERC (D      DARLENE LOVE     V     (D     ORRIN WATERS       V     (D
JULIA TILLMAN    V     (D      ED WATKINS       B     (D     MAGGIE HENRY       V     (D
ED GREENE        D     (D      PAUL WARREN      G     (D     CORKY HALE         HARP  (D
OLIVER LEIBER    G PERC (D     MARCIA LEVY      V     (D     FRED TACKETT       G     (D
BRIAN GAROFALO   B     (D      LENNY PICKETT    FLT   (D     EDNA WRIGHT        V     (D
```

B227

PAUL BROOKS

```
PAUL BROOKS                    ( ) STEPS FROM BEYOND       19     STATE             ETAT  21
```
B228

BROTHER BUNG

```
BOB PEARCE     V G HCA  (A     (A) BLUES CRUSADE (EP)      1968   AVENUE ARTISTS    BEV   1055
BOB GORMAN       G V    (A
KEVIN FRANCIS    B V    (A     ROGER CHANTLER     D     (A
```
B229

BROTHERHOOD OF BREATH

```
CHRIS McGREGOR   K     (C      (A) BROTHERHOOD OF BREATH   1971   NEON              NE    2
HARRY MILLER     B     (C      (B) BROTHERHOOD             1972   RCA               SF8269
EVAN PARKER      SAX   (C      (C) LIVE AT WILLISAU        1974   OGUN              OG    100
NICK EVANS       TROM  (C      (D) PROCESSION              1978   OGUN              OG    524
MONGEZI FEZA     TPT   (C
DUDU PUKWANA     SAX   (C
```

EDGAR BROUGHTON BAND(THE BROUGHTONS) B230

EDGAR BROUGHTON G V K B HCA(ALL	(A) WASA WASA	1969	HARVEST	UK	SHVL	757
STEVE BROUGHTON D V K B G (ALL	(A) WASA WASA	1969	EMI		IC038	04083
ARTHUR GRANT G B V K (ABCDEFGH1	(B) SING BROTHER SING	1970	HARVEST	UK	SHVL	772
JOHNNY VAN DERRICK VLN (C	(C) EDGAR BROUGHTON BAND	1971	HARVEST	UK	SHVL	791
VICTOR UNITT V G HCA K (CDE	(D) INSIDE OUT	1972	HARVEST	UK	SHTC	252
P HAROLD FATT V (C	(E) OORA	1973	HARVEST	UK	SHVL	810
DAVID BEDFORD PNO (CE	(F) BANDAGES	1975	NEMS	UK	NEL	6006
MIKE OLDFIELD MAND G HARP (CF	(G) PARLEZ VOUS ENGLISH	1979	BABY		Z	80007
JOHN THOMAS G (FH	(H) LIVE HITS HARDER	1979	BB		BB201009	
LEI ALOAH MEI V (F	( ) MASTERS OF ROCK	1975	EMI		IC054	9548
PETE KNUDSEN K (F	( ) BUNCH OF 45s	1975	HARVEST	UK	SHSM	2001
DUNCAN BRIDGEMAN K (1	(G) PARLEZ VOUS ENGLISH	1979	INFINITY		INS	3027
DIGGER DAVIS G (F	(1) BROUGHTONS 1979/80					
MADELINE BELL V (E						
DORIS TROY V (E	LISA STRIKE V (E	MAGGIE THOMAS		V	(E	
RICHARD DE BASTION K V (G	PETE TOLSEN G (G	TOM NORDEN		G V	(G1	
ALLAN SMITH SAX (G	PETER HOPE EVANS HCA (G	VICKI GAFFEE		CELLO(G		
SUSIE O'LIST V (G	LOZ BROUGHTON V (G	SHAZZI SCOOT		V	(G	
SALLY BROUGHTON V (G	ALI KIMBALL V (G	TAMARA KIMBALL		V	(G	
SHELLEY WATSON V (G	KAY KARNERA V (G	TERRY COTTAM		G	(H	

ARTHUR BROWN B231

ARTHUR BROWN V (ALL	(A) THE CRAZY WORLD OF ARTHUR BROWN	19	TRACK	UK	2407	012
VINCENT CRANE K (A	(A) THE CRAZY WORLD OF ARTHUR BROWN	1968	TRACK	UK	613	005
DRACHEN THEAKER D (AE	(B) GALACTIC ZOO DOSSIER	1972	POLYDOR	UK	2310	130
CARL PALMER D (	(C) KINGDOM COME	1973	POLYDOR	UK	2310	178
ANDY DALBY G (BCDE	(C) KINGDOM COME	19	TRACK	US	GUD2003/4	
KEITH TIPPETT K (E	(D) THE JOURNEY	1973	POLYDOR	UK	2310	254
CHARLIE CHARLES D (E	(E) DANCE	1974	GULL	UK	GULP 1008	
LEE ROBINSON B (E	(F) LOST EARS (PUDDLETOWN EXPRESS) 1976		GULL	UK	G 2003/4	
PETE SOLLEY K (E	(G) CHISHOLM IN MY BOSOM	1978	GULL	UK	GULP 1023	
MALCOLM FLYNN PERC (E						
LLOYD PARKS B (E	CHARLIE DUNBAR D (E	THUNDERTHIGHS		V	(E	
GEORGE KAHN SAX (E	PAT LEWIS PERC (E	JAMES MORGAN		B	(E	
STEVE YORK B (E	RANCHIE McCLEAN G (E	ERROL NELSON		K	(E	
PHIL SHUTT B (BCD	MARTIN STEER D (BC	MICHAEL HARRIS		K	(BC	
SEAN NICHOLAS B (A	DESMOND FISHER B (B	JULIAN BROWN		V	(B	
VICTOR PERAINO K (D						

BUSTER BROWN B232

BUSTER BROWN	(A) RAISE A RUCKUS TONIGHT	1976	DJM		DJM 22037

CLARENCE 'GATEMOUTH' BROWN B233

CLARENCE GATEMOUTH BROWN HCA FDL(ALL(A) SINGS LOUIS JORDAN	1974	BLACK & BLUE		33053		
WITH	(B) GATES ON THE HEAT	1975	BARCLAY		80603	
JACK McVEA SAX (D	(C) DOWN SOUTH IN BAYOU COUNTRY	1975	BARCLAY		90002	
GEORGE ALEXANDER TPT (D	(D) SAN ANTONIO BALLBUSTER	1975	RED LIGHTNING	RL	0010	
WILMER SHAKESLINER SAX (D	(D) SAN ANTONIO BALLBUSTER	1979	CHARLY		CR 30169	
GERALDINE CARELL V (C	(E) BOGALUSA BOOGIE MAN	1976	BARCLAY		90035	
BILL EVANS V (C	(F) HOUSE OF THE BLUES VOL 3	19	BLUE STAR	US	80603	
CLARENCE GREEN PNO (D	(G) THE BLUES AINT NOTHIN'	19	BLACK & BLUE		33033	
GARY BARDWELL V (C	(H) MAKIN' MUSIC(ROY CLARK)	1979	ABC	UK	MCF	3009
HAROLD EASTON D (D						
IRVIN REASON SAX (D	CARL OWENS PNO (D	DUKE BARKER	D	(D	
BILL HARVEY SAX (D	FRED FORD SAX (D	JOHNNY PARKER	B	(D	
PLUMA DAVIS TROM (D	JIMMY McCRACKIN PNO (D	HENRY BOOZIER	TPT	(D	
JOE TOUSSAINT B (D	SAN FRISCO JEFF D (D	JOE SCOTT	TPT	(D	
AL GREY TROM (D	ALLEN CLARK SAX (D	CARL LOTT	B	(D	
JOHNNY BOARD SAX (D	BOB LITTLE SAX (D	PAUL MONDAY	PNO	(D	
RAY JOHNSON B (D	ELLIS BARTES D (D	EMILE RUSSELL	D	(D	
NAT DOUGLAS G (D	NATHAN WOODARD TPT (D	DON BUZZARD	STEEL	(C	
RED LANE G (C	JIM EHINGER PNO (C	JULIUS FARMER	B	(C	
DOUG MORGANO G (C	JACK HUFFMAN D (C	DAVID CRAIG	V	(C	
CHARLIE GRESSETT V (C	HOYT GARRICK (C				

DENNIS BROWN B234

DENNIS BROWN V (ABCD	(A) MEETS HIPPY HARRY	19	GOLDEN AGE	UK	PIOLP 2	
HIPPY HARRY V (A	(B) SUPER HITS	19	TROJAN	UK	TRLS	57
SLY DUNBAR D (D	(C) JUST DENNIS	1975	TROJAN	UK	TRLS	107
LLOYD PARKS B (D	(D) VISIONS OF	1978	LIGHTNING	UK	LIP 7	
FRANKLYN WAUL K (D	(E) WESTBOUND TRAIN	1978	THIRD WORLD	UK	TWS	934
CLIVE HUNT TPT (I	(F) WORDS OF WISDOM	1979	LASER	UK	LASL	1
DANNY WALTERS SAX (I	(G) LIVE IN MONTREUX	1979	LASER	UK	LASL	5
DEAN FRASER SAX (I	(H) WOLF & LEOPARDS	1979	EMI	UK	EMC	330
SKULLEY PERC (I	(I) SPELLBOUND	1980	LASER	UK	LASL	8
KEITH STIRLING K (I						
VIN GORDON TROM (D	ERROL NELSON K (D	HAROLD BUTLER	K	(D	
TOMMY McCOOK SAX (D	BOBBY ELLIS TPT (D	ERIC LAMONT	G	(D	
STICKIE PERC (D	ROBBIE SHAKESPEARE G (D	LENNOX GORDON	G	(D	
HERMAN MARQUIS SAX (D	ROBERT XYN K (I	GLADSTONE ANDERSON	K	(I	
STYLE SCOTT D (I	ANSEL COLLINS K (I	NOEL BAILEY	G	(I	
WILLIE LINDO G (I	DAVID MADDENS TPT (I	TAMLINS	V	(I	

JAMES BROWN B235

JAMES BROWN V (ALL	AMAZING JAMES BROWN	196	KING	US	743	
	AT THE APOLLO	196	KING	US	826	
	AT THE APOLLO	196	LONDON	UK	HA 8184	
	AT THE APOLLO	196	POLYDOR	UK	583729/30	
	AT THE APOLLO	19	POLYDOR	U	2612	005
	AT THE APOLLO	19	POLYDOR	UK	657	107
	AT THE APOLLO	1975	POLYDOR		2482	184
	AT THE APOLLO	19	POLYDOR		2659	011
	PURE DYNAMITE	196	KING	US	883	

JAMES BROWN

Title	Year	Label	Country	Catalog
PURE DYNAMITE	196	LONDON	UK	HA 8177
UNBEATABLE HITS	19	KING	US	919
UNBEATABLE HITS	196	LONDON	UK	HA 8203
PLEASE PLEASE	196	LONDON	UK	HA 8231
TOURS THE USA	1965	LONDON	UK	HA 8240
PAPAS GOT A BRAND NEW BAG	196	LONDON	UK	HA 8262
PAPAS GOT A BRAND NEW BAG	19	POLYDOR		657 001
PAPAS GOT A BRAND NEW BAG	196	KING	US	938
PAPAS GOT A BRAND NEW BAG	1966	PYE	UK	NPL 28099
PAPAS GOT A BRAND NEW BAG	19	POLYDOR	UK	2334 009
NIGHT TRAIN	196	POLYDOR	UK	657 106
GRITS & SOUL	1965			
SHOWTIME	196	SMASH	US	MGS 27054
PLAYS JAMES BROWN	1966	PHILIPS		BL 7697
PLAYS RHYTHM & BLUES	19	PHILIPS	US	14575
PLAYS JAMES BROWN	1966	SMASH	US	MGS 27072
I GOT YOU	1966	PYE INT	UK	NPL 29074
ITS A MANS WORLD	1966	PYE INT	UK	NPL 28079
ITS A MANS WORLD	1966	POLYDOR		657 111
CHRISTMAS ALBUM	1966	PYE INT	UK	NPL 28097
RAW SOUL	196	POLYDOR		657 123
RAW SOUL	196	PYE INT	UK	NPL 28103
RAW SOUL	196	KING	US	1016
LIVE AT THE GARDEN	196	POLYDOR		658 041
LIVE AT THE GARDEN	196	PYE INT	UK	NPL 28104
COLD SWEAT	196	POLYDOR		658 043
PRESENTS HIS SHOW OF TOMORROW	19	POLYDOR		658 073
I CAN'T STAND MYSELF	196	POLYDOR		658 077
HANDFUL OF SOUL	1967	PHILIPS		SBL 7761
PLAYS THE REAL THING	1967	PHILIPS		SBL 7823
PLAYS THE REAL THING	1967	SMASH	US	67093
JAMES BROWN SHOW	1967			
22 GIANT HITS		SMASH	US	67109
PLAYS THE NEW BREED	1968	SMASH	US	MGS 27080
NOTHING BUT SOUL	1968	POLYDOR		658 101
I GOT A FEELING	196	POLYDOR		658 105
I GOT A FEELING	196	KING	US	1031
SOUL PARTY	19	POLYDOR		658 106
OUT OF SIGHT	1968			
SAY IT LOUD I'M BLACK & I'M PROUD	19	KING	US	1047
SAY IT LOUD I'M BLACK & I'M PROUD	19	POLYDOR	UK	583 741
GETTIN' DOWN TO IT	19	KING	US	1051
GETTIN' DOWN TO IT		POLYDOR		658 151
GETTIN' DOWN TO IT	19	POLYDOR	UK	583 742
REVOLUTION OF THE MIND	1972	POLYDOR US 25 3003 UK 2675034		
THE POPCORN	19	KING	US	1055
THE POPCORN	19	POLYDOR		184 319
THE POPCORN	19	POLYDOR		658 172
GET ON THE GOOD FOOT	1973	POLYDOR		2675 054
GET ON THE GOOD FOOT	1973	POLYDOR		2659 018
GET ON THE GOOD FOOT	1973	POLYDOR	US	PD 23004
SOUL BROTHER No 1	1973	POLYDOR		
HOT PANTS	197	POLYDOR	US	PD 4054
ITS A MOTHER	19	POLYDOR		658 371
SLAUGHTERS BIG RIP OFF	1973	POLYDOR	UK	2391 084
SLAUGHTERS BIG RIP OFF	1973	POLYDOR		2490 119
THERE IT IS	19	POLYDOR US 5028		2391 033
THE PAYBACK	1974	POLYDOR US23007 UK		2659 030
THE PAYBACK		POLYDOR		2675 082
HELL	1974	POLYDOR US29001 UK		2659 036
HELL	1974	POLYDOR		2669 018
REALITY	1974	POLYDOR US 6039 UK		2391 164
SOUL CLASSICS	1974	POLYDOR US 5401		2391 057
BLACK CAESAR	1974	POLYDOR	UK	2490 117
MISTER DYNAMITE	197	POLYDOR		2357 004
SOUL ON TOP	19	POLYDOR	UK	2310 022
SOUL ON TOP	19	KING	US	KS 1100
IT'S A NEW DAY	197	POLYDOR	UK	2310 029
IT'S A NEW DAY	197	KING	US	1095
SHE IS FUNKY	197	POLYDOR	UK	2310 089
SUPER BAD	197	KING	US	KS 1127
SEX MACHINE	19	POLYDOR	UK	2625 004
SEX MACHINE TODAY	1975	POLYDOR US 6042 UK		2391 175
EVERYBODYS DOIN' THE HUSTLE	1975	POLYDOR US 6054 UK		2391 197
HOT	197	POLYDOR	US	PD 6059
SEX MACHINE LIVE	197	POLTDOR	US	PD29004
SOUL CLASSICS VOL 2	1975	POLYDOR	UK	2391 116
SOUL CLASSICS VOL 3	1975	POLYDOR	UK	2391 166
THE BEST OF JAMES BROWN	1975	POLYDOR	UK	2343 036
GET UP OFFA THING	1976	POLYDOR US 6071 UK		2391 228
BODY HEAT	1976	POLYDOR	UK	2391 258
POP HISTORY	19	POLYDOR		2625 009
MUTHAS NATURE	1977	POLYDOR US16111 UK		2391 300
SOLID GOLD	1977	POLYDOR	UK	2679 044
JAM 1980'S	1978	POLYDOR US16140 UK		2391 343
TAKE A LOOK AT THOSE CAKES	197	POLYDOR US16181 UK		2391 384
ORIGINAL DISCO MAN	1979	POLYDOR	UK	2391 412
SOUL SYNDROME	1980	RCA PL25334		ALP 5006

JOE BROWN

```
JOE BROWN            G V   (ALL    (A) PICTURE OF YOU            1962   GOLDEN GUINEA  UK   GGL  0146
                                   (B) LIVE                      1963   PICCADILLY     UK   NPL 38006
                                   (C) HERE COMES JOE BROWN      196    GOLDEN GUINEA  UK   GGL  0231
                                   (D) PICTURE OF YOU            19     ACE OF CLUBS   UK   ACL  1127
                                   (E) BROWNS HOME BREW          1972   BELL           UK   BELLS 208
                                   (F) TOGETHER                  1974   VERTIGO        UK   6360  114
                                   (G) JOE BROWN COLLECTION      1974   GOLDEN HOUR    UK   GH  583
                                   (H) JOE BROWN LIVE            1977   POWER EXCHANGE UK   PXLS 2002
                                   (EP) HIT PARADE              196    PICCADILLY     UK   NEP 34025
                                   (EP) ALL THINGS BRIGHT       196    PICCADILLY     UK   NEP 34026
```

PETE BROWN
B237

```
PETE BROWN   V PERC LYRICS(ALL   (A) MANTLEPIECE                      1969   HARVEST    UK   SHVL  758
WITH                             (B) A MEAL YOU CAN SHAKE HANDS WITH  1969   HARVEST    UK   SHVL  752
DICK HECKSTALL SMITH SAX  (F     (C) ART SCHOOL DANCE GOES ON FOREVER 1970   HARVEST    UK   SHVL  768
JIM MULLEN         G B   (CDF    (D) THOUSANDS ON A RAFT              1970   HARVEST    UK   SHVL  782
ROGER BRUNN        B     (CF     (E) NOT FORGOTTEN ASSOCIATION        1973   DERAM      UK   SML  1103
DAVE THOMPSON      D     (CDF    (F) MY LAST BAND                     1977   HARVEST    UK   SHSM 2017
ROB TAIT           D     (ACDF   (G) BACK TO FRONT LINE UP 1977
CHRIS SPEDDING     G     (AF
PETE BAILEY        PERC  (AF     ROGER BUTCH POTTER   B      (AF     CHARLIE HART   K    (F
BUMBO ALCOCK       SAX   (       BRIAN BREEZE         G      (F      PHIL RYAN      K    (F
LYN MAKINELL       K     (G      JOHN WEATHERS        D      (F      BOB EMMINES         (
DILL KATZ          B     (G      IAN LYNN             K      (G      HELEN HARDY    V    (G
STEVE GLOVER       PERC B(DF     ED SPEVOCK           D      (E      GEORGE KAHN  ]             (AF
JEFF CLYNE         B     (E      MAX MIDDLETON        K      (E      NISAR AHMED  ]  SAX
DEREK FOLEY        G     (E      TAFF WILLIAMS        G      (E      TONY HUDD      G    (E
HENRY LOWTHER      TPT   (E      JACK LANCASTER      WIND    (E      VIV STANSHALL  TUBA (E
```

RANDY BROWN
B238

```
RANDY BROWN                       (A) WELCOME TO MY ROOM        1978   PARACHUTE         RRL  1005
                                  (B) INTIMATELY                1979   PARACHUTE         RRL  2007
```

RAY BROWN
B239

```
RAY BROWN            B    (ALL    (A) SOMETHING FOR LESTER      19     CONTEMPORARY   US   7641
                                  (B) BROWN'S BAG               19     CONCORD JAZZ   US   19
```

ROY BROWN
B240

```
ROY BROWN            V    (ALL    (A) HARD TIMES               1973   BLUESWAY          BLS  6056
WITH                              (B) HARD LUCK BLUES          19     STARDAY/KING      KS   1130
FREDDIE HILL       TPT   (A       (C)BLUES ARE ALL BROWN       19     BLUESWAY       US  BLS  6019
GARY COLEMAN       PERC  (A       (D) & WYNONIE HARRIS         19     KING           US       607
EARL PALMER        D     (A       (E) SINGS 24 HITS            19     KING           US       956
DON RANDI          PNO   (A       (F) GOOD ROCKING TONIGHT     1978   ROUTE 66       US  KIK    6
ARTHUR WRIGHT      B     (A       (G) CHEAPEST PRICE IN TOWN   19     FAITH                91020
DENNIS BUDIMIR     G     (A       (H) LAUGHING BUT CRYING      1978   ROUTE 66          KIX 2
JEFF KAPLIN        G     (A
MEL MOORE          TPT   (A       JOHN EWING          TROM   (A      JIM HORN       SAX  (A
JOHNNY WILLIAMS    SAX   (A       HERMAN RILEY        SAX    (A      JIMMY CARMICHAEL PNO (A
MEL BROWN          G     (A       CHARLES WRIGHT      G      (A      BOB WEST       B    (A
ABE MILES          D     (A       ALAN ESTES          PERC   (A      CLIFFORD SCOTT SAX  (A
CAROL KAYE         B     (A       TONY TERRAN         TPT    (A      RICHARD LEITH  TROM (A
```

RUTH BROWN
B241

```
RUTH BROWN           V    (ALL    (A) THE BEST OF RUTH BROWN   19     ATLANTIC          8080
                                  (B) MISS RHYTHM              19     ATLANTIC          8026
                                  (C) RUTH BROWN               19     ATLANTIC          8004
                                  (D) SUGAR BABE               1976   PRESIDENT         1067
```

SHIRLEY BROWN
B242

```
SHIRLEY BROWN        V    (ALL    (A) WOMAN TO WOMAN           1978 STAX UK STX3005  US TRUTH  4206
                                  (B) SHIRLEY BROWN            1977 ARISTA US 4129   UK SPARTY 1017
                                  (C) FOR THE REAL FEELING     1979 STAX UK STX3014
```

THE STANLEY BROWN BAND
B242A

```
JAMES BROWN        K V   (AB      (A) STANLEY BROWN            19     SIRE           US  SRIX 6053
RICHARD BUNKIEWICZ B     (B       (B) OUR PLEASURE TO SERVE YOU 1976  SIRE               9147 7516
JERRY CORPASCO     D     (B
JEFFREY LEYNOR     G     (B       ALLAN ROW           SAX    (B
```

DUNCAN BROWNE
B243

```
DUNCAN BROWNE      G V   (ALL     (A) GIVE ME TAKE YOU         19     IMMEDIATE      IMP Z12 52012
WITH                              (A) GIVE ME TAKE YOU         1968   IMMEDIATE      UK  IMSP  018
TONY HYMAS         K     (CD      (B) DUNCAN BROWNE            1973   RAK            UK  SRKA 6754
JOHN GIBLIN        B     (CD      (C) WILD PLACES              1978   LOGO           UK  LOGO 1007
SIMON PHILLIPS     D     (CD      (D) STREETS OF FIRE          1979   LOGO           UK  LOGO 1016
DICK MORRISSEY     SAX   (D
JOHN BUNDRICK      K     (B       SUZI QUATRO         V      (B      ROBERT HENRIT  D    (B
JOHN CAMERON       PNO   (B       KEITH HODGE         V      (B      JIM RODFORD    B    (B
TONY CARR          V     (B
```

JACKSON BROWNE
B244

```
JACKSON BROWNE     V G   (ALL     (A) FIRST ALBUM  (UNRELEASED)  1967   ELEKTRA
WITH                              (B) JACKSON BROWNE            1972   ASYLUM      UK   5YL  9002
RUSS KUNKEL        D     (CEF      (B) JACKSON BROWNE            1972   ASYLUM      UK   K  53022
JIM GORDON         D     (E        (B) JACKSON BROWNE            1973   ASYLUM      US   SD  5051
CHUCK RAINEY       B     (E        (C) FOR EVERYMAN             1973   ASYLUM      US   SD  5067
JOYCE EVERSON      V     (D        (C) FOR EVERYMAN             1975   ASYLUM      UK   K  43003
BILL PAYNE         K     (CE       (C) FOR EVERYMAN             1973   ASYLUM                4003
LOWELL GEORGE      G     (E        (D) LATE FOR THE SKY         1974   ASYLUM      UK   K  43007
FRED TACKETT       G     (E        (D) LATE FOR THE SKY         1974   ASYLUM           5YL  9018
JOHN HALL          G     (E        (D) LATE FOR THE SKY         1974   ASYLUM      US   7E   1017
MIKE UTLEY         K     (CE       (E) THE PRETENDER           1976   ASYLUM      UK   K  53048
JIM HORN           HRNS  (E        (E) THE PRETENDER           1976   ASYLUM      US   7E   1079
ALBERT LEE         G     (BE       (F) RUNNING ON EMPTY        1978   ASYLUM      UK   K  53070
LELAND SKLAR       B     (EF       (F) RUNNING ON EMPTY        1978   ASYLUM      US   6E   1131
ROY BITTAN         PNO   (E        (G) HOLD OUT                1980   ASYLUM US 5E511 UK   K52226
                                                                             (CONTINUED)
```

JACKSON BROWNE

ARTHUR GERST		(E	BOB GLAUB	B	(E	BONNIE RAITT	V	(CE
JON LANDAU	V	(E	JEFF PORCARO	D	(E	GARY COLEMAN	PERC	(E
ROSEMARY BUTLER	V	(EF	DON HENLEY	V	(CDE	CHUCK FINDLEY	HRNS	(E
J D SOUTHER	V	(E	QUITMAN DENNIS	HRNS	(E	DAVID CROSBY	V	(BE
DICK HYDE	HRNS	(E	MARK JORDAN	K	(	JOHN MAUCERN	D	(E
GRAHAM NASH	V	(E	DANNY KORTCHMAR	G	(F	DOUG HAYWOOD	B V	(CDF
BRIAN GAROFALO	B	(E	MICKY McGEE	D	(C	JIM KELTNER	D	(C
SNEAKY PETE KLeiNOW	STEEL	(BC	GARY MALLABER	D	(C	BETH FICHET	V	(D
SPOONER OLDHAM	ORG	(C	ROCKADAY JOHNNIE	PNO	(C	GLENN FREY	V	(C
DAVID PAICH	PNO	(C	WILTON FELDER	B	(C	LARRY ZACK	D	(D
JONI MITCHELL	PNO	(C	CLARENCE WHITE	G	(B	DAVID JACKSON	PNO	(B
JAI WINDING	K	(D	JIM GORDON	ORG	(B	JIM FADDEN	HCA	(B
JESSE ED DAVIS	G	(B	LEAH KUNKEL	V	(B	DAVID LINDLEY	G VLN	(CDEF
DAVID CAMPBELL	VIOLA	(BE	LEWIS F DAMIAN	G V	(E	JOEL BERNSTEIN	V	(F
CRAIG DOERGE	K	(BEF	DAN FOGELBERG	V	(D	TERRY REID	V	(D
ROBERT GUTIERREZ	G V	(D	FRITZ RICHMOND	JUG	(D			
PERRY LINDLEY	V	(D						

B245

SEVERIN BROWNE

SEVERIN BROWNE	V PNO G	(ALL						
WITH								
JOHN GUERIN	D	(A	MERLE BREGANTE	D	(A	JEFF PORCARO	D	(B
EMORY GORDY	B	(A	DAVID HUNGATE	B	(B	DAVID PAICH	ACC	(B
SNEAKY PETE KLEINOW	STEEL	(A	ALAN LINDGREN	K SYN	(AB	JOE PORCARO	PERC	(B
RUSS KUNKEL	D	(B	STEVE LEEDS	SAX	(B	ROBERT GRINNEDGE	STDRUM	(B
RICHARD BENNETT	G STEEL	(AB	JENNIFER WARREN	V	(B	CAROL CARMICHAEL	V	(B
BOBBY TORRES	PERC	(B	JULES SHEAR	V	(B	DENNIS CONWAY	D	(A
DEAN WEBB	MAND	(B	RAY KELLY	CELLO	(A	MAURY MANSEAU	G	(A
BOBBI THOMAS	V	(B	KING ERRISON	CONGAS	(A			
STEVE LE FEVER	B	(A						
BRUCE BUELL	B	(A						

(A) SEVERIN BROWNE	1973	MOWEST	US	M774L
(B) NEW IMPROVED	1974	MOTOWN	US	6 779
(B) LOVESONGS	1974	MOWEST	UK	MWS 7005

B246

BROWNSVILLE STATION

HENRY WEEK	D V	(H
CUBBY KODA	G HCA	(H
MICHAEL LUTZ	G V K	(H
BRUCE NAZARIAN	G SYN	(H
TONY DRIGGINS	B	(
T J CRONLEY	D	(

(A) BROWNSVILLE STATION	19	PALLADIUM	US	1004
(A) BROWNSVILLE STATION	19	PRIVATE STOCK	US	2026
(B) A NIGHT ON THE TOWN	19	BELL	US	BTS 2010
(C) YEAH!	19	BELL	US	BT 2101
(D) SCHOOL PUNKS	19	BIG TREE	US	89600
(E) SMOKIN' IN THE BOYS ROOM	19	PHILIPS		6369 804
(F) MOTOR CITY CONNECTION	1975	BIG TREE		89510
(G) BROWNSVILLE STATION	19	PRIVATE STOCK		PVLP 1021
(H) AIR SPECIAL	1980	EPIC	UK	EPC 83161

B247

ANNETTE & VICTOR BROX

VICTOR BROX	V K	(A	GLEN CARTLIDGE	G SAX	(A	HARVEY ROSE	B V	(A
ANNETTE BROX	V PERC	(A	RAY WARLEIGH	SAX	(A	BRUCE MITCHELL	PERC	(A
JEFF WALTERS	WIND	(A	GORDON REED	V	(A	TONY MOSS	B	(A
CHARLENE COLLINS	V	'A	JOHN MORSHEAD	G	(A	ALEX DMOCHCWSKI	B	(A
LOUIS HUTCHINSON	V	(A	LARRY GANNON	G	(A	PETE WAUGH	G V	(A
PAUL BURGESS	PERC D	(A	KEITH BAILEY	D	(A	LOL CREME	D	(A
RAY RUSSELL	G	(A	GERALDINE CONNOR	V	(A	JOYCE HOBSON	V	(A
JOHN PORTER	G	(A	TOSH RYAN-CARTER	SAX	(A	DAVE LOWARCH	G	(A
BRIAN KEITH	TROM V	(A						
JUNE LEWIS	V	(A						

(A) ROLLIN' BACK	1974	SONET	UK	SNTF 663

B248

JACK BRUCE

JACK BRUCE	B V	(ALL	(A) SONGS FOR A TAYLOR		1969	POLYDOR	UK	583 058
DICK HECKSTALL SMITH	SAX	(AB	(A) SONGS FOR A TAYLOR		1969	ATCO	US	33306
CHRIS SPEDDING	G	(AC	(A) SONGS FOR A TAYLOR		1969	POLYDOR		1843 20
JOHN McLAUGHLIN	G	(B	(B) THINGS WE LIKE		1970	POLYDOR	UK	2343 033
JON HISEMAN	D	(AB	(B) THINGS WE LIKE		1970	ATCO	US	33349
JOHN MARSHALL	D	(AC	(B) THINGS WE LIKE		1970	POLYDOR		2310 077
ART THEMEN	SAX	(A	(C) HARMONY ROW		1971	POLYDOR	UK	2310 107
HENRY LOWTHER	HRNS	(A	(C) HARMONY ROW		1971	ATCO	US	33365
HARRY BECKETT	HRNS	(A	(C) HARMONY ROW		1971	POLYDOR		2385 065
JOHN MUMFORD	HRNS	(	(D) OUT OF THE STORM		1974	POLYDOR	UK	2394 143
MITCH MITCHELL	D	(	(D) OUT OF THE STORM		1974	RSO		4805 0698
LARRY CORYELL	G	(	(D) OUT OF THE STORM		1974	RSO		2479 123
MIKE MANDEL	K	(	(E) HOWS TRICKS		1977	RSO	UK	2394 180
GRAHAM BOND	K	(	(E) HOWS TRICKS		1977	RSO	US	1-3021
MICK TAYLOR	G	(1	( ) POP GIANTS No. 14		19	BRUNSWICK	IMP	2911 525
JIM GORDON	D	(D	( ) AT HIS BEST		1974	RSO		2659 024
SIMON PHILLIPS	D	(E	( ) AT HIS BEST		1972	POLYDOR	US	PD 3505
HUGH BURNS	G	(E	(1) JACK BRUCE BAND 1977					
RONNIE LEAHY	K	(1	(F) IVE ALWAYS WANTED TO DO THIS		1980	EPIC	UK	84672
CLEM CLEMSON	G	(F						
JIM KELTNER	D	(D	FELIX PAPPALARDI	V PERC	(A	TONY HYMAS	K	(E
CARLA BLEY	K V	(1	BRUCE GARY	D	(1	STEVE HUNTER	G	(D
BILLY COBHAM	D	(F	DAVIS SANCIOUS	K G	(F			

B249

BILL BRUFORD

BILL BRUFORD	D	(ALL
WITH		
DAVE STEWART	K	(AB
JEFF BERLIN	B	(AB
ALLAN HOLDSWORTH	G	(AB
NEIL MURRAY	B	(A
ANNETTE PEACOCK	V	(A
JOHN GOODSALL	G	(A

(A) FEELS GOOD TO ME	1978	POLYDOR		2310 579
(A) FEELS GOOD TO ME	1978	POLYDOR		2302 075
(B) BRUFORD	1979	POLYDOR		2302 091
(B) BRUFORD	1979	POLYDOR	US	POLD 5020
(C) BRUFORD TAPES	1979	POLYDOR		BRUBOOT28
(D) GRADUALLY GOING TORNADO	1979	EG	UK	EGLP 104

BRUNNING HALL SUNFLOWER BLUES BAND   B250

```
BOB BRUNNING            B    (ABC    (A) BULLEN STREET BLUES      1968  SAGA    FID  2118
BIG SUNFLOWER(BOB HALL)PNO(ABC       (B) SUNFLOWER BLUES BAND     196   GEMINI  GM   2010
MICK HALLS              G    (A      (C) TRACKSIDE BLUES          1969  SAGA    EROS 8132
COLIN JORDAN            G    (AC
PETER FRENCH            V    (A      JEFF RUSSELL    D     (A   PAT GROVER    V G   (B
LEO MANNING             D    (B      JO ANNE KELLY   V     (B   JOHN O'LEARY  HCA   (B
STEVE RYE               HCA  (B      KEITH NELSON    BANJO (B   BARRY GUARD   D     (B
PETE BANHAM             D    (C      PETER GREEN     G V   (C
```

BRUSH ARBOR   B250A
```
                                     (A) STRAIGHT
```

BEABO BRYSON   B251
```
PEABO BRYSON      V    (ALL          (A) REACHING FOR THE SKY     1978  CAPITOL  EST 11729
WITH                                 (B) CROSSWINDS               1978  CAPITOL  ST  11875
PAUL LIBMAN       K    (A
TERRY FRYER       SYN  (A            BOBBY CHRISTIAN  PERC (A   DAN LEAKE       G  (A
ROSS TRAUT        G    (A            LARRY BALL       B    (A   MORRIS JENNINGS D  (A
SONNY SEALS       SAX  (A

ROD PRINCE             (A
```

BUBBLE PUPPY   B252
```
                                     (A) BUBBLE PUPPY                    IA
```

ROY BUCHANAN   B253
```
ROY BUCHANAN      G V  (ALL          (A) ROY BUCHANAN             1972  POLYDOR  UK 2391 042
WITH                                 (A) ROY BUCHANAN             1972  POLYDOR  US   PD 5033
STEVE CROPPER     G    (G            (B) SECOND ALBUM             1973  POLYDOR  UK 2391 062
DIVA GRAY         V    (G            (B) SECOND ALBUM             1973  POLYDOR  US   PD 5046
RHETTA HUGHES     V    (G            (C) THATS WHAT I'M HERE FOR  1974  POLYDOR  UK 2391 114
LAURA WILLIAMS    V    (G            (C) THATS WHAT I'M HERE FOR  1974  POLYDOR  US   PD 6020
RON FOSTER        V    (G            (D) RESCUE ME               1975  POLYDOR  UK 2391 152
RAY GOMEZ         G    (G            (E) LIVE STOCK              1975  POLYDOR  US   PD 6048
STANLEY CLARKE    G    (G            (F) A STREET CALLED STRAIGHT 1976  POLYDOR  UK 2391 233
NARADA MICHAEL WALDEN D (G           (F) A STREET CALLED STRAIGHT 1976  ATLANTIC US  SD 18170
MALCOLM LUKENS    K    (G            (G) LOADING ZONE            1977  POLYDOR  UK 2391 295
JAN HAMMER        K    (G            (G) LOADING ZONE            1977  POLYDOR  US   PD 8219
SCOTT MUSMANNO    V    (G            (H) NOT ALONE               1978  ATLANTIC US  SD 19170
DENNIS PARKER     B    (G            ( ) ROY BUCHANAN            1976  POLYDOR  UK 2482 275
DAVID GARIBALDI   D    (G            ( ) IN THE BEGINNING       19    POLYDOR  US   PD 6035
DONALD DUCK DUNN  B    (G
WILL LEE          B    (G
DICK HEINTZE      K    (BC           TOM FLYE      PERC (D   ARMANDO PERAZA  CONGA(D
DON PAYNE         B    (B            TEDDY IRWIN   G    (B   JERRY MERCER    D    (B
BILLY PRICE       V    (C            CHUCK TILLEY  V    (B   NED DAVIS       D    (B
BILL SHEFFIELD    V    (D            JOHN HARRISON B V  (C   ROBBIE MAGRUDER D    (C
BILL STEWART      D    (D            NEIL LARSEN   K    (D   KENNY TIBBETTS  B    (D
MIMI CASTILLO     SAX  (D            GREG ADAMS    TPT  (D   LENNY PICKETT   SAX  (D
ED FREEMAN        K    (D            MIC GILLETTE  HRNS (D   STEPHEN KUPKA   SAX  (D
                                     VENETTA FIELDS V   (D   CARLENE WILLIAMS V   (D
```

BUCKACRE   B254
```
ALAN THACKER      G FDL  (AB         (A) MORNING COMES           1976  MCA  UK  MCF 2771
DICK HALLEY       B BANJ (AB         (A) MORNING COMES           1976  MCA  US  MCA 2216
DICK VERUCCHI     D PERC (AB         (B) BUCKACRE                1978  MCA  US  MCA 2365
DARRELL DATA      STEEL G V(AB
LES LOCKRIDGE     G      (A          DAVID ANSON     PNO K V(B
```

BUCKEYE   B254A
```
RONN PRICE        V B G  (A          (A) BUCKEYE                 1970  POLYDOR   2391 416
THOM FOWLE        G V    (A
GABRIEL KATONA    K V    (A          BEAVER PARKER   D PERC V(A
```

BUCKINGHAM NICKS   B255
```
STEVIE NICKS         V    (A         (A) BUCKINGHAM NICKS        1973  POLYDOR  US   PD5058
LINDSEY BUCKINGHAM   G V  (A         (A) BUCKINGHAM NICKS        1977  POLYDOR  UK 2391 093
GARY 'HOPPY' HODGES  D    (A
JIM KELTNER          D    (A         JERRY SCHEFF  B   (A   ROBERT 'WADDY'WACHTEL G (A
MARK TULIN           B    (A         RON TUTT      D   (A   PEGGY SANDVIG  K   (A
JORGE CALDERON       PERC (A         MONTY STARK   SYN (A   XAVIER PACHECO K V (
BRIAN KANE           G    (          BOB GEARY     D   (    TOM CRIEFF     B   (
```

TIM BUCKLEY   B256
```
TIM BUCKLEY       G V  (ALL          (A) TIM BUCKLEY             1966  ELEKTRA   US  EKS 74004
WITH                                 (A) TIM BUCKLEY             1971  ELEKTRA   UK   K 42010
LEE UNDERWOOD     G K  (ABCDEFHJ     (B) GOODBYE & HELLO         1967  ELEKTRA   US  EKS 7318
VAN DYKE PARKS    PNO  (A            (B) GOODBYE & HELLO         1971  ELEKTRA   US  EKS 74028
BILLY MUNDI       D    (A            (B) GOODBYE & HELLO         1971  ELEKTRA   UK   K 42070
JIMMY BOND        B    (B            (C) HAPPY SAD              1969  ELEKTRA   US  EKS 74045
DON RANDI         K    (B            (C) HAPPY SAD              1971  ELEKTRA   UK   K 42072
JERRY YESTER      K    (B            (D) LORCA                  1970  ELEKTRA   US  EKS 74074
JIMMY MADISON     D    (E            (D) LORCA                  1971  ELEKTRA   UK   K 42053
BRIAN HARTZLER    G    (B            (E) BLUE AFTERNOON         1970  STRAIGHT  US  STS 1060
CARTER COLLINS    CONGAS(CDE         (E) BLUE AFTERNOON         1970  WB        US   WS 1842
DAVID FRIEDMAN    PERC (CE           (F) STARSAILOR            1971  STRAIGHT  UK  STS 1064
JIM FIELDER       B    (ABJ          (F) STARSAILOR            1971  WB        US   WS 1881
JOHN MILLER       B    (CE           (F) STARSAILOR            197   ELECTROLA GERM IC06292094
EDDIE HOH         PERC (B            (G) GREETINGS FROM L A    1972  WB        US   BS 2631
DAVE GUARD        PERC (B            (G) GREETINGS FROM L A    1972  WB        UK   K 46176
BERNIE MYSIOR     B    (H            (H) SEFRONIA              1974  DISCREET  UK   K 49201
BUDDY HELM        D    (H            (H) SEFRONIA              1974  WB        US   MS 2157
MARK TIERNAN      K    (HJ           (J) LOOK AT THE FOOL      1974  DISCREET  UK   K 59204
JOE FALSIA        G    (HJB          (J) LOOK AT THE FOOL      1974  DISCREET  US   DS 2201
MIKE MELVOIN      PNO  (J
CHUCK RAINEY      B    (J            EARL PALMER     D    (J   KING ERRISON    PERC (HJ
JESSE EHRLICH     CELLO (J           DAVID BLUEFIELD K    (J   JIM HUGHART     B    (J
CARY COLEMAN      PERC (J            ANTHONY TERRAN  HRNS (J   WILLIAM PETERSON HRNS (J
```

(CONTINUED)

B256 (CONTINUED)

RICHARD NASH	HRNS	(J
CLYDIE KING	V	(J
BUZZ GARDNER	HRNS	(F
BOB RAFKIN	G	(H
FRED SELDON	FLT	(H
LISA ROBERTS	V	(H
MARCIA WALDORF	V	(H

TIM BUCKLEY

JOHNNY ROTELLA	HRNS	(J
SHIRLEY MATTHEWS	V	(J
BUNK GARDNER	HRNS	(F
KENNETH WATSON	PERC	(H
MYRNA MATTHEWS	V	(H
TOM SCOTT	SAX	(H
LARRY BUNKER	PERC	(H

VENETTA FIELDS	V	(J
JOHN BALKIN	B	(DF
MAURY BAKER PERC	PERC	(F
ERIC DUMLER	HRNS	(H
SHARON BEARD	V	(H
DENNY RANDELL	K	(H
TERRY HARRINGTON	SAX	(J

B257 BUCKWHEAT

(A) BUCKWHEAT	1972	LONDON		SHU 8423
(B) MOVING ON	1972	LONDON		SHU 8429
(C) CHARADE	1973	LONDON		SHU 8444
(D) HOT TRACKS	1975	LONDON		SHU 8470

B258 BUDGIE

BURKE SHELLEY	B V	(ABCDEFGH
TONY BOURGE	G V	(ABCDEFGH
RAY PHILLIPS	D	(ABC
PETE BOOT	D	(D
STEVE WILLIAMS	D	(E
ROB KENDRICK	G	(

(A) BUDGIE	1971	MCA	UK	MKPS 2018
(A) BUDGIE	1974	MCA	UK	MCF 2506
(B) SQUAWK	1972	MCA	UK	MKPS 2023
(B) SQUAWK	1974	MCA	UK	MCF 2502
(C) NEVER TURN YOUR BACK ON A FRIEND	1973	MCA	UK	MDKS 8010
(C) NEVER TURN YOUR BACK ON A FRIEND	1974	MCA	UK	MCG 3513
(D) IN FOR THE KILL	1974	MCA	UK	MCF 2546
(D) IN FOR THE KILL	1974	BARCLAY	FR	410026
(D) IN FOR THE KILL	1974	MCA	US	429
(E) BANDOLIER	1975	MCA	UK	MCF 2723
(E) BANDOLIER	1975	A&M	US	4618
(F) IF I WAS BRITANNIA I'D WAIVE...	1976	A&M	UK	AMLH68377
(F) IF I WAS BRITANNIA I'D WAIVE...	1976	A&M	US	4593
(G) IMPECKABLE	1978	A&M	UK	AMLH64675
(G) IMPECKABLE	1978	A&M	US	4675
( ) THE BEST OF	1976	MCA	UK	MCF 2766

B259 NORTON BUFFALO

NORTON BUFFALO	V HCA PERC	(AB
WITH		
DAVE SHAPIRO	G MAND	(A
FRED JONES	STEEL	(A
KIRK HARWOOD	D	(A
BYRON ALLRED	K	(A
BOB McFEE	B	(A
MICKEY HART	PERC	(A

(A) LOVING IN THE VALLEY	1977	CAPITOL		ST 11625
(B) DESERT HORIZON	1978	CAPITOL		SW 11847

PHIL RICHARDSON	VLN	(A
TRAMAINE HAWKINS	V	(A
DAVID LADD	FLT	(A
SEAN HOPPER	K	(A
FEDDIE SMITH	V	(A

GARY CRELLER	B	(A
JOHN McFEE G VLN STEEL		(A
JOHN CIAMBOTTI	B	(A
LYNETTE HAWKINS	V	(A
STRING SECTION		(A

B260 BUFFALO SPRINGFIELD

NEIL YOUNG	G V	(ALL
STEPHEN STILLS	G V	(ALL
DEWEY MARTIN	D	(ALL
RICHIE FURAY	G V	(ABC
BRUCE PALMER	B	(AB
KEN KOBLUN	B	(
BOBBY WEST	B	(B
DOUG HASTINGS	G V	(
JIM FIELDER	B	(B
JIM MESSINA	B	(C
CHARLIE CHIN	BANJO	(B
JAMES BURTON	G	(B
JACK NITZSCHE	K	(B
DON RANDI	PNO	(B

(A) BUFFALO SPRINGFIELD	1967	ATCO	US	SD 33200
(A) THE BEGINNING (REISSUE)	1973	ATLANTIC	UK	K 30028
(B) BUFFALO SPRINGFIELD AGAIN	1967	ATLANTIC	US	SD 33226
(B) BUFFALO SPRINGFIELD AGAIN	1968	ATLANTIC	UK	587 091
(B) BUFFALO SPRINGFIELD AGAIN	1971	ATLANTIC	UK	K 40014
(C) LAST TIME AROUND	1969	ATCO	US	228 024
(C) LAST TIME AROUND	1971	ATLANTIC	UK	K 40077
(C) LAST TIME AROUND	1969	ATCO	US	SD 33250
(D) EXPECTING TO FLY	1970	ATLANTIC	UK	2462 012
(E) THE BEST OF/ RETROSPECTIVE	1972	ATLANTIC	US	SD 33283
(E) THE BEST OF/ RETROSPECTIVE	1972	ATLANTIC	UK	K 40071
(E) THE BEST OF/ RETROSPECTIVE	1972	ATCO	US	SD 38105
(F) BUFFALO SPRINGFIELD (DBL)	1973	ATLANTIC	UK	K 70001
(F) BUFFALO SPRINGFIELD (DBL)	1973	ATCO	US	SD 2 806
( ) STAR COLLECTION	19	WEA MIDI	UK	K 30037

B261 JIMMY BUFFETT

JIMMY BUFFETT	G V	(ALL
WITH		
REGGIE YOUNG	G	(BCD
LANNY FIEL	G	(ACGK
DOYLE GRISHAM	STEEL	(BCDE
TOMMY COGBILL	B	(CD
MIKE UTLEY	K	(BCDFHIJLM
SAM CREASON	D	(BCDF
BRENDA BRYANT	V	(M
GREG TAYLOR	HCA	(BCDFHIJLM
FARRELL MORRIS	PERC	(BCDFHI
DAVID BRYANT	V	(CDF
DON GANT	V	(BCDF
BUZZ CASON	V	(ABCDFGK
BERGEN WHITE	V	(CDFGK
BILL PUETT	HRNS	(CH
STEVE GOODMAN	G	(BDFI
PAULETTE BROWN	V	(M
JAY SPELL	K	(IJL
DEBBIE McCALL	V	(IJM
ROGER BARTLETT	G	(DFH
PHILLIP FAJARDO	D	(E
JERRY McGEE	G	(F
JOHNNY GIMBLE	FDL	(F
MUSCLE SHOALS HORNS		(F
MICHAEL GARDNER	D	(H
SHELLEY KURLAND	STRINGS	(H
STEVE SYKES	G V	(M
HARVEY THOMPSON	SAX	(I
PENNY NICHOLS	V	(I
JAMES TAYLOR	G V	(M
SHANE KEISTER	SYN	(B
BOBBY THOMPSON	BANJ	(GK
SANDY GOODRUM	K	(GK

(A) DOWN TO EARTH	1972	BARNABY	US	Z 30093
(B) A WHITE SPORTS COAT & A PINK..	1973	PROBE	UK	SPB 1078
(B) A WHITE SPORTS COAT...	1973	DUNHILL	US	X 60150
(B) A WHITE SPORTS COAT.....	1974	ABC	UK	ABCL 5036
(C) LIVING & DYING IN 3/4 TIME	1974	ABC	UK	ABCL 5047
(C) LIVING & DYING IN 3/4 TIME	1974	DUNHILL	US	D 50132
(D) A.1.A	1975	ABC	UK	ABCL 5065
(D) A.1.A	1975	DUNHILL	US	D 50187
(E) RANCHO DELUXE (SOUNDTRACK)6TRACKS	1975	UA	US	LA 466G
(F) HAVANA DAYDREAMING	1976	ABC	US	ABCD 915
(F) HAVANA DAYDREAMING	1976	ABC	UK	ABCL 5148
(G) HIGH CUMBERLAND JUBILEE(1972)	1976	BARNABY	US	BR 6014
(H) CHANGES IN LATITUDES	1977	ABC	UK	ABCL 5218
(H) CHANGES IN LATITUDES	1977	ABC	US	ABC 990
(I) SON OF A SAILOR	1978	ABC	UK	ABCL 5242
(I) SON OF A SAILOR	1978	ABC	US	ABC 1046
(J) YOU HAD TO BE THERE (DBL)	1979	ABC		AK 1008/2
(J) YOU HAD TO BE THERE (DLE)	1979	MCA		MCDW 451
(K) BEFORE THE SALT (A/G COMP)	1979	BARNABY	US	2BR 6019
(M) VOLCANO	1979	MCA	US	5102
(M) VOLCANO	1979	MCA	UK	MCG 4005

JOE OSBORN	B	(F
GINGER HOLLADAY	V	(FI
HARRY DAILEY	B	(FHIJLM
KENNY BUTTREY	D	(H
RUSS KUNKEL	D	(M
BARRY CHANCE	G	(JLM
JANIE FRICKE	V	(I
LARRY LEE	V	(I
JAMES ELMER	B	(M
PHIL ROYSTER	CONGAS	(B
PAUL TABET	D	(GK
JACKIE DANGLER	PERC	(M

STEVE FORMAN	PERC	(M
ANITA BALL	V	(F
BARRY CHANCE	G	(J
MIKE JEFFREY	G	(H
ANDY McMAHON	K V	(M
NORBERT PUTNAM	B	(IM
LEA JANE BERINATI	V	(I
VANETTA FIELDS	V	(M
TIM KREKEL	G	(IL
ED WILLIAMS	B	(B
RICK FIEL	B	(GK
BILL JONES	REC	(M

(CONTINUED)

JIMMY BUFFETT
B261

DAVE LOGGINS	V	(M	HUGH TAYLOR	V	(M	ALEX TAYLOR	V	(M
VASSAR CLEMENTS	FDL	(B	DON KLOETZE	V	(GK	TRAVIS TURK	D	(AK
KARL HIMMEL	D	(AK	BOB COOK	B G	(AK	DAVE HANEY	B	(AK
WILFRED TUILT	G	(M	JUAN CADIZ	V	(M	MARVIN GARDENS	PERC	(B
JOHNNY MONTEZUMA	PERC	(M	DON DOUGLAS	BANJ	(M			

BULL
B262

(A) THIS IS BULL

			1970	PARAMOUNT	US	PA	5028

BARRY BULL GORDON	G B V	(A				
ANDY MUSON	B	(A				
PAUL GRIFFIN	K	(A	HERB LOVELLE	D	(A	CARLA CALRWELL	V	(A
HILDA HARRIS	V	(A	EILEEN GILBERT	V	(A	TASHA THOMAS	V	(A
STRINGS		(A				

BULLDOG
B262A

BILLY HOCHER	B V	(A	(A) BULLDOG	1972	MCA US 5370	UK MCF	2662
ERIC THORNGREN	G	(A	(A) BULLDOG	1972	MCA		510072
JOHN TURK	K V	(A	(B) SMASHER	1974	BUDDAH		840 031
GENE CORNISH	G	(A	(B) SMASHER	197	BUDDAH US 5600	UK BDLP	4007
DINO DANELLI	D	(A				

BULLDOG BREED
B262B

(A) MADE IN ENGLAND

	1970	NOVA	UK		SDN 5

BULLDOZER
B262C

(A) BULLDOZER

197	RCA	FR	PL	37161

BULLFROG
B262D

SEBASTIAN LEITNER	G	(	(A) BULLFROG	1976	SKY		006
GERD HOCH	V	(	(B) HIGH IN SPIRITS	1977	SKY		012
VINCENT TROST	B	(				
HARALD KALTENECKER	K	(	BRUNO PEROSA	PERC	(		

CINDY BULLENS
B263

CINDY BULLENS	V G	(ALL	(A) DESIRE WIRE	1978	UA	UK	UAG	30217
WITH			(A) DESIRE WIRE	1978	UA	US	LA	933H
JEFF MIRANOV	G	(A				
MARK DOYLE	G	(A	DAVID MANSFIELD	G	(A	LOU MARINI	SAX	(A
LANCE QUINN	G	(A	DANNY GATTON	G	(A	GEORGE YOUNG	SAX	(A
LEON PENDARVIS	K	(A	BILLY MERNIT	K V	(A	ROB MOUNSEY	K	(A
PAUL SCHAEFFER	K	(A	NEIL JASON	B	(A	BOB BABITT	B	(A
JERRY PETERSON	SAX	(A	JERRY MAROTTA	D	(A	ALLEN SCHWARZBERG	D	(A
KENNY BISCHEL	SYN	(A	JIMMY MAELEN	PERC	(A	JAN JOYCE	V	(A

BULLET
B264

BARRY LANG	V G	(				
PAUL GOODING	K					
STEVE THOMAS	B V	(	JOHN SHAW	G V	(	GRAHAM SPEARS	D	(

BUMBLE BEE SLIM
B265

(A) EVERYBODY'S FISHING

AMOS EASTON[BUMBLE BEE SLIM]		1977	MAGPIE		PY	1808

B266

THE BUNCH
B266

(A) THE BUNCH

SANDY DENNY	V	(A		1972	ISLAND	UK	ILPS 9189
RICHARD THOMPSON	G V	(A				
TREVOR LUCAS	G V	(A	ASHLEY HUTCHINGS	V	(A	GERRY CONWAY	D	(A
IAN WHITEMAN	PNO	(A	ROGER BALL	SAX	(A	LINDA PETERS	V	(A
TONY COX	PNO	(A	PAT DONALDSON	B	(A	DAVE MATTACKS	D	(A
MALCOLM DUNCAN	SAX	(A	MIKE ROSEN	TPT	(A			

BUOYS
B267

CHRIS HANLON	D	(A	(A) THE BUOYS	1971	WAND		WNS	15
BILL KELLY	G FLT	(A	(A) THE BUOYS	197	SCEPTRE		SPS 24001
CARL SIRACUSE	G K	(A				
GERRY HLUDZIK	B	(A	FRAN BROZENA	G K	(A			

ERIC BURDON
B268

ERIC BURDON	V	(ALL	(A) GUILTY	1971	UA	UK	UAG 29251
WITH			(A) GUILTY	1971	MGM	US	SE 4791
JIMMY WITHERSPOON	V	(A	(B) SUN SECRETS	1975	CAPITOL		EST 11359
BOB MERCEREAU	HCA	(A	(C) STOP	1975	CAPITOL		EST 11426
LEE OSKAR	HCA	(A	(D) POP HISTORY	197	POLYDOR		2625 011
PAPA DEE ALLEN	PERC	(A	(E) STAR PORTRAIT	197	VERVE		2629 001
HAROLD BROWN	D	(A	(E) STAR PORTRAIT	197	MGM		2624 024
GEORGE SURANOVICH	D	(AC	(F) SURVIVOR	1978	POLYDOR		2302 078
CHARLES MILLER	SAX	(A	(F) SURVIVOR	1978	POLYDOR		2310 577
HOWARD SCOTT	G	(A	(1) 1978 MARCH TOUR			
JOHN STERLING	G	(AC	(G) MADMAN	1976	KARUSSELL	GERM	2674 004
LONNIE JORDAN	K	(A				
GLENN PENNISTON	D	(1	TERRY RYAN	K	(AC	B B DICKERSON	B	(A
GEOFF WHITEHORN	G	(	ALVIN TAYLOR	D	(BC	LARRY STEELE	G	(1
MORRIS WHEELOCK	PERC	(C	KIM KESTERSON	B	(AC	KENNY PARRY	G	(
AALON BUTLER	G	(B	DELISLE HARPER	B	(1	ZOOT MONEY	K	(
DAVE DOVER	D	(	RANDY RICE	B	(BC			

SONNY BURGESS
B269

SONNY BURGESS		(	(A) LEGENDARY SUN PERFORMERS	19	CHARLY		CR 30136
			(B) OLD GANG	1977	LAKE COUNTY		LP 503
			(EP)SONNY BURGESS	19	CHARLY		CEP 103

KEN BURIGAN
B269A

(A) THE BIG WOW WOW STRAIN

KEN BURGAN		(A		1974	BLUE THUMB	US	BTS 6016
GUS CONTOS		(A				
JOHN GIRTON		(A	WILTON FELDER		(A	HARVEY MASON		(A
HILARY HAMBERG		(A	PAUL HUMPHREY		(A	MIKE SALTSBERG		

KEVIN BURKE
B270

KEVIN BURKE	FDL	(	(A) IF THE CAT FITS	1978	ROCKBURGH		ROC 105
			(A) IF THE CAT FITS	1979	MULLIGAN		LUN 021
			(B) PROMENADE	1979	MULLIGAN		LUN 028

B271   **SOLOMON BURKE**

SOLOMON BURKE	V	(ALL	( ) GREATEST	19	LONDON	UK	HAK	8018
			( ) GREATEST HITS	19	ATLANTIC			8067
			( ) IF YOU NEED ME	19	ATLANTIC			8085
			( ) ROCK'N'SOUL	1964	ATLANTIC			8096
			( ) ROCK'N'SOUL	1964	ATLANTIC	UK	ATL	5009
			( ) THE BEST OF	19	ATLANTIC			8109
			( ) KING OF ROCK'N' SOUL	1966	ATLANTIC	UK	590	004
			( ) PROUD MARY	1969	BELL		SBLL	118
			( ) ELECTRONIC MAGNETISM	19	POLYDOR		2315	048
			( ) MUSIC TO MAKE LOVE BY	1975	CHESS		9109	102
			( ) MUSIC TO MAKE LOVE BY	197	CHESS	US		60042
			( ) STAR COLLECTION	1975	ATLANTIC	UK	K 20064	
			( ) GET UP AND DO SOMETHING...	197	MGM			
			( ) BACK TO MY ROOTS	19	CHESS	US		19002
			( ) FROM THE HEART	1980	CHARLY	UK	CRB	1024

B272   **BURLESQUE**

IAN TRIMMER	SAX V	(AB	(A) ACUPUNCTURE	1977	ARISTA		ARTY	151
BILLY JENKINS	G V	(AB	(B) BURLESQUE	1977	ARISTA		SPARTY 1028	
STEVE PARR	K	(AB						
STEVE HUGHES	B V	(AB	PAUL WARREN	D	(A	KEVIN CURRIE	D	(B

B272A   **DORSEY BURNETTE**

DORSEY BURNETTE	V	(A	(A) DORSEY BURNETTE	1963	LONDON	UK	HAD	8050

B273   **HANK C BURNETTE**

HANK C BURNETTE	G V	(ALL	(A) SPINNIN' ROCK BOOGIE	1974	SOUTHERN SOUND	UK		
			(B) DONT MESS WITH MY DUCKTAIL	1976	SONET	UK	SNTF	693
			(C) ROCKABILLY GASSEROONIE	1978	SONET	UK	SNTF	750
			(D) HOT LICKS & FANCY TRICKS	1979	SONET	UK	SNTF	792

B274   **JOHNNY BURNETTE**

JOHNNY BURNETTE	G V	(ALL	(A) DREAMIN'	196	LONDON	UK	HAG	2306
DORSEY BURNETTE	B V	(	(A) DREAMIN'	196	LIBERTY	US	LRP	3183
PAUL BURLISON	D	(	(A) DREAMIN'	19	SUNSET	UK	SLS	50007
			(A) DREAMIN'	19	SUNSET	US	SUS	6179
			(B) ROCK'N'ROLL TRIO	196	CORAL 10"		LVC	10041
			(B) ROCK'N'ROLL TRIO	1971	CORAL		CP	61
			(B) ROCK'N'ROLL TRIO	1974	CORAL MCA		CRLM	1043
			(B) ROCK'N'ROLL TRIO	1978	CORAL MCA		CDLM	8054
			(C) TEAR IT UP	1969	CORAL		CP	10
			(C) TEAR IT UP	1974	CORAL		CRLM	1022
			(C) TEAR IT UP	1975	MCA		COPS	6355
			(C) TEAR IT UP	1978	SOLID SMOKE	US		3001
			( ) JOHNNY BURNETTE	196	LONDON		HAG	2349
			( ) JOHNNY BURNETTE SINGS	196	LONDON		HAG	2375
			( ) JOHNNY BURNETTE SINGS	196	LONDON		SAH	6175
			( ) JOHNNY BURNETTE SINGS	196	LIBERTY	US	LST	7190
			( ) JOHNNY BURNETTE SINGS MONO	196	LIBERTY	US	LRP	3190
			( ) BEST OF	19	SUNSET	CAN	SS	4028
			( ) HITS & OTHER FAVOURITES	19	LIBERTY	UK	LBY	1006
			( ) HITS & OTHER FAVOURITES	19	LIBERTY	US	LST	7206
			( ) 10th ANNIVERSARY ALBUM	1974	U A		UAS	29643
			( ) 10th ANNIVERSARY ALBUM	1978	SUNSET		SLS	50413
			( ) STARS OF ROCK'N'ROLL VOL 1	1979	MCA	FR	410	074

B274A   **ROCKY BURNETTE**

ROCKY BURNETTE	V	(A	(A) SON OF ROCK'N'ROLL	1979	EMI	UK	EMC	3323
STEVE DEUTSH	B	(A						
RON COLEMAN	G	(A	RICK CROY	D	(A	BIFF DAWES	B	(A
DAVE EDMUNDS	G	(A	MIKE PORTER	D	(A	BILL HOUSE B PERC	K	(A
JOHN HUNT	G	(A	STEVE TURNER	D	(A	CURTIS STONE	B	(A
BILLY WALKER	G	(A	CHRIS BROSIUS	G V	(A	BILLY BURNETTE	G	(A
JOHN HOBBS	K	(A	RANDY STERN	K	(A	MEL COLLINS	HRNS	(A
DENNIS DREITH	HRNS	(A	JOE RAMANO	HRNS	(A	STANLEY BEHRENS	HCA	(A
JIM SEITER	PERC	(A	BILLY GRAHAM	V	(A			

B275   **BURNIN' RED IVANHOE**

KIM MENZER	WIND VLN	(AC	(A) M144 DBL	1969	SONET	DK	SLPS1512/3	
OLE FICK	G V	(C	(B) KOKSI LADY (EP)	1969	SONET	DK		6092
KARSTEN VOGEL	SAX K	(C	(C) BURNIN' RED IVANHOE	1970	SONET	DK	SLPS	1522
JESS STAEHR	B PERC	(C	(C) BURNIN' RED IVANHOE	1970	WB	UK	K 44062	
BO THRIGE ANDERSEN	D	(C	(C) BURNIN' RED IVANHOE	1970	WB	US		3013
			(D) 6 ELEFANTSKOVCIKADEVISER	1971	SONET	DK	SLPS	1528
			(E) WWW	1971	SONET	DK	ALSP	1530
			(E) WWW	1971	DANDELION	UK	2310	145
			(E) WWW	1980	TELDEC	GERM		
			(F) MILEY SMILE	1972	SONET	DK	SLPA	1540
			(F) MILEY SMILE	1972	TELEFUNKEN	GERM	SLE	14687
			(F) MILEY SMILE	1980	TELDEC			
			(G) RIGHT ON	1974	SONET	DK	SLPS	1549
			(H) BURNIN' LIVE 1970-72 (CASSETTE)	1974	INSTANT		INS	2

B276   **BURNING SPEAR**

WINSTON RODNEY	V PERC	(ABCDEFG	(A) MARCUS GARVEY	1975	ISLAND		ILPS	9377
DELROY HINES	V	(AC	(B) MAN IN THE HILLS	1976	ISLAND		ILPS	9412
RUPERT WILLINGTON	V	(AC	(C) GARVEY'S GHOST	1976	ISLAND/MANGO		ILPS	9382
PHILIP FULLWOOD	CONGA	(E	(D) DRY & HEAVY	1977	ISLAND MANGO		MLPS	9431
GEORGE LEE	SAX	(E	(E) LIVE	1977	ISLAND		ILPS	9513
ANGUS GAYE	D	(E	(E) LIVE	1977	PHONOGRAM	IMP	9101	680
EARL SMITH	G	(ACD	(F) HARDER THAN THE REST	1979	ISLAND		ILPS	9567
BRINSLEY FORDE	G	(E	(G) HAIL H.I.M.	1980	TAMMI		RDC	2003

(CONTINUED)

```
ROBBIE SHAKESPEARE  B    (ACD     COURTNEY HEMMINGS  K     (E     DONALD GRIFFITHS  G     (E
BOBBY ELLIS         TPT  (ACDEG   ASTON BARRETT      PERC B (ACDG   TONY CHIN         G     (AC
GEORGE OBAN         B    (E       TYRONE DOWNIE      K     (ACG    CARLTON SAMUELS   FLT   (AC
LEROY WALLACE       D    (ACD     EGBERT EVANS       HRNS  (G      ROOTS KINSLEY     G     (D
WIRE LINDO          K    (DG      HERMAN MARQUIS     SAX   (ACDG   RANCHIE           G     (D
NELSON MILLER       D    (G       RICHARD HALL       SAX   (ACD    SKULLY            PERC  (D
JUNIOR MARVIN       G    (G       STICKY             PERC  (D      VIN GORDON        TROM  (ACD
BERNARD HARVEY      K    (ACD
```

EDDIE GUITAR BURNS   B277

```
EDDIE GUITAR BURNS  G V  (AB      (A) BOTTLE UP & GO              1972   ACTION      UK  ACMP  100
WITH                              (B) DETROIT BLACKBOTTOM         1975   BIG BEAR    UK  BEAR    7
PAT GROVER          G    (A
BOB HALL            PNO  (AB      ERWIN HELFER   PNO  (A          BOB BRUNNING  B    (A
JOHN HUNT           D    (A       JIMMY JEWELL   SAX  (A          DAVE GELLY    SAX  (A
BOB WILSON          B G  (B       ROGER HILL     G    (B          PETER YORK    D    (B
```

RANDY BURNS   B278

```
RANDY BURNS         V G  (ALL     (A) OF LOVE & WAR              1966   E.S.P.            ESP  1039
WITH                              (B) EVENING OF MAGICIAN        1968   E.S.P.            ESP  1089
BRUCE SAMUELS       V B  (DEF     (C) SONG FOR UNCERTAIN LADY    1970   E.S.P.            ESP  2007
MATT KASTNER        V G K (DEF    (D) SKYDOG BAND                1971   MERCURY           SR 61329
JOHN O'LEARY        D    (D       (E) I'M A LOVER NOT A FOOL     1972   POLYDOR      US   PD 5039
A J MULHERN         V    (DEF     (F) STILL ON OUR FEET          1973   POLYDOR      US   PD 5049
DAVID BROMBERG      G    (D
OZ                  PNO  (D       DAVID MOHN   D PERC V(EF       DAVID TWEEDY  K V  (F
BEN KEITH           STEEL (E
```

JAMES BURTON   B279

```
JAMES BURTON        G V  (AB      (A) GUITAR SOUNDS OF JAMES BURTON   1971  A&M      UK  AMLS64293
RALPH MOONEY             (B       (B) CORN PICKIN' & SLICK SLIDIN     196   CAPITOL  US
```

BUSH   B279A

```
ROY KENNER          CONGAS V(A    (A) BUSH                       1970   PROBE       UK  SPB  1012
DOM TROIANO         G V  (A       (A) BUSH                       1970   DUNHILL     US       50086
PRAKASH JOHN        B V  (A
PENTTI J GLAN       D    (A
```

KATE BUSH   B280

```
KATE BUSH           V K  (AB      (A) THE KICK INSIDE            1978   EMI         UK  EMC  3223
PRESTON HEYMAN      D    (C       (B) LIONHEART                  1978   EMI         UK  EMA   787
DEL PALMER          B    (C       (C) NEVER FOR EVER             1980   emi         UK  EMA   794
BARRY DE SOUZA      D    (A
DAVID PATON         B    (AB      IAN BAIRNSON    G    (ABC      DUNCAN MACKAY   K        (ABC
BRUCE LYNCH         B    (A       PAUL KEOGH      G    (A        ALAN PARKER     G        (A
ANDREW POWELL       K    (AB      ALAN SKIDMORE   SAX  (A        MORRIS PERT     PERC     (AC
PADDY BUSH  V HCA MAND   (AB      CHARLIE MORGAN  D    (B        BRIAN BATH      G        (BC
DEL PALMER          B    (B       FRANCIS MONKMAN K    (B        RICHARD HARVEY  RECORDER (B
STUART ELLIOTT      D    (ABC     JOHN GIBLIN     B    (C        MAX MIDDLETON   K        (C
ALAN MURPHY         G    (C       GARY HURST      V    (C        ANDREW BRYANT   V        (C
MIKE MORAN          K    (C       ROY HARPER      V    (C        ROLAND          PERC     (C
MARTYN FORD ORCH         (C       ADAM SKEAPING   VLA  (C        JO SKEAPING     LIRONI(C
```

JERRY BUTLER   B281

```
JERRY BUTLER        V    (ALL
WITH                              HE WILL BREAK YOUR HEART     1963 STATESIDE    UK SL 10032
BETTY EVERETT       V    (*       HE WILL BREAK YOUR HEART     1963 VEE JAY      US    1029
THELMA HOUSTON      V    (+       FOLK SONGS                   1963 STATESIDE    UK SL 10050
                                  FOLK SONGS                   1963 VEE JAY      US    1057
                                  THEY'RE DELICIOUS TOGETHER19      VEE JAY      US    1099
                                  THEY'RE DELICIOUS TOGETHER19      JOY          JOYS 123
                                  ALL TIME HITE                19   TRIP         US    8011
                                  16 GREATEST HITS             19   TRIP         US TOP16-45
                                  JUST BEAUTIFUL               19   KENT         US     536
                                  STARRING BETTY EVERETT (*)19      TRADITION US  2073
                                  FOR YOUR PRECIOUS LOVE       19   JOY          JOY  104
                                  LOVE ME                      19   JOY          JOS  126
                                  VERY BEST OF                 19   UA           US UASLA498
                                  SUITE FOR A SINGLE GIRL      19   TAMLA        UK STML12052
                                  SUITE FOR A SINGLE GIRL      19   MOTOWN       US   M7878
                                  IT ALL COMES OUT             19   TAMLA        UK STML12073
                                  IT ALL COMES OUT             19   MOTOWN       US   M7892
                                  LOVE'S ON THE MENU           1976 TAMLA        UK STML12032
                                  LOVE'S ON THE MENU           1976 MOTOWN       US   M7850
                                  THELMA HOUSTON & JERRY (+)197     MOTOWN       US   M7887
                                  THELMA HOUSTON & JERRY (+)197     PATHE        FRC066 9911Z
                                  SPICE OF LIFE                1972 MERCURY      6338 102
                                  BEST OF                      1972 MERCURY      6430 401
                                  BEST OF                      1972 MERCURY           61281
                                  THE SOUL GOES ON             19   MERCURY      US SR 61171
                                  THE SAGITTARIUS MOVEMENT     19   MERCURY      US SR 61347
                                  MAKE IT EASY ON YOURSELF     1976 DJM          DJD 28027
                                  NOTHING SAYS I LOVE YOU      1978 PHILADELPHIA PIR83810
                                  NOTHING SAYS I LOVE YOU      1978 PHIL LA      US   35510
                                  THEMLA HOUSTON & JERRY       1977 MOTOWN       UK STML12063
                                  TWO TO ONE                   1978 MOTOWN       UK STML12092
```

B282 — PAUL BUTTERFIELD & THE BUTTERFIELD BLUES BAND

Name	Instr	Group
PAUL BUTTERFIELD	V HCA	(ALL
SAM LAY	D	(AB
JERONE ARNOLD	B	(ABC
SMOKEY SMOTHERS	G	(A
ELVIN BISHOP	G	(BCDE
MIKE BLOOMFIELD	G	(BC
MARK NAFTALIN	K	(BCDE
BILLY DAVENPORT	D	(C
BUGSY MAUGH	B	(DE
PHIL WILSON	D	(DEF
DAVE SANBORN	SAX	(DEFGHJ
KEITH JOHNSON	TPT	(DEF
GENE DINWIDDIE	SAX	(DEFGHJ
STEVE MADAIO	TPT	(FGH
BUZZY FEITEN	G V K	(F
ROD HICKS	V B	(FG
BIG BLACK	V PERC	(H
RALPH WASH	V G	(GH
DENNIS WHITTED	D	(HJ
BOBBYE HALL	PERC	(H
GEORGE DAVIDSON	D	(GH
TREVOR LAWRENCE	SAX	(FH
TED HARRIS	PNO	(FGH
RONNIE BARRON	K V	(JK
BOBBY CHARLES	V	(JK
GEOFF MULDAUR	V G VIBES	(JK
AMOS GARRETT	G	(JK
CHRISTOPHER PARKER	D	(JK
MARIA MULDAUR	V	(JK
BILLY RICH	B	(JK
PETE ECKLUND	TPT	(J
VANETTA FIELDS	V	(GH
GARY BROCKS	TROM	(J
FRED BECKMAIER	B	(F
HOWARD JOHNSON	HRNS	(JK
AL KOOPER	ORG	(E
OMA DRAKE	V	(GH
JERRY RAGOVOY	PNO	(F
J D PARRAN	SAX	(J
SAM BURTIS	TROM	(J
CLYDIE KING	V	(GH
MERRY CLAYTON	V	(GH
STAN SHAFRAN	TPT	(J

	Title		Year	Label	Country	Cat
(A)	OFFER YOU CANT REFUSE(1SIDE 1963)		1972	RED LIGHTNIN		R 008
(B)	BUTTERFIELD BLUES BAND		1965	ELEKTRA	US	EKS 7294
(B)	BUTTERFIELD BLUES BAND		1965	ELEKTRA	UK	K 42004
(B)	BUTTERFIELD BLUES BAND		1975	MIDI		22004
(C)	EAST WEST		1866	ELEKTRA	US	EKS 7315
(C)	EAST WEST		197	ELEKTRA	UK	K 42006
(D)	RESURRECTION OF PIGBOY CRABSHAW		1967	ELEKTRA	US	EKS 4015
(D)	RESURRECTION OF PIGBOY CRABSHAW		19	ELEKTRA		EKS 74015
(D)	RESURRECTION OF PIGBOY CRABSHAW		1971	ELEKTRA	UK	K 42017
(E)	IN MY OWN DREAM		1968	ELEKTRA	US	EKS 4025
(E)	IN MY OWN DREAM		1976	ELEKTRA	UK	K 42042
(F)	KEEP ON MOVING		1969	ELEKTRA	US	EKS 74053
(F)	KEEP ON MOVING		1971	ELEKTRA	UK	K 42033
(G)	LIVE		1970	ELEKTRA	US	7E 2001
(G)	LIVE		1976	ELEKTRA	UK	K 62001
(H)	SOMETIMES I JUST FEEL LIKE SMILIN'		1971	ELEKTRA	US	EKS 75013
(H)	SOMETIMES I JUST FEEL LIKE SMILIN'		1971	ELEKTRA	UK	K 42095
(J)	BETTER DAYS		1973	BEARSVILLE	US	BR 2119
(J)	BETTER DAYS		1973	BEARSVILLE	UK	K 45515
(K)	IT ALL COMES BACK		1974	BEARSVILLE	US	BR 2170
(K)	IT ALL COMES BACK		1974	BEARSVILLE	UK	K 45517
(L)	PUT IT IN YOUR EAR		1976	BEARSVILLE	US	BR 6960
(L)	PUT IT IN YOUR EAR		1976	BEARSVILLE	UK	K 55509
(M)	WHATS SHAKIN'		19	ELEKTRA	US	EKS 4002
(N)	GOLDEN BUTTER	(BEST OF)	1972	ELEKTRA	US	7E 2005
(N)	GOLDEN BUTTER	(BEST OF)	1972	ELEKTRA	UK	K 62011
(EP)	WITH JOHN MAYALL		196	DECCA	UK	DFE 8673

B283 — THE BUTTS BAND

Name	Instr	Group
JOHN DENSMORE	D	(AB
BOBBY KRIEGER	G	(AB
JESS RODEN	V G	(A
PHIL CHEN	B	(A
ROY DAVIES	K	(A
ALLAN SHARP	CONGA	(A
MICK WEAVER	K	(A
ALEX BERKOWITZ	D	(A
BOBBYE HALL	CONGAS	(B
LARRY McDONALD	CONGA	(A
KARL RUCKER	B	(B
MICHAEL STULL	V G	(B
ALEX RICHMAN	V K	(B

	Title	Year	Label	Country	Cat
(A)	THE BUTTS BAND	1974	BLUE THUMB	UK	ILPS 9260
(A)	THE BUTTS BAND	1974	BLUE THUMB	US	BTY 28011
(B)	HEAR & NOW	1975	ABC		ABCL 5117
(B)	HEAR & NOW	1975	VOGUE	FR	10042
(B)	HEAR & NOW	1975	BLUE THUMB	US	BT 6018

B284 — BUZZCOCKS

Name	Instr	Group
HOWARD DEVOTO	V	(1
PETE SHELLEY	G V	(AB1
STEVE DIGGLE	B G	(AB
STEVE GARVEY	B	(AB
GARTH SMITH	B	(B
JOHN MAHER	D	(AB1

	Title		Year	Label	Country	Cat
(1)	SPIRAL SCRATCH	(EP)	1977	NEW HORMONES	UK	ORG 1
(A)	ANOTHER MUSIC IN A DIFFERENT KITCHEN		1977	UA	UK	UAG 30519
(B)	LOVE BITES		1978	UA	UK	UAG 30197
(B)	LOVE BITES		1978	SONOPRESSE	FR	062 61897
(C)	DIFFERENT KINDS OF TENSION		1979	UA	UK	UAG 30260
(D)	SINGLES GOING STEADY		1979	UA	UK	UAG 30279

B285 — BYRDS

Name	Instr	Group
ROGER McGUINN	V G BANJO	(ALL
GENE CLARK	G V	(ABCDOP
MIKE CLARKE	D	(BCDEFGOP
CHRIS HILLMAN	B V MAND	(BCDEFGHOP
DAVID CROSBY	G V	(ABCDEOP
KEVIN KELLEY	D	(HP
GRAM PARSONS	G V	(HP
SNEAKY PETE KLEINOW	STEEL	(M
DOUG DILLARD	G V	(
CLARENCE WHITE	G V	(HJKLMNP
JOHN YORK	B	(JKP
SKIP BATTIN	B	(LMNP
GENE PARSONS	D	(JKLMNP
JOHN GUERIN		(
EARL P BALL	PNO	(H
JIMMI SEITER	PERC	(M
PAUL POLENA	HRNS STRGS	(M
BYRON BERLINE	FDL	(M
LARRY KNECHTEL	K	(M
TERRY MELCHER	PNO	(M
JON CORNEAL	D	(H
LLOYD GREEN	STEEL	(H
JAYDEE MANESS	STEEL	(H
JOHN HARTFORD	BANJ G	(H
ROY M HUSKEY	B	(H

	Title		Year	Label	Country	Cat
(A)	EARLY FLIGHT	(JET SET)	19	CBS		ST 1014
(A)	EARLY FLIGHT	(JET SET)	19	TOGETHER		SST 1001
(B)	PREFLYTE		1964	BUMBLE	US	GEXP 8001
(B)	PREFLYTE		19	CBS		KC 32183
(B)	PREFLYTE		19	ARIOLA	HOLL	86468
(C)	MR TAMBOURINE MAN		1965	CBS	UK	62571
(C)	MR TAMBOURINE MAN		1965	CBS	US	CS 9172
(C)	MR TAMBOURINE MAN		19	EMBASSY		31057
(C)	MR TAMBOURINE MAN		19	EMBASSY		31503
(D)	TURN TURN TURN		1966	CBS	UK	62652
(D)	TURN TURN TURN		1966	CBS	US	CS 9254
(D)	TURN TURN TURN		19	EMBASSY		31526
(D)	TURN TURN TURN		19	EMBASSY		31257
(CD)	MR TAMBOURINE/TURN TURN TURN		19	CBS		22018X2
(E)	FIFTH DIMENSION		1966	CBS	UK	62783
(E)	FIFTH DIMENSION		1966	CBS	US	9349
(F)	YOUNGER THAN YESTERDAY		1967	CBS	UK	62988
(F)	YOUNGER THAN YESTERDAY		1967	CBS	US	CS 9442
( )	GREATEST HITS		1967	CBS	UK	63107
( )	GREATEST HITS		196	CBS	IMP	66298
(G)	NOTORIOUS BYRD BROTHERS		1968	CBS	UK	63169
(G)	NOTORIOUS BYRD BROTHERS		1968	CBS	US	CS 9575
(H)	SWEETHEART OF THE RODEO		1968	CBS	UK	63353
(H)	SWEETHEART OF THE RODEO		1968	CBS	US	CS 9670
(H)	SWEETHEART OF THE RODEO		19	EMBASSY		EMB 31124
(GH)	SWEETHEART / NOTORIOUS BYRD BROS		1976	CBS		22040
(J)	DR BYRDS & MR HYDE		1969	CBS	UK	63545
(J)	DR BYRDS & MR HYDE		1969	CBS	US	CS 9755
(K)	BALLAD OF EASY RIDER		1970	CBS	UK	63795
(K)	BALLAD OF EASY RIDER		1970	CBS	US	CS 9942
(L)	UNTITLED	(DBL)	1970	CBS	UK	66253
(L)	UNTITLED	(DBL)	1970	CBS	US	G 30127
(M)	BYRDMANIAX		1971	CBS	UK	64389
(M)	BYRDMANIAX		1971	CBS	US	KC 30640

(CONTINUED)

BYRDS
B285

Album		Year	Label	Country	Cat. No.
(N) FARTHER ALONG		1972	CBS	UK	KC 64676
(N) FARTHER ALONG		1972	CBS	US	KC 31050
( ) GREATEST HITS	VOL 2	1972	CBS	UK	64650
( ) GREATEST HITS	VOL 2	1972	CBS	US	PC 31795
(O) THE BYRDS		1973	ASYLUM	UK	SYLA 8754
(O) THE BYRDS		1973	ASYLUM	US	SD 5058
(O) THE BYRDS		19	WEA		K 53006
( ) HISTORY OF THE BYRDS		1973	CBS	UK	68242
( ) L A FULL CIRCLE		19	WEA	HOLL	23000
( ) L A FULL CIRCLE		19	MERCURY	US	SRM 11074
( ) GREATEST HITS	VOL 3	19	CBS	UK	64966
( ) MR TAMBOURINE MAN(COMP DBL)		19	CBS	UK	66298
( ) SINGLES 1965 67		1980	CBS		31851
(P) PLAY DYLAN		1980	CBS	UK	31795

DAVID BYRON
B286

DAVID BYRON	V	(AB	
LOU STONEBRIDGE	K	(A	
DENNY BALL	B	(A	
LEE KERSLAKE	D PERC	(A	
PETE THOMPSON	PERC	(A	
LESTER FRY	PERC	(B	

Album		Year	Label	Country	Cat. No.
(A) TAKE NO PRISONERS		1975	BRONZE	UK	ILPS 9342
(B) BABY FACED KILLER		1978	ARISTA	UK	SPARTA 1077

STUART ELLIOTT	D	(B	BARRY DE SOUZA	D	(B
ALAN JONES	B	(B	DANIEL BOONE	G K	(B

BYSTANDERS
B287

VIC OAKLEY	V	(1	
RAY WILLIAMS	B	(1	
JEFF JONES	D	(1	

(1) 1968

CLIVE JOHN	K V	(1	MICKEY JONES	G V	(1

BYZANTIUM
B288

NICO RAMSDEN	G V	(A	
CHAS JANKEL	G V	(AB	
ROBIN LAMBLE	B V G	(AB	
STEVE CORDUNER	D	(AB	
DAVID HENTSCHEL	SYN	(B	
ROBIN SYLVESTER	SYN	(B	

Album	Year	Label	Cat. No.
(A) BYZANTIUM	1972	A&M	AMLS89104
(B) SEASONS CHANGING	1973	A&M	AMLH68163

MICK BARAKAN	G V	(B	FRANK RICOTTI	PERC	(B
JAMIE RUBINSTEIN	G V	(B	B J COLE	STEEL	(B

ROY C
C1

ROY C	V	'A

Album	Year	Label	Cat. No.
(A) SEX & SOUL	1975	MERCURY	9100 017

C C P P
C1A

A CECCARELLI	D	(
M CHANTEREAU	PNO	(
C PADOVAN	B	(

Album	Year	Label	Cat. No.
(A) C.C.P.P.	19	FLAMOPHONE	2933 104

SLIM PEZIN   G   (

C C S
C2

ALEXIS KORNER	G V	(ALL
LES CONDON	TPT	(D
PETER THORUP	V	(D
GREG BOWEN	TPT	(D
HAROLD BECKETT	TPT	(D
HENRY LOWTHER	TPT	(D
KENNY WHEELER	TPT	(D
DON LUSHER	TROM	(D
HAROLD McNAIR	WIND	(D
DANNY MOSS	WIND	(D
ALAN PARKER	G	(D
BARRY MORGAN	D	(D
BILL LE SAGE	VIBES	(D

Album	Year	Label	Country	Cat. No.
(A) C C S	1970	RAK	UK	SRKA 6751
(A) C C S	19	RAK	US	SR Z30559
(B) C C S 2	1972	RAK	UK	SRAK 503
(C) THE BEST BAND IN THE LAND	1973	RAK	UK	SRAK 504
(D) THE BEST OF C C S	1977	RAK	UK	SRAK 527

JOHN MARSHALL	TROM	(D	BRIAN PERRIN	TROM	(D
BILL GELDARD	TROM	(D	NEIL SANDERS	HRNS	(D
TONY COE	WIND	(D	PETE KING	WIND	(D
BOB EFFORD	WIND	(D	RON MOSS	WIND	(D
HERBIE FLOWERS	B	(D	SPIKE HEATLEY	B	(D
TONY CARR	D	(D	JIM LAWLESS	PERC	(D
TONY FISHER	TPT	(D			

C M U
C3

LARRAINE ODELL	V	(A
RICHARD JOSEPH	V G	(A
IAN HAMLETT	G	(A

Album	Year	Label	Cat. No.
(A) SPACE CABARET	1972	TRANSATLANTIC	TRA 259

LEARY HASSON	K	(A	ROGER ODELL	D	(A

C O B
C4

CLIVE PALMER BANJO V G		(AB
JOHN BIDWELL BANJO K V		(AB
MICK BENNETT PERC V K		(AB
RALPH McTELL	G D	(A
GENEVIEVE BAKER		(B

Album	Year	Label	Cat. No.
(A) THE SPIRIT OF LOVE	1971	CBS	69010
(B) MOYSHE McSTIFF	1972	POLYDOR	2383 161

STEVE BONNETT	B	(A	URSULA SMITH	CELLO	(A
DEMELZA VAL BAKER		(B			

CABOOSE
C4A

GARY JOHNS	V	(A
WALTER RAMSEY	K	(A
TOMMY CATHEY	B V	(A
PAT KARR	V	(A

Album	Year	Label	Country	Cat. No.
(A) CABOOSE	19	ENTERPRISE	US	ENS 1015

JACKIE COOK	G	(A	JOEL WILLIAMS	PERC	(A

CACTUS
C5

RUSTY DAY	V	(ABC
JIM McCARTY	G	(ABC
TIM BOGERT	B	(ABCD
CARMINE APPICE	D	(ABCD
PETER FRENCH	V	(D
DUANE HITCHINGS	K	(D
WERNER FRITZSCHINGS	G	(D

Album	Year	Label	Country	Cat. No.
(A) CACTUS	1970	ATLANTIC	UK	2400 020
(A) CACTUS	1970	ATCO	US	SD 33340
(B) ONE WAY OR ANOTHER	1971	ATLANTIC	UK	2460 114
(B) ONE WAY OR ANOTHER	1971	ATCO	US	33340
(B) ONE WAY OR ANOTHER	1972	ATLANTIC	UK	K 40216
(C) RESTRICTIONS	1972	ATLANTIC	UK	K40307
(C) RESTRICTIONS	1972	ATCO	US	SD 33577
(D) 'OT & SWEATY	1972	ATLANTIC	UK	K 50013
(D) 'OT & SWEATY	1972	ATCO	US	SD 7011

VINCE CADILLAC
C6

VINCE CADILLAC	G V	(A
TIGGER LYONS	B	(A
TIM FRANKS	D	(A
TONY TODD	G	(A
PAUL JENKINS	G	(A
PETE WINGFIELD	K V	(A
PETER LEMER	PNO	(A

Album	Year	Label	Country	Cat. No.
(A) MODERN BOY	1978	SATRIL	UI	SATL 4010

DAVE EPPEL	G	(A	LARRY BARTLETT	K	(A
MIKE SMITH	V	(A	JOHN PORTER	V	(A
PAUL WESTWOOD	B	(A	RICK HITCHCOCK	G	(A
BARRY MORGAN	D	(A	BARRY DE SOUZA	D	(A

C7
```
COLIN TULLY          SAX   (BA
DAVY ROY             D     (AB
STUART MACKILLOP     K     (AB
GAVIN HODGSON        B     (AB
PADDY McHUGH         V     (A
```

CADO BELLE
```
(A) CADO BELLE                      1976   ANCHOR      UK    ANCL 2015
(B) CADO BELLE    (EP)              1977   ANCHOR      UK      AN  1

MAGGIE REILLY        V     (AB    ALAN DARBY      G     (AB
FRANK COLLINS        V     (A
```

C8
```
CHRISTOPHER THOMPSON G V   (B
PHIL COLLINS         D     (B
MICHAEL OGLETREE     D G   (B
COLIN NELSON         B     (B
PETER VEITCH         K     (B
```

CAFE JACQUES
```
(A) ROUND THE BACK                  1977   EPIC        UK       82315
(A) ROUND THE BACK                  1977   CBS         US   JC  35294
(C) CAFE JACQUES INTERNATIONAL      1978   EPIC             83042

GEOFFREY RICHARDSON G FLT   (B    JOHN PERRY      B     (A
```

C9
```
RAPHAEL DOYLE        G V       (A
HEREWARD KAYE    V PNO G       (A
TOM ROBINSON     V B G NPO     (A
JOHN BEECHAM         HRNS      (A
NICK SOUTH           B         (A
LOUIS STEWART        G         (A
```

CAFE SOCIETY
```
(A) CAFE SOCIETY                    1975   KONK             KONK  102

JOHN GOSLING         K     (A    MICK AVORY      D     (A
JIM FRANKS           D     (A    ROBIN WILLIAMS  FDL   (A
PHIL PALMER          G     (A    PAT DONALDSON   B     (A
ROY DYKE             D     (A
```

C10
```
ALLAN TAYLOR         G V   (A
JOHN GILLASPIE       K WIND(AB
BRIAN GOLBEY         FDL G (AB
DIK CADBURY          G V   (B
```

CAJUN MOON
```
(A) CAJUN MOON                      1976   CHRYSALIS   UK    CHR  1116
(B) LATER LINE UP
```

C11
```
BARBARA MORILLO      V     (AB
JANETTE JACOBS       V     (AB
ELEANOR BAROOSHIAN   V     (AB
WITH
DR JOHN              PNO   (
DAVID COHEN          G     (
LESLIE MILTON        D     (
```

CAKE
```
(A) CAKE                            1967   DECCA            DL  74927
(A) CAKE                            1968   MCA              MUPS  303
(B) A SLICE OF CAKE                 1968   DECCA            DL  75039
(B) A SLICE OF CAKE                 1969   MCA              MUPS  390

MIKE DEASY           G     (    CAROL KAYE      B     (
MIKE MELVOIN         ORG   (
```

C11A
```
JOHN ATKINS          SYN K (A
TOBY SAKS            CELLO (A
```

CALDARA
```
(A) A MOOG MASS                     197    KAMA SUTRA       2319  020
```

C11B
```
JORGE CALDERON       V G   (A
WADDY WACHTEL    V G K     (A
HOPPY HODGES         D     (A
PAT RIZZO            HRNS   (A
TESSE COEN          PERC V (A
JAMES GADSON         D     (A
RUSS TITELMAN       PERC   (A
BOBBY LYLE           K     (A
BOBBYE HALL         PERC   (A
```

JORGE CALDERON
```
(A) CITY MUSIC                      1975   WB          US    BS  2904

WILLIE WEEKS         B     (A    MAYUTO         PERC  (A
STEVE MADAIO        HRNS   (A    WILLIAM SMITH  V K   (A
YVONNE RANKIN        V     (A    ANDY NEWMARK    D    (A
VICTOR FELDMAN      PERC   (A    PAUL PAYDOS    PERC  (A
VALERIE CARTER       V     (A    PAUL STALLWORTH V    (A
JIM KELTNER          D     (A    NICK DE CARO   SYN   (A
```

C12
```
BOBBY CALDWELL B G K SYN V(AB
WITH
ED GREENE            D
HAROLD SEAY          D     (A
STEVE MEALY          G     (A
RICHIE VELASQUEZ     B     (A
```

BOBBY CALDWELL
```
(A) BOBBY CALDWELL                  1978   CLOUDS              8804
(A) BOBBY CALDWELL                  1978   TKR (CBS)           83362

JOE GALDO            D     (A    BENNY LATIMORE  K    (A
ALFONS KETTNER       G     (A    GEORGE PERRY    B    (A
```

C13
```
JOHN CALE            G K B V(ALL
WITH
TERRY RILEY      SAX K     (B
PHIL MANZANERA       G     (EF
BRIAN ENO            K     (EFGJ
NICO                 V     (J
CHRIS SPEDDING       G     (FG
TIM DONALD           D     (FG
PAT DONALDSON        B     (FG
CHRIS THOMAS         K     (F
GERRY CONWAY         D     (F
GEOFF MULDAUR        V     (F
PHIL COLLINS         D     (G
OLLIE HALSALL        G     (J
JOHN RABBIT BUNDRICK K     (J
ADAM MILLER          V     (B
ARCHIE LEGGET        B     (EJ
ROBERT WYATT        PERC   (J
DOREEN CHANTER       V     (EJ
BRIAN TURRINGTON     B     (E
JUDY NYLON           V     (E
```

JOHN CALE
```
(A) VINTAGE VIOLENCE                1970   CBS              64256
(A) VINTAGE VIOLENCE                1970   CBS         US   CS   1037
(B) CHURCH OF ANTHRAX               1971   CBS         UK       64259
(B) CHURCH OF ANTHRAX               1971   CBS         US   CS  30131
(C) ACADEMY OF PERIL                1972   REPRISE     UK    K 44212
(B) ACADEMY OF PERIL                1972   REPRISE     US   MS  2079
(D) PARIS 1919                      1973   REPRISE     UK    K 44239
(D) PARIS 1919                      1973   REPISE      US   MS  2131
(E) FEAR                            1974   ISLAND      UK   ILPS 9301
(F) SLOW DAZZLE                     1975   ISLAND      UK   ILPS 9317
(G) HELEN OF TROY                   1975   ISLAND      UK   ILPS 9350
(G) HELEN OF TROY                   1975   PHONOGRAM   EUR  9123  002
(H) GUTS                            1977   PHONOGRAM   EUR  9101  672
(H) GUTS                            1977   ISLAND      UK   ILPS 9459
(J) JUNE 1 1974 (NICO ENO KEVIN AYERS)1974  ISLAND     UK   ILPS 9291

KEVIN AYERS          B     (J    EDDIE SPARROW   D    (J
LIZA STRIKE          V     (EJ   IRENE CHANTER   V    (EJ
MIKE OLDFIELD        G     (J    RICHARD THOMPSON G   (E
BOBBY COLOMBY        D     (B    BRYN HAWORTH    G    (E
MICHAEL DESMARAIS    D     (E
```

C14
```
J J CALE   PNO B D G V     (ALL
WITH
KARL HIMMEL          D     (ACDE
CHUCK BROWNING       G D   (AD
TIM DRUMMOND         D     (AC
CARL RADLE           B     (AE
NORBERT PUTNAM       B     (AB
BOB WILSON           PNO   (A
DAVID BRIGGS         K     (ABE
JERRY WHITEHURST     K     (AC
WELDON MYRICK        STEEL (AC
BUDDY SPICHER        FDL   (A
```

J J CALE
```
(A) NATURALLY                       1971   A&M         UK   AMLS68105
(A) NATURALLY                       1973   SHELTER     UK   ISA  5003
(A) NATURALLY                       197    CAPITOL     US        8508
(A) NATURALLY                       197    CARRERE     FR       67614
(A) NATURALLY                       197    SHELTER     US       52009
(B) REALLY                          1972   A&M         UK   AMLS68157
(B) REALLY                          197    SHELTER     UK   ISA  5002
(B) REALLY                          197    SHELTER     US       52015
(B) REALLY                          197    CARRERE     FR       67613
(C) OKIE                            197    A&M         UK   AMLS68261
(C) OKIE                            1974   SHELTER     UK   ISA  5004
(C) OKIE                            197    SHELTER     US       52015
                                                       (CONTINUED)
```

[64]

J J CALE — C14

SHORTY LAVENDER	FDL	(A			197	CARRERE	FR	67608
WALTER HAYES	DOBRO	(A			1976	SHELTER	UK	ISA 5011
MAC GAYDEN	G	(ABC			1976	CARRERE	FR	67618
ED COLIS	HCA	(A			1976	SHELTER	US	52002
DIANE DAVIDSON	V	(A			1979	SHELTER	UK	ISA 5018
ROGER HAWKINS	D	(B						
DAVID HOOD	B	(B						
BARRY BECKETT	K	(B	BILL KENNER	MAND	(E	PAUL DAVIS	G	(C
DON SHEFFIELD	TPT	(BE	JIMMY JOHNSON	G	(B	JOAN SWEENEY	V	(B
NORM RAY	SAX	(B	BOB PHILLIPS	TPT	(B	BILL HUMBLE	TROM	(B
KENNY BUTTREY	D	(BDE	FARRELL MORRIS	D VIBES	(BCDE	BOBBY WOODS	K	(BD
ROBERT TARRANT	PERC	(B	GEORGE SOULE	D	(B	BOB RAY	B	(B
JOE ZINKAN	B	(B	JIMMY CAPPS	G	(B	KOSSIE GARDNER	ORG	(B
CHARLIE McCOY	HCA	(B	JOSH GRAVES	DOBRO	(B	VASSAR CLEMENTS	FDL	(B
BILL BOATMAN	G	(BDE	JIMMY KARSTEIN	D	(BDE	GARY GILMORE	B	(B
LLOYD GREEN	STEEL	(D	CHARLES DUNGEY	B	(D	REG YOUNG	G	(CD
JOE OSBORN	B	(D	TOMMY COGBILL	B	(CD	HAROLD BRADLEY	G	(CD
BUDDY HARMON	D	(DE	AUDIE ASHWORTH	PERC	(D	DON TWEEDY	K	(D
J J ALLISON	PERC	(D	BUDDY EMMONS	STEEL	(D	BILL RAFFENSPEGER	B	(D
DENNIS GOODE	TROM	(CDE	GORDON PAYNE	G	(D	GEORGE TIDWELL	TPT	(CDE
GARY PAXTON	V	(D	BILLY PUETT	SAX	(CD	KENNY MALONE	D	(CD
RED SPIVEY	K	(C	BILL PURCELL	K	(D	MIKE LEECH	B	(C
JERRY SMITH	K	(C	BEEGIE CRUZER	K	(C	JOEL GREEN	B	(C
TERRY PERKINS	D	(C	GRADY MARTIN	G	(C	PIG ROBBINS	K	(C
SHERRY PORTER	V	(E	BILLY COX	B	(E	CHRISTINE LAKELAND	K V	(E
NICK RATHER	B	(E	STRING SECTION		(E	TERRY WILLIAMS	HRNS	(E
			LARRY BELL	K	(E			

CALICO — C15

JERRY OATES	G V	(	(A) CALICO		19	UA	US	UALA 454
KEITH IMPELLITIER	G V	(	(B) CALICO 2		19	SONOPRESSE	FR	UALA 659
BULL MINOR	D V	(						
TOM MORREL	STEEL	(	JOHN McCLURE	K	(	MIKE REDEN	D	(
DAVE KIRBY	G	(						

RANDY CALIFORNIA — C15A

RANDY CALIFORNIA	G V	(A	(A) KAPTAIN KOPTER & THE TWIRLY BIRDS 1972 EPIC UK EPC 65381
CHARLY BUNDY	B	(A	
TIM McGOVERN	D	(A	ED(CASS STRANGE)CASSIDY D (A NOEL(CLIT McTORIUS)REDDING B (A
LARRY KNIGHT	B	(A	MITCH(HENRY MANCHOVITZ)MITCHELL D(A

MISSISSIPPI JOE CALLICOTT — C16

MISSISSIPPI JOE CALLICOTT (	( ) PRESENTING THE COUNTRY BLUES	19 BLUE HORIZON 8 63227

TERRY CALLIER — C17

TERRY CALLIER			(F) FIRE ON ICE	1978	ELEKTRA	UK	K 52096
MINNIE RIPERTON	V	(F	(F) FIRE ON ICE	19	ELEKTRA	US	6E 143
SIDNEY BARNES	V	(F	( ) I JUST CANT HELP MYSELF	19	CADET	US	50041
JYNEAN BELL	V	(F	( ) OCCASIONAL RAIN	19	CADET	US	50007
ELLIE WILLIS	V	(F	( ) WHAT COLOUR IS LOVE	19	CADET	US	50019
CYNTHIA WHITE	V	(F	( ) TURN YOU TO LOVE	1979	ELEKTRA	UK	K 52140
PHIL UPCHURCH	G	(F					
CHARLES FEARING	G	(F	LARRY WADE	G	(F	EDDIE HARRIS	SAX	(F
FRED JACKSON	SAX	(F	CHARLES OWEN	SAX	(F	CORINNE ALBRIGHT	SAX	(F
GARNETT BROWN	TROM	(F	GEORGE BOHANON	TROM	(F	JIMMY CLEVELAND	TROM	(F
PAUL SERRANO	TPT	(F	KENNETH MASON	TPT	(F	EUGENE YOUNG	TPT	(F
REGINALD BURKE	K	(F	MICHAEL BODDICKER	SYN	(F	SCOTT EDWARDS	B	(F
PAUL N HUMPHREY	D	(F	JAMES GADSON	D	(F	FRED WALKER	PERC	(F
MORRIS JENNINGS	PERC	(F'	STRINGS		(F	W ROSS TRAUT	G	(F
DANNY LEAKE	G	(F						

ROBERT CALVERT — C18

ROBERT CALVERT	PERC V TPT	(AB	(A) CAPTAIN LOCKHEED & THE STARFIGHTERS 74	UA		UK	UAG 29507
PAUL RUDOLPH	B G	(AB	(B) LUCKY LEIF & THE LONGSHIPS	1975 UA		UK	UAG 29852
SIMON KING	D	(A					
NIK TURNER	SAX	(A	LEMMY	G B	(A	ANDY ROBERTS	G	(B
DEL DETTMAR	SYN	(A	DAVE BROCK	G	(A	TWINK	D	(A
ARTHUR BROWN	V	(A	ADRIAN WAGNER	K	(A	VIV STANSHALL	V	(A
JIM CAPALDI	V	(A	TOM MITTELDORF	V	(A	RICHARD EALING	V	(A
SIMON HOUSE	VLN	(B	MIKE NICHOLS	D PERC	(B	MICHAEL MOORCOCK	BANJO	(A
SAL MAIDA	B	(B	BRIAN TURRINGTON	PNO	(			

CAMEL — C19

PETER BARDENS	K	(ABCDEFG	(A) CAMEL	1973	MCA		MAPS 6477
ANDY LATIMER	V G FLT	(ABCDEFGHJ	(A) CAMEL	1973	MCA		MUPS 473
DOUG FERGUSON	B	(ABCDF	(A) CAMEL	1974	MCA		MCF 2665
ANDY WARD	D PERC	(ABCDEFGHJ	(B) MIRAGE	1974	DERAM	UK	SML 1107
RICHARD SINCLAIR	B V	(EFG	(B) MIRAGE	1974	DECCA		278135
COLIN BASS	B V	(HJ	(B) MIRAGE	19	JANUS	US	7009
MEL COLLINS	SAX	(FGHJ	(C) SNOW GOOSE	1975	DERAM	UK	SKLR 5207
DUNCAN MACKAY	K	(J	(C) SNOW GOOSE	1975	DECCA		278136
JAN SCHELHAAS	PNO	(JH	(C) SNOW GOOSE	1975	JANUS	US	7016
CHRIS GREEN	CELLO	(J	(D) MOONMADNESS	1976	DERAM	UK	TXSR 115
GASPAR LAWAL	PERC	(J	(D) MOONMADNESS	1976	DECCA		278115
HERBIE FLOWERS	TUBA	(J	(D) MOONMADNESS	1976	JANUS	US	7024
KIT WATKINS	K FLT	(H	(E) RAIN DANCE	1977	GAMA	UK	TXSR 124
PHIL COLLINS	PERC	(H	(E) RAINDANCE	1977	DECCA		260015
RUPERT HINE	V	(H	(F) A LIVE RECORD	1978	DECCA	UK	DBCR 7/8
			(G) BREATHLESS	1978	DECCA	UK	TXSR 132
			(H) I CAN SEE YOUR HOUSE FROM HERE	1979	DECCA	UK	TXSR 137
			(J) NUDE	1981	DECCA	UK	SKL 5323

C20 — CAMEO

LARRY BLACKMON	D	(BC	(A) CARDIAC ARREST			1977	CASABLANCA	CAL	2015
GREGORY JOHNSON	K V	(BC	(B) WE ALL KNOW WHO WE ARE			1978	CASABLANCA	CAL	2026
TOMI JENKINS	V	(BC	(C) UGLY EGO			1978	CASABLANCA	CAL	2038
NATHAN LEFTENANT	TPT	(BC	(D) SECRET OMEN			1979	CASABLANCA	CAL	2058
CHARLES SAMBOW	G	(B							
ARNETT LEFTENANT	SAX	(BC	ERIC DURHAM	G	(BC	WAYNE COOPER		V	(BC
GARY DOW	B	(BC	ANTHONY COCKETT		(C				

C21 — JOHN CAMERON

JOHN CAMERON	PNO	(AB	(A) COVER LOVER	1967	COLUMBIA	UK	SCX 6116
DANNY THOMPSON	B	(B	(B) OFF CENTRE	1969	DERAM	UK	SML 1044
TONY CARR	D	(B					
HAROLD McNAIR	SAX	(B					

C21A — JEFF CAMPBELL

JEFF CAMPBELL	V G	(A	(A) LIVE ON THE WIRE			1979	ONEINE		
DAVID JAUREQUI	G	(A							
DAVID KOPPENHAUER	G	(A	BILLY LISKA	B	(A	KEVIN REDDING	D	(A
TONY TANNER	PERC	(A	DOUG FREEMAN	G	(A	CHARLIE	G	(A
ROB LIEBERMAN	G	(A	RICK STURBINS	PNO	(A	SUE RUEDA	V	(A

C22 — JUNIOR CAMPBELL

JUNIOR CAMPBELL	V	(A	(A) SECOND TIME AROUND	1974	DERAM	UK	SML 1106

C23 — PATRICK CAMPBELL-LYONS

PATRICK CAMPBELL-LYONS		(A	(A) ME & MY FRIEND	1973	SOVEREIGN	UK	SVNA 7258
BOBBY HARRISON		(A					
PETER DENNIS		(A	DANNY DEMON		(A	SYLVIA SCHUSTER	(A
BOB SARGEANT		(A	JIM FRANK		(A	CHOIRS	V	(A

C24 — ROBERT CAMPBESS

ROBERT CAMPBESS		(A	(A) LIVING IN THE SHADOW	1977	DECCA	UK	SHL 5285

C25 — CAN

MALCOLM MOONEY	V	(A	(A) MONSTER MOVIE		1970	UA	UK	UAS 29094
JAKI LIEBEZEIT	D	(ABCDFHKLMN	(B) TAGO MAGO	DBL	1971	UA	UK	UAD 60009/0
IRMIN SCHMIDT	V K	(ABCDFHKLMN	(B) TAGO MAGO	DBL	1971	SONOPRESSE	FR	19211/2
MICHAEL KAROLI	G VLN	(ABCDFHKLMN	(C) EGE BAMYASI		1972	UA	UK	UAS 29414
HOLGER CZUKAY	B	(ABCDFHKL	(D) DEEP END	(SOUNDTRACKS)	1973	UA	UK	UAS 29283
KENJI 'DAMO' SUZUKI	V	(BCDK	(E) FUTURE DAYS		1973	UA	UK	UAS 29505
ROSKO GEE	B	(MN	(F) SOON OVER BABALUMA		1974	UA	UK	UAG 29673
PETER GILMORE	V	(L	(G) LIMITED EDITION		1974	UA	UK	USP 103
RENE TINNER	V	(L	(H) LANDED		1975	VIRGIN	UK	V 2041
REEBOP KWAKU BAAH	PERC	(MN	(J) UNLIMITED EDITION		1976	CAROLINE	UK	CAD 3001
OLAF KUBLER	SAX	(H	(K) OPENER		1976	SUNSET	UK	SLS 50400
			(L) FLOW MOTION		1976	VIRGIN	UK	V 2071
			(L) FLOW MOTION		1976	POLYDOR		2473 712
			(M) SAW DELIGHT		1977	VIRGIN	UK	V 2079
			(M) SAW DELIGHT		1977	POLYDOR		2473 712
			(N) OUT OF REACH		1978	LIGHTNING		LIG 4
			( ) CANNIBALISMS (BEST OF)		1978	UA	UK	UDM 105/6
			( ) CLASSIC GERMAN ROCK SCENE		19	SONOPRESSE	FR	29772 /73
			( ) CAN		1979	LASER	UK	LASL 2

C25A — CANDYMEN

JOHN RAINEY ADKINS	G	(AB	(A) THE CANDYMEN			1967			
RODNEY JUSTO	V	(AB	(B) BRING YOU CANDYPOWER			1968	ABC	US	ABCS 633
DEAN DAUGHTRY	K	(AB							
BILLY GILMORE	B	(AB	BOB NIX	D	(AB				

C26 — CANNED HEAT

BOB HITE	V	(ABCDGLMN	(A) CANNED HEAT		1967	LIBERTY	US	LST 7526
HENRY VESTINE	G	(ABCDLMN	(A) CANNED HEAT		1967	LIBERTY	UK	83059
AL WILSON	G V	(ABCDG	(A) CANNED HEAT		1972	U A	UK	UAG 29304
LARRY TAYLOR	B	(ABCDG	(B) BOOGIE WITH CANNED HEAT		1968	LIBERTY	UK	LBS 83103
FRANK COOK	D	(A	(B) BOOGIE WITH CANNED HEAT		1968	LIBERTY	US	LST 7541
FITO DE LA PARRA	D	(BCDGLMN	(B) BOOGIE WITH CANNED HEAT		197	UA	UK	UAG 29298
JAMES SHANE	G	(MN	(C) LIVING THE BLUES	DBL	1969	LIBERTY	UK	LDS 84001
ED BEYER	K	(MN	(C) LIVING THE BLUES	DBL	1968	LIBERTY		27200
RICHARD HITE	B	(MN	(C) LIVING THE BLUES	DBL	1969	UA	US	9955
HARVERY MANDEL	G	(GL	(C) LIVING THE BLUES	DBL	19	UA		29258/9
JOEL SCOTT HILL	V G	(L	(D) HALLELUJAH		1969	LIBERTY	UK	LBS 83239
ANTONIO BARREDA	B	(L	(D) HALLELUJAH		1969	LIBERTY	US	LST 7618
CHRIS MORGAN	G	(	(E) VINTAGE HEAT		1970	JANUS	US	JSL 3009
GENE TAYLOR	K	(	(F) LIVE IN EUROPE		1970	LIBERTY	UK	LBS 83333
STAM WEBB	G	(	(F) LIVE IN EUROPE		1970	LIBERTY		5509
MEMPHIS SLIM		(K	(G) FUTURE BLUES		1970	LIBERTY	UK	LBS 83364
JOHN LEE HOOKER	V	(J	(G) FUTURE BLUES		1970	LIBERTY	US	LST 11002
SUNNYLAND SLIM	PNO	(B	(H) COOKBOOK		1970	LIBERTY	UK	LBS 83303
MARK NAFTALIN	K	(D	(H) COOKBOOK		1970	LIBERTY	US	LST 11000
SKIP DIAMOND	V	(D	(H) COOKBOOK		1975	SUNSET		SLS 50377
ELLIOT INGBER	V	(D	(J) HOOKER & HEAT	DBL	1971	LIBERTY	UK	LPS 031/2
JAVIER BATISE	V	(D	(J) HOOKER & HEAT	DBL	1971	LIBERTY	US	35002-1/2
MIKE PACHECO	PERC	(D	(K) MEMPHIS HEAT		1971	BARCLAY		80607
ERNEST LANE	K	(DGL	( ) LIVE AT THE TOPANGA CORRAL		1971	WAND		693
DR JOHN	K	(G	( ) LIVE AT THE TOPANGA CORRAL		1976	DJM		DJS 26072
LITTLE RICHARD	PNO	(L	( ) LIVE AT THE TOPANGA CORRAL		197	PICKWICK		SPC 3364
CLIFFORD SOLOMON	SAX	(L	(L) HISTORICAL FIGURES		1972	UA	UK	UAG 29304
CHARLES LLOYD	FLT	(L	(L) HISTORICAL FIGURES		1972	UA	US	5557
KEVIN BURTON	ORG	(L	( ) PORTRAIT VOL 1 & 2		19	UA		29320 /21
RAY BUSHBAUM	PNO	(L	(M) NEW AGE		1973	UA	UK	UAS 29455
CLARA WARD SINGERS	V	(M	(M) NEW AGE		1973	UA	US	UALA 049F
HARRISON CALLOWAY	TPT	(N	(N) ONE MORE RIVER TO CROSS		1974	ATLANTIC	UK	K 50026
CHARLES ROSE	TROM	(N	(N) ONE MORE RIVER TO CROSS		1974	ATLANTIC	US	SD 7289

(CONTINUED)

CANNED HEAT   C26

RONNIE EADES	SAX	(N	(O) ROLLIN' & TUMBLIN'	1973	SUNSET		SLS 50321
HARVEY THOMPSON	SAX		(N) HUMAN CONDITION	197	SONET	UK	SNTF 783
			( ) COLLAGE	19	SUNSET		SLS 50225
			( ) COLLAGE	19	SUNSET	US	5298
			( ) ORIGINAL CANNED HEAT	19	SPRINGBOARD	US	SPB 4026
			( ) BOOGIE WITH HOOKER & HEAT	19	SPRINGBOARD	US	TSX 3501
			( ) BOOGIE WITH HOOKER & HEAT	19	MUSIDISC		ALB 202
			( ) HISTORY OF	19	SONOPRESSE/UA		29862/63
			( ) VERY BEST OF	19	UA		UASLA431E

CANNED ROCK   C26A

DOUGIE KENNARD	G SYN V	(AB	(A) KINETIC ENERGY	1978	CANNED ROCK	UK	CAN 002
PETE BUCKBY	D PERC V	(AB	(B) LIVE	1979	CANNED ROCK	UK	CAN 003
DON MAXWELL	B G V	(AB					

ACE CANNON   C27

ACE CANNON	SAX	(ALL	( ) ACE OF SAX	1970	LONDON	UK	SHU 8407
			( ) TUFF	197	HI	US	SHL 32007
			( ) INCOMPARABLE SAX OF ACE CANNON	197	HI	US	SHL 32048
			( ) COUNTRY CANNON ACE THAT IS	1972	HI	US	SHL 32071
			( ) BABY DONT GET HOOKED ON ME	1973	HI	US	SHL 32076
			( ) COUNTRY COMFORT	197	LONDON	US	SHXL 32080
			( ) THAT MUSIC CITY FEELING	1974	HI	US	SHL 32086
			( ) THAT MUSIC CITY FEELING	1974	LONDON	US	SHU 8478
			( ) SUPER SAX	1975	LONDON	US	32090
			( ) VERY BEST OF ACE CANNON	1975	LONDON	US	SHU 8486
			( ) SAX MAN	1978	LONDON	US	HLP 8003

FREDDY CANNON   C28

FREDDY CANNON	V	(ALL	( ) THE EXPLOSIVE FREDDY CANNON	1960	TOP RANK	UK	25 / 018
			( ) THE EXPLOSIVE FREDDY CANNON	1960	SWAN	US	502
			( ) THE EXPLOSIVE FREDDY CANNON	1976	SONIC		SON 007
			( ) HAPPY SHADES OF BLUE	1962	TOP RANK	UK	35 / 106
			( ) HAPPY SHADES OF BLUE	1962	SWAN	US	504
			( ) FREDDY CANNON FAVOURITES	1961	TOP RANK	UK	35 / 113
			( ) FREDDY CANNON FAVOURITES	1961	SWAN	US	505
			( ) BANG ON	1963	STATESIDE	UK	SL 10013
			( ) BANG ON	1963	SWAN	US	507
			( ) STEPS OUT	1964	STATESIDE	UK	SL 10062
			( ) STEPS OUT	1964	SWAN	US	511
			( ) HITS	19	WB	US	WS 1544

CAPABILITY BROWN   C29

TONY FERGUSON	V G B	(B	(A) FROM SCRATCH	1972	CHARISMA	UK	CAS1056
DAVE NEVIN	K V G B	(B	(B) VOICE	1973	CHARISMA	UK	CAS1068
ROGER WILLIS	V D K	(B	(C) LIAR	1976	CHARISMA	UK	CS5
GRAHAME WHITE	V K G	(B					
KENNY ROWE	B V PERC	(B	JOE WILLIAMS	V PERC	(B		

JIM CAPALDI   C30

JIM CAPALDI	V D	(ALL	(A) OH HOW WE DANCED	1972	ISLAND	UK	ILPS 9187
ROGER HAWKINS	D	(ABCD	(A) OH HOW WE DANCED	1972	PHONOGRAM	EURO	6896 015
DAVID HOOD	B	(ABCD	(B) WHALE MEAT AGAIN	1974	ISLAND	UK	ILPS 9254
PETE CARR	G	(BCD	(B) WHALE MEAT AGAIN	1974	PHONOGRAM	EURO	9101 634
JIMMY JOHNSON	G	(ABCD	(C) SHORT CUT DRAW BLOOD	1975	ISLAND	UK	ILPS 9336
BARRY BECKETT	PNO	(ABCD	(C) SHORT CUT DRAW BLOOD	1975	PHONOGRAM	EURO	6396 045
STEVE WINWOOD	K B G	(ABC	(D) THE CONTENDER	1978	POLYDOR	UK	2383 490
MUSCLE SHOALS	HRNS	(ABC	(E) THE SWEET SMELL OF...SUCCESS	1980	CARRERE	UK	CAL 116
RABBIT BUNDRICK	K	(BC	( ) DAUGHTER OF THE NIGHT	19	RSO	US	1- 3037
JEAN ROUSSEL	B K	(BC	( ) PLAY IT BY EAR	1977	ISLAND	UK	ILPS 9497
POTATO SMITH	V	(B	( ) ELECTRIC NIGHTS	1979	POLYDOR	UK	2383 534
JOHN BARNES	K	(D					
LAURENCE PEABODY	V	(A	CHRIS STAINTON	K	(B	REMI KABAKA	PERC (C
REBOP KWAKU BAAH	PERC	(AC	RAY ALLEN	SAX	(CD	PHILIP CHEN	B (C
JESS RODEN	G	(C	GERRY CONWAY	D	(C	ROSKO GEE	B (C
CHRIS SPEDDING	G	(C	PETER YARROW	G	(C	RICK GRECH	B (A
PAUL KOSSOFF	G	(ACD	RICO RODRIGUES	TROM	(C	SUE GLOVER	V (A
SUNNY LESLIE	V	(A	CHRIS WOOD	WIND	(AC	DAVE MASON	HCA (A
JIM GORDON	D	(A	TREVOR BURTON	B	(A	MIKE KELLIE	D (A
BOB GRIFFIN	PNO	(A	TREVOR MORAIS	D	(D	ALAN SPENNER	B (D
PETER BONAS	G	(D	PHIL CAPALDI	V PERC	(D	RALPH RICHARDSON	D (D
JACKIE McAULEY	G	(D	CHRIS PARREN	K	(D	ED GREENE	D (D
DAVID SHIELDS	B	(D	CHUCK RAINEY	K	(D	RAY PARKER	G (D
DEAN PARKS	G	(D					

CAPTAIN BEYOND   C31

LARRY 'RHINO' RHEINHART	G	(ABC	(A) CAPTAIN BEYOND	1972	CAPRICORN	UK	K 47503
LEE DORMAN	B V K	(ABC	(A) CAPTAIN BEYOND	1972	CAPRICORN	US	CP 0105
ROD EVANS	V	(AB	(B) SUFFICIENTLY BREATHLESS	1973	CAPRICORN	US	CP 0115
BOBBY CALDWELL	D V K	(AC	(C) DAWN EXPLOSION	1977	WB	US	BS 3047
GUILLE GARCIA	PERC	(B					
MARTY RODRIGUEZ	D	(B	REESE WYNANS	PNO	(B	PAUL HORNSBY	K (B
WILLY DAFFERN	V	(C					

CAPTAIN RUGELEYS BLUES BAND   C32

CLIVE TIMPERLEE	G	(	(NO ALBUMS)
MARTIN LAMBLE	D	(	

GILBERT CARAHNAC   C33

GILBERT CARANHAC		(A) THE DOBRO	1975	CHANT DU MONDE	LDX 74508

CARAVAN

RICHARD COUGHLAN	D	(ALL	(A) CARAVAN		1968	VERVE		6011
PYE HASTINGS	G V	(ALL	(A) CARAVAN		1968	MGM		2353 058
DAVE SINCLAIR	K	(ABCEFG145L	(A) CARAVAN		1972	POLYDOR	UK	2353 058
RICHARD SINCLAIR	B	(ABCD12	(B) IF I COULD DO IT ALL OVER AGAIN...	1970	DECCA	UK	SKL 5052
GEOFF RICHARDSON	V G VLN	(EFGK34567	(B) IF I COULD DO IT ALL OVER AGAIN...	1970	METRONOME	FR	MLP15 375
STEVE MILLER	K	(D2	(B) IF I COULD DO IT ALL OVER AGAIN...	1970	CARRERE	FR	44002
BROTHER JAMES	WIND	(B	(B) IF I COULD DO IT ALL OVER AGAIN...	1970	LONDON	US	PS 582
MIKE WEDGWOOD	B	(GK567	(C) IN THE LAND OF THE GREY & PINK	1971	DERAM	UK	SDL 1
JOHN G PERRY	B V	(EF4	(C) IN THE LAND OF THE GREY & PINK	1971	LONDON	US	PS 593
JIM HASTINGS	WIND	(CDE	(C) IN THE LAND OF THE GREY & PINK	197	CARRERE	FR	44007
DEREK AUSTIN	K	(3	(D) WATERLOO LILY	1972	DERAM	UK	SDL 8
STUART EVANS	B	(3	(D) WATERLOO LILY	1972	LONDON	US	PS 615
DEK MESSECAR	B V	(K7	(D) WATERLOO LILY	197	VOGUE		HV 6001
JAN SCHELHAAS	K	(6	(E) FOR GIRLS WHO GROW PLUMP IN NIGHT	1973	DERAM	UK	SKLR 12
DAVE GRINSTEAD	PERC	(C	(E) FOR GIRLS WHO GROW PLUMP IN NIGHT	1973	LONDON	US	PS 627
FRANK RICOTTI	PERC	(E	(E) FOR GIRLS WHO GROW PLUMP IN NIGHT	197	VOGUE		KV 6006
RUPERT HINE	SYN	(E	(F) & THE NEW SYMPHONIA	1974	DERAM	UK	SKLR 1110
TONY COE	WIND	(E	(F) & THE NEW SYMPHONIA	1974	LONDON	US	PS 650
TOMMY WHITTLE	WIND	(E	(F) & THE NEW SYMPHONIA	197	VOGUE		KV 6008
HARRY KLEIN	WIND	(E	(G) CUNNING STUNTS	1975	DERAM	UK	SKLR 5210
PETE KING	WIND	(E	(G) CUNNING STUNTS	1975	BTM		BTM 5000
BARRY ROBINSON	WIND	(E	(G) CUNNING STUNTS	197	RCA		26 21544
HENRY LOWTHER	HRNS	(E	(G) CUNNING STUNTS	197	BTM		BTM 1003
CHRIS PYNE	TROM	(E	(H) CANTERBURY TALES (DBL COMP)	1976	DECCA	UK	DKLR81/82
JOHN BEECHAM	TROM	(E	(J) BLIND DOG AT ST DUNSTANS	1976	BTM	UK	BTM 1007
MIKE COTTON	TPT	(E	(K) BETTER BY FAR	1977	ARISTA	UK	SPARTY 1008
			(K) BETTER BY FAR	1977	ARISTA	US	AB 434
			(K) BETTER BY FAR	1977	PATHE	FR	0C64 99089
			(L) THE ALBUM	1980	KINGDOM	UK	KVL 9003
			( ) THIS IS CARAVAN	19	BRAIN	GERM	200164
			( ) CARAVAN VOL1	19	POLYDOR		2445 202
			( ) CARAVAN VOL2	19	POLYDOR		2445 203
			( ) PROFILE	19	TELDEC	GERM	624017 AL

( ) JAN 68/JULY 71   (2) AUG 71/ JULY 72   (3) JULY 72/ EARLY 73
(4) 73 / JUNE 74   (5) JUNE74/ JULY 75   (6) JULY75/ DEC 76
(7) APRIL 77>

GLENN CARDIER

GLENN CARDIER			(A) GLENN CARDIER	1976	EMI	UK	EMC 3115

CARGO

MIKE PROUDFOOT	G	(A	(A) SIMPLE THINGS	1969	RINGSIDE		RS 104
NORM FOSTER	D	(A					
RAY PARKER	ORG	(A	GARTH VAGAN	B	(A		

CARGOE

BILL PHILLIPS	(		(A) CARGOE	1972	ARDENT	US	ADS 2802
TOMMY RICHARD	(						
MAX WISLEY	(		TIM BENTON	(			

CARILLO

DAVID DONEN	D	(A	(A) RINGS AROUND THE MOON	1978	ATLANTIC	US SD	19176
KEVIN KEANE	B V	(A					
LUKE SPAGNUDO	LYRICS(A		FRANK CARILLO	V G	(A	JAN MULLANEY	K V (A
KRISTI BARTON	V	(A	YVONNE ELLIMAN	V	(A	RICK SILECHIO	G (A

DAVE CARLSEN

DAVE CARLSEN		(A	(A) A PALE HORSE	1973	SPARK	UK	SRLP 110
KEITH MOON	D	(A					
HENRY McCULLOUGH	G	(A	NOEL REDDING	B	(A		

LARRY CARLTON

LARRY CARLTON	G	(ALL	(A) SINGING PLAYING	1973	BLUE THUMB	US	BST 46
GREG MATHESON	K	(B	(B) LARRY CARLTON	1978	WB	UK	K 56548
ABE LABORIEL	B	(B	(B) LARRY CARLTON	1978	WB	US	BSK3221
JEFF PORCARO	D	(B	(C) LIVE IN JAPAN	1979	?	JAP	P 10643
PAULINHO DA COSTA	PERC	(B					
WILLIAM'SMITTY' SMITH	V	(B					

CARMEN

DAVID ALLEN	G V	(AB	(A) FANDANGOS IN SPACE	1973	REGAL ZONOPHONE	UK	SRZA 8518
ANGELA ALLEN	V K	(AB	(A) FANDANGOS IN SPACE	1973	DUNHILL	US	DP 50192
ROBERTO AMARAL	V PERC	(B	(B) DANCING ON A COLD WIND	1975	REGAL ZONOPHONE	UK	SLRZ1040
PAUL FENTON	D	(A	(C) THE GYPSIES	1976	MERCURY	US	SRM1 1047
JOHN GLASCOCK	B V	(A					

ERIC CARMEN

ERIC CARMEN	V K D	(ALL	(A) ERIC CARMEN	1976	ARISTA	UK	ARTY 120
DAVE WINTOUR	B	(B	(A) ERIC CARMEN	1976	ARISTA	US	AQ 4057
JEFF PORCARO	D	(B	(B) BOATS AGAINST THE CURRENT	1977	ARISTA	UK	SPARTY 1015
GENE ESTES	PERC	(B	(B) BOATS AGAINST THE CURRENT	1977	ARISTA	US	A 4124
ANDREW GOLD	G V	(B	(C) CHANGE OF HEART	1978	ARISTA	UK	SPARTI068
NIGEL OLSSON	D	(BC	(C) CHANGE OF HEART	1978	ARISTA	US	4184
MICHAEL BODDIKER	K	(C	(D) TONIGHT YOU'RE MINE	1980	ARISTA	UK	SPARTI134
CURT BOETCHER	V	(C					
TOMMY MORGAN	HCA	(C	BRUCE JOHNSTON	V	(C	JOE CHEMAY	V (C
JAMES NEWTON HOWARD	SYN	(C	BURTON CUMMINGS	PNO	(C	RICHARD REISING	G V (BC
MIKE PORCARO	B	(C	VALERIE CARTER	V	(C	BOBBY KEYS	SAX (B
JAI WINDING	K	(C	DONNY GERRARD	V	(C	RUSS KUNKEL	D (C
TOM SCOTT	SAX	(B	DANIEL KORTCHMAR	G	(C	LEE SKLAR	B (C
RICHIE ZETO	G	(BC	PAULINHO DA COSTA	PERC	(C	CRAIG DOERGE	K (C
JIM HORN	SAX	(C	LAURA ALLEN	V	(C	FRED TACKETT	G (C
OLLIE BROWN	PERC	(B	JOE PORCARO	PERC	(C	DAVID PAICH	K (C
STEVE MADAIO	TPT	(B	BRIAN RUSSELL	V	(C	BRENDA RUSSELL	V (C
SAMANTHA SANG	V	(C	MIKE BOTTS	D	(C		

CARPENTERS — C39

Personnel			Album	Year	Label	Country	Catalog
RICHARD CARPENTER	K V	(ALL	(A) CLOSE TO YOU	1970	A&M		AMLS 998
KAREN CARPENTER	D V	(ALL	(A) CLOSE TO YOU	1970	A&M	US	4271
JOE OSBORN	B	(ABDE	(B) THE CARPENTERS	1971	A&M		6 3502
BOB MESSENGER	B WIND	(ABDEL	(C) TICKET TO RIDE	1972	A&M		6 4205
RON GORDON	D	(E	(C) TICKET TO RIDE	1972	HAMLET	UK	AMLP8001
DOUG STRAWN	K WIND V	(ABEL	(D) A SONG FOR YOU	1972	A&M		6 3511
JIM HORN	WIND	(AB	(E) NOW & THEN	1973	A&M		6 3519
HAL BLAINE	D	(ABDE	(F) THE SINGLES 69 73	1974	A&M		6 3601
TIM WEISBERG	FLT	(D	(G) HORIZON	1975	A&M		6 4530
LOUIE SHELTON	G	(D	(H) A KIND OF HUSH	1976	A&M		6 4581
TONY PELUSO	G B K V	(DEL	(J) CARPENTER COLLECTION	197	A&M		CARP 1000
RED RHODES	STEEL	(D	(L)K) LIVE IN JAPAN	1975	A&M		GSW301/02
EARL DUMLER	WIND	(DE	(L) LIVE AT THE PALLADIUM	1977	A&M		6 8403
NORM HERZBERG	WIND	(D	(M) PASSAGE	1977	A&M		6 4703
DANNY WOODHAMS	B	(D	(N) THE SINGLES 74 78	1978	A&M		19748
CUBBY O'BRIEN	D	(L					
TOM SCOTT	WIND	(E					
GARY SIMS	G	(E					
BUDDY EMMONS	STEEL	(E	JAYDEE MANESS	STEEL	(E		

PAUL CARRACK — C39A

Personnel			Album	Year	Label	Country	Catalog
PAUL CARRACK	V	(A	(A) THE NIGHTBIRD	1980	VERTIGO		6359 016
RICHAR BAILEY	D	(A					
ANDY NEWMARK	D	(A	JEFF SEOPARDIE	D	(A	ALAN SPENNER	B	(A
KUMA HARADA	B	(A	TIM RENWICK	G	(A	NEIL HUBBARD	G	(A
WINSTON DELANDRO	G	(A	NEVILLE MURRAY	PERC	(A	DYAN BIRCH	V	(A
ALAN BAM KING	V	(A	NOEL McCALLA	V	(A	MEL COLLINS	HRNS	(A
MARTIN DROVER	HRNS	(A	MALCOLM GRIFFITHS	HRNS	(A	GUY BARKER	HRNS	(A

JOE 'KING' CARRASCO — C39B

Personnel			Album	Year	Label	Country	Catalog
JOE 'KING' CARRASCO	V G	(A	(A) JOE KING CARRASCO & THE CROWNS	1980	STIFF	UK	SEEZ 28
MIKE NAVARRP		(A					
KRIS CUMMINGS		(A	BRAD KIZER		(A		

BARBARA CARROLL — C40

Personnel			Album	Year	Label	Country	Catalog
BARBARA CARROLL	PNO K	(A	(A) FROM THE BEGINNING	1977	UA	US	UALA 778H
EUGENE BIANCO	HARP	(A	(A) FROM THE BEGINNING	1978	UA	UK	UAG 30168
IRWIN MARKOWITZ	HRNS	(A					
MARVIN STAMM	HRNS	(A	JAY LEONHART	B	(A	STEVE GADD	D	(A
STEVE THORNTON	PERC	(A	RUSSELL GEORGE	B	(A	HUGH McCRACKEN	G	(A
BOB ROSE	G	(A	CRUSHER BENNETT	PERC	(A	GEORGE DEVENS	VIBES	(A
JAY BERLINER	G	(A	RICHARD DAVIS	B	(A	BILL LAVORGNA	D	(A
RON CARTER	B	(A					

CARS — C41

Personnel			Album	Year	Label	Country	Catalog
RIC OCASEK	G	(ABC	(A) THE CARS	1978	ELEKTRA	UK	K52088
ELLIOT EASTON	G	(	(A) THE CARS	1978	ELEKTRA	US	6E 135
DAVID ROBINSON	D	(	(B) CANDY O	1979	ELEKTRA	UK	K 52148
BEN ORR (ORZECHOWSKI)	B	(	(C) PANORAMA	1980	ELEKTRA	UK	K 52240
GREG HAWKES	K	(					

CARSON — C41A

Personnel			Album	Year	Label	Country	Catalog
BRODERICK SMITH	V HCA	(	(A) BLOWN	19	HARVEST	UK	SHVL 608
SLEEPY GREG LAWRIE	G	(	(B) ON THE AIR(LIVE)	19	PATHE	FR 064	81774
IAN WINTER	G	(					
GARY CLARKE	B	(	TONY LUNT	D	(		

CARLENE CARTER — C42

Personnel			Album	Year	Label	Country	Catalog
CARLENE CARTER	V G PNO	(A	(A) CARLENE CARTER	1978	WB US BSK3204	UK	K 56502
DAVE EDMUNDS	G V	(B	(B) MUSICAL SHAPES	1980	F BEAT	UK	XXLP3
ANDREW BODNAR	B	(A					
STEVE GOULDING	D	(A	BRINSLEY SCHWARZ	G V	(A	BOB ANDREWS	K V	(AB
CHRIS GOWER	TROM	(A	JOHN EARLE	SAX	(A	NICK LOWE	B	(AB
GRAHAM PARKER	G	(A	TERRY WILLIAMS	D	(AB	RAY BEARIS	SAX	(A
DICK HANSON	HRNS	(A	KEVIN WELLS	D	(B	BILLY BREMNER	G	(B
JOHN McFEE	G	(B	JOHN CIAMBOTTI	B	(B	SEAN HOPPER	K	(B
ROGER RETTIG	STEEL	(B					

CLARENCE CARTER — C43

Personnel			Album	Year	Label	Country	Catalog
CLARENCE CARTER	V	(ALL	(A) THIS IS	1968	ATLANTIC	UK	588 152
			(A) THIS IS	1968	ATLANTIC	US	SD 8192
			(B) THE DYNAMIC	1968	ATLANTIC	UK	588 172
			(B) THE DYNAMIC	1968	ATLANTIC	US	SD 8199
			(C) TESTIFYIN'	1969	ATLANTIC	UK	588 191
			(C) TESTIFYIN'	1969	ATLANTIC	US	SD 8238
			(D) PATCHES	1970	ATLANTIC	UK	2400 027
			(D) PATCHES	1970	ATLANTIC	US	SD 8267
			(E) SIXTY MINUTES	1974	FAME		186
			(F) REAL	1974	ABC	US	ABCD 833
			(F) REAL	1974	ANCHOR	UK	ABCL 5060
			(G) LONELINESS & TEMPTATION	1975	ABC	US	ABCD 896
			(H) HEART FULL OF SONG	1976	ABC	US	ABCD 943
			( ) THE BEST OF	19	ATLANTIC	US	40245

RON CARTER — C44

Personnel			Album	Year	Label	Country	Catalog
RON CARTER	B	(ALL	(A) BLUES FARM	1973	CTI	US	6027
WITH			( ) ALL BLUES	19	CTI	US	6037
BILLY COBHAM	D	(AJ	( ) ALONE TOGETHER	19	MILESTONE	US	904
BOB JAMES	K	(A	( ) MAGIC	19	PRESTIGE	US	24053
GENE BERTONCINI	G	(A	( ) OUT FRONT	19	PRESTIGE	US	7397
SAM BROWN	G	(A	( ) SPANISH BLUE	19	CTI	US	6051
STEVE GADD	D	(G	(G) ANYTHING GOES	1975	KUDU		KU 25
JIMMY MADISON	D	(G	( ) WHERE	19	PRESTIGE	US	7843
BARRY ROGERS	TROM	(G	( ) UPTOWN CONVERSATION	197	EMBRYO		SD 521
ERIC GALE	G	(G	(J) YELLOW & GREEN	1976	CTI		63004

(CONTINUED)

C44 (CONTINUED)   RON CARTER

GEORGE DEVENS	PERC	(G	(J) YELLOW & GREEN			1976	CTI	US	6064
RALPH McDONALD	PERC	(AG	(K) PASTELS			1977	MILESTONE		9073
HUBERT LAWS	FLT	(AG	( ) SONG FOR YOU			1979	MILESTONE		9086
RANDY BRECKER	HRNS	(G	( ) PARADE			1979	MILESTONE		9088
HARVEY MASON	D	(K							
ALAN RUBIN	HRNS	(G	DON GROLNICK	K	(GJ	RICHARD TEE	K	(AG	
MICHAEL BRECKER	HRNS	(G	DAVE SANBORN	SAX	(G	PHIL WOODS	SAX	(G	
PATTI AUSTIN	V	(G	MARILYN JACKSON	V	(G	MAERETHA STEWART	V	(G	
KENNY BARRON	PNO	(JK	HARVEY MANDEL	G	(J	HUGH McCRACKEN	G	(JK	
ARTHUR JENKINS	PERC	(G	DOM UM ROMAO	PERC	(J	BEN RILEY	D	(J	

C45   VALERIE CARTER

VALERIE CARTER	V	(ALL	(A) JUST A STONES THROW AWAY			1977	CBS	US	PC	34155
WITH			(A) JUST A STONES THROW AWAY			1977	CBS	UK		81958
BILL PAYNE		(A	(B) WILD CHILD			1978	CBS	US	JC	35084
LOWELL GEORGE	G	(A	(B) WILD CHILD			1978	CBS	UK		82556
JEFF PORCARO	D	(AB								
BOB GLAUB		(A	FRED TACKETT	G	(AB	SAM CLAYTON	PERC	(A		
CHARLES RAINEY	B	(AB	JOHN HALL		(A	ERNIE WATTS	SAX	(A		
TOM JANS		(A	HERB PEDERSEN		(A	MIKE UTLEY	K	(AB		
JOHN SEBASTIAN		(A	JACKSON BROWNE		(A	OSCAR BRASHEAR	HRNS	(A		
MIKE HARRIS		(A	LOUIS SATTERFIELD		(A	DON MYRICK	SAX	(A		
DAVID CAMPBELL		(A	LARRY DUNN		(A	AL McKAY		(A		
VERDINE WHITE	B	(AB	FRED WHITE		(A	ANDREW WOOLFOLK		(A		
JERRY PETERS		(A	SKIP SCARBOROUGH		(A	GEORGE BOHANON		(A		
PAUL BARRERE		(A	COLIN CAMERON		(A	VICTOR FELDMAN	PERC	(B		
DAVID HUNGATE	B	(B	STEVE LUKATHER	G	(B	JAMES NEWTON HOWARE	K	(B		
STEVE PORCARO	SYN	(B	RAY PARKER	G	(B	JAY GRAYDON	G	(B		
VINI PONCIA	V	(B	WENDY HAAS	V	(B	DAVID LASLEY	V	(B		
TOMMY SAVIANO	SAX	(B	DAVEY JOHNSTONE	G	(B	LENNY CASTRO	PERC	(B		
CHUCK FINDLEY	HRNS	(B	STEVE MADAIO	HRNS	(B	JIM HORN	HRNS	(B		

C46   CARTER LEWIS & THE SOUTHERNERS

JOHN(JOHN SHAKESPEARE)CARTER	V B G	
KEN (KEN JAMES) LEWIS	V K	
JIMMY PAGE	G	
VIV PRINCE	D	

C47   MARTIN CARTHY

MARTIN CARTHY	V G	(ALL	(A) MARTIN CARTHY	1965	FONTANA	STL	5269
WITH			(A) MARTIN CARTHY	1977	TOPIC	12TS	340
DAVE SWARBRICK	VLN	(ABCDEHI	(B) SECOND ALBUM	196	FONTANA	STL	5362
MADDY PRIOR	V	(K	(B) SECOND ALBUM	1977	TOPIC	12TS	341
LEON ROSSELSON		(F	(C) BYKER HILL	196	FONTANA	STL	5434
			(C) BYKER HILL	1977	FONTANA	12TS	342
			(D) BUT TWO CAME BY	1968	FONTANA	STL	5477
			(D) BUT TWO CAME BY	1977	TOPIC	12TS	343
			(E) PRINCE HEATHEN	1969	FONTANA	STL	5529
			(E) PRINCE HEATHEN	1977	TOPIC	12TS	344
			(F) THE WORD IS	19	TRAILER	LER	3015
			(G) LANDFALL	1971	PHILIPS	6309	049
			(G) LANDFALL	1977	TOPIC	12TS	345
			(H) SELECTIONS	1971	PEGASUS		PEG 6
			(I) THIS IS MARTIN CARTHY	1972	PHILIPS	6282	022
			(J) SWEET WIVELSFIELD	1974	DERAM	SML	1111
			(K) SHEARWATER	1975	MOONCREST	CREST	25
			(K) SHEARWATER	197	PEGASUS	PEG	12
			(L) CROWN OF HORN	1976	TOPIC	12TS	300
			(M) BECAUSE ITS THERE	1979	TOPIC	12TS	289

C48   CASABLANCA

BARRY CLARKE	V G	(A	(A) CASABLANCA			1974	ROCKET	PIGL	7
DAVID COSTA	G V	(A							
JUANITA FRANKLIN	V	(A	ALIKI ASHMAN	V	(A	BILLY LIVSEY	K	(A	
STEVE BINGHAM	B	(A	TERRY STANNARD	D	(A	LOL COXHILL	WIND	(A	
BRUCE ROWLAND	D	(A	TREVOR VALLIS	B	(A	NICK JUDD	K	(A	
GRAHAM PRESKETT	VLN	(A	JOHNNY WILSON	D	(A	BIAS BOSHELL	B	(A	
LUIS JARDIM	PERC	(A	PAUL VIGRASS	V	(A	GARY OSBORNE	V	(A	
PHILIP CHEN	B	(A							

C49   AL CASEY

AL CASEY	G	(AB	(A) JUMPIN' WITH AL	1974	BLACK & BLUE		33056
			(B) GUITAR ODYSSEY	1976	JAZZ ODYSSEY	JO	012

C50   JOHNNY CASH

JOHNNY CASH
WITH
JUNE CARTER CASH

CARLENE CARTER	V	ANITA CARTER	V	ROSANNE CASH	V	CINDY CASH	V
STATLER BROTHERS		KRIS KRISTOFFERSON	V	BILLY LEE RILEY	G	LARRY BUTLER	
LARRY GATLIN		JAN HOWARD		RON TUTT		REINIE PRESS	
DAVID FOSTER		LARRY MUHOBERAC		RON ELLIOTT		RY COODER	G
JAMES BURTON	G	RUSS TITELMAN		JERRY COLE		VICTOR FELDMAN	PERC
JOE PORCARO	PERC	GENE ESTES		NICK DE CARO		GENE CIPRIANO	SAX
REGGIE YOUNG		KENNY MALONE		HENRY STRZELECKI		SHANE KEISTER	K
TEDDY IRWIN		DAVID ALAN COE	V	JACKIE WARD	V	RON HICKLIN SINGERS	V
JIMMY CAPPS	G	ROSEY NIX	V	MARSHALL GRANT	B	JORDANAIRES	V
WES HOLLAND	D	BOB WOOTTON	G	CARL PERKINS	V	LUTHER PERKINS	G
CHARLIE McCOY	HCA	CHUCK COCHRAN		JOE ALLEN		EARL SCRUGGS	BANJO
OAKRIDGE BOYS	V	LARRY McCOY		RAY EDENTON		JERRY HENSLEY	G
JACK ROUTH	G	EARL BALL	PNO	MARK MORRIS	PERC	MICHAEL BACON	CELLO
SAM MULLINS	STRINGS	KATHLEEN BRIMM	V	RED LANE	G	BILL PURSELL	
TOMMY ALSUP	G	JACK CLEMENT	G	JACK HALE	HRNS	BOB LEWINS	HRNS
JOEL SONNIER	HCA	DENNIS GOODE	TROM	BILLY PUETT	WIND	WAYNE JACKSON	TPT
GENE LOWERY SINGERS	V	RICH SCHULMAN	V	JIMMY WILSON	PNO	JAMES VAN EATON	D
RODNEY CROWELL	V	THE CARTER FAMILY		HELEN CARTER	V	(CONTINUED)	

Title	Year	Label		Cat. No.	Title	Year	Label		Cat. No.
WITH HIS HOT & BLUE GUITAR	1957	SUN		SLP 1220	A MAN IN BLACK	1971	CBS		64331
SONGS THAT MADE HIM FAMOUS	1958	SUN	US	SLP1235	MAN IN BLACK	1971	CBS	US	30550
SONGS THAT MADE HIM FAMOUS	1967	LONDON		HAS 2157	THE LEGEND	197	SUN	US	2 118
FABULOUS JOHNNY CASH	1959	CBS		62042	ROUGH CUT KING OF COUNTRY	197	SUN	US	122
GREATEST JOHNNY CASH	1959	SUN	US	SLP1240	THE MAN THE WORLD HIS MUSIC	197	SUN	US	126
HYMNS BY JOHNNY CASH	1959	CBS	US	CS8125	PORTRAIT	197	CBS		64516
HYMNS BY JOHNNY CASH	1971	HALLMARK		SHM 739	GIVE MY LOVE TO ROSE	1972	CBS	US	31256
SINGS HANK WILLIAMS	1960	SUN	US	SLP1245	INTERNATIONAL SUPERSTAR	1972	CBS	GERM	67284
SINGS HANK WILLIAMS	196	LONDON	NZ	HAM6195	A THING CALLED LOVE	1972	CBS		64898
SINGS HANK WILLIAMS	196	SUN	US	125	JOHNNY CASH	197	EMBASSY		31495
SONGS OF OUR SOIL	1959	CBS	US	CS 8148	JOHNNY CASH	1974	EMBASSY		31039
NOW THERE WAS A SONG	1960	PHILIPS		BBL 7358	SHOWTIME	197	SUN		6467 016
NOW THERE WAS A SONG	1960	CBS	US	CS 8254	JOHNNY CASH SONG BOOK	1972	HARMONY	US	31602
NOW THERE WAS A SONG	1960	CBS		62028	CHRISTMAS & THE CASH FAMILY	1972	CBS	US	31764
RIDE THIS TRAIN	1960	CBS		62575	ORIGINAL GOLDEN HITS 3	1972	SUN		6467 022
NOW HERES JOHNNY CASH	1961	SUN	US	SLP1255	ORIGINAL GOLDEN HITS 3	197	SUN	US	127
RIDE THIS TRAIN	1960	CBS	US	CS 8255	GOSPEL ROAD	1973	CBS	US	32253
HYMNS FROM THE HEART	1962	CBS	US	CS8522	GOSPEL ROAD	1973	CBS	UK	68243
ALL ABOARD THE BLUE TRAIN	1962	SUN	US	SLP1270	SUNDAY MORNING COMING DOWN	197	CBS	US	32240
SOUND OF JOHNNY CASH	1962	CBS	US	CS 8602	MAGNIFICENT JOHNNY CASH	1972	HALLMARK		SHM 777
BLOOD SWEAT & TEARS	1963	CBS	US	CS 8730	COUNTRY & WESTERN SUPERSTAR	1973	CBS	GERM	68224
BLOOD SWEAT & TEARS	1963	CBS	UK	65163	AMERICA	1973	CBS		65163
RING OF FIRE	1963	CBS		62171	SUNDAY DOWN SOUTH	1973	SUN	US	6467024
RING OF FIRE	1963	CBS	US	CS 8853	ANY OLD WIND THAT BLOWS	1973	CBS		65431
CHRISTMAS SPIRIT	1963	CBS		62284	ANY OLD WIND THAT BLOWS	197	CBS	US	KC32091
KEEP ON THE SUNNYSIDE	1964	CBS	US	CS 8952	J CASH & HIS WOMAN	1973	CBS		65689
I WALK THE LINE	1964	CBS	US	CS8990	J CASH & HIS WOMAN	1973	CBS	US	KC32443
I WALK THE LINE	196	CBS	UK	62371	MIGHTY JOHNNY CASH	1973	HALLMARK		SHM 804
I WALK THE LINE	1974	CBS		70083	FIVE FEET HIGH & RISING	1974	CBS	US	32951
I WALK THE LINE	1974	HALLMARK	UK	SHM 849	AT OSTERAKER PRISON	1974	CBS	HOLL	65308
BITTER TEARS	1964	CBS		62463	FOLSOM PRISON BLUES	1974	HALLMARK		SHM 822
LORENA	1964	CBS	GERM	52705	SOUND OF J CASH	197	EMBASSY		31081
ORIGINAL SUN SOUND OF J C	1964	SUN	US	SLP1275	BALLADS OF AMERICAN INDIANS	1974	HARMONY	US	32388
ORIGINAL SUN SOUND OF J C	1967	LONDON		HA58220	BLUE TRAIN	197	SHARE	US	5002
ORANGE BLOSSOM SPECIAL	1965	CBS		62501	JUNKIE & JUICEHEAD	1974	CBS		80347
ORANGE BLOSSOM SPECIAL	1965	CBS	US	CS 9109	JUNKIE & JUICEHEAD	1974	CBS	US	33086
TRUE WEST	1965	CBS		62538	ROUGH CUT KING	1974	SUN		6870 605
TRUE WEST	1965	CBS	US	C2S 838	GENTLE GIANT OF COUNTRY	1974	SUN		6641 161
MEAN AS HELL	1966	CBS	US	CS 9246	PRECIOUS MEMORIES	197	CBS	US	33087
TRUE WEST 2	196	CBS		62591	RAGGED OLD FLAG	1974	CBS		80113
EVERYBODY LOVES A NUT	1966	CBS		62717	RAGGED OLD FLAG	1974	CBS	US	32917
EVERYBODY LOVES A NUT	1966	CBS	US	CS 9292	FOLSOM & SAN QUENTIN	197	CBS DBL	US	33639
HAPPINESS IS YOU	1966	CBS		62760	JOHN R CASH	1974	CBS		80634
GREATEST HITS	1967	CBS		63062	RIDING THE RAILS	1975	CBS		88153
GREATEST HITS 1	1967	CBS	US	CS 9478	CHILDRENS ALBUM	1975	CBS	US	32898
CARRYIN' ON	1967	CBS		63105	LOOK AT THEM BEANS	1975	CBS		81012
OLD GOLDEN THROAT	1968	CBS		63318	LOOK AT THEM BEANS	1975	CBS	US	34193
OLD GOLDEN THROAT	1975	CHARLY		CR 30005	I FORGOT TO REMEMBER	1975	HALLMARK		SHM 884
THE HOLY LAND	1968	CBS		63428	BALLAD OF TEENAGE QUEEN	1975	HALLMARK		SHM 862
THE HOLY LAND	196	CBS	US	KCS9726	STORY OF A BROKEN HEART	1976	HALLMARK		SHM 897
LEGENDS OF LOVE SONGS	1968	CBS	CAN	DS 363	KING OF COUNTRY	1975	MUSIDISC		174
MORE OLD GOLDEN THROAT	1969	CBS		63521	SPOTLIGHT ON JOHNNY CASH	1975	SUN	NL	SPL01
SINGING STORY TELLER	1969	SUN	US	115	COLLECTION	1976	PICKWICK		PDA 005
SINGING STORY TELLER	19	BUCKBOARD	US	BB51021	DESTINATION VICTORIA STATION	1976	CBS	US	VS150
JACKSON	1969	CBS	US	CS 9528	MAKING A LEGEND	1976	CHARLY		18051
FROM SEA TO SHINING SEA	1968	CBS		62972	JOHNNY CASH	19	PICKWICK	US	2052
AT FOLSOM PRISON	1968	CBS		63308	KINGS OF COUNTRY DBL	19	FESTIVAL	US	174
AT FOLSOM PRISON	1968	CBS	US	CS 9639	SONGBOOK	19	CBS		EUR51357
AT SAN QUENTIN	1969	CBS		63629	IN SWEDEN	1976	CBS		65308
AT SAN QUENTIN	1969	CBS	US	CS 9827	STRAWBERRY CAKE	1976	CBS		81211
HELLO IM JOHNNY CASH	1969	CBS		63796	ONE PIECE AT A TIME	1976	CBS		81416
WORLD OF JOHNNY CASH	1970	CBS		66237	ONE PIECE AT A TIME	1976	CBS	US	34193
WORLD OF JOHNNY CASH	1970	CBS		CG 29	LAST GUNFIGHTER BALLAD	1977	CBS		81566
HIS GREATEST HITS VOL 2	19	CBS	US	30887	LAST GUNFIGHTER BALLAD	1977	CBS	US	34314
JOHNNY CASH SHOW	1970	CBS		64089	THE RAMBLER	1977	CBS	US	34833
ORIGINAL GOLDEN HITS 1	1970	SUN		6467 001	THIS IS JOHNNY CASH	197	HARMONY	US	11342
ORIGINAL GOLDEN HITS 1	19	SUN	US	100	I WOULD LIKE TO SEE YOU	1978	CBS UNISSUED		82676
ORIGINAL GOLDEN HITS 2	1970	SUN		6467 007	I WOULD LIKE TO SEE YOU	1978	CBS	US	35313
ORIGINAL GOLDEN HITS 2	19	SUN	US	101	GONE GIRL	1978	CBS		83323
THE GREAT JOHNNY CASH	1970	HALLMARK		SHM 696	UNISSUED JOHNNY CASH	1878	BEAR FAM	GER	15016
ORIGINAL JOHNNY CASH	1970	CHARLY		CR 30113	JOHNNY & JUNE	1978	BEAR FAM	GER	15030
LITTLE FAUSS & BIG HALSY	1970	CBS		70087	ITCHY FEET 20 FOOT TAPPERS	1978	CBS		10009
THE MAN & HIS WORLD	1971	SUN		6641 008	COLLECTION VOL 2	1978	PICKWICK		PDA 033
TRAINS & RIVERS	1971	SUN		6467012	RING OF FIRE	1979	HALLMARK		SHM 998
TRAINS & RIVERS	197	SUN	US	104	GREATEST HITS VOL 3	1979	CBS	US	35637
SHOWTIME	197	SUN	US	106	JOHNNY CASH TODAY	1978	K TEL	CAN	NC424
GET RHYTHM	1971	SUN		6467 014	HOT'N'BLUE GUITAR RI	1980	CHARLY		CRM 2013
UNDERSTAND YOUR MAN	1971	HARMONY	US	30916					

TERRY CASHMAN	V	(ABC	(A) SONG OR TWO		1972				
TOMMY WEST	V K G	(ABC	(B) MOONDOG SERENADE		1973	DUNHILL	US	DSX 50141	
RAY POHLMAN	B	(B	(B) MOONDOG SERENADE		1973	PROBE	UK	SPBA 6226	
GARY KATZ	V	(A	(C) LIFESONG		1974	ABC	UK	ABCL 5058	
MIKE OMARTIAN	K	(B							
JEFF BAXTER	STEEL	(B	STEVE BARRI	PERC	(B	BEN BENAY	HCA G	(B	
GARY COLEMAN	PERC	(B	JIMMIE HASKELL	ACC	(B	EDDIE LAMBERT	V	(B	
LOUIS SHELTON	G	(B	JIM GORDON	D	(B				

CASINO

(A) CASINO		1976	STATE	ETAT	5
(A) CASINO		1976	MCA	US	2191

C52

JEAN PIERRE CASTELAIN G (ALL

JEAN PIERRE CASTELAIN

(A) DE MES YEUX VU		19	WEA		46155
(B) ALBERIA		19	WEA		46285
(C) LA SOURIS S'EN VA EN GUERRE		19	WEA		56188
(D) LE MIROIR	DBL	19	WEA		86011

C52A

DAVID CASTLE (AB

DAVID CASTLE

(A) CASTLE IN THE SKY	1977	PARACHUTE		RRL2001
(B) LOVE YOU FOREVER	1979	PARACHUTE		RRL2009

C53

JIMMY CASTOR (ALL

JIMMY CASTOR BUNCH

( ) DIMENSION 3		1973	RCA		APDI 0103
( ) THE EVERYTHING MAN		1974	ATLANTIC	UK	K 50052
( ) THE EVERYTHING MAN		197	ATCO	US	SD 1305
( ) SUPER SOUND		1975	ATLANTIC	UK	K 50190
( ) SUPER SOUND		1975	ATCO	US	SD 18150
( ) BUTT OF COURSE		1975	ATLANTIC	UK	K 50120
( ) BUTT OF COURSE		1975	ATCO	US	SD 18124
( ) E MAN GROOVIN		1976	ATLANTIC	UK	K 50295
( ) E MAN GROOVIN		1976	ATCO	US	SD 18186
( ) HEY LEROY		197	SMASH	US	MGS 27091
( ) MAXIMUM STIMULATION		197	ATCO	US	SD 19111

C54

TESSA POLLITT	G
ANGELA RISNER	G
BUDGIE CAROLL	B LOUISE K

CASTRATORS

C55

CASUALS

( ) HOUR WORLD	1969	DECCA	UK	SKL 5001

C56

CAT MOTHER

ROY MICHAELS	B G V	(ABD
MICHAEL EQUINE	D G V	(ABD
LARRY PACKER	G V	(AB
BOB SMITH	K D V	(ABD
CHARLIE CHIN	BANJO G V	(A
JAY UNGAR	G V	(B
PAUL JOHNSON	G	(B
LYNDON LEE HARDY	V	(B
CHARLIE HARCOURT		(D
STEVE DAVIDSON	PERC	(D
CHARLIE PRITCHARD	G	

(A) THE STREET GIVETH		1969	POLYDOR		184 300
(A) THE STREET GIVETH		1969	POLYDOR		24 4001
(B) ALBION DOOWAH		1970	POLYDOR		2425 021
(B) ALBION DOOWAH		1970	POLYDOR		24 4023
(C) LAST CHANCE DANCE		1973	UA		UAG 29481
(C) LAST CHANCE DANCE		1973	POLYDOR		5042
(D) CAT MOTHER		1974	BARCLAY		920 285
(D) CAT MOTHER		1974	UA		UAG 29313
(D) CAT MOTHER		1974	POLYDOR		24 5017

C57

CATAPILLA

THIERRY REINHARDT	WIND	(A
ANNA MEEK	V	(A
HUGH EAGLESTONE	SAX	(A
ROBERT CALVERT	SAX	(A
GRAHAM WILSON	G	(A

(A) CATAPILLA		1971	VERTIGO		6360 029
(B) CHANGES		1972	VERTIGO		6360 074

DAVE TAYLOR   B   (A   MALCOLM FRITH   D   (A

C57A

CATCH

ANN LENNOX	V K
DAVE STEWART	G
JIM TOOMEY	D

PETE COMBES   G V

C58

THE CATE BROTHERS

ERNIE CATE	V K	(ALL
EARL CATE	V G	(ALL
NIGEL OLSSON	D	(A
ED GREENE	D	(A
LELAND SKLAR	B	(A
SCOTT EDWARDS	B	(A
STEVE CROPPER	G	(AB
MICHAEL BAIRD	D	(AB
KLAUS VOORMANN	B	(A
DAVID FOSTER	K	(B
DONALD DUNN	B	(B
STEVE FORMAN	PERC	(B
TERRY CAGLE	D V	(BCD
JIM HORN	SAX	(B
BROOKS HUNNICUTT	V	(B
WILLIE HALL	PERC	(B
TIM SCHMIT	V	(C
JERRY JUMONVILLE	SAX	(C
JOEL PESKIN	SAX	(C
MAXINE WILLARD	V	(A
LEVON HELM	D V	(AD

(A) THE CATE BROTHERS		1975	ASYLUM	UK	SYL 9030
(A) THE CATE BROTHERS		1975	ASYLUM	US	7E 1050
(A) THE CATE BROTHERS		1975	ASYLUM		24 4001
(A) THE CATE BROTHERS		1976	ASYLUM	UK	K 53019
(B) IN ONE EYE		1976	ASYLUM	UK	K 53049
(B) IN ONE EYE		1976	ASYLUM	US	7E 1080
(C) THE CATE BROTHERS BAND		1977	ASYLUM	UK	K 53064
(C) THE CATE BROTHERS BAND		1977	ASYLUM	US	7E 1116
(D) FIRE ON THE TRACKS		1979	ATLANTIC	US	SD 19240
(D) FIRE ON THE TRACKS		1979	ATLANTIC	GERM	ATL 50627

GEORGE TERRY	G	(D	PAUL HARRIS	K	(D				
ALBERT SINGLETON	V	(B	JAY GRAYDON	K	(B				
BOBBY KEYS	HRNS	(B	SID SHARP	VLN	(B				
VERNA RICHARDSON	V	(B	LISA ROBERTS	V	(B				
RON EOFF	B	(CD	JOE LALA	PERC	(CD				
STEVE MADAIO	TPT	(C	MARK UNDERWOOD	TPT	(C				
JOHN PHILLIPS	SAX	(C	LINDA SMALL	TROM	(C				
KING ERRISON	PERC	(A	CARL MARCH	SYN	(A				
JULIA TILLMAN	V	(A	GARY COLEMAN	PERC	(A				
WILLIAM SMITTY SMITH	K	(A	BOB GLAUB	B	(A				

C58A

CATFISH

BOB HODGE   V G K   (AB

(A) GET DOWN		19	EPIC	UK	EPC 64006
(B) LIVE CATFISH		1971	EPIC	UK	EPC 64408

C59

CATFISH HODGE

BOB 'CATFISH' HODGE	V G K	(AB
LARRY ZACK	D	(A
JOHN BADANJEK	D	(A
DENNIS KOVARIK	B	(A
SNEAKY PETE KLEINOW	STEEL	(A
BOB SCARF	WIND	(A
JIM THACKERY	G	(B
DAVID NAMERDY	G	(B
DIXIE D BALLIN	V	(B
JAMIE MACKINNON	SAX	(B

(A) SOAP OPERA'S		1975	20th CENTURY		W 202
(B) EYEWITNESS BLUES		1979	ADELPHI		AD 4113

DR JOHN	K	(A	WAYNE COOK	K	(A			
BONNIE RAITT	G	(A	JAMES MONTGOMERY	HARP	(A			
COTTON KENT	K	(B	FREEBO	V	(B			
JOHN LEE	D	(B	DUANE CAMPBELL	B	(B			
JIMMY POWERS	HCA	(B	DIANA CRAWFORD	V	(B			
JAMES COTTON	HCA	(B	DOUG FAGAN	SAX	(B			
SAVOY BEARD	SAX	(B	GEORGE McWHIRTER	TROM	(B			

CATHARSIS   C60

PATRICK MOULIA	G K V	(ABC
CHARLIE EDDI	D	(ABCF
YVES DE ROUBAIX	G V	(ABC
ROLAND BOCQUET	K V	(ABCF
ALAIN GEOFFROY	K V	(AC
CHARLOTTE	V VLN	(AC
NILES BROWN	G VLN	(A
CLAUDE	G SITAR	(F
MICHEL	B	(F

(A) CATHARSIS	19	DISCODIS	FR	AZSH 1025
(A) CATHARSIS	19	SARAVAH		10025
(B) CATHARSIS 2	19	DISCODIS	FR	AZSH 1035
(B) CATHARSIS 2	19	SARAVAH		10035
(C) CATHARSIS	19	EXPLOSIVE		558 004
(D) POP POEMS	19			528002
(E) RIMBAUD C'EST TOI	19	PATHE	FR	064 11473
(F) LE BOLERO DU VEAU DES DAMES	19	SONOPRESSE	FR	ST 69612
(G) 32 MARS	19	MUSIDISC	FR	600507
(H) ET S'AIMER ET MOURIR	19	MUSIDISC	FR	FLD 678

PHILIP CATHERINE   C61

PHILIP CATHERINE	G B K	(ALL
LARRY CORYELL	G	(DE
PALLE MIKKELBORG	TPT	(B
CHARLIE MANANO	WIND	(BC
JOHN LEE	B	(BC
GERRY BROWN	D	(BC
ROB FRANKEN	K	(C

JASPER VAN HOF   K   (BC

(A) STREAM	1972	WB	FR	46049
(B) SEPTEMBER MAN	1974	WB	GERM	46562
(C) GUITARS	1975	ATLANTIC	UK	K 50193
(D) TWIN HOUSE	1977	ATLANTIC	UK	K 50342
(E) SPLENDID	1978	ATLANTIC	UK	K 52086

CATS   C61A

DANNY WESTON	G	(A
DENNIS TILLI	B	(A
FRED ZARRA	K SYN V	(A
TOMMY STEWART	D V	(A

MICHAEL CORR   V   (A   PETER KELTZ   G   (A

(A) CATS	1980	ELEKTRA	US	6E 275

FELIX CAVALIERE   C62

FELIX CAVALIERE	V K	(AB
EARL FORD	TROM	(B
ED LOGAN	SAX	(B
EN BISCHEL	SYN	(B
BUZZ FEITEN	G	(B
JACK SCARANGELLLA	D	(B
RICK MAROTTA	D	(B
TONY FARRELL	SAX	(B
EDGAR MATTHEWS	TPT	(B
WILL LEE	B	(B
DAVE SANBORN	SAX	(B
LESLIE WEST	G	(B
EDDIE RIVERA	B	(B

STEVE KHAN	G	(B
GEORGE YOUNG	SAX	(B
ALAN RUBIN	TPT	(B
TONY JIMINEZ	PERC	(B
LAURA NYRO	V	(B
DINO DANELLI	D	(B
TOM MALONE	TROM	(B
VICTOR MATTSON	SAX	(B
NANCY O'NEILL	V	(B

MERVIN BRONSON	B	(B
GAIL BOGGS	V	(B
WAYNE ANDRE	SAX	(A
DIANE SCANLON	V	(B
DARCY MILLER	V	(B
MICHAEL BRECKER	SAX	(B
JEFF SOUTHWORTH	G	(B
ELLIOT RANDALL	G	(B

(A) FELIX CAVALIERE	1974	BEARSVILLE		US	6955
(B) DESTINY	1975	BEARSVILLE	UK K55505	US	6958
(C) CASTLES IN THE AIR	1979	EPIC	UK		83817

ANDRE CECCARELLI   C62A

ANDRE CECCARELLI	D	(A
JANIK TOP		
HENRI GIORDANO		(A
CHRISTIAN ESCOUDE		(A

FRANCOIS JEANNEAU   (A   DIDIER LOCKWOOD   (A
JEAN CLAUDE CHAVANAT   (A   ALEX LIGERTWOOD   (A

(A) ANDRE CECCARELLI	19	SONOPRESSE	FR	500 002

CENTIPEDE   C63

JOHN MARSHALL	D	(A
TONY FENNELL	D	(A
ROBERT WYATT	D	(A
BRIAN GODDING	G	(A
JULIE TIPPETT	V	(A
MONGESI FEZA	HRN	(A
MARK CHARIG	CORNET	(A
MICK COLLINS	TPT	(A
PETER PARKES	TPT	(A
ELTON DEAN	SAX	(A
JAN STEEL	SAX	(A
IAN McDONALD	SAX	(A
DUDU PUKWANA	SAX	(A

BRIAN BELSHAW	B	(A
MIKE PATTO	V	(A
ALAN SKIDMORE	SAX	(A
LARRY STABBINS	SAX	(A
GARY WINDO	SAX	(A
BRIAN SMITH	SAX	(A
DAVE WHITE	SAX	(A
KARL JENKINS	SAX	(A
JOHN WILLIAMS	SAX	(A
LARGE STRING SECTION		(A

MAGGIE NICHOLLS	V	(A
BOZ BURRELL	V	(A
ROY BABBINGTON	B	(A
JILL LYONS	B	(A
HARRY MILLER	B	(A
JEFF CLYNE	B	(A
DAVE MARKEE	B	(A
KEITH TIPPETT	PNO	(A
IAN CARR	TPT	(A

(A) SEPTOBER ENERGY	1971	NEON		NE9
(A) SEPTOBER ENERGY REISSUE	1974	RCA	DPS	2054

CHA LAWA   C64

CAH LAWA   (A

(A) EXODUS DUB	1978	SKYNOTE

CHACALS DE BETHUNE   C64A

(A) LA MALEDICTION DES ROCKERS	197	BARCLAY	FR	521194

CHAIN   C65

JAMES MADISON	G V	(A
PHIL MANNING	G	(A
IAN CLYNE	K	(A
GREG LAWRIE	G	(A

GEORGE BEAUFORD   HCA V   (A   BARRY SULLIVAN   B   (A
BARRY HARVEY   D   (A   MAL CAPEWELL   WIND   (A

(A) TWO OF A KIND	1973	MUSHROOM	AUST	35017

CHAIN REACTION   C66

(A) INDEBTED TO YOU	1977	GULL	GULP1021

CHAIRMEN OF THE BOARD   C67

GENERAL NORMAN JOHNSON	V	(
EDDIE CUETIS	V	(
HARRISON KENNEDY	V	(
DANNY WOODS	V	(

(A) CHAIRMEN OF THE BOARD	1970	INVICTUS	UK	SVT 1002
(A) CHAIRMEN OF THE BOARD	1970	INVICTUS	US	7300
(B) IN SESSION	1971	INVICTUS	UK	SVT 1003
(B) IN SESSION	1971	INVICTUS	US	7304
(C) BITTERSWEET	1972	INVICTUS	UK	SVT 1006
(D) GREATEST HITS	1973	INVICTUS	UK	SVT 1009
(E) SKIN I'M IN	1974	INVICTUS	UK	65868
(E) SKIN I'M IN	1974	INVICTUS	US	32526

CHALLENGERS   C68

( ) SURFBEAT	1963	STATESIDE	UK	SL 10030
( ) SURFBEAT	1963	VAULT	US	
( ) WIPE OUT	1967	VOCALION		SAVN 8069

C69 CHAMBERS BROTHERS

LESTER CHAMBER	V HCA	(ALL	(A) PEOPLE GET READY	1965	VAULT	US		9003
WILLIE CHAMBERS	G V	(ALL	(A) PEOPLE GET READY	1966	VOCALION	UK	SAVL	8058
GEORGE CHAMBERS	B	(ALL	(B) NOW	1966	VAULT	US		115
JOE CHAMBERS	G V	(ALL	(C) SHOUT	1968	VAULT	US		120
WITH			(D) THE TIME HAS COME TODAY	1968	CBS	US		9522
BRIAN KEENAN	D	(	(D) THE TIME HAS COME TODAY	1968	DIRECTION	UK		63407
			(E) A NEW TIME A NEW DAY	1968	CBS	US		9671
			(E) A NEW TIME A NEW DAY	1968	DIRECTION	UK		63451
			(E) A NEW TIME A NEW DAY	1968	CBS	US		33642
			(F) LIVE AT FILLMORE EAST	1970	CBS	US		20
			(G) FEELING THE BLUES	1970	LIBERTY	UK		LBS83276
			(G) FEELING THE BLUES	1970	VAULT	US		128
			(H) A NEW GENERATION	1971	CBS	US		30032
			(H) A NEW GENERATION	1971	CBS	UK		64156
			(I) OH MY GOD	1972	CBS	US		31158
			(J) UNBOUNDED	1973	AVCO	US		11013
			(K) LOVE PEACE & HAPPINESS	1974	CBS	US		KGP20
			(K) LOVE PEACE & HAPPINESS	1974	CBS	US		66228
			(L) RIGHT MOVE	1975	AVCO	US		69003
			( ) BEST OF	19	MUSIDISC	FR		6018
			(DE) TIME HAS COME/NEW DAY DBL	19	CBS	US		33642
			( ) THE BEST OF	19	FANTASY	US		24718
			( ) GREATEST HITS	19	CBS	US		30871

C70 CHAMPION

GARY BELL	V G	(A	(A) CHAMPION	1978	EPIC	UK		83179
CLEM CLEMPSON	G	(A	(A) CHAMPION	1978	EPIC	US		35438
DAMON BUTCHER	K							

C71 CHAMPS

GLEN CAMPBELL	G	(	( ) EVERYBODY'S ROCKIN'	1960	CHALLENGE	US		2500
CHUCK RIO	SAX		( ) GO CHAMPS GO	196	LONDON	UK	HAH	2152
DAVE BURGESS	G		( ) GREAT DANCE HITS	196	LONDON	UK	HAH	2451
DALE NORRIS	G		( ) BEST OF THE CHAMPS	1977	LONDON	UK	ZGH	141
DEAN BEARD	PNO		( ) PLAY ALL AMERICAN	19	CHALLENGE	US		2514
GENE ALDEN	D		( ) PLAY JOSHUA LOGAN ALL AMERICAN	19	CHALLENGE	US		614
VAN NORMAN	B							
DASH CROFTS	D		JIMMY SEALS SAX	BOBBY MORRIS				

C72 GENE CHANDLER

GENE CHANDLER	V	(ALL	THERE WAS A TIME	197	MCA	UK	MUPS	367
			THERE WAS A TIME	19	BRUNSWICK	US		754131
			ALBUM	1974	JOY		JOYS	136
			DUKE OF EARL	1976	DJM		DJB	26077
			GET DOWN	19	20TH CENTURY	US		578
			SITUATION	1970	MERCURY	US	SR	61304
			THE GIRL DONT CARE	19	BRUNSWICK	US		54124
			TWO SIDES OF	19	BRUNSWICK	US		754149
			WHEN YOU'RE No1	1979	20th CENTURY	UK		T 598

C73 BRUCE CHANNEL

BRUCE CHANNELL	V	(ALL	HEY BABY	19	SMASH	US		27008
			GOIN BACK TO LOUISIANA	19	SONET		SNT	301

C74 CHANTAYS

			PIPELINE	1974	CONTOUR	UK		2879 389

C75 CHANTERS SISTERS

DOREEN CHANTER	K V	(ALL	(A) BIRDS OF A FEATHER	1970	PAGE ONE	UK	POLS	027
IRENE CHANTER	K V	(ALL	(B) FIRST FLIGHT	1976	POLYDOR UK6075	UK	2383	382
RAY WARLEIGH	WIND	(D	(C) READY FOR LOVE	1978	SAFARI		LONG	3
PETE WINGFIELD	K	(D	(D) SHOULDER TO SHOULDER	1978	SAFARI		LONG	4
HENRY SPINETTI	D	(D						
DAVE MARKEE	B	(D	RAY RUSSELL	G	(D	MICK MOODY	G	(D
SIMON PHILLIPS	D	(D	JOHN GIBLIN	B	(D	TONY HYMAS CLAR PNO		(D
RAY COOPER	PERC	(D	HUGH BURNS	G	(D	CHRIS MERCER	SAX	(D
MARTIN DROVER	WIND	(D	JIMMY CHAMBERS	V	(D	TONY JACKSON	V	(D

C76 HARRY CHAPIN

HARRY CHAPIN	G V	(ALL	(A) HEADS & TALES	1971 ELEKTRA US EKS75023	UK K42107
TIM SCOTT	CELLO	(CEGH	(B) SNIPER & OTHER LOVE SONGS	1972 ELEKTRA US EKS75042	UK K42125
JOHN WALLACE	B V	(BCEGHKL	(C) SHORT STORIES	1973 ELEKTRA US EKS75065	UK K42155
PAUL LEKA	K	(CEG	(D) VERITIES & BALDERDASH	1974 ELEKTRA US 7E 1012	UK K52007
JEANNE FRENCH	V	(C	(E) PORTRAIT GALLERY	1975 ELEKTRA US 7E 1041	UK K52023
BUDDY SALZMAN	D	(C	(F) ON THE ROAD TO KINGDOM COME	1976 ELEKTRA US 7E 1082	UK K52040
HOWIE FIELDS	D	(HGKL	(G) GREATEST STORIES LIVE	1976 ELEKTRA US K62015	UK K52021
JOHN TROPEA	G	(EG	(H) DANCE BAND ON THE TITANIC	1977 ELEKTRA us 9E 301	UK K62021
TOM CHAPIN	G BANJ	(GHL	(J) LIVING ROOM SUITE	1978 ELEKTRA US 6E 142	UK K52089
STEVE CHAPIN	PNO V	(EGH	(K) LEGENDS OF THE LOST & FOUND	1979 ELEKTRA	UK K62026
ALLEN SCHWARZBERG	D	(EG			

ED BEDNARSKI	CLAR	(EG	FRANK PORTO	ACC	(E	DONNA D REILLY	V	(H
ROB WHITEWHISTLE		(E	KEN SMITH	PERC MAND	(EG	BOB SPRINGER	PERC	(EG
KRIS KRISTOFFERSON	V	(E	RITA COOLIDGE	V	(E	BILLY SWAN	V	(E
GEORGE SIMS		(EG	ELLIOT RANDALL	G	(H	DOUG WALKER	G B	(GH
DON PEAK	SYN	(E	DAVE KONZIELA	V	(E	FRANK SIMMS	V	(E
RON BACCHIOCCHI	PERC	(EG	SCOTT SPRAY		(EG	BOB SMITH		(EG
PAUL GABRIEL		(EG	JIMMY KEYES		(EG	GENE BIANCO	HARP	(E
SUE WHITE	V	(EG	KATHY RAMOS	V	(EG	KATHY PORTER	V	(E
CAROLYN WILLIS	V	(E	MARTY McCALL	V	(E	JACKIE WARD	V	(E
CHERYL FERRIO	V	(G	JEFF GROSS	V	(EH	TOM SMITH		(G
TIM MOORE	K	(EG	SHEILA TURNER	V	(E	J FLOOD	V	(E
GEOFF PARKER	V	(E	JOAN FISHMAN	V	(E	JUDI PARKER	V	(E
PAUL HUBINON	WIND	(E	BUD BRISBOIS	WIND	(E	JACKIE KELSO	WIND	(E
								(CONTINUED)

HARRY CHAPIN

C76

JAY MIGLIORI	WIND	(E	JIM HORN	SAX	(E	GEORG BOHANON	WIND	(E
CHRISTINE FAITH	V	(G	MARY MUNDY	V	(G	BETSY WAGER	V	(G
STEVE GADD	D	(H	NEIL JASON	B	(H	BUZZ BRAUNER	SAX	(H
HARRY DEVITO	TROM	(H	ARTHUR JENKINS	PERC	(H	CHRIS WAITE	PERC	(H
VICTORIA	CONGA	(H	NANCY NEWMAN	V	(H	CRAIG MITCHELL	V	(H
THEODORE MARNEL	V	(H	STEVE RANDALL	V	(H	MARSH LYNN GOLDBERG	V	(H
JOHN QUAYLE	V	(H	ART KRAHULCK	V	(H	BARBRA CARR	V	(H
MIKE SOLOMON	V	(H	BARBARA LINDQUIST	V	(H	BERNIE KEISING	V	(H
STEVE CHAPIN	PNO V	(EGHKL	DAVE ARMSTRONG	HCA	(C	DON PAYNE	B	(EG
BOBBY CARLIN	D	(C	TOMI LEE BRADLEY	V	(C	KIM SCHOLES	CELLO	(HK
MICHAEL MASTERS	CELLO	(CEG	RON PALMER	G V	(CEGH	YVONNE CABLE	CELLO	(L
JOE LALA	PERC	(L	CHUCK KIRKPATRICK	V	(L	HOWARD ALBERT	SYN	(L
CHARLES CHALMERS	V	(L	SANDRA RHODES	V	(L	DONNA RHODES	V	(L
STRING SECTION	V	(L						

BLONDIE CHAPLIN

C77

BLONDIE CHAPLIN	V G B PERC	(A	(A) BLONDIE CHAPLIN			1977	ASYLUM	UK	K53062
RICKY FATAAR	D PERC	(A							
DAVID MASON	PNO	(A	RICHARD TEE	K	(A	GARTH HUDSON	ACC	(A
JOHN HARTMAN	PNO	(A	STEVE LAWRENCE	SAX	(A	KENNY WALTER	TROM	(A
HOWARD TSUKAMOTO	B	(A	TOM BRAY	HRNS	(A	CAR MUNOL	ORG	(A
BRYAN GAROFALO	B	(A	CLYDIE KING	V	(A	VANEETA FIELDS	V	(A
KENNY GRADNEY	B	(A	DANIEL MOORE	V	(A	CAROL HOLMES	V	(A
MATTHEW MOORE	V	(A	RITA JEAN BODINE	V	(A			

MICHAEL CHAPMAN

C78

MICHAEL CHAPMAN	G K V	(ALL	(A) RAINMAKER		1969	HARVEST	UK	SHVL	755
WITH			(B) FULLY QUALIFIED SURVIVOR		1969	HARVEST	UK	SHVL	764
RAY LAIDLAW	D	(N	(B) FULLY QUALIFIED SURVIVOR		1979	CRIMINAL	UK		STEAL3
RICK KEMP	B	(ABCDEFGK	(C) WINDOW		1971	HARVEST	UK	SHVL	786
BARRY MORGAN	D	(ABK	(D) WRECKED AGAIN		1971	HARVEST	UK	SHVL	798
ANDY LATIMER	G	(HJ	(D) WRECKED AGAIN		1971	POLYDOR	GERM	2310	192
DANNY THOMPSON		(A	(E) MILLSTONE GRIT		1973	HARVEST	UK	SML	1105
CLEM CLEMPSON	G	(AK	(F) DEAL GONE DOWN		1974	HARVEST	UK	SML	1114
NORMAN HAINES		(AK	(G) PLEASURES OF THE STREET		1975	NOVA	GERM		622321
ALEX DMOCHOWSKI	B	(AK	(H) SAVAGE AMUSEMENT		1976	GAMA DECCA	UK	SKLR	5242
AYNSLEY DUNBAR	D	(AK	(J) THE MAN WHO HATED MORNINGS		1977	DECCA	UK	SKLR	5290
MICK RONSON	G	(ABJK	(J) THE MAN WHO HATED MORNINGS		1978	CRIMINAL	UK		STEAL3
GUS DUDGEON		(B	(K) LIVED HERE		1977	CUBE	UK	GNAT	1
PAUL BUCKMASTER	CELLO	(B	(L) PLAYING GUITAR THE EASY WAY		19	CRIMINAL	UK		STEAL2
JOHNNY VAN DERRICK	VLN	(BCJ	(M) LIFE ON THE CEILING		1978	CRIMINAL	UK		STEAL5
ANDRU CHAPMAN	V	(N	(N) LOOKING FOR ELEVEN		1980	CRIMINAL	UK		STEAL9
B J COLE	STEEL	(J						
AROLD FATT	G	(CK	PETE WINGFIELD	K	(J	JOHN McBURNIE	V	(J
RICHIE DHARMA	D	(CK	VIV McAULIFFE	V	(J	PRELUDE	V	(F
ALEX ATTERSON	PNO	(CE	PIQUE WITHERS	D	(DK	RAY MARTINEZ	G	(DK
JACK EMBLOW	ACC	(D	LIZA STRIKE	V	(D	CLAUDETTE HOUCHEN	V	(D
NEIL LANCASTER	V	(D	ALBERT HAMMOND	V	(D	KEEF HARTLEY	D	(EGHJ
NIGEL PEGRUM	D	(F	MADDY PRIOR	V	(F	BRIDGET ST JOHN	V	(F
PETER WOOD	K	(H	LEO LE BLANC	STEEL	(H	MUTT		(GH
STEVIE	V	(GH	FUZZ	V	(GH	STEFFI STEFAN		(G
ACHIM REICHEL		(G	PAUL SUTTON	G	(G	ROD CLEMENTS	B	(J
ANDY ROBERTS	G	(	HENRY McCULLOUGH	G	(	TIM RENWICK	G	(H

ROGER CHAPMAN

C79

ROGER CHAPMAN	V	(ALL	(A) CHAPPO		1979	ARISTA	UK	SPART1083
WITH			(B) LIVE IN HAMBURG		1979	ACROBAT	UK	ACRO 6
DAVE MARKEE	B	(A	(C) MAIL ORDER MAGIC		1980	LINE		LLP5080
BRIAN ODGERS	B	(A						
BILLY LIVSEY	K	(A	JOHN HALSEY	D	(C	LES BINKS	D	(C
GEOFF WHITEHORN	G	(ABC	MICK MOODY	G	(A	HENRY SPINETTI	D	(A
SIMON MORTON	PERC	(A	RAY COOPER	PERC	(A	RON ASPERY	SAX	(A
POLI PALMER	SYN	(AC	PETER HOPE EVANS	HCA	(A	JOY YATES	V	(A
VICKI BROWN	V	(A	JIMMY CHAMBERS	V	(	GEORGE CHANDLER	V	(A
MEL COLLINS	SAX	(B	TIM HINKLEY	K	(BC	JEROME RIMSON	B V	(BC
JOHN WETTON	B	(C	STRETCH	D	(B	HELEN HARDY	V	(B
KATHI O'DONOGHUE	V	(B	MITCH MITCHELL	D	(C			

CHARGE

C80

ROSETTA HIGHTOWER	V	(A	(A) CHARGE		1974	FRESH AIR		6308 900
LEE VANDERBILT	V	(A						
MIKE WOODS	G	(A	NEIL HUBBARD	G	(A	ALAN SPENNER	B	(A
GODFREY MACLEAN	D	(A	SMILEY DE JONNES	PERC	(A	CHRIS STAINTON	ORG	(A
CHRIS MERCER	SAX	(A	STEVE GREGORY	SAS	(A	RON CARTHY	TPT	(A

MARK CHARIG

C80A

MARK CHARIG	TPT	(A	(A) PIPEDREAM		1977	OGUN	

CHARIOT

C80B

MICHAEL KOPLAN	G V	(A	(A) CHARIOT		1968	NATIONAL GENERAL	NG2003
LARRY GOULD	B V						
PUG BAKER	D						

CHARLATANS

C81

DAN HICKS	V D G	(12	(A) THE CHARLATANS		1969	PHILIPS	US	600 309
RICHARD OLSEN	B	(A123	(B) THE CHARLATANS		1979	GROUCHO	IT	MAR X
GEORGE HUNTER	V	(12						
MICHAEL FERGUSON	K	(1	(1) 64 67	(2) 67 68	(C) 68 69			
MIKE WILHELM	V G	(A123						
PATRICK BOGERTY	PNO	(2	TERRY WILSON	D	(A23	DARRYL DEVORE	K	(A3
SAM LINDE	D	(1						

BOBBY CHARLES

C82

BOBBY CHARLES (ROBERT GUIDRY)	(A	(A) BOBBY CHARLES		1972	BEARSVILLE	K 45516
AMOS GARRETT	G	(A					
DR JOHN	K	(A					

CHILLI CHARLES	D V K (AB	(A) BUSY CORNER		1974 VIRGIN	UK V2009
DEL RICHARDSON	G (AB	(B) QUICKSTEP		1975 VIRGIN	UK V2028
ROBERT BAILEY	K (AB				
JOE JAMMER	G (B	MEL COLLINS	SAX (A	GORDON SMITH	G (A
FUZZY SAMUELS	B (A	PAT ARNOLD	V (A	KENNY COLE	V (A
PHIL BECQUE	B (A	JEAN ROUSSEL	B K (B	BROTHER JAMES	V (B
VICKY BUSISWE MHLONGO	V (B	GEORGE LARNYOH	SAX (B	EDDIE QUANSAH	TPT (B
PETE VANDER PUIJE	SAX (B	JON PIRANA	V (B	SUZY SHUTE	V (B

C84   RAY CHARLES

RAY CHARLES   K V (ALL

(EPs)			
HIT THE ROAD JACK	19	HMV	7EG 8729
I CANT STOP LOVING YOU	19	HMV	7EG 8781
BALLAD STYLE OF RAY CHARLES	19	HMV	7EG 8783
BALLAD STYLE OF RAY CHARLES	19	HMV	GES 5864
SWINGING STYLE	19	HMV	7EG 8801
SWINGING STYLE	19	HMV	GES 5871
BABY ITS COLD OUTSIDE	19	HMV	7EG 8807
TAKE THESE CHAINS	19	HMV	7EG 8812
BUSTED	19	HMV	7EG 8841
RAY CHARLES SINGS	19	HMV	7EG 8861

(LPs)

RAY CHARLES	1957	ATLANTIC	8006	CINCINNATI KID	1965	MGM	US	SE4313
RAY CHARLES (HALLELUJAH)	19	ATLANTIC UK	587056	CRYING TIME	1966	HMV	UK	3533
THE GREAT R C	1958	ATLANTIC US	1259	CRYING TIME	1966	HMV	US	344
THE GREAT R C	1958	LONDON UK	15134	RAYS MOOD	1966	HMV	UK	3574
RAY CHARLES AT NEWPORT	1958	ATLANTIC	1289	RAYS MOOD	1966	ABC	US	550
RAY CHARLES AT NEWPORT	1958	LONDON UK	6008	LISTEN	1967	HMV	UK	3630
RAY CHARLES AT NEWPORT	197	ATLANTIC UK	K30032	LISTEN	1967	ABC	US	595
ORIGINAL RAY CHARLES	19	LONDON UK	8022	A MAN & HIS SOUL	1967	ABC		590
YES INDEED	1958	ATLANTIC	8025	LE GRAND	196	ATLANTIC FR	332030
YES INDEED	1958	LONDON UK	2168	IN THE HEAT OF THE NIGHT	1967	U A	US	5160
WHAT'D I SAY	1959	ATLANTIC	8029	GREAT HITS (5LP SET)	19	LONGINES US	95647
WHAT'D I SAY	1959	LONDON UK	2226	14 ORIGINAL HITS	19	STARDAY US K	5011
WHAT'D I SAY	19	ATLANTIC UK	588161	GREATEST HITS VOL 2	19	STATESIDE	UK10241
WHAT'D I SAY	1971	ATLANTIC UK	K40029	LOVE COUNTRY STYLE	1969	PROBE		1015
GENIUS OF R C	1959	ATLANTIC	1312	LOVE COUNTRY STYLE	19	ABC		707
RAY CHARLES	1959	XTRA	1103	IM ALL YOURS BABY	1969	ABC		675
SOUL BROTHERS	1959	LONDON UK	6030	IM ALL YOURS BABY	1969	STATESIDE		10281
RAY CHARLES SEXTET	1960	LONDON UK	15178	DOING HIS THING	1959	ABC	US	695
RAY CHARLES SEXTET	1960	ATLANTIC	1304	THE ARTISTRY OF	19	BARONET	US	111
IN PERSON	1960	ATLANTIC US	8039	3 OF A KIND	19	DESIGN	US	909
IN PERSON	1960	LONDON UK	2284	PORTRAIT OF RAY	1969	STATESIDE UK	10269
GENIUS SINGS THE BLUES	1960	ATLANTIC	8052	PORTRAIT OF RAY	1969	ABC	US	625
GENIUS SINGS THE BLUES	1960	LONDON UK	15238	MY KIND OF JAZZ	1970	TANGERINE 6495 001
DEDICATED TO YOU	1960	HMV UK	1362	FOCUS ON	1975	LONDON		F051/2
DEDICATED TO YOU	1961	HMV UK	1449	MY KIND OF JAZZ	1970	TANGERINE TRCS1512
DEDICATED TO YOU	1961	ABC UK	355	VOLCANIC ACTION	1971	PROBE		1039
GENIUS+SOUL=JAZZ	1960	ATLANTIC	A2	VOLCANIC ACTION	1971	ABC	US	726
GENIUS+SOUL=JAZZ	1961	HMV UK	1384	PRESENTS THE RAELETTES	1972	TANGERINE US	1515
GENIUS+SOUL=JAZZ	1961	HMV UK	1475	JAZZ NUMBER TWO	1973	TANGERINE US	1516
DO THE TWIST	196	ATLANTIC	8054	MESSAGE FROM THE PEOPLE	1972	PROBE		1060
GENIUS HITS THE ROAD	1960	ABC US	335	MESSAGE FROM THE PEOPLE	1972	ABC	US	755
GENIUS HITS THE ROAD	1960	HMV UK	1387	25th ANNIVERSARY(DBL)	1972	ATLANTIC UK	K60014
GENIUS HITS THE ROAD	1960	HMV UK	1320	25th ANNIVERSARY(DBL)	1971	ABC	US	731
& BETTY CARTER	1960	COLUMBIA	340742	ORIGINAL RAY CHARLES	1972	BOULEVARD		4005
& BETTY CARTER	1960	HMV US	385	GENIUS IN CONCERT L A	1973	BLUESWAY		6053
& BETTY CARTER	196	ABC US	385	ALLTIME GREAT C&W HITS	1973	PROBE	UK	108
& BETTY CARTER	196	HMV UK	1414	THE FANTASTIC	19	MUSIDISC		ALB103
MODERN SOUNDS IN C&W	196	HMV UK	1580	MEMORIES OF MOVIE FAN	19	ATLANTIC		SD 263
MODERN SOUNDS IN C&W	196	ABC US	410	INCOMPARABLE	19	MUSIDISC		CV 964
MODERN SOUNDS IN C&W 2	196	HMV UK	1613	STAR COLLECTION	1978	MIDI	FR	20015
MODERN SOUNDS IN C&W 2	196	ABC US	435	BEST OF	19	POLYDOR	2472 044
SOUL MEETING(MILT JACKSON)	1962	ATLANTIC	1360	THROUGH THE EYES OF LOVE	1973	PROBE	UK	1066
SOUL MEETING(MILT JACKSON)	197	ATLANTIC	K50234	THROUGH THE EYES OF LOVE	1973	ABC	US	765
SOUL MEETING(MILT JACKSON)	1963	LONDON UK	8046	COME LIVE WITH ME	1974	LONDON	UK	8467
GREATEST HITS	1962	ABC US	415	COME LIVE WITH ME	1974	CROSSOVER		9000
GREATEST HITS	196	HMV UK	1482	WORLD OF RAY CHARLES VOL 2	1975	DECCA	UK	422
GREATEST HITS	196	HMV UK	1626	WORLD OF RAY CHARLES	1974	ARGO	UK	SPA361
STORY VOL 1	1962	ATLANTIC	8063	LIVE IN JAPAN	DBL	1975	CROSSOVER		535/6
STORY VOL 1	1962	LONDON UK	8023	RENAISSANCE	1975	LONDON	UK	8485
STORY VOL 2	1962	ATLANTIC	8064	RENAISSANCE	1975	CROSSOVER		9005
STORY VOL 2	1962	LONDON UK	8024	MY KIND OF JAZZ VOL 3	1975	CROSSOVER		9007
STORY VOL 3	1963	ATLANTIC	8083	THE GREAT R C	19	MUSIDISC		1232
GREAT HITS	1963	HMV UK	1482	HONEY HONEY	19	XTRA		1103
GREAT HITS	1963	ATLANTIC	7101	PORGY & BESS(CLEO LAINE)	1976	RCA	US 2	1831
RECIPE FOR SOUL	1963	ABC US	465	PORGY & BESS(CLEO LAINE)	1976	LONDON		D 31/2
RECIPE FOR SOUL	1963	HMV UK	1678	THE BEST OF	19	MCP		8029
SWEET & SOUR TEARS	1963	ABC US	480	RAY CHARLES	19	EVEREST	US	244
SWEET & SOUR TEARS	1963	HMV UK	1728	RAY CHARLES VOL2	19	EVEREST	US	292
SWEET & SOUR TEARS	1963	HMV UK	1537	RAY CHARLES	19	UPFRONT	US UPF170
C&W MEETS R&B	196	HMV UK	1630	RAY CHARLES	19	UPFRONT	US UPF192
C&W MEETS R&B	196	HMV UK	1914	TRUE TO LIFE	1977	LONDON		8509
STORY VOL 4	1964	ATLANTIC	8094	TRUE TO LIFE	1977	ATLANTIC		19142
HAVE A SMILE WITH ME	1964	HMV UK	1566	WHAT HAVE DONE TO THEIR SONG	1977	LONDON		ZGU 139
HAVE A SMILE WITH ME	1964	HMV UK	1795	LOVE & PEACE	1978	LONDON		8519
LIVE	196	ATLANTIC US	2503	BLUES	1978	EMBER	UK CJS854
IN CONCERT	1965	HMV UK	1872	LOVE & PEACE	1978	ATCO		19199
IN CONCERT	1965	HMV UK	1606	FABULOUS RAY CHARLES	1978	MUSIDISC		CV1288
IN CONCERT	1965	ABC US	500	AIN'T IT SO	1979	LONDON	UK SHL8537
TOGETHER AGAIN	1965	ABC US	520	SUPERDISC OF R C	1979	A&M		GXM9012
TOGETHER AGAIN	1965	HMV UK		20 GOLDEN PIECES OF R C	1979	BULLDOG	BDL2012
SENSATIONAL	1965	SOCIETY	998					

CHARLIE C85

JOHN ANDERSON	B V	(ABCD	(A) FANTASY GIRLS	1976	POLYDOR	UK	2382 373
TERRY THOMAS	G V	(ABCD	(A) FANTASY GIRLS	1976	CBS	US	33081
STEVE GADD	D PERC	(ABCD	(B) NO SECOND CHANCE	1977	POLYDOR	UK	2383 422
JULIAN COLBECK	K	(CD	(B) NO SECOND CHANCE	1977	JANUS	US	7032
EUGENE ORGAN	G V	(CD	(C) LINES	1978	POLYDOR	UK	2383 487
GRAEME QUINTON-JONES	K	(A	(C) LINES	1978	JANUS	UK	7036
MARTIN SMITH	G V	(A	(D) FIGHT DIRTY	1979	POLYDOR	UK	2443 161
SHEP LONSDALE	D	(D	(D) FIGHT DIRTY	1979	POLYDOR		POLD 5017
VICTOR PAZ	TPT	(D					
ARNIE LAWRENCE	SAX	(D	LAWRENCE FELDMAN	SAX	(D	PETE THOMS	TROM (D
PHILLIP TODD	FLT	(D	DAVID POTTS	FLT	(D	RAY COOPER	PERC (D

CHARLIE & THE PEP BOYS C86

CHARLIE WOODS-PEARSON	V	(A	(A) DADDY'S GIRL	1976	A&M	UK	AMLH64563
MICHAEL STERN	G	(A	(A) DADDY'S GIRL	1976	A&M	US	SP 4563
ALAN ADKINS	G	(A					
BOBBY MANRIQUEZ	G	(A	ROLF HANSON	B	(A	MICHAEL ZACK	D (A
MICHAEL S	SAX	(A	CRAIG RYAN	TPT	(A	LEFTY POTOMAC	K (A

CHARLIE & THE WIDE BOYS C87

CHARLIE AINLEY	V	(AB	(A) CHARLIE & THE WIDE BOYS (EP)	1974	ANCHOR		ANCE 1007
RICHARD WORTHY	G	(AB	(B) GREAT COUNTRY ROCKERS	1976	MFP ANCHOR		50293
GREG PHILLIPS	V PERC	(AB					
NIGEL CHAPPELL	B	(AB	GUY EVANS	D	(AB	SIMON FRASER	G (AB

CHARLIE BOY C87A

CHARLIE NEWPORT	G V	(A	(A) INTRODUCING CHARLIE BOY	19	RELEASE		BRL 4076
EDDY WILLIAMS	B V	(A					
STEVE HODGES	V	(A	BRIAN ROPER	D V	(A	BILLY ROPER G STEEL V (A
FRED LLOYD	K	(A	BRENDAN BONASS	G	(A	

CHARTREUSE C88

PAUL JEFFREYS	B				
MILTON REAME-JAMES	K				
JEFF FAULKNER	G	MALCOLM ASHMAN	D	ROB ELLIOT	V

CHAS & DAVE C89

CHAS HODGES		(A) ONE FING 'N'ANUVVER	1975	RETREAT RT6004	NUT	NUT17
DAVE PEACOCK		(B) CHAS & DAVE	1978	ROCKNEY		OCKNEY 1
		(C) ROCKNEY	1978	EMI		EMC 3288
		(D) MUSTN'T GRUMBLE	1981	ROCKNEY		909

CHASE C90

BILL CHASE	TPT	(ABCD	(A) CHASE	1971	EPIC/CBS	UK	64544
TED PIERCEFIELD	TPT V	(A	(A) CHASE	1971	EPIC	US	33737
ALAN WARE	TPT	(A	(A) CHASE	197	EPIC	US	30472
JERRY VAN BLAIR	TPT V	(A	(B) ENNEA	1972	EPIC/CBS	UK	64710
PHIL PORTER	K	(A	(B) ENNEA	1972	EPIC	US	31097
DENNIS JOHNSON	B V	(A	(C) PURE MUSIC	1974	EPIC	UK	80017
ANGEL SOUTH	G V	(A	(C) PURE MUSIC	1974	EPIC	US	32572
JAY SOLLENBERGER	TPT	(C	(D) GET IT ON	197	EPIC	US	26297
DARTANYAN BROWN	B V	(A					
JAY BURRID	PERC	(A	JIM OATTS	TPT	(C	JOHN EMMA	G (C
TERRY RICHARDS	V	(A	JOE MORRISSEY	TPT	(C	JIM PETERIK	V (C
WALLY YOHN	K	(C	TOM GORDON	D	(C	

CHEAP FLIGHTS C91

JOHN GRIMALDI	G				
PETER ARNESEN	K				
PETE ERNEST	G	DAN BROWN	B	CLIFF VENNER	PERC

CHEAP TRICK C92

RICK NIELSEN	G	(ABCDEF	(A) CHEAP TRICK	1977	EPIC	US	34400
TOM PETERSSON	B	(ABCDEF	(B) IN COLOR	1977	EPIC	UK	82214
ROBIN ZANDER	V	(ABCDEF	(B) IN COLOR	1977	EPIC	US	34884
BUN E CARLOS	D	(ABCDEF	(C) HEAVEN TONIGHT	1978	EPIC	UK	82679
XENO	V	(	(C) HEAVEN TONIGHT	1978	EPIC	US	35312
			(D) LIVE AT BUDOKAN	1978	EPIC	UK	86083
			(D) LIVE AT BUDOKAN	1978	EPIC	US	35795
			(D) LIVE AT BUDOKAN	1978	EPIC		253P5
			(E) DREAM POLICE	1979	EPIC	UK	85322
			(F) ALL SHOOK UP	1980	EPIC	UK	86124

CHEATERS C92A

NEIL COSSAR	G		
MICK BROPHY	G		
JON MARTIN	K	STUART BURNETT D	

CHUBBY CHECKER C93

CHUBBY CHECKER	V	(ALL	CHEQUERED	19	LONDON	UK	SHZ 8419
			TWIST	1962	COLUMBIA	UK	
			DONT KNOCK THE TWIST	1962			
			TWIST WITH	1962	PARKWAY	US	P7001
			ITS PONY TIME	1962			
			LETS TWIST AGAIN	1962	PARKWAY	US	P7004
			YOUR TWIST PARTY	1962	PARKWAY	US	P7007
			TWISTIN' AROUND THE WORLD	1962	PARKWAY	US	P7008
			FOR TEEN TWISTERS ONLY	19	PARKWAY	US	P7009
			TWISTIN' AROUND THE WORLD	1962	GOLDEN GUINEA	UK	GGL 0236
			ALL THE HITS	1963	PARKWAY		P7014
			LIMBO PARTY	1963	PARKWAY	US	P7020
			BIGGEST HITS	1963			
			LETS LIMBO SOME MORE	1963			
			BEACH PARTY	1963			
			TWIST IT UP	196			
			CHUBBY CHECKER & BOBBY RYDELL	19	CAMEO		C1013

(CONTINUED)

CHUBBY CHECKER

DISCOTHEQUE	19			
FOLK ALBUM	1964	PARKWAY		P7040
DOWN TO EARTH	1963	CAMEO		C1029
GOLDEN HITS	196	CAMEO	US	C1063
DANCIN' PARTY (EP)	1963	CAMEO		CPE 550
GREATEST HITS	1976	LONDON	UK	HAU 8492

CHEECH & CHONG

RICHARD CHEECH MARIN
THOMAS CHONG

CHEECH & CHONG	1971	A&M	UK	AMLS67010
CHEECH & CHONG	1971	WB	US	K3250
BIG BAMBU	1972	A&M	UK	AMLH67014
BIG BAMBU	1972	WB	US	K3251
LOS COCHINOS	1973	ODE	UK	ODE 77019
LOS COCHINOS	1973	WB	US	K3252
WEDDING ALBUM	1974	ODE	UK	ODE 77025
WEDDING ALBUM	1974	WB	US	K3253
SLEEPING BEAUTY	1976	ODE	UK	ODE 77040
SLEEPING BEAUTY	1976	WB	US	K3254

CHELSEA

GENE OCTOBER	V G	(A) CHELSEA	1979	STEP FORWARD	UK	SFLP 2
BRIAN JAMES	G	(B) ALTERNATIVE HITS	1980	STEP FORWARD	UK	SFLP 5
BILLY IDOL	V					
JOHN TOWE	D	TONY JAMES B	BOY CARIE		D	
BOB JESSIE	B	MARTI STACEY G	GARY FORTUNE		D	
JAMES STEVENSON	G	GEOFF MYLES B	STEVE L JONES		D	

CHER

CHER	V	(ALL	ALL I REALLY WANT TO DO	1965	LIBERTY	UK	SLBY 3058
		ALL I REALLY WANT TO DO	196	IMPERIAL	US	12292
		SONNY SIDE OF CHER	1966	LIBERTY	UK	SLBY 3072
		SONNY SIDE OF CHER	196	IMPERIAL	US	12301
		CHER	1967	LIBERTY	UK	SLBY 3081
		CHER	196	IMPERIAL	US	12320
		WITH LOVE	1968	IMPERIAL	US	12358
		BACKSTAGE	1968	IMPERIAL	US	12373
		GOLDEN GREATS	1968			
		3614 JACKSON HIGHWAY	19	ATCO	US	33298
		CHER	1971	MCA	UK	MUPS 438
		CHER	1974	MCA	UK	MCF 2508
		CHER	19	UA	US	UXS 88
		CHER	19	UA	US	UXS 94
		CHER	19	CBS	US	3649
		SINGS THE HITS	19	SPRINGBOARD	US	4029
		GREATEST HITS	19	SPRINGBOARD	US	4028
		FOXY LADY	1972	MCA		MUPS 459
		FOXY LADY	197	KAPP	US	KRS 5514
		FOXY LADY	197	MCA	UK	MCF 2521
		HITS OF CHER	1972	UA	UK	UAS 29317
		BITTERSWEET WHITE LIGHT	1973	MCA	UK	MUPS 484
		BITTERSWEET WHITE LIGHT	1974	MCA	UK	MCF 2511
		HALF BREED	1974	MCA	UK	MCF 2501
		HALF BREED	1974	MCA	US	2104
		DARK LADY	1974	MCA	UK	MCF 2559
		DARK LADY	1974	MCA	US	2113
		STARS	1975	WB	US	2850
		STARS	1975	WB	UK	K 56111
		GOLDEN HITS	1975	SUNSET	UK	SLS 50378
		GOLDEN HITS	19	UA	UK	UAS 29317
		THIS IS CHER	197	SUNSET	US	5276
		GREATEST HITS	1975	MCA	UK	MCF 2597
		GREATEST HITS	197	MCA	US	2127
		I'D RATHER BELIEVE IN YOU	1977	WB	US	BS 2898
		I'D RATHER BELIEVE IN YOU	1977	WB	UK	K 56292
		CHERISHED	1977	WB	US	S 3046
		CHERISHED	1977	WB	UK	K 56401
		TAKE ME HOME	19	CASABLANCA	US	7133
		TAKE ME HOME	1979	CASABLANCA	UK	CAL 2047

CHEYNES

PETER BARDENS	K V				
ROGER PEACOCK	V				
PHIL SAWYER	G	MICK FLEETWOOD D	EDDIE LYNCH G	PETER HOLLIS	B

CHI LITES

EUGENE RECORD
MARSHALL THOMPSON
ROBERT LESTER
CREADEL JONES

GIVE IT AWAY	1968	MCA	UK	MUPS 397
GIVE IT AWAY	1968	BRUNSWICK	US	754152
GIVE MORE POWER TO THE PEOPLE	1971	MCA	UK	MUPS 437
GIVE MORE POWER TO THE PEOPLE	1971	BRUNSWICK	US	7541??
GIVE MORE POWER TO THE PEOPLE	1976	BRUNSWICK		BRLS 3011
A LONELY MAN	1972	MCA	UK	MUPS 457
A LONELY MAN	1972	BRUNSWICK	US	754179
A LONELY MAN	1972	BRUNSWICK		BRLS 3012
A LETTER TO MYSELF	1973	BRUNSWICK	UK	BRLS 3007
A LETTER TO MYSELF	1973	BRUNSWICK	US	754118
THE CHI LITES	1974	BRUNSWICK	UK	BRLS 3009
TOBY	1974	BRUNSWICK	UK	BRLS 3010
TOBY	1974	BRUNSWICK	US	754200
HALF A LOVE	1975	BRUNSWICK	UK	BRLS 3015
				(CONTINUED)

CHI LITES   C98

HALF A LOVE	1975	BRUNSWICK	US	754204
HALF A LOVE	1978	LONDON	UK	SHU 8521
HAPPY BEING LONELY	1976	MERCURY	UK	9100 027
HAPPY BEING LONELY	1976	MERCURY	US	SRM1 1118
VERY BEST OF THE CHI LITES	1976	BRUNSWICK	UK	BRLS 3023
CHILITETIME (COMP)	1976	LONDON	UK	SHU 8520
GREATEST HITS VOL 2	19	BRUNSWICK	US	754208
THE FANTASTIC CHI LITES	1977	MERCURY	UK	9100 041
THE FANTASTIC CHI LITES	1977	MERCURY	US	SRM1 1147

CHIC   C99

NORMA JEAN	V	(A
ALFA ANDERSON	V	(AB
BERNARD EDWARDS	V K	(AB
TONY THOMPSON	D	(AB
DIVA GRAY	V	(AB
LUCI MARTIN	V	(B
VALERIE HAYWOOD	VLN	(
DAVID LASLEY	V	(AB
LUTHER VANDROSS	V	(AB
ANDY SCHWARTZ	K	(AB
JON FADDIS	HRNS	(AB
KENNY LEHMAN	WIND	(A
GEORGE YOUNG	WIND	(A
MARIANNE CARRoll	VLN	(B
ELLEN SEELING	HRNS	(B

(A) CHIC	1978	ATLANTIC UK K 50441
(A) CHIC	1978	ATLANTIC US SD 19153
(B) C'EST CHIC	1978	ATLANTIC UK K 50565
(B) C'EST CHIC	1978	ATCO US SD 19209
(C) RISQUE	1979	ATLANTIC UK K 50634
(D) GREATEST HITS	1979	ATLANTIC UK K 50686
(E) REAL PEOPLE	1980	ATLANTIC UK K 50711

NILE RODGERS	G	(AB	ROBERT SABINO	K	(AB
RAYMOND JONES	K	(B	SAMMY FIGUEROA	PERC	(AB
BARRY ROGERS	TROM	(AB	ROBIN CLARK	V	(A
DAVID FRIEDMAN	PERC	(A	TOM COPPOLA	K	(A
GLORIA AGOSTINI	HARP	(A	JOE ROSSY	PERC	(B
CHERYL HONG	VLN	(B	KAREN MILNE	VLN	(B
ALEX FOSTER	HRNS	(B	JEAN FINEBERG	HRNS	(B

CHICAGO   C100

PETER CETERA	B G V	(ALL	(A) CHICAGO TRANSIT AUTHORITY(DBL)	1968	CBS UK 66221	US	PG8
ROBERT LAMM	K V	(ALL	(B) CHICAGO	(DBL)	1970	CBS UK 66233	US 2G24
TERRY KATHBS	G V	(A7TO'L	(C) CHICAGO 3	(DBL)	1971	CBS UK 66260	US 30110
JAMES PANKOW		(ALL	(D) CHICAGO 4	(LIVE)	1971	CBS UK 66405	US 30865
LEE LOUGHNANE V PERC TPT		(ALL	(E) CHICAGO 5		1972	CBS UK 69018	US 31002
WALTER PARAZEIDER	WIND	(ALL	(F) CHICAGO 6		1973	CBS UK 69041	US 32400
DANIEL SERAPHINE	D	(ALL	(G) CHICAGO 7	(DBL)	1974	CBS UK 88015	US 32810
LAUDIR DE OLIVEIRA	PERC	(I	(H) CHICAGO 8		1975	CBS UK 69130	US 33130
DONNIE DACUS	G	(M	(I) GREATEST HITS		1975	CBS UK 69222	US 33900
			(J) LIVE IN JAPAN 1972		1975	CBS/SONY JAP	SCP531/32
			(K) CHICAGO 10		1976	CBS UK 86101	US 34260
			(L) CHICAGO XI		1977	CBS UK 86031	US 34860
			(M) HOT STREETS		1978	CBS UK 86069	US 35512
			(N) No13		1979	CBS UK 86093	
			(O) CHICAGO XVI		1980	CBS UK 86118	

CHICKEN SHACK   C101

STAN WEBB	G V	(ALL	(A) 40 BLUE FINGERS	1968	BLUE HORIZON UK 7 63203
CHRISTINE PERFECT	K V	(ABK	(B) O.K. KEN	1968	BLUE HORIZON UK 7 63209
ANDY SYLVESTER	B	(ABCDK	(C) 100 TON CHICKEN	1969	BLUE HORIZON UK 7 63218
DAVE BIDWELL	D	(ABCDK	(D) ACCEPT	1970	BLUE HORIZON UK 7 63861
PAUL RAYMOND	V K	(CDK	(E) IMAGINATION LADY	1972	DERAM UK SDL5
JOHN GLASCOCK	B	(E	(E) IMAGINATION LADY	1972	DERAM US 18063
PAUL HANCOX	D	(E	(F) UNLUCKY BOY	1973	DERAM UK SML1100
ED SPEVOCK	D	(H1	(G) GOODBYE	(LIVE)	1974	NOVA SDL8008
STEVE YORK	B	(1	(G) GOODBYE	(LIVE)	197	NOVA GERM 6 21579
ROBBIE BLUNT	G	(1H	(FG) STAN THE MAN	DBL	1977	NOVA GERM 6 28375
DAVE WINTHROP	SAX	(1H	(H) THE CREEPER	1978	EURODISC 913 203
PAUL MARTINEZ	B	(H	(H) THE CREEPER	1978	ARIOLA 25891
ALAN ELLIS	TPT	(AK	(J) THATS THE WAY WE ARE	1978	SHARK GERM 148 501
DAVE WILKINSON	K	(F	(K) IN THE CAN	(COMP)	1980	CBS UK 31811
ROB HULL	B	(F	( ) GOLDEN ERA OF POP MUSIC(DBL)	1977	CBS UK 68252
ALAN POWELL	D	(F	( ) CHICKEN SHACK	1979	GULL UK GULP 1034
BUD BEADLE	SAX	(B	(1) LIVE 78 GIG			
ALISON YOUNG	V	(D				

DICK HECKSTALL SMITH SAX		(ALL	RODERICK LEE	TPT	(B	TERRY NOONAN	TPT	(B
WALTER HORTON	HCA	(B	JOHNNY ALMOND	SAX	(AB	STEVE GREGORY	SAX	(B
DON FEY	SAX	(B	TONY ASHTON	K	(H	

CHIEFTAINS   C102

PADDY MOLONEY	PIPES	(ABCDE	(A) CHIEFTAINS 1	1965 CLADDAGH IRL CC2 ISLAND 76 RI ILPS9364
SEAN POTTS	WHISTLE	(EH	(A) CHIEFTAINS 1	1978 CBS RI 82986
SEAN KEANE	FDL	(EH	(B) CHIEFTAINS 2	1969 CLADDAGH IRL CC7 ISLAND 76 RI ILPS9365
MARTIN FAY	FDL	(EH	(B) CHIEFTAINS 2	1978 CBS RI 82988
MICK TUBRIDY	FLT	(EH	(C) CHIEFTAINS 3	1971 CLADDAGH IRL RRC10 ISLAND 76 RI ILPS9379
PEADAR MERCIER	BODHRAN	(E	(C) CHIEFTAINS 3	1978 CBS RI 82987
DEREK BELL	HARP	(EH	(D) CHIEFTAINS 4	1975 CLADDAGH IRL RRC14 ISLAND 76 RI ILPS9380
KEVIN CONNEFF	BODHRAN	(H	(D) CHIEFTAINS 4	1978 CBS RI 82989
RONNIE McSHANE	PERC	(E	(E) CHIEFTAINS 5	1975 CLADDAGH IRL CC16 ISLAND 76 RI ILPS9334
			(E) CHIEFTAINS 5	1978 CBS RI 82991
			(F) BONAPARTES RETREAT	1976 ISLAND UK ILPS9432
			(G) LIVE	1977 ISLAND UK ILPS9501
			(H) CHIEFTAINS 7	1978 CLADDAGH IRL CC24
			(H) CHIEFTAINS 7	1978 CBS UK 82814 US 35612
			(J) CHIEFTAINS	1979 CBS UK 83262

CHIFFONS

C103

JUDY CRAIG	V	(
BARBARA LEE	V	(
PATRICIA BENNET	V	(
SYLVIA PETERSON	V	(

(A) THE CHIFFONS	1963	STATESIDE	UK	S1	10040
(A) THE CHIFFONS	196	LAURIE	US		2018
(B) ONE FINE DAY	196	LAURIE	US		2020
(C) SWEET TALKIN GUY	1966	STATESIDE	UK	SSL	10190
(C) SWEET TALKIN GUY	196	LAURIE	US		2036
(C) SWEET TALKIN GUY	1972	LONDON	UK	ZGP	125
(D) SWEET TALKIN	1972	PHASE 4		PFS	4256
(E) EVERTHING YOU ALWAYS WANTED	19	LAURIE	US		4001
(EP) THEY'RE SO FINE	19	STATESIDE	UK	SE	1012
( ) PICK HITS	1976	SONIC	UK	SON	005

C103A

CHILDREN

(A) REBIRTH	19	ATCO	US		SD33271

C104

CHILDREN OF GOD

GERRY MOORE	V G WIND	(1
EDDIE VERNON	V K HCA	(1
TOM EVERETT	V G K	(1

(1) 1969 US

C105

CHILLI WILLI & THE RED HOT PEPPERS

MARTIN STONE	G MAND	(AB
SNAKEFINGERS LITHMAN	G	(AB
PETE THOMAS	D	(B
BOB ANDREWS	SAX K	(AB
RED RHODES	STEEL	(B
SOPHIE ISRAEL	V	(B
BILLY RANKIN	D	(A
DAVE VORHAUS	SYN	(A

(A) KINGS OF THE ROBOT RHYTHM	1972	REVELATION	UK	REV	002
(B) BONGOS OVER BALHAM	1974	MOONCREST	UK	CREST	21

P C BAILEY	BANJO SAX G	(B	WILL STALLIBRASS	HCA	(B
JO ANN KELLY	V	(AB	JACQUI McSHEE	V	(B
CAROL GRIMES	V	(B	NICK LOWE	B	(A
ENGLISH JOHN FOX	B	(A	BARRY EVERITT	PERC	(A
PAUL RILEY	B	(B			

C106

CHILLIWACK

BILL HENDERSON	V G	(
HOWARD FROESE	V G K	(
CLAIRE LAWRENCE WIND B K	(
GLENN MILLER	V B	(
ROSS TURNEY	D	(

(A) CHILLIWACK	1971	LONDON UK SHU8418 PARROT			71040
(B) CHILLIWACK	197	A&M UK AMLH63509	US		3509
(C) CHILLIWACK	197	SIRE	US		7506
(D) ROCKERBOX	197	SIRE UK 9103 250	US		7511
(C) DREAMS DREAMS DREAMS	1977	MUSHROOM		MRS	5006
(D) ALL OVER YOU	1972	A&M	US		4375
(E) LIGHTS FROM THE VALLEY	197	MUSHROOM	US	MRS	5011

C107

CHINA

DAVEY JOHNSTONE	G	(A
JAMES NEWTON HOWARD	K	(A
COOKER LOPRESTI	B	(A

(A) CHINA	1977	ROCKET	UK		ROLL9

DENNIS CONWAY	D	(A	JO PARTRIDGE	G	(A

C107A

CHOCOLATE & CLAY

GEORGE 'CHOCOLATE' PERRY B	(A
CLAY CROPPER	G K	(A
JOE MILLER	SAX	(A

(A) CHOCOLATE & CLAY	1977	CAT	US		2610

C107B

HAROLD SEAY	D	(A

CHOCOLATE WATCHBAND

(A) NO WAY OUT	19	TOWER	US	ST	5096
(B) THE INNER MYSTIQUE	19	TOWER	US	ST	5106
(C) ONE STEP BEYOND	19	TOWER	US	ST	5153

C108

CHOPYN

ANN ODELL	V K	(A
DENNY McCAFFREY	V	(A
RAY RUSSELL	G V	(A
SIMON COLCLOUGH	V PERC	(A

(A) GRAND SLAM	1975	JET	UK		LP 08

KLYDE McMULLIN	G V	(A	SIMON PHILLIPS	D PERC	(A

C109

KEITH CHRISTMAS

KEITH CHRISTMAS	G V PERC	(ALL
WITH		
PAT DONALDSON	B	(B
GERRY CONWAY	D	(B
IAN WHITEMAN	K	(B
BOB STEWART	K	(B
ROGER POWELL	D	(B
SHELAGH McDONALD	V	(B
ALAN SPENNER	B	(D
EDDIE MORDUE	SAX	(D
MALCOLM GRIFFITHS	TROM	(D
DARRYL RUNSWICK	B	(D
TOMMY REILLY	HCA	(D
STEVE CROPPER	G	(E
DONALD DUNN	B	(E
PETER BERNSTEIN	V SYN	(E
KEITH TIPPETT	PNO	(E

(A) STIMULUS	1969	RCA		SF	8059
(B) FABLE OF THE WINGS	1970	B+C		CAS	1015
(C) PIGMY	1971	B+C		CAS	1041
(D) BRIGHTER DAY	1974	MANTICORE		K	53503
(D) BRIGHTER DAY	1974	MANTICORE	US		MA6
(E) STORIES FROM A HUMAN ZOO	1976	ATLANTIC		K	13515
(E) STORIES FROM A HUMAN ZOO	1976	ATLANTIC	UK	K	53509

IAN WALLACE	D	(D	NEIL HUBBARD	G	(D
RAY WARLEIGH	SAX	(D	MEL COLLINS	SAX	(D
HENRY LOWTHER	TPT	(D	MARTIN DROVER	TPT	(D
IAN McDONALD	K	(D	PETE SOLLEY	K	(D
SKAILA KANGA	HCA	(D	WILL WATSON	HRNS	(D
SNUFFY WALDEN	G	(E	DAVID NICHTERN	G	(E
WILLIAM SMITH	K	(E	DAVID KEMPER	D	(E
WENDY WALDMAN	V	(E	DANIEL MOORE	V	(E
MIKE EVANS	B	(B			

C110

CHROME

JOHN L CYBORG	DATA	(ABC
DAMON EDGE	V G K	(ABC
GARRY SPAIN	B G V	(ABC
HELIOS CREED	V G B	(ABC

(A) THE VISITATION	1976	SIREN			DE1000
(B) ALIEN SOUNDTRACKS	1977	SIREN			DE2200
(C) HALT MACHINE LIP MOVES	197	SIREN			DE 333

C110A

CHRONICLE

NOBLIO HOICHI	G V	(A
KEII SHIKAWA	B V	(A
KENJI MISHIRO	K V	(A

(A) LIKE A MESSAGE FROM THE STORM	1977	ALL EARS			CH 11477

OSAMU TAKEDA	D V	(A			

C111

CHRYSALIS

PAUL ALBUM	B	(A
J SPIDER BARBOUR	V	(A
RALPH KOTKOV	K V	(A
DAHAUD SHAAR	D	(A

(A) DEFINITION	1968				

NANCY NAIN	V	(A	JOHN SABIN	G	(A

CHICK CHURCHILL C112

CHICK CHURCHILL	K V	(A	(A) YOU & ME			1973	CHRYSALIS UK CHR 1051
LEO LYONS	B	(A					
RIC LEE	D	(A	MARTIN BARRE	G	(A	BERNIE MARSDEN	G (A
BILL JACKMAN	SAX	(A	COZY POWELL	D	(A	GARY PICKFORD HOPKINS	V (A
ROGER HODGSON	G B	(A	RICK DAVIES	D	(A		

CHURLS C113

BRAD FOWLES	D	(	(1968 CANADA)		
HARRY SOUTHWORTH AMES	G	(			
SAM HURRIE	G	(	JOHN BARR	B (	BOB O'NEILL V (

CHUTE LIBRE C113A

GILLES DOUIEB	B	(	(A) CHUTE LIBRE	19	PATHE 066 14359
OLIVIER HUTMAN	K	(	(B) ALI BABA	19	PATHE 068 14522
PATRICE CINILU	G				
MINO CINILU	PERC	(	DENNIS BARBIER	FLT (	ERIC LETOURNEUX SAX (A
PIERRE JEAN GIDEN	SAX	(			

CIMARONS C114

CARL LEVY	K G V	(D	(A) IN TIME	1974	TROJAN TRLS 87
FRANKLYN DUNN	B K V	(D	(B) ON THE ROCK	1976	VULCAN VULA 501
WINSTON REID	V PERC	(D	(C) LIVE AT THE ROUNDHOUSE	1978	POLYDOR 2383 489
LOCKSLEY GICHIE	G V	(D	(D) MAKA	1978	POLYDOR 2383 512
MAURICE ELLIS	D	(D			

CIRCUS C115

PHILIP GOODHAND TAIT	K	(A	(A) CIRCUS	1969	TRANSATLANTIC TRA 207
MEL COLLINS	SAX	(A			
IAN JELTS		(A	CHRIS BURROWS	(A	ALAN BUNN (A
KIRK RIDDELL		(A	** PREVIOUSLY THE STORMVILLE SHAKERS		

CIRCUS MAXIMUS C116

BOB BRUNO	G V K	(AB	(A) CIRCUS MAXIMUS	1967	VANGUARD VSD 79260
DAVID SCHERSTROM	D	(AB	(B) NEVERLAND REVISITED	1968	VANGUARD VSD 79274
GARY WHITE	B V	(AB			
PETER TROUTNER	G V	(AB	JERRY JEFF WALKER	V G (A	

CITY C117

CAROLE KING	K V	(A	(A) NOW THAT EVERYTHINGS BEEN SAID	1969	ODE US Z12 44012
DANNY KORTCHMAR	G V	(A			
JIM GORDON	D	(A	CHARLES LARKEY	B (A	

CITY BOY C118

LOL MASON	V	(ABCDE	(A) CITY BOY	1976	VERTIGO	UK 6360 126
MIKE SLAMER		(ABCDE	(A) CITY BOY	1976	MERCURY	US 1098
STEVE BROUGHTON	V	(ABCDE	(B) DINNER AT THE RITZ	1976	VERTIGO	UK 6360 136
CHRIS DUNN	G B	(ABCDE	(B) DINNER AT THE RITZ	1976	MERCURY	US 1121
MAX THOMAS	V K	(ABCDE	(C) YOUNG MEN GONE WEST	1977	VERTIGO	UK 6360 151
FIACHRA TRENCH	PNO	(B	(C) YOUNG MEN GONE WEST	1977	PHONOGRAM	9102 018
R J LANGE	B	(B	(D) BOOK EARLY	1978	VERTIGO	UK 9102 028
B J COLE	STEEL	(B	(E) DAY THE EARTH CAUGHT FIRE	1979	VERTIGO	UK 9102 036
ROGER KENT	D	(AB	(F) HEAD ARE ROLLING	1980	VERTIGO	UK 6359 024
ROY WARD	D	(DE				
DAVE JACKSON	SAX	(B	VANDERGRAAF GENERATOR V (B	JACK HOLSTEIN	FDL (B	

CLANCY C119

DAVE SKINNER	K V	(AB	(A) SERIOUSLY SPEAKING	1975	W B UK K 56103
GASPAR LAWAL	PERC V	(AB	(B) EVERYDAY	1975	W B UK K 56206
ERNIE GRAHAM	G V	(AB			
DAVE VASCO	G V	(AB	COLIN BASS	B V (AB	SAM MITCHELL DOBRO (B
JIM CUOMO	SAX	(AB	BARRY FORD	D V (AB	

CLANNAD C120

MAIRE BRENNAN	HARP V	(A	(A) CLANNAD	1973	PHILIPS 6392 013
PAUL BRENNAN	G V PERC FLT	(ABC	(B) CLANNAD 2	197	GAEL LINN CEF 041
CIARAN BRENNAN	B G V K	(ABC	(C) IN CONCERT	1978	OGHAM BLB 5001
NOEL DUGGAN	G V	(ABC	(D) DULAMAN	1977	GAEL LINN CEF 058
PADRAIG DUGGAN	G V MAND	(ABC			
JOHN WADHAM	D	(A	GRAINNE McMONAGLE	WHISTLE (A	

ERIC CLAPTON C121

ERIC CLAPTON	G V	(ALL	(A) ERIC CLAPTON	1970	POLYDOR US PD13008 UK 2383 021	
WITH			(A) ERIC CLAPTON	1976	RSO	UK 2394 186
CARL RADLE	B	(EFGKLN	(B) HISTORY OF	1972	RSO 2659 012 RI	2671 107
JAMIE OLDAKER	D	(EFGKLN	(B) HISTORY OF	197	ATCO	US 501 803
DICK SIMS	K	(EFGKLN	(B) HISTORY OF	197	POLYDOR	2668 011
GEORGE TERRY	G	(EFGKLN	(C) AT HIS BEST	1972	POLYDOR	2659 025
YVONNE ELLIMAN	V	(EF	(D) RAINBOW CONCERT	1973	RSO	UK 2394 116
MARCY LEVY	V	(FGKN	(D) RAINBOW CONCERT	1973	RSO	US 50 877
SERGIO RODRIGUEZ	PERC	(	(E) 461 OCEAN BOULEVARD	1974	RSO	2479 118
ALBHY GALUTEN	PNO	(EF	(E) 461 OCEAN BOULEVARD	1974	RSO	QD 4801
AL JACKSON	D	(E	(E) 461 OCEAN BOULEVARD	1974	RSO	US 1 3023
TOM BERNFELD	V	(E	(F) THERE'S ONE IN EVERY CROWD	1974	RSO	UK 2479 132
PETE TOWNSHEND	G V	(D	(F) THERE'S ONE IN EVERY CROWD	1974	RSO	US 50 4806
RICK GRECH	B	(D	(G) E C WAS HERE	1975	RSO	UK 2394 160
JIM CAPALDI	D	(D	(G) E C WAS HERE	1975	RSO	2479 154
JIM KARSTEIN	D	(D	(H) BLUES WORLD OF E C	1975	DECCA	UK SPA 387
RONNIE WOOD	G	(D	(I) THE BEST OF E C	1975	POLYDOR	2482 143
STEVE WINWOOD	K V	(D	(J) NO REASON TO CRY	1976	RSO	UK 2479 179
REBOP	PERC	(D	(J) NO REASON TO CRY	1976	RSO	US 1 3004
BOBBY WHITLOCK	K V	(	(L) SLOWHAND	1977	RSO	UK 2479 201
DELANEY BRAMLETT	G V	(	(L) SLOWHAND	1977	RSO	US 1 3030
GRAHAM LYLE	V	(N	(M) CLAPTON	1978	RSO	UK 2479 702
JIM FOX	D	(E	(N) BACKLESS	1978	RSO	UK 2479 221
SONNY CURTIS	V	(	(N) BACKLESS	1978	RSO	RSD 5001
						(CONTINUED)

C121 (CONTINUED)

			ERIC CLAPTON					
JERRY ALLISON	V	(	(N) BACKLESS		1978	RSO	US	1 3039
ALBERT LEE	G	(O1P	(O) JUST ONE NIGHT		1980	RSO	UK	2479 240
LEON RUSSELL	PNO	(A	( ) POP GIANTS		19	BRUNSWICK		2911 518
JIM GORDON	D	(	( ) POP HISTORY		19	POLYDOR		2668 001
BENNY GALLAGHER	V	(N	( ) CLAPTON BECK & PAGE		1973	ELECTROLA		048 51780
HENRY SPINETTI	D	(O1P	( ) GREATEST HITS		1976	TELDEC	GER	622282
CHRIS STAINTON	K	(OP	( ) POP MUSIC		19	POLYDOR	FR	2458 111
DAVE MARKEE	B	(O1P	(P) ANOTHER TICKET		1981	RSO	UK	2479 285
GARY BROOKER	K	(1P	(1) 1980 TOUR					

C122

			DAVE CLARK FIVE					
DAVE CLARK	D V	(ALL	A SESSION WITH	1963	COLUMBIA	UK		33SX 1598
MIKE SMITH	K V	(ALL	A SESSION WITH	1968	M F P	UK		MFP 1260
LENNY DAVIDSON	G B	(ALL	GLAD ALL OVER	1964	EPIC	US MON LN24093	STER BN 26093
RICK HUXLEY	G	(ALL	AMERICAN TOUR	1964	EPIC	US MON LN24104	STER BN 26117
DENNIS PAYTON	SAX K	(ALL	RETURN	1964	EPIC	US MON LN24104	
			COAST TO COAST	1965	EPIC	US		STER BN 26128
			CATCH US IF YOU CAN	1965	COLUMBIA	UK		SX 1756
			WILD WEEKEND	1965	EPIC	US MON LN24162	STER BN 26162
			I LIKE IT LIKE THAT	1966	EPIC			
			GREATEST HITS	1966	COLUMBIA	UK		SX 6105
			GREATEST HITS	1966	EPIC	US		STER BN 26185
			TRY TO HARD	1966	EPIC	US MON LN24198	STER BN 26198
			SATISFIED WITH YOU	1966	EPIC	US MON LN24212	STER BN 26212
			MORE GREATEST HITS	1966	EPIC	US MON LN24221	STER BN 26221
			5 BY 5	1967	EPIC	US		
			YOU GOT WHAT IT TAKES	1967	EPIC	US		STER BN 26312
			EVERYBODY KNOWS	1968	COLUMBIA	UK		SX 6207
			14 TITLES BY DAVE CLARK	1968	COLUMBIA	UK		SCX 6309
			WEEKEND IN LONDON	1968	EPIC	US MON LN24139	STER BN 26139
			BEST OF	1970	STARLINE	UK		SRS 5037
			IF SOMEBODY LOVES YOU(SOLO)	1971	COLUMBIA	UK		SCX 6437
			GOOD OLD ROCK'N'ROLL	1971	STARLINE	UK		SRS 5090
			GOOD OLD ROCK'N'ROLL	1975	MFP	UK		MFP 90197
			25 THUMPING HITS	1978	POLYDOR	UK		POLTV 7
			DAVE CLARK FIVE (DBL)	19	EPIC	US		EG 30434
			BEAT BATTLE OF THE WORLD	19	GROOVEMASTER US		BR 140
			ACROSS CANADA	19	CAPITOL	CAN		
			ON STAGE	19	CAPITOL	CAN		
			OVER & OVER	19	CAPITOL	CAN		
			& FRIENDS	1972	COLUMBIA	UK		SCX 6494
			EPS					
			DAVE CLARK FIVE	1964	COLUMBIA	UK	SEG 8289	
			HITS OF THE D CLARK FIVE	1964	COLUMBIA	UK	SEG 8381	

C123

				GENE CLARK							
GENE CLARK	G V	(ALL	(A) GENE CLARK & THE GOSDIN BROTHERS	1967	CBS	US 9418	US	CL2618
LEON RUSSELL	K	(A	(B) FANTASTIC EXPEDITION	1969	A&M	US 4159	UK	AMLS 939
LELAND SKLAR	B	(F	(B) FANTASTIC EXPEDITION	1975	ARIOLA			86027
BUTCH TRUCKS	D	(F	(C) THROUGH THE MORNING	1969	A&M	US 4203	UK	AMLS 966
RUSS KUNKEL	D	(F	(D) WHITE LIGHT	1972	A&M	US 4292	UK	AMLS64297
MICHAEL UTLEY	K	(DFH	(D) WHITE LIGHT	1974	ARIOLA			88172
CRAIG DOERGE	K	(F	(E) ROAD MASTER	1973	ARIOLA			87584
JOE LALA	PERC	(F	(F) NO OTHER	1974	ASYLUM US 7E1016 UK	SYL 9020
RICHARD GREENE	VLN	(F	(F) NO OTHER	1974	ELEKTRA		UK	K53005
CHRIS HILLMAN	MAND	(AF	(G) KANSAS CITY SOUTHERN	1975	ARIOLA			86436
TED MACHELL	CELLO	(F	(H) TWO SIDES TO EVERY STORY	1977	RSO	US 1 3011 UK	2394 176
JESSE ED DAVIS	G	(DF	( ) COLLECTORS CLASSICS	1976	CBS		US	32998
BILL CUOMO	K	(F	( ) EARLY L A SESSIONS	1975	CBS		US	31123
JERRY McGEE	G	(FH	( ) GENE CLARK (COMP)	19	TOGETHER		US	ST 1001
DANNY KOOTCH	G	(F						

STEVE BRUTON	G	(F	BUZZY FEITEN	G	(F	RONNIE BARRON	V	(F	SHIRLEY MATTHEWS V	(F
CALENE WILLIAMS	V	(F	TIM SCHMIT	V	(F	AL PERKINS	G	(H	JEFF BAXTER	G	(H
DOUG DILLARD		(ABH	EMMYLOU HARRIS	V	(H	BYRON BERLINE	FDL	(H	CHRIS ETHRIDGE	B	(D
BOBBYE HALL	PERC	(D	GARY MALLABER	D	(D	JOHN SELK	G	(D	BEN SIDRAN	K	(D
BILL RHEINHART	G	(A	CLARENCE WHITE	G	(A	GLEN CAMPBELL	G	(A	JERRY COLE	G	(A
MIKE CLARKE	D	(A	SAMMY CREASON	D	(A	JIM FIELDER	B	(H	STEVE SOLES	V	(H
PEPPER WATKINS	V	(H	JOHN HARTFORD	V	(H	THOMAS JEFFERSON KAYE V	(H	DANIEL MOORE	V	(H
MATTHEW MOORE	V	(H									

C124

			GUY CLARK					
GUY CLARK	G V	(ABC	(A) OLD NUMBER ONE		1976	RCA		APLI 1303
MIKE LEECH	B	(AB	(B) TEXAS COOKIN'		1976	RCA		RS 1097
JERRY KROON	D	(AB	(C) GUY CLARK		1978	WB US 3241	UK	K 56565
JERRY CARRIGAN	D	(A						

LARRIE LONDIN	D	(A	CHIP YOUNG	G	(A	PAT CARTER	G V	(A	STEVE GIBSON	G	(A
DICK FELLER	G	(A	JIM COLVARD	G	(A	REGGIE YOUNG	G	(A	HAL RUGG	DOB STEEL(A
DAVID BRIGGS	K V	(AB	CHUCK COCHRAN	PNO	(AB	SHANE KEISTER	PNO	(A	LEA JANE BERINATI K V(AB
JOHNNY GIMBLE	FDL	(A	BRIAN AHERN	G	(B	DANNY ROWLAND	G V	(B	MICKEY RAPHAEL	HCA (A
RODNEY CROWELL	V	(AB	EMMYLOU HARRIS	V	(AB	GARY B WHITE	V	(B	FLORENCE WARNER	V	(A
STEVE EARLE	V	(A	SAMMI SMITH	V	(A	STEVE KEITH	FDL	(B	TOMMY WILLIAMS	FDL	(A
JACK HICKS	BANJO	(B	PETE GRANT	STEEL	(B	CHRIS LAIRD	PERC	(B	BYRON BACH	CELLO	(B
JERRY JEFF WALKER	G V	(B	WAYLON JENNINGS	G V	(B	CHIP MOMAN	G	(B	NICOLETTE LARSON	V	(B
SUSANNA CLARK	V	(B	CHARLIE BUNDY	V	(B	TRACY NELSON	V	(B	HOYT AXTON	V	(B

C125

			SANFORD CLARK				
SANFORD CLARK			( ) THEY CALL ME COUNTRY	19	EMBER		CW 131

C126

			CLARK HUTCHINSON				
ANDY CLARK	V K	(ABC	(A) A=MH²	1970	NOVA		SDNR2
MICHAEL HUTCHINSON	G	(ABC	(B) RETRIBUTION	1970	DERAM	UK	SML 1076
DEL COVERLY	PERC	(C	(C) GESTALT	1971	DERAM	UK	SML 1090
STEPHEN AMAZING	B	(AB	(AB)A=MH²/RETRIBUTION	1973	TELDEC	GERM SDM3015/ 2

ALLAN CLARKE — C127

ALLAN CLARKE	V	(ALL	(A) MY REAL NAME IS 'AROLD	1972 RCA		UK	SF	8283
WITH			(B) HEADROOM	1973 EMI		UK	EMA	752
HERBIE FLOWERS	B	(A	(C) ALLAN CLARKE	1974 EMI		UK	EMC	3041
GARY BROOKER	K	(A	(D) I'VE GOT TIME	1976 EMI		UK	EMC	3130
ROGER COULAM		(A	(D) I'VE GOT TIME	1976 ASYLUM		US	7E	1056
JOE EGAN		(A	(E) I WASN'T BORN YESTERDAY	1978 AURA		UK	UAL	704
JOE MORRETTI		(A	(E) I WASN'T BORN YESTERDAY	1979 ATLANTIC		US	SD	19175
ERIC DILLON		(A						
ALAN PARKER		(A	DEE MURRAY	K V	(AB	MARGO NEWMAN	V	(B	KIRK DUNCAN	K V (B
TONY NEWMAN	D V	(B	RAY GLYNN	V G	(B	STEVE KIPNER	V	(E	DAVID KEMPER	D (E
LARRY BROWN	PERC	(E	JAY GRAYDON	G	(E	BEN BENAY	G	(E	TOM HENSLEY	K (E
MIKE PORCARO	B	(E	ROBBIE BUCHANAN	K	(E	DEAN WEBB	MAND	(E	TONY BERG	G (E
RANDY BISHOP	G V	(E	MIKE STATON	STEEL	(E	DAVID WOLFERT	G	(E	HERB PEDERSEN	V (E

JOHNNY CLARKE — C128

JOHNNY CLARKE	(A) ENTER INTO HIS GATES	1975 ATTACK ATLP 1015
	(B) PUT IT ON	1975 VULCAN VULP 001
	(C) ROCKERS TIME NOW	1976 VIRGIN V 2058
	( ) AUTHORISED VERSIONS	1977 VIRGIN V 2076
	( ) UP PARK CAMP	1977 JUSTICE JUS 001
	( ) DONT STAY OUT LATE	1977 PARADISE PDL 001
	( ) GIRL I LOVE YOU	1978 JUSTICE JUS 006
	( ) SWEET CONVERSATION	1978 THIRD WORLD TWS 914
	( ) KING OF THE ARENA	1978 THIRD WORLD TWS 932
	( ) SATISFACTION	1979 THIRD WORLD TWSD 4

STANLEY CLARKE — C129

STANLEY CLARKE	B PNO	(ALL	(A) STANLEY CLARKE	1974 NEMPEROR US 431 UK K50101
JEFF BECK	G	(BCDE	(B) JOURNEY TO LOVE	1975 NEMPEROR US 433 UK K50187
CHICK COREA	K	(BC	(C) SCHOOLDAYS	1976 NEMPEROR US 900 UK K50296
GEORGE DUKE	K	(BCE	(D) MODERN MAN	1978 NEMPEROR US 35303 EPIC UK 82674
DAVID SANCIOUS	G	(BC	(E) I WANNA PLAY FOR YOU	1979 EPIC UK 88331
LENNY WHITE	D	(BC	(F) ROCKS PEBBLES & SAND	1980 EPIC UK 84342
JON FADDIS	TPT	(ABC	( ) CHILDREN OF FOREVER	1972 POLYDOR US PD 5531
LEW SOLOFF	TPT	(ABC		

CARMINE APPICE	D	(D	PETER GORDON	HRNS(ABC	ALAN RUBIN	TPT	(BC	DAVID TAYLOR	TROM (ABC
TOM MALONE	TROM	(BC	JOHN CLARK	HRNS(BC	EARL CHAPIN	HRNS	(BC	WILMER WISE	HRNS (BC
JEFF BAXTER	G	(D	JEFF PORCARO	D	(D	RAY GOMEZ	G	(DE	MICHAEL GARSON	K (DE
JAMES TINSLEY	TPT	(DE	AL HARRISON	TPT	(DE	DEE DEE BRIDGEWATER	V(DE	BOBBY MALACH	TPT (DE
ALFIE WILLIAMS	SAX	(DE	DALE DEVOE	TROM(D	MAXINE WILLARD	V	(D	JULIA TILLMAN	V (D
GERRY BROWN	D	(DE	JOHN McLAUGHLIN	G	(BC	STEVE GADD	D	(BCDE	JAN HAMMER	K (A
TONY WILLIAMS	D	(A	BILL CONNORS	G	(A	AIRTO MOREIRA	PERC	(AE	JAMES BUFFINGTON	HRNS(A
GARNET BROWN	HRNS	(A	DARRYL BROWN		(E	CATHY CARSON	V	(E	TODD COCHRAN	K (E
JUANITA CURIEL		(E	RONNIE FOSTER		(E	STAN GETZ	SAX	(E	FREDDIE HUBBARD	(E
HARVEY MASON	D	(E	GWEN OWENS	V	(E	LEE RITENOUR	G	(E	PETER ROBINSON	K (E
TOM SCOTT	SAX	(E							

THE CLASH — C130

TERRY CHIMES	D	(12A	(A) THE CLASH	1977 CBS UK 82000
KEITH LEVINE	G	(1	(B) GIVE THEM ENOUGH ROPE	1978 CBS US 35543 UK 82341
MICK JONES	G V	(123ABC	(C) LONDON CALLING	1979 CBS CLASH3
JOE STRUMMER	G V	(123ABC	(D) SANDINISTA (TRP)	1980 CBS FSLN 1
NICKY HEADON	D	(3BC	(E) BLACK MARKET	1980 EPIC US
PAUL SIMONON	B	(123ABC	(F) PEARL HARBOUR	19 JAP
			(1) APR/SEP 1976 (2) SEP76/MARCH 77	(3) MAR77/>>

CLAT THYGER — C131

BAM KING	G	(A	(A) 1972 NO ALBUMS
PHIL HARRIS	G	(A	
REG KING	G V	(A	

CLAYSON & THE ARGONAUTS — C132

ALAN CLAYSON	V					
MIC BARWISE	G					
SANDY MONTEITH	B	HAYDN MEDDICK	K	ALAN WETLOR	SAX	ALAN BARWISE

LEE CLAYTON — C133

LEE CLAYTON	HCA V G	(ABC	(A) LEE CLAYTON	1973 MCA
COLIN CAMERON	B	(B	(B) BORDER AFFAIR	1978 CAPITOL ST 11751
JIMMY DAY	STEEL	(B	(C) NAKED CHILD	1979 CAPITOL EST 11942
PHILIP DONNELLY	G	(B		
DANNY LANE	D	(B	ANDY McMAHON	K	(B	WAYNE JACKSON	TPT (B
ANDREW LOVE	SAX	(B		

MERRY CLAYTON — C134

MERRY CLAYTON	V	(ALL	(A) GIMME SHELTER	1970 A&M AMLS 995
WITH			(A) GIMME SHELTER	1970 ODE US ODE 77001
CAROLE KING	PNO	(B	(B) MERRY CLAYTON	1971 A&M UK AMLS67012
			(B) MERRY CLAYTON	1972 ODE US 77012
			(B) MERRY CLAYTON	197 EPIC US PE 34948
			(C) KEEP YOUR EYE ON THE SPARROW	1975 ODE US ODE 77030
			(C) KEEP YOUR EYE ON THE SPARROW	1975 EPIC US PE 34957
			(D) CELEBRATION	197 ODE US X 77008

PETER CLAYTON — C135

PETER CLAYTON	V	(A	(A)PEARL HARBOUR BLUES (1 SIDE ONLY)	1970 RCA INT INT 1176
BLIND JOHN DAVIS	PNO	(A		
RANSOM KNOWLING	B	(A	WILLIE LACEY	G	(A	ALFRED ELKINS	B (A

DAVID CLAYTON THOMAS — C136

DAVID CLAYTON THOMAS	V	(ALL	DAVID CLAYTON THOMAS	1969 DECCA DL 75146
			DAVID CLAYTON THOMAS	1972 CBS US 31000
			DAVID CLAYTON THOMAS	1972 CBS UK 65755
			HARMONY JUNCTION	1973 RCA UK SF 8381
			DAVID CLAYTON THOMAS	1973 RCA APLI 0173
			TEQUILA SUNRISE	1972 CBS US 30700
			TEQUILA SUNRISE	1973 CBS UK 65237
			CLAYTON	19 ABC 1104

[83]

C136A   CLEAR BLUE SKY

JOHN SIMMONS	G	(A	(A) CLEAR BLUE SKY		19	VERTIGO	UK	6360 013
MARK SHEATER	B	(A						
KEN WHITE	D	(A						

C137   CLEARLIGHT

STEVE HILLAGE	G	(A	(A) CLEARLIGHT SYMPHONY		1975	VIRGIN	V	2029
DIDIER MALHERBE	SAX	(A	(B) FOREVER BLOWING BUBBLES		1975	VIRGIN	V	2039
MARTIN ISAACS	B	(A	(C) LES CONTES DU SINGE FOU		1976	ISADORA	ISA	9009
CHRISTIAN BOULE	G	(AB						
GILBERT ARTMAN	D PERC	(AB	CYRILLE VERDEAUX	K	(ABC	TIM BLAKE	SYN	(AC
FRANCOIS JEANNEAU	WIND	(B	BOB BOISADAN	K	(B	JOEL DUGRENOT	B V	(BC
JEAN CLAUDE AGOSTINI	GFLT	(B	CHRISTIAN STAPINOPOULOS	D	(B	BRUNO VERDEAUX	SYN	(B
BRIGITTE ROY	V	(B	FRANCIS MANDIN	SYN	(C	YVES CHOUARD	G	(C
IAN BELLAMY	V	(C	DIDIER LOCKWOOD	VLN	(C	SERGE AOUZI	D PERC	(C
DAVID CROSS	VLN	(A						

C138   CLEAR LIGHT (US)

CLIFF DE YOUNG	V	(A	(A) CLEAR LIGHT		1967	ELEKTRA	US	EKS 74011
DOUGLAS LUBAHN	B	(A						
MICHAEL NEY	D	(A	BOB SEAL	G	(A	DALLAS TAYLOR	D	(A
RALPH SHUCKETT	K	(A	DANNY KOOTCH	G	(			

C139   JIMMY CLIFF

JIMMY CLIFF	V	(ALL	(A) HARD ROAD		1967	ISLAND	UK	ILPS 962
WITH			(A) HARD ROAD		1967	PHONOGRAM	EUR	9101 675
JACKIE JACKSON	B	(E	(B) JIMMY CLIFF		1969	TROJAN		TRLS 16
WINSTON GRENNAN	D	(E	(B) JIMMY CLIFF		1977	ISLAND	UK	ILPS 9414
RAD BRYAN	G	(E	(C) ANOTHER CYCLE		1971	ISLAND	UK	ILPS 9159
HUX BROWN	G	(E	(D) HARDER THEY COME		1972	ISLAND	UK	ILPS 9202
WINSTON WRIGHT	ORG	(E	(E) UNLIMITED		1973	EMI	UK	EMA 757
GLADSTONE ANDERSON	K	(E	(E) UNLIMITED		197	PATHE	FR	064 05404
LESLIE BUTLER	K FLT	(E	(F) STRUGGLING MAN		1974	ISLAND	UK	ILPS 9235
HEPTONES	V	(E	(G) HOUSE OF EXILE		1974	EMI	UK	EMC 3035
RITA MARLEY	V	(E	(H) BRAVE WARRIOR		1975	EMI	UK	EMC 3078
JUDY MOWATT	V	(E	(H) BRAVE WARRIOR		1975	PATHE	FR	066 05873
NEVILLE GRANT	V	(E	(I) BEST OF JIMMY CLIFF		1975	ISLAND	UK	ICD 6
BINGI BUNNY	PERC	(E	(J) FOLLOW MY MIND		1976	REPRISE	UK	K 54061
TOMMY McCOOK	WIND	(E	(K) GOODBYE YESTERDAY		197	ISLAND	IMP	85568
JEAN WATT	V	(E	(L) OH JAMAICA		1976	EMI	UK	NUT 3
BOB TAYLOR	V	(E	(M) POP CHRONIK	VOL 9	(DBL) 1975	ISLAND	IMP	
DENSIL LAING	PERC	(E	(N) LIVE IN CONCERT		1976	REPRISE	UK	K 54086
BOBBY ELLIS	TPT	(E	(N) LIVE IN CONCERT		1976	REPRISE	US	2256
RALSTON WEBB	V	(E	(O) WONDERFUL WORLD		197	A&M	US	4251
ZOOT SIMS		(E	(P) GIVE THANX		1978	WB	UK	K 56558
RON WILSON	WIND	(E	( ) SENSE OF DIRECTION		197	SIRE	US	7501
NORA DEAN	V	(E	( ) CANT GET ENOUGH		197	VEEP	US	VPS 16536
BONGO HERMAN	PERC	(E	(O) WONDERFUL WORLD		197	ISLAND	IMP	86488
STICKIE	PERC	(E						
TESFA McDONALD	V	(E	GLENTON TAYLOR	V	(E	BARRY BECKETT	K	(C
ROGER HAWKINS	D	(C	DAVID HOOD	B	(C	JIMMY JOHNSON	C	(C
TIPPY ARMSTRONG	G	(C	JOSEPH HIGGS	V	(N	EDDY HINTON	G	(C
ERNEST RANGLIN	G	(N	EARL 'BAGA'WALKER	B	(N	NOEL BAILEY	G	(N
SANTA	D	(N	ERNEST McCLEOD	K	(N			

C139A   BUZZ CLIFFORD

BUZZ CLIFFORD	V	(	(A) BABY SITTIN' WITH BUZZ		19	CBS	US	1616
			(A) BABY SITTIN' WITH BUZZ		19	CBS	US	S 8416
			(B) SEE YOUR WAY CLEAR		19	DOT	US	25965

C139B   DOUG CLIFFORD

DOUG CLIFFORD	D	(A	(A) DOUG'COSMO' CLIFFORD		19	FANTASY	US	9411

C140   LINDA CLIFFORD

LINDA CLIFFORD	V	(AB	(A) IF MY FRIENDS COULD SEE ME NOW		1978	CURTOM		56498
			(A) IF MY FRIENDS COULD SEE ME NOW		1978	CURTOM	US	5021
			(B) LINDA		197	CURTOM	US	5016
			( ) LET ME BE YOUR WOMAN		1979	RSO	UK	RSD 5005
			( ) I'M YOURS		1980	RSO	US	RS 13087

C140A   CLIMAX

SONNY GERACI	V	(A	(A) CLIMAX		1972	BELL	US	RR 3506
JOE OSBORN	B	(A						
STEVE LAFEVER	B	(A	REINIE PRESS	B	(A	JOE BELLAMY	B	(A
EARL PALMER	D	(A	JON GUTTMAN	D PERC	(A	JOHN RAINES	D	(A
WILT NIMS	G	(A	JOHN STEVENSON	K	(A	LARRY KNECHTEL	K	(A
NICK D'AMICO	K	(A	ALAN ESTES	PERC	(A	LARRY COX	PERC	(A
GORDON MacKINNON	HRNS	(A						

C141   CLIMAX BLUES BAND

ARTHUR WOOD	K	(BCD	(A) CLIMAX CHICAGO BLUES BAND		1969	PARLOPHONE	UK	PCS 7069
GEORGE NEWSOME	D	(BCD	(A) CLIMAX CHICAGO BLUES BAND		19	SIRE	US	SES 97013
PETE HAYCOCK	V G	(ALL	(B) PLAYS ON		1969	PARLOPHONE	UK	PCS 7084
COLIN COOPER	SAX	(ALL	(B) PLAYS ON		19	SIRE	US	SES 97023
DEREK HOLT	B	(ALL	(B) PLAYS ON		19	SIRE	US	6003
RICHARD JONES	K	(ABHJK	(C) A LOT OF BOTTLE		1970	HARVEST	UK	SHSP 4009
JOHN CUFFLEY	D	(AEFJHGKLM	(C) A LOT OF BOTTLE		19	SIRE	US	6004
HUMPTY FARMER	K	(C	(D) TIGHTLY KNIT		1971	HARVEST	UK	SHSP 4015
BOB WALTERS	TPT	(G	(D) TIGHTLY KNIT		197	SIRE	US	6008
PETER FILLEUL	V K	(KL	(D) TIGHTLY KNIT		197	SIRE	US	15903
PETE RILEY	PER	(K	(E) RICH MAN		1972	HARVEST	UK	SHSP 4024
COLIN FAIRLEY	V	(K	(E) RICH MAN		197	SIRE	US	7402
MADELINE BELL	V	(K	(F) FM/LIVE		1974	POLYDOR	UK	2383 229
JOY YATES	V	(K	(F) FM/LIVE		197	SIRE	US	2X5 6013
LIZA STRIKE	V	(K	(G) SENSE OF DIRECTION		1974	POLYDOR	UK	2883 291

(CONTINUED)

CLIMAX BLUES BAND C141

(G) SENSE OF DIRECTION	1974	SIRE		SAS	7501
(H) STAMP ALBUM	1975	B T M	UK	BTM	1004
(H) STAMP ALBUM	1975	SIRE	US		6016
(H) STAMP ALBUM	19	SIRE	US		7507
(I) 1969 72	1975	HARVEST	UK	SHSM	2003
(J) GOLD PLATED	1976	B T M	UK	BTM	1009
(J) GOLD PLATED	197	SIRE	US		7523
(K) SHINE ON	1978	WB	UK	K	56461
(K) SHINE ON	1978	SIRE	US		6056
(L) REAL TO REEL	1979	WB	UK	K	56642
(M) FLYING THE FLAG	1980	WB US BSK3493	UK		K56871

Personnel (CONTINUED):

HELEN CHAPPELLE	V	(K
NICKY HOPKINS	PNO	(M
GABRIEL KATONA	SYN	(M
MAXINE WILLARD	V	(M
JULIA TILLMAN	V	(M
CLYDENE JACKSON	V	(M

CLIQUE C141A

(A) THE CLIQUE	197	WHITE WHALE	US	WW	7126

CLOCKWORK C141B

(A) CLOCKWORK	19	GREEN BOTTLE	US	1013

CLOUDS C142

HARRY HUGHES	D	(AB
IAN ELLIS	G B V	(AB
BILLY RITCHIE	K B G V	(AB

(A) SCRAPBOOK	1969	ISLAND	UK	ILPS	9100
(A) UP ABOVE OUR HEADS	1969	DERAM	US	DES	18044
(B) WATERCOLOUR DAYS	1971	ISLAND	UK	ILPS	9151
(B) WATERCOLOUR DAYS	1971	DERAM	US	DES	18058

CLOUT C143

(A) SUBSTITUTE	1978	CRRERE		EMC

CLOVER C144

JOHN McFEE	VLN G V	(ALL
HUEY LOUIS	HCA V	(ALL
JOHNNY CIAMBOTTI	B V	(ALL
SEAN HOPPER	K V	(ALL
ALEX CALL	V G	(ALL
MICKY SHINE	D V	(AC
ED BOGAS	FDL	(A
TONY BRAUNAGEL	D	(D

(A) CLOVER	1970	FANTASY US 8395	LIBERTY UK 83340
(A) CLOVER	197	MERCURY US SRM1 1169	
(B) FOURTY NINER	1971	FANTASY US 8405	LIBERTY UK 83487
(C) UNAVAILABLE	1977		VERTIGO UK 6360 145
(D) LOVE ON THE WIRE	1977	MERCURY US SRMI 3708	VERTIGO UK 6360 155
(E) CHRONICLE (COMP AB)	1979	FANTASY	UK FT550

MITCH HOWIE D (AB

THE CLOVERS C144A

JOHN BUDDY BAILEY	V	(
BILLY MITCHELL	V	(
BILL HARRIS	G	(
HAROLD LUCAS	V	(
MATTHEW McQUATER	V	(
HAROLD WINLEY	V	(
THOMAS WOODS	V	(
BILLY SHELTON	V	(

(A) THE CLOVERS	19	ATLANTIC US 1248		US	8009
(B) DANCE PARTY	19	ATLANTIC		US	8034
(C) IN CLOVER	19	UA	US 3033	US POPLAR	1001
(D) LOVE POTION No9	19	UA	US 6099		
(E) THE ORIGINAL LOVE POTION No9	19	GRAND PRIX		US	K428
(F) THEIR GREATEST RECORDINGS	19	ATCO		US	SD33374
(EP) THE CLOVERS	19	ATLANTIC		US	590
(EP) GOOD LOVIN'	19	ATLANTIC		US	537
(EP) ONE MINT JULEP	19	ATLANTIC		US	504

CLUSTER C145

HANS JOACHIM ROEDELIUS	SYN	(ALL
DIETER MOEBIUS	SYN	(ALL
CONRAD SCHNITZLER	SYN	(AB
CONRAD PLANK		(D
MICHAEL ROTHER	G	(E
HOLGER CZUKAY	B	(G
BRIAN ENO	SYN	(G

(A) KLOPFZEICHEN	(KLUSTER)	1970	SCHWANN	GERM	STUDIO511
(B) ZWEI OSTEREI	(KLUSTER)	1970	SCHWANN	GERM	STUDIO512
(C) CLUSTER		1971	PHILIPS		6305 074
(D) CLUSTER 2		1972	BRAIN/LOGO		0001 006
(E) ZUCKERZEIT		1974	BRAIN	GERN	1065
(E) ZUCKERZEIT		1980	BRAIN	UK	0040 116
(F) SOWIESO		1976	RCA SKY		005
(G) CLUSTER & ENO		1977	RCA SKY		010
( ) CLUSTER 71		1980	SKY		047

THE COASTERS C146

CARL GARDNER	V
BILLY GUY	V
BOBBY NUNN	V
LEON HUGHES	V
YOUNG JESSIE	V
CORNEL GUNTER	V
WILL 'DUB' JONES	V
EARL CARROLL	V
JIMMY NORMAN	V

THE COASTERS	19	ATCO	US	33101
COASTERS GREATEST HITS	19	ATCO	US	33111
COASTERS GREATEST HITS	19	LONDON	UK	HAE 2237
ONE BY ONE	19	ATCO	US	33123
COAST ALONG	19	ATCO	US	33135
GREATEST RECORDINGS	19	ATCO	US	33371
THATS ROCK 'N' ROLL	19	CLARION	US	605
THE EARLY YEARS	19	ATLANTIC	UK	K 30031
ON BROADWAY	19	KING	US	1146
ON BROADWAY	1974	LONDON	UK	SHZ 8460
WORLD FAMOUS COASTERS	1976	DJM	UK	DJM22053
HUNGRY	19	JOY	UK	JOYS 189
20 GREAT ORIGINALS	1978	ATLANTIC	UK	K 30057

WITH

PLAS JOHNSON	SAX
KING CURTIS	SAX
BUDDY LUCAS	SAX HCA
SELDON POWELL	SAX
HAYWOOD HENRY	SAX
JIMMY POWELL	SAX
PAUL WILLIAMS	SAX
NOBLE WATTS	SAX

EPS

ROCK'N'ROLL WITH	19	ATCO	US	4501
KEEP ROCKIN WITH	19	ATCO	US	4502
THE COASTERS	19	ATCO	US	4506
TOP HITS	19	ATCO	US	4507

ALVA McCAIN	SAX	STEVE DOUGLAS	SAX	GRADY GAINES	SAX	CLIFFORD BURKS	SAX
BARNEY KESSEL	G	KENNY BURRELL	G	AL CAIOLA	G	ALAN HANLON	G
PHIL SPECTOR	G	CORNELL DUPREE	G	THOMAS PALMER	G	CARL LYNCH	G
EVERETT BARKSDALE	G	VINCENT BELL	G	AL GORGONI	G	BILLY BUTLER	G
MIMI ROMAN	G	BUCKY PIZZARELLI	G	JOE RICHARDSON	G	SONNY FORRIEST	G
GEORGE BARNES	G	RENE HALL	G	ART RYERSON	G	ADOLPH JACOBS	G
MICKEY BAKER	G	TONY MOTTOLA	G BAN	DON ARNONE	G	CLIFFTON BEST	G
ALVIN STOLLER	D	JOE MARSHALL	D	FRED BELOW	D	BUDDY SALZMAN	D
RAY LUCAS	D	PANAMA FRANCIS	D	GARY CHESTER	D	EMILE RUSSELL	D
BOB ROSENGARTEN	D	MELVIN POLLAN	D	DON LAMOND	D	ALFRED DREARES	D
JESSIE SAILES	D	WILLIE DIXON	B	MIKE STOLLER	PNO	RED SOLOMAN	TPT
WENDEL MARSHALL	B	LAMAR WRIGHT	TPT	JOE NEWMAN	TPT	BILL BERRY	TPT
BERT KEYES	PNO	BILL WINSTON	B	BOBBY DONALDSON	D	JAMES CLEVELAND	TROM
LEROY GLOVER	ORG	HARACE OTT	PNO	RUSS SAUNDERS	B	ELMON WRIGHT	TPT
GEORGE MATTHEWS	TROM	GEORGE STUBBS	PNO	JIMMY LEWIS	B	ART BUTLER	PNO

(CONTINUED)

C146 (CONTINUED) — THE COASTERS

DUD BASCOMBE	TPT	HARRY DEVITO	TROM	AL LUCAS	B	OLSIE ROBINSON	B	
GARY BELL		SANDY NELSON	D	JAMES DAVIDS		MICHAEL ADAMS		
LLEWELLYN KLASS		ABIE BAKER	B	JEWEL GRANT	B	ERNIE FREEMAN	PNO	
EDDIE WILLIAMS	B	GEORGE DUVIVIER	B	PHIL KRAUS	PERC	WILL RODRIGUEZ	PERC	
STICK EVANS	D	MILT HINTON	B	LLOYD TROTMAN	B	HARRY BREUER		
FRANCISCO POZO	PERC	JOE OLIVERA	PERC	RALPH HAMILTON	B			

C147 — BILLY COBHAM

BILLY COBHAM	D PERC(ALL	(A) SPECTRUM	1973	ATLANTIC	UK	K	40506
WITH		(A) SPECTRUM	1973	ATLANTIC	US	SD	7268
TOMMY BOLIN	G (A	(B) TOTAL ECLIPSE	1974	ATLANTIC	UK	K	50098
JAN HAMMER	K (A	(B) TOTAL ECLIPSE	1974	ATLANTIC	US	SD	18121
LELAND SKLAR	B (A	(C) CROSSWINDS	1974	ATLANTIC	UK	K	50037
JOE FARRELL	WIND (A	(C) CROSSWIND	1974	ATLANTIC	US	SD	7300
JIMMY OWENS	HRNS (A	(D) SHABAZZ	1975	ATLANTIC	UK	K	50147
JOHN TROPEA	G (A	(D) SHABAZZ	1975	ATLANTIC	US	SD	18139
RON CARTER	B (A	(E) A FUNKY THIDE OF SINGS	1975	ATLANTIC	UK	K	50189
RAY BARRETO	PERC (A	(E) A FUNKY THIDE OF SINGS	1975	ATLANTIC	US	SD	18149
JOHN ABERCROMBIE	G (BCD	(F) LIFE & TIMES	1976	ATLANTIC	UK	K	50253
MICHAEL BRECKER	HRNS (BCDE	(F) LIFE & TIMES	1976	ATLANTIC	US	SD	18166
RANDY BRECKER	HRNS (BCDE	(G) LIVE IN EUROPE	1976	ATLANTIC	UK	K	50316
MILCHO LEVIEV	K (BDE	(G) LIVE IN EUROPE	1976	ATLANTIC	US	SD	18194
ALEX BLAKE	B (BDE	(H) MAGIC	1977	CBS	UK		82277
GLEN FERRIS	TROM (BDE	(J) INNER CONFLICTS	1978	ATLANTIC	US	SD	19174
JOHN SCOFIELD	G (DEFG	(K) SIMPLICITY OF EXPRESSION	1978	CBS	UK		82967
WALT FOWLER	TPT (E	(L) A LIVE MUTHA FOR YA	1978	CBS	UK		82813
LARRY SCHNEIDER	SAX (E	(M) B C	1979	CBS	UK		83641
TOM MALONE	TROM (E	(N) THE BEST OF	1980	CBS	UK		84325
STEVE KHAN	G (L						
DAWILLI GONGA	K (F	DOUG RAUCH	B (F	ALAN ZAVOD	K (F
PHIL BODNER	REEDS B(F	AL BROWN	VIOLA (F	KERMIT MOORE	CELLO(F
GENE ORLOFF	VLN (F	GARNETT BROWN	TROM (CM	GEORGE DUKE	K V (CGM
LEE PASTORA	PERC (C	JOHN WILLIAMS	B (C	ALFONSO JOHNSON	B V (GL
TOM SCOTT	SAX (L				

C148 — COCHISE

B J COLE	STEEL G(AB	(A) COCHISE	1970	UA	UK	UAS	29117
MICK GRABHAM	G K V (AB	(B) SWALLOW TALES	1971	LIBERTY	UK	LBG	83428
WILLIE WILSON	D (AB	(B) SWALLOW TALES	1971	U A	US		5518
STEWART BROWN	V G (AB	(C) SO FAR	1972	U A	UK	UAS	29286
RICK WILLS	B V (AB	(EP) SWALLOW TALES	1971	UA	US	SP	50
ROY OTEMPO							
JOHN GILBERT	V (B	CALEB QUAYE	PNO (B	STEVE MARRIOTT	PNO V (B
NIGEL OLSSON	V (B	TIM RENWICK	G (B	CAL BATCHELOR	G (B

C149 — EDDIE COCHRAN

EDDIE COCHRAN	D G V B (ALL	EDDIE COCHRAN	1960	LIBERTY	US	LST	7172
GENE VINCENT	V (*	EDDIE COCHRAN	1960	LIBERTY	US	LRP	3172
JOE BROWN	G (*	CHERISHED MEMORIES	1962	LIBERTY		LBY	1109
		CHERISHED MEMORIES	196	LIBERTY		LBS	83072
		CHERISHED MEMORIES	1972	SUNSET	UK	SLS	50289
		MEMORIAL ALBUM	19	LIBERTY		LBY	1127
		MEMORIAL ALBUM	19	LIBERTY		LBS	83009
		MEMORIAL ALBUM	19	LONDON	UK		
		SINGING TO MY BABY	19	LIBERTY		LBY	1158
		SINGING TO MY BABY	19	LIBERTY	MONO LRP	3061
		SINGING TO MY BABY	19	LONDON	UK		
		SINGING TO MY BABY	1968	LIBERTY	UK	LBS	83152
		MY WAY	1964	LIBERTY	US	LBY	1205
		MY WAY	19	LIBERTY	UK	LBS	83104
		NEVER TO BE FORGOTTEN	1963	LIBERTY	US	LRP	3220
		SUMMERTIME BLUES	19	SUNSET	GERM	SLS	50094
		SUMMERTIME BLUES	19	SUNSET	US	SUS	5123
		SUMMERTIME BLUES	19	SUNSET	MONO US	SUM	1123
		C'MON EVERYBODY	1970	SUNSET	UK	SLS	50155
		10th ANNIVERSARY ALBUM	1970	LIBERTY	UK	LBS	83337
		STORY VOL 1	1970	SONOPRESSE	FR		83430
		STORY VOL 2	1970	SONOPRESSE	FR		83431
		STORY VOL 3	1970	SONOPRESSE	FR		83432
		STORY VOL 4	1970	SONOPRESSE	FR		83433
		LEGENDARY	1971	U A	UK	UAS	29163
		STORY VOL 5	1971	SONOPRESSE	FR		29167
		LEGENDARY MASTERS DBL	1972	UA	UK		60017/18
		LEGENDARY MASTERS DBL	1972	UA	US		9959
		ON THE AIR (*)	1972	UA	UK	UAS	29380
		VERY BEST OF (15th ANNIVERSARY)	1975	UA	UK	UAG	29760
		MANY SIDES OF	1975	ROCKSTAR	JGR		1001
		EDDIE COCHRAN DBL	197	SUNSET			55003/4
		VERY BEST OF	19	UA	US	LA	428E
		A LEGEND IN OUR TIME	19	UNION PACIFIC	US		UP001
		COFFRET 5 ALBUMS	19	UA	FR		25003/7
		CREST SESSIONS	19	RAVE ON	FR		5001
		SINGLES ALBUM	1979	UA	UK	UAK	30244
		20th ANNIVERSARY ALBUM	1980	UA	UK	UCSP	20
		MANY SIDES OF	1979	ROLLER COASTER			RSRLP1001

EPS

NEVER TO BE FORGOTTEN	19	LIBERTY	UK	LEP	2052
CHERISHED MEMORIES	19	LIBERTY	UK	LEP	2111
C'MON EVERYBODY	19	LIBERTY	UK	LEP	2111
SOMETHIN' ELSE	19	LIBERTY	UK	LEP	2122
CHERISHED MEMORIES OF EDDIE COCHRAN	19	LIBERTY	UK	LEP	2123
EDDIES HITS	19	LIBERTY	UK	LEP	2124
C'MON AGAIN	19	LIBERTY	UK	LEP	2165
STOCKINGS N SHOES	1964	LIBERTY	UK	LEP	2180

WAYNE COCHRAN
C150

WAYNE COCHRAN	V	(ALL	(A) HIGH & RIDIN'	19	KING	US	KS	1116
			(B) ALIVE & WELL	19	BETHLEHEM	US		10002
			(C) OLD KING GOLD	19	KING	US		16001
			(D) WAYNE COCHRAN	19	CHESS	US		1519
			(E) COCHRAN	19	EPIC	US		30989
			(E) COCHRAN	19	EPIC	UK		64933

BRUCE COCKBURN
C151

BRUCE COCKBURN	G DULC V	(ALL	(A) BRUCE COCKBURN	1970	TRUE NORTH	CAN		TN1
ROBERT BOUNDER	B	(I	(A) BRUCE COCKBURN	19	EPIC	US		30812
PAT GODFREY	PNO V PERC	(I	(B) HIGH WINDS WHITE SKY	1971	TRUE NORTH	CAN		TN3
BILL USHER	PERC V	(I	(C) SUNWHEEL DANCE	1972	EPIC	UK		65187
RAY MACKAY	PIPES	(I	(C) SUNWHEEL DANCE	1972	TRUE NORTH	CAN		TN7
			(C) SUNWHEEL DANCE	1972	EPIC	US		31768
			(D) NIGHT VISION	1973	TRUE NORTH	CAN		TN11
			(E) HAND DANCING	197	TRUE NORTH	CAN		TN13
			(F) SALT SUN AND TIME	1974	TRUE NORTH	CAN		TN16
			(G) JOY WILL FIND A WAY	1975	TRUE NORTH	CAN		TN23
			(H) IN THE FALLING DARK	197	TRUE NORTH	CAN		TN26
			(H) IN THE FALLING DARK	1977	ISLAND/TN	US	ILTA	9463
			(I) CIRCLES IN THE STREAM DBL	1977	ISLAND/TN	US	ILTA	9475
			(J) FURTHER ADVENTURES	197	TRUE NORTH	CAN		TN33
			(J) FURTHER ADVENTURES	197	ISLAND/TN	US	ILTA	9528
			(K) DANCING IN THE DRAGONS JAW	1979	TRUE NORTH	CAN		TN37
			(K) DANCING IN THE DRAGONS JAW	1979	MILLENNIUM	UK	BXLI	7747
			(L) HUMANS	1980	MILLENNIUM	UK	FL	17752

PETER & CHRIS COE
C152

PETER COE		(AB	(A) OPEN THE DOOR	1972	LEADER		LER	2077
CHRIS COE		(AB	(B) OUT OF THE SEASON	1976	LEADER		LER	2098
DAVE BLAND	V	(A	(C) GAME OF ALL FOURS	1979	HIGHWAY		SHY	7007
CLIVE WOOLF	V	(A						
DOUG SHERRIFF	V	(A	STEVE ASHLEY V (A					

COEUR MAGIQUE
C152A

CLAUDE OLMOS	G PERC	(A	(A) WANKAN TANKA	197	BYG	FR		529018
HARRY SEUR	V	(A						
DIDIER LESSAGE	D	(A	LAURENT MURINO B PERC (A					

DENNIS COFFEY & THE DETROIT GUITAR BAND
C153

DENNIS COFFEY	G	(ALL	(A) EVOLUTION	19	SUSSEX	US		7004
WITH			(A) EVOLUTION	19	A&M	UK		AMLS68035
ANDREW SMITH	D	(BC	(B) GOIN' FOR MYSELF	1972	SUSSEX	US		7010
BOB BABBITT	B	(BC	(B) GOIN' FOR MYSELF	1972	A&M	UK		AMLS68072
ERIC MORGANSON	K	(BC	(C) ELECTRIC COFFEY	1972	SUSSEX	US		7021
JACK ASHFORD	PERC	(BCD	(D) INSTANT COFFEY	1974	SUSSEX	UK		8031
EDDY BROWN	PERC	(C	(E) DANCE PARTY	1974	SUSSEX	US		8152
BRUCE NAZARIAN	G	(G	(E) DANCE PARTY	1974	A&M		AM	212
EDDIE WILLIS	G	(G	(F) GETTIN' IT ON	1975	CARRERE	FR		67605
RUDY ROBINSON	PNO	(G	(G) BACK HOME	19	WESTBOUND	US		300
GARY SCHUNK	PNO	(G	(G) BACK HOME	1977	ATLANTIC	UK	K	50371
RODERICK CHANDLER	B	(G	(H) LONG TASTE OF SIN	19	WESTBOUND	US		6105
LEE NATHAM	D	(G						

LORENZO BROWN	PERC	(G	JOHN TRUDELL	TPT	(G	MAURICE DAVIS	TPT	(G
STU SANDERS	TROM	(G	LARRY NOZERO	SAX	(G	BRANDY	V	(G
JAMES BARNES	PERC	(B	TONY NEWTON	B	(B	ART WRIGHT	G	(D
MELVIN WAH WAH RAGIN	G	(D	ED GREENE	D	(D	JAMES GADSON	D	(D
JOE SAMPLE	K	(D	CLARENCE McDONALD	K	(D	MELVIN MELVOIN	K	(D
STEPHANIE SPRUILL	PERC	(D	KING ERRISON	CONGAS	(D	JOE CLAYTON	CONGAS	(D
JAMES JAMERSON	B	(D	GARY COLEMAN	VIBES	(D	RONALD LANGINGER	HRNS	(D
BUD SHANK	HRNS	(D	LLOYD HILDERBRAND	HRNS	(D	GENE CIPRIANO	HRNS	(D
CHUCK FINDLEY	HRNS	(D	VINCENT DEROSA	HRNS	(D	ARTHUR MAEBE	HRNS	(D
GEORGE BOHANON	HRNS	(D	DICK HYDE	HRNS	(D	BOBBY BRYANT	HRNS	(D
ERNIE WATTS	HRNS	(D	STRING SECTION		(DB			

DAVID COHEN
C154

DAVID COHEN	G	(A	(A) HOW TO PLAY FOLK GUITAR	1976	KICKING MULE		SNKF	118

JOE COCKER
C155

JOE COCKER	V	(ALL	(A) BACKING BANDS 1968/69 PRE RECORDS					
WITH			(B) WITH A LITTLE HELP FROM MY FRIEND	1969	REGAL ZONOPHONE		SLRZ	1006
ALAN SPENNER	B	(ACK	(B) WITH A LITTLE HELP FROM MY FRIEND	19	A&M	US	AM	4182
NEIL HUBBARD	G	(AK	(B) WITH A LITTLE HELP FROM MY FRIEND	19	POLYDOR	EURO	2326	015
CHRIS STAINTON	B K	(ABCDK	(B) WITH A LITTLE HELP FROM MY FRIEND	1972	MFP		MFP	52757
HENRY McCULLOUGH	G	(ABCGH	(C) JOE COCKER	1970	REGAL ZONOPHONE	UK	SLRZ	1011
BRUCE ROWLAND	D	(AC	(C) JOE COCKER	197	A&M	US	AM	4224
PAUL HUMPHREY	D	(BC	(C) JOE COCKER	197	A&M	US	AM	4368
CAROL KAYE	B	(B	(C) JOE COCKER	197	CUBE POLYDOR	EURO	2326	014
DAVID COHEN	G	(B	(BC) WITH A LITTLE HELP/JOE COCKER	1972	FLY		TOOFA	1/2
ARTIE BUTLER	PNO	(B	(BC) WITH A LITTLE HELP/JOE COCKER	1975	CUBE		TOOFA	1/2
LAUDIR DE OLIVIRA	PERC	(B	(D) MAD DOGS & ENGLISHMEN	1971	A&M	US/UK	AMLD	6002
CLEM CATTINI	D	(B	(E) COCKER HAPPY	1971	FLY	UK	HIFLY	3
TONY VISCONTI	G	(B	(E) COCKER HAPPY	1971	CUBE	EUR	2338	009
JIMMY PAGE	G	(B	(F) SOMETHING TO SAY	1973	CUBE	UK	HIFLY	13
MIKE KELLIE	D	(B	(F) SOMETHING TO SAY	1973	CUBE	EUR	2338	022
ALBERT LEE	G	(BJ	(G) I CAN STAND A LITTLE RAIN	1974	CUBE	UK	HIFLY	18
B J WILSON	D	(B	(G) I CAN STAND A LITTLE RAIN	1974	A&M	US	AM	3633
TOMMY EYRE	K	(AB	(G) I CAN STAND A LITTLE RAIN	1974	CUBE	EUR	2338	027
MATTHEW FISHER	ORG	(B	(H) JAMAICA SAY YOU WILL	1975	CUBE	UK	HIFLY	20
STEVE WINWOOD	K	(B	(H) JAMAICA SAY YOU WILL	1975	A&M	US	AM	4529
KENNY SLADE	D	(B	(H) JAMAICA SAY YOU WILL	1975	CUBE	EUR	2326	040
LEON RUSSELL	V K G	(CD	(J) STINGRAY	1976	A&M	UK	AMLH64574
MILT HOLLAND	PERC	(C	(J) STINGRAY	1976	A&M	US	AM	4574

(CONTINUED)

C155 (CONTINUED)

JOE COCKER

SNEAKY PETE KLEINOW	STEEL (C	(K) LIVE IN L A		1976	CUBE	UK	HIFLY 23
CLARENCE WHITE	G (C	(K) LIVE IN L A		1976	CUBE	EUR	2326 041
DON PRESTON	G (D	(L) LUXURY YOU CAN AFFORD		1978	ASYLUM US 6E145 UK		K 53087
CARL RADLE	B (D	(L) LUXURY YOU CAN AFFORD		1978	ELEKTRA		K 52092
JIM GORDON	D (D	( ) JOE COCKER(BEST OF)		19'	IMPACT	FR	6886 554
JIM KELTNER	D (D	( ) GREATEST HITS		19	A&M	US	AM 4670
CHUCK BLACKWELL	D PERC(D						
SANDY KONIKOFF	PER (D						
BOBBY TORRES	PERC (D	JIM PRICE V K HRNS (DGHK		BOBBY KEYS	SAX (DK		
STU BLUMBERG	TPT (G	STEVE MADAIO	TPT (GH	JIM HORN	SAX (GHK		
TREVOR LAWRENCE	SAX (GH	MAYO TIANA	TROM (G	DAVID PAICH	PNO (G		
RAY PARKER	G (G	RALPH HAMMER	G (G	DAVE McDANIEL	B (GH		
OLLIE BROWN	D (G	NICKY HOPKINS	PNO (GH	JAY GRAYDON	G (G		
JEFF PORCARO	D (G	RICHARD TEE	K (GH	CORNELL DUPREE	G (GHJ		
CHUCK RAINEY	B (GH	BERNARD PURDIE	D (GH	CHRIS STEWART	B (GH		
JIM KARSTEIN	D (GHK	JIMMY WEBB	PNO (G	PEGGY SANDVIG	GH (GH		
GREG MATHESON	PNO (G	RANDY NEWMAN	PNO (G	JEAN ROUSSEL	ORG (H		
BEN BENAY	G HCA (H	SID SHARP	STRINGS(H	DAN SAWYER	G (H		
JOE CORRERO	D (H	DON PONCHER	PERC (H	STEVE GADD	D (J		
GORDON EDWARDS	B (J	ERIC GALE	G (J	SAM RIVERS	SAX (J		
FLACO FALCON	PERC (JK	ERIC CLAPTON	G (J	ROSETTA HIGHTOWER	V (B		
BRENDA HOLLOWAY	V (B	MERRY CLAYTON	V (BCG	PATRICE HOLLOWAY	V (BC		
MADELINE BELL	V (B	SUE GLOVER	V (B	SONNIE LESLIE	V (B		
BONNIE BRAMLETT	V (CJ	RITA COOLIDGE	V (CD	SHIRLEY MATTHEWS	V (CGH		
CLAUDIA LENNEAR	V (D	DANIEL MOORE	V (DGH	DONNA WEISS	V (D		
PAMELA POLLAND	V (D	MATTHEW MOORE	V (DH	DONNA WASHBURN	V (D		
NICOLE BARCLAY	V (D	BOBBY JONES	V (D	CLYDIE KING	B (GH		
VANETTA FIELDS	V (GH	CAROL STALLINGS	V (H	BUZZ CLIFFORD	V (H		
JOANNE BELL	V (H	CYNTHIA BARCLAY	V (H	LANI GROVES	V (J		
DENIECE WILLIAMS	V (J	PHYLLIS LINDSAY	V (J	MAXINE WILLARD	V (J		
BRENDA WHITE	V (J	PATTI AUSTIN	V (J	GWEN GUTHRIE	V (J		
VIOLA WILLS	V (K	BEVERLY GARDNER	V (K	VIRGINIA AYERS	V (K		

C156

LEONARD COHEN

LEONARD COHEN	V (ALL	(A) SONGS OF LEONARD COHEN	1968	CBS	UK	63241
		(A) SONGS OF LEONARD COHEN	1968	CBS	US	9533
JENNIFER WARNES	V (G	(B) SONGS FROM A ROOM	1968	CBS	UK	63587
		(B) SONGS FROM A ROOM	1968	CBS	US	9767
		(C) SONGS OF LOVE & HATE	1970	CBS	UK	69004
		(C) SONGS OF LOVE & HATE	1970	CBS	US	30103
		(D) LIVE SONGS	1973	CBS	UK	65224
		(D) LIVE SONGS	1973	CBS	US	31724
		(E) NEW SKIN FOR OLD CEREMONY	1974	CBS	UK	69087
		(E) NEW SKIN FOR OLD CEREMONY	1974	CBS	US	33167
		(F) GREATEST HITS	1975	CBS	UK	69161
		( ) BEST OF	197	CBS	US	34077
		(F) DEATH OF A LADIES MAN	1977	CBS	UK	86042
		(F) DEATH OF A LADIES MAN	1977	WB	US	BS 3125
		(G) RECENT SONGS	1979	CBS	UK	86097

C157

MARK COLBY

MARK COLBY	SAX (A	(A) SERPENTINE FIRE	1978	CBS	UK	82668
ERIC GALE	G (A	(A) SERPENTINE FIRE	1978	CBS	US	35298
STEVE KHAN	G (A					
BOB JAMES	(A	STEVE GADD D (A				

C158

COLD BLOOD

CARL LEACH	TPT (A	(A) COLD BLOOD (FIRST BLOOD)	1970	SAN FRANCISCO US		200
RAUL MATUTE	K (ABCDEF	(A) COLD BLOOD (FIRST BLOOD)	1970	ATLANTIC	UK	588 218
LARRY JONUTZ	TPT (AB	(B) SISYPHUS	1971	SAN FRANCISCO US		205
ROD ELLICOTT	B (ABDE	(B) SISYPHUS	1971	ATLANTIC	UK	2400 102
FRANK J DAVIS	D (A	(C) FIRST TASTE OF SIN	1972	REPRISE	US	2074
DANNY HULL	SAX V (ABF	(D) THRILLER	1973	REPRISE	US	2130
DAVID PADRON	TPT (A	(E) LYDIA	1974	WB	US	2806
LARRY FIELD	G (AB	(E) LYDIA	1974	WB	UK	K56047
LYDIA PENSE	V (ABCDEF	(F) LYDIA PENSE & COLD BLOOD	1976	ABC	US	ABCD 917
MIC GILLETTE	HRNS (AB	(F) LYDIA PENSE & COLD BLOOD	1976	ABC	UK	ABCL 5172
SANDY McKEE	D (B					
JOSE CHEPITO AREAS	PERC (B	POINTER SISTERS V (BD	MIKE ANDREAS	SAX (D		
RIGBY POWELL	TPT (D	MEL MARTIN SAX (D	HOLLY TIGARD	V (D		
GAYLORD BIRCH	D (DE	BILL ATWOOD TPT FLT(D	MAX HASKETT	TPT V(DEF		
SKIP MESQUITE	WIND V(D	BOB FERREIRA WIND (D	MICHAEL SASAKI	G (DEF		
TOMMY CATHEY	B (E	PAT OHARA TROM (D	PETER WELKER	TPT (D		
JOE WILLIAMS	D (E	JOHN MEWBORN HRNS (D	PAUL CANNON	G (D		
STEVE CROPPER	G (E	BENNY MAUPIN WIND (D	MEMPHIS HORNS	(E		
SMITH DOBSON	PNO V (E	DANNY KOOTCH G (E	BOBBYE HALL	PERC (E		
DAVID LUELL	SAX (E	CHUCK BENNETT TROM (E	PAUL HUBINON	TPT (E		
CHUCK FINDLEY	TPT (E	BOBBY SHEW TPT (E	JIM HORN	WIND (E		
DON MENZA	WIND (E	PETER CHRISTLIEB WIND (E	BROOKS HUNNICUTT	V (E		
GWEN EDWARDS	V (E	BRENDA GORDON V (E	TISH SMITH	V (E		
PAT COULTER	V (E	JERRY JONUTZ SAX (A	HARVEY HUGHES	D (F		
DOMINGO BALINTON	B (F	SKIP KONTE SYN (F				

C158A

COLD CHISEL

		(A) YOUR'E 13	1978	ELEKTRA EP US	EP 12001

C159

COLD COMFORT

DAVE PRICE	V G K (A	(A) IN THE CAN	1978	JET	UK JET LP211
DEREK SODEN	V B G (A				
NIGEL BAGGE	V G (A	IAN BYRON D (A	ROD EDWARDS	K VLN (A	
GRAHAM MATTHEWS	PERC V(A	HENRY LOWTHER TPT (A	GEOFF DALY	SAX (A	
CHRIS MERCER	SAX (A				

COLD STEEL   C160

DAVID LOVELACE	K	(A	(A) COLD STEEL		1974	ARIOLA	IMP	87736
GREG ATTAWAY	V D	(A
RICHARD BOWDEN	G V	(A	MIKE BOWDEN	B V (A	SNEAKY PETE		STEEL	(A
GIB GUILBEAU	FDL	(A

B J COLE   C161

B J COLE STEEL G K	(A	(A) NEW HOVERING DOG		1972	UA	UK	UAS 29418
ROBERT KIRBY	PNO	(A
GRAHAM PRESKETT	VLN	(A	TRISTRAM FRY	PERC	(A	KEITH BAKER	B	(A
CRISPIAN STEEL PERKINS TPT	(A	LAURIE JELLYMAN	D	(A	MICK AUDSLEY	G V	(A
DANNY THOMPSON	B	(A	MIKE GILES	D	(A	FRANCIS MONKMAN	K	(A
ANDY BABYNCHUK	VLN	(A	ROY GILLARD	VLN	(A	SUE SHEPPARD	CELLO	(A
BRIAN HAWKINS	VIOLA	(A

JERRY COLE & THE SPACEMEN   C161A

JERRY COLE	G		A GO GO GUITARS	19	CROWN	US	539
			OUTER LIMITS	19	CAPITOL	US	2044
			HOT ROD DANCE	19	CAPITOL	US	2061
			SURF AGE	19	CAPITOL	US	2112

THE COLLECTORS   C161B

| | | | (A) THE COLLECTORS | 19 | WB | US | WS 1746 |
| | | | (B) GRASS & WILD STRAWBERRIES | 19 | WB | US | WS 1774 |

ALBERT COLLINS   C162

ALBERT COLLINS	G V	(ALL	(A) TRUCKIN	19	BLUE THUMB	US	BTS8
WITH			(B) COOL SOUND OF	19	T C F HALL	US	8002
LARRY BURTON	G	(F	(C) LOVE CAN BE FOUND	19	IMPERIAL	US	12428
ALAN BATTS	K	(FG	(D) COMPLETE ALBERT COLLINS	19	IMPERIAL	US	12445
A C REED	SAX	(FG	(E) THERE'S GOTTA BE A CHANGE	19	TUMBLEWEED	UK	TW 3501
CASEY JONES	D	(F	(E) THERE'S GOTTA BE A CHANGE	19	TUMBLEWEED	UK	TWS 103
CHUCK SMITH	SAX	(F	(F) ICE PICKIN'	1978	SONET	UK	SNTF 707
ARON BURTON	B	(F	(F) ICE PICKIN'	197	ALLIGATOR		4713
MARVIN JACKSON	G	(G	(G) FROSTBITE	1980	SONET	UK	SNTF 837
JOHNNY GAYDEN	B	(G	(G) FROSTBITE	19	ALLIGATOR	US	
PAUL HOWARD	TPT	(G	(H) ALIVE & COOL	197	RED LIGHTNIN	UK	RL 004
JERRY WILSON	SAX	(G
BILL McFARLAND	TROM	(G	HENRI FORD	SAX	(G

DAVE & ANSELL COLLINS   C163

DAVE COLLINS			(A) DOUBLE BARREL	19	TROJAN		TRL 162
ANSELL COLLINS			(A) DOUBLE BARREL	19	BLUE THUMB	US	2005
			(B) IN THE GHETTO	1976	TROJAN		TRLS 124

JUDY COLLINS   C164

JUDY COLLINS	V G K (ALL		(A) MAID OF CONSTANT SORROW	1962	ELEKTRA	US	EKS 7209
WITH			(A) MAID OF CONSTANT SORROW	1975	ELEKTRA	UK	K 52032
MICHAEL SAHL	K	(H	(B) GOLDEN APPLES OF THE SUN	1963	ELEKTRA	US	EKS 7222
STEPHEN STILLS	G	(H	(B) GOLDEN APPLES OF THE SUN	1975	ELEKTRA	UK	K
CHRIS ETHRIDGE	B	(H	(C) 3RD ALBUM	1963	ELEKTRA	US	EKS 7243
JAMES GORDON	D	(H	(C) 3RD ALBUM	19	CHANT DU MONTE	FR	4324
MICHAEL MELVOIN	K	(H	(D) CONCERT	1964	ELEKTRA	US	EKS 7280
JAMES BURTON	G	(H	(E) FIFTH ALBUM	1965	ELEKTRA	US	EKS 7300
BUDDY EMMONS	STEEL	(H	(E) FIFTH ALBUM	19	CHANT DU MONTE	FR	74333
VAN DYKE PARKS	K	(H	(F) WILD FLOWERS	1967	ELEKTRA	US	EKS 74012
FRED HELLERMAN	G	(A	(F) WILD FLOWERS	197	ELEKTRA	UK	K 42014
ERIK DARLING	BANJO	(A	(F) WILD FLOWERS	19	VOGUE	FR	217
WALTER RAIM	G BANJO(BC		(G) IN MY LIFE	1968	ELEKTRA	US	EKS 74027
ROGER McGUINN	G BANJO(C		(G) IN MY LIFE	197	ELEKTRA	UK	K 42009
BILL TAKAS	B	(CE	(G) IN MY LIFE	1968	ELEKTRA	US	7320
CHUCK ISRAELS	B CELLO(DE		(G) IN MY LIFE	19	VOGUE	FR	155
STEVE MANDELL	G BANJO(D		(H) WHO KNOWS WHERE THE TIME GOES	1968	ELEKTRA	US	EKS 74033
RICHARD FARINA	DULCIMER (E		(H) WHO KNOWS WHERE THE TIME GOES	197	ELEKTRA	UK	K 42044
ERIC WEISSBERG	G V	(E	(H) WHO KNOWS WHERE THE TIME GOES	197	VOGUE	FR	322
JERRY DODGION	FLT	(E	( ) RECOLLECTIONS(BEST OF)	1969	ELEKTRA	US	74055
BOB SYLVESTER	CELLO	(E	( ) RECOLLECTIONS(BEST OF)	197	ELEKTRA	UK	K 42035
BILL LEE	B	(E	(I) BOTH SIDES NOW	1971	ELEKTRA		EKS 75030
DANNY KALB	G	(E	(I) BOTH SIDES NOW	1971	ELEKTRA	UK	K 42098
JOHN SEBASTIAN	HCA	(E	(J) WHALES & NIGHTINGALES	1971	ELEKTRA	US	EKS 75010
			(J) WHALES & NIGHTINGALES	1971	ELEKTRA	UK	K 42059
			(K) LIVING	1972	ELEKTRA	US	EKS 75014
			(K) LIVING	1972	ELEKTRA	UK	K 42102
			( ) COLOURS OF DAY (BEST OF)	1972	ELEKTRA	UK	75030
			( ) AMAZING GRACE (BEST OF)	1972	ELEKTRA	UK	K 42110
			(L) TRUE STORIES & OTHER DREAMS	1973	ELEKTRA	US	EKS 75053
			(L) TRUE STORIES & OTHER DREAMS	1973	ELEKTRA	UK	K 42132
			(M) JUDITH	1975	ELEKTRA	US	1032
			(M) JUDITH	1975	ELEKTRA	UK	K 52019
			(N) BREAD & ROSES	1976	ELEKTRA	US	7E 1076
			(N) BREAD & ROSES	1976	ELEKTRA	UK	K 52039
			(O) SO EARLY IN SPRING	1977	ELEKTRA	US	8E 6007
			(O) SO EARLY IN SPRING	1977	ELEKTRA	UK	K 62019
			(P) SAVE THE CHILDREN	197	WOMAN	US	W001
			( ) MOST BEAUTIFUL SONGS OF	1979	ELEKTRA	UK	K 62006
			( ) HARD TIME FOR LOVERS	1979	ELEKTRA	UK	K 52121
			) RUNNING FOR MY LIFE	1980	ELEKTRA US 6E253	UK K	52205

```
C165                                    SHIRLEY COLLINS
SHIRLEY COLLINS  V G BANJO(ALL   (A) THE SWEET PRIMEROSES              1967 TOPIC      UK        12TS 170
WITH                             (B) POWER OF THE TRUE LOVE KNOT       1968 POLYDOR    UK        583  025
DOLLY COLLINS    V    (ALL       (C) ANTHEMS IN EDEN                   1969 HARVEST    UK        SHVL 754
CHRIS HOGWOOD    K    (DG        (D) LOVE DEATH & THE LADY             1970 HARVEST    UK        SHVL 771
ALLAN LUMSDEN    SACK (DG        (E) NO ROSES                          1971 PEGASUS    UK        PEG 7
ADAM SKEAPING    VLN  (DG        (E) NO ROSES                          1974 MOONCREST  UK        CREST 11
ROD SKEAPING     VLN  (DG        (F) ADIEU TO  OLD ENGLAND             1974 TOPIC      UK        12T  238
ELEANOR SLOAN    REBEC(D         ( ) A FAVOURITE GARLAND   (BEST OF)   1975 DECCA      UK        SML 1117
JOHN FORDHAM     REC  (DG        (G) AMARANTH                          1976 HARVEST    UK        SHSM2008
TERRY COX        PERC (D         (H) FOR AS MANY AS WILL               1978 TOPIC      UK        12T  380
PETER WOOD       CONC (D
SIMON NICOL      V G  (EFG  IAN WHITEMAN      PNO  (E   DAVE BLAND       CONC (E   ASHLEY HUTCHINGS B     (EG
ROGER POWELL     D    (E    RICHARD THOMPSON  G    (E   LOL COXHILL      SAX  (E   ALAN CAVE    BASSOON (E
TONY HALL        MEL  (E    DAVE MATTACKS     D    (EG  JOHN KIRKPATRICK ACC  (EG  NIC JONES       V FDL (E
BARRY DRANSFIELD V FDL(EH   TIM RENWICK       G    (E   FRANCIS BAINES   G    (E   COLIN ROSS   PIPES   (E
MADDY PRIOR      V    'E    LAL WATERSON      V    (E   ROYSTON WOOD     V    (E   STEVE MIGDEN       HRNS(E
MIKE WATERSON    V    (E    GREGG BUTLER      SERP (E   TREVOR CROZIER        (F   JOHN WATCHAM       CONC(FG
TERRY POTTER     HCA  (FG   BILL MOLAN        V MEL(F   GEOFF SINGLETON  V FDL(F   JOHN HARRINGTON V CONC(F
IAN HOLDER       ACC  (F    BOB STEWART       PSALT(F   ROGER SWALLOW    D    (F   JOHN RODD          CONC(G
PAT DONALDSON    B    (F    ROGER BRENNER     SACK (G   COLIN SHEEN      SACK (G   PAUL BEER          SACK(G
MARTIN NICHOLLS  SACK (G    JOHN SOTHCOTT     VIELL(E   DAVID MURROW     WIND (G   STEVE ASHLEY     V    (G
RAY WORMAN       V    (G    JOHN MORGAN       V    (G   DAVID BUSBY      V    (G   MIKE CLIFTON     V    (G
DOTS DAULTREY    V    (G    STUART HOLLYER    V    (G   ROGER RIGDEN     V    (G   ADA TURNHAM      V    (G
OLIVER BROOKES   VLN  (G    MICHAEL LAIRD     CORNET(G  RICHARD LEE      REC  (G   GILLIAN REID       BELL(G
PHIL PICKETT     WIND (H    MICHAEL GREGORY   PERC (H   PAUL NIEMAN      HRNS (H   TONY ENGLE         CANC(H
C166                                      COLOSSEUM
JON HISEMAN            D    (ALL   (A) THOSE WHO ARE ABOUT TO DIE   1969 FONTANA          UK        STLS 5510
DICK HECKSTALL SMITH  SAX  (ALL   (A) THOSE WHO ARE ABOUT TO DIE   1969 DUNHILL          US        50062
TONY REEVES           B    (A     (B) VALENTYNE SUITE              1969 VERTIGO UK V01 BRONZE       HELP4
JAMES LITHERLAND      G    (AE    (B) VALENTYNE SUITE              1    BRONZE           UK        BRNA 214
DAVE GREENSLADE       K    (ALL   (C) DAUGHTER OF TIME             1970 VERTIGO          UK        6360 017
MARK CLARKE           B    (BCD   (C) DAUGHTER OF TIME             1970 DUNHILL          US        50101
DAVE CLEMPSON         G    (BCDE  (D) LIVE                         1971 BRONZE           UK        ICD 1
CHRIS FARLOWE         V    (CDE   (D) LIVE                         197  WB               US        2XS 1942
LOUIS CENNAMO         B    (C     (E) COLLECTORS COLOSSEUM         1971 BRONZE           UK        ILPS 9173
BARBARA THOMPSON      WIND (C     (F) POP CHRONIK                  1975                            V012
                                  ( ) GRASS IS GREENER             1969 DUNHILL          US        DS 50079
C167                                     COLOSSEUM II
JON HISEMAN      D    (ABC   (A) STRANGE NEW FLESH    1976 BRONZE   UK        ILPS 9356
NEIL MURRAY      B    (A     (A) STRANGE NEW FLESH    1976 WB       US        2016
JOHN CARY        K    (      (B) ELECTRIC SAVAGE      1977 MCA      UK   MCF  2800
DON AIREY        K    (ABC   (B) ELECTRIC SAVAGE      1977 MCA      US        2293
MIKE STARR       V    (      (C) WARDANCE             1977 MCA      UK   MCF  2817
GARY MOORE       G    (ABC   (C) WARDANCE             1977 MCA      US        2310
JOHN MOLE        B    (BC
C168                                      COLOURS
CARL RADLE        B    (A     (A) COLOURS       19   DOT   US        25854
CHUCK BLACKWELL   D    (A     (B) ATMOSPHERE    19   DOT   US        25935
GARY MONTGOMERY   PNO  (A
JACK DALTON       G    (A     ROB EDWARDS       G    (A
C168A                                      P J COLT
P J COLT          V    (A     (A) P J COLT           1976 POLYDOR            2489  011
WITH
FRANCISCO SERRANO  B    (A     JIM WILKINS      D    (A    JEFF BAXTER       G    (A
VALERIE ROBINSON   V    (A     CYNTHIA OUTLAW   V    (A    GWEN ROGERS       V    (A
ROSALIND ROGERS    V    (A     ED COSTA         K    (A    PEE WEE ELLIS     HRNS (A
HANK CRAWFORD      HRNS (A     BARRY ROGERS     HRNS (A    JULIAN PRIESTER   HRNS (A
JOANNE BENNETT     V    (A     MONICA WILLIAMS  V    (A
C169                                      JESSI COLTER
JESSI COLTER      V K (ALL    (A) A COUNTRY STAR IS BORN        1970 RCA      US   LSP  4333
WITH                         (B) I'M JESSI COLTER              1975 CAPITOL  US   ST11363
WAYLON JENNINGS   G V  (BCDEF (C) JESSI                        1975 CAPITOL  US   ST11477
JOHN LESLIE HUG   G    (D     (D) DIAMOND IN THE ROUGH         1976 CAPITOL  US   ST11543
RITCHIE ALBRIGHT  D    (BCDEF (D) DIAMOND IN THE ROUGH         1976 CAPITOL  US   SM11822
SHERMAN HAYES     B    (CDEF  (E) MIRRIAM                      1977 CAPITOL  US   ST11583
RALPH MOONEY      STEEL (BCDEF (F) THATS THE WAY A COWBOY ROCKS 1978 CAPITOL US   ST11863
BILLY GRAHAM      FDL MAND (D
CRAIG WARE        HRNS (D     ROBERT WARE      HRNS (D    TODD MILLER       HRNS (D
DON ROBERTSON     K    (D     BARNEY ROBERTSON K V  (DEF  CARTER ROBERTSON  V    (DEF
JOHN BUCK WILKIN  G    (D     REGGIE YOUNG     G    (BC   LARRY MUHOBERAC   PNO  (BC
DUKE GOFF         B    (BC    TOMMY COGBILL    B    (B    WELDON MYRICK     STEEL(B
JOHNNY GIMBLE     FDL  (BF    JIM GORDON       HRNS (BCE  RANDY SCRUGGS     G BANJ(C
DICK HYDE         TROM (BCE   MAC JOHNSON      TPT  (CE   LARRY MURRAY      DULC (C
GORDON PAYNE      G    (EF    G MERLIN         DULC (E    JOHN CHRISTOPHER  G    (E
GAYLE LEVANT      HARP (E     RANCE WASSON     G    (E    FRED CARTER       G    (F
TONY JOE WHITE    G HCA (F    J J CALE         G    (F
C170                                     ALICE COLTRANE
ALICE COLTRANE          COSMIC MUSIC                     1967 IMPULSE            AS   9148
                        MONASTIC TRIO                    197  IMPULSE            AS   9156
                        MONASTIC TRIO                    1976 IMPULSE       UK   IMPL 8031
                        HUNTINGTON ASHRAM MONASTERY      1969 IMPULSE            AS   9185
                        PTAH THE EL DAOUD                197  IMPULSE            AS   9196
                        JOURNEY IN SATCHIDANANDA         197  IMPULSE            AS   9203
                        UNIVERSAL CONSCIOUSNESS          197  IMPULSE            AS   9210
                        WORLD GALAXY                     197  IMPULSE            AS   9218
                        LORD OF LORDS                    1973 IMPULSE            AS   9224
                                                                            (CONTINUED)
```

ALICE COLTRANE   C170

LORD OF LORDS	1975	IMPULSE	UK	IMPL 8009
REFLECTION ON CREATION	1973	IMPULSE		AS 9232/2
ILLUMINATIONS	1974	CBS	UK	69063
ETERNITY	1976	WB	K	56198
RADWA KRSRA NANA MONASTERY	1977	WB	BS	2986
TRANSCENDENCE	1977	WB		

CHI COLTRANE   C171

CHI COLTRANE   V PERC K(ALL
WITH

JIM GORDON	D	(BC
JIM KELTNER	D	(B
BARRY DE SOUZA	D	(B
STEVE PARSONS	D	(B
CHRIS KARAN	D	(B
LARRY KNECHTEL	B	(B
CHRIS LAURENCE	B	(B
BOBBYE HALL	PERC	(B
LEE RITENOUR	G	(B
ALAN ESTES	PERC	(B
JEFF PORCARO	D	(C
MICHAEL BOTTS	D	(C
GREG PRESTOPINO	V	(C
BRIAN RUSSELL	V	(C
QUITMAN DENNIS	HRNS	(C

(A) CHI COLTRANE	1972	CBS	US	31275
(A) CHI COLTRANE	197	CBS	UK	65043
(B) LET IT RIDE	1973	CBS	UK	65639
(B) LET IT RIDE	1974	CBS	US	32463
(C) ROAD TO TOMORROW	1977	TK		82501

KENNY EDWARDS	B	(C	WILLIE WEEKS	B	(C
EMORY GORDY	B	(B	KLAUS VOORMAN	B	(B
MARK CIPOLA	B	(B	JOE PUERTA	B	(B
PAUL BUCKMASTER	SYN	(B	JOHN GUSTAFSON	B	(B
BEB BENAY	G	(BD	LARRY BYROM	G	(B
PAUL ESSARD	CLAR	(B	MERRY CLAYTON	V	(B
STEPHANIE SPRUILL	V	(B	CLYDIE KING	V	(C
ABE LABORIEL	B	(C	VICTOR FELDMAN	PERC	(C
JENNIFER WARNES	V	(C	IAN UNDERWOOD	SYN	(C
JIM HORN	HRNS	(C	CHUCK FINDLEY	HRNS	(C

COLWELL WINFIELD BLUES BAND   C172

MIKE WINFIELD	B	(A
BILL COLWELL	G	(A
MOOSE SORRENTO	V	(A
COLLIN TILTON	WIND	(A

(A) COLD WIND BLUES	1968		US

CHUCK PURRO	D	(A	JACK SHROER	SAX	(A

COMMANDER CODY & THE LOST PLANET AIRMEN   C173

GEORGE FRAYNE	K V	(ALL
BILLY C FARLOW	HCA V	(ABCDEFG
LANCE DICKERSON	D V	(ABCDEFG
ANDY STEIN	FDL SAX	(ABCDEFG
BILL KIRCHEN	G V	(ABCDEFG
BRUCE BARLOW	B V	(ABCDEFGJ
BOBBY BLACK	STEEL V	(BCDFGJ
JOHN TICHY	G	(ABCDEF
ERNIE HAGAR	STEEL	(E
RICK HIGGINBOTHAM	G	(G
MIC GILLETTE	TPT	(EF
GREG ADAMS	TPT	(EF
DAVID BROMBERG	G	(F
HOYT AXTON	G V	(F
RONEE BLAKLEY	B V	(F
MIMI FARINA	B V	(F
NORTON BUFFALO	HRNS V	(G
FRED MYER	D	(J
DARIUS JAVAHER	G	(J
ROB GREER	B	(J
CISCO G	SAX	(J
CRAIG CHAQUICO	G	(J
RENEE ARMAND	V	(F
MARC EDELSTEIN	V	(F
NICOLETTE LARSON	V	(FJ
GRAHAM BROAD	PERC	(J
DEBORAH ANDERSON	V	(F
CHARRA PENNY	V	(J
TOM FLYE	PERC	(J
KEVIN FARRELL	V	(F

(A) LOST IN THE OZONE	1971	PARAMOUNT	US	PAR 6017
(A) LOST IN THE OZONE	197	PARAMOUNT		SPFL 276
(A) LOST IN THE OZONE	197	CARRERE	FR	68020
(A) LOST IN THE OZONE	1976	ANCHOR	UK	ABC 5074
(B) HOT LICKS COLD STEEL	1972	PARAMOUNT	US	PAS 6031
(B) HOT LICKS COLD STEEL	197	PARAMOUNT		SPFL 281
(B) HOT LICKS COLD STEEL	197	CARRERE	FR	68019
(B) HOT LICKS COLD STEEL	1976	ANCHOR	UK	ABCL 5079
(C) COUNTRY CASANOVA	1973	PARAMOUNT	US	PAS 6054
(C) COUNTRY CASANOVA	197	PARAMOUNT		SPFL 287
(C) COUNTRY CASANOVA	197	CARRERE	FR	68002
(C) COUNTRY CASANOVA	1976	ANCHOR	UK	ABCL 5083
(D) LIVE DEEP IN THE HEART OF TEXAS	1974	PARAMOUNT	US	PAS 1017
(D) LIVE DEEP IN THE HEART OF TEXAS	197	PARAMOUNT		SPFL 295
(D) LIVE DEEP IN THE HEART OF TEXAS	197	CARRERE	FR	68001
(D) LIVE DEEP IN THE HEART OF TEXAS	1976	ANCHOR	UK	ABCL 5088
(E) COMM' CODY HIS LOST PLANET AIRMEN	1975	WB	US	BS 2847
(E) COMM' CODY HIS LOST PLANET AIRMEN	1975	WB	UK	K 56108
(F) TALES FROM THE OZONE	1975	WB	US	BS 2883
(F) TALES FROM THE OZONE	1975	WB	UK	K 56158
(G) WEVE GOT A LIVE ONE HERE	1976	WB	US	BS 2939
(G) WEVE GOT A LIVE ONE HERE	1976	WB	UK	K 66043
(H) MIDNIGHT MAN (CODY SOLO)	19	ARISTA	US	AB 4125
(J) ROCK'N'ROLL AGAIN	1977	ARISTA	US	SPART1018
(J) ROCK'N'ROLL AGAIN	1977	ARISTA	US	AL 4125
(J) ROCK'N'ROLL AGAIN	1977	PATHE	FR	068 99251
(K) FLYING DREAMS	1978	ARISTA	US	AB 4183
(K) FLYING DREAMS	1978	ARISTA	US	SPART1067

WEST VIRGINIA CREEPER STEEL   (A

COMMODORES   C174

LIONEL RICHIE
WILLIAM KING
WALTER ORANGE
TOMMY McCLARY
RON LAPRAED
MILAN WILLIAMS

(A) MACHINE GUN	1974	TAMLA MOTOWN	US	M7 798
(A) MACHINE GUN	1974	TAMLA MOTOWN	UK	STML11273
(B) CAUGHT IN THE ACT	1975	TAMLA MOTOWN	US	M7 820
(B) CAUGHT IN THE ACT	1975	TAMLA MOTOWN	UK	STML11286
(C) HOT ON THE TRACKS	1976	TAMLA MOWTOWN	UK	STM 12031
(D) MOVIN ON	197	TAMLA MOTOWN	US	M7 848
(D) MOVIN ON	1975	TAMLA MOTOWN	UK	STML12001
(E) ZOOM	1977	TAMLA MOTOWN	UK	STML12057
(F) COMMODORES	197	TAMLA MOTOWN	US	M7 884
(G) LIVE	1978	TAMLA MOTOWN	UK	TMSP 6007
(G) LIVE	1978	TAMLA MOTOWN	US	M9 894
(H) NATURAL HIGH	1978	TAMLA MOTOWN	UK	STML12087
(H) NATURAL HIGH	1978	TAMLA MOTOWN	US	M7 902
(I) GREATEST HITS	1978	TAMLA MOTOWN	UK	STML12100
(I) GREATEST HITS	1978	TAMLA MOTOWN	US	M7 912
(J) MIDNIGHT MAGIC	1979	TAMLA MOTOWN	UK	STMA 8032

COMUS   C175

ROGER WOOTON	G V	(AB
BOBBIE WATSON	V	(AB
COLIN PEARSON	VLN	(A
ROB YOUNG	PERC	(A
LINDSAY COOPER	WIND	(B
DIDIER MALHERBE	SAX	(B

(A) FIRST UTTERANCE	1971	DAWN	UK	DNLS 3019
(B) TO KEEP FROM CRYING	1974	VIRGIN	UK	V 2018

KEITH HALE	K	(B	ANDY HELLABY	B	(B
GORDON CAXON	D	(B	PHIL BARRY	PERC	(B
TIM KRAEMER	CELLO	(B

CONGO   C176

(A) HEART OF THE CONGO	1978	BLACK ART
(B) CONGO	1979	CBS		83796

C176A			CONGRESS OF WONDERS					
			(A) REVOLTING	19	FANTASY	US		7016
C176B			ARTHUR CONLEY					
ARTHUR CONLEY			(A) SOUL DIRECTION	19	ATCO	US		33243
			(B) SHAKE RATTLE & ROLL	19	ATCO	US		33220
			(C) SWEET SOUL MUSIC	19		US		
C177			BILLY CONNOLLY					
BILLY CONNOLY			LIVE	197	TRANSATLANTIC	UK	TRA	258
			LIVE	RI	1981	TRANSATLANTIC	UK	TRS	103
			SOLO CONCERT	1974	TRANSATLANTIC	UK	TRA	279
			WORDS & MUSIC	1975	TRANSATLANTIC	UK	TRASAM	32
			COP YER WHACK FOR THIS	1974	POLYDOR	UK	2383	310
			GET RIGHT INTAE HIM	1975	POLYDOR	UK	2383	368
			ATLANTIC BRIDGE	197	POLYDOR	UK	2383	419
			RAW MEAT FROM THE BALCONY	1977	POLYDOR	UK	2383	464
			BILLY CONNOLLY	1977	HALLMARK	UK	SHM	927
			B C COLLECTION	1978	PICKWICK		PDA	035
			THE BIG YIN	1976	TRANSATLANTIC	UK	TRASAM	38
			GOLDEN GIFT BOX	1976	TRANSATLANTIC	UK		GAR1
			ANTHOLOGY	1978	TRANSATLANTIC	UK	MTRA	2008
			RIOUTOUS ASSEMBLY	1979	POLYDOR	UK	2383	543

C177A			ROBERT CONNOLLY				
ROBERT CONNOLLY	G B K	(A	(A) PLATEAU	1978	TUBE		TSH	352
GREG McILVEEN	D	(A					
DAVE BEATLY	G	(A	PETER CROLLY	B V FLT	(A	FRANK RUSSELL	D	(A
HOWIE STRUTT	V	(A	SHEILA WILLICK	V	(A	SANDRA WILLICK	V	(A
C177B			BILL CONNORS				
BILL CONNORS			(A) THEME TO THE GUARDIAN	1975	ECM		1057
			(B) OF THE MIST & MELTING	1978	ECM		1120
C177C			CONTOURS				
BILLY GORDON			(A) DO YOU LOVE ME	19	GORDY	US		901
JOE BILLINGSLEA			(B) BABY HIT & RUN	1974	M F P	UK		50054
SYLVESTER POTTS							
BILLY HOGGS		HUBERT JOHNSON		HUEY DAVIS	G		

C178			CONTRABAND				
MAE McKENNA	V G	(A	(A) CONTRABAND	1974	TRANSATLANTIC	UK	TRA 278
PETER CAIRNEY	B G	(A					
JOHN MARTIN	VLN	(A	GEORGE JOHNSON	MAND G K	(A	BILLY JACKSON	B	(A
ALEC BAIRD	D G	(A					

C179			RY COODER				
RY COODER	G V B MAND	(ALL	(A) RY COODER	1971	REPRISE	US 6402	UK K44093
JIM KELTNER	D	(BCDEHIJ	(B) INTO THE PURPLE VALLEY	1972	REPRISE	US 2052	UK K44142
MILT HOLLAND	PERC	(ABCDEHJ	(C) BOOMERS STORY	1972	REPRISE	US 2117	UK K44224
ROGER HAWKINS	D	(C	(D) PARADISE & LUNCH	1974	REPRISE	US 2179	UK K44260
CHARLES LAWING	CLAR	(C	(E) CHICKEN SKIN MUSIC	1976	REPRISE	US 2254	UK K54083
RANDY NEWMAN	PNO	(C	(F) SHOWTIME	1977	WB	US 3059	UK K56386
GEORGE BOHANON	HRNS	(BCEGJ	(G) JAZZ	1978	WB	US 3197	UK K56488
FLACO JIMINEZ	ACC	(EF	( ) YOU SEND ME	197	CAMDEN	US	ACS1 0445
ATTA ISAACS	G	(E	(H) BOP TILL YOU DROP	1979	WB	US 3358	UK K56691
TOMMY McCLURE	B	(C	(I) BORDERLINE	1980	WB	US 3489	UK K56864
GENE FINNEY	HCA	(C	(J) LONG RIDERS (SOUNDTRACK)	1980	WB	US 3448	UK K56826
SLEEPY JOHN ESTES	G V	(C					
JIM DICKINSON	PNO	(BCJ					
ISAAC GARCIA	D	(F	HENRY BIG RED OJEDA B	(EF	FRANK VILLAREAL	SAX	(F	ELDRIDGE KING	V	(F
BOBBY KING	V	(DEFHI	TERRY EVANS	V	(EF	PAT RIZZO	SAX	(EFG	JESSE PONCE BANJO	(F
EARL HINES	PNO	(DG	RITCHIE HAYWARD	D	(A	ROY ESTRADA	B	(A	JOHN BARBEDA	(A
MAX BENNETT	B	(A	BOBBY BRUCE		(A	GEORGE McCURN	V	(D	WALTER COOK	V	(D
RICHARD JONES	V	(D	KARL RUSSELL	V	(D	TOM PEDRINI	B	(G	RANDY ALLCROFT	TROM(G
DAVID SHERR	CLAR	(A	HARVEY PITTEL	WIND	(G	TOM COLLIER	PERC	(G	BARBARA STARKEY	K	(G
CHUCK DOMANICO	B	(G	MARIO GUARNERI	CORNET(G	RED CALLENDER	TUBA	(DEG	MARK STEVENS	D	(G
DAVID LINDLEY	G MAND(GHJ	CHRIS ETHRIDGE	B	(ABCE	FRITZ RICHMOND	B	(B	JERRY JUMONVILLE HRNS(B
JOE DAVIS	HRNS (B	IKE WILLIAMS	HRNS	(B	JOHN CRAVIOTTO	D	(B	VAN DYKE PARKS	K	(AB
GLORIA JONES	V	(AB	DONNA WASHBURN	V	(B	DONNA WEISS	V	(B	CLAUDIA LENNEAR	V	(B
SIMON PICO PAYNE	V	(G	BILL JOHNSON	V	(DG	JIMMY ADAMS	V	(G	CHUCK BERGHOFFER	B	(G
WILLIE SCHWARTZ	CLAR	(G	BILL HOOD	SAX	(G	JOHN RODBY	K	(G	FRED JACKSON	SAX(E
STUART BROTMAN	CYMB	(G	OSCAR BRASHEAR CORNET(DEGJ	CLIFF GIVENS	V	(EGH	RUSS TITELMAN	B V(DE
BENNY POWELL	TROM	(E	GABBY PAHINUI	STEEL(E	RONNIE BARRON	K	(DH	HERMAN JOHNSON	V	(EH
JOHN DUKE	B	(D	PLAS JOHNSON	SAX	(D	GENE MUMFORD	V	(D	RANDY LORENZO	V	(H
TIM DRUMMOND	B	(HI	PATRICK HENDERSON K	(H	PICO PAYNE	V	(HJ	GREG PRESTOPINO	V	(H
JIMMY ADAMS	V	(H	CHAKA KHAN	V V	(I	GEORGE McFADDEN V	(I	GEORGE PIERRE	PERC(IJ
REGGIE McBRIDE	B	(H	WILLIAM D SMITH	K V	(I	JOHN HIATT	G V	(I	JESSE HARMS	SYN(I
WILLIE GREEN	V	(I	CURT BOUTERSE	DULC (J	BILL BRYSON	B	(J	TOM SAUBER BAN G	(J
MITCH GREENHILL	G V	(J	JOE CHAMBERS	V	(J	JIM KEACH	V	(J	LESTER CHAMBERS	V	(J
HARRY CAREY JRN	V	(J	DAN PENN	V	(C			

C179A				SAM COOKE				
COOKES TOUR		1960 RCA		2221	AINT THAT GOOD NEWS	1964 RCA	US	2899
HITS OF THE 50s		1960 RCA	US	2236	AINT THAT GOOD NEWS	1964 SPECIALTY		2115
SAM COOKE		196 RCA	US	2293	GOSPEL SOUL OF SAM COOKE	196 SPECIALTY	US	2116
MY KIND OF BLUES		1961 RCA	US	2392	2 SIDES	19 SPECIALTY	US	2119
TWISTIN THE NIGHT AWAY		1961 RCA	US	2555	2 SIDES	1971 SONET UK		SNTF5009
TWISTIN THE NIGHT AWAY		1976 STARCALL	UK	1034	GOSPEL SOUL VOL 2	196 SPECIALTY	US	2128
BEST OF SAM COOKE VOL1		1962 RCA	US	2625	AT THE COPA	1964 RCA	US	2970
MR SOUL		1962 RCA	US	2673	ORIGINAL SOUL STIRRERS	196 SPECIALTY	US	2137
3 GREAT GUYS (ANKA SEDAKA)		196 RCA	US	2720	THATS HEAVEN TO ME	196 SPECIALTY	US	2146
NIGHT BEAT		1963 RCA	US	2709	GOLDEN SOUND	196 TRIP	US	8030
SOUL STIRRERS		1964 SAR	US	105	16 GREATEST HITS	196 TRIP	US	15 2
SOUL STIRRERS		1964 LONDON			SHAKE	1965 RCA	US	3367

(CONTINUED)

SAM COOKE

Title	Year/Label	Cat
BEST OF VOL 2	1965 RCA	US 3373
SAMS SONGS	196 FAMOUS	US 502
ONLY SIXTEEN	196 FAMOUS	US 505
SO WONDERFUL	196 FAMOUS	US 508
YOU SEND ME	196 FAMOUS	US 509
YOU SEND ME	19 CAMDEN	US ACL10445
CHA CHA CHA	196 FAMOUS	US 512
RIGHT ON	196 CHERIE	US 1001
TRY A LITTLE LOVE	1965 RCA	US 3435
HIT KIT	196 KEEN	US 86101
I THANK GOD	196 KEEN	US 86103
SAM COOKE	196 KEEN	US 2001
ENCORE	196 KEEN	US 2003
TRIBUTE TO THE LADY	196 KEEN	US 2004
ENCORE VOL 2	196 KEEN	US 2008
WONDERFUL WORLD(50s)	1966 IMMEDIATE	UKIMLP002
WONDERFUL WORLD(50s	1966 KEEN	US 86106
UNFORGETTABLE SAM COOKE	1966 RCA	US 3517
UNFORGETTABLE SAM COOKE	196 CAMDEN	US 2610
MAN WHO INVENTED SOUL	1968 RCA	US 3991
GOLDEN AGE	196 RCA	UK 1054
THE LATE SAM COOKE	1969 RCA INT	UKINT1080
THIS IS SAM COOKE	1971 RCA	UK 2007
THIS IS SAM COOKE	197 RCA	US 6027
SINGS BILLIE HOLIDAY	1976 STARCALL	UK 1030
SINGS BILLIE HOLIDAY	197 UPFRONT	US 160
INTERPRETS BILLIE HOLIDAY	19 RCA	APLI0899
INTERPRETS BILLIE HOLIDAY	1976 RCA	UK HY1030
FOREVER	1976 RCA	7194
ANOTHER SATURDAY NIGHT	19 RCA	US 4375
WHEN I FALL IN LOVE	1979 NUT	UK NUTM23

CALVIN COOL & THE SURF KNOBS

| CALVIN COOL | | (A) THE SURFERS BEAT | 19 CHARTER | US 103 |

RITA COOLIDGE

RITA COOLIDGE	V (ALL	(A) RITA COOLIDGE	1971 A&M	US 4291	UK AMLS 2015
WITH		(B) NICE FEELIN'	1971 A&M	US 4325	UK AMLS64325
LEON RUSSELL	K (A	(C) LADY'S NOT FOR SALE	1972 A&M	US 4370	UK AMLS64370
SPOONER OLDHAM	K (A	(D) FALL INTO SPRING	1974 A&M	US 3627	UK AMLS63627
CLARENCE WHITE	G (A	(E) ITS ONLY LOVE	1975 A&M	US 4531	UK AMLS64531
MARC BENNO	G (AC	(F) ANYTIME ANYWHERE	1977 A&M	US 4616	UK AMLH64616
CHRIS ETHRIDGE	B (A	(G) LOVE ME AGAIN	1978 A&M	US 4699	UK AMLH64699
JIM KELTNER	D (ACH	(H) SATISFIED	1979 A&M		UK AMLH64781
FRED TACKETT	G (H				

Musician	Inst	Codes
FRED TACKETT	G	(H
STEPHEN STILLS	G	(A
DONALD DUNN	B	(A
JERRY McGEE	G	(ACEG
FUZZY SAMUELS	B	(A
DON MENZA	SAX	(A
GEORGE BOHANON	HRNS	(A
JACK REDMAN	TROM	(A
CHUCK FINDLEY	TPT	(A
VINCE DE ROSA	HRNS	(A
DAVID DUKE	HRNS	(A
SHIRLEY MATTHEWS	V	(ACE
GRAHAM NASH	V	(A
MIKE UTLEY	K	(CEGH
RUSS KUNKEL	D	(D
STEPHEN BRUTON	V G	(GH
AL KOOPER	G	(C
TOMMY McCLURE	B	(CH
BROOKS HUNNICUTT	V	(E
STEVE FORMAN	PERC	(G
BARBARA CARROLL	PNO	(E
MIKE BAIRD	D	(G
ORRIN WATERS	V	(G
DEAN PARKS	G	(H
JOHN SEITER	V	(H
DONNY GARRARD	V	(H
BOOKER T JONES	B K	(ACEFGH
BOBBYE HALL	PERC	(AEF
PLAS JOHNSON	SAX	(A
JIM HORN	SAX	(A
CLIFFORD SCOTT	SAX	(A
LEW McCREARY	TROM	(A
DICK HYDE	TROM	(A
AL AARONS	TPT	(A
BILL HENSHAW	HRNS	(A
CLYDIE KING	V	(AE
PRISCILLA COOLIDGE	V	(ACH
BOB SEGARINI	V	(A
CARL RADLE	B	(C
JAY GRAYDON	G	(G
BERNIE LEADON	G	(C
JOHN SEBASTIAN	HCA	(C
SAMMY CREASON	D	(CEH
JENNIFER WARNES	V	(E
MAXINE WILLARD	V	(CG
CHUCK DOMANICO	B	(E
DENNIS BELFIELD	B	(G
LUTHER WATERS	V	(G
BOB GLAUB	B	(H
MICHAEL McDONALD	V	(H
BOBBY WOMACK	G	(A
LARRY LEE	V	(G
RY COODER	G	(A
JOHN KELSO	SAX	(A
PETER CHRISTLIEB		(A
ERNIE TACK	TROM	(A
OLLIVER MITCHELL	HRNS	(A
DALTON SMITH	HRNS	(A
ARTHUR MAEBE	HRNS	(A
VANETTA FIELDS	V	(A
DONNA WEISS	V	(AC
RANDY BISHOP	V	(A
AL PERKINS	G	(CE
JIM HAAS	V	(G
LEE SKLAR	B	(CE
CHARLIE FREEMAN	G	(C
SNEAKY PETE	STEEL	(C
PETSYE POWELL	V	(E
KRIS KRISTOFFERSON	V	(C
COLIN BAILEY	D	(E
JULIA TILLMAN	V	(G
CORY WELLS	V	(G
DOROTHY ASHBY	HARP	(H
RICHIE CANNATA	HRNS	(H

ALICE COOPER

[ALICE COOPER VINCENT FURNIER]	V (ALL	(1) SPIDERS (2) EARWIGS(EARLY GROUPS)			
		(A) PRETTIES FOR YOU	1969 STRAIGHT		STS 1051
GLEN BUXTON	G (12ABCDEF	(A) PRETTIES FOR YOU	1969 WB	US	1840
JOHN TATUM	(1	(B) EASY ACTION	1969 STRAIGHT		STS 1061
JOHN SPEAR	(1	(B) EASY ACTION	1969 WB	US	1845
MICHAEL BRUCE	K G (2ABCDEF	(AB)SCOOLDAYS(PRETTIES/EASY ACTION	1973 STRAIGHT	UK	K 66021
STEVE HUNTER	G (JKLM	(C) LOVE IT TO DEATH	1971 STRAIGHT		STS 1065
PRAKASH JOHN	B (JLM	(C) LOVE IT TO DEATH	1971 WB	UK	K 46177
PENTTI GLAN	D (JM	(C) LOVE IT TO DEATH	1971 WB	US	1883
JOSEF CHIROWSKI	K (JL	(C) LOVE IT TO DEATH	197 MIDI		20633
DICK WAGNER	G (EFJKLMO	(D) KILLER	1971 WB	UK	K 56005
NEAL SMITH	D (ABF	(D) KILLER	1971 WB	US	2567
FRED MANDEL	K (MP	(E) SCHOOLS OUT	1972 WB	UK	K 56007
DENNIS DUNAWAY	B (ABCDEF	(E) SCHOOLS OUT	1972 WB	US	2623
DAVID BRIGGS	PNO (B	(F) BILLION DOLLAR BABIES	1973 WB	UK	K 56013
VANETTA FIELDS	V (L	(F) BILLION DOLLAR BABIES	1973 WB	US	2685
JULIA TILLMAN	V (L	(G) MUSCLE OF LOVE	1974 WB	UK	K 56018
LORNA WILLARD	V (L	(G) MUSCLE OF LOVE	1974 WB	US	
ERNIE WATTS	SAX (L	(G) MUSCLE OF LOVE (QUAD)	1975 WB	US	CD4 2748
ALLEN SCHWARZBERG	D (KL	(H) GREATEST HITS	1974 WB	UK	K 56043
JIM GORDON	D (KL	(H) GREATEST HITS	1974 WB	US	3107
AL McMILLAN	PNO (KL	(J) WELCOME TO MY NIGHTMARE	1975 ANCHOR	UK	ANCL 2011
AL KOOPER	K (L	(J) WELCOME TO MY NIGHTMARE	1975 ATCO	US	19157
MARCY LEVY	V (O	(J) WELCOME TO MY NIGHTMARE	1975 CARRERE	FR	68051
DAVEY JOHNSTONE	G (OP	(K) GOES TO HELL	1976 WB	UK	K 56171
RICK NIELSEN	G (O	(K) GOES TO HELL	1976 WB	US	2896
TONY LEVIN	B (JKL	(L) LACE & WHISKEY	1977 WB	UK	K 56365
BOB BABITT	B (LK	(L) LACE & WHISKEY	1977 WB	US	3027
JIM KELTNER	D (O	(M) ALICE COOPER SHOW	1977 WB	UK	K 56439
BOB EZRIN	K V (JKL	(M) ALICE COOPER SHOW	1977 WB	US	3138
DONOVAN	G (F	(N) ALICE COOPER	19 CHARTERLINE		CTR 46177
JOHNNY BADANJEK	D (J	(O) FROM THE INSIDE	1978 WB	UK	K 56577
GERRY LYONS	V (J	(O) FROM THE INSIDE	1978 WB	US	3263
REGGIE VINCENT	G V (E	(P) FLUSH THE FASHION	1980 WB	UK	K 56805

(CONTINUED)

C182 (CONTINUED)

SHARON LEE WILLIAMS	V	(K
COLINA PHILLIPS	V	(K
BILL MISENER	V	(K
MICHAEL SHERMAN	V	(K
LAUREL WARD	V	(K

C183

MIKE COOPER	V	(ALL
WITH		
ALAN COOK	K	(
TIM RICHARDSON	PERC	(
LES CALVERT	BASS	(
STEFAN GROSSMAN	G	(D
THE HERON	V	(D
ALAN SKIDMORE	SAX	(D
JOHN TAYLOR	PNO	(D
BILL BOAZMAN	G	(D
ROY BABBINGTON	B	(D
HARRY MILLER	DBL B	(C

C183A

BRIAN COOPER	B V	(A
RICHARD COOPER	G V	(A
TERRY KING	STEEL V	(A
GLEN BELL	D V	(A
KEITH JOLLIMORE	SAX	(A
LENNY SOLOMON	STRINGS	(A

C184

JOHN COOPER CLARKE	V	(ALL
PAUL BURGESS	D	(A
LYN OAKLEY	G	(A
BILL NELSON	G	(A
PETE SHELLEY	G	(A
STEVE HOPKINS	K	(A

C185

JOHN CIPOLLINA	G	(A
GARY PHILIPPET	V G K	(A
JIM McPHERSON	V G B	(A

C185A

JOHN COPPIN	V G K	(A
PHIL BEAR	VLN G V	(A
TONY BENNETT	G V	(A

C185B

PHIL CORDELL	G B	(A
BARRY DE SOUZA	D	(A
CHRIS HUNT	D	(A
PAUL KENDRICK	B V	(A
REV STOCKDALE	K	(A
DOREEN CHANTER	V	(A
JIMMY HELMS	V	(A
ROBIN WILLIAMS	STRGS HRNS	(A

C185C

C185D

KENNETH KNUDSEN	K	(AB123
CLAUS BOHLING	G	(3B
OLE STREENBERG	D	(B23
PETER FRIIS NIELSEN	B	(123AB
CLAUS BOJE	D	(A1

C186

ALICE COOPER

DENNY VOSBURGH	V	(K
JIM MAELEN	PERC	(K
SHAUN JACKSON	V	(K
DENNIS CONWAY	D	(P

JOE GANNON	V	(K
JOHN TROPEA	G	(K
SHEP GORDON	V	(K
JOHN LOPRESTI	B	(P

MIKE COOPER

(A) INVERTED WORLD	1968	MATCHBOX		SDM 159
(B) OH REALLY	1969	PYE		NSPL18281
(C) DO I KNOW YOU	1970	DAWN	UK	DNLS 3005
(D) TROUT STEEL	1970	DAWN	UK	DNLS 3011
(E) PLACES I KNOW	1971	DAWN	UK	DNLS 3026
(F) MACHINE GUN COMPANY	1972	DAWN	UK	DNLS 3031
(G) LIFE & DEATH IN PARADISE	1974	FRESH AIR	UK	6370 500

GERRY FIELD	VLN	(D
MIKE OSBORNE	WIND	(D
NICK PICKETT	VLN	(D
IAN A ANDERSON		(A

ALAN JACKSON	D	(D
GEOFF HAWKINS	WIND	(D
POOR LITTLE ANN	V	(C

COOPER BROTHERS

(A) THE DREAM NEVER DIES	1978	CAPRICORN	UK	2429 171

DON BREGG	V	(A
DARRYL ALGUIRE	PERC V	(A
GLOVES McGUINTY	PNO	(A
CHARLIE ROBERTSON	FLT	(A

AL SERWA	K V	(A
JOHN SAUNDERS	BANJO	(A
AL BRISCOE	DOBRO	(A
STEVE HOLLINGSWORTH	D V	(A

JOHN COOPER CLARKE

(A) DISGUISE IN LOVE	1978	CBS	UK	83132
(B) OU EST LA MAISON DE FROMAGE	197	EPIC	US	
(B) OU EST LA MAISON DE FROMAGE	197	RABID	UK	NOZE1
(C) WALKING BACK TO HAPPINESS(LIVE)	1979	CBS	UK	JCC1

MARTIN HANNETT	B	(A	JOHN SCOTT	G	(A

COPPERHEAD

(A) COPPERHEAD	1973	CBS	US	32250

HUTCH HUTCHINSON	V B	(A	DAVID WEBER	D	(A

JOHN COPPIN

(A) NO GOING BACK	1979	ROLA		R002

MICK CANDLER	D	(A	STEVE HUTT	B V	(A

PHIL CORDELL

(A) BORN AGAIN	1977	PRODIGAL		PDL 2006

CHAS O'BRIEN	D	(A
DAVE MARKEE	D	(A
MADELINE BELL	V	(A
LIZA STRIKE	V	(A
TONY BURROWS	V	(A

RAY FENWICK	G	(A
LENNIE WATTS	K	(A
R & J STONE	V	(A
GEORGE CHANDLER	V	(A
WESLEY MAGOOGAN	SAX	(A

CORNELLS

(A) BEACH BOUND	196	GAREX	US	LPGA 100

CORONARIAS DAN

(1) 1969 71	(2) 71 72	(3) 73+		
(A) BREATHE	1971	PARLOPHONE	EUR	MOCK 1018
(B) VISITOR	1975	STEEPLECHASE		SCS 1032

CHICK COREA & RETURN TO FOREVER

CHICK COREA	K	(ALL	(A) TONES FOR JOANS BONES	1968 VORTEX	IMP	2004
FLORA PLURIM	V PERC	(INj	(A) TONES FOR JOANS BONES	1978 ATLANTIC	UK	K50302
AIRTO MOREIRA	D PERC	(INj	(B) IS	1969 SOLID STATE	US	18055
JOE FARRELL	WIND	(AJNThj	(C) NOW HE SINGS	1969 SOLID STATE	US	7011
STANLEY CLARKE	B	(JKONTUWahj	(D) SONG OF THE SINGING	1971 BLUENOTE 84353	RI 7B	40030
ANTHONY BRAXTON	WIND	(Tf	(E) COREA	19 BLUENOTE		39542
DAVE HOLLAND	B	(DFTf	(F) ARC	1971 ECM		1009
BARRY ALTSCHUL	D	(DFT	(G) PIANO IMPROVISATIONS	1972 ECM		1014
BILL CONNORS	G	(K	(H) CRYSTAL SILENCE	1972 ECM		1024
LENNY WHITE	D	(KOUWh	(I) LIGHT AS A FEATHER	1972 POLYDOR US 5525	UK	2310 247
AL DIMEOLA	G	(OUWh	(J) CHILDREN OF FOREVER	1972 POLYDOR	UK	2310 267
GAYLE MORAN	V	(Yah	(K) HYMN OF THE SEVENTH GALAXY	1972 POLYDOR US 5536	UK	2310 286
STEVE GADD	D	(ah	(K) HYMN OF THE SEVENTH GALAXY	1972 POLYDOR	EURO	2302 028
EDDIE GOMEZ	B	(Y	(L) PIANO IMPROVISATIONS 2	1972 ECM		1020
ANTHONY JACKSON	B	(Y	(M) BLISS	1973 MUSE		5011
BILL WATRONS	TROM	(Y	(N) RETURN TO FOREVER	1972 ECM		1022
WAYNE ANDRE	TROM	(Y	(O) WHERE HAVE I KNOWN YOU BEFORE	1974 POLYDOR US 6509	UK	2310 354
DANNY CAHN	TPT	(Y	(O) WHERE HAVE I KNOWN YOU BEFORE	197 POLYDOR	EURO	2302 030
BOB MILLIKAN	TPT	(Y	(P) ROUND TRIP	1974 EPIC	UK	65559
JOHN GATCHELL	TPT	(Y	(Q) SUNDANCE	1974 PEOPLE UK 09 US G MERCHANT		2202
JEAN LUC PONTY	VLN	(a	(R) INNER SPACE	1974 ATLANTIC US 2305	UK	K60081
DON ALIAS	PERC	(aj	(S) WITH UNDERSTANDING	1975 MUSE		5083
JOHN THOMAS	TPT	(a	(T) LIVE IN NEW YORK 74	1975 OXFORD	US	3005
JOHN ROSENBURG	TPT	(a	(U) NO MYSTERY	1975 POLYDOR US 6512	UK	2310 378
RON MOSS	TPT	(a	(V) CAPTAIN MARVEL	1975 VERVE		2304 225
NARADA MICHAEL WALDEN	D	(a	(W) ROMANTIC WARRIOR	1976 CBS US 34076	UK	81221
WOODY SHAW	TPT	(a	(X) CIRCLING IN (DBL)	1976 BLUENOTE		BLNAD 472
STEVE SWALLOW	B	(A	(Y) LEPRECHAUN	1976 POLYDOR	UK	2391 217
JOE CHAMBERS	D	(A	(Z) MUSIC MAGIC	1977 CBS	UK	81959

(CONTINUED)

CHICK COREA & RETURN TO FOREVER
C186

GERRY BROWN	D	(	(a) MY SPANISH HEART	1977	POLYDOR	UK	2672	031
PETE LA ROCCO	D	(M	(b) MAD HATTER	1978	POLYDOR US 16130	UK	2490	114
STAN GETZ	SAX	(V	(c) LIVE	1978	CBS	UK		82808
SADAO WATANABE		(P	(d) SECRET AGENT	1979	POLYDOR	UK	2391	381
STUART BLUMBERG	TPT	(A	(e) DELPHI VOL 1	1979	POLYDOR	UK	2490	150
HERBIE HANCOCK	K	(g	(f) CIRCLES PARIS CONCERT (DBL)	197	ECM			1018/19
JIM PUGH	TROM	(h	(g) COREA/HANCOCK	1979	POLYDOR	UK	2672	049
LAUDIR DE OLIVEIRA	PERC	(j	(h) BEST OF RETURN TO FOREVER	1980	CBS	UK		84292
HUBERT LAWS	FLT	(j	(j) TAP STEP	1980	WB	US 3425 UK		K56801
BUNNY BRUNEL	B	(j						
TOM BRECHTLEIN	D	(j	AL VIZZUTTI TPT (j	JAMIE FAUNT	B	(j	JOE HENDERSON	SAX (j
STRING SECTION		(aY						

DAVE 'BABY' CORTEZ
C186A

DAVE 'BABY' CORTEZ	ORG	(ALL	RINKY DINK	19	CHESS	US	1473
			ORGAN SHINDIG	19	ROULETTE	US	25298
			MUSIC AROUND THE CLOCK	19	CLOCK	US	CX201
			IN ORBIT WITH	19	ROULETTE	US	25328
			HAPPY ORGAN	19	RCA	US	2099
			FABULOUS ORGAN	19	METRO	US	550
			& JERRYS HOUSE ROCKERS	19	CROWN	US	357
			DAVE BABY CORTEZ	19	CLOCK	US	331

CORTINAS
C187

JEREMY VALENTINE	V	(A) TRUE ROMANCES	1978	CBS	UK	82831
MIKE FEWINS	G					
NICK SHEPPARD	G					

DEXTER BALWOOD   B   DAN SWARM   D

CORVETTES
C188

JOHN WARE	D	(1	(1) 1969		
JOHN LONDON	B	(1			
BERNIE LEADON	G	(1	CHRIS DARROW	(1	

C189
LARRY CORYELL
C189

LARRY CORYELL	G	(ALL	(A) FREE SPIRIT	1967	ABC		062 90593
WITH			(B) BAREFOOT BOY	1972	PHILIPS		6369 407
BILLY COBHAM	D	(	(B) BAREFOOT BOY	197	FLYING DUTCHMAN		10139
CHICK COREA	K	(	(C) FAIRYLAND	197	FLYING DUTCHMAN		51500
JACK BRUCE	B	(	(C) FAIRYLAND	1972	PHILIPS		6369 411
WILL LEE	B	(V	(C) FAIRYLAND	19	MEGA		607
JOHN MARSHALL	D	(	(D) OFFERING	197	VANGUARD		VSD 79319
MICHAEL LAWRENCE	TPT	(NW	(D) OFFERING	197	MUSIDISC	FR	23001
MIROSLAV VITOUS		(	(E) SPACES	197	VANGUARD		VSD 79345
JOHN LEE	B	(NPT	(E) SPACES	197	VANGUARD 6359 005		VSD 6558
MIKE MANDEL	K	(JNOPQW	(E) SPACES	197	MUSIDISC		23002
ALPHONSE MOUZON	PERC	(TJNW	(F) THE REAL GREAT ESCAPE	197	VANGUARD		VSD 79329
STEVE KHAN	G	(NPV	(F) THE REAL GREAT ESCAPE	197	MUSIDISC		23019
PHILIP CATHERINE	G	(RST	(G) LADY CORELL	1969	VANGUARD		SVRL19051
CHERYL ALEXANDER	V	(T	(G) LADY CORYELL	1972	VANGUARD		6509
TAWATHA AGEE	V	(T	(G) LADY CORYELL	197	MUSIDISC		23017
DANNY TRIFAN	B	(JW	(H) CORYELL	1970	VANGUARD		SVRL19059
RANDY BRECKER	HRNS	(JP	(H) CORYELL	1972	VANGUARD		VSD 6547
MICHAEL BRECKER	HRNS	(PV	(H) CORYELL	197	MUSIDISC		23020
MERVIN BRONSON	B	(I	(I) AT THE VILLAGE GATE	197	VANGUARD		VSD 6573
HARRY WILKINSON	D	(I	(I) AT THE VILLAGE GATE	197	MUSIDISC		23024
JULIE CORYELL	V	(I	(J) INTRODUCING 11TH HOUSE	197	VANGUARD		VSD 79342
MITCH MITCHELL	D	(	(K) PLANET END	1976	VANGUARD		VSD 79367
JIM PEPPER	SAX	(A	(K) PLANET END	1976	MUSIDISC		23022
CHRIS HILLS	B	(A	(L) ESSENTIAL	1975	VANGUARD		VSD 75/76
BOB MOSES	D	(A	(M) RESTFUL MIND	1975	VANGUARD		VSD 79353
CHIP BAKER	G	(A	(M) RESTFUL MIND	1975	MUSIDISC		23013
RON CARTER	B	(O	(N) LEVEL ONE	1976	ARISTA	UK	ARTY 113
CHUCK RAINEY	B	(O	(N) LEVEL ONE	1976	ARISTA	US	4052
BERNARD PURDIE	D	(O	(O) BASICS	197	VANGUARD		VSD 79375
STEVE HAAS	D	(O	(P) ASPECTS	1976	ARISTA US4077	UK	ARTY 133
RAY MANTILLA	PERC	(O	(Q) LION & THE RAM	1977	ARISTA	UK	ARTY 154
GERRY BROWN	D	(P	(Q) LION & THE RAM	1977	ARISTA	US	4108
TERUMASA HINO	TPT	(P	(R) TWIN HOUSE	1977	ATLANTIC	UK	K 50342
MTUME	PERC	(P	(S) SPLENDID	1978	ELEKTRA	UK	K 52086
DANNY TOAN	G	(P	(T) BACK TOGETHER AGAIN	1977	ATLANTIC	UK	K 50382
DAVID SANBORN	SAX	(PV	(U) TWO FOR THE ROAD	1977	ARISTA	UK	SPARTI1050
ARTHUR RHAMES	G	(V	(V) DIFFERENCE	1978	BARCLAY	FR	900 558
GLEN MOORE	B	(V	(W) AT MONTREUX	1978	VANGUARD		VSD 79410
STEVE GADD	D	(V	(X) LIVE IN EUROPE	1978	LC	IMP	
TONY WILLIAMS	D	(V	(Y) FREE SMILE	1979	ARISTA	US	
DON GROLNICK	K	(V	(Z) OTHER SIDE OF	1975	VANGUARD		VSD 79360

COSMIC COWBOYS
C190

(A) COSMIC COWBOYS	1973	EMI		EMA 754

COSMIC EYE
C191

(A) DREAM SEQUENCE	1972	REGALZONOPHONE UK		SLRZ 1030

COSMIC JOKERS
C192

DIETER DIERKS		(A) COSMIC JOKERS	1974	METRONOME	KM 58008
JURGEN DOLLASE		(B) PLANET SIT IN	1974	METRONOME	KM 58013
MANUEL GOETTSCHING					
HARALD GROSSKOPF		KLAUS SCHULZE	STERNEN MADCHEN GILLE		

COSMIC SOUNDS
C192A

PAUL BEAVER	SYN ELEC(A	(A) THE ZODIAC	1967	ELEKTRA	EKS 74009

C193 ELVIS COSTELLO

Personnel		
ELVIS COSTELLO	G V	(ALL
JOHN McFEE	G V	(A
HUEY LOUIS	HCA V	(A
JOHNNY CIAMBOTTI	B V	(A
SEAN HOPPER	K V	(A
ALEX CALL	G V	(A
MICKY SHINE	D V	(A
NICK LOWE	B	(1
STEVE MASON (NAIVE)	K	(CBF
PETER THOMAS	D	(CBEF
BRUCE THOMAS	B	(BCEF
GLENN TILBROOK	V	(F

	Album	Year	Label	Country	Cat#
(A)	MY AIM IS TRUE	1977	STIFF	UK	SEEZ 3
(A)	MY AIM IS TRUE	1977	CBS	US	35037
(B)	THIS YEARS MODEL	1978	RADAR	UK	RAD 3
(B)	THIS YEARS MODEL	1978	CBS	US	35331
(C)	ARMED FORCES	1979	RADAR	UK	RAD14
(C)	ARMED FORCES	1979	CBS	US	35709
(D)	LIVE AT MOCAMBO	1978	CBS	CAN	PROMO
(1)	LIVE FOR A WEEK IN 1978				
(E)	GET HAPPY	1980	F BEAT	UK	XXLP 1
(F)	TRUST	1981	F BEAT	UK	XXLP 11

MARTIN BELMONT G (F

C194 GENE COTTON

Personnel		
GENE COTTON	G V	(ALL
WITH		
PETE WADE	G	(B
BILLY SANFORD	G	(B
REGGIE YOUNG	G	(BC
JOHNNY CHRISTOPHER	G	(BC
B G CRUZER ADAIR	K	(BCD
SANDY COTTON	FLT	(B
CHARLIE McCOY	HCA	(BCDF
JACK WILLIAMS	B	(BCDF
KENNY BUTTREY	D	(BCF
RON OATES	K	(D
JOE OSBORN	B	(C
FARRELL MORRIS	PERC	(DF
TOMMY WELLS	D	(F
BOBBY OGDIN	K SYN	(F
GUNNAR SCRIVENOR	AUTOHARP	(F
BOBBY THOMPSON	G BANJ	(C

	Album	Year	Label	Country	Cat#
(A)	GREY OF THE MORNING	1974	MYRRH	US	MST 6511
(B)	LIBERTY	1974	MYRRH	US	MST 6524
(C)	FOR ALL THE YOUNG WRITERS	1976	ABC	US	AB 933
(D)	RAIN ON	1976	ABC	US	AB 983
(D)	RAIN ON	1976	ABC	UK	ABCL 5213
(E)	SAVE THE DANCER	1978	ARIOLA	US	SW 50031
(E)	SAVE THE DANCER	1978	ARIOLA	UK	ARL 5015
(E)	SAVE THE DANCER	1978	EMI INT		INS 3018
(F)	NO STRINGS ATTACHED	1979	ARIOLA	US	SW 50070

Personnel					
SHANE KEISTER	K SYN	(DF	JIM COLVARD	G	(C
LARRIE LONDIN	D	(D	KENNY MALONE	D	(D
TED REYNOLDS	B	(D	STEVE GIBSON	B G MAND	(CDF
DIANNE DARLING	SYN PERC V	(F	MARC SPEER	G STEEL V	(F
JAMES OWMBY	K SAX V	(F	MIKE JOYCE	B V	(F
BUDDY SKIPPER	SYN	(F	MIKE LAWLER	SYN	(F
DOYLE GRISHAM	STEEL	(F	BILL JONES	SAX	(F

C195 JAMES COTTON BLUES BAND

JAMES COTTON	V HCA	(ALL
WITH		
MATT MURPHY	G	(EF
JAMES BOOKER	PNO	(
LUTHER TUCKER	G	(
BOB ANDERSON	B	(
ALBERT GIANQUINTO	PNO	(
FRANCIS CLAY	D	(
WAYNE TALBERT	K	(D
MARTIN FIERRO	SAX	(D
MIKE FENDER	TPT	(D
EDDIE ADAMS	B	(D
CHARLES CALMESE	B	(F
PHIL JEKANOWSKI	PNO	(F
TODD RUNDGREN	PERC G V	(E
MARK KLINGMAN	V K	(E
RITCHIE HAYWARD	D	(E
TOM COSGROVE	V	(E
RONELLE STAFFORD	V	(E
TREVOR LAWRENCE	HRNS	(D

	Album	Year	Label	Country	Cat#
(A)	JAMES COTTON BLUES BAND	1967	VERVE FVS9507	US	3023
(B)	PURE COTTON	1968	VERVE FVS9512	US	3038
(C)	COTTON IN YOUR EARS	1968	VERVE	US	3060
(D)	CUT YOU LOOSE	1968	VANGUARD		VSD 79283
(D)	CUT YOU LOOSE	1968	VANGUARD		SVRL19035
(E)	TAKING CARE OF BUSINESS	19	CAPITOL		SM814
(F)	100% COTTON	1974	BUDDAH		BDS 5620
(G)	HIGH ENERGY	1978	BUDDAH		BDLP 4048
(G)	HIGH ENERGY	1978	BUDDAH		5650
(H)	LIVE	197	BUDDAH		5661

Personnel					
JOE RODRIGUEZ	D	(D	LITTLE BO	SAX	(F
KENNY JOHNSON	D	(F	LENNY KING	SAX	(F
JAMES COOK	G	(D	MIKE BLOOMFIELD	G	(E
DOMENIC TROIANO	G	(E	JOHNNY WINTER	G	(E
RALPH SCHUCKETT	PNO	(E	STU WOODS	B	(D
JOEL BISHOP OBRIEN	D	(E	N D SMART	D V	(E
CISSY HOUSTON	V	(E	VENERIT SIMS	V	(E
DEIRDRE TUCK	V	(E	GENE DINWIDDIE	HRNS	(E
DAVE SANBORN	HRNS	(E	STEVE MADAIO	HRNS	(E

C196 JOHNNY COUGAR

JOHNNY COUGAR MELLENCAMP		(AB
JIMMY HOROWITZ		(B
ROBERT FRANK	B	(AB
TOM KNOWLES	D	(AB
JOHN SMITH		(B
MIKE WANCHIC		(B
PAUL HARRIS	K	(B

	Album	Year	Label	Country	Cat#
(A)	BIOGRAPHY	1978	RIVA		RVLP6
(B)	JOHNNY COUGAR	1979	RIVA		RVLP9
(C)	NOTHING MATTER'S & WHAT IF IT DID	1980	RIVA		RVLP10

Personnel					
ANDY MACKAY	SAX	(B	LARRY CRANE	G	(AB
BRIAN BEC VAR		(B	JOE LALA	PERC	(B
BLUE WEAVER	K	(B	MIKE LEWIS		(B

C197 DENNIS COULSON

DENNIS COULSON

	Album	Year	Label	Country	Cat#
(A)	DENNIS COULSON	1973	ELEKTRA	US	K 42148

C198 COUNT

	Album	Year	Label	Country	Cat#
(A)	IM A STAR	1978	FLAMINGO		67291

C199 COUNT BISHOPS

JOHNNY GUITAR	G V	(ABC
PAUL BALBI	D	(ABC
STEVE LEWINS	B	(AB
ZEN DEFLEUR HIEROWSKI	G V	(ABC
MIKE SPENCER	V	(
DAVE TICE	V	(BC
PAT McMULLEN	B	(C
JULIAN HOLLAND	PNO	(B

	Album		Year	Label	Country	Cat#
(A)	THE COUNT BISHOPS		1977	DYNAMITE	HOLL	33001
(B)	COUNT BISHOPS		1977	CHISWICK	UK	WIK 1
(C)	LIVE	12"	1978	CHISWICK	UK	CH7
(C)	LIVE	10"	1978	CHISWICK	UK	CHT7
(C)	LIVE	12"	1979	CHISWICK	UK	CWK 3006
(C)	LIVE	10"	1979	CHISWICK	UK	CWM 2001
(D)	CROSSCUT(BISHOPS)		1979	CHISWICK	UK	CWK 3009

C199A COUNT FIVE

KENN ELLNER	V HCA	'A
SEAN BYRNE	G	(A
JOHN MICHALSKI	G	(A

	Album	Year	Label	Country	Cat#
(A)	PSYCHOTIC REACTION	1966	DOUBLE SHOT	US	DSM 1001

ROY CHANEY B (A   CRAIG ATKINSON D (A

C200 COUNTRY GAZZETTE

BYRON BERLINE	FDL V	(ABCDE
ROGER BUSH	B V	(ABCDE
ALAN MUNDE	BANJ V	(ABCDE
KENNY WERTZ	G V	(ABCDE
HERB PEDERSEN	V G	(AC
SKIP CONOVER	DOBRO	(A
CHRIS SMITH	G	(A
CLARENCE WHITE	G	(C

	Album	Year	Label	Country	Cat#
(A)	TRAITOR IN OUR MIDST	1972	U A	UK	UAG 29404
(B)	LIVE IN AMSTERDAM	1972	BUMBLE		GEXD 301
(C)	DONT GIVE UP YOUR DAY JOB	1973	U A	UK	UAS 29491
(D)	BLUEGRASS SPECIAL	1973	ARIOLA		86 501HT
(E)	BANJO SANDWICH	197	ARIOLA	NL	27239
(F)	LIVE	1975	TRANSATLANTIC	UK	TRA 291
(F)	LIVE	1975	ARIOLA	NL	88558
(G)	MILESTONES	1975	EMI INT		COPS7418D1/2
					(CONTINUED)

AL PERKINS	STEEL	(C	
ROLAND WHITE		(F	
LEE SKLAR	B	(C	

COUNTRY GAZZETTE — C200

(H) SUNNY SIDE OF THE MOUNTAIN	1976	TRANSATLANTIC	UK	TRA	318
(J) OUT TO LUNCH	197	FLYING FISH		FF027	
(K) WHAT A WAY TO EARN A LIVING	1977	TRANSATLANTIC	UK	TRA	347
(L) FROM THE BEGINNING	1978	SUNSET	UK	SNS	50414
(M) ALL THIS AND MONEY TOO	1979	RIDGE RUNNER	US	RRR	017
(AC)TRAITOR/DONT GIVE UP	19	UA		184 52064/5	

PIERRE COURBOIS — C201

PIERRE COURBOIS	D	(A	(A) ASSOCIATION	1970	MUNICH 6802634
JASPER VANTHOF	PNO	(A			
SIGGI BUSCH	B	(A			

PETER KRIJNEN	B	(A	TOTO BLANKE G (A

DAVID COURTNEY — C201A

DAVID COURTNEY	V PNO	(A	(A) FIRST DAY	1975	EMI UK EMC3094 US UA LA 553G
BARRY MORGAN	D	(A			
BRIAN ODGERS	B	(A	STEVE GAY	PNO	(A
ALAN PARKER	G	(A	SKAILA KANGA	HARP	(A
MIKE MORAN	K	(A	BARRY DE SOUZA	D	(A
FRANCIS MONKMAN	SYN K	(A	JEAN ROUSSEL	PNO	(A
FRANK RICOTTI	PERC	(A	BRUCE LYNCH	B	(A
JANE POWELL		(A	B J COLE	STEEL G	(A
ALF DUKES	FLEXATONE	(A	PILOT	V	(A
BERNARD THOMAS	WIND	(A	DAVE GILMOUR	G	(A

PAUL KEOGH	G	(A	
TONY BURROWS	V	(A	
ANDREW POWELL	B K	(A	
RUSS BALLARD	G	(A	
AIXA COURTNEY	V	(A	
MORRIS PERT	PERC	(A	
RICHARD HARVEY	WIND	(A	
ENGLISH CORALE	V	(A	

DAVE COUSINS — C202

DAVE COUSINS	PER V G PNO	(A	(A) TWO WEEKS LAST SUMMER	1972	A&M AMLS68118
ROGER GLOVER	B	(A			
TOM ALLOM	ORG	(A	MILLER ANDERSON	G	(A
JON HISEMAN	D	(A	RICK WAKEMAN	K	(A
KIDDINGTON COSSACKS		(A	ROBERT KIRBY	WIND	(A

DAVE LAMBERT	G	(A	
LAMPOON		(A	

DON COVAY — C203

DON COVAY	V	(ALL	(A) MERCY	1964	ATLANTIC	US 8104
WITH			(B) SEE SAW	1966	ATLANTIC	US 8120
JOE RICHARDSON	G V	(C	(C) HOUSE OF BLUE LIGHT	1969	ATLANTIC	US 8237
MARGARET WILLIAMS	G V	(C	(C) HOUSE OF BLUE LIGHT	1969	ATLANTIC	UK K 50225
JOHN HAMMOND	HCA G	(C	(D) DIFFERENT STROKES	1970	JANUS	US 3038
BUTCH VALENTINE	B	(C	(E) SUPERDUDE	1973	MERCURY	UK 6338 211
DANNY JONES	D	(C	(E) SUPERDUDE	1973	MERCURY	US SRM1 653
JERRY JEMMOTT	B	(CF	(F) HOT BLOOD	1975	MERCURY	UK 9100 010
CHARLES OTIS	D	(C	(G) TRAVELLIN' IN HEAVY TRAFFIC	1976	PHILAD INT	PIR 81492
SREDNI VOLLNER	HCA	(F	(G) TRAVELLIN' IN HEAVY TRAFFIC	1976	PHILAD INT	33957
TONY VON COVAY		(F	( ) COUNTRY FUNK	19	POLYDOR	2482 018
RODNEY BEYTHAM	K	(F				
BILLY CADIEUX	G	(F				

COVEN — C203A

(A) BLOOD ON THE SNOW	19	BUDDAH 5614	BDLH 5011

DAVID COVERDALE & WHITESNAKE — C204

DAVID COVERDALE	V	(ALL	(A) WHITESNAKE	1977	PURPLE	UK TPS 3509
MICK MOODY	G	(ABCDE	(A) WHITESNAKE	1977	VOGUE	FR 20257
SIMON PHILLIPS	D	(A	(B) NORTHWIND	1978	PURPLE	UK TPS 3513
TIM HINKLEY	K	(A	(C) TROUBLE	1978	SUNBURST	INS 3022
RON ASPERY	SAX	(AB	(D) SNAKEBITE (EP)	1978	SUNBURST	INEP 751
DELISLE HARPER	B	(AB	(E) SNAKEBITE (LP)	1978	SUNBURST NL62 61290	USUA 915
ROGER GLOVER	K B PERC	(AB	(F) LOVEHUNTER	1979	UA	UK UAG 30264
DAVID DOWLE	D	(CDE	(G) LIVE	1980	UA	SNAKE 1
BERNIE MARSDEN	G	(CD	(H) READY & WILLING	1980	UA	UAG 30302
BRIAN JOHNSTON	K	(				
NEIL MURRAY	B	(CDE	JON LORD	K	(C	BARRY ST JOHN V (A
IAN PAICH	D	(E	PETE SOLLEY	K	(D	ALAN SPENNER B (B
TONY NEWMAN	D	(B	LEE BRILLEAUX	HCA	(B	HENRY LOWTHER HRNS (B
MALCOLM GRIFFITHS	TROM	(B	GRAHAM PRESKETT	K	(B	LIZA STRIKE V (AB
IRENE CHANTER	V	(B	DOREEN CHANTER	V	(B	HELEN CHAPPELLE V (A

JOEY COVINGTON — C205

JOEY COVINGTON	D V	(A	(A) FAT FANDAGO	1973	GRUNT BFL1 0149
PATRICK CRAIG	K	(A			
STEVE MIDNITE	G	(A	JACK PRENDERGAST	B	(A

JULIE COVINGTON — C206

JULIE COVINGTON	V	(AB	(A) BEAUTIFUL CHANGES	1971	COLUMBIA UK SCX 6466
RICHARD THOMPSON	G	(B	(B) JULIE COVINGTON	1978	VIRGIN UK V 2107
NEIL LARSEN	K	(B			
WILLIE WEEKS	B	(B	RAY COOPER	PERC	(B	JOHN KIRKPATRICK ACC (B
TREVOR LUCAS	G	(B	SIMON NICOL	G	(B	CHRIS SPEDDING G (B
RUSS TITELMAN	G	(B	STEVE WINWOOD	K	(B	ANDY FAIRWEATHER LOW V (B
IAN MATTHEWS	V	(B	GARY TRAVERS	V	(B	GREG PRESTOPINO V (B
PLAS JOHNSON	SAX	(B	ANDY NEWMARK	D	(B	JOHN CALE K (B

COWBOY — C207

SCOTT BOYER	G	(AB	(A) REACH FOR THE SKY	1971	ATLANTIC	UK 2466 022
TOMMY TALTON	G V	(AB	(B) 5'LL GET YOU TEN	1972	ATLANTIC	UK K 40312
BILL PILLMORE	K G V	(A	(AB)WHY QUIT WHEN YOU'RE LOSING	1975	CAPRICORN	US 2CX 0121
TOMM WYNN	D PERC	(A	(C) BOYER & TALTON	1975	CAPRICORN	US CPO 113
GEORGE CLARK	B V	(AB	(D) COWBOY	197	CAPRICORN	US CP 0127
PETE KOWALKE	G V	(AB	(D) COWBOY	1977	CAPRICORN	US CO 0190
DUANE ALLMAN	G DOBRO	(B				
CHUCK LEAVELL	PNO	(A				

BILLY COX — C208

BILLY COX	B	(A	(A) NITRO FUNCTION	1971	PYE UK NSPL28158
CHAR VINNEDGE	G	(A			
ROBERT TARRANT	D	(D			

C209 — LOL COXHILL

Personnel		
LOL COXHILL	SAX	(ALL
STEVEN MILLER	PNO	(C
DAVID BEDFORD	ORG	(A
MIKE OLDFIELD	G	(A
ROBERT WYATT	PERC V	(AD
PIERRE COURBOIS	D	(AB
JASPER VANT HOF	PNO	(AB
PIP PYLE	PERC	(C
RICHARD SINCLAIR	B	(C
PHIL MILLER	G	(AD
LAURIE ALLEN	CYMB	(CD
ARCHIE LEGGETT	BASS	(CD
KEVIN AYERS	G	(AD
PHIL MINTON	TPT	(E
STEVE GUMBLEY	PERC	(E
JANE DURRANT	SAX	(E
LIZ LOCKHART	FLT	(E
BORIS HOWARTH	VLN G	(E
G F FITZGERALD	G	(F
JOHN MITCHELL	D	(G
KEN SHAW	G	(H

Title			Year	Label		Cat
(A) EAR OF THE BEHOLDER			1971	DANDELION 69001 +		DSD 8008
(A) EAR OF THE BEHOLDER			1971	AMPEX	US	10132
(B) TOVERBAL SWEET			1972	MUSHROOM		150 MR 23
(C) COXHILL MILLER/MILLER COXHILL			1973	CAROLINE		C 1503
(D) STORY SO FAR...OH REALLY			1974	CAROLINE		C 1507
(E) LOL COXHILL & WELFARE STATE			1975	CAROLINE		C 1514
(F) FLEAS IN CUSTARD			1975	CAROLINE		C 1515
(G) DIVERSE			1976	OGUN		OG 510
(H) THE JOY OF PARANOIA			1978	OGUN		OG 525
(I) MOOT			1978	ICTUS		0008
(J) LID			1978	ICTUS		0011

JOHN FOX	SAX	(E	LOU GLANDFIELD	TROM	(E
COLIN WOOD	CELLO	(EG	CATHY KIDDLE	CLAR	(E
PENNY GLANDFIELD	PERC	(E	WARNER VAN WELY	V	(E
PETER KIDDLE	WHISTLE	(E	JOHN CHAPMAN	WHISTLE	(E
SUE FOX	V	(E	DIANA DAVIES	ORG	(E
MICK AUDSLEY	V	(F	KEN ELLIS	V	(F
DAVE GREEN	B	(G	ANDREA CEMTAZZO	D	(I
MICHAEL GARRICK	PNO	(H	PAUL MITCHELL DAVIDSON	B	(H
VERYAN WESTON	PNO	(H	RICHARD WRIGHT	G	(H

C210 — KEVIN COYNE

KEVIN COYNE	V G	(ALL
WITH		
GORDON SMITH	G	(BCD
JEAN ROUSSEL	K	(B
TONY COUSINS	B	(BC
CHILI CHARLES	D	(BC
STEVE VERROCA	PERC K	(C
RUAN O'LOCHLAINN	SAX G K	(C
FI TRENCH	K	(C
RICK DODD	SAX	(C
TERRY SLADE	D	(C
ARCHIE LEGGET	B	(D
PETER WOOLF	D	(DEF
TIM PENN	K	(D
JOANNE WILLIAMS	V	(C
STEVE THOMPSON	B	(EF
VIC SWEENEY	D	(H

Title			Year	Label		Cat
(A) CASE HISTORY			1972	DANDELION		2310 228
(B) MARJORY RAZORBLADE			1973	VIRGIN		VD 2501
(C) BLAME IT ON THE NIGHT			1974	VIRGIN		V 2012
(D) MATCHING HEAD & FEET			1975	VIRGIN		V 2033
(E) HEARTBURN			1976	VIRGIN		V 2047
(F) IN LIVING BLACK & WHITE	(DBL)		1976	VIRGIN		VD 2505
(F) IN LIVING BLACK & WHITE	(DBL)		1976	POLYDOR	EUR	2676 710
(G) DYNAMITE DAZE			1978	VIRGIN		V 2095
(G) DYNAMITE DAZE			1978	POLYDOR	EUR	2933 746
(H) MILLIONAIRES & TEDDY BEARS			1978	VIRGIN		V 2110
(I) BEAUTIFUL EXTREMES			1978	VIRGIN		V 25527
(J) BABBLE			1979	VIRGIN		V 2128

ANDY SUMMERS	G	(DEF	LISA STRIKE	V	(C
BARRY ST JOHN	V	(C	ZOOT MONEY	K V	(EF
BOB WARD	G	(H	PAUL WICKENS	K	(H
AL JAMES	B	(H	DAGMAR KRAUSE		(J

C211 — CRABBY APPLETON

Personnel		
MICHAEL FENNELLY	G V	(AB
PHIL JONES	D	(AB
CASEY FOUTZ	K	(AB
FLACO FALCON	PERC	(AB
BYRON BERLINE	FDL	(B
JESSICA SMITH	V	(B

Title			Year	Label		Cat
(A) CRABBY APPLETON			1970	ELEKTRA		EKS 74067
(B) ROTTEN TO THE CORE			1971	ELEKTRA		EKS 74106

HANK HARVEY	B	(AB	DAVID GRISMAN	MAND	(B
CLYDIE KING	V	(B	OMA DRAKE	V	(B

C212 — CRACK THE SKY

JOHN PALUMBO	K V	(AB
RICK WITKOWSKI	G	(ABC
JIM GRIFFITHS	G V	(ABC
JOE MACRE	B V	(ABC
JOEY D'AMICO	D V	(ABC
GARY LEE CHAPPELL	V	(C
ROB STEVENS	K	(C

Title			Year	Label		Cat
(A) CRACK THE SKY			1975	LIFESONG		6000
(A) CRACK THE SKY	(RI)		197	LIFESONG	US	34994
(B) ANIMAL NOTES			1976	LIFESONG		6005
(B) ANIMAL NOTES	(RI)		197	LIFESONG	US	34996
(C) SAFETY IN NUMBERS			1978	LIFESONG		6015
(C) SAFETY IN NUMBERS	(RI)		19	LIFESONG	US	35041

C213 — CRACKIN'

Personnel		
PETER BUNETTA	D	(AB
RICK CHUDACOFF	B	(AB
ARNO LUCAS	V PERC	(AB
LESLIE O SMITH	V PERC	(AB
LESTER ABRAMS	V K	(AB
VICTOR FELDMAN	PERC	(A
STEVE MADAIO	HRNS	(B
FRED SELDON	STRGS	(B

Title			Year	Label		Cat
(A) MAKINGS OF A DREAM			1977	WB	US	BS2989
(B) CRACKIN			1977	WB	US	BS3123

G T CLINTON	K	(AB	BOB BORDY	G	(AB
BRIAN RAY	G	(B	GENE DINWIDDIE	HRNS	(AB
MILT HOLLAND	PERC	(A	DAVID SANBORN	HRNS	(A
CHUCK FINDLEY	HRNS	(B	JACKIE KELSO	HRNS	(B
MICHAEL OMARTIAN	K	(B	STEMSY HUNTER	SAX	(B

C213A — CRASS

STEVE IGNORANT	V	
PENNY RIMBAUD	D	(A
EVE LIBERTINE	V	(A
PETE WRIGHT	V B	(A

Title			Year	Label
(A) STATION OF CRASS	(DBL)		1980	SMALL WONDER

JOY DE VIVRE	V K G	(A	N A PALMER	G V	(A
PHIL FREE	G V	(A			

C214 — CRAWLER

TONY CARR	PERC	(A
TERRY WILSON SLESSER	G	(AB
TERRY WILSON	B V	(AB
TONY BRAUNAGEL	D V	(AB
CHRIS WOOD	FLT	(A

Title			Year	Label			Cat
(A) CRAWLER			1977	EPIC US 34900	UK		EPC 82083
(B) SNAKE RATTLE & ROLL			1979	EPIC US 35482	UK		EPC 82965

JOHN BUNDRICK	K	(AB	TED BUNTING	SAX	(A
STEVIE LANGE	V	(A	GEOFF WHITEHORN	G	(A

C214A — PEE WEE CRAYTON

PEE WEE CRAYTON

Title		Year	Label		Cat
PEE WEE CRAYTON		1975	BULLDOG		BDL 1004
PEE WEE CRAYTON		197	CROWN	US	CLPS 5175
THINGS WE USED TO DO		1976	VANGUARD	US	VSD 6566
THINGS WE USED TO DO		197	CHARLY	UK	CR 30014
BLUE GUITAR GENIUS VOL 1 (10")		19	ACE	UK	10CH 23

C215 — CRAZY CAVAN & THE RHYTHM ROCKERS

CRAZY CAVAN GROGAN	V	(
LYNDON NEEDS	G	(
TERRY WALLEY	G	(
GRAHAM PRICE	B	(
MICK COFFEY	D	(

Title		Year	Label		Cat
CRAZY RHYTHM		19	ROCKHOUSE		7510
ROCKABILITY		19	CHARLY	UK	CR 5001
ROCKABILITY		19	POLYDOR		2445 210
IS STILL ALIVE		19	CHARLY	UK	CR 5002
IS STILL ALIVE		19	POLYDOR		2445 211

(CONTINUED)

CRAZY CAVAN & THE RHYTHM ROCKERS — C215

OUR OWN WAY OF ROCKIN'	19	CHARLY	UK	CR	5004
OUR OWN WAY OF ROCKIN'	19	POLYDOR		2933	214
LIVE AT THE RAINBOW	19	CHARLY	UK	CR	30139
CRAZY RHYTHM	19	CHARLY	UK	CR	30156
RED HOT 'N' ROCKABILLY	1979	CHARLY	UK	CR	30174

CRAZY ELEPHANT — C215A

LARRY ALUFER	K V	(A	(A) CRAZY ELEPHANT	19	BELL	US	6034
BOB AVERY	D	(A					
RONNIE BRETONE	B	(A	KENNY COHEN	K SAX V	(A	HAL HING	V	(A

CRAZY HORSE — C216

BILLY TALBOT	B	(ALL	(A) CRAZY HORSE	1971	REPRISE	US	RSLP 6438
RICK CURTIS	G V	(C7	(A) CRAZY HORSE	1980	REPRISE RI	GERM	REP 24026
RALPH MOLINA	D	(ALL	(A) CRAZY HORSE	1972	REPRISE	UK	K 44114
DANNY WHITTEN	G V	(A123456	(B) LOOSE	1972	REPRISE	US	MS 2059
BOBBY NOTKOFF	VLN	(CD1234	(B) LOOSE	1972	REPRISE	UK	K 44171
LEON WHITSELL	G V	(1	(C) AT CROOKED CREEK	1973	EPIC	US	KE 31710
GEORGE WHITSELL	G V	(B17	(C) AT CROOKED CREEK	1973	EPIC	UK	EPC 65223
NILS LOFGREN	G V	(A4568	(D) CRAZY MOON	1978	RCA		AFL1 3054
JACK NITZSCHE	K	(A6					
GREG LEROY	G V	(BCD67	(1) 1962 68 ROCKETS				
JOHN BLANTON	K	(B67	(2) 69 +NEIL YOUNG LP(EVERYBODY)				
MICHAEL CURTIS	G K V	(CD7	(3) 1969				
BEN KEITH	STEEL	(8	(4) 1969 70				
FRANK SAMPEDRO	G	(D9	(5) MID 70 NEIL YOUNG LP(GOLDRUSH)				
PACHECO	CONGA	(C	(6) JULY70 DEC71				
SNEAKY PETE KLEINOW	STEEL	(C	(7) 1972 73				
PATTI MOAN	V	(C	(8) LATE 73 + NEIL YOUNG LPs(TONIGHTS +ON THE BEACH)				
STEVE LAWRENCE	SAX	(D	(9) FEB 75 + NEIL YOUNG LP (ZUMA)				
KIRBY	PNO	(D					
NEIL YOUNG	G V	(D2589	RY COODER	G	(A	GIB GUILBEAU	FDL	(A
BARRY GOLDBERG	K	(D	TOM BRAY	TPT	(D	JOEL TEPP	HCA	(B
JAY GRAYDON	G	(D	KENNY WALTER	TROM	(D	MICHAEL KOWALSKI	D	(D

PAPA JOHN CREACH — C217

PAPA JOHN CREACH	VLN V	(ALL	(A) PAPA JOHN CREACH	1971	GRUNT		FTR 1003
BIG JOE TURNER	V	(B	(B) FILTHY	1972	GRUNT		FTR 1009
HARMONICA FATS	HCA	(B	(C) ZULU PLAYING MY FIDDLE FOR YOU	1974	GRUNT		BFL1 0418
CARL BYRD	D	(B	(D) IM THE FIDDLE MAN	1975	BUDDAH	US	5649
KEVIN MOORE	G	(N	(D) IM THE FIDDLE MAN	1975	BUDDAH	UK	BDLP 4039
JACK CASADY	B	(AB	(E) ROCK FATHER	1976	BUDDAH	US	BDS 5660
JORMA KAUKONEN	G	(AB	(E) ROCK FATHER	1976	VOGUE	FR	60007
JOHN PARKER	K	(B	(F) THE CAT & FIDDLE	1977	DJM		DJM11
HOLDEN RAPHAEL	PERC	(B	(F) THE CAT & FIDDLE	1977	DJM		DJF 20515
SAM WILLIAMS	B	(B	(G) INPHASION	1978	DJM	UK	DJF 20545
HENRY COKER	TROM	(B	(G) INPHASION	1978	DJM		DJM18
SAMMY PIAZZA	D	(AB					
JOHN EWING	TROM	(B	BLUE MITCHELL	TPT	(B	JOE LANE DAVIS	SAX	(B
JERRY JUMONVILLE	SAX	(B	MAURICE SIMON	SAX	(B	MAXINE WILLARD	V	(B
VANETTA FIELDS	V	(B	SHIRLEY MATTHEWS	V	(B	MARTI McCALL	V	(B
LUTHER WATERS	V	(B	ORRIN WATERS	V	(B	GREG ADAMS	TPT	(A
JACK BONUS	SAX	(A	JOHN CIPOLLINA	G	(A	JOEY COVINGTON	D	(A
MIC GILLETTE	TROM	(A	MIKE LIPKIN	K	(A	PETE SEARS	B	(A
GRACE SLICK	V	(	STAN MONTEIRO	CLAR	(A	BOB WILSON	G	(A
NICK BLACK	PNO	(A	BRUCE CONTE	G	(A	DOUGLAS RAUCH	B	(A
STEVE HABERMAN	K	(FG	BRIAN TILFORD	B V	(FG	MARK LEON	D V	(FG
JOE BRASLER	G	(FG	REID KING	V G	(FG	TONY SMITH	D	(A
CARLOS SANTANA	G	(A	ART HILLERY	PNO	(A	PAUL KANTNER	G	(A
BOBBY HAYES	B	(A	AL STAEHELY	V	(F	SCOTT CUSHNIE	K	(F
BOB ZIMMITTI	D	(G	JOHNNY GUITAR WATSON	G	(G	CHARLIE DANIELS	FDL	(G
DR JOHN	K	(G	DAVID LAFLAMME	FDL	(G	RUFUS ANDERSON	G	(A
DAVID BROWN	B	(A	JERRY GARCIA	G	(A	GREGG ROLIE	ORG	(A

CREAM — C218

ERIC CLAPTON	G V	(ALL	GOODBYE	1969	POLYDOR	GERM 184	203
JACK BRUCE	HCA	K B V	(ALL	BEST OF CREAM	1969	POLYDOR	UK	583	060
GINGER BAKER	D V	(ALL	BEST OF CREAM	1969	POLYDOR	GERM 184	298
FELIX PAPPALARDI	B K VLA	(*	I FEEL FREE	1969	KARUSSELL	GERM 2499	002
			BEST OF	(DBL)	1969	POLYDOR	GERM 2499	010
FRESH CREAM	1966	REACTION	UK 594 001	SWLABR	19	KARUSSELL	GERM 2499	013
FRESH CREAM	1966	ATCO	US 33206	ROCK SENSATION	1969	KARUSSELL	GERM 2499	112
FRESH CREAM	1966	POLYDOR	GERM 623 031	CREAM LIVE	1970	POLYDOR	UK 2383	016
FRESH CREAM	197	RSO	US 1 3009	CREAM LIVE	1970	ATCO	US 33328
FULL CREAM	1966	REACTION	UK 2447 010	CREAM LIVE	197	RSO	US 1 3014
DISRAELI GEARS	1967	REACTION	UK 594 003	CREAM LIVE 2	1972	POLYDOR	UK 2383	119
DISRAELI GEARS	1967	POLYDOR	GERM 184 105	CREAM LIVE 2	197	RSO	US 1 3015
DISRAELI GEARS	1967	ATCO	US 33232	OFF THE TOP	1972	POLYDOR	US 5529
DISRAELI GEARS	19	POLYDOR	UK 2442 114	HEAVY CREAM	1973	POLYDOR	UK 2659	022
DISRAELI GEARS	197	RSO	US 1 3010	HEAVY CREAM	1973	POLYDOR	US 3502
WHEELS OF FIRE	(DBL)*	1968 POLYDOR	UK 583 031/2	CREAM	1975	POLYDOR	UK 2384	067
WHEELS OF FIRE	(DBL)*	1968 ATCO	US 2/700	PORTRAIT OF CREAM	1975	POLYDOR	US 2482	142
WHEELS OF FIRE	(DBL)*	1972 POLYDOR	UK 2612 001	THE BEST VOL 2	1975	POLYDOR	UK 2675	087
WHEELS OF FIRE	(DBL)*	1972 POLYDOR	2658 110	POP GIANTS	19	BRUNSWICK	2911	528
WHEELS OF FIRE	(DBL)*	197 RSO	US 2 3802	BEST OF CREAM LIVE	19	POLYDOR	2674	018
WHEELS OF FIRE	(STUDIO)*	1968 POLYDOR	UK 583 033	POP HISTORY	197	POLYDOR	2675	014
WHEELS OF FIRE	(LIVE)	1968 POLYDOR	UK 583 040	CREAM VOL 2	1978	RSO	UK 2479	701
GOODBYE		1969 POLYDOR	UK 583 053	EARLY CREAM	19	SPRINGBOARD	US 4037
GOODBYE		1969 ATCO	US 7001				

C219
				CREATION					
JACK JONES	D	(ABC	(A) WE ARE THE PAINTERMEN	1967	SONET		DK	SLPS 1251
KENNY PICKETT	V	(ABC	(A) WE ARE THE PAINTERMEN	1970	SONET	RI	DK	1933
EDDIE PHILLIPS	G	(ABC	(A) WE ARE THE PAINTERMEN	1967	HIT TON		GERM	340 037
BOB GARNER	B	(ABC	(B) BEST OF CREATION	1968	POP		GERM	ZS 10 168
			(C) 1966 67 CREATION	1973	CHARISMA		UK	CS8

C219A
CREATIVE ROCK
HEIKO STEINSIEK	D PERC(A	(A) LADY PIG	1974	BRAIN		1061
M M MAASS	B G K V (A					
APOSTOLOS PAPANIKOLAOU	G (A					
RAINER ERBEL	V (A					

RUDIGER STREMMEL   SAX V (A   KLUBERTUS KREUTNER   TPT V(A

C220
CREATIVE SOURCE
MELVIN RAGIN	G	(B	(A) CREATIVE SOURCE	1974	SUSSEX		LPSX6
RAY PARKER	G	(B	(A) CREATIVE SOURCE	1974	SUSSEX	US	8027
JAMES JAMESON	B	(B	(B) MIGRATION	1974	SUSSEX		LPSX7
KENNETH RICE	D	(B	(B) MIGRATION	1974	SUSSEX	US	8035
CLARENCE McDONALD	K	(B	(C) PASS THE FEELING ON	1976	POLYDOR		2391 196
SKIP SCARBOROUGH	K	(B	(C) PASS THE FEELING ON	1976	POLYDOR	US	6052
BOBBYE HALL	PERC	(B	(D) CONSIDER THE SOURCE	1976	POLYDOR		2391 221
MIKE STOKES	K	(B	(D) CONSIDER THE SOURCE	1976	POLYDOR	US	6065
CARL AUSTIN	STINGS(B						
RALPH TERRANA	SYN	(B	JOHN TRADEL HRNS (B				

C220A
CREATURES
	MONSTER RALLY	19	RCA	US	1923

C220B
CREDIBILITY GAP
	A GREAT GIFT IDEA	19	REPRISE	US	2154

C221
CREEDENCE CLEARWATER REVIVAL

				FANTASY UK	FANTASY US	LIBERTY UK	MUSIDISC FR
TOM FOGERTY	G V	(ALL	(A) CREEDENCE CLEARWATER REVIVAL	1969 506	8382	83259	6049
JOHN FOGERTY	G V	(ALL	(B) BAYOU COUNTY	1969 507	8387	83261	6048
STU COOK	D	(ALL	(C) GREEN RIVER	1969 504	8393		6047
DOUG CLIFFORD	B	(ALL	(D) WILLIE & THE POOR BOYS	1970 503	8397	83338	6046
			(E) COSMOS FACTORY	1970 502	8402	83388	6043
			(F) PENDULUM	1971 508	8410	83400	6042
			(G) MARDI GRAS	1972 505	9404		6036
			(H) CREEDENCE GOLD	1973 501	8402		6029
			(H) CREEDENCE GOLD	197	9418		
			(I) MORE CREEDENCE GOLD	1973 512	9430		6019
			(J) LIVE IN EUROPE	1974 520	FCCR 1		6009
			(K) MASTERS OF ROCK	1975 EMI IMP	SC054		
			(L) CHRONICLE	1976 528	FCCR 2		235
			(L) CHRONICLE	1978 FESTIVAL ALB 235 IMP			
			(M) LIVE AT THE ALBERT HALL	1981			

C222
LOL CREME & KEVIN GODLEY
LOL CREME	G B V K PERC (ALL	(A) CONSEQUENCES	1977	MERCURY	CONS017	6641658
KEVIN GODLEY	D V PERC B K(ALL	(A) CONSEQUENCES	1977	MERCURY	US	SRM3 1700
		(B) "L"	1978	MERCURY		9109 611
JONATHAN HANDELSMAN	SAX (B	(C) MUSIC FROM CONSEQUENCES	1978	MERCURY		9109 615
ANDY MACKAY	SAX (B					
PAUL GAMBACCINI	V (B					

C222A
CRESCENDOS
DALE WARD	V	(A	(A) OH JULIE	196	GUEST STAR	US	1453

C223
CRESSIDA
ANGUS CULLEN	V G	(AB	(A) CRESSIDA	1970	VERTIGO		V07
PETER JENNINGS	K	(AB	(B) ASYLUM	1971	VERTIGO		6360 025
KEVIN McCARTHY	B	(AB					
IAIN CLARK	D	(AB	HAROLD McNAIR FLT (B	JOHN CULLEY	G	(B
				JOHN HEYWORTH	G	(A

C223A
CRESTS
JOHNNY MAESTRO	V	(	CRESTS SING	19	POST	US	3000
JAY CARTER	V	(	CRESTS SING ALL BIGGIES	19	COED	US	901
HARROLD TORRES	V	(	BEST OF THE CRESTS	19	COED	US	904
TOMMY GOUGH	V	(					

C224
CRICKETS
BUDDY HOLLY	G V	(	CHIRPIN CRICKETS	1958	CORAL	UK	LVA 9081
JERRY ALLISON	D		CHIRPIN CRICKETS	1969	CORAL	UK	CP 20
LARRY WELBORN	B	(	CHIRPIN CRICKETS	1974	MCA	UK	CRLM 1023
NIKI SULLIVAN	G	(	CHIRPIN CRICKETS	197	MCA	IMP	CDLM 8035
JOE MAULDIN	B		CHIRPIN CRICKETS	19	BRUNSWICK	US	54038
JERRY NAYLOR			CHIRPIN CRICKETS	19	BRUNSWICK	US	71036
GLEN D HARDIN	G K		BOBBY VEE MEETS THE CRICKETS	196	LIBERTY	UK	SLBY 1086
SONNY CURTIS	G V		BOBBY VEE MEETS THE CRICKETS	197	SUNSET	UK	SLS 50357
RICK GRECH	B		IN STYLE WITH	196	CORAL	UK	LVA 9142
			IN STYLE WITH	196	CORAL		57320
ALBERT LEE	G		CALIFORNIA SUN	19	LIBERTY	US	7372
NICKY HOPKINS	K		REMNANTS	19	VERTIGO	US	VEL 1020
			SOMETHING OLD SOMETHING NEW ...	19	LIBERTY	UK	SLBY 1120
			SOMETHING OLD SOMETHING NEW	19	LIBERTY	US	7272
			WE GOTTA GET TOGETHER	19	LIBERTY	US	55742
			ROCKIN 50s ROCK'N'ROLL	1971	CBS	UK	64301
			ROCKIN 50s ROCK'N'ROLL	1971	BARNABY	US	30268
			ROCK REFLECTIONS	1971	SUNSET	UK	SLS 50207
			BUBBLEGUM, POP , BALLADS & BOOGIE	1973	PHILIPS	UK	6308 149
			LONG WAY FROM LUBBOCK	1974	MERCURY	UK	6310 007
			BACK IN STYLE	1975	M C A	UK	MCFM 2710
							(CONTINUED)

```
EPS
STRAIGHT NO STRINGS                              19    LIBERTY      UK   SLEP 2094
THE CRICKETS                                     19    CORAL        US   81192
CHIRPING CRICKETS                                19    BRUNSWICK    US   71036
SOUND OF THE CRICKETS                            19    BRUNSWICK    US   71038
BOBBY VEE & THE CRICKETS                         19    LIBERTY      UK   LEP 2084
A FOREVER KIND OF LOVE                           19    LIBERTY      UK   LEP 2089
BOBBY VEE MEETS THE CRICKETS                     19    LIBERTY      UK   LEP 2116
BOBBY VEE MEETS THE CRICKETS  2                  19    LIBERTY      UK   LEP 2149
COME ON                                          19    LIBERTY      UK   LEP 2173
```

                                    CRIME   C225

```
BRITTLEY BLACK      D     (1     (1) EARLY LINE UP    (2) 1977 78
FRANKIE FIX         G V   (1 2
JOHNNY STRIKE       G V   (1 2   RON THE RIPPER    B    (1 2    HANK RANK      D    (2
```

                                  CRIMINALS   C226

```
SYLVAIN SYLVAIN     V G   (1     (1) 1977 LINE UP
BOBBY BLAIN         K     (1
TONY MACHINE        D     (1     MIKE PAGE          G        (1
```

                                  PETE CRISS   C227

```
PETE CRISS                       PETE CRISS                       1978  CASABLANCA        NBLP 7122
```

                                   CRITTERS   C228

```
CHRIS DARWAY  AUTOHARP   (       ( ) TOUCH'N GO WITH THE CRITTERS   196   PROJECT 3   US   PB 4001
KENNY GORKA         B     (       ( ) THE CRITTERS                   1966  PROJECT 3   US   PB 4002
BOB SPINELLA        K     (       ( ) YOUNGER GIRL                   1966  KAPP        US         1485
JIM RYAN            G     (       ( ) YOUNGER GIRL                   1966  KAPP        US STEREO 3485
JEFF PELOSI         D     (
```

                                   JIM CROCE   C229

```
JIM CROCE           G V   (ALL   (A) CROCE                            19    CAPITOL     US          ST315
INGRID CROCE              (A     (B) YOU DONT MESS AROUND WITH JIM    1971  VERTIGO     UK   6360  700
MAURY MUEHLEISEN    G V   (B     (B) YOU DONT MESS AROUND WITH JIM    19    ABC         US          756
GARY CHESTER        D     (B     (B) YOU DONT MESS AROUND WITH JIM    19    COMMAND     US          40006
H J BOYLE           G     (B     (B) YOU DONT MESS AROUND WITH JIM    19    LIFESONG    US          34993
ELLIE GREENWICH     V     (B     (C) LIFE & TIMES                     1973  VERTIGO     UK   6360  701
TOMMY WEST      K V B     (B     (C) LIFE & TIMES                     197   ABC         US          769
TASHA THOMAS        V     (B     (C) LIFE & TIMES                     197   COMMAND     US          40007
JOE MACHO           B     (B     (C) LIFE & TIMES                     197   LIFESONG    US          35008
TERRY CASHMAN       V     (B     (D) I GOT A NAME                     1973  VERTIGO     UK   6360  703
JIM RYAN            B     (B     (D) I GOT A NAME                     197   ABC         US          797
                                 (D) I GOT A NAME                     197   COMMAND     US          40008
                                 (D) I GOT A NAME                     197   LIFESONG    US          35009
                                 (E) PHOTOGRAPHS & MEMORIES           1975  LIFESONG    UK   ELSLP5000
                                 (E) PHOTOGRAPHS & MEMORIES           197   ABC         US          835
                                 (E) PHOTOGRAPHS & MEMORIES           197   COMMAND     US          40020
                                 (E) PHOTOGRAPHS & MEMORIES           197   LIFESONG    US          35010
                                 (F) THE FACES I'VE BEEN              19    LIFESONG    US   ELSDP 900
                                 (G) JIM CROCE COLLECTION             197   TEE VEE     US   TVLP77024
                                 (H) TIME IN A BOTTLE                 197   LIFESONG    US          35000
                                 (I) HIS GREATEST SONGS               1980  K TEL       UK   NE  1059
```

                              ANDREW CRONSHAW   C230

```
ANDREW CRONSHAW          (       (A) A IS FOR ANDREW                  1974  TRANSATLANTIC UK  XTRA 1139
                                 ( ) EARTHED IN CLOUD VALLEY          1977  TRAILER       UK  LER  2104
                                 ( ) WADE IN THE FLOOD                1978  TRANSATLANTIC UK  LTRA 508
```

                                STEVE CROPPER   C231

```
STEVE CROPPER       G     (       (A) WITH A LITTLE HELP FROM MY FRIENDS 1971  STAX      UK   SXATS1008
WITH                             (A) WITH A LITTLE HELP FROM MY FRIENDS 1971  VOLT      US   VOS  6006
ALBERT KING         G     (B     (B)JAMMED TOGETHER                  1971  STAX        UK   STX  3009
POP STAPLES         G     (B     (C) PLAYING MY THANG                1980  MCA         US
DUCK DUNN           B     (C
MEMPHIS HORNS             (C
```

                                DAVID CROSBY   C232

```
DAVID CROSBY        G V   (A     (A) IF I COULD ONLY REMEMBER MY NAME  1971  ATLANTIC   UK   K 40320
WITH                             (A) IF I COULD ONLY REMEMBER MY NAME  1971  ATLANTIC   UK   2401  005
GRAHAM NASH         G V   (A     (A) IF I COULD ONLY REMEMBER MY NAME  1971  ATLANTIC   US          7203
BILL KREUTZMANN           (A
PHIL LESH                 (A     DAVID FREIBERG          (A    ETHAN CROSBY         (A
MICKEY HART               (A     HENRY DILTZ             (A    LAURA ALLEN          (A
PAUL KANTNER              (A     JERRY GARCIA            (A    MICHAEL SHRIEVE      (A
JACK CASADY               (A     JORMA KAUKONEN          (A    GRACE SLICK          (A
GREGG ROLIE              (A     JONI MITCHELL           (A    GARY BURDEN          (A
STEPHEN BARNCARD          (A     ROBERT HAMMER           (A    DAVID GEFFEN         (A
RONALD STONE              (A     ELLIOT ROBERTS          (A    NEIL YOUNG           (
```

                               CROSBY & NASH   C233

```
DAVID CROSBY        G V   (ALL   (A) CROSBY & NASH                    1972  ATLANTIC    UK   K 50011
GRAHAM NASH         G V   (ALL   (A) CROSBY & NASH                    1972  ATLANTIC    US          7220
RUSS KUNKEL         D     (CDE   (B) WIND ON THE WATER                1975  POLYDOR     UK   2310  428
TIM DRUMMOND        B     (CDE   (B) WIND ON THE WATER                1975  POLYDOR     EUR  2302  038
DANNY KORTCHMAR     B     (CDE   (B) WIND ON THE WATER                1975  ABC         US          902
CRAIG KINLERS       G     (C     (C) WHISTLE DOWN THE WIRE            1976  POLYDOR     UK   2310  468
DAVID LINDLEY   VLN G     (CDE1  (C) WHISTLE DOWN THE WIRE            1976  ABC         US          956
CRAIG DOERGE        K     (CDE1  (D) LIVE                             1977  POLYDOR     UK   2310  565
JOEL BERNSTEIN      G     (C     (D) LIVE                             1977  ABC         US          1042
BEN KEITH           G     (C     (E) BEST OF                          1978  POLYDOR     UK   2310  626
STAN SZELESTE       K     (C     (1) 1976 BRITISH TOUR
LEE SKLAR           B     (CE
BILL KREUTZMANN     D     (E     LEAH KUNKEL       V     (E    JERRY GARCIA      G     (E
JACKSON BROWNE            (E     JOHN BARBATA      D     (E    JONI MITCHELL     V     (E
JAMES TAYLOR        V     (CE    CAROLE KING       K     (CE
```

C234 CROSBY STILLS NASH & YOUNG

DAVID CROSBY	G V	(ABCDE1234
STEPHEN STILLS	G V K	(ABCDE1234
GRAHAM NASH	G V	(ABCDE1234
NEIL YOUNG	G V	(BCD234
WITH		
DALLAS TAYLOR	D	(AB12
GREG REEVES	B	(B2
CALVIN SAMUELS	B	(B2
JOHN BARBATA	D	(C3
JOE LALA	PERC	(4
TIM DRUMMOND	B	(4
RUSS KUNKEL	D	(4
JERRY GARCIA	STEEL	(B
JOHN SEBASTIAN	HCA	(B

(A) CROSBY STILLS & NASH	1969	ATLANTIC	UK	K 40033
(A) CROSBY STILLS & NASH	1969	ATLANTIC	UK	588 189
(A) CROSBY STILLS & NASH	1969	ATLANTIC	US	8229
(B) DEJA VU	1970	ATLANTIC	UK	2401 001
(B) DEJA VU	1970	ATLANTIC	UK	K 50001
(B) DEJA VU	1970	ATLANTIC	US	7200
(B) DEJA VU	1972	ATLANTIC	US	19118
(C) FOUR WAY STREET	1972	ATLANTIC	UK	2657 007
(C) FOUR WAY STREET	1972	ATLANTIC	UK	K 60003
(C) FOUR WAY STREET	1972	ATLANTIC	US	2902
(D) SO FAR	1974	ATLANTIC	UK	K 50023
(D) SO FAR	1974	ATLANTIC	US	18100
(E) C S N	1977	ATLANTIC	UK	K 50369

(1) 1968/1969   (2) 1969/70   (3) 1970   (4) 1974/75

C234A CROSS COUNTRY

JAY SIEGEL	V PERC	(A
MITCH MARGO	V PERC K G	(A
BOB MANN	G	(A
PHIL MARGO	V PERC	(A
JERRY FRIEDMAN	G	(A
RICK McGRATH	STEEL	(A
GREG WALKER	B	(A
GEORGE DEVENS	PERC	(A

(A) CROSS COUNTRY	1973	ATLANTIC	UK	K 40516
(A) CROSS COUNTRY	1973	ATCO	US	SD 7024

AL GORGONE	G	(A		HUGH McCRACKEN	G	(A
LOREN KOREVEC	G	(A		ERIC WEISSBERG	STEEL	(A
KIRK HAMILTON	B	(A		STU WOODS	B	(A
ALLEN SCHWARZBERG	D	(A		JIM MAELEN	PERC	(A
MAX HOLLANDER	STRINGS	(A				

C234B CROSSFIRES

(A) LIMBO ROCK	196	STRAND	US	1083
(B) GUITARS IN MOTION	19	EDGEMONT	US	

C235 CROW

DAVE WAGNER	V	(ABCDE
DICK WIEGAND	G	(ABCDE
LARRY WIEGAND	B	(ABCDE
KINK MIDDLEMIST	K	(ABCDE
DENNY CASSWELL	D V	(BCD
BROOKS HUNNICUTT	V	(B
MAXINE WILLARD	V	(B
JULIA TILLMAN	V	(B
MARK'CHICO' PEREZ	PERC	(B

(A) CROW MUSIC	1969	AMARET		5001
(A) CROW MUSIC	1969	STATESIDE	UK	SSL 10301
(B) CROW BY CROW	1970	AMARET	1970	5006
(B) CROW BY CROW	1970	STATESIDE	UK	SSL 10310
(C) MOSAIC	1981	AMARET	US	5009
(D) BEST OF	1972	AMARET	US	5012
(E) CROW	1972	AMARET	US	5-13

C236 CROWBAR

SONNIE BERNARDI	D	(ABCDEF
JOZEF CHIROWSKI FLT PERC K		(ABCDEF
JOHN GIBBARD	G V	(EF
KELLY JAY	K V	(ABCDEF
ROLAND GREENWAY	B V	(ABCDEF
RHEAL LANTHIER	G V	(ABCDE
RAY FENNELL	PERC	(C
SKIP PROKOP	PERC	(C
LEIGH ROBINSON	PERC	(C
KING BISCUIT BOY	V	(B
THE GHETTO	V G	(CC
BOB BRYDEN	V	(B
BRIAN LE BLANC	HRNS	(C
GREG MUDRY	HRNS	(C
PETE SIMPSON	HRNS	(C
THE ROCK		(E
STEVE HUNTER	G	(E
WADE MARCUS		(E
JOHN PEARSON		(E

(A) OFFICIAL MUSIC(KING BISCUIT BOY)	1970	PARAMOUNT	US	PAS 5030
(B) BAD MANORS	1970	CAPITOL		SBA 16004
(B) BAD MANORS	1971	PARAMOUNT	UK	SPLA 272
(B) BAD MANORS	1971	PARAMOUNT	US	PAR 6007
(C) LARGER THAN LIFE	1971	PARAMOUNT		SPLA 7002
(D) HEAVY DUTY	1972	DAFFODIL	AUST	DDL 34665
(D) HEAVY DUTY	1973	PARAMOUNT		SPFL 283
(E) CROWBAR	1973	EPIC	UK	80040
(E) CROWBAR	1973	EPIC	US	KE 32746
(F) CROWBAR CLASSICS	1972	CAPITOL		16030

RITCHIE YORK	PERC	(B		BRUCE FLYNN	HRNS	(C
STEVE KENNEDY	HRNS K	(BC		BRUCE CASSIDY	HRNS	(B
KEITH JOLLIMORE	HRNS	(C		HOWARD SHORE	HRNS	(C
LARRY GREEN	HRNS	(C		MICHAEL BRECKER	HRNS	(E
PAUL PRESTOPINO		(E		RANDY BRECKER	HRNS	(E
SNEAKY PETE KLEINOW	STEEL	(E		HUGH McCRACKEN	G	(E
JAY MESSINA		(E		ED SPRIGG		(E
TERRY BERRY CHOIR	V	(BC		LARRY SMITH		(E

C237 RODNEY CROWELL

RODNEY CROWELL		(A
LARRY LONDIN	D	(B
EMORY GORDY	B	(AB
ALBERT LEE	G V PNO MAN	(AB
RY COODER	G	(A
JIM KELTNER	D	(A
RICKY SKAGGS	FDL V	(A
GLEN D HARDIN	PNO	(A
HANK DEVITO	STEEL	(AB
WILLIE NELSON	V	(A
TOM SAUBER	BANJO	(A
STEVE WOOD	K V	(B
TOWER OF POWER	HRNS	(B

(A) AINT LIVING LONG LIKE THIS	1978	WB US BSK3228	UK	K 56564
(B) BUT WHAT WILL THE NEIGHBORS THINK	1980	WB US BSK3407	GERM	56776

JAMES BURTON	G DOBRO	(A		AMOS GARRETT	G	(AB
JOHN WARE	D	(A		HAL BLAINE	D	(A
EMMYLOU HARRIS	V G	(A		MAC REBENNACK	K	(A
BYRON BERLINE	FDL	(A		BRIAN AHERN	G PERC	(A
JERRY JUMONVILLE	HRNS	(A		RICHARD GREENE	STRINGS	(A
MICKEY RAPHAEL	HCA	(A		NICOLETTE LARSON	V	(A
LARRY WILLOUGHBY	V	(AB		DONIVAN COWART	V	(A
TONY BROWN	V	(B		FRANK RECKARD	G	(B
DON WHALEY	V	(B		CRAIG LEON	PNO FLT	(B

C238 CROWFOOT

RUSSELL DASHIELL	G K B V	(A
SAM McGUIRE	G V	(A
DON FRANCISCO	D PERC V	(A

(A) FIND THE SUN	1971	PROBE	UK	SPB 1042
(A) FIND THE SUN	1971	ABC	US	ABCS 745

C238A CRUCIFICTION

PETER MORGAN	D
GEOFF FORD	G

C239 ARTHUR 'BIG BOY' CRUDUP

ARTHUR'BIG'BOY' CRUDUP		(ALL
RANSOM KNOWLING	B	(AC
EDWARD EL	G	(AC
DAVE MYERS	B	(AC
LAWRENCE 'JUDGE' RILEY	D	(AC
WILLIE DIXON	B	(C

(A) LOOK ON YONDERS WALL	1968	DELMARK		DS	614
(B) MEAN OLE FRISCO	1969	TRIP	US		7501
(B) MEAN OLE FRISCO	1969	BLUE HORIZON	UK		763855
(C) CRUDUPS MOOD	1970	DELMARK		DS	621
(D) FATHER OF ROCK'N'ROLL	1971	RCA UK RD 8224 US			537
(E) ROEBUCK MAN	1974	LIBERTY	UK		UAS 29092
(F) THATS ALL RIGHT MAMA	1976	DJM	UK		DJM 22025
HARPIN' ON IT	197	POLYDOR			2941 001
ARTHUR BIG BOY CRUDUP	19	FIRE	US		103

R CRUMB & THE CHEAP SUIT SERENADERS   C240

R CRUMB	BANJO	(AB	(A) CHEAP SUIT SERENADERS VOL 1	1974	BLUE GOOSE		BG 2014
ROBERT ARMSTRONG	G	(AB	(B) CHEAP SUIT SERENADERS VOL 2	1976	BLUE GOOSE		BG 2019
ALLAN DODGE	FDL MAND	(AB	(C) CHEAP SUIT SERENADERS VOL 3	1978	BLUE GOOSE		BG 2025
TERRY ZWIGOFF	CELLO	(AB					

CRUSADERS   C241

WILTON FELDER	SAX	(ALL	FREEDOM SOUND	1961	PACIFIC JAZZ			PJ 27
			LOOKING AHEAD	1962	PACIFIC JAZZ			PJ 43
JOE SAMPLE	K	(ALL	AT THE LIGHTHOUSE	1963	PACIFIC JAZZ			PJ 57
			TOUGH TALK	1963	PACIFIC JAZZ			PJ 58
LARRY CARLTON	G	(ABCDEFGHI	HEAT WAVE	1965	PACIFIC JAZZ			PJ 87
STIX HOOPER	D	(ABCDEFGHIJKLY	CHILE CON SOUL	1966	PACIFIC JAZZ			PJ 20092
			LIGHTHOUSE 66	1966	PACIFIC JAZZ			PJ 20098
WAYNE HENDERSON	TROM	(ABCDEFGY	TALK THAT TALK	1966	PACIFIC JAZZ			pj 20106
ROY GAINES	G	(	FESTIVAL JAZZ	1967	PACIFIC JAZZ			PJ 20115
JIMMY BOND	B	(Y	LIGHTHOUSE 68	1968	PACIFIC JAZZ			PJ 20131
JOE PASS	G	(Y	UH HAH	1968	PACIFIC JAZZ			PJ 20175
MONK MONTGOMERY	B	(Y	POWERHOUSE	1969	PACIFIC JAZZ			PJ 20136
LARRY GOSKIN		(	LIGHTHOUSE 69	1969	PACIFIC JAZZ			PJ 20165
BILLY ROGERS	G	(J	BEST OF THE JAZZ CRUSADERS	1969	PACIFIC JAZZ			PJ 20175
POPS POPWELL	B	(GHIJ	GIVE PEACE A CHANCE	19	LIBERTY			LIB11005
ARTHUR ADAMS	G	(ABCGH	(Y) YOUNG RABBITS	1976	BLUE NOTE UK BND4028 BNLA 530			
MAX BENNETT	B	(C	OLD SOX NEW SHOES	19	CHISA			804
DAVID T WALKER	G	(AB	OLD SOX NEW SHOES	1971	RARE EARTH		SRE	3001
DEAN PARKS	G	(JHL	PASS THE PLATE	19	CHISA			807
PAULINHO DA COSTA	PERC	(JHL	HOLLY WOOD	1973	MOWEST			118
ROLAN BAUTISTA	G	(JHL	HOLLYWOOD	1973	MOWEST			7004
CHUCK RAINEY	B	(A	AT THEIR BEST	19	MOWEST			796
BILL WITHERS	V	(L	(A) CRUSADERS (DBL)	1971 ABC		US	ABCD	609
RANDY CRAWFORD	V	(K	(A) CRUSADERS (DBL)	1971 BLUE THUMB US BTS6001 UK			ILPS	9218
VICTOR GASKIN	B	(Y	(B) SECOND CRUSADE (DBL)	1972 ABC ABCD 610			BTS	7000
LEROY VINNEGAR	B	(Y	(C) UNSUNG HEROES	1973 ABC ABCL 5180 BLUE THUMB			BTS	6007
CHARLES WILLIAMS	B	(Y	(D) SCRATCH	1975 ABC ABCL 5181 BLUE THUMB			BTS	6010
BOBBY HAYNES	B	(Y	(E) SOUTHERN COMFORT (DBL)	1975 ABC ABCD 607 BLUE THUMB			BT	9002
CLARE FISCHER	K	(Y	(F) CHAIN REACTION	1975 ABC ABCL 5144 BLUE THUMB			BT	6022
CARLOS VIDAL	CONG	(Y	(G) THOSE SOUTHERN KNIGHTS	1976 ABC ABCL 5164 BLUE THUMB			BTS	6024
RALPH MACDONALD	PERC	(H	(H) FREE AS THE WIND	1977 ABC ABCL 5226 BLUE THUMB			BT	6029
ALPHONSO JOHNSON	B	(L	(I) BEST OF THE CRUSADERS(DBL)	1976 ABC ABCL 612 BLUE THUMB			BT	6027
BOB MANN	G	(L	(J) IMAGES	1978 ABC ABCL 5250 BLUE THUMB			BT	6030
HUBERT LAWS	FLT	(Y	(K) STREET LIFE	1979 MCA		UK	MCF	3008
AL McKIBBON	B	(Y	(L) RHAPSODY & BLUES	1980 MCA		UK	MCG	4010
HUNGRIA GARCIA	PERC	(Y						
PHIL UPCHURCH	G	(L	SHEILA ESCOVEDO PERC (L	ABRAHAM LABORIEL B (L				
RALF RICKERT	TPT	(L	(NOTE) RECORDS LISTED BEFORE (A) ARE BY THE JAZZ CRUSADERS					

CRYAN SHAMES   C241A

(A) A SCRATCH IN THE SKY	196	CBS	US	2786
(A) A SCRATCH IN THE SKY	196	CBS	US	9586
(B) SUGAR & SPICE	196	CBS	US	2589
(C) SYNTHESIS	19	CBS	UK	9719

CRYSTAL MANSION   C241B

ERIC FAULKNER	V	(A	(A) CRYSTAL MANSION FEATURING J CASWELL19	CAPITOL	US	SKAO	227
JOHNNY CASWELL	V PNO	(A	(B) CRYSTAL MANSION	19	RARE EARTH	US		R540L
JERRY MARLOW	B	(A					
RONNIE GENTILE	G B	(A	RICKEY MORLEY D (A	DAVE WHITE	PNO V	(A	
SAN ROTA	K	(	MARIO SANCHEZ V PERC (	BILL CRAWFORD	B	(	

CRYSTALS   C242

MARY THOMAS	V	(	WALL OF SOUND VOL3 THE CRYSTALS	1975	PHIL SPECTOR	2307 006
DEE DEE KENNIEBREW	V	(	HES A REBEL	196	PHILLES	4001
LALA BROOKS	V	(	TWIST UPTOWN	196	PHILLES	4000
BARBARA ALSTON	V	(	GREATEST HITS	196	PHILLES	4003
VICKI ALSTON	V	(				
PAT WRIGHT	V	(				

CUBY & THE BLIZZARDS   C243

HENRY 'CUBY' MUSKIE	V HCA	(ALL	(A) DESOLATION	1966	PHILIPS		SBL	7874
EELCO GELLING	G	(GH	(B) WITH REGARDS FROM GROLLO	1967	PHILIPS	NL	6343	227
HANS KINDS	G	(AFM	(B) WITH REGARDS FROM GROLLO	1967	PHILIPS		855	040
WILLY MIDDEL	B	(ABDFM	(B) GROETEN UIT GROLLO	1967	PHILIPS		9286	131
HENK HILBRANDIE	PNO	(A	(C) TRIPPIN'THRU' A MIDNIGHT BLUES	1967	PHILIPS	NL	6343	228
EDDIE BOYD	PNO	(D	(D) PRAISE THE BLUES	1968	PHILIPS	NL	6440	308
HERMAN BROOD	K V	(BCFGMOPQ	(D) PRAISE THE BLUES	1968	PHILIPS	US	665	033
JAAP VAN EIK	B	(CDFGPQ	(E) SOUL	1968				
DICK BEEKMAN	D	(CFGPQ	(F) BEST OF (66 68)	1968	PHILIPS	NL	6677	023
EDWARD NINCK BLOK	TPT	(C	(G) LIVE	1968	PHILIPS	NL	6440	091
ROEL HEMMES	SAX	(C	(G) LIVE	1968	PHILIPS	US	600	307
JENNE MEINEMA	SAX	(C	(H) APPLEKNOCKERS FLOPHOUSE	1969	PHILIPS	UK	SBL	7918
ALEXIS KORNER	G V	(G	(H) APPLEKNOCKERS FLOPHOUSE	1969	PHILIPS	NL	849	0167
HELMIG VANDER VEGT	K	(HIKLPQ	(I) TOO BLIND TO SEE	1969	PHILIPS	NL	6440	312
HERMAN DEINUM	B	(BHIKLPQ	(I) TOO BLIND TO SEE	1969	PHILIPS		6413	002
BAS MUNNINKSNA	WIND	(I	(J) KING OF THE WORLD	1970	PHILIPS	NL	6314	002
RUDI VAN DIJK	SAX	(I	(J) KING OF THE WORLD	1970	PHILIPS	US	600	331
FRANK NUYENS	G	(NO	(K) SIMPLE MAN	1971	PHILIPS		6413	014
LOURENS LEEUW	B	(NO	(K) SIMPLE MAN	1971	PHILIPS	NL	6440	306
HERMAN VAN BOEYEN	D	(N	(L) SOMETIMES	1972	PHILIPS		6413	026
GEORGE KOOYMANS	G V	(N	(L) SOMETIMES	1972	PHILIPS	NL	6440	311
ROBERT JAN STIPS	K	(N	(M) AFSCHEIDSCONCERT	1974	PHILIPS	NL	6343	229
EGON JANSEB	PERC	(N	(N) RED WHITE BLUE	1975	POLYDOR	NL	2925	034
MELS BOL	D	(O	(N) RED WHITE BLUE	1975	VERTIGO	NL	6360	631
MAGGIE McNEAL	V	(O	(O) KID BLUE	1976	CNR	NL	660	002

(CONTINUED)

```
C243  (CONTINUED)                           CUBY & THE BLIZZARDS
  MARGRIET ESHUIS    V    (0    (P) OLD TIMES GOOD TIMES      1977 PHILIPS    NL  6416 111
  NEPPY NOVA         PERC (0    (Q) FORGOTTEN TAPES           1977 PHILIPS    NL  6401 107
  JAN SCHUURMAN      PERC (0    (R) LOVE VENDETTA             1977 NEGRAM     NL       NN3
  ROB HOEKE          PNO  (P
  MARTIN VAN DIJK    PNO  (R    BERNARD PEINKE    G    (R     JAN GROENINK    D   (R
  PIET VAN BLAUW     D    (R
C244                                              CULT
                              THE MAIL MUST GO THROUGH        19   STARBURST  US  SLT  500
C245                                            CULTURE
  JOSEPH HILL         V    (ABCDE   (A) 2 7S CLASH            1978 LIGHTNING  UK       LIP1
  KENNETH LLOYD DAYES V    (ABCDE   (B) AFRICA STAND ALONE    1978 APRIL       ADI     735
  ALBERT WALKER       V    (ABCDE   (C) HARDER THAN THE REST  1978 FRONT LINE UK     FL1016
  ROBBIE SHAKESPEARE  B    (AC      (D) CUMBOLO               1979 FRONT LINE UK     FL1040
  ANSEL COLLINS       K    (C       (E) INTERNATIONAL HERB    1979 FRONT LINE UK     FL1047
  WIRE LINDO          K    (C       (F) BALDHEAD BRIDGE       1980 LASER      UK     LASL 1
  WILLIE LINDO        G    (C
  RANCHIE             G    (C   SLY DUNBAR    D    (AC STICKY       PERC (AC DAVID MADDEN   TPT (C
  VIN GORDON          TROM (AC  ERROL NELSON  K    (A  CEDRIC BROOKS SAX (C  ERIC LAMONT    G   (A
  FELIX HEADLEY       SAX  (C   LENNOX GORDON G    (A  LLOYD PARKS  B    (A  HERMAN MARQUIS SAX (A
  FRANKLIN WAUL       K    (A   BOBBY ELLIS   TPT  (A  TOMMY McCOOK SAX  (A
C246                                         BURTON CUMMINGS
  BURTON CUMMINGS   K V  (ALL    (A) BURTON CUMMINGS    1976 PORTRAIT UK 81573 US 34261
  DICK WAGNER       G    (C      (B) MY OWN WAY TO ROCK 1977 PORTRAIT UK 82012 US 34698
  RANDY BACHMAN     G V  (BC     (C) DREAM OF A CHILD   1978 PORTRAIT UK 82962 US 35481
  IAN GARDINER      B    (BC
  JIM GORDON        D    (C   JEFF BAXTER    G   (C  BOBBY KING      V  (B  E L KING       V   (B
  RICK SCHLOSSER    D    (BC  TERRY EVANS    V   (B  PHYLLIS ST JAMES PERC (BC STEVE MADAIO HRNS(C
  BECKY LOPEZ       V    (C   VANETTA FIELDS V   (C  PLAS JOHNSON   SAX (C  SHIRLEY MATTHEWS V (C
  JIMMY PHILLIPS    K SYN(BC  JEFF PORCARO   D   (BC JIM HORN       SAX (BC DANNY WEIS     G   (B
  LENNY CASTRO      PERC (B   RAY PARKER     G   (B  SCOTT EDWARDS  B   (B  OLLIE E BROWN  D   (B
  TREVOR LAWRENCE   SAX  (B
C247                                           RICK CUNHA
  RICK CUNHA     G V  (AB   (A) CUNHA SONGS      1973 GRC          GA 5004
  JERRY CARRIGAN D    (A    (B) MOVING PICTURES  1977 CBS            33697
  TOMMY COGBILL  B    (A   BILL CUNNINGHAM   (A LARRY MUHOBERAC  (A REGGIE YOUNG G (A
  LARRY CARLTON  G    (A   JEFF GILKENSON    (A DON BROOKS    HCA (A DAVID BRIGGS K (A
  JOHN GUERIN         (A   WAYLON JENNINGS   (A CATES SISTERS    (A WELDON MYRICK  (A
  GARY SCRUGGS        (A   NASHVILLE EDITION (A DAVID DAWSON     (A RANDY SCRUGGS  (A
  STEVE NORMAN        (A   DONNA WEISS       (A DONNA WASHBURN   (A JOE OSBORN   B (A
C247A                                             CURE
  ROBERT SMITH      G  (B   (A) CURE             1979 FICTION UK FIX001
  MATTIEU HARTLEY   K  (B   (B) SEVENTEEN SECONDS 1980 FICTION UK FIX004
  LAURENCE TOLHURST D  (B
  SIMON GALLUP      B  (B
C248                                        CHERIE CURRIE
  CHERIE CURRIE     V  (A   (A) BEAUTY'S ONLY SKIN DEEP  197 MERCURY
C249                                          TIM CURRY
  TIM CURRY     V    (AB   (A) READ MY LIPS   1978 A&M   AMLH64717
  DICK WAGNER   G    (B    (B) FEARLESS       1979 A&M   AMLH64773
  MICHAEL KAMEN K    (B
  BOB BABITT    B    (B   CHARLES COLLINS D (B DAVID LASLEY V (B ARNOLD McCULLER  V  (B
  ULA HEDWIG    V    (B   BOB KULICK        (B BETTE SUSSMAN K (B MICHAEL TSCHUDIN SYN(B
  DAVE SANBORN  SAX  (B   ALLEN SCHWARZBERG D (B JIM MAELEN   PERC (B
C250                                        LITTLE JOE CURTIS
  LITTLE JOE CURTIS V (A   (A) LITTLE JOE CURTIS  19 MARBLE ARCH      MAL 772
                          (B) SOUL              19 ALSTON              5082
C250A                                          MAC CURTIS
  MAC CURTIS   V  (ALL   (A) GOOD ROCKIN TOMORROW 19 ROLLIN ROCK US LP007
                        (B) RUFFABILLY          19 ROLLIN ROCK US LP002
                        (C) SUNSHINE MAN        19 EPIC       US 26419
                        (D) ROCKABILLY KINGS    1974 POLYDOR   UK 2310 293
                        (E) ROCKIN' MOTHER      1979 RADAR     UK RAD22
C250B                                        SONNY CURTIS
  SONNY CURTIS G V  (ALL  (A) 1ST OF SONNY CURTIS 19 VIVA     US V 36012
                          (B) SONNY CURTIS STYLE 19 VIVA     US V 36021
                          (C) BEATLE HITS       19 imperial  US 12276
C251                                          CURVED AIR
  SONJA KRISTINA  V       (ABCDEFG (A) AIR CONDITIONING 1970 WB          UK K 56004
  DARRYL WAY      VLN     (ABCDEFG (A) AIR CONDITIONING 1970 WB          US    1903
  FLORIAN PILKINGTON MIKSA D (ABCE (A) AIR CONDITIONING 1970 WB PIC DISC    3012
  FRANCIS MONKMAN K       (ABCE   (B) SECOND ALBUM      1971 WB          UK K 46092
  IAN EYRE        B       (AB     (B) SECOND ALBUM      1971 WB          US    1951
  MIKE WEDGWOOD   B       (CD     (C) PHANTASMAGORIA    1972 WB          UK K 46158
  EDDIE JOBSON    K       (D      (C) PHANTASMAGORIA    1972 WB          US    2628
  KIRBY           G       (D      (D) AIR CUT           1973 WB          UK K 46224
  JIM RUSSELL     PERC    (D      (E) LIVE              1975 DECCA       UK SML 119
  STEWART COPELAND D      (FG     (F) MIDNIGHT WIRE     1975 BTM         UK BTM 1005
  MIKE JAQUES     G       (FG     (G) AIRBORNE          1976 BTM         UK BTM 1008
  PHILIP KOHN     B G     (E      ( ) BEST OF           1976 WB             K 36015
  TONY REEVES     B       (G      ( ) CURVED AIR        197  MIDI        UK   20021
  HENRY LOWTHER   HRNS    (G
  COLIN CALDWELL  PERC    (C   ALEX RICHARDSON K    (   JEAN AKERS    PERC (C
  MAL LINWOOD ROSE PERC   (C   STEVE SAUNDERS  TROM (C  DAVID PARKER  TROM (C
  ALAN GOUT       TROM    (C   CHRIS PYNE      TROM (C  FRANK RICOTTI PERC (CG
  JACK EMBLOW     ACC     (G   BOB SARGEANT    K    (G  ANNIE STEWART FLT  (C
  CRISPIAN STEEL PERKINS TPT(C JIM WATSON      TPT  (C  PAUL KOSH     TPT  (C
  GEORGE PARNABY  TPT     (C   JOHN PERRY      B    (F  PETER WOODS   K    (F
  DEREK DAMIAN    V       (F   ROBIN LUMLEY    PNO  (G  ALAN SKIDMORE SAX  (G
```

IVOR CUTLER

| IVOR CUTLER | V K (ALL | | | | | |

IVOR CUTLER
C252

WHO TORE YOUR TROUSERS	19	DECCA		LK 4405
LUDO	19	DECCA		
DANDRUFF	1974	VIRGIN		V 2021
VELVET DONKEY	1975	VIRGIN		V 2937
JAMMY SMEARS	1976	VIRGIN		V 2065
LIFE IN A SCOTCH SITTING ROOM	1978	HARVEST		SHSP4084

CYANIDE
C253

BOB DE VRIES	V (A				
DAVE STEWART	G (A				
DAVE THOMPSON	B (A				

| (A) CYANIDE | 1978 | PYE | UK | NSPL18554 |

MICK STEWART   D   (A

JOHN L CYBORG
C253A

JOHN L CYBORG	SYNS (A				
AKISI YAMANAKA	V (A				
MASANI WADA	D (A				

(A) SATORI THE FLOWER TRAVELLING BAND 198   GTR   CAN 9230 1005

HIDEKI SHIMA   G   (A   SHIGEYUKI KOBAYASHI   B   (A

CYMANDE
C254

RAY KING	V PERC(A				
PETER SERREO	SAX (A				
MIKE ROSE WIND PERC (A					
PABLO GONSALES	CONGA (A				
SAM KELLY	D (A				
JOEY DEE	V PERC(A				
PATRICK PATTERSON	G (A				

(A) CYMANDE	1973	JANUS	US	JSL 3044
(A) CYMANDE	1973	ALASKA		ALKA 100
(B) SECOND TIME AROUND	1973	JANUS	US	JLS 3054
(C) PROMISED HEIGHTS	1974	CONTEMPO		CLP 508

DEREK GIBBS   SAX   (A   STEVE SCIPIO   B   (A

CYRKLE
C255

TOM DAWES	SITAR G B (AB				
MICHAEL LOSEKAMP	K (AB				
MARTY FRIED	D PERC(AB				
DON DANNEMAN	G (AB				
BOBBY GREGG	PERC (B				
BUDDY SALZMAN	PERC (B				
JOHN SIMON	K (B				

(A) RED RUBBER BALL	1966	CBS MONO	US	2544
(A) RED RUBBER BALL	1966	CBS	STEREO	9344
(B) NEON	1967	CBS MONO	US	2632
(B) NEON	1967	CBS	STEREO	2977
(B) NEON	1967	CBS	UK	62977

RAY BARRETTO   PERC   (B

HOLGER CZUKAY
C256

HOLGER CZUKY	V G K SYN (A				
JAKI LIEBEZEIT	D (A				
MICHAEL KAROLI	G (A				
IRMIN SCHMIDT	PNO (A				

| (A) MOVIES | 1979 | ELECTROLA | EUR | 064 45754 |
| (A) MOVIES | 1979 | EMI | UK | EMC 3319 |

REBOP KWAKU BAAH   PERC   (A

D C NIGHTHAWKS
D1

| (A) THE D C NIGHTHAWKS | 1980 | MERCURY | | 6337 111 |

D F K BAND
D1A

LES DUDEK	G (A				
MIKE FINNIGAN	K (A				
JIM KRUEGER	G (A				
MIKE HOSSACK	D (A				

| (A) SPECIAL TOUR SAMPLER | 1978 | CBS | US | AS430 |

MAX GRONENTHAL   K   (A   TREY THOMPSON   B   (A
BILL MEEKER   D   (A

D M Z
D1B

RICK CORACCIO	B (A				
PAUL MURPHY	D (A				
JAI RASSLER	G (A1				
PETER GREENBERG	G (A1				
MIKE LEWIS	B (1				

| (A) DMZ | 1978 | SIRE | | SRK 6051 |
| (1) 1976 | | | | |

DAVE ROBINSON   D   (1   MONO MANN   V K PERC(1

MICHAEL D'ABO
D2

MICHAEL D'ABO	V K (ALL				
WITH					
GRAHAM NASH	V (C				
DENNY SEIWELL	(C				
MIKE BLOOMFIELD	G (C				
TEDDY IRWIN	(C				
RAB NOAKES	(A				
TONY	V (A				
GARY TAYLOR	B (C				
BOBBY THOMPSON	(C				
GRANT SERPELL	D (B1				
MIKE JOPP	G (B1				
LYN DOBSON	HCA FLT SAX(B				
ALBERT LEE	G (A				
ROY BABBINGTON	B (A				
MATTHEW	HCA (A				
SUE GLOVER	V (A				
NANETTE	V (A				
JACK LANCASTER	SAX (D				

(A) D'ABO	1970	UNI		6369 601
(A) D'ABO	1970	MCA		MAPS 2040
(B) DOWN AT RACHEL'S PLACE	1972	A&M	UK	AMLH68097
(B) DOWN AT RACHEL'S PLACE	1972	RCA	FR	SP 4346
(C) BROKEN RAINBOWS	1974	A&M	UK	AMLH63634
(D) SMITH & D'ABO	1976	CBS	uk	81583
(1) TOURING BAND 1971 ??				

MARK NAFTALIN	K (C		JORDANAIRES	V (C
BEN KEITH	(C		MO FOSTER	B (B1
JIMMY ROBERTSON	ACC (B		MIKE MORAN	K (B
JOHN KONGOS	G (B		RAY COOPER	PERC (B
MIKE LENTIN	G (B		KEITH CHRISTIE	TROM (B
CHRIS SPEDDING	G (A		PAT DONALDSON	B (A
GERRY CONWAY	D (B		JOHN MARSHALL	D (A
LEW WARBURTON	STRINGS		MIKE LEANDER	STRING(A
SUNNY LESLIE	V (A		DORIS TROY	V (A
HUGH	V (A		JOHN NEIL	V (A

PAULINHO DACOSTA
D3

| PAULINHO DACOSTA | PERC V(A | | | | |

| (A) AGORA | 1977 | POLYDOR | UK | 2335 747 |
| (B) HAPPY PEOPLE | 1979 | POLYDOR | UK | 2312 102 |

DADA
D4

ELKIE BROOKS	V (A				
ROBERT PALMER	V (				
PAUL KORDA	V (A				
ERNIE LAUCHLAN	HRNS (A				
STEVE YORK	B (				

| (A) DADA | 1970 | ATCO | | 2400 030 |

JIMMY CHAMBERS	V PERC (A		MARTYN HARRYMAN	D (A
PETE GAGE	G B (A		BARRY DUGGAN	WIND (A
DON SHINN	K (A		MALCOLM CAPEWELL	WIND (A

DADDY COOL
D4A

ROSS WILSON	HCA G V (				
ROSS HANNAFORD	G V (				
WAYNE DUNCAN	B V (				
GARY YOUNG	D V (				

| DADDY COOL | 19 | REPRISE | US | 6471 |
| TEENAGE HEAVEN | 19 | REPRISE | US | 2088 |

IAN WINTERS   G   (

D5

KURT PALOMAKI   B V CLAR (ABC
CLIFF CARRISON   D   (ABCD
STEVE HAYTON   G V   (AC
MOE ARMSTRONG   V   (A
STEVE MILLER   K   (AC
IVAN CHANDLER   K   (C

D5A

PATTI DAHLSTROM   V   (ABCD
LARRY KNECHTEL   K   (BC
MICHAEL UTLEY   K   (B
ANDY CAHAN   K   (B
GEORGE CLINTON   K   (B
JACK CONRAD   B   (BC
DAVID KEMPER   D   (B
DEAN PARKS   G   (B
FRED TACKETT   G   (B
AL CASEY   G   (B
JIM HORN   HRNS   (BC
LON VAN EATON   HRNS   (B

D5B

D6

ROBIN McDONALD   G   (
MIKE MAXFIELD   G
RAY JONES   B

D6A

WES DAKUS

D7

MICHAEL D'ALBUQUERQUE

D7A

D8

KATHY DALTON   V   (A
WITH
LOWELL GEORGE   G V   (A
PAUL BARRERE   G   (A
BILL PAYNE   K   (A
RICHIE HAYWARD   D   (A
CLYDIE KING   V   (A
BILLY HINSCHE   V   (A
TONY MARTIN   V   (A
GABRIEL FLEMMING   HRNS   (A
JAY MIGLIORI   HRNS   (A

D8A

SCOTT ENGEL   V   (A
JOHN 'MAUS' STEWART   V

D9

ROGER DALTREY   V   (ALL
WITH
RUSS BALLARD   V G   (AB
PADDY McHUGH   V   (B
DYAN BIRCH   V   (B
FRANK COLLINS   V   (B
DAVE WINTOUR   B   (AB
PHILIP GOODHAND TAIT PNO   (B
CLEM CLEMPSON   G   (B
STEWART FRANCIS   D   (B
DAVE ARBUS   VLN   (B
BRIAN ODGERS   B   (C
JIMMY McCULLOCH   G   (C
PHIL KENZIE   SAX   (C
JOHN PERRY   V   (C

D9A

D10

DAVE VANIAN   V   (AB
BRIAN JAMES   G V   (AB
CAPTAIN (RAY BURNS) SENSIBLE B(AB
RAT SCABIES   D   (AB
LU   G   (B

D10A

LOU STONEBRIDGE   V G   (A
STEVE VAN DeLLER   G   (A
ROB TOWNSEND   D   (A
DICK HANSON   TPT   (A

D11

MARTIN JENKINS   V MAND VLN(D
POLLY BOLTON   V   (D
DAVE COOPER   G V   (D
KEVIN DEMPSEY   G V B (D
TED KAY   PERC   (D
ROGER BULLEN   B   (
PAUL DUNMALL   SAX   (D

DADDY LONGLEGS

(A) DADDY LONGLEGS	1970	WB	US	3004
(B) OAKDOWN FARM	1971	VERTIGO	UK	6360 038
(C) THREE MUSICIANS	1972	POLYDOR	UK	2371 261
(D) SHIFTING SANDS	1972	POLYDOR	UK	2371 323

GARY NORTON HOLDERMAN G V (BD   PETER ARNESEN   K   (BC

PATTI DAHLSTROM

(A) THE WAY I AM	1973	20th CENTURY	US	T 421
(A) THE WAY I AM	1973	20th CENTURY	CAN 9209	421
(B) YOUR PLACE OR MINE	1975	20th CENTURY	US	T 461
(C) LIVIN' IT THRU'	1976	20th CENTURY	US	T 521

DAVID HUNGATE   B   (B   KLAUS VOORMANN   B   (B
GARY MALLABER   D   (B   JIM KELTNER   D   (B
AL STAEHELY   G   (B   ART MUNSON   G   (B
STEVE CROPPER   G   (B   JAY GRAYDON   G   (B
DAVID LINDLEY BANJ FDL G   (B   NICK DE CARO   ACC   (B
CHUCK FINDLEY   HRNS   (BC   JACKIE KELSO   HRNS (BC

DON DAILEY

SURF STOMPIN'	19	CROWN	US	CST 314

DAKOTAS

(A) MEET THE DAKOTAS (EP)	196	PARLOPHONE		GEP 888

TONY MANSFIELD   D

WES DAKUS & THE REBELS

WES DAKUS REBELS	19	KAPP	US	3536
WES DAKUS ALBUM	19	CAPITOL	US	6120

MICHAEL D'ALBUQUERQUE

(A) WE MAY BE CATTLE	1974	RCA	UK	SF 8383
(B) STALKING THE SLEEPER	1976	WB	UK	K 56276

DALLAS COUNTY

(A) DALLAS COUNTY	19	ENTERPRISE	US	1011

KATHY DALTON

(A) AMAZING	197	DISCREET UK K59202 US	DS2168
(A) BOOGIE BANDS & ONE NIGHT STANDS	1974	DISCREET	US	DS2208
(ONE TRACK DIFFERENT)				

SAM CLAYTON   PERC   (A   KENNY GRADNEY   B   (A
VAN DYKE PARKS   PNO V   (A   SNEAKY PETE   STEEL (A
JIMMY GILSTRAP   V   (A   LOULIE JEAN NORMAN   V   (A
CARL WILSON   V   (A   JEAN JUDSON   V   (A
VANILLA GRITS   V   (A   JOHN RAYFORD   HRNS (A
LARRY WILSON   HRNS   (A   JIMMY REED   HRNS (A
ERIC HORD   G   (A   STAN AYEROFF   G   (A

DALTON BROTHERS

(A) I ONLY CAME TO DANCE	1964	TOWER	US	T5026

ROGER DALTREY

(A) DALTREY	1973	TRACK	UK	2406 207
(A) DALTREY	1973	POLYDOR		2409 202
(A) DALTREY	1973	MCA	US	328
(B) RIDE A ROCK HORSE	1975	POLYDOR	UK	2442 135
(B) RIDE A ROCK HORSE	1975	MCA	US	2147
(C) ONE OF THE BOYS	1977	POLYDOR	UK	2441 146
(C) ONE OF THE BOYS	1977	MCA	US	2271

HENRY SPINETTI   D   (B   ALAN BROWN   (B
DAVE COURTNEY   PNO   (A   BOB HENRIT   D   (A
B J COLE   STEEL   (A   ROY YOUNG BAND   HRNS (A
JOHN ENTWISTLE   B   (C   STUART TOSH   D   (C
PAUL KEOGH   G   (C   ROD ARGENT   K   (C
JIMMY JEWELL   SAX   (C   TONY RIVERS   V   (C
STUART CALVER   V   (C

DAMNATION

( ) WHICH IS THE JUSTICE	19	UA	US	UAS 5533
( ) SECOND DAMNATION	19	UA	US	UAS 6773
( ) THE DAMNATION OF ADAM BLESSING	19	UA	US	UAS 6738

DAMNED

(A) DAMNED DAMNED DAMNED	1977	STIFF	UK	SEEZ1
(B) MUSIC FOR PLEASURE	1977	STIFF	UK	SEEZ5
(C) MACHINE GUN ETIQUETTE	1979	CHISWICK	UK	CWK 3011

LOL COXHILL   SAX   (B

DANCE BAND

(A) FANCY FOOTWORK	1980	DOUBLE D	UK	DDLP1

STEVE MULLENS   B   (A   PETER HOPE EVANS   HCA (A
JOHN IRISH EARLE   SAX   (A

DANDO SHAFT

(A) AN EVENING WITH DANDO SHAFT	1970	YOUNGBLOOD	UK	SSYB6
(A) AN EVENING WITH DANDO SHAFT	197	DECCA	US	75217
(B) DANDO SHAFT	1971	NEON	UK	NE5
(C) LANTALOON	1972	RCA	UK	SF 8256
(D) KINGDOM	1977	RUBBER	UK	RUB 034

JON STEVENS   D   (D   ROD CLEMENTS   B   (D
TOMMY KEARTON   K   (D   DANNY THOMPSON   B   (D

CHARLIE DANIELS
D12

D12

CHARLIE DANIELS	G FDL V	(ALL	(A) TE JOHN,GREASE & WOLFMAN	1970	KAMA SUTRA	US		2060
WITH			(A) TE JOHN,GREASE & WOLFMAN	1978	EPIC	RI	SU	34665
JOEL DIGREGORIO	K V	(ABCDEFGHIJKL1	(B) CHARLIE DANIELS	1970	CAPITOL		ST 11414
EARL'TE JOHN' GRIGSBY	B V(ABC		(C) HONEY IN THE ROCK	1970	KAMA SUTRA	US		2071
JEFF 'WOLFMAN' MYER	D	(AB	(D) WAY DOWN YONDER	1970	KAMA SUTRA	US		2076
BUDDY DAVIS	D	(CD	(D) WHISKEY	1977	EPIC	RI	US	34664
FRED EDWARDS	D	(CDEFGHI*JKL1	(E) FIRE ON THE MOUNTAIN	1975	KAMA SUTRA	US		2603
HOLLADAY SISTERS	V	(C	(E) FIRE ON THE MOUNTAIN	1975	KAMA SUTRA	UK		7007
TIM DRUMMOND	B	(B	(E) FIRE ON THE MOUNTAIN	197	EPIC	RI	US	34365
BILLY COX	B	(BD	(F) NIGHTRIDER	1975	KAMA SUTRA	US		2607
KARL HIMMEL	D	(B	(F) NIGHTRIDER	1975	KAMA SUTRA	US		7009
BOB WILSON	K	(B	(F) NIGHTRIDER	197	EPIC	US		34402
BEN KEITH	STEEL	(B	(G) SADDLE TRAMP	1976	EPIC	UK		81335
JERRY CORBITT	V G	(B	(G) SADDLE TRAMP	1976	EPIC	US		34150
BARRY BAINES	G V	(D	(H) UNEASY RIDER	197	EPIC	US		34369
GARY ALLEN	D	(DE	(I) HIGH & LONESOME	1977	EPIC	US		34377
MARK FITZGERALD	B V	(DE	(I) HIGH & LONESOME	1977	EPIC	UK		81666
LEA JANE BERINATI	V	(DK	(J) MIDNIGHT WIND	1977	EPIC	US		34970
TED REYNOLDS		(D	(*) ESSENTIAL CHARLIE DANIELS	197	KAMA SUTRA			
CHARLIE HAYWARD	B	(FGHIJ*1KL	(*) VOLUNTEERS JAM	1976	CAPRICORN	UK	2429 143
DICKIE BETTS	G	(E*	( ) VOLUNTEERS JAM 3/4	1978	EPIC	US	E2 35368
TOY CALDWELL	G STEEL	(FGI*	( ) VOLUNTEERS JAM (EP)	197	KAMA SUTRA		EP10
JAMES MARSHALL	D	(1KL	(1) NOV 1979 GIG				
MARIE CAIN		(D	(K) MILLION MILE REFLECTIONS	1979	EPIC	UK		83446
TOM CRAIN	G V	(FGHI*KL	(L) FULL MOON	1980	EPIC	UK		84461
PAUL HORNSBY	K	(FG					
SHARON VAUGHN		(D	JAIMIE NICHOLS	PERC	(E*	GEORGE McCORKLE	G	(I*
BANJO BANJO	G	(E	JAI JOHANNY JOHANSON	D	(FG	TOM CALDWELL	B	(*
DOUG GRAY	V PERC(*		JERRY EUBANKS	SAX	(*	PAUL RIDDLE	D	(*
CHUCK LEAVELL	PNO	(*	JIMMY HALL	HCA	(*	DAVID BROWN	B	(*
GARY PEACEMAKER	D	(*	RONNIE STONEMAN	BANJO	(*	MYLON LEFEVRE	V PERC(*
DON MURRAY	D	(FGHI*						

RICK DANKO
D13

RICK DANKO	B G	(A	(A) RICK DANKO	1978	ARISTA	UK SPARTY 1037
WITH			(A) RICK DANKO	1978	ARISTA	US		4141
DENNY SEIWELL	D	(A						
TERRY DANKO	D	(A	LEVON HELM	V	(A	ROBBIE ROBERTSON	G	(A
MICHAEL DE TEMPLE	G	(A	LEWIS BUSTOS	HRNS	(A	ROCKY MORALES	HRNS	(A
DOUG SAHM	G	(A	ROB FRABONI	PERC	(A	GERRY BECKLEY	V G	(A
JIM ATKINSON	G	(A	BLONDIE CHAPLIN	G B	(A	WAYNE NEUENDORF	V	(A
WALT RICHMOND	PNO	(A	RON WOOD	G	(A	TIM DRUMMOND	B	(A
JIM GORDON	K HRNS(A		ERIC CLAPTON	G	(A	KEN LAUBER	PNO	(A
JIM PRICE	HRNS	(A	JOE LALA	PERC	(A	GEORGE WEBER	ORG	(A
CHARLIE McBURNEY	HRNS	(A	RICHARD MANUEL	K	(A	DAVID PAICH	K	(A
GARTH HUDSON	ACC	(A						

DANNY & THE JUNIORS
D14

DANNY RAPP			( ) ROCK AND ROLL IS HERE TO STAY	19	SINGULAR	US	569
DAVE WHITE							
BILL CARLUCCI			FRANK MAFFEI		JOE TERRANOVA		

DARLING
D15

ALICE SPRINGS	V	(A	(A) PUT IT DOWN TO EXPERIENCE	1979	CHARISMA	UK	CAS 1144
MICK HOWARD	B	(A					
PAUL VARLEY	D	(A	HAL LINDES	G	(A		

JENNY DARREN
D16

JENNY DARREN	V	(ABC	(A) CITY LIGHTS	1977	DJM	UK	DJF 20497
CLIFF WADE	G B V	(ABC	(B) JENNY DARREN	1978	DJM	UK	DJF 20523
GEOFF GILL	PERC V(ABC		(C) QUEEN OF FOOLS	1978	DJM	UK	DJF 20547
WILL MALONE	PNO V	(A	(D) JENNY DARREN	1980	DJM	UK	DJF 20569
STUART BUCKLEY	SAX	(C						
BRIAN JONES	SAX	(A	TONY SPATH		(A	MIKE ASHCROFT	G	(
BEAU CHEMIN	K	(	COLIN ELLAR	B	(	KELLY CONOVER	D	(
LEE PATRICK	G V	(BC	DES TONGUE	B	(BC			

CHRIS DARROW
D17

CHRIS DARROW BAN G V MAND VLN(ALL			(A) CHRIS DARROW	1973	UA UK UAG29453	US UALA 048
WITH			(B) UNDER MY OWN DISGUISE	1974	UA UK UAG29634	US UALA 242
CALEB QUAYE	PNO G	(A	(C) FRETLESS	1979	PACIFIC ARTS	US PAC7 132
CLIVE CHAMAN	B	(A						
ROGER POPE	D	(A	STEVE CAHILL G V AUTOHARP	(AC	EARL DANN	G	(A
SONNY BRICE	K	(A	TREVOR WHITE	B	(A	DANNY SMITH	D	(A
DAVE PEGG	B	(A	DAVE MATTACKS	D	(A	ALAN STIVELL	HARP FLT (A
DOLLY COLLINS	K	(A	ALAN LUMSDEN	SACK	(A	RODERICK SKEAPING	VLA	(A
JOSEPH SKEAPING	REBEC	(A	THERESA CAUDLE	WIND	(A	ANDREW VANDER BEEK	HRNS	(A
RANDY STERLING	B	(C	JOHN RUSSELL	D	(C	LOREN NEWKIRK	PNO	(C
STEVEN DARROW	PERC	(C	JERRY WALLER	TPT K	(C	BOB SIGGINS	V STEEL(C
MAX BUDA	HCA	(C	ROBB STRANDLUND	G V	(C	FRANK RECKARD	G	(C
STEVE MORK	HRNS	(C	CINDY EDWARDS	V	(C	CORKY CARROLL	V	(C
EARL SHAKELFORD	V	(C	GREG PRESTOPINO	V	(C	DAVID JONES	PERC	(C
TITO LLOYD	PERC	(C	BABATUNDE OLATUNJI	CONGA	(C			

DARTS
D18

HORATIO HORNBLOWER	SAX	(AB	(A) DARTS	1977	MAGNET	UK	MAG 5020
GEORGE CURRIE	G	(AB	(B) EVERYBODY PLAYS DARTS	1978	MAGNET	UK	MAG 5022
GRIFF FENDER	V	(AB	( ) AMAZING DARTS	1978	MAGNET		062 61889
JOHN DUMMER	D	(AB	( ) AMAZING DARTS	1978	K TEL	UK	DLP 7901
DEN HEGARTH	V	(AB	(C) DART ATTACK	1979	MAGNET	UK	MAGL 5030
RITA RAY	V	(AB	( ) GREATEST HITS	1980	MAGNET	UK	MAGL 5037
THUMP THOMPSON	B	(AB					
MIKE DEACON	K	(	HAMMY HOWELL	K	(AB	BOB FISH	V	(AB	KENNY EDWARDS	V	(

D18A

DARTS(US)

( ) HOLLYWOOD DRAG   19   DELFI   US   DFST 1244

D18B

RUSSELL DASHIELL

RUSSELL1 DASHIELL	V G K PERC(A
STU COOK	B (A
DOUG CLIFFORD	D (A
JOHN TANNER	PNO (A

(A) ELEVATOR   1978   EPIC   UK   35074
(A) ELEVATOR   1978   EPIC   UK   82637

D19

| GREG DEMPSEY | (A |
| KATHLEEN YESSE | (A |

DAUGHTERS OF THE ALBION

(A) DAUGHTERS OF THE ALBION   1968   FONTANA   67586
(A) "   "   "   1968   FONTANA NL 887806 UK STL 5486

D19A

WOLFGANG DAUNER

WOLFGANG DAUNER	K FLT (ALL
FRED BRACEFUL	D (AB
EBERHARD WEBER	B CELLO(AB
ROLAND WITTICH	D (A
SIEGFRIED SCHWAB	G (A

(A) RISCHKAS SOUL   1972   BRAIN   1016
(B) OUTPUT   19   ECM   1006
(C) GIRL FROM MARTINIQUE   19   ECM   1008
(D) CHANGES   1979   MOOD   GER   23333

D20

DAVE DEE(HARMAN)	V (ALL
TREVOR 'DOZY' DAVIES	B (
JOHN'BEAKY' DYMOND	G D (
MICHAEL'MICK' WILSON	D (
IAN 'TICH' AMEY	G (
PETER LUCAS	G (

DAVE DEE,DOZY,BEAKY,MICK & TICH

DAVE DEE,DOZY,BEAKY MICK & TICH	1966	FONTANA		STL	5350
IF MUSIC BE THE FOOD OF LOVE	1966	FONTANA		STL	5388
IF MUSIC BE THE FOOD OF LOVE	1967	FONTANA		858	030
GOLDEN HITS	1967	FONTANA		STL	5441
WHATS IN A NAME	1967	FONTANA		858	000
IF NO ONE SANG	1968	FONTANA		886	478
IF NO ONE SANG	1968	FONTANA		STL	5471
GREATEST HITS	1968	FONTANA		SFL	13002
TOGETHER	1969	FONTANA		701	751
TOGETHER	1969	FONTANA		SFL	13173
LEGEND OF	1969	FONTANA		SFL	13063
FRESH AIR	1970	PHILIPS		6308	029
ATTENTION	19	FONTANA		6438	058
GREATEST HITS	1971	PHILIPS		6382	018
GREATEST HITS	19	FONTANA	US		67567
GREATEST HITS	19	FONTANA	US		27567
GREATEST HITS	1976	PHILIPS	UK	SON	015
TIME TO TAKE OFF	19	IMPERIAL	US		12402

D20

DAVEY & THE BADMEN

WANTED   19   KRW   US   63 054

D21

DIANNE DAVIDSON

DIANNE DAVIDSON	V G (AB
WITH	
MAC GAYDEN	G.V (A
JOHN HARRIS	PNO (A
TIM DRUMMOND	B (A
KENNY MALONE	D (A
BRENT DAVIDSON STEEL DRUM (A

(A) MOUNTAIN MAMA   1972   JANUS   US   JLS   3048
(B) BACKWOODS WOMAN   1972   JANUS   UK   6310   209

KARL HIMMEL	D (A	KENNETH BUTTREY	D (A
WELDON MYRICK	STEEL (A	RUTH PFAU	VIOLA(A
ANITA BALL	G V (A	TRACY NELSON	V (A

D22

ALUN DAVIES

ALUN DAVIES	V G (A
JEREMY TAYLOR	G (A
CAT STEVENS	K (A
CHARLIE GAINSFORD	BANJO (A
JEAN ROUSSEL	K (A

(A) DAYDO   1972   CBS   US   31469
(A) DAYDO   1972   CBS   UK   65108

| GERRY CONWAY | D (A | CHRIS LAURENCE | B (A |
| LARRY STEELE | B (A | HARVEY BURNS | D (A |

D23

CYRIL DAVIES

CYRIL DAVIES	HCA V (A
WITH	
ALEXIS KORNER	V G (A
LISA TURNER	V BANJ(A
MIKE COLLINS	PERC (A
TERRY PLANT	B (A

(A) THE LEGENDARY CYRIL DAVIES   1957 PRIVATE PRESSING UK
(A) THE LEGENDARY CYRIL DAVIES   1970   FOLKLORE   UK   FLEUT   9
(EP) THE SOUND OF DAVIES   19   PYE
( ) CYRIL DAVIES   19   ACE OF CLUBS   UK   ACL   1130

JEFF BRADFORD   G MAND (A   REG TURNER   JUG (A

D23A

RON DAVIES

RON DAVIES	G (A
MIKE DEASY	G (A
DIMITRI CALLAS	G (A
CHAD STUART	B (A
LEON RUSSELL	PNO (A
MERRY CLAYTON	V (A

(A) SILENT SONG THROUGH THE LAND   1970   A&M   UK   AMLS   933

MIKE LANG	PNO (A	LARRY KNECHTEL	ORG (A
JIM KELTNER	D (A	VICKI DAVIES	V (A
DOUG DILLARD	BANJO (A	BYRON BERLINE	MAND (A
CLYDIE KING	V (A	VANETTA FIELDS	V (A

D24

BETTY DAVIS

BETTY DAVIS	V (ALL
WITH	
GREGG ERRICO	D (A
HERSHALL KENNEDY	K V (AB
VICTOR PANTOJA	PERC (AB
DAVID RODRIGUES	G (A
MERL SAUNDERS	K (AB
DOUG RAUCH	B (A
SKIP MESQUITE	SAX (A
POINTER SISTERS	V (A
WILLY SPARKS	D V (AB
CARLOS MORALES	G V (B
JAMES ALLEN SMITH	K (B
TRUDY PERKINS	V (B
CORDELL DUDLEY	V G (B
JIMMY GODWIN	G (B

(A) BETTY DAVIS   1973   JUST SUNSHINE   JSS5
(B) THEY SAY IM DIFFERENT   1974   JUST SUNSHINE US   JSS 3500
(B) THEY SAY IM DIFFERENT   1974   POLYDOR   UK   2933   402
(C) NASTY GAL   1975   ISLAND   UK   ILPS 9329

NEAL SCHON	G (A	BUDDY MILES	G (B
LARRY GRAHAM	B (A	RICHARD KERMODE	K (A
PETE SEARS	PNO (A	GREG ADAMS	HRNS (A
MIC GILLETTE	TROM (A	JULES BROUSSARD	SAX (A
KATHI McDONALD	V (A	PATRYCE BANKS	V (A
LARRY JOHNSON	B (BC	FRED MILLS	K V (B
NICKY NEAL	D V (B	ERROL BENNETT	PERC (B
DEBBIE BURRELL	V (B	ELAINE CLARK	V (B
MARY JONES	V (B	TONY VAUGHN	K V (B
PETE ESCOVEDO	PERC (B	MIKE CLARKE	D (B

EDDIE DAVIS
D25

EDDIE DAVIS			LIVE AT MINTONS	1964	STATESIDE	UK	SL	10102
JOHNNY GRIFFIN	SAX	(	LIVE AT MINTONS	196	PRESTIGE	US		7309
SHIRLEY SCOTT	K	(	COOKBOOK	1974	PRESTIGE		PR	24039
			LEAPIN' ON LENNOX	1976	BLACK'N'BLUE			33072
			TOUGHESS TENORS	1976	MILESTONES		M	47135
			EDDIE LOCKJAW DAVIS	1976	MAHOLNY		558	104

FRANK DAVIS
D25A

FRANK DAVIS		METAMORPHOSIS	(UNRELEASED)	

JESSE ED DAVIS
D26

JESSE ED DAVIS	G V	(ALL	(A) JESSE ED DAVIS		1971	ATCO	US	33346
WITH			(A) JESSE ED DAVIS		1971	ATCO	UK	2400 106
ALBHY GALUTEN	PNO	(B	(B) ULULU		1972	ATLANTIC	UK	K 40329
MAC REBENNACK	PNO	(B	(B) ULULU		1972	ATCO	US	33382
LEON RUSSELL	PNO	(AB	(C) KEEP ON COMING		1973	EPIC	US	32133
STAN SZELESTE	PNO	(AB	(C) KEEP ON COMING		1973	CBS	UK	65649
LARRY KNECHTEL	K	(AB						
DONALD DUNN	B	(B	BILLY RICH	B	(AB	ARNOLD ROSENTHAL	B	(B
JIM KELTNER	D	(B	MAXINE WILLARD	V	(A	GRAM PARSONS	V	(A
MERRY CLAYTON	V	(AB	VANETTA FIELDS	V	(AB	CLYDIE KING	V	(AB
CHUCK KIRKPATRICK	V	(B	CHARLES CHALMERS SINGERS	V	(B	ERIC CLAPTON	G	(A
JOEL SCOTT HILL	G	(A	LARRY PIERCE	K	(A	BEN SIDRAN	K	(A
JOHN SIMON	K	(A	STEVE THOMPSON	B	(A	CHUCK BLACKWELL	D	(A
STEVE MITCHELL	D	(A	BRUCE ROWLAND	D	(A	ALAN WHITE	D	(A
PATT DALEY	PERC	(A	SANDY KONIKOFF	PERC	(A	JACKIE LOMAX	PERC	(A
PETE WADINGTON	PERC	(A	JOHNNIE WARE	PERC	(A	ALAN YOSHIDA	PERC	(A
JIM GORDON	HRNS	(A	JERRY JUMONVILLE	HRNS	(A	DARRELL LEONARD	HRNS	(A
FRANK MAYES	HRNS	(A	NIKKI BARCLAY	V	(A	BOBBY JONES	V	(A
GLORIA JONES	V	(A						

MILES DAVIS
D27

MILES DAVIS	TPT	(ALL	KIND OF BLUE	1959	CBS	US 163		UK	62066
WITH			PORGY & BESS	1959	CBS	US		UK	62108
WAYNE HENDERSON	TROM	(	SKETCHES OF SPAIN	1959	CBS			UK	62327
JOE ZAWINUL		(	ROUND ABOUT MIDNIGHT	19	CBS			UK	62323
TONY WILLIAMS	D	(	FRIDAY AT THE BLACKHAWK	19	CBS			UK	62306
HERBIE HANCOCK	K	(	FRIDAY AT THE NIGHTHAWK VOL2	19	CBS			UK	62307
KEITH JARRETT	K	(	IN PERSON AT THE BLACKHAWK	19	CBS	US C2S 820(DBL)			
JOHN McLAUGHLIN	G	(	MILESTONES	1959	CBS	US 9428		UK	62308
CHICK COREA	K	(	MILES & MONK AT NEWPORT	19	CBS			UK	62389
LARRY CORYELL	G	(	SOMEDAY MY PRINCE WILL COME	1962	CBS	US 8465		UK	62104
GEORGE PAULIS	K	(	SEVEN STEPS TO HEAVEN	1963	CBS	US 8851		UK	62170
AL FOSTER	D	(	IN EUROPE	1964	CBS	US 8983	EMBASSY	UK	31103
T M STEVENS	B	(	MY FUNNY VALENTINE	1965	CBS	US 9106		UK	62510
MASUBUMBI KIKUCHI	K	(	FOUR & MORE	1966	CBS	US 9253		UK	62655
WAYNE SHORTER	SAX	(	MILES AT ANTIBES	19	CBS			UK	62390
DAVE HOLLAND	B	(	MILES AHEAD	19	CBS	US 8633		UK	62496
RON CARTER	B	(	FACETS	19	CBS			UK	62637
JOHN COLTRANE	SAX	(	IN BERLIN	19	CBS			UK	62976
DIZZY GILLESPIE	TPT	(	TRUMPET GIANTS	1964	NEWJAZZ	US 8296	STATESIDE	UK	10103
CHARLIE PAKER	SAX	(	PLAYS RICHARD RODGERS	1964			STATESIDE	UK	10111
GIL EVANS		(	PLAYS RICHARD RODGERS	1976	PRESTIGE	US 7332	CBS	UK	88029
CANNONBALL ADDERLEY	SAX	(	ESP	1965	CBS	US 9150		UK	62577
TADD DAMERON	PNO	(	PLAYS FOR LOVERS	1966	PRESTIGE	US 7352	STATESIDE	UK	10168
			GREATEST HITS	1966	PRESTIGE	US 7457			
			MILES SMILES	1967	CBS	US 9401		UK	62933
			THE SORCERER	1967	CBS	US 9832		UK	63097
			NEFERTITI	1968	CBS	US 9594		UK	63248
			MILES IN THE SKY	1968	CBS	US 9628		UK	63352
			AT NEWPORT	19	CBS			UK	63417
			FILLES OF KILIMANJARO	1968	CBS	US 9750		UK	63551
			GREATEST HITS	19	CBS			UK	63620
			IN A SILENT WAY	1969	CBS	US 9857		UK	63630
			BITCHES BREW	1970	CBS	US PG26		UK	66236
			BITCHES BREW	197	CBS				30997
			LIVE AT THE FILLMORE(DBL)	1971	CBS			UK	66257
			JACK JOHNSON(SOUNDTRACK)	1971	CBS	US 30455		UK	70089
			LIKE EVIL (DBL)	1972	CBS	US 30954		UK	67219
			CN THE CORNER	1973	CBS	US 31906		UK	65246
			IN CONCERT (DBL)	1973	CBS			UK	68222
			ESSENTIAL MILES DAVIS	1973	CBS			UK	66310
			AT NEWPORT	197	CBS			UK	66417
			MILES DAVIS	197	PRESTIGE				24001
			TALLEST TREES (DBL)	1973	PRESTIGE				24012
			COLLECTORS ITEMS (DBL)	1973	PRESTIGE				24022
			WORKIN' & STEAMIN' (DBL)	1974	PRESTIGE				24034
			BASIC MILES	197	CBS	US 32025		UK	65343
			JAZZ AT THE PLAZA	1974	CBS	US 32470		UK	65778
			BIG FUN	1974	CBS	US 32866		UK	88024
			BLACK BEAUTY	1974	CBS				
			GET UP WITH IT	1975	CBS	US 33236		UK	88092
			CLASSICS (DBL)	1975	CBS			UK	88138
			AGHARTA (DBL)	1975	CBS	US 33967		UK	88159
			BIRD & MILES	1975	DJM	DJB26062		DJML	062
			EARLY MILES	1975	PRESTIGE	US 7674		UK	PR7674
			MILES DAVIS	1975	BLUENOTE				81501/2
			ALL STARS	1976	BEPPO			BEP	502
			AT THE BIRDLAND	1976	BEPPO			BEP	501

(CONTINUED)

D27 (CONTINUED)

MILES DAVIS

Title	Year	Label	Country	Cat.
DAVIS PARKER GILLESPIE	1976	VOGUE		VKD5529
GREEN HAZE	1976	PRESTIGE		24064
WATER BABIES	1977	CBS	US	34396
ARCHIVES OF JAZZ VOL 3	19	PATHE		FR 062 95819
AT CARNEGIE HALL	19	CBS		153 005
BIRTH OF THE COOL	19	CAPITOL		40678
BLUE HAZE	19	PRESTIGE		054 10134
BLUE MOODS	19	FANTASY		6051
COMPLETE BIRTH OF THE COOL	19	PATHE		FR 062 80798
CONCEPTION	19	PRESTIGE	US	7744
COOKING	19	PRESTIGE		240530
DIG	19	PRESTIGE		24054
MILES AHEAD	19	PRESTIGE	US	7822
MILES OF JAZZ	19	TRIP		5015
MODERN JAZZ GIANTS	19	PRESTIGE	US	7650
ODYSSEY	19	PRESTIGE	US	7540
OLEO	19	PRESTIGE	US	7847
SOMETHING ELSE	19	CBS		81595
SOULIN'	19	PRESTIGE		240757
STEAMIN'	19	PRESTIGE	US	7580
WALKIN'	19	PRESTIGE	US	7608
LIVE AT THE PLUGGED NICKEL	19	CBS		
PONGAEA	19	CBS		
JAZZ TRACK	19	CBS	US	1268
MOUNTAINS IN THE SKY	19	ATCO	US	SD1622

D27A

PAUL DAVIS

Personnel			Album	Year	Label	Country	Cat.
PAUL DAVIS	V	(ALL	(A) LITTLE BIT OF P D	197	BANG	US	223
JIMMY JOHNSON	G	(D	(B) PAUL DAVIS	197	BANG	US	226
DAVID HOOD	B	(D	(C) RIDE 'EM COWBOY	197	BANG	US	401
BARRY BECKETT	K	(D	(D) SOUTHERN TRACKS & FANTASIES	1976	BANG	US	405
ROGER HAWKINS	D	(D	(E) PAUL DAVIS	1977	bang US 410	UK	SHOT 002
BARRY BAILEY	G	(C					
CHARLIE OWEN	STEEL	(C					
TOM ROBB	B	(C	CHRIS ETHRIDGE B (C		ROY YEAGER D (C		
AUBURN BURRELL	G	(C					

D28

SPENCER DAVIS

Personnel			Album	Year	Label	Country	Cat.
SPENCER DAVIS	G V	(ALL	(A) EVERY LITTLE BIT HURTS	1965	WING	UK	WL 1165
MUFF WINWOOD	G V B	(ABCFKNDE	(A) 1ST ALBUM	1965	SONET	SW	1401
STEVE WINWOOD	K G V	(ABCDEFKNI	(A) 1ST ALBUM	196	FONTANA	UK	5242
PETER YORK	D	(ABCDELJKM	(B) SECOND ALBUM	1966	FONTANA	UK	TL 5295
EDDIE HARDIN	K	(JLM	(C) AUTUMN 66	1966	FONTANA	UK	STL 5359
PHIL SAWYER	G	(	(D) GIMME SOME LOVIN'	1967	UA	US	3578
RAY FENWICK	G	(JLM1	(D) GIMME SOME LOVIN'	1967	UA	US	6578
NIGEL OLSSON	D	(	(E) I'M A MAN	1967	UA	US	3589
NEIL MURRAY	B	(1	(E) I'M A MAN	1967	UA	US	6589
GARY COOPER	G	(L	(F) THE BEST OF SPENCER DAVIS	1968	ISLAND	UK	ILPS 9070
CHARLIE McCRACKEN	B	(LM	(G) VERY BEST OF	1968	UA	US	443E
TONY COE	CLAR	(M	(H) HERE WE GO ROUND THE MULBERY BUSH	1968	UA (SOUNDTRACK)	UK	SULP 1186
BRIAN DEXTER	ACC	(M	(I) GREATEST HITS	1968	UA	US	3461
MARTYN FORD	HRNS	(M	(I) GREATEST HITS	1968	UA	US	6641
DORIS TROY	V	(M	(J) WITH THEIR NEW FACE ON	1968	UA	US	6652
LIZA STRIKE	V	(M	(J) WITH THEIR NEW FACE ON	1968	UA		1192
RUBY JAMES	V	(M	(J) LETS DANCE WITH	19	SUNSET	GERM	50141
DAVE HYNES	D	(1	(K) HEAVIES	1969	UA	US	6691
TRAFFIC		(H	(L) GLUGGO	1973	VERTIGO	UK	6360 088
ANDY ELLISON		(H	(L) GLUGGO	1973	VERTIGO	US	1015
PETER JAMESON		(X	(M) LIVING ON A BACK STREET	1974	VERTIGO	UK	6360 105
SNEAKY PETE	STEEL	(Y	(M) LIVING ON A BACK STREET	197	VERTIGO		6499 978
JIM KELTNER	D	(Y	( ) POP CHRONIK (DBL)	1975	ISLAND	IMP	VOL4
			( ) POP CHRONIK (DBL)	1977	ISLAND	IMP	87213
			( ) SPENCER DAVIS GROUP	19	SONET		GP 9916
			( ) BEST OF	19	SONET		GP 9992
			(EP) SPENCER DAVIS	1978	ISLAND	UK	1EP10
SPENCER DAVIS SOLO			(1) 1967/68				
			(X) ITS BEEN SO LONG	1971	UA	UK	UAS 29177
			(Y) MOUSETRAP	1972	UA	UK	UAS 29361

D29

BRIAN DAVISON

Personnel			Album	Year	Label	Country	Cat.
BRIAN DAVISON	D V	(A	(A) EVERY WHICH WAY	1970	CHARISMA	UK	CAS 1021
GRAHAM BELL	V K	(A	(A) EVERY WHICH WAY	1970	MERCURY	US	SR 61340
GEOFF PEACH	WIND	(A					
ALAN CARTWRIGHT	B	(A	JOHN HEDLEY G (A				

D29A

TIM DAWE

Personnel			Album	Year	Label	Country	Cat.
TIM DAWE		(A	(A) PENROD	19	STRAIGHT	US	S1058

D30

JIMMY DAWKINS

Personnel			Album	Year	Label	Country	Cat.
JIMMY DAWKINS	G V	(ALL	(A) TRANSATLANTIC 770	1972	BLUE HORIZON	UK	
WITH			(A) TRANSATLANTIC 770	1975	CONTEMPO		CLP 513
JOE JAMMER	G	(A	(A) TRANSATLANTIC 770	1978	SONET		SNTF 758
ROSA DOTSON	V	(A	(A) TRANSATLANTIC 770	197	EXCELLO	US	8024
BOB BRUNNING	B	(A	(B) FAST FINGERS	19	DELMARK		DS 623
CECIL MOSS	TPT	(A	(C) ALL FOR BUSINESS	19	DELMARK		DS 634
MIKE VERNON	PERC	(A	(D) BLISTERING	1978	DELMARK	US	641
PETE WINGFIELD	K	(A	(E) I WANT TO KNOW	1977	MCM	IMP	900 290
TONY STEVENS	B	(A	(F) COME BACK BABY	19	MCM	FR	900 295
BILLY GRAHAM	TROM	(A					
NOVELLE WILLIAMS	V K	(A	REG ISADORE D (A		AG'BUBBLES' WHITE G (A		
DICK PARRY	SAX	(A	VELMA SMITH V (A		CHRIS MERCER SAX (A		

D30A

BOBBY DAY

Personnel			Album	Year	Label	Country	Cat.
BOBBY DAY	V	(A	(A) ROCKIN' WITH ROBIN	19	CLASS	US	LP 5002

DAY BLINDNESS
D30B

DAVE MITCHELL	V D	(A
GARY PIHL	G V	(A
FELIX BRIA	V B K	(A

(A) DAY BLINDNESS   19   STUDIO 10   DBX   101

HANS LAURIDSEN	V	(AB
ERIK RASMUSSEN	B V	(AB
HENRIK FRIIS NIELSEN	D	(AB
KARSTEN LYNG	G	(AB
OLE PREHN	G V	(AB
KENNETH KNUDSEN	PNO	(A

DAY OF THE PHOENIX
D31

(A) WIDE OPEN N WAY	1970	SONET		SLPS 1510
(A) WIDE OPEN N WAY	197	GREENWICH	UK	GSLPR1002
(B) THE NEIGHBOUR'S SON	1972	SONET		SLPS 1541
(B) THE NEIGHBOUR'S SON	197	CHAPTER ONE	UK	CNSR 812

PETER FRIIS NIELSEN   B   (A   TONY REEVES   B   (B

DAYLIGHT
D31A

MIKE SILVER	G V	(A
STEVE HATTON	G MAND V	(A
CHRISSIE QUAYE	G	(A
LYN DOBSON	WIND	(A

(A) DAYLIGHT   1971   RCA   UK   SF 8194

TONY CARR   D   (A   SPIKE HEATLEY   B   (A

DEAD BOYS
D32

STIV BATORS	V	(A
JOHNNY BLITZ	D	(A
CHEETAH CHROME	G	(A
JIMMY ZERO	G	(A
JEFF MAGNUM	B	(A

(A) YOUNG LOUD & SNOTTY	1977	SIRE	UK	9103 329
(A) YOUNG LOUD & SNOTTY	1978	SIRE	UK	SRK 6038
(B) WE HAVE COME FOR YOUR CHILDREN	1978	SIRE	UK	SRK 6054

DEAD FINGERS TALK
D33

BOBO PHOENIX	V	(A
ANDY LINKLATER	B	(A
JEFF PARSONS	G	(A

(A) STORM THE REALITY STUDIOS   1978   PYE   UK   NSPH   24

TONY CARTER   D   (A

DEAD KENNEDYS
D33A

EAST BAY RIDE	G	(A
TED	D	(A
KLAUS FLOURIDE	B V	(A
JELLO BIAFRA	V	(A
ROCKY MOUNTAIN ARSENAL CHOIR		(A

(A) FRESH FRUIT FOR ROTTING VEGETABLES 1980   CHERRY RED   RED   10

PAUL ROESSLER   K   (A   NINOTCHKA   K   (A

DEAD SEA FRUIT
D33B

DAVE 'BEANO' LASHMAR	G V	(A
CLIVE KENNEDY	V	(A
CHRISTOPHER HALL	B G V	(A

(A) DEAD SEA FRUIT   1967   CAMP   UK   603001

JOHN TOWNSEND   PERC V   (A   SI CLIFFORD   K   (A

DEAF SCHOOL
D34

TIM WHITTAKER	D	(C
ENRICO CADILLAC	V	(ABC
CLIFF LANGER	G	(ABC
MAX RIPPLE	K	(ABC
ERIC SHARK	V	(C
BETTE BRIGHT	V	(ABC
PAUL PILNICK	G B ACC	(
FRANKIE AVERAGE	B	(

(A) DONT STOP THE WORLD	1975	WB	UK	K 56364
(B) SECOND HONEYMOON	1976	WB	UK	K 56280
(AB) DONT STOP/2ND HONEYMOON	197	WB	US	2LS 3011
(C) ENGLISH BOYS WORKING GIRLS	1978	WB	UK	K 56450
(C) ENGLISH BOYS WORKING GIRLS	197	WB	US	3169

IAN RITCHIE   SAX   (C   STEVE LINDSEY   B   (C

DEALER
D34A

IAN KING	B	(1
JOHN METCALFE	D	(1
TAMMI COLLINS	V	(1

(1) 1979 OCT

TEM COLLINS   V   (1   ROGER LEWIS   G   (A

ELTON DEAN
D35

ELTON DEAN	SAX	(ALL
PHIL HOWARD	D	(A
MARK CHARIG	CORNET	(A
NEVILLE WHITEHEAD	B	(A
MIKE RATLEDGE	K	(A
ROY BABBINGTON	B	(A
ALAN SKIDMORE		(D
HUGH HOPPER	B	(C
KEITH TIPPETT	PNO	(C
JOE GALLIVAN		(C

(A) ELTON DEAN	1971	CBS	UK	64539
(B) THEY ALL BE ON THIS OLD ROAD	1977	OGUN		OG 410
(C) CRUEL BUT FAIR	1977	COMPENDIUM	NOR	FID 4
(D) EL SKID	1978	VINYL		VS 103
(E) ROGUE ELEMENTS	1978	OGUN	UK	OG 527
(F) CHEQUE IS IN THE POST	1977	OGUN	UK	OG 610
(G) NINESENSE	1977	OGUN	UK	OG 900
(H) HAPPY DAYS	1978	OGUN	UK	OG 910

DEBRIS
D35A

(A) DEBRIS   19   STATIC DISPOSAL   PIGOOOO

CHRIS DE BURGH
D36

CHRIS DE BURGH		(ALL
RAY JACKSON	MAND/HCA	(A
CHRIS LAWRENCE	B	(AB
LIZA STRIKE	V	(A
JOY YATES	V	(A
KEN FREEMAN	SYN	(AB
MADELINE BELL	V	(A
MICK EVE	SAX	(B
STUART ELLIOTT	D	(D
BARRY DE SOUZA	D	(AB
RONNIE LEAHY	K	(A
TONY HYMAS	K	(B
GLENN MORROW	K	(E
JOHN HELLIWELL	SAX	(E
LISA DEL BELLO	V	(E

(A FAR BEYOND THESE CASTLE WALLS	1975	A&M US 4516	UK	AMLH68284
(B) SPANISH TRAIN	1975	A&M US 4508	UK	AMLH68343
(C) AT THE END OF A PERFECT DAY	1977	A&M	UK	AMLH64647
(D) CRUSADER	1979	A&M	UK	AMLH64746
(E) EASTERN WIND	1980	A&M	UK	AMLH64815

TONY REEVES	B	(B	CHRIS MERCER	SAX	(B
IAN BAIRNSON	G	(B	DAVID PATON	B	(D
MIKE MORAN	K	(D	ANDREW POWELL	PNO	(D
BRIAN ODGERS	B	(A	LENNOX LAINGTON	PERC	(AB
RAY GLYNN	G	(AB	B J COLE	STEEL	(A
PHILIP GOODHAND TAIT	K	(AB	TIM WYNVEEN	G V	(E
AL MARNIE	B V	(E	JEFF PHILLIPS	D	(E
DICK SMITH	PERC	(E	ERIC ROBERTSON	K	(E
COLLEENA PHILLIPS	V	(E	SHARON LEE WILIAMS	V	(E

DECAMERON
D37

DAVE BELL	G	(BCDE
DIK CADBURY	B G V	(BCDE
JOHNNY COPPIN	G K	(BCDE
AL FENN	G B	(BCDE
GEOFF MARCH	K V	(BCDE
JOHN HALSEY	D	(BC
FRANK RICOTTI	PERC	(B
MONGEZI FEZA	PERC	(B
SHAMSI SARUMI	PERC	(B

(A) DECAMERON	1973	VERTIGO	UK	6360 097
(B) MAMMOTH SPECIAL	1974	MOONCREST	UK	CREST 19
(C) THIRD LIGHT	1975	TRANSATLANTIC	UK	TRA 304
(D) BEYOND THE LIGHT	1975	MOONCREST	UK	CREST 28
(E) TOMORROWS PANTOMIME	1976	TRANSATLANTIC	UK	TRA 375

JOHN MEALING	K	(C	DUDU PUKWANA	PERC	(B
MIKE WINFIELD	HRNS	(C	GASPAR LAWAL	PERC	(B
BOB CRITCHLEY	D	(E		

D37A			DECEMBERS CHILDREN					
			DECEMBERS CHILDREN	19	MAINSTREAM	US		6128
D37B			DECENNIUM					
GER BRANDS	D	(A	(A) SONG OF SAD TIMES	1974			NR	501
FRITS VAN UDEN	ORG V	(A						
JACK KESSELS	G V	(A	KOOS KOSTER	B V	(A	PIETER KOSTER	G K V	(A
D38			DE DANANN					
			(A) DE DANANN	1977	DECCA	UK	SKL	5287
			(B) MIST COVERED MOUNTAIN	1980	GAELLINN	IR	CEF	087
D38A			JOEY DEE & THE STARLIGHTERS					
JOEY DEE			PEPPERMINT TWISTERS	196	SCEPTER	US		503
CARLTON LATIMORE	K SAX	(	DOIN' THE TWIST	196	ROULETTE	US		RS25166
WILLIE DAVIS	D V	(	HEY LETS TWIST	196	ROULETTE	US		RS25168
LARRY VERNIERI	V	(	ALL THE WORLD IS TWISTIN'	196	ROULETTE	US		RS25171
DAVID BRIGATI	V SAX	(	BACK AT THE PEPPERMINT LOUNGE	196	ROULETTE	US		RS25173
JIMI HENDRIX	G	(1	TWO TICKETS TO PARIS	196	ROULETTE	US		RS25182
			JOEY DEE (SOLO)	19	ROULETTE	US		RS25197
			DANCE DANCE DANCE (SOLO)	19	ROULETTE	US		RS25221
			(1) LIVE 1966					
D39			KIKI DEE					
KIKI DEE	V	(ALL	(A) I'M KIKI DEE	1968	FONTANA	UK	STL	5455
BIAS BOSHELL	K	(CG	(B) GREAT EXPECTATIONS	1970	TAMLA US TS303	UK	STM	11158
ROGER POPE	D	(D	(C) LOVING & FREE	1973	ROCKET US 3040	UK	PIGL	5
JO PARTRIDGE	G	(D	(C) LOVING & FREE	1973	MCA	UA		395
BRIAN HOLLAWAY	G	(G	(D) IVE GOT THE MUSIC IN ME	1974	ROCKET US 3042	UK	PIGL	10
ANDY DALBY	G	(G	(D) IVE GOT THE MUSIC IN ME	1974	MCA	US		458
B J COLE	STEEL	(CD	(E) KIKI DEE	1974	SOUNDS SUPERB	UK	SPR	90030
ROGER BALL	SAX	(C	(F) PATTERNS	1974	PHILIPS	UK	6382	079
DAVEY JOHNSTONE	G	(CG	(F) PATTERNS	1974	LIBERTY	US	LST	763
NIGEL OLSSON			(G) KIKI DEE	1977	ROCKET US BXLI225	UK	ROLA	3
DOREEN CHANTER	V	(C	(H) STAY WITH ME	1979	ROCKET US BXLI3011	UK	TRAIN	3
DAVE MATTACKS	D	(C	(I) GREATEST HITS	1980	WARWICK	UK	WW	5092
DEE MURRAY	B	(CG						
KAY GARNER	V	(CD	PAUL KEOGH	G	(C	JIMMY HALL	K	(C
IRENE CHANTER	V	(CD	JIM RYAN	G	(C	JOHN McBERNIE	G	(
GERRY CONWAY	D	(C	ELTON JOHN	K	(C	LESLEY DUNCAN	V	(C
RONNIE LEAHY	K	(C	LIZA STRIKE	V	(C	PETE CLARKE	D	(D
MIKE DEACON	K	(D	CISSY HOUSTON	V	(D	JOSHIE ARMSTEAD	V	(D
MAERETHA STEWART	V	(D	BARRY MORGAN	PERC	(D	JEFF TITMUS	PERC	(D
CLIVE FRANKS	V	(D	STUART EPPS	V	(D	BARRY ST JOHN	V	(D
BILLY LAWRIE	V	(D	PAUL VIGRASS	V	(D	GARY OSBORNE	V	(D
PHIL CURTIS	B	(DG	MELVIN GALE	PERC	(G	HUGH McDOWELL	CELLO	(G
RAY COOPER	PERC	(G	DAVID SANBORN	HRNS	(G	MICHAEL BRECKER	HRNS	(G
RANDY BRECKER	HRNS	(G	R & J STONE	V	(G	SUNNY LESLIE	V	(G
STEVE HOLLY	D	(G	JAMES NEWTON HOWARD		(G	RICHARD TANDY	SYN	(G
TONY BURROWS	V	(G						
D39A			DEEP					
			PSYCHEDELIC MOODS	196	PARKWAY	US		7051
D40			DEEP PURPLE					
JON LORD	K	(ALL	(A) SHADES OF DEEP PURPLE	1968	PARLOPHONE	UK	PCS	7055
IAN PAICE	D	(ALL	(A) SHADES OF DEEP PURPLE	1977	HARVEST	UK	AHSM	2016
RITCHIE BLACKMORE	G	[(ABCDEFGHIJ	(A) SHADES OF DEEP PURPLE	19	PATHE	FR	066	04175
		(KLNOPQST*	(A) SHADES OF DEEP PURPLE	1968	TETRAGRAMMATON	US		102
NICK SIMPER	B	(ABC*SIT	(B) BOOK OF TALIESYN	1969	HARVEST	UK	SHVL	751
ROD EVANS	V	(ABCTSI	(B) BOOK OF TALIESYN	196	TETRAGRAMMATON	US		107
ROGER GLOVER	B	(DEFGHIJNOQ*ST	(B) BOOK OF TALIESYN	19	PATHE	FR	066	04000
IAN GILLAN	V	(DEFGHIJNOQ*ST	(C) DEEP PURPLE	1969	HARVEST	UK	SHVL	759
DAVID COVERDALE	V	(KLMPR	(C) DEEP PURPLE	19	TETRAGRAMMATON	US		119
GLEN HUGHES	B	(KLMPRT	(C) DEEP PURPLE	19	PATHE	FR	066	90505
TOMMY BOLIN	G	(MRT	(D) CONCERTO FOR GROUP & ORCHESTRA	1970	HARVEST	UK	SHVL	767
$ RANDY CALIFORNIA	G		(D) CONCERTO FOR GROUP & ORCHESTRA	1970	WB	US		1860
			(D) CONCERTO FOR GROUP & ORCHESTRA	19	PATHE	FR	066	90749
$ REPLACED BLACKMORE IN US 1 NIGHT			(E) DEEP PURPLE IN ROCK	1970	HARVEST	UK	SHVL	777
			(E) DEEP PURPLE IN ROCK	1970	WB	US		1877
			(F) FIREBALL	1971	HARVEST	UK	SHVL	793
			(F) FIREBALL	197	WB	US		2564
			(G) MACHINE HEAD	1972	PURPLE	UK	TPSA	7504
			(G) MACHINE HEAD	197	WB	US		2607
			(G) MACHINE HEAD	197	PATHE	FR	066	83261
			(H) MADE IN JAPAN	1972	PURPLE	UK	TPSP	351
			(H) MADE IN JAPAN	197	PURPLE	US		2701
			(I) BEST OF	1972	SCEPTER	US		18010
			(J) WHO DO WE THINK WE ARE	1973	PURPLE	UK	TPSA	7508
			(J) WHO DO WE THINK WE ARE	197	WB	US		2678
			(J) WHO DO WE THINK WE ARE	197	PATHE	FR	066	94140
			(K) BURN	1974	PURPLE	UK	TPS	3505
			(K) BURN	197	WB	US		2766
			(L) STORMBRINGER	1974	PURPLE	UK	TPS	3508
			(L) STORMBRINGER	197	WB	US		2832
			(L) STORMBRINGER	197	PATHE	FR	066	96004
			(*) Mk 1 & 2	1974	ELECTROLA	FR	188	94865
			(M) COME TASTE THE BAND	1975	PURPLE	UK	TPSA	7515
			(M) COME TASTE THE BAND	197	WB	US		2895
			(M) COME TASTE THE BAND	197	PATHE	FR	066	97044
			(N) 24 CARAT PURPLE	1975	PURPLE	UK	TPSM	2002
			(N) 24 CARAT PURPLE	197	PATHE	FR	066	96424
			(O) PURPLE PASSAGES	1975	WB	US		2644
			(CONTINUED)					

DEEP PURPLE

D40

(P) MADE IN EUROPE	1976	PURPLE	UK	TPSA 7517
(P) MADE IN EUROPE	197	WB	US	2995
(P) MADE IN EUROPE	197	PATHE	FR	068 98181
(Q) POWER HOUSE	1977	PURPLE	UK	TPS 3510
(Q) POWER HOUSE	197	PATHE	FR	068 60072
(R) LAST CONCERT IN JAPAN	1977	PURPLE	UK	P 10370
(S) THE SINGLES	1978	HARVEST	UK	SHSM 2026
(T) WHEN WE ROCK WE ROCK	1978	WB	US	3223
( ) LIVE IN JAPAN	197	PURPLE		55067
(EP) NEW LIVE & RARE	1978	PURPLE	UK	PUR 137

DEEP SIX

D40A

( ) DEEP SIX	19	LIBERTY	US	LRP 3475

DEF LEPPARD

D40B

STEVE CLARK	G	(
RICK SAVAGE	B	(A
PETE WILLIS	G	(A

(A)ON THROUGH THE NIGHT	1980	VERTIGO	UK	9102 040

RICK ALLEN   D   (A   JOE ELLIOTT   V   (A

DEFENDERS

D40C

( ) PLAY THE BIG ONES(WILD WEEK END)	19	WORLD PACIFIC	US	WP 1810
( ) DRAG BEAT	19	DEL FI	US	DFLP 1242

JACK DeJOHNETTE

D40D

JACK De JOHNETTE	D	(ALL
KEITH JARRETT	PNO	(I
JOHN ABERCROMBIE	G	(
MIROSLAV VITOUS		(
GARY PEACOCK		(I

( ) COSMIC CHICKEN	19	PRESTIGE		10094
( ) THE DE JOHNETTE COMPLEX	1968	MILESTONE		9022
( ) HAVE YOU HEARD	19	MILESTONES		9029
( ) JACK DE JOHNETTE	19	ECM		ECM 1021
( ) SORCERY	19	MILESTONE		9061
( ) SORCERY	19	PRESTIGE		10081
( ) UNTITLED	1976	ECM		ECM 1074
( ) PICTURES	1977	ECM		ECM 1079
( ) NEW RAGS	1977	ECM		ECM 1103
( ) GATEWAY	1975	ECM		ECM 1061
(I) TALES OF ANOTHER	1977	ECM		ECM 1101
( ) NEW DIRECTION	1978	ECM		ECM 1118

DESMOND DEKKER

D41

DESMOND DEKKER	V	(ALL
WITH		
BARRY HOWARD	V	
SAMMY JONES	V	

(A) ISRAELITES	1975	CACTUS		CTLP 111
(A) ISRAELITES	19	UNI	US	73059
(B) DOUBLE DEKKER	19	TROJAN		TRLD 401
(C) YOU CAN GET IT	19	TROJAN		TRL 146
(D) SWEET 16 HITS	1978	TROJAN	UK	TRLS 154

DELFONICS

D42

WILLIAM HART	V	(ALL
WILBERT HART	V	(ALL
RANDY CAIN	V	(
RITCHIE DANIELS	V	(
MAJOR FARRIS	V	(
BRUCE PETERSON	V	(

(A) LA MEANS I LOVE YOU	1968	BELL	UK	SBLL 106
(B) SOUND OF SEXY SOUL	1969	BELL	UK	SBLL 121
(C) DELFONICS	1971	BELL	UK	SBLL 137
(D) SUPER HITS	1972	BELL	UK	BELLS 204
(D) SUPER HITS	197	PHILLY GROOVE	US	1152
(E) TELL ME THIS IS A DREAM	1973	BELL	UK	BELLS 217
(F) ALIVE & KICKING	1974	BELL	UK	BELLS 245
(G) LET IT BE ME	1975	SOUNDS SUPERB	UK	SPR 90078

DEL VIKINGS

D43

NORMAN WRIGHT	V	(
CORINTHIAN JOHNSON	V	(
DONALD BAKUS	V	(
DAVID LERCHEY	V	(
CLARENCE E QUICK	V	(

COME GO WITH ME	19	DOT	US	DLP 3695
COME GO WITH ME	19	LUNAVERSE	US	LP 1000
COME GO WITH ME	19	CONTOUR	UK	2870 388
AND THE SONNETS	19	CROWN	US	CLP 5368
NEWIES & OLDIES	19	FEE BEE	US	205
SWINGING SINGING RECORD SESSION	19	MERCURY	US	MG 20353
THEY SING THEY SWING	19	MERCURY	US	MG 20314
(EPS)				
COME GO WITH US	19	DOT	US	DEP 1058
DEL VIKINGS	19	MERCURY	US	MEP 35A
THEY SING THEY SWING	19	MERCURY	US	EP1 3362

DELLS

D44

MARVIN JUNIOR	V	(
CHUCK BARKSDALE	V	(
VERN ALLISON	V	(
JOHNNY CARTER	V	(
MIKE McGILL	V	(

THERE IS	19	CADET	US	804
GREATEST HITS	19	CADET	US	824
MUSICAL MENU	19	CADET	US	822
LOVE IS BLUE	19	CADET	US	829
LIKE IT IS	19	CADET	US	837
FREEDOM MEANS	19	CADET	US	50004
SING DIONNE WARWICK	19	CADET	US	50017
SWEET AS FUNK CAN BE	19	CADET	US	
CORNERED DBL	1977	DJM	UK	DJD 28032
BEST OF	1973	CHECKER	US	6467 303
MIGHTY MIGHTY	1975	CHESS	UK	9109 100
OH WHAT A NITE	19	VEE JAY	US	1010
OH WHAT A NIGHT	19	JOY	UK	JOYS 186
NO WAY BACK	19	MERCURY	US	SRM 11084
ITS NOT UNUSUAL	19	VEEJAY	US	1141
FACE TO FACE	19	ABC	US	AA 1113
LOVE CONNECTION	19	MERCURY	US	SRM1 3711
THEY SAID IT COULN'T BE DONE BUT WE DID		MERCURY	US	SRM1 1145
I TOUCHED A DREAM	1980	20TH CENTURY	UK	T 618

DELTA

D45

JUDE ALLEN	K V
TONY LEE	G V
DENNY BALL	B V

EIKE ERZMONEIT   D

D45A
ROD PRINCE

DEMIAN

(A) DEMIAN		19	ABC	US	718

D45B

DEMIAN

(A) ROCK STAR FARM		19	STARBURST		ARC 3301

D45C
MAX DEMIAN   (

MAX DEMIAN BAND

(A) TAKE IT TO MAX		1979	RCA		PL 13273

D46
HERBIE ARMSTRONG	V G	(AB
ROD DEMICK	V G STEEL HCA	(AB
WITH		
GORDON SMITH	G V	(AB
DAVID WATKINS	PNO	(A
SUNNY LESLIE	V	(

DEMICK & ARMSTRONG

(A) LITTLE WILLIE RAMBLE		1971	MAM	UK	MAM 1001
(B) LOOKING THROUGH		1972	A&M 2504	UK	AMLH68098

HENRY SPINETTI	D PERC	(B	TONY KNIGHT	D	(A
ALICE PEPPER	V	(	SUE GLOVER	V	
KAY GARNER	V	(			

D47
SMOKEY ADAMS	V	(A
STEVEN JOHN	D	(A
RAY RHODES	K	(A
SLEEPY JACK JOSEPH	B	(A
W RAPHAEL JOSEPH	G	(A
AYINDE FOLARON	CONGA	(A

DEMON FUZZ

(A) AFREAKA		1971	JANUS	US	JLS 3029
(A) AFREAKA		1971	DAWN	UK	DNLS 3013
(EP) I PUT A SPELL ON YOU		1970	DAWN	UK	DNX 2504

CLARENCE BROOMS CROSDALE TROM	(A		PADDY COREA	WIND	(A

D48
DEMON FORTMAN	V	(AB
STEPHEN NUESCH	K	(B
GEFF HARRISON	V	(
VEIT MARCUS	K	(

DEMON THOR

(A) ANNO 1972		1974	UA	UK	UAS 29393
(B) WRITTEN IN THE SKY		1974	UA	UK	UAS 29496

D48A
IAN DEVLIN	G K
JOHN EVERETT	B V
PHILIP ALLCHIN	G

DENIGH

JOHN NEAGAN   D

D48B
G P LAWSON	B
TOEMAN IRMAK	K
ANDY DOWNER	G

DENIZENS

ROB BRIGHT   D   CLIVE LICHFIELD (SOUND)

D49

SANDY DENNY

SANDY DENNY	V	(ALL	(A) ALL OUR OWN WORK	1968	PICKWICK	UK SHM 813
TONY HOOPER	G V	(A	(B) FOTHERINGAY	1970	ISLAND UK ILPS9125 US A&M4269	
DAVE COUSINS	G V K	(A	(C) SANDY DENNY	1970	SAGA	UK 8153
RON CHESTERMAN	B	(A	(C) SANDY DENNY	1977	NOVA	GERM 6 22968AK
KEN GUDMAND	D	(A	(C) SANDY DENNY (*)	1978	MOONCREST	UK CREST 28
TREVOR LUCAS	G V	(BDF	(D) NORTHSTAR GRASS MAN & THE RAVENS	1971	ISLAND	UK ILPS 9165
JERRY DONAHUE	G V	(BDFG	(D) NORTHSTAR GRASS MAN & THE RAVENS	19	A&M	US 4317
GERRY CONWAY	D	(BDF	(E) SANDY DENNY	1972	ISLAND	UK ILPS 9207
PAT DONALDSON	B V	(BDEFG	(E) SANDY DENNY	1972	A&M	US 4371
LINDA (THOMPSON) PETERS	V	(BE	(F) LIKE AN OLD FASHIONED WALTZ	1973	ISLAND	UK ILPS 9258
RICHARD THOMPSON	G V	(DEFG	(F) LIKE AN OLD FASHIONED WALTZ	1973	ISLAND	US SW 9340
IAN WHITEMAN	K	(D	(G) RENDEZVOUS	1977	ISLAND	UK ILPS 9433
TONY REEVES	B	(D				
BARRY DRANSFIELD	V	(D	(*) HAS 1 EXTRA TRACK			
ROBIN DRANSFIELD	V	(D				
ROYSTON WOOD	V	(D	ROGER POWELL	D (D	LADYBIRDS	V (G
BUDDY EMMONS	STEEL	(D	TIMI DONALD	D (EG	DAVE SWARBRICK	VLN (E
SNEAKY PETE KLEINOW	STEEL	(E	RABBIT BUNDRICK	K (EFG	DAVE PEGG	B (FG
DAVE MATTACKS	D	(FG	DANNY THOMPSON	B (F	ALAN SKIDMORE	(F
IAN ARMIT	B	(F	JEAN ROUSSEL	K (F	DIZ DISLEY	G (F
STEVE WINWOOD	K	(G	JUNIOR MARVIN	G (G	BROTHER JAMES	G (G
JIMMY HAINES		(G	FRANK RICOTTI	G (G	JOHN GILLASPIE	(G
DICK CUTHELL		(G	BILLIE LIVSEY	K (G	BOB WESTON	G (G
JESS RODEN	V	(G	SUE GLOVER	V (G	SUNNY LESLIE	V (G
KAY GARNER	V	(G	CLAIRE TORRY	V (G	BENNIE GALLAGHER	V (G
GRAHAM LYLE	V	(G				

D50

DEODATO

EUMIR DEODATO	K	(ALL	(A) PRELUDE	1973	CTI		CTL 10
JOHN TROPEA	G	(ABCFD	(A) PRELUDE	1976	CTI		CTI 6021
RON CARTER	B	(AB	(B) DEODATO 2	1973	CTI		CTL 17
JOHN GIULINO	B	(BD	(B) DEODATO 2	1976	CTI		CTI 6029
STANLEY CLARKE	B	(AB	(C) IN CONCERT	1974	CTI		CTL 21
JAY BERLINER	G	(A	(C) IN CONCERT	1976	CTI		CTO 6041
BILLY COBHAM	D	(ABD	(D) WHIRLWINDS	1974	MCA	UK	MCG 3518
RICK MAROTTA	D	(BF	(D) WHIRLWINDS	1974	MCA		410021
AIRTO MOREIRA	PERC	(AC	(E) VERY TOGETHER	1976	MCA	UK	MCG 2774
GILMORE DEGAP	PERC	(BD	(E) VERY TOGETHER	197	MCA	US	410
JOHN FROSK		(A	(E) VERY TOGETHER	19	BARCLAY	FR	414004
RUBENS BASSINI	PERC	(BD	(F) LOVE ISLAND	1978	WB	UK	K 56416
RAY BARRETTO	CONGA	(A	(F) LOVE ISLAND	1978	WB	US	BSK 3132
MARVIN STAMM	TPT	(ABD	(G) ARTISTRY	1975	MCA MCF2587	US	457
GARNETT BROWN	TROM	(AB	(H) FIRST CUCKOO	1975	MCA MCF 2728	US	491
WAYNE ANDRE	TROM	(ABF	(H) FIRST CUCKOO	197	BARCLAY	FR	410039
GEORGE STRAKEY	TROM	(A	(I) 2001	19	CTI		CTI 7081
MARKY MARKOWITZ	TPT	(A	(J) NIGHT CRUISER	1980	WB US BSK3467 GERM		56848
BILL WATRONS	TROM	(A					
PAUL FAULISE	HRNS	(A	JOE SHEPLEY	TPT (AB	BILL BUFFINGTON	HRNS (ABDF	
PETER GORDON	HRNS	(A	GERRY CHAMBERLAIN	TROM (F	TONY LEVIN	B (D	
HUBERT LAWS	FLT	(AB	PHIL BODNER	WIND (AD	GEORGE MARGE	WIND (ABD	
ROMEO PENQUE	WIND	(ABDF	BURT COLLINS	HRNS (B	JON FADDIS	HRNS (BD	
VICTOR PAZ	HRNS	(BD	ALAN RUBIN	HRNS (BD	TONY STUDD	HRNS (B	
BROOKS TILLOTSON	HRNS	(BFD	JOE TEMPERLEY	HRNS (BD	LARRY CARLTON	G (F	

(CONTINUED)

DEODATO   D50

RAY GOMEZ	G	(FJ
JIMMY MAELEN	PERC	(FJ
RAY ARMONDO	PERC	(F
VERDINE WHITE	B	(F
JERRY DODGION	FLT	(F
JOHN GATCHELL	TPT	(F
SAM BURTIS	TROM	(DF
JOHN ECKERT	TPT	(D
ARTIE KAPLAN	WIND	(D
GEORGE PARRISH	G	(J
DAVID BRAVO	K	(J
RONALD BELL	SAX	(J
LOU MARINI	SAX	(J

POPS POPWELL	B	(F
CHARLIE CONRAD	PERC	(F
JOE CORRERO	D	(F
PHILIP BAILEY	PERC	(F
JOEL KAYE	FLT	(F
RANDY BRECKER	TPT	(F
TONY PRICE	TUBA	(DF
LARRY SPENCER	TPT	(D
GARY GRANGER	B	(J
PLATINUM HOOK	V	(J
SKIPP INGRAM	B	(J
KEITH O'QUINN	TROM	(J
STRING SECTION		(DJ

HARVEY MASON	D	(F
VICTOR FELDMAN	PERC	(F
AL McKAY	G	(F
GORDON EDWARDS	B	(F
WALLY KANE	FLT	(F
BOB MILLIKAN	TPT	(F
NICK REMO	D	(D
URBIE GREEN	TROM	(D
STEPHEN DANIELS	PERC	(J
SERGIO DIAS	G	(J
VICTOR JONES	G	(J
HARVEY ESTRIN	FLT	(J

DEPRESSIONS   D51

'AMMER SMITH	G	(A					
RICO THE KNIFE	G	(A					
DAVE BARNARD	B V	(AB					
KROBAR GARVEY	D	(AB	ERIC WRIGHT	G V	(B	TONY MAYBERRY	G V (B

(A) THE DEPRESSIONS		1978	BARN	UK	2314 105
(B) IF YOU KNOW WHAT I MEAN(AS D Ps)		1978	BARN	UK	2314 107

DEREK & THE DOMINO'S   D52

ERIC CLAPTON	G V	(AB
CARL RADLE	B	(AB
BOBBY WHITLOCK	K	(AB
JIM GORDON	D	(AB
DAVE MASON	G V	(LIVE
DUANE ALLMAN	G	(A

(A) LAYLA & OTHER ASSORTED LOVE SONGS	1971	ATCO	US	SD2	704
(A) LAYLA & OTHER ASSORTED LOVE SONGS	1971	POLYDOR		2625	005
(A) LAYLA & OTHER ASSORTED LOVE SONGS	1977	RSO US 3801	UK	2671	110
(A) LAYLA & OTHER ASSORTED LOVE SONGS	197	POLYDOR	US		3501
		POLYDOR		2612	014
(B) LIVE IN CONCERT	1973	POLYDOR	UK	2659	020
(B) LIVE IN CONCERT	1973	POLYDOR	IMP	2671	101
(B) LIVE IN CONCERT	197	RSO	US	SO	28800

RICK DERRINGER   D53

RICK DERRINGER	G V	(ALL
VINNY APPICE	D	(CDE
DANNY JOHNSON	G	(CDE
KENNY AARONSON	B	(CDEFG
MYRON GROMBACHER	D	(FG
TASHA THOMAS	V	(C
MAERETHA STEWART	V	(C
NEIL GERALDO	PNO	(G
JIMMY WILCOX	D V	(H
BENJY KING	K V	(H
KASIM SULTON	B V	(G

(A) ALL AMERICAN BOY	1973 BLUE SKY	US 32481	UK	EPC 65831
(B) SPRING FEVER	1975 BLUE SKY	US 33423	UK	SKY 80733
(C) DERRINGER	1976 BLUE SKY	US 34181	UK	SKY 81458
(D) SWEET EVIL	1977 BLUE SKY	US 34470	UK	SKY 81847
(E) LIVE	1977 BLUE SKY	US 34848	UK	SKY 82130
(F) IF YOU WEREN'T SO ROMANTIC	1978 BLUE SKY	US 35075	UK	SKY 82464
(G) GUITARS & WOMEN	197 BLUE SKY	US	UK	SKY 83746
(H) FACE TO FACE	1980 BLUE SKY		UK	SKY 84462

ROGER POWELL	SYN	(G	DONNIE KISSELBACH	B V	(H
TODD RUNDGREN		(G			

ANDY DESMOND   D54

ANDY DESMOND	V G	(AB
RON LAWRENCE	B	(B
NICK TREVISICK	D	(B
TOM KING	V G	(B
PAUL CARTWRIGHT	PERC	(B
BONNIE WILKINSON	V	(B
DEBI DOSS	HCA	(B
BARRY ST JOHN	V	(B
GRAHAM COLLYER	G	(B
SHIRLEY RODEN	V	(B
GINNY KLEE	V	(B

(A) LIVING ON A SHOE STRING		1975	KONK	KONK 103
(B) ANDY DESMOND		1978	ARIOLA	ARL 5001

MICK WEAVER	K	(B	LOZ NETTO	G	(B
DYAN BIRCH	V	(B	FRANK COLLINS	V	(B
NICKY PAYN	HCA SAX(B	KEITH NELSON		BANJO(B
JACK EMBLOW	ACC	(B	IAN LYNN	SYN V(B
DAVE MARKEE	B	(B	TERRY JONES	HRNS (B
NOEL McCALLA	V	(B	GRAHAM SMITH	VLN (B
IAIN WHITMORE	V	(B	LUCY KLEE	V	(B

DESPERATE BICYCLES   D55

DANNY WIGLEY		(A
NICKY STEPHENS		

(A) REMORSE CODE		1980	REFILL	UK	RR6

DESTROY ALL MONSTERS   D56

CARY LOREN		(123
JIM SHAW		(1
MIKE KELLY		(1
LARRY MILLER	G	(234
MIKE DAVIS	B	(34

(1) 1973	(2) 1977	(3) 1977	(4) 1978

NIAGARA		(1	BEN MILLER	SAX	(234
RON ASHETON	G	(34	ROB KING	D	(34

DESTROYERS   D56A

TERRY VISION	V	
DAVE ROBERTSON	B	
TOM WORDSWORTH	G V	

JOHN RIDLEY	G		MARKO FALCINI	D

D57

DETECTIVE   D57

BOBBY PICKETT	B	(A
TONY KAYE	K	(A
MICHAEL DES BARRES	V	(A
JON HYDE	D	(A

(A) DETECTIVE	1977	SWANSONG	US 558417 UK 59405
(B) IT TAKES ONE TO KNOW ONE	1978	SWANSONG	US 558504 UK 59406

MICHAEL MONARCH	G	(A

DETERGENTS   D57A

(A) THE MANY FACES OF THE DETERGENTS	19	ROULETTE	US	25308

DEVIANTS   D58

MICK FARREN	V	(AB
SID BISHOP		(A1
DUNCAN SANDERSON		(A1C
RUSS HUNTER	D	(AB1C
M J McDONNELL		(A
DENNIS HUGHES		(A
PAUL RUDOLPH	G	(AC
STEPHEN SPARKES		(A
DICK HECKSTALL SMITH	SAX	(A
GEORGE		(A
PETE BROWN		(A
KARL DALLAS		(A

(A) DISPOSABLE	1968	STABLE	UK	SLP 7001
(A) DISPOSABLE	1968	SIRE	US	97005
(B) PTOOFF	1969	UNDERGROUND IMPRESARIOS		IMP1
(B) PTOOFF	19	SIRE	US	97001
(B) PTOOFF	1969	DECCA	UK	SKLR 4993
(C) DEVIANTS	1968	TRANSATLANTIC	UK	TRA 204
(C) DEVIANTS	1978	LOGO	UK	MOGO 4001
( ) 33	19	SIRE	US	97016
( ) SCREWED UP(EP)	19	STIFF	UK	LAST 4

TONY FERGUSON		(A	JENNY ASHWORTH		(A
ANDREW JOHNS		(A	CORD REES	B G V(A

DEVILS ANVIL   D58A

(A) HARD ROCK FROM THE MIDDLE EAST	19	CBS	US	9464

D59

JERRY CASALE	B V	(
BOB	G V	(
MARK	K V	(
BOB	G V	(
ALAN	D	(

D59A

KEVIN ROWLAND	V	(
GROEK	D	
PETE WILLIAMS	B	(
JIMMY PATERSON	HRNS	(

D59B

CLIFF DE YOUNG	V	(A
JOE OSBORN	B	(A
VICTOR FELDMAN	PERC	(A
LARRY MUHOBERAC	PNO	(A
DAVID KEMPER	D	(A
GEORGE BOHANON	TROM	(A
VALERIE CARTER	V	(A

D59C

D60

DYAN DIAMOND	V G	(A
CRAIG MAGEE	G	(A
JERRY ACKERMAN	B	(A
CHRIS DARROW	G MAND	(A

D61

MIKE PRINCE	K V	(
JEFF POOLE	D	(
MICHAEL DIAMOND	B	(
RICK SANFORD	V FLT	(
ROGER ROMEO	G V	(A

D62

DAVE SOMERVILLE	V	(AB
MIKE DOUGLAS	V	(B
JOHN FELTON	V	(B
EVAN FISHER	V	(B
BILL REED	V	(A
TED KOWALSKI	V	(Z
PHIL LEAVITT	V	(A

D63

MANU DIBANGO		
ROBBIE SHAKESPEARE	B	(H
VAL DOUGLAS	B	(H
GEOFF CHUNG	B G K	(H
CLYDE BULLARD	B	(H
SLY DUNBAR	D	(H
MIKEY BOO RICHARDS	D	(H
CRUSHER BENNETT	PERC	(H
STICKY	PERC	(H
MIKEY MAO CHUNG	G	(H
WILLIE LINDO	G	(H
LOU MARINI	SAX	(H
ED BYRNE	TROM	(H
MIKE LAWRENCE	TPT	(H
GWEN GUTHRIE	V	(H
YVONNE LEWIS	V	(H

D63A

DICK ST JOHN	V	(
DEE DEE SPERLING	V	(

D63B

GERRY'DICKEY DOO'GRANAHAN	V	(
JERRY GRANT	V	(
HARVEY DAVIS	V	(
AL WAYS	V	(

D64

LEONARD PHILIPS	K V	(B
STAN LEE	G V	(B
BILLY CLUB	V B	(B
KARLOS KABALLERO	D	(B

D65

HANDSOME DICK MANITOBA	V	(ABC
ANDY SHERNOFF	B K V	(ABC
SCOTT KEMPER	G	(
ROSS FUNICELLO	G V	(ABC
RITCHIE TEETER	D V	(BC
TOP TEN	G	(A

D66

BO DIDDLEY(ELIAS McDANIEL	G V	(ALL
JEROME GREEN	MARACAS	
OTIS SPANN	PNO	(
BILLY BOY ARNOLD	HCA	(
FRANK KIRKLAND	D	(

DEVO

(A) ARE WE NOT MEN WE ARE DEVO	1978	VIRGIN	UK	V	2106
(A) ARE WE NOT MEN WE ARE DEVO	1978	WB	US		723
(B) DUTY NOW FOR THE FUTURE	1979	VIRGIN	UK	V	2125

DEXY'S MIDNIGHT RUNNERS

(A) SEARCHING FOR THE YOUNG SOUL REBELS	1980	PARLOPHONE	UK		PCS 7213

STEVE SPOONER	HRNS	(	J B	HRNS	(

CLIFF DE YOUNG

(A) CLIFF DE YOUNG		1975	MCA	US	432

DENNIS BUDIMIR	G	(A	BEN BENAY	G	(A		
BROOKS HUNNICUTT	V	(A	NORMAN KURBAN	PNO V	(A		
DAVID HUNGATE	B	(A	ART MUNSON	G	(A		
OSCAR BRASHAR	TPT	(A	JACKIE KELSO	SAX	(A		

DIAMOND

(A) DIAMOND	19	PARAMOUNT	US	1021

DYAN DIAMOND

(A) IN THE DARK	1978	MCA	UK	MCF 2875

JOSEPH FITZGERALD	K	(A	RANDY WHELPLEY	D	(A

LEGS DIAMOND

(A) FIRE POWER	1978	CREAM	US	CR	1010
(B) LEGS DIAMOND	197	MERCURY	US	SRMI	1136
(C) A DIAMOND IS A HARD ROCK	197	MERCURY	US	SRMI	1191

THE DIAMONDS

POP HITS	19	WING	CAN		12178
AMERICA'S No 1 SINGING STYLISTS	19	MERCURY	US	MG	20309
MEET PETE RUGOLO	19	MERCURY	US	MG	20368
OLD WEST	19	MERCURY	US	MG	60159
STROLL	19	MERCURY	US	EP	13390
DIAMONDS	19	BRUNSWICK	US	EP	71031
(A) 1955/58 (B) 1959>					

MANU DIBANGO

O BOSO	1973	LONDON	UK	SH	8451
MAKOSSA MUSIC	1975	CREOLE	UK	CRLP	503
MANU 76	1976	DECCA	FR	362	001
SUPER KUMBA	1976	DECCA	FR	360	052
AFROVISION	1976	DECCA	UK	SKLR	5296
AFROVISION	1978	ISLAND	US		9526
A L'OLYMPIA	DBL	1978	FIESTA	FR	360 099/100
SUN EXPLOSION	1978	DECCA	UK	SKLR	5303
(H) GONE CLEAR	1980	ISLAND	UK	ILPS	9539

ANSEL COLLINS	K	(H	BARRY ROGERS	TROM	(H		
RANDY BRECKER	TPT	(H	JON FADDIS	TPT	(H		
WAYNE ARMOND	G	(H	PETER ASHBOURNE	K	(H		
ROBBIE LYN	K	(H	CLIVE HUNT	K	(H		
YOLLANDA McCULLOUGH	V	(H	BRENDA WHITE	V	(H		
FRANK FLOYD	V	(H	JOCELYN BROWN	V	(H		

DICK & DEE DEE

YOUNG & IN LOVE	19	WB	US	1500
TURN AROUND	19	WB	US	1538
THOU SHALT NOT STEAL	19	WB	US	1586
SONGS WEVE SUNG	19	WB	US	1623
TELL ME	19	LIBERTY	US	7236

DICKEY DOO & THE DONTS

( ) THE MADISON	196	UA	US	UAS	6094
( ) TEEN SCENE	196	UA	US	UAS	6097

RAY GANGI	V	(	

DICKIES

(A) THE INCREDIBLE SHRINKING DICKIES	1979	A&M	UK	AMLH64742
(B) DAWN OF THE DICKIES	1979	A&M	UK	AMLE68510

CHUCK WAGON	K G	(B	

DICTATORS

(A) GO GIRL CRAZY	1975	EPIC	US 33348	UK	80767
(B) MANIFEST DESTINY	1977	ASYLUM	US 7E1109	UK	53061
(C) BLOOD BROTHERS	1978	ASYLUM		UK	K53083

MARK MENDOZA	B	(B	STU BOY KING	D	(A

BO DIDDLEY

HAVE GUITAR WILL TRAVEL	196	CHECKER	US	2974
IN THE SPOTLIGHT	196	CHECKER	US	2976
IN THE SPOTLIGHT	1964	PYE	UK	NPL 28034
IS A GUNSLINGER	1963	PYE INT	UK	280
IS A GUNSLINGER	196	CHECKER	US	2977
				(CONTINUED)

(CONTINUED)

THE DUCHESS	G̶	(
CHUCK BERRY	G	(
HOWLIN' WOLF	V HCA	(*
MUDDY WATERS	G V	(*
COOKIE LEE	V	(X
RICHARD EVANS	B	(X
CLIFFORD DAVIS	SAX	(X
WILLIE HENDERSON	SAX	(X
GENE BARGE	SAX	(X
STEVE GALLOWAY	TROM	(X
FRANK GORDON	TPT	(X
MURRAY WATSON	TPT	(X
ARTHUR HOYLE	TPT	(X
PHILIP UPCHURCH	G	(X
GERALD SIMS	G	(X
TENNYSON STEPHENS	PNO	(X
DERF REKLAN RAHEEM	CONGA	(X
ROBERT CROWDER	D	(X
BRIAN GRICE	D	(X
MARY ANN STEWART	V	(X
MARYLYN HAYWOOD	V	(X
VIVIAN HARRELL	V	(X
ROY WOOD	B	(X
EDDIE HARDIN	ORG	(X
RAY FENWICK	G	(X
KEITH SMART	D	(X
CHARLES GRIMAR	CONGA	(X
NIGEL GRAINGE	PERC	(X
GREGORY TAYLOR	V	(X
CHARISE TAYLOR	V	(X
JUANITA BUCKNER	V	(X
CRYSTAL BRAKE	V	(X
ANGELA SMITH	V	(X
LYNN MOORE	V	(X

BO DIDDLEY — D66

A LOVER	196	CHECKER	US		2980
IS A TWISTER	196	CHECKER	US		2982
BO DIDDLEY	1963	PYE	UK		28026
BO DIDDLEY	196	CHESS	UK		704
BO DIDDLEY	196	CHECKER	US		2984
BO DIDDLEY	196	CHECKER	US		1431
BO DIDDLEY RIDES AGAIN	1963	PYE	UK		28029
BEACH PARTY	1963	PYE	UK		28032
TWO GREAT GUITARS	1964	PYE	UK		28047
HEY GOOD LOOKING	1964	CHESS	UK	CRL	4002
BO DIDDLEY & COMPANY	196	CHECKER	US		2985
SURFIN' WITH BO DIDDLEY	196	CHECKER	US		2987
SURFIN' WITH BO DIDDLEY	196	MARBLE ARCH	UK	MAL	751
ROAD RUNNER	196	CHECKER	US		2988
16 ALL TIME HITS	1964	PYE INT	UK		28049
16 ALL TIME HITS	196	CHECKER	US		2989
LET ME PASS	1965	CHESS	UK	CRL	4507
HEY BO DIDDLEY	196	PYE	UK		28025
HEY BO DIDDLEY	1967	GOLDEN GUINEA	UK	GGO358	
HEY BO DIDDLEY	1968	MARBLE ARCH	UK	MAL814	
HEY BO DIDDLEY	196	CHECKER	US		2992
500% MORE MAN	196	CHECKER	US		2996
ORIGINATOR	196	CHECKER	US		3001
GO BO DIDDLEY	196	CHECKER	US		3006
GO BO DIDDLEY	196	CHECKER	US		1436
BOSS MAN	196	CHECKER	US		3007
(*) SUPER BLUES BAND	1968	CHECKER	US		3010
BLACK GLADIATOR	196	CHECKER	US		3013
BLACK GLADIATOR	196	CHECKER	US		50004
(X) LONDON SESSIONS	1972	CHECKER	UK	6499	476
(X) LONDON SESSIONS	197	CHECKER	US		50029
GOT ANOTHER BAG OF TRICKS	1973	CHECKER	UK	6467	304
GOT ANOTHER BAG OF TRICKS	197	CHESS	US		2CH60005
GOLDEN DACADE	1973	CHESS	UK	6310	123
ANOTHER DIMENSION	1975	CHECKER	US		50001
20thANNIVERSARY	1976	RCA			1042
20thANNIVERSARY	1976	RCA		APLI	1225
WHERE IT ALL BEGAN	197	CHESS	US		50016
BIG BAD BO	197	CHECKER	US		50047

EPS

CHUCK & BO	1963	PYE	UK	NEP	44009
HEY BO DIDDLEY	1963	PYE	UK	NEP	44014
THE STORY OF BO DIDDLEY	1964	PYE	UK	NEP	44019
IS A LUMBERJACK	1964	PYE		NEP	44031
DIDDLING	1964	PYE	UK	NEP	44036
IM A MAN	1965	CHESS	UK	CRE	6008
ROOSTER STEW	1966	CHESS	UK	CRE	6023
BO DIDDLEY	19	CHESS	UK		5125

DIGA RHYTHM BAND — D67

MICKEY HART	D	(A
JIM LOVELESS	PERC	(A
RAY SPIEGEL	PERC	(A
JOY SCHULMAN	PERC	(A
ARSHAD SYED	PERC	(A
TOR DIETRICHSON	PERC	(A

(A) DIGA RHYTHM BAND	1976	UA ROUND	UK	UAS 29975
(A) DIGA RHYTHM BAND	1976	UA ROUND	US	RXLA 600G

ZAKIR HUSSAIN	PERC	(A	PETER CARMICHAEL	PERC (A
JORDAN AMARANTHA	PERC	(A	VINCE DELEACHO	PERC (A
ASHIM CHAUDHURI	PERC	(A		

RICHARD DIGANCE — D68

RICHARD DIGANCE	G V	(ALL
JOHN O'CONNOR	G V	(ACF
BARRIEMORE BARLOW	D V	(F
RICK KEMP	B V	(F
DOUG MORTER	G V	(CDF
MIKE LEWIS	K	(F
DAVE COOKE	PNO	(C
ENGLISH TAPESTRY	V	(D
PETER CURTIS	B K	(C
NIGEL PEGRUM	PERC	(D
ALEX ATTERSON V HARMONIUM	(D
PAUL RODRIGUEZ	K	(D

(A) PISCES	1971	TRAILER	UK	LER	2025
(B) IN CONCERT 74	1976	TRANSATLANTIC	UK	TRASAM	35
(C) ENGLANDS GREEN & PLEASANT LAND	1974	TRANSATLANTIC	UK	TRA	277
(D) HOW THE WEST WAS LOST	1975	TRANSATLANTIC	UK	TRA	289
(E) TREADING THE BOARDS	1975	TRANSATLANTIC	UK	TRA	306
(F) LIVE AT QUEEN ELIZABETH HALL	1978	CHRYSALIS	UK	CHR	1187
(G) COMMERCIAL ROAD	1979	CHRYSALIS	UK	CHR	1262

ALAN BROOKS	D	(C	PHIL MILNER	B V	(D
MICHAEL CHAPMAN	G	(D	MARTIN JENKINS	BANJO FDL	(D
DIK CADBURY	B V	(D	GERRY MORRIS	B	(D
MIKE BIEVENEU	PNO	(D	JOHN REDPATH	D	(D

DIGNITY — D68A

STONEWALL JACKSON	V	(1
TONY WOOL	D	(1
DANNY EDWARDS	SAX K V	(1
TONY BRIAN	G	(1

(1) 1980					

| COTA | B | (1 | VINCE GORDON | PERC | (1 |
| GERARD ROLFE | G V | (1 | KIERAN BUCKLEY | K | (1 |

DOUG DILLARD — D68B

DOUG DILLARD	BANJO G				

( ) THE BANJO ALBUM	19	TOGETHER	US		1003
( ) DUELLING BANJOS	19	20th CENTURY	US	T	409
( ) DOUGLAS FLINT DILLARD	19	20th CENTURY	US	T	426
( ) HEAVEN	1979	FLYING FISH	US		FF086

DILLARD & CLARK — D69

DOUG DILLARD	BANJO G	(ALL
GENE CLARK	G V	(ALL
DAVID JACKSON	B V	(AB
BERNIE LEADON	G V	(A
JON CORNEAL	D	(B
BYRON BERLINE	FDL	(B
MICHAEL CLARK	D	(A
DON BECK	G HCA	(A
DONNA WASHBURN	V G	(B

(A) FANTASTIC EXPEDITION	1968	A&M	US	AMLS	939
(A) FANTASTIC EXPEDITION	1975	A&M	US	SP	4158
(B) THROUGH THE MORNING	1969	A&M	UK	AML	966
(B) THROUGH THE MORNING	1975	A&M	US	SP	4203
(C) DILLARD CLARK	1975	ARIOLA			86027
(D) KANSAS CITY SOUTHERN	1975	ARIOLA			86436
( ) GRASS ROOTS (½ ALBUM ½BURRITOES)	1972	MAYFAIR	UK	AMLB51038	

DILLARD HARTFORD DILLARD

DOUG DILLARD	BAJO G(A	
ROD DILLARD	(A	
JOHN HARTFORD	(A	
SAM BUSH	MAND (A	
HARGUS ROBBINS	PNO (A	
KENNY MALONE	D (A	
PEPPER WATKINS	V (A	

(A) DILLARD HARTFORD DILLARD	1977	SONET	UK	SNTF 730
(B) GLITTER GLASS	1977	FLYING FISH	US	FF036

JIM COLVARD	G	(A	BUDDY EMMONS	STEEL	(A
HENRY STRZELECKI	B	(A	JEFF GILKENSON	HCA	(A
BENNY MARTIN	V	(A	MICHAEL MELFORD	MAND	(A

THE DILLARDS

DOUG DILLARD	BAN G (ABC	
ROD DILLARD	G (ABCDEFGJ	
DEAN WEBB	MAND (ABCDEFGJ	
MITCH JAYNE	B V (ABCDEFG	
BYRON BERLINE	FDL (CE	
HERB PEDERSEN	BANJO (DE	
BILLY RAY LATHAM	G BANJO(FGJ	
ANDREW BELLING	K (G	
PAUL YORK	D (EFGJ	
COLIN CAMERON	B (G	
GARY ITRI	B (G	
JOHN HARTFORD	FDL (G	
BUCK GRAVES	DOBRO G (G	
DON GALLESE	PERC (G	
BUDDY EMMONS	STEEL (D	
JOE OSBORN	B (D	
TOXEY FRENCH	D (D	
IRV DUGAN	G (G	
DOUG HAYWOOD	B V (J	
GABRIEL KATONA	K (J	

(A) BACK PORCH BLUE GRASS	1963	ELEKTRA	US	EKS 7232
(B) LIVE ALMOST	1964	ELEKTRA	US	EKS 7265
(C) PICKIN' & FIDDLIN'	1965	ELEKTRA	US	EKS 7285
(D) WHEATSHEAF STRAW	1968	ELEKTRA	US	EKS 74035
(D) WHEATSHEAF STRAW	1972	ELEKTRA	UK	K 42045
(E) COPPERFIELDS	1970	ELEKTRA	US	EKS 74054
(E) COPPERFIELDS	1972	ELEKTRA	UK	K 42034
(F) ROOTS & BRANCHES	1972	UA	UK	UAS 29366
(F) ROOTS & BRANCHES	1972	ANTHEM	US	ANS 5091
(G) TRIBUTE TO THE AMERICAN DUCK	1973	UA	UK	UAS 29516
(G) TRIBUTE TO THE AMERICAN DUCK	197	POPPY	US	LA 175
(H) BEST OF THE DILLARDS	1976	ELEKTRA	UK	K 52035
(J) Vs THE INCREDIBLE L A TIME MACHINE	77	SONET	UK	SNTF 743
(J) Vs THE INCREDIBLE L A TIME MACHINE	77	FLYING FISH	US	FF040
(K) DECADE WALTZ	1979	FLYING FISH	US	FF082

JIM GORDON	D	(D	JOHN RAINES	D	(G
LINDA DILLARD	V	(G	JEFF GILKENSON	B V	(J
JOEY SCARBURY	V	(J	JEFF SILVERMAN	G	(J

DILLINGER

DILLINGER	(ALL	
SLY DUNBAR	D (*	
EARL CHINNA SMITH	G (*	
ASTON BARRETT	B (*	
STICKY	PERC (*	
TOMMY McCOOK	HRNS (*	
NOEL BENBOW	D (*	
VIN GORDON	HRNS (*	
TRINITY	V (*	
BOBBY ELLIS	HRNS (*	

TALKING BLUES	1977	MAGNUM		DEAD 1001
TOP RANKING DILLINGER	1977	THIRD WORLD		TWS 919
ANSWER ME QUESTION	1978	THIRD WORLD		TWS 928
MARIJUANA MY BRAIN	1978	JAMAICA SOUND		JSLP 002
LIVE AT THE MUSIC MACHINE	1978	JAMAICA SOUND		JSLP 004
BABYLON FEVER	19	UA	US	UALA 795R
(*) CB 200	1978	ISLAND		9385
BIONIC DREAD	1978	ISLAND		9455

AL DIMEOLA

AL DIMEOLA	G (ALL	
MINGO LEWIS	PERC K(ABCD	
STEVE GADD	D (ABCD	
ANTHONY JACKSON	B (ABCD	
ROBBIE GONZALES	D (1D	
CHICK COREA	K (AD	
LENNY WHITE	D (AB	
STANLEY CLARKE	B (A	
PACO DE LUCIA	G (B	
WILODEK GULGOWSKI	K (1	
PHILLIPE SAISSE	K (D1	

(A) LAND OF MIDNIGHT SUN	1976	CBS	US 34076	UK	81220
(B) ELEGANT GYPSY	1977	CBS	US 34461	UK	81845
(C) CASINO	1978	CBS	US 35277	UK	82645
(D) SPLENDIDO HOTEL	1979	CBS		UK	88468
(1) 1978 UK TOUR					

BARRY MILES	K	(AC	EDDIE COLON	PERRC	(CD1
JAN HAMMER	K	(BD	PATTI BIYAKAS	V	(A
ALPHONSE MOUZON	D	(A	JACO PASTORIUS	B	(A
LES PAUL	G	(D	TIM LANDERS	B	(D1
PETER CANNAROZZI	K	(D	STRINGS		(D

MICHAEL DINNER

MICHAEL DINNER	G V (AB	
WADDY WACHTEL	G V (B	
DAVID FOSTER	K (B	
BILL CHAMPLIN	K V (B	
LAURA ALLEN	V (B	
GARY ROWLES	V (B	
TIM SMITH	V (B	
RICHIE HAYWARD	V (B	

(A) PRETENDER	197	FANTASY	US	9454
(B) TOM THUMB	1976	FANTASY	UK	FTA 3006
(B) TOM THUMB	197	FANTASY	US	9512

CHUCK FINDLEY	TPT	(B	LENNY PICKETT	SAX	(B
DEE MURRAY	B V	(B	NIGEL OLSSON	D V	(B
ALAN ESTES	PERC	(B	DICK HYDE	TROM	(B

DINGOES

BRODERICK SMITH	V HCA (A	
CHRIS STOCKLEY	G (A	
KERRYN TOLHURST	G MAND(A	
NICKY HOPKINS	PNO (A	

(A) FIVE TIMES THE SUN	1977	A&M	UK	AMLH64636

JOHN DU BOIS	B	(A	JOHN LEE	D	(A
GARTH HUDSON	K	(A			

DIODES

PAUL ROBINSON	V
JOHN CATTO	G
IAN McKAY	B
JOHN HAMILTON	D

DION

DION DI MUCCI	V (ALL	
FRED MILANO	V (	
ANGELO D'ALEO	V (	
CARLO MASTRANGELO	V (	
RON FRANGIPANE	PNO (S	
JOE MACK	B (S	
AL ROGERS	D (S	
SAL DITROIA	G (S	
GEORGE DEVENS	PERC (S	
DAVE BROMBERG	G (S	
SELDON POWELL	SAX (S	
MIKE OMARTIAN	K V (*	
LEE SKLAR	B (*	
DAVID KEMPER	D (*	
DEAN PARKS	G (*	
BEN BENAY	G (*	

PRESENTING DION & THE BELMONTS	196	LAURIE	US		2002
DION ALONE	196	LAURIE	US		2004
TOPPERMOST VOL 1	1960	TOP RANK	UK		25/027
WISH UPON A STAR	196	LAURIE	US		2006
RUNAROUND SUE	196	LAURIE	US		2009
RUNAROUND SUE	196	HMV	UK	CLP	1539
LOVERS WHO WONDER	196	LAURIE	US		2012
LOVERS WHO WONDER	196	STATESIDE	UK	SL	10034
DIONS GREATEST HITS	196	LAURIE	US		2013
LOVE CAME TO ME	196	LAURIE	US		2015
TOGETHER WITH BELMONTS	196	LAURIE	US		2016
SONGS TO SANDY	1966	LAURIE	US		2017
15 MILLION SELLERS	1966	LAURIE	US		2019
MORE GREATEST HITS DION	19	LAURIE	US		2022
			(CONTINUED)		

VICTOR FELDMAN	PFRC	(*
GARY COLEMAN	PERC	(*
STEVE BARRI	PERC	(*
CHUCK FINDLEY	TPT	(*
STEVE MADAIO	TPT	(*
NINO TEMPO	SAX	(*
ERNIE WATTS	SAX	(*
STEVE DOUGLAS	SAX	(*
DICK HYDE	TROM	(*
SID SHARP	STRINGS	(*
PHIL EVERLY	V	(*
ORRIN WATERS	V	(*
ANN WHITE	V	(*
LUTHER WATERS	V	(*
CAROLYN WILLIS	V	(*
KERRY CHATER	V	(*
MYRNA MATTHEWS	V	(*
JIM HAAS	V	(*
STORMIE OMARTIAN	V	(*

Title	Year	Label	Country	Catalog
DONNA THE PRIMA DONNA	19	CBS	US	2107
DONNA THE PRIMA DONNA	19	CBS	US	8907
WONDER WHERE IM BOUND	19	CBS	US	9773
TOGETHER AGAIN	1967	ABC	US	599
TOGETHER AGAIN	1967	HMV	UK	CSD 3618
TOGETHER AGAIN	19	B+C	UK	CAS 1007
DION	1969	LONDON	UK	SHP 8390
DION	196	LAURIE	US	2047
SIT DOWN OLD FRIEND	1970	WB	US	WS 1826
YOU'RE NOT ALONE	1971	WB	US	WS 1872
(S)SANCTUARY	1972	WB	US	WS 1945
(S)SANCTUARY	1972	WB	UK	K 46122
SUITE FOE LATE SUMMER	1972	WB	US	WS 2642
LIVE AT MADISON SQUARE GARDENS 1972	1972	WB	US	2664
SUITE FOR LATE SUMMER	1972	WB	UK	K 46199
REUNION	1973	WB	UK	K 46208
BORN TO BE WITH YOU	1975	PHILLES	UK	2307 002
BORN TO BE WITH YOU	197	PHIL SPECTOR	US	002
(*) STREET HEART	1976	WB	UK	K 56279
(*) STREET HEART	197	WB	US	BS 2954
PICK OF THE RADIO GOOD GUYS	1976	SONIC	UK	SON 19
PICK OF THE RADIO GOOD GUYS 2	197	SONIC	UK	SON 004
RETURN OF THE WANDERER	1978	LIFESONG	US	35356
60 HITS BOX SET	19	LAURIE	US	SLP 6000
DOOWOP	19	PICKWICK	US	VSP 3521
EVERYTHING YOU WANTED TO HEAR BY DION	19	LAURIE	US	4002
20 HITS	19		US	ENY 8
DIONS GREATEST HITS	19	CBS	US	31942
OLDIES BUT GOODIES	1979	TELDEC	GER	623646

DIRE STRAITS　　D75

MARK KNOPFLER	G V	(ALL
DAVID KNOPFLER	G V	(AB
JOHN ILLSLEY	B V	(AB1
PICK WITHERS	D	(AB1
B BEAR	K	(B
HAL LINDES	G	(1

ALAN CLARK　　K　　(1

Title	Year	Label	Country	Catalog
(A) DIRE STRAITS	1978	VERTIGO	UK 9102 021 US WB	3266
(B) COMMUNIQUE	1979	VERTIGO	UK	9102 031
(C) MAKING MOVIES	1980	VERTIGO	UK	6359 034
(1) 1980 TOUR				

DIRTY ANGELS　　D76

CHARLIE KARP	V G	(A
DAVID HULL	K B V MANS	(A
GEORGE MAHER	G	(A
JIMMY MAHER	D V	(A

Title	Year	Label	Country	Catalog
(A) KISS TOMORROW GOODBYE	1977	PRIVATE STOCK	UK	PVLP 1019
(A) KISS TOMORROW GOODBYE	197	PRIVATE STOCK	US	PS 2020

RICHARD GOTTEHRER　K V　(A　　　ARTIE KAPLAN　SAX　(A

DIRTY BLUES BAND　　D77

ROD PIAZZA	V HCA	(AB
GLEN ROSS CAMPBELL	G	(A
ROBERT SANAELL	STEEL	(A
PAT MALONE	K	(AB
LES MORRISON	B	(A
JOHN MILLIKEN	D	(A
GREG ANDERSON	B	(B
FREDDIE HILL	TPT	(B

Title	Year	Label	Country	Catalog
(A) DIRTY BLUES BAND	1967	BLUESWAY	US	BLS 6010
(A) DIRTY BLUES BAND	196	STATESIDE	UK	SSL 10234
(B) STONE DIRT	1969	BLUESWAY	US	BLS 6020
(B) STONE DIRT	1969	STATESIDE	UK	SSL 10268

DAVE MITER　D　(B　　　RICK LUNETTA　G　(B
JIMMY FORREST　SAX　(B　　　WILLIE GREEN　SAX　(B

DIRTY DOG　　D77A

Title	Year	Label	Country	Catalog
LET GO OF MY HAND　(EP)	1977	LIGHTNING	GIL	511

DIRTY DOGS　　D77B

Title	Year	Label	Country	Catalog
7 LIVES FOR ROCK'N'ROLL	1979	CBS	UK	83929

DIRTY TRICKS　　D78

TERRY HORBURY	B	(ABC
ANDY BEIRNE	D	(C
KENNY STEWART	V	(ABC
JOHN FRASER BINNIE	G K	(ABC
JOHN LEE	D	(A

Title	Year	Label	Country	Catalog
(A) DIRTY TRICKS	1976	POLYDOR	UK	2383 351
(B) NIGHT MAN	1977	POLYDOR	US 16082 UK	2383 398
(C) HIT & RUN	1977	POLYDOR	US 16104 UK	2383 466

DIXIE CUPS　　D78A

Title	Year	Label	Country	Catalog
(A) CHAPEL OF LOVE	1964	RED BIRD	US	20 100
(B) IKO IKO	196	RED BIRD	US	20 103
(C) RIDIN' HIGH	196	ABC PARAMOUNT	US	ABCS 525

DIXIE DREGS　　D79

ROD MORGENSTEIN	D	(ABC
ANDY WEST	B	(ABC
ALLEN SLOAN	VLN	(ABC
STEVE MORSE	G	(ABC
STEVE DAVIDOWSKI	K	(A

Title	Year	Label	Country	Catalog
(A) FREE FALL	1977	CAPRICORN	US 0189 UK	2429 154
(B) WHAT IF	1978	CAPRICORN	US 0203 UK	2429 165
(C) NIGHT OF LIVING DREGS	1979	CAPRICORN	UK	2429 181

MARK PARRISH　K　(BC

ERROL DIXON　　D79A

ERROL DIXON　(A

Title	Year	Label	Country	Catalog
(A) BLUES IN A POT	19	LONDON	US	P5550

FLOYD DIXON　　D80

FLOYD DIXON　(ALL

Title	Year	Label	Country	Catalog
(A) OPPORTUNITY BLUES	1978	ROUTE 66		KIX1
(B) ROCKIN' THIS JOINT TONITE	1978	JSP	UK	1002
(C) HOUSTON JUMP	1979	ROUTE 66	SWED	KIX11

WILLIE DIXON　　D80A

WILLIE DIXON　B V　(ALL
MEMPHIS SLIM　PNO　(AE

Title	Year	Label	Country	Catalog
(A) WILLIES BLUES	19	PRESTIGE	US	1003
(B) I AM THE BLUES	19	CBS	US	9987
(C) AUX TROIS MAILOTS	19	POLYDOR	US	658148
(D) CATALYST	19	PATHE	FR	064 9603
(D) CATALYST	19	OVATION	UK	QD 1433
(E) AT THE VILLAGE GATE	19			
(F) WHAT HAPPENED TO MY BLUES	19	OVATION		QD 1441
(G) EARTHQUAKE & HURRICANE	19	SPOONFUL	US	

LYN DOBSON　　D81

LYN DOBSON

Title	Year	Label	Country	Catalog
(A) JAM SANDWICH	1974	FRESH AIR		6370 501

D82   DR ALIMANTADO

GREGORY ISAACS	V	(A	(A) BEST DRESSED CHICKEN IN TOWN		1978	GREENSLEEVES	UK	GREL1
HORACE ANDY	V	(A						
JACKIE EDWARDS	V	(A	JAH WOOSH	V	(A	JIMMY RADWELL	V	(A
DROPPY	V	(A						

D83   DR BUZZARD'S ORIGINAL SAVANNAH BAND

CORY DAYE	V	(AB	(A) DR BUZZARD'S ORIGINAL SAVANNAH BAND	1976	RCA	RS 1072	US APLI	1504
AUGUST DARNELL	V B	(AB	(B) DR BUZZARD MEETS KING PENETT		1978	RCA		APLI 2402
ANDY HERNANDEZ	ACC PERC	(AB						
MICKEY SEVILLA	D	(AB	PAULINHO DA COSTA	PERC	(B	SUSANDRA MINSKY	V	(B
DON ARMANDO BONILLA	PERC	(A	STONY BROWDER	V G K	(AB			

D83A   DR DOPO JAM

K POMMER	K G V	(A	(A) FAT DOGS & DANISHMEN		1974	ZEBRA	DENM 2949	012
J KNUDSEN	G	(A						
S SNITKER	HRNS	(A	A GAARDMAN	WIND	(A	J NORDAL	TROM	(A
B C LAUSEN D G VIBES		(A	E WEISGARD	D PERC	(A	V HANSEN	B	(A
LARS BISGAARD	V	(A	BORGE LYSHOLMORTENSEN	V	(A	BIRGIT SMIDT	V	(A
BIRGILE HOLM SORENSEN	V	(A						

D84   DR FEELGOOD

LEE BRILLEAUX	V G HCA	(ALL	(A) DOWN BY THE JETTY		1975	UA	UK	UAS 29727
JOHN B SPARKS	B	(ALL	(B) MALPRACTICE		1975	UA	UK	UAS 29880
FIGURE MARTIN	D	(ALL	(B) MALPRACTICE		1975	CBS	US	34098
WILKO JOHNSON	G V	(ABCD	(C) STUPIDITY		1976	UA	UK	UAS 29990
HENRY McCULLOUGH	G	(1	(D) SNEAKIN' SUSPICION		1977	UA	UK	UAS 30075
JOHN MAYO	G	(EFGHJ	(D) SNEAKIN' SUSPICION		1977	CBS	US	34806
TIM HINKLEY	K	(D	(E) BE SEEING YOU		1977	UA	UK	UAS 30123
BOB ANDREWS	K SAX	(AB	(F) PRIVATE PRACTICE		1978	UA	UK	UAG 30184
BRINSLEY SCHWARZ	SAX	(A	(G) AS IT HAPPENS		1979	UA	UK	UAS 30239
			(H) LET IT ROLL		1979	UA	UK	UAS 30269
			(J) CASE OF SHAKES		1980	UA	UK	UAG 30311
			(1) 1977 TOUR					

D85   DR HOOK & THE MEDICINE SHOW

RAY SAWYER	V G	(ALL	(A) DR HOOK & THE MEDICINE SHOW		1971	CBS	US	30898
			(A) DR HOOK & THE MEDICINE SHOW		1971	CBS	UK	65754
DENNIS LOCORRIERE	V G	(ALL	(B) SLOPPY SECONDS		1972	CBS	US	31622
			(B) SLOPPY SECONDS		1972	CBS	UK	65132
WILLIAM FRANCIS	K	(BGHK	(C) BELLY UP		1973	CBS	US	32270
			(C) BELLY UP		1973	CBS	UK	65560
RICHARD ELSWIT	G	(BGHK	(D) FRIED FACE		1974	CBS	UK	80372
GEORGE CUMMINGS	STEEL	(B	(E) BALLAD OF LUCY JORDAN		1975	CBS	UK	80114
JANCE GARFAT	B	(BGK	(F) BANKRUPT		1976	CAPITOL		11397
JOHN DAVID	D	(B	(G) A LITTLE BIT MORE		1976	CAPITOL		11522
JOHN WOLTERS	D	(GHK	(H) MAKIN' LOVE & MUSIC		1977	CAPITOL		11632
BOB HENKE		(HK	(I) STREET PEOPLE		197	CBS	US	32920
			(J) REVISITED		197	CBS	US	34147
			(K) PLEASURE & PAIN		1978	CAPITOL		11859
			( ) SYLVIAS MOTHER		1977	EMBASSY	UK	31458
			( ) BEST OF		197	CBS	US	34147
			( ) BEST OF	(DBL)	1980	CBS		22102

D86   DR JOHN

Dr JOHN(MAC REBENNACK)	K V	(ALL	(A) DrJOHN AND HIS NEW ORLEANS CONG		19	ACE	US	2020
WITH			(B) GRIS GRIS		1968	ATLANTIC	UK	588 147
ERIC CLAPTON	G	(E	(B) GRIS GRIS		1968	ATCO	US	33234
SHIRLEY GOODMAN	V	(EF	(B) GRIS GRIS		1972	ATLANTIC	UK	K 40168
RONNIE BARRON	V K	(EFL	(C) BABYLON		1969	ATLANTIC	UK	228 018
VICTOR BROX	HRNS K	(E	(C) BABYLON		1969	ATCO	US	33270
P P ARNOLD	V	(E	(D) REMEDIES		1970	ATLANTIC	UK	2400 015
DORIS TROY	V	(E	(D) REMEDIES		1970	ATCO	US	33316
STEVE YORK	B	(E	(E) SUN MOON & HERBS		1971	ATLANTIC	UK	2400 161
CALVIN SAMUELS	PERC	(E	(E) SUN MOON & HERBS		1971	ATCO	US	33362
GRAHAM BOND	SAX	(E	(E) SUN MOON & HERBS		1971	ATLANTIC	UK	K 40250
JIM PRICE	TPT	(E	(F) GUMBO		1972	ATLANTIC	UK	K 40384
JOHN BOUDREAUX	D	(EL	(F) GUMBO		1972	ATCO	US	7006
TAMMY LYNN	V	(EFL	(G) IN THE RIGHT PLACE		1973	ATLANTIC	UK	K 50017
ALVIN BISHOP ROBINSON	G	(FL	(G) IN THE RIGHT PLACE		1973	ATCO	US	7018
ROBBIE MONTGOMERY	V	(FJL	(H) TRIUMVIRATE(BLOOMFIELD HAMMOND)		1974	CBS US 32172	UK	65659
TOMMY FERRONNE	G	(E	(J) DESITIVELY BONAROO		1974	ATLANTIC	UK	K 50035
RAY DRAPER	TUBA V	(E	(J) DESITIVELY BONAROO		1974	ATCO	US	7043
FRED STAEHLE	D PERC	(EF	(K) CUT ME WHILE I'M HOT		1975	DJM UK DJM22019		DJSLM 019
MICK JAGGER	V	(E	(L) HOLLYWOOD KNOW THY NAME		1975	UA	UK	UAG 29902
JONI JONZ	FLT	(E	(L) HOLLYWOOD KNOW THY NAME		1975	UA	US	UALA 552
KEN TERROADE	FLT	(E	(M) ONE LATE NIGHT		19	KARATE	US	5402
CHRIS MERCER	SAX	(E	(N) Dr JOHN SUPERPAH		19	TRIP	US	3507
WALTER DAVIS	PNO	(E	(O) ZU ZU MAN		19	TRIP	US	9518
BOBBY WHITLOCK	V	(E	(P) Dr JOHN		19	SPRINGBOARD	US	4018
JIM GORDON	PERC	(E	(Q) 16 GREATEST HITS		19	TRIP	US	TOP 16/1
JESSIE BOYCE	B	(E	(R) CITY LIGHTS		1978	HORIZON		AMLJ 732
WAYNE JACKSON	HRNS	(E	( ) ANYTIME ,ANYPLACE		19	BAROMETER	US	BRM67001
BOB EZRIN	K V	(L						
ROGER HOPPS	TPT	(E	FREEMAN BROWN	PERC	(E	ANDREW LOVE	SAX	(E
BOBBY KEYS	SAX	(E	CARL RADLE	B	(E	JULIUS FARMER	B	(L
JACK HALE	TROM	(E	ED LOGAN	SAX	(E	JAMES MITCHELL	SAX	(E
RON JOHNSON	B	(E	ED HOERNER	TPT	(E	JERRY JUMONVILLE	SAX	(E
MELVIN LASTIE	CORNET	(F	SIDNEY GEORGE SAX HCA		(F	LEE ALLEN	SAX	(F
DAVID LASTIE	SAX	(F	MOE BECHAMIN	SAX V	(F	HAROLD BATTISTE	WIND	(F
KEN KLIMAK	G	(F	JIMMY CALHOUN	B	(F	RICHARD WASHINGTON	PERC	(F
JESSIE SMITH	V	(FJ	ALLEN TOUSSAINT	K	(GJ	DAVID SPINOZZA	G	(G
RALPH McDONALD	PERC	(G	GARY BROWN	SAX	(GJ	LEO NOCENTELLI	G	(GJ

DR JOHN
D86

ARTHUR NEVILLE	K	(GJ	GEORGE PORTER	B	(GJ	JOSEPH MODELISTE	D	(GJ
STEVE HUNTER	G	(L	THE METERS		(J	MARK COLBY	WIND	(J
WHIT SIDENER	SAX	(J	KEN FAULK	HRNS	(J	PETER GRAVES	HRNS	(J
JOHNNY BADANJEK	D	(L	LEROY COOPER	SAX	(J	ERNIE WATTS	SAX	(L
CHAUNCEY WELSH	TROM	(L	BOBBY TORRES	CONGAS	(L	VENETTA FIELDS	V	(L
WARREN LUENING	TPT	(L	JAMES SMITTY SMITH	G	(L	CLIFFORD SOLOMON	SAX	(L
KENNY ASCHER	K	(L	TOMMY VIG	PERC	(L	STEVE GADD	D	(Q
WILL LEE	B	(M	RICHARD TEE	K	(Q	HUGH McCRACKEN	G	(Q
JOHN TROPEA	G	(Q	ARTHUR JENKINS	PERC	(Q			

DR K's BLUES BAND
D86A

GEOFF KRIVIT	G B	(A	(A) DR K'S BLUES BAND		19	WORLD PACIFIC	US	WPS 21903
ROGER ROLT	G	(A						
DR K(RICHARD KAY)	PNO	(A	HAROLD VICKERS	B	(A	ERIC PEACHEY	D	(A
MICK HASSE	V HCA	(A						

DR MARIGOLDS PRESCRIPTION
D87

DAVE		(A) PICTURES OF LIFE		1969	MARBLE ARCH	UK	MALS 1222
FRED RADLEY		(B) HELLO GIRL		1973	SANTA PONSA	UK	PNL 501
ALAN							
BILL							

DR ROSS
D87A

CHARLES ISAIAH 'DOCTOR' ROSS G V HCA	(A) DOCTOR ROSS THE HARMONICA BOSS		19	FORTUNE	US	3011
	(B) DOCTOR ROSS		19	TESTAMENT	US	2206
	(C) THE HARMONICA BOSS		197	BIG BEAR	UK	BEAR2
	(D) JIVIN' THE BLUES		197	BIG BEAR	UK	BEAR15

DR STRANGELY STRANGE
D88

TIM GOULDING	V K	(B	(A) KIP OF THE SERENES		1969	ISLAND	UK	ILPS 9106
TIM BOOTH	V G	(B	(B) HEAVY PETTING		1970	VERTIGO	UK	6360 009
IVAN PAWLE	V B K	(B						
JOHNNY MOYNIHAN	BAZ	(B	DAVE MATTACKS	D	(B	GARY MOORE	G	(B
JAY MYRDAL	GLOCK	(B	HEATHER WOOD	V	(B	ANDY IRVINE	MAND	(B
LINUS	PERC	(B	JOHANNA	V K	(B	ANNIE CHRISTMAS	V K	(B
BRENDAN SHIELS	B	(B						

DR WEST'S MEDICINE SHOW & JUNK BAND
D88A

NORMAN GREENBAUM	(A) THE EGGPLANT THAT ATE CHICAGO	19	GOGO	US	17001

DOCTORS OF MADNESS
D89

DAVE VANIAN	V	(ABC2	(1) 1978 (2) 1978 APRIL	(3) MAY 1978>				
KID STRANGE		(ABC123	(A) LATE NIGHT MOVIES		1976	POLYDOR	UK	2383 378
STONER		(123	(B) FIGMENTS OF EMANCIPATION		1976	POLYDOR	UK	2383 403
PETER DILEMMA		(ABC123	(C) SONS OF SURVIVAL		1978	POLYDOR	UK	2383 472
JILL MACKINTOSH	V	(B						
URBAN BLITZ	G VLN	(ABC	CLAIRE TORRY	V	(B	STEPHANIE DE SYKES	V	(B

DODGERS
D90

JOHN WILSON	G B V	(A	(A) LOVE ON THE REBOUND		1978	POLYDOR	UK	2391 379
ROGER LOMAS	G B V	(A	(A) LOVE ON THE REBOUND		1978	POLYDOR	US	PD1 6174
BOB JACKSON	K V G	(A	(A) LOVE ON THE REBOUND		1978	POLYDOR	UK	2383 513
PAUL HOOPER	D V	(A						

DOG SOLDIER
D91

KEEF HARTLEY	D	(A	(A) DOG SOLDIER		1975	UA	UK	UAS 29769
MILLER ANDERSON	G V	(A1	(A) DOG SOLDIER		1975	UA	US	UALA 405
PAUL BLISS	B	(A1	(1) LATER LINE UP					
MEL SIMPSON	K	(A1						
DEREK GRIFFITHS	G	(A1	ERIC DILLON	D	(1			

BUNK DOGGER
D92

BUNK DOGGER	V G SYN	(A	(A) FIRST OFFENCE		1978	RCA	UK	PL 25138
ANDY ROBERTS	G	(A						
JIMMY JEWELL	SAX	(A	LESLEY DUNCAN	V	(A	TONY BURROWS	V	(A
PETE WINGFIELD	K	(A	ALAN HODGE	G	(A	IAN WILSON	G	(A
NACHUM HEIMAN	ACC	(A	RUSSELL STONE	V	(A	TOM WILDY	SAX	(A
PHIL CURTIS	B	(A	JOHN ATKINSON	B	(A	MARY CARROLL	V	(A
FRANK RICOTTI	PERC	(A	LUIS JARDIM	PERC	(A	ALUN EDEN	D	(A
TONY COX	PNO	(A	GERRY CONWAY	D	(A			

DOGGEREL BANK
D93

WILLIAM BEALBY WRIGHT V		(AB	(A) SILVER FACES		1973	CHARISMA	UK	CAS 1079
SUSAN BAKER VLN MAND HCA		(AB	(B) MISTER SKILLICORN DANCES		1975	CHARISMA	UK	CAS 1102
GARY BOYLE	G	(AB						
ANDREW STEELE	D	(A	TONY CAMPO	B	(A	RAY COOPER	PERC	(A
JIM PARKER	K	(AB	TOM PARKER	K	(AB	RICHARD MORCOMBE	G	(B
DAVE OLNEY	B	(B	MARTIN FRY	TUBA	(B	JONATHAN ADAMS	V	(B
JOE CASTALDINI	BASSOON	(B	TINA CHARLES	V	(B	CLAIRE TORRY	V	(B
MARTIN JAY	V	(B						

DOLL
D94

MARION VALENTINE	V G	(A	(A) LISTEN TO THE SILENCE		1979	BEGGARS BANQUET		BEGA12
DENNIS HAINES	K	(A						
JAMES WEST-ORAM	G	(A	CHRISTOPHER YIANNI	B	(A	PAUL TURNER	D	(A

DOLL BY DOLL
D95

JACKIE LEVEN	V G	(AB	(A) REMEMBER		1979	AUTOMATIC		K 56618
JO SHAW	V G K	(AB	(B) GYPSY BLOOD		1979	AUTOMATIC		K 56755
TONY WAITE	V B	(B						
ROBIN SPREAFICO	B	(A	DAVID McINTOSH	V D	(AB	B J COLE		STEEL G(B
GRAHAM PRESKETT	VLN K	(B						

DOLPHIN
D95A

ROY DAVIES	K	(A	(A) GOODBYE		1977	PRIVATE STOCK		PVLP 1055
GERRY CONWAY	D	(A	(B) MOLECULES		1980	GALE		LP 02
JOHN GIBLIN	B	(A						
JIMMY JEWELL	SAX	(A	ROGER CHURCHYARD	VLN	(A	PAUL CARMAN	B BANJO V	(A
GLEN LEFLEUR	D	(B	DAVE ROSE	SYN	(B	PRESTON HEYMAN	D	(B

FATS DOMINO

ANTOINE 'FATS' DOMINO PNO V(ALL
WITH

LEE ALLEN	SAX	DAVE BARTHOLOMEW	TPT	SMOKEY JOHNSON	D
JOE HARRIS	SAX	HERB HARDESTY	SAX	ALVIN RED TYLER	SAX
CLARENCE HALL	SAX	ERNEST McLEEN	G	FRANK FIELDS	B
EARL PALMER	D	WENDEL DUCONGE	SAX	ROBERT BUDDY HAGANS	SAX
WALTER NELSON	G	BILLY DIAMOND	B	CORNELIUS COLEMAN	D
HARRISON VERRETT	G	JUSTIN ADAMS	G	CHARLES WILLIAMS	D
WALDRON JOSEPH	TROM	CLARENCE FORD	SAX	ROY MONTRELL	G
JIMMY DAVIS	B	FREDRICK KEMP	SAX	FRED SHEPPARD	SAX
WALTER LASTIE	D	WALTER KIMBLE	SAX	ROGER HAYWARD LOUIS	SAX
DAVID DOUGLAS	B	MORRIS SIMON	SAX	THOMAS JOHNSON	TPT
CARLTON MACWILLIAMS	B	JOSEPH JOHNSON	D		

LPS

		US	US	US RI	UK	UK RI	UK
CARRY ON ROCKIN	19	IMPERIAL	9004		LONDON		2041
ROCK AND ROLLIN'	19	IMPERIAL	9009	12387	LONDON		2028
THIS IS FATS DOMINO	1956	IMPERIAL	9028	12389	LONDON		2073
HERE STANDS FATS DOMINO	1957	IMPERIAL	9038	12390	LONDON		2052
THIS IS FATS	1958	IMPERIAL	9040	12391	LONDON		2087
FABULOUS MR D	1958	IMPERIAL	9055	12394	LONDON		2135
FATS DOMINO SWINGS	19	IMPERIAL	9062	12091			
LETS PLAY FATS DOMINO	1959	IMPERIAL	9065		LONDON		2223
FATS DOMINO SINGS	1960	IMPERIAL	9103	12103			
A LOT OF DOMINO'S	1960	IMPERIAL	9127	12066	LONDON		2312
I MISS YOU SO	1961	IMPERIAL	9138	12398	LONDON		2364
LET THE 4 WINDS BLOW	1961	IMPERIAL	9153	12073	LONDON		2420
WHAT A PARTY	1961	IMPERIAL	9164		LONDON		2426
TWISTIN' THE STOMP	1962	IMPERIAL	9170		LONDON		2447
JUST DOMINO	1963	IMPERIAL	9206				
LETS DANCE	1963	IMPERIAL	9239				
HERE HE COMES AGAIN	1963	IMPERIAL	9248				
WALKING TO NEW ORLEANS	1963	IMPERIAL	9227	12227	LONDON		8084
HERE COMES FATS	1963	ABC	455		HMV		1690
FATS ON FIRE	1963	ABC	479		HMV		1740
GETAWAY WITH FATS	1966	ABC	510		HMV		1821
FANTASTIC FATS	196	ABC			STATESIDE		10240
FATS DOMINO	196	SUN	5103				
AINT THAT A SHAME	19	SUN	5130				
WHEN IM WALKING	19	HARMONY	11343				
FATS DOMINO	19	GRAND AWARD	267				
FATS DOMINO	19	EVEREST	280				
TROUBLE IN MIND	196	SUN	5200				
FATS IS BACK	1968	REPRISE	6304		VALIANT		107
FATS	1970	REPRISE	6439				
MILLION SELLERS	1962	IMPERIAL	9195	12195	LIBERTY	3303	83023
MILLION SELLERS VOL 2	19				LIBERTY	3046	83024
MILLION SELLERS VOL 3	19				LIBERTY		83101
FAT SOUND	19				LIBERTY		83142
'65	1965	MERCURY	20070(M) 62039				
VERY BEST OF	19	UA	223	380	LIBERTY		83331
SOUTHWIND USA	19	MERCURY	21065 (M)61065(S)				
RARE DOMINO'S	19				LIBERTY		83174
30 HITS	19	UA	104				
COOKING WITH FATS	1966	UA	122		UA		60061/2
BE MY GUEST	1971				SUNSET		50252
RARE DOMINOS VOL 2	1972				UA		29152
LEGENDARY MASTERS (DBL)	1972	UA	9958		UA		60015/6
PLAY IT AGAIN FATS	1973				UA		29467
LIVE IN LAS VEGAS	1973				PHILIPS		6336 217
LIVE AT MONTREUX	1974				ATLANTIC		K 50107
FATS DOMINO STORY (DBL)	1974				LIBERTY		83456/7
LIVE IN NEW YORK	1976				PHILIPS		6336 275
20 GREATEST HITS	1976				UA		29967
STAR COLLECTION	19				WB MIDI		MD2 4006
BLUEBERRY HILL	19	PICKWICK	3111				
MY BLUE HEAVEN	19	PICKWICK	3295				
STORY VOL1	1977				UA		30067
STORY VOL2	1977				UA		30068
STORY VOL 3	1977				UA		30069
STORY VOL 4	1977				UA		30070
STORY VOL 5	1977				UA		30117
STORY VOL 6	1977				UA		30118
LIVE IN EUROPE	1978				UA		30121
SLEEPING ON THE JOB	1979	POLYDOR	PD 3215		SONET		SNTF 793
GOLDEN GREATS	1979				HAMMER		HMR 9002

DON & DEWEY

DON 'SUGARCANE' HARRIS VLN(AB	(A) DON & DEWEY			19	SPECIALTY	UK	SNTF 5006
DEWEY TERRY K V (AB	(B) THEY'RE ROCKIN TILL MIDNIGHT			19	SPECIALTY	US	SPS 2131
PLAS JOHNSON SAX							
JACKIE KELSO SAX (	RENE HALL	B	(	EARL PALMER	D	(	
PETE SMITH B (	SONNY GILLETTE	D	(				

RAL DONNER

RAL DONNER	V	(ALL	( ) TAKIN CARE OF BUSINESS 196	GONE US	5012
			( ) TAKIN CARE OF BUSINESS VOL1	19 RONDO	US RLP 22436
			( ) TAKIN CARE OF BUSINESS VOL2	19 RONDO	US RLP 22437
			( ) ELVIS SCRAPBOOK 1977	GONE US	5033
			( ) YOU DONT KNOW WHAT YOU GOT	1978 PYE	UK NSPL28269

DONOVAN LEITCH	V G HCA	(ALL	(A) WHAT'S BIN DID		1965	PYE		UK	NPL 18117
WITH			(A) WHAT'S BIN DID		1968	MARBLE ARCH		UK	MAL 795
LESLEY DUNCAN	V	(QL	(B) CATCH THE WIND		1965	HICKORY		US	123
SUZI QUATRO	V	(Q	(B) CATCH THE WIND		1971	HALLMARK		UK	HMA 200
VALERIE CARRINGTON	V	(Q	(C) FAIRYTALE		1965	PYE		UK	NLP 18128
JILL UTTING	V	(Q	(C) FAIRYTALE		1965	HICKORY		US	127
NICK CURTIS	V	(Q	(C) FAIRYTALE		1969	MARBLE ARCH		UK	MAL 867
CARY WILSON	V	(Q	(D) SUNSHINE SUPERMAN		1967	PYE		UK	NPL 18181
GAYNOR STEWART	V	(Q	(D) SUNSHINE SUPERMAN		1966	EPIC		US	BN 26217
JULIE FORSYTHE	V	(Q	(E) THE REAL DONOVAN		1966	HICKORY		US	LP 135
LESLIE ASH	V	(Q	(F) MELLOW YELLOW		1967	EPIC		US	BN 26239
JOHN McCARTHY	V	(Q	(G) FOR LITTLE ONES		1967	EPIC		US	BN 26350
LESLIE FYSON	V	(Q	(H) WEAR YOUR LOVE LIKE HEAVEN		1967	EPIC		US	BN 26349
CHRIS SPEDDING	V	(Q	(I) UNIVERSAL SOLDIER		1967	MARBLE ARCH		UK	MAL 718
COZY POWELL	D	(Q	(J) IN CONCERT		1968	PYE		UK	NSPL18237
ALAN WHITE	D	(Q	(J) IN CONCERT		1968	EPIC		US	BN 26386
CLIVE CHAMAN	B	(Q	(DJ) IN CONCERT/SUNSHINE SUPERMAN(DBL)		19	EPIC		US	33731
DENNIS WALL	B	(Q	(K) HURDY GURDY MAN		1968	EPIC		US	BN 26420
PHIL CHEN	B	(Q	(L) BARABAJAGAL		1968	EPIC		US	BN 26481
JOHN BUNDRICK	K	(Q	(KL) HURDY GURDY/BARABAJAGAL(DBL)		19	EPIC		US	33734
BOBBY KEYS	SAX	(Q	(M) FROM A FLOWER TO A GARDEN(DBL)		1968	PYE		UK	NSPL20000
JIM HORN	SAX	(Q	(M) FROM A FLOWER TO A GARDEN(DBL)		1968	EPIC		US	B2N 171
PETE HALLING	VLN	(Q	(N) LIKE IT IS		1968	HICKORY		US	143
JACK EMBLOW	ACC	(Q	( ) GREATEST HITS		1969	PYE		UK	NSPL18283
TONY CARR	PERC	(GJLQ	( ) GREATEST HITS		1969	EPIC		US	BN 26836
RONNIE LEAHY	K	(V	( ) BEST OF DONOVAN		19	HICKORY		US	149
NICK SOUTH	B	(V	( ) DONOVAN P LEITCH		19	JANUS		US	3022
COLIN ALLEN	D	(V	( ) WORLD OF DONOVAN		1969	MARBLE ARCH		UK	MAL 1168
ISAAC GUILLORY	G	(V	( ) WORLD OF DONOVAN		19	EPIC			66289
JOHNNY CHRISTOPHER	G	(T	( ) WORLD OF DONOVAN		19	EPIC			64494/5
DAVID BRIGGS	K	(T	( ) WORLD OF DONOVAN		19	EPIC		US	31210
HARVEY THOMPSON	HRNS	(T	(O) OPEN ROAD		1970	DAWN		UK	DNLS 3009
HARRISON CALLOWAY	HRNS	(T	(O) OPEN ROAD		1970	EPIC		US	30125
BEN CAULEY	HRNS	(T	( ) GOLDEN HOUR		1971	PYE		UK	GH 506
CHARLIE ROSE	HRNS	(T	(P) H M S DONOVAN (DBL)		1971	DAWN		UK	DNLD 4001
RONNIE EADES	HRNS	(T	( ) COLOURS		1972	HALLMARK		UK	HMA 241
BUFFY SE MARIE	V	(T	(Q) COSMIC WHEELS		1973	EPIC		UK	65450
LEA JANE BERINATI	V	(T	(R) ESSENCE TO ESSENCE		1973	EPIC		UK	69050
GINGER HOLLADAY	V	(T	(R) ESSENCE TO ESSENCE		1973	EPIC		US	32800
DAVID HUNGATE	B	(U	(S) LIVE IN JAPAN		1973	EPIC SONY			ECPM 25
MARY HOLLADAY	V	(U	(T) 7 TEASE		1974	EPIC		UK	69104
FLORENCE WARNER	V	(T	(T) 7 TEASE		1974	EPIC		US	33245
BYRON WARNER	V	(T	(T) 7 TEASE		1974	EPIC		NL	80531
WILTON FELDER	B	(U	( ) DONOVAN		1974	JOKER		IT	13730
KLAUS VOORMANN	B	(U	( ) DONOVAN		197	ARISTA		US	4143
LELAND SKLAR	B	(U	( ) DONOVAN		19	VOGUE		FR	687
JIM KELTNER	D	(U	(U) SLOW DOWN WORLD		1976	EPIC		UK	86011
DOUG DAVIS	CELLO	(U	(U) SLOW DOWN WORLD		1976	EPIC		US	33945
TOM SCOTT	WIND	(U	(U) SLOW DOWN WORLD		1976	EPIC		NL	81371
DAVID FOSTER	K	(U	(V) DONOVAN		1977	RAK		UK	SRAK 528
EMIL RICHARDS	PERC	(U	(W) DONOVAN FILE		1977	PYE		UK	FILD 004
BOBBYE HALL	PERC	(U	( ) TROUBADOUR		19	MODE		IMP	MD 9034
CHUCK FINDLEY	HRNS	(U							
PHILLIP DONNELLY	G	(U							

JESSE ED DAVIS	G	(U	LEW McCREARY	HRNS	(U	B J COOK	V	(U
DONNY GERRARD	V	(U	ED WHITTING	V	(U	JENNETTE CLINGER	V	(U
STACY JO CLINGER	V	(U	ALLAN DELORY	V	(U	RON HICKLIN	V	(U
JENNIFER HICKLIN	V	(U	SUSIE IVES	V	(U	JOHN MERLINO	V	(U
MAXINE WILLARD	V	(U	JULIA TILLMAN	V	(U	CLIFF BARTON	B	(H
JACK BRUCE	B	(H	MIKE O'NEIL	K	(H	KEITH WEBB	D	(H
CANDY JOHN CARR	PERC	(GH	HAROLD McNAIR	FLT	(GHJL	MIKE CARR	VIBES	(H
ERIC LEESE	G	(H	BRIAN LOCKING	B	(A	SKIP ALLEN	D	(A
GYPSY DAVE	KAZOO	(H	DANNY THOMPSON	B	(L	ALAN HAWKSHAW	PNO	(L
MADELINE BELL	V	(L	JEFF BECK GROUP		(L	KEN BALDOCK	B	(G

LONNIE DONEGAN	BANJ V G	(ALL	(A) SHOWCASE		1956	PYE NIXA		UK	NPT 19012
			(A) SHOWCASE		1968	MARBLE ARCH		UK	MAL 797
WITH			(B) LONNIE		195	PYE NIXA		UK	NPT 19027
DENNY WRIGHT	G	(A	(C) TOPS WITH LONNIE		19	PYE		UK	NPL 18034
MICKY ASHMAN	B	(A	(D) RIDES AGAIN		19	PYE		UK	NPL 18043
NICK NICHOLLS	D	(A	(D) RIDES AGAIN		1969	MARBLE ARCH		UK	MAL 1153
DAVE WINTOUR	B	(T	(E) MORE TOPS WITH LONNIE		1961	PYE		UK	NPL 18063
RAY COOPER	PERC	(T	(F) SING HALLELUJAH		1962	PYE		UK	NPL 18073
HENRY SPINETTI	D	(T	(F) SING HALLELUJAH		19	ABC		US	433
RINGO STARR	D	(T	(G) GOLDEN AGE OF DONEGAN		1962	GOLDEN GUINEA		UK	GGL 0135
NICKY HOPKINS	K	(T	(G) GOLDEN AGE OF DONEGAN		1965	MARBLE ARCH		UK	MAL 636
BRUCE GARY	D	(T	(H) GOLDEN AGE OF DONEGAN VOL 2		1963	GOLDEN GUINEA		UK	GGL 0170
GARY BROOKER	K	(T	(H) GOLDEN AGE OF DONEGAN VOL 2		1967	MARBLE ARCH		UK	MAL 698
FRANK GIBSON	D	(T	(I) FOLK ALBUM		1965	PYE		UK	NPL 18126
PETE WINGFIELD	K	(T	(I) FOLK ALBUM		1967	GOLDEN GUINEA		UK	GGL 0382
JIM KELTNER	D	(T	(J) AN ENGLISHMAN SINGS AMERICAN FOLK		19	MERCURY		US	20229
ALAN JONES	B	(T	( ) HITS OF LONNIE DONEGAN		1978	MFP		UK	50389
KLAUS VOORMANN	B	(T	(K) LONNIE POPS		19	DECCA		UK	SKL 5068
MICK RALPHS	G B	(T	(L) GOLDEN HOUR		197	PYE		UK	GH 514
PETER JAMESON	G	(T	(M) GOLDEN HOUR VOL2		1973	PYE		UK	GH 564
RORY GALLAGHER	G	(T	(N) GREATEST HITS		19	RONCO		UK	RTL 2017

(CONTINUED)

D100 (CONTINUED)

ROGER McKEW	G B	(T	(O) MY OLD MANS A DUSTMAN		1971	HALLMARK	UK	HMA	204
ALBERT LEE	G	(T	(P) LONNIE DONEGAN		19	HALLMARK	UK	HMA	252
PETER BANKS	G	(T	(Q) LONNIE DONEGAN		19	DOT	US		3394
BRIAN MAY	G	(T	(R) SKIFFLE FOLK MUSIC		19	ATLANTIC	US		8038
RON WOOD	G	(T	(S) LONNIE DONEGAN FILE	(DBL)	1977	PYE	UK FILD 0111/2		
LEO SAYER	HCA V	(T	(T) PUTTIN' ON THE STYLE		1977	CHRYSALIS	UK	CHR	1158
ZOOT MONEY	PNO	(T	(T) PUTTIN' ON THE STYLE		1977	UA	US	UALA	827
ELTON JOHN	PNO	(T	(T) PUTTIN' ON THE STYLE		197	PHONOGRAM	EUR	6367	618
WILLIAM D SMITH	ORG	(T	(U) SUNDOWN		1978	CHRYSALIS	UK	CHR	1205
COLIN FAIRLEY	D	(T							
MICHELLE PHILLIPS	V	(T							
REV JAMES CLEVELAND	PNO	(T							

D101   DOOBIE BROTHERS

JOHN HARTMAN	D	(ABCDEFH*	(A) DOOBIE BROTHERS	1972	WB	US	1919	UK K	46090
TOM JOHNSTON	G V	(ABCDEFH*	(B) TOULOUSE STREET	1973	WB	US	2634	UK K	46183
DAVE SHOGREN	K B G B	(A	(C) THE CAPTAIN & ME	1974	WB	US	2694	UK K	46217
PAT SIMMONS	G V	(ABCDEFGH	(D) WHAT ONCE WERE VICES	1974	WB	US	2750	UK K	56026
MICHAEL HOSSACK	D	(BCD	(E) STAMPEDE	1975	WB	US	2835	UK K	56094
TIRAN PORTER	B V	(BCDEFGH	(F) TAKING IT TO THE STREETS	1976	WB	US	2899	UK K	56196
KEITH KNUDSEN	D V	(DEFGH	(G) BEST OF	1976	WB	US	2978	UK K	56308
JEFF BAXTER	G	(CDEFGH	(H) LIVING ON THE FAULT LINE	1977	WB	US	3045	UK K	56383
BILL PAYNE	K	(CDE	(J) MINUTE BY MINUTE	1979	WB	US	3193	UK K	56486
MILT HOLLAND	PERC	(D	( ) STAR COLLECTION	1974	MIDI				26022
MIKE McDONALD	K V	(FGHJ	(K) ONE STEP CLOSER	1980	WB			UK K	56824
BOBBY LAKIND	CONGA	(FH	(*) 1970 LINE UP NO ALBUMS						
MARIA MULDAUR	V	(EF							
WAYNE JACKSON	HRNS	(DF	ANDREW LOVE	HRNS	(DF	NOVI		VLA	(D
JAMES MITCHELL	HRNS	(DF	LEWIS COLLINS	HRNS	(F	JACK HALE		TROM	(DF
RITCHIE HAYWARD	D	(F	JESSE BUTLER	ORG	(F	DAN ARMSTRONG		SITAR	(H
NORTON BUFFALO	HCA	(H	VICTOR FELDMAN	VIBES PERC	(EH	ROSEMARY BUTLER	V		(H
MAUREEN McDONALD	V	(H	RY COODER	G	(E	KARL HIMMEL		D	(E
BOBBYE HALL	PERC	(E	SHIRLEY MATTHEWS	V	(E	VANETTA FIELDS		V	(E
JESSICA SMITH	V	(E	CONTE CONDOLI	TPT	(E	PETE CONDOLI		TPT	(E
EDDIE GUZMAN	PERC	(D	ARLO GUTHRIE	HCA	(D				

D102   DOOMED

DAVE VANIAN
RAT SCABIES
CAPT SENSIBLE   HENRI BADOWSKI

D103   THE DOORS

JIM MORRISON	V	(ABCDEFGJMNO	(A) THE DOORS	1967	ELEKTRA	US		74007
RAY MANZAREK	K V	(ALL	(A) THE DOORS	1971	ELEKTRA	UK	K	42012
BOBBY KRIEGER	G	(ALL	(B) STRANGE DAYS	1968	ELEKTRA	US		74014
JOHN DENSMORE	D	(ALL	(B) STRANGE DAYS	1971	ELEKTRA	UK	K	42016
JERRY SCHEFF	B	(GHMN	(C) THE SOFT PARADE	1969	ELEKTRA	US		75005
MARC BENNO	G	(GN	(C) THE SOFT PARADE	1971	ELEKTRA	UK	K	42079
DOUGLAS LUBAHN	B	(BCDN	(D) WAITING FOR THE SUN	1969	ELEKTRA	US		74024
HARVEY BROOKS	B	(CN	(D) WAITING FOR THE SUN	1971	ELEKTRA	UK	K	42041
CURTIS AMY	SAX	(CN	(E) MORRISON HOTEL	1970	ELEKTRA	US		75007
GEORGE BOHANON	TROM	(C	(E) MORRISON HOTEL	1971	ELEKTRA	UK	K	42080
CHAMP WEBB	HRNS	(C	(F) ABSOLUTELY LIVE	1970	ELEKTRA	US	2 9002	
JESSE McREYNOLDS	MAND	(C	(F) ABSOLUTELY LIVE	1971	ELEKTRA	UK	K	62005
JIMMY BUCHANAN	FDL	(C	(G) LA WOMAN	1971	ELEKTRA	US		75011
REINOL ANDINO	PERC	(C	(G) LA WOMAN	1971	ELEKTRA	UK	K	42090
KERRY MAGNESS	B	(D	(H) OTHER VOICES	1971	ELEKTRA	US		75017
LEROY VINEGAR	B	(D	(H) OTHER VOICES	1971	ELEKTRA	UK	K	42104
RAY NEAPOLITAN	B	(EH	(J) WEIRD SCENES INSIDE THE GOLDMINE	1971	ELEKTRA	US	2 6001	
LONNIE MACK	B	(EN	(J) WEIRD SCENES INSIDE THE GOLDMINE	1971	ELEKTRA	UK	K	62009
G PUGLESE	HARP	(E	(K) DOORS 13	197	ELEKTRA	US		74079
JACK CONRAD	B	(HL	(K) DOORS 13	1971	ELEKTRA	UK	K	42062
WILLIE RUFF	B	(H	(L) FULL CIRCLE	1972	ELEKTRA	US		75038
FRANCISCO AQUABELLA	PERC	(H	(L) FULL CIRCLE	1972	ELEKTRA	UK	K	42116
EMIL RICHARDS	PERC	(H	(M) AN AMERICAN PRAYER	1978	ELEKTRA	US		5E502
WOLFGANG MELTZ	B	(H	(M) AN AMERICAN PRAYER	1978	ELEKTRA	UK	K	52111
CHRIS ETHRIDGE	B	(L	(N) GREATEST HITS	1980	ELEKTRA	GERM		52254
CHARLES LARKEY	B	(L	( ) BEST OF	1974	ELEKTRA	US	EQ	5035
BOBBYE HALL	PERC	(L	( ) BEST OF	1974	ELEKTRA	UK	K	42143
CHARLES LLOYD	WIND	(L	( ) STAR COLLECTION	1975	MIDI	UK		22001
LELAND SKLAR	B	(L	( ) STAR COLLECTION 2	1975	MIDI	UK		22019
CHICO BATERA	PERC	(L	(AB) DOORS /STRANGE DAYS	1975	ELEKTRA	GERM		621013
CLYDIE KING	V	(L						
VANETTA FIELDS	V	(L	MELISSA MACKAY	V	(L	BOB GLAUB	B	(M
JOHN SEBASTIAN	HCA	(N						

D104   CHARLIE DORE

CHARLIE DORE		(A	(A) WHERE TO NOW	1979	ISLAND	UK	ILPS 9559

D105   RAY DORSET

RAY DORSET	G V	(A	(A) COLD BLUE EXCURSION	1972 DAWN		UK	DNLS 3033	
MIKE McNAUGHT	PNO	(A						
DAVE MARKEE	B	(A	MIKE TRAVIS	D	(A	JOE RUSH	PERC (A	SUNNY LESLIE	V (A
SUE GLOVER	V	(A	COLIN EARL		(A	JOHN GODFREY	B	(A

D106   LEE DORSEY

LEE DORSEY	V	(ALL	(A) LEE DORSEY	1966	AMY US 8010 UK STATESIDE				10177
ALLEN TOUSSAINT	PNO	(	(B) NEW LEE DORSEY	1966	AMY US 8011 UK STATESIDE				10192
CHARLES WILLIAMS	D	(	(C) YES WE CAN	1970	POLYDOR 2482 280 +			2489	006
ROY MONTRELL	G	(	(C) YES WE CAN	1970	POLYDOR		GERM		244042
NAT PERILLAT	SAX	(	(D) GREATEST HITS	19	SUE ISLAND		UK	ILP	924
			( ) GREATEST HITS	1974	SOUNDS SUPERB		UK	SPR	90045
			( ) BEST OF	19	STARLINE		UK	SRS	5023

```
                          DOUCETTE                                                      D106A
                          (A) MAMA LET HIM PLAY          19    MUSHROOM       US    5009
                          EARLE DOUD                                                     D106B
EARLE DOUD        V PERC(ALL    (A) LYNDON JOHNSONS LONELY HEARTS CLUB BAND  19  ATCO  US  SD33230
ALEN ROBIN                     (B) HONEST TO GOD WE REALLY MEANT IT     19  BRUNSWICK  US  754201
                               (C) WELCOME TO L B J RANCH              19  CAPITOL   US  2423
              STEVE DOUGLAS & THE REBEL ROUSERS                                          D106C
STEVE DOUGLAS      (A        (A) TWIST                    19    CROWN         US    5254
                          DOVELLS                                                        D106D
LEN BARRY         V  (        (A) BRISTOL STOMP           1961  PARKWAY       US    7006
JERRY SUMMERS     V  (        (B) ALL THE HITS            1962  PARKWAY       US    7010
MIKE DENNIS       V  (        (C) FOR YOUR HULLY GULLY PARTY  1962  PARKWAY   US    7020
ARNIE SATIN       V  (        (D) YOU CANT SIT DOWN       1962  PARKWAY       US    7025
DANNY BROOKS      V  (        (E) BIGGEST HITS            196   WYNCOTE       US    9114
                             (F) DISCOTHEQUE             19    WYNCOTE       US    9052
                             (G) CAMEO PARKWAY SESSIONS   1979  LONDON        UK    HAU 8515
                          BRENTON DOWE                                                   D107
BRENTON DOWE      V  (A       (A) BUILD ME UP             19    TROJAN        UK    TRLS  76
                          BOB DOWNES                                                     D108
BOB DOWNES        V WIND(ALL   (A) DREAM  JOURNEY         1970  PHILIPS             SBL 7922
CHRIS SPEDDING    G  (BC      (B) ELECTRIC CITY           1970  VERTIGO       UK    6360  005
RAY RUSSELL       G  (BC      (C) DEEP DOWN HEAVY         1970  M F P         UK    MFP 1412
PETER BILLAM      G  (C       (D) DIVERSIONS              1974  OPENIUM             BDOM  001
ROBERT COCKBURN   V  (C       (E) EPISODE AT 4 AM         1974  OPENIUM             BDOM  002
DEREK HOBBS       D  (C       (F) HELLS ANGELS            1975  OPENIUM             BDOM  003
ALAN RUSHTON      D  (C
HARRY MILLER      B  (BC  LAURIE ALLEN      D  (C   DAVE BROOKS    SAX  (B  HERBIE FLOWERS   B  (B
DARRYL RUNSWICK   B  (B   DENNIS SMITH      D  (B   ALAN RUSHTON   D   (B  CLEN CATTINI    D  (B
DOM FAY           SAX (B   NIGEL CARTER     TPT (B  KENNY WHEELER  TPT (B  BUD PARKES      HRNS (B
HAROLD BECKETT    HRNS (B  IAN CARR         HRNS (B  ROBIN JONES   PERC (B
                          DOWNLINER SECT                                                 D109
DON CRAINE        V  (        ( ) THE SECT               1964  COLUMBIA      UK    33SX 1658
PAUL TITLER       HCA (       ( ) THE SECT               1977  CHARLY        UK    CR  30122
KEITH GRANT       V B (       ( ) THE COUNTRY SECT       1965  COLUMBIA      UK    33SX 1745
TERRY GIBSON      G  (        ( ) THE COUNTRY SECT       1979  CHARLY        UK    CR  30137
JOHN SUTTON       D  (        ( ) THE ROCK SECTS IN      1966  COLUMBIA      UK    SCX  6028
PIP HARVEY        V  (        ( ) THE ROCK SECTS IN      1978  CHARLY        UK    CR  30140
JOHN PAUL JONES   PNO (       ( ) SHOWBIZ                1979  RAW           UK    RWLP 106
MICHAEL SUTTON    PERC D(     ( ) THE DOWNLINERS SECT    19    HMV           SWED  SGLP 534
RAY SONE          HCA (       (EP) NITE AT GT NEWPORT STREET  1964  RBC      UK    001
                             (EP) SECT SING SICK SONGS   1965  COLUMBIA      UK    SEG  8438
                          PETER DOYLE                                                    D110
PETER DOYLE       G V  (A     (A) SKIN DEEP              1977  RCA                 PL  25113
ALAN TARNEY V G B K   (A
GEOFF WHITEHORN   G   (A   PAUL KEOGH        SLIDE (A  TREVOR SPENCER  D  (A
SIMON PHILLIPS    D   (A   B J COLE          STEEL (A  TONY HYMAS      K  (A
MAC TONTOH        TPT (A   JOY YATES         V   (A  JEAN GILBERT    V  (A
VAL STOKES        V   (A
                          DRAGON                                                         D110A
NEIL STORY        D   (       ( ) SCENTED GARDENS FOR THE BLIND  19  PHONOGRAM         6360  903
IVAN THOMPSON     K   (       ( ) SAME OLD BLUES         19    PORTRAIT           32636
MARC HUNTER       V   (       ( ) RUNNING FREE           1977  CBS           UK    33005
ROBERT TAYLOR     G V (       ( ) DRAGON                 1977  PORTRAIT      UK    PRT 82636
KERRY JACOBSON    D   (
PAUL HEWSON       K V ((   TODD HUNTER        B V   (
                          NICK DRAKE                                                     D111
NICK DRAKE   V G PNO  (ALL    (A) FIVE LEAVES LEFT       19    ANTILLES      US    AN   7010
WITH                         (A) FIVE LEAVES LEFT        1969  ISLAND        UK    ILPS 9105
PAUL HARRIS       PNO (AB     (B) BRYTER LAYTER          1970  ISLAND        UK    ILPS 9134
RICHARD THOMPSON  G   (AB     (B) BRYTER LAYTER          1977  ANTILLES      US    AN   7028
DANNY THOMPSON    B   (A      (C) PINK MOON              1972  ISLAND        UK    ILPS 9084
ROCKY DZIDZORNU   PERC (A     (ABC)FRUIT TREE(+ EXTRA TRACKS)  1979  ISLAND  UK    NDSP  100
CLARE LOWTHER     CELLO (A
TRISTAM FRY   D VIBES (A   DAVE PEGG         B    (B  DAVE MATTACKS   D  (B
RAY WARLEIGH      SAX  (B   ED CARTER        B    (B  MIKE KOWALSKI   D  (B
LYN DOBSON        FLT  (B   JOHN CALE        VLA K (B  CHRIS McGREGOR  V  (B
P P ARNOLD        V   (B   DORIS TROY        V    (B
                          PETE DRAKE                                                     D112
PETE DRAKE        STEEL (ALL  FOREVER                    1964  SMASH         US    SRS 67053
                             PETE DRAKE & HIS TALKING GUITAR  19  MOUTAIN DEW  US   S  7042
                             THE HITS I PLAYED ON        1969  AMBASSADORE   US    S  98061
                             PLAYS ALL TIME COUNTRY FAVOURITES  19  HOLLYWOOD  US  HLP  506
                             STEEL AWAY                 1973  CANAAN        UK    CGS  8502
                          THE DRANSFIELDS                                                D113
ROBIN DRANSFIELD  V G  (ABDEG  (A) ROUT OF THE BLUES     1970  TRAILER       UK    LER 2011
BARRY DRANSFIELD  V G FDL (ABCDEF (B) LORD OF ALL I BEHOLD  1971  TRAILER    UK    LER 2026
BRIAN HARRISON    D   (D      (C) BARRY DRANSFIELD       1972  POLYDOR       UK    2383  160
CHARLIE SMITH     V B K (D     (D) THE FIDDLERS DREAM    1976  TRANSATLANTIC UK    TRA  322
                             (E) POPULAR TO CONTRARY BELIEF  1977  FREE REED  UK   FRR  018
                             (F) BOWIN' & SCRAPIN'       1978  TRANSATLANTIC UK    TRA  386
                             (G) TIDEWAVE                1981  TOPIC         UK    12TS 414
                          DREAM                                                          D114
DEKE LEONARD      G V  (A     (A) 1967/ 68
MARTIN ACE        G V  (A
WES REYNOLDS      B    (A   TERRY WILLIAMS     D    (A
```

D115 — DREAMS

JEFF KENT — K G V (A1
DOUG LUBAHN — B V (A1
MARK WHITTAKER — D (1
RANDY BRECKER — HRNS (AB
MICHAEL BRECKER — HRNS (AB
BOB MANN — G WIND V (B
BARRY ROGERS — TROM (AB
TONI TORRENCE — V (B
STEVE GADD — D (2

(1) 1969   (2) LATER LINE UPS

(A) DREAMS	1970	CBS US 30225	UK	64203
(B) IMAGINE MY SUPRISE	1971	CBS US 30960	UK	64597

BILLY COBHAM — D (AB
EDWARD VERNON — V (AB
DON GROLNICK — K (B
ANGEL ALLENDE — CONGA (A
CHUCK RAINEY — B (2

JOHN ABERCROMBIE — G (A
WILL LEE — B (B
STEVE CROPPER — G (B
ALLEN SCHWARZBERG — D (2

D116 — DRIFTERS

CLYDE McPHATTER — V (
BEN E KING — V (
DAVID BAUGHN — V (
ELSBEARY HOBBS — V (
RUDY LEWIS — V (
BILLY LEWIS — V (
CLYDE BROWN — V (
DIONNE WARWICK — V (
JO BLUNT — V (

DEE DEE WARWICK — V (
CISSY HOUSTON — V (
DORIS TROY — V (
JIMMY OLIVER — G (
TOMMY EVANS — V (
CHARLES HUGHES — V (
ANDREW THRASHER — V (

BOBBY HENDRICKS — V (
JOHNNY MOORE — V (
BILL PINKNEY — V (
GERHARD THRASHER — V (
CHARLIE THOMAS — V (
DOC GREEN — V (

( ) CLYDE McPHATTER & THE DRIFTERS	195	ATCO	US		8003
( ) ROCKIN' & DRIFTIN'	1958	ATCO	US		8022
( ) DRIFTERS GREATEST HITS	1960	ATCO	US		8041
( ) SAVE THE LAST DANCE FOR ME	1962	ATCO	US		8059
( ) SAVE THE LAST DANCE FOR ME	1962	ATLANTIC	UK	587	063
( ) I'LL TAKE YOU WHERE THE MUSIC'S..	1965	ATCO	US		8113
( ) I'LL TAKE YOU WHERE THE MUSIC'S..	1965	ATLANTIC	UK	587	061
( ) I'LL TAKE YOU WHERE THE MUSIC'S..	1971	ATLANTIC	UK RI	K40009
( ) GOLDEN HITS	1966	ATCO	US		8153
( ) GOLDEN HITS	1966	ATLANTIC	UK	588	013
( ) GOLDEN HITS	1972	ATLANTIC	UK		K40018
( ) THE DRIFTERS	197	ATLANTIC	UK		K40412
( ) STAR COLLECTION	197	MIDI	UK		20027
( ) THE DRIFTERS NOW	1973	BELL	US		219
( ) LOVE GAMES	1975	BELL UK BELLS246	US		246
( ) THERE GOES MY FIRST LOVE	1975	BELL UK BELLS280	US		260
( ) 24 ORIGINAL HITS	1975	ATLANTIC	UK		K60106
( ) THE DRIFTERS STORY	1975	ATLANTIC	UK		K40565
( ) SAVE THE LAST DANCE	1975	SOUNDS SUPERB	UK	SPR 90083
( ) EVERY NIGHT IS SATURDAY NIGHT	1976	ARISTA	AB		4140
( ) UP ON THE ROOF	1963	ATCO	US		8073
( ) UP ON THE ROOF	1963	ATLANTIC	UK	588	160
( ) OUR BIGGEST HITS	196	ATCO	US		8093
( ) OUR BIGGEST HITS	196	ATLANTIC	UK	587	038
( ) UNDER THE BOARDWALK	1964	ATCO	US		8099
( ) GOOD LIFE	1965	ATCO	US		8103

D117 — DRIFTWOOD

( ) DRIFTWOOD	1970	DECCA	UK	SKL 5069

D118 — JULIE DRISCOLL

JULIE DRISCOLL — V (ALL
WITH
KEITH TIPPETT — K (A
CHRIS SPEDDING — G B (A
BOB DOWNES — FLT (A
JEFF CLYNE — B (A
ELTON DEAN — SAX (A
KARL JENKINS — OBOE (A
DEREK WADSWORTH — TROM (A
JIM CREGAN — G (A

(A) JULIE DRISCOLL	1971	POLYDOR		2480 074
(A) JULIE DRISCOLL	1971	POLYDOR		2383 077
(B) STARPORTRAIT	197	POLYDOR		2625 008
(C) SUNSET GLOW	1976	UTOPIA		UTS 601
(D) JULIE DRISCOLL	19	SPRINGBOARD	US	SPB 4043

NICK EVANS — TROM (A
BUD PARKES — TPT (A
BRIAN GODDING — V G (A
BARRY REEVES — D (A

TREVOR TOMKINS — D (A
STAN SULZMANN — SAX (A
BRIAN BELSHAW — B V (A

D119 — DRIVERS

LAURIE DRIVER — D
CHRIS HALSALL — G V

SID — G   ANDY — B

D120 — DRONES

M J DRONE — V G (A
PETE PURRFECT — D (
STEVE CUNDALL — B (

(A) FURTHER TEMPTATIONS	1977	VALER	UK	VLRP1

GUS CALLENDER — G (

D121 — DRUICK & LORANGE

DWIGHT DRUICK
KIRK LORANGE

(A) DRUICK & LORANGE	1974	GOODEAR		EARLH5001

D122 — DRUID

NEIL BREWER — B (AB
ANDREW McCRORIE SHAND — K (AB
CEDRIC SHARPLEY — D PERC (AB
DANE — G V (AB

(A) TOWARDS THE SUN	1975	EMI	UK	EMC 3081
(B) FLUID DRUID	1976	EMI	UK	EMC 3128

D122A — DRUIDS OF STONEHENGE

(A) CREATION	19	UNI	US	73004

D122B — DRY CITY SCAT BAND

( ) DRY CITY SCAT BAND	19	ELEKTRA	US	7292

D122C — DUCKS

BRUCE BRYMEN — D V (A
KENT HOLWEMAN — G V (A
DENNIS LANIGAN — V K SAX FLT (A

(A) DUCKS	1973	JUST SUNSHINE	US	JSS6

DONALD LUTHER — B V (A
JIM GORDON — D (A

D123 — DUCKS DELUXE

SEAN TYLA — G V K (AABC12
MARTIN BELMONT — G (ABC12
NICK GARVEY — B (AB1
TOM ROPER — D (ABC1
BOB ANDREWS — K (A
GEORGE LARNYOH — SAX (A
PETER VANDER PUIJE — SAX (A
ANDY McMASTERS — K V (1
MICK GROOM — B (2C

(A) DUCKS DELUXE	1974	RCA		LPI 5008
(B) TAXI TO THE TERMINAL ZONE	1974	RCA	UK	SF 8402
(C) JUMPIN' (EP)	1975	SKYDOG		005
( ) DONT MIND ROCKIN' (COMPILATION)	1978	RCA		PL 25132

(1) 1974   (2) FINAL LINE UP 1975

EDDIE QUANSAH — TPT (A
BILLY RANKIN — D (2

DAVE EDMUNDS — G (B
BRINSLEY SCHWARZ — G V (2

LES DUDEK	G V	(ALL	(A)LES DUDEK			1976	CBS US 33702	UK 81380
WITH			(B)SAY NO MORE			1977	CBS US 34397	UK 81758
JEFF PORCARO	D	(ABC	(C)GHOST TOWN PARADE			1978	CBS US 35088	UK 82562
GERALD JOHNSON	B	(ABC						
DAVID PAICH	K	(ABC	MAXINE GREEN	V	(A	PEPPER SWENSON	V	(A
JERI STEVENS	V	(A	JIM HUGHART	B	(A	CAROLYN WILLIS	V	(A
MYRNA MATTHEWS	V	(A	DAVID HUNGATE	B	(A	REBECCA LOUIS	V	(AB
CHUCK RAINEY	B	(AB	BOZ SCAGGS	V	(A	DAVID FOSTER	K	(A
MAILTO CORREA	CONGA	(A	GLEN CHRONCHITE	PERC	(A	JIM KELTNER	D	(C
ANDREW FEINGOLD	K	(B	JOACHIM YOUNG	K	(B	TEA STRAON	K	(B
DAVID SANCIOUS	K	(B	TONY WILLIAMS	D	(B	KEVIN COLHOUN	PERC	(B
SHIRLEY MATTHEWS	V	(B	CLYDIE KING	V	(B	REYMONDO	PERC	(B
PAT MURPHY	PERC	(BC	JIM KRUEGER	G	(C	MIKE FINNIGAN	K V	(C
GARY MALLABER	D	(C	JACK BRUCE	V	(C	ROBERT 'POPS' POPSWELL	B	(BC
MAX GRONENTHAL	K	(C	CARMINE APPICE	D	(C	TOM SCOTT	LYRICON	(A

BRIAN GREENWAY	G V	(A	(A) WERE NO ANGELS			1975	CBS	US	33577
DAVID HENMAN	G V	(A	(EP) WANNA DANCE			19	CBS	US	156
WAYNE CULLEN	D V	(A						
BOB SEGARINI	G V	(A	RITCHIE HENMAN	D V	(A	KOOTCH TROCHIM	B V	(A

DUFFO	V	(AB	(A) DUFFO			1979	BEGGARS BANQUET	UK	BEGA5
MIKE HOWLETT	B	(A	(B) THE DISAPPEARING BOY			1980	PVK	UK	PVK 2
NICHOLAS COLA	PNO	(A						
DAVID HERZOG	G	(A	PETER DOBSON		D	(A			

DUFFY			(A) SCRUFFY DUFFY		19	CHAPTER ONE	UK	CHSR 814

GEORGE DUKE	K V	(ALL	(A) THE GEORGE DUKE QUARTET(1966)	19	MPS		0068233
WITH			(B) SAVE THE COUNTRY (1969)	1978	PICKWICK		SPC 3588
JOHN HEARD	B	(ABCE	(C) GEORGE DUKE (1969)	1978	PACIFIC JAZZ	UK	PJLA 891
DAVID SIMMONS	TPT	(A	(D) LIVE IN LA	1971	SUNSET		SLS 50232
GEORGE WALKER	D	(A	(E) FEEL	1974	MPS BASF 6802US		21223124
JAY GRAYDON	G	(BC	(F) FACES IN REFLECTION	1975	BASF		MC 22018
ERNIE WATTS	SAX	(BC	(G) I LOVE THE BLUES	1975	BASF		BAP 5071
RICHARD BERK	D	(BC	(H) THE AURA WILL PREVAIL	1975	BASF		BAP 5064
ERNIE TACK	TROM	(BC	(I) LIBERATED FANTASIES	1976	BASF		G 22835
JAY DAVERSA	TPT	(BC	(J) LIVE TOUR IN EUROPE	1976	ATLANTIC US18194		UK K50316
CHARLES FINDLEY	TPT	(BC	(K) FROM ME TO YOU	1977	EPIC UK 81850	US	34469
GLENN FERRIS	TROM	(BC	(L) REACH FOR IT	1977	EPIC US 34883		UK 82216
LEON NDUGU CHANCLER	D PERC(EGHIK		(M) DONT LET GO	1978	EPIC US 35366		UK 82821
AIRTO MOREIRA	PERC	(EGHI	(N) FOLLOW THE RAINBOW	1979	EPIC		UK 83336
JOHNNY GUITAR WATSON	G(G		(O)MASTER OF THE GAME	1979	EPIC		UK 83951
FLORA PURIM	V	(EGNO	(P) BRAZILIAN LOVE AFFAIR	1980	EPIC		UK 84311
FRANK ZAPPA	G	(E					

TOM FOWLER	B	(G	LEE RITENOUR	G	(G	BYRON MILLER	B	(GKNO GEORGE JOHNSON	G	(GI
DARYL STUERMER	G	(GI	EMIL RICHARDS	PERC(G		JOHN WITTENBERG	VLN(G		JANET FERGUSON HOFF V(GI
RUTH UNDERWOOD	PER V(GI		BRUCE FOWLER	TROM(G		ALPHONSO JOHNSON	B	(HJS SYLVIA ST JAMES	V	(H
KATHY WOEHRLE	V	(H	GEE JANZEN	V	(H	EMBAMBA	B	(I NAPOLEON M BROCK	V	(INO
DAVID AMARO	G	(I	RASHID DUKE	V	(I	BILLY COBHAM	D	(J JOHN SCOFIELD	G	(J
STANLEY CLARKE	B	(K	MIKE SEMBELLO	G	(K	DIANE REEVES	V	(K MAXINE WILLARD	V	(K
JULIA TILLMAN	V	(K	JESSICA SMITH	V	(K	RICKY LAWSON	D	(NO CHARLES JOHNSON	G	(N
SHEILA ESCOVEDO	PERC	(NO	LYNN JAMES	V	(NO	JOSIE JAMES	V	(NO MILTON BAUTISTA		(O
GARY GRANT		(O	GARY HERBIG	SAX	(O	JERRY HEY	HRNS(O	DAVID MYLES		(O
RAY OBIEDO	G	(O	BILL REICHENBACH	TROM(O		FRED WASHINGTON		(O		

RHINESTONE MUDFLAPS	V SAX	(	(A) CRUISIN'		19	ABC	US	911
MAD MISSISSIPPI BUFFALO	V K(		(B) ROLLIN ON		1975	ABC	US	942
SAM DELUXE	G V	(						
CADILLAC JACK	G V	(	BOBBY BLUE SKY	D	(			

DON MARACLE	G	(A	(A) TASTE THE NIGHT		1979	MERCURY	US	SRM 13756
GEORGE BARAJAS	B	(A						
GREG WALKER	G V	(A	MARSHALL STYLER	K V	(A	DAVID HANLON	D PERC	(A
YVONNE M LEWIS	V	(A	JANET WRIGHT	V	(A	DIVA GRAY	V	(A

MILLER ANDERSON	G V	(A12	(A) THE DUKES		1979	WB US BSK 3376	UK K56710
RONNIE LEAHY	K	(A12	(1) 1979 (2) 1980				
JIMMY McCULLOCH	G	(A1					
CHARLIE TUMAHAI	B V	(A12	STUART ELLIOTT	D	(A	BARRY DE SOUZA	D	(A
MORRIS PERT	PERC	(A	GREG JACKMAN	D	(A	MICK GRABHAM	G	(2
NICK TREVISICK	D	(12						

JOHN DUMMER	D	(ALL	(A) CABAL	1969	MERCURY	UK	SMCL20136
BOB HALL	PNO	(AB	(B) JOHN DUMMERS BLUES BAND	1969	MERCURY	UK	SMCL20167
DAVE KELLY	G V	(ABH12	(B) JOHN DUMMERS BLUES BAND	1969	MERCURY	NZ	MCY138166
ADRIAN PIETRYGA	G	(2BDHAC	(C) FAMOUS MUSIC BAND	1970	VERTIGO	UK	6382 040
IAIN THOMPSON	B	(AB12DHC	(D) BLUE	1972	VERTIGO	UK	6360 055
NICK PICKETT V VLN G K		(1BCD	(E) THIS IS	1972	PHILIPS		6382 039
KINGSLEY WARD	PNO	(H	(F) TRY ME ONE MORE TIME	197	VERTIGO	UK	6382 040
MIKE EVANS	VLN		(G) VOL 2	1973	PHILIPS		6382 083
JO ANN KELLY	V	(ABH1	(H) OOBLEEDOOBLEEJUBILEE	1973	VERTIGO	UK	6360 083
MIKE COOPER	G	(1	(H) OOBLEEDOOBLEEJUBILEE	1974	MERCURY		2360 083
ELLIOTT JACKSON		(1	(1) 1968 (2) 1969				
ROGER BROWN	V	(H					
KEITH TILLMAN	B	(A	TONY McPHEE	G V	(A	JOHN O'LEARY	HCA	(A
STEVE MILLER	PNO	(A	JOHN FAIRWEATHER	HARMONIUM(C		CHRIS TRENGROVE	SAX	(C

D129 — AYNSLEY DUNBAR

Personnel				Release	Year	Label	Country	Cat. No.
AYNSLEY DUNBAR	D	(ALL	(A)	AYNSLEY DUNBAR RETALIATION	1968	BLUE THUMB	US	BTS 4
VICTOR BROX HRNS K	G V	(ABCD1	(A)	AYNSLEY DUNBAR RETALIATION	1968	LIBERTY	UK	LBL 83154
JOHN MOORSHEAD	G V	(ABCD1	(A)	AYNSLEY DUNBAR RETALIATION	19	BYG	FR	529501
ALEX DMOCHOWSKI	B	(ABCD	(B)	DOCTOR DUNBARS PRESCRIPTION	1969	LIBERTY	UK	LBS 83223
TOMMY EYRE	K	(CE	(B)	DOCTOR DUNBARS PRESCRIPTION	1969	BLUE THUMB	US	BTS 6
ANNETTE BROX	V	(D	(C)	TO MUM FROM AYNSLEY & THE BOYS	1969	LIBERTY	UK	LBS 83223
KEITH TILLMAN	B	(1	(C)	TO MUM FROM AYNSLEY & THE BOYS	19	BYG	FR	529506
PAUL WILLIAMS	B	(E	(D)	REMAINS TO BE HEARD	1970	LIBERTY	UK	LBS 83316
PAT HICKS	TPT	(E	(E)	BLUE WHALE	1970	WB	UK	K 46062
IVAN ZAGNI	G	(E	(E)	BLUE WHALE	1978	CHARLY	UK	CR 30142
NORMAN LEPPARD	SAX	(E	( )	CLASSIC BRITISH ROCK	19	SONOPRESSE	FR	2978889
ROGER SUTTON	B	(E						
EDWARDS REAY-SMITH	TROM	(E						

D130 — SLY DUNBAR

Personnel				Release	Year	Label	Country	Cat. No.
SLY DUNBAR	D	(AB	(A)	SIMPLE SLY MAN	1978	FRONT LINE	UK	FL 1008
ROBBIE SHAKESPEARE	B	(B	(B)	SLY WICKED & SLICK	1979	FRONT LINE	UK	FL 1042
MIKEY CHUNG	K G B	(B						

ANSEL COLLINS	K	(B	KEITH STERLING	K	(B	RAD BRYAN	G	(B
ROBERT LYN	K	(B	DEAN FRASER	SAX	'B	TOMMY McCOOK	SAX	(B
VIN GORDON	TROM	(B	HERMAN MARQUIS	SAX	(B	ELNATHAN BRACKENRIDGE TPT	(B
BERES HAMMOND	V	(B	CALMAN SCOTT	V	(B	TAMLINS	V	(B
TOUTER	V	(B	STICKY	PERRC	(B	SCULLY	PERC	(B
BARNABAS	PERC	(B						

D131 — LESLEY DUNCAN

Personnel				Release	Year	Label	Country	Cat. No.
LESLEY DUNCAN V G MAND		(ALL	(A)	SING CHILDREN SING	1971	CBS	UK	64202
WITH			(B)	EARTH MOTHER	1972	CBS	UK	64807
ELTON JOHN	PNO	(A	(C)	EVERYTHING CHANGES	1974	GM	UK	GML 1007
TERRY COX	D	(A	(D)	MOONBATHING	1975	GM	UK	GML 1017
TRISTAN FRY	PERC	(A	(E)	MAYBE IT'S LOST	1977	GM	UK	GML 1019
TONI CAMPO	B	(A						

JOE MORETTI	G	(A	RAY COOPER	PERC	(A	DAVID KATZ	STR	(A	CHRIS SPEDDING	G BOUZ	(ABDE
BOB COHEN	G	(C	LARRY STEELE	B	(C	LIZA STRIKE	V	(CD	JIMMY HOROWITZ	K	(ABCDE
SUE GLOVER	V	(C	ANDY BOWN	G	(BC	PETER FRAMPTON	G	(C	PETE DENNIS	B	(DE
GLEN LEFLEUR	D	(DE	BARRY DE SOUZA	D	(BC	JOANNA NEWMAN	V	(D	DEREK GROSSMITH	WIND	(D
JACK ROTHSTEIN	STR	(B	ROBERT AHWAI	G	(E	NICO RAMSDEN	G V	(E	ALAN MURPHY	G	(E
BOBBY KEYS	SAX	(E	LAURIE ANDREW	V	(E	JOHN PERRY	V	(E	MADELINE BELL	V	(E

D132 — DAVID DUNDAS

Personnel				Release	Year	Label	Country	Cat. No.
DAVID DUNDAS	V K	(AB	(A)	DAVID DUNDAS	1977	CHRYSALIS	UK	CHR 1141
WITH			(B)	VERTICAL HOLD	1978	CHRYSALIS	UK	CHR 1197
ALAN TARNEY	B	(B						

GERRY CONWAY	D	(B	GRAHAM PRESKETT K MAND V	(B	FRANK RICOTTI	PERC	(B
KEN FRIEDMAN	SYN	(B	JIMMY JEWELL	SAX	(B	RON ASPERY	SAX	(B
DOREEN CHANTER	V	(B	JOHN GREEN	HRNS	(B	IRENE CHANTER	V	(B
RICKY HITCHCOCK	G	(B	EDDIE HOWELL	V	(B			

D133 — CHAMPION JACK DUPREE

Personnel				Release	Year	Label	Country	Cat. No.
CHAMPION JACK DUPREE V K D		(ALL		SINGS THE BLUES	19	KING	US	735
WITH				CHAMPION JACK DUPREE	19	STORYVILLE		SLP 107
MICKEY BAKER	G	(EFJ		CHAMPION JACK DUPREE	19	EVEREST	US	217
HAL SINGER	SAX	(J		BLUES FOR EVERYONE	19	KING STARDAY	US	KS 1084
MICHEL CARRAS	ORG	(M	(A)	CHAMPION JACK DUPREE	19	STORYVILLE		SLP 824
LARRY MARTIN	G	(ML		PLAYS & SINGS THE BLUES	19	STORYVILLE		SLP 145
PAUL PECHANAERT	G	(M		BEST OF THE BLUES	19	STORYVILLE		SLP 151
ZOX	B	(LM		BARREL HOUSE BLUES	19	STORYVILLE		SLP 155
JACQUES MAHIEUX	D	(LM		CHAMPION JACK DUPREE	19	STORYVILLE		SLP 161
RICHARD STUDT	VLN	(H		BOOGIE BLUES & BARRELHOUSE BLUES	19	STORYVILLE		SLP 183
REG COLE	VLN	(H		PIANO BLUES VOL 2	19	STORYVILLE		SLP 187
PETER OXER	VLN	(H		JACK DUPREE	19	STORYVILLE		SLP 193
TERRY NOONAN	HRNS	(H		JACK DUPREE	19	STORYVILLE		SLP 194
BUD PARKES	HRNS	(H		BLUES IN EUROPE	19	STORYVILLE		SLP 214
ALAN SKIDMORE	SAX	(H		CHAMPION JACK DUPREE	19	STORYVILLE		SLP 216
LES WINGFIELD	SAX	(H		FROM NEW ORLEANS TO CHICAGO	1966	DECCA	UK	LK 4747
JIM CHESTER	SAX	(H		FROM NEW ORLEANS TO CHICAGO	196	LONDON	US	553
WALLACE TRING	B	(H	(E)	& HIS BLUES BAND	1967	DECCA	UK	SKL 4871
MIKE VERNON	PERC	(H		BLUES FROM THE GUTTER	196	ATCO	US	8019
BIG CHIEF DRUMSTICK D PERC		(H		BLUES FROM THE GUTTER	1975	ATLANTIC	UK	K 40526
CHRISTOPHER TURNER	HCA	(G		CHAMPION OF THE BLUES	19	ATCO	US	8056
STAN WEBB	G	(G	(F)	ANTHOLOGIE DU BLUES	1968	VOGUE	FR	CLVLX 271
MICK TAYLOR	G	(H3	(G)	WHEN YOU FEEL THE FEELING	1968	BLUE HORIZON UK CBS US 763206
EDUARDO GIVEZANO	B	(H	(H)	SCOOBY DOOBY DOO	1969	BLUE HORIZON UK CBS US 763214
HARRIS DUNDEE	D	(G		NATURAL & SOULFUL BLUES	196	ATCO	US	8045
PAUL KOSSOFF	G	(12G		CHAMPION OF THE BLUES	196	ATCO	US	8056
STUART BROOKS	B	(12G		TRICKS	19	GNP		10001
SIMON KIRKE	D	(12G	(J)	IM HAPPY TO BE FREE	1971	GNP		10005
GARY THAIN	B	(3		CHAMPION JACK DUPREE	1971	FESTIVAL		FLD 653
KEEF HARTLEY	D	(3		INCREDIBLE	1970	SONET		SNTF 614
DUSTER BENNETT	HCA	(3G		LEGACY OF THE BLUES VOL 3	197	GNP		10013
HORST LANGE	G	(A		LEGACY OF THE BLUES VOL 3	1972	SONET	UK	SNTF 626
MOGENS SEIDELIN	B	(A	(N)	BLUES FROM MONTREUX	19	ATCO	US	1637
KING CURTIS	SAX	(N	(N)	BLUES FROM MONTREUX	1972	ATLANTIC	UK	K 40434
				WOMAN BLUES	19	FOLKWAYS		3825
				TROUBLE TROUBLE	19	MUSIDISC	FR	ST 21001
				FINE & MELLOW	19	MUSIDISC	FR	ST 21009
				HAMBURG SESSIONS	1974	HAPPYBIRD		HAPB 5011
				BLUES OF C J DUPREE	1976	STORYVILLE		SLP 240
			(L)	SHAKESPEARE SAYS	1976	SARAVAH		SH 10065
			(M)	1977	1977	ISADORA		ISL 6405

(1) 1968 APRIL   (2) 1968 LIVE BAND   (3) 1969 SESSION

D134			SIMON DUPREE & THE BIG SOUND						D134
DEREK SHULMAN	V	(	(A) WITHOUT RESERVATIONS		1967	PARLOPHONE	UK	PCS	7029
PHIL SHULMAN	SAX	(A	(A) WITHOUT RESERVATIONS		1967	CAPITOL	US	T	5097
RAY SHULMAN	B G V	(A							
PETER O'FLAHERTY	B	(A	TONY RANSLEY	D	(A	MARTIN SMITH	D	(	
GEARY KENWORTHY		(	ERIC HINE		(				

D135			TERRY DURHAM						D135
TERRY DURHAM		(A	(A) CRYSTAL TELEPHONE		1969	DERAM	OK	SML	1042
WITH									
EVAN PARKER	SAX	(A	CHRIS KARAN	D	(A	ALAN PARKER	G	(A	JOHN COLEMAN PNO(A

D136			DURUTTI COLUMN						D136
TONY BOWERS	B G	(	(A) RETURN OF DURUTTI COLUMN		19				
VINNIE RILEY	G K	(							
DAVE ROWBOTHAM	G B	(	CHRIS JOYCE	D	(	PHIL RAYNHAM	V	(	

D137			IAN DURY & THE BLOCKHEADS						D137
IAN DURY	V	(ALL	(A) NEW BOOTS & PANTIES	1977	STIFF	US	0001	IMP 002	UK SEEZ4
CHARLEY CHARLES	D	(AB	(B) DO IT YOURSELF	1979	STIFF				UK SEEZ14
NORMAN WATT ROY	B	(AB							
CHAZ JANKEL	G K	(AB	DAVEY PAYNE	SAX	(AB	EDWARD SPEIGHT	G	(A	
GEOFF CASTLE	K	(A	MICK GALLAGHER	K	(B	JOHN TURNBULL	G	(B	

D138			DUST						D138
			(A) DUST		19	POLYDOR	UK	2319	014
			(A) DUST		19	KAMA SUTRA	US	KSBS	2041
			(B) HARD ATTACK		19	KAMA SUTRA	US	KSBS	2059

D139 — BOB DYLAN — D139

BOB DYLAN	HCA V G	(ALL					
ROBBIE ROBERTSON	G V(GKOPR	RICK DANKO	B V VLN (KOPR	LEVON HELM	D V MAND (KOPR	RICHARD MANUEL	K V D (KOPR
GARTH HUDSON	K SAX(KOPR	AL KOOPER	G K HRNS (KLG	CHARLIE McCOY	HCA(GHJK	KENNY BUTTREY	D (GHJK
JOHNNY CASH	V (J	JIM KELTNER	D (M	EMMYLOU HARRIS	V (S	MICK RONSON	G (T
ROGER McGUINN	G (M	PETE DRAKE	STEEL (HJK	CHARLIE DANIELS	(JKL	NORMAN BLAKE	(JK
BOB WILSON	(JK	TONY BROWN	B (Q	BUDDY CAGE	STEEL(Q	PAUL GRIFFIN	K (Q
ERIC WEISSBERG	(Q	DELIVERANCE	(Q	STEVEN SOLES	G (1ST	ALAN PASQUA	K (1U
CAROLYN DENNIS	(1U	WAYNE MOSS	G V (G	BILLY CROSS	G (1U	JERRY SCHEFF	B (1U
IAN WALLACE	D (1U	JO ANN HARRIS	V (1U	DAVID MANSFIELD	MAND G(1TU	STEVE DOUGLAS	SAX (1U
BOBBYE HALL	PERC (1U	HELENA SPRINGS	V (1U	JOAN BAEZ	G V(	PAUL BUTTERFIELD	HCA (
JESSE ED DAVIS	G (	FRED KATZ	CELLO(M	DAVID BROMBERG	G (KL	BILLY DAVENPORT	(
ROB STONER	B (ST	ALBERT W BUTLER	(K	RINGO STARR	D (	RONNIE BLAKLEY	V (S
FRED CARTER	(K	MARK NAFTALIN	(K	LUTHER	PERC (S	MARVIN D CHANTRY	VIOLA(K
MIKE BLOOMFIELD	G (	HOWARD WYETH	D PNO (ST	RON CORNELIUS	G (KL	BILLY PRESTON	K (
GARY BURKE	D (T	DOTTIE DILLARD	V (K	ELVIN BISHOP	G (	SCARLET RIVERA	VLN (ST
DELORES EDGIN	(K	LEON RUSSELL	K (	TED MICHEL	CELLO(M	SOLIE J FOTT	(K
JEROME ARNOLD	(	DOM CORTESE	MAND (S	BUBBA FOLLER	(K	KLAUS VOORMANN	B (
GEORGE BARNES	B (B	DENNIS A GOODE	TROM (K	SAM LAY	D (	DICK WELLSTOOD	PNO (B
EMANUEL GREEN	VLN (K	GEORGE HARRISON	G V (	HERB LOVELL	D (B	HILDA HARRIS	V (KL
ERIC CLAPTON	G (	HOWIE COLLINS	G (B	FREDRICK HILL	TPT(K	BYRON BERLINE	FDL (M
LEONARD GASKIN	B (B	KARL HIMMEL	D (K	TERRY PAUL	B (M	BRUCE LANGHORNE	G (BM
LILIAN HUNT	(K	BRENDA PATTERSON	V (M	BYRON BACH	VLN(K	MARTIN KATAHN	(K
CARL FORTINA	K (M	BRENTON BANKS	VLN (K	DOUG KERSHAW	(K	GARY FOSTER	WIND (M
GEORGE BINKLEY	VLN (K	MILLIE KIRKHAM	(K	MARTHA McCRORY	(K	BARRY McDONALD	(K
SHELDON KURLAND	VLN (K	OLIVER MITCHELL	TPT (K	CAROL MONTGOMERY	(K	BOB MOORE	B (K
GENE A MULLINS	(K	JUNE PAGE	(K	REX PEER	(K	GARY VAN OSDALE	VIOLA(K
BILL PURSELL	(K	ALBERTINE ROBERTSON	V(KL	ALVIN ROGERS	D (K	FRANK C SMITH	(K
MAERETHA STEWART	V (KLOPR	ANTHONY FERRON	(K	STU WOODS	B (K	STEVE MADAIO	TPT (U
HAPPY TRAUM	B G V BANJ(*	HARVEY BROOKS	B (L	BUZZY FEITEN	G (L	RUSS KUNKEL	D (LM
BILL MUNDI	D (L	BOOKER T JONES	K (M	CAROL HUNTER	(M	DONNA WEISS	V (M
PRISCILLA JONES	V (M	VINCENT BELL	BAZ (S	T BONE BURNETT	G PNO(T	JOE SOUTH	(G
HENRY STRZELECKI	B (G	BILL ATKINS	K (G	JERRY KENNEDY	G (G	HARGUS ROBBINS	K (G

	DATE	US	STEREO	MONO	JAPAN				UK
(A) BOB DYLAN	1962	CBS	8579	1779	CBS SONY	25AP 268	CBS	62022
(B) FREEWHEELIN' BOB DYLAN	1963	CBS	8786	1986	CBS SONY	25AP 269	CBS	62193
(C) TIMES THEY ARE A CHANGIN'	1964	CBS	8905	2105	CBS SONY	25AP 270	CBS	62251
(D) ANOTHER SIDE OF BOB DYLAN	1964	CBS	8993	2193	CBS SONY	25AP 271	CBS	62429
(E) BRINGING IT ALL BACK HOME	1965	CBS	9128	2328	CBS SONY	25AP 272	CBS	62515
(F) HIGHWAY 61 REVISITED	1965	CBS	9189	2389	CBS SONY	25AP 273	CBS	62572
(G) BLONDE ON BLONDE (DBL)	1966	CBS	C25841	C2841	CBS SONY	40 AP 274/5	CBS	66012
(H) JOHN WESLEY HARDING	1968	CBS	9604	2804	CBS SONY	25AP 277	CBS	63252
(J) NASHVILLE SKYLINE	1969	CBS	9825		CBS SONY	25AP 278	CBS	63601
(K) SELF PORTRAIT (DBL)	1970	CBS	30050		CBS SONY	40AP279/80	CBS	66250
(L) NEW MORNING	1970	CBS	30290		CBS SONY	25AP 281	CBS	69001
(M) PAT GARRETT & BILLY THE KID	1973	CBS	32460		CBS SONY	25AP 284	CBS	69042
(N) DYLAN	1973	CBS	32747		CBS SONY	25AP 285	CBS	69049
(O) PLANET WAVES	1974	ASYLUM	7E1003				ISLAND ILPS9261	
(P) BEFORE THE FLOOD (DBL)	1974	ASYLUM	AB 201				ISLAND	IBD 1
(Q) BLOOD ON THE TRACKS	1974	CBS	33235				CBS	69097
(R) BASEMENT TAPES	1975	CBS	33682		CBS SONY	40AP287/8	CBS	88147
(S) DESIRE	1975	CBS	33893		CBS SONY	25AP 289	CBS	86003
(T) HARD RAIN	1976	CBS	34349		CBS SONY	25AP 290	CBS	86016
(U) STREET LEGAL	1978	CBS	35453		CBS SONY	25AP 1099	CBS	86067
(V) AT BUDOKAN	1978	CBS			CBS SONY	40AP 2200	CBS	96004
(W) SLOW TRAIN COMING	1979	CBS					CBS	86095
( ) GREATEST HITS	1967	CBS	9463	2663	CBS SONY	25AP 276	CBS	62847
( ) GREATEST HITS VOL 2	19	CBS	31120				CBS	62911
( ) GREATEST HITS VOL 3	19	CBS					CBS	63111
(*) MORE GREATEST HITS	1972	CBS					CBS	67239
( ) NOBODY SINGS LIKE BOB DYLAN	19	CBS					CBS	62694
( ) 11 YEARS IN THE LIFE OF BOB DYLAN	197	CBS					SOPI	11/12
( ) BROADSIDE BALLADS	19	BROADSIDE	BR301					
(EP) DYLAN	19	CBS						6051
(EP) I WANT YOU	19	CBS	4 43683					
(1) 1978 TOUR								

E1
EAGLE
(A) EAGLE 19 JANUS US JLS 3011

E2
EAGLES

					US	UK	UK
RANDY MEISNER	V B	(ABCDE	(A) THE EAGLES	1972	ASYLUM 5054	SYTC101 +	K 53009
GLENN FREY	V G	(ABCDE	(B) DESPARADO	1973	ASYLUM 5068	SYLA9011+	K 53008
DON HENLEY	D V	(ABCDE	(C) ON THE BORDER	1974	ASYLUM 7E1004	SYL9016 +	K 43005
BERNIE LEADON	G V	(AB	(D) ON OF THESE NIGHTS	1975	ASYLUM 7E1039	SYLA 8759+	K 53014
DON FELDER	G V	(CDE	(E) HOTEL CALIFORNIA	1976	ASYLUM 6E103A		K 53051
JOE WALSH	G V	(EFG	(F) THE LONG RUN	1979	ASYLUM BB705		K 52181
TIM SCHMIT	B V	(	(G) EAGLES LIVE	1980	ASYLUM		K 62032
J D SOUTHER	V G	(G	( ) GREATEST HITS	1975	ASYLUM 6E105A		K 53017
JOE VITALE	K D	(G					
PHIL KENZIE	SAX	(G	VINCE MELAMED	K	(G JAGE JACKSON	G	(G

E3
BOBBY EAGLESHAM

BOBBY EAGLESHAM	G V	(A	(A) BOBBY EAGLESHAM	1974	XTRA	UK	XTRA 1137
SID CAIRNS	B	(A					

E4
EARTH & FIRE

JERNEY KAAGMAN	V	(BDCEF	(A) EARTH & FIRE	197			6437 004
GERARD KOERTS V FLT VIBES K(CDEF			(A) EARTH & FIRE	197	REDBULLET	US	PRBLP3000
CHRIS KOERTS	V G	(DCEF	(B) ATLANTIS	1973	POLYDOR	IMP	2419 059
TON VANDER KLAY	V D	(CDEF	(B) ATLANTIS	1975	POLYDOR	UK	2310 216
HANS ZIECH	B	(CD	(C) SONG OF THE MARCHING CHILDREN	197	POLYDOR	IMP	2925 003
THEO HURTS	B	(EF	(D) MEMORIES	1975	POLYDOR	UK	2310 209
			(E) TO THE WORLD A FUTURE	1975	POLYDOR		2374 121
(C) & (D) THE SAME ALBUM			(E) TO THE WORLD A FUTURE	1975	POLYDOR		2925 033
			(F) GATE TO INFINITY	1977	POLYDOR		2925 065

E5
EARTH OPERA

PETER ROWAN V SAX G		(A	(A) EARTH OPERA	1968	ELEKTRA		EKS 74016
DAVID GRISMAN	K SAX	(A	(B) GREAT AMERICAN EAGLE TRADEDY	1969	ELEKTRA		EKS 74038
JOHN NAGY	B	(A					
BILL STEVENSON	K	(A	BILL MUNDI	PERC	(A WARREN SMITH	PERC (A
PAUL DILLON	D G V	(A					

E6
EARTH QUAKE

JOHN DOUKAS	V PNO	(DEF	(A) WHY DONT YOU TRY ME	1972	A&M	US	SP 4337
ROBBIE DUNBAR	G V	(DEF	(B) EARTHQUAKE	1975	A&M	US	SP 4308
STAN MILLER	B V	(DEF	(C) EARTHQUAKE LIVE	1975	U A	UK	UAS 29853
STEVE NELSON	D	(DEF	(D) ROCKIN' THE WORLD	1975	BESERKLEY	US	0045
GARY PHILLIPS	G V	(DEF	(D) ROCKIN' THE WORLD	197	BESERKLEY	US RI	34752
			(D) ROCKIN' THE WORLD	1978	BESERKLEY	UK	BSERK 3
			(E) 8.5	197	BESERKLEY	US	0047
			(E) 8.5	197	BESERKLEY	US RI	34754
			(E) 8.5	1976	BESERKLEY	UK	BSERK5
			(F) LEVELED	197	BESERKLEY	US	0054
			(F) LEVELED	197	BESERKLEY	US RI	34801
			(F) LEVELED	1977	BESERKLEY	UK	BSERK7

E7
EARTH WIND & FIRE

MAURICE WHITE	D V	(ALL	(A) EARTH WIND & FIRE	1971	WB	US	1905	
VERDINE WHITE	B V	(FKM	(B) THE NEED OF LOVE	1972	WB	US	1958	
FRED WHITE	D PERC(KM		(C) ANOTHER TIME	1972	WB	US	2798	
ANDY WOOLFOLK	WIND	(FKM	(D) LAST DAYS & TIME	1973	CBS	US	31702	UK 65208
PHILIP BAILEY	V PERC(FKMN		(E) HEAD TO THE SKY	1974	CBS	US	32104	UK 65604
RONALD BATTISTA	(		(F) OPEN YOUR EYES	1974	CBS	US	32712	UK 65844
LARRY DUNN	K	(FMKN	(G) THATS THE WAY OF THE WORLD	1975	CBS	US	33280	UK 80575
RON WAYNE LAWS	(		(H) GRATITUDE	1975	CBS	US	33694	UK 88160
RALPH JOHNSON	D PERC(FKM		(J) SPIRIT	1977	CBS	US	34241	UK 81451
AL McKAY	G PERC(FKMN		(K) ALL AND ALL	1978	CBS	US	34905	UK 86051
JOHNNY GRAHAM	G	(FKM	(L) BEST OF VOL 1	1978	CBS	US	35647	UK 83284
DAVID FOSTER	K	(M	(M) I AM	1979	CBS	US	35730	UK 86084
EDDIE DEL BARRIO	PERC	(KM	(N) EARTH WIND & FIRE	1980	CBS			UK 86498
MARLO HENDERSON	G	(M	( ) EARTH WIND & FIRE (TRIPLE BOX)	1979	CBS			UK 66350
SKIP SCARBOROUGH	PERC	(K	(EP) SING A SONG(PROMO EP)	1977	CBS		EWF1	
PAULINHO DA COSTA	PERC	(KM						
DONALD MYRICK	SAX	(KM	LOUIS SATTERFIELD	TROM	(KMN MICHAEL HARRIS	TPT	(KM
RAHMLEE DAVIS	TPT	(MMN	JESSICA CLEAVES	V	(STEVE LUKATHER	G	(M
BILLY MYERS	K	(M	SHEILA WHITT	V	(M BENJAMIN POWELL	TROM	(M
STEVE PORCARO	SYN	(M	JEANETTE HAWES	V	(M BILL REICHENBACH	TROM	(M
WANDA HUTCHINSON	V	(M	ELMER BROWN	TPT	(M MAURICE SPEARS	TROM	(M
OSCAR BRASHEAR	TPT	(M	FRED JACKSON	SAX	(M BOBBY BRYANT	TPT	(M
HERMAN RILEY	SAX	(M	JEROME RICHARDSON	SAX	(M JERRY HEY	TPT	(M
BARBARA KORN	HRNS	(M	DOROTHY ASHBY	HARP	(M RICHARD LEPORE	PERC	(M
STEVE MADAIO	TPT	(M	GEORGE BOHANON	TROM	(M GARNETT BROWN	TROM	(M
SIDNEY MULDRON	HRN	(M	RICHARD PERISSI	HRNS	(M MARILYN ROBINSON	HRN	(M

E7A
EARTHQUAKE

ULI ROTH	G V	(A	(A) ELECTRIC SUN	1979	BRAIN		0060 196

E7B
EARTHQUIRE

TATA VEGA	V	(A	(A) EARTHQUIRE	1972	NATURAL RESOURCES	NR	106L
GREG MATHESON	K	(A					
MARK KOFSTEIN	WIND	(A	BOB CROSBY	WIND	(A LAURIE ANNE BALL	V	(A
JIM VARLEY	D	(A	MIKE GORFAINE	V	(A CHARLIE STEPHENS	B	(A
BRIE BRANDT	V	(A					

E7C
EARTHSTAR

DENNIS REA	G	(A	(A) FRENCH SKYLINE	1979	SKY		SKY 031
TIM FINNEGAN	FLT	(A					
CRAIG WOEST	K	(A	NORMAN PEACH	B	(A DARYL TRIVIERI	VLN	(A
MARLA THOMSON	HRNS	(A	DIRK SCHMALENBACH	SITAR	(A		

CHRIS EAST   E7D

CHRIS EAST	G	(A	(A) HOTEL IN THE COUNTRY		1978	GTO	UK	GTLP 034
MO WITHAM	G B	(A					
PA THOMPSON	D	(A	KEVIN MORRIS	D	(A	IAN GIBSONS	(K
B J COLE	STEEL	(A	ALAN HAWKSHAW	K	(A		

EAST OF EDEN   E8

DAVE ARBUS	WIND VLN	(12ABCEG	(A) MERCATOR PROJECTED	1969	DERAM	UK	SML 1038
RON CAINES	V SAX	(12ABE	(B) SNAFU	1970	DERAM	UK	SML 1050
GEOFF NICHOLSON	G V	(12ABE	(B) SNAFU	19	DREAM	US	18043
PETER FILLEUL	K	(F	(AB)SNAFU/MERCATOR	1975	DERAM	UK	SDM3013 1/2
STEVE YORK	B	(AE	(C) NEW LEAF	1971	HARVEST	UK	SNVL 796
DAVE DUFONT	D	(AE	(D) EAST OF EDEN	1971	HARVEST	UK	SHVL 792
GEOFF BRITTON	D	(1BE	(D) EAST OF EDEN	197	HARVEST	US	SW 806
ANDY SNEDDON	B	(12BE	(E) WORLD OF	1971	DECCA	UKSPA34+SPA751
JEFF ALLEN	D	(2CEFG	(F) HERE WE GO AGAIN	1976	EMI	EURO 062 98065
JOE O'DONNELL	VLN	(	(G) MASTERS OF ROCK	1975	EMI	EURO 062 95117
DAVID JACKS	B	(CEFG	(H) THINGS	1976	NOVA		628367
JIM ROCHE	G	(CH	(I) JIG A JIG	197	DECCA		210006
DAVE WELLER	SAX	(CF				
LES DAVIDSON		(F	(1) 1969 (2) 1970			

EAST SIDE KIDS   E8A

DAVE POTTER			(A) TIGER & THE LAMB	19	UNI	73032

EASY STREET   E9

PETER MARSH	G	(ABC	(A) EASY STREET	1974	EPIC	UK	80468
KEN NICOL	G	(ABC	(B) EASY STREET	1976	POLYDOR	UK	2383 415
JIM HALL	B	(BC	(C) UNDER THE GLASS	1977	POLYDOR	UK	2383 444
KEVIN SAVIGAR	K	(C	(C) UNDER THE GLASS	1977	CAPRICORN	US	0184
BARRY DE SOUZA	D	(A					
PETE ZORN	B SAX	(AB	RAY DUFFY	D	(A	DOUG WRIGHT	D	(A
B J COLE	STEEL	(A	GRAHAM SMITH	HCA	(A	PADDIE McHUGH	G	(A
FRANK COLLINS	V	(A	DYAN BIRCH	V	(A	BILL ZORN	BANJO	(A
CHRISTOPHER	PNO	(B	RICHARD BURGESS	D	(BC	ROD ARGENT	K	(B
DICK PEARCE	HRNS	(B	PETER THOMS	HRNS	(B	ROGER WILLIAMS	HRNS	(B
KENNY KING	HRNS	(B	JOHN WALTERS	SAX	(B		

EASYBEATS   E10

GEORGE YOUNG	G V		( ) FRIDAY ON MY MIND	1967	UA	US	UAS 6588
DICK DIAMONDE	B		( ) GOOD FRIDAY	1967	UA	UK	SULP 1167
HARRY VANDA	G V		( ) GOOD FRIDAY	1967	UA	US	UA 29627
STEVE WRIGHT	V		( ) FALLING OFF THE EDGE OF THE WORLD	1968	UA	US	UAS 6667
GORDON FLEET	D		( ) VIGIL	1968	UA	UK	SULP 1199
TONY CAHILL	D		( ) FRIENDS	1970	POLYDOR	UK	2482 010
			( ) ABSOLUTE ANTHOLOGY (DBL)	19		AUST	

EATER   E11

ANDY BLADE	V	(A	(A) THE ALBUM	1977	THE LABEL	UK	TLRLP 001
BRIAN CHEVETTE	G	(A					
IAN WOODCOCK	B	(A	DEE GENERATE	D	(A		

EBERSON GRAF HOVENSJO CHRISTENSEN   E11A

JON EBERSON	G	(A	(A) BLOW OUT	1977	COMPENDIUM	NOR	FID10
HAKON GRAF	K	(A					
SVEINUNG HOVENSJO	B	(A	JON CHRISTENSEN	D	(A	MIKI NDOYE	CONGA	(A
FRODE HOLM							

ECHO & THE BUNNYMEN   E11B

			A) CROCODILES	1980	KOROVA	UK	KODE1

ECLECTION   E12

KERRILEE MALE	V	(A	(A) ECLECTION	1968	ELEKTRA	EKS 74023
MICHAEL ROSEN	V G TPT	(A				
TREVOR LUCAS	G V	(A	GERRY CONWAY	D V	(A	GEORG HULTGREEN	V G	(A
DORRIS HENDERSON	V	(	POLI PALMER	V VIBES	(	MICK WOODS	D	(
KEVIN WESTLAKE	PERC G	(	GARY BOYLE	G	(	ERIC JOHNS	G	(

ECLIPSE   E12A

PIERRE GAUTHIER	K V	(A	(A) NIGHT & DAY	1977	CASABLANCA	NBLP 7097
JESSE OTTEN	G V	(A				
MIKE DINARDO	D PERC	(A	CLAUDE LAFERRIERE	B G	(A		

EDDIE & THE HOT RODS   E13

BARRY MASTERS	V	(ABCD	(A) LIVE AT THE MARQUEE	(EP)	19	ISLAND	UK	IEP 2
DAVE HIGGS	G	(ABCD	(B) TEENAGE DEPRESSION	19	ISLAND	UK	ILPS 9457
STEVE NICOL	D	(ABCD	(B) TEENAGE DEPRESSION	1976	PHONOGRAM	EURO 9101 671
PAUL GRAY	B	(ABCD	(C) LIFE ON THE LINE	1977	ISLAND	UK	ILPS 9509
GRAEME DOUGLAS	G V K	(CD	(C) LIFE ON THE LINE	1977	PHONOGRAM	EURO 9123 025
			(D) THRILLER	1979	ISLAND	UK	ILPS 9563
			( ) FISH & CHIPS	19		US	

DUANE EDDY   E14

DUANE EDDY   G
WITH

AL CASEY	B G	LARRY KNECHTEL	K	STEVE DOUGLAS	SAX	IKE CLANTON	B
BUDDY WHEELER	B	BOB TAYLOR	D	CORKY CASEY	G	JIM HORN	SAX
DON OWEN	G	JIMMY TROXEL	D	BEN DEMOTTO	V		

HAVE TWANGY GUITAR WILL TRAVEL	1958	JAMIE	US	3000	LONDON UK (M) HAW 2160
ESPECIALLY FOR YOU	1958	JAMIE	US	3006	LONDON UK (M) HAW 2191 (S) SAHW 6045
TWANGS THE THANG	1959	JAMIE	US	3009	LONDON UK (M) HAW2236 (S) SAHW 6068
SONGS FOR OUR HERITAGE	1960	JAMIE	US	3011	LONDON UK (M) HAW 2285 (S) SAHW 6119
1,000,000 DOLLARS OF TWANG	1961	JAMIE	US	3014	LONDON UK (M) HAW 2325
GIRLS GIRLS GIRLS	1961	JAMIE	US	3019	LONDON UK (M) HAW 2373 (S) SAHW 6173
1,000,000 DOLLARS OF TWANG 2	1962	JAMIE	US	3021	LONDON UK (M) HAW 2435
TWISTIN' & TWANGIN'	1962	RCA	US	LSP2525	

(CONTINUED)

D14 (CONTINUED)

DUANE EDDY

TWANGY GUITAR SILKY STRINGS	1962	RCA	US	LSP2576
TWISTIN'	196	JAMIE	US	3022
SURFIN'	196	JAMIE	US	3024
IN PERSON	196	JAMIE	US	3025
16 GREATEST HITS	196	JAMIE	US	3026
DANCE WITH THE GUITAR MAN	1963	RCA	US	LSP2648
PURE GOLD	19	RCA	US	ANL2671
TWANGS A COUNTRY SONG	1963	RCA	US	LSP2681
TWANGIN' UP A STORM	1963	RCA	US	LSP 2700
LONELY GUITAR	1964	RCA	US	LSP2798
WATERSKIING	196	RCA	US	LSP2918
TWANGIN' GOLDEN HITS	196	RCA	US	LSP2993
DUANE A GO GO	1965	COLPIX	US	PXL490
DUANE DOES DYLAN	1965	COLPIX	US	PXL494
TWANGSVILLE	1965	RCA	US	LSP3432
BEST OF	1965	RCA	US	LSP3477
BIGGEST TWANG OF ALL	1966	REPRISE	US	6218
ROARIN' TWANGIES	1967	REPRISE	US	6240
MOVIN' & GROOVIN'	1970			
TWANGY GUITAR	1970			
LEGEND OF ROCK	1974			
LEGEND OF ROCK 2	1974			
LEGEND OF ROCK 3 RARE ITEMS	1974			
YESTERDAYS POP SCENE	1975			
GUITAR MAN	1975			
GUITAR MAN	197			
VINTAGE YEARS	197	SIR	US	3707/2
DUANE EDDY	1979			
GREATEST HITS	1979			
OLDIES BUT GOODIES	1979			
DUANE EDDY COLLECTION	1978			
(EPS)				
MOVIN' & GROOVIN'	19	JAMIE US		JEP 100
YEP	19	JAMIE US		JEP 300
DETOUR	19	JAMIE US		JEP 301
SHAZAM	19	JAMIE US		JEP 303
BECAUSE THEY'RE YOUNG	19	JAMIE	US	JEP 304

RCA	UK	SF	7560
RCA	UK	RD	7568
RCA INT	UK	INT	1057
CAMDEN	UK	CDS	1109
VALIANT	UK	VS	108
LONDON	UK	ZGW	105
CAMDEN	UK	CDS	1072
DERAM		DLL5033/4	
TELDEC	GER	LS	3259
LONDON		LS	3281
TELEFUNKEN	AF	622002	
GTO		GTLP	002
HALLMARK			947
RCA UKAPL	12671		
RONCO	UK	RTL	2035
TELDEC	GERM	623647	
PICKWICK	UK	PDA	043

E15

RANDY EDELMAN

RANDY EDELMAN	K V	(ALL	
WITH			
NIGEL OLSSON	D V	(B	
REINIE PRESS	B	(B	
GARY COLEMAN	PERC	(B	
DEAN PARKS	G	(B	
LEE RITENOUR	G	(B	
AL KOOPER	G	(B	
STEVE CROPPER	G	(B	
ANDREW GOLD	G	(B	
TOM BAHLER	V	(B	
VINI PONCIA	V	(B	

(A) PRIME CUTS			1976	20th CENTURY		BT	448
(B) FAREWELL FAIRBANKS			1976	20th CENTURY		BT	494
(C) IF LOVE IS REAL			1977	20th CENTURY	UK	BT	542
(C) IF LOVE IS REAL			1977	ARISTA	US	AL	4139
(D) UPTOWN UPTEMPO			1979	20th CENTURY		T	601
( ) LAUGHTER & TEARS			19	LION	US		1013
( ) YOUR'E THE ONE			1979	20TH CENTURY		BT	581

ART MUNSON	G	(B	BEN BENAY	G	(B
DEE MURRAY	V	(B	JIMMY HAAS	V	(B
MELISSA MANCHESTER	V	(B	JACKIE DeSHANNON	V	(B

E16

EDENS CHILDREN

RICHARD SCHAMACH	G	(AB	
JIMMY STURMAN	D	(AB	
LARRY KIELY	B	(AB	

(A) EDENS CHILDREN	1968	ABC	US	ABCS 624
(A) EDENS CHILDREN	1968	STATESIDE	UK	SSL 10235
(B) SURE LOOKS REAL	1969	ABC	US	ABCS 652

E17

EDGE

JOHN MOSS	D	(A
LU EDM UNDS	G	(A
GAVIN POVEY	K	(A

(A) SQUARE ONE	1980	HURRICANE	UK	FLAK 102

GLYN HAVARD	B	(A

E18

GRAEME EDGE

GRAEME EDGE	D V	(AB
ADRIAN GURVITZ	G V	(AB
PAUL GURVITZ	B	(AB
MICK GALLAGHER	K	(A
BRIAN PARRISH	V	(B
RUBY JAMES	V	(A
BARRY ST JOHN	V	(A
ANN ODELL	K	(B
REBOP	PERC	(B
BILL EASLEY	HRNS	(B
EDGAR MATTHEWS	HRNS	(B

(A) KICK OFF YOUR MUDDY BOOTS	1974	THRESHOLD	UK	TH S15
(B) PARADISE BALLROOM	1977	DECCA	UK	TXS 121
(B) PARADISE BALLROOM	1977	LONDON	US	PS 686

RAY THOMAS	V	(A	SUNNY LESLIE	V	(A
NICKY JAMES	V	(A	LESLEY DUNCAN	V	(A
JOANNE WILLIAMS	V	(A	GINGER BAKER	D	(A
TONY HYMAS	K	(B	BLUE WEAVER	K	(B
LAWRIE McMILLAN	HRNS	(B	B J COLE	STEEL	(B
KEN SPAIN	HRNS	(B	BEN CAULEY	HRNS	(B

E18A

EDISON ELECTRIC BAND

DAN'FREEBO'FRIEDBERG	G B	(A
T J TINDALL	G V	(A
MARK JORDAN	K G	(A
NORMAN PRIDE	CONGA	(A

(A) BLESS YOU, DR WOODWARD	1970	COTILION	US	SD 9022

RIP STOCK	V D	(A	MICHAEL ZIEGLER	G	(A
BROOKMEAD MUMBLE CHOIR	V	(A

E18B

EDITION SPECIALE

ANN BALLISTER	K	(
MIMI LORENZINI	G V	(
JOSQUIN TURENNE B G V		(
J J BOUCHET D'ANGELY	D	(

ALLEE DES TILLEULS	19	SONOPRESSE	FR	UAS 29965
ALIQUANTE	19	RCA		PL 37069

DAVE EDMUNDS
LOVE SCUPTURE & ROCKPILE   E19

DAVE EDMUNDS G K V B (ALL
WITH
NICK LOWE B V (CDEFG
BILLY BREMNER G V (CDEFG
TERRY WILLIAMS D (4ACDEFG
JOHN WILLIAMS B V PNO(A
MICKEY GEE G (
BOB JONES D V (14
B J COLE STEEL (4A
ANDY FAIRWEATHER LOW G (4A
BILLY RANKIN D (D
STEVE GOULDING D (D
PAUL RILEY B (D
BOB ANDREWS K (CD
GERRY HOGAN STEEL (E
PETE KELLY PNO (E
BRINSLEY SCHWARZ G (C
IAN GOMM G V (C
PICK WITHERS D (C
ALBERT LEE G (F
BILLY RANKIN D V (C

	Title	Year	Label		Cat. No.
(1)	BLUES HELPING(LOVE SCULPTURE)	1968	PARLOPHONE	UK	PCS 7059
(2)	FORMS & FEELINGS (LOVE SCULPTURE)	1969	PARLOPHONE	UK	PCS 7090
(3)	CLASSIC TRACKS (LOVE SCULPTURE)	1974	ONE UP		OU 2047
(4)	ROCKERS (LOVE SCULPTURE)	197	PARLOPHONE	IMP	15099466/7
(5)	SINGLES A's & B's	1980	HARVEST	UK	SHSM 2032
(A)	ROCKPILE	1972	REGAL ZONOPHONE	UK	SLRZ 1026
(A)	ROCKPILE	1972	MAM	US	MAM3
(A)	ROCKPILE	197	PATHE	FR	064 93282
(B)	STARDUST (SOUNDTRACK 1 SIDE)	1974	RONCO	UK	RG2009/10
(C)	SUBTLE AS A FLYING MALLET	1975	ROCKFIELD	UK	RRL 101
(C)	SUBTLE AS A FLYING MALLET	1978	RCA	UK	PL 25129
(C)	SUBTLE AS A FLYING MALLET	197	RCA	US	APLI 5003
(D)	GET IT	1977	SWANSONG	UK	SSK 59404
(D)	GET IT	1977	SWANSONG	US	8418
(E)	TRACKS ON WAX	1978	SWANSONG	UK	SSK 59407
(E)	TRACKS ON WAX	1978	SWANSONG	US	8505
(F)	REPEAT WHEN NECESSARY	1979	SWANSONG	UK	SSK 59409
(G)	SECONDS OF PLEASURE(ROCKPILE)	1980	F BEAT	UK	XXLP7

EDWARD BEAR   E19A

( ) EDWARD BEAR   19 PENNYFARTHING UK PELS 532

EDWARD BEAR   E19B

DANNY MARKS G V BAN(A
PAUL WELDON K PNO B V (A
LARRY EVOY D V (A

(A)	ECLIPSE	1970	CAPITOL	CAN	SKAO 6349
(A)	ECLIPSE	1970	CAPITOL	US	ST 580
(B)	BEARINGS	19	CAPITOL	US	SKAO 426
( )	EDWARD BEAR	19	CAPITOL	US	ST 11157
( )	CLOSE YOUR EYES	19	CAPITOL	US	SMAS11192

JACKIE EDWARDS   E19C

JACKIE EDWARDS V (ALL

( )	PREMATURE GOLDEN SANDS	1967	ISLAND	UK	ILP 960
( )	PUT YOUR TEARS AWAY	19	VEEP	US	VPS 16533
( )	I DO LOVE YOU	19	TROJAN	UK	TRL 47
( )	DO YOU BELIEVE IN LOVE	1976	KLIK	UK	KLP 9009
( )	BEFORE THE NEXT TEARDROP	1977	THIRD WORLD		TWS 928
( )	LET'S FALL IN LOVE	1978	THIRD WORLD		TDWD 3
( )	COME TO ME SOFTLY	1979	THIRD WORLD		TDWD 10

JONATHAN EDWARDS   E20

JONATHAN EDWARDS B G HCA V(ALL
WITH
STUART SCHULMAN B VLN K(ABCD
BILL KEITH STEEL BANJO (ABCD
BILL ELLIOTT PNO ORG(CD
GEORGE GRANTHAM D V (C
R DAVIES B (C
DAVID BROMBERG G MAND DOBRO(C
AL ANDERSON G (D
ERIC LILLEQUIST G V (ABD
DAVE CONRAD B (D
JAMES BURTON G (E
EMMYLOU HARRIS V G (EF
CHANDLER TRAVIS MARACAS(B
RODNEY CROWELL G (EF
DAVID GRISMAN MAND (E
MIKE AULDRIDGE DOBRO (F

(A)	JONATHAN EDWARDS	1971	CAPRICORN	US	8021
(A)	JONATHAN EDWARDS	1971	CAPRICORN		S 862
(A)	JONATHAN EDWARDS	1971	ATLANTIC	UK	K 40282
(B)	HONKY TONK STARDUST COWBOY	1972	ATCO	US	SD 7015
(C)	HAVE A GOOD TIME FOR ME	1973	ATCO	US	SD 7036
(D)	LUCKY DAY	1974	ATCO	US	SD 36104
(E)	ROCKIN' CHAIR	1976	REPRISE	US	2238
(F)	SAILBOAT	1977	WB	US	BS 3020

DEAN ADRIAN PERC (BD   ROB CHOINARD D (D
JOHN WARE D (EF   GLEN D HARDIN PNO (EF
HANK DE VITO STEEL (EF   EMORY GORDY B MAND(EF
JEFF LABES K (A   RICHARD ADELMAN D (AB
BILL PAYNE PNO (E   BRIAN AHERN G (EF
BYRON BERLINE FDL (E   HERB PEDERSEN BANJ V(EF
DIANNE BROOKS V (EF   LYNNIE (DALL) EDWARDS V (DE
ALBERT LEE G MAND (F

EDWARDS HAND   E21

ROY EDWARDS K V (AB
ROGER HAND G V (AB
JAMES LITHERLAND G (B
JOHN WETTON B (B

(A)	EDWARDS HAND	19	GTO	US	1005
(B)	STRANDED	1971	RCA	UK	SF 8154

CLEM CATTINI D (B

EELA CRAIG   E21A

HUBERT BOGNERMAYR K V (A
HUBERT SCHNAUER K (
HARALD ZUSCHRADER K G (
WILL ORTHOFER V (
FRANK HUEBER D (

(A)	ONE NITER	1976	VERTIGO		6360 635
(B)	HATS OF GLASS	1977	VERTIGO		6360 638

FRITZ RUDELBERGER G K V (GERHARD ENGLISCH B PERC (

JOE EGAN   E22

JOE EGAN G V (A
WITH
HENRY SPINETTI D (A
PAUL PILNICK G (A
CHARLES SPITTERI PERC (A
SYLVIA V (A
GEORGE CHANDLER V (A

(A)	OUT OF NOWHERE	1979	ARIOLA	UK	ARL 5021

DAVE MARKEE B (A   BILLY LIVSEY K (A
PHIL PALMER G (A   ALAN PARKER G (A
BENNY GALLAGHER ACC (A GRAHAM LYLE MAND (A
JOY YATES V (A   VICKY BROWN V (A
JIMMY ELLIS V (A

WALTER EGAN   E23

WALTER EGAN V (AB
WITH
ANNIE McCLOONE V (B
TOM MONCRIEFF G V (B
LINDSEY BUCKINGHAM G (B
MICK FLEETWOOD D (B
EARL SHAKLEFORD V (B
STEVE HAGUE K V (B
JOHN ZAMBETTI V (B

(A)	FUNDAMENTAL ROLL	1977	POLYDOR	UK	2310 614
(A)	FUNDAMENTAL ROLL	1977	UA	UK	UAG 30032
(A)	FUNDAMENTAL ROLL	1977	CBS	US	34679
(B)	NOT SHY	1978	CBS	US	35077
(B)	NOT SHY	1978	POLYDOR	UK	2310 609

JOHN SELK B V G (B   MIKE HUEY D PERC (B
STEVIE NICKS V (B   DEAN TORRANCE V (B

```
E24                                                  EGG
    HUGH MONTGOMERY CAMPBELL  K(AB     (A) EGG                        1970   NOVA              SDN    14
    DAVE STEWART           K   (AB     (A) EGG                        1970   DERAM      UK           18039
    CLIVE BROOKS           D   (AB     (B) POLITE FORCE               1970   DERAM      UK    SML   1074
                                       (C) CIVIL SURFACE              1974   CAROLINE   UK    C     1510
E25                                       EIGHTEEN CARAT GOLD
                                       ( ) ALL BUMM                   1974   UA         UK    UAS  29559
E26                                       EIRE APPARENT
    MICHAEL COX            G   (        (A) SUNRISE                    1969   BUDDAH            203   021
    CHRIS STEWART          B   (        (A) SUNRISE                    1969   BUDDAH                  5031
    DAVE LUTTON            D   (        (B) ROCK'N'ROLL BAND           19     POLYDOR
    ERNIE GRAHAM           B   (
    JIMI HENDRIX          G   (
E27                                        EKSEPTION
    RICK VAN DER LINDEN   K   (ALL      (A) EKSEPTION                  1968   PHILIPS    NL    873   003
    REIN VAN DER LINDEN  HRNS  (ALL     (A) EKSEPTION                  1970   PHILIPS    UK    6314  005
    PETER DE LEEUWE       D   (DE       (A) EKSEPTION                  197    PHILIPS          600   344
    COR DEKKER            B   (DE       (B) BEGGAR JULIA'S TIME TRIP   1969   PHILIPS          6314  001
    DICK REMELINK        SAX  (DE       (C) 3                          1971   PHILIPS          6423  005
    PETER VOOGT           D   (         (D) 00.04                      1971   PHILIPS          6423  019
    JAN VANNIK           WIND  (         (E) EKSEPTION 5                1972   PHILIPS          6423  042
    DENNIS WHITBREAD      D   (         (E) EKSEPTION 5                197    PHILIPS          700   002
                                        ( ) BEST OF                    197    PHILIPS          6423  053
                                        (F) TRINITY                    1973   PHILIPS    NL    6423  056
                                        (G) BINGO                      1974   PHILIPS    NL
                                        (H) CLASSICS IN POP            197    PHILIPS          6423  079
                                        (I) MIND MIRROR                1975   PHILIPS    NL    6423  082
                                        (J) CLASSICS                   1975   PHILIPS          6410  044
                                        (K) REFLECTION SERIES          1976   PHILIPS    NL    6428  111
                                        (L) GREATEST HITS              197    PHILIPS          6677  025
                                        (M) BACK TO THE CLASSICS       197    POLYDOR          2393  167
                                        (N) LA CINQUIEME               197    PHILIPS          6440  217
E28                                        ELASTIC BAND
    ANDY SCOTT                          (A) EXPANSIONS ON LIFE         1969   NOVA              SND 6
    DAVE SCOTT
    TED YEADON              SEAN JENKINS
E29                                        DONNIE ELBERT
    DONNIE ELBERT         V   (ALL      ( ) ROOTS OF DONNIE ELBERT     1973   EMBER      UK    EMB   3421
                                        ( ) STOP IN THE NAME OF LOVE   1976   D JM       UK    DJM  22014
                                        ( ) WHERE DID OUR LOVE GO      19     ALL PLATINUM US          3007
                                        ( ) DONNIE ELBERT SINGS        19     KING       US            629
                                        ( ) HAVE I SINNED              19     DELUXE     US    DLP  12003
E30                                        EL CHICANO
    BOBBY ESPINOSA       K V  (C        (A) EL CHICANO                 19     MCA        UK    MUPS   445
    MICKEY LESPRON        G   (C        (A) EL CHICANO                 19     MCA        US    MCA     69
    ENRIQUE BAEZA        PERC (C        (B) CELEBRATION                19     MCA        UK    MUPS   456
                                        (B) CELEBRATION                1974   MCA        UK    MCF   2659
    HECTOR REGALADO     D PERC(C        (C) CINCO                      1974   MCA        UK    MAPS  7262
    BRIAN MAGNESS         B   (C        (C) CINCO                      197    MCA        UK    MCF   2556
    JERRY SALAS         G V  (C        (C) CINCO                      197    MCA        US    MCA    401
    EDDIE RODRIGUEZ     D PERC(C        (D) REVOLUTION                 1974   MCA        UK    MCF   2654
    SHERRY WILLIAMS       V   (C        (E) LOOK OF LOVE               197    MUSIDISC         CU    1183
    FREDDIE SANCHEZ      V B  (         (F) PYRAMID OF LOVE & FRIENDS  1975   MCA        US    MCA   2150
    JOHN DE LUNA          D   (         (G) THE BEST OF EVERYTHING     1975   MCA        US    MCA    437
                                        ( ) VIVA TIRADO                19     MCA        US    MCA    548
E31                                        EL COCO
    W MICHAEL LEWIS     K SAX (ABC      (A) LET'S GET IT TOGETHER      1976   PYE        UK    NSPL28229
    LAURIN RINDER      V D SAX (ABC     (B) COCOMOTION                 1978   PYE        UK    NSPL28237
    JOE BELLAMY           B   (A        (C) DANCING IN PARADISE        1978   PYE        UK    NSPL28268
    JOHN HUNT             G   (A
    HARRY KIM            TPT  (ABC    DOUG RICHARDSON    WIND  (ABC   DAVE CAHOUN      PNO  (A
    JACK WEBER            G   (A      CHRIS BOCCHINO     V     (A     JERRI BOCCHINO   V    (A
    MARSHA THACKER        V   (AB     ADRIENNE WILLIAMS  V     (AB    KATHY NIXON      V    (A
    MERRIA ROSS           V   (ABC    PAT POWDRILL       V     (A     CLEO KENNEDY     V    (B
    BILL HENDERSON       VLN  (B      PAM TOMKINS        VLN   (B     JIMBO ROSS       VIOLA(B
    MIKE JACOBSEN       CELLO (B      DAVID STOUT        TROM  (C     BOB ETOLL        G    (C
    SHAMSI SARUMI        PERC  (C      ALEX BROWN         V     (C     MORTONETTE JENKINS V  (C
E32                         WAYNE/JAYNE COUNTY & THE ELECTRIC CHAIRS
    WAYNE/JAYNE COUNTY    V   (ABCD     (A) EP THE ELECTRIC CHAIRS     1977   ILLEGAL    UK           IL002
    GREG VAN COOK         G   (BC       (B) ELECTRIC CHAIRS            1978   SAFARI     UK           LONG1
    VAL HALLER            B   (BCD      (B) ELECTRIC CHAIRS            1978   SAFARI     UK    SPA  20308
    J J JOHNSON           D   (BCD      (C) STORM THE GATES OF HEAVEN  1978   SAFARI     UK           GOOD1
    JOOLS HOLLAND         K   (B        (D) THINGS YOUR MOTHER NEVER TOLD 1979 SAFARI    UK           GOOD2
    ELLIOT MICHAELS       G   (D        (EP) BLATANTLY OFFENSIVE       197    SAFARI     UK           WC 2
    HENRI PADOVANI        G   (D
E33                                        ELECTRIC FLAG
    NICK GRAVENITES       V   (ABCD     (A) A LONG TIME COMIN'         1968   CBS        UK           63294
    MIKE BLOOMFIELD      G V  (AC       (A) A LONG TIME COMIN'         1968   CBS        US    CS    9597
    BUDDY MILES           D   (ABCD     (A) A LONG TIME COMIN'         1974   EMBASSY    UK RI        31061
    BARRY GOLDBERG        K   (ABCD     (B) ELECTRIC FLAG              1969   CBS        UK           63462
    HARVEY BROOKS        G B  (AB       (B) ELECTRIC FLAG              1969   CBS        US    CS    9714
    HERBIE RICH       SAX K G (AB       (C) THE BAND KEPT PLAYING      1974   ATLANTIC   UK    K    50090
    MARCUS DOUBLEDAY     TPT  (AB       (C) THE BAND KEPT PLAYING      1974   ATLANTIC   US           18112
    STEMSY HUNTER       V SAX (AB       ( ) THE BEST OF                1971   CBS        US           30422
    PETER STRAZZA        SAX  (A        ( ) THE BEST OF                1971   CBS        UK           64337
    SIVUCA                G   (A

                                                                                        (CONTINUED)

                                                 [134]
```

ELECTRIC FLAG   E33

MIKE FONFARA	K	(A
JOE CHURCH	PERC	(A
JOHN SIMON	PNO	(B
VIRGIL GONSALVES	WIND	(B
NICK MARRERO	PERC	(C
ALBHY GALUTEN	K	(C

JOHN COURT	V PERC	(A
PAUL BEAVER	K	(A
HOSHAL WRIGHT	G	(B
GEORGE TERRY	G	(C
RICHARD NEWELL	HCA	(C

RICHIE HAVENS	PERC	(A
ROGER TROY	B	(BC
TERRY CLEMENTS	SAX	(B
BARRY BECKETT	K	(C
RICHARD TEE	K	(C

ELECTRIC LIGHT ORCHESTRA   E34

ROY WOOD	G V	(A	(A) ELECTRIC LIGHT ORCHESTRA	1971	HARVEST	UK	SHVL 797
RICK PRICE	(		(A) ELECTRIC LIGHT ORCHESTRA	197	SONOPRESSE	FR	69670
JEFF LYNNE	G V	(ALL	(A) ELECTRIC LIGHT ORCHESTRA	197	UA	US	5573
BEV BEVAN	D V	(ALL	(A) NO ANSWER(RI OF(A)	197	JET	US	35524
RICHARD TANDY	K (BCDEFGHJKLMN		(A) NO ANSWER (RI OF (A)	197	UA	US	UALA 040
MICHAEL D'ALBUQUERQUE B V	(B		(B) ELO 2	1973	HARVEST	UK	SHVL 806
MIKE EDWARDS	CELLO	(B	(B) ELO 2	197	JET	US	35533
COLIN WALKER	CELLO	(B	(B) ELO 2	197	SONOPRESSE	FR	69671
WILF GIBSON	VLN	(B	(C) ON THE THIRD DAY	1973	WB	UK	K 56021
HUGH McDOWELL	CELLO	(J	(C) ON THE THIRD DAY	197	SONOPRESSE	FR	30091
MIK KAMINSKI	VLN	(J	(C) ON THE THIRD DAY	197	JET UK LP202	US	35525
MELVYN GALE	CELLO	(J	(C) ON THE THIRD DAY	197	UA	US	UALA 188
KELLY GROUCOTT	B	(JN	(D) SHOWDOWN	1974	HARVEST	UK	SHSP 4037
BILL HUNT	HRNS	(A	(E) THE NIGHT THE LIGHTS WENT ON	1974	WB	UK	K 56058
STEVE WOOLAM	VLN	(A	(E) THE NIGHT THE LIGHTS WENT ON	197	UA	US	UALA 318
			(F) FACE THE MUSIC	1975	JET	UK	LP 11
			(E) FACE THE MUSIC	1975	JET	UK	LP 201
			(F) FACE THE MUSIC	197	SONOPRESSE	FR	30034
			(F) FACE THE MUSIC	197	UA	US	UALA 546
			(F) FACE THE MUSIC	197	POLYDOR	GREECE	2310 414
			(F) FACE THE MUSIC	197	JET	US	35526
			(G) ELDORADO	1975	WB	UK	K 56090
			(G) ELDORADO	197	SONOPRESSE	FR	30092
			(G) ELDORADO	197	JET UK LP203	US	35526
			(G) ELDORADO	197	UA	US	UALA 339
			(H) OLE' ELO	1976	JET	UK	LP 19
			(H) OLE' ELO	197	JET	US	35528
			(H) OLE' ELO	197	JET	NL	LP 903
			(H) OLE' ELO	197	UA	US	UALA 630
			(J) NEW WORLD RECORD	1976	JET	UK	30034
			(J) NEW WORLD RECORD	197	UA	US	UALA 679
			(J) NEW WORLD RECORD	197	JET UK LP200	US	35529
			(J) NEW WORLD RECORD	197	SONOPRESSE	FR	30017
			(K) OUT OF THE BLUE	1977	JET	UK	UAR 100
			(K) OUT OF THE BLUE	197	JET	DP	400
			(K) OUT OF THE BLUE	197	JET	US	35530
			(K) OUT OF THE BLUE	197	JET	US	JTLA 823
			(L) THE LIGHT SHINES ON	1977	HARVEST	UK	SHSM 2015
			(M) THE LIGHT SHINES ON VOL2	1979	HARVEST	UK	SHSM 2027
			(N) DISCOVERY	1979	JET		LX500
			(N) DISCOVERY	1979	JET	US	45769
			(N) DISCOVERY	1979	CBS SONY	JAP	25AP 1600
			(O) GREATEST HITS	1979	JET	UK	LX525

ELECTRIC PRUNES   E35

JIM LOWE AUTOHARP V	(A	(A) ELECTRIC PRUNES	1967	REPRISE	US	RLP 6248
JOHN HERREN	K	(C	(A) ELECTRIC PRUNES	1967	REPRISE	IMP	24033
MARK TULIN	B	(A	(B) UNDERGROUND	1967	REPRISE	US	RLP 6262
KEN WILLIAMS	G	(A	(C) MASS IN F MINOR	1968	REPRISE	US	RLP 6275
PRESTON RITTER	D	(A	(C) MASS IN F MINOR	1972	REPRISE	UK	K 34003
WEASEL SPAGNOLA	G	(A	(C) MASS IN F MINOR	197	MIDI	UK	24010
RON MORGAN	G	(C	(D) RELEASE OF AN OATH	1968	REPRISE	US	RLP 6316
MARK KINCAID	G V	(C	(E) JUST GOOD OLD ROCK'N'ROLL	1969	REPRISE	US	RSLP 6342
RICHARD WHETSTONE	D G V	(C					
BRETT WADE	B V FLT	(C					

DENNY LAINE	V G	(
ANDY LEIGH	B V	(
VIV PRINCE	D	(

ELECTRIC STRING BAND   E35A

THE ELECTRIC TOILET   E35B

(A) ELECTRIC TOILET	19	NASCO	US	NASCO

ELECTROPHON   E35C

(A) ZYGOAT	1974	POLYDOR		2383 270
( ) ELECTROPHON	197	POLDOR		2383 210
( ) FURTHER THOUGHTS ON THE CLASSICS	1977	POLYDOR		2482 335

BIG MOJO ELEM   E35D

BIG MOJO ELEM	V B	(A	(A) MOJO BOOGIE	1978	MCM	FR	900303
FRED BELOW	D	(A					
WAYNE BENNETT	G	(A					

WILLIE JAMES LYONS   G   (A

ELEPHANT   E36

(A) ELEPHANT	1973	CAPITOL		SMAS11154

DICK GLASS	V G	(A	
RUSS KUNKEL	D	(A	
CHARLES LARKEY	B	(A	GEOFF LEVIN G (A AMBROSE CAMPBELL PERC (A

E37   **ELEPHANTS MEMORY**

```
RICK FRANK            D V    (ABCDE    (A) ELEPHANTS MEMORY                 1969  BUDDAH                         5033
STAN BRONSTEIN        V SAX  (ABCDE    (A) ELEPHANTS MEMORY                 1969  BUDDAH               203  022
GARY VAN SCYOC        B V    (ABCDE    (B) MIDNIGHT COWBOY  (SOUNDTRACK)    1969  BUDDAH                         5038
WAYNE TEX GABRIEL     G V    (D        (C) TAKE IT TO THE STREETS           1971  METRONOME            MD   1052
JOHN LENNON     V G K PERC   (D        (C) TAKE IT TO THE STREETS           1971  METRONOME                 1035
CHRIS ROBISON         V K G  (E        (D) ELEPHANTS MEMORY                 1972  APPLE                SMAS 3389
ADAM IPPOLITO       K TPT V  (D        (D) ELEPHANTS MEMORY                 1972  APPLE                SAPCOR.22
THUNDERTHIGHS         V      (E        (E) ANGELS FOREVER                   1974  POLYDOR              2383 260
TERRY & THE PIRATES   V      (E        (E) ANGELS FOREVER                   1974  RCA                  APLI 0569
YOKO ONO              V      (D        (F) OUR ISLAND MUSIC                 197   MUSE          US     MR   5072
MARTHA VELEZ          V      (D
HILDA HARRIS          V      (D
TONI WINE             V      (D        KEITH JOHNSON     TPT    (D     DAVID PEEL          V    (D
JON SACHS             G V    (D        LINDA NOVEMBER    V      (D     MYRON YULES         V    (D
                                       JOHN WARD         B      (      RICHARD SUSSMAN     K    (
```

E38   **ELF**

```
RONNIE JAMES DIO  ]SAME V B(ABC        (A) ELF                              19    EPIC          US           31789
RON PADAVONA      ]                    (B) CAROLINA COUNTRY BALL            1974  PURPLE        UK     TPSA 3506
MICKEY LEE SOULE      K G    (ABC      (B) CAROLINA COUNTRY BALL (LA59)     197   MGM           US     M3G  4974
GARY DRISCOLL        D       (ABC      (C) TRY TO BURN THE SUN              1975  MGM           US     M3G  4994
DAVE FEINSTEIN       G       (A
GRAIG GRUBER         B       (BC       STEVE EDWARDS     G      (BC    MARK NAUSEEF        PERC (C
```

E39   **ELIZABETH**

```
STEVE WEINGARTEN     G ORG   (A        (A) ELIZABETH                        1968  VANGUARD             VSD  6501
JIM DAHME            V FLT G(A
BOB PATTERSON        G V     (A        STEVE BRUNO       B K    (A     HANK RANSOME        D G B(A
```

E40   **YVONNE ELLIMAN**

```
YVONNE ELLIMAN       V       (ALL      (A) I DON'T KNOW HOW TO LOVE HIM     1972  POLYDOR              2383 141
WITH                                   (B) FOOD OF LOVE                     1973  PURPLE        UK     TPS  3504
DAVID SPINOZZA       G       (A        (B) FOOD OF LOVE                     1973  MCA           US            356
HUGH McCRACKEN       G       (A        (C) RISING SUN                       1975  RSO           UK     2393 149
STU WOODS            B       (A        (D) LOVE ME                          1977  RSO     US 3018 UK  2394 182
RICK MAROTTA         D       (A        (E) NIGHT FLIGHT                     1978  RSO     US 3031 UK  2394 197
MICHAEL OMARTIAN     K       (F        (F) YVONNE                           1979  RSO                  RS   16
JIM KELTNER          D       (FE
JEFF PORCARO         D       (F        STEVE CROPPER     G      (FE    JAY GRAYDON        G       (F
RICHIE ZETO          G       (F        MARTY WALSH       G      (F     DAVEY JOHNSTONE    G SITAR(FE
MIKE PORCARO         B       (F        LEE RITENOUR      G      (F     VICTOR FELDMAN     PERC    (F
PAUL STALLWORTH      B       (FE       STEVE BARRI       PERC   (F     LEE SKLAR         B        (FE
JIM HORN             WIND    (FE       BUELL NEIDLINGER  B      (F     MAXINE WILLARD    V        (FE
DAVID PAICH          K       (F        JULIA TILLMAN     V      (F     TOM SNOW          K        (F
JIM HAAS             V       (F        TOM CANNING       K      (F     JON JOYCE         V        (F
BILL PAYNE           K       (F        STAN FARBER       V      (F     CRAIG DOERGE      K        (FE
JOHN HENRY KURTZ     V       (F        DR JOHN           K V    (F     GARY COLEMAN      PERC     (EF
JOE PORCARO          PERC    (F        FRED STAEHLE      PERC   (F     CHUCK FINDLEY     HRNS     (FE
ERIC CARMEN          V K     (EF       JACKIE KELSO      HRNS   (EF    MATTHEW MOORE     V        (F
KATHY COLLIER        V       (FE       CARMEN TWILLIE    V      (EF    VENNETTE GLOUD    V        (EF
MIKE BAIRD           D       (E        SONNY BURKE       K      (E     BOB BOWLES        G        (E
JAMES GADSON         D       (E        JAMES NEWTON HOWARD K    (E     LOWELL GEORGE     G        (E
RITCHIE HAYWARD      D       (E        WILLIAM SMITH     K      (E     STEVE HUNTER      G        (E
RUSS KUNKEL          D       (E        KIKI DEE          V      (E     DANNY KORTCHMAR   G        (E
BABOO PIERRE         PERC    (E        DONNY GERRARD     V      (E     DEAN PARKES       G        (E
PAULINHO DA COSTA    PERC    (E        SCOTT EDWARDS     B      (E     HENRY KAPONO      V        (E
BOB ZIMITTI          PERC    (E        DEE MURRAY        B      (E     MARTI McCALL      V        (E
FRED PERREN          SYN     (D)       BEN BENAY         G      (E     CECILIO RODRIGUEZ V        (E
```

E41   **MARC ELLINGTON**

```
MARC ELLINGTON V G BAGPIPES(ALL        (A) MARC ELLINGTON                   1969  PHILIPS       UK     SBL  7883
WITH                                   (B) RAINS/ REINS OF CHANGE           1971  B&C           UK     CAS  103
KAREN ELLINGTON      V       (ABC      (C) A QUESTION OF ROADS              1972  PHILIPS       UK     6308 120
RICHARD THOMPSON     G       (ABE      (D) RESTORATION                      1972  PHILIPS       UK     6308 143
DAVE PEGG            B       (B        (E) MARC TIME                        1972  XTRA          UK     XTRA 1154
CHRIS HILLMAN        V MAND(B
DAVE MATTACKS    D   (BDE    IAN MATTHEWS    V   (BD    SNEAKY PETE KLEINOW STEEL(B   TONY COX        K   (BDE
MIKE DIEGHAN G BANJO(BCD    PAT DONALDSON   B   (BDE   GERRY CONWAY      D   (BE    GORDON HUNTLEY  B   (AB
RAY DUFFY        D   (BC     SANDY DENNY     V   (B     FRITZ FRYER       V   (B     STEVE RYE       HCA (B
MICK FRENCH      VLN(B       RICK ROBERTS    V   (B     GERRY FIELD       VLN (B     TIM RENWICK     G   (C
BRUCE THOMAS     B   (C      ANDY LEIGH      B   (C     JOHN WILSON       D   (C     DAVE RICHARDS   B PNO(CDE
ANDY ROBERTS     G K(CDE     ERIC ELLINGTON  V   (C     JERRY DONAHUE     G   (DE    DAVE PEACOCK    B   (D
DAVE HEPBURN     B   (D      TIMI DONALD     D   (DE    BARRY DE SOUZA    D   (D     PHIL CHESTERTON D   (D
TOM PARKER       PNO(D       ZOOT MONEY      PNO(D      DOLLY COLLINS     PNO (D     BOB RONGA       G   (D
SIMON NICOL      G   (ADE    PHIL PICKETT    G   (D     RAY WARLEIGH      SAX (D      IAN WHITEMAN    K   (DE
SUE DRAHEIM      VLN(D       MAC KISSOON     V   (DE    SANDY ROBERTSON   G   (E     LONGDANCER      V   (D
KATHY KISSOON    V   (DE     ROGER SWALLOW   D   (AE    LINDA THOMPSON    V   (E     B J COLE        STEEL(E
STEVE ASHLEY     HCA(E       REG POWELL      K   (A     JAMIE OGILVY FORBES PIPES(D   MARK GRIFFITHS  B   (AB
```

E42   **CASS ELLIOT**

```
CASS ELLIOT          V       (ALL      (A) CASS ELLIOT                             1968 RCA          US     LSP 4619
DAVE MASON           G V(F             (B) DREAM A LITTLE DREAM                    1968 DUNHILL      US         50040
                                       (B) DREAM A LITTLE DREAM                    1968 STATESIDE    UK          5004
                                       (C) BUBBLE GUM LEMONADE & SOMETHING         1969 DUNHILL      US         50055
                                       (C) BUBBLE GUM LEMONADE & SOMETHING         1969 STATESIDE    UK          5014
                                       (D) MAKE YOUR OWN MUSIC                     19   DUNHILL
                                       (E) MAMA'S BIG ONES                         1971 PROBE        UK     SPB 1020
                                       (E) MAMA'S BIG ONES                         1974 ABC UK ABCL5011 DUNHILL US50093
                                       (F) DAVE MASON & CASS ELLIOT                1971 PROBE UK SPB6259 US B THUMB8825
                                       (G) ROAD IS NO PLACE FOR A LADY             1974 RCA   US LSA 3194 UK SF  8306
                                       (H) DON'T CALL ME MAMA ANYMORE              1974 RCA          UK     APLI 0303
```

COLONEL ELLIOT
E43

COLONEL ELLIOT		(A) INTERSTELLA REGGAE DRIVE	1974	RHINO		SRNP 9001

DAVE ELLIOTT
E44

DAVID ELLIOTT		(A) SOLID GROUND	1973	ATLANTIC	UK	K 40527

RON ELLIOTT
E45

RON ELLIOTT		(A) CANDELSTICK MAKER	19	WB		WS 1833

ELLIS
E46

STEVE ELLIS	V	(AB	(A) RIDING ON THE CREST OF A SLUMP	1972	EPIC	UK	EPC 64878
ZOOT MONEY	K V	(AB	(B) WHY NOT?	1973	EPIC	UK	EPC 65650
ANDY GEE	G	(AB					
DAVE LUTTON	D	(AB	COLIN ALLEN	D PERC (B	GARY FARR	HCA	(
JIM LEVERTON	B	(A	MAGGIE BELL	V	(AB	MICK WEAVER	K (
NICK SOUTH	B	(B	JULIE TIPPETTS	V	(B	ROGER CHAPMAN	V (B
MIKE PATTO	V	(B	MAGGIE NICHOLLS	V	(B		

DAVE ELLIS
E47

DAVE ELLIS	G	(A	(A) ALBUM	1973	SONET	UK	SNTF 646
GORDON GILTRAP	G	(A					

MATTHEW ELLIS
E48

MATTHEW ELLIS	V G K (ALL	(A) MATTHEW ELLIS	1971	REGAL ZONOPHONE UK	SRZA 8501
CHRIS SPEDDING g	(B	(B) AM I	1971	REGAL ZONOPHONE UK	SRZA 8505
TONI CAMPO	B	(B					
CLEM CATTINI D	(B	BARRY MORGAN	D	(B	CHRIS WALKER	K	(B	REX MORRIS	SAX (B
PAUL SCHERMAN VLN	(B	TOMMY REILLY	HCA	(B	SUNNY LESLIE	V	(B	KAY GARNER	V (B
LESLEY DUNCAN	V	(B					

PEE WEE ELLIS
E49

PEE WEE ELLIS SAX K V PERC(A	(A) HOME IN THE COUNTRY	1977	SAVOY	IMP SJL 3301

ROLAND HANNA	K (A					
JON SCHOLLE	G (A	JEFF BERLIN	B (A	IDRIS MUHAMMAD	D (A	JIMMY STRASSBURG	D (A
JUMMA SANTOS CONGA	(A	CHARLOTTE CROSSLEY V (A	LILLIAN TYNES	V (A	CHARLES BROWN	G (A
ANTHONY JACKSON B	(A	BABATUNDE	CONGA	(A	GORDON EDWARDS	B (A	MELANIE JORDIN	V (A
JOHN GATCHELL TPT	(A	BARRY ROGERS	TROM	(A	ERNIE HAYES	K (A	CORNELL DUPREE	G (A
ERIC GALE	G (A	BERNARD PURDIE	D (A	RAY MANTILLA	PERC (A	LEON THOMAS	V (A
LANI GROVES	V (A	WAYMON REED	TPT	(A	GEORGE BENSON	G (A	CHRIS PARKER	D (A
VIVIAN CHERRY	V (A	DWAIN JONES	V (A	DAVE LIEBMAN	SAX (A	ELEANA STEINBERG	V (A

LORRAINE ELLISON
E49A

LORRAINE ELLISON	V	(AB	(A) LORRAINE ELLISON	19	WB	US BS 2780	UK K	46296
			(B) HEART & SOUL	19	WB	US BS 1821		
			(C) BEST OF PHILADELPHIAS QUEEN	1976	WB		UK K	56230

ELMER GANTY'S VELVET OPERA
E50

ELMER GANTRY	V	(AB	(A) ELMER GANTRY'S VELVET OPERA	1968	DIRECTION	UK	8 63300
COLIN FORSTER	G	(A	(B) 1968 LIVE LINE UP				
JOHN FORD	B	(AB					
RICHARD HUDSON	D	(AB	PAUL BRETT	G	(B		

ELOY
E50A

FRANK BORNEMANN	V G	(AB	(A) INSIDE	1973	ELECTROLA	GERM 064 29479
KLAUS PETER MATZIOL V B	(	(A) INSIDE	197	JANUS	US	3062
FRITZ RANDOW	D G	(AB	(B) FLOATING	1974	ELECTROLA	GERM 072 29521
DETLEV SCHMIDTCHEN	K SYN	(	(C) POWER & THE PASSION	1975	ELECTROLA	GERM 062 29602
JURGEN ROSENTHAL	D	(	(D) DAWN	1976	ELECTROLA	GERM 064 31787
MANFRED WIECZORKE	K G V (AB	(E) OCEAN	1977	ELECTROLA	GERM 064 32596
WOLFGANG STOCKER	B	(B	(F) SILENT CRIES AND MIGHTY ECHOES	1978	ELECTROLA	GERM 064 45269
LUITJEN JANSSEN	B	(A	(G) LIVE	1978	ELECTROLA	GERM 164 32934
			(H) COLOURS	1980	ELECTROLA	GERM 064 45936

JOE ELY
E51

JOE ELY	G V	(ALL	(A) JOE ELY	1977	MCA US 2242	UK MCF 2808
LLOYD MAINES STEEL V	(BC	(B) HONKY TONK MASQUERADE	1978	MCA US 2333	UK MCF 2832
JESSE TAYLOR	G V	(BC	(C) DOWN IN THE DRAG	1979	MCA	UK MCG 3532
GREGG WRIGHT	B V	(BC	(D) LIVE SHOTS	1980	MCA	UK MCF 3064
STEVE KEETON	D	(BC					
PONTI BONE	K	(BC	CHIP YOUNG	G	(B	SHANE KEISTER	K	(B
FARRELL MORRIS	PERC	(B	ED CIZARD	SAX	(C	RICHARD BOWDEN	FDL	(C
DAVID MASON	K	(C	DINK THOMAS	WHISTLE(C	PETER WEST	V	(C
LEA JANE BERINATI	V	(B	GINGER HOLLADAY	V	(B	LISA SILVER	V	(B
BUTCH HANCOCK	V	(B					

EMBRYO
E52

CHRISTIAN BURCHARD	V D K (12E	( ) OPAL	1970	OHR	GERM OMM556003
EDGAR HOFMANN	V WIND(12	(B) EMBRYO'S RACHE	1971	UA		UAS 29239
JOHN KELLY	G V	(1	(C) STEIG AUS	1973	BRAIN	GERM	1023
RALPH FISHER	B G V K (1	(D) THIS IS	197	BRAIN		201109
UWE MULLRICH	B	(2	(E) ROCK SESSION	1973	BRAIN	GERM	1036
ROMAN BUNKA	G V CLAR(2	(E) ROCK SESSION	197	BRAIN		201190
JIMMY JACKSON	K	(E	(F) WE KEEP ON	1974	BASF	GERM 21865/1
SIEGFRIED SCHWAB	G	(E	(G) SURFIN'	1975	BASF	GERM 22385/3
MAL WALDRON	K	(E	(H) FATHER SON HOLY GHOST	1975	UA		29344
JORG EVERS	B	(E	(J) EMBRYO LIVE	1976	TRIKONT		0003
			(1) 1969 (2) 1977				

EMERGENCY
E52A

HANUS BERKA	SAX	(AB	(A) GOLD ROCK	1973	BRAIN	201 104
JOHN REDPATH	D	(A	(B) NO COMPROMISE	1974			
FRANK DIEZ	G B	(AB					
HANS STOER	G B	(A	PETER BISCHOF	B	(A	RICHARD PALMER JAMES	G	(A
MARTIN HARRISON		(A	ELMAR SCHMIDT	D	(	RALF TOURSEL	K SYN(

BILLY THE KID EMERSON
E52B

BILLY THE KID EMERSON V PNO (A	(A) LITTLE HEALTHY THING	19	CHARLY	UK	CR 30187

EUGENE FOX	SAX	(A					
OLIVER SAIN	SAX	(A	IKE TURNER	G	(A	JESSE KNIGHT	B	(A	CHARLES SMITH	TPT (A
MOSES REED	SAX	(A	CALVIN NEWBORN G	(A	ROBERT PRINDELL	D	(A	WILLIE SIMS	D	(A
BOBBY FIELD	SAX	(A	LUTHER TAYLOR	SAX	(A	JEWEL BRISCOE	SAX	(A	KENNETH BANKS	B	(A
RAYMOND HILL	SAX	(A	BENNIE MOORE	SAX	(A	ELVEN PARR	G	(A	PHINEAS NEWBORN D	(A

EMERSON LAKE & PALMER

KEITH EMERSON	K	(ALL	(A) EMERSON LAKE & PALMER	1970	ISLAND	UK	ILPS 9132
GREG LAKE	B G V	(ALL	(A) EMERSON LAKE & PALMER	1973	MANTICORE	UK	K 43503
CARL PALMER	D	(ALL	(A) EMERSON LAKE & PALMER	197	COTILLION	US	9040
WITH			(A) EMERSON LAKE & PALMER	197	MANTICORE	US	19120
			(A) EMERSON LAKE & PALMER	197	ARIOLA	GERM	87 224ET
JOE WALSH	G	(G	(B) TARKUS	1971	ISLAND	UK	ILPS 9155
			(B) TARKUS	1973	MANTICORE	UK	K 43504
			(B) TARKUS	197	COTILLION	US	9900
			(B) TARKUS	197	MANTICORE	US	19121
			(B) TARKUS	197	ARIOLA	GERM	87225XOT
			(C) PICTURES AT AN EXHIBITION	1971	ISLAND	UK	HELP1
			(C) PICTURES AT AN EXHIBITION	1973	MANTICORE	UK	K 33501
			(C) PICTURES AT AN EXHIBITION	197	MANTICORE	US	66666
			(C) PICTURES AT AN EXHIBITION	197	MANTICORE	US	19122
			(C) PICTURES AT AN EXHIBITION	197	ARIOLA	GERM	87 226.ET
			(D) TRILOGY	1972	ISLAND	UK	ILPS 9186
			(D) TRILOGY	1973	MANTICORE	UK	K 43505
			(D) TRILOGY	197	COTILLION	US	9903
			(D) TRILOGY	197	MANTICORE	US	19123
			(D) TRILOGY	197	ARIOLA	GERM	87 227XOT
			(E) BRAIN SALAD SURGERY	1973	MANTICORE	UK	K 53501
			(E) BRAIN SALAD SURGERY	197	MANTICORE	US	66669
			(E) BRAIN SALAD SURGERY	197	ATLANTIC	US	19124
			(E) BRAIN SALAD SURGERY	197	ARIOLA	GERM	87 302XOT
			(F) WELCOME MY FRIENDS	1974	MANTICORE	UK	K 63500
			(F) WELCOME MY FRIENDS	1974	MANTICORE	US	MC3 200
			(F) WELCOME MY FRIENDS	197	ARIOLA	GERM	88 150XET
			(G) WORKS	1977	MANTICORE	UK	K 80009
			(G) WORKS	1977	ATLANTIC	US	SD2 7000
			(G) WORKS	197	ARIOLA	GERM	28 614XDU
			(H) WORKS VOL 2	1977	ATLANTIC	UK	K 50422
			(H) WORKS VOL 2	1977	ATLANTIC	US	19147
			(H) WORKS VOL 2	197	ARIOLA	GERM	25 553XOT
			(J) LOVE BEACH	1978	ATLANTIC	UK	K 50552
			(J) LOVE BEACH	1978	ATLANTIC	US	19211
			(J) LOVE BEACH	1978	ARIOLA	GERM	200249420
			(K) IN CONCERT	1979	ATLANTIC	UK	K 50757
			(K) IN CONCERT	1979	ATLANTIC	US	19283
			(L) BEST OF	1980	ATLANTIC	UK	K 50652

BUDDY EMMONS

BUDDY EMMONS	STEEL	(ALL	(A) 2 ACES BACK TO BACK(I SIDE)	1971	K ARK	US	K6028
BUDDY SPICHER	FDL	(E	(B) EMMONS GUITAR INC	197	EMMONS	US	
LENNY BREAU		(	(C) STEEL GUITAR	1975	FLYING FISH	UK	SNTF 708
			(C) STEEL GUITAR	1975	FLYING FISH	US	FF 007
			(D) SINGS BOB WILLS	1976	FLYING	UK	SNTF 706
			(D) SINGS BOB WILLS	1977	FLYING FISH	US	FF 017
			(E) BUDDIES	1977	FLYING FISH	US	FF 041
			(E) BUDDIES	1977	FLYING FISH	UK	SNTF 741
			(F) EMMONS LIVE VOL 1	197	MIDLAND	US	ISGC1
			(G) EMMONS LIVE VOL 2	197	MIDLAND	US	ISGC2
			(H) MINORS ALOUD	1979	FLYING FISH	US	FF 088
			(H) MINORS ALOUD	1979	FLYING FISH	UK	SNTF 799

EMOTIONS

JEANETTE HAWES	V	(E	(A) SO I CAN LOVE YOU	19	VOLT	US	6008	
SHEILA HUTCHINSON	V	(EFG	(B) SONGS OF LOVE	19	VOLT	US	6921	
WANDA HUTCHINSON	V	(EFG	(C) UNTOUCHED	19	VOLT	US	6015	
PAMELA	V	(F	(D) CHRONICLE	19	STAX	US	4121	
THERESA DAVIS	V	(G	(E) FLOWERS	1976	CBS US 34163		UK	81639
VERDINE WHITE	B	(EF	(F) REJOICE	1977	CBS US 34762		UK	82065
LARRY DUNN	K	(EF	(G) SUNSHINE	1977	STAX US 4100		UK	3003
AL McKAY	G	(EF	(H) SUNBEAM	1978	CBS		UK	82864
JOE HUTCHINSON	G	(E	(J) BEST OF	1979	STAX US 4121		UK	3008
MICHAEL HARRIS	TPT	(E						

FRED WHITE	D	(EF	DON MYRICK	D	(EF	OSCAR BRASHEAR	TPT	(EF	RICHARD BROWN	SAX	(E
DAVID SHIELDS	B	(F	JAMES GADSON	D	(F	MAURICE WHITE	D	(F	JERRY PETERS	K	(F
PAULINHO DACOSTA	PERC	(F	SKIP SCARBOROUGH	K	(F	MARLO HENDERSON	G	(F	CLARENCE McDONALD	K	(F
LOUIS SATTERFIELD	TROM	(EF	MICHAEL TOLES	G	(F	BOBBY MANUEL	G	(G	MARVELL THOMAS	K	(G
LESTER SNARE	K	(G	RONNIE WILLIAMS	K	(G	EARL THOMAS	B	(G	DONALD DUCK DUNN	B	(G
AL JACKSON	D	(G	WILLIE HALL	D	(G						

EMPEROR

JOE ALEXANDER	G V	(A	(A) EMPEROR			1977	PRIVATE STOCK UK	2029
JOE MARQUES	B V	(A						
MIKE LOBBETT	K V	(A	STEVE WATTS	D V	(A	RANDY BUDIKAS	D V	(A

END

(A) INTROSPECTION	1969	DECCA	UK	SKL 5015
(A) INTROSPECTION	1969	LONDON	US	PS 560

ENGLAND

MARTIN HENDERSON	B V	(A	(A) GARDEN SHED		1977	ARISTA	UK	ARTY 153
FRANC HOLLAND	G V	(A					
ROBERT WEBB	K V	(A	JODE LEIGH	B V	(A		

```
ENGLAND DAN SEALS    V G   (ALL    (A) ENGLAND DAN & JOHN FORD COLEY   197    A&M      US 4305   UK AMLS64305
JOHN FORD COLEY      V G K (ALL    (B) FABLES                          197    A&M      US 4350   UK AMLS64350
WITH                              (C) I HEAR MUSIC                    1976   A&M      US 4616   UK AMLH64613
BOBBY THOMPSON    G   (F          (D) NIGHTS ARE FOREVER              1976 BIG TREE US 89517  UK K  50297
JOHNNY CHRISTOPHER G(F            (E) DOWDY FERRY ROAD                 197 BIG TREE US 50362  UK K  50362
STEVE GIBSON      G   (FG         (F) SOMETHINGS DONT COME EASY       1978 BIG TREE US 70006  UK K  50470
LEE RITENOUR      G   (G          (G) DR HECKLE & MR JIVE             1979 BIG TREE US 76015  UK K  50602
STEVE LUKATHER    G   (G
DAN FERGUSON      G   (G    WAH WAH WATSON   G   (G    DOYLE GRISHAM  STEEL (F   JACK WILLIAMS  B  (F
JOE OSBORN        B   (F    WILTON FELDER    B   (G    DEE MURRAY     B    (G    DAN GORMAN     D  (G
JOHN LELAND       B   (G    LEE SKLAR        B   (G    SHANE KEISTER  K    (FG   JOEY CARBONE   PNO (G
BOBBY EMMONS      ORG (F    GREG PHILLINGANES PNO (G   MICHAEL BODDIKER SYN (G   STEVE PORCARO  SYN (G
MICHAEL VERNACCHIO K(G      BILL PAYNE       SYN (G    FARREL MORRIS  PERC (F    CYNDI REYNOLDS HARP(F
MIKE MILLER       SAX (F    BILLY PUETT      WIND(F    GOVE SCRIVENER AUTOHARP (F HARRISON CALLOWAY HRNS(F
HARVEY THOMPSON   HRNS(F    RONNIE EADES     HRNS(F    DENNIS GOODE   HRNS (F    SHELLEY KURLAND STR(F
LISA SILVER       V   (F    SHERI KRAMER     V   (F    DIANE TIDWELL  V    (F    VICKI LEHNING  V  (F
DENISE PERALTA    V   (F    STEVE FORMAN     PERC(G    ERNIE WATTS    SAX  (G    GARY MALLABER  D  (G
RALPH HUMPHREY    D   (G    JEFF PORCARO     D   (G    RICHIE ZETO    G    (G    JIM GILSTRAP   V  (G
JAI WINDING       PNO (G    LESLIE BULKIN    V   (G    KELLY BULKIN   V    (G    OVID STEVENS   G  (G
ED GREENE         D   (G    BUBBA KEITH      HCA (G    GARY TORPS     G    (G    LARRIE LONDIN  D  (F
```

THE ENID   E58

```
ROBERT GODFREY    K   (CDE    (A) THE ENID                   1976   BUK              BULP 2014
FRANCIS LICKERISH G   (CDE    (B) IN THE REGION OF THE STARS 1977   EMI              INS 3005
STEPHEN STEWART   G   (CDE    (C) AERIE FAERIE NONSENSE      1977   EMI              INS 3012
DAVID STOREY      D   (CD     (D) TOUCH ME                   1979   PYE        UK    NSPH18593
CHARLIE ELSTON    K   (C      (E) SIX PIECES                 1979   PYE        UK    N  116
TERRY PACK            (CD
WILLIAM GILMOUR   K   (DE     TONY FREER   HRNS   (D      MARTIN RUSSELL    K B (E
ROBBIE DOBSON     D   (E
```

BRIAN ENO   E59

```
BRIAN ENO         V K SYN (ALL   (A) NO PUSSYFOOTIN'                         1973   ISLAND      UK HELP  16
WITH                             (A) NO PUSSYFOOTIN'                         197    PHONOGRAM   EURO 9101  629
ROBERT FRIPP      G    (ABEFHJ   (B) HERE COME THE WARM JETS                 1974   ISLAND      UK ILPS 9268
KURT SCHWITTERS   V    (H        (B) HERE COME THE WARM JETS                 197    PHONOGRAM   EURO 6396  032
FREDDIE SMITH     D    (H        (C) JUNE 1ST 1974                           1974   ISLAND      UK ILPS 9291
SHIRLEY WILLIAMS  PERC (H        (D) TAKING TIGER MOUNTAIN BY STRATEGY 1974   ISLAND      UK ILPS 9309
JAKI LIEBEZEIT    D    (H        (D) TAKING TIGER MOUNTAIN BY STRATEGY 197    POLYDOR     UK 2302  068
RHELL DAVIES      PERC (H        (D) TAKING TIGER MOUNTAIN BY STRATEGY 197    ISLAND      US    1-3001
PAUL RUDOLPH      G    (BEHJ     (E) ANOTHER GREEN WORLD                     1974   ISLAND      UK ILPS 9351
FRED FRITH        G    (HJ       (E) ANOTHER GREEN WORLD                     1974   POLYDOR     UK 2302  069
PERCY JONES       B    (EHJ      (F) EVENING STAR                            1975   ISLAND      UK HELP  22
BILL McCORMICK    B    (HJB      (G) DISCREET MUSIC                          1975   OBSCURE        OBSCURE 4
PHIL COLLINS      PERC (HJ       (H) BEFORE & AFTER SCIENCE                  1977   POLYDOR     UK 2302  071
DAVE MATTACKS     PERC (HJ       (H) BEFORE & AFTER SCIENCE                  1977   POLYDOR     EURO 2310  547
ROD MELVIN        K    (EJ       (H) BEFORE & AFTER SCIENCE                  1977   ISLAND      US     9478
ANDY FRASER       B    (H        (J) MUSIC FOR FILMS                         1978   POLYDOR     UK 2310  623
ACHIM ROEDELIUS   K    (HK       (K) AFTER THE HEAT                          1978   SKY            021
MOBI MOEBIUS      K    (HK       (L) MUSIC FOR AIRPORTS                      1979   AMBIENT     AMB  001
BRIAN TURRINGTON  B    (DEH      (M) POSSIBLE MUSIC                          1980   EDITIONS       EGED7
RABBIT BUNDRICK   K    (C        (N) THE PLATEAUX OF MIRRORS                 1980   EDITIONS       EGAMB 002
EDDIE SPARROW     D    (C
MIKE OLDFIELD     G    (C    JOHN CALE   VIOLA K  (CE   OLLIE HALSALL G PNO (C   ARCHIE LEGGET B   (C
KEVIN AYERS       B    (C    ROBERT WYATT PERC(CDL  NICO     V HARMONIUM(C  JOHN HASSEL       (M
HAROLD BUDD            (N    INGE ZEININGER   V  (L  NICK JUDD   K    (B   ANDY MACKAY   SAX K(BD
PHIL MANZANERA    G    (BD   SWEETFEED         V  (B  CHRIS THOMAS B    (B   LLOYD WATSON  G   (B
PAUL THOMPSON     PERC (B    MARTY SIMON      PERC(B  SIMON KING  PERC (B   JOHN WETTON   B   (B
BUSTA CHERRY JONES B   (B    CHRIS SPEDDING   G  (B  CHRISTA FAST V    (L   CHRISTINE GOMEZ V (L
PORTSMOUTH SINFONIA    (C    POLLY ELTES      V  (D  SIMPLISTICS V    (D   RANDI & PYRAMIDS V (D
```

JOHN ENTWISTLE   E60

```
JOHN ENTWISTLE    B V K (ALL    (A) SMASH YOUR HEAD                 1971   TRACK     UK 2406  005
GRAHAM DEACON     D PERC(CD     (a) SMASH YOUR HEAD                 197    MCA       US     2024
TONY ASHTON       PNO  (CD      (A) SMASH YOUR HEAD   (DIFF MIX)    197    DECCA     US    79183
JIM RYAN          G    (D       (B) WHISTLE RHYMES                 1972   TRACK     UK 2406  104
HOWIE CASEY       SAX  (CD      (B) WHISTLE RHYMES                 197    DECCA     US    79190
DAVE CASWELL      TPT  (D       (C) RIGOR MORTIS SETS IN           1973   TRACK     UK 2406  106
JOHN MUMFORD      TROM (D       (C) RIGOR MORTIS SETS IN           197    EPIC         34467
DICK PARRY        SAX  (D       (D) MAD DOG                        1975   TRACK     UK TX 5114
DOREEN CHANTER    V    (D       (D) MAD DOG                        197    MCA       US     2129
BRYAN WILLIAMS    TROM (C       (D) MAD DOG                        197    LONDON    JAP LAX 1034
IRENE CHANTER     V    (D       (E) BACKTRACK 14 ( THE OX)         1971   TRACK     UK 2407  014
MIKE WEDGEWOOD    G    (D
EDDIE JOBSON      K    (D       JOHN MEALING  PNO   (D    JUANITA FRANKLIN  V   (D
ALAN ROSS         G    (C       LADYBIRDS     V     (C
```

EON   E60A

```
EON                                                19     SCEPTER    US     5122
```

EPISODE SIX   E61

```
SHEILA CARTER DIMMOCK K V (1234   (1) 1965  (2) 1965/7  (3) 1967  (4) 1967/8
GRAHAM CARTER DIMMOCK G V (1234
TONY LANDER       G V  (1234   HARVEY SHIELDS   D V  (12   IAN GILLAN     V   (234
ALAN ROSS         V G  (1      JOHN KERRISON    D    (3    MICK UNDERWOOD D   (4
ROGER GLOVER      B V  (1234
```

PRESTON EPPS   E61A

```
BONGOLA                                   19     TOP RANK      US  RM  349
BONGO ROCK                              1959     ORIGINAL SOUND US     1001
SURFIN' BONGOS                            19     ORIGINAL SOUND US 5009M+8872S
```

E61B

MICHAEL WINZKOWSKI	G V	(AB						
HARTMUT PFANNMULLER	D PERC	(AB						
WALTER ORTEL	K	(AB						
MICHAEL ERTL	B	(AB						

EPSILON

(A) EPSILON	1971	BELLAPHON	GERM	BLPS19070
(B) MOVE ON	197	BELLAPHON	GERM	BLPS19078

E62

DERVIN GORDON	V	(1234
DAVE MARTIN	G	(CD
LINCOLN GORDON	G	(1234
EDDIE GRANT	G	(1
PAT LLOYD	G	(1234
JOHN HALL	D	(123
JIMMY HAYNES	G	(B
NEIL McBAIN	D	(4

(1) 1966   (2) 1971
(3) 19673   (4) 1975

EQUALS

UNEQUALLED	1967	PRESIDENT		PTL 1006
UNEQUALLED	196	LAURIE	US	2045
EQUAL SENSATION	1968	PRESIDENT		PTL 1015
SENSATIONAL EQUALS	1968	PRESIDENT		PTLS 1020
EQUALS SUPREME	1968	PRESIDENT		PTLS 1025
BABY COME BACK	1968	RCA	US	LSP 4078
EQUALS STRIKE BACK	1969	PRESIDENT		PTLS 1030
BEST OF THE EQUALS	1969	PRESIDENT		PTLS 1050
BEST OF THE EQUALS	1969	JOY PRESIDENT		JOYS 137
AT THE TOP	1970	PRESIDENT		PTLS 1038
EQUALS ROCK AROUND THE CLOCK	1974	PRESIDENT		PTLS 1054
GREATEST HITS	1974	M F P	UK	MFP 50153
DOIN' THE 45's	1975	RHAPSODY		RHAS 9017
BORN YA	1976	MERCURY	UK	9109 601
MYSTIC SYNSTER	1978	ICE	UK	ICEL 1002

E62A

LIONEL LEDISSEZ	V	(
JEAN GUERIN	K	(
MAX TOUAT	B	(
BRUTUS	D	(

ERGO SUM

(A) MEXICO	19	THELEME	FR	6332 500

ROLAND MEYNET   VLN   (MICHEL LEONARDI   G   (

E62B

ROCKY ERICKSON	G V	(
DUANE ASLAKSEN	G	(
BILL MILLER	AUTOHARP	(

ROCKY ERICKSON & THE ALIENS

(A) ROCKY ERICKSON & THE ALIENS	197	CBS	UK	84463

JEFF SUTTON   D   (BOBBY GORMAN   B   (

E63

JOACHIM H EHRIG K SYN G D VLN	(ABCD	
CARLOS BOTTICH	G	'C
KASI KLASSEN	B V HCA	(C
VOLKER KAHRS	K	(C
WOLFGANG JAGER	B	(C
GERD KUHN	G V	(C
BERNHARD UHLEMANN	B V	(C

EROC

(A) EROC	1975	BRIAN	EURO	1069
(A) EROC	1977	BRAIN	UK	201 109
(B) ZWEI	1976	BRAIN		006 0007
(C) 3 (RECORDED 1969 79)	1979	BRAIN		0060 197

STEPHEN DANIELAK   G V   (C   EDD HUBER   B   (C

E64

ERUPTION

(A) ERUPTION	1978	ATLANTIC	UK	K 50454
(B) LEAVE A LIGHT	1979	ATLANTIC	UK	K 50595

E65

COKE ESCOVEDO	PERC	(ALL
WITH		
ERROL KNOWLES	V	(B
FRANK MERCURIO	K	(B
GLEN SYMMONDS	D	(B
JOE HENDERSON	SAX	(B

COKE ESCOVEDO

(A) COKE	1975	MERCURY	US	SRM1 1041
(B) COMIN' AT YA	197	MERCURY	US	SRM1 1085
(C) DISCO FANTASY	1977	MERCURY	US	SRM1 1132

MARG PHILLIPS   B   (B   ABEL ZARATE   G   (B
GABOR SZABO   G   (B

E66

RAYMOND VINCENT	VLN	(B
TONY MALISAN	D	(B
GINO MALISAN	B	(B
TONY HARRIS	VIOLA	(B
BRUNO LIBERT	K V	(B
TIMOTHY KRAEMER	CELLO	(B
BRIGETTE DU DOIT	V	(B

ESPERANTO ROCK ORCHESTRA

(A) ESPERANTO ROCK ORCHESTRA	1973	A&M US 4399	UK	AMLH68175
(B) DANSE MACABRE	1974	A&M US 3624	UK	AMLH63624
(C) LAST TANGO	1975	A&M US 4524	UK	AMLH68294

KEITH CHRISTMAS   V   (B   GODFREY SALMON   VLN V   (B
GLEN SHORROCK   V   (B   BRIAN HOLLAWAY   G   (B

E66A

RICH TEA		(A
LORA LOGIC		(A
ASHLEY BUFF		(A

ESSENTIAL LOGIC

(A) BEAT RHYTHM NEWS	1979	ROUGH TRADE	UK	ROUGH 5

MARK TURNER   (A   DAVE WRIGHT   (A

E67

SLEEPY JOHN ESTES	G V	(ALL
WITH		
HAMMIE NIXON	HCA	(ABDCI
YANK RACHELL	G	(BD
ED WILKENSON	B	(AD
RANSOM KNOWLING	B	(D
SUNNYLAND SLIM	PNO	(F
JIMMY DAWKINS	G	(F
ODIE PAYNE	D	(F
CAREY BELL	HCA	(F
EARL HOOKER	B	(F
JOE HARPER	B	(F

SLEEPY JOHN ESTES

(A) LEGEND OF	19	DELMARK		DL 603
(A) LEGEND OF	19	TRIO	JAP	PA 6212
(B) BROKE & HUNGRY	19	DELMARK		DL 608
(C) IN EUROPE	19	DELMARK		DL 611
(D) BROWNSVILLE BLUES	19	DELMARK		DL 613
(E) ELECTRIC SLEEP	19	DELMARK		DL 619
(F) 1929 1940	19	FOLKWAYS		RF8
(G) DOWN SOUTH BLUES	1974	MCA		510 091
(H) SLEEPY JOHN ESTES	19	COLLECTORS CLASSICS		CC.24
(I) & HAMMIE NIXON	19	STORYVILLE		SLP 172

MIKE BLOOMFIELD   G   (B   JOHN'KNOCKY' PARKER   PNO   (A

E67A

ETERNITYS CHILDREN

(A) ETERNITYS CHILDREN	19	TOWER	US	ST 5223

E68

ETHIOPIANS

(A) WOMAN CAPTURE MAN	197	TROJAN		TBL 112
(B) SLAVE CALL	1977	THIRD WORLD		TWS 15

E69

CHRIS ETHRIDGE	B V	(A
JOEL SCOTT HILL	G V	(A
JOHN BARBATA	D	(A

CHRIS ETHRIDGE

(A) L A GETAWAY	1971	ATLANTIC	UK	K 40310

```
GUIGOU CHENEVIER     D     (AB1234   (A) BATELAGES                          1976   GRATTE CIEL    FR   CIEL 2001
JEAN BAPTISTE MOULU  K     (1       (B) LES TROIS FOUS PERDEGAGNENT         1978   9H17 RECORDS   FR        7001
MOREY                B     (1       (B) LES TROIS FOUS PERDEGAGNENT         197    TAPIOCA             TP 10020
CHRIS(EULALIE RYNAT)CHANET SAX(123A (1) 1971 (2) 1972  (3) 1973  (4) 1977
FERDINAND RICHARD    B     (34AB
FRANCIS'PICHENETTE' GRAND SAX(B4    JEAN PIERRE GRASSET   G      (B   MICHAEL GREZES           (B
```

```
BART LIBBY           K     (A       (A) EUPHONIOUS WAIL                     19     KAPP           US        3668
STEVE TRACY          G V   (A
GARY VIOLESTTI       B V   (A       SUZANNA REY           V      (A   DOUG HOFFMANN        D    (A
```

```
                                    (A) EUPHORIA                           19     HERITAGE       US   HTS35,005
```

```
MARIA D'AMATO(MULDAUR) V  (A        (A) EVEN DOZEN JUG BAND                 1964   ELEKTRA        US   EKS  7246
STEVE KATZ           G V   (A       (A) JUG BAND SONGS OF SOUTHERN MOUNTAINS       LEGACY         US   LEG   119
PETE SIEGEL          G V   (A
JOHN SEBASTIAN       G V   (A       JOSHUA RIFKIN         PNO    (A   STEFAN GROSSMAN      G V  (A
```

```
BETTY EVERETT        V     (ALL     (A) THERE'LL COME A TIME               1974   MCA            UK   MCF  2676
JOE SAMPLE           K     (B       (A) THERE'LL COME A TIME               197    UNI                 UNLS  109
GENE PAGE            K     (B       (B) HAPPY ENDINGS                      1975   FANTASY        FT    524
GARY COLEMAN         PERC  (B       (B) HAPPY ENDINGS                      1975   FANTASY        US        9480
RAY PARKER           G     (B       (C) ITS IN HIS KISS                    19     JOY                 JOYS  106
DEAN PARKS           G     (B       (C) ITS IN HIS KISS                    1976   DJM                 DJM 22042
MELVIN WAH WAH RAGIN G     (B       (D) THEY'RE DELICIOUS TOGETHER         197    JOYS                JOYS  123
DAVID T WALKER       G     (B       (E) BETTY EVERETT STARRING             197    TRADITION      US        2073
SCOTT EDWARDS        B     (B       (F) & KETTY LESTER                     19     GRAND PRIX     US   K 125
KETTY LESTER         V     (F
BOBBYE HALL          PERC  (B       CAROLYN WILLIS        V      (B   ED GREENE            D    (B
MARTI McCALL         V     (B       EDNA WRIGHT           V      (B   JACKIE WARD          V    (B
JERRY BUTLER         V     (B
```

```
                                    (A) 7 DO ELEVEN                        19     MERCURY        US   SR 61157
```

```
SKIP BATTIN          B V   (A       (A) THE BALLAD OF EVERGREEN BLUESHOES 1969   LONDON         UK   SHU  8399
LANNY MATHIJSSEN     G     (A       (A) THE BALLAD OF EVERGREEN BLUESHOES 1969   AMOS           US        7002
AL ROSENBERG         G     (A
KEN KLEIST           K     (A       CHESTER McCRACKEN     D      (A
```

```
BRUCE MILNER         K     (A       (A) EVERY MOTHER'S SON                 19     MGM            SE   4471
DENNIS LARDEN  V G BANJO   (A       (B) BACK                               1968   MGM            SE   4505
LARY LARDEN          G V   (A
CHRISTOPHER AUGUSTINE D            (A  SCHUYLER LARSEN    B      (A   DON KERR             B    (
```

```
DON EVERLY           G V   (ALL     (A) DON EVERLY                         1971   ODE US  2007   UK   77005
JEAN ROUSSEL         B     (B       (B) SUNSET TOWERS                      1974   ODE            UK   77023
BUDDY EMMONS         STEEL (BC      (C) BROTHER JUKE BOX                   1977   DJM            UK   20501
PETE GAVIN           D PERC(B       (C) BROTHER JUKE BOX                   1977   HICKORY        US   44003
ALBERT LEE           G B K (B
JOE OSBORN           B     (BC   RAY SMITH         G      (B   LANI GROVES       V      (B   JUNE WILLIAMS     V (B
SHIRLEY BREWER       V     (B    STEPHANIE SPRUILL V      (B   JESSICA CLEAVES V        (B   CYNTHIA BULLENS   V (B
REGGIE YOUNG         G     (C    JOHN LEE CHRISTOPER G    (C   JERRY STEMBRIDGE G       (C   LOUIS NUNLEY      V (C
BOBBY R WOOD         PNO   (C    MICHAEL LEECH     B      (C   KENNY MALONE      D      (C   LEA JANE BERINATI V (C
JANIE FRICKE         V     (C    GINGER HOLLADAY   V      (C   BOBBY HARDEN      V      (C   J ALAN MOORE V K STR(C
DAVID VANDERPOOL   STR(C         MARILYN SMITH     STR    (C   PAUL YANDELL      G      (C   TONY MIGLIORE       PNO(C
RALPH GALLANT        D     (C    THOMAS MARTIN     G      (C   HARGUS ROBBINS    PNO    (C   JEANINE WALKER    V (C
WILLIAM WRIGHT       V     (C    DOROTHY DILLARD   V      (C
```

```
PHIL EVERLY          V G   (ALL     (A) STAR SPANGLED SPRINGER             1973   RCA            UK   SF 8370
WITH                                (A) STAR SPANGLED SPRINGER             1973   RCA            US   APLI 0092
WARRON ZEVON         G K   (AD      (B) NOTHINGS TOO GOOD FOR MY BABY      1974   PYE            UK   NSPL18448
JAMES BURTON         G     (A       (C) PHILS DINER                        197    PYE            US   12040
DUANE EDDY           G     (A       (D) MYSTIC LINE                        1975   PYE            UK   NSPL18473
DONNIE LANIER        G     (A       (D) MYSTIC LINE                        1975   PYE            US   12121
NEIL LEVANG          G     (A       (E) PHIL EVERLY                        1979   ELEKTRA   US        6E213
KENNY CLAYTON        PNO   (B
SAMMY McCUE  G K STEEL(A          DEAN PARKS      G      (A   BUDDY EMMONS    STEEL (A   JAY DEE MANESS STEEL(A
REINIE PRESS         B     (A     LYLE RITZ       B      (A   JOHN GUERIN     D     (A   EARL PALMER    D (A
VICTOR FELDMAN    PERC(A          JIM HORN        SAX    (A   MARTIN KERSHAW  G     (D   FOGGY LITTLE   G (DB
FRANK McDONALD       B     (D     RONNIE VERRELL  D      (D   CLEM CATTINI    D     (D   RICHARD BENNETT G (A
BARRY MORGAN         D     (B     TONY CAMPO      B      (B   JOE MORETTI     G     (B
```

```
DON EVERLY           G V   (ALL     THE EVERLY BROTHERS                    1958   LONDON         UK   HA A 2001
PHIL EVERLY          G V   (ALL     THE EVERLY BROTHERS                    1958   CADENCE        US   CLP  3003
WITH                                THE EVERLY BROTHERS                    19     HARMONY        US        11304
CHET ATKINS          G     (*       SONGS OUR DADDY TAUGHT US              1958   LONDON         UK
PAUL YANDELL         G     (*       SONGS OUR DADDY TAUGHT US              1958   CADENCE        US   CLP  3016
DALE SELLERS         G     (*       SONGS OUR DADDY TAUGHT US              1975   PHILIPS             6467  500
PETE WADE            G     (*       THEIR BEST                             19     CADENCE        US   CLP  3025
BOBBY THOMPSON     G BANJ.(*        FABULOUS STYLE OF THE EVERLY BROTHERS  1960   CADENCE US CLP3040  (S) 25040
WELDON MYRICK        STEEL (*       FABULOUS STYLE OF THE EVERLY BROTHERS  1960   LONDON         UK
HAROLD RUGG          STEEL (*       FOLK SONGS                             196    CADENCE US CLP3059  (S) 25059
HARGUS ROBBINS       PNO   (*       15 HITS                                196    CADENCE US CLP3062  (S) 25062
DAVID BRIGGS         PNO   (*       ITS EVERLY TIME                        1960   WB   US            1381
STEVE SCHAFFER       B     (*       ITS EVERLY TIME                        1960   WB   UK(M)4012    (S) 8012
RALPH GALLANT  ]     D     (*       A DATE WITH THE EVERLY BROTHERS        1961   WB   US            1395
LARRY LONDIN   ]                    A DATE WITH THE EVERLY BROTHERS        1961   WB   UK(M)4028    (S) 8028
JOHNNY GIMBLE        FDL MAN(*                                                                (CONTINUED)
```

THE EVERLY BROTHERS

BOTH SIDES OF AN EVENING		1961	WB	US	1418
INSTANT PARTY		1962	WB	US	1430
GOLDEN HITS		1962	WB		1471
GOLDEN HITS		1971	WB	UK RI K	46005
CHRISTMAS WITH		196	WB		1483
CHRISTMAS WITH		19	HARMONY	US	11350
SING GREAT COUNTRY HITS		1963	WB	US	1513
VERY BEST OF		1965	WB		1554
VERY BEST OF		197	WB	UK RI K	46008
ROCK'N'SOUL		1965	WB		1578
CHAINED TO A MEMORY		19	HARMONY	US	11388
GONE GONE GONE		1965	WB	US	1585
GONE GONE GONE		197	VALIANT	UK VS	109
IN OUR IMAGE		1965	WB		1620
TWO YANKS IN LONDON		1965	WB		1646
HIT SOUNDS OF		1967	WB		1676
THE EVERLY BROTHERS SING		1967	WB		1708
ROOTS		1968	WB		1752
ROOTS		1971	WB	UK RI K36002	
THE EVERLY BROTHERS SHOW	(DBL)	1970	WB		1858
THE EVERLY BROTHERS SHOW	(DBL)	1971	WB	UK RI K	66003
MOST BEAUTIFUL SONGS		19	WB	UK K	66016
THE EVERLY BROTHERS		197	WB	UK K	16209
HISTORY OF		19	BARNABY	US	15008
GREATEST HITS		19	BARNABY	US	4004
GREATEST HITS		19	BARNABY	US	4005
ORIGINAL GREATEST HITS		1970	BARNABY US 6006	UK CBS	66255
END OF AN ERA		1970	BARNABY US 80260	UK CBS	66259
STORIES WE COULD TELL		1974	RCA	US	4620
STORIES WE COULD TELL		1974	RCA	UK SF	8270
STORIES WE COULD TELL		197	RCA INT	INT	1474
FABULOUS 50s TREASURY		1974	JANUS	6310	300
(*)PASS THE CHICKEN		1975	RCA	UK SF	8332
(*)PASS THE CHICKEN		1975	RCA	US LSP	4781
(*)EXCITING EVERLY BROS(PASS THE CHICKEN)		1975	CAMDEN	RI CDS	1136
WALK RIGHT BACK		1975	WB	UK K	56168
BYE BYE EVERLYS		1975	MIDI	66032	
NEW ALBUM		1977	WB	UK K	56415
COKE CHRYSLER & COUNTRY	BOOT??	1977	GRIN	US G	5173
EVERLY BROTHERS		197	GTE	US GTR	7702
GREATEST HITS		1979	PICKWICK	UK PDA	063
ORIGINAL HITS		197	MUSIDISC		256
20 SUPERHITS		197	TELDEC	GERM AP6	23484
LIVING LEGENDS		1977	WARWICK	UK WW	5027
(EPs)					
THE EVERLY BROTHERS		19	CADENCE	US CEP	104
THE EVERLY BROTHERS		19	CADENCE	US CEP	105
THE EVERLY BROTHERS		19	CADENCE	US CEP	107
THE EVERLY BROTHERS		19	CADENCE	US CEP	111
THE EVERLY BROTHERS		19	CADENCE	US CEP	118
SONG OUR DADDY TAUGHT US		19	CADENCE	US CEP	108
SONGS OUR DADDY TAUGHT US		19	CADENCE	US CEP	109
SONGS OUR DADDY TAUGHT US		19	CADENCE	US CEP	110
ROCKIN WITH		19	CADENCE	US CEP	333
ROCKIN WITH		19	CADENCE	US CEP	334
ESPECIALLY FOR YOU		19	CADENCE	US CEP1381/1	
ESPECIALLY FOR YOU		19	CADENCE	US CEP1381/2	
VERY BEST OF		19	CADENCE	US CEP	121
EVERLY BROTHERS		19	WB	US	5501
THE PRICE OF LOVE		196	WB	UK WEP	604
LOVE IS STRANGE		196	WB	UK WEP	610
PEOPLE GET READY		196	WB	UK WEP	612
WHAT AM I LIVING FOR		196	WB	UK WEP	618
SOMEBODY HELP ME		196	WB	UK WEP	623

EVERYONE

E76

ANDY ROBERTS	G V VLN	(A	
BOB SARGEANT	G V K HCA	(A	
JOHN PEARSON	D	(A	

(A) EVERYONE		1971	B&C	UK CAS	1028

DAVE RICHARDS   V B K (A   JOHN PORTER   G   (A

EXCITERS

E76A

BRENDA REID	V	(
CAROL JOHNSON	V	(
LILIAN WALKER	V	(
HERBERT ROONEY	V	(

(A) TELL HIM	19	UA US MONO 3264	US STER	6264
(B) EXCITERS	19	ROULETTE US		25326
(C) CAVIAR & CHITLINS	19	RCA US	LSP	4211
(D) BLACK BEAUTY	19	TODAY US	TLP	1001

EXILE

E77

J P PENNINGTON	G V	(BC
JIMMY STOKEY	V	(BC
BUZZ CORNELISON	K V	(BC
MARLON HARGIS	K V	(BC
SONNY LEMAIRE	B V	(BC
SUE RICHMAN	V	(C
ANDREA ROBINSON	V	(B

(A) EXILE	19	WOODEN NICKEL US		1020
(B) MIXED EMOTIONS	1978	RAK	UK SRAK	533
(C) ALL THERE IS	1979	RAK	UK SRAK	535

STEVE GOETMAN   D   (BC   DANNY WILLIAMS   V B   (B
RUSTY BUCHANAN   V   (C   LYNDA LAWLEY   V   (C

EXILED

E77A

SVOLTA	V	(A
SEIKO BROTHERS	V	(A
LESLEY DUNCAN	V	(A
BERNIE FROST	V	(A
PAUL THOMPSON	D	(A

(A) EXILED	1980	RCA	PL	25297

TERRY CASSIDY	V	(A	DAN McCAFFERTY	V (A	FRANCIS ROSSI	V	(A
COLIN BLUNSTONE	V	(A	NIGEL MARTINEZ	D (A	STUART ELLIOTT	D	(A
DELISLE HARPER	B	(A	JOHN GIBLIN	B (A	ANDY PASK	B	(A

(CONTINUED)

(CONTINUED)

EXILED   E77A

JOE JAMMER	G (A	PAUL KEOGH	G (A	RAY RUSSELL	G (A	MITCH DALTON	G (A
LAWRENCE JUBER	G (A	STEVE COE	K (A	DAVE LAWSON	K (A	ROBIN LUMLEY	K (A
CHRIS PARREN	K (A	CRAIG PRUESS	K (A	TOMMY EYRE	K (A	LUIS JARDIM	PERC(A
JOHN EARLE	SAX (A	ROBERT POWELL	NARRATIVE(A				

EXMAGMA   E77B

FRED BRACEFUL	D PERC(A	(A) GOLDBALL	19	DISJUUCTA	FR	000 00009
ANDY GOLDNER	G B SAX(A					
THOMAS BALLUFF	K TPT WIND(A					

EXUMA   E78

EXUMA	G V PERC(ALL	(A) EXUMA	19	BARCLAY		920 208
YOGI BEN MAUSEL	V PERC (	( ) EXUMA	19	BARCLAY		920 291
O'NEIL GUIMUNGIE	SAX V (	( ) EXUMA	19	VERTIGO		6338 018
K SMITH	D (	( ) EXUMA	19	MERCURY	US	61314
BARON SAMEDI	PERC(	( ) SNAKE	19	POLYDOR		2319 016
R WISE	G (	( ) REINCARNATION	19	POLYDOR		2319 026
K AARONSON	D (	( ) REINCARNATION	19	KAMA SUTRA	US	2052
PAUL CARPENTER	K (	( ) LIFE	19	KAMA SUTRA	US	2074
F GUMBS	D (	( ) THE OBEAH MAN	19	MERCURY	US	61265
		( ) DO WAH NANNY	19	KAMA SUTRA	US	2041

EYES   E79

DOUG KANE	V			
REG MARSHALL	B			
MICK PORTER	G	JOHN STUART MILLS G	STEVE SIMMONS	D

EYES OF BLUE   E80

GARY PICKFORD HOPKINS	V (B1	(A) CROSSROADS OF TIME	1968	MERCURY US 61184	UK 20134
JOHN WEATHERS	F (B	(A) CROSSROADS OF TIME	1968	MERCURY	134 087
RITCHIE FRANCIS	G (B1	(B) IN FIELDS OF ARDATH	1969	MERCURY US 61220	UK 20164
R BENNETT	B (B	(1) 1967			
PHIL RYAN	K (AB1				
RAY WILLIAMS	B (1	WYNDHAM REES	D (1		

F B I   F1

BONNIE WILKENSON	V (A	(A) F B I	1976	GOODEARTH	UK GDS 802
ROOT JACKSON	V (A				
JOANE BLACK	V (A	HERSCHEL HOLDER PERC (A	LLOYD SMITH	HRNS (A

F WORD   F2

| ( ) F WORD LIKE IT OR NOT | 1978 | PBS | 101 |

FABIAN   F2A

( ) HOLD THAT TIGER	19	CHANCELLOR	US	5003
( ) FABULOUS FABIAN	19	CHANCELLOR	US	5005
( ) GOOD OLD SUMMERTIME	19	CHANCELLOR	US	5012
( ) ROCKIN' HOT	19	CHANCELLOR	US	5019
( ) 16 GREATEST HITS	19	CHANCELLOR	US	5024
( ) 16 GREATEST HITS	19	ABC	US	806
( ) 16 GREATEST HITS	19	TRIP	US	TOP 1620
( ) VERY BEST OF FABIAN	19	UA	US	UA LA 449
( ) FACADE	19	CHANCELLOR	US	68902
( ) FABIAN	1974	EMI	NL 5C 05095031

FABULOUS POODLES   F3

TONY DE MEUR	G V (ABC	(A) FABULOUS POODLES	1977	PYE	UK NSPL18530
BOBBY VALENTINO	VLN (ABC	(B) UNSUITABLE	1978	PYE	UK NSPH 25
RICHIE ROBERTSON	B (AB	(C) THINK PINK	1979	BLUEPRINT	UK BLUP 5001
BRYN B BURROWS	D (AB	(D) MIRROR STARS	19	EPIC	US 35666
JOHN PARSONS	(C				

FABULOUS RHINESTONES   F2A

MARTY GREBB SAX K V G	(A	(A) FREEWHEELIN'	1973	JUST SUNSHINE	US	JSS9
KAL DAVID	G V (A					
TERRY EATON	SAX (A	HARVEY BROOKS	B V (A	GREG THOMAS	D (A
DAVE SANBORN	SAX (A	REINOL ISAAC ANDINO	CONGA (A	RANDY BRECKER	HRNS (A
MICHAEL BRECKER	HRNS (A	BARRY ROGERS	TROM (A	DENNIS WHITTED	D (A
JEAN'TOOTS' THIALEMANS	HCA(A	TITO PUENTE	PERC (A	KAT McCORD	V (A

FABULOUS THUNDERBIRDS   F3B

JIMMY VAUGHAN	G (AB	(A) GO GIRL CRAZY	1979	CHRYSALIS	UK CHR 1250
KIM WILSON	V HCA (AB	(B) WHATS THE WORD	1980	CHRYSALIS	UK CHR 1287
KEITH FERGUSON	B (AB				
MIKE BUCK	D (AB	FRAN CHRISTINA	D PERC (B		

FACES   F4

RONNIE LANE	B (ABCDE	(A) FIRST STEP	1970	WB US	UK K 46053
IAN MACLAGAN	K (ABCDE	(B) LONG PLAYER	1971	WB US 1892	UK K 46064
KENNY JONES	D (ABCDE	(C) A NOD5 AS GOOD AS A WINK	1972	WB US 2574	UK K 56006
ROD STEWART	V (ABCDE	(D) OOH LA LA	1973	WB US 2665	UK K 56011
RON WOOD	G (ABCDE	(E) OVERTURE /COAST TO COAST	1974	MERCURY US 1 697	UK 9100 011
TETSU YAMAUCHI	B (E	(AB) FIRST STEP/LONG PLAYER	1977	WB	UK K 66027
BOBBY KEYS	SAX (B	( ) BEST OF	19	RIVA	UK RVLP.3
HARRY BECKETT	TPT (B	( ) SNAKES & LADDERS (BEST OF)	19	WB US2897	UK K 56172
		( ) ROD STEWART & THE FACES	19	SPRINGBOARD	US 4030

FAD GADGET   F4A

FAD GADGET	V SYN (A	(A) FIRESIDE FAVOURITES	1980	MUTE	STUMM 3
ERIC RADCLIFFE	G B BAN (A				
JOHN FRYER	PERC (A	NICK CASH D (A	DANIEL MILLER PERC SYN (A
PHIL WAUQUAIRE	B (A			

[143]

JOHN FAHEY		1966	US VANGUARD VSD 79259					
TRANSFIGURATION OF BLIND JOE DEATH		1967	US TAKOMA	9015	UK 19	SONET	SNTF 607	
TRANSFIGURATION OF BLIND JOE DEATH		19	US TAKOMA	1002	UK 19	SONET	SNTF 774	
TRANSFIGURATION OF BLIND JOE DEATH		19	US RIVER	RB1	UK TRANSATLANTIC TRA173			
DEATH CHANTS & BREAKDOWNS		1968	US TAKOMA	1003	UK 1969 SONET		SNTF 608	
(Y)YELLOW PRINCESS		1968	US VANGUARD VSD 79293	UK 19				
REQUIA		19	VANGUARD		UK		SVRL 19033	
DANCE OF DEATH		196	US TAKOMA	1004			SVRL 19055	
GREAT SAN BERNADINO BIRTHDAY PARTY		196	US TAKOMA	1008				
DAYS HAVE GONE BY		1967	US TAKOMA	1014				
VOICE OF THE TURTLE		1968	US TAKOMA	1019				
NEW POSSIBILITY		19	US TAKOMA	1020				
FARE FORWARD VOYAGERS		19	US TAKOMA	1035	UK 1974 SONET		SNTF 656	
FAHEY, LEO KOTTKE , PETER LANG		19	US TAKOMA	1040	UK 197	SONET	SNTF 675	
(O)OLD FASHIONED LOVE		19	US TAKOMA	1043	UK 1975 SONET		SNTF 688	
CHRISTMAS ALBUM		19	US TAKOMA	1045	UK 1976 SONET		SNTF 702	
BEST OF 1959 77		19	US TAKOMA	1058	UK 197	SONET	SNTF 733	
OF RIVERS & RELIGION		197	US REPRISE		UK 197	REPRISE	K 44213	
AFTER THE BALL		1973	US REPRISE	2145	UK 197	REPRISE	K 44246	
FAHEY,KELLY ,MANN,MILLER,SEIDLER		19	US BLUE GOOSE BG 2009					
ESSENTIAL JOHN FAHEY		19	VANGUARD VSD 55/56					

JOHN FAHEY   G   (ALL
WITH

JAY FERGUSON	K	(Y	MARK ANDES	B	(Y	MATT ANDES	G	(Y
KEVIN KELLEY	D	(Y	WOODROW MANN	G	(O	JACK FEIERMAN	TPT V	(O
ALLAN REUSS	G BANJO	(O	JOE DARENSBOURG	CLAR	(O	IRA WESTLEY	TUBA	(O
JOHN ROTELLA	SAX	(O	BRITT WOODMAN	TROM	(O	DICK CARY	PNO	(O
NICK FATOOL	D	(O	BOBBY BRUCE	V VLN	(O			

F 5A   FAIRFIELD PARLOUR

PETER DALTREY	V K (A	(A) FROM HOME TO HOME		1970	VERTIGO	UK	6360 001
EDDY PUMER	V K G(A						
STEVE CLARK	B FLT(A	DAN BRIDGMAN V D	(A				

F 6   FAIRPORT CONVENTION

(A) 1966(ETHNIC SHUFFLE ORCH)	(1) FAIRPORT CONVENTION	1968	POLYDOR		UK	583 035
(B) 1967 SPRING (1 GIG)	(1) FAIRPORT CONVENTION	1968	COTILLION		US	SD 9024
(C) 1967 JULY NOV	(1) FAIRPORT CONVENTION	1975	POLYDOR	RI	UK	2384 047
(D) 1967 NOV/MAY 1968	(1) FAIRPORT CONVENTION	197	POLYDOR		EURO 2383 355	
(E) 1968 MAY/FEB 1969	(2) WHAT WE DID ON OUR HOLIDAYS	1969	ISLAND		UK	ILPS 9092
(F) 1969 FEB/JUNE 1969	(2) WHAT WE DID ON OUR HOLIDAYS	19	ARIOLA		88 183XAT	
MOTORWAY ACCIDENT KILLED	(2) FAIRPORT CONVENTION	1969	A&M		US	4185
MARTIN LAMBLE.	(3) UNHALFBRICKING	1969	ISLAND		UK	ILPS 9102
(G) 1969 SEPT/NOV	(3) UNHALFBRICKING	19	A&M		US	4206
(H) 1969 DEC/JAN1971	(4) LIEGE AND LIEF	1969	ISLAND		UK	ILPS 9115
(i) 1971 JAN/DEC	(4) LIEGE AND LIEF	19	A&M		US	4257
(J) 1971 DEC RAINBOW GIG	(5) FULL HOUSE	1970	ISLAND		UK	ILPS 9130
(K) 1971 DEC/FEB 1972	(5) FUL HOUSE	1970	A&M		US	4265
(L) 1972 FEB /JUNE	(6) ANGEL DELIGHT	1971	ISLAND		UK	ILPS 9162
(M) 1972 JUNE/AUTUMN. RECORDED	(6) ANGEL DELIGHT	1971	A&M		US	4316
MANOR ALBUM NOT RELEASED.	(7) BABBACOMBE LEE	1971	ISLAND		UK	ILPS 9176
(N) 1972 AUTUMN/SUMMER 1973	(7) BABBACOMBE LEE	1971	A&M		US	4333
(O) 1973 SUMMER/MARCH 1974	(8) HISTORY OF (DBL)	1972	ISLAND		UK	ICD 4
(P) 1974 MARCH/ JAN 1975	(8) HISTORY OF (DBL)	197	PHONOGRAM		EURO 6405 004	
(Q) 1975 JAN/FEB	(9) ROSIE	1973	ISLAND		UK	ILPS 9208
(R) 1975 FEB /DEC	(9) ROSIE	1973	A&M		US	4383
(S) 1976 JAN/FEB	(10) FAIRPORT NINE	1973	ISLAND		UK	ILPS 9246
(T) 1976 MARCH	(10) FAIRPORT NINE	1973	A&M		US	4407
(U) 1976 MARCH	(10) FAIRPORT NINE	197	A&M		US	3603
(V) 1976 APRIL/SEPT. SHORTENED	(11) FAIRPORT LIVE A MOVEABLE FEAST	1974	ISLAND	US UK	ILPS 9285
NAME TO 'FAIRPORT'.	(12) RISING FOR THE MOON	1975	ISLAND	US UK	ILPS 9312
(W).1976 MAY/AUG 1979 RESTORED	(13) FAIRPORT CONVENTION(TOUR SAMPLER)1975	ISLAND		UK	ISS2
NAME TO 'FAIRPORT CONVENTION'	(14) GOTTLE O' GEER	1976	ISLAND		UK	ILPS 9389
(X) 1979 AUG SWARBRICK ADVISED	(14) GOTTLE O' GEER	1976	PHONOGRAM		EURO 9101 665	
TO GIVE UP ON MEDICAL GROUNDS	(15) CHRONICLES	1976	A&M		US	3530
GROUP ABANDONED.	(16) LIVE AT L A TROUBADOUR	1976	ISLAND		UK	HELP 28
	(17) HEYDAY (CASSETTE ONLY)	1976				
N.B. (13) MARKED	(18) BONNY BUNCH OF ROSES	1977	VERTIGO		UK	9102 015
"FOR RADIO USE ONLY" ALSO USED	(18) BONNY BUNCH OF ROSES	1977	PHONOGRAM		EURO 6360 152	
AS A PRIZE IN N.M.E. COMPETITION.	(19) TIPPLERS TALES	1978	VERTIGO		UK	9102 022
	(20) FAREWELL FAREWELL	1979	SIMONS		UK	GAMA 1
	(20) FAREWELL FAREWELL	1979	WOODWORM		UK	BEAR22

DAVE SWARBRICK VLN V MAND	(GHiJKLMNOPQRSTUVWX 3.4.5.6.7.8.9.10.11.12.13.14.15.16.17.18.19.20.				
DAVE PEGG	B V	(HiJKLMNOPQRSTUVWX 5.6.7.8.9.10.11.12.13.14.15.16.17.18.19.20.			
SIMON NICOL	V G	(ABCDEFGHiJWX 1.2.3.4.5.6.7.8.13.14.15.16.17.18.19.20.			
DAVE MATTACKS	D	(GHiJKOPN 4.5.6.7.8.9.10.11.12.13.15.16.			
RICHARD THOMPSON	V G	(ABCDEFGHJ 1.2.3.4.5.8.9.13.15.16.17.	TONY COX	PNO	(15.
ASHLEY HUTCHINGS	B V	(ABCDEFG 1.2.3.4.8.13.15.17.	PAT DONALDSON	B	(15.
SANDY DENNY	V G PNO	(EFGJPQR 2.3.4.8.9.11.12.13.15.17.	IAN WHITEMAN	PNO	(15.
JERRY DONAHUE	G V	(NOPQR 9.10.11.12.13.15.	IAN WILSON	V	(14.
TREVOR LUCAS	V G PERC	(NOPQR 3.8.9.10.11.12.13.15.	ERIC JOHNS	G	(14.
BRUCE ROWLAND	D	(RSTUVWX 12.13.14.18.19.20.	HENRY LOWTHER	HRNS	(14.
MARTIN LAMBLE	D VLN	(1.2.3.8.13.15.17.	JIMMY JEWELL	SAX	(14.
IAN MATTHEWS	V PERC(DE 1.2.3.8.13.17.	NICK JUDD	PNO	(14.	
JUDY DYBLE	V AUTOHARP	(BCD1	GRAHAM LYLE	V G ACC	(14
IAN FRATER	D	(B	BENNY GALLAGHER	V G ACC	(14.	MARTIN CARTHY	G	(14.
CLARE LOWTHER	CELLO	(1.2.8.	DAN AR BRAS	G	(V	BOB BRADY	K V	(UV 14.
MARC ELLINGTON	V	(3	ROGER BURRIDGE	V VLN	(TUV 14.	PAUL WARREN	D	(Q
A L LLOYD	V	(7	TIMI DONALD	D	(9	GERRY CONWAY	D	(9.13.15.
PHILIP STIRLING WALL V	(7	ROGER HILL	G V	(KL	TOM FARNELL	D	(LM
DAVID REA	V G BANJO	(M	LINDA THOMPSON	V	(9.13.15.	RALPH McTELL	G	(9

[144]

ANDY FAIRWEATHER LOW G V (ALL	(A) BEGINNING FROM AN END(FAIRWEATHER	1971	NEON	UK	NE1
WITH	(B) SPIDER JIVING	1974	A&M US 3646	UK AMLH68263
HENRY McCULLOUGH G (B	(C) LA BOOGA ROOGA	1975	A&M US 4542	UK AMLH68328
MARK NAFTALIN K (B	(D) BE BOP & HOLLA	1976	A&M US 4602	UK AMLH64602
MICK WEAVER K (BD	(E) ANDY FAIRWEATHER LOW (COMP)	1976	RCA	HY 1033
BLUE WEAVER K (A	(F) MEGA SHEBANG	1980	WB	US BSK3450 UK K 56820
CHRISSY STEWART B (B				

DENNY SEIWELL D (B	JOHN KAHN G (B	JIMMY JEWEL SAX (C	CHARLIE McCOY HCA (B
WELDON MYRICK STEEL(B	BUDDY SPICHER FDL (B	VASSAR CLEMENTS FDL (B	BOBBY THOMPSON BANJ(B
LEA JANE BERINATI V (B	MEMPHIS HORNS (B	JOHN DAVID B V (CDF	B J COLE STEEL (ACD
GERRY RAFFERTY V (C	JOE EGAN V (C	EDDIE THORNTON TPT (CD	STEVE GREGORY HRNS(CDF
BUD BEADLE SAX (CDF	NEIL JONES G (A	CLIVE TAYLOR B (A	GEORGIE FAME K (CD
BENNY GALLAGHER V (C	GRAHAM LYLE V (C	DAVE MATTACKS D (C	BRUCE ROWLANDS D (C
BERNIE LEADON G (CD	DOREEN CHANTER V (C	IRENE CHANTER V (C	BARRY ST JOHN V (C
LIZA STRIKE V (C	JOANNE WILLIAMS V (C	HENRY SPINETTI D (DF	KENNY BUTTREY D (B
MARY HOLLADAY V (B	GINGER HOLLADAY V (B	DIANE DAVIDSON V (B	DENNIS BRYON D (A
JULIAN DIGGLE PERC(D	RABBIT BUNDRICK K (CD	KENNEY JONES D (CD	TUNJI OMOSHETI PERC(D
MALCOLM GRIFFITHS TROM(D	MARTIN DROVER TPT (D	GLYN JOHNS PERC (D	BRYN HAWORTH G (D
BUD PARKES TPT (A	TERRY NOONAN (A	DEREK WADSWORTH HRNS(F	DAVE CHARLES B (F
LINCOLN CARR D (F	GERAINT WATKINS K (F	MICKEY GEE G (F	GEORGE CHISHOLM HRNS(F
MEL COLLINS SAX (F			

MANFRED VON BUTTLAR K (A	(A) BACK ON MY HILL	1980	SKY	SKY 038
HORST STABENOW B (A				
JURGEN WERITZ D (A	HEINZ MIKUS G V (A	JURGEN RENFORDT V (A	

MARIANNE FAITHFULL V (ALL	(A) COME MY WAY	1965	DECCA UK LK 4688	
WITH	(B) MARIANNE FAITHFULL	1965	DECCA UK LK 4689	US LONDON 3423
THE GREASE BAND (*	(C) GO AWAY FROM MY WORLD	1965		US LONDON 3452
	(D) NORTH COUNTRY MAID	1966	DECCA UK LK 4778	
	(E) FAITHFULL FOREVER	1966		US LONDON 3482
(*) HAVE SIMILAR TRACK LISTING	(F) LOVE IN A MIST	1967	DECCA UK LK 4854	
RECORDED AT SAME TIME	(G) GREATEST HITS	196	DECCA UK LK	US LONDON 3547
	(H) WORLD OF	1969	DECCA UK SPA 17	
	(*I) DREAMIN' MY DREAMS	1976	NEMS UK NEL 6007	
	(*J) FAITHLESS	1978	NEMS UK NEL 6012	
	(K) BROKEN ENGLISH	1979	ISLAND UK+US	ILPS 9570
	( ) AS TEARS GO BY (COMP)	1981	DECCA UK TAB 13	
	(EP) MARIANNE FAITHFULL	1965	DECCA UK DFE 8624	

BILLY FALCON G V (AB	(A) BILLY FALCONS BURNING ROSE	1978	PHILIPS	UK 9103 450
MICHAEL VISAGGIO K FLT V(A	(B) FALCON AROUND	1980	MCA	UK MCF 3065
RICK ZOLLO G V (A				
BILLY MILNE D V (A	GLENN EICHLER B HCA (A	GREG MEADE	V (A	
RICHIE MEADE V (A	PAGE TO THE WIND CHOIR(A			

RODERICK FALCONER SYN V G(A	(A) NEW NATION	1976	UA	UK UAG 29992
HIRAM BINGHAM B (A	(B) VICTORY IN ROCK CITY	1977	UA	UK UAG 30100
MIKE KELLIE D (A				
MIKE JAPP G (A	MATTHEW FISHER K (A			

1950s EARLY 60S				
JOE STUBBS V				
MACK RICE V	LANCE FINNIE V	WILLIE SCHOFIELD V	EDDIE FLOYD V	WILSON PICKETT V

KARL BURNS D (A345	(A) LIVES AT THE WITCH TRIALS	1979	STEP FORWARD	SFLP 1
MARK SMITH V (a12345	(B) DRAGNET	1979	STEP FORWARD	SFLP 4
ERIC B (4	(C) TOTALES TURNS	1980	STEP FORWARD	
MARTIN BRAMAH G (A1234	(1) 1976 (2) 1977 (3) 1978 (4) 1978 (5) 1979			
UNA BAINES K (234				
JONNIE BROWN B (3	TONY FRIEL B (12	MARC RILEY G B (A5	
CRAIG SCANLON G (5	STEVE HANLEY B (5	YVONNE FAWLETT K (A	

JIM KATZIN VLN (A	(A) EARLY FALL	1979	PARACHUTE	P 009
BOB OSTERTAG SYN (A				
NED ROTHENBERG WIND (A	RICHARD ROGERS PNO (A	DAVID WILES PERC (A	

LARRY KEITH	(A) WATCH FOR FALLENROCK	1974	CAPRICORN US 0143 UK 2429 122
STEVE PIPPIN			
RAFE VAN HOY			

ROGER CHAPMAN V HCA (ALL	(A) MUSIC IN A DOLLS HOUSE	1968	REPRISE	UK/US 6312
CHARLIE WHITNEY G (ALL	(A) MUSIC IN A DOLLS HOUSE	1971	REPRISE	RI UK K 44057
ROB TOWNSEND D (ALL	(B) FAMILY ENTERTAINMENT	1969	REPRISE	UK/US 6340
JIM KING WIND V(AB	(B) FAMILY ENTERTAINMENT	1971	REPRISE	UK RI K 44069
JOHN WEIDER B V (CD	(C) A SONG FOR ME	1970	REPRISE	US 6384
	(C) A SONG FOR ME	1970	REPRISE	UK 9001
POLI PALMER K VIBES(CDEF	(C) A SONG FOR ME	1971	REPRISE	UK RI K 44104
JOHN WETTON B V (EF	(D) ANYWAY	1970	REPRISE	UK 9005
RICK GRECH B V VLN (AB	(D) ANYWAY	1971	REPRISE	UK RI K 54002
JIM CREGAN G B (G	(D) ANYWAY	1970	UA	US 5527
TONY ASHTON K (G	(E) FEARLESS	1971	REPRISE	UK K 54003
CHARLIE McCRACKEN G (G	(E) FEARLESS	1971	UA	US 5562
PETER HOPE EVANS (G	(F) BANDSTAND	1972	REPRISE	UK K 54006
ROY DYKE (G	(F) BANDSTAND	1972	UA	US 5644
LADBROKE HORNS (E	(G) ITS ONLY A MOVIE	1973	RAFT	UK RA 58501
	(G) ITS ONLY A MOVIE	1973	UA	US UALA 181
	(H) OLD SONGS NEW SONGS	1971	REPRISE	UK K 34001
	(J) BEST OF FAMILY	1974	REPRISE	UK K 54023

F13

FAMILY DOGG

STEVE ROWLAND	(	(A) A WAY OF LIFE	1969	BELL		SP 22122
ALBERT HAMMOND	G V (B	(B) VIEW FROM ROWLANDS HEAD	1972	POLYDOR	UK	2318 061
MIKE HAZELWOOD	(B	(B) VIEW FROM ROWLANDS HEAD	197	BUDDAH	US	BDS 5100
JIMMY PAGE	G (A					

JOHN PAUL JONES	(	CHRISTINE HOLMES	B	(	IREEN SHERR	V	(B	GARY TAYLOR	B V (B
ANDREW STEEL	D (B	ALAN PARKER	G	(B	B J COLE	DOB G	(B	BARRY MORGAN	D (B
LIZA STRIKE	V (B	DORIS TROY	V	(B	MIKE MORGAN	K	(B	CHRIS SPEDDING G	(B
MADELINE BELL	V (B	PHIL DENNYS	PNO	(B	TONY CARR	PERC	(B	SUE LYNN	V (B
PAT ARNOLD	V (B	CLARE TORRY	V	(B					

F13A

FAMILY TREE

BOB SEGARINI	G V (A	(A) THE FAMILY TREE	196	RCA	US	LSP 3955
VANN SCATER	(A					
MICHAEL DURE	(A	BILL TROCHIM	B (A	JIMMY DE COCQ	G K	(A

F14

GEORGIE FAME

GEORGIE FAME(CLIVE POWELL) K V(ALL		(A) R& B AT THE FLAMINGO	1964	COLUMBIA	UK	SX 1599
WITH		(B) FAME AT LAST	1964	COLUMBIA	UK	33SX 1638
COLIN GREEN	G (CDR1	(C) SWEET THING	1966	COLUMBIA	UK	SX 6043
TED MAKINS	B (	(D) SOUND VENTURE	1966	COLUMBIA	UK	SX 6076
GEORGE KISH	G (G	( ) YEH YEH	1966	IMPERIAL	US	12282
JOHN McLAUGHLIN	G (G	( ) GET AWAY	1966	IMPERIAL	US	12331
RED PREECE	D (	(E) HALL OF FAME	1967	COLUMBIA	UK	SX 6120
AL WATSON	SAX (	(F) TWO FACES OF FAME	1967	CBS	UK	63018
CLIFF BARTON	B (C	(G) THIRD FACE OF FAME	1968	CBS	UK	63293
PHIL BATES	B (DFG	(H) SEVENTH SON	1969	CBS	uk	63786
RIK BROWN	B (F	(J) GEORGIE FAME	1969	STARLINE	UK	SRS 5002
FRANK CLARKE	B (G	(K) DOES HIS OWN THING WITH STRINGS	1970	CBS	UK	63650
RONNIE SEABROOK	B (G	(L) GOING HOME	1971	CBS	UK	64350
JEFF CLYNE	B (F	(M) FAME & PRICE	1971	CBS	UK	64392
JOHN MITCHELL	D (C	(N) ALL ME OWN WORK	1972	REPRISE	UK	K 44183
PHIL SEAMAN	D (D	(O) FAME AGAIN	1972	STARLINE	UK	SRS 5107
BILL EYDEN	D (DFG	(P) BALLAD OF BONNIE & CLYDE	1973 EMBASSY UK 31033 EPIC US			26368
HUGHIE FLINT	D (F	(Q) GEORGIE FAME	1974	ISLAND	UK	ILPS 9293
HAYDEN JACKSON	D (G	(R) RIGHT NOW	1979	PYE	UK	NSLP18600
SPEEDY ACQUAYE	D (CRS	(S) THATS WHAT FRIENDS ARE FOR	1979	PYE	UK	N 119
J SCOTT	D (F	(T) CLOSING THE GAP	1980	PICCADILLY	UK	N 137
JIM MULLEN	G (S	(1) 1969 LIVE BAND				
TONY OXLEY	D (F					

TERRY SMITH	G (GR	ARTHUR GREENSLADE K (G	GORDON BECK	K (DFG	ERNIE SHEARS	G (G
STAN TRACY	K (D	PETER COE	SAX (G	GLEN HUGHES	SAX (C	ROY WILCOX	SAX (D
RAY WARLEIGH	SAX (DR	RONNIE SCOTT	SAX (DFG	TUBBY HAYES	SAX (D	HARRY KLEIN	SAX (DFG
ALAN BRANSCOMBE	SAX (DF	TONY COE	SAX (DFG	DICK MORRISSEY	SAX (DFS	LYN DOBSON	SAX (F
TOMMY WHITTLE	SAX (G	ART ELLEFSON	SAX (G	CYRIL REUBENS	SAX (G	JOHNNY MARSHALL SAX(FG
PETER KING	SAX (F	ED THORNTON	TPT (CFST	GREG BOWEN	TPT (DFG	BERT COURTLEY	TPT (D
IAN HAMMER	TPT (DFGS	JIMMY DEUCHER	TPT (D	LES CONDON	TPT (DGH	KENNY WHEELER	TPT (D
TONY FISHER	TPT (D	DEREK WATKINS	TPT (FG	DEREK HEALEY	TPT (G	ALBERT HALL	TPT (G
BOB HAUGHEY	TPT (G	KEITH CHRISTIE	TROM (DF	ALAN PARKER	G (RS	CHRIS SMITH	TROM(DF
KEN GOLDE	TROM(D	GIB WALLACE	TROM (DFG	DEREK WADSWORTH	TROM (F	MORRIS PLATT	TROM(G
BERNIE HOLLAND	G (R	BRIAN ODGERS	B (RS1	BARRY MORGAN	D (RS	HENRY LOWTHER	TPT (R
STEVE GREGORY	SAX (SR	MALCOLM GRIFFITHS TROM(RS	FRANK RICOTTI PERC	SAX (1	ALAN SKIDMORE	SAX (1
JOHN WARREN	SAX (1	HAROLD BECKETT TPT (1	CHRIS PYNE	TROM (1	HARVEY BURNS	D (1
HENRY SPINETTI	D (S	MIKE DAVIS	TPT (S	BRIAN SMITH	WIND (S	REGGAE PHILHARMONIC ORCH(T
JAMES LASCELLES HRNS(T		GUARDIAN ANGELS V (T	JACKIE SHARP	SAX (D		

F15

FAMOUS JUG BAND

JILL JOHNSON	V G (AB	(A) SUNSHINE POSSIBILITIES	1969	LIBERTY	UK	LBS 83263
PETE BERRYMAN	G V (AB	(B) CHAMELEON	1970	LIBERTY	UK	LBS 83355
CLIVE PALMER	G V (A					
HENRY VIII BARTLETT V JUG (AB						

F16

FANCY

RAY FENWICK	G (C	(A) FANCY MEETING YOU HERE	19	POISON RING	US	2238
MO FOSTER	B (C	(B) WILD THING	1974	ATLANTIC	UK	K 51502
LES BINKS	D (C	(B) WILD THING	1974	BIG TREE	US	89502
ANNIE KAVANAGH	V (C	(C) SOMETHING TO REMEMBER	1975	ARISTA	US	ARTY 102
		(D) TURNS YOU ON	1976	RCA	US	APLI 1482

F16A

FANDANGO

NICK SIMPER	B (A	(A) SLIPSTREAMING	1979	GULL	UK	GULP 1033
PETE PARKS	G (A					
JIM PROOPS	V (A	RON PENNEY	D (A	NEIL McARTHUR	ORG (A

F17

FANIA ALL STARS

JOHNNY PACHECO FLT PERC	(B	(A) FANIA ALL STARS	1975	ISLAND	UK	ILPS 9331
STEVE WINWOOD	G (A	(A) FANIA ALL STARS	1976	CBS	US	
RAY BARRETTO	PERC (B	(B) SALSA LIVE	1976	ISLAND	UK	ILPS 9447
BOBBY VALENTIN	B (B	(C) DELICATE & JUMPY	197	ISLAND	UK	HELP.21
NIKKY MARRERO	PERC (B	( ) LIVE AT THE CHEETA	1971	FANIA	US	SLP 00415
ROBERTO ROENA	PERC (B	( ) LATIN SOUL ROCK	1973	FANIA	US	SLP 00470
PAPO LUCCA	PNO (					

WILLIE COLON	TROM (B	LARRY HARLOW	K (B	RICHARD RAY	K (B	MONGO SANTAMARIA PERC(B
CELIA CRUZ	V (B	JUSTO BETANCOURT	V (B	SANTOS COLON	V (B	BOBBY CRUZ	V (B
CHEO FELICIANO	V (B	HECTOR LAVOE	V (B	ISMAEL MIRANDA	V (B	ISHMAEL QUINTANA V (B
PETE RODRIGUEZ	V (B	RAY MALANALDO	TPT (B	LUIS ORTIS	TPT (B	VICTOR PAZ	TPT(B
LEWIS KAHN	TROM (B	BARRY ROGERS	TROM (B	YOMO TORO	TRES (B		

F18

FANNY

JEAN MILLINGTON	G B V (ABCDE12	(A) FANNY	1970	REPRISE US 6416		
JUNE MILLINGTON	G V (ABCD2	(B) CHARITY BALL	1971	REPRISE US 6456	UK	K44144
NICOLE BARCLAY	K V (ABCDE	(C) FANNY HILL	1972	REPRISE US 2058	UK	K44174
ALICE DE BUHR	D V (E1	(D) MOTHERS PRIDE	1973	REPRISE US 2137	UK	K44233
PATTI QUATRO	B (E1	(E) ROCK'N'ROLL SURVIVORS	1975 CASABLANCA US 7007		UK	4001
BRIE HOWARD	D (E2	(E) ROCK'N'ROLL SURVIVORS	19	PATHE FR	064	96062
CAM DAVIES	D (1	(1) 1974 (2) 1975				
BOBBY KEYS	SAX (C	JIM PRICE WIND (C	JAMES NEWTON HOWARD K (E			

```
                        FANNY ADAMS                                          F18A
                   (A) FANNY ADAMS              19      KAPP  US            3644
                        FANTASTIC BAGGIES                                     F18B
PHIL SLOAN          (A   (A) TELL 'EM I'M SURFIN'   196   IMPERIAL    US    12270
STEVE BARRI         (A

                        RICHARD & MIMI FARINA                                 F19

RICHARD FARINA      V   (ABCD  (A) CELEBRATIONS FOR A GREY DAY  1965 FONTANA 6060 VANGUARD VSD 79281
MIMI FARINA         V   (ALL   (B) REFLECTIONS IN A CRYSTAL WIND 1965 FONTANA 6075 VANGUARD VSD 79204
TOM JANS            V   (E     (C) MEMORIES            1968 VANGUARD19047        VSD 79263
JOAN BAEZ           G V (C     (D) RICHARD FARINA      1968 VANGUARD            VSD 79281
RUSS SAVAKUS        B   (C     (E) MIMI FARINA & TOM JANS 1971 A&M US 4310   UK  AMLS64310
BRUCE LANGHORNE     G   (C     ( ) THE BEST OF RICHARD & MIMI FARINA 70 VANGUARD  VSD 21/2
CHARLES SMALL       PNO (C
AL ROGERS           D   (C     JOHN HAMMOND     HCA  (C    FRITZ RICHMOND    B   (C
KYLE GRAHAN         HCA (C    (RICHARD DIED 1966 MIMI IS JOAN BAEZ SISTER)
                        FAR CRY                                               F20

JERE WHITING        V HCA (A   (A) FAR CRY          19 VANGUARD US VSD 6510 UK SVRL 19041
PAUL LENART         G     (A
DICK MARTIN         SAX PERC(A  DAVID PERRY        G V  (A    LARRY LUDDECKE    K    (A
SEAN HUTCHINSON     B     (A   VICTOR McGILL      D PERC (A
                        FAR EAST FAMILY BAND                                  F20A
FUMIO MIYASHTA V G K SYN (     (A) NEPPORJIN          1975   VERTIGO          6370  850
HIROHITO FUKUSHIMA  G V  (     (B) THE CAVE DOWN TO EARTH 1975 MULAND         CD 7139M
YUJIN HARADA        D PERC(     (C) PARALLEL WORLD     1976   MULAND          LQ 7002M
AKIRA FUKAKUSA      B    (      (D) TENKEYIN          1977   ALL EARS
                        CHRIS FARLOWE                                         F21
CHRIS FARLOWE       V    (ALL  (A) CHRIS FARLOWE & THE THUNDERBIRDS 1966 COLUMBIA  UK  SCX  6034
ALBERT LEE          G    (AB   (B) STORMY MONDAY      1966   M F P           UK  MFP 1186
IAN HAGUE           D    (     (B) CHRIS FARLOWE & THE THUNDERBIRDS 1978 CHARLY  UK  CR 30021
DAVE GREENSLADE     K    (     (C) OUT OF TIME        1966   IMMEDIATE         Z12 52010
BRUCE WADDELL       B    (H    (C) OUT OF TIME        1976   IMMEDIATE       UK RI IML 1002
RICKY CHARMAN       B    (     (D) 14 THINGS TO THINK ABOUT 1966 IMMEDIATE   UK  IMLP  005
PAUL CARSON         SAX  (     (E) THE ART OF CHRIS FARLOWE 1966 IMMEDIATE   UK  IMLP  006
CARL PALMER         D    (     (F) THE BEST OF CHRIS FARLOWE 1968 IMMEDIATE  UK  IMCP  010
PETE SHELLEY        D    (     (G) THE LAST GOODBYE   1969   IMMEDIATE       UK  IMLP  021
STEVE HAMMOND       G    (H    (H) FROM HERE TO MAMA ROSA 1970 POLYDOR       UK  2425  029
JOANNE WILLIAMS     V    (J    (H) FROM HERE TO MAMA ROSA 1970 POLYDOR       US   20  4041
COLIN DAVY          D    (H    (J) CHRIS FARLOWE BAND LIVE 1975 POLYDOR      UK  2460  225
PETER ROBINSON      K    (H    (K) OUT OF TIME/PAINT IT BLACK 1976 CHARLY    UK  CR 300020
PAUL BUCKMASTER     CELLO (H   (C) GREATEST HITS      1977   IMMEDIATE       UK  IML  2002
PAT DONALDSON       B    (J    ( ) FABULOUS CHRIS FARLOWE & THUNDERBIRDS  CBS  US   9393
JEAN ROUSSEL        K    (J
GERRY CONWAY        D    (J    CHRIS MERCER     SAX  (J   MADELINE BELL    V   (J
RON CARTHY          HRNS (J
                        MARK FARNER                                          F22
MARK FARNER         G V  (A    (A) MARK FARNER        1978   ATLANTIC US 18232 UK K50419
PHIL AABERG         K    (A
BOB BABITT          B    (A    BOB KULICK       G    (A   AL WOTTON        D   (A
JIM MAELEN          PERC (A    DICK WAGNER      G    (A   RICKY FARNER     V   (A
DENNIS BALLINGER    V    (A
                        FARQUAHR                                             F22A
BARNSWALLOW FARQUAHR G V (AB   (A) FABULOUS FARQUAHR  19     VERVE FORECAST  FTS  3053
HUMMINGBIRD FARQUAHR G V (AB   (B) FARQUAHR           1970   ELEKTRA      US EKS 74083
CONDOR FARQUAHR     G V  (AB
FLAMINGO FARQUAHR   G V  (AB   JERRY RAGOVOY    K    (B   GARY CHESTER     D   (B
ERIC  WEISSBERG     BANJO (B   JOE MACK         B    (B   LOU MAURO            (B
                        GARY FARR                                           F23
GARY FARR           V G  (ALL  (A) TAKE SOMETHING WITH YOU 1969 MARMALADE   UK  608  013
MIKE STEPHENS       G    (A    (B) STRANGE FRUIT      1971   CBS            UK       64138
ROGER POWELL        D    (A    (C) ADDRESSED TO THE CENSORS OF LOVE 1973 ATCO US 5D 7034
IAN WHITEMAN        WIND K(A    (D) LONDON 1964/65     1977   CHARLY         UK  CR 300015
ANDY LEIGH          B    (A    (E) ROCK GENERATION VOL 7 (1 SIDE) 19 BYG    FR  529  707
MARTIN STONE        G    (A
BRIAN BELSHAW       B    (A    NICK JONES PERC  (A   RICHARD THOMPSON  G  (B  VINCE WETHERALL  G   (D
MICHAEL EVANS       B    (A    ANDY McKECHNIE G  (D   STU PARKS         B  (D  BRIAN WALKELEY   D   (D
ANDY STEELE         D    (D    HARVEY THOMPSON WIND(C  MIKE LEWIS     WIND  (C  RONNIE EADES     SAX (C
HARRISON CALLOWAY TPT(C        BEN CAULEY       TPT (C  CHARLES ROSE   TROM  (C  GEORGE TERRY     G   (C
JIMMY JOHNSON       G    (C    PETE CARR        G   (C  BARRY BECKETT    K  (C  DAVID HOOD       B   (C
JERRY MASTERS       B    (C    ROGER HAWKINS    D   (C
                        MICK FARREN                                         F24
MICK FARREN         V    (AB   (A) CARNIVOROUS CIRCUS(MONA)  1970 TRANSATLANTIC UK TRA  212
WILKO JOHNSON       G    (B    (B) VAMPIRES STOLE MY LUNCH MONEY 1978 LOGO  UK  LOGO 1010
ALAN POWELL         D    (B
WILL STALLIBRASS HCA(B         ANDY COLQUHOUN B  (B   CHRISSIE HYNDE   V  (B  SONJA KRISTINA   V   (B
SUSIE               V    (B    MARIA            V   (B
                        FAST                                                F25
PAUL ZONE           (
MIKI ZONE           (
ARMAND ZONE         (          PETER HOFFMAN    (     TOMMIE MODNIL    (
                        FAST BUCK                                           F26
DAVID KERR CLEMSON  (          (A) FAST BUCK          1976   JET            UK  JETLP 16
ANDREW LOCKE        (
JEFF BROWN          (          EDWIN HAMILTON   (    MIKE HOUGH  ( JAMIE PEARCE  ( STEPHEN FORREST (
                        FAST EXIT                                           F26A
SAM SAMPSON   V HCA (1          (1) 1979
ANDY JOHNSON  G    (1
JEFF BROWN    B    (1          JAMES BIZZY   D   (1   NOSFERATU   SAX   (1

                              [147]
```

```
F27                               FAT
   PETER NEWLAND     V HCA (A   (A) FAT                        1970  RCA              LSA3009
   JAMES KAMINSKI    G V   (A
   MICHAEL BENSON    G     (A   GUY DE VITO      V    (A   WILLIAM BENJAMIN  D V (A
F27A                              FAT CITY
                              (A) REINCARNATION             19    PROBE        US   CPLI 4508
F28                           FAT MAN RIDDIM SECTION
                              (A) ISRAEL TAFARI            1978  TOP RANKING   UK
F29                               FAT MATTRESS
   NOEL REDDING G B V  (A1   (A) FAT MATTRESS          1969 POLYDOR UK 583 056  ATCO US  33309
   STEVE HAMMOND  G    (2    (B) FAT MATTRESS 2        1970 POLYDOR UK 2383 025 ATCO US  33347
   NEIL LANDON    V    (12A  (1) 1969   (2)1970
   JIM LEVERTON K B V  (12A
   ERIC DILLON    D    (12A  CHRIS WOOD  FLT   (A   MICK WEAVER    K   (
F29A                              FAUN
                              (A) FAUN                    19    GREGAR       US   GG  7000
F30                               FAUST
   WERNER DIERMAIER      (ABC  (A) FAUST                  1972  POLYDOR      UK   2310 142
   JEAN HERVE PERON      (ABC  (A) FAUST                  1979  RECOMMENDED            RR1
   RUDOLF SOSNA          (ABC  (B) SO FAR                 1972  POLYDOR      UK   2310 196
   TONY CONRAD           (C    (B) SO FAR                 1972  RECOMMENDED            RR2
   HANS JOACHIM IRMLER   (AB   (C) OUTSIDE DREAM SYNDICATE 1973 CAROLINE     UK        C1501
   GUNTHER WUSTHOFF      (AB   (D) FAUST 4                1973  VIRGIN       UK        V2004
   ARMULF MEIFERT        (A    (E) FAUST TAPES            1973  VIRGIN       UK        VC501
F30A                              BILL FAY
   BILL FAY       V PNO (AB   (A) BILL FAY                1970  DERAM NOVA         SDN..12
   GEORGE BIRD    B     (A    (B) TIME OF LAST PERSECUTION 1971 DERAM             SML1079
   JOHN MARSHALL  D     (A
   TREVOR TAYLOR  D     (A    RICHARD MILLS     G    (A   RAY RUSSELL    G   (A
F30B                              FEAR ITSELF
                              (A) FEAR ITSELF             19    DOT          US   DLP 25942
F31                               CHARLIE FEATHERS
   CHARLIE FEATHERS G V  (ALL  (A) ROCKABILLY KING        1974  POLYDOR      UK   2310 293
   QUINTON CLAUCH  G    (C     (B) CHARLIE FEATHERS (EP)  1977  CHARLY       UK   CEP  116
   BILL CANTRELLI  FDL  (C     (C) ROCKABILLY MAN         1978  CHARLY       UK   CR 30161
   STAN KESTER     STEEL (C    ( ) GOOD ROCKIN' TONIGHT   19    BARRELHOUSE  US    BH  03
   BILL BLACK      B    (C     ( ) LIVE IN MEMPHIS TENNESSEE 197 BARRELHOUSE US    BH.06
   JEFF TODD       B    (C     ( ) THAT ROCKABILLY CAT    1979  BARRELHOUSE  US    BH014
   BILLY RILEY     B    (C     ( ) CHARLIE FEATHERS VOL 1 1979  FEATHERS     US    FR101
   MARCUS VAN STORY B   (C     ( ) CHARLIE FEATHERS VOL 2 1979  FEATHERS     US    FR102
   BUBBA FEATHERS  G    (C     ( ) ROCK'N'ROLL            19    STAR         US
   MACK SELF       V    (C
   JIMMY VAN EATON D    (C   JACK SMITH D   (C  WILLIAM DIEHL   B   (C  BRAD SUGGS   G   (C
F32                               DR FEELGOOD
   DR FEELGOOD                 ( ) R& B WITH DR FEELGOOD(EP) 196 COLUMBIA     UK   SEG 8310
                              ( ) PERCUSSIVE PIANO       19    EUPHONIC     US        1212
                              ( ) JUMPIN' THE BOOGIE     19                 US    1 2821
                              ( ) PIANO RED              19    BLACK LION        BLP 30171
F32A                              FEELIES
                              (A) CRAZY RHYTHMS          1980  STIFF        UK   SEEZ  20
F33                               WILTON FELDER
   WILTON FELDER  HRNS B(AB   (A) WE ALL HAVE A STAR     1978  ABC          UK   ABCL 5265
   DEAN PARKS     G     (B    (B) INHERIT THE WIND       1980  MCA          UK   MCG 4013
   ARTHUR ADAMS   G     (B
   ROLAND BAUTISTA G    (B  JOE SAMPLE   K SYN (B  ABRAHAM LABORIEL B  (B NDUGU CHANCLER D  (B
   RICKY LAWSON   D     (B  PAULINHO DA COSTA PERC (B  BOBBY WOMACK    V  (B MERRY CLAYTON  V  (B
   PAT POWDRILL   V     (B  GWEN EVANS      V     (B  GERRY GARRETT   V  (B ALEX BROWN     V  (B
   JIM GILSTRAP   V     (B  ZEDRIC TURNBOUGH V    (B  AUGIE JOHNSON   V  (B
F34                               VICTOR FELDMAN
   VICTOR FELDMAN PERC PNO VIBES(ALL (A) ROCKAVIBABE     1977  DJM          UK   DJM 22058
   JOHN GUERIN    D     (A    ( ) SUITE 16               19                      C3541
   TOM SCOTT      SAX   (A    ( ) THE ARRIVAL OF VICTOR FELDMAN 19 CONTEMPORARY S7549 + LAC 12172
   CHUCK DOMANICO B     (A    ( ) LATINSVILLE            19    CONTEMPORARY      LAC  580
   TERRY GIBBS          (*    ( ) ARTFUL DODGER          19    CONCORD JAZZ US        .38
   LARRY BUNKER         (*    (*) VIBES TO THE POWER OF 3 1960 TOP RANK     UK    30 007
                              (*) VIBES TO THE POWER OF 3 19   INTERLUDE    US
                              ( ) IN MY POCKET(DIRECT CUT) 1978 COHEARANT   US   CER 1001
F35                               JULIE FELIX
   JULIE FELIX    V G   (ALL  (A) JULIE FELIX            1964  DECCA        UK   SKL  4626
   WITH                       (B) SINGS DYLAN & GUTHRIE  1965  DECCA        UK    LK  4683
   STEVE HAYTON   G V   (P    (C) 2ND ALBUM              1965  DECCA        UK    LK  4724
   DANNY THOMPSON B     (P    (D) 3RD ALBUM              1967  DECCA        UK    LK  4820
   BILLY STEVENS  HCA   (P    (E) CHANGES                1966  FONTANA      UK TL/STL 5368
   KESH SATHIE    TABLA (P    (F) FLOWERS                1967  FONTANA      UK TL/STL 5437
   TED LAZER      ACC   (P    (F) FLOWERS                1974  CONTOUR      UK   6870  507
                              (G) THIS WORLD GOES ROUND & ROUND 1968 FONTANA UK TL/STL 5473
                              (H) THE WORLD OF JULIE FELIX 1969 DECCA       UK   SPA     6
                              (I) GOING TO THE ZOO       1969  DECCA             SFL 13117
                              (J) THE WORLD OF VOL 2     1970  DECCA        UK   SPA    76
                              (K) THIS IS JULIE FELIX    1970  PHILIPS      UK   6382  019
                              (L) CLOTHO'S WEB           1972  RAK          UK   SRKA 6752
                              (M) THIS IS JULIE FELIX VOL 2 1974 PHILIPS    UK   6382  049
                              (N) LIGHTNING              1974  EMI          UK   EMC  3030
                              (O) LONDON PALLADIUM       1974  RCA               LSP  6021
                              (P) HOT CHOCOLATA          1979  GULL         UK   GULP 1032
```

[148]

DICK FELLER F35A

DICK FELLER	V	(ALL	( ) NO WORDS ON ME	19	ASYLUM	US		CM1
CHARLIE McCOY	HCA	(	( ) SOME DAYS ARE DIAMONDS	19	ASYLUM	US	7E	1044
JOHNNY GIMBLE	FDL	(						
PETE DRAKE	STEEL	(						

NARVEL FELTS F35B

NARVEL FELTS	V	(ALL	(A) DRIFT AWAY	19	CINNAMON	US	5000
			( ) NARVEL FELTS	19	DOT	US	DOSD 2025
			( ) GREATEST HITS	19	DOT	US	DOSD 2036

FENDERMEN F35C

JIM SUNDQUIST		(A	( ) MULE SKINNER BLUES	19&	SOMA	US	MG 1240
PHIL HUMPHREY		(A					

MICHAEL FENNELLY F36

MICHAEL FENNELLY	G V	(ALL	(A) LANE CHANGER	1974	EPIS	UK 80230	US 32703	
CASEY FOUTZ	K	(A	(B) STRANGERS	1975	MERCURY		US 1-1043	
NICK NEWELL	SAX(A							
JIM RODFORD	B	(A	ROBERT HENRIT	D	(A	HENRY SPINETTI	D	(A	DAVE WINTOUR	B	(A
MIKE COTTON	TPT(A		JOHN BEECHAM	TROM	(A	ALAN HOLMES	SAX	(A	ROD ARGENT	V	(A
RUSS BALLARD	V	(A	GASPAR LAWAL	PERC	(A	MIKE GILES	D	(A			

SHANE FENTON & THE FENTONES F37

SHANE FENTON	V	(A	(A) GOOD ROCKIN TONIGHT	1974	CONTOUR	UK	2870 409
(LATER ALVIN STARDUST)							

RAY FENWICK F38

RAY FENWICK	G V	(A	(A) KEEP AMERICA BEAUTIFUL	1971	DECCA	UK	SKL 5090

FERGUS F38A

FERGUS	G V	(A	(A) FERGUS	1978	RONDERCREST	ROND LP1

JAY FERGUSON F39

JAY FERGUSON	K V(A		(A) ALL ALONE IN THE END ZONE	1976	ASYLUM US 1063	UK K53040	
JOE WALSH	G	(AB	(B) THUNDER ISLAND	1977	ASYLUM US 1115	UK K53046	
JOE VITALE	D PERC	(A	(C) REAL LIFE AINT THIS WAY	1979	ASYLUM US 6E 158	UK K53086	
JOEY MURCIA	G	(AB					
GEORGE PERRY	B V(A	JOE LALA	PERC	(A	STAN SKIPPER	D	(A	TONY BATTAGLIA	B	(B
ED BROWN	B	(B	HAROLD COWART	B	(B	BILL SZYMCZYK	PERC(B	BOB WEBB	G	(B

ANDY FERNBACH F40

ANDY FERNBACH	G V	(A1	(A) IF YOU MISS YOUR CONNEXION	1969	LIBERTY	UK	LBS 83233
DAVE FERNBACH	K	(A	(1) 1969 BAND CALLED CONNEXION				
PETE CRUICKSHANK	B	(A					
KEN PUSTELNIK	D	(A	CHRIS ELVIN	HCA	(A	J D FANGER	G	(A1	BOB ROWE	B	(1
PHILLIP CROWTHER	D	(1					

AL FERRIER & HIS BOPPIN' BILLIES F40A

AL FERRIER		(A) BIRTH OF ROCKABILLY	19	GOLDSTAR	US
		(B) SOUND OF ROCKABILLY	19	SHOWTIME	US 1000
		(C) BOPPIN' TONIGHT	1977 FLYRIGHT	UK	LP525

FERRIS WHEEL F41

MICHAEL SNOW	V K G	(AB	(A) CANT BREAK THE HABIT	1967	PYE	UK	NPL 18203
LINDA LEWIS	V	(AB	(B) FERRIS WHEEL	1970	POLYDOR	UK	588 066
DAVID SWEETNAM/FORD	SAX (AB						
GEORGE SWEETNAM/FORD	B V(AB	DENNIS ELLIOTT	D	(AB	TERRY EDMUNDS	G	(B	BERNIE HOLLAND	G	(B
DIANA FERREZ	V	(A	MICKY LISTON		(A	KEITH ANTHONY		(A			

BRIAN FERRY F42

BRIAN FERRY	V PNO	(ALL	(A) THESE FOOLISH THINGS	1973 ISLAND	UK ILPS9249	ATLANTIC US 7304
WITH			(A) THESE FOOLISH THINGS	1977 POLYDOR	RI2302 046	2310 507
ANN ODELL	V	(1	(B) ANOTHER TIME ANOTHER PLACE	1974 ISLAND	UK ILPS9284	ATLANTIC US18113
CHRIS SPEDDING	G	(CD1	(B) ANOTHER TIME ANOTHER PLACE	1977 POLYDOR	RI 2302 047	2310 508
JOHN WETTON	B	(BCD1	(C) LET'S STICK TOGETHER	1976 ISLAND	UK ILPS9367	ATLANTIC US18187
PHIL MANZANERA	G	(ACD1	(C) LET'S STICK TOGETHER	1977 POLYDOR	RI 2302 045	2310 045
DYAN BIRCH	V	(D1	(D) IN YOUR MIND	1977 POLYDOR	RI 2302 055	ATLANTIC US18216
PADDY McHUGH	V	(D1	(E) BRIDE STRIPPED BARE	1978 POLYDOR	POLD 5003	
FRANK COLLINS	V	(D1	(EP) PRICE OF LOVE	1976 ISLAND	UK IEP 1	
PAUL THOMPSON	D	(ABCD1	(1) 1977 LIVE TOUR			
MARTIN DROVER	HRNS	(BCD1				

NEIL HUBBARD	G	(CED	ALAN SPENNER	G	(E	WADDY WACHTEL	K G	(E	RICK MAROTTA	D	(E
CHRIS MERCER	SAX	(BCD	MEL COLLINS	SAX	(CD	EDDIE JOBSON	VLN K	(AC	MORRIS PERT	PERC(BC
JOHN GUSTAFSON	B	(C	RICK WILLS	B	(C	JOHN PORTER	G B	(ABCD	DAVID O'LIST	G	(BC
HENRY LOWTHER	HRNS	(BA	RUAN OLOCHLAINN	SAX	(BA	CHRIS PYNE	TROM	(B	TONY CARR		(B
TONY CHARLES		(B	PAUL KOSH		(B	GEOFF DALEY		(B	BOB EFFORD		(B
MALCOLM GRIFFITHS		(B	JIMMY HASTINGS		(B	JOHN PUNTER	D	(AB	ALF REECE		(B
PETER ROBINSON		(B	RONNIE ROSS		(B	BRUCE ROWLAND		(B	STEVE SAUNDERS		(B
ALAN SKIDMORE		(B	WINSTON STONE		(B	DAVID SKINNER	PNO	(AD	VICKI BROWN	V	(B
RAY COOPER	PERC	(D	MARK WARNER		(B	JACQUIE SULLIVAN	V	(D	HELEN CHAPPELLE	V	(BD
DOREEN CHANTER	V	(D	PRESTON HEYMAN		(D	BARRY ST JOHN	V	(B	LIZA STRIKE	V	(B
DON CIRILO	V	(B	ROGER BALL	SAX	(A	MALCOLM DUNCAN	SAX	(A	JESSIE DAVIS	V	(B
ANGELETTES	V	(A	ROBBIE MONTGOMERY	V	(A						

FEVERTREE F43

E E WOLFE	B	(A	(A) FEVER TREE	1968	UK UNLS 102 US	73024	
JOHN TUTTLE	PERC(A		(A) FEVER TREE	19	MCA	US 551	
ROB LANDES	WIND K	(A	(B) ANOTHER TIME ANOTHER PLACE	1968	UNI US 73040 UK MCA MUPS 347		
DENNIS KELLER	V	(A	(C) CREATION	19	UNI	US 73067	
MICHAEL	G	(A	(D) FOR SALE	19	AMPEX	US A 10113	

KAREL FIALKA F43A

KAREL FIALKA	V SYN	(A	(A) STILL LIFE	1980	BLUEPRINT	U BULP 5003
ROBERT LANGRIDGE	K	(A				
MARTIN DEEGAN	D	(A	HAMTONES	V	(A	ANDY BROWN	B	(A	DEREK TULLOCH	SAX (A

FIELDS F44

GRAHAM FIELD	K	(A	(A) FIELDS	1971	CBS	69009
ALAN BARRY	G V B SYN(A		(A) FIELDS	197	UNI	US 73050
ANDY McCULLOCH	D	(A				
FRANK FARRELL	B	(A				

FINCH

JOOP VAN NIMWEGEN	G (A	(A) GALLEON OF PASSION	1977	ROCKBURGH	UK	ROC	103
AD WAMMES	K (A	( ) FINCH	19				
HANS BASBOOM	D (A	( ) BEYOND EXPLOSION	19				
PETER JINK	B (	( ) GLORY OF THE INNER FORCE	1975				
BEER KLAASSE	D (						
CLEEM DETERMEIER	K (						

F46
PETER FINGER

PETER FINGER	G (ALL	( ) DETLEF & FINGER	197	KICKING MULE	UK	SNKF	104
		( ) BOTTLENECK GUITAR SOLOS	197	KICKING MULE	UK	SNKF	105
		( ) ACCOUSTIC ROCK GUITAR	1977	KICKING MULE	UK	SNKF	144

F47
FINGERPRINTZ

JIMME O'NEIL	V G (AB	(A) THE VERY DAB	1979	VIRGIN	UK	V2119
CHA BURNZ	V G (AB	(B) DISTINGUISHING MARKS	1980	VIRGIN	UK	V2170
KENNY ALTON	B V (AB					
BOB SCHILLING	D (AB	PAUL RYAN	SAX (A	BERNIE CLARKE	K (B

F48
MIKE FINNIGAN

MIKE FINNIGAN	B (AB	(A) MIKE FINNIGAN	1976	WB US 2944	UK	K56257
ROGER HAWKINS	D (A	(B) BLACK & WHITE	1978	CBS	US	35259
DAVID HOOD	B (B					

BARRY BECKETT	K (A	PETE CARR	G (A	JIMMY JOHNSON	G (A	AMOS GARRETT	G (B
TOM ROADY	PERC(A	JOHNNY GIMBLE	FDL (A	TEX WEX	PERC (A	HARRISON CALLOWAY	HRNS(A
RON EADES	SAX (A	CHARLES ROSE	TROM (A	PEE WEE ERWIN	TPT (A	BUDDY MORROW	TROM (A
BOB WILBUR	CLAR(A	DON BUTTERFIELD TUBA (A	ED SAUTER STRINGS	(A	STAMPS QUARTET	V (A
FRANCES BARNETTE	V (A	PRISCILLA THOMAS	V (A	JACKIE DIXON	V (A	SUZY STORM	V (A
BARBARA WYRICK	V (A	AVA ALDRIDGE	V (A	JAMES GRIFFIN	V (A	MARIA MULDAUR	V (A

F48A
FINNIGAN & WOOD

MIKE FINNIGAN	V K HCA(A	(A) CRAZED HIPSTERS	1972	BLUE THUMB	US	BTS	.35
JERRY WOOD	V G (A						
DON CLAREY	D (A	RAY BAGBY D (A	DAVE GATES	B (A	RAY LOECKLIE	SAX (A

F48B
FIRE

DAVID LAMBERT	V G K(A	(A) MAGIC SHOEMAKER	1970	PYE	UK	NSPL18343
BOB VOICE	D V (A					
DICK DUFALL	B V (A					

F48C
FIRE ESCAPE

( ) PSYCHOTIC REACTION	19	GNP CRESENDO	US	2034

F49
FIREBALLS

JIMMY GILMER	K (	(A) VAQUERO	1961	TOP RANK UK 105	US(M)343(S)643
GEORGE TOMSCO	G (	( ) TORQUAY	1963	DOT	US	25512
STAN LARK	B (	( ) SUGAR SHACK	196	DOT	US	25545
ERIC BUDD	D (	( ) FIREWATER	196	DOT	US	25856
		( ) SUGER SHACKERS	19	CROWN	US	
		( ) JIMMY GILMER & FIREBALLS	19	CROWN	US	5376
		( ) HERE WE ARE	19	WARWICK	US	W2042
		( ) BOTTLE OF WINE	1968	STATESIDEUK10237	US ATCO 33239
		( ) COME ON REACT	1969	LONDON UK 8396	US ATCO 33275
		( ) CAMPUSOLOGY	19	DOT	US	

F50
FIREFALL

RICK ROBERTS	G V (ABC	(A) FIREFALL	1976	ATLANTIC US 18174 UK K	50260
MIKE CLARKE	D (ABC	(B) LUNA SEA	1977	ATLANTIC US 19101 UK K	50355
MARK ANDES	B (ABC	(C) ELAN	1978	ATLANTIC US 19183 UK K	50494
JOCK BARTLEY	G (ABC					

LARRY BURNETT	V G (ABC	DAVID MUSE	K WIND (ABC	PETER GRAVES	TROM (A	WHIT SIDENER	SAX (A
ANDREW LOVE	SAX (B	KEN FAULK	TPT (A	WAYNE JACKSON	HRNS (A	JACK HALE	TROM (A
LEWIS COLLINS	SAX (B	JAMES MITCHELL	SAX (B	CLYDIE KING	V (B	VANETTA FIELDS	V (B
SHIRLEY MATTHEWS	V (B	JOE LALA	PERC(A	FLACO PADRON	PERC(B	ALAN ESTES	PERC (B
SKIP EDWARDS	PNO (B	TIM SCHMIT	V (B	JERRY AIELLO	ORG(B		

F50A
FIREFLIES

RITCHIE ADAMS	( ) YOU WERE MINE	19	TAURUS	US	1002
LEE REYNOLDS					
JOHNNY VICELLI	PAUL GIACALONE				

F51
FIRESIGN THEATRE

PETER BEGMAN	(A) JUST FOLKS	19	BUTTERFLY	UK	001
PHIL AUSTIN	( ) WAITING FOR THE ELCTRICIAN	1968	CBS UK 65129	US	9518
PHIL PROCTOR	( ) HOW CAN YOU BE IN TWO PLACES..	1968	CBS UK 65130	US	9884
DAVID OSSMAN	( ) DON'T CRUSH THAT DWARF	1972	CB	US	30102
	( ) DEAR FRIENDS	1972	CBS	US	31099
	( ) NOT INSANE	1972	CBS	US	31585
BAND KNOW AS PARTY PIECE IN UK	( ) GIANT RAT OF SUMATRA	1974	CBS	US	32730
	( ) EVERYTHING YOU KNOW	1975	CBS	US	33141
	( ) IN THE NEXT WORLD	1972	CBS	31383 + US	33475
	( ) FORWARD INTO THE PAST	1977	CBS	US	34391
	( ) I THINK WERE ALL BOZOS ON THIS BUS	1970	CBS	US	30737
	( ) TV OR NOT TV	1972	CBS	UK	32199
	( ) HOW TIME FLIES	19	CBS	US	
	( ) PINK PUFFINS IN A PELICANS WORLD	19	CBS	US	
	( ) LENIN & MARX	19	CBS	US	

F51A
FIRST AID

ALAN WORMALD	G V (A	(A) NOSTRADAMUS	1977	DECCA	UK	TXS 117
KEITH PARKINSON	K (					
DAVE FREEMAN	PERC (A	NORRIE TENNENT	B (A			

F52
FIRST CHOICE

( ) SO LET US ENTERTAIN YOU	1976	WB UK K56226	US	2934
( ) SMARTY PANTS	19	PHILLYGROOVE	US	
( ) ARMED AND EXTREMELY DANGEROUS	1973	BELL	BELLS 299
( ) DELUSIONS	1978	SALSOUL	SSLP 1503
( ) HOLD YOUR HORSES	1979	SALSOUL	UK	SSLP!%!$

FIRST CLASS   F53

CHAS MILLS	V	(
TONY BURROWS	V	(
JOHN CARTER	V	(
DEL JOHN	V	(
ROBIN SHAW	B V	(

| ( ) FIRST CLASS | 1974 | 53109 US | UK UKAL 1008 |
| ( ) S S T | 1976 | | UK UKAL 1022 |

SPENCER JAMES   G V   (EDDIE RICHARDS   D V (
CLIVE BARRETT   K V   (

WILD MAN FISCHER   F54

LARRY 'WILD MAN' FISCHER	V(ALL
DON BUCHANAN	G	(B
JOE STODDARD	D	(B
STUART DEAL	B	(B
FRANK ZAPPA	PERC	(A

| (A) AN EVENING WITH WILD MAN FISCHER | 1970 | REPRISE 6332 | BIZARRE 6332 |
| (B) WILDMANIA | 1977 | RHINO | RNLP 001 |

LEONARD SAMARTINO   G V   A(B   SANDRA SAMARTINO   V   (B

FISCHER Z   F54A

JOHN WATTS	G V	(AB
STEVE SKOLNIK	K V	(AB
STEVE LIDDLE	D PERC(AB
DAVID GRAHAM	B	(AB

| (A) WORD SALAD | 1979 | UA | UK UAG 30232 |
| (B) GOING DEAF FOR A LIVING | 1980 | UA | UK UAG 30295 |

FISHBAUGH FISHBAUGH ZORN   F55

GARY FISHBAUGH	V G PERC	(A
PAULA FISHBAUGH	V PNO PERC(A
PETE ZORN	V B G WIND PERC(A
JUNIOR CAMPBELL	G K	(A
RAYMOND DUFFY	D	(A
GRAHAM PRESKETT	VLN	(A

| (A) FISHBAUGH FISHBAUGH & ZORN | 1972 | CBS | UK 64783 |

RICK WEST   G   (A   BRIAN DALY   G   (A
STUART COWELL   G   (A   TERRY COX   D   (A
REG GUEST   K   (A   GORDON HUNTLEY   STEEL(A
MIKE STONE   PERC   (A

MATTHEW FISHER   F56

MATTHEW FISHER	PERC V K G HCA(ABC
GEOFF SWETTENHAM	D	(A
MICK HAWKSWORTH	B	(A
BOBBY HARRISON	V	(A
JOHN CARTER	V	(A
JIM RYAN	B G(B
BARRY DE SOUZA	D	(C
MICK GRABHAM	G	(C
ROD ARGENT	V	(C

(A) JOURNEYS END	1973	RCA UK SF8380	APLI 0195
(B) I'LL BE THERE	1974	RCA	APLI 0325
(C) MATTHEW FISHER	1980	VERTIGO	9198 652

MIKE JAPP   G   (B   ALAN COULTER   D PERC (B   STEVE BINGHAM   B (BC
JAMES FRANK   D   (B   DAVE MATTACKS   D   (C   HENRY SPINETTI   D (C
DIL KATZ   B   (C   PAUL WESTWOOD   B   (C   TIM RENWICK   G (C
JIM DEWAR   V   (C   PETE ZORN   V   (C   JOHN VERITY   V (C
KEN LEWIS   V   (B   TONY BURROWS   V   (A

FIST   F56A

HARRY HILL	D	(A
KEITH SATCHFIELD	G V	(A
JOHN WYLIE	B V	(A

| (A) TURN HELL ON | 1980 | MCA | UK MCF 3082 |

DAVE IRWIN   G V   (A

G F FITZGERALD   F57

G F FITZGERALD

| (A) MOUSEPROOF | 1970 | UNI | UNLS 115 |

FIVE AMERICANS   F57A

( ) I SEE THE LIGHT	19	ABNAK	US	8503
( ) WESTERN UNION	19	ABNAK	US	2067
( ) PROGRESSIONS	19	ABNAK	US	2069
( ) NOW & THEN	19	ABNAK	US	2071

FIVE DOLLAR SHOES   F58

GREGG DIAMOND	D V	(A
TOM GRAVES	K V	(A
JIM GREGORY	B V	(A

| (A) FIVE DOLLAR SHOES | 1972 | NEIGHBORHOOD | UK NH 3001 |

MIKE MILLIUS   V HCA   (A   SCOTT WOODY   G V   (A

FIVE HAND REEL   F59

BOBBY EAGLESHAM	V G	(ABCD
DICK GAUGHAN	G V	(ABC
TOM HICKLAND	K VLN V	(ABCD
BARRY LYONS	PERC B K	(ABCD
DAVE TULLOCH	D	(ABCD
SAM BRACKEN	V G	(D

(A) FIVE HAND REEL	1976	RUBBER 019	RCA PL 25065
(B) FOR A' THAT	1977	RCA	PL 25085
(C) EARL O'MORAY	1978	RCA	PL 25150
(D) BUNCH OF FIVES	1979	TOPIC	12TS 406

FIVE MAN ELECTRICAL BAND   F59A

LES EMERSON	G V	(
BRIAN RADING	V B	(
RICK BELANGER	D V	(
TEDDY GEROW	SAX K V(
MIKE BELANGER	V PERC(

( ) FIVE MAN ELECTRICAL BAND	1969	CAPITOL	US	ST165
( ) FIVE MAN ELECTRICAL BAND	19	PICKWICK	US	SPC 3289
( ) COMING OF AGE	19	LIONEL		1101
( ) GOODBYE & BUTTERFLIES	19	LIONEL		1100
( ) SWEET PARADISE	19	LIONEL		1009
( ) FIND THE ONE	1972	LIONEL	US	

FIVE ROYALES   F59B

LOWMAN PAULING	V	(
CLARENCE PAULING	V	(
JOHNNY MOORE	V	(
OBEDIAH CARTER	V	(
JOHNNY TANNER	V	(

( ) DEDICATED TO YOU	19	KING	580
( ) FIVE ROYALES	19	KING	678
( ) ALL TIME HITS	19	KING	955
( ) ROCKIN'	19	APOLLO	488

ROBERTA FLACK   F60

ROBERTA FLACK	V PNO(ALL
WITH	
JOHN PIZZARELLI	G	(A
RON CARTER	B	(A
RAY LUCAS	D	(A
FRANK WESS	SAX	(A
SELDON POWELL	SAX	(A
BENNIE POWELL	TROM	(A
JOE NEWMAN	TPT	(A
JIMMY NOTTINGHAM	TPT	(A
REGGIE LUCAS	G	(GHJ
HOWARD KING	D V	(GHJ
DAVID SPINOZZA	G	(GH
HARRY WHITTAKER	K	(GHJ
RONNIE FOSTER	K	(GHJ
DAVE CAREY	PERC	(GH

(A) FIRST TAKE	1969	ATLANTIC US 8230	UK588 204
(A) FIRST TAKE	1971	ATLANTIC	RI UK K40040
(B) CHAPTER TWO	1970	ATLANTIC US 1569	UK 2400 023
(B) CHAPTER TWO	1971	ATLANTIC	RI UK K40097
(C) QUIET FIRE	1971	ATLANTIC US 1594	UK K40297
(D) & DONNIE HATHAWAY	1972	ATLANTIC US 7716	UK K40380
(E) KILLING ME SOFTLY	1973	ATLANTIC US 7271	
(E) KILLING ME SOFTLY	1973	ATLANTIC US 19154	UK K50021
(F) FEEL LIKE MAKIN LOVE	1975	ATLANTIC US 18131	UK K50049
(G) BLUE LIGHTS IN THE BASEMENT	1977	ATLANTIC US 19149	UK K50440
(H) ROBERTA FLACK	1978	ATLANTIC US 19186	UK K50495
(J) FEATURING DONNIE HATHAWAY	1980	ATLANTIC	UK K50696
(AB) FIRST TAKE / CHAPTER TWO	1975	ATLANTIC	RI UK K60062
( ) FIRST TIME I SAW YOU	19	PICKWICK	SHM 3022

(CONTINUED)

ROBERTA FLACK

GARY KING	PERC	(G	DON GROLNICK	K	(G	PAUL GRIFFIN	K	(GH	MICHAEL KAMEN	OBOE	(G
ROB MOUNSEY	K	(GH	LEON PENDARVISK	V	(GH	GWEN GUTHRIE	V	(GHJ	ANTHONY JACKSON	B	(GHJ
BRENDA WHITE	V	(GHJ	BASIL FEARRINGTON	B	(GHJ	WILL LEE	B	(GH	LANI GROVES	V	(GH
JIMMY MAELEN	PERC	(G	STEVE GADD	D	(GH	JIMMY WONG	D	(G	IDRIS MUHAMMAD	D	(G
ALLEN SCHWARZBERG	D	(G	MTUME	PERC	(GH	ERROL BENNETT	PERC	(GHJ	DONNY HATHAWAY	V	PNO(DJ
EUGENE McDANIELS	V	(G	ZACK SANDERS	V	(GH	HIRAM BULLOCK	G	(HJ	CLIFF MORRIS	G	(H
MONTY ALEXANDER	K	(H	HOWARD SCHNEIDER	K	(H	BRIAN ALLSOP	B	(H	YOLLANDA McCULLOUGH	V	(H
ELEANORE MILLS	V	(J	JOCELYN SHAW	V	(J	ERIC MERCURY	V	(J	ED WALSH	SYN	(J
HUBERT EAVES	SYN	(J	STEVE FERRONE	D	(H	GARY MURE	D	(H	WARREN CHIASSON	PERC	(H
ANGELO DIBRACCIO	SAX	(H	LARRY ALEXANDER	PERC	(H	SHERRY WILSON	FLT	(H	FRANK LLOYD	V	(H
LUTHER VANDROSS	V	(HJ	YVONNE LEWIS	V	(GH	TAMMY SMITH	V	(H	ELURIEL BARFIELD	B	(J
RAY JONES	K	(J	RAY CHEW	K	(J	HUGH McCRACKEN	G	(GH	JEFF MIRONOV	G	(GHJ
JOHN TROPEA	G	(GJ	DENIECE WILLIAMS	V	(G	JIM GILSTRAP	V	(G			

F60A

JIMMY CRESPO	G	(A
FRANK RUBY	G	(A
MARGE RAYMOND	V	(A

FLAME

(A) QUEEN OF THE NEIGHBOURHOOD		1977	RCA	PL 12160

F61

FLAMIN' GROOVIES

CYRIL JORDAN	G V	(123ABDEK	(A) SNEAKERS	10" LP	1969	SNAZZ	US	2371
GEORGE ALEXANDER	B	(123ABCEK	(A) SNEAKERS	10" LP	1975	SKYDOG	US	FGG 803
TIM LYNCH	G	(ABDE	(B) SUPER NAZZ		1970	EPIC	US	26487
RON GRECO	D	(	(C) FLAMIN' GROOVIES	DBL	19	POLYDOR	UK	2683 003
DANNY MIHM	D	(12ABDE	(D) FLAMINGO		1971	KAMA SUTRA	US	KSBS 2021
			(D) THIS IS (FLAMINGO)		1975	METRONOME	EURO	201 707
JAMES FARRELL	G	(23	(E) TEENAGE HEAD		1971	KAMA SUTRA	US	KSBS 2031
CHRIS WILSON	G V	(23K	(E) TEENAGE HEAD		1976	KAMA SUTRA	UK	KSMD101/1
			(DE)COLLECTORS ITEMS (HEAD/FLAMINGO	1976	KAMA SUTRA		940 106/7
TERRY RAE	D	(	(F) GREASE (EP)		197	SKYDOG	US	66001
DAVID WRIGHT	D	(3K	(G) SHAKE SOME ACTION		1976	SIRE	UK	9103 251
MIKE WILHELM	G	(K	(G) SHAKE SOME ACTION		197	KAMASUTRA	US	7521
ROY A LONEY	V	(1ABDE	(G) SHAKE SOME ACTION		197	PHILIPS	EURO	6370 804
			(H) MORE GREASE(EP)		19	SKYDOG	US	66002
(1) 1970 (2) 1872 (3) 1976			(I) STILL SHAKIN'		1976	BUDDAH	US	5683
			(I) STILL SHAKIN'		1976	PHILIPS	EURO	940541
			(J) NOW		1978	SIRE	US	K6059
			(J) NOW		1978	SIRE		9103 333
			(J) NOW		1978	SIRE		7222 103
			(K) JUMPIN IN THE NIGHT		1979	SIRE	UK	SRK 6067
			(EP) SLOW DEATH		197	UA	UK	
			(EP) SHAKE SOME ACTION		197	SIRE	UK	6198 086
			(EP) ABSOLUTELY SWEET MARY		197	SIRE	UK	SIR 4018

F62

FLAMING YOUTH

RONNIE CARYL	B	(A	(A) ARK 2		19	UNI	73075
GORDON SMITH	G	(A	(A) ARK 2		1969	FONTANA	UK	STL 5533
PHIL COLLINS	D	(A					
BRIAN CHATTON	K	(A					

F63

FLASH

TONY KAYE	K	(A	(A) FLASH	1972 SOVEREIGN UK SVNA 7251 US CAPITOL 11040
PETER BANKS BAN G V SYN	(ABC	(B) FLASH IN THE CAN	1972 SOVEREIGN UK SVNA 7255 US CAPITOL 11115
COLIN CARTER	V D	(ABC	(C) OUT OF OUR HANDS	1973 SOVEREIGN UK SVNA 7260 US CAPITOL 11218
RAY BENNETT K B G V SYN	(ABC	(C) OUT OF OUR HANDS	1973 SOVEREIGN IMP XHVL 1026
MIKE HOUGH	D PERC	(ABC		

F64

FLASH CADILLAC

FLASH CADILLAC	GV	(A	(A) FLASH CADILLAC & THE CONTINENTAL	1973	EPIC US 31787	UK 65438
WARREN'BUTCH'KNIGHT	B	V(A	(B) NO FACE LIKE CHROME	1974	EPIC US 32488	UK 65870
SAM McFADIN	G V	(A	(C) SONS OF BEACHES	1975	PRIVATE STOCK 2003+1002 +2012
ANGELO	K V	(A	(D) ROCK'N'ROLL FOREVER	19	EPIC US 33465
GEORGE ROBINSON	SAX	(A				
JOHN MASION	D V	(A				
LINN PHILLIPS	G V	(				

F65

FLASH FEARLESS

ELKIE BROOKS	V	(A	(A) FLASH FEARLESS Vs THE ZORG WOMEN	1975	CHRYSALIS	UK	CHR 1081
FRANKIE MILLER (US)	V	(A					

ALICE COOPER	V	(A	JAMES DEWAR	V	(A	JIM DANDY	V	(A	KAY GARNER	V	(A
MADDY PRIOR	V	(A	DOREEN CHANTER	V	(A	LESLEY DUNCAN	V	(A	KEITH MOON	V	(A
THUNDERTHIGHS	V	(A	JOHN ENTWISTLE	V B	(A	MICK GRABHAM	G	(A	CARMINE APPICE	D	(A
NICKY HOPKINS	K	(A	MIKE DEACON	K	(A	GRAHAM DEACON	PERC	(A	ROBERT JOHNSON	G	(A
JOHN WEIDER	G	(A	BILL BRUFORD	D	(A	JUSTIN HAYWARD	G	(A	JIM FRANK	HCA	(A
EDDIE JOBSON	K VLN	(A	STEVE PETTICAN	G	(A	CHICK CHURCHILL	K	(A	HOWIE CASEY	SAX	(A
JILL MACKINTOSH	V	(A	KIRK DUNCAN	K	(A	KENNEY JONES	D	(A			

F65A

FLASH AND THE PAN

GEORGE YOUNG	SYN V	(A	(A) FLASH AND THE PAN	1979	ENSIGN	UK	ENVY 6
HARRY VANDA	G V	(AB	(B) LIGHTS IN THE NIGHT	1980	ENSIGN	UK	ENVY 13
RAY ARNOTT	D	(B					
LES KARSKI	B	(B	WARREN MORGAN	PNO	(B		

F66

FLEETWOOD MAC

MICK FLEETWOOD	D	(ALL	(A) FLEETWOOD MAC	1968	BLUE HORIZON		UK	7 63200
JOHN McVIE	B	(ALL	(A) FLEETWOOD MAC	1973	EMBASSY		31036 +	31494
CHRISTINE McVIE	V K(BGHJKLMNOPQXY	(B) MR WONDERFULL	1968	BLUE HORIZON		UK	7 63205
PETER GREEN	G V	(ABCDEGWXYZ	(B) BLUES JAM AT CHESS	1969	BLUE HORIZON US 3801	UK	7 66227
JEREMY SPENCER	G V	(ABCDEFGXYZ	(C) FLEETWOOD MAC IN CHICAGO	1969	SIRE	US 3715+2XS	6009
BOB BRUNNING	B	(A	(D) THEN PLAY ON	1969	REPRISE	US 6368	UK MIDI24001
BOB WELCH	G V	(HKLMJ	(D) THEN PLAY ON	1970	REPRISE		UK	K 44103
STEVE GREGORY	SAX	(B	(E) PIOUS BIRD OF GOOD OMEN	1969	BLUE HORIZON (COMP)	UK	7 63215
JOHNNY ALMOND	SAX	(B	(F) KILN HOUSE	1970	REPRISE	US 6408 UK 9004 +	K 54001
ROLAND VAUGHAN	SAX	(B	(G) ORIGINAL FLEETWOOD MAC	1971	SIRE	US 6045	UK CBS 63875

(CONTINUED)

(CONTINUED)

FLEETWOOD MAC
F66

DUSTER BENNETT	HCA	(B	(H) FUTURE GAMES		1971	REPRISE UUS6465	UK		K 44153
DAVE HOWARD	SAX	(J	(J) BARE TREES		1972	REPRISE US 2080+2278	UK		K 44181
DANNY KIRWAN	V	(CDEFHX	(K) PENGUIN		1973	REPRISE US 2138	UK		K 44235
BOB WESTON	G	(LK	(L) MYSTERY TO ME		1973	REPRISE US 2158+2279	UK		K 44248
MARTIN BIRCH	G	(L	(M) HEROES ARE HARD TO FIND		1974	REPRISE US 2196	UK		K 54026
DAVE WALKER	HCA V(K		(N) FLEETWOOD MAC		1975	REPRISE US 2225 +2281	UK		K 54043
STEVE NYE	K	(K	(O) ROUMORS		1977	WB US 3016	UK		K 56344
RALPH RICHARDSON PERC		(K	(P) TUSK	DBL	1980	WB	UK		K 66088
RUSSEL VALDEZ	PERC	(K	(Q) LIVE	DBL	1980	WB US 3500	UK		K 66097
FRED TOTESAUT	PERC	(K							
STEVE NICKS	V	(NOPQ	(U) ENGLISH ROSE		1969	EPIC US26446	UK CBS		22025
LINDSEY BUCKINGHAM G		V(NOPQ	(V) BLACK MAGIC WOMAN		197	EPIC US 30632			
OTIS SPANN	PNO	(C	(W) GREATEST HITS		1971		UK CBS		69011
WILLLIE DIXON	B	(C	(X) VINTAGE YEARS		1977	SIRE 3706+ 6006	UK CBS		88227
WALTER HORTON	HCA	(C	(Y) ALBATROSS		1977	EMBASSY	UK		31569
GUITAR BUDDY	G	(C	(Z) MAN OF THE WORLD		1978	CBS	UK		83110
HONEYBOY EDWARDS G		(C	( ) BEST OF		1978	REPRISE	UK		K 44138
SP LEARY	D	(C							
SNEAKY PETE	STEEL(M		J T BROWN V SAX (C	EDDIE BOYD	V PNO (E				

FLICKS
F67

TOMMY WILLIS	G	(A	(A) GO FOR THE EFFECT	1979	ARIOLA	ARL	5024
JOHN BUTLER	G V	(A					
DAVE SMITH	D V	(A	JOHNNY KAPP G V (A	LEE STRZELCZYK	B (A		

FLO & EDDIE
F68

FLO(MARK VOLMAN)	V	(ALL	(A) PHLORESCENT LEECH & EDDIE	1972	REPRISE US 2097	UK	K44201
EDDIE (HOWARD KAYLAN)V		(ALL	(B) FLO & EDDIE	1973	REPRISE US 2141	UK	K44234
JIM PONS	B	(AB	(C) IMMORAL ILLEGAL & FATTENING	1974	CBS US 33554		
AYNSLEY DUNBAR	D	(ABC	(D) MOVING TARGETS	1976	CBS US 33262	UK	81509
GARY ROWLES	G	(AB					
DON PRESTON	K	(A	DANNY KOOTCH G (C	LEE SKLAR	B (C	IAN UNDERWOOD K (C	
JOHN HERREN	K	(B	LYNN BLESSING (A	CLAUDE WILLIAMS	(A	ERIC SCOTT B (C	
ANDY CAHAN	D	(C	PHILL REED G (C				

FLOATING BRIDGE
F69

RICK DANGEL	G	(A	(A) FLOATING BRIDGE	1969	LIBERTY	UK	LPS 83271
JOE JOHANSEN	G	(A	(B) BROUGHT UP WRONG	19	VAULT	US	124
JOE JOHNSON	B	(A					
MIKE MARINELLI	D	(A					

FLOCK
F70

JERRY GOODMAN	VLN	(A	(A) FLOCK	1969	CBS US 9911	UK	63733
FRED GLICKSTEIN	G V	(ABC	(B) DINOSAUR SWAMPS	1971	CBS US30007	UK	64055
JAMES L HIRSEN	K V	(C	(C) INSIDE OUT	1975	MERCURY US1 1035	UK 9100	016
JERRY SMITH	B V	(ABC	(AB) FLOCK (DBL)	1972	CBS NL 67278		
RON KARPMAN	D V	(ABC					
MIKE ZYDOWSKY	VLN	(C	RICK CANOFF SAX (A TOM WEBB (A		FRANK POSA (A FELIX PAPPALARDI V(C		

FLOH DE COLOGNE
F70A

HANSI FRANCK	D	(	(A) FLIESSBANDBABYS BEAT SHOW	19	OHR		OMM556000
DIETER KLEMM	V	(	(B) ROCKOPER PROFITGEIER LIVE	19	OHR		OMM556010
MARKUS SCHMIDT	G K	(	(C) GEYER SYMPHONIE	19	OHR		OMM556033
DICK STADTLER	B	(	(D) LUCKY STREIK LIVE	19	OHR		OMM556029
GERD WOLLSCHON	V	(					

HERBIE FLOWERS
F70B

HERBIE FLOWERS	B	(AB	(A) PLANT LIFE	1975	PHILIPS		9109 204
			(B) A LITTLE POTTY	1980	NOTE	NTS	216

FLOWERS OF ROMANCE
F71

SID VICIOUS	V	(A	(A) WINTER 1976/7 NO RECORDS				
STEVE WALSH	G	(A					
KEITH LEVINE	G	(A	SARAH B (A PALMOLIVE D (A		VIV ALBERTINE G (A		

EDDIE FLOYD
F72

EDDIE FLOYD	V	(ALL	( ) KNOCK ON WOOD	1967	ATCO	UK	228 014	
			( ) KNOCK ON WOOD	1967	STAX	US	714	
			( ) NEVER FOUND A GIRL	19	STAX	US	2002	
			( ) RARE STAMPS	19	STAX	US	2011	
			( ) CALIFORIA GIRL	19	STAX	US	2029	
			( ) DOWN TO EARTH	19	STAX	US	2041	
			( ) THINK ABOUT IT	19	ATCO	US	7023	
			( ) YOU'VE GOT TO HAVE EDDIE	19	POLYDOR	UK	2363 010	
			( ) SOUL STREET	1974	STAX US 5512	UK	1002	
			( ) EXPERIENCE	1977	MALACO		6352	
			( ) CHRONICLE	1978	STAX	UK	7005	

FLYING ACES
F73

MARTIN ACE	G B V	(AB	(A) 1975 (B) 1977		
GEORGINA ACE	G B V	(AB			
RICHARD TREECE	G	(B	MICK GIBBON D (B		

FLYING BURRITO BROTHERS
F74

CHRIS ETHRIDGE	K B V(AF		(A) GILDED PALACE OF SIN	1969	A&M US	4175	UK	931	
CHRIS HILLMAN G V B		(ABD	(B) BURRITO DELUXE	1970	A&M US	4258	UK	983	
JON CORNEAL	D	(A	(C) FLYING BURRITO BROTHERS	1971	A&M US	4295	UK	64295	
GRAM PARSONS G V MAND (ABFK			(D) LAST OF THE RED HOT BURRITOS	1971	A&M US	4343	UK	64343	
PETE KLEINOW	STEEL(ABF		(E) CLOSE UP THE HONKY TONKS	1974	A&M US	3631	UK	63631	
BERNIE LEADON	G V	(D	(F) FLYING AGAIN	1975	CBS US	33817	UK	61984	
RICK ROBERTS	G V	(D	(G) HOT BURRITO	1975	ARIOLA		NL	85272	
MIKE CLARKE	D	(BD	(H) LIVE IN AMSTERDAM	1975	BUMBLE US 301 ARIOLA NL 86439				
BYRON BERLINE	FDL	(D	(H) LIVE IN AMSTERDAM	1975	PHONOGRAM	6641 144			
ROGER BUSH	B	'D	(J) AIRBORNE	1976	CBS US	34222	UK	81433	
KENNY WERTZ	G V	(D	(K) SLEEPLESS NIGHTS	1976	A&M US	4578	UK	64578	
AL PERKINS	D	(D	(L) BLUEGRASS SPECIAL	19	ARIOLA		NL	86501	

(CONTINUED)

F74 (CONTINUED) FLYING BURRITO BROTHERS

```
ALAN MUNDE      G V (         (M) LIVE FROM TOKYO              1978  REGENCY           US  79001
ERIC DALTON     G   (         (N) POP CHRONIK      (DBL)       19    ARIOLA            NL  89136
DON BECK        STEEL(        (O) HONKY TONK HEAVEN (DBL)       19    ARIOLA            NL  87585
SKIP BATTIN     B   (
GENE PARSONS    D   (F  EDDIE HOH      D   (A    SAM GOLDSTEIN D   (A   POPEYE PHILLIPS       D   (A
SPOONER OLDHAM  K   (F  GIB GUILBEAU G FDL(F    JOEL SCOTT HILL G V (F   ED PONDER            D   (
LEON RUSSEL     PNO (B  LEOPOLD CARBAJAL ACC(B  FRANK BLANCO   PERC (B   TOMMY JOHNSON        HRNS(B
BUDDY CHILDERS  HRNS (B
```

F74A FLYING CIRCUS

```
                          (A) FLYING CIRCUS              19    CAPITOL           US  ST 11147
```

F74B FLYING ISLAND

```
JEFF BOVA    K TPT(       (A) FLYING ISLAND              19    VANGUARD          US  79359
RAY SMITH    G   (        (B) ANOTHER KIND OF SPACE      1976  vANGUARD          US  79368
BILL BARON   D   (
FAITH FRAIOLI VLN (   THOM PREL        B    (A
```

F74C FLYING LIZARDS

```
                          (A) FLYING LIZARDS             1980  VIRGIN            UK  V2150
```

F75 FLYING SAUCERS

```
                          (A) KEEP ON COMING             1978  ALASKA            UK  ALKA 101
```

F75A FLYING SAUCERS

```
                          ( ) WATERGATE                  19    IX CHAINS         US  9000
```

F75B FLYING SQUAD

```
IAN MUIR        G   (A    (A) FLYING SQUAD               1978  EPIC              UK  82875
MONTY McMONAGLE G   (A
GEORGE CROSSAN  B K V(A   ALEX CALDER G V (A    JIM KELLY   D    (A
```

F76 FLYS

```
                          (A) WAIKIKI BEACH REFUGEES     1978  EMI               UK  EMC 3249
                          (B) OWN                        198   EMI               UK  EMC 3316
```

F77 FOCUS

```
THIJS VAN LEER FLT SYN K V(ABCDEFGHI (A) IN & OUT OF FOCUS    1971  POLYDOR UK 2344 003    UK SIRE  7404
JAN AKKERMANN G PERC  (ABCDEFG       (B) MOVING WAVES         1971  POLYDOR UK 2931 002    US SIRE  7401
HANS ERIC CLEUVER    D(AE            (C) FOCUS THREE          1972  POLYDOR UK 2659 016    US SIRE  3901
MARTIN DRESDEN       B(AE            (D) AT THE RAINBOW       1973  POLYDOR UK 2443 118    US SIRE  7408
PIERRE VAN DER LINDEN D(BCEF         (E) HAMBURGER CONCERTO   1974  POLYDOR UK 2442 124    US ATCO 36100
CYRIL HAVERMANS      B(B             (F) SHIP OF MEMORIES     1974  HARVEST UK SHSP4068    US SIRE  7531
BERT RUITER     PERC B(CDEFG         (G) MOTHER FOCUS        1975  POLYDOR UK 2302 036    US ATCO 36117
COLIN ALLEN     PERC D(EFG           (G) MOTHER FOCUS         197   POLYDOR    ABCR 266        2310  408
DAVID KEMPER         D(FG            (H) FOCUS                1975  POLYDOR UK 2384 070
PHILIP CATHERINE     G(I             (I) FOCUS CON PROBY      1978  HARVEST    SHSP11721  IMP EMI 064 25713
STEVE SMITH          D(I             (J) DUTCH MASTERS        19                          US SIRE  7505
P J PROBY            V(I             ( ) MASTERS OF ROCK      1975  EMI                       054 25130
EEF ALBERS           G(I
```

F78 DAN FOGELBERG

```
DAN FOGELBERG    V K G(ALL   (A) HOME FREE                   1973  CBS   US 31751
WITH                        (B) SOUVENIRS                    1975  EPIC  US 33137    UK  80623
NORBERT PUTNAM   B   (ABCD   (C) CAPTURED ANGEL              1975  EPIC  US 34499    UK  69189
DON HENLEY       V   (BDE    (D) NETHERLANDS                 1977  EPIC  US 34185    UK  69189
KENNY BUTTREY    D   (ADF    (E) TWIN SONS OF DIFFERENT MOTHERS 1978 EPIC US         UK  82774
JOE WALSH        G   (BD     (F) PHEONIX                     1980  EPIC              UK  83317
FRANK MAROCCO    ACC (D
WELDON MYRICK STEEL G (A  BUDDY SPICHER       FDL (A  GLENN FREY         V     (B  DAVID BRIGGS   PNO (A
GLENN SPREEN     STRINGS(A RUSS KUNKEL         D   (BCD FARRELL MORRIS PERC (A  AL PERKINS     STEEL(BC
JOE VITALE       D   (D   JOHN DAVID SOUTHER  V   (DC JOE LALA       PERC (CDE TIM WEISBERG   FLT (DE
JOHN STRONACH    PERC (D  HOT DAMN BROTHERS   V   (C  KENNY PASSARELLI B   (B  GRAHAM NASH    V   (B
JIMMY HASKELL    ACC (B   PAUL HARRIS         K   (F  BRYAN GAROFALO  G    (B  NEIL LARSEN    K   (E
BOBBYE HALL      PERC (E  ANDY NEWMARK        D   (E  WILLIE WEEKS    B    (E  JIM KELTNER    D   (E
EARL DUMLER      HRNS (E  DAVID BREINENTHAL BASSOON(E JOHN HUG        G    (E  ANN MASON STOCKTON HARP(E
JOHN ELLIS       OBOE (E  VINCENT DE ROSA    HRNS(E  GARY COLEMAN   PERC (E  FLORENCE WARNER V (E
RANDY MEISNER    V   (B   JODY BOYER          V   (B  MARIE OUHRABKA  V    (B  MIKE UTLEY     K   (F
GERRY BECKLEY    G   (B   JODY LINSCOTT      CONGA(F MARTY LEWIS    PERC (F  TOM SCOTT      SAX (F
JERRY HEY        HRNS (F  GAIL LEVANT        HARP(F
```

F79 JOHN FOGERTY

```
JOHN FOGERTY    G V  (ALL   (A) BLUE RIDGE RANGERS        1973  FANTASY UKFT511    US  9415
                           (B) JOHN FOGERTY               1975  FANTASY UKFT526
                           (B) JOHN FOGERTY               197   ASYLUM            US7E 1046
                           (C) HOODOO                     197   ASYLUM            US 7E1081
```

F80 TOM FOGERTY

```
TOM FOGERTY    G V  (ALL    (A) TOM FOGERTY               1972  FANTASY           US  9407
STU COOK   B G V SYN (D     (B) EXCALIBUR                 1973  FANTASY           US  9413
J C FOGERTY    G V  (D      (C) MYOPIA                    1974  FANTASY           US  9469
DOUG CLIFFORD  D V  (D      (D) ZEPHYR NATIONAL           1975  FANTASY           US  9448
MERL SAUNDERS  K V  (A
JOHN KAHN      B    (A   BILL VITT     D PERC  (A    RUSS GARY        G V (AD  BILLY MUNDI    PERC (A
ROGER COLLINS  V    (A   TOM PHILLIPS        G    (D  GARY POTTERTON   G   (D  STEPHEN MILLER  K(D
STEPHEN FUNK   K    (D   JEFF NERELL  STEEL DRUM (D  REV RON STALLINGS SAX (D
LILLIAN,NETTA & JO=THE STOVELLS V(D
```

F81 FOGHAT

```
ROD PRICE   V DOBRO G  (ABCDEFGHJK  (A) FOGHAT             1972  BEARSVILLE US 2077 UK  K45503
DAVE PEVERETT   V G  (ABCDEFGHJK    (B) FOGHAT ROCK'N'ROLL 1973  BEARSVILLE US 2136 UK K 45514
NICK JAMESON K G B V (E             (C) ENERGISED         1974  BEARSVILLE US 6950 UK K 55500
ROGER EARL      D   (ABCDEFGHJK     (D) ROCK'N'ROLL OUTLAWS 1974 BEARSVILLE US 6956 UK K 55502
TONY STEVENS    B   (ABCD           (E) FOOL FOR THE CITY  1975  BEARSVILLE US 6959 UK K 55507
CRAIG MACGREGOR B   (FGHJK          (F) NIGHT SHIFT        1977  BEARSVILLE US 6962 UK K 55511
DAVE EDMUNDS    G   (A              (G) LIVE               1977  BEARSVILLE US 6971 UK K 55518
                                                                                (CONTINUED)
```

FOGHAT   F81

TODD RUNDGREN	(A	(H) STONE BLUE	1978	BEARSVILLE US 6977	
JOHN WILLIAMS	(A	(J) BOOGIE MOTEL	1979	BEARSVILLE US 6990	
ANDY FAIRWEATHER LOW V(A		(K) TIGHT SHOES	1980	BEARSVILLE US	UK ILPS9637

ELLEN FOLEY   F81A

ELLEN FOLEY	V	(A) NIGHT OUT	1979	EPIC	UK	83718

MICK RONSON G K V PERC(A

IAN HUNTER K V PERC (A	TOM MANDEL	K	(A	HILLY MICHAELS	D	(A	MARTIN BRILEY B	(A
KERRYN TOLHURST G (A	RORY DODD	V	(A					

FOODBAND   F81B

WOL MAAHN   V G   (A   (A) FOODBAND   1979   TRIX   TRIX   10

AXEL MANRICO HEILHECKER G V(A

MATHIAS KEUL B K V (A	JUMPY ZERLETT	K V	(A	JAN DIX	D V	(A	WOLFGANG BULLMEYER B(A
LYN DOBSON SAX (A	ZWIEBEL	B	(A	PACO SAVAL	V	(A	MIDNIGHT HANDCLAP SEC V(A

THE FOOL   F81C

SEEMON POSTHUMA	(A	(A) FOOL	1969	MERCURY US 61178	UK 20138
MARIJKE KOGER	(A				
JOSJE LEEGER	(A	BARRY FINCH (A			

THE FOOLS   F81D

(A) SOLD OUT   1980   EMI   UK   AML   3008

FOOLS GOLD   F82

TOM KELLY	V G B(A	(A) FOOLS GOLD	1976	ARISTA	UK	ARTY 131
DENNY HENSON	G V (A	(B) MR LUCKY	1977	CBS	US 34828 UK	82148
DOUG LIVINGSTON	G K (A					
RON GRINEL	D (A					

FOOT IN COLD WATER   F83

BOB HORNE	K (A	(A) FOOT IN COLD WATER	1974	ELEKTRA	UK	K 52011
HUGHIE LEGGAT B G V (A						
ALEX MACHIN	V (A	PAUL NAUMANN	G	(A	DANNY TAYLOR	D V	(A

STEVE FORBERT   F83A

STEVE FORBERT HCA G V (ALL	(A) ACIVE ON ARRIVAL	1978	EPIC	UK 83308
STEVE BURGH	G (A	(B) JACKRABBIT SLIM	1979	EPIC	UK 83879
BARRY LAZAROWITZ D (AC	(C) LITTLE STEVIE ORBIT	1980	EPIC	UK 84501

HUGH McDONALD   G B   (AC

ROBBIE KONDOR	K	(AC	HARVEY SHAPIRO	STEEL	(A	DAVID SANBORN	SAX	(A	BRIAN TORFF	B(A
BOBBY OGDIN	PNO	(B	PAUL ERRICO	K	(BC	JOHN GOIN	G	(B	GUNNAR GELLOTE	D(B
BOB WRAY	B	(B	ALAN FREEDMAN	G	(B	JACK WILLIAMS	B	(B	ROGER CLARK	D(B
JERRY BRIDGES	B	(B	BILL JONES	SAX	(BC	MIKE LEECH	B	(B	RON KELLER	TPT(B
DENNIS GOOD	TROM	(B	AVA ALDRIDGE	V	(B	CINDY RICHARDSON	V	(B	MARIE TOMLINSON	V(b
SHANE FONTAYNE	G	(C	KEN KOSEK	FDL	(C	BOBBY LLOYD HICKS D		(C		

FRANKIE FORD   F83B

FRANKIE FORD	V	(	(A) ON A SEA CRUISE	19	ACE	US	LP	1005
			(B) FRANKIE FORD	19	BRIARMEADE	US	BR	5002
			(EP) BEST OF FRANKIE FORD	19	ACE	US		EP105

FOREIGNER   F84

MICK JONES	K V G	(AB	(A) FOREIGNER	1977	ATLANTIC US 18215	UK K50356
IAN McDONALD	K G D V	(AB	(B) DOUBLE VISION	1978	ATLANTIC US 19999	UK K50476
LOU GRAMM	V	(AB	(C) HEAD GAMES	1979	ATLANTIC US 29999	UK K50651
DENNIS ELLIOTT	D	(AB	(EP) FEELS LIKE THE FIRST TIME	1978	ATLANTIC	UK K11086
AL GREENWOOD	SYN K(AB					
ED GAGLIARDI	V B	(AB	IAN LLOYD	V	(B		

FOREST   F85

MARTIN WELHAM G V K PERC(AB	(A) FOREST	1969	HARVEST	UK	SHVL 760
DEREK ALLENBY K V HCA PERC(AB	(B) FULL CIRCLE	1970	HARVEST	UK	SHVL 784

HADRIAN WELAHM G K V HCA PERC(A

GORDON HUNTLEY   STEEL   (B

FOREVER MORE   F85A

ALAN GORRIE	K B	(AB	(A) WORDS ON BLACK PLASTIC	19	RCA US LSP 4435	
STEWART FRANCIS	D V	(AB	(B) PAINT IT YOURSELF	19	RCA US LSP 4272	UK SF8016
ONNIE MAIR	G V B(AB					
MICK TRAVIS	G	(AB				

DAVID FORMAN   F85B

DAVID FORMAN   (A) DAVID FORMAN   1976   ARISTA   US   4084

FORMERLY FAT HARRY   F85C

PHIL GREENBERG   V G   (A   (A) FORMERLY FAT HARRY   1971   HARVEST   UK   SHSP 4016

GARY PETERSON V G K PERC(A

BRUCE BARTHOL   B   (A   LAURIE ALLEN   D   (A   NISAR AHMAD GEORGE KHAN   SAX   (A

SHARON FORRESTER   F86

SHARON FORRESTER V   (A   (A) SHARON   1974   ASHANTI SHAN105+ VULCAN

GEOFFREY CHUNG   K V G(A

ROBERT BAILEY	K	(A	PHIL CHEN	B	(A	RICHARD BAILEY	D	(A	WINSTON DELANDRO	G	(A
ALLAN SHARP	PERC	(A	DEL RICHARDSON	HCA	(A	MIKE MORAN	K	(A	HENRY LOWTHER TPT		(A
RON CARTHY	TPT	(A	RAY WARLEIGH	HRNS	(A	GRAHAM PRESKETT	MAND	(A	VAL DOUGLAS	B	(A
MICHAEL RICHARDS	D	(A	ROBERT LYN	PNO	(A	EARL LINDO	K	(A	MALCOLM GRIFFITHS TROM(A		
CHRIS MERCER	SAX	(A	MEL COLLINS	SAX	(A	MARTIN DROVER	TPT	(A	MARTYN FORD HRNS		(A
30 PIECE ORCHESTRA		(A	NINE BACKING SINGERS		(A						

FORTUNES   F87

BARRY PRITCHARD	G V	(	(A) FORTUNES	1965	DECCA	LK	4736
DAVID CARR	K	(	(B) FORTUNES	1972	CAPITOL	ST	21891
ROD ALLEN	B	(	(C) REMEMBERING THE FORTUNES	1976	DECCA		REM 2
ANDY BROWN	D	(					
GLEN DALE	G V	(	SHEL McCRAE	(			

F87A

			RONNIE FOSTER					
RONNIE FOSTER	V K	(A	(A) LOVE SATELLITE	1978	CBS		UK	83037
DENNIS DAVIS	D	(A						
LEON CHANCLER	PERC	(A	ALPHONSO JOHNSON B (A PAULINHO DA COSTA		PERC(A	HARVEY MASON	D	(A
BYRON MILLER	B	(A	JERRY PETERS V PNO (A STEVE WONDER		D (A	ROY AYERS	VIBES(A	

F88

			FOSTER BROTHERS					
GRAHAM FOSTER	G V SYN(A		(A) ON THE LINE	1977	ROCKET		UK	ROLL10
MALCOLM FOSTER	G V							
EDDIE WILLIAMS	D PERC(A		ROB McINTOSH V K (A PETE WINGFIELD K		(A	STEVE GREGORY HRNS	(A	
BUD BEADLE	SAX (A		GEORGE CHISHOLM TPT (A MALCOLM GRIFFITHS TROM (A					

F89

			FOTHERINGAY					
SANDY DENNY	V	(A	(A) FOTHERINGAY	1970	ISLAND UK ILPS9125 US A&M4269			
TREVOR LUCAS	G	(A						
JERRY DONAHUE	G	(A	PAT DONALDSON B (A GERRY CONWAY		D (A	LINDA THOMPSON	V (A	
TOD LLOYD	V	(A						

F90

			FOTOMAKER					
WALLY BRYSON	G V	(A	(A) FOTOMAKER	1978	ATLANTIC US 19165		UK K50450	
GENE CORNISH	B V	(A						
DINO DANELLI	D	(A	LEX MARCHESI G V (A FRANKIE VINCI		K V (A			

F90A

			FOUNDATIONS					
CLEM CURTIS	V	(A	(A) FROM THE FOUNDATIONS	1967	PYE		UK	NPL 18206
COLIN YOUNG	V	(D	(A) BABY NOW THAT IVE FOUND YOU	1967	UNI		US	73016
ALAN WARNER	G	(AD	(B) FROM THE FOUNDATION	196	PYE		UK	NPL 18227
ERIC ALLENDALE	TROM	(AD	(C) BUILD ME UP BUTTERCUP	196	UNI		US	73043
TONY GOMEZ	ORG	(AD	(D) DIGGING THE FOUNDATIONS	1969	PYE		UK	NPL 18290
TIM HARRIS	D	(AD	(D) DIGGING THE FOUNDATIONS	1969	UNI		US	73058
PETER MACBETH	B	(AD	( ) THE FOUNDATIONS	1968	MARBLE ARCH		UK	MALS11571
PAT BURKE	WIND	(AD	(EP) ITS ALL RIGHT	19	PYE		UK	NEP 24297
MIKE ELLIOTT	SAX	(A	( ) GOLDEN HOUR	1973	PYE		UK	GH574
			( ) ROCK FROM BRITAIN VOL 2	197	MODE		US	9040

F91

			FRANKIE VALLI & THE FOUR SEASONS					
FRANKIE VALLI	V	(X	SHERRY	1963	VEE JAY US	1053	UK STATESIDE	10033
TOMMY DEVITO			GREETINGS	1963	VEE JAY US	1055	UK STATESIDE	10051
NICK DEVITO			BIG GIRLS	1963	VEE JAY US	1056		
NICK MASSI			AINT THAT A SHAME	1963	VEE JAY US	1059	UK STATESIDE	10043
BOB GAUDIO			STAY	1964	VEE JAY US	1082		
JOEY LONG			GOLDEN HITS	196	VEE JAY US	1088		
GERRY POLCI	D	(X	WE LOVE GIRLS	196	VEE JAY US	1121		
DON CICCIONE	B	(X	LIVE ON STAGE	196	VEE JAY US	1154		
LEE SHAPIRO	K		DAWN	1964	PHILIPS US	600124	BL	7621
JOHN PAIVA	G		BORN TO WANDER	1964	PHILIPS US	600129	BL	7611
JERRY CORBETTA	K V	(X	RAG DOLL	1964	PHILIPS US	600146	BL	7643
LARRY LINGLE	G V	(X	SING BIG HITS	1965	PHILIPS US	600150	BL	7687
REX ROBINSON	K	(X	ENTERTAIN YOU	1965	PHILIPS US	600164	BL	7663
ROBBY ROBINSON	K	(X	BIG HITS BY BACHARACH,DAVID & DYLAN		PHILIPS US	600193		
RICHARD GARCIA	PERC	(X	GOLD VAULT HITS	1965	PHILIPS US	600196	BL	7719
TOBEE TYLER	V	(X	WORKING MY WAY BACK TO YOU	1965	PHILIPS US	600201	BL	7699
TONY WALTHERS	V	(X	2ND VAULT	196	PHILIPS US	600221		
			LOOKING BACK	196	PHILIPS US	600222	BL	7752
			CHRISTMAS ALBUM	1966	PHILIPS US	600223	BL	7753
			NEW GOLD HITS	196	PHILIPS US	600243		
			GENUINE IMITATION LIFE GAZETTE	1968	PHILIPS US	600290		
			HALF & HALF	196	PHILIPS US	600341		
			EDIZIONE D'ORO	1969	PHILIPS US	2 6501	UK	6640 002
			SEASONED HITS	1968	FONTANA		UK	SFJL 952
			BIG ONES	1971	PHILIPS		UK	6336 208
			CHAMELEON	1972	MOWEST US	108	UK	MWAS 5501
			CHAMELEON	1975	MOWEST		UK RI MWS 7006	
			GOLD	1975	PRIVATE STOCK			
			OUR DAY WILL COME	1975	PRIVATE STOCK			
			CLOSE TO YOU	1975	PRIVATE STOCK		UK	PVLP 1001
			FALLEN ANGEL	1975	PRIVATE STOCK		UK	PVLP 1005
			WHO LOVES YOU	1975	WB US	2900	UK	K 56179
			INSIDE YOU	1975	MOWEST		UK	MWS 7007
			STORY	1976	PRIVATE STOCK US 7000			
			HELICON	1977	WB US	3016	UK	K 56350
			FRANKIE VALLI IS THE WORD	1978	WB US		UK	
			(X) REUNITED LIVE (DBL)	1981	WB US	3497	UK	K 66098
			GREATEST HITS	1976	K TEL		UK	NE952
			GREATEST HITS(4 RECORD SET	19	LONGINES US	95833		
			BROTHER HOOD OF MAN	19	PICKWICK US	3223		
			BROTHERHOOD OF MAN	19	SEARS US	609		
			(EPS)					
			GENUINE IMITATION LIFE GAZETTE	19	PHILIPS US	2704		
			FOUR SEASONS SING	19	VEE JAY US	902		
			PEANUTS	19	VEE JAY US	901		

F92

			FOUR TOPS					
LEVI STUBBS	V	(ALL	FOUR TOPS	1965	TAMLA MOTOWN US	622	UK	STML 11010
RENALDO BENSON	V	(ALL	SECOND ALBUM	1966	TAMLA MOTOWN US	647	UK	STML 11021
LAWRENCE PAYTON	V	(ALL	ON TOP	1966	TAMLA MOTOWN US	634	UK	STML 11037
ABDUL FAKIR	V	(ALL	LIVE	1967	TAMLA MOTOWN US		UK	STML 11041
WITH			REACH OUT	1967	TAMLA MOTOWN US		UK	STML 11056
ED GREENE	D	(*	LIVE AT THE ROOSTER TAIL	196	TAMLA MOTOWN US	654		
MAX BENNETT	B	(*	ON BROADWAY	1967	TAMLA MOTOWN US	657		
WILTON FELDER	B	(*	GREATEST HITS	1968	TAMLA MOTOWN US	662	UK	STML 11061
BEN BENAY	G	(*	YESTERDAYS DREAM	1969	TAMLA MOTOWN US	669	UK	STML 11087
DAVID T WALKER	G	(*	FOUR TOPS NOW	1969	TAMLA MOTOWN US	675	UK	STML 11113
LEE RITENOUR	G	(*	SOUL SPIN	1970	TAMLA MOTOWN US	695		
DEAN PARKS	G	(*						

(CONTINUED)

FOUR TOPS

												F92

(CONTINUED)

JAY GRAYDON	G	(*	STILL WATERS RUN DEEP	1970	TAMLA MOTOWN	US	704			UK	STML	11149
MICHAEL OMARTIAN	K	(*	CHANGING TIMES	1971	TAMLA MOTOWN	US				UK	STML	11173
CLIFFORD CARTER	K	(*	GREATEST HITS VOL 2	1971	TAMLA MOTOWN	US	740			UK	STML	11195
VICTOR FELDMAN	PERC	(*	DYNAMITE (SUPREMES)	1972	TAMLA MOTOWN	US	745			UK	STML	11203
KING ERRISSON	PERC	(*	NATURE PLANNED IT	1972	TAMLA MOTOWN	US	748			UK	STML	11206
ERNIE WATTS	HRNS	(*	BEST OF	197	TAMLA MOTOWN	US	764					
CHUCK FINDLEY	HRNS	(*	KEEPER OF THE CASTLE	1972	DUNHILL	US	50129	PROBE	UK	SPB	1064	
PAUL HUBINON	HRNS	(*	KEEPER OF THE CASTLE	1974	ABC					UK	ABCL	5023
JACKIE KELSO	HRNS	(*	FOUR TOPS STORY	1973	TAMLA MOTOWN					UK	TMSP	1124
LEW McCREARY	HRNS	(*	MAIN STREET PEOPLE	1973	DUNHILL	US	50144	PROBE	UK	SPBA	6277
FRED SELDON	HRNS	(*	MAIN STREET PEOPLE	1974	ABC					UK	ABCL	5037
SID SHARP	STRINGS	(*	MEETING OF THE MINDS	1974	DUNHILL	US	50166	PROBE	UK	SPBA	6283
GINGER BLAKE	V	(*	MEETING OF THE MINDS	1974	ABC					UK	ABCL	5046
			SHAFT IN AFRICA(SOUNDTRACK)	1974	PROBE		UK	SBP1077	ANCHOR UK	ABCL	5035	
			LIVE IN CONCERT	1974	DUNHILL	US	50188	ANCHOR UK	ABCL	5062	
			(*) NIGHT LIGHTS HARMONY	1974	ABC	US	862	ANCHOR UK	ABCL	5130	
			SUPER HITS	1976	TAMLA MOTOWN					UK	STML	8028
			CATFISH	1976	ABC	US	968					
			ANTHOLOGY	197	TAMLA MOTOWN	US	M9809					
			MOTOWN SPECIAL	1977	TAMLA MOTOWN					UK	STMX	6004
			SHOW MUST GO ON	1977	ABC	US	1014	ANCHOR UK	ABCL	5223	
			AT THE TOP	1978	ABC					UK	ABCL	5262
			ITS ALL IN THE GAME	1979	MFP					UK		50253

FOURMOST

F93

BRIAN O'HARA	G V	(A	(A) FIRST & FOURMOST	1965	PARLOPHONE	UK	PMC	1259
MIKE MILLWARD	G V	(A	(EP)FOURMOST SOUND	1964	PARLOPHONE	UK	GEP	8892
BILLY HATTON	B	(A	(EP)FOURMOST	1964	PARLOPHONE	UK	GEP	8917
DAVE LOVELADY	D	(						

KIM FOWLEY

F94

KIM FOWLEY	V K	(ALL	LOVE IS ALIVE AND WELL	1967	TOWER	US	DT	5080
MIKE ALLSUP	G	(*	IN THE UNDERGROUND	1968				
EDDIE HOH	PERC	(*	BORN TO BE WILD	1968	IMPERIAL	US	LP	12413
MARS BONFIRE	G	(*G	(*) OUTRAGEOUS	1969	IMPERIAL	US	LP	12423
JIMMY GREENSPOON	K	(*	GOOD CLEAN FUN	1969	IMPERIAL	US	LP	12443
JOE SCHERMIE	B	(*	THE DAY THE EARTH STOOD STILL	1970	MNW	SWED MNWL	7P	
ORVILLE RHODES	STEEL	(G	(G) I'M BAD	1972	CAPITOL		ST	11075
WAYNE TABERT	K	(*	OUTLAW SUPERMAN (NOT RELEASED)	1971	RCA	US		
CARMAN RIALE	B	(*	INTERNATIONAL HEROES	1973	CAPITOL		ST	11159
BEN BENAY	G	(*G	SUNSET BOULEVARD	197	ILLEGAL	UK	ILP	002
JOE TORRES	PERC	(*	AUTOMATIC	197	CAPITOL			11248
PETE SEARS	B K	(G	LIVING IN THE STREETS	1978	SONET	UK	SNTF	733
WARREN KLEIN	G	(G	ANIMAL GOD OF THE STREETS	1979	CAPITOL			24636
			LEGENDARY DOG DUKE SESSIONS	19	B F D		BFD	5012
			SNAKE DOCUMENT MASQUERADE	1979	ISLAND		ILPS	9572

FOX

F95

NOOSHA FOX	V	(AB	(A) FOX	1975	GTO	UK	GTLP	001
HERBIE ARMSTRONG	G V	(A	(A) TALES OF ILLUSION	1975	GTO	UK	GTLP	006
KENNY YOUNG	G V	(A	(C) BLUE HOTEL	1977	GTO	UK	GTLP	020
GARY TAYLOR	B V	(A						
JIM FRANK D PERC V		(A	PETE SOLLEY	K V	(A	JIM GANNON	G V	(A

FOX

F95B

STEVE BRAYNE	G	(A	(A) FOR FOX SAKE	1970	FONTANA	UK	6309	007
WINSTON WEATHERILL G SITAR		(A						
TIM REEVES	D	(A	DAVID WINDCROSS	B PNO	(A	ALEX LANE	K	(A

FOXX

F96

| | | | (A) REVOLT OF EMILY YOUNG | 1971 | MCA | UK | MUPS | 419 |

INEZ & CHARLES FOXX

F97

CHARLES FOXX	V	(ALL	(A) MOCKINGBIRD	1964	SUE	US 1027		UK ILP911
INEZ FOXX	V	(ALL	(B) INEZ & CHARLES FOXX	196	SUE	US 1037	LONDON UK	8241
			(C) AT MEMPHIS	19	VOLT	US 6022		
			(D) COME BY HERE	19	DYNAMO	8000		
			(E) GREATEST HITS	19	PYE		UK	4406

JOHN FOXX

F97A

JOHN FOXX	SYN V	(A	(A) METAMATIC	1980	VIRGIN	UK	V2146
JOHN BARKER	SYN	(A					
JAKE DURANT	B	(A					

FOXY

F98

| | | (A) GET OFF | 1978 | TK | | TKR 82544 |
| | | (B) HOT NUMBERS | 1979 | TK | UK | TKR 83353 |

GARLAND FRADY

F99

| GARLAND FRADY | | (A) PURE COUNTRY | 1973 | COUNTRYSIDE | US | CS101 |

PETER FRAMPTON

F100

PETER FRAMPTON	G V B K	(ALL	(A) WIND OF CHANGE	1972	A&M	US 4348	UK	AMLS68099
RICK WILLS	B	(BC	(B) FRAMPTONS CAMEL	1973	A&M	US 4389	UK	AMLH68150
MICK GALLAGHER	K	(B	(C) SOMETHINGS HAPPENING	1974	A&M	US 3617	UK	AMLH63619
MIKE KELLIE	D	(	(D) FRAMPTON	1975	A&M	US 4512	UK	AMLH64512
JOHN SIOMOS	D	(BDEF	(E) COMES ALIVE	1975	A&M	US 3703	UK	AMLG63703
ANDY BOWN	K	(D	(F) I'M IN YOU	1977	A&M	US 4704	UK	AMLK64704
BOB MAYO	V K G	(EF	(G) WHERE I SHOULD BE	1979	A&M	US	UK	AMLK63710
STANLEY SHELDON	B	(EF						
STEVIE WONDER	HCA	(F	FRANK CARILLO	G V	(B	POLI PALMER	VIBES	(D	RITCHIE HAYWARD	PERC	(F
JOHN HEADLEY DOWN	D	(C	NICKY HOPKINS	PNO	(C			

RITCHIE FRANCIS

F101

RITCHIE FRANCIS	PNO V	(A	(A) SONGBIRD	1971	PEGASUS UK PEG 1+ INTERCORD 26006-7U		
MIKE KELLIE	D	(A					
BARRY MORGAN	D	(A	WILL MALONE	D	(A	PHIL CURTIS	B	(A	JOHN ROSTILL	B	(A
TAFF WILLIAMS	G	(A	JIM SULLIVAN	G	(A			

F101A

BOB FRANK	G V	(A

BOB FRANK

(A) BOB FRANK	19	VANGUARD	US	6582

F102

FRANK RUBY	G V	(A
JOHN PAUL FETTA	B V	(A
BARRY BAILEY	G	(A
DEAN DAUGHTRY	K	(A

FRANKIE & JOHNNY

(A) SWEETHEART SAMPLER	1973	WB	US	2675

EDDIE BARBATO	G	(A	AL KOOPER	GK	(A	J R COBB	G	(A
ROBERT NIX	D	(A	MIKE GATELY	V	(A			

F103

ARETHA FRANKLIN	PNO V	(ALL
WITH		
CORNELL DUPREE	G	(*
JACK CAVARI	G	(*
TOM HANLON	G	(*
RICHARD TEE	K	(*
KEN ASCHER	K	(*
PAUL GRIFFIN	K	(*
VAN McCOY	V K	(*
GORDON EDWARDS	B	(*
BRIAN ALLSOP	B	(*
CHRIS PARKER	D	(*
CRUSHER BENNETT	PERC	(*
GEORGE DEVENS	PERC	(*
KEN BISCHEL	SYN	(*
DESTRY	V	(*
ZULEMA CUSSEAUX	V	(*
ALBERT BAILEY	V	(*
BRENDA HILLIARD	V	(*
JEROME JACKSON	V	(*
RICHARD HARRIS	V	(*
PETE MARSHALL	V	(*
CAROLYN FRANKLIN	V	(*
SHARON BROWN	V	(*
PAT WILLIAMSON	V	(*

ARETHA FRANKLIN

ARETHA	1961	CBS	US 1612(M)			8402(S)
ELECTRIFYING	1962	CBS	US 1761(M)			8561(S)
TENDER MOVING & SWINGING	1962	CBS	US 1876(M)			8676(S)
LAUGHING ON THE OUTSIDE	1963	CBS	US			8897(S)
UNFORGETTABLE	1964	CBS	US			8963(S)
SONGS OF FAITH	1964	CHECKER	US 10009			
RUNNING OUT OF FOOLS	1964	CBS	US GP4			
YEAH	1965	CBS	US 2351(M)			9151(S)
SOUL SISTER	1966	CBS	US 2521(M)			9321(S)
QUEEN OF SOUL	196	CBS		UK		52562
TAKE IT LIKE YOU GIVE IT	1967	CBS		UK		62969
LEE CROSS	196	CBS		UK		63160
GREATEST HITS	1967	CBS	US 9601+31355	UK		64536
I NEVER LOVED A MAN	1967	ATLANTIC	US 8139	UK		80007
ONCE IN A LIFETIME	19	HARMONY	US 11349			
GREATEST HITS 1960 65	19	HARMONY	US 30606			
ARETHA ARRIVES	1967	ATLANTIC	US 8150			
LADY SOUL	1968	ATLANTIC	US 8176	UK	588 099	
GREATEST HITS VOL 2	1968	CBS	US 9601	UK		63064
BEST OF	19	ATLANTIC	US 8305			
LIVE AT PARIS OLYMPIA	1968	ATLANTIC	US 8207 UK588149 +RI K40024			
ARETHA NOW	1968	ATLANTIC	US 8186	UK	588 114	
SOUL 69	1969	ATLANTIC		UK	588 163	
TODAY I SING THE BLUES	1969	CBS				
SOFT & BEAUTIFUL	19	CBS	US 9776			
ARETHAA GOLD	1969	ATLANTIC	UK 588 192 UK RI		K40036	
SATISFACTION	19	ATLANTIC	US 8215			
I SAY A LITTLE PRAYER	1969	ATLANTIC		UK	2464 007	
THIS GIRLS IN LOVE WITH YOU	1970	ATLANTIC	US	UK	2400 004	
SPIRIT IN THE DARK	1970	ATLANTIC	US 8265	UK	K 40095	
DONT PLAY THAT SONG	1970	ATLANTIC	US	UK	2400 021	
LIVE AT FILLMORE WEST	1971	ATLANTIC	US 7295	UK	K 40222	
YOUNG GIFTED & BLACK	1971	ATLANTIC	US 7213	UK	K 40323	
ARETHAS GREATEST HITS	1971	ATLANTIC	US 8295	UK	K 40279	
AMAZING GRACE	1972	ATLANTIC	US 2 906	UK	K 60023	
HEY HEY NOW	1973	ATLANTIC	US 7265	UK	K 40504	
STAR COLLECTION	1978	MIDI		UK	K 20016	
FIRST 12 SIDES	1973	CBS	US 31953 EMBASSY UK		31006	
LET ME INTO YOUR LIFE	1974	ATLANTIC	US 7292	UK	K 50031	
WITH EVERY THING I FEEL IN ME	1975	ATLANTIC	US 18116	UK	K 50093	
YOU	1975	ATLANTIC	US 18151	UK	K 50159	
SPARKLE	1976	ATLANTIC	US 18176	UK	K 56248	
TEN YEARS OF GOLD	1976	ATLANTIC	US 18204	UK	K 50326	
SWEET PASSION	1977	ATLANTIC	US 19102	UK	K 50368	
ALMIGHTY FIRE	1978	ATLANTIC	US 19161	UK	K 50445	
(*)LA DIVA	1979	ATLANTIC		UK	K 50637	
ARETHA	1980	ARISTA		UK SPART1147		

F103A

CAROLYN FRANKLIN	V	(

CAROLYN FRANKLIN

(A) CAROLYN FRANKLIN	1976	RCA	UK	APLI 0420
( ) CHAIN REACTION	19	RCA	US	LPS 4317
( ) FIRST TIME I CRIED	19	JOY	UK	JOYS 180

F103B

ERMA FRANKLIN	V	(

ERMA FRANKLIN

(A) SOUL SISTER	19	BRUNSWICK		754147
( ) HER NAME IS ERMA	19	EPIC	US	3824

F103C

RODNEY FRANKLIN	K B V	(AB
VINCENT SPAULDING	G	(AB
HAROLD FOREMAN	B	(A
TONY ST JAMES	D	(AB
RANDY MERRITT	D	(A
LISA ROBERTS	V	(A
DAVID LUELL	HRNS	(B
BOBBY BRYANT	HRNS	(B
DENNIS BUDIMIR	G	(B
ERNIE WATTS	SAX	(B
IAN UNDERWOOD	SYN	(B

RODNEY FRANKLIN

(A) YOU'LL NEVER KNOW	1980	CBS	UK	83812
(B) RODNEY FRANKLIN	1980	CBS	UK	84528

KENNETH NASH	PERC	(A	DEAN HOLZKAMP	WIND	(a	MEL MARTIN	WIND	(A
PAUL JACKSON	B	(A	RAY PIZZI	CLAR	(A	PHYLLIS ST JAMES	V	(AB
BROOKS HUNNICUTT	V	(A	AUDREY FRANKLIN	V	(A	OSCAR BRASHEAR	HRNS	(B
SEAWIND	HRNS	(A	PHIL UPCHURCH	G	(B	NATHAN EAST	B	(B
PAULINHO DA COSTA	PERC	(B	MARTI McCALL	V	(B	CARMEN TWILLIE	V	)B
DAVID SHIELDS	B	(B	JEFF PORCARO	D	(B	VICTOR FELDMAN	PERC	(B
LEONARD GIBBS	PERC	(B	DON MYRICK	SAX	(B	FREDDIE HUBBARD	HRNS	(B

F103D

MICHAEL FRANKS		(ABC
JOE SAMPLE	K	(B
WILTON FELDER		(B
JOHN GUERIN		(B
LARRY CARLTON	G	(B
RICK ZUNIGAR		(D
RAY ARMANDO		(D
DENNIS BELFIELD		(D
EDDIE GOMEZ		(D
RICK MAROTTA	D	(D
DAVID SPINOZZA	G	(D

MICHAEL FRANKS

(A) THE ART OF TEA	197	REPRISE	US	MS 2230	
(B) SLEEPING GYPSY	1977	WB	US 3004	UK K56346	
(C) BURCHFIELD NINES	197	WB	US 3167		
(D) ONE BAD HABIT	1980	WB	US 3427		

DAVID SANBORN		(B	MICHAEL BRECKER	HRNS	(B	LARRY BUNKER		(B
JOAO PALMA		(B	JOAO DONATO		(B	HELIO DELMIRO		(B
LENNY CASTRO		(D	ANDRE FISHER		(D	ERIC GALE	G	(D
DON GROLNICK	K	(D	JERRY HEY	HRNS	(D	NEIL JASON	B	(D
HUGH McCRACKEN	G	(D	GEORGE SOPUCH		(D	LARRY WILLIAMS		(D
TENNISON STEPHENS		(D						

F103E

FRANTIC

(A) FRANTIC	19	LIZARD	US	20103

ANDY FRASER   F104

ANDY FRASER	B V	(AB1	(A) ANDY FRASER BAND	1975	CBS	UK	80731
NICK JUDD	K	(A1	(B) IN YOUR EYES	1975	CBS	UK	81027
KIM TURNER	D	(A	(1) 1974 MILLER FRASER BAND				
FRANKIE MILLER	V	(1					
HENRY McCULLOUGH	G	(1	MIKE KELLIE D	(1			

FRATERNITY OF MAN   F104A

ELLIOT INGBER	G	(AB	(A) THE FRATERNITY OF MAN	19	ABC	US	ABCS 647
WARREN KLEIN G SITAR		(AB	(B) GET IT ON	19	DOT	US	25955
RICHIE HAYWARD	D V	(AB					
MARTIN KIBBEE	B	(AB	LAWRENCE WAGNER	G V	(AB		

JOHN FRED & HIS PLAYBOYS   F105

JOHN FRED	V HCA	(ALL	(A) JOHN FRED & HIS PLAYBOYS	1968	PAULA	US	2191
ANDREW BERNARD	SAX	(	(B) 34.40 OF JOHN FRED	196	PAULA	US	2193
RONNIE GOODSON	TPT	(	(C) AGNES ENGLISH	19	PAULA	US	2197
CHARLIE SPIN	TPT	(	(C) JUDY IN DISGUISE	19	PAULA	US	2197
JIMMY O'ROURKE	G	(	(D) PERMANENTLY STATED	1968	PAULA	US	2201
HAROLD COWART	B	(	(E) LOVE IN MY SOUL	19	UNI	US	73077
TOMMY DE GENERES	ORG	(					
JOE MICELY	D	(					

FREDDIE & THE DREAMERS   F106

FREDDIE GARRITY	V	(ALL	FREDDIE & THE DREAMERS	1963	COLUMBIA	UK	33SX 1577
ROY CREWSDON	G	(	YOU WERE MADE FOR ME	1964	COLUMBIA	UK	33SX 1663
PETE BIRRELL	D	(	SING ALONG	1965	COLUMBIA	UK	SX 1785
BERNIE DWYER	D	(	IN DISNEYLAND	1966	COLUMBIA	UK	SCX 6069
DEREK QUINN	G	(	FREDDIE & THE DREAMERS	1966	MERCURY	US	61017
			DO THE FREDDIE	196	MERCURY	US	61026
			SEASIDE SWINGERS	1966	MERCURY	US	61031
			FRANTIC FREDDIE	196	MERCURY	US	61053
			FUN LOVIN'	196	MERCURY	US	61061
			KING FREDDIE & DREAMING KINIGHTS	1967	COLUMBIA	UK	SX 6177
			I'M TELLING YOU	19	TOWER	UK	5003
			OLIVER IN UNDERWORLD	19	STARLINE	UK	SRS 5019
			BEST OF	1977	EMI	UK	NUT11

EPs
IF YOU MAKE A FOOL	1963	COLUMBIA	UK	SEG 8275
CRAZY WORLD	1964	COLUMBIA	UK	SEG 8287
YOU WERE MADE FOR ME	1964	COLUMBIA	UK	SEG 8302
FREDDIE & THE DREAMERS	1965	COLUMBIA	UK	SEG 8323
JUST FOR YOU	196	COLUMBIA	UK	SEG 8349

BILL FREDERICKS   F107

BILL FREDERICKS	(A) LOVE WITH YOU	1978	POLYDOR	UK	2382 470

FREE   F108

PAUL RODGERS	V	(ABCDEGH13456	(A) TONS OF SOBS	1969	A&M US 4198	UK ISLAND	ILPS 9089
PAUL KOSSOFF	G	(ABCDEFGH1235	(B) FREE	1969	A&M US 4204	UK ISLAND	ILPS 9104
ANDY FRASER	B	(ABCDEG13	(C) FIRE & WATER	1970	A&M US 4268	UK ISLAND	ILPS 9120
SIMON KIRKE	D	(ABCDEFGH123456	(D) HIGHWAY	1970	A&M US 4287	UK ISLAND	ILPS 9138
TETSU YAMAUCHI	B	(FH2456	(E) LIVE	1971	A&M US 4306	UK ISLAND	ILPS 9160
RABBIT BUNDRICK	K	(FH2456	(F) KOSSOFF,KIRKE,TETSU & RABBIT 1971			UK ISLAND	ILPS 9188
SNUFFY WALDEN	G	(H	(G) FREE AT LAST	1972	A&M US 4349	UK ISLAND	ILPS 9192
WENDEL RICHARDSON	G(6		(H) HEARTBREAKER	1973		UK ISLAND	ILPS 9217
STEVE MILLER	PNO	(A	(J) THE FREE STORY (DBL)	1973		UK ISLAND	ISLD4
B J COLE	STEEL	(F					
REBOP	PERC	(H	(K) BEST OF FREE	1975	A&M US 3663		
			(L) FREE & EASY ROUGH READY	1976		UK ISLAND	ILPS 9453
(1) 1968/71	(2) MAY71/JAN72		(M) POP CHRONIK (DBL)	1977		EURO ISLAND	89236

(3) 71 /72   (4) JUL72/SEP72
(5) SEPT 72 (6) JAN73/JUNE73

FREE BEER   F108A

SANDY ALLEN	V G B	(ABC	(A) FREE BEER	1975	SOUTHWIND	SWS 6402
MICHAEL PACKER	V G B	(ABC	(B) HIGHWAY ROBBERY	1976	RCA	APLI 1733
CALEB POTTER V G PERC		(A	(C) NOUVEAU CHAPEAU	1977	RCA	APLI 2072
NED ALBRIGHT	PNO	(A				

RICHARD CROOKS	D	(A	JOE X DUBE	D	(A	LARRY GONSKY K SYN	(A	RICHARD HARBERT	PNO (A
BRENDAN HARKIN	G V	(A	PATTIE DARDY HARKIN	V	(A	JACK JENNINGS PERC	(A	GEORGE MARGE	SAX(A
JON HARRIS	HCA	(A	BERNARD PURDIE	D	(A	RONNIE RENNINGER G	(A	PAUL SCHWARZ	D (A
ERIC WEISSBERG FDL DOB	(A		DANIEL BEN ZEBULON PERC	(AB	MARKY MARKOWITZ HRNS	(A	BOB MINTZER	SAX(A
JERRY MAROTTA	D	(B	DAN DALEY	STEEL	(A	WERNER FRITZSCHING G	(B	RALPH SCHUCKETT	K (BC
HUGH McCRACKEN	G	(C	STEVE KHAN	G	(C	KEN ASCHER K	(C	WILL LEE	B (C
CHRISTOPHER PARKER D	(C		STU WOODS	B	(C				

FREE CREEK   F108

TODD RUNDGREN	G	(A	(A) MUSIC FROM FREE CREEK	1973	CHARISMA	UK CADS 101
ROY MARKOWITZ	D	(A	(A) SUMMIT MEETING	1976	CHARISMA	C53
MOOGY KLINGMAN	ORG	(A				

STU WOODS	B	(A	LEW DELGATTO	TROM(A	BOBBY KELLER TROM(A	MECO MONARDO	TROM(A
LEW SOLOFF	TPT	(A	ALAN RUBIN	TPT (A	BILL CHASE TPT (A	BUZZY FEITEN	G (A
ERIC CLAPTON	G	(A	KEITH EMERSON	ORG (A	MITCH MITCHELL D (A	CHUCK RAINEY	B (A
DELANEY BRAMLETT	G	(A	CHRIS WOOD	FLT (A	JOE FARRELL FLT (A	TOM MALONE	TROM(A
ELLIOTT RANDALL	G	(A	RED RHODES	STEEL(A	JOHN LONDON B (A	JOHN WARE	D (A
MAERETHA STEWART	V	(A	HILDA HARRIS	V (A	VALERIE SIMPSON V (A	HARVEY MANDEL	G (A
JACK WILKINS	G	(A	JIMMY GREENSPOON K	(A	LARRY TAYLOR B (A	LARRY PACKER	VLN (A
FITO DE LA PARRA	D	(A	BILLY CHESBORO	CONGA(A	EARLE DOUD V CONGA(A	DIDYMUS	PERC(A
CAROL HUNTER	G	(A	RICHARD DAVIS	B (A	DOCTOR JOHN PNO (A	KING COOL	G (A
RICHARD CROOKS	D	(A	TOMMY COSGROVE	B (A	DOUGIE RODRIGUEZ G (A	BOBBY DEAN	TROM(A
HARRY HALL	TPT	(A	LINDA RONSTADT	V (A	BERNIE LEADON G (A	CHRIS DARROW	VLN (A
TIMMY HARRISON	V	(A	ERIC MERCURY	V (A	BOB SMITH ORG (A	GERI MILLER	V (A

F109A   **FREE SPIRIT**

```
F109A                              FREE SPIRIT
   LARRY CORYELL    G   (A      (A) OUT OF SIGHT & SOUND       19    ABC          US           593
   JIM PEPPER       SAX (A
   CHRIS HILL       B V (A    CHIP BAKER    G  (A    BOB MOSES D   (A
F110                                FREEDOM
   BOBBY HARRISON   V D (ABC     (A) FREEDOM                  1970  PROBE        UK   SPBA 6252
                                 (B) AT LAST                  1970  METRONOME    UK   MLP 15371
   PETER DENNIS     V B K(ABC    (C) THROUGH THE YEARS        1971  COTILLION    US   SD   9048
   ROGER SAUNDERS   V G K(ABC    (D) FREEDOM                  1971  VERTIGO      UK   6360 049
                                 (E) IS MORE THAN A WORD      1972  VERTIGO      UK   6360 072
F110A                            BOBBY FREEMAN
   BOBBY FREEMAN    V   (ALL     (A) DO YOU WANNNA DANCE      1958  JUBILEE      US          1086
                                 (B) C'MON & SWIM            1964  AUTUMN       US           102
                                 (C) GET IN THE SWIM         1959  JOSIE        US          4007
                                 (D) TWIST WITH               19   JUBILEE      US          5010
                                 (E) LOVABLE SIDE OF         1960  KING         US           930
F110B                             FREEPORT
                                 (A) FREEPORT                 19   MAINSTREAM   US          6130
F110C                             FREEWAY
   JOHN HOBBS K B G    (A        (A) FREEWAY                 1979  DECCA        UK   TXS  131
   J D MANESS       STEEL(A
   TERRY MELCHER    V PNO(A    MEL COLLINS SAX  (A     RICKY FATAAR D PERC(A    JIM SEITER    PERC (A
F111                             ACE FREHLEY
   ACE FREHLEY V B G SYN (A      (A) ACE FREHLEY             1978  CASABLANCA        NBLP 7121
   ANTON FIG        D   (A
   WILL LEE         B   (A    CARL TALLARICO   D    (A   LARRY KELLY   V   (A    DAVID LASLEY  V  (A
   BILL SCHENIMAN   V   (A    SUSAN COLLINS    V    (A
F112                               FRESH
   MILO MARTIN      B   (A        (A) GET FRESH              1977  MCA    US 2241  UK MCF 2797
   BILL PRATT       V   (A
   FRED ALLEN       D   (A    ELAINE MAYO G   (A    PAUL MARSHALL   G(A   DAVID KAFFINETTI   K(A
F113                               FRESH
   BOB GORMAN       G V (AB       (A) FRESH OUT OF BORSTAL   1970  RCA   US 4328   UK      8122
   KEVIN FRANCIS    B V (AB       (B) FRESH TODAY            1971  RCA   US 3027
   ROGER CHANTLER   D   (AB
F113A                           FRESH START
                                 (A) FRESH START             19   DUNHILL      US         50175
F114                         FRESHLY LAYED BAND
   TIM HOLT         G V (A        (A) A LOW VOLUME(2007?) CASSETTE RELEASED BY THE GROUP THEMSELVES
   BOB PENDRY       G V (A
   RICHARD FURTER   B   (A    NICK BUCKLER    D    (A   ROGER HUNT    V   (A
F115                            DEAN FRIEDMAN
   DEAN FRIEDMAN                  (A) DEAN FRIEDMAN          1978  LIFESONG US 35001  UK    6008
                                 (B) WELL WELL SAID THE ROCKING CHAIR  1978  LIFESONG      UK    6019
F116                            KINKY FRIEDMAN
   KINKY FRIEDMAN   V   (ALL      (A) SOLD AMERICAN          1974  VANGUARD     US         79333
   JIM ATKINSON     G   (C        (B) KINKY FRIEDMAN         1975  ABC   US 829 UK ANCHOR 5134
   T BONE BURNETT   G   (C        (C) LASSO FROM EL PASO     1976  EPIC  US 34304         81640
   MICK RONSON      G   (C
   TOM CULPEPPER    G   (C    BILL HAM      G     (C   LEVON HELM    G   (C    RON WOOD      G   (C
   STEVE SOLES      G   (C    ERIC CLAPTON DOBRO(C   MICHAEL DE TEMPO G (C    BRIAN CLARKE  B   (C
   TERRY DANKO      B   (C    ROB STONER B        (C   IRA WILKES   B   (C    MAJOR BOLES   D   (C
   GARY BURKE       D   (C    TEDDY JACK EDDY D   (C   RICHARD MANUEL  D (C    DAHRELL NORRIS D  (C
   HOWIE WYETH      D   (C    DR JOHN       K     (C   KEN LAUBER   K   (C    JEWFORD SHELBY K  (C
   RED YOUNG        K   (C    DAVID MANSFIELD STEEL(A  RUSTY YOUNG  STEEL(C   SNAKEBITE JACOBS HRNS(C
   ROGER McGUINN    BANJO(C    AL GARTH     FDL    (C   FRENCHIE BOURKE FDL (C   RINGO STARR      V (C
   TRACY BALIN      V   (C    RICK DANKO B V      (C   RONNIE HAWKINS V  (C    ROSCOE WEST      V (C
F117                             BRIAN FRIEL
   BRIAN FRIEL      V G (ABC      (A) BRIAN JOSEPH FRIEL     1974  DAWN  UK 3054 US  PYE 12102
   COLIN PINCOTT    G   (B        (B) ARRIVEDERCI ARDROSSAN  1975  DAWN  UK 3064
   MICK DEVONPORT   G   (B        (C) ASHES & MATCHSTICKS     19   PYE   US
   TIM RENWICK      G   (B
   ANDY ROBERTS     G   (B    ARTHUR RODMAN   G    (B   ZOOT MONEY    K   (AB   CRAIG PRUESS     K(B
   DE LISLE HARPER  B   (B    PAUL FRANCIS    D    (B   BILLY LAWRIE  V   (A    PAUL VIGRASS  V  (AB
   STEVE THOMPSON   B   (A    GARY OSBORNE    V    (A   COLIN ALLEN   D   (A    THE PHANTOM   G  (A
   B J COLE         STEEL(A    MAGS McGLINT    V    (A
F118                             TERRY FRIEND
   TERRY FRIEND                  (A) COME THE DAY           1978  TRAMP
F119                               FRIENDS
   MARC COHEN       SAX (A        (A) FRIENDS                1975  CAROLINE     UK         C1511
   CLINT HOUSTON    B   (A
   JOHN ABERCROMBIE G   (A    JEFF WILLIAMS   D    (A
F119A                           FRIENDSHIP
   ALEX ACUNA       D   (A        (A) FRIENDSHIP             1979  ELEKTRA US 6E 241  UK K52185
   ERNIE WATTS      WIND (A
   DAVE GRUSIN      K   (A    ABRAHAM LABORIEL B   (A   LEE RITENOUR  G (A
F120                            FRIJID PINK
   TOM BEUDRY       B   (        (A) FRIJID PINK            1970  DERAM UK 1062 US PARROT 71033
   RICH STEVERS     D   (        (B) DEFROSTED              1970  DERAM UK 1077 US PARROT 71041
   KELLY GREEN      V   (        (C) ALL PINK INSIDE         197  FANTASY      US          9464
   GARY THOMPSON    G   (
F120A                          FRINGE BENEFIT
   JOHN JONES       G V (A        (A) FRINGE BENEFIT         1977  CAPRICORN    US      CP 0183
   CHRIS HAINES     B   (A
   DAVE GRAY        G   (A    STEVEN LAURIE   D    (A   MIKE MORAN    K   (A
```

ROBERT FRIPP   F121

ROBERT FRIPP	G	(ALL	(A) NO PUSSY FOOTIN'	1972	ISLAND	UK	HELP	16
BRIAN ENO	K	(ABC	(A) NO PUSSY FOOTIN'	1977	POLYDOR EG	UK	2343	095
BARRY ANDREWS	K	(A	(B) EVENING STAR	1975	ISLAND	UK	HELP	22
PETER HAMMILL	V	(C	(B) EVENING STAR	1977	POLYDOR EG	UK	2343	094
PHIL COLLINS	D PERC	(C	(C) EXPOSURE	1979	EG	UK	EGLP	101
MICHAEL WALDEN	D	(C	(D) GOD SAVE THE QUEEN/MANNERS	1980	EG	UK	EGLP	105
TERRE ROCHE	V	(C	(E) FRIPPERTRONICS/LET THE POWER FALL	1981	EG	UK	EGED	

LORRAINE FRISAURA   F122

LORRAINE FRISAURA	V G	(A	(A) BE HAPPY FOR ME	1976	RCA		PL 13034
STEVE KHAN	G	(A					
DON GROLNICK	K	(A	MICHAEL BRECKER HRNS (A	MERLE MILLER V (A	ERIN DICKINS V (A		
WILLIAM F LEE	B	(A	MIKE MANDEL SYN (A	GAIL KANTOR V (A	CHRIS HILLS D (A		
MTUME	PERC	(A	KAY T OSLIN V (A				

FRED FRITH   F123

FRED FRITH	G	(ABCD	(A) GUITAR SOLS	1974	CAROLINE	UK	C1508
DEREK BAILEY		(B	(B) GUITAR SOLOS 2	1976	CAROLINE	UK	C1518
HANS REICHEL		(B	(C) GUITAR SOLOS 3	1979	RIFT		RIFT1
HENRY KAISER		(C	(D) GRAVITY	1980	RALPH	US	
G F FITZGERALD		(B					
CHIP HANDY		(C	PETER CUSACK (C	DAVEY WILLIAMS (C	KEITH ROWE (C		
EUGENE CHADBURNE		(C	AKIRA HIJIMA (C				

DONNIE FRITTS   F123A

DONNIE FRITTS	V PNO	(A	(A) PRONE TO LEAN	1974	ATLANTIC	US	SD 18117
PETE CARR	G DOB	(A					
JIMMY JOHNSON	G	(A	EDDIE HINTON G HCA(A	BARRY BECKETT K VIBES(A	MIKE UTLEY ORG(A		
DAVID HOOD	B	(A	ROGER HAWKINS D (A	SAMMY CREASON D (A	JERRY McGEE G (A		
TONY JOE WHITE	G B V	(A	JERRY MASTERS B (A	SPOONER OLDHAM VIBES (A	MICKEY RAPHAEL HARP(A		

EDGAR FROESE   F124

EDGAR FROESE	MULTI INST	(ALL	(A) AQUA	1974	VIRGIN	UK	V2016
KLAUS KRIEGER	D	(C	(B) EPSILON IN MALAYSIAN PALE	1975	VIVGIN	UK	V2060
			(C) AGES	1977	VIRGIN	UK	V2507
			(D) MACULA TRANSFER	19	IMP		
			(E) STUNT MAN	1979	VIRGIN	UK	V2139
			(F) ELECTRONIC DREAMS	197	BRAIN	GER	0040 148

WYNDER K FROG   F125

WYNDER K FROG(MICK WEAVER)	K		(A) SUNSHINE SUPER FROG	1967	ISLAND	UK	ILPS 944
CHRIS MERCER	SAX	(	(B) OUT OF THE FRYING PAN	1968	UA US 6695 UK ISLAND	ILPS 9082	
REBOP	PERC	(	(C) INTO THE FIRE	1970	UA US 6749		
NEIL HUBBARD	G	(					
ALAN SPENNER	B	(	BRUCE ROWLAND D (	DICK HECKSTALL SMITH SAX(			

RAYMOND FROGGATT   F126

RAYMOND FROGGATT	V	(ABCD	(A) VOICE AND WRITING OF	1969	POLYDOR	UK	583 044
LOUIS CLARK	K	(	(B) BLEACH	1972	BELL	UK	BELLS 207
LEONARD ABLETHORPE		(	(C) ROGUES & THIEVES	1974	REPRISE	UK	K 44257
HARTLEY CAIN		(	(D) SOUTHERN FRIED FROG	1978	JET	UK	JATLP 209
JORDANAIRES	V	(D					
BILLY SANFORD	G	(D	PETE DRAKE STEEL (D	BUDDY HARMON D (D	LARRY BUTLER PNO (D		
JAMES CAPPS	G	(D	TOMMY ALSUP B (D				

FROGMORTON   F127

MIKE SMITH	G V	(A	(A) FROGMORTON AT LAST	1976	PHILIPS	UK	6308 261
LUCY SHARPE	G PERC V	(A					
CHRIS TULLOCH	K MAND V	(A	DAVE HARDY ACC PERC(A	BILL LYNN B (A	TERRY NEWBURY D (A		

STEVEN FROMHOLZ   F128

STEVEN FROMHOLZ	G V	(ALL	(A) FROMMOX	1969	PROBE	US	CPLP45115
JOHN BEAL	B	(A	(B) HOW LONG IS THE ROAD TO KENTUCKY	1973 NOT RELEASED			
DON BROOKS	HCA	(A	(C) A RUMOR IN MY TIME	1976	CAPITOL	US	11521
BOB JAMES	PNO	(A	(D) FROLICKING IN THE MYTH	1977	CAPITOL	US	11611
OMAR CLAY	D	(A	(E) MUSIC FROM OUTLAW BLUES(3SONGS)	1977	CAPITOL	US	11691
EVERETT BARKSDALE	B	(A	(F) JUS' PLAYIN' ALONG	1978	LONE STAR	US	L4601
ERIC WEISSBERG FDL G STEEL B	(A		(G) FROMHOLZ LIVE	1979	FELICITY RECORDS	US	FR001
KENNY ALTMAN	B	(A					
GARY BARRY	G	(A	RANDY BEAVERS (A	BILL BROWDER (C	MICHAEL CAMPBELL (C		
DOUG DILLARD	BANJO G	(CE	DONNY DOLAN D PERC (C	KELLY DUNN K SYN (C	DAVE FERGUSON K (C		
PAUL HARRIS	PNO	(C	ROGER HARRIS (C	JOHN INMON G V (C	MICHAEL JEFFREY G (C		
FRED KRC D PERC		(C	ROBERT LIVINGSTON G B V (C	REX LUDWICK (C	WILLIE NELSON V (C		
GARY NUNN G K B V SYN		(C	JODY PAYNE (C	GARY PELFRY (C	JOE PORCARO PERC (C		
MICKEY RAPHAEL	HCA	(C	RED RHODES STEEL (CD	JOHN SEBASTIAN G V (C	BEE SPEARS B (C		
B W STEVENSON	G V	(C	CASSELL WEBB V (C	KIRK BRUNER D (D	MIKE McKINNEY B V(D		
STEVE FORMAN	PERC	(D	JIM SCHULMAN PERC G V(D	STANLEY SCHWARTZ PNO (D	LARRY NYE G (D		
JOE RENZETTI	G	(D	JAY GRAYDON G (D	JOHN BARNES K SYN (D	DAVID LUELL SAX (D		
ANDY MUSON	B	(D	JIM KELTNER D (E	JEFF BAXTER G (E	ROBBEN FORD G(E		
GEORGE CLINTON	PNO	(E	ARNIE MOORE B (E	RICHARD GREENE FDL (E	J J WALKER PERC (E		
MARK DAWSON	HCA	(E	PETE GRANT STEEL (E	BAMBI ROBERTS K (E			

FRONT   F129

GREGG VAN COOK	G			
DREW BLOOD	G V	(		
BEN E FICIAL	B	(	TOM TOMM D (	

FROST   F129A

DICK WAGNER	G V	(ABC	(A) FROST MUSIC	19	VANGUARD	US	6520
DON HARTMAN	G V	(ABC	(B) ROCK'N' ROLL MUSIC	19	VANGUARD	US	6541
GERDY GARRIS D K V		(ABC	(C) THROUGH THE EYES OF LOVE	19	VANGUARD	US	6556
BOB RIGGS	D	(ABC					

FRUIT EATING BEARS

CHRIS CRASH		(A	(A) 1970
NEVILLE CROZIER		(A	
GARY CROUDACE		(A	

F130A   FRUMPY

Personnel			Albums	Year	Label	Country	Cat. No.
CARSTEN BOHN	B PERC(		(A) FRUMPY	19	VERTIGO		6305 067
KARL HEINZSCHOTT	B (		(B) FRUMPY 2	19	VERTIGO		6305 098
RAINER BAUMANN	K STEEL (		(C) BY THE WAY	19	VERTIGO		6360 604
EUVIN RAMIAN	K (		(C) BY THE WAY	1974	BILLINGSGATE		BG 1003
INGA RUMPF	V G (		(D) LIVE	19	VERTIGO		6623 022
JEAN JACQUES KRAVETZ	K(						

F131   FRUUP

Personnel		Albums	Year	Label	Country	Cat. No.
PETER FARELLY	B G V(AB	(A) FUTURE LEGENDS	1973	DAWN	UK	DNLS 3053
STEPHEN HOUSTON	K OBOE V(AB	(B) PRINCE OF HEAVENS EYES	1974	DAWN	UK	DNLH 2
MARTIN FOYE	D PERC(AB	(C) SEVEN SECRETS	1974	DAWN	UK	DNLS 3058
VINCE McCUSKER	G V (AB	(D) MODERN MASQUERADES	1975	DAWN	UK	DNLS 3070

F132   FUCHIA

Personnel		Albums	Year	Label	Country	Cat. No.
TONY DURANT	G V (A	(A) FUCHSIA	1971	PEGASUS		PEG 8

F132A   FUGITIVES

Albums	Year	Label	Country	Cat. No.
(A) FUGITIVES AT DAVES HIDEOUT	19	HIDEOUT	US	HLP 1001

F133   FUGS

Personnel		Albums	Year	Label			Cat. No.
ED SANDERS	V (CED	(A) FIRST ALBUM	1965	ESP US 1018 UK FONTANA			5513
EN WEAVER	V D (ACED	(B) THE FUGS(KILL FOR PEACE)	1966	ESP	US		1028
PETER STAMPFEL	G STEEL (	(B) THE FUGS	1970	FONTANA	UK		STL 5524
TILI KUPFERBERG	V PERC(ABCDEFGH	(C) VIRGIN FUGS	1966	ESP US 1038 UK FONTANA			5501
KEN PINE	G V (ED	(D) TENDERNESS JUNCTION	1966	TRANSATLANTIC	UK		TRA 180
CHARLES LARKEY	B (ED	(D) TENDERNESS JUNCTION	1968	REPRISE	US		6280
BOB MASON	D (E	(E) IT CRAWLED INTO MY HAND HONEST	196	TRANSATLANTIC	UK		TRA 181
BETSY KLEIN	(	(E) IT CRAWLED INTO MY HAND HONEST	19	REPRISE	US		6305
PETE KEARNEY	(	(F) GOLDEN FILTH	1968	REPRISE	US		6396
LEE CRABTREE	(ABC	(G) BELLE OF AVENUE A	1969	REPRISE	US		6359
STEVE WEBER	G (ABC	(H) FUGS 4 ROUNDERS SCORE	1975	ESP	US		2018
VINNY LEARY	G (ABC						

JOHN ANDERSON	B V (ACB	DOUG FRANKLIN	V (E	JENNIFER BROWN	V (E	EARL BAKER	V (E
KENNETH BATES	V (E	BILL WOLF	B (	LESLIE DORSEY	V (E	BOB DOROUGH	V (E
BARBARA CALABRIA	V (E	MARLYS TRUNKHILL	V (E	BOB HANSON	V (E	JAMES JARVIS	B (E
ALLEN GINSBERG	V HCA(D	DANNY KORTCHMAR	G (ED	MARETTA GREER	V (D	CARL LYNCH	G (
RICHARD LEE	K (	HOWARD JOHNSON	HRNS(	JULIUS WATKINS	HRN(		

F133A   FULL MOON

Personnel		Albums	Year	Label	Cat. No.
LUCAS AMOR	VLN (AB	(A) MOON FOOLS	1976	FULL MOON	FM001
JOHANNES LUTTICK	G V (AB	(B) NOTHING VENTURED NOTHING GAINED	1977	FULL MOON	FM002
NORMAN HASSALL	PERC (A				
BERT KLEYN	D PERC(B	MAX BRUNET	G SYN (AB	GERARD AMMERLAAN	B STRINGS(AB

F133B   BOBBY FULLER FOUR

Personnel		Albums	Year	Label	Country	Cat. No.
BOBBY FULLER	(	(A) I FOUGHT THE LAW	196	MUSTANG	US	901
RANDY FULLER	(	(B) K R L A KING OF THE WHEELS	196	MUSTANG	US	900
WAYNE QUIRICO	(	(C) CIVIL DEFENSE	19	?	US	
JIM REESE	(					

F134   LOWELL FULSON

Personnel		Albums		Year	Label	Country	Cat. No.
LOWELL FULSON	G V (ALL	(A) BLUES MASTERS	(DBL)	19	CHESS		2ACMB 205
TOMMY CATHEY	(E	(B) HUNG DOWN HEAD		19	CHESS	US	408
STEVE CROPPER	G (E	(C) IN A HEAVY BAG		19	POLYDOR UK 2384038 US JEWEL		5003
AL JACKSON	D (E	(D) LOWELL FULSON (EARLY RECORDINGS)		1975	ARHOOLIE	US	2003
MARVELL THOMAS	(E	(E) THE OL' BLUES SINGER		1975	JET	UK	LP9
MICHAEL TOLES	(E	(F) SOUL		19	KENT	US	516
BEN BENAY	G (E	(G) TRAMP		19	KENT	US	520
REINIE PRESS	(E	(H) NOW		19	KENT	US	531
MIKE HENDERSON	(E	(J) LETS GO GET STONED		19	KENT	US	558
DONALD MENZA	(E	(K) IVE GOT THE BLUES		19	JEWEL	US	5009
DALTON SMITH	(E	(L) EVERYDAY I HAVE THE BLUES		19	NASHVILLE	US	2030
LEONARD MALARSKY	(E	(M) LOWELL FULSON		19	KENT	US	5020
JULIA TILLMAN	V (E	(N) SAN FRANCISCO BLUES		19	VOGUE	FR	512508
CARL LAMAGNA	(E	(O) MAN OF MOTION		1980	CHARLY	UK	CRB 1018
EDDIE CHAMBLEE	SAX (E						

RAY KELLEY	(E	MAXINE WILLARD	V (E	JOHN KELSON	HRNS (E	BUD BRISBOIS	(E
LOU McCREARY	(E	THOMAS SHEPARD	(E	CAROLYN WILLIS	V (E	BOBBYE HALL	PERC(E
JAMES GETZOFF	(E	HARRY WESTONE	(E	LOU KLASS	(E	MURRAY ADLER	(E
BONNIE DOUGLAS	(E	GARETH NUTTYCOMBE	(E	SAM BOGHOSSIAN	(E	JAN KELLEY	(E
HARRY BLUESTONE	(E	EARL BROWN	SAX (E	LLOYD GLENN	PNO (EN	ELDRIDE McCARTHY	PNO(N
BIG DAD	B (N	RUFUS J RUSSELL	PNO (N	ARTHUR ROBINSON	N (N	ASAL CARSON	D (N
ELLIS SOLOMON	PNO (N	EARL BROWN	(N	RALPH HAMILTON	B (E	BOB HARVEY	D (N
ROGER HAWKINS	D (C	EDDIE HINTON	G (C	BARRY BECKETT	K (C	DAVID HOOD	B (C

F135   FUMBLE

Personnel		Albums	Year	Label	Country	Cat. No.
DES HENLY	G V (B	(A) FUMBLE	1972	SOVEREIGN	UK	SVNA 7254
DAVE CHRISTOPHER	G V (B	(B) POETRY IN LOTION	1974	RCA	UK	SF 8403
SEAN MAYES	V PNO(B					
MARIO FERRARI	B V (B	BARRY PIKE	D (B			

F135A   FUN & GAMES

Albums	Year	Label	Country	Cat. No.
(A) ELEPHANT CANDY	19	UNI	US	73042

F136   FUNGUS

Personnel		Albums	Year	Label	Country	Cat. No.
FRED PIEK	G V (A	(A) LIEF ENDE LEID	1975	NEGRAM	NL	NR 115
BOB DEKENGA	K (A					
KOOS PAKVIS	B V (A	LOUIS DEBIJ	D (A	RENS VANDER ZALM	VLN G(A	SIDO MARTENS	G(A

F136A   FUNK FACTORY

Albums	Year	Label	Country	Cat. No.
(A) FUNK FACTORY	1976	ATCO	US	36116

FUNKADELIC F137

```
GARY SHIDER      G V  (FK     (A) FUNKADELIC                            1970 WESTBOUND  US 216   PYE UK 28137
MIKE HAMPTON     G    (K      (B) FREE YOUR MIND YOUR ASS WILL FOLLOW 71 WESTBOUND  US 2001  PYE UK 28144
BOBBY LAVIS      G    (K      (C) MAGGOT BRAIN                          1971 WESTBOUND  US 2007      UK6310200
WALTER MORRISON  K SYN(K      (D) COSMIC SLOP                           1973 WESTBOUND  US 223
BERNARD WORRELL  K V  (KF     (E) AMERICA EATS ITS YOUNG                19
TYRONE LAMPKIN   D    (FK     (F) STANDING ON THE VERGE OF TIME         19   WESTBOUND  US 208
BOOTSY COLLINS   D    (K      (G) LETS TAKE IT TO THE STAGE             1975 WESTBOUND  US 215
JEROME BRAILEY   D    (K      (G) LETS TAKE IT TO THE STAGE             1975 20TH CENTURY UK 215
LARRY FRATANGELO D    (K      (H) TALES OF KIDD FUNKADELIC              197  WESTBOUND  US 227
RAYMOND DAVIS    V    (KF     (J) HARDCORE JOLLIES                      1978 WB         US 2973      UK K56299
LYNN MABRY       V    (K      (K) ONE NATION UNDER A GROOVE             1978 WB         US           UK K56539
RON FORD         V    (K      ( ) BEST OF THE EARLY YEARS               197  WESTBOUND  US 303
DAWN SILVA       V    (K      ( ) UNCLE SAM WANTS YOU                   1979 WB                      UK K56539
LEON PATILLO     PNO  (F
DEBBIE WRIGHT    V    (K   GARY SHIDE      V    (K   JEANETTE WASHINGTON V  (K   MULLIN FRANKLIN V  (K
CORDELL MOSSON   V    (K   GEORGE CLINTON  V    (KF  GRADY THOMAS       V  (KF  CALVIN SIMON   V PERC(K
CLARENCE HASKINS V    (F   C MOSSON         B V  (F   EDDIE HAZEL       G V  (F   R FULWOOD      V PERC (F
RON BRYLOWSKI    G    (F   GARY BRONSON     D    (F   JIMMY CALHOUN     B    (F
```

FUNKY COMMUNICATION COMMITTEE F137A

```
                    (A) BABY I WANT YOU                  1979 FREE FLIGHT     US  AHLI 3405
```

FUNKY KINGS F138

```
JACK TEMPCHIN V G HCA(A     (A) FUNKY KINGS                         1976 ARISTA       US  AL  4078
RICHARD STEKOL V G PNO(A
JULES SHEAR      G V(A   FRANK COTINOLA   D   (A   BILL BODINE   B V  (A   GREG LEISZ  G STEEL V (A
MIKE FINNIGAN    V K(A   BARRY BECKETT    PNO (A   KATY MOFFATT  V    (A
```

RICHIE FURAY F139

```
RICHIE FURAY     V G  (AB     (A) I'VE GOT A REASON      1976 ASYLUM US 7E1067 UK  K 53043
JAY TRUAX        B V  (A      (B) DANCE A LITTLE         1978 ASYLUM US  E115  UK  K 53074
JOHN MEHLER      D    (A
TOM STIPE        K V  (A   MICHAEL OMARTIAN K V  (A   STORMIE OMARTIAN V  (A   AL PERKINS    G  (A
STEVE CROPPER    G    (A   ANN WADE          V   (A   MYRNA MATTHEWS  V  (A   CAROLYN WILLIS V  (A
? MacDOUGALL     PERC (A   DON BARBER        BANJO (A
```

BILLY FURY F140

```
BILLY FURY       V    (ALL    (A) THE SOUND OF FURY        1960 DECCA           UK   LF   1329
JOE BROWN        G    (A      (B) BILLY FURY               1960 ACE OF CLUBS UK  ACL  1047
ARTHUR GREENSLADE K   (A      (C) HALFWAY TO PARADISE      1961 ACE OF CLUBS UK  ACL  1083
                             (D) BILLY                    1963 DECCA           UK   LK   4533
                             (E) WE WANT BILLY            1963 DECCA           UK   SKL  4548
                             (F) BEST OF                  1967 ACE OF CLUBS UK  ACL  1229
                             ( ) THE BILLY FURY STORY DBL 1977 DECCA           UK   DPA  3033
                             ( ) GOLDEN YEARS             1979 K TEL           UK   NE   1020
                             ( ) WORLD OF                 1972 DECCA           UK   SAA  108
```

FUSE F140A

```
RICK NIELSEN     G K  (A      (A) FUSE                     1968 EPIC         US        26502
CRAIG MEYERS     G    (A
CHIP GREENMAN    D    (A   JOE SUNDBERG V   (A   TOM PETERSON   B   (A
```

FUSION ORCHESTRA F140B

```
COLIN DAWSON     G    (A      (A) SKELETON IN ARMOUR       1973 EMI          UK   EMA  758
DAVE BELL        D    (A
JILL SAWARD G SYN FLT V (A  STEN LAND G SYN PERC HCA(A   DAVE COWELL   B HCA(A
```

FUZZY DUCK F141

```
MIKE HAWKSWORTH  B    (1      (A) FUZZY DUCK               1971 MAM          UK   MAM 1005
PAUL FRANCIS     D    (1      (1) POST LP LINE UP  DIFFERENT GUITARIST ON LP
GARTH WATT ROY   G V  (1
ROY SHARLAND     ORG  (1
```

FYNN McCOOL F142

```
CHRIS STONE      G V  (A      (A) FYNN McCOOL             1970 RCA          UK   SF 8112
MICK CARTER      D    (A
ALAN ESCOMBE     B    (A   MICK FOWLER K V  (A
```

JOHNNY G G1

```
JOHNNY G         G V  (A      (A) G SHARP G NATURAL       1979 BEGGARS BANQUET UK  BEGA 6
GRAHAM HINE      G    (A      (B) G BEAT                  1980 BEGGARS BANQUET UK  BEGA16
TAFFY DAVIES     K    (A
KEITH TRUSSELL        (A   JOHN RANDALL   D PERC(A  CHAS AMBLER   V    (AB  MALCOLM BENNETT B  (A
CHRIS GOWER      TROM (A   DICK HANSON   HRNS  (A  RAY BEAVIS   SAX  (A   JOHN EARLE     SAX (A
DAVE BELLOTTI         (A   ANGUS GAYE     D    (A  TERRY BARKHAM B    (A   NICK HOWELL    D  (A
STEVE LILLYWHITE  D   (A   NICK GLENNIE SMITH PNO (A  MARK HOLLIS  V  (A   JOHN SPENCER      (A
PAUL HUGHES      B V  (B   JOHN EVERY      HCA (B  BRETT         V    (B  FIN            V  (B
```

G FORCE G1A

```
GARY MOORE       G K V(A      (A) G FORCE                 1980 JET          UK   JETLP 229
MARK NAUSEEF     D PERC(A
WILLIE DEE       B K V(A   TONY NEWTON V   (A
```

GABRIEL G1B

```
FRANK BUTORAC    G V  (A      (A) THIS STAR ON EVERY HEEL  1975 ABC         US   ABCD 885
MICHAEL KINDER   D PERC(A     (B) SWEET RELEASE            197  ABC         US   AB   922
STACY CHRISTENSON K V (A
GARY RUHL        B    (A   TERRY LAUBER G STEEL V (A   MARK PENNICK   CONGA(A
```

PETER GABRIEL G2

```
PETER GABRIEL    V K  (ABC    (A) PETER GABRIEL           1977 CHARISMA   UK  CAS  4006
ALLEN SCHWARZBERG D   (       (A) PETER GABRIEL           1977 PHONOGRAM  EURO 9103 115
TONY LEVIN       B V  (AB     (A) PETER GABRIEL           1977 ATCO       US        36147
JIM MAELEN       G    (       (B) PETER GABRIEL           1978 CHARISMA   UK  CAS  4013
STEVE HUNTER     G    (       (B) PETER GABRIEL           1978 ATLANTIC   US        19181
ROBERT FRIPP     G    (B      (B) PETER GABRIEL           1978 PHONOGRAM  EURO 9103 123
JOSEF WAGNER     G    (       (C) PETER GABRIEL           1980 CHARISMA   UK  CAS  4019
JERRY MAROTTA    V D  (AB
SIDNEY McGINNIS  G V  (AB  LARRY FAST     SYN  (AB  TIM CAPELLO   K   (AB  BAYETE        K  (B
ROY BITTAN       K    (B   GEORGE MARGE RECORDERS (B
```

[163]

G2A   GABRIEL BONDAGE

```
REX BUNDY           G V (
TONY STRAM          B V (
L JAMES BIERACKI    G MAND V( RON SCHWARTZ    K SYN(   BILL WISNIEWSKI    WIND V (   NOEL LEVITT D V      (
```

G3   GAGS

```
GERRY MacLOUGHLIN   G   (A         (A) DEATH IN BUZZARD GULCH       1978 GAG
BREN GORE           K V (A
JOHN KELLY          B   (A   NIGEL COATMAN    D   (A
```

G3A   GALACTIC SUPERMARKET

```
GILLE                              (A) GALACTIC SUPERMARKET        1974 KOMISCHE        KM  58010
ROSI
DIETER DIERKS            (     JURGEN DOLLASE      (A  MANUEL GOETTSCHING (    HARALD GROSSKOPF         (
KLAUS SCHULZE            (
```

G3B   ARLYN GALE

```
ARLYN GALE          G V (A         (A) BACK TO THE MIDWEST NIGHT   1978 ABC         UK          ABCL 5261
ALONA TUSEL         K SYN(A
OMAR HAKIM          D V (A   IVAN ELLIS    B       (A  STEVE CAVARETTA    G   (A
```

G4   ERIC GALE

```
ERIC GALE           G   (ALL        (A) FORECAST            1973 KUDU      UK          KUL .8
BOB JAMES           K   (B          (B) GINSENG WOMAN       1977 CBS       UK          82958
RICHARD TEE         K   (B          (C) MULTIPLICATION      1978 CBS       UK          82283
ANTHONY JACKSON     B   (B          (D) TOUCH OF SILK       1980 CBS       UK          84509
STEVE GADD          D   (B          (E) BEST OF             1980 CBS       UK          84201
RALPH MACDONALD     PERC (B
GROVER WASHINGTON   SAX (BD  ALLEN TOUSSAINT   K   (D    ROBERT DABON    K   (D   GARY KING       B  (B
ANDREW SMITH        D   (B   GEORGE YOUNG SAX      (B    GARY BROWN      SAX (D   ARTHUR BLYTHE   SAX (D
HAROLD VICK         SAX (D   WAYNE ANDRE  TROM     (B    DAVE TAYLOR     TROM (B   LOU SOLOFF      TPT (B
BILL EATON          V   (B   ZACK SANDERS     V    (B    RAY SIMPSON     V   (B   FRANK FLOYD     V   (B
VIVIAN CHERRY       V   (B   LANI GROVES      V    (B    PATTI AUSTIN    V   (B   RANDY BRECKER   TPT (B
ALAN RUBIN          TPT (B   JON FADDIS       TPT  (B    EDDIE DANIELS   SAX (B   MICHAEL BRECKER SAX (B
CHARLES EARLAND     K   (D   IDRIS MUHAMMAD   D    (D    KENNETH WILLIAMS PERC (D  JAMES BLACK     D   (D
DAVID BARARD        B   (D
```

G5   RORY GALLAGHER

```
RORY GALLAGHER      G V (ALL        (A) RORY GALLAGHER      1971 POLYDOR        UK    2383  044
GERRY McAVOY        B   (ALL        (A) RORY GALLAGHER      1975 POLYDOR        UK    2384  066
WILGAR CAMPBELL     D   (ABCJ       (B) DEUCE               1971 POLYDOR        UK    2383  076
ROD DeATH           D   (EDFJK      (C) LIVE IN EUROPE      1972 POLYDOR US 5513 UK    2383  112
LOU MARTIN          K   (EDFJK      (D) BLUEPRINT           1973 POLYDOR US 5522 UK    2383  189
TED McKENNA         D   (MN         (E) TATTOO              1973 POLYDOR US 5539 UK    2383  230
VINCENT CRANE       K   (A          (F) IRISH TOUR 1974     1974 POLYDOR US 9501 UK    2659  031
                                    (G) IN THE BEGINNING    1974 EMERALD GEM    UK    GES1  101
                                    (H) AGAINST THE GRAIN   1975 CHRYSALIS      UK    CHR   1098
                                    (H) AGAINST THE GRAIN   1975 POLYDOR        EURO  6307  563
                                    (I) SINNER .......& SAINT 197 POLYDOR US 6510     2383  315
                                    (J) THE STORY SO FAR    1975 POLYDOR US 6519 UK    2383  376
                                    (K) CALLING CARD        1976 CHRYSALIS      UK    CHE   1124
                                    (K) CALLING CARD        1976 PHONOGRAM      EURO  6307  586
                                    (L) THE BEST YEARS      1976 POLYDOR              2664  303
                                    (M) PHOTO FINISH        1978 CHRYSALIS      UK    CHR   1170
                                    (N) TOP PRIORITY        1979 CHRYSALIS      UK    CHR   1235
                                    (O) STAGE STRUCK        1980 CHRYSALIS      UK    CHR   1280
                                    ( ) LIVE  TRACKS FROM (C) (F) 1977 POLYDOR         2384  079
```

G6   GALLAGHER & LYLE

```
BENNY GALLAGHER     G V (ALL        (A) GALLAGHER & LYLE    1972 CAPITOL US 11-16 UK      21906
GRAHAM LYLE         G V (ALL        (A) GALLAGHER & LYLE    1972 A&M                 AMLS68125
WITH                                (B) WILLIE & THER LAP DOG 1973 A&M    US 4384 UK  AMLH68148
JIMMY JEWELL        SAX (1DEF       (C) SEEDS               1973 A&M      US 4425 UK  AMLS68207
JOHN MUMFORD        HRN (1EF        (D) LAST COWBOY         1974 A&M      US 3665 UK  AMLS68273
IAIN RAE            K   (1F         (E) BREAKAWAY           1976 A&M      US 4566 UK  AMLH68348
ALAN HORNALL        B   (12EFG      (F) LOVE ON THE AIRWAVES 1976 A&M     US 4620 UK  AMLH64620
RAY DUFFY           D   (12EFG      (G) SHOWDOWN            1978 A&M      US 4675 UK  AMLH68461
BILLY LIVSEY        K   (2DEG       (H) LONESOME NO MORE    1979 MERCURY          UK  9109 628
STEVE GREGORY       WIND (2         (I) BEST OF             1980 WARWICK          UK  WW   5080
PAUL NIEMAN         TROM (2         (1) 1977 TOUR  (2) 1978 TOUR
PHIL RYAN           K   (2
BRYN HAWORTH        G   (2   PETE TOWNSHEND   HCA (B   RAY COOPER    PERC (G   BRUCE ROWLAND    D PERC(ABD
JIM HORN            SAX (G   HUGHIE FLINT     D   (B   CHRIS STEWART  B  (A
```

G7   GALLIARD

```
RICHARD PANNELL     G   (          (A) STRANGE PLEASURE    1969 NOVA         UK       SDN4
GEOFF BROWN         V   (          (B) NEW DAWN            1970 DERAM        UK   SML  1075
ANDREW ABBOTT       B   (
LESLIE PODRAZA      D   (    JOHN SMITH   WIND     (    DAVE CASWELL    WIND (
```

G7A   GAMBLER

```
NATHAN SHAFFER      V G (A         (A) TEENAGE MAGIC       1979 LIBERTY         AML  3005
WARREN MAYS         G V (A         (B) LOVE AND OTHER CRIMES 1980 U A           AML  3010
DEL BRECKENFELD     B V (A
CHUCK SCHWARTZ      D   (A   BRUCE BRECKENFELD     K V (A
```

G7B   GAMMA

```
RONNIE MONTROSE     G   (          (A) 1                   1980 ELEKTRA US 6E 129 UK K 52163
JIM ALCIVAR         SYN (          (B) 2                   1980 ELEKTRA US 6E 228 UK K 52245
DAVEY PATTISON      V   (
ALAN FITZGERALD     B   (    SKIP GILLETTE     PERC (
```

G7C   GANG OF FOUR

```
JOHN KING           V   (A         (A) ENTERTAINMENT       1979 EMI            EMC  3313
ANDY GILL           G   (A         (B) SOLID GOLD          1981
HUGO BURNHAM        D   (A
DAVE ALLEN          B   (A
```

GANGSTERS   G7D

RICHARD HOLGARTH	G V	(A		(A) GANSTERS		1979 STORTBEAT		BEAT2
BILL MEADOWS	G V	(A						
TERRY HANDS	D	(A	MARTIN HOLDEN	B	(A	STEVE HORTON	K	(A

G8
CECIL GANT   G8

CECIL GANT	PNO V(ALL	(A) INCOMPARABLE	19	SOUND	US	601
		(B) ROCK LITTLE BABY	1974 FLYRIGHT	UK	4710
		(C) CECIL BOOGIE	1976 FLYRIGHT	UK	4714
		(D) KILLER DILLER BOOGIE	1979 MAGPIE	UK	PY1816

JERRY GARCIA   G9

JERRY GARCIA	G V	(ALL	(A) GARCIA	1972 WB	US 2582	UK K46139
HOWARD WALES	K	(B	(B) HOOTEROLL	1972 DOUGLAS		69013
JOHN KAHN	B	(BCF	(C) LIVE AT THE KEYSTONE	1973 FANTASY		79002
CURLY COOKE	G	(D	(D) GARCIA	1974 GARCIA ROUND 59301		102
BILL VITT	D	(BC	(E) REFLECTIONS	1976 UA	US LA565	UK 29921
MICHAEL MARINELLI	D	(B	(F) CATS UNDER THE STARS	1978 ARISTA	UK SPART1053	US AB4160
KEN BALZALL	TPT	(B				
MARTIN FIERRO	WIND	(B	KEITH GODCHAUX	V K	(F	DONNA GODCHAUX	V K	(F	BRIAN GODCHAUX	VLN (F
CANDY GODCHAUX	VLN	(F	RON TUTT	D	(F	MERL SAUNDERS	K	(FC	MARIA MULDAUR	V (F
STEVE SCHUSTER	WIND	(F				

ART GARFUNKEL   G10

ART GARFUNKEL	V	(ALL	(A) ANGEL CLARE	1973 CBS	US 31474	UK 69021
LARRY CARLTON	G	(A	(B) BREAKAWAY	1975 CBS	US 33700	UK 86002
DEAN PARKS	G	(A	(C) WATERMARK	1977 CBS	US 34975	UK 86054
STEVE CROPPER	G	(B	(D) FATE FOR BREAKFAST	1979 CBS	US	UK 86082
MAX BENNETT	B	(B	(E) ART GARFULKEL	1879 CBS	TRIPLE	UK 66351
LON VAN EATON	G	(B				

LOUIE SHELTON	G	(B	MIKE OMARTIAN	K	(A	JIM GORDON	D	(A	JOE CLAYTON	PERC (B
PETE CARR	G	(BC	LARRY KNECHTEL	K	(AB	RUSS KUNKEL	D	(B	TOM ROADY	PERC (C
PAUL SIMON	G V	(BC	BRUCE JOHNSTON	PNO	(B	DENNY SEIWELL	D	(B	THOMAS LA TONDRE	PERC (C
JIMMY JOHNSON	G	(C	BILL PAYNE	K	(BC	JIM KELTNER	D	(BC	CRAIG KRAMPF	PERC (C
HUGH McCRACKEN	G	(C	NICKY HOPKINS	K	(B	RICK SCHLOSSER	D	(BC	TOMMY VIG	VIBES(C
ANDREW GOLD	G	(C	JIMMY WEBB	K	(C	JOHN GUERIN	D	(B	DEREK BELL	HARP (C
STEPHEN BISHOP	G V	(BC	RICHARD TEE	K	(C	ROGER HAWKINS	D	(BC	MICHAEL TUBRIDY	FLT (C
JOE OSBORN	B	(ABC	BARRY BECKETT	PNO	(BC	STEVE GADD	D	(C	SEAN KEANE	FDL (C
LEE SKLAR	B	(B	JOHN JARVIS	PNO V	(B	HAL BLAINE	D	(A	PADDY MOLONEY	WIND (C
KLAUS VOORMANN	B	(B	PAUL DESMOND SAX		(C	RALPH McDONALD	PERC (C	JOE FARRELL WIND	(C
DAVID HOOD	B	(B	MARTIN FAY	FDL	(C	GRAHAM NASH	V	(B	DAVID CROSBY	V (BC
REINIE PRESS	B	(B	TONI TENNILLE	V	(B	JAN JOYCE	V	(B	JAY CLAYTON	V (B
TONY LEVIN	B	(C	SHELLEY HIRSCH	V	(C	ED HASSELBRINK	V	(C	FRED FARELL	V (C
CAROL FLAMM	V	(C	ALEXANDRA STAVROU V		(C	JAMES TAYLOR	V	(C	BOB DOROUGH	V (C
LEAH KUNKEL	V	(C	OKLAHOMA UNI CHORALE		(C			

GARRISON & VAN DYKE   G10A

MICHEL VANDYKE	V	(A		(A) GARRISON & VAN DYKE	1979 ATCO	US	38119
RISON	G B K HCA(A							
SHELL SHELLEKENS	D	(A	EELCO GELLING	G	(A	DANNY LADEMACHER	G	(A	KOKO KAUWSOLEA	PERC (A

GARUDA   G11

TONY COE	WIND (A		(A) GARUDA		1977 EMI	UK	EMC 3174
JEFF DALEY	WIND (A							
HENRY LOWTHER	HRNS (A	DAVE HORTER TROM	(A	ZACK LAWRENCE	K	(A	TONI CAMPO	B G (A
BARRY MORGAN	D (A	HAROLD FISHER	D	(A	FRANK RICOTTI	PERC (A		

GASOLIN   G12

FRANZ BECKERLEE G K SYN V	(ALL	(A) ANGAENDE LONE (EP)	1970 SONET		T 7259
WILI JONSSON	B K V	(ALL	(B) GASOLIN	1971 CBS		64685
KIM LARSEN	G V	(ALL	(C) GASOLIN 2	1972 CBS		65229
TOM BAILEY	G	(	(D) GASOLIN 3	1973 CBS		65798
TOM McEWAN	G	(	(E) GASOLIN	1974 CBS	UK	80099
NIELS HARRIT	SAX	(E	(F) STAKKELS JIM (LAST JIM)	1974 CBS	80549 UK	80470
BJORN UGLEBJERG	D	(A	(G) GAS 5	1975 CBS		80993
SOREN BERLEV	D	(ALL	(H) LIVE SADAN DBL	1976 CBS		88207
			(J) LEMON (US GASOLIN)	1976 CBS US 34149	UK	81436
			(K) EFTER ENDNU EN DAG	1976 CBS		81650

GASS   G13

BOB TENCH	B V	(A		(A) GASS		1970 POLYDOR	UK	2383 022
GODFREY McLEAN	D	(A						
ERROL McLEAN	PERC (A	FRANK CLARK	K	(A	HUMPHREY OKAN	SAX (A	ALAN ROSKAMS	G (A
DELISLE HARPER	B PERC(A	MICHAEL PIGGOTT	VLN (A	DEREK AUSTIN	K	(A	PETER GREEN	G (A

DAVID GATES   G14

DAVID GATES	V G	(ALL	(A) FIRST ALBUM	1973 ELEKTRA US 75066	UK K 42150
MIKE BOTTS		(A	(B) NEVER LET HER GO	1975 ELEKTRA US 1028	UK K 52012
LARRY CARLTON	G	(A	(C) GOODBYE GIRL	1978 ELEKTRA US 6E148	UK K 52091
JAMES GETZOFF	STRING(A	(D) SONGBOOK	197 ELEKTRA US 6002	
RUSS KUNKEL	D	(A	(E) FALLING IN LOVE AGAIN	1980 ELEKTRA	UK K 52206
JOHN GUERIN	D	(A			
JIM GORDON	D	(A	JIM HORN	SAX (A	LARRY KNECHTEL	K	(A	LOUIE SHELTON	G (A

GATOR CREEK   G15

ALLAN BEUTLER	WIND (A		(A) GATOR CREEK		1970 MERCURY		6338 085
DEE BARTON	V K	(A						
MIKE DEASY	G V	(A	RAY NEAPOLITAN	B	(A	MERRY CLAYTON	V	(A	LOUIE SHELTON	V (A
CHUCK FINDLEY	TPT	(A	NICK CEROLI	D	(A	LARRY KNECHTEL	G	(A	VANETTA FIELDS	V (A
MIKE OMARTIAN	K	(A	KATHY DEASY	V PERC	(A	KENNY LOGGINS	G V	(A	GENE PELLO	D (A
CLYDIE KING	V	(A	LOUIS GASCA	TPT	(A	JOHN BANISTER	K	(A		

G16 — MAC GAYDEN

Personnel:
```
MAC GAYDEN       V G BANJO MAND(ALL
BILL CHEATHAM    G    (C
VIC MASTRIANNI   D    (C
MIKE MILLER      WIND V(C
BILL AIKENS      K    (C     NELSON M PADRON  PERC (C   BUZZ CASON      V    (C   RANDY MEISNER   V    (C
ANITA BALL       V    (C     KEN BUTTREY      D    (A   PHILLIP ROYSTER CONGA(A   KARL HIMMEL     PERC (A
BOB JOHNSTON     HCA  (A      JAMES MOON       V    (A   CHARLES MYERS   V    (A   PAUL EASLEY     V    (A
JAMES CLEMMONS   V    (A
```

Album	Year	Label	US	UK	Cat
(A) McGAVOCK GAYDEN	1973	EMI		UK	EMA 760
(B) SKYBOAT	1976	ABC	US 927	UK	ABCL 5169
(C) HYMN TO THE SEEKER	1976	ABC	US 960		

G17 — MARVIN GAYE

Personnel:
```
MARVIN GAYE          V K D(ALL
WITH
KIM WESTOM           V
DIANA ROSS           V
TAMMY TERRELL        V
MARY WELLS           V
RAYMOND CROSSLEY     K     (Z
GORDON BANKS         G     (Z
CURTIS NOLEN         G     (Z
ROBERT AHWAI         G     (Z
SUNSHIP              PERC  (Z
JOE MAYO             PERC  (Z
NOLAN SMITH          TPT   (Z
GEORGE SHAW          TPT   (Z
KENNY MASON          TPT   (Z
RAY BROWN            TPT   (Z
FRANK BLAIR          D B   (Z
BUGSY WILCOX         D     (Z
NIGEL MARTINEZ       D     (Z
ELMIRA COLLINS       VIBES (Z
GARY JONES           PERC  (Z
FLEEDY JOE JAMES     PERC  (Z
SIDNEY MULDREW       HRNS  (Z
RAPHAEL RAVENSCROFT  SAX   (Z
FRANK BATES                (Z
LEE KENTLE                 (Z
```

Album	Year	Label	US	UK	Cat
SOULFUL MOOD	1961	TAMLA	US 221		
THAT STUBBORN KINDA FELLOW	1963	TAMLA	US 239		
LIVE ON STAGE	1963	TAMLA	US 242		
WHEN I'M ALONE I CRY	1964	TAMLA	US 251		
GREATEST HITS	1964	TAMLA	US 252		
HOW SWEET IT IS	1964	TAMLA	US 258		
HELLO BRAODWAY	1964	TAMLA	US 259		
TOGETHER (MARY WELLS)	1964	TAMLA	US 613	STATESIDE UK	10097
MARVIN GAYE	1964			STATESIDE UK	10100
TRIBUTE TO NAT KING COLE	1965	TAMLA	US 261		
MOODS OF MARVIN GAYE	1966	TAMLA	US 266	UK	STML11033
TAKE TWO	1966	TAMLA	US 270	UK	STML11049
UNITED (TAMMY TERRELL)	1966	TAMLA	US 277	UK	STML11062
GREATEST HITS	196	TAMLA		UK	STML11065
YOU'RE ALL I NEED TO GET BY	1968	TAMLA	US 284	UK	STML11084
IN THE GROOVE	1968	TAMLA	US 285		
M.P.G.	1969	TAMLA	US 292		
& HIS GIRLS(TERRELL WELLS KIM WESTON)	196	TAMLA	US 293		
EASY	1969	TAMLA	US 294		
THATS THE WAY LOVE IS	1969	TAMLA	US 299		
SUPERHITS	19	TAMLA	US 300		
GREATEST HITS	1970	TAMLA		UK	STML11153
WHATS GOING ON	1971	TAMLA	US 310	UK	STML11190
HITS OF MARVIN GAYE	1972	TAMLA		UK	STML11201
TROUBLED MAN (SOUNDTRACK)	1972	TAMLA	US 322	UK	STML11225
LETS GET IT ON	1973	TAMLA	US 329	UK	STMA 8013
MARVIN ' DIANA	1974	TAMLA	US 803	UK	STMA 8015
LIVE	1974	TAMLA	US 333	UK	STML 8018
ANTHOLOGY	1974	TAMLA	US 790/1	UK	TMSP 1128
I WANT YOU	1976	TAMLA	US 342	UK	STML12025
THE BEST OF	1976	TAMLA		UK	STML12042
LIVE AT LONDON PALLADIUM	1977	TAMLA	US 352	UK	TMSP 6006
HERE MY DEAR	1978	TAMLA	US 364	UK	TMSP 6008
HOW SWEET IT IS	1979	M F P		UK	50423
(Z) IN OUR LIFETIME	1981	TAMLA		UK	STML12149

G18 — RON GEESIN

Personnel:
```
RON GEESIN    V K SYN BANJO(ALL
ROGER WATERS            (A
```

Album	Year	Label	UK	Cat
(A) THE BODY	1970	HARVEST	UK	SHSP 4008
(B) ELECTROSOUND	197	KPM		1102
(C) AS HE STANDS	197	GEESIN	UK	RON 28
(D) PATRUNS	197	GEESIN	UK	RON 31
(E) RIGHT THROUGH	197	GEESIN	UK	RON 323

G19 — J GEILS BAND

Personnel:
```
J GEILS          G    (ALL
PETER WOLF       V    (ALL
SETH JUSTMAN     K    (ALL
MAGIC DICK       HCA  (ALL
DANNY KLEIN      B    (ALL
STEPHEN BLADD    D    (ALL
BARBARA INGRAM   V    (J
EVETTE BENTON    V    (J
HARRIET THARPE   V    (J
LUTHER VANDROSS  V    (J
G DIANE SUMLER   V    (J
MICHELLE COBBS   V    (J
THERESA REED     V    (J
MICHAEL BRECKER  HRNS (J   RON CUBER  SAX (J   LEW DEL GATTO  SAX (J
RANDY BRECKER    HRNS (J   ALAN RUBIN TPT (J   LEW SOLOFF     TPT (J   FRANK VICARI SAX (J   JUK JOINT JIMMY G (H
```

Album	Year	Label	US	UK	Cat
(A) J GEILS BAND	1971	ATLANTIC	US 8275	UK	k 40108
(B) MORNING AFTER	1972	ATLANTIC	US 8297	UK	K 40293
(AB) J GEILS /MORNING AFTER	1975	ATLANTIC		UK	K 60061
(C) LIVE FULL HOUSE	1972	ATLANTIC	US 7241	UK	K 40426
(D) BLOODSHOT	1973	ATLANTIC	US 7260	UK	K 40479
(E) LADIES INVITED	1974	ATLANTIC	US 7286	UK	K 40536
(F) NIGHTMARES	1974	ATLANTIC	US 18107	UK	K 50073
(G) HOT LINE	1975	ATLANTIC	US 18147	UK	K 50175
(H) BLOW YOUR FACE OUT	1976	ATLANTIC	US 507	UK	K 60115
(J) MONKEY ISLAND	1977	ATLANTIC	US 19130	UK	K 50381
(K) SANCTUARY	1978	EMI	US 17006	UK	AMS 2004
(L) LOVE STINKS	1980	EMI		UK	AML 3004

G20 — GENERATION X

Personnel:
```
BILLY IDOL    V G  (AB1
BOB ANDREWS   G V  (AB1
TONY JAMES    B    (AB1
JOHN TOWE     D    (1
MARK LAFF     D    (AB
```

Album	Year	Label	UK	Cat
(A) GENERATION X	1978	CHRYSALIS	UK	CHR 1169
(B) VALLEY OF DOLLS	1979	CHRYSALIS	UK	CHR 1193
(1) 1976/77				
(C) KISS ME DEADLY	1981	CHRYSALIS	UK	CHR 1327

G21 — GENESIS

Personnel:
```
JOHN MAYHEW       D       (AB
ANTHONY PHILLIPS  G       (AB
TONY BANKS        K       (ALL
MIKE RUTHERFORD   G B     (ALL
PETER GABRIEL     V FLT PERC(ABCDEFG
PHIL COLLINS      D PERC V (CDEFGHJKLMN12
STEVE HACKETT     G B     (CDEFGHJKL
BILL BRUFORD      D PERC(
CHESTER THOMPSON  D PERC(12
DARYL STUERMER    G       (12
CHRIS STEWART     D       (*
JIM SILVER        D       (*
DAVE HENTSCHEL    V       (N
```

Album	Year	US	US Cat	UK	Cat
(A) FROM GENESIS TO REVELATION	1969	US LONDON	643	UK DECCA	4990
(A) IN THE BEGINNING	1974	US LONDON	50006	UK DECCA	4990
(B) TRESPASS	1970	US ABC	816	UK CHARISMA	CAS 1020
(C) NURSERY CRYME	1971			UK CHARISMA	CAS 1052
(BC) TRESPASS/NURSERY CRYME	1975			UK CHARISMA	CGS 102
(D) FOXTROT	1972			UK CHARISMA	CAS 1058
(E) SELLING ENGLAND BY THE POUND	1973	US	6060	UK CHARISMA	CAS 1074
(DE) FOXTROT /SELLING ENGLAND	1975			UK CHARISMA	CGS 103
(F) LIVE	1973			UK CHARISMA	CLASS 1
(G) THE LAMB LIES DOWN ON BROADWAY	1974	US ATCO	2401	UK CHARISMA	CGS 101
(H) TRICK OF THE TAIL	1976	US ATCO	38101	UK CHARISMA	CDS 4001
(J) WIND & WUTHERING	1977	US ATCO	36144	UK CHARISMA	CDS 4005
(K) SECONDS OUT	1977	ATLANTIC	20002	UK CHARISMA	GE 2001

(CONTINUED)

GENESIS — G21

(L)	SPOT THE PIGEON (EP)	1977		UK CHARISMA	GEN 001
(M)	AND THEN THERE WERE THREE	1978	ATLANTIC 19173	UK CHARISMA	CDS 4010
(N)	DUKE	1980		UK CHARISMA	BRA 101
( )	ROCK ROOTS	1975		UK DECCA	ROOTS.1
( )	REFLECTION	1975		FONTANA	9299 515
( )	THE BEST OF	1976	US BUDDAH 56592		
( )	STORY OF GENESIS	1978		JAP FLYOVER	10061/2

(1) 1978 TOUR   (2) 1980 TOUR   (*) PRE RECORDING MUSICIANS

GENTLE GIANT — G22

PHIL SHULMAN	SAX	(ABCD	(A)	GENTLE GIANT	1970		UK VERTIGO 6360 020
DEREK SHULMAN	V G B	(ALL	(B)	ACQUIRING THE TASTE	1971		UK VERTIGO 6360 041
RAY SHULMAN	V B VLN PERC	(ALL	(C)	THREE FRIENDS	1972	US CBS 31649	UK VERTIGO 6360 070
KERRY MINNEAR	K V	(ALL	(D)	OCTOPUS	1973	US CBS 32022	UK VERTIGO 6360 080
GARY GREEN	G V	(ALL	(E)	IN A GLASS HOUSE	1973		UK W W A WWA 002
MARTIN SMITH	D	(AB	(F)	THE POWER & THE GLORY	1974	UK W W A	UK W W A WWA 010
JOHN WEATHERS	D V	(DEFGHJKLMNO	(G)	FREE HAND	1975	US CAPITOL 11428	UK CHRYSALIS 1093
MIKE VICKERS	SYN	(D	(H)	A GIANT STEP (DBL)	1975		UK VERTIGO 6641 334
MARTIN RUSHENT	SYN	(D	(J)	INTERVIEW	1976	US CAPITOL 11532	UK CHRYSALIS 1115
CHRIS THOMAS	SYN	(B	(K)	PLAYING THE FOOL (LIVE DBL)	1976	US CAPITOL 11592	UK CHRYSALIS 1133
PAUL KOSH	TPT	(B	(L)	THE MISSING PIECE	1977	US CAPITOL 11696	UK CHRYSALIS 1152
MALCOLM MORTIMER	D	(A	(M)	PRETENTIOUS DBL	1977		UK VERTIGO 6641 629
			(N)	GIANT FOR A DAY	1978	US CAPITOL 11813	UK CHRYSALIS 1186
			(O)	CIVILIAN	1980		UK CHRYSALIS 1285

GEORDIE — G23

BRIAN JOHNSON	V	(A	(A)	HOPE YOU LIKE IT	1973	EMI	UK	EMC 3001
TOM HILL	B	(	(B)	MASTERS OF ROCK	1974	EMI	UK	054 95689
BRIAN GIBSON	D	(	(C)	DONT BE FOOLED BY THE NAME	1974	EMI	UK	EMA 764
VIC MALCOLM	G	(	(D)	SAVE THE WORLD	1976	EMI	UK	EMC 3134

LOWELL GEORGE — G24

LOWELL GEORGE	G V	(A	(A) THANKS I'LL EAT IT HERE	1979	WB US 3194	UK	K 56487	

JIM GORDON	D	(A									
JIM KELTNER	D	(A	JIM PRICE	HRNS (A	MIKE BAIRD	D	(A	DARRELL LEONARD	HRNS(A
CHUCK RAINEY	B	(A	FRED TACKETT	G	(A	BILL PAYNE	K	(A	DAVID FOSTER	K	(A
JIMMY GREENSPOON	PNO	(A	JEFF PORCARO	D	(A	BONNIE RAITT	V	(A	CHILLI CHARLES	D	(A
DENNIS BELFIELD	B	(A	GORDON DE WITTE	K	(A	JAMES HOWARD	K	(A	NICKY HOPKINS	K	(A
PAUL STALLWORTH	B	(A	JERRY JUMONVILLE	HRNS (A	STEVE BRUTON	G	(A	DEAN PARKS	G	(A
FLOYD SNEED	D	(A	ROBERTO GUTIERREZ	G	(A	LUIS DAMIAN	G	(A	RICHIE HAYWARD	D	(A
HERB PEDERSEN	V	(A	J D SOUTHER	V	(A	MAXINE WATERS	V	(A	BOBBY BRUCE	FDL	(A
PEGGY SANDVIG	K	(A	BRUCE PAULSON	(A	MAXAYN LEWIS	V	(A	JOEL PESKIN	SAX	(A
JOHN PHILLIPS	SAX	(A									

GERONIMO BLACK — G25

JIMMY CARL BLACK	D	(AB	(A) GERONIMO BLACK	1972	UNI 127	1974 MCA	MCF 2683
TJAY CANTRELLI	G	(A	(B) WELCOME BACK GERONIMO BLACK	19	HELIOS	US	
DENNY WALLEY	G	(A					
BUNK GARDNER	WIND	(A	ANDY CAHEN	K	(A	TOM LEAVEY	B	(A	BUZZ GARDNER	(A
DON PRESTON	K	(B	RAY COLLINS	V	(B	MEATBALL	D	(B		

DENNY GERRARD — G25A

DENNY GERRARD		(A	(A) SINISTER MORNING	1970	DERAM NOVA	SDN10
TONY HILL	G	(A				
SIMON HOUSE	VLN	(A	PETER PAVLI	B	(A	ROGER HADDEN	D	(A

GERRY & THE PACEMAKERS — G26

GERRY MARSDEN	G V	(ALL	HOW DO YOU DO IT	1963	COLUMBIA	1546(M)	SCX 3492(S)
FREDDIE MARSDEN	D	(ALL	FERRY ACROSS THE MERSEY	1964	COLUMBIA	SCX3544	US UA3387
LES McGUIRE	B V	(ALL	DONT LET THE SUN CATCH YOU CRYING	196	LAURIE	US	2027
LES CHADWICK	PNO	(ALL	SECOND ALBUM (US)	196	LAURIE	US	2037
			I'LL BE THERE	196	LAURIE	US	2030
			GREATEST HITS	196	LAURIE	US	2031
			GIRL ON A SWING	196	LAURIE	US	2037

EPS

HOW DO YOU DO IT	19663	COLUMBIA	SEG 8257	YOU'LL NEVER WALK ALONE	1964	COLUMBIA	SEG8295
I'M THE ONE	1964	COLUMBIA	SEG 8311	DONT LET THE SUN	1964	COLUMBIA	SEG8346
IT'S GONNA BE ALL RIGHT	1964	COLUMBIA	SEG 8367	GERRY IN CALIFORNIA	1964	COLUMBIA	SEG8388
FERRY ACROSS THE MERSEY	1965	COLUMBIA	SEG 8397	RIP IT UP	1965	COLUMBIA	SEG8426

RENEE GEYER BAND — G26A

RENNE GEYER	V	(AB	(A) READY TO DEAL	1975	RCA AUSTRALIA	VPLI 0105
BARRY SULLIVAN	B	(A	(B) IT'S A MAN'S WORLD	1975	RCA UK	SF8450
MARK PUNCH	G V	(A	GREG TELL	D	(A	MAL LOGAN	K	(A	RUSSELL SMITH	TPT (A
TONY BUCHANAN	WIND	(A						

GIANT CRAB — G26B

ERNIE OROSCO	V G	(A	(A) A GIANT CRAB COMES FORTH	1968	UNI	US	73037
RAY OROSCO	B K	(A	(B) COOL IT HELIOS	196	UNI	US	73057
RUBEN OROSCO	B D SAX	(A					
DENNIS FRICIA	D HRNS	(A	KENNY FRICIA	K HRNS VIBES	(A			

GIANTS — G26C

KARL RUCKER	B	(A	(A) THANKS FOR THE MUSIC	1976	CASABLANCA	US	NBLP 7027
JOHN COHEN	V	(A					
JOHN PLATANIA	G V	(A	LAURIE COHEN	V	(A	BRUCE GARY	B PERC (A	RON ELLIOTT G	(A

STEVE GIBBONS — G27

STEVE GIBBONS	G V	(ALL	(A) SHORT STORIES	1971	WIZARD		UK	SWZA 5501
TREVOR BURTON	B V G	(BCDEFG	(B) ANY ROAD UP	1976	MCA	US 2183	POLYDOR UK 2383 381
BOB WILSON	G K V	(BCDEF	(C) ROLLING ON	1977	MCA	US 2243	POLYDOR UK 2383 433
DAVE CARROLL	G	(BCDEF	(D) CAUGHT IN THE ACT	1977	MCA	US 2305	POLYDOR UK 2478 112
BOB LAMB	D	(BCDEF	(E) DOWN IN THE BUNKER	1978	POLYDOR US 6154		UK 2391.358
ALBERT LEE	G	(A	(F) BEST OF	1980	POLYDOR SWE2383 339		UK 2383 110
GARY WRIGHT	K	(A	(G) STREET PARADE	1980	RCA		UK LP 5005

(CONTINUED)

G27 STEVE GIBBONS

MIKE KELLIE	D	(A						
DORIS TROY	V	(A	PAT DONALDSON	B	(A	MADELINE BELL V	(A	JERRY DONAHUE	G	(A
JIMMY MILLER	PERC	(A	GREG RIDLEY B	(A	HUGH McCRACKEN G	(A	NICK PENTELOW	SAX(E
TONY VISCONTI	SYN B(A	LONDON SYMPHONY ORCH	(E	HARRY RIX	D V	(G	BILL PAUL	SAX	(G
GINGER JOHNSON	PERC (A	IAN WHITEMAN PNO	(A	LARRY FALLON	WIND (A	ALAN WHITE PERC FLT	(A
GERRY CONWAY	STEEL(A	ROCKY DZIDZORNU	PERC (A	JOHNNY VAN DERRICK (A	CLAIRE DENIZ	CELLO(A
BILL POVEY	CLAR (A							

G28 MIKE GIBBS

MIKE GIBBS	(A	(A) THE ONLY CHROME WATERFALL ORCH	1975	ISLAND	UK	ILPS	9353
PHILIP CATHERINE	G	(						

G29 NICK GILDER

NICK GILDER	V	(ABC	(A) YOU KNOW WHO YOU ARE	1977	CHRYSALIS UK	CHR	1147
JAMES McCULLOCH	G	(ABC	(B) CITY NIGHT	1978	CHRYSALIS UK	CHR	1202
JAMES HERNDON K SYN G V(BC	(C) FREQUENCY	1979	CHRYSALIS UK	CHR	1219
ERIC NELSON	B V	(ABC						
STEVE KALTER	K	(A	CRAIG KRAMPF	D PERC V	(BC CHET McCRACKEN	D (A

G29A GILES GILES & FRIPP

MIKE GILES	D	(A	(A) CHEERFUL INSANITY	1968	DERAM	UK	SPA	423
PETER GILES	B	(A						
ROBERT FRIPP	G	(A	JUDY DYBLE	V	(A			

G30 GILGAMESH

PHIL LEE	G	(AB	(A) GILGAMESH		1975 CAROLINE	UK	CA	2007
ALAN GOWEN	K	(AB	(B) ANOTHER FINE TUNE YOU'VE GOT ME INTO	1978 CHARLY	UK	CRL	5009
JEFF CLYNE	B	(A						
MICHAEL TRAVIS	D	(A	HUGH HOPPER	B	(B	AMANDA PARSONS	V	(A	TREVOR TOMKINS	D	(B

G31 IAN GILLAN

IAN GILLAN	V	(ALL	(A) IAN GILLAN BAND	19	OYSTER	US	11602
COLIN TOWNS	K	(12BDE	(A) CHILD IN TIME	1976	OYSTER	UK	2490 136
MARK NAUSEEF	D PERC(AB	(A) CHILD IN TIME	1976	POLYDOR	UK	ACBR 261
JOHN GUSTAFSON	B V	(AB	(B) CLEAR AIR TURBULANCE	1977	ISLAND	UK	ILPS 9500
RAY FENWICK	G V	(AB	(C) SCARABUS	1977	ISLAND	UK	ILPS 9511
BERNIE TORME	G	(2de	( ) LIVE	1978	ISLAND	UK	ILPS 9545
MIKE MORAN	K	(A	(D) MR UNIVERSE	1979	ACROBAT	UK	ACRO 3
PHIL KENZIE	SAX	(B	(E) GLORY ROAD	1980	VIRGIN	UK	V 2171
JOHN HUCKRIDGE	TPT	(B	(1) 1978 BAND	(2) 1979 OCT BAND			
DEREK HEALEY	TPT	(B						
MALCOLM GRIFFITHS TROM (B	MARTIN FRITH	SAX	(B	ROGER GLOVER SYN V(A	STEVE TOWNES	K	(1
JOHN McCOY	B	(12DE PETER BARNACLE	D	(1	LIAM GENOCHEY D	(1D STEVE BYRD	D	(D
MICK UNDERWOOD	D	(2DE						

G32 DANA GILLESPIE

DANA GILLESPIE	V G SYN(ABC1	(A) BOX OF SURPRISES	1969 DECCA	UK	SKL 5012
DAVE WINTOUR	B	(B	(B) WERE'NT BORN A MAN	1973 RCA	UK	APLI 0354
PAT DONALDSON	B	(B	(C) AIN'T GONNA PLAY NO SECOND FIDDLE	1974 RCA	UK	APLI 0682
BRIAN ODGERS	B	(B	(A?) FOOLISH SEASONS	19	LONDON	US	540
MIKE MORAN	K	(B	(1) 1978 TOUR				
PAUL KEOGH	G	(B	CHRIS RAY	G	(B	RONNIE LEAHY	K	(B	RAY GLYNN	G	(B
JIM RYAN	G	(B	RICK WAKEMAN	K	(B | BARRY DE SOUZA | D |)B	TERRY COX	D	(B
BOBBY KEYS	SAX	(B	RAY COOPER	PERC (B	FRANK RICOTTI	PERC (B	ROSETTA HIGHTOWER V (B
LIZA STRIKE	V	(B	JOANNE WILLIAMS	V	(B	JOHN HAWKEN	K	(1	JOHN KNIGHTSBRIDGE G(1
BARBARA SPITZ	G	(1	NEIL KORNER	B	(1	JOHN BARKER	D	(1	TONY HALL	SAX(1
JOHN PORTER	G	(C	BRYN HAWORTH	G	(C	DAVE SKINNER	K	(C	PHIL CHEN	B	(C
BOB WESTON	G	(C	SIMON PHILLIPS	D	(C	MEL COLLINS	SAX	(C	ROBIN SYLVESTER B	(C
EDDIE JOBSON	SYN VLN(C JOHN TURNBULL	G	(C	MICK GALLAGHER	PNO	(C	JODY LINSCOTT	CONGA(C
RABBIT BUNDRICK	K	(B	FRANK COLLINS	V	(C	DYAN BIRCH	V	(C	PADDY McHUGH	V	(C
MALCOLM DUNCAN	HRNS (C	ROGER BALL	HRNS	(C	HENRY LOWTHER	HRNS (C

G33 STEVE GILLETTE

STEVE GILLETTE		(A) STEVE GILLETTE	1967	VANGUARD	US	VSD79251

G34 DAVE GILMOUR

DAVE GILMOUR	G V	(A	(A) DAVID GILMOUR	1978 US CBS 35388 UK HARVEST SHVL817
MICK WEAVER	K	(A					
WILLIE WILSON	D	(A	RICK WILLS	B	(A		

G35 GORDON GILTRAP

GORDON GILTRAP	G	(ALL	(A) TESTAMENT OF TIME	1971 MCA	MKPS 2020 +	MCF 2688
CLIVE BUNKER	D	(E	(B) GILTRAP	1973 PHILIPS	6308 175
JOHN G PERRY	B	(CE	(C) VISIONARY	1974 ELECTRIC	UK	TRIX.2
ROD EDWARDS	K V	(EC	(D) PERILOUS JOURNEY	1977 ELECTRIC	UK	TRIX.4
ROGER HAND	G V	(E	(E) FEAR OF THE DARK	1978 ELECTRIC	UK	TRIX.7
EDDIE SPENCE	K	(	(F) PEACOCK PARTY	1980 PVK	UK	GIL 1
RIC SANDERS	VLN	(F					
SIMON PHILLIPS	D	(EC GRAHAM PRESKETT	VLN	(E	SHIRLEY RODEN	V	(E	RICHARD HARVEY	RECORDER(EF
TONY CARR	PERC (E	JOHN BAILEY	G	(C	BIMBO ACOCK	WIND (F	JOHN GUSTAFSON	B	(F
MORRIS PERT	PERC (F	IAN MOSLEY	D	(F				

G35 GINA X PERFORMANCE

GINA KIKOINE	V	(A	(A) GINA X PERFORMANCE	1979 EMI	UK	EMC 3314
ZEUS B HELD	K	(A	(B) X TRA ORDINAIRE	1980 EMI	UK	EMC 3336
LASZLO CXIGANY	D	(A					
HEINZ TREWER	SYN	(A	MARTIN HAMBERG	SYN (A			

G36 GINHOUSE

GEOFF SHARKEY	G V	(A	(A) GINHOUSE	1971 B&C	UK	CAS 1031
STEWART BURLISON	B V	(A					
DAVE WHITAKER	D	(A					

G36A GIRL

SIMON LAFFY	G	(A	(A) SHEER GREED	1980	JET	UK	JETLP224
GERRY LAFFY	B V	(A					
PHILIP LEWIS	V	(A	PHIL COLLEN	G	(A	DAVE GAYNOR	G	(A

GIRL SCHOOL   G37

ENID WILLIAMS	B V (A		(A) DEMOLITION	1980	BRONZE	UK	BRONX 525
KELLY JOHNSON	G V (A						
KIM McAULIFFE	G V (A	DENISE DUFORT D (A					

GIRLS TOGETHER OUTRAGEOUSLY   G38

(A) PERMANENT DAMAGE   1969 STRAIGHT   UK   STS 1059

GLACIER   G38A

(A) FROM SEA TO SKY   19   MERCURY   US   MG 20895

GLAD   G38B

(A) FEELIN' GLAD   19   ABC   US   665

GLADIATORS   G39

CLINTON FEARON	B V (ABCDE	(A) TRENCH TOWN MIX UP	197	VIRGIN	UK	V 2062
ALBERT GRIFFITHS	V G (ABCDE	(B) PROVERBIAL REGGAE	1978	FRONT LINE	UK	FL1002
LLOYD PARKS	B (AC	(C) NATURALITY	1978	FRONT LINE	UK	FL1035
GALLIMORE SUTHERLAND	V G(ABCDE	(D) SWEET SO TILL	1979	FRONT LINE	UK	FL1048
SCULLY	PERC (C	(E) GLADIATORS	1980	VIRGIN	UK	V 2161
ANSEL COLLINS	K (BD					

STICKIE THOMPSON	PERC (BCD	EARL LINDO	K (B	SLY DUNBAR	D (B	PABLOV BLACK	K (D
RICHARD ACE	K (D	EARL BAGGA	B (D	BONGO HERMAN	PERC (D	SKY JUICE	PERC (D
TOMMY McCOOK	WIND (D	HEADLEY BENNETT	HRNS (D	LEROY WALLACE	D (CD	ERNEST RANGLIN	G (D
JIMMY BECKMAN	HCA (D	SOJIE	PERC (D	BOBBY ELLIS	HRNS (D	RANCHIE McLEAN	G (C
WINSTON WRIGHT	K (C	ANGUS GAYE	D (E	EDDIE GRANT	K G (E	DONALD BENJAMIN	G (E
TONY ZAP EDMUNDS	K (E	TONY KING	K (E	MARK JAMES	B (E	COACH HOUSE HORNS	(E

GLADSTONE   G40

H L VOELKER	V (B		(A) GLADSTONE	1972	PROBE	UK	SPBA 6264
DOUG RHONE	G V (B		(B) LOOKIN' FOR A SMILE	1973	ABC	US	ABCX 778
JERRY SCHEFF	B (B						
RON TUTT	D (B	RANDY FOUTS	K (B	BOBBY TUTTLE	STEEL (B	MICK RAPHAEL	HCA (B
ROBIN BRIANS	V PERC(B	DAVID STANLEY	B (B	PAUL LEIM	D (B	GARY CRAPSTER	D (B
LARRY WHITE	DOBRO(B	A D WASHINGTON	CONG (B	LYNN GROOM	K (B	TOM RUSSELL	V (B
DALE BAKER	V (B						

GLASS MENAGERIE   G41

LOU STONEBRIDGE	(1		(1) 1968				
AL KENDALL	(1						
BILL ATKINSON	(1	JOHN MEDLEY	(1				

GLASS PRISM   G42

(A) ON JOY & SORROW   1970 RCA   US   LSP 4270

GLASSHARP   G43

(A) GLASSHARP   1972 MCA UK MUPS431 US DECCA 75261
(B) SYNERGY   1972 MCA UK MUPS449 US DECCA 75306
(C) IT MAKES ME GLAD   1973 MCA UK MUPS470 US DECCA 5358

GLASSHOUSE   G44

(A) THANKS I NEEDED THAT   19   INVICTUS   US   T9810

GLENCOE   G45

GRAHAM MAITLAND	K V (AB		(A) GLENCOE	1972	EPIC	UK	65207
NORMAN WATT ROY	B V (AB		(B) THE SPIRIT OF GLENCOE	1973	EPIC	UK	65717
STEWART FRANCIS	D (AB						
JOHN TURNBULL	G V (AB	GERALD JOHNSON	B (B	KOFI AYIVOR	PERC (B	BEN SIDRAN K	(B

GLOBAL VILLAGE TRUCKING COMPANY   G46

JON OWEN	G V (AB	(A) GREASY TRUCKER LIVE AT DINGWALLS	1973 GREASY TRUCKERS	UK	GT 4997
JOHN McKENZIE	B (AB	(B) GLOBAL VILLAGE TRUCKING COMPANY	1976 CAROLINE	UK	C 1516
JIMMY LASCELLES	K (AB				
SIMON STEWART	D (AB	MIKE MEDORA	HCA G V (AB	PETE KIRTLEY	G V (B	CAROMAY DIXON	V (B
JIM CUOMO	SAX (B	JEREMY LASCELLES	PERC (B	MONICA GARELTS	V (B		

GLOBE UNITY   G47

ENRICO PAVA			LIVE IN WUPPERTAL	1973 FMP	0160
MANFRED SCHAF			EVIDENCE	1976 FMP	0220
PETER BROTZMANN			INTO THE VALLEY	1976 FMP	0270
EVAN PARKER			PEARLS	1977 FMP	0380
KENNY WHEELER			JAHRMARKET	1977 POTORCH	JWB3
TONY BRAXTON			IMPROVISATIONS	1978 JAPO	60021

GLORIA MUNDI   G48

EDDIE MAELOV	V (AB		(A) I INDIVIDUAL	1978	RCA	UK PL 25157
MIKE NICHOLLS	D (AB		(B) WORD IS OUT	1979	RCA	UK PL 25244
SUNSHINE	K V (AB					
BEETHOVEN	G (A	KIRBY	G (B	CC	SAX (AB	NIGEL ROSS SCOTT B (B
ICE	B (A					

GLORY   G48A

(A) A MEAT MUSIC   1969 TEXAS REVOLUTION US   69

JOHN GLOVER   G49

JOHN GLOVER	G V (A		(A) MIDNIGHT OVER ENGLAND	1978	ELECTRIC	UK	TRIX9
PETE VAN HOOKE	D (A						
PAUL WESTWOOD	B (A	JOHN MEALING	K (A	STEVE O'DONNELL	K (A	PETER ARNESEN	PNO (A
TONY HICKS	G (A	JOHN IRISH EARLE	SAX (A	STEVE GREGORY	WIND (A	GEOFF RICHARDSON	VLA (A
COLIN JENNINGS	PERC (A	DICK HANSON	TPT (A	JACKIE SULLIVAN	V (A	JOY YATES	V (A
B J COLE	STEEL(A	ROGER SAUNDERS	G (A				

ROGER GLOVER   G50

ROGER GLOVER	B V (ABC		(A) BUTTERFLY BALL	1974 PURPLE	UK	TPSA 7514
SIMON PHILLIPS	D (C		(B) ROGER GLOVER	197 OYSTER US 1605		
GRAHAM PRESKETT	VLN (C		(C) ELEMENTS	1978 OYSTER US 1637 UK POLYDOR 2391 306		
RONNIE ASPERY	WIND (C					
MICKY LEE SOULE	K V (AC	MARTIN BIRCH	(C	LIZA STRIKE	V (AC	HELEN CHAPPELLE	V (AC
EDDIE HARDIN	K SYN(A	LES BINKS	D (A	RAY FENWICK	G (A	MO FOSTER	B (A
MIKE MORAN	K (A	BARRY ST JOHN	V (A	JUDY KUHL	V (A	KAY GARNER	V (A
JOANNE WILLIAMS	V (A	ANN ODELL	PNO (A	MIKE GILES	D (A	NIGEL WATSON	SAX (A
EDDIE JOBSON	VLN (A	JACK EMBLOW	ACC (A	CHRIS KARAN	TABLA(A	ROBIN THOMPSON	BASSOON (A
GLENN HUGHES	V (A	NEIL LANCASTER	V (A	JOHN GOODISON	V (A	DAVID COVERDALE	V (A
RONNIE DIO	V (A						

G51 SUE GLOVER

SUE GLOVER	V	(A	(A) SOLO			1976 DJM	DJF 20469 + DJLPS 469
EDDIE BAIRD		(A					
TONY BRAUNAGEL	D	(A	IRENE CHANTER	V (A	DOREEN CHANTER	V (A	MICK FEAT	B (A
PAUL KOSSOFF	G	(A	DAVE MATTACKS	D (A	RABBIT BUNDRICK	K (A	TONY WILLIAMS	D (A
TERRY WILSON	B	(A	SUNNY LESLIE	V (A				

G51A GLAXO BABIES

ROB CHAPMAN	V	(C	(A) THIS IS YOUR LIFE (EP)	1979	HEARTBEAT	12PULSE3
DAN CATSIS	G V	(C	(B) NINE MONTHS TO THE DISCO	1980	HEARTBEAT	HB2
TONY WRAFTERS	SAX	(C	(C) PUT ME ON THE GUEST LIST	1980	HEARTBEAT	HB3
TOM NICHOLS	B V	(C				
GEOFF ALSOPP	D	(C	CHARLES LLEWELLYN D (C			

G52 GNIDROLOG

STEWART GOLDRING	G	(AB	(A) IN SPITE OF HARRY'S TOENAIL	1971	RCA	UK	SF8261
COLIN GOLDRING	G V SAX	(AB	(B) LADY LAKE	1972	RCA	UK	SF8322
NIGEL PEGRUM	D FLT OBOE	(B					
JOHN EARLE	V WIND	(B	PETER COWLING B CELLO(B CHARLOTTE FENDRICH PNO (B			

G52A GOBLIN

CLAUDO SIMONETTI	K	(A	(A) SUSPIRIA(SOUNDTRACK)	1979	EMI	UK	3222
MASSIMO MORANTE	G V	(A					
FABIO PIGNATELLI	B G PERC V	(A	AGNOSTINO MARANGOLA D V (A			

G53 KEITH & DONNA GODCHAUX

KEITH GODCHAUX	K V	((A	(A) KEITH & DONNA GODCHAUX	1975	ROUND	UK	RX 104
DONNA GODCHAUX	V	(A						
JERRY GARCIA	G V	(A	BRIAN GODCHAUX	VLN (A	JOHN KAHN	B (A	DENNY SEIWELL	D (A
MERL SAUNDERS	ORG	(A	JIM BRERETON	D (A	CHRISSY STEWART	B (A	BERNARD PURDIE	D (A
BILL WOLF	B	(A						

G53A GODDO

GREG GODOVITZ	V B	(	(A) GODDO	1976	POLYDOR	2424 901
GINO SCARPELLI	G	(	(B) WHO CARES	1978	POLYDOR	2424 902
DOUG INGLIS	D	(	(C) AN ACT OF GODDO	1979	POLYDOR	2424 189

G54 ROBERT JOHN GODFREY

ROBERT JOHN GODFREY		(A	(A) FALL OF HYPERION	1974	CHARISMA	UK	CAS 1084

G55 GODIEGO

YUKIHIDE TAKEKAWA	G	(A	(A) WATER MARGIN	1978	SATRIL	UK	SATL 4009
MICKIE YOSHINO	K	(A	(B) ROAD OF BROODY CLAP	197		UK	
TAKAMI ASANO	G	(A					
TAKAHIKO ISHIKAWA	G	(A	MEGUNI SAKAMOTO V (A	JUNKO KAMIMURA	V (A	STEVE FOX	B (A
RYOJI ASANO	D	(A	YUJIN HARADA D (A				

G56 GODS

KEN HENSLEY	K G V PERC	(ABC1	(A) GENESIS	1968	COLUMBIA	UK	SCX 6286
LEE KERSLAKE	D	(ABC1	(B) TO SAMUEL A SON	1970	COLUMBIA	UK	SCX 6372
JOE KONAS	G V	(ABC1	(C) GODS	1976	HARVEST	UK	SHSM 2011
JOHN GLASCOCK	B V	(ABC	(1) PRE LP LINE UP				
GREG LAKE	B V	(1					

G56A GODS GIFT

STEVE EDWARDS	V	(A	(A) MANCHESTER 1979 GROUP
PAUL LEDBETTER	D	(A	
STEPHEN MURPHY	G	(A	LAURA PLANT B (A

G57 THE GODZ

ERIC MOORE	B V	(AB	(A) GODZ	1978 MILLENNIUM	8003 + RCA XL13051
GLEN CATALINE	D V	(AB	(B) NOTHING IS SACRED	1979 CASABLANCA	7134 + RCA XL13072
MARK CHATFIELD	G V	(AB			
BOB HILL	G K V	(AB			

G58 THE GODZ

PAUL THORNTON	D	(ABCD	(A) CONTACT HIGH	1967	ESP	US	1037
JAY DILLON	K	(ABCD	(B) GODZ TWO	1968	ESP	US	1047
LARRY KESSLER	G VLN	(ABCD	(B) GODZ TWO	1969	FONTANA	UK	STL 5512
JIM McCARTHY	G V	(ABCD	(C) THIRD TESTAMENT	19	ESP	US	1077
			(D) GODZHUNHEIT	19	ESP	US	2017

G58A GERRY GOFFIN

GERRY GOFFIN			(A) IT AINT EXACTLY ENTERTAINMENT	19	ADELPHI	US	4102

G59 HERBIE GOINS

HERBIE GOINS			(A) No ONE IN YOUR HEART	1967	PARLOPHONE	UK	PMC 7026

G60 ANDREW GOLD

ANDREW GOLD	G V K B D	(ALL	(A) ANDREW GOLD	1975 ASYLUM US 7E 1047 UK SYL 9028
KENNY EDWARDS	G VB	(ABD	(A) ANDREW GOLD	1975 ASYLUM	UK K 53020
DON FRANCISCO	V	(A	(B) WHAT'S WRONG WITH THIS PICTURE	1976 ASYLUM US 7E 1086 UK K 53052
GENE GARFIN	V D	(A	(C) ALL THIS & HEAVEN TOO	1978 ASYLUM US 6E 116 UK K 53072
MIKE BOTTS	D	(ABD	(D) WHIRLWIND	1980 ASYLUM US 6E 264 UK K 52219
LINDA RONSTADT	V	(AB		
TREVOR LAWRENCE	HRNS	(A	BOBBY KEYS HRNS (A	PETER BERNSTEIN B (A	DAVID KEMPER D (A
DAN DUGMORE	G STEEL	(A	BROCK WALSH K V (BD	WADDY WACHTEL G (BD	RUSS KUNKEL D (B
LEE SKLAR	B	(B	DONALD MENZA SAX (B	DANNY KORTCHMAR G (B	PETER ASHER V PERC(B
VAL GARAY	V	(B	TESSIE COEN PERC (B	CLARENCE McDONALD K (B	BRYAN GAROFALO B (D
RICK MAROTTA	D	(D	DON GROLNICK K (D		

G60A JIM GOLD

JIM GOLD	V	(A	(A) HOMETOWN HERO	1978	TABU	US	JZ 35520
JOHN STEVENSON	B V	(A					
DAVE THOMPSON	K	(A	MIKE EVERSOLE G (A	DAVE EVERSOLE B STEEL V(A	SCOTT THOMPSON D (A
MIKE IRISH	G MAND	(A				

BARRY GOLDBERG

BARRY GOLDBERG	V G K	(ALL	(A) CHICAGO ANTHOLOGY	1966	TOGETHER	US	ST1024
DAVID HOOD	B	(HJK	(B) BLOWING MY MIND	1966	EPIC	US	26199
ROGER HAWKINS	D	(J	(C) REUNION	1968	BUDDAH		5012
PETE CARR	G V	(J	(D) TWO JEWS BLUES	1969	BUDDAH	US	5029
JIMMY JOHNSON	G	(EJ	(D) TWO JEWS BLUES	1969	BUDDAH	UK	203 020
EDDIE HINTON	G	(DHJ	(E) STREETMAN	1970	BUDDAH	US	5051
RULE YARBOROUGH	BANJO	(J	(F) BARRY GOLDBERG AND	1972	RECORD MAN	US	CR5105
HARVEY THOMPSON	WIND	(J	(G) IVAR AVENUE REUNION	197	RCA	US	LSP 4442
WAYNE HILL	TPT	(J	(H) BLAST FROM MY PAST	1974	BUDDAH	US	5081
ARTHUR JENKINS	PERC	(J	(H) BLAST FROM MY PAST	1974	POLYDOR	UK	2318 938
TEX BERNFELD	V	(J	(J) BARRY GOLDBERG	1974	ATCO	US	7040
MARGARET BRANCH	V	(J	(K) &FRIENDS RECORDED LIVE	1976	BUDDAH	US	5684
GEORGE TERRY	G	(J					

AL LESTER	FDL	(J	BARRY BECKETT	K	(J	JIMMY EVANS	CONGA	(J	RONNIE EADES	SAX	(J
HARRISON CALLOWAY	TPT	(J	CHARLES ROSE	TROM	(J	RALPH MACDONALD	PERC	(J	BOB DYLAN	V PERC	(J
JERRY WEXLER	PERC	(J	TOM BERNFELD	V	(J	BRENDA BRYANT	V	(J	PAT SMITH	V	(J
MIKE BLOOMFIELD	G	(DFHK	DANNY WHITTED	G	(H	DUANE ALLMAN	G	(DH	HARVEY MANDEL	G	(ABCDFHK
MARKEYS	HRNS	(H	DON McCALLISTER	G	(CDH	PETE STRAZZA	SAX	(H	CHARLIE MUSSELWHITE	HCA	(ABCDGHK
NETTIE 'MAMA' GOLDBERG	K	(CH	EDDY HOH	D	(CDF	RON WOODS	PERC	(C	RONALD MINSKY	PERC	(C
SOULVILLE HORNS		(D	GREAT	G HRNS	(D	NEIL MERRYWEATHER	B	(GK	LYNN CAREY	V	(G
JOHN RICHARDSON	G	(J	BOERS	D	(G	RON RUBY	B	(AB	BOBBY JONES	G	(A
VINNIE BELL	G	(K	MAURICE McKINLEY	D	(B	BILLY BUTLER	G	(E	ERIC GALE	G	(E
JERRY JEMMOTT	B	(E	BOBBY GREGG	D	(E						

GOLDBRIARS

	(A) GOLDBRIARS	19	EPIC	US	BN	26087
	(B) STRAIGHT AHEAD	19	EPIC	US	BN	26114

GOLDEN DAWN

TOM RAMSEY	(	(A) GOLDEN DAWN	19	UA	
GEORGE KINNEY	(				
BILL HALLMARK	(	BOBBY RECTOR (A BIRD (			

GOLDEN EAGLE

WOODY WOODMANSEY	D	(A	(A) 1978 LINE UP
GRAHAM FORBES	D	(A	
FRANKIE MARSHALL	K	(A	PHIL PLANT B (A

GOLDEN EARRING

GEORGE KOOYMANS	G V	(CELPQS	(A) JUST EARRING	1964			POLYDOR NL	736 007		
RINUS GERRITSEN	B K	(CELPQS	(B) WINTER HARVEST	196	CAPITOL US	2823	POLYDOR NL	736 068		
BARRY HAY	V FLT	(ELPQS	(C) MIRACLE MIRROR	196	CAPITOL US	164	POLYDOR NL	1236 283	+ 2459 330	
ROBERT JAN STIPS	K	(Q	(D) ON THE DOUBLE	196			POLYDOR NL	2653 001	+2236 823/4	
CESAR ZUIDERWIJK	D	(LPQS	(E) EIGHT MILES HIGH	1969	MAJ/MIN UKSM	65	POLYDOR NL	1656 015	UK 658 900	
EELCO GELLING	G	(LPQS	(F) GOLDEN EARRING	197	CAPITOL US	11315	POLYDOR	2499 009	+ 2482 329	
PAT PAAY	V	(LQ	(F) GOLDEN EARRING	197	DWARF	US PDLP 9000				
BERTUS BORGERS	SAX	(L	(G) SING MY SONG	1971			KARUSSELL		2499 009	
KEVIN NANCE	K	(S	(H) SEVEN TEARS	1971			POLYDOR	2344 008	UK 2310 135	
LANI GROVES	V	(S	(I) TOGETHER	1972			POLYDOR NL	2925 009	UK 2310 210	
JIM MAELEN	PERC	(S	(J) BEST OF	1973	KARUSSELL 2499 053		POLYDOR	2459 259		
JOHN ZANGRANDO	SAX	(S	(K) HEARING EARRING	1973			TRACK		UK 2406 109	
JAAP EGGERMONT	D	(C	(L) MOONTAN	1974	MCA	US 2354	POLYDOR		UK 2310 288	
NEPPIE NOYA	PERC	(Q	(L) MOONTAN	1973	TRACK	US 396	TRACK		UK 2406 112	
FRANS KRASSENBURG	V	(C	(M) SWITCH	1975	MCA	US 2139	POLYDOR		UK 2310 381	
SIEB WARNER	D PERC	(E	(M) SWITCH	1975			TRACK		UK 2406 117	
			(N) TO THE HILT	1976	MCA	US 2183	POLYDOR		2430 330	
			(O) MAD LOVE	1977	MCA	US 2254				
			(P) LIVE (DBL)	1977			POLYDOR		2625 034	
			(Q) CONTRABAND	1977			POLYDOR	2344 059	UK 2310 491	
			(R) STORY	1977			POLYDOR		2664 372	
			(S) POTRAIT OF	1977			POLYDOR	EURO	2482 192	
			(T) GRAB IT FOR A SECOND	1979			POLYDOR		UK 2310 639	

GOLIATH

JOSEPH ROSBOTHAM	WIND	(A	(A) GOLIATH	1970	CBS UK 64229	US	ABC702
MALCOLM GRUNDY	G	(A					
LINDA ROTHWELL	V	(A	JOHN WILLIAMSON B (A NICK GLENNIE SMITH	ERIC EASTMAN	D PERC(A		

GOLLIWOGS

JOHN FOGERTY	G V	(A	(A) GOLLIWOGS(PRECREEDENCE)	1975	FANTASY F9474	US FAN	5996
TOM FOGERTY	G V	(A					
STU COOK	B	(A	DOUG CLIFFORD D (A				

RAY GOMEZ

RAY GOMEZ	G V	(A	(A) VOLUME	1980	CBS	UK	84134

IAN GOMM

IAN GOMM	V G	(AB	(A) GOMM WITH THE WIND]SAME	1978	STIFF 36103	ALBION UK DAI 1	
HERBIE FLOWERS	B	(AB	(A) SUMMER HOLIDAY	1978	ALBION	UK	ALBG 100
CHRIS PARREN	K	(AB	(B) WHAT A BLOW	1980	ALBION	UK	ALB 102
BARRY DE SOUZA	D	(AB					
TAFF WILLIAMS	G V	(B	ROD DEMICK B V (B NICK GLENNIE SMITH	K V (B	B J COLE STEEL	(B	
ALAN COULTER	D V	(B	MARTIN RUSHENT V (B MALCOLM MORLEY	K (B	RAPHAEL RAVENSCROFT	BRASS(B	

GONG

DAEVID ALLEN	G V	(ABCDHIJ	(A)THE FLYING TEAPOT	1973	VIRGIN	UK 2002 +	BYG	FR 529027
GILLIE SMYTH	V	(ABCEI	(B) ANGELS EGG	1973	VIRGIN	UK 2007		
DIDIER MALHERBE	WIND	(ABCEFGHIJL	(C) CONTINENTAL CIRCUS	1974			PHILIPS	6332330
CHRISTIAN TRITSCH	B G	(	(D) CAMEMBERT ELECTRIQUE	1974	CAROLINE UK 1052+	BYG	FR	529353
PIP PYLE	D	(	(E) YOU	1974	VIRGIN	UK 2019	BARCLAY	FR 840065
CHARLES HAYWARD	D	(I	(F) SHAMAL	1976	VIRGIN	UK 2046 +	BARCLAY	FR 940521
LAURIE ALLEN	D	(A	(G) GAZEUSE	1977	VIRGIN	UK 2074 +	POLYDOR	2473 711
BOB TAIT	D	(	(H) LIVE	1977	VIRGIN	UK 3501 +	POLYDOR	2676 723
FRANCIS MOSE	B	(G	(I) MAGICK BROTHER	1977	AFFINITY UK AFF4			
DI BOND	D	(	(I) MAGICK BROTHER	197	BYG	FR 529305 +	METRONOME	15372
STEVE HILLAGE	G	(ABEFH	(J) GONG EST MORT DBL	1977	TAPIOCA	10002/3		

G66 GONG

TIM BLAKE	K	(BEJH	(K) EXPRESSO 2		1978	VIRGIN	UK 2099	POLYDOR	2473 742
MIKE HOWLETT	B V	(BEFH	(L) DOWNWIND		1979	ARISTA UK SPART 1080
BILL BRUFORD	D	(	(M) TIME IS THE KEY		1979	ARISTA UK SPART 1105
BRIAN DAVISON	D	(	(N) P MOERLENS GONG LIVE		1979	ARISTA UK SPART 1130
MIREILLE BAUER	PERC	(BFGHLK
PIERRE MOERLEN D	(BEFGHKLMN

PATRICE LEMOINE	K	(F	JORGE PINCHEVSKY	VLN	(F	EARL FREEMAN	(I	SANDY COLLEY	(F
DARRYL WAY	VLN	(LK	FRANCOIS CHAUSSE	PERC	(L	ALLAN HOLDSWORTH	G(GLK	MICK TAYLOR	G	(LK
HANNY ROWE	B	(LK	MIKE OLDFIELD	G	(L	BENOIT MOERLEN	PERC(GKL	STEVE WINWOOD	K	(L
MAC POOLE	D	(	ROSS RECORD	G	(L	MINO CINELON	PERC(G	RACHID HOUARI	D	(I
DIETER GEWISSLER	(I	BURTON GREEN	(I	TAMSIN	(I	MIQUETTE GIRAUDY	V K(FI
FRANCIS BACON	(A	DIDIER LOCKWOOD	VLN	(L	FRANCOIS COUSSE	CONGA(LK	BON LOZAGA	(K
PERE CUSHION DE	D	(J	MISTER T BEING	B	(J

G67 GONZALEZ

MICK EVE	SAX	(ABCDE	(A) GONZALEZ		1974	EMI	UK	EMC 3046
BUD BEADLE	SAX	(ABCDE	(B) OUR ONLY WEAPON IS OUR MUSIC		1975	EMI	UK	EMC 3100
RON CARTHY	TPT	(ABCDE	(B) OUR ONLY WEAPON IS OUR MUSIC		197	CAPITOL	US	ST 11644
ROY DAVIES	K	(ABCDE	(C) HAVEN'T STOPPED DANCIN'		1979	SIDEWALK	UK	SWK 2001
STEVE GREGORY	SAX	(ABCE	(D) MOVE IT TO THE MUSIC		1979	SIDEWALK	UK	SWK 2003
GORDON HUNTE	G	(ABCE	(E) SHIPWRECKED(SOME TRACKS AS C)		1977	CAPITOL	US	SW 11855
CHRIS MERCER	SAX	(ABCDE

BOBBY STIGNAC	D	(BCDE	COLIN JACAS	TROM	(CDE	STEVE WALLER	G V	(CE	GEORGE CHANDLER	V	(CE
JOHN GIBLIN	B	(CE	DE LISLE HARPER	B	(A	GLEN LE FLEUR	D	(AB	PRESTON HEYMAN	D	(B
ALAN SHARPE	PERC	(AB	RICHARD BAILEY	D	(ACE	LENNY ZAKATEK	G	(BCE	BOBBY JOHN	PERC(A
LINDA TAYLOR	V	(CDE	MARTIN DROVER	HRNS	(CDE	LARRY STEELE	B	(B	ROBERT AHWAI	G	(B
KEN FREEMAN	SYN	(B	MALCOLM GRIFFITHS	TROM(B	LANCE DIXON	SYN	(B	GODFREY McLEAN	PERC(B
VIOLA WILLS	V	(B	ALAN MARSHALL	V	(D	TIM CANSFIELD	V G	(D	HUGH BULLEN	B	(D
SERGIO CASTILO	D	(D

G67A GOOD MISSIONARIES

	(A) FIRE FROM HEAVEN		1979	DEPTFORD FUN CITY	UK DLP 04

G68 GOOD OLD BOYS

PATRICK CAMPBELL	B	(AB	(A) PISTOL PACKIN' MAMA		1976	UA UK UAS 29951 US ROUND LA57G
DAVID NELSON	G V	(AB	(B) BLUEGRASS		1978	FLYING FISH	US	FF 049
DON RENO	BAN V(AB
FRANK WAKEFIELD	MAND V(AB	CHUBBY WISE	FDL	(AB

G69 GOOD RATS

JOE FRANCO	D	(D	(A) GOOD RATS		1968	KAPP	US	3580
LENNY KOTKE	B	(D	(B) TASTY		1974	WB	US	2813
PEPPI MARCHELLO	V	(D	(C) RAT CITY IN BLUE		1976	PLATINUM	US	RCR 8001
MICKEY MARCHELLO	G V	(D	(C) RAT CITY IN BLUE		1976	PHILIPS		6310 625
TOM JULIANO	SAX	(D	(D) RATS TO RICHES		1978	RADAR	UK	RAD.5
BRIAN CUOMO	PNO	(D	(D) RATS TO RICHES		1978	PATHE	FR	068 60615
HOWARD KAYLAN	V	(D
MARK VOLMAN	V	(D	JOHN GATTO	K G	(D

G70 GOOD THUNDER

JAMES CAHOON LINDSAY	V PERC(A	(A) GOOD THUNDER		1972 ELEKTRA UK K 42123 US EKS 75041
JOHN DESAUTELS	D	(A
DAVID HANSON	G V	(A	BILL RHODES	B	(A	WAYNE COOK	K(A

G70A GOODGUYS

	(A) SIDEWALK SURFIN'		19	GNP CRESCENDO	US 2001

G71 PHILLIP GOODHAND TAIT

PHILLIP GOODHAND TAIT	K V(ALL	(A) REHEARSAL		1971	DJM	UK	DJLPS 411
ANDY LATIMER	G	(B	(B) I'LL WRITE A SONG		1971	DJM	UK	DJLPS 416
DOUG FERGUSON	B	(B	(C) SONGFALL		1972	DJM	UK	DJLPS 425
ANDY WARD	D	(B	(D) PHILIP GOODHAND TAIT		1973	DJM	UK	DJLPS 432
			(E) JINGLE JANGLE MAN		1975	DJM	UK	DJLPS 453
			(F) OCEANS AWAY		1976	CHRYSALIS	UK	CHR 1113
			(G) TEACHING AN OLD DOG		1977	CHRYSALIS	UK	CHR 1146

G72 STEVE GOODMAN

STEVE GOODMAN	G V	(ALL	(A) STEVE GOODMAN		1971	BUDDAH	US	BDS 5096
DONNIE FRITTS	ORG	(A	(A) STEVE GOODMAN		1972	BUDDAH	US	BDLH 5007
NORBERT PUTNAM	B	(A	(B) SOMEBODY ELSE'S TROUBLE		1973	BUDDAH UK4019 US	5121
DAVID BRIGGS	PNO	(A	(C) JESSIE'S JIG & OTHER FAVOURITES		1975	ASYLUM	UK	SYL 9017
CHARLIE McCOY	HCA	(A	(C) JESSIE'S JIG & OTHER FAVOURITES		1875	ASYLUM UK K53025 US	7E 1061
BILLY SANFORD	G BAN(A	(D) WORDS WE CAN DANCE TO		1976	ASYLUM UK K53038 US	7E 1061
BEN KEITH	STEEL(A	(E) SAY IT IN PRIVATE		1978	ASYLUM UK K53067 US	7E 1118
BUCKY WILKIN	G	(A	( ) THE ESSENTIAL		19	BUDDAH	US	5665

STEPHEN BRUNTON	PERC	(A	GRADY MARTIN	(A	VASSAR CLEMENTS	FDL	(A	PETE WADE	G	(A
GEORGE TIDWELL	TPT	(A	WILLIAM PUETT	CLAR	(A	GENE MULLINS	TROM	(A	DENNIS GOODE	TROM(A
MARTHA McCRORY	CELLO(A	STEVE BURGH	G	(D	STEVE MOSLEY	D	(D	SID SIMS	B	(D
SAUL BROUDY	HCA	(D	WINNIE WINSTON	BAN STEEL(D	JEFF GUTCHEON	K	(D	BILL SWOFFORD	V	(D
HUGH McDONALD	B	(D	RUAN MacKINNON	V	(D	DIANE HOLMES	V	(D	MARY GAFFNEY	V	(D
JIM ROTHERMEL	SAX	(D	PETER ECKLUND	CLAR	(D	JETHRO BURNS	MAND	(D	KENNY KOSEK	FDL (D
LEW LONDON	DOBRO(D	TOM RADTKE	TIMBALES	(D	JOHN FRIGO	B VLN(D	BOBBY ROSSI	ACC (D
KEN BUTTREY	PERC	(A

G72A GOOSE CREEK SYMPHONY

RITCHIE HART	V G	(A	(A) GOOSE CREEK SYMPHONY		19	CAPITOL US M444 UK ST 690
PAUL HOWARD	G V	(A	(B) WORDS OF EARNEST		1972	CAPITOL		EST 11044
BOB HENKE	G K V(A	(C) WELCOME TO GOOSE CREEK		19		US
ELLIS SCHWEID	FDL	(	(D) DO YOUR THING		1974		US
DENNIS KENMORE	D	(

DAVE BIRKETT	B	(A	MIKE McFADDEN	G	(A	CHARLES GEARHART	G	(B	PAUL SPRADLIN	G	(B
JIM TOLLES	VLN	(B	FRED	VLN	(B	FROGGY	B	(B	FLASH	D	(B
WILLARD	G	(B	RANDALL	SAX	(B	HAROLD	SAX	(B	PAT MOORE	B	(
CHRIS MOSTERT	SAX	(

SAM GOPAL G73

SAM GOPAL	PERC (A	(A) SAM GOPAL	1969	STABLE	UK	SLE	8001	
IAN 'LEMMY'WILLIS	G V (A							
ROGER DIELIA	G (A	PHIL DUKE	B (A	SUNNY LESLIE	V (A	SUE GLOVER	V (A	

GORDIAN KNOT G73A

	(A) GORDIAN KNOT	19	VERVE	US	V6 5062	

JIM GORDON G73B

JIM GORDON	(A	(A) PLAYS HEAVY	19	CREAM	US	9007	

ROBERT GORDON G74

ROBERT GORDON	V (A	(A) ROBERT GORDON & LINK WRAY	1977	PRIVATE STOCK	PVLP1027+PS	2030	
LINK WRAY	G (A	(B) FRESH FISH SPECIAL	1978	PRIVATE STOCK	PS	7008	
BILLY CROSS	G (A	(B) FRESH FISH SPECIAL	1978	PRIVATE STOCK	PVLP	1038	
HOWIE WYETH	D (A	(C) ROCK BILLY BOOGIE	1979	RCA	APLI	3294	
ROB STONER	B PNO(A	(D) LIVE AT DJ PARADISE BOSTON	197	RCA	3411		
CHARLIE MESSING	G (A						
RICHARD GOTTEHRER	PNO (A						

GORILLAS G75

ALAN BUTLER	B (A	(A) MESSAGE TO THE WORLD	1978	RAW	UK	RWLP	103
GARY ANDERSON	D (A						
JESSE HECTOR	G V (A						

GOSPEL OAK G76

	(A) GOSPEL OAK	1970	UNI	UNLS	113	

GRAHAM GOULDMAN G76A

GRAHAM GOULDMAN	(B	(A) GRAHAM GOULDMAN THING	197	RCA	US		
		(B) ANIMALYMPICS	1980	MERCURY	UK	9109	630

MICK GRABHAM G77

MICK GRABHAM	G V (A	(A) MICK THE LAD	1972	U A	UK	UAS 29341	
NIGEL OLSSON	D (A						
MIKE STOREY	PNO (A	DICK PARRY	SAX (A	CALEB QUAYE	G (A		

GRACIOUS G77A

PAUL DAVIS	G V (A	(A) GRACIOUS!	1970 VERTIGO UK 6360 002 CAPITOL US 602			
MARTIN KITCAT	K (A					
ALAN COWDEROY	G V (A	TIM WHEATLEY	B (A	ROBERT LIPSON	D (A	

GRADUATE G77B

CURT SMITH	B V (A	(A) ACTING MY AGE	1980	PRECISION	UK PART 001	
STEVE BUCK	K FLT(A					
ANDY MARSDEN	D (A	ROLAND ORZABAL	G V (A	JOHN BAKER	G V (A	

GRAFFITI G77C

GEORGE STRUNZ	G (A	(A) GRAFFITI	1968	ABC	US	ABCS 663
JOHN ST JOHN	G (A					
RICHIE BLAKIN	D (A	STEVE BENDEROTH	K B (A	TONY TAYLOR	V (A	

DAVEY GRAHAM G78

DAVEY GRAHAM	G V (ALL	(A) GUITAR PLAYER	1963 GOLDEN GUINEA	UK	GGL 0224	
WITH		(B) FOLK ROOTS NEW ROUTES	1964 DECCA UK LK4652 RI RIGHTEOUS001			
SHIRLEY COLLINS	BANJO(B	(C) FOLK BLUES & BEYOND	1965 DECCA	UK	LK 4649	
		(D) MIDNIGHT MAN	1966 DECCA	UK	LK 4780	
		(E) LARGE AS LIFE & TWICE AS NATURAL	1968 DECCA	UK	SKL 4969	
		(F) HAT	1969 DECCA	UK	SKL 5011	
		(G) GODINGTON BOUNDARY	19	PRESIDENT	PTLS 1039	
		(H) 3/4 AD	19	TOPIC	UK	TOP 70
		(I) HOLLY KALEIDOSCOPE	1970 DECCA	UK	SKL 5056	
		(J) COMPLETE GUITARIST	1978 KICKING MULE	UK	SNKF 138	
		(K) DANCE FOR TWO PEOPLE	1979 KICKING MULE	UK	SNKF 158	

ERNIE GRAHAM G79

ERNIE GRAHAM	G V (A	(A) ERNIE GRAHAM	1971	LIBERTY	UK	LBS 83485
BOB ANDREWS	G V K(A					
C CUNNINGHAM	VLN (A	J EICHLER	V (A	IAN GOMM	G V (A	NICK LOWE B V (A
MALCOLM MORLEY	G V (A	BILLY RANKIN	D (A	BRINSLEY SCHWARZ	G (A	RICHARD TREECE G (A
DAVE CHARLES	D V (A	KEN WHALEY	B (A			

LARRY GRAHAM G79A

LARRY GRAHAM B D G K V (A		(A) ONE IN A MILLION	1980	WB	US	BSK 3447
ERIC DANIELS	K V (A					
WILTON RABB	G V (A	TINA GRAHAM	V (A			

TOMMY GRAHAM G79B

TOMMY GRAHAM	G SITAR (A	(A) PLANET EARTH	1972	CAPITOL	EAST21956	
SKIP BECKWITH	B (A					
JOSH COLLINS	D (A	RON BULLY	D (A	EUGENE AMARO	FLT (A	MIKE LEWIS PNO (A
BILLY SPEER	PNO (A	BUDDY CAGE	STEEL (A	KATHY MOSES	FLT (A	MILES WILKINSON (A
JENNY BABOOLA	TAMB (A	BRIAN AHERN	G (A			

GRAHAM CENTRAL STATION G80

TOMMY GRAHAM	V B G (ALL	(A) GRAHAM CENTRAL STATION	1974	WB UK K 46286	US	2763
PATRYCE BANKS	D V (ABD	(B) RELEASE YOURSELF	1974	WB UK K 56062	US	2814
HERSHALL KENNEDY	WIND (ABDE	(C) AINT NO BOUT ADOUT IT	1975	WB UK K 56147	US	2875
WILLIE SPARKS	D (AB	(D) MIRROR	1976	WB UK K 56235	US	2937
DAVID VEGA	G (ABDE	(E) NOW DO U WANNA DANCE	1977	WB UK K 56359	US	3041
ROBERT SAM	K V (ABDE	(F) MY RADIO SURE SOUNDS GOOD	1978	WB	US	3175
MILT HOLLAND	PERC (A					
LENNY WILLIAMS	V (A	FREDDIE STONE	G (A	GAYLORD BIRCH	D (DE	GAIL MULDROW G V (E

BILLY GRAMMER G80A

BILLY GRAMMER	G V (A	(A) TRAVELLIN' ON	1959 MONUMENT	US	4000	

GRAND FUNK RAILROAD

MARK FARNER	K G V	HCA(ALL	(A) ON TIME	1970	CAPITOL			EST	307
MEL SCHACHER	V B	(ALL	(B) GRAND FUNK	1970	CAPITOL			EST	406
DON BREWER	D V	(ALL	(C) CLOSER TO HOME	1970	CAPITOL			EST	471
CRAIG FROST	K V	(LK	(D) LIVE	1971	CAPITOL UK ESTDW1/2 EST				633
TODD RUNDGREN	G	(K	(E) SURVIVAL	1971	CAPITOL			ESW	764
FRANK ZAPPA	G	(P	(F) E PLURIBUS FUNK	1972	CAPITOL			EAS	853
			(G) MARK,DON & MEL 1969 71	1972	CAPITOL UK ESTSP10				11042
			(H) PHOENIX	1973	CAPITOL				11099
			(J) WE'RE JUST AN AMERICAN BAND	1973	CAPITOL				11207
			(K) SHININ' ON	1974	CAPITOL				11278
			(L) MASTERS OF ROCK	1975	EMI	054 81479 EMI			81580
			(M) ALL THE GIRLS IN THE WORLD	1975	CAPITOL				11356
			(N) CAUGHT IN THE ACT	1975	CAPITOL UK ESTSP 15				11445
			(O) BORN TO DIE	1976	CAPITOL				11482
			(P) GOOD SINGING, GOOD PLAYING	1976	EMI	UK 1503 MCA US 2216			
			( ) HITS	1977	CAPITOL				11579

GRAND HOTEL

COL CAMPSIE	V	(A	(A) DO NOT DISTURB	1979	CBS			UK	83134
IVAN PENFOLD	G K V(A								
ROB GREEN	G V	(A	MEL COLLINS SAX (A GEORGE McFARLANE B K V(A GRAHAM BROAD D PERC(A						
DANNY McINTOSH	G	(A	NICKY GRAHAM STRINGS (A						

GRAND PRIX

PHIL LANZON	K V	(A	(A) GRAND PRIX FIRST ALBUM	1980	RCA			UK	PL 25321
MICHAEL O'DONAGHUE	G V	(A							
RALPH HOOD	B V	(A	ANDY BEIRNE D PERC (A BERNIE SHAW V (A						

GRANNY'S INTENTION

PAT NASH	D	(A	(A) HONEST INJUN	1970	DERAM			UK	SML 1060
PETE CUMMINGS B FLT		(A							
JOHN RYAN	K	(A	JOHNNY DUHAN V (A JOHNNY HOCKEDY G MAND(A						

GRAPEFRUIT

GEOFF SWETTENHAM	D	(A	(A) DEEP WATER	1969	RCA US LSP4215			ST	8030
GEORGE ALEXANDER	B	(AB	(B) AROUND GRAPEFRUIT	1969	DUNHILL		US		50050
JOHN PERRY	G	(AB	(B) AROUND GRAPEFRUIT	1969	STATESIDE		UK	SSL	5008
PETE SWETTENHAM	G	(B							
BOB HALE		(	MICK FOWLER (						

GRASS ROOTS

JOEL LARSON	D	(I	(A) GRASS ROOTS	19	HAVEN		US		9204
WARREN ENTNER	G	(ABCDEFGHI	(B) LETS LIVE FOR TODAY	19	DUNHILL		US		50020
ROB GRILL	V	(ABCDEFGHI	(C) FEELINGS	19	DUNHILL		US		50027
VIRGIL WEBER		(I	(D) GOLDEN GRASS	1969	DUNHILL		US		50047
REED KAILING		(I	(E) LOVIN' THING	1969	DUNHILL		US		50052
ERIK MICHAEL COONCE	D	(ABCDEFGH	(F) LEAVING IT BEHIND	1969	DUNHILL		US		50067
CREED BRATTON	G	(ABCDEF	(F) LEAVING IT BEHIND	1969	STATESIDE		UK	SSL	5012
DENNIS PROVISOR	V	(	(G) MORE GOLDEN GRASS	19	DUNHILL		US		50087
TERRY FURLONG	G	(	(H) 16 GREATEST HITS	19	DUNHILL		US		50107
			(I) MOVE ALONG	1972	DUNHILL		US		50112
			(J) A LOT OF MILEAGE	197	DUNHILL		US		50137

GRATEFUL DEAD

JERRY GARCIA	G V(ABCDEFGHPRTV		(A) GRATEFUL DEAD	1967	WB	US	1689		
ROD'PIGPEN'McKERNAN	K V(ABCDEFGHI		(B) ANTHEM FOR THE SUN	1968	WB	US	1749	UK	K 46021
BOB WEIR	G	(ABCDEFGHPRTV	(C) AOXOMOXOA	1969	WB	US	1790	UK	K 46027
PHIL LESH	B V	(ABCDEFGHPRTV	(D) LIVE/DEAD(DBL)	1970	WB	US	1830	UK	K 66002
MICKEY HART	D	(BCDFPRTV	(E) WORKINGMANS DEAD	1970	WB	US	1869	UK	K 46049
BILL KREUTZMANN	D	(ABCDEFGHPRTV	(F) AMERICAN BEAUTY	1970	WB	US	1893	UK	K 46074
TOM CONSTANTEN	K	(CD	(G) GRATEFUL DEAD LIVE(DBL)	1971	WB	US	1935	UK	K 66009
ROBERT HUNTER		(EFGHPT	(H) EUROPE 72 (TRIPLE)	1972	WB	US 3X2662		UK	K 66019
KEITH GODCHAUX	K	(HPRTV	(I) VINTAGE DEAD	1972	POLYDOR			UK	2310 172
DONNA GODCHAUX	V	(HPRTV	(I) VINTAGE DEAD	197	SUNFLOWER		US	SNF	5001
DAVE NELSON		(EF	(J) HISTORY OF	1973	WB	US	2721	UK	K 46246
DAVE TORBERT	B	(F	(J) HISTORY OF	197	PRIDE	US	0016		
DAVE GRISMAN	MAND(F		(L) HISTORIC DEAD	197	POLYDOR			UK	2310 171
HOWARD WALES	K	(F	(L) HISTORIC DEAD	197	SUNFLOWER		US		5004
NED LAGIN	K	(F	(M) WAKE OF THE FLOOD	1973	G DEAD US		01	Uk	K 49301
MERL SAUNDERS	K	(G	(M) WAKE OF THE FLOOD	1976	UA			UK RI	29903
JOHN DAWSON	G V	(	(N) FROM MARS HOTEL	1974	G DEAD US		102	UK	K 59302
BOB MATTHEWS	G V	(	(N) FROM MARS HOTEL	1976	UA			UK RI	29904
STEVEN SCHUSTER		(P	(MN) WAKE /MARS HOTEL	1977	UA				UDM103/4
BILL ATWOOD	TPT	(MN	(O) SKELETONS FROM THE CLOSET	1974	WB	US	2764	UK	K 56024
VASSAR CLEMENTS	VLN(MN		(P) BLUES FOR ALLAH	1975	G DEAD US		494	UK	UAS 29895
PAT OHARA	TROM	(MN	(Q) STEAL YOUR FACE(DBL)	1976	G DEAD US		629	UK	UAD60131/2
JOE ELLIS	TPT	(MN	(R) TERRAPIN STAAION	1977	ARISTA US		7001	UK	1016
MARTIN FIERRO	SAX	(MN	(S) WHAT A LONG STRANGE TRIP	1978	WB	US	3091	UK	K 66073
SARAH FULCHER	V	(MN	(T) SHAKEDOWN STREET	1978	ARISTA US		4198	UK	ARTY 159
BRENT MYDLAND		(V	(U) POP HISTORY 13	197	POLYDOR				2612019
MATTHEW KELLY	HCA (MNT		(V) GO TO HEAVEN	1980	ARISTA			UK	1115
FRANK MORIN	SAX	(NM	( ) POP HISTORY 23	1976	POLYDOR				2679003
DOUG SAHM	G(MN		(X) RECKONING	1981	ARISTA			UK DARTY	9
BENNY VELARDES	PERC(MN								
JORDAN AMARANTHA		PERC (T							

NICK GRAVENITES

NICK GRAVENITES	G V	(ALL	(A) MY LABOURS	1969	CBS			UK	63818
PETE SEARS	B K	(C	(B) JUNKYARD IN MALIBU	1980	LINE			GERM	6 24264
JOEY COVINGTON	D	(C	(C) BLUE STAR	1980	LINE			GERM	LLP 5039
HUEY LOUIS	HCA	(C							
GREG DOUGLAS	G	(C	WILLY TROST G (C ROGER TROY B V (C JOHN CIPOLLINA G (C						
MARLA HUNT	V	(C	DIANE HURST V (C						

GRAVY TRAIN G85

NORMAN BARRETT	V G	(AB	(A) GRAVY TRAIN	1970	VERTIGO	UK	6360	023
BARRY DAVENPORT	D	(AB	(B) BALLAD OF A PEACEFUL MAN	1971	VERTIGO	UK	6360	051
J D HUGHES WIND	K V	(AB	(C) SECOND BIRTH	1973	DAWN	UK	DNLS	3046
LES WILLIAMS	B V	(AB	(D) STAIRCASE TO THE DAY	1974	DAWN	UK	DNLH	1

GREASE BAND G86

HENRY McCULLOUGH	G	(AB	(A) THE GREASE BAND	1971	HARVEST	UK	SHVL	790
ALAN SPENNER	B	(AB	(B) AMAZING GREASE	1975	GOODEAR	UK	EAR	2902
BRUCE ROWLAND	D	(AB						
NEIL HUBBARD	G	(AB CHRIS STAINTON K (B TERRY STANNARD D (B MEL COLLINS SAX (B						
MICK WEAVER	K	(B TOMMY EYRE K (JOHN WEATHERS D (						

GREAT BEAR G86A

(A) GREAT BEAR	1971	WAND	UK	WNS8
(A) GREAT BEAR	197	SCEPTER	US	SPS 585

GREAT JONES G87

BILLY CADIEUX	G	(A	(A) ALL BOWED DOWN	197	TONSIL	US	T 4002
GARY KOLLARUS	D	(A					
DAVID TOLMIE	B	(A JEFF GUTCHEON K (A MERRY CLAYTON V (A VANETTA FIELDS V (A					
CLYDIE KING	V	(A					

GREAT METROLPOLITAN STEAM BAND G87A

(A) GREAT METROPOLITAN STEAM BAND	1969 MCA	UK MUPS 403 + MAPS 2162		

GREAT SOCIETY G88

GRACE SLICK	V	(	(A) GREAT SOCIETY	196	CBS US 30459	UK 63476
JERRY SLICK	D	(	(B) CONSPICUOUS ONLY IN ITS ABSENCE	1968	CBS US 9624	
DARBY SLICK	G	(	(C) HOW IT WAS	1968	CBS US 9702	30461
DAVID MINOR	G	(	(D) SOMEBODY TO LOVE	19	HARMONY US	30391
PETER VAN DEGILDER	B	(				

GREATEST SHOW ON EARTH G89

COLIN HORTON JENNINGS	V G D(	(A) HORIZONS	1970	HARVEST	UK	SHVL	769
GARTH WATT ROY	VG (	(B) THE GOING'S EASY	1970	HARVEST	UK	SHVL	783
NORMAN WATT ROY	V B (	(C) GREATEST SHOW ON EARTH	1975	HARVEST	UK	SHSM	2004
MIKE DEACON	K (						
RON PRUDENCE	CONGA D(DICK HANSON HRNS (TEX PHILPOTTS SAX (IAN AITCHISON SAX (						

JOHN GREAVES & PETER BLEGVAD G90

JOHN GREAVES	B V K PERC(A	(A) KEW RHONE	1977	VIRGIN	UK	V 2082	
PETER BLEGVAD	V G SAX(A						
LISA HERMAN	V (A ANDREW CYRILLE D PERC(A MIKE MANTLER HRNS (A CARLA BLEY V SAX(A						
MICHAEL LEVINE	VLN V(A VITO RENDACE WIND (A APRIL LANG V (A DANA JOHNSON V (A						
BORIS KINBERG	CLAVE (A						

RICH GRECH G91

RICK GRECH	B VLN V(A	(A) THE LAST FIVE YEARS(COMP)	1973	RSO	UK	2394	111

GREEN G91A

GARY CASEBEER	K HRNS V(A	(A) GREEN	1969	ATCO	UK	33282
RICHARD GARDZINA	K V HRNS(A					
WILSON FISHER	V HCA(A JOHN MARTIN K V (A JAMES NEEL V K WIND (A BOBBY BLOOD HRNS (A					

AL GREEN G92

AL GREEN	V	(ALL	(A) BACK UP TRAIN	19	ACTION US		
WAYNE JACKSON	TPT	(H	(B) GREEN IS BLUES	1970	HI US 32055		
ANDREW LOVE	SAX	(H	(C) GETS NEXT TO YOU	1971	HI US 32062	LONDON UK	8424
ED LOGAN	SAX	(H	(D) LETS STAY TOGETHER	1972	HI US 8007	LONDON UK	8430
JAMES MITCHELL	SAX	(H	(E) I'M STILL IN LOVE WITH YOU	1972	HI US 32074	LONDON UK	8443
JACK HALE	TROM	(H	(F) CALL ME	1973	HI US 32077	LONDON UK	8457
HOWARD GRIMES	D PERC(H	(G) LIVING FOR YOU	1974	HI US 32082	LONDON UK	8464
LEROY HODGES	B	(H	(H) EXPLORES YOUR MIND	1974	HI US 32087	LONDON UK	8479
CHARLES HODGES	K	(H	(I) AL GREEN IS LOVE	1975	HI US 32092	LONDON UK	8488
TEENIE HODGES	G	(H	(J) FULL OF FIRE	1976	HI US 32097	LONDON UK	8493
ARCHIE TURNER	PNO	(H	(K) HAVE A GOOD TIME	1976	HI US	LONDON UK	8505
MICHAEL ALLEN	PNO	(H	(L) BELLE ALBUM	1977	HI US 6004	CREAM UK	6004
MEMPHIS STRINGS		(H	(M) TRUTH & TIME	1978	HI US 6009		
REUBEN FAIRFAX	B	(L	(N) CREAM OF	1980	CREAM HLP101		
JAMES BASS	G	(L					
MARGARET FOXWORTH	V	(L LINDA JONES V (L HARVEY JONES V (L LEON THOMAS K (L					
DARRYL NEELY	HRNS (L JOHNNY BROLIN V (L FRED JORDAN TPT K (L JOHN TONEY D (L					
RON ECHOLS	SAX (L ROB PAYNE PERC (L ARDIS HARDIN D (L BUDDY JARRETT SAX(L					

BUNKY GREEN G92A

BUNKY GREEN	(ALL	(A) THE LATINIZATION OF..	19	CADET	US LP 780
		(B) TESTIFYIN' TIME	19	CADET	US LP 753
		(C) PLAYING FOR KEEPS	19	CADET	US LP 766

DANNY GREEN G92B

DANNY GREEN	G V	(A	(A) NIGHT DOG	1978	ABC	UK ABCL 5259
DON BARRETT	B	(A				
GINO ZIMMERMAN	G	(A CARSON WHITSETT K (A KAREN TAYLOR V (A JOE HARDY V (A				
JAMES STROUD	D PERC(A ED FORESMAN B V (A WALTER POLK D (A JUDY RODMAN V (A				
JERRY McKINNEY	HRNS (A DR JOHN PNO (A WILLIAM C BROWN V (A DUNCAN SISTERS V (A				
JOE MULHERIN	HRNS (A MIKE PLUNKETT K (A				

LLOYD GREEN G93

LLOYD GREEN	STEEL	(ALL	( ) THE BIG STEEL GUITAR	1965	TIME		
		( ) HIT SOUNDS	1966	LITTLE DARLIN'	US SLD		
		( ) MR NASHVILLE SOUND	1968	CHART	US		
		( ) GREEN COUNTRY	1969	LITTLE DARLIN'	US SLD	8021
		( ) MOODY RIDER	1969	CHART	US CHS	1024
		( ) DAY FOR DECISION	196	LITTLE DARLIN	US LD	4002
		( ) AND HIS STEEL GUITAR	1971	MONUMENT	UK	1003
		( ) STAINLESS STEEL	19	PYE	UK	28249
		( ) COOL STEEL MAN	1973	CHART	US CHS	2003
		( ) SHADES OF STEEL	1973	MONUMENT	US	32532
		( ) STEEL RIDES	1976	MONUMENT	UK	81245
		( ) TEN SHADES OF GREEN	1977	CHECK MATE	UK CMLF	1001
		( ) FEELINGS	1977	GRT	US GRT	8018

G94 PETER GREEN

PETER GREEN	G V	(	(A) THE END OF THE GAME	1970 REPRISE K RSLP 9006+RI K44106
ZOOT MONEY	PNO	(A	(A) THE END OF THE GAME	1970 REPRISE US 9436
GODFREY MACLEAN	D	(A	(B) IN THE SKIES	1979 PVK UK PVLS 101
NICK BUCK	K	(A	(C) LITTLE DREAMER	1980 PVK UK PVLP 102+CREOLE 6 24300
ALEX DMOCHOWSKI	B	(A	(D) WHATCHA DONNA DO?	1981 PVK UK PET 1
JOHN EDWARDS	B	(C
KUMA HARADA	B	(BC	REG ISADORE	D	(B	RON JOHNSON	G	(C	PAUL WESTWOOD	B (C
DAVE WILKEY	PNO	(C	SNOWY WHITE	G	(B	LENNOX LAINGTON	D	(B	PETER BARDENS	K (B
ROY SHIPSTON	K	(CD	PETER VERNON KELL PNO	(C	DAVE MATTACKS	D	(CD	MORRIS PERT	PERC (C
CAROL INGRAM	V	(C	PAM DOUGLAS	V	(C

G95 GREEN BULLFROG

RITCHIE BLACKMORE	G	(B	(A) GREEN BULLFROG	19 MCA MKPS 2021 RI 74 MCF 2689
ALBERT LEE	G	(B	(B) GREEN BULLFROG	19 ECY STREET ECY 16
ROGER GLOVER	B	(B
IAN PAICE	D	(B	JIM SULLIVAN V (B

G96 NORMAN GREENBAUM

NORMAN GREENBAUM	(ALL	(A) SPIRIT IN THE SKY	1969 REPRISE US 6365
		(B) BACK HOME AGAIN	1972 REPRISE US 6422
		(C) PETALUMA	1973 REPRISE US 2084

G97 GREENSLADE

DAVE GREENSLADE	K	(ABCD	(A) GREENSLADE	1973 WB UK K 46207+ PHILIPS 6325 500
TONY REEVES	B	(ABC	(B) BEDSIDE MANNERS ARE EXTRA	1973 WB UK K 46259+
DAVE LAWSON	K	(ABCD	(C) SPYGLASS GUEST	1974 WB UK K 56055+ MERCURY US 1015
ANDY McCULLOCH	D	(ABCD	(D) TIME & TIDE	1975 WB UK K 56126+ MERCURY US 1025
MARTIN BRILEY	G B	(D
DAVE CLEMPSON	G	(C	GRAHAM SMITH VLN	(C	MICK ROGERS	G V	(	BARRY MORGAN	PERF (D
JILL MACKINTOSH	V	(D	DAVE MARKEE B	(C	ANN SIMMONS	V	(D	TREVERVA MALE CHOIR	(D
JEREMY ENSOR EFFECTS	(C	GREG JACKMAN EFFECTS	(C	ANDY ROBERTS	G	(C

G97A DAVE GREENSLADE

DAVE GREENSLADE	K	(AB	(A) CACTUS CHOIR	1976 WB UK K 5630&
TONY REEVES	B	(A	(B) PENTATEUCH OF THE COSMOGONY(DBL)	1979 EMI UK EMC3321/2
SIMON PHILLIPS	D	(A
JOHN PERRY	B	(A	STEVE GOULD V	(A	BILL JACKMAN	WIND (A	MICK GRABHAM	G (A

G98 MICK GREENWOOD

MICK GREENWOOD	V G K	(ABC	(A) LIVING GAME	1971 MCA UK 8003+RI MCA 74 MCG 3520
JERRY DONAHUE	G V	(AB	(B) TO FRIENDS	1972 MCA UK 2026+RI MCA UK MCF 8692
TONY COX	K V	(AB	(C) MIDNIGHT DREAMER	1974 WB UK K56059
PAT DONALDSON	B	(A
GERRY CONWAY	D	(A	LYN DOBSON WIND SITAR	(A	DAVE PEGG	B	(A	ANDY SMITH BANJO	(A
CHRISTINE QUAILE	V	(A	DUDU PUKWANA SAX	(A	KARL JENKINS	SAX	(A	BUD PARKES TPT	(A
DEREK WADSWORTH	TROM	(A	NED BALEN PERC	(A	BARRY DE SOUZA	D	(A	DAVE PEACOCK B V VLN	(B
BARRY ST JOHN	V	(B	DORIS TROY V	(A	JIMMY HELMS	V	(B

G99 GREEP

COLIN FLETCHER	G	(
ANDY WINFIELD	G	(
JOHN McKENZIE	B	(	NIGEL WATSON	D	(	TINO TURVILLE	K	(

G100 GREEZY WHEELS

CLEVE HATTERSLEY	V G	(AB	(A) JUST LOVE DEM 'OL GREEZY WHEELS	1975 LONDON US PS 657
LISSA HATTERSLEY	G V	(AB	(B) RADIO RADIALS	1976 LONDON UK SHU 8497
MARY EGAN	FDL	(AB
PAT PANKRATZ	G	(AB	TONY AIROLDI	G	(AB	MIKE PUGH	B	(AB	TONY LAIER D	(AB
MADRILLE WILSON	CONGA	(AB	JIMMY DAY STEEL	(A	ALFRED ROBERTS	PERC	(A	RILEY OSBORNE	PERC(A

G100A ZAINE GRIFF

ZAINE GRIFF	SYN	(A	(A) ASHES & DIAMONDS	1980 AUTOMATIC UK K 56834
ANDY DUNCAN	D	(A
STEVE BOLTON	G	(A	ANDY CLARK K	(A	TONY VISCONTI B V PERC(A

G101 GRIFFIN

GRAHAM BELL	V	(1	(1) 1969
ALAN WHITE	D	(1
COLIN GIBSON	B	(1	PETE KIRTLEY	G	(1	KEN CRADDOCK	K	(1

G101A JAMES GRIFFIN

JAMES GRIFFIN	G V	(A	(A) JAMES GRIFFIN	1978 POLYDOR UK 2391 274
DAVID PAICH	K	(A	(B) EAGLE	197 POLYDOR US 6018
DAVE BUDAMEYER	B	(A	( ) BREAKING UP IS EASY	1974 POLYDOR UK 2391 113
JIM GORDON	D	(A
JACK HALE	TROM	(A	DEAN PARKS	G	(A	JIM HORN	HRNS	(A	LARRY KNECHTEL	B(A
MIKE BOTTS	D	(A	CAROL CARMICHAEL	V	(A	DAVID GATES	D	(A	JOE LAMANO	B (A
ED LOGAN	SAX	(A	BARRY BURTON	G	(A	ANDREW LOVE	SAX	(A	JAMES MITCHELL	SAX (A
WAYNE JACKSON	HRNS	(A

G101B ROB GRILL

ROB GRILL	V	(A	(A) UPROOTED	1980 MERCURY 9111 055 US SRM1 3798
ROBBIE BUCHANAN	K	(A
STEVE HUNTER	G	(A	JOHN McVIE	B	(A	MICK FLEETWOOD	D	(A	MARK LEONARD	B (A
LINDSEY BUCKINGHAM	G	(A	MIKE HUEY	D	(A	DENNIS PROVISOR	K	(A	ANNIE McCLOONE	V (A
DONNIE GERRARD	V	(A	BILL CHAMPLIN	V	(A	JAY GRUSKA	V	(A	CARL GRAVES	V (A
KATHY COLLIER	V	(A	BRIAN NAUGHTON	G	(A

G102 CAROLE GRIMES

CAROL GRIMES	V	(ALL	(A) FOOLS MEETING	1970 B+C CAS 1023
STEVE MILLER	PNO	(A	(B) WARM BLOOD	1974 CAROLINE UK CA 2001
ROY BABBINGTON	B	(A	(C) CAROLE GRIMES	1976 DECCA UK SKLR5258
PHIL MILLER	G	(A	(1) MAY 1978 TOUR
PIP PYLE	D	(A	(2) 1980 F.A. RECORDING IN SWEDEN
LOL COXHILL	SAX	(A	(C) CAROLE GRIMES	1979 CHARLY 30164
TONY HICKS	D	(2
BOB WILSON	K	(B	RON CORNELIUS	G	(BC	MAC GAYDEN	G	(B	KENNY BUTTREY	D (B

(CONTINUED)

CAROLE GRIMES   G102

TOMMY COGBILL	B	(B	KARL HIMMEL	D	(B	GRAHAM BELL	HCA V(B	SAM MITCHELL	G	(B
RABBIT BUNDRICK	K	(B	TOMMY EYRE	K	(B	ARCHIE LEGGET	V	(B	JESS RODEN	V	(B
ROGER BALL	SAX	(B	MALCOLM DUNCAN	SAX	(B	HENRY LOWTHER	TPT	(B	JOHN McKENZIE	B	(1
NIGEL WATSON	D	(1	COLIN FLETCHER	G	(1	ANDY WINFIELD	G	(1	TINO TURVILLE	K	(1
MICHAEL BRECKER	HRNS	(C	MEMPHIS HRNS		(C	WESTETTES	V	(C	GINGER HOLLADAY	V	(C
MARY HOLLADAY	V	(C	BOB MANUEL	G	(C	BUDDY DAVIES	G	(C	HUGH McCRACKEN	G	(C
NEIL HUBBARD	G	(C	DONALD DUNN	B	(C	JOE DAVIES	B	(C	WILLIE HALL	D	(C
LLOYD PERRATA	D	(C	BOBBY EMMONS	PNO	(C	JAY SPELL	PNO	(C	BOB CLAIRE	HRNS PNO	(C
FREDERICK KNIGHT		(C	OLLIE MALLARD	K V	(2	PETE KIRTLEY	G V	(2	GARY TWIGG	B	(2

GRIMMS   G103

NEIL INNES	G K V(ABC		(A) GRIMMS	1973	ISLAND	UK	HELP	1
ROGER McGOUGH	V	(ABC	(B) ROCKING DUCK	1973	ISLAND	UK	ILPS 9248	
JOHN GORMAN	V	(ABC	(C) SLEEPERS	1976	D J M	UK	DJLPS 470	
ANDY ROBERTS	G	(BC						
DAVE RICHARDS	B V	(BC	JOHN MEGGINSON	B V K(ABC	OLLIE HALSALL	G V	(B	ZOOT MONEY K		(AC
MIKE McGEAR	V	(AB	GERRY CONWAY	D	(B	ADRIAN HENRI	V	(A	BRIAN PATTEN		V(AB
TIMI DONALD	D	(C	MIKE GILES		(A					

GRINDERSWITCH   G104

DRU LOMBAR	G V	(ABCD	(A) HONEST TO GOODNESS	1974	CAPRICORN	US	CP 0135	
STEPHEN MILLER	K V	(CD	(B) MACON TRACKS	1975	CAPRICORN	US	CP 0150	
LARRY HOWARD	G V	(ABCD	(C) PULLIN' TOGETHER	1977	CAPRICORN UK2429 144 US CP 0173			
JOE DAN PETTY	B V	(ABCD	(D) REDWING	1977	ATCO	US		36152
RICK BURNETT	D	(ABCD						
PAUL HORNSBY	K	(B	CHARLIE DANIELS FDL	(B	JIMMY HALL	HCA	(C	JERRY JOSEPH	CONGA(C

GRINGO   G105

| (A) GRINGO | 1971 | MCA | UK | MKPS 2017 |

GROBSCHNITT   G106

JOACHIM H EHRIG(EROC)D V SYN(ALL	(A) GROBSCHNITT	1972	BRAIN		1008
AXEL HARLOS(FELIX) D PERC	(A	(B) BALLERMANN	1974	BRIAN 2/1050 BRAIN	0021	050
STEFAN DANIELAK(WILDSCHWEIN) G V(ALL	(C) JUMBO	ENGLISH LYRICS	1975	BRAIN		1076
BERNARD UHLEMANN(BAER) B FLR PERC(AB	(C) JUMBO	GERMAN LYRICS	1976	BRAIN		1081
GERD KUHN (LUPO)	G V	(ALL	(D) ROCKPOMMELS LAND	1977	BRAIN	0060	041
HERMANN QUETTING(QUECKSILBER)K PERC(A(E) SOLAR MUSIC LIVE	1978	BRAIN	0060	139
WOLFGANG JAEGER(PEPE)		(CDEFG	(F) MERRY GO ROUND	1979	BRAIN	0060	224
VOLKER KAHRS(MIST) K V		(BCDEFG	(G) VOLLE MOLLE	1980	BRAIN	0060	291
MILLA KAPOLLKE	B	)H	(H) ILLEGAL	1981	BRAIN		

MAX GRONENTHAL   G106A

MAX GRONENTHAL	K V	(AB	(A) WHISTLING IN THE DARK	1979	CHRYSALIS	UK	CHR 1231	
BILLY MEEKER	D	(A	(B) MAX	1980	CHRYSALIS	UK	CHR 1278	
TREY THOMPSON	B	(A						
TIMMY GOODMAN	G	(A	WILL McFARLANE	G	(A	MICHAEL O'NEILL	G	(A	JAMES N HOWARD	SYN (A
ROCKE GRACE	V	(A	KENNY LOGGINS	V	(A	GERARD McMAHON	V	(A	MICHAEL McDONALD V	(A
PATRICK SIMMONS	V	(A	RICKY FATAAR D PERC V G(B	JERRY WILSON	B V	(B	RICK BEILKE G V	(B
RENEE GEYER	V	(B	MIKE FINNIGAN	V	(B	MARCY LEVY	V	(B	RUSTY ANDERSON	G	(B

GROOTNA   G107

ANNA RIZZO	V	(A	(A) GROOTNA	1972	CBS	US		31033
KELLY BRYAN	B	(A						
SLIM CHANCE	G	(A	GREG DEWEY DA GREASE D (A	RICHARD SUSMAN	PNO	(A	VIC SMITH	G	(A

WINSTON GROOVY   G108

| WINSTON GROOVY | | (A | (A) PRESENTING WINSTON GROOVY | 1974 | TROJAN | UK | TRLS 88 |
| | | | (B) WINSTON GROOVY | 1978 | LIGHTNING | UK | PIL 6 |

HENRY GROSS   G109

HENRY GROSS	V G	(ALL	(A) PLUG ME INTO SOMETHING	1970	A&M	US 4502 UK AMLS 64502
CARL WILSON	V	(A	(B) HENRY GROSS	1974	A&M	US 4426 UK AMLH 64416
RICKY FATAAR	V	(A	(C) SHOW ME THE STAGE	197	LIFESONG	US 6016 RI	35002
CARLOS MUNOZ	V	(A	(D) RELEASE	1976	LIFESONG	6002 RI	34995
TERRY CASHMAN	V	(AD	(E) LOVE IS THE STUFF	197	LIFESONG		35280
TOMMY WEST	V	(ABD				
STEVE GADD	D	(BD	WARREN NICHOLS	B	(AD	PHIL AABERG	K	(AD	ALLEN SCHWARZBERG	D (AD
ANN E SUTTON	V	(AD	MICHAEL KAMEN	SYN	AB	MARTY NELSON	V	(ABD	RICHIE SCHMIERER	V (A
TASHA THOMAS	V	(ABD	DAVE SANBORN	SAX	(D	ELLIE GREENWICH	V	(D	HUGH McCRACKEN	G (D
GEORGE DEVENS	PERC	(BD	BUCKY PIZZARELLI	G	(D	LARRY PACKER	FDL	(D	MIKE CORBETT	V (D
STU WOODS	B	(B	ARNIE LAWRENCE	FLT	(B	TYRONE BABBOZZA	V	(B	JOE MACHO	B (B
ERIC WEISSBERG	VLN	(B	RONDO RAPPONE	V	(B	ZELDA GROSS	V	(B	EUGENE BIANCO	HARP (B

STEFAN GROSSMAN   G110

STEFAN GROSSMAN	G	(ALL	(A) YAZOO BASIN BOOGIE	1970	TRANSATLANTIC	UK	TRA 217
WITH			(A) YAZOO BASIN BOOGIE	197	KICKING MULE	UK	SNKF 134
DANNY KALB		(U	(A) YAZOO BASIN BOOGIE	1975	KICKING MULE	US	102
PAUL ROWAN	HCA	(Q	(B) RAGTIME COWBOY JEW	1971	TRANSATLANTIC	UK	TRA 223
SON HOUSE	V	(Q	(C) HOW TO PLAY BLUES	1971	TRANSATLANTIC	UK	XTRA 1113
JO ANN KELLY	V	(Q	(C) HOW TO PLAY BLUES	197	KICKING MULE US 109 UK SNKF 150
MIKE COOPER	G	(KQ	(D) THOSE PLEASANT DAYS	1972	TRANSATLANTIC	UK	TRA 246
SAM MITCHELL	G	(QT	(E) HOT DOGS	1972	TRANSATLANTIC	UK	TRA 257
DUCK BAKER	G	(ST	(E) HOT DOGS	197	KICKING MULE	US	131
TONY ROBERTS	WIND	(T	(F) GRAMERCY PARK SHEIK	1972	SONET	UK	SNTF 627
JOHN RENBOURN	G	(RS	(G) ANN MOLLY'S MURRAY FARM	1973	SONET	UK	SNTF 640
RORY BLOCK	G	(C	(H) LIVE	1973	TRANSATLANTIC	UK	TRA 264
			(I) MEMPHIS JELLYROLL	1973	TRANSATLANTIC	UK	TRA 274
			(J) FINGER PICKIN'	1974	TRANSATLANTIC	UK	XTRA 1138
			(K) BOTTLENECK SERENADE	1975	TRANSATLANTIC	UK	TRA 293
			(L) HOW TO PLAY RAGTIME GUITAR	1975	TRANSATLANTIC	UK	XTRA 1151
			(M) MY CREOLE BELLE	1976	TRANSATLANTIC	UK	TRA 326
			(N) ACOUSTIC MUSIC FOR BODY & SOUL	1976	KICKING MULE	US	105
			(O) BOX SET	(TRIPLE)	1977	TRANSATLANTIC	UK	GRS 6
			(P) HOW TO PLAY RAGTIME	197	KICKING MULE	US	115

(CONTINUED)

STEFAN GROSSMAN

(Q) COUNTRY BLUES GUITAR	1977	KICKING MULE	UK	SNKF	129
(R) AND JOHN RENBOURN	1978	KICKING MULE	UK	SNKF	139
(R) AND JOHN RENBOURN	197	KICKING MULE	US		152
(S) UNDER THE VOLCANO	1979	KICKING MULE	UK	SNKF	161
(T) THUNDER ON THE RUN	1980	KICKING MULE	UK	SNKF	170
(U) CROSSCURRENTS	19	COTILLION	US	SD	9007

G111 LUTHER GROSVENOR

LUTHER GROSVENOR B G V (A   (A) UNDER OPEN SKIES   1971 ISLAND   ILPS 9168
MIKE KELLIE D (A
JOHN HAWKEN PNO (A   JIM CAPALDI V (A   MICK RALPHS V (A   MIKE GILES D (A
TREVOR BURTON B (A   TREVOR LUCAS V (A   PAUL BENNETT V (A

G112 GROUNDHOGS

TONY McPHEE G B SYN V (A11	(A) SCRATCHING THE SURFACE	1968	LIBERTY	UK	LBS 83199
PETER CRUICKSHANK B (ABCDEFGH	(A) SCRATCHING THE SURFACE	197	WORLD PACIFIC US		21892
DAVE BOORMAN D (	(B) BLUES OBITUARY	1969	LIBERTY UK 83253		
BOB HALL PNO (	(B) BLUES OBITUARY	196	IMPERIAL	US	12452
KEN PUSTELNIK D (ABCDEH	(C) THANK CHRIST FOR THE BOMB	1970	LIBERTY UK 83295 US		7644
STEVE RYE HCA (A	(C) THANK CHRIST FOR THE BOMB	1975	SUNSET UK		50376
DAVE WELLBELOVED G (KL	(D) SPLIT	1971	LIBERTY UK 83401+1017+US UA5513		
MARTIN KENT B (KL	(E) LIVE AT LEEDS	1971	(LTD ED? OR BOOT?)		
MICK COOK D (KL	(F) WHO WILL SAVE THE WORLD	1972	UA	UK 29237	US UA5570
CLIVE BROOKS D (GH	(G) HOGWASH	1972	UA	UK 29419	US UA 008
RICK ADAMS G (K	(H) SOLID	1974	WWA	UK 004	
	(J) BEST OF 1969 72	1974	UA	UK 60063/4	
	(K) CROSSCUT SAW	1976	UA	UK 29917	
	(L) BLACK DIAMOND	1976	UA	UK 29994	
	( ) JOHN LEE HOOKER,JOHN MAYALL	19	CLEVE	US	82871

G112A GROWL

MICK SMALL G (A   (A) GROWL   1974 DISCREET   US   DS 2209
DENNIS RODRIGUEZ V (A
RICHARD MANUPUTI V (A   DANNY McBRIDE D (A   HARRY BRENDER BRANDIS G V(A   GENO LUCERO B (A

G113 GRUPPO SPORTIVO

HANS VANDENBURG G V (AB   (A) 10 MISTAKES   1977 ARIOLA 25464+1978 EPIC UK 82793
MAX MOLLINGER D (AB   (B) BACK TO 78   1978   EPIC UK 83263
ERIC WEHRMEYER B (AB
PETER CALICHER K (AB   JOSEE VAN IERSEL V (AB   MEIKE TOUW V (AB   JANKEES TANS SAX (B
ROB KRUISMAN HRNS (B   REIN VANDER BROEK HRNS (B   MAARTEN VAN NORDEN HRNS (B

G114 GRYPHON

BRIAN GULLAND REC HRNS (B	(A) GRYPHON	1973	TRANSATLANTIC	UK	TRA 262
RICHARD HARVEY WIND HRNS(B	(B) MIDNIGHT MUSHRUMPS	1974	TRANSATLANTIC	UK	TRA 282
GRAEME TAYLOR G (B	(C) RED QUEEN TO GRYPHON 3	1974	TRANSATLANTIC	UK	TRA 287
DAVID OBERLE PERC (B	(C) RED QUEEN TO GRYPHON 3	197	ARISTA	US	4018
MALCOLM BENNETT (	(D) RAINDANCE	1975	TRANSATLANTIC	UK	TRA 302
BOB FOSTER G (	(E) TREASON	1977	HARVEST	UK	SHSP 4063
ALEX BAIRD D (					
JON DAVIE B (	PHILIP NESTOR B (B	PETER AIREY	G	(	

G115 GUESS WHO

BURTON CUMMINGS V K (N	( ) SHAKIN ALL OVER	1968	SCEPTER US 533+ SPRINGBAORD4022			
GARRY PETERSON D (N	(A) GUESS WHO	19	MGM	US	4654	
RANDY BACHMAN G V (	(B) PLAY THE GUESS WHO	1976	PIP	US	6804	
CHAD ALLAN V (	(C) WHEATFIELD SOUL	1969	RCA	US LSP 4141		ANLI 1171
	(C) WHEATFIELD SOUL	1969	RCA		UK SF	8037
JIM KALE B (T	(D) CANNED WHEAT	19	RCA	US LSP 4157		ANLI 0986
KURT WINTER G (	(E) AMERICAN WOMAN	19	RCA	US LSP 4574	UK SF	8107
GREG LESKIW G (	(F) SHARE THE LAND	19	RCA	US LSP 4359	UK SF	8153
BILLY WALLACE B (N	(G) SO LONG BANNATYNE	19	RCA	US LSP 4574	UK SF	8216
DOMENIC TROIANO G (N	(H) ROCKIN'	19	RCA	US LSP 4602	UK SF	8269
DON McDOUGAL G (T	(H) ROCKIN'	197	RCA			ANLI 2683
ALLAN McDOUGALL V (T	(I) LIVE AT THE PARAMOUNT	1973	RCA	US LSP 4779	UK SF	8329
DAVID PARASZ HRNS (T	(J) TEN	1974	RCA	US APLI 0130		
DAVID INGLIS G (T	(K) ARTIFICIAL PARADISE	1974	RCA	US LSP 4830	UK SF	8349
VANCE MASTERS V D (T	(L) ROAD FOOD	1974	RCA	US APLI 0405		
	(M) FLAVOURS	1975	RCA	US APLI 0636	UK SF	8399
	(N) POWER IN THE MUSIC	1975	RCA	US APLI 0995	UK RS	1017
	(O) BEST OF THE GUESS WHO	1971	RCA	US LSPX 1004	UK AFLI2594	
	(P) BEST OF VOL 2	1974	RCA	US APLI 0269		
	(Q) GREATEST	19	RCA	US APLI 2253		
	(R) BORN IN CANADA	1976	WAND		691	
	(S) HISTORY OF	19	PRIDE		0012	
	(T) ALL THIS FOR A SONG	1979	AQUARIUS		AQR 522	
	(U) WILD ONE	19	PICKWICK US 3246			
	(V) GUESS WHO	19	PICKWICK US 3240			

G116 GIB GUILBEAU

GIB GUILBEAU FDL (ALL	GIB GUILBEAU	1973	ALSHIRE	US	AS 209
	CAJUN COUNTRY	197	ALSHIRE	US	S 5121
	CAJUN COUNTRY	1975	ARIOLA		87147
	TOE TAPPIN' MUSIC	1979	SHILOH	US	4085

G116A ISAAC GUILLORY

ISAAC GUILLORY G V B K (A   (A) ISAAC GUILLORY   1974 ATLANTIC   UK   K 40521
SAM GOPAL TABLAS(A
JIM CAREY D (A   FRED GANDY B (A   MOX HCA (A   JIM COLE B V (A
CATHY HALL FLT (A   JIM FAIRS G DULC (A   JOHNSE HOLT G (A   PETE GAVIN D (A
ROGER POPE D (A

G116B GUITAR SLIM

JAMES(GUITAR SLIM) STEPHENSON G V(ALL	(A) THINGS I USED TO DO	19	SPECIALTY	US	2120
ALSO USED NAME GUITAR SLIM GREEN	(B) STONE DOWN BLUES	19	UNITED	US	7764
	(C) GREENSBORO ROUNDER	1977	FLYRIGHT	UK	LP 538

GULLIVER

DARYL HALL	K V	(A	(A) GULLIVER		1969 ELEKTRA US 74070+1970 UK 2410006	
JIM HELMER	D	(A				
TIM MOORE	G V	(A	TOM SELLERS	B K	(A	

GUN

ADRIAN CURTIS(GURVITZ)	G	(AB	(A) GUN	1968 CBS	US 26468	+ UK	63552
PAUL CURTIS(GURVITZ)	B	(AB	(B) GUNSIGHT	1969 CBS	US 26551	+ UK	62683
LOUIS FARRELL	D	(A			
PETER DUNTON	D	(	TIM MYCROFT	(

ARTHUR GUNTER

ARTHUR GUNTER		(A) BLACK & BLUES	19	CONTEMPO UK119+EXCELLO US 8017
		(B) BLUES AFTER HOURS	19	BLUE HORIZON 2431 012

GURU GURU

MANI NEUMEIER	D K	(CFJLMN	(A) UFO	19	OHR	GERM	556005
ULI TREPLE	B	(C	(B) HINTEN	19	OHR	GERM	556027
AX GENRICH	G	(CFJM	(C) KAN GURU	1972	BRAIN		1007
SEPP JANDRISITS	G	(JLM	(D) GURU GURU	197	BRAIN		1025
JOGI KARPENKIEL	B	(JLM	(E) LIVE	1973	BRAIN		0080 018
HELMUT HATTLER	B	(JM	(F) THIS IS GURU GURU	1973	BRAIN		200 145
PETER WOLFBRANDT	G	(J	(G) DER ELEKTROLURCH	1974	BRAIN		2 1057
JAN FRIDE	K	(J	(H) DANCE OF THE FLAMES	1974	ATLANTIC		K50044
INGO BISCHOF	K	(JLMN	(J) MANI UND SEINE FREUNDE	1975	ATLANTIC		K50157
TOMMY GOLDSCHMIDT PERC	(JLM		(K) DONT CALL US	1975	ATLANTIC		K50022
MOEBI MOEBIUS	K	(J	(L) TANGO FANGO	1976	BRAIN		1089
ACHIM RODELIUS	K	(J	(M) GLOBETROTTER	1977	BRAIN		0060 039
GERD DUDECK	WIND	(J	(N) HEYDU	1979	BRAIN		0060 187
CHAMPION JACK DUPREE K	(J					
CHRISTA FAST	(	PETER KUHMSTEDT	B	(MN ROLAND SCHAEFFER	SYN G(LMN HOUSCHANG NEJADEPOUR G(H	
CONNY PLANK	G K	(HANS HARTMANN	B	(H GERALD LUCIANO HARTWIG B(N MICHAEL PITZ	CLAR(M	
KARLA VON SINNEN B	(N BUTZE FISCHER	D PERC(N BRUNO SCHABB	B	(F		

ADRIAN GURVITZ

ADRIAN GURVITZ	G V	(A	(A) SWEET VENDETTA	1979	JET	UK	JETLP 220
JOE PORCARO	PERC	(A	(B) IL ASSASSINO	1980	JET	UK	JETLP 226
JEFF PORCARO	D	(A				
ED GREENE	D	(A RICK SCHLOSSER	D	(A DAVID HUNGATE	G (A DAVID SHIELDS	B (A
FRED TACKETT	G	(A STEVE PORCARO	K	(A DAVID PAICH	PNO (A STEVE LEEDS SAX FLT(A	
DICK HYDE	TROM	(A CHUCK FINDLEY	TPT	(A STEVE MADAIO	TPT (A JERRY HEY TPT	(A
EARL LON PRICE	SAX	(A PAUL GURVITZ	V	(AB JOE PORCARO	PERC (A	

ARLO GUTHRIE

ARLO GUTHRIE	G V	(ALL	(A) ALICES RESTAURANT	1967 REPRISE	US 6267	UK K44045	
KEVIN BURKE	FDL	(H	(B) ARLO	1968 REPRISE	US 6299	UK K44052	
JIM KELTNER	D	(H	(C) RUNNING DOWN THE ROAD	1969 REPRISE	US 6246	UK K44071	
BOB GLAUB	B	(H	(D) WASHINGTON COUNTY	1970 REPRISE	US 6411	UK K44099	
JESSE ED DAVIS	G	(H	(E) ALICES RESTRAURANT (SOUNDTRACK)	1970 UA		UAS 29061	
JIM GORDON	K	(H	(F) ARLO GUTHRIE (COMP)	1972 CHARTER LINE	IT 24003		
GEORGE BOHANON	HRNS	(H	(G) HOBOES LULLABYE	1972 REPRISE	US 2060	UK K44169	
DICK HYDE	TROM	(H	(H) LAST OF THE BROOKLYN COWBOYS	1973 REPRISE	US 2142	UK K44236	
GENE COE	HRNS	(H	(I) ARLO GUTHRIE	1974 REPRISE	US 2183	UK K54019	
NICK DECARO	ACC	(H	(J) TOGETHER (DBL) LIVE)	1975 REPRISE	US 2214	UK K64023	
JERRY WIGGINS	D	(H	(K) AMIGO	1975 REPRISE	US 2239	UK K54077	
PETE SEEGER	G V	(J	(L) OUTLASTING THE BLUES	1979 WB	US 3336	UK K56658	
DOYLE SINGER	B MAND(H		( ) THE BEST OF	1977 WB	US 3117	UK K56431	
DON RICH	G FDL(H		( ) STAR COLLECTION	197 MIDI		UK 4003	
BUDDY ALAN	G	(H				
BOB MORRIS	G	(H JIM SHAW	PNO	(H DON CHRISTLIEB	WIND (H BUDDY COLLETTE	CLAR (H
JERRY BRIGHTMAN STEEL	(H WILLIAM GREEN	OBOE	(H ERNIE WATTS	FLT (H LEE SKLAR	B (H
RY COODER	G	(H JOHN PILLA	G	(H GENE PARSONS	D (H THAD MAXWELL	B (H
DOUG DILLARD	BANJO(H	GIB GUILBEAU	FDL	(H CLARENCE WHITE	G (H GRADY MARTIN	G (H
RICHARD HAYWARD	D	(H CHUCK RAINEY	B	(H MIKE UTLEY	ORG (H JESSIE SMITH	V (H
CLYDIE KING	V	(H VANETTA FIELDS	V	(H GENE MERLINO	V (H THURLE RAVENSCROFT	V (H
ROBERT TEBOW	V	(H BILL COLE	V	(H TERRY A LA BERRY	(L STEVE IDE	(L
DAVID GROVER	(L	DAN VELIKA		(L CAROL IDE	(L	

BUDDY GUY

BUDDY GUY	G V	(ALL	(A) HOODOO MAN BLUES	1966	DELMARK		612
JUNIOR WELLS	HCA V(JKM		(B) ITS MY LIFE BABY	1966	VANGUARD		VSD 79231
ERIC CLAPTON	G	(J	(C) COMING AT YOU	1968	VANGUARD 5VRL19001	VSD 79262	
DR JOHN	PNO	(J	(D) A MAN AND HIS BLUES	1968	VANGUARD 5VRL19002	VSD 79272	
J GEILS BAND		(J	(E) I LEFT MY BLUES IN SAN FRANCISCO	1968	CHESS 1527 BELLAPHON	4069	
LONNIE TAYLOR	D	(DH	(F) BLUES TODAY	1968	VANGUARD 5VRL 19004		
MIKE UTLEY	K	(J	(G) THIS IS BUDDY GUY } SAME?	196	VANGUARD 5VRL 19008 VSD 79290		
TIM KAIHATSU	G	(DH	(H) HOT & COOL	1979	VANGUARD		VSD 79290
JACK MYERS	D	(DHJKLM	(I) HOLD THAT PLANE	1972	VANGUARD		VSD 79323
GLENWAY McTEER	D	(GH	(J) & JUNIOR WELLS PLAY THE BLUES	1972	ATLANTIC	K 40240	
NORMAN SPILLER	TPT	(GH	(K) I WAS WALKING THROUGH THE WOODS	19	CHESS	LP 409	
BOBBY FIELD	SAX	(DGH	(L) IN THE BEGINNING(58/64)	1971	RED LIGHTNING	RL 001	
JUNIOR MANCE	PNO	(H	(M) GOT TO USE YOUR HEAD	1979	BLUES BALL	2005	
GARY BARTZ	SAX	(HI	(N) DOLLAR DONE FELL	1980	JSP	1009	
MARK JORDAN	K	(I	(EP) CRAZY MUSIC	1965	CHESS	CRE 6004	
LEROY STEWART	B	(J	(EP) WITH THE BLUES	1965	CHESS	CRE 6009	
BARRY ALTSCHUL	D	(IJ				
JUKE JOINT JIMMY	(J	LESLIE CRAWFORD	SAX	(GH SETH JUSTMAN	PNO (J GEORGE ALEXANDER	TPT(GH
J W WILLIAMS	B	(N ERNEST JOHNSON	B	(M WAYNE BENNETT	G (DG AL DUNCAN	D (M
CLIFTON JAMES	D	(M ROBERT NIGHTHAWK	G	(M FRED BELOW	D (DKLHM SONNY BOY WILLIAMSON HCA(LM	
FREEBO	B	(I ROOSEVELT SHAW	D	(J CARL RADLE	B (JL STEPHEN BLADD	D (J
MAGIC DICK	HCA	(I LAFAYETTE LEAKE	PNO	(MKL A C REED	SAX (GHIJ PHILIP GUY	G (HJN
JESSE LEWIS	D	(HI OTIS SPANN	PNO(DHKLM	AARON CORTHEN	SAX (DH PHIL THOMAS	D (LM
DAVID RIP STOCK	D	(I BILL FOLWELL	B	(I JIM GORDON	D (J DANNY KLEIN	B (J

(CONTINUED)

G122 (CONTINUED)   BUDDY GUY

GERRY GIBSON	SAX	(KLM	BOB NEELY	SAX	(LM	MACK EASTER	B	(L	OTIS RUSH		G	(L
WILLIE DIXON	B	(L	ODIE PAYNE	D	(L	DONALD HANKINS	SAX(DHLM		SONNY TURNER		TPT(LM
MURRAY WATSON	TPT	(LM	ABE LOCKE	SAX	(LM	LEFTY BATES	G	(LM	LITTLE PHIL SMITH		G	(N
RAY ALLISON	D	(N										

G122A   DENNY GUY

DENNY GUY	V	(A	(A) DENNY GUY				1972	DAY BREAK		DR	2008
RANDALL ATON	B	(A									
JOHN MILLIKEN	D	(A	JAMES JEFFERS	G	(A	THOMAS GUY	G	(A	EMPERADOR ATON	D	(A

G123   GWENDAL

BRUNO BARRE	VLN	(AB	(A) GWENDAL		1974	PATHE	FR	064 12725
JEAN MARIE RENARD	G	(AB	(B) GWENDAL 2		1975	PATHE	FR	064 13075
YOUENN LEBERRE	WIND	(AB						
PATRICE GRUPALLO	MAND PERC(AB	ROGER SCHAUB	B G	(AB				

G124   GYPSY

ROBIN PIZER	G V	(AB	(A) GYPSY				1971	UA	UK	UAS 29155
MOTH SMITH	D	(AB	(B) BRENDA & THE RATTLESNAKE				1972	UA	UK	UAS 29420
ROD READ	G V	(A								
DAVID McCARTHY	B V	(AB	JOHN KNAPP	V G K	(AB	RAY MARTINEZ	G V	(B	RAY COOPER	PERC (B

H1   H P LOVECRAFT

GEORGE EDWARDS	V G B(AB		(A) H P LOVECRAFT				1967	PHILIPS	BL 7830+6336210+600252
DAVE MICHAELS	K V	(AB	(B) H P LOVECRAFT2				1968	PHILIPS	SBL7872+6336213+600279
TONY CAVALLARI	V G	(AB							
JERRY McGEORGE	V B	(A	MICHAEL TEGZA	V D	(ABC	JEFF BOYAN	B	(B	LEN DRUSS	HRNS(A
RALPH CRAIG	TROM	(A	HERB WEISS	TROM	(A	CLYDE BACHAND	TUBA	(A	BILL TRAUB	WIND(A
EDDIE HIGGINS	VIBES(A		PAUL TERVELT	HRNS	(A	JACK HENNINGBAUM	HRNS	(A		

H2   HABIBIYYA

ROGER POWELL		(A	(A) IF MAN BUT KNEW		1972	ISLAND	HELP.7
IAN WHITEMAN		(A					
MIKE EVANS		(A					

H3   HACKENSACK

PAUL MARTINEZ	B	(A	(A) UP THE HARDWAY		1974	POLYDOR	2383 263
RAY SMITH	G	(A						
NICKY MOORE	V	(A	SIMON FOX	D	(A			

H4   STEVE HACKETT

STEVE HACKETT	V G K(ALL		(A) VOYAGE OF THE ACOLYTE		1975	CARHISMA	UK	CAS1111	US	1176
PHIL COLLINS	D V	(A	(A) VOYAGE OF THE ACOLYTE		197	PHONOGRAM			EURO	9103 106
JOHN HACKETT	FLT K(ABC1		(B) PLEASE DONT TOUCH		1978	CHARISMA	UK	CAS4012	US	1112
JOHN ACOCK	K	(AB	(B) PLEASE DONT TOUCH		197	PHONOGRAM			EURO	9103 122
MIKE RUTHERFORD	B	(A	(C) SPECTRAL MORNINGS		1979	CHARISMA	UK	CDS4017		
SALLY OLDFIELD	V	(A	(D) DEFECTOR		1980	CHARISMA	UK	CDS4018		
PETER HICKS	V	(1C	(1) 1978 TOUR							
DIK CADBURY	B	(1C								
ROBIN MILLER	WIND	(A	NIGEL WARREN-GREEN	CELLO(A	PERCY JONES	B	(A	JOHN GUSTAFSON	B	(A
RANDY CRAWFORD	V	(B	RICHIE HAVENS	V PERC(B	STEVE WALSH	V	(B	DAVE LEBOLT	K	(B
JOHN SHEARER	D	(C1	HUGH MALLOY	CELLO(B	CHESTER THOMPSON	PERC(B		PHIL EHART	PERC(B
JAMES BRADLEY	PERC (B		TOM FOWLER	B	(B	GRAHAM SMITH	VLN	(B	NICK MANUS	K	(C

H5   SAMMY HAGAR

SAMMY HAGAR	G V	(ALL	(A) NINE ON A TEN SCALE		1976	CAPITOL	UK	EST 11489
BILL CHURCH	B	(ABC	(B) SAMMY HAGAR		1977	CAPITOL	UK	EST 11599
ALAN FITZGERALD	K	(ABC	(C) MUSICAL CHAIRS		1978	CAPITOL	UK	EST 11706
DENNIS CARMASSI	D	(C	(D) ALL NIGHT LONG(LIVE)		1978	CAPITOL	UK	EST 11812
SCOTT QUICK	G	(A	(E) STREET MACHINE		1979	CAPITOL	UK	EST 11983
JERRY SHIRLEY	D	(A	(F) HARDER,FASTER		1979	CAPITOL	UK	EST 12013
JIM HODDER	D	(A	(G) DANGER ZONE		1979	CAPITOL	UK	EST 12069
AYNSLEY DUNBAR	D	(A	(H) LOUD & CLEAR (COMP)		1980	CAPITOL	UK	EST 25330
DALLAS TAYLOR	D	(A						
VANETTA FIELDS	V	(A	SHIRLEY MATTHEWS	V	(A	MAXAYN LEWIS	V	(A	WIZARD STAN	K	(A
JOE CRANE	K	(A	DAVID LEWARK	G	(B	JOHN BLAKELEY	G	(A	MIC GILLETTE	HRNS(A
GREG ADAMS	HRNS (A		EMILIO CASTILLO	HRNS	(A	STEVE KUPKA	HRNS	(A	LENNY PICKETT	HRNS(A
SCOTT MATTHEWS	D	(B	GARY PIHL	G	(				

H5A   NINA HAGEN BAND

NINA HAGEN	V	(	(A) NINA HAGEN BAND		1978	CBS	UK	83136
HEIL	K V	(	(B) UNBEHAGEN		1979	CBS	UK	84159
MITTEREGGER	D V	(					
POTSCHKA	G V	(	PRAEKER	B G V	(		

H5B   HAIR

PETER ROINAES	D	(A	(A) PIECE		1970	COLUMBIA	SCX 6452
ALLEN SORENSEN	B	(A					
BENNY DYHR	G	(A	PADDY GYTHFELDT	K G	(A		

H6   BILL HALEY

BILL HALEY	G V	(							
RUDY POMPELLI	SAX	(							
FRANCIS BEECHER	G	(	JOHN GRANDE	K	(	BILLY WILLIAMSON	STEEL(	AL REX	B	(
DON RAYMOND		(							

BILL HALEY & THE COMETS	19	DECCA	US	2670	TWISTING KNIGHTS	196	ROULETTE	US	25174
" " " "	19	WB	US	1378	ROCKIN' THE OLDIES	1962	ACE OF HEARTS	UK	AH 35
HALEYS JUKE BOX	19	WB	US	1391	ROCKIN' AROUND THE WORLD	19	DECCA	US	8569
SHAKE RATTLE & ROLL 10"	19	DECCA	US	5560	ROCKIN' AROUND THE WORLD	19	DECCA	US	8692
ROCK AROUND THE CLOCK	195	BRUNSWICK UK			ROCKIN' THE JOINT 10"	19	DECCA	US	8775
" " " "	19	DECCA	US	8225	" " "	1979	ROLLERCOASTER UK		2002
" " " "	1970	HALLMARK	UK	SHM 668	" " "	196	LONDON	US	HAF 2037
" " " "	1971	CORAL		CP 55	CHICKS	1964	ACE OF HEARTS	UK	AH 66
" " " "	1974	CORAL		CDL 8017	"	19	BRUNSWICK UK	STA	3011
" " " "	1974	CORAL	UK	CRLM 1039	"	19	DECCA	US	8821
" " " "	19	ACE OF HEARTS	UK	AH 13	HE DIGS ROCK'N'ROLL	19	DECCA	US	8315
ROCK 'N' ROLL STAGE SHOW	19	DECCA	US	8345	STRICTLY INSTRUMENTAL	196	BRUNSWICK UK	LAT	8326
									(CONTINUED)

BILL HALEY

STRICTLY INSTRUMENTAL	196	DECCA	US		8964	RAZZLE DAZZLE	19	JANUS	US	7003
GREATEST HITS	1968	MCA	US		161	ROCK 'N' ROLL DANCE PARTY	19	SUMMERSET	US	4600
ON STAGE	1970	HALLMARK	UK	SHM	694	ROCK WITH	19	TRANSWORLD	US	202
ROCK'N'ROLL	19	GNP	US		2077	JUST ROCK'N'ROLL MUSIC	1973	SONET	UK	SNTF 645
ROCK AROUND THE COUNTRY	1971	SONET	UK	SNTF	623	KING OF ROCK'N'ROLL MUSIC	1973	MUSIDISC		ALB 137
" " " "	197	GNP CRESCENDO	US		2097	LIVE IN LONDON 74	1974	ATLANTIC	UK	K 51501
" " " "	1974	HALLMARK	UK	SHM	837	RARE ITEMS	1975	MCA		COPS72741/2
GOLDEN KING OF ROCK'N'ROLL	1972	HALLMARK	UK	SHM	773	ROCK ROCK ROCK	1975	MUSIDISC	CV	1072
KING OF ROCK	1973	EMBER	UK	EMB	3396	GOLDEN HITS	1974	MCA	UK	MCF 2555
" "	197	ALSHIRE	US		5313	" "	197	DECCA	US	7211
BILL HALEY & THE COMETS	19	VALIANT	UK	VS	103	R O C K	1976	SONET	UK	SNTF 710
RIP IT UP	19	MCA	UK	MUPS	318	ARMCHAIR ROCK'N'ROLL	1978	MCA	UK	MCF 2838
Mr ROCK'N'ROLL	19	EMBER	UK	EMB	3401	20 GOLDEN PIECES OF	1979	BULLDOG	UK	BDL 2002
TRAVELLING BAND	19	JANUS	US		3035	EVERYONE CAN ROCK'N'ROLL	1979	SONET	UK	SNTF 808

HALFBREED

MICK WHITTAKER	V	(A	(A) HALFBREED			1975	U A	UK UAG 29877
TOM FARRIER	G	(A						
JIM LOWERY	K	(A	GEOFF HUTCHINSON D	(A	FRANKIE GIBBON	B	(A	

DARYL HALL

DARYL HALL	V	(A	(A) SACRED SONGS	1980	RCA	PL 13573
ROBERT FRIPP		(A				

JOHN HALL

JOHN HALL	G V	(AB	(A) JOHN HALL	1978	ASYLUM	US 6E 117 UK K 53075
MICHAEL BRECKER	HRNS	(A	(B) POWER	197	ARC	US
LYNN PITNEY	V	(A				

GARLAND JEFFREYS	V	(A	JOEL TEPP	HCA	(A	JERRY LAWSON	V	(A	CHUCK RAINEY	B	(A
STEVE GADD	D	(A	JOE SAMPLE	K	(A	JIMMY HAYES	V	(A	BILL PAYNE	K	(A
SONNY BURKE	K	(A	DAVID LASLEY	V	(A	ARNOLD McCULLER	V	(A	TUBO	V	(A
ED GREENE	D	(A	PHILIP BALLOU	V	(A	DAVID SANBORN	SAX	(A	DAVID HUNGATE	B	(A
JAMES TAYLOR	V	(A	CARLY SIMON	V	(A	WILTON FELDER	V	(A	MILT HOLLAND	PERC	(A
DAVID PAICH	PNO	(A	LOWELL GEORGE	G V	(A	JAY OTIS WASHINGTON	V	(A	BONNIE RAITT	V	(A
JOSEPH RUSSELL	V	(A									

LANI HALL

LANI HALL	V	(ALL	(A) SUNDOWN LADY	1974	A&M	UK AMLS64359
CHARLES LOPER	TROM	(C	(B) HELLO ITS ME	1975	A&M	UK AMLS64508
LEW McCREARY	TROM	(C	(C) SWEETBIRD	1977	A&M	UK AMLH64647
TONY TERRAN	TPT	(B	(D) DOUBLE OR NOTHING	1979	A&M	UK AMLH64760
JOHN PISANO	G	(B				

PAPITO HERNANDEZ	B	(B	STEVE SCHAEFFER	D	(B	CLARENCE McDONALD	K	(B	VINCE CHARLES	PERC	(B
LARRY CARLTON	G	(BC	BOB FINDLEY	TPT	(B	WILTON FELDER	B	(B	MARK STEVENS	D	(B
PETE JOLLY	ACC	(B	HERB ALPERT	TPT PNO	(BC	JIM HUGHART	B	(B	MICHEL COLOMBIER	B	(BC
EMIL RICHARDS	PERC	(B	JULIUS WECHTER	PERC	(B	DAVE FRISHBERG	PNO	(B	BOB EDMONDSON	TROM	(B
MIKE MELVOIN	PNO	(B	JIM GORDON	D	(B	ERNIE McDANIELS	B	(B	NICK CEROLI	D	(B
JOHN AUDINO	TPT	(C	BOBBY SHEW	TPT	(C	LEE RITENOUR	G	(C	DENNIS BUDIMIR	G	(C
CHUCK DOMANICO	B	(CD	STAN CLARKE	B	(C	JIM KELTNER	D	(C	MILT HOLLAND	PERC	(C
MICHAEL BODDICKER	SYN	(C	GAYLE LEVANT	HARP	(C	DAVID DUKE	HRNS	(C	NEIL LARSEN	K	(D
BUZZ FEITEN	G	(D	PETER DONALD	D	(D	MANOLO BADRENA	PERC	(D	JERRY KNIGHT	B	(D
LERRY TOLBERT	D	(D	VINCENT DEROSA	HRNS	(C	ROBERT HENDERSON	HRNS	(C	EARL DUMLER	OBOE	(C
LANNY MORGAN	WIND	(C	CLIFFORD SHANK	FLT	(C	JEROME RICHARDSON	FLT	(C	STRING SECTION		(C

HALL & OATES

DARYL HALL	K V G	(ALL	(A) WHOLE OATES	1972	ATLANTIC	US 7242	UK 76 K50306
JOHN OATES	G V K	(ALL	(B) ABANDONED LUNCHEONETTE	1973	ATLANTIC	US 7269	UK K40534
CHRIS BOND	G K	(BDEG	(B) ABANDONED LUNCHEONETTE	197	ATLANTIC	US 19139	
TOM SCOTT	SAX	(EG	(C) WAR BABIES	1974	ATLANTIC	US 18109	UK K50086
GARY COLEMAN	PERC	(DEG	(D) HALL & OATES	1975	RCA	US APL1 1144	UK PL11144
GORDON EDWARDS	B	(B	(E) BIGGER THAN BOTH OF US	1976	RCA	US APL1 1467	UK PL11467
LELAND SKLAR	B	(DEG	(F) NO GOODBYES	1977	ATLANTIC		UK K50347
JIM GORDON	D	(DE	(F) NO GOODBYES	197	RCA	US AFLI 2802	UK PL12802
ED GREENE	D	(DE	(G) BEAUTY ON A BACK STREET	1977	RCA	US AFLI 2300	UK PL12306
EDDIE ZYNE	D	(	(H) ALONG THE RED LEDGE	1978	RCA	US AFLI 2894	UK PL12804
DAVE KENT	K V	(J	(I) PAST TIME BEHIND	1977	CHELSEA	US	547
TODD SHARP	G	(	(J) LIVE TIME	1978	RCA	US AFLI 2802	UK PL12802
STEPHEN DEAN	B	(	(K) X STATIC	1979	RCA	US AFLI 3494	UK PL13494
JIM GETZOFF	K	(E	(L) VOICES	1980	RCA		UK PL 13646
TOM HENSLEY	PNO	(E					

TODD RUNDGREN	G	(C	DON YORK	K	(C	JOHN SIEGLER	B	(C	JOHN WILCOX	D	(C
MIKE McCARTY	B	(A	JIM HELMER	D	(A	HUGH McCRACKEN	G	(B	BERNARD PURDIE	D	(B
RALPH McDONALD	PERC	(B	LARRY PACKER	FDL	(B	JOE FARRELL	SAX	(B	RICK MAROTTA	D	(B
RICHARD TEE	K	(B	GLORIA AGOSTINI	HARP	(B	JOHN BLAIR	VLN	(B	CLARENCE McDONALD	K	(D
SCOTT EDWARDS	B	(DEG	STEVE GELSAND	G B	(B	JERRY RICKS	G	(B	PANCHO MORALES	D	(B
PAT REBILLOT	K PERC	(B	MARK HORWITZ	BANJO	(B	MARVIN STAMM	HRNS	(B	MIKE BAIRD	D	(D
C O B	SYN	(	SANDY ALLEN	V	(D	JEFF PORCARO	D	(G	TONI MOTTOLA	V	(G
GAIL BOGGS	V	(C	KENNY PASSARELLI	B	(J	CALEB QUAYE	G	(J	ROGER POPE	D	(J
CHARLES DE CHANT	SAX K V	(J									

FERGUS HAMBLETON

FERGUS HAMBLETON	V K G B SAX	(A	(A) ALL THE RIGHT NOISES	1971	CAPITOL	CAN ST 6370
GREG HAMBLETON	V	(A				
ALVIN FALL	HRNS	(A	JACK TAYLOR	HRNS (A	STAN THERIAULT	B (A PAUL CLINCH D (A
+ STRINGS						

CHICO HAMILTON

CHICO HAMILTON	PERC D	(ALL	(A) PASSIN' THRU	19	IMPULSE	AS 29
BILL PAYNE	PNO	(I	(B) MAN FROM TWO WORLDS	19	IMPULSE	AS 59
LOWELL GEORGE	G	(I	(C) CHIC CHIC CHICO	19	IMPULSE	AS 82
KENNY GRADNEY	B	(I	(D) EL CHICO	19	IMPULSE	AS 9102
PAUL BARRERE	G	(I	(E) THE DEALER	19	IMPULSE	AS 9130
STU GARDNER	K	(I	(F) BEST OF	19	IMPULSE	AS 9174

(CONTINUED)

H10   CHICO HAMILTON

SAM CLAYTON	D	(I	(G) HIS GREAT HITS	19	IMPULSE		AS9213/2
JERRY AIELLO	K	(I	(H) WITH GERRY MULLIGAN	19	FANTASY		8082
ERIC DONALDSON	WIND	(K	(I) CHICO THE MASTER	1973	STAX		ENS 5701
DENNIS BUDIMIR	G	(K	(J) MONTREUX FESTIVAL	1975	STAX		STX 1029
CHARLES LLOYD	SAX	(K	(K) THAT'S JAZZ	1976	WB	UK	K 56239
ALBERT STINSON	B	(K					
WYATT RUTHER	G	(K	GABOR SZABO G (K NATHAN GERSHMAN CELLO (K GEORGE BOHANON TROM(K				

H11   CLAIRE HAMILL

CLAIRE HAMILL	V G K(ALL		(A) ONE HOUSE LEFT STANDING	1971	ISLAND	UK	ILPS9182
JOHN MARTYN	G	(A	(B) OCTOBER	1973	ISLAND	UK	ILPS9225
PAUL BUCKMASTER	CELLO(A		(C) STAGE DOOR JOHNNIES	1974	KONK	UK	101
DAVID LINDLEY	G	(A	(D) ABRACADABRA	1975	KONK	UK	104
JOHN HAWKEN	K	(A					
RAY WARLEIGH	FLT	(A	JACK EMBLOW ACC (A JOHN PIGNEGNY HRNS (A AUBREY JOHNSON OBOE(A				
PHIL BATES	B	(A	TERRY REID G V (A SIMON KIRKE D (A TETSU YAMAUCHI B (A				
RABBIT BUNDRICK	K	(A	WAYNE PERKINS G V (B JEAN ROUSSEL K (B TIM SMITH G V (B				
STEVE SMITH	K V	(B	CHRIS LAURENCE B (B ALAN WHITE D (B GERRY CONWAY D (B				
PAT DONALDSON	B	(B	HENRY SPINETTI PERC (B NICK SOUTH B (C PHILIP CHEN B (CD				
PAUL WESTWOOD	B	(C	DAVE ROWEBERRY K (C TIM HINKLEY K (C JIM FRANKS D (C				
CLEM CATTINI	D	(C	NEIL McBAIN D (C PHIL PALMER G (CD DIZ DISLEY G (C				
ROY NEVE	G	(C	LAURIE BROWN TPT (C ALAN HOLMES FLT (C JOHN HARTMANN K (D				
GARY RAY	D	(D	MEL COLLINS SAX (D DOREEN CHANTER V (D VICKY BROWN V (D				
TOM ROBINSON	V	(D	RAPHAEL DOYLE V (D HEREWARD KAYE V (D ALEX WELSH BAND (A				

H11A   HAMILTON FACE BAND

LENNY LAKS	V	'A	(A) AIN'T GOT NO TIME	1970	BELL		SBLL 132
RUTH UNDERWOOD	D	(A					
STEVEN MARGOSHES	PNO	(A	RONNIE SELDIN G (A ALAN COOPER B (A				

H12   JAN HAMMER

JAN HAMMER	K	(ALL	(A) LIKE CHILDREN	1974	ATLANTIC	UK K 50092 US NEMPEROR 430	
JERRY GOODMAN	VLN	(A	(B) FIRST SEVEN DAYS	1975	ATLANTIC	UK K 50184 US NEMPEROR 432	
JEFF BECK	G	(E	(C) OH YEAH	1976	NEMPEROR	UK K 50276 US	437
STEVE KINDLER	VLN	(BC	(D) MAKE LOVE	1976	BASF	GERM 20688	
FERNANDO SAUNDERS	B V	(CH	(E) LIVE WITH JEFF BECK	1977	CBS	UK 86025 US EPIC	34433
TONY SMITH	D V	(CH	(F) TIMELESS	197		US ECM	1047
DAVID EARLE JOHNSON	PERC(B		(G) MELODIES	197	EPIC	UK 82405 US NEMPEROR35003	
COLIN HODGKINSON	V	(H	(H) BLACK SHEEP	197)	ASYLUM	UK K 53089 US ASYLUM 6E173	
BOB CHRISTIANSON	V	(H					
GREGG GEYA CARTER	V	(H					

H13   PETER HAMMILL

PETER HAMMILL	V G K(ALL		(A) FOOLS MATE	1972	CHARISMA	UK	CAS 1037
GUY EVANS	D	(BCD	(B) CHAMELEON IN THE SHADOW	1972	CHARISMA	UK	CAS 1067
DAVID JACKSON	SAX	(BCEJ	(C) THE SILENT CORNER	1974	CHARISMA	UK	CAS 1083
HUGH BANTON	K	(BC	(D) IN CAMERA	1974	CHARISMA	UK	CAS 1089
NIC POTTER	B	(B	(E) NADIRS LAST CHANCE	1975	CHARISMA	UK	CAS 1099
PAUL WHITEHEAD	D	(D	(F) OVER	1977	CHARISMA	UK	CAS 1125
RANDY CALIFORNIA	G	(C	(G) FUTURE NOW	1978	CHARISMA	UK	CAS 1137
GRAHAME SMITH	VLN	(FJ	(H) VISION	1978	GTR	US	9211 1016
CHRIS SMITH	PERC V	(D	(J) P H 7	1979	CHARISMA	UK	CAS 1146
ROBERT FRIPP	G	(A					

H14   ALBERT HAMMOND

ALBERT HAMMOnD	G V	(ALL	(A) IT NEVER RAINS IN SOUTHERN CALIFORNIA	1973	MUM		MUM 65320
MIKE OMARTIAN	K	(B	(B) FREE ELECTRIC BAND	1973	MUM		MUM 65554
JIM GORDON	D	(B	(C) ALBERT HAMMOND	1974	MUM		MUM 80026
JOE OSBORN	B	(B	(D) 99 MILES FROM LA	1975	EPIC		80961
JAY LEWIS	G	(B	(E) WHEN I NEED YOU	1977	EPIC		81983
LARRY CARLTON	G	(B	(F) GREATEST HITS	1978	EMBASSY		31643
CAROL CARMICHAEL	V	(B					
SID SHARP	STRING(B						

H15   JOHN HAMMOND

JOHN HAMMOND	HCA G V	(ALL	(A) JOHN HAMMOND	1963	VANGUARD	US	2148
BILLY BUTLER	G	(BEQ	(B) BIG CITY BLUES	1964	VANGUARD	US	VSD 79153
JAMES SPRUILL	G	(BEQ	(B) BIG CITY BLUES	1964	FONTANA	UK	TFL 6046
JIMMY LEWIS	B	(BCEFQ	(C) SO MANY ROADS	1965	VANGUARD	US	VSD 79178
BOBBY DONALDSON	D	(BEQ	(C) SO MANY ROADS	1965	FONTANA	UK	TFL 6059
CHARLIE MUSSELWHITE	HCA(CEQ		(D) COUNTRY BLUES	1965	VANGUARD	US	VSD 79198
JAIME R ROBERTSON	G	(CEFQ	(E) MIRRORS	1968	VANGUARD	US	VSD 79245
LEVON HELM	D	(CEQ	(F) I CAN TELL	1968	ATLANTIC	US	SD 8152
MIKE BLOOMFIELD	G PNO	(CEQL	(G) SOONER OR LATER	1968	ATLANTIC	US	SD 8206
DR JOHN	K	(O	(H) SOUTHERN FRIED	1970	ATLANTIC	US	SD 8251
BILLY NICHOLS	B	(K	(K) SOURCE POINT	1971	CBS US 30458	UK	64365
EDDIE HINTON	G PNO(R		(L) LITTLE BIG MAN (SOUNDTRACK)	197	CBS US 30545		
RANDALL BRAMBLETT	K	(R	(M) WHEN I NEED	197	CBS US 30549		
KENNY BUTTREY	D	(R	(N) I'M SATISFIED	1972	CBS	UK	65051
TOMMY COGBILL	B	(R	(O) TRIUMVIRATE	1973	CBS	UK	65659
SPOONER OLDHAM	PNO	(R	(P) SPIRITUALS TO SWING	19	VANGUARD		VRS8523/4
LEONARD FEATHER	G	(F	(Q) BEST OF (SOUTHERN FRIED)	1974	VANGUARD		VSD 11/2
ROGER HAWKINS	D	(R	(R) CANT BEAT THE KID	1975	CAPRICORN	US	CP 0153
RICK DANKO	B	(F	(S) MY SPANISH ALBUM	19	CAYTRONICS	US	1493
BILL WYMAN	B	(F	(T) JOHN HAMMOND SOLO	197	VANGUARD	US	VSD 79380
JAN ZUKOWSKI	B	(V	(U) FOOTWORK	197	VANGUARD	US	VSD 79400
JIMMY THACKERY	G	(V	(V) HOT TRACKS	197	VANGUARD	US	VSD 79424
MARK WEINER	HCA	(V	(W) MILEAGE	1979	SONET	UK	SNTF 835
PETE RAYUSA	D	(V					
ERIC 'GARTH' HUDSON	ORG(CEQ	CHARLES OTIS D (FKW BOB MONSLTO PNO (W ROBBIE KONDOR PNO (W					
SHERMAN HOLMES	B	(W	SEE MIKE BLOOMFIELD ENTRY FOR FULL LINE UP ON(O)				

M15A   HANGMEN

	(A) BITTER SWEET	19	MONUMENT	US	MLP 8077

HANNIBAL   H16

ALEX BOYCE	V	(A	(A) HANNIBAL	1970	B&C	UK	CAS	1022
BILL HUNT	K HRNS(A							
ADRIAN INGRAM	G	(A	JACK GRIFFITHS	B	(A	JOHN PARKES	D	(A

RANDY HANSEN   H16A

RANDY HANSEN	G V	(A	(A) RANDY HANSEN	1980	CAPITOL	EST	12119
SCOTT ROSBURG	B V	(A					
CHARLES TAPP	D V	(A					

JUNIOR HANSON   H17

JUNIOR HANSON	G V	(AB	(A) NOW HEAR THIS	1973	MANTICORE	UK	K 43507
JEAN ROUSSEL	K	(A	(B) MAGIC DRAGON	1974	MANTICORE	US	MC 66677
CLIVE CHAMAN	B	(A					
CONRAD ISADORE	D	(A	LISLE HARPER	B	(A	REBOP KWAKU BAAH	PERC (A	JIMMY THOMAS	V	(A
KEN CUMBERBATCH	PNO	(A	CHRIS WOOD	FLT	(A	BOB TENCH	G V	(A	GODFREY MACLEAN	D V(A
NEIL MURRAY	B	(B	BROTHER JAMES	PERC	(B	GLEN LEFLEUR	D	(B	ANDRE LEWIS	K	(B
MARLO HENDERSON	G	(B	CASSANDRA	V	(B			

BO HANSSON   H18

BO HANSSON	G K B	(ALL	(A) LORD OF THE RINGS	1972		CHARISMA UK	1059
RUNE CARLSSON	D	(ABC	(B) MAGICIANS HAT	1973		CHARISMA UK	1073
GUNNAR BERGSTEN	WIND	(ABC	(C) ATTIC THOUGHTS	1975 SIRE US 7525	CHARISMA UK	1113
STEN BERGMAN	FLT	(ABC	(D) WATERSHIP DOWN	1977 SIRE US 6044	CHARISMA UK	1132
KENNY HAKANSSON	B G	(BCD					
ROLF SCHERRER	G	(BC	BOBO STENSSON	K	(B	OWE GUSTAVSSON	B	(B	PELLE EKMAN	D	(B
GORAN FREESE	SAX	(B	BILL OHRSTROM	CONGA(B	GORAN LAGERBERG	B G	(CD	THOMAS NETZLER	B	(CD
MATS GLENNGARD	VLN	(C	BO SKOGLUND	D	(D	TORBJORN EKLUND	FLT	(D	FREDRIK NOREN	D	(D
PONTUS OLSSON	PNO	(D					

HANSSON & KARLSSON   H18A

BO HANSSON	ORG	(AB	(A) SWEDISH UNDERGROUND	1967	POLYDOR	184 196
JAN KARLSSON	D	(AB	(B) GOLD (COMPILATION)	19	KARUSSELL	2468 009

HERBIE HANCOCK   H19

HERBIE HANCOCK	K V	(ALL	(A) MWANDISHI	1971 WB	US 1898	UK K 46077
EDDIE HENDERSON	TPT PERC(ACH1		(B) CROSSING	1972 WB	US 2617	UK K 46164
BILLY HART	D PERC(ACH		(C) SEXTANT	1972 CBS	US 32212	UK 65582
JULIAN PRIESTER	TROM	(AC1	(D) HEAD HUNTERS	1974 CBS	US 32731	UK 65928
BUSTER WILLIAMS	B PERC(ACH1		(E) THRUST	1974 CBS	US 32965	UK 80193
BENNY MAUPIN	WIND PERC(AC14		(F) TREASURE CHEST(DBL)	1974 EMI IMP	2WS 2807	
JACO PASTORIUS	B	(C	(G) BLOW UP (SOUNDTRACK+ YARDBIRDS)	19	MGM	US 4447
PATRICK GLEASON	SYN	(C	(H) FAT ALBERT ROTUNDA	1974 WB	US 1834	UK K 46039
VICTOR PONTOJA	CONGA(C		(I) MY POINT OF VIEW	197 BLUENOTE	BST84126
CANDY LOVE	V	(C	(J) INVENTIONS & DIMENSIONS	197 BLUENOTE	BST84147
SANDRA STEVENS	V	(C	(K) EMPYREAN ISLES	1964 BLUENOTE	BST84175
DELTA HORNE	V	(C	(L) HERBIE HANCOCK	1964 BLUENOTE US LA399	BST84190
VICTOR DOMAGALSKI	V	(C	(M) MAIDEN VOYAGE	197 BLUENOTE BNS 40020	BST84195
SCOTT BEACH	V	(C	(N) SPEAK LIKE A CHILD	1978 BLUENOTE BNS 40025	BST84279
RON CARTER	B	(Z14	(O) PRISONER	197 BLUENOTE	BST84321
TONY WILLIAMS	D	(Z14	(P) THE BEST OF	197 BLUENOTE	BST89907
FREDDIE HUBBARD	TPT	(1	(Q) DEATH WISH	1975 CBS	US 33199 UK	80546
WAYNE SHORTER	SAX	(1	(R) MAN CHILD	1975 CBS	US 33812 UK	69185
WAH WAH WATSON	G	(14	(S) LIVE IN JAPAN(DBL)	1975 CBS /SONY	SOP 98/99
RAY PARKER	B	(1	(T) SUCCOTASH	1975 BLUENOTE US LA152	
JOHNNY COLES	HRNS	(4	(U) WATER BABIES	197 CBS	UK	81741
PAUL JACKSON	B	(14	(V) HANCOCK	1975 BLUENOTE US LA399	
FREDDIE WASHINGTON	B	(4	(W) SECRETS	1976 CBS	US 34280 UK	81591
SHEILA ESCOVEDO	V	(4	(X) KAWAIDA	1976 DJM	UK	22008
JAMES LEVI		(1	(Y) FLOOD	1977 CBS	
KENNETH NASH	PERC	(1	(Z) HERBIE HANCOCK TRIO	1977 CBS	JAP25AP650
LEON CHANCLER	D	(A4	(1) V S O P (DBL)	1977 CBS	US 34976 UK	88235
JOSE AREAS	PERC	(A	(2) SUNLIGHT	1978 CBS	UK	82240
RONNIE MONTROSE	G	(A	(3) TAKIN' OFF	197 CBS		84109
JOHNNY COLES	HRNS	(H	(4) MR HANDY	1980 CBS	UK	84638
GARNETT BROWN	TROM	(H	(5) QUINTET	1977 CBS	UK	88273
TOOTIE HEATH	D	(H	(6) TEMPEST IN THE COLOSSEUM	1978 CBS/SONY	JAP 40 AP771/2
HARVEY MASON	D	(4	( ) FEETS DONT FAIL ME NOW	1979 CBS	UK	83491
ALPHONSE MOUZON	D	(4	( ) AN EVENING WITH	1979 CBS	UK	88329
BILL SUMMERS	PERC	(4	( ) LIVE UNDER THE SKY	1976 CBS/SONY JAP40AP 1037/875	
BYRON MILLER	B	(	( ) WITH DON CHERRY	1976 DJM	UK DJM22008

HAPPY THE MAN   H19A

KIT WATKINS	SYN K	(A	(A) HAPPY THE MAN	1976	ARISTA US 4120 UK	SPART1057
MICK BECK	PERC	(A				
RICK KENNELL	B	(A	STANLEY WHITAKER G V (A FRANK WYATT	WIND K V	(A

HAPSHASH & COLOURED COAT   H19B

TONY McFEE	G V	(A	(A) WESTERN FLYER	1969	LIBERTY	UK	83212
MICHAEL RAMSDEN	V	(A	(A) WESTERN FLYER	1969	IMPERIAL	US	LP 12430
ANDY RENTON	D	(A	(B) HUMAN HOST & THE HEAVY METAL KIDS	19	LIBERTY	UK	40001
MICHAEL MAYHEW	G	(A					
HEAVY METAL KIDS	PERC	(A	EDDIE TRIPP B (A FREDDIE BALLERINI	VLN(A	MIKE BATT	K	(A

HARCOURTS HEROS   H20

CHARLIE HARCOURT	G V	(A	(A) 1977 LINE UP
RAY JACKSON	V	(A	
MARTIN CRAGGS	SAX PERC (A	COLIN MASON	D (A BARRY SPENCE B V (A LES DODDS G (A

HARD ROAD   H20A

JOHN SPENCER	G	(A	(A) NO PROBLEM	1979	GOODSTUFF	UK	LP1002
KRIS GRAY	G V	(A				
HEANOR HUCKNALL	B	(A	RORY O'CARROLL	(A

HARD STUFF   H21

JOHN GUSTAFSON	B	(A	(A) BULLET PROOF	1972	PURPLE	UK	TPSA 7505
JOHN CANN	G	(A	(B) BOLEX DEMENTIA	1973	PURPLE	UK	TPSA 7507
PAUL HAMMOND	D	(					

H22 EDDIE HARDIN

```
EDDIE HARDIN      V K  (A      (A)YOU CANT TEACH AN OLD DOG NEW TRICKS 1977 ATTIC        UK   LAT  1023
LIZA STRIKE       V    (A      ( ) HOME IS WHERE YOU FIND IT           1972 DECCA        UK   TXS  106
HENRY SPINETTI    D    (A
IAN PAICE         D    (A  B J COLE    STEEL    (A  MO FOSTER    B  (A  HELEN CHAPELLE  V  (A
BARRY DE SOUZA    D    (A  ROGER GLOVER  PERC V (A  DORIS TROY   V  (A  RAY FLEMING    G V(A
DEE MURRAY        B    (A
```

H23 TIM HARDIN

```
TIM HARDIN        K V G(ALL    (A) TIM HARDIN 1                       1966 VERVE  UK 5018    US   3004
WARREN BERNHARDT  K    (F       (B) TIM HARDIN 2                       1967 VERVE  UK 6002    US   3022
BOB COHEN         G    (K       (C) THIS IS TIM HARDIN                 1967 ATCO   UK 588 082 US   33210
GARY KLAIN        K    (F       (D) LIVE IN CONCERT                    1968 VERVE  UK         US   3049
DONALD McDONALD   D    (F       (E) TIM HARDIN 4                       1969 VERVE  UK 6016    US   3064
MONTE DUNN        G    (F       (F) SUITE FOR SUSAN MOORE & DAMIAN     1970 CBS    UK 63571   US   9787
KEITH             TPT  (F       (G) THE BEST OF                        1970 VERVE  UK 2317003 US   3078
DAVID             SAX  (F       (H) BIRD ON A WIRE                     1970 CBS    UK 64335   US   30551
BUZZ              CELESTE (F    (I) PAINTED HEAD                       1973 CBS    UK 65209   US   31764
ANDY BOWN         B    (K       (J) ARCHETYPES                         1973 MGM               US   4952
PHILIPE           CONGA(F       (K) NINE                               1974 ANTILLES US 7023 GM UK  1004
JOHN MEALING      K    (K       (AB) TIM HARDIN 1&2                    1974 VERVE  UK 2683 048
BOB BUSHWELL      B    (A
MIKE DRISCOLL     D    (K  JIMMY HOROWITZ   K   (K  PETER FRAMPTON  G  (K  LESLEY DUNCAN   V  (K
LIZA STRIKE       V    (K  MADELINE BELL    V   (K  SUSAN GLOVER    V  (K  DAVID KATZ    STRINGS(K
JOHN SEBASTIAN    HCA  (A  GARY BURTON  VIBES  (A  PHIL KRAUSS   VIBES(A  BUDDY SALZMAN   D  (A
EARL PALMER       D    (A  WALTER YOST        B   (A
```

H24 HARDIN & YORK

```
EDDIE HARDIN      K V  (A      (A) TOMORROW TODAY                      1969 BELL  US 6043          UK SBLL 125
PETER YORK        D    (A      (B) WORLDS SMALLEST BIG BAND            1970 BELL                    UK SBLL 136
HERBIE FLOWERS    B    (A      (C) FOR THE WORLD                       1971 LONDON US 602 DECCA UK SKL 5095
MIKE HURST        G    (A      (D) POP HISTORY                         1972 POLYDOR               2625 021
MEL THORPE        HRNS (A      (E) AIN'T NO BREEZE                     197  PHONOGRAM              6360 622
VIC FLICK         G    (A
```

H25 HARDMEAT

```
MICK CARLESS      D PERC(A     (A) HARDMEAT                            1970 WB                     WS  1852
MICK DOLAN     G HCA V (AB     (B) THROUGH A WINDOW                    1970 WB WS 3008 US  UK  WS  1879
STEVE DOLAN       B G V(AB
IAN WHITEMAN    PNO FLT(A  BRUCE HOWARD      PNO  (A  PETE WESTBROOK  FLT  (B  PHIL JUMP  K  (B
```

H26 LINDA HARGROVE

```
LINDA HARGROVE    G V  (ALL    (A) MUSIC IS YOUR MISTRESS              1973 ELEKTRA   US  EKS 75063
BUDDY HARMON      D    (BA     (B) BLUE JEAN COUNTRY QUEEN             1974 ELEKTRA   US    7E1013
KENNY MALONE      D    (B      (C) LOVE,YOU'RE THE TEACHER             1975 CAPITOL   US  ST 11463
JERRY CARRIGAN    D    (BA     (D) JUST LIKE YOU                       1976 CAPITOL   US  ST 11564
BOB MOORE         B    (BA     (E) IMPRESSIONS                         1977 CAPITOL   US  ST 11685
TOMMY COGBILL     B    (B
LARRY BUTLER      PNO  (B  HARGUS'PIG'ROBBINS PNO (AB  BOBBY WOOD   PNO  (B  PETE DRAKE  STEEL   (AB
BOBBY BLACK       STEEL(B  PETE WADE     G    (B  JIMMY CAPPS   G  (B  DAVE KIRBY    G  (AB
REGGIE YOUNG      G    (B  RONNIE LIGHT  G    (B  LARRY BLACK   G  (B  GRADY MARTIN  G  (AB
JIMMY COLVARD     G    (BA  BUDDY SPICHER  FDL  (B  BOBBY THOMPSON  BANJO(BA  MARY HOLLADAY  V  (B
GINGER HOLLADAY   V    (B  LEA JANE BERINATI V  (B  JERRY SMITH   PNO  (A  JOE ALLEN     B  (A
MELBA MONTGOMERY  V    (A  GARY S PAXTON SINGERS (A  CHIP YOUNG    G  (A  JACK SOLOMON  G  (A
EARL BALL         K    (A  HENRY STRZELECKI  B  (A  ANITA GROUPS SINGERS (A  KARL HIMMEL  D  (A
HAROLD BRADLEY    G    (A  SHELLEY KURLAND STRINGS(A
```

H26A STEVE HARLEY & COCKNEY REBEL

```
STEVE HARLEY      V    (ALL    (A) THE HUMAN MENAGERIE                 1974 EMI            UK  EMA  759
STUART ELLIOTT    D    (ABEFGK1 (B) PSYCHOMODO                         1974 EMI US 11330   UK  EMC 3033
JEAN PAUL CROCKER VLN (ABEFK   (C) BEST YEARS OF OUR LIVES            1975 EMI US 11394   UK  EMC 3068
PAUL JEFFREYS     B    (ABFK    (D) TIMELESS FLIGHT                    1976 EMI US 11500   UK  EMA  775
MILTON REAME JAMES K  (ABFK    (E) LOVE IS A PRIMA DONNA              1976 EMI US 11596   UK  EMC 3156
JIM CREGAN        G    (EFK     (F) A CLOSER LOOK                      1976 EMI US 11456
GEORGE FORD       B    (EFGK    (G) FACE TO FACE                      1977 EMI US 11661   UK  EMSP 320
DUNCAN McKAY      K    (EFGK    (H) HOBO WITH A GRIN                  1978 EMI            UK  EMC 3254
LINDSAY ELLIOTT   PERC (EGK1    (J) CANDIDATE                         1979 EMI            UK  EMC 3311
JO PARTRIDGE      G    (EK1     (K)BEST OF STEVE HARLEY & COCKNEY R   1980 EMI            UK  EMC 3345
STUART CALVER     V    (G       (1) 1979 OCT CONCERT LINE UP
TONY RIVERS       V    (G
JOHN PERRY        V    (G  BILL PAYNE     PNO  (K  BOBBY KIMBALL   V  (K  JIMMY HOROWITZ  K  (1
BOB GLAUB         B    (K  GREG POREE     G    (K  BILL CHAMPLIN   V  (K  TOMMY KELLY     V  (K
JOHN GIBLIN       B    (1  NICO RAMSDEN   G    (1
```

H26B HARLIS

```
CHARLY MAUCHER    B V  (AB     (A) HARLIS                              1975 SKY                     001
WERNER LOHR       D V  (AB     (B) NIGHT MEETS THE DAY                 1976 SKY                     008
WOLFGANG KRANTZ   G    (AB
ARNDT SCHULZ      G    (AB
```

H27 HARMONIA

```
DIETER MOEBIUS    K    (AB     (A) HARMONIA                            1973    BRAIN               1044
JOACHIM ROEDELIUS K   (AB     (B) DE LUXE                             1975    BRAIN               1073
MICHAEL ROTHER    K    (AB     ( ) DINO                                197     BRAIN     GER  0040 116
```

H28 HARMONIUM

```
                               (A) L'HEPTADE                           19   CBS                 88234
```

H29 ROY HARPER

```
ROY HARPER        V    (ALL    (A) SOPHISTICATED BEGGAR                1967 STRIKE              SYB.7
BILL BRUFORD      D    (J       (A) SOPHISTICATED BEGGAR                1970 YOUNGBLOOD           SYB.7
HENRY McCULLOUGH  G    (K       (A) SOPHISTICATED BEGGAR                1972 BIRTH RAB.3 1977 BIGBEN 502
KEITH MOON        D    (        (B) COME OUT FIGHTING GHENGIS SMITH    1967 CBS          UK          63184
DAVE COCHRAN      G    (JK      (C) FOLKJOKEOPUS                       1969 LIBERTY      UK  LBS 83231
JIMMY PAGE        G    (        (C) FOLKJOKEOPUS                       1975 SUNSET       UK  SLS 50373
                                                                                         (CONTINUED)
```

```
JOHN HALSEY        D    (K       (C) FOLKJOKEOPUS                  19     WORLD PACIFIC   US            21888
RONNIE LANE        G B  (K       (D) FLAT BAROQUE & BERSERK        1970   HARVEST US 418  UK   SHVL     776
DAVE LAWSON        K    (K       (E) STORMCOCK                     1971   HARVEST         UK   SHVL     789
CHRIS SPEDDING     G    (J       (F) LIFE MASK                     1973   HARVEST         UK   SHVL     808
ANDY ROBERTS       G    (K       (G) VALENTINE                     1974   HARVEST         UK   SHSP     4027
KEITH EMERSON      K    (D       (G) VALENTINE                     1974   PATHE           FR   062      05531
BRIAN DAVISON      D    (D       (H) FLASHES FROM THE ARCHIVES     1974   HARVEST         UK   SHDW     405
LEE JACKSON        B    (D       (H) FLASHES FROM THE ARCHIVES     197    PATHE           FR   162      05736
TONY VISCONTI  RECORDER(D        (J) H Q                           1975   HARVEST         UK   SHSP     4046
STEVE BROUGHTON    K    (K        (J) H Q                          1975   PATHE           FR   066      05883
B J COLE        STEEL(K           (K) BULLINAMINGVASE              1977   HARVEST         UK   SHSP     4060
HERBIE FLOWERS     B    (K        (K) BULLINAMINGVASE              1977   PATHE           FR   068      06336
BRIAN GOFF              (K        (L) COMMERCIAL BREAK             1977   HARVEST         UK   SHSP     4077
PERCY JONES        B    (K        (M) THE EARLY YEARS             1977   EMBASSY         UK            31544
JIMMY McCULLOCH    G    (K        (N) ROY HARPER 70/75            1978   HARVEST         UK   SHSM     2025
WINGS                   (K        (O) WHEN AN OLD CRICKETER(J)    1975   CHRYSALIS       US            1105
RUSS               B    (C        (P) ONE OF THOSE DAYS IN ENGLAND(K)  19  CHRYSALIS      US            1138
DAVID BEDFORD      K    (EGJ      (Q) UNKNOWN SOLDIER             1980   HARVEST         UK   SHVL     820
MOX                     (C
CLEM               D    (C       (K) WITHDRAWN AFTER LEGAL ACTION(FEB 1979) ONE TRACK REMOVED
NICKY             PNO   (C
JOHN PAUL JONES         (C    SKAILA KANGA      (K    ALVIN LEE    G   (K    MAX MIDDLETON  K  (K
DAVE PLOWMAN            (K    DAVID GILMOUR     (J    STEVE BROUGHTON G V (J  RAY WARLEIGH   WIND(J
JANE                    (C   S FLAVIUS MERCURIUS G (E   GRIMETHORPE COLLIERY BAND(J
```

HARPERS BIZARRE   H30
```
TED TEMPLEMAN      G V  (ABCDE    (A) FEELIN' GROOVY                1967   WB              US   WS       1693
DICK SCOPPETTONE   G    (ABCDEF   (B) ANYTHING GOES                 1967   WB              US   WS       1716
EDDIE JAMES        G    (ABCDEF   (C) SECRET LIFE OF HARPERS BIZARRE 1968  WB              US   WS       1739
JOHN PETERSEN      D    (ABCDEF   (D) HARPERS BIZARRE 4             1969   WB              US   WS       1784
DICK YOUNT         B    (ABCDEF   (E) BEST OF                       1974   WB              US            K56044
                                  (F) AS TIME GOES BY               1976   FOREST BAY CO   US            7545
```

SLIM HARPO   H31
```
SLIM HARPO V HCA G(DIED 1970)ALL  (A) A LONG DRINK OF THE BLUES     1965   STATESIDE       UK   SL       10135
GUITAR GABLE       G    (DF       (B) HE KNEW THE BLUES             19     BLUE HORIZON    UK            763844
WARREN STORM       D    (F        (B) HE KNEW THE BLUES             19     EXCELLO         US            8013
FATS PERRODIN      B    (DF       (B) HE KNEW THE BLUES             1978   SONET           UK   SNTF     769
JERRY WEST         D    (D        (C) TIP ON IN                     19     PRESIDENT       US   PTS      1017
BOBBY McBRIDE      B    (F        (C) TIP ON IN                     19     EXCELLO         US            8008
JAMES JOHNSON      G    (D        (D) TRIGGER FINGER                1971   BLUE HORIZON    UK   2431     013
SAMMY K BROWN      D    (D        (E) BLUES HANGOVER                1976   FLYRIGHT        UK   LP       520
RUDOLPH RICHARD    G    (D        (F) GOT LOVE IF YOU WANT IT       1980   FLYRIGHT        UK   FLY      558
GEESE AUGUST       B    (D        (G) BABY SCRATCH MY BACK          19     EXCELLO         US            8005
CLARENCE ETIENNE   D    (F        (H) RAINING IN MY HEART           19     EXCELLO         US            8003
AUSTIN BROUSSARD   D    (F        (I) THE BEST OF                   19     EXCELLO         US            8010
AL FOREMAN         G    (F
MERTON THIBODEAUX PNO  (F    RUFUS THIBODEAUX  B   (F
```

CAREY BELL HARRINGTON   H32
```
CAREY BELL HARRINGTON V HCA(AB    (A) BLUES HARP                    19     DELMARK              DS       622
DAVE MYERS         B    (B        (B) LAST NIGHT                    1973   BLUESWAY             BLS      6079
WILLIE SMITH       D    (B
EDDIE TAYLOR       G    (B    JOE PERKINS K   (B
```

DERRICK HARRIOTT   H33
```
DERRICK HARRIOTT        (ALL      (A) UNDERTAKER                    19     TROJAN               TBL      114
                                  (B) PSYCHEDELIC TRAIN             19     TROJAN               TBL      141
                                  (C) REGGAE HITS                   1975   TROJAN               TRLS     116
```

DON 'SUGARCANE' HARRIS   H34
```
DON SUGARCANE HARRIS V FDL(ALL    (A) KEEP ON DRIVING               19     MUSIDISC 15060 +     MPS      68027
VOLKER KRIEGEL     G    (A        (B) FIDDLER ON THE ROCK           1970   BASF878         POLYDOR  2120878
TERJE RYPDAL            (A        (B) FIDDLER ON THE ROCK           19     MUSIDISC 15062 +     MPS      68028
NEVILLE WHITEHEAD  B    (A        (C) GOT THE BLUES                 19     POLYDOR              2121     283
ROBERT WYATT            (A        (C) GOT THE BLUES                 19     MUSIDISC 15079 +     MPS      68029
PAUL LAGOS         D    (BE       (D) CUPFUL OF DREAMS              19     POLYDOR              2121     792
HARVEY MANDEL      G    (B        (D) CUPFUL OF DREAMS              19                          MPS      68030
LARRY TAYLOR       B    (B        (E) I'M YOUR CASE                 19     MPS 2121912/7        MPS      68031
JOHNNY OTIS             (H        (F) FLASHIN' TIME                 19     SONOPRESSE064060204+ MPS      68032
SHUGGIE OTIS       G B  (H        (G) SUGARCANE                     19     EPIC     26524    +           30027
CLIFTON EDDIE      D    (E        (H) DON'SUGARCANE 'HARRIS         1970   EPIC     26286
DEWEY TERRY        K    (E
JAMES BRADSHAW     G    (E    RANDY RESNICK   G   (E    RICHARD APLANALP  SAX  (E    BILL SPRAGUE  TPT (E
DALNE VAIL         V    (E    ELSIE LEWIS         V   (E
```

EMMYLOU HARRIS   H35
```
EMMYLOU HARRIS     V G  (ALL      (A) GLIDING BIRD                  1969   JUBILEE         US   JGS      0031
BEN KEITH       STEEL(BC          (A) GLIDING BIRD                  1979   PYE             UK   PKL      5577
BYRON BERLINE FDL MAND (BC        (A) GLIDING BIRD                  19     AMOS            US            12052
JAMES BURTON       G    (BCDE     (B) PIECES OF THE SKY             1975   REPRISE US 2213 UK   K 54037
GLEN D HARDIN      K    (BCDE     (B) PIECES OF THE SKY             197    WB RI   US 2284
EMORY GORDY        B    (CDE      (C) ELITE HOTEL                   1976   REPRISE US 2236 UK   K 54060
JOHN WARE          D    (CDE      (D) LUXURY LINER                  1977   REPRISE US 2998
HANK DE VITO    STEEL(CDE         (D) LUXURY LINER                  1977   WB      US 3115 UK   K 56334
RODNEY CROWELL     G V  (CDE      (E) 1/4 MOON IN A TEN CENT TOWN   1978   WB      US 3141 UK   K 56443
ALBERT LEE         G V  (DE       (F) PROFILE          (COMP)       1978   WB      US 3258 UK   K 56570
RAY POHLMAN        G    (B        (G) BLUE KENTUCKY GIRL            1979   WB              UK   K 56627
RON TUTT           D    (BC       (H) CHRISTMAS ALBUM               19
HERB PEDERSEN G BANJ V (BCD       (J) HER BEST SONGS                1980   K TEL           UK   NE 1058
BERNIE LEADON V G BANJ (BC        (K) EVANGELINE                    1981   WB      US 3508 UK   K 56880
BRIAN AHERN        B G  (BCDE
RICK CUNHA         G    (BCD   RICHARD GREENE  FDL (B   FAY5SOUL STARLING V (BCDE  BILL PAYNE   K  (BC
                                                                                            (CONTINUED)
```

H35 (CONTINUED)

EMMYLOU HARRIS

BRUCE ARCHER	G	(AB	TOM GUIDERA	B	(B	DANNY PENDLETON	STEEL(B	RICKY SKAGGS FDL MAND(BD
DUKE BARDWELL	B	(B	AMOS GARRETT	G	(BC	MARK CUFF	D	(B	LINDA RONSTADT	V	(BC
DIANNE BROOKS	V	(CDE	JOHN STARLING	V	(C	JONATHAN EDWARDS	V	(C	MIKE AULDRIDGE	G	(CD
DOLLY PARTON	V	(D	NICOLETTE LARSON	V	(DE	MICK RAPHAEL	HCA (CDE		

H35A

HI TIDE HARRIS

HI TIDE HARRIS	V G	(AB	(A) CELEBRATING WITH HI TIDE HARRIS	1978	RCA	JAP	RVL 8031
JUNJI YAMAGISHI	G	(A	(B) GENTLEMANS BLUES	197	RCA	JAP	RVL
OSAMU ISHIDA	G	(A					
SHINJI SHIOTSUGU	G	(A	TADASHI KOBORI	B	(A	YU FUJII	B	(A	TERUO MATSUMOTO	D	(A
CHARLES SHIMIZU	K	(A	YASUHARU NAKANISHI	K	(A	TATSURO KONDO	K	(A	SHUICHI CHINO	K	(A
RYUICHIRO SENOO	HCA	(A	TETSU NAKAMURA	SAX	(A	JUNICHI KANEKAZI	TPT	(A	ICHIRO ARAI	HRNS (A

H36

JET HARRIS

| JET HARRIS | B | (A | (A) REMEMBERING | 1976 | DECCA | UK | REM.1 |
| TONY MEEHAN | D | (A | | | | | |

H37

SHAKEY JAKE HARRIS

SHAKY JAKE HARRIS	HCA V(AB	(A) FURTHER ON UP THE ROAD	1969	LIBERTY	UK	83217
KENNY COURTNEY	HCA	(A	(B) THE DEVIL'S HARMONICA	1972	POLYDOR	US 5014 UK	2391 015
WANDERING JOHN	PNO	(A					
LUTHER ALLISON	G	(A	ROBERT MOJO ELEM	B	(A	SUNNYLAND SLIM	PNO	(A	DENNY BRUCE	PERC(A
FRANCIS CLAY	D	(A	STEVE CUMMINS	PERC	(A	FREDDY ROBINSON	G	(B	LARRY TAYLOR	B	(B
RON SELICO	D	(B	PHIL PARKER	D	(B	ELLIOT INGBER	G	(B	JOHN MAYALL	G PNO(B

H37A

SHAUN HARRIS

SHAUN HARRIS	G V B(A	(A) SHAUN HARRIS	1973	CAPITOL	ST 11168
DAN HARRIS	G V	(A				
BEN BENAY	G	(A	DEAN PARKS	G	(A	BOBBY PHILLIPS	G	(A	HAL BLAINE	D	(A
JIM GORDON	D	(A	JOHN GUERIN	D	(A	JOHANNA HARRIS	K	(A	LARRY KNECHTEL	K	(A
MICHAEL OMARTIAN	K	(A	CAROL KAYE	B	(A	JOE OSBORN	B	(A	BRUCE JOHNSTON	V	(A

H37B

BILLY HARRISON

BILLY HARRISON	V G	(A	(A) BILLY WHO?;	1980	VAGABOND	GERM VRLP 8 80001
NIELS TABY	D	(A				
PETER URBAN	K	(A	MARTIN TIEFENSEE	B	(A	HANNES BAUER	G	(A	RAINER BAUMANN	G	(A

H38

DON HARRISON BAND

DON HARRISON	V G	(ABC	(A) DON HARRISON BAND	1976 ATLANTIC US 18111 UK K 50263
STU COOK	B V	(ABC	(B) RED HOT	1976 ATLANTIC US 18208 UK K 50340
DOUG CLIFFORD	D V	(ABC	(C) NOT FAR FROM FREE	1977 MERCURY US SRM11185 UK9100 044
RUSSELL DASHIELL	G V	(ABC		
JOHN TANNER	K	(B	MICHAEL CARROLL	B	(C	JEFF MORROW	K	(C	JOEL PESKIN SAX	(C
GARY GOSSETT	D	(C	KAREN FRIEDMAN	V	(C	NOVI NOVAG	VILA (C	DAN STICKLER	G	(C
PAT MATA	V	(C	MEMPHIS HRNS	(A		

H38A

GEFF HARRISON

GEFF HARRISON	V	(A	(A) TOGETHER	19	JUPITER	25595
PETER OEHLER	G V	(A				
ALAN WROE	B V	(A	ASTOR ASTOR	D V	(A	CHRIS KLOBER	K V	(A

H39

GEORGE HARRISON

GEORGE HARRISON	G V	(ALL	(A) WONDERWALL	1968 APPLE FRO66 90490	SAPCOR 1
ERIC CLAPTON	G	(CDFK	(B) ELECTRONIC SOUNDS	1969 ZAPPLE	ZAPPLE 1
JESSE ED DAVIS	G	(D	(C) ALL THINGS MUST PASS	1971 APPLE STCH639+PATHE 192 040789
RINGO STARR	D	(CDF	(D) CONCERT FOR BANGLA DESH	1972 APPLE STCX3385
JIM KELTNER	D	(DF	(E) LIVING IN A MATERIAL WORLD	1973 APPLE PAS10006	US 3410
KLAUS VOORMANN	B	(CDF	(F) DARK HORSE	1974 APPPLE PAS 10008	US 3418
BILLY PRESTON	K	(CDF	(F) DARK HORSE	1974 PATHE	FR 068 05774
LEON RUSSELL	K	(D	(G) EXTRA TEXTURE	1975 APPLE PAS 10009	US 3420
STEVE WINWOOD	K V	(K	(G) EXTRA TEXTURE	1975 PATHE	FR 068 05952
WILLIE WEEKS	B	(FK	(H) 33 1/3	1976 DARK HORSE K 56319+	US DH3005
ANDY NEWMARK	D	(FK	(J) BEST OF	1976 PARLOPHONE	UK 10011
GARY WRIGHT	K	(CF	(J) BEST OF	1976 PATHE	FR 068 06249
MICK JONES	G	(F	(J) BEST OF	1976 CAPITOL	US 11578
CHUCK FINDLEY	HRNS (F	(K) GEORGE HARRISON	1979 DARK HORSE K 56562+	US 3255
DERREK VAN EATON	V	(F		
ROGER KELLAWAY	PNO	(F	NICKY HOPKINS	PNO	(F	DAVE MASON	G V	(C	BOBBY KEYS SAX	(C
JIM PRICE	B	(C	BOBBY KEYS	SAX	(C	GINGER BAKER	D	(C	RON WOOD	G	(F
JIM HORN	FLT	(F	ROBBEN FORD	G	(F	PATTI HARRISON	V	(F	TOM SCOTT SAX	(F
LON VAN EATON	V	(F	EMIL RICHARDS	PREC (F	MAX BENNETT	B	(F	ALAN WHITE	D	(C
ALVIN LEE	G	(F	JOHN GUERIN	D	(F		

H40

MIKE HARRISON

MIKE HARRISON	V K HCA (ABC	(A) MIKE HARRISON	1971 ISLAND	UK	ILPS 9170
KEN IVERSON	D V	(A	(B) SMOKESTACK LIGHTNING	1972 ISLAND	UK	ILPS 9209
PETER BATEY	B	(A	(C) RAINBOW RIDER	1975 GOODEAR UK 7002+SONOPRESSE37007
IAN HERBERT	G V K(A		
FRANK KENYON	G V	(A	ARTHUR BELCHER	SAX	(A	PETER CARR	G	(B	JIMMY JOHNSON	G	(B
WAYNE PERKINS	G	(B	LUTHER GROSVENOR	G	(B	BARRY BECKETT	K	(B	CLAYTON IVEY	K	(B
DAVID HOOD	B	(B	HARRISON CALLOWAY	TPT	(B	MIKE STACEY	TPT	(B	HARRY THOMPSON	SAX (B
RONNIE EADES	SAX	(B	CHARLES ROSE	TROM (B	MORGAN FISHER	K	(C	KENNY BUTTREY	D	(C
MICKY JONES	G	(C	BOB COHEN	G	(C	WAYNE JACKSON	HRNS (C	KIRK LORANGE	G	(C
MEMPHIS HRNS	(C	NORBERT PUTNAM	B	(C	20TH CENTURY SINGERS	(C	CORONA STAGE SCHOOL	V(C

H41

WILBERT HARRISON

WILBERT HARRISON	V G	(ALL	(A) LETS WORK TOGETHER	1969	SUE US 8801	LONDON UK SH8415
			(B) BATTLE OF THE GIANTS(1 SIDE)	1962	JOY	JOYS191
			(C) KANSAS CITY	19	SPHERE	US 7000
			(D) WILBERT HARRISON	19	BUDDAH	US 5092
			(E) SOUL FOOD MAN	19	CHELSEA	US 523
			(F) ANYTHING YOU WANT	19	WET SOUL	US 1001
			(G) SHOOT YOU FULL OF LOVE	19	JUGGERNAUT	US 8803

MELANIE HARROLD

```
MELANIE HARROLD    V   (AB      (A) FANCY THAT(AS JOANNA CARLIN)   1977  DJM            DJF 20508
JERRY DONAHUE      G   (A       (B) BLUE ANGEL                     1979  DJM            DJF 20550
PAT DONALDSON      B   (A
JOHNNY VAN DERRICK VLN (A   TOMMY EYRE  K    (A   BOB HIRSCHMAN   TROM (A   HENRY SPINETTI  D    (A
GLEN LE FLEUR      D   (A   PETE ZORN  SAX FLT (A  KEITH NELSON    BANJO(A   PETE SOLLEY     K    (A
MICK MOODY         G   (A   MARTIN JAY  V    (A   GRAHAM SMITH    FDL  (B   JULIAN LITTMAN  G    (B
PAUL DI VINCI      V   (A   RICHARD BRUNTON G (A  BILL SKEET      K FLT(B   SIMON MORTON    PERC (B
MALCOLM GRIFFITHS TROM (B   BETSY COOKE  V   (B   ALBERT WING     SAX  (B   LIAM GENOCKEY   D    (B
```

HARSH REALITY

```
MARK GRIFFITHS    G  (A      (A) HEAVEN & HELL       1969  PHILIPS        SBL  7891
CARL BARNWELL     G  (A
ROGER SWALLOW     D  (A   CLIFF JENKINS      (A   STEVE MILLER   (A
```

BILLY HART

```
BILLY HART           (A      (A) ENCHANCE           1978  HORIZON        AMLJ 725
```

MICKEY HART

```
MICKEY HART     D V  (A      (A) ROLLING THUNDER    1972  WB   US 2635   UK   K 46182
STEPHEN STILLS  G V  (A
JOHN CIPOLLINA  V    (A   JERRY GARCIA  G   (A   CARMELO GARCIA TIMBALES (A   BOB WEIR   G V (A
STEVE SHUSTER   FLT  (A   BARRY MELTON  G   (A   BILL CHAMPLIN      K    (A   ALLA RAKHA       (A
TOWER OF POWER  HRNS (A   DAVID FREIBERG K G V B(A  ROBBIE STOKES   G    (A   GRACE SLICK  V   (A
PHIL LESH       V    (A   MIKE HINTON  MARIMBA (A   ZAKIR HUSSAIN   TABLA(A   SAM ANDREW   G   (A
PAUL KANTNER    V    (A   GREG ERRICO  D    (A   TERRY HAGGERTY     B    (A   NANCY HINTON MARIMBA(A
```

MIKE HART

```
MIKE HART            (AB     (A) MIKE HART BLEEDS           1970  DANDELION   UK     63756
                             (B) BASHER CHALKY PONGO & ME   1972  POLYDOR     UK   2310 211
```

TIM HART

```
TIM HART        G V  (A      (A) TIM HART             1979 CHRYSALIS   UK    CHR
RICK KEMP       B    (A
NIGEL PEGRUM    D    (A   VIC EMERSON  SYN  (A
```

TIM HART & MADDY PRIOR

```
TIM HART        G V  (ALL    (A) FOLK SONGS OF OLDE ENGLAND 1   1968  B&C         TE PEE TRM105
MADDY PRIOR     V    (ALL    (A) FOLK SONGS OF OLDE ENGLAND 1   19    ADRHYTHM         ARP 53
ANDY IRVINE     MAND (C      (A) FOLK SONGS OF OLDE ENGLAND 1   1974  MOONCREST      CREST 23
JOHN RYAN       B    ( C     (B) FOLK SONGS OF OLDE ENGLAND 2   19    ADRHYTHM         ARP 54
GERRY CONWAY    D    (C      (B) FOLK SONGS OF OLDE ENGLAND 2   1976  MOONCREST      CREST 26
PAT DONALDSON   B    (C      (B) FOLK SONGS OF OLDE ENGLAND 2   1968  TE PEE
                             (C) SUMMER SOLSTICE              1972  B&C            CAS 1035
                             (C) SUMMER SOLSTICE              1974  MOONCREST      CREST 12
```

JOHN HARTFORD

```
JOHN HARTFORD G FDL BAN(ALL  (A) LOOKS AT LIFE                  1967  RCA        US  LSP  3687
BENNY MARTIN       FDL  (KM  (B) EARTHWORDS & MUSIC             1967  RCA        US  LSP  3796
KENNY MALONE       D    (KM  (C) THE LOVE ALBUM                 1968  RCA        US  LSP  3884
DALTON DILLINGHAM  B    (K   (D) HOUSING PROJECT                1968  RCA        US  LSP  3998
ROY HUSKY JR       B    (MK  (E) GENTLE ON MY MIND              1968  RCA        US  LSP  4068
JIMMY COLVARD      G    (MK  (F) JOHN HARTFORD                  1969  RCA        US  LSP  4156
DALE SELLERS       G    (K   (G) IRON MOUNTAIN DEPOT            1970  RCA        US  LSP  4337
DAVID BRIGGS       K    (KM  (H) AERO PLAIN                     1971  WB         US        1916
BUDDY EMMONS       STEEL(KM  (I) MORNING BUGLE                  1972  WB         US        2651
SAM BUSH           V MAND(KM (J) MARK TWANG                     1976  FLYING FISH US       FF 020
MAC WISEMAN        V    (K   (J) MARK TWANG                     1976  SONET      UK  SNTF  700
LARRIE LONDIN      D    (M   (K) NOBODY KNOWS WHAT YOU DO       1976  FLYING FISH US       FF 028
CURLY SECKLER      V    (M   (K) NOBODY KNOWS WHAT YOU DO       1977  SONET      UK  SNTF  727
HENRY STRZELECKI   B    (M   (L) DILLARD HARTFORD DILLARD       1977  FLYING FISH US       FF 036
PIG ROBBINS        PNO  (M   (L) DILLARD HARTFORD DILLARD       1977  SONET      UK  SNTF  727
JACK GREENE        V    (N   (M) ALL IN THE NAME OF LOVE        1977  FLYING FISH US       FF 044
JEANNIE EELY       V    (N   (M) ALL IN THE NAME OF LOVE        1978  SONET      UK  SNTF  747
DIANE TIDWELL      V    (N   (N) HEADING DOWN INTO THE MYSTERY BELOW 78  FLYING FISH  US   FF 063
BILLY RAY REYNOLDS V    (N   (O) SLUMBERIN' ON THE CUMBERLAND   1979  FLYING FISH US       FF 095
LISA SILVER        V    (N

                             (L) FULL LINE UP IN DILLARD HARTFORD DILLARD ENTRY)
```

KEEF HARTLEY

```
KEEF HARTLEY     D   (ALL     (A) HALFBREED              1969 DERAM  UK SML 1037   US 18037
MILLER ANDERSON  G V (ABCDE   (B) BATTLE OF N W 6        1970 DERAM  UK SML 1054   US 18035
PETER DINES      K   (AD      (C) THE TIME IS NEAR       1970 DERAM  UK SML 1071   US 18047
SPIT JAMES       G   (AB      (D) OVERDOG                1971 DERAM  UK DSL    2   US 18057
GARY THAIN       B   (ABCDEF  (E) LITTLE BIG BAND        1971 DERAM  UK SDL    4
HENRY LOWTHER  VLN TPT(ABC    (F) SEVENTY SECOND BRAVE   1972 DERAM  UK SDL    9   US 13070
HARRY BECKETT    TPT (ABE     (G) LANCASHIRE HUSTLER     1973 DERAM  UK SDL   13
LYN DOBSON       WIND (ABE    (H) THE BEST OF    (DBL)   1974 DERAM  UK DPA 3011/2
CHRIS MERCER     SAX (ABEF    (I) THROUGHOUT THE YEARS (DBL)  197 LONDON          US 2 6001
MICK WEAVER      K   (BDFG
RAY WARLEIGH     FLT (B   MICK TAYLOR      G   (B   MIKE DAVIS     TPT (BE  DAVE CASWELL   TPT (CD
LYLE JENKINS     SAX (CD  BARBARA THOMPSON WIND (BE  STUART WICKS  K  (C   DEL ROLL       PERC(C
JOHNNY ALMOND    FLT (D   JON HISEMAN      D  (D    INGRID THOMAS  V  (D   JOAN KNIGHTON   V  (D
VALERIE CHARRINGTON V (D  PETE WINGFIELD  K V (F   JUNIOR KERR    G V (FG  NICK NEWELL WIND   (F
JESS RODEN       V   (G   JEAN ROUSSEL     K  (G    PHIL CHEN      B  (G   PETE GAGE       G  (G
ELKIE BROOKS     V   (G   ROBERT PALMER    V  (G    JIMMY JEWELL   SAX (BC  PETE YORK      PERC(E
DEREK AUSTIN     K   (E   ROGER WADE      SAX (E    MIKE ROSEN     TPT (E   TERRY NOONAN   TPT (E
MARTIN DROVER    TPT (E   DANNY ALLMARK   TROM (E   DEREK WADSWORTH TROM(E  JOHN MAYALL    V   (A
```

DAN HARTMAN

```
DAN HARTMAN V K G B  (ALL     (A) IMAGES            1976  BLUE SKY US 34322
EDGAR WINTER    HRNS (ABC      (B) INSTANT REPLAY   1978  BLUE SKY US 35641   UK 83265
HILLY MICHAELS  D    (BC       (C) RELIGHT MY FIRE  1979  BLUE SKY            UK 84073
BLANCHE NAPOLEON V   (BC
GE SMITH        G    (BC   LARRY WASHINGTON  CONGA(BC  VINNIE CUSANO  G V (B   JOHN WILCOX   D (A
JOHN SIEGLER    B    (A    RONNIE MONTROSE   G   (A   RICK DERRINGER G   (A   CARL HARTMAN    (A
```

(CONTINUED)

DAN HARTMAN

```
CLARENCE CLEMMONS SAX  (A   REVELATION      V     (A   TOM STROHMAN     FLT  (A   RANDY BRECKER     HRNS(A
GEORGE YOUNG      HRNS  (A   TONY POGANO  HRNS    (A   LARRY SADLER     D    (A   JOE ABBONDANZA    B   (A
JIMMY MAELEN      PERC  (C   STEVIE WONDER   HCA  (C   PHIL HOUGHTON    CONGA(C   LOLEATTA HOLLOWAY V  (C
BRIAN BRAKE       D     (C   CRAIG PEYTON    VIBES(C   OOGAH BUNCH      V    (C   SCHOOLHOUSE KIDS  V  (C
```

ALEX HARVEY

ALEX HARVEY	G V	(ALL	(A) ALEX HARVEY SOUL BAND	1964 POLYDOR		237	624
ZAL CLEMINSON	G	(DEFGHIJKL	(B) THE BLUES	1964 POLYDOR		5LPHM237641	
CHRIS GLEN	B	(DEFGHIJKL	(C) ROMAN WALL BLUES	1969 FONTANA		UK STL 5534	
HUGH McKENNA	K	(DEFGHIJKL	(D) FRAMED	1972 VERTIGO		UK 6360 081	
TED McKENNA	D	(DEFGHIJKL	(E) NEXT	1974 VERTIGO	US 1017	UK 6360 103	
TOMMY EYRE	K	(L1	(F) IMPOSSIBLE DREAM	1974 VERTIGO	US 2000	UK 6360 112	
PHIL KENZIE	SAX	(D	(G) TOMORROW BELONGS TO ME	1975 VERTIGO	US 2004	UK 6360 120	
BUD BEADLE	SAX	(D	(H) LIVE	1975 ATLANTIC	US18184 VERTIGO	UK6360 122	
DAVID BATCHELOR	V	(E	(I) PENTHOUSE TAPES	1975 VERTIGO EURO 9103 205		UK 9102 007	
VICKI SILVA	V	(F	(J) STORIES	1976 MOUNTAIN		UK TOPS 112	
VICKY BROWN	V	(G	(K) BIG HITS & CLOSE SHAVES	1977 VERTIGO		UK 6360 147	
LIZA STRIKE	V	(G	(L) FOURPLAY	1977 MOUNTAIN 4		UK TOPC5006	
BARRY ST JOHN	V	(G	(M) PRESENTS THE LOCK NESS MONSTER	1977 K TEL		NE 984	
B J COLE	STEEL	(I	(N) ROCK DRILL	1978 MOUNTAIN		UK TOPS 114	
SIMON CHATTERTON	D	(1Q	(O) VAMBO ROOLS	197 VERTIGO EURO 6370422			
MATTHEW LANG	G	(1Q	(P) COLLECTORS ITEMS	1980 MOUNTAIN		UK TOPS 129	
DON WELLER	SAX	(1Q	(Q) MAFIA STOLE MY GUITAR	1979 RCA		UK PL 25257	
GORDON SELLARS	B	(1Q	(1) LIVE LINE UP				

ALEXANDER HARVEY

ALEXANDER HARVEY	V	(AB	(A) ALEX HARVEY	1973		CAPITOL	US ST 789
CRAIG DOERGE	PNO	(A	(B) SOUVENIRS	1973		CAPITOL	US EST 11128
HONEY COMBS	V	(A	(C) PRESHUS CHILD	197		KAMA SUTRA	US KSBS 2618
JOHN HOBBS	PNO	(A					

```
DAVID JACKSON    B    (A   DENNIS ST JOHN   D     (A   KEN VASSEY      G    (A   DANNY ROWLAND    G    (A
RANDY STERLING   B G  (A   AL PERKINS    STEEL    (A   KENNY ROGERS    V    (A   CAROL CARMICHAEL V    (A
LARRY CANSLER    STRING(A   VANGIE CARMICHAEL V   (A   JOHN HARRIS     PNO  (A   KENNETH BUTTREY  D    (A
MAC GAYDEN       G    (A   WELDON MYRICK    STEEL(A   WAYNE MOSS       G    (A   BROOKS HUNNICUTT V    (A
KIM GARNES       V    (A   DAVID ELLINGTON V     (A   BUDDY SPICHER    VLN  (A   JOE ALLEN        B    (A
JIMMY ISBELL     D    (A   KEN MALONE      D     (A   JOHN DARNALL     G    (A   BOBBY THOMPSON   G    (A
TRACY NELSON     V    (A   DIANNE DAVIDSON V     (C
```

RICHARD HARVEY

RICHARD HARVEY	WIND	(A	(A) DIVISION ON A GROUND	1975	TRANSATLANTIC	TRA 292

GORDON HASKELL

GORDON HASKELL	G V	(AB	(A) SAIL IN MY BOAT	1969	CBS	UK 63741
JOHN WETTON	B K V	(B	(B) IT IS AND IT ISN'T	1974	ATLANTIC	UK K 40311
DAVE KAFFINETTI	K	(B				
BILL ATKINSON	D	(B				
NEAL ROSENGARDEN	PNO	(B				

```
ALAN BARRY       G    (B   ARIF MARDIN     K    (B   DAVID SPINOZZA   G    (B
EDDIE BRIGATI    V    (B   DAVID BRIGATI   V    (B
```

ANNIE HASLAM

ANNIE HASLAM	V	(A	(A) ANNIE IN WONDERLAND	1978 SIRE US 6040+ WB UK		K 56453
JON CAMP	G B	(A				
DAVE DONOVAN	D	(A	LOUIS CLARK SYN (A ROY WOOD G B K D WIND(A			

HASSLES

JOHN EDWARD DIZEK V PERC		(A	(A) HASSLES	19	US	US UAS 6631
WILLIAM JOSEPH JOEL V K		(A	(B) HOUR OF THE WOLF	19	UA	US UAS 6699
HOWARD ARTHUR BLAUVELT B		(A				
JONATHAN SMALL	D	(A	RICHARD McKENNER G (A			

TORU HATANO

TORU HATANO	ALL INST	(A	(A) LOVE FOR YOU	1976	MULAND	LX 7024M

GEORGE HATCHER

GEORGE HATCHER	V	(ABC	(A) DRY RUN	1976	UA	UK UAG 29997
JOHN THOMAS	G	(ABC	(B) HAVE BAND WILL TRAVEL(10")	1977	UA	UK EXP 100
STEVE WREN	K	(ABC	(C) TALKIN' TURKEY	1977	UA	UK UAS 30090
HARRIS JOANNOU	B V	(ABC				
PHIL SWAN	G	(ABC	TERRY SLADE D (ABC JOHN McFEE STEEL (C HUEY LOUIS HCA (C			
TONY CARR	PERC	(C	DYAN BIRCH V (C FRANK COLLINS V (C PADDY McHUGH V (C			

HATFIELD & THE NORTH

RICHARD SINCLAIR	B V	(AB	(A) HATFIELD & THE NORTH	1974	VIRGIN	UK V2008
PIP PYLE	D	(AB	(B) THE ROTTERS CLUB	1975	VIRGIN	UK V2030
STEVE MILLER	K	(	(C) AFTERS	1979	VIRGIN	UK VR5
PHIL MILLER	G	(AB				
DAVID SINCLAIR	K	(	DAVE STEWART K (AB AMANDA PEARSON V (AB BARBARA GASKIN V (AB			
ANN ROSENTHAL	V	(AB	GEOFF LEIGH WIND (A JEREMY BAINES WIND (A ROBERT WYATT V D(A			
JIMMY HASTINGS	WIND	(B				

DONNIE HATHAWAY

DONNIE HATHAWAY	V	(ALL	(A) EVERYTHING IS EVERYTHING	1970 ATLANTIC US	33332	UK 2465 019	
ROBERTA FLACK	V	(DF	(A) EVERYTHING IS EVERYTHING	1971 ATLANTIC		UK K40063	
ERIC GALE	G	(F	(B) DONNIE HATHAWAY	1970 ATLANTIC US	33360	UK 503 068	
DAVID SPINOZZA	G	(F	(B) DONNIE HATHAWAY	1971 ATLANTIC US		UK K40241	
CORNELL DUPREE	G	(F	(C) LIVE	1972 ATLANTIC US	33386	UK K40369	
PHIL UPCHURCH	B G	(F	(D) FLACK & HATHAWAY	197 ATLANTIC		UK K40380	
MIKE HOWARD	G	(F	(E) EXTENSION OF MAN	1973 ATLANTIC US	7029	UK K40487	
KEITH LOVING	G	(F	(F) BEST OF	19 ATLANTIC US	38107	UK K50525	
HERB SMITH	B	(F					

```
CHUCK RAINEY     B    (F   DEREK GRAVES     B    (F   BERNARD PURDIE   D    (F   STEVE NOVOSEL    B    (F
WILLIE WEEKS     B    (F   BILLY COBHAM     F    (F   AL JACKSON       D    (F   MORRIS JENNINGS  D    (F
FRED WHITE       D    (F   RAY LUCAS        D    (F   BILLY JOHNSON    D    (F   RALPH McDONALD   PERC(F
EARL DEROUEN     PERC (F   JACK JENNINGS    PERC (F   LEONARD GIBBS    PERC (F   JOE GENTLE       WIND(F
KING CURTIS      SAX  (F   DAVE SANBORN     WIND (F
```

RICHIE HAVENS G V SITAR(ALL	(A) RICHIE HAVENS RECORD	1965	TRANSATLANTIC 199UK US DOUGLAS	779
JERRY FRIEDMAN	G	(L	(B) ELECTRIC HAVENS	1966	TRANSATLANTIC 187 US DOUGLAS	780
ERIC WEISSBERG	STEEL(L	(C) MIXED BAG	1967	VERVE	UK 2317002 US MGM	4698
ERIC OXENDINE	B	(JL	(D) SOMETHING ELSE AGAIN	1978	VERVE	UK 2317030 US VERVE	3034
PAUL WILLIAMS	G	(CDEJLO	(E) RICHARD D HAVENS 1983	1969	VERVE	UK 2620001 US VERVE	3047
DANIEL BEN ZEBULON D	(DEL	(F) STONEHENGE	1970	POLYDOR UK 2317004 US STORMY FOREST 6001
PAUL HOFFERT	ORG	(L	(G) A STATE OF MIND	1971	VERVE	UK 2304050
BILLIE MITCHELL	G	(L	(H) ALARM CLOCK	1971	POLYDOR UK 2310080 US STORMY FOREST 6005
WARREN BERNHARDT	K	(DE	(J) GREAT BLIND DEGREE	1972	POLYDOR UK 2480049 US STORMY FOrest 6016
JEREMY STEIG	FLT	(DE	(K) LIVE ON STAGE	1972	POLYDOR UK 2659015 US STORMY FOREST 6012
DONALD MACDONALD	D	(DE	(L) PORTFOLIO	1973	POLYDOR UK 2480166
EDDIE GOMEZ	B	(D	(M) MIXED BAG 2	1974	POLYDOR UK 2310356 US STORMY FOREST 6201
DON PAYNE	B	(D	(N) END OF THE BEGINNING	1976	A&M UK AMLH64598 US A&M	4598
ADRIAN GUILLERY	G	(D	(O) MIRAGE	1977	A&M UK AMLH64641 US A&M	4641
JOHN BLAIR	VLN	(D	(P) RICHIE HAVENS	19	POLYDOR UK 2482273
SKIP PROKOP	D	(C	(Q) POP HISTORY	197	POLYDOR UK 2612017
DARRYL JOHNSON	G K	(O
HERMAN ERNEST	D	(O	TONY BROUSSARD	B	(O	DAVID LEBOLT	K	(O	WILLIAM SMITTY SMITH	K V (O
TOM SCOTT	WIND	(O	GARY COLEMAN	PERC	(O	DUITCH HELMER	V	(O	CHRISTOPHER BOND	G	(O
DENNY GERRARD	B	(F	EMILE LATIMER	CONGA(J	BOB MARGOULEFF	SYN	(J	MALCOLM CECIL	SYN	(J
PAUL HARRIS	K	(C	HARVEY BROOKS	B	(C	BILL LAVORGNA	D	(C	HOWARD COLLINS	G	(C
JOE PRICE	PERC	(C	JOHN ORD	K	(E	BRAD CAMPBELL	B	(E	KEN LAUBER	K	(E
TEDDY IRWIN	G	(E	WELDON MYRICK	STEEL(E	CAROL HUNTER	B	(E	BRUCE LANGHORN	G	(E
COLLIN WALCOTT	SITAR(E	CHARLIE SMALLS	K	(E	STEVE STILLS	B	(E	MARK ROTH	(E
BOB CHASE	PERC (E	DIANE COMINS HARP	(E	CHARLES HOWALL	V	(E	JYMM FAIRS	B	(E
ARNE MOORE	B	(E	CARTER COLLINS	CONGA(E

CYRIL HAVERMANNS   H60

CYRIL HAVERMANS	V G B(AB	(A) CYRIL	1973 MGM 2315 261	+ MGM SE 4926
PIERRE VANDER LINDEN	D(A	(B) MIND WAVE	1974 MGM 2315 311
THIJS VAN LEER	K FLT(A
JACKIE WARD	V	(A	ANDREA WILLIS	V	(A	MAXINE WILLARD	V	(A	CHUCK DOMANICO	B	(A
EMILE RICHARDS	PERC	(A	BOBBY BRUCE	VLN	(A	JOHN D'ANDREA	PERC	(AB	HERMAN DEINUM B PERC(B
RUDY DE QUELJOU	G	(B	HANS LAFAILLE	PERC	(B	CAROLYN WILLIS	V	(A

H61 DALE HAWKINS   H61

DALE HAWKINS	V	(ALL	( ) LETS TWIST AT THE PEPPERMINT LOUNGE 196	ROULETTE	US	25175
JAMES BURTON	G	(	( ) DALE HAWKINS	19	CHESS	703
			( ) SUSIE Q	19	CHECKER	UK6467310
			( ) SUSIE Q	1958	CHESS	US	1429
			( ) LA MEMPHIS & TYLER TEXAS	19	BELL	US	6036

RONNIE HAWKINS   H62

RONNIE HAWKINS	V	(ALL	(A) RONNIE HAWKINS	1959	ROULETTE	US	R25078
KING BISCUIT BOY	HCA	(J	(B) Mr DYNAMO	1960	ROULETTE	US	R25102
BARRY BECKETT	K	(J	(C) FOLK BALLADS	1960	ROULETTE	US	R25120
SCOTT CUSHNIE	K	(J	(D) SINGS HANK WILLIAMS	1961	ROULETTE	US	R25137
DUANE ALLMAN	G	(J	(E) SINGS HANK WILLIAMS	19	GRAND PRIX	SWED	GP 9970
EDDIE HINTON	G	(J	(F) THE BEST OF	1963	ROULETTE	US	R25255
JIMMY JOHNSON	G	(J	(F) THE BEST OF	19	ROULETTE	US	SR42045
DAVID HOOD	B	(J	(G) MOJO MAN	1964	ROULETTE	US	R25390
ROGER HAWKINS	D	(J	(H) RRRRACKET TIME	1965	WLW	CAN	WLW101
JAMES COTTON	HCA	(H	(H) RRRRACKET TIME	1980	CHARLY	UK	CR 30180
LEVON HELM	D	(ABCDGH	(I) RONNIE HAWKINS	1968	YORKVILLE	US	YVS 33002
FRED CARTER	G	(HL	(I) HAWK IN WINTER(REISSUE OF ABOVE) 1976	POLYDOR	CAN	2424 121
DAVE KIRBY	G	(L	(J) RONNIE HAWKINS	1970	COTILLION	US	SD 9019
JERRY CARRIGAN	D	(L	(J) RONNIE HAWKINS	1970	ATLANTIC	UK	2400 009
DAVID BRIGGS	ORG	(L	(K) THE HAWK	1971	COTILLION	US	SD 9030
BOOTS RANDOLPH	SAX	(L	(L) ROCK & ROLL RESURRECTION	1972	MONUMENT	US	KZ 31330
DON SHEFFIELD	TPT	(L	(L) ROCK & ROLL RESURRECTION	1972	MONUMENT	UK	65122
DAVID DARLING	STRINGS(L	(M) GIANT OF ROCK'N'ROLL	1974	MONUMENT	US	KZ 32940
JAMES CASON	V	(L	(N) ROCKIN	197	MODE	FR	MO 9028
MARY HOLLADAY	V	(L	(N) ROCKIN	1977	PYE	UK	NSPL28238
TIM DRUMMOND	B	(L	(O) THE HAWK	1979	UA US LA968	UK	UAG 30283
STAN SZELEST	PNO	(LO
CHARLIE McCOY	HCA	(L	NORMAN RAY	SAX	(L	BYRON BACH	STRINGS	(L	MARVIN CHANTRY STRINGS(L
JUNE PAGE	V	(L	GINGER HOLLADAY	V	(L	GRADY MARTIN	G	(L	KENNETH BUTTREY D (L
FARRELL MORRIS	PERC	(L	PETE DRAKE	STEEL(L	BILL PUETT	SAX	(L	GARY VANOSDALE STRINGS(L
D BERGEN WHITE	V	(L	JEANNIE GREENE	V	(A	KEITH ALLISON V G B	(O	JAMES BURTON	G	(O
WADDY WACHTEL	G	(O	DEE MURRAY	B	(O	JERRY SOMMERS	D	(O	RICK SHLOSSER	D	(O
GARTH HUDSON	ACC SYN	(O	GABRIEL KATONA	SYN	(O	CARL MATHERS	FDL	(O	JERRY PETERSON SAX	(O
PAUL BUTTERFIELD	HCA	(O	RYELAND ALLISON	PERC	(O	BOBBY LAKIND	CONGAS(O	BROOKS HUNNICUTT V	(O
LISA ROBERTS	V	(O	PHYLLIS ST JAMES	V	(O	TERRY DANKO	V	(O	JAMES G EVANS	B	(B
ROBBIE ROBERTSON	G	(G	WILL JONES	PNO	(AB	RAY PAULMAN	G	(AB

SCREAMING JAY HAWKINS   H63

SCREAMING JAY HAWKINS	V(ALL	(A) AT HOME WITH	1957	EPIC	US	3448
GINNY HAWKINS	V	(F	(B) THE NIGHT & DAY OF	19	PLANET	US	1001
RED PRYSTOCK	SAX	(H	(C) A NITE AT THE FORBIDDEN CITY	19	SOUND OF HAWAII	US	50158
TINY GRIMES	G	(H	(D) WHAT THAT IS	1969	PHILIPS	US 600319
LEROY KIRKLAND BAND	(H	(E) SCREAMIN' JAY HAWKINS	1970	PHILIPS	US 600336
TEDDY McRAE ORCHESTRA	(H	(F) PORTRAIT OF A MAN & HIS WOMAN	1972	HOT LINE	US	10024
SAMMY LOWE'S ORCHESTRA	(H	(G) I PUT A SPELL ON YOU	1969	EPIC	US	26457
WALTER YOUNG ORCHESTRA	(H	(H) SCREAMIN' THE BLUES	1979	RED LIGHTNING	UK RL0025

HAWKWIND & HAWKLORDS

DAVE BROCK	HCA V G V K(ABCDEFHHJKLPQ(A)	HAWKWIND	1970	LIBERTY	US	5519	UK LBA 83348
NIK TURNER	V SAX(ABCDEFHJ	(A) HAWKWIND	1975	SUNSET			UK SLS 50374
TERRY OLLIS	D	(ABJ	(B) IN SEARCH IN SPACE	1971	U A	US	5567	UK UAG 29202
DAVE ANDERSON	B	(J	(C) DOREMI FARSOLATIDO	1972	U A	US LA 001	UK UAG 29364
BOB CALVERT		(DHJKL	(D) SPACE RITUAL	1973	U A	US LA 120	UK UAD600378
DIK MIK	K	(ABCDJ	(E) HALL OF THE MOUNTAIN GRILL	1974	U A		UK UAG 29672
ADRIAN SHAW	B	(K	(F) WARRIOR ON THE EDGE OF TIME	1975	U A		UK UAG 29766
LLOYD LANGTON	G	(APJPQ	(G) ROAD HAWKS	1976	U A		UK UAK 29919
IAN'LEMMY' KILMISTER	B G V(CDEFJ	(H) ASTOUNDING SOUNDS	1976	CHARISMA		UK CDS 4004
SIMON KING	D	(CDEFHJKLP	(J) MASTERS OF THE UNIVERSE	1977	U A		UK UAG 30025
DEL DETTMAR	K	(BCDEJ	(K) QUARK STRANGENESS & CHARM	1977	CHARISMA US	4008	US SIRE 6047
SIMON HOUSE	K	(EFHJKL	(L) 25 YEARS (HAWKLORDS)	1978	CHARISMA		UK CDS 4014
PAUL RUDOLPH	B	(H	(M) HAWKWIND(ROCKFILE)	197	LIBERTY		UK LBR 1012
ALAN POWELL	D	(FH	(N) PXR 5	1979	CHARISMA		UK CDS 4016
JOHN HARRISON	B	(AJ	(O) REPEAT PERFORMANCE (COMP)	1980	CHARISMA		UK BG2
MICHAEL MOORCOCK	V	(F	(P) LIVE 79	1980	BRONZE		UK BRON 527
HARVEY BAINSBRIDGE	B V	(LOP	(Q) LEVITATION	1980	BRONZE		UK BRON 530
LES McCLURE	B	(L					
STEVE SWINDELLS	K V	(L	MARTIN GRIFFIN	D	(L	HENRY LOWTHER	TPT (L	TIM BLAKE	K (PQ

BRYN HAWORTH

BRYN HAWORTH	G V	(ALL	(A) LET THE DAYS GO BY	1974	ISLAND	UK	ILPS 9287
BRUCE ROWLAND	D	(AB	(B) SUNNY SIDE OF THE STREET	1975	ISLAND	UK	ILPS 9332
TERRY STANNARD	D	(AB	(C) GRAND ARRIVAL	1978	A&M	UK	AMLH68462
FRAN BYRNE	D	(1	(D) KEEP THE BALL ROLLING	1979	A&M	UK	AMLH68507
BUGS PEMBERTON	D	(A	(1) 1978 TOUR				
KARL HIMMEL	D	(C					
BUDDY HARMON	D	(C	ALAN SPENNER	B	(AB	CHRIS STAINTON	K	(BD	BUDDY EMMONS	G (C
DAVE MATTACKS	D	(B	JOHN COWAN	B	(C	RABBIT BUNDRICK	K	(A	JIM MULLEN	G (B
KEVIN KELLEY	D	(A	DAVE PEGG	B	(B	PETE WINGFIELD	K	(ABD	JOHN PORTER	G (A
JERRY CARRIGAN	D	(C	PAT DONALDSON	B	(B	TONY O'MALLEY	K	(B	BILLY SANFORD	G (C
HENRY SPINETTI	D	(D	FREEBO	B	(A	MICK WEAVER	K	(1	HAROLD BRADLEY	G (C
DAVE SWARBRICK	FDL	(C	GORDON HASKELL	B	(A	BOBBY WOODS	K	(C	BAM KING	G (1
SHELLEY KURLAND STRINGS(C			JESSIE BOYCE	B	(C	RON OATES	K	(C	RONNY LIGHT	G (C
COURTNEY JOHNSON	BANJO(C		TEX COMER	B	(1	PIG ROBBINS	K	(C	CURTIS BURCH	G (C
ALAN MUNDE	BANJO(B		JOE OSBORN	B	(C	GRAHAM MAITLAND	K	(A	TERRY HELLYER	TROM (D
FARRELL MORRIS	PERC (C		NICK RATHER	B	(C	BILLY PUETT	SAX	(C	DENNIS GOODE	TROM (C
SAM BUSH	MAND (C		TOMMY COGBILL	B	(C	ANDREW LOVE	SAX	(C	GEORGE TIDWELL	TPT(C
SIMON MORTON	PNO	(D	DAVE MARKEE	B	(D	MEL COLLINS	SAX	(ABD	WAYNE JACKSON	TPT(C
IMPERIALS	V	(C	MADELINE BELL	V	(B	STEVE GREGORY SAX FLT	(D	MARTIN DROVER	TPT(D
LEE VANDERBILT	V	(C	JOANNE WILLIAMS	V	(B	BUD BEADLE	SAX	(D	PADDY McHUGH	V (B
FRANK COLLINS	V	(B	HOLLADAY SISTERS	V	(C	JIM CUOMO	SAX	(D	DYAN BIRCH	V (B
DON EVERLY	V	(C	CLIFF RICHARD	V	(D	JOHN PERRY	V	(D	TONY RIVERS	V (D
STU CALVER	V	(D					

JUSTIN HAYWARD

JUSTIN HAYWARD	G V	(AB	(A) SONGWRITER	1977	DERAM US 18073 DECCA UK SDL 15
AJ WEBBER		(A	(B) NIGHT FLIGHT	1980	DECCA UK TXS 138
KEN FREEMAN		(A			
CLEM CATTINI	D	(A	TERRY ROWLEY	(A	PETE MORGAN	(A	MEL GALLEY G	(A
DAVE HOLLAND		(A	DAVID SNELL	HARP (A			

HAZZARD & BARNES

TONY HAZZARD	G	(A	(A) HAZZARD & BARNES	1977	WB US 4670	uk k56233
RICHARD BARNES	G	(A				
HERBIE FLOWERS	B	(A	BARRY DE SOUZA	D	(A	TONY HYMAS	K	(A	ROGER McKEW	G BAN(A
PETER SWETTENHAM	K	(A	JACK EMBLOW	ACC	(A	JOHNNY VAN DERRICK FDL	(A	CHRIS NEIL	HCA (A
TONY ASHTON	K	(A	DAVE LAWSON	SYN	(A	FRANK RICOTTI	PERC	(A	LESLEY DUNCAN	V (A
LIZA STRIKE	V	(A	+HRNS & STRINGS		(A			

EDDIE HAZEL

EDDIE HAZEL		(A	(A) GAMES, DAMES & GUITAR THANGS	1977	WB US BS 3958

HEAD

BILL KYLE	D	(A	(A) BLACKPOOL COOL	1978	HEAD	HSLP 330
JOHN DAVIES	TPT K(A					
GORDON CRUICKSHANK SAX (A		LACHLAN McCOLL	G	(A	GRAHAM MINCE	B	(A

HEAD (US)

			(A) HEAD	19	BUDDAH	BDS 5062

MURRAY HEAD

MURRAY HEAD	G V	(AB	(A) NIGEL LIVED	1973	CBS	UK	65503
BOB WESTON	G V	(B	(B) SAY IT AINT SO	1975	ISLAND FR 9101 655 UK ILPS 9347
ALUN DAVIES	G V	(B					
JIM CREGAN	G	(B	BRUCE LYNCH	B	(B	GLENN LE FLEUR	D	(B	PAM KEEVIL	V (B
ARTHUR WATTS	B	(B	LIZA STRIKE	V	(B	PETE THOMPSON	D	(B	BROTHER JAMES	CONGA(B
CHILLI CHARLES	PERC (B		MICKEY FINN	G	(B	NICKY SOUTH	B	(B	SIMON PHILLIPS	D (B
P J CROTTY	WIND	(B	BILLY DAY	K	(B	MORRIS PERT	PERC	(B	BRIAN JOHNSTON	K (B
CHAS JANKEL	K	(B	ANN O'DELL	K	(B	GERRY CONWAY	D	(B	SUE LYNCH	V (B
ANTHONY HEAD	V	(B	VICKY BROWN	V	(B	GRAHAM PRESKETT	MAND (B	TROPIC ISLES STEEL BAND(B

HEAD EAST

ROGER BOYD	K V	(ABCDE	(A) FLAT AS A PANCAKE	1975	A&M US 4537	UK	AMLH64537
DAN BIRNEY	B V	(ABCDE	(B) GET YOURSELF UP	1976	A&M US 4579	UK	AMLH64579
MIKE SOMERVILLE	G V	(ABCDE	(C) GETTIN' LUCKY	1977	A&M US 4624	UK	AMLH64624
JOHN SCHLITT	V	(ABCDE	(D) HEAD EAST	1978	A&M US 46680	UK	AMLH64680
STEVE HUSTON	D V	(ABCDE	(E) LIVE	(DBL)	1979	A&M US 6007	UK	AML 66007
RICHARD PODOLOR	G	(C					
STAN GILL	ORG	(E					

HEADBOYS

LOU LEWIS	G V	(A	(A) HEADBOYS	1980	RSO	RSS 13
GEORGE BOYTER	B V	(A				
CALUM MALCOLM	K V	(A	DAVY ROSS	D V	(A	ROBIN MORTON	PERC (A	ALY BAIN	FDL (A
BOB HEATLIE	SAX	(A				

HEADHUNTERS

BENNIE MAUPIN	WIND V(AB	(A) SURVIVAL OF THE FITTEST	1975	ARISTA US AL4038 UK ARTY 116
MICHAEL CLARK	D (B	(B) STRAIGHT FROM THE GATE	1977	ARISTA US AL4146 UK SPART1048
PAUL JACKSON	B V (B			

OBSIDITION BLACKBYRD]G B V(B   PAUL PORTYEN K V (B   DERRICK YOUMAN   V (B   BILL SUMMERS   PERC(B
DWAYNE McKNIGHT

HEADSTONE

MARK ASHTON	G V (AB	(A) BAD HABITS	1974	EMI	UK	EMA 766
STEVE BOLTON	G (AB	(B) HEADSTONE	1975	EMI	UK	EMC 3073
PHILIP CHEN	B (A	(B) HEADSTONE	19	20TH CENTURY	US	T483
CHILLI CHARLES	D (A					

JOE O'DONNELL VLN G(AB STEVE GOULD V (A SPARKIE V (A JUANITA FRANKLIN V(AB
CARL DOUGLAS V (A TONY LUKYN SYN (A DAVE KAFFINETTI K (A PETER VAN HOOKE D (B
JEROME RIMSON B (A

HEADS HANDS & FEET

ALBERT LEE	G V (ABC	(A) HEADS HANDS & FEET	1971		UK ISLAND ILPS9149
PETE GAVIN	D V (ABC	(B) TRACKS	1972	CAPITOL US11051	UK ISLAND ILPS 9185
CHAS HODGES B G FDL V(ABC		(C) OLD SOLDIERS NEVER DIE	1973	ATLANTIC US 7025 UK	K40465
MIKE O'NEIL	K (A	(AB) HEADS HANDS & FEET	197	CAPITOL US	680
TONY COLTON	V (BCA				

RAY SMITH B G V(BAC JERRY DONAHUE V (BC RAY OSBORNE V (B BARRY ST JOHN V (B
LINDA THOMPSON V (C GERRY HOGAN STEEL (B LINDA LEWIS V (C NORMA WINSTONE V (C
JIM DONNELLY V (C DAVE SWARBRICK V (C JACKIE LYNTON V (C PAM SUILICON V (C
SYLVIA KING V (C

HEART

NANCY WILSON	V G (ALL	(A) DREAMBOAT ANNIE	1976 MUSHROOM US 5005	ARISTA UK ARTY139
ANN WILSON	K V (ALL	(B) LITTLE QUEEN	1977 PORTRAIT US 34799	UK 82075
MICHAEL DEROSIER	D (ABCDEF	(C) MAGAZINE	1978 MUSHROOM US 5008	ARISTA UK 1024
HOWARD LEESE G K SYN (ABCDEF		(D) DOG AND BUTTERFLY	1978 PORTRAIT US 35555	UK 83080
STEVE FOSSEN B PERC(ABCDEF		(E) BEBE LE STRANGE	1980 EPIC	UK 84135
ROGER FISHER STEEL G (ABCD		(F) HEART	1981 EPIC	UK 84829
KAT HENDRIKSE	D (A	(G) GREATEST HITS LIVE	1980 EPIC IMP	
BRIAN NEWCOMBE	B (A			
DURIS MAXWELL	D (A	ROB DEANS	K SYN(A MIKE FLICKER PERC (A DAVE WILSON D (A
ROY AYOTTE	PERC (A	GEOFF FOUBERT	BANJO(A

HEARTBREAKERS

JOHNNY THUNDERS	G V (AB	(A) L A M F	1977	TRACK	2400 218
JERRY NOLAN	V D (A	(B) LIVE AT MAX'S KANSAS CITY	1979	BEGGARS BANQUET	BEGA9
WALTER LURE	G (AB				
RICHARD HELL	B V (A	BILLY RATH B (AB TY STYX D (B			

HEARTS & FLOWERS

DAVE LAWSON V AUTOHARP (AB		(A) NOW IS THE TIME	1967	CAPITOL US	ST 2762
LARRY MURRAY	G V (AB	(B) OF OLD HORSES,KIDS & FORGOTTEN	1968	CAPITOL US	ST 2868
RICK CUNHA	G V (AB				
BERNIE LEADON	G (B	DAVID JACKSON B (			

HEARTSFIELD

ARTIE BALDACCI D SYN K V(ABCD		(A) HEARTSFIELD	1973	MERCURY US	SRM1 688
GREG BIELA	B V (ABCD	(B) WONDER OF IT ALL	1974	MERCURY US	SRM1 1003
FRED DOBBS	G BAN V (ABCD	(C) FOOLISH PLEASURES	1975	MERCURY US	SRM1 1034
J C HARTSFIELD G MAN FDL V(ABCD		(D) HEARTSFIELD COLLECTORS ITEM	1977	CBS US	34456
PHIL LUCAFO	G STEEL V(ABCD				
PERRY CORDELL JORDAN	G V(ABCD				

FLACO FALCON PERC (A TOM GEVING SAX PNO (AC BRIAN PRICE FDL (C CHEPITO AREAS PERC (C
KURT McGETTRICK HRNS (D TED ASHFORD PNO (D TERRY ADAMS CELLO(D JACK KRAMMER TPT (B
BILL DINWIDDIE TROM (B BRANDON LEAVITT PERC (B

HEARTWOOD

BYRON PAUL	G V (A	(A) NOTHING FANCY	1975	GRC	GA 10008

CARTER MINOR V HCA PERC(A
T M HILDEBRANDT G V (A JOE McGLOHON STEEL SAX(A BUDDY BLACKMAN BANJO(A JERRY JOSEPH CONGA (A
BILL BUTLER V G K(A DAVID BLACKMAN MAND (A ROBERT HUDSON V B (A PAUL HORNSBY K (A
DAVIS CAUSEY G (A GARY JOHNSON V B (A

HEAT

JEFF FORMOSA D (
JEFF LI B G (
DWYTT DAYAN V D (ALVIN ROBERTSON D (TALLY TALIOFERRO G (

HEATERS

MERCY BERMUNDEZ V SAX(
MAGGIE CONNELL K (
MISSY CONNELL B V (

HEATWAVE

JOHNNY WILDER	V CONGA(ABCD	(A) TOO HOT TOO HANDLE	1976 GTO UK GTLP 013	EPIC US 34761
ROD TEMPERTON	K (ABC	(B) CENTRAL HEATING	1978 GTO UK GTLP 027	EPIC US 35260
KEITH WILDER	V (ABD	(C) HOT PROPERTY	1979 GTO UK GTLP 039	
J D NICHOLAS	V (D	(D) CANDLES	1980 GTO UK GTLP 047	
MARIO MANTESE	B (AB	ERIC JOHNS G (AB ERNEST BERGER D (ABD ROY CARTER B PNO (A
CALVIN DUKE	K (D	DEREK BRAMBLE D (D WILLIAM L JONES G V (D

HEAVEN

TERRY SCOTT	V G K(A	(A) BRASS ROCK 1 (DBL)	1971	CBS UK	66293
EDDI HARNETT	G V (A				

JOHN JAMES GORDON V B (A VIC GLOVER D (A DAVE GANTREY HRNS (A BUTCH HUDSON HRNS(A
DAVID HORLER TROM K(A RAY KING HRNS (A DEREK SOMERVILLE HRNS (A

H84
HEAVY JELLY

```
JOHN MOORSHEAD    G (ABCDEFG   JIM CAPALDI    D  (BC    STEVE THOMPSON  B (GF    CHRIS WOOD   WIND    (BC
ALEX DMOCHOWSKI   B (ABCDE     JACKIE LOMAX   V G(CDEFG  DAVEY LUTTON   D (G     BARRY JENKINS  D       (D
BRUCE ROWLAND     D (EF        ROCKY          (A        CARLO LITTLE   D (A
```

THE HEAVY JELLY ON THE ISLAND SAMPLER(NICE ENOUGH TO EAT'(I KEEP SINGING THAT SAME OLD SONG) WAS REALLY SKIP
BIFFERTY. THE NAME HEAVY JELLY BEGAN AS A REVIEW HOAX BUT WAS REGISTERED BY JOHN CURD OF HEAD RECORDS AND
APPLIES TO THE LINE UPS HERE.
ONE SINGLE 'CHEWN IN/TIME OUT' ON HEAD 4001. AN ALBUM WAS PREPARED BUT WAS NOT RELEASED. ALSO A SESSION FOR THE
B.B.C. WAS RECORDED MID 1970.

(A) EARLY 1969   (B)   1969   (C) JULY 1969   (D) JAN 1970   (E) MARCH 1970   (F) MID 1970   (G) LATE 1970.

H85
HEAVY METAL KIDS

```
GARY HOLTON      V    (AB12    (A) HEAVY METAL KIDS        1974    ATLANTIC    UK    K50047
RONNIE THOMAS    B V  (AB12    (B) ANVIL CHORUS            1975    ATLANTIC    UK    K50143
KEITH BOYCE      D    (ABC12   (C) KITSCH                  1977    RAK         UK    SRAK 523
JOHN SINCLAIR    K V  (1       (1) 1976       (2) 1977/78
BARRY PAUL       G V  (12
JAY WILLIAMS          (2       MICKEY WALLER    G   (A    DANNY PEYRONEL   K V  (AB    PHIL KENZIE SAX      (B
MADELINE BELL    V    (B       IRENE CHANTER    V   (B    DOREEN CHANTER   V    (B    COSMO        G      (2
```

H86
DICK HECKSTALL SMITH

```
DICK HECKSTALL SMITH SAX(A     (A) A STORY ENDED           1972    BRONZE      UK    ILPS 9196
PAUL WILLIAMS    V    (A
CALEB QUAYE      G    (A        DAVE GREENSLADE  K   (A    JON HISEMAN      D    (A    MARK CLARKE B    (A
GORDON BECK      PNO  (A        CHRIS SPEDDING   G   (A    ROB TAIT         D    (A    GRAHAM BOND K V  (A
CHRIS FARLOWE    V    (A
```

H86A
DASHIELL HEDAYAT

```
DASHIELL HEDAYAT G V K(AB      (A) MELMOTH   LA DEVANTURE DES IVRESSES1969  ARION      FR        30 T079
RICHARD RAUX     WIND (A        (B) OBSOLETE                1971    SHANDAR FR 10009 CBS UK 83512
ROBERT BALESTER  D    (A
JOSE B FADLA     G    (A        DIDIER DE ST JORES  K  (A    DAEVID ALLEN    G   (B    WILLIAM BURROUGHS   V(B
DIDIER MALHERBE  WIND (B        PIP PYLE         G D (B    GILLI SMYTH      V   (B    CHRISTIAN TRITSCH   G B(B
```

H87
HEDGEHOG PIE

```
MARGI LUCKLEY    V    'BC       (A) HIS ROUND              1972    RUBBER      UK    RUB  002
JED GRIMES       G    (BCD      (B) HEDGEHOG PIE           1975    RUBBER      UK    RUB  009
MARTIN JENKINS V MAND VLN(BC    (C) GREEN LADY             1975    RUBBER      UK    RUB  014
STU LUCKLEY      V B  (BC       (D) JUST ACT NORNAL        1978    RUBBER      UK    RUB  024
DIK              D    (C        (EP) WONDERFUL LEGEND OF LAMBTON  1977  RUBBER    UK    TUB  12
WALTER FAIRBAIRN G    (D
TONY CAPSTICK         (A        TOM DUFFY        B   (D    DAVE BURLAND         (D    MICHAEL DOONAM  FLT (BCD
PHIL MURRAY      B    (
```

H88
HEINZ

```
                               (A) TRIBUTE TO EDDIE        1964    DECCA       UK    LK   4599
                               (B) REMEMBERING             1977    DECCA       UK    REM.7
```

H89
ZEUS B HELD

```
ZEUS B HELD                    (A) ZEUS AMUSEMENT          1978    BRAIN             0060  120
```

H89A
HELDON

```
RICHARD PINHAS   G K  (ABCDEFG  (A) ELECTRONIC GORILLA     1974    DISJUNCTA         000  001
PATRICK GAUTHIER K SYN(ACDEFG   (A) ELECTRONIC GORILLA     1979    COBRA             37019
GEORGES GRUNBLATT SYN K(ABC     (B) ALLEZ TEIA             1975    DISJUNCTA         000  002
PIERROT ROUSSEL  B    (A        (C) ITS ALWAYS ROCK AND ROLL 1975  DISJUNCTA         000 006/7
COCO ROUSSEL     PERC (AD       (D) AGNETA NILSSON         1976    URUS              000  011
GILLES DELEUZE   V    (A        (E) UN REVE SANS CONSEQUENCE SPECIALE 1976  COBRA      37002
ALAIN BELLAICHE  G    (BD       (F) INTERFACE              1976    COBRA             37013
ALAIN RENAUD     G    (BC       (G) STAND BY               1979    EGG               900  578
JEAN MY TRUONG   D    (C
GILBERT ARTMAN   D    (C        ARIEL KALMA      K   (C    PHILIBERT ROSSI  SYN (D    MICHEL ETTORI   G  (D
GERARD PREVOST   B    (D        FRANCOIS AUGER D PERC(EFG  DIDIER BATARD    B   (EG   JANIK TOP       B  (E
KLAUS BLASQUIZ   V    (G
```

H89B
ERWIN HELFER

```
ERWIN HELFER     PNO  (A        (A) BOOGIE PIANO CHICAGO SYTLE 1976 BIG BEAR        BEAR   11
```

H90
RICHARD HELL

```
RICHARD HELL     B V  (ALL      (A) BLANK GENERATION       1976    STIFF       UK         BUY7
MARC BELL        D    (B1       (B) BLANK GENERATION       1977    SIRE  US 6037 UK  9103  327
IVAN JULIAN      G    (B1       (1) MAY 1978
ROBERT QUINE     G    (B1
JERRY ANTONIUS   K B  (1        FRANK MAURO      D   (1
```

H91
HELL PREACHERS

```
RUMOURED TO BE                  (A) SUPREME PSYCHEDELIC UNDERGROUND 1968 MARBLE ARCH  UK  MAS  1169
RITCHIE BLACKMORE G
JON LORD         K              IAN PAICE    D    IN PRE DEEP PURPLE DAYS BUT ALWAYS DENIED BY THEM ALL.
```

H91A
HELLFIELD

```
RICK LAMB        K G V(A        (A) HELLFIELD              1978    EPIC        US         36005
MITCH HELLFIELD  D G V(A
JAMIE LARSEN     B V  (A        BILL SMITH   D    (A
```

H92
LEVON HELM

```
LEVON HELM       D V  (AB       (A) LEVON HELM  & THE RCO ALL STARS 1977 ABC US 1017 UK  ABCL 5236
PAUL BUTTERFIELD HCA  (A        (B) LEVON HELM             1978    ABC   US 1089
FRED CARTER      G    (A
DONALD DUNN      B    (A        STEVE CROPPER    G   (AB   BOOKER T JONES   K   (A    JOHN FLAMINGO   V  (A
JEANETTE BAKER   V    (A        ROBBIE ROBERTSON G   (A    GARTH HUDSON     ACC (A    CHARLES MILLER  SAX (A
ALAN RUBIN       TPT  (AB       LOU MARINI       SAX (AB   WILLIE HALL      D   (B    TOM MALONE      TROM(B
HOWARD JOHNSON   HRNS (AB       ROGER HAWKINS    D   (B    DR JOHN          K G (A    EMMARETTA MARKS V  (A
BARRY BECKETT    K    (B        RANDY McCORMICK  K   (B    ERNIE CATE       V   (B    DAN FERGUSON    G  (B
LARRY BYROM      G    (B        EARL CATE        V   (B    JIMMY JOHNSON    G   (B    SCOTT EDWARDS   B  (B
DAVID HOOD       B    (B        LOU DEL GATTO    SAX (B    MARY BERRY       V   (B
```

HELP YOURSELF

MALCOLM MORLEY	G V	(ABCDE	(A) HELP YOURSELF	1971 LIBERTY		UK		83484
RICHARD TREECE	G V	(ABCDE	(B) STRANGE AFFAIR	1972 U A	US 5591	UK	UAS 29287
KEN WHALEY	B	(ADE	(C) BEWARE OF THE SHADOW	1972 U A		UK	UAS 29413
DAVE CHARLES	D V	(ABCDE	(D) RETURN OF KEN WHALEY	1973 U A		UK	UAS 29487
PAUL BURTON	B G	(BCDE	(E) HAPPY DAYS	1973 U A		UK	FREE1
MARTIN ACE	V B	(E	(DE) RETURN/HAPPY DAYS	1973 U A		UK	UDG 4001
GEORGINA ACE	V G	(E					
VIV MORRIS	G V	(E	ERNIE GRAHAM V G (B JOJO GLEMSER G (B				

HEMLOCK

MILLER ANDERSON	G V	(A	(A) HEMLOCK	1973	DERAM	UK	SML 1102
JIM LEVERTON	B V	(A					
ERIC DILLON	D	(A	MICK WEAVER K (A PETER DINES K G V(A CHRIS MERCER SAX (A				
PETE WILLSHER	STEEL(A		CHRIS STEWART V (A				

DORRIS HENDERSON

DORRIS HENDERSON ACC V	(ABC		(A) THERE YOU GO	1965	COLUMBIA	UK	SX 6001
JOHN RENBOURN	G	(AB	(B) WATCH THE STARS	1967	FONTANA	UK	STL 5385
TIM WALKER	G	(B	(C) ROTTERDAM BLUES(EP)	196	SHR	NL	VR 108
DANNY THOMPSON	B	(B					

WAYNE HENDERSON

WAYNE HENDERSON	TROM	(AB	(A) LIVING ON A DREAM	1978 POLYDOR US 16145	UK 2391 343
RONNIE LAWS	SAX	(A	(B) FREEDOM SOUNDS	19 ATLANTIC US 1512	
DEBORAH SHOTLOW	V	(A	( ) AT BIG DADDY'S PLACE	1977 ABC US	
ALEXANDRA BROWN	V	(A	( ) STEP INTO YOUR LIFE	1978 POLYDOR POLS 1004	UK 2391 380
AUGIE JOHNSON	V	(A	( ) EMPHASISED	1979 POLYDOR	
BOBBY LYLE	K	(A			
ROLAND BAUTISTA	G	(A	STEVEN GUITIERREZ D (A DONNIE BECK B (A MARLON McLAIN G (A
NATHANIEL PHILLIPS B	(A		BRUCE CARTER D (A VANCE TENORT PERC (A DEAN GANT SYN (A
VICTOR FELDMAN	PERC	(A	JAY GRAYDON G (A GEORGE DEL BARRIO K (A GEORGE BOHANON TROM(A
DONALD COOKE	TROM	(A	JOHN ERVIN WIND (A EARL DUMLER OBOE (A JACK MARSH WIND (A
OSCAR BRASHEAR	TPT	(A	STEVE MADAIO TPT (A DAVE GROVER TPT (A BOB GREVE WIND (A
CHUCK BROOKE	WIND	(A	SYLVIA ST JAMES V (A SAUNDRA ALEXANDER V (A JIM GILSTRAP V (A
MYRNA MATTHEWS	V	(A	SYREETA WRIGHT V (A

EDDIE HENDERSON

EDDIE HENDERSON	HRNS	(ALL	(A) INSIDE OUT	1974 CAPRICORN US CP0122	UK 2429 106
PATRICE RUSHEN	B K	(E	(A) INSIDE OUT	1974 CAPRICORN	UK K 5750L
GEORGE CABLES	K	(E	(B) REALIZATION	1974 CAPRICORN US CP0118	UK K 57505
CHARLES MIMMS	K	(E	(C) SUNBURST	1975 BLUENOTE	BNLA 464
MTUME	K V PERC	(E	(D) HERITAGE	197 BLUENOTE	BNLA 636
LEE RITENOUR	G	(E	(E) COMIN' THROUGH	1977 CAPITOL	EST 11671
AL McKAY	G	(E	(F) MAHAL	1978 CAPITOL	EST 11846
MANI BOYD	WIND	(E	(G) RUNNING TO YOUR LOVE	1979 TOWER	EST 11984
CONNIE HENDERSON	WIND	(E			
JULIAN PRIESTER	TROM	(E	PHILIP BAILEY V PERC(E HOWARD KING D (E PAUL JACKSON B (E
SKIP DRINKWATER	PERC	(E	DIANE REEVES V (E

MICHAEL HENDERSON

			(A) SOLID	1976 BUDDAH		BDS5662
MICHAEL HENDERSON V B K(ALL			(B) GOIN' PLACES	1977 BUDDAH		BDLH 5018
ROZ RYAN	V	(E	(C) IN THE NIGHT TIME	1978 BUDDAH		BDLH 4055
ELI FONTAINE	SAX	(E	(D) DO IT ALL	1979 BUDDAH		BDLP 4062
KATHY KOSINS	V	(E	(E) WIDE RECEIVER	1980 BUDDAH		BDLP 4065
SHEILA HORNE	V	(E			
CAROL HALL	V	(E	JEANETTE McFRUDER V (E VENNA KEITH V (E RANDALL JACOBS G PNO(E
RAY PARKER	G	(E	OLLIE E BROWN D (E CORY HEATH D (E BOBBY FRANKLIN D (E
CHERYL NORTON	V	(E	ERIK WALLACE D (E RON PANGBORN D (E ERNESTRO WILSON K (E
GARY NESTER	K	(E	MANON SAULSBY K (E SYLVESTER RIVERS PNO (E MICHAEL IACOPELLI SYN (E
LORENZO BROWN	PERC	(E	MIGUEL FUENTES PERC (E

JIMI HENDRIX

JIMI HENDRIX	G V	(ALL
NOEL REDDING	B	(ABCDIMN
MITCH MITCHELL	D(ABCDHIKLMNU
BILLY COX	B(GHIJKLNOU
JACK CASADY	B	(
BUDDY MILES	D	(FLWU BUDDY MILES (JIM MORRISON V HCA(W JIM McCARTY G (W
ROLAND ROBINSON	B	(U LARRY YOUNG K (U LARRY LEE G (U STEVE WINWOOD K (H
JEFF MIRANOV	G	(OS ALLEN SCHWARZBERG D (OS LANCE QUINN G (OS JIMMY MAELEN PERC (OS
MAERETHA STEWART	V	(S HILDA HARRIS V (S VIVIAN CHERRY V (OS BUDDY LUCAS HCA (S
CHRIS WOOD	WIND	(H LINDA NOVEMBER V (O JUMA EDWARDS PERC (I RONETTES V (I
GHETTO FIGHTERS	V	(HI EMERETTA MARKS V (H BUZZY LINHART VIBES(H BARBARA MASSEY V (O
JOHNNY WINTER	G	(W RANDY HOBBS B (W RANDY ZEHRINGER D (W BOB BABITT B (OS

***** THIS ALBUM WITHDRAWN BEFORE
       PUBLIC RELEASE A FEW DJ COPIES
       CAN BE BOUGHT.

(A) ARE YOU EXPERIENCED	1967 TRACK	2407 004		(D) ELECTRIC LADYLAND	1968 TRACK	UK	2657 001
(A) " " "	1967 POLYDOR GER	184 085		(D) " "	1968 REPRISE US	2RS 6307
(A) " " "	1970 BACKTRACK	2407 010		(D) " "	197 POLYDOR US	2657 012
(A) " " "	19 REPRISE US	RS6261		(D) " "	19 BARCLAY FR	80583/4
(A) " " "	19 TRACK	612 001		(D) " " PT1	1968 TRACK UK	613 010
(B) AXIS BOLD AS LOVE	1967 REPRISE US	RS6281		(D) " " PT1	1974 POLYDOR UK	2310 271
(B) " " " "	1967 TRACK UK	2407 011		(D) " " PT2	1968 TRACK UK	613 017
(B) " " " "	19 POLYDOR GER	184 110		(D) " " PT2	1968 POLYDOR UK	2310 272
(B) " " " "	19 TRACK GER	239 000		(E) ELECTRIC HENDRIX*****	1968 TRACK UK	2856 002
(C) SMASH HITS	1968 REPRISE US	MS2025		(F) MONTEREY	1970 REPRISE UK	K40430
(C) " "	1968 TRACK UK	613 004		(F) " "	1970 REPRISE US	MS 2029
(C) " "	1973 POLYDOR UK	ACD 219		(G) BAND OF GYPSYS	1970 TRACK UK	2406 002
(C) " "	1968 POLYDOR GER	184 138		(G) " " "	1970 CAPITOL US	STA0472
						(CONTINUED)

JIMI HENDRIX

(G) " " "	1970	BARCLAY FR	92922		
(G) " " "	1974	POLYDOR UK	2480 005		
(H) CRY OF LOVE	1971	POLYDOR UK	2302 023		
(H) " " "	1971	BARCLAY FR	80433		
(H) " " "	1971	REPRISE US	RS 2034		
(H) " " "	197	POLYDOR	2406 002		
(H) " " "	197	POLYDOR	2408 101		
(I) RAINBOW BRIDGE	1971	REPRISE UK	K44159		
(I) " "	1971	REPRISE US	RS 2040		
(J) ISLE OF WIGHT	1971	BARCLAY FR	80462		
(J) " " "	1971	POLYDOR UK	2302 016		
(K) IN THE WEST	1972	POLYDOR UK	2302 018		
(K) " " "	1972	BARCLAY FR	80448		
(K) " " "	1972	REPRISE US	RS 2049		
(L) WAR HEROES	1973	POLYDOR UK	2302 020		
(L) " "	1973	BARCLAY FR	80448		
(L) " "	1973	REPRISE US	RS 2103		
(M) JIMI HENDRIX	1973	REPRISE UK	K64017		
(N) LOOSE ENDS	1973	POLYDOR UK	2310 301		
(N) " "	1973	BARCLAY FR	80491		
(O) CRASH LANDING	1975	POLYDOR UK	2310 398		
(O) " " "	1975	REPRISE US	RS 2204		
(P) JIMI HENDRIX(SPECIAL)	1975	POLYDOR UK	2343 080		
(Q) JIMI HENDRIX 2	1975	POLYDOR UK	2343 086		
(R) LEGACY	1975	POLYDOR UK	MP9357/8		
(S) MIDNIGHT LIGHTNING	1976	POLYDOR UK	2310 415		
(S) " "	197	POLYDOR	2302 039		
(S) " "	1976	REPRISE US	RS 2229		
(T) THE ESSENTIAL	1978	POLYDOR UK	2612 034		
(U) 9 TO THE UNIVERSE	1980	POLYDOR	POLS1023		
(U) " " " "	1980	POLYDOR UK	2344 155		
(V) STONE FREE	1981	POLYDOR UK	2343 114		
(W) WOKE UP THIS MORNING	1980	RED LIGHTNIN'	0015		
(W) SKY HIGH(BOOTLEG ?)	1972	SKYDOG	SGSH20/7378		
(W) SKY HIGH(BOOTLEG ?)	197	KUSTOM	SJSH 1		

JIMI HENDRIX	1968	SAGA	6307
AT HIS BEST 1	1972	SAGA	6313
AT HIS BEST 2	1972	SAGA	6314
AT HIS BEST 3	1972	SAGA	6315
LOOKING BACK	1974	EMBER	EMB3428
EXPERIENCE (SOUNDTRACK)	1971	EMBER	NR 5057
EXPERIENCE (SOUNDTRACK)	1971	VOGUE	30148
EXPERIENCE (SOUNDTRACK)	1978	MODE	9011
MORE EXPERIENCE	197	EMBER	NR 5061
MORE EXPERIENCE	1972	VOGUE	782
MORE EXPERIENCE	1972	BULLDOG	BDL4003
JIMI HENDRIX	197	TRIP	3505
JIMI HENDRIX	197	TRIP	3509
ROOTS OF HENDRIX	197	TRIP	9501
IN THE BEGINNING	1973	EMBER	NR 5068
IN THE BEGINNING	197	SHOUT	502
THE EARLY YEARS	19	MFP	
BIRTH OF SUCCESS	1970	MFP	50053
FRIENDS(LITTLE RICHARD)	1977	EMBER	EMB3434
JIMI HENDRIX	1973	BOULEVARD	41060
JIMI HENDRIX VOL1	1973	PAN	6313
JIMI HENDRIX VOL2	1973	PAN	6314
JIMI HENDRIX VOL3	1973	PAN	6315
HENDRIX 66	197	ENTERPRISE	1030
VERY BEST OF	1975	UA	LA 505
FOR REAL	1976	DJM	DJLMD8011
THE BEST OF	19	MUSIDISC	CV 1208
RARE HENDRIX	1975	ENTERPRISE	3000
RARE HENDRIX	1975	EXPLOSIVE	558002
HENDRIX STORY	197	WB	K64017
SUPER HENDRIX	197	MUSIDISC	1354
ETERNAL	197	HALLMARK	732
IN CONCERT	197	SPRINGBOARD	4031
THE WILD(CURTIS KNIGHT)	1973	HALLMARK	SHM 791
GET THAT FEELING (C KNIGHT)	1968	LONDON	SH 8349
STRANGE THING	1968	LONDON	SH 8369
BACKTRACK 4(1 SIDE)	19	TRACK	2407 004
BACKTRACK 5(1 SIDE)	19	TRACK	2407 005
GENIUS OF HENDRIX	1978	FESTIVAL	ALB 204
STAR PORTRAIT	197	POLYDOR	2672 002
POP HISTORY	197	POLYDOR	2675 013

H100   PIERRE HENRY

PIERRE HENRY	K SYN(A	(A) MESSE DE LIVERPOOL		19	PHILIPS		6510 001
(LINE UP FOR (B) SEE SPOOKY TOOTH		(B) CEREMONY (WITH SPOOKY TOOTH)		1969	ISLAND	UK	ILPS9107

H101   HENRY COW

TIM HODGKINSON	K (BCE	(A) LEGEND		1973	VIRGIN	UK	V 2005
FRED FRITH	G VLN K (BBCE	(B) UNREST		1974	VIRGIN	UK	V 2011
JOHN GREAVES	B PNO(BC	(C) IN PRAISE OF LEARNING		1975	VIRGIN	UK	V 2027
PETER BLEGVAD	G V CLAR(C	(D) CONCERTS		1976	CAROLINE	UK	CAD 3002
CHRIS CUTLER	V (BCE	(D) CONCERTS		1978	COMPENDIUM		FIDARO 1
ANTHONY MOORE	K (C	(E) WESTERN CULTURE		1978	BROADCAST		BC 1
LINDSAY COOPER	WIND (BCE						
GEOFF LEIGH	SAX (C	MONGEZI FEZA	TPT (C	DAGMAR KRAUSE	(	GEORGIE BORN	B (B
ANNEMARIE ROELOFS	TROM (E						

H102   HENSKE YESTER

JUDY HENSKE	V (AB	(A) FAREWELL ALDEBARAN		1969	STRAIGHT		STS 1052
JERRY YESTER	G B V(AB	(B) ROSEBUD		1971	REPRISE		RS 6426
GRAIG DOERGE	K V (B						
JOHN SEITER	D V (B	DAVID VAUGHT	B (B	RAY BROWN	B (B	BUDDY EMMONS	STEEL(B
BARRY ZWEIG	G (B	MIKE DEASY	G (B				

H103   JUDY HENSKE

JUDY HENSKE	V (ALL	(A) JUDY HENSKE	1963	ELEKTRA		EKS 7231
JOHN FORSAY	G (C	(B) HIGH FLYING BIRD	1964	ELEKTRA		EKS 7241
TOM TEDESCO	G (C	(C) DEATH DEFYING	1965	REPRISE	UK	RS 6203
		(D) A LITTLE BIT OF SUNSHINE	1965	MERCURY	US	SR 61010

H104   KEN HENSLEY

KEN HENSLEY	V G K(AB	(A) PROUD WORDS ON A DUSTY SHELF	1973	BRONZE UK ILPS 9223+RI		BRON 223
DAVE PAUL	B(A	(B) EAGER TO PLEASE	1975	BRONZE UK ILPS 9307+RI		BRON 307
GARY THAIN	B(A	(B) EAGER TO PLEASE	197	WB	US	2863
LEE KERSLAKE	D(A					
MARK CLARKE	B(B	BUGS PEMBERTON	D (B	B J COLE	STEEL(B	

H105   HEPTONES

EARL MORGAN	G V (D	(A) HEPTONES & FRIENDS	1972	TROJAN		TBL 183
LEROY SIBBLES	B V (D	(B) NIGHTFOOD	1976	ISLAND		ISPS 9381
BARRY LLEWELLYN	V (D	(C) COOL RASTA	1976	TROJAN		TRLS 128
WILLIE LINDO	G (D	(D) PARTY TIME	1977	ISLAND		ISLP 9456
PHILL	G (D	(E) IN LOVE WITH YOU	1978	UA		LA 805
R WILLIAM	G (D	(F) BETTER DAYS	1978	THIRD WORLD		TDWD 1
DAVID MADEN	HRNS (D	(G) HEPTONES & FRIENDS VOL 2	197	ATTACK		ATLP 1001
GLEN DA COSTA	HRNS (D	(H) GOOD LIFE	1979	GREENSLEEVES		GREL 6
VIN GORDON	HRNS (D					
BORIS GARDINER	B (D	KEITH STERLING	PNO (D	WINSTON WRIGHT	K (D	
MIKEY BOO	D (D	SKULLY	PERC (D			

HERD
H106

PETER FRAMPTON	G V (A	(A) PARADISE LOST	1968	FONTANA	UK	STL	5458
ANDY BOWN	K (A	(B) LOOKIN' THRU YOU	1968	FONTANA	US		67579
GARY TAYLOR	B (A	(C) NOSTALGIA	1972	BUMBLE	US	GEMP	5001
ANDREW STEELE	D (						
RIC ROTHWELL	D (	HENRY SPINETTI	D (	TONY CHAPMAN	D (TERRY CLARKE	G (
LEWIS RICH	V (	MICK UNDERWOOD	D (	LOUIS CENNAMO	B (

H107
HERE & NOW

(A) WHAT YOU SEE IS WHAT YOU GET	(A TV)1978	DEPTFORD FUN CITY		DLP	02
(B) GIVE & TAKE	1978	CHARLY	UK	NOW	1
(C) ALL OVER THE SHOW	197	CHARLY	UK	NOW	2
(EP) A DOG IN HELL	1978	CHARLY	UK	CEP	122

H108
HERMANS HERMITS

PETER NOONE	V (ALL						
DEREK LECKENBY	G (	KEITH HOPWOOD	G (	KARL GREEN B (	BARRY WHITWAM D (
FRANK RENSHAW	(						

HERMANS HERMITS	1965 COLUMBIA UK 33SX1727	HOLD ON(SOUNDTRACK)	1966 MGM	US SE 4342
HERMANS HERMITS	1965 COLUMBIA GERM C 73994	BEST OF VOL 2	1966 MGM	US SE 4416
HERMANS HERMITS	196 H M V SW SGLP 532	THERE'S A KIND OF HUSH	1967 COLUMBIA UK SCX 6174
HERMANS HERMITS	197 M F P AUST A 8148	THERE'S A KIND OF HUSH	1967 COLUMBIA UK SCXC 34
THE BEST OF	1965 COLUMBIA UK SCXC 27	THERE'S A KIND OF HUSH	1967 MGM US SE 4438
HERMANS HERMITS HITS	1965 COLUMBIA GERM C 74030	X15	1967 COLUMBIA GERM SMC74317
BRITISH GOGO (ANIMALS)	1965 MGM US SE 4306	BLAZE	1967 MGM US SE 4478
THE BEST OF	1965 MGM US SE 4315	MRS BROWN (SOUNDTRACK)	1968 COLUMBIA UK SCX 6303
INTRODUCING	1965 MGM US SE 4282	MRS BROWN (SOUNDTRACK)	1968 MGM US SE 4548
ON TOUR	1965 MGM US SE 4295	BEST OF VOL 3	1968 MGM US SE 4505
WHEN THE BOYS MEET THE GIRL	65 MGM US SE 4334	THE BEST OF UK	1969 COLUMBIA UK SCX 6332
BOTH SIDES OF	1966 COLUMBIA UK SX 6084	THE MOST OF	1972 M F P UK MFP 5216
BOTH SIDES OF	1966 MGM US SE 4386	MOST OF VOL 2	1973 M F P UK MFP50008
AGAIN	1966 COLUMBIA GERM SMC74150	XX THEIR GREATEST HITS	1973 ABKOC US AB 4227
LUCKY 13	1966 COLUMBIA GERM SMC74232	20 GREATEST HITS	1977 K TEL UK NE 1001

H109
HERON

ROY APPS	V G K(B	(A) HERON	1970	DAWN	UK	DNLS 3010
STEVE JONES	K (B	(B) TWICE AS NICE	1972	DAWN	UK	DNLS 3025
TONY POOK	V PERC(B					
GERALD T MOORE	V G K(B	MIKE FINESILVER B (B	TERRY GITTINS D (B	MIKE COOPER G V (B
WILLIE BOAZMAN	G V (B				

H110
MIKE HERON

MIKE HERON	G G K (ABC	(A) SMILING MEN WITH BAD REPUTATIONS	1971	ISLAND	UK	ILPS59146
DUDU PUKWANA	SAX (A	(A) SMILING MEN WITH BAD REPUTATIONS	197	ELEKTRA	US	EKS74093
MALCOLM LE MAISTRE	C(A	(B) MIKE HERONS REPUTATION	1975	NEIGHBOURHOOD	UK	NBH 80637
SIMON NICOL	G (A	(C) DIAMOND OF DREAM	1977	BRONZE UK ILPS9460+RI BRON460
DAVE PEGG	B (A					
MIKE KOWALSKI	D (A	RICHARD THOMPSON G (A	GERRY CONWAY D (A	SUE GLOVER V (A
SUNNY LESLIE	V (A	LIZA STRIKE V (A	VEMU MUKUNDA (A	MOHANA LAKSHMIPATHY (A
VSHAILENDRA	(A	P R MONEY (A	HEATHER WOOD V (A	DR STRANGELY STRANGE V(A
PAT DONALDSON	B (A	TONY COX SYN (A	FRANK USHER G (C	DAVID SAMS K (C
MIKE TOMICH	B (C	JOHN GILSTON D (C	SUSIE WOTSON TELLY V (C	DAVID BARKER K (A
PETE TOWNSHEND	G (A*	JOHN ENTWISTLE B (A*	KEITH MOON D (A*	KRYSIA KOCJAN V (C
ROSE SIMPSON	B (A	DAVE MATTACKS D (A	JOHN CALE B G K V VLN (A	

*CREDITS ON ALBUM AS TOMMY & THE BIJOUX

H111
GARTH HEWITT

GARTH HEWITT	G V (ALL	(A) THE LION & THE LAMB	1973	MYRRH	MYR1001
GRAHAM JARVIS	D PERC(A	(B) I NEVER KNEW LIFE	1974	MYRRH	MYR1017
DAVE WINTOUR	B (A	(C) LOVE SONGS TO THE EARTH	1976	MYRRH	MYR1051
JO PARTRIDGE	G (A	(D) I'M GRATEFUL	1979	MYRRH	MYR1078
MIKE MORAN	K (A	(E) DID HE JUMP OR...	1979	PATCH	UK WOOF1001
KEVIB PEEK	G (A				
CLIFF RICHARD	V (A	DAVE LAWSON K (A ADRIAN LEE SYN (A BRYN HAWORTH G(A

H111A
JOHN HIATT

JOHN HIATT	VG (ALL	(A) HANGING ROUND THE OBSERVATORY	197	EPIC	US
JON PARIS	B G (C	(B) OVERCOAT	1975	EPIC	US 33190
DOUG YANKUS	G (C	(C) SLUG LINE	1979	MCA	UK MCF 3005
BRUCE GARY	D (C	(D) TWO BIT MONSTERS	1980	MCA	UK
B J WILSON	D (C				
GERRY CONWAY	D (C	THOM MOONEY D (C TODD COCHRAN K (C ETAN McELROY PNO V(C
VEYER HILDEBRAND	B (C				

H111B
JIMMY HIBBERT

JIMMY HIBBERT	PERC (A	(A) HEAVY DUTY	1980	LOGO	LOGO 1021
MANFRED MANN	SYN (A				
GEOFF WHITEHORN	G V (A	PAT KING B V (A	JOHN LINGWOOD D V (A	GRAHAM PRESKETT SYN (A
ED CROSS	V (A	LAURIE CATHAM V PERC(A DAVE PHEE V (A	STEVE WALLER V (A
STEVE BOLTON	V (A				

H112
DAN HICKS & HIS HOT LICKS

DAN HICKS V G HCA	(ALL	(A) ORIGINAL RECORDINGS	1969 EPIC	US 26464
JON WEBER	G (A	(B) WHERES THE MONEY	1971 BLUE THUMB	BTS29
SID PAGE	V VIOLA(ABCDF	(C) STRIKING IT RICH	1972 BLUE THUMB US 36 UK ILPS 9204
SHERRY SNOW	V (A	(D) LAST TRAIN TO HICKSVILLE	1973 BLUE THUMB	BTS51
CHRISTINA GANCHER V K	(A	(E) HEY GOOD LOOKIN'	1975 WB	UK K 56157
JAIME LEOPOLD	VLN B(ABCD	(F) IT HAPPENED ONE BITE	1978 WB	US BSK 3158
MARYANN PRICE	V PERC(BCDF				
NAOMI EISENBERG V VLN PERC(BCD	JOHN L GIRTON G (CDF GERRY STEINHOLTZ D PERC(F BOB SCOTT D (D
MICHAEL FRANKS	BANJO(F	LYLE RITZ B (F CLARENCE McDONALD K (F BILL DICKENSON B (F
JOHN PISANO	G (F	RICHARD BORD D PERC(E

H113
JOE HIGGS

JOE HIGGS	(A	(A) LIFE OF CONTRADICTION	1976	VULCAN	GROL 508
		(B) UNITY IS POWER	1979	ISLAND	ILPS 9535

[195]

H114
HIGH COUNTRY

		(A) HIGH COUNTRY		19	WARNER /RACCOON		RACCOON 7

H115
HIGH TIDE

TONY HILL	G	(	(A) SEA SHANTIES		1969	LIBERTY US 7638	UK	LBS 83264
SIMON HOUSE	VLN	(	(B) HIGH TIDE		1970	LIBERTY		UK	LBS 83294
PETER PAVLI	B	(						
ROGER HADDEN	D	(						

H116
HIGHWAY

DARYL BRAITHWAITE	V	(A	(A) HIGHWAY 1		1979	EPIC	UK	83760
GARTH PORTER	K V	(A						
TONY MITCHELL	B V	(A	HARVEY JAMES G V	(A	ALAN SANDON	D	(A	JIM HORN	SAX (A
DAVID FOSTER	SYN	(A	JAY LEWIS	G SIT(A	BILL CUOMO	K	(A	STEVE FORMAN PERC(A
MICHAEL BODDICKER	SYN	(A	CARMEN TWILLIE	V (A	VENNETTE GLOUD	V	(A	SHARON ROBINSON V(A

H116A
HIGHWAY (UK)

RAY MINHINNIT	G V	(AB	(A) HIGHWAY		1974	EMI	UK	EMA 3019
JIM HALL	K V	(AB	(B) SMOKING AT THE EDGE		197	EMI	UK	EMA 770
JOHN GORDON	B G V(AB							
JON ELSTAR	V HCA PERC(AB	IAN BYRON	D V (AB					

H117
DAN HILL

DAN HILL	G V	(ALL	(A) DAN HILL		1976	20th CENTURY	BTH	500
LARRY LONDIN	D	(BC	(B) HOLD ON		197	20th CENTURY	BTH	526
RICK HOMME	B	(ABC	(C) LONGER FUSE		1978	20th CENTURY BTH	8005+BT	547
DON POTTER	V G	(ABC	(D) FROZEN IN THE NIGHT		1978	20th CENTURY	BT	558
JOHN CAPEK	K	(BC						
FRED MOLLIN	G V	(ABC	MATTHEW McAULEY	V K	(ABC	CATHY SMITH	V	(B	BOB MANN	G	(BC
BRIAN RUSSELL	G	(AB	BOBBY OGDIN PNO	(C	BEN MINK	MAND (C	ERICA GOODMAN	HARP(C
TON SZCZESNIAK	B	(ABC	JORN ANDERSEN	D	(BC	DENNIS PENDRITH	B	(C	RON LAURIE CELLO	B(C
BOB BOUCHER	B	(B	BRIAN LEONARD	D	(A	BARRY KEANE	D	(A	STEPHANIE TAYLOR V	(C
ERIC ROBINSON	K	(ABC						

H118
ROY HILL

ROY HILL	V	(A1	(A) ROY HILL		1978	ARISTA	UK	SPART1034
MIKE TAYLOR	K	(1	(1) 1978 TOUR					
JAMIE WEST ORHAM	G	(1						
STEVE SHONE	B	(1	COLIN WILKINSON	D	(1			

H119
STEVE HILLAGE

STEVE HILLAGE G SYN V	(ALL	(A) FISH RISING		1975		VIRGIN UK V2031
MIQUETTE GIRAUDY	K	(BCDEF	(B) "L"		1975	ATLANTIS US18205VIRGIN UK V2066
DON CHERRY	HRNS	(B	(C) MOTOVATION RADIO		1977	ATLANTIC US19144VIRGIN UK V2777
ROGER POWELL	K	(B	(D) GREEN		1978		VIRGIN UK V2098
JOHN WILCOX	D	(B	(E) LIVE HERALD (DBL)		1978		VIRGIN UK 3502
KASIM SULTON	B	(B	(F) OPEN		1979		VIRGIN UK V2135
LARRY KARUSH	TABLA(B	(G) RAINBOW DOME MUSICK		1979		VIRGIN UK VR1
SONJA MALKINE	K	(B					
COLIN BASS	B	(E	PHILIP HODGE	K	(E	BASIL BROOKS	K	(E	JAHIB	PERC	(E
CHRISTIAN BOULE	PERC (E	CLIVE BUNKER	D	(E	CURTIS ROBERTSON	B	(DE	JOE BLOCKER D	(CDE
CHUCK BYNUM	K G	(	JOHN McKENZIE	B	(E	ANDY ANDERSON	D	(E	DAVE STEWART	G V (F
JEAN PHILIPPE RYKIEL SYN(F	REG McBRIDE	B	(C	MALCOLM CECIL	SYN	(C	DAVE STEWART	SYN (F
PAUL FRANCIS	B	(C					

H120
CHRIS HILLMAN

CHRIS HILLMAN	G V B(AB	(A) SLIPPIN' AWAY		1976	ASYLUM US 7E 1062 UK	K 53041
AL GARTH	SAX FDL(	(B) CLEAR SAILIN'		1977	ASYLUM US 7E 1104 UK	K 53060
MEREL BREGANTE	D	(				
FUZZY SAMUELS	B	(	RICHARD MARTS	G V	(A	SKIP EDWARDS	STEEL	(	JOHN BRENNEN	G	(
JOE LALA	PERC (A	JIM GORDON	D	(A	PAUL HARRIS	K	(A	GEORGE TERRY	G	(A
STEVE CROPPER	G	(A	TIM SCHMIT	V	(A	HERB PEDERSEN	V	(A	MARK VOLMAN	V	(A
HOWARD KAYLAN	V	(A	JIM FIELDER	B	(A	RUSS KUNKEL	D	(A	LEE SKLAR	B	(A
AL PERKINS	STEEL(A	ALBHY GALUTEN	SYN	(A	DONNIE DACUS	G	(A	RICK ROBERTS	V	(A
DONALD DUNN	B	(A	SAM BROUSSARD	G	(A	DAVID GARIBALDI	D	(A	HOWARD ALBERT	PERC(A
IVORY JOE HARRIS	K	(A	BYRON BERLINE	V FDL(A	BERNIE LEADON	G V	(A		

H121
RUPERT HINE

RUPERT HINE G V HCA	(AB	(A) PICK UP A BONE		1971	PURPLE	UK	TPSA 7502
SIMON JEFFES	G	(A	(B) UNFINISHED PICTURE		1973	PURPLE	UK	TPSA 7509
DAVID MACIVER	G	(A	(C) IMMUNITY		1981	A&M	UK	AMLH68519
BARRY DE SOUZA	D	(A						
PETER ROBINSON	K	(A	PETE MORGAN	B	(A	TERRY COX	D	(A	CLIVE HICKS G	(A
RAUL MAYORA	PERC (A	ERIC FORD	G	(A	JOE MORETTI	G	(A	STEVE HAMMOND G BAN(A
PAUL BUCKMASTER	CELLO(A	EDDIE MORDUE	WIND (A	ROY WILCOX	WIND (A	ROGER GLOVER	PERC(A

H122
JUSTIN HINES

JUSTIN HINES	V	(AB	(A) JEZEBEL		1976	ISLAND	UK	ILPS 9416
			(B) JUST IN TIME		1979	MANGO	UK	MLPS 9532

H122A
MARCIA HINES

MARCIA HINES	V	(A	(A) OOH CHILD		1980	LOGO	UK	LOGO 1023
MIKE PORCARO	B	(A						
DAVID HUNGATE	B	(A	LEE RITENOUR	G	(A	TIM MAY	G	(A	FRED TACKETT	G	(A
ROBBIE PORTER	PERC (A	RICK SPRINGFIELD	G	(A	BOB MACK	G	(A	PAUL SABU	G	(A
WILLIE ORNELAS	D	(A	ED GREENE	D	(A	STEVE FORMAN	PERC (A	JAI WINDING	K	(A
AL CAPPS	K	(A	TERRY YOUNG	K	(A	JULIUS WECHTER	PERC (A	BOB CONTI	PERC	(A
CARL FRIBERG	PERC (A						

H123
HINKLEYS HERO'S

TIM HINKLEY	K	(12	PICK UP BAND WHICH FORMS FROM TIME TO TIME FOR ODD GIGS PERSONNEL VARIES
MIKE PATTO	V	(1	(1) 1976/JAN 77
BOZ BURRELL	B	(12	(2) JULY 1980
HENRY McCULLOUGH	D	(1	
POLI PALMER	VIBES(12	CHARLIE WHITNEY	G	(1	BRIAN ROBERTSON	G	(1	MICK RALPHS	G	(1
JOHN HALSEY	D	(12	BERNIE HOLLAND	G	(1	BOB TENCH	G V	(1	ROGER CHAPMAN	V	(12
STEVE SIMPSON	G	(2	MITCH MITCHELL	D	(12	MEL COLLINS	SAX (12	JIM CREGAN	G	(1
ERIC BURDON	V	(1	KIKI DEE	V	(2			

```
                    HITCH HIKERS                                              H124
                (A) HITCH HIKERS              1977   ABC              ABCL 5209
                    HITMEN                                                   H124A
BEN WATKINS     G V (A      (A) AIM FOR THE FEET      1980   URGENT          ZIP 84888
PETE GLENISTER  G V (A
NEIL BROCKBANK  B   (A   STAN SHAW    K  (A   MIKE GAFFEY    D V (A
                    HOBO                                                     H125
STUART HARRISON V G (A      (A) HOBO                  1976   ROCKFIELD       UAS 29909
COLIN DUGGAN    V G (A
JOHN MORRIS     V G (A   PAUL COBBOLD     B K (A   STEVE BULL   D  (A   ROGER DAVIES   V (A
                    TOMMY HOEHN                                              H125A
TOMMY HOEHN     V K G(A     (A) LOSING YOU TO SLEEP  1978   LONDON          SHU 8536
GENE NUNEZ      G B (A
JOHN HAMPTON    D PERC(A  KEITH YOUNG      B   (A
                    MICHAEL HOENIG                                           H126
MICHAEL HOENIG  K SYN(A     (A) DEPARTURE FROM THE NORTHERN WASTELAND 1978 WB US BSK3152   UK K56464
LUTZ ULBRICH    G   (A
MICKY DUWE      V   (A   USCHI    V  (A
                    SILAS HOGAN                                              H127
SILAS HOGAN                (A) TROUBLE AT HOME        19     CONTEMPO        CRM   117
                           (A) TROUBLE AT HOME        1971   BLUE HORIZON    2431  008
                    SMOKEY HOGG                                              H128
SMOKEY HOGG                (A) SINGS THE BLUES        19     EMBER           EMB  3405
                           (B) JOHN LEE HOOKER,LIGHTNING HOPKINS 1973 SPECIALTY   SNTF 5013
                           (C) U BETTER WATCH THAT JIVE  1974 SPECIALTY      SNTF 5018
                    HOKUS POKE                                               H129
CLIVE BLENKHORN G V (A      (A) EARTH HARMONY         1972   VERTIGO     UK  6360 064
SMITH CAMPBELL  B   (A
ROGER CLARKE    G STEEL(A  JOHNNIE MILES       D   (A
                    RAM JAM HOLDER                                           H130
RAM JAM HOLDER     (ALL     (A) BOOTLEG BLUES         1974   BEACON          BEA   17
                           (B) BLACK LONDON BLUES     1974   BEACON          BEA   2
                           (C) YOU SIMPLY ARE         1975   FRESH AIR       9299  470
                    ALLAN HOLDSWORTH                                         H131
ALLAN HOLDSWORTH G  (A      (A) VELVET DARKNESS       1977   CTI             6068
                    MARC HOLLANDER                                           H131A
MARC HOLLANDER K CLAR SAX(A (A) ONZE DANSES POUR COMBATTRE LA MIGRAINE1977 KAMIKAZE    KAM1
PAOLO RADONI    G    (A
JEANNOT GILLIS  VLN  (A   VINCENT KENIS    ACC (A  CATHERINE JAUNIAUX V  (A  LUCY GRAUMAN    V (A
CHRIS JORIS     K SAX(A   DAVID LEE SCHLOSS SAX (A
                    THE HOLLIES                                              H132
TONY HICKS      G    (ALL   ( ) STAY WITH THE HOLLIES  1964 PARLOPHONE UK (S)3054 (M) 1220
ALLAN CLARKE    V    (      ( ) IN THE HOLLIES STYLE   1965 PARLOPHONE UK         (M) 1235
TERRY SYLVESTER G V  (      ( ) HERE I GO             1965 IMPERIAL   US          12265
MICHAEL RICKFORS B   (      ( ) HEAR HERE             1965 IMPERIAL   US          12299
GRAHAM NASH     G/V  (      ( ) THE HOLLIES           1965 PARLOPHONE UK      (M) 1261
DON RATHBONE    D    (      ( ) THE HOLLIES           1965 IMPERIAL   US          12312
ERIC HAYDOCK    B    (      ( ) WOULD YOU BELIEVE     1966 PARLOPHONE UK          7008
BOBBY ELLIOTT   D    (      ( ) FOR CERTAIN BECAUSE   1966 PARLOPHONE UK          7011
BERNIE CALVERT  B    (      ( ) EVOLUTION             1967 EPIC US 26315 PARLOPHONE UK7022
                           ( ) EVOLUTION             1978 PARLOPHONE UK      RI   7175
PETE WINGFIELD  K    (XYZ   ( ) BUTTERFLY             1967 PARLOPHONE UK          7039
PETER ARNESEN   K    (YZ    ( ) BUTTERFLY             1978 PARLOPHONE UK      RI   7177
JIMMY JEWELL    SAX  (Y     ( ) HOLLIES GREATEST      1968 EPIC US 32061 PARLOPHONE UK7057
TONY COE        SAX  (Y     ( ) HOLLIES GREATEST      19   ODEON             SM074 236
REG BROOKS      HRNS (Z     ( ) KING MIDAS            1968 EPIC       US          26344
SOL AMARFIO     CONGA(Y     ( ) SING DYLAN            1969 EPIC US 24447 PARLOPHONE UK7028
HOWIE CASEY     HRNS (Z     ( ) SING HOLLIES          1969 PARLOPHONE UK          7092
DAVE CASWELL    HRNS (Z     ( ) MOVING FINGER         196  EPIC       US          30255
RON ASPERY      HRNS (Z     ( ) REFLECTION            1969 STARLINE   UK      SRS  5008
DON HARPER      VLN  (Z     ( ) CONFESSIONS OF THE MIND 1970 PARLOPHONE UK 7116+RI 1978 7178
                           ( ) BUS STOP              19   IMPERIAL   US          12330
                           ( ) BUS STOP              19   EMIDISC    EURO        048 50732
                           ( ) DISTANT LIGHT          1971 EPIC US 30958 PARLOPHONE  10005
                           ( ) STOP STOP STOP        197  IMPERIAL  US12339 STARLINE 5088
                           ( ) POP CHRONIK           19   POLYDOR    GER         VOL 3
                           ( ) ROMANY                1972 EPIC US 31992 POLYDOR 2383 144
                           ( ) HOLLIES               1972 M F P      UK          5252
                           ( ) GREATEST HITS VOL 2   1972 PARLOPHONE             7148
                           ( ) GREATEST HITS VOL 2   1974 BOVEMA     EURO        054 05432
                           ( ) THE HOLLIES           1974 EPIC US 32574 POLYDOR 2383 262
                           ( ) I CANT LET GO         1974 M F P                  50094
                           ( ) ANOTHER NIGHT         1975 EPIC US 33387 POLYDOR 2441 128
                           ( ) HISTORY OF THE HOLLIES 1975 EMI                  EMSP 650
                           ( ) WRITE ON              1976            POLYDOR 2442 141
                           ( ) RUSSIAN ROULETTE      1976            POLYDOR 2382 421
                           ( ) VINTAGE RARE          19   WRC        US          979
                           ( ) VERY BEST OF          19   UA         US          LA 329
                           (X) LIVE HITS             1977 POLYDOR UK2383 428+GERM2374 123
                           ( ) BEST OF THE HOLLIES   1978 PARLOPHONE UK          7174
                           ( ) THE OTHER SIDE OF     1978 PARLOPHONE UK          7176
                           ( ) 20 GOLDEN GREATS      1978 EMI        UK      EMTV  11
                           (Y) CRAZY STEAL           1978 POLYDOR                2383 474
                           ( ) DOUBLE SEVEN O FOUR   1979 POLYDOR    UK          2442 160
                           (Z) BUDDY HOLLY           1980 POLYDOR    UK          POLTV 12

                              [197]
```

H132A LAURIE HOLLOWAY

LAURIE HOLLOWAY	K	(A
DAVE MARKEE	B	(A
HUGH BURNS	G	(A
NORMA WINSTONE	V	(A
JOHN GIRVAN	G	(A
BARRY MORGAN	D	(A

(A) CUMULUS — 1979 HOBO — HO503

H133 LOLEATTA HOLLOWAY

LOLEATTA HOLLOWAY	V	(A
EARL YOUNG	D	(A
MADELINE STRICKLAND	V	(A
SCOTTY MILLER	D	(A
GORDON EDWARDS	B	(A
DENNIS RICHARDSON	V	(A
KIM MILLER	G	(A
JIMMY SIGLER	K	(A
LARRY WASHINGTON	CONGA	(A
MOTO	PERC	(A
STEVE GADD	D	(A
NORMAN HARRIS	G	(A
MIKKI FARROW	V	(A
BUNNY SIGLER	K	(A
RICHARD TEE	K	(A
JAMES WALKER	CONGA	(A
CARLA BENSON	V	(A
JIMMY WILLIAMS	B	(A
T J TINDALL	G	(A
CORNELL DUPREE	G	(A
RON KERSEY	K	(A
GEORGE BUSSEY	K	(A
EMANUEL WILLIAMS	CONGA	(A
EVETTE BENTON	V	(A
RAYMOND EARL	B	(A
EDWARD MOORE	G	(A
ERIC GALE	G	(A
BRUCE GARY	K	(A
RON TYSON	V	(A
BUNNY HARRIS	PERC	(A
BARBARA INGRAM	V	(A

(A) QUEEN OF THE NIGHT — 1978 SALSOUL UK1509 GOLDMINE US 9501
( ) LOLAETTA — 1977 SALSOUL — SZS 5513

H134 BUDDY HOLLY

BUDDY HOLLY	G V	(ALL
BOB MONTGOMERY		(
TOMMY ALSUP	G	(
JERRY ALLISON	D	(
NIKI SULLIVAN	G	(
JOE MAULDIN	B	(

Title	Year	Label		Cat	Title	Year	Label		Cat
CHIRPIN CRICKETS	1957	BRUNSWICK	US	54038	LISTEN TO ME	1968	MCA	UK MUPS	312
CHIRPIN CRICKETS	1958	CORAL	UK	9081	LISTEN TO ME	1974	MCA	UK MCF	2613
CHIRPIN CRICKETS	1969	CORAL	UK CP	20	THE GREAT BUDDY HOLLY	196	CORAL	US	57492
CHIRPIN CRICKETS	1975	MCA	UK CD	8035	THE GREAT BUDDY HOLLY	196	VOCALION	UA VL	3811
BUDDY HOLLY	1958	CORAL	UK	9085	RAVE ON	1968	MCA	UK MUPS	313
BUDDY HOLLY	19	CORAL	US	57210	RAVE ON	1974	MCA	UK MCF	2614
BUDDY HOLLY	1975	MCA	UK CP	8034	RAVE ON	1975	M F P	UK	50176
BUDDY HOLLY STORY	1959	CORAL	UK	9105	BROWN EYED HANDSOME MAN	1968	MCA	UK MUPS	314
BUDDY HOLLY STORY	19	CORAL	US	57279	BROWN EYED HANDSOME MAN	1974	MCA	UK MCF	2615
BUDDY HOLLY STORY	19	CORAL	US	81182	HE'S THE ONE	1968	MCA	UK MUPS	315
BUDDY HOLLY STORY 2	1960	CORAL	UK	9127	TRUE LOVE WAYS	1968	MCA	UK MUPS	319
BUDDY HOLLY STORY 2	196	CORAL	US	57326	TRUE LOVE WAYS	1974	MCA	UK MCF	2616
THAT'LL BE THE DAY	1961	ACE OF HEARTS		AH3	WISHIN'	1968	MCA	UK MUPS	320
THAT'LL BE THE DAY	1974	CORAL	UK CP	24	GIANT	1969	MCA	UK MUPS	371
THAT'LL BE THE DAY	197	DECCA	US	8707	GIANT	196	CORAL	US	57504
THAT'LL BE THE DAY	1974	CORAL	UK CRL	1024	GIANT	1974	MCA	UK MCF	2625
REMINISCING	1963	CORAL	UK LVA	9212	REMEMBER	1971	CORAL	UK CPS	71
REMINISCING	1963	CORAL	US	57426	REMEMBER	1974	CORAL	UK CRL	1087
SHOWCASE	1964	CORAL	UK LVA	9222	GOOD ROCKIN'	1971	VOCALION	US	73923
SHOWCASE	1964	CORAL	US	57450	ROCK'N'ROLL COLLECTION	1972	MCA		2 4009
HOLLY IN THE HILLS	1965	CORAL	UK LVA	9227	ROCK'N'ROLL COLLECTION	1972	DECCA	US DSXE	7207
HOLLY IN THE HILLS	1965	CORAL	US	57463	LEGEND	1974	MCA	UK CDMSP	802
BEST OF	1966	CORAL	UK	CXB 8	COMPLETE B H (9LP SET)	1974	MCA UK COPS		7100H1/9
GREATEST HITS	1967	ACE OF HEARTS		AH148	NASHVILLE SESSIONS	1975	MCA	UK CDLM	8038
GREATEST HITS	1969	CORAL	UK	CP8	PORTRAIT IN MUSIC	1975	TELDEC	EURO	4408
GREATEST HITS	1974	MCA	UK CDLM	8007	PORTRAIT IN MUSIC (DBL)	1975	CORAL	UK	5616/7
GREATEST HITS	1974	CORAL	UK CRLM	1001	WESTERN & BOP	1978	MCA	UK CDLM	8055
GREATEST HITS	1974	CORAL	UK CRL	1005	20 GREATEST HITS	1978	MCA	UK	CMTV8
GREATEST HITS 2	1970	CORAL	UK CPS	47	20 GOLDEN GREATS	19	MCA	UK	3040
					BUDDY HOLLY (6LP SET)	1979	CORAL	CDMSP	807
					BUDDY HOLLY LIVES	1978	MCA		EMTV 8
					BUDDY HOLLY STORY	1979	WARWICK		WW 5064

H134A HOLLYWOOD ARGYLES

GARY PAXTON	V	(
BOBBY REY	V	(
TED MARSH	V	(
GARY WEBB	D	(
DEARY WEAVER	G	(
TED WINTERS	B	(A

(A) ALLEY OOP — 196 LUTE US — L9001

H135 HOLLYWOOD BRATS

ANDREW MATHESON	V	(A
EUNON BRADY	G	(AB
WAYNE MANOR	B	(AB
LOUIS SPARKS	D	(AB
CASINO STEEL	G V K	(AB

(A) GROWN UP WRONG — 1975 US
(B) HOLLYWOOD BRATS (RECORDED 73) — 1980 CHERRY RED UK — ARED 6

H135A HOLLYWOOD STARS

TERRY RAE	V D	(A
RUBEN DE FUENTES	G	(A
BOBBY DRIER	D	(A
STEVE DeLACY	G	(A
MARK ANTHONY	V G	(A
OLLIVER E BROWN	CONGA	(A
NICKY HOPKINS	PNO	(A
MICHAEL RUMMANS	B	(A

(A) HOLLYWOOD STARS — 1977 ARISTA — AL4119

H136 JAKE HOLMES

JAKE HOLMES	G K V	(ALL
TED IRWIN	G	(A
WELDON MYRICK	STEEL	(A
DAVID BRIGGS	PNO	(A
KENNY BUTTREY	D	(A

(A) JAKE HOLMES — 1969 POLYDOR UK — 583 578
(B) SO CLOSE SO VERY FAR TO GO — 1970 POLYDOR UK — 2425 036
(C) HOW MUCH TIME — 1972 CBS UK — 64905
( ) ABOVE GROUND SOUND OF JAKE HOLMES — 19 TOWER US — ST 5079

H137 RUPERT HOLMES

RUPERT HOLMES	V K SYN	(ALL
DEAN BAILIN	G	(F
BENNY GRAMM	D PERC	(F
JOHN CARUSO	B	(F
CHRISSY FAITH	V	(F
PHIL BUDHOS	PNO	(F
SETH GLASSMAN	B	(F

(A) RUPERT HOLMES — 1975 EPIC UK 80942 US 33443
(B) WIDESCREEN — 1975 EPIC UK 80323 US 32864
(C) PURSUIT OF HAPPINESS — 1978 PRIVATE STOCK UK1034 US 7006K
(D) SINGLES — 197 EPIC US 34283
(E) PARTNERS IN CRIME — 1979 MCA UK MCF 3051
(F) ADVENTURE — 1980 MCA UK MCF 3088

H138 ROOSEVELT HOLTS

ROOSEVELT HOLTS	G V	(

(A) PRESENTING THE COUNTRY BLUES — 19 BLUE HORIZON UK 763201+US 7704
(B) AND HIS FRIENDS — 19 ARHOOLIE US 1057

HOLY MODAL ROUNDERS   H139

```
JOHN WESLEY ANNIS B  (          ( ) MORAY EELS EAT HOLY MODAL ROUNDERS 1969 ELEKTRA        EKL 74026
STEVE WEBER        G V  (       ( ) GOOD TASTE IS TIMELESS      1969 MEROMEDIA    US   740
RICHARD TYLER      PNO  (       ( ) ALLEGED IN THEIR OWN TIME   1976 ROUNDER           3004
SAM SHEPARD        D    (       ( ) HOLY MODAL ROUNDERS VOL1    1968 PRESTIGE US 7451 +  7720
PETER STAMPFEL FDL BANJ V(      ( ) INDIAN WAR WHOOP            1967 ESP          US  1068
ROBIN REMAILLY          (       ( ) STAMPFEL & WEBER(COMP)(DBL) 19   FANTASY      US  24711
MICHAEL HURLEY          (       ( ) HOLY MODAL ROUNDERS VOL 2   1968 PRESTIGE     US  7410
LUKE FAUST              (       ( ) LAST ROUND                  1979 ADELPHI      US  MD 1030
```

HOLY MOSES   H139A

```
BILLY BATSON       K V  (A      (A) HOLY MOSES                  1971 RCA          UK   SF8204
DAVID VITTEK       G B V(A
TEDDY SPELEOS      G V  (A   MARTY DAVID  B SAX V(A    CHRISTOPHER PARKER PERC (A
```

HOME   H140

```
LAURIE WISEFIELD   G V (ABC     (A) PAUSE FOR A HOARSE HORSE    197  EPIC US 31146 UK  64365
MICK STUBBS        K V G(ABC     (B) HOME                       1972 CBS          UK   64752
CLIFF WILLIAMS     B V (ABC     (C) ALCHEMIST                   1973 CBS          UK   65550
MICK COOK          V D (ABC
JIMMY ANDERSON     K   (C    DAVID SKILLIN LYRICS   (C   WILL WEIDER   FDL (A   CLIVE JOHN K  (A
```

HOMETOWN BAND   H141

```
SHARI ULRICH V VLN FLT (A      (A) FLYING                       1976 A&M          UK   AMLH 64605
CLAIRE LAWRENCE    WIND (A
GEOFF EYRE         D V  (A   ROBBIE KING K V  (A     DOUG EDWARDS  K B V G(A
```

HONEY BOY   H142

```
                                (A) SWEET CHERRIES             1974 CACTUS           CTLP 101
                                (B) A TASTE OF HONEY           1975 CACTUS           CTLP 105
                                (C) LOVERS                     1977 THIRD WORLD      TWLP 108
                                (D) STRANGE THOUGHTS           1977 TROJAN           TRLS 125
                                (E) DARK END OF THE STREET     1978 DIAMOND          DMLP 402
```

HONEYBUS   H143

```
PETER DELLO        V    (       (A) STORY                       1970 DERAM        UK   SML 1056
JIM KELLY          G V  (A
RAY CANE V G K V        (A   PETE KIRCHER       (     COLIN HARE     V G B (A
```

HONEYDEW   H144

```
                                (A) HONEYDEW                    1971 ARGO              ZFB 15
```

HONKY   H145

```
RAY OTHEN          V PERC(A     (A) HONKY                       1978 CREOLE       UK   CRLP513
BOB WHITE          D    (A
TREVOR CUMMINS     G    (A   CLIFF BARKS  B  (A   MALCOLM BAGGOTT   SAX (A   CLARK NEWTON SAX (A
RON TAYLOR         SAX  (A
```

HOODOO RHYTHM DEVILS   H146

```
JOHN REWIND        G    (C      (A) BARBEQUE OF THE DEVILLE     197  BLUE THUMB     US   BTS 42
JOE CRANE          V    (CE     (B) RACK JOBBERS BLUES          1972 CAPITOL        US   ST 842
BOB PLUMES         G    (C      (C) WHAT THE KIDS WANT          1973 BLUE THUMB BTS 57+VOGUE FR  10029
GLENN WALTERS PERC V    (CE     (D) SAFE IN THEIR HOMES         1976 FANTASY 9522+WORLD JAZZ  9201
DEXTER C PLATES    B    (C      (E) ALL KIDDING ASIDE          1978 FANTASY FTC 540 +      F 9543
SKIP MESQUITE      SAX  (C      ( ) TOO HOT TO HANDLE          1973
JEROME             D    (C
BOB WRAY           B    (E   MUSCLE SHOALS HRNS   (E   CLAYTON IVEY   K    (E   BARBARA WYRICK  V  (E
ROGER CLARK        D    'E   LARRY BYROM        G (E   SUZY STORM     V    (E   TOM ROADY      PERC(E
```

HOOK   H146A

```
                                (A) THE HOOK WILL GRAB YOU      19   UNI          US   73023
                                (B) HOOKED                     19   UNI          US   73038
```

EARL HOOKER   H147

```
EARL HOOKER        G    (ALL    (A) DON'T HAVE TO WORRY         1969 BLUESWAY       US   6034
REGGIE BOYD        G    (J      (B) SWEET BLACK ANGEL          1970 BLUE HORIZON   UK   763850
BIG MOOSE          PNO  (J      (B) SWEET BLACK ANGEL          1970 BLUE THUMB     US   BTBB12
LILLIAN OFFITT     V    (J      (C) THERES A FUNGUS            1972 RED LIGHTNING  UK   RL 009
RICK ALLEN         V    (J      (D) DO YOU REMEMBER            1973 BLUESWAY       US   BLS6072
A C REED           V    (J      (E) 2 BUGS & A ROACH           1975 ARHOOLIE            F 1044
STEVE MILLER       PNO V(G      (G) HOOKER & STEVE             1975 ARHOOLIE       US   F 1051
LOUIS MYERS        HCA  (G      (H) FIRST & LAST               1975 ARHOOLIE       US   F 1066
GENE SKAGGS        B V  (AG     (J) LEADING BRAND              1977 RED LIGHTNING  UK   RL 0018
BOBBY JOHNSON      D    (G      (K) THE LAST OF THE GREAT EARL HOOKER 197 ANTILLES US   7024
JOHNNY WALKER      K V  (A      (L) THE GENIUS                 197  CUCU           US   3400
ANDREW OLDHAM      V    (A
JEFFREY M CARP     HCA  (A   PAUL ASBELL        G  (A   ROOSEVELT SHAW    D  (A
```

HOOKFOOT   H148

```
CALEB QUAYE        G V K(ADE    (A) HOOKFOOT                    1971 DJM          UK   DJLPS 413
DAVE GLOVER        B    (AE     (B) GOOD TIMES A COMIN'        1972 A&M US SP4338  UKDJM DJLPS 422
IAN DUCK           HCA V(ADE    (C) COMMUNICATIONS             1973 DJM          UK   DJLPS 428
ROGER POPE         D V  (ADE    (D) ROARING                    1974 DJM          UK   DJLPS 435
PETER ROSS         HCA V(AE     (E) HEADLINES (DBL)(COMP)      1975 DJM DJLPS28013+     DJLMD 8013
FREDDY GANDY       B V  (DE
BOB KULICK         G V  (E
```

MARSHALL HOOKS & CO   H149

```
MARSHALL HOOKS     G V  (A      (A) MARSHALL HOOKS & CO        1970 BLUE HORIZON      2431 003
JOHN GOINES        D    (A
RON SIMPKINS       K    (A   JIM SUARD        B   (A
```

JOHN LEE HOOKER

JOHN LEE HOOKER	V	(ALL					
ROBERT HOOKER	K	(DH	QUINN WILSON	B		(K	
CLIFF COULTER	K	(DH	FRANKIE BRADFORD	PNO		(K	
BENNY ROWE	G	(D	EVERETT McCRARY	B		(K	
LUTHER TUCKER	G	(DEH	RICHARD JOHNSON	D		(K	
GINO SCAGGS	B	(DBH	JOE HUNTER	PNO		(K	
RON BECK	D	(DH	EARL PHILLIPS	D		(K	
KEN SWANK	D	(DEH	OSCAR BRASHEAR HRNS			(H	
CHARLIE MUSSELWHITE	HCA	(D	GEORGE BOHANON	TROM		(H	
CHUCK GRIMMELL	D	(DH	JOHN KLEMMER	SAX		(H	
MICHAEL WHITE	VLN	(DH	DON MENZA	SAX		(H	
MARK NAFTALIN	K	(DH	STEVE MILLER	PNO		(H	
PAUL WOOD	G	(DH	DON SUGARCANE HARRIS	VLN		(H	
MEL BROWN	G	(DH	JOHN KAHN	B		(H	
RAY McCARTY	G	(DH	RON BECK	D		(H	
ELVIN BISHOP	G	(DH	BENNY ROWE	G		(H	
VAN MORRISON	V	(DH	MARTI McCALL	V		(H	
EDDIE KIRKLAND	G	(DH	BLINKY WILLIAMS	V		(H	
MEMPHIS SLIM	PNO	(A	OMA DRAKE	V		(H	
JIMMY REED	V G	(AK	TONY McPHEE	G		(G	
ALAN WILSON G HCA PNO		(C	GROUNDHOGS			(G	
HENRY VESTINE	G	(C	CHARLIE GRIMES	G		(E	
ANTONIO BARRADA	B	(C	LEX SILVER	B		(E	
ADOLFO DE LA PARRA	D	(C	EARL HOOKER	G		(B	
EDDIE TAYLOR	G	(K	PAUL ASBELL	G		(B	
GEORGE WASHINGTON	B	(K	JOHNNY WALKER	K		(B	
TOM WHITEHEAD	D	(K	JEFFREY CARP	HCA		(B	
OTIS FINCH	SAX	(K	ROOSEVELT SHAW	D		(B	

(H)BORN IN MISSISSIPPI	1973	ABC	ABCX	768
JOHN LEE VOL 1	1973	GREENBOTTLE	GN4002	
THE BLUES	197	MUSIDISC	AM 6078	
LIVE AT SUGAR HILL	19	MUSIDISC	AM 6094	
I WANNA DANCE ALL NIGHT	19	MUSIDISC	AM 6101	
LIVING WITH BLUES	19	MUSIDISC	CV 955	
KING OF FOLK BLUES	19	MUSIDISC	AM 6074	
GREAT BLUES SOUND OF	19	MUSIDISC	AM 6077	
BLACK R&B	1975	MUSIDISC	ALB 186	
(J) MAD MAN BLUES	1973	CHECKER	6467 305	
(J) MAD MAN BLUES	197	CHESS US	2 60011	
BEST OF	1974	CRESCENDO	210007	
ENDLESS BOOGIE	197	ABC	US ALLD 720	
FREE BEER & CHICKEN	1974	ABC	ABCL 5059	
ALONE	1974	SPECIALTY	SNTF 5005	
ALONE	197	SPECIALTY US	2125	
DONT TURN ME FROM YOUR DOOR	74	ATLANTIC UK	K40507	
DONT TURN ME FROM YOUR DOOR	74	ATCO	US SD33151	
BIG MACEO MERRIWEATHER	19	FORTUNE US	3002	
BLUES BEFORE SUNRISE	1976	BULLDOG	1011	
(K) DIMPLES	1977	DJM	DJD 28026	
LIVE	1978	LUNARZ	LZS 2008	
THE CREAM (DBL)	1978	TOMATO	US 2 7009	
THIS IS HIP	1980	CHARLY	CRB 1004	
SITTIN' HERE THINKING	19	MUSE	US MR5205	
EVERYBODY ROCKIN	1980	CHARLY UK	CRB 1014	

HOUSE OF THE BLUES	1960			
PLAYS & SINGS THE BLUES	1961			
TUPELO BLUES	1962	RIVERSIDE		673020
FOLKLORE OF JOHN L HOOKER	1962	STATESIDE	UK	10014
FOLKLORE OF JOHN L HOOKER	1962	VEE JAY	US	1033
FOLKLORE	19	JOY		JOYS133
(A) PREACHIN THE BLUES	1964	STATESIDE	UK	10053
(A) BIG SOUL	1964	VEE JAY	US	1088
(A) BIG SOUL	19	JOY		JOYS147
I WANT TO SHOUT THE BLUES	1964	STATESIDE	UK	10074
I WANT TO SHOUT THE BLUES	1964	VEE JAY	US	1066
SEVEN NIGHTS	1966			
IT SERVES YOU RIGHT	1966	HMV	UK	CSD3542
IT SERVES YOU RIGHT	1966	IMPULSE	US	9103
LIVE AT CAFE AU GO GO	1966	HMV	UK	CSD3612
LIVE AT CAFE AU GO GO	1973	BLUESWAY		BLS6002
REAL FOLK BLUES	1968			
URBAN BLUES	1968	STATESIDE		10246
URBAN BLUES	1973	BLUESWAY		BLS6012
(B) IF YOU MISS 'IM	1969	BLUESWAY		BLS6038
SIMPLY THE TRUTH	1969	STATESIDE		10280
SIMPLY THE TRUTH	1969	BLUESWAY US		BLS6023
I'M JOHN LEE HOOKER	196	JOY		JOYS101
I'M JOHN LEE HOOKER	19	VEE JAY		VJLP1007
BURNIN'	196	JOY		JOYS124
TRAVELLIN'	19	JOY		JOYS129
CONCERT AT NEWPORT	196	JOY		JOYS142
IN PERSON	196	JOY		JOYS155
BEST OF	196	JOY		JOYS156
THATS WHERE ITS AT	1970	STAX	2362	017
THATS WHERE ITS AT	197	STAX	US	2013
FOLK BLUES	19	CROWN	US	CLP5295
MOANIN' & STOMPIN THE BLUES	19	STARDAY US		SK 1085
I FEEL GOOD	1972	JEWEL	US	5005
NO FRIEND AROUND	1970	RED LIGHTNIN'	RL 003	
NO FRIEND AROUND	1979	CHARLY	UK	CR30170
COAST TO COAST	1971	U A		29235
(C) HOOKER & HEAT	1971	LIBERTY	UK	103/4
(C) HOOKER & HEAT	19	TRIP	US	3501
WHISKEY & WIMMEN	19	TRIP	US	X 9504
REAL BLUES	19	TRADITION US		2089
BOOGIE CHILLIN'	19	FANTASY	US	24706
BLACK SNAKE	19	FANTASY	US	24722
ENDLESS BOOGIE	1971	PROBE	UK	SPB1034
(D) NEVER GET OUT OF BLUES	1972	PROBE	UK	SPB1057
(E) LIVE AT SOLEDAD PRISON	72	ABC	UK	ABCX761
DETROIT SPECIAL	197	ATLANTIC	UK	K40405
SLIMS STOMP	197	POLYDOR	UK	2310256
JOHN LEE HOOKER	19	XTRA		XTRA114
JOHN LEE HOOKER	19	EVEREST	US	222
JOHN LEE HOOKER	19	KENT	US	525
GREATEST HITS	19	KENT	US	559
JOHN LEE HOOKER	1975	NEW WORLD		NW 6003
(F) DUSTY ROAD (DBL)	19	BELLAPHON	BLS	5523
(G) DON'T WANT NOBODY	19	INTERCORD		128607
KABUKI WUKI	1973	BLUESWAY		BLS6052

STIX HOOPER

STIX HOOPER	D	(A	(A) WORLD WITHIN				1979 MCA MCF3042	MCG 4006	
ALPHONSO JOHNSON	B	(A							
BOBBY HUTCHERSON	PERC	(A	PAULINHO DA COSTA	PERC V(A	DEAN PARKS	G	(A	BARRY FINNERTY	G (A
ROLAND BAUTISTA	G	(A	KIM HUTCHCROFT	HRNS (A	LARRY WILLIAMS	HRNS (A		JERRY HEY	HRNS(A
OSAMU KITAJIMA	KOTO	(A	KAZU MATSUI	PERC (A	TODD COCHRAN	SYN	(A	FRANK MAROCCO	MUSETTE(A

MARY HOPKIN

MARY HOPKIN	V G HCA	(ALL	(A) POSTCARD	1969	APPLE SW 3381 US	UK SAPCOR 5				
KEVIN PEEK	G	(B	(B) EARTH SONG	1971	APPLE SW 3381 US	UK SAPCOR 21				
BRIAN DALY	G	(B	(C) THOSE WERE THE DAYS	1972	APPLE SW 3395 US	UK SAPCOR 23				
RALPH McTELL	G	(B	(D) WELSH WORLD OF (RECORDED 1968)	1979	DECCA	UK SPA 546				
TERRY WEIL	CELLO	(B	(E) KIDNAPPED	19	AIR	US 1042				
DAVE COUSINS	G BANJO									
CLIVE ANSTEE	CELLO	(B	DANNY THOMPSON	B	(B	TONY VISCONTI	V	(B		

LIGHTNIN' HOPKINS

SAM LIGHTNIN' HOPKINS	G V	(ALL		
EARL PALMER	D	(		
JIMMY BOND	B	(		

CALIFORNIA MUDSLIDE	19	VOLT US	129	
KEEPS ON RAININ'	19	SUPERSCOPE US		
LIGHTNING STRIKES	1963	STATESIDE UK	10031	
LIGHTNING STRIKES	196	VERVE	5014	
LIGHTNING STRIKES	196	TRADITION US	2013	
LIGHTNING STRIKES	19	VEE JAY US	1044	
LIGHTNING STRIKES	19	MAYFAIR	4000	
LIGHTNING STRIKES	19	JOY	5115	
COFFEE HOUSE BLUES	19	JOY	5175	
BLUES HOOT	1964	STATESIDE	10076	
BLUES HOOT	196	HORIZON	US	1617
HOOTIN' THE BLUES	1965	STATESIDE UK	10110	

HOOTIN' THE BLUES	196	PRESTIGE	US	14021
HOOTIN' THE BLUES	196	PRESTIGE		7806
DOWN HOME BLUES	1965	STATESIDE UK		10155
DOWN HOME BLUES	1965	PRESTIGE	US	1086
& SPIDER KILPATRICK	196	ARHOOLIE		F1011
& BARBARA DANE	1965	ARHOOLIE		F1022
TEXAS BLUES MAN	1965	ARHOOLIE		F1034
LIGHTNIN' HOPKINS	1966	SAGA		ERO8001
THE BLUES	1969	ACE OF HEARTS		183
LIGHTNIN' VOL 1	1970	POPPY		11000
LIGHTNIN'	197	POPPY		60002
IN NEW YORK	19	BARNABY US		30247
SHAKE IT BABY	19	VOGUE		891
BLUES UNDERGROUND	19	"D"		8000
LIGHTNIN' HOPKINS VOL 1	19	TIME	US	
LETS WORK AWHILE	1971	BLUE HORIZON	2431005	

(CONTINUED)

EARTH BLUES	19	UA		40006	ROOTS OF	19	XTRA	XTRA 1127
FAST LIFE WOMAN	19	VERVE	US	8453	ROOTS OF	19	FOLKWAYS US	31011
SINGS THE BLUES	19	CROWN	US	5224	ROOTS OF	19	VERVE	5003
AT HIS NATURAL BEST	19	RHAPSODY	US	RHAP8	ROOSTER CROWED IN ENGLAND	19	77	LA 12/200
FREE FORM PATTERNS	19	INT ARTISTS		AT6	LEGACY OF THE BLUES	19	SPECIALTY	SNTF 672
BURNIN' IN L A	19	FONTANA		688 801ZL	LEGACY OF THE BLUES	19	GNP US	10022
BLUE BIRD BLUES	19	FONTANA		688 803ZL	LONESOME LIGHTNIN'	1972	CARNIVAL	2941005
AUTOBIOGRAPHY	19	TRADITION		1040	BLUE LIGHTNIN'	197	JEWEL	5000
BEST	19	TRADITION		2056	BLUE LIGHTNIN'	197	DISCODIS	155 505
GREATEST HITS	19	PRESTIGE		7592	TALKING SOME SENSE	197	JEWEL	5001
BEST OF TEXAS BLUES BAND	19	PRESTIGE		7714	TALKING SOME SENSE	197	PATHE FR	C240842
DOUBLE BLUES	19	FANTAGE		24702	GREAT ELECTRIC SHOW	1973	MUSIDISC FR AM013/4
GOIN' AWAY	19	PRESTIGE		1073	GREAT ELECTRIC SHOW	197	JEWEL US	5002
HIS GREATEST HITS	19	BLUESVILLE US		1084	DIRTY BLUES	1973	MAINSTREAM	MSL1001
COUNTRY BLUES	19	TRADITION		1035	DIRTY BLUES	197	MAINSTREAM	326
LAST OF THE GREAT BLUES	19	TIME	US	70004	THE BLUES	1974	MAINSTREAM	MSL1020
MOJO HAND	19	FIRE	US	104	THE BLUES	197	MAINSTREAM US	311
ON STAGE	19	IMPERIAL	US	9180	THE BLUES	197	PRESTIGE US	7811
SOUL BLUES	19	PRESTIGE	US	7377	LOWDOWN DIRTY BLUES	1975	MAINSTREAM	MSL1031
LIGHTNIN' HOPKINS	19	TRIP		8015	LOWDOWN DIRTY BLUES	197	MAINSTREAM US	405
LIGHTNIN' HOPKIN	19	ARCHIVES		241	IN BERKELEY	1975	ARHOOLIE	F1063
GOTTA MOVE YOUR BABY	19	PRESTIGE		7831	EARLY RECORDINGS	1975	ARHOOLIE	F2007
REALLY THE BLUES	19	MUSIDISC		AM 6080	EARLY RECORDINGS 2	1975	ARHOOLIE	F2010
PENITENTIARY BLUES	19	CHANT DU MONDE 53822			LEGEND IN HIS OWN TIME	1976	BLUE ANTHOLOGY	5608
LIGHTNIN' HOPKINS	19	PATHE FR		40005	ALL THEM BLUES	1976	DJM	28016
LIGHTNIN' HOPKINS	19	VOGUE		68130	KING OF DOWLING STREET	19	PATHE	83254
LIGHTNIN' HOPKINS	19	TRIUMPH		240036				
A JOHN LEE HOOKER	19	STORYVILLE		SLP 174				

NICKY HOPKINS   H153

NICKY HOPKINS	K	(ALL	(A) REVOLUTIONARY PIANO	1966	CBS	UK	62679
			(B) TIN MAN WAS A DREAMER	1973	CBS	UK	65416
			(C) NO MORE CHANGES	1975	MERCURY	US	SRM1 1028

HUGH HOPPER   H154

HUGH HOPPER	B PNO(ALL		(A) 1984	1973	CBS	UK	65466
JOHN MARSHALL	D	(A	(A) 1984	1980	ATMOSPHERE	US	IRI 5010
PYE HASTINGS	G	(A	(B) CRUEL BUT FAIR	1976	COMPENDIUM		FIDARDO 4
LOL COXHILL	SAX	(A	(C) HOPPER TUNITY BOX	1977	COMPENDIUM		FIDARDO 7
GARY WINDO	SAX	(AC	(D) ROUGE ELEMENT	197	OGUN		OG 527
MALCOLM GRIFFITHS	TROM	(A	(E) MONSTER BAND	1979	ATMOSPHERE		IRI 5003
NICK EVANS	TROM	(A					

ELTON DEAN   SAX   (BCDE KEITH TIPPETT   PNO   (B   JOE GALLIVAN   D SYN(B   MARK CHARIG   CORNET(C
FRANK ROBERTS   PNO   (C   DAVE STEWART   ORG   (C   MIKE TRAVIS   D   (CE   RICHARD BRUNTON   G   (C
NIGEL MORRIS   D   (C   ALAN GOWAN   ORG   (D   SHEEN   (D   JEAN PIERRE CAROLFI   K   (E
JEAN PIERRE WEILLER B   (E

HOPSCOTCH   H155

ONNIE McINTYRE	V G	(A	(A) 1967		
STEWART FRANCIS	D	(A			
GRAHAM MAITLAND	K	(A	ALAN GORRIE V B (A		

HORDE CATALYTIQUE POUR LA FIN   H155A

RICHARD ACCART	WIND (A		(A) GESTATION SONORE	1971	FUTURA	FR	SON 003
FRANCKY BOURLIER	HARP VIBES(A					
JACQUES FASSOLA	B BAN G(A	GIL STERG D PERC	(A			

PAUL HORN   H156

PAUL HORN	(		(A) INSIDE	1973	EPIC	UK	65201
			(B) SPECIAL EDITION	1974	ISLAND	UK	ISLD 6
			(C) PAUL HORN & NEXUS	1976	EPIC	UK	69219
			(D) IN INDIA	1976	BLUENOTE	UK	BNLAD 519
			(E) DREAM MACHINE	1978	MUSHROOM		5010

JIMMY BO HORNE   H157

JIMMY BO HORNE	V	(A	(A) DANCE ACROSS THE FLOOR	1978	TK	TKR82533
HARRY CASEY	K	(A	(B) BEST OF	1980	TK	TKR83391
SNOOPY DEAN	G	(A				

MIKE LEWIS   SAX   (A   ROBERT JOHNSON   D   (A   RONALD ZIEGLER   D   (A   RICHARD FINCH   B   (A
WHIT SIDENER   SAX   (A   VINNIE TANNO   TPT   (A   KEN FAULK   TPT   (A   FERMIN GOYTISLO PERC(A
JEROME SMITH   G   (A

HORSE   H157A

ROD ROACH	G	(A	(A) HORSE	1970	RCA	SF 8109
COLIN STANDRING	B	(A				
RIC PARNELL	D	(A	ADRIAN HAWKINS V (A			

HORSES   H157B

		(A) HORSES	19	WHITE WHALE US WW 7121

HORSESHOE   H157C

ARTO BORG	G	(A	(A) FIRST KICK	19	BASF GERM 20 25727.4
TIMO JUUTI	B PERC(A				
HANS RANTIO	D PERC V (A	ARI TALKAMO V G PNO(A			

HORSLIPS   H158

EAMONN CARR	D V	(ABDGJ	(A) HAPPY TO MEET	1973	OATS	M003
CHARLES O'CONNOR	VLN	(ABDGJ	(A) HAPPY TO MEET	197	ATLANTIC GERM 20119+US7030
			(A) HAPPY TO MEET	1978	DJM	UK DJF 20544
JIM LOCKHART	FLT VLN K	(ABDGJ	(B) THE TAIN	1973	OATS	M005
BARRY DEVLIN	V B	(ABDGJ	(B) THE TAIN	197	ATLANTIC	US	7039
JOHN FEAN	V G	(ABDGJ	(B) THE TAIN	1978	DJM	UK DJF 20543
			(C) DANCEHALL SWEETHEARTS	1974	OATS	M007
			(C) DANCEHALL SWEETHEARTS	1974	RCA	APLI0709
			(D) UNFORTUNATE CUP OF TEA	1975	OATS	M008
			(D) UNFORTUNATE CUP OF TEA	1975	RCA	SF 8432

(CONTINUED)

HORSLIPS
```
                    (E) DRIVE THE COLD WINTER AWAY   1976 OATS                      MOO9
                    (F) HORSLIPS                     1976 OATS                      MOO10
                    (G) CELTIC SYMPHONY/BOOK OF INVASIONS 1977 DJM  DJM10 US UK DJF 20498
                    (H) ALIENS                       1977 DJM  DJM16 US UK DJF 20519
                    (I) TRACKS FROM THE VAULTS       1978 OATS                      MOO13
                    (J) MAN WHO BUILT AMERICA        1979 DJM  DJM20 US UK DJF 20546
                    (K) SHORT STORIES -TALL TALES    1980 MERCURY         9100 070
```

H159   WALTER HORTON
```
WALTER HORTON      V HCA(ALL   (A) SOUL OF BLUES HARMONICA      1964 ARGO              US          4037
ROBERT NIGHTHAWK   G    (B     (B) AN OFFER YOU CANT REFUSE(1SIDE) 1972 RED LIGHTNIN' UK        RL008
JIMMY DE BERRY     G    (C     (C) COTTON PATCH HOTFOOTS  (1SIDE) 1973 POLYDOR           2383 200
WILLIE NIX         D    (C     (D) AND HOT COTTAGE             1974 EXTRA                       1135
CAREY BELL HARRINGTON HCA(E    (E) WITH CAREY BELL     1972 ALLIGATOR 4702+UK SONET SNTF 677
EDDIE TAYLOR       G    (E     (F) PRIME CUTS                  19   BLIND PIG          US           006
JOE HARPER         B    (E
BUDDY GUY          G    (A  BOBBY BUSTER    ORG  (A   JACK MYERS    B  (A   WILLIE SMITH   D (A
FRANK SWAN         D    (E
```

H160   HOT DOGS
```
BILL RENNIE        V    (A     (A) SAY WHAT YOU MEAN           19   ARDENT               ADS    2805
GREG REDING        PNO G V(A
TERRY MANNING      G    (A  JACK HOLDER   G  (A  ROBERT JOHNSON  G  (A  FRED PROUTY    D (A
STEVE HOLT         D    (A  RICHARD ROSEBROUGH D (A  STEVE SMITH   K  (A  CARGOE         V (A
```

H161   HOT TUNA
```
JORMA KAUKONEN     G V  (ALL   (A) HOT TUNA                    1970 RCA   UK SF 8125  US   LSP  4353
JACK CASADY        B V  (ALL   (B) FIRST PULL UP(ELECTRIC)     1971 RCA               US   LSP  4550
WILL SCARLETT      HCA  (      (C) BURGERS                     1972 GRUNT UK FTR1004  US   BFLI 0921
PAPA CREACH        V VLN(C      (D) PHOSPHORESCENT RAT         1974 GRUNT             US   BFLI 0348
JOEY COVINGTON     D    (       (E) AMERICA'S CHOICE           1975 GRUNT             US   BFLI 0820
SAMMY PIAZZA       D V  (CD     (F) YELLOW FEVER               1975 GRUNT             US   BLFI 1238
NIKKI BUCK         K    (CFGH   (G) HOPPKORV                   1976 GRUNT UK FTR2006  US   BFLI 1920
BOB STEELER        D    (EFGH   (H) DOUBLE DOSE   (DBL LIVE)   1977 GRUNT UK FL02545  US   CYL  22545
JOHN SHERMAN       G    (FG     (I) FINAL VINYL                1979 GRUNT UK FL13357
MARTY BALIN        G    (
PAUL ZEIGLER       G    (   DAVE CROSBY     V  (C  RICHARD TALBOTT  V G (C  KAREN TOBIN   V (G
```

H162   HOT VULTURES
```
IAN A ANDERSON     G V  (AB     (A) CARRION ON                 1976 RED RAG          UK      RRR 005
MAGGIE HOLLAND     B V  (AB     (B) EAST ST SHAKES             1978 RED RAG          UK      RRR 015
MARTIN SIMPSON     G BAN(B
RAGGY FARMER       PERC V(B  DAVE GRIFFITHS VLN MAND(A  AL JONES   G  (A  JOHN PILGRIM    PERC(A
DAVE PEABODY       HCA  (A  SIMON MAYOR   FDL MAND(B  HILARY JONES  V  (B
```

H162A   HOTEL
```
TOMMY CALTON       G V  (A     (A) HOTEL                       1979 MCA              UK      MCF  3036
MARC PHILLIPS      K V  (A
MICHAEL REID       G V  (A  GEORGE CREASMAN  B V (A  LEE BARGERON  K V (A  MICHAEL CADENHEAD D PERC(A
FARRELL MORRIS     PERC (A  SHANE KEISTER  SYN (A  JOHN NUCKOLS   D  (A
```

H163   HOTLEGS
```
ERIC STEWART       G B V(ABC    (A) THINK SCHOOL STINKS        1971 PHILIPS 6308 057+    6308 047
KEVIN GODLEY       D V  (ABC    (A) THINK SCHOOL STINKS        1971 CAPITOL              US ST 378
LOL CREME          G B K V(ABC  (B) SONGS                      197  PHILIPS              6308 080
BAZ BARKER         VLN  (C      (C) YOU DIDN'T LIKE IT         1976 SONIC                SON  009
GRAHAM GOULDMAN    B    (C
MIKE TIMONEY       ORG  (C
```

H164   THE HOURGLASS
```
GREGG ALLMAN       K V  (ALL    (A) HOURGLASS                  1968 LIBERTY US 7536  UK  LBL 83219
PAUL HORNSBY       K    (A      (B) POWER OF LOVE              19   LIBERTY US 7555
DUANE ALLMAN       G    (ALL    (C) HOURGLASS (DBL)            1973 UA     US 013G2 UK  USD 303/4
JESSE WILLARD CARR      (
MABRON McKINNEY         (    JOHNNY SANDLIN    (    PETE CARR     B  (A
```

H164A   DIXON HOUSE BAND
```
DIXON HOUSE        K V  (A      (A) FIGHTING ALONE             1979 INFINITY            INS   2006
CHRISSY SHEFTS     G    (A
HOWARD LEESE       G    (A  CHUCK GARDNER   G  (A  JAMES KENFIELD  B  (A  FRED ZEUFELDT  B(A
```

H165   HOUSESHAKERS
```
                                (A) DEMOLITION ROCK            1974 CONTOUR          UK   2870   160
```

H166   CHUCK HOWARD
```
CHUCK HOWARD       V    (A      (A) CHUCK HOWARD               1977 CREAM            US     CR1005
KEN PARK           D    (A
JERRY COLE         G    (A  BEN BENAY    G  (A  ROB WALSH     G  (A  DAVE McDANIELS   B (A
MARK GIBBONS       K    (A  RAY PIZZI  WIND (A  JONATHAN LEE  HCA (A  JEFF TWEED       V (A
JOHN NICOLS        V    (A
```

H167   CATHERINE HOWE
```
CATHERINE HOWE     V K  (ALL    (A) HARRY                      1975 RCA LPI 5091 +      SF 8407
PETER BOITA        D    (C      (B) SILENT MOTHER NATURE       1976 RCA                 RS 1041
ALAN PARKER        G    (C      (C) DRAGONFLY DAYS             1977 ARIOLA            ARL 5013
CHRIS REA          G    (C      (EP) TRUTH OF THE MATTER       1977 RCA                 PE 5004
FOGGY LITTLE       G    (C
PAUL KEOGH         G    (C  LES HURDLE    B  (C  MELT KINGTON   B  (C  CHRIS KARAN PERC  (C
RICHARD HEWSON     SYN  (C  DAVID HANCOCK HRNS (C  PETE WINGFIELD K  (C  DICK HOLMES    K (C
```

H168   STEVE HOWE
```
STEVE HOWE G V B K SYN PERC(AB  (A) BEGINNINGS                 1977 ATLANTIC US 18514  UK K 50151
PATRICK MORAZ      K    (AB     (B) STEVE HOWE ALBUM           1979 ATLANTIC          UK K 50621
ALAN WHITE         D    (AB
JOHN MECK          VIOLA(A  PATRICK HALLING  VLN (A  WILLIAM REID  VLN (A  PETER HALLING CELLO (A
CHRIS LAURENCE     B    (A  JAMES GREGORY  FLT (A  MALCOLM BENNETT FLT (A  BUD BEADLE    SAX (A
SIDNEY SUTCLIFFE   OBOE (A  BILL BRUFORD    D  (AB  MICK EVE    SAX  (A  GWYN BROOKE BASSOON (A
COLIN GIBSON       B    (A  RONNIE LEAHY    K  (B  CLIVE BUNKER  D  (B  CLAIRE HAMILL    V (B
GRAHAM PRESKETT    VLN  (B  GRAEME TAYLOR   G  (A  DAVID OBERLE  D  (A
```

EDDIE HOWELL
H169

EDDIE HOWELL	G V K(A		(A) GRAMOPHONE RECORD			1975	WB		UK	K 56154
PHIL COLLINS	D	(A								
JOHN GOODSALL	G	(A	PERCY JONES	B	(A	GARY MOORE	G	(A	ROBIN LUMLEY	K (A
JACK LANCASTER	WIND	(A	GASPAR LAWAL	PERC	(A	TONY SADLER	G	(A	CHARMING LEMMINGS	PERC(A
DAVID MINNS	V	(A	MARTIN KITCAT	V	(A	JEROME RIMSON	B	(A		

HOWLIN' WOLF
H170

HOWLIN' WOLF(CHESTER BURNETT)	V G HCA	(A) MOANING IN THE MOONLIGHT	1964 CHESS	UK 4006	US		1434
HUBERT SUMLIN	G	(MNPQUVWZY	(A) " " " "	196	MARBLE ARCH	UK		MAL 665
WILLIE JOHNSON	G	(EFQSTUWX	(A) EVIL	196	CHESS	US		1540
WILLIE DIXON	B	(QUVWY	(B) POOR BOY	1965	CHESS	UK		CRL4508
SAM LAY	D	(UVXY	(C) REAL FOLK BLUES	1966	CHESS	US		1502
HOSEA LEE KENNARD	PNO	(QTUVWXY	(D) BIG CITY BLUES	1966	EMBER	UK		EMB3370
EARL PHILLIPS	G D	(QTUVXYW	(E) CITY BLUES	19	UNITED US 7717	+ US CUSTOM 2055		
JODY WILLIAMS	G	(QXYW	(F) ORIGINAL FOLK BLUES	19	UNITED US 7747	+ US KENT		526
SP LEARY	D	(NUVXY	(G) SINGS THE BLUES	19	CROWN	US		5240
FRED BELOW	D	(NWX	(H) MORE REAL FOLK BLUES	1967	CHESS	US		1512
IKE TURNER	PNO	(EFSTWVX	(I) SUPER SUPER BLUES BAND	1968	CHECKER UK 3010	+ US CHESS		4537
HENRY GRAY	PNO	(VWY	(J) THE HOWLIN' WOLF ALBUM	1969	CADET	UK LPS319+US CHESS		4543
WILLIE STEEL	D	(EFQSTVWX	(K) AKA CHESTER BURNETT	1971	CHESS			
JAMES COTTON	HCA	(TVW	(L) MESSAGE TO THE YOUNG	1971	CHESS UK 6310108	+US CHESS		50002
JOHNNY JONES	PNO	(UVY	(M) LONDON SESSIONS	1971	ROLLSTONES 49101	+US CHESS		60008
J T BROWN	SAX	(UXY	(N) LIVE & COOKIN' AT ALICES REVISITED	197	CHESS	US		50015
BILLY DOBKINS	SAX	(TUV	(O) BACK DOOR WOLF	1973	CHESS	US		50045
OTIS SMOTHERS	G	(TUWX	(P) LONDON REVISITED	1974	CHESS	US		60006
DON HANKINS	SAX	(UY	(Q) BLUES MASTERS	197	CHESS	UK		2ACBM 201
JUNIOR BLACKMAN	D	(XY	(R) SAM'S BLUES	197	CHARLY	UK	CR	30102
BUDDY GUY	G	(V	(S) LEGENDARY SUN PERFORMERS	197	CHARLY	UK	CR	30134
WILLIE WILIAMS	D	(WX	(T) HEART LIKE A RAILROAD STEEL	19	BLUES BALL	US		2001
L D McGHEE	G	(VYU	(U) CANT PUT ME OUT	19	BLUES BALL	US		2002
LAYFAYETTE LEAKE	PNO	(MU	(V) FROM EARLY TO LATE	19	BLUE NIGHT		BN	0731667
DAVE MYERS	B	(N	(W) GOIN' BACK HOME	19	SYNDICATE CHAPTER US		SC	003
JEROME ARNOLD		(X	(X) HOWLIN' WOLF	19	PYTHON	US		PLP KM 13
ALBERT LUANDREW	PNO	(N	(Y) CHANGIN MY WAY	1977	CHESS		CHV	418
OTIS SPANN	PNO	(Q						
BRYCE ROBERSON	G	(L	SONNY THOMPSON	PNO	(L	ALFRED ELKINS	B	(UT	ERIC CLAPTON	G (M
STEVE WINWOOD	K	(M	BILL WYMAN	B	(MP	CHARLIE WATTS	D	(MP	JEFFREY M CARP	HRNS(MP
KLAUS VOORMAN	B	(M	JOHN SIMON	K	(M	PHIL UPCHURCH	B	(MJ	DENNIS LANSING	HRNS(M
DONALD MYRICK	FLT	(J	GENE BARGE	HRNS	(J	JOE MILLER	HRNS	(M	JORDON SANDKE	HRNS(M
MORRIS JENNINGS	D	(J	ROLAND FAULKNER	G	(J	JOHN STOCKLIN	G	(L	TYRONE SMITH	D (L
LOUIS SATTERFIELD	B	(J	MUDDY WATERS	G V	(I	PETE COSEY	G	(J	BOB CROWDER	D (L
ALBERT WILLIAMS	PNO	(Q	JOHN JERIMIAH	ORG	(L	BO DIDDLEY	G V	(I	JIMMY ROGERS	G (Y
ABE LOCKE	SAX	(WY	LV WILLIAMS	B	(U	ERNIE SHAW	SAX	(U	ANDREW PALMER	B (Y
ARNOLD ROGERS	SAX	(Y	ADOLPH DOLLINS	SAX	(W					

LINDA HOYLE
H171

LINDA HOYLE	V	(A		(A) PIECES OF ME		1971 VERTIGO	UK	6360	060
CHRIS SPEDDING	G	(A							
JOHN MARSHALL	D	(A	JEFF CLYNE	B	(A	KARL JENKINS	OCBE K (A	COLIN PURBROOK	PNO(A

KEITH HUDSON
H172

KEITH HUDSON			(A) TOUCH OF FREEDOM	1975 ATRA			1001
SLY DUNBAR	D	(C	(B) TOO EXPENSIVE	1976 VIRGIN		V	2056
ERIC CLARKE	D	(C	(C) RASTA COMMUNICATIONS	1978 JOINT			JT0003
ROBBIE SHAKESPEARE	G	(C	(D) RASTA COMMUNICATION	1979 GREENSLEVES	UK		GREL 5
EARL SMITH	G	(C					
RANCHIE McLEAN	B G	(C	GITSIE	G	(C	PAGET KING	K V (C	TONY BROTHER	PERC (C
STICKMAN	V	(C	LIZA STRIKE	V	(C	THEO BECKFORD	K (C	TARZAN NELSON	K (C
KEITH STIRLING	K	(C	WILLY BARRETT	G	(C	KEN ELLIOT	K (C		

HUDSON BROTHERS
H172A

BILL HUDSON	G V	(ALL	(A) HOLLYWOOD SITUATION	1974	CASABLANCA US 9008	UK	7004
MARK HUDSON	G V	(ALL	(B) BA FA	1976	ROCKET	US	PIG2169
BRETT HUDSON	V B	(ALL	(C) TOTALLY OUT OF CONTROL	197	ROCKET	US	460
CRAIG KRAMPF	D	(A	( ) HUDSON	197	PLAYBOY	US	PB 102
PHIL REED	G	(A					
MIKE PARKER	K	(A	BARRY PULMAN SYN (A				

HUDSON FORD
H173

RICHARD HUDSON	V G PERC	(ABCD	(A) NICKELODEON	1973 A&M	US 3616	UK	AMLH 68208
JOHN FORD	G B	(ABCD	(B) FREE SPIRIT	1974 A&M	US 3652	UK	AMLH 68274
KEN LAWS	D	(D	(C) WORLDS COLLIDE	1975 A&M	US 4535	UK	AMLH 64535

HUG
H174

MIKE HUGG	V K	(A	(A) NEON DREAM	1975 POLYDOR	UK	2383	330
RON TELEMAK	D V	(A					
MARCUS JAMES	D V	(A	JOHN KNIGHTSBRIDGE	G V (A			

MIKE HUGG
H175

MIKE HUGG	V K	(AB	(A) SOMEWHERE	1972	POLYDOR	UK	2383 140
MICKY WALLER	D	(AB	(B) STRESS & STRAIN	1973	POLYDOR	UK	2383 213
KIM GARDNER	B	(B					
DAVE KING	G	(AB	SONNY CORBETT	HRNS (B	DAVID HEATH HADFIELD G (B	EDDIE GRANT	G (B
LYN DOBSON	HRNS	(B	PAUL WESTWOOD	B	(B	KEVIN PEEK	G (AB	ELTON DEAN	SAX(AB
IAN CARR	HRNS	(B	TONY RIVERS	K V	(B	ANDY BOWN	B (A	TOM McGUINESS	G (A
LIZA STRIKE	V	(A	JUDITH POWELL	V	(A	ALAN TARNEY	B (A	BRIAN HUGG	V (A
MANFRED MANN	ORG	(A	TWEED HARRIS	STRINGS(A	ROGER POPE	D (A	BARRY ST JOHN	V (A
GRAHAM PRESKETT	B	(A	TERRY BRITTON	G	(A	CALEB QUAYE	G (A	MICK ROGERS	G (A
HENRY SPINETTI	D	(A	GERRY BECKLEY	G	(A			

GLEN HUGHES
H176

GLEN HUGHES	V G B K(A		(A) PLAY ME OUT		SAFARI 1977 LONG2	+1978	6/23085
MEL GALLEY	G	(A					
BOB BOWMAN	G	(A	PAT TRAVERS	G	(A	DAVE HOLLAND	D (A	TERRY ROWLEY	PNO (A
ROBERT BAILEY	PNO	(A	RON ASPERY	SAX	(A	HENRY LOWTHER	TPT (A	MARK NAUSEEF	PERC(A
LIZA STRIKE	V	(A	JOY WRIGHT	V	(A	HELEN CHAPPELLE	V (A		

H176A   **JIMMY HUGHES**

JIMMY HUGHES	(A	(A) A SHOT OF RHYTHM & BLUES	1980	CHARLY		CTD	103

H177   **ALAN HULL**

ALAN HULL V G PERC K	(ABC	(A) PIPEDREAM	1973	CHARISMA	UK	CAS 1069	
KEN CRADDOCK G V K PERC	(ABC	(B) SQUIRE	1975	WB US WS4587	UK	K 56121	
COLIN GIBSON	B PERC(ABC	(C) PHANTOMS	1979	ROCKET	UK	TRAIN 6	
RAY LAIDLAW	D (ABC						
MICK MOODY	G (B	LESLEY DUNCAN	V	(BC	JOHN TURNBULL	G (A	RAY JACKSON HCA MAND (A
BRIAN CHATTON	K (B	JO NEWMAN	V	(BC	DAVE BROOKS	SAX (A	TERRY POPPLE D (B
ALBERT LEE	G (B	JEAN ROUSSEL	K	(B	PETER KIRTLEY	G (C	STEVE GREGORY HRNS(C
BUD BEADLE	HRNS (C	LIZA STRIKE	V	(C	RAB NOAKES	V (C	

H178   **HUMAN BEAST**

	( ) HUMAN BEAST	1970	DECCA	UK	SKL	5053

H178A   **HUMAN LEAGUE**

IAN CRAIG MARSH	SYN V(AB	(A) REPRODUCTION	1979	VIRGIN	UK	V 2133	
PHILIP OAKLEY	SYN V(AB	(B) TRAVELOGUE	1980	VIRGIN	UK	V 2160	
MARTYN WARE	SYN V(AB						
PHILIP ADRIAN WRIGHT SYN(AB							

H179   **HUMBLE PIE**

STEVE MARRIOTT G V K HCA(ALL		(A) AS SAFE AS YESTERDAY IS	1969	IMMEDIATE US 101	UK	IMSP025	
PETER FRAMPTON	G V (ABCDELKMN	(B) TOWN & COUNTRY	1969	IMMEDIATE	UK	IMSP027	
JERRY SHIRLEY	D (ALL	(B) TOWN & COUNTRY	1978	CHARLY	UK	CR 300016	
GREG RIDLEY	B (ABCDEFGHJKLMN	(C) HUMBLE PIE	1970	A&M US 4270	UK	AMLS 986	
DAVE CLEMPSON	G (FGHJN	(D) ROCK ON	1971	A&M US 4301	UK	AMLS 2013	
B J COLE	STEEL(CDGN	(E) ROCKIN' AT FILLMORE (DBL)	1971	A&M US 3502	UK	AMLH 63506	
WILLIE WILSON	D (C	(F) SMOKIN'	1972	A&M US 4342	UK	AMLS 64342	
ALEXIS KORNER	V (DF	(G) EAT IT	1973	A&M US 3701	UK	AMLS 6004	
BOBBY KEYS	SAX (D	(H) THUNDERBOX	1974	A&M US 3611	UK	AMLH 63611	
DORIS TROY	V (DF	(J) STREET RATS	1975	A&M US 4514	UK	AMLS 68282	
P P ARNOLD	V (D	(K) CRUST OF IT	1975	EMI		IMP C048 50720	
CLAUDIA LENNEAR	V (D	(L) BACK HOME AGAIN	1976	IMMEDIATE	UK	IML 1005	
MADELINE BELL	V (F	(M) GREATEST HITS	1977	IMMEDIATE	UK	IML 2005	
STEPHEN STILLS	(F	(N) POP CHRONIK	19	A&M		IMP 88771	
RICKY WILLS	(F	(O) FAMOUS POP GROUPS OF THE 60s (+NICE	19	MFP		GERM 14694319/2	
SIDNEY GEORGE	SAX (GN	(P) ON TO VICTORY	1980	JET	UK	231	
BILLY BARNUM	V (GHN	(AB) LOST & FOUND (DBL)	1976	A&M US 3513			
TIM HINKLEY	K (J						
BOB TENCH	G V (P	ANTHONY JONES	B V (P	LYN DOBSON	WIND (ALM CLYDIE KING	V (GN
CARLENA WILLIAMS	V (H	VANETTA FIELDS	V (GHN	MEL COLLINS	HRNS (HJ	

H180   **HUMBLEBUMS**

BILLY CONNOLLY	V G (ABC	(A) FIRST COLLECTION....	1969	TRANSATLANTIC	UK	TRA 186	
TAM HARVEY V G MAND	(A	(B) HUMBLEBUMS	1969	TRANSATLANTIC	UK	TRA 201	
RONNIE RAE	B (A	(B) HUMBLEBUMS	1969	LIBERTY	US	7636	
GERRY RAFFERTY	G V (BC	(C) OPEN UP THE DOOR	1970	TRANSATLANTIC	UK	TRA 218	
BERNIE HOLLAND	G (C	(C) OPEN UP THE DOOR	1970	LIBERTY	US	7656	
TERRY COX	D (C	(ABC) THE COMPLETE..	1974	TRANSATLANTIC	UK	TRAT288	
JIMMY TAGFORD	(C						
BARRY DRANSFIELD FDL (C	REG GUEST	(C					

H181   **HUMMINGBIRD**

BOB TENCH	G V (ABC	(A) HUMMINGBIRD	1975	A&M US 4536	UK	AMLS 68292	
MAX MIDDLETON	K (ABC	(B) WE CANT GO ON MEETING LIKE THIS	1976	A&M US 4595	UK	AMLH 68383	
CLIVE CHAMAN	B (ABC	(C) DIAMOND NIGHTS	1977	A&M US 4661	UK	AMLH 64661	
BERNIE HOLLAND	G (AB						
BERNARD PURDIE	D (BC	ROBERT AHWAI	G (BC	CONRAD ISADORE	D (A	JIM HORN WIND (C
QUITMAN DENNIS	HRNS (C	CHUCK FINDLEY	HRNS (C	AIRTO MOREIRA	PERC (C	PANCHO MORALES PERC(C
VANETTA FIELDS	V (C	MAXINE WILLARD	V (C	JULIA TILLMAN	V (C	STEPHANIE SPRUILL V(C
PAULETTE McWILLIAMS V (C	LISA FREEMAN ROBERTS V (C	LINDA LEWIS	V (A	SANDRA ISADORE V (A
GODFREY McCLEAN	CONGA(A	MADELINE BELL	V (B	JOANNE WILLIAMS	V (B	LIZA STRIKE V (B

H182   **HUNGRY CHUCK**

PETER ECKLUNS	WIND (A	(A) HUNGRY CHUCK	1972	BEARSVILLE		BR 2071

H183   **HUNGRY WOLF**

ALAN HAWKSHAW	K (A	(A) HUNGRY WOLF	1970	PHILIPS		6308 009
ALAN PARKER	G (A						
CLEM CATTINI	D (A	BOBBY HAUGHEY	TPT (A	DEREK WATKINS	TPT (A	HERBIE FLOWERS B (A
PETER LEE STIRLING V (A	TONY FISHER	TPT (A	CLIFF HARDY	TROM (A	KEN GOULDIE TROM (A
JOHNNIE EDWARDS	TROM (A						

H183A   **HUNT**

PAUL DICKINSON	G V (A	(A) BACK ON THE HUNT	1980	VISA		7013
BRIAN GAGREN	B V K G (A						
PAUL KERSEY	D (A						

H184   **MARSHA HUNT**

MARSHA HUNT	V (A	(A) WOMAN CHILD	1971	TRACK	UK	2410 101
		(A) ATTENTION WOMAN CHILD)	1974	FONTANA	GERM RI	

H184A   **HUNTER**

LES HUNT	G V (A	(A) ROCK ON	1978	PATHE	FR	068 61882
LES CRITCHLOW	D (A						
P G CORNELL VLN TROM K(A	NICK EGAN	B (A	CHRIS ELLIS	K (A		

H185   **IAN HUNTER**

IAN HUNTER	G V (ALL	(A) IAN HUNTER	1975	CBS US 33480	UK	80710	
EARL SLICK	G (C	(B) ALL AMERICAN ALIEN BOY	1976	CBS US 34142	UK	81310	
MICK RONSON	G V (ABDEF	(C) OVERNIGHT ANGELS	1977	CBS US	UK	81993	
ROB RAWLINSON	B (C	(D) SHADES OF (COMP DBL)	1978	CBS	UK	88476	
CURLY SMITH	D (C	(E) YOU'RE NEVER ALONE WITH A SCHIZO'	1979	CHRYSALIS	UK	CHR 1214	
PETER OXENDALE	K (C	(F) LIVE WELCOME TO THE CLUB(DBL)	1980	CHRYSALIS	UK	CJT6	
DENNIS ELLIOTT	D (AC						
AYNSLEY DUNBAR	D (B	PETER ARNESEN	K (A	DAVID SANBORN	SAX (B	FREDDIE MERCURY V (B

(CONTINUED)

IAN HUNTER   H185

CHRIS STAINTON	K	(B	GEOFF APPLEBY B HCA	V	(A	BRIAN MAY	V	(B	ROGER TAYLOR	V	(B
MILLER ANDERSON	V	(C	ROY BAKER	PERC	(C	LEM LUBIN	V	(C	ROY BITTAN	K	(E
GARRY TALLENT	B	(E	MAX WEINBERG	D	(E	JOHN CALE	K	(E	GEORGE YOUNG	SAX	(E
LEW DEL GATTO	SAX	(E	ELLEN FOLEY	V	(EF	RORY DODD	V	(E	ERIC BLOOM	V	(E
ERIC PARKER	D V	(F	MARTIN BRILEY	B V	(F	TOMMY MORRONGIELLO	G V	(F	TOMMY MANDEL	K	V(F
GEORGE MEYER	K V	(F	SUSIE RONSON	V	(F						

ROBERT HUNTER   H186

ROBERT HUNTER	V G	(ABC	(A) TALES OF GREAT RUM RUNNERS	1974 ROUND	RX 101
MICKEY HART	D	(AB	(B) TIGER ROSE	1975 ROUND	RX 105
BARRY MELTON	G	(A	(C) JACK O' ROSES	1980 DARK STAR	DSLP 8001
JERRY GARCIA	G	(AB		

DAVID FREIBERG	B	(AB	PETER ALBIN	B	(A	KEITH GODCHAUX	K	(A	DONNA GODCHAUX	V	(A
STEVEN SCHUSTER	SAX	(A	SNOOKY FLOWERS	SAX	(A	MARLO CIPOLLINA		(A	BRUCE GAPINSKI		(A
MILT FARROW		(A	JOHN FAREY		(A	DAVID KESSNER		(A	RAY SCOTT		(A
JEFF SLATTERY		(A	RANDALL SMITH		(A	BILL STEELE		(A	HADI EL SADOON	TPT(A
RODNEY ALBIN	V FDL	(A	T WILL CLAIRE	V	(A	MAUREEN AYLETT		SPOONS(A	BUDDY CAGE	STEEL	(A
RICKY SHUBB	BANJ	(A	MARKEE SHUBB	MAND	(A	ROBBIE STOKES	G	(A	JAMIE PARIS		(A
PETE SEARS		(A	CHRISTIE BOURNE	PERC	(A	DAVE TORBERT		(B		

STEVE HUNTER   H187

| STEVE HUNTER | G V | (A | (A) SWEPT AWAY | 1977 ATCO US | SD 36148 |
| PRAKASH JOHN | B | (A | | |

| JIM GORDON | D | (A | BOB EZRIN | K PERC V | (A | JIM MAELEN | PERC | (A | JOSEF CHIROWSKI | K | (A |
| C EZRIN | B | (A | CAROL POPE | V | (A | JOANNE BROOKS | V | (A | TONY D'AMICO | V | (A |

HUNTER MUSKETT   H188

| DOUG MORTER | G | (| (A) EVERYTIME YOU MOVE | 1970 DECCA NOVA | SND 20 |
| | | | (B) HUNTER / MUSKETT | 1973 BRADLEYS | BRADL 1003 |

MICHAEL HURLEY   H189

MICHAEL HURLEY	G V FDL	(ABC	(A) ARMCHAIRBOOGIE	1971 WB	US	WS 1915
JEFFREY FREDERICKS	V PERC	(B	(B) HAVE MOICY	1976 ROUNDER	US	3010
ROBERT IWASKIEWICZ	G V B	(BC	(C) LONG JOURNEY	19 ROUNDER	US	3011
ROBERT NICKSON	D	(BC				

PETER STAMPFEL V BAN FDL	(BC	JOHN NAGY	MAND	(B	MORGAN HUBER		B PNO(C	DEREK SEMLER	B V	(C
ROB HYKYS	STEEL	(C	AL ZANZLER	TPT	(C	ELVIN WOODS		FDL	(C	CHRISTOPHER L'ESTRANG G	(C
MEDULLA	V	(C	JOHN KEYES	V	(C	PAUL PRESTI		G V	(B	DAVE REISCH	B V	(BC
ROBIN REMAILY V FDL MAND	(B										

HURRIGANES   H190

AALTONEN	(A) ROCK & ROLL ALL NIGHT LONG	19 LOVE	SW	LRLP 84
HAKKINEN	(B) ROAD RUNNER	19 LOVE	SW	LRLP 117
STALEY	(C) CRAZY DAYS	19 LOVE	SW	LRLP 141
	(D) HOT WHEELS	19 LOVE	SW	LRLP 206
	(E) HURRIGANES	1977 SONET FR STA 20311 UK	SNTF 732
	(F) USE NO HOOKS	1978 SONET FR STA 20345 UK	SNTF 754

PHIL HURTT   H192

PHIL HURTT	V PNO	(AB	(A) GIVING IT BACK	1978 FANTASY	F 546
EVETTE BENTON	V	(AB	(B) P H FACTOR	1979 FANTASY	FT 561
BARBARA INGRAM	V	(AB		

CARLA BENSON	V	(AB	BABBS STEWART	V	(A	RICHIE ROME	K	(A	GREG POREE	G	(A
DAVID WILLIAMS	G	(A	GREG MIDDLETON	B	(A	LARRY TOLBERT	D	(A	SHONDON AKIEM	PERC(A
CARL HELM	V	(B	RON TYSON	V	(B	ANN S CLARK	PNO	(B	LARRY WASHINGTON	PERC(B
MIGUEL FUENTES	PERC	(B									

HUSTLER   H193

(A) HIGH STREET	1974 FIREFLY US 4504	UK AMLS 68276
(B) PLAY LOUD	1975 FIREFLY US 4556	UK AMLH 33001
(EP) JUKEBOX QUEEN ?SAME GROUP?	19 REFINED	UK RR1

ASHLEY HUTCHINGS   H194

ASHLEY HUTCHINGS	V B	(ALL	(A) MORRIS ON	1972 ISLAND	UK	HELP 5
RICHARD THOMPSON	G V	(A	(B) COMPLEAT DANCING MASTER	1974 ISLAND	UK	HELP17
BARRY DRANSFIELD	G V VLN	(A	(C) RATTLEBONE & PLOUGHJACK	1976 ISLAND	UK	HELP24
JOHN KIRKPATRICK	V ACC	(AB	(D) SON OF MORRIS ON	1976 HARVEST	UK SHSM 2012
DAVE MATTACKS	D	(ABD	(E) KICKIN' UP THE SAWDUST	1977 HARVEST	UK SHSP 4073
SHIRLEY COLLINS	V	(AD		

BERT CLEAVER	PIPE	(AB	PHIL PICKETT	WIND	(BD	SIMON NICOL	G	)BD	ROGER SWALLOW	D	(B
ROD SKEAPING	VLN	(B	JEREMY MONTAGU	PERC	(B	SUE HARRIS	OBOE	(B	RICHARD HARVEY	CLAR(B
ADAM SKEAPING	VLN	(B	ALAN LUMSDEN SERPENT	(B	TERRY POTTER	HCA	(BE	DAVE KETTLEWELL	WIND(B
ALAN WARD	CELLO(B	FANNY WARLOCK SPINET	(B	PETER KNIGHT	VLN	(B	RAY WARLEIGH	SAX	(B
FRANCIS BAINES	VLN	(B	ELIZABETH BAINES VLN	(B	LONI PATT	VLN	(B	PETER VEL	VLN	(B
JOHN WATCHAM	CONC	(D	MICHAEL GREGORY D PERC	(DE	MARTIN CARTHY	G	(D	JOHN TAMS	CONC V	(DE
JAMES PLESTER	VLN	(D	JOHN RODD	CONC	(DE	IAN CUTLER	VLN	(D	BOB CANN	MELODEON (E
JIMMY COOPER	DULC	(E	MICHAEL HEBBERT	CONC K(E	PETER BULLOCK	WIND SYN	(E	GRAEME TAYLOR	G	(E

J B HUTTO   H194A

J B HUTTO	V G	(ALL	(A) HAWKSQUAT	19 DELMARK	US	IMP	DS617
BREWER PHILLIPS	G V	(C	(B) SLIDEWINDER	19 DELMARK	IMP	DS 636
MARK HARRIS	B	(C	(C) LIVE VOLUME ONE	1977 CHARLY	UK	CR 30182
TED HARVEY	D	(C	(D) BLUES FOR FONESSA	1979 AMUGO	AMLP 823
MIKE ALLEN	PNO	(C	(E) LIVE AT SANDY'S JAZZ REVUE	1979 BARON	101
SUNNYLAND SLIM	PNO	(A	(F) MASTER OF MODERN BLUES	19 TESTAMENT	US	2213

HYBRID KID   H194B

| LOL COXHILL | SAX | (B | (A) A COLLECTION OF CLASSIC MUTANTS | 1980 CHERRY RED | UK | ARED 5 |
| | | | (B) CLAWS | 1980 CHERRY RED | UK | BRED 11 |

HYDRA   H195

WAYNE BRUCE	V K	(AB	(A) HYDRA	1974 CAPRICORN US 0130	UK 2429120
SPENCER KIRKPATRICK G	(AB	(B) LAND OF MONEY	1975 CAPRICORN US 0157	UK 2429130
ORVILLE DAVIS	V	(AB	(C) ROCK THE WORLD	1977 CAPRICORN PD 6996	
STEVE PACE	D	(AB		

DAN TURBEVILLE	K	(A	RANDALL BRAMBLETT SAX	(A	WILL BOULWARE	K	(B	EARL FORD	TROM(A
JOHNNY SANDLIN	PERC	(B	OSCAR JACKSON	SAX	(A	TODD LOGAN	TPT	(A	CHUCK LEAVELL	K	(B
BILL STEWART	PERC	(B									

H196 HYDRAVION

PHILIPPE BESOMBES K G V(A		(A) HYDRAVION		1978	SONET	UK	SNTF 766
PIERRE BATTAILLET D (A							
DOMINIQUE ESNAULT D (A	PATRICK VERBEKE G (A COOKY RHINOSCEROS G (A CHRIS SAINT ROCK B (A						
CHRISTIAN WERBROUCK EFFECT(A							

H197 PHYLIS HYMAN

PHYLLIS HYMAN (A	(A) PHYLLIS HYMAN	1978	BUDDAH		BDLP	4046
	(B) SING A SONG	1979	BUDDAH		BDLP	4058

I1 I DON'T CARE

GARY BOGGESS K SYN(A	(A) ASK ANYONE	1976	BUDDAH		KSBS 2617
FRANK PELLINE G K V(A					
PETER KNAPP HRNS V(A JOSE ORTIZ D V (A TIM GRAZIANO B (A PAUL McDONALD WIND(A					
FRANK BONZIE V (A DOUG THOMAS V (A					

I1A I ROY

I ROY (ALL	(A) PRESENTING I ROY	19	TROJAN		TRLS 63
ROBBIE SHAKESPEARE B (I	(B) HELL & SORROW	19	TROJAN		TRLS 71
LEROY WALLACE D (I	(C) I ROY	1974	TROJAN		TRLS 91
EARL LINDO K (I	(D) VERSIONS GALORE	19	TROJAN		TBL 161
EARL SMITH G (I	(E) DREAD BALDHEAD	1976	KLIK		KLP 9020
CARLTON DAVIS D (I	(F) CRISUS TIME	1976	CAROLINE	UK	CA 2011
SCIENTIST PERC (I	(G) CANT CONQUER RASTA	1977	JUSTICE		JUSTLP 008
SCULLY PERC (I	(H) MUSICAL SHARK ATTACK	1977	VIRGIN	UK	V 2075
PABLO BLACK SYN (I	(I) HEART OF A LION	1978	FRONT LINE	UK	FL 1001
	(J) TEN COMMANDMENTS	1978	FRONT LINE	UK	FL 1028
	(J) TEN COMMANDMENTS	1980	BUTT		ONLY..1
	( ) CANCER	1979	FRONT LINE	UK	FLX4001
	( ) THE GENERAL (DBL)	1978	FRONT LINE	UK	FLD6002
	( ) WORLD ON FIRE	1978	FRONT LINE	UK	FL 1033

I2 JANIS IAN

JANIS IAN G V (ALL	(A) JANIS IAN	1967	VERVE FORECAST		US FTS3017
AL ROGERS D (D	(A) JANIS IAN	197	POLYDOR		PD 6058
BOB BUSHNELL B (D	(B) FOR ALL THE SEASONS	1968	VERVE		US FTS3024
DICK HYMAN ORG (D	(C) SECRET LIFE OF EDDIE FINK	1968	VERVE		US FTS3048
HUGH McCRACKEN G (D	(D) WHO REALLY CARES	1969	VERVE MGS 1850		US FTS3063
MARVIN STAMM VLN (D	(E) PRESENT COMPANY	1971	CAPITOL SM683		VMP 1014
STU SCHARF G (D	(F) STARS	1974	CBS US 32857	UK	80224
RALPH CASALE G (D	(G) BETWEEN THE LINES	1975	CBS US 33394	UK	80635
TONY STUD TROM (D	(H) AFTERTONES	1975	CBS US 33919	UK	69220
BERNIE GLOW TPT (D	(J) MIRACLE ROW	1977	CBS US 34440	UK	81879
RAY ALONGE HRNS (D	(K) JANIS IAN	1978	CBS US 35325	UK	82700
BRAD SPINNEY PERC (D	(L)NIGHT RAINS	1979	CBS	UK	83802
GENE ORLOFF VLN (D	(M) BEST OF	1980	CBS	UK	84711
HAROLD COLETTA VIOLA(D					
GEORGE RICCI CELLO(DFG CLAIRE BAY V (HJ PHIL BODNER WIND (FGH GONZALO FERDINDEZ (H					
LARRY HARLOW K (H ODETTA (H JEFF LAYTON G (HJ AL GORGONI G(AGH					
BUCKY PIZZARELLI G (H STU WOODS B (HJ RICHARD DAVIS B (FGH BARRY LAZAROWITZ PERC(FGHJ					
JOE FARRELL SAX (D ROMEO PENQUE SAX (DFH MANNY GREEN VLN (D JOE MALIN VLN (D					
AARON ROSAND VLN (D JULES SCHACTER VLN (D ARTIE BUTLER K (A VINNIE BELL G (A					
SAL DE TROIA G (AGL JOE MARK B (A ARTIE KAPLAN FLT (A KEN KOSEK FDL (G					
RUSSELL GEORGE B (G BUDDY SALZMAN D (A ALAN RAPH TROM (G JESSE LEVY STRINGS(H					
PHOEBE SNOW V (H RAY BECKENSTEIN WIND (F JOE SHEPLEY HRNS (F DON PAYNE B (G					
BURT COLLINS TPT (G RUBENS BASSINI CONGA(G PHIL KRAUS PERC (J CLARENCE CLEMONS SAX(L					
MIKE MAINIERI VIBES(L RICHARD CROOKS D (L JIM MAELEN PERC (L JOHN CROWDER B V (L					
RON GETMAN G (L STEVE LOVE G (L GARY HERBIG SAX (L CHICK COREA PNO (L					
LES HURDLE B (L STEVE MADAIO TPT (L KEITH FORSEY D (L HAROLD FACTERMEYER K(L					
STEPHANIE SPRUILL V (L LISA ROBERTS V (L FRANK OWENS K (L BOB KULICK G (L					
SCOTT ZITO G (L MATS BJOERKLUND G (L GORDON GRODY V (L FRANK FLOYD V (L					
ALLAN SCHWARZBERG D (L NEIL JASON B (L JOE D'ELIA (L JOCELYN BROWN V (L					
LANI GROVES V (L DINO SOLERA SAX (L GLORIA AGOSTINI HARP(L					

I3 IAN & SYLVIA

IAN TYSON G V	(A) IAN & SYLVIA	1962	VANGUARD US 79215	+ VSD 2113
SYLVIA TYSON AUTOHARP V(	(B) FOUR STRONG WINDS	1964	VANGUARD	VSD 2149
MONTE DUNN G (D	(C) NORTHERN JOURNEY	1964	VANGUARD	VSD 79154
RUSS SAVAKUS B (D	(D) EARLY MORNING RAIN	1965	VANGUARD US 79175 FONTANA TF6053
	(E) PLAY ONE MORE	1966	VANGUARD	VSD 79215
	(F) SO MUCH DREAMING	1967	VANGUARD	VSD 79241
	(G) NASHVILLE	1968	VANGUARD	VSD 79284
	(H) FULL CIRCLE	1968	VANGUARD	
	(I) BEST OF	1968	VANGUARD	SVRL 19004
	(J) IAN & SYLVIA (GREATEST HITS)	19	VANGUARD	VSD 5/6
	(K) BEST OF	19	CBS US 32516	UK 64634
	(L) LOVIN' SOUND	19	POLYDOR	2353 063
	( ) OL'OEN(SOLO IAN)	19	A&M	SP 9017
	( ) WOMANS WORLD (SOLO SYLVIA)	19	CAPITOL	ST 11434
	( ) ONE JUMP AHEAD OF THE DEVIL(IAN)	1979	BOOT	CAN BOS 7189

I4 ICE

JOHN CARTER (	(A) ICE	19	PASSPORT	US	10075
STEVE TURNER B (	(B) IMPORT	19	PASSPORT	US	10096
GLYN JAMES (					
LYNTON NAIFF K (GRANT SERPELL D (					

I5 ICEBREAKERS

	(A) PLANET MARS DUB	1978	FRONT LINE	UK	FL 1010

I6 IDES OF MARCH

JOHN LARSON TPT (A	(A) VEHICLE	1970	WB	US	WS1863
RAY HERR G B V(A	(B) COMMON BOND	197	WB	US	WS1896
JAMES PETERIK G V (ABCD	(C) WORLD WOVEN	197	RCA	US	LSP 4812
LARRY MILLAS G B FLT V (ABCD	(D) MIDNIGHT OIL	1973	RCA	US	APLI 0143
MIKE BORCH D VIBES (ABCD					
BOB BERGLAND B V (ABCD CHUCK SOUMAR PERC HCA V(ABCD DAVE ARELLANO K (D RUSTY YOUNG STEEL/DOB(D					

[206]

IDLE RACE

```
JEFF LYNNE      G V  (1AB      (A) BIRTHDAY PARTY              1968 LIBERTY US 7603    UK LBS 83132
GREG MASTERS    B    (1ABC     (A) BIRTHDAY PARTY              197  SUNSET            UK SLS 50381
DAVE WALKER          (C        (B) IDLE RACE                   1969 LIBERTY            UK LBS 83221
BOB WILSON           (         (C) TIME IS                     1971 REGAL ZONOPHONE    SLRZ 1017
BOB LAMB             (         (D) IMPOSTERS OF LIFE MAGAZINE  19
RITCHIE WALKER       (         (E) ON WITH THE SHOW            1973 SUNSET            UK SLS 50354
DAVE PRITCHARD  G    (1ABC        (1) 1967
MIKE HOPKINS         (C
ROGER SPENCER   D    (1ABC
```

IF

```
TERRY SMITH      G    (ABCD      (A) IF                        1970 CAPITOL US 539    UK ISLAND ILPS 9129
DICK MORRISSEY   SAX  (ABCDEHI   (B) IF2                       1970 CAPITOL US 676    UK ISLAND ILPS 9137
JOHN MEALING     K    (ABCD      (C) IF3                       1971 CAPITOL US 820    UK U A   UAG 29158
JIM RICHARDSON   B    (ABCD      (D) IF4                       1972                   UK U A   UAG 29315
DENNIS ELLIOTT   F    (ABCD      (E) NOT JUST A BUNCH OF PRETTY.. 1974 CAPITOL US 11299 UK GULL GULP 1004
J W HODGKINSON        (ABCD      (F) TEA BREAK IS OVER         1975                   UK GULL GULP 1007
DAVE QUINCY      SAX  (ABCD      (G) THIS IS IF                1973 BRAIN                201  005
DAVE GREENSLADE  K    (          (H) GOLD ROCK                 1974 BRAIN                201  103
DAVE WINTOUR     B    (I         (I) WATERFALL                 19   METROMEDIA   IMP      1057
CLIFF DAVIS      D    (EHI       (J) DOUBLE DIAMOND            19   METROMEDIA          1 0174
WALT MONAGHAN    V B  (EHI
FI TRENCH        K    (      KURT PALOMAKI   PERC (   PETE ARNESEN    K   ( GEOFF WHITEHORN   G (EHI
GABRIEL MAGNO    K    (EHI
```

IGGINBOTTOM

```
                 (A) IGGINBOTTOM'S WRENCH       1969  DERAM    UK   SML 1051
```

IGGY POP & THE STOOGES

```
IGGY POP         V    (ALL      (A) THE STOOGES               1972 ELEKTRA US EKS74051 UK  K 42032
SCOTT THURSTON B V G K(EGHJ     (B) FUN HOUSE                 197  ELEKTRA             UK  K 42055
SCOTT ASHETON    D    (ACE      (C) RAW POWER                 1973 CBS      US 32111   UK   65586
FRED SONIC SMITH G    (         (C) RAW POWER                 1977 EMBASSY             UK   31464
TONY SALES       B    (FGH      (D) IDIOT                     1976 RCA                     PL12275
RICKY GARDINER   G    (FH       (E) METALLIC K O              1976 SKYDOG          US      IMP1015
GARY RASMUSSEN   B    (         (F) LUST FOR LIFE             1977 RCA                     PL12488
HUNT SALES       D    (FGH      (G) KILL CITY                 1978 RADAR      K56467   +   RAD  2
DAVID BOWIE      PNO V(FH       (H) T V EYE                   1978 RCA                     PL12796
STACEY HAYDEN    G    (H        (J) NEW VALUES                1979 ARISTA              UK APART1092
DAVE ALEXANDER   B    (A        (K) SOLDIER                   1079 ARISTA              UK SPART1117
STEVE TRANIO     B    (G        (L) NO FUN                    1980 ELEKTRA US EF 7095  UK  K 52234
JAMES WILLIAMSON G V  (CEGJ
RON ASHETON    V B G(ACE  CARLOS ALOMAR   G V  (F   GAYNIA         V(G    BRIAN GLASCOCK D   (G
JOHN HARDEN    SAX   (GJ   DAVE BROCK   STRINGS (J   GLEN MATLOCK  G V(K   IVAN KRAL          (K
STEVE NEW           (K    BARRY ANDREWS       (K    EARL SHAKELFORD V  (J  ALFONO SISTERS   V (J
KLAUS KRUGER   D    (JK   JACKIE CLARK   B    (J    DOUGLAS BROWNE D (    MICHAEL PAGE   B   (
ROBER\ DUPREE  G    (
```

IGUANA

```
BRUCE ROBERTS    G V  (A        (A) IGUANA                    1974  POLYDOR     UK   2383 108
PETE HUNT        D    (A
JOHN CARTWRIGHT  B    (A    RON TAYLOR    SAX   (A   CHRIS GOWER   TROM (A
```

IJAHMAN

```
IJAHMAN          V G(AB         (A) HAILE I HYMN              1978  ISLAND      ILPS 9521
JONI             G    (A        (B) ARE WE A WARRIOR          1979  ISLAND      ILPS 9557
BO PE            G    (A
WILLIE LINDO     G    (A   EARL SMITH    G    (A  DEL RICHARDSON    G   (A  GEOFFREY CHUNG  K G (A
STEVE WINWOODJANE K   (A   EARL LINDO    K    (A  ERROL NELSON    PNO   (A  ROBERT LYN PNO     (A
OSSIE HIBBERTELF PNO  (A   VAL DOUGLAS   B    (A  ROBBIE SHAKESPEARE B  (A  LLOYD PARKS    B  (A
MICKY RICHARDSV  D    (A   SLY DUNBAR    D    (A  BOBBY ELLIS     TPT   (A  HERMAN MARQUIS SAX (A
RICHARD HALL     SAX  (A   EDDIE BLAIR   HRN  (A  ADRIAN BRETT    WIND  (A  ALAN BEEVER FLT   (A
HI HO SILVER     PERC (A   SONS OF NEGUS PERC    (A  GROCO           PERC (A
```

ILLUSION

```
JANE RELF        V    (AB       (A) OUT OF THE MIST          1977  ISLAND      ILPS 9489
JIM McCARTY      G V  (AB       (B) ILLUSION                 1978  ISLAND      ILPS 9519
JOHN HAWKEN      K    (AB
EDDIE McNEIL     D    (AB  LOUIS CENNAMO   B   (AB  JOHN KNIGHTSBRIDGE G  (A  PAUL SAMWEEL SMITH V(B
```

ILLUSTRATION

```
                 (A) ILLUSTRATION              1970  PYE INTERNATIONAL   NSPL28140
```

IMAN CALIFATO INDEPENDIENTE

```
KIKO GUERRERO    D    (A        (A) CAMUNO DEL AGIULA         19    CBS       SPAIN  584277
MARCOS MANTERO   K    (A
MANUEL RODRIGUES, G V (A   URBANO MORALES   B   (A
```

IMPALAS

```
JOE FRAZIER      V    (         (A) SORRY(I RAN ALL THE WAY HOME) 19   CUB       US     8003
TONY CARLUCCI    V    (
LENNY RENDA      V    (    RICHIE WAGNER    V   (A
```

IMPERIALS

```
                 TIME TO GET IT TOGETHER      19    KEY               KL  012
                 FOLLOW MAN WITH MUSIC        19    KEY               KL  025
                 THE IMPERIALS NOW            19    IMPACT      US    HWS1990
                 WHO'S GONNA LOVE ME          1978  POWER EXCHANGE    PXL 029
                 SAIL ON                      1978  DAYSPRING   UK    DAY4001
```

IMPRESSIONS

```
JERRY BUTLER     V        THE IMPRESSIONS         1964 ABC   US   450
CURTIS MAYFIELD  V        NEVER ENDING IMPRESSIONS 1963 ABC  US   468
SAMUEL GOODEN    V        KEEP ON PUSHING         1964 ABC   US   493
FRED CASH        V        PEOPLE GET READY        1965 ABC   US   505
LEROY HUGHES     V        GREATEST HITS           1965 ABC   US   515
REG TORAIN       V        ONE BY ONE              1965 ABC   US   523
RALPH JOHNSON    V        BIG 16                  1965 HMV   UK (M) CLP 1935    (S)CSD1642
                                                                              (CONTINUED)
```

IMPRESSIONS

RIDIN' HIGH	196	ABC	US	545	UK HMV		CSD3548
FABULOUS IMPRESSIONS	1967	ABC	US	607	UK HMV		CSD3631
WE'RE ON A WINNER	1968	ABC	US	635	UK STATESIDE		10239
THIS IS MY COUNTRY	1968	CURTOM	US	8001			
YOUNG MOD'S FORGOTTEN STORY	1969	CURTOM	US	8003	UK POLYDOR	2359	003
BEST IMPRESSIONS	196	CURTOM	US	8004			
BIG 16 VOL 2	1969				UK STATESIDE		10279
AMEN	196				UK POLYDOR	2359	009
BEST OF	19	ABC	US	654			
VERSATILE	19	ABC	US	668			
CHECK OUT YOUR MIND	197	CURTOM	US	8006	UK POLYDOR	2318	017
TIMES HAVE CHANGED	1972	CURTOM	US	8012	UK POLYDOR	2310	059
16 GREATEST HITS	197	ABC	US	727			
EARLY YEARS	1973				UK PROBE		GTSP 201
PREACHER MAN	1973	CURTOM	US	8016			
FINALLY GOT MYSELF TOGETHER	1974	CURTOM	US	8019	UK BUDDAH		4003
FIRST IMPRESSIONS	1975	CURTOM	US	5003	UK		K 56143
FIRST IMPRESSIONS	197	RSO					RSS 009
BIG 16 RI	1975	ABC			UK		ABCL 5104
FOR YOUR PRECIOUS LOVE	1976	VEE JAY	US	1075	UK DJM		DJB 26086
FOR YOUR PRECIOUS LOVE	197	JOY					JOYS 104
IT'S ABOUT TIME	1976	COTILLION	US	9912			
ORIGINALS (DBL)	1976	ABC	US	303			
LOVING POWER	1976	CURTOM	US	5009	UK		K 56211
VINTAGE YEARS	197	SIRE	US	3717			
THREE THE HARD WAY	197	CURTOM	US	8602			
COLLECTION	197	ABC	US	30009			

IN CAMERA

115A

PETE MOORE	B		1980	
ANDY GRAY	G			
JEFF WILLMOTT	D	DAVE STEINER	V	

116

INCREDIBLE STRING BAND

ROBIN WILLIAMSON G V K VLN+(ALL	(A) INCREDIBLE STRING BAND	1966	ELEKTRA				EKS 7322
MIKE HERON K G V B HCA FLT+(ALL	(B) THE 5000 SPIRITS	1967	ELEKTRA	EKS 74010+RI	K	42001
CLIVE PALMER V G BANJO (A	(C) HANGMANS BEAUTIFUL DAUGHTER	1968	ELEKTRA	EKS 74021+RI	K	42002
ROSE SIMPSON B PERC(CDEGJ	(D) THE BIG HUGE	1968	ELEKTRA	EKS 74037+RI	K	42022
LICORICE McKECHNIE VLN K(BCDGJK	(E) WEE TAM	1968	ELEKTRA	EKS 74036+RI	K	42021
MALCOLM LeMAISTRE V K B+(KLMN	(F) CHANGING HORSES	1969	ELEKTRA	EKS 74057+RI	K	42037
GERALD DOTT CLAR K (LM	(G) I LOOKED UP	1970	ELEKTRA	EKS 74061+RI	K	42046
JOHN GILSTON D (	(H) 'U'	1970	ELEKTRA		K	62002
STAN LEE B V STEEL (KMN	(I) RELICS OF I S B	1970	ELEKTRA	K62008+	K	42060
GRAHAM FORBES G (N	(J) BE GLAD FOR THE SONG	1970	ISLAND			ILPS 9140
MIKE TOMICH (	(K) LIQUID ACROBAT	1971	ISLAND	UK		ILPS 9172
DAVID BARKER (	(L) EARTH SPAN	1972	ISLAND	UK		ILPS 9211
JACK INGRAM V D (MN	(M) NO RUINOUS FEUD	1973	ISLAND	UK		ILPS 9229
DANNY THOMPSON B (BN	(N) HARD ROPE & SILKEN TWINE	1974	ISLAND	UK		ILPS 9270
JOHN HOPKINS PNO (B	(O) SEASONS THEY CHANGE	1976	ISLAND	UK		ISLD 9
SUSIE WATSON TAYLOR FLT(M						

B J WILSON   D   (M   STAN SCHNIER   B V (M   ALUN EDEN   D   (M   JANET WILLIAMSON FLT (M
SOMA   SITAR TAMBOURA (B   GERRY CONWAY   D   (K

117

INCREDIBLES

(A) HEART & SOUL	1974	CONTEMPO		CLP	512
(A) HEART & SOUL	19	AUDIO ARTS		AAS	7000

117A

INDIAN SUMMER

BOB JACKSON	K V	(A	(A) INDIAN SUMMER	1971	NEON	NE 3
COLIN WILLIAMS	G V	(A				
PAUL HOOPER D PERC V		(A	MALCOLM HARKER B VIBES V (A			

117B

INDUSTRIALS

DANNY STAG	V G K B	(A	(A) INDUSTRIALS	1980	CBS	UK	84399
J B FRANK	V G K D	(A				
JAN MACKENZIE	V	(A	MIKE BOLT V G K(A CALVIN TEARDROP B (A CYCLOPS D (A			

117C

INFERNAL BLUES MACHINE

WARREN RAY	V	(A	(A) INFERNAL BLUES MACHINE	1976	LONDON	UK	SHU 8496
GREG MIDDLETON	B	(A				
MIKE CAVANAUGH	K	(A	GREGG PARKER G (A			

118

INFLIKTORS

GARRY COOK	D V	(A	(A) 1976
KIT DENNIS	B	(A	
LEE RITTER	G V	(A	J D SKY G V (A

118A

INMATES

PETER GUNN	G V	(AB	(A) FIRST OFFENCE	1979	RADAR	RAD	25
BILL HURLEY	V	(AB	(B) SHOT IN THE DARK	1980	RADAR	RAD	28
BEN DONNELLY	B	(AB				
TONY OLIVER	G V	(AB	LAURIE GARMAN HCA (A JOHN BULL D (A EDDIE D (A			
JOHN EARLE	SAX	(A	DICK HANSON TPT (A RAY BEAVIS SAX (A GAVIN POVEY K (A			
JIM RUSSELL	D V	(A				

119

INNER CIRCLE

ROGER LEWIS	G	(	(A) ROCK THE BOAT	1974	TROJAN	TRLS	93
JACOB MILLER		(	(B) BLAME IT ON THE SUN	1975	TROJAN	TRLS	114
BERNARD 'TOUTER' HARVEY K(			(C) REGGAE THING	1976	CAPITOL	EST	11574
IAN LEWIS	B	(	(D) READY FOR THE WORLD	1977	CAPITOL	EST	11664
CALVIN McKENZIE	D	(	(E) EVERYTHING IS GREAT	1979	ISLAND	ILPS	9558
CHARLES FARQUHARSON K		(	(F) NEW AGE MUSIC	1980	ISLAND	ILPS	9608
EVERALD 'BLACKSPY' JAHSON PERC(						
JOE ORTIZ		(	LESTER ADDERLEY G V (			

INNER CITY UNIT   119A

NIK TURNER	V SAX(A	(A) PASS OUT	19	RIDDLE	RID	002
TREN THOMS	G V (A					
DEAD FRED	V K (A	BAZ MAGNETO B V (A MICK STUPP D (A				

NEIL INNES   120

NEIL INNES	G V HCA K (ABCD	(A) LUCKY PLANET	1970	LIBERTY	LBG	83419
IAN WALLACE	D (A	(B) HOW SWEET TO BE AN IDIOT	1973	U A	UAG	29492
ROGER McKEW	G (A	(C) RUTLAND TIMES	1976	BBC	REB	233
ROGER ROWAN	B (A	(D) TAKING OFF	1977	ARISTA	SPARTY1004	
JOHN HALSEY	D (CD	(E) INNES BOOK OF RECORDS	1979	POLYDOR	2383	556
TIMMI DONALD	D (D					
ROGER SWALLOW	D (C					

JON FIELD   CONGA(CD   BRIAN HODGSON   B (CD   ALAN JAMES   B (D   BILLY BREMNER   G (CD
ROGER RETTIG   G STEEL(CD   JOHN MEGGINSON   K (D   JULIAN SMEDLEY   VLN V(D   KEITH NELSON   BANJO(D
WILLIE FAHEY   WIND (D   BRIAN BOWLES   V (D   SUE JONES DAVIS   V (D   GERRY CONWAY   D (B
ANDY ROBERTS   G (BC   MIKE KELLIE   D (B   DAVE RICHARDS   B (BC   OLLIE HALSALL   G (B
ERIC IDLE   V (C   DAVE BALLBY   V (C

INSECT TRUST   121

LUKE FAUST HCA G V (AB		(A) INSECT TRUST	1968	CAPITOL	US	SKAO 109
TREVOR KOEHLER WIND D (AB		(B) HOBOKEN SATURDAY NIGHT	1970	ATCO	US	SD 33313
ROBERT PALMER	WIND (AB					
NANCY JEFFRIES	V (AB	BILL BARTH G STEEL(AB HUGH McCRACKEN G (ELVIN JONES D (				

INTERGALACTIC TOURING BAND   122

DAVID SCANCE	G (A	(A) INTER GALACTIC TOURING BAND	1977	CHARISMA	UK	CDS 4009
BRIAN CUOMO	K (A					

STEVE BARTH   V (A   ROD ARGENT   V (A   PETER SABEL   B (A   LARRY FAST   K SYN(A
RYCHE CHLANDA   G (A   PERCY JONES   B (A   DAVE COUSINS   V (A   JEFFREY LEYNOR   V (A
JIM CUOMO   V (A   MR SNIPS   V (A   JOHN TROPEA   G (A   MARGE RAYMOND   V (A
PAUL MARCHETTI   PERC (A   FRANCIS ROSSI   V (A   ANNIE HASLAM   V (A   JOEL KRATZ   V (A
ANTHONY PHILLIPS   G (A   FRANK PRESCOD   B (A   DAVID BEDFORD   (A   MIGHTY JOE YOUNG   (A
FRANK D'AGOSTINO   (A   CLARENCE CLEMONS   SAX (A   RICK PARFITT   (A   ARTHUR BROWN   (A
MEATLOAF   V (A   BEN E KING   V (A   WILL MALONE   (A

INTERNATIONAL SUBMARINE BAND   123

GRAM PARSONS	G V (A	(A) SAFE AT HOME	1968	LHI US	411+	LHIS 12001
BOB BUCHANAN	G V (A					
IAN DUNLOP	B (A	JOHN NUESE G (A JON CORNEAL D (A				

INTERVIEW   123A

JEFF STARRS	V (A	(A) BIG OCEANS	1979	VIRGIN	UK	V2123
PETE ALLERHAND	G V K(A					
ALAN BRIAN	G V (A	MANNY ELIAS D (A PHIL CROWTHER B (A				

INVISIBLE MANS BAND   123B

	(A) INVISIBLE MANS BAND	1980	ISLAND	UK	ILPS 9537

IRON BUTTERFLY   124

RON BUSHY	D (ABCDEFH	(A) HEAVY	1967 ATCO	US 33227	US 2465 015	
DOUG INGLE	K V (ABCDEH	(B) IN A GADDA DA VIDA	1968 ATCO	US 33250	UK 588 116	
JERRY PENROD	(A	(B) IN A GADDA DA VIDA	196 ATCO	UK K40022	FR WE341	
DANNY WEIS	(A	(C) BALL	1969 ATLANTIC	US 33280	UK 228 011	
DARRYL DELOACH	(A	(D) LIVE	1970 ATLANTIC	US 33318	UK 2400 014	
ERIC BRAUNN	G V (BCFGH	(E) METAMORPHOSIS	1970 ATLANTIC	US 33339	UK 2401 003	
MIKE PINERA	G (E	(F) METAMORPHOSIS	1972 ATLANTIC		UK K 40294	
LARRY RHEINHART	G (E	(F) SUN & STEEL	1975 MCA	US 2164	UK MCF 2738	
PHIL KRAMER	B (FG	(F) SUN & STEEL	1975 MCA	IMP 32869		
HOWARD REITZES	K (G	(G) SCORCHING BEAUTY	1975 MCA	US 465	UK MCF 2694	
LEE DORMAN	B (BCDEH	( ) EVOLUTION (BEST OF)	1970 ATLANTIC		UK K 40298	
BILL DEMARTINES	K V (F	( ) STAR COLLECTION	1973 MIDI	30038 +	20021	
RICHARD PODOLOR	G SITAR(E	(CE) BALL METAMORPHOSIS (DBL)	1975 ATLANTIC		UK K 80003	
BILL COOPER	G (E					
JEROME JUMMONVILLE HRNS(F		JULIA TILLMAN V (F MAXINE WILLARD V (F DENIECE WILLIAMS V (F				

IRON CITY HOUSEROCKERS   124A

JOE GRUSHECKLY	G V (A	(A) LOVES SO TOUGH	1979	MCA	UK MCF 3031
NED E RANKIN	D (A				

GIL SNYDER   K (A   BILLY CROSS G   (A   RICHARD REISING   V (A   SUSAN LYNCH V (A
RODNEY PSYKA   V (A   MARC REISMAN   HCA (A   PAUL GLANZ   PNO (A   ART NADINI B (A
GARY SCALESE   G (A   DENNY MARTIN   ACC (A   TAMPA LANN   V (A

IRON MAIDEN   125

PAUL DI'ANNO	V (AB	(A) IRON MAIDEN	1980	EMI	UK EMC 3330
DAVE MURRAY	G (AB	(B) KILLERS	1981	EMI	UK EMC 3357
ADRIAN SMITH	G (B				
STEVE HARRIS	B V (A	DENNIS STRATTON G V (A CLIVE BURR D (A			

IRONHORSE   125A

RANDY BACHMAN	G SYN V (AB	(A) IRONHORSE 1979		SCOTTI BROS US 7103	UK K 50598
TOM SPARKS	G V (AB	(B) EVERYTHING IS GREY	1980	SCOTTI BROS	UK K 50730
JOHN PIERCE	B (A				
MIKE BAIRD	D (A	FRANK LUDWIG V K (B RON FOOS B (B CHRIS LEIGHTON D (B			
MAVIS McCAULEY	V (A	BARRY ALLEN V (A			

GREGORY ISAACS   126

GREGORY ISAACS	(ALL	( ) IN PERSON	1975	TROJAN	TRLS 102
		( ) ALL I HAVE IS LOVE	1976	TROJAN	TRLS 121
		( ) COOL RULER	1978	FRONT LINE	UK FL 1020
		( ) BEST OF	1978	G G	
		( ) LONELY LOVER	1980	PRE	X1
		( ) SOON FORWARD	1979	FRONT LINE	UK FL 1044

ISIS   127

CAROLE MACDONALD	G V (AB	(A) ISIS	1974	BUDDAH BDS5605 +	BDLP 4002
GINGER BIANCO	D (AB	(B) AIN'T NO BACKIN' UP NOW	1975	BUDDAH BDS5626	
STELLA BASS	B (AB				

LIBERTY MATA   PERC (AB   JEANIE FINEBERG   WIND (AB   LOLLIE BIENENFIELD TROM V(A   JUNE MILLINGTON G (B
EDITH DANKOWITZ   WIND V(B   ELLEN SEELING   TPT (B   RENATE FERRER   G (B   LEWIS SOLOFF   TPT(B
MARGO LEWIS   K V (B   LAUREN DRAPER   HRNS (A   SUZI GHEZZI   G (A

```
RUDOLPH ISLEY      V    (ALL      SHOUT                        1959 RCA    US LSP 2156
RONALD ISLEY       V    (ALL      TWIST & SHOUT                1962 WAND   US     653 UK DJM        2628
KELLY ISLEY        V    (ALL      TWISTING & SHOUTING          196  UA     US    6313 UK UA    ULP  1064
MARVIN ISLEY       B    (ABCDEFGH TAKE SOME TIME OUT           1966                  UK MARBLEARCH 894
ERNIE ISLEY        G D  (ABCDEFGH THIS OLD HEART OF MINE       1966 TAMLA  US     269 UK     STML 11034
CHRIS JASPER       K    (ABCDEFGH SOUL ON THE ROCKS            1966 TAMLA  US     275
ROCKY DZIDZORNU    CONGA(A        DOIN' THEIR THING            1969 TAMLA  US     289 UK SUNSET     5257
TRUMAN THOMAS      K    (A        IT'S OUR THING               1969 TNECK  US    3001
GEORGE MORELAND    D    (A        THE BROTHERS ISLEY           1969 TNECK  US    3002 UK STATESIDE10300
                                  LIVE AT YANKEE STADIUM       1970 TNECK  US    3004
                                  GET INTO SOMETHING           1970 TNECK  US    3006
                                  IN THE BEGINNING             1970 TNECK  US    3007
                                  GIVING IT BACK               1971 TNECK  US    3008
                                  BROTHER BROTHER BROTHER      1972 TNECK  US    3009
                                  LIVE                         197  TNECK  US    3010
                                  GREATEST HITS                197  TNECK  US    3011 UK STARLINE   5043
                                  ROCK AROUND THE CLOCK        19   CAMDEN US ACLI0861
                                  (A) THREE + THREE            1973 TNECK  US   32453 UK EPIC       65740
                                  BEST OF                      19   BUDDAH US 2 5652
                                  VERY BEST OF                 19   UA     US LA 500G
                                  LIVE IT UP                   1974 TNECK  US   33070 UK EPIC       80317
                                  (B) THE HEAT IS ON           1975 TNECK  US   33536 UK EPIC       69139
                                  (C) HARVEST FOR THE WORLD    1976 TNECK  US   33809 UK EPIC       81268
                                  SUPER HITS                   1976               UK TAMLA STMA8024
                                  (D) GO FOR YOUR GUNS         1977 TNECK  US   34432 UK EPIC       86027
                                  (E) FOREVER GOLD   (COMP)    1977 TNECK  US   34452 UK EPIC       86040
                                  (F) SHOWDOWN                 1978 TNECK  US   34930 UK EPIC       86039
                                  TIMELESS                     1978               UK EPIC       88327
                                  (G) WINNER TAKES ALL         1979               UK EPIC       88460
                                  (H) GO ALL THE WAY           1980               UK EPIC       65740
```

129   ISOTOPE

```
GARY BOYLE    G   (ABCD                                  (A) ISOTOPE      1974 POLYDOR FR 2933 701 UK GULL 1002
BRIAN MILLER  K   (A                                     (B) ILLUSION     1974 POLYDOR FR 2933 704 UK GULL 1006
JEFF CLYNE    B   (A                                     (C) DEEP END     1976                     UK GULL 1017
LAURENCE SCOTT K  (BC                                    (D) BEST OF      1978                     UK GULL 1024
HUGH HOPPER   B   (BC
ZOE KRONBERGER K V (C  FRANK ROBERTS  K   (C  NIGEL MORRIS    D   (ABC AUREO DE SOUZA  D   (
DAN K BROWN   B   (C   MORRIS PERT    PERC (C  NEVILLE WHITEHEAD B  (C
```

130   ISRAEL VIBRATION

```
(A) SAME SONG     1978 TOP RANKING IMP+HARVEST UK SHSP409
```

131   ITS A BEAUTIFUL DAY

```
DAVID LAFLAMME F FLT VLN V(ALL   (A) ITS A BEAUTIFUL DAY       1968 CBS US 9768      UK        63722
LINDA LA FLAMME K (A             (A) ITS A BEAUTIFUL DAY       196  ALLIED PRODUCTION (PROMO)    364
PATTI SANTOS    V PERC(ABCDE     (B) MARRYING MAIDEN           1970 CBS US 1058      UK        64065
BILL GREGORY    G   (CDE         (C) CHOICE QUALITY STUFF      1971 CBS US 30734     UK        64314
TOM FOWLER      B   (CD          (D) LIVE AT CARNEGIE HALL     1972 CBS US 31338     UK        64929
HAL WAGENET     G V (ABC         (D) LIVE AT CARNEGIE HALL     1979 CBS            RI          83907
MITCHELL HOLMAN HCA V B(ABC      (E) TODAY                     1973 CBS US 32181    UK        65483
ROLF STUART     FLT (C           (F) 1001 NIGHTS               1974 CBS US 32660    UK        65812
JOSE AREAS      PERC (C          (G) ITS A BEAUTIFUL DAY (COMP)1979 CBS            UK          83797
FRED WEBB       K V (BCDE
VAL FUENTES   D V(ABCDE COKE ESCOVEDO  PERC (C   SID PAGE      VLN (BC BRUCE STEINBERG HCA (AC
VAN HUGHES    TROM  (C  BILL ATWOOD    TPT (C    ROBERT FERREIRA SAX (C CHARLES PETERSON SAX (C
GREGG ROLIE   K    (C   BUD COCKRELL   B V (E    RICHARD OLSEN CLAR (B JERRY GARCIA G BANJO (B
GREG BLOCH VLN MAND (E  DON WALDROP    TUBA (E
```

J1   J A L N

```
(A) LIFE IS A FIGHT                      1976 MAGNET      MAG 5017
(B) JUST ANOTHER LONELY NIGHT            1977 MAGNET      MAG 5018
(C) MOVIN' CITY HIGH                     1978 MAGNET      MAG 5023
(EP)    NOTHING EVER COMES THAT EASY     1977 MAGNET      MAG  901
```

J2   J J BAND

```
(A) JJ BAND                              1971 CBS         UK 64396
```

J3   JSD BAND

```
DES COFFIELD MAND G K V(ABCD     (A) COUNTRY OF THE BLIND  1971 REGAL ZONOPHONE UK SLRZ 1018
SEAN O'ROURKE   G V FDL (ABCD    (B) TAKE OFF YOUR HEAD    1972 RUBBER          UK RUB   001
JIM DIVERS   B CELLO V  (ABCD    (C) J S D BAND           1972 FLY             UK HIFLY 11
CHUCK FLEMING FDL MAND(D         (D) TRAVELLING DAYS       1973 CUBE            UK HIFLY 14
COLIN FINN      D   (CD
LINDSAY SCOTT   VLN V(D
```

J3A   J T B

```
JUKKA TOLONEN   G   (A           (A)J T B                  1979 PICK UP         PULP 79 302
COSTE APETREA   G   (A
CHRISTER EKLUND SAX (A  BILL CARSON  D   (A  HARRI MERICAHTI B  (A  JOACHIM KUHN   K  (A
```

J4   JABULA

```
VICKY BUSISWE MHLONGO V(A        (A) JABULA                1975 CAROLINE   UK  CA 2004
GRAHAM MORGAN    D   (AB         (B) THUNDER INTO OUR HEARTS 1976 CAROLINE  UK  CA 2009
KEN ELY          SAX (AB         (C) IN AMSTERDAM          1979 JABULA         JBL2003
MADUMETJA RANKU  G PERC(AB
EDDI QUANSAH    TPT (A  WILLIE CHEETHAM PERC V(A GEORGE LARNYOH WIND (A  JEAN ROUSSEL       K  (A
SEBOTHANE BAHULA PERC (AB SPARTACUS R   B   (B  MIKE ROSE      FLT (B  MAUREEN KOTO LEMBEDE V(A
FRANK ROBERTS   K   (B  BOB HOWSE     WIND (B  JIM CHAMBERS   V   (B  DUDU PUKWANA     SAX (AB
PETER VANDER PUIJE SAX (A MOGOTSI MOTHLE B V (AB NICK EVANS    TROM (B  JIM DVORAK       TPT (B
JIM THOMAS      V   (B
```

ALAN JACK CIVILIZATION

```
ALAN JACK            K V  (A        (A) BLUESY MIND                  19    BYG                      529011
CLAUDE OLMOS         G V  (A
RICHARD FONTAINE     B V  (A    JEAN FALISSARD      D V  (A
```

JACK KNIFE

```
JOHN WETTON          B V K(A        (A) I WISH YOU WOULD            1979   POLYDOR         UK   POLS 1010
RICHARD PALMER-JAMES G (A
JOHN HUTCHESON       K V  (A    CURT CRESS      D PERC(A  PETER BISCHOF    V   (A   MICHAEL LOHMANN  SAX (A
CKRISTIAN SHULZE     K    (A
```

JACK THE LAD

```
RAY LAIDLAW          D V  (ABC      (A) JACK THE LAD              1974   CHARISMA        UK   CAS  1085
PHIL MURRAY          B V  (BCD      (B) OLD STRAIGHT TRACK        1974   CHARISMA        UK   CAS  1094
BILLY MITCHELL       G V  (ABCD     (C) ROUGH DIAMONDS            1975   CHARISMA        UK   CAS  1110
WALTER FAIRBAIRN     G V  (BCD      (D) JACKPOT                   1976   UA              UK   UAS  29999
RAY JACKSON          HCA  (CD
MADDY PRIOR          V    (A    TOMMY EYRE      K    (A  CHRIS MERCER    HRNS (D  JOHN KIRKPATRICK ACC (C
JIMMY WRIGHTSON      CONC (A    STEVE GREGORY   HRNS (D  ROD CLEMENTS         (A  ANDY BOWN        K   (D
BUD BEADLE           HRNS (D    SIMON COWE      G V  (AB
```

CHARLES JACKSON

```
CHARLES JACKSON      V    (AB      (A) PASSIONATE BREEZES        1978   CAPITOL                  11775
BRUCE CONTE          G    (B       (B) GONNA GETCHA LOVE         1979   TOWER            EST 12002
MICHAEL McGLOIRY     G    (B
COLEMAN HEAD         G    (B    VICTOR CONTE    B    (B  JERRY KNIGHT    B V  (B  JULIA TILLMAN    V  (B
MELVIN BRITT         V    (B    WELTON GITE     B    (B  HARVEY HUGHES   D    (B  DENNIS DAVIS     D  (B
GAVIN CHRISTOPHER    K V  (B    GREG LEVIAS     K    (B  MAXINE WILLARD  V    (B  JUDY JONES       V  (B
NATE GINSBERG        K    (B    CHESTER THOMPSON K   (B  RONNIE FOSTER   K    (B  ROBERT THE ROOT  HCA(B
SYLVIA COX           V    (B    ORREN WATERS    V    (B
```

GORDON JACKSON

```
GORDON JACKSON G V SITAR(A       (A) THINKING BACK             1969   MARMALADE       UK    608 012
(NOT THE ACTOR)
REMI KEBAKA         PERC (A    STEVE WINWOOD   B K  (A  POLI PALMER     V K  (A  JIM CAPALDI      V   (A
LUTHER GROSVENOR    V    (A    ROCKY DZIDZORNU PERC (A  RICK GRECH      B    (A  CHRIS WOOD      WIND (A
JULIE DRISCOLL      V    (A    DAVE MASON      B    (A  ROB BLUNT    SITAR G   (A  JIM KING        SAX  (A
REG KING            V    (A
```

JOE JACKSON

```
JOE JACKSON V K HCA (ALL        (A) LOOK SHARP                 1979   A&M             UK   AMLH 64743
GARY SANFORD         G    (A    (A) LOOK SHARP (10" DOUBLE)    1979   A&M             US   SP   3666
GRAHAM MABY          B    (ABC  (B) I'M THE MAN                1979   A&M             UK   AMLH 64794
DAVE HOUGHTON        D    (A    (C) BEAT CRAZY                 1980   A&M             UK   AMLH 64837
```

MICK JACKSON

```
MICK JACKSON         V    (A       (A) MICK JACKSON            1979   ATLANTIC        UK   K 50605
KEITH FORSEY         D    (A
CURT CRESS          PERC (A    MATS BJORKLUND   G    (A  GUNTHER GEBAUER  B    (A  SYLVESTER LEVAY  K   (A
PATRICIA SHOKLEY     V    (A    TIM TOUCHTON     V    (A  ERIK THONER     V    (A  GABOR CRISTIF   TPT  (A
GUISEPPE SOLERA     SAX  (A    GEOFF BASTOW     K    (A  PATRICK GAMMON  K V  (A  MAX GREGOR       K   (A
KRISTIAN SCHULZE    SYN  (A    TOOTS THIELEMANS HCA  (A  VICTORIA MILES  V    (A  JERRY RIX        V   (A
WOLFGANG EMPERHOFF   V    (A    BOBBY STERN     SAX  (A  BENNY GEBAUER   SAX  (A  HERMANN BREUER  TROM(A
```

MILLIE JACKSON

```
MILLIE JACKSON       V    (ALL     (A) MILLIE JACKSON          1972 POLYDOR UK 2391 025 US SPRING 5703
JIMMY JOHNSON        G    (DEJFK    (B) IT HURTS SO GOOD        1972 POLYDOR UK 2391 091 US SPRING 5706
PETE CARR            G    (EFK      (C) MILLIE                  197                     US SPRING 6701
BARRY BECKETT        K    (DFJK     (D) CAUGHT UP               197  POLYDOR UK 2391 147 US SPRING 6703
DAVID HOOD           B    (DFJK     (E) STILL CAUGHT UP         197  POLYDOR UK 2391 183 US SPRING 6708
ROGER HAWKINS        D    (DEJFK    (F) FREE & IN LOVE          197  POLYDOR UK 2391 215 US SPRING 6709
BRAD SHAPIRO        PERC (D         (G) BEST OF                 1976 POLYDOR UK 2391 247
TOM ROADY           PERC (DEJFK     (H) LOVINGLY YOURS          197  POLYDOR UK 2391 252 US SPRING 6712
CHARLES CHALMERS     V    (EF       (J) FEELIN' BITCHY          1977 POLYDOR UK 2391 301 US SPRING 6715
SANDY RHODES         V    (EF       (K) GET IT OUTCHA SYSTEM    1978 POLYDOR UK 2391 336 US SPRING 6719
DONNA RHODES         V    (EF       (L) ROYAL RAPPIN'S          1979 POLYDOR UK 2480 516
ISAAC HAYES               (L
JANE FRICKY          V    (JF   KEN BELL       G    (JF  SPIDERMAN HARRISON V  (JK  MARY LOU VAN DE PITTE V(K
RON EADES           HRNS (F    CYNTHIA DOUGLAS      (K  THE MOMENTS     V    (H  HARRISON CALLOWAY    HRNS(F
DONNA DAVIS          V    (K    STEVE MELTON         (K  HARVEY THOMPSON HRNS (F  SHELDON KIRKLAND STRINGS(K
BRANDY               V    (JH   TIM HENSON      K    (J  PAM VINCENT     V    (K  CHARLES ROSE         HRNS(F
LARRY BYROM          G    (J    MIKE MEYERS          (K
```

WANDA JACKSON

```
WANDA JACKSON        V    (ALL     ROCKIN WITH WANDA            1960   CAPITOL         US   TS   1384
BILLY SANFORD        G    (*       ROCKIN WITH WANDA            1977   CAPITOL         UK   CAPS 1007
RAY EDENTON          G    (*       RIGHT OR WRONG               1061   CAPITOL         US   ST   1596
RUSSELL HICKS        G    (*       WONDERFUL WANDA              1962   CAPITOL         US   ST   1776
JERRY SHOOK          G    (*       THERE'S A PARTY GOING ON     19     CAPITOL         US   ST   1511
JAMES CAPPS          G    (*       WANDA JACKSON                19     CAPITOL         US   T    1041
WELDON MYRICK      STEEL (*        LOVE ME FOREVER              19     CAPITOL         US   ST   1911
CHARLIE McCOY       HCA  (*        I GOT TO SING                19     CAPITOL         US   ST   669
JERRY SMITH         PNO  (*        2 SIDES OF WANDA             19     CAPITOL         US   ST   2030
JACK WILLIAMS        B    (*       WANDA JACKSON                19     PICKWICK        UK        2053
HENRY STRZELECKI     B    (*       BLUES IN MY HEART            19     CAPITOL         US   ST   2306
KENNY MALONE         D    (*       SINGS COUNTRY SONGS          1966   CAPITOL         US   ST   2438
JERRY CARRIGAN       D    (*       COUNTRY MUSIC HALL OF FAME   1967   CAPITOL         US   ST   2606
FARRELL MORRIS      PERC (*        YOU'LL HAVE MY LOVE          19     CAPITOL         US   ST   2812
DELORES EDGIN        V    (*       CREAM OF THE CROP            1969   CAPITOL         US   ST   2976
JUNE PAGE            V    (*       BEST OF                      19     CAPITOL         US   ST   2883
BERGEN WHITE         V    (*       BEST OF                      19     CAPITOL         US   ST   11166
HURSHAL WIGGINTON    V    (*       A PORTRAIT OF                1970   CAPITOL         US   ST   21530
JOSEPH BABCOCK       V    (*       A WOMAN LIVES TO LOVE        1970   CAPITOL         US   ST   554
                                   COUNTRY                      1970   CAPITOL         US   ST   434
                                   PRAISE THE LORD              1972   CAPITOL         US   ST   11023
                                   PIONEERS OF ROCK             1972   STARLINE        UK   SRS  5120
```

(CONTINUED)

WANDA JACKSON

COUNTRY KEEPSAKES	1973	CAPITOL	US	ST	11161
I WOULD'NT WANT YOU ANY OTHER WAY	1973	CAPITOL	US	ST	11096
COUNTRY CLASSICS	1973	CAPITOL	EURO	5C 052 81215	
WHEN IT'S TIME TO FALL IN LOVE AGAIN	1974	CAPITOL	US	ST	6513
COUNTRY GOSPEL	1974	WORD		WST	9514
NOW I HAVE EVERYTHING	1975	MYRRH		MYR	1021
MAKE ME A CHILD AGAIN	1976	MYRRH		MYR	1043
(*)I'LL STILL LOVE YOU	1976	DJM	UK	DJF	20493
PLEASE HELP ME I'M FALLING	19	HILLTOP	US	JS	6058
LEAVE MY BABY	19	HILLTOP	US	JS	6074
WE'LL SING IN SUNSHINE	19	HILLTOP	US	JS	6116
BY THE TIME I GET TO PHOENIX	19	HILLTOP	US	JS	6123
TEARS AT GRAND OLE OPRY	19	HILLTOP	US	JS	6184
NOBODY'S DARLIN'	19	VOCALION	US	VL	73861
CLOSER TO JESUS	1978	WORD		WST	9580
ROCK'N'ROLL HISTORY	1979	CAPITOL	US	038 82098	
GREATEST HITS	1979	CAPITOL	US	134 53025/6	

JACKSON HEIGHTS

LEE JACKSON	B V G(ABCD	(A) KING PROGRESS	1970	CHARISMA	UK	CAS	1018
CHARLIE HARCOURT	(A	(A) KING PROGRESS	197	MERCURY	US	SR	61331
TOMMY SLOANE	D (A	(B) 5TH AVENUE BUS	1972	VERTIGO	UK	6360	067
MARIO ENRIQUE	B (A	(C) RAGAMUFFINS FOOL	1973	VERTIGO	UK	6360	077
COVARRURAS TAPIA	(A	(C) JACKSON HEIGHTS	1973	VERVE	US	V6	5089
PATRICK MORAZ	K (	(D) BUMP & GRIND	1973	VERTIGO	UK	6360	092
MIKE GILES	D (BCD						
BRIAN CHATTON	K V (BCD	JOHN McBURNIE	G V K(BCD	TONY CONNOR	(C	LAWRIE WRIGHT	PNO (B
DAVE WATTS	PNO (B	IAN WALLACE	D (D	ROGER McKEW	G (D	JOHNNY VAN DERRICK	FDL(D
BILLY BELL	BANJO(D	CHRIS LAURENCE	B (D	JOHNNY TOOGOOD	SAX (C	RACE McLEOD	D (C
MO FLETCHER	B (C	MOX	HCA (C	KEITH HARRIS	BANJO(C	OLI OLIVER	FDL (C
LAURIE JAY	D (C						

JACKSON HIGHWAY

DENNIS GULLEY	V G K(A	(A) JACKSON HIGHWAY	1980	CAPITOL	US	ST	12044
BRITT MEACHAM	G V (A						
TOMMY PATERSON	K V (A	RUSSELL GULLEY	B V (A	RONNIE VANCE	D V (A	ROGER HAWKINS	D (A
DAVID HOOD	B (A	JIMMY JOHNSON	G (A	RANDY McCORMICK	K (A	RICKY MEDLOCKE	D (A
GREG T WALKER	(A	DUNCAN CAMERON	(A				

THE JACKSONS

MICHAEL JACKSON	V (	I WANT YOU BACK	1969	TAMLA US			
JACKIE JACKSON	V (	DIANA ROSS PRESENTS	1970	TAMLA US 700	UK	STML	11142
TITO JACKSON	V (	A B C	1970	TAMLA US 709	UK	STML	11156
JERMAINE JACKSON	V (	CHRISTMAS ALBUM	1970	TAMLA	UK	STML	11168
MARLON JACKSON	V (	THIRD ALBUM	1971	TAMLA US 718	UK	STML	11174
RANDY JACKSON	V (	MAYBE TOMORROW	1971	TAMLA US 735	UK	STML	11188
		GREATEST HITS	1972	TAMLA	UK	STML	11212
		LOOKIN' THROUGH WINDOWS	1972	TAMLA US 750	UK	STML	11214
		SKYWRITER	1973	TAMLA	UK	STML	11231
		DANCING MACHINE	1973	TAMLA US 780	UK	STML	11275
		GET IT TOGETHER	1973	TAMLA US 783	UK	STML	11243
		MOVING VIBRATIONS	1975	TAMLA	UK	STML	11290
		JACKSONS	1976	EPIC US 34229	UK		86009
		MOTOWN SPECIAL	1977	TAMLA	UK	STMX	6006
		ANTHOLOGY	1977	TAMLA US M7868	UK	TMSM	6004
		JOYFUL JUKEBOX MUSIC	1977	TAMLA US 865	UK	STML	12046
		GOIN' PLACES	1977	EPIC US 34835	UK		86035
		DESTINY	1978	EPIC US 35520	UK		83200
		ZIP A DEE DOO DAH	1979	MFP	UK		50418
		20 GOLDEN GREATS	1979	TAMLA	UK	STML	12121

DALE JACOBS

DALE JACOBS	K (A	(A) COBRA	1979	EPIC	UK		83761
JOEL WADE	B (A						
BRETT WADE	G (A	JIM VALLANCE	D (A	JIM McGILLEVRAY	PERC(A	DOUG LOUIE	K (A
WAYNE KOSAK	WIND (A	LOU HOOVER	D (A	TOM LAVIN	G (A	BRIAN HARRISON	B (A
CAT HENDRIKSE	D (A	DOUG CUTHBERT	D (A	RALPH DYCK	VIBES(A		

JADD FAIR

(A) ZOMBIES OF MORA TAM	1980	ARMAGEDDON	UK	AEP	003

JADE WARRIOR

TONY DUHIG	G B K(ALL	(A) JADE WARRIOR	1971	VERTIGO US 1007	UK	6360	033
JON FIELD PERC G K	(ALL	(B) RELEASED	1971	VERTIGO US 1009	UK	6360	062
COLERIDGE GOODE	B (DF	(C) AUTUMNS DREAM	1972	VERTIGO US 1012	UK	6360	079
GLYN HAVARD	B G V(ABC	(D) FLOATING WORLD	1974	ISLAND	UK	ILPS	9290
DAVID DUHIG	G (CDE	(E) WAVES	1975	ISLAND	UK	ILPS	9318
ALAN PRICE	D (BC	(F) KITES	1976	ISLAND	UK	ILPS	9393
SKAILA KANKA	HARP(DG	(G) WAY OF THE SUN	1978	ISLAND	UK	ILPS	9552
CHRIS KARAN	D (D	(H) REFLECTIONS (COMP)	1980	BUTT		BUTT	001
GRAHAM DEACON	D (D						
MARTHA MDENGE	V (D	STEVE WINWOOD	K (E	CLODAGH SIMMONDS	V (F	ROGER BRYSON	PNO (F
JOE O'DONNELL	VLN (F	GOWAN TURNBULL	SAX (F	DAVE CONNERS	WIND (B	GRAHAM MORGAN	D (FG
DEBBIE HALL	VLN (F	GEOFF WESTLEY	PNO (F	JOHN DENTITH	D (G	DICK CUTHELL	HRNS(G
PETE GIBSON	HRNS(F	WILLIE	PERC (F	FRED FRITH	VLA (F	BILL SMITH	B (G

JAGS

NICK WATKINSON	G V (A	(A) BACK OF MY HAND (EP)	1979	ISLAND	UK	12SWIP6501
JOHN ALDER	G V (A					
ALEX BAIRD	D (A	STEVE PRUDENCE	B V (A			

JAGUAR

ROY HOWELL G MAND B	(A	(A) JAGUAR	1977	RCA		APLI 2420
ED FORESMAN	B V (A					
WALTER POLK	D PERC(A	RANDY COPELAND	B (A	DREW HAYS	V PERC(A	PAT TAYLOR G V (A
DOUG MAYO	K PERC(A	BEVERLEY BAXTER	V (A			

```
                              JAH LION                                                    J17A
JAH LION              (A      (A) COLUMBIA COLLIE              1976    ISLAND          ILPS 9386
                              JAH LLOYD                                                   J17B
JAH LLOYD        V    (AB      (A) THE HUMBLE ONE              1978 FRONT LINE      UK  FL  1005
SLY DUNBAR       D    (B       (B) BLACK MOSES                 1979 FRONT LINE      UK  FL  1031
ROBBIE SHAKESPEARE B  (B
ANSEL COLLINS    ORG  (B   BOBBY KALPHAT    PNO  (B   ERIC LAMONT      G   (B   RAD BRYAN      G (B
STICKY THOMPSON  PERC (B   HUNTLEY          FLT  (B
                              JAH STITCH                                                  J17C
JAH STITCH           (AB      (A) MY PRECIOUS LOCKS           1978 CANCER          CAN LPOO2
                              (B) WATCH YOUR STEP             1979 THIRD WORLD      TWLP  701
                              JAH THOMAS                                                  J17D
JAH THOMAS           (AB      (A) STOP YU LOAFIN'             1978 GREENSLEEVES     GREL    3
                              (B) DANCE HALL STYLEE           1980 DADDY KOOL       DKLP16
                              JAH WOOSH                                                   J17E
JAH WOOSH            (AB       (A) THE WORLD MARIJUANA TOUR   1977    CARIB GEMS
                              (B) LICK HIM WITH THE DUSTBIN   1977    KAB
                              ( ) JAH WOOSH                   1974    CACTUS        CTLP 103
                              ( ) JAH JAH DEY DEY             1976    CACTUS        CTLP 116
                              ( ) DREADLOCK AFFAIR            1976    TROJAN        TRLS 113
                              ( ) PSALMS OF WISDOM            1977    BLACKWAX      LP2
                              ( ) RELIGIOUS DREAD             1979    TROJAN        TRLS 157
                         JAKE & THE FAMILY JEWELS                                         J18
JAKE(ALLAN JACOBS) V G (A     (A) JAKE & THE FAMILY JEWELS   19     POLYDOR US 24 4029 UK  2425  027
MIKE ROSA            D    (A
JEREMIAH BURNHAM FLT B V(A  DAN MANSOLINO    K V  (A  DANIEL BEN ZEBULON °ERC (A  KENNY PINE    G V (A
KATHLEEN WHELEN  PERC (A  VITO JACOBS      G V  (A  MYLES ARONOWITZ JEWSHARP(A  JON LIND      G V (A
JIM STARSES      G    (A  BOB SMITH        PNO  (A  PERRY ROBINSON    CLAR(A  LARRY PACKER      FDL(A
CHARLIE CHIN     BANJ (A  DON BROOKS       HCA  (A  BUZZY LINHART     V   (A  BUNKY ROCHELLE SKINNER V(A
                              THE JAM                                                     J19
PAUL WELLER      G V  (ALL     (A) IN THE CITY               1977 POLYDOR US 6110  UK    2383 447
RICK BUCKLER     D    (ALL     (B) THIS IS THE MODERN WORLD  1977 POLYDOR US 6129  UK    2383 475
BRUCE FOXTON     B V  (ALL     (C) ALL MOD CONS              1978 POLYDOR US 6118  UK    2442 155
MICK TALBOT      PNO  (D       (C) ALL MOD CONS              1978 POLYDOR          UK    POLD 5008
STEVE RUDI       SAX  (D       (D) SETTING SONS              1979 POLYDOR          UK5018  2442 168
                              (E) SOUND AFFECTS              1980 POLYDOR          UK5035
                              (AB) IN THE CITY/MODERN WORLD  1980 POLYDOR          UK    2683 074
                              BOB JAMES                                                   J20
BOB JAMES        K    (ALL     (A) ONE                       1975    CTI                  6043
GARY KING        B    (ABCDEFGHI (B) TWO                     1975    CTI                  6057
STEVE GADD       D    (ABDEFI  (C) THREE                     1976    CTI                  6063
RALPH McDONALD   PERC (ABCDEFGHI (D) FOUR                    1977    CTI                  7074
GROVER WASHINGTON SAX (ACEHI   (E) HEADS                     1977    CBS US 34896  UK     82271
JON FADDIS      HRNS  (ACEHI   (F) TOUCHDOWN                 1978    CBS           UK     83175
LEW SOLOFF      TPT   (ABCDEI  (G) ONE ON ONE                1979    CBS           UK     83931
WAYNE ANDRE     TROM  (ABCEI   (H) 'H'                       1980    CBS           UK     84238
EDDIE DANIELS   WIND  (BCDEHI  (I) BEST OF                   19      CTI           UK    00630034
GEORGE MARGE    WIND  (ADEHI   (J) EXPLOSIONS                19      ESP           US     1009
ROMEO PENQUE    WIND  (ADHJ
ERIC GALE       G     (BCDEI  ARTHUR JENKINS PERC(BI  HUBERT LAWS    FLY  (BCDEI  RANDY BRECKER HRNS (BEHI
MARVIN STAMM    TPT   (ABCI   DANNY CAHN     TPT  (H   MICHAEL LAWRENCE TPT (H    IDRIS MUHAMMAD D   (AEH
RICHIE RESNICOFF G    (ABI    ERIC WEISSBERG STEEL(AI  DAVE FRIEDMAN  VIBES(AI    HUGH McCRACKEN HCA(ACI
THAD JONES      HRNS  (AI     VICTOR PAZ     TPT  (ABI ALAN RUBIN     TPT  (ABI   PAUL FAULISE  TROM (AHI
JACK GALE       TROM  (AFI    ALAN RAPH      TROM (AI  ANDREW SMITH   D    (BI    JOHN FROSK   HRNS(BCDEI
JIMMY BUFFINGTON HRNS (BEI    PETER GORDON   HRNS (BIE AL RICHMOND    HRNS (BI    EDDIE BERT   TROM (BI
TOM MITCHELL    TROM  (BEI    TONY STUDD     TROM (BI  PATTI AUSTIN   V    (BEI   FRANK FLOYD   V   (IB
LANI GROVES     V     (BEI    ZACHARY SANDERS V   (BI  SIDNEY WEINBERG WIND (DI   EARL KLUGH    G   (FG
BARRY ROGERS    TROM  (H      LIBERTY DE VITO D   (BI  DAVID BROWN    G    (H     HIRAM BULLOCK G   (HF
BUDDY WILLIAMS  D     (H      HARVEY MASON   D    (CGI ANDY NEWMARK   D    (CE    WILL LEE      B   (CE
JEFF MIRANOV    G     (CE     JERRY DODGION FLT   (CHI DAVE BARGERON  HRNS (CI    DAVE TAYLOR  TROM (CEI
GLORIA AGOSTINI HARP (CEI     ART FARMER     HRNS (DI  JOHN GATCHELL  TPT  (D     JIM PUGH     TROM (H
DOUG STEGMEYER  B     (H      LEONARD GIBBS PERC  (H   AIRTO MOREIRA  PERC (H     BRUCE DUNLAP  G   (H
MICHAEL MAINERI VIBES(E       DAVE SANBORN   SAX  (EF  VIVIAN CHERRY  V    (E     GWEN GUTHRIE  V   (E
ALLEN SCHWARZBERG D  (E       ALPHONSO JOHNSON B  (E   STEVE KHAN     G    (E     JEFF LAYTON   G   (E
BROOKS TILLOTSON HRNS(E       PHIL BODNER   WIND  (EH  MICHAEL BRECKER SAX (E     GERRY NIEWOOD WIND (E
RON CARTER      B     (FG     NEIL JASON          (G   MONGO SANTAMARIA    (F
                              ELMORE JAMES                                               J21
ELMORE JAMES    G V  (ALL      (A) TOUGH                     197  BLUE HORIZON   UK   7 63204
JOHN BRIM            (AK       (B) TO KNOW A MAN             1969 BLUE HORIZON   UK   7 66230
JOHNNY JONES    PNO  (DELMN    (C) LEGEND OF                 1970 UA            UK   UAS  29109
HOMESICK JAMES WILLIAMSON(E    (D) COTTON PATCH(1 SIDE)      1973 POLYDOR       UK    2383 200
J T BROWN       SAX  (DELMN    (E) ALL THEM BLUES            1975 DJM           UK   DJLMD 8008
ODIE PAYNE      D    (DE L     (F) RESURRECTION OF ELMORE JAMES 1976 BLUES ANTHOLOGY UK AB  5610
BOYD ATKINS     SAX  (D        (F) RESURRECTION OF ELMORE JAMES 197  KENT       US      9010
IKE TURNER      PNO  (D        (G) LEGEND OF ELMORE JAMES    1976 BLUES ANTHOLOGY UK  AB  5601
JAMES PARR      TPT  (D        (G) THE LEGEND OF ELMORE JAMES 1976 KENT          US     9001
MAXWELL DAVIS   SAX  (D        (H) BEST OF                   19   SUE           UK   ILP 918
JEWELL GRANT    SAX  (D        (J) MEMORIAL ALBUM            19   SUE           UK   ILP 927
JESSE SAILES    D    (D        (K) WHOSE MUDDY SHOES         19   CHESS               1537
EDDIE TAYLOR    G    (M        (L) THE BLUES IN MY HEART     19                 US      7716
WILLIAM McDANIEL     (         (M) STREET TALKIN'            19   MUSE          MR 5087
BUSHY HEAD      PNO  (B        (N) DUST MY BLUES             19   GLOBE         VIP 5004M
CHUCK HAMILTON       (         (O) ELMORE JAMES              19   KENT          US      522
                              (P) HISTORY OF VOL 1           19   TRIP          US     8007
                              (Q) HISTORY OF VOL 2           19   TRIP          US     9511
                              (R) ONE WAY OUT                1980 CHARLY        UK   CRB 1008
                              (S) SKY IS CRYING              19   SPHERE SOUND  US     7002
                                                                               (CONTINUED)
```

ELMORE JAMES

			(T) SCREAMING BLUES	19	HARLEM HIT PARADE			5014
			(U) BLUES MASTERS VOL 1	19	BLUE HORIZON	US		46021
			(V) I NEED YOU	19	SPHERE SOUND	US		7008

J22 ETTA JAMES

ETTA JAMES	V	(ALL	AT LAST	1961	CADET	US		4003
WITH			SECOND TIME AROUND	1961	CADET	US		4011
JEFF PORCARO	D	(*	ETTA JAMES	1963	CADET	US		4013
CHUCK RAINEY	B	(*	SINGS FOR LOVERS	1963	CADET	US		4018
LARRY CARLTON	G	(*	TOP TEN	1963	CADET	US		4025
CORNELL DUPREE	G	(*	ROCKS THE HOUSE	1963	CADET	US		4032
BRIAN RAY	G	(*	QUEEN OF SOUL	1965	CADET	US		4040
RICHARD TEE	K	(*	CALL MY NAME	196	CADET	US		4055
KEITH JOHNSON	PNO	(*	TELL MAMA	1969	CADET	US		802
ALEXANDER HAMILTON	V	(*	TELL MAMA	1969	CHESS		CRL	4536
MERRY CLAYTON	V	(*	FUNK	1970	CADET	US		
JOYCE AUSTIN	V	(*	MISS ETTA JAMES	19	CROWN	US	CLP	5209
GILBERT IVEY	V	(*	BEST OF	19	CROWN	US	CLP	5234
REUBEN FRANKLIN	V	(*	TWIST WITH	19	CROWN	US	CLP	5250
HENRY JACKSON	V	(*	GOLDEN DECADE	1972	CHESS	UK	6310	126
THE SNAKES	V	(*	ETTA JAMES	1973	CHESS			50042
TOM ROADY	PERC	(*	COME A LITTLE CLOSER	19	CHESS			60029
RICK SCHLOSSER	D	(*	ETTA IS BETTA THAN EVAH	1975	CHESS			19003
JIM HORN	SAX	(*	PEACHES	19	CHESS		2CH	60004
RON STOCKERT	K	(*	(*) DEEP IN THE NIGHT	1978	WB US BSK 3156		UK K	56492
ALIMASH SHANANDA	PERC	(*						
STEVE CROPPER	G	(* PLAS JOHNSON SAX (*						

J23 GARY JAMES

GARY JAMES		(A) THIRDS	19	ABC DUNHILL	US	ABCX	721

J24 JIMMY JAMES & THE VAGABONDS

JIMMY JAMES	V	(ABC	(A) NEW RELIGION	1966	PICCADILLY		NPL	38027
COUNT MILLER	V	(A	(B) OPEN UP YOUR SOUL	1968	PYE		NSPL	18231
WALLACE WILSON	G	(A	(C) THIS IS JIMMY JAMES	1968	MARBLE ARCH		MAL	823
RUPERT BALGOBIN	D	(A	(D) LONDON SWINGS (1SIDE)	1968	PYE		NSPL	18156
MATT FREDERICK	SAX	(A	(E) YOU DONT STAND A CHANCE	1975	PYE		NSPL	18457
PHIL CHEN	B	(A	(F) NOW	1976	PYE		NSPL	18495
PAT GRAVESEND	SAX	(	(G) COME SOFTLY TO ME	19	ATCO	US	SD	33222
ARTHUR REGIS	ORG	(						
CARL NOEL	ORG	(A MILTON JAMES SAX (A						

J25 JOHN JAMES

JOHN JAMES	G V	(ALL	(A) MORNING BRINGS THE LIGHT	1970	TRANSATLANTIC	UK	TRA	219
PETE BERRYMAN	G	(C	(B) JOHN JAMES	1971	TRANSATLANTIC	UK	TRA	242
JOHN RENBOURN	G	(DEF	(C) SKY IN MY PIE	1972	TRANSATLANTIC	UK	TRA	250
CHRIS BILLINGS	G	(F	(D) HEAD IN THE CLOUDS	1975	TRANSATLANTIC	UK	TRA	305
DUCK BAKER	G	(E	(E) DESCRIPTIVE GUITAR INSTRUMENTALS	1977	KICKING MULE	UK	SNKF	128
			(F) IN CONCERT	1978	KICKING MULE	UK	SNKF	136

J26 KEEF JAMES

KEEF JAMES		(A	(A) ONE TREE OR ANOTHER	1973	RARE EARTH		SRE	3007

J27 NICKY JAMES

NICKY JAMES	V PERC G	(ABC	(A) NICKY JAMES	1971	PHILIPS		6308	069
KIRK DUNCAN	PNO V	(C	(B) EVERY HOME SHOULD HAVE ONE	1973	THRESHOLD	UK	THS	10
MIKE WEDGWOOD	B V	(C	(C) THUNDERTHROAT	1976	THRESHOLD	UK	THS	19
GRAHAM DEACON	D	(C						
LYNDON GREEN	G	(C RAY GLYNN G (C RAY THOMAS (C GERRY HOFF V (C						
DAVID KATZ	STRINGS	(C NASHVILLE KATZ STRINGS(C JUSTIN HAYWARD G (C MOX FLT HCA (C						
B J COLE	STEEL	(C ALAN FELDMAN K (C BROTHER FATAAR B (CHICO GREENWOOD D (C						
BARRY MARTIN	WIND V	(C JOHN WEIDER G VLN (C MAGGIE CAIRNES V (C HIROSHI KATO G (C						
IRENE CHANTER	V	(C DOREEN CHANTER V (C						

J28 RICK JAMES

RICK JAMES		(A	(A) COME GET IT	1978	TAMLA	UK	STML	12085
STONE CITY BAND		(A						

J29 SKIP JAMES

SKIP JAMES	G V	(ALL	A TRIBUTE	19	BIOGRAPH	BLP	12016	
			THIS OLD WORLD	19	BIOGRAPH	BLP	12027	
			EARLY RECORDINGS	19	BIOGRAPH	BLP	12029	
			THEY SANG THE BLUES	19	HISTORICAL	HLP	22	
			SKIP JAMES TODAY	1965	VANGUARD SVRL 19001+VSD		79219	
			DEVIL GOT MY WOMEN	1968	VANGUARD	VSD	79273	
			GREATEST OF THE DELTA BLUES SINGERS	19	MELODEON	US	7321	
			I'M SO GLAD	1978	VANGUARD	VPD	20001	

J30 TOMMY JAMES & THE SHONDELLS

TOMMY JAMES	V	(ALL	(A) HANKY PANKY	1966	ROULETTE	US	25336
RONNIE ROSMAN	K	(K	(B) ITS ONLY LOVE	196	ROULETTE	US	25344
PETER LUCIA	D	(K	(C) I THINK WE'RE ALONE NOW	196	ROULETTE	US	25353
MIKE VALE	B	(K	(D) SOMETHING SPECIAL	196	ROULETTE	US	25355
EDDIE GRAY	G	(K	(E) GETTING TOGETHER	196	ROULETTE	US	25357
			(F) MONY MONY	1968	ROULETTE	US	25012
			(G) CRIMSON & CLOVER	1969	ROULETTE	US	42012
			(H) CELLOPHANE SYMPHONY	1969	ROULETTE	US	42030
			(J) BEST OF	1970	ROULETTE	US	42040
			(K) TRAVELIN'	1970	ROULETTE	US	42044
			(L) TOMMY JAMES	197	ROULETTE	US	42051
			(M) CHRISTIAN OF THE WORLD	197	ROULETTE	US	3001
			(N) MY HEAD,MY BED & MY RED GUITAR	197	ROULETTE	US	3007
			(O) AT THE SATURDAY HOP	19	LOUISIANNE	US	
			(P) IN TOUCH	19	FANTASY	US	9509
			(Q) MIDNIGHT RIDER	19	FANTASY	US	9532

JIM FOX	D V	(ABCDEFHJL	(A) YER ALBUM	1969	STATESIDE UK 10295	ABC US	688
DALE PETERS	B V	(BCDFHL	(A) YER ALBUM	1969	BLUESWAY	US	6034
GLENN SCHWARTZ	G	(	(B) JAMES GANG RIDES AGAIN	1970	PROBE UK 6253	ABC US	711
TOM KRISS	B	(A	(B) JAMES GANG RIDES AGAIN	1970	ABC UK 5009	MCA GERM	52075
DOMENIC TROIANO	G	(E	(C) THIRDS	1971	PROBE UK 038	ABC US	721
ROY KENNER	V	(EHJ	(D) LIVE IN CONCERT	1971	PROBE UK 1045	ABC US	733
TOMMY BOLIN	G	(HJ	(D) LIVE IN CONCERT	1974	ABC UK 5016		
BUBBA KEITH	G V	(L	(E) STRAIGHT SHOOTER	1972	PROBE UK 1056	ABC US	741
RICHARD SHACK	G	(L	(F) PASSIN' THROUGH	1972	PROBE UK 1065	ABC US	760
ALBHY GALUTEN	K	(J	(G) BEST OF	1972	PROBE UK 1070	ABC US	774
RUSTY YOUNG	STEEL	(B	(G) BEST OF	1973	ABC UK 5027		
SHELLY KURLAND	VLN	(E	(H) BANG	1973	ATLANTIC UK K50028	US	7939
DAVID BRIGGS	ORG	(L	(I) GOLD RECORD	1973	ABC	EURO	68303
TOM DOWD	K	(L	(J) MIAMI	1974	ATLANTIC UK K50068	US	36102
KEN HAMANN	SYN	(L	(K) 16 GREATEST HITS	1974		ABC US	801/2
GEORGE RICCI	CELLO	(L	(L) NEWBORN	1975	ATLANTIC UK K50148	US	36112
DONNY BROOKS	HCA	(L	(M) JESSE COME HOME	1976	ATCO	US	36141
AL PERKINS	STEEL	(L					
BOB WEBB	V G	(	PHIL GIALLOMARDO K V (				

NICK JAMESON	V G B K D	(A	(A) ALREADY FREE	1977 BEARSVILLE US 6972	UK K 55519
ERIC PARKER	D	(A			
PAUL BUTTERFIELD	HCA	(A			

(A) JAMESTOWN SHEIKS	19 CHAPTER ONE UK	CMS 1001

JOE JAMMER	G V	(A	(A) BAD NEWS	1973 REGAL ZONOPHONE UK SRZA 8515
TONY STEVENS	B	(A		
REG ISADORE	D	(A	SAPPHO KORNER V (A JEAN ROUSSEL K (A CHRIS MERCER HRNS (A
DANNY LEWINSON	V	(A		

MICK JAGGER	V	(A	(A) JAMMING WITH EDWARD	1972 ROLLING STONES COC 39100
NICKY HOPKINS	K	(A		
RY COODER	G	(A	BILL WYMAN B (A CHARLIE WATTS D (A

JAN BERRY	V	(ALL	GOLDEN HITS	1962 LIBERTY US (M) 3248	(S)7248
DEAN TORRENCE	V	(ALL	TAKE LINDA SURFIN'	1963 LIBERTY US (M) 3294	(S)7294
HAL BLAINE	D	(*	(*) SURF CITY	1963 LIBERTY US (M) 3314	(S)7314
RAY POHLMAN		(*	(*) SURF CITY	1963 LIBERTY UK	LBY 1163
LEON RUSSELL	K	(*	DRAG CITY	1963 LIBERTY US (M) 3339	(S)7339
LARRY KNECHTEL	B	(*	DEAD MANS CURVE/NEW GIRL IN SCHOOL	1964 LIBERTY US (M) 3361	(S)7361
STEVE DOUGLAS	SAX	(*	RIDE THE WILD SURF	1964 LIBERTY US (M) 3368	(S)7368
TOMMY TEDESCO	G	(*	LITTLE OLD LADY FROM PASADENA	1964 LIBERTY US (M) 3377	(S)7377
BILL PITMAN		(*	COMMAND PERFORMANCE	1965 LIBERTY US (M) 3403	(S)7403
BILLY STRANGE		(*	GOLDEN HITS VOL 2	1965 LIBERTY US (M) 3417	(S)7417
GLEN CAMPBELL	G V	(*	FOLK & ROLL	1965 LIBERTY US (M) 3431	(S)7431
			FILET OF SOUL	1966 LIBERTY US (M) 3441	(S)7441
			MEET BATMAN	1966 LIBERTY US (M) 3444	(S)7444
			POPSICLE	1966 LIBERTY US (M) 3458	(S)7458
			GOLDEN HITS VOL 3	1966 LIBERTY US (M) 3460	(S)7460
			SAVE FOR A RAINY DAY	1967 J &D US	JDS 101
			JAN & DEAN	19 SUNSET US (M) 1156	(S)5156
			LEGENDARY MASTERS	1971 UA	UAS 9961
			REMEMBER (EP)	1973 UA US REM401	
			GOTTA TAKE THAT ONE LAST RIDE	1974 UA US	UALA 341H2
			JAN & DEAN (DBL)	197 SUNSET NL	12860020/1
			20 ROCK'N'ROLL HITS	1979 UA SWED ROCK10	
			STORY	1980 CREOLE UK PAST 1	US KTEL502

DEREK NOY	G TPT TROM	(B	(A) SORCERERS	1970	NOVA UK	SDN 8
DENIS CONLAN	D	(B	(B) MICE & RATS IN THE LOFT	1971	TRANSATLANTIC UK	TRA234
MICHAEL BAIRSTOW	WIND	(B				

BERND PULST	V	(A	(A) JANE TOGETHER	1972	BRAIN	1 002
KLAUS HESS	G V	(ABCD	(B) HERE WE ARE	1973	BRAIN	1 032
WERNER NADOLNY	K FLT	(AB	(C) JANE 3	1974	BRAIN	1 048
CHARLY MAUCHER	B V	(AC	(D) LADY JANE	1975	BRAIN	1 066
PETER PANKA	D V	(ABCD	(E) FIRE, WATER , EARTH & WIND	1975	BRAIN	1 084
MARTIN HESSE	B	(D	(F) LIVE	1976	BRAIN	0080 001
GOTTFRIED JANKO	K V	(D	(G) BETWEEN HEAVEN & HELL	197	BRAIN	0060 055
WOLFGANG KRANTZ	G PNO	(BC	(H) AGE OF MADNESS	1978	LOGO UK	1005
DIETER DIERKS	SYN	(B	(J) SIGN No NINE	1979	BRAIN	0060 218

LU JANIS	V K	(A	(A) OR DURVS	1978 INPHASION 3900
AL CINER	G	(A		
JOEY BRASLER	G	(A	PHIL REED G (A DENNIS BELFIELD V B (A BUTCH RILLERA D (A
BOBBY RUFFINO	D	(A	CRAIG KRAMPF D (A ROY BRAVERMAN K (A BECKY LEWIS V (A
VINCE POULOS	EFFECTS	(A	SILKY MAYER G (A

CHAS JANKEL	V K PERC G	(A	(A) CHAS JANKEL	1980 A&M UK AMLH 68518
PETER VAN HOOKE	D	(A		
CHRIS WARWICK	SYN	(A	MARK ISHAM TPT SAX SYN(A KUMA HARADA B (A CHRIS HUNTER SAX (A
PAUL WESTWOOD	B	(A	

(A) GRAVEDIGGER	1974 ELECTROLA	IC062 29433

J39B   NOEL JANUS

NOEL JANUS		(A	(A) HEROES OF THE WORLD			1977	DJM		UK	DJF 20509
KIRBY	G	(A								
JEFF RICH	D	(A	STEVE EMERY	B	(A	JOHN COOK		K SYN(A		

J40   JAPAN

DAVID SYLVIAN	V G	(ABCD	(A) ADOLESCENT SEX	1978	ARIOLA		AHAL	8004
MICK KARN	B V	(ABC	(B) OBSCURE ALTERNATIVES	1979	ARIOLA		AHAL	8007
STEVE JANSEN	D V	(ABC	(C) QUIET LIFE	1979	ARIOLA		AHAL	8011
ROB DEAN	G V	(ABC	(D) GENTLEMEN TAKE POLAROIDS	1980	VIRGIN		V	2180
RICHARD BARBIERI	K V	(ABC						
RAY SINGER	V	(A						

J41   BERT JANSCH

BERT JANSCH	G V PNO(ALL		(A) BERT JANSCH	1965	TRANSATLANTIC	UK	TRA	125
JAY LACY	G	(N	(B) IT DON'T BOTHER ME	1965	TRANSATLANTIC		TRA	132
JIM BAKER	G V	(N	(C) JACK ORION	1966	TRANSATLANTIC	UK	TRA	143
DON WHALEY	B V	(N	(C) JACK ORION	196	VANGUARD	US	VSD	6544
ERNIE McDANIELS	B	(N	(D) BERT & JOHN RENBOURN	1966	TRANSATLANTIC	UK	TRA	144
DAVID HUNGATE	B HRNS(N		(E) LUCKY THIRTEEN	1966	VANGUARD		VSD79212	
DANNY R LANE	D	(N	(F) NICOLA	1967	TRANSATLANTIC	UK	TRA	157
TRIS IMBODEN	D	(N	(G) BIRTHDAY BLUES	1968	TRANSATLANTIC	UK	TRA	179
ROBERT GREENIDGE	D	(N	(H) STEPPING STONES	1969	VANGUARD US 6506	UK	VSD79292	
CRAIG BULHER	HNRS (N		(I) SAMPLER	1969	TRANSATLANTIC		TRASAM	10
DARRYL LEONARD	HRNS (N		(J) ROSEMARY LANE	1971	TRANSATLANTIC	UK	TRA	235
JIM GORDON	HRNS (N		(K) BOX OF LOVE (COMP)	1972	TRANSATLANTIC	UK	TRASAM	27
BILL SMITH	K	(N	(L) MOONSHINE	1973	REPRISE	UK	K 44225	
DAVID BARRY	K	(N	(M) L.A. TURNAROUND	1974	CHARISMA	UK	CAS	1090
GEORGE SEYMOUR	K	(N	(N) SANTA BARBARA HONEYMOON	1975	CHARISMA	UK	CAS	1107
RAY WARLEIGH	FLT	(K	(O) EARLY BERT	1976	XTRA	UK	XTRA	1163
BETH FICHET	V	(N	(P) EARLY BERT VOL 2	1976	XTRA	UK	XTRA	1164
RON McGUIRE	V	(N	(Q) EARLY BERT VOL 3	1976	XTRA	UK	XTRA	1165
STEVE WOOD	V	(N	(R) EARLY BERT VOL 4	1977	XTRA	UK	XTRA	1170
MICHAEL NESMITH	G	(M	(S) A RARE CONUNDRUM	1977	CHARISMA	UK	CAS	1127
RALPH McTELL	HCA	(S	(T) ANTHOLOGY	1978	TRANSATLANTIC	UK	MTRA	2007
DAVE BAINBRIDGE	K	(S	(U) AVOCET	1979	CHARISMA	UK	CLASS	6
PICK WITHERS	D	(S						
ROD CLEMENTS G B MAND (S			DANNY THOMPSON	B	(U	MIKE PIGGOTT	VLN (S	JOHN RENBOURN	G (BCDK
NIGEL PORTMAN SMITH B K(			LUCE LANGRIDGE	D	(	JACQUI McSHEE	V	(	MARTIN JENKINS FLT VLN MAND(KU

J42   JEAN MICHEL JARRE

JEAN MICHEL JARRE	K SYN(AB	(A) OXYGENE	1977	POLYDOR	UK	2310 555
		(B) EQUINOXE	1978	POLYDOR	UK	POLD 5007

J43   AL JARREAU

AL JARREAU	V	(ALL	(A) WE GOT BY	1975	WB US 2224		UK K 54045	
TOM CANNING	K	(AB	(B) GLOW	1976	WB US 2248		UK K 54073	
JOE CORRERO	D	(AB	(C) LOOK TO THE RAINBOW(DBL) LIVE)	197	WB US 3052		UK K 66059	
WILTIN FELDER	B	(B	(D) ALL FLY HOME	1979	WB US 3229		UK K 56546	
LARRY CARLTON	G	(B						
LARRY NASH	K	(B	JOE SAMPLE	PNO (B	LARRY BUNKER	VIBES(A	STEVE FORMAN	PERC (B
RALPH MACDONALD	PER	(A	DAVE GRUSIN	K	(A	WILLIE WEEKS	B	(B	PAUL STALLWORTH	B (AB
ARTHUR ADAMS	G	(A						

J44   JAY & THE AMERICANS

JAY BLACK	V	(ALL	(A) SHE CRIED	1962	UA		US	6222
KENNY VANCE		(	(B) AT THE CAFE WHA	1963	UA		US	6300
SANDY YAGUDA		(	(C) COME A LITTLE BIT CLOSER	1965	UA		US	6407
MARTY SANDERS		(	(D) BLOCKBUSTERS	1965	UA		US	6417
WALTER BECKER	B G	(	(E) GREATEST HITS VOL 1	1965	UA		US	6453
DONALD FAGEN	K	(	(F) SUNDAY & ME	1966	UA		US	6474
HOWIE KANE	G	(	(G) LIVING ABOVE YOUR HEAD	1966	US		US	6534
JAY TRAYNOR	V	(A	(H) GREATEST HITS VOL 2	1967	UA		US	6555
			(J) TRY SOME OF THIS	1967	UA		US	6562
			(K) SAND OF TIME	1969	UA		US	6671
			(L) WAX MUSEUM VOL 1	1970	UA		US	6719
			(M) WAX MUSEUM VOL 2	197	UA		US	6751
			(N) VERY BEST OF(COMP)	197	UA UK LBR1000	US>	UALA	357
			(O) CAPTURE THE MOMENT	19	UA		US	6762

J45   JAZZ ROCK EXPERIENCE

		(A) JAZZ ROCK EXPERIENCE	1970	NOVA	SDN 19

J46   JEFFERSON AIRPLANE & STARSHIP

PAUL KANTNER G V			(A) JEFFERSON AIRPLANE TAKES OFF	1966	RCA US LSP 3584		UK SF	8195
	(ABCDEFGHJKLMNOPQRST		(A) JEFFERSON AIRPLANE TAKES OFF	1974	RCA INTERNATIONAL		INT	1476
JORMA KAUKONEN	G V		(B) SURREALISTIC PILLOW****	1967	RCA US LSP 3766		UK SF	7889
	(ABCDEFGHJKLP		(B) SURREALISTIC PILLOW****	1975	RCA		AYLI	3738
MARTY BALIN	G V		(C) AFTER BATHING AT BAXTERS	1967	RCA US LSO 1511		UK SF	7926
	(ABCDEFJLMNOPQR		(C) AFTER BATHING AT BAXTERS	197	RCA		AFLI	4545
SIGNE ANDERSON	V	(ALP	(D) CROWN OF CREATION	1968	RCA US LSP 4058		UK SF	7976
SKIP SPENCE	D	(ALP	(E) BLESS ITS POINTED LITTLE HEAD	1969	RCA US LSP 4133		UK SF	8019
SPENCER DRYDEN	D	(ABCDEFJLP	(E) BLESS ITS POINTED LITTLE HEAD	197	TELDEC SR 3012 +RCA		AFLI	4133
BOB HARVEY	B	(	(F) VOLUNTEERS	1969	RCA US LSP 4238		UK SF	8076
JACK CASADY	B	(ABCDEFGHJKLP	(G) BARK	1971	GRUNT		FTR	1001
GRACE SLICK	K V		(H) LONG JOHN SILVER	1972	GRUNT		FTR	1007
	(BCDEFGHJKLMNOPQ		(J) THE WORST OF (COMP)	1970	RCA US LSP 4459		UK SF	8164
JOEY COVINGTON	D	(GHL	(K) 30 SECONDS OVER WINTERLAND	1973	GRUNT		BFLI	0147
JERRY GARCIA	G	(L	(L) EARLY FLIGHT	1974	GRUNT		APLI	0437
PAPA JOHN CREACH	VLN V(GHKMNR		(M) DRAGONFLY	1974	GRUNT		BFLI	0717
JOHN HAMMOND	HCA	(L	(N) RED OCTOPUS	1975	GRUNT FTR 2002		BFLI	0999
JOHN BARBATA	D	(HKMNOQR	(O) SPITFIRE	1976	GRUNT		BFLI	1557
SAMMY PIAZZA	D	(H	(P) FLIGHT LOG	1976	RCA US LSP 3766		UK SF	7889

(CONTINUED)

[216]

```
DAVID FREIBERG      V  (KMNOQRS   (P) FLIGHT LOG              1976 GRUNT                  CYL2 1255
IRV COX             SAX (N        (Q) EARTH                   1978 GRUNT                  BXLI  215
PETER KAUKONEN      B  (          (R) GOLD (COMP)             1979 GRUNT                  FL  13247
BOBBYE HALL         PERC (N       (S) FREEDOM AT POINT ZERO   1979 GRUNT                  FL  13452
CRAIG CHAQUICO      G  (MNOQRS    (T) BEST OF                 1980 RCA INT US 42727   UK    5030
PETER SEARS         B K (MNOQRS   (AB) SURREALISTIC AIRPLANE (DBL)  19
AYNSLEY DUNBAR      D  (S
MICKEY THOMAS       V  (S

                 **** DIFFERENT TRACKS ON US/UK LPS
```

GARLAND JEFFREYS   J48

```
GARLAND JEFFREYS PERC G V   (ALL   (A) GARLAND JEFFREYS          1973 ATLANTIC US SD 7253
STEVE GADD          D  (BC         (B) GHOST WRITER             1977 A&M US   4629      UK AMLH 64629
DON GROLNICK        K  (BC         (C) ONE EYED JACK            1978 A&M US   4681      UK AMLH 64681
DR JOHN             K  (ABC        (D) AMERICAN BOY & GIRL      1979 A&M US   4778      UK AMLH 64778
JEFF MIRANOV        G  (C
RICHARD TRIFAN      K  (C    DAVID SANBORN      SAX (BC   LUTHER VANDROSS    V   (C   HUGH McCRACKEN G HCA (BC
MICHAEL BRECKER     SAX (BC  PHOEBE SNOW        V   (C    PAUL PRESTOPINO   MAND (D   DAVID SPINOZZA K G   (BC
RANDY BRECKER       TPT (BC  DAVID LASLEY       V   (BC   ALAN FREEDMAN      G   (ABD PAT AUSTIN      V   (A
DAVID BROMBERG      DOBRO(A  DONALD BROOKS      HCA (A    HUX BROWN          G   (A   LORI BURTON      V   (A
GEOFFREY CHUNG      G   (A   RICHARD DAVIS      B   (A    WINSTNON GRENNAN   D   (A   PAUL GRIFFIN     K   (A
NEVILLE HINDS       ORG (A   JACKIE JACKSON     B   (A    JIMMY JOHNSON      D   (A   DENZIL LAING     PERC(A
RALPH MACDONALD     PERC(A   MIKE MAINIERI      VIBES(A   ADAM MILLER        V   (A   DAVID NEWMAN     SAX (A
CHRIS OSBORNE       G   (A   LARRY PACKER       VLA VLN(A THE PERSUASIONS    V   (A   BERNARD PURDIE   D   (A
CHUCK RAINEY        B   (A   ALBERTINE ROBINSON V   (A    JOHN SIMON        PNO  (A   MAERETHA STEWART V   (A
WINSTON WRIGHT      PNO (A   ANTHONY JACKSON    B   (BC   RUBENS BASSINI    PERC (A   ARNOLD McCULLER  V   (B
JAMES TAYLOR        V   (A   JOHN BOUDREAUX     D   (B    PHIL MESSINA      TROM (B   SUGARBEAR        G   (B
DANNY CAHN          TPT (B   LYNNE PITNEY       V   (B    AL COHN           SAX  (B   LEON PENDARVIS   K   (B
DAVID PEEL          V   (B   BURT COLLINS       TPT (B    ROBERT ATHAS      G B  (D   TIMMY CAPELLO K SAX V(D
ANTON FIG           D   (D   RAFAEL GOLDFIELD   B   (D    RORY DODD          V   (D   ERIC TROYER      V   (D
HERB ALPERT         TPT (D
```

JELLY   J49

```
FRED BLIFFERT       V  (A         (A) TRUE STORY              1977 ASYLUM      US    7E 1096
JESSE ROE           V  (A
AMY MADIGAN         V  (A
```

JELLYBREAD   J50

```
PAUL BUTLER         G V (ABC      (A) FIRST SLICE             1969 BLUE HORIZON US 4801  UK 7 63853
PETE WINGFIELD      K V (AB       (B) 65 PARKWAY              1970 BLUE HORIZON          2431 002
JOHN BEST           B   (ABC      (C) BACK TO BEGIN AGAIN     1972 BLUE HORIZON          2931 004
CHRIS WATERS        D   (AB
RICK HAYWARD        G   (C   KENNY LAMB   D PERC   (C
```

JELLYROLL   J51

```
                                  (A) JELLYROLL              1971 MCA UK MUPS 420 + US KAPP 3626
```

JOHNNY JENKINS   J52

```
JOHNNY JENKINS  V G HCA   (A      (A) TON TON MACOUTE        1970 ATLANTIC UK 2400 033+ RI  K40105
DUANE ALLMAN        G    (A       (A) TON TON MACOUTE        1970 ATCO     US SD 33331+ FR  503056
PETE CARR           G    (A
PAUL HORNSBY        G K  (A   ROBERT 'POPS' POPWELL B(A   BERRY OAKLEY    B    (A   BUTCH TRUCKS     D  (A
JOHNNY SANDLIN      D    (A   JAI JOHANNY JOHANSON PERC(A  EDDIE HINTON   PERC  (A   JOHNNY WYKER    PERC(A
TIPPY ARMSTRONG     PERC (A   SOUTHERN COMFORT      (A  ELLA BROWN        V    (A
```

BILL JENNINGS   J52A

```
BILL JENNINGS            (A      (A) GUITAR MOODS           19   KING         US   KEP  342
```

WAYLON JENNINGS   J53

```
WAYLON JENNINGS   G V (ALL    FOLK COUNTRY                 1965 RCA            US LSP 3523
BILLY SANFORD     G   (OM     LEAVIN TOWN                  1966 RCA            US LSP 3620
DALE SELLERS      G   (O      NASHVILLE REBEL              1966 RCA            US LSP 3736
REGGIE YOUNG      G   (OPZX   SINGS OL' HARLAN             1966 RCA            US LSP 3660
GERRY GROPP       G   (O      JEWELS                       1967 RCA            US LSP 4035
EDDIE HINTON      G   (O      LOVE OF THE COMMON PEOPLE    1967 RCA            US LSP 3825
BILLY REYNOLDS    G   (OQMUS  HANGIN' ON                   1968 RCA            US LSP 3918
RANDY SCRUGGS     G   (OQS    ONLY THE GREATEST            1968 RCA    UK SF 8003 US LSP 4023
LARRY WHITMORE    G   (OPQUS  COUNTRY FOLK                 1969 RCA            US LSP 4180
STEVE YOUNG       G   (O      JUST TO SATISFY YOU          1969 RCA            US LSP 4137
RALPH MOONEY STEEL G  (OPMSTUXZ WAYLON JENNINGS           1969 VOCALION        US VL  73873
JOE ALLEN         B   (OQ     BEST OF                      1970 RCA    UK LSA 3000 US LSP 4341
BEE SPEARS        B   (OZ     WAYLON                       1970 RCA            US LSP 4260
HENRY STRZELECKI  B   (OM     SINGER OF SAD SONGS          1970 RCA    UK LSA 3025 US LSP 4418
TOMMY WILLIAMS        (O      DONT THINK TWICE             1969 A&M            US   S  4238
BYRON BACH        CELLO(      COUNTRY STYLE OF             1970 A&M                AMLB 1006
MARTHA McCRORY    CELLO(O     THE TAKER                    1970 RCA            US LSP 4487
DAVID BRIGGS      PNO (O      THE ONE & ONLY WAYLON        19   CAMDEN             CAS  2183
ANDY McMAHON      ORG (OQ     CEDARTOWN GEORGIA            1970 RCA    UK LSA 3053 US LSP 4567
DON BROOKS        HCA (OPZ    (M)LADIES LOVE OUTLAWS       1971 RCA    UK LSA 3142 US LSP 4751
WILLIE ACKERMANN  D   (O      GOOD HEARTED WOMAN           1972 RCA            US LSP 4647
RICHIE ALBRIGHT   D   (OPQSTUXZ HEARTACHES BY THE NUMBER   1972 CAMDEN             CAS  2556
BUDDY HARMAN      D   (OM     LONESOME ON'RY & MEAN        1972 RCA            US LSP 4854
FRED NEWELL       G   (PQ     (O ) HONKY TONK HEROES       1973 RCA            US   APL1 0240
WILLIE NELSON     V B (P      RUBY DONT TAKE YOUR LOVE TO TOWN  1973 CAMDEN         CAS  2608
JESSI COLTER      K   (P      (P) THIS TIME                1974 RCA            US APL0 539
DEE MOELLING      K   (P      (Q ) RAMBLING MAN            1974 RCA    UK LSA 3136 US APL1 0734
DUKE GOFF         B   (OPQSTU NED KELLY                    1975 U A            US UALA 3066
KYLE LEHMING      K TPT(OPQ   OUTLAWS                      1976 RCA    UK RS  1070 US APL1 1321
CHARLIE McCOY     HCA (S      (S)DREAMING MY DREAMS        1975 RCA    UK LSA 3247US APL1 1062
ROGER CRABTREE    HCA (QSU    (T)ARE YOU READY FOR COUNTRY 1976 RCA    UK RS  1067 US APL1 1816
CHARLES LOCHRAN   PNO (S      (U)LIVE                      1976 RCA    UK PL 11108 US APL1 1108
MERLE WATSON      G   (S      MACKINTOSH & TJ (SOUNDTRACK) 1976 RCA            US APL1 1520
                                                                            (CONTINUED)
```

WAYLON JENNINGS

JOHN WILKIN	G	(MRS	HITS OF	1977	RCA	UK PL 42211		
JOE PALLEN	G	(S	(X)OL' WAYLON	1977	RCA	UK PL 12317 US	APL1 2317	
JIMMY COLVARD	G	(S	WAYLON & WILLIE	1978	RCA	UK PL 12686 US	APL1 2686	
KENNY MALONE	D	(S	(Z) I'VE ALWAYS BEEN CRAZY	1978	RCA	UK PL 12959 US	APL1 2959	
BUDDY SPICHER	FDL	(S	WAYLON AT JDs	1978	BEAR FAMILY	GERM JD	1001	
STRING SECTION		(S	A SOUVENIR OF ARIZONA	19		LJR	114	
DAVE KIRBY	G	(MQ	ONLY DADDY THAT'LL WALK THE LINE	19	RCA	ACLI 0306		
BUNKY KEELS	PNO	(Q	DARK SIDE OF FAME	19	RCA	ACLI 7019		
LARRIE LONDIN	D	(MQ	GREATEST HITS OF WAYLON	1979	RCA	UK PL 13378		
THOMAS JACKSON	FDL	(Q	WHAT GOES AROUND COMES AROUND	1979	RCA	UK PL 13493		
LEON RHODES	B	(Q	EARLY YEARS	1979	CAORAL	CDL 8501		
CARL GAY	G	(Q						
SHERMAN HAYES	B	(Q	JOHN LESLIE HUG G	(T	BARNEY ROBERTSON	PNO/V(T	GRAHAM NASH	(T
JIM GORDON	HRNS	(T	MAURICE SPEARS HRNS	(T	MACK JOHNSON	HRNS (T	CARTER ROBERTSON	V(TXZ
GORDON PAYNE	V	(Z	RANCE WASSON V	(TXZ	JERRY STEMBRIDGE	G (M	FRED CARTER	(Z
TONY JOE WHITE		(Z	STAN REECE	(Z	CLIFF ROBERTSON	K (XZ	JOHNNY GIMBLE G	(S
KENNY BUTTREY	D	(M	WILLY ACKERMAN D	(M	NORBERT PUTNAM	B (M	HARGUS 'PIG' ROBBINS	PNO(M
JIM PIERCE	PNO	(M	GORDON PAYNE V/G	(X	JOHN CHRISTOPHER	G (X	BOBBY DYSON B	(N
BILLY GRAHAM	FDL	(T	DON ROBERTSON	(T	BOBBY THOMPSON	G (Q	'RICK POWELL SYN	(M

JEREMY & THE SATYRS

JEREMY STEIG	FLT	(A	(A) JEREMY & THE SATYRS	1968	REPRISE	US	RS	6282
DONALD McDONALD	D	(A						
EDGAR GOMEZ	B	(A	ADRIAN GUILLERY G (A WARREN B BERNHARDT K (A					

JERICHO

ROBB HUXLEY	G	(B	(A) JUNKIES MONKEYS AND DONKEYS	1971	A&M	UK	AMLH 68050
AMI TRIEBICH	D	(B	(B) JERICHO	1972	A&M	UK	AMLS 68079
DANNY SHOSHAN	V	(B					
MICHAEL GABRIELLO	B	(B	HAIM ROMANO G (B				

JERONIMO

RINGO FUNK	D V	(A	(A) TIME RIDE	1972	BELLAPHON		BLPS 19095
MICHAEL KOCH	G V	K(A					
GUNNAR SCHAEFER	V B	G(A	DIETER DIERKS V (A PETER HAUKE	V	(A		

JACK JERSEY

JACK JERSEY		(A	(A) FOREVER	19	EMI	IMP 064	25560

JET

DAVY O'LIST	G	(A	(A) JET	1975	CBS	UK	80699
CHRIS TOWNSON	D	(A					
PETER OXENDALE	K	(A	MARTIN GORDON B (A ANDY ELLISON	V	(A		

JETHRO TULL

IAN ANDERSON	FLT G V	(ALL	(A) THIS WAS JETHRO TULL	1968	ISLAND	UK	ILPS 9085	
CLIVE BUNKER	D	(ABCDE	(A) " " " "	1973	CHRYSALIS	UK	CHR 1041	
MICK ABRAHAMS	G	(AE	(A) " " " "	197	REPRISE	US	6336	
GLEN CORNICK	B	(ABCE	(A) " " " "	197	PHONOGRAM	EURO 6307	517	
JEFFREY HAMMOND HAMMOND	B	(DEFH	(B) STAND UP	1969	ISLAND	UK	ILPS 9103	
MARTIN BARRE	G	(1BCDEFGHJKLMNOPQR	(B) " "	1973	CHRYSALIS	UK	CHR 1042	
TONY IOMMI	G	(	(B) " "	197	REPRISE	US	6360	
BARRIEMORE BARLOW	D	(1FHMOPQ	(B) " "	197	PHONOGRAM	EURO 6307	519	
JOHN EVAN	K	(1CDEFMPOQ	(C) BENEFIT	1970	ISLAND	UK	ILPS 9123	
JOHN GLASCOCK	B	(MOPQ	(C) " "	1973	CHRYSALIS	UK	CHR 1043	
HARRY HUGHES	D	(	(C) " "	197	REPRISE	US	6400	
DAVID PALMER	K	(1MOPQ	(C) " "	197	PHONOGRAM	EURO 6307	516	
TONY WILLIAMS	B	(1M	(D) AQUALUNG	1971	ISLAND	UK	ILPS 9145	
FRANCIS WILSON	V	(Q	(D) " "	1973	CHRYSALIS	UK	CHR 1044	
DAVE PEGG	B	(R	(D) " "	197	REPRISE	US	2035	
MARK CRAWEY	D	(R	(D) " "	197	PHONOGRAM	EURO 6307	515	
EDDIE JOBSON	K VLN	(R	(E) LIVING IN THE PAST	1972	CHRYSALIS	UK	CJT1	
			(E) " " " "	197	CHRYSALIS	US	1035	
			(E) " " " "	197	CHRYSALIS	US	2106	
			(F) THICK AS A BRICK	1972	CHRYSALIS	UK	CHR 1003	
			(F) " " " " "	197	REPRISE	US	2071	
			(F) " " " " "	197	PHONOGRAM	EURO 6307	502	
			(G) PASSION PLAY	1973	CHRYSALIS	UK	CHR 1040	
			(G) " " " "	197	PHONOGRAM	EURO 6307	518	
			(H) WAR CHILD	1974	CHRYSALIS	US+UK	CHR 1067	
			(H) " " "	197	PHONOGRAM	EURO 6307	537	
			(J) MINSTREL IN THE GALLERY	1975	CHRYSALIS	US+UK	CHR 1082	
			(J) " " " "	197	PHONOGRAM	EURO 6307	559	
			(K) TOO OLD TO ROCK'N'ROLL	1976	CHRYSALIS	US+UK	CHR 1111	
			(K) " " " "	197	PHONOGRAM	EURO 6307	572	
			(L) THE BEST OF JETHRO TULL	1976	CHRYSALIS	UK	CHR 1078	
			(M) SONGS FROM THE WOOD	1977	CHRYSALIS	US+UK	CHR 1132	
			(M) " " " "	197	PHONOGRAM	EURO 6307	591	
			(N) REPEAT (BEST OF VOL 2)	1977	CHRYSALIS	UK	CHR 1135	
			(O) HEAVY HORSES	1978	CHRYSALIS	US+UK	CHR 1175	
			(O) " " "	197	PHONOGRAM	EURO 6307	622	
			(P) LIVE BURSTING OUT	1978	CHRYSALIS	US 21201 UK	CJT4	
			(Q) STORMWATCH	1979	CHRYSALIS	UK	CDL 1238	
			(R) "A"	1980	CHRYSALIS	UK	CDL 1301	
			(1) LIVE TV SHOW VIA SATELLITE					
			(EP) LIFE IS A LONG SONG	1971	CHRYSALIS	UK	WIP 6106	
			(EP) RING OUT SOLSTICE BELLS	1976	CHRYSALIS	UK	CPX2	

JETS

		(A) ROCK'N'ROLL MUSIC	1974	SEVEN SUN	SBLP	100

JOAN JETT

JOAN JETT	V	(A	(A) JOAN JETT	1980	ARIOLA	ARL	5058

JIMMY JEWELL   J60

JIMMY JEWELL	SAX (AB	(A) I'M AMAZED	1977	AFFINITY	AFF2
JOHN MUMFORD	TROM (AB	(B) FROM THE FIRST TIME I MET YOU	1978	AFFINITY	AFF5
BILLY LIVSEY	PNO (AB				
RICHARD BRUNTON	G (AB	STEVE BINGHAM	B	(AB RAY DUFFY	D (AB

JIVA   J62

MICHAEL LANNING	G V (A	(A) JIVA	1975	DARK HORSE/A&M	UK AMLH 22003
JAMES STRAUSS	B V (A				
THOMAS HILTON	G V (A	MICHAEL REED D PERC(A			

JIVE BUREAUX   J63

TONY MESSENGER G V HCA (A		(A) STICK IT	1978 GULL	UK	GULP 1025
SHAM	V (A				
TIM MATTHEWMAN	B V (A	BOB WILSON	K (A	IAN STEPHENSON	PERC (A JOE SLYTHE D (A
ROGER QUESTED	PERC (A	SUE GLOVER	V (A	SUNNY LESLIE	V (A J STONE V (A
GARY WINDO	SAX (A	HARRY BECKETT	TPT (A	NICK EVANS	TROM (A BARRY MORGAN PERC (A
FRANK RICOTTI	VIBES(A				

JO JO GUNNE   J64

MARK ANDES	B V (A	(A) JO JO GUNNE	1972	ASYLUM US	SD 5053 UK SYLA	8752
JAY FERGUSON	K V (ABCD	(B) BITE DOWN HARD	1973	ASYLUM US	SD 5065 UK SYL	9005
MATT ANDES	G V (ABC	(C) JUMPIN' THE GUNNE	1973	ASYLUM US	5071 UK SYL	9015
CURLY SMITH	D (ABCD	(D) SO...WHERE'S THE SHOW	1974	ASYLUM US	7E 1022 UK SYL	9019
JIMMIE RANDALL	B (BCD					
JOHN STAEHELY	G V (D					

JO JO ZEP & THE FALCONS   J64A

JOE CAMILLERI	SAX V(ALL	(A) DON'T WASTE IT	1976	EMI AUSTRALIA	062	61153
JEFF BURSTIN	G (ALL	(B) WHIP IT OUT	1977	OZ AUSTRALIA		OZS 1004
JOHN POWER	B V (ALL	(C) SO YOUNG	1978	OZ " "		OZS 1002
GARY YOUNG	D (ALL	(D) LIVE IN CONCERT	1978	OZ " "		OZS 1013
TONY FAEHSE	G (BCDEFGH	(E) SCREAMING TARGETS	1979	MUSHROOM	UK	K99094
WILBUR WILDE	SAX (BCDEFGH	(F) JO JO ZEP & THE FALCONS	1979	ROCKBURGH	UK	ROC 108
WAYNE BURT	G V (ABEFG	(G) TAKIN' THE WRAPS OFF (DBL)	1979	ROCKBURGH	UK	ROCD 110
		(H) HATS OFF, STEP LIVELY	1980	MUSHROOM	UK	K37321

JO MAMA   J65

BOB WILLIAMS	TPT (A	(A) JO MAMA(O SOLE MIO)	1971	ATLANTIC US	SD 8269 UK 2400	129
MICHAEL DUBKIN	SAX (A	(B) J IS FOR JUMP	1971	ATLANTIC US	SD 8288 UK 2400	174
OLLIE MITCHELL	TPT (A					
MAYO TIANA	TROM (A	ABIGALE HANESS V (AB	CHARLES LARKEY	B (AB CAROLE KING V (B		
JOEL BISHOP-O'BRIEN D (AB	RALPH SCHUCKETT K V (AB	DANNY KOOTCH	G V (AB			

JOBRIATH   J65A

BARDEN JOBRIATH	(AB	(A) JOBRIATH	1973	BARCLAY FR 80514 ELEKTRA US 75070	
STEVE LOVE	G (	(B) CREATURES OF THE STREET	1974	ELEKTRA	US 7E 1010
ANDY MUSON	B (				
JOHN SIOMOS	D (				

JO'BURG HAWK   J66

BRAHAM MALBERBE	G (A	(A) JO'BURG HAWK	1973	CHARISMA	UK CAS 1064
JULIAN LAXTON	G (A				
DAVE ORNELLAS	V (A	LES GOODE	B (A SPOOK KAHN	G (A IVOR BACK D (A	
BILLY KNIGHT	PERC V(A	AUDREY MOTAUNG	PERC V(A PETE KUBHAKA	PERC V(A	

JODY GRIND   J67

TIM HINKLEY	K V (AB	(A) ONE STEP ON	1969	UA	US UAS 6774
BARRY WILSON	D (A	(B) FAR CANAL	1970	TRANSATLANTIC UK	TRA 221
IVAN ZAGNI	G (A	(B) FAR CANAL	1970	METRONOME	EURO MLP15 388
BERNIE HOLLAND	G (B				
LOUIS CENNAMO	B (A	PETE GAVIN	D(B		

JOE   J68

GORDON HASKELL	B (
JIM RUSSELL	D (
HIROSHI KATO	G (

BILLY JOEL   J69

BILLY JOEL	V K (ALL	(A) PIANOMAN	1973 CBS	US 32544	JAP 25AP952	UK 80719
RICHIE CANNATA	K WIND(EF	(B) COLD SPRING HARBOUR	1974 PHONOGRAM			6369 150
LIBERTY DEVITO	D (D	(C) STREET LIFE SERENADE	1975 CBS	US 33146	JAP 25AP1078 UK	80766
DOUG STEGMEYER	B (D	(D) TURNSTILES	1976 CBS	US 33848	JAP 25AP953 UK	81195
RUSSEL JAVORS	G (D	(E) STRANGER	1977 CBS	US 34987	JAP 25AP843 UK	82311
STEVE KHAN	G (F	(F) 52nd STREET	1978 CBS	US 35609	JAP 25AP1152 UK	83181
HOWIE EMERSON	G (D	(G) GLASSHOUSES	1980 CBS		UK	86108
JAMES SMITH	G (D					
DEAN PARKS	G (A	RON TUTT	D (AC	ERIC WEISSBERG	BANJ (A LAURA CREAMER V (A
LARRY CARLTON	G (A	WILTON FELDER	K (AC	RHYS CLARK	D (A FRED HEILBRUN BANJO(A
MARK CREAMER	V (A	RICHARD BENNETT	G (ABC	MIKE OMARTIAN ACC	(ABC MIKE OMARTIAN ACC (
BILLY ARMSTRONG	FDL (A	SUSAN STEWARD	V (A	LARRY KNECHTEL	B (C TOM WHITEHORSE STEEL(C
GARY DALTON	G (C	MINGO LEWIS PERC	(D	JOE CLAYTON	CONGA(C MIKE DEASY G (C
ROJ RATHOR	G (C	AL HERTZBERG	G (C	DON EVANS	G (C ART MUNSON G (C
MICHAEL STEWART	G (C	WILLIAM SMITH	K (C	FREDDIE HUBBARD	TPT (F MIKE MAINIERI PERC (F
ZACK SANDERS	V (F	MILT GRAYSON	V (F	RAY SIMPSON	V (F GEORGE MARGE RECORDER(F
DAVID SPINOZZA	G (F	DONNIE DACUS	V (F	PETER CETERA	V (F DAVID FRIEDMAN PERC (F
RALPH MACDONALD	PERC (F	ERIC GALE	G (F	FRANK FLOYD	V (F BABI FLOYD V (F
HUGH McCRACKEN	G (F				

DAVID JOHANSEN   J70

DAVID JOHANSEN	V K (AB	(A) DAVID JOHANSEN	1978	BLUE SKY US 34926 UK	82335
JOHNNY RAO	G (A	(B) IN STYLE	1979	BLUE SKY	UK 83745
THOMAS TRASK	G (A				
BUZ VERNO	B (A	SARA DASH	V (A	SCARLET RIVERA	VLN (A STAN BRONSTEIN HRNS (A
TONY MACHINE	PERC (A	FELIX CAVALIERE	ORG (A	BOBBIE BLAIN	ORG (A NONA HENDRYX V (A
JOE PERRY	K (A	FRANKIEN LAROCKA	D (A		

J70A   ANDREW JOHN

```
ANDREW JOHN  V G B K D WIND(A      (A) THE MACHINE STOPS          1972 CBS              UK        64835
MIKE WOODS      G B    (A
CLIVE SARSTEDT  B      (A   RIC LEE      D   (A  CARSTEN SMEDEGAARD D  (A
```
J71   CLIVE JOHN

```
CLIVE JOHN(CLINT SPACE)G K V(A   (A) YOU ALWAYS KNOW WHERE YOU STAND WITH A BUZZARD 1975 UA   UK UAS 29733
MARTIN ACE      B      (A
DAVE CHARLES    D      (A   TOMMY RILEY       D   (A  PHIL RYAN        K   (A   BRIAN BREEZE    G   (A
ANDY FAIRWEATHER LOW G V(A  PETE HURLEY       B   (A  JOHN WILLIAMS    V   (A   TED CROOK       HCA (A
```
J72   ELTON JOHN

```
ELTON JOHN       V K  (ALL     (A) EMPTY SKY                    1969 MCA   US  3008 UK  DJM DJLPS  403
CALEB QUAYE      G    (ABCFMO   (B) ELTON JOHN                   1970 MCA   US  3000 UK  DJM DJF  20406
DAVEY JOHNSTONE  G    (FGHJKMO  (C) TUMBLEWEED CONNECTION        1970 MCA   US  3001 UK  DJM DJLPS  410
FRANK CLARK      G    (B        (D) 17.11.70                     1971 MCA 2015+3002 UK  DLM DJLPS  414
COLIN GREEN      G    (B        (E) FRIENDS                      1971 PARAMOUNT 420+       SPFL   269
CLIVE HICKS      G    (B        (F) MADMAN ACROSS THE WATER      1971 MCA   US  3003 UK  DJM DJH  20420
ROLAND HARKER    G    (B        (G) HONKY CHATEAU                1972 MCA   US  3004 UK  DJM DJLPH  423
ALAN PARKER      G    (F        (H) DONT SHOOT ME, I'M ONLY THE PIANO'1973 MCA US 3005 UK DJM DJLPH  427
LES THATCHER     G    (F        (J) GOODBYE YELLOW BRICK ROAD    1973 MCA US210003 UK  DJM DJLPD 1001
CHRIS SPEDDING   G    (F        (J) GOODBYE YELLOW BRICK ROAD    1973                 UK  DJM DJE  29001
TIM RENWICK      G    (P1       (K) CARIBOU                      1974 MCA   US  3006 UK  DJM DJLH   439
B J COLE      STEEL(F           (L) CAPTAIN FANTASTIC            1974 MCA   US  3009 UK  DJM DJLPX    1
RICHIE ZITO      G    (1        (M) ROCK OF THE WESTIES          1975 MCA   US  3010 UK  DJM DJLPH  464
TONY MURRAY      B    (A        (N) HERE & THERE                 1976               UK  DJM DJH  20473
DAVE RICHMOND    B    (B        (O) BLUE MOVES                   1976 MCA US211004 UK  ROCKET    ROLL12
LES HURDLE       B    (B        (P) SINGLE MAN                   1978 MCA   US  3065 UK  ROCKET TRAIN  1
BRIAN ODGERS     B    (F        (Q) VICTIM OF LOVE               1979               UK  ROCKET HISPD125
HERBIE FLOWERS   B    (F        (R) 21 AT 33                     1980 ROCKET 9103 511+UK     HISPD126
CHRIS LAURENCE   B    (F
DEE MURRAY       B    (CFGHJK1  ( ) ELTONS GREATEST HITS         1974 MCA   US  3007 UK  DJM DJLPH  442
KENNY PASSARELLI B    (MO       ( ) POP CHRONIK                  1975 DJM                       VOL7
DAVID GLOVER     B    (CF       ( ) GREATEST HITS VOL 2          1977 MCA   US  3027 UK  DJM DJH  20520
ALAN WEIGHELL    B    (B        ( ) LIVE COLLECTION (DBL)        1979 PICKWICK                PDA  047
BARRY MORGAN     D    (BF       ( ) LIVE (NEW YORK NOV 70)       1978 HALLMARK              SHM  942
TERRY COX        D    (BF       ( ) LONDON & NEW YORK LIVE       1978 HALLMARK              SHM  966
ROGER POPE       D    (ACFMO    ( ) LADY SAMANTHA(COMP)          1980              DJM        22085
STEVE HOLLY      D    (P        ( ) VERY BEST OF                 1980 K TEL                 NE 1094
DENNIS LOPEZ   PERF  (B         (EP) FOUR FROM FOUR EYES         1977              DJM DJR  18001
RAY COOPER     PERC (FGJKMO     (1) ELTON JOHN BAND AUTUMN 1980
NIGEL OLSSON     D    (ACFGHJK1
TEX NAVARRA    PERC (B    IAN DUCK      HCA (C  SKAILA KANGA    HARP (B  GRAHAM VICKERY   HCA (A
PAUL BUCKMASTER CELLO(B   GENE PAGE     STRINGS (O  MICHAEL HURWITZ CELLO(O MADELINE BELL    V   (BG
TONY BURROWS     V   (BF  SUE GLOVER    V   (F  SUNNY LESLIE    V   (F  CLYDIE KING      V   (K
DUSTY SPRINGFIELD V  (K   TONI TENILLE  V   (KO CLIVE FRANKS    V   (MP GRAHAM NASH      V   (O
JAN JOYCE        V   (O   GENE MORFORD  V   (O  BRIAN DEE       K   (BD DIANA LEWIS      SYN (EF
RICK WAKEMAN     K   (F   DAVID HENTSCHEL K (GJK CHESTER THOMPSON K  (K JAMES NEWTON HOWARD K (MO1
JACK EMBLOW     ACC  (F   CARL FORTINA  ACC (K  MARTYN FORD ORCHESTRA (O  DON FAY        WIND (K
LEROY GOMEZ     SAX  (O   STEVE KUPKA   SAX (K  EMILIO CASTILLO SAX (K  MIC GILLETTE     HRNS (K
GREG ADAMS      HRNS (K   RANDY BRECKER HRNS (K MICHAEL BRECKER HRNS (O  BARRY ROGERS    HRNS (O
DAVID SANBORN   HRNS (K   LENNY PICKETT WIND (K LESLEY DUNCAN   V  (BCF TONY HAZZARD      V  (BG
BARRY ST JOHN    V   (F   TERRY STEELE  V   (F  SHIRLEY MATTHEWS V  (K  CARL WILSON       V  (K
BILLY HINSCHE    V   (K   ANN ORSON     V   (M  JOE CHEMAY      V   (O  CINDY BULLENS     V  (O
CURT BOETCHER    V   (O   KAY GARNER    V   (B  ROGER COOK      V   (BF LIZA STRIKE       V  (FG
KIKI DEE         V   (JM  JESSIE MAY SMITH V (K BRUCE JOHNSTON   V  (KO LABELLE           V  (M
DAVID CROSBY     V   (O   CLARK BURROUGHS V (O  RON HICKLIN     V   (O  CORNERSTONE CHIOR V  (O
JACQUES BOLOGNESI TROM (G  IVAN JULIAN   TPT (G  JEAN LOUIS CHAUTEMPS SAX(G ALAIN HATOT   V  (G
JEAN LUC PONTY   VLN (G   LEGS LARRY SMITH   (G  LARRY STEELE    V   (G  GUS DUDGEON  V WHISTLE(G
```
J73   JOHNNY LITTLE JOHN

```
JOHNNY LITTLE JOHN  G V(ALL   (A) JOHNNY LITTLE JOHN & CHICAGO BLUES BAND 197  ARHOOLIE      F 1043
DAVE MYERS       B    (B       (B) FUNKY FROM CHICAGO           1973 BLUESWAY            BL  6069
EDDIE TAYLOR     G    (B       (C) JOHNNY LITTLE JOHN           197  MCM           FR    900 300
FRED BELOW       D    (B
```
J73A   ROBERT JOHN

```
ROBERT JOHN      V    (A       (A) ROBERT JOHN                  1979 EMI AMERICA         AML 3003
ED GREENE        D    (A
HAL BLAINE       D    (A   H LEE WOLEN  D PERC  (A  SCOTT EDWARDS   B   (A  DAVID SHIELDS B  (A
DENNIS BELFIELD  B    (A   MIKE PICCIRILLO  G V (A  BILL NEALE      G   (A  STEWART LEVIN  K(A
MIKE THOMPSON    K    (A   EDNA WRIGHT      V   (A  DARLENE LOVE    V   (A  GEORGE TOBIN  V (A
```
J74   JOHNNY & THE HURRICANES

```
JOHNNY PARIS    SAX  (      JOHNNY & HURRICANES              1960 WARWICK    US            W2007
PAUL TESLUK     ORG  (      STORMSVILLE                     1960 WARWICK US W2010 +LONDON UK 2269
DAVE YORKO      G    (      BIG SOUND                       1960 LONDON   HAX 2322 BIG TOP US 1302
LIONEL MATTICE  B    (      BEATNIK FLY                     19   TWIRL        US          5002
DON STACZEK     D    (      BEST OF                         19   BIRCHMOUNT   US           565
BILL SAVICH     D    (      RED RIVER ROCK                  196  LONDON       UK    HA    2227
TONY KAYE       D    (      PROFILE                         19   TELDEC       GERM      624008
                           LIVE AT THE STAR CLUB HAMBURG   196  ATILA        US          1030
                       (EP)REMEMBER                         1973 UA                    REM 401
                           VERY BEST OF                     1975 CONTEMPO             CRMD 1002
                           LEGEND OF ROCK VOL 1 (DBL)       19   LONDON             DP628 329
                           LEGEND OF ROCK VOL 2 (DBL)       19   LONDON             DP628 318
                       (EP) JOHNNY & THE HURRICANES         19   WARWICK     US           700
```
J74A   JOHNNY & THE JAILBIRDS

```
                           (A) OUT ON BAIL                  19   CHARLY       UK     cr 30184
```
J75   JOHNS CHILDREN

```
ANDY ELLISON    V    (A     (A) ORGASM                      19   WHITE WHALE  US     WW  7128
MARC BOLAN      G V  (A
JOHN HEWLETT    B    (A   CHRIS TOWNSON     D   (A
```

ALPHONSO JOHNSON

ALPHONSO JOHNSON	B V	(AB	(A) MOONSHADOWS	1976	EPIC	US	34118
DAWILLI GONGA	K V	(A	(B) YESTERDAYS DREAMS	1976	EPIC	US	34364
PATRICE RUSHEN	K	(AB	(C) SPELLBOUND	1978	EPIC	UK	82197

CHRIS BOND   G   (A
IAN UNDERWOOD   K   (AB   FLORA PURIM   V   (AB   BENNIE MAUPIN   WIND (A   NARADA MICHAEL WALDEN D K(A
LEON CHANCLER   D   (A   BLACKBIRD McKNIGHT G (A   ALEJANDRO ACUNA PERC (A   AIRTO MOREIRA   PERC (A
GARY BARTZ   SAX (A   ALPHONSE MOUZON   K   (A   GROVER WASHINGTON SAX (B   RAY GOMEZ   G   (B
LEE RITENOUR   G   (AB   MARK JORDAN   KRG (B   DAVID FOSTER   ORG (B   RUTH UNDERWOOD   PERC (B
CHESTER THOMPSON D   (B   MIKE CLARK   G   (B   SHEILA ESCOVEDO PERC (B   GARNETT BROWN   TROM (B
JON LUCIEN   V   (B   PHILIP BAILEY   V   (B   DIANE REEVES   V   (B   ERNIE WATTS   SAX   (B
ERNIE FIELDS   SAX (B   CHUCK FINDLEY   TPT (B   GARY GRANT   HRNS (B   GEORGE BOHANON   TROM (B

BOB JOHNSON & PETER KNIGHT

BOB JOHNSON		(A	(A) KING OF ELFLAND'S DAUGHTER	1977	CHRYSALIS	UK CHR1137

PETER KNIGHT   (A
CHRISTOPHER LEE   V   (A   MARY HOPKIN   V   (A   FRANKIE MILLER   V   (A   ALEXIS KORNER   V (A
P P ARNOLD   V   (A   DEREK BRIMSTONE V   (A   CHRIS FARLOWE   V   (A

DAVID EARLE JOHNSON

DAVID EARLE JOHNSON		(A	(A) TIME IS FREE	1978	VANGUARD	VSD 79401

JAN HAMMER   K   (A

JIMMY JOHNSON

JIMMY JOHNSON		(AB	(A) JIMMY JOHNSON & LUTHER JOHNSON	1977	MCM	900 294
LUTHER JOHNSON	G	(A	(B) JIMMY JOHNSON	1978	MCM	900 302

LARRY JOHNSON

LARRY JOHNSON	G V	(ALL	(A) PRESENTING THE COUNTRY BLUES	1970	BLUE HORIZON	7 63851
JOHN PAUL HAMMOND		(B	(B) COUNTRY BLUES	197	BIOGRAGHICAL	US	BLP 12028
			(C) FAST & FUNKY	19	BLUE GOOSE	BG 2001

LONNIE JOHNSON

LONNIE JOHNSON   K VLN (ALL   (A)LONNIE JOHNSON   19   STORYVILLE   SLP 162
ELMER SNOWDEN   G   (LONNIE JOHNSON   19   COLLECTORS CLASSICS   CC   30
VICTORIA SPIVEY V   (K   BLUES GUITAR VOL 2   1970 PARLOPHONE   PMC 7106
OTIS SPANN   PNO (K   ANOTHER NIGHT TO CRY   19   BLUESVILLE   US   1062
JOHN HUGHES   PNO (K   TOMORROW NIGHT   196   STARDAY/KING SK1083+ GD   5039X
ROY COULTER   B   (K   MR JOHNSONS BLUES   197   MAMUSH   3807
ALLEN SMITH   PNO (K   BLUES & BALLADS   19   PRESTIGE   US   1011
MONTE MORRISON   B   (K   BLUES BY LONNIE JOHNSON   19   PRESTIGE   US   1007
HERMAN SMITH   PNO (K   IDLE HOURS   19   PRESTIGE   US   1044
                               WOMAN BLUES   19   PRESTIGE   US   1054
                 (K)LONESOME ROAD   19   KING   US   520
                               SINGS 24 12 BAR BLUES   19   KING   US   958
                               LOSING GAME   19   PRESTIGE   US   1024

LUTHER 'GEORGIA BOY SNAKE' JOHNSON

LUTHER JOHNSON   G V (ABC   (A) WITH THE MUDDY WATERS BLUES BAND 1969 TRANSATLANTIC UK   TRA 188
GEORGE 'MOJO' BUFORD HCA(A   (A) WITH THE MUDDY WATERS BLUES BAND 1969 DOUGLAS   US   SD 789
MUDDY WATERS   G   (A   (B) BORN IN GEORGIA   1974 BLACK & BLUE   FR   33503
OTIS SPANN   PNO (A   (C) ON THE ROAD AGAIN   1976 BLACK & BLUE   FR   33509
SAMMY LAWHORN   G   (A
FRANCIS CLAY   D   (A

ROBERT JOHNSON

ROBERT JOHNSON   G V (ALL   KING OF THE DELTA BLUES SINGERS   1966 CBS US CL1654 UK   62456
                               KING OF THE DELTA BLUES SINGERS VOL 2 1970 CBS US 30034 UK   64102
                               LEGACY   19   CBS US 33904

ROBERT JOHNSON

ROBERT JOHNSON   G V (AB   (A) CLOSE PERSONAL FRIEND   1979 ENSIGN   ENVY 4
DAVID COCHRAN   V B D(AB   (B) MEMPHIS DEMOS   1980 ENSIGN   ENRJ 12
BLAIR CUNNINGHAM   V D (AB

WILKO JOHNSON & SOLID SENDERS

WILKO JOHNSON   G V (A   (A) SOLID SENDERS   1978 VIRGIN   UK V 2105
JOHN POTTER   K   (A   (A) LIVE (FREE WITH V 2105)   1978 VIRGIN   UK VDJ 26
STEVE LEWINS   B   (A
ALAN PLATT   D   (A   DAVE BROOKS   SAX (A   JOHN DENTON   PNO (A   RUSSELL STRUTHER B (
ALEX BINES   D   (

BROTHERS JOHNSON

		(A) LOOK OUT FOR NO 1	197	A&M	UK AMLH 64567
		(B) RIGHT ON TIME	1977	A&M	UK AMLH 64644
		(C) BLAM	1978	A&M	UK AMLH 64714

ADRIENNE JOHNSTON

ADRIENNE JOHNSTON V   (A   (A) ADRIENNE JOHNSTON OF THE JOHNSTONS 1975 RCA   UK   SF 8416
DON FRASER   PNO (A
PAT DONALDSON   B   (A   BARRY MORGAN   D   (A   GERRY CONWAY   D   (A   GREG BARON CELLO (A
MICHAEL HURWITZ   CELLO(A   BARRY CASTLE   HRNS (A   CHRIS ANDREETY   V   (A   TOM MADDEN   V   (A
WILF GIBSON   VLN (A   HOWARD DAVIS   VLN (A   GEORGE ROBERTSON VLA (A   CLIVE ANSTEE CELLO (A
JOHN HORNET   HRNS(A   FRANK RYECROFT HRNS (A   MIRIAM KEOGH   HARP (A   SIMON NICOL G   (A

BRUCE JOHNSTON

BRUCE JOHNSTON   G V (ABC   (A) SURFIN' PAJAMA PARTY   196   DELFI   US   634
                               (B) SURFIN' AROUND THE WORLD   196   CBS   US 2057 +   8857
                               (C) GOING PUBLIC   1977 CBS   US 34459 UK   81854

TOM JOHNSTON

TOM JOHNSTON   V G (A   (A) EVERYTHING YOU'VE HEARD IS TRUE 1979 WB US BSK 3304 UK K 56632
JIM KELTNER   D   (A
RICK SCHLOSSER   D   (A   DAVID GARIBALDI D   (A   KEITH KNUDSEN   D   (A   PAUL STALLWORTH B (A
BOB GLAUB   B   (A   RICK CHUDACOFF   B   (A   PAUL BARRERE   G   (A   BILL PAYNE   K (A
DAVID PAICH   K   (A   MARK JORDAN   K   (A   MICHAEL McDONALD K   (A   NICOLETTE LARSON V (A
TED TEMPLEMAN   V   (A   ANDREW LOVE   SAX (A   LEWIS COLLINS   HRNS (A   BEN CAULEY   HRNS(A
JERRY JUMONVILLE   SAX (A   JACK HALE   HRNS (A   LENNY PICKETT   HRNS (A   EMILIO CASTILLO HRNS (A
STEVE KUPKA   HRNS (A   MIC GILLETTE   HRNS (A   GREG ADAMS   HRNS (A   TOWER OF POWER HRNS(A

J86

DAVEY JOHNSTONE

DAVEY JOHNSTONE	G V	(A		(A) SMILING FACE			1973	ROCKET	UK		PIGL2
DAVE HENTSCHEL	SYN	(A									
JOAN ARMATRADING	PNO	(A	B J COLE	STEEL(A	MOHAMMED AMIR	HCA (A	RICK BATEMAN	HCA (A		
CHRIS LAURENCE	B	(A	MICHAEL HINTON TPT(A		GRAHAM MORGAN	D (A	MICK FLYNN	WHISTLE(A		
JO PARTRIDGE	G	(A	CHRIS KARAN	TABLA(A	RAY COOPER	PERC (A	GUS DUDGEON	PERC(A		

J86A

JOLLIVER ARKANSAW

| LESLIE WEST | G | (A | | (A) HOME | 1969 | BELL | US | | 119 |
| FELIX PAPPALARDI | | (A | | | | | | | |

J87

JOLT

JIM DOAK	B V	(A		(A) JOLT	1978	POLYDOR	UK	2383 504
ROBERT COLLINS	G V	(A						
IAIN SHEDDEN	D	(A						

J88

JONAH

ROBERT GENGO	G V	(A		(A) JONAH		1974 CAPITOL		T 456
MICHAEL GREGORIO	PERC V(A							
VINCENT LA FATA	G V	(A	JOE GENGO	PERC (A	DON GROLNICK	ORG (A	BOB MANN	G (A
EDDIE BRIGATI	PERC	(A	TOMMY WEST	K (A	TONY SANTARELLA	B (A	MIKE BRECKER	SAX (A
ALLEN SCHWARZBERG	D	(A						

J88A

BOOKER T JONES

BOOKER T JONES	K V	(A		(A) TRY AND LOVE AGAIN	1978 A&M		UK	AM 64720
JAY GRAYDON	G	(A						
DENNIS BELFIELD	B	(A	MIKE BAIRD	D (A	MIKE UTLEY	K (A	JIM GILSTRAP	V (A
JOHN LEHMAN	V	(A	MARLENA TETER	V (A	PATRICIA HENDERSON V	(A		

J89

BRIAN JONES

| BRIAN JONES | | (A | | (A) PRESENTS THE PIPES OF PAN AT JOUJOUKA 1971 ROLLING STONES COC 49100 |

J90

CHRISTOPHER JONES

| CHRISTOPHER JONES | | (A | | (A) NO MORE RANGE TO ROAM | 1978 TRANSATLANTIC | UK | TRA 503 |

J91

CURTIS JONES

CURTIS JONES	PNO V(AB		(A) NOW RESIDENT IN EUROPE	1968 BLUE HORIZON	UK	7 63207
BRIAN BROCKLEHURST	B(A		(B) TROUBLE BLUES	19 PRESTIGE	US	1022
DOUGIE WRIGHT	D (A		(C) LONESOME BEDROOM BLUES	19 DELMARK		DL 605
ALEXIS KORNER	G (					

J92

GRACE JONES

GRACE JONES	V	(ALL		(A) WINDSTORM		1977 CAPITOL SW 11854+SIDEWALK 1002
DAN FERGUSON	G	(A		(B) PORTFOLIO		1977 ISLAND	UK	ILPS 9470
ROBERT WHITE		(A		(C) FAME		1978 ISLAND	UK	ILPS 9525
LAWRENCE HILL	V	(A		(D) MUSE		1979 ISLAND	UK	ILPS 9538
DARRYL MOORE		(A						
PAUL HUMPHREY	D	(A	OMA DRAKE	V (A	T YOUNG	V (A	M YOUNG	V (A
RAY PARKER	G	(A	JOE SAMPLE	K (A	SCOTT EDWARDS	B (A	JACK ASHFORD	PERC(A
EDDIE BROWN		(A	JAMES GADSON	D (A	EMMANUEL GREEN	VLN (A	SYLVESTER RIVERS	K(A
WAH WAH WATSON	G	(A	TIM MAY		RON COLEMAN	(A	GARY COLEMAN	PERC(A
JIMMY WALKER	PERC	(C	LARRY WASHINGTON	PERC (BC	CRAIG SNYDER	G (C	JIMMY WILLIAMS	B (C
J SINGLETON	V	(A	JOE GREEN	V (A	JESSE KIRKLAND	V (A	SHARON MINGUS	V (A
NANIS NORMAN	V	(A	CARLA BENSON	V (BC	SWEETHEARTS OF SIGMA V	(BC	BARBARA INGRAM	V (BC
EVETTE BENTON	V	(BC	ALLAN SCHWARZBERG	D (B	WILBUR BASCOMB	B (B	LANCE QUINN	G (B
CLIFF MORRIS	G	(B	BOBBY ELI	G (B	CARLTON KENT	(B	RON KERSEY	K (B
VINCE MONTANA	VIBES(B		MOTO	TAMB (C	DON RENALDO	STRINGS (BC	KEITH BENSON	D (C
PIGGY PIGERINO	VLN	(C	JOHN DAVIS	K (C				

J93

MICKEY JONES BAND

MICKY JONES	G V	(				
TWEKE LEWIS	G	(				
STEVE DIXON	D	(	STEVE GURL	K (A	ALAN McKENNA	B	(

J93A

NIGEL MAZLYN JONES

| NIGEL MAZLYN JONES | G V(A | | (A) SHIP TO SHORE | 1976 ISLE OF LIGHT | | IOL 666/1 |
| | | | (B) SENTINEL | 1978 AVADA | | AVA 105 |

J93B

PAUL JONES

PAUL JONES	V HCA(A		(A) LOVE ME LOVE MY FRIENDS	1967 H M V	UK	CSD 3602
			(B) CRUCIFIX IN A HORSESHOE	1971 VERTIGO	UK	6360 059
			(C) SINGS PRIVILEGE & OTHERS	19 CAPITOL	US	ST 2795

J93C

RICKIE LEE JONES

RICKIE LEE JONES	G K V PERC(A			(A) RICKIE LEE JONES		1979 WB US BSK 3296	UK K 56628
STEVE GADD	D	(A					
ANDY NEWMARK	D	(A	VICTOR FELDMAN PERC K D(A	MARK STEVENS	D PERC(A	JEFF PORCARO	D (A
TOM SCOTT	HRNS	(A	ARNO LUCAS	V (A	MATTHEW WIENER	V (A	WILLIE WEEKS	B (A
RED CALLENDER	B	(A	BUZZY FEITEN	G (A	FRED TACKETT	G (A	NEIL LARSEN	K (A
CHUCK FINDLEY	HRNS	(A	LESLIE SMITH	V (A	MICHAEL McDONALD	V (A	RANDY KERBER	K (A
RALPH GRIERSON	K	(A	DR JOHN	K (A	RANDY NEWMAN	SYN (A	MICHAEL BODDICKER	SYN(A
ERNIE WATTS	HRNS	(A	JOE TORANO	V (A	NICK DE CARO	ACC (A		

J94

JONESY

ALAN BOWN	TPT PERC(BC		(A) NO ALTERNATIVE	1972 DAWN	UK	DNLS 3042
PLUG THOMAS	D V	(BC	(B) KEEPING UP	1973 DAWN	UK	DNLS 3048
JAMIE KALETH	K V	(ABC	(C) GROWING	1973 DAWN	UK	DNLS 3055
JOHN EVAN JONES	G V	(ABC1	(1) JONESY 1978			
GYPSY JONES	G V	(BC				
JACK JONES		(1	MORRIS PERT	PERC (C	PAUL STARK	(1	DAVID PAULL	B V (A
JIM PAYNE	D	(A	PHIL CLARKE	(1	KEN ELLIOT	SYN (C	CLIVE LONIE	(1
BERNIE HAGLEY	SAX	(C					

J94A

JOOK

| | | | (A) WATCH YOUR STEP(EP) | 197 CHISWICK | UK | SW30 |

JANIS JOPLIN

JANIS JOPLIN	G V	(ALL	(A) I GOT DEM OL' KOZMIC BLUES AGAIN	1969	CBS	US	9913	UK	63546
BRAD CAMPBELL	B	(ABCF	(B) PEARL	1971	CBS	US	30322	UK	64188
CLARK PIERSON	D	(BCF	(C) IN CONCERT (DBL)	1972	CBS	US	31160	UK	67241
KEN PEARSON	ORG	(BCF	(D) GREATEST HITS	1973	CBS	US	32168	UK	65470
JOHN TILL	G	(BCF	(E) JANIS (SOUNDTRACK)	1974	CBS	US	33345	UK	88115
RICHARD BELL	PNO	(BCF	(F) ANTHOLOGY (DBL)	1980	CBS				22101
SANDRA CROUCH	TAMB	(B	(G) JANIS JOPLIN	19	SUPRAPHON	IMP	1 13 2215		
BOBBYE HALL	PERC	(B							
BOBBY WOMACK	G	(B	VINCE MITCHELL	V	(B	PHIL BADELLA	V	(B	JOHN COOKE V (B
SAM ANDREW	G V	(ACF	RICHARD KERMODE	K	(AF	GABRIEL MEKLER	K	(AF	MAURY BAKER D (A
LONNIE CASTILLE	D	(AF	SNOOKY FLOWERS	SAX	(AF	TERRY CLEMENTS	SAX	(AF	LUIS GASCA TPT (AF
JAMES GURLEY	G	(CF	PETER ALBIN	B	(CF	DAVE GETZ	D	(CF	

LONNIE JORDAN

LONNIE JORDAN	K B D V	(A	(A) DIFFERENT MOODS OF ME	1978	MCA		UK	MCG	3526
EUGENE PALMER	V	(A						
DAROLD MATHEW	V	(A	MOSES WHEELOCK	PERC (A	CAMEO ROSS	V	(A	LARRY BROWN G (A
ANDY SHAPHIN	SYN	(A	TOM LETONDRE	TPT (A	JOE ROBB	SAX	(A	SUSAN BUCKNER V (A
DEBORAH PRATT	V	(A	LEM TAYLOR	V (A	MILTON MYRICK	V	(A	DOUGLAS PARKS V (A
DAWN PARKS	V	(A	MICHAEL PARKS	V (A	GREGORY PARKS	V	(A	CAROL WILSON V (A
KEVIN FARMER	V	(A	KIMBERLY FARMER	V (A	ROBIN PARKS	V	(A	

LOUIS JORDAN

LOUIS JORDAN	V SAX	(ALL	(A) SOMEBODY UP THERE LIKES ME	19	WING US 16126+MERCURY	US	20242
SHUGGIE OTIS	G B K	(I	(B) GREATEST HITS	19	MCA US 274 + DECCA	US	75033
JOHNNY OTIS	D PNO	(I	(C) LOUIS JORDAN VOL 1	19	DECCA	US	2029
IRV COX	SAX	(I	(D) LOUIS JORDAN VOL 2	19	DECCA	US	A645
BOB MITCHELL	TPT	(I	(E) MAN WERE WAILIN'	19	MERCURY	US	20331
CHRIS BARBER		(N	(F) & HIS TYMPANI FIVE	19	JAZZ CLUB US 123+ PERFORMANCE	3001	
BUD JOHNSON		(	(G) HALLELUJAH	1964	TANGERINE		1503
ERNIE ROYAL		(	(H) LET THE GOOD TIMES ROLL	1970	CORAL CP 59 +CP 54 + CRLM		1042
JIMMY CLEVELAND		(	(H) LET THE GOOD TIMES ROLL	19	DECCA	US	8551
SAM TAYLOR		(	(I) GREAT RHYTHM & BLUES	1973	BULLDOG	BDL	1000
TEDDY EDWARDS	SAX	(	(J) BEST OF	1975	MCA US 2 4079 +UK MCFM	2715	
			(K) I BELIEVE IN MUSIC	1975	BLACK & BLUE		33059
			(L) CHOO CHOO CH BOOGIE	1975	PHILIPS	6336	246
			(M) IN MEMORIAM	1975	MCA	PCO	7837
			(M) IN MEMORIAM	1975	CORAL		622175
			(N) LOUIS JORDAN SWINGS	1976	BLACK LION	BLP	30175
			(O) & HIS ORCHESTRA	1976	MCA	PCO	8332

JORDANAIRES

HOYT HAWKINS	V	(1	WE'D LIKE TO TEACH THE WORLD TO SING	1972	EMBER	UK CW	141
NIAL MATTHEWS	V	(1	SPOTLIGHT ON THE JORDANAIRES	19	CAPITOL	US ST	1742
LOVIS NUNLEY	V	(1	BIG COUNTRY HITS	19	CBS	US	9258
GORDON STOKER	V	(1	MONSTER MAKERS	19	STOP	US	10010
			CHURCH IN THE WILDWOOD	19	VOCALION	US	73854
			THE JORDANAIRES	19	CBS	US	
			(1)1978				

JOURNEY

GREGG ROLIE	G V	(ALL	(A) JOURNEY	1975	CBS	US	33388	UK	80724
NEAL SCHON	G	(ALL	(B) LOOK INTO THE FUTURE	1976	CBS	US	33904	UK	69203
AYNSLEY DUNBAR	D	(ABCDF	(C) NEXT	1977	CBS	US	34311	UK	81554
GEORGE TICKNER	G	(AF	(D) INFINITY	1978	CBS	US	34912	UK	82244
ROSS VALORY	B	(ALL	(E) EVOLUTION	1979	CBS			UK	83566
ROBERT FLEISHMAN	V	(	(F) IN THE BEGINNING(DBL) (COMP)	1979	CBS				22073
STEVE PERRY	V	(DEG	(G) DEPARTURE	1980	CBS			UK	84101
STEVE SMITH	D	(EG						

JOY DIVISION

		(A) UNKNOWN PLEASURES	19	FACTORY	UK FACT	10
		(B) CLOSER	19	FACTORY	UK FACTXXV	

JOY OF COOKING

TONI BROWN	V K G	(ABC	(A) JOY OF COOKING	1970	CAPITOL	EST	661
TERRY GARTHWAITE	V G	(ABC	(B) CLOSER TO THE GROUND	1971	CAPITOL	EST	828
FRITZ KASTEN	D SAX	(ABC	(C) CASTLES	1972	CAPITOL	EST	11050
JEFF NEIGHBOR	B TROM	(BC					
RON WILSON	PERC HCA	(ABC	JIM HORN SAX (C DAVID GARTHWAITE	B G (A			

JUBAL

DENNIS LINDE	G V	(A	(A) JUBAL	1972	ELEKTRA

JUDAS PRIEST

K K DOWNING	G	(ALL	(A) ROCKA ROLLA	1974	GULL		UK	GULP	1005
GLEN TIPTON	G	(ALL	(B) SAD WINGS OF DESTINY	1976	GULL		UK	GULP	1015
ROB HALFORD	V	(ALL	(B) SAD WINGS OF DESTINY	1976	JANUS		US		7019
IAN HILL	B	(ALL	(C) SIN AFTER SIN	1977	CBS	US 34587	UK		82008
JOHN HINCH	D	(AD	(D) THE BEST OF	1978	GULL		UK	GULP	1026
ALAN MOORE	D	(BD	(E) STAINED CLASS	1978	CBS	US 35296	UK		82430
SIMON PHILLIPS	D	(C	(F) KILLING MACHINE	1978	CBS		UK		83135
LES BINKS	D	(FG	(G) UNLEASHED IN THE EAST	1979	CBS		UK		83852
DAVE HOLLAND	D	(H	(H) BRITISH STEEL	1980	CBS		UK		84160

JUDE

ROBIN TROWER	G	(
FRANKIE MILLER	V	(
JIMMY DEWAR	B	(

JUDGE DREAD

JUDGE DREAD		(A) DREADMANIA	1973	TROJAN	TRLS	60
		(B) WORKING CLASS 'ERO	1974	TROJAN	TRLS	100
		(C) BEDTIME STORIES	1975	CACTUS	CTLP	1130
		(D) LAST OF THE SKINHEADS	1976	CACTUS	CTLP	123
		(E) BEST OF	1976	KLIK	KLP	9008
		(EP) JAMAICA JERK	1977	CACTUS	CT	98

```
J105                              JUICY LUCY
  RAY OWEN          V   (A      (A) JUICY LUCY                    1969 VERTIGO   UK 847 901 US ATCO 33367
  GLENN CAMPBELL    V G (ABC     (B) LIE BACK & ENJOY IT          1970 VERTIGO   UK 6360014 US ATCO 33345
  CHRIS MERCER      SAX K(ABC    (C) GET A WIFF A THIS            1971 BRONZE    UK ILPS9157 US ATCO 33367
  NEIL HUBBARD      G   (A       (D) PIECES                       1972 POLYDOR        UK 2310 160
  KEITH ELLIS       B   (AB
  PETE DOBSON       D   (A   MICK WEAVER    K   (D   IAN MACLAGAN      K   (D   REMI KEBAKA      PERC   (A
  JEAN ROUSSEL      K   (D   RON BERG       D   (D   LOUGHTY AMAO     PERC (A   ANDY PYLE       B      (D
  JIM LEVERTON      B   (C   MICK MOODY     G   (BCD PAUL WILLIAMS   V PERC(BCD ROD COOMBES     D      (BC
J105A                         JULES & THE POLAR BEARS
  JULES SHEAR       G V (AB      (A) GOT NO BREEDING              1978 CBS            US   35601
  JIM GORDON        D   (A       (B) PHONETICS                    1979 CBS            UK   83865
  RICHARD BREDICE   G   (AB
  STEPHEN HAGUE     K SYN(AB DAVID BEEBE    D   (AB  DAVID WHITE      B   (B   KENNY ALTMAN     B   (B
  LARRY HIRSCH      PERC (A   JERRY PETERSON SAX (A  JERRY JUMONVILLE SAX (A   MIKE HENDERSON   SAX (A
  LEE THORNBERG     TPT  (A   DARRELL LEONARD TPT (A  BILL EDWARDS    TROM(A   MARK UNDERWOOD   TPT (A
  JAY PRUITT        TPT  (A   SKIP WIESNER TROM  (A  LINDA SMALL      TROM(A
J105B                               JULVERNE
  PIERRE COULON     FLT  (AB      (A) A NEUF                      19   CRAMMED DISCS     CRA    274
  MICHEL DURET      CLAR (A       (B) COULONNEUX                  19   IBC/EMI            058 99069
  MICHEL BERCKMANS BASSOON(A
  JEAN PAUL LAURENT PNO (AB  CHARLES LOOS   PNO (A  BAUDOUIN DEHAYE  VIBES(A   JOSE BEDEUR      B   (A
  DENIS VAN ECKE    CELLO(A   JEAN FRANCOIS LACROIX SAX(A JEANNOT GILLIS VLN (AB MICHEL DAYEZ    G   (B
  RICHARD ROUSSELET TPT (B   ANNE DENIS     VLN (B  JEAN COULON      TROM(B
J106                                 JUMBO
                                (A) CITY GIRLS                    1978 PYE INT        UK         28234
J107                            JUNCO PARTNERS
  RONNIE BARKER         (1       (A) JUNCO PARTNERS               197  BARCLAY        FR         920193
  JOHN WOODS        D   (1B      (B) JUNCO PARTNERS               1971 PHILIPS             6308 032
  DAVE SPROAT       B   (1B      (1) 1978  REFORMED
  KENNY BARKER      G   (1
  BOB SARGEANT      K V (B   NEIL PERRY   SAX    (1   MAV LANDERS   V  (1   CHARLES HARCOURT  G  (B
J108                            JUNIOR  EYES
  MICK WAYNE            (        (A) JUNIOR'S EYES                196  A&M        US         SP  4189
  JOHN REDFERN          (        (B) BATTERSEA POWER STATION      1969 REGAL ZONOPHONE  UK SLRZ 1008
  STEVE CHAPMAN         (
  GROM KELLY           (    TIM RENWICK  G   (    JOHN CAMBRIDGE          (
J109                           JUNKYARD ANGELS
  KEN IVERSON       D V (A       (A) APPEARED ON  MIKE HARRISON LP 1971 ISLAND     UK         ILPS 9170
  PETER BATEY       B   (A
  IAN HERBERT       G V K(A  FRANK KENYON G V (A
J110                             MICKEY JUPP
  MICKEY JUPP       G V K(ABC    (A) JUPPANESE                    1978 STIFF      UK         SEEZ   10
  DAVE EDMUNDS      G V (A       (B) LEGEND (COMP OF 'LEGEND'TRACKS) 1978 STIFF   UK         GET     2
  BILLY BREMNER     G   (A       (C) LONG DISTANCE ROMANCER       1979 CHRYSALIS  UK         CHR  1261
  NICK LOWE         B   (A       (1) 1975 BAND
  TERRY WILLIAMS    D   (A
  GARY BROOKER      K   (AB  BRUCE LYNCH    B   (A   CHRIS SPEDDING  G   (A   DAVE MATTACKS    D   (A
  MO WITHAM         G   (B   BOB CLOUTER    D   (B1  BILL FIFIELD    D   (B   CHRIS EAST       G   (B
  STEVE GEERE       B   (B   NIGEL DUNBAR   D   (B   CHRIS COPPING   B   (B   B J WILSON       D   (B
  TIM RENWICK       G   (B   MICK MOODY     G   (B   COLIN GIBSON    B   (B   HENRY SPINETTI   D   (B
  JIMMY JEWELL      SAX (B   PETE SOLLEY    PNO (B   GLEN LE FLEUR   PERC (B  KEVIN GODLEY     D V (C
  GARY TIBBS        B   (C   LOL CREME      G V (C   ANDY MACKAY     SAX (C   PETRINA LORDAN   V   (C
  ERIN LORDAN       V   (C   JOHN PUGH      SAX (1   BOB FISH        V   (1   COLIN MAXWELL    D   (1
  PETE ZEAR         G   (1   JOY SARNEY     V   (1   PAUL MITCHELL   B   (1   FRANK MEAD       SAX (1
  PETE THE HAT      V   (1   RON TELEMACQUE D   (    JOHN GORDON     B   (    MICK GRABHAM     G   (
J111                              BILL JUSTIS
  BILL JUSTIS       SAX  (       RAUNCHY & OTHER GUITAR INSTRUMENTALS 1974 SUN   UK      6467 010
  SID MANKER        G    (       RAUNCHY                          19   SUN        US         109
                                 SOLID & RAUNCHY                  19   PHILIPS INTERNATIONAL US 1950
J112                              JUSTWATER
  GUSKIN MARTIN     D   (A       (A) THE RIFF                     1977 BRANDED
  TOM KORBA         B   (A
  MITCHELL DANCIK   V K (A   DANNY RUBIN      G   (A
J113                           PATRICK JUVET
  PATRICK JUVET     V K (ABC     (A) PARIS BY NIGHT               1977 BARCLAY            90098
  SONNY BURKE       K   (A       (B) GOT A FEELING                1978 CASABLANCA     CAL 2028
  HENRY DAVIS       B   (A       (C) LADY NIGHT                   1979 CASABLANCA     CAL 2049
  SCOTT EDWARDS     B   (A
  JIM GORDON        D   (A   JAMES GADSON   D   (A   ED GREENE       D   (A   GARY COLEMAN     PERC(A
  RAY PARKER        G   (A   LEE RITENOUR   G   (A   ERNIE WATTS     HRNS (A  JIM HORN         SAX (A
  MIKE BODDIKER     K   (A   K SCHAEFFER  STRINGS (A GEORGES RODI    SYN (A   RUSSELL DABNEY   D   (A
  ALFONSO CAREY     B   (B   JIMMY LEE      G   (B   ROGER LEE       G   (B   NATHANIEL WHITE  K   (B
  ERROL BENNETT     CONGA(B   M GRILLO      PERC (B   PHIL KRAUS      PERC (B  BABATUNDE OLATUNJI PERC(B
  GEORGE DEVENS     PERC (B
K1                         K C & THE SUNSHINE BAND
  HARRY WAYNE CASEY K   (G       (A) DO IT GOOD                   1974 JAYBOY JSL  9   + US TK  500
  ROBERT JOHNSON    D   (G       (A) DO IT GOOD                   197  TK     UK TK 82505 + US TK  600
  RICHARD FINCH     B D (G       (B) K C & THE SUNSHINE BAND      1975 JAYBOY  JSL 9   + US TK  603
  JEROME SMITH      G   (G       (C) SOUND OF SUNSHINE            1975              US TK  604
  FERMIN GOYTISOLO  PERC (G      (D) PART THREE                   1977 TK     UK TK 82507 + US TK  605
  MIKE LEWIS        SAX  (G      (E) THE BEST OF                  197  JAYBOY UK JSB 101
  VINNIE TANNO      TPT  (G      (F) I LIKE TO DO IT              1977 PRESIDENT         JRE 500
  KEN FAULK         TPT  (G      (G) WHO DO YA LOVE               1978 TK     UK TK 86100 + US TK  607
  WHIT SIDENER      SAX  (G
  BEVERLEY CHAMPION V   (G   JEANETTE WILLIAMS  V  (G
```

```
RAY KENNEDY        V   (AB        (A) K G B                     1976 MCA   UK MCF  2749   US    2166
MIKE BLOOMFIELD    G   (A         (B) MOTION                    1976 MCA   UK MCF  2773   US    2221
RICK GRECH         B   (A
CARMINE APPICE     D   (AB  BARRY GOLDBERG    K  (AB  BEN SCHULTZ   G   (B   GREG SUTTON    B   (B
```

KAJANUS PICKETT   K3

```
GEORG KAJANUS          (A         (A) HI HO SILVER             1973  SIGNPOST        UK  SGZ 500
PHIL PICKETT           (A
```

HARRY KAKOULLI   K3A

```
HARRY KAKOULLI V B SYN G D(A      (A) EVEN WHEN I'M NOT        1980  OVAL        UK       OVLP 505
GARRELL REDFEARN   SYN (A
NIGEL SHARPE       G   (A    NICK ROBBINS    D    (A
```

KALA   K4

```
JOHNNIE MILES      D V (A         (A) KALA                     1973  BRADLEYS    UK   BRADL  1002
PERRY SINCLAIR     G V (A
SID GARDNER        B V (A    DAVE COOLING      G V (A  DAVE SKINNER   PNO (A  PAUL BENNETT    V  (A
LES NICOL          G V (A    JACK STEVENSON   PERC (A  PETER ARNESEN  PNO (A  SHIVA JONES   V K  (A
CAROL GRIMES       V   (A    JOHN BARHAM     CELLO (A
```

KALEIDOSCOPE   K5

```
PETE DALTREY       K   (          (A) TANGERINE DREAM         1967  FONTANA        UK  TL 5448
EDDIE PUMER        G   (          (B) FAINTLY BLOWING         1969  FONTANA        UK  STL 5491
DANNY BRIDGMAN     F   (
STEVE CLARK        B   (
```

KALEIDOSCOPE   K6

```
FENRUS EPP         VLN K(AB       (A) SIDE TRIPS              1967  EPIC            US  26304
JOHN VIDICAN       PERC (AB       (B) BEACON FROM MARS        1968  EPIC            US  26333
SOLOMON FELDTHOUSE G V (ABCDE     (C) INCREDIBLE KALEIDOSCOPE 1969  EPIC            US  26467
DAVID LINDLEY      VLN G V(ABCD   (D) BERNICE                 1970  CBS  UK 64005   US  26508
CHRIS DARROW       FDL G V (ABE   (E) WHEN SCOPES COLLIDE     1976  ISLAND UK       ILPS 9462
STUART BROTMAN     B V (CDE       (E) WHEN SCOPES COLLIDE     1976  PACIFIC ARTS    US   102
PAUL LAGOS         D   (CDE       (F) BROTHER MARY            19    POLYDOR         2315  002
TEMPLETON PARCELY  K V (CE
MAXWELL BUDA       HARM (C    RICHARD APLAN    FLT (D  JEFF KAPTON   G V (D  CONNIE CRILL    V  (D
```

AMORY KANE   K7

```
AMORY KANE         G V (AB        (A) MEMORIES OF TIME UNWOUND 1968 MCA        UK   MUPS  348
DAVE PEGG          B   (B         (B) JUST TO BE THERE        1970  CBS        UK         63849
NED BALEN          D   (B
```

KANGAROO   K8

```
JOHN HALL          B   (A         (A) KANGAROO                1968  ?          US
TEDDY SPELEOD      G   (A
N D SMART II       D   (A    BARBARA KEITH    V    (A
```

KANSAS   K9

```
PHIL EHART         D   (          (A) MASQUE                  1975  KIRSHNER US 33806
STEVE WALSH        K V (          (B) KANSAS                  1975  KIRSHNER US 32817  UK   80174
ROBBIE STEINHARDT  VLN (          (C) SONG FOR AMERICA        1976  KIRSHNER US 33385  UK   80740
DAVE HOPE          B   (          (D) LEFTOVERTURE            1976  KIRSHNER US 34224  UK   81728
RICH WILLIAMS          (          (E) POINT OF KNOW RETURN    1977  KIRSHNER US 34929  UK   82234
KERRY LIVGREN      G K (          (F) TWO FOR THE SHOW        1978  KIRSHNER US 35660  UK   88318
                                  (G) MONOLITH               1979  KIRSHNER           UK   83644
                                  (H)AUDIO VISIONS           1980  KIRSHNER           UK   84500
```

PAUL KANTNER   K10

```
PAUL KANTNER       G V (ABC       (A) ITS A FRESH WIND THAT BLOWS .... 1970 RCA US LPS 4448  UK SF 8163
GRACE SLICK        K V (AB         (B) SUNFIGHTER            1971  GRUNT                 FTR 1002
DAVID FREIBERG     V   (AC         (C) BARON VON TOLLBOOTH   1973  GRUNT                 BFLI 0148
JACK CASADY        B   (ABC
POINTER SISTERS    V   (C    PAPA JOHN CREACH  VLN (BC  JOHN BARBATA   D  (C  CRAIG CHAQUICO     G (C
MICKEY HART        D   (AC   PETER KAUKONEN     G   (A  PHIL SAWYER       (AB  BILL KREUTZMANN   D (A
CHRIS ETHRIDGE     B   (C    DAVID CROSBY      V G (ABC  JORMA KAUKONEN  G  (ABC RON DUDLEY        (A
JOEY COVINGTON     D PERC(AB BILL THOMPSON         (A  JERRY GARCIA   G BAN(ABC JACK TRAYLOR     V (C
HARVEY BROOKS      B   (A    GRAHAM NASH       V PERC(AB SPENCER DRYDEN      (B
```

KARTHARGO   K11

```
JOEY ALBRECHT      V G (ABCDE      (A) KARTHARGO             1971  BASF        GERM  20 211851
GLENN CORNICK      B   (C          (B) SECOND STEP           1973  BASF        GERM  20 211801
INGO BISCHOF       K V (ABCDE      (C) ROCK'N'ROLL TESTAMENT 1974  BELLAPHON   GERM BLPS 19201
TOMMY GOLDSCHMIDT  D   (ABCDE      (D) LIVE AT THE ROXY      1976  BELLAPHON   GERM BDA  7506
NORBERT LEHEMANN   D   (B          (E) LIVE                  1976  BELLAPHON   GERM B  15190
KONNI BOMMARIUS    D   (C
GERALD HARTWIG B V PERC(ABD  WOLFGANG BROCK  D PERC (A  RINGO FUNK   D  (D  REINHARD BOPP    G V (D
VICKI BROWN        V   (C    BARRY ST JOHN       V  (C  JOANNE WILLIAMS  V  (C  TOM CUNNINGHAM   V (C
```

JORMA KAUKONEN   K12

```
JORMA KAUKONEN     G V (A         (A) QUAH                   1975  GRUNT       US    BLFI 0209
TOM HOBSON             (A
```

PETER KAUKONEN   K13

```
PETER KAUKONEN     G V (A         (A) BLACK KANGAROO         1971  GRUNT       US    FTR 1006
SHELLEY SILVERMAN  D   (A
TERRY ADAMS        CELLO(A   DIANE EARL        V    (A  LARRY WEISBERG  B   (A  NICK BUCK     K  (A
PETER MARSHALL     B   (A    MARK RYAN         B    (A  JOEY COVINGTON  D V (A
```

JOHN KAY   K14

```
JOHN KAY    V G HCA   (ALL    (A) FORGOTTEN SONGS & UNSUNG HEROES 1972 DUNHILL US 50120 UK PROBE  1054
KENT HENRY         G   (B     (B) MY SPORTIN' LIFE        1973 DUNHILL US 50147  UK PROBE  8011
GEORGE BIONDO      B   (B     (B) MY SPORTIN' LIFE        1973               UK PROBE  6274
PENTTI GLAN        D   (B     (C) ALL IN GOOD TIME        1978 MERCURY US 1 3715 UK   9110 054
HUGH SULLIVAN      K   (B     (D) JOHN KAY & SPARROW      19   CBS          UK         63564
LARRY KNECHTEL     K   (B
BILL COOPER        B   (B  ALAN O'DAY      K   (B  DANNY KORTCHMAR  G  (B  RUSS KUNKEL    D  (B
LEE SKLAR          B   (B  MIKE UTLEY    PNO   (B  DARRYL DRAGON    K  (B  RICHARD PODOLOR PNO MAND(B
SHIRLEY MATTHEWS   V   (B  GLORIA JONES    V   (B  VANETTA FIELDS   V  (B  STAN FARBER    V  (B
GENE MORFORD       V   (B
```

```
K16                             KAYAK
    CEES VAN LEEUWEN  B   (AB        (A) SEE SEE THE SUN            1973 HARVEST      UK       SHSP  4033
    TOM SCHERPENZEEL  K   (AB        (B) KAYAK                      1974 HARVEST      UK       SHSP  4036
    MAX WERLEROFZOIETS V  (ABD       (C) THE LAST ENCORE           19
    JOHAN SLAGER      G   (ABD       (D) ROYAL BED BOUNCER          1975 VERTIGO UK 6360 53 +US JANUS7023
    PIM KOOPMAN       D   (ABD       (D) ROYAL BED BOUNCER          1975 EMI          N L     5C 064 25271
    CHARLES SCHOUTEN  D   (          (E) STARLIGHT DANCER           1977 VERTIGO UK 6360 856 US JANUS7034
    BERT VELDKAMP     B   (AD        (F) THE BEST OF                1978 EMI          N L     5C 050 25828
    THEO DEJONG       B   (          (G) PHANTOM OF THE NIGHT       1978             US JANUS7039
    GERRIT JAN LEENDERS V (A         (H) PERISCOPE LIFE             1979 MERCURY      US       SRM1  3824
    ERNST REIZIGER    CELLO(A
    GINNY BUSCH       VLN  (A   MARTIN  KOEMAN   VLN  (A   RIJN PETER DE KLERK      (A
K17                             ERIC KAZ
    ERIC KAZ V G K HCA SYN (ABC      (A) IF YOU'RE LONELY           1972 ATLANTIC UK K 40468 US  SD  7246
    BOB BABITT        B   (B         (B) CUL DE SAC                 1974 ATLANTIC            US  SD  7290
    PAUL BARRERE      G   (B         (C) FULLER/KAZ                 1978 CBS                 US      35324
    MALCOLM CECIL     SYN (B
    GORDON EDWARDS    B   (B   BOOKER T JONES HRNS K G(B   JOHN  KELSO    HRNS (B   JIM KELTNER      D   (B
    RAY LUCAS         D   (B   TIM MOORE        V   (B   BERNARD PURDIE   D   (B   JEROME RICHARDSON SAX (B
    ROCKY DZIDZORNU   PERC (B  SNEAKY PETE KLEINOW STEEL(B  DAVID T WALKER  G   (B   CRAIG FULLER    G V  (C
    DAN DUGMORE       G   (C   LEE SKLAR        B   (C   RUSS KUNKEL    D PERC(C   CRAIG DOERGE     K   (C
    DON GROLNICK      K   (C   STEVE LUKATHER   G   (C   CHARLES VEAL    VLN (C   ROLLICE DALE     VLA (C
    DENNIS KARMAZYN   CELLO(C  LEAH KUNKEL      V   (C   LEO SAYER      V   (C   JAMES NEWTON HOWARD K (C
K19                             LINDA KEEL
    LINDA KEEL        V   (A         (A) LADY ROCK'N'ROLL           1978 PYE          UK       NSPL  28273
    JACKY CHALARD     B   (A
    PATRICK VERBEC    G   (A   MOREAU SERRI     G   (A   JEAN PIERRE PREVOTAT   D (A JEAN YVES D'ANGELO  K  (A
    ROLLY             HCA (A   RENE MORIZURE    SAX (A   PIERROT PLOQUIN   TPT(A  FREDDY OMEZIAN      TPT(A
    ERIC BAMI         V   (A
K20                             JOHN 'SPEEDY' KEEN
    JOHN'SPEEDY'KEEN V G K D(AB      (A) PREVIOUS CONVICTIONS       1971     TRACK    UK       2406  105
    JIMMY McCULLOCH   G   (B         (B) Y' KNOW WOT I MEAN         1975     ISLAND   UK       ILPS 9338
    DAVE McDOUGALL    K   (
    BUTCH SANDFORD    G   (B   TERRY WILSON     B   (B   EMANUEL RENTZOS   K   (B   TONY BRAUNAGEL   D   (B
    RABBIT BUNDRICK   K   (B   B J COLE        STEEL(B   PETER VANDER PUIJE HRNS (B  LIZA STRIKE      V   (B
    GEORGE LEE        HRNS (B   EDDIE QUANSAH   HRNS (B
K21                             ACE KEFFORD
    ACE KEFFORD       B   (1         (1) ACE KEFFORD STAND 1969
    COZY POWELL       D   (1
    DAVE BALL         G   (1   DENNIS BALL        (1
K22                             CASEY KELLY
    CASEY KELLY   V G HCA   (AB      (A) CASEY KELLY               1972 ELEKTRA US 75040    UK K 42121
    LEE SKLAR         B   (A         (B) FOR SALE                  197  ELEKTRA
    RUSS KUNKEL       D   (A
    CRAIG DOERGE      K   (A   SNEAKY PETE KLEINOW STEEL(A   AL GARTH     FDL (A    DANNY COHEN ACC      (A
    JIM MESSINA       G   (A
K22A                            DAVE KELLY
    DAVE KELLY        G V PERC(AB    (A) SURVIVORS                 1979     APPALOOSA  ITALY   AP 001
    PAUL JONES        HCA (B         (B) WILLING                   1979     APPALOOSA  ITALY   AP 003
    GARY FLETCHER     B   (B
    BOB HALL          PNO V(B   STEVE GURL    K     (B
K23                             JO ANN KELLY
    JO ANN KELLY      G V (ABCD      (A) SAME THING ON THEIR MINDS  1971     SUNSET   UK       SLS  50209
    JOHN FAHEY        G   (B         (B) WITH FAHEY,MANN & MILLER  19       BLUE GOOSE         BG    2009
    ALAN SEIDLER          (B         (C) JO ANN KELLY             1969     CBS      UK           63841
    WOODY MANN            (B         (D) DO IT                    1976     RED RAG            RRR  006
    PETE EMERY           (D
    TONY McPHEE       G V (A   JOHN MILLER     G V (A
K24                             JONATHAN KELLY
    JONATHAN KELLY    V G K D(ABCD   (A) TWICE AROUND THE HOUSES    1972 RCA          UK       SF  8262
    MARK GRIFFITHS    B   (B         (B) WAIT TILL THEY CHANGE THE BACKDROP 73  RCA  UK       SF  8353
    ROY BABBINGTON    B   (B         (C) WAITING ON YOU            1974 RCA          UK       LPL 15022
    RAY DUFFY         D   (B         (D) TWO DAYS IN WINTER        1865 RCA          UK       SF  8415
    PETER WOODS       K   (AB
    THUNDERTHIGHS     V   (B   BARRY DESOUZA    D   (B   BRUCE THOMAS    B   (B   WILLIE WILSON    D   (B
    TIM RENWICK G FLT V  (AB  IAN SUTHERLAND   V   (B   GAVIN SUTHERLAND V   (B   MICHAEL OLIVER   D   (B
    LENNOX JAMES      PERC (B  LUCIANO BRAVO    D   (B   KEN SCOTT      PERC (B   TREVOR WILLIAMS  B   (C
    CHAS JANKEL       G   (C   DAVE SHEEN       D   (CD  SNOWY WHITE     G   (C   LARRY STEELE     D   (A
    GERRY CONWAY      D   (A   RICK KEMP        B   (A   HARVEY BURNS    D   (A   DONAL LUNNY      G   (A
    DAVE BALL         G   (A   JIM TOOMEY       D   (A   BYRON LYEFOOT   D   (A   JERRY DONAHUE    G   (A
    KUMA HARADA     B G PERC(D  DARRYL LEE QUE  CONGA (D  PIZZA QUARTET       (D  BRIAN GASCOIGNE MARIMBA(D
K25                             TONY KELLY
    TONY KELLY        G V (A         (A) BRING ME BACK             1972 POLYDOR      UK       2383  123
    PAUL MILLINS      K   (A
    JACK MILLS        G   (A   KEITH EVANS      B   (A   CODY         PERC HCA(A   TERRY STANNARD D PERC (A
    CLAUDIA LENNEAR   V   (A   KATHI MacDONALD  V   (A   LINDA NOVEMBER V (A      HELEN MILES      V    (A
    HILDA HARRIS      V   (A
K26                             EDDIE KENDRICKS
    EDDIE KENDRICKS   V   (ALL       (A) ALL BY MYSELF             1971 TAMLA  US  309    UK STML 11186
                                     (B) PEOPLE HOLD ON            1973 TAMLA  US  315    UK STML 11213
                                     (C) EDDIE HENDRICKS           1973 TAMLA               UK STML 11245
                                     (D) BOOGIE DOWN               1974 TAMLA  US  330    UK STML 11266
                                     (E) FOR YOU                   1975 TAMLA  US  335    UK STMA  8020
                                     (F) THE HIT MAN               1975 TAMLA  US  338    UK STML 12001
                                     (G) HE'S A FRIEND             1976 TAMLA  US  343    UK STML 12016
                                     (H) GOING UP IN SMOKE         1976 TAMLA  US  346    UK STML 12043
                                     (J) SLICK                     1977 TAMLA  US  350    UK STML 12071
                                     (K) AT HIS BEST               1978 TAMLA  US  354    UK STML 12080
                                     (L) VINTAGE 78                1978 ARISTA US 4170    UK SPART 1040
```

CHRIS KENNER   K27

CHRIS KENNER   V   (A   (A) LAND OF A THOUSAND DANCES   1963 ATLANTIC   US   SD 8117
KENNY & THE CASUALS   K27A

KENNY DANIELS   V   (AB   (A) IMPACT   1965 MARK US
TOMMY NICHOLS   B   (B   (B) LIVE AT THE STUDIO CLUB   1966 MARK US   MARK 5000
LEE LIGHTFOOT   B   (AB
DAVID BLACKLEY   D   (AB   PAUL ROACH   K   (AB JERRY SMITH   G   (A
KENSINGTON MARKET   K28

ALEX DAROU   B   ((A) KENSINGTON MARKET, AVENUE ROAD 1968 WB   US   WS 1754
LUKE GIBSON   V   ((B) AARDVARK   1969 WB   US
GENE MARTYNEC   V G PNO(
KEITH McKIE   G V (JIMMY WATSON   D (
KLARK KENT   K28A

KLARK'STEWART COPELAND'KENT   (A) KLARK KENT 10"   1980 A&M   UK   AMLE 68511
PAUL KENT   K28B

PAUL KENT   V K (AB   (A) P C KENT   1970 RCA   UK   SF 8083
DAVID RICHARDS   V G K(A   (B) PAUL KENT   1971 B&C   UK   CAS 1044
GAVIN WATSON   V G B(AB
JOHN WARD   D   (A   PAT DONALDSON   B   (B   TIM RENWICK   G   (B   TONY REEVES   B   (B
KATHY KISSOON   V   (B   MIKE LONDON   V   (B   GERRY CONWAY D   (B   RAY WARLEIGH WIND (B
ROGER POWELL   D   (B   CHRIS TURNER   HCA   (B   MAC KISSOON   V   (A   ANDY ROBERTS   G   (B
KENTUCKY COLONELS   K29

CLARENCE WHITE   G V ((A) LIVIN' IN THE PAST   19   SIERRA/BRIAR   US 7202
ROLAND WHITE   V MAND((B) KENTUCKY COLONELS   1974 UA UK UAS 29514 US ROUNDER 0070
BILLY RAY LATHAM   BAN ((C) WHITE BROTHERS   19   US ROUNDER 0073
ERIC WHITE   B   (
LEROY MACK   DOB (DENIS MORRIS   G   (BOBBY SLONE   FDL (SCOTT STONEMAN FDL (
BOB WARFORD   BAN (
DOUG KERSHAW   K30

DOUG KERSHAW   G V (ALL   (A) THE CAJUN WAY   1969 WB   US WS 1820
JOHN CHRISTOPHER   G   (EF   (B) SPANISH MOSS   1970 WB   US WS 1861
JIMMY COLVARD   G   (E   (C) DOUG KERSHAW   1971 WB   US WS 1906
TROY SEALS   G   (E   (D) SWAMP GRASS   1972 WB   US BS 2581
BUDDY KILLEN   PERC (E   (E) DEVILS ELBOW   1972 WB UK K 46196   US BS 2649
WILLIE ACKERMAN   D   (E   (F) DOUGLAS JAMES KERSHAW   1973 WB UK K 46264   US BS 2725
STU BASORE   STEEL(E   (G) MAMA KERSHAWS BOY   1974 WB   US BS 2793
CURLY CHALKER   STEEL(E   (H) ALIVE & KICKIN'   1975 WB   US BS 2851
BOBBY EMMONS   K   (EF   (I) RAGIN' CAJUN   1976 WB   US BS 2910
BOBBY WOOD   K   (EF   (J) FLIP FLOP FLY   1977 WB   US BS 3025
KARL HIMMEL   D   (E   (K) LOUISIANA MAN   1978 WB   US BS 3166
JOE ALLEN   B   (EF   (L) LOUISIANA CAJUN COUNTRY   1979 STARFLITE   US   2003
JERRY CARRIGAN   D   (E
CHARLIE McCOY   HCA (E   TOMMY COGBILL   B   (E   KENNY MALONE   D   (EF JORDANAIRES   V   (EF
CHIP MOMAN   G   (F   RICHARD MAINEGRA G V   (F   REGGIE YOUNG   G   (F   MIKE LEECH   B   (F
LARRIE LONDON   D   (F   DON SHEFFIELD   TPT   (F   DWAYNE WEST   V   (F   GORDON STOKER   V   (F
RAY WALKER   V   (F   HOYT HAWKINS   V   (F   DOTTIE DELEONIBUS V   (F   BILL STEWART   D   (J
MARTY VADALABENE   D   (J   CALVIN ARLINE   B   (J   MAX PAUL SCHWENNSEN G V (J JOHNNY SANDLIN G   (J
JIMMY NALLS   G   (J   ELVIN BISHOP   G   (J   NEIL URPEN   K   (J   JOHN HUGHEY   STEEL (J
BONNIE BRAMLETT   V   (J   RONNIE EADES   SAX   (J   CHARLES ROSE   TROM (J   PETE PENDRAS   G   (J
AL KAATZ   G   (J   DR JOHN   K   (J   ANNIE ROSE DEARMAS V (J   RANDALL BRAMBLETT SAX(J
HARRISON CAOWAY   TPT (J   HARVEY THOMPSON SAX(J
RUSTY KERSHAW   K31

RUSTY KERSHAW   (A   (A) CAJUN IN BLUES COUNTRY   1970 COTILLION   US   SD 9030
RUSTY & DOUG KERSHAW   K32

DOUG KERSHAW   FDL V(ABC   (A) LOUISIANA MAN   1971 LONDON   UK LGE 114
RUSTY KERSHAW   G V (ABC   (B) LOUISIANA MAN   1976 DJM   UK DJB 26080
TOMMY JACKSON   FDL (B   (C) CAJUN COUNTRY ROCKERS   1979 BEAR FAMILY   GERM BRX 15036
HOWARD JOHNSON   D   (B
CHET ATKINS   G   (B   EDDIE HILL   G   (B   HAROLD RAY BRADLEY G (B   HANK GARLAND   G   (B
RAY EDENTON   G   (B   FLOYD CHANCE   B   (B   WOODY WOODHAMS   B   (B   ERNIE NEWTON   B   (B
JIMMY DAY   STEEL(B   BOB FOSTER   STEEL   (B   PETE DRAKE   STEEL (B   CHARLES THERIOT STEEL (B
LOUIS FOURNERAT   STEEL(B   FLOYD CRAMER PNO   (B   WILEY BARKDULL   PNO V(B   MURREY H HARMAN D   (B
CAROLEE COOPER   V   (B
KESTREL   K32A

DAVE BLACK   G V (A   (A) KESTREL   1975 CUBE   HIFLY 19
JOHN COOK   G V SYN (A
DAVID WHITTAKER   D PERC(A   FENWICK MOIR   B   (A   TOM KNOWLES   V   (A
KEY   K32B

VOLKER LANGEFELD   V(MULTI INST)A   (A) FIT ME IN   1978 ELECTROLA   EURO IC 064 45137
ALAN WARREN   D   (A
KEY LARGO   K33

PAT McAULIFFE   V   (A   (A) KEY LARGO   1970 BLUE HORIZON   UK   7 63859
LAURENCE GARMAN   HCA (A
BOB SAVAGE   K   (A   LAURIE SANFORD   G   (A   TOM STEAD   B   (A   KENNY LAMB   D (A
BOBBY KEYS   K34

BOBBY KEYS   SAX (A   (A) BOBBY KEYS   1972 WB   UK K46141
KHAN   K35

STEVE HILLAGE   G   (12A   (A) SPACE SHANTY   1972 DERAM   UK SDLR 11
ERIC PEACHEY   D   (12A   (1) APRIL 1971 JULY 1972   (B) JULY 1972 NOV 1972
NICK GREENWOOD   B   (A1
NIGEL SMITH   B   (2   DICK HENNINGHAM   K   (1   DAVE STEWART   K   (2A

K36

CHAKA KHAN

CHAKA KHAN	V	(A		(A) CHAKA			1978	WB	US	BSK 3245	UK		K56560
RICHARD TEE	K	(A		(B) NAUGHTY			1980	WB	US	BSK 3385	UK		K56713
KERMIT MOORE	CELLO(A			(C) WHATTA GONNA DO TO ME			1981	WB			UK		K56888
TERRI GONZALES	V	(A											
STEVE FERRONE	D	(A	PHIL UPCHURCH	G	(A	HAMISH STUART	G V	(A	WILL LEE	B V	(A
ANTHONY JACKSON	B	(A	BROOK TILLOTSON	HRNS	(A	JIM BUFFINGTON	HRNS	(A	ARTHUR JENKINS	K	(A
ONNIE McINTYRE	G	(A	MARK STEVENS	B V	(A	SAMMY FIGUEROA	CONGA(A		TONY MAIDEN	G	(A
RICHARD BOCK	CELLO(A		CISSY HOUSTON	V	(A	DAVID LASLEY	V	(A	RANDY BRECKER	TPT	(A
GEORGE YOUNG	SAX	'A	MICHAEL BRECKER	SAX	(A	GENE BIANCO	HARP	(A	ALAN GORRIE	V	(A
GEORGE BENSON	V	(A	RAPHAEL CRUZ	CONGA(A		DAVID SANBORN	SAX	(A	JOHN CLARK HRNS		(A
PAUL FAULISE	TROM	(A	JESSE LEVY	CELLO(A		BARRY ROGERS	TROM	(A	RONNIE CUBER SAX		(A
LEON PENDARVIS	K	(A	RICK MAROTTA	D	(A	CORNELL DUPREE	G	(A	KEN BISCHEL	SYN	(A
EDDIE DANIELS	FLT	(A	PHIL BODNER	FLT	(A	GEORGE MARGE	FLT	(A	AIRTO MOREIRA	PERC	(A
ANDREW KASTNER	G	(A										

K37

STEVE KHAN

STEVE KHAN	G	(AB		(A) TIGHTROPE	1978	CBS		UK	82230
				(B) BLUE MAN	1978	CBS		UK	83146
				(C) BEST OF	1980	CBS		UK	84234

K38

KICKS

PAUL RUDOLPH	G	(				
CAL BATCHELOR	G V	(				
STEVE YORK	B	(	ALAN POWELL	D	(

K39

JOHNNY KIDD & THE PIRATES

JOHNNY KIDD(FRED HEATH)	V(ALL		(A) SHAKIN' ALL OVER		1971	STARLINE	UK		SRS 5100
ALAN CADDY	G	(12	(B) YOUR CHEATIN' HEART		197	PATHE	IMP		2C062 04731
TOMMY DOCHERTY	G	(1	(C) MEMORIAL ALBUM		197	PATH	IMP		2C062 04422
JOHNNY GORDON	B	(1	(D) BEST OF		1978	EMI	UK		NUT M12
CLEM CATTINI	D	(1	(EP) PLEASE DONT TOUCH		1960	HMV	UK		7EG 8628
KEN McKAY	D	(2	(EP) I'LL NEVER GET OVER YOU		1963	HMV	UK		7EG 8834
BRIAN GREGG	B	(2	(1) 1958/9	(2) 1959	(3) 1962	(4) 1962/65			
JOE MORETTI	G	(2	(5) 1965	(6) 1966	(7) 1966	(8) 1966/67			
THUNDERCLAP JONES	PNO	(2							
JOHNNY PATTO	G	(3	JOHNNY SPENCER	B	(345	FRANK FARLEY	D	(345	MICK GREEN G (345
JOHN WEIDER	G	(5	ROGER TRUTH	D	(678	NICK SIMPER	B	(678	JOHNNY CARROL ORG (8
RAY SOAPER	ORG	(6	MICKY STEWART	G	(678				

K40

GREG KIHN

GREG KIHN	G V	(ALL	(A) GREG KIHN	1976	BESERKLEY	US 0046	UK	BSERK 4
STEVE WRIGHT	B V	(ABCDE	(B) GREG KIHN AGAIN	1977	BESERKLEY	US 0052	UK	BSREK 8
LARRY LYNCH	D V	(ABCDE	(C) NEXT OF KIHN	1978	BESERKLEY	US 0056	UK	BSERK13
ROBBIE DUNBAR	V K G(A		(D) GREG KIHN /RUBINOOS LIVE	1978	BESERKLEY		UK	GIG1
DAVE CARPENDER	G V	(BCDE	(E) WITH THE NAKED EYE	1979	BESERKLEY		UK	BSERK20
GARY PHILLIPS	G V	(A	(F) POWERLINES	1980	BESERKLEY		UK	BSERK20
MARK JORDAN	K	(A						
JOHN DOUKAS	K	(A						

K41

KILBURN & THE HIGH ROADS

IAN DURY	V	(A	(A) HANDSOME	1975	DAWN	UK	DNLS	3065
KEITH LUCAS	G	(A	(A) HANDSOME	1977	PYE	UK	NSPL	18541
DAVEY PAYNE	SAX	(A	(B) WOT A BUNCH	1978	WB	UK	K	56513
RODERICK MELVIN	PNO	(A	(EP) KILBURN & THE HIGH ROADS	19	BONAPARTE	UK		BONE1
CHARLES SINCLAIR	B	(A						
CLAIRE TORRY		(A	MARIO GIBBINGS	(A	CLYDE DIAS	(A	MATTHEW EMMANUEL	(A
DAVID NEWTON ROHOMAN	D	(A	PETE WILLSHER	(A	LES THATCHER	(A	DAVE MATTACKS D	(A
JON FIELD		(A	ROD KING	(A	MARTIN JAY	(A	TONY CHARLES	(A
TREVOR CUMBERBATCH		(A	TINA CHARLES	V	(A			

K42

KILLERS

SUCHARD THITTICHAI	G	(A	(A) KILLER	1978	ARIOLA	ARL	5003
JOHN CLAY	G V	(A					
TONY MAYBERRY	B	(A	STUART GREEN	D	(A	PHIL KENZIE	SAX (A

K43

KILLING FLOOR

MICK CLARKE		(	(A) KILLING FLOOR	1970	SPARK	SRLP 102+1973 SRLM 2004	
BILL THORNYCROFT		(	(A) KILLING FLOOR	197	SIRE	US	97019
BAS SMITH		(	(B) OUT OF URANUS	197	PENNY FARTHING	UK	PELS 511
LOU MARTIN		(					
STU McDONALD		(					

K43A

KILLING JOKE

JAZZ COLEMAN	K V	(A	(A) KILLING JOKE	1980	EG	UK	EGMD	5.45
PIG YOUTH	B V	(A					
PAUL	D	(A	GEORDIE	G	(A		

K44

KILLJOYS

BOB PEACH	D	(			
KEITH RIMELL	G	(			
KEVIN ROWLAND	G V	(	GHISLAINE WESTON	B V	(

K44A

KIND HEARTS & ENGLISH

TONY BIRD	V	(	(A) A WISH FOR A SEASON	1976	DJM	UK	DJF 20490
JOHN TIPPET	G PNO(		(B) BEACHCOMBER	1977	DJM	UK	DJM 20512
PAUL KEOGH	G	(					
LEE FOTHERGILL	G	(	PAUL BIRCHIL	G	(	FRANK MacDONALD	B (	KEVIN WELLS D (
DOUGLAS KEAN	SYN	(					

K45

B B KING

BB KING	G V PNO(ALL								
CHUCK FINDLEY	HRNS	(EJ	JIM KELTNER	D	(E	MAC REBENNNACK	PNO	(E	JOHN URIBE	(E
KENNY SANDS	TPT	(A	HENRY BOOZIER	TPT	(A	PLUMA DAVIS	TROM	(A	LAWRENCE BURDINE SAX(A
JOHNNY BOARD	SAX	(A	BARNEY HUBERT	SAX	(ADFH	MILLARD LEE	PNO	(A	MAYALL YORK B (A
SONNY FREEMAN	D	(ADFH	JOHN BROWNING	TPT	(DF	BROOKER WALKER	SAX	(DL	RON LEVY SYN PNO(DFLH
ALEXIS KORNER	G	(E	RINGO STARR	D	(E	JIM PRICE	HRNS	(E	BOBBY KEYS HRNS(E
GARY WRIGHT	K	(E	KLAUS VOORMANN	B	(E	DUSTER BENNETT	HCA	(E	STEVE MARRIOTT G (E
GREG RIDLEY		(E	JERRY SHIRLEY		(E	PETE WINGFIELD	K	(E	PAUL BUTLER (E
JOHN BEST		(E	JIM GORDON	D	(E	BILL PERKINS		(E	OLLIE MITCHELL (E

(CONTINUED)

BARRY FORD		(E	RICK WRIGHT		(E	DAVID SPINOZZA		(E	CARL HALL		(E
JOE SAMPLE	K	(J	WILTON FELDER	SAX	(J	STIX HOOPER	D	(J	POPS POPWELL	B	(J
DR RAGOVOY		(E	JOSHIE ARMSTEAD	V	(E	TASHA THOMAS	V	(E	CAROLE KING	PNO	(C
BRYAN GAROFALO	B	(CF	RUSS KUNKEL	D	(C	LEON RUSSELL	PNO	(C	JOE WALSH	G	(FC
PAUL HARRIS	K	(FC	HUGH McCRACKEN	G	(C	JERRY JEMMOTT	B	(C	HERB LOVELL	D	(C
SHIRLEY MATTHEWS	V	(C	MERRY CLAYTON	V	(C	CLYDIE KING	V	(C	VANETTA FIELDS	V	(C
BOBBY BRYANT	TPT	(FK	PLAS JOHNSON	SAX	(F	BOB MORIN	D	(F	MEL BROWN	G	(FH
JOHN TURK	ORG	(F	EARL PALMER	D	(F	RONNIE BAKER	B	(G	ELLI TARKESTY	G	(G
WILL BOULWARE	K	(G	VINCE MONTANA	VIBES	(G	MEMPHIS HRNS	HRNS	(G	MELVIN JACKSON		(H
CATO WALKER		(H	CHARLES POLK		(H	THEODORE ARTHUR		(H	JOSEPH HARDIN		(H
DEAN PARKS	G	(J	ROLAND BAUTISTA	G	(J	KURT McGETRICK	SAX	(J	LUTHER WATERS	V	(J
JULIA TILLMAN	V	(J	RED CALLANDER	TUBA	(F	JESSE ED DAVIS	G	(F	JOE BURTON	TROM	(FH
CLIFF COULTER	K PERC	(F	RANDY WOLFE	G	(F	SANDY KONIKOFF	PERC	(F	DERYLL INMAN	G	(G
ROLAND CHAMBERS	G	(G	RON KERSEY	K	(G	ANDREW LOVE	SAX	(G	DON RENALDO STRINGS		(G
BEN BENAY	G	(H	BOBBY FORTE	SAX	(HL	TOMMY PUNKSON		(H	THEODORE REYNOLDS		(H
ALFRED THOMAS		(H	JAMES GADSON	D	(J	GEORGE BOHANON	HRNS	(J	GARY HERBIG	FLT	(J
ORRIN WATERS	V	(J	MAXINE WILLARD	V	(J	RED HOLLOWAY	SAX	(F	VICTOR FELDMAN	PERC K	(F
EARL TURBINTON	SAX	(F	TAJ MAHAL	HCA G	(F	RON BROWN		(K	EARL YOUNG	D	(G
NORMAN HARRIS	G	(G	DAVE CRAWFORD	K	(G	LARRY WASHINGTON	PERC	(G	WAYNE JACKSON	TPT	(G
PHILADELPHIA STRINGS		(G	MILTON HOPKINS	G	(KHL	EDWARD ROWE	HRNS	(HL	HAROLD POTIER JR		(H
LEO PENN		(H	MICHAEL OMARTIAN	K	(H	STEVE MADAIO	TPT	(J	QUITMAN DENNIS	HRNS	(J
ABE MOST	CLAR	(K	LEE RITENOUR	G	(K	JAMES TONEY	ORG	(KL	RONNIE BARRON	ORG	(K
SONNY BURKE	K	(K	JOE TURNER	B	(K	SCOTT EDWARDS	B	(K	JOHN STARKS	D	(KL
ED GREENE	D	(K	EARL NASH	PERC	(K	EDDIE BROWN	PERC	(K	AL AARONS	TPT	(K
ROY POPER	TPT	(K	GARNETT BROWN	TROM	(K	JIMMY FORREST	SAX	(K	FRED JACKSON	WIND	(K
ERNIE WATTS	SAX	(K	JEROME RICHARDSON	SAX	(K	JOE LIGON	V	(K	JOHNNY MARTIN	V	(K
ELMEO FRANKLIN	V	(K	RICHARD WALLACE	V	(K	CALVIN OWENS	TPT	(M	CALEP EMPHREY	D	(M
EDGAR SYNIGAL	SAX	(M	LEONARD GILL	G	(M	STEVE SHERARD	TROM	(M	HILTON JOSEPH	SAX	(M
PHIL BLACKMAN	K	(M	JOHN WILLIE COOK	TPT	(M	JON JONES	G	(M	NANA VASCONCELOS	PERC	(M
RUDY AIKELS	B	(L	MARCUS BARNETT	PERC	(L	JOSEPH BURTON	TROM	(L	JESS DANIELS	G	(L
HERBERT HARDESTY	SAX	(L	RUSSELL JACKSON	B	(M	WILBERT FREEMAN	B	(DFM	EDDIE MILLER	WIND	(J

(A) LIVE AT THE REGAL	1965	ABC	US	ABCS	724
(A) " "	19	ABC	US	ABCD	509
(A) " "	1965	HMV	UK		
(B) BLUES ON TOP OF BLUES	1967	BLUESWAY US	BLS	6011	
(B) " "	1968	STATESIDE UK		10238	
(B) " "	19	ABC	US	ABC	709
(C) INDIANOLA MISSISSIPPI	1970	PROBE	UK	SPB	6255
(C) " "	197	ABC	US		713
(D) LIVE AT COOK COUNTY	1971	PROBE	UK	SPB	1032
(D) " "	197	ABC	US		723
(E) B B KING IN LONDON	1971	PROBE	UK	SPB	1041
(E) " "	197	ABC	UK	ABC	5015
(E) " "	197	ABC	US		730
(F) L A MIDNIGHT	1972	PROBE	UK	SPB	1051
(F) " "	1977	ABC			743
(G) FRIENDS	1974	ABC	UK	ABCL	5051
(G) " "	1977	ABC	US	AB	825
(H) TOGETHER	1974	DUNHILL	US		751096
(H) " "	1974	ANCHOR	UK	ABCD	605
(J) MIDNIGHT BELIEVER	1978	ABC	UK	ABCL	5246
(K) KINGSIZE	19	ABC	US		977
(K) KINGSIZE	19	EMI EUROICO54		95148	
(L) LUCILLE TALKS BACK	1975	ABC	US		5149
(L) LUCILLE TALKS BACK	197	ABC	US		909
(M) NOW APPEARING AT O'MISS	80	MCA		MCA28016	
B B KING STORY	1968	BLUE HORIZON		7 63216	
B B KING STORY VOL 2	1969	BLUE HORIZON		7 63226	
LIVE & WELL	1970	STATESIDE	UK		10297
" "	1973	BLUESWAY	US	BLS56031	
" "	19	ABC	US		819
COMPLETELY WELL	1970	STATESIDE	UK		10299
" "	19	ABC	US		868
" "	1974	BLUESWAY	US	BLS56037	
" "	19	NEW WORLD		NW6005	
GUESS WHO	1973	PROBE			1063
" "	19	ABC			5021
" "	197	ABC	US		759
TO KNOW YOU IS TO LOVE YOU	1973	PROBE	UK		1083
" " "	1974	ABC			5038
" " "	19	ABC	US		794
BACK IN THE ALLEY	1973	BLUESWAY	US		6050
" "	1977	ABC			878
GREATEST HITS	1973	PROBE	UK		1069
GREATEST HITS VOL 1	19	UNITED	US		7766
" "	19	KENT	US		552
LUCILLE	1969	STATESIDE	UK		10272
" "	1973	BLUESWAY	US		6016
" "	1977	ABC	US		712
MR BLUES	19	ABC	US		456
BEST OF	1973	ABC			5026
" "	19	ABC	US		767
B B KING	19	NEW WORLD			6004
B B KING VOL 2	19	NEW WORLD			6006
SOUL OF B B KING	19	FESTIVAL			532
" " "	19	KENT	US		5-16
" " "	19	KENT	US		516
" " "	19	CUSTOM	US		2052
" " "	19	CUSTOM	US		1052
" " "	19	UNITED	US		7714

BLUES IS KING	19	ABC	US	704
" "	196	HMV	UK	3608
CONFESSIN' THE BLUES	19	ABC	US	528
" "	19	HMV	UK	3514
BLUES ON TOP OF BLUES	1968	STATESIDE	UK	10238
" "	19	BLUESWAY	US	6011
" "	19'	ABC	US	868
THE ELECTRIC B B KING	1977	ABC	US	813
" "	19	ABC	US	1061
" "	1969	STATESIDE	UK	10284
" "	1969	BLUESWAY	US	6022
KING OF THE BLUES	1976	M F P	UK	50259
" "	19	CROWN	US	5167
" "	19	UNITED	US	7730
TOGETHER AGAIN	1976	IMPULSE		8027
" "	1976	IMPULSE	US	9317
TAKE A SWING WITH ME	19	BLUE HORIZON	2431	004
B B KING ANTHOLOGY	1976	ABC		5611
" "	19	KENT		9011
FEELING THEY CALL THE BLUES	19	TRIO	JAP	PA 6220
FEELING THEY CALL VOL2	19	TRIO	JAP	PA 6221
B B KING LIVE	19	KENT	US	565
LIVE	19	KENT	US	515
LIVE	19	UNITED	US	7771
ON STAGE LIVE	19	UNITED	US	7736
ON STAGE LIVE	19	KENT	US	5015
BETTER THAN EVER	19	KENT	US	561
BOSS OF THE BLUES	19	KENT	US	5029
BOSS OF THE BLUES	19	UNITED	US	7750
DOING MY THING LORD	19	KENT	US	563
FROM THE BEGINNING	19	KENT	US	533
INCREDIBLE SOUL OF	19	KENT	US	539
INCREDIBLE SOUL OF	19	UNITED	US	7756
B B KING STORY	19	JOKER	ITALY	3727
SINGIN' THE BLUES	19	CROWN	US	5020
SINGIN' THE BLUES	19	UNITED	US	7726
MORE	19	CROWN	US	5230
MY KIND OF BLUES	19	CROWN	US	5188
MY KIND OF BLUES	19	UNITED	US	7724
SPANISH HARLEM	19	ATCO	US	33133
THE BLUES	19	CROWN	US	5063
THE BLUES	19	UNITED	US	7732
LET ME LOVE YOU	19	KENT	US	513
LET ME LOVE YOU	19	UNITED	US	7734
ORIGINAL SWEET 16	19	KENT	US	568
ORIGINAL SWEET 16	19	UNITED	US	7773
PURE SOUL	19	KENT	US	517
THE JUNGLE	19	KENT	US	521
THE JUNGLE	19	UNITED	US	7742
TURN ON WITH B B KING	19	KENT	US	548
TURN ON WITH B B KING	19	UNITED	US	7763
UNDERGROUND BLUES	19	KENT	US	535
9 X 9.5	19	UNITED	US	7788
WAILS	19	CROWN	US	5115
WAILS	19	CROWN	US	147
BLUE FOR ME	19	UNITED	US	7708
BLUE FOR ME	19	CUSTOM	US	2046
BLUES IN MY HEART	19	CROWN	US	309
EASY LISTENING BLUES	19	CROWN	US	5286
EASY LISTENING BLUES	19	UNITED	US	7705

(CONTINUED)

B B KING

GREAT B B KING	19	CROWN	US	5143
THE GREAT	19	UNITED	US	7728
HEART FULL OF BLUES	19	UNITED	US	7703
I LOVE YOU SO	19	CUSTOM	US	2049
I LOVE YOU SO	19	UNITED	US	7711
ROCK ME BABY	19	KENT	US	5012
ROCK ME BABY	19	UNITED	US	7733
TWIST WITH B B KING	19	CROWN	US	5248

K46   ALBERT KING

ALBERT KING	G V	(ALL	(A) THE BIG BLUES	1962	KING	US		852
DONALD 'DUCK' DUNN	B	(FHO	(B) TRAVELLING TO CALIFORNIA	1967	KING	US		K1060
STEVE CROPPER	G	(F	(B) TRAVELLING TO CALIFORNIA	1967	POLYDOR	UK		2343 026
AL JACKSON	D	(EFGO	(C) BORN UNDER A BAD SIGN	1967	STAX US	+IMPULSE US		7723
JIM KELTNER	D	(H	(D) KING OF THE BLUES GUITAR	1968	ATLANTIC	UK 588 173	US	SD8213
ROGER HAWKINS	D	(H	(D) KING OF THE BLUES GUITAR	197	ATLANTIC	UK RI		K40494
WILLIE HALL	D	(O	(E) LIVE WIRE BLUES POWER	1968	STAX US 2003		UK	1002
JAMES GADSON	D	(L	(F) DOES THE KINGS THING	1968	STAX US 2015		UK	1017
DAVID HOOD	B	(H	(G) YEARS GONE BY	1969	STAX US 2010		UK	1022
EARL THOMAS	B	(O	(H) LOVEJOY	1971	STAX US 2040		UK	2325
HENRY DAVIS	B	(L	(I) I'LL PLAY THE BLUES FOR YOU	197	STAX US 3009		UK	1019
CHUCK RAINEY	B	(L	(I) I'LL PLAY THE BLUES FOR YOU	197	POLYDOR		UK	2325089
JESSE ED DAVIS	G	(H	(J) I WANNA GET FUNKY	1974	STAX US 5505		UK	1003
TIPPY ARMSTRONG	G	(H	(K) MONTREUX FESTIVAL	197	STAX US 5520			
WAYNE PERKINS	G	(H	(L) TRUCKLOAD OF LOVIN'	1976	UTOPIA US 1 1387		UK	UTS 602
MICHAEL TOLES	G	(H	(M) LIVE (DBL)	1977	UTOPIA US 2 2205			
VERNON BURCH	G	(O	(N) ALBERT	1977	UTOPIA US 1 1731			
BOBBY MANUEL	G	(O	(O) THE PINCH	1978	STAX	US 4101	UK	3001
WAH WAH WATSON	G	(L	(P) DOOR TO DOOR	19	CHESS			1538
BILLY FENDER	G	(L	(Q) CHRONICLE (1 SIDE)	1979	STAX	US 4123		
GREG POREE	G	(L	(R) KING ALBERT	1977	TOMATO	US 6002		
LESTER SNELL	K	(O						

JOE SAMPLE	K	(L	SANDY KONIKOFF	PERC (H	KING ERRISSON	PERC (L	DENIECE WILLIAMS	V (L
JEANIE ARNOLD	V	(L	OTIS RUSH	G V (P	JOHN GALLIE	K (H	WINSTON STEWART	K (O
BERT DECOTEAUX	K	(L	JEANNE GREEN	V (H	LANI GROVES	V (L	JULIA TILLMAN	V (L
MEMPHIS HORNS		(O	BARRY BECKETT	K (H	MARVELL THOMAS	K (O	JERRY PETERS	K (L
WILLIAM C BROWN	V	(O	MAXINE WILLARD	V (L	DEE IRVIN	V (L	MOUNT ZION SINGERS	V (H
RUDY ROBINSON	K	(R	ANTHONY WILLIS	B (R	AARON WILLIS	G (R	RAY TINI JR	G (R
DWAYNE LOMAX	D	(R	BARBARA HUBY	PERC (R	LARRY FRATANGELO	PERC (R	BRANDYE	V (R
JOHN FRAGA	B	(R	JAMES McCARTY	G (R	DENNIS ROBBINS	G (R	JOHN BADANJEK	D (R
FRED WESLEY	HRNS	(R	RONALD WRIGHT	D (R	EDDIE WILLS	G (R	GLEN GOINS	G (R

K47   BEN E KING

BEN E KING	V	(ALL	(A) SPANISH HARLEM	1961	ATCO	US 33133		
JEFF MIRANOV	G	(N	(B) SINGS FOR SOULFUL LOVERS	1962	ATCO	US 33137		
KEN HATFIELD	G	(N	(C) DONT PLAY THAT SONG	1962	ATCO	US 33142		
KEN KIRKLAND	K	(N	(D) GREATEST HITS	1964	ATLANTIC US 33165	UK	2464 010	
MARCUS MILLER	B	(N	(E) ROUGH EDGES	19	MAXWELL	US 88001 UK CREWE	203	
BEN E KING JR	B	(N	(F) BEGINNING OF IT ALL	1971	MANDALA	US 3007 UK CBS	64570	
JIMMY YOUNG	D	(N	(G) SEVEN LETTERS	1965	ATCO	US 33174		
SAMMY FIGUEROA	PERC	(N	(H) SUPERNATURAL THING	1975	ATLANTIC US 18132 UK			K50118
YVONNE LEWIS	V	(N	(J) BEN E KING STORY	1975	ATLANTIC		UK	K50139
JANET PENDARVIS	V	(N	(K) I HAD A LOVE	1976	ATLANTIC US 18169 UK			K50264
CRYSTAL DAVIS	V	(N	(L) LET ME LIVE IN YOUR LIFE	1978	ATLANTIC US 19200 UK			K50527
DEIRDRE TUCK-COREL	V	(N	(M) STAR COLLECTION	197	MIDI		GERM	20040
RODNEY PHELPS	G	(N	(N) MUSIC TRANCE	1980	ATLANTIC US 19269 UK			K50713
KEVIN DOUGLAS	V	(N						
RICARDO WILLIAMS	D	(N	EMMANUEL REDDING	D (N	TYRONE WILLIAMS	K (N	GREGORY McCOY	K (N
JAMES DRUMGOLE	TPT	(N	RENNELLE STAFFORD	V (N	JAMILLAR MUHAMMAD	V (N		

K47A   BOBBY KING

BOBBY KING		(A	(A) CHASER	197	MCM	FR	900 292

K48   CAROLE KING

CAROLE KING	G PNO V	(ALL	(A) NOW THAT EVERYTHINGS BEEN SAID	1969	ODE	Z1244 012(BY GROUP CITY)		
RALPH SCHUCKETT	K	(BCDL	(B) WRITER	1970	ODE US 77066	US RI EPIC 34944		
CHARLES LARKEY	B	(BCDEFGL	(B) WRITER	1970	A&M UK		AMLS	996
DANNY KOOTCH	G V	(BCDEFGIL	(C) TAPESTRY	1972	ODE US 77006	US RI EPIC 34956		
JAMES TAYLOR	G V	(BCDIL	(C) TAPESTRY	197	A&M UK 2025	UK RI EPIC 82308		
BOBBYE HALL	PERC	(DEFL	(D) MUSIC	197	ODE US 77013	US RI EPIC 34949		
THERESA CALDERONE	PERC	(DL	(D) MUSIC	197	A&M UK		AMLH	67013
ABIGALE HANESS	V	(BDG	(E) RHYMES & REASONS	1972	ODE	77016	US RI EPIC 34950	
MERRY CLAYTON	V	(CDL	(F) FANTASY	1973	ODE	77018	US RI EPIC 34962	
WILLIAM GREEN	WIND	(DL	(G) WRAP AROUND JOY	1974	ODE	77024	US RI EPIC 34953	
WILLIAM COLLETTE	WIND	(DL	(H) REALLY ROSIE	1975	ODE	77027	US RI EPIC 34955	
ERNIE WATTS	WIND	(DEFGJKL	(I) THOROUGHBRED	1976	ODE	77034	US RI EPIC 34963	
PLAS JOHNSON	WIND	(DL	(J) SIMPLE THINGS	1977	CAPITOL		11667	
MIKE ALTSCHUL	WIND	(DFG	(K) WELCOME HOME	1978	CAPITOL		11785	
OSCAR BRASHEAR	WIND	(DJ	(L) GREATEST HITS	1978	ODE	86043	US EPIC 34967	
CURTIS AMY	WIND	(CDFL	(M) TOUCH THE SKY	1979	CAPITOL		11953	
RON COBB	V WIND	(M						

HARVEY MASON	D	(EFL	DAVID T WALKER	G (DEL	RED RHODES	STEEL(E	HARRY EDISON	HRNS (E
ROBERT BRYANT	HRNS	(E	GEORGE BOHANON	TROM(EFGJKL	CHARLIE LOPER	TROM (EL	DICK HYDE	TROM (FGL
OLLIE MITCHELL	HRNS	(F	CHUCK FINDLEY	TPT (FGL	ALBERT AARONS	TPT (EL	TOM SCOTT	SAX (FGJL
ANDY NEWMARK	D	(GL	DEAN PARKS	G (GL	FRED JACKSON	HRNS (G	GENE COE	HRNS (G
JIM HORN	SAX	(G	EDDIE KENDRICKS	SINGERS(F	LOUISE GOFFIN	V (GJL	SHERRY GOFFIN	V (GLJ
WADDY WACHTEL	G	(IL	RUSS KUNKEL	D (CIL	LEE SKLAR	B (LI	RALPH MACDONALD	PERC(IL
DAVID CROSBY	V	(I	GRAHAM NASH	V (I	J D SOUTHER	V (I	ROBERT McENTEE	V G K(JK
MARK HALLMAN	G V K(JKM		ROB GALLOWAY	B (KJ	MICHAEL WOOTEN	D (JK	MIGUEL RIVERA	PERC (JKM
RICHARD HARDY	WIND	(JKM	CLARK SPANGLER	SYN (JK	NOLAN SMITH	HRNS (JK	MAURICE SPEARS	TROM (J

(CONTINUED)

CAROLE KING

(CONTINUED)

TERRY HARRINGTON	SAX	(J	JOEL O'BRIEN	D	(CL	PERRY STEINBERG	B	(C	JULIA TILLMAN	V	(BL
JOHN FISCHBACH	SYN	(B	DOLORES HALL	V	(B	LEO LEBLANC	G V	(M	REESE WYNANS	K	(M
FRED KRC	D V	(M	DAVE PERKINS	G V	(K	BOBBY RAMBO	G V	(M	TOMAS RAMIREZ	WIND V	(M
STEPHANIE SPRUILL	V	(K	ALEXANDRA BROWN	V	(K	ANN WHITE	V	(K	BOB HARRINGTON	DULC	(K
ANNE GOLIA	TAMB	(K	GEORGIA KELLY	HARP	(J	RICK EVERS	PERC	(K	STRING SECTION		(KFEC

CLYDIE KING

CLYDIE KING	V	(A	(A) BROWN SUGAR	1974	POLYDOR	UK	2310 231

EARL KING

EARL KING		(AB	(A) NEW ORLEANS ROCK'N'ROLL	1978	SONET	UK	SNTF 719
			(B) EARL KING	19	VIVID	JAP	1012

FREDDIE KING

FREDDIE KING	G V	(ALL	(A) FREDDIE KING SINGS	196	KING US	762				
SONNY THOMPSON	PNO	(ABC	(B) LETS HIDEAWAY & DANCEAWAY	196	KING US	773				
FRED JORDAN	G	(ABC	(C) FREDDIE KING GOES SURFIN'	196	KING US	856				
WILLIAM WILLIS	B	(ABC	(D) BONANZA OF INSTRUMENTALS	196	KING US	928				
PHILIP PAUL	D	(ABC	(E) HIDEAWAY	196	KING US	1059+ 1977 RI STARDAY	5033			
BUD BEADLE	SAX	(NPR	(F) KING OF R&B VOL 2	1969	POLYDOR UK	2343 009				
RON CARTHY	TPT	(NPR	(G) IS A BLUES MASTER	1969	ATLANTIC UK 588 186 + RI	K 40496				
ROY DAVIES	K	(NPR	(G) IS A BLUES MASTER	1969	COTILLION	US	SD9004			
MICK EVE	SAX	(NPR	(H) HIS EARLY YEARS	197	POLYDOR	UK	2343 047			
STEVE FERRONE	D	(NPR	(J) MY FEELING FOR THE BLUES	1970	COTILLION	US	SD9016			
STEVE GREGORY	SAX	(NPR	(J) MY FEELING FOR THE BLUES	1975	ATLANTIC	UK RI	K 40947			
DELISLE HARPER	B	(NPR	(K) GETTING READY	1971	A&M UK AMLS65004	US SHELTER	8905			
CHRIS MERCER	SAX	(NPR	(L) TEXAS CANNONBALL	1972	A&M UK AMLS68113					
BOB TENCH	G V	(NPR	(M) WOMAN ACROSS THE WATER	1973	A&M UK AMLS68919	US SHELTER	8919			
MIKE VERNON	PERC	(NR	(N) BURGLAR	1974	RSO UK 2394 140	US RSO	4803			
PETE WINGFIELD	K	(NPR	(O) BEST OF FREDDIE KING	1974	A&M UK AMLS68313	US SHELTER	2140			
BRIAN AUGER	ORG	(N	(P) LARGER THAN LIFE	1975	RSO UK 2394 163	US RSO	4811			
MISTY BROWNING	V	(N	(Q) ORIGINAL HITS	1977	STARDAY/KING	US	5012			
P P ARNOLD	V	(N	(R) 1934 TO 1976	1977	RSO UK 2394 192	US RSO	1 3025			
VIE	V	(N	(S) BEST OF FREDDIE KING	1976	ISLAND	UK	ISA 5001			
ERIC CLAPTON	G V	(NR								

JAMIE OLDAKER	D	(NR	CARL RADLE	B	(NMLR	DICK SIMS	K	(NR	GEORGE TERRY	G	(NR
SERGIO PASTORA	PERC	(R	MELVIN JONES	ORG	(R	LOUIS STEPHENS	PNO	(RP	KING CURTIS	SAX	(J
JERRY JEMMOTT	B	(J	ERNIE ROYAL	TPT	(J	FRANK WESS	SAX	(J	JOHN GALLIE	K	(KL
DON PRESTON	G V	(KLM	CLAUDIA LENNEAR	V	(K	SONNY BURKE	K	(P	JIM KELTNER	D	(M
HENRY DAVIS	B	(NR	JIM GORDON K	SAX	(P	ANDREW JONES	G	(P	MIKE O'NEILL	G	(P
BENNY TURNER	B	(PR	KENNY PASSARELLI	B	(R	ROBERT WILSON	B	(P	WILLIE BRIDGES	SAX	(J
GEORGE COLEMAN	SAX	(J	TREVOR LAWRENCE	SAX	(J	KENNY RICE	D	(J	CHUCK BLACKWELL	D	(KLM
JIM GORDON	D	(L	LEON RUSSELL	K	(LKM	KATHI McDONALD	V	(K	SAM CLAYTON	PERC	(P
O'NEILL TWINS		(M	BIG JOHN ETHOMASSIE	D	(P	ALVIN HEMPHILL	K	(P	DARRYL LEONARD	TPT	(P
MELVIN WAH WAH RAGIN	G	(P	K O THOMAS	PNO	(P	SAM WYLE	G	(P	CHARLES ROBINSON	D	(R
MARTIN BANKS	TPT	(J	CORNELL DUPREE	G	(J	HUGH McCRACKEN	HCA	(J	GEORGE STUBBS	PNO	(J
DONALD DUCK DUNN	B	(KL	AL JACKSON	D	(L	JOEY COOPER	V	(K	CHARLES MYERS	D	(KP
JOE DAVIS	SAX	(P	REV PAT HENDERSON	K	(M	JAMES GADSON	D	(P	JERRY JUMONVILLE	SAX	(P
DAVID NEWMAN	SAX	(P	JOHN THOMAS	TPT	(P	LONNIE MACK	G	(D	GENE REDD	SAX	(ABC
CLIFFORD SCOTT	SAX	(ABC	BOBBY KING	G	(D	BENNY TURNER	B	(D			

REG KING

REG KING	G V	(A	(A) REG KING	1971	UA	UK	UAS 29157

MICK EVANS	B	(A								
ROGER POWELL	D	(A	IAN WHITEMAN K B FLT	(A	BRIAN GODDING	G V	(A	DORIS TROY	V	(A
PETER DALE	V	(A	NICK JONES	PERC	(A	MARTIN STONE	G	(A	BRIAN BELSHAW	B V	(A
PETER SWALES	V	(A	BRENDA FRENCH	V	(A	ALAN KING	G	(A	KEVIN WESTLAKE	D G	(A
DICK THOMAS	D	(A	FRANK FARRELL	B	(A	JO WRIGHT	G	(A	GEORGE BARKER	TPT	(A
PAUL NIEMAN	TROM	(A	BARRY JENKINS	D	(A	MICK TAYLOR	G	(A	BRIAN AUGER	K	(A
DANNY McCULLOCH	B	(A	ELTON DEAN	SAX	(A	MARK CHARIG	TPT	(A	STEVE WINWOOD	K	(A

KING BISCUIT BOY

KING BISCUIT BOY	HCA G V	(ALL	(A) GOOD UNS	1971	PARAMOUNT US PAS 6023+SPFA 7001			
(RICHARD NEWELL)			(A) GOOD UNS	19	DAFFODIL	IMP	934 505	
LARRY ATAMANUIK	D	(AB	(B) OFFICIAL MUSIC	1971	PARAMOUNT US PAS 5030+SPFL	270		
ROLY GREENWAY	B	(AB	(C) KING BISCUIT BOY	1974	EPIC	US	32891	
SONNIE BERNARDI	D	(AB						
DIANNE BROOKS	V	(AB	BRIAN RUSSELL	V	(A	RHONDA SILVER	V	(A	RICK BELL	K	(AB
RHEAL LANTHIER	G	(AB	KELLY JAY	K	(AB	STEVE KENNEDY	HRNS	(AB	SLIDE TALLMAN	HRNS	(A
ALLEN TOUSSAINT	K V	(C	ARTHUR NEVILLE	K	(C	LEO NOCENTELLI	G	(C	GEORGE PORTER JR B	(C
JOSEPH MODELISTE	D	(C	ALFRED ROBERTS	CONGA	(C	CLYDE KERR JR	HRNS	(C	LESTER CALISTE	HRNS	(C
CARL BLOUIN	HRNS	(C	ALVIN THOMAS	HRNS	(C	JOAN HARMON	V	(C	DR JOHN	G	(C
DANNY McBRIDE	G	(C	JOHN GIBBARD	G	(B	DOUG RILEY	K	(B	MOE KOFFMAN	HRNS	B
GREGG MUDRI	HRNS	(B						

KING CREOLE & THE COCONUTS

		(A) OFF THE COAST OF ME	1980	ZE		ILPS 7012

KING CRIMSON

ROBERT FRIPP	G K	(ALL	(A) IN THE COURT OF THE CRIMSON KING	1969	ISLAND	UK ILP59111		
MIKE GILES	D	(A	(A) IN THE COURT OF THE CRIMSON KING	1969	ATLANTIC US 8245	+RI	SD19155	
GREG LAKE	B V	(AB	(A) IN THE COURT OF THE CRIMSON KING	1969	POLYDOR	UK 2302 057 +FR	2310 516	
IAN McDONALD	FLT K	(A	(B) IN THE WAKE OF POSEIDON	1970	ISLAND	UK ILP59127 +US ATLANTIC	8266	
MEL COLLINS	SAX	(BCDEH	(B) IN THE WAKE OF POSEIDON	197	POLYDOR	UK 2302 058 +FR	2310 517	
PETE SINFIELD LYRICS		(ABCDE	(C) LIZARDS	1970	ISLAND	UK ILP59141 +US ATLANTIC	8278	
PETE GILES	B	(AB	(C) LIZARDS	197	POLYDOR	UK 2302 059 +FR	2310 518	
GORDON HASKELL	B V	(BC	(D) ISLANDS	1971	ISLAND	UK ILP59175 +US ATLANTIC	7212	
ANDY McCULLOCH	D	(C	(D) ISLANDS	1971	POLYDOR	UK 2302 060 +FR	2310 519	
BOZ BURRELL	B V	(DE	(E) EARTHBOUND	1972	ISLAND	UK HELP 6		
IAN WALLACE	D V	(DE	(E) EARTHBOUND	1977	POLYDOR	UK 2343 092 +FR	2344 074	
BILL BRUFORD	D	(FGHJ	(F) LARKS TONGUES IN ASPIC	1973	ISLAND	UK ILP59230 +US ATLANTIC	7263	
JOHN WETTON	B	(FGHJ	(F) LARKS TONGUES IN ASPIC	1977	POLYDOR	UK 2302 061 +FR	2310 520	
DAVID CROSS	VLN K	(FGHJ	(G) STARLESS & BIBLE BLACK	1974	ISLAND	UK ILP59275 +US ATLANTIC	7298	
KEITH TIPPETT	K	(BCD	(G) STARLESS & BIBLE BLACK	1977	POLYDOR	UK 2302 065 +FR	2310 521	

(CONTINUED)

KING CRIMSON

ROBIN MILLER	WIND (CDH	(H) RED	1974	ISLAND	UK ILPS9308	+US ATLANTIC 18110
MARK CHARIG	CORNET(CDH	(H) RED	1977	POLYDOR	UK 2302 066	+FR 2310 522
HARRY MILLER	B (D	(J) U S A	1975	ISLAND	UK ILPS9316	+US ATLANTIC 18136
JON ANDERSON	V (C	(J) U S A	1977	POLYDOR	UK 2302 067	+FR 2310 523
NICK EVANS	TROM (C	(K) YOUNG PERSONS GUIDE TO K C	1975	ISLAND	UK ISLD 7	
EDDIE JOBSON	K VLN(J	(K) YOUNG PERSONS GUIDE TO K C	1977	POLYDOR	UK 2612 036	+FR 2625 035
PAULINA LUCAS	V (D	(L) GREATEST	197	PHONOGRAM	FR 6641 356
JAMIE MUIR	PERC (F				

KING CURTIS

KING CURTIS	SAX (ALL	HAVE TENOR WILL BLOW	1959	ATCO	US 33113
(CURTIS OUSLEY)		SAX IN MOTION	1963		US
WILLIE BRIDGES	SAX (L	SOUL SERENADE	1964	CAPITOL	US 2095
MELVIN LASTIE	CORNET(L	PLAYS HITS OF SAM COOKE	1965		US
CHARLES RAINEY	B (L	THAT LOVIN' FEELIN'	1966	ATCO US 33189
CORNELL DUPREE	G (L	(L) LIVE AT SMALLS PARADISE	1966	ATCO US 33198 UK ATLANTIC K30029
PAUL GRIFFIN	PNO (L	PLAYS GREAT MEMPHIS HITS	1967	ATCO US 33211 UK ATLANTIC 588 067
RAY LUCAS	D (L	KINGSIZE SOUL	1967	ATCO US 33231 UK ATLANTIC 587 043
NOBLE KNIGHTS	(S	SWEET SOUL	1968	ATCO US 33247 UK ATLANTIC 588 115
SHIRELLES	V (E	BEST OF KING CURTIS	1968	ATCO US 33266+US PRESTIGE 7709
		BEST OF KING CURTIS	19	ATLANTIC UK 228 002 + K40067
CHAMPION JACK DUPREE V K(B		INSTANT GROOVE	1968	ATCO US 33292 UK ATLANTIC 2228027
		ONE MORE TIME(BEST OF)	196	PRESTIGE US 7775
		GET READY	196	ATCO US 33338
		LIVE AT FILLMORE	19	ATCO US 33359 UK ATLANTIC K40214
		EVERYBODY'S TALKIN'	19	ATCO US 33385 UK ATLANTIC K40360
		(E) ETERNALLY SOUL	1970	WAND WNS4
		(S) SOUL SERENADE	1972	EMBER SPE 6600
		MR SOUL	1972	EMBER SPE 6607
		(B) BLUES AT MONTREUX	197	ATLANTIC UK K40430
		SOUL TWIST	19	ENJOY US 2001
		SOUL TIME	19	UPFRONT US UPF 157
		KING SOUL	19	PRESTIGE US 7789
		SOUL MEETING	19	PRESTIGE US 7833
		JAZZ GROOVE	1974	PRESTIGE US 24033
		STAR COLLECTION	1974	ATLANTIC UK K30049
		SAX ROCK	1976	MUSIDISC EURO CV 1334

KING EARL BOOGIE BAND

COLIN EARL	(A	(A) TROUBLE AT MILL	1972	DAWN	DNLS 3040
PAUL KING	(A				

KING ERRISSON

KING ERRISSON	PERC (ALL	(A)THE KING ARRIVES	197	CANYON	US 7703
PAMELA VINCENT	V (C	(B) MAGIC MAN	197	WESTBOUND	US 224
CYNTHIA DOUGLAS	V (C	(C) L A BOUND	1977	WESTBOUND	US WT 307
FREDDIE HILL	TPT (A	(C) L A BOUND	1977	WEA	50426
JACK WALRATH	TPT (A	PRESTON LOVE	WIND (A	MAURICE SPEARS	TROM (A
GEORGE BOHANON	TROM (A	BENNY PARKS	D (A	WASHINGTON RUCKER	D (A
CLARENCE McDONALD	PNO (A	JYMM YOUNG	PNO (A	CALVIN KEYS	G (A
DAVID T WALKER	G (A	WILTON FELDER	B (A	BILL UPCHURCH	B (A
CHARLES CLARK	V (C	CLEVELAND HORNE	V (C	DONNA DAVIS	V (C

KING HARRY

HAROLD KING	D (A	(A) DIVIDED WE STAND	1977	EMI	UK EMC 3188
JOHN DICKERSON	K V (A				
ALAN BOWERY	G B V(A	TINO LICINIO G B V (A			

KING HARVEST

PETER CETERA	(	(A) DANCING IN THE MOONLIGHT	1973	PYE UK NSPL28174 US PERCEPTION36
MIKE LOVE	(	(B) KINGHARVEST	1975	A&M	US SP 4540
CARL WILSON	(				

KING OF HEARTS

ROBERT FITOUSSI	V (A	(A) CLOSE BUT NO GUITAR	1978	CAPITOL	11873
MARC TOBALY	V G (A								
ELLIOTT RANDALL	G (A	STEVE PORCARO	K (A	STU WOODS	B (A	RICK SCHLOSSER	D (A
JAI WINDING	K (A	MICHAEL BRAUN	D (A	PEPPI CASTRO	B (A	DEAN KRAUS	K (A
JEFF LAYTON	G (A	TONY WELLS	V (A	LENNY ROBERTS	V (A	JIM HAAS	V (A
LEE SKLAR	B (A	IVAN ELIAS	B (A	DAVID BROWN	G (A	JIM MAELEN	PERC (A
PAUL GRIFFIN	ORG (A	MARTY NELSON	V (A	JON JOYCE	V (A	LOREN FARBER	V (A

KINGFISH

DAVE TORBERT	V B (ABC	(A) KINGFISH	1976	ROUND US LA 564	UK UAG 29922
MATTHEW KELLY	V G (ABC	(B) LIVE & KICKIN'	1977	JET US LA 732	UK UAG 30080
BOB WEIR	G (AB	(C) TRIDENT	1978	JET US 35479	UK JETLP 215
ROBBY HODINOTT	G (AB								
CHRIS HEROLD	D (AB	DAVE PEPPER	D V (AC	MICHAEL O'NEILL	G V (C	BOB HOGINS	K V (C
BARRY FLASH	PNO (A	JOE ENGLISH	D (C	JOHN HUG	G (C	JOHNNY SANDLIN	B (C

KINKS

RAY DAVIES	V G (ALL	(A) THE KINKS	1964	PYE UK NPL 18096(M) 83021(S)
DAVE DAVIES	G V (ALL	(B) YOU REALLY GOT ME	1965	REPRISE US 6143
MICK AVORY D	(ABCDEFGHVY6AADDJL	(C) KINKSIZE	1965	REPRISE US 6158
PETER QUAIFE B	(AABCDEFGHIJKL	(D) KINDA KINKS	1965	PYE UK NPL 18112 REPRISE US 6173
JOHN DALTON	B (VY36	(D) KINDA KINKS	1969	MARBLE ARCH UK MAL1100
JOHN GOSLING	K (VYAA36	(E) KINKS KINGDOM	1966	REPRISE US 6184
ALAN HOLMES	HRNS (VY36	(F) KINKS KONTROVERSY	1966	PYE UK NPL 18131 REPRISE US 6197
LAURIE BROWN	HRNS (Y3	(G) KINKS GREATEST HITS	1966	REPRISE US 6217
JOHN BEECHAM	HRNS (VY36	(H) FACE TO FACE	1966	PYE UK NPL 18149 REPRISE US 6228
ANDY PYLE	B (AA	(I) THE KINKS (COMP)	1966	GOLDEN GUINEA UK GGL0357
JIM RODFORD	B (DD	(J) WELL RESPECTED KINKS	1966	MARBLE ARCH UK MAL 612
GORDON EDWARDS	K (	(K) LIVE AT KELVIN HALL	1967	PYE UK NSPL18191 REPRISE US 6260
NICK TREVISIK	D (AA	(L) SOMETHING ELSE	1967	PYE UK NSPL18193 REPRISE US 6279
RON LAWRENCE	B (AA	(M) SUNNY AFTERNOON (COMP)	1967	MARBLE ARCH UK MAL 716
				(CONTINUED)

KINKS

(CONTINUED)

PAMELA TRAVIS	V	(Y3	(N) VILLAGE GREEN PRESERVATION SOC	1968	PYE UK NSPL18233	REPRISE US 6327
SHIRLEY RODEN	V	(3	(O) ARTHUR OR DECLINE OF BRITISH EMP	1969	PYE UK NSPL18317	REPRISE US 6366
LYNDSEY MOORE	V	(3	(P) KINKS PART 1 (LOLA Vs POWERMAN	1970	PYE UK NSPL18359	REPRISE US 6423
JUNE RITCHIE	V	(3	(Q) THE KINKS (COMP DBL)	1970	PYE UK NPL 18326	
NICK NEWELL	K SAX	(6DD	(R) PERCY (SOUNDTRACK)	1971	PYE UK NSPL18365	
LEE PAVEY	V	(Y	(S) MUSWELL HILLBILLIES	1971	RCA UK SF 8423	US LSP4644
KRYSIA KOCJAN	V	(Y	(T) GOLDEN HOUR	1971	PYE UK GH 501	
MIKE COTTON	TPT	(SV	(U) LOLA	1971	HALLMARK UK	HMA 201
SUE BROWN	V	(Y	(V) EVERYBODY'S IN SHOWBIZ	1972	RCA UK DPS 2035	US 6065
DAVEY JONES	WIND	(V	(W) KINK KRONIKLES	1972		REPRISE US 6454
LEWIS RICH	V	(Y	(X) GREAT LOST KINKS ALBUM	1973		REPRISE US 2127
IAN GIBBONS	K	(DD	(Y) PRESERVATION ACT 1	1973	RCA UK SF 8392	US LPL5002
			(Z) ALL THE GOOD TIMES	1973	PYE UK	
			(1) GOLDEN HOUR VOL 2	1973	PYE UK GH 558	
			(2) PRESERVATION ACT 2	1974	RCA UK 5040	US CPL5040
			(3) SOAP OPERA	1975	RCA UK SF 8411	US LPL5081
			(4) POP CHRONIK	1975	PYE	VOL1
			(5) CELLULOID HEROES (COMP)	1976	RCA UK RS 1059	US LPL1743
			(6) SCHOOLBOYS IN DISGRACE	1976	RCA UK RS 1028	US FLI5102
			(7) KINKS (FILE DBL)	1977	PYE UK FILD 001-1/2	
			(8) SLEEPWALKER	1977	ARISTA UK 1002	US AL 4106
			(9) ALL THE GOOD TIMES	197	PYE UK ILPP 100/4	
			(AA) MISFITS	1978	ARISTA UK 1055	US AL 4167
			(BB) 20 GOLDEN GREATS	1978	RONCO UK RPL2031	
			(CC) LOW BUDGET	1979	ARISTA UK 1099	US AB 4240
			(DD) ONE FOR THE ROAD (LIVE DBL)	1980	ARISTA UK DARTY6	
			(EE) YOU REALLY GOT ME (COMP)	1980	PYE UK NSPL18615	FR MODE 9017
			(FF) ALL DAY & ALL OF THE NIGHT	19		FR MODE 9054
			(EPs)			
			KINKSIZE HITS	1964	PYE	UK NEP 24203
			KWIET KINKS	1965	PYE	UK NEP 24221
			FOUR TIMES FOUR	1965	PYE	UK NEP 24228
			KINKSIZE SESSION	1966	PYE	UK NEP 24200
			DEDICATED KINKS	1966	PYE	UK NEP 24258

KIPPINGTON LODGE

BARRY LANDERMAN	K V		1965/69		
BOB ANDREWS	K V				
NICK LOWE	B V	BRINSLEY SCHWARZ	G V	PETER WHALE	D

KIRBY

KIRBY	G	(A	(A) COMPOSITION	1978	HOT WAX		HW2			
FRAN BYRNE	D	(A								
IAN PAICE	D	(A	STEVE EMERY	B	(A	JOHN COOK	K	(A	CHRIS FLETCHER	PERC(A
ROBIN JAMES	PERC	(A	NIGEL WATSON	G	(A	TONY RIVERS	V	(A	STUART CALVER	V (A
JOHN PERRY	V	(A	MICK EVE	HRNS	(A	NORMAN NEWELL	HRNS	(A	BUD BEADLE	HRNS (A
COLIN JACAS	HRNS	(A	MIKE BAILEY	HRNS	(A	RON ASPERY	SAX	(A		

BASIL KIRCHIN

BASIL KIRCHIN		(A	(A) WORLDS WITHIN WORLDS	1974	ISLAND UK	HELP18

JOHN KIRKPATRICK & SUE HARRIS

JOHN KIRKPATRICK	K WIND	V(ABCDE	(A) JUMP AT THE SUN	1972	TRAILER		LER 2033			
SUE HARRIS	WIND DULC	V (ABCDE	(B) ROSE OF BRITAINS ISLE	1974	TOPIC		12TS 247			
TONY ROSE	WIND	V(A	(C) AMONG THE ATTRACTIONS......	1976	TOPIC		12TS 295			
BERI CROWE	V	(A	(D) SHREDS & PATCHES	1977	TOPIC		12TS 355			
ROS LENNOX	V	(A	(E) GOING SPARE	1978	FREE REED		FRR 030			
ANGELA McNEILL	V	(A								
TERRY ROBINSON	V	(A	DAVE WIGHT	V	(A	DENIS SHEEHAN	V	(A	AGNES MIRREN	G (A
ASHLEY HUTCHINGS	B	(A	PENNIE HARRIS	DULC	(D	TUFTY SMITH	MELOD(D		DEREK PEARSE	BAN PERC(DE
GEOFF HARRIS	G	(D	STEWART GOLDRING	G	(E	ALAN HARRIS	BAN	(E	BILL CADDICK	G (E
COLIN GOLDRING	B	(E	NIGEL PEGRUM	D	(E	FI FRASER	V	(E	MARTIN BRINSFORD	V (E

DANNY KIRWAN

DANNY KIRWAN	V G	(ALL	(A) SECOND CHAPTER	1975	DJM UK DJLPS 454	US DJM 1				
GEOFF BRITTON	D	(A	(B) MIDNIGHT IN SAN JUAN	1976	DJM UK DJF 20481					
JIM RUSSELL	D	(A	(C) HELLO THERE BIG BOY	1979	DJM UK DJF 20555					
ANDY SYLVESTER	B	(A	(D) DANNY KIRWAN	19	DJM US DJM 9					
PAUL RAYMOND	K	(A								
JOHN COOK	PNO	(BC	TEX COMER	B	(C	STUART CALVER	V	(C	JOHN PERRY	V (C
STEVE EMERY	B	(B	KIRBY	G	(C	FRAN BYRNE	D	(C	KEVIN KITCHEN	K (C
DANA GILLESPIE	V	(C	JEFF RICH	D	(B	BOB WESTON	G	(C	TONY RIVERS	V (C
CHRIS FLETCHER	PERC	(C								

KISS

ACE FREHLEY	G	(ALL	(A) KISS	1975	CASABLANCA US 7001	UK CBC 4003
PAUL STANLEY	G	(ALL	(A) KISS	1977	CASABLANCA	UK RI CAL 2006
GENE SIMMONS	B	(ALL	(B) HOTTER THAN HELL	1974	CASABLANCA US 7006	UK 77 CAL 7007
PETE CRISS	D	(ALL	(C) DRESSED TO KILL	1975	CASABLANCA US 7016	UK CBC 4004
BRUCE FOSTER	PNO	(A	(C) DRESSED TO KILL	1977	CASABLANCA	UK RI CAL 2008
			(D) ALIVE	197	CASABLANCA US 7020	UK RI CAS 5001
			(E) DESTROYER	1976	CASABLANCA US 7025	UK 77 CAL 2009
			(F) THE ORIGINALS	197	CASABLANCA US 7032	
			(G) ROCK'N'ROLL OVER	197	CASABLANCA US 7037	UK 77 CAL 2001
			(H) LOVE GUN	197	CASABLANCA US 7057	UK 77 CAL 2027
			(J) ALIVE 2	1978	CASABLANCA US 7076	UK CAL 5004
			(K) DOUBLE PLATINUM (DBL)	1978	CASABLANCA US 7100-2	UKCALD5005
			(L) DYNASTY	1979	CASABLANCA US	UK CALH2051
			(M) UNMASKED	1980	MERCURY	UK 6302 032
			(N) THE BEST OF THE SOLO ALBUMS	1981	CASABLANCA	UK 6302 060

KITE

			(A) KITE	19	SOLENT SS 050

KLAATU

(A) KLAATU		1976	CAPITOL	11542
(B) HOPE		1977	CAPITOL	11633
(C) SIR ARMY SUIT		1978	CAPITOL	11836
(D) ENDANGERED SPECIES		1980	CAPITOL	12080

K68A

KLEER

WOODY CUNNINGHAM	D V	(AB
RICHARD LEE	G	(AB
YVETTE FLOWERS		(B
PAUL CRUTCHFIELD	PERC V(BA	
MARVIN STAMM	HRNS	(A
LOUISE FISCHER	V	(A

NORMAN DURHAM	B V	(BA
TERRY DOLPHIN	PNO	(AB
ERIC ROHRBAUGH		

ISABELLE COLES	V	(AB
RICHARD CUMMINGS	K	(A
MELANIE MOORE		(B

| RANDY BRECKER | HRNS (A |
| ANGEL NATER | PERC (A |

(A) I LOVE TO DANCE		1979	ATLANTIC US SD 19237	UK K50614
(B) LICENSE TO DREAM		1981	ATLANTIC US SD 19288	

K68B

KLEENEX

REGULA SING	V	(A
MARLENE MARDER	G	(A
KLAUDIA SCHIFF	B	(A

LISLOT HA   D   (A

(A) AIN'T YOU (EP)		1978	SUNRISE

K69

EARL KLUGH

EARL KLUGH	G	(ALL
GREG PHILLINGANES	K	(E
CHARLES MEEKS	B	(E
RALPH MACDONALD	PERC	(E
VICTOR LEWIS	D	(E
PHIL UPCHURCH	G	(E
GLORIA AGOSTINI	HARP	(G
DR GIBBS	PERC	(G
PHIL BODNER	WIND	(G
SAM BURTIS	TROM	(G
JAY ELFENBEIN	B	(G
GINO BIONDO	B	(G
DAVID SPINOZZA	G	(G

WALTER KANE	WIND	(G
JOSE MADERA	PERC	(G
RON CUBER	SAX	(G
MARCUS MILLER	B	(G

DAVID FRIEDMAN	PERC	(G
LEWIS PEAR	B	(G
KEN ASCHER	PNO	(G
JOHN GATCHELL	TPT	(G

JOSEPH SHEPLEY	TPT	(G
JACK KULOWITCH	B	(G
MICHAEL COLLAZO	PERC(G
DAVID TOFANI	SAX	(G

(A) EARL KLUGH		197	BLUENOTE	US LA 596
(B) LIVING INSIDE YOUR LOVE		1977	UA UK UAG 20009	BLUENOTE US 667
(C) FINGER PAINTING		1977	UA UK UAG 20011	BLUENOTE US 737
(D) MAGIC IN YOUR EYES		1978	UA UK UAG 30171	
(E) HEART STRING		1979	UA UK UAG 30233	
(F) DREAM COME TRUE		1980	UA UK UAG 30092	LIBERTY US 1026
(G) LATE NIGHT GUITAR		1980	UA UK UAG 30332	LIBERTY US 1079

K69A

THE KNACK

DOUG FIEGER	G	(AB
BERTON AVERRE	G	(AB
BRUCE GARY	D	(AB
PRESCOTT NILES	B	(AB

(A) GET THE KNACK		1979	CAPITOL	11948
(B) BUT THE LITTLE GIRLS UNDERSTAND		1980	CAPITOL	

K70

CURTIS KNIGHT

CURTIS KNIGHT		(ALL
JIMI HENDRIX	G	(BCD

(A) DOWN THE VILLAGE		19	PARAMOUNT	US5023
(B) GET THAT FEELING		1968	LONDON UK SH 8349	DECCA US195002
(C) STRANGE THINGS		1968	LONDON UK SH 8369	DECCA US185005
(D) THE WILD ONE		1973	HALLMARK	UK 791
(E) SECOND COMING		1974	DAWN UK	DNLS3060

K71

JEAN KNIGHT

JEAN KNIGHT	(A) Mr BIG STUFF	1977	STAX US ST2045 UK	STX 1004

K72

GLADYS KNIGHT & THE PIPS

GLADYS KNIGHT	V	(ALL
WITH		
THE PIPS		
MERALD KNIGHT	V	(
BRENDA KNIGHT	V	(
WILLIAM GUEST	V	(
ELENOR GUEST	V	(
EDWARD PATTEN	V	(

EVERYBODY NEEDS LOVE	1967	SOUL	US 706	TAMLA UK STML 11058
FEELIN BLUESY	1968	SOUL	US 707	
TASTIEST HITS	1968	BELL	US 6013	
SILK & SOUL	1969	SOUL	US 711	TAMLA UK STML 11100
NITTY GRITTY	1970	SOUL	US 713	
GREATEST HITS	1970	SOUL	US 723	TAMLA UK STML 11148
ALL IN A KNIGHTS WORK	197	SOUL	US 730	
IF I WERE YOUR WOMAN	1971	SOUL	US 731	TAMLA UK STML 11187
STANDING OVATION	1972	SOUL	US 736	TAMLA UK STML 11208
HELP ME MAKE IT THROUGH THE NIGHT	1973			TAMLA UK STML 11226
NEITHER ONE OF US	1973	SOUL	US 737	TAMLA UK STML 11230
ALL I NEED IS TIME	1974	SOUL	US '39	TAMLA UK STML 11264
ANTHOLOGY	1974	TAMLA	US 792	UK TMSP 1127
GLADYS KNIGHT & THE PIPS	1974	HALLMARK		UK SHM 833
IMAGINATION	1974	BUDDAH	US 5141	UK BDLP 4005
CLAUDINE	1974	BUDDAH	US 5602	UK BDLP 4010
I FEEL A SONG	197	BUDDAH	US 5612	UK BDLP 4030
2ND ANNIVERSARY	1975	BUDDAH	US 5639	UK BDLP 4038
2ND ANNIVERSARY	1975	BUDDAH		UK 2318 111
KNIGHT TIME	1975	SOUL	US 741	TAMLA UK STML 11279
A LITTLE KNIGHT MUSIC	1975	SOUL	US 744	TAMLA UK STML 12013
BEST OF	1975	STAX		UK STX 1042
GLADYS KNIGHT & THE PIPS	1975	DJM		UK DJMLD 8010
SUPER HITS	1976	TAMLA		UK STMA 8026
PIPE DREAMS	1976	BUDDAH	US 5676	UK BDLP 5017
TAKE ME IN YOUR ARMS	1976	MFP		UK 50304
STILL TOGETHER	1977	BUDDAH	US 5689	UK BDLP 5014
BEST OF	1977	BUDDAH		UK BDLP 5013
BLESS THIS HOUSE	1978	BUDDAH	US 5651	UK BDLP 4050
GLADYS KNIGHT	1979	CBS		UK 83341
MISS GLADYS KNIGHT	1979	BUDDAH	US 5714	UK BDLP 4056
LETTER FULL OF TEARS	19	FURY	US 1003	
VERY BEST OF	19	UA	US LA503	
EARLY HITS	19	SPRINGBOARD		US 4035
HOW DO YOU SAY GOODBYE	19	SPRINGBOARD		US 4050
BEST OF	19	MODE		FR 9021
GLADYS KNIGHT & THE PIPS	19	TRIP		US 3500
" " " " "	19	UP FRONT		US 130
" " " " "	19	UP FRONT		US 185
" " " " "	19	SPHERE SOUND		US 7006
" " " " "	19	MAXX		US 3000
20 GOLDEN GREATS	1979	MOTOWN		UK STML12122
30 GREATEST HITS	1979	K TEL		UK NE1004

REGGIE KNIGHTON

REGGIE KNIGHTON	G V (AB	(A) REGGIE KNIGHTON		1977	CBS US 34685		
BRIAN RAY	G (B	(B) REGGIE KNIGHTON BAND		1978	CBS US 35286		UK 82627
GLENN SYMMONDS	D (B						
JOHN STAEHELY	G (B	KURTIS TEEL	B (B	GEOFF WORKMAN	STRINGS(B	JON LIND	V (B
RICHARD HOVEY	V (B						

BUDDY KNOX

BUDDY KNOX	G V (ALL	BUDDY KNOX	1957	ROULETTE US	25003
DON LANIER	G (	BUDDY KNOX & JIMMY BOWEN(1 SIDE EACH 19		ROULETTE US	25048
DAVE ALLDRED	D (	BUDDY KNOX	19	POINT US	201
JIMMY BOWEN	B (	BUDDY KNOX IN NASHVILLE	19	POINT US	289
		GOLDEN HITS	196	LIBERTY US	LST 7251
		GYPSY MAN	1970	U A US	UAS 6689
		ROCK REFLECTIONS	1971	SUNSET UK	SLS 50206
		BUDDY KNOX ROCKS	1973	SWEETWATER CAN	SW 1001
		PARTY DOLL	1978	PYE INT UK	NSPL28243
		FOUR ROCK LEGENDS (8 TRACKS)	1978	HARVEST HERITAGE UK	SHSM 2024

KRYSIA KOCJAN

KRYSIA KOCJAN	G V (A	(A) KRYSIA		1974	RCA		UK	LPLI 5052
STEVE HAYTON	G (A							
JERRY DONAHUE	G (A	RABBIT BUNDRICK	K (A	ALAN SHEARER	VLV (A	JOHN McLEVY	TPT (A	
ROY SIDWELL	SAX (A	DAVE PEGG	B (A	RAY COOPER	PERC(A	ROGER CHURCHYARD	VLN (A	
DAVE SHARMAN	TROM (A	DAVE MATTACKS	D (A	MOX	FLT (A	TONY COE	CLAR (A	
HARRY KLEIN	SAX (A							

JOHN KOERNER

'SPIDER' JOHN KOERNER	(ALL	(A) MUSIC IS JUST A BUNCH OF NOTES	19	SWEETJANE US	SJL 5872	
WILLIE MURPHY	(C	(B) SPIDER BLUES	19	ELEKTRA US	7290	
		(C) RUNNING JUMPING STANDING STILL	19	ELEKTRA US 74041	UK K42026	

KOERNER,RAY & GLOVER

JOHN KOERNER	G (ALL	(A) BLUES RAGS & HOLLERS	19	ELEKTRA US	240
DAVE RAY	G (ALL	(B) GOOD OLD KOERNER, RAY & GLOVER	19	MILL CITY US	MCR 172
TONY GLOVER	HCA (ALL	(C) LOTS MORE BLUES RAGS & HOLLERS	19	ELEKTRA US	7267
		(D) RETURN OF KOERNER ,RAY & GLOVER	19	ELEKTRA US	7305

KOKOMO

TONY O'MALLEY	V K (AB	(A) KOKOMO		1975	CBS US 33442	UK 80670		
PADDY McHUGH	V (AB	(B) RISE & SHINE		1975	CBS US 34031	UK 69229		
DYAN BIRCH	V (AB							
FRANK COLLINS	V (AB	MEL COLLINS	SAX (AB	TERRY STANNARD	D (A	JIM MULLEN	G (A	
ALAN SPENNER	V B (AB	JOHN SUSSEWELL	D (B	NEIL HUBBARD	G (AB	JODY LINSCOTT	PERC(A	

BONNIE KOLOC

BONNIE KOLOC	G V (ALL	(A) AFTER ALL THIS TIME	1971 LONDON UK 8432 OVATION	US 14 21	
NORMAN CHRISTIAN	D (ABC	(B) HOLD ON TO ME	1972 LONDON UK 8440 OVATION	US 14 26	
RON SCROGGIN G HCA B V (ABC		(C) BONNIE KOLOC	1973 OVATION	US 14 29	
STU HEISS	G (A	(D) YOU'RE GONNA LOVE YOURSELF	1974 OVATION	US 14 38	
PHIL UPCHURCH	B G (AB	(E) CLOSE UP	1976 EPIC	US 34184	
ALLEN BARCUS	PNO (AB	(F) WILD RECLUSE	1978 EPIC	US 35254	
SID SIMMS	B (A	(G) AT HER BEST	19 OVATION	US 17 01	
TREVOR VEITCH	G DOB(B				
BOB LEWIS	G (B	BOBBY CHRISTIAN PERC (BC	PHIL THOMAS CONGA(B	WALLY PILLICH	B (B
CHUCK DE MEYER	K V (C	JONATHAN PEARTHREE G V(C	HAROLD KRITZ B (C	DAVID VAN DELINDER	G (C
LONNIE KNIGHT	G (C	DANNY LONG PNO (C	DAVID BRIGGS PNO (D	MIKE LEECH	B (D
NORBERT PUTNAM	B (D	HENRY STRZELECKI B (D	REGGIE YOUNG G (D	JOHNNY CHRISTOPHER	G (D
BILLY SANFORD	G (D	JIMMY COLVARD G (D	PETE WADE G (D	STEVE GOODMAN	G (DE
KENNY MALONE	D (D	LARRY LONDIN D (D	JERRY CARRIGAN D (D	FARRELL MORRIS	PERC(D
RUSTY YOUNG	STEEL(E	DAVID LINDLEY G (E	PAUL HARRIS K (E	BRYAN GAROFALO	B (E
GARY MALLABER	D (E	GUILLE GARCIA CONGA(E	PHILIP DONNELLY G (E	JAI WINDING	PNO(E
DONNIE FRITTS	PNO (E	CHUCK DOMANICO B (E	CORKY SIEGEL HCA (E	MIKE CAMPBELL	G (E
DON MENZA	WIND (E	RAY NEOPOLITAN B (E			

KOMINTERN

SERGE CATTALANO	D (A	(A) LE BAL DU RAT MORT	1971 HARVEST PATHE FR	2C 062 11774		
RICHARD AUBERT	VLN (A					
OLIVIER ZDRZALIK B G V (A		FRANCIS LEMONNIER SAX V(A	MICHEL MUSAC G (A	PASCAL CHASSIN	G (A	

JOHN KONGOS

JOHN KONGOS V G PERC (AB		(A) CONFUSIONS ABOUT GOLDFISH	1969 JANUS US 3032 DAWN UK DNLS 3002		
CALEB QUAYE	G (B	(B) JOHN KONGOS	1971 ELEKTRA US 75019 FLY UK HIFLY 7		
DAVE GLOVER	B (B				
ROGER POPE	D (B	RAY COOPER PERC (B	MIKE NOBLE PERC(B	DAVID CHAMBERS	HRNS (B
LOL COXHILL	SAX (B	MIKE MORAN K (B	RALPH McTELL G (B	GUS DUDGEON	PERC(B
SUE GLOVER	V (B	SUNNY LESLIE V (B	CLAIRE DENIZ CELLO(B		

KOOBAS

ROY MORRIS	(A		
STU LEATHERWOOD	(A		
KEITH ELLIS	B (A	TONY O'RILEY (A	

KOOL & THE GANG

ROBERT 'KOOL' BELL B V(ALL		(A) KOOL & THE GANG	19	DE LITE US 2003		
CHARLES 'CLAYDES'SMITH G V(OQR		(B) MUSIC IS THE MESSAGE	19		POLYDOR 2347 004	
GEORGE BROWN	D V K(OQR	(C) LIVE AT THE SEX MACHINE	19	DELITE US 2008 POLYDOR 2343 083		
ROBERT MICKENS	TPT V(OQR	(D) BEST	19	DE LITE US 2009		
OTHA NASH	V HRNS(O	(E) LIVE AT PJs	19	DE LITE US 2010		
DENNIS THOMAS	WIND K V (OQR	(F) GOOD TIMES	19	DE LITE US 2012		
RON'KHALIS BAYYAN' BELL WIND K V(OQR		(G) WILD & PEACEFUL	1974 DE LITE US 2013	POLYDOR US 2310 299		
DONAL BOYCE	V (O	(H) LIGHT OF WORLDS	1974	POLYDOR US 2310 357		
KEVIN LASSITER	K V (O	(J) GREATEST HITS	1975 DE LITE US 2015	POLYDOR UK 2310 401		
RENEE CONNEL	V (O	(K) SPIRIT OF THE BOOGIE	1975	POLYDOR UK 2310 416		
ARTHUR CAPEHART	TPT (O	(L) LOVE & UNDERSTANDING	1976	POLYDOR UK 2310 441		
BEVERLEY OWENS	V (O	(M) BEHIND THE EYES	197	POOYDOR		
CYNTHIA HUGGINS	V (OQ	(N) OPEN SESAME	197 DE LITE US 2025			

(CONTINUED)

KOOL & THE GANG

M.F.S.B. STRINGS	(0	(O) THE FORCE		1977 DE LITE US 9501	MERCURY	6372 700
JOAN MOTLEY	V (OQ	(P) SPIN THEIR TOP HITS		1978 DE LITE US 9507		
CHRIS ALBERT	TPT (Q	(Q) LADIES NIGHT		1979 DE LITE		UK 6372 763
JON FADDIS	TPT (Q	(R) CELEBRATE		1980 DE LITE		UK 6359 029
EARL TOON	K V (RQ					
DIANE CAMERON	V (Q	CEDRIC TOON	V (RQ	KEVIN BELL	K (R	JAMES J T TAYLOR	V (QR
MEEKAEEL MUHAMMAD V	(R	ADAM IPPOLITO	K (RQ	EUMIR DEODATO	K (Q	CLIFF ADAMS	TROM (Q

K81 AL KOOPER

AL KOOPER	K G V(ALL	(A) SUPER SESSION		1969	CBS US 9701	UK 63396
MIKE BLOOMFIELD	G (ACL	(A) SUPER SESSION		1973	EMBASSY RI 31493	UK 31029
STEPHEN STILLS	G (AL	(B) I STAND ALONE		1969	CBS US 9718	UK 63538
HARVEY BROOKS	B (AGL	(C) LIVE ADVENTURES (DBL)		1969	CBS US PG6	UK 66216
EDDIE HOH	D (AL	(D) YOU NEVER KNOW WHO YOUR FRIENDS...	1969	CBS US 9855	UK 63651
BARRY GOLDBERG	K (AL	(E) KOOPER SESSIONS		1970	CBS US 9951	UK 63797
SHUGGIE OTIS	G (EL	(F) EASY DOES IT		1970	CBS US 30031	UK 66252
WELLS KELLY	D (EGL	(G) LANDLORD		1971	U A	UK 29120
STU WOODS	B (EL	(H) NEW YORK CITY		1971	CBS US 30506	UK 64340
MARK KLINGMAN	K (E	(J) POSSIBLE PROJECTION OF FUTURE		1972	CBS US 31118	UK 64208
CARLOS SANTANA	G (C	(K) NAKED SONGS		1973	CBS US 31793	UK 65193
RALPH CASALE	G (D	(L) AL'S BIG DEAL (COMP DBL)		1975	CBS US 33169	UK 88093
ERIC GALE	G (DG	(N) ACT LIKE NOTHINGS WRONG		1976	UA	UK 30020
ERNIE HAYES	K (D	(O) AL KOOPER & STEVE KATZ		19	VERVE UK	2304010
PAUL GRIFFIN	K (D					

FRANK OWENS	K (DG	CHUCK RAINEY	B (DG	JERRY JEMMOTT	B (D	JOHN MILLER	B (DG
BERNARD PURDIE	D (D	AL RODGERS	G D (DG	BERNIE GLOW	TPT (DG	ERNIE ROYAL	TPT(D
MARVIN STAMM	TPT (DG	RAY DESIO	TROM (D	JIMMY KNEPPER	TROM (D	BILL WATRONS	TROM(D
TONY STUDD	TROM (D	GEORGE YOUNG	SAX (DG	SOL SCHLINGER	SAX (D	SELDON POWELL	SAX (D
JOE FARRELL	SAX (DG	MANNY GREEN	VLN (D	JERRY KUSHNICK	STRINGS(D	STAN POLLEY	STRINGS(D
AARON SCHECTER	STRING(D	HILDA HARRIS	V (DL	CONNIE ZIMET	V (D	ALBERTINE ROBERTSON	V(DL
MIKE GATELY	V (D	ROBERT JOHN	V (DL	LOU CHRISTIE	V (D	CHARLIE CALELLO	V(D
MAERETHA STEWART	V((GL	LORRAINE ELLISON	V (G	STAPLES SINGERS	V (G	JOHN HALL	G(G
PHIL BODNER	WIND (G	PAUL HARRIS	PNO (G	JOE BECK	G (G	STEVE KATZ	G(LO
FRED LIPSIUS	SAX (L	BOBBY COLOMBY	D V (L	JERRY WEISS	HRNS (L	RANDY BRECKER	HRNS(L
DICK HALLIGAN	HRNS (L	JIM FIELDER	B (L	AL GORGONI	G (L	JOHN SIMON	PNO (L
VALERIE SIMPSON	V (L	MELBA MOORE	V (L	BOB DYLAN	G V (L	RON CORNELIUS	G(L
CHARLIE DANIELS	G B (L	RUSS KUNKEL	D (L	JOHN KAHN	B (L	SKIP PROKOP	D(L
PAUL SIMON	V (L	J R COBB	G (L	BARRY BAILEY	G (L	DEAN DAUGHTRY	PNO(L
PAUL GODDARD	B (L	ROBERT NIX	D (L	EILEEN GILBERT	V (L	LINDA NOVEMBER	V(L
TASHA THOMAS	V (L	PATTI AUSTIN	V (L	JERRY KENNEDY	V (L	WAYNE MOSS	G (L
CHARLIE McCOY	HCA (L	KENNY BUTTREY	D (L	RICK MAROTTA	D (L	HERBIE FLOWERS	B (L
KEN SCOTT	(L	BLOSSOMS	V (L	RALPH CASALE	G (D		

K82 PAUL KORDA

PAUL KORDA	V K G(A	(A) PASSING STRANGER		1971	MAM	MAM AS 1003
ALAN GORRIE	B K G V(A					
ROB TAIT	D (A	ONNIE McINTYRE	G (A	RAY RUSSELL	G (A	DORIS TROY	V (A
MADELINE BELL	V (A	NANETTE NEWMAN	V (A	ANDY ROBERTS	G (A	CHRIS SPEDDING	G (A
JONATHAN COUDRILLE	K (A	MIKE STOREY	K (A				

K83 KORGIS

ANDY DAVIS	V K D MAND (A	(A) THE KORGIS		1979	RIALTO	TENOR 101
JAMES WARREN	V B (A	(B) DUMB WAITERS		1980	RIALTO	TENOR 104
PHIL HARRISON	K PERC(A					
GLENN TOOMEY	K (A	DAVID LORD	K (A	BILL BIRKS	D (A	AL POWELL	D (A
STUART GORDON	PERC VLN MAND(A	KEITH WARMINGTON	HCA(A	KENNY LACEY	PERC (A	JO MULLEY	V (A
JO POMEROY	V (A						

K84 ALEXIS KORNER

ALEXIS KORNER	G V (ALL	(A) R & B AT THE MARQUEE		1962 ACE OF CLUBS	UK	ACL 1130
ERIC CLAPTON	G (1	(B) AT THE CAVERN		1964 ORIOLE	UK	
ZOOT MONEY	K (1G	(C) RED HOT WITH ALEX		1964 TRANSATLANTIC	UK	TRA 117
CHRIS FARLOWE	V (1	(D) BLUES INC		1965 ACE OF CLUBS	UK	ACL 1187
IAN STEWART	V (1	(D) BLUES INC		1967 POLYDOR	UK	236 206
PAUL JONES	V (1	(E) I WONDER WHO		1967 FONTANA	UK	STL5381
ART THEMAN	WIND (1CG	(F) NEW GENERATION OF BLUES		1968 SONET		SLP 64
MEL COLLINS	HRNS (1N	(F) NEW GENERATION OF BLUES		1968 LIBERTY		LBS 83147
DICK MORRISSEY	SAX (1	(G) ALEXIS KORNERS ALL STARS BLUES INC	69 TRANSATLANTIC	UK	TRASAM 7
DICK HECKSTALL SMITH	SAX(1GM	(H) BOTH SIDES		1969 METRONOME		MLP 15364
JOHN SURMAN	SAX (1M	(J) THE NEW CHURCH		1970 METRONOME		
MIKE ZWERIN	TROM (1M	(K) ALEXIS		1971 RAK	UK	SRAK 501
COLIN HODGKINSON	B (1M	(L) WHATS THAT SOUND I HEAR		1971 SUNSET	UK	SLS 50245
STU SPEAR	(1	(M) BOOTLEG HIM		1972 RAK UK SRAKSP 51 US WB		1966
JIMMY LITHERLAND	G (1	(N) ACCIDENTALLY BORN IN NEW ORLEANS	1973 TRANSATLANTIC	UK	TRA 269
GUS JOHNSON	(1	(N) ACCIDENTALLY BORN IN NEW ORLEANS	1973 WB	US	2647
IAN WALLACE	D (N	(O) SNAPE LIVE ON TOUR		1974 BRAIN		2/ 1039
BOZ BURRELL	B (N	(P) GET OFF MY CLOUD		1975 CBS US 33427	UK	69155
STEVE MARRIOTT	ORG (N	(Q) JUST EASY		1978 INTERCORD		INT 60099
DAVE CASTLE	WIND (CG	(R) ME (DIRECT CUT)		1979 JETON		100 3305
HERBIE GOINS	V (CMG	(1) 50th BIRTHDAY PARTY JAM				
RON EDGEWORTH	V (GC					

DANNY THOMPSON	B (CGM	BARRY HOWTEN	D (CG	CYRIL DAVIES	HCA V(CM	KEITH SCOTT	PNO (MA
COLIN BOWDEN	D (M	DAVE STEVENS	PNO (M	CHARLIE WATTS	D (M	JACK BRUCE	B (M
TERRY COX	D (M	CHRIS PYNE TROM	PNO (M	RAY WARLEIGH	SAX (M	DAVE HOLLAND	B (M
ALAN SKIDMORE	SAX (M	GINGER BAKER	D (M	GRAHAM BOND	SAX (M	JOHNNY PARKER	PNO (M
NIGEL STANGER	SAX (M	BRIAN SMITH	SAX (M	PETER THORUP	V G (M	PAUL RODGERS	V (M
ANNETTE BROX	V (M	ANDY FRASER	B (M	LOL COXHILL	SAX (M	JOHN MARSHALL	D (M
MALCOLM GRIFFITHS	TROM (M	HAROLD BECKETT	TPT (M	HENRY LOWTHER	TPT (M	VICTOR BROX PNO TPT V(M
ROBERT PLANT	V HCA(M	STEVE MILLER	PNO (M	PETER FENSOME	V (M	ROY BABBINGTON	B (M
CHRIS McGREGOR	PNO (M	LARRY POWER	G (M	JACK BROOKS	D (M	JOHN CAMERON	K (M

(CONTINUED)

ALEXIS KORNER   K84

ALAN PARKER	G	(M	HERBIE FLOWERS	B	(M	BARRY MORGAN	D	(M	TONY CARR	D	(M
SPIKE HEATLEY	B	(AM	JIM LAWLESS	PERC	(M	BILL LESAGE	PERC	(M	HAROLD McNAIR	FLT	(M
TONY COE	WIND	(M	PETE KING	WIND	(M	DANNY MOSS	WIND	(M	BOB EFFORD	WIND(M
RON ROSS	WIND	(M	NEIL SANDERS	HRNS	(M	KENNY WHEELER	TPT	(M	GREG BOWEN	TPT	(M
TONY FISHER	TPT	(M	LES CONDON	TPT	(M	DON LUSHER	TROM	(M	JOHN MARSHALL	TROM(M
BRIAN PERRIN	TROM	(M	BILL GELDARD	TROM	(M	SAPPHO KORNER	V	(J	GRAHAM BURBRIDGE	D(A
LONG JOHN BALDRY	V	(A

ARTIE KORNFELDS TREE   K84A
(A) A TIME TO REMEMBER   1970   PROBE   UK   SPB 1022

KORPS   K85
(A) HELLO WORLD   1979   LIMP   IMP   1002

DANNY KORTCHMAR   K86
DANNY KORTCHMAR   G V   (A   (A) KOOTCH   1973   WB   US   BS 2711
(B) INNUENDO   19   US

PAUL KOSSOFF   K87

PAUL KOSSOFF	G	(AB
ALAN WHITE	D	(A
RABBIT BUNDRICK	K	(AB
ALAN SPENNER	B	(A	JEAN ROUSSEL	K	(A	JESS RODEN	V	(A	TETSU YAMAUCHI	B (AB
SIMON KIRKE	D	(AB	JOHN MARTYN	G	(AB	PAUL RODGERS	V	(AB	ANDY FRASER	B	(AB
CONRAD ISADORE	D	(A	CLIVE CHAMAN	B	(A	TREVOR BURTON	B	(A	DAVID HOOD	B	(B
ROGER HAWKINS	D	(B	BARRY BECKETT	K	(B	PETE CARR	G	(B	JIMMY JOHNSON	G	(B
MIKE KELLIE	D	(B	DAVID ELLIOTT	PNO	(B	TONY BRAUNAGEL	D	(B	TERRY WILSON	B	(B
MIKE MONTGOMERY	PNO	(B	PETER COX	V	(B	JIM CAPALDI	V	(B	SUE GLOVER	V	(B
EDDIE BAIRD	G K V(B	TERRY WINCOTT	G V	(B	WILLY MURRAY	D	(B	SUNNY LESLIE	D	(B
MICK FEAT	B	(B	TERRY WILSON SLESSER V	(B	GEORGE LARNYOH	HRNS	(B	PETER VANDER PUIJE HRNS(B
EDDIE QUANSAH	HRNS (B

(A) BACK STREET CRAWLER   1973   ISLAND   UK   ILPS 9264
(B) KOSS (COMP DBL)   1977   DJM   UK   DJE 29002

LEO KOTTKE   K88

LEO KOTTKE	G	(ALL	(A) CIRCLE AROUND THE SUN	1970 SYMPOSIUM		2001
MIKE JOHNSON	G	(G	(B) MUDLARK	1971 CAPITOL		682
BILL BERG	PERC	(FGH	(C) LEO KOTTKE 6 & 12 STRING GUITAR	1972 SONET UK SNTF 629 TAKOMA US1024
BILL PETERSON	B	(FGH	(D) GREENHOUSE	1973 CAPITOL		11000
BILL BARBER	SYN	(FGH	(E) MY FEET ARE SMILING	1973 CAPITOL		11164
CAL HAND	STEEL(FG	(F) ICE WATER	1974 CAPITOL		11262
HERB PILHOFER	PNO	(G	(G) DREAMS & ALL THAT STUFF	1974 CAPITOL		11335
JACK SMITH	PNO	(G	(H) CHEWING PINE	1974 CAPITOL		11446
ROY ESTRADA	B	(B	(H) BEST OF	1976 CAPITOL	UK	CAPS1003
PAUL LAGOS	D	(B	(H) LEO KOTTKE	1976 CHRYSALIS	UK	CHR 1106
WAYNE MOSS	B	(B	(K) BURNT LIPS	1978 CHRYSALIS	UK	CHR 1191
KEN BUTTREY	D	(BN	(L) THE BEST	1978 CAPITOL		ESTSP 21
JOHN HARRIS	PNO	(BN	(M) LEO KOTTKE 1971/76	1976 CAPITOL		11576
MIKE LEECH	B	(N	(N) BALANCE	1979 CHRYSALIS	UK	CHR 1234
BOBBY OGDIN	PNO	(N	(O) LIVE IN EUROPE	1980 CHRYSALIS	UK	CHR 1284
LARRY TAYLOR	B	(B
KIM FOWLEY	V	(B

KRAAN   K89

PETER WOLBRANDT	G V	(ABCDEFG	(A) WINTHRUP	1972 SPIEGELEI		28523/9
HELLMUT HATTLER	B	(ABCDEFG	(B) KRAAN	1973 SPIEGELEI		28778/9
JAN FRIDE	D	(ABCDEF	(C) ANDY NOGGER	1975 GULL UK 1009 PASSPORT US 98006
JOHANNES PAPPERT	SAX	(ABCDE	(D) KRAAN LIVE	1975 GULL UK		2001/2
INGO BISCHOF	K	(EFG	(D) KRAAN LIVE	1975 SPIEGELEI		26440/8
TOMMY GOLDSCHMIDT	PERC	(F	(E) LET IT OUT	1975 GULL UK 1013 PASSPORT US 98015
UDO DATIMEN	D	(G	(E) LET IT OUT	1975 SPIEGELEI		24548/1
			(F) WIEDERHOREN	1977 HARVEST ELECTROLA GER 064 32110
			(G) FLYDAY	1978 HARVEST ELECTROLA	064 45210

KRACKER   K90

CARL DRIGGS	V PERC(A	(A) KRACKER BRAND	1973 ROLLING STONES		COC 49102
CHUCK FRANCOUR	K V	(A
VICTOR ANGULO	G V	(A	CARLOS GARCIA	B V	(A	ARTHUR CASADO	D PERC V(A	MALCOLM CECIL	SYN(A
ROBERT MARGOULEFF	SYN	(A	BOBBY KEYS	SAX	(A

KRACQ   K91
(A) CIRCUMVISION   1978   UAP   003

KRAFTWERK   K92

			(A) KRAFTWERK 1	1971 PHILIPS		6305 058
			(B) KRAFTWERK 2	1972 PHILIPS		6305 117
RALF HUTTER V K D(ABCDEFGHI	(C) KRAFTWERK	1973 VERTIGO	UK	6641 077
FLORIAN SCHNEIDER D K(ABCDEFGHI	(D) RALF & FLORIAN	1973 VERTIGO	UK	6360 616
KLAUS ROEDER	VLN G(E	(E) AUTOBAHN	1974 VERTIGO US 2003 UK	6360 620
WOLFGANG FLUR	PERC(EFGHI	(E) AUTOBAHN	1974 MERCURY US 1 3704
KARL BARTOS	PERC(FGHI	(F) RADIOACTIVITY	1975 CAPITOL		11457
			(G) EXCELLER 8	1975 VERTIGO	UK	6360 629
			(H) TRANS EUROPE EXPRESS	1977 CAPITOL		11603
			(I) MAN MACHINE	1978 CAPITOL		11728

BILLY J KRAMER & THE DAKOTAS   K93

BILLY J KRAMER	V	(ALL	LISTEN TO	1963 PARLOPHONE UK (M) 1209 (S) 3047
MIKE MAXFIELD	G	(	I'LL KEEP YOU SATISFIED	196 IMPERIAL US (M) 9273 (S)12273
ROBIN McDONALD	G	(	LITTLE CHILDREN	196 IMPERIAL US (M) 9287 (S)12267
RAY JONES	B	(	TRAINS BOATS & PLANES	196 IMPERIAL US (M) 9291 (S)12291
TONY MANSFIELD	D	(	THE BEST OF	1977 EMI UK	NUT9
			(EP) HITS	1963 PARLOPHONE UK	GEP 8885
			(EP) I'LL KEEP YOU SATISFIED	1964 PARLOPHONE UK	GEP 8895
			(EP) LITTLE CHILDREN	1964 PARLOPHONE UK	GEP 8907
			(EP) FROM A WINDOW	1964 PARLOPHONE UK	GEP 8921
			(EP) PLAYS FROM THE STATES	1965 PARLOPHONE UK	GEP 8928

K94 KRAZY KAT

GRAHAME WHITE	G V	(AB	(A) CHINA SEA		1976	MOUNTAIN		TOPC 5004
TONY FERGUSON	G V	(AB	(B) TROUBLED AIR		1977	MOUNTAIN		TOPC 5009
ROGER BRADLEY-WILLIS	D(AB							
RAY LEWIS	B V	(AB	HENRY MACDONALD	K V	(AB			

K94A ROBBIE KRIEGER

ROBBIE KRIEGER	G V K(A	(A) ..AND FRIENDS			1977	BLUE NOTE		LA 664
ED GREENE	D	(A						
REGGIE McBRIDE	B	(A	RON STOCKERT	K	(A	SAL MARQUEZ HRNS K (A	JOCK ELLIS	TROM (A
JOEL PESKIN	SAX	(A	BRUCE GARY	D	(A	KENNY WILD	B (A	GREG MATHIESON ORG (A
SHARON ROBINSON	V	(A	AFREEKA TREES	V	(A	JIMMY SMITH	ORG (A	JOHN DENSMORE D (A
STU GOLDBERG	SYN K(A	PERICO	CONGA(A	EDDIE TALAMANTES TIMBS(A	GARY BARONE	TPT (A
BOB GLAUB	B	(A						

K94B SONJA KRISTINA

SONJA KRISTINA	V	(A	(A) SONJA KRISTINA		1980	CHOPPER		CHOPE5
LIAM GENOCKEY	D	(A						
ALFIE AGIUS	B	(A	STEVE BYRD	G	(A	COLIN TOWNS	FLT K (A	GASPAR LAWAL PERC (A
NIGEL GRAY	SYN	(A	DARRYL WAY	VLN	(A	ALEXANDER SKEAPING	K(A	LAWRENCE JUBER G (A
IAIN DUNNET	SYN	(A	DAVE SMITH	B	(A	TONY HENDRICKS	D (A	BOB BARNETT G (A
DAVID WALKER	K	(A	BRIAN DEVITO	B	(A	PETER VAN HOOKE	D (A	DAVE OLNEY B (A
IAN MILNE	K	(A	PETE ACOCK	SAX	(A	TONY CARR	PERC (A	CORONA STAGE SCHOOL V(A

K95 KRIS KRISTOFFERSON

KRIS KRISTOFFERSON	V G	(ALL	(A) KRISTOFFERSON	1970	MONUMENT UK 5042		
JERRY KENNEDY	G	(AC	(A) ME & BOBBY McGEE(RI)	1973	MONUMENT UK 64631	US	30817
NORBERT PUTNAM	B	(CE	(B) CISCO PETE	197	CBS	US	9154
JERRY CARRIGAN	D	(C	(C) SILVER TONGUED DEVIL & I	1971	MONUMENT UK 64636	US	30679
DAVID BRIGGS	K	(CE	(D) BORDER LORD	1972	MONUMENT UK 64963	US	31302
JERRY SHOOK	G	(CE	(E) JESUS WAS A CAPRICORN	1973	MONUMENT UK 65391	US	31909
NORMAN BLAKE	G	(C	(F) SPOOKY LADY'S SIDESHOW	1974	MONUMENT UK 69074	US	32914
BOBBY DYSON	B	(C	(G) WHO'S TO BLESS & WHO'S TO BLAME	1975	MONUMENT UK 69158	US	33379
CHARLIE McCOY	HCA	(C	(H) SURREAL THING	1976	MONUMENT UK 81496	US	35254
FARRELL MORRIS	PERC	(C	(J) SONGS OF KRISTOFFERSON	1977	MONUMENT UK 82002	US	34254
BILLY SWAN	B V	(CEH	(K) A STAR IS BORN (SOUNDTRACK)	1977	CBS	UK 86021	
CHRIS GANTRY	G	(C	(L) EASTER ISLAND	1978	MONUMENT UK 86056	US	35310
DONNIE FRITTS	K V	(C	(M) HELP ME MAKE IT THROUGH THE NIGHT	1980	CBS		31839
RITA COOLIDGE	V	(CFH					

LARRY GATLIN	V	(E	BENNY WHITEHEAD	V	(E	RANDY CULLERS	V	(E	ALAN RUSH	V (E
TERRY DEARMORE	V	(E	ALLEN WALD	V	(H	TERRY PAUL	V	(H	GARY BUSEY	V (H
KENNY BUTTREY	D	(E	ANDY NEWMARK	D	(E	JOSH GRAVES	G	(E	JERRY McGEE	G V(FH
LEE SKLAR	B	(FH	BARBARA STREISLAND V	(K	SAMMY CREASON	D	(FH	BOBBYE HALL	PERC(F
JIM HORN	SAX	(F	JACKIE KELSO	SAX	(F	CHUCK FINDLEY	TPT	(F	DICK HYDE	TROM(F
HERB PEDERSEN	V	(FH	LARRY MURRAY	V	(F	JOHN BELAND	V	(F	BOBBY NEUWIRTH	V (F
CLYDIE KING	V	(H	SHIRLEY MATTHEWS	V	(H	BYRON BERLINE	V	(H	JACK SKINNER	V (H
CHARLES CHALMERS	V	(E	SANDRA CHALMERS	V	(E	DONNA RHODES	V	(E	D BERGEN WHITE	V (E
JAMES E CASON	V	(E	JUNE PAGE	V	(E	JORDANAIRES	V	(E	RAYMOND WALKER	V (E
HOYT HAWKINS	V	(E	JOHN HARRIS	K	(E	GORDON STOKER	V	(E	DON GANT	V (E
MILDRED KIRKHAM	V	(E	STEPHEN BRUTON	G V	(E	DENNIS LINDE	G	(E	TOM COGBILL	B (E
MAC GAYDEN	G	(E	CHIP YOUNG	G	(E	JOHN BUCK WILKIN	G	(E	JAMES COLVARD	G (E
GRADY MARTIN	G	(E	FRED CARTER	G	(E	JOHN L CHRISTOPHER	G	(E	WELDON MYRICK	STEEL(E
MIKE UTLEY	K V	(E	BOBBY WOOD	K	(E	BOBBY EMMONS	K	(E		

K96 KRIS KRISTOFFERSON & RITA COOLIDGE

KRIS KRISTOFFERSON	V	(ABC	(A) FULL MOON		1973	A&M	US 4403 UK AMLH64403	
RITA COOLIDGE	V	(ABC	(B) BREAKAWAY		1974	MONUMENT	US 33278 UK	80547
STEPHEN BRUTON	G V	(AC	(C) NATURAL ACT		1978	A&M	UK AMLH64690	
CHIP YOUNG	G	(B						
JIM COLVARD	G	(B	JOHN L CHRISTOPHER G	(B	JERRY SHOOK	G	(B	WELDON MYRICK STEEL(B
MIKE UTLEY	K	(ABC	BOBBY WOOD	K	(B	BOBBY EMMONS	K	(B	TOMMY COGBILL B (B
JOSH GRAVES	G	(A	JERRY McGEE	G	(AC	LEE SKLAR	B	(A	SAMMY CREASON D (ABC
BOBBYE HALL	PERC	(A	TERRY PAUL	V	(A	GENE CHRISMAN	D	(B	BUDDY SPICHER FDL (B
REGGIE YOUNG	G	(B	RAY EDENTON	G	(B	SHANE KEISTER	K	(B	FARRELL MORRIS PERC (B
CHARLIE McCOY	HCA	(B	RON EADES	HRNS	(B	HARRISON CALLOWAY HRNS(B	CHARLES ROSE HRNS (B
DON SHEFFIELD	HRNS	(B	DAVID BROMBERG	G	(A	NICK DE CARO	D	(A	DAVID SMITH (A
GARY SCRUGGS		(A	RANDY SCRUGGS		(A	VASSAR CLEMENTS	FDL	(A	BOOKER T JONES K (A
HERB ALPERT	TPT	(A	BILLY SWAN	V	(C	DONNIE FRITTS	K	(C	JERRY JUMONVILLE SAX(C
DENNIS BELFIELD	B	(C						

K96A KROKUS

MARC STORACE	V	(AB	(A) METAL RENDEZVOUS		1980	ARIOLA		ARL 5056
TOMMY KIEFFER	G V	(AB	(B) HARDWARE		1981	ARIOLA		ARL 5064
FERNANDO VON ARB	G V	(AB	(C) PAINKILLER		1981	PHONOGRAM	NL	6326 800
CHRIS VON ROHR	B V	(AB						
FREDDY STEADY	D V	(AB	JUERG NAEGELI	K V	(A			

K96B JIM KRUEGER

JIM KRUEGER		(A	(A) SWEET SALVATION		1978	CBS	US	35295

K97 DAVID KUBINEC

DAVID KUBINEC	G V PNO (A	(A) SOME THINGS NEVER CHANGE		1978	A&M	UK	AMLH68501
CHRIS SPEDDING	G	(A						
JIM BAIN	B	(A	JOHN CALE	K	(A	OLLIE HALSALL	G	(A	ALAN MACLEOD PIPES (A
TIMI DONALD	D	(A	PAT DONALDSON	B	(A			

K98 JOACHIM KUHN

JOACHIM KUHN	K	(ALL	(A) BOLD IS WONDERFUL		19	MPS		15239
PHILIP CATHERINE	G	(L	(B) CINEMASCOPE		19	MPS BASF		2122270 5
JOHN LEE	B	(L	(C) IMPRESSION OF NEW YORK		19	IMPULSE		9158
GERRY BROWN	D	(L	(D) INTERCHANGE		19	MPS		21328 5
ZBIGNIEW SEIFERT	VLN	(L	(E) PARIS IS WONDERFUL		19	BYG		529 346
CURT CRESS	D	(L	(F) PIANO		1971	MPS BASF		2121330 7
ROLF KUHN		(CK	(G) SOLOS		1974	FUTURA		GER 18
PETER WARREN		(J	(H) SOUNDS OF FEELING		19	BYG		519 317
							(CONTINUED)

			JOACHIM KUHN				K98
DANIEL HUSSAIN	(J		(J) THIS WAY OUT	19	BASF	2921752 3	
GERD DUDEK	(J		(K) TRANSFIGURATION	19	MPS	15118	
			(L) SPRING FEVER	1977	ATLANTIC	K50280	
			(M) CHARISMA	19	ATLANTIC	K50352	
			(N) MONDAY MORNING	19	ELECTROLA	SHZE 909B	

			STEVE KUHN				K99
STEVE KUHN	PNO	(ALL	CHILDHOOD IS FOREVER	1969	BYG	529136	
			TRANCE	1974	ECM	1052	
			ECSTASY	1974	ECM	1058	
			MOTILITY	1977	ECM	1094	
			NON FICTION	1978 ECM		1124	
			WATCH WHAT HAPPENS	19	MPS	15193	

			KURSAAL FLYERS				K100
PAUL SHUTTLEWORTH	V	(ALL	(A) CHOCS AWAY	1975	UK	UK	2330 101
RICHIE BULL	B V	(ALL	(B) GREAT ARTISTE	1975	UK	UK	UKAL 1018
GRAEME DOUGLAS	G	(ABC	(C) GOLDEN MILE	1976	CBS	UK	81622
VIC COLLINS G V STEEL	(ALL		(D) FIVE LIVE KURSAALS	1977	CBS	UK	82253
WILL BIRCH	D	(ALL					
BARRY MARTIN	G V	(D					

			JIM KWESKIN				K101
JIM KWESKIN	G V	(ALL	(A) UNBLUSHING BRASSINESS	1963 VANGUARD		VSD 2158	
MARIA(D'AMATO) MULDAUR	V(F		(B) JUG BAND MUSIC	1965 VANGUARD		VSD 79163	
GEOFF MULDAUR	G V	(F	(C) RELAX YOUR MIND	1966 VANGUARD		VSD 79188	
BILL KEITH	STEEL(F		(D) SEE REVERSE SIDE FOR TITLE	1966 VANGUARD VSD 79234 FONTANA 6080			
MEL LYMAN	HCA (		(E) JUMP FOR JOY	1967 VANGUARD		VSD 79243	
FRITZ RICHMOND	B	(F	(F) GARDEN OF JOY	1967 REPRISE	US	6266	
RICHARD GREENE	FDL	(F	(G) BEST OF	1968 VANGUARD		VSD 79270	
			(H) WHATEVER HAPPENED TO THOSE DAYS	1968 VANGUARD		VAS 79278	
			(J) AMERICAN AVIATOR	1969 REPRISE	US	6353	
			(K) GREATEST HITS(DBL)	1970 VANGUARD		VSD 13/14	
			(L) JIM KWESKIN'S AMERICA	1971 REPRISE	US	6464	
			(M) JIM KWESKIN	1978 MOUNTAIN RAILROAD		MR 52780	
			(N) LIVES AGAIN	1978 MOUNTAIN RAILROAD		MR 52782	

			L A EXPRESS				L1
DAVID LUELL	SAX	(AB	(A) L A EXPRESS	1976 CARIBOU	US 33940	UK	81267
ROBBEN FORD	G	(AB	(B) SHADOW PLAY	1976 CARIBOU	US 34355	UK	81671
VICTOR FELDMAN	PERC K	(AB					
PETER MAUNU G (AB MAX BENNETT B (AB JOHN GUERIN D K (AB JONI MITCHELL V (B							
PAULETTE McWILLIAMS V (B							

			L A JETS				L1A
KAREN LAWRENCE	V	(A	(A) L A JETS	1976 RCA	US	APLI 1547	
HARLIN McNEES	G V	(A					
RON CINDRICH B (A JOHN DESAUTELS D (A SILVER HANSON G (A WAYNE COOK K(A							
JAMES LINDSEL	PERC	(A					

			L T D				L2
BILLY OSBORNE	K	(C	(A) LOVE TOGETHERNESS & DEVOTION	197 A&M	US 3602		
JEFF OSBORNE	D V	(C	(B) GITTIN' DOWN	1975 A&M	US 3660	UK	AMLS63660
HENRY DAVIS	B V	(C	(C) LOVE TO THE WORLD	1976 A&M	US 4589	UK	AMLH64589
JIMMIE DAVIS	K V	(C	(D) SOMETHING TO LOVE	1977 A&M	US 4646	UK	AMLH64646
ROBERT SANTIEL	PERC	(C	(E) TOGETHERNESS	1978 A&M	US 4705	UK	AMLH64705
JOHN McGEE	G	(C	(F) DEVOTION	1979 A&M	US 4771		AMLH64771
ABRAHAM MILLER	SAX V(C		(G) SHINE ON	1980 A&M	US 4819	UK	AMLH64819
CARLE VICKERS	HRNS (C						
LORENZO CARNEGIE SAX (C JAKE RILEY TROM(C TOBY WYNN SAX (C							

			JOAN LA BARBARA				L2A
JOAN LA BARBARA	V	(A	(A) VOICE IS THE ORIGINAL INSTRUMENT	1976 WIZARD	US	RVW 2266	

			SLEEPY LA BEEF				L3
SLEEPY LA BEEF	G V	(ALL	(A) BULLS NIGHT OUT	1976 SUN	US	130	
TERRY DUNCAN	PNO	(E	(B) EARLY RARE & ROCKIN	19 BARON	US	102	
LONNIE SEABOLT	B	(E	(B) EARLY RARE & ROCKIN	1979 CHARLY	RI UK	CR 30181	
CLETE CHAPMAN	D	(E	(C) WESTERN GOLD	1977 SUN	US	138	
BUCKY MEADOWS	G ORG(E		(D) ROCKABILLY 77	1977 SUN	US	1004	
CLIFF PARKER	G	(E	(E) BEEFY ROCKABILLY	1978 CHARLY	UK	CR 30145	
GORDON TERRY	FDL	(E	(F) DOWN HOME ROCKABILLY	1979 CHARLY	UK	CR 30172	
RUFUS THIBODEAUX	FDL	(E	(G) ROCKABILLY HEAVYWEIGHT	1979 CHARLY	UK	CRL 5017	
			(H) SLEEPY LA BEEF & FRIENDS(10")	1979 ACE		10 CH16	
			(EP) TORE UP	1978 CHARLY	UK	CEP 123	

			LABELLE				L4
PATTI LABELLE	V	(ALL	(A) OVER THE RAINBOW(BLUEBELLS)	196	ATLANTIC	US 5D8119	
SARAH DASH	V	(HAJ	(B) DREAMER	1967	ATLANTIC	US 8147	
NONA HENDRYX	V	(HAJ	(C) LA BELLE	1971	WB	US 1943	
ALLEN TOUSSAINT	K	(H	(D) MOON SHADOWS	1972	WB	US 2618	
JAMES ELLISON	K	(H	(E) MERRY CHRISTMAS	19	MISTLETOE	US 1204	
JAMES BOOKER	K	(H	(F) PRESSURE COOKIN'	1974	RCA US LSA 3223 UK APLI0205		
HERMAN ERNEST	D	(H	(G) NIGHT BIRDS	197	EPIC US 33075		
GEORGE PORTER	B	(H	(H) PHOENIX	1975	EPIC US 33579	UK	69167
CARMINE ROJAS	B	(H	(J) C'EST LA VIE	1975	DJM	UK DJSL 050	
LEO NOCENTELLI	G	(H	(K) CHAMELEON	1976	EPIC US 34189	UK	81422
TEDDY ROYAL	G	(H	(L) PATTI LABELLE	1977	EPIC US 34847	UK	82226
LON PRICE	WIND	(H	(M) EARLY HITS	19	TRIP US	9525	
JOHN LONGO	TPT	(H	(N) TASTY	197	EPIC US 35335		
CINDY BIRDSONG	V	(AJ	(O) ITS ALL RIGHT WITH ME	1979	EPIC	UK	83524
EDWARD BATTS	G	(H					
JEFFREY SHANNON PERC (H JIM MOORE WIND (H LESTER CALISTE TROM (H STEVE HUGHES G (H							
STEVE HOWARD HRNS (H CARL BLOUIN SAX (H							

L4A — JERRY LACROIX

```
JERRY LACROIX        V    (A        (A) SECOND COMING          1974   MERCURY      US    SRM 1 701
LAUREL ANNE MASSE    V    (A        ( ) LA CROIX               1972                US
DAVID SPINOZZA       G    (A
JOHNNY WINTER        G    (A    BOB MANN          G    (A   EDGAR WINTER      K    (A   JERRY FRIEDMAN G   (A
BOB ROSE             G    (A    HUGH McCRACKEN    G    (A   STU WOODS         B    (A   JOHN TROPEA    G   (A
PAUL GRIFFIN         K    (A    RICK MAROTTA      D    (A   RALPH MACDONALD   PERC (A   TASHA THOMAS   V   (A
CARL HALL            V    (A    HILDA HARRIS      V    (A   CHARLOTTA GILBERT V    (A   RALPH SCHUCKETT K  (A
RICHARD CROOKS       D    (A    RANDY BRECKER     HRNS(A   ROBERT MILLIKAN   HRNS (A   DAVID SANBORN  HRNS(A
LEW DEL GATTO        HRNS (A    JAMES MAELIN      PERC (A   RICK DERRINGER    G    (A   GAIL KANTOR    V   (A
MERLE MILLER         V    (A
```

L5 — LA DUSSELDORF

```
KLAUS DINGER         G V  (AB       (A) LA DUSSELDORF          1976   DECCA        UK    SKLR3252
THOMAS DINGER        PERC V (AB      (A) LA DUSSELDORF          1978   RADAR        UK    RAD 7
HANS LAMPE           PERC SYN K(AB   (B) VIVA                   1978   RADAR        UK    RAD10
NIKOLAUS VAN RHEIN   K    (AB
HARALD KONIETZKO     B    (AB   ANDREAS SCHELL    PNO  (A
```

K5A — LADY JUNE

```
LADY JUNE            V    (A        (A) LINGUISTIC LEPROSY     1974   CAROLINE     UK    C1509
KEVIN AYERS          G B SYN(A
BRIAN ENO            K G V(A    KIM SOLOMON       PNO  (A   DAVID VORHAUS          (A   MARTHA         V   (A
PIP PYLE             D    (A
```

L6 — LAFAYETTE AFRO ROCK BAND

```
                                    (A) SOUL MAKOSSA           1973   MUSIDISC     FR    CV1269
                                    (B) MALIK                  19     AMERICA            30AM6137
```

L7 — DENNY LAINE

```
DENNY LAINE          G K V(ABC      (A) AAH LAINE              1973   WIZARD US 2190   UK  2001
PAUL McCARTNEY       V B G D K(BC    (B) HOLLY DAYS            1976   CAPITOL US 11588 UK EMI781
LINDA McCARTNEY      K V  (B         (C) JAPANESE TEARS        1980   SCRATCH          UK  5001
JOHN MORESHEAD       G    (A
STEVE THOMPSON       B    (A    MACEY McCREARY    V    (A   PHOEBE LAOB       V    (A   COLIN ALLEN    D   (A
JO JO LAINE          V    (C    STEVE HOLLY       D V  (C   BUDDY EMMONS      STEEL(C   THADIUS RICHARDS FLT(C
LAWRENCE JUBER       G    (C    GORDON SELLAR     G    (C   ANDY RICHARDS          (C   MIKE PIGGOTT       (C
HOWIE CASEY          SAX  (C    DENNY SEIWELL     D    (C   HENRY McCULLOUGH  G    (C
```

L8 — DAVID LAFLAMME

```
DAVID LAFLAMME       V VLN(AB       (A) WHITE BIRD            1977   AMHERST      us    AMH 1007
MITCHELL FROOM       K TPT VIBES(AB  (B) INSIDE OUT           1978   AMHERST      US    AMH 1012
JAMES RALSTON        G    (AB
DOUG KILMER          D    (AB   MICHAEL BAIRD     D    (B   DOMINIQUE DELLACROIX (AB  PETER MILIO    D   (AB
MITCHELL HOLMAN      B    (A    TOM MARKEN        D    (A   JEFF DAMBRAU      BANJO(A   ROGER GLENN    FLT (A
CARL TASSI           PERC (A    GREG ADAMS        HRNS (A   MIC GILLETE       HRNS (A   EMILIO CASTILLO SAX(A
LENNY PICKETT        SAX  (A    STEVE KUPKA       SAX  (A
```

L9 — CORKY LAING

```
CORKY LAING          V D G(A        (A) MAKIN' IT ON THE STREET  1977  ELEKTRA    US    7E 1097
CLYDIE KING          V    (A
PETE CARR            G    (A    NEIL LARSEN       K    (A   HARVEY THOMPSON   HRNS (A   RANDALL BRAMBLETT HRNS(A
VANETTA FIELDS       V    (A    TOMMY TALTON      G    (A   CHARLES ROSE      HRNS (A   FRANK VICARI   HRNS (A
SHIRLEY MATTHEWS     V    (A    CALVIN ARLINE     B    (A   RON EADES         HRNS (A   HARRISON CALLOWAY HRNS(A
MIKE MONTGOMERY      K    (      DONNY KRIETER    B    (    BOB KULICK        G    (    TUPPER LIENICE PNO  (
```

L10 — LAKE

```
JAMES HOPKINS-HARRISON V(ABC      (A) LAKE                   1976   CBS US  34763  UK  81661
DEITER AHRENDT       D V  (ABC       (B) LAKE 2                1978   CBS US  35289  UK  82651
GEOFF PEACEY         G K V(ABC       (C) PARADISE ISLAND       1979   CBS US  35817  UK  83480
ALEX CONTI           G V  (ABC
CARL WILSON               (B    DETLEF PETERSEN   K V  (BC  MARTIN TIEFENSEE B   (ABC  OTTO WAALKEN   CONGA(C
JAMES WILLIAM GUERCIO     (C
```

L10A — LAKESIDE

```
FRED ALEXANDER       D    (C        (A) LAKESIDE              197    ABC          US    AB 999
NORMAN BEAVERS       K    (C        (B) SHOT OF LOVE          1979   RCA          UK    FL12937
MARVIN CRAIG         B    (C        (C) ROUGH RIDERS          1979   SOLAR US 3490 UK RCA FL13490
FRED LEWIS           PERC (C        (D) FANTASTIC VOYAGE      1980   RCA          US    BXLI3720
TIEMEYER McCAIN      PERC V(C
MARK A WOOD          K V  (C    THOMAS SHELBY     V    (C   STEPHEN SHOCKLEY  G K (C   OTIS STOKES    K B GV(C
```

L11 — KEVIN LAMB

```
KEVIN LAMB           V    (A        (A) SAILIN' DOWN THE YEARS  1978 ARISTA US  AB 4166 UK SPART1026
STEVE GOULD          G    (A
MICK FEAT            B    (A    BILLY LIVSEY      K    (A   DAVID DOWLE       D    (A   RAY COOPER     PERC (A
ANDY SUMMERS         G    (A    B J COLE          STEEL(A   GEOFF DALY        SAX  (A   CHRIS THOMPSON V    (A
STEVIE LANGE         V    (A    JUNIOR MARVIN     G    (A
```

L12 — DAVE LAMBERT

```
DAVE LAMBERT         G V  (A        (A) FRAMED                1979   POLYDOR  PD 1 6193 UK 2391  391
JOHN ENTWISTLE       B    (A
RICHARD BENNETT      G    (A    LEE SKLAR         B    (A   TOM HENSLEY       K    (A   LARRY BROWN    PERC(A
DENNY SEIWELL        D    (A    ROBBIE BUCHANAN   PNO  (A
```

L12A — LAMBRETTAS

```
                                    (A) BEAT BOYS IN THE JET AGE  1980  ROCKET    UK    TRAIN 10
```

L13 — ROBERT LAMM

```
ROBERT LAMM               (A        (A) SKINNY BOY            1975   CBS US  33095  UK 80359
TERRY KATH           G B  (A
ROSS SALOMONE        D    (A    JAMES VINCENT     G    (A   ALAN DE CARLO     G    (A   POINTER SISTERS V   (A
GUILLE GARCIA        PERC (A    STRING SECTION         (A   WILLIAM COLLETTE  WIND (A
```

L14 — LAMP OF CHILDHOOD

```
JAMES HENDRICKS      V    (
FRED OLSEN           G    (
MICK TANI                 (     BILLY MUNDI       D    (
```

```
JACK LANCASTER     WIND (AB        (A) MARSCAPE                    1976 RSO     US  3020  UK   2394 170
ROBIN LUMLEY       K    (A         (B) WILD CONNECTIONS           1979 ACROBAT         UK         ACRO 2
RICK VAN DER LINDEN K  (B
JOHN GOODSALL      G    (A   SIMON JEFFES    KOTO (A   PERCY JONES   B   (A    BERNIE FROST  V  (A
PHIL COLLINS       D    (A   MORRIS PERT  PERC    (A   BARRY MORGAN  D   (B
```

LANDSCAPE   L16

```
JOHN WALTERS       WIND K(A        (A) LANDSCAPE                   1979 RCA     UK             PL 25248
RICHARD BURGESS    D    (A         (B) FROM THE TEAROOMS OF MARS   1981 RCA     UK
ANDY(CAPT WHORLIX)PASK B(A
CHRIS HEATON       K    (A   PETER THOMAS TROM    (A
```

RONNIE LANE & SLIM CHANCE   L16A

```
RONNIE LANE        V B G(ALL       (A) ANYMORE FOR ANYMORE        1974 GM GML 1017 US +   UK 1024
CHARLIE HART       VLN K(BC         (B) RONNIE LANE'S SLIM CHANCE  1975 ISLAND UK ILPS 9321 US A&M 3638
BRIAN BELSHAW      B    (BC         (C) ONE FOR THE ROAD           1976 ISLAND UK ILPS 9366
COLIN DAVY         D    (C          (D) SEE ME                     1979 GEM              UK GEM107
STEVE SIMPSON      G K  (BC
RUAN O'LOCHLAINN   SAX  (B   KEVIN WESTLAKE   G   (A   KEN SLAVEN   FDL  (A   GLEN LEFLEUR  D  (B
BENNY GALLAGHER G B ACC(A   BILLY LIVSEY     K   (A   THE TANNERS  V    (A   BRUCE ROWLAND D  (A
GRAHAM LYLE G BAN MAND (A   STEVE BINGHAM    B   (A   JIMMY JEWELL SAX  (A
```

PETER LANG   L16B

```
PETER LANG         G V  (AB        (A) LYCURGUS                   19   FLYING FISH  US    FF014
                                   (B) THE THING AT THE NURSERY WINDOW  19  TAKOMA  US    1034
```

CLIVE LANGER & THE BOXES   L16C

```
CLIVE LANGER       G V  (A         (A) I WANT THE WHOLE WORLD     1978 RADAR     UK        RDR 2
BUDGIE             B D  (A         (B) SPLASH                     1980 F BEAT    UK        XXLP2
STEVE ALLEN        V    (AB
BETTE BRIGHT       V    (AB  BEN BARSON     K   (AB   JAMES ELLER  B   (B   MARTIN HUGHES D  (B
RUMOUR BRASS       HRNS (B
```

HIP LANKCHAN   L16D

```
HIP LANKCHAN       G V  (A         (A) I AM ON MY WAY            197  MCM        FR        900299
JIMMIE MILLER      G    (A
ERNEST GATEWOOD    B    (A   TYRONE CENTURY   D   (A
```

LARD FREE   L17

```
GILBERT ARTMAN     D K  (ABC       (A) LARD FREE                 1973 VAMP      FR    VP 59500
PHILIPPE BOLLIET   SAX  (A         (B) I'M AROUND ABOUT MIDNIGHT 1975 VAMP      FR    VP 59502
FRANCOIS MATIVET   G    (A         (C) LARD FREE                 1977 COBRA     FR       37007
HERVE EYHANI       B SYN(A
RICHARD PINHAS     G SYN(A   JEAN JACQUES MIETTE B (A  ALAIN AUDAT  SYN SAX(B  ANTOINE DUVERNET  WIND(B
XAVIER BAULLERET   G    (C   YVES LANES     SYN (C    JEAN PIERRE THIRAUT CLAR (C
```

NEIL LARSEN   L18

```
NEIL LARSEN        K    (A         (A) JUNGLE FEVER              1978 HORIZON   UK   AMLJ 733
BUZZ FEITEN        G    (A         (B) HIGH GEAR                 1979 HORIZON   US   SP  3117
LARRY WILLIAMS     WIND (A
RALPH MACDONALD    PERC (A   JERRY HEY       HRNS (A   WILLIE WEEKS  B  (A   MICHAEL BRECKER  HRNS(A
ANDY NEWMARK       D    (A
```

LARSEN/ FEITEN BAND   L18A

```
NEIL LARSEN        K    (A         (A) LARSEN/FEITEN BAND        1980 WB        US   BSK 3468
BUZZ FEITEN        G    (A
WILLIE WEEKS       B    (A   KIM HUTCHCROFT  SAX  (A   LENNY CASTRO  V PERC(A  ART RODRIGUEZ D  (A
BILL REICHENBACH   HRNS (A   LARRY WILLIAMS  SAX  (A
```

NICOLETTE LARSON   L19

```
NICOLETTE LARSON V G PERC(AB       (A) NICOLETTE               1978 WB    US BSK 3243 UK  K56569
BILL PAYNE         K    (A         (B) IN THE NICK OF TIME     1979 WB    US BSK 3370 UK  K56750
JAMES BURTON       G    (A         (C) RADIOLAND               19    US
BOB GLAUB          B    (A
PAUL BARRERE       G    (A   HERB PEDERSEN   V G  (A   RICK SCHLOSSER  D  (A   MARK JORDAN   K  (A
DAVID KALISH       G    (A   ANDREW LOVE     SAX  (A   PLAS JOHNSON   FLT (A   TED TEMPLEMAN V  (A
JIM HORN           HRNS (A   CHUCK FINDLEY   HRNS (A   STEVE MADAIO  HRNS (A   VALERIE CARTER V  (A
MIKE McDONALD      V    (A   LINDA RONSTADT  V    (A   KLAUS VOORMANN  B  (A   FRED TACKETT  G  (A
ALBERT LEE         MAND (A   PATRICK SIMMONS G    (A
```

LA SEINE   L20

```
TOM SEUFERT        G V  (A         (A) LIKE THE RIVER          1976 ARIOLA  UK AAA752  US  50008
DON WHALEY         B    (A
TRIS IMBODEN       D    (A   STEVE HAGUE     K    (A   BOB EASTON  G SYN (A   MARK CREAMER  V  (A
LAURA CREAMER      V    (A
```

LASO   L21

```
FRANK OWENS        K    (A         (A) LASO                    1977 MCA           UK  MCF 2804
GORDON EDWARDS     B    (A
ALLEN SCHWARZBERG  D    (A   GEORGE DEVENS  VIBES(A   EUGENE BIANCO  HARP (A   GERRY CHAMBERLAIN TROM(A
RAY CADLE          G    )A   JOE BATAAN     PNO  (A   ADRIAN ALBERT   V   (A   MAERETHA STEWART  V  (A
HILDA HARRIS       V    (A   JIM MAELEN  CONGA    (A   PETER QUINTERO CONGA(A   BOB PORCELLI  SAX   (A
LOU MARINI         WIND (A   LEW SOLOFF     TPT  (A   VICTOR PAZ     TPT  (A   BARRY ROGERS  TROM  (A
LOUIE DEVIS        B    (A   JULIAN LLANOS   V   (A   JOCELYN SHAW    V   (A   BIG B         V     (A
```

LAST   L21A

```
JOE NOLIE          G V  (A         (A) L A EXPLOSION           1979 LONDON           SHZ 8540
MIKE NOLTE         V    (A
DAVID NOLTE        B V  (A   VITUS MATARE  K FLT (A   JACK REYNOLDS  D   (A
```

THE LAST POETS   L22

```
ALAFIA PUDIM       V    (          THE LAST POETS             1970 DOUGLAS              US  30811
OMAR BEN HASSEN    V    (          THIS IS MADNESS            1971 DOUGLAS  UK 69012   US  30583
NILIJAH            PERC (          CHASTISEMENT               1972 BLUE THUMB
ABIO DUN OYEWOLE   V    (          RIGHT ON                  19   JUGGERNAUT           US  8802
SULIAMAN EL HADI   V    (          THE REVOLUTION WILL NOT BE TELEVISED  197
                                   JAZZOETRY                  197
                                   DELIGHTS OF THE GARDEN    19   CASABLANCA           US  7501
```

L22A — LAST WORDS

JOHNNY IOMBARDO	V	(A	(A) LAST WORDS	1968	ATCO	US	SD 33235
MIKE BYRNES	G	(A					
STEVE SECHAK	K	(A	RICKY COOK	D	(A

L23 — LATE SHOW

BILL CLIFT	G V	(A	(A) SNAP	1979	DECCA	UK	TXS134
DAVE HEAD	G V	(A					
MIKE JELLY	G V VLN	(A	TIM JOYCE	B V	(A	NIX F PLONK	K	(A	BRUISER CLIVE	(A
DON WELLER	SAX	(A	GEORGE CHISHOLM	TPT	(A	MALCOLM GRIFFITHS TROM	(A	ALAN PRICE	G	(

L24 — LATIMORE

BENNY LATIMORE	PNO	(ABC	(A) LATIMORE	1974	PRESIDENT	UK 1058	GLADES	US6502
FREDDIE SCOTT	D	(A	(B) IT AIN'T WHERE YOU BEEN	1977	TK	UK XL14034	GLADES	US7509
VAN OLANDER	D	(A	(C) LATIMORE 3	1977	PRESIDENT	UK 1065	GLADES	US7505
BOBBY RADELOFF	D	(A	(D) MORE MORE MORE	19			GLADES	US6503
BETTY WRIGHT	V	(A	(E) DIG A LITTLE DEEPER	19			GLADES	US7515
MIKE LEWIS	FLT	(A						
RON BOGDON	B	(A	GWEN McCRAE	V	(A	AL KOOPER	K	(A	JOEY MURCIA	G	(A
GEORGE McCRAE	V	(A						

L24A — LAUGHING DOGS

MOE POTTS	D V	(A	(A) LAUGHING DOGS	1979	CBS	UK	83807
RONNIE CARLE	B HCA V	(A					
CARTER CATHCART	K G V	(A	JAMES LEONARD	G V	(A

L24B — LAVA

THOMAS KARRENBACH	K V	(A	(A) TEARS ARE GOING HOME	1973	BRAIN		1031
STEFAN OSTERTAG	G V	(A					
JURGEN KRAAZ	G B FLT B K	(A	CHRISTIAN OSTERTAG B	(A	ARCHER WEAVER	D HCA V	(A	PETER MOSES	PERC	(A

L25 — LAVENDER HILL MOB

NICKY CRIGENO	V B	(A	(A) LAVENDER HILL MOB	1977	UA		UAS 30043
RONNY JONES	G V	(A					
GERRY HARDY	V WIND	(A	HECTOR JACOB	G V	(A	CHUCK CHANDLER	K V	(A	VITO FIORY	D	(A

L26 — LAW

TOM POOL	D	(A	(A) LAW	1975	GRC	US		GA 10017
RONNIE LEE CUNNINGHAM	K V	(AB	(B) BREAKIN' IT	1977	MCA	US 2240	UK	2785
STEVE ACKER	G V	(AB	(C) HOLD ON TO IT	19	MCA	US 2306		
JOHN McIVERS	B	(AB						
JOE LALA	PERC	(A	ALBHY GALUTEN	SYN	(A	MEMPHIS HRNS		(A	STEVE LAWRENCE D V	(B
ROY KENNER	V	(B	JOEY MURCIA	G	(B	MIAMI HRNS		(B	BILL COLANTONE PERC	(B
FLACO PADRON	PERC	(B						

L26A — DOMINIQUE LAWARLEE

DOMINIQUE LAWARLEE	K	(ALL	(A) INFINITUDES	197	WALRUS		WLS 001
MARC HOLLANDER	PNO	(C	(B) LE CHOIX DU TITRE EST UN FAUX	1977	WALRUS		WLS 003
CHARLES LOOS	PNO	(C	(C) TRACES	1978	WALRUS		WLS 004
			(D) BRINS D'HERBE	1978	WALRUS		WLS 005
			(E) VIS A VIS	1979	WALRUS		WLS 006

L26B — CLAIRE LAWRENCE

CLAIRE LAWRENCE	V WIND	(A	(A) LEAVING YOU FREE	1973	HAIDA	CAN	HL 5103
JIM GORDON	D	(A					
MAX BENNETT	B	(A	LARRY CARLTON	G	(A	DEAN PARKS	G	(A	BRETT WADE	G	(A
CLARENCE McDONALD	PNO	(A	RON TUTT	D	(A	LOUIS SHELTON	G	(A	KATHY STACK	V	(A
STEPHANIE SPRUILL	V	(A	BEVERLEY JACKSON	V	(A	LISA ROBERTS	V	(A	STRING SECTION		(A

L27 — BILLY LAWRIE

BILLY LAWRIE	V	(A	(A) SHIP IMAGINATION	1973	RCA	UK	SF 8395
RONNIE LEAHY	K	(A					
JIMMY McCULLOCH	G	(A	COLIN ALLEN	D	(A	TIM RENWICK	G	(A	STEVE THOMPSON B	(A
WILLIE WILSON	D	(A	BRUCE THOMAS	B	(A	GARY OSBORNE	G V	(A	PAUL VIGRASS	V	(A
ROGER BALL	HRNS	(A	MALCOLM DUNCAN	HRNS	(A	RAY COOPER	PERC	(A	LULU	V	(A
LIZA STRIKE	V	(A	MAGGIE BELL	V	(A	KIM GARDNER	B	(A	KENNY JONES	D	(A
BARRY CLARKE	G	(A	LUIS JARDIM	PERC	(A	JUANITA FRANKLIN V	(A	PETER WOOD	K	(A
LES HARVEY	G	(A	JOHN COLEMAN	PNO	(A	JO PARTRIDGE	G	(A

L28 — RONNIE LAWS

RONNIE LAWS	V	(ALL	(A) PRESSURE SENSITIVE	1975	BLUENOTE 452	UK 76	UAG20002
MARLOW THE MAGICIAN	G	(B	(B) FEVER	1976	UA		UAG20007
NATHANIEL PHILLIPS	B	(BD	(C) FLAME	1978	UA		UAG30204
BRUCE CARTER	D	(B	(D) EVERY GENERATION	1980	LIBERTY	US LT 1001	UA UAG30289
DONALD HEPBURN	K	(B					
MICHAEL HEPBURN	K	(B	BRUCE SMITH	PERC	(B	BOBBY LYLE	K	(BD	STEVE GUITIERREZ	D	(B
WILTON FELDER	B	(B	TONY BEN	CONGA	(B	STRING SECTION		(BD	ELOISE LAWS	V	(D
ALEXANDRA BROWN	V	(D	JEAN THOMPSON	V	(D	MIKE HOWARD	V	(D	DOROTHY ASHBY	HARP	(D
PAT KELLY	G	(D	BARNABY FINCH	SYN	(D	LARRY DUNN		(CD	RONNIE FOSTER		(D
HUBERT LAWS		(D	PATRICE RUSHEN		(D	JOE SAMPLE	K	(D	PHILIP BAILEY		(C
ROLAND BAUTISTA		(C						

L28A — LAZARUS

SHELBY SINGLETON		(A	LAZARUS	1970	AMAZON	US	AM 1001
THOMAS BOMBACI		(A					
RAYMOND CICHON		(A	RONALD STABLINI		(A	TONY BERTOLLOTTI	(	STEVE McNICOL		(A

L29 — KEN LAZARUS

KEN LAZARUS	V	(ALL	REGGAE SCORCHERS	1970	LONDON	UK	ZGJ102
			REGGAE GREAT HITS VOL1	1970	LONDON	UK	ZGJ107
			REGGAE GREAT HITS VOL 2	1970	LONDON	UK	ZGJ108

L30 — LAZY RACER

TIM RENWICK	G V	(AB	(A) LAZY RACER	1979	A&M	UK	AMLH64768
HENRY SPINETTI	D	(AB	(B) FORMULA 2	1980	A&M	UK	AMLH64808
DAVE MARKEE	B	(A					
TIM GORMAN	V K	(AB	BILL LAMB	G V	(AB	KELLY HARLAND	V	(AB	PAT DONALDSON	D	(B

L31 — BERNIE LEADON & MICHAEL GEORGIADES

BERNIE LEADON	G V BAN	(A	(A) NATURAL PROGRESSION	1977	ASYLUM	US 7E1107	UK K53063
MICHAEL GEORGIADES	G V	(A					
BRYAN GAROFALO	B	(A	DAVID KEMPER	D	(A	STEVE GOLDSTEIN	K	(A

```
                          LEAFHOUND                                                      L32
                    (A) GROWERS OF MUSHROOMS          1971  DECCA         UK   SKLR 5094
                          LEAGUE OF GENTLEMEN                                             L32A
ROBERT FRIPP     G  (A    (A) LEAGUE OF GENTLEMEN     1981  EG    UK
BARRY ANDREWS    K  (A
JOHNNY TOOBAD    D  (A   SARAH LEE    B  (A
                          LEATHER COATED MINDS                                            L33
J J CALE         G  (A    (A) TRIP DOWN SUNSET STRIP  19   FONTANA UK 5412 VIVA US 36003
                          LEATHER NUN                                                    L33A
                    (A) SLOW DEATH (EP)               19   INDUSTRIAL          IR 0006
                          LEAVES                                                         L34
JIM PONS         (        (A) HEY JOE                 1966  MIRA       US           3005
BILL RINEHART    (A       (B) ALL THE GOOD THAT'S HAPPENING 1967 CAPITOL US     ST 2638
JOHN BECK        (
BOBBY ARLIN      (      TOM RAY       (    ROBERT REINER       (
                          LENNIE LEBLANC                                                 L34A
LENNIE LEBLANC   G V (A   (A) HOUND DOG MAN           1977  BIG TREE      US      76003
                          LEBLANC & CARR                                                 L35
LENNIE LEBLANC   G V (A   (A) MIDNIGHT LIGHT          1978  BIG TREE US 89521 UK K50474
PETE CARR        G V (A
BUTCH LEADFORD   B  (A   BOB WRAY      B  (A    RANDY McCORMICK  K  (A    TIM HENSON     K (A
CLAYTON IVEY     K  (A   ROBERT BYRNE  G  (A
                          LED ZEPPELIN                                                   L36
JIMMY PAGE       G  (ALL  (A) LED ZEPPELIN          1968 ATLANTIC US  8216  UK 588171
ROBERT PLANT     V HCA(ALL (A) LED ZEPPELIN         1971 ATLANTIC US 19126  UK K40031
JOHN BONHAM      D  (ALL  (B) LED ZEPPELIN 2        1969 ATLANTIC US  8236  UK 588198
JOHN PAUL JONES  B K (ALL (B) LED ZEPPELIN 2        1971 ATLANTIC US 19127  UK K40037
WITH                     (C) LED ZEPPELIN 3         1970 ATLANTIC US  7201  UK2401002
VIRAM JASANI     TABLAS(A (C) LED ZEPPELIN 3        1971 ATLANTIC US 19128  UK K50002
SANDY DENNY      V  (D    (D) LED ZEPPELIN 4        1971 ATLANTIC US 7203   UK2401012
                         (D) LED ZEPPELIN 4         1971 ATLANTIC        UK K50008
                         (E) HOUSES OF THE HOLY     1973 ATLANTIC US  7255  UK K50014
                         (F) PHYSICAL GRAFFITI      1975 SWANSONG US SS2 200 UK K89400
                         (G) PRESENCE               1976 ATCO     US  7255
                         (G) PRESENCE               1976 SWANSONG US SS 8416 UK K59402
                         (H) THE SONG REMAINS THE SAME 1976 SWANSONG US SS2 201 UK K89402
                         (I) LIVE                   197  JOKER     ITALY       SM3721
                         (J) IN THROUGH THE OUT DOOR 1979 SWANSONG        UK K59410
                          ALBERT LEE                                                     L36A
ALBERT LEE   V G K MAND(A  (A) HIDING               1979  A&M            UK    AMLH64750
JOHN WARE        D  (A
EMORY GORDY      B  (A   HANK DEVITO STEEL V (A  GLEN D HARDIN   PNO  (A   RICKY SKAGGS   V FDL(A
EMMYLOU HARRIS   V  (A   MICKEY RAPHAEL   HCA (A  BRIAN AHERN    G    (A   DON EVERLY     V    (A
PETE GAVIN       D  (A   DAVE PEACOCK     B   (A  CHAS HODGES    PNO  (A   BRUCE GARY     D    (A
BUDDY EMMONS     STEEL(A GERRY CONWAY     D   (A  PAT DONALDSON  B    (A   JERRY JUMONVILLE HRNS(A
RODNEY CROWELL   V  (A   DONIVAN COWART   V   (A
                          ALVIN LEE                                                      L37
ALVIN LEE        G V (ALL  (A) ROAD TO FREEDOM       1973 CHRYSALIS UK 1054 US CBS 32729
MYLON LEFEVRE  G V PERC(A  (B) IN FLIGHT       (DBL) 1974 CHRYSALIS UK 1069 US CBS 33187
STEVE WINWOOD    K  (A    (C) PUMP IRON            1975 CHRYSALIS UK 1094 US CBS 33796
JIM CAPALDI      D  (A    (D) LET IT ROCK          1978 CHRYSALIS UK 1190
REBOP BAAH       PERC(A   (E) FREE FALL            1980 AVATAR    UK AALP5002
MIKE PATTO       V  (A
TIM HINKLEY      K  (ABC GEORGE HARRISON  G  (A   RON WOOD       G B D(A   MICK FLEETWOOD  G (A
ANDY STEIN       FDL (A  IAN WALLACE      D  (ABC BOBBY BLACK  STEEL(A    BOZ BURRELL     B (AC
MEL COLLINS      SAX (A  ALAN SPENNER     B  (B   NEIL HUBBARD   G   (B    DYAN BIRCH      V (B
FRANK COLLINS    V   (B  PADDY McHUGH     V  (B   BRYSON GRAHAM  D   (C    JACK LANCASTER HRNS (C
HAROLD BURGON    K   (C  RONNIE LEAHY     K  (C   STEVE THOMPSON B   (C    BROTHER JAMES  PERC(C
RON BERG         D   (C  ANDY PYLE        B  (C   COLIN GIBSON   B   (C    STEVE GOULD    G V (E
MICK FEAT        B V (E  TOM COMPTON  D PERC (E   DEREK AUSTIN   K   (E    AL KOOPER      ORG (E
RAPHAEL RAVENSCROFT SAX(E PETER THOMS     TROM (E
                          ARTHUR LEE                                                     L38
ARTHUR LEE       G V (A   (A) VINDICATOR            1972  A&M US 4356   UK   AMLS64356
DON PONCHER      D  (A
CHARLES KARP     G  (A   DAVID HULL      B  (A   CRAIG TARWATER  G  (A    FRANK FAYAD     B (A
CLARENCE McDONALD K  (A
                          BRENDA LEE                                                     L39
BRENDA LEE       1960 DECCA   US   74039   BY REQUEST          1964 DECCA    US    74509
GRANDMA WHAT GREAT SONGS  BRUNSWICK UK LAT  8319   "       "   1964 BRUNSWICK UK STA 8576
 "    "     "     "       DECCA     US   78873   MERRY CHRISTMAS 1964 DECCA   US   74583
MISS DYNAMITE    196  BRUNSWICK UK LAT 8347   "       "        1964 BRUNSWICK UK STA 8590
LOVE YOU         196  ACE OF HEARTS UK AH 59  TOP TEEN HITS    1965 DECCA    US   74626
THIS IS BRENDA LEE 1961 BRUNSWICK UK LAT 8360  "       "       1965 BRUNSWICK UK STA 8603
 "       "       1961 DECCA    US   74082   VERSATILE          1965 DECCA    US   74661
EMMOTIONS        1961 DECCA    US   74104   "       "          1965 BRUNSWICK UK STA 8614
 "       "       1961 BRUNSWICK UK LAT 8376  TOO MANY RIVERS   1965 DECCA    US   74684
 "       "       1961 BRUNSWICK UK STA 3044  "       "         1965 BRUNSWICK UK STA 8622
ALL THE WAY      1961 DECCA    US   74176   BYE BYE BLUES      1966 DECCA    US   74755
 "       "       1961 BRUNSWICK UK LAT 8383  "       "         1966 BRUNSWICK UK STA 8649
 "       "       1961 BRUNSWICK UK STA 3048  10 GOLDEN YEARS   1966 DECCA    US   74757
SINCERELY        1961 DECCA    US   74216   "       "          19   MCA      US   107
 "       "       1961 BRUNSWICK UK LAT 8396  COMING ON STONG   1967 DECCA    US   74825
 "       "       1961 BRUNSWICK UK STA 3056  REFLECTIONS IN BLUE 1967 DECCA  US   74941
 "       "       197  MCA      US   477     "       "    "     19   MCA      UK MUPS 306
THAT'S ALL       1962 DECCA    US   74326   CALL ME BRENDA     196  MCA      UK MUPS 321
 "       "       1962 BRUNSWICK US   8516   GOOD LIFE          196  MCA      UK MUPS 322
ALL ALONE AM I   1962 DECCA    US   74370   HERE'S BRENDA LEE  1967 VOCALION US VL 7 3795
 "       "       1962 BRUNSWICK UK STA 8530 LET IT BE ME       19   VOCALION US VL 7 3890
LET ME SING      1964 DECCA    US   74439   "       "    "     19   CORAL    US CB 20044
 "       "       1964 BRUNSWICK UK STA 8548 FOR THE FIRST TIME 1968 MCA      UK MUPS 332
```

[243]

L39 (CONTINUED)

BRENDA LEE

FOR THE FIRST TIME	196	DECCA	US		74955	NEW SUNRISE	1974	MCA	US		373
JOHNNY ONE TIME	1969	DECCA	US		75111	" "	1974	MCA	UK	MCF	2527
" " "	1970	MCA	UK	MUPS	396	NOW	1975	MCA	US		433
" " "	1974	MCA	UK	MCF	2633	"	1975	MCA	UK	MCF	2593
MEMPHIS PORTRAIT	1970	DECCA	US		75232	SINCERELY	1975	MCA	US		477
" " "	1971	MCA	UK	MUPS	423	" "	1975	MCA	UK	MCF	2709
" " "	1974	MCA	UK	MCF	2519	FUNNY HOW TIME SLIPS	1975	SOUNDS SUPERB	UK		90067
A WHOLE LOTTA	1972	MCA	UK	MUPS	460	LITTLE MISS DYNAMITE	1976	MCA	UK	MCF	2729
" "	1974	MCA	UK	MCF	2660	L A SESSION	1977	MCA	UK	MCF	2783
BRENDA	197	MCA	US		305	" "	1977	MCA	US		2233
"	1973	MCA	UK	MUPS	485	LEGENDS OF ROCK (DBL)	19	CORAL	US		61141/2
"	1974	MCA	UK	MCF	2507	MISS DYNAMITE	1979	MCA	FR		414030
BRENDA LEE STORY	1974	MCA	UK	MCDW	428	LITTLE MISS DYNAMITE	1980	WARWICK	WW		5083
" " "	197	DECCA	US		74012						

L39A

BYRON LEE & THE DRAGONAIRES

BYRON LEE (ALL

SOUNDS OF JAMAICA	19	TOWER HALL	US	LP 006
REGGAE	19	TROJAN		TRLS 18
REGGAE SPLASH DOWN	19	TROJAN		TRL 28
REGGAE HOT COOL EASY	19	TROJAN		TRLS 40
REGGAE BLASH OFF	19	TROJAN		TBL 110
REGGAE FEVER	1974	POLYDOR		2460 229
DISCO REGGAE	1975	MERCURY	US	SRMI 1063
MIDAS TOUCH	1975	DRAGON		DRLS 5006
& MIGHTY SPARROW	1976	DYNAMIC		DYLP 3002
THIS IS CARNIVAL	1976	DYNAMIC		DYLP 3006
REGGAE INTERNATIONAL	1976	DYNAMIC		DYLP 3008
ART OF MAS	1977	DYNAMIC		DYLS 1002
BYRON LEE & THE DRAGONAIRES	19	JAD	US	JAS 1004
MORE CARNIVAL	1978	DYNAMIC		DYLP 3012
CARNIVAL EXPERIENCE	1979	DYNAMIC		DYLP 3014
JAMAICA'S GOLDEN HITS VOL 1	1979	STATE		ETMP 14
JAMAICA'S GOLDEN HITS VOL 2	1979	STATE		ETMP 17
DANCE THE SKY	19	B M N		BLP 004

L40

FREDDY FINGERS LEE

FREDDY FINGERS LEE (AB

(A) FREDDY FINGERS LEE	1978	CHARLY		CR 30160
(B) OL' ONE EYE IS BACK	1979	CHARLY		CR 30178

L41

JOHN LEE & GERRY BROWN

JOHN LEE	K B PERC	(ABC
GERRY BROWN	D PERC	(ABC
PHILIP CATHERINE	G	(B
EEF ALBERS	G	(BC
ERIC TAGG	K	(B
WAH WAH WATSON	G	(B
BOBBY MALACH	SAX	(C
MTUME	V PERC	(A
DAVID SANBORN	SAX	(A
DONALD SMITH	V	(A
GARY BARTZ	SAX	(A

(A) STILL CAN'T SAY ENOUGH	1976	BLUENOTE	US	BNLA 701				
(B) MANGO SUNRISE	1976	BLUENOTE	US	BNLA 541	UK	20004		
(C) CHASER	1979	CBS	US	36212				

JASPER VANT HOF	K	(B	ROB FRANKEN	K	(AB	MIKE MANDEL	K	(B
DARRYL THOMPSON	G	(C	PALLE MIKKELBORG	TPT PERC	(C	KENNETH KNUDSEN	K	(C
REGGIE LUCAS	G	(A	RAY GOMEZ	G	(A	HUBERT EAVES	K	(A
TAWATHA AGEE	V	(A	RANDY BRECKER	HRNS	(A	MICHAEL BRECKER	SAX	(A
BARRY ROGERS	TROM	(A	HAROLD WILLIAMS	K	(A	IAN UNDERWOOD	SYN	(A
C P ALEXANDER	V	(A	JON FADDIS	TPT	(A	ERNIE WATTS	SAX	(A
RON CUBER	SAX	(A						

L42

RANDY LEE

RANDY LEE	V	(A
PETE DRAKE	STEEL	(A
LARRY SASSER	STEEL	(A
DON TWEEDY	HRNS	(A
KENNY BUTTREY	D	(A
LEA JANE BERINATI	V	(A
JACK SOLOMON	G	(A

(A) SOAKIN' WITH TEARS	1974	ELEKTRA	US	EKS 75081

JERRY CARRIGAN	D	(A	PIG ROBBINS	PNO	(A	JAMES M JOHNSON	G	(A
GEORGE CUNNINGHAM	HRNS	(A	WENDELLYN SUITS	V	(A	TOMMY COGBILL	B	(A
EARL BALL	PNO	(A	JIMMY COLVARD	G	(A	BOB PHILLIPS	HRNS	(A
GARY S PAXTON SINGERS		(A	HOYET HENRY	B	(A	KEN MALONE	D	(A
BILLY SANFORD	G	(A	LOUIS BROWN	HRNS	(A	SHARON VAUGHN	V	(A

L42A

LEE RIDERS

ROBERT LEE	G V	(A
MIKE O'CONNOR	K	(A
MATT PRESBY	G	(A

(A) LEE RIDERS	1972	UA		UAS 29312

MIKE REILLY	B V	(A	ROY OTEMRO	D PERC G	(A	B J COLE	STEEL	(A

L42B

THOMAS LEER & ROBERT RENTAL

THOMAS LEER	V SYN G	(A
ROBERT RENTAL	V G SYN B	(A

(A) THE BRIDGE	1979	INDUSTRIAL	UK	1R0007

L43

JOHN LEES

JOHN LEES		(A
SKIP ALLEN	D	(A
ROD ARGENT	K	(A
ERIC STEWART	G	(A
REX MORRISON	SAX	(A

(A) A MAJOR FANCY	1973	HARVEST	UK	SHVL 811
(A) A MAJOR FANCY	1977	HARVEST	RI UK	SHSM 2018

WALLY WALLER	B	(A	KEVIN GODLEY	(A	GORDON EDWARDS	PNO	(A

L44

MYLON LEFEVRE

MYLON LEFEVRE	G V	(ALL
PIERCE LEFEVRE		(CE
AUBURN BURRELL	G	(AB
ALVIN LEE	G V	(D
J P LAUZON	G	(B
MARTY SIMON	D	(B
LESLIE WEST	G	(B
DR JOHN	K	(B
TINA BLOUNT	V	(B
RENAY GARVIN	V	(B
PAT CUMMINGS	V	(B
MERRY CLAYTON	V	(B

(A) MYLON	1971	ATLANITC		2400 104
(A) MYLON	197	COTILLION	US	SD 9026
(B) OVER THE INFLUENCE	1972	CBS	US	31472
(C) PIERCE & MYLON LEFEVRE	1972	CANAAN	UK	CAS 9673
(D) ROAD TO FREEDOM	1973	CHRYSALIS	UK	CHR 1054
(E) LEFEVRES GREATEST HITS	197	STARDAY	US	SD 3006
(F) WEAK AT THE KNEES	19	WB	UK	K56407

TOM ROBB	B	(B	ALLEN TOUSSAINT	K	(B	BARRY BAILEY	G	(AB
LESTER LANGDALE	K	(B	RICHARD PENNIMAN	V	(B	STEVE SANDERS	V	(B
KIM VENABLE	D	(A	DEAN DAUGHTRY	K	(A	RON GRAYBEAL	B	(A
VANETTA FIELDS	V	(A	CLYDIE KING	V	(A	SHIRLEY MATTHEWS	V	(A

** FOR FULL LINE UP OF D SEE ALVIN LEE ENTRY

L45

LEFT BANKE

RICK BRAND	G BAN	(A
STEVE MARTIN	V	(AB
TOM FINN	B	(AB
MIKE BROWN	K	(A
GEORGE CAMERON	D	(AB

(A) WALK AWAY RENEE	1967	PHILIPS		SBL 7773
(A) WALK AWAY RENEE	1967	SMASH US (M)	27088	(S) 67088
(B) TOO	1969	SMASH US		(S) 67113

LEGEND

MICKEY JUPP	G K V(ALL	(A) LEGEND	1969	BELL	UK	SBLL	115
NIGEL DUNBAR	D (A	(A) LEGEND	1969	BELL	US		6027
STEVE GEARE	B V (A	(B) RED BOOT ALBUM	1971	VERTIGO	UK	6360 019
CHRIS EAST	G V (A	(C) MOONSHINE	1972	VERTIGO	UK	6360 063
MO WITHAM	G (BCD	(D) MICKEY JUPPS LEGEND (COMP)	1978	STIFF		GET2
JOHN BOBIN	B (BCD						
BILL FIFIELD	D (B	BOB CLOUTER	D (C	BARNEY JAMES	D (	TIM RENWICK	G (D
MICK MOODY	G (D	COLIN GIBSON	B (D	HENRY SPINETTI	D (D	JIMMY JEWELL	SAX (D
PETE SOLLEY	K (D	GARY BROOKER	PNO (D	CHRIS COPPING	B (D	B J WILSON	D (D
GLEN LEFLEUR	D (D						

LEGOVER

RAPHAEL RAVENSCROFT	WIND(A	(A) WAIT TILL NIGHTTIME	1978	SMACK	UK	SL1001
DAVID ULM	PERC V(A					
LINDSAY SCOTT	VLN V (A	SEAN BYRNE	G V (A	DAVE ROSE	K (A	MICKEY FEAT	B (A
DEREK AUSTIN	K (A	DELISLE HARPER	B (A	PHIL CHEN	B (A	THEODORE THUNDER	D(A
GLEN LEFLEUR	D (A	JOHN DENLITH	D V (A	BILL SKEAT	WIND (A	ALAN BOWN	TPT(A
GEORGE HOWDEN	TROM (A	MICK PACE	HCA	JOHN WELLS	V (A		

ANDY LEIGH

ANDY LEIGH	B V G K PERC(A	(A) MAGICIAN	1970	POLYDOR	UK	2343 034
BRYN HAWORTH	G (A	(A) MAGICIAN	197	SIRE	US	SES97025
KEVIN WESTLAKE	D V (A					
REG KING	K V(A	GORDON JACKSON SITAR(A	GARY FARR	HCA G(A	MIKE KELLIE	D (A
BRIAN GODDING	G (A	TONY PRIESTLAND WIND(A	GARY WRIGHT	K (A		

LEMON KITTENS

KARL BLAKE	G V (A	(A) WE BUY A HAMMER FOR DADDY	1980	UNITED DAIRIES UK	UD02
DANIELLE DAX	SAX (A				
MIKE BARNES	D (A	IAN STURGESS	B (A		

LEMON PIPERS

BILL ALBAUGH	D (A	(A) GREEN TAMBOURINE	1968	BUDDAH	UK	2349 006
REG NAVE	ORG (A	(B) JUNGLE MARMALADE	1968	BUDDAH	US	BDS 5016
BILL BARTLETT	G (A				
STEVE WALMSLEY	B (A	IVAN BROWNE G V (A			

CLAUDIA LENNEAR

CLAUDIA LENNEAR	V (A	(A) PHEW	1973 WB	US BS2654	UK	K 46204
RY COODER	G (A					
JOHN CRAVIOTTO	D (A	JIM DICKINSON	G K (A	CHARLES GRIMES	G (A	MILT HOLLAND	PERC (A
MIKE UTLEY	K (A	DICK HYDE	TROM (A	JIM KELTNER	D (A	RICK LITTLEFIELD	G (A
LEW McCREARY	TROM (A	SPOONER OLDHAM	K (A	WILLIAM SMITH	K (A	ARTHUR ADAMS	G (A
HAROLD BATTISTE JR	SAX (A	TESSIE CALDERON	CONGA(A	GENE CIPRIANO	SAX (A	MARLINE GREENE	G (A
PAUL HUBINON	TPT (A	WARREN LUENING JR	TPT (A	DON MENZA	WIND (A	CHUCK RAINEY	B (A
ALLEN TOUSSAINT	K V (A						

JOHN LENNON & YOKO ONO

JOHN LENNON	G K V(ALL	(A) TWO VIRGINS	1968 APPLE	US 5001	UK SAPCOR 2
YOKO ONO	V WIND	(B) LIFE WITH THE LIONS	1969 APPLE	US 3357	UK ZAPPLE 01
KLAUS VOORMANN	B (DEHJN	(C) WEDDING ALBUM	1969 APPLE	US 3361	UK SAPCOR 11
STEVE BRENDELL	B (H	(D) LIVE PEACE IN TORONTO	1969 APPLE	US 3362	UK CORE 2001
ALAN WHITE	D (EH	(E) PLASTIC ONO BAND	1970 APPLE	US 3372	UK SAPCOR 17
GEORGE HARRISON	G (HJ	(F) PLASTIC ONO BAND	1971 APPLE		UK PCS 7124
NICKY HOPKINS	K (HJN	(H) IMAGINE	1971 APPLE	US 3379	UK PAS 10004
TED TURNER	G (H	(J) SOMETIME IN NEW YORK CITY	1972 APPLE	US 3392	UK PCSP 7161
ROD LINTON	G (H	(K) MIND GAMES	1973 APPLE	US 3414	UK PCS 8165
JOHN TOUT	(H	(L) APPROXIMATELY INFINITE UNIVERSE	1973 APPLE		UK SAPD01001
JIM KELTNER	D (HJKN	(M) FEELING THE SPACE	1973 APPLE		UK SAPCOR 26
JOHN BARHAM	K (H	(N) WALLS & BRIDGES	1974 APPLE	US 3416	UK PCTC 253
JIM GORDON	D (H	(O) ROCK'ROLL	1975 APPLE	US 3419	UK PCS 7169
KING CURTIS	SAX (H	( ) SINGS ROCK'ROLL (ROOTS)	1975 ADAM	US 8018	
TOM EVANS	G (H	(P) SHAVED FISH	1975 APPLE	US 3421	UK PCS 7173
JOEY MOLLAND	G (H	(Q) DOUBLE FANTASY	1980 GEFFEN	US 2001	UK K 99131
MIKE PINDER	PERC (H				
KEN ASCHER	K (KN	GORDON EDWARDS	B (K	RICK MAROTTA	D (K	MICHAEL BRECKER	SAX(K
SNEAKY PETE	STEEL(K	JESSE ED DAVIS	G (N	ERIC CLAPTON	G (DJ	RINGO STARR	D (E
JULIAN LENNON	D (N	FRANK ZAPPA	G V (J	MARK VOLMAN	V (J	HOWARD KAYLAN	V (J
JIM PONS	B V (J	STAN BRONSTEIN	SAX (J	DON PRESTON	SYN (J	RICHARD FRANK	D (J
IAN UNDERWOOD	WIND K V(J	BOB HARRIS	K V (J	ADAM IPPOLITO	K (J	WAYNE GABRIEL	G (J
BOBBY KEYS	SAX (JN	GARY VAN SCYOC	B (J	AYNSLEY DUNBAR	D (J	BILLY PRESTON	K (J
KEITH MOON	D (J	JOHN LA BOSCA	PNO (J	ARTHUR JENKINS	PERC (N	EDDIE MOTTAU	G (N
ELTON JOHN	K V (N	LORI BURTON	V (N	MAY PANG	V (N	HARRY NILSSON	V (N
STEVE MADAIO	HRNS (N	HOWARD JOHNSON	HRNS (N	RON APREA	HRNS (N	FRANK VICARI	HRNS(N
DAVID SPINOZZA	G (K						

J B LENOIR

J B LENOIR	G V (ALL	(A) CRUSADE	1970 POLYDOR	UK	2482 014
ALEX ATKINS	SAX (BC	(B) NATURAL MAN	19 CHESS	US	410
ERNEST COTTON	SAX (BC	(C) BLUESMASTER	1976 CHESS		2A CMB208
JOE MONTGOMERY	PNO (BC	(D) ALABAMA BLUES	1979 L+R		42 001
LORENZO SMITH	SAX (BC	(E) DOWN IN MISSISSIPPI	1980 L+R		42 012
ALFRED WALLACE	D (BCF	(F) THE TAY MAY CLUB	1980 FLYRIGHT	UK	FLY 564
WILLIE DIXON	B (ABCDE					
FRED BELOW	D (DAE	LEROY FOSTER	G (BC	J T BROWN	SAX (F	AL GAVIN	D (BC
SUNNYLAND SLIM	PNO (BCF					

THE LENS

MIKE HOLMES	G			
BRIAN MARSHALL	D			
LESLIE MARSHALL	B	MARTIN ORFORD	K FLT	KEVIN SHARP	SYN

KLAUS LENZ BAND

KLAUS LENZ		(A) WIEGENLIED	1978	VINYL	UK	VS001

L 53 DEKE LEONARD

DEKE LEONARD	G K V(ALL	(A) ICEBERG				1973	UA	US LA150	UK	UAG 29464
MARTIN ACE	B	(AB	(B) KAMIKAZE				1974	UA		UK	UAG 29544
DAVE CHARLES	D V	(AB	(C) BEFORE YOUR VERY EYES				1981	UA		UK	UAG 30240
MICKY JONES	G	(AB	(A) ICEBERG(ROCKFILE)				1980	UA LIBERTY RI		UK	LBR 1042
PAUL BURTON	B V	(A									
TOMMY RILEY	D	(AB	BEAU ADAMS	D	(A	RICHARD TREECE	G	(A	DAVE PHILLIPS	VLN	(A
BRIAN BREEZE	G	(B	KEITH HODGE	D	(B	LINCOLN CARR	B G	(B	KEN WHALEY	B	(B
TERRY WILLIAMS	D	(B	BYRON BERLINE	FDL	(AB						

L54 LEOPARD

(A) KANSAS CITY SLICKERS	1978	MOON	IMP

L 54A LE ORME

ANTONIO PAGLIUCA	K	(ABCDEFGHJ	(A) COLLAGE	1971	PHILIPS	6323 007
ALDO TAGLIAPIETRA	B V G(ABCDEFGHJ		(B) UOMO DI PEZZA	1972	PHILIPS	6323 013
MIKI DEI ROSSI	PERC (ABCDEFGHJ		(C) FELONA & SERONA	1973	PHILIPS	6323 023
GERMANO SERAFIN	G	(GHJ	(C) FELONA & SERONA	1973	CHARISMA	CAS 1072
			(D) IN CONCERT	1974	PHILIPS	6323 028
			(E) CONTRAPPUNTI	1974	PHILIPS	6323 035
			(F) BEYOND LENG	1975	COSMOS	PILP 9008
			(G) SMOGMAGICA	1975	PHILIPS	6323 041
			(H) VERITA NASCOSTE	1976	PHILIPS	6323 045
			(J) STORIA O LEGGANDA	1977	PHILIPS	6323 052
			(K) FLORIAN	1979	PHILIPS	6323 086
			(L) PICCOLA RAPSODIE DELL APE	1980	PHILIPS	6323 102

L 55 LE PAMPLEMOUSSE

W MICHAEL LEWIS	K	(AB	(A) LE SPANK			1978	PYE		NSPL28244
LAURIN RINDER	D V	(AB	(B) SWEET MAGIC			1978	AV		AVLP 501
DAVE WILLIAMS	B	(AB							
GIL KARSON	B	(A	SHIRLEY JONES	V	(A	BRENDA JONES	V	(A	VALORIE JONES	V (A
DOUG RICHARDSON	SAX	(AB	HARRY KIM	TPT	(AB	JEFF SIGMAN	B	(B	DAVID STOUT	TROM (A
ALEX BROWN	V	(B	PATTI HALL	V	(B	MORTONETTE JENKINS	V	(B		

L 56 LE ROUX

(A) LOUISIANA'S LE ROUX	1978	CAPITOL	11734
(B) KEEP THE FIRE BURNIN'	1979	CAPITOL	11926

L 56A MIKE LESLEY

MIKE LESLEY		(A) MIKE LESLEY	1976	BIG TREE	89516

L 56B SUNNY LESLIE

SUNNY LESLIE	V	(A	(A) DOCTORS ORDERS	1974	CBS	80219

L 57 LES VARIATIONS

ROBERT FITOUSSI	G V	(A	(A) CAFE DE PARIS				1975	BUDDAH	BDS5625
JACQUES GRANDE	B	(A	( ) TAKE IT OR LEAVE IT				1974	PATHE FR	064 12628
JACKY BITTON	D PERC V	(A	(B) MOROCCAN ROLL				1974	BUDDAH	BDS5601
MARC TOBALY	G V	(A							
MAURICE MAIMOUN	VLN	(A	JIM MORRIS	K V	(A	PATRICK ADAMS	STRINGS	(A	JIM LAELEN	PERC (A
MICHAEL MONTGOMERY	K	(A	PHIL BATES		(A	GARY DORN			MICHAEL WENDROFF	V	(A

L 57A LEVY & THE RIPCORDS

LEVI DEXTER	V	(A	(A) CAT FIGHT (EP)			1980	GUN	
DANNY B HARVEY	G	(A						
JIMMY REED	G	(A	DAVE CURRY	B	(A	PAT BROWN	D	(A

L 58 LEVITT McCLURE

DAN LEVITT		(A	(A) LIVING IN THE COUNTRY	19	CASABLANCA	WS 1807
DOUG McCLURE		(A				

L 58A BARRINGTON LEVY

BARRINGTON LEVY		(A	(A) ENGLISHMAN			1979	GREENSLEEVES	GREL 9
ERROL 'FLABBA' HOLT	B	(C	(B) BOUNTY HUNTER			1979	JAH LIFE	
CARLTON 'SANTA' DAVIS	D(C		(C) ROBIN HOOD			1980	GREENSLEEVES	GREL 14
GLADSTONE ANDERSON	K	(C						
ANSEL COLLINS	K	(C	ERIC LAMONT	G	(C	EARL SMITH	G	(C	CHRISTOPHER BLAKE PERC(C
HEADLEY BENNETT	TROM (C		BOBBY ELLIS	TPT	(C			

L 59 JONA LEWIE

JONA LEWIE	K V D G PNO	(AB	(A) ON THE OTHER HAND THERE'S A FIST	1978	STIFF	UK	SEEZ 8
MALCOLM MORTIMER	D	(A	(B) ALIAS JONA LEWIE			1980	SONET	UK	SNTF 794
CLIVE CHAPPEL	G B	(A						
TIM BRANSTON	G	(A	MALCOLM HINE	G	(A	JOHN RANDALL	PERC (A	KEITH TRUSSELL PERC (A
ROB CAROL	D	(A	MICK SMYTHE	D	(A	KEN BUTCHER	SAX (A	HELEN ROBINSON V (A
CATHY CLELAND	V	(A	DENNIS BOVELL	V	(A	DICK HANSON	TPT (A	JOHN EARLE SAX (A
JOHN STONE	PNO	(A	MIKE DAY	V	(A	DORRIS HENDERSON	V (A	

L 60 DAVE LEWIS

DAVE LEWIS	G K	(ABC	(A) FROM TIME TO TIME	1976	POLYDOR	UK	2383 420
PRESTON HEYMAN	D	(B	(B) A COLLECTION OF HIS SHORT DREAMS	1978	POLYDOR	UK	2383 522
FELIX KRISH	B	(B	(C) THE LATE SHOW	1978	POLYDOR	UK	2383 493
STEVE BRANTLEY	B V PERC(B						
BRUCE DEES	G V	(B	JAMIE BRANTLEY	G	(B	ANDY McMAHON	K V	(B	MAGGIE RYDER	V (B

L 61 FURRY LEWIS

FURRY LEWIS	G V	PRESENTING THE COUNTRY BLUES	1969	BLUE HORIZON		763228
		IN MEMPHIS	1970	MATCHBOX	SDR	190
		FURRY LEWIS	1971	XTRA		XTRA 1116
		FABULOUS FURRY LEWIS	19	SOUTHLAND	US	3
		FURRY LEWIS BAND	19	FOLKWAYS		3823
		BEALE STREET BLUES	19	BARCLAY	FR	920 352
		FOURTH & BEALE	19	BARCLAY	FR	80602
		& FRED McDOWELL	19	BIOGRAPH		BLP12017
		IN HIS PRIME	19	YAZOO		L 1050
		BLUES MASTERS VOL 5	19	BLUE HORIZON	US	BM 4605
		HOUSE OF BLUES VOL 2	19	BLUE STAR	FR	80 602
		ON THE ROAD AGAIN	19	ADELPHI		1007
		BACK ON MY FEET AGAIN	19	PRESTIGE	US	7810
		SHAKE 'EM ON DOWN	19	FANTASY		24703
		LIVE AT THE GAS LIGHT	19	AMPEX		A10140

HUEY LEWIS & THE NEWS

HUEY LEWIS	V (A	(A) HUEY LEWIS & THE NEWS	1980	CHRYSALIS		CHR 1292	
CHRIS HAYES	G V (A						
SEAN HOPPER	K V (A	MARIO CIPOLLINA	B (A	BILL GIBSON	D V (A	JOHNNY COLLA	G SAX V(A

LEW LEWIS & REFORMER

LEW LEWIS	V HCA(A	(A) SAVE THE WAIL	1979	STIFF	UK	SEEZ 16	
PETE ZEAR	G (1	(1) 1977 LIVE (2) 1979 REFORMER					
LEE GREEN	G (1						
JOHNNY OCEAN	B (1	BOB CLOUTER	D (1	JOHNNY SQUIRREL	B (2A	RICK TAYLOR	G (2A
BUZZ BARWELL	D (2A	GAVIN POVEY	PNO	(A			

LINDA LEWIS

LINDA LEWIS	V G (ALL	(A) SAY NO MORE	1971	REPRISE	UK	K44130
CHRIS SPEDDING	G (A	(B) LARK**	1972	REPRISE	UK	K44208
RAY COOPER	PERC (A	(C) FATHOMS DEEP	1973	RAFT	UK	RA 48501
SHAWN PHILLIPS	G (A	(D) NOT A LITTLE GIRL ANYMORE	1975	ARISTA US 4047 UK ARTY		109
IAN McDONALD	FLT (A	(E) WOMAN OVERBOARD	1977	ARISTA	UK	SPARTY1003
MIKE EGAN	G (A	( ) HEART STRINGS	197	REPRISE US 2192		
SKAILA KANGA	HARP (A	(F) HACIENDA VIEW	1970	ARIOLA	UK	ARL 5033
FIACHRA TRENCH	K (A	(1) 1975 OCT GIG	**TWO VERSIONS WITH SLIGHTLY DIFFERENT TRACKS			
LOUIS CENNAMO	B (A					

TONY CAMPO	B (A	GEORGE FORD	B (A	TERRY COX	D (A	PETE GAVIN	D (A
JIMMY HOROWITZ	K (A	JIM CREGAN	G V (BCDE1	EMILE LATIMER	PERC (B	PAT DONALDSON	B (B
GERRY CONWAY	D (BD	JEAN ROUSSEL	K (BDE	ERIC OXENDINE	B (B	POLI PALMER FLT VIBES(BC	
PAUL WILLIAMS	G (B	MICK EVE	SAX (BC	BOB TENCH	G (C	MAX MIDDLETON	K (CDE
CLIVE CHAMAN	B (CD	CONRAD ISADORE	D (C	ROBERT AHWAI	G (CD	PHIL CHEN	B (CDE1
RICHARD BAILEY	D (CDE	ALAN SHARPE	PERC (C	DANNY THOMPSON	B (C	LARRY STEELE	PERC(C
STEVE GREGORY	WIND K(CDE1	RON CARTHY	TPT (C	CHRIS MERCER	SAX (C	ANNA PEACOCK	V (DE
DEREK SMITH	K (DE	JEFF MIRANOV	G (DE	JERRY FRIEDMAN	G (DE	LANCE QUINN	G (DE
BOB BABITT	B (DE	PHIL KRAUS	PERC (DE	TED SOMMERS	PERC (DE	JACK JENNINGS	PERC(DE
CARLOS MARTIN	PERC (DE	DUNCAN McKAY	K (D	CAPABILITY BROWN	V (D	TOWER OF POWER HRNS(D	
DOMINO	V (D1	DARRYL LEE QUE	PERC (DE1	LENNY PICKETT	FLT (D	BERNIE HOLLAND G (D	
LOWELL GEORGE	G (D	LISA STRIKE	V (DE	SNOWY WHITE	B (DE	GEOFF SEOPARDI	D (1
DEREK AUSTIN	K (E1	CLYDE TOVAL	B (E	ALEX BROWN	V (E	HERMAN ERNEST	D (E
JIM GILSTRAP	V (E	KIM JOSEPH	PERC (E	PAUL BATISTE	G (E	TONY RIVERS	V (E
WALTER HARRIS	G (E	STU CALVER	V (E	JAMES BOOKER	K (E	JOHN PERRY	V (E
ALLEN TOUSSAINT	K (E	TIM RENWICK	G (E	WINSTON DELANDRO	G (E	BARRY ST JOHN	V (E
VICKY BROWN	V (E	ALUN DAVIES	G (E	WILLIE WEEKS	B (E	PETER HOPE-EVANS HCA(E	
OLLIE BROWN	D (E	BOB BARTON	V (E	BOBBYE HALL	PERC (E	RAY PARKER	G (E
JUNE D WILLIAMS	V (E						

JERRY LEE LEWIS

JERRY LEE LEWIS	PNO V(ALL	JERRY LEE LEWIS	196	LONDON	UK HAS2138	SUN	US	1230
LEO LODNER	G (N	GREATEST	196			SUN	US	1265
ROLAND JANES	G (N	JERRY LEE LEWIS VOL 2	196	LONDON	UK HAS2440			
JIMMY VAN EATON	D (N	WHOLE LOTTA SHAKIN' GOIN' ON	196	LONDON	UK HAS8251			
BILLY RILEY	G B (N	BREATHLESS	196	LONDON	UK HAS8323			
JACK CLEMENTS	B (	GOLDEN HITS	1964	PHILIPS	UK SBL7622+	SMASH	US	67040
OTIS JETT	D (	LIVE AT THE STAR CLUB HAMBURG	1964	PHILIPS	UK SBL7646			
J W BROWN	B (	GREATEST LIVE SHOW ON EARTH	1964	PHILIPS	UK SBL7650	SMASH	US	67056
SCOTTY MOORE	G (N	RETURN OF ROCK	1963			WING	US	16340
HANK GARLAND	G (	RETURN OF ROCK	1967	PHILIPS	UK SBL7668	SMASH	US	67063
KEN LOVELACE	G (	COUNTRY SONGS FOR CITY FOLKS	1965	PHILIPS	UK SBL7688	SMASH	US	67071
ROBBY BROWN	D (	MEMPHIS BEAT	196	PHILIPS	UK SBL7706	SMASH	US	67079
JOEL SHUMAKER	B (	BY REQUEST	1967	PHILIPS	UK SBL7746	SMASH	US	67086
DELANEY BRAMLETT	G V (L	SOUL MY WAY	196			SMASH	US	67097
ALBERT LEE	G (L	ANOTHER PLACE ANOTHER TIME	1968	MERCURY	UK 21011	SMASH	US	67104
GARY WRIGHT	K (L	SHE STILL COMES AROUND	1968	MERCURY	UK 20147	SMASH	US	67112
PETER FRAMPTON	G V (L	COUNTRY HITS	196			SMASH	US	67118
ANDY BROWN	K (L	TOGETHER	1969	PHILIPS	UK 20172	SMASH	US	67126
TONY ASHTON	K (L	SHE EVEN WOKE ME UP TO SAY G'BYE	1970			SMASH	US	67128
KENNY JONES	D (L	BEST OF	196			SMASH	US	67131
KLAUS VOORMANN	B (L	I'M ON FIRE	1969	MERCURY	UK 20156			
RORY GALLAGHER	G (L	COUNTRY MUSIC HALL OF FAME	19	MERCURY	UK 20157			
MIKE KELLIE	D (L	COUNTRY MUSIC HALL OF FAME 2	19	MERCURY	UK 20158			
BRAD SUGGS	G (N	BEST OF	1970	MERCURY	UK 6338014			
CLIFF ACRED	D (N	ORIGINAL GOLDEN HITS	1970	SUN	UK 6467002	SUN	US	102
CHARLIE RICH	PNO (N	THERE MUST BE MORE TO LOVE	1971	MERCURY	UK 6338043			
JEFF DAVIS	D (N	ORIGINAL GOLDEN HITS VOL 2	1970	SUN	UK 6467008	SUN	US	103
ALBERT JACKSON	D (N	ROCKIN RHYTHM & BLUES	1971	SUN	UK 6467017	SUN	US	107
R W McGHEE	D (N	GOLDEN CREAM OF COUNTRY	1971	SUN	UK 6467011	SUN	US	108
HERMAN HAWKINS	B (N	TASTE OF COUNTRY	1971	SUN	UK 6467015	SUN	US	114
GEORGE WEBB	G (N	MEMPHIS ROCK'N'ROLL	197			SUN	US	116
WILLIAM RAY FELTS	ORG (N	SUNDAY DOWN SOUTH(JOHNNY CASH)	1971	SUN	UK 6467024	SUN	US	119
MORRIS TARRANT	D (N	MEMPHIS COUNTRY	1971			SUN	US	120
BUDDY HARMAN	B (N	OLD TYME COUNTRY MUSIC	1971	SUN	UK 6464020	SUN	US	121
FLOYD CHANCE	B (N	MONSTERS	1971	SUN	UK 6467019	SUN	US	124
LITTLE JOHNNY DEMPSEY	G(N	SINGS WITH HANK WILLIAMS	1971	SUN	UK 6467018	SUN	US	125
CARL PERKINS	G V (	IN LOVING MEMORIES	1971			MERCURY	US	61338
JOHNNY CASH	V (	ORIGINAL GOLDEN HITS VOL3	1972	SUN	UK 6467023	SUN	US	128
		ROCKIN' UP A STORM	1972	SUN (DBL)UK 6641162				
		THE KILLER ROCKS ON	1972	MERCURY	UK 6338088			
		WILL YOU TAKE ANOTHER CHANCE	1972	MERCURY	UK 6338071			
		WILL YOU TAKE ANOTHER CHANCE	1975	CONTOUR	UK 6870620			
		ROCKIN'	1973	MERCURY	UK 6336300			
		LIVE AT THE INTERNATIONAL	1973	MERCURY	UK 6338148			
		WHO'S GONNA PLAY THE OLD PIANO	1973			MERCURY	US	61366
		SOLID GOLD ROCK'N'ROLL VOL 2	197			MERCURY	US	61372
		SOMETIMES A MEMORY AINT ENOUGH	1973			MERCURY	US	1 677
		(L) LONDON SESSION	1973	MERCURY	UK 6672008	MERCURY	US	2 803
		1 40 COUNTRY	1974			MERCURY	US	1 710
						(CONTINUED)		

JERRY LEE LEWIS

Title	Year	Label	Country/Cat			
COUNTRY STYLE	197	MERCURY	UK 6851001			
ROCKIN' & FREE	1974	SUN	UK 6467029			
FAN CLUB CHOICE	1974	MERCURY	UK 6338496			
SOUTHERN ROOTS	1974	MERCURY	UK 6338452			
JERRY LEE LEWIS	197	IMPACT	UK 6886402			
SUNSTROKE(CARL PERKINS)	197	EMBER	UK NR 5038			
RARE VOL1	1975	CHARLY	UK CR30006			
RARE VOL2	1975	CHARLY	UK CR30007			
24 ORIGINAL HITS	1975	MUSIDISC	FR ALB 170			
BOOGIE WOOGIE COUNTRY MAN	1975			MERCURY	US 1 1030	
ORIGINAL SUPER ROCK	1975	MUSIDISC	FR ALB 184			
I'M A ROCKER	1975	MERCURY	UK 6338602			
ODD MAN IN	197			MERCURY	US 1 1064	
EXPLOSIVE	19	CONTOUR	UK 6870533			
GOOD ROCKIN' TONIGHT	1975	HALLMARK	UK SHM 867			
COUNTRY CLASS	1976			MERCURY	US 1 1109	
GOLDEN HITS	1976	PHILIPS INT 6336245				
& HIS PUMPING PIANO	1975	CHARLY	UK CR30002			
THE ORIGINAL	1976	CHARLY	UK CR30111			
NUGGETS	1977	CHARLY	UK CR30121			
(N)NUGGETS VOL 2	1977	CHARLY	UK CR30129			
COUNTRY MEMORIES	1977			MERCURY	US 1 5004	
BEST OF VOL 2	1978			MERCURY	US 1 5006	
KEEPS ON ROCKIN'	1978			MERCURY	US 1 5010	
BACK TO BACK	1978	MERCURY	UK 6641869			
SHAKIN' JERRY LEE	1978	ARCADE	UK ADEP 34			
ESSENTIAL JERRY LEE LEWIS	1978	CHARLY	UK CRM2001			
JERRY LEE LEWIS	1978	IMPACT	6995401			
JERRY LEE LEWIS	1978	FESTIVAL	ALB 233			
DUETS	1978	CHARLY	UK SUN1002			
20 GREATEST HITS	1979	ARCADE	FR FR18			
COLLECTORS EDITION	19	SUN	NL NY6			
JERRY LEE LEWIS	1979	ELEKTRA	UK K52132			
FROM THE VAULTS OF SUN	19	STARDAY			US PO 247	
HIGH HEELED SNEAKERS	19			PICKWICK	US 3224	
ROLL OVER BEETHOVEN	19			PICKWICK	US 6110	
RURAL ROUTE No1	19			PICKWICK	US 6120	
COLLECTION	19	PICKWICK	UK PDA 007			
BREATHLESS(DBL)	19			PICKWICK	US 2055	
BEST OF J L L	19			TRIP DBL	US 8501	
GREAT BALLS OF FIRE	19	HALLMARK	UK SHM 823			
WHOLE LOTTA SHAKIN'	19	HALLMARK	UK SHM 851			
DRINKIN' WINE SPO DEE O DEE	19			PICKWICK	US 3344	
GOT YOU ON MY MIND	19	FONTANA	UK SFJL964			
JERRY LEE LEWIS	19			ELEKTRA	US 6E 184	
JERRY LEE LEWIS	19			EVEREST	US 298	
GREATEST HITS VOL1	19	IMPACT	6886402			
GREATEST HITS VOL2	19	IMPACT	6886408			
LIVE AT THE STAR CLUB HAMBURG	1980	PHILIPS	UK			
JERRY LEE'S GREATEST	1980	CHARLY	CRM 2008			

RAMSEY LEWIS

Personnel			Title	Year	Label		Cat
RAMSEY LEWIS	K	(ALL	SOUND OF CHRISTMAS	1964		US CADET	LPS693
ELDEE YOUNG	B	( ]TRIO	SOUND OF SPRING	1964		US CADET	LPS693
ISAAC HOLT	D	(	POT LUCK	1964		US CADET	LPS715
			BAREFOOT SUNDAY BLUES	1964		US CADET	LPS723
DERF REKLAW RAHEEM PERC V (O			AT THE BOHEMIAN CAVERNS	1965 PYE	UK NJL 55	US CADET	LPS741
BYRON GREGORY	G	(OQ	MORE SOUNDS OF CHRISTMAS	1965 CHESS	UK 4504	US CADET	LPS745
RON HARRIS	B	(OQ	THE IN CROWD	1965 CHESS	UK 4511	US CADET	LPS757
KEITH HOWARD	D	(O	HANG ON RAMSEY	1966 CHESS	UK 4517	US CADET	LPS761
JIMMY BRYANT	K V	(O	SWINGIN'	1966		US CADET	LPS771
TERRY FRYER	K	(OQ	CHOICE(BEST OF)	1966 CHESS	UK 4518		
RAHM LEE	HRNS	(OR	WADE IN THE WATER	1966 CHESS	UK 4522	US CADET	LPS774
MICHAEL DAVIS	V TPT	(OR	GOIN' LATIN	1967 CHESS	UK 4528		
MIKE McGLOIRY	G	(Q	MOVIE ALBUM	1967 CHESS	UK 4531	US CADET	LPS782
ED REDDICK	B	(Q	DANCIN' IN THE STREET	1968 CHESS	UK 4533	US CADET	LPS794
JAMES GADSON	D	(QR	RAMSEY LEWIS TRIO	1968		US CADET	LPS796
VANCE TENORT	PERC	(Q	UP POPS RAMSEY	1968 CHESS	UK 4535	US CADET	LPS799
ALEXANDRA BROWN	V	(Q	MAIDEN VOYAGE	1968 CHESS	UK 4539	US CADET	LPS811
JIM GILSTRAP	V	(Q	MOTHER NATURES SON	1969 CHESS	UK 4545		
STEPHANIE SPRUILL	V	(Q	UPENDO NI PAMOJA	197	UK 64718		
ANGELA WINBUSH	V	(Q	BACK TO THE ROOTS	1971 CHESS	UK 6310 106		
JOHN REASONS	K G	(Q	BEST OF	1972 CHESS	UK 6310 114		
BOBBY LYLE	K	(Q	TOBACCO ROAD	1972 CHESS	UK 6310 124		
MORRIS JENNINGS	D	(Q	FUNKY SERENITY	1973 CBS	UK 65307		
KEITHN CARTER	V	(Q	GREATEST HITS	1973 CBS	UK 65759		
CYNTHIA HARRELL	V	(Q	GROOVER	1974 CHESS	UK 6467 305		
KITTY HAYWOOD	V	(Q	SOLAR WIND	1974 CBS	UK 80083		
VIVIAN HAYWOOD	V	(Q	DON'T IT FEEL GOOD	1975 CBS	UK 81006		
KENNETH WILLIAMS	PERC	(R	SUN GODDESS	1975 CBS	UK 80677		
LEO NOCENTELLI	G	(R	SOLID IVORY	1975 CHESS	UK 6641 328		
DAVID BARARD	B	(R	LIVE IN TOKYO	1975		US CADET	SMS7501
ZURI RAHEEM	V	(O	SALONGO	1976 CBS	UK 81406		
DARLENE KOLDENHOVEN V		(Q	(O) LOVE NOTES	1977 CBS	UK 82024		
PAT FERRARI	G	(Q	(P) TEQUILA MOCKINGBIRD	1977 CBS	UK 83270		
LARRY DUNN	K	(R	LEGACY	1978 CBS	UK 82964		
AL McKAY	G	(R	(Q) RAMSEY	1979 CBS	UK 83584		
BYRON MILLER	B	(R	(R) ROUTES	1980 CBS	UK 84243		
LEO CHANCLER	D	(R	DOWN TO EARTH	19		US MERCURY	36150
KENNY BURKE	B	(R	AN HOUR WITH	19		US ARGO	645

(CONTINUED)

```
ROLAND BAUTISTA      G    (R
PAULINHO DA COSTA PERC (R    FRED WHITE       PERC(R    DON MYRICK    SAX (R    LOUIS SATTERFIELD  TROM(R
MAURICE WHITE        V    (R    JON LIND         V   (R    WARREN WEINBERG V (R    ALLEN TOUSSAINT    K   (R
SAM HENRY            G    (R    HERMAN V ERNEST  D   (R
```

SMILEY LEWIS   L66

```
SMILEY LEWIS         V   (ALL        SHAME SHAME SHAME         1970 LIBERTY     UK           LBS 83308
                                     I HEAR YOU KNOCKING       1978 UA   UK UAS 30167 US IMPERIAL9141
                                     THE BELLS ARE RINGING     1978 UA   UK UAS 30186
```

WEBSTER LEWIS   L66A

```
WEBSTER LEWIS     K V  (A        (A) 8 FOR THE 80's            1980 EPIC        UK           EPC 84283
JAMES GADSON        D    (A
NATHANIEL WATTS     B    (A    PAUL JACKSON       G    (A    WAH WAH WATSON  G   (A    TOWER OF POWER HRNS (A
OSCAR BRASHEAR   HRNS (A    D J ROGERS         V    (A    SYLVIA COX      V   (A    CHERYL PITTS   B    (A
JOHNNY BAKER        V    (A    BOBBY BRYANT     HRNS (A    GARNETT BROWN  HRNS (A    BENNY POWELL   HRNS (A
BILL GREEN       HRNS (A    HERBIE HANCOCK     K    (A    CARMEN TWILLIE  V   (A    YOLANDA HOWARD V    (A
VENETTE GLOUD       V    (A    JUDITH JONES       V    (A    BILL CHAMPLIN   V   (A
```

LEWIS & GILBERT   L66B

```
G LEWIS                          (A) DOME                     1980   DOME (ROUGH TRADE)   DOME1
B C GILBERT
```

LIAR   L67

```
CLIVE BROOKS        D    (AB        (A) STRAIGHT FROM THE HIP   1977   DECCA      UK    SKL  5275
DAVE BURTON         G    (AB        (B) SET THE WORLD ON FIRE   1979   BEARSVILLE UK    K   55524
PAUL TRAVIS         G    (AB
STEVE MANN        G K  (AB    DAVID TAYLOR       B    (AB
```

LIBRA   L67A

```
                                 LIBRA                        197    TAMLA MOTOWN  US    M 6847
                                 WINTER DAYS NIGHTMARE        19     TAMLA MOTOWN  US    M 6864
```

DAVID LIEBMAN   L67B

```
DAVID LIEBMAN    SAX  (ABC       (A) SWEET HANDS              19     HORIZON    US    SP  702
RICHARD BEIRACH  PNO  (BC        (B) FORGOTTEN FANTASIES      19     HORIZON    US    SP  709
LINK CHAMBERLAND    G    (C        (C) LIGHT'N UP PLEASE       1977   HORIZON    US    SP  721
PEE WEE ELLIS    PNO  (C        (D) FATHER TIME             1976   ENJA       GERM       2056
SONNY BROWN      PERC (C
CHRIS HAYES         G    (C    TONY SAUNDERS      B    (C    JIMMY STRASSBURG D (C    JUMMA SANTOS    CONGAS(C
LEON THOMAS         V    (C    HAROLD WILLIAMS    K    (C    AL FOSTER       D  (C    JEFF BERLIN     B    (C
```

LIEUTENANT PIGEON   L68

```
ROB WOODWARD              (        (A) MOULDY OLD MUSIC        1973   DECCA      UK    SKL  5154
NIGEL FLETCHER           (        (B) PIGEON PIE              1974   DECCA      UK    SKL  5174
Mrs FLETCHER             (        (C) PIGEON PARTY            1974   DECCA      UK    SKL  5196
STEVE.....?
```

LIFE   L68A

```
ROGER COTTON      K V  (A        (A) LIFE AFTER DEATH         1974   POLYDOR          2383 295
IAN GIBBONS       K FLT (A
RICHARD THORPE    B V  (A    PAUL THORPE        D V(A
```

LIFESTYLE   L69

```
JERRY JAY FERGUSON K V (A        (A) LIFESTYLE               1977 MCA UK MCF 2809    US    2246
JOHNNY MATHIS        V    (A
WADE 'HOLMES' DAVIS V (A    SHEDRICK SWEET     V    (A    RICHIE ROME     K   (A    DENNIS HARRIS   G  (A
GEORGE BERG      SAX  (A    JON FADDIS       TPT  (A    CHARLES LEE     V   (A    MICHAEL FOREMAN B  (A
LARRY WASHINGTON CONGA(A    ARTHUR CLARKE    SAX  (A    VICTOR PAZ     TPT  (A    MEL DAVIS       TPT(A
PAUL GRIFFIN        K    (A    CHARLES COLLINS    D    (A    RICHARD DAVIS   B   (A    BILLY JACKSON   PERC(A
ROMEO PENQUE     SAX  (A    BUDDY TERRY      SAX  (A    JANICE ROBINSON TROM(A    STRING SECTION     (A
```

LIFETIME   L70

```
TONY WILLIAMS       D    (ALL        (A) LIFETIME              1965   BLUENOTE              84180
JACK BRUCE          B    (            (B) EMERGENCY             1969   POLYDOR  583 574 ++  25/30001
JOHN McLAUGHLIN     G    (            (B) EMERGENCY             197    POLYDOR              2673 002
ALLAN HOLDSWORTH    G    (H        (C) TURN IT OVER           1970   POLYDOR              2425 019
ALAN PASQUA         K    (H        (D) EGO                    197o   POLYDOR  2425 070 ++ 2440 065
TONY NEWTON       B V  (H        (E) THE OLD BUMS RUSH      1972   POLYDOR              2391 052
RON CARTER    B CELLO  (D        (F) LIFETIME               1975   POLYDOR              2482 179
KHALID YASIN      ORG  (D        (G) BELIEVE IT             1976   CBS  UK 69201  US  33836
TOM DUNBAR          G    (D        (H) MILLION DOLLAR LEGS    1976   CBS  UK 81510  US  34263
DON ALIAS        PERC (D        (J) LIFETIME               1978   BLUENOTE             40018
WARREN SMITH     PERC (D        (K) JOY OF FLYING          1979   CBS  UK 83338
```

JOE & JIMMY LIGGINS   L71

```
JOE LIGGINS             (AB        (A) JOE LIGGINS            1975   BULLDOG              BDL 1005
JIMMY LIGGINS           (AB        (B) JOE & JIMMY LIGGINS    1976   SONET      UK    SNTF5020
```

LIGHT   L71A

```
JIM ARMSTRONG       G    (A        (A) LIGHT                  1977   MINT             MINT11
ALBERT MILLS      B V  (A
BRIAN SCOTT     K FLT V (A    GEORGE O'HARA    G V  (A    BERTIE MACDONALD    D (A
```

LIGHT OF THE WORLD   L71B

```
NEVILLE McKRIETH  G V  (A        (A) ROUND TRIP             1980   ENSIGN           ENVY 14
PATRYCE BANKS        V    (A        ( ) LIGHT OF THE WORLD     1979   ENSIGN           ENVY  7
PAUL WILLIAMS     B V  (A
PETER HINDS         K    (A    EVERTON McCALLA    D    (A    GANIYU BELLO   PERC V(A    NATHANIEL AUGUSTIN TROM(A
CANUTE WELLINGTON HRNS V(A    DAVID BAPTISTE   WIND V(A    WAYNE HENDERSON TROM(A    BOBBY LYLE      PNO(A
VICTOR FELDMAN   VIBES(A    MIKI HOWARD      TPT  (A    STEVE MADAIO    TPT (A    JOHN ERVIN      TROM(A
CHUCK BROOKE     SAX  (A    BOB GREAVES      SAX  (A    VANCE TENORT    PERC(A    STEVE BECKMEIER G  (A
GREG PRECLES     HRNS (A    MEL GAYNOR         D    (A    AUGIE JOHNSON    V  (A    STRING SECTION     (A
```

GORDON LIGHTFOOT   L72

```
GORDON LIGHTFOOT G PNO V(ALL        (A) LIGHTFOOT              1966 UA     US 6487
TERRY CLEMENTS G   (JLMNORSV        (B) WAY I FEEL            1967 UA     US 6587SUNSET UK  50231
RICK HAYNES         B    (HJLMNORSV        (C) LIGHTFOOT             1968
PEE WEE CHARLES STEEL(NORSV        (D) DID SHE MENTION MY NAME 1968 US    US 6649     UK SULP 1199
BARRY KEANE         D    (LORSV        (E) BACK HERE ON EARTH    1969 UA     US 6672     UK SULP 1239
                                                                                         (CONTINUED)
```

GORDON LIGHTFOOT

```
GENE MARTYNEC      SYN   (MR        (F) EARLY LIGHTFOOT              1969 UA                    UK UAS 29012
JIM GORDON         D     (MNOR      (G) SUNDAY CONCERT              1969 UA                    UK UAS 29040
RED SHEA           G     (HJLMNOS   (H) SIT DOWN YOUNG STRANGER     1970 REPRISE US 6392       UK   K 44091
DAVID BROWN        PERC  (L         (J) DON QUIXOTE                 1972 REPRISE US 2056       UK   K 44166
JOHN STOCKFISH     B     (MNO       (K) SUMMERSIDE OF LIFE          1971 REPRISE US 2037       UK   K 44132
CATHERINE SMITH    V     (M         (L) OLD DANS RECORDS            1972 REPRISE US 2116       UK   K 44219
BRUCE GOOD   AUTOHARP  (LOV         (M) SUNDOWN                     1974 REPRISE US 2177       UK   K 44258
NICK DE CARO       ACC   (LMNOV     (N) COLD ON THE SHOULDER        1975 REPRISE US 2206       UK   K 54033
MILT HOLLAND       PERC  (MNO       (O) GORD'S GOLD                 1975 REPRISE US 2237       UK   K 64033
JACK ZAZA          WIND  (NS        (P) VERY BEST OF                1975 UA         US LA445EMI 5C 05096474
SUSIE McCUNE       V     (N         (Q) EARLY MORNING RAIN          1976 SUNSET               UK SLS 50398
TOM SZCZESNIAK     B     (S         (R) SUMMERTIME DREAM            1976 REPRISE US 2246       UK   K 54067
LARRY GOOD         BAN   (LO        (S) ENDLESS WIRE                1978 WB         US 3149     UK   K 56444
MITCH CLARKE   BASSOON  (S          (T) CLASSIC LIGHTFOOT           19   UA                    UK UAS  5510
OLLIE STRONG       STEEL (LO        (U) GORDON LIGHTFOOT HUDBA A SLOVA 19 SUPRAPHON
DOUG RILEY         PNO   (S          (V) DREAM STREET ROSE          1980 WB         US 3426     UK   K 56802
DAVID BROMBERG     G     (L         (JK) 2 ORIGINALS OF GORDON LIGHTFOOT 19 REPRISE           UK   K 64022
JUNIOR HUSKY       B     (O
PIG ROBBINS        PNO   (O
LENNY CASTRO       PERC  (V    BOB GLAUB       B   (V    KEN BUTTREY   D  (O   GAYLE LEVANT     HARP (V
CHARLIE McCOY      HARM  (O    MICHAEL OMARTIAN K  (V    HERB PEDERSEN BAN(V   JACKIE WARD       V   (N
```

L73 PAPA GEORGE LIGHTFOOT

```
PAPA GEORGE LIGHTFOOT V HCA(ALL    (A) RURAL BLUES VOL 2           19   LIBERTY             UK LBL 83214
CARSON WHITSETT    PNO   (B         (B) NATCHEZ TRACE              1969 LIBERTY             UK LBS 83353
RON JOHNSON        B     (B
JERRY PUCKETT      G     (B    TOMMY TATE      D   (B
```

L74 LIGHTHOUSE

```
SKIP PROKOP        G D V(BCDGJ      (A) LIGHTHOUSE                 1969 RCA        US LSP4173
PAUL HOFFERT       K     (BCDG       (B) PEACING IT ALL TOGETHER    1970 RCA        US LSP4225 UK SF 8121
RALPH COLE         G V   (BCDGJ      (C) SUITE FEELING              1970 RCA        US LSP4241 UK SF 8103
DON DINOVO         VLA   (BCDGJ      (D) ONE FINE MORNING           1971 EVOLUTION US    3007
DICK ARMIN         CELLO (BCDGJ      (D) ONE FINE MORNING           1971 VERTIGO             UK 6342010
LOUIS YACKNIN      B     (DG         (E) THOUGHTS OF MOVING ON      197  EVOLUTION US    3010
KEITH JOLIMORE     WIND V(D          (E) THOUGHTS OF MOVING ON      197  VERTIGO             UK 6342011
LARRY SMITH        TROM V(DGJ        (F) LIVE                       197  EVOLUTION US    3014
HOWARD SHORE       SAX   (BCDG       (G) SUNNY DAYS                 1972 EVOLUTION US    3016
DALE HILLARY       SAX V(J           (G) SUNNY DAYS                 1972 MOONCREST           UK CREST 2
RICK STEPTON       TROM  (J          (H) ONE FINE LIGHT             1972 RCA        US    6047
PAUL ARMIN         VLN   (BC         (J) CAN FEEL IT                1974 POLYDOR    US PD 5056 UK 2391088
PAUL ADAMSON       TPT   (C          (K) GOOD DAY                   19   POLYDOR    US    6028
ARNIE CHYCOSKI     TPT   (B          (L) BEST OF                    19   JANUS      US JXS7025
JOHN CAPON         TROM  (B
PETE PANTALUK      TPT   (D    JOHN NASLEN  TPT    (GJ  PINKY DAUVIN   V  (BC  MYRON MOSKALYK   VLN(C
BRUCE CASSIDY      TPT   (BC   BOB McBRIDE PERC V  (DG  ALAN WILMOT    B  (GJ  GRANT FULLERTON  B V(BC
LES SNIDER         CELLO (BC   RUSS LITTLE      TROM (BC
```

L75 LIGHTNIN' SLIM

```
LIGHTNIN' SLIM(OTIS HICK G V (ALL   (A) ROOSTER BLUES              196  EXCELLO      US          8000
PETE WINGFIELD     K     (E         (A) ROOSTER BLUES              196  BLUE HORIZON UK       7 63863
LAURIE GARMAN      HCA   (E         (B) BELL RINGER                196  EXCELLO      US          8004
RICK HAYWARD       G     (E         (C) HIGH & LOW DOWN            196  EXCELLO      US          8018
PAUL BUTLER        G     (E         (C) HIGH & LOW DOWN            197  CONTEMPO              CRM118
KENNY LAMB         D     (E         (C) HIGH & LOW DOWN            1978 SONET        UK   SNTF 770
JOHN BEST          B     (E         (D) A LONG DRINK OF BLUES(1 SIDE) 1964 EMI       UK   SL10135
DICK PARRY         SAX   (E         (E) LONDON GUMBO               1972 BLUE HORIZON UK   2931 005
WILL THAKE         HCA   (E         (E) LONDON GUMBO               1975 CONTEMPO     UK   CLP  514
CECIL MOSS         TPT   (E         (E) LONDON GUMBO               1978 SONET        UK   SNTF 757
MIKE VERNON        G D   (E         (F) THE EARLY YEARS            1977 FLYRIGHT          CLP  524
ROGER BROOKS       TROM  (E         (G) TRIP TO CHICAGO            1978 FLYRIGHT          CLP  533
LAZY LESTER        HCA   (A
WARREN STORM       D     (AB   AL FOREMAN      G   (B    BOBBY McBRIDE  G  (B   KATIE WEBSTER    PNO (B
AUSTIN BROUSSARD   D     (B    RUFUS THIBODEAUX B  (B    JESSE CARR     G  (C   CLAYTON IVEY     K   (C
STACY GOSS         HRNS  (C    MIKE STOUGH     HRNS (C   SONNY ROYAL    HRNS(C  CHARLES ROSE     HRNS(C
FRED PROUDLY       D     (C    BOB WARY        B   (C    TIPPY ARMSTRONG HCA(C
```

L76 LILIENTAL

```
                                    (A) LILIENTAL                  19   BRAIN                 0060 117
```

L76A LIMELIGHT

```
MIKE SCRIMSHAW   V B G K(A          (A) LIMELIGHT                  1980 FUTURE EARTH          FER  008
GLENN SCRIMSHAW    G K V (A
PAT COLEMAN        D V   (A
```

L76B LIMEY

```
BRIAN ENGEL        G V   (AB        (A) LIMEY                      1976  RCA         UK   SF  8463
JOHN KNIGHTSBRIDGE G     (B         (B) SILVER EAGLE               1977  RCA              PL 25032
PAUL KEOGH         G     (B
GARTH WATT-ROY     G     (B    TOM WILLIS      G   (B    ALAN SPENNER   B  (B   BOB HENRIT       D   (B
JIM RODFORD        B     (B    TOMMY EYRE      K FLT(B   DAVE BOWKER    B  (AB  IAN KEWLEY       K   (AB
ROBIN LE MESURIER  G     (AB   MAC McINERNEY   D PERC(A
```

L77 DENNIS LINDE

```
DENNIS LINDE B G V D K(ALL          (A) LINDE MANOR                1970 INTREPID     US   IT 74004
WAYNE MOSS         G B   (AB        (B) DENNIS LINDE               1973 ELEKTRA      UK   K 42149
DOODLES LANCASTER  D     (A         (C) TRAPPED IN THE SUBURBS     1974 ELEKTRA      UK   K 52013
BERGEN WHITE       HRNS  (A         (D) SURFACE NOISE              197  MONUMENT     US
BUDDY SPICHER  STRINGS  (ABE        (E) UNDER THE EYE              1977 MONUMENT     US   MG 7608
FARRELL MORRIS     PERC  (AC
JERRY SMITH        K     (A    BENNY WHITEHEAD  HRN V(B   RANDY CULLERS D B G V(BCE  TERRY DEARMORE  G V (B
BOBBY OGDIN FDL K FLT  (BCE    ALAN RUSH  V G BANJO  (BCE  ROBERT GALBRAITH K V(BC   LLOYD GREEN     STEEL(BC
CHIP YOUNG         V     (BC   BILLY SWAN      V   (B    JOHN HARRIS    K  (B   KENNY MALONE     D   (B
WELDON MYRICK      STEEL (B    BOBBY THOMPSON  BANJ (E   RUSS HICKS     STEEL(B RON EADES        SAX (B
HARRISON CALLOWAY  HRNS(C     JOHNNY CHRISTOPHER G  (C   JIMMY COLVARD  G  (C   BOBBY EMMONS     K   (CE
HURSHAL WIGGINTON  V    (C     SHANE KEISTER   SYN K(E   JERRY CARRIGAN D  (E   THOMAS CAIN      PNO (E
MAC GAYDEN         G    (E     MARY HOLLADAY   V   (E    GINGER HOLLADAY V  (E
```

UDO LINDENBERG   L78

UDO LINDENBERG	V D PERC(ALL	(A) LINDENBERG	1971	TELEFUNKEN	GERM	SLE14637
THOMAS KRETSCHMER	G	(H	(B) DAUMEN IM WIND	1972	TELEFUNKEN	GERM	62830
KARL ALLANT	G	(H	(C) ALLES KLAR AUF DER ANDREA DORIA	1973	TELEFUNKEN	GERM	SLE14719
HELMUT FRANKE	G	(H	(D) BALL POMPOS	1974	TELEFUNKEN	GERM	SLE14790
STEFFI STEPHAN	B	(H	(E) VOTAN WAHNWITZ	1975	TELEFUNKEN	GERM	6 22223
GOTTFRIED BOTTGER	K (	(H	(F) DAS SIND DIE HERRN VOM ANDERN STERN 76	TELEFUNKEN	GERM	6 22460
JEAN JACQUES KRAVETZ	K	(H	(G) SISTER KING KONG	1976	TELEFUNKEN	GERM	6 22609
KEITH FORSEY	D PERC(H	(H) NO PANIC	1976	DECCA	UK	TXSR116
DIETER AHRENDT	D PERC(H					
LONZO WESTPHAL	VLN (H	PETER HERBOLZHEIMER HRNS(H				

JAYSON LINDH   L79

BJORN JAYSON LINDH	FLT(AB	(A) JAYSON LINDH	1977	ATLANTIC	UK	K50337
ERNIE WATTS	SAX (A	(B) DAY AT THE SURFACE	1980	SONET	UK	SNTF 833
NAGI EL HABASHI	CELLO(B					

DON GRUSIN	PNO (A	LEE RITENOUR	G	(A	KEN WILD	B	(A	JOE CORRERO	D	(A
JOE LALA	PERC (A	LARS CARLSSON	SAX (A		JIM JOHNSON	G	(A	TOM ROADY	PERF	(A
BERTIL LOVGREN	TPT (A	JAN KLING	WIND (A		JIM GILSTRAP	V	(A	AUGIE JOHNSON	V	(A
JAN KOHLIN	TPT (A	ULF ADAKER	TPT (A	ULF ANDERSSON	SAX	(A	JOHAN STENGARD	SAX(A
BARRY BECKETT	K (A	DAVID HOOD	B	(A	LARS OLOF KYNDEL	K	(A	SVEN LARSSON	TROM(A
PETER SUNDELL	PERC (B	PETE ROBINSON	K	(B	GEORG WADENIUS	B	(B	OKAY TEMIZ	PERC(B
JAN BANDEL	VLN (B	LENNART ABERG	SAX (B	JON CHRISTENSEN	D	(B	JANNE SCHAFFER	G	(AB
STEFAN BROLUND	B	(AB	MALANDO GASSAMA	D	(AB	MATS GLENNGARD	VLN (A	AKE ERIKSSON	D	(A
KEN BELL	G	(A	ROGER HAWKINS	D	(A	AMERICO BELLOTTO TPT	(A	LARS OLOFSSON	TROM(A

LINDISFARNE   L80

ALAN HULL	K G(ALL	(A) NICELY OUT OF TUNE	1970	CHARISMA	UK	CAS 1025
ROD CLEMENTS	V G K	(ABCDHIJK	(B) FOG ON THE TYNE	1971	CHARISMA	UK	CAS 1050
RAY JACKSON	V G MAND(ABCDEFGHIJK	(C) DINGLY DELL	1972	CHARISMA	UK	CAS 1057
SIMON COWE	V G MAND(ABCDGHIJK	(D) LINDISFARNE LIVE	1973	CHARISMA	UK	CLASS 2
RAY LAIDLAW	D	(ABCDGHIJK	(E) ROLL ON RUBY	1973	CHARISMA	UK	CAS 1076
PAUL NICHOLS	D	(EF	(F) HAPPY DAZE	1974	WB	UK	K56070
TOM DUFFY	B	(EF	(G) FINEST HITS	1975	CHARISMA	UK	CAS 1108
KEN CRADDOCK	K G	(EF	(H) LADY ELEANOR	1976	PICKWICK		SHM 919
CHARLIE HARCOURT	G	(EF	(I) BACK & FOURTH	1978	MERCURY UK 9109609+ATCO US108
BUD BEADLE	HRNS (F	(J) MAGIC IN THE AIR	1978	MERCURY UK 6641877
STEVE GREGORY	HRNS (F	(K) THE NEWS	1979	MERCURY UK 9109626
FRANK RICOTTI	PERC (K					
PETE WINGFIELD	PERC (K	NICK ROWLEY	HRNS(K	STRING SECTION	(K

LINER   L80A

TOM FARMER	V B (A	(A) LINER	1979	ATLANTIC	K50553
EDDIE GOLGA	G V (A				
ARIF MASDIN	SYN (A	IAN LYNN	K	(A	MEL COLLINS	SAX (A	DICK MORRISSEY	SAX (A
KEN BISCHEL	K (A	MARVIN STAMM	TPT (A	JON FADDIS	TPT (A	GEORGE YOUNG	SAX (A
FRANK VICARI	SAX (A	CISSY HOUSTON	V	(A	BARRY ROGERS	TROM (A	RONNIE CUBER	SAX (A
MAERETHA STEWART	V (A	BEVERLY INGRAM	V	(A			

LINES   L80B

RICHARD CONNING	V (A	(A) COOL SNAP (EP)	1980	RED

LINN COUNTY   L81

SNAKE McANDREW	D	(A	(A) PROUD FLESH SOOTHSEER	1968	MERCURY UK 20142	US 61181
DINO LONG	B	(A	(B) FEVER SHOT	1969	MERCURY UK 20165	US 61218
FRED WALK	SITAR G (A	(C) TILL THE BREAK OF DAWN	1970	PHILIPS	US 600326
LARRY EASTER	WIND (A					
STEPHEN MILLER	V ORG(A					

LION   L81A

STEVE WEBB	G V (A	(A) RUNNING ALL NIGHT	1980	A&M	UK	AMLH64755
ROBIN LE MESURIER	G	(A				
GARY FARR	V	(A	ERIC DILLON	D	(A	STEVE HUMPHREYS	B	(A	JOHN SINCLAIR	K V (A

(JENNIE HAANS) LION   L82

JENNIE HAAN	V	(	
DAVE HEWITT	B	(	
GEOFF LAYTON BENNOT	G	(	GLEN FRASER	G	(	CHRIS WADE	G	(A

BOOKER LITTLE   L83

BOOKER LITTLE	TPT (A	(A) THE LEGENDARY QUARTET ALBUM	1977	ISLAND	UK	ILPS 9454
TOMMY FLANAGAN	PNO (A					
WYNTON KELLY	PNO (A	SCOTT LA FARO	B	(A	ROY HAYNES	D	(A

MARIE LITTLE   L84

MARIE LITTLE	V	(AB	(A) FACTORY GIRL	1972	ARGO	FB 19
ROBIN DRANSFIELD	(A	(B) MARIE LITTLE	1973	LEADER	LER2084
BARRY DRANSFIELD	(A				
SMILEY MOSES	G	(A	DAVE MOSES B RECORDER(A		

LITTLE ANTHONY & THE IMPERIALS   L85

ANTHONY GOURDINE	V	(	(A) OUT OF SIGHT OUT OF MIND	1969	UA US 6720
CLARENCE COLLINS	(	(B) FOREVER YOURS	19	ROULETTE
TRACY LORD	(	(C) GREATEST HITS	19	ROULETTE US 25292
ERNEST WRIGHT	(	(D) GOIN' OUT OF MY HEAD	1965	DCP	US 6808
NAT ROGERS	(	(E) ON A NEW STREET	1974	AVCO	US 11012
SAM STRAIN	(	(F) WE ARE THE IMPERIALS	19	END	US 303
		(G) SHADES OF THE 40's	19	END	US 311
		(H) I'M ON THE OUTSIDE LOOKIN' IN	1964	DCP	US 3801
		(I) PAYIN' OUR DUES	1967	VEEP	US 16513
		(J) REFLECTIONS	1967	VEEP	US 16514
		(K) SING THEIR HITS	19	FORUM	US 9107
		(L) MOVIE GRABBERS	19	VEEP	US 16516
		(M) BEST OF	19	VEEP	US 16519
		(EP) REMEMBER	1976	UA	UK REM 405

L86   LITTLE BEAVER

WILLIE' LITTLE BEAVER'HALE	G V(ABC	(A) LITTLE BEAVER	1974	PRESIDENT		PTLS1060
RON BAGDON	B	(AB	(B) PARTY DOWN	1975	PRESIDENT		PTLS1063
EDMUND COLLINS	B	(A	(C) BLACK RHAPSODY	19	CAT		CAT 1602
FREDDIE SCOTT	D	(A				
ROBERT FERGUSON	D	(AB	BENNY LATIMORE	K	(AB	GEORGE PERRY	B	(B	NELSON PADRON	B	(B
TIMMY THOMAS	K	(B	GLEN HOLMES	PERC (B	WILLIE CLARKE	PERC (B	BETTY WRIGHT	V	(B

L86A   LITTLE BO BITCH

DERMOT MOUGHAN	K	(A	(A) LITTLE BO BITCH	1979	COBRA	CBR 1002
BOB WAINWRIGHT	B	(A				
STEVE CARROLL	G	(A	TERRY REECE	D	(A	TONY WATSON	V	(A

L87   LITTLE BOB STORY

BOB PIAZZA	V	(AB	(A) OFF THE RAILS	1977	CHISWICK	UK	WIK 6
GUY GREMY	G	(AB	(B) LITTLE BOB STORY	1978	CRYPTO	FR	ZAL6415
DOMINIQUE GUILLON	G	(AB	(EP) I'M CRYING	1977	CHISWICK	UK	SW7
DOMINIQUE QUERTIER	D	(AB	(C) HIGH TIME	1977	ARCANE	FR	9103 076
DOMINIQUE LELAN	B	(AB				

L88   LITTLE EVA

LITTLE EVA	V	(ALL	(A) LLLLLOCOMOTION	1962	DIMENSION	US	6000
			(A) LLLLLOCOMOTION	196	LONDON		UKHAU8036
			(B) LOCOMOTION	1972	LONDON		UKSHU8437

L89   LITTLE FEAT

LOWELL GEORGE	G V	(ALL	(A) LITTLE FEAT	1971	WB US WS 1890	UK K46072
RITCHIE HAYWARD	D V	(ALL	(B) SAILIN' SHOES	1972	WB US BS 2600	UK K46156
RY COODER	G	(A	(C) DIXIE CHICKEN	1973	WB US BS 2686	UK K46200
PAUL BARRERE	G V	(CDEFGH	(D) FEATS DONT FAIL ME NOW	1974	WB US BS 2784	UK K56030
SAM CLAYTON	V PERC	(CDEFGH	(E) LAST RECORD ALBUM	1976	WB US BS 2884	UK K56156
KEN GRADNEY	B	(CDEFGH	(F) TIME LOVES A HERO	1977	WB US BS 3015	UK K56349
BILL PAYNE	K V PERC	(ALL	(G) WAITING FOR COLUMBUS(DBL LIVE)	1978	WB US 2 3140	UK K66075
ROY ESTRADA	B	(AB	(H) DOWN ON THE FARM	1979	WB US HS 3345	UK K56667
JEFF BAXTER	G	(F	(BC) TWO ORIGINALS	1975	WB	UK K66038
FRED TACKETT	G	(AFH				
PAT SIMMONS	G V	(F	MIKE McDONALD	V	(F	GREG ADAMS	TPT	(FG	EMILIO CASTILLO	SAX	(AFG
MIC GILLETTE	HRNS	(AFG	STEVE KUPKA	SAX	(AFG	LENNIE PICKETT	SAX	(AFG	ELLIOT INGBER		(AG
DEBBIE LINDSEY	V	(B	EMMYLOU HARRIS	V	(D	JOHN HALL	G	(E	DAVID LINDLEY		(E
RUSS TITELMAN	PNO	(AB	MILT HOLLAND	PERC (B	FRAN TATE	V	(DE	VALERIE CARTER	V	(E
JULIA TILLMAN	V	(H	JERRY JUMONVILLE		(H	SNEAKY PETE	STEEL(BCH	RON ELLIOTT	G	(B
BONNIE RAITT	V	(DH	FRAN PAYNE	V	(H	EARL PALMER		(H	MAXINE WILLARD	V	(H
ROBBEN FORD		(H	ROSEMARY BUTLER	V	(H	DAN SMITH		(H	LUTHER WATERS	V	(H
ORRIN WATERS	V	(H	LEE THORNBERG		(H						

L90   LITTLE MILTON

LITTLE MILTON CAMPBELL	G V(ALL	(A) WERE GONNA MAKE IT	19	CHECKER	US	2995
BOBBY MANUEL	G	(F	(B) SINGS BIG BLUES	19	CHECKER	US	3002
MICHAEL TOLES	G	(F	(C) IF WALLS COULD TALK	1969	CHECKER	US	3012
LESTER SNELL	PNO	(F	(D) GRITS & GROCERIES	1969	CHESS		CRLS 4552
WILLIAM MURPHY	B	(F	(E) FRIEND OF MINE	19	GLADES	US	7508
DAVID WEATHERSPOON	B	(F	(F) BLUES & SOUL	1974	STAX UK STX1013	US	5514
WILLIE HALL	D	(F	(G) GOLDEN DECADE	1974	PHONOGRAM		6310 120
MEMPHIS HRNS		(F	(H) MONTREUX FESTIVAL	1974	STAX	UK	STX 1029
LAWRENCE TAYLOR	SAX	(J	(J) RAISE A LITTLE SAND	1975	RED LIGHTNIN'	UK	RL 0011
EUGENE TURNER	PNO	(J	(K) BLUES MASTERS	1976	CHESS		2A CMB204
JERRY WALKER	D	(J	(L) SAMS BLUES	1976	CHARLY	UK	CR 30102
LARRY PROTO	TPT	(J	(M) WAITIN' FOR	19	STAX	UK	SAS 3012
FONTELLA BASS	PNO	(J	(N) GREATEST HITS	19	CHESS		CH 50113
C W TATE	SAX	(J	(O) CHRONICLE	1979	STAX	UK	STX 4123
CLEOPHUS ROBINSON	B	(J				
IKE TURNER	PNO	(J	OLIVER SAIN	SAX	(J	LONNIE HAYES	D	(J	VERN HARRELL	SAX	(J
JESSE KNIGHT	B	(J	JAMES CARR	SAX	(J						

L91   LITTLE RICHARD

LITTLE RICHARD (PENNIMAN)PNO V(ALL		HERE'S LITTLE RICHARD	1958	SPECIALTY	US 2100	UK LONDON	2055
WITH			LITTLE RICHARD 2	1958	SPECIALTY	US 2103	UK LONDON	2126
JIMI HENDRIX	G V	(*	THE FABULOUS	1959	SPECIALTY	US 2104	UK LONDON	2193
			BIGGEST HITS	196	SPECIALTY	US 2111	
			GREATEST HITS	196	SPECIALTY	US 2113	
			WELL ALRIGHT	1959	SPECIALTY	US 2136	
			SINGS GOSPEL	1964	STATESIDE	UK	SL10054
			LITTLE RICHARD IS BACK	196	JOY	US 100	
			LITTLE RICHARD IS BACK	196	FONTANA	UK	TL5235
			LITTLE RICHARD IS BACK	196	VEEJAY	US 1107	
			LITTLE RICHARD	196	JOY	US 107	
			MR BIG	196	JOY	US 195	
			RIP IT UP	196	JOY	US 260	
			SLIPPIN' & SLIDIN'	196	JOY	US 270	
			GREAT HITS	196		UK FONTANA 5314	
			ITS REAL	196		UK FONTANA 13010	
			LITTLE RICHARD STORY	196	JOY	US 5003/4	
			COMING HOME	1964	CORAL	US 757446 UK	LVA9220
			SINGS FREEDOM SONGS	1963	CROWN	US 5362	
			GREATEST HITS LIVE	19	MODERN	US 100	
			KING OF GOSPEL SONGS	1965	MERCURY	US 12288	
			WILD & FRANTIC	1965	MODERN	US 103	
			WILD & FRANTIC	19	UNITED	US 7777	
			THE EXPLOSIVE	1967	OKEH	US 14117 UK COLUMBIA 6136	
			GREATEST HITS LIVE	19	OKEH	US 14121	
			& ROY ORBISON	1970	RCA	UK	CDS 1077
			THE RILL THING	1971	REPRISE	US 6406	
			KING OF ROCK 'N' ROLL	1971	REPRISE	US 6462 UK	K 44156
			SECOND COMING	1971	REPRISE	US 2107 UK	K 44204
			THE GREAT ONES	197		UK MFP 50096	

(CONTINUED)

LITTLE RICHARD

ALL TIME HITS	1972	SONET	UK	SNTF 5000
ROCK HARD ROCK HEAVY	1972	SONET	UK	SNTF 5001
THE ORIGINAL	1972	SONET	UK	SNTF 5011
LITTLE RICHARD SINGS	19	20TH CENTURY	5010	
LITTLE RICHARD	19	KAMA SUTRA US	2023	
LITTLE RICHARD	19	BUDDAH US	7501	
BEST OF	19	SCEPTER US	18020	
RECORDED LIVE	19	EMBASSY	UK	31065
THE INCREDIBLE	19	CONTOUR	UK	2870 150
YOU CANT KEEP A GOOD MAN DOWN	1972	UNION PACIFIC	UK	UP 003
SINGS SPIRITUALS	19	UNITED US	7723	
GREATEST HITS	19	UNITED US	7775	
RIGHT NOW	19	UNITED US	7791	
THE BEST OF	19	UPFRONT US	123	
KEEP A KNOCKIN	19	RHAPSODY US	9013	
EVERY HOUR WITH	19	RCA US	2430	
KING OF GOSPEL SINGERS	19	WING US	12288	
CLAP YOUR HANDS	19	SPINORAMA US	S 119	
BIG HITS	19	GNP	US	9033
THE ONE & ONLY	1974	POLYDOR	UK	2482 440
STAR COLLECTION	1975	REPRISE	UK	K24009
THE VERY BEST OF	1975	UA	US LA4976	
DOLLARS DOLLARS & MORE DOLLARS	1975	CHARLY	UK	CR 30009
CAST A LONG SHADOW	197	EPIC	UK	66285
LITTLE RICHARD	197	EPIC	US 26260	
GREATEST HITS	197	EPIC	US 24257 UK EMBASY	31504
& SISTER ROSETTA THARPE	19	MARBLE ARCH	UK	MALS1319
(*) FRIENDS FROM THE BEGINNING	197	EMBER	UK	EMB 3434
GOOD GOLLY MISS MOLLY	19	HALLMARK	UK	SHM 858
22 ORIGINAL HITS	1977	WARWICK	UK	WW5034
20 ORIGINAL HITS	1976	SPECIALTY	UK	SNTF5017
NOW	1977	CREOLE		CRLP 510
(EP)				
HERE'S LITTLE RICHARD	195	SPECIALTY US	SEP 400	
" " " " 2	195	SPECIALTY US	SEP 401	
" " " " 3	195	SPECIALTY US	SEP 402	
LITTLE RICHARD 1	195	SPECIALTY US	SEP 403	
" " " 2	195	SPECIALTY US	SEP 404	
" " " 3	195	SPECIALTY US	SEP 405	
ROCKS	19	RCA US	CAE 446	
LITTLE RICHARD	19	RCA CAMDEN US	CAE 4111	
LONG TALL SALLY	1977	SPECIALTY UK	SONE 1	
LITTLE RICHARD	19	SPECIALTY UK	SON 5016	

LITTLE RIVER BAND

GRAHAM GOBLE	G V	(ABCD	(A) LITTLE RIVER BAND	1975 EMI	UK EMC3144 US CAPITOL 11512	
DAVID BRIGGS	G	(BCD	(B) AFTER HOURS	1976 EMI	UK EMC2546	
GLENN SHORROCK HCA V	(ABCD		(C) DIAMANTINA COCKTAIL	1977 EMI	UK EMC3187 US CAPITOL 11645	
GEORGE McARDLE	B	(BCD	(D) SLEEPER CATCHER	1978 EMI	UK EMA 786 US CAPITOL 11782	
DEREK PELLICCI	D	(ABCD	(E) IT'S A LONG WAY THERE	1978 EMIIMP 064 82516		
BEEB BIRTLES	G	(ABCD	(F) FIRST UNDER THE WIRE	1979 CAPITOL	11954	
RICK FORMOSA	G	(AC	(G) BACKSTAGE PASS	1980 CAPITOL	12061	
IAN MASON	PNO	(AC				
COL LAUGHNAN	SAX	(A	PETER SULLIVAN PNO (C TONY BUCHANAN	SAX (C ROGER McLACHLAN B (A		
STEPHEN COONEY	MAND	(A	GARY HYDE PERC (A EDDIE DENTON	(C GRAHAM LYALL FLT (C		
PETER JONES	PNO	(A	GEOFF SKEWES K (A			

LITTLE TINA & FLIGHT 56

(A) THIS GIRL GONNA ROCK	1978	CHARLY	UK	CR 30155	

LITTLE WALTER

LITTLE WALTER JACOBS HCA A(ALL		(A) LITTLE WALTER	1964 PYE INT	UK NPL 28043	
LOUIS MYERS	G	(AGHLMN	(A) LITTLE WALTER	1968 MARBLE ARCH	UK RI MAL 815
DAVE MYERS	G	(AGHLMN	(B) SUPER BLUES	1967 CHESS	UK CRL 4529
WILLIE DIXON	B	(AGHLMN	(C) BEST	196 CHESS US 1428 +CHECKER	3004
FRED BELOW	D	(AGHLMN	(D) BOSS OF BLUES HARMONICA	196 CHESS	US 60014
ROBERT LOCKWOOD	G	(GHLMN	(E) BLUES MASTERS	196 CHESS	UK 2A CBM 202
FRED ROBINSON	G	(AGHLMN	(F) HATE TO SEE YOU GO	19 CHESS	US 1535
OTIS SPANN	PNO	(AGHLMN	(G) & HIS JUKES	19 PYTHON	US PLPKM 20
MUDDY WATERS	G	(AGLMN	(H) QUARTER TO TWELVE	1970 RED LIGHTNIN'	UK RL 002
GEORGE HUNTER	D	(AGHLMN	(J) THUNDERBIRD	1971 SYNDICATE CHAPTER	SC 004
LUTHER TUCKER	G	(AGHLMN	(K) CONFESSIN' THE BLUES	1976 CHESS	FR CH 50043
JIMMY LEE ROBINSON G		(G	(L) BLUE & LONESOME	19 ROI DU BLUES	CAN 33 2007
LEONARD CASTON	G	(G	(M) SOUTHERN FEELING	19 ROI DU BLUES	CAN 33 2012
BILL STEPNEY	D	(G	(N) BLUE MIDNIGHT	19 ROI DU BLUES	CAN 33 2017
BO DIDDLEY	G	(G			
JIMMY ROGERS	G	(L	ELGIN EVANSIDE D (L HENRY GRAY	PNO (L ANDREW STEPHENSON B (M	
JARRETT GIBSON	SAX	(MH	JACK MYERS B (MN J T BROWN	SAX (N FRANCIS CLAY D (M	
LAFAYETTE LEAKE	PNO	(MN	AL DUNCAN D (MN PAT HARE	G (M BUDDY GUY G (MN	
BILLY EMERSON	K	(MN	ERNEST 'BIG' CRAWFORD B (N THE CORONETS	V (M	

LITTLE WILLIE LITTLEFIELD

LITTLE WILLIE LITTLEFIELD	(A) LITTLE WILLIE LITTLEFIELD VOL 1(10")	1980 ACE	10CH 24
	(B) IT'S MIDNIGHT	19 ROUTE 66 SWED	KIX 10

LIVERPOOL SCENE

ANDY ROBERTS	G V	(ABCDEF1	(A) INCREDIBLE NEW LIVERPOOL SCENE	1967 CBS UK EPIC US	BN 26336
ADRIAN HENRI	V	(ABCDEF1	(B) AMAZING ADVENTURES OF	1968 RCA US LSP4109	UK SF 7995
MIKE EVANS	V SAX(BCDE1		(C) BREAD ON THE NIGHT	1969 RCA US LSP4267	UK SF 8057
MIKE HART	V G	(BE1	(D) ST ADRIAN & CO	1969 RCA	UK SF 8100
PERCY JONES	B HCA(BCDE		(E) HEIRLOON	1970 RCA	UK SF 8134
BRIAN DODSON	D	(BCDE	(F) RECOLLECTIONS	1972 CHARISMA	UK CS 3
PETE CLARKE		(E	(1) 1974 REFORM		
ROGER McGOUGH	V	(A			
TOM KEMPINSKI	V	(E	DAVE RICHARDS B (1 MIKE KELLIE D (1 FRANK GARRETT (E		

LIVE WIRE

L95A

GERMAN GONZALES	D V	(AB	(A) PICK IT UP	1979	A&M	UK	AMLH	64793
MIKE EDWARDS	V G	(AB	(B) NO FRIGHT	1980	A&M	UK	AMLH	64814
JEREMY MEEK	B V	(AB						
CHRIS CUTLER	G V	(A	SIMON BOSWELL	G K V(B				

LIVIN' BLUES

L95B

NICKO CHRISTIANSEN	V SAX(ABCDE	(A) HELLS SESSION	1969	PHILIPS		6440	315
TED OBERG	G (ABCDEFG	(B) WANG DANG DOODLE	1970	PHILIPS		6440	125
JOHN LA GRAND	HCA (ABCDE	(C) BAMBOOZLE	1971	PHILIPS		6413	024
HENK SMITSKAMP	B K (AF	(D) ROCKIN' AT THE TWEEDMILL	1972	PHILIPS		6423	052
CESAR ZUIDERWIJK	D (A	(E) RAM JAM JOSEY	1973	ARIOLA		88525	
RUUD VAN BUUREN	B (BCDE	(F) LIVE '75	1975	ARIOLA		89243	
DICK BEEKMAN	D (B	(G) BLUE BREEZE	1976	ARIOLA		28430	
ARJEAN KAMMINGA	D (D						

PETE WINGFIELD PNO (DE MIKE VERNON V (D KENNY LAMB D (E JOHN FREDRIKSZ V (FG
COR VAN DER BEEK D (F ANDRE REIJNEN B (G JACOB VAN HEININGEN D (G MARGRIET ESHUYS V (G
MAGGIE McNEAL V (G MARTIN AGTERBERG K (G JONNY LE JEUNE D (D

DANDY LIVINGSTONE

L96

DANDY LIVINGSTONE	(ALL	(A) RETURNS	19	TROJAN		TRL	2
		(B) DANDY LIVINGSTONE	19	TROJAN		TRL	45
		(C) MORNING SIDE OF THE MOUNTAIN	19	TROJAN		TBL	118
		(D) CONSCIOUS	19	MOONCREST		CREST 5	
		(E) SOUTH AFRICAN EXPERIENCE	1978	NIGHT OWL	NORLP	1001	

CHARLES LLOYD

L97

CHARLES LLOYD	WIND (ALL	(A) MOONMAN	1972	MCA MUPS 421 UK+1974 UK MCF 2643				
MIKE LOVE	(E	(B) LOVE IN	19	ATLANTIC		US SD	1481	
CARL WILSON	(E	(C) IN EUROPE	19	ATLANTIC		US SD	1500	
AL JARDINE	(E	(D) SOUNDTRACK	19	ATLANTIC		US SD	1519	
ROGER McGUINN	(E	(E) WAVES	1972	A&M		US SP	3044	

IAN LLOYD

L98

IAN LLOYD	V (AB	(A) IAN LLOYD	19	POLYDOR		US	1 6066	
JIM VALLANCE	(B	(B) GOOSE BUMPS	1979	SCOTTI BROS UK K50655 US SB 7104				
STEVE BUSLOWE	(B							

JIMMY CRESPO (B MICK JONES (B LOU GRAMM (B DENNIS ELLIOTT (B
RICK OCASEK (B BENJAMIN ORR (B JIMMY MAELEN (B DAVID SINCLAIR (B
MICHAEL BRECKER HRNS (B LINDSAY MITCHELL (B LARRY FAST (B GREGG DIAMOND D (A
IAN McDONALD SAX (A

RICHARD LLOYD

L98A

RICHARD LLOYD	G V PNO HCA(A	(A) ALCHEMY	1979'	ELEKTRA	UK K52196
MATTHEW MACKENZIE	G PNO V(A				
JIM MASTRO	G (A	FRED SMITH	B V (A VINNY DENUNZIO	D V (A MICHAEL YOUNG G SYN(A

ANDREW LLOYD WEBBER

L99

ANDREW LLOYD WEBBER	(A	(A) VARIATIONS	1977	MCA	UK MCF 2824
DON AIREY	K (A				
ROD ARGENT	K (A	GARY MOORE	G (A JON HISEMAN	D (A BARBARA THOMPSON WIND (A
JOHN MOLE	B (A	JULIAN LLOYD WEBBER CELLO(A			

LOADING ZONE

L100

LINDA TILLERY	V B D HCA(A	(A) LOADING ZONE	1968	RCA	US	LSP	3959
PAUL FAUERSO	V K (A	(B) ONE FOR ALL	19	UMBRELLA	US		101
PETER SHAPIRO	G (A						

TODD ANDERSON WIND K(A PAT O'HARA TROM (A STEVE DOWLER G (A BOB KRIDLE B (A
GEORGE NEWCOM D (A

LOCAL HEROES

L100A

KEVIN ARMSTRONG	V G (A	(A) DRIP DRY ZONE	1980	OVAL	UK	OVLP	504
KIM BARTI	D (A						
MATTHEW SELIGMAN	B (A						

GERRY LOCKRAN

L101

GERRY LOCKRAN	V (ALL	(A) HOLD ON I'M COMING	1967	PLANET		PLL 1002
KIRK LORANGE	G V (D	(B) THE ESSENTIAL	1969	SPARK		SRLP104
NEIL HUBBARD	G (D	(C) WUN	1972	POLYDOR		2383 122
HENRY McCULLOUGH	G (D	(D) RAGS TO GLADRAGS	1976	DECCA	UK	SKLR5257
ISRAEL ZACUTO	G (D	(E) BLUES VENDETTA	19	WAVERLEY		ZLP 2091
CHRIS STEWART	B (D	(1) BLUES BAND 1968				
BRUCE ROWLAND	D (D					

MEL COLLINS SAX (D CLIFF AUNGIER (1 PHIL CHEN B (D LOUIE MARTIN PERC (D
DWIGHT DRUICK V (D HARVEY BURNS D (1 TERRY STANNARD D (D PETE WINGFIELD PNO (D
JOHNNY PARKER (1 BRIAN HOPKINS (1

ROBERT LOCKWOOD

L102

ROBERT 'JUNIOR'LOCKWOOD	G V(ALL	(A) STEADY ROLLIN' MAN	19	DELMARK		630
GENE SCHWARTZ	B (DF	(B) COUNTRY BLUES CLASSICS	19	BLUES CLASSICS		7
GEORGE COOK	D (D	(C) LONESOME ROAD BLUES	19	YAZOO		1038
MAURICE REEDUS	SAX (DF	(D) CONTRASTS	1974	TRIX		330 7
LOUIS MYERS	G HCA(E	(E) BLUES LIVE	1975	ADVENT US 2807 +TRIO JAP 6024		
DAVE MYERS	B (E	(F) DOES 12	1976	TRIX		331 7
FRED BELOW	D (E	(G) HANGIN' ON	19	ROUNDER	US	2023
MARK HAHN	G (F					
JIMMY JONES	D (F	JOHNNY SHINES	G V (G			

LOCOMOTIV GT

L103

TAMAS BARTA	G V HCA (A	(A) LOCOMOTIV GT	1974 ABC ABCX 811	+EPIC UK80229	
JOSEPH LAUX	D (A	(B) ALL ABOARD	1975	US	
GABOR PRESSER	K V (A				
THOMAS SOMLO	B V SAX VLN(A	JACK BRUCE	HCA (A JIMMY MILLER	PERC (A

LOCOMOTIVE

L104

MICK HINCKS	B (	(A) WE ARE EVERYTHING YOU SEE	1969 PARLOPHONE	UK	PCS 7093
MIKE TAYLOR	(					
NORMAN HAINES	(	CHRIS WOOD WIND (A BILL MADGE	(	BOB LAMB	D (

LOCOMOTIVE (US)

L104A

		(A) LOCOMOTIVE	19	MGM	US	SE4653

```
                        LOCUST                                    L105
                   (A) PLAYGUE              1977  ANNUIT COEPTIS    AC1004
                      JOHN LODGE                                   L106
JOHN LODGE      V G  (A    (A) NATURAL AVENUE   1977 DECCA UK TXS 120 LONDON US  683
KENNEY JONES         (A
BRIAN ROGERS         (A   MEL COLLINS      (A   JOHN RICHARDSON    (A  STEVE SIMPSON   (A
CHRIS SPEDDING   G   (A   MARTIN DOBSON    (A   ALAN WILLIAMS      (A  MICK WEAVER     (A
JIMMY JEWELL    WIND (A   GARY OSBORNE     (A   BILLY LAWRIE       (A
                   NILS LOFGREN & GRIN                            L107
NILS LOFGREN    G VK(ALL   (A) GRIN               1971 EPIC UK 64272 US SPINDIZZY 30321
BOB BERBERICH   D V  (ABCDL  (B) ONE PLUS ONE     1972 EPIC UK 64652 US SPINDIZZY 31038
BOB GORDON      B V  (ABCDL  (C) ALL OUT          1972 EPIC UK 65166
TOM LOFGREN     G V  (CDFHJKL1  (D) GONE CRAZY    1975 A&M  UK 64415 US A&M  SP4415
REV PAT HENDERSON K  (HJ    (E) NILS LOFGREN      1975 A&M  UK 64509 US A&M  SP4509
WORNELL JONES   B    (EFHJ   (F) CRY TOUGH        1976 A&M  UK 64573 US A&M  SP4573
KATHY McDONALD  V    (CL     (G) BACK IT UP(AUTHORIZED BOOTLEG) 1976 A&M  US A&M  SPB362
AYNSLEY DUNBAR  D    (EF     (H) I CAME TO DANCE  1977 A&M  UK 64628 US A&M  SP4628
STU GARDNER     V    (E      (J) NIGHT AFTER NIGHT 1977 A&M  UK 69439 US A&M  SP3707
CHUCK RAINEY    B    (F      (K) NILS             1979 A&M  UK 64756
JIM GORDON      D    (F      (L) NILS LOFGREN & GRIN 1979 CBS      US       31770
BOB EZRIN   PERC V K (K      (AB) GRIN/ONE PLUS ONE 1976 CBS UK 88204
DOUG RILEY      ORG  (K      (1) LIVE TOUR 1975 LINE UP
EMIL RICHARDS   PERC (F
AL KOOPER       K    (F  RON HICKLIN SINGERS (F  P P ARNOLD      V  (F  CLAUDIA LENNEAR  V (F
BUDDY MILES     V    (F  RALPH MOLINA    V   (F  MIKE ZACK       D  (1  BOBBYE HALL   PERC (D
PAUL STALLWORTH B    (F  SCOTT BALL      B  (F1  DAVID PLATSHON  D  (1  ANDY NEWMARK    D  (H
HOLDEN RAPHAEL  PERC (F  GRAHAM NASH     V   (B  CLYDIE KING     V  (D  SHIRLEY MATTHEWS V (K
MERRY CLAYTON   V    (D  ALLEN SCHWARZBERG D (K  JODY LINSCOTT CONGA(K  DAVID SANBORN  SAX (K
STU DAYE        G V  (K  BOB BABITT          B (K
                      DAVE LOGGINS                                L108
DAVE LOGGINS    G V  (ALL  (A) PERSONAL BELONGINGS  1972 VANGUARD    UK VSD  6580
JERRY CARRIGAN  D    (B    (B) APPRENTICE         1974 EPIC US 32833 UK  80622
JOHN GUERIN     D    (B    (C) COUNTRY SUITE       1976 EPIC US 33946
KENNY MALONE    D    (B    (D) ONE WAY TICKET TO PARADISE 1977 EPIC US 34713
NORBERT PUTNAM  B    (B    (E) DAVID LOGGINS       1977 EPIC
WILLIAM SMITH   PNO  (B
BILLY SANFORD   G    (B  BYRON BACH     CELLO(B  FARRELL MORRIS PERC (B  JOHN RAINES     D(B
LEE SKLAR       B    (B  DAVID BRIGGS   PNO  (B  MIKE NOBLE      G  (B  AL DELEONIBUS ACC(B
LARRY LONDIN    D    (B  SHANE KEISTER  K    (B  STEVE GIBSON    G  (B  MAC GAYDEN  FDL G (B
WELDON MYRICK   STEEL(B
                      KENNY LOGGINS                               L109
KENNY LOGGINS   G V  (ALL  (A) CELEBRATE ME HOME  1977 CBS US 34655  UK  81882
ROBBEN FORD     G    (A    (B) NIGHTWATCH         1978 CBS US 35387  UK  82865
STEVE GADD      D    (A    (C) KEEP THE FIRE      1979 CBS US        UK  83869
LAUDIR DE OLIVEIRA PERC(A  (D) ALIVE(DBL)         1980 CBS US        UK  88500
ERIC GALE       G    (A
GEORGE HAWKINS  B V  (D  VINCE DENHAM WIND V (D  MIKE HAMILTON  G V (D  BRIAN MANN   K V (D
TRIS IMBODEN    D V  (D  JON CLARKE  WIND PERC (D
                    LOGGINS & MESSINA                             L110
KENNY LOGGINS   G V  (ALL  (A) SITTIN' IN          1971 CBS US 31044  UK  64902
JIM MESSINA     G B V(ALL  (B) LOGGINS & MESSINA   1972 CBS US 31748  UK  65194
LARRY SIMS      B    (CDJK  (C) FULL SAIL          1973 CBS US 32540  UK  65775
AL GARTH   HRNS FDL (CDJK   (D) ON STAGE           1974 CBS US 33848  UK  88014
MEREL BREGANTE  D    (CDJK  (E) MOTHERLODE         1975 CBS US 33175  UK  80431
JON CLARKE    HRNS  (CDJK   (F) SO FINE            1975 CBS US 33810  UK  69169
MIKE OMARTIAN   K    (      (G) NATIVE SONS        1976 CBS US 33578  UK  69227
JACK LENZ       FLT  (J     (H) BEST OF FRIENDS    1977 CBS US 34388  UK  81692
VINCE DENHAM    SAX  (J     (J) FINALE             1978 CBS US 34167  UK  88205
DON ROBERTS     SAX  (J     (K) BEST OF            1980 CBS US 31826
RICHARD GREENE  VLN  (J
STEVE FOREMAN   PERC (J  WOODY CHRISMAN   G   (J  GEORGE HAWKINS  B V (J  DOUG LIVINGSTON K (J
WILLIE ORNELAS  D    (J
                      JACKIE LOMAX                                L111
JACKIE LOMAX    G V        (A) IS THIS WHAT YOU WANT  1969 APPLE US 3354 UK SAPCOR 6
(AKA RICK RED STREAK)      (B) HOME IS IN MY HEAD   1971 WB   US 1914 UK  K 46091
JOHN BARHAM          (A    (C) THREE               1972 WB   US 2591 UK  K 46151
HAL BLAINE      D    (A    (D) LIVIN' FOR LOVIN'   1976 CAPITOL        11558
ALAN BRANSCOMBE      (A    (E) DID YOU EVER        1977 CAPITOL        11668
ERIC CLAPTON    G    (A
PETE CLARKE          (A  NICKY HOPKINS   K   (A  BISHOP O'BRIEN    (A  RINGO STARR   D V (A
BRYN HAWORTH    G V  (B  PAUL GRIFFIN    K   (B  LINDA NOVEMBER V (B  BILLY RICH    B  (C
ROBBIE ROBERTSON G   (C  RICHARD MANUEL      (C  RON STOCKERT  K V (DE STEVE BECKMAIER G (D
HARVEY MASON    D    (D  IAN MATTHEWS    V   (D  GEORGE HARRISON G (A  LARRY KNECHTEL   (A
TONY NEWMAN          (A  KLAUS VOORMANN  B   (A  BUGS PEMBERTON  D (BDE EDDIE BRIGATI  V (B
SELDON POWELL   SAX  (B  MAERETHA STEWART V  (B  JOHN HALL     G  (C  LEVON HELM    V D (C
MARTY GREBB     SAX  (D  WILLIAM D SMITH K   (D  MARTY DAVID   B  (DE CHRISTOPHER PARKER D (D
DON WHALEY      V    (A  SPIKE HEATLEY       (A  PAUL McCARTNEY    (A  JOE OSBORN       (A
ISRAEL ZACUTO   G    (B  TOMMY CACCETTA  B   (B  DAVID BRIGATI V (B  HELENE W MILES  V (B
BERNARD PURDIE  D    (C  RICK DANKO          (C  GARTH HUDSON     (C  JIMMY ROBERTS SAX (DE
RANDY ZACUTO    G    (D  RITCHIE HAYWARD D   (E  JOE CORRERO   D  (D  AL STAEHELY    V (D
ANDRE FISCHER   D    (E  AL CINER       G    (E  MAX MIDDLETON SYN (E  GENE DINWIDDIE WIND(E
DEBORAH LINDSEY V    (E  STEVE MADAIO  TPT   (E  JIM PRICE   TROM (E  PAT MURPHY    PERC(E
BROOKS HUNNICUTT V   (E  LISA FREEMAN ROBERTS V (E
                     LOMAX ALLIANCE                              L112
JACKIE LOMAX    V G  (
BUGS PEMBERTON  D    (
TOM CACCETTA    B    (
```

L113   LONDON

```
RIFF REGAN       V  (A        (A) ANIMAL GAMES           1978  MCA                MCF  2823
STEVE VOICE      B  (A
JOHN MOSS        D  (A   DAVE WIGHT     G  (A
```

L113A   LONE GROOVER

```
                              (A) WHO CARES (EP)         1978  CHARLY      UK     CEP  124
```

L114   LONE STAR

```
KEN DRISCOLL     V  (A        (A) LONE STAR             1976  CBS US 34475  UK EPIC 81545
TONY SMITH       G  (AB       (B) FIRING ON ALL SIX     1977               UK EPIC 82213
PAUL CHAPMAN     G  (AB
PETE HURLEY      B  (AB  DIXIE LEE      D  (AB  RICK WORSNOP   K  (AB  JOHN SLOMAN      V  (B
```

L115   LONESOME SUNDOWN

```
LONESOME SUNDOWN              (A) LONESOME LONELY BLUES  1970  EXCELLO       US         8012
(CORNELIUS GREEN) V G (AB     (A) LONESOME LONELY BLUES  1970  BLUE HORIZON  UK    7  63864
LIONEL PREVO     SAX (A       (B) BEEN GONE TOO LONG     1979  JOLIET        US         6002
AUSTIN BROUSSARD D  (A
KATIE WEBSTER    PNO (A  MERT THIBODEAUX  PNO (A  LAZY LESTER   HCA (A  DEE DEE GRADNIER  HCA(A
BOBBY McBRIDE    B  (A   RUFUS THIBODEAUX B  (A   WARREN STORM  D  (A
```

L115A   ROY LONEY & THE PHANTOM MOVERS

```
ROY LONEY        V  (A        (A) PHANTOM TRACKS         1980  SOLID SMOKE
DANNY MIHM       D  (A        ( ) OUT AFTER DARK         1979  SOLID SMOKE   US    9001
JAMES FERRELL    G  (A
MAURICE TANI     B  (A   LARRY LEA      G  (A
```

L116   LONGBRANCH PENNYWHISTLE

```
J D SOUTHER      G V (A       (A) LONGBRANCH PENNYWHISTLE 1970 AMOS         US     AAS 7007
GLENN FREY       G V (A
JAMES BURTON     G   (A  RY COODER      G  (A  JIM GORDON    D  (A  BUDDY EMMONS    STEEL(A
LARRY KNECHTEL   PNO (A  JOE OSBORN     B  (A  DOUG KERSHAW  G V (A
```

L117   LONGDANCER

```
MATT IRVING      K G V(B      (A) IF IT WAS SO SIMPLE    1973  ROCKET              PIGL  1
STEVE SPROXTON   G V (AB      (B) TRAILER FOR A GOOD LIFE 1974 ROCKET              PIGL  6
BRIAN HARRISON   G B V(AB
DAVE STEWART     G B V(AB CHARLIE SMITH   D V (AB  JIMMY HALL    PNO (A  ROGER POWELL      D(A
VIRAM JASANI     SITAR(B  TOMMY McCARTHY  PIPES(B  POPART STRINGS      (B  KAI OLSSON      G V (A
BOB RONGA        B   (A   ANDY ROBERTS    DULC (A  KESH SATHIE   PERC (B  BONES             V (B
DAVE MATTACKS    F   (B   TONY ASHTON     K   (A   DEL NEWMAN    K  (B  JUDD PROCTOR     BANJ(B
CHARLES YOUNG    CHOIR (B
```

L117A   LONG HELLO

```
                              (A) LONG HELLO             1979  BUTT                NOTT  002
```

L118   PROFESSOR LONGHAIR

```
PROFESSOR LONGHAIR  V PNO(ALL (A) NEW ORLEANS PIANO      1972  ATLANTIC  US 7225 UK  K 40402
LEE ALLEN        SAX (A       (A) NEW ORLEANS PIANO      197   PIONEER    JAP       P4582A
RED TYLER        SAX (A       (B) ROCK'N' ROLL GUMBO     1975  BARCLAY             80606
EDGAR BLANCHARD  B   (A       (C) LIVE ON THE QUEEN MARY 1978  HARVEST    UK SHSP 4086
EARL PALMER      D   (A       (D) CRAWFISH FIESTA        1980  SONET      UK SNTF  830
ROBERT PARKER    SAX (A       (D) CRAWFISH FIESTA        1980  ALLIGATOR  US  AL 4718
DAVID LEE WATSON B   (D
CHARLIE BURBECK  SAX (A   AL MILLER       D   (A   JOHN WOODROW  D  (A  DR JOHN         G  (D
ANDY KASLOW      SAX (D   TONY DAGRADI    SAX (D   JOHN VIDACOVICH D (D  JIM MOORE      SAX(D
ALFRED ROBERTS   CONGA(D
```

L119   WILBERT LONGMIRE

```
WILBERT LONGMIRE G V (ABC     (A) SUNNY SIDE UP          1978  CBS                UK  82845
BOB JAMES        K   (ABC     (B) CHAMPAGNE              1979  CBS                UK  83257
DAVE SANBORN     SAX (A       (C) WITH ALL MY LOVE       1980  CBS                UK  84155
ERIC GALE        G   (AB
HARVEY MASON     D   (AB  RICHARD TEE    K  (AB  RANDY BRECKER  TPT (B  JON FADDIS     TPT (B
WAYNE ANDRE      TROM(BC   RON CUBER      SAX (B  EDDIE DANIELS  FLT (BC GORDON GRODY    V  (B
STEVE KHAN       G   (C   GILMORE DIGAP  PERC(C  PETER GORDON   HRNS(C  GLORIA AGOSTINI HARP(C
JOCELYN SHAW     V   (C   GARY KING      B  (BC  JIM MAELEN     PERC(BC IDRIS MUHAMMAD  D  (B
LEWIS SOLOFF     TPT (B   MIKE LAWRENCE  TPT(BC  PAUL FAULISE   TROM(B  GEORGE MARGE    WIND(BC
PHIL BODNER      FLT (BC  LANI GROVES    V  (BC  BARRY MILES    K  (C   MARVIN STAMM    HRNS(C
JIM BUFFINGTON   HRNS(C   BABBI B FLOYD  V  (C   EARL McINTYRE  TROM(B  BARRY ROGERS    TROM(B
MICHAEL BRECKER  SAX (C   GEORGE YOUNG   SAX(B   DIVA GRAY      V  (BC  ZACK SANDERS    V  (BC
BUDDY WILLIAMS   D   (C   DAVE TAYLOR    HRNS(C  FRANK FLOYD    V  (C
```

L119A   LOOK

```
JOHNNY FONTAINE  V G  (
MICK BASS        G V K(
GUS GOAD         B V  (   TREVOR WALTERS  D  (
```

L119B   LOOKING GLASS

```
ELLIOT LURIE     G V (A       (A) LOOKING GLASS          1972  EPIC       UK  EPC 65041
LARRY GONSKY     K V (A
PIET SWEVAL      B V (A   JEFF GROB      D  (A  BARBARA MASSEY  V  (A  CAROLYN DAVIS    V (A
TASHA THOMAS     V   (A
```

L119C   JEFF LORBER FUSION

```
JEFF LORBER      K   (ALL     (A) SOFT SPACE             197   INNER CITY  US      IC1056
TERRY LAYNE      WIND(A        (B) WATER SIGN            1979  ARISTA      US   AB 4234
LESTER McFARLAND B   (A       (C) WIZARD ISLAND          1980  ARISTA      US   AL 9516
DENNIS BRADFORD  D   (ABC
RON YOUNG        PERC(A   DANNY WILSON   B  (BC  DOUG LEWIS     G  (B  KENNY GORELICK  WIND(C
CHICK COREA      K   (AC  JOE FARRELL    SAX(AB  DENNIS SPRINGER SAX(B  JAY KODER       G  (BC
PAULINHO DA COSTA PERC(C  BRUCE SMITH    PERC(AB DEAN REICHERT  G  (A  FREDDY HUBBARD  HRNS(B
```

L120   JON LORD

```
JON LORD         K   (ALL     (A) GEMINI SUITE          1971  PURPLE     UK  TPSA 7501
TONY ASHTON      K V (AB      (B) WINDOWS                1974  PURPLE     UK  TPSA 7513
DAVID COVERDALE  V   (A       (C) SARABANDE              1976  PURPLE     UK  TPSA 7516
RAY FENWICK      G   (B
GLENN HUGHES     V G B(B  EBERHARD SCHOENER K (B  ROGER GLOVER  B  (A  ALBERT LEE      G  (A
PETE YORK        D   (B   YVONNE ELLIMAN  V  (A   IAN PAICE     D  (A  ORCHESTRAS      (AB
```

LORDS L121

(A) ULLEOGAMAXBE 19 COLUMBIA SMC 74343

LOST & FOUND L121A

JAMES HARRELL (A
PETE BLACK (A
JIMMY FROST (A
STEVE WEBB (A

(A) EVERYBODY'S HERE 19 INTERNATIONAL ARTISTS IALP3

LOST GONZO BAND L122

GARY NUNN PNO V B G (A
ROBERT LIVINGSTON B K V(B
JOHN INMON G V (B
KELLY DUNN SYN K(B
DONNY DOLAN D PERC(B

(A) LOST GONZO BAND 1975 MCA UK MCF 2727 US MCA 487
(B) THRILLS 1976 MCA US MCA2232
(C) SIGNS OF LIFE 197 CAPITOL US 11788

LOTHAR & THE HAND PEOPLE L122A

JOHN EMELIN EFFECTS(A
KIM KING G (A
TOM FLYE D (A
PAUL CONLEY G (A
RUSTY FORD B (A

(A) PRESENTING LOTHAR & THE HAND PEOPLE 1968 CAPITOL US 2997
(B) SPACE HYMN 19 CAPITOL US 247

J D LOUDERMILK L123

J D LOUDERMILK

LANGUAGE OF LOVE 196 RCA US LSP 2434
12 SIDES OF 196 RCA US LSP 2539
SINGS A BIZARRE COLLECTION 1966 RCA UK RD7890 US LSP 3497
SURBURBAN ATTITUDES 1967 RCA US LSP 3807
COUNTRY LOVE SONGS 1968 RCA US LSP 4040
THE OPEN MIND OF J D LOUDERMILK 1969 RCA US LSP 4097
ELLOREE VOL 1 1971 WB UK K46124 US 1922
BEST OF 1973 RCA US LSA 3159
ENCORES 1975 RCA US LSA 3220
JUST PASSING THROUGH 1978 MIM US MIMLP9009

LOUDSPEAKERS L124

RICHARD RAE D (A
CHRIS THOMAS G V (A
IAN GAIR K V (A
BRIAN ENGEL V (A
BRENDAN WALSH B G (A

(A) LOUDSPEAKERS 1978 EBONY UK EBY 1004

JOE HILL LOUIS L125

JOE HILL LOUIS G V HCA(A
WILLIE NIX D V (A
BILLY 'RED' LOVE PNO (A
WILLIE JOHNSON G (A

(A) BLUE IN THE MORNING 1973 POLYDOR 2383 214

LOUISIANA RED L126

LOUISIANA RED G V (ALL
BILL DICEY HCA (C
TOMMY TUCKER PNO (C
DAVE'BABY 'CORTEZ ORG (C
ROBERT BANKS PNO (C
NAPOLEON ALLEN G (C
EARL WILLIAMS D (C
PAUL MARTINEZ B (C
KEN MIMMS G (C
DICK BUNN B (C
DON COOK PNO (C
SID BARNES D (C
SUNNYLAND SLIM PNO (J
SUGAR BLUE HCA (F
JIM EVANS D (C
ELAINE MONK V (G
BOB STROGER B (J
BOB MALENKY G (C
VIVIAN MINTER V (G
ODIE PAYNE D (J
LEONARD GASKIN B (C
HUBERT SUMLIN G (J
CAREY BELL HARRINGTON HCA(J

(A) SEVENTH SON 1963 CARNIVAL RI 2941 002
(A) LOW DOWN BACK PORCH BLUES 196 ROULETTE US 25200
(C) SINGS THE BLUES 1972 ATLANTIC UK K40436 US 33389
(D) SWEET BLOOD CALL 1975 BLUE LABOR US BL 104
(E) DEAD STRAY DOG 1976 BLUE LABOR US BL 107
(F) RED FUNK & BLUE 1978 BLACK PANTHER UK BP1001
(G) NEW YORK BLUES 1979 L&R 42 002
(H) KING BEE 1979 JSP 1006
(J) REALITY BLUES 1980 L&R 42 011

LOUNGE LIZARDS L126A

JOHN LURIE SAX (1
ATRO LINDSAY G (1
STEVE PICCOLO B (1
ANTON FIER D (1

(1) 1980 US

LOU'S L127

PAMELA POPO G V (
SACHA DEJONG D (
RAPHAELE DEVINS G (A
TOLIM TOTO B (

LOVE L128

ARTHUR LEE G V (ABCDF
JOHN ECHOLS G (BC
BRYAN MACLEAN G V (BC
KEN FORSSI B (BC
ALBAN PFISTERER D (B
DON CONKA D (
MICHAEL STUART PERC (BC
TJAY CANTRELLI PERC (B
JAY DONNELLAN G (DF
FRANK FAYAD B (DF
GEORGE SURANOVICH D (DF
GARY ROWLES G (F
DRACHEN THEAKER D (DF
JOEY BLOCKER D (J
BUZZY FEITEN G (J
WILBER BROWN HRNS (J
ART FOX G (J
ALAN DE VILLE HRNS (J
JESSIE SMITH V (J
SHERWOOD AKUNA B (J
JOEY DEAGUERO VIBES(J
PAUL MARTIN G (F
BOBBY LYLE K (J
HERMAN McCORMICK CONGA(J
FRED CARTER HRNS (J
ROBERT ROZELLE B (J
VANETTA FIELDS V (J
JIM HOBSON K (F
CARLENE WILLIAMS V (J
HARVEY MANDEL G (J
BILLY SPRAGUE HRNS (J
MELVAN WHITTINGTON G (J
CLIFFORD SOLOMON HRNS (J
JOHN STIRLING G (J
JOHN CLAUDER HRNS(J
GARY BELL SYN(J

(A) LOVE 1966 ELEKTRA EKS 74001
(B) DA CAPO 1967 ELEKTRA UK K42011 EKS 74005
(C) FOREVER CHANGES 1967 ELEKTRA UK K42015 EKS 74013
(D) FOUR SAIL 1969 ELEKTRA UK K42030 EKS 74049
(E) LOVE REVISTITED 1970 ELEKTRA 2469 009 EKS 74058
(E) LOVE REVISITED 1971 ELEKTRA UK K42091
(F) OUT HERE 1969 BLUE THUMB US BTS 9000
(F) OUT HERE 1969 HARVEST UK SHDW 3/4
(G) FALSE START 1970 BLUE THUMB US BTS 8822
(G) FALSE START 1970 HARVEST UK SHVL 787
(H) LOVE MASTERS 1972 ELEKTRA UK K32002
(J) REEL TO REAL 1974 RSO 2394 145 US 4804

CLAYTON LOVE L128A

CLAYTON LOVE V PNO(A
SID WALLACE V (A
EUGENE WASHINGTON D (A
GEORGE BRAZIER B (A
NAT RIGGINS G (A

(A) COME ON HOME BLUES(10") 197 RED LIGHTNING RL0029

MIKE LOVE L129

MIKE LOVE V (A
CHARLES LLOYD WIND (A
RON ALTBACH PNO V(A
MIKE KOWALSKI D (A
ED CARTER G (A
GARY GRIFFIN K (A
DAVE ROBINSON B (A
WELLS KELLY G (A

(A) CELEBRATION 197

L130 LOVE COMMITTEE

NORMAN FRAZIER	V	(A		(A) LAW & ORDER				1978 SALSOUL UK 1506 GOLDMINE US9500			
LARRY RICHARDSON	V	(A									
JOE FREEMAN	V	(A	RON TYSON	V PERC(A	EARL YOUNG	D	(A	KEITH BENSON	D	(A	
RON BAKER	B	(A	JIMMY WILLIAMS	B	(A	NORMAN HARRIS	G	(A	BOBBY ELI	G	(A
ROLAND CHAMBERS	G	(A	T J TINDALL	G	(A	EDDIE MOORE	G	(A	RON KERSEY	K	(A
COTTON KENT	K	(A	BRUCE GRAY	K	(A	T G CONWAY	K	(A	BRUCE HAWES	K	(A
LARRY WASHINGTON	CONGAS(A		ALLAN FELDER PERC		(A	DON RENALDO	STRINGS	(A	EVETTE BENTON	V	(A
BARBARA INGRAM	V	(A	CARLA BENSON	V	(A						

L130A LOVECRAFT

MICHAEL TEGZA	D V	(AB		(A) VALLEY OF THE MOON	1970	REPRISE		6419
LALOMIE WASHBURN	V PERC(B			(B) WE LOVE YOU WHOEVER YOU ARE	1975	MERCURY	US	SRMI 1031
FRANK CAPEK	G	(B						
JORGE RODRIGUEZ	G	(B	CRAIG GIGSTAD	B	(B	GEORGE AGOSTO	PERC (B	MARK JUSTIN	K SYN(B

L130B LOVERBOY

MIKE RENO	V	(A		(A) LOVERBOY	1980	CBS	US	36762
PAUL DEAN	G V	(A						
MATT FRENETTE	D	(A	DOUG JOHNSON	K	(A	SCOTT SMITH	B	(A

L131 LENE LOVICH

LENE LOVICH	V SAX(AB			(A) STATELESS	1978	STIFF	UK	SEEZ 7
LES CHAPPELL	G	(B		(B) FLEX	1979	STIFF	UK	SEEZ 19
MARK CHAPLIN	B	(B						
JUSTIN HILDRETH	D	(B	DEAN KLAVETT	K	(B	NICK PLYTAS	K	(B CHRIS JUDGE-SMITH V (B

L132 LOVING AWARENESS

CHARLIE CHARLES	D	(A		(A) LOVING AWARENESS	1976	MORE LOVE		ML 001
NORMAN WATT-ROY	B	(A						
MICK GALLAGHER	K	(A	JOHN TURNBULL	G	(A			

L133 LOVING SPOONFUL

JOHN SEBASTIAN	G V	(	(A) DO YOU BELIEVE IN MAGIC	1965 PYE UK 28069 KAMA SUTRA	US 8050
ZAL YANOVSKY	V G	(	(B) DAYDREAMS	1966 PYE UK 28078 KAMA SUTRA	US 8051
JOE BUTLER	D	(	(C) WHATS UP TIGER LILY	1966 KAMA SUTRA	US 8053
STEVE BOONE	B	(	(D) HUMS	1966 KAMA SUTRA UK 401	US 8054
JERRY YESTER	G	(	(D) HUMS	196 KAMA SUTRA GERM	2319 034
GLEN COVE	D	(	(E) BEST OF VOL 1	1967 KAMA SUTRA UK 403	US 2608
WOODY ALLEN		(C	(E) BEST OF VOL 1	1967 KAMA SUTRA GERM 620004	US 8056
			(F) YOU'RE A BIG BOY NOW	1967 KAMA SUTRA UK 402	US 8058
			(G) EVERYTHING PLAYING	1967 KAMA SUTRA UK 404	US 8061
			(G) EVERYTHING PLAYING	1967 KAMA SUTRA GERM 620006	
			(H) BEST OF VOL 2	1968 KAMA SUTRA UK 405	US 8064
			(H) BEST OF VOL 2	1968 KAMA SUTRA GERM 620007	
			(J) REVELATION REVOLUTION	1968 KAMA SUTRA	US 8073
			(K) THE VERY BEST OF (COMP)	19 KAMA SUTRA	US 2013
			(L) GREATEST HITS	1970 KAMA SUTRA	2361 002
			(M) POP HISTORY	19 POLYDOR	2625 010
			(N) MORE GOLDEN SPOONFUL	1974 KAMA SUTRA	KSMD 9002
			(O) GOLDEN HOUR	1975 PYE UK	GH 838
			(P) THE GREAT YEARS	19 MODE FR	MD 9022
			(Q) LOVING SPOONFUL	19 PROFILE GERM	624 018
			(R) FILE	1977 PYE UK	FILD009
			(EP)		
			DID YOU EVER	1966 KAMA SUTRA	KEP 300
			JUG BAND MUSIC	1966 KAMA SUTRA	KEP 301
			SUMMER IN THE CITY	1966 KAMA SUTRA	KEP 302
			DAY BLUES	1967 KAMA SUTRA	KEP 303
			NASHVILLE CATS	1967 KAMA SUTRA	KEP 304
			LOVING YOU	1967 KAMA SUTRA	KEP 305
			SOMETHING IN THE NIGHT	1967 KAMA SUTRA	KEP 306

L134 LOW NUMBERS

(A) TWIST AGAIN WITH THE LOW NUMBERS   1978   RHINO   RNLP 004

L135 NICK LOWE

NICK LOWE	B V G(ALL		(A) JESUS OF COOL	1978 RADAR RAD 1	+ RADAR K56466
DAVE EDMUNDS	G	(	(A) PURE POP FOR NOW PEOPLE	1978 CBS	US 35329
BILLY BREMNER	G	(	(B) LABOUR OF LUST	1979 RADAR	RAD21
TERRY WILLIAMS	D	(	(EP) BOWI	1977 STIFF	LAST 1

L136 HENRY LOWTHER

HENRY LOWTHER	HRNS VLN(A			(A) CHILD SONG	1970	DERAM	UK	SML 1070
TONY ROBERTS	WIND (A							
MIKE McNAUGHT	K	(A	DARYL RUNSWICK	B	(A	MIKE TRAVIS	D	(A JIMMY JEWELL SAX (A
NEIL SLAVEN	PERC (A							

L137 TREVOR LUCAS

TREVOR LUCAS	V G	(A		(A) OVERLANDER	1966	REALITY	RY1002
ALF EDWARDS	CONC (A						
CYRIL HARLING	FDL (A		GEORGE GIBBS	B	(A		

L138 LUCIFER

			(A) BIG GUN	19		LLP 1
			(B) EXIT	19		LLP 2
			(C) MARGRIET	19 EMI	IMP	064 25655

L139 LUCIFERS FRIEND

PETER HECHT	K	(ABCDEFG	(A) LUCIFERS FRIEND	1971	PHILIPS		6305 068
DIETER HORNS	B V	(ABCDEFG	(A) LUCIFERS FRIEND	1973	BILLINGSGATE		1002
JOHN LAWTON	V	(ABCDE	(B) WHERE GROUPIES KILLED THE BLUES	1972	PASSPORT	US	98008
JOACHIM RIETENBACK	D	(ABC	(C) I'M JUST A ROCK'N'ROLL SINGER	1974	BILLINGSGATE		1008
PETER HESSLEIN	G V	(ABCDEFG	(D) BANQUET	1975	PASSPORT	US	98012
HERBERT BORNHOLDT	PERC V(CDEFG		(E) MIND EXPLODING	1976	VERTIGO 6360	633 +JANUS 7030	
ADRIAN ASKEW	K V	(G	(F) GOOD TIME WARRIOR	1978	ELEKTRA		63 159
MIKE STARRS	V	(FG	(G) SNEAK ME IN	1980	ELEKTRA	GERM	52203
KARL HERMANN LUER	WIND	(E					
HERB GELLER	WIND	(CD	BOB LANESE	TPT	(CD		

LUDUS
L139A

(A) THE VISIT (EP)　19　NEW HORMONE　ORG 4

LULU
L140

LULU(MARIE LAWRIE	V	(ALL	(A) SOMETHING TO SHOUT ABOUT	1965	DECCA	UK	LK	4719	
JIM DEWAR	B	(	(B) LULU	1967	ACE OF CLUBS	UK	ACL	1232	
ROSS NELSON		(	(C) TO SIR WITH LOVE	1967	EPIC US 26339	FONTANA UK		5446	
ALEC BELL		(	(D) ITS LULU	196	EPIC US 26536				
JIMMY SMITH		(	(E) LOVE LOVES TO LOVE LULU	1967	COLUMBIA	UK	SCX	6201	
TONY TIERNEY		(	(F) LULU'S ALBUM	1969	COLUMBIA	UK	SCX	6365	
DAVID MILLER		(	(G) WORLD OF LULU	1969	DECCA	UK	SPA	8	
DUANE ALLMAN	G	(J	(H) WORLD OF LULU	1969	DECCA	UK	SPA	94	
			(J) NEW ROUTES	1970	ATLANTIC US 33310 UK			228031	
			(K) MELODY FAIR	1970	ATLANTIC US 33330 UK		2400	017	
			( ) LULU	19	PICKWICK	US		3237	
			( ) TO LOVE SOMEBODY	19	HARMONY	US		30449	
			( ) FROM LULU WITH LOVE	19	PARROT	US		71016	
			(P) DONT TAKE LOVE FOR GRANTED	1979	ROCKET	UK		TRAIN8	

BOB LUMAN
L141

BOB LUMAN	G V	(ALL	LETS THINK ABOUT LIVING	1960	WB			WS1396	
			WHEN YOU SAY LOVE	196	EPIC			31375	
			GETTING BACK TO NORNA	1970	EPIC			26541	
			IS IT ANY WONDER THAT I LOVE YOU	197	EPIC	US		30617	
			A CHAIN DONT TAKE TO ME	19	EPIC LE10187			30923	
			LIVIN LOVIN SOUNDS	1971	LONDON UK ZGE115 US HSP 124006				
			LONELY WOMEN MAKE GOOD LOVERS	1972	EPIC	US		31746	
			BOB LUMAN	1973	HARMONY	US		32006	
			NEITHER ONE OF US	1973	EPIC	US		32192	
			GREATEST HITS	1974	EPIC	US		32759	
			RED CADILLAC & BLACK MUSTACHE	197	EPIC	US		33177	
			STILL LOVING YOU	1974	HICKORY	US		4508	
			WHEN YOU SAY LOVE/LONELY WOMEN (DBL)	197	EPIC	US		33755	
			A SATISFIED MIND	1976	EPIC	US		33942	
			ALIVE & WELL	1977	EPIC	US		34445	
			BOB LUMAN ROCKS	1977	DJM	UK		DJM 22057	
			THE PAY PHONE	1978	POLYDOR	US		PDI6135	
			THE ROCKER	1979	BEAR FAMILY	GERM		15037	
			MORE OF THE ROCKER	1979	BEAR FAMILY	GERM		15039	

LYDIA LUNCH
L141A

LYDIA LUNCH　(A) QUEEN OF SIAM　1980　ZE　?

LURKERS
L142

PETE STRIDE	G	(ABC	(A) FULHAM FALL OUT	1978	BEGGARS BANQUET	UK	BEG2
HOWARD WALL	V	(ABC	(B) GODS LONELY MEN	1979	BEGGARS BANQUET	UK	BEGA8
MANIC ESSO	D	(ABC	(C) GREATEST HITS LAST WILL & TESTAMENT 80		BEGGARS BANQUET	UK	BOPA2
NIGEL MOORE	B	(ABC	(EP) SHADOW	1979	BEGGARS BANQUET	UK	BACK1
KYM BRADSHAW	B	(	(EP) I DONT NEED TO TELL HER	1979	BEGGARS BANQUET	UK	BACK3
PETE EDWARDS	V HCA(A						
JOHN PLAIN	G	(C	ARTURO BASSICK	B	(C		

WILLIAM LYALL
L142A

WILLIAM LYALL V PERC K SYN(A			(A) SOLO CASTING	1976	EMI	UK	EMA 780
PHIL CHEN	B	(A					
RONNIE LEAHY	PNO	(A	PHIL COLLINS D (A DAVID PATON G (A ROBERT AHWAI G (A				
IAN BAIRNSON	G	(A	PATATO CONGA(A				

BOBBY LYLE
L143

BOBBY LYLE	K V	(A	(A) NEW WARRIOR	1978	CAPITOL/TOWER	11809
ANGELA WINBUSH	V	(A				
NATHANIEL PHILLIPS B		(A	HARVEY MASON D (A STEPHANIE SPRUILL V (A JOE BLOCKER PERC (A			
RON BANKS	V	(A	JIM GILSTRAP V (A VANCE TENORT V (A ALEXANDRA BROWN V (A			
MIKE BODDIKER	SYN	(A	PAULINHO DA COSTA PERC (A GREGORY MATTA V (A DAVID T WALKER G (A			
MARTINETTE JENKINS V		(A	SUNSHIP PERC (A ROLAND BAUTISTA G (A AUGIE JOHNSON V (A			
WAYNE HENDERSON	PERC V(A		STRING SECTION (A			

FRANKIE LYMON & THE TEENAGERS
L144

FRANKIE LYMON	V	(ALL	(A) WHY DO FOOLS FALL IN LOVE	1956	GEE US + UK PYE 1978	28251	
SHERMAN GARNES		(	(B) ROCK'N' ROLL PARTY	19	GUEST STAR US	GS 1406	
JOE NEGRONI		(	(C) AT THE LONDON PALLADIUM	19	ROULETTE US	R 25013	
HERMAN SANTIAGO		(	(D) GREATEST HITS	19	ROULETTE US	R 25250	
JIMMY MERCHANT		(	(EP) FRANKIE LYMON WITH THE TEENAGERS	19	SONET DK	5XP 3025	
			(EP AT THE LONDON PALLADIUM	19	ROULETTE US	EPR 1304	

BARBARA LYNN
L144A

BARBARA LYNN　V　(A　(A) HERE IS　1976　OVAL　UK　OVLM5002

PHIL LYNOTT
L144B

PHIL LYNOTT　V B　(A　(A) SOLO IN SOHO　1980　VERTIGO　UK　9102 038

JACKIE LYNTON
L145

JACKIE LYNTON	V	(AB	(A) THE JACKIE LYNTON ALBUM	1974	WWA	WWA 012
TONY LEACH	V PNO(B		(B) JACKIE LYNTON BAND (DBL)	1980	SCRATCH	SCRL 5002
GRAHAME WHITE	G V	(B				
GREG TERRY-SHORT	D V	(B	KIRK RIDDLE B (B			

WILLIE JAMES LYONS
L145A

WILLIE JAMES LYONS G		(A	(A) W J LYONS & W KENT GHETTO	197	MCM	FR	900 291
WILLIE KENT		(A					

LYNYRD SKYNYRD
L146

RONNIE VAN ZANT	V	(ALL	(A) PRONOUNCED LEHNERD SKINNERD	1974	MCA US 363	US RI	3019	
STEVE GAINES	G	(EF	(A) " " " " "	1974	MCA UK 3502 FR BARCLAY		410010	
GUY ROSSINGTON	G	(ALL	(B) SECOND HELPING	1974	MCA US 413 US RI		3020	
ALLEN COLLINS	G	(ALL	(B) " " " "	1974	MCA US 2547 FR BARCLAY		410020	
LEON WILKESON	B	(ALL	(C) NUTHIN' FANCY	1975	MCA US 2137 US RI		3021	
BILLY POWELL	K	(ALL	(C) " " " "	1975	MCA US 2700 FR BARCLAY		410042	
ARTIMUS PYLE	D	(E	(D) GIMME BACK MY BULLETS	1976	MCA US 2170 US RI		3022	
CASSIE GAINES	V	(EG	(D) " " " " "	1976	MCA UK 2744 FR BARCLAY		410048	

(CONTINUED)

LYNYRD SKYNYRD

```
JO BILLINGSLEY      V    (EG           (E) ONE MORE FOR THE ROAD          1976 MCA  US              2/8001
LESLIE HAWKINS      V    (EG           (E)  "    "    "    "               1976 MCA  UK 279  FR BARCLAY410060/1
SAM McPHERSON       HCA  (E            (F) STREET SURVIVORS               1977 MCA  US              3029
JIMMY JOHNSON       G    (G            (F)  "    "    "                   1977 MCA  UK 3525 FR BARCLAY 511002
RICKY MEDLOCKE      D    (G            (G) SKYNYRDS FIRST & LAST          1978 MCA  US 3047 UK       3529
RANDY McCORMICK     K    (G            (H) GOLD & PLATINUM BAND    (DBL)  1979 MCA  UK             MCSP 308
MERRY CLAYTON       V    (B            (EP) DOWN SOUTH JUKIN'             1978 MCA  UK            MCEP 101
TREVOR LAWRENCE     SAX  (B
ED KING             G    (ABG  ROOSEVELT GOOK   B K V(A  BOBBYE HALL       PERC (A  WAYNE PERKINS   G  (G
GREG WALKER         B    (G    TIM SMITH        V   (G  MIKE PORTER       D    (B  STEVE MADAIO    TPT(B
ROBERT BURNS        D    (ABG  ROBERT NIX       D   (A  STEVE KATZ        HCA  (A  RON EADES       SAX (G
GIMMER NICHOLS      G    (G    CLYDIE KING      V   (B  BOBBY KEYS        SAX  (B
```

M C 5

```
ROB TYNER           HCA V(ABC           (A) KICK OUT THE JAMS            1969 ELEKTRA US 74042 UK 1977 K42027
FRED SMITH V K G HCA     (ABC           (B) BACK IN THE USA              1970 ATLANTIC US 8247 UK      2400 016
MIKE DAVIS          B V   (ABC          (B) BACK IN THE USA              1977 ATLANTIC         UK      K50346
DENNIS THOMPSON     D V   (ABC          (C) HIGH TIME                    1971 ATLANTIC US 8285 UK      K40223
WAYNE KRAMER        G V K(ABC
PETE KELLY          K    (B
CHARLES MOORE       HRN V(C    JOANNE HILL      V   (C  BRENDAN KNIGHT    V    (C  MERLENE DRISCOLL  V (C
DAVID OVERSTEAK     TUBA (C    LARRY HORTON     TROM (C  BOBBY WAYNE DERMINER PERC(C  BUTCH O'BRIEN  PERC (C
LEON HENDERSON      SAX  (C    RICK FERRETTI    SAX  (C  SKIP KNAPP       ORG   (C  KINKI LE PEW    PERC (C
DAN BULLOCK         TROM (C    BOB SEGER    PERC   (C  SCOTT MORGAN       PERC  (C  TERRY TRABANDT  PERC (C
DAVE HELLER         PERC (C    DAVE MORGAN      PERC (C  ELLIS DEE         PERC  (C  DANNY JORDAN    K   (B
```

M1A

'M'

```
ROBIN SCOTT         G V    (B            (A) NEW YORK, LONDON ,PARIS ,MUNICH  1979  MCA        UK   MCF  3046
PHILIP GOULD        D      (B            (B) OFFICIAL SECRETS ACT           1980  MCA        UK   MCF  3085
MARK KING           G B D(B
JULIAN SCOTT        B      (B    DAVID VORHAUS    SYN  (B  GARY BARNACLE    SAX  (B  PADDY KEENAN    PIPES(B
BRIGIT VINCHON      V      (B    DENIS BLACKHAM   V    (B  MOG AHERNE       V    (B  JOHN KEOGH      V   (B
BILLY BROWN         V      (B    DES SMITH        V    (B  DEIRDRIE COSTELLO V   (B
```

M2

M.F.S.B.

```
DEXTER WANSEL       K      (J            (A) M.F.S.B.                      1973 T S O P UK 65903      US 32046
JAMES HERB SMITH    G      (J            (B) T S O P                       1974 T S O P UK 80154
LARRY MOORE         B      (J            (C) LOVE IS THE MESSAGE           197  T S O P                US 32707
EVAN SOLOT          TPT    (J            (D) UNIVERSAL LOVE                1975 T S O P UK 80410      US 33158
LARRY McKENNA       SAX    (J            (E) PHILADELPHIA FREEDOM          1976 T S O P UK 69206      US 33845
CLIFFORD RUDD       D      (J            (F) SUMMERTIME                    1976 T S O P UK 81459      US 34238
MIGUEL FUENTES      PERC   (J            (G) END OF PHASE ONE              1978 T S O P UK 81889      US 34658
EVETTE BENTON       V      (J            (H) M F S B & GAMBLE HUFF ORCHESTRA 1978 T S O P UK 83010
JOHN L USRY         K      (J            (J) MYSTERIES OF THE WORLD        1980 T S O P UK 84251
DENNIS HARRIS       G      (J
DON RENALDO         VLN    (J    ZAHMU            V    (J  CARLETON KENT    K    (J  DAVID CRUSE     PERC (J
MARC RUBIN          G      (J    ALPHONSO CAREY   B    (J  QUINTON JOSEPH   D    (J  STEVE GOLD      K    (J
DERRICK GRAVES      B      (J    BILLY JOHNSON    D    (J  CARLA BENSON     V    (J  BARBARA INGRAM  V    (J
LENNY PAKULA        K      (J    STEVE GREEN      B    (J  BOB MALACH       SAX  (J  JOEL BRYANT     K    (J
JOHN R FAITH        FLT    (J    LEON HUFF        K    (J
```

M3

THE M Gs

```
DONALD DUNN         B      (A            (A) THE M Gs                     1973        STAX             STS 3024
AL JACKSON          D      (A
BOBBY MANUEL        G      (A    CARSON WHITSETT  K    (A
```

M4

MX 80 SOUND

```
BRUCE ANDERSON      G      (A            (A) HARD ATTACK                  1977 ISLAND        UK    ILPS9529
RICH STIM           G K    (A            (B) OUT OF THE TUNNEL            1980 RALPH
DALE SOPHIEA        B      (A
JEFF ARMOUR         D      (A    DAVE MAHONEY     D    (A
```

M5

WILLIE MABON

```
WILLIE MABON        V PNO(ALL            (A) THE COMEBACK                 196  AMERICA            AM   6126
MICKEY BAKER        G      (D            (B) CHICAGO 63                   1963 AMERICA            AM   6136
DAN ARMSTRONG       B      (D            (C) WILLIE MABON                 19   CHESS       US          1439
PETE  YORK          D      (D            (D) COMEBACK                     1973 BIG BEAR           BEAR   9
DYAN BIRCH          V      (D            (E) COLD CHILLY WOMAN            1975 BLACK & BLUE            33501
COLIN SMITH         TPT    (D            (F) SHAKE THAT THING             1975 BLACK & BLUE            33506
BILL WARREN         D      (EG           (G) SINGS "I DONT KNOW"          1976 ANTILLES    US
EMMET SUTTON        B      (AE           (H) CHICAGO BLUES SESSION        1979 L & R               42 003
JIMMY ROGERS        G      (F
LOUIS MYERS         G      (F    DAVE MYERS       B    (F  FRED BELOW       D    (F  FRANK COLLINS   V  (D
JOHNNY BARNES       SAX   'D    PADDIE McHUGH    V    (D  EDDY TULEJA      G    (A  TONY CAHILL     D  (A
CLIFTON JAMES       D      (B    WILLIE HUDSON    G    (B  AL DUNCAN        D    (B  EARL CROSSLEY   SAX (
JOHNNIE CAMERON     SAX    (B    BILLY THE KID EMERSON K(B  JIMMY RICHARDS   B    (G  MALCOLM SIMMONS HCA (G
MIGHTY JOE YOUNG    G      (G    EUGENE PEARSON   G    (G  HUBERT SUMLIN    G    (H  EDDIE TAYLOR    G  (H
AARON BURTON        B      (H    CASEY JONES      D    (H
```

M6

JACKIE McAULEY

```
JACKIE McAULEY      V G K(A            (A) JACKIE McAULEY               1971 DAWN        UK    DNLS 3023
MIKE McNAUGHT       K      (A
HENRY LOWTHER VLN HRNS (A    MIKE TRAVIS      D    (A  TONY ROBERTS     FLT  (A  ROY BABBINGTON  B  (A
PETE HOSSEL         JUG    (A
```

M7

DAN McCAFFERTY

```
DAN McCAFFERTY      V      (A            (A) DAN McCAFFERTY              1975 MOUNTAIN UK TOPS108 US AM4553
MANNY CHARLTON      G      (A
HUGH McKENNA        K      (A    CHRIS MERCER     SAX  (A  HELEN CHAPPELLE   V   (A  JOHN PERRY      V  (A
ZAL CLEMINSON       G      (A    TED McKENNA      D    (A  LIZA STRIKE       V   (A  JOANNE WILLIAMS V  (A
ROGER GLOVER        B      (A    GRAHAM PRESKETT  VLN  (A  BARRY ST JOHN     V   (A  TONY RIVERS     V  (A
```

M7A

NOEL McCALLA

```
NOEL McCALLA        V PERC(A            (A) NIGHT TIME EMOTION          1979 EPIC          UK        83838
TREVOR RABIN        G K B(A
PRESTON HEYMAN      D      (A    NICK PAYNE       SAX  (A  TONY BEARD        D    (A  VICKI BROWN     V  (A
CHRIS THOMPSON      V      (A    DOUG BAINBRIDGE  SAX  (A  MEL COLLINS       SAX  (A  JOHN McKENZIE   B  (A
GRAHAM BROAD        D      (A    STEVIE LANGE V        (A
```

JIM McCARTHY

JIM McCARTHY (A   (A) GUIDE ME TO YOUR LOVE   1974 ESP US ESP 3008

PAUL McCARTNEY & WINGS

Personnel		Albums	Releases
PAUL McCARTNEY	B V G K (ALL	(A) McCARTNEY	1970 APPLE UK 7102 US CAPITOL 3363
LINDA McCARTNEY	V K (ALL	(B) RAM	1971 APPLE UK 10003 US CAPITOL 3375
DENNY LAINE	G V K (CDEFGHJKL	(C) WILD LIFE	1971 APPLE UK 7142 US CAPITOL 3386
DENNY SEIWELL	D (BCD	(D) RED ROSE SPEEDWAY	1972 APPLE UK 251 US APPLE 3409
HENRY McCULLOUGH	G (D	(E) BAND ON THE RUN	1974 APPLE UK 10007 US CAPITOL 3415
JIMMY McCULLOCH	G (FGHJ	(E) BAND ON THE RUN	1974 CAPITOL 11901
GEOFF BRITTON	D (F	(F) VENUS & MARS	1975 EMI UK 254 US CAPITOL 11419
JOE ENGLISH	D (GHJ	(G) WINGS AT THE SPEED OF SOUND	1976 EMI UK 10010 US CAPITOL 11525
DAVE MASON	G (F	(H) WINGS OVER AMERICA	1976 EMI UK 720 US CAPITOL 11593
AFRO	PERC (F	(J) LONDON TOWN	1978 EMI UK 10012 US CAPITOL 11777
TONY DORSEY	TROM (H	(K) WINGS GREATEST	1978 EMI UK 256
HUGH McCRACKEN	G (B	(L) BACK TO THE EGG	1979 PARLOPHONE UK PCTC 257
THADIUS RICHARD	WIND (B	(M) McCARTNEY II	1980 MPL UK 258
DAVID SPINOZZA	G (B	(N) McCARTNEY INTERVIEW	1981 EMI UK CHAT1
STEVE HOWARD	HRNS (H		
ALLEN TOUSSAINT	K (F		

HOWIE CASEY SAX (EH TOM SCOTT SAX (F

DELBERT McCLINTON

Personnel		Albums	Releases
DELBERT McCLINTON	(ALL	(A) DELBERT & GLEN	1972 CLEAN US CN6010598
GLEN CLARK	(AB	(B) SUBJECT TO CHANGE	1973 CLEAN US CN6020598
ROGER HAWKINS	D (I	(C) VICTIM OF LIFE'S CIRCUMSTANCES	1975 ABC US AB 907
DAVID HOOD	B (I	(D) GENUINE COWHIDE	1976 ABC US ABC 959
BARRY BECKETT	K (I	(E) LOVE RUSTLER	1977 ABC UK ABCL5217 US AB 991
JIMMY JOHNSON	G (I	(F) SECOND WIND	1978 CAPRICORN US CP 0201
BONNIE BRAMLETT	V (I	(G) VERY EARLY DELBERT McCLINTON	1978 LECAM US LCS 404A
WAYNE PERKINS	G (I	(H) KEEPER OF THE FLAME	1979 CAPRICORN US CP 0223
HARRISON CALLOWAY	SAX (I	(I) JEALOUS KIND	1980 CAPITOL 12115

CHARLIE McCOY

Personnel		Albums	Releases
CHARLIE McCOY	HCA V (ALL	(A) HARPIN' THE BLUES	1970 MONUMENT UK 69204 US 33802
JIM ISBELL	D (FAJK	(A) HARPIN' THE BLUES	197 MONUMENT US 6629
KENNETH BUTTREY	D (AFJK	(B) CHARLIE McCOY	1972 MONUMENT UK 5034 US 31910
JERRY WHITE	D (FA	(B) CHARLIE McCOY	197 MONUMENT US 6624
KENNY MALONE	PERC (AF	(C) REAL McCOY	1972 MONUMENT US 6623 US 31329
SI EDWARDS	PERC (FAJK	(D) GOOD TIME CHARLIE	1973 MONUMENT US 6625 US 32215
FARRELL MORRIS	VIBES (FAJK	(E) FASTEST HARP IN THE SOUTH	1973 MONUMENT US 6626 US 32749
BUDDY SKIPPER	K V CLAR (FAJ	(F) NASHVILLE HIT MAN	1974 MONUMENT UK 80115 US 6627
GEORGE BINKLEY	VLN (F	(G) CHARLIE MY BOY	1975 MONUMENT US 6628 US 33384
RUSS HICKS	STEEL V G (FAJK	(H) CHRISTMAS ALBUM	1975 MONUMENT US 6645 US 33176
BUDDY SPICHER	FDL (AF	(I) GREATEST HITS	197 MONUMENT US 7622
BRENTON BANKS	VLN (F	(J) PLAY IT AGAIN CHARLIE	197 MONUMENT US 6630
LENNIE HAIGHT	VLN (F	(K) COUNTRY COOKIN'	1977 MONUMENT UK 81559 US 7612
BERGEN WHITE	V (F	(L) STONE FOX CHASE	1977 MONUMENT UK 82444 US 81886
WENDY SUITS	V (F	(M) APPALACHIAN FEVER	1979 MONUMENT UK 83516
LARRY BUTLER	PNO (F		

DON SMITH B (AFJK LEON RHODES B G (F JOHNNY GIMBLE FDL (FK BTRON BACH CELLO (F
BOBBY THOMPSON G BAN(AFJK RAY EDENTON G (AFJK HAROLD BRADLEY VLN (F PIG ROBBINS PNO (AFJK
JOSH GRAVES DOBRO(FAJK CARL GORODETZKY VLN (F GARY VANOSDALE VLA (F STEPHANIE WOOLF VLN (F
BILLY LINNEMAN B (F JOE ZINKAN B (FA BOBBY DYSON B (FA BILLY SANFORD G (F
MARTHA McCRORY CELLO(F DAVE KIRBY G (FJ CHIP YOUNG G (F MARVIN CHANTRY VIOLA (F
JIMMY WILKERSON G (FA SHELDON KURLAND VLN (F CAROL MONTGOMERY V (F HAL RUGG STEEL (F
JOHN PROBST PNO (FA WAYNE MOSS B AFJK JOHNNY JOHNSON B (FA FRED NEWELL G (AFJK
STEVE SMITH VLN (F TOMMY ALSUP G (F TERRY DEARMORE G (FJ
DALE SELLERS G (FA WELDON MYRICK STEEL(FAJK

VAN McCOY

Personnel		Albums	Releases
VAN McCOY	V PNO(ALL	(A) DISCO BABY	1975 AVCO UK 9109 004
ALBERT BAILEY	V (E	(B) DISCO KID	1975 AVCO UK 9109 007
DESTRY	V (E	(C) THE REAL McCOY	1976 H&L UK 9109 009
ZULEMA	V (E	(D) THE HUSTLE	1976 H&L US 69016
BRENDA HILLIARD	V (E	(E) MY FAVOURITE FANTASY	1978 MCA UK MCF 2843 US 3036
DIANE WILSON	V (E	(F) LONELY DANCER	19 MCA US 3071
BERNIE GLOW	TPT (E	(G) DANCIN'	19 SSS US 33
URBIE GREEN	TROM (E	(H) FROM DISCO TO LOVE	19 BUDDAH US 5648 FR MODE 9026
MICKEY GRAVINE	TROM (E	(J) SWEET RHYTHM	1979 H&L 6467 651
PHIL BODNER	FLT (E		

BOB ADAMS D (E SKIP FENSELL K (E DAVID CAREY PERC (E ARTHUR JENKINS PNO (E
CHARLIE KIPPS D (E CORNELL DUPREE G (E STEVE GADD D (E LEON PENDARVIS K (E
PRISCILLA BASKERVILLE V/E MEL DAVIS TPT (E WAYNE ANDRE TROM (E TOM MALONE TROM(E
JIM BUFFINGTON HRNS (E DENNIS RICHEY G D (E JAMES FUNCHES B (E PAT REBILLOT PNO (E
BERT JONES G (E GORDON EDWARDS B (E RICHARD TEE PNO (E JOHN TROPEA G (E
MIKE MANIERI PERC (E JON FADDIS TPT (E VICTOR PAZ TPT (E BOB ALEXANDER TROM(E
PAUL FAULISE TROM (E BROOKS TILLOTSON HRNS (E ARTHUR LISI K (E JON WARE PERC (E
STEVE JORDAN D (E CRUSHER BENNETT PERC (E CHRIS PARKER D (E GEORGE DEVENS PERC(E
HUGH McCRACKEN G (E

McCOYS

Personnel		Albums	Releases
RICK DERRINGER	G V (ALL	(A) HANG ON SLOOPY	1965 BANG US 212 JOY JOYS 196
RANDY ZEHRINGER	D (ALL	(A) HANG ON SLOOPY	196 IMMEDIATE UK IMLP 001
RANDY HOBBS	B (ALL	(B) YOU MAKE ME FEEL SO GOOD	1966 BANG US 213
BOBBY PETERSON	K (ALL	(C) INFINITE McCOYS	1968 MERCURY US 61163
PETE DRAKE	STEEL(D	(D) HUMAN BALL	1968 MERCURY US 61207
DICK HALLIGAN	TROM (C		
FRED LIPSIUS	SAX (C		

RANDY BRECKER TPT (C JERRY WEISS TPT (C

JIMMY McCRACKLIN

Personnel		Albums	Releases
JIMMY McCRACKLIN	PNO V(ALL	MY ANSWER	19 IMPERIAL US LP 12306
DAVID BLUNSTON	PNO (	EVERYNIGHT EVERYDAY	19 IMPERIAL US LP 12285
JOHN HENRY	B (	THINK	19 IMPERIAL US LP 12297
ALRAY KIDD	D (	I JUST GOTTA KNOW	19 IMPERIAL US LP(M)9219
ROBERT KELTON	G (	JIMMY McCRACKLIN SONGS	19 CHESS US LP 1464
LITTLE RED	D (	LETS GET TOGETHER	19 MINIT US LP 24011
			(CONTINUED)

M13A (CONTINUED)

JIMMY McCRACKLIN

JOE CONWRIGHT	SAX (	NEW SOUL OF	19	IMPERIAL	US LP 12316
CHARLES SUTTER	SAX (	(H) TWIST WITH	19	CROWN US CLP5244	US CUSTOM 2057
LAFAYETTE THOMAS	G (H	ROCKIN' MAN	19	ROUTE 66	SWED KIX 12
SAN FRISCO JEFF	D (	AND HIS BLUESBLASTERS	1981	ACE	CH 28
JOHNNY PARKER	SAX (				

M14

MARY McCREARY

MARY McCREARY	V (AB	(A) JEZEBEL	19	SHELTER
		(B) BUTTERFLIES IN HEAVEN	19	SHELTER

M15

HENRY McCULLOUGH

HENRY McCULLOUGH	G V (A	(A) MIND YOUR OWN BUSINESS			1975	DARK HORSE		UK	AMLH22005
ALAN SPENNER	B (A								
STEVE CHAPMAN	D (A	MICK WEAVER	K (A	JOHN HALSEY	D	(A	LLOYD SMITH	SAX (A	
NEIL HUBBARD	G (A	CHARLIE HARRISON	B (A	TIM HINKLEY	K	(A	FRANKIE MILLER	V (A	
LIONEL KINGHAM	SAX (A	BRUCE ROWLAND	D (A	JIM LEVERTON	B	(A	JOE O'DONNELL	VLN (A	
HERSCHEL HOLDER	TPT (A								

M16

KATHI McDONALD

KATHI McDONALD	V (A	(A) INSANE ASYLUM			1974	CAPITOL	US	ST 11224	
NILS LOFGREN	G (A								
PETE SEARS	G B K(A	BOBBYE HALL	PERC (A	RONNIE MONTROSE	G	(A	GREG DOUGLAS	G	(A
NEAL SCHON	G (A	MARK UNOBSKI	G (A	PAPA JOHN CREACH	FDL	(A	JIM McPHERSON	B	(A
JOHN CIPPOLLINA	G (A	GARY PHILIPPET	G (A	BOOTS HOUSTON	HRNS	(A	AYNSLEY DUNBAR	D	(A
TOWER OF POWER	HRNS (A	SLY STONE	V (A	POINTER SISTERS	V	(A			

M17

RALPH MACDONALD

RALPH MACDONALD	PERC (ALL	(A) SOUND OF A DRUM	1976	MARLIN US 2202+	XL	XL14030
GROVER WASHINGTON JR	SAX(ABC	(B) THE PATH	1978	MARLIN UA 2210+	TK	TKR82515
CHUCK RAINEY	B (AB	(C) COUNTERPOINT	1979	TK	UK	TKR83373
ERIC GALE	G B (ABC					

RICHARD TEE	PNO (ABC	ARTHUR JENKINS	K (ABC	DAVID FRIEDMAN	VIBES(AB	CLINTON THOBOURNE CLAR(AB
JOE FARRELL	HRNS (A	JIMMY OWENS	HRNS (A	PATTI AUSTIN	V (AB	RAYMOND SIMPSON V (A
RICK MAROTTA	D (AB	WILLIAM EATON	V (A	NICHOLAS MARRERO	PERC (AB	URIAS FRITZ BOTTLE(A
SELDON POWELL	HRNS (A	VERGIL JONES	HRNS (A	ZACHARY SANDERS	V (AC	GWEN GUTHRIE V (AB
JEAN THIELEMANS	HCA (AB	BOB JAMES	SYN (AB	WILLIAM SALTER	B (AB	HAROLD VICK HRNS (AC
KIANE ZAWADI	HRNS (A	VIVIAN CHERRY	V (A	FRANK FLOYD	V (AC	STEVE GADD D (BC
HARVEY MASON	D (C	ROBERT GREENIDGE	PERC (C	MICHAEL BRECKER	HRNS (CB	RANDY BRECKER HRNS (CB
BARRY ROGERS	HRNS (CB	JOE BROWN	B PERC (C	WILL LEE	B (CB	TOM SCOTT WIND (C
JON FADDIS	HRNS (C	RON CUBER	HRNS (C	DAVE SANBORN	HRNS (CB	KEN WILLIAMS V (C
HOWARD JOHNSON	HRNS (C	TOM MALONE	HRNS (C	STRING SECTION	(ABC	

M18

COUNTRY JOE McDONALD & THE FISH

JOE McDONALD	HCA C G(ALL	(A) ELECTRIC MUSIC FOR THE MIND	1967	VANGUARD US VSD 79244	UK SVRL19026
JOHN LEHMAN	V (W	(A) ELECTRIC MUSIC FOR THE MIND	1967	FONTANA	UK STFL 6081
BARRY MELTON	G (ABCG	(B) I FEEL LIKE I'M FIXIN TO DIE	1967	VANGUARD US VSD 79266	UK SVRL19029
DAVID COHEN	K (ABC	(B) I FEEL LIKE I'M FIXIN TO DIE	1967	FONTANA	UK STFL 6087
BRUCE BARTHOL	B (ABCQ	(C) TOGETHER	1968	VANGUARD US VSD 79277	UK SVRL19006
CHICKEN HIRSH	D (AB	(D) HERE WE GO AGAIN	1969	VANGUARD US VSD79299	UK STVL19048
DAVID GETZ	D (M	(E) THINKING OF WOODY GUTHRIE	1969	VANGUARD US VSD 6546	UK VRL 19057
PETER ALBIN	B (M	( ) GREATEST HITS	1969	VANGUARD US VSD 6545	UK SVRL19058
JEFF PORCARO	D (W	(F) TONIGHT I'M SINGING FOR YOU	1970	VANGUARD US VSD 6557	UK 6359 004
MIKE PORCARO	B (W	(G) C J FISH	1970	VANGUARD US VSD 6555	UK 6359 004
MAC CRIDLIN	B (WZ	(H) QUIET DAY IN CLICHY	1971	SONET	UK SNTF 622
STEVE MADAIO	HRNS (QW	(I) FROM ASHBURY TO WOODSTOCK	1971	VANGUARD	VSD 27/28
JAY GRAYDON	G (WZ	(J) HOLD ON ITS COMING	1971	VANGUARD US VSD 79314	
JOHN BLAKELEY	G (WQZ	(K) WAR WAR WAR	1971	VANGUARD US VSD 79315	
DAVID FOSTER	K (W	(L) INCEDIBLE LIVE	1972	VANGUARD US VSD 79316	
BILL CUOMO	K (W	(M) PARIS SESSIONS	1973	VANGUARD US VSD 79328	
MICHAEL BODDIKER	K (W	(O) THE BEST OF	1973	VANGUARD US VSD 79000	UK SVRL19058
CHILI CHARLES	D (W	(P) COUNTRY JOE	1975	VANGUARD US VSD 79348	
STEPHANIE SPRUILL	V (W	(Q) PARADISE WITH AN OCEAN VIEW	1975	FANTASY US 9495	UK FTA 3002
MARTI McCALL	V (W	(R) THE ESSENTIAL (DBL)	1976	VANGUARD	VSD 85/86
LISA ROBERTS	V (W	(T) LOVE IS A FIRE	1976	FANTASY US 9511	UK FTA 3005
JAN JOYCE	V (W	(U) GOLDEN HOUR	1977	PYE	UK GH 865
JIM GILSTRAP	V (QW	(V) GOODBYE BLUES	1977	FANTASY US 9525	UK FT 529
PETE WALSH	V (VW	(W) ROCK'N'ROLL FROM PLANET EARTH	1978	FANTASY US 9544	UK FT 539
ROGER KENERLY SAINT	V (W	(X) REUNION	1977	FANTASY US 9530	
ANDREA ROBINSON	V (W	(Y) TRIBUTE TO WOODY	19	WB US 2W 3007	
CHUCK FINDLEY	HRNS (W	(Z) LEISURE SUITE	1979	FANTASY	UK FT 565
JOHN MITCHELL	HRNS (W				

TREVOR LAWRENCE	HRNS (QW	SAROD ASHISH KHAN TAMB (W	GREG DEWEY	D (G	DOUG METZNER	B (G
MARK KAPNER	K (G	DAVID HAYES	B (QZ	PETER MILIO	D (QV	TED ASHFORD	K (QV
STEVE GABOURY	PNO (Q	VANETTA FIELDS	V (Q	SALLY STEVENS	V (Q	MARLEENA JETTER	V (Q
SID SHARP	STRING(Q	PHIL MARSH	G (MQ	BOBBY KEYS	SAX (Q	CARLENA WILLIAMS	V (Q
MAXINE ANDERSON	V (Q	AUGIE JOHNSON	V (Q	RON MARABUTO	D (Q	JOHNNY ROTELLA	SAX (Q
SHIRLEY MATTHEWS	V (Q	MICHAEL IRWIN	V (Q	GERALD GARRETT	V (Q	RICHARD CORSELLO	G (Z
SCOTT LAWRENCE	PNO (Z	GREG DOUGLAS	G (Z	JIM HOBSON	PNO (Z	HERB JIMMERSON	SYN (Z
TIP WIRRICK	G (Z	CHUCK DAY	G (Z	PETER WALSH	B (Z	DAHUD SHAAR D (Z
BOB KINGSON	B (Z	JEFFREY MEYER	D (Z	MICHAEL HERBICK	D (Z	KELVIN DIXON	D (Z
PERSUASIONS	V (Z	FISCHLERS	V (Z	BILL COLLINS	V (Z	DANIEL GUNNIP	V (Z
BOBBI VANDERVOORT	V (Z	DAVID GUNNIP	V (Z	SEBASTIAN	CONG (M	JOHN REWIND	G (M
DIANE RASCONIA	V (Z	DAVID BROMBERG	DOBRO(V	JERRY CORBITT	V (V	NATHAN RUBIN	VLN (V
MALVINA REYNOLDS	V (V	BILL SUMMERS PERC (V	MARTY BALIN	V (V	ANNE RIZZO	V (VM
TERRY ADAMS	CELLO(V	DOROTHU MOSKOWITZ V PNO(M	TUCKI BAILEY	WIND (M	JOHN VIERRA	SYN (M

M19

SHELAGH McDONALD

SHELAGH McDONALD	G V K(AB	(A) SHELAGH McDONALD			1970	B & C		CAS 1019
JOHN RYAN	B (B	(B) STARGAZER			1971	B & C		CAS 1043
DANNY THOMPSON	B (B							
KEITH CHRISTMAS	G (AB	HARVEY BURNS	D (B	RAY WARLEIGH	SAX (B	IAN WHITEMAN	K (AB
DAVE RICHARDS	B (B	KATHY KISSOON	V (B	MAC KISSOON	V (B	MIKE LONDON	V (B
RICHARD THOMPSON	G (B	DAVE MATTACKS	D (B	PAT DONALDSON	B (AB	ANDY ROBERTS	G (A
ROGER POWELL	D (A	KEITH TIPPETT	PNO (A	GERRY CONWAY	D (A	MIKE EVANS	B (A
GORDON HUNTLEY	STEEL(A	TRISTAN FRY	VIBES(A				

[262]

McDONALD & GILES

IAN McDONALD	K SAX(A	(A) McDONALD & GILES	1970 ISLAND	UK	ILPS 9126
MIKE GILES	D (A	(A) McDONALD & GILES	1977 POLYDOR	UK	2302 070
MICHAEL BLAKESLEY TROM (A		(A) McDONALD & GILES	197 COTILLION	US	9042
PETER GILES	B (A				
STEVE WINWOOD	(A				

BROTHER JACK McDUFF

JACK McDUFF	ORG (AB	(A) NATURAL THING	196 CADET		LPS 812
JERRY BYRDE	G (B	(B) GIN & ORANGE	1969 CADET	US	LPS 831
GENE BARGE	SAX (B				
BEN BRANCH	SAX (B	MORRIS JENNINGS D (B	PHIL UPCHURCH B (B	RICHARD POWELL PERC (B
CASH McCALL	G (B	JOE BURKE D (B	BILL PHIPPS SAX (B	CLIFF DAVIS SAX (B

KATE & ANNA McGARRIGLE

KATE McGARRIGLE	K V G BAN(ALL	(A) KATE & ANNA McGARRIGLE	1975 WB	US BS2862	UK K 56218
ANNA McGARRIGLE	V K BAN(ALL	(B) DANCER WITH BRUISED KNEES	1977 WB	US BS3014	UK K 56356
TONY LEVIN	B (AC	(C) PRONTO MONTO	1978 WB	US BS3248	UK K 56561
STEPHEN GADD	D (ABC				
DAVID SPINOZZA	G (AC	GREG PRESTOPINO G V K(A	BOBBY KEYS SAX (A	TONY RICE G (A
JOEL TEPP	CLAR HCA (A	DAVID GRISMAN MAND (A	RED CALLENDER B (A	AMOS GARRETT G (A
JANIE McGARRIGLE-DOW V K(AB		PETER WELDON V HCA BAN(ABC	DANE LANKEN V (ABC	CHAIM TANNENBAUM V G HCA(ABC
JAY UNGAR	FDL (A	FLOYD GILBEAU FDL (A	ANDREW GOLD G (A	DENSIL LANG PERC(A
PLAS JOHNSON	WIND (A	RUSS KUNKEL D (A	NICK DECARO ACC (A	DIMMY DIMBUSTER PERC(A
SCOT LANG	G (A	JOHN CALE K (A	MIKE VISCIGLIA B (B	GRADY TATE D (BC
TOMMY MORGAN	HCA (B	RICHARD DAVIS B (B	PAT DONALDSON B (BC	DAVE MATTACKS D (B
KENNY PEARSON	K (BC	WARREN SMITH PERC (B	RON DOLEMAN VLN (B	SUSAN EVANS PERC(BC
GORDIE FLEMING ACC (B		GILLES LOSIER B (B	ANDREW COWAN G (B	GEORGE BOHANON HRNS(AB
LOWELL GEORGE	G (A	HUGH McCRACKEN G (B	JEFF MIRANOV G (C	JERRY DONAHUE G (C
GEORGE YOUNG	CLAR (C	BOB GLAUB B (C	VICTOR FELDMAN PERC (C	BRYAN CUMMING SAX (C
GEORGE DEVENS	PERC (C	BERNARD PURDIE D (C	GORDON EDWARDS B (C	JOHN SCHOLLE G (C
MICHAEL MOORE	B (C	FREEBO TUBA (C	DAVID NICHTERN G (C	DAVID WOODFORD SAX (C
KEn KOSEK	FDL (C	GARY MALLABER D (C	GARY MURE	

MISSISSIPPI FRED McDOWELL

MISSISSIPPI FRED McDOWELL	G V(ALL	(A) MISSISSIPPI DELTA BLUES	1964	ARHOOLIE	US	F1021
MIKE RUSSO	G (E	(A) MISSISSIPPI DELTA BLUES	19	POLYDOR	UK	2460 193
JOHN KAHN	B (E	(B) MY HOME IS IN THE DELTA	1964	TESTAMENT	US	2208
BOB JONES	D (E	(C) AMAZING GRACE	1964	TESTAMENT	US	2219
FANNIE DAVIS	(	(D) MISSISSIPPI DELTA BLUES VOL 2	1966	ARHOOLIE	US	F 1027
MILES PRATCHER	(	(E) & HIS BLUES BOYS	19	ARHOOLIE	US	F 1046
ANNIE MAE McDOWELL	V (ABC	(F) LONDON 1	19	TRANSATLANTIC	UK	TRA 194
ELI GREEN	V (D	( ) LONDON 2	19	TRANSATLANTIC	UK	TRA 203
		( ) LONG WAY FROM HOME	19	CBS UK 63735 MILESTONE US 93003
		( ) & FURRY LEWIS	19	BIOGRAPH		BLP 12017
		( ) KEEP YOUR LAMP TRIMMED	19	ARHOOLIE	US	F1068
		( ) I DONT PLAY NO ROCK'N' ROLL	19	CAPITOL	US	409
		( ) 1904 72	1974	XTRA	UK	XTRA 1136
		( ) MISSISSIPPI FRED McDOWELL	19	EVEREST	US	253
		( ) LIVE IN NEW YORK	19	OBLIVION	US	OBL1
		( ) SOMEBODY KEEPS CALLIN' ME	19	ANTILLES	US	7022

MIKE McGEAR

MIKE McGEAR	V (AB	(A) WOMAN	1972 ISLAND	UK	ILPS 9191
ZOOT MONEY	K (A	(B) McGEAR	1974 WB	US 2825 UK	K 56051
JOHN MEGGINSON	K (A				
NORMAN YARDLEY	HCA (A	CHRIS PYNE HRNS (A	MALCOLM DUNCAN HRNS (A	PAUL KORDA V (A
GINGER JOHNSON	PERC (A	DENNY LAINE G V (B	PADDY MOLONEY PIPES(A	ANDY ROBERTS G (A
DAVE RICHARDS	B (A	GERRY CONWAY D (AB	CENTIPEDE STRINGS (A	CECIL MOSS HRNS(A
MIKE ROSEN	HRNS (A	ROGER BALL HRNS (A	TONY COE SAX (AB	ALAN GORRIE V (A
STEVE GOULD	V (A	BRIAN AUGER K (A	LINDA McCARTNEY V K (B	JIMMY McCULLOCH G (B
BRIAN JONES	SAX (B	DENNY SEIWELL D (B		

DONNA McGHEE

DONNA McGHEE	(A	(A) MAKE IT LAST FOREVER	1978 ANCHOR	UK	ANCL 2027

ROGER McGOUGH

ROGER McGOUGH	V (A	(A) A SUMMER WITH MONIKA	1978 ISLAND	UK	ILPS 9551
PAT DONALDSON	B (A				
JOHN MEGGINSON	K (A	DAVE OLNEY B (A	TIMI DONALD D (A	JACK EMBLOW ACC (A
DAVE LAWSON	SYN (A	ZOOT MONEY K (A	ANDY ROBERTS G (A	

BAT McGRATH

BAT McGRATH	(AB	(A) FROM THE BLUE EAGLE	1977 AMHERST	US	1005
ETHAN POTTER	G (	(B) THE SPY	1978 AMHERST	US	1011

JIMMY McGRIFF

JIMMY McGRIFF	ORG(ALL	(A) CHERRY	196	SOLID STATE	US	SM 17006
ERIC GALE	G (A	(B) THE BIG BAND	1968	SOLID STATE	US	LAS 1800
GRADY TATE	D (A	(C) ELECTRIC FUNK	19	BLUENOTE	US	BST 84350
MILT HINTON	B (A	(D) SOMETHING TO LISTEN TO	19	BLUENOTE	US	BST 84364
EVERETT BARKSDALE	G (A	(E) BLACK PEARL	19	BLUENOTE	US	BST 84374
GROOVE HOLMES	K (KP	(F) GOOD THING DONT HAPPEN,....	1973	GROOVEMERCHANT	US	GM 2205
O'DONEL LEVY	G (K	(G) GROOVE GREASE	19	GROOVEMERCHANT	US	GM 503
GEORGE FREEMAN	G (K	(H) BLACK & BLUES	19	GROOVEMERCHANT	US	GM 2203
BERNARD PURDIE	D (K	(H) BLACK & BLUES	19	PEOPLE		PLED 501
KWASI JAYOURBA	CONGA(K	(J) FLYDUDE	1974	GROOVEMERCHANT	US	GM 509
ERNEST JONES	SYN (N	(J) FLYDUDE	1974	PEOPLE		PLEO 14
LEO JOHNSON	SAX (N	(K) COME TOGETHER	1974	GROOVEMERCHANT	US	GM 520
JIMMY PONDER	G (RSN	(K) COME TOGETHER	1974	PEOPLE		PLEO 16
JESSE MORRISON	SAX (N	(L) LETS STAY TOGETHER	1974	PEOPLE		PLEO 19
JOE THOMAS	SAX (N	(M) IF YOU'RE READY	1974	PEOPLE		PLEO 23
RALPH BYRD	G (N	(N) STUMP JUICE	1975	GROOVEMERCHANT	US	GM 3309
ANDREW McCLOUD	B (N	(O) FLYIN' TIME	19	GROOVEMERCHANT	US	GM 4403
LAWRENCE KILLIAN	PERC (N	(P) GIANT OF THE ORGAN	19	GROOVEMERCHANT	US	GM 3300
BOBBY CRANSHAW	B (N	(Q) SUPA COOKIN'	19	GROOVEMERCHANT	US	GM 4409
ALLAN SCHWARZBERG	D (R	(R) TAIL GUNNER	1977	L R C		LRC 9316

(CONTINUED)

M26 (CONTINUED)

JIMMY McGRIFF

| JIMMY YOUNG | D | (RS | (S) OUTSIDE LOOKIN' IN | 1978 L R C | LRC 9330 |

JIMMY YOUNG	D	(RS
RON ZITO	D	(RS
PAT REBILLOT	K	(RS	FRANCISCO CENTENO	B	(R	JERRY FRIEDMAN	G	(R	JIMMY MAELEN	PERC	(RS
LEW DELGATTO	HRNS	(RS	EDDIE DANIELS	HRNS	(RS	GEORGE YOUNG	HRNS	(R	ALAN RUBIN	HRNS	(R
RANDY BRECKER	HRNS	(R	JACK FROSK	HRNS	(R	MARVIN STAMM	HRNS	(R	JOE SHEPLEY	HRNS	(R
DAVE TAYLOR	HRNS	(R	DOMINIC MENARDO	HRNS	(R	BARRY ROGERS	HRNS	(R	JOE RANDAZZO	HRNS	(R
PAUL GRIFFIN	K	(R	RALPH SCHUCKETT	K	(R	BOB BABITT	B	(RS	WILL LEE	B	(R
LANCE QUINN	G	(RS	RUBENS BASSINI	PERC	(R	AL DOWNING	V	(R	DENISE WOOTEN	V	(R
PATRICIA JOHNSON	V	(R	HANK CRAWFORD	SAX	(S	NEIL JASON	B	(S	JEFF MIRANOV	G	(S
BARRY MILES	K	(S

M27

ROGER McGUINN

ROGER McGUINN	G V B(ALL	(A) ROGER McGUINN	1973 CBS	US 31946	UK	65274
BUDDY EMMONS	STEEL (A	(B) PEACE ON YOU	1974 CBS	US 32956	UK	80171
BRUCE JOHNSTON	PNO (A	(C) ROGER McGUINN & HIS BAND	1975 CBS	US 33341	UK	80877
DAVID CROSBY	G V (A	(D) CARDIFF ROSE	1976 CBS	US 34154	UK	81369
JOHN GUERIN	D (A	(E) THUNDERBYRDS	1977 CBS	US 34656	UK	81883
DAVID VAUGHT	B (A	(1) THUNDERBYRDS 1976 (2) UK TOUR 1974 AUG
LELAND SKLAR	B (A
JIM GORDON	D (A	JERRY COLE	G (A	CHRIS ETHRIDGE	B (A	SPOONER OLDHAM	K (A
SPANKY McFARLANE	V (A	HAL BLAINE	D (A	BOB DYLAN	HCA (A	CHRIS HILLMAN	B (A
MICHAEL CLARKE	D (A	CHARLES LLOYD	SAX (A	GENE CLARK	V (A	JIMMY JOYCE CHILDRENS CHOIR(A
RICK VITO	G (E	GREG THOMAS	D (E	CHARLIE HARRISON	B (E	MICK RONSON	G V K(D
ROB STONER	B V (D	HOWIE WYETH	D (D	TIM SCHMIT	V (D	RICHARD BOWDEN	(2
JAMES SMITH	G (1	MARTY GREBB	K (E	JANIS OLIVER	V (E	DAVID MANSFIELD	G K (D
KIM HUTCHCROFT	SAX (D	GREG ATTAWAY	(2	DAVID LOVELACE	(2	STEVE LOVE	B (2
BRUCE BARLOW	B (1E	LANCE DICKERSON	D (1	TOM SCOTT	SAX (E	JENNIFER O'NEILL	V (E
KRISTINE OLIVER	V (E	STEVE FORMAN	PERC (E

M28

McGUINN HILLMAN CLARK

ROGER McGUINN	G V (ABC	(A) McGUINN,HILLMAN & CLARK	1979	CAPITOL	11910
CHRIS HILLMAN	V G B(ABC	(B) CITY	1980	CAPITOL EURO 06486075	12043
GENE CLARK	V (AB	(C) SAME	1980	CAPITOL EURO 06486237
JOE LALA	PERC (AC
DONNA RHODES	V (A	GREG THOMAS	D (A	PAUL HARRIS	K (A	SANDRA CHALMERS	V (A
GEORGE TERRY	G (A	JOHN SAMBARATO	G V (ABC	CHARLES CHALMERS	V (A	SCOTT KIRKPATRICK	D V(BC
CHUCK CRANE	G (B	SKIP EDWARDS	K STEEL (B	WAYNE PERKINS	G (C	BARRY BECKETT	K (C

M29

McGUINNESS FLINT

TOM McGUINNESS	G B V(ABCDEF	(A) McGUINNESS FLINT	1971 CAPITOL	US SMAS625	UK EST 22625
HUGH FLINT	D V (ABCDEF	(B) HAPPY BIRTHDAY RUTHIE BABY	1971 CAPITOL	ST 22794
DENNIS COULSON	K G V(ABC	(C) LO & BEHOLD	1972 DJM UK DJLPS 424	SIRE US SAS 7405
BENNY GALLAGHER	V G (AB	(D) RAINBOW	1973 BRONZE	UK ILPS 9244	UK RI 87330
GRAHAM LYLE	V G (AB	(E) CEST LA VIE	1974 BRONZE	UK ILPS 9302
DIXIE DEAN	V B K(CDE	(F) GREATEST HITS	197 SOUNDS SUPERB	UK SPR 80537
LOU STONEBRIDGE HCA G V K(DE
JIM EVANS STEEL FDL G (DE	PAUL RUTHERFORD	HRNS (A	NICKY HOPKINS	K (B	JOHN MUMFORD	(B
JIMMY JEWELL	SAX (B

M30

BARRY McGUIRE

BARRY McGUIRE	V G B(ALL	(A) EVE OF DESTRUCTION	1965 DUNHILL	US 50003	UK ABC	ABCL 5110
MICHAEL CLARKE	D (D	(A) EVE OF DESTRUCTION	19 RCA	UK	RD 7751
ERIC HORD	G V (D	(B) THIS PRECIOUS TIME	1966 DUNHILL	US 50005 UK
CHRIS HILLMAN	B (D	(C) WORLDS LAST PRIVATE CITIZEN	1968 DUNHILL	US 50033
BERNIE LEADON	G (D	(D) BARRY McGUIRE & THE DOCTOR	1971 ODE	US 77004 UK A&M AMLS	2008
ROCKIE HILTON	G (D	(E) SEEDS	1974 MYRRH	US 6519 UK MYRRH	1006
BILLY MUNDI	D (D	(F) NARNIA	1974 MYRRH	UK	1007
BYRON BERLINE	FDL (D	(G) LIGHTEN UP	1975 MYRRH	US 6531 UK MYRRH	1020
SNEAKY PETE KLEINOW STEEL(D	(H) TO THE BRIDE	1976 MYRRH	US 6548 UK MYRRH	1044
RILEY WILDFLOWER	B (D	(I) EVE OF DESTRUCTION MAN	197 EMBER	UK	EMB 3362
NICKY WOODS	PERC (D	(J) C'MON ALONG	1976 SPARROW	UK	BIRD 105
MERLE BOATMAN	D (D	(K) HAPPY ROADS	19 DJM	UK DJM	22071
		(L) HAVE YOU HEARD	1976 SPARROW	BIRD 3+	BIRD 111
		(M) COSMIC COWBOY	1979 SPARROW	UK	BIRD 117
		(N) JUBILATION	19 MYRRH	US 6555
		(O) JUBILATION TOO	19 MYRRH	US 6568
		(P) BARRY McGUIRE ALBUM	19 HORIZON US 1636 US MIRA US	3000

M30A

MACHIAVEL

MARIO GUCCIO	V (A	(A) MECHANICAL MOONBEAMS	1978 EMI HARVEST	EURO 064 23805
ROLAND DE GREEF	B (A
MARC YSAYE	D V (A	ALBERT LETECHEUR K (A	JEAN PAUL DEVAUBE	G (A

M30B

MACHINES

| | | (EP) MACHINES | 19 WAX | EAR1 |

M31

MACHINE GUN

RANDY HANSEN	G (A	(A) 1978
LARRY EPPERLY	B (A
TIM KELIHER	D (A

M31A

ELLEN McILWAINE

ELLEN McILWAINE	G V (ABC	(A) HONKY TONK ANGEL	19 POYLDOR	US	5021
		(B) WE THE PEOPLE	19 POLYDOR	US	5044
		(C) THE REAL ELLEN McILWAINE	19 KOT'AI	US	3306

M31B

JIMMIE MACK

| JIMMIE MACK | (A | (A) JIMMIE MACK | 19 BIG TREE | US | 76007 |

M32

LONNIE MACK

LONNIE MACK	G V (ALL	(A) THE WHAM OF THE MEMPHIS MAN	1964 FRATERNITY	US	1014
WAYNE BULLOCK	K B (AF	(A) THE WHAM " " "	1967 PRESIDENT	US	PTL 1004
TRUMAN FIELDS	K (A	(A) FOR COLLECTORS ONLY (THE WHAM)	1970 ELEKTRA	US	EKS74077
RON GRAYSON	D (AC	(A) THE WHAM	1973 ELEKTRA	UK	K 42056
MARV LIEBERMAN	SAX (A	(B) GLAD I'M IN THE BAND	1969 ELEKTRA	US 74040 UK	K 42025
IRV RUSSOTTO	SAX (A	(C) WHATEVER'S RIGHT	1969 ELEKTRA	US 74050 UK	K 42031
BILL JONES	B (A	(D) THE HILLS OF INDIANA	1972 ELEKTRA	US 74102 UK	K 42097
DAVID BYRD	K (AC	(E) HOME AT LAST	1977 CAPITOL	US 11619
TIM DRUMMOND	B (CF	(F) LONNIE MACK WITH PISMO	1978 CAPITOL	US 11703

                    (CONTINUED)

```
IAN WALLACE        (F
TROY SEALS      V  (F    DAVID LINDLEY      G   (F    BEN KEITH      STEEL(F   DAVID BRIGGS     K  (F
BILLY McINTOSH     (F    STAN SZELESTE      K   (F    TERRY ADAMS    CELLO(F   GRAHAM NASH      V  (F
TIMOTHY HEDDING  ORG(C   DENZIL RICE       PNO  (C    JERRY LOVE     D   (C    RUSTY YORK      HCA(C
JACK BRICKLES   HCA (C   ROY CHRISTIANSEN  CELLO(C    SHIRLEY MATTHEWS SINGERS(C
```

WARNER MACK   M33

```
WARNER MACK    G V (ALL        (A) GOLDEN COUNTRY HITS          1963   LONDON        UK      SHU   8025
LLOYD GREEN    STEEL(J         (B) DRIFTING APART               1968   BRUNSWICK UK 8684 US DECCA 74883
                               (C) THE COUNTRY TOUCH            196                    US DECCA 74766
                               (D) MANY COUNTRY MOODS           196                    US DECCA 74995
                               (E) THE CONTRY BEAT OF WARNER MACK 1969                 US DECCA 75092
                               (F) WARNER MACK VOL 1            196                    US KAPP  8002
                               (G) WARMER MACK VOL 2            196                    US KAPP  8025
                               (H) I'LL STILL BE MISSING YOU    1970                   US DECCA 75165
                               (I) LOVE HUNGRY                  1970                   US DECCA 75219
                               (J) YOU MAKE ME FEEL LIKE A MAN  1971                   US DECCA 75272
                               (K) GREAT COUNTRY                197                    US MCA   20001
                               (L) THE BEST OF THE BEST         1979                   US GUSTO 0042
```

ANDY MACKAY   M34

```
ANDY MACKAY     SAX (AB        (A) IN SEARCH OF EDDIE RIFF      1974 ISLAND        UK      ILPS9278
PHIL MANZANERA  G   (AB        (A) IN SEARCH OF EDDIE RIFF      1977 POLYDOR       UK      2302 064
JOHN PORTER     B   (A         (B) RESOLVING CONTRADICTIONS     1978 BRONZE        UK      BRON  510
JOHN GUSTAFSON  B   (A
LLOYD WATSON    G   (A    ROGER GLOVER     B   (A    PAUL THOMPSON    D   (AB  EDDIE JOBSON    VLN K(A
BRIAN CHATTON   K   (A    BRUCE ROWLAND    D   (A    SADIE MACKENZIE  VLN (A   JANE RIFF       VLN (A
MO FOSTER       B   (B    TONY STEVENS     B   (B    PETER VAN HOOKE  D   (B   TIM WHEATER     FLT (B
CHRIS PARREN    K   (B    GAVYN WRIGHT     VLN (B    MICHAEL LAIRD    TPT (B
```

DUNCAN MACKAY   M35

```
DUNCAN MACKAY   K   (AB        (A) SCORE                        1977 EMI          UK      EMC   3168
STEVE HARLEY    V   (A         (B) VISA                         1980 EDGE         UK      HOG   2
JOHN WETTON     B   (A
CLIVE CHAMAN    B   (A    ANDY McCULLOCH    D PERC(A  MEL COLLINS    WIND (A   YVONNE KEELY    V  (A
SIMON PHILLIPS  D   (B    ALAN JONES             (B
```

JOANNE MACKELL   M36

```
JOANNE MACKELL  V   (A         (A) JOANNE MACKELL               1978 UA           UK      UAG 30180
```

McKENDREE SPRING   M37

```
FRAN McKENDREE V B G K(ALL      (A) McKENDREE SPRING            19   DECCA US75104          MCA   277
FRED HOLMAN    B V (CD          (B) SECOND THOUGHTS             197  DECCA US75230
MICHAEL DREYFUSS VLN K(CDEFG    (C) SECOND THOUGHTS             1971 MCA     UK MUPS 433 RI 74 MCF 2651
MARTIN SLUTSKY G   (CDEFG       (C) THREE                       1972 MCA     UK MUPS 454 RI 74 MCF 2658
HANK DEVITO    STEEL(O          (C) THREE                       197  MCA     US MCA  44
ANDY NEWMARK   D   (CD          (D) TRACKS                      1973 MCA     UK MUPS 476 RI 74 MCF 2666
RAUN MACKINNON K   (CD          (D) TRACKS                      197  DECCA   US 75385
ARTIE KAPLAN   SAX (D           (E) SPRING SUITE                1973 MCA     US    370
DAVID WOODS    G   (D           (F) GET ME TO THE COUNTRY       1975 DAWN    UK DNLS3076  IMP PYE 12108
JO ANN VENT    V   (D           (G) TOO YOUNG TO FEEL THIS OLD  1976                      IMP PYE 12124
BOB HIPWELL    V   (D
JOHN MONTGOMERY V  (D     CARSON MICHAELS   D V (EG  CHRISTOPHER BISHOP B V K(EFG VALERIE ROSA  V  (F
HOWARD WYETH   K   (F     CHILLI CHARLES    PERC (F  BOBBY GREGG      D   (C   ELLEN KEARNEY   V  (C
JERRY BURNHAM  FLT (C     RUSSELL GEORGE    B   (C   JOHN DEVOE       V   (C   SUZANNE FRENCH  V  (C
WARREN BERNHARDT K (G
```

MAE McKENNA   M38

```
MAE McKENNA    V   (ABC         (A) MAE McKENNA                 1975 TRANSATLANTIC UK     TRA   297
TREVOR SPENCER D   (A           (B) EVERYTHING THAT TOUCHES ME  1976 TRANSATLANTIC UK     TRA   321
MARTIN BRILEY  G B (A           (C) WALK ON WATER               1977 TRANSATLANTIC UK     TRA   345
GRAHAM PRESKETT B  (A
B J COLE       STEEL(A    SKAILA KANGA      HARP (A   ISAAC GUILLORY   G   (BC  ELLIOT RANDALL  G(BC
RONNIE LEAHY   K   (BC    PETE WILLSHER     STEEL(BC  TIMI DONALD      D   (B   PAT DONALDSON   B(B
RITCHIE GOLD   V   (B     PETE WINGFIELD    K   (C    JOHN GIBLIN      B   (C   GLEN LEFLEUR    D(C
COLIN BLUNSTONE V  (C     ROD ARGENT        V   (C    ALAN JAMES       B   (C   GERRY CONWAY    D(C
MORRIS PERT    PERC (C
```

McKENNA MENDELSON MAINLINE   M39

```
MIKE McKENNA    G   (AB        (A) STINK                        1969    LIBERTY    UK    LBS 83251
JOE MENDELSON G V K HCA(AB      (B) NO SUBSTITUTE               1975    TAURUS    CAN    TR    103
TONY VOLASCO    D   (A
MIKE HARRISON   B   (A    ADAM MITCHELL   MAND V PERC(B  T TOTH   VLN (B   JØRN ANDERSEN   PERC (B
EDWARD PURDIE   K   (B
```

SCOTT McKENZIE   M39A

```
SCOTT McKENZIE  V   (AB         (A) VOICE OF SCOTT McKENZIE     1967 ODE           US     44002
                               (B) STAINED GLASS MORNING        1970 ODE           US     77007
```

IAN McLAGAN   M39B

```
IAN McLAGAN    V K G(A          (A) TROUBLEMAKER                1979 MERCURY        US     SRM 13786
JOHNNY LEE SCHELL G V (A
RON WOOD        G   (A    KEITH RICHARDS    G   (A    JIM KELTNER     D   (A   RINGO STARR     D  (A
JOSEPH MODELISTE D  (A    PAUL STALLWORTH   B   (A    STANLEY CLARKE  B   (A   FLAP WORKMAN    ACC(A
BOBBY KEYS      HRNS(A    RON WOOD               V HRNS(A  STEVE MADAIO HRNS (A   JAIME SEGEL   D  (A
```

JOHN McLAUGHLIN & THE MAHAVISHNU ORCHESTRA   M40

```
JOHN McLAUGHLIN G  (ALL         (A) EXTRAPOLATION         1969 MARMALADE  UK 608007 RI70 2343 012
TONY OXLEY      D   (A           (A) EXTRAPOLATION        1972 POLYDOR    UK 2310018 US   PD6074
BRIAN ODGERS    B   (A           (B) MY GOALS BEYOND      1971 DOUGLAS    UK 69014 US CBS  30766
JOHN SURMAN     SAX (AE          (C) DEVOTION             1971 DOUGLAS    UK 65075
JERRY GOODMAN   VLN (BCDFM       (D) INNER MOUNTING FLAME 1971 CBS        UK 64717 US CBS  31067
BILLY COBHAM    D   (BDFGM       (E) WHERE FORTUNE SMILES 1972 DAWN       UK DNLS3018
JAN HAMMER      K   (DFG          (F) BIRDS OF FIRE       1973 CBS        UK 65321 US      31996
JEAN LUC PONTY  VLN (IJ          (G) LOVE DEVOTION & SURRENDER 1973 CBS   UK 59037 US      32034
RICK LAIRD      B   (DF          (H) BETWEEN NOTHINGNESS & ETERNITY 1974 CBS UK 69046 US   32766
CARLOS SANTANA  G   (G           (I) APOCALYPSE          1974 CBS        UK 69076 US       32957
TONY WILLIAMS   D   (M           (J) VISIONS OF THE EMERALD BEYOND 1975 CBS UK 69108 US    33411
                                                                          (CONTINUED)
```

JOHN McLAUGHLIN & THE MAHAVISHNU ORCHESTRA

MILES DAVIS	TPT	(	(K) INNER WORLDS	1976 CBS	UK 69216 US	33908
JACK BRUCE	B	(M	(L) IN RETROSPECT	1976 POLYDOR	UK 2675 091	
CHICK COREA	K	(M	(M) ELECTRIC GUITARIST	1978 CBS	UK 82702	
STANLEY CLARKE	B	(M	(N) ELECTRIC DREAMS (ONE TRUTH BAND)	1979 CBS	UK 83256	
ALPHONSO JOHNSON		(M	(O) BEST OF MAHAVISHNU ORCHESTRA	1980 CBS	UK 84232	
PATRICE RUSHEN	V	(M	(P) BEST OF JOHN McLAUGHLIN	1980 CBS	UK 84455	
DAVID SANBORN	SAX	(M	(1) ONE TRUTH BAND 1978 LIVE			
FERNANDO SAUNDERS	B	(1				
BUDDY MILES	D	(C	LARRY YOUNG	K	(CG	BILLY RICH	B	(C	STU GOLDBERG	K (K1
ANTHONY ALLEN SMITH	D	(1	L SHANKAR	VLN PERC	(1	ARMANDO PERAZA	CONGA(G	DON ALIAS	D (G
DOUG RAUCH	B	(FG	MINGO LEWIS	PERC	(G	RALPH ARMSTRONG	B	(KJ	GAYLE MORAN	K (J
NARADA MICHAEL WALDEN	D(JK	STU MARTIN		(E	STEVE KINDLER	VLN	(J	DAVE HOLLAND	(E
KARL BERGER	(E	CAROL SHIRE	VLN	(J	PHILLIP HIRSCHI	CELLO(J	BOB KNAPP	WIND(J
AIRTO MOREIRA	PERC	(B	CHARLIE HAYDEN	B	(B	MAHALAKSHMI	SITAR(B	BADAL ROY	PERC(B

M41
DON McLEAN

DON McLEAN	G V	(ALL	(A) TAPESTRY	1972 UA	UK UAS 29350	US	5522
GEORGE RICCI	CELLO(A		(B) AMERICAN PIE	1972 UA	UK UAS 29285	US	5535
RALPH MACDONALD	PERC³(D		(C) DON McLEAN	1972 UA	UK UAS 29399	US	5651
DON BROOKS	HCA	(D	(D) PLAYIN' FAVOURITES	1973 UA	UK UAS 29528	US	LA161 G
DICK HYMAN	PNO	(D	(E) HOMELESS BROTHER	1974 UA	UK UAG 29646	US	LA315 G
WARREN BERNHARDT	PNO	(D	(F) SOLO (LIVE DBL)	1976 UA	UK UAD 60139/40 US	LA652H2
TONY LEVIN	B	(D	(G) PRIME TIME	1977 EMI	UK INS 3011	ARISTA US	4149
ED TRICKETT	DULC	(D	(H) CHAIN LIGHTNING	1979 EMI	UK INS 3025	
BUZZY FEITEN	G	(D	(J) VERY BEST OF	1980 UA	UK UAG 30314	
CHRIS PARKER	D	(D				
NEIL LARSEN	K	(D	RUSS SAVAKUS	VLN	(D	BOB ROTHSTEIN	B V(D	YUSEF LATEEF	(E
KENNY VANCE	(E	BOB MOORE	G	(H	KEN ASCHER	K	(G	PAT REBILLOT	K (G
JOHN FARRELL	G	(D	ROBBIE STONER	V B	(G	HOWIE WYETH	K V(G	DAVE SANBORN	SAX(G
RONA WYETH	V	(G	CHRISTINE FAITH	V	(G	ANGELA HOWELL	V	(G	GENE ORLOFF	STRING (G
RUBENS BASSINI	PERC	(G	DOM CORTESE	ACC	(G	BILLY SANFORD	G	(H	JAMES CAPPS	G (H
JOSEPH CHRISMAN	D	(H	JORDANAIRES	V	(H	RAY EDENTON	G	(H	PETE DRAKE	STEEL (H
TOMMY ALSUP	G	(H	EDDY ANDERSON	D	(H	PIG ROBBINS	PNO(H	CHUCK COCHRAN	PNO(H
BOBBY WOODS	K	(H	JERRY CARRIGAN	D	(H	PERSUASIONS	V	(E		

M41A
SANDY McLELLAND & THE BACKLINE

SANDY McLELLAND	V	(A	(A) SANDY McLELLAND & THE BACKLINE	1979 MERCURY	UK	9109 620
DAVID BATES	PERC	(A	(B) McLELLAND	1981 action	UK	AL 1000
PAUL KAMOWSKI	G	(A				
ROBIN RANKIN	K	(A	ANDY HAMILTON	SAX	(A	ROBERT PATERSON	B	(A	PETER COE	D (A
MARK KNOPFLER	G	(A	JIM MULLEN	G	(A	DICK HANSON	HRNS	(A	JOHN EARLE	HRNS(A
CHRIS GOWER	TROM	(A	RAY BEAVIS	HRNS	(A	FRANK COLLINS	V	(A	DYAN BIRCH	V (A
COLLETTE WILKINSON	V	(A	ANDY LUNN	PERC	(A	JON ASTLEY	PERRC(A		

M41B
ANDREW McMAHON

ANDREW'BLUEBLOOD' McMAHON	(A	(A) GO GET MY BABY	1978	MCM	FR	900 301

M42
HAROLD McNAIR

HAROLD McNAIR	FLT	(ALL	(A) HAROLD McNAIR	1968	RCA	UK	SF 7969
RICK GRECH	B	(B	(B) THE FENCE	1970	B&C	UK	CAS 1016
KEITH TIPPETT		(B	(C) HAROLD McNAIR	1971	B&C	UK	CAS 1045
			(D) AFFECTION FINK	19	ISLAND	UK	
			(E) FLUTE & NUT	19	RCA	UK	INTS1096

M43
CLYDE McPHATTER

CLYDE McPHATTER	V	(ALL	CLYDE McPHATTER & THE DRIFTERS	195	ATLANTIC	US	SD 8003
			LOVE BALLADS	1958	ATLANTIC	US	SD 8024
			CLYDE	1959	ATLANTIC	US	SD 8031
			BEST OF CLYDE McPHATTER	1963	ATLANTIC	US	SD 8077
			TA TA	19	MERCURY	US (M)20597 (S)	60252
			GOLDEN BLUES HITS	19	MERCURY	US (M)20665 (S)	60665
			LOVER PLEASE	19	MERCURY	US (M)20711 (S)	60711
			RHYTHM & SOUL	19	MERCURY	US (M)20750 (S)	60750
			GREATEST HITS	1963	MERCURY	US (M)20783 (S)	60783
			SONGS OF THE BIG CITY	1964	MERCURY	US (M)20902 (S)	60902
			LIVE AT THE APOLLO	1964	MERCURY	US (M)20915 (S)	60915
			MAY I SING FOR YOU	1966	MERCURY	US (M)12224 (S)	16224
			LETS START OVER	19	MGM	US	3775
			GREATEST HITS	19	MGM	US	3866
			WITH BILLY WARD & THE DOMINOES	19	KING	US	559
			18 ORIGINAL HITS	19	KING	US	5006
			WELCOME HOME	1971	MCA	UK MCPS 418	RI 74 MCF2642
			WELCOME HOME	19	DECCA	US	75231
			A TRIBUTE TO CLYDE McPHATTER	19	ATLANTIC UK	K30033

M44
TONY McPHEE

TONY McPHEE	G K V(ALL	(A) ME & THE DEVIL	1968 LIBERTY	UK	LBS83190
JO ANN KELLY	V G	(ABC	(B) I ASKED FOR WATER(VAR ARTIST)	1969 LIBERTY	UK	LBS83252
GROUNDHOGS		(B	(C) SAME THING ON THEIR MINDS	1971 SUNSET	UK	SLS50209
BRETT MARVIN & THUNDERBOLTS(B		(D) TWO SIDES OF	1973 WWA	UK	WWA 001
			(***) C FEATURES TRACKS FROM A+B			

M45
RALPH McTELL

RALPH McTELL	G V	(ALL	(A) 8 FRAMES A SECOND	1968 TRANSATLANTIC	UK	TRA 165
MIKE PIGGOTT	FDL	(1GH	(B) SPIRAL STAIRCASE	1969 TRANSATLANTIC	UK	TRA 177
NIGEL SMITH	K	(1	(C) MY SIDE OF YOUR WINDOW	1969 TRANSATLANTIC	UK	TRA 209
DAVE PEGG	B	(1HL	(D) REVISITED	1970 TRANSATLANTIC	UK	TRA 227
DAVE MATTACKS	D	(1G	(E) YOU WELL MEANING BROUGHT ME HERE	1971 FAMOUS 5753 UK	+ ABC ABCL 5084
BRIAN BROCKLEHURST	B	(C	(F) NOT TILL TOMORROW	1972 REPRISE	UK	K44210
FOLK WEAVERS	V	(C	(G) EASY	1973 REPRISE	UK	K54013
HENRY VIII	JUG	(ABC	(H) STREETS	1975 WB	UK	K56105
PETE BERRYMAN	G	(ABH	(I) STREETS OF LONDON	1975 TRANSATLANTIC	UK	TRASAM34
ROD CLEMENTS	B	(HL	(K) STAR COLLECTION	1975 MIDI		MID26030
GOLDRUSHERS	V	(H	(L) RIGHT SIDE UP	1976 WB	UK	K56296

(CONTINUED)

(CONTINUED)   RALPH McTELL

DANNY THOMPSON	B	(GHL	(M) COLLECTION	1977 TRANSATLANTIC	UK		TRASAM39
DANNY LANE	D	(H	(N) RALPH,ALBERT,SYDNEY	1977 WB	UK		K56399
BOB KERR	SAX	(H	(O) MAGINOT WALTZ (EP)	1977 WB	UK		K17008
JERRY DONAHUE	G	(H	(P) RALPH McTELL	1978 PICKWICK			SHM 962
WIZZ JONES	G	(G	(Q) SLIDE AWAY THE SCREEN	1979 WB	UK		K56599
ANDY CRONSHAW ZITHER		(H					

STEVE BONNETT   MAND (G   JOHN KONGOS   V   (G   RABBIT BUNDRICK   K   (H   LINDSAY SCOTT   VLN (G
SANDY SPENCER   CELLO(H   ALAN HARRIS   PERC (H   ROD EDWARDS   PNO (H   MADDY PRIOR   V   (H
GERRY CONWAY   G   (H   BERT JANSCH   G   (G   PICK WITHER   D   (L   JON STEVENS   D   (L
GRAHAM PRESKETT K   (L   PETER SWETENHAM K   (L   SAMMY MITCHELL   DOBRO(L   TONY RIVERS   V   (L
KEN GOLD   V   (L   JOHN PERRY   V   (L   JOHN MARTYN   V   (L   MAC MACGANN   G   (A
WHISPERING MICK PERC (AB   BOB STRAWBRIDGE MAND (L

M45A
DAVID McWILLIAMS G V (ALL   DAVID McWILLIAMS

(A) DAYS OF PEARLY SPENCER	1971 STARLINE	UK	SRS 5075
(B) LORD OFFALY	1972 DAWN	UK	DNLS 3039
(C) BEGGAR & THE PRIEST	1973 DAWN	UK	DNLS 3047
(D) LIVING JUST A STATE OF MIND	1974 DAWN	UK	DNLS 3059
(E) DAVID McWILLIAMS	1977 EMI	UK	EMC 3169

MAD RIVER   M46

TOM MANNING	V	(ALL	(A) MAD RIVER	1968 CAPITOL		ST 2985
DAVID ROBINSON	G	(ALL	(B) PARADISE BAR & GRILL	1969 CAPITOL		ST 185
RICK BOCHNER	G	(ALL	(EP) MAD RIVER	1967 WEE		10021
LAURIE HAMMOND	B	(ALL				
GREG DEWEY	D	(ALL				

MADNESS   M46A

MIKE BARSON HCA PERC K   (AB   (A) ONE STEP BEYOND   1979 STIFF   UK   SEEZ 17
CHRIS FOREMAN   G   (AB   (B) ABSOLUTELY   1980 STIFF   UK   SEEZ 29
GRAHAM McPHERSON V   (A
MARK BEDFORD   B   (AB LEE THOMPSON SAX V(AB DAN WOODGATE   D (AB CHAS SMASH TPT V(AB
SUGGS   V PERC(B

JIMMY MAELEN   M46B

JIMMY MAELEN PERC V(A   (A) BEATS WORKIN'   1980 CBS   UK   84211
NEIL JASON   V   (A
FRANK MAELEN   V   (A   RANDY BRECKER   TPT (A   BARRY ROGERS   TROM(A   ELLIOT RANDALL G   (A
LANI GROVES   V   (A   IRENE CARA   V   (A   STEVE LOVE   HRNS (A   ROBIN BECK   V   (A
VICKI SUE ROBINSON V (A ANNIE SUTTON   V   (A   LUTHER VANDROSS V (A   GEORGE YOUNG   SAX(A
JOHN TROPEA   G   (A   ROB MOUNSEY   K   (A   PAT REBILLOT   K   (A   JOHN LONGO   TPT(A
LEW SOLOFF   TPT (A   KEN ASCHER   K   (A   ALLEN SCHWARZBERG D (A PAUL SHAFFER   K (A
RONNIE CUBER   SAX (A   LAWRENCE FELDMAN SAX (A
                                  MAGAZINE   M47

HOWARD DEVITO	V K	(ABCD	(A) REAL LIFE	1978 VIRGIN	UK		V 2100
BARRY ADAMSON	G B	(ABCD	(B) SECONDHAND DAYLIGHT	1979 VIRGIN	UK		V2121
DAVE FORMULA	K	(ABCD	(C) CORRECT USE OF SOAP	1980 VIRGIN	UK		V2156
MARTIN JACKSON	D	(A	(D) PLAY LIVE	1980 VIRGIN	UK		V2184
SUPER MAGS	V	(B					

JOHN McGEOCH G K SAX (ABC JOHN DOYLE   D   (BCD LAURA TERESA   V   (C   ROBIN SIMON G   (D
                                  MAGIC SAM   M48

MAGIC SAM MAGHETT G V (ALL   (A) MAGIC SAM 1937/69   1970 BLUE HORIZON UK   763223
LITTLE BRO MONTGOMERY K(ADE   (B) BLACK MAGIC   19   DELMARK DS 620 JAP TRIO PA 6216
MACK THOMPSON   B   (ABCDEF   (C) WEST SIDE SOUL   19   DELMARK DS 615 JAP TRIO PA 6214
WILLIE DIXON   B   (ADE   (D) MAGIC ROCKER   1980 FLYRIGHT   UK   FL 561
BILLY STEPNEY   D   (ABE   (E) OTIS RUSH & MAGIC SAM 1980 FLYRIGHT UK   FL 562
EDDIE SHAW   SAX (B   (F) LATE GREAT MAGIC SAM 1980 L&R   42014
LAFAYETTE LEAKE PNO (B   (G) BLUES MASTERS VOL 3 19   BLUE HORIZON US   BN 4603
MIGHTY JOE YOUNG G   (BC
ODIE PAYNE   D   (ABCDE SHAKEY JAKE HARRIS V (ADE SYL JOHNSON   B   (ADE HARRY BURRAGE PNO (ADE
STOCKHOLM SLIM PNO (C   ERNEST JOHNSON   B   (C   ROBERT ST JULIEN D (EF BOYD ATKINS   SAX (
JOHNNY JONES   PNO (ODELL CAMPBELL   B   (E   S P LEARY   D (FOUR DUCHESSES V   (
AMMONS SISTERS V   (
                                  MAGIC SAND   M48A

(A) MAGIC SAND   1970 UNI   US   73094
                                  MAGIC SLIM   M48B

MAGIC SLIM   G V (ALL   (A) BORN UNDER A BAD SIGN   197 MCM   FR   900 298
JUNIOR PETTIS   G   (A   (B) VOL 2   197 MCM   FR   900 305
NICK HOLT   B   (A   (C) LIVE AT THE ZOO BAR   1980 CANDY APPLE US
DOUGLAS HOLT   D   (A
                                  MAGITS   M48C
                     (A(FULLY COHERENT (EP)   19   OUTER HIMALAYAN   ?
                                  MAGMA   M49

CHRISTIAN VANDER D PERC V K(ALL   (A) MAGMA (DBL)   1970 PHILIPS   63595 001/2
JANNIK TOP   B   (CDF   (B) 1001 CENTIGRADE   1971 PHILIPS 9101 286 +   6397 031
KLAUS BLASQUIZ   V PERC(ABCDF   (C) KOHN TARK05Z   1974 A&M   US 3650 UK AMLH6B260
TEDDY LASRY   WIND (ABD   (C) KOHN TARK05Z   1974 VERTIGO   EURO 6325 750
JEAN LUC MANDERLIER K (D   (D) MEKANIK DESTRUKTIW KOMMANDOH 1974 A&M US 4397 UK AMLH64397
RENE GARBES   CLAR V(D   (D) MEKANIK DESTRUKTIW KOMMANDOH 197 VERTIGO EURO 6499 729
CLAUDE OLMOS   G   (D   (E) LIVE (DBL)   1975 UTOPIA   CYL21245 + 5PC 0002
BENOIT WIDEMANN   K   (HD   (F) UDU WUDU   1976 TOMATO   6001 RCA FPLA 7332
BERNARD PAGANOTTI B   (F   (G) EDITS   1977 TAPIOCA
DOM REINHARDT   V   (D   (H) ATTAHK   197 WEA   EURO   913213
LOUIS SARKISSIAN SAX (ABC
GABRIEL FEDERON   G   (LIZA DELUXE   V   (D   DIDIER LOCKWOOD VLN (JEAN POL ASSELINE K (
STELLA VANDER   V   (DCH EVELYNE RAZYMOVSKI V (D MURIEL STREIFELD V (D LOUIS TOESCA   TPT(B
CLAUD ENGEL   G V (D   FRANCIS MOZE   B   (D   FRANCOIS COHEN   K   (AB JEFF SEFFER   SAX(B
ALAIN HATOT   FLT (F   PATRICK GAUTHIER K   (F   PIERRE DU TOUR   TPT (F RICHARD RAUX   WIND (A
ALAIN CHARLERY   TPT (C   GERLAD BIKAILO   K   (C   MICHEL GRAILLIER K   (C BRIAN GODDING G (C
MICHELLE SANTHIER V   (STEELE VANDER   V   (A

MAGNA CARTA

CHRIS SIMPSON	G V	(ALL	(A) MAGNA CARTA	1969	MERCURY			SMCL20166
DAVEY JOHNSTONE	G V	(BEF	(B) SEASONS	1970	VERTIGO			6360 003
GLEN STUART	V	(ABEFGH	(C) TIMES OF CHANGE	197	FONTANA	NL		6438 080
LYELL TRANTER	(AB		(D) BEST OF MAGNA CARTA	197	VERTIGO	NL		9107 100
STAN GORDON	G V	(GH	(D) BEST OF MAGNA CATRA	197	VERTIGO	NL RI		9199 737
BARRY MORGAN	D	(B	(E) SONGS FRON WASTIES ORCHARD	1971	VERTIGO	UK		6360 040
TONY CARR	D	(AB	(F) IN CONCERT	1972	VERTIGO	UK		6360 068
TONY VISCONTI	B PERC	(BE	(G) LORD OF THE AGES	1973	VERTIGO	UK		6360 093
SPIKE HEATLEY	B	(B	(H) MARTINS CAFE	197	VERTIGO	NL		6360 146
RICK WAKEMAN	K	(BE	(J) PUTTING IT BACK TOGETHER	1976	POLYDOR 2321 012		GTO GTLP 012	
ALASTAIR ANDERSON	(E		(K) TOOK A LONG TIME	197	GTO			2321 112
RON CHESTERMAN	(E		(L) SPOTLIGHT ON	1977	PHILIPS			6625 031
GUS DUDGEON	(E		(M) PRISONERS ON THE LINE	1978	PHILIPS			9109 229
CHRIS LAURENCE	(E		(N) LIVE IB BERGEN 8/10/78	1978	FONTANA	NL		6438 080
DANNY THOMPSON	B	(AE						

FRANK HODGES	PERC	(A	PETER WILLISON	CELLO(B	DAVE ARTHUR	(E	HEATHER CORBETT	(E
HOOKFOOT	(E	NICK POTTER	(E	TIM RENWICK	RECORDER	(B	DEREK GROSSMITH	FLT(B
TONI ARTHUR	(C	JOHNNY VAN DERRICK	(E	HAROLD McNAIR	FLT(A	DAVE MARKEE	B	(M
GRAHAM SMITH	B V HCA	(H	LES CYRCLE	D	(M	HENNIE BEKKER	K	(M	MIKE FINDLEY	G	(M
DAVE BARKER	(	TOMMY HOY	(M	NIGEL SMITH	ACC(M	LEE ABBOT	(
ROBIN THYNE	(M	TOM McCONVILLE	(	GEORGE MORRIS	(	AL FENN	(
ROY BABBINGTON	B	(M	ROBIN ELLIS	V	(M	EMIL ZJHBZ	V	(M	CHRIS KARAN	(C
GRAHAM STUART	(							

MAGNETS

BOB BARNETT	G	(		
STEVE CLEAR	G V	(		
NICK DODD	D	(	BRIAN DIVITO B	(

MAGNUM

TONY CLARKIN	G V	(ABC	(A) KINGDOM OF MADNESS	1978	JET	UK	LP	210
RICHARD BAILEY	K V FLT	(ABC	(B) MAGNUM 2	1979	JET	UK	LP	222
BOB CATLEY	G V	(ABC	(C) MARAUDER	1980	JET	UK	LP	230
KEX GORIN	D	(ABC						
COLIN LOWE	B V	(ABC						

TAJ MAHAL

TAJ MAHAL	G V HCA BANJ	(ALL	(A) TAJ MAHAL	1967	DIRECTION	UK		863279	
RY COODER	G	(A	(A) TAJ MAHAL	1967	CBS	US	(M) 2779	(S) 9579	
JESSE ED DAVIS	G	(ABCE	(B) NATCH'L BLUES	1978	DIRECTION	UK 863397	US CBS	9698	
JAMES THOMAS	B	(A	(C) GIANT STEP/DE OLE FOLKS (DBL)	1969	CBS	UK 866226	US CBS	18	
SANFORD KONIKOFF	D	(A	(D) THE REAL THING (DBL)	1971	CBS	UK	66288	US CBS 30619	
BILL BOATMAN	G	(A	(E) HAPPY JUST TO BE LIKE I AM	1971	CBS	UK	64447	US CBS 30767	
GARY GILMORE	B	(ABC	(F) RECYCLING THE BLUES	1973	CBS	UK	65090	US CBS 31605	
CHUCK BLACKWELL	D	(ABC	(G) OOH SO GOOD 'N' BLUES	1973	CBS	UK	65814	US CBS 32600	
AL KOOPER	K	(B	(H) MO ROOTS	1974	CBS	UK	80346	US CBS 33051	
EARL PALMER	D	(B	(J) MUSIC KEEPS ME TOGETHER	1975	CBS	UK	80972	US CBS 33801	
JAMES CHARLES OTEY	D	(E	(K) SATISFIED N TICKLED TOO	1976	CBS	UK	81346	US CBS 34103	
JOHN SIMON	K	(ED	(L) ANTHOLOGY VOL 1 1966/76	1976	CBS			US CBS 34466	
BILL RICH	B	(EHDPQ	(M) MUSIC FUH YA	1977	WB	UK K56324	US	2994	
HOSHAL WRIGHT	G	(EH	(N) BROTHERS	197	WB		US	3024	
ROCKY DZIDZORNU	PERC	(EHMND	(O) EVOLUTION	197	WB		US	3094	
HOWARD JOHNSON	HRNS	(ED	(P) & INTERNATIONAL RHYTHM BAND LIVE	1979	CRYSTAL CLEAR		CCX 5011		
BOB STEWART	HRNS	(ED	(Q) & INTERNATIONAL RHYTHM BAND	1980	MAGNET		MAGL 5035		
ANDY NARELL	STEEL DRUM	(E	(R) GOING HOME (COMP)	1980	CBS			31844	
MERLE SAUNDERS	K	(H							

CLAUDIA LENNEAR	V	(HN	LARRY McDONALD	PERC K(MN	BISMARK FRANCO	PERC	(M	JONI HAASTRUP	V	(M
RASHAIDA NIROBE	V	(M	JOSEPH DALEY	HRNS	(DE	EARL MacINTYRE	HRNS	(DE	KESTER SMITH	PERC(HMN
RUDY COSTA	WIND	(MHN	ASTON BARRETT	K	(H	CAROLE FREDERICKS	V	(MH	TOMMY HENDERSON	V	(H
MERRY CLAYTON	V	(H	ROBERT GREENIDGE	D V	(MPQ	RAY FIZPATRICK	B G K V	(MN	INSHIRAH MAHAL	V	(M
MONA RAM	V	(M	YVONNE FIMBRES	V	(M	ALISON MILLS	V	(N	JOHN HALL	G	(D
GREG THOMAS	D	(D	JUMMA SANTOS	PERC	(PQ	RUDY COSTA	WIND	(PQ	KESTER SMITH	D	(PQ
ELLA JAMERSON	V	(PQ	GERI JOHNSON	V	(PQ	BIANCA ODEN	V	(PQ	VERLIN SANDLES	V	(PQ
OLA MARIE TYLER	V	(PQ	CAREY WILLIAMS	V	(PQ						

MAHOGANY RUSH

FRANK MARINO	G VK	(ALL	(A) CHILD OF THE NOVELTY	1975	20TH CENTURY		US T	451
PAUL HARWOOD	B	(ALL	(B) MAXOOM	1975	20TH CENTURY		US T	463
JIMMY AYOUB	D	(ALL	(C) STRANGE UNIVERSE	1975	20TH CENTURY		US T	482
NANETTE WORKMAN	V	(G	(D) MAHOGANY RUSH	1976	CBS	UK 81417	US	34190
VINCE MARINO	G	(H	(E) WORLD ANTHEM	1977	CBS	UK 81978	US	34677
			(F) LIVE	1978	CBS	UK 82625	US	35257
			(G) TALES OF THE UNEXPECTED	1979	CBS		US	35753
			(H) WHATS NEXT	1980	CBS	UK 83897		

MAINHORSE

PATRICK MORAZ	K	(A	(A) MAINHORSE	1971	POLYDOR UK 2383049+VISA IMP		1001
PETER COCKETT	G VLN V	(A					
BRYSON GRAHAM	D	(A	JEAN RISTON B CELLO V(A				

MIKE MAINIERI

MIKE MAINIERI	VIBES	(A	(A) JOURNEY THRU AN ELECTRIC TUBE	1969	UA		UAS	29051	
JEREMY STEIG	FLT	(A							
JOE BECK	G	(A	SALLY WARING	V	(A	SAM BROWN	G	(A	WARREN BERNHARDT PNO (A
DONALD MACDONALD	D	(A	HAL TAYLOR	B	(A	CHUCK RAINEY	B	(A	

MAINLAND

LES PAYNE	G V	(A	(A) EXPOSURE	1979	CHRISTY MUSIC		AMCL 0200
ANDY NYE	V K	(A					
ADE WALKER	B	(A	JAKE JACOBS	G	(A		

MAJOR LANCE

MAJOR LANCE	(ALL	RHYTHM OF	19	OKEH	UK		33SX 1728
		GREATEST HITS	1973	CONTEMPO			COLP 1001
		BEST OF	1976	EPIC	UK		81519
		LIVE AT THE TORCH	1977	CONTEMPO		CLP	523
		NOW ARRIVING	1978	TAMLA	UK		STMC 12094

MAJOR SURGERY M57

(A) FIRST CUT   1977   NEXT   NEXT 1

MALACHI M57A

MALACHI	G	(A	(A) CHEVROLET	19	VERVE	?	
STEVE CUNNINGHAM		(A					

MALICORNE M57B

LAURENT VERCAMBE VLN K V(A		(A) MALICORNE	1974 HEXAGONE FR 883002+SHANNON 76 8001
HUGHES DE COURSON G B V (A		(B) MALICORNE TWO	197 HEXAGONE FR 883004
GABRIEL YACOUB	G V	(A		
MARIE YACOUB V DULC		(A		

MALLARD M58

BILL HARKLROAD	G	(AB	(A) MALLARD	1976 VIRGIN	UK	V 2045			
MARK BOSTON	G V B(AB		(B) IN A DIFFERENT CLIMATE	1977 VIRGIN US 34489	UK	V 2077			
ARTIE TRIPP	D	(A							
SAM GALPIN	V	(AB	BARRY MORGAN PERC (A	JOHN THOMAS	K V (B	GEORGE DRAGGOTA	D	(B
JOHN JAMES	K	(	RABBIT BUNDRICK K (A	JOHN McFEE	STEEL(B			

MALO M59

JORGE SANTANA	G	(ALL	(A) MALO	1972 WB	US BS 2584	UK K46142				
RON SMITH	HRNS	(CD	(B) DOS	1972 WB	US BS 2652	UK K46179				
WILLIE G	V	(D	(C) EVOLUTION	1973 WB	US BS 2702	UK K46221				
TONY SMITH	PERC V(CD		(D) ASCENSION	1974 WB	US BS 2769	UK K56033				
FRANCISCO AQUABELLA PERC V(BCD										
STEVE SHERARD	TROM (CD	MIKE FUGATE	TPT (D	ABEL ZARATE	G (A	RICHARD SPREMICH	D	(AB
ROY MURRAY	HRNS (A	ARCELIO GARCIA V PERC (ABC		FORREST BUCHTEP	TPT (BC	RICK QUINTANAL	D	(B
RON DEMASI	K V (CD	LUIS GASCA	TPT (A	PAUL REKOW	PERC (B	COKE ESCOVEDO	PERC	(A
CARLOS FEDERICO	PNO (C	AL ZULAICA	PNO (C	JOHN WATSON	V (B	PABLO TELLEZ	B PERC	(ALL
RICHARD KERMODE	K	(AB	LEO ROSALES	PERC (B	VICTOR PANTOJA	PERC (A	RICHARD BEAN	V PERC	(A
HADLEY CALIMAN	WIND (B	GEORGE BERMUDEZ	CONGA(B	BILL ATWOOD	TPT (B	MIKE HEATHMAN	TROM	(B
JOSE SANTANA	VLN (B	TOM POOLE	TPT (B	ALEX RODRIGUEZ	TPT (B			

MAMA LION M60

LYNN CAREY	V	(A	(A) MAMA LION	1972 PHILIPS	6369 153	
NEIL MERRYWEATHER V B		(A				
COFFI HALL	D	(A	RICK GAXIOLA G (A	JIM HOWARD	K V (A

MAMA'S & THE PAPA'S M61

CASS ELLIOT	V	(ALL	IF YOU CAN BELIEVE YOUR EYES	1966 DUNHILL US 50006 UK RCA RD 7803
MICHELLE GILLIAM PHILLIPS(ALL			CASS,JOHN,MICHELLE & DENNY	1966 DUNHILL US 50010 UK RCA SF 7834
JOHN PHILLIPS	V	(ALL	DELIVER	1967 DUNHILL US 50014 UK RCA SF 7880
DENNY DOHERTY	V	(ALL	BOOK OF SONGS	196 DUNHILL US 50022
			FAREWELL TO 1ST GOLDEN ERA	1968 DUNHILL US 50025
HAL BLAINE	D	(	PAPAS & MAMAS	1968 DUNHILL US 50031 UK RCA SF 7960
LARRY KNECHTEL	K	(	GOLDEN ERA VOL 2	1968 DUNHILL US 50038 UK STATESIDE 5002
JOE OSBORN	B	(	HITS OF GOLD	1969 ABC (74) 5003 UK STATESIDE 5007
			16 OF THE GREATEST	19 DUNHILL US 50064
			A GATHERING OF FLOWERS	1970 DUNHILL US 50073 UK PROBE 1003/4
			MONTEREY INTERNATIONAL POP FESTIVAL	1971 DUNHILL US 50100
			PEOPLE LIKE US	1972 DUNHILL US 50106 UK PROBE 1048
			PEOPLE LIKE US	1974 RI UK ABC ABCL 5017
			20 GOLDEN HITS	1972 DUNHILL US 50145 UK PROBE 200
			20 GOLDEN HITS	1974 RI UK ABC ABCL 604
			BIGGEST HITS	197 PICKWICK 2076
			MONDAY MONDAY	1973 PICKWICK US 3380 UK MFP 90025
			CALIFORNIA	1974 PICKWICK US 3357 UK MFP 90050
			BEST OF	1977 ARCADE UK

MAMAS PRIDE M62

DON LISTON	G V	(AB	(A) MAMAS PRIDE	1976 ATLANTIC US 36122	UK K 50197			
PAT LISTON	G V	(AB	(B) UPTOWN..LOWDOWN	1977 ATLANTIC US 36146	UK K 50348			
MAX BAKER	K	(AB						
KEVIN SANDERS		(AB	JOE TUREK	B V (AB	DICKIE STETTENPOHL B V (B	FRANK GAGLIANO	K SYN (A
JOE LALA	PERC	(B	JIM MASON	HRNS (B	DENNIS DREITH	HRNS (B	PAUL WILLETT	K V (B
JERRY JUMONVILLE	HRNS	(B						

MAN M63

MICKY JONES	G V	(ALL	(A) REVELATION	1969 PYE	UK 18275			
CLIVE JOHN	G K V(ABCDFGJ		(B) 2OZ OF PLASTIC WITH A HOLE	1969 DAWN	UK 3003			
DEKE LEONARD G V(ABCSEGJKLMNOP			(C) MAN	1970 LIBERTY UK 83464	US 9803			
TERRY WILLIAMS D(CDEFHJKLMOP			(C) MAN	1976 SUNSET RI	UK 50380			
JEFF JONES	D	(ABG	(D) DO YOU LIKE IT HERE,ARE YOU...	1971 LIBERTY US 1032	UK UA 29236			
RAY WILLIAMS	B	(ABG	(E) LIVE AT THE PADGET ROOMS PENARTH	1972 UA	UK USP 100			
MARTIN ACE	B G V(CDEJMP		(F) BE GOOD TO YOURSELF...	1972 UA US LA 077	UK US 29417			
TWEKE LEWIS	G	(H	(G) GOLDEN HOUR	1973 PYE	UK GH 569			
WILL YOUATT	B	(FHJ	(H) BACK INTO THE FUTURE	1973 UA US LA 179	UK 60053/4			
PHIL RYAN	K	(FHJNO	(J) CHRISTMAS AT THE PATII(10" DBL)	1973 UA	UK UDX205/6			
KEN WHALEY	B	(KL	(K) RHINOS, WINOS & LUNATICS	1974 UA US LA 247	UK 29631			
MALCOLM MORLEY	K G	(JK	(L) SLOW MOTION	1974 UA US LA 345	UK 29675			
JOHN McKENZIE	B	(NO	(M) MAXIMUM DARKNESS	1975 UA	UK 29872			
JOHN CIPOLLINA	G	(M	(N) THE WELSH CONNECTION	1976 MCA	UK MCF 2753			
DAVE CHARLES		(J	(O) ALL'S WELL THAT ENDS WELL	1977 MCA	UK MCF 2815			
GEORGINA ACE	B	(J	(P) ALSO APPEARED ON GREASY TRUCKERS	1972 UA	UK UDX203/4			
PLUM HOLLIS	V	(J	(EP) BANANAS	1976 UA	UK REM 408			
DAVE EDMUNDS	G V	(J						
MICKEY GEE	G	(J	B J COLE	STEEL(J	STAN PHIFER	V (J	SEAN TYLA	G V(J
RICHARD TREECE	G	(J	PAUL BURTON	B (J	MARTIN BELMONT	G V (J	TIM ROPER	D (J
NICK GARVEY	B	(J						

MANASSAS M64

STEPHEN STILLS	G V K(AB		(A) MANASSAS (DBL)	1972 ATLANTIC US 2/903	UK K60021				
AL PERKINS	STEEL(AB		(B) DOWN THE ROAD	1973 ATLANTIC US 7250	UK K40440				
PAUL HARRIS	K	(AB							
ROGER BUSH	B	(A	JOE LALA PERC	(AB	KENNY PASSARELLI B V	(	JOE WALSH	G (B
DALLAS TAYLOR	D	(AB	BOBBY WHITLOCK K V	(B	SYDNEY GEORGE	FLT (AB	CALVIN SAMUELS	B (AB
JERRY AIELLO	ORG	(AB	CHARLIE GRIMES G	(B	CHRIS HILLMAN	B G V(AB	GUILLE GARCIA	PERC(B
LACHY ESPINOL	PERC	(B	PAT ARNOLD V	(B	BILL WYMAN	B (A	BYRON BERLINE	FDL (A

M65 — MANCHILD

ANTHONY JOHNSON	B	(A	(A) POWER & LOVE				1977	CHINA TOWN US LA765	UK UA 30134
KENNY EDMONDS	G V	(A	(B) FEEL THE PHUFF				19	CHINA TOWN US LA 872	
DARYL SIMMONS	PERC V(A								
FLASH FERRELL	V	(A	ROBERT PARSON	D	(A	CHUCKIE BUSH	K(A	REGGIE GRIFFIN	SAX G(A

M66 — MANDALA

GEORGE OLLIVER	V	(A	(A) SOUL CRUSADE			1968	ATLANTIC US	SD 8184
DOMENIC TROIANO	G	(A						
HUGH SULLIVAN	K	(A	ROY KENNER	V	(A	JOEY CHIROWSKI	K (A	DON ELLIOTT	B (A
WHITEY GLAN	D	(A						

M67 — MANDALABAND

DAVID DURANT	V	(A	(A) MANDALABAND				1975	CHRYSALIS	UK CHR 1095
ASHLEY MULFORD	G	(A	(B) THE EYE OF WENDOR				1978	CHRYSALIS	UK CHR 1181
JOHN STIMPSON	B G	(A							
TONY CRESSWELL	D	(A	VIC EMERSON	K	(A	RITCHIE CLOSE	PNO (B	DAVY ROHL	PNO (B
KIM TURNER	G D	(B	MEL PRITCHARD	D	(B	GRAHAM GOULDMAN	B (B	PETE GLENNON	B (B
ALF TRAMONTIN	B	(B	NOEL REDDING	B	(B	LES HOLROYD	B (B	STEVE BROOMHEAD	G (B
JIMMY McDONNELL	G	(B	JOHN LEES	G	(B	MADDY PRIOR	V (B	MARK GILBANKS	TPT (B
ANDY CROMPTON	TROM (B		MIKE CARLTON	TROM (B		ERIC STEWART	V (B	TONY SPATH	OBOE (B
JOHN GILSTON	PERC (B		GERRY MURPHY	PIPES(B		RICHARD SCOTT	RECOD(B	MICKY PURTON	HRNS(B
RUSSELL HAYWARD	HRNS (B		PAUL BRYAN FARR	HRNS (B		ANDY WARDAUGH	TPT (B	MARTIN LAWRENCE	PERC(B
DAVID HASSALL	PERC (B		PHIL CHAPMAN	WIND (B		JOHN TURNER	K (B	STEWART WOLSTENHOLME	K(B
NORMAN BARRETT	G	(B	GERALD BROWN SINGERS	V	(B	DAVE GORTON	TROM (B	KEVIN GODLEY	V (B
PAUL YOUNG	V	(B	JUSTIN HAYWARD	V	(B	LOL CREME	V (B	IAN WILSON	V (B
FRIDAY BROWN	V	(B	GILLY ROHL	V	(B	FIONA PARKER	V (B		

M68 — HARVEY MANDEL

HARVEY MANDEL	G	(ALL	(A) CRISTO REDENTOR		1968	PHILIPS	UK SBL 7873 RI	706336009
PETE DRAKE	STEEL(A		(A) CRISTO REDENTOR		1968	PHILIPS	US	600281
KENNY BUTTREY	D	(A	(B) RIGHTEOUS		1969	PHILIPS UK SBL 7904	US	600306
BOB MOORE	B	(A	(C) GAMES GUITARS PLAY		1970	PHILIPS UK SBL 7915	US	600325
HARGUS ROBBINS	K	(A	(D) BABY BATTER		1971	DAWN	UK DNLS3015 US JANUS	3017
GRAHAM BOND	K	(A	(E) GET OFF IN CHICAGO		1972	LONDON	UK SHO 8426 US OVATION1415	
EDDIE HOH	D	(AB	(F) THE SNAKE		1972	JANUS	UK 6310 210 US	3037
CHIP MARTIN	G	(A	(G) SHANGRENADE		1973	JANUS	UK 6499 831 US	3047
BOB JONES	G	(AB	(H) FEEL THE SOUND OF		1974	JANUS	US	3067
CATHERINE GOTTHOFER	HARP(A		(J) BEST OF		1975	JANUS	US	7014
BARRY GOLDBERG	K	(A						
ARMANDO PERAZA	CONGA(A		CAROLYN WILLIS	V	(A	JACQUELINE MAY ALLEN V(A	STEVE MILLER	K (A
CARTER COLLINS	CONGA(A		DUANE HITCHINGS	K	(B	ART STAVRO	B (AB	LARRY EASTER	SAX (A
JULIA TILLMAN	V	(A	FREDDIE FOX	V	(E	VICKI HUBLEY	V (E	G E STINSON	G (E
NORM WAGNER	G	(E	DAVE COOK	K	(E	IRA KART	K (E	DON CODY	B (E
PETER MILIO	D	(E	KEN LITTLE	B V	(E	BOBBY DAVIS	D (E	JUDY ROBERTS	K V (E
JOHN BISHOP	G	(E	NICK TOUNTAS	B	(E	RUSTY JONES	D (E	PHIL JOHNSON	D (E
EARL PALMER	D	(B	BUDDY CHILDERS	TPT	(B	JOHN AUDINO	TPT (B	STAN FISHELSON	TPT (B
OLLIE MITCHELL	TPT	(B	LEW McCREARY	TROM	(B	MIKE BARONE	TROM (B	PETE MYERS	TROM (B
DICK LEITH	TROM	(B	ERNIE WATTS	SAX	(B	PLAS JOHNSON	SAX (B	BILL PERKINS	SAX (B
GENE CIPRIANO	SAX	(B	JACK NIMITZ	SAX	(B	PETE JOLLY	K (B	BOB WEST	B (B
HOWARD ROBERTS	G	(B	VICTOR FELDMAN	PERC	(B	NICK DECARO	K (A	CHARLIE MUSSELWHITE	HCA (A
CRAIG RASBAND	B	(E	COLEMAN HEAD	G	(G	PAUL LAGOS	D (G	VICTOR CONTE	G (G
BOBBY LYLE	K	(G	BOBBY NOTKOFF	STR	(G	FRED ROULETTE	STEEL(G	DON 'SUGARCANE'HARRIS	VLN(G

M69 — MIKE MANDEL

MIKE MANDEL	K	(A	(A) SKY MUSIC		1978	VANGUARD	VSD 79409	
DAVE SANBORN	SAX	(A						
GARY ANDERSON	SAX	(A	DARRYL THOMPSON	G	(A	BERT KHAN	G (A	WILBUR BASCOMB	B (A
JOHN LEE	B	(A	CHRISTOPHER PARKER D		(A	GERRY BROWN	D (A	CRUSHER BENNETT	PERC(A
CHRIS HILLS	PERC	(A	JON FADDIS	HRNS(A		LOU SOLOFF	HRNS (A	DAVE TAYLOR	HRNS(A
GEORGE YOUNG	SAX	(A	ALEX FOSTER	SAX	(A	BARRY ROGERS	TROM (A	LOU MARINI	SAX (A

M70 — MANDRAKE MEMORIAL

KEVIN LALLY	D	(ABC	(A) MANDRAKE MEMORIAL		19		US POPPY	40002
RANDY MONACO	V B	(ABC	(B) MEDIUM		1969	RCA UK SF 8028 US POPPY	40003	
CRAIG ANDERTON	G	(ABC	(C) PUZZLE		1970	POPPY UK 11003 US POPPY	40006	
MICHAEL KAC	K V	(B						

M71 — MANDRAKE PADDLESTEAMER

MARC BRIERLEY		(A	(A) 1969 LINE UP				
BRIAN MARTIN		(A					
PAUL RIBB		(A	JOHN WHITEHEAD	(A	PAUL WHITEHEAD	(A	

M72 — MANDRILL

CLAUDE CAVE	K V	(	(A) MANDRILL IS		1972	POLUDOR UK 2391 030 US	5025	
ANDRE LOCKE	D V	(	(B) COMPOSITE TRUTH		19	POLYDOR UK 2391 061 US	5043	
BRIAN ALLSOP	B V	(	(C) JUST OUTSIDE OF TOWN		1975	POLYDOR UK 2391 092		
TOMMY TRUSILLO	G V	(	(D) BEST OF		19	POLYDOR UK 2391 186 US	6047	
RICK WILSON	SAX	(	(E) SOLID		1975	UA UK UAG29786 US	UA LA409	
LOU WILSON	TPT PERC V(		(F) BEAST FROM THE EAST		1976	UA UK UAS29920 US	UA LA577	
CHARLES WILSON	HRNS PERC V(		(G) MANDRILLAND		1976	POLYDOR UK 2672 023		
OMAR MESA	G PERC V	(	(H) MANDRILL		197	POLYDOR UK 2489 028		
CHARLES PADRO	D PERC V(		(J) WE ARE ONE		1978	ARISTA UK SPART1035 US	4144	
FUDGIE KAE	B	(	(K) NEW WORLD		1978	ARISTA UK ARTY 162 US	4195	
			(L) GREATEST		19	ARISTA US	7000	
			(M) GETTING IN THE MOOD		1980	ARISTA US	9527	

M73 — MANDRE

ANDRE LEWIS MANDRE		(	(A) MANDRE		1977	TAMLA UK STML23062 US	882
			(B) MANDRE 2		1978	TAMLA UK STML12084 US	7900

M74 — GAP MANGIONE

GAP MANGIONE	K	(A	(A) SUITE LADY		1978	A&M	UK AMLH 64694	
LARRY CARLTON	G	(A						
POPS POPWELL	B	(A	GREG MATHESON	PNO (A	ABRAHAM LABORIEL	B (A	RALPH HUMPHREY	D (A
JEFF PORCARO	PERC (A		CHUCK FINDLEY	TPT (A	PETER DONALD	D (A	VINCENT DE ROSA	HRNS(A
JOE PORCARO	PERC (A		BILL REICHENBACH	TROM (A	DAN SAWYER SAX HCA	(A		

TIM HAUSER	V	(ABCDEF	(A) JUKIN'	1971 CAPITOL		E ST	11405
MICKEY ROKER	D	(A	(A) MANHATTAN TRANSFER	1978 MFP RI		UK	50387
ERIN DICKINS	V	(A	(B) MANHATTAN TRANSFER	1975 ATLANTIC US 18133		UK K50138	
PAT ROSALIA	V	(A	(C) COMING OUT	1976 ATLANTIC US 18183		UK K50291	
MARTY NELSON	V CLAR(A		(D) PASTICHE	1978 ATLANTIC US 19163		UK K50444	
ALAN PAUL	V	(BCDEF	(E) LIVE	1978 ATLANTIC		UK K50540	
LAUREL MASSE	V	(BCDE	(F) EXTENSIONS	1979 ATLANTIC US 19258		UK K50674	
JANIS SIEGEL	V	(BCDE					
CHERYL BENTYNE	V	(F					

GENE PISTILLI	V G	(A	NORBERT PUTNAM	B	(A	MIKE ROD	SAX	(B	KENNY BUTTREY	D	(A
TOMMY WEST	K	(A	MURRAY WEINSTOCK	K	(B	DAVID BRIGGS	K	(A	GARY CHESTER	D	(A
JERRY FRIEDMAN	G	(A	GEORGE EDWARDS	STEEL(A		HAYWOOD HENRY	SAX	(A	RICHARD TEE	K	(B
BUDDY SPICHER	FDL	(A	IRA NEWBORN	G	(BC	MICHAEL BRECKER	SAX	(BC	ADAM MITCHELL	G	(A
DON GROLNICK	K	(B	JERRY DODGION	SAX	(AB	RANDY BRECKER	TPT	(BC	ANDY MUSON	B	(BC
DANIEL BEN ZEBULON	PERC(B		AL GIBBONS	SAX	(A	ROY MARKOWITZ	D	(BC	ZOOT SIMS	SAX	(B
EARL WILLIAMS	D	(A	PAUL FAULISE	TROM	(B	SELDON POWELL	WIND	(B	BOB BUSHNELL	B	(A
MICKEY GRAVINE	TROM	(B	LEW DELGATTO	SAX	(B	BIG AL WILLIAMS	K	(A	QUENTIN JACKSON	TROM(B	
MEL DAVIS	TPT	(B	LEW TABACKIN	SAX	(A	ALAN RAPH	TROM	(B	JON FADDIS	TPT	(B
FRANK BEROWSKI	SAX	(A	PHIL BODNER	SAX	(B	BOB McCOY	TPT	(B	BURT COLLINS	TPT	(A
GEORGE DORSEY	SAX	(A	MARKY MARKOWITZ	TPT	(B	GARNETT BROWN	TROM	(AB	HARVEY ESTRIN	SAX	(B
MARVIN STAMM	TPT	(B	WAYNE ANDRE	TROM	(AB	DAVE SANBORN	SAX	(B	ALAN RUBIN	TPT	(B
SABER	G	(A	FRANK VICARI	SAX	(B	GEORGE YOUNG	SAX	(B	RON CARTER	B	(A
WALLY KANE	WIND	(B	PAUL GRIFFIN	K	(C	BOBBYE HALL	PERC	(C	RINGO STARR	D	(C
MAC REBENNACK	K	(C	DOUG THORNGREN	PERC	(C	JIM GORDON	D	(C	JOHN BARNES	PNO	(C
BEN BENAY	G	(C	STEVE PAIETTA	ACC	(C	JAY MIGLIORI	SAX	(C	RICK SHLOSSER	D	(C
CLARENCE McDONALD	PNO	(C	RALPH MACDONALD	PERC	(C	JACKIE KELSO	SAX	(C	JIM NELSON	D	(C
BILL PAYNE	PNO	(C	ROGER STEINMAN	PNO	(C	ARTHUR JENKINS	PNO	(C	NICK MARRERO	PERC(C	
JOHN RODRIGUEZ	PERC	(C	DAVID KEMPER	D	(C	BOB BOWLES	G	(C	JIM KELTNER	D	(C
DAVID FRISHBERG	K	(C									

	DEDICATED	19	CARNIVAL	US		201
	FOR YOU & YOURS	19	CARNIVAL	US		202
	WITH THESE HANDS	19		US DELUXE 12000		
	MILLION TO ONE	19	LONDON UK SHB 8449 US DELUXE 12004			
	THERE'S NO ME WITHOUT YOU	19	CBS	US		32444
	THATS HOW MUCH I LOVE YOU	19	CBS	US		33064
	MANHATTANS	1976 CBS	UK	81513 US		33830
	I WANNA BE YOUR EVERYTHING	1976 DJM	UK DJM26084			
	THERE'S NO GOOD IN GOODBYE	1978 CBS	UK	82567 US		35252
	LOVE TALK	1979 CBS	UK	83342 US		
	AFTER MIDNIGHT	1980 CBS	UK	84223		
	IT FEELS SO GOOD	1980 CBS	UK	84828		

CARL MANN	G V	(ALL	(A) LIKE MANN	1959 PHILIPS INT	US	PLP1960	
			(B) CARL MANN	19 SONET	SWED	SPO 13	
			(C) LEGENDARY SUN PERFORMERS	1977 CHARLY	UK	CR 30130	
			(D) GONNA ROCK'N' ROLL TONIGHT	1978 CHARLY	UK	CR 5008	
			(EP) CARL MANN	1977 CHARLY	UK	CEP 114	
			( ) LIKE MANN	1980 charly	UK	CRM 2006	

HERBIE MANN	FLT	ALL	WITH JOAO GILBERTO & ANTONIO JOBIM	19	ATLANTIC		US	SD	8105
BILL EVANS	PNO	(N	THE COMMON GROUND	19	ATLANTIC		US	SD	1343
CHUCK ISRAELS	B	(N	THIS IS MY BELOVED	19	ATLANTIC		US	SD	1367
PAUL MOTIAN	D	(N	FAMILY OF MANN	19	ATLANTIC		US	SD	1371
CHICK GANIMIAN		(I	AT THE VILLAGE GATE	19	ATLANTIC	UK 588 054	US	SD	1380
ROY AYERS	VIBES(IM		RIGHT NOW	19	ATLANTIC		US	SD	1384
BRUNO CARR	D	(IM	DO THE BOSSA NOVA	19	ATLANTIC		US	SD	1397
REGGIE WORKMAN	B	(I	RETURN TO THE VILLAGE GATE	19	ATLANTIC		US	SD	1407
CARLOS VALDES	PERC	(IL	(L)LIVE AT NEWPORT	1963	ATLANTIC		US	SD	1413
THOMAS KAZANAN	PERC	(I	LATIN FEVER	196	ATLANTIC		US	SD	1422
GERALDINE SWEE	PERC	(I	(N)NIRVANA	1964	ATLANTIC	UK K 50238	US	SD	426
JIMMY OWENS	TPT	(I	MY KINDA GROOVE	19	ATLANTIC		US	SD	1433
JULIAN PRIESTER	SAX	(I	THE SMELL OF THE CROWD,ROAR OF G PAINT	196	ATLANTIC		US	SD	1437
JOE ORANGE	SAX	(I	STANDING OVATION AT NEWPORT	196	ATLANTIC		US	SD	1445
MOHAMED ELEKLAD	ZITHER	(I	TODAY	196	ATLANTIC		US	SD	1454
ATTILA ZOLLER	G	(IL	MONDAY NIGHT AT THE VILLAGE GATE	196	ATLANTIC		US	SD	1462
RICHARD DAVIS	B	(I	OUR MANN FLUTE	196	ATLANTIC		US	SD	1464
GLORIA AGOSTINI	HARP	(I	NEW MANN AT NEWPORT	196	ATLANTIC		US	SD	1471
DAVE PIKE	VIBES(L		(I)IMPRESSIONS OF THE MIDDLE EAST	1967	ATLANTIC		US	SD	1475
DON FRIEDMAN	PNO	(L	BEAT GOES ON	196	ATLANTIC		US	SD	1483
BEN TUETHE	B	(L	STRING ALBUM	196	ATLANTIC		US	SD	1490
BOB THOMAS	D	(L	WAILING DERVISHES	196	ATLANTIC		US	SD	1497
WILLIE BOBO	PERC	(L	(U) MEMPHIS UNDERGROUND	196	ATLANTIC	UK 588 200	US	SD	1522
MELVIN LASTIE	HRNS	(M	(U) MEMPHIS UNDERGROUND	197	ATLANTIC	UK K 40038	RI UK K50520		
IKE WILLIAMS	HRNS	(M	LIVE AT THE WHISKY	196	ATLANTIC		US	SD	1536
GEORGE BOHANAN	TROM	(M	BEST OF	19	ATLANTIC		US	SD	1544
AL VESCOVO	G	(M	TURTLE BAY	19	ATLANTIC	UK K 50020	US	SD	1642
JOHN BARNES	K	(M	GLORY OF LOVE	1969	A&M			AMLS	944
DARREL CLAYBORN	B	(M	EVOLUTIONOF MANN	19	ATLANTIC	UK K 60020	US	SD 2	300
RICHARD WATERS	D	(M	BEST OF	19	PRESTIGE		US		7432
VICTOR PANTOJA	PERC	(M	BIG BOSS MAN	19	CBS		US		1068
LARRY CORYELL	G	(M	ET TU FLUTE	19	VERVE			2V6	8821
REGGIE YOUNG	G	(M	LATIN MANN	19	CSP		US	JCS	9188
BOBBY EMMONS	K	(M	MANN IN SWEDEN	19	PRESTIGE		US		7659
BOBBY WOOD	K	(M	SUPER MANN	19	TRIP		US		5031
MICK LEECH	B	(M	WITH FLOOT TO BOOT	19	SPRINGBOARD		US		4055
GENE CHRISTMAN	D	(M	CONCERTO GROSSO IN D BLUES	196	ATLANTIC	UK 2465005			
ERIC WEISSBERG	G	(M	STONE FLUTE	19	ATLANTIC	UK 2465088	US	SD	520
SONNY SHARROCK	G	(M	MUSCLE SHOALS NITTY GRITTY	19	ATLANTIC	UK 2400022	UK RI K40096		

(CONTINUED)

M78 (CONTINUED)   HERBIE MANN

```
    CHARLIE BROWN         G     (M      MUSCLE SHOALS NITTY GRITTY        19    EMBRYO                          US   SD    526
    MIROSLAV VITOUS       B     (M      (M)MEMPHIS TWO STEP               1971  EMBRYO                          US   SD    531
    RON CARTER            B     (M      (P)PUSH PUSH                      1971  EMBRYO                          US   SD    532
    RICHIE RESNICOFF      G     (M      (P)PUSH PUSH                      1971  ATLANTIC   UK 2400191 UK RI K40283
    PAT REBILLOT          K     (G      BRAZIL BLUES                      197   UA         UK UAS 5631
    SAM BROWN             G     (G      MISSISSIPPI GAMBLER               1974  ATLANTIC   UK K 40385
    TONY LEVIN            B     (G      HOLD ON IM COMING                 197   ATLANTIC   UK K 40467
    STEVE GADD            D     (G      LET ME TELL YOU                   1974  MILESTONE                       ML   47010
    MINURO MURAOKA              (G      LONDON UNDERGROUND                1974  ATLANTIC   UK K 50032 US  SD  1648
    MODERN SHOMYO STUDY GROUP(G         REGGAE                            1974  ATLANTIC   UK K 50053 US  SD  1655
    ONO GAGAKU SOCIETY          (G      STAR COLLECTION                   1975  MIDI       UK K 20018
    DUANE ALLMAN          G     (P      DISCOTHEQUE                       1975  ATLANTIC   UK K 50128 US  SD  1670
    CORNELL DUPREE        G     (P      WATER BED                         1975  ATLANTIC   UK K 50174
    BERNARD PURDIE        D     (P      (G) GAGAKU & BEYOND               1976  FINNADAR                        SR   9014
    JERRY JEMMOTT         B     (P      SURPRISES                         19    ATCO                       US        1682
    AL JACKSON            D     (P      BIRD IN A SILVER CAGE             1977  ATLANTIC   UK K 50338 US  SD  18209
    GENE BIANCO           HARP  (P      BRASIL                            1978  ATLANTIC   UK
    RICHARD TEE           K     (P      BE BOP SYNTHESIS                  1977  SAVOY                      US   SJL1102
    CHUCK RAINEY          B     (P
    RALPH MACDONALD   PERC (P  DONALD DUNN    B   (P  RAY BARRETTO   PERC (   BABATHNDE OLATUNJI PERC(
    RAY MANTILLA      PERC (    ARMANDO PERAZA    PERC (
```

M79   MICHAEL MANTLER

```
    MICHAEL MANTLER       TPT   (ALL    (A) JAZZ COMPOSERS ORCHESTRA      1974  VIRGIN                    UK   JD   3001
    DON CHERRY            HRNS  (AB     (B) NO ANSWER                     1974  VIRGIN                    UK        WATT 2
    STEVE LACY            SAX   (A      (C) 13 3/4                        1975  VIRGIN                    UK        WATT 3
    AL GIBBONS            SAX   (A      (D) THE HAPLESS CHILD             1976  VIRGIN                    UK        WATT 4
    GENE HULL             SAX   (A      (E) SILENCE                       1976  VIRGIN                    UK        WATT 5
    BOB DONOVAN           SAX   (A      (F) MOVIES                        1978  VIRGIN                    UK        WATT 7
    LEW TABACKIN          SAX   (A
    GEORGE BARROW     SAX   (A  CHARLES DAVIS    SAX (A  LLOYD MICHAELS  HRNS (A  RANDY BRECKER    HRNS(A
    BOB NORTHERN      HRNS )A   JULIUS WATKINS   HRNS(A  JIMMY KNEPPER   TROM (A  JACK JEFFERS     TROM(A
    STEPHEN FURTADO        (A   HOWARD JOHNSON   TUBA (A  EDDIE GOMEZ    B    (A  STEVE SWALLOW    B   (ADF
    CARLA BLEY      K V(ALL     KENT CARTER      B   (A  BEAVER HARRIS   D    (A  RON CARTER       B   (A
    ROSWELL RUDD    TROM (A     RICHARD DAVIS    B   (A  PHAROAH SANDERS SAX  (A  CHARLIE HADEN    B   (A
    CECIL TAYLOR    PNO  (A     REGGIE WORKMAN   B   (A  JIMMY LYONS     SAX  (A  ANDREW CYRILLE   D   (A
    BOB CUNNINGHAM  B    (A     LARRY CORYELL    G   (A  REGGIE JOHNSON  B    (A  STEVE MARCUS     SAX (A
    ALAN SILVA      B    (A     FRANK WESS       SAX (A  JACK BRUCE      B V  (AB ROBERT WYATT     V   (DE
    JACK DEJOHNETTE D    (D     TERJE RYPDAL     G   (D  KEVIN COYNE     V    (E  CHRIS SPEDDING   G   (E
    RON McCLURE     B    (E     CLARE MAHER      CELLO(E TONY WILLIAMS   D    (F
```

M80   MANFRED MANN

```
    MANFRED MANN K V(ALL               (A)MANFRED MANN ALBUM             1964                              US ASCOT    16015
    MIKE HUGG      D (ABCDEFGHIJKLMO3   (B) FIVE FACES OF MANFRED MANN   1964  HMV CLP 1731                US ASCOT    16018
    MIKE VICKERS   SAX  (ABCD3          (C) MANN MADE                    1964  HMV CLP 1911/1628           US ASCOT    16024
    DAVE RICHMOND  B    (               (C) MANN MADE                    1969  STARLINE          UK        SRS 5007
    PAUL JONES     V    (ABCD3          (D) MY LITTLE RED BOOK OF WINNERS 1965                             US ASCOT    16021
    TOM McGUINNESS B G  (ABCDEFG3       (E) MANN MADE HITS               1966  HMV CLP 3559
    JACK BRUCE     B    (3              (F) PRETTY FLAMINGO              1966                              US UA       6549
    MIKE D'ABO     V    (G3             (G) AS IS                        1966  FONTANA STL 5377
    BERNIE LIVING  WIND (NO             (H) GREATEST HITS                1966                              US UA       6551
    STEVE YORK     B    (NO             (I) SOUL OF MANN                 1967  HMV    CLP 3594   US CAPITOL 6199
    CRAIG COLLINGE D    (NO             (J) UP THE JUNCTION              1968  FONTANA STL 5460
    SONNY CORBETT  TPT  (NO             (K) MIGHTY GARVEY                1968  FONTANA STL 5470
    IAN FENBY           (N              (L) WHAT A MAN                   1968  FONTANA SFL13003
    HAROLD BECKETT TPT  (N              (M) MIGHTY QUINN                 1968                              US MERCURY  61168
    DAVID COXHILL  SAX  (NO             (N) CHAPTER THREE                1969  VERTIGO UK VO3    US POLYDOR 4013
    DEREK WADSWORTH     (G              (O) CHAPTER THREE VOL 2          1970  VERTIGO UK 6360 012
    CHRIS PYNE          (N              (P) THIS IS MANFRED MANN         1971  PHILIPS UK 6382 020
    DAVE QUINCY         (N              (Q) EARTH BAND                   1972  PHILIPS UK 6308 086   US POLYDOR 5015
    PHIL KENZIE         (N              (Q) EARTH BAND                   1977  BRONZE  UK BRON 252
    DAVE POTTER         (N              (R) GLORIFIED MAGNIFIED          1972  PHILIPS UK 6308 125   US POLYDOR 5031
    GEOFF DRISCOLL      (N              (R) GLORIFIED MAGNIFIED          1977  BRONZE  UK BRON 257
    MICK EVANS          (N              (S) MESSIN'                      1973  PHILIPS UK 6360 087   RI 77 BRONZE  261
    MADELINE BELL  V    (N              (S) GET YOUR ROCKS OFF           1973                              US POLYDOR  5050
    SUNNY LESLIE   V    (N              (U) SOLAR FIRE                   1973  BRONZE  UK ILPS9265   US POLYDOR 6019
    SUE GLOVER     V    (N              (U) SOLAR FIRE                   1977  BRONZE  UK BRON 265
    BRIAN HUGG     G    (NO             (V) THE GOOD EARTH               1974  BRONZE  UK ILPS9306   US WB  BS 2826
    DAVE BROOKS    SAX  (O              (V) THE GOOD EARTH               1977  BRONZE  UK BRON 306
    CLIVE STEVENS  SAX  (O              (W) NIGHTINGALES & BOMBERS       1975  BRONZE  UK ILPS9337   US WB  BS 2877
    GERRY FIELDS   FDL  (O              (W) NIGHTINGALES & BOMBERS       1977  BRONZE  UK BRON 337
    CONRAD ISADORE D    (O              (X) ROARING SILENCE              1976  BRONZE  UK ILPS9357   US WB  BS 2965
    ANDY McCULLOCH D    (O              (X) ROARING SILENCE              1977  BRONZE  UK BRON 357
    COLIN PATTENDEN B   (QRSUVVWZ       (Y) THE BEST OF MANFRED MANN     1977  EMI     UK NUT 7
    CHRIS SLADE    D    (QRSUVVWZ1      (Z) THE EARTH BAND 1971 /73      1977  VERTIGO UK 9199 107
    MICK ROGERS    G V  (QRSUVWZ24      (1) WATCH                        1978  BRONZE  UK BRON 507   US WB  BS 3157
    DAVE FLETT     G    (X1             (2) ANGEL STATION                1979  BRONZE  UK BRON 516
    LIZA STRIKE    V    (S              (3) SEMI DETATCHED SUBURBAN      1979  EMI     UK EMTV 19
    RUBY JAMES     V    (SW             (4) CHANCE                       1980  BRONZE  UK BRON 529
    GRAHAM ELLIOTT CELLO(W              ( ) THE BEST OF MANFRED MANN     197   CAPITOL            US        11688
    MARTHA SMITH   V    (W              ( ) THE BEST OF MANFRED MANN     197   JANUS              US        3064
    VICKY SILVA    V    (1              ( ) ONE WAY                      1968  FONTANA            NL        858 037
    STEVE WALLER   G V  (24             ( ) ATTENTION                    19    FONTANA                      6438 063
    ANTHONY MOORE  G K  (12             ( ) MANNERISMS                   1976  SONIC                        SON 016
    DAVID BOSWELL-BROWN CELLO(W         (EP) GROOVIN' WITH               1964  HMV  (EP)          UK        7EG8876
    DAVID CULPAN   RECORDER(X           (EP) MANFRED MANN                1964  HMV  (EP)          UK        7EG8848
    BARBARA THOMPSON SAX (X4            (EP) INSTRUMENTAL ASSASSINATION  1967  FONTANA            UK        TE 17483
    KLAUS VOORMANN B    (G              (EP) INSTUMENTAL ASYLUM          1966  HMV                UK        7EG8949
    CHRIS THOMPSON G    (X124
    IRENE CHANTER    V   (1  KIM GOODY      V   (2  JIM O'NEILL      G   (2  DOREEN CHANTER   V  (W1
    DAVID MILLMAN    STRINGS (WX  TONY ROWELL    RECORDER (X  PAT KING   B   (124 LAURIE BAKER    D  (2
    STEVIE LANGE     V   (1  GEOFF BRITTON  D   (2  DYAN BIRCH       V   (24 MARGARET WOOD RECORDER(X
```

(CONTINUED)

MANFRED MANN M80

(CONTINUED)							
CHRIS WARREN-GREEN	VLN (W	NIGEL WARREN-GREEN	CELLO(W	JOHN LINGWOOD	D (4	TREVOR RABIN	G (4
GRAHAM PRESKETT	VLN (4	ROBBIE McINTOSH	G (4	GEOFF WHITEHORN	G (4	WILLY FINLAYSON	V (4
PETER MARSH	V (4	CAROL STOCKER	V (4				

PHIL MANZANERA M81

PHIL MANZANERA	G V (ABCD	(A) DIAMOND HEAD	1975	ISLAND ILPS 9315	US ATC036113	
BRIAN ENO	K (AB	(A) DIAMOND HEAD	1977	POLYDOR UK RI	2302 062	
LLOYD WATSON	G (B	(B) 801 LIVE	1976	ISLAND ILPS 9444	US POLYDOR6178	
FRANCIS MONKMAN	K (B	(B) 801 LIVE	1977	POLYDOR UK RI	2302 044	
BILL MACCORMICK	B (ABC	(C) LISTEN NOW	1977	POLYDOR UK 2302 074		
SIMON PHILLIPS	D (B	(D) K SCOPE	1978	POLYDOR UK 2302 074 US	6147	
PAUL THOMPSON	D (AC					
SONNY AXPAN	PERC (A	CHYKE MADU	PERC (A	DOREEN CHANTER	V (A	JOHN WETTON PERC (A
DAVE SKINNER	K V (C	ROBERT WYATT	(A	BRIAN TURRINGTON	B (A	ANDY MACKAY WIND (A
EDDIE JOBSON	K VLN(A	DANNY HEIBS	PERC (A	CHARLES HAYWARD	PERC (A	DAVE JARRETT K (A
IAN MACDONALD	PIPES(A					

RAY MANZAREK M82

RAY MANZAREK	K V (ABC	(A) THE GOLDEN SCARAB	1975	MERCURY UK 6398 007 US SRM1 203	
LARRY CARLTON	G (A	(B) THE WHOLE THING STARTED WITH R'N'R	1975	MERCURY UK 6338 552 US SRMI1024	
JERRY SCHEFF	B (A	(C) NITE CITY	1977	20TH CENTURY US 528	
TONY WILLIAMS	D (A				
TONY SALES	(C	STEVE FORMAN	PERC (AB	NIGEL HARRISON	(C	HUNT SALES D (C
MAILTO CORREA	PERC (A	OSCAR BRASHEAR	TPT (A	MARK PINES	G (B	MILT HOLLAND PERC(A
GARY MALLABER	D PERC (B	MIKE FENNELLY	G (B	TIM DOWNS	D (A	ERNIE WATTS SAX (A
NOAH JONES	V (A	PAUL WARREN	G V (C	MARK VOLMAN	V (B	HOWARD KAYLAN V (B
JOE WALSH	G (B	GEORGE SEGAL	BANJO(B	JOHN KLEMMER	SAX (B	PAUL DAVIS PERC(B

MIKE MARAN M83

MIKE MARAN	(A	(A) FAIR WARNING	1971 BRONZE	ILPS 9221	

MARCUS M84

MARCUSMALONE	V (A	(A) MARCUS	1978 UA	UK UAS 30000	US UA LA 668	
GENE BLOCH	G (A					
RANDALL DAVID	G (A	TIM BOGERT	B (A	JACK WEBER	G (A	DANDY HOLMES D (A

BENNY MARDONES M84A

BENNY MARDONES	V (A	(A) THANK GOD FOR GIRLS	1978 PRIVATE STOCK	US PS 7007		
MICK RONSON	G (A					
JERRY SHIRLEY	D (A	MIKE NEVILLE	B (A	HAYDEN WAYNE	K V (A	RON FRANGIPANE K (A
JOEY STANN	SAX (A	MERLE MILLER	V (A	KIMBERLEY CARLSON	V (A	D L BYRON V (A

MARIAH M84B

	(A) MARIAH	197 UA US	UALA 493

JON MARK M84C

JON MARK	G V (A	(A) SONGS FOR A FRIEND	1975 CBS	US 33339		
TOMMY EYRE	K (A					
SALLI TERRI	V (A	RON CARTER	B (A	LARRY KNECHTEL	B (A	HAL BLAINE D (A
DONALD REINBERG	TPT (A	GAYLE LEVANT	HARP (A	VICTOR FELDMAN	PERC (A	ANDREW NARELL STEEL D(A
PATRICK GLEASON	SYN (A					

THE MARKEYS M85

STEVE CROPPER	G (	(A) THE MARKEYS	1961	ATLANTIC	US	8055
DONALD DUCK DUNN	B (	(B) DO THE POPEYE	1962	ATLANTIC	US	8062
TERRY JOHNSON	D (	(C) GREAT MEMPHIS SOUND	1965	STAX US 707	UK ATLANTIC587024	
AL JACKSON	D (	(D) BACK TO BACK	196	STAX US 720		
PACK AXTON	SAX (	(E) DAMIFIKNEW	1969	COTILLION	US	SD 9014
DON NIX	SAX (	(F) MEMPHIS HORNS	1970	COTILLION	US	9014
BOO ER T JONES	ORG (	(G) MEMPHIS EXPERIENCE	1970	STAX	US	2036
WAYNE JACKSON	TPT (	(H) HIGH ON MUSIC	1976	RCA	US	1056
ANDREW LOVE	SAX (	(I) MELLOW JELLY	19	ATLANTIC	UK	587 135
ISAAC HAYES	PNO (					
JERRY LEE SMITH	K (	FLOYD NEWMAN SAX (				

MARK ALMOND M86

JON MARK	V G B PERC (ALL	(A) MARK ALMOND	1971 HARVEST UK SHSP 4011	US BLUETHUMB BTS 27	
JOHN ALMOND	SAX V PERC (ALL	(B) MARK ALMOND 2	1972 BLUE THUMB US BT 32		
TOMMY EYRE	K G PERC (AB	(C) RISING	1972 HARVEST UK SHVL 809	US CBS 31917	
ROGER SUTTON	G V PERC (AB	(D) MARK ALMOND 73 (DBL)	1973 NOVA GERM 628448	US CBS 32486	
JOHN TROPEA	G (F	(E) TO THE HEART	1976 ABC UK ABCL 5183	US ABC ABCD 945	
LEON PENDARVIS	K (F	(F) OTHER PEOPLES ROOMS	1978 HORIZON UK AMLJ 730	US A&M AM 730	
RALPH MACDONALD	PERC (F				
DANNY RICHMOND	D (B	JEFF CONDON	FLT V(	KEN CRADDOCK	K V G(	COLIN GIBSON G V PERC(
WILL LEE	B (F	LARRY WILLIAMS	SYN (F	STEVE GADD	D (F	JERRY HEY HRNS (F

BOB MARKLEY M86A

BOB MARKLEY	(	(A) MARKLEY	1969	FORWARD	US STF 1007
SHAUN HARRIS	(				
DAN HARRIS	(	MICHAEL LLOYD (			

ALAIN MARKUSFELD M87

ALAIN MARKUSFELD	G V (ALL	(A) LE DESERT NOIR	1978	EGG	900 528
JOEL DUGRENEAU	B (	(B) PLATOCK	1978	EGG	900 556
LAURENT THIBAULT	K (	(C) LE MONDE EN ETAGES	19	BARCLAY	920 179
DOMINIQUE FRANCARD	SYN(	(D) LE SON TOMBE DU CIEL	19	BARCLAY	920 327
GERA FRENZI	D (	(E) CONTEMPORUS	1979 EGG		900 581

BOB MARLEY M88

BOB MARLEY	G V (ALL	(A) SOUL REBEL	1971 TROJAN		TBL 126
PETER TOSH	(BDN	(B) CATCH A FIRE	1972 ISLAND	UK	ILPS 9241
BUNNY LIVINGSTONE	(BDN	(C) AFRICAN HERBSMAN	1973 TROJAN		TRL 62
EARL LINDO	K (DFQS	(D) BURNIN'	1973 ISLAND	UK	ILPS 9256
JUNIOR BRAITHWAITE	(	(E) RASTA REVOLUTION	1974 TROJAN	UK	TRLS 89
BEVERLEY KELSO	(	(F) NATTY DREAD	1975 ISLAND	UK	ILPS 9281
CARLTON BARRETT	D (BDFJPTQS	(G) LIVE	1975 ISLAND	UK	ILPS 9376
ASTON BARRETT	G B (BDFJPTQS	(H) JAH LIVE	1975 ISLAND	UK	IDJ 8
AL ANDERSON	G (FJTQS	(J) RASTA MAN VIBRATION	1976 ISLAND	UK	ILPS 9383
BERNARD HARVEY	K (F	(K) EXODUS	1977 ISLAND	UK	ILPS 9498
TYRONE DOWNIE	K (QS	(L) BIRTH OF A LEGEND	1977 EPIC	UK	82066

(CONTINUED)

BOB MARLEY

ALVIN PATTERSON	PERC	(FJPQS	(M) BIRTH OF A LEGEND (DBL)	1977 CALLA			CAS 1240
CHINNA SMITH	G	(J	(N) EARLY MUSIC	1977 EMBASSY	UK		31584
JUDY MOWATT	V	(FJPQS	(O) REFLECTION	1977 FONTANA	FR		
MARCIA GRIFFITHS	V	(FJPTQS	(P) KAYA	1978 ISLAND	UK		ILPS9517
RITA MARLEY	V	(FJPQS	(Q) BABYLON BY BUS (DBL)	1978 ISLAND	UK		ILPD 11
JUNIOR MARVIN	G	(FPQS	(R) BOB MARLEY & THE WAILERS	1979 HAMMER			MHR 9006
DONALD KINSLEY	G	(J	(S) SURVIVAL	1979 ISLAND	UK		ILPS9542
			(T) UPRISING	1980 ISLAND	UK		ILPS9596
			(U) IN THE BEGINNING	1979 PSYCHO			PLP 6002

M88A

RITA MARLEY

RITA MARLEY	V	(A	(A) RITA MARLEY	1980 TRIDENT		TLP 001

M89

MARMALADE

PAT FAIRLEY	B	(E	(A) THERE'S A LOT OF IT ABOUT	1968 CBS		UK	63414
JUNIOR CAMPBELL	G	(E	(B) BEST OF	1969 CBS	US 26553	UK	SPB36
DEAN FORD	G HCA V	(EF	(C) REFLECTIONS	1970 LONDON	US 575	UK DECCA	SKL5047
GRAHAM KNIGHT	B V	(EFH	(D) SONGS	1971 DECCA		UK	SKL5111
ALAN WHITEHEAD	D	(EH	(E) OB LA DI	1973 EMBASSY		UK	EMB31032
MIKE JAPP	G V K	(F	(F) OUR HOUSE IS ROCKING	1974 EMI		UK	EMC 3047
DOUGLAS HENDERSON	D	(F	(G) THE WORLD OF MARMALADE	1976 DECCA		UK	SPA 470
JOE BREEN	B	(F	(H) ONLY LIGHT ON MY HORIZON NOW	1977 TARGET		UK	TGS 501
HOWIE CASEY	HRNS	(F	(I) DOING IT ALL FOR YOU	1979 SKY			LP1
SANDY NEWMAN	G K V	(H					
GARTH WATT ROY	G V	(H					

M89A

STEVE MARRIOTT

STEVE MARRIOTT	G V	(A	(A) MARRIOTT	1976	A&M	US 4572	UK AMLH64572
GREG RIDLEY	B V	(A					
IAN WALLACE	D	(A	MICKEY FINN	G	(A	DAVID FOSTER	K	(A	DENNIS KOVARIK	B	(A
BEN BENAY	G	(A	MIKE BAIRD	D	(A	RED RHODES	STEEL(A	ALAN ESTES CONGA	(A
ERNIE WATTS	SAX	(A	DAVID SPINOZZA	G	(A	MAXINE WILLARD	V	(A	VANETTA FIELDS	V	(A
CARLEENA WILLIAMS	V	(A					

M90

JOHNNY MARS

JOHNNY MARS	HCA V	(AB	(A) BLUES FROM MARS	1972	POLYDOR	UK	2460 168
BOB HALL	PNO MAND	(A	(B) OAKLAND BOOGIE	1976	BIG BEAR	UK	BEAR 12
BOB BRUNNING	B	(A	(C) MIGHTY MARS	1980	JSP	UK	1023
BOOGIE WOOGIE RED	V	(A					
PAT GROVER	G	(A	BABY BOY WARREN	V	(A	JOHN HUNT	D	(A

M91

MARSEILLE

PAUL DALE	V	(AB	(A) RED WHITE & SLIGHTLY BLUE	1978 MOUNTAIN		UK	TOPC5012
NEIL BUCHANAN	G	(AB	(B) MARSEILLE	1979 MOUNTAIN		UK	TOPS 125
ANDY CHARTERS	G	(AB					
STEVE DINWOODIE	B	(AB	KEITH KNOWLES	D	(AB			

M92

MARSHALL HAIN

			(A) FREE RIDE	1978	HARVEST	UK	SHSP 4087

M93

MARSHALL TUCKER

TOY CALDWELL	G V	(ABCDEFGHIJ	(A) A NEW LIFE	1974 CAPRICORN	US 0124	UK 2429 101
TOMMY CALDWELL	B V	(ABCDEFGHIJ	(A) A NEW LIFE	197 CAPRICORN		UK K 57501
GEORGE McCORKLE	G	(BCDEFGHIJ	(B) MARSHALL TUCKER BAND	1974 CAPRICORN	US 0112	UK 2429 114
JERRY EUBANKS	SAX	(BCDEFGHIJ	(B) MARSHALL TUCKER BAND	197 CAPRICORN		UK K 47509
PAUL RIDDLE	D	(BCDEFGHIJ	(C) SEARCHIN' FOR A RAINBOW	1975 CAPRICORN	US 0161	UK 2429 129
DOUG GRAY	G V	(BCDEFGHIJ	(D) WHERE WE ALL BELONG	1975 CAPRICORN	US 1045	UK 2659 042
PAUL HORNSBY	K	(ABCF	(E) LONG HARD RIDE	1976 CAPRICORN	US 0170	UK 2429 140
CHARLIE DANIELS	FDL	(ACEF	(F) CAROLINA DREAMS	1977 CAPRICORN	US 0180	UK 2476 130
JOHN McEUEN	BANJO	(E	(G) TOGETHER FOREVER	1978 CAPRICORN	US 0205	UK 2476 139
JEROME JOSEPH	PERC	(CE	(H) GREATEST HITS	1978 CAPRICORN	US 0214	
RICHARD BETTS	G	(C	(I) BEST OF	1978 CAPRICORN		UK 2429 190
CHUCK LEAVELL	K	(CFJ	(J) RUNNING LIKE THE WIND	1979 WB	US BA3317	UK K 56621
AL McDONALD	MAND	(C				
LEO LABRANCHE	HRNS	(B	JAIMOE JOHANSON	CONGA(FB	BUDDY THORNTON	(B	FRED WISE	FDL (B
DONNA HALL	V	(B	ERNESTINE JONES	V	(B	ELLA BROWN	V	(B	OSCAR JACKSON	SAX (B
SAM DIXON	TPT	(B	STEVE MADAIO	HRNS	(J	GARY GRANT	HRNS	(J	DAVID LUELL	HRNS(J
GARY HERBIG	HRNS	(J	BILL REICHENBACH	HRNS	(J			

M94

JOHN MARTYN

JOHN MARTYN	G V K HCA	(ALL	(A) LONDON CONVERSATION	1967 ISLAND	UK ILPS 952
HAROLD McNAIR	FLT	(B	(B) THE TUMBLER	1968 ISLAND	UK ILPS 9091
BEVERLEY MARTYN	V G	(CDEH	(C) STORMBRINGER	1970 ISLAND	UK ILPS 9113
PAUL HARRIS	K	(CD	(D) THE ROAD TO RUIN	1970 ISLAND	UK ILPS 9133
HARVEY BROOKS	B	(C	(E) BLESS THE WEATHER	1971 ISLAND	UK ILPS 9167
LEVON HELM	D	(C	(F) SOLID AIR	1973 ISLAND	UK ILPS 9226
WELLS KELLY	D	(D	(G) INSIDE OUT	1973 ISLAND	UK ILPS 9253
BILLY MUNDI	D	(C	(H) SUNDAYS CHILD	1975 ISLAND	UK ILPS 9296
HERBIE LOVELL	D	(C	(J) SO FAR SO GOOD	1976 ISLAND	UK ILPS 9484
JOHN SIMON	K	(C	(K) LIVE AT LEEDS	1975 ISLAND	UK ILPS 9343
MIKE KOWALSKI	D	(D	(L) ONE WORLD	1977 ISLAND	UK ILPS 9492
ROCKY DZIDZORNU	PERC	(D	(M) GRACE & DANGER	1980 ISLAND	UK ILPS 9560
DAVE PEGG	B	(DL			
ALAN SPENNER	B	(D	DANNY THOMPSON	B	(DEGHL	LYN DOBSON	FLT	(D	RAY WARLEIGH	SAX (D
STEVE WINWOOD	K B	(GL	REMI KEBAKA	PERC	(G	CHRIS STEWART	(G	CHRIS WOOD	WIND(G
KESH SATHIE	TABLA	(GHL	BOBBY KEYS	SAX	(G	LIAM GENOCHEY	D	(H	TONY BRAUNAGEL	D	(H
TERRY WILSON	B	(H	AL ANDERSON	B	(H	RABBIT BUNDRICK	K	(H	DUDU PUKWANA	SAX (D
JON FIELD	FLT	(L	TRISTRAM FRY	PERC	(L	GEORGE LEE	SAX	(L	NEIL MURRAY	B	(L
ANDY NEWMARK	D	(L	MORRIS PERT	PERC	(L	RICO RODRIGUES	TROM	(L	HANSFORD ROWE	B	(L
BRUCE ROWLAND	D	(L	JON STEVENS	D	(L	PAUL WHEELER	G	(B	DAVE MOSES	B	(B
TONY REEVES	B	(E	IAN WHITEMAN	K	(E	SMILEY DE JONNES	PERC	(E	RICHARD THOMPSON	G	(E
ROGER POWELL	D	(E	PHIL COLLINS	D V	(M	TOMMY EYRE	K	(M	JOHN GIBLIN	B	(M
DAVE LAWSON	SYN	(M					

MARSUPILAMI M95

DAVE LAVEROCK	G	(A	(A) MARSUPILAMI	1970	TRANSATLANTIC		UK	TRA 213
LEARY HASSON	K	(A	(B) ARENA	1971	TRANSATLANTIC		UK	TRA 230
FRED HASSON	V HCA	(A						
MIKE FOURACRE	D	(A	JESSICA STANLEY-CLARKE FLT V(A RICHARD LATHAN HICKS B (A

MARTHA & THE MUFFINS M95A

MARTHA JOHNSON	V K	(AB	(A) METROMUSIC	1980	DINDISC	UK		DID 1
MARTHA LADLY	K V TROM	(A	(B) TRANCE & DANCE	1980	DINDISC	UK		DID 5
ANDY HAAS	SAX	(A						
CARL FINKLE	B	(A	MARK GANE G (A TIM GANE D (A

MARTIAN DANCE M95B

JERRY LAMONT	V	(A	(A) 1980
KEVIN ADDISON	G	(A	
DUNCAN GRIEG	D	(A	DANIEL GRAHAME B (A

MIKE MARTIN M95C

MIKE MARTIN		(A	(A) ON THE ROAD	1979 FLYRIGHT			FLY 301

MOON MARTIN M96

MOON MARTIN	G V	(ALL	(A) SHOTS FROM A COLD NIGHTMARE	1979	CAPITOL		11787
HOWIE WYETH	D	(B	(B) ESCAPE FROM DOMINATION	1979	CAPITOL		11933
GARY VALENTINE	B	(A	(C) STREET FEVER	1980	CAPITOL		12099
CRAIG LEON	K	(AC					
PHIL SEYMOUR	D V	(A	SUSAN HALL PERC (A CHARLIE MERRIAM V (A WILLIE ALEXANDER PNO (A
JIM LEITH	V	(A	JUDE COLE V (BC DENNIS CROY B (BC RICK CROY D (BC
JEFF FARGUS	K V	(C	STEVE DOUGLAS SAX (C DANA FERRIS G (C ROBERT WRIGHT V (C
P ROBINSON	V	(C	P MAROSHEK V (C S HESS V (C ROB STONER B (B

HIRTH MARTINEZ M96A

HIRTH MARTINEZ		(AB	(A) HIRTH FROM EARTH	19	WB		US	B 2867
			(B) BIG BRIGHT STREET	19	WB	UK K56400	US	B 3031

NIGEL MARTINEZ M97

NIGEL MARTINEZ		(A	(A) BETTER THINGS TO COME	1978 STATE		UK	ETAT 17

MARVELETTES M98

WANDA YOUNG	V	(	(A)PLEASE MR POSTMAN	1961	TAMLA	US TS 228		
KATHERIN SCHAFFNER	V	(	(B) MARVELETTES SING	196	TAMLA	US TS 229		
ANN BOGAN	V	(	(C) PLAYBOY	1963	TAMLA	US TS 231		
GLADYS HORTON	V	(	(D) MARVELOUS MARVELETTES	1963	TAMLA	US TS 237	UK 65	STML11008
GEORGEANNA TILLMAN	V	(	(E) LIVE ON STAGE	196	TAMLA	US TS 243		
KATHY ANDERSON	V	(	(F) GREATEST HITS	196	TAMLA	US TS 253		
JUANITA COWART	V	(	(G) MARVELETTES	1967	TAMLA	US TS 274	UK 67	STML11052
			(H) SOPHISTICATED SOUL	1968	TAMLA	US TS 286	UK 69	STML11090
			(I) IN FULL BLOOM	1970	TAMLA	US TS 288	UK	STML11145
			(J) RETURN OF THE MARVELETTES	197	TAMLA	US TS 305		
			(K) BEST OF	1975	TAMLA		UK	STML11258
			(L) ANTHOLOGY	197	TAMLA	US M7 827		

BRETT MARVIN & THE THUNDERBOLTS M99

GRAHAM HINE	G V	(AB	(A) BRETT MARVIN & THE THUNDERBOLTS	1970 SONET	UK SNTF 616 METRONOME 15380
DAVE ARNOT	D	(A	(B) 12 INCHES OF	1971	SONET	UK	SNTF 619
JIM PITTS G V HCA		(AB	(C) BEST OF FRIENDS	1971	SONET	UK	SNTF 620
PETE GIBSON PERC V TROM	(AB		(D) ALIAS TERRY DACTYL	1972	SONET	UK	SNTF 630
JOHN LEWIS	K V	(AB	(E) TEN LEGGED FRIEND	1973	SONET	UK	SNTF 651
KEITH TRUSSELL	PERC	(AB	(F) BRETT MARVIN	19	BARCLAY	FR	920 242
BIG JOHN RANDALL	PERC	(AB					
DAVE ELLIS	G	(A					

HANK MARVIN M100

HANK MARVIN	G V B	(ALL	(A) HANK MARVIN	1969 COLUMBIA	UK	SCX 6352
BRUCE WELCH	G V	(BCD	(B) MARVIN WELCH & FARRAR	1971 REGAL ZONO UK 8502 US CAPITOL 760
JOHN FARRAR	G V B	(BCD	(C) SECOND OPINION	1971 REGAL ZONO UK 8504 US SIR 7403
BRIAN BENNETT	D PERC	(CD	(D) MARVIN & FARRAR	1973 EMI UK EMA 755 US CAPITOL11403
DAVE RICHMOND	B	(C	(E) GUITAR SYNDICATE	1977 EMI UK EMC3215
AL HAWKSHAW	K	(C					
JOHNNY VAN DERRICK FDL (C	OLIVIA NEWTON JOHN REC (D TREVOR SPENCER D PERC(D ALAN TARNEY B (D
ALAN PARKER	G	(E	KEVIN PEEK G (E PAUL KEOGH G (E ALAN SPARKS G (E
LES THATCHER	G	(E	VIC FLICK G (E COLIN GREEN G (E RICKIE HITCHCOCK G (E
CHRIS REA		(E	CLEM CATTINI D (E HERBIE FLOWERS B (E FRANK RICCOTTI PERC(E

MARZ & EPERJESSY M100A

		(A) MARZ & EPERJESSY	1971 BELLAPHON	BLPS19072

CAROLYNE MAS M100B

CAROLYNE MAS		(AB	(A) CAROLYNE MAS	1979	MERCURY	UK	9100 068
			(B) HOLD ON	1980	MERCURY	UK	6337 105

MASCARA M100C

			(A) DESOLATED WORLD (EP)	19	OPTIMISTIC	OPT 006

MASHMAKHAN M100D

			(A) MASHMAKHAN	197	EPIC	US	30235
			(B) THE FAMILY	197	EPIC	US	30813

MASKED MARAUDERS M100E

BOB DYLAN	A		(A) THE MASKED MARAUDERS	1969	REPRISE	US	RS 6378
JOHN LENNON		(A					
PAUL McCARTNEY		(A	GEORGE HARRISON (A MICK JAGGER (A

**** THE ABOVE WERE REPORTED BY ROLLING STONE TO BE INCLUDED IN THE LINE UP BUT THE BASIC BAND WERE CANADIAN AND THE MENTION OF THESE WELL KNOWN NAMES MAY WELL HAVE BEEN A HOAX.

DAVE MASON M101

DAVE MASON	G V	(ALL	(A) ALONE TOGETHER	1970 HARVEST	UK SHTC251 UK	ABC 197	5191
LEON RUSSELL	K	(A	(A) ALONE TOGETHER	1975 BLUE THUMB US BTS 29	+	BT	8819
JIM CAPALDI	D	(A	(B) DAVE MASON & CASS ELLIOT	1971 PROBE	UK 6259	US BLUE THUMB	8825
JOHN SIMON		(A	(C) HEADKEEPER	1072 BLUE YHUMB UK ILPS9203 US		BTS 34
JIM KELTNER	D	(A	(C) HEADKEEPER	1973 ABC RI UK ABCL5189
JIM GORDON	D	(AF	(D) 15 ALIVE	1972 BLUE THUMB	US	BTS 54
CHRIS ETHRIDGE		(A	(E) SCRAPBOOK	1972 ISLAND	UK ICD 5

(CONTINUED)

M101 (CONTINUED) — DAVE MASON

Album	Year	Label	US		UK	
(F) IT'S LIKE YOU NEVER LEFT	1974	CBS	US 31721		UK 65258	
(G) BEST OF	1974	BLUE THUMB	US BTSD6013			
(H) DAVE MASON	1975	CBS	US 33096		UK 80360	
(J) SPLIT COCONUT	1975	CBS	US 33698		UK 69163	
(K) AT HIS BEST	1975	ABC	US TD880	UK	ABCL5122	
(L) CERTIFIED LIVE	1976	CBS	US 34174		UK 88293	
(M) LET IT FLOW	1977	CBS	US 34680		UK 81984	
(N) MARIPOSA DE ORO	1978	CBS	US 35285		UK 82625	
(O) OLD CREST ON A NEW WAVE	1980	CBS			UK	83828

Musician	Inst	Code	Musician	Inst	Code	Musician	Inst	Code	Musician	Inst	Code
CARL RADLE	B	(A									
LARRY KNECHTEL		(A									
MICK DE TEMPLE		(A									
JOHN BARBATA	D	(A									
DELANEY BRAMLETT	G V	(A									
BONNIE BRAMLETT	V	(A									
CLAUDIA LENNEAR	V	(A									
RITA COOLIDGE	V	(AC									
JACK STORTI		(A									
LOU COOPER		(A									
CASS ELLIOT	V	(B	MIKE COOLIDGE	D	(CFHJO	MARK JORDAN	K	(CJ	BOB NORWOOD		(A
LONNIE TURNER	B	(CF	RICK JAEGER	D	(CFHJO	FELIX FLACO FALCON	PERC	(C	SPENCER DAVIS	V	(C
GRAHAM NASH	V G	(CJ	KATHY McDONALD	V	(C	JIM KRUEGER	G	(HJLMO	CHUCK RAINEY	B	(F
ROCKY DZIDZORNU	PERC	(F	MAXINE WILLARD	V	(F	CLYDIE KING	V	(F	JULIA TILLMAN	V	(F
KATHLEEN SAROYAN	V	(F	SON OF HARRY	G	(F	CHARLES FLETCHER	B	(F	GREG REEVES	B	(F
JOHN BATDORF	V	(F	STEVE MADAIO	HRNS	(F	DENNIS MOROUSE	HRNS	(F	NORMA BELL		HRNS(F
STEVIE WONDER	HCA	(F	NASTYEE		(F	MIKE FINNIGAN	K V	(HLMO	BOB GLAUB	B	(HO
GARY BARONE	HRNS	(H	JERRY JUMONVILLE	HRNS	(H	JOCK ELLIS	HRNS	(H	SAL MARQUEZ		HRNS(H
TIM WEISBERG	FLT	(H	EMIL RICHARDS	PERC	(J	DAVID CROSBY	V	(J	GERALD JOHNSON		(LJM
JAY WINDING	K	(J	MANHATTAN TRANSFER	V	(J	DON PRESTON		(A	STEPHEN STILLS	V	(M
YVONNE ELLIMAN	V	(M	ERNIE WATTS	SAX	(M	BOBBYE HALL	PERC	(M	BROOKS HUNNICUTT	V	(M
VERNA RICHARDSON	V	(M	KAREN PATTERSON	V	(M	BRYAN GAROFALO	B	(B	RUSS KUNKEL	D PERC	(B
PAUL HARRIS	K	(B	MICHAEL JACKSON	V	(O	RAY REVIS	PERC	(O	MARK STEIN	K V	(O

M102 — HARVEY MASON

Album	Year	Label			US	
(A) MARCHING IN THE STREET	1976	ARISTA			US AL 4054	
(B) EARTHMOVER	1976	ARISTA			US AL 4096	
(C) FUNK IN A MASON JAR	1977	ARISTA	UK SPART	1049	US AL 4175	
(D) GROOVIN' YOU	1979	ARISTA	UK ARTY	166		
(E) WORLD CLASS	1981	ARISTA			US AB 4283	

Musician	Inst	Code
HARVEY MASON	D	(ALL
JAN HAMMER	K	(B
GREG ADAMS	HRNS	(C
DOROTHY ASHBY		(C
STANLEY BANKS	B	(C
WILFREDO WILSON		(D

Musician	Inst	Code	Musician	Inst	Code	Musician	Inst	Code	Musician	Inst	Code
GEORGE BENSON	G V	(C	EMILIO CASTILLO	HRNS	(C	MERRY CLAYTON	V	(C	JORGE DALTO	K	(C
BOB JAMES	K	(CD	KENNY MASON	TPT	(CD	AL McKAY	G	(C	RAY PARKER	G	(CD
MIKE PORCARO	B	(CD	TOM SCOTT	HRNS	(C	TOWER OF POWER	HRNS	(C	CHARLES VEAL		VLN(CD
MAXINE WILLARD	V	(B	VERDINE WHITE	B	(CD	DENNIS BELFIELD	B	(D	STANLEY CLARKE	B	(D
VICTOR FELDMAN	PERC	(D	VANETTA FIELDS	V	(C	CHUCK FINDLEY	HRNS	(C	DAVID FOSTER	B	(CD
RONNIE FOSTER	K	(CD	MICK GILLETTE	HRNS	(C	LOUIS JOHNSON	B	(C	MARVIN MASON		(C
PAULETTE McWILLIAMS	V	(C	JERRY PETERS	K	(CD	LEE RITENOUR	G	(CD	IAN UNDERWOOD		(C
DAVID T WALKER	G	(C	BILL WATRONS	TROM	(C	LARRY WILLIAMS	WIND	(C	BILL CHAMPLIN	V	(D
TONY DUMAS		(C	GARY GRANT	HRNS	(C	JAY GRAYDON	G	(CD	DAVE GRUSIN	K	(C
JERRY HEY	HRNS	(C	KIM HUTCHCROFT	V	(C	DICK HYDE	HRNS	(C	ANTHONY JACKSON	B	(C
HOPPY MASON		(CD	RALPH MACDONALD	PERC	(C	DAVID PAICH	K	(C	LENNY PICKETT		HRNS(C
SEAWIND	HRNS	(C	STEPHANIE SPRUILL	V	(CD	PHIL UPCHURCH	G	(CD	JULIA TILLMAN	V	(C
NATE WATT	B	(C	ART WILSON		(C	PETER CHAIKIN		(D	SHEILA ESCOVEDO		(D
JAMES GILSTRAP	V	(D	BUNNY HULL		(D	ROGER ST KENNERLY	V	(D	PHIL MOORES		(D
RICHARD TEE	K	(D	JERRY WHITMAN	V	(D	JAI WINDING	PNO	(D	JIM HAAS	V	(D
NEIL JASON	B V	(D	STEVE LUKATHER	G	(D	DAVID SHIELDS	B	(D	RANDY WALDMAN		(D
DAVID WILLIAMS	D	(D	BOB WERTZ		(D	RON HICKLIN		(D	MORRIS PAUL KENNEDY		(D
BILL MEYERS		(D	DAVID SPINOZZA	D	(D	WAH WAH WATSON	G	(D			

M102A — JAE MASON

Musician	Inst	Code
JAE MASON		

Album	Year	Label	US	
(A) CROSSROADS	19	BUDDAH	US	BDS 5604
(B) TENDERMAN	19	BUDDAH	US	BDS 5640

M102B — MASON PROFFIT

Musician	Inst	Code
JOHN TALBOT	V G	(
TERRY TALBOT	G V	(
TIM AYERS	B	(
BRUCE KURNOW	HCA	(
BYRON BERLINE	VLN	(

Album	Year	Label	US	
ROCKFISH CROSSING	19	WB	US	BS 2657
BAREBACK RIDER	19	WB	US	BS 2704
COME & GONE	19	WB	US	BS 2746
MASON PROFFIT WANTED	19	HAPPY TIGER	US	009
MOVING TOWARDS HAPPINESS	19	HAPPY TIGER	US	1019
LAST NIGHT I HAD THE STRANGEST DREAM	19	AMPEX	US	100138

M102C — MASON WOOD CAPALDI & FROG

Musician	Inst	Code	Musician	Inst	Code
DAVE MASON	G B V	(A			
CHRIS WOOD	WIND	(A			
JIM CAPALDI	D V	(A	MICK WEAVER	K	(A

M102D — MASQUERADERS

Album	Year	Label	US	
(A) EVERYBODY WANNA LIVE ON	19	ABC	US	ABCD921
(B) LOVE ANONYMOUS	1977	ABC UK ABCL5222	US	ABC 962

M103 — MASS PRODUCTION

Album	Year	Label	UK	US
(A) WELCOME TO OUR WORLD	1977	COTILLION	UK K 50331	US SD9910
(B) BELIEVE	1977	COTILLION	UK K 50400	US SD9918
(C) THREE MILES HIGH	1978	COTILLION	UK K 50510	US SD5205
(D) IN THE PUREST FORM	1979	COTILLION	UK K 50601	US SD5211

M103A — MASTERS

Musician	Inst	Code	Musician	Inst	Code
JIMMY BERICK	G V	(A			
RANDY RAND	B G	(A			
DAVE RADA	D V	(A	JON FLAK	V	(A

Album	Year	Label	UK	US
(A) MASTERS OF THE AIRWAVES	1974	EPIC	UK X598	US 33060

M104 — MASTERSWITCH

Musician	Inst	Code	Musician	Inst	Code
STEVE WILKIN		(A			
MARK LOUIS		(A			
MARTIN LEE		(A	JAMES EDWARDS		(A

M105 — MATCHBOX

Musician	Inst	Code	Musician	Inst	Code
BOB BURGOS	D	(			
GRAHAM FENTON	V	(			
FRED POKE	B	(			
GORDON WATERS	G V	(			
STEVE BLOOMFIELD	G MAND	(	JIMMY REDHEAD	D	(

Album	Year	Label	UK	
(A) SETTIN' THE WOODS ON FIRE	1978	CHISWICK	UK	WIK 10
(B) RIDERS IN THE SKY	1978	CHARLY	UK CR 30157	
(C) MATCHBOX	1979	MAGNET	UK MAGL5031	

MATCHING MOLE

```
ROBERT WYATT     D V  (AB         (A) MATCHING MOLE              1972  CBS              UK   64850
PHIL MILLER      K G  (AB         (B) LITTLE RED RECORD          1973  CBS              UK   65260
BILL MACCORMICK  B    (AB
DAVE McRAE       K    (AB  ENO      SYN (B   DAVE SINCLAIR     K (A
```

ANDREW MATHESON
M106A

```
ANDREW MATHESON  V   (A          (A) MONTEREY SHOES             1979  ARIOLA           ARL  5025
PETE KIRCHER     D   (A
ANDY PASK        B   (A   RAPHAEL RAVENSCROFT  SAX (A  TOMMY EYRE    K  (A   NIGEL JENKINS    G  (A
E S BRADY        G   (A   HOWIE CASEY          SAX (A  BILL STREET   HRNS (A
```

MATRIX
M106B

```
NICK ZESSES         (A          (A) MATRIX                     1972  RARE EARTH       US   R542L
DINO FEKARIS        (A
TOM BAIRD           (A
```

DAVE MATTHEWS
M107

```
DAVE MATTHEWS    K   (AB         (A) SHOOGIE WANNA BOOGIE       1976  KUDU                  KU 30
DON GROLNICK     K   (A          (B) DUNE                       1977  CTI                   5005
ANDY NEWMARK     D   (AB
BARRY MILES      K    (A   JERRY FRIEDMAN    G   (A  STEVE KHAN     G    (A   ANTHONY JACKSON  B   (A
SUE EVANS        PERC (AB  RANDY BRECKER     TPT (AB  JON FADDIS     TPT  (AB  MICHAEL BRECKER  SAX (A
RON CUBER        SAX  (A   BURT COLLINS      TPT (AB  ALAN RUBIN     TPT  (A   JOE SHEPLEY      TPT (AB
TOM MALONE       TROM (AB  SAM BURTIS        TROM(AB  DAVE TAYLOR    TROM (AB  PATTI AUSTIN     V   (A
VIVIAN CHERRY    V    (A   GWEN GUTHRIE      V   (A   JIM BUFFINGTON HRNS (A   PETER GORDON     HRNS(A
JOE FARRELL      SAX  (A   FRED WESBY        TROM(A   LANCE QUINN    G    (A   JOHN TROPEA      G   (A
CARLOS MARTIN    PERC (A   KEN ASCHER        K   (A   WILL LEE       B    (A   NICKY MARRERO    PERC(A
PAT REBILLOT     K    (A   JEFF BERLIN       B   (A   CLIFF CARTER   K    (B   MARK EGAN        B   (B
GARY KING        B    (B   JIM BOSBY         HRNS(B   JOHN GATCHELL  HRNS (B   LEW SOLOFF       HRNS(B
STEVE GADD       D    (B   HIRAM BULLOCK     G   (B   ERIC GALE      G    (B   GORDON GOTTLIEB  PERC(B
WAYNE ANDRE      TROM (B   JERRY CHAMBERLAIN TROM(B   DAVID SANBORN  SAX  (B   GROVER WASHINGTON SAX(B
LEW DEL GATTO    WIND (B   DAVID TOFANI      WIND(B   GOOGIE COPPOLA V    (B   SANFORD ALLEN  STRINGS(B
```

IAN MATTHEWS & MATTHEWS SOUTHERN COMFORT
M108

```
IAN MATTHEWS      G V   (ALL        (A) MATTHEWS SOUTHERN COMFORT    1970  UNI                 UNLS 108
GERRY CONWAY      D     (AD         (A) "     "     "      "        1970  MCA                 MAPS1641
ROGER COULAM      K     (AC         (A) "     "     "      "        1974  MCA RI              MCF 2675
SIMON NICOL       G     (A          (B) SECOND SPRING               1970  UNI                 UNLS 112
MARC ELLINGTON    PERC  (A          (B) "     "     "      "        1970  MCA                 MAPS2038
ANDY LEIGH        B V   (BC         (B) "     "     "      "        1974  MCA                 MCF 2677
CARL BARNWELL     G V   (BC3        (B) "     "     "      "        197   UNI             FR  6369 600
KEITH NELSON      BANJO (C          (C) LATER THAT SAME YEAR        1970  MCA                 MKPS2015
KEITH TIPPETT     K     (D          (C) "     "     "      "        1970  MCA                 MAPS3976
CAL BATCHELOR     G     (E          (C) "     "     "      "        1974  MCA                 MCF 2686
BRUCE THOMAS      B     (E          (C) "     "     "      " DIFF TRACKS 197  DECCA   US      75264
WOLFE J FLYWHEEL  ACC   (E          (C) "     "     "      " DIFF TRACKS 197  PICKWICK       CAN SPC 3698
BILLY GRAHAM      B FDL (FG         (D) IF YOU SAW THROUGH MY EYES  1971  VERTIGO US VEL 1002 UK 6360 034
MICHAEL NESMITH   G     (F          (E) TIGERS WILL SURVIVE         1972  VERTIGO US VEL 1010 UK 6360 056
BYRON BERLINE     FDL   (F          (E) "     "     "      "  (POP LEGEND) 1980 VERTIGO       NL 9199 139
JEFF BAXTER       G     (G          (F) VALLEY HI                   1973  ELEKTRA US EKS75061 UK K 42144
DANNY WEIS        G     (G          (G) SOME DAYS YOU EAT THE BEAR....  1974 ELEKTRA US EKS75078 UK K 42160
B J COLE          STEEL (G          (H) JOURNEYS FROM GOSPEL OAK    1974  MOONCREST           UK CREST 18
JERRY DONAHUE     G     (H          (H) "     "      "     "        1979  BOULEVARD           BD 3009
MIKE PORTER       D     (J          (J) GO FOR BROKE                1976  CBS     US   34102  UK   81316
KENNY EDWARDS     B     (J          (K) HIT & RUN                   1977  CBS     US   34671  UK   81930
PETER WOOD        K     (J          (L) STEALIN' HOME               1978  ROCKBURGH           UK ROC 106
SHANE KEISTER     K     (J          (L) "     "    "                1978  MUSHROOM            MRS 5012
MUSCLE SHOALS     HRNS  (J          (M) SIAMESE FRIENDS             1979  ROCKBURGH           UK ROC 107
BONNIE MURRAY     V     (K          (N) SHAKE IT (12" EP)           1978  ROCKBURGH           UK ROCS209
MICK WEAVER       K     (1M         (O) SPOT OF INTERFERENCE        1980  ROCKBURGH           UK 2383 582
PETE WINGFIELD    K     (LN         ( ) BEST OF MATTHEWS SOUTHERN COMFORT 1975 MCA            UK MCF 2574
SIMON MORTON      PERC  (LMN        (1) 1978 TOUR   (2) 1979 FEB TOUR    (3) 1970 LIVE
BOB METZGER       G     (2MO
ASHLEY HUTCHINGS  B     (A
RICHARD THOMPSON  G     (AD  GORDON HUNTLEY STEEL(ABC3   PETE WILLSHER  G  (A   DOLLY COLLINS  K  (A
POLI PALMER       FKT   (A   RAY DUFFY      D    (BC   MARK GRIFFITHS B G V(123BCMO TOM PALEY   BAN (B
ROGER CHURCHYARD  FDL   (B   MARTIN JENKINS MAND (B    TRISTRAM FRY   VIBES(C  PAT DONALDSON  B  (DH
TIM RENWICK       G     (DE  ANDY ROBERTS   G    (DEGH SANDY DENNY    K V (D   TIMI DONALD    D  (EGH
WILLIE WILSON     D     (E   IAN WHITEMAN   K    (E    BOB RONGA      K B (E   RAY WARLEIGH   SAX (E
DANNY LANE        D     (FG  JAY LACY       G    (FGJK BOBBY WARFORD  G   (FG  RED RHODES     STEEL(F
DAVID BARRY       K     (FG  WILLIE LEACOX  D    (G    DAVID DICKEY   B   (G   MICHAEL FONFARA K (G
STEVE GILLETTE    G     (G   JOEL TEPP   HCA G   (12GJM LYN DOBSON    SAX (G   AL GARTH       SAX (G
DAVID LINDLEY     STEEL (G   TRIS IMBODEN   D    (JK   KENNY BUTTREY  D   (J   DON WHALEY     B  (JK
NORBERT PUTNAM    B     (J   MIKE LEECH     B    (J    STEVE WOOD     K   (J   DAVID BRIGGS   K  (J
GLEN SPREEN       K     (J   REG YOUNG      G    (J    HARRY ROBINSON G   (J   STEVE HOOKS    WIND(K
CHARLIE HARWOOD   K V   (K   PHIL PALMER    G    (1LN  JIM RUSSELL    D   (1LMN BRYN HAWORTH  G MAND(LN
RICK KEMP         B     (LN  MEL COLLINS    SAX  (LMN  DUFFY POWER    HCA (L   PETER WATKINS  B  (3
ROGER SWALLOW     D     (3   CRAIG BUHLER   SAX  (M    DAVE WINTOUR   B   (O   ROBERT HENRIT  D  (O
```

MILT MATTHEWS
M108A

```
MILT MATTHEWS        (A          (A) MILT MATTHEWS INC           1971  EMBER                NR 5056
NORMAN HARRISON  K   (A
RANDY B WINGY    G   (A   TOMMY BYRD      D   (A   CARL MATTHEWS    B   (A
```

MATUMBI
M109

```
DENNIS BOVELL    V G K(BC         (A) BEST OF MATUMBI            1977  TROJAN           TRLS  145
BEVIN FAGAN      B V  (ABC        (B) SEVEN SEALS               1978  HARVEST          SHSP 4090
EUTON JONES      PERC (ABC        (C) POINT OF VIEW             1979  M R              RDC  2001
GLAISTER VENN    V    (ABC        (D) AH WHO SEH ? GO GO DEH!   197   RAMA             R
EATON BLAKE      B    (ABC
LLOYD DONALDSON  D    (ABC  WEBSTER JOHNSON  K V (ABC  PATRICK TENYUE  HRNS (C   HENRY TENYUE  HRNS  (C
NICK STRAKER     K    (C    ANDY             G   (C    JULIO FINN      HCA  (C
```

M110   BENNIE MAUPIN
    BENNIE MAUPIN   SAX (ALL   (A) THE JEWEL IN THE LOTUS   1975 ECM   ECM1043
                                  (B) MOONSCAPES   1978 MERCURY
                                  (C) SLOW TRAFFIC TO THE RIGHT   197   MERCURY US   SRM11148
                                  (D) AKMANAC   1978 IMPROVISING   IAI373851
M111   JOHN MAYALL & THE BLUESBREAKERS
    JOHN MAYALL G V HCA K (ALL   (A) JOHN MAYALL PLAYS JOHN MAYALL 1964 DECCA UK LK 4680
    JOHN McVIE   B   (ABCDLOak (B) BLUESBREAKERS   1965 DECCA UK SLK4804 US LONDON PS492
    KEITH TILLMAN   B   (GH   (B) BLUESBREAKERS   1965 DECCA GER   SLK 16547
    MICK FLEETWOOD   D   (LO   (C) A HARD ROAD   1967 DECCA UK SKL4853 US LONDON PS502
    PETE WARD   D   (A   (D) CRUSADE   1967 DECCA UK SKL4890 US LONDON PS529
    HENRY LOWTHER   TPT (LJa   (D) CRUSADE   196 DECCA GER   SLK16499
    CHRIS MERCER   SAX (DGHOa   (E) BLUES ALONE   1967 ACE   UK SCL1243 US LONDON PS534
    HUGHIE FLINT   D   (DRJLa1   (F) RAW BLUES   1967 ACE   UK SCL1220 US LONDON PS543
    JON HISEMAN   D   (Ja   (EP)WITH PAUL BUTTERFIELD   1967 DECCA UK DFE8673
    ERIC CLAPTON   G   (BOXdp   (G) DIARY OF A BAND VOL 1   1968 DECCA UK SKL4918
    DICK HECKSTALL SMITH SAX(GHJOa   (H) DIARY OF A BAND VOL 2   1968 DECCA UK SKL4919
    JIMMY McCULLOCH   G   (3   (GH) DIARY OF A BAND VOL 1/2   196   US LONDON PS570
    PAUL WILLIAMS   B   (Oa   (I) BLUES GIANT   1968 DECCA IMP   3117
    COLIN ALLEN   D   (K   (J) BARE WIRES   1968 DECCA UK SKL4945 US LONDON PS537
    JOHNNY ALMOND   SAX (BPQXk   (J) BARE WIRES   1968 DECCA GER   SLK 16558
    ALEX DMOCHOWSKI   B   (k   (K) LAUREL CANYON   1969 DECCA UK SKL4972 US LONDON PS545
    HARVEY MANDEL   G   (RXY   (K) LAUREL CANYON   196 DECCA GER   SLK 16573
    PAUL LAGOS   D   (X   (L) SO MANY ROADS   1969 DECCA GER   SLK 16590
    AYNSLEY DUNBAR   D   (CLOa   (M) LIVE   1969 DECCA GER   SLK 16615
    BERNIE WATSON   G   (OLa   (N) BEST OF JOHN MAYALL   1969 DECCA GER   SLK 16632
    ANDY FRASER   B   ((O) LOOKING BACK   1970 DECCA UK SKL5010 US LONDON PS562
    KEEF HARTLEY   D   (GHOEabcX3 (P) TURNING POINT   1970 POLYDOR UK 583 571 US PD 4004
    ROGER DEAN   G   (ALOa   (Q) EMPTY ROOMS   1970 POLYDOR UK 583 580 US
    JACK BRUCE   B   (O1   (PQ)TURNING POINT/EMPTY ROOMS 1974 POLYDOR UK 2683 039
    MICK TAYLOR   G   (DGHJKOQXad (R) USA UNION   1970 POLYDOR UK 2425 020
    TONY REEVES   B   (Ja   (S) LIVE IN EUROPE   1970 LONDON   US   PS589
    RIP KANT   HRNS (D   (T) WORLD OF VOL1   1970 DECCA UK SPA 47
    JEFF KRIBBETT   G   (1   (U) WORLD OF VOL2   1971 DECCA UK SPA 138
    PETER GREEN   G   (CLOad   (V) DOWN THE LINE   197 LONDON   US   PS618/9
    STEVE THOMPSON   B   (KPQX6   (W) MEMORIES   1971 POLYDOR UK 2425 085
    JON MARK   ACC G(PQk   (X) BACK TO THE ROOTS   1971 POLYDOR UK 2657 005
    LARRY TAYLOR   B   (RWXZbghik3 (Y) BEYOND THE TURNING POINT 1971 POLYDOR UK 2483 016
    DON SUGARCANE HARRIS VLN(RXehik   (Z) JAZZ BLUES FUSION   1972 POLYDOR UK 2425 103 US   PD 5027
    JERRY McGEE   G   (WX   (a) THROUGH THE YEARS   1972 DECCA UK SKL5086 US LONDON PS600/1
    BLUE MITCHELL   TPT (Zbek   (b) MOVING ON   1973 POLYDOR UK 2391 047 US   PD 5036
    CLIFFORD SOLOMON   SAX (Zb   (c) BEST OF   197 POLYDOR   US   PD 23006
    RON SELICO   D   (Z   (d) JOHN MAYALL PROFILE   197 TELDEC GER   624010
    FREDDY ROBINSON   G   (Zbe   (e) TEN YEARS ARE GONE   1973 POLYDOR UK 2683 036 US   PD 3005
    VICTOR GASKIN   B   (be   (f) STAR PORTRAIT   1973 POLYDOR IMP 2675019
    RED HOLLOWAY   SAX (egk   (f) POP HISTORY   1973 POLYDOR IMP 2675017
    ERNIE WATTS   SAX (b   (g) LATEST EDITION   1975 POLYDOR UK 2391 141 US   PD 6030
    CHARLES OWEN   SAX (b   (h) NEW YEAR NEW BAND NEW COMPANY 1975 ABC UK ABCL5115 US   6019
    HIGHTIDE HARRIS   G   (g   (i) NOTICE TO APPEAR   1975 ABC   UK ABCL5142 US ABCD 926
    SOKO RICHARDSON   D   (ghik56   (j) JOHN MAYALL   1976 POLYDOR UK 2482 272
    RANDY RESNICK   G   (g   (k) BANQUET IN BLUES   1976 ABC   UK ABCL5187 US ABCD 958
    DEE McKINNIE   V   (hik   (m) LOTS OF PEOPLE   1977 ABC   UK ABCL5126 US ABCD 992
    NOLAN SMITH   TPT (4   (n) A HARD CORE PACKAGE   1977 ABC   US ABCD 1039
    ANN PATERSON   SAX (4   (p) PRIMAL SOLOS   1977 LONDON   US LC 50003
    JIMMY ROBERTS   SAX (4   (q) BLUES ROOTS   1978 DECCA UK ROOTS 8
    BILL LAMB   TPT (4   (r) LAST OF THE BRITISH BLUES 1978 ABC   US ABCD 1086
    WARREN BRYANT   PERC (4   (s) BOTTOM LINE   1979 DJM   UK DJF20556
    DAVID LI   SAX (4   (t) NO MORE INTERVIEWS   1979 DJM   UK DJF20564
    FRANK WILSON   D   (4   ( ) HIGHLIGHTS   1977 POLYDOR GER 2674 013
    EDMOND LEE   B   (5   (1) 1969 (2) 1971 (3) 1977 (4) 1977 (5) 1977
    BRAD THOELKE   TROM (t
    JESSE ED DAVIS   G   (ALLAN TOUSSAINT K   (i   RICK VITO   G (hikt JAY SPELL   K (hik
    LARRY BLOUIN   SAX (i   LON PRICE   WIND   (i   NICK MESSINA   G   (i   HERMAN ERNEST   D (i
    JAMES CARROLL BOOKER K (i   TONY BROSSARD   B   (i   KIM JOSEPH   CONGA(i   STEVE HUGHES   G (i
    ALAN SKIDMORE   SAX (B   DENNIS HEALEY   TPT (B   BUCK CLARK   PERC (k   BENNY POWELL   TROM(k
    RONNIE BARRON   K V (kt   RON McCURDY   D   (k   DOUG BARE   K   (k   MIKE COOLEY   G (k
    LENNY McDANIEL   B   (k   PHIL DESPOMMIER D   (k   NOVI NOVAG   VLA (k   PAT SMITH   V (
    PEPPER WATKINS   V   (s4   JAMES SMITH   G   (56 LEON PENDARVIS K   (s   BOB BABITT   B (s
    FRANCISCO CENTENO B   (s   JEFF MIRANOV   G   (s   SIDNEY McGINNIS G   (s   JOHN TROPEA   G (s
    STEVE JORDAN   D   (s   ERROL BENNETT   PERC (s ARTHUR JENKINS PERC (s ROB MOUNSEY   K (s
    JON FADDIS   HRNS (s   VERGIL JONES   HRNS (s STEVE FORMAN   PERC (s LEE HOLDRIDGE STRING(s
    CHERYL LYNN   V   (s   DELBERT LANGSTON V   (s   ALAN RAPH   TROM (s HOWARD JOHNSON   HRNS(s
    VIVIAN CHERRY   V   (s   YOLANDA McCULLOUGH V (s   GORDON EDWARDS B   (s   JANICE PENDARVIS V (s
    CORNELL DUPREE   G   (s   JEFF LAYTON   G   (s   PAUL SCHAEFFER K   (s   RUBENS BASSINI   PERC(s
    ALEJANDRO ACUNA   PERC (s   JOHN JARVIS   K   (s   JEFF PORCARO   D   (s   STEVE LUKATHER   G (s
    BEN BENAY   G   (s   RANDY BRECKER   HRNS (s MICHAEL BRECKER HRNS (s RON CUBER   WIND (s
    LEW SOLOFF   TPT (s   BERNARD KRAUSE   SYN (s   DAVID SHIELDS   B   (s   TIM DRUMMOND   B (s
    LEE RITENOUR   G   (s   NIGEL STANGER   SAX (AL MARTIN HART   D   (LOa NICK NEWELL   SAX (L
    MAGGIE PARKER   V   (t   JAMES QUILL SMITH G (t   CHRIS CAMERON   K   (t   CHRISTIAAN MOSTERT WIND)t
    ANGUS THOMAS   B   (t   RUBIN ALVAREZ   D   (t   BECKIE BURNS   V   (t   BUDDY McDANIELS SAX (t
    GEORGE SHAW   TPT (t
M111A   MAX
                                  (A) MAX   1980 CHRYSALIS   UK CHR 1278
M112   MAX WEBSTER
    DAVE MYLES   B V (D   (A) MAX WEBSTER   1975 ANTHEM   US   ANR 1006
    KIM MITCHELL   G V (D   (B) HIGH CLASS & BORROWED SHOES 1977 ANTHEM   US   ANR 1007
    TERRY WATKINSON D V (D   (C) MUTINY UP MY SLEEVE   1978 CAPITOL   11776
    GARY McCRACKEN D V (D   (D) MILLION VACATIONS   1979 CAPITOL   11937
                                   (E) LIVE MAGNETIC AIR   1979 CAPITOL   12042
                                   (F) UNIVERSAL JUVENILES   1980 MERCURY   US   SRM1 3855

[278]

MAXFIELD PARRISH
M113

```
DAVID BIASOTTI        (A      (A) IT'S A CINCH TO GIVE LEGS....   1972   CURNON        US        CNL  721
PERRIN MUIR           (A
DAVID McCLELLAN       (A      RANDY GROENKE      (A   CHRIS DARROW   G   (A   DAVID LINDLEY   FDL V(A
BERNIE LEADON    G    (A      JOHN LONDON     B  (A   JOHN WARE      D   (A   CHESTER CRILL          (A
```

PHIL MAY
M114A

```
PHIL MAY       G V   (A      (A) PHIL MAY & THE FALLEN ANGELS   1978 PHILIPS       NL        6410 969
WALLY WALLER   B     (A
CHICO GREENWOOD  D   (A      BILLY LOVELADY    G   (A   ED DEAN     G   (A   BRIAN JOHNSTON  K  (
MICKEY FINN    G     (A      JACK JOHNSTON     K   (A   JOHN POVEY  V   (A   JOHN PORTER     G  (A
FRAN BYRNE     D     (A      L SHANKAR       VLN (A
```

MAY BLITZ
M114B

```
TONY NEWMAN   VIBES D(AB1     (A) MAY BLITZ          1970   VERTIGO       UK 6360  007
REID HUDSON   B V    (AB      (B) SECOND OF MAY      1971   VERTIGO       UK 6360  037
JAMES BLACK   G V    (AB1     (1) 1969 LINE UP
TERRY POOLE   B      (1
KEITH BAKER   D      (1
```

CURTIS MAYFIELD
M115

```
CURTIS MAYFIELD   V   (ALL    EARLY YEARS                 1973 PROBE UK GTSP 201 UK ABC ABCD780
                              SWEET EXORCIST              1974 BUDDAH  BDLH 5001   UK  2318 099
                              SWEET EXORCIST              1976 CURTOM              UK  K 56284
                              ROOTS                       1974 BUDDAH  BDLH 5006   UK  2318 045
                              ROOTS                       1976 CURTOM              UKRI K 56249
                              CURTIS                      1974 BUDDAH  BDLH 5005   UK  2318 015
                              CURTIS                      1976 CURTOM              UK  K 56252
                              BACK TO THE WORLD           1974 BUDDAH  BDLH 5008   UKRI K 56251
                              IN CHICAGO LIVE             1974 BUDDAH  BDLH 5009
                              IN CHICAGO LIVE             1976 CURTOM  US 8018     UK  K 56250
                              SHORT EYES                  197  CURTOM  US  5017
                              DO IT ALL NIGHT             197  CURTOM  US  5022
                              MOVE ON UP                  1974 BUDDAH  BDLP 4015
                              SUPERFLY                    1974 BUDDAH  BDLH 4018
                              GOT TO FIND A WAY           1974 BUDDAH  BDLP 4029 CURTOM US   8604
                              AMERICA TODAY               1974 BUDDAH  BDLP 4033 CURTOM US   5001
                              GIVE GET TAKE HAVE          1976 BUDDAH  BDLP 4042 CURTOM US   5007
                              CURTIS LIVE                 1974 BUDDAH  BDLD 2001 CURTOM UK K66047
                              NEVER SAY YOU CANT SURVIVE  1977 CURTOM    CU 5013       UK K56352
                              HEARTBEAT                   1979 CURTOM  US   3053
```

PERCY MAYFIELD
M116

```
PERCY MAYFIELD   V PNO(ALL    (A) PERCY MAYFIELD           1969 TANGERINE      UK        TRC 1505
                              (B) BOUGHT BLUES            1969 TANGERINE      US        TRS 1510
                              (C) TIGHTROPE              1969 BRUNSWICK                  754145
                              (D) SINGS                  1970 RCA VICTOR     US          4269
                              (E) WEAKNESS IS A THING CALLED MAN 1970 RCA VICTOR US      4444
                              (F) BLUES & THEN SOME      1971 RCA VICTOR     US          4558
                              (G) THE INCREDIBLE         1972 SPECIALTY  US 5010 UK SNTF 5010
                              (H) BEST OF                197  SPECIALTY      US          2126
```

MAZE
M117

```
FRANKIE BEVERLY        (      (A) ARMAGEDDON             197  MTA           US        MTS 5012
                              (B) MAZE                   1977 CAPITOL                   11607
                              (C) GOLDEN TIME OF DAY     1978 CAPITOL                   11710
```

MEAL TICKET
M118

```
CHRIS HUNT     D PERC (AB     (A) CODE OF THE ROAD       1977 EMI           UK        INS 3008
JACK BRAND     B V    (AB     (B) THREE TIMES A DAY      1978 EMI           UK        INS 3010
RAY FLACKE     G V    (AB     (C) TAKEAWAY               1978 LOGO          UK          1008
STEVE SIMPSON FDL G V (ABC
RICK JONES     K V    (ABC KEITH NELSON    BANJO(BC  DAVE PIERCE      (   WILLY FINLAYSON G V K(ABC
DON WELLER     SAX    (B    ALAN COULTER         D  (C   ROD DEMICK    B   (C
```

MEAN STREET DEALERS
M119

```
MARK BRISTOW    G    (A       (A) BENT NEEDLES           1979 MEAN ST DEALERS         MSD  001
NIGEL DARVILLS  K    (A       (A) BENT NEEDLES           1979 GRADUATE                GRAD LP1
JAMES LANGSTON  V    (A
JIM SIMPSON     D    (A    BOB BOUCHER    B   (A
```

MEATLOAF
M120

```
MEATLOAF      V    (AB        (A) STONEY & MEATLOAF       1971 RARE EARTH              SRE 3005
KARLA DEVITO  V    (          (A) MEATLOAF(FEATURING STONEY) 1979 PRODIGAL US 10029 UK PDL 2010
ED KING       G    (          (B) BAT OUT OF HELL        1978 EPIC    US 34974 UK     82419
TODD RUNDGREN      (B
JOHN STEINMAN      (     ELLEN FOLEY       (   ROY BITAN      (A   KASIM SULTON     (A
ROGER POWELL       (     JOHN WILCOX          EDGAR WINTER   (
```

MEDICINE HEAD
M121

```
JOHN FIDDLER     G V (ALL     (A) NEW BOTTLES OLD MEDICINE  1970 DANDELION       UK          63757
PETER HOPE EVANS HCA V (ABDEFG (B) HEAVY ON THE DRUM      1971 DANDELION  DAN 8005 K 49005
KEITH RELF      B V  (C       (C) DARK SIDE OF THE MOON   1971 DANDELION       UK         2310 166
JOHN DAVIES     D    (C       (D) ONE & ONE IS ONE       1972 POLYDOR         UK         2310 248
ROB TOWNSEND    D    (E       (E) THRU A FIVE            1974 POLYDOR         UK         2383 272
ROGER SAUNDERS  G    (E       (F) MEDICINE HEAD (COMP)   1975 POLYDOR         UK         2384 069
IAN SAINTY      B    (        (G) TWO MAN BAND           1976 BARN           UK          2314 102
CHARLIE McCRACKEN B  (        ( ) POP HISTORY VOL XXV    1973 POLYDOR                    2625 026
GEORGE FORD     B V  (E
TONY ASHTON     K    (DE CLIVE THACKER    D   (D   ROY DYKE    D   (D   PAT DONALDSON   B  (D
MIKE LIBER      G    (D  BRIAN PARRISH    G   (D
```

MEDITATIONS
M122

```
                              (A) WAKE UP                 1978 THIRD WORLD             TWS  929
                              (B) A MESSAGE FROM THE MEDITATIONS 1978 UA  US LA 802 UK UAS30178
```

BILL MEDLEY

LAY A LITTLE LOVIN' ON ME	19	UA	US	LA	929H
WINGS	19	A&M	US		3506
A SONG FOR YOU	19	A&M	UK	AMLH	63505
SMILE	19	A&M	US		3517
BILL MEDLEY 100%	19	MGM	US	SE	4583
SOFT & SOULFUL	19	MGM	US	SE	4603

M123 — RANDY MEISNER

RANDY MEISNER	G V(ALL		(A) RANDY MEISNER		1978	ASYLUM	US 6E140	UK	K53079
KELLY SHANAHAN	D (A		(B) ONE MORE SONG		1980	EPIC		UK	84531
STEVE EDWARDS	G (A								
KERRY MORRIS	B (A	JOHN HOBBS	PNO (A	JERRY SWALLOW	G (A	TITA KERPAN		V (A	
BYRON BERLINE	FDL (A	DONNY ULLSTROM	V (A	ERNIE WATTS	SAX (A	ALAN BRACKETT		V (A	
GEOFFREY LEIB	PNO (A	RICHIE WALKER	V (A	J D SOUTHER	V (A	BILL LAMB		V (A	
DAVID CASSIDY	V (A	DON FRANCISCO	PERC V(B	CRAIG HULL	G (B	BRYAN GAROFALO		B (B	
CRAIG KRAMPF	D (B	STERLING SMITH	K (B	WENDY WALDMAN	G V (B	BILL CUOMO		SYN (B	
MICHAEL JACOBSON	SAX (B	KIM CARNES	V (B	DON HENLEY	V (B	GLENN FREY		V (B	

M124 — MEKONS

JON LANGFORD	D (		(A) THE QUALITY OF MERCY IS NOT STRNEN	1979	VIRGIN	UK	V 2143
ROSS ALLEN	B (		(B) MEKONS	1980	REDMEK	UK	1
ANDY CARRIGAN	V (						
MARK WHITE	V (	KEVIN LYCETT	G (	TOM GREENHALGH	G (		

M125 — MELANIE

MELANIE SAFKA	V (ALL	(A) BORN TO BE	1969	BUDDAH	203 019		BDLH	5002
RON FRANGIPANE	K (GJ	(B) AFFECTIONATELY	1969	BUDDAH	203 028		BDLP	4016
JOE MACK	B (G	(C) CANDLES IN THE RAIN	1970	BUDDAH	2318 009		BDLP	5003
SAL DE TROIA	G (GJV	(C) CANDLES IN THE RAIN	1970	BUDDAH		US		5060
ERIC WEISSBERG	FDL (G	(D) LEFTOVER WINE	1970	BUDDAH	2318 011		BDLH	5004
VINNIE BELL	G (G	(E) ALL THE RIGHT NOISES	1971	BUDDAH	2319 034			
HUGH McCRACKEN	G (GJU	(F) GARDEN IN THE CITY	197	BUDDAH	2318 054		BDLP	4017
GEORGE DEVENS	D (G	(F) GARDEN IN THE CITY	197	BUDDAH		US		5095
BUDDY SALZMAN	D (G	(G) GOOD BOOK	1971	BUDDAH	2322 001		BDLH	5010
GEORGE MARCH	WIND (G	(G) GOOD BOOK	197	BUDDAH	US 5006	MODE FR	MD9024	
DAVE SANBORN	SAX (U	(H) GATHER ME	1971	NEIGHBORHOOD	US 4700	BUDDAH	4022	
RANDY BRECKER	HRNS (U	(I) FOUR SIDES OF (COMP DBL)	1974	BUDDAH		UK	BDLD	2002
MICHAEL BRECKER	HRNS (U	(J) STONEGROUND WORDS	1972	NEIGHBORHOOD	US 47005	UK	NHTC	251
RICHARD TEE	K (U	(J) STONEGROUND WORDS	1975	ABC	RI			
WILL LEE	B (U	(K) AT CARNEGIE HALL	1973	NEIGHBORHOOD	US 49001	UK	NHSP	301
CHRIS PARKER	D (U	(K) AT CARNEGIE HALL	1975	ABC	RI	UK	ABCL	606
JOHNNY PACHECO	CONGA (U	(L) VERY BEST OF	1974	BUDDAH		UK	BDLP	4001
BILL KEITH	STEEL (J	(M) PLEASE LOVE ME	1974	BUDDAH	US 5132	UK	BDLP	4021
DON PAYNE	B (J	(N) MADRUGADA	1974	NEIGHBORHOOD	US 48001	UK	NH	3003
CHUCK DOMANICO	B (J	(N) MADRUGADA	1975	ANCHOR		UK	ABCL	5085
ROGER KELLAWAY	PNO (J	(O) AS I SEE IT NOW	1975	NEIGHBORHOOD	US 3000	UK	NBH	80636
DONALD McDONALD	D (J	(P) SUNSET & OTHER BEGINNINGS	1975	NEIGHBORHOOD	US 3001	UK	NBH	69168
MEL LEWIS	D (J	(Q) FROM THE BEGINNING (COMP)	1975	ABC		UK	ABLC	5124
RICHARD DAVIS	B (J	(R) PROFILE (COMP)	197	TELDEC		GER		624022
ROBBIE GEORGIA	(W	(S) GOLDEN HOUR (COMP)	1977	PYE		UK	GH	861
BOB LEONE	(W	(T) BEST OF (COMP)	197	BUDDAH	US 5664	UK	BDLP	5705
MARY McCAFFREY	V (W	(U) PHONOGENIC	1978	MIDSONG	US 3033	MCA UK	MCF	8033
LOUIS CABAZA	(W	(V) PHOTOGRAPH	1979	ATLANTIC	US 18190			
TONY BATTAGLIA	(W	(W) BALLROOM STREETS	1979	RCA			XL	03073
STAN KIPPER	D (W							

M125A — TERRY MELCHER

TERRY MELCHER	V K (A	(A) TERRY MELCHER	1974	REPRISE	US MS 2185	UK	k54016
JIM KELTNER	D (A						
HAL BLAINE	D (A	MICHAEL CLARKE	D (A	JOE OSBORN	B (A	CHRIS HILLMAN	B (A
CLARENCE WHITE	G (A	RY COODER	G (A	MIKE DEASY	G (A	TONY MARTIN JR	G (A
SNEAKY PETE	STEEL(A	J D MANESS	STEEL(A	LARRY KNECHTEL	K (A	SPOONER OLDHAM	K (A
JIM HORN	HRNS (A	SLYDE HYDE	HRNS (A	CHUCK FINDLEY	HRNS (A	JACKIE KELSO	HRNS(A
JIMMIE HASKELL	STRING(A	BRUCE JOHNSTON	V (A	SPANKY MACFARLANE	V (A	DORIS DAY	V (A

M126 — BARRY MELTON

BARRY MELTON	G V (ALL	(A) BRIGHT SUN IS SHINING	1970	VANGUARD	US	VSD	6551
DONNIE HATHAWAY	PNO (A	(B) MELTON,LEVY & THE DEY BROTHERS	1972	CBS	US		31279
PHIL UPCHURCH	B (A	(C) THE FISH	1975	UA	UK	UAS	29908
JAY LEVY	K V (B	(D) WE ARE LIKE THE OCEAN	1977	MUSIC IS MEDICINE	US	MIM	9007
RICK DEY	B V (B	(E) LEVEL WITH ME	1981	RAG BABY			1004
JIM BOYES	V (D						
TONY DEY	D (B	DAVE CHARLES	D (C	TOMMY EYRE	K (C	RAY MARTINEZ	G (CD
KEN WHALEY	B (C	ROB PIZER	G (D	BOB FLURIE	G (D	ELMO SHROPSHIRE	BAN(D
PAUL COBBOLD	B (D	MOTH SMITH	D (D	BOB HOGINS	PNO (D	DAVE BRADY	V (D
HEATHER BRADY	V (D						

M127 — MEMBERS

NICKY TESCO	V (AB	(A) AT THE CHELSEA NIGHTCLUB	1979	VIRGIN		V	2120
NIGEL BENNETT	G V (AB	(B) 1980 THE CHOICE IS YOURS	1980	VIRGIN		V	2153
CHRIS PAYNE	B V (AB						
ADRIAN LILLYWHITE	D PERC(AB	STEVE 'RUD' THOMPSON SAX(A	JOE JACKSON	PNO (B	DICK CUTHELL	HRNS (B
JEAN CARROLL	G V (AB	RUPERT HINE	K (B	ALBE DONNELLY	SAX (B	RICO RODRIGUEZ	TROM (B

M128 — MEMPHIS BEND

MICKY GEE	G V (A	(A) GOOD ROCKIN TONITE	1977	UA	UK	UAS	30036
LINCOLN CARR	B (A						
TOM RILEY	D V (A	JOHN JENKINS	PNO (A	B J COLE	STEEL (A	JOHN DAVID	B (A
MICK WEAVER	K (A						

MEMPHIS SLIM	PNO V(ALL	ALL THEM BLUES	1976	DJM	DJD	28012
CHRIS SPEDDING	G (B	CLASSICAL AMERICAN MUSIC	1973	BARCLAY	FR	920 407
PETER GREEN	G (B	AT LAUSANNE	1974	MUSIDISC	EURO CV	1289
DUSTER BENNETT	HCA (B	AT THE GATE OF HORN	19	BARNABY US 31291 JOY UK		143
PETE WINGFIELD	K (B	AT THE GATE OF HORN	19	VEE JAY		1012
LARRY STEELE	B (B	AT THE VILLAGE GATE	19	FOLKWAYS	US	2386
CONRAD ISADORE	D (B	BAD LUCK & TROUBLE	1972	CBS	UK	67248
ROOSEVELT SYKES	K G (N	BLUE MEMPHIS	1971	BARCLAY FR 920214	US	WB1899
BUDDY GUY	G (NS	BLUES IN EUROPE	19	STORYVILLE	SLP	188
JUNIOR WELLS	HCA (N	BLUES IN EUROPE	19	STORYVILLE	SLP	214
PHILIP GUY	G (N	BLUES IS EVERYWHERE	19	GNP CRESCENDO	US	10002
ERNEST JOHNSON	B (N	BLUES MAN	1975	MUSIDISC	FR	ALB187
ROOSEVELT SHAW	D (N	BORN WITH BLUES	19	JEWEL	US	5004
A C REED	SAX (N	BOOGIE WOOGIE	1978	FESTIVAL		ALB247
JIMMY CONLEY	SAX (N	BROKEN SOUL BLUES	19	UA	US LA	6137
ALEXIS KORNER	G (CF	CHICAGO BLUES	19	FOLKWAYS US 3536	UK XTRA	1085
STAN GRIEG	D (CF	CHICAGO BOOGIE	1976	BLACK LION	BLP	30196
LEROY BATCHELOR	B (M	() FRISCO BAY BLUES	1960	FONTANA	UK	688 315
ALFRED ELKINS	B (M	FATTENIN FROGS FOR SNAKES	1976	MELODISC		MLPS12149
		FAVOURITE BLUES	19	FOLKWAYS	US	2387
		GREAT MEMPHIS SLIM	19	AMERICA	AM	6076
		GOIN' BACK TO TENNESSEE	1975	BARCLAY	FR	90034
		HOUSE OF THE BLUES VOL1	19	BLUE STAR	FR	80601
		HOUSE OF THE BLUES VOL 7	19	BLUE STAR	FR	80607
		JUST BLUES	19	PRESTIGE	US	1018
		LEGACY OF THE BLUES	1973	GNP CRESCENDO	US	10017
		LEGACY OF THE BLUES	1973	SONET	UK SNTF	647
		LIVE	1974	STORYVILLE	UK SLP	219
		LEGEND OF THE BLUES VOL 2	19	BEACON	BEAS	6
		LONESOME BLUES	19	SPINERAMA	US	149
		MEMPHIS SLIM	19	B&B		33002
		MEMPHIS SLIM	19	STORYVILLE	UK SLP	118
		MEMPHIS SLIM	19	BARCLAY	FR	920214
		MEMPHIS SLIM	1974	AMERICA	AM	6130
		MEMPHIS SLIM	19	KING	US	885
		MEMPHIS SLIM	19	EVEREST	US	215
		MEMPHIS SLIM	19	CHESS	US	1455
		MEMPHIS SLIM	19	BLACK & WHITE	FR	730 581
		MEMPHIS SLIM (BLUEBIRD No 3)	19	RCA	FXMI	7215
		MEMPHIS SLIM VOL 2	19	EVEREST	US	286
		MEMPHIS SLIM & MATTHEW MURPHY	1974	BLACK & BLUE		33 002
		MEMPHIS SLIM & WILLIE DIXON(PARIS)19		BATTLE	US	6122
		MEMPHIS SLIM & WILLIE DIXON	19	FOLKWAYS	US	2385
		MEMPHIS SLIM & S BOY WILLIAMSON	19	GNP CRESCENDO	US	GNP10003
		MEMPHIS SLIM STORY	19	VOGUE		LD 58330
		MESSIN' AROUND WITH THE BLUES	19	KING	US	1082
		MOTHER EARTH	1972	BUDDAH	BDS	7505
		NO STRAIN	19	PRESTIGE	US	1031
		OLD TIMES NEW TIMES	1972	BARCLAY	FR	920332 3
		PIANO BLUES	19	STORYVILLE	UK SLP	168
		RAINING THE BLUES	19	FANTASY	US	24705
		REAL FOLK BLUES	19	CHESS	US	1510
		REAL HONKY TONK	19	FOLKWAYS	US	3535
		RIGHT NOW	19	TRIP	US	8025
		ROCK ME BABY	1975	BLACK LION		2460 155
		SELF PORTRAIT	19	SCEPTER	US	535
		SOUL BLUES	1973	EMBER	UK	3422
		(S)SOUTH SIDE REUNION	1975	BARCLAY	FR	80501
		(S)SOUTH SIDE REUNION	19	WB	US	2646
		USA	19	CANDID	US	9024
		WORLDS FOREMOST BLUES SINGER	19	STRAND	US	1046
		BLUES & WOMEN	1981	ISABEL	FR 900	506

WAYNE JACKSON	HRNS (C	(A) MEMPHIS HORNS	197	COTILLION	US SD	9014
ROGER HOPPS	HRNS (	(B) HIGH ON MUSIC	1976	RCA RS 1056	APLI	1355
ANDREW LOVE	HRNS (C	(C) GET UP & DANCE	1977	RCA	APLI	2198
ED LOGAN	SAX (	(D) MEMPHIS HORNS BAND 2	19	RCA	APLI	2643
JACK HALE	TROM (C					

JAMES MITCHELL SAX (C   LEWIS COLLINS   SAX (C   CLARENCE McDONALD   K   (C   JAMES GADSON   D (C
MARLO HENDERSON G (C   DAVID SHIELDS   B   (C   JAY GRAYDON   G   (C   BOBBY EATON   B (C
PATRICK MOTEN SYN (C   PAULINHO DA COSTA PERC (C

NOEL MARTIN   D
MORGAN WEBSTER V
STEVE TANNET   G   CHARLEY CASSEY   B

ANDY MENDELSON V K G B(A		(A) ANDY MENDELSON	1978	ARISTA	US AB	4207

RICHARD MENDELSON D   (A
FRANK DE FONDA D   (A   DAVID SHAPIRO   B   (A   GAIL HEIDEMAN   V   (A   GWEN OWENS   V (A
GREG HAWKES   WIND (A   TOM SCOTT   WIND   (A   JOE FARRELL   SAX (A   ERNIE WATTS   SAX (A
ANDY PRATT   V   (A   MARY HASLIM   V   (A   LAURA CREAMER   V   (A

JOE MENDELSON V G B D K HCA(AB   (A) MR MIDDLE OF THE ROAD   19   NOBODY   9230 1027
                                  (B) SOPHISTO JOE MENDELSON   19   TAURUS

(A) GOD FOR A DAY   19   KAMIKAZE

(A) MENTAL AS ANYTHING   1980   VIRGIN   UK

M133
MERGER

BARRY FORD V G WIND D (A1		(A) EXILES IN A BABYLON		1977	SUNSTAR		SUN 1001
IVOR STEADMAN B (A1		(B) ARMAGEDDON TIME		1980	EMERGENCY		
WINSTON BENNETT G V (A12		(!) 1978 (2) LATE 1978					
RAS DANJUMA G (2							
MIKE OSEI D (12 EVER WELLINGTON B (2 TONY OSEI				ORG (12 FAR I PERC (2			
MICHAEL DAN K V (A ADETOKUMBO ILLORIN G (A JIMMY THOMAS				V PERC(A EUNICE GREEN V (A			
PAM NESTOR V PERC(A STRECKER CATIOUS V (A							

M134
MAX MERRITT & THE METEORS

MAX MERRITT G V (ALL		(A) A LITTLE EASIER		1975	ARISTA		UK ARTY 108
STEWART SPEER D (B		(B) OUT OF THE BLUE		1976	ARISTA		UK ARTY 134
LANCE DIXON K SAX V (B		(C) KEEPING IN TOUCH		1978	POLYDOR		UK 2383 514
MARTIN'FUZZ' DENIZ B V (B							
JOHN GOURD G (B							

M135
NEIL MERRYWEATHER

NEIL MERRYWEATHER B G V(ALL		(A) NEIL MERRYWEATHER & THE BOERS		19	KENT		US KST 546
MICHAEL WILLIS G (E		(B) WORD OF MOUTH		1969	CAPITOL		US STBB 278
TIM McGOVERN D (E		(C) IVAR AVENUE REUNION		1970	RCA		US LPS 4442
ED GEMONT SYN (E		(D) VACUUM CLEANER		1971	RCA	UK SF 8210	US LSP 4485
STEVE MILLER G V (B		(E) SPACE RANGERS		1974	MERCURY	UK 9100008	US SRMI 1007
BARRY GOLDBERG K (B		(F) KRYPTONITE		1975	MERCURY		US SRMI 1024
DAVE MASON G (B							
CHARLIE MUSSELWHITE HCA(B HOWARD ROBERTS G (B DAVE BURT				G V (B SIDNEY GEORGE HRNS (D			
COFFI HALL D (BD EDWARD ROTH FDL FLT K(BD KAL DAVID				G (D HUEY SULLIVAN PNO (D			
ROBIN BOERS D (AD J J VELKER K (D JOHN RICHARDSON				G (DA LYNN CAREY V (D			

M136
MERSEYBEATS

TONY CRANE G V (A		(A) MERSEYBEATS		1964	FONTANA		UK TL 5210
AARON WILLIAMS G V (A		(B) MERSEYBEATS		1965	WING		WL 1163
BILLY KINSLEY B V (A		(C) ENGLANDS BEST SELLERS		19	ARC INTERNATIONAL	US ARC 834	
JOHN BANKS D (A		(EP) MERSEYBEATS		1964	FONTANA		UK TE 17423
JOHN GUSTAFSON B (		(EP) ON STAGE		1964	FONTANA		UK TE 17422
BOB GARDNER B (		(EP) WISHIN' & HOPIN'		1964	FONTANA		UK TE 17432

M136A
MERTON PARKAS

MICK TALBOT PNO (A		(A) FACE IN THE CROWD		1979	BEGGARS BANQUET	UK	BEGA 11
DANNY TALBOT G (A							
SIMON SMITH D (A NEIL HURRELL B V (A							

M136B
MESSAGE

ALLAN MURDOCH G (ABCDE		(A) THE DAWN ANEW IS COMING		197	BELLAPHON		BLPS19081
TOM McGUIGAN V WIND SYN(ABCD		(B) FROM BOOKS AND DREAMS		1973	BELLAPHON		BLPS19159
HORST STACHELHAUS B (ABCD		(C) MESSAGE		1975	NOVA 622213 DECCA UK SKLR5213		
GERHARD SCHABER PERC V(A		(D) SYNAPSE		1976	NOVA 622523		
ALLAN'TAFF' FREEMAN SYN V(AE		(E) ASTRAL JOURNEY 1978		BRAIN	0060 165		
BILLY TABBERT G V (A							
GUNTHER KLINGER D (B MANFRED VON BOHR D PERC(CD TONY GREAVES				WIND (D SAMMY KUNIG V SAX PERC(E			
PETER SCHMIDT D PERC(E FRITZ GROGER G PERC(E JEANETTE MACLEOD				V (E MANFRED KNEIL VIBES (E			
REINER NAGEL B K (E UTE NAGEL V (E							

M136C
JIM MESSINA

JIM MESSINA V (A		(A) OASIS		1979	CBS	UK	83803

M137
METABOLIST

ANTON LOACH K (		(A) METABOLIST (EP)		19	DROMM		DR01
MALCOLM LANE G (		(B) HANSTEN KLORK		19	DROMM		DR02
SIMON MILLWARD B (JED KINGSFORD D (							

M137A
METEORS

HUGO SINZHEIMER V (A		(A) TEENAGE HEART		1979	EMI		EMC 3315
FERDINAND BAKKER G V (A							
JOHN VEE B (A AKE DANIALSON K (A ERIC DE ZWAAN				G V (A JOB TARENSKEEN V D SAX(A			

M138
THE METERS

ART NEVILLE K (ABCDEFGHI		(A) THE METERS		1971	JOSIE	US	4010
CYRIL NEVILLE PERC (FGHI		(B) LOOK KA PY PY		1972	JOSIE	US	4011
LEO NOCENTELLI G V (ABCDEFHIG		(C) CABBAGE ALLEY		1972	REPISE UK K33242	US	MS 2076
GEORGE PORTER B (ABCDEFGHI		(D) REJUVENATION		1974	REPRISE UK K54027	US	MS 2200
JOE MODELISTE D (EFHIABCDG		(E) CISSY STRUT		1974	ISLAND UK ILPS9250		
EARL KING V (H		(E) SECOND LINE STRUT		1980	CHARLY RI CRB 1009		
KURT McGETTRICK SAX (I		(F) FIRE ON THE BAYOU		1975	REPRISE UK K54044	US	MS 2228
SWAMP TABERNACLE CHOIR (I		(G) BEST OF THE METERS		1975	REPRISE UK K54076		
		( ) BEST OF THE METERS		1975	VIRGO		SV12002
		(H) TRICK BAG		1976	REPRISE UK K54078	US	MS 2252
		(I) NEW DIRECTION		1977	WB UK K56378	US	MS 3042
		(J) GOOD OLD FUNKY MUSIC		1979	PYE UK PKL5578		
		(EP) LOOK KA PY PY		1980	CHARLY	UK	CTD 113

M138A
PAT METHENY

PAT METHENY G B (ALL		(A) BRIGHT SIZE LIFE		1975	ECM		1073
JACO PASTORIUS B (A		(B) WATERCOLOURS		1977	ECM		1097
BOB MOSES D (A		(C) PAT METHENY GROUP		1978	ECM		1114
LYLE MAYS K (BCE		(D) NEW CHAUTAUQUA		1978	ECM		1131
EBERHARD WEBER B (B		(E) AMERICAN GARAGE		1979	ECM		1155
DAN GOTTLIEB D (BCE		(F) 80 81		1980	ECM		
MARK EGAN B (CE							
MICHAEL BRECKER SAX (F JACK DEJOHNETTE D (F CHARLIE HADEN				B (F			

M139
METHOD

MICK BRASSINGTON V (A		(A) METHOD		1976	UK	UK	UKAL1020
JOHN HUGHES G (A							

M139A
METHUSALEM

BUBU HIFIKER D V (A		(A) FOR OUR FRIENDS		1979	METHUSALEM		METH7901
ANDY SABER G V (A							
RICK HOCHULI B V (A FERNANDO PALENCIAS G V (A ROBY WURGLER				G V (A MARCO RAUBER K (A			

SEAN LYONS   G   (AB   (A) METRO   1977 TRANSATLANTIC   UK TRAG 340
PETER GODWIN V SAX SYN(AB   (B) NEW LOVE   1979 EMI   UK EMC 3295
DUNCAN BROWNE V G K B (A
JOHN GIBLIN   B   (A   SIMON PHILLIPS   D   (A GRAHAM PRESKETT   VLN (A BARRY HUSBAND   V (A
TONY ADAMS   B V (B   COLIN WIGHT   G   (B JOHN LAFORGE   D   (B
                                    AUGIE MEYER   M141

AUGIE MEYER   (ALL   (A) YOU AINT ROLLIN YOUR ROLL   1973 PARAMOUNT   US
DOUG SAHM   (D   WESTERN HEAD MUSIC CO   19 POLYDOR   US   24 4069
                                    LIVE AT THE LONGNECK   197 TEXAS   US   1002
                                (D) FINALLY IN LIGHTS   1977 TEXAS   US TRC 1005
                                    FREDDI MEYER   M141A
FREDDI MEYER   (A   (A) FREDDI MEYER   19   BARN   NARB 002
                                    MI SEX   M141B
                                (A) COMPUTOR GAMES   1980 CBS   UK 84157
                                    MIAMIS   M141C

JIMMY WYNBRANDT   G V (
TOMMY WYNBRANDT   G V (
DALE POWERS   B V (TOM MANDEL   K V (GEORGE DAY   D V (
                                    STEPHEN MICAS   M142
STEPHEN MICAS   (A) ARCHAIC CONCERTS   1976 CAROLINE   UK C 1517
                                (B) IMPLOSIONS   1977 JAPO   60017
                                    GORDON MICHAELS   M143
GORDON MICHAELS V G K (A   (A) STARGAZER   1979 HORIZON   US SP 737
HUGH McCRACKEN   G HCA(A
RICK MAROTTA   D   (A   TONY LEVIN   B   (A RICHARD TEE   K   (A MIKE MAINIERI   PERC(A
GEORGE YOUNG   FLT (A   ED WALSH   SYN (A DAVID SANBORN   SAX (A GEORGE MARGE   WIND(A
LISA GILKYSON   V   (A   ARTHUR JENKINS PERC (A BILL BROWN   HRNS (A LINDA REDDOWOLF V (A
                                    LEE MICHAELS   M144
LEE MICHAELS   V B K(ALL   (A) CARNIVAL OF LIFE   1968 A&M   US   4140
KEITH KNUDSEN   D   (GH   (B) RECITAL   1969 A&M   UK AMLS 928 US   4152
JOEL CHRISTIE   B   (G   (C) LEE MICHAELS   1969 A&M   UK AMLS 956 US   4199
DRAKE LEVIN   G   (G   (D) BARREL   1970 A&M   UK AMLS 991 US   4249
NORMA KINNEY   PERC (E   (E) FIFTH   1971 A&M   UK AMLS64302 US   4302
RICHARD MADRID   PERC (E   (F) LIFE   1972 ARIOLA   86725   US A&M 3518
HENRY LEWY   PERC (E   (G) SPACE & FIRST TAKES   1972 A&M   UK AMLS64336 US   4336
JOEL LARSEN   SAX (E   (H) NICE DAY FOR SOMETHING 1973 CBS   UK   65651 US   32275
BARTHOLOMEW SMITH-FROST D(C   (J) TAILFACE   1974 CBS   UK   US   32846
                                    SATURN RINGS   197 ABC   US ABCD 684
                        MAX MIDDLETON & ROBERT AHWAI   M145
MAX MIDDLETON   K   (A   (A) ANOTHER SLEEPER   1979 HARVEST   SHSP 4103
ROBERT AHWAI   G   (A
RICHARD BAILEY   D   (A   KUMA HARADA   B   (A DARRYL LEE QUE   PERC (A STEVE GREGORY   WIND (A
BUD BEADLE   WIND (A GEORGE CHISHOLM TPT (A TREVOR BARBER   TPT (A CHRIS RAINBOW   V (A
LINDA TAYLOR   V   (A   CHRISTIE THOMPSON V (A
                                    MIDNIGHT OIL   M146
ROB HIRST   D V (A   (A) HEAD INJURIES   1979 POWDER WORKS   AUST MLF 322
PETER GARRETT   V   (A
JAMES MOGINIE   G K (A   ANDREW JAMES   B V (A MARTIN POTSEY   G   (A
                                    MIDNIGHT RAGS   M146A
PAUL ROLAND   (A) WEREWOLF OF LONDON   1980 ACE
                                    MIDNIGHT SUN   M147
BENT HESSELMANN   WIND (ABCD   (A) RAINBOW BAND   1970 SONET   SLPS 1523
NIELS BRONDSTED   K   (ABCD   (B) RAINBOW BAND (DIFF VOCALS) 1971 SONET   SLPS1523A
CARSTEN SMEDGAARD D   (ABCD   (B) MIDNIGHT SUN   1972 MCA   MKPS 2019
PEER FROST   G   (ABC   (C) WALKING CIRCLES   1972 SONET SLPS 1536 UK MCA MKPS 2024
BO STIEF   B   (ABC   (D) MIDNIGHT DREAM   1974 SONET   SLPS 1547
LARS BISGAARD   V   (A
HANS LAURIDSEN   V   (C   JENS ELBØL   B   (D TOM HEATH   G   (D ALLAN MORTENSEN V (B
                                    MIGHTY BABY   M148
PETE WATSON   G   (1   (A) MIGHTY BABY   1969 HEAD   UK HDLS6002
MIKE EVANS   B   (12345A (B) A JUG OF LOVE   1971 BLUE HORIZON UK   2931 001
ROGER POWELL   D   (12345A (1) 1963   (2) ACTION 1966 (3) ACTION   (4) ACTION (5) 1968 71
REG KING   G   (123
ALAN 'BAM 'KING   G   (12345A IAN WHITEMAN V WIND K(245A MARTIN STONE   G (345A
                                    MIGHTY DIAMONDS   M149
DONALD SHAW   V   (BCDEF   (A) RIGHT TIME   1976 VIRGIN   US 34235 UK V 2078
FIZTROY SIMPSON   V   (BCDEF   (B) ICE ON FIRE   1977 VIRGIN   US 34235 UK V 2078
LLOYD FERGUSON   V   (BCDEF   (C) PLANET EARTH   1978 VIRGIN   UK V 2102
DWIGHT RICHARDS   D   (B   (D) STAND UP   1978 CHANNEL ONE
KENNETH WILLIAMS PERC (B   (E) DEEPER ROOTS   1979 FRONT LINE   UK FLD 6001
STEVE HUGHES   G   (B   (F) TELL ME WHAT'S WRONG   1980 J&J   US
HERMAN MARQUIS   SAX (CF
DAVE BARARD   B   (B   ROBERT DABON   PNO (B CLYDE KERR JNR   TPT (B JOHN LONGO   TPT (B
ALVIN THOMAS   SAX (B   MICHAEL PIERCE SAX (B CARL BLOUIN   SAX (B THEODORE ROYAL G (B
WARDELL QUEZERGUE K   (B   RAYMOND JONES   PNO (B ISAAC BOLDEN   PNO (B CARLTON DAVIS   D (B
EARL CHINNA SMITH G   (B   SLY DUNBAR   D   (CF STICKY   PERC (CF TOMMY McCOOK   SAX (CF
                                    MIGHTY FLEA   M149A
GENE'MIGHTY FLEA'CONNERS V TROM(A   (A) LET THE GOOD TIMES ROLL 1973 BIG BEAR 19 + POLYDOR79 2460185
                                    MIGIL FIVE   M150
                                (A) MOCKINGBIRD HILL   1964 PYE   UK NPL 18093
                                (B) COME DANCE WITH   1969 JOY   JOYS 138
                                    MIKE, SLOT & BUMPER   M150A
                                (A) AMAZIN' R&B   (EP)   1979 BLUEPORT   BLU3

M151
BUDDY MILES

```
BUDDY MILES    V D G K B   (ALL     (A) EXPRESSWAY TO YOUR SKULL      1968  MERCURY    US SR61196   UK SMCL 20137
HERBIE RICH    ORG SAX    (A       (B) ELECTRIC CHURCH                1969  MERCURY    US SR61222   UK SMCL 20163
JIM McCARTY    G          (ABC     (C) THEM CHANGES                   1970  MERCURY    US SR61280   UK    6338 016
BILL RICH      B          (A       (D) WE GOT TO LIVE TOGETHER        1970  MERCURY    US SR61313   UK    6338 028
RON WOODS      D          (A       (E) MESSAGE TO THE PEOPLE          1970  MERCURY    US SRM1608   UK    6338 048
TERRENCE CLEMENTS SAX     (A       (F) LIVE                           1971  MERCURY    US SRM7500   UK    6641 033
MARCUS DOUBLEDAY TPT      (A       (G) WITH CARLOS SANTANA            1972  CBS        US    31308   UK       65142
VIRGIL GONSALVES WIND     (A       (H) CHAPTER VII                    1973  CBS        US    32048   UK       65406
BILL McPHERSON WIND       (AD      (J) BOOGER BEAR                    1973  CBS        US    32694   UK       65820
DUANE HITCHINGS ORG       (BCH     (K) ALL THE FACES OF BUDDY MILES   1974  EPIC       US    33089   UK       80349
TOBIE WYNN     SAX        (BC      (L) MORE MILES PER GALLON          1975  CASABLANCA US     7019   UK        4006
JAMES TATUM    SAX        (BC      (M) BICENTENNIAL GATHERING         1976  CASABLANCA US     7024
BOBBY ROCK     SAX        (B
PETER CARTER   TPT        (BC
TOM HALL       TPT        (BCF  BOB PARKINS      ORG  (C    WALLY ROSSUNOLO  G    (C   BILLY COX      B    (C
ROBERT PITTMAN SAX        (C    TEDDY BLANDIN    TPT  (C    CHARLIE KARP     G    (CDEF BOB HOGINS    K TROM(CDF
ROBIN McBRIDE  K          (C    ANDRE LEWIS      ORG  (CDEH MARLO HENDERSON  G    (CDEH DAVID HULL    B    (CDEF
LEE ALLEN      SAX        (CD   PHIL WOOD        HRNS (CD   MARK WILLIAMS    WIND (CD  ROLAND ROBINSON B   (CJ
FRED ALLEN     PERC       (DE   JOE PORTER       TPT  (D    DICK GABRIEL     SAX  (D   MICHAEL FUGATE  TPT (E
HANK REDD      SAX        (EF   STEMSY HUNTER    SAX  (EFL  DONNIE BECK      ORG  (FJM ADRIAN CURTIS  G V (H
RON JOHNSON    B          (H    ROBERT HOGGINS   G V  (H    RICHARD APLANALP SAX  (H   BILLY SPRAGUE   HRNS(H
DAVID DHALSTON HRNS       (H    DENISE PANTOS MILES D (H    WILLIE BOBO      PERC (H   VICTOR PANTOJA  CONGA(H
JAMES BRADSHAW G          (H    PAUL GURVITZ(CURTIS) V (H   STEVE BUSHFIELD  G    (J   BOB FERREIRA    SAX (J
PAT O'HARA     TROM       (J    PETER WALKER     TPT  (J    BILL ATWOOD      TPT  (J   MINGO LEWIS     PERC(J
JERRY PETERS   K          (K    CLARENCE McDONALD K   (K    JAMES JAMERSON   B    (K   EDWARD GREENE   D   (K
KEN HAWKINS    G          (K    RAY PARKER       G    (K    MELVIN RAGIN     G    (K   JOE CLAYTON     PERC(K
GENE ESTES     PERC       (K    ERNIE WATTS      SAX  (K    BEN SCHULTZ      G K  (LM  BOBBY BERGE     D   (LM
STEVE LAWRENCE SAX        (LM   KEN WALTER       TROM (LM   TOM BRAY         TPT  (LM  PAUL CACRA      TPT (LM
STEVIE WONDER  K          (L    AL BROWN         D    (L    JOHN MALLER      D    (M   DANNY HULL      SAX (M
RON PERRY      B          (M    BOYD ALBRITTON   G    (M    DICKIE BETTS     G    (M
```

M152
JOHN MILES

```
JOHN MILES     G V K(ALL    (A) REBEL                1976  DECCA  UK SKL 5231  US LONDON 660
BOB MARSHALL   B    (ABCD   (B) STRANGER IN THE CITY 1976  DECCA  UK TXS  118  US LONDON 682
BARRY BLACK    D    (ABCD   (C) ZARAGON              1978  DECCA  UK TXS  126  US ARISTA4176
GARY MOBERLEY  K    (B      (D) MMMMMPH              1979  DECCA  UK TXSR 135
BRIAN CHATTON  K    (D
ORCHESTRA           (D
```

M153
CHRISTOPHER MILK

```
CHRISTOPHER MILK    (A      (A) SOME PEOPLE WILL DRINK ANYTHING  1977  REPRISE       US MS 2111
```

M154
MILK & COOKIES

```
IAN NORTH      K G  (A      (A) MILK & COOKIES      1977  ISLAND    UK  ILPS 9320
JUSTIN STRAUSS V    (A
SAL MAIDA      B    (A   MIKE RUIZ   D   (A   JIM GREGORY   B   (
```

M155
MILKWOOD

```
BEN ORR             (       (A) MILKWOOD          1972  PARAMOUNT   US
RICHARD OCASEK      (       (B) HOW'S THE WEATHER  19   PARAMOUNT   US          6046
```

M156
MILLENIUM

```
CURT BOETCHER    V    (A       (A) BEGIN          1968  CBS    US  CS 9663
MICHAEL FENNELLY G V  (A
LEE MALLORY      (A   JOE STEC      (A   RED RHODES    STEEL(A   DOUG RHODES     (A
KEITH OLSEN      (A   PAT SHANAHAN  (A   RON EDGAR     (A        DOUG DILLARD    (A
JIM RYAN         (A
```

M157
FRANKIE MILLER

```
FRANKIE MILLER V G  (ALL     (A) ONCE IN A BLUE MOON   1973  CHRYSALIS  UK  CHR 1036
ALLEN TOUSSAINT K   (B       (B) HIGH LIFE             1974  CHRYSALIS  UK  CHR 1052
JOE WILSON     G    (B       (C) THE ROCK              1975  CHRYSALIS  UK  CHR 1088
BOB ANDREWS    K V  (A       (D) FULL HOUSE            1977  CHRYSALIS  UK  CHR 1128
BRINSLEY SCHWARZ G  (A       (E) DOUBLE TROUBLE        1978  CHRYSALIS  UK  CHR 1174
BILLY RANKIN   D    (A       (F) FALLING IN LOVE       1979  CHRYSALIS  UK  CHR 1220
IAN GOMM       G    (A       (G) EASY MONEY            1980  CHRYSALIS  UK  CHR 1268
NICK LOWE      B V  (A       (EP) JEALOUS GUY          1977  CHRYSALIS  UK  CHS 2184
TOM ROBB       B    (B       (1) FEB 1978 TOUR   (2) MARCH 1978 TOUR
MIKE HUEY      D    (B       (3) MAY 1978 TOUR  (4) SEPT  1978 TOUR
G C COLEMAN    D    (B
AUBURN BURRELL G    (B    BARRY BAILEY    G    (B   LESTER CALISTE  TROM (B   CLYDE KERR JR     TROM(B
GARY BROWN     SAX  (B    JOHN LONGO  TPT      (B   ALVIN THOMAS    SAX  (B   HENRY McCULLOUGH   G   (C
MICK WEAVER    K    (C    CHRIS STEWART  B(CDE123   STU PERRY       D    (C   RAY MINHINNIT     G   (D
JAMES HALL     K    (D    GRAHAM DEACON   D    (D   KAREN LAWRENCE  V    (E   HUGH BURNS        G   (3
FRAN BYRNE     D    (F4   RICHARD SUPA    V    (E   STEPHEN TYLER   V HCA(E   MARTIN DROVER     TPT (E12
CHRIS MERCER   SAX  (E123 PAUL CARRACK    K V(EF12  B J WILSON      D    (E123 RAY RUSSELL      G   (E2
MICK MOODY     G    (1    LANI GROVES     V    (E   ERIC TROYER     V    (E   CHRIS SLADE       D   (F
TEX COMER      B    (F4   DAVE WINTOUR    B    (F   BARRIE GUARD    PERC (F   TIM RENWICK       G   (F
ED DEAN        G    (F4   TERRY BRITTON   G    (F   STEVE SIMPSON   G    (F4  LINDA TAYLOR      V   (F
RON ASPERY     HRNS (F    CHRIS HALL      K    (F   CHRIS SPEDDING  G    (D   RABBIT            K   (D
GARY BROOKER   K V  (D    MEMPHIS HORNS   HRNS (D   LARRY LONDIN    D PERC(G   REG YOUNG         G   (G
BOBBY THOMPSON G    (G    JOE OSBORN      B    (G
```

M158
JACOB MILLER

```
JACOB MILLER        (A      (A) DREAD DREAD      1978  UA    US   UALA 806
                            ( ) WANTED          1979
```

M158A
STEPHEN MILLER

```
STEPHEN MILLER K    (AB     (A) MILLER & COXHILL  1974  CAROLINE  UK  C 1503
LOL COXHILL   WIND  (A      (B) STORY SO FAR      1974  CAROLINE  UK  C 1507
LAURIE ALLEN  PERC  (B
```

STEVE MILLER BAND

STEVE MILLER	G K V(ALL	(A) CHILDREN OF THE FUTURE	1968	CAPITOL	2920	718
LONNIE TURNER	B(13456ABCDEHJK	(B) SAILOR	1969	CAPITOL	2984	719
TIM DAVIS	B (12ABCDE	(AB) LIVING IN USA(DBL)	1973	CAPITOL		717
JAMES COOKE	G (1EJK	(C) BRAVE NEW WORLD	1969	CAPITOL		184
JIM PETERMAN	K (AB	(D) YOUR SAVING GRACE	1970	CAPITOL		331
BOZ SCAGGS	G V (AB	(E) NUMBER FIVE	1970	CAPITOL		436
BEN SIDRAN	K (CDEG	(F) ROCK LOVE	1971	CAPITOL		748
NICKY HOPKINS	K (CDE	(G) RECALL THE BEGINNING	1972	CAPITOL		11022
JIMMY MILLER	G (E	(H) THE JOKER	1973	CAPITOL		11235
BOBBY THOMPSON	B (E	(J) FLY LIKE AN EAGLE	1976	MERCURY UK 9286177	US CAPITOL	11497
BOBBY WINKLEMAN	B (2	(K) BOOK OF DREAMS	1977	MERCURY UK 9286455	US CAPITOL	11630
ROSS VALORY	B (F					
JOHN KING	D (45H	( ) REVOLUTION(QUICKSILVER,MOTHER EARTH)1968 UA		UK 29069	US UA	UAS5185
JACK KING	D (FG3	( ) TRIPLE SET(QUICKSILVER,BAND)	19	CAPITOL		STCR 288
GERALD JOHNSON	B (345GH	( ) ANTHOLOGY	1973	CAPITOL UK ESTSP12 US		11114
JIM KELTNER	D (G	( ) BEST OF	1973	ELECTROLA	EURO SHZE 901	
DICKY THOMPSON	K (345GH	( ) MASTERS OF ROCK	1974	EMI	EURO 054 81583	
GARY MALLABER	D (GJK	( ) PROFILES	1974	EMI	EURO 284 81581	
LES DUDEK	G (6JK	( ) THE LEGEND	1975	CAPITOL	VMP 1008	
DOUG CLIFFORD	D (6	( ) ADVENTURES OF A SPACE COWBOY	1975	CAPITOL	EURO 054 81645	
NORTON BUFFALO	V HCA(K	( ) BEST OF 1968 73	1977	CAPITOL	EST 24058	
DAVID DENNY	G (K	( ) GREATEST HITS 1974/78	1978	MERCURY UK 9199916	US CAPITOL	11822
BYRON ALLRED	K (K					
JOHN McFEE	G (J	(1) NOV 1966	(2) NOV 1969/70	(3) JAN 1972		
JOACHIM YOUNG	K (KJ	(4) MAR 1972	(5) OCT 1972	(6) JULY 1975		
BUD BILLINGS	TPT (K					

KENNY JOHNSON	D (JK	SNEAKY PETE KLEINOW STEEL(H GREG DOUGLAS	G (K	BUDDY SPICHER	FDL (E
JAMES COTTON	HCA (J	ROGER CLARK D (34G CHARLIE McCOY	HCA (E	WAYNE MOSS	G B (E
LEE MICHAELS	K (E	JIMMY TILLMAN B (E CHARLIE CALMESE	B (K	BOB GLAUB	B (K
JESSE ED DAVIS	G (G	PAUL McCARTNEY B D V(C			

MILLINGTON

JEAN MILLINGTON	B V (A	(A) LADIES ON THE STAGE	1978	UA	US LA 821	UK UAG 30158
JUNE MILLINGTON	G V (A					

LEO ADAMIAN	D V (A	TONY RAMOS V (A	IRENE CARA	V (A	VICKI RANDLE	V (A
FAITH FUSILLO	V (A	GORDON GRODY V (A	CHRIS WILLIAMSON	V (A	FLEMING WILLIAMS	V (A
TOM SCOTT	WIND (A	DEBBY GABER G (A	SNEAKY PETE	STEEL(A	RALPH SCHUCKETT	K (A
COLLEEN STEWART	K (A	TOM SELLERS K (A	MARGO LEWIS	V (A	ED GREENE	D (A
SCOTT EDWARDS	B (A	BRIE HOWARD V (A	ROLAND ROZZELLE	K (A	LARRY CARLTON	G (A
KENNY NEMIROFF	K (A	GARY COLEMAN PERC (A	JUNE ADAMIAN	V (A	BRYAN PARRIS	D (A
ELLEN SHIPLEY	V (A	NEGRA V (A	LEE RIENOUR	G (A	DEAN PARKS	G (A
CHRISTOPHER BOND	G (A	EARL SLICK G (A				

GARNET MIMMS

GARNET MIMMS	V (ALL	REMEMBER (EP)	1973	UA		UK REM 403
SAM BELL	V (	HAS IT ALL	1978	ARISTA		UK SPART1032
ZOLA PEARNELL	V (	AS LONG AS I HAVE YOU	1964	UA	US	UAS 6396
CHARLES BOYER	V (	CRY BABY	1963	UA	US	UAS 6305
		I'LL TAKE GOOD CARE OF YOU	1966	UA	US	UAS 6498

(WAYNE FONTANA) & THE MINDBENDERS

WAYNE FONTANA	V (	(A) WAYNE FONTANA & THE MINDBENDERS	1965	FONTANA	UK	TL 5230
ERIC STEWART	G V (	(A) WFATM(SAME AS ABOVE +3 TRACKS)	1967	FONTANA SPEC		SFL 13106
		(A) WFATM(SAME AS A +2 TRACKS)	1967	WING		WL 1166
BOB LAND	B (	(B) ERIC RICK WAYNE BOB	1966	FONTANA	UK	TL 5257
RICK ROTHWELL	D (	(C) WAYNE ONE(WAYNE SOLO)	196	FONTANA	UK	STL 5351
PAUL HANCOX	D (	(D) THE MINDBENDERS	1966	FONTANA	UK	SFL 13045
GRAHAM GOULDMAN	G (	(E) WITH WOMAN IN MIND	1967	FONTANA	UK	STL 5403
JAMES O'NEIL	G (	(F) A GROOVY KIND OF LOVE	1967	FONTANA US(M) 27554 (S)		67554
		( ) TO SIR WITH LOVE(ON SOUNDTRACK)	1967	FONTANA	UK STL	5446

MINK DEVILLE

WILLY DE VILLE	V G (ABC	(A) MINK DEVILLE	1977	CAPITOL		11631
BOBBY LEONARDS	K (AB	(B) RETURN TO MAGENTA	1978	CAPITOL		11780
VAL HERON	V (A	(C) LE CHAT BLEU	1980	CAPITOL		25390
RUBIN SIQUENZA	B SAX(AB					

LOUIE ERLANGER	G V (ABC	THOMAS R ALLEN D (A	STEVE DOUGLAS	SAX (BC	RITCH COLBERT	K (
JACKIE KELSO	SAX (B	DR JOHN PNO (A	DAVID FORMAN	V (B	LEON DOUGLAS	V (B
MIKE JOHNSON	V (A	MAX BOWMAN V (AB	JAKE		V (C	

MIRAGE

GEORGE KHAN	SAX FLT(A	(A) NOW YOU SEE IT	1977	COMPENDIUM	NORWAY FIDARO 9	
BRIAN GODDING	G (A					
STEVE COOK	B (A	DAVE SHEEN D (A				

STEVE MIRO & THE EYES

STEVE MIRO	V G (A	(A) RUDE INTRUSIONS	1980	OBJECT		OBJ008
JIMMY CARTER	B V (A					
BRIAN MARTIN	D V (A	DUNCAN PRESTBURY K V (A	STEVE SOLAMAR	HCA (A	FREDRICK BURROWS	TPT (A

MR BIG

JEFF DICKEN	HCA B G V (AB	(A) SWEET SILENCE	1975	EMI	UK	EMC 3101
PETE CROWTHER	G B (AB	(B) MR BIG	1977	EMI	UK	EMC 3171
EDDIE CARTER	G V (B					
VINCE CHAULK	V D (AB	JOHN MARTER D V (	JOHN BURNIP	D (A	IAN BLUNSDON	K (A
JOHN PUNTER	SYN (A	ROBERT HIRSCHMAN B TROM(A				

MR BLOE

		(A) GROOVIN WITH MR BLOE	1973 SILVERLINE 036 + DJM 1974	DJLPS409	

MR FOX

BOB PEGG	V G B K (AB	(A) MR FOX	1970	TRANSATLANTIC	UK	TRA226
CAROLE PEGG	V FDL (AB	(B) THE GYPSY	1971	TRANSATLANTIC	UK	TRA236
ALUN EVANS	D (AB	(AB THE COMPLETE MR FOX	1975	TRANSATLANTIC	UK	TRA303
BARRY LYONS	B DULC (AB					
ANDREW MASSEY	CELLO(A	JOHN MYATT WIND(A RICHIE BULL	B BANJ(	GRIDLEY TABERNACLE ORCH (B	
NICK STRUTT	MULTI(					

M167　　　　　　　　　　　　　　　　MISTRESS
```
CHARLIE WILLIAMS  G V  (A              (A) MISTRESS                    1979    RSO                      RSS 14
DAVID BROWN       B    (A
KENNY HOPKINS     G V  (A   DANNY CHAUNCEY   G V (A   MIKE UTLEY       K    (A   DOUG DILLARD     BAN (A
CHRIS PAULSEN     D    (A   JOHN McFEE       STEEL(A   RICK CLARK       V    (A   GREG DOUGLAS     G   (
DAVE WALKER       V    (    SKIP OLSEN       B    (
```
M167A　　　　　　　　　　　　　　　　MISTY
```
                                      (A) IN ROOTS(LIVE)             1979    PEOPLE UNITE             PU003
```
M168　　　　　　　　　　　　　　　MISUNDERSTOOD
```
GLEN FERNANDO CAMPBELL STEEL(AB   (A)MISUNDERSTOOD 1966 1967   (B) 1969
TONY HILL        G V  (A
GREG TREADWAY    G V  (A   RICK BROWN       V   (A   STEVE WHITING    B    (A   RICK MOE    D    (A
STEVE HOARD      V    (B   DAVY D'LIST      G   (B   NICK POTTER      B    (B   CHRIS MERCER     SAX(B
NEIL HUBBARD     G    (B   GUY EVANS        D   (B
```
M169　　　　　　　　　　　　　　　BLUE MITCHELL
```
BLUE MITCHELL    HRNS (A              THING TO DO              19    BLUENOTE             BST 84178
                                     BRING IT HOME TO ME      19    BLUENOTE             BST 84228
                                     BOSS HORN                19    BLUENOTE             BST 84257
                                     HEADS UP                 19    BLUENOTE             BST 84272
                                     COLLISION IN BLACK       19    BLUENOTE             BST 84300
                                     BANTU VILLAGE            19    BLUENOTE             BST 84324
                                     GRAFFITI BLUES           1974  MAINSTREAM           MSL  1026
                                     MANY SHADES OF BLUE      1975  MAINSTREAM           MSL  1028
```
M169A　　　　　　　　　　　　　　IAN MITCHELL BAND
```
IAN MITCHELL    V G K B  (A          (A) LONELY NIGHTS         1979  WB              UK   K 58070
JON JAY         B V G(A
NICKY DIAMOND   K V  (A   PAUL JACKSON G K V(A   LINDSAY SIMON HONEY D V K(A
```
M170　　　　　　　　　　　　　　　　JONI MITCHELL
```
JONI MITCHELL     V G K(ALL         (A) JONI MITCHELL          1968 REPRISE US   6293   UK  K 44051
TOM SCOTT         WIND (EJ          (B) CLOUDS                 1969 RERPISE US   6341   UK  K 44070
WILTON FELDER     B    (EFGH        (C) LADIES OF THE CANYON   1970 REPRISE US   6376   UK  K 44085
RUSS KUNKEL       D    (DE          (D) BLUE                   1971 REPRISE US   2038   UK  K 44128
BOBBYE HALL       PERC (EJK         (E) FOR THE ROSES          1972 ASYLUM  US   5056   UK SYLA 8753
GRAHAM NASH       V HCA(EFGH        (E) FOR THE ROSES          1975 ASYLUM           RI UK  K 53007
JAMES BURTON      G    (E           (F) COURT & SPARK          1974 ASYLUM  US 7E1001   UK SYLA 8756
STEPHEN STILLS    G B  (DE          (F) COURT & SPARK          1975 ASYLUM           RI UK  K 53002
JAMES TAYLOR      G V  (DH          (G) MILES OF AISLES        1974 ASYLUM  US    202   UK SYSP 902
SNEAKY PETE KLEINOW STEEL(D         (G) MILES OF AISLES        1975 ASYLUM           RI UK  K 63001
JOHN GUERIN       D    (FGHJK       (H) HISSING OF SUMMER LAWNS 1975 ASYLUM US 7E1051  UK SYLA 8763
MAX BENNETT       B    (FGHJ        (H) HISSING OF SUMMER LAWNS 1975 ASYLUM          RI UK  K 53018
JIM HUGHART       B    (F           (J) HEJIRA                 1976 ASYLUM  US 7E1087   UK  K 53053
MILT HOLLAND      PERC (CF          (K) DON JUANS RECKLESS DAUGHTER 1977 ASYLUM US  107 UK  K 63003
CHUCK FINDLEY     TPT  (FGHJ        (L) MINGUS                 1979 ASYLUM  US 5E505    UK  K 53091
JOE SAMPLE        K    (FGH         (M) SHADOWS & LIGHT (DBL)  1980 ASYLUM  US    704   UK     62030
DAVID CROSBY      V    (FGH
SUSAN WEBB        V    (F   WAYNE PERKINS    G   (F   DENNIS BUDIMIR   G   (F   ROBBIE ROBERTSON G  (F
JOSE FELICIANO    G    (F   ROBBEN FORD      G   (GH  CHEECH & CHONG   V   (F
VICTOR FELDMAN    PERC K (FGJ BUD SHANK      WIND (GH  JACO PASTORIUS   B   (JKLM NEIL YOUNG     HCA (J
ABE MOST          CLAR (J   CHUCK DOMANICO   B   (J   TERESSA ADAMS    CELLO(C   PAUL HORN       WIND(C
JIM HORN          SAX  (C   SASHATUNES       V   (C   WAYNE SHORTER    SAX (   HERBIE HANCOCK   K  (L
PETER ERSKINE     D    (L   DON ALIAS        CONGA(LKM EMIL RICHARDS   PERC (L   MANOLO BADRENA  PERC(K
AIRTO MOREIRA     PERC (K   GLENN FREY       V   (K   LYLE MAYS        K   (M   PERSUASIONS     V  (K
LARRY CARLTON     G (FGHJK  MICHEL COLOMBIER PNO (K   ALEJANDRO ACUNA  PERC (K   CHAKA KHAN      V  (K
J D SOUTHER       V    (K   PAT METHENY      G   (M   MICHAEL BRECKER  SAX (M
```
M171　　　　　　　　　　　　　　　　SAM MITCHELL
```
SAM MITCHELL     G V  (AB            (A) BOTTLENECK & SLIDE GUITAR  1978  KICKING MULE         SNKF  121
                                     (B) FOLLOW YOU DOWN           1978  KICKING MULE         SNKF  147
```
M172　　　　　　　　　　　　　　　　WILLIE MITCHELL
```
WILLIE MITCHELL  TPT  (ALL           (A) SOUL SERENADE         1968  LONDON          UK  SHU  8365
JAMES MITCHELL   SAX  (D             (B) LIVE                  1968  LONDON          UK  SHU  8368
LEROY HODGES     B    (D             (C) SOLID SOUL            1969  LONDON          UK  SHU  8372
HOWARD GRIMES    D    (D             (D) ON TOP                1969  LONDON          UK  SHU  8388
MABON HODGES     G    (D             (E) SOUL BAG              1970  LONDON          UK  SHU  8408
CHARLES HODGES   K    (D             (F) HOLD IT               197   HI              US       32021
AL JACKSON       D    (              ( ) BEST OF               19    HI              US    2 32068
MICHAEL TOLES    G K  (G             (G) LISTEN DANCE          1981  BEARSVILLE      US  BRK 3520
```
M173　　　　　　　　　　　　　　　　HANK MIZELL
```
HANK MIZZELL     G V  (ALL           (A) JUNGLE ROCK           1976  CHARLY          UK  CRL 5000
JIMMY DEMPSEY    G    (A             (EP) HIGHER               1977  CHARLY          UK  CEP  115
JAMES BOBO       G    (A
LEO JACKSON      G    (A   BILL COLLINS     D   (A   JERRY KROON      D    (A   EDDIE            B  (A
JACK ROSS        B    (A   D J FONTANA      D   (A   BOB DEAN              (A   BILL HUMBLE      B  (A
ALAN MOORE       PNO SAX (A
```
M173A　　　　　　　　　　　　　　　MO DETTES
```
                                     (A) STORY SO FAR          1980  DERAM           UK  AML 1120
```
M174　　　　　　　　　　　　　　　　MOBY GRAPE
```
PETER LEWIS      G    (ABEF          (A) MOBY GRAPE            1967 CBS US CS 9498(S)  CL 2698 (M)
JOEL SCOTT HILL  V    (              (A) MOBY GRAPE            196  CBS US   30392   UK   63090
KENT DUNBAR      D    (              (B) WOW                   1968 CBS US    9613   UK   63271
BOB MOSLEY       B    (ABEF          (B) WOW/GRAPE JAM (FREE LP WITH WOW) 1968 CBS US MGC1   +    66209
SKIP SPENCE      G D  (ABEF          (C) MOBY GRAPE 69         1969 CBS US    9696   UK   63430
BOB NEWKIRK      D    (              (D) TRULY FINE CITIZEN    1970 CBS US    9912   UK   63698
DON STEVENSON    G D  (ABEF          (E) 20 GRANITE CREEK      1972 REPRISE US  6460 UK   K 44152
JERRY MILLER     G    (ABEF          (F) GREAT GRAPE           1974 CBS     US 31098 UK   64743
BOB MOORE        B    (              (G) BEST OF               1976 CBS             EURO  53371
GORDON STEVENS   VLN G(E             (H) GRAPE LIVE            1979             IMP
ANDY NARELL      PERC (E
DAVID RUBINSTEIN PNO PERC(E JEFFREY COHEN    B   (E
```

```
CLIFF FOX        G V (
MARCO PIRRONI    G   (
MICK ALLEN       B   (    TERRY DAY         D   (
```
```
                 (A) FETISHES (EP)                19    OPEN EYE           0E1001
                     MODERN MAN                                M175B
DANNY MITCHELL   G SYN(A   (A) CONCRETE  SCHEME    1980  MAM                LP 5001
JIM COOK         V   (A
MIKE MORAN       B   (A   ALI McLEOD        G   (A   COLIN KING    D V (A
```
```
DIETER MOEBIUS   K SYN    (A   (A) RASTAKRAUT      1980  SKY                039
CONNIE PLANK     K SYN    (A
```
```
JAMES LITHERLAND G   (A   (A) MOGUL THRASH        1971  RCA         UK     SF 8156
JOHN WETTON      B   (A
BILL HARRISON    D   (A   ROGER BALL    SAX (A   MAL DUNCAN   SAX (A   MIKE ROSEN   TPT (A
BRIAN AUGER      PNO (A
```
```
ESSRA(SANDY HURVITZ)MOHAWK K V(ALL  (A) SANDYS ALBUM IS HERE AT LAST  1969 VERVE      US   V6 5064
JIM PEPPER       SAX  (A        (B) PRIMORDIAL LOVERS          1970 REPRISE     US   RS 6377
LARRY CARLTON    G    (C        (C) ESSRA MOHAWK               1975 MOONCREST UK CREST24 US ASYLUM1023
TOM SELLERS      K B G(C        (D) ESSRA                      1977 PRIVATE STOCK PS 2024 + PVLP 1016
WILTON FELDER    B    (V
DENNIS PARKER    B    (C   KING ERRISSON    PERC (C   ED GREENE     D   (C   GENE ESTES     PERCI(C
ZITRO            D    (C   GENE PELLO       D    (C   KENNY JENKINS FLT (C   SKIP SWITZER   D   (C
DEAN PARKS       G    (C   TOM HENSLEY      K    (C   ERIC GALE     G   (D   JONATHAN KALB  G   (D
DAVID STONE      G    (D   SONNY BURKE      K    (D   RICHARD DAVIS B   (D   ANDY NEWMARK   D   (D
BERNARD PURDIE   D    (D   HOWIE WYETH      D    (D   PAUL GRIFFIN  K   (D   JERRY RAGOVOY  K   (D
JEREMY STEIG     FLT  (AD  DAVID LASLEY     V    (D   ULA HEDWIG    V   (D   ARNOLD McCULLER V  (D
IAN UNDERWOOD         (A   RUETTA HUGHES         (D
```
```
MIKE STEWART     G V  (A   (A) SIX DAYS ON THE ROAD       1972  KINGDOM UK     KVL  9001
PAUL MACCULLUM   B V  (A
MIKE FUDGE       MAND VLN (A   CHRIS HUNT      D   (A   JOE GILLINGHAM   K   (A
```
```
DUANE ROLAND     G    (ABC  (A) 'MOLLY HATCHET         1978  EPIC      UK   83250
DAVE HLUBEK      G    (ABC  (B) FLIRTIN' WITH DISASTER 1979  EPIC      UK   83791
STEVE HOLLAND    G    (ABC  (C) BEATIN' THE ODDS       1980  CBS       UK   84471
BRUCE CRUMP      D    (ABC
JIMMY FARRAR     V    (C   BANNER THOMAS     B   (ABC DANNY JOE BROWN   V (A
```
```
TONY GIGLIOTTI   V    (A   (A) MUSIC                  1973  BROWN BAG US BB LA 073
BOB FIORINO      V    (A   (B) MOMS APPLE PIE         197   BROWN BAG US    14200
BOB MILLER       G    (A
DAVE MAZZOCHI    K V  (A   JOE AHLADIS      G   (A   PAT AULIZIA   D   (A   GREG YOCHMAN   B  (A
ROGER FORCE      WIND (A   BOB PINTA       TPT  (A   FRED MARZULLA TROM(A
```
```
LARRY PHILLIPS   B V  (A   (A) FIRST INVESTMENT      1979  GULL      UK GULP1031
DAVID WEST-MULLEN VPERC(A
JOHN OVERTON     G V  (A   TONY BODEN   D PERC V (A   CHRIS TSANGARIDES  K  (A
```
```
EDDIE MONEY      V K SAX(ABC  (A) EDDIE MONEY        1977  CBS              UK 82434
JIMMY LYON       G    (ABC  (B) LIFE IS FOR THE TAKING 1978 CBS   US 35598  UK 83159
GARY MALLABER    D    (ABC  (C) PLAYING FOR KEEPS    1980  CBS              UK 84371
LONNIE TURNER    B    (ABC
GENE PARDUE      D    (A   POPS POPWELL     B   (A   ALAN PASQUA   K   (AB EMILIO CASTILLO HRNS(C
STEVE KUPKA      HRNS (C   MAUREEN McCORMICK V (C   RANDY NICHOLS K   (ABC FREDDIE WEBB    K  (A
KEVIN CALHOUN    PERC (C   TOM SCOTT      SAX  (AB  JO BAKER      V   (A   MYRNA MATTHEWS  V  (C
JULIA TILLMAN    V    (C   MARTI McCALL     V   (C   VALERIE CARTER V  (C   DAVID LEWARK    G  (C
JOHN NELSON      G    (C   GREG DOUGLAS     G   (C   BOB GLAUB     C   (C   KENNY LEWIS     B  (C
NICKY HOPKINS    K    (B   LLOYD CHIATE     G   (B   JOHN WHITNEY  G   (B   DAVE DANZA      D  (B
GREGORY PHILLINGANES K (B  DAVID LINDLEY    G   (B   TIM SHERIDAN  B   (B   STEVE PORCARO   SYN(B
DARRELL VERDUSCO V    (B   K WINBUSH        V   (B
```
```
ZOOT MONEY       K V  (ALL  (A) IT SHOULD HAVE BEEN ME      1965  COLUMBIA  UK SX 1734
PAUL WILLIAMS    B V  (2    (B) ZOOT                        1966  COLUMBIA  UK SCX 6075
COLIN ALLEN      D    (12   (C) TRANSITION                 1968  DIRECTION UK 863231
NICK NEWELL      SAX  (23   (D) WELCOME TO MY HEAD          1969  CAPITOL   US    318
ANDY SUMMERS     G    (12   (E) ALL HAPPENING AT KLOOKS KLEEK 19  EPIC     US  24241
CLIVE BURROWS    SAX  (2    (F) ZOOT MONEY                 1970  POLYDOR   UK 2482 019
PAT DONALDSON    B    (1    (G) MR MONEY                   1980  MAGIC MOON   LUNE 1
BARRY WILSON     D    (4    (1) DANTALIONS CHARIOT   (2) BIG ROLL BAND
JOHNNY ALMOND    SAX  (     (3) MUSIC BAND 1969     (4) MUSIC BAND
BERNIE BYRNES    D    (3
JOHN DEAN        B    (4    MIKE COTTON     TPT (3   JOHN BEECHAM   TROM (3   LEN LUBIN   B  (3
MICK MOODY       G    (34
```
```
ROBERT BRADY     K V  (A   (A) GET YOUR TEETH INTO THIS   1973 POLYDOR  UK 2383  182
STUART SCOTT     G    (A
RICK PRICE       B    (A   KEITH SMART     D   (A   CHARLIE GRIMA  PERC (A  MEGAN DAVIES   B  (A
TOM FARNELL      D    (A   ROGER HILL      G   (A
```
```
MEREDITH MONK    V ORG (A   (A) KEY                       1977 LOVELY MUSIC US LML 1051
DANIEL IRA SVERDLIK  (A
DICK HIGGINS         (A   COLLIN WALCOTT       (A   LANNY HARRISON   (A   MARK MONSTERMAKER (A
```

M181 THE MONKEES

DAVY JONES	V	(ALL	THE MONKEES	19	RCA	UK SF7844	COLGEMS US	101
MICKEY DOLENZ	D V	(ALL	MORE OF THE MONKEES	19	RCA	UK SF7868	COLGEMS US	102
PETER TORK	G B V(ALL EX*		HEADQUARTERS	1967	RCA	UK SF7886	COLGEMS US	103
MICHAEL NESMITH	G V	(ALL EX *	PISCES,AQUARIUS, CAPRICORN & JONES	1967	RCA	UK SF 7912	COLGEMS US	104
			THE BIRDS THE BEES & THE MONKEES	1968	RCA	UK SF7948	COLGEMS US	109
TOMMY BOYCE	(*		INSTANT REPLAY	1969	RCA	UK SF8016	COLGEMS US	113
BOBBY HART	(*		GREATEST HITS 196	196			COLGEMS US 115
			CHANGES	19			COLGEMS US	119
			HEAD	1969	RCA	UK SF8015	COLGEMS US	5008
			GOLDEN HITS	19			COLGEMS US	329
			BARREL FULL OF MONKEES	19			COLGEMS US	1001
			THE MONKEES (DBL)	19	LAURIE HOUSE		US	8009
			THE MONKEES	1973	SOUNDS SUPERB		UK	90032
			RE FOCUS	19	BELL		US	6081
			GREATEST HITS	19	ARISTA		GERM	201115
			GREATEST HITS	19	ARISTA			4089
			(*)JONES DOLENZ BOYCE & HART	1976	CAPITOL			11513
			40 TIMELESS HITS	1980	EMI		UK	

M181A MONKS (1960s)

GARY BURGER	G	(A	(A) BLACK MONK TIME	1966	POLYDOR	UK	2417129
LARRY CLARK	ORG	(A					
EDDIE SHAW	B	(A	ROGER JOHNSTON D (A				

M181B MONKS(1979)

JOHN FORD	(A		(A) BAD HABITS	1979	EMI	UK	EMC 3309
RICHARD HUDSON	(A						
TERRY CASSIDY	(A						

M181C MONOCHROME SET

LESTER SQUARE	G V	(AB	(A) STRANGE BOUTIQUE	1980	DINDISC	UK	DID4
BID	V G	(AB	(B) LOVE ZOMBIES	1980	DINDISC	UK	DID8
ANDY WARREN	B V	(AB					
J D HANEY	D V	(AB	BOB SARGEANT K V (A ALVIN CLARK K (B				

M181D MONROE

STEVE BUTLER	V	(A	(A) MONROE	1980	POLYDOR	UK	2383 597
GARY SHARPE	G	(A					
PETE HUMPHRIES	G	(A	JAN TAYLOR B (A STEVE GIBSON D (A				

M182 MONTAGE

BOB STEURER	V	(A	(A MONTAGE	1969	LAURIE	US	SLP 2049
VANCE CHAPMAN	D V	(A					
MIKE SMYTH	G V	(A	LANCE CORNELIUS B V (A MICHAEL BROWN K (A				

M182A MONTE CAZAZZA

			(A) SOMETHING FOR NOBODY (EP)	19	INDUSTRIAL		IR 0010

M183 CHRIS MONTEZ

CHRIS MONTEZ	V	(ALL	THE MORE I SEE YOU	1966	PYE	UK NPL23080	MAYFAIR	AMLB1011
			THE MORE I SEE YOU	19	A&M	US 4115		
			TIME AFTER TIME	1967	PYE	UK NSPL28187	HAMLET	AMLP8006
			TIME AFTER TIME	19	A&M	US 4120		
			FOOLIN' AROUND	1967	A&M	UK		AML 906
			WATCH WHAT HAPPENED	1968	A&M	UK		AML 925
			LETS DANCE	19	CBS	UK 65408	LONDON UK HAU8079
			LETS DANCE	19	MONOGRAM US 100	M F P	UK 50122

M184 JAMES MONTGOMERY BAND

JAMES MONTGOMERY	V HCA(AB		(A) HIGH ROLLER	1974	CAPRICORN	US	CP 0142
BILLY MATHER	B V	(A	(B) JAMES MONTGOMERY BAND	1977	ISLAND	UK	ILPS9419
PETER MALICK	G V STEEL (A						
DAVE CASE	K V	(A	CHUCK PURRO D V (A PETER BELL G V (A				

M185 LITTLE BROTHER MONTGOMERY

EURREAL MONTGOMERY	V PNO(ALL		LITTLE BROTHER MONTGOMERY	1960	DECCA	UK	LK 4664
LEE COLLINS	TPT	(	LITTLE BROTHER MONTGOMERY	1960	COLUMBIA	UK	33SX 1289
OLIVER ALCORN	WIND	(	TASTY BLUES	1960	BLUESVILLE	US	BNLP 1012
ERNEST CRAWFORD	B	(	AFTER HOURS BLUES	19	BIOGRAPH		BLP 12010
JEROME SMITH	D	(	& SUNNYLAND SLIM	19	77		LA 1211
ALEXIS KORNER	G	(	FARRO STREET JIVE	19	XTRA		XTRA 1115
LAYFAYETTE THOMAS	G	(	1972	1972	MATCHBOX		SDM 223
JULIAN EULL	B	(	DEEP SOUTH PIANO	1975	STORYVILLE		SLP 228
KEN COLYER	TPT	(	1930/69	1971	MATCHBOX		SDR 213
JACK FALCON	B	(	NO SPECIAL RIDER	19	ADELPHI	US	1001
ROB GUTHRIE		(	BLUES	19	FOLKWAY	US	3527
LONNIE JOHNSON	G	(	SPIRITUALS	19	FOLKWAYS	US	31042
SONNY GREER	D	(	SOUTH SIDE BLUES	19	REV	US	403
MAMA YANCEY		(	TISHOMINGO BLUES	1980	JSP		1015
			LITTLE BROTHER MONTGOMERY	19	COLLECTORS CLASSICS	US	CC 35

M187 MONTROSE

RONNIE MONTROSE	G	(ALL	(A) MONTROSE	1974	WB	US 2740	UK K46276
BOB JAMES	V	(CD	(B) PAPER MONEY	1974	WB	US 2823	UK K56069
JIM ALCIVAR	K	(CDE	(C) WB PRESENTS	1975	WB	US 2892	UK K56170
ALAN FITZGERALD	B	(BCE	(D) JUMP ON IT	1976	WB	US 2963	UK K56291
DENNY CARMASSI	D	(ABCD	(E) OPEN FIRE	1978	WB	US 3134	UK K56451
BILL CHURCH	B	(A					
SAMMY HAGAR	V	(AB MARK JORDAN K (B NICK DE CARO K (B NOVI NOVAG VLA (C
RANDY JO HOBBS	B	(D RICK SCHLOSSER D (E EDGAR WINTER K (E

M188 MONTY PYTHON'S FLYING CIRCUS

JOHN CLEESE		(	(A) MONTY PYTHON'S FLYING CIRCUS	1970	BBC		REB 73M
ERIC IDLE		(	(b) ANOTHER MONTY PYTHON RECORD	1971	CHARISMA	UK	CAS 1049
MICHAEL PALIN		(	(C) PREVIOUS RECORD	1972	CHARISMA	UK	CAS 1063
TERRY WILLIAMS		(	(D) MATCHING TIE & HANKERCHIEF	1973	CHARISMA	UKCAS1080 US ARISTA	4039
GRAHAM CHAPMAN		(	(E) LIVE AT DURY LANE	1974	CHARISMA	UK	CLASS 4
TERRY GILLIAM		(	(F) MONTY PYTHON & THE HOLY GRAIL	1975	CHARISMA	UKCAS1102 US ARISTA	4050

(CONTINUED)

MONTY PYTHON'S FLYING CIRCUS

DOUGLAS ADAMS	(	(G) LIVE AT THE CITY CENTRE	1976 ARISTA	US	4073
JOHN YOUNG	(	(H) INSTANT RECORD COLLECTION	1977 CHARISMA UK CAS1134		
BEE DUFFELL	(	(I) WORST OF MONTY PYTHON	19 BUDDAH	US	5656/2
CONNIE BOOTH	(	(J) LIFE OF BRIAN	1979 WB	UK	K56757
CAROL CLEVELAND	(				

MONUMENT

STEVEN LOWE	V K (A	(A) MONUMENT	1971 BEACON	BEAS15
WES TRUVOR	G (A			
JAKE BREWSTER	D (A MARVE FLETCHLEY B (A			

MOODY BLUES

DENNY LAINE	G V (AB	(A) GO NOW , THE MOODY BLUES	1965 LONDON	US LP 428
CLINT WARWICK	B (AB	(B) MAGNIFICENT MOODIES	1966 DECCA	UK LK 4711
MIKE PINDER	K V(ABCDEFGHJKLMN	(C) DAYS OF FUTURE PAST	1967 DERAM	US 18012 UK SML 707
GRAEME EDGE	D (ABCDEFGHJKLMN1	(D) IN SEARCH OF THE LOST CHORD	1968 DERAM	US 18017 UK SML 717
RAY THOMAS	FLT V (ABCDEFGHJKLMN1	(E) ON THE THRESHOLD OF A DREAM	1969 DERAM	US 18025 UK SML 1035
JUSTIN HAYWARD	G V(CDEFGHJKLMN1	(F) TO YOUR CHILDRENS CHILDREN	1969 THRESHOLD	UK/US THS 1
JOHN LODGE	B V(CDEFGHJKLMN1	(G) QUESTION OF BALANCE	1970 THRESHOLD	UK/US THS 3
PATRICK MORAZ	K (1	(H) EVERY GOOD BOY DESERVES FAVOUR	1971 THRESHOLD	UK/US THS 5
		(J) SEVENTH SOJOURN	1972 THRESHOLD	UK/US THS 7
(1) 1978 TOUR		(K) THIS IS THE MOODY BLUES	1974 THRESHOLD US 2 12/13 UK MB1/2	
		(K) THIS IS THE MOODY BLUES	19 TELDEC GERM	DX6 28316
		(L) IN THE BEGINNING	1975 DERAM	US 18051 TELDEC GERM 769
		(M) CAUGHT LIVE PLUS FIVE	1977 LONDON US 2PS6901 UK DECCA MB3/4	
		(M) CAUGHT LIVE PLUS FIVE	1977 TELDEC GERM	DP& 24812
		(N) DREAM	1977 TELDEC GERM	DP6 28362
		(O) OCTAVE	1978 LONDON US PS 708 UK DECCA TXS 129	
		(P) OUT OF THIS WORLD (COMP)	1979 K TEL	NE1051
		( ) MOODY BLUES (PROFILE)	19 TELDEC GERM	624004
		(EP) MOODY BLUES(EP)	1965 DECCA	UK DFE8622

MOON(UK)

NOEL McCALLA	V (AB	(A) TOO CLOSE FOR COMFORT	1976 EPIC	UK 81456
LOZ NETTO	G V (AB	(B) TURNING THE TIDE	1977 EPIC	UK 82084
GRAHAM COLLYER	G (AB			
DOUG BAINBRIDGE	WIND (AB NICKY PAYN WIND (AB JOHN SHEARER	(B RON LAWRENCE B (AB		
LUIGI SALVONI	D (A GARY MOBERLEY K (A BOB JACKSON	K (A DAVE DENNIS V (A		

MOON(US)

MATTHEW MOORE	V PNO(A	(A) MOON WITHOUT EARTH	196 IMPERIAL	US LP 12381
DAVID MARKS	G (	(B) MOON	196 IMPERIAL	US LP 12444
DAVE JACKSON	B (			
LARRY BROWN	D (			

KEITH MOON

KEITH MOON	D V PERC(A	(A) TWO SIDES OF THE MOON	1975 POLYDOR UK 2442 134 MCA US 2136				
CURLY SMITH	D (A						
CAM DAVIES	D (A	MIGUEL FERRER	D (A	MICKEY McGEE	D (A	RON GRINEL	D (A
JIM KELTNER	D (A	RINGO STARR	D V (A	JIMMIE RANDALL	B . (A	PAUL STALLWORTH	B (A
JEAN MILLINGTON	B (A	DAVID BIRKETT	B (A	KLAUS VOORMANN	B (A	SPENCER DAVIS	G (A
AL STAEHELY	G (A	MIKE CONDELLO	G (A	DANNY KOOTCH	G (A	JOHN STAEHELY	G (A
JESSE ED DAVIS	G (A	PATTI QUATRO	G (A	JOE WALSH	G SYN(A	BEAU GUSS	G (A
JOHN SEBASTIAN	G (A	STEVE ADAMICK	G (A	JAMES ED HAYMER	D (A	DICK DALE	G (A
PAUL LENART	G (A	JAY FERGUSON	K (A	NICKEY BARCLAY	K (A	BLAIR AARONSON	K (A
DAVID FOSTER	K (A	NORMAN KURBAN	K (A	HARRY NILSSON	V (A	SHIRLEY MATTHEWS V (A	
LORNA WILLARD	V (A	JULIA TILLMAN	V (A	JAMES GILSTRAP	V (A	CLYDIE KING	V (A
MARK VOLMAN	V (A	HOWARD KAYLAN	V (A	DENNIS LARDEN	V (A	JAY WHITE	V (A
RON HICKLIN	V (A	AUGUST JOHNSON	V (A	GREG MATTA	V (A	IRMA ROUTEN	V (A
ANDREA WILLIS	V (A	IRA HAWKINS	V (A	GERALD GARRETT	V (A	CAROLYN WILLIS	V (A
SKIP EDWARDS	STEEL(A	OLLIE MITCHELL	HRNS(A	STEVE DOUGLAS	HRNS (A	BOBBY KEYS	SAX(A
ROBERT GREENIDGE	PERC (A						

MOONDOG

LOUIS HARDIN	V PERC HCA(ALL	(A) MOONDOG	19 CBS	US 7335	UK63906
FRITZ STORFINGER		(B) MOONDOG 2	19 CBS	US 30897	
		(C) MOONDOG IN EUROPE	19 KOPF		RRF 33014
		(D) H'ART SONGS	19 KOPF		RRF 33016

JOHN MOONEY

JOHN MOONEY	G V (A	(A) COMIN' YOUR WAY	19 BLIND PIG	US	BP 779
BRIAN WILLIAMS	B (A				
BOB COOPER	PNO (A NICK LANGAN	HCA K(A TOM McDERMOTT	D (A STEVE NARDELLA	HCA(A
GREG PICCOLO	SAX (A DOUG JAMES	SAX (A RICH LATAILLE	SAX (A DAVID SWAIN SECTION	(A

MOONQUAKE

HOVANESS HAGOPIAN	G V (B	(A) MOONQUAKE	197 FANTASY	US	9450
JACK AUGUST	B V (B	(B) STARSTRUCK	197 FANTASY	US	9486
DEREK KENDRICK	D V (B				

MOONRIDER

KEITH WEST	G V (A	(A) MOONRIDER	1975 ANCHOR	US ANCL 2010
CHICO GREENWOOD	D (A			
JOHN WEIDER	G V (A BRUCE THOMAS B (A			

MICHAEL MOORCOCK & DEEP FIX

MICHAEL MOORCOCK	G V MAND(A	(A) THE NEW WORLDS FAIR	1975 UA	UK UAG 29732
STEVE GILMORE	G (A			
DEBI ROSS	V (A ALAN POWELL	D (A KUMA HARADA	B (A GRAHAM CHARNOCK G (A
SIMON HOUSE	VLN K(A DAVE BROCK	G (A PETE PAVLI	CELLO(A SHIRLEY RODEN	V (A
SIMON KING	D (A SNOWY WHITE	G (A HERBERT NORTH	G (A	

G T MOORE & THE REGGAE GUITARS

G T MOORE	G V (AB	(A) G T MOORE & THE REGGAE GUITARS	1974 CHARISMA	UK CAS 1095
TOM WHYTE	B (AB	(B) REGGAE BLUE	1975 CHARISMA	UK CAS 1105
MARTIN HAYWARD	G (AB			
TIM JONES	K (AB TOM ROBINSON V PERC (A RABBIT BUNDRICK	K (A PETER VAN DER PUIJE SAX (A
TONY HANNAFORD	V PERC(A EDDIE QUANSAH TPT (A TONY REDUNZO	D V (B MALCOLM MORTIMER	D (A
GEORGE LARNYOH	SAX (A CHRIS MERCER SAX (B			

M196

GARY MOORE

GARY MOORE	G V	(AB		(A) GRINDING STONE		1973	CBS		UK		65527
PHIL LYNOTT	B V	(B		(B) BACK ON THE STREETS		1978	MCA		UK		MCF 2853
BRIAN DOWNEY	D	(B									
DON AIREY	K	(B	SIMON PHILLIPS	D	(B	JOHN MOLE	B	(B			

M197

MERRILL MOORE

MERRILL MOORE	PNO	(ALL		(A) TREE TOP TALL	1969	B &C		CAS 1001
				(B) BELLYFULOF BLUE THUNDER	1972	EMBER		EMB 3392
				(C) ROUGH HOUSE 88	1972	EMBER		EMB 3394
				(D) MERRILL MOORE	19	CAPITOL	US	1 608
				(E) 20 GOLDEN PIECES OF	1979	BULLDOG		BDL2011

M197A

SCOTTY MOORE

SCOTTY MOORE	G	(A		(A) GUITAR THAT CHANGED THE WORLD	1973	EPIC	US 26103
BOOTS RANDOLPH	SAX	(A		(B) BIG ELVIS HITS	1976	CBS	NL 53343
BILL PURSELL	PNO	(A					
JERRY KENNEDY	G	(A	BOB MOORE	B	(A	D J FONTANA	G (A BUDDY HARMAN	D (A
JORDANAIRES	V	(A					

M198

TIM MOORE

TIM MOORE	V	(ALL		(A) A FOOL LIKE YOU	1974 MOONCREST	UK	CREST 16
RUSS KUNKEL		(B		(B) TIM MOORE	1975 POLYDOR 2310 363 UK US	ASYLUM	7E 1019
ROY MANKOWITZ	D	(B		(C) BEHIND THE EYES	1975 POLYDOR 2310 412 UK US	ASYLUM	7E 1042
BERNARD PURDIE	D	(B		(D) WHITE SHADOWS	1977 POLYDOR 2310 512 UK US	ASYLUM	7E 1088
BILL McCORD	D	(B					
BILL PAYNE	K	(D	MARK VOLMAN	V (D	JEFF PORCARO	D (D	ELLIOT RANDALL	G (D
HOWARD KAYLAN	V	(D	FRED TACKETT	G (D	MIKE UTLEY	K (D	LEE SKLAR	B (D
MICHAEL McDONALD	V	(D					

M199

JOHNNY MOPED

JOHNNY MOPED(PAUL HALFORD)V(A		(A) CYCLEDELIC	1978	CHISWICK	UK	WIK8
SLIMEY TOAD	G	(A					
FRED BERK	D	(A	PHIL BURNS	B (A	DAVE BERK	B	(A	RAY BURNS	G	(A

M200

PATRICK MORAZ

PATRICK MORAZ	K	(A		(A) "I"	1976	CHARISMA		CDS 4002
VIVIENNE McAULIFFE	V	(A		(A) "I"	1976	ATLANTIC	US	18175
JOHN McBURNIE	V	(AB		(B) OUT OF THE SUN	1977	CHARISMA		CDS 4007
RAY GOMEZ	G	(AB		(B) OUT OF THE SUN	1977	VISA	US	1015
JEFF BERLIN	B	(A		(C) PATRICK MORAZ	1978	CHARISMA	UK	CDS 4015
ALPHONSE MOUZON	D	(A		(D) FUTURE MEMORIES LIVE ON TV	1979	CARRERE	FR	67435
ANDY NEWMARK	D	(AB		(E) CO EXISTENCE	1980	CARRERE	FR	CAL 117
JEAN RISTORI	B	(A					
VERONIQUE MUELLER	V	(A	FRANCOIS ZMIROU	V (B	RICHIE MORALES	D (E	JEAN LUC BOURGEOIS	PERC (A
AUGUSTE DE ANTHONY	G	(A	PHILIPPE STAEHLI	PERC (A	RENE MORAZ	PERC (A	WORNELL JONES	B (B
SYRINX		(E	JOHN WOOLOFF	G (E			

M200A

A MORE

| A MORE | | | | (A) FLYING DOESN'T HELP | 1979 | QUANGO | | HMG 98 |

M201

MORGAN

MORGAN FISHER	K	(AB		(A) THE SLEEPER WAKES	1979	CHERRY RED	UK	A RED1
MAURICE BACON	D	(AB		(B) NOVA SOLIS	19	RCA		
TIM STAFFELL	G V	(AB					
BOB SAPSTEAD	B	(B					

M202

RON PAUL MORIN

RON PAUL MORIN	G V	(A		(A) PEACEFUL COMPANY	1972	SOVEREIGN		SVNA 7252
LUKE P WILSON	G V BAN	(A					
GRAHAM TODD	K	(A	JOHNNY VAN DERRICK	FDL (A	JOHN PEARSE	G V (A	RICK KEMP	B (A
CAMILLA DE CRESPIGNY	V	(A	CHRIS LAURENCE	B (A	PETE WILLSHER	STEEL(A	SUSAN JAMES	V (A

M202A

ROGER MORRIS

ROGER MORRIS	G V	(A		(A) FIRST ALBUM	1972	REGAL ZONOPHONE	UK SRZA 8509
LISLE HARPER	B	(A				
BRUCE ROWLAND	D	(A	TERRY STANNARD	D (A	ROD COOMBES	D (A	TOMMY EYRE	PNO (A
JOHN WEIDER	G	(A	KEITH WEST	G (A	GLEN CAMPBELL	STEEL(A	JOHNNY ALMOND	SAX (A
CHRIS MERCER	SAX	(A	KEN BURGESS				

M202B

MORRIS & THE MINORS

| | | (A) STATE THE OBVIOUS(EP) | 19 | ROUND | UK | MOR 1 |

M202C

TOMMY MORRISON

TOMMY MORRISON	V	(A		(A) PLACE YOUR BETS	1979	REAL		RAL 2
PAUL RODGERS	V	(A					
JOHN WATCHMAN		(A	ROD DEATH	D (A	DAVE RAMSEY	(A	BOB MARSHALL	(A JAMES HONEYMANSCOTT(A
KUMA HARADA	B	(A	STUART McDONALD	(A	GARY WINDO	(A	LOU MARTIN	K(A PETE FARNDON (A

M203

VAN MORRISON

VAN MORRISON	V SAX G	(ALL		(A) BLOWIN' YOUR MIND	1967 BANG	US BLB21 LONDON UK	8346
RICHARD DAVIS	B	(B		(B) ASTRAL WEEKS	1968 WB	US	WS 1768	UK K46024
CONNIE KAY	D	(BFG		(C) BEST OF	1970 BANG	US	BLP222
WARREN SMITH	PERC	(B		(C) BEST OF	1970 PRESIDENT		UK 1045
JOHN PAYNE	FLT	(D		(D) MOONDANCE	1970 WB	US	WS 1835	UK K46040
JOHN PLATANIA	G	(DEHJ		(E) HIS BAND & STREET CHOIR	1970 WB	US	WS 1884	UK K46066
JOHN KLINGBERG	B	(DE		(F) TUPELO HONEY	1971 WB	US	WS 1950	UK K46114
GARY MALLABER	D PERC	(DFGH		(G) ST DOMINICS PREVIEW	1972 WB	US	BS 2633	UK K46172
JACK SCHROER	SAX PNO	(DEFGHJL		(H) HARD NOSE THE HIGHWAY	1973 WB	US	BS 2712	UK K46242
COLLIN TILTON	WIND	(D		(J) ITS TOO LATE TO STOP NOW	1974 WB	US	BS 2760	UK K86007
JEFF LABES	K	(DHJL		(K) TB SHEETS	1974 BANG US BLP400	LONDON UK HSM5008
EMILY HOUSTON	V	(D		(L) VEEDON FLEECE	1974 WB	US	BS 2805	UK K56068
JUDY CLAY	V	(D		(EF) HIS BAND/TUPELO HONEY	1975 WB		UK K86009
JACKIE VERDELL	V	(D		(M) THIS IS WHERE I CAME IN(COMP)	1977 BANG	UK	6467 625
DAVID SHAW	PERC CLAR	(DEJL		(N) PERIOD OF TRANSITION	1977 WB	US	BS 2987	UK K56322
BILL CHURCH	B	(FG		(O) WAVELENGTH	1978 WB	US BSK3212	UK K56526
KEITH JOHNSON	TPT K	(E		(P) INTO THE MUSIC	197 MERCURY	JAP 7630	UK 9102 852
ALAN HAND	PNO SAX	(E		(Q) CHAIRFELLOWS(BOOTLEG ?)	1978 IMPOSSIBLE		IMP118
ELLEN SCHROER	V	(EFG		(R) COMMON ONE	1980 MERCURY		UK 6302 021
JAY BERLINER	G	(B		(1) 1979 TOUR			

(CONTINUED)

```
MARTHA  JELEZ       V   (E      ANDY ROBINSON      V   (E      JANET PLANET       V   (EFG  JIM ROTHERMEL      WIND(L
LARRY GOLDSMITH     V   (E      LUIS GASCA         TPT (F      RONNIE MONTROSE    G V (FG   TED TEMPLMAN       ORG (F
MARK JORDAN         PNO (FGP    BRUCE ROYSTON      FLT (F      BOOTS STUART HOUSTON V FLT(F JULES BROUSSARD    SAX(GH
JOHN McFEE          STEEL(FG    DOUG MESSENGER     G   (G      MARK SPRINGER      V   (G    PAT O'HARA         HRNS(G
TOM SALISBURY       K   (G      RICK SCHLOSSER     D   (FGH    ROLF HOUSTON           (G    BERNIE KRAUSE      SYN (G
MARK NAFTALIN       PNO (G      MARTY DAVID        B   (H      DAVID HAYES        B   (HJLPR BILL ATWOOD       HCA (H
RON ELLIOTT         G   (G      JACKIE DE SHANNON  V   (H      RALPH WASH         G   (L    JAMES TRUMBO       K   (L
JOSEPH ELLIS        HRNS (H     NATHAN RUBIN   STRINGS (HJL    ZAVEN MALIKIAN     VLN (H    NANCY ELLIS        VLA (HJ
JOE MACHO           B   (H      MICHAEL GIRLING    VLN (H      TIM KOVATCH        VLN (J    TOM HAPLIN         VLN (J
JOHN TENNEY         VLN (H      JOHN TROPEA        G   (L      DR JOHN            K   (N    REGGIE McBRIDE     B   (N
ALLEN SCHWARZBERG   D   (L      MARLO HENDERSEN    G   (N      JERRY JUMONVILLE   SAX (N    ROBBIE MONTGOMERY  V   (N
OLLIE BROWN         D   (N      GARY GARRETT       V   (N      CARLENA WILLIAMS   V   (N    GREGORY WRIGHT     V   (N
JOE POWELL          V   (N      CANDY NASH         V   (N      PAULETTE PARKER    V   (N    ROGER KENERLY SAINT V(N
TONY McVEY          V   (N      MARK UNDERWOOD     TPT (N      BOB TENCH          G   (1Q0Q JOHN ALTMAN        SAX (1
JOEL PESKIN         SAX (N      TONI MARCUS        VLN (P      PEE WEE ELLIS      SAX (PR   MARK ISHAM         TPT (PR
KATIE KISSOON       V   (1PQ    ROBIN WILLIAMSON   WHISTLE(P    KURT WORTMAN       D   (P    MICK COX           G   (R
PETER VAN HOOKE     D   (OPQR   RY COODER          G   (P      JOHN ALLAIR        K   (R    PETE BREWIS        V   (R
ZAKIR HUSSAIN       PERC (P     MITCH DALTON       G   (O      GINGER BLAKE       V   (O    LAURA CREAMER      V   (O
GARTH HUDSON        K SYN(O     MICKEY FEAT        B   (OQ     ANNA PEACOCK       V   (Q    LEE CHARLTON       D   (R
LINDA DILLARD       V   (O
HERBIE ARMSTRONG    G V (OPQR
```

MORNING
M204

```
JAY LEWIS          G V (A        (A) MORNING                1970 LIBERTY            LBS 83463
JIM HOBSON         K V (A        (B) STRUCK LIKE SILVER     1974 UA                 UAS 29337
BARRY BROWN        G D (A
BRUCE WALLACE      B   (A    AL PERKINS     STEEL(A    JIM KEHN     D V (A   TERRY JOHNSON   G B (A
JAY DONNELLAN      G   (
```

MORNING GLORY
M205

```
JOHN SURMAN        SAX (A        (A) MORNING GLORY          1973    ISLAND      UK     ILPS 9237
JOHN MARSHALL      D   (A        (B) 2 SUNS WORTH           19      FONTANA            67573
TERJE RYPDAL       G   (A
MALCOLM GRIFFITHS  TROM (A   CHRIS LAURENCE    B   (A    JOHN TAYLOR    K   (A
```

MORNING STAR
M205A

```
RICK BACUS         G K V(AB       (A) MORNING STAR          1978    CBS         US     35316
JERRY CHAMBERS     G V (AB        (B) VENUS                 1979    CBS         US     35713
MICHAEL EDMUNDS    G V (AB
GREG HARRIS        D PERC (AB  GREG LEECH     B   (AB
```

DICK MORRISSEY & JIM MULLEN
M206

```
DICK MORRISSEY     SAX (AB        (A) UP                    1977    EMBRYO      US     SD  536
JIM MULLEN         G   (AB        (B) CAPE WRATH            1979    FUSION      UK     SHSP 4098
MALCOLM DUNCAN     SAX (A
HAMISH STUART      G   (A    ONNIE McINTYRE   G   (A    PAT REBILLOT   K   (A    ROGER BALL    K (A
ALAN GORRIE        B   (A    STEVE FERRONE    D   (A    SAMMY FIGUEROA PERC (A   RAFAEL CRUZ   PERC (A
RICHARD BAILEY     D   (B    TONY CARR      PERC (B    MAX MIDDLETON  K   (B    KUMA HARADA   B   (B
ROBERT AHWAI       G   (B
```

PABLO MOSE
M207

```
PABLO MOSES              (ALL      (A) REVOLUTIONARY DREAM   1976 SOUNDTRACS   + DIFF 1978  GETL 104
                                   (B) I LOVE I BRING        1978 UA                        LA 798
```

MOSE JONES
M208

```
RANDY LEWIS        B V (AC        (A) MOSE KNOWS             1974 MCA                MCA 394
JIMMY O'NEILL      G V (A         (B) GET RIGHT              1974 MCA                MCF 2673
BRYAN GLENNCOLE    D V (A         (C) BLACKBIRD              1978 RCA                PL 12793
STEVE McRAY        K V (AC
CHRIS SEYMOUR      D V (C     MARTIN TAYLOR     G V (C
```

BOB MOSLEY
M209

```
BOB MOSLEY         G V (A         (A) BOB MOSLEY             1972    WB       US       MS 2068
ED BLACK           STEEL(A
WOODIE BERRY       V   (A     FRANK SMITH       V   (A    WAYNE JACKSON  HRNS (A   ALLEN WEHR     V (A
ANDREW LOVE        HRNS (A
```

ELTON MOTELLO
M210

```
ELTON MOTELLO      V   (A         (A) POP ART                1980 EDGE               RKM HOG1
MIKE BUTCHER       G V (A
WALTER MEYER       D V (A     PAUL KIDSLEY      V   (A    ANDREW GOLDBERG K V (A   J P MARTIN  G B (A
```

MOTELS
M210A

```
MARTHA DAVIS       V G (A         (A) CAREFUL                1980 CAPITOL            EST 12070
MARTIN JOURARD     K SAX(A
TIM McGOVERN       G   (A     MICHAEL GOODROE   B   (A    BRIAN GLASCOCK  D  (A
```

MOTHER EARTH
M211

```
TRACY NELSON       K V (ALL       (A) REVOLUTION(+ STEVE MILLER ETC)  1968  UA                    US   5185
MARTIN FIERRO      SAX (A1        (B) LIVING WITH THE ANIMALS        1968  MERCURY               US  SR 61194
MARK NAFTALIN      K   (A         (C) MAKE A JOYFUL NOISE            1969  MERCURY UK SMCL 20173 SR61226
BOB ARTHUR         B V (ACD       (D) TRACY NELSON COUNTRY           1969  MERCURY UK SMCL 20179 US  61230
JOHN ANDREWS       G   (ABDEFG    (E) SATISFIED                      1970  MERCURY UK  6338 023  SR61270
GEORGE RAINS       D SAX(A        (F) BRING ME HOME                  1971  REPRISE UK K44133  US    6431
TIM DRUMMOND       B   (BF        (G) POOR MANS PARADISE             1973  CBS                   US   31759
KARL HIMMEL        D   (BEF       (1) EARLY LINE UP
IRV KANE           TROM (G
JOHN GIMBLE        FDL (BCDF   SAMMY DODGE    FDL (BF   BEN KEITH      G   (BCF  TERRY BURNSIDE  SAX (G
BILLY PUETT        SAX (G      REV STALLINGS  V   (C    JOSEPH ARNOLD  SAX (C   PETE DRAKE     STEEL(CD
PIG ROBBINS        K   (C      R P ST JOHN    HCA V(CA1 CLAYBORNE BROTHER COTTON(C SHORTY LAVENDER FDL (CD
ANDREW MACMAHON    K   (EFG    BOB CARDWELL   G   (EF   JAMES DAY      STEEL(E   DAVE ZETTNER   B   (E
IRMA JEAN ROUTEN   V   (CF     SADIE CANTRELL V   (CF   LADY CORDER    V   (CF   LONNIE CASTILLE D  (1
SCOTTY MOORE       G   (D      JORDANAIRES    V   (D    JACK DRAKE     B   (D    DENNIS GOODE   TROM (G
JACK LEE           G V (G      STEVE MANDELL  B   (G    BEAU DOLLAR    D   (G    JERRY CARRIGAN  D  (G
MAC GAYDEN         G   (G      RANDY SCRUGGS  G   (G    TOMMY SMITH    TPT (G
```

M211A

MOTHER GONG

GILLI SMYTH	V	(A	(A) FAIRY TALES			19	CHARLY		UK	CRL	5018
HARRY WILLIAMSON	G	(A									
DIDIER MALHERBE	WIND	(A	RONNIE WATHEN PIPES	(A	NICK TURNER	WIND	(A	TREVOR DARKS	B	(A	
MO VICARAGE	K	(A	EDUARDO NIEBLA	G	(A	MARIANNE OBERASHER HARP	(A	CORRINA		V	(A
ERMANO GHISIO ERBA	D	(A									

M212

MOTHERS FINEST

JOYCE BABY	V PERC(ABC	(A) MOTHERS FINEST	1976	EPIC	US	34179	UK	81595	
JEAN KENNEDY	V PERC(ABC	(B) ANOTHER MOTHER FURTHER	1977	EPIC	US	34695	UK	82037	
GLENN MURDOCK	V (ABC	(C) MOTHER FACTOR	1978	EPIC	US	35546	UK	83011	
JAMES CUNNINGHAM	PERC (C								
SKIP SCARBOROUGH	PNO (C	MOSES MO	G V (ABC	WIZZARD	B V (ABC B B BORDEN	D (ABC			
MIKE	K (ABC								

M213

MOTORHEAD

LEMMY	B V (ABCDE	(A) MOTORHEAD	1977	CHISWICK	UK	WIK2 +	CWK 3008	
LARRY WALLIS	G (AE	(B) OVERKILL	1979	BRONZE		UK	BRON 515	
LUCAS FOX	D (AE	(C) BOMBER	1979	BRONZE		UK	BRON 523	
PHIL TAYLOR	D (ACDE	(D) ACE OF SPADES	1980	BRONZE		UK	BRON 531	
EDDIE CLARKE	G (ACDE	(E) ON PAROLE (ROCKFILE)	1980	LIBERTY			LBR 1004	
GIRL SCHOOL	(EP	(EP) ST VALENTINES DAY MASSACRE	1981	BRONZE	UK		BROX116	

M214

MOTT THE HOOPLE

PETE OVEREND WATTS	B (ABCDEFGHJKLMN	(A) MOTT THE HOOPLE	1969	ISLAND UK ILPS9108	US	ATLANTIC	8258	
DALE GRIFFIN	D (ABCDJK	(B) MAD SHADOWS	1970	ISLAND UK ILPS9119	US	ATLANTIC	8272	
MICK RALPHS	G (ABCD	(C) WILD LIFE	1971	ISLAND UK ILPS9144	US	ATLANTIC	8284	
VERDEN ALLEN	K (ABCD	(D) BRAIN CAPERS	1971	ISLAND UK ILPS9178	US	ATLANTIC	8304	
STAN TIPPENS	V (CJ	(E) ROCK'N' ROLL QUEEN	1972	ISLAND UK ILPS9215	US	ATLANTIC	7297	
IAN HUNTER	V K G(ABCDEFGHJLN	(F) ALL THE YOUNG DUDES	1972	CBS UK	65184	US		31750
ARIEL BENDER	G (J	(G) MOTT	1973	CBS UK	69038	US		32425
BLUE WEAVER	K (J	(H) THE HOOPLE	1974	CBS UK	69062	US		32871
MORGAN FISHER	K (JK	(J) MOTT THE HOOPLE LIVE	1974	CBS UK	69093	US		33282
MICK RONSON	G V (	(K) DRIVE ON	1975	CBS UK	69154	US		33705
RAY MAJOR	G (K	(L) POP CHRONIK	1975	ISLAND IMP VOL 11				
NIGEL BENJAMIN	V (KM	(M) SHOUTING & POINTING	1976	CBS UK	81289	US		34236
STEVE HYMANS	V (	(N) GREATEST HITS	1976	CBS UK	81225	US		34368
MICK BOLTON	ORG (J							
GUY STEVENS	PNO (B	JAMES ARCHER	VLN (C	GERRY HOGAN	STEEL (C	JESS RODEN	V (C	
JIM PRICE	TPT (D	PAUL BUCKMASTER	CELLO(G	GRAHAM PRESKETT VLN	(G	THUNDERTHIGHS	V (G	
ANDY MACKAY	SAX (G							

M215

MOTORS

ANDY McMASTER	V B K(ABC	(A) MOTORS 1	1977	VIRGIN	UK	V2089	US 34924	
NICK GARVEY	G V (ABC	(B) APPROVED BY THE MOTORS	1978	VIRGIN	UK	V2101	US 35348	
BRAM TCHAIKOVSKY	G V (AB	(C) TENEMENT STEPS	197	VIRGIN	UK	V2151		
RICHARD SLAUGHTER WERNHAM D(AB								

M216

MOUNTAIN

LESLIE WEST	G V (ALL	(A) MOUNTAIN	1970	WINDFALL US	4500			
FELIX PAPPALARDI	B (ALL	(B) MOUNTAIN CLIMBING	1970	WINDFALL US	4501	UK BELL SBLL133		
STEVE KNIGHT	K PERC(ABCDH	(C) NANTUCKET SLEIGHRIDE	1971	WINDFALL US	5500	UK ISLAND 9148		
CORKY LAING	D (BCDEFHJ	(D) FLOWERS OF EVIL	1971	WINDFALL US	5501	UK ISLAND 9179		
NORMAN SMART	D (	(E) MOUNTAIN LIVE	1972	WINDFALL US	5502	UK ISLAND 9199		
DAVID PERRY	G (J	(F) ROAD GOES ON FOREVER	1972	WINDFALL US	5503			
BOB MANN	G K (K	(G) POP HISTORY	1972	POLYDOR		2625 022		
ALLEN SCHWARTZBERG D (K	(H) BEST OF	1973	CBS	US	32079 UK ISLAND 9236			
		(J) AVALANCHE	1974	EPIC	US	33088 UK	80492	
		(K) TWIN PEAKS (DBL)	1977	CBS	US	32818 UK	88095	

M216A

MOUNTAIN BUS

	(A) SUNDANCE	19	GOOD		US	G101

M217

MOUSE

	(A) LADY KILLER	1974	SOVEREIGN		SVNA 7262	

M218

ALPHONSE MOUZON

ALPHONSE MOUZON	D K (ALL	(A) THE ESSENCE OF MYSTERY	1975	BLUENOTE		BNLA 059	
TOMMY BOLIN	G (C	(B) FUNKY SNAKEFOOT	1975	BLUENOTE		BNLA 222	
JAY GRAYDON	G K (C	(C) MIND TRANSPLANT	1975	BLUENOTE		BNLA 398	
LEE RITENOUR	G (C	(D) THE MAN INCOGNITO	1976	UA	UK	UAG 20005	
JERRY PETERS	K (C	(E) BACK TOGETHER AGAIN	1977	ATLANTIC	UK	K 50382	
HENRY DAVIS	B (C	(F) ALPHONSE MOUZON	19	SONOPRESSE	FR	056 99408	
LARRY CORYELL	G (E						
PHILIP CATHERINE	G (E	JOHN LEE	B (E	CHERYL P ALEXANDER V	(E	TAWATHA AGEE	V (E

M219

THE MOVE

ROY WOOD	G V (ALL	(A) THE MOVE	1966	REGAL ZONOPHONE	UK	SLRZ1002	
BEV BEVAN	D (ALL	(A) THE MOVE	1974	M F P	UK	50158	
ACE KEFFORD	B (A	(A) THE BEST OF MOVE (REPACKAGE)	19	A&M	UK	SP3625	
TREVOR BURTON	G (A	(B) SHAZAM	1970	REGAL ZONOPHONE	UK	SLRZ1012	
CARL WAYNE	V B (AB	(B) SHAZAM	197	A&M	US	SP4259	
RICK PRICE	B (B	(B) SHAZAM	197	POLYDOR		2310 012	
JEFF LYNNE	G V (E	(C) BEST OF	1970	FLY	UK	TON 3	
		(D) LOOKING ON	1971	FLY UK FLY1 CAPITOL US ST658			
		(E) MESSAGE FROM THE COUNTRY	1971	HARVEST		UK SHSP 4013	
		(E) MESSAGE FROM THE COUNTRY	197	CAPITOL	US	ST811	
		(E) SHINES ON	1979	HARVEST		UK SHSM 2029	
		(F) FIRE BRIGADE	1971	M F P	UK	5276	
		(G) SPLIT ENDS	1972	US		US UAS 5666	
		(AB) MOVE /SHAZAM	1972	CUBE		UK TOOFA 5/6	
		(H) CALIFORNIA MAN	1974	HARVEST		UK SHSP 4035	
		(I) MASTERS OF ROCK	1974	HARVEST		EURO 054 05696	
		(EP) SOMETHING ELSE	1968	REGAL ZONOPHONE	UK	TR2 2001	
		(J) GREATEST HITS VOL 1	1978	HALLMARK UK		SHM 952	

MOVIES (UK)

```
JON COLE          G V  (ABCD      (A) THE MOVIES                  1975  FIREFLY   UK    AMLH33002
GREG KNOWLES      G V  (ABCD      (B) DOUBLE A                    1977  GTO       UK    GTLP 026
DAG SMALL         K V  (A         (C) BULLETS THROUGH THE BARRIER 1978  GTO       UK    GTLP 031
JULIAN DIGGLE     PERC V(ABCD     (D) INDIA                       1980  GEM       UK    GEMLP 105
JAMIE LANE        D V  (ABCD
DURBAN LAVERNE    B V  (A   STAN SULZMANN    SAX (B   MICK PARKER    K CLAR (BC   DAVE QUINN   B V (BC
COLIN GIBSON      B V  (D   RAY WARLEIGH     SAX (B
```

MOVIES(US)

```
TED MEDBURY       (A       (A) MOVIES                            1976  ARISTA US         AL 4085
PETER BARNES      (A
MICHAEL MORGAN    (A
```

MOVING FINGER

```
KEN ELLIOT        V K  (A         (A) REALITY                    1969  POLYDOR           583045
NICK SOUTH        B    (A
KIERAN O'CONNOR   D    (A   BOB GIBBONS       G    (A
```

MOVING GELATINE PLATES

```
GERARD BERTRAM    G V  (AB        (A) MOVING GELATINE PLATES     19    CBS               64399
MAURICE HELMINGER K FLT(AB        (B) THE WORLD OF GENIUS HANS   1971  CBS               64146
DIDIER THIBAUT    B V  (AB
GERARD PONS       D    (AB  MICHEL CAMICAS   TROM (B   JEAN PIERRE LAROQUE BASSOON (B  GUY BOYER  VIBES (B
CLAUDE DELCLOO    V    (B
```

MOVING SIDEWALKS

```
BILLY GIBBONS     G V  (A         (A) FLASH                      19    TANTARA   US    TS 6919
DON SUMMERS       B    (A
DAN MITCHELL      D    (A   TOM MOORE         K    (A
```

JUDY MOWATT

```
JUDY MOWATT       V    (A         (A) BLACK WOMAN                1980  GROVE MUSIC       ILPS 9649
FREDDIE McGREGOR  D K V(A
DALTON BROWNE     V    (A   LEROY WALLACE     D    (A   HOWARD SPREAD BADESSIE B(A  TONY CHIN     G    (A
EWAN LEWIS        B    (A   EARL SMITH        G    (A   MASKEL I         B   (A  CAT COORE     G    (A
MIKEY HEWLETTE    K    (A   GEOFFREY CHUNG    K    (A   TYRONE DOWNIE    K   (A  WIRE          K    (A
STELLEY           K    (A   ARNOLD BRACKENRIDGE TPT(A   HEADLEY BENNETT  SAX (A  DONALD GREAVES TPT   (A
HERBERT CHANG     FLT  (A   ENROY GRANT       SAX  (A   SCULLY           PERC(A  EVERTON CARRINGTON PERC (A
ORVILLE WOOD      PERC (A   RAS INEFIRE TROI  PERC (A   ANICEA BANKS     V   (A  HAROLD BUTLER MELODICA (A
JOY TULLOCH       V    (A   SHARON TUCKER     V    (A   PAM HALL         V   (A
```

MOXY

```
BUDDY CAINE       G    (BCD       (A) MOXY 1                     19    MERCURY   US    SRMI 1087
BILL WADE         D    (BC        (B) MOXY 2                     1976  MERCURY   US    SRMI 1115
BUZZ SHERMAN      V    (BC        (C) RIDIN HIGH                 1977  MERCURY   US    SRMI 1161
TERRY JURIC       B    (DBC       (D) UNDER THE LIGHTS           19    MERCURY   US    SRMI 3723
EARL JOHNSON      G    (DBC
MICHAEL RYNOSKL   V    (D   DANNY BELAN       D    (D
```

MTUME

```
MTUME             V K PERC(A      (A) IN SEARCH OF THE RAINBOW SEEKERS 1980 EPIC   UK    EPC 84629
TAWATHA AGEE      V PERC(A
REGGIE LUCAS      G V  (A   HOWARD KING       D V  (A   SINCLAIR ACEY    HRNS (A  DANNY COLEMAN  HRNS   (A
GWEN GUTHRIE      V    (A   BRENDA    WHITE   V    (A   BASIL FEARRINGTON B V (A  ED TREE MOORE  G      (A
HUBERT EAVES      K V  (A   ED WALSH          SYN  (A   PETE CANNAROZZI  SYN  (A  LUTHER VAN DROSS V   (A
```

MU

```
MERREL FRANKHAUSER G V (A         (A) MU                         19    RTV US 300  + UK  UA  UAG29709
JEFF COTTON       SAX G V (A
RANDY WIMER       PERC (A   LARRY WILLEY      B V  (A
```

MUCKRAM WAKES

```
JOHN ADAMS FDL BAN TROM(AB        (A) MUCKRAM WAKES              1976  TRAILER   UK    LER2093
SUZIE ADAMS       D    (AB        (B) WARBLES,JANGLES & REEDS    1980  HIGHWAY   UK    SHY7009
PETER COE         DULC (A
HELEN WATSON      K    (AB  ROGER WATSON      CONC (AB  BILL LEADER  PERC (A  SONIA JACKSON  CELLO (A
CHRIS COE         DULC (A
```

MUD

```
LES GRAY          V    (ALL       (A) MUD ROCK                   1974  RAK       UK    SRAK 508
ROB DAVIS         G    (ALL       (B) USE YOUR IMAGINATION       1975  PRIVATE STOCK UK PVLP 1003
ROY STILES        B    (ALL       (C) GREATEST HITS              1975  RAK       UK    SRAK 6755
DAVE MOUNT        D    (ALL       (D) MUD ROCK  VOL 2            1975  RAK       UK    SRAK 513
                                  (E) ITS BETTER THAN WORKING    1976  PRIVATE STOCK UK PVLP 1011
                                  (F) ROCK ON                    1978  RCA             PL25170
                                  (G) MUD PACK                   1977  PRIVATE STOCK UK PVLP 1022
```

MUFFINS

```
                                  (A) MANNA/MIRAGE              19    RANDOM RADAR      RRR003
```

MUGWUMPS

```
CASS ELLIOT       V    (          (A) MUGWUMPS                   1967  WB        US    W 1697
DENNY DOHERTY     V    (          (B) HISTORICAL RECORDINGS      197   VALIANT   UK    VS 134
ZAL YANOVSKY           (
JAMES HENDRICKS        (
```

IDRIS MUHAMMAD

```
IDRIS MUHAMMAD    D V  (ALL       (A) BLACK RHYTHM REVOLUTION    19    PRESTIGE  US    10005
JERRY HEY         HRNS (J         (B) YOU TALK THAT TALK         19    PRESTIGE  US    10019
LARRY HALL        HRNS (J         (C) PEACE & RHYTHM             19    PRESTIGE  US    10036
BILL REICHENBACH  HRNS (J         (D) POWER OF SOUL              1975  KUDU            KU 17
CARLBERG JONES    HRNS (J         (E) IDRIS MUHAMMAD             1976  KUDU            KU 27
HERB JIMMERSON    K    (J         (F) TURN THIS MUTHA OUT        1977  KUDU            KU 36
ROLAND BAUTISTA   G    (J         (G) BOOGIE TO THE TOP          1978  KUDU            KU 38
TIP WIRRICK       G    (J         (H) YOU AIN'T NO FRIEND OF MINE 1978 FANTASY         FT 552
NATHANIEL PHILLIPS      B   (J    (I) FOX HUNTIN'                1979  FANTASY         F 562
CLAY TOVEN        V    (J         (J) MAKE IT COUNT              1980  FANTASY   US    F 9598
MAXINE WATERS     V    (J
JULIA TILLMAN     V    (J   CLYDENE JACKSON   V    (J   PAUL SMITH    K V (J   DAVID FRAZIER  PERC   (J
                                                                                       (CONTINUED)
```

IDRIS MUHAMMAD

Name	Inst		Name	Inst		Name	Inst		Name	Inst	
PAT HENDERSON	V	(J	KEITH HATCHER	B	(J	DAVID STONE	FLT	(J	WILL LEE	B	(G
CLIFF CARTER	K	(G	DAVID FRIEDMAN	VIBES	(G	RONNIE CUBER	SAX	(G	HIRAM BULLOCK	G	(G
DANIEL CAHN	TPT	(G	JEREMY STEIG	FLT	(G	FRANK FLOYD	V	(G	SAM FIGUEROA	PERC	(G
JOHN GATCHELL	HRNS	(G	HUGH McCRACKEN	HCA	(G	ZACHARY SANDERS	V	(G	NICKY MARRERO	PERC	(G
RAY DAVIS	SAX	(G	GLORIA AGOSTINI	HARP	(G	RAY SIMPSON	V	(G	KEN WILLIAMS	V	(G

M226

MUMPS

LOUD LANCE
SABLE STAR   PAUL RATNER   KRISTIAN

M227

GEOFF MULDAUR

Name	Inst		Album	Year	Label	Country	Cat
GEOFF MULDAUR	V G K	(ALL	(A) GEOFF MULDAUR	1964	PRESTIGE	US	14004
JAMES JAMESON	B	(D	(B) SLEEPY MAN BLUES	1965	PRESTIGE	US	7727
KLAUS VOORMANN	B	(D	(C) IS HAVING A WONDERFUL TIME	1975	REPRISE	UK	K54046
AMOS GARRETT		(CE	(D) MOTION	1976	REPRISE	US	MS 2255
DOC CHEATHAM	TPT	(C	(E) GEOFF MULDAUR & AMOS GARRETT	197	FLYING FISH	US	061
JIMMY NOTTINGHAM	TPT	(C	(F) BLUES BOY	1979	FLYING FISH	US	FF 210
TAFT JORDON	TPT	(C					

Name	Inst		Name	Inst		Name	Inst		Name	Inst	
RON CARTER	B	(C	STEPHEN BRUTON	G V	(C	ED DANIELS	FLT	(C	JAMES BOOKER	K	(C
DENSIL LANG	V PERC	(C	BENNY MORTON	TROM	(C	QUENTON JACKSON	TROM	(C	BILL BUTLER	G	(C
PETER GORDON	HRNS	(C	KENNETH BERGER	CLAR	(C	JOHN CALE	VLN	(C	BOB WILBUR	WIND	(C
RUSSELL PROCOPE	SAX	(C	BOB SIGGINS	BANJ	(C	FRANK WESS	SAX	(C	ROMEO PENQUE	CLAR	(C
JOHN CLARK	HRN	(C	GEORGE DORSEY	SAX	(C	HOWARD JOHNSON	SAX	(C	DAVID SIMON	HCA V	(C
HERSCHEL HOLDER	TPT	(C	DON BUTTERFIELD	TUBA	(C	JENNY MULDAUR	V	(C	JERRY JEMMOTT	B	(C
GUS BIVONA	CLAR	(A	EARL MACINTYRE	TROM	(A	MARIA MULDAUR	FDL V	(C	RICHARD THOMPSON	G	(C
BERNARD PURDIE	D	(C	HAROLD VICK	SAX	(C	LLOYD SMITH	SAX	(C	MERLE SAUNDERS	K	(C
CHARLES WILLIAMS	SAX	(C	CORNELL DUPREE	G	(C	JIMMY SHIRLEY	BANJO	(C	LIONEL KINGHAM	SAX	(C
FRITZ RICHMOND	JUG	(C	BILLY RICH	B	(CD	GRAHAM LYONS	BASSOON	(C	SELDON POWELL	SAX	(C
EDDIE LOCKE	D	(C	PAUL HUMPHREY	D	(C	CHRIS PARKER	D	(C	BILL KEITH	STEEL	(C
GREG PRESTOPINO	V	(CD	PATTI BONE	K	(C	LEWIS SOLOFF	HRNS	(C	JOE FARRELL	OBOE	(C
ED GREENE	D	(D	MIKE BAIRD	D	(D	STEVE MADAIO	HRNS	(D	BOBBY KEYS	HRNS	(D
TREVOR LAWRENCE	HRNS	(D	LYNDA LAURENCE	V	(D	JIM KELTNER	D	(D	ABIGAIL HANESS	V	(D
DAVID KEMPER	D	(D	CINDY BULLENS	V	(D	DR JOHN	K	(D	DEIDRA ASKEY	V	(D
TOM COSTER	K	(D	SUSAN MOORE	V	(D	JAMES GETZ	K	(D	MARTIN MULL	V	(D
DENNIS COFFEY	G	(D	BONNIE RAITT	V	(D	JAY GRAYDON	G	(D	SID SHARP STRINGS		(D
JESSE ED DAVIS	G	(D	DEAN PARKS	G	(D	MIKE ANTHONY	G	(D	JOHN MORELL	G	(D
DAVID WOLFERT	G	(D	MICHAEL BODDICKER	SYN	(D	BOBBYE HALL	PERC	(D	JIM PRICE	HRNS	(D

M228

GEOFF & MARIA MULDAUR

Name	Inst		Album	Year	Label	Country	Cat
GEOFF MULDAUR	V G K	(AB	(A) POTTERY PIE	1970	REPRISE	US	RS 6350
MARIA MULDAUR	V	(AB	(B) SWEET POTATOES	1972	WB	US	MS 2073
BILL KEITH	STEEL	(A					

Name	Inst		Name	Inst		Name	Inst		Name	Inst	
AMOS GARRETT	G	(A	BILLY WOLF	B	(A	RICK MARCUS	D	(A	BILLY MUNDI	D	(A
BETSY SIGGINS	V	(A	HAL GROSSMAN	HRNS	(A	PETER ECKLUND	TPT	(A			

M229

MARIA MULDAUR

Name	Inst		Album	Year	Label	UK	US	
MARIA MULDAUR	V	(ALL	(A) MUD ACRES	1972	ROUNDER		US	3001
RY COODER	G	(B	(B) MARIA MULDAUR	1974	REPRISE	UK K44255	US	2148
DAVID LINDLEY	G	(BC	(C) WAITRESS IN A DONUTSHOP	1974	REPRISE	UK K54925	US	2194
JIM KELTNER	D	(B	(D) SWEET HARMONY	1976	REPRISE	UK K54059	US	2235
JIM DICKINSON	K	(B	(E) SOUTHERN WINDS	1978	WB	UK K56463	US	2162
MARK JORDAN	K	(BC	(F) OPEN YOUR EYES	1979	WB	UK K56634	US	
KLAUS VOORMANN	B	(B						

Name	Inst		Name	Inst		Name	Inst		Name	Inst	
RAY BROWN	B	(BC	AMOS GARRETT	G B V	(BCDE	GLORIA JONES	V	(B	DAVID NICHTERN	G	(BCDF
CHRIS ETHRIDGE	B	(B	SPOONER OLDHAM	K	(BC	BILL KEITH	BANJ STEEL	(B	LARRY PACKER	VLN	(BC
DAVE HOLLAND	B	(B	KAREN ALEXANDER	V	(B	ANDREW GOLD	G	(B	ED SHAUGHNESSY	D	(B
JAMES CALHOUN	B	(B	BETTY LAVETTE	V	(B	GREG PRESTOPINO	V K	(BCE	CHRIS PARKER	D	(B
CLARENCE WHITE	G	(B	DAVID GRISMAN	MAND	(BC	RICHARD GREENE	VLN	(B	ELLEN KEARNEY	V	(BCD
MAC REBENNACK	K	(BC	JIM GORDON	SAX CLAR K	(BD	FREEBO	B	(C	JOHN BOUDREAUX	D	(B
JESSIE M SMITH	V	(B	PAUL BUTTERFIELD	HCA	(C	JEFF GUTCHEON	K	(C	BOBBYE HALL	PERC	(CF
JIM GORDON	D	(C	BOBBY KING	V	(C	PAUL HUMPHREY	D	(C	DENNIS BUDIMIR	G	(C
JOHN KAHN	B	(C	ROSENDO CERVANTES	TPT	(C	RED CALLENDER	B	(C	DOC WATSON	G	(C
JAMES BOOKER	K	(CD	BUD SHANK	SAX	(C	TERRY LEE EVANS	V	(C	HARRY SWEETS EDISON	TPT	(C
SNOOKY YOUNG	TPT	(C	GEORGE BOHANON	TROM	(C	KATE McGARRIGLE	V	(C	LOWELL GEORGE	G	(C
MILT HOLLAND	PERC	(C	JOSE ORDAZ DURANTE	TPT	(C	EARL PALMER	D	(CD	MERLE WATSON	G	(C
JOHN COLLINS	G	(C	ABE MOSS	SAX	(C	PLAS JOHNSON	SAX	(CD	SHAHIB SHIHAB	SAX	(CD
ROGER KELLAWAY	K	(C	LINDA RONSTADT	V	(CD	TOM TEDESCO	REQUINTO	(C	EMIL RICHARDS	PERC	(C
PAUL HARRIS	K	(C	ANNA McGARRIGLE	V	(C	ALVIN BISHOP ROBINSON	G	(C	FRED STAEHLE	D	(C
VI REDD	SAX	(D	WADDY WACHTEL	G	(C	BILL PAYNE	K	(D	WILLIE WEEKS	B	(D
FRED JACKSON	SAX	(D	HOWARD JOHNSON	SAX	(D	AL AARONS	TPT	(D	BENNY POWELL	TROM	(D
JOHN GIRTON	G	(D	MICHAEL FINNIGAN	K V	(DE	MICHAEL MOORE	B	(D	VICTOR FELDMAN	PERC	(D
DAVID WILCOX	G	(D	BILL DICKINSON	B	(D	MARY ANN PRICE	V	(D	TREVOR LAWRENCE	SAX	(D
JOHNNY ROTELLA	WIND	(D	STEVE MADAIO	TPT	(D	LEW McCREARY	TROM	(DE	MARSHAL ROYAL	SAX	(D
GENE COE	TPT	(D	OSCAR BRASHEAR	TPT	(D	WENDY WALDMAN	V	(DE	ARTHUR ADAMS	V	(D
WILLIAMS SMITH	K	(D	J J CALE	G	(D	LARRY GALES	B	(D	JOE HARNELL	PNO	(D
KENNY BURRELL	G	(D	BRITT WOODMAN	TROM	(D	CHRISTOPHER BOND	G SYN	(E	THOM ROTELLA	G	(E
JOHN HUG	G	(E	ED GREENE	D	(E	SCOTT EDWARDS	B	(E	LES DUDEK	G	(E
GARY COLEMAN	PERC	(E	DAVE BURGIN	HCA	(E	PHIL AABERG	K	(E	PEPPER WATKINS	V	(E
ROSEMARY BUTLER	V	(E	JIM ANDERSON	V	(E	ERNIE WATTS	HRNS	(E	DON MENZA	HRNS	(E
JIM HORN	HRNS	(E	CHUCK FINDLEY	HRNS	(E	ROBERT BRYANT	HRNS	(E	GARY MALLABER	D	(E
STEVIE WONDER	HCA	(F	JUNIOR WALKER	SAX	(F	PAT HENDERSON		(F	TOMMY McCLURE	B	(AB

M230

MUNGO JERRY

Name	Inst		Album	Year	Label	Country	Cat
RAY DORSET	G V PERC	(ALL	(A) MUNGO JERRY	1970	DAWN	UK	DNLS 3008
COLIN EARL	PNO V	(ABCJ	(B) ELECTRONICALLY TESTED	1971	DAWN	UK	DNLS 3020
PAUL KING	BAN G V	(ABC	(C) YOU DONT HAVE TO BE IN THE ARMY	1971	DAWN	UK	DNLS 3028
MIKE COLE	B	(A	(D) BOOT POWER	1972	DAWN	UK	DNLS 3041
JOHN GODFREY	V G K	(BCD	(E) GREATEST HITS	1973	DAWN	UK	DNLS 3045
JOE RUSH	PERC	(C	(F) LONG LEGGED WOMAN	1974	DAWN	UK	DNLS 3051
TIM REEVES	D	(D	(G) GOLDEN HOUR	1974	PYE	UK	GH 586
JON POPE	K	(D	(H) IMPALA SAGA	1976	POLYDOR	UK	2383 364
CHRIS WARNES	B	(J	(I) FILE	1977	PYE	UK	FILD 003
PETE SULLIVAN	D	(J	(J) LOVE IN THE ALLEY	1977	POLYDOR	UK	2383 435
			(K) IN THE SUMMERTIME	197	PYE	UK	H121/6
			(L) RAY DORSET & MUNGO JERRY	1978	POLYDOR	UK	2383 485

MICHAEL MURPHEY

MICHAEL MURPHEY	G V HCA PNO(ALL	(A) GERONIMO'S CADILLAC	1972 A&M US SP4358	UK REGAL ZONO8512
LEONARD ARNOW	G STEEL (A	(B) COSMIC COWBOY SOUVENIR	1973 A&M US SP4388	UK EMI EMA 754
GARY NUNN	G B K V (AB	(C) MICHAEL MURPHEY	1974 EPIC US 32835	UK EMI EMC2037
ROBERT LIVINGSTON	B V G (AB	(D) BLUE SKY NIGHT THUNDER	1975 EPIC US 33290	UK EPIC 80741
BOOMER CASTLEMAN	G (A	(E) SWANS AGAINST THE SUN	1975 EPIC US 33851	UK EPIC 69224
KENNY BUTTREY	D PERC(AC	(F) FLOWING FREE FOREVER	1976 EPIC US 34220	UK EPIC 81713
KARL HIMMEL	D (A	(G) LONE WOLF	1978 EPIC US 35013	
CHARLES JOHN QUARTO	V (A	(H) PEAKS, VALLEYS,HONKY-TONKS & ALLEYS 79 EPIC US 35742		
MICHAEL McGEARY	D (B			

HERB STEINER	STEEL (BC	CRAIG HILLIS	G (BC	W ALAN RAMSEY	V (B	TOMMY COGBILL	B (C
JOHN HILL	D (C	BILL FARMER	PNO (C	BUDDY SPICHER	FDL (C	BOB HOLMES	ORG(C
CLYDIE KING	V (C	MERRY CLAYTON	V (C	PATTIE HENDERSON	V (C	PAT POWDRILL	V (C
ANDY JOHNSTON	V (C	CHARLIE DANIELS FDL G V(E		RICHARD DEAN	V (E	JOHN DENVER	G V(E
JAMES GUERCIO	B (E	JEFF HANNA	V (E	JOHN McEUEN BAN FDL G (EF		MICHAEL McKINNEY	B V(EF
JERRY MILLS	MAND (E	JAC MURPHY	K SYN(EF	TRACY NELSON	V (E	WILLIE NELSON	V (E
EARL PALMER	D (E	MICKEY RAPHAEL	HCA (E	STEVE WEISBERG	G V (FGH	SAM BROUSSARD	G V (FGH
JAI WINDING	K (GH	HARRY WILKINSON PERC D(EF		BOB GLAUB	B (GH	JOHN MACY	STEEL(F
RAY BONNERVILLE	HCA (GH	DAVID LUELL	SAX (F	DEBORAH McCOLL	V (F	STEVE FROMHOLZ	V (H
MIKE BOTTS	D (GH	DENNIS CHRISTIANSON HRNS(G		DICK HYDE	HRNS (G	JERRY JUMONVILLE	HRNS(G
STEVE MADAIO	HRNS (G	BILL PAYNE	K SYN HRNS(G	LON PRICE	HRNS (G	VICTOR FELDMAN	PERC(FG
ROBERT GREENIDGE	PERC(G	JOEY DE LAURO	V (G	JOHN BOYLAN	V (G	WENDY WEBB	V (G
ROD PHILLIPS	K (H	DON BROOKS	HCA (H	BYRON BERLINE	FDL (H	DAN DUGMORE	STEEL(H
DOUG DILLARD	BANJO(H	GARY COLEMAN	PERC (H	KATY MOFFATT	V (H	TOM KELLY	V (H
BOBBY KIMBALL	V (H	TIM SCHMIT	V (H				

ELLIOTT MURPHY

ELLIOTT MURPHY	V G K HCA(ALL	(A) AQUASHOW	1974 POLYDOR US 5061 2391 100
MATTHEW MURPHY	B V (A	(B) LOST GENERATION	1975 RCA US APLIO916
GENE PARSONS	D V (A	(C) NIGHT LIGHTS	1976 RCA US APLI1318
PAT REBILLOT	K (A	(D) JUST A STORY FROM AMERICA	1977 CBS US 34653 UK 81881
LINDA NOVEMBER	V (A		

DENNIS FERRANTE	V (A	JIM MASON	V (A	EDDIE MOTTAU	V (A	MAERETHA STEWART	V (A
TEDDY IRWIN	G (A	FRANK OWENS	K (A	DICK WAGNER	V (A	TASHA THOMAS	V (A
MICK TAYLOR	G (D	GORDON EDWARDS	B (B	JACKIE CLARK	G (B	SONNY LANDRETH	G (B
JIM GORDON	D PERC(B	WAYNE DEVILLIER	K (B	RICHARD TEE	K (B	JON SMITH	SAX (B
BOBBY KIMBALL	V (B	TERRY HARRISON	K (C	ANDY PALEY	D (C	ERNIE BROOKS	B (C
BILLY JOEL	PNO (C	MIKE BRAUN	D (C	RALPH SCHUCKETT	ORG (C	DOUG YULE	G (C
RICHARD DAVIS	B (C	STEVE KATZ	V (C	MARK HOROWITZ	STEEL(C	LEW SOLOFF HRNS	(C
LOU MARINI	HRNS (C	TOM MALONE	HRNS (C	MICHAEL BRECKER	HRNS (C	HOWARD JOHNSON	HRNS(C
HARRY LOOKOFSY	VLN (D	PHIL COLLINS	D (D	DAVE MARKEE	B (D	PETER OXENDALE	V (D
CHRIS MERCER	SAX (D	STEVE GREGORY	SAX (D	MORRIS PERT	PERC(D	BARRY DE SOUZA	D (D
MIKE MORAN	K (D	NICKY HARRISON RECORDER	(D	NICK CARAWAY	V (D	STRINGS	(D

PAULINE MURRAY

PAULINE MURRAY	V (A	(A) & THE INVISIBLE GIRLS	1980 ILLUSIVE 2394 277
MARTIN HANNETT	(A		
STEVE HOPKINS	(A		

JUNIOR MURVIN

JUNIOR MURVIN	G (A	(A) POLICE & THIEVES	1977 MANGO/ISLAND ILPS 9499

MUSCLE SHOALS

SPOONER OLDHAM	G (	(A) DOIN' IT TO THE BONE	1971 ARIOLA ST 50021
BARRY BECKETT	K (ABC	(B) CREAM OF MUSCLE SHOALS	197 ATLANTIC UK K 50283
JIMMY JOHNSON	G (BC	(C) BORN TO GET DOWN	1976 BANG BLP 403 + SHOT 001
DAVE HOOD	B (AB		

CHARLES ROSE	HRNS (ABC	ROGER HAWKINS	D (ABC	HARRISON CALLOWAY	HRNS (ABC	HARVEY THOMPSON	HRNS(ABC
RONNIE EADES	HRNS (ABC	CLAYTON IVEY	K (B	PETE CARR	G (B	TRAVIS WAMMACK	G (B
ROGER CLARK	D (A	BOB WRAY	B (AC	TIM HENSON	K (A	KEN BELL	G (AC
LARRY BYROM	G (A	TOM ROADY	PERC (AC	ANTHONY PARSONS	FLT (A	RANDY McCORMICK	K (C
KATHERINE HILL	V (C						

MUSCLES

	(A) MUSCLES	197 BIG BEAR BEAR 24
	( ) MUSCLES	1978 BIG BEAR BBR 1001

MUSIC EXPLOSION

JAMES LYONS	V (A	(A) LITTLE BIT O' SOUL	1967 LAURIE US SLLP 2040
DON ATKINS	G (A		
RICK NESTA	G (A	BUTCH STAHL B ORG(A BOB AVERY D HCA(A	

MUSIC MACHINE

SEAN BONNIWELL	G (A	(A) TURN ON THE MUSIC	1966 ORIGINAL SOUND US OSRLPS8875
KEITH OLSEN	B (A		
RON EDGAR	D (A	DOUG RHODES ORG (A MARK LANDON G (A	

HARRY MUSKEE BAND

HARRY MUSKEE	V HCA(A	(A) HARRY MUSKEE BAND	1977 NEGRAM NN3
MARTIN VAN DIJK	K (A		
BERNARD REINKE	G (A	LOURENS LEEUW B (A JAN GROENINK	D (A PETER SCHON SYN (A
PIET VAN BLAUW	PERC (A	CARL KALFF HRNS (A FRANS MIJTS	HRNS (A FRED LEEFLANG HRNS(A
BART VAN LIER	HRNS (A	JAN SCHUURMAN BELLS(A MONICA	V (A FLOUR V (A
JOSEE VAN IERSEL	V (A		

CHARLIE MUSSELWHITE

CHARLIE MUSSELWHITE	V G HCA(ALL	(A) STAND BACK	1966 VANGUARD US VSD 79232
TIM KAIHATSU	G (A	(B) STONE BLUES	1968 VANGUARD UK SVRL19012
CLAY COTTON	K V (A	(C) CHARLIE MUSSELWHITE	1968 VANGUARD US VSD 79287
CARL SEVEREID	B (A	(D) LOUISIANA FOG	1968 CHERRY RED US CR 5102
EDDIE HOH	D (A	(E) BLUES FROM CHICAGO	1968 CHERRY RED US CR 5104
ROBBIN FORD	G V (G	(F) TENNESSEE WOMAN	1969 VANGUARD US VSD 6528
JACK MYERS	B (H	(G) TAKIN' MY TIME	1971 ARHOOLIE US 1056
LANCE DICKERSON	D (G	(H) MEMPHIS TENNESSEE	197 PARAMOUNT PAR 5012
GERALD PEDERSEN	B (G	(J) GOIN' BACK DOWN SOUTH	1974 ARHOOLIE US 1074
BOB HALL	PNO (L	(K) LEAVE THE BLUES TO US	1975 CAPITOL US 11450
SAM MITCHELL	G (L	(L) HARMONICA ACCORDING TO CHARLIE	1978 KICKING MULE UK SNKF

(CONTINUED)

CHARLIE MUSSELWHITE

EUGENE BLACKNELL	G	(M	(M) TIMES GETTIN TOUGHER THAN TOUGH	1978 CRYSTAL CLEAR	US		CCS	005	
PEE WEE ELLIS	SAX	(M							
BIG JOHN EVANS	D	(M	BOBBY FORTE	SAX	(M	JOHNNY HEARTSMAN	G	(M	STEVEN B JONES D (M
JOHN TURK	TPT	(M	DARRELL BROADNAX	B	(M	PAT FORD		(D	STU FELDMAN B (D
WORIN BELLAS	ORG	(D	MIKE OSBORN	G	(D	STAN POPLIN	G	(D	VICTOR VIGEANT B (D
MICHAEL KONCALSKI	D	(D	DARYL DRAGON	PNO	(D	ED CARTER	G	(D	SKIP ROSE PNO (FK
FRED ROULETTE	STEEL	(F	LARRY MARTIN	D	(K	RAY ARBIZU	HRNS	(K	MIKE BLOOMFIELD G (K
LYNN CAREY'MAMA LION'	V	(K	STEVE YORK	B	(L	LONNIE CASTILLE	D	(H	PATRICK FORD D (G
JEFF RICH	D	(L							

MUTANTS

ART LYZAK	V	(A						
JOHN AMORE	B	(A	TOM MORWATTS G	(A	PASADENA	G K	(A	STEVE SORTER V D (A

LOUIS MYERS

LOUIS MYERS	V G HCA	(A	(A) I'M A SOUTHERN MAN	1978	ADVENT	US	2809
FREDDY ROBINSON	G	(A					
NATHANIEL DOVE	PNO	(A	DENNIS WALKER	B	(A	BUSTER JONES	D (A

SAM MYERS

SAM MYERS	HCA V	(A	(A) DOWN HOME IN MISSISSIPPI	19	TJ	US	1030
TOMMY LEE THOMPSON	G	(A					

RICHARD MYHILL

RICHARD MYHILL	V	(AB	(A) RICHARD MYHILL ALBUM	1974	EMI	UK	EMC3024
PAUL KEOGH	G	(A	(B) 21 DAYS IN SOHO	1974	EMI	UK	EMC3051
GRAHAM PRESKETT	B MAND	(A					
BRIAN COLE	STEEL	(A	MIKE MORGAN	G	(A	FRANK RICOTTI	PERC (A TONY CARR PERC(A
HENRY SPINETTI	D	(A					

MYOFIST

RON CHENIER	G V	(A	(A) HOT SPIKES	1980	A&M	UK	AMLH64823
ED EAGAN	K	(A					
JOHN CHENIER	D V	(A	JEFF NYSTROM	B V	(A		

MYSTERY GIRLS

	(A) FAMOUS MEN (EP)	19	STRANGE	UK	HAM 001

MYSTERYS

	(A) MYSTERYS (EP)	1979	DEAD GOOD	UK	DEAD 4

MYTHOS

STEPHAN KASKE V K SYN D G(A	(A) QUASAR	1980	SKY		SKY 046

N C C U

(A) SUPER TRICK	1977	UA	UK	UAS30122

N R B Q

TERRY ADAMS L WIND	V	(AD	(A) N R B Q	197	CBS	UK	63653
STEVE FERGUSON	G V	(A	(B) SCAPS	1974	POLYDOR	UK	2329018
FRANK GADLER	V	(	(C) AT YANKEE STADIUM	1978	MERCURY	US	3712
JODY ST NICOLAS	B V	(A	(D) ALL HOPPED UP	1978	RED ROOSTER 101	+ROUNDER	3029
G T STALEY	D	(A	(E) KICK ME HARD	1979	ROUNDER	US	3030
DON ADAMS	TROM	(A					
AL ANDERSON	G V	(D	TOM ARDOLINI D	(D	JOE SAMPINAIO	B G V(D	

N Y C C

ARTHUR FREEMAN		(A	(A) MAKE EVERY DAY COUNT	1978	RCA		PL12782
BENNY DIGGS		(A					
JOSEPH JOUBERT		(A	GREG COLE	PNO	(A	RICHARD TEE	K	(A PAUL SCHAEFFER PNO (A
LEON PENDARVIS	K	(A	WILL LEE	B	(A	JOHN TROPEA	G	(A WILLIAM SEADMAN G(A
CLIFF MORRIS	G	(A	JEFF MIRANOV	G	(A	STEVE GADD	D	(A GEORGE DEVENS PERC(A
ERROL BENNETT	PERC	(A						

NA FILI

TOMAS O CANAINN V PIPES(A	(A) CHANTERS TUNE	1977	TRANSATLANTIC UK		TRA353
TOM BARRY	WIND(A				
MATT CRANITCH	FDL (A				

NAPOLEON XIV

JERRY SAMUELS	V	(A	(A) THEY'RE COMING TO TAKE ME AWAY	1966	WB	US	W1661

GRAHAM NASH

GRAHAM NASH	G V	(AB	(A) SONGS FOR BEGINNERS	1971 ATLANTIC UK 2401 011	US	SD 7204
JOHN BARBATA	D	(AB	(A) SONGS FOR BEGINNERS	1971 ATLANTIC		UK IR K40237
CALVIN SAMUELS	B	(A	(B) WILD TALES	1973 ATLANTIC UK K50025	US	SD 7288
JOEL BERNSTEIN	K	(AB	(C) EARTH & SKY	1980 EMI	UK SWAK12014	
DAVID MASON	G	(AB				
DALLAS TAYLOR	D	(A	RITA COOLIDGE	V	(A JOE YANKEE PNO (AB PAT ARNOLD V (A
PHIL LESH	B	(A	JERRY GARCIA	G	(A DAVID CROSBY G V (AB DAVID LINDLEY FDL G V(AB
CHRIS ETHRIDGE	B	(A	BOBBY KEYS	SAX	(A VANETTA FIELDS V (A SHIRLEY MATTHEWS V (A
CLYDIE KING	V	(A	DOROTHY MORRISON	V	(A DORIAN RUDNYTSKY CELLO (A LARRY COX (A
TIM DRUMMOND	B	(B	BEN KEITH	STEEL	(B HARRY HALEX PNO (B JONI MITCHELL V (B

NASHVILLE TEENS

ARTHUR SHARP	V	(	(A) TOBACCO ROAD	19	LONDON	US	3407
RAY PHILLIPS	V B	(	(B) NASHVILLE TEENS	19	NEW WORLD		AW 6002
JOHN ALLEN	G	(	(C) REMEMBERING	19	DECCA		
PATER SHANNON	B G	(	(D) NASHVILLE TEENS (EP)	1964 DECCA	UK	DFE8600
BARRY JENKINS	D	(				
JOHN HAWKEN	K	(	ROGER GROOM D	(	NEIL KORNER	B (

NASTY POP

TONY WILMSHURST	G V	(AB	(A) NASTY POP	1975	ISLAND	UK	ILPS 9340
KEITH WILKINSON	B V	(AB	(B) MISTAKEN IDENTITY	1977	POLYDOR	UK	2302 056
STEVE GRACE	G HCA(AB					
JON FITZPATRICK	V	(AB	STEVE CORDUNER D	(B	CHRIS MERCER	SAX (B MARTYN FORD HRNS (B
JOHN HEATH	D	(A				

NANETTE NATAL

NANETTE NATAL	G V	(A	(A) THE BEGINNING	19	EVOLUTION	US	3009
JERRY FRIEDMAN	G	(A				
KEN ASCHER	K	(A	ANDY MUSON B	(A	ALLAN SCHWARZBERG	D (A

NATCHEZ TRACE

(A) TO NASHVILLE	197	PINE RIDGE	6414 104
(B) BEST OF	1975	SWEETFOLK	SFA 048

NATIONAL HEAD BAND

LEE KERSLAKE	D K V(A	(A) ALBERT ONE	1971	WB	UK	K46094
JAN SCHELHAAS	K (A					
DAVE PAUL	B G K V(A NEIL FORD	G V (A				

NATIONAL HEALTH

AMANDA PARSONS	V (12A	(A) NATIONAL HEALTH	1978	AFFINITY	UK	AFF 6
DAVE STEWART	K (1345AB	(B) OF QUEUES & CURES	1978	CHARLY	UK	CRL5010
RICK BIDDULPH	B (B	(1) 1977 (2) 1977 (3) 1978 (4) 1978 (5) 1978				
BILL BRUFORD	D (1					
ALAN GOWAN	K (12A PHIL MILLER	G (ALL NEIL MURRAY	B (123A PIP PYLE	D (AB2345
JOHN GREAVES	B (45B GEORGE BORN CELLO B V (45B LINDSAY COOPER	WIND (5 JOHN MITCHELL PERC(A
JIMMY HASTINGS	WIND (AB PAUL NIEMAN TROM (B PHIL MINTON	TPT (B SELWUN BAPTISTE (B
KEITH THOMPSON	OBOE (B PETER BLEGVAD V (B

NATIONAL LAMPOON

JOHN BELUSHI	(*	(A) RADIO DINNER	1972	ISLAND UK HELP 8 BLUE THUMB US 38		
CHRISTOPHER CERF	(*	(B) LEMMINGS	1973	BLUE THUMB	US	BTS6006
CHEVY CHASE	(*	(C) MISSING WHITE HOUSE TAPES	1974	BLUETHUMB	US	BTS6008
RHONDA COULLET	(*	(D) GOLD TURKEY	1975	EPIC	US	33410
BRIAN DOYLE-MURRAY	(*	(E) GOODBYE POP	1976	EPIC	US	33956
TONY HENDRA	(*	(F) THATS NOT FUNNY THATS SICK	1978	RADAR	UK	RAD 4
MARK HOROWITZ	(*	(G) ANIMAL HOUSE	1979	MCA UK MCF 2868	US	3046
DAVID HURDON	(*	(*) GREATEST HITS	1978	VISA	IMP	
HAROLD RAMIS	(*					
PAUL JACOBS	(*	BILL MURRAY (* ALICE PLAYTEN	(* NORMAN ROSE (*
MELISSA MANCHESTER	(*	JOSEPH O'FLAHERTY (* GILDA RADNER	(* PAUL SHAFFER (*
CHRISTOPHER GUEST	(*					

NATURAL ACOUSTIC BAND

KRYSIA KOCJAN	V (	(A) LEARNING TO LIVE	1972	RCA	UK	SF 8272
		(B) BRANCHING IN	1974	RCA	UK	SF 8314

NATIVE

WAYNE JOBSON	G V (A	(A) 1ST ALBUM	1979	ARISTA	UK	NEW 2
BRIAN JOBSON	G (A					
WARREN MENDES	B (A PETER COUCH K (A PERRY TOLE	G (A CHRIS LOPEZ PERC (A
RICHARD SINCLAIR	D (A					

NATURAL GAS

JERRY SHIRLEY	D (A	(A) NATURAL GAS	1976	PRIVATE STOCK	PVLP 1007
PETER WOOD	K (A				
MARK CLARKE	B V (A JOEY MOLLAND G V (A FELIX PAPPALARDI	V (A

NAVARRO

ROBERT McENTEE	G V (B	(A)LISTEN	197	CAPITOL	US	SW 11670
MARK HALLMAN	G V K(B	(B) STRAIGHT TO THE HEART	197	CAPITOL	US	SW 11784
RICHARD HARDY	WIND (B					
MICHAEL WOOTEN	D (B STEVE SIROTKIN K (B ROB GALLOWAY	B (B MIGUEL RIVERA PERC (B
JOEY CONWAY	PNO (B					

NAVASOTA

JEFF BAXTER	G (A	(A) ROOTIN'	1972	ABC	US	ABCX 757
RAY PAWLIK	G (A					
STEVE LONG	G (A PAUL MINTER B (A LINDSEY MINTER	D (A DICKY SONY PNO (A
CLYDIE KING	V (A SHIRLEY MATTHEWS V (A JACKIE WARD	V (A DONALD FAGEN K (A
BYRON BERLINE	FDL (A MARK VOLMAN V (A HOWARD KAYLAN	V (A

NAZARETH

DAN McCAFFERTY	V (ALL	(A) NAZARETH	1971	PEGASUS UK PEG 10 MOONCREST CREST 10
PETE AGNEW	G B (ALL	(A) NAZARETH	197	MOUNTAIN TOPC5001 US WB BS 2615
MANNY CHARLTON	G (ALL	(B) EXERCISES	1972	MOONCREST CREST14
DARRELL SWEET	D (ALL	(B) EXERCISES	19	MOUNTAIN TOPS103 US WB BS 2629
PETE WINGFIELD	K (A	(C) RAZAMANAZ	1973	MOONCREST CREST 1
PETE YORK	PERC (A	(C) RAZAMANAZ	197	MOUNTAIN TOPS104 US A&M SP 4396
B J COLE	STEEL (A	(D) LOUD & PROUD	1974	MOONCREST CREST 4
DAVE STEWART	K (A	(D) LOUD & PROUD	1974	MOUNTAIN TOPS105 US A&M SP 3609
ZAL CLEMINSON	SYN G(MN	(E) HAIR OF THE DOG	1975	MOONCREST CREST27
MAX MIDDLETON	K (E	(E) HAIR OF THE DOG	197	MOUNTAIN TOPS107 US A&M SP 4511
VICKI BROWN	V (E	(F) RAMPANT	1975	MOONCREST CREST15
SIMON PHILLIPS	PERC (E	(F) RAMPANT	197	MOUNTAIN TOPS106 US A&M SP 3641
LISA STRIKE	V (E	(G) GREATEST HITS	1975	MOUNTAIN TOPS108
BARRY ST JOHN	V (E	(H) CLOSE ENOUGH FOR ROCK'N'ROLL	1976	MOUNTAIN TOPS109 US A&M SP 4562
VICKY SILVA	V (E	(J) PLAY 'N' THE GAME	1977	MOUNTAIN TOPS113 US A&M SP 4610
JEFFREY BAXTER	SYN (O	(K) EXPECT NO MERCY	1977	MOUNTAIN TOPS115 US A&M SP 4666
JOHN LOCKE	K (O	(L) HOT TRACKS (EP)	1977	MOUNTAIN NAZ 001 US A&M 4643
		(M) NO MEAN CITY	1978	MOUNTAIN TOPS123 US A&M SP 4741
		(N) MALICE IN WONDERLAND	1980	MOUNTAIN TOPS126
		(O) FOOL CIRCLE	1981	NEMS UK NEL 6019

NAZTY

(A) I GOT TO MOVE	197	CONTEMPO	CLP 542

NAZZ

TODD RUNDGREN	G (AB	(A) NAZZ	1968	SGC	US	SD 5001
THOM MOONEY	D (AB	(B) NAZZ NAZZ	1969	SGC	US	SD 5002
ROBERT ANTONI	K V (AB	(C) NAZZ 3	1969	SGC	US	SD 5004
CARSON VAN OSTEN	B V (AB					

TED NEELEY

TED NEELEY	V (A	(A) 1974 AD	1973	RCA	US	APLI 0317
MICHAEL OMARTIAN	K (A					
LEW McCREARY	TROM (A JIM GORDON D (A MARK TULIN	B (A DEAN PARKS G (A
BEN BENAY	G (A KING ERRISSON CONG (A BARRY FASMAN	K (A PAUL HUBINON TPT(A
JACKIE KELSO	SAX (A DAVID DUKE HRNS(A BARBARA CARLSON	HRNS (A CHUCK FINDLEY TPT(A
FRED SELDON	SAX (A SID SHARP SAX (A

FRED NEIL

FRED NEIL	G V (ALL	(A) HOOTENANNY LIVE AT THE BITTER END	1964	FM RECORDS	US	FM 309
		(B) WORLD OF FOLK MUSIC	1964	FM RECORDS	US	FM 319
		(C) TEAR DOWN THE WALLS	1964	ELEKTRA	US	EKS 7248
		(D) BLEECKER & MACDOUGAL	196	ELEKTRA	US	EKS 7293
		(D) LITTLE BIT OF RAIN	1970	ELEKTRA	US	EKS 74073
		(E) FRED NEIL	1966	CAPITOL	US	ST 2665
		(E) EVERYBODY'S TALKIN'	1969	CAPITOL	US	ST 2665
		(F) SESSIONS	1971	CAPIT0l	US	ST 2862
		(G) OTHER SIDE OF THIS LIFE	1971	CAPITOL	US	ST 657

NEKTAR

MICK BROCKETT	(ALL	(A) JOURNEY TO THE CENTRE OF THE EYE	1972	BELLAPHON		BLPS19064
ALLAN FREEMANN	K (ALL	(A) TAB IN THE OCEAN	1972	BELLAPHON		BLPS19118
ROY ALBRIGHTON	G V (ABCDEFGH	(B) " " " "	1974	UA		UAS 29499
BEN HOWDEN	D (ALL	(B) " " " "	197	PASSPORT	US	98017
DEREK MOORE	B V (ALL	(C) REMEMBER THE FUTURE	1973	BELLAPHON		BLPS19164
DAVE NELSON	G V (J	(C) " " " "	1974	UA		UAS 29545
CHRIS MERCER	SAX (E	(C) " " " "	197	PASSPORT	US	98002
LARRY FAST	(J	(D) SOUNDS LIKE THIS	1973	BELLAPHON		BDA 7506
STEVE GREGORY	SAX (E	(D) " " " "	1973	UA		UAD60041/2
ROBERT CALVERT	V (E	(E) DOWN TO EARTH	1973	BELLAPHON		BLPS19190
P P ARNOLD	V (E	(E) " " "	1973	UA		UAG29680
KEN COLE	V (E	(E) " " "	197	PASSPORT		98005
PHIL BROWN	B (E	(F) LIVE AT THE ROUNDHOUSE	1974	BELLAPHON		BLPS19182
STEPHEN WICK	TUBA (E	(F) " " " "	197	BACILLUS		BAC 2028
BUTCH HUDSON	TPT (E	(G) RECYCLED	1976	BELLAPHON		BLPS19219
RON CARTHY	TPT (E	(G) " "	1976	DECCA	UK	SKLR 5250
CHRIS PYNE	TROM (E	(H) NEKTAR	1976	BELLAPHON		BLPS19224
		(J) MAGIC IS A CHILD	1977	BELLAPHON		BAC 2050
		(J) " " "	1977	POLYDOR	US	PD 6115
		(K) LIVE IN NEW YORK	1977	BELLAPHON		BAC 2004
		(L) MORE LIVE IN NEW YORK	1978	BELLAPHON		BAC 2058
		(M) THRU THE EARS	1978	IMPORT		IMP 9001
		(N) MAN IN THE MOON	19			

BILL NELSON

BILL NELSON	G V (A	(A) NORTHERN DREAM	1971	SMILE		LAF 2182
		(A) NORTHERN DREAM	1980	BUTT RI		BUTT002

BILL NELSONS RED NOISE

BILL NELSON	G V	(A) SOUND ON SOUND	1979 HARVEST UK SHSP 4095 US ST 11931
ANDREW CLARK	K (A		
IAN NELSON	SAX (A RICK FORD B (A STEVE PEER D (A		

RICK NELSON

RICK NELSON	G V (ALL	RICKY	1957	US IMPERIAL 9048	UK LONDON	HAP 2080
JAMES BURTON	G (	RICKY (RI 2 TRACKS LESS)	1979	US IMPERIAL M1004		
JOE OSBORN	B (	RICKY NELSON	1958	US IMPERIAL 9050	UK LONDON	HAP 2119
JAMES KIRKLAND	B (	RICKY SINGS AGAIN	1959	US IMPERIAL 9061	UK LONDON	HAP 2159
RICHIE FROST	D (	SONGS BY RICKY	1959	US IMPERIAL 9082	UK LONSDON	HAP 2206
RAY JOHNSON	PNO (	SONGS BY RICKY	1959	US IMPERIAL 12030		
JOE MAPHIS	G (	MORE SONGS BY RICKY	1960	US IMPERIAL 9122	UK LONDON	HAP 2290
BARNEY KESSEL	G (	MORE SONGS BY RICKY	1960	US IMPERIAL 12059		
GENE GARTH	PNO (	RICK IS 21	1961	US IMPERIAL 9152	UK LONDON	HAP 2379
		RICK IS 21	1961	US IMPERIAL 12071		
JIM CETERA	B V (J	ALBUM SEVEN	1962	US IMPERIAL 9167	UK LONDON	HAP 2445
TOM BRUMLEY	STEEL (JKLMN	ALBUM SEVEN	1962	US IMPERIAL 12082		
ALLEN KEMP	G V (JKL	BEST SELLERS BY RICK NELSON	1963	US IMPERIAL 9218	US IMPERIAL	12218
PATRICK SHANAHAN	D (JKL	ITS UP TO YOU	1963	US IMPERIAL 9223	US IMPERIAL	12223
RANDY MEISNER	B V (K	ITS UP TO YOU (DIFF TRACKS)	1963		UK LONDON	HAP 8066
ANDY BELLING	K (K	MILLION SELLERS	1963	US IMPERIAL 9232	US IMPERIAL (S)	12232
STEPHEN A LOVE	B V (L	MILLION SELLERS(DIFF TRACKS)	1964	UK	BRUNSWICK LBY 3027
DON NELSON	FLT (L	HELLO MARY LOU (SAME AS ABOVE)	197	NL SUNSET		DA 5026
DENNIS LARDEN	G (MN	ROCK 'N' ROLL CLASSICS(AS ABOVE)	197	NL U A		52 92968
JAT DE WITT WHITE	B V (MN	STORY OF R'N'R (RI OF IMP 9232)	19	GERM U A	UA	30050
TY GRIMES	D (M	A LONG VACATION	1963	US IMPERIAL 9244	US	(S) 12244
RICHIE HAYWARD	D (	SINGS FOR YOU	1964	US IMPERIAL 9251	US	(S) 12251
SNEAKY PETE KLEINOW	STEEL(	FOR YOUR SWEET LOVE	1963	US DECCA DL 74419	UK BRUNSWICK LAT 8545
BUDDY EMMONS	STEEL(	SINGS FOR YOU	1964	US DECCA DL 74479	UK BRUNSWICK LAT 8562
STEVE DUNCAN	D PERC V(N	THE VERY THOUGHT OF YOU	1964	US DECCA DL 74559	UK BRUNSWICK LAT 8581
JAI WINDING	K (N	SPOTLIGHT ON RICK	1964	US DECCA DL 74608	UK BRUNSWICK LAT 8596
ROGER BUSH	B (N	BEST ALWAYS	1965	US DECCA DL 74660	UK BRUNSWICK LAT 8615
		LOVE & KISSES	1965	US DECCA DL 74678	UK BRUNSWICK LAT 8630
		BRIGHT LIGHTS & COUNTRY MUSIC	1966	US DECCA DL 74779	UK BRUNSWICK LAT 8657
		ON THE FLIP SIDE (4 TRACK BY RICK)	66	US DECCA DL 74836		
		COUNTRY FEVER	1967	US DECCA DL 74837	UK BRUNSWICK LAT 8680
		ANOTHER SIDE OF RICK	1968	US DECCA DL 74944	UK MCA	MUPS 302
		PERSPECTIVE	1969	US DECCA DL 75162		
		RICK NELSON IN CONCERT	1970	US DECCA DL 75162	UK MCA	MUPS 409
		RICK NELSON IN CONCERT	197	US MCA RI MCA 3		
		(J)RICK SINGS NELSON	1970	US DECCA DL 75236	UK MCA	MUPS 442
		(J)RICK SINGS NELSON	197	US MCA RO MCA20	UK MCA RI	MCF 2644
		(K)RUDY THE FIFTH	1971	US DECCA DL 75297	UK MCA	MUPS 440
		(K)RUDY THE FIFTH	197	US MCA RI MCA37	UK MCA RI	MCF 2535
		(L)GARDEN PARTY	1972	US DECCA DL 75391	UK MCA	MDKS8009
		(L)GARDEN PARTY	1974	US MCA RI MCA62	UK MCA RI	NCG 3515
		(M)WINDFALL	1974	US MCA 383	UK MCA	MCG 3516
		(N)INTAKES	1977	US EPIC 34420	UK EPIC	81802
		VERY BEST OF	1970	SUNSET	UK	SLS 50164
		VERY BEST OF (DIFF TRACKS)	197	UA	US	UALA 330E
		LEGENDARY MASTERS	1971	UA US 9960	UK UA	UAD 60029/30
		POP CHRONICLE (RI OF ABOVE)	197	UA	GERM	UA 29962
		RICK NELSON COUNTRY	1973	MCA		MCA 24004

RICK NELSON

RICK NELSON	197	SUNSET	US	SUS 5118
I NEED YOU	197	SUNSET	US	SUS 5205
RICKY NELSON STORY (TRIPLE)	197	ARI	US	ARI 1003
RICKY NELSON SINGLES	1977 MCA US	CDL 8053	UK RI MFP	MFP 50411
RICKY NELSON ALBUMS	1979 UK UA			UAK 30246
STARS OF THE 60s	19	NL UA		50 94953
RICK NELSON STORY	19	JAP JET		JET 7070
BIG HITS	19	JAP UA		UA GXH18
PLAYING TO WIN	1981 CAPITOL			12109

SANDY NELSON   N22

SANDY NELSON   D   (ALL

TEENBEAT	1960	IMPERIAL US	(M)9105(S)12044	
HES A DRUMMER BOY	1961	IMPERIAL US	(M)9136(S)12159	
LET THERE BE DRUMS	1961	IMPERIAL US	(M)9159(S)12080	
DRUMS ARE MY BEAT	1962	IMPERIAL US	(M)9168(S)12083	

SUPERDRUMS	196	IMPERIAL US	(M)9314(S)12914	DRUMMING UP A STORM	196	IMPERIAL US	(M)9189(S)12189
SUPERDRUMS	196	LIBERTY UK	LBY 3080	GOLDEN HITS	196	IMPERIAL US	(M)9202(S)12202
IN BEAT	196	IMPERIAL US	(M)9305(S)12305	ON THE WILD SIDE	196	IMPERIAL US	(M)9203(S)12203
BEAT THAT *?!! DRUM	196	IMPERIAL US	(M)9329(S)12329	AND THEN THERE WERE DRUMS	196	IMPERIAL US	(M)9204(S)12204
SOUL DRUMS	196	IMPERIAL US	(M)9362(S)12362	TEENAGE HOUSE PARTY	196	IMPERIAL US	(M)9215(S)12215
BOOGALOO BEAT	196	IMPERIAL US	(M)9367(S)12367	BEST OF THE BEATS	196	IMPERIAL US	(M)9224(S)12224
ROCK'N'ROLL REVIVAL	196	IMPERIAL US	(M)9400(S)12400	BEAT THAT DRUM	196	IMPERIAL US	(S)12237
MANHATTAN SPIRITUAL	196	IMPERIAL US	(M)9439(S)12439	SANDY NELSON PLAYS	196	IMPERIAL US	(M)9249(S)12249
GROOVY	196	IMPERIAL US	(M)9451(S)12451	SANDY NELSON PLAYS	1964	LIBERTY UK	BY 3007
WALKING BEAT	19	SUNSET US	1114	BE TRUE TO YOUR SCHOOL	196	IMPERIAL US	(M)9258(S)12258
TEENDRUMS	19	SUNSET UK	SLS50061	LIVE IN LAS VEGAS	196	IMPERIAL US	(S)12272
& THEN THERE WERE	19	SUNSET UK	SUS 5224	LIVE IN LAS VEGAS	196	LIBERTY UK	LBY 3035
THE BEST OF	1974	LIBERTY UK	LBS83387	TEENBEAT 65	196	IMPERIAL US	(M)9278(S)12278
HOCUS POCUS	1976	EMI IMP	UAS29509	DISCOTHEQUE DRUMS	196	IMPERIAL US	(M)9283(S)12283
VERY BEST OF	19	UA US	LA 440	DRUMS A GOGO	196	LIBERTY UK	LBY 3061
VERY BEST OF	1978	SUNSET UK	SLS50411	BOSS BEAT	196	IMPERIAL US	(M)9298(S)12298

TRACY NELSON   N23

TRACY NELSON	G K	(ALL	(A) DEEP ARE THE ROOTS	1966	PRESTIGE	US	7726
RON CORNELIUS	G	(CD	(B) POOR MAN'S PARADISE	1972	CBS	US	31759
REGGIE YOUNG	G	(CD	(C) TRACY NELSON	1974	ATLANTIC US SDD7310	UK K50091	
MAC GAYDEN	G	(BC	(D) SWEET SOUL MUSIC	1975	MCA	US MCA 494	
BOBBY EMMONS	K	(C	(E) TIME IS ON MY SIDE	1976	MCA	US 2203	UK MCF2765
BOBBY WOODS	K	(C	(F) HOMEMADE SONGS	197	FLYING FISH	US	FF 052
JOM GORDON	D	(E	(G) COME SEE ME ABOUT IT	1980	FLYING FISH	US	FF 209
ED GREENE	D	(E					

JIM HUGHART	B	(E	DAVID FOSTER	K	(E	CLARENCE McDONALD	K	(E	LARRY MUHOBERAC	K	(E
LARRY CARLTON	G	(E	DEAN PARKS	G	(E	JESSE ED DAVIS	G	(E	DANNY KORTCHMAR	G	(E
JIM HORN	SAX	(E	LAURA CREAMER	V	(E	GERALD GARRETT	V	(CE	MAXINE WILLARD	V	(E
JULIA TILLMAN	V	(E	MARK CREAMER	V	(E	IRMA ROUTEN	V	(E	SUSAN STEWARD	V	(E
OMA DRAKE SINGERS	V	(E	DARLENE GRONCKI	V	(E	LEON PENDARVIS	K	(CD	JACK LEE	G V K(BC
TOMMY COGBILL	B	(C	KENNY MALONE	D	(C	STEVE HOWARD	TPT	(C	MARSHALL CYR	TPT	(C
LON PRICE	SAX	(C	MICHAEL PIERCE	SAX	(C	CLARENCE FORD	HRNS	(C	CLYDIE KING	V	(C
BEAU CECCHINO	V	(C	MERRY CLAYTON	V	(C	JIM GILSTRAP	V	(C	JOE GREEN	V	(C
PAT POWDRILL	V	(C	WILLIE NELSON	V	(C	LINDA RONSTADT	V	(C	BEAU DOLLAR	PERC	(B
JERRY CARRIGAN	PERC	(B	ANDY MACMAHON	K V	(BG	TOAD ANDREWS	G	(B	STEVIE MENDELL	B	(B
TERRY BURNSIDE	SAX	(B	BILLY PUETT	SAX	(B	TOMMY SMITH	TPT	(B	IRV KANE	TROM	(B
DENNIS GOODE	TROM	(B	SADIE CANTRELL	V	(B	ANITA BALL	V	(B	RICHARD KROUSE	V	(B
REV JOSEPH CANTRELL	V	(B	SYLVIA TEPPER	V	(D	BOB BABITT	B	(D	WILLIE HALL	D	(D
MYRNA SMITH	V	(D	SYLVIA SHEMWELL	V	(D	JOHNNY GIMBLE	FDL	(D	RICHARD TEE	K	(D
ESTELLE BROWN	V	(D	PETE DRAKE	STEEL	(D	HARVEY THOMPSON	HRNS	(D	CHARLES ROSE	HRNS	(D
RON EADES	HRNS	(D	HARRISON CALLOWAY	HRNS	(D	LANNY BOLES	PERC	(D	LARRY CHANEY	G	(D
BARRY CHANCE	G	(G	CHRIS LEUZINGER	G	(G	LISA SILVER REYNOLDS	V	(G	SHERRY KRAMER	V	(G
DONNA McELROY	V	(G	JAMIE BRANTLEY	V	(G	JACK GROCHMAL	V	(G	TED REYNOLDS	B	(G
WAYNE JACKSON	HRNS	(G	ANDREW LOVE	HRNS	(G	PEBBLE DANIEL	V	(G	MARCIA ROUTH	V	(G
SHERRY GROOMS	V	(G	YVONNE HODGES	V	(G	STEVE BRANTLEY	V	(G	BRUCE DEES	V	(G

WILLIE NELSON   N23A

...AND THAN I WROTE	1962	LIBERTY	US	LST7239	RED HEADED STRANGER	1975	CBS	US	33482
HERE'S WILLIE NELSON	1963	LIBERTY	US	LST7308	RED HEADED STRANGER	1975	CBS	UK	69200
COUNTRY WILLIE	1965	RCA	US	LSP3418	FAMOUS COUNTRY (DBL)	1975	RCA	UK	DPS2062
HELLO WALLS	1966	SUNSET	US	SUS5138	SOUND IN YOUR MIND	1976	CBS	US	34092
HELLO WALLS	197	PICKWICK	US	SPC3584	SOUND IN YOUR MIND	1974	CBS	UK	81252
COUNTRY FAVOURITES	1966	RCA	US	LSP3528	SOUND IN YOUR MIND	1980	EMBASSY	UK	31828
COUNTRY MUSIC CONCERT	1966	RCA	US	LSP3659	TROUBLEMAKER	1976	CBS	US	34112
MAKE WAY FOR	1967	RCA	US	LSP3748	TROUBLEMAKER	1976	CBS	UK	81565
THE PARTYS OVER	1967	RCA	US	LSP3858	WANTED THE OUTLAWS	1976	RCA	US	APL11321
TEXAS IN MY SOUL	1968	RCA	US	LSP3937	WANTED THE OUTLAWS	1976	RCA	UK	RS 1048
TEXAS IN MY SOUL	1968	RCA	UK	RD 7997	WILLIE NELSON LIVE	1976	RCA	US	APL11487
GOOD TIMES	1968	RCA	US	LSP4057	WILLIE NELSON LIVE	1976	RCA	UK	LSA3277
MY OWN PECULIAR WAY	1969	RCA	US	LSP4111	& FRIENDS	1976	PLANTATION US	PLP214
BOTH SIDES NOW	1970	RCA	US	LSP4294	& FRIENDS	1976	CHARLY	UK	CR 30120
LAYING MY BURDENS DOWN	1970	RCA	US	LSP4404	WILLIE NELSON 1961	1977	DOUBLE BARREL	LT1961
COLUMBUS STOCKADE	1970	CAMDEN	US	CAS2444	BEFORE HIS TIME	1977	RCA	US	APL12210
COLUMBUS STOCKADE	197	CAMDEN	US	ACL 7018	TEXAS COUNTRY (DBL)	1976	U A	US	LA 574H2
WILLIE NELSON & FAMILY	1971	RCA	US	LSP4489	TO LEFTY FROM WILLIE	1977	CBS	US	34695
YESTERDAYS WINE	1971	RCA	US	LSP4568	WAYLON & WILLIE	1978	RCA	UK US A PL12686
YESTERDAYS WINE	197	CAMDEN	US	ANL1102	STARDUST	1978	CBS	US	35305
YESTERDAYS WINE	1980	INTERNATIONAL	INT5014	STARDUST	1978	CBS	UK	82710
THE WORDS DONT FIT	1972	RCA	US	LSP4653	FACE OF A FIGHTER	1978	LONE STAR	US	L4602
THE WILLIE WAY	1972	RCA	US	LSP4760	THERE'LL BE NO TEARS	1978	UA	US	UAL A930
COUNTRY WINNERS	1973	CAMDEN	US	ACL10326	THERE'LL BE NO TEARS	1978	UA	UK	UAS30215
THE BEST OF(RI LST7239)	1973	UA	US	UAL A086	WILLIE & FAMILY LIVE	1978	CBS	US	35642
SPOTLIGHT ON	1974	CAMDEN	US	ACL10705	WILLIE & FAMILY LIVE	1978	CBS	UK	88333
COUNTRY WILLIE	1973	UA	UA	UAL A420	PRETTY PAPER	1979	CBS	US	36189
SHOTGUN WILLIE	1973	ATLANTIC	US	SD 7262	SINGS KRISTOFFERSON	1979	CBS	US	36158
PHASES & STAGES	1974	ATLANTIC	US	SD 7291	SINGS KRISTOFFERSON	1979	CBS	UK	83877
WHAT CAN YOU DO TO ME	1975	RCA	US	APL11234	SWEET MEMORIES	1979	RCA	US	AHL13243

WILLIE NELSON

SWEET MEMORIES	1979 RCA	US	AHLI 3243
CLASSIC WILLIE NELSON	1979 SUNSET		SLS 50430
ONE FOR THE ROAD	1979 CBS	US	36064
ONE FOR THE ROAD	1979 CBS	UK	88461
ELECTRIC HORSEMAN	1979 CBS	US	36327
ELECTRIC HORSEMAN	1979 CBS	UK	70177
SAN ANTONIO ROSE	1980 CBS	US	36476
SAN ANTONIO ROSE	1980 CBS	UK	84358
HONEYSUCKLE ROSE	1980 CBS	US	36752
HONEYSUCKLE ROSE	1980 CBS	UK	22080
FAMILY BIBLE	1980 SONGBIRD	US	MCA 3258

N24 NEO

IAN NORTH	V	
ROBIN SIMON	G	
PAUL SIMON	D	GEORGE DYNER	B

N24A NEON HEARTS

PAUL RAVEN	B	(A	(A) POPULAR MUSIC	1979	SATRIL	UK	SATL 4012
KEITH ALLEN	D	(A				
STEVE HEART	SAX	(A	MARTIN RATCLIFFE	G	(A

N25 MICHAEL NESMITH

MICHAEL NESMITH	G V	(ALL	(A) WICHITA TRAIN WHISTLE SINGS	1968	DOT	US	SLPD 516
RED RHODES	STEEL	(ABCDEFG	(A) WICHITA TRAIN WHISTLE SINGS	1978	PACIFIC ARTS	US RI	PACB 7113
JAMES BURTON	G	(AD	(B) MAGNETIC SOUTH	1970	RCA	US LSP4371 UK SF8136
SHORTY ROGERS	D	(A	(C) LOOSE SALUTE	1970	RCA	US LSP4415
HAL BLAINE	D	(A	(D) NEVADA FIGHTER	1971	RCA	US LSP4497 UK SF8209
JOHN AUDINO	TPT	(A	(E) TANTAMOUNT TO TREASON	1972	RCA	US LPS4563 UK SF8276
CHUCK BERGHOFFER	B	(A	(F) AND THE HITS JUST KEEP ON COMING	1972	RCA	US LSP4695
MILT BERNHART	TROM	(A	(F) AND THE HITS JUST KEEP ON COMING	1977	ISLAND	UK	ILPS 9439
BUD BRISBOIS	TPT	(A	(F) AND THE HITS JUST KEEP ON COMING	197	PACIFIC ARTS	US	PAC 116
FRANK CAPP	PERC	(A	(G) PRETTY MUCH YOUR STANDARD STASH	1973	RCA	US	APLI 0164
BUDDY CHILDERS	TPT	(A	(G) PRETTY MUCH YOUR STANDARD STASH	1977	ISLAND	UK	ILPS 9440
GENE CIPRIANO	WIND	(A	(G) PRETTY MUCH YOUR STANDARD STASH	197	PACIFIC ARTS	US	PAC 117
GARY COLEMAN	PERC	(A	(H) THE PRISON	1975	PACIFIC ARTS	US	PAC 101
BUDDY COLLETTE	WIND	(A	(J) FROM A RADIO ENGINE TO PHOTON WING	1977 ISLAND	UK	ILPS 9486
JIM DECKER	HRNS	(A	(J) FROM A RADIO ENGINE TO PHOTON WING	197	PACIFIC ARTS	US	PAC 107
DOUG DILLARD	BANJO	(A	(K) BEST OF	1976	RCA	US	RS 1064
VICTOR FELDMAN	PERC	(A	(L) LIVE AT THE PALAIS	1978	PACIFIC	US	PAC 7118
JUSTIN GORDON	WIND	(A	(M) COMPILATION	197	PACIFIC ARTS	US PAC106 +PAC 7106
BILL HINSHAW	HRNS	(A	(N) INFINITE RIDER ON THE BIG DOGMA	1979	PACIFIC ARTS	US	PAC 7130
JOE HOWARD	TROM	(A				

DICK HYDE	TROM	(A	JULES JACOB	TROM	(A	JOHN KITZMILLER	TUBA	(A	MANNY KLAIN	TPT	(A
LARRY KNECHTEL	PNO	(A	JOHN LOWE	WIND	(A	LEW McCREARY	TROM	(A	JACK NIMITZ	WIND	(A
BARRETT O'HARA	TROM	(A	EARL PALMER	D	(A	LONNIE MACK	G	(J	DICK PERISSI	HRNS	(A
DON RANDI	PNO	(A	SAM RICE	TUBA	(A	KENNY SHROYER	TROM	(A	TOMMY TEDESCO	G	(A
TONY TERRAN	TPT	(A	JIMMY ZITO	TPT	(A	LOUISE BLACKBURN	TROM	(A	JULES CHAIKEN	TPT	(A
JIM HORN	WIND	(A	OLLIE MITCHELL	TPT	(A	JOHN WARE	D	(BCDL	JOHN LONDON	B	(BCD
EARL P HALL	K	(B	AL CASEY	G	(D	JACK PANELLI	D	(E	JOHNNY MEEKS	B	(E
DAVID MACKAY	B	(JLM	LARRIE LONDIN	D	(J	JERRY CARRIGAN	D	(J	GLEN D HARDIN	K	(CD
JOSE FELICIANO CONGAS	(E	DAVID BRIGGS	K	(J	JOE OSBORN	B	(D	JAY LACY	G	(G
JOHN SHANE KEISTER	K	(J	MAX BENNETT	B	(D	DAVID BARRY	K	(G	JOE CHEMAY	V	(M
MICHAEL COHEN	K	(DE	BILL GRAHAM	B FDL	(G	LISA SILVER	VLN	(J	GREG TAYLOR	HCA	(J
DANNY LANE	D	(G	WELDON MYRICK	STEEL	(J	LINDA HARGROVE	V	(J	MARCIA ROUTH	V	(J
PEBBLE DANIEL	V	(J	JACK RANELLI		(J	AL PERKINS	STEEL	(LM	JAMES TRUMBO	K	(L
RON TUTT	D	(D	PAUL LEIM	D	(M	LENNY CASTRO	PERC	(M	JOHN HOBBS	K V	(M
TOM SAVIANO	SAX	(M									

N26 NEU

KLAUS DINGER	G V D	(ALL	(A) NEU	1972 UA UK UAS 29396	BRAIN	000 1004
MICHAEL ROTHER	G B	(ALL	(B) NEU 2	1973 UA UK UAS 29500	BRAIN	000 1028
			(C) NEU 75	1977 UA UK UAS 29782	BRAIN	000 1062
			(D) HALLOGALLO	197	BRAIN	0040 145
			(AB) 2 ORIGINALS	197	BRAIN	008 0114

N26A RICK NEUFELD

RICK NEUFELD	G V	(A	(A) PRAIRIE DOG	1974	RCA	UA APLI 0074	UK	SF 8413
DON ZUEFF FDL MAND V G	(A						
HUMPHREY DUMPTRUCK BAN V	(A	BURTON CUMMINGS	K FLT V	(A	BILL WALLACE	B HRNS V	(A	GARY PETERSON D PERC	(A
AL BRISCOE	STEEL	(A	TERRY BUSH	G V	(A	TOM JACKSON	V	(A	LORNA HIBBERT	V	(A
LUCILLE LEPING	V	(A	GRAEME GARD	V	(A			

N27 NEUTRONS

WILL YOUATT	G B	(AB	(A) BLACK HOLE STAR	1974	UA	UK	UAG 29652
MARTIN WALLACE	G V	(AB	(B) TALES FROM THE BLUE COCOONS	1975	UA	UK	UAG 29726
PHIL RYAN	K	(AB					
STUART HALLIDAY	D	(B	CAROMAY DIXON	V	(AB	JOHN WEATHERS	D	(A	RAY TAFF WILLIAMS	G	(AB
STUART GORDON	VLN	(A	DAVID CHARLES	D	(AB	PICK WITHERS	PERC	(A

N27A NEVILLE BROTHERS

| | | | (A) THE NEVILLE BROTHERS | 1979 CAPITOL | UK US | 11865 |

N27B NEW ADVENTURE

PETER BOOTSMAN	G V	(A	(A) NEW ADVENTURE	1980	POLYDOR	2925 098
HARRY DE WINTER	K B V	(A				
HENK TORPEDO	D PERC	(A				

N27C NEW BARBARIANS

RON WOOD	G V	(A	(A) LIVE 1979 NO RECORDS
PHIL CHEN	B	(A	
KEITH RICHARDS	G	(A	BOBBY KEYS	SAX	(A	SUGAR BLUE	HCA	(A	IAN MACLAGAN	K	(A

N28 NEW BIRTH

MELVIN WILSON		(A	(A) BIRTHDAY	1973 RCA UK SF 8368	US	LSP 4797
CARL McDONALD		(A	(A) BIRTHDAY	197 RCA		APLI 2145
JAMES BAKER		(A	(B) ITS BEEN A LONG TIME	1974 RCA		ALPI 0285
TONY CHURCHILL		(A	(C) BLIND BABY	1975 BUDDAH UK 4034	US	5636

(CONTINUED)

NEW BIRTH

VERNON BULLOCK	(A	(D) COMIN' FROM ALL ENDS	19	RCA		US	APLI 0494
ROBERT JACKSON	(A	(E) REINCARNATION	197	RCA		US	APLI 1801
		(F) BEST OF	197	RCA		US	AHLI 1021
		(G) BEHOLD(THE MIGHTY ARMY)	197	WB		US	BS3071
		(H) LOVE POTION	197	WB		US	BS2953

NEW CACTUS BAND
N29

DUANE HITCHINGS K V FLT(A	(A) SON OF CACTUS	1973 ATLANTIC US SD7917 UK	K40488
ROLAND ROBINSON	B V	(A			
MANNY BERTEMATTI	D V	(A	MIKE PINERA	G V (A	JERRY NORRIS	D V (A

NEW ENGLAND
N29A

JOHN FANNON	G V	(AB	(A) NEW ENGLAND	1979	INFINITY	INS 2005
JIMMY WALDO	K V	(AB	(B) EXPLORER SUITE	1980	ELEKTRA	6E 307
HIRSH GARDNER	D V	(AB				
GARY SHEA	B	(AB				

NEW HEARTS
N30

MATT McINTYRE	D	(1	(1) 1977/78 (2) JULY 1978
IAN PAIN	V	(12	
DAVE CAIRNS	G	(12	JOHN HARTY B (12 JAMIE D (2

NEW MUSIK
N30A

TONY MANSFIELD	V G K(B	(A) FROM A TO B	1980	GTO	UK	GTLP 041
TONY HIBBERT	B	(B	(B) ANYWHERE	1981	GTO	UK	GTLP 044
CLIVE GATES	K	(B				
PHIL TOWNER	D	(B				

NEW ORDER
N31

RON ASHETON	G	(A	(A) NEW ORDER	1978 RCA/FUN	ISL 6443
DENNIS THOMPSON	D	(A			
RAY GUNN	G	(A	JIMMY RECCA B (A SCOTT THURSTON K (A JEFF SPREY V (A
DAVE GILBERT	V	(A			

NEW RIDERS OF THE PURPLE SAGE
N32

JOHN DAWSON	G V	(ALL	(A) NEW RIDERS OF THE PURPLE SAGE	1971	CBS	US 30888	UK	64843
DAVID NELSON	G V MAND	(ALL	(B) POWERGLIDE	1972	CBS	US 31284	UK	64843
DAVE TORBERT	B G V(ABCDE	(C) GYPSY COWBOY	1973	CBS	US 31930	UK	65008
SPENCER DRYDEN	D V	(ALL	(D) ADVENTURES OF PANAMA RED	1973	CBS	US 32450	UK	65687
MICKEY HART	D	(	(E) HOME HOME ON THE ROAD	1974	CBS	US 32870	UK	80060
JERRY GARCIA	G	(ABG	(F) BRUJO	1975	CBS	US 33145	UK	80405
PHIL LESH	B	(	(G) OH WHAT A MIGHTY TIME	1975	CBS	US 33688	UK	69182
COMMANDER CODY	PNO	(	(H) NEW RIDERS	1976	MCA	US 2196	UK MCF2758
BUDDY CAGE	STEEL	(BCDEFGHK	(J) BEST OF	1976	CBS	US 34367	UK	81742
BILLY KREUTZMAN	PERC	(B	(K) WHO ARE THESE GUYS	1977	MCA	US 2248	UK MCF2793
NICKY HOPKINS	K	(B	(L) MARIN COUNTY LINE	1978	MCA	US 2307	UK MCF2830
SKIP BATTIN	B V	(FGH						

NORBERT PUTNAM	B	(	SLY STONE	K V	(G	JOHN HUG	G	(K	BILL STEWART	D (K
JEFF NARELL	PERC	(G	PEPPER WATKINS	V	(G	BOOTCHE ANDERSON	V	(G	MARILYN SCOTT	V (G
PAY PARK	FDL	(G	DONNA GODCHAUX	V	(CD	BUFFY ST MARIE	V	(D	MEMPHIS HORNS	HRNS (D
STEPHEN LOVE	B	(K	PENE BLANCA	V	(G	JACK SCHROER	HRNS (C	LUCHA CARDENAS	V (G
RICHARD GREENE	VLN	(C	PATTIE SANTOS	V	(G	ANDREA AHLGREN	V	(G	DARLENE DIDOMENICO	V (C
MARK NAFTALIN	PNO	(C						

NEW VICTORY BAND
N33

JOHN ADAMS TROM FDL	(A	(A) ONE MORE DANCE & THEN	1978	TOPIC	12 TS 382
SUZIE ADAMS	BANJO(A				
CHRIS COE	DULCIMER(A	PETER COE MELODEON(A HELEN WATSON K (A IAN WORDSWORTH PERC (A
ROGER WATSON	TUBA (A	LINDA WORDSWORTH (A

NEW YORK DOLLS
N34

DAVID JOHANSEN	V	(12345AB	(A) NEW YORK DOLLS	1973 MERCURY	UK 6338 270 US SRM1 675
JOHNNY THUNDERS	G	(1234AB	(B) TOO MUCH TOO SOON	1974 MERCURY	UK 6338 498 US SRMI 1001
RICK RIVETS	G	(1	(AB)N Y DOLLS/TOO MUCH	1977 MERCURY	UK 6641 631
ARTHUR KANE	B	(123A	(1) 1972 (2) 1972 (3) 1972/73 (4) 1974 1975 (5) 1975/77
BILLY MURCIA	d	(12			
TONY MACHINE		(5	CHRIS ROBINSON K (5 SYLVAIN SYLVAIN G(2345G JERRY NOLAN D (34AB
PETER JORDAN	B	(45B BOBBY BLAIN K (5

NEW YORK GONG
N34A

	(A) ABOUT TIME	19	CHARLY	CRL 5021

NEW YORK MARY
N35

BRUCE JOHNSTONE	WIND (B	(A) NEW YORK MARY	197	FREEDOM	US	1019
RICK PETRONE	B	(B	(B) A PIECE OF THE APPLE	1977 FREEDOM	UK 41035	US	1035
JOE CORSELLO	D	(B				
ROBERT FRIEDMAN	HRNS (B	GENE BERTONCINI G (B DON ELLIOTT SINGERS V(B PETE LEVIN SYN (B

NEW YORK ROCK & ROLL ENSEMBLE
N36

DORIAN RUDNYTSKY K H HRNS(BD	(A) NEW YORK ROCK AND ROLL ENSEMBLE	1968	ATCO	US	33240
MARTIN FULTERMAN	D OBOE (BD	(B) FAITHFUL FRIENDS	1969	ATCO UK 228 932	US	33294
BRIAN CORRIGAN	G V	(B	(C) REFLECTIONS	1970	ATCO	US	33312
CLIFFORD NIVISON	G	(BD	(D) ROLL OVER	1971	CBS UK 64126	US	30033
MICHAEL KAMEN K G V WIND(BD	(E) FREEDOMBURGER	1972	CBS UK 64324	US	31317
LARRY PACKER	FDL	(				
DAVID SANBORN	SAX	(	HANK DE VITO STEEL(D DENNIS WHITTED D (

MICKEY NEWBURY
N37

MICKEY NEWBURY	G V	(ALL	(A) HARLEQUINN MELODIES	1968	RCA	US LSP 4043
JERRY KENNEDY	S SITAR (B	(B) LOOKS LIKE RAIN	1969	MERCURY	US SR 61236
KENNY BUTTREY	D	(B	(B) LOOKS LIKE RAIN	197	ELEKTRA	UK K72001
CHARLIE McCOY	HCA G(BEG	(C) FRISCO MABEL JOY	1971	ELEKTRA UK K42105	US EKS574107
WAYNE MOSS	G	(BEJ	(D) SINGS HIS OWN	1972	RCA UK SF B268	US LPS 4675
FARRELL MORRIS	PERC (BEIJG	(E) HEAVEN HELP THE CHILD	1973	ELEKTRA UK K42137	US EKS575055
DENNIS LINDE	G V	(E	(F) LIVE AT MONTEZUMA	1973	ELEKTRA	US 7E 2007
KENNY MALONE	D	(EG	(G) I CAME TO HEAR THE MUSIC	1974	ELEKTRA UK K42162	US 7E 1007
WELDON MYRICK	STEEL(E	(H) LOVERS	1975	ELEKTRA UK K52017	US 7E 1030
CHET ATKINS	G	(E	(I) RUSTY TRACKS	1977	HICKORY	US AH44002
NORBERT PUTNAM	B	(EI	(I) RUSTY TRACKS	1977	ABC	UK ABCL 5215

(CONTINUED)

MICKEY NEWBURY

BOB SEYMOUR		(E		(J) HIS EYE ON THE SPARROW			1978	HICKORY			US	HA44011	
BUDDY SPICHER	FDL	(EG		(K) THE SPARROW			1979	HICKORY			US	HB44017	
VASSAR CLEMENTS	FDL	(E		(L) FUNNY FAMILIAR FORGOTTEN FEELINGS		19	RCA	UK					
EMORY GORDY	B	(E											
RICHARD BENNETT	G	(E	DENNIS ST JOHN	D	(E	DON RANDI	PNO	(E	MARLINE GREENE	G	(E	
JOE OSBORN	B	(E	BOBBY WOOD	K	(EIK	BOBBY THOMPSON G BAN	(EIJK	TOMMY COGBILL	B	(EG
BOB BECKHAM		(E	DAVID BRIGGS	K	(EG	JIMMY HASKELL ACC/STRINGS(E		JIMMY GETZOFF	VLN(E
TOM BAYLOR	V	(E	BILLY SANFORD		(EIK	STAN FARBER	V	(E	JOE ALLEN	B	(I
HENRY STRZELECKI	B'	(IG	HAYWARD BISHOP	D PERC(IJ	JIM ISBELL	D PERC(I	LARRIE LONDIN	D PERC(I
BOBBY EMMONS	K	(IG	ALAN MOORE	K	(IJK	RON OATES	K	(I	PHIL BAUGH	G	(I
JOHNNY CHRISTOPHER	G	(I	DAVE KIRBY	G	(I	REGGIE YOUNG	G	(I	BUDDY EMMONS	STEEL(I
LLOYD GREEN	STEEL(IG	TERRY McMILLAN	HCA	(IJK	EVERHARD RAMM	HRNS	(I	CINDY REYNOLDS	HARP (I
ROBERT S GALBRAITH	K	(J	THOMAS G CAIN	K	(J	DONALD L POTTER	G	(J	STEVE COLLOM	G	(J
JESSE BOYCE	B	(J	JOHN C WILLIAMS	B	(J	DAN ECKLEY	MAND (J	RAFE VAN HOY	G	(K
DON ROTH	G	(K	RAY EDENTON	G	(KG	BARRY BURTON	G	(K	JOSEPH PELLECHIA	SAX	(K
BOB L MOORE	B	(K	JERRY CARRIGAN	D	(KG	MARK B MORRIS	PERC (K	MIKE LEECH	B	(G
SHANE KEISTER	SYN	(G	PETE WADE	G	(G	JERRY SHOOK	G	(G	GORDON STOKER	V	(G
LAVERNA MOORE	V	(G	WENDY SUITS	V	(G	REGGIE YOUNG	G	(G	GEORGE TIDWELL	HRNS (G
DON GANT	V	(G	BUDDY HARMON	D	(G	HOYT HAWKINS	V	(G	DOTTIE DELEONIBUS	V (G
BERGEN WHITE	V	(G	DENNIS GOODE	HRNS (G	HAROLD BRADLEY	B	(G	RAY WALKER	V (G
NEAL MATTHEWS	V	(G	DIANE TIDWELL	V	(G	CHIP YOUNG	G	(G	DON SHEFFIELD	HRNS (G
BILLY PUETT	HRNS (G												

N38   ANDY NEWMAN

ANDY NEWMAN	K	(A		(A) RAINBOW		1971	TRACK		UK 2406 103

N39   DAVID FATHEAD' NEWMAN

DAVID FATHEAD NEWMAN	SAX(ALL		(A) BEST OF		1971	ATLANTIC		US SD 1590			
CLAUDE JOHNSON	PNO G(F		(B) THE WEAPON		19	ATLANTIC		US SD 1638			
ROGER BOYKIN	G B	(F	(C) CAPTAIN BUCKLES		19	ATLANTIC		US SD 18002			
GEORGE CABLES	K	(G	(D) STRAIGHT AHEAD		19	ATLANTIC		US SD 1366			
HILTON RUIZ	K	(G	(E) MR FATHEAD		1976	W B		UK K56201			
GEORGE DAVIS	G	(G	(F) FRONT MONEY		1977	W B		US BS 2984			
LEE RITENOUR	G	(G	(G) KEEP THE DREAM ALIVE		1978	PRESTIGE		US P10106			
BILL SUMMERS	PERC (GH		(H) SCRATCH MY BACK		1979	PRESTIGE		US P10108			
JEFF DAVIS	TPT	(G									
LARRY MOSES	TPT	(G	JANICE ROBINSON	TROM (G	EARL McINTYRE	TROM (GH	KENNETH HARRIS	FLT	(GH
ED XIQUES	SAX	(G	RENE MANNING	V	(G	YVONNE FLETCHER	V	(G	RANDY BRECKER	TPT	(H
JERRY DODGION	FLT	(G	JAMES BUFFINGTON	HRNS (H	BEN CARTER	V	(H	KEVIN TONEY	K	(H
RICHARD TEE	K	(H	ERIC GALE	G	(H	CORNELL DUPREE	G	(H	RON CARTER	B	(H
WILBUR BASCOMB	B	(H	HARVEY MASON	D	(H	TANYETTE	V	(H	BESSIE RUTH SCOTT	V	(H
JON FADDIS	TPT	(H	GEORGE MARGE	FLT	(H	FLAME BRAITHWAITE	V	(H	DEBORAH McGRIFF	V	(H
IDRIS MUHAMMAD	D	(G									

N39A   JIMMY C NEWMAN

JIMMY C NEWMAN		(A		(A) HAPPY CAJUN		19	CHARLY		UK CR 30177
				(B) PROGRESSIVE CC		1977	CHARLY		UK CRL 5005

N40   RANDY NEWMAN

RANDY NEWMAN	PNO V(ALL		(A) RANDY NEWMAN		1968	REPRISE	US	6286				
RY COODER	G	(DEF	(B) 12 SONGS		197	REPRISE	US	6373	UK	K44084	
RUSS TITELMAN	G B	(DE	(C) LIVE		1971	REPRISE	US	6459	UK	K44151	
JIM KELTNER	D	(DEF	(D) SAIL AWAY		1972	REPRISE	US	2064	UK	K44185	
GENE PARSONS	D	(D	(E) GOOD OLD BOYS		1974	WB	US	2193	UK	K54022	
EARL PALMER	D	(D	(F) LITTLE CRIMINALS		1977	WB	US	3079	UK	K56404	
CHRIS ETHRIDGE	B	(D	(G) BORN AGAIN		1979	WB	US	3346	UK	K56663	
WILTON FELDER	B	(D										
JIMMY BOND	B	(D	MILT HOLLAND	PERC (DEF	ABE MOST	SAX	(D	RED CALLENDER	B	(E
DON HENLEY	V	(EF	J D SOUTHER	V	(F	KLAUS VOORMANN	B	(F	TIM SCHMIT	V	(F
DAVID SHIELDS	B	(G	VICTOR FELDMAN	K PERC (G	CHUCK FINDLEY	TPT	(G	STEPHEN BISHOP	V	(G
VALERIE CARTER	V	(G	ARNO LUCAS	V	(G	ANDY NEWMARK	D	(EFG	BOBBYE HALL	PERC(E
RON ELLIOTT	G	(D	JOHN PLATANIA	G	(G	DENNIS BUDIMIR	G	(E	AL PERKINS	STEEL(E
WILLIE WEEKS	B	(EFG	GLENN FREY	G V	(EF	RICK MAROTTA	D	(F	WADDY WACHTEL	G	(FG
JOE WALSH	G	(F	RALPH GRIERSON	PNO	(F	MICHAEL BODDICKER	SYN	(FG	LENNY CASTRO	PERC(G
TOM SCOTT	HRNS (G	BUZZY FEITEN	G	(G								

N41   TOM NEWMAN

TOM NEWMAN	G V K(ALL		(A) FINE OLD TOM		1975	VIRGIN	UK			V2022	
MIKE OLDFIELD	G	(A	(B) LIVE AT THE ARGONAUT (NOT RELEASED)197		VIRGIN	UK			V2042	
FRED FRITH	G B	(A	(C) FAERIE SYMPHONY		1977	DECCA	UK			TXS 123	
CHRIS BUTLER	D	(A										
JOHN VARNOM	G	(A	HUGH FLINT	D	(A	MIKE STOREY	K	(A	DAVID DUHIG	G	(A
NED CALLAN	B	(A	JON FIELD	D WIND PERC V(AC	PETER COOK	HCA	(A	LOL COXHILL	SAX(A
SUZI SHUTE	V	(A	JOHN OBYTON	V	(A	TED MACDOWELL	G	(A	NEIL INNES	K G(A
MICK TAYLOR	G	(A	TOM NORDEN	G	(C	PETE GIBSON	TROM D(C	DEBBIE HALL	VLN(C
TERRY EDWARDS	V	(C	JOE O'DONNELL	VLN	(C	TINA JONES	V	(C	GEOFF WESTLEY	PNO(C
WARD KELLY CONOVER	D	(C	JON COLLINS	VLN	(C	JANE GIBSON	D	(C			

N42   NEWS

SAM SMITH	G V	(A		(A) 1978 MARCH					
GRAHAM CULPIN	B	(A							
LINDSAY ELLIOT	D	(A	MICHAEL TAYLOR	K	(A	ALAN RICHARDS	G	(A

N43   JUICE NEWTON

JUICE NEWTON	G V	(ABCD	(A) & SILVER SPUR		1975	RCA			APLI1004	
TOM KEALEY	G B V(AC		(B) AFTER DUST SETTLED		1977	RCA			APLI1722	
OTHA YOUNG	G V	(AC	(C) COME TO ME		1977	CAPITOL			11682	
JEFF PORCARO	D	(A	(D) WELL KEPT SECRET		1978	CAPITOL			11811	
HAL BLAINE	D PERC(A									
MIKE MELVOIN	PNO	(A	RUSTY YOUNG	STEEL(A	R GILLMAN	K V	(C	BUZZY BUCHANAN	D	(C
SMIGGY	G	(C	MICHAEL O'NEILL	G	(C	TONY SAUNDERS	B	(C	BOB HOGINS	K	(C
MATTHEW KELLY	HCA	(C	TEDDY IRWIN	G	(C	DENNY SEIWELL	D	(C			

NICE

			(A) THOUGHTS OF EMERLIST DAVJACK	1967 IMMEDIATE IMSP016	US	52004
KEITH EMERSON	V K	(ALL	(A) " " " " "	1973 CBS	IMP	11633
BRIAN DAVISON	D	(ALL	(A) " " " " "	1978 CHARLY	UK	CR300021
LEE JACKSON	B G V	(ALL	(B) ARS LONGA VITA BREVIS	1968 IMMEDIATE IMSP020	US	52020
DAVY O'LIST	G	(A	(B) " " " "	1973 CBS	IMP	11634
SINFONIA OF LONDON		(D	(B) " " " "	1978 CHARLY	UK	CR300019
GORDON LONGSTAFF	G	(1	(C) NICE	1969 IMMEDIATE IMSP026	US	52022
			(C) " "	1973 CBS	IMP	11635
(1) 1968			(C) " "	1978 CHARLY	UK	CR300014
			(D) FIVE BRIDGES SUITE	1970 CHARISMA	UK	CAS1014
			(D) " " " "	1970 MERCURY	US	SR61295
			(E) ELEGY	1971 CHARISMA	UK	CAS1030
			(E) ELEGY	1971 MERCURY	US	SR61324
			(F) AUTUMN 67, SPRING 68	1972 CHARISMA	UK	CS1
			( ) BEST OF NICE	197 ELECTROLA	IMP	04890674
			( ) IN MEMORIAM	197 PATHE	FR	05491951
			( ) VINTAGE YEARS	1975 SIRE	IMP	3710
			( ) HANG ON TO A DREAM	197 EMI IMP		04850722
			( ) AMOENI REDIVIVI	1976 IMMEDIATE		IML1003
			( ) NICE WITH KEITH EMERSON	1976 PHONOGRAM		6641 119
			( ) KEITH EMRSON & THE NICE	197 MERCURY	US	SRM26500
			( ) AMERICA	1976 PICKWICK	US	SHM 917
			( ) POP GROUPS OF THE 60s (WITH H PIE)	197 MFP	GERM	14694319/20

NICO

NICO	V HARMONIUM	(ALL	(A) CHELSEA GIRL	1968	MGM		2353 025
PHIL MANZANERA	G	(D	(B) MARBLE INDEX	1968	ELEKTRA	US EKS 74029	K 42065
BRIAN ENO	SYN	(D	(C) DESERT SHORE	1971	REPRISE		K 44102
JOHN CALE	K B G	(BCD	(D) THE END	1974	ISLAND		ILPS9311
ADAM MILLER	V	(C	(E) JUNE 1st 1974	1974	ISLAND		ILPS9291
VICKI WOOD	V	(C					
ANNAGH WOOD	V	(C					

NIEMEN

CZESLAW NIEMEN	K	(	(A) STRANGE IS THE WORLD	19	CBS		64896
JAN HAMMER	D	(B	(B) MOURNERS RHAPSODY	1975	CBS		80557
DAVE JOHNSON	PERC	(B					
RICK LAIRD	B	(B	MICHAEL URBANIAK VLN (B ERIN DICKENS V (B GAIL CANTOR V (B
TASHA THOMAS	V	(B	SELDON POWELL FLT (B STEVE KHAN G (B DON GROLNICK PNO (B
JOHN ABERCROMBIE	G	(B	

NIGHT

CHRIS THOMPSON	G V	(AB	(A) NIGHT	1979	PLANET		K 52200
STEVIE LANGE	V	(AB	(B) LONG DISTANCE	1980	PLANET		K 52251
NICKY HOPKINS	PNO	(A					
ROBBIE McINTOSH	G	(AB	BILLY KRISTIAN B (A RICK MAROTTA D (A BOBBY GUISOTTI D (B
BOBBY WRIGHT	K	(B	

NIGHTCAPS

(A) WINE WINE WINE	197	CHARLY	UK CR30183

ROBERT NIGHTHAWK

ROBERT NIGHTHAWK	G V	(ALL	(A) BRICKS ON MY PILLOW	19	PEARL US	P11
JOHNNY YOUNG	G	(C	(B) MASTERS OF MODERN BLUES	19	TESTAMENT US	T 2215
ROBERT WHITEHEAD	D	(C	(C) LIVE ON MAXWELL STREET 1964	1979	ROUNDER US	2022
CAREY BELL	HCA	(C				
HOUSTON STACKHOUSE		(B				

NIGHTLIFE

IAN ELLIS	B V	(
JIMMY ROCHE	G	(
MAC POOLE	D	(

MAXINE NIGHTINGALE

MAXINE NIGHTINGALE	V	(ALL	(A) RIGHT BACK WHERE WE STARTED	1976	UA	US LA 626	UK UAG29953
			(B) LOVE HIT ME	1977	UA		UK UAS30076
			(C) NIGHT LIFE	1977	UA	UA LA 731	UK UAS30105
			(D) LOVE LINES	1978	UA		UK UAG30179
			(E) BITTERSWEET	1981	LIBERTY		UK LBG30323

NIGHTRIDERS

MIKE SHERIDAN	V	(	(PRE IDLE RACE CIRCA 1963)
ALAN JOHNSON	G	(	
BRIAN COPE	B	(	DAVE PRITCHARD G (JEFF LYNNE G V (ROGER SPENCER D (
GREG MASTERS		(	ROY WOOD G (

WILLIE NILE

WILLIE NILE	G PNO V	(A	(A) WILLIE NILE	1980	ARISTA	US AB4260 UK SPART1126
CLAY BARNES	G V	(A				
PETER HOFFMAN	G	(A	TOM ETHRIDGE B (A JAY DEE DAUGHERTY D (A MARK JOHNSON V (A

NINE BELOW ZERO

DENNIS GREAVES	G V	(ABC	(A) PACKED FAIR & SQUARE (EP)	1979	M&L	UK ML 1
PETER CLARK	B V	(ABC	(B) LIVE AT THE MARQUEE	1980	A&M	UK AMLE68515
MARK FELTHAM	V HCA	(ABC	(C) DON'T POINT YOUR FINGER	1981	A&M	UK AMLH68521
STIX BURKEY	D	(BC				
KENNY BRADLEY	D	(A				

NINE NINE NINE (999)

NICK CASH	G V	(ABC	(A) 9 9 9	1978	UA	UK	UAG 30199
PABLO LABRITAIN	D	(ABC	(B) SEPARATES	1978	UA	UK	UAG 30209
JOHN WATSON	B	(ABC	(C) BIGGEST PRIZE IN SPORT	1980	POLYDOR		POLS 1013
GUY DAYS	G	(AB	(D) CONCRETE	1981	ALBION	UK	ITS 999
ED CASE	V D	(C					

NINE SENSE

ELTON DEAN	SAX	(B	(A) OH! FOR THE EDGE	1976	OGUN		OG 900
ALAN SKIDMORE	SAX	(B	(B) HAPPY DAZE	1977	OGUN		OG 910
HARRY BECKETT	HRNS	(	LOUIS MOHOLO D (B RADU MALFATI TROM (
NICK EVANS	TROM	(	MARK CHARIG HRNS (B KEITH TIPPETT PNO (B HARRY MILLER B (B

```
N50A                                        1994
    KAREN LAWRENCE     V    (         (A) 1994              1978   A&M              UK AMLH64709
    JOHN DESAUTELS     D    (
    STEVE SCHIFF       G    (    BILL RHODES      B    (
N50B                                    90 DEGREES INCLUSIVE
    HUGH FRANCIS      G V  (AB         (A) 90' INCLUSIVE      1976   VERTIGO          UK  6360 139
    HENRY BARNES      G V  (AB         (B) FIRE OVER YONDER   1978   ICE                  ICEL 1005
    WEBSTER DYER       K   (AB
    WINSTON HENRY      B   (AB  DELFORD DAVIS   D   (AB  EDDY GRANT   SYN HCA(A   LLOYD TYRELL   V (B
N51                                          NIRVANA
    PATRICK CAMPBELL-LYONS (ABC        (A) SIMON SIMOPATH     1967   ISLAND       UK      ILPS9059
    ALEX SPRYOPOULOS  PNO  (ABC        (B) ALL OF US          1968   ISLAND       UK      ILPS9087
    BRIAN HENDERSON    B   (A          (C) DEDICATED TO MARKOS III 1970 PYE               28132
    RAY SINGER        G V  (A          (D) LOCAL ANAESTHETIC  1971   VERTIGO          6360 031
    SYLVIA SCHUSTER   CELLO(A          (E) SONGS OF LOVE & PRAISE 1972 PHILIPS          6308 089
    PETER KESTER       D   (A
    BILLY BREMNER      G   (C   LESLEY DUNCAN   V   (C   SPOOKY TOOTH          (C
N52                                         NITE CITY
    RAY MANZAREK       K   (AB         (A) NITE CITY          1977   20TH CENTURY         T 528
    NOAH JONES         V   (A          (B) GOLDEN DAYS DIAMOND NIGHTS 1978 20TH CENTURY  6370 263
    PAUL WARREN       G V  (AB
    NIGEL HARRISON     B   (AB  JIMMY HUNTER D V  (AB
N53                              NITTY GRITTY DIRT BAND (DIRT BAND)
    JEFF HANNA        G V  (ALL        (A) NITTY GRITTY DIRT BAND 1967 LIBERTY  US    LST 7501
    JIMMIE FADDEN     G HCA(ALL
    BRUCE KUNKEL          (ACE         (C) RICOCHET           1967   LIBERTY  US    LST 7516
    GLEN CROSLOSE         (            (D) RARE JUNK          1967   LIBERTY  US    LST 7540
    STEVE PRYKA          (             (E) PURE DIRT          1968   LIBERTY  UK       83122
    MICHAEL WHITTAKER    (             (F) ALIVE              1969   LIBERTY  US    LST 7611
    RALPH BARR        G V (ACDEFG      (G) DEAD & ALIVE       1969   LIBERTY  UK    LBS83286
    WILLIAM McEUEN        (            (H) UNCLE CHARLIE & HIS DOG 1970 LIBERTY US LST7642 UK LBGB3345
    LES THOMPSON      B G V(ACDEFGHJK  (J) ALL THE GOOD TIMES 1972   UA   US UAS5553 UK UAS29284
    JACKSON BROWNE     V  (            (K) WILL THE CIRCLE BE UNBROKEN 1973 UA US UAT9801
    JOHN McEUEN STEEL G V (DEFHJKLMNOP (L) STARS & STRIPES FOREVER 1974 UA US LA 184 UK UAS29570
    DUANE ALLMAN       G  (            (M) DREAM              1975   UA   US LA469  UK UAS29850
    GREGG ALLMAN      K V (            (N) DIRT SILVER & GOLD(TRIPLE) 1977 UA US 9802 + LA 670
    STEVE GILLETTE       (             (O) DIRT BAND          1978   UA   US LA 854 UK UAK30174
    STEVE MARTIN         (             (P) AMERICAN DREAM     1979   UA   US LA 974 UK UAG30271
    JIM IBBOTSON  G V K D (HJKLMN
    CHRIS DARROW  G V VLN (DFG JOHN LONDON        (H  MIKE RUBINI        (H  BYRON BERLINE  FDL (H
    RUSS KUNKEL          (H  JOHN CABLE   G V (HJKLMN JACKIE CLARK  B (AJLMN BILL CUNNINGHAM    (H
    MAURICE MANSEAU II   (H  AL GARTH     VLN V SAX(OP MEREL BREGANTE D V (OP RICHARD HATHAWAY B (OP
    MICHAEL McDONALD  V  (O  JAN GARRETT      V  (O  HADEN GREGG     V  (O  ROSEMARY BUTLER  V (O
    BOB CARPENDER   V K (OP  MICKEY THOMAS    V  (O  LEON MEDICA     B  (OP BRYAN SAVAGE  HRNS (O
    DENNY CHRISTENSEN HRNS(O AL KOOPER      SYN  (O  BOBBY MASON     G  (O  GREG TAYLOR   HARP (O
    JEFF POLLARD      G  (P  TONY HASELDON    G  (P  JIM GORDON   HRNS K (H DAVID PETERS    D  (P
    ROD RODDY         K  (P  LINDA RONSTADT   V  (P  LEAH KUNKEL     V  (P FUNKY LESTER  HRNS (P
    MARTY GUINN       V  (P  BOBBY LAKIND    PERC (P
N53A                                         NITZINGER
    JOHN NITZINGER    G V  (ABC        (A) NITZINGER          1972   CAPITOL       SMAS 11091
    LINDA WARING      V D  (AB         (B) ONE FOOT IN HISTORY 1973  CAPITOL       SMAS 11122
    CURLY BENTON      B V  (AB         (C) LIVE BETTER ELECTRICALLY 1976 20TH CENTURY 6370 251
    BUGS HENDERSON     G   (B
    PAUL LEIM          D   (C   JERRY HARRIS    B   (C   KENNETH WHITFIELD  K  (C  LAYTON DE PENNING  V (C
    THE AUSTIN SINGERS     (C   DARRELL NORRIS  D   (C   LARRY WHITE   STEEL(C  RANDY REEDE      D (C
    MARIANNE LINDSEY  V   (C   PHYLLIS LINDSEY  V   (C   WHITEY THOMAS  K  (C
N54                                        JACK NITZSCHE
    JACK NITZSCHE      K   (ALL        (A) THE LONELY SURFER  1963   REPRISE    US     6101
    DAVID MEASHAM         (E           (B) HITS OF THE BEATLES 1964  REPRISE    US     6115
    LONDON SYPHONY ORCHESTRA(E         (C) CHOPIN' 66         1966   REPRISE    US     6200
                                       (D) PERFORMANCE        1970   WB             WS 2554
                                       (E) ST GILES CRIPPLEGATE 1972 REPRISE    US     2092
                                       (F) ONE FLEW OVER THE CUCKOO'S NEST 1976 FANTASY UK FTA 3004
N55                                           DON NIX
    DON NIX               (ALL        (A) IN GOD WE TRUST     1971   SHELTER        SHE 8902
    BARRY BECKETT      K  (BC          (B) LIVING BY THE DAYS 1971   ELEKTRA UK K 42096 US EKS74101
    CHRIS STAINTON     K  (B           (C) HOBOS HEROES & STREET CORNER CLOWNS 74 ENTERPRISE ENS 1032
    WAYNE PERKINS     G V (BC          (D) GONE TOO LONG      197    CREAM      US     1001
    JIMMY JOHNSON      G  (B
    ROGER HAWKINS      D  (BC  DAVID HOOD      B   (BC  DONALD DUCK DUNN  B (B  LON PRICE          (C
    TIPPY ARMSTRONG    G  (B   GIMMER NICHOLSON G  (B   CLAUDIA LENNEAR V (B  JOEY COOPER     V (B
    MARLINE GREENE     V  (B   KATHI McDONALD  V   (B   DON PRESTON     V (B  JEANNIE GREENE  V (B
    FURRY LEWIS        V  (BC  PETE CARR          (C    EDDIE HINTON    G (C  KLAUS VOORMANN  B (C
    STEVE SMITH           (C   TIM SMITH          (C    LARRY RASPBERRY   (C  BOBBY MANUEL      (C
    ORCHESTRA             (C
N56                                          NO DICE
    ROGER FERRIS       V  (B1         (A) NO DICE            1977   EMI  UK EMC 3195 US CAPITOL11236
    DAVE MOORE         G  (B1         (B) TWO FACED          1979   EMI  UK EMC 3282
    DAVE MARTIN        G  (B1         (1) 1979 SEPT
    GARY STRANGE       B  (B1
    CHRIS WYLES      D PERC(B   TONY FERNANDEZ   D PERC(1
N56A                                       NO ENTRY BAND
    KENNETH TURLEWICZ V   (A          (A) COLD & LONELY LIVES(EP) 1978 KUBE ARTS      KA 1
    ILONA TURLEWICZ  G V  (A
    KENNETH LITTLE   G V  (A   DOUGIE BURNS    D   (A   ROBERT KIRK     B (A
```

RAB NOAKES — N57

```
RAB NOAKES      G V  (ALL      REGGIE YOUNG     G   (C    WAYNE JACKSON   TPT  (C    JACK HALE        TROM (C
GERRY RAFFERTY  V   (BCD       ANDREW LOVE      HRNS(C    SHEL TALMY      TAMB (C    JOHN CHRISTOPHER G    (C
JOE EGAN        V   (BCD       WELDON MYRICK    G   (CD   JOHN HARRIS     K    (CD   TOMMY COGBILL    B    (C
SID CAIRNS      B   (B         ED LOGAN         SAX (C    JAMES MITCHELL  SAX  (C    DANNY SEIWELL    D    (D
DAVIE CRAIG     FDL V(B        BEN KEITH     V G K D (D   RALPH MOLINA    V    (D    ARTIE TRAUM      G    (D
ROBIN McKIDD    G HCA(AB       MIKE DEACON      K   (D    JACK EMBLOW     ACC  (D    RICKY FATAAR     D PERC(E
ALAN NOAKES     G   (B         RICHARD BRUNTON  G   (EF   JEFF ALLEN      D PERC(E   PETE ZORN        B    (E
RAY JACKSON     HCA (C         ALY BAIN         FDL (E    TERRY MELCHER   K V  (E    MEL COLLINS      HRNS (E
TOMMY JACKSON   HCA (C         SUZANNE LYNCH    V   (E    BARBARA DICKSON V    (E    CHARLIE DORE     V    (E
TEDDY IRWIN     G   (CD        ROGER BROWN      V   (E    TOMMY EYRE      K    (F    ROD CLEMENTS     B    (F
KENNY BUTTREY   D   (C         KARL HIMMEL      D   (B    BIL KEMP        D    (A    ALLAN TRAJAN     K    (A
CHRISSY STEWART B   (D
BOB BERTLES     SAX (D
JOHN PERRY      B   (E
MARTIN JENNER   G   (E
TOMMY McCARTHY  PIPES(E
BARRY ST JOHN   V   (E
LIAM GENOCKEY   D   (F
RONNIE RAE      B   (A
```

	Title	Year	Label	Country	Cat. No.
(A)	DO YOU SEE THE LIGHT	1970	DECCA	UK	SKL 5061
(B)	RAB NOAKES	1972	A&M	UK	AMLS68119
(C)	RED PUMP SPECIAL	1974	WB	UK	K46284
(D)	NEVER TOO LATE	1975	WB	UK	K56114
(E)	RESTLESS	1978	RING O RECORDS	UK	2339 201
(F)	RAB NOAKES	1980	MCA	UK	MCA 3251

STEVE NOONAN — N58

```
STEVE NOONAN    (A
```

	Title	Year	Label	Country	Cat. No.
(A)	STEVE NOONAN	196	ELEKTRA	US	EKS 74017

IAN NORTH — N58A

```
IAN NORTH   G V SYN  (AB
```

	Title	Year	Label	Country	Cat. No.
(A)	NEO	1979	AURA		AUL 706
(B)	MY GIRLFRIENDS DEAD	1981	CACHALOT	US	CA

NORTHWIND — N59

	Title	Year	Label	Country	Cat. No.
(A)	SISTER BROTHER LOVER	1971	REGAL ZONOPHONE	UK	SLRZ 1020

NOTATIONS — N59A

	Title	Year	Label	Country	Cat. No.
(A)	NOTATIONS	1976	GEMIGO US 5501 UK WB		K56212

NOVA — N60

```
CORRADO RUSTICI  G MARIMBA V(ABC
ELIO D'ANNA      WIND      (ABC
RENATO ROSSET    K   (AB
PERCY JONES      B   (B
NARADA MICHAEL WALDEN G(B
PHIL COLLINS     D   (B     ZAKIR HUSSAIN  CONGA(A    RICK PARNELL   D (A    BARRY JOHNSON  B V (A
LUCIANO MILANESE B V (A     FRANCO LOPREVITE    (A    DANIELO RUSTICI G (A
```

	Title	Year	Label	Country	Cat. No.
(A)	BLINK	1976	ARISTA	UK	ARTY 118
(B)	VIMANA	1976	ARISTA US 4110 UK		ARTY 138
(C)	WINGS OF LOVE	1977	ARISTA US 4150 UK		SPARTY 102
(D)	SUN CITY	197	ARISTA US 4203		

NOVAKS KAPELLE — N60A

```
ERWIN NOVAK      D   (A
HARRY STOJKA     G   (A
WALLA MAURITZ V SAX HCA(A   PAETER TRAVNICEK B V (A    PAUL BRAUNSTEINER G V (A    GITTA WALTHER  V (A
RENATE MAUERER   V   (A     MARIA NEUHAUSE   V   (A
```

	Title	Year	Label	Country	Cat. No.
(A)	NAKED	1978	ARIOLA	GERM	25 784

NOVALIS — N61

```
DETLEF JOB       G V  (F
FRED MUHLBOCK    G V  (F
LUTZ RAHN        K SYN(F
HARTWIG BIEREICHEL D  (F
HEINO SCHUNZEL   B V  (F
```

	Title	Year	Label	Cat. No.
(A)	BANISHED BRIDGE	1973	BRAIN	0001029
(B)	NOVALIS	1975	BRAIN	0001070
(C)	SOMMERABEND	1976	BRAIN	0001087
(D)	KONZERTE	1977	BRAIN	0060065
(E)	BRANDUNG	1977	BRAIN	0060094
(F)	VIELLEICHT BIST DU EIN CLOWN	1978	BRAIN	0060164

NOYES BROTHERS — N61A

	Title	Year	Label	Cat. No.
(A)	SHEEP FROM GOATS	19	OBJECT MUSIC	OBJ009/0010

NUCLEUS — N62

```
IAN CARR         PTP (ALL
KARL JENKINS     SAX K(C
JOHN MARSHALL    D   (C
CHRIS SPEDDING   G   (C
BOB BERTLES      SAX (GHJ
KEN SHAW         G   (GHJ
GEOFF CASTLE     K   (GHJ
ROGER SUTTON     B   (GHJ
ROGER SELLERS    D   (HJ
KENNY WHEELER    TPT (C
BRIAN SMITH      WIND(CD
TONY ROBERTS     WIND(C
CHRIS KARAN      PERC(C
KEITH WINTER     K   (C     JEFF CLYNE       B   (C    DAVE MacRAE    K (D    ALLAN HOLDSWORTH G (D
RON MATHESON     B   (C     ROY BABBINGTON   B   (D    CLIVE THACKER  D (D    GORDON BECK      K (DG
TREVOR TOMKINS   PERC(DJ    JOCELYN PITCHER  G   (G    BRYAN SPRING   D (G    KIERAN WHITE     V (D
HARRY BECKETT    TPT (C
```

	Title	Year	Label	Country	Cat. No.
(A)	ELASTIC ROCK	1970	VERTIGO	UK	6360 065
(B)	WE'LL TALK ABOUT IT LATER	1970	VERTIGO	UK	6360 027
(C)	SOLAR PLEXUS	1971	VERTIGO	UK	6360 039
(D)	BELLADONNA	1972	VERTIGO	UK	6360 076
(E)	LABYRINTH	1973	VERTIGO	UK	6360 091
(F)	ROOTS	1973	VERTIGO	UK	6360 100
(G)	UNDER THE SUN	1974	VERTIGO	UK	6350 110
(H)	SNAKE HIPS ETCETERA	1975	VERTIGO	UK	6360 119
(J)	ALLEY CAT	1975	VERTIGO	UK	6360 124
(K)	DIRECT HITS	1976	VERTIGO	UK	9286 019
(L)	IN FLAGRANTE DELICTO	1978	CAPITOL	UK/US	11771
(M)	OUT OF THE LONG DARK	1979	CAPITOL		EST 11916

TED NUGENT & AMBOY DUKES — N63

```
TED NUGENT       G    (ALL
DAVE PALMER      D    (ABC
STEVE FARMER     G    (AB
RICK LOBER       K    (A
BILL WHITE       B    (A
JOHN DRAKE       V    (AB
ANDY JEZOWSKI    V    (FG
GREG ARAMA       B    (BCD
ANDY SOLOMAN     K    (BC
ROB ROESGER           (E
K J KNIGHT       D    (E
JOHN ANGELOS     V    (
ROB GRANGE       B    (EFHJKL
JOE VITALE       D    (
CLIFF DAVIS           (IJKL
DEREK ST HOLMES  V    (IJKL
VIC MASTRIANNI   D    (FG
BRIAN STAFFELD   PERC (I
```

	Title	Year	Label	Country	Cat. No.	UK Cat. No.
(A)	THE AMBOY DUKES	1968	MAINSTREAM	US 6104		
(B)	JOURNEY TO THE CENTRE OF THE MIND	1969	LONDON		UK	8378
(B)	" " " " "	1969	MAINSTREAM	US 6112		
(C)	MIGRATION	1969	LONDON		UK	8392
(C)	" "	1969	MAINSTREAM	US 6118		
(D)	MARRIAGE ON THE ROCKS	1970	POLYDOR	US 6073		24 4012
(BC)	JOURNEYS & MIGRATIONS	1975	MAINSTREAM	US 2/ 801		
(E)	SURVIVAL OF THE FITTEST	1974	POLYDOR	US 4035 UK		2675 141
(DE)	MARRIAGE/SURVIVAL	1977	POLYDOR		UK	2664 344
(F)	CALL OF THE WILD	1974	DISCREET	US 2181	UK	K59203
(G)	TOOTH FANG & CLAW	1975	DISCREET	US 2203	UK	K59205
(FG)	CALL/TOOTH	1977	WB		UK	K69202
(H)	DR SLINGSHOT	1975	MAINSTREAM	US 414		
(I)	TED NUGENT	1976	EPIC	US 33692	UK	81196
(J)	FREE FOR ALL	1976	EPIC	US 34121	UK	81397
(K)	CAT SCRATCH FEVER	1977	EPIC	US 34700	UK	82010
(L)	DOUBLE LIVE GONZO	1978	EPIC	US 35069	UK	88282
(M)	WEEKEND WARRIOR	1978	EPIC	US 35551	UK	83036

(CONTINUED)

N63 (CONTINUED) TED NUGENT & AMBOY DUKES

Name	Role		Album	Year	Label	Country	Cat#
CHARLIE HUHEN	G V	(	(N) STATE OF SHOCK	1979	EPIC	UK	86092
JOHN SAUTER	B	(	(O) SCREAM DREAM	1980	EPIC	UK	86111
GABE MAGNO	K FLT(EF		( ) BEST OF AMBOY DUKES	19	MAINSTREAM US 6125		
MEATLOAF	V	(J					
STEVE McRAY	K	(IJ BOZ BURRELL	V (K RORY DODD	V	(K ALAN SPENNER	V (K	
MONTEGO JOE	PERC (K	TOM WERMAN	PERC (IJK				

N63A GARY NUMAN

Name	Role		Album	Year	Label	Country	Cat#
GARY NUMAN	K V G(ALL		(A) PLEASURE PRINCIPLE	1979	BEGGARS BANQUET	UK	BEGA10
PAUL GARDINER	B	(A	(B) TELEKON	1980	BEGGARS BANQUET	UK	BEGA19
CHRISTOPHER PAYNE	K VLA(A		(C) LIVING ORNAMENTS '79	1981	BEGGARS BANQUET	UK	BEGA24
GARRY ROBSON	V	(A	(D) LIVING ORNAMENTS '80	1981	BEGGARS BANQUET	UK	BEGA25
CEDRIC SHARPLEY	D	(A	(CD)BOX SET +SINGLE	1981	BEGGARS BANQUET	UK	BRX 1
BILL CURRIE	VLN	(A	(NB) C & D DELETED AFTER ONE MONTH AFTER ISSUE				

N63B CRAIG NUTTYCOMBE

Name	Role		Album	Year	Label	Country	Cat#
CRAIG NUTTYCOMBE	G V	(A	(A) ITS JUST A LIFETIME	1978	A&M	US	SP 4683
HENRY SPINETTI	D	(A					
DAVE PEGG	B	(A ANDY FAIRWEATHER LOW V G(A	TIM RENWICK	G	(A DICK MORRISSEY	SAX (A	
DAVE MARKEE	B	(A GLYN JONES	G (A PETER HOPE EVANS	HCA	(A DAVE MATTACKS	D (A	
PAT DONALDSON	B	(A GEORGIE FAME	K (A TONY CARR	PERC	(A STEVE GREGORY	SAX (A	
BUD BEADLE	SAX	(A MALCOLM GRIFFITHS TROM	(A BERNIE LEADON	G	(A		

N64 NUTZ

Name	Role		Album	Year	Label	Country	Cat#
MICK DEVONPORT	G V	(ABCD	(A) NUTZ	1974	A&M	US 3648	UK AMLS68256
DAVID LLOYD	G V	(ABCD	(B) NUTZ TOO	1975	A&M		UK AMLS68306
KEITH MULHOLLAND	B	(ABCD	(C) HARD NUTZ	1977	A&M	US 4623	UK AMLH64623
JOHN MYLETT	D	(ABCD	(D) NUTZ LIVE CUTZ	1977	A&M		UK AMLH68453
RABBIT	K	(A					
CHRIS HUGHES	HRNS (A	PAUL CARRACK	K (B NEIL KERNON	K	(B KENNY NEWTON	K (D	

N64A NYL

Name	Role		Album	Year	Label	Country	Cat#
STEPHANE ROSSINI	D	(A	(A) NYL	1976	URUS	FR	000 013
MICHEL PETEAU	G	(A					
OLIVER PAMELA	V B	(A BERNARD LAVALLE	G (A ELIZABETH WIENER	V	(A ARIEL KALMA	SAX (A	
PATRICK QUENTIN	SAX	(A LOY	K (A JANIK TOP	B	(A		

N65 LAURA NYRO

Name	Role		Album	Year	Label	Country	Cat#
LAURA NYRO	G V K(ALL		(A) MORE THAN A NEW DISCOVERY	1966	VERVE	US FTS3020	
JOHN TROPEA	G	(GHJ	(B) ELI & 13TH CONFESSION	1968	CBS	US 9621	UK 63346
MICHAEL MAINIERI	VIBES(H		(C) NEW YORK TENDABERRY	1969	CBS	US 9737	UK 63510
ANDY NEWMARK	D	(HJ	(D) XMAS & THE BEADS OF SWEAT	1970	CBS	US 30259	UK 64157
RICHARD DAVIS	B	(DGH	(E) GONNA TAKE A MIRACLE	1971	CBS	US 30987	UK 64770
NYDIA MATA	PERC (EGHJ		(F) THE FIRST SONGS	1973	CBS	US 31440	UK 64991
ELLEN SEELING	TPT	(H	(G) SMILE	1976	CBS	US 33912	UK 81171
JEFF KING	SAX	(H	(H) SEASON OF LIGHT	1977	CBS	US 34786	UK 82183
JEANIE FINEBERG	WIND	(H	(J) NESTED	1978	CBS	US 35449	UK 82917
CARTER COLLINS	PERC (GH		(K) IMPRESSIONS (COMP)	1980	CBS		31864
LABELLE	V	(E					
JIM HELMER	D	(E LARRY WASHINGTON	PERC (E RONNIE BAKER	B	(E ROLAND CHAMBERS	G (E	
NORMAN HARRIS	G	(E LENNY PAKULA	ORG (E VINCE MONTANA	PERC	(E ROGER HAWKINS	D (D	
EDDIE HINTON	G	(D BARRY BECKETT	VIBES(D DAVID HOOD	B	(D FELIX CAVALIERE	K (DJ	
STU SHARF	G	(D DINO DANELLI	D (D CHUCK RAINEY	B	(D CORNELL DUPREE	G (D	
RALPH McDONALD	PERC (D ASHAD GARABEDIAN	OUD (D MICHAEL SZITTAI	CIM	(D ALICE COLTRANE	HARP(D		
JOE FARRELL	WIND	(DG DUANE ALLMAN	G (D WILL LEE	B	(GJ CHRIS PARKER	D (G	
PAUL MESSING	PERC (G HUGH McCRACKEN	G (G BOB BABITT	B	(G ALLEN SCHWARZBERG	G (G		
JEFF MIRANOV	G	(G JERRY FRIEDMAN	G (G DAVID FRIEDMAN	VIBES	(G JIMMY MAELEN	PERC(G	
MICHAEL BRECKER	WIND (G RANDY BRECKER	TPT (G JOE BECK	G	(G GEORGE YOUNG	FLT(G		
RUBENS BASSINI	PERC (G GREG BENNETT	G (G RICK MAROTTA	D	(G REIKA KAMOTA	KOTO(G		
VINNIE CUSANO	G	(J JOHN SEBASTIAN	HCA (J CYRIL CIANFLONE	B	(J TONY LEVIN	B (J	
JACK JENNINGS	PERC (D NISAKO KOSHIDA	KOTO (G					

N66 NYTRO

Name	Role		Album	Year	Label	Country	Cat#
RONALD A SMITH	K	(A	(A) RETURN TO NYTROPOLIS	1979	WHITFIELD US WHK3275	UK K56614	
CHRIS POWELL	SAX	(A					
ROBERT JUSTICE	V	(A THEODORE WILLINGHAM B	(A JOHN JACKSON	D	(A EARNEST REDD	G (A	
KENNETH SCOTT	TPT	(A LAMORRIS PAYNE	TPT (A JAMES GADSON	D	(A TREY STONE	G (A	
TERRY SANTIEL	PERC (A MARK ENGEL	HCA (A					

O1 'O' BAND

Name	Role		Album	Year	Label	Country	Cat#
PIX	G V	(ABCD	(A) A BAND CALLED O	1974	EPIC	UK	80120
PETER FILLEUL	K	(AB	(B) OASIS	1975	EPIC	UK	80596
MARK ANDERS	B	(ABCD	(C) WITHIN REACH	1976	UA	UK UAG29942	
DEREK BALLARD	D	(ABCD	(D) THE KNIFE	1977	UA	UK UAG30077	
CRAIG ANDERS	G	(ABCD					
JEFF BANNISTER	K V	(CD					

O1A O LEVEL

Name	Role		Album	Year	Label	Country	Cat#
			(A) WE LOVE MALCOLM McLAREN(EP)	19	KINGS ROAD		002

O2 OAKDALE

Name	Role				
MARCUS THOMPSON	V	(			
KEN HART	G V	(			
JOHN BROOKS	G	(DAVE GIBBS	B (ANDY PEGG	D (

O3 OAKLEY

Name	Role		Album	Year	Label	Country	Cat#
RITCHIE OAKLEY	G	(A	(A) OAKLEY	1980	NOVA		WRCI 957
WAYNE NICHOLSON	V	(A					
BRUCE DIXON	B	(A BILL McCAULEY	K (A DOUG MACKAY	D	(A		

O4 OBSERVER ALL STARS

	Album	Year	Label	Cat#
	(A) DUBBING WITH THE OBSERVER	1978	ATTACK	ATLP1017

O5 OCCASIONAL WORD ENSEMBLE

	Album	Year	Label	Country	Cat#
	(A) THE YEAR OF THE GREAT LEAP SIDEWAYS	1970	DANDELION	UK	63753

PHIL OCHS

PHIL OCHS	G V (ALL	(A) ALL THE NEWS THATS FIT TO SING	1964	ELEKTRA		US		7269
VAN DYKE PARKS	(E	(A) " " " "	19	CHARTERLINE		ITALY		22016
JACK ELLIOT	(E	(B) I AINT MARCHIN' ANYMORE	1965	ELEKTRA		US		7287
LINCOLN MAYORGA	PNO (EH	(C) IN CONCERT	1966	ELEKTRA		US		7310
BOB RAFKIN	G (H	(D) PLEASURE OF THE HARBOUR	1967	A&M	US 4133 UK	AML	913
KENNY KAUFMAN	B (H	(E) TAPE FROM CALIFORNIA	1968	A&M	US 4148 UK	AMLS	919
KEVIN KELLEY	D (H	(F) REHEARSALS FOR RETIREMENT	1969	A&M	US 4181 UK	AMLS	934
		(G) GREATEST HITS	1970	A&M	US 4253 UK	AMLS	973
		(H) GUNFIGHT AT CARNEGIE HALL	1971	A&M	US 9010
		(J) CHORDS OF FAME	1974	A&M	US 4599 UK	AMLM64599
		(K) PHIL OCHS SINGS	19	FOLKWAYS	US 5320
		(L) INTERVIEWS	19	FOLKWAYS	US 5321

HAZEL O'CONNOR

HAZEL O'CONNOR	K V (AB	(A) BREAKING GLASS	1980	A&M		UK	AMLH64820
BOB CARTER	G K V(A	(B) SONS & LOVERS	1980	ALBION		UK	ALB 104
WESLEY McGOOGAN	SAX (AB						
RICK FORD	B (A	ANDY QUNTA	K (B	NEIL O'CONNOR	G (B	ANDY DUNCAN	D (A
TONY VISCONTI	K V (A	ED CASE	D (B	WILD OSCAR	B (B	GARY TIBBS	B (B

OCTOBER CHERRIES

PHIL TOWNER	D (A	(A) BAKING HOT	1980	BAAL	BAL89014
STEVE COOPER	D (A	( ) WORLD HITS '76	1976	BAAL	BE 603
JOHN EDMED	STEEL(A				
CHRIS GOULSTONE	G (A	PETER DIAZ	G V (A	JAY SHOTAM	V B (A	JEREMIAH STAR	K VIBES (A

OCTOPUS

WERNER LITTAU	K (ABC	(A) THE BOAT OF THOUGHTS	1976	SKY	SKY009
SEPP NIEMEYER	D PERC(B	(B) AN OCEAN OF ROCKS	1978	SKY	SKY016
JENNIFER HENSEL	V (ABC	(C) RUBBER ANGEL	1979	SKY	SKY035
CLAUS D KNIEMEYER	B (ABC				
PIT HENSE+	G (ABC	FRANK EULE D (A			

MARTIN O'CUTHBERT

MARTIN O'CUTHBERT	(A	(A) NAVIGATOR THROUGH NOWHERE	19	ESOTERIC	EEE3

ANN ODELL

ANN ODELL	K V (A	(A) A LITTLE TASTE	1973	DJM	DJLPS 434
MADELINE BELL	V (A				
LIZA STRIKE	V (A	DORIS TROY	V (A	BRUCE ROWLAND	D (A	BARRY DE SOUZA	V (A
RAY COOPER	PERC (A	RAY FENWICK	G (A	GARY BOYLE	G (A	CALEB QUAYE	G (A
JOHN GUSTAFSON	B (A	CHRISTOPHER NEAL HARP (A	RICHARD TAYLOR	REC (A	PETER ROBINSON	K (A
ANDREW CAUTHENY	WIND (A						

ANDREW ODOM

ANDREW ODOM	V (AB	(A) GOING TO CALIFORNIA	197	MCM	FR	900 297
EARL HOOKER	G (B	(B) FARTHER ON THE ROAD	1973	BLUESWAY	US	6055
JOHNNY WALKER	K (B					
JIMMY BOND	B (B	DAVID FRANCIS D (B				

JOE O'DONNELL BAND

JOE O'DONNELL	VLN (A	(A) GAODHAL'S VISION	1978	POLYDOR	2383 465
THEODORE THUNDER	D (A				
STEVE BOLTON	G (A	DAVE LENNOX	K (A	BILL SMITH	B (A

ODYSSEY

GENE PELLO	D (A	(A) ODYSSEY	1972	MOWEST	US	MW 115
BILLY PIERCE	V (A					
KATHLEEN WARREN	K V (A	WARNER SCHWEBKE	B (A	DON DACUS	G (A	DON PEAKE	G (A
ROYCE JONES	V (A	CHRIS DARROW FDL BANJ (A	BUDDY EMMONS	STEEL(A	DAVID T WALKER	G (A
CARTER C C COLLINS CONGA(A		ROBERT JAMES FLT (A				

OFF BROADWAY

CLIFF JOHNSON	V (A	(A) QUICK TIMES	1980	ATLANTIC	US	SD 19286
JOHN IVAN	G (A					
ROB HARDING	G (A	KEN HARCK	D (A	MIKE GORMAN	B (A

OFFENBACH

GERALD BOULEL	V K G(A	(A) NEVER TOO TENDER	1976	A&M	US SP9025	UK AMLH69025
JEAN GRAVEL	G V (A					
ROGER BELVAL	D V (A	MICHEL LAMOTHE	B V (A			

OHIO EXPRESS

DALE POWERS	G (	(A) OHIO EXPRESS	1968	BUDDAH	US	BDS 5018
DEAN KASTRAN	B (	(A) OHIO EXPRESS	1968	PYE	UK	NSPL 28117
JIM PFAYLER	K (	(B) SALT WATER TAFFY	1968	BUDDAH	US	BDS 5021
TIM CORWIN	D (	(C) CHEWY CHEWY	1968	BUDDAH UK203015	US	BDS 5026
DOUGALAS GRASSEL	G (	(D) MERCY	1969	BUDDAH	US	BDS 5037
		(E) VERY BEST OF THE OHIO EXPRESS	196	BUDDAH	US	BDS 5058
		(F) BEG, BORROW & STEAL	1968	CAMEO	US	20000

OHIO KNOX

PAUL HARRIS	K (A	(A) OHIO KNOX	1971	REPRISE	US	6435
PETER GALLWAY	V G (A					
RAY NEOPOLITAN	B (A	DALLAS TAYLOR	D (A	RUSS KUNKEL	CONGAS (A LYNN BLESSING	VIBES (A
JOHN SEBASTIAN G V HCA (A		DANNY WEIS	G (A			

OHIO PLAYERS

CLARENCE SATCHELL SAX V(MR		FIRST IMPRESSIONS	1968 TRIP		US	8029
		(A) FIRST IMPRESSIONS	1976 DJM		UK	DJM22015
LEROY BONNER	G V (MR	OHIO PLAYERS	19 TRIP		US	3506
JAMES WILLIAMS	D V (MR	OBSERVATIONS IN TIME	1969 CAPITOL		US	192
MERVIN PIERCE	TPT (MR	OHIO PLAYERS 19	CAPITOL			11291
MARSHALL JONES	B (MR	PAIN	1972 WESTBOUND		US	2015
RALPH MIDDLEBROOKS TPT (MR		PLEASURE	1973 WESTBOUND		US	2017
WILLIE BECK	K V (MR	ECSTACY	197 WESTBOUND		US	2021
RUBENS BASSINI	PERC (R	PAIN+PLEASURE=ECSTACY	1974 WESTBOUND		UK	6309 103
CLARENCE WILLIS	G V (R	BEST OF	19 WESTBOUND		US	304
AZZEDIN WESTON	PERC (R	SKIN TIGHT	1974 MERCURY	UK SRM1 705 UK 6338		497

(CONTINUED)

OHIO PLAYERS

FIRE	1974 MERCURY	US SRM1 1013 UK 9100 009
HONEY	1975 MERCURY	US SRM1 1038 UK 9100 014
CONTRADICTION	1976 MERCURY	US SRM1 1088 UK 9100 .024
(M) GOLD	1976 MERCURY	US SRM1 1122 UK 9100 030
ANGEL	1977 MERCURY	US SRM1 3701 UK 9100 037
MR MEAN	197 MERCURY	US SRM1 3717
JASS AY LAY DEE	1978 MERCURY	US SRM1 3730
(R) EVERYBODY UP	1979 ARISTA	US AB 4226

O14

O JAYS

EDDIE LAVERT	V	(ALL	COMIN' THROUGH	1965 IMPERIAL	US 9290
WALTER WILLIAMS	V	(ALL	SOUL SOUNDS	1967 MINIT	US 40008
WILLIAMS POWELL	V	(ALL	BACKSTABBER	1972 EPIC	UK 65257
BOBBY MASSEY	V	(LEFT 72	BACKSTABBER	1973 PHILADELPHIA US 31712	UK 65932
BILL ISLES	V	(LEFT 66	IN PHILADELPHIA	1973 EPIC	UK 65469
			IN PHILADELPHIA	1973 PHILADELPHIA US 34482	UK 65933
WITH			LIVE IN LONDON	1974 PHILADELPHIA US 32953	UK 80169
LEON CHANCLER	PERC	(MN	LIVE	1974 MFP	UK 50124
MTUME	PERC	(MN	SHIP AHOY	1974 PHILADELPHIA US 32408	UK 65860
LEON HUFF	K	(N	SURVIVAL	1975 PHILADELPHIA US 33150	UK 80765
VICTOR CARSTARPHEN	K	(N	PEACE	1975 POWER EXCHANGE	PXL 2001
DENNIS WILLIAMS	K	(N	FAMILY REUNION	1976 PHILADELPHIA US 33807	UK 69196
MIKE JACKSON	K	(N	MESSAGE IN THE MUSIC	1976 PHILADELPHIA US 34245	UK 81460
ROLAND CHAMBERS	G	(N	O'JAYS	1976 DJM	UK 22009
RAYMOND EVIL	B	(N	SO FULL OF SOUL	1978 PHILADELPHIA US 35355	UK 86066
CHARLES COLLINS	D	(N	GREATEST HITS	1978 PHILADELPHIA	UK 86058
SHORTY MILLER	V	(N	(M) IDENTIFY YOURSELF	1979 PHILADELPHIA	UK 83666
DAVID CRUSE	PERC	(N	(N) YEAR 2000	1980 T S O P	UK 84221
WALTER SIGLER	PNO	(N			
JAMES SIGLER	K	(N			
LENNY PAKULA	K	(N DENNIS RICHARDSON K (N DENNIS HARRIS G (N KIM MILLER G (N
WILLIE ROSS	G	(N MICHAEL FOREMAN B (N JAMES WILLIAMS B (N QUINTON JOSEPH D (N
LARRY WASHINGTON	PERC	(N CHARLES WILLIAMS CONGA(N

O15

DANNY O'KEEFE

DANNY O'KEEFE	G V	(ALL	(A) DANNY O'KEEFE	1971 ATLANTIC	UK 2466001
DOUG HASTINGS	G	(A	(A) DANNY O'KEEFE	1971 COTILLION	US 9036
BILL McPHERSON	WIND	(A	(B) O'KEEFE	1972 SIGNPOST	US 8404
BOB NIXON	K	(A	(B) O'KEEFE	1972 SIGNPOST	UK 4252
CHRIS ETHRIDGE	B	(A	(B) O'KEEFE	1979 CRIMINAL RI	UK TAKE 1
RICH CROOKS	D	(A	(C) BREEZY STORIES	1973 ATLANTIC	US SD 7264
EDDIE HINTON	G	(A	(D) SO LONG HARRY TRUMAN	1975 ATLANTIC	US SD18125
JIMMY JOHNSON	G	(A	(E) AMERICAN ROULETTE	1977 WB	US BS 3050
ROGER HAWKINS	D	(A	(F) SEATTLE TAPES	1977 FIRST AMERICAN	US
BARRY BECKETT	K	'A	(G) GLOBAL BLUES	1978 WB	US BS 3314
DAVID HOOD	B	(A			
REGGIE YOUNG	G	(B JOHN CHRISTOPHER G (B BOBBY WOOD K (B SHANE KEISTER K (B
BOBBY EMMONS	K	(B MIKE LEECH B (B GENE CHRISMAN D (B HAYWARD BISHOP D (B
HOWARD McNATT	VLN	(B LEO LEBLANC STEEL(B MARKIE MARKOWITZ TPT (B PHIL OLIVELLA CLAR(B
EDDIE BRIGATI	V	(B DAVID BRIGATI V (B HUGH McCRACKEN G (C DONNY HATHAWAY K (C
GORDON EDWARDS	B	(C BERNARD PURDIE D (C NORMAN PRIDE PERC (C AIRTO MOREIRA PERC(C
DOMINIC CORTESE	ACC	(C MONTEGO JOE CONGA(C ARIF MARDIN VIBES(C DAVID BROMBERG G (C
RICHARD DAVIS	B	(C CISSY HOUSTON V (C MYRNA SMITH V (C SYLVIA SHEMWELL V (C
ANDY STATMAN	MAND	(C KEN KOSEK FDL (C DR JOHN K (C HUGH McDONALD G (C
STEVE MOSLEY	D	(C GENE ORLOFF VLN (C EMANUEL GREEN VLN (C RICHARD DICKLER VLA (C
NORMAN FOREST	VLA	(C CHARLES McCRACKEN CELLO(C PETR ECKLUND TPT (C JOHN PAYNE SAX (C
TOM SCOTT	WIND	(D DAVID GRISMAN MAND (D LARRY VANOVER JUG (D RANDY MEISNER B (D
LARRY KNECHTEL	K B	(D DON HENLEY D V (D BERNIE LEADON V (D LINDA RONSTADT V (D
ANDREW GOLD	K	(D JIM FIELDER B (D GARY MALLABER D (DE SNEAKY PETE STEEL(D
JOHN BOYLAN	K	(D ROGER KELLAWAY K (DEG CHUCK DOMANICO B (D JOHN GUERIN D (D
JOYCE EVERSON	V	(D RICHARD GREENE VLN (D JIMMY BOND B (D GLENN FREY G (D
DAVID LINDLEY	STEEL(DE VEYLER HILDEBRAND B (D MIKE MELVOIN PNO (E REGGIE McBRIDE B (E
ALVIN TAYLOR	D	(E OLIVER BROWN CONGA(E SCOTT STRONG G (E KING ERRISSON CONGA(E
CHARLES IRWIN	K	(EG VINCE MELAMED K (EG DAVE PARLATO B (E ROGER BETHELMY D (E
LAUDIR DE OLIVEIRA	PERC(E BOBBYE HALL PERC (E STEVE SCHAEFFER D (E PETER WOODFORD G (E
JOHN HOBBS	K	(E TOM SCOTT SAX (E TONY WILLIAMS D (E BILL CUOMO PNO (G
JIM GORDON	D	(E STEVE FORMAN PERC (E VENETTE GLOUD V (G JIM KELTNER D (G
SHARON ROBINSON	V	(G LARRY MUHOBERAC PNO (G CARMEN TWILLIE V (G BOBBY KING V (G
FRANK MAROCCO	ACC	(G 'BIGGY' McFADDEN V (G KAZU MATSUI SHAKAHACHI (G RONNIE BARRON V (G
CHARLE IRWIN	SYN	(G JIM EWING TROM (G BILL BRAUN PERC (G RICHARD NASH TROM(G
RUSTY BUCHANAN	B	(G MIKE BAIRD CLAR (G SUE RICHMAN V (G JOHN ROTELLA CLAR(G
LYNDA LAWLEY	V	(G JOHN COAN CORNET (G PAUL WOLTZ TUBA (G JAY LEWIS G (G
THOM MOONEY	D	(G MIKE BODDIKER SYN (G JOEL TEPP G (G

O16

OKLAHOMA MAFIA

LEON RUSSELL	K V	(					
LEVON HELM	MAND	V(					
BOBBY KEYS	SAX	(	CARL RADLE B (JESSE ED DAVIS G (JIMMY MARKHAM (

O17

OLD & IN THE WAY

JERRY GARCIA	BANJ G V	(A	(A) OLD & IN THE WAY	1975 ROUND	RX 103
DAVID GRISMAN	MAND	V(A			
PETER ROWAN	G V	(A	JOHN KAHN B (A VASSAR CLEMENTS VLN (A

O18

MIKE OLDFIELD

MIKE OLDFIELD	G B K+++(ALL	(A) TUBULAR BELLS	1973 VIRGIN US 13135	UK V 2001
STEVE BROUGHTON	D	(A	(B) HERGEST RIDGE	1974 VIRGIN US 13109	UK V 2013
MUNDY ELLIS	V	(A	(C) OMMADAWN	1975 VIRGIN US 33913	UK V 2043
JON FIELD	FLT	(A	( ) BOX SET (4LP SET)	1976 VIRGIN	UK VBOX1
VIV STANSHALL	V	(A	(D) INCANTATIONS	1978 VIRGIN	UK VDT 101
JABULA	PERC	(A	(E) EXPOSED (LIVE DBL)	1979 VIRGIN	UK VD 2511
SALLY OLDFIELD	V	(ABD	(F) PLATINUM	1979 VIRGIN	UK V 2141
TERRY OLDFIELD	FLT	(D	(G) Q E 2	1980 VIRGIN	UK V 2181
LINDSAY COOPER	B OBOE	(AB		(CONTINUED)

MIKE OLDFIELD

JUNE WHITING	OBOE (B	TED HOBART	TPT (B	CHILI CHARLES	D (B	CLODAGH SIMMONDS	V (B
PIERRE MOERLEN	D (D	MIKE FRYE PERC	(E	BENOIT MOERLEN	PERC (E	DAVID BEDFORD	PERC (E
RINGO McDONOUGH	BOD (E	NICO RAMSDEN	G (E	PHIL BEER	G V (E	PEKKA POHJOLA	B (E
PETE LEMER	K (E	TIM CROSS	K (E	MADDY PRIOR	V (DE	RAY GAY	TPT (E
RALPH IZEN	TPT (E	SIMO SALMINEN	TPT (E	COLIN MOORE	TPT (E	SEBASTIAN BELL	FLT (DE
CHRIS NICHOLLS	FLT (E	DEBRA BRONSTEIN	V (E	EMMA ACHESON	V (E	DIANA COULSON	V (E
MARY ELLIOTT	V (E	MARY CREED	V (E	CECILY HAZELL	V (E	WENDY LAMPITT	V (E
CLARA HARRIS	V (E	EMMA SMITH	V (E	CATHERINE LOEWE	V (E	MIKE LAIRD	TPT (D
STRING SECTION	(E						

SALLY OLDFIELD

SALLY OLDFIELD V G K WIND(ABC		(A) WATER BEARER	1978	BRONZE	UK	BRON 511
FRANK RICOTTI	PERC (A	(B) EASY	1979	BRONZE	UK	BRON 522
BRIAN BURROWS	SAX (A	(C) CELEBRATION	1980	BRONZE	UK	BRON 528
JEAN PRICE	HARP (A					
TIM WHEATER	PERC (A TREVOR SPENCER PERC (A DAVE LAWSON		SYN (A			

KAI OLSSON

KAI OLSSON	G V (A	(A) CRAZY LOVE	1979	CHRYSALIS	UK	CHR 1226
TERRY BRITTEN	G (A					
MICK GRABHAM	G (A TAFF WILLIAMS G (A DAVE WINTOUR R (A HERBIE FLOWERS B (A					
COLIN PATTENDEN	B (A ALAN COULTER D (A STUART ELLIOTT D (A CHRIS SLADE D (A					
BARRIE GUARD	G K (A CLIFF HALL K (A DAVID MACKAY K (A RON ASPERY SAX (A					
STUART BROOKS	TPT (A TERRY JOHN HRNS (A STEPHEN NYE OBOE (A ANDREW JACKMAN MAND(A					
STEVE SIMPSON	VLN (A TONY HARRIS VLA (A DIGBY RICHARDS V (A LINDA TAYLOR V (A					
WAYNE OLSSON	V (A					

NIGEL OLSSON

NIGEL OLSSON	D V PERC(ABC	(A) DRUM ORCHESTRA	1972	DJM UK DJLPS417	US UNI 73113
		(B) NIGEL OLSSON	1975	ROCKET UK ROLL 2	US PIG 2158
		(C) DRUMMERS CAN SING TOO	197	ROCKET	US PIG 1932

OLYMPIC RUNNERS

PETE WINGFIELD	K V (BDEFG	(A) PUT YOUR MONEY WHERE YOUR MOUTH IS	1974	LONDON US PS653	
GLEN LEFLEUR	D (BDEG	(B) OUT IN FRONT	1975	LONDON US PS658	UK SHU 8483
JO JAMMER	G (BDEFG	(C) DONT LET UP	1975	LONDON US PS668	
GEORGE CHANDLER	V (BDEFG	(D) HOT TO TROT	1977	LONDON US PS678	
DELISLE HARPER	B (BDEFG	(D) HOT TO TROT	1977	CHIPPING NORTON	UK NOR 1
MIKE VERNON	PERC (BDEFG	(E) KEEPING IT UP	1978	RCA	PL 25124
PEARLY GATES	V (B	(F) PUTTIN' IT ON YOU	1978	POLYDOR	POLD5015
JIMMY HAYNES	V (B	(G) OUT OF THE GROUND	1979	RCA	PL 25195
GLEN PENNISTON	D (F	(H) ITS A BITCH	1979	POLYDOR	2383 549
STEVE GREGORY	WIND (F				
JOY YATES	V (D SIMON PHILLIPS D (F JACQUIE SULLIVAN V (D GEORGE CHISHOLM HRNS (F				

OLYMPICS

WALTER WARD	V (ALL	HULLY GULLY	19	ARVEE	US	423
EDDIE LEWIS	V (ALL	DANCE BY THE LIGHT OF THE MOON	19	ARVEE	US	424
CHARLES FIZER	V (ALL	PARTY TIME	19	ARVEE	US	429
MELVIN KING	V (ALL	OLYMPICS	19	JAYBOY		SSX 2008
		DO THE BOUNCE	19	TRIDISC	US	1001
		SOMETHING OLD SOMETHING NEW	19	MIRWOOD	US	7003
		OLYMPICS SING	19	POST	US	8000

OMAHA SHERRIFF

PAUL MUGGLETON	G V (A	(A) COME HELL OR HIGH WATER	1977	GOODEARTH	GDS 803
BOB NOBLE	K (A				
CHRIS BIRKETT	G V PERC(A TONY VISCONTI B (A MICHAEL SPENCER ARSCOTT D HCA V(A				

MICHAEL OMARTIAN

MICHAEL OMARTIAN	K (ALL	(A) ONWARD	197	ABC	ABC 903
STORMIE OMARTIAN	(D	(B) WHITE HORSE	197	MYRRH	MYRA1048
		(C) ADAM AGAIN	1979	MYRRH	MYR 1058
		(D) SEASONS OF THE SOUL	1979	MYRRH	MYR 1073

OMEGA

JANOS KABOR	V (ALL	OMEGA	1973	BELLAPHON	BAC 2017
GYORGY MOLNAR	G (ALL	OMEGA	1973	PASSPORT US	98007
LASLO BENKO K SYN	(ALL	ON TOUR	197	BELLAPHON	BBS 2527
TAMAS MIHALY	B (ALL	III	197	BELLAPHON BLPS 19191+	BAC 2030
FERENC DEBRECENI	D PERC(ALL	2000 YEARS AFTER PAST WAR	1974	BELLAPHON BLPS 19175	
		RED STAR	197	DECCA	UK SKL 4974
		HALL OF FLOATERS IN THE SKY	1976	DECCA	UK SKLR5219
		TIME ROBBER	1976	DECCA	UK SKLR5243
		SKYROVER	1978	BELLAPHON	BAC 2052
		GANNAPOLIS	1978	BELLAPHON	BAC 2061

ONE(UK)

ALAN MARSHALL	G V HCA (A	(A) ONE	1969	FONTANA	UK STL 5539
BOBBY SASS	G K (A				
NORMAN LEPPARD	WIND (A KEVIN FOGARTY G (A BRENT FORBES B (A CONRAD ISADORE D (A				

ONE (US)

MARK BAKER	D (A	(A) ONE	1972	GRUNT	US	FTR 1008
REALITY D BLIPCROTCH V PERC(A						
ROGER CRISSINGER	K (A FRANK TREVOR FEE B (A DONALD ENSSLIN G BAN(A THEODORE TEIPEL FLT HCA K(A					
MARV GRANAT G SITAR DULC(A SARAH OPPENHEIM AUTOHARP(A LAURIE PAUL V (A						

ONE O ONERS (101ERS)

CLIVE TIMPERLEY	G (A	(A) ELGIN AVE BREAKDOWN	1981 ANDALUCIA	UK	AND101
RICHARD DUDANSKI	D V (A				
DAN KELLEHER	B K V(A JOE STRUMMER G V (A MOLE B (A				

ONLY ONES

MIKE KELLIE	D (ABC	(A) THE ONLY ONES	1978	CBS	UK 82830
ALAN MAIR	B (ABC	(B) EVEN SERPENTS SHINE	1979	CBS	UK 83451
JOHN PERRY	G (ABC	(C) BABY'S GOT A GUN	1980	CBS	UK 84089
PETER PERRETT	G V (ABC				
KOULLA KAKOULLI	V (B ADAM MAITLAND K SAX(B RABBIT BUNDRICK K (B				

YOKO ONO

YOKO ONO	V	(AB	(A) FLY			1971 APPLE			SPTU 101/2
JOHN LENNON	G V	(A	(B) FEELING THE SPACE			1973 APPLE SW3412			SAPCOR 26
ERIC CLAPTON	G	(A							
RINGO STARR	D	(A	KLAUSS VOORMANN	B	(A	JIM KELTNER	D	(AB	JIM GORDON	D	(A
BOBBY KEYS	SAX	(A	CHRIS OSBORNE		(A	JOE JONES		(A	DAVID SPINOZZA	G	(A
KEN ASCHER	K	(B	BOB BABITT	B	(B	ANDREW SMITH	D	(B	JEREMY STEIG	FLT	(B
GORDON EDWARDS	B	(B	ARTHUR JENKINS	PERC	(B	DAVID FRIEDMAN	VIBES	(B	RICK MAROTTA	D	(B
DON BROOKS	HCA	(B	SNEAKY PETE STEEL		(B	MICHAEL BRECKER	SAX	(B	JOHN O'CEAN	G	(B

O27A   OPA

HUGO FATTORUSO	K V	(AB	(A) GOLDEN WINGS		1976 MILESTONE		M9069
GEORGE FATTORUSO	D V	(AB	(B) MAGIC TIME		1977 MILESTONE		M9078
RINGO THIELMANN	B V	(AB					
HERMETO PASCOAL	FLT	(AB	DAVID AMRO	G	(AB		

O28   OPEN ROAD

JOHN CARR	D	(A	(A) WINDY DAZE	1971 GREENWICH	GSLP 1001
MIKE THOMSON	B	(A			
SIMON LANZON	K	(A	BARRY HUSBAND	G V	(A

O29   ROY ORBISON

ROY ORBISON   G V   (ALL

LONELY & BLUE	1963	LONDON		SHU2342	VERY BEST OF	19	MONUMENT		18045
LONELY & BLUE	196	MONUMENT		14002	VERY BEST OF	19	MONUMENT		6622
CRYING	1963	LONDON		SHU6229	AT THE ROCKHOUSE	196	SUN	US	1260
CRYING	19	MONUMENT	US	14007	AT THE ROCKHOUSE	1980	CHARLY	UK	CRM2007
CRYING	19	MONUMENT	US	6620	MANY MOODS OF	1969	MGM	US	4636
IN DREAMS	1963	LONDON	UK	SHU8108	GREAT SONGS	1969	MGM	US	4659
IN DREAMS	196	MONUMENT	US	18003	HANK WILLIAMS SONGS	1969	MGM	US	4683
IN DREAMS	196	MONUMENT	US	6620	THE BIG O	1970	LONDON		8496
EXCITING SOUNDS	1964	EMBER			THE ORIGINAL SOUND	1970	SUN	US	113
OH PRETTY WOMAN	1964	LONDON	UK	8207	THE ORIGINAL SOUND	197	SUN	UK	6467 005
THERE IS ONLY ONE	1965	LONDON	UK	8252	ROY ORBISON SINGS	1972	LONDON	UK	8435
THERE IS ONLY ONE	1965	MGM	US	4683	ROY ORBISON SINGS	197	MGM	US	4835
THE ORBISON WAY	1966	LONDON	UK	8279	MEMPHIS	1973	LONDON	UK	8445
THE ORBISON WAY	1966	MGM	US	4322	MEMPHIS	1973	MGM	US	4867
THE CLASSIC	1966	LONDON	UK	8297	THE BEST OF	1973	BOVEMA	EURO	05491411
THE CLASSIC	1966	MGM	US	4379	THE BEST OF	19	TRIP	US	
SINGS DON GIBSON	1967	LONDON	UK	8318	ALL TIME GREATEST HITS	1973	MONUMENT		67290
SINGS DON GIBSON	1967	MGM	US	4424	ALL TIME GRESTEST HITS	19	MONUMENT		8600
CRY SOFTLY LONELY ONE	1968	LONDON	UK	8357	ALL TIME GREATEST HITS	19	MONUMENT		31484
CRY SOFTLY LONELY ONE	1968	MGM	US	4514	THE EXCITING	1974	HALLMARK	UK	SHM 824
FASTEST GUITAR ALIVE	1968	LONDON	UK	8358	MILESTONES	19	MGM	US	4934
ORBISONGS	196	MONUMENT		5004	IM STILL IN LOVE WITH YOU	19	MERCURY	US	SRMI1045
ORBISONGS	196	MONUMENT		18035	ORBITING	19	DESIGN	US	DLP 164
EARLY ORBISON	196	MONUMENT		5013	STARS OF THE 60s	1974	EMI	EURO	05092542
EARLY ORBISON	196	MONUMENT		18023	THE BIG O	1975	CHARLY	UK	CR300008
GREATEST HITS	19	MONUMENT		5007	THE BEST OF	1975	ARCADE	UK	ADE P19
GREATEST HITS	19	MONUMENT		64663	MONUMENTAL HITS	1975	MONUMENT	UK	69147
GREATEST HITS	19	MONUMENT	US	6619	MONUMENTAL HITS VOL2	1975	MONUMENT	UK	69188
GREATEST HITS	19	MONUMENT		14009	FOCOS ON	1976	DECCA		FOS/U15/6
MORE GREATEST HITS	19	MONUMENT		5014	REGENERATION	1977	MONUMENT	UK	81809
MORE GREATEST HITS	19	MONUMENT		6621	REGENERATION	1977	MONUMENT	US	7600
MORE GREATEST HITS	19	MONUMENT		18024	LAMINAR FLOW	1979	ASYLUM	UK	K53092
					LAMINAR FLOW	1979	ELEKTRA	US	6E 198

O29A   ORCHESTRAL MANOEUVRES IN THE DARK

PAUL HUMPHREYS	V K PERC	(AB	(A) ORCHESTRAL MANOEUVRES IN THE DARK		1980 DINDISC UK	DID2
ANDY McCLUSKEY	V B K PERC	(AB	(B) ORGANISATION		1980 DINDISC UK	DID6
DAVE FAIRBAIRN	G	(A				
MALCOLM HOLMES	PERC D	(AB	MARTIN COOPER	SAX	(A	

O29B   ORCHIDS

LAURIE E BELL	D V	(A	(A) ORCHIDS		1980 MCA	UK MCF 3067
JAN KING	V G K	(A				
LAURIE McALISTER	B V	(A	SUNBIE SINN	G PNO V	(A	CHE ZURO	G K V	(A

O30   OREGON

PAUL McCANDLESS	(E	(A) MUSIC OF ANOTHER PRESENT ERA	1974 VANGUARD	VSD79326
GLEN MOORE	(E	(B) DISTANT HILLS	1974 VANGUARD	VSD79341
RALPH TOWNER	(E	(C) WINTER LIGHT	1975 VANGUARD	VSD79350
COLLIN WALCOTT	(E	(D) IN CONCERT	1975 VANGUARD	VSD79358
ELVIN JONES	(F	(E) TOGETHER	1977 VANGUARD	VSD79377
		(F) OUT OF THE WOODS	1978 ELEKTRA	K52101

O30A   ORGANISATION

RALF HUTTER	ORG	(A	(A) TONE FLOAT		1970 RCA	SF8111
BASIL HAMMOUDI	PERC V	(A				
FLORIAN SCHNEIDER-ESLEBEN	FLT	(A	BUTCH HAUF	B PERC	(A	FRED MONICKS	D PERC	(A

O31   ORIGINALS

WALTER GAINES	(	(A) GREEN GROW THE LILACS	1969 SOUL	US	716	
C P SPENCER	(A	(B) PORTRAIT	1970 SOUL	US	724	
HENRY DIXON	(	(C) NATURALLY TOGETHER	1971 SOUL	US	729	
FREDERICK GORMAN	(	(D) DEFINITIONS	1972 SOUL	US	734	
JOE STUBBS	(	(E) GAME CALLED LOVE	1974 SOUL	US	740	
TY HUNTER	(	(F) CALIFORNIA SUNSET	1975 MOTOWN	US	826	UK	11287
		(G) COMMUNIQUE	1976 SOUL	US	746	UK TAMLA12034
		(H) DOWN TO LOVE TOWN	1977 SOUL	US	749	UK TAMLA12054
		(J) ANOTHER TIME ANOTHER PLACE	1978 FANTASY	US 9546	UK	FT542
		(K) COME AWAY WITH ME	1978 FANTASY	US 9577	

O31A   ORION

	(A) REBORN	197 CHARLY	CRL 5020

```
LARRY HOPPEN      G V  (ABCDE      (A)  ORLEANS                1975 ABC     US ABCX  795 UK ABCL 5107
LANCE HOPPEN      B V  (ABCDE      (B)  LET THERE BE MUSIC     1975 ASYLUM US 7E 1029 UK SYL 9023
JOHN HALL         G V  (ABCD       (B)  LET THERE BE MUSIC     1975 ASYLUM           UK   K53011
WELLS KELLY       D V K(ABCDE      (C)  WAKING & DREAMING      1976 ASYLUM US 7E 1070 UK   K53044
JERRY MAROTTA     D    (C          (D)  BEFORE THE DANCE       1977 ABC         US  1058 UK ABCL 6224
MICHAEL BRECKER   SAX  (C          (E)  FOREVER                1979 INFINITY US 9006 UK   2004
BLUE MITCHELL     TPT  (C
LINDA RONSTADT    V    (C  BOB LEINBACH     K V (E   R A MARTIN      HRNS K V(AE   JIMMY MAELEN    PERC(E
RUBENS BASSINI    PERC (E  STRING SECTION        (E
```

ORLONS   O33

```
STEVE CALDWELL     V  (12     ALL THE HITS              19 CAMEO       US      1033
MARLEN DAVIS       V  (12     SOUTH STREET              19 CAMEO       US      1041
ROSETTA HIGHTOWER  V  (12     NOT ME                    19 CAMEO       US      1054
AUDREY BRICKLEY    V  (1      BIGGEST HITS              19 CAMEO       US      1061
SHIRLEY BRICKLEY   V  (1      GOLDEN HITS              196 CAMEO       US      1067
                             DOWN MEMORY LANE           19 CAMEO       US      1073
                             THE BEST OF              1977 LONDON      UK   HAU 8594
                             (1) PRE 1959  (2) POST 1959
```

ORPHAN   O33A

```
ERIC LILLEQUIST    V G  (        (A)  EVERYONE LOVES TO SING   1972  LONDON  US PS 614 UK SHU 8438
STUART SCHULMAN    B K V(        (B)  ROCK & REFLECTION        1973  LONDON           UK SHU 8452
RICHARD ADELMAN    D    (        (C)  MORE ORPHAN THAN NOT     1974  LONDON           UK SHU 8475
BILL KEITH         STEEL(
DAVE CONRAD        B    (   BILL ELLIOTT K   (   BOB CHOUINARD      D  (
```

ORPHAN EGG   O33B

```
                                 (A)  ORPHAN EGG               19    CAROLE   US    CARS8004
```

ORPHEUS   O33C

```
ERIC GULLIKSEN     B V  (A        (A)  ASCENDING              1968   MGM      US    SE4569
JACK McKENES       G V  (A
BRUCE ARNOLD       G V  (A   HARRY SANDLER      D V (A
```

OSANNA   O33D

```
ELIO D'ANNA       SAX  (ABCDE     (A)  L'UOMO               197  FONIT  LPX 10 +1976    MF 103
DANIEL RUSTICI    G    (ABCDE     (B)  MILANO CALIBRO 9     1974 FONIT  LPX 14 +COSMOS PILPS9001
MASSIMO GUARINO   D    (ABCD      (C)  PALEPOLI             197  FONIT  LPX 19
LELLO BRANDI      B    (ABCD      (D)  LANDSCAPE OF LIFE    197  FONIT  LPX 32 +COSMOS PILPS9007
LINO VAIRETTI     K SYN V(ABCD    (E)  UNO                  1974 FONIT  LPX 26 +MOTORS MT 44027
ENZO VALICELLI    D    (E
```

OZZY OSBOURNE   O33E

```
OZZY OSBOURNE     D   (A          (A)  BLIZZARD OF OZ       1980  JET     UK    JETLP234
BOB DAISLEY       B   (A
RANDY RHODES      G   (A
```

OSCAR   O33F

```
BRIAN McGLADDERY  G V  (          (A)  TWILIGHT ASYLUM      1976  DJM     UK    DJF 20494
TONY BANFORD      K    (          (B)  COBBLESTONE HEROES   1977  DJM     UK    DJF 20516
KEVIN PARROT      G    (
ROGER TWEEDALE    PERC (   GARY McDOUGAL     B   (
```

OSAMU   O33G

```
OSAMU KITAJIMA G KOTO V(A         (A)  OSAMU               1977  ISLAND    UK   ILPS 9426
JOHN HUG    G MAND    (A
GEOFFREY HALES  D PERC(A  DENNIS BELFIELD   B   (A   BRIAN WHITCOMB G K SYN(A   TATSUYA SANO     (A
GEORGE MARINELLI  G   (A  MINNIE RIPERTON   V   (A
```

WAVIS O'SHAVE   O33H

```
WAVIS O'SHAVE     V   (           (A)  DENNIS SMOKES TABS(EP)   19  COMPANY            CR  003
                                  (B)  ANNA FORD'S BUM   (EP)   19  ANTI POP           AP 2
```

OSIBISA   O34

```
TEDDY OSEI FLT PERC   (ALL        (A)  OSIBISA              1971 MCA   UK MDKS8001 +74 MCG 3508
LOUGHTY AMAO      SAX  (ABCD       (A)  OSIBISA              197  DECCA US   75285 +MCA  MCA32
ROBERT BAILEY     K    (ABCDGK     (B)  WOYAYA               1971 MCA   UK MDKS8005 +74 MCD 3506
SPARTACUS R       B    (ABCD       (B)  WOYAYA               197  DECCA US   75327 +MCA  MCA43
WENDEL RICHARDSON G    (ABCDHK     (C)  HEADS                1972 MCA   UK MDKS8007 +74 MCG 3514
MAC TONTOH        TPT  (ALL        (C)  HEADS                197  DECCA US   75368
SOL AMARFIO       D    (ALL        (D)  BEST OF              1974 MCA   US            MCF 2575
KIKI GYAN         K    (FH         (E)  HAPPY CHILDREN       1973 WB    US  BS 2732 UK K56022
KOFI AYIVOR       PERC (EFGH       (F)  OSIBIROCK            1974 WB    US  BS 2802 UK K56048
PAUL GOLLY        G    (FH         (G)  SUPER FLY TNT        1974 BUDDAH US   5136 UK 2318 087
GORDON HUNTE      G V  (G          (G)  SUPER FLY TNT        197  BUDDAH           UK BDLP4020
JEAN ROUSSEL      K    (E          (H)  WELCOME HOME         1975 BRONZE UK ILPS9355 RI BRNA355
MIKE ODUMUSU      B    (HK         (H)  WELCOME HOME         197  ANTILLES         US   7051
JEAN MANDENGUE    B    (EFGH       (J)  OJAH AWAKE           1976 BRONZE UK ILPS9411 RI BRNA 411
DAKU 'POTATO'     K    (KL         (J)  OJAH AWAKE           197  ANTILLES         US   7058
SONIA LEKHELA     V    (K          (K)  BLACK MAGIC NIGHT    1977 BRONZE UK BRSP 3
NTOBI MDUDU       V    (K          (L)  MYSTIC ENERGY        1980 CALIBRE          UK CAB1002
TINY CONCO        V    (K
LINDA CONCO       V    (K   KARI BANNERMAN    G   (L   DIKOTO MANDENGUE   B  (L   EMA YAWKOBA RENTZOS K V(L
ROBERT ABIA       G B  (L   ALTON EDWARDS     V   (L   REBOP KWAKU BAAH   PERC (L   PAM DOUGLAS    V  (L
MIQUEL BROWN      V    (L   CANDY McKENZIE    V   (L   KATHY T            V  (L
```

LEE OSKAR   O35

```
LEE OSKAR         HCA V   (AB      (A)  LEE OSKAR            1976 UA       US      UALA  594
(OSKAR LEVETIN HANSEN)             (B)  BEFORE THE RAIN      1978 MCA UK MCF2870 US ELEKTRA 6E150
GREG ERRICO       K D   (A
ROBERT VEGA       B    (A   STEVE BUSFELD   G   (A   CHEPITO AREAS   CONGA(A   WENDY HAAS      V  (A
HERMAN EBERITZSCH PNO  (A   MOSES WHEELOCK  CONGA(A   HAROLD BROWN    D   (A   MONTY STARK   PERC (A
JULIA TILLMAN     V    (A   MAXINE WILLARD  V   (A   LANI GROVES     V   (A   EDNA WRIGHT     V  (A
CHARLES MILLER    SAX  (A   JERRY FISHER    V   (A   CONNIE FISHER   V   (A   NITO MEDINA     G  (A
LONNIE JORDAN     PERC K (A  PAPA DEE ALLEN  PERC (A   HOWARD SCOTT    G V (A   B B DICKERSON   B  (A
```

O36 OSMOSIS

CHARLIE MARIANT	WIND (A		(A) OSMOSIS				1970 RCA		US	1sa 3010
BOBBY KNOW	V (A									
DANNY COMFORT	B (A	LOU PETERSON	D (A	BOBBY CLARK		PERC (A	CHARLIE BECHLER	K (A		
ANDY STENBORN	G (A									

O37 OTGER DICE

ANTON VERHAGEN	V (A		(A) GARDEN OF PLEASURE			19 TRIANGLE		150 330020
OTGER COOYMANS	K V (A							
FRED BERGER	G (A	DAVID KEMPER	D (A	PAUL HAPPENER	B (A	EEF ALBERS	G (A
JAN PIJNENBERG	D (A	DEAN PARKS	G (A	VICTOR FELDMAN	PERC (A		

O37A OTHER HALF

RANDY HOLDEN	G (		(A) THE OTHER HALF	19 ATCA	A38004
MIKE PORT	(				

O38 JOHNNY OTIS

JOHNNY OTIS	D V PNO(ALL	(A) COLD SHOT	1969 SONET UK SNTF613 US KENT	534
SHUGGIE OTIS	G B (A	(B) CUTTIN' UP	1970 EPIC	US	26524
MIGHTY MOUTH EVANS	V (A	(C) LIVE AT MONTEREY	1971 EPIC UK 66295 US	30473
AL RIVERA	B (A	(D) GREAT R & B	19 BLUES SPECTRUM US	BS 103
HOOTIE GALVAN	V (A	(E) ROCK'N'ROLL HIT PARADE	197 DIG	US	104
DON SUGARCANE HARRIS	VLN(A	(F) FORMIDABLE	19 EMBER	UK	SPE 6604
BROADWAY THOMAS	B (A	(G) THE JOHNNY OTIS SHOW	19 BOVEMA	EURO 052 80676
BUDDY REDD	D (A	(H) THE JOHNNY OTIS SHOW	19 SAVOY	US	2221
ESTHER PHILLIPS	V (	(I) THE JOHNNY OTIS SHOW	19 CAPITOL	US	940
MEL WALKER	(	(J) PIONEERS OF ROCK	1973 STARLINE	UK	SRS 5129
CLIFFORD SOLOMON	(	(K) JOHNNY OTIS	1975 BULLDOG	BDL1002
MIGHTY FLEA	TROM (	(L) ROCK'N'ROLL HISTORY	1979 CAPITOL	FR 038 85085
LADY DEE WILLIAMS	(	(M) ROCK'N'ROLL	1979 FLYRIGHT	UK	550
PETE LEWIS	(			
ROBINS	V (	BIG JIM WYNN	(OTISETTES	V (MARGIE EVANS	V (
BIG DADDY RUCKER	(	EDDIE VINSON	G V (BIG JOE TURNER	V (

O39 SHUGGIE OTIS

SHUGGIE OTIS	G B V(ALL	(A) AL KOOPER INTRODUCES	1969 CBS US 9951 UK	63797
JOHNNY OTIS	D PNO(BC	(B) HERE COMES SHUGGIE OTIS	1970 CBS US 26511 UK	63996
AL KOOPER	K V (A	(C) FREEDOM FLIGHT	1971 EPIC US 30752
RAY JOHNSON	K (B	(D) INSPIATION INFORMATION	1975 EPIC US 33059
LEON HAYWOOD	K (B	(E) OMAHA BAR B Q	19 KENT US 540
WILTON FELDER	B (BC	(1) 1969 LIVE	
AL McKIBBON	B (B		
STIX HOOPER	D (B	PAUL LAGOS	D (B	ABE MILLS	D (B	PRESTON LOVE	WIND (B1
PLAS JOHNSON	SAX (B	TANK JERNIGAN	WINS (AB	JIM HORN	SAX (B	JACK KELSO	SAX (BD1
MELVIN MOORE	TPT (B	BOB MITCHELL	TPT (B	GENE'MIGHTY FLEA'CONNERS(B	WILLIE RUFF	HRNS (B
WELLS KELLY	D (A	STU WOODS	B (A	MARK KLINGMAN	PNO (A	CLIFFORD SOLOMON	SAX (1
ED PLEASANCE	SAX (1	WALLACE BRODIE	SAX (1	JOE EPPS	SAX (1	BILL CATER	SAX (1
RON SELICO	D (1	MIKE KOWALSKI	D (C	GEORGE DUKE	K (C	AYNSLEY DUNBAR	D (C
JIM BRADSHAW	HCA V(C	RICHARD APLANALP	FLT (C	CLYDIE KING	V (C	VANETTA FIELDS	V (C
SHIRLEY MATTHEWS	V (C	CURT SLETTEN	TPT (D	RON ROBBINS	TPT (D	DOUG WINTZ	TROM (D
JIM PRINGLE	TROM (D	JEFF MARTNEY	HRNS (D	STRINGS SECTION	(AD RICHARD MACKAY	HRNS (B

O40 JOHN OTWAY

JOHN OTWAY	G V (ALL	(A) JOHN OTWAY & WILD WILLY BARRETT	1977 EXTRACKED ELP1+POLYDOR 2383 453
WILD WILLY BARRETT	G V (A	(B) DEEP & MEANINGLESS	1978 POLYDOR	2383 501
PETE TOWNSHEND	G (A	(C) WHERE DID I GO RIGHT	1979 POLYDOR	2383 532
PAUL WARD	(ABD	(D) WAY & BAR	1980 POLYDOR	2383 581
NIGEL PEGRUM	D (ABD		
PHIL CUTLER	(A	STUART EATON	(A	LYN FLETCHER	(A	FIONA BUTT	(B
MARTIN LOVEDAY	(A	MILTON REAME JAMES	(A	LISA STRIKE	V (A	MORGAN FISHER	K (C
OLLIE HALSALL	G (A	PAUL MARTINEZ	B (C	CHARLIE MORGAN	D (C	MAGGIE RYDER	V (CD
JULIAN SMEDLEY	FDL (C	MARK FREEMAN	(BD	MAURICE BACON	(D	LOL COXHILL	(D
DAVE HOLMES	(B	YVONNE GRECH	(B	SIMON HANSON	(B	ROGER CAREY	(D

O40A OUTCASTS

	(A) SELF CONSCIOUS OVER YOU	19 GOOD VIBRATIONS	BIG 1

O41 OUTLAW BLUES BAND

LEON RUBENHOLD	(A	(A) BREAKING IN	1969 STATESIDE UK	SSL10290
PHILLIP JOHN	(A	(A) BREAKING IN	1969 BLUESWAY US	BLS 6030
VICTOR ALEMAN	(A			
LAWRENCE DICKENS	(A	JOE WHITEMAN	(A		

O42 THE OUTLAWS (UK)

MIKE BERRY	V (	(A) DREAM OF THE WEST	1961 EMI
CHAS HODGES	B (		
REG HAWKINS	G (	BILLY KUY	G (	BOBBY GRAHAM	D (	DON GROOM	D (
KEN KUNGREN	G (	ROGER MINGAY	G (	LORNE GREENE	G (	RITCHIE BLACKMORE G (
MICK UNDERWOOD	D (	HARVEY HINSLEY	G (		

O43 OUTLAWS(US)

BILLY JONES	G V (ABCDE	(A) THE OUTLAWS	1975 ARISTA US AL 4042 UK ARTY 115
FRANK O'KEEFE	B (AB	(B) LADY IN WAITING	1976 ARISTA	UK ARTY 126
HENRY PAUL	G V (ABC	(C) HURRY SUNDOWN	1977 ARISTA US AL 4135 UK SPARTI1010
HUGHIE THOMASSON	G V (ABCDE	(D) BRING IT BACK ALIVE	1978 ARISTA	UK DARTY 5
MONTE YOHO	D (ABCDE	(E) PLAYING TO WIN	1978 ARISTA	UK ARTY 156
JOE LALA	PERC (B	(F) IN THE EYE OF THE STORM	1979 ARISTA US AL 9507
HARVEY ARNOLD	B V (CDE	(G) GHOST RIDERS IN THE SKY	1981 ARISTA	UK SPART1160
JOE VITALE	SYN STRING(C		
MANUAL LABOUR	PERC (C	DAVID DIX	D PERC(DE	FREDDIE SALEM	G V(DE

O44 OUTSIDERS

ADRIAN BORLAND	G V (AB1	(A) CALLING ON YOUTH	1977 RAW EDGE	RER 001
ADRIAN JANES	D V (AB1	(B) CLOSE UP	1978 RAW EDGE	RER 003
BOB LAWRENCE	B (AB	(1) 1979	
GRAHAM GREEN	B (1		

OUTSIDERS (US)
O44A

TOM KING	G	(A) TIME WONT LET ME IN	19	CAPITOL	US	2501
BILL BRUNO		(B) ALBUM 2	19	CAPITOL	US	2568
MERDIN MADSEN	B G HCA	(C) IN	19	CAPITOL	US	2636
SONNY GERACI	V	(D) HAPPENING LIVE	19	CAPITOL	US	2745
RICKY BAKER	D					

OVARY LODGE
O45

KEITH TIPPETT	K (AB	(A) OVARY LODGE	1973	RCA	UK	SF8372
JULIE TIPPETT	V (B	(B) OVARY LODGE	1976	OGUN		OG 600
HARRY MILLER	B (B					
FRANK PERRY	V PERC(AB ROY BABBINGTON B (A					

OZARK MOUNTAIN DAREDEVILS
O46

JOHN DILLON	G V K(ABCD	(A) OZARK MOUNTAIN DAREDEVILS	1973	A&M	US 4411	UK AMLH64411
RANDLE CHOWNING G V HCA(ABCD		(B) IT'LL SHINE WHEN IT SHINES	1974	A&M	US 3654	UK AMLH63654
STEVE CASH	HCA V(ABCD	(B) CAR OVER THE LAKE ALBUM	1975	A&M	US 4549	UK AMLH64549
BUDDY BRAYFIELD	K (ABCD	(D) MEN FROM EARTH	1976	A&M	US 4601	UK AMLH64601
LARRY LEE	D (ABCD	(E) DONT LOOK DOWN	1978	A&M	US 4662	UK AMLH64662
MICHAEL GRANDA	B V (ABCD	(F) ITS ALIVE	1978	A&M		UK AMLH66006
NICK DE CARO	ACC (A	(G) OZARK MOUNTAIN DAREDEVILS	1980	CBS		UK 84193
WELDON MYRICK	STEEL(C						
FARRELL MORRIS	PERC (C JODY TROUTMAN V (B NANCY BLAKE CELLO (C BILL JONES WIND K V(C
GLYN JOHNS	G (B STEVE CANADY G D V (JERRY MILLS MAND (RUNE WALLE G (
RUSSELL CHAPPELL	K V (

OZO
O47

JOHN MIZEROLLO	G (AB	(A) LISTEN TO THE BUDDAH	1976	DJM	UK	20488
BETH KUSTRA	V (A	(B) MUSEUM OF THE WORLD	1978	DJM	UK	20517
VAL MACDONALD	D PERC (A					
VERNON CUMMINGS	PERC V(A EDDIE DAVIES K V (A MARTIN ABRAHAMS G (A FRANZ KOCK WIND(A
TREVOR STEPHENS	B (A HELEN DENISTON V (A KIM WENDELS V (A DEREK MANDL G (A
HUGH ASHTON	G (A MICK WAYNE G (A KATHY TONTO V (B

OZZ
O48

ALEXIS T ANGEL	V (A	(A) NO PRISONERS	1980	CBS		36198
GREGG PARKER	G V (A					
DONNELL HAGAN	D (A CRAIG GRUBER B (A WILLIE BASS B (A MICHAEL CAVANAUGH K SYN(A

PFM
P1

FLAVIO PREMOLI	K V (ALL	(A) STORIA DI UN MINOTO	1972	NUMERO UNO	IT ZSLN55055
FRANZ DI CIOCCIO	D V (CFGH	(B) PER UN AMICO	1972	NUMERO UNO	IT ZSLN55155
FRANCO MUSSIDA	G V (CFGH	(C) PHOTO'S OF GHOSTS	1973	MANTICORE ANTI2003 UK	K43502
MAURO PAGANI	FLT V VLN(CFH	(D) WORLD BECAME THE WORLD	1974	MANTICORE	UK K53502
PATRIC DJIVAS	B (FH	(E) COOK	1975	MANTICORE US MA6502 UK	K53506
BERNARDO LANZETTI G V (FH		(F) CHOCOLATE KINGS	1976	MANTICORE	UK K53508
GIORGIO PIAZZA	B (CG	(F) CHOCOLATE KINGS	1976	NUMERO UNO	IT 55684
GREGORY BLOCH	VLN (G	(F) CHOCOLATE KINGS	1976	ASYLUM	US 7E1071
		(G) MARCONI BAKERY	1976	PETERS INT	9014
		(H) JET LAG	1977	MANTICORE	UK K53511
		(H) JET LAG	1977	ASYLUM	US 7E1101
		(J) PASS PARTU	197	ZOO	34032
		(K) SUONARESUONARE	197	ZOO	34092
		(L) LIVE USA	197	ZOO	55676

AUGUSTOS PABLO
P2

AUGUSTOS PABLO	V K (ABC	(A) ITAL DUB	1975	TROJAN	TRLS 115
BAGGA	B (B	(B) EAST OF THE RIVER NILE	1978	MESSAGE	
ROBERT SHAKESPEARE	B (B	(C) ORIGINAL ROCKERS	1979	GREENSLEEVES	GREL 8
CARLTON BARRETT	D (B					
EARL 'CHINNA'SMITH G (B C DOWNIE B (B MAX EDWARDS D (B EVERTON DA SILVA PERC (B
ASTON BARRETT	B (B NOEL BENBOW D (B

PABLO CRUISE
P3

DAVE JENKINS	G B V(ABCDE	(A) PABLO CRUISE	1975	A&M	US 4528	AMLH64528
CORY LERIOS	PNO (ABCDE	(B) LIFE LINE	1976	A&M	US 4575	AMLH64575
STEPHEN PRICE	D PERC(ABCDE	(C) A PLACE IN THE SUN	1977	A&M	US 4625	AMLH64625
BRUCE DAY	B V (E	(D) WORLDS AWAY	1978	A&M	US 4597	AMLH64697
BUD COCKRELL	B V (ABC	(E) PART OF THE GAME	1980	A&M		AMLK63712
GENE MEROS	SAX (E					
MIKE PORCARO	B (E VICTOR FELDMAN PERC (E DAVID FOSTER SYN (E MICHAEL BODDICKER SYN(E
STEVE PORCARO	SYN (E

TOM PACHECO
P3A

TOM PACHECO	(	(A) SWALLOWED UP IN AMERICAN HEARTLAND	1976	RCA	APLI 1254
		(B) THE OUTSIDER	1977	RCA	APLI 1887

PACIFIC DRIFT
P4

LAWRENCE ARENDS	D PERC V(A	(A) FEELIN' FREE	1970	NOVA UK SND13	US DECCA 18040
BARRY REYNOLDS	G V (A				
BRIAN SHAPMAN	K V (A GRAHAM HARROP B G (A JACK LANCASTER FLT (A DAVE DAVANI HRNS(A
SUE GLOVER	V (A SUNNY LESLIE V (A

PACIFIC EARDRUM
P5

DAVE MACRAE	K (AB	(A) PACIFIC EARDRUM	1977	CHARISMA	CAS1133
ISAAC GUILLORY	G (AB	(B) BEYOND PANIC	1978	CHARISMA	CAS1136
GEOFF SEOPARDIE	D (AB				
JOY YATES	V (AB BILLY KRISTIAN B (AB BRIAN SMITH WIND PERC(B JIM CUOMO SAX (A
MORRIS PERT	PERC (A SIMON MORTON PERC (B

PACIFIC GAS & THE ELECTRIC
P6

CHARLIE ALLEN	V (ALL	(A) PACIFIC GAS & THE ELECTRIC	1969	CBS	US 9900	UK 63822
BRENT BLACK	B (AC	(B) GET IT ON	1969	KENT	US 547	UK B&C CAS100b
FRANK COOK	D (AC	(B) GET IT ON	19	ORANGE	US 701	METRONOME15379
TOM MARSHALL	G (AC	(C) ARE YOU READY	1970	CBS	US 1017	UK 64026
GLENN SCHWARTZ	G (AB	(D) P G & E (HARD BURN)	1971	CBS	US 30362	UK 64295
FREDDY HILL	TPT (AC	(E) P G & E WITH CHARLIE ALLEN	1973	DUNHILL US 157	
BUD BRISBOIS	TPT (A	(F) BEST	1973	CBS	US 32019	
WAYNE HENDERSON	TROM (A	(G) LIVE & KICKING AT LEXINGTON	187	CBS		UK 66264

(CONTINUED)

PACIFIC GAS & THE ELECTRIC

ALLEN SCHWARZBERG	D	(E									
WILTON FELDER	SAX	(E	GORDON EDWARDS	B	(E	JOHN HILL	K	(E	BOB MANN	G	(E
CHARLIE BROWN	G	(E	JON STROLL	PNO	(E	GEORGE YOUNG	SAX	(E	ARTIE KAPLAN	SAX	(E
JOE GRIMM	SAX	(E	SELDON POWELL	SAX	(E	MICHAEL BRECKER	SAX	(E	PHIL BODNER	SAX	(E
CORNELL DUPREE	G	(E	ERNIE HAYES	K	(E	LOU SOLOFF	HRNS	(E	AL DE RISI	HRNS	(E
BURT COLLINS	HRNS	(E	MICKEY GRAVINE	HRNS	(E	RAY ROLLARD	V	(E	J R BAILEY	V	(E
JIM MADEN	TAMB V	(E	TASHA THOMAS	V	(E	BARBARA MASSEY	V	(E	CARL HALL	V	(E
KENNY WILLIAMS	V	(E	LOU COURTNEY	V	(E	JERRY FRIEDMAN	G	(E	SAMMY TURNER	V	(E
SHERMAN LEWIS	V	(E	TROY KEYES	V	(E	BILL FOSTER	V	(E	JOHN LUCAS	V	(E
RON MARSHALL	V	(E	LANI GROVES	V	(E	GLORIA BARLEY	V	(E	SHIRLEY BREWER	V	(E
MANNY SEYMOUR	V	(E	MELVIN KENT	V	(E	JOHN BROWN	V	(E	CHARLOTTE GILBERT	V	(E
JAMES RYAN	V	(E	DELORES HARVIN	V	(E	ALBERTINE ROBERTSON	V	(E	JOSHIE ARMSTEAD	V	(E
VANETTA FIELDS	V	(C	DELORES HALL	V	(C	GINGER SCHACKNE	V	(C	RUSTY YOUNG	G	(C
SHERRILL ATWOOD	V	(C	CLYDIE KING	V	(C	LORNA WILLARD	V	(C	MERRY CLAYTON	V	(C
SHIRLEY MATTHEWS	V	(C	ALFRED GALLEROS	SAX	(D	KEN UTTERBACK	G	(D	RON WOODS	SAX	(D
JERRY AIELLO	K	(D	JOE LALA	PERC	(D	STANLEY ABERNATHY	TPT	(D	FRANK PETRICCA	B	(D
BLACKBERRIES	V	(D									

CLEO PAGE

(A) LEAVING MISSISSIPPI	!)')	JSP		UK	1003

GENE PAGE

GENE PAGE						
	BLACULA	197	RCA	US		LSP 4806
	HOT CITY	1975	ATLANTIC	US 18111	UK	K50105
	LOVELOCK	1976	ATLANTIC	US 18161	UK	K50221
	CLOSE ENCOUNTERS	1978	ARISTA	US 4174		SPART1052

JIMMY PAGE

JIMMY PAGE	G	(A	(A) DONT SEND ME NO FLOWERS	1969	MARMALADE		UK	608004
SONNY BOY WILLIAMSON	V	(A	(A) SONNY BOY WILLIAMSON	1975	SPRINGBOARD			4038
BRIAN AUGER	K	(A	(A) JAM SESSION	1975	CHARLY		UK	CR 30011
JOE HARRIOT	SAX	(A						
ALAN SKIDMORE	SAX	(A	MICK WALLER	D	(A			

PAICE ASHTON & LORD

IAN PAICE	D	(A	(A) MALICE IN WONDERLAND	1977	WB	JAPAN P10360		US	BS3088
JON LORD	K	(A	(A) MALICE IN WONDERLAND	1977	OYSTER		UK	2391 269	
TONY ASHTON	K V	(A							
PAUL MARTINEZ	B	(A	BERNIE MARSDEN	G	(A	HOWIE CASEY	SAX	(A	REG BROOKS	TROM (A
SHEILA McKINLEY	V	(A	DAVE CASWELL	HRNS (A	GILBERT DALL'ENESE	SAX	(A	JEANETTE McKINLEY	V (A

RONNIE PAISLEY BAND

RONNIE PAISLEY	V	(A	(A) SMOKING MIRROR	1979	PYE	UK		NSPL18582
ANDY BROWN		(A						
STEVE GREGORY	HRNS	(A	JOHN MARK	(A	TONY HILL	(A	KIM HAKINSSON	(A
PETE KELLY		(A	DAVID PAISLEY	(A	ALAN PARK	(A	PETE PAVLI	(A
FRANK RICOTTI	PERC	(A	JIM TOOMEY	(A	PAUL TURNER	(A	DIGGER DAVIES	(A
LADYBIRDS	V	(A						

PALADIN

KEITH WEBB	D	(AB1	(A) PALADIN	1971	BRONZE		ILPS 9150
PETE SOLLEY	K V VLN	(AB1	(B) CHARGE	1972	BRONZE		ILPS 9190
PETE BECKETT	B V	(AB1	(1) 1972				
LOU STONEBRIDGE	K V	(AB					
DEREK FOLEY	G V	(AB	JOE JAMMER	G	(1		

PALEY BROTHERS

ANDY PALEY	V G HCA	(A	(A) PALEY BROTHERS	1978	SIRE		SRK 6052
JONATHAN PALEY	G V	(A					
JEFF LASS	K	(A					
ERIC ROSENFELD	G	(A	JAN UVENA	D	(A	LEIGH FOXX	B	(A	JIM HASLIP	B	(A
RAMONES	G B D	(A	PAUL JUSTICE	B	(	JEFF WILKINSON	D	(

BRUCE PALMER

BRUCE PALMER		(A	(A) THE CYCLE IS COMPLETE	1971	VERVE/FORECAST		VRF 3086

ROBERT PALMER

ROBERT PALMER	V PERC	(ALL	(A) SNEAKIN' SALLY THROUGH THE ALLEY	1974	ISLAND	UK	ILPS 9294
SPIDER WEBB	D	(C	(B) PRESSURE DROP	1975	ISLAND	UK	ILPS 9374
JEFF PORCARO	D	(C	(C) SOME PEOPLE CAN DO WHAT THEY LIKE	1976	ISLAND	UK	ILPS 9420
ALLEN SCHWARZBERG	D	(D	(D) DOUBLE TROUBLE	1978	ISLAND	UK	ILPS 9476
KEITH BENSON	D	(D	(E) SECRETS	1979	ISLAND	UK	ILPS 9544
CHRIS PARKER	D	(D	(F) CLUES	1980	ISLAND	UK	ILPS 9595
RITCHIE HAYWARD	D	(BCD					
ED GREENE	D	(B	FREDDIE HARRIS	G	(CD	CHUCK RAINEY	B	(C	BILL PAYNE	K V	(BCD
SAM CLAYTON	PERC	(BC	PAUL BARRERE	G V	(BCD	PIERRE BROCK	B	(CDE	JAMES ALAN SMITH	K	(CD
CHILI CHARLES	PERC	(C	CAROL KAYE	G	(C	JAMES JAMESON	B	(B	JEAN ROUSSEL	K	(B
JODY LINSCOTT	CONGA	(C	FREDDIE WALL	G	(C	KEN GRADNEY	B	(D	LOUIS JOHN DAVIS	K	(D
ROBERT GREENRIDGE	PERC	(CD	LOWELL GEORGE	G	(B	BOB BABITT	B	(D	STEVE ROBBINS	K	(DE
LENNY CASTRO	PERC	(D	JAMES MAHONEY	G	(D	JIMMY WILLIAMS	B	(D	RON KERSEY	K	(D
DAVID SNELL	HARP	(B	DONOVAN McKITTY	G	(D	ANDY FRASER	B	(F	EDWARD PUTMON	K	(D
DONY WYNN	D	(EF	NEIL HUBBARD	G	(D	PAUL GARDINER	B	(F	GARY NUMAN	K	(F
GREG CARROLL	HCA	(C	T J TINDALL	G	(D	RANDY BRECKER	HRNS	(D	WILLIAM SMITH	K	(C
CHRIS FRANTZ	PER	(F	ALAN MANSFIELD	G	(F	MICHAEL BRECKER	HRNS	(B	JACK WALDMAN	K	(EF
STEVE YORK	HCA	(B	KENNY MAZUR	G	(EF	MEL COLLINS	SAX	(B	ART SMITH	OCARINA	(C
BRIAN RUSSELL	V	(B	BRENDA RUSSELL	V	(D	MARTIN FRY	TUBA	(B	RAY ALLEN		HRNS (B
FRAN TATE	V	(B	VICKI BROWN	V	(B	MONGEZI FEZA	HRNS	(B	MUSCLE SHOALS		HRNS (B
GORDON DEWITTE	K	(B	JOE BROWN	BANJO	(B					

PAN

RON ELLIOTT		(A	(A) PAN	1973	CBS	US	32062

PANAMA FRANCIS BLUES BAND

(A) TOUGH TALK	196	STATESIDE		SL 10070

PANAMA LIMITED JUG BAND

DENNIS PARKER		(A	(A) PANAMA LIMITED JUG BAND	1969	HARVEST	UK	SHVL 753
LIZ HANNS		(A					
BRIAN STRACHAN		(A	GARY COMPTON	(A	RON NEEDS	(A

PANDEMONIUM P18A

JEAN BAPTISTE BARRIERE	SYN(AB	(A) VILLE OUVERTE	1979	ATEM	7003
JEAN MARIE BARRIERE	SYN(AB	(B) NON JAMAIS L'ESPERANCE	1979	ATEM	7004

PANTIES P19

KIM LESLEY	V	(							
MAZ ROBERTS	V	(							
HAMISH STEWART	D	(	SAM HARLEY	B	(A	PETER FLASHETT	G	(	PHIL HAMMOND K (
ROBIN BIHI	G	(							

FELIX PAPPALARDI & CREATION P20

FELIX PAPPALARDI	B V K(A	(A) FELIX PAPPALARDI & CREATION	1976	A&M	US 4586	UK AMLH64586		
PAUL BUTTERFIELD	HCA (A							
RALPH MOSS	PERC (A	SHIGERU MATSUMOTO	B	(A	KAZUO TAKEDA	G	(A	YOSHIAKI IIJIMA G (A
MASAYUKI HIGUCHI	D	(A						

PARADISE EXPRESS P21

VI ANN	V	(A	(A) PARADISE EXPRESS	1979	FANTASY	FT557			
HERB JIMMERSON	K	(A							
KENNETH ELLIOTT	D	(A	DAVID PRUITT	G	(A	DAVID FRAZIER	PERC (A	ROMEO WILLIAMS B (A
BRIAN CABANAS	D	(A	FRED BERRY	HRNS (A	AL BENT	HRNS (A	CHARLES McCARTHY HRNS(A
MARTHA WASH	V	(A	IZORA RHODES	V	(A	SHARON HYMES	V	(A

PARAFFIN JACK FLASH LTD P22

	(A) MOVERS & GROOVERS	1968	PYE	NSPL18252

PARAMOUNTS P23

GARY BROOKER	V K (A12	(A) PARAMOUNTS (EP)	196	PARLOPHONE	GEP8908
B J WILSON	D	(A12	(A) 1962 (2) 1963/66		
ROBIN TROWER	G	(A12			
CHRIS COPPING	B	(1 DIZ DERRICK	B (A2		

PARIS P24

HUNT SALES	D	(B	(A) PARIS	1976 CAPITOL	ST 11464
ROBERT WELCH	G V	(AB	(B) BIG TOWNE 2061	1976 CAPITOL 2061	ST 11560
GLEN CORNICK	K B	(AB			
BERNIE MARSDEN	G	(THOM MOONEY	D (A		

PARISH HALL P24A

GARY WAGNER G PNO	V	(A	(A) PARISH HALL	1970 LIBERTY	LBS 83374
STEVE ADAMS	D	(A			
JOHN HADEN	B	(A			

DENNIS PARKER P24B

DENNIS PARKER	V	(A	(A) LIKE AN EAGLE	1979 MERCURY	UK 9109 622			
RUSSELL DABNEY	D	(A						
ALFONSO CAREY	B V	(A	JIMMI LEE	G	(A	RODGER LEE	G (A BARRY FINNERTY G (A
TOM POLITE	K	(A	NATHANIEL WILKIE	K	(A	RICHARD TRIFAN	SYN (A PHIL HURTT V (A
MILT GREGSON	V	(A	FRANK FLOYD	V	(A	ARTHUR WILLIAMS	V (A TONY WELLS V (A
LENNY ROBERTS	V	(A	MARTY NELSON				

GRAHAM PARKER & THE RUMOUR P25

GRAHAM PARKER	V G	(ALL	(A) HOWLIN' WIND	1976 MERCURY	US	SRM1 1095
STEVE GOULDING	PERC	(ABCDEFGH	(A) "	1976 VERTIGO	UK	6360 129
BRINSLEY SCHWARZ	G	(ABCDEFGH	(B) HEAT TREATMENT	1976 MERCURY	US	SRM1 1117
ANDREW BODNAR	D	(ABCDEFG	(B) " "	1976 VERTIGO	UK	6360 137
MARTIN BELMONT	G	(ABCDEFGH	(C) AT MARBLE ARCH	1976 VERTIGO	UK	GP1
BOB ANDREWS	K	(ABCDEFG	(D) STICK TO ME	1977 MERCURY	US	SRM1 3706
STEWART LYNAS	SAX	(A	(D) STICK TO ME	1977 VERTIGO	UK	9102 017
HERSCHEL HOLDER	TPT	(A	(E) PARKERILLA	1978 MERCURY	US	SRM 2100
DAVE CONNERS	SAX	(A	(E) PARKERILLA	1978 VERTIGO	UK	6641 797
DANNY ELLIS	TROM	(AB	(F) SQUEEZING OUT SPARKS	1979 VERTIGO	UK	9102 030
JOHN EARLE	SAX	(ABE	(G) BEST OF	1980 VERTIGO	UK	9102 042
ALBE DONNELLY	SAX	(B	(H) THE UP ESCALATOR	1980 STIFF	UK	SEEZ23
DAVE EDMUNDS	G	(A	(EP) PINK PARKER	1977 VERTIGO	UK	PARK 001
NOEL BROWN	G	(A	(EP) PINK PARKER	1977 MERCURY	US	6831 040
DICK HANSON	TPT	(BE				
ED DEAN	G	(A	CHRIS GOWER TROM (E RAY BEAVIS	SAX (E NICKY HOPKINS	K (H
DANNY FEDERICI	K	(H	PETER WOODS SYN (H JIMMY MAELEM	PERC (H BRUCE SPRINGSTEEN	V(H

JUNIOR PARKER P26

JUNIOR PARKER	HCA V(ALL	DRIVING	19	DUKE	US	DLP 76
MATT MURPHY	G	(BLUES CONSOLIDATED	19	DUKE	US	
PAT HARE	G	(BEST OF	19	DUKE	US	DLP 83
JOHN BOWERS	D	(JUNIOR PARKER	19	BLUESWAY	US	6066
KENNETH BANKS	B	(OUTSIDE MAN	19	CAPITOL	US	ST 564
JAMES WHEELER	SAX	(LIKE IT IS	19	MERCURY	UK	SMCL20097
BILL JOHNSON	PNO	(BLUE SHADOWS FALLING	1972	GROOVE MERCHANT		GM 502
RAYMOND HILL	SAX	((X) GOOD THINGS DONT HAPPEN EVERYDAY	1972	GROOVE MERCHANT		GM2205
HOUSTON STOKES	D	(YOU DONT HAVE TO BE BLACK	1973	PEOPLE		PLEO 4
IKE TURNER	PNO	(LOVE AIN' NOTHIN' BUT BUSINESS	1974	PEOPLE		PLEO18
JIMMY McGRIFF	ORG	(X BLUES FOR MR CRUMP (APPEARED ON)	1974	POLYDOR	UK	2383 257
L C DRANES	D	((EP) JUNIOR PARKER(LOVE MY BABY)	1976	CHARLY	UK	CEP 104
FLOYD MURPHY	G	(LEGENDARY SUN PERFORMERS(1 SIDE)	1978	CHARLY	UK	CR 30135
JIM STEWART	TPT	(				
JOE FRITZ	SAX	(JIMMY JOHNSON SAX (RAY FIELDS	SAX (JOE SCOTT	TPT (
DALE McJOWN	PNO	(HAMP SIMMONS B (BILL HARVEY	SAX (PLUMA DAVIS	TROM(
SONNY FREEMAN	D	(OTIS JACKSON B (AL SMITH	B (CONNIE McBOOKER	PNO (

ROBERT PARKER P27

ROBERT PARKER	V	(ALL	(A) BAREFOOTIN'	1966 ISLAND	UK ILP942
			(B) BAREFOOTIN'	196 NOLA	US LP1001
			(EP) BAREFOOTIN'	1980 CHARLY	UK CTD123

VAN DYKE PARKS P28

VAN DYKE PARKS	V	(ALL	(A) SONG CYCLE	1968 WB	US	WS 1727
HUGH BORDE		(C	(B) DISCOVER AMERICA	1972 WB NL 26043	US	WS 2589
MALCOLM CECIL		(C	(C) CLANG OF YANKEE REAPER	1975 WB UK K56161	US	BS 2878
CHILLI CHARLES	D	(C				
JESSE ED DAVIS	G	(C	HOLLIS DURITY (C ROBERT GREENIDGE	(C FRED TACKETT	G (C
JIM KELTNER	D	(C	KLAUS VOORMANN B (C BOBBY KEYS	SAX (C NOBLE WILLIAMS	(C

[315]

PARLIAMENT

```
GEORGE CLINTON  V  (ALL      (A) OSMUIM                              1970 INVICTUS              US  7304
CALVIN SIMON    V  (E        (B) UP FOR THE DOWN STROKE             1974 CASABLANCA UK CAL2011 US  7002
FUZZY HASKINS   V  (E        (C) CHOCOLATE CITY                     1975 CASABLANCA UK CAL2012 US  7014
RAYMOND DAVIS   V  (E        (D) MOTHERSHIP CONNECTION              1976 CASABLANCA UK CAL2013 US  7022
GRADY THOMAS    V  (E        (E) CLONES OF DR FUNKENSTEIN           1976 CASABLANCA UK CAL2001 US  7032
GARRY SHIDER    V  (E        (F) GET DOWN & BOOGIE                  197  CASABLANCA              US  7042
EDDIE HAZAL     G V (E       (G) LIVE (DBL)                         1977 CASABLANCA UK CALD5002 US  7053
MICHAEL HAMPTON G V (E       (H) FUNKENSTEIN VsTHE PLACEBO SYNDROME 1977 CASABLANCA UK CALN2021 US  7084
GLEN COLLINS    G V (E       (J) MOTOR BOOTY AFFAIR                 1)'( CASABLANCA UK CALH2044 US  7125
WILLIE NELSON   G  (
BERNIE WORRELL  K  (E    JEROME BRAILEY   D   (E   BOOTSY COLLINS  B D G(E   GARY COOPER   D   (E
GARY BRONSON    D  (     TIKI FULWOOD     D   (    FRED WESLEY     HRNS (E   MACEO PARKER  HRNS(E
RICK GARDNER    HRNS (E  MICHAEL BRECKER  HRNS (E  RANDY BRECKER   HRNS (E   CORDELL MOSSON   B(
PETER CHASE     WHISTLE(
```

BRIAN PARRISH

```
BRIAN PARRISH      (A       (A) LOVE ON MY MIND                    1976 BARN       UK        2314 101
```

ALAN PARSONS PROJECT

```
ALAN PARSONS   K V (ALL     (A) TALES OF MYSTERY & IMAGINATION     1976 CHARISMA CDS 4003 US 2OCENT 339
B J COLE       STEEL(A      (B) I ROBOT                            1977 ARISTA  US 7002   UK SPARTY1012
STUART TOSH    D  (A        (C) PYRAMID                            1978 ARISTA  US 4180   UK SPART 1054
IAN BAIRNSON   G  (ACE      (D) EVE                                1979 ARISTA                UK SPART1100
DAVID PATON    V B (ACE     (E) TURN OF A FRIENDLY CARD            1980 ARISTA                UK DLART    1
STEVE HARLEY   V  (
ALLAN CLARKE   V  (    ERIC WOOLFSON   K   (CE  COLIN BLUNSTONE   V   (C   JACK HARRIS       V (C
DUNCAN MACKAY  K  (C   LENNY ZAKATEK   V   (CE  DEAN FORD         V   (C   STUART ELLIOTT    D (CE
JOE PUERTA     B  (A   DARRYL RUNSWICK  B   (A  BURLEIGH DRUMMOND D   (A   DAVID PACK        G (C
ARTHUR BROWN   V  (A   CHRIS RAINBOW   V   (E   ELMER GANTRY      V   (E   MUNICH CHAM OPERA ORCH(E
```

GENE PARSONS

```
GENE PARSONS  V G B D(A     (A) KINDLING                           1974  WB               UK  K46257
RED CALLENDER   TUBA (A     (B) MELODIES                           1979  SIERRA           US  8703
CLARENCE WHITE  G MAND(A
VASSAR CLEMMENTS FDL (A  GIB GUILBEAU  FDL  (A  ROGER BUSH    B (A
RALPH STANLEY   SAX  (A  BILL PYNE     SYN  (A  NICK DECARO   ACC (A  ANDY NEWMARK   D  (A
```

GRAM PARSONS

```
GRAM PARSONS   G V (ALL     (A) G P                                1973 REPRISE US MS 2133 UK  K44228
GEORGE WRIGLEY BAN G(D      (B) GRIEVOUS ANGEL                     1974 REPRISE US MS 2171 UK  K54018
PAUL SURRATT   G BAND       (C) SLEEPLESS NIGHTS                   1976 A&M     US     4578 UK AMLH64578
JOE KELLY      V B (D       (D) EARLY YEARS                        1979 SIERRA  US     8702 ARIOLA200750
LEWIS MORFORD  V  (A
MITCH WRIGLEY  V  (A   GLEN D HARDIN   K   (ABC RICK GRECH    B  (BC  N D SMART      D  (B
HERB PEDERSEN  G  (BC  BERNIE LEADON   G V (BC  JAMES BURTON  G  (ABC AL PERKINS  STEEL (ABC
BYRON BERLINE  FDL (ABC STEVE SNYDER   VIBES(A  CHRIS HILLMAN V  (B   CHRIS HILLMAN  B  (C
SNEAKY PETE    STEEL(C MICHAEL CLARKE  D   (C   EMORY GORDY   B  (BC  RONNIE TUTT    D  (ABC
EMMYLOU HARRIS V  (ABC JOHN CONRAD     B   (A   JOHN GUERIN   D  (A   SAM GOLDSTEIN  D  (A
BARRY TASHIAN  G V (A  BUDDY EMMONS    STEEL(A  ALAN MUNDE  BANJO(A   HAL BATTISTE   SAX (A
RON HICKLIN    V  (A   TOM BAHLER      V   (A
```

PASSAGE

```
                            (A) BAG OF NERVES                      19   OBJECT            OBJ0011
                            (EP) NEW LOVE SONGS                    19   OBJECT            OM   02
                            (EP) ABOUT TIME                        19   OBJECT            OM   08
```

PASSIONS

```
BARBARA GOGAN  G V (12      (A) MICHAEL & MIRANDA                  1980 FICTION   FIX 003  2383  573
CLIVE TIMPERLEY  G  (12     (1) 1978   (2) 1981
RICHARD WILLIAMS D  (12
CLAIRE BIDWELL   B  (1   DAVID AGAR   B  (2
```

PASSPORT

```
KLAUS DOLDINGER SAX K(ALL   (A) PASSPORT                           1971 ATLANTIC                40299
OLAF KUBLER    WIND (       (B) SECOND                             1972 ATLANTIC                40417
LOTHAR MEID    B  (         (C) HAND MADE                          1973 ATLANTIC                40483
JIMMY JACKSON  ORG (        (D) LOOKING THROUGH                    1973 ATLANTIC US 7042   UK K50024
UDO LINDENBERG D  (         (E) DOLDINGER JUBILEE(TRIPLE)          1973 ATLANTIC                60073
JOHN MEALING   K  (         (F) DOLDINGER                          1973 ATLANTIC           UK K44243
BRYAN SPRING   D  (         (G) DOLDINGER JUBILEE CONCERT          1974 ATLANTIC                50070
FRANK ROBERTS  K  (         (H) CROSS COLLATERAL                   1975 ATLANTIC US 36107      50111
VOLKER KRIEGER G  (         (J) DOLDINGER JUBILEE 75               1975 ATLANTIC US 18162      50186
ALEXIS KORNER  G  (         (K) INFINITY MACHINE                   1976 ATLANTIC US 36132  UK K50354
BRIAN AUGER    K  (         (L) IGUACU                             1977 ATLANTIC US 36149
WOLFGANG SCHMIDT B G (K     (M) SKY BLUE                           1978 ATLANI  US 19177
CURT CRESS     D  (K        (N) ATARAXIA                           1978 ATLANTIC           UK K50456
KRISTIAN SCHULTZE K  (K     (O) GARDEN OF EDEN                     1979 ATLANTIC           UK K50586
WILLY KETZER   D  (MO       (P) OCEANLINER                         1980 ATLANTIC                50688
HENDRIK SCHAPER K  (MOP
ELMER LOUIS    PERC (M  DIETER PETEREIT  B   (MOP ROY LOUIS    G  (M  GUILLERMO MARCHENA V PERC(M
KEVIN MULLIGAN G V (OP  HORST RAMTHOR    HCA (O   KATHY BARTNEY V  (O  DAVID CRIGGER      D  (P
```

JACO PASTORIUS

```
JACO PASTORIUS B  (AB       (A) JACO PASTORIUS                     1976 EPIC       US 33949 UK  81453
DON ALIAS      CONGA (A     (B) JACO                               1978 IMPRO ARTS           IAI373846
RANDY BRECKER  HRNS (A
RON TOOLEY     TPT  (A  PETER GRAVES     TROM (A  DAVID SANBORN   SAX (A  MICHAEL BRECKER HRNS (A
HOWARD JOHNSON SAX  (A  HERBIE HANCOCK   K   (A   NARADA MICHAEL WALDEN D (A  SAM MOORE     V    (A
ALEX DAROU     K    (A  LENNY WHITE      D   (A   BOBBY ECONOMOU  D   (A  STRING SECTION       (A
WAYNE SHORTER  SAX  (A  OTHELLO MOLINEAUX PERC (A LEROY WILLIAMS  PERC(A  PETER GORDON    HRNS (A
HUBERT LAWS    WIND (A  PAUL BLEY        (B       DAVE PRATER     V   (A
```

BRIAN PATTEN

BRIAN PATTEN	V	(ABC	(A) BRIAN PATTEN			1970	CAEDMON		TC 1300
ROGER McGOUGH	V	(C	(B) VANISHING TRICK			1971	TANGENT		TGS 116
LINDA THOMPSON	V	(b	(C) PATTEN & McGOUGH			1976	ARGO		ZLP 1190
DAVE RICHARDS	B	(B							
GERRY CONWAY	D	(B	JOHN TAYLOR	K	(B	NEIL INNES	K	(B	JONNO DELMAR	G (B
RICHARD THOMPSON	G	(B	NORMA WINSTONE	V	(B	ANDY ROBERTS	G	(B	ALAN DALZIEL	CELLO(B
PHIL LEE	G	(B	STAN SULZMANN	FLT	(B					

BOBBY PATTERSON

BOBBY PATTERSON		(A) SHE DONT HAVE TO SEE YOU(EP)	1980	CHARLY	CTD 112

PATTO

MIKE PATTO	V	(ABC	(A) PATTO	1970	VERTIGO VEL 1001 +	6360 016	
OLLIE HALSALL	G K	(ABC	(B) HOLD YOUR FIRE	1971	VERTIGO VEL 1008	6360 032	
CLIVE GRIFFITHS	B	(A	(C) ROLL EM SMOKE EM	1972	ISLAND	ILPS9210	
JOHN HALSEY	D	(A					

LES PAUL

LES PAUL	G	(ALL	NEW SOUND	10 INCH	19	CAPITOL		226
MARY FORD	V	(	NEW SOUND VOL2	10 INCH	19	CAPITOL		286
CHET ATKINS	G	(*	BYE BYE BLUES	10 INCH	19	CAPITOL		356
			HIT MAKERS		19	CAPITOL		416
			LES & MARY		19	CAPITOL		577
			TIME TO DREAM		19	CAPITOL		802
			LOVER		19	CAPITOL		1276
			HITS OF LES & MARY		19	CAPITOL		1476
			LES PAUL NOW		1968	DECCA	UK LK 4924 +	PFS 4138
			LES PAUL NOW		1968	LONDON	US	SP44101
			VERY BEST OF		1974	CAPITOL		23321
			STORY VOL 1		1974	CAPITOL EURO	052	81050
			STORY VOL 2		1974	CAPITOL EURI	052	81359
			LES & MARY		1975	CAPITOL		11308
			GUIAR TAPESTRY		19	PROJECT 3		US6-19/20
			(*) GUITAR MONSTERS		1978	RCA		PL 12786
			(*) CHESTER & LESTER		1977	RCA		LSA 3290

PAUPER

SKIP PROKOP	D V	(AB	(A) MAGIC PEOPLE			1967	VERVE	FTS 3026
ADAM MITCHELL	G V	D(AB	(B) ELLIS ISLAND			1968	VERVE	FTS 3051
CHUCK BEAL	G MAND	(AB						
DENNY GERRARD	B	(A	BRAD CAMPBELL	G B D V(B				

PAVLOVS DOG

DAVID SURKAMP	G V	(AB	(A) PAMPERED MENIAL			1975	CBS US 33552	UK 80872
DOUG RAYBURN FLT	B K	(AB	(B) THE SOUND OF THE BELL			1976	CBS US 33694	UK 81163
STEVE SCORFINA	G	(AB						
DAVID HAMILTON	K	(AB	RICHARD STOCKTON	B	(AB	TOM NICKESON	G V (B	MIKE SAFRON	D (A
SIEGFRIED CARVER	VLN	(AB	BILL BRUFORD	D	(B	MIKE ABABE	ORG (A	MICHAEL BRECKER	SAX(B
GEORGE GENCH	ORG	(B	ANDY MACKAY	SAX	(B	LES NICOL	G (B	PAUL PRESTOPINO	MAND(B
ELLIOT RANDALL	G B	(B	GAVYN WRIGHT	VLN	(B				

TOM PAXTON

TOM PAXTON	G V	(ALL	(A) RAMBLIN BOY	1964	ELEKTRA US EKS 7277	UK	K42003
JACK BONUS	WIND	(E	(B) AIN'T THAT NEWS	1965	ELEKTRA US EKS 7289	UK	K42005
ALBERT BOUCHARD	D	(E	(C) OUTWARD BOUND	1966	ELEKTRA US EKS 7317	UK	K42007
DAVID BROMBERG	G	(EF	(D) MORNING AGAIN	1968	ELEKTRA US EKS74019	UK	K42019
HERB BUSHLER	B	(EFO	(E) THINGS I NOTICE NOW	1969	ELEKTRA US EKS74043	UK	K42028
JOHNNY COLES	HRNS	(E	(F) NUMBER 6	1970	ELEKTRA US EKS74066	UK	K42047
RICHARD GRAND	WIND	(E	(G) THE COMPLEAT TOM PAXTON	1971	ELEKTRA US 7E 2003	UK	K62004
DAVID HOROWITZ	K	(EFH	(H) HOW COME THE SUN	1971	REPRISE US RS 6443	UK	K44129
HUBERT LAWS	FLT	(E	(J) PEACE WILL COME	1972	REPRISE US RS 2096	UK	K44182
JIMMY MADISON	D	(E	(K) NEW SONGS OLD FRIENDS	1973	REPRISE US RS 2144	UK	K44237
MAX POLLIKOFF	VLN	(E	(L) CHILDRENS SONG BOOK	1974	BRADLEYS	UK	BRADN601
ROBERT SYLVESTER	CELLO(E		(M) SOMETHING IN MY LIFE	1975	MAM	UK	MAM 1002
STEVE GOODMAN	G V	(O	(M) SOMETHING IN MY LIFE	1975	PRIVATE STOCK	US	2002
ANGEL ALLENDE	V	(O	(N) SATURDAY NIGHT	1976	MAM	UK	MAMS1003
IAN HUNT	G	(M	(O) NEW SONGS FROM THE BRIAR PATCH	1977	MAM	UK	MAMS1005
DAVE WILLIS	B	(KMH	(O) NEW SONGS FROM THE BRIAR PATCH	1977	VANGUARD	US	VSD79395
PETER WOOD	K	(M	(P) HEROES	1978	VANGUARD		VSD79411
BARRY DE SOUZA	D	(M					
CHRIS KARAN	PERC	(KM	NANCY LEE BAXTER	V	(P	KENNETH KOSEK	VLN (P	ERIC WEISSBERG	G MAND (P
GARY CHESTER	D	(P	PETER SARSTEDT	V	(K	RALPH McTELL G V HCA	(K	GARY MURE	D (P
TONY VISCONTI	G	(K	MARY VISCONTI	V	(K	RAYMOND MANTILLA	PERC (K	JENNIFER PAXTON	V (K
DANNY THOMPSON	B	(K	PAUL PRESTOPINO	G	(F	TEDDY SOMMER	D (F	MARK HOROWITZ	G BAN (H
MIKE MORGAN	G	(H	JULIAN CUMMINGS	VLN	(H	BRIAN ODGERS	B (H	SUE EVANS	D (H
CHRIS SLADE	D	(H	DIANA CUMMINGS	VLN	(H	HARRY PITCH	HCA (H	LUCIANO JORIO	VLN (H
DOUGLAS CUMMINGS	CELLO(H		KATY PAXTON	V	(K	MIKE BRITTAIN	B (H	CHRIS LAURENCE	B (H
JEFF CLYNE	B	(H							

JOHN PAYNE

JOHN PAYNE		(AB	(A) BEDTIME STORIES	19	ARISTA	AL 1025
			(B) RAZOR'S EDGE	1977	ARISTA	AL 1036

PAZ

BRIAN SMITH	FLT	(A	(A) KANDEEN LOVE SONG			1977	SPOTLIGHT	SPJ 507
GEOFF CASTLE	K	(A						
PHIL LEE	G	(A	RON MATTHEWSON	B	(A	DICK CROUCH	PERC (A	DAVE SHEEN	D (A
SIMON MORTON	PERC	(A	RAY WARLEIGH	FLT	(A	CHRIS FLETCHER	CONGA(A		

PEACE

'PAUL RODGERS	V	(	MICK UNDERWOOD	D	(	STEWART McDONALD	B (

PEACHES & HERB

FRANCINE 'PEACHES' HURD	V(A		(A) LETS FALL IN LOVE	19	CBS	UK	62966
HERB FAME	V	(ALL	(B) FOR YOUR LOVE	1967	CBS	UK	63119
PETE ROBINSON	K	(FG	(C) GOLDEN DUETS	19	DATE	US	TES 4007
FREDDIE PERREN PNO VIBES(FG			(D) PEACHES & HERB	1977	MCA	UK	MCF 2802
DOIE WATKINS	B	(FG	(E) 2 HOT	1979	POLYDOR US 1 6172 UK 2391		378

(CONTINUED)

PEACHES & HERB

```
JAMES GADSON       D    (FG            (F) TWICE THE FIRE                1979 POLYDOR  US 1 6239 UK   2391  433
BOB BOWLES         G    (FG            (G) WORTH THE WAIT                1980 POLYDOR           UK   2391  484
WAH WAH WATSON     G    (FG
PAULINHO DA COSTA  PERC (FG  BOB ZIMITTI  PERC      (FG  CLARENCE McDONALD  K   (G  JOSE FELICIANO    G  (G
EDDIE BROWN        CONGA(G  KATIE KIRKPATRICK HARP  (G  GARY HERBIG        SAX  (G  MAXINE WILLARD    V  (G
JULIA TILLMAN      V    (G  LUTHER WATERS           V  (G  OREN WATERS       V   (G
```

P45
ANNETTE PEACOCK

```
ANNETTE PEACOCK    V K  (ALL           (A) BLEY/PEACOCK SYNTHESIZER SHOW  1971 POLYDOR             2425 043
MICK RONSON        G    (               (B) I'M THE ONE                   1972 RCA     US LSP 4578 UK  SF 8255
BILL BRUFORD       D    (               (C) IMPROVISE                     1973 AMERICA            FR    6121
GEORGE KHAN        SAX  (               (D) DUAL UNITY                    1973 FREEDOM Uk 40109 GERM 2383  105
DAVE CHAMBERS      HRNS (               (E) X DREAMS                      1978 AURA               AUL   702
TOM COSGROVE       G    (B              (F) PERFECT DREAMS                1979 AURA               AUL   707
JEFF CLYNE         B    (               (1) 1974 DANISH TOUR
SAM PHIPPS         SAX  (1  ROBBIE SCHWIMMER  K    (1  PETE LA ROCCA     D   (1  PAUL BLEY          (C
STU WOODS          B    (B  RICK MAROTTA      D    (B  MICHAEL GARSON    K   (B  GLEN MOORE       B  (B
LAURENCE COOK      D    (B  MICHAEL MOSS     SAX   (B  BARRY ALTSCHUL   PERC (B  AIRTO MOREIRA   PERC(B
ORESTES VILATO     PERC (B  DOMUN ROMAO      PERC  (B  APACHE BLEY      PNO  (B  CHRIS SPEDDING   G  (E
```

P46
PEANUT BUTTER CONSPIRACY

```
JIM VOIGHT         D    (AB             (A) IS SPREADING                  1968 CBS               US    9454
AL BRACKETT        B    (AB             (B) GREAT CONSPIRACY              1968 CBS               US    9590
LANCE FENT         G    (AB             (C) FOR CHILDREN OF ALL AGES      196  CHALLENGE         US    2000
JOHN MERRILL       G    (AB
SANDI ROBINSON     V    (AB  BILL WOLF       G HCA (AB
```

P47
BOB PEARCE BLUES BAND

```
BOBPEARCE  G V HCA (ALL           (1) BLUES CRUSADE   (EP)               1968      AVENUE          BEV 1054
BOB GORMAN         G V  (1        (2) LET'S GET DRUNK AGAIN(SOLO)        1974      WESTWOOD        WRS 040
ROGER CHANTLER     D    (1        (3) COLOUR BLIND                       1979      FOREST TRACKS   FT  3015
PETE HARRIS        G V K(4        (4) I'M A BLUEMAN   (EP)               1981 WHITE ELEPHANT  UK  RIOCH 2
KEVIN FRANCIS      B V  (1        (A)   68/FEB 69   (B) FEB 69/JUL 70    (C) JUL 70/OCT 70  (D) OCT 70/NOV 70
GLENN'JUDGE'LEE D(ACDEFGHJKLMVWX  (E) NOV 70/NOV 71  (F) NOV 71/FEB 72   (G) FEB 72/OCT 74  (H) OCT 74/NOV 74
TONY BURNETT       D    (NO       (J) NOV 74/DEC 74  (K) DEC 74/FEB 75   (L) FEB 75/NOV 75  (M) NOV 75/APR 76
JOHN PICKEN        D    (PQ       (N) APR 76/JUL 76  (O) JUL 76/AUG 76   (P) AUG 76/OCT 76  (Q) OCT 76/NOV 76
CHRIS NEWMAN       D    (R        (R) NOV 76/JUL 77  (S) JUL 77/AUG 77   (T) AUG 77/SEP 77  (U) SEP 77/JAN 78
BARRY FREEMAN      D    (ST       (V) JAN 78/JUL 78  (W) JUL 78/DEC 78   (X) DEC 78/FEB 79  (Y) FEB 79/
HENRY WRIGHT       D    (UY34
BIG JOHN McATEE    B    (CD  BOB WILLIAMS      B    (H  PETE 'BALDY' WARD  B(MNOPQR  ERNEST FAGG    B  (ST
KEN WHEELER        B    (UVW  JOSS JONES        B    ((XY34CHRIS GODDEN  G   (F  MICK WILLIAMS   G  (H
DEREK GARDENER     G    (J  DOUG WALKER       G    (K  VERNON CHUTER     G   (MNOP  JOHN MARSHALL  SAX (O
LEE GOODALL        SAX  (N  PAPA JOHN LIVERMORE G K(BY3 PAUL BRYER G (NOPQRSTUVWXY3  DAVE 'DOMINO'WARD HCA(TUV
JOHN CARTWRIGHT    B    (*  PETE HUNT         D    (*  (*) INVALUABLE ASSISTANCE THROUGH THE YEARS
CARL'SONNY'LEYLAND PNO  (4
```

P48
PEARL

```
DEBBIE PEARL       V    (A              (A) PEARL                        1977 LONDON            UK   SHU 8508
LESLIE PEARL       V    (A
DEAN PARKS         G    (A  RUSS KUNKEL       D    (A  MARK LEVINE       B   (A
```

P48A
PEARL HARBOUR

```
PEARL E GATES      V PERC (AB           (A) AND THE EXPLOSIONS            1980 WB  US BSK 3404 UK     K56769
PETER BILT         G V  (A              (B) DON'T FOLLOW ME, I'M LOST TOO 1980 WB  US BSK 3515 UK     K56885
HILARY STENCH      B V  (A
JOHN STENCH        D    (A
```

P49
PEARLS BEFORE SWINE

```
TOM RAPP           G V  (ALL            (A) ONE NATION UNDERGROUND        1967 ESP               US    1054
WAYNE HARLEY       BAN V(ABC            (B) BALAKLAVA                     1968 ESP               US    1075
LANE LEDERER       B G HRNS (AB         (C) THESE THINGS TOO             1969 REPRISE            RSLP 6364
ROGER CRISSINGER   K    (A              (D) THE USE OF ASHES             1970 REPRISE            RSLP 6405
WARREN SMITH       D    (A              (E) CITY OF GOLD                 1971 REPRISE            RSLP 6442
JIM BOHANNON       K    (B              (F) BEAUTIFUL LIES YOU COULD LIVE 1971 REPRISE           RSLP 6467
JOE FARRELL        WIND (B
LEE CRABTREE       K FLT(B  BILL SALTER       B    (BC  AL SHACKMAN      G   (B  DAVID NOYES     V  (E
ELIZABETH          V    (CDEF  RICHARD GREENE    VLN  (C  MORRIE E BROWN    B   (F  GRADY TATE      D  (C
GORDON HAYES       B    (F  MICHAEL KRAWITZ   PNO  (F  BILLY MUNDI       D   (F  BOB DOROUGH    PNO(F
STU SCHARF         G    (F  AMOS GARRETT      G    (F  HERB LOVELL       D   (F  JOHN DUKE      WIND(D
JERRY JEMMOTT      B    (F  CHARLIE McCOY  V G B HCA(D  BUDDY SPICHER    VLN  (D  HUTCH DAVIE    WIND(D
NORBERT PUTNAM     B    (D  BILL PIPPIN     WIND  (D  KEN BUTTREY       D   (D  MAC GAYDEN      G  (D
DAVID BRIGGS       K    (D  JOHN TOOKER       G    (F  JIM FAIRS        G V K(C  STEVE GRABLE    K  (F
```

P49A
KEITH PEARSON

```
KEITH PEARSON      G V BAN(A             (A) RIGHT HAND BAND              1976   ERON                  014
PAUL CRASWELL      B V  (A
DAVE CRASWELL      G V PERC(A  DAVE ARBUS    VLN SAX V (A
```

P50
HERB PEDERSEN

```
HERB PEDERSEN      V    (AB             (A) SOUTHWEST                    1976 EPIC              US    34225
CHRIS SMITH        G    (A              (B) SANDMAN                      1977 EPIC              US    34933
ED CARTER          (A
JIM GORDON         D    (A  JOHN GUERIN       D    (A  LARRY CARLTON    G   (A  JOSH GRAVES DOBRO  (A
AL PERKINS         G    (A  MIKE BAIRD        D    (A  ROY DEAN WEBB         (A  DAVID LINDLEY      (A
GARY COLEMAN       PERC (A  EMMYLOU HARRIS    V    (A  LEE SKLAR        B   (AB  LINDA RONSTADT  V (AB
DOLLY PARTON       V    (B  LOWELL GEORGE     G    (B  JOEY SCARBURY        (B  JOHNNY RIVERS     (AB
```

P51
ANN PEEBLES

```
ANN PEEBLES        V    (ALL            (A) THIS IS                      1969 HI  US 32053
HOWARD GRIMES      D    (D              (B) PART TIME LOVE               1971 HI  US 32059
LEROY HODGES       B    (D              (C) STRAIGHT FROM THE HEART      1972 HI  US 32065 UK LONDON SHU8434
CHARLES HODGES     K    (D              (D) CANT STAND THE RAIN          1974 HI  US 32079 UK LONDON SHU8468
ED LOGAN           SAX  (D              (E) TELLIN' IT                   1976          UK LONDON SHU8490
WAYNE JACKSON      TPT  (D              (F) IF THIS IS HEAVEN            1978 HI  US  6002
JAMES MITCHELL     SAX  (B              (G) HANDWRITING IS ON THE WALL   197  HI  US  6007
TEENIE HODGES      G    (D
ANDREW LOVE        SAX  (D  JACK HALE       TROM (D  ARCHIE TURNER     K   (D
```

P53   DAVID PEEL & THE LOWER EAST SIDE   P53

```
DAVID PEEL        V    (ALL      (A) HAVE A MARIJUANA           1969 ELEKTRA              US EKS74032
HAROLD C BLACK    TAMB (A         (B) AMERICAN REVOLUTION        1971 ELEKTRA UK 2410 001  US EKS74069
LARRY ADAM        G    (A         (C) THE POPE SMOKES DOPE       1972 APPLE                US SW 3391
BILLY JOE WHITE   G    (A         (D) AN EVENING WITH            1975 ORANGE               US ORA 713
GEORGE CORI       B    (A
CHRIS OSBORNE     (C   EDDIE MOTTAU    (C   EDDIE RYAN        (C
```

P54   BOB PEGG   P54

```
BOB PEGG        G V WIND(ABC     (A) BOB PEGG & NICK STRUTT    1973  TRANSATLANTIC    TRA 265
NICK STRUTT     G MAND(AB         (B) SHIPBUILDER               1974  TRANSATLANTIC    TRA 280
STEVE SIMPSON   G VLN(B           (C) ANCIENT MAPS              1975  TRANSATLANTIC    TRA 299
RICHIE BULL     B    (B
DAVE HAMMEL     D    (B   CHRIS TAYLOR  RECORDER(C   RICHARD McNICOL RECORDER (C ADRIAN BRETT RECORDER(C
ROGER BRENNER SACKBUT (C  MALCOLM FISHER SACKBUT (C  JOHN EDNEY       SACKBUT(C DAVID PURSER SACKBUT (C
TONY COE      CLAR (C     DAVID CROPPER  HRNS (C    MIKE LAIRD   CORNETTO (C IAN WILSON   CORNETTO(C
BILL STOKES   CORNETTO (C RAY WARLEIGH   FLT (C     PAUL HARVEY     CLAR (C NORMAN WEBB   HARP(C
BRENT FORBES  B   (C      GRAHAM FIELD   K   (C     HAROLD FISHER  D  (C   RICK RUSSELL   G  (C
B J COLE      STEEL(A     MICK YARROW        (B
```

P55   BOB & CAROLANNE PEGG   P55

```
BOB PEGG        G V WIND(A    (A) HE CAME FROM THE MOUNTAIN  1971 TRAILER   UK  LER 3016
CAROLANNE PEGG  V    (A
```

P56   CAROLANNE PEGG   P56

```
CAROLANNE PEGG  V    (A     (A) CAROLANNE PEGG   1973 TRANSATLANTIC UK TRA 266
ALBERT LEE      G K  (A
KEITH NELSON    BANJO(A   MICHAEL LAVELLE  CELLO(A  ALUN EDEN   D  (A  PAUL ROWAN   HCA(A
DAVE PEACOCK    B G  (A
```

P56A   JIM PEMBROKE   P56A

```
JIM PEMBROKE       (ABC    (A) WICKED IVORY                           19
                            (B) ??
                            (C) CORPORAL CAULIFLOWERS MENTAL FUNCTION  1977
```

P57   ALVARO PENA ROJAS   P57

```
ALVARO PENA ROJAS K V B FLT(A   (A) DRINKING MY OWN SPERM   197 SQUEAKY SHOE   SSRDR 1
ANTONIO NARVAEZ   D V   (A
CATHY WILLIAMS    V     (A
```

P58   PENETRATION   P58

```
PAULINE MURRAY   V    (A       (A) MOVING TARGETS            1978 VIRGIN   UK  V 2149
FRED PURSER      G K  (ABC      (B) DANGER SIGNS      (EP)    1979 VIRGIN   UK  V25712
GARY SMALLMAN    D    (ABC      (C) COMING UP FOR AIR         1979 VIRGIN   UK  V 2131
NEALE FLOYD      G    (ABC      (D) RACE AGAINST TIME(OFFICIAL BOOT) 1980 CLIFDAYN
ROBERT BLAMIRE   B    (ABC
STEVE JACOBS     D    (
```

P59   PENGUINS   P59

```
CLEVELAND DUNCAN V    (       (A) COOL COOL PENGUINS   19 DOOTONE   US  DTE 242
DEXTER TISBY     V    (
CURTIS WILLIAMS  V    (   BRUCE TATE    V   (   RANDY JONES   V  ( TEDDY HARPER   V  (
```

P60   PENTANGLE   P60

```
BERT JANSCH      G V   (ALL     (A) THE PENTANGLE          1968 TRANSATLANTIC UK  TRA162
JOHN RENBOURNE G V SITAR(ALL    (A) THE PENTANGLE          1968 REPRISE       US  6315
JACQUI McSHEE    V     (ALL      (B) SWEET CHILD            1968 TRANSATLANTIC UK  TRA178
DANNY THOMPSON   B     (ALL      (B) SWEET CHILD            1968 REPRISE       US  6334
TERRY COX        D PERC(ALL      (C) BASKET OF LIGHT        1969 TRANSATLANTIC UK  TRA205
                                 (C) BASKET OF LIGHT        1969 REPRISE       US  6372
                                 (D) CRUEL SISTER           1970 TRANSATLANTIC UK  TRA228
                                 (D) CRUEL SISTER           197  XTRA          UK  XTRA1172
                                 (D) CRUEL SISTER           1970 REPRISE       US  6430
                                 (E) REFLECTIONS            1971 TRANSATLANTIC UK  TRA240
                                 (E) REFLECTIONS            1971 REPRISE       US  6463
                                 (F) SOLOMANS SEAL          1972 REPRISE US 2100 UK K44197
                                 (G) HISTORY BOOK           1972 TRANSATLANTIC UK  TRASAM23
                                 (H) PENTANGLING            1973 TRANSATLANTIC UK  TRASAM29
                                 (J) PENTANGLE COLLECTION   1975 TRANSATLANTIC UK  89503/4
                                 (K) ANTHOLOGY              1978 TRANSATLANTIC UK  MTRA 2013
```

P60A   JIM PEPPER   P60A

```
JIM PEPPER       V SAX D(A     (A) PEPPERS POW WOW   1971 ATLANTIC  UK  2400 149
RAVIE PEPPER     FLT V(A
LARRY CORYELL    G    (A   TOM GRANT   PNO V(A  CHUCK RAINEY   B  (A  BILLY COBHAM   D (A
JERRY JEMMOTT    B    (A   SPIDER RICE D  (A   GIB PEPPER     V D (A
```

P60B   VICTOR PERAINO'S KINGDOM COME   P60B

```
VICTOR PERAINO   K V  (A    (A) NO MANS LAND   1975 MKC   5121 N10
DAVID WILD       D    (A
EDWARD HOWLEHAN  D    (A  PAUL ROGERSON   B V (A  JON LAFLOTTE FLT G V (A  DAVID CHRISTIAN G (A
HERMAN DALDIN    B    (A
```

P61   PERE UBU   P61

```
DAVID THOMAS      V    (1234ABC    (A) MODERN DANCE               1978 BLANK US 001 UK MERCURY 9100052
ALLEN RAVENSTINE  K    (134AC       (A) MODERN DANCE          RI   198  ROUGH TRADE   UK  ROUGH 22
THOMAS LAUGHNER   G    (1234C        (B) DUB HOUSING               1978 CHRYSALIS     UK  CHR 1207
TOM HERMAN        G    (2134AC        (C) DATAPANIK IN THE YEAR ZERO(EP) 1978 RADAR UK RDR1
TIM WRIGHT        B    (123C           (D) DATAPANIK IN THE YEAR ZERO(LP) 1979 ATLANTIC UK  K50587
SCOTT KRAUSS      D    (1234AC         (E) NEW PICNIC TIME           1979 CHRYSALIS UK  CHR 1248
TONY MAIMONE      B    (AC             (F) ART OF WALKING            1980 ROUGH TRADE UK ROUGH 14
ALAN GREENBLATT   G    (4C             (G) 390' SIMULATED STEREO     198  ROUGH TRADE UK ROUGH 23
DAVID TAYLOR      K    (2C             (1) 1975    (2) 1976    (3) 1976  (4) 1977
```

P62   CHRISTINE PERFECT   P62

```
CHRISTINE(McVIE) PERFECT K V(ALL  (A) CHRISTINE PERFECT        1970 BLUE HORIZON UK 7 63860
TOP TOPHAM       G    (AC          (B) ALBATROSS (1 SIDE)        1977 EMBASSY      UK  31569
RICK HAYWARD     G    (AC          (C) THE LENGENDARY CP ALBUM   1978 SIRE            SASD 7522
MARTIN DUNSFORD  B    (A
DANNY KIRWAN     G    (AC  JOHN McVIE    B    (AC  ANDY SYLVESTER  B  (B  STAN WEBB   G (B
DAVE BIDWELL     D    (B   CHRIS HARDING D    (A
```

CARL PERKINS

CARL PERKINS	G V	(ALL	(A) DANCE ALBUM	1959	LONDON	UK HA 2202	US	SUN	1225
W S HOLLAND	D	(1	(B) WHOLE LOTTA SHAKIN'	1959	CBS		US		1234
JAY PERKINS	G	(1	(C) COUNTRY BOY DREAMS	1968	LONDON	UK SHP8366	US	DOLLIE4001
CLAYTON PERKINS	B	(1	(D) ON TOP	1969	CBS		US		9931
STAN PERKINS	D	(2	(E) BLUE SUEDE SHOES	1969	LONDON	UK HAS2202	US	SUN	112
GREG PERKINS	B	(2	(E) BLUE SUDE SHOES	1974	SUN	UK		6467	009
DAVID SEA	SAX	(2	(F) ORIGINAL GOLDEN HITS	1970	SUN	UK	6467 004	US	111
LEE McALPIN	PNO	(2	(G) KING OF ROCK	19	CBS	UK	63309		
HAROLD BRADLEY	G	(P	(H) BOPPIN THE BLUES	19	CBS	UK	63826	US	9981
RAY EDENTON	G	(P	(I) CARL PERKINS	19	HARMONY		US		11385
JERRY KENNEDY	G	(P	(J) BROWN EYED HANDSOME MAN	19	HARMONY		US		31179
JERRY SHOOK	G	(PV	(K) GREATEST HITS	19	HARMONY		US		31792
PETE WADE	G	(P	(K) GREATEST HITS	19	CBS		UK		63676
CHIP YOUNG	G	(P	(L) MATCHBOX	19	PICKWICK		US		JS6103
BUDDY HARMON	D	(P	(M) MAN BEHIND JOHNNY CASH	1972	CBS				64892
BOB MOORE	B	(P	(N) BEST OF	19	TRIP		US		TLX8503
HENRY STRZELECKI	B	(P	(O) GREATEST HITS	197	EMBASSY		UK		31527
PIG ROBBINS	K	(P	(P) MY KIND OF COUNTRY	1974	MERCURY	US SRM1681	UK	6338 475
MICHAEL LEECH	B	(V	(Q) ROCKIN GUITAR MAN	1975	CHARLY		UK		CR30081
GAYLE WHITFIELD	SAX	(V	(R) ORIGINAL CARL PERKINS	1976	CHARLY		UK		CR30110
HOYT HAWKINS	V	(V	(S) CARL PERKINS SHOW	1976	SUEDE		US		NR 6778
GINGER HOLLADAY	V	(V	(T) LONG TALL SALLY	1977	EMBASSY		UK		31554
N R B Q		(H	(U) FROM JACKSON TENNESSEE	1977	LAKE COUNTY		US		LC 505
PETE DRAKE	STEEL	(P	(V) OL' BLUE SUEDES BACK	1978	JET	JTLA 856	UK		30146
CHARLIE McCOY	HCA	(P	(W) OL' BLUE SUEDES BACK	1978	JET US		35604		
HAYWARD BISHOP	D	(V	(X) SUN SOUNDS SPECIAL	1978	CHARLY		UK		CR30152
DAVID BRIGGS	PNO	(V	(Y) SUN STORY VOL 3	1979	SUN		US		9330 903
WELDON MYRICK	STEEL	(V	(Z) TENNESSEE	19	DESIGN		US		DLP 611
HUGH STOKER	V	(V							
NEAL MATTHEWS	V	(V	RAYMOND L WALKER V	(V	LEA JANE BERINATI	V	(V	LISA SILVER	V (V

(1) EARLY BANDS (2) 1978 TOUR

JOE PERRY

JOE PERRY	G V	(A	(A) LET THE MUSIC DO THE TALKING	1980	CBS		UK	84213
RALPH MORMAN	V	(A						
DAVID HULL	V B	(A	RONNIE STEWART	D	(A			

JOHN PERRY

JOHN PERRY		(A	(A) SUNSET WADING	1976	DECCA		UK	SKL 5233
RUPERT HINE		(A						

LEE PERRY

LEE PERRY		(ALL	AFRICA BLOOD	19	TROJAN		TBL 166
			REVOLUTION DUB	1979	CACTUS		CTLP 112
			BEST OF LEE PERRY & UPSETTERS	19	JET STAR		PTLP1023
			SUPER APE	1976	ISLAND		ILPS ?

PERSUADERS

		PERSUADERS	1974	ATLANTIC	UK K40476	US	7021
		BEST THING THATS HAPPENED TO ME	19	ATLANTIC		US	7046
		THIN LINE BETWEEN LOVE & HATE	1974	ATLANTIC	UK K40370	US	33387
		ITS ALL ABOUT LOVE	19	CALLA		US	34802

PERSUASIONS

JERRY LAWSON	V	(BD	(A) WE CAME TO PLAY	19	CAPITOL		US	791
JIMMY HAYES	V	(BD	(B) STREET CORNER SYMPHONY	1972	CAPITOL		US	872
JOSEPH RUSSELL	V	(BD	(B) STREET CORNER SYMPHONY	1972	ISLAND	UK	ILPS 9201
WILLIE C DANIELS	V	(D	(C) SPREAD THE WORD	197	CAPITOL		US	11101
HERBERT RHOAD	V	(BD	(D) MORE THAN BEFORE	1974	A&M	UK AMLS 63635	US SP3635
BENORCE BLACKMON	G	(D	(E) I JUST WANNA SING	197	A&M		US SP3656
HENRY DAVIS	B	(D	(F) ACAPELLA	19	STRAIGHT		STS1062
JAY OTIS WASHINGTON	V	(B	(G) CHIRPIN'	1977	ELEKTRA		US 7E1099
JEFF BARRY	PERC	(D	(H) WE STILL AIN'T GO NO BAND	197	MCA		US	326
RICK BEILKE	G	(D						
OLLIE BROWN	D	(D	RANDY KOONTZ	B	(D	JOE AGLIO	D (D	CLARENCE McDONALD	K (D

PERTH COUNTY CONSPIRACY

		(A) ALIVE	19	COLUMBIA		IMP	GES 90037

PESKY GEE

		(A) EXCLAMATION MARK	1969	PYE		UK	NSPL18293

JIM PETERIK

JIM PETERIK	(A	(A) DON'T FIGHT THAT FEELING	19	EPIC		US	34196

COLLEEN PETERSON

COLLEEN PETERSON	V	(ALL	(A) BEGINNING TO FEEL LIKE HOME	1976	CAPITOL			
			(B) COLLEEN	1977	CAPITOL		US	ST 11714
			(C) TAKIN' MY BOOTS OFF	1978	CAPITOL		UK/US	11835

PETS

GREG SUTTON	B V	(A	(A) WET BEHIND THE EARS	1978	ARISTA	UK SPART 1061	US AB4154
GREG LEROY	G WIND	(A					
VINCE MELAMED	K V	(A	DEANE HAGEN	D	(A	IRA INGBER	G V (A	ALAN ESTES	PERC (A
STEVE FORMAN	PERC	(A	EDDIE TUDURI	D	(A	MIKE BAIRD	D (A	SCOTT STRONG	G (A
JOANNE HARRIS	V	(A					

TOM PETTY & THE HEARTBREAKERS

TOM PETTY	G V	(ALL	(A) TOM PETTY & THE HEARTBREAKERS	1977	ISLAND	UK ISA5014	US SHELTER 52006
BENJMONT TENCH	K V	(ABCD	(B) YOURE GONNA GET IT	1978	ISLAND	UK ISA5017	US SHELTER 52029
RON BLAIR	B	(ABCD	(C) OFFICIAL LIVE BOOTLEG	197			US SHELTER 12677
STAN LYNCH	D K	(ABCD	(D) DAMN THE TORPEDOES	1979	BACKSTREET	UK	MCF 3044
MIKE CAMPBELL	G	(ABCD	(E) HARD PROMISES	1981	MCA	UK MCF3098

PEZBAND

MIMI BETINIS	G K V	(B	(A) PEZBAND	1977	PASSPORT	US 9821		
MIKE GORMAN	B V	(B	(B) LAUGHING IN THE DARK	1978	PASSPORT	US 9826	UK RADAR RAD 6
TOMMY GAWENDA	G	(B					
MICK RAIN	D V	(B	MEL COLLINS	SAX	(B	TOMMY EYRE	PNO (B

PHANTOM BAND

JAKI LIEBEZEIT	D	(A	(A) PHANTOM BAND	1980 SKY	SKY 048
ELEK GELBA	PERC	(A			
HELMUT ZERLETT	K	(A	DOMINIK VON SENGER G (A ROSKO GEE	V B (A	

ANTHONY PHILLIPS

ANTHONY PHILLIPS G V (ABCD   (A) THE GEESE & THE GHOST   1977 HIT & RUN   UK   001
MICHAEL RUTHERFORD G B K D(A   (B) WISE AFTER THE EVENT   1978 ARISTA   UK SPARTY 1063
PHIL COLLINS   V   (A   (C) PRIVATE PARTS AND PIECES   1978 APL UK AFLP 1   PASSPORT US 7905
ROB PHILLIPS   OBOE (AB   (D) SIDES   1979 ARISTA   UK SPART 1085
LAZA MOMULOVICH   OBOE (A

JOHN HACKETT   FLT (A   WIL SLEATH   FLT (A   JACK LANCASTER FLT (A   CHARLIE MARTIN   CELLO(A
KIRK TREVOR   CELLO(A   NICK HAYLEY   VLN (A   MARTIN WESTLAKE PERC (A   VIV McAULIFFE   V (A
THE VICAR   G V K(BD   MIKE GILES   D (BD   JOHN G PERRY   B (BD   FRANK RICOTTI   PERC (D
RALPH BERNASCONE   V (D   VIC STENCH   B (BD   JEREMY GILBERT   K (B   RUPERT HINE   V PERC (B
DALE NEWMAN   OBOE (A   DAN OWEN   V (D   RAY COOPER   PERC (D   MORRIS PERT   PERC (D
HUMBERT RUSE   PERC HRNS(BD   MEL COLLINS   SAX (BD   PERKIN ALANBECK SYN (B

GLENN PHILLIPS

GLENN PHILLIPS   G V (AB   (A) LOST AT SEA   1975 CAROLINE UK C1519 US SNOWSTAR SSR1
JOHN CARR HARRIMAN CELLO(A   (B) SWIM IN THE WIND   1977 VIRGIN   UK   V2087
MIKE HOLBROOK   B (A
JIM PRESMANES   D (A   BILL REA   G (AB   SANT RAM SINGH KHALSA K (AB   JERRY FIELDS   D (AB
DAVID LANDSBERG   D (B   JANIE GEISER REA   V (B   BILLY McPHERSON   WIND (B   CHUCK MOON   V (B
JOHN CURRIE   (B   DANA HOWARD NELSON K V (B   BILLY McKINLEY   BANJO (B   PHOEBE   PNO (B
DAVID BYRD   STEEL(B   JIM MARETT   PNO (B   BILL SHEFFIELD   HCA V (B

JOHN PHILLIPS

JOHN PHILLIPS   G V (A   (A) WOLFKING OF L A   1970 STATESIDE UK 5027 US DUNHILL 50077

MICHELLE PHILLIPS

MICHELLE PHILLIPS V (A   (A) VICTIM OF ROMANCE   1977   A&M   UK   AMLH64651
JACK NITZSCHE   K PERC(A
SCOTT FREE   D G ACC V (A   DAVID C ALLEN   G (A   GREGORY LEE   B (A   TIM DRUMMOND   B (A
DON RANDI   PNO (A   JOHN MOON MARTIN   G V (A   STEVE DOUGLAS   WIND PERC(A   RON NAGLE   PERC (A
GENE ESTES   PERC (A   BEN BENAY   G MAND   (A   JERRY DONAHUE   G (A   MIKE BODDIKER   SYN(A
SID SHARP   STRINGS (A   JERRY JUMONVILLE   WIND (A   JAY MIGLIORI   WIND   (A   DENNIS DREITH   WIND(A
JACK NIMITZ   WIND (A   BOB FINDLEY   TPT (A   BILL PETERSON   TPT (A   MARK UNDERWOOD   TPT(A
TRICIA JOHNS   V (A   LAURA CREAMER   V (A   CHERIE ENGLISH   V (A   MYRNA MATTHEWS   V (A
MAXINE WILLARD   V (A   KATHY WARD   V (A   BILLY GUY   V (A   GRADY CHAPMAN   V (A
JEROME EVANS   V (A

SHAWN PHILLIPS

SHAWN PHILLIPS   V (ALL   (A) CONTRIBUTION   1970   A&M US 4241   UK   AMLS 978
SNEAKY PETE   STEEL(FJ   (B) SECOND CONTRIBUTION   1971   A&M US 4282   UK   AMLS 2006
JIM PRICE   HRNS (F   (C) COLLABORATION   1972   A&M US 4323   UK   AMLS64324
JIM HORN   SAX (FJ   (D) FACES   1973   A&M US 4363   UK   AMLS64363
CRAIG DOERGE   (F   (E) FURTHERMORE   1974   A&M US 3662   UK   AMLH68278
BOBBY KEYS   SAX (F   (F) BRIGHT WHITE   1974   A&M US 4402   UK   AMLH64402
LEE SKLAR   B (J   (G) DO YOU WONDER   1975   A&M US 4539   UK   AMLH64539
RUSS KUNKEL   D (J   (H) RUMPLESTILTSKIN'S RESOLVE   1976   A&M US 4582   UK   AMLH64582
JOE SAMPLE   K (J   (J) SPACED   1977   A&M US 4650   UK   AMLH64650
PETER ROBINSON   K (H   (K) TRANSCENDENCE   1978   RCA US   APLI13028
MICHAEL BAIRD   D (J
CHUCK RAINEY   B (J   MIKE MILLER   G B (HJ   AL WING   SAX (HJ   STEVE NEILEN   D (J
ANTHONY NEDZA   K (J   JOSEPH GAETA   G B (J   DANIEL TIMMS   G (J   BRUCE ROWLAND   D (J
BRIAN ODGERS   B (J   CHRIS MERCER   SAX (J   JOHNNY ALMOND   SAX (J   MIKE CLARKE   D (HJ
PAUL JACKSON   B (HJ   BOBBY LICHTIG   B (H   STEVE HAMMOND   G (H   JOHN GUSTAFSON   B (H
BARRY DE SOUZA   D (H   CALEB QUAYE   G (H   PAUL BUCKMASTER   K (H   JOHN PULLEN   OBOE(H
BILL SUMMERS   PERC (H

PHILLIPS MACLEOD

ROBERT PHILLIPS   G V (A   (A) LE PARTIE DU COCKTAIL   1979 POLYDOR   US PD1 6198
SEAN MacLEOD   G V (A
JIM DIVISEK   (A
ANDREW STEELE   (A   BRIAN WHITCOMB   (A   BOB CONTI   (A   DAVID KEMPER   (A

PHOENIX

JOHN VERITY   V B G(AB   (A) PHOENIX   1976   CBS   UK   81621
ROBERT HENRIT   D (AB   (B) IN FULL VIEW   1980   CHARISMA   UK   CAS 1150
ROD ARGENT   K (B
JIM RODFORD   D (A   MICHAEL DES BARRES V   (A   RAY MINHINNIT   G V (B   RUSS BALLARD   V (B
BRUCE TURGON   V (B   RONNIE LEE CUNNINGHAM K V(B

PHOTOS

WENDY WU   V (AB   (A) PHOTOS   1980   EPIC   UK   PHOTO 5
STEVE EAGLES   G V (AB   (B) BLACKMAIL TAPES[FREE WITH (A)]
DAVE SPARROW   B V (AB
OLLY HARRISON   D (AB

PICCADILLY LINE

ROD EDWARDS   V G K(A   (A) HUGE WORLD OF EMILY SMALL   19   CBS   63129
ROGER HAND   G V (A
NORRIE McLEAN   B (A   KEITH HODGE   D (A

BOBBY 'BORIS' PICKETT

BOBBY 'BORIS' PICKETT V(A   (A) MONSTER MASH   1973 LONDON   UK   ZGU 133
    ( ) MONSTER MASH   1962 GARPAX   US SGP 67001
    ( ) ORIGINAL MONSTER MASH   1973 PARROT   UK   71063

COURTLAND PICKETT

COURTLAND PICKETT V B (A   (A) FANCY DANCER   1973 ELEKTRA UK K42147 US EKS 75060
DAVID HOOD   B (A
ROGER HAWKINS   D (A   BARRY BECKETT   K (A   PETE CARR   G (A   JIMMY JOHNSON   G (A
CHARLES STRATFORD TROM (A   BOBBY BRUCE   VLN (A   SONNY ROYAL   CLAR (A   WAYNE HILL   TPT(A
HARVEY THOMPSON   SAX (A   RONNIE EADES   SAX (A   CHARLES ROSE   TROM (A   JO ANN CARR   V (A
LAURA STRUZICK   V (A   SUZY STORM   V (A

P80

WILSON PICKETT

Personnel			Album	Year	Label		Country	Number
WILSON PICKETT	V	(ALL	(A) IN THE MIDNIGHT HOUR	196	ATLANTIC		US	8114
JEAN ROUSSEL	K	(Z	EXCITING WILSON PICKETT	196	ATLANTIC		US	8129
MARTY SIMON	D	(Z	WICKED PICKETT	196	ATLANTIC	UK 588 057	US	8138
JERRY KNIGHT	B V	(Z	THE SOUND OF	196	ATLANTIC	UK 588 050	US	8145
WALTER ROSSI	G	(Z	THE BEST OF	196	ATLANTIC	UK 588 092	US	8151
GARY BROWN	SAX	(Z	I'M IN LOVE	196	ATLANTIC		US	8183
CLYDE KERR	TPT	(Z	MIDNIGHT MOVER	196	ATLANTIC		US	8183
JIMMY TANAKA	PERC	(Z	GREAT HITS	196	WAND		US	672
GARY WILSON	V	(Z	HEY JUDE	196	ATLANTIC	UK 588 170	US	8215
BILLY NELSON	V	(Z	RIGHT ON	196	ATLANTIC	UK 2465 002	US	8250
PETSYE POWELL	V	(Z	IN PHILADELPHIA	1970	ATLANTIC		US	8270
			BEST OF VOL 2	1971	ATLANTIC		US	8290
			IF YOU NEED ME	19	JOY			JOYS181
			BEST OF	197	ATLANTIC	UK K40015	US	2 501
			MR MAGIC MAN	1973	RCA	UK SF 8344		
			DONT KNOCK MY LOVE	1974	ATLANTIC	UK K40319	US	8300
			TONIGHT I'M MY BIGGEST AUDIENCE	1974	RCA		US LSP 4858	
			MIZ LENAS BOY	1974	RCA	UK SF 8390		
			LIVE IN JAPAN	1974	RCA		APL 20669	
			PICKETT IN POCKET	1974	RCA		APL1 0495	
			JOIN ME & LETS BE FREE	1975	RCA	UK SF8439	USAPL1 0856	
			PEACE BREAKER	1975	DJM	UK DJSL064		
			ITS TOO LATE	19	DOUBLE L		US	2300
			KEEP THE DREAM ALIVE	19	RCA			VSPX 6097
			STAR COLLECTION	1978	WEA	UK MID26001	FR	20017
			FUNKY SITUATION	19	BIG TREE		IMP	76011
			(Z) I WANT YOU	1979	EMI AMERICA	UK AML3007	US	17019
			RIGHT TRACK	1981	EMI AMERICA	UK AML3016		

P80A

PIERCE ARROW

DOUG LUBAHN (A
JEFF KENT (A
DAVID BUSKIN (A   ROBIN BATTEAU (A   WERNER FRITZSCHING (A   BOBBY CHOUINARD (A

(A) PIERCE ARROW   197 CBS US 34805

P80B

PIECES

GEOFFREY LEIB K SYN(A
MIKE LINGLE D V (A
KENNY LEE LEWIS B V (A   LARRY LINGLE G V (A

(A) PIECES   1979 UA US UALA 966 UK UAG 30252

P80C

MARIE PIERRE

MARIE PIERRE V (A
JAH BUNNY D (A
DENNIS BOVELL K B (A   WEBSTER JOHNSON PNO (A   JOHN KPIAYE G (A   PATRICK TENYUE TPT (A
HENRY TENYUE TROM (A

(A) LOVE AFFAIR   1979 TROJAN TRLS 177

P81

PIGSTY HILL LIGHT ORCHESTRA

ANDY LEGGETT V G SAX (A
DAVID CREECH V TPT(AC
BARRY BLACK G V (A
BILL COLE B (A
JON HAYS PERC V(C   ROBERT GREENFIELD G V (C   CHRIS NEWMAN G B (C

(A) PIGGERY JOKERY   1971 VILLAGE THING VTS 8
(B) CUSHION FOOT STOMP   197 VILLAGE THING VTS 1
(C) PIGSTY HILL LIGHT ORCHESTRA   1976 PHLO 001

P81A

PIIRPAUKE

SAKARI KUKKO SAX PNO(ALL
HASSE WALL G PERC (ALL
ANTTI HYTTI B V (ALL
JUKKA WASAMA D (ALL

(A) I   19 LOVE LRLP 148
(B) II   19 LOVE LRLP 192
(C) LIVE   19 LOVE LRLP 251

P81B

PILOT

DAVID PATON B V (
BILLY LYALL K V (
STUART TOSH D V (
IAN BAIRNSON G (

(A) FROM THE ALBUM OF THE SAME NAME   1974 EMI EMC 3045
(B) MORIN HEIGHTS   1976 EMI EMA 779
(C) TWOS A CROWD   1977 ARISTA SPARTY 1014
(D) BEST OF   1980 EMI NUT 29

P82

PILTDOWN MEN

ED COBB
LINCOLN MAYORGA

(EP) PILTDOWN RIDES AGAIN   19 CAPITOL EAP 1 20155

P83

MICHAEL PINDER

MICHAEL PINDER G K V(A
BILL BERG D (A
FLYN J JOHNSON B (A   MAXINE WILLARD V (A   JEANIE KING V (A   JULIA TILLMAN V (A
JIM DILLAN G V (A   FRED BECKMEIER B (A   SMITTY SMITH ORG (A   SUSAN McDONALD HARP(A
JOEL DIBARTELLO B (A   TOM PETERSON WIND (A   MICHAEL AZEVEDO CONGA(A   DEAN OLCH WIND(A
STEVE MADAIO TPT (A   BOBBY KEYS SAX (A

(A) THE PROMISE   1976 THRESHOLD UK THS 18

P83A

MIKE PINERA

MIKE PINERA G V (A

(A) ISLA   19 CAPRICORN US 0202

P83B

RICHARD PINHAS

RICHARD PINHAS SYN G (ALL
FRANCOIS AUGER D (C
JEAN PHILIPPE GOUDE SYN(C

(A) RHIZOSPERE   1979 COBRA FR COB37005
(B) CHRONOLYSE   1979 COBRA FR COB37015
(C) ICE LAND   1980 PULSE 001
(D) EAST WEST   1980 PULSE 003

P84

PINK FAIRIES

DUNCAN SANDERSON B (ABC
RUSSEL HUNTER D (ABC
MARTIN STONE G (
LARRY WILLIS G V (C
PAUL RUDOLPH G (AB
TWINK D (A1
MICK FARREN (1   STEVE TOOK (1

(A) NEVER NEVER LAND   1971 POLYDOR UK 2383 045
(B) WHAT A BUNCH OF SWEETIES   1972 POLYDOR UK 2383 132
(C) KINGS OF OBLIVION   1975 POLYDOR US5537 UK 2383 212
(D) PINK FAIRIES   1975 POLYDOR UK 2384 071
(1) 1969 70

PINK FLOYD

ROGER WATERS	B V G(ALL	(A) PIPER AT THE GATES OF DAWN	1967	TOWER	US	5093	UK	COLUMBIA	SCX 6157
RICHARD WRIGHT	K V (ALL	(B) SAUCERFUL OF SECRETS	1968	TOWER	US	5131	UK	COLUMBIA	SCX 6258
NICK MASON	D (ALL	(C) MORE	1969	HARVEST	US	11198	UK	COLUMBIA	SCX 6346
SYD BARRETT	G V (ABG	(D) UMMAGUMMA	1969	HARVEST	US	388	UK	HARVEST	SHDW 1/2
DAVE GILMOUR	G V (BCDEFGHJKLM	(E) ATOM HEART MOTHER	1970	HARVEST	US	382	UK	HARVEST	SHVL 781
ROY HARPER	V (K	(F) MEDDLE	1971	HARVEST	US	832	UK	HARVEST	SHVL 795
SNOWY WHITE	G (	(G) RELICS	1971	HARVEST	US	759	UK	STARLINE	SRS 5071
PETER WOOD	K (	(G) RELICS	1978				UK	MFP	50397
WILLIE WILSON	D (	(H) OBSCURED BY CLOUDS	1972	HARVEST	US	11078	UK	HARVEST	SHSP4020
ANDY BOWN	B (	(J) DARK SIDE OF THE MOON	1973	HARVEST	US	11163	UK	HARVEST	SHVL 804
DICK PARRY	SAX (J	(K) WISH YOU WERE HERE	1976	CBS	US	33453	UK	HARVEST	SHVL 814
LESLEY DUNCAN	V (J	(L) ANIMALS	1977	CBS	US	34474	UK	HARVEST	SHVL 815
CLAIRE TORRY	V (J	(M) THE WALL	1979				UK	HARVEST	SHDW 411
LIZA STRIKE	V (J								
DORIS TROY	V (J	(AB) A NICE PAIR	1973	HARVEST	US	11257	UK	HARVEST	SHDW 403
BARRY ST JOHN	V (J	( ) MASTERS OF ROCK	1975	EMI IMP	EURO	054 04299	1976	062	04299
BRUCE JOHNSTON	V (M	(*) ZABRISKIE POINT (SOUNDTRACK)	1970	MGM	2315	002		2354	040
JON JOYCE	V (M	(*) TONIGHT LETS ALL MEK LOVE	1968	INSTANT ANALYSIS				INLP	002
TONI TENNILLE	V (M								
STAN FARBER	V (M	(*) BOTH SOUNDTRACK LPS WITH OTHER ARTISTS							
JOE CHEMAY	V (M								
JIM HAAS	V (M	ISLINGTON GREEN SCHOOL V (M							

PINK MILITARY

JAYNE	V (A	(A) DO ANIMALS BELIEVE IN GOD	1980	VIRGIN		UK	ERIC5004
NICKY	G SYN(A						
CHARLIE	K (A	MARTIN B G (A	NEIL PERC (A	CHRIS JOYCE	D (A		

PINPOINT

ARTURO BASSICK	G (
DAVE ALLEN	B (
HUGH GRIFFITHS	D (

PIONEERS

LONGSHOT	1970	TROJAN	TBL	103
BATTLE OF THE GIANTS	197	TROJAN	TBL	139
YEAH	1971	TROJAN	TRL	24
I BELIEVE IN LOVE	1972	TROJAN	TRLS	48
FREEDOM FELING	1973	TROJAN	TRLS	64
I'M GONNA KNOCK ON YOUR DOOR	1974	TROJAN	TRLS	98
FEEL THE RHYTHM	1976	MERCURY	9286	172
ROLL ON MUDDY RIVER	1877	TROJAN	TRLS	144
PUSHER MAN	1979	TROJAN	TRLS	156
GREATEST HITS	1979	TROJAN	TRLS	172

PIPER

BILLY SQUIRE	V G PERC(A	PIPER	19	A&M	US	SP 4615
ALAN LAINE NOLAN	G PERC(A	CANT WAIT	19	A&M	US	SP4654
TOMMY GUNN	G (A					
DANNY McGARY	B (A	RICHIE FONTANA D (A				

PIPS

(A) AT LAST THE PIPS	1978	CASABLANCA	CAL 2022
(B) CALLIN'	1978	CASABLANCA	CAL 2031

PIRANA

JIM YONGE	D (AB	(A) PIRANA	19	HARVEST	SHVL 603
GRAEME THOMPSON	B (AB	(B) PIRANA II	1972	HARVEST	SHVL 609
TONY HAMILTON G B V PERC(AB					
STAN WHITE	K V (A	COL LAUGHNAN FLT (A	KEITH GREIG	K PERC(B	

PIRANHAS

DICK SLEXIA	D (A	(A) PIRANHAS	1980	SIRE	SRK 6098
BOB GROVER	(A				
JOHNNY HELMER	G (A	ZOOT SAX (A	RICHARD MYHILL	K (A MIKE COOK	VLN (A
REG	(A	GRAHAM PRESKETT VLN (A			

PIRATES

MICK GREEN	G (ABC	(A) OUT OF THEIR SKULLS	1977	WB	US 3155	UK	K56411
JOHN SPENCER	B V (ABC	(B) SKULL WARS	1978	WB	US 3224	UK	K56468
FRANK FARLEY	D (ABC	(C) HAPPY BIRTHDAY ROCK'N'ROLL	1980	CUBE		UK	HIFLY33

PLAIN SAILING

PAUL STEWART	V HCA(A	(A) DANGEROUS TIMES	1980	CHARISMA	UK	CHR 1282
ROBERT FREEMAN	G V (A					
ALAN STEWART	G V (A	COLIN STEWART K V (A	DAVE WINTOUR	B (A ALAN COULTER	D (A	

PLAINSONG

IAN MATTHEWS	G V (AB	(A) IN SEARCH OF AMELIA EARHART	1972	ELEKTRA	NL ELK 22013 UK	K42120
ANDY ROBERTS	G V (AB	(B) PLAINSONG III RELEASED AS A WHITE LABEL PROMOTION BUT NOT GENERALLY				
DAVE RICHARDS	G V (AB	RELEASED. THE TRACKS LATER APPEARED ON IAN MATTHEWS 'VALLEY HI' &				
BOB RONGA	B V (AB	'SOMEDAYS YOU EAT THE BEAR' & ALSO ON ANDY ROBERTS ' URBAN COWBOY'.				
WITH						
TIMI DONALD	D (A	THE FIRST PLAINSONG RECORDING 'ALONG COMES MARY' HAD VOCAL OVERDUBBED BY				
DAVE MATTACKS	D (A	MARC ELLINGTON & ISSUED ON HIS RESTORATION ALBUM.				
MARTIN JENKINS	MAND (A					

PLANET EARTH

COLIN GREEN	G (A	(A) PLANET EARTH	1978	PYE	UK	NSPL18556
KEVIN PEEK	G (A					
BILLY CHRISTIAN	B (A	TREVOR BARTON K (A	RONNIE ASPERY	SAX (A BARRY MORGAN	D (A	
MIKE RATLEDGE	K (A	TRISTRAM FRY PERC (A	KARL JENKINS	K (A		

PLANET GONG

DAEVID ALLEN	G V (A	(A) FLOATING ARNACHY LIVE 77	1978	CHARLY	UK	CRM 2000
GILLI SMYTH	V (A					
PEPSI MILAN	G V (A	JUANE BIBLIONI G V (A	SAM GOPAL PERC SYN(A			

PLANETS

(A) GOONHILLY DOWN	1979	RIALTO	TENOR102
(B) SPOT	1980	RIALTO	TENOR10?

PLANXTY

CHRISTY MOORE	G V	(EF	(A) PLANXTY		1973	POLYDOR	UK	2383 186
MATT MOLLOY	FLT	(EF	(B) WELL BELOW THE VALLEY		1973	POLYDOR	UK	2383 232
DONAL LUNNY	G SYN	(EF	(C) COLD BLOW & THE RAINY NIGHT		1974	POLYDOR	UK	2383 301
PAUL BRADY	(		(D) PLANXTY COLLECTION		1976	POLYDOR	UK	2389 397
ANDY IRVINE	(ALL		(E) AFTER THE BREAK		1979	TARA		3001
LIAM O'FLYNN	WIND	(ALL	(F) WOMAN I LOVED SO WELL		1980	TARA		3005
JOHNNY MOYNIHAN	(							
NOEL HILL	CONC	(F TONY LINNANE FDL	(F BILL WHELAN	K (F				

P93A

PLASMATICS

WENDY 'O' WILLIAMS	V	(	(A) NEW HOPE		198	
STU DEUTSCH		(				
RICHIE STOTTS		(				

P94

PLASTIC BERTRAND

PLASTIC BERTRAND	V	(A	(A) AN 1	1978	SIRE		9103 258

P94A

PLASTIC PEOPLE OF THE UNIVERSE

(A) EGON BONDY'S HAPPY HEART CLUB BANNED	19	INVISIBLE	SCOPA 10001

P95

PLASTIC PENNY

PAUL RAYMOND	ORG	(					
NIGEL OLSSON	D	(TONY MURRAY B (BRIAN KEITH	V (MICK GRABHAM	G (

P96

PLATINUM HOOK

(A) PLATINUM HOOK	1978	TAMLA	UK	STML12086
(B) IT'S TIME	1979	TAMLA	UK	STML12140

PLATTERS

P97

DAVID LYNCH	V	(ABCDE	ALL TIME MOVIE HITS	19	MERCURY	US	SR 60782
HERB REED	V	(ABCDE	BEST OF VOL 1	1973	PHILIPS	UK	6336 218
TONY WILLIAMS	V	(ABC	BEST OF VOL 2	1973	PHILIPS	UK	6336 219
ALEX HODGE	V	(AB	CHRISTMAS WITH THE PLATTERS	19	MERCURY	US	SR 60841
PAUL ROBI	V	(BCD	COLLECTION	1976	HALLMARK	UK	PDA 003
ZOLA TAYLOR	V	(CD	DOUBLE GOLD PLATTERS	19	MUSICOR	US	4601
SONNY TURNER	V	(DE	ENCORE OF BROADWAY GOLDEN HITS	19	MERCURY	US	SR 60613
SANDRA DAWN	V	(E	ENCORE OF GOLDEN HITS	19	MERCURY	US	SR 60243
NATE NELSON	V	(E	ENCORE OF GOLDEN HITS OF THE GROUPS	19	MERCURY	US	SR 60893
			ENCORES	19	WING	US	SRW 16112
(A) 1953			THE FLYING PLATTERS	19	MERCURY	US	MG 20298
(B) 1954			FLYING PLATTERS AROUND THE WORLD	19	MERCURY	US	SR 60043
(C) 1955			GOING BACK TO DETROIT	19	MUSICOR	US	MS 3125
(D) 1961			GOING BACK TO DETROIT	1967	STATESIDE	UK	SSL 10208
(E) 1963			GOLDEN HOUR	19	PYE	UK	GH 808
			GREAT PRETENDER	1974	HALLMARK	UK	SHM 843
			I GET THE SWEETEST FEELING	19	MUSICOR	US	MS 3171
			I LOVE YOU A THOUSAND TIMES	19	MUSICOR	US	MS 3091
			IN THE STILL OF THE NIGHT	19	PICKWICK	US	3120
			LIVE	1974	CONTOUR	UK	6870 627
			LIFE IS JUST A BOWL OF CHERRIES	19	MERCURY	US	MG 20589
			MOONLIGHT MEMORIES	19	MERCURY	US	SR 60759
			MORE ENCORE OF GOLDEN HITS	19	MERCURY	US	SR 60252
			MUSIC FROM ACROSS THE WAY	1975	PHILIPS	UK	6382 117
			MY PRAYER	1975	HALLMARK	UK	SHM 876
			NOW	1975	CONTOUR	UK	6870 640
			NEW GOLDEN HITS OF THE PLATTERS	19	MUSICOR	US	MS 3141
			NEW GOLDEN HITS OF THE PLATTERS	1968	STATESIDE	UK	SSL 10227
			NEW SOUL OF THE PLATTERS	19	MERCURY	US	SR 60983
			ONLY YOU	19	GUEST STAR	US	NG 1419
			OUR WAY	19	PYE	UK	NSPL28149
			PLATTERS	19	SPRINGBOARD		4059
			THE ORIGINAL	1978	FESTIVAL		ALB 281
			THE ORIGINAL	1978	PHILIPS	UK	9100 049
			PLATTERS	19	KING	US	LP 549
			THE PLATTERS	19	STARDAY	US	K5002
			THE PLATTERS	19	MERCURY	US	MG 20146
			THE PLATTERS	19	IMPACT		6886 401
			THE PLATTERS	19	MERCURY	US	SR 60245
			PLATTERS HITS	1976	SONIC		SON 002
			PLATTERS HAVE THE MAGIC TOUCH	19	MUSICOR	US	MS 3111
			REFLECTIONS	19	MERCURY	US	SR 60160
			REFLECTIONS	19	WING RI	US	SRW 16672
			REFLECTIONS	1968	WING	UK	WL1174
			REMEMBER WHEN	19	MERCURY	US	SR 60087
			SING LATINO	19	MERCURY	US	SR 60808
			SING LATINO	1968	FONTANA	UK	SFL13040
			SIXTEEN GREATEST HITS	19	TRIP		TOP 1611
			SONG FOR THE LONELY	19	MERCURY	US	SR 60669
			SPOTLIGHT ON	1974	PHILIPS	UK	6641 202
			SUPER HITS	19	PICKWICK	US	3236
			SWEET SWEET LOVIN'	19	MUSICOR	US	MS 3156
			SWEET SWEET LOVIN'	1968	STATESIDE	UK	SSL 10245
			TWO DECADES OF HITS	19	PYE	UK	PKL 4411
			TWENTY CLASSIC HITS	1976	MERCURY	UK	9100 048
			TEHTH ANNIVERSARY ALBUM	1968	WING	UK	WL 1174
			WONDER OF YOU	1976	HALLMARK	UK	SHM 896

P98

PLAYER

J C CROWLEY	K G V	(A	(A) PLAYER	1978	RSO US 1 3036	UK	2394 193
PETER BECKETT	G V	(A	(B) DANGER ZONE	1978	RSO US 1 3026	UK	2394 208
JOHN FRIESEN	D	(A	(B) DANGER ZONE	1978	RSO	UK	RSS 3
RON MOSS	B	(A	(C) ROOM WITH A VIEW	19	CASABLANCA	UK	NBLP7217
WAYNE COOK	K	(A					

PLAYER ASSOCIATION

CHRIS HILLS	G V K B D	(AC	(A) BORN TO DANCE		1978	VANGUARD			VSD 79398
MICHAEL BRECKER	SAX	(A	(B) TURN THE MUSIC UP		1979	VANGUARD			VSD 79421
DAVE SANBORN	SAX	(A	(C) WE GOT THE GROOVE		1980	VANGUARD			VSD 79431
JON FADDIS	TPT	(A							
STEVE KHAN	G	(A							
WILBUR BASSCOMB	B	(A	MTUME	CONG (A	LORRAINE MOORE	V (A	WAYNE ANDRE	TROM(A	
MIKE MANDEL	SYN	(A	LEON PENDARVIS	K (A	FREDDIE HARRIS	G (A	DANNY TRIFAN	B (A	
NICKY MARRERO	CONG	(A	DAVID EARLE JOHNSON	PERC(A	ED'EASY' ZANT	V (A	JIM McELWAINE	K (C	
CALEB MARTIN	G	(C	LUCIO HOPPER	B (C	RAY MANTILLA	PERC (C	BOB BERG	SAX(C	
RONNIE CUBER	SAX	(C	TOM HARREL	HRNS (C	JOHN DEARTH	TPT (C	VICTOR PAZ	TPT(C	
WENDELL MORRISON	V	(C	MARIAN ROLLE	V (C					

COUSIN JOE PLEASANT

COUSIN JOE PLEASANT	V PNO(A		(A) BLUESMAN FROM NEW ORLEANS		1974	BIG BEAR			BEAR3
ROGER HILL	G	(A							
GRAHAM GALLERY	B	(A	PETE YORK	D (A	DYAN BIRCH	V (A	FRANK COLLINS	V (A	
PADDY McHUGH	V	(A	GEORGE CHISHOLM	TROM (A	COLIN SMITH	TPT (A	JOHNNY BARNES	CLAR(A	

PLEASERS

DAVE ROTCHELLE	D	(	
STEVE McNERNEY	G WIND	(	
NICK POWELL	G	(	BO BENHAM K B (

PLEASURE

(A) DUST YOURSELF OFF	19	FANTASY	9473
(B) ACCEPT NO SUBSTITUTES	19	FANTASY	9506
(C) JOYOUS	19	FANTASY	9526
(D) GET TO THE FEELING	1978	FANTASY FT 543	9550

PLUGS

(A) PLUGROCK (EP)	19	CATHEDRAL	CATH1

PLUMMET AIRLINES

DARRYL HUNT	(1	(1) 1977			
RICHARD BOOTH	(1	(A) ON STONEY GROUND	1981 HEDONICS	UK	HEDON1/2
DUNCAN KERR	(1				
KEITH GOTHERIDGE	(1	HARRY STEPHENSON (1			

PLUTO

(A) PLUTO	197	DAWN UK	DNLS 3030

POACHER

TIM FLAHERTY	G (A	(A) POACHER	1978	RK	RKLP 5002
PETE ALLEN	STEEL (A				
PETE LONGBOTTOM	BANJ (A	ADRIAN HART G (A ALLAN CROOKES	B (A	STAN BENNETT	D (A

POCKETS

(A) COME GO WITH US	1977	CBS US 34879	UK	82288
(B) TAKE IT ON UP	19	CBS US 35384		

POCO

RUSTY YOUNG	V STEEL (ABCDEFGHIJKLMN	(A) PICKING UP THE PIECES	1969	EPIC	US 26460	UK	65327
GEORGE GRANTHAM	D (ABCDEFGHIJKLMN	(B) POCO	1970	EPIC	US 26522	UK	64082
RICHIE FURAY	G V(ABCDEH	(C) DELIVERIN'	1971	EPIC	US 30209	UK	64204
RANDY MEISNER	B V G(A	(D) FROM THE INSIDE	1971	EPIC	US 30753	UK	64543
JIM MESSINA	G V (ABC	(E) GOOD FEELIN' TO KNOW	1973	EPIC	US 31601	UK	65126
TIM SCHMIT	B V(BCDEFGHIJKLM	(F) CRAZY EYES	1973	EPIC	US 32354	UK	65631
PAUL COTTON	G V (DEFGHIJKLMN	(G) SEVEN	1974	EPIC	US 32895	UK	80082
CHARLIE HARRISON	B V (M	(H) CANTAMOS	1975	EPIC	US 33192	UK	80596
STEVE CHAPMAN	D (M	(I) THE VERY BEST OF POCO	1975	EPIC	US 33537	UK	88135
MILT HOLLAND	PERC (JL	(J) HEAD OVER HEELS	1975	ABC	US 890	UK	ABCL 5137
STEVE FORMAN	PERC (JN	(K) LIVE	1975	EPIC	US 33336	UK	80705
DONALD FAGEN	SYN (N	(L) ROSE OF CIMARRON	1976	ABC	US 946	UK	ABCL 5166
MARK HENRY HARMAN	K (JN	(M) INDIAN SUMMER	1977	ABC	US 989	UK	ABCL 5220
AL GARTH	VLN (JL	(N) LEGEND	1978	ABC	US 1099	UK	ABCL 5264
VICTOR FELDMAN	PERC (J	(O) UNDER THE GUN	1980	MCA		UK	MCF 3076
MICHAEL VON VERDICK V	(J						
CHRIS HILLMAN	MAND (F	PAUL HARRIS PNO (F JOE LALA	PERC (F	BILL GRAHAM	FDL (F		
SID SHARP STRINGS	(L	JOHN LOGAN BANJO(L STEVE FERGUSON	PNO (L	GARTH HUDSON	K (J		
JIM HASKELL	STRING(J	BARRY FAST PNO (E					

POET & THE ONE MAN BAND

TONY COLTON	V PERC(A	(A) POET & THE ONE MAN BAND	1969	VERVE FORECAST	UK		SVLP6012
RAY SMITH	G V (A	(A) POET & THE ONE MAN BAND	1969	PARAMOUNT	US		5010
BARRY MORGAN	D (A						
PAT DONALDSON	B V (A	ALBERT LEE G V (A NICKY HOPKINS	PNO (A	ROGER COULAM	ORG (A		
WILLIAM DAVIES	ORG (A	SPEEDY ACQUAYE CONGA(A JERRY DONAHUE	V (A	JOHN BELL	CLAR (A		
MIKE O'NEIL	K (	PETE GAVIN V D (					

POET & THE ROOTS

P108

LINTON KWESI JOHNSON	V(A	(A) DREAD BEAT AN' BLOOD	1978	FRONT LINE UK	FL1017
VIVIAN WEATHERS	B G V(A				
DENNIS BOVELL	G K (A	WINSTON CURNIFFE D (A JAH BUNNY	D (A	DESMOND CRAIG	K (A
EVERALD FORREST	PERC (A	LILA WEATHERS V (A JOHN VARNOM	G (A		

PEKKA POHJOLA

PEKKA POHJOLA	(ALL	(A) PIHKASILMA KAARNAKORVA	1972	LOVE	LRLP 71
		(B) HARAKKA BIALOIPOKKU	1975	LOVE	LRLP 118
		(B) B THE MAGPIE	1975	VIRGIN UK	V 2036
		(C) KEESOJEN LEHTO	1977	LOVE	LRLP 219
		(C) MATHEMATICIANS AIR DISPLAY	1977	VIRGIN UK	V 2084
		(D) VISITATION	1980	DIG IT	DIGLP 4

POINT BLANK

RUSTY BURNS	G V (ABC	(A) POINT BLANK	1976	ARISTA US AL 4087 UK ARTY 135
KIM DAVIS	G V (ABC	(B) SECOND SEASON	1977	ARISTA UK SPARTY1019
PETER GRUEN	D (ABC	(C) AIRPLAY	1979	MCA UK MCF 3049
JOHN O'DANIEL	V (ABC	(D) THE HARD WAY	1980	MCA US 5114
PHILIP PETTY	B (AB			
BILL RANDOLPH	B V (C	STEVE HARDIN K V HCA (C		

```
P110                              POLECAT
  GRAHAM BROAD   D PERC V  (A        (A) MONEY TALKIN            1976   DJM              UK   DJH 40475
  BERNIE LEE       G V    (A
  GEOFF KNOWLES    G V    (A    DAVE GOODMAN      B  (A   STEPHEN COTTON   K V  (A   ROGER DELL        PERC V(A
  ROBIN LAWRENCE   SAX    (A    MARTIN HAYES TPT V   (A
P110A                             POLECATS
  TIM WORMAN              (A        (A) CULT HEROES             1981   NERVOUS               NERD 001
  BOZ BOORER             (A
  PHIL BLOOMBERG         (A    NEIL ROONEY         (A
P111                              POLICE
  GORDON 'STING'SUMNER  V B(ALL      (A) OUTLANDOS D'AMOUR       1978   A&M   US  4753   UK   AMLH68502
  ANDY SUMMERS         (ALL         (B) REGATTA DE BLANC        1979   A&M               UK   AMLH64792
  STEWART COPELAND   D V (ALL        (C) ZENYATTA MONDATTA       1980   A&M               UK   AMLH64831
P112                              PAMELA POLLAND
  PAMELA POLLAND    K V  (A         (A) PAMELA POLLAND          1972   CBS  US 31116    UK   64934
  TAJ MAHAL         G    (A
  MARC McCLURE      V    (A    DENNIS LOCORRIERE V  (A   RAY SAWYER      V   (A   GEORGE CUMMINGS  V  (A
  ROWAN BROS        V    (A    GEORGE DALY      V   (A   JIMMY SPHEERIS  V   (A   MARC McCALLEN    V  (A
  MEMPHIS HRNS           (A    ART ROSCH      PERC  (A   PAUL FALLERSO   K   (A   ROSCOE HIRSCHBERG PERC(A
  NICKY HOPKINS     K    (A    DAVID BRIGGS   K     (A   JOHN SHINE      G   (A   EDDIE HINTON     G  (A
  RICHARD SCHLOSSER D    (A    KENNY BUTTREY  D     (A   BING NATHAN     B   (A   NORBERT PUTNAM   B  (A
  TOMMY COGBILL     B    (A    BOBBY WOOD     K     (A
P113                              BONNIE POINTER
  BONNIE POINTER    V    (A         (A) BONNIE POINTER          1978   MOTOWN US M7 911 UK   STML12101
  TRUMAN THOMAS     K    (A         (B) BONNIE POINTER 2        1980   MOTOWN
  NIGEL OLSSON      D    (A
  OLLIE BROWN       D    (A    EDDIE HAZEL    G    (A   JACK ASHFORD    PERC (A   JAMES JAMESON    B  (A
  DONALD BALDWIN    G B  (A
P114                              POINTER SISTERS
  ANITA POINTER     V    (ABCDFGH    (A) THE POINTER SISTERS     1973  BLUE THUMB US BT 48   UK  ILPS 9243
  RUTH POINTER      V    (ABCDFGH    (B) THATS A PLENTY          1974  BLUE THUMB US 6009    UK  ILPS 9276
  JUNE POINTER      V    (ABCDFGH    (C) LIVE AT THE OPERA HOUSE 1974  ABC         US 8002   UK  ABCD  608
  BONNIE POINTER    V    (ABCDF      (D) STEPPIN'               1975  BLUE THUMB US 6021 UK  ANCHOR  5133
  GAYLORD BIRCH     D    (ACDF       (E) BEST OF                1976  BLUE THUMB US 6026 UK  ABC ABCD  611
  TOM SALISBURY     K    (ACDF       (F) HAVING A PARTY         1978  BLUE THUMB US 6023 UK  ABC ABCL 5163
  RON McCLURE       B    (A          (G) ENERGY                 1978  PLANET      US  P1  UK       K52107
  WILLIE FULTON     G    (A          (H) PRIORITY               1979  PLANET      US 9003 UK       K52161
  JOHN REWIND       G    (A          (J) SPECIAL THINGS         1980  PLANET      US  P9  UK       K52242
  SKIP MESQUITE     SAX  (A
  JOHN NEWMAN       B    (C    CHRIS MICHIE    G   (CDF SONNY BURKE    K   (F  STEVIE WONDER    K  (DF
  JAMES GADSON      D    (F    ED GREENE       D   (F   LOUIS JOHNSON   B   (F  CHUCK DOMANICO   B  (F
  JAMES JAMESON     B    (F    WILLIE WEEKS    B   (F   GENE SANTINI    B   (FD WAH WAH WATSON   G  (DF
  RAY PARKER        G    (F    DAVID T WALKER  G   (F   ROBERT BOWLES   G   (F  ERNIE WATTS      SAX(F
  ANDY NARELL       STEEL(F    ED MARSHALL     D   (A   ROD ELLICOTT    B   (A  NORMAN LANDSBERG K  (A
  JOE CRANE         K    (A    DEXTER C PLATES B   (A   JEROME KIMSEY   B   (A  KENNETH NASH     PERC(F
  GERALD JOHNSON    B    (G    MICHAEL BAIRD   D   (G   ABRAHAM LABORIEL B  (G  RANDY BACHMAN    G  (G
  EDDIE WATKINS JNR      (G    BRYAN CUMMING   SAX (G   JEFF PORCARO    D   (G  DAVID HUNGATE    B  (G
  WADDY WACHTEL     G    (GH   DANNY KORTCHMAR G   (G   DAVID PAICH     K   (G  LENNY CASTRO     PERC(G
  JIMMY PHILLIPS    K    (G    MIKE PORCARO    B   (G   STEVE PORCARO   K   (G  JAMES NEWTON HOWARD K(G
  DAVEY JOHNSTONE   G    (G    JAI WINDING     K   (G   RICHARD PERRY   PERC(G  RICK JAEGER      D  (G
  FRED TACKETT      G    (G    HERBIE HANCOCK  K   (D   PAUL JOHNSON    B   (D  BILL SUMMERS     PERC(D
  JIM ROTHERMEL     CLAR (D    DAVID SPINOZZA  G   (H   RICK MAROTTA    D   (H  DAN DUGMORE      G  (H
  BILL PAYNE        PNO  (H    WILLIAM 'SMITTY' SMITH K(H SCOTT CHAMBERS B   (H  BOBBY GUIDOTTI   PERC(H
  NICKY HOPKINS     PNO  (H
P114A                             POISON GIRLS
                                   (A) FATAL MICROBES MEET THE POISON GIRLS(EP 1979 SMALL WONDER  UK WEENY3
                                   (B) HEX   (EP)                         1979 SMALL WONDER  UK WEENY4
P114B                             MICHEL POLNAREFF
  MICHEL POLNAREFF                  (A) MICHEL POLNAREFF        1976   ATLANTIC US SD 18153  UK K50195
  LEE RITENOUR      G    (A         (B) LIPSTICK               1976   ATLANTIC              UK K50281
  CLIFF GIVINGS     V    (A
  ANDREW GOLD       G V  (A    STEVE CROPPER   G   (A   GARY STOVALL    G   (A  FRED TACKETT     G  (A
  DONNIE DACUS      G    (A    DAVID HENSCHEL  K   (A   LEE SKLAR       B   (A  DAVID HUNGATE    B  (A
  REINY PRESS       B    (A    WILLIE WEEKS    B   (A   NIGEL OLSSON    D   (A  JIM GORDON       D  (A
  JIM KELTNER       D    (A    DAVID KEMPER    D   (A   RUSS KUNKEL     PERC(A  STAR RICHARDS    SAX(A
  ELLEN KEARNEY     V    (A    LEAH KUNKEL     V   (A   JENNIFER WARNES V   (A  VALERIE CARTER   V 'A
  BROOKS HUNNICUTT  V    (A    EUGENE GARFIN   V   (A   LEWIS FUREY     V   (A  BOBBY KING       V  (A
  TERRY EVANS       V    (A
P115                              JEAN LUC PONTY
  JEAN LUC PONTY    VLN  (ALL        (A) SUNDAY WALK            1967   MPS   0068 226             15045
  WOLFGANG DAUNER   PNO  (A          (A) SUNDAY WALK            1975   BASF  BAP 5070            20645
  NIELS HENNING PEDERSEN B(AE        (B) ELECTRIC CONNECTION    1968   PACIFIC JAZZ 20156 UK LIBERTY 83262
  DANIEL HUMAIR     D    (A          (C) EXPERIENCE             1969   PACIFIC JAZZ 20168
  GEORGE DUKE       PNO  (BCD        (C) EXPERIENCE             1971   SUNSET             UK        SLS 50232
  WILBERT LONGMIRE  G    (B          (D) KING KONG              1970   PACIFIC JAZZ 20172 UK LIBERTY 83375
  BUD SHANK         SAX  (B          (E) ASTRORAMA             1970   FAR EAST                     65016
  TONY ORTEGA       FLT  (B          (F) OPEN STRINGS           1972   MPS         68088   BASF 75 21288
  RICHARD APLAN     SAX  (B          (G) LIVE IN MONTREUX       1972   INNER CITY                 IC1003
  TONY RISCH        TPT  (B          (H) PONTY/GRAPPELLI        1973   AMERICA                    6139
  LARRY McGUIRE     TPT  (B          (J) UPON THE WINGS OF MUSIC 1975  ATLANTIC US 18138  UK       K50149
  WILLIAM PETERSON  TPT  (B          (K) IMAGINARY VOYAGE       1976   ATLANTIC US 18195  UK       K50317
  PAUL HUBINON      TPT  (B          (L) CANTELOUPE ISLAND      1976   BLUENOTE US BNLA 632 UK     BND 4018
  THURMAN GREEN     TROM (B          (M) AURORA                1977   ATLANTIC           UK        K50228
  FRANK STRONG      TROM (B          (N) ENIGMATIC OCEAN        1977   ATLANTIC           UK        K50409
  MIKE WIMBERLEY    TROM (B          (O) COSMIC MESSENGER       1979   ATLANTIC           UK        K50505
  BOB WEST          B    (B          (P) CIVILIZED EVIL         1980   ATLANTIC US 16020  UK       K50744
  PAUL HUMPHREY     D    (B
  JOHN HEARD        B    (CL   DICK BERK       D   (CL  GENE ESTES VIBES PERC (DL  BUELL NEIDLINGER B (DL
  ARTHUR TRIPP      D    (DL   IAN UNDERWOOD   SAX (DL  WILTON FELDER    B   (DL   JOHN GUERIN      D (DL
  ERNIE WATTS       SAX  (DL   FRANK ZAPPA     G   (DL  DONALD CHRISTLIEB WIND(DL  GENE CIPRIANO  WIND(DL
                                                                                   (CONTINUED)
```

JEAN LUC PONTY

(CONTINUED)								
VINCENT DE ROSA	HRNS (DL	ARTHUR MAEBE	HRNS (DL	JONATHAN MEYER	FLT(DL	HAROLD BEMKO	CELLO(DL	
MILTON THOMAS	VLA (DL	MASAHIKO SATO	PNO (E	YOSHIAKI MASUO	G (E	MOTOHIKO HINO	D (E	
JOACHIM KUHN	PNO (FG	PHILIP CATHERINE	G (FH	OLIVER JOHNSON	D (FG	PETER WARREN	B (F	
J F JENNY CLARKE	B (G	NANA	PERC (G	STEPHANE GRAPPELLI	VLN(H	MAURICE VANDER	PNO(H	
TONY BONFILS	B (H	ANDRE CECCARELLI	D (H	DARRYL STUERMER	G(KMNP	PATRICE RUSHEN	K (M	
TOM FOWLER	B (KM	NORMAN FEARRINGTON	D (M	ALLAN HOLDSWORTH	G (N	RALPHE ARMSTRONG	B (NO	
ALLAN ZAVOD	K (KNO	STEVE SMITH	D (K	MARK CRANEY	D (OP	CASEY SCHEUERELL	D (O	
PETER MAUNU	G (O	JOAQUIN LIEVANO	G (OP	CHRIS RHYNE	K (P	RANDY JACKSON	B (P	

THE POP

DAVID SWANSON	(B	(A) THE POP		1977	ARISTA	ARTY	170
ROGER PRESCOTT	(B	(B) THE POP		1978	AUTOMATIC	SA	101
JOEL MARTINEZ	D (B	(C) GO!		1979	ARISTA	SPART	1107
TIM HENDERSON	B (B						
IVAN KRAL	(	TIM McGOVERN	G (B	DAVID ROBINSON	(	STEPHEN T	(

THE POP GROUP

MARK STEWART	V (A	(A) THE POP GROUP 'Y'		1979	RADAR	UK	RAD 20
GARETH SAGER	G (A	(B) WE ARE TIME		1980	ROUGH TRADE		ROUGH 12
PAUL STEWART	D (	(C) FOR HOW MUCH LONGER MUST WE STAND	1980	ROUGH TRADE		
BRUCE SMITH	D (A						
SIMON UNDERWOOD	B (A	JOHN WADDINGTON	G (A				

POPOL ACE

ARNE SCHULZE	G (	(A) POPOL ACE	1973	POLYDOR	2480	270
THOR ANDREASSEN	D (	(B) STOLEN FROM TIME	1975	POLYDOR	2480	332
TERJE METHI	G (	(C) CURLY SOUNDS	1978	POLYDOR	2483	498
PETE KNUDSEN	G K SYN (					
JOHN TEIGEN	V (					

POPOL VUH

FLORIAN FRICKE	PNO (	DISCOVER COSMIC (DBL)	1973	OHR	94011920	
DANIEL FISCHELSCHER	G (	AFFENSTUNDE	1971	LIBERTY	83460	
TED DE JONG	PERC (	DAS HOHENLIED SALOMOS	1975	UA	UAS 29781	
BOB ELISCU	OBOE (	LETZTETAGE NACHTE	1976	UA	UAS 29916	
MATTIAS V TIPPELSKIRCH	FLT(	SELIGPREISUNG	1974	KOSMISCHE 58009 ARON	EU 093	
		COEUR DE VERRE	1977	EGG	900 536	
ALOIS GROMER	SITAR(	HEART OF GLASS (HERZ AUS GLAS)	1977	BRAIN	0060 079	
		IN DEN GARTEN PHARAOS	1972	BASF	21276 9	
		HOSIANNA MANTRA	1973	BASF	29143 1	
		EINSJAGER AND SIEBENJAGER	1975	KOSMISCHE	58009	
		OSFERATU	1979	EGG		
		BRUEDER DES SCHATTENS SOEHNE DES LICHTS	78	BRAIN	0060 167	
		SEI STILLE	1981	INNOVATIVE COMMUNICATION 80007		

POTTER ST CLOUD

DAVE POTTER	(A	(A) POTTER ST CLOUD	19	MEDIARTS	41 7
ENDLE ST CLOUD	(A				
JAMES HARRELL	(A				

POUSSETTE DART BAND

JOHN POUSSETTE DART	G (ABC	(A) POUSSETTE DART	1976	CAPITOL	EST 11507	
JOHN CURTIS	G (ABC	(B) AMNESIA	1977	CAPITOL	EST 11608	
JOHN TROY	B (CB	(C) 3	1978	CAPITOL	SW 11781	
MICHAEL DAWE	D (C					
NORMAN PRIDE	PERC (C	DAVE APPELL STRINGS (C	HANK MEDRESS	PERC (C	DAVID LASLEY	V (C
STAN SCHWARTZ	K (C	ARNOLD McCULLER V (C				

POWDER BLUES BAND

TOM LAVIN	G V (A	(A) POWDER BLUES	1980	RCA	PL 10365	
JACK LAVIN	B V (A					
WILL MAC CALDER	K V (A	DURIS MAXWELL	D (A	DAVE WOODWARD	SAX V(A WAYNE KOZAK	SAX (A
GORD BERTRAM	SAX (A	MARK HASSELBACH	TPT (A			

COZY POWELL

COZY POWELL	D (A	(A) OVER THE TOP	1979	ARIOLA	ARL 5038
JACK BRUCE	B (A				
DON AIREY	K (A				
GARY MOORE	G (A	CLEM CLEMPSON G (A MAX MIDDLETON	K (A BERNIE MARSDEN	G (A

ROGER POWELL

ROGER POWELL	K (A	(A) AIR POCKET	1980	BEARSVILLE	ILPS 9607

DUFFY POWER

DUFFY POWER	V (ALL	(A) INNOVATIONS	1971	TRANSATLANTIC	TRA229
		(B) DUFFY POWER	1973	SPARK	SRLM 2005
		(C) DUFFY POWER	1973	GSF	GS 502
		(D) POWERHOUSE	1976	BUK	BULP2110

POWERHOUSE

GRAHAM FORBES	G (	ALEX O'DONNELL	(ALISTAIR BRADSHAW	BAIN B(IAN McDONALD	D (

POWERHOUSE FOUR

ERIC CLAPTON	G	STEVE WINWOOD	K V (PAUL JONES	V HCA(JACK BRUCE	B V (

PRAGVEC

	(A) NO COWBOYS	1980	5REC	UK

ANDY PRATT

ANDY PRATT	V PNO(ALL	(A) RECORDS ARE LIKE LIFE	1969	POLYDOR UK	2489 003	
ANDY MENDELSON	K (D	(B) ANDY PRATT	1973	EPIC US 31722	UK 65646	
GARY LINK	B V (D	(C) RESOLUTION	1976	NEMPEROR US NE438	UK K50279	
RICK SCHLOSSER	D (D	(D) SHIVER IN THE NIGHT	1977	NEMPEROR US NE443	UK K50386	
MARK DOYLE	G V (D					
LUTHER VANDROSS	V (D	G DIANE SUMLER V (D	DAVID LASLEY	V (D	MICHAEL BRECKER	SAX (D
LOUIS MARINI	SAX (D	LEWIS DEL GATTO SAX (D	RANDY BRECKER	TPT (D	RUBENS BASSINI	PERC(D
ANDY NEWMARK	D (D	HUGH McDONALD B (D	GENE ORLOFF	STRINGS (D		

PRELUDE

BRIAN HUME	G V (ABCDE			(A) HOW LONG IS FOREVER		1973	DAWN	UK		DNLS 3052
IAN VARDY	G V (ABCDE			(B) AFTER THE GOLDRUSH		1974	ISLAND			ILPS 9282
IRENE HUME	V PERC(ABCDE			(C) DUTCH COURAGE		1974	DAWN	UK		DNLS 3061
TONY HYMAS	K (E			(D) OWLCREEK INCIDENT		1975	DAWN DNLH 3	PYE		12120
HUGH BURNS	G (E			(E) BACK INTO THE LIGHT		1976	PYE			NSPL19448
DAVE MATTACKS	D (E									
DAVE PEACOCK	B (A	ISAAC GUILLORY	B K G(D	MIKE DRISCOLL	D (D	ALAN CARNEY	B (E			
JIM HORNSBY	BANJO(D	PATRICE LEMOINE	K (D	ROGER RETTIG	G STEEL (D	LINDA CURTIS	PERC (D			
STEVE GREGORY	SAX (D	ROD CLEMENTS	B (D	PICK WITHERS	D (D					

ELVIS PRESLEY

ELVIS PRESLEY	G V (ALL					
BILL BLACK	B	SCOTTY MOORE	G	D J FONTANA	D	FLOYD CRAMER	PNO
JAMES BURTON	G	HANK GARLAND	G	CHET ATKINS	G	KENNY BURRELL	G
HAL BLAINE	D	JORDANAIRES	V	BUDDY HARMON	D	RONNIE TUTT	D
JOHN WILKINSON	G	JERRY SCHEFF	B	GLEN D HARDIN	K	SONNY BROWN	PNO
DAVID BRIGGS CLAR	K	CHARLIE HODGES	G V	BOOTS RANDOLPH	SAX	MARVIN HUGHES	PNO
SHORTY LONG	PNO	NEIL MATTHEWS	SAX	HUGH JARRETT	V	HOYT HAWKINS	V
DUDLEY BROOKS	PNO	MIKE STOLLER	PNO	MILLIE KIRKHAM	V	KITTY WHITE	V
H J TRIMBRELL	G	BOB MOORE	B	HAROLD BRADLEY	G	CHIP YOUNG	G
PETE DRAKE	G	TEDDY TEDESCO	G	DON RANDI	K	LARRY KNECHTEL	B
MIKE DEASY	G	TOMMY COGBILL	B G	BOBBY EMMONS	PNO	GLEN SPREEN	ORG
MIKE LEECH	B	HENRY SLAUGHTER	ORG	CHARLIE McCOY	HCA	GRADY MARTIN	G
PETE HALLIN	K	JERRY REED	G	DARLENE LOVE	V	FANITA JAMES	V
JEAN KING	V	JEANNIE GREEN	V	LARRY MUHOBERAC	PNO	RON TUTT	D
NORBERT PUTNAM	B	JERRY CARRIGAN	D	TEMPLE RISER	V	KEN BUTTREY	D
EMORY GORDY	B	KATH WESTMORELAND	V	J D SUMNER	V	STAMPS	V
RONNIE MILSAP	V	ED LOGAN	HRNS	MARY HOLLADAY	V	GINGER HOLLADAY	V
BOB TAYLOR	HRNS	WAYNE JACKSON	HRNS	GENE CHRISMAN	V	JUBILEE FOUR	V
CAROLE LOMBARD QUARTET		BOB WOOD	PNO	REGGIE YOUNG	G	SANDY POSEY	V
JOHN CHRISTOPHER	G					

			MONO UK	STER UK	MONO US	STER US
ELVIS (ROCK'N'ROLL No1)	HMV	1956	CLP 1093			
" " " "	RCA				LPM 1254	LSP 1254
ELVIS (ROCK'N'ROLL No2)	HMV	1956	CLP 1105			
" " " "	RCA	1956	RD 7528	SF 7526	LPM 1382	LSP 1382
THE BEST OF ELVIS	HMV	1956	DLP 1159			
LOVING YOU	RCA	1957	RC 24001		LPM 1515	LSP 1515
LOVING YOU RI 12"	RCA	1977		PLG 2358		
ELVIS CHRISTMAS ALBUM	RCA	1957	RD 27052		LOC 1035	
" " " "	RCA	195			LPM 1951	LSP 1951
" " " "	CAMDEN	19	INT 1126		CAS 2428	
KING CREOLE	RCA	1958	RD 27088	SF 8231	LPM 1884	LSP 1884
GOLDEN RECORDS VOL 1	RCA	1958	RD 16069	SF 8129	LPM 1707	LSP 1707
ELVIS FOR LP FANS ONLY	RCA	1959	RD 27120	SF 8378	LPM 1990	LSP 1990
A DATE WITH ELVIS	RCA	1959	RD 27128		LPM 2011	LSP 2011
ELVIS GOLDEN RECORDS VOL 2	RCA	1959	RD 27159	SF 8151	LPM 2075	LSP 2075
ELVIS IS BACK	RCA	1960	RD 27171	SF 5060	LPM 2231	LSP 2231
G I BLUES	RCA	1960	RD 27192	SF 5078	LPM 2256	LSP 2256
HIS HAND IN MINE	RCA	1960	RD 27211	SF 5094	LPM 2328	LSP 2328
" " "	RCA RI	19		SF 8207		
SOMETHING FOR EVERYBODY	RCA	1961	RD 27244	SF 5106	LPM 2370	LSP 2370
BLUE HAWAII	RCA	1961	RD 27238	SF 5115	LPM 2426	LSP 2426
" "	RCA RI	19		SF 8145		
POT LUCK	RCA	1962	RD 27265	SF 5135	LPM 2523	LSP 2523
GIRLS GIRLS GIRLS	RCA	1963	RD 7534	SF 7534	LPM 2621	LSP 2621
IT HAPPENED AT THE WORLD FAIR	RCA	1963	RD 7565	SF 7565	LPM 2697	LSP 2697
" " " " "	RCA RI	19		1025		APLI2568
FUN IN ACAPULCO	RCA	1963	RD 7609	SF 7609	LPM 2756	LSP 2756
GOLDEN RECORDS VOL 3	RCA	1964	RD 7630	sf 7630	LPM 2765	LSP 2765
KISSIN COUSINS	RCA	1964	RD 7645	SF 7645	LPM 2894	LSP 2894
GIRL HAPPY	RCA	1965	RD 7714	SF 7714	LPM 3338	LSP 3338
FLAMING STAR	RCA	1965	RD 7723		PRS 279	
" "	RCA	19		INT 1017		
" "	CAMDEN			CAS 2304		
ELVIS FOR EVERYONE	RCA	1965	RD 7751	SF 7751	LPM 2450	LSP 3450
" " "	RCA	19		SF 8232		
HARUM SCARUM	RCA	1965			LPM 3468	LSP 3468
HAREM HOLIDAY	RCA	1965	RD 7767	SF 7767		
HAREM HOLIDAY	RCA	19		46 1022		
FRANKIE & JOHNNY	RCA	1966	RD 7793	SF 7793	LPM 3553	LSP 3553
" " "	RCA	19		46 1024		ACL 7007
" " "	RCA	19				APLI2559
PARADISE HAWAIIAN STYLE	RCA	1966	RD 7810	SF 7810	LPM 3643	LSP 3643
CALIFORNIA HOLIDAY	RCA	1966	RD 7820	SF 7820		
" " "	RCA	19		46 1020		
SPIN OUT	RCA	1966			LPM 3702	LSP 3702
" "	RCA	197				APLI2560
HOW GREAT THOU ART	RCA	1967	RD 7867	SF 7867	LPM 3758	LSP 3758
" " " "	RCA	19		SF 8206		
DOUBLE TROUBLE	RCA	1967	RD 7892	SF 7892	LPM 3787	LSP 3787
" " "	RCA	196				AFLI2564
CLAMBAKE	RCA	1967	RD 7917	SF 7917	LPM 3893	LSP 3893
" "	RCA	19		46 1021		APLI2568
GOLDEN RECORDS VOL 4	RCA	1968	RD 7924	SF 7924	LPM 3921	LSP 3921
SPEEDWAY	RCA	1968	RD 7957	SF 7957	LPM 3989	LSP 3989
NBC TV SPECIAL	RCA	1968	RD 8011		LSP 4088	
FROM ELVIS IN MEMPHIS	RCA	1969	RD 8029	SF 8029		LSP 4155
FROM MEMPHIS TO VEGAS	RCA	1970		SF 8080		LSP 6020

(CONTINUED)

			MONO UK	STER UK	MONO US	STER US
ON STAGE FEB 1970	RCA	1970		SF 8128		LSP 4362
WORLDWIDE 50 GOLD HITS VOL 1	RCA	1970	LPM 6401		LPM 6401	
IN PERSON AT THE INTERNATIONAL	RCA	1970				LSP 4428
BACK IN MEMPHIS	RCA	1970				LSP 4429
LETS BE FRIENDS	RCA INT	1970		INT 1103		
" " "	CAMDEN	1970				CAS 2408
ALMOST IN LOVE	RCA INT	1970		INT 1023		
" " "	CAMDEN	1970				CAS 2440
THATS THE WAY IT IS	RCA	1971		SF 8162		LSP 4445
ELVIS COUNTRY I'M 10,000 YEARS OLD	RCA	1971		SF 8172		LSP 4460
LOVE LETTERS FROM ELVIS	RCA	1971		SF 8202		LSP 4530
50 GOLD AWARD (THE OTHER SIDES)	RCA	1971	LPM 6402		LPM 6402	
C'MON EVERYBODY	RCA INT	1971		INT 1280		
" " "	CAMDEN	1971				CAS 2518
I GOT LUCKY	RCA INT	1971		INT 1322		CAS 2533
" "	CAMDEN	1971		CDS 1154		CAS 2611
YOU'LL NEVER WALK ALONE	CAMDEN	1971		CMD 1088		CAS 2472
WONDERFUL WORLD OF CHRISTMAS	RCA	1971		SF 8221		LSP 4579
" " " "	RCA	197				ANI 1936
ELVIS NOW	RCA	1972		SF 8266		LSP 4671
LIVE AT MADISON SQUARE GARDENS	RCA	1972		SF 8296		LSP 4776
HE TOUCHED ME	RCA	1972		SF 8275		LSP 4690
HITS FROM THE MOVIES	CAMDEN	1972		CDS 1110		CAS 2567
ALOHA FROM HAWAII	RCA	1973		DPS 2040		VPSX6089
ELVIS	RCA	1973		PL 10283		APL 10283
BURNING LOVE	RCA INT	1973		INT 1414		
" "	CAMDEN	1973				CAS 2595
RAISED ON ROCK	RCA	1973		PL 10388		APL 10388
SEPARATE WAYS	CAMDEN	1973		CDS 1118		CAS 2611
LEGENDARY PERFORMER 1	RCA	1974		LP 10341		CPL 10341
GOOD TIMES	RCA	1974		PL 10475		APL 10475
LIVE ON STAGE IN MEMPHIS	RCA	1974		PL 10606		APL 10606
HAVING FUN ON STAGE	RCA	1974		PM 10828		AFM 10818
40 GREATEST HITS	ARCADE	1975		ADEP 12		
HITS OF THE 70s	RCA	1974		FL 17527		
PROMISED LAND	RCA	1974		PL 10873		APL 10873
PURE GOLD	RCA	1975				ANL 10971
TODAY	RCA	1975		PL 11039		APL 11039
LEGENDARY PERFORMER VOL 2	RCA	1975				CLP 11349
US MALE	CAMDEN	1974		CDS 1150		
PICTURES OF ELVIS	RCA	1975		HY 1023		
DOUBLE DYNAMITE	PICKWICK	1975				DL 25001
THE SUN COLLECTION	RCA	1975		HY 1001		
THE SUN SESSIONS	RCA	1976		PM 11675		APL 11675
FROM ELVIS PRESLEY BOULEVARD	RCA	1976		PL 11506		APL 11506
WELCOME TO MY WORLD	RCA	1976		PL 12274		APL 12274
MOODY BLUE	RCA	1977		PL 12428		APL 12428
THE SUN YEARS	CHARLY	1977		SUN 1001		
IN DEMAND	RCA	1977		PL 42003		
THE '56 SESSIONS	RCA	1978		PL 42101		
40 GREATEST HITS	RCA	1978		PL 42691		
ELVIS TAPES	CHISWICK /ACE	197		RED 1		
ELVIS PRESLEY COLLECTION	PICKWICK	1978		PDA 042		
HE WALKS BESIDE ME	RCA	1978		PL 12772		APL 12772
TV SPECIAL	RCA	1978		PL 42370		
LEGENDARY PERFORMER VOL 3	RCA	1978		PL 13082		
RETURN TO SENDER	PICKWICK	19		CDS 1200		
ELVIS	PICKWICK	19		CDS 1201		
WONDERFUL WORLD	PICKWICK	19		PDA 073		
THE '56 SESSIONS VOL 2	RCA	1979		PL 42102		
ELVIS AARON PRESLEY (8 RECORD SET)	RCA	1980		CPL 83699		
INSPIRATION	K TEL	1980		NE 1101		
GUITAR MAN	RCA	1980		RCALP5010		

OTHER RELEASES

PORTRAIT IN MUSIC	RCA	1975	SRS 558
SOLID ROCKS	RCA	1975	RJS27120
GOLD THITY	RCA	1975	6176 77
GOOD ROCKIN' TONIGHT 10"	RCA	19	130 252
ELVIS GOLDEN RECORDS 10"	RCA	19	HP 50X
PANEL DELUXE	RCA	19	9201
ON STAGE FEB 1970	RCA	19	R4P 5009
GREAT HITS	RCA	19	SR1 9062
CHRISTMAS ALBUM	RCA	19	5028
GIRL HAPPY	RCA	19	5436
GOLDEN BOY	HORZU	19	SHZT521
ROCKIN' ON VOL 1	RCA	19	135
ROCKIN' ON VOL 2	RCA	19	141
MAGICAL ROCKIN' SOUND	JUBILEE	19	MLP1956
BLUE CHRISTMAS	RCA	19	KNL17047
ELVIS PRESLEY 10"	RCA	19	CML 3009
ELVIS PRESLEY	IMPACT	1978	6886007
GREATEST HITS (7 RECORD SET)	RCA	19	GELV 6A

P125A   PRESSURE   P125A

				(A) PRESSURE			1979	MCA		UK	MCF 3055	
MELVIN ROBINSON	G	(A										
BARNABY FINCH	K	(A										
BOBBY VEGAS		(A	PAT KELLY		G V	(A	ART RODRIGUEZ	D	(A	RONNIE LAWS SAX V	(A	
JOHNNY LAWS	V	(A	SAMUEL MOORE		V	(A	REGGIE ALEXANDER	V	(A	SANDRA	V	(A

BILLY PRESTON

BILLY PRESTON	K V	(ALL	(A) THE WILDEST ORGAN IN TOWN	1966	CAPITOL			ST 2532		
OLLIE BROWN	D	(P	(B) MOST EXCITING ORGAN EVER	1967	SUE	UK	ILP 935	US V	JAY1123	
KEN BURKE	B	(P	(B) MOST EXCITING ORGAN EVER	196	JOY	UK	JOYS 112			
TRUMAN THOMAS	K	(P	(C) GOSPEL IN MY SOUL	19	JOY	UK	JOYS 174			
MANUEL KELLOUGH	D	(HKLP	(D) THE APPLE OF THEIR EYE	1969	PRESIDENT			PTLS1034		
BOBBY WATSON	B	(K	(E) THAT'S THE WAY GOD PLANNED IT	1969	APPLE	UK	SAPCOR 9	US	ST 3359	
TONY MAIDEN	G	(KP	(F) ENCOURAGING WORDS	1969	APPLE	UK	SAPCOR14	US	ST 3370	
JOE WALSH	G	(K	(G) I WROTE A SIMPLE SONG	1971	A&M	UK	AMLH6350'	US	3507	
ALBERT PERKINS	BANJ	(K	(H) MUSIC IS MY LIFE	1972	A&M	UK	AMLS63516	US	3516	
KENNETH LUPPER	K	(KL	(J) EVERYBODY LIKES SOME KIND OF MUSIC	1973	A&M	UK	AMLH63526	US	3526	
HUBERT HEARD	K	(HKL	(K) THE KIDS & ME	1974	A&M	UK	AMLH63645	US	3645	
ALVIN TAYLOR	D	(P	(L) LIVE EUROPEAN TOUR	1974	A&M	UK	AMLH68265	US	3657	
WELTON GITE	B	(P	(M) ITS MY PLEASURE	1975	A&M	UK	AMLH64532	US	4532	
WYNELL MONTGOMERY	SAX	(P	(N) BILLY PRESTON	1976	A&M	UK	AMLH64587	US	4587	
EUGENE HENDERSON	G	(P	(O) BILLY'S BAG	1976	DJM	UK	DJB 26082			
MICHAEL McGLOIRY	G	(P	(P) WHOLE NEW THING	1977	A&M	UK	AMLH64656	US	4656	
CHARLES GARNETT	TPT	(GP	( ) THE GENIUS OF	1975	SPRINGBOARD		US	4034		
KENNETH L MOORE	K	(P	( ) SIXTEEN YEAR OLD SOUL	19						
BOBBYE HALL	PERC	(P	( ) SOUL'D OUT	1977	GNP		US	2 2071		
ANGELO RICHARDS	TPT	(P	( ) GREAZEE SOUL	1969	SOUL CITY			SCM 002		
GLORIA JONES	V	(P	( ) ORGAN TRANSPLANT	19	PICKWICK			SPC 3315		
GWEN GUTHRIE	V	(H	(Q) BEHOLD	197	MYRRH			MYR 1070		
SYREETA WRIGHT	V	(R	(R) & SYREETA	1979	MOTOWN		UK	STML12107		
JESSE KIRKLAND	V	(G	(S) LATE AT NIGHT	1979	MOTOWN		UK	STML12116		
ANDRE CROUCH	V	(P								

FRANKIE SPRING	V	(P	CLYDIE KING	V	(GHP	JOE GREEN	V	(P	VANETTA FIELDS	V	(GH
OMA DRAKE	V	(H	TOM SCOTT	HRNS	(H	JIM HORN	HRNS	(H	GEORGE BOHANON	HRN(H
BUCK MONARI	HRNS	(H	PAUL HUBINON	HRNS	(H	LOUIS JOHNSON	B	(H	GEORGE JOHNSON	G	(H
DAVID T WALKER	G	(G	GEORGE HARRISON	G	(G	MERRY CLAYTON	V	(G	PATRICE HOLLOWAY	V	(G
MYRNA MATTHEWS	V	(G	KING ERRISSON	CONGA	(G	ROCKY PEOPLES	SAX	(G	SHERRILL ATWOOD	V	(G
EUGENE BRYANT	V	(G	DOUG GIBBS	V	(G	DUANE ROGERS	V	(G		

PRETENDERS

CHRIS HYNDE	G V	(A	(A) PRETENDERS	1979	REAL	UK	RAL 3
PETE FARNDON	B V	(A					
MARTIN CHAMBERS	D V	(A	JAMES HONEYMAN-SCOTT G K V(A CHRIS THOMAS K (A				

PRETTY THINGS

PHIL MAY	B G V	(ALL	(A) THE PRETTY THINGS	1965	FONTANA	US 67544	UK	TL5239
DICK TAYLOR	B G V	(ABCDEFGHV	(A) THE PRETTY THINGS	1967	WING		RI UK	WL1167
BRIAN PENDLETON	G	(AB	(B) GET THE PICTURE	1965	FONTANA		UK	TL5280
JOHN STAX	B	(AB	(B) WE WANT YOUR LOVE	1967	FONTANA			858039
PETE TOLSON	G B	(1KLM	(C) EMOTIONS	1967	FONTANA	UK 13140	UK	TL5425
VIV PRINCE	D	(AB	(D) ELECTRIC BANANA	1967	DE WOLF			3040
JOHN POVEY PERC V K	(1CDEFHJKLMV		(E) MORE ELECTRIC BANANA	1968	DE WOLF			3069
SKIP ALLEN	D V	(1CJKLMV	(F) EVEN MORE ELECTRIC BANANA	1969	DE WOLF			3284
JACK GREEN	G B V	(LM	(G) HOT LICKS	1970	DE WOLF			3284
GORDON EDWARD	V G B K	(LM	(H) S F SORROW	1968	COLUMBIA	UK		SCX 6306
WALLY ALLEN	B V	(CH	(H) S F SORROW	1969	RARE EARTH		US	506
JOHN ADLER (TWINK)	D	(CH	(H) S F SORROW	1973	ELECTROLA			062 04004
STUART BROOKS	B	(K1	(J) PARACHUTE	1970	HARVEST	UK		SHVL 774
WALLY WALLER	B G V	(V	(J) PARACHUTE	1970	RARE EARTH		US	515
VICTOR UNITT	G	(J	(HJ) S F SORROW/ PARACHUTE	1975	HARVEST	UK		SHDW 406
			(K) FREEWAY MADNESS	1973	W B	US 2680	UK	K46190
			(L) SILK TORPEDO	1974	SWANSONG	US 8411	UK	SSK 59400
			(M) SAVAGE EYE	1975	SWANSONG	US 8414	UK	SSL 59401
(1) 1973 LIVE GIG			(N) GREATEST HITS	1975	PHILIPS			6625 015
			(O) ATTENTION	1975	VERTIGO		UK	6438 202
			(O) ATTENTION	1975	FONTANA			6438 059
			(P) VINTAGE YEARS	1976	SIRE		US	SASH37132
			(Q) THE SINGLES	1977	HARVEST		UK	SHSM 2022
			(R) LIVE	1978	JADE		US	
			(S) REAL PRETTY	197	RARE EARTH		US	R7 549
			(T) ELECTRIC BANANA	1979	BUTT		NOTT	001
			(U) ELECTRIC BANANA	1980	BUTT		NOTT	003
			(V) CROSS TALK	1980	WB		UK	K56842
			(EP) PRETTY THINGS	1964	FONTANA		UK	TE 17434
			(EP) RAINING IN MY HEART	1965	FONTANA		UK	TE 17442
			(EP) ON FILM	1966	FONTANA		UK	TE 17472
			(EP) PRETTY THINGS	1965	WING			WL1167
			(EP) PRETTY THINGS	1965	FONTANA		UK	TL 17434
			(EP) RAINING IN MY HEART	1965	FONTANA		UK	TL 17442
			(EP) ON FILM	1966	FONTANA		UK	TE 17472

DORY PREVIN

DORY PREVIN	G V.	(ALL	(A) MYTHICAL KINGS & IGUANAS	1972	UA	US 4110	UK	UAG 29186
PETER JAMESON	G	(AC	(B) REFLECTIONS IN A MUD PUDDLE	1972	UA		UK	UAG 29346
DAVID COHEN	G	(ACD	(C) MARY C BROWN	1972	UA	US 5657	UK	UAG 29435
LAURINDO ALMEIDA	G	(C	(D) ON MY WAY TO WHERE	1973	UA		UK	UAG 29176
BUDDY COLLETTE	WIND	(D	(D) ON MY WAY TO WHERE	1976	SUNSET RI		UK	SLS 50385
BRYAN GAROFALO	B	(C	(E) LIVE AT CARNEGIE HALL	1973	UA	US 1082	UK	UAD 60043
JOE OSBORN	B	(AC	(F) DORY PREVIN	1974	WB	US 5336	UK	K56066
REINHOLD PRESS	B	(C	(G) WERE CHILDREN OF COINCIDENCE	1976	WB	US 2908	UK	K56213
PEGGY SANDVIG	K	(C	(H) ONE AM PHONE CALLS	1977	UA		UK	UAS 30070
TOM KEENE	K	(AC						

MICHAEL LANG	K	(CD	EARL PALMER	D	(C	RON TUTT	D	(ACD	BRIAN DAVIES	G (A
JOHN P GUERIN	D	(C	CLARK MAFFITT	G	(A	LAWRENCE W KNECHTEL	K	(AD	LOUIE SHELTON	G (A
HAMILTON WESLEY WATT	G	(A	DENNY BROOKS	V	(A	MICHAEL McGINNIS	V	(A	PETER MORSE	V (A
B G DAVIES	V	(A	FLOYD C MAFFITT	V	(A	JUDY MAYHAN	V	(A	WEST VENET	V (A
D VERONICA LANGDEN	V	(A	JIMMY BOND		(D	JOHN WILKIN	G	(D	BERNIE LEADON	G (D
CAROL KAYE	B	(D	JOE SAMPLE	K	(D	FRANK CAPP	PERC	(D	DENNIS BUDIMIR	G (D
HERB ELLIS		(D	DON RANDI	K	(D	JOHN MORELL	G	(D	TOM TEDESCO	G (D

JIM PRICE

JIM PRICE	V K HRNS	(AB	(A) KIDS NOWADAYS AINT GOT NO SHAME	1971 A&M	UK	AMLS64321
JOHN URIBE	G V	(AB	(B) SHINDEGOS TRAVELLING ORCHESTRA	1974 DUNHILL	US	50126
DAVE FARRELL	B	(B	(B) SHINDEGOS TRAVELLING ORCHESTRA	1974 CBS	UK	65245
KLAUS VOORMANN	B	(A				
JIM KELTNER	D	(A BOBBY KEYS	SAX (AB NICKY HOPKINS	K (A DON PONCHER D	(B	

ALAN PRICE

ALAN PRICE	K V	(ALL	(A) THE PRICE TO PLAY	1966 DECCA	UK	LK4839
CLIVE BURROWS D B WIND	(		(B) A PRICE ON HIS HEAD	1967 DECCA	UK	LK4907
STEVE GREGORY	WIND	(J	(C) THE AMAZING (EP)	1967 DECCA	UK	8670
JOHN WALTERS	HRNS	(	(D) PRICE IS RIGHT	1968 PARROT	US	PAS 71018
ROD 'BOOTS'SLADE	B	(1	(E) THE WORLD OF ALAN PRICE	1970 DECCA	UK	SPA 77
LITTLE ROY	WIND	(	(F) FAME & PRICE	1971 CBS	UK	64392
RICK MORCOMBE	G V	(L	(G) O LUCKY MAN	1973 WB US 2710 UK		K46227
THEODORE THUNDER	B V	(L	(H) BETWEEN YESTERDAY & TODAY	1974 WB	UK	K56032
JOHN GORDON	B V	(L	(J) METROPOLITAN MAN	1975 POLYDOR	UK	2442 133
COLIN GREEN	G B	(HJ	(K) PERFORMING PRICE	1975 POLYDOR	UK	2683 062
DAVE MARKEE	B	(H	(L) SHOUTS ACROSS THE STREET	1976 POLYDOR	UK	2383 410
GRAHAM SMITH	HCA	(J	(M) RAINBOWS END	1977 JET	UK	UAG 30133
LYN DOBSON	WIND	(1	(N) ENGLAND MY ENGLAND	1978 JET	JET	DL 300
HARRY BECKETT	TPT	(1	(O) ALAN PRICE	1978 JET US LA809G UK		JETLP 207
BERNIE GEORGE	WIND	(1	(P) FOCUS ON	1979 DECCA	UK	FOS 65/6
HUGHIE FLINT	D	(1	(1) FLOATING BAND			
DEREK WADSWORTH	HRNS	(1				
JOHN MUMFORD	HRNS	(1 WILLY PAINE	(1 DENIS ANDRE	(1 TONY CARR	D PERC(J	
BARRY MORGAN	D	(J ALAN PARKER	G (J PAUL KEOGH	G (J DAVE MARKEE	B(J	
CLIVE THACKER	D	(J KENNY BAKER	TPT (J KENNY WHEELER	TPT (J ALAN DOWNEY	TPT(J	
CHRIS PYNE	TROM	(J CLIFF HARDY	TROM (J BILL GELDARD	TROM (J PETER CIVIL	HRNS(J	
FRED CROSSMAN	HRNS	(J VIC ASH	WIND (J			

LLOYD PRICE

LLOYD PRICE	V	(ALL	A B C COLLECTION	19 ABC	US	AC 30006
			BEST OF	1970 STARLINE	UK	SRS 5025
			COME TO ME	19 GUEST STAR	US	1910
			COOKIN'	19 ABC	US	382
			EXCITING LLOYD PRICE	19 ABC	US	277
			FANTASTIC	19 ABC	US	346
			LLOYD PRICE	19 SPECIALTY US 2105 UK		SNTF5007
			LLOYD AT ANY PRICE	19 JOY	UK	JOYS 179
			LLOYD SWINGS FOR SAMMY	19 MONUMENT	US	8032
			LLOYD PRICE ORCHESTRA	19 DOUBLE	US	8301
			MR PERSONALITY	19 ABC	US	297
			MR PERSONALITY SINGS THE BLUES	19 ABC	US	315
			MR PERSONALITYS BIG 15	19 ABC	US	324
			MISTY	19 DOUBLE	US	8308
			MISTY	1976 DJM	UK	DJB26074
			MISTY	19 UPFRONT	US	UPF 126
			MR RHYTHM & BLUES	19 GRAND PRIX	US	422
			NOW	19 TURNTABLE	US	5001
			NOW	19 JAD	US	1002
			ROCK'N'ROLL CLASSICS	1973 PATHE	FR 052	91361
			SINGS THE MILLIONS SELLERS	19 ABC	US	366
			SIXTEEN GREATEST HITS	19 ABC	US	AC 30006
			SIXTEEN GREATEST HITS	19 STRIP	US	TOP16/5
			STAGGER LEE	19 JOY	UK	JOY 202
			THIS IS MY BAND	19 DOUBLE	US	2301

PRINCE BUSTER

PRINCE BUSTER	V	(ALL	FABULOUS GREATEST HITS	19 MELODISC		M 51
			SISTERS BIG STUFF	19 MELODISC		M12156
			BIG 5	19 MELODISC		M12157
			WRECK A PUM PUM	19 BLUE BEAT		BBLP 821
			TEN COMMANDMENTS	19 RCA	US	LSP 3792
			SHE WAS A ROUGH RIDER	1978 BLUE BEAT		BBLP 820

PRINCE FAR I

PRINCE FAR I	V PERC(ALL		(A) MESSAGE FROM THE KING	1978 FRONT LINE	UK	FL 1013
CHINNAAS MELCHEZ INICK G(BE			(B) LONG LIFE	1978 FRONT LINE	UK	FL 1021
BINGY BUNNY	G	(BDF	(C) CRY TUFF DUB ENCOUNTER	1978 FRONT LINE	UK	
BOBBY KALPHAT	K	(BDF	(D) FREE FROM SIN	1979 TROJAN	UK	TRLS 125
TARZAN	K	(B	(E) DUB TO AFRICA	1979 HIT & RUN		APLP 9006
SNAPPY	K	(BD	(F) SHOWCASE	1979 PRE		PREFIX 3
ROBBIE SHAKESPEARE B		(B	(G) CRY TUFF DUB ENCOUNTER II	1979 FRONT LINE	UK	FL 4002
GEORGE FULLWOOD	B	(B	(H) CRY TOUGH DUB ENCOUNTER III	1980 DADDY COOL		
SLY DUNBAR	D	(B				
SANTA	D	(B BONGO HERMAN	PERC (BD DIRTY HARRY	HRNS (B DON DRUMMOND	HRNS (B	
STYLE SCOTT	D	(DEF ERROL HOLT	B (DEF SOWELL	G VLN(DEF EARL CHINNA SMITH	G (D	
DEADLEY HEADLEY	HRNS	(D RAS MILLINER	PERC (D SCULLY	PERC (F GLADSTONE ANDERSON	K (F	
ROY JOHNSTON KONGO PERC(F						

PRINCE HAMMER

PRINCE HAMMER		(A	(A) BIBLE	1978 FRONT LINE	UK	FL 1004
ERROL NELSON	K	(A				
FRANKLIN WAUL	K	(A ERIC LAMONT	K (A BO PE	G (A SLY DUNBAR	D (A	
LLOYD PARKS	B	(A ROBBIE SHAKESPEARE B	(A STICKY	PERC (A TOMMY McCOOK	HRNS(A	
VIN GORDON	HRNS	(A HERMAN MARQUIS	HRNS (A			

PRINCE JAMMY

		(A) KAMIKAZI DUB	1979 TROJAN	UK	TRLS 174

PRINCE MOHAMMED

PRINCE MOHAMMED	(A	(A) PEOPLE ARE YOU READY	1978 BALLISTIC	UK	UAS30192

PRINCIPAL EDWARDS MAGIC THEATRE

BELINDA BOURQUIN	K VLN V(ABC		(A) SOUNDTRACK			1969 DANDELION	US D9103	UK S63752
DAVID JONES	PERC (ABC		(B) THE ASMOTO RUNNING BAND			1971 DANDELION		UK DAN8002
JEREMY ENSOR	B (AB		(C) ROUND ONE			1973 DERAM		UK SML1108
MARTIN STELLMAN	V (AB							
ROGER SWALLOW	D (B	JOHN HILL	DANCE	(A	CHRIS RUNCIMAN	LIGHTS(A	ROOT CARTWRIGHT	G (ABC
LESLIE ADEY	LIGHTS (A	MONICA NETTLES	V (A	VIVIENNE McAULIFFE	V (AB	DAVID WEEKS	(A
GILLIAN HADLEY	(	EVA DARLOW	DANCE (A	HARRY HOUSMAN	STAGE (A	LYN EDWARDS	PERC(A
RICHARD JONES	B V (C	NICK PALLETT	G V (C	GEOFF NICHOLS	D (C		

JOHN PRINE

JOHN PRINE	G V (ALL	(A) JOHN PRINE	1972 ATLANTIC	US SD 8296	UK K40357
REGGIE YOUNG	G (ACE	(B) DIAMONDS IN THE ROUGH	1973 ATLANTIC	US SD7240	UK K40427
STEVE GOODMAN	G (BCDEF	(C) SWEET REVENGE	1974 ATLANTIC	US SD 7274	UK K40524
DAVID BRIGGS	K (CE	(D) COMMON SENSE	1975 ATLANTIC	US SD18127	UK K50137
MIKE LEECH	B (ACE	(E) PRIME PRINE	1976 ATLANTIC	US SD18202	
KENNY MALONE	D (CE	(F) BRUISED ORANGE	1978 ASYLUM	US 6E 139	UK K53084
JOHN CHRISTOPHER	G (ACE	(G) PINK CADILLAC	1979 ASYLUM	US 6E 222	UK K52164
DAVE PRINE	G (CDE				

GRADY MARTIN	G (C	JERRY SHOOK	HCA (C	STEVE BURGH	G (C	KENNY ASCHER	K (C
HUGH McDONALD	B (C	STEVE MOSLEY	D (C	RALPH McDONALD	PERC (C	JOHN BURNS	G V(F
DOYLE GRISHAM	STEEL(C	BOBBY WOODS	K (ACE	BILL SLATER	B (C	RAUN McKINNON	V (CE
JUDY CLAY	V (CE	DEIRDRE TUCK	V (CE	CISSY HOUSTON	V (CE	SID SIMS	B V(F
TOM RADTKE	D PEEC (F	JIM ROTHERMEL	WIND V (F	RICK VITO	G (DE	LEN DRESSLAR	V (F
DON SHELTON	V (F	BOB BOWKER	V (F	LEO LEBLANC	STEEL G(ACDEF	CORKY SIEGEL	HCA(F
BONNIE HERMAN	V (F	JACKSON BROWNE	V (DF	MIKE UTLEY	K (F	VICKI HUBLEY	V (F
KITTY HAYWOOD	V (F	DIANE HOLMES	V (F	BONNIE KOLOC	V (F	HOWARD LEVY	ACC(F
BOB HOBAN	PNO V(F	HARRY WALLER	V (F	MIKE JORDAN	V (F	STEVE RODBY	B (F
SAM BUSH	G V (F	JETHRO BURNS	MAND V (F	DAN CRONIN	V (DF	RAMBLIN' JACK ELLIOT	V(F
JOHN COWAN	V (F	FRED HOLSTEIN	V (F	BRYAN BOWERS	V (F	TOM HANSON	V (F
HANK NEUBERGER	V (F	EARL PIONKE	V (F	JAMES TALLEY	V (F	ED HOLSTIEN	V (F
ALDO BOTTALLA	V (F	MIKE URSCHEL	V (F	JAMES McNAMARA	V (F	AL BUNETTA	V (F
TYLER WILSON	V (F	TIM MESSER	V (F	PETER BUNETTA	D V (DE	TOMMY CATHEY	B (DE
JAMES BROWN	K (DE	PAUL CANNON	G (DE	WAYNE JACKSON	HRNS (DE	ANDREW LOVE	HRNS(DE
JACK HALE	HRNS (DE	JAMES MITCHELL	HRNS (DE	LEWIS COLLINS	HRNS (DE	LARRY MUHOBERAC	PNO(DE
JOHN DAVID SOUTHER	V (D	GLENN FREY	V (D	BONNIE RAITT	V (DE	HERB PEDERSEN	V (D
DUCK DUNN	B (DE	ALAN HAND	V PNO(DE	MAILTO CORREA	PERC (DE	BROOKS HUNNICUTT	V (DE
PAT COULTER	V (DE	GWENN EDWARDS	V (DE	JIM HORN	HRNS (D	CHUCK FINDLEY	HRNS(D
JACKIE KELSO	HRNS (D	GREG JACKSON	V (D	CARL MARSH	STR (D	STEVE SPEAR	B (D
BOBBY EMMONS	K (A						

MADDY PRIOR

MADDY PRIOR	V (AB	(A) WOMAN IN THE WINGS	1978 CHRYSALIS	UK	CHR 1185
CHRIS STAINTON	K (B1	(B) CHANGING WINDS	1978 CHRYSALIS	UK	CHR 1203
PAT DONALDSON	B (1	(1) 1978 TOUR			
JOHN LINGWOOD	D (1B				

KEVIN SAVIGAR	SYN (1B	ANDY ROBERTS	G (A	BARRIEMORE BARLOW	D (A	JOHN GLASCOCK	B (A
DAVID PALMER	K (A	DAVID OLNEY	B (A	MARTIN BARRE	G (A	IAN ANDERSON	FLT(A
JOHN HALSEY	D (A	BARRY BOOTH	PNO (A	SHONA ANDERSON	V (A	CHERRY GILLESPIE	V (A
BOB GILL	G (A	RAY FLACKE	G (1	RICHIE CLOSE	K (B	SARAH DECO	V PNO (B
DOUG MORTER	G V (B	JOHN O'CONNOR	G V (B	RICK KEMP	B V (B	B J COLE	STEEL (B
DAVID HASSALL	PERC (B	GLYN THOMAS	PERC (B	MALCOLM PEET	G (B	PHILIP TODD	WIND(B
BARBARA DICKSON	V (B						

PRISM

RON TABAK	B (ABC	(A) PRISM	1978 EMI UK INS 3014	ARIOLA US 50020
LINDSAY MITCHELL	G V (ABC	(B) SEE FOREVER EYES	1978 ARIOLA ARL 5014	US 50034
JOHN HALL	K V (ABC	(C) ARMAGEDDON	1979 CAPITOL	12051
ALLEN HARLOW	B G (BC	(D) YOUNG & RESTLESS	1980 CAPITOL	12072
ROCKET NORTON	D (BC			
A B BRYANT	B (A	RODNEY HIGGS	K D (A	TOM KEENLYSIDE	HRNS (A	BRUCE FAIRBAIRN	HRNS(A

PRISONAIRES

JOHNNY BRAGG	V (A	(A) FIVE BEATS BEHIND BARS	1979 CHARLY	UK	CR 30176
ED THURMAN	V (A				

PRIVATE EYE

HUGHIE LEGGAT	G V (A	(A) PRIVATE EYE	1979 CAPITOL		EST 11980
HOWARD WARDEN	B (A				
GORDY LEGGAT	G (A	PAUL 'BOOMER' STAMP	D V (A			

PRIVATE SECTOR

	(A) I WANNA STAY FREE (EP)	19	TJM	UK	TJM 8

PROCESSION

CRAIG COLLINGE	D (A	(A) PROCESSION	19 MERCURY	UK SMCL 20132
TREVOR GRIFFIN	K V (A			
MICK ROGERS	V G B(A	BRIAN PEACOCK	B G K(A		

PROCOL HARUM

GARY BROOKER	K V (ALL	(A) PROCOL HARUM	1967 REGAL ZONOPHONE	UK	LRZ 1001
KEITH REID	LYRICS (ABCDEFG1	(A) PROCOL HARUM	1967 DERAM	US	18008
B J WILSON	D (ABCDEFGHJ	(B) SHINE ON BRIGHTLY	1969 REGAL ZONOPHONE	UK	SLRZ 1004
CHRIS COPPING	K B (DEFGHJ	(B) SHINE ON BRIGHTLY	1969 A&M	US	SP 4151
DAVE KNIGHTS	B (ABC1	(C) A SALTY DOG	1969 REGAL ZONOPHONE	UK	SLRZ 1009
B J COLE	STEEL(H	(C) A SALTY DOG	1969 A&M	US	SP 4179
RAY ROYER	G (1	(C) A SALTY DOG(RI DIFF TRACKS)1972 M F P		UK	MFP 5275
BOBBY HARRISON	D (1	(D) HOME	1970 REGAL ZONOPHONE	UK	SLRZ 1014
BILL EYDEN	D (1	(D) HOME	1970 A&M	US	SP 4261
MATTHEW FISHER	K (ABC1	(E) BROKEN BARRICADES	1971 CHRYSALIS UK ILPS 9158	US A&M SP 4294
ALAN CARTWRIGHT	B (FGHJ	(E) BROKEN BARRICADES	1974 CHRYSALIS UK RI CHR1056	
MICK GRABHAM	G (GHJ	(F) LIVE IN CONCERT	1972 CHRYLALIS UK CHR 1004	US A&M SP 4335
ROBIN TROWER	G (E	(G) GRAND HOTEL	1973 CHRYSALIS UK CHR 1037	US CHR 1037
DAVE BALL	G (F	(H) EXOTIC BIRDS & FRUIT	1974 CHRYSALIS UK CHR 1058	US CHR 1058
PETE SOLLEY	K (K	(J) PROCOL NINTH	1975 CHRYSALIS UK CHR 1080	US CHR 1080
CHRISTIANNE LEGRAND	V (G	(K) SOMETHING MAGIC	1977 CHRYSALIS UK CHR 1130	US CHR 1130
DA CAMERA SINGERS	V (F				

(CONTINUED)

PROCOL HARUM

(CONTINUED)						
EDMONTON SYN ORCH	(F	(AC) WHITER SHADE/SALTY DOG	1972 CUBE	UK		TOOFA 7
		(BD) SHINE ON/HOME	1972 CUBE	UK		TOOFA 10
(1) 1967		( ) WHITER SHADE OF PALE	19 INTERCORD			126 300
		( ) WHITER SHADE OF PALE	19 A&M	US		SP 4373
		( ) ROCK ROOTS	1976 DECCA	UK		ROOTS 4
		( ) BEST OF	1971 FLY	UK		TON 4
		( ) PORTRAIT	1975 POLYDOR			2434 059
		( ) HITS (DBL)	1976 POLYDOR	GER		2647 102
		( ) GREATEST HITS	1977 IMPACT	FR		6886 555
		( ) GREATEST HITS	1978 HALLMARK	UK		SHM 956

PRODUCT
P140A

(A) STYLE WARS(45 RPM LP)   1981 CLAY RECORDS   UK   PLATE 1

PROLES
P140B

(A) CONDEMNED (EP)   198 ROCK AGAINST RACISM

MICHAEL PROPHET
P140C

MICHAEL PROPHET	V (A	(A) SERIOUS REASONING	1980 GROVE MUSIC	UK		ILPS9606
SANTA	D (A					
CLINTON FERRON	B (A	ALBERT GRIFFITHS G (A CHINNA SMITH	G (A	BERNARD HARVEY	K (A	
ANSEL COLLINS	K (A	PATRICK ANDY V (A SCULLY	PERC (A	TOMMY McCOOK	HRN(A	
BOBBY ELLIS	HRNS (A	TONY TUFF V (A YABBY U(VIV JACKSON) V (A				

BRIAN PROTHEROE
P141

BRIAN PROTHEROE	V K G(ALL	(A) PINBALL	1974 CHRYSALIS	UK/US	CHR 1065
BRIAN ODGERS	B (B	(B) PICK UP	1975 CHRYSALIS	UK/US	CHR 1090
BARRY MORGAN	D (B	(C) I.YOU	1976 CHRYSALIS		CHR 1108
		(D) LEAVE HIM TO HEAVEN	1976 CHRYSALIS		CHR 1118

PROVIDENCE
P141A

JIM COCKNEY	VLN V(A	(A) EVER SENSE THE DAWN	1972 THRESHOLD	UK	THS 9
BARTHOLOMEW BISHOP	K V(A			
TIM TOMPKINS CELLO V PERC(A BOB BARRIATUA	B V (A TOM TOMPKINS	VLN V(A ANDY GUZIE G V (A		

SNOOKY PRYOR
P142

SNOOKY JAMES PRYOR HCA V(ALL	(A) SNOOKY	19 MAGPIE	US		1813
HOMESICK JAMES G V (C	(B) SNOOKY PRYOR	19 FLYRIGHT	UK		LP 100
BOB HALL PNO (C	(C) HOMESICK JAMES & SNOOKY PRYOR	1973 CAROLINE	UK		C 1502
JOHN HUNT D (B	(C) HOMESICK JAMES & SNOOKY PRYOR	1979 BIG BEAR	UK		BEAR21
BOB BRUNNING B (C	(D) DO IT IF YOU WANT	19 BLUEWAY	US		6076
MOODY JONES G (E	(E) SNOOKY & MOODY	1980 FLYRIGHT	UK		FLY565
EARL PHILLIPS D (	( ) SHAKE YOUR BOOGIE	1976 BIG BEAR	UK		BEAR14
LEE COOPER G (	( ) CHAKE YOUR BOOGIE	1979 INTERCORD	GER		146406
SUNNYLAND SLIM PNO (E					
ALFRED ELKINS B (E ALFRED WALLACE D (E LEROY FOSTER	G (EDDIE TAYLOR	G (			

ARTHUR PRYSOCK
P142A

ARTHUR PRYSOCK (ALL	ARTHUR PRYSOCK'74	1973 OLDTOWN	US	12001
	LOVE MAKES IT RIGHT	1974 OLDTOWN	US	12002
	ALL MY LIFE	1974 OLDTOWN	US	12004
	ALL MY LIFE	1977 POLYDOR	UK	2383 441
	BEST OF ARTHUR PRYSOCK	19 VERVE		6 5011
	THIS IS MY BELOVED	19 VERVE		6 5070
	SILK & SATIN	19 POLYDOR	US	2 8901
	DOES IT AGAIN	1978 POLYDOR	UK	2383 481

PSEUDO EXISTERS
P142B

NICK ARMSTRONG	G (123A	(A) STAMP OUT NORMALITY(EP)	1979 DEAD GOOD UK	DEAD 2
GES HALL	B (12	(1) JULY 1978 (2) AUTUMN 1978	(3) DECEMBER 1978	
PAUL STEEL	G V (123A			
JOHN CARTWRIGHT	V (1 MARK SIDDY D (123A JOHN LOONAM	G B (23A		

PSYCHEDELIC FURS
P142C

BUTLER REP	V (A	(A) PSYCHEDELIC FURS	1980 CBS UK	84084
JOHN ASHTON	G (A			
DUNCAN KILBURN	SAX (A ROGER MORRIS G (A VINCE ELY	D (A TIM BUTLER B (A		

PSYCHOTIC PINEAPPLE
P142D

(A) WHERE'S THE PARTY   19   US

PUBLIC FOOT THE ROMAN
P143

DAG SMALL	K V (A	(A) PUBLIC FOOT THE ROMAN	1973 SOVEREIGN UK	SVNA 7259
SEAN BYRNE	G V (A			
JAMIE LANE	D V (A GREG KNOWLES G (A WARD	B (A		

PUBLIC IMAGE LTD
P144

JOHN LYDON	V (A	(A) PUBLIC IMAGE LTD	1978 VIRGIN	UK	V2114
KEITH LEVINE	G (A	(B) SECOND EDITON	1979 VIRGIN	UK	VD2512
JIM WALKER	D (A	(C) METAL BOX	1979 VIRGIN	UK	METAL1
JAH WOBBLE	B (A	(D) PARIS AU PRINTEMPS	1980 VIRGIN	UK	V2183
		(E) FLOWERS OF ROMANCE	1981 VIRGIN		

GARY PUCKETT & THE UNION GAP
P145

GARY PUCKETT	V (ALL	WOMAN WOMAN	1968 CBS	US 9612	
DWIGHT BEMENT	SAX (ALL	YOUNG GIRL	1968 CBS	US 9664	UK 63342
KERRY CHATER	B (ALL	INCREDIBLE	1968 CBS	US 9715	UK 63429
PAUL WHEATBREAD	D (ALL	NEW ALBUM	1970 CBS	US 9935	UK 63794
GARY WITHEM	PNO (ALL	GREATEST HITS	1970 CBS		UK 64115

PUDDLETOWN EXPRESS
P145A

ARTHUR BROWN	V (AB	(A) APRIL 1969 (B) JULY 1969
DRACHEN THEAKER	SYN D(AB	
DENNIS TAYLOR	B (AB GEORGE KHAN SAX (B JOHN MARSHALL	D (A JONAH MITCHELL ORG (B
McCULLOCH	ORG (A ANDROID FUNNEL G (A	

P146   DUDU PUKWANA

DUDU PUKWANA	SAX V	K PERC(ABC	(A) IN THE TOWNSHIPS				1974	CAROLINE		UK	C 1504	
MONGEZI FEZA	TPT PERC V(AC		(B) FLUTE MUSIC				1975	CAROLINE		UK	CA2005	
LOUIS MOHOLO	D	(AC	(C) DIAMOND EXPRESS				1978	FREEDOM			FLP 41044	
BIZO MNGQIKANA	SAX PERC V(A											
HARRY MILLER	B	(A	ELTON DEAN	SAX	(C	NICK EVANS	TROM (C	KEITH TIPPETT	PNO (C
LUCKY RANKU	G	(C	VICTOR NTONI	B	(C	FRANK ROBERTS	K (C	ERNEST MOTHLE	B (C
JAMES MENE	D	(C							

P147   PULSAR

JACQUES ROMAN	K B	(AB	(A) POLLEN		1976	DECCA	UK	SKLR 5228
VICTOR BOSCH	D PERC(AB		(B) THE STRANDS OF THE FUTURE		1976	DECCA		TXS R 119
GILBERT GANDIL	G V	(AB						
PHILIPPE ROMAN	B V	(A	ROLAND RICHARD	FLT	(AB			

P148   PUNISHMENT OF LUXURY

NEVILLE LUXURY	G	(	(A) LAUGHING ACADEMY		1979	UA	UK	UAG 30258
BRIAN BOND	V	(						
RED HELMIT	G	(	JIMMY GIRO	B	(	LES DENHAM	D (

P149   BERNARD PURDIE

BURNARD PURDIE	D V	(ALL	(A) SOUL FINDERS		1968	CAMDEN		CAS 2170
RALPH McDONALD	CONGA(E		(B) SOUL DRUMS		1968	DIRECTION		8 63290
HORACE OTT	K	(E	(C) STAND BY ME		1971	MEGA		51 5001
CORNELL DUPREE	G	(E	(D) PURDIE GOOD		1971	PRESTIGE	US	10013
LLOYD DAVIS	G	(E	(E) SOUL IS ... PRETTY PURDIE		1972	PHILIPS		6369 421
GARNETT BROWN	TROM (E		(F) SHAFT		1974	PRESTIGE	US	10038
BILLY NICHOLS	G	(E	(G) DELIGHTS OF THE GARDEN		19	CASABLANCA	US	7051
NORMAN PRIDE	PERC (E	MAERETHA STEWART	V	(E	RICHARD TEE	K (E	JAY BERLINER	G (E
PAUL MARTINEZ	B	(E	DANNY MOORE	TPT	(E	SELDON POWELL	SAX (E	JAMES POWELL	SAX(E
HILDA HARRIS	V	(E	CHARLIE BROWN	SAX	(E	GORDON POWELL	PERC (E	JERRY JEMMOTT	B (E
EILEEN GILBERT	V	(E	PAUL GRIFFIN	K	(E	ERNIE ROYAL	TPT (E	HAROLD VICK	SAX (E
CARL HALL	V	(E	BARBARA MASSEY	V	(E				

P150   PURE FOOD & DRUG ACT

HARVEY MANDEL	G	(A	(A) CHOICE CUTS		1972	EPIC	US	31401
DON 'SUGARCANE 'HARRIS	VLN(A							
PAUL LAGOS	D	(A	VICTOR CONTE B	(A	COLEMAN HEAD	G V (A	RANDY RESNICK	G V (A

P151   PURE PRAIRIE LEAGUE

CRAIG FULLER	G V	(AB	(A) PURE PRAIRIE LEAGUE		1972	RCA	UK SF 8320	RI 73 SF8453
GEORGE POWELL	G V	(ABCDEFG	(A) PURE PRAIRIE LEAGUE		1972	RCA	US	LSP4650
JOHN CALL	STEEL (ACDE		(B) BUSTIN' OUT		1972	RCA	UK SF 8417	US LSP 4769
JIM LANHAM	B V	(A	(C) TWO LANE HIGHWAY		1975	RCA	UK SF 8445	US APLI 0933
BILLY HINDS	D	(BCDEGJ	(D) IF THE SHOE FITS		1976	RCA	UK RS 1040	US AFLI 1249
MICK RONSON	G V	(B	(E) DANCE		1976	RCA	UK PL 11924	US APLI 1924
MICHAEL O'CONNOR	K	(CDEGJ	(F) LIVE TAKIN' THE STAGE		1977	RCA		US CPLL 2404
JAMES ROLLESTON	B	(B	(G) JUST FLY		1978	RCA	UK PL 12590	US AFLI 2590
LARRY GOSHORN	G	(CDEG	(H) HOLD BACK		1979	RCA	UK PL 13335	US APLI 3335
MICHAEL REILLY	B	(CDEGJ	(J) FIRIN' UP		1980	CASABLANCA		NBLP 7212
AL BRISCO	STEEL(B							
ANDY STEIN	FDL	(E	TIM GOSHORN	G V	(G	DAVID SANBORN	SAX (J	GARY MIELKE SYN (J
JANIS GILL	V	(J	KRISTINE ARNOLD	V	(J	VINCE GILL G V FDL BAN (J	JEFF WILSON G V (J
JIM CAUGHLAN	D	(A	DIANNE BROOKS	V	(B	LITTLE BOBBY RING PERC (B	

P152   PURIFY BROTHERS

JAMES PURIFY	V	(AB	(A) JAMES & BOBBY PURIFY		1977	MERCURY UK 9110 028	US	SRM11134
BOBBY PURIFY	V	(ALL	(B) YOU & MEE TOGETHER FOREVER		1978	CASABLANCA		CAL 2025
			( ) PURE SOUND OF		19	BELL	US	6010

P153   PURPLE GANG

	( ) PURPLE GANG STRIKES	1968	TRANSATLANTIC UK SIRE US	97006

P154   PURPLE HEARTS

	(A) BEAT THAT	19	FICTION	UK	FIX2

P155   JIMMY PURSEY

JIMMY PURSEY		(A	(A) IMAGINATION CAMOUFLAGE	1980	POLYDOR	UK	2442 180

P156   PUSSYCAT

	(A) SOUVENIRS	19	EMI	NL	064 25565
	(B) FIRST OF ALL	1976	SONET		SNTF 725

P157   PYLON

	(A) GYRATE	1980	ARMAGEDDON	UK	ARM5

P158   PYRAMID

IAN MATTHEWS	V	(A	(A) 1968
ANDY LEIGH			

P159   PYTHON LEE JACKSON

DAVE BENTLEY	K V	(A	(A) IN A BROKEN DREAM		1974	YOUNGBLOOD 3001	US GNP	2066
DAVE MONTGOMERY	D	(A						
MICK LIBER	G	(A	TONY CAHILL	B	(A	GARY BOYLE	G (A	ROD STEWART	V (A

Q1   EDDIE QUANSAH

EDDIE QUANSAH	HRNS PERC V(A		(A) CHE CHE KULE		1977	ISLAND	UK	ILPS 9446
DICK CUTHELL	TPT	(A						
MAC TONTOH	TPT	(A	GEORGE LARNYOH	SAX	(A	RAY ALLEN	SAX (A	PETE VANDER PUIJE SAX(A
CHRIS MERCER	SAX	(A	GRAEME MORGAN	D	(A	KOFI AYIVOR	D PERC(A	TERRY WILSON	B (A
COLIN BASS	B	(A	WILLY CHEETA	CONGA(A		JIMMY CHAMBERS	V (A	PATRICE EBIGWE	V (A
JOANNA WHYTE	V	(A	ESTHER BYRD	V	(A	WINSTON DELANDRO	G V (A	JUNIOR KERR	G (A
JANOS BAJTALA	K	(A	KIKI GYAN	K	(A	EMMANUEL RENTZOS	K V (A	JOE SCOTT	K (A
PETE WINGFIELD	K	(A	TONY BRAUNAGEL	D	(A	REMI KEBAKA	D (A	SPARTACUS R	B (A
JEROME RIMSON	B	(A	REEBOP KWAKU BAAH PERC (A			IAN GREEN	SYN (A	CLIFFORD MATAYA	V (A
PAMELA DOUGLAS	V	(A	ROSETTA HIGHTOWER	V	(A				

Q1.A   'Q'

	(A) DANCIN' MAN	1977	EPIC	US	34691

```
FRANK NUYENS        G    (A                               1966   DECCA          NL  6440675
PETER VINK          B    (A              (A) REVOLUTION
WILLIAM BIELER      HCA V(A   JOOP ROELOFS    G   (A   JAY BAAR     D   (A
```

'Q TIPS'

```
PAUL YOUNG          V    (A              (A) Q TIPS           1980 CHRYSALIS      UK   CHR 1255
BARRY WATTS         D    (A
MICK PEARL          B    (A   GARTH WATT ROY   G V (A   IAN KEW     K   (A   TONY HUGHES TPT (A
STEVE FARR          SAX V(A   STEWART BLANDMER SAX V(A
```

QUANTUM JUMP

```
MARK WARNER         G V  (AC             (A) QUANTUM JUMP     1976   ELECTRIC      UK   TRIX1
TREVOR MORAIS       D    (ABC            (B) BARRACUDA        1977   ELECTRIC      UK   TRIX3
JOHN PERRY          B    (ABC            (C) MIXING           1979   ELECTRIC      UK   TRIX11
ROY ALBRIGHTON      G    (
RUPERT HINE         K V  (ABC GEOFFREY RICHARDSON G VLN(B MORRIS PERT     PERC (A   RAY COOPER  PERC (AB
PAUL KEOGH          G    (B   ELKIE BROOKS     V       (B GEOFF DALY      HRNS (B   HENRY LOWTHER HRNS(B
PENGUIN CAFE STRINGS     (B   GAVIN WRIGHT STRINGS     (B HELEN LIEBMANN  STR  (B
```

QUARTZ

```
DEREK ARNOLD        B    (ABCDE          (A) QUARTZ           1977 JET            UK   UAG 30081
MALCOLM COPE        D    (ABCDE          (B) QUARTZ           1978 PYE            UK   NSPL28261
MICK HOPKINS        G    (ABCDE          (C) DELETED          1979 JET            UK   JETLP 223
MIKE 'TAFFY' TAYLOR V    (ABCDE          (D) LIVE COUNT DRACULA 1980 REDDINGTON   UK   REDD 001
                                         (E) STAND UP & FIGHT 1980 MCA            UK   MCF 3080
```

BILL QUATEMAN

```
BILL QUATEMAN       G V  (A              (A) NIGHT AFTER NIGHT 1977 RCA UK PL12027 US AFLI 2027
CALEB QUAYE         G V  (A              (B) SHOT IN THE DARK  197  RCA            US AFLI 2434
DENNY SEIWELL       D    (A
JOHN MARSH          B    (A   IRA KART       PNO  (A   TERRY REID      V    (A   RICHARD SUPA    V  (A
LENNY CASTRO        CONGA(A   IAN UNDERWOOD  K    (A   BRUCE JOHNSTON  V    (A   CINDY BULLENS   V  (A
JIMMY HAAS          V    (A   ERNIE WATTS    HRNS (A   NOLAN SMITH     HRNS (A   SHIRLEY MATTHEWS V (A
GEORGE BOHANON      HRNS (A   OSCAR BRASHEAR HRNS (A   VANETTA FIELDS  V    (A   MAXAYN LEWIS    V  (A
JACKIE KELSO        HRNS (A   JON JOYCE      V    (A   STRING SECTION       (A
```

QUATERMASS

```
JOHN GUSTAFSON      B V  (A              (A) QUATERMASS       1970 HARVEST        UK   SHVL  775
PETE ROBINSON       K    (A              (A) QUATERMASS       1975 HARVEST RI     UK   SHSM 2002
MICK UNDERWOOD      D    (
```

MICHAEL QUATRO

```
MICHAEL QUATRO      K    (A              (A) IN COLLABORATION WITH THE GODS 1975 UA  US LA 420 UK UAS 29785
TEDDY HALE          G    (A              (B) DANCERS ROMANCERS & DREAMERS   1976 PRODIGAL         UK   PDL 2001
RICK DERRINGER      G    (A              (C) GETTING READY                  197  PRODIGAL         US   P7 10016
DAVE KISWINEY       B V  (A
KIRK TRACHSEL       D    (A   HOWARD KAYLAN     V   (A   MARK VOLMAN      V (A
```

SUZI QUATRO

```
SUZI QUATRO         B V  (ALL            (A) SUZI QUATRO        1973 RAK UK SRAK505 US BELL   1302
KEITH HODGE         D    (               (B) QUATRO             1974 RAK UK SRAK509 US BELL   1313
LENNIE TUCKEY       G    (BCDE           (C) YOUR MAMA WON'T LIKE ME 1975 RAK UK SRAK514 US ARISTA 4035
MIKE DEACON         K    (DE             (D) AGGRO PHOBIA       1977 RAK UK SRAK525
BILL HURD           K    (               (E) IF YOU KNEW SUZI   1978 RAK UK SRAK532
ALASTAIR McKENZIE   K    (B              (F) GREATEST HITS      1980 RAK UK EMTV24
DAVE NEAL           D    (BDE
```

QUAZAR

```
                                         (A) QUAZAR            1978 ARISTA         UK   ARTY 157
```

QUEEN

```
                                                          UK   UK    US     US    JAP    JAP
FREDDIE MERCURY   V PNO(ALL   (A) QUEEN                    1973 EMI EMC 3006 ELEKTRA 75064 ELEKTRA P10118E
BRIAN MAY G K V BANJO (ALL    (B) QUEEN II                1974 EMI EMC  767 ELEKTRA 75082 ELEKTRA P10119E
JOHN DEACON       G B (ALL    (C) SHEER HEART ATTACK      1974 EMI EMC 3061 ELEKTRA 7E1026 ELEKTRA P10137E
ROGER TAYLOR      D V (ALL    (D) A NIGHT AT THE OPERA    1875 EMI EMTC 103 ELEKTRA 7E1053 ELEKTRA P10075E
                              (E) A DAY AT THE RACES      1976 EMI EMTC 104 ELEKTRA 6E 101 ELEKTRA P10300E
                              (F) NEWS OF THE WORLD       1977 EMI EMA  784 ELEKTRA 7E 112 ELEKTRA P10430E
                              (G) JAZZ                    1978 EMI EMA  788 ELEKTRA 6E 166 ELEKTRA P10601E
                              (H) LIVE KILLERS            1979 EMI EMSP 330
                              (J) THE GAME                1980 EMI EMA  795
                              (K) FLASH GORDON (S TRCK)1980 EMI EMC 3351
                              (EP) GOOD OLD FASHIONED  1977 EMI EMI 2623
```

QUESTION MARK & THE MYSTERIANS

```
RUDY MARTINEZ       V    (               (A) 99 TEARS          1966   CAMEO          US   C2004
ROBERT MARTINEZ          (               (B) ACTION            1966   CAMEO          US   C2006
BOBBY BALDERAMMA    G    (
EDDIE SERRATI       D    (    FRANK LUGO      B   (   FRANK RODRIGUEZ   ORG  (   LARRY BORJAS     (
```

QUICK

```
DANNY WILDE         V    (A              (A) MONDO DECO        1977 MERCURY         US   SRM1 1114
DANNY BENAIR        D    (A
BILLY BIZEAU        K V  (A   IAN AINSWORTH    B   (A   STEVE HUFSTETER   G   (A
```

QUICKSAND

```
JIMMY DAVIES             (A              (A) HOME IS WHERE I BELONG 1974 DAWN       UK   DNLS 3056
PHIL DAVIES              (A
ROBERT COLLINS           (A   ANTHONY STONE       (A
```

QUICKSILVER MESSENGER SERVICE

```
GREG ELMORE         D    (ALL         (A) QUICKSILVER MESSENGER SERVICE 1968 CAPITOL    UK/US      2904
GARY DUNCAN         V G B(ABDEFGHJ1    (B) HAPPY TRAILS            1969 CAPITOL    UK/US       120
JOHN CIPOLLINA      G    (ABCDEJ1      (C) SHADY GROVE            1969 CAPITOL    UK/US       391
DAVID FREIBERG      B V G(ABCDEJ1      (D) JUST FOR LOVE          1970 CAPITOL    UK/US       498
JIM MURRAY          V HCA(1            (D) JUST FOR LOVE          197  EMI        GERM 038 80543
NICKY HOPKINS       K    (CDEJ         (E) WHAT ABOUT ME          1971 CAPITOL    UK/US       630
DINO VALENTI   FLT G V   (DEFGJ        (E) WHAT ABOUT ME          19   CAPITOL    US RI   16092
JOSE REYES          PERC (E            (F) QUICKSILVER            1972 CAPITOL    UK/US       819
MARK RYAN           B    (FG           (G) COMIN' THRU'          1972 CAPITOL    UK/US     11002
CHUCK STEAKS        K    (FG           (H) ANTHOLOGY             1973 CAPITOL UK ESTSP 13  US  11165
                                                                              (CONTINUED)
```

QUICKSILVER MESSENGER SERVICE

```
PETE SEARS          PNO (J        (J) SOLID SILVER              1975 CAPITOL          UK/US     11462
MICHAEL LEWIS       K   (J        (K) BEST OF                   197  CAPITOL          EURO 054 80691
SKIP OLSON          B   (J        (L) HIT ROAD                  1976 EMI              EURO 048 51874
MARIO CIPOLLINA     B   (J        (1) 1965/67
KEN BALZALL         TPT (E
KATHI McDONALD      V   (J   MARK NAFTALIN   PNO (J  MARTIN FIERRO    WIND (E   RON TAERMINA    SAX (E
FRANK MORIN         SAX (E   PAT O'HARA   TROM        (E
```

Q13

QUIET SUN

```
PHIL MAZANERA       G K (A        (A) MAINSTREAM               1975 ISLAND           UK        HELP19
DAVE JARRETT        K   (A        (A) MAINSTREAM               1977 POLYDOR RI        UK   2343 093
BRIAN ENO           K   (A        (A) MAINSTREAM               1975 ANTILLES          US        7008
IAN MACCORMICK      V   (A
BILL MACCORMICK     B V (A   CHARLES HAYWARD   D K V(A
```

Q14

QUIET WORLD

```
                                  (A) THE ROAD                 1970 DAWN             UK DNLS 3007
```

Q15

QUILL

```
                                  (A) QUILL                    19   COTILLION        US SD   9017
```

Q15

QUINAIMES BAND

```
DAVID PALMER        V   (A        (A) QUINAIMES BAND           1971 ELEKTRA          US   EKS 74096
KENNY PINE          G V (A
MIKE ROSA           D   (A   JERRY BURNHAM    B V (A  DANNY MANSOLINO   K V (A   DANIEL BEN ZEBULON CONGA(A
DANNY KOOTCH        G   (A   ALLAN JACOBS     G   (A  RICHARD GREENE    FDL (A    BILL KEITH  STEEL       (A
RICHARD GRANDO      SAX (A
```

Q16

QUINTESSENCE

```
RAJA RAM      FLT V PNO  (        (A) IN BLISSFUL COMPANY      1969 ISLAND           UK   ILPS 9110
SHIVA SHANKAR       V K  (        (B) QUINTESSENCE             1970 ISLAND           UK   ILPS 9128
SAMBHU BABAJI       B    (        (C) DIVE DEEP                1970 ISLAND           UK   ILPS 9143
JAKE MILTON         D    (        (D) SELF                     1971 RCA             UK     SF8273
MAHA DEV            G    (        (E) INDWELLER                1972 RCA             UK     SF8317
ALAN MOSTERT        G    (
```

Q17

QUIVER

```
TIM RENWICK         G    (AB       (A) QUIVER                  1971 WB      US  1939  UK   K46089
WILLIE WILSON       D    (AB       (B) GONE IN THE MORNING     1972 WB      US  2630  UK   K46153
CAL BATCHELOR       V G K(AB
BRUCE THOMAS        B    (AB  DICK PARRY   SAX  (A
```

R1

R A F

```
DAVID VALENTINE     V K  (A        (A) R.A.F.                  1980 A&M           UK       AMLH64816
DOUGLAS A BOGIE     G    (A        (B) THE HEAT'S ON           1981 A&M           UK       AMLH68525
BILLY McGHEE        B    (A
TOM ANNAN           PERC (A   BOBBY HEATLIE    SAX  (A   ANDY GROSSART   B   (A   WENDY BOGIE V    (A
```

R1A

REO SPEEDWAGON

```
TERRY LUTTRELL      V    (ABD      (A) R E O SPEEDWAGON        1971 EPIC   US 31089  uk       64813
KEVIN CRONIN        G V  (DEFHJL    (B) R E O 2                 1972 EPIC   US 31745
ALAN GRATZER        D    (EHJLABDEFG (D) RIDING THE STORM       1973 EPIC   US 32378
GARY RICHRATH       G V  (EHJL      (E) LOST IN A DREAM         1974 EPIC   US 34143
NEAL DOUGHTY        K    (EHJLABDFG (F) THIS TIME WE MEAN IT    1975 EPIC   US 33338
MIKE MURPHY         V    (E        (G) R E O                   1976 EPIC   US 34143
SLY STONE           G B K(E        (H) YOU GET WHAT YOU PLAY FOR 1977 EPIC  US 34494  UK       88265
LON PRICE           SAX  (J        (J) YOU CAN TUNE A PIANO .....1978 EPIC  US 35083  UK       82554
BRUCE HALL          B    (JL       (K) NINE LIVES              1979 EPIC            UK       83647
                                   (L) DECADE OF ROCK'N'ROLL (DBL COMP) 1980 EPIC   UK       88488
```

R2

R M O

```
                                   (A) BEYOND THE LIMIT        19   BRAIN                  0060 115
                                   (B) GET THE BALL            19   BRAIN                  0001 083
                                   (C) GARUDA                  19   BRAIN                  0001 072
```

R3

RABBIT

```
JOHN 'RABBIT' BUNDRICK V K G B(AB  (A) BROKEN ARROWS           1973 ISLAND          UK   ISPS 9238
TETSU YAMAUCHI      B    (AB       (B) DARK SALOON             1974 ISLAND          UK   ILPS 9289
SNUFFY WALDEN       G    (AB
REEBOP              PERC (A   RANDY            D   (A   GEORGE LARNYOH    HRNS (AB EDDY QUANSAH    HRNS (AB
PETER VANDER PUIJE  (AB  CHRIS LAURENCE   B   (A   JERRY MASTERS     B   (A   JIM CAPALDI     D   (A
PETE CARR           G    (A   RICHARD REEVES   G   (A   DUNDEE HORNS          (A   ALAN GERRI      G B (AB
SIMON KIRKE         D    (A   JUNIOR KERR      G   (A   CONRAD ISADORE    D   (A   TERRY WILSON    B   (B
TONY BRAUNAGEL      D    (B   DAVID KEELEY     G   (B   JANNE SCHAFFER    G   (B   OLA BRUNKERT    D   (B
MIKE                B    (B   BRYSON GRAHAM    D   (B
```

R3A

RABBITT

```
TREVOR RABIN   G V K SYN (AB       (A) BOYS WILL BE BOYS       1976 CAPRICORN       US       0175
RONNIE ROBOT        B    (AB       (A) BOYS WILL BE BOYS       1976 JET            UK   JETLP 17
NEIL CLOUD   D PERC (AB            (B) CROAK & GRUNT IN THE NIGHT 1977 CAPRICORN    US       0190
DUNCAN FAURE        K V  (
```

R4

EDDIE RABBITT

```
EDDIE RABBITT       G V  (ALL      (A) EDDIE RABBITT           1975 ELEKTRA         US      CM3
MIKE LEECH          B    (A        (B) ROCKY MOUNTAIN MUSIC    1976 ELEKTRA UK K52037 US 7E1065
JACK WILLIAMS       B    (BC       (C) RABBITT                 1977 ELEKTRA UK K52054 US 7E1105
JOE OSBORN          B    (B        (D) VARIATIONS              1978 ELEKTRA         US 6E 127
LARRY LONDIN        D    (BC       (E) LOVELINES               1979 ELEKTRA UK K52135 US 6E 181
HARGUS ROBBINS      PNO  (BC       (F) BEST OF                 1979 ELEKTRA         US 6E 235
NORBERT PUTNAM      B    (E        (G) HORIZONS                1981 ELEKTRA UK K52225
SHANE KEISTER       PNO  (B
DAVID BRIGGS        PNO  (B   MICHAEL SPRIGGS   G   (B   PETE WADE       G   (B   JOHN CHRISTOPHER G  (B
BOBBY THOMPSON      G    (BC  STEVE GIBSON      G   (BC  REGGIE YOUNG    G   (BC  SONNY GARRISH   STEEL(BC
HAL RUGG            STEEL(B   BUDDY SPICHER     FDL (B   FARRELL MORRIS  PERC (BC LEA JANE SINGERS     (B
NASHVILLE EDITION   (B   KENNY MALONE     D   (C   MIKE SUTTLE     V   (C   DAVID HOOD      B   (E
DENNIS BELFIELD     B    (E   ROGER HAWKINS    D   (E   RANDY McCORMICK K   (E   STEVE FORMAN    PERC (E
MICHELE GRUSKA      V    (E   DAVID HUNGATE    B   (E   BARRY BECKETT   K   (E   LARRY BYROM     G   (E
JIMMY JOHNSON       G    (E   TIM MAY          G   (E   ERNIE WATTS     FLT (E   SARAH TAYLOR    V   (E
SHERRY GROOMS       V    (E
```

TREVOR RABIN
R5

```
TREVOR RABIN  G B K V   (ABC              (A) TREVOR RABIN          1978 CHRYSALIS      UK   CHR  1196
KEVIN KRUGER  D       (AB              (B) FACE TO FACE          1979 CHRYSALIS      UK   CHR  1221
SIMON PHILLIPS D      (C               (C) WOLF                 1981 CHRYSALIS      UK   CHR  1295
JACK BRUCE    B       (C
MO FOSTER     B       (C   MANFRED MANN      V    (C   CHRIS THOMPSON   V  (C   STEVIE LANGE    V (C
RABBIT        K       (C   NOEL McCALLA      V    (C
```

RACING CARS
R6

```
RAY ENNIS        G V  (AB              (A) DOWNTOWN TONIGHT      1976 CHRYSALIS      UK   CHR  1099
GRAHAM WILLIAMS  G V  (AB              (B) WEEKEND RENDEZVOUS    1977 CHRYSALIS      UK   CHR  1149
GARETH MORTIMER  G V  (AB              (C) BRING ON THE NIGHT    1978 CHRYSALIS      UK   CHR  1178
DAVE LAND        B V  (AB
ROBERT WILDING   D V  (AB  ROY EDWARDS       K    (A   ROGER HAND       K  (A   BOWLES BROTHERS BAND V(A
TONY CARR        PERC (A   GERAINT WATKINS   K    (A
```

MAXIM RAD
R6A

```
MAXIM RAD           G V  (A            (A) TIMES AINT THAT BAD   1980   DISQUES MOTORS       MTO 77016
CLAUDE ANGEL        G    (A
DOMINIQUE PERRIER   PNO  (A   SAUVEUR MALLIA    B    (A   JEAN PAUL PRATT  D V (A  RICHARD PRATT    SAX (A
YVONNE JONES        V    (A
```

RADIATOR
R7

```
ALAN HULL       G V  (A               (A) ISN'T IT STRANGE      1977 ROCKET         UK   ROLL  14
RAY LAIDLAW     D    (A
KENNY CRADDOCK  K    (A   PETE KIRTLEY      G    (A   COLIN GIBSON     B  (A   TERRY POPPLE    D (A
```

RADIATORS FROM SPACE
R8

```
PETER HOLIDAI   G V  (AB               (A) T V TUBE HEART       1977 CHISWICK       UK        WIK 4
PHILIP CHEVRON  G V  (AB               (B) GHOSTOWN             1979 CHISWICK       UK   CWK  3003
MARK MEGARAY    B V  (AB
JAMES CRASH     D    (AB  STEVE RAPID       V    (A
```

RADIO BIRDMAN
R9

```
ROB YOUNGER     V    (A                (A) RADIOS APPEAR        1978 SIRE UK 9103 332 UK  RI  6050
WARWICK GILBERT B    (A
CHRIS MANSUAK   G    (A   DENIZ TEK         G    (A   JOHNNY KANNIS    V  (A   RON KEELEY  D  (A
PIP HOYLE       K    (A
```

RADIO STARS
R10

```
ANDY ELLISON    V    (                 (A) SONG FOR SWINGING LOVERS  1977 CHISWICK WIK5   +   CWK 3005
MARTIN GORDON   B V  (                 (B) HOLIDAY ALBUM        1978 CHISWICK            CWK 3001
STEVE PERRY     D    (                 (EP) STOP IT             19   CHISWICK            SW   17
IAN MACLEOD     G    (
```

GERRY RAFFERTY
R11

```
GERRY RAFFERTY  V G K(ALL              (A) CAN I HAVE MY MONEY BACK      1971 TRANSATLANTIC  UK   TRA  241
ROGER BROWN     G V  (AD1              (A) CAN I HAVE MY MONEY BACK      197  BLUE THUMB US BTS 58 +  6031
TOM PARKER      K    (A                (B) GERRY RAFFERTY REVISITED     1974 TRANSATLANTIC  UK   TRA  270
GARY TAYLOR     B V  (ADE1             (C) GERRY RAFFERTY               1978 LOGO           UK   MOGO 4002
HENRY SPINETTI  D    (AD               (D) CITY TO CITY                 1978 UA             UK   UAS 30104
JOE EGAN        V    (A                (E) NIGHT OWL                    1979 UA   US LA840  UK   UAS 30238
ROD KING        STEEL(A                (F) SNAKES & LADDERS            1980 UA             UK   UAS 32098
ALAN PARKER     G    (A                (1) 1978 TOUR BAND
VIV McAULIFFE   V    (D
GLEN LEFLEUR    PERC (D   BARBARA DICKSON   V    (DE  RAB NOAKES       G V (AD  HUGH MURPHY V   (AD
JOHN VANDERRICK FDL  (A   ANDREW STEELE     D    (A   ANDY FAIRWEATHER LOW G (D  HUGH BURNS  G   (DE
GRAHAM PRESKETT K FDL V(DE TOMMY EYRE       K    (DE1 RAPHAEL RAVENSCROFT SAX (DEF1LIAM GENOCKEY D (EF1
BRIAN COLE      STEEL(D   MICK MOODY        G    (D   NIGEL JENKINS    G   (D   WILLY RAY   ACC (D
JERRY DONAHUE   G    (DF  PAUL JONES   HCA       (D   JOHN McBURNIE    V   (D   RICHARD BRUNTON G(EF
RICHARD THOMPSON G MAND(E PETE WINGFIELD   ORG    (EF  MO FOSTER        B   (EF  FRANK RICOTTI PERC(EF
JOHN KIRKPATRICK ACC (E   RICHARD HARVEY WIND SYN(EF BETSY COOKE       V   (EF  LINDA THOMPSON V(E
IAN LYNN        K    (F   BRYN HAWORTH      G    (F   BILLY LIVSEY     K   (F   PETE ZORN   B   (F
```

JIM RAFFERTY
R12

```
JIM RAFFERTY     G V  (AB              (A) DONT TALK BACK       1978 DECCA          UK   SKL  8291
HENRY SPINETTI   D    (A               (B) SOLID LOGIC          1979 DECCA          UK   SKLR5314
PICK WITHERS     D    (A
DAVE MATTACKS    D    (A   PETER VAN HOOKE   D    (A   LYNTON NAIFF     PNO (A   BRIAN ODGERS    B  (A
GRAHAM PRESKETT  FDL K(AB  ROD CLEMENTS      B    (A   HUGH BURNS       G   (AB  LAWRENCE JUBER  G  (A
FRANK BOGIE      G    (AB  B J COLE        STEEL(A    GARY TAYLOR      B   (A   FRANCIS MONKMAN K  (A
BARRY MORGAN     D    (A   MIKE DAY        D PERC (A   TIM RENWICK      G   (A   GERRY RAFFERTY G V SYN(AB
HERBIE FLOWERS   B    (A   JOHN JAMES        G    (A   MADELINE BELL    V   (A   KAY GARNER      V  (A
PETE SWETTENHAM       (A   CHRIS MERCER    SAX    (A   JOHN NIVEN       CONC(A   GEORGE McCRAE   PIPES(A
FRANK SHERPAS    V    (A   MIKE SHERPAS      V    (A   BILL McGEACHY    V   (A   FIONA McGEACHY  V  (A
RAB NOAKES       V    (AB  PRESTON HEYMAN    D    (B   BEN BARSON       K   (B   DON AIREY       K  (A
JOHN GIBLIN      B    (B   MEL COLLINS     SAX    (B   MORRIS PERT      PERC(B   MARTIN LEVAN    PERC(B
PEPE LEMER       V    (B   RICKY HITCHCOCK   G    (B   TERRY JONES      HRNS(B
```

RAH BAND
R13

```
                                       (A) THE CRUNCH & BEYOND  1978 EBONY               EBY1001
```

(RITCHIE BLACKMORES)RAINBOW
R14

```
RITCHIE BLACKMORE G   (ALL             (A) RITCHIE BLACKMORE'S RAINBOW  1975 OYSTER            OYA 2001
COZY POWELL       D   (BCDE1           (A) RITCHIE BLACKMORE'S RAINBOW  1978 POLYDOR     RI    2490 141
GARY DRISCOLL     D   (A               (B) RAINBOW RISING              1976 OYSTER            2490 137
CRAIG GRUBER      B   (A               (C) ON STAGE                    1977 OYSTER            OYA21801
MICKY LEE SOULE   K   (A               (C) ON STAGE                    1977 POLYDOR           2490 016
TONY CAREY        K   (B1              (D) LONG LIVE ROCK'N'ROLL       1978 POLYDOR POLD 5002 2490 142
JIM BAIN          B   (B               (E) DOWN TO EARTH               1979 POLYDOR POLD 5023
RONNIE DIO        V   (BCD1            (F) DIFFICULT TO CURE           1981 POLYDOR POLD 5036
MARK CLARKE       B   (1               (1) 1977
GRAHAM BONNET     V   (E
DAVID STONE       K   (D   BOB DAISLEY       B    (D   ROGER GLOVER     B   (EF  DON AIREY       K  (E
BOB RONDINELLI    D   (F   JOE LYNN TURNER   V    (F
```

R15 CHRIS RAINBOW

CHRIS RAINBOW	V	(ABC	(A) HOME OF THE BRAVE			1975 POLYDOR	UK		2383 467
SIMON PHILLIPS	D	(C	(B) LOOKING OVER MY SHOULDER			1978 POLYDOR	UK		2383 338
PETE ZORN	B	(C	(C) WHITE TRAILS			1979 EMI	UK		EMC 3305
MO FOSTER	B	(C							
DAVE LAWSON	SYN	(C	IAN BAIRNSON	G (C	LINDA TAYLOR	V (C	SHUG BARR	G (C	
MART JENNER	G	(C	MAX MIDDLETON	K (C	DEREK QUINN	PERC (C	DICK MORRISSEY	SAX(C	
MARLYN BAIRNSON	V	(C	CHRISTY THOMPSON	V (C					

R16 RAINBOW FFOLLY

		(A) SALLIES FORTH	1967 PARLOPHONE	PCS 7050

R16A RAINBOW RED OXIDISER

ED CASSIDY	D	(A	(A) RECORDED LIES	19
MARS BONFIRE	G	(A		

R17 RAINCOATS

JEREMIE FRANK	G V	(123	(A) RAINCOATS			1979 ROUGH TRADE	UK	ROUGH 3
RICHARD DUDANSKI	D	(3	(1) 1978	(2) 1978	(3) 1978 JULY	(4) 1979		
NICK TURNER	D	(12	(EP) FAIRYTALE IN THE SUPERMARKET			1979 ROUGH TRADE	UK	
KATE KORUS	G	(1						
ANA DA SILVA	G V	(1234A GINA BIRCH B V (1234A PALMOLIVE				D (4A VICKI ASPINALL VLN (4A		
LORA LOGIC	SAX	(A						

R18 MARVIN RAINWATER

MARVIN RAINWATER	V	(ALL	(A) GONNA FIND ME A BLUEBIRD		196	MGM	US	4046
			(B) SONGS		196	MGM	US	3534
			(C) WITH A HEART		19	MGM	US	3721
			(D) MARVIN RAINWATER		19	CROWN	US	5307
			(E) GETS COUNTRY FEVER		1972	PHILIPS	UK	6414 110
			(F) NEW COUNTRY SOUND		1974	GEM		GES 1108
			(G) ESPECIALLY FOR YOU		1976	WESTWOOD		WRS 101

R19 RAM JAM

PETER CHARLES	D	(A	(A) RAM JAM	1977 EPIC US 35387		UK 82215
BILL BARTLETT	G V	(A	(B) PORTRAIT OF THE ARTIST	19 EPIC US 34885		
HOWIE BLAUVELT	B V	(A				
MYKE SCAVONE	V PERC	(A				

R20 RAMASES (UK)

RAMASES		(AB	(A) SPACE HYMNS		1971 VERTIGO	UK	6360 046
SEL		(AB	(A) SPACE HYMNS		1980 VERTIGO	NL	9199 134
ERIC STEWART	G SYN	(A	(B) GLASS TOP COFFIN		1975 VERTIGO	UK	6360 115
LOL CREME	G SYN	(A					
KEVIN GODLEY	D FLT	(A	GRAHAM GOULDMAN	G B (A	MARTIN RAPHAEL	SITAR(A	PETE KINGSMAN B (B
ROGER HARRISON	D	(B	BARRY KIRSCH	K (B	JO ROMERO	G (B	SUE GLOVER V (B
BOB BERTLES	SAX	(B	COLIN THURSTON	B (B	SUNNY LESLIE	V (B	KAY GARNER V (B
EDDIE LESTER CHORALE	V	(B					

R20A RAMASES(GER)

WINFRIED LANGHORST	K V	(	(A) LA LEYLA		1975 SKY	SKY 002
HANS KLINKHAMMER	B	(	(B) ETERNITY RISE		1978 SKY	SKY 020
NORBERT LANGHORST	G	(				
HERBERT NATHO	V	(	REINHARD SCHROTER	D (A		

R21 RAMATAM

APRIL LAWTON	G B V HCA	(AB	(A) RAMATAM		1972 ATLANTIC	UK K40415	US SD7236
TOMMY SULLIVAN	K G V WIND	(AB	(A) IN APRIL CAME THE DAWNING		1973 ATLANTIC		US SD7261
MITCH MITCHELL	D	(A					
MIKE PINERA	G V	(A	RUSS SMITH	B V (A	JIMMY WALKER	V PERC(B	BRUCE MORGENHEIM VLN (A
SELDON POWELL	HRNS	(B	GARNETT BROWN	HRNS (B	ARTHUR KAPLAN	HRNS (B	JOE NEWMAN HRNS(B
MARVIN STAMM	HRNS	(B	RAYMOND BECKENSTEIN	HRN(B	JOE SHEPLEY	HRNS (B	DOMINICK GRAVINE HRNS(B
STRING SECTION		(B					

R22 BONNIE RAITT

BONNIE RAITT	G V	(ALL	(A) BONNIE RAITT		1971 WB	US WS 1953 UK	K56255
JUNIOR WELLS	HCA	(A	(B) GIVE IT UP		1972 WB	US BS 2643 UK	K46189
A C REED	SAX	(A	(C) TAKIN' MY TIME		1973 WB	US BS 2729 UK	K46261
WILLIE MURPHY	V K	(A	(C) TAKIN' MY TIME		1975 WB	RI UK	K56254
FREEBO	B V	(ABCDEFG	(D) STREET LIGHTS		1974 WB	US BS 2818 UK	K56075
PETER BELL	G	(A	(E) HOME PLATE		1975 WB	US BS 2864 UK	K56160
DOUGLAS SPURGEON	TROM	(A	(F) SWEET FORGIVNESS		1977 WB	US BS 2990 UK	K56323
PETER ASHER	V	(G	(G) THE GLOW		1979 WB	US 3369 UK	K56706
RUSSELL HAGEN	G	(A					
STEPHEN BRADLEY	D	(A	VOYLE HARRIS	TPT (A	MAURICE JACOX	WIND (A	EUGENE HOFFMAN SAX (A
PAUL BARRERE	G	(C	JOHN HALL	G (BCDE	BILL PAYNE	K V (CEFG	JIM KELTNER D (C
MILT HOLLAND	PERC	(C	EARL PALMER	D (C	TAJ MAHAL	B V HCA (C	GEORGE BOHANON TROM(CE
OSCAR BRASHEAR	HRNS	(C	ERNIE WATTS	SAX (C	SAM CLAYTON	CONGA(CF	VAN DYKE PARKS K V (C
ANTHONY TERRAN	HRNS	(C	GLEN FERRIS	HRNS (C	JOEL PESKIN	HRNS (C	MARTIN KRYSTALL HRNS(C
ROBERT HARDAWAY	HRNS	(C	BUD BRISBOIS HRNS	(C	LOWELL GEORGE	G (C	DON GROLNICK K (DG
STEPHEN GADD	D	(D	DAVID SPINOZZA	G (D	ARTHUR JENKINS	PERC (D	LEON PENDARVIS K (D
BOB KREINAR	B	(D	CHARLES BROWN	G (D	JEFF MIRANOV	G (D	DAVID LASLEY V (D
LOU COURTNEY	V	(D	JERRY FRIEDMAN	G (D	CARL HALL	V (D	SHARON REDD K (D
TASHA THOMAS	V	(D	JOHN TROPEA	G (D	RALPH McDONALD	PERC (D	PAUL GRIFFIN K (D
JOHN MAYER	K	(D	RICHARD DAVIS	B (D	ROBERT MANN	G (D	TERRY REID V (D
EMMYLOU HARRIS	V	(E	GREG PRESTOPINO	V (E	WILLOW VANDER HOEK	V (E	JEFF LABES K (F
MICHAEL McDONALD	V	(F	CARLENA WILLIAMS	V (E	NATALIE VENABLE	V (E	GARY MALLABER D (E
WILL McFARLANE	G	(EF	FRED TACKETT	K G (EF	JAY WINDING	K (E	DENNIS WHITTED D (BEF
WILLIAM SMITH	K	(E	JOE PORCARO	PERC (E	JEFF PORCARO	PERC (E	JOHN SEBASTIAN A'HARP(E
JERRY JUMONVILLE	SAX	(E	JIM GORDON	SAX (E	DICK HYDE	HRNS (E	VANETTA FIELDS V (E
ROBBIE MONTGOMERY	V	(E	MAXAYN LEWIS	V (EFG	JACKSON BROWNE	V (E	ROSEMARY BUTLER V (EFG
JOHN D SOUTHER	V	(EFG	DEBBIE GREENE	V (E	JOHN HERALD	V (E	TOM WAITS V (E
DAVID GRISMAN	MAND	(F	LESTER CHAMBERS	V (F	TERRY EATON	SAX (B	TIM MOORE V (B
PAUL BUTTERFIELD	HCA	(BG	GENE STASHUK CELLO	(B	MARTY GREBB	SAX (B	MERL SAUNDERS PNO (B
KAL DAVID	G	(B	AMOS GARRETT	G (B	ERIC KAZ	VIBES(B	WELLS KELLY CONGA(B
T J TINDALL	G	(B	MARK JORDAN	K (B	JACKIE LOMAX	V (B	JACK VIERTEL G (B
DAVE HOLLAND	B	(B	LOU TERRICIANO	PNO (B	CHRIS PARKER	D (B	JOHN PAYNE WIND(B
PETER ECKLUND	CORNET	(B	WADDY WACHTEL	G V (G	DANNY KORTHCHMAR	G V (G	BOB GLAUB B (G
							(CONTINUED)

BONNIE RAITT   R22

RICK MAROTTA	D	(G	KEN EDWARDS	V	(G	TREVOR LAWRENCE	SAX (G	LARRY WILLIAMS	SAX (G
DAVID SANBORN	SAX	(G	STEVE MADAIO	TPT	(G	CRAIG FULLER	V	(G	JOHN GUERIN	D (G
BOB MAGNUSSON	B	(G							

PHIL RAMBOW   R23

PHILIP RAMBOW	G V	(ALL		(A) SHOOTING GALLERY	1979	EMI	UK	EMC 3304
MICK RONSON	G	(1		(1) 1977 TOUR				
MAGGIE RONSON	V	(1						
DAVE DRILL	B	(1	LAURIE JELLYMAN	D	(1	HUGH BURNS	G	(A	DAVE COCHRAN	B (A
JOHN MACKENZIE		(A	BLAIR CUNNINGHAM	D	(A	PETE WINGFIELD	K V	(A	JOE BREEN	(A
JOHN KIRKPATRICK		(A	TONY BEARD		(A	DAVE DONEN	D PERC(	PETER GORIN	B (
TOM SPAHN	K	(						

RAMONES   R24

JOHNNY RAMONE	G	(ABCDE	(A) RAMONES	1976 MERCURY	UK 9103 253
JOEY RAMONE	V	(ABCDE	(A) RAMONES	1976 SIRE	US 7520	RI 1977 6020
DEE DEE RAMONE	B	(ABCDE	(B) RAMONES LEAVE HOME	1976 MERCURY	UK 9103 254
TOMMY RAMONE	D	(ABCE	(B) RAMONES LEAVE HOME	1976 SIRE	US 7528	RI 1977 6031
MARC BELL RAMONE	D	(D	(C) ROCKET TO RUSSIA	1977 SIRE	US 6042	UK 9103 255
			(D) ROAD TO RUIN	1978 SIRE	SRK 6063
			(E) ITS ALIVE (DBLE)	1979 SIRE	SRK26074
			(F) END OF THE CENTURY	1980 SIRE	SRK 6077

ELLIOTT RANDALL   R25

ELLIOTT RANDALL	G V	(ABC	(A) RANDALLS ISLAND	1970 POLYDOR	UK 2489 004
BOB PIAZZA	B V	(A	(B) ROCK'N'ROLL CITY	1973 POLYDOR	5026
ALLEN HERMAN	D PERC(A	(C) RANDALLS NEW YORK	1977 KIRSHNER	US 34351
PAUL FLEISHER	WIND (A			
GEORGE ANDREWS	PNO	(A	ANDY ALISON	B	(A	TERRY ADAMS	K	(A	RICHARD BOCK	CELLO(A
POT	PNO	(A	BOB BABITT	B	(C	RUBENS BASSINI	PERC (C	GENE BIANCO	HARP (C
KEN BISCHEL	K	(C	SUZANNE CIANI	K	(C	JERRY FRIEDMAN	G	(C	STEVE GADD	D (C
PAUL GRIFFIN	K	(C	WILL LEE	B	(C	TONY LEVIN	B	(C	JESSE LEVY	CELLO(C
RALPH MACDONALD	PERC (C	JIMMY MAELEN	PERC (C	MITCH MARGO	V G K(C	LESLIE MILLER	V (C
JEFF MIRANOV	G	(C	JEFF PORCARO	D	(C	ALLEN SCHWARZBERG	D	(C	JAY SIEGEL	V (C
THE TOKENS	V	(C						

BOOTS RANDOLPH   R26

BOOTS RANDOLPH	SAX	(ALL	YAKETY SAX	19	MONUMENT US 18002	US RI MC6600
MAYBELLE CARTER		(*	HIP BOOTS	19	MONUMENT UK 5002	US RI MC6601
CHET ATKINS	G	(*	MORE YAKETY SAX	19	MONUMENT US 18037	RI MC6602
JOSH GRAVES	G	(*	THE FANTASTIC BOOTS RANDOLPH	19	MONUMENT UK 5012	US RI MC6603
			BOOTS WITH STRINGS	19	MONUMENT UK 5003	US RI MC6604
			SAX-SATIONAL	19	MONUMENT UK 5022	US RI MC6605
			VOICES & STRINGS	19	MONUMENT	US RI MC6606
			SUNDAY SAX	19	MONUMENT	US RI MC6607
			THE SOUND OF BOOTS	19	MONUMENT	US RI MC6608
			WITH LOVE	19	MONUMENT	US RI MC6609
			BOOTS & STOCKING	19	MONUMENT	US RI MC6610
			YAKETY REVISITED	19	MONUMENT UK 5040	US RI MC6611
			HIP BOOTS	19	MONUMENT	US RI MC6612
			BOOTS WITH BRASS	19	MONUMENT	US RI MC6613
			HOMER LOUIS RANDOLPH	19	MONUMENT	US RI MC6614
			GREAT HITS OF TODAY	19	MONUMENT US 31908	US RI MC6615
			SENTIMENTAL JOURNEY	19	MONUMENT	US RI MC6616
			(*)COUNTRY BOOTS	1974 MONUMENT US 32912	US RI MC6617
			COOL BOOTS	19	MONUMENT	US RI MC6618
			GREATEST HITS	1976 MONUMENT UK 80548	US RI MG7602
			PARTY BOOTS (DBL)	1976 MONUMENT US 34082	US RI MPB604
			COOL BOOTS	1976 MONUMENT US 33803	
			THE YANKIN SAX MAN	196 CAMDEN	CAS 825
			SAX APPEAL	19 MERCURY	US MG7611
			THE WORLD OF	1973 MONUMENT UK 68203	

ERIC RANDOM   R26A

ERIC RANDOM		(A) THAT'S WHAT I LIKE ABOUT ME	19 NEW HORMONE	ORG 6

RANDOM HOLD   R27

RANDOM HOLD	V	(A	(A) THE VIEW FROM HERE	1980 POLYDOR POLS1015	2383 564
DAVE FERGUSON	K	(A	(EP)RANDOM HOLD	1979 POLYDOR	RHX 1
DAVID RHODES	G	(A			
BILL MACCORMICK	B	(A	PETER PHIPPS	D	(A	DAVID LEECH	D	(	SIMON AINLEY	G V	(

RANDY PIE   R28

DICKY TARRACH	D	(ABCD	(A) SIGHTSEEING TOUR	1974 POLYDOR	2371 491
MANFRED THIERS	B V	(ABC	(B) HIGHWAY DRIVER	1974 POLYDOR	2371 555
WERNER BECKER	K V	(ABC	(C) KITSCH	1975 POLYDOR	2371 666
PETER FRENCH		(D	(D) ENGLAND ENGLAND	1976 POLYDOR	2664 160
BERND SCHULZ		(E	(E) FAST FORWARD	1977	
BERND WIPPICH	G V	(ABC			
RAINER BAUMANN	G	(A	JEAN JACQUES KRAVETZ	K (BC	JOCHEN PETERSEN	V G SAX(BC	GEORGE MEYER	(D
HERBERT HILDEBRAND	G V	(D			

RANK STRANGERS   R28A

CHRIS DARROW	G V MAND	(A	(A) RANK STRANGERS	1977 PACIFIC ARTS	US PAC7 112
JOHN SELK	V B	(A			
ROBB STRANDLUND	G V	(A	TEMPLETON PARCELY	VLN (A	CINDY EDWARDS	V	(A	MAX BUDA	HCA (A
POPE TERMAN	B	(A			

RANKING JOE   R29

RANKING JOE	V	(ABC	(A) WEAKHEART FADE AWAY	1978 GREENSLEEVES	GREL2
SLY DUNBAR	D	(C	(B) DUB IT IN A DANCE	1980 TROJAN	TRLS 194
SANTA	D	(C	(C) SATURDAY NIGHT JAMDOWN STYLE	1980 GREENSLEEVES	GREL 16
STYLE	D	(C			
FLABBA	B	(C	STEELIE	K	(C	ANSEL COLLINS	K	(C	GLADSTONE ANDERSON	K (C
SOREL	G	(C	BINGY BUNNY	G	(C	BONGO HERMAN	PERC (C	SKY JUICE	PERC (C
STICKY	PERC (C	HEADLEY BENNETT	SAX (C	VAL BENNETT	TROM (C	BOBBY ELLIS	TPT (C
JIMMY BECKER	HCA (C				

R30
RANKING TREVOR

RANKING TREVOR	V	(ABC	(A) IN FINE STYLE		1978 FRONT LINE	UK	FL 1015
SLY DUNBAR	D	(A	(B) 3 PIECE CHICKEN		1978 CHA CHA		CHALP 001
RANCHIE McLEAN	G B	(A					
ROBBIE SHAKESPEARE	B	(A	ANSEL COLLINS	K (A	TOUTER HARVEY	K (A	DUGGIE	G	(A
STICKY	PERC (A	BARNABAS		PERC (A			

R30A
RAPED

		(A) PRETTY PAEDOPHILES(EP)	19 PAROLE	UK	KNIT 1

R31
TOM RAPP

TOM RAPP	G V	(ABC	(A) TOM RAPP (FAMILIAR SONGS)	1972 REPRISE	US	MS 2.109
ART ELLIS FLT CONC	V	(BC	(B) STARDANCER	1972 BLUE THUMB	US	BTS 44
BILL ROLLINS	CELLO(BC		(C) SUNFOREST	1973 BLUE THUMB	US	BTS 56
STEVE McCORD	G	(BC				
JIM COLVARD	G DOBR(BC	CHARLIE McCOY HCA V G K(BC	BUZZ CASON	B (C	DIANE HARRIS	V (C
CHUCK COCHRAN	PNO (C	BUDDY SPICHER	VLN (BC	DAVID BRIGGS	PNO (BC	MIKE LEECH	B (BC
FARRELL MORRIS	PERC (C	BOBBY WOOD	PERC (BC	REGGIE YOUNG	PNO (BC	KARL HIMMEL	D (C
BOBBY THOMPSON	G BANJ(C	CHIP YOUNG	G (C	BOB MOORE	B (C	KENNY BUTTREY	D (C
BOB DOROUGH	PNO (C	BILL SALTER	B (C	WARREN SMITH	PERC (C	JIM ISBELL	D PERC(B
WELDON MYRICK	STEEL(B	FLORENCE WARNER	V (B	HARRY ORLOVE	G V MAND (B	STRING SECTION	(B

R32
RARE EARTH

GIL BRIDGES FLT V SAX	(ABCDEF	(A) GET READY	1970	TAMLA UK	STML11156 RARE EARTH US	507
PETE RIVERA	D V	(ABCDEF	(B) ECOLOGY	1971	TAMLA UK	STML11180 RARE EARTH US	514
JOHN PERSH	B V	(ABC	(C) ONE WORLD	1971	RARE EARTH UK	4001	US	520
ROD RICHARDS	G V	(A	(D) IN CONCERT	1972	RARE EARTH UK	301	US	534
KENNY JAMES	K	(A	(E) WILLIE REMEMBERS	1973	RARE EARTH UK	3008	US	543
RAY MONETTE	G V	(CEF	(F) MA	1973	RARE EARTH UK	3010	US	546
PETE HOORELBEKE	D V	(EF	(G) BACK TO EARTH	1975	TAMLA		US 6 548
MIKE URSO	B V	(EF	(H) MIDNIGHT LADY	1976	RARE EARTH UK	3013	US	550
ED GUZMAN	PERC (CE	(J) RARE EARTH	1977	PRODIGAL	UK	2007	US 10019
MARK OLSON	K V	(CEF	(K) BAND TOGETHER	1978	PRODIGAL	UK	2008	US 10025
			(L) GRAND SLAM	1978	PRODIGAL	UK	2009	
			( ) DREAM ANSWERS	19	VERVE		US 5056
			( ) DISQUE DO'R	1976	PATHE	FR	064 95295

R33
RAREBIRD

STEVE GOULD	V SAX B(ALL	(A) RAREBIRD	1969 CHARISMA	UK	CAS 1005
FRED KELLY	PERC (CDEF	(B) AS YOUR MIND FLIES BY	1970 CHARISMA	UK CAS1011 US ABC	716
DAVE KAFFINETTI	K	(ALL	(C) EPIC FOREST	1972 POLYDOR	UK 2442 101 US	5530
ANDY RAE	B	(	(D) SOMEBODYS WATCHING	1973 POLYDOR	UK 2383 211 US	6502
KEVIN LAMB	ORG	(AG	(E) BORN AGAIN	1974 POLYDOR	UK 2383 274 US	6506
GRAHAM FIELD	ORG	(AG	(F) RAREBIRD	1975 POLYGRAM	UK 9299 008 US	4514
MARK ASHTON	D V	(AG	(G) SYMPATHY	1976 CHARISMA	UK	CS 4
ANDY CURTIS	G	(CDH	(H) RARE BIRD(POLYDOR SPECIAL)	1977 POLYDOR	UK 2384 078
AL MATTHEWS	PERC (D			
NICK POTTER	B	(DH	SAMMY ABU	PERC (D	PAUL HOLLAND	PERC (D	PAUL KORDA	V (D
PAUL KARAS	B	(CH	NICKY JAMES	V (D	JOHN WETTON	B (D

R33A
RAS MICHAEL

RAS MICHAELS	(AB	(A) NYAHBINGHI	1975 TROJAN	TRS 113
		(B) TRIBUTE	1976 TROJAN	TRS 132
		(C) FREEDOM SOUND	1979 DYNAMIC	DYLP3004

R34
THE YOUNG RASCALS

FELIX CAVALIERE	K V	(ALL	(A) THE YOUNG RASCALS	1966 ATLANTIC	US SD8122
DINO DANELLI	D	(ALL	(B) COLLECTIONS	1966 ATLANTIC	US SD8134
GENE CORNISH	G	(ABCDEFGH	(C) GROOVIN'	1967 ATLANTIC	US SD8148
EDDIE BRIGATI	V	(ABCDEFG	(D) ONCE UPON A DREAM	1968 ATLANTIC	UK 588 098 US SD8169
ROBERT POPWELL	B	(JK	(E) GREATEST HITS (TIMEPEACE)	1968 ATLANTIC	US SD8190
ANN SUTTON	V	(JK	(F) FREEDOM SUITE	1969 ATLANTIC	UK 588 183 US SD8901
BUZZY FEITEN	G	(JK	(G) SEARCH & NEARNESS	1969 ATLANTIC	UK 2400113 US SD8246
HAROLD COWART	B	(G	(H) SEE	1970 ATLANTIC	US SD8246
CHUCK RAINEY	B	(GH	(J) PEACEFUL WORLD	1971 CBS	UK 66292 US 30462
JOE NEWMAN	TPT	(G	(K) ISLAND OF REAL 1972	CBS	UK 64756 US 31103
JOE FARRELL	SAX	(G	(L) STAR COLLECTION	1973 MIDI	UK 30049 GERM 20022
SELDON POWELL	SAX	(G		
MOLLY HOLT	V	(J	HUBERT LAWS	FLT (H	RON CARTER	B (H	DANNY LABBATE	SAX (H
JOE BUSHKIN	PNO (H			

R35
RASPBERRIES

WALLY BRYSON	G	(AB	(A) RASPBERRIES	1972 CAPITOL	UK/US	11036
ERIC CARMEN	G V K(ABE	(B) FRESH	1973 CAPITOL	UK/US	11123
DAVE SMALLEY	G B	(AB	(C) SIDE THREE	1974 CAPITOL	UK/US	11220
JIM BONFANTI	D	(AB	(D) STARTING OVER	1974 CAPITOL	UK/US	11329
SCOTT McCARL	B	(	(E) BEST OF	1975 CAPITOL	UK/US	11524
MIKE McBRIDE	D	(	(E) BEST OF	1976 CAPITOL		CAPS 1026

R35A
RASPUTIN S STASH

		(A) RASPUTIN'S STASH	19 COTILLION	US	9046
		(B) RASPUTIN'S STASH	19 GEMIGO	US	5500

R35B
RASSES

LINCOLN THOMPSON	G V	(BC	(A) HUMANITY	1979 BALLISTIC	UAG 30227
KEITH PETERKIN	V	(B	(B) EXPERIENCE	1979 BALLISTIC	UAG 30259
CLINTON HALL	V	(B	(C) NATURAL WILD	1980 BALLISTIC	UAG 30309
LEROY WALLACE	D	(BD	(D) HARDER NA RASS	1980 BALLISTIC	LBR 1031
MIKEYBOOTH	D	(BCD		
BOBBY ELLIS	TPT	(BD	STICKY	PERC (BD	VAL DOUGLAS	B (BD	WIRE LINDO	K (BD
PABLO BLACK	K	(BD	GEOFFREY CHUNG	K (BD	CECIL LLOYD	K (BD	BUBBLER	HRNS(BD
BROTHER JOMO	PERC (BD	JOE JACKSON	K (BC	GEORGE MILLER	G (BD	DIGGLES	G (BD
ERNEST RANGLIN	G	(BD	TOMMY McCOOK	HRNS (BD	HEADLEY BENNETT	SAX (BD	BAGGA	B (BD
GRAHAM MABY	B	(C	RANCHIE McLEAN	D (C	GARY SANFORD	G (C	WILLIE LINDO	G (BC
DOUGIE	G	(C	DAVE HOUGHTON	D (C	ANSEL COLLINS	K (C	TONY GAD	SYN	(C
GEORGE OBAN	PERC (C	CRIS ALNE	DUB SOUNDS(C	MO	PERC(C		

R36
RASTUS

	(A) STEAMIN'	1972 NEIGHBORHOOD	NH3002

RATS   R37

(A) RATS FIRST   1974 GOODEAR   EARLH5003

RATTLES   R38

ACHIM REICHEL	G V (1	(A) TWIST AT THE STAR CLUB	1964 PHILIPS	BL 7614

ACHIM REICHEL   G V (1   (A) TWIST AT THE STAR CLUB   1964 PHILIPS   BL   7614
HERBERT HILDEBRAND   K B(1   (B) THE RATTLES   1965 FONTANA
DICKY TARRACH   D   (1   (C) HURRA! DIE RATTLE KOMMEN 1966 FONTANA
RUGY RUGINSTEIN   G   (1   (D) ATTENTION   19   FONTANA   6434 162
DIETER SADLOWSKI   D   ((E) GREATEST HITS   1969 FONTANA 701707 US MERCURY 61127
HAJO KREUTZFELD   G   ((F) THE RATTLES   1971 DECCA   UK SKL 5008
ZAPPO LUNGEN   B   (23   (G) TONIGHT STARRING EDNA   1972 PHILIPS   6305 176
FRANK MILLER   G   (23   (H) GIN MILL   1974 RCA   PPLI 4016
HERBERT BONHOLD   D   (2   (EP) TEENBEAT   19   ARIOLA   541174
EDNA BEJARANO   V   (2G   (EP) TEENBEAT 2   19   DECCA   DFE 8568
LINDA FIELDS   V   (3   (EP) RATTLES   19   PHILIPS   423 560
GEORGE MEYER   G V (3   (EP) RATTLES   19   FONTANA   466 030
LUDE LAFAYETTE   K   (3   (1) 1961   (2) 1970   (3) 1975
AL BROCK   D   (3

GENYA RAVAN   R39

GENYA RAVAN V HCA PERC(ALL   (A) GENYA RAVAN WITH BABY   1972 CBS   UK 64872 US 31001
BOBBY KEYS   SAX (C   (B) THEY LOVE ME /THEY LOVE ME NOT 1973 DUNHILL   US 50143
KENNETH RICE   D   (C   (C) GOLDIE ZELKOWITZ   1974 JANUS   US 3060
FRED BECKMIER   B   (C   (D) URBAN DESIRE   1978 20th CENTURY BTH8007   T 562
KEN MARCO   G   (C   (E) AND I MEAN IT   1979 20th CENTURY   T 595
DANNY KORTCHMAR   G   (C
STEVE BECKMIER G   (C   LARRY NASH   K   (C   GABRIEL MAKLER   K   (C   TREVOR LAWRENCE K HRNS(C
WILLIAM SMITH   K   (C   MAILTO CORREA   PERC (C STEVE MADAIO   HRNS (C ABIGALE HANESS   V   (C
GWENDOLYN EDWARDS V (C C C WILLIAMSON   V   (C   CHARLIE GIORDANO K   (DE CONRAD TAYLOR   G   (DE
RITCHIE FLIEGLER G MAND(D DON NOSSOV   B   (D   BOBBY CHEN   D   (DE STUART DAYE   G   (D
JOEY RIBAUDO   V   (D   PAUL OPALACH   B   (D   JOHN PAUL FETTA B   (D   DAVID LASLEY   V   (D
IVAN KRAL   V   (D   LOU REED   V   (D   MITCH STYLES   G   (A   NICK OLIVA   K   (A
JOHN PLATANIA   G   (A   PETER HODGSON   B   (A   BRIAN KEENAN   D   (A   BERNARD WILLIAMS CONGA(A
MIKE LOMBARDI   B   (E   IAN HUNTER   V   (E   MICK RONSON   G   (E

RAVEN   R40

JOHN CIPOLLINA   G   (A   (A) 1976
ANDY KIRBY   D V (A
DAVID WEBER   D   (A   SKIP OLSEN B (A   NICKY HOPKINS   K (A GREG DOUGLAS G (A HUTCH HUTCHINSON K (A
DAVE WALKER

RAVEN   R40A

(A) LIVE AT THE INFERNO   19   DISCOVERY   US   36133

RAPHAEL RAVENSCROFT   R40B

RAPHAEL RAVENSCROFT   SAX FLT(A (A) HER FATHER DIDN'T LIKE ME ANYWAY 1979 PORTRAIT   35683
GARY TAYLOR   B   (A
KUMA HARADA   B   (A   PETE ZORN   B FLT(A STEVE YORK   B   (A   LIAM GENOCKEY   D   (A
PRESTON HEYMAN D   (A   STRETCH   D   (A   GEOFF BRITTON   D   (A   TOMMY EYRE   K   (A
JEFF BANNISTER K   (A   BETSY COOKE   K V (A   PETE SOLLEY   K   (A   NIGEL JENKINS   G   (A
JULIAN LITTMAN G   (A   RICHARD BRUNTON G   (A   STEVE WALLER   G   (A   BRIAN HOLLOWAY   G   (A
FRANK RICOTTI   PERC (A DAVID ULM   PERC (A CHARLES BOROMEO V   (A   PAUL DA VINCI   V   (A
MAGGIE RYDER   V   (A   VIVIAN   V   (A   DENNIS O'BRIEN   V   (A   ALBERT WING   WIND (A
BIL SKEAT   WIND (A VIC ASH   SAX (A   MANNY WINTER   SAX (A   KEITH BIRD   SAX(A
JOHN WILBRAHAM TPT (A   DEREK WATKINS   TPT (A   EDDIE BLAIR   TPT (A   KENNY BAKER   TPT(A
DEREK HEALEY   TPT (A   JOHN HUCKRIDGE TPT (A   DON LUSHER   TROM (A WALLY SMITH   TROM(A
BOBBY LAMB   TROM (A KEN GOLDIE   TROM   (A   JIM BROWN   HRNS (A JOHN PIGNEGNY   HRNS(A

RAVERS   R41

(A) PUNK ROCK CHRISTMAS (EP)   1978   RHINO   RNEP 503

RAW MATERIAL   R42

(A) TIME IS   1971   NEON   NE 8

JAMES RAY   R43

JAMES RAY   V   (A   (A) JAMES RAY   1961   CAPRICE   US   1002

RAY OWEN'S MOON   R44

RAY OWEN   G V PNO(A (A) RAY OWEN'S MOON   1971   POLYDOR   UK   2425 061
SID GARDNER   G B K(A
DICK STUBBS   G   (A   L ES NICOL   G   (A IAN McLEAN   D   (A

RAYDIO   R45

RAY PARKER   G   (ABC (A) RAYDIO   1978 ARISTA US 4163 UK SPART 1041
VINCENT BONHAM   (A   (B) ROCK ON   1979 ARISTA US 4212 UK SPART 1087
JERRY KNIGHT   B   (A   (C) TWO PLACES AT THE SAME TIME 1980 ARISTA   UK SPART 1121
NORMA JEAN BELL SAX (B   (D) JUST LOVE   1981 ARISTA US)%$£ UK SPART 1152
ARNELL CARMICHAEL   (ABC
CHARLES FEARING G (ABC LARRY TOLBERT   (BC DARREN CARMICHAEL   (BC OLLIE BROWN D V (BC
SYLVESTER RIVERS PNO (C JACK ASHFORD PERC (C KEN PETERSON V TPT(BC HORATIO GORDON SAX (BC
VALORIE JONES   V   (B   FRANCIS PEARMAN V   (B   CHERYL BROWN V   (B   HERBIE HANCOCK K   (C
GARY COLEMAN   VIBES(C DEBORAH THOMAS V   (C   NORMA JEAN BELL SAX (B

CHRIS REA   R46

CHRIS REA   V   (ABC (A) WHATEVER HAPPENED TO BENNY SANTINI 1978 MAGNET UK MAG5021 US UALA 879
ROD ARGENT   K   (A   (B) DELTICS   1979 MAGNET UK   MAGL5028
PETE WINGFIELD K   (A   (C) TENNIS   1980 MAGNET UK   MAGL5032
DAVE MATTACKS   D   (A

DAVID REA   R47

DAVID REA   G V BANJO (AB (A) MAVERICK CHILD   19
                              (B) BY THE GRACE OF GOD   19

JOHN DAWSON READ   R48

JOHN DAWSON READ G V (AB (A) A FRIEND OF MINE   1975 CHRYSALIS UK   CHR 1075
ALAN HODGE   G   (A   (B) READ ON   1976 CHRYSALIS UK   CHR 1102
B J COLE   STEEL(A
LES HURDLE   B   (A   TERRY COX   D   (A   ALBERT HALL   HRNS (A RAY SWINFIELD   FLT (A
DEAN FORD   V   (A   GUY FLETCHER   V   (A

READYMADES

R49
JONATHAN POSTAL   B V (A
RICKY SLUDGE   G   (
BRITTLEY BLACK   D   (MOREY GOLDSTEIN SAX K(A   WAYNE DIZEL   G   (
R50
REAL KIDS

JOHN FELICE   G V (A1   (A) THE REAL KIDS   1978 BRONZE BRON 509 RED STAR RS2
ALAN PAULINO   B V (A1   (1) 1976
HOWARD FERGUSON   D   (A1
BILL BORGEOLLI   G   (A1
R50A
ROGER C REALE & RUE MORGUE

ROGER C REALE   B V (A   (A) ROGER C REALE & RUE MORGUE   1979 LONDON/BIG SOUND   SHY 8528
BILLY MICHAELS   D V (A
G E SMITH   G   (A   MICHAEL CAVADINI PNO (A
R51
REBEL

TONY RIVERS   V
STUART ELLIOTT   D
GEORGE FORD   B   DUNCAN MACKAY   K
R51A
RECORD PLAYERS

(A) GIVE AN INCH   (EP)   1979 WRECKORD   UK   AERO1004
R52
RECORDS

JOHN WICKS   G V (A   (A) SHADES IN BED   1979 VIRGIN   UK   V2122
HUW GOWER   G V (A   (B) CRASHES   1980 VIRGIN   UK   V2155
PHIL BROWN   B V (A   (EP) HIGH HEELS(FREE WITH A)   1979 VIRGIN
WILL BIRCH   D   (A
IAN GIBBONS   K   (A
R52A
RED CLAY RAMBLERS

BILL HICKS   FDL V(CD   (A) THE RED CLAY RAMBLERS   19   FOLKWAYS   US   31039
TOMMY THOMPSON   G V (CD   (B) STOLEN LOVE   19   FLYING FISH US 009
MIKE CRAVER   D K G(CD   (C) TWISTED LAUREL   1977 FLYING FISH US 030 SONET UK 731
JIM WATSON   MAND G V B(CD   (D) MERCHANTS LUNCH   1978 FLYING FISH US   SONET UK 745
JACK HERRICK B V HCA TPT(CD   (E) CHUCKIN' THE FRIZZ   1979 FLYING FISH US 089

R53
RED CRAYOLA

MAYO THOMPSON   (ABC   (A) PARABLE OF ARABLE LAND   1967 INTERNATIONAL ARTISTS US IALP 2
STEVE CUNNINGHAM   (AB   (A) PARABLE OF ARABLE LAND   1978 RADAR   UK RAD12
TOMMY SMITH   D   (AB   (B) GOD BLESS THE RED CRAYOLA   1968 INTERNATIONAL ARTISTS US IALP 7
RICK BARTHELME   (A   (B) GOD BLESS THE RED CRAYOLA   1978 RADAR   UK RAD16
HOLLY PRITCHARD   V   (B   (C) SOLDIER TALK   1979 RADAR   UK RAD18
JESSE CHAMBERLAIN   (C
DICK CUTHELL   (C   SCOTT KRAUSS   (C   CHRISTINE THOMPSON   (C   TOM HERMAN   (C
LORA LOGIC   SAX (C   DAVID THOMAS   (C   TONY MAIMONE   (C   ALLEN RAVENSTINE (C
R53A
RED EYE

DAVE HODGKINS   G V (A   (A) ONE MANS POISON   19   PENTAGRAM   US   PE 10006
BOB BEREMAN   D   (A
BILL KIRKHAM   B V (A   DOUGLAS 'RED'MARK G V (A
R53B
RED HELICOPTER

(EP) BRACKNELL   19   PAY FOR
R53C
RED NOISE

PATRICK VIAN   G V (A   (A) SARCELLES LOCHERES   1970 FUTURA   FR   RED01
JEAN CLAUDE CENCU WIND V(A
DANIEL GEOFFROY   B V (A   PHILIP BARRY   D G (A   JOHN LIVENGOOD   ORG (A   AUSTIN BLUE   PERC (A
R54
REDBONE

TONY BELLAMY   G V (ABCDEF   (A) REDBONE   1970 CBS   US   501   UK   64069
PAT VEGAS   B   (ABCDEF   (B) POTLATCH   1971 EPIC US 30109   UK   64198
LOLLY VEGAS   G V (ABCDEF   (C) WITCH QUEEN OF NEW ORLEANS   1971 EPIC   UK   64709
PETER DEPOE   D   (ABCD   (C) MESSAGE FROM A DRUM   1971 EPIC US 30815
DON BRANKER   (C   (D) ALREADY HERE   1973 EPIC US 31598   UK   65072
WARREN WINSTON   (C   (E) WOVOKA   1973 EPIC US 32462   UK   65500
EDDIE CAICEDO   (C   (F) BEADED DREAMS   1974 EPIC US 33053   UK   80429
JOHN D'ANDREA   (C   (G) COME & GET YOUR REDBONE   1975 EPIC US 33456   UK   22003
RASMUSSEN TOWER   (C   (H) CYCLES   19   RCA   AFLI 2352
CLARENCE McDONALD   (C   (J) BEST OF   19   EPIC   UK   65678
BUTCH PILLERA   D V (EF
RED RHODES   STEEL(D   TERRY FURLONG   G   (D   GORDON DE WITTE PNO (D   ELIJAH HORN SECTION (D
CHIPPER LAVERGNE PERC (D   RONNIE BARRON   PERC (D   DAVID OLIVER   V   (D   MICHAEL FREDA   V (D
BONNIE BRAMLETT   V   (F   MERRY CLAYTON   V   (F   CLYDIE KING   V   (F   ED GREENE   (C
R55
NOEL REDDING

NOEL REDDING   G V B(AB   (A) CLONAKILTY COWBOYS   1975 RCA UK RS 1030   APLI 1237
ERIC BELL   G V (AB   (B) BLOWIN'   1976 RCA UK RS 1084   APLI 1863
LES SAMSON   D   (AB
DAVE CLARKE   K V (AB   DON MICHAEL YOUNG K   (B   STANLEY SCHNIER B   (B   ANDY KEELY   V (B
R56
OTIS REDDING

OTIS REDDING   V   (ALL   (A) THE PAIN IN MY HEART   1965 ATLANTIC   US 33161 UK 587042
(1941/1967)   (B) OTIS BLUE   1966 ATLANTIC   US 33284 UK 588036
STEVE CROPPER   G   (B   (B) OTIS BLUE   19   ATLANTIC RIUK K40003 US VOLT412
JOE CURTIS   V   (QS   (C) DICTIONARY OF SOUL   1966 ATLANTIC US 33284   UK 588 050
JIMMY KING   ((C) DICTIONARY OF SOUL   19   US VOLT416
RON CALDWELL   ((D) LIVE IN EUROPE   1966 ATLANTIC US 33286 US 228 017
PHALIN JONES   ((D) LIVE IN EUROPE   19   US VOLT416
CARL CUNNINGHAM   ((E) DOCK OF THE BAY   1968 ATLANTIC US 33288 US 228 022
BEN CAULEY   ((E) DOCK OF THE BAY   19   ATLANTIC UKRI K40076 US VOLT419
CARLA THOMAS   V   (P   (F) IMMORTAL OTIS REDDING   1968 ATLANTIC US 33252   UK 588 113
SAMMIE COLEMAN   TPT (G   (F) IMMORTAL OTIS REDDING   19   ATLANTIC UKRI K40019
                                   (G) IN PERSON AT THE WHISKEY   1968 ATLANTIC UK 588 148 US   33265
JOHN FARRIS   TPT (G   (H) LOVE MAN   1969 ATLANTIC US 33289   UK 228 025
CLARENCE JOHNSON TROM (G   (H) LOVE MAN   19   ATLANTIC UKRI K40078
BOB HOLLOWAY   SAX (G   (I HISTORY OF OTIS REDDING   1969 ATLANTIC US 33261   UK 228 001
                                                                                             (CONTINUED)

OTIS REDDING

(CONTINUED)			
BOBBY PITTMAN	SAX (G	(I) HISTORY OF OTIS REDDING	197 ATLANTIC UKRI K40066 US VOLT418
DONALD HENRY	SAX (G	(J) TELL THE TRUTH	1970 ATLANTIC UK 2400 018 US 33333
JAMES RANDOLF YOUNG G((G		(K) THE BEST OF	1972 ATLANTIC UK K 60016 US 31801
ELBERT WOODSON	D (G	(L) SINGS SOUL BALLADS	197 VOLT US 411
		(M) SOUL ALBUM	19 ATLANTIC UK 588 011 US 33285
		(N) REMEMBERING	19 ATLANTIC UK 2464 003
		(P) KING & QUEEN	19 STAX US 716
		(Q) HERE COMES SOME SOUL	19 ATLANTIC
		(R) MONTEREY POP (1 SIDE)	19 REPRISE US 2029
		(S) SOUL AS SUNG BY	19 ALLSHIRE US 5082
		(T) OTIS REDDING STORY (DBL)	19 ATCO FR 60013
		(U) OTIS REDDING STORY VOL 2	19 ATCO FR 60016

THE REDS

(A) THE REDS	1979 A&M	UK AMLH64772

REDUCERS

(A) MAN WITH GUN(EP)	19 VIBES	UK VR 003

REDWING

RON FLOEGEL	G V (ABC	(A) REDWING	1971 FANTASY US 8409
ANDREW SAMUELS	G V B(ABC	(A) REDWING	1971 UA UK UAS29188
GEORGE HULLIN	D V (ABC	(B) WHAT THIS COUNTRY NEEDS	1972 FANTASY US 9405
TOM PHILLIPS G K STEEL (AC		(C) TAKE ME HOME	1973 FANTASY UK FT518 US 9405
JOHN MYERS	B (C	(D) DEAD OR ALIVE	1974 FANTASY US 9459
		(E) BEYOND THE SUN & STARS	1975 FANTASY US 9488

HERB REED

HERB REED	(A	(A) SWEET RIVER	197 PVK	UK PVK002

JIMMY REED

JIMMY REED	G V (ALL	(A)I'M JIMMY REED	19 USVEEJAY1004
PHIL UPCHURCH	B (KLCEDMR	(B)ROCKIN WITH JIMMY REED	19 US VEEJAY1008
LEFTY BATES	G (BCEFJKLMDRQ	(C) FOUND LOVE	19 US VEEJAY1022
AL DUNCAN	D (KMR	(D)NOW APPEARING	19 US VEEJAY1025
JIMMY REED JR	B (KMR	(E)AT CARNEGIE HALL	1962 STATESIDE UK SL10012 US VEEJAY1035
EDDIE TAYLOR	G (KLQABEFJMCDNP	(E)AT CARNEGIE HALL	19 BLUESWAY BLX60732 JOY JOYS 120
WAYNE BENNETT	G (L	(O) PREACHIN THE BLUES(4 TRACKS) 1963 STATESIDE UK SL10046
JIMMY TILLMAN	D (L	(F)THE BEST OF	196 US VEEJAY1039
JOHN LEE HOOKER	(O	(R)JUST JIMMY REED	1964 STATESIDE UK SL10055 US VEEJAY1050
MEMPHIS SLIM	(O	(R)JUST JIMMY REED	196 RI JOY JOYS146
MORRIS WILKERSON	D (QABEFJP	(G)T'AINT NO BIG THING	196 US VEEJAY1067
W C DALTON	G (QACEFM	(H)SINGS THE BEST OF THE BLUES	196 STATESIDE UK SL10069 US VEEJAY1072
HENRY GRAY	PNO (ACEFMQ	(J)PLAYS 12 STRING GUITAR BLUES	1964 STATESIDE UK SL10086 US VEEJAY1073
MILTON RECTOR	B (QAEFMC	(J)PLAYS 12 STRING GUITAR BLUES	1968 JOY JOYS132
EARL PHILLIPS	D (ACEDFBJMQ	(M)BOSS MAN OF THE BLUES	1964 STATESIDE UK SL10091 US VEEJAY1080
VERNELL FOURNIER	D (Q	(N)AT SOUL CITY	196 JOY JOYS 127 US VEEJAY1095
REMO BIONDI	G (QABEFM	(P)THE LEGEND,THE MAN	196 JOY JOYS 111 US VEEJAY8501
LEE BAKER	G (QCEFM	(K) SOULIN'	1968 STATESIDE UK SL10221
WILLIE DIXON	B (QCEFM	(K) SOULIN'	19 BLUESWAY US BLS 6009
MARY LEE REED	V (QEJM	NEW JIMMY REED	19 HMV UK CLP 3611
MARCUS JOHNSON	B (CEFJM	WAILIN' THE BLUES	19 MUSIDISC FR 6088 TRADITIOn US2069
CURTIS MAYFIELD	B (E	(L) BIG BOSS MAN	1973 BLUESWAY US BLS 6015
JOHNNY JONES	PNO (N	DOWN IN VIRGINIA	197 BLUESWAY US BLS 6024
HUBERT SUMLIN	G (N	I AIN'T FROM CHICAGO	1973 BLUESWAY US BLS 6054
		THE ULTIMATE	197 BLUESWAY US BLS 6067
		THE BEAT OF JIMMY REED	1974 G N P CRESENDO US GNP 10006
		JIMMY REED IS BACK	1976 JOY JOYS 264
		(Q)MEMORIAL ALBUM VOL 1	1976 DJM 28033
		LET THE BOSSMAN SPEAK	19 BLUE ON BLUES US 10001
		AS JIMMY IS	197 ROKER US 6067
		COLD CHILLS	19 ANTILLES US 7007
		HISTORY OF	19 TRIP US 8012
		JIMMY REED	19 EVEREST US 234
		UPSIDE YOUR HEAD	1980 CHARLY UK CRB 1003
		HIGH & LONESOME	1980 CHARLY UK CRB 1013
		SHAME SHAME SHAME (EP)	1980 CHARLY UK CTD 105

LOU REED

LOU REED	G V K(ALL	(A) LOU REED	1972 RCA US LSP 4701 UK SF8281
CLEM CATTINI	PERC (A	(B) TRANSFORMER	1972 RCA US LSP 4807
RICK WAKEMAN	K (A	(B) TRANSFORMER	1980 RCA INT UK INTS5061
CALEB QUAYE	G PNO(A	(C) BERLIN	1973 RCA UK RS1002
STEVE HOWE	G (A	(D) ROCK'N'ROLL ANIMAL	1974 RCA US APLI0472 UK PL 10472
PAUL KEOGH	G (A	(E) SALLY CANT DANCE	1974 RCA US APLI0611 UK PL 10611
LES HURDLE	B (A	(F) LOU REED LIVE	1975 RCA US APLI0959 UK RS1007
BRIAN ODGERS	B (A	(G) METAL MACHINE MUSIC	1975 RCA CPL2 1101
DAVID BOWIE	V (B	(H) CONEY ISLAND BABY	1976 RCA US APLI0915 UK RS1035
MICK RONSON	G (B	(H) CONEY ISLAND BABY	197 RCA US ANLI2480
THUNDERTHIGHS	V (B	(J) ROCK'N'ROLL HEART	1976 ARISTA US 4100 UK ARTY 142
KLAUS VOORMANN	B (B	(K) WALK ON THE WILD SIDE (BEST OF)	1977 RCA US APLI2001 UK PL 12001
HERBIE FLOWERS	B (B	(L) STREET HASSLE	1978 ARISTA US 4169 UK 5PARTY1045
JOHN HALSEY	D (B	(M) LIVE TAKE NO PRISONERS	1978 ARISTA US 8502 UK XL 03066
BARRY DE SOUZA	D (B	(N) VICIOUS	1979 RCA NL 42731
RONNIE ROSS	SAX (B	(O) THE BELLS	1979 ARISTA UK SPART 1093
STEVE HUNTER	G (CDF	(P) GROWING UP IN PUBLIC	1980 ARISTA UK SPART 1131
ALLAN MacMILLAN	K (C	(Q) ROCK'N'ROLL DIARY	1980 ARISTA UK DART 8
MICHAEL BRECKER	SAX (C		

RANDY BRECKER	TPT (C	JACK BRUCE	B (C	AYNSLEY DUNBAR	D (C	BOB EZRIN	K V (C
TONY LEVIN	B (C	GENE MARTYNEC	G K V(C	JON PIERSON	TROM (C	DICK WAGNER	G V (CDF
BLUE WEAVER	K (C	B J WILSON	D (C	STEVE WINWOOD	K (C	DENNIS FERRANTE	V (C
STEVE HYDEN	V (C	ELIZABETH MARSH	V (C	RAY COLCORD	K (DF	PENTTI GLAN	D (DEF
PRAKASH JOHN	B V (DEF	MICHAEL WENDROFF	V (EH	DANNY WEIS	G V (E	MICHAEL FONFARA	K (EJMP
RITCHIE DHARMA	D (BE	PAUL FLEISHER	SAX (E	JOANNE VENT	B V (E	STEVE KATZ	HCA (E
GODFREY DIAMOND	V (H	BOB KULICK	G (H	MICHAEL SUCHORSKY	D (HJPM	BRUCE YAW	B (HJ

(CONTINUED)

R60 (CONTINUED)

LOU REED

GARLAND JEFFREYS	V	(J	KAY GARNER	V	(A	HELENE FRANCOIS	V	(A	STUART HEINRICH G V (PM
CHUCK HAMMER	SYN G(P	ELLARD BOWLES	B	(PM	MARTY FOGEL		SAX	(M	ANGELA HOWELL V (M
CHRISSY FAITH	V	(M							

R61

REFUGEE

LEE JACKSON	B	(A	(A) REFUGEE		1974	CHARISMA	UK	CAS 1087
BRIAN DAVISON	D	(A						
PATRICK MORAZ	K	(A						

R61A

REGULARS

ALLAN'KINGPIN'KING	V	(A	(A) VICTIM	1978 CBS	UK	83541
ANTHONY ROOKWOOD	V	(A				
NORMAN EBANKS	G	(A	PATRICK DONEGAN G (A GEORGE CLARKE	K (A	TREVOR SALMON	B (A
ERROLL FRANCIS	D	(A	ERROLL FORREST PERC (A GEORGE CHISHOLM	TPT (A	DEREK WADSWORTH	TROM(A
STEVE GREGORY	SAX	(A				

R61B

JOHN REID

			(A) FACADE	19	CBS	US	PC 34298

R61C

ROY REID

ROY REID	V	(A	(A) WHAP'N BAP'N	1980	VIRGIN	UK	V2164
ANGUS GAYE	D	(A					
JAH BUNNY	D	(A	NICK BAILEY	V	(A		
WEBSTER JOHNSON	PNO	(A	JOHN KPIAYE G (A EUTON JONES	PERC (A	GLAISTER VENN	PERC (A
ZENON		(A	DELROY CLARKE FLT (A BAGGA FAGAN	PERC B V (A	TONY ROBINSON	B (A
DENNIS BOVELL	K B G(A	PATRICK TENYUE HRNS (A HENRY TENYUE	HRNS (A	PHIL TOWNER	D (A

R62

TERRY REID

TERRY REID	G V	(ALL	(A) TERRY REID	1969	EMI		UK	SCX 6370
ERIC LEESE	K	(A	(A) THE MOST OF TERRY REID	1971	MFP		UK	5220
KEITH WEBB	D	(AD	(B) BANG BANG YOU'RE TERRY REID	1969	EPIC		US	26427
CONRAD ISADORE	D	(D	(C) MOVE OVER FOR TERRY REID	1969	EPIC		US	26477
WILLIE BOBO	PERC	(D	(D) RIVER	1973	ATLANTIC	US 7259 UK	K40340
AL VIOLA		(F	(E) SEED OF MEMORY	1976	ABC	US 935	UK	ABCL5162
ETE SOLLEY	K	(D	(F) ROGUES WAVES	1979	CAPITOL		UK	11857
LEE MILES	B	(DF1	(1) 1973 JUNE TOUR					
DAVID LINDLEY	G VLN(DF							
SOKO RICHARDSON	D	(D1	BEN KEITH STEEL (F JOEL BERNSTEIN	G (F	JESSE ERLICH	CELLO(F
BLUE MITCHELL	HRNS	(F	FRED WESLEY HRNS (F PLAS JOHNSON	SAX (F	GRAHAM NASH	V (F
TIM WEISBERG	FLT	(F	CLIFFORD SOLOMON HRNS (F JAMES GADSON	D (F		

R63

RELEASE MUSIC ORCHESTRA

NORBERT	PNO	(A	(A) LIFE	1974	BRAIN	1056
ZABBA	D V	(A	(B) GET THE BALL	1977	BRAIN	1083
BERND	B V	(A				
MANNE	K V	(A				

R63A

RELUCTANT STEREOTYPES

	(A) THE LABEL	1980	WEA	UK	K58201

R63B

REMA REMA

	(A) WHEEL IN THE ROSES(EP)	1980	UAD	UK	BAD5

R64

REMAINS

BARRY TASHIAN	G V	(A	(A) REMAINS	1967	SPOONFED	US	3305
CHIP DAMIANI	D	(A	(A) REMAINS	19	EPIC	US	24214
VERN MILLER	B G HRNS(A						
WILLIAM BRIGGS	K	(A					

R65

RENAISSANCE

KEITH RELF V G HCA		(A	(A) RENAISSANCE	1969	ISLAND UK ILPS 9114 US ELEKTRA 74068
JIM McCARTY	D	(A	(B) ILLUSION	19	ISLAND UK HELP 27NOT RELEASED
JANE RELF	V	(A	(C) PROLOGUE	1972	SOVEREIGN UK 7253 US CAPITOL 11116
JOHN HAWKEN	K	(A	(D) ASHES ARE BURNING	1973	SOVEREIGN UK 7261 US CAPITOL 11116
LOUIS CENNAMO	B	(A	(E) TURN OF THE CARDS	1975	BTM UK 1000 US SIRE 6015
ANNIE HASLAM	V	(CDEFGHJL	(F) SCHEHERAZADE & OTHER STORIES	1975	BTM UK 1006 US SIRE 6017
MIKE DUNFORD	G V	(DEFGHJL	(G) LIVE AT CARNEGIE HALL	1976	BTM UK 2001 US SIRE 6029
JON CAMP	V B	(CDEFGHJL	(H) NOVELLA	1977	WB UK K56422 US SIRE 6024
JOHN TOUT	K	(CDEFGHJL	(J) A SONG FOR ALL SEASONS	1978	WB UK K56460 US SIRE 6049
TERENCE SULLIVAN	D	(CDEFGHJL	(K) IN THE BEGINNING	19	CAPITOL US 11871
ROB HENDRY	V	(C	(L) AZURE D'OR	1979	WB UK K56633
ANDY POWELL	G	(D			
FRANCIS MONKMAN	SYN	(C			

R66

JOHN RENBOURN

JOHN RENBOURN	G V	(ALL	(A) JOHN RENBOURN	1965	TRANSATLANTIC UK TRA135 US REPRISE 6482
BERT JANSCH	G	(AB	(B) BERT & JOHN	1966	TRANSATLANTIC UK TRA144
JACQUI McSHEE	V	(CLN	(C) ANOTHER MONDAY	1967	TRANSATLANTIC UK TRA149
JENNIFER DE MONTFORTE JONES OBOE(C			(D) SIR JOHN ALOT OF M ENGLAND	1968	TRANSATLANTIC UK TRA167 US REPRISE 6344
TERRY COX	PERC	(DG	(E) LADY & THE UNICORN	1970	TRANSATLANTIC UK TRA224 US REPRISE 6407
RAY WARLEIGH	FLT	(D	(F) JOHN RENBOURN SAMPLER	1971	TRANSATLANTIC UK TRASAM20
DOMINIQUE TREPEAU	G	(K	(G) FARO ANNIE	1972	TRANSATLANTIC UK TRA247 US REPRISE 2082
JOHN JAMES	G	(K	(H) SO CLEAR	1973	TRANSATLANTIC UK TRASAM28
TONY ROBERTS	V WIND(LNO		(J) HEADS & TAILS	1974	TRANSATLANTIC UK TRASAM18
SUE DRAHEIM	V FDL(GL		(K) THE HERMIT	1977	TRANSATLANTIC UK TRA 336
KESH SATHIE	PERC	(LO	(L) MAID IN BEDLAM	1977	TRANSATLANTIC UK TRA 348
GLEN TOMMY	D	(O	(M) JOHN RENBOURN & S GROSSMAN	1978	KICKING MULE UK SNKF139
JOHN MOLINAUX V DULC MAND(O			(N) BLACK BALLOON	1979	TRANSATLANTIC UK TRA 355
STEFAN GROSSMAN	G	(M	(O) ENCHANTED GARDEN	1980	TRANSATLANTIC UK TRA 356
STUART GORDON	TABLA(N				
PETE DYER	HCA	(G	DORRIS HENDERSON V (G DANNY THOMPSON	B (G

R66A

RENIA

PETER SUTHERLAND	K V	(A	(A) FIRST OFFENDERS	1973	TRANSATLANTIC	UK	TRA261
KENNY STEWART	V	(A					
JOHN ROBINSON	G V	(A	MALCOLM SUTHERLAND B K V(A DAVE MATTHEWS	D (A

R66B

ROBERT RENTAL & THE NORMAL

	(A) LIVE AT WEST RUNTON PAVILLION	1980	ROUGH TRADE	UK	ROUGH 17

```
PETER McCANN        V G K(A        (A) REPAIRS                    1972 MOWEST          US    MW1211
SUKIE HONEYCUTT V K PERC(A
LARRY TREADWELL V K G HCA(A  MIKE FOLEY    V B G TROM(A JIM HONEYCUTT   B G (A   ACE HOLLERAN    D PERC(A
DAVID McCANN        FDL (A    BOB BONEFANT       HRNS   (A BARRY MARSHALL  HRNS (A   MICHAEL KAMEN   HRNS (A
```

THE RESIDENTS   R67

```
THE RESIDENTS V G K B D VLN HRNS  (A) MEET THE RESIDENTS      1974 RALPH RECORDS   US   RRO274
WITH                              (A) MEET THE RESIDENTS      1977 RALPH RECORDS   US   RRO677
PAMELA ZEIBAK       V   (CD        (B) NOT AVAILABLE           197  RALPH RECORDS   US   RR1174
SNAKEFINGER LITHMAN G V VLN(C      (C) 3RD REICH & ROLL        1976 RALPH RECORDS   US   RR1075
D JACKOVICH         PERC (D        (D) FINGER PRINCE           1977 RALPH RECORDS   US   RR1276
A DEKBAR            VLN (D         (E) DUCK STAB /BUSTER & GLEN 197  RALPH           US
T LOGAN             PERC (D        (F) NIBBLES   (COMP)        1979 VIRGIN          UK        VR3
```

RESISTANCE   R68

```
MARTIN SAUNDERS     D   (
MARK DAMRON         G V  (
JOHN O'LEARY        B   (  IAN REID K V (A
```

RETAINERS   R69

```
PAUL CARRACK        K   (1        (A) MAY 1978
TONY O'MALLEY       K   (1
ALAN SPENNER        B   (1  NEIL HUBBARD    G   (1  MEL COLLINS    SAX (1
```

MARTIN REV   R69A

```
MARTIN REV          V   (A        (A) MARTIN REV              1980 INFIDELITY             ?
```

REVELATION   R69B

```
BENNY DIGGS         V   (A        (A) REVELATION             1976 RSO            US    4810
                                  (A) REVELATION             1976 RSO            UK    2394 161
```

PAUL REVERE & THE RAIDERS   R70

```
PAUL REVERE         ORG (ALL      (A) PAUL REVERE & THE RAIDERS  19  SANDE            US  1001
MARK LINDSAY        K SAX V(K      (A) IN THE BEGINNING       1966 JERDEN           US  7004
DRAKE LEVIN         G   (          (B) HERE THEY COME         1965 CBS              US  9107
MICHAEL SMITH       D   (          (C) JUST LIKE US           1966 CBS              US  9251
JOE CORRERO         D V (K         (D) MIDNIGHT RIDE          1966 CBS   UK 62397   US  9308
PHILIP VOLK         B   (          (E) SPIRIT OF 67           1967 CBS              US  9395
CHARLIE COE         B   (          (F) GREATEST HITS          1967 CBS              US  9462
JIM VALLEY          G   (          (G) REVOLUTION             1967 CBS   UK 63093   US  9521
FREDDY WELLER       G V (K         (H) CHRISTMAS PAST & PRESENT 1968 CBS            US  9555
KEITH ALLISON       G V K(K        (I) GOIN' TO MEMPHIS       1968 CBS   UK 63265   US  9605
                                   (J) SOMETHINGS HAPPENING    1968 CBS            US  9665
                                   (K) HARD & HEAVY           1969 CBS   UK 63649   US  9753
                                   (L) SPIRIT OF 69           1969 CBS              US  GP12
                                   (M) ALIAS PINK PUZZ         19  CBS             US  9905
                                   (N) COLLAGE (RAIDERS)       19  CBS   UK 63973   US  9964
                                   (O) PAUL REVERE & THE RAIDERS  19 HARMONY       US  30089
                                   (P) GREATEST HITS VOL 2     19  CBS             US  30386
                                   (Q) INDIAN RESERVATION     1971 CBS             US  30768
                                   (R) GOOD THING              197 CBS   UK 62923 HARMONY US 30975
                                   (S) MOVIN' ON               197 HARMONY        US  31183
                                   (T) COUNTRY WINE            19  CBS             US  31196
                                   (U) ALL TIME GREATEST HITS 1972 CBS             US  31464
```

REVILLOS   R70A

```
FAY FIFE            V   (A        (A) REV UP                 1980 DINDISC         UK   DID 3
EUGENE REYNOLDS     K V (A
HI FI HARRIS        G   (A  D K SMYTHE      B  (   ROCKY RHYTHM   D  (A  KID KRUPA   G  (A
BABS & CHERRY HANDJIVE (A   WILLIAM MYSTERIOUS B  (A
```

REVOLUTIONAIRES   R71

```
                                   (A) REACTION IN DUB        1978 CHACHA          CHALP 002
                                   (B) GOLDMINE DUB           1979 GREENSLEEVES     GREL  4
                                   (C) REVOLUTIONAIRES SOUNDS VOL2 1978 BALLISTIC   UAG 30237
                                   (D) NEGREA LOVE DUB        1979 TROJAN           TRLS 153
                                   (E) OUTLAW DUB             1979 TROJAN           TRLS 169
```

REVOLUTIONARY BLUES BAND   R72

```
                                   (A) REVOLUTIONARY BLUES BAND  19 MCA UK MUPS402 CORAL US 757506
```

REX   R73

```
REX SMITH           V   (A        (A) WHERE DO WE GO FROM HERE 1978 CBS            UK   82186
ORVILLE DAVIS       B   (A
LARS HANSON         G   (A  LOU VANDORA G  (A  MIKE RATTI        D (A
```

REXY   R73A

```
                                   (A) RUNNING OUT OF TIME    1981 ALIEN    UK     BEALIEN2
```

REZILLOS   R74

```
FAY FIFE            V   (AB       (A) CANT STAND THE REZILLOS 1978 SIRE 9103 257    K56530
EUGENE REYNOLDS     V   (AB       (B) MISSION ACCOMPLISHED   1979 SIRE             SRK  6069
ANGEL PATERSON      D   (AB
LUKE WARM           G   (B  SIMON TEMPLAR    B  (B   JO CALLIS     (A  GAIL WARNING   V  (B
WILLIAM MYSTERIOUS SAX (AB  D K SMYTHE    B  (   HI FI HARRIS   G  (
```

RHINOCEROS   R75

```
BILL MUNDI          D   (AB       (A) RHINOCEROS             1968 ELEKTRA US 74030 71RI UK K42042
MIKE FONFARA        K   (ABC      (B) SATIN CHICKEN          1969 ELEKTRA US 74056 71RI UK K42036
DANNY WEIS          K G (ABC      (C) BETTER TIMES ARE COMING 1970 ELEKTRA US 74075  UK  2469 006
DOUG HASTINGS       G   (AB       (C) BETTER TIMES ARE COMING 1971 ELEKTRA         UK RI K42049
JERRY PENROD        B   (A
JOHN FINLEY         V   (ABC ALAN GERBER  K V    (AB DUKE EDWARDS     D (C PETER HODGSON   B  (BC
LARRY LEISHMAN      G   (C
```

EMITT RHODES   R76

```
EMITT RHODES ALL INST (ALL        (A) AMERICAN DREAM         1971 A&M    US SP4254  UK    AML564254
CHUCK BERGHOFFER    B   (A         (B) EMITT RHODES          1971 DUNHILL US 50089  UK PROBE SPBA6256
HAL BLAINE          D   (A         (C) MIRROR                1971 DUNHILL US 50111  UK PROBE SPBA6262
DAVID COHEN         G   (A         (D) FAREWELL TO PARADISE  1972 DUNHILL US 50122  UK PROBE SPBA6266
JIM GORDON          D   (A         (D) FAREWELL TO PARADISE  1974 ABC RI            UK    ABCL 5041
JOHN GUERIN         D   (A                                                          (CONTINUED)
```

R76 (CONTINUED) — EMITT RHODES

PETE JOLLY		(A	LARRY KNECHTEL	K	(A	GARY KATO		(A	MICHAEL RICE	(A
JOEL LARSON	D	(A	JAMES LEITCH		(A	DRAKE LEVIN		(A	DON PEAK	(A
JOE PORCARO	PERC	(A	EMIL RADOCCHIA		(A	DON RANDI	K	(A	TOM REYNOLDS	(A
BILL RHEINHART		(A	LYLE RITZ	B	(A					

R77 — RED RHODES

ORVILLE J 'RED'RHODES STEEL(ALL	(A) ONCE A DAY	19	CROWN	US	CST	520
JAY LACY	G	(F	(B) BLUE BLUE DAY	19	CROWN	US	CST	528
ROBERT K WARFORD	G	(F	(C) STEEL GUITAR RAG	19	CROWN	US	CST	535
COLIN CAMERON	B	(F	(D) GUITARS GO COUNTRY	19	CROWN	US	
DANNY LANE	D	(F	(E) LIVE AT THE PALOMINO	19	HAPPY TIGER	US	HT10035
DAVID BARNY	PNO	(F	(F) VELVET HAMMER IN A COWBOY BAND	1973 COUNTRYSIDE	US	CS 102
JIM STALLINGS	B	(F			

R77A — RHYTHM CATS

(A) ROCK WITH THE RHYTHM(EP)	19	TYGER		TYG 3

R77B — RHYTHM DEVILS

MICKEY HART	D	(A	(A) PLAY RIVER MUSIC	1980 PASSPORT	US	PB 9844
BILLY KREUTZMANN	D	(A				
AIRTO MOREIRA	PERC	(A	MIKE HINTON		(A	JIM LOVELESS		PERC (A	GREGG ERRICO	(A
JORDAN AMARANTHA	PERC	(A	PHIL LESH		(A					

R77C — RHYTHM HAWKS

(A) WALK OUT ON YOU(EP)	19	REDBALL		RR 011

R78 — RHYTHM HERITAGE

MICHAEL OMARTIAN	K V	(AB	(A) DISCO FIED	1976 ABC	UK ABCL 5174	US ABCD 934
ED GREENE	D	(AB	(B) SKY'S THE LIMIT	1978 ABC	US	1037
STEVE MADAIO	TPT	(B	(C) LAST NIGHT ON EARTH	1977 ABC	US	987
DEAN PARKS	G	(A				
SCOTT EDWARDS	B	(AB	TONY TERRAN	TPT	(A	TOM SCOTT	WIND (A	ERNIE WATTS	SAX (AB
FRED SELDON	WIND	(AB	LEW McCREARY	TROM	(A	SID SHARP	STRINGS(AB	LEE RITENOUR	G (A
DAVID DUKE		(A	GALE ROBINSON		(A	ORRIN WATERS	V (AB	LUTHER WATERS	V (AB
MICHAEL PRICE	V	(A	MARVIN DEANE	PERC	(A	PAT McCOY	PERC (A	RAY PARKER	G (A
BEN BENAY	G	(A	VICTOR FELDMAN	PERC	(AB	PAUL HUBINON	TPT (A	JAY GRAYDON	G (B
CHUCK FINDLEY	B	(B							

R79 — RICH KIDS

GLEN MATLOCK	B V	(A	(A) GHOSTS OF PRINCES IN TOWERS	1978	EMI	UK	EMC 3263
RUSTY EGAN	D	(A					
MIDGE URE	G V	(A	STEVE NEW	G	(A	IAN McLAGAN	PNO (A

R80 — CLIFF RICHARD

CLIFF RICHARD(HARRY WEBB)	V(ALL	CLIFF	1959 COLUMBIA UK	33SX1147
HANK MARVIN	G	(	CLIFF SINGS	1959 COLUMBIA UK	33SX1192
BRIAN BENNETT	D	(	CLIFF SINGS	19 ABC US	ABC 321
BRUCE WELCH	G V	(	ME & MY SHADOWS	1960 COLUMBIA UK SCX3330	33SX1261
TONY MEEHAN	D	(	LISTEN TO CLIFF	1961 COLUMBIA UK SCX3375	33SX1320
IAN SAMWELL		(	LISTEN TO CLIFF	19 ABC US	ABC 391
JET HARRIS	B	(	THE YOUNG ONES	1961 COLUMBIA UK SCX3397	
TERRY SMART		(	21 TODAY	1961 COLUMBIA UK SCX3409	33SX1368
JOHN ROSTILL	B	(	32 MINUTES 17 SECONDS	1962 COLUMBIA UK SCX3436	33SX1431
JOHN FARRAR	G B	(	WHEN IN SPAIN	1963 COLUMBIA UK SCX3488	33SX1541
			IN SPAIN WITH THE SHADOWS	196 EPIC US	24115
			SUMMER HOLIDAY	1963 COLUMBIA UK SCX3462	
			SUMMER HOLIDAY	1963 EPIC US	24063
			WONDERFUL LIFE	1963 COLUMBIA UK SCX3515	33SX1628
			HIT ALBUM	1963 COLUMBIA UK	33SX1512
			IT'S ALL IN THE GAME	19 EPIC US	26089
			SWINGERS PARADISE	19 EPIC US	26145
			ALADDIN & HIS WONDERFUL LAMP	1965 COLUMBIA UK SCX3522	33SX1676
			WONDERFUL TO BE YOUNG	19 DOT US	3474
			CLIFF RICHARD	1965 COLUMBIA UK SCX3546	33SX1709
			WHEN IN ROME	1965 COLUMBIA UK	SX1762
			MORE HITS	1965 COLUMBIA UK SCX3555	SX1737
			LOVE IS FOREVER	1965 COLUMBIA UK SCX3569	SX1769
			KINDA LATIN	1966 COLUMBIA UK SCX6039	SX6039
			FINDERS KEEPERS	1966 COLUMBIA UK SCX6079	SX6079
			CINDERELLA	1967 COLUMBIA UK SCX6103	SX6103
			DON'T STOP ME NOW	1967 COLUMBIA UK SCX6133	
			GOOD NEWS	1967 COLUMBIA UK SCX6167	
			CLIFF IN JAPAN	1968 COLUMBIA UK SCX6244	
			TWO A PENNY	1968 COLUMBIA UK SCX6262	
			ESTABLISHED 1958	1968 COLUMBIA UK SCX6282	
			BEST OF	1969 COLUMBIA UK SCX6343	
			SINCERELY	1969 COLUMBIA UK SCX6357	
			IT'LL BE ME	1969 STARLINE UK	5011
			ABOUT THAT MAN	1970 COLUMBIA UK SCX6408	
			ALL MY LOVE	1970 MFP UK	MFP1420
			LIVE AT THE TALK OF THE TOWN	1970 STARLINE UK	5031
			TRACKS & GROOVES	1970 COLUMBIA UK SCX6435	
			HIS LAND	1970 COLUMBIA UK SCX6443	
			BEST OF VOL 2	1972 COLUMBIA UK SCX6519	
			CLIFF & THE SHADOWS	197 ELECTROLA EURO	048 04318
			HISTORY OF	1973 EMI IMP EURO	052 05019
			TAKE ME HIGH	1973 EMI UK	EMC3016
			POWER TO ALL MY FRIENDS	1973 EMI IMP EURO	062 05355
			EDITION 2000	19 CONTEMPORARY	C2027/8
			HELP IT ALONG	1974 EMI	EMA 768
			31ST OF FEBRUARY	1974 EMI	EMC 3048
			JAPAN TOUR 1974	1975 IRL IMP	EMS67037
			LIVE	1976 MFP UK	MFP50307
			I'M NEARLY FAMOUS	1976 EMI UK	EMC 3122
			I'M NEARLY FAMOUS	1976 ROCKET US	3004
			EVERY FACE TELLS A STORY	1977 EMI UK	EMC 3172

(CONTINUED)

CLIFF RICHARD R80

EVERY FACE TELLS A STORY	1977 ROCKET US	2268
MY KIND OF LIFE	1977 EMI UK	EMI12584
40 GOLDEN GREATS	1977 EMI UK	EMTVS 6
SMALL CORNERS	1978 EMI UK	EMC 3219
GREEN LIGHT	1978 EMI UK	EMC 3231
ROCK'N'ROLL JUVENILE	1979 EMI UK	EMC 3307
STARS OF R'N'R	1978 EMI EURO	052 04740
THANK YOU VERY MUCH	1979 EMI UK	EMTV 15

DIGBY RICHARDS R80A

DIGBY RICHARDS G V (A   (A) WHISKEY SUNDOWN   1978 RCA   UK   PL 25154
TAFF WILLIAMS G (A
PETE KING STEEL(A   ROGER BARA   K   (A   KEVIN DUNN   B (A   MICKEY GIBBONS D PERC(A

TURLEY RICHARDS R81

TURLEY RICHARDS V (AB   (A) EXPRESSIONS   1971 WB UK   K 46086
DANNY KORTCHMAR G (A   (B) WEST VIRGINIA SUPERSTAR   19 EPIC US   34306
BRYAN GAROFALO B (A
RUSS KUNKEL D (A   JIM HORN   FLT (A   LEE SKLAR   B (A

DEL RICHARDSON R82

DEL RICHARDSON G B V(A   (A) A PIECES OF A JIGSAW   1973   MCA UK MUPS 491 +RI MCF 2513
CHILI CHARLES D (A
REMI KABAKA PERC (A   ROSETTA HIGHTOWER V (A   JEAN ROUSSEL   K (A   ROGER BALL HRNS (A
DONNY PERKINS V (A   ALAN SPENNER   B (A   MALCOLM DUNCAN   HRNS (A

JONATHAN RICHMAN & THE MODERN LOVERS R83

JONATHAN RICHMAN G V (ALL   (A) MODERN LOVERS   1977 BESERKLEY US 0048 UK BSERK 1
ERNIE BROOKS B (A   (B) MODERN LOVERS   1977 BESERKLEY US 0041 UK BSERK 2
JERRY HARRISON K V (A   (C) ROCK'N' ROLL WITH THE MODERN LOVER 1977 BESERKLEY US 0052 UK BSERK 9
DAVID ROBINSON D V (AB   (D) MODERN LOVERS LIVE   1977 BESERKLEY US 055 UK BSERK12
LEROY RADCLIFFE G V (BCDE   (E) MODERN LOVE SONGS   1979 BESERKLEY UK BSERK17
GREG KERANEN B V (BC
ASA BREBNER B (DE   D SHARPE   D V (CDE JOHN FELICE   G (RALPH ANDERSON   B (

RICO R84

RICO RODRIGUES TROM (A   (A) MAN FROM WAREIKA   1977 ISLAND   UK   ILP59485
SLY DUNBAR D (A
BUNNY McKENZIE B (A   ROBBIE SHAKESPEARE B (A   JACKO   D (A   DUGGIE BRYAN   G (A
KARL PITTERSON G K PERC(A   JUNIOR HANSON MARVIN G (A   LLOYD PARKS   G (A   PHIL CHEN   G (A
TOUTER HARVEY K (A   ANSEL COLLINS   K (A   TARZAN NELSON   K (A   TONY WASHINGTON K (A
SKULLY PERC (A   TONY UTER   PERC (A   SATCH DIXON   PERC (A   FLICK   PERC(A
CANDY McKENZIE V (A   DICK CUTHELL   HRNS (A   VIV TALENT HALL   TPT (A   BOBBY ELLIS   TPT(A
EDDIE THORNTON TPT (A   DIRTY HARRY   SAX (A   GEORGE LEE   SAX (A   KEITH GEMMELL   SAX(A
HERMAN MARQUIS SAX (A   RAY ALLEN   SAX (A

RICOTTI & ALBUQUERQUE R85

FRANK RICOTTI (A   (A) FIRST WIND   1971 PEGASUS   UK   PEG 2
MICHAEL D'ALBUQUERQUE (A

BOB RIEDY BLUES BAND R85A

BOB RIEDY PNO (A   (A) JUST OFF HALSTED   1974 FLYING FISH US   006
JOHN REDA G (A   (B) LAKE MICHIGAN   1977 ROUNDER US   2005
MIKE COGAN SAX (A
DAN DRAHER G (A   MARK GASTON   TPT (A   BOB FALVEY   B (A   RICHARD ROBINSON D (A
CAREY BELL HARRINGTON HCA(A   EDDY CLEARWATER   V (A   MIKE WILLENS   SAX (A

RIFF RAFF R86

AUREO DE SOUZA D (AB   (A) RIFF RAFF   1973 RCA   UK   SF 8351
TOMMY EYRE K V (AB   (B) ORIGINAL MAN   1974 RCA   LPLI5023
PETE KIRTLEY G V (AB
ROGER SUTTON B V (AB   BUD BEADLE   SAX (AB   JOE O'DONNELL   VIOLA(B   STEVE GREGORY   WIND (B
JO NEWMAN V (B

RIFF RAFF R86A

(A) COSMONAUT (EP)   19 CHISWICK   UK   SW 34

RIGHTEOUS BROTHERS R87

BOBBY HATFIELD	V	RIGHT NOW	1964 MOONGLOW US 1001 UK PYE NPL 28059
BILL MEDLEY	V	SOME BLUE EYED SOUL	1965 MOONGLOW US 1002 UK PYE NPL 28056
JIMMY WALKER	V	THIS IS NEW	196 MOONGLOW US 1003
WITH		BEST OF THE RIGHTEOUS BROTHERS	196 MOONGLOW US 1004
DAVID PAICH	K (5	YOU'VE LOST THAT LOVIN FEELIN'	1966 PHILLES US 4007 UK LONDON HA 8226
TOM SELLERS	K (5	JUST ONCE IN MY LIFE	1965 PHILLES US 4008 UK LONDON HA 8245
DENNIS LAMBERT	K (5	BACK TO BACK	1965 PHILLES US 4009 UK LONDON HA 8278
DAVID HUNGATE	B (5	SOUL & INSPIRATION	1966 VERVE US 5001 UK VERVE SVLP9131
DEAN PARKS	G (5	GO AHEAD & CRY	1966 VERVE US 5004 UK VERVE SVLP9140
ED GREENE	D (5	IN ACTION	1966 GNP US 2029 UK SUE ILP 937
GARY COLEMAN	PERC (5	SAYIN' SOMETHIN'	1967 VERVE US 5010 UK VERVE SVLP9168
BRIAN POTTER	PERC (5	GREATEST HITS	1967 VERVE US 5020 UK VERVE SVLP9183
CHUCK FINDLEY	HRNS (5	GREATEST HITS	197 VERVE UK RI 2352 018
PAUL HUBINON	HRNS (5	GREATEST HITS VOL 2	1967 VERVE UK SVLP9240
ERNIE WATTS	SAX (5	GREATEST HITS VOL 2	197 VERVE UK RI 2352 019
TOM SCOTT	SAX (5	SOULED OUT	1967 VERVE US 5031
DON MENZA	HRNS (5	STANDARDS	1967 VERVE US 5051
DICK HYDE	TROM (5	ONE FOR THE ROAD	1968 VERVE US 5058
GINGER BLAKE	V (5	REBIRTH	1970 VERVE US 5076 UK VERVE SVLP9249
JULIA TILLMAN	V (5	RIGHTEOUS BROTHERS	1970 MGM US 102
MAXINE WILLARD	V (5	2 BY 2	1973 POLYDOR UK 2683 033
CARLENA WILLIAMS	V (5	KINGSTON ROCK	1974 RCA UK INTS1487
STRING SECTION	(5	GIVE IT TO THE PEOPLE	1974 HAVEN US 9201 UK CAPITOL 9201
		(5)SONS OF MRS RIGHTEOUS	1975 HAVEN US 9203 UK CAPITOL 9203
		PORTRAIT	1975 POLYDOR UK 2348 119
		UNCHAINED MELODY	1975 METRONOME 200 115

R88   **RIKKI & THE LAST DAYS**

(A) FOUR MINUTE WARNING	1978	DJM	UK	DJF 20526

R89   **BILLY LEE RILEY**

BILLY LEE RILEY   (ALL

FUNK HARMONICA	19	CRESCENDO	US	2020
IN ACTION	19	CRESCENDO	US	2028
HARMONICA & THE BLUES	19	CROWN	US	5277
HARMONICA BEATLEMANIA	19	MERCURY	US	SR60974
BIG HARMONICA SPECIAL	19	MERCURY	US	SR60965
WHISKEY A GO GO PRESENTS	19	MERCURY	US	SR60985
SOUTHERN SOUL	19	MAJO	US	1933
LEGENDARY SUN PERFORMER	1978	CHARLY	UK	CR30131
SUN SOUNDS SPECIAL	1978	CHARLY	UK	CR30151
(EP) BILLY LEE RILEY	1977	CHARLY	UK	CEP 112

R89A   **JIMMY RILEY**

(A) TELL THE YOUTHS THE TRUTH	19	TROJAN		TRLS 167
(B) JIMMY RILEY EXPLOSIVE SHOW	1978	BURNING SOUNDS		BS 1011

R90   **TERRY RILEY**

TERRY RILEY   K   (ALL
JOHN CALE   (D

(A) REED STREAMS	1967	MASS,ART,INC	US	M131
(B) KEYBOARD STUDIES	1969	BYG		
(C) IN 'C'	1970	CBS	UK	64565
(D) CHURCH OF ANTHRAX	1971	CBS	UK	64259
(E) RAINBOW IN CURVED AIR	1971	CBS	UK	64564
(F) PERSIAN SURGERY DERVISHES	1972	SHANDAR		83501/2
(G) LE SECRET DE LA VIE	1975	PHILIPS		9120 037
(H) SHRI CAMEL	1980	CBS		73929

R91   **LAURIN RINDER & W MICHAEL LEWIS**

LAURIN RINDER   D SAX(AB
W MICHAEL LEWIS   K SAX(AB
ADAM STRANGE   G   (B
DAVID TURNER   G   (B   VENETTE GLOUD   V   (B   AZAR LAWRENCE   SAX (B   JIMBO ROSS   VLA (B
CARMEN TWILLIE   V   (B

(A) SEVEN DEADLY SINS	1978	PYE	UK	NSPL28252
(B) WARRIORS	1979	AVI	US	6073

R92   **RING OF TRUTH**

VICTOR BROX   K V   (A
ANNETTE BROX   V   (A
JIM KING   SAX   (A   ANNIE MATTHEWS   PNO   (A   GERRY FIELDS   VLN   (A   FLOYD LAWSON   B   (A
RAY DRAPER   V   (A   JOHN PEARSON   D   (A

(A) 1970				

R93   **RINGS**

TWINK   D V   (
PAUL RUDOLPH   G   (
SANDY ROBERTSON   B   (RUSSELL HUNTER   D   (

R93A   **RINKY DINK & THE CRYSTAL SETS**

ALLAN BLACK   G   (A
NIGEL WARD   K V   (A
JANE HUTCHINSON   V   (A   BILL WARD   D   (A   KEN COOK   B   (A   GRAHAM BLYTH   K   (A
RON ASPERY   SAX   (A

(A) CAMEO ROLES	1975	HARVEST	UK	SHSP 4047

R94   **RIOT**

GUY SPERANZA   V PERC(AB
MARK REALE   G V   (AB
PETER BITELLI   D   (AB
JIMMY IOMMI   B   (AB   RICK VENTURA   G   (B   L A KOUVARIS   G   (A

(A) RIOT CITY	1978	ARIOLA			ARL 5007
(B) NARITA	1979	CAPITOL	UK	12081 +ATTIC	1067

R95   **RIOT ROCKERS**

(A) RIOT ROCKERS	1978	CHARLY	UK	CR 30158

R96   **RIOT SQUAD**

MITCH MITCHELL   (
JON LORD   (
TERRY CLIFFORD   (GRAHAM BONNET   (DELL ROLL   (ROGER CRISP   (
BUTCH DAVIS   (BOB EVANS   (NERO   (

(A) 1965/67				

R96A   **RIP CHORDS**

(A) HEY LITTLE COBRA	196	CBS	UK	8951
(B) THREE WINDOW COUPE	196	CBS	UK	9016

R97   **MINNIE RIPERTON**

MINNIE RIPERTON   V   (
JOSE FELICIANO   (E
HUBERT LAWS   FLT   (EF
TOM SCOTT   SAX   (EF
DAVID HUNGATE   (E
CHUCK RAINEY   B   (E
PHIL UPCHURCH   B   (E
HARVEY MASON   D   (EF   GERRY VINCI   VLN (EF   OSCAR NEVES   (E   CLAUDIO SLOAN   (E
STEVE FORMAN   (E   ART PHILLIPS   (E   LARRY WILLIAMS   HRNS (E   KIM HUTCHCROFT   HRNS(E
VICTOR FELDMAN   PERC   (E   LEON CHANCLER   HRNS (E   ABE LABORIEL   B   (EF   BILL REICHENBACH   (E
MARLO HENDERSON   (E   LEON CHANCLER   (E   RANDY WALDMAN   (E   BUDDY COLLETTE   (E
JEREMY LUBBOCK   (E   BILL GREEN   (E   PAULINHO DA COSTA   PERC (EF   SHERIDAN STOKES   (E
HENRY GIBSON   (E   VINCE DE ROSA   (E   RICHARD PERISSI   (E   DAVID DUKE   (E
LENNY CASTRO   PERC   (F   GREG PHILLINGANES K   (F   PAUL JACKSON   G   (F   LEE RITENOUR   G   (F
TENNYSON STEPHENS PNO   (F   GAYLE LEVANT   HARP (F   MAXINE WILLARD   V   (F   ROBERTA FLACK   V   (F
JULIA TILLMAN   V   (F   PEABO BRYSON   V   (F   STEPHANIE SPRUILL   V   (F   MICHAEL JACKSON   V   (F
MICHAEL BODDICKER SYN   (F   STEVIE WONDER   HCA (F   GEORGE BENSON   V   (F   PATRICE RUSHEN   V K(F

(A) COME TO MY GARDEN	19	JANUS	US	7011
(B) PERFECT ANGEL	1974	EPIC US 32561	UK	80426
(C) ADVENTURES IN PARADISE	1975	EPIC US 33454	UK	69142
(D) STAY IN LOVE	1977	EPIC US 34191	UK	81457
(E) MINNIE	1979	CAPITOL		11936
(F) LOVE LIVES FOREVER	1980	CAPITOL		12097

R98   **RISING SONS**

ED CASSIDY   D
TAJ MAHAL   V
RY COODER   G   JESSE ED DAVIS   G   JESSE LEE KINCADE   PNO   KEVIN KELLEY D   GARY MARKER   B

LEE RITENOUR

LEE RITENOUR	G	(ALL	(A) FIRST CHOICE		1976 EPIC		US	33847
PATRICE RUSHEN	K	(ABC	(B) CAPTAIN FINGERS		1977 EPIC		US	34426
DAVID GRUSIN	SYN	(ABCFG	(C) CAPTAINS JOURNEY		1978 ELEKTRA UK K52094			
STEVE GADD	D	(CF	(D) GENTLE THOUGHTS		1978 JVC		JAP	VIDC1
DAVID NADIEN	STRINGS	(E	(E) SUGAR LOAF EXPRESS		1978 JVC		JAP	VIDC2
ALEX ACUNA	PERC	(BCFG	(F) FEEL THE NIGHT		1979 ELEKTRA UK K52141		US 6E192	
CARMEN TWILLIE	V	(C	(G) FRIENDSHIP		1979 JVC		JAP	VIDC3
DAVID FOSTER	C	(BCF	(H) RIT		1981 ELEKTRA UK K52273			
LARRY WILLIAMS	HRNS	(F						

SUE EVANS	PERC	(C	PAULINHO DA COSTA	PERC	(C	RAY BECKENSTEIN	FLT	(C	IAN UNDERWOOD	SYN	(ABFC
JAY GRAYDON	G	(BC	BILL REICHENBACH	HRNS	(F	VENETTE GLOUD	V	(C	STEVE THORNTON	PERC	(C
PATTI AUSTIN	V	(CF	DAVE VALENTIN	FLT	(B	ABRAHAM LABORIEL	B	(CFG	ANTHONY JACKSON	B	(BC
BILL CHAMPLIN	V	(BC	MITCH HOLDER	G	(BC	ERNIE WATTS	SAX	(ABCFG	TOM BAYLOR	V	(C
EDDY DANIELS	FLT	(C	STEVE FORMAN	PERC	(FBC	JERRY STEINHOLTZ	PERC	(A	JERRY PETERS	K	(A
LARRY NASH	K	(A	MIKE OMARTIAN	K	(A	CHUCK RAINEY	B	(A	LOUIS JOHNSON	B	(A
ED GREENE	D	(A	TOM SCOTT	SAX	(A	JEROME RICHARDSON	SAX	(A	CHUCK FINDLEY	TPT	(AF
FRANK ROSELINO	TROM	(A	DAWILLI GONGA	K	(B	DENNIS BUDIMIR	G	(B	RAY PARKER	G	(B
ALPHONSO JOHNSON	B	(B	BILL DICKINSON	B	(AB	CHARLES MEEKS	B	(B	MIKE PORCARO	B	(B
HARVEY MASON	D	(AB	JEFF PORCARO	D	(B	MIKE BODDICKER	SYN	(F	VICTOR FELDMAN	PERC	(F
ALEX ACUNA	PERC	(FG	STEVE LUKATHER	G	(F	JOE SAMPLE	PNO	(F	TOM BAHLER	V	(F
JERRY HEY	HRNS	(F	GARY GRANT	HRNS	(F	LOU McCREARY	HRNS	(F			

SCARLET RIVERA

SCARLET RIVERA	VLN	(A	(A) SCARLET FEVER		1978	WB		US	BSK3174
DOMINIC CARDINALE	K	(A							

BERNARD PURDIE	D	(A	MIKE MAINIERI	VIBES	(A	GARY BURKE	D	(A	FRANCISCO SANTANA	B	(A
URBIE GREEN	TROM	(A	ED MIKENAS	B	(A	PAUL GRIFFIN	K	(A	PAUL PRESTOPINO	MAND	(A
LANI GROVES	V	(A	ULLANDA McCULLOUGH	V	(A	MICHELLE LEWIS	V	(A	JAMIE LEE	V	(A
REGGIE YOUNG	G	(A	VINNIE BELL	G	(A	ELLIOTT RANDALL	G	(A	CLARENCE CLEMONS	SAX	V(A
SREDNI VOLLNER	HCA	(A	DAVE SANBORN	SAX	(A	MICHAEL BRECKER	SAX	(A	RANDY BRECKER	SAX	(A
BURT COLLINS	TPT	(A	ARTIE KAPLAN	WIND	(A	VIVIAN CHERRY	V	(A	DEDE WASHBURN	V	(A
HELENE MILES	V	(A	KRISTIN PIMPINELLA	V	(A						

JOHNNY RIVERS

JOHNNY RIVERS	V	(ALL	AT THE WHISKY A GO GO	1964 LIBERTY UK LBY3031	US IMPERIAL	12264
WITH			AT THE WHISKY A GO GO	1970 SUNSET UK 50157 US		5157
JIM GORDON	D	(ABLMO	HERE WE GOGO AGAIN	1964 LIBERTY UK LBY3036	US IMPERIAL	12274
JOE OSBORN	B	(ABHM	IN ACTION	196	US IMPERIAL	12280
LARRY KNECHTEL	PNO	(ABHNS	BACK AT THE WHISKY	196	US IMPERIAL	12284
MICHAEL OMARTIAN	K	(ABMO	ROCKS THE FOLK	1965 LIBERTY UK LBY3064	US IMPERIAL	12293
JIM WEBB	K	(A	AND I KNOW YOU WANNA DANCE	1966	US IMPERIAL	12307
JERRY ALLISON	D	(A	(C)CHANGES	196 LIBERTY UK LBY3087	US IMPERIAL	12334
MICHAEL GEORGIADES	V	(ABMO	GOLDEN HITS	196	US IMPERIAL	12324
HERB PEDERSEN	V	(ABLMO	REWIND	196	US IMPERIAL	12341
KEITH ALLISON	B	(A	REALIZATION	196	US IMPERIAL	12372
DEAN PARKS	G	(ABLMO	A TOUCH OF GOLD	1970 LIBERTY UK 83141	US IMPERIAL	12427
LARRY CARLTON	G	(ABM	JOHN LEE HOOKER	1970 SUNSET UK 50025		
BOBBYE HALL	PERC	(A	(S) SLO SLIM SLIDER	19	US IMPERIAL	16001
GARY COLEMAN	PERC	(ABMO	WILD NIGHT	19	US UA	LA486
JIM HORN	SAX	(ABHLMS	JOHNNY RIVERS	19	US UA	LA593
CHUCK FINDLEY	HRNS	(ABLMO	(A) LA REGGAE	1973 UA UK 29298	US UA	LA5650
JACKIE KELSO	SAX	(ABM	(H) HOME GROWN	197	US UA	LA5532
JACK CONRAD	B	(L	HISTORY OF	197 LIBERTY UK 83461		
MICHAEL MELVOIN	K	(L	GO JOHNNY GO	19	UA UA	LA3386
MICKEY JONES	D	(L	(B) BLUE SUEDE SHOES	1973 UA UK 29473	US	LA 075
JAMES HENDRICKS	V	(B	(L) LAST BOOGIE IN PARIS	1974 ATLANTIC UK K50033		
RON TUTT	D	(HS	ROAD	1974 ATLANTIC UK K50063		
GLEN TOWNSEND	G	(H	(M) HELP ME RHONDA	1975 EPIC UK 80987		
RITA COOLIDGE	V	(H	NEW LOVES AND OLD FRIENDS	1975 CBS UK 80946 US		33681
CLYDIE KING	V	(H	(O) OUTSIDE HELP	1978 POLYDOR UK 2310603	US SOULCITY	76004
RON MICO DUQUETTE	G V	(H	MR TEENAGE	19	US SEARS	417
CHARLES D HARRIS	V	(H	SENSATIONAL	19	US CAPITOL	2161
MIKE DEASY	G V	(H	JOHNNY RIVERS	19	US PICKWICK	3191
FRANK KINSEL	V	(H	VERY BEST OF	19		
CHRIS ETHRIDGE	B	(H	SUPER PAK	197 UA UK UX593		
VANETTA FIELDS	V	(H	SWINGING SHINDIG	19	US CORNET	246
KATHY DEASY	V	(H	20 GREATEST HITS	19	CAN TEEVEE	1062
JIM KELTNER	D	(HO				
MICHAEL AMILIUS	V	(H				

JAMES BURTON	G	(HS	JERRY SCHEFF	B	(HS	WAYNE MINCY	V HCA(H	TOMMY COE	G V	(H
MIKE SHANKLIN	G V	(H	GURU RAMDAS SINGERS		(H	SCOTT EDWARDS	B	(MO	GINGER BLAKE	V	(MO
JULIA TILLMAN	V	(MO	MAXINE WILLARD	V	(MO	JOHN RAINES	D	(M	JIM HUGHART	B	(M
TAY UHLER	G	(MO	BEN BENAY	G	(M	TOM SCOTT	SAX	(MO	BRIAN WILSON	V	(M
MARK BOOKIN	STRINGS	(M	BARRY BOOKIN	V	(M	TOM LEADON	G	(M	ED GREENE	D	(MO
BOB ALCIVER	HRNS	(S	MARTY PAICH	HRNS	(M	GARY ILLINGSWORTH	PNO	(S	JOE SAMPLE	PNO	(O
WAYNE BERRY	G V	(O	RICHARD CUOMO	K	(O	M L BENOIT	PERC	(O	LUTHER WATERS	V	(O
ORRIN WATERS	V	(O	JERRY JUMONVILLE	HRNS	(O	JOHN PHILLIPS	HRNS	(O	JOEL PESKIN	HRNS	(O
FRED TACKETT	G	(O	HAL BLAINE	D	(OS	DAVID HUNGATE	B	(O	JON DOUGLAS HAYWOOD	V	(O
JAMES E HAAS	V	(O	DAVID KEMPER	D	(M	NED DOHENY	G	(M	DAVID T WALKER	G	(M
JIM HELMER	D	(M	SKIP EDWARDS	K	(M	DUITCH HELMER	V	(M	MARTY GWINN	V	(M
PLAS JOHNSON	SAX	(M	GARY HERBIG	HRNS	(O	GARY GRANT	HRNS	(O	MILT HOLLAND	PERC	(O
MARC F LEVINE	B	(O	HARLAN ROGERS	K	(O						

RIVITS

JESS RODEN	D V	(A	(A) MULTIPLAY		1980 ISLAND	UK		ILPS 9617
PETER WOOD	K V	(A							
STEVE DWIRE	B	(A	DOANE PERRY	D	(A	LEE GOODALL	SAX	(A

ROAD

NOEL REDDING	B V	(A	(A) ROAD		1972 NATURAL RESOURCES		NR105L
ROD RICHARDS	G V	(A	(B) ROAD		1973 RARE EARTH		SRE 3006
LESLIE SAMPSON	D V	(A	(C) COGNITION		19 KAMA SUTRA		2032

R102A ROADMASTER

BOBBY JOHNS	D	(BC	(A) ROADMASTER		19			
RICK BENICK	G	(BC	(B) FORTRESS		1979 MERCURY	US		SRMI3814
STEPHEN McNALLY	V	(BC	(C) HEY WORLD		1979 MERCURY	US		SRMI3774
TOBY MYERS	B	(BC						
MICHAEL READ	K	(BC						

R103 HARGUS ROBBINS

HARGUS 'PIG' ROBBINS PNO(ALL	(A) HARGUS ROBBINS		196 CHART	US		
	(B) COUNTRY INSTRUMENTALIST		1977 ELEKTRA	US		7E1110
	(C) A PIG IN A POKE		1978 ELEKTRA	UK K52071 US	6E 129
	(D) UNBREAKABLE HEARTS		1979 ELEKTRA	US		6E 185

R104 TEX ROBERG BAND

TEX ROBERG	V	(A1	(A) FIRST PRESSING		1979 ARNIES SHACK	UK	AS 029			
BRUCE ROBERTS	G V	(A1	(1) 1979 SPRING							
VERNON CHUTER	G	(A								
DAVE NASH	STEEL(A	MICK WILLIAMS	G	(A	BOB PHILLIPS	B	(A	CHRIS BROWN	G V (1
CHRIS	PNO	(A	DAVE WARD	HCA	(1	BOB WILLIAMS	B	(1	PETE HUNT	D (A1

R105 AL ROBERTS JR

AL ROBERTS JR		(AB	(A) ROCKABILLY GUITAR MAN		1978 FROG	001
			(B) FROGABILLY		1979 FROG	002

R106 ANDY ROBERTS

ANDY ROBERTS G V PERC FLT(ALL	(A) HOME GROWN		1971 B&C CAS 1034 AMPEX US		10120
IAN WHITEMAN	K V	(A	(B) NINA & THE DREAM TREE	1971 PEGASUS		PEG 5
MIKE EVANS	K V	(A	(C) URBAN COWBOY	1973 ELEKTRA	UK	K42139
DAVE RICHARDS	B V	(ABC	(D) & THE GREAT STAMPEDE	1973 ELEKTRA	UK	K42151
ROGER POWELL	D V	(AB	(E) ANDY ROBERTS	1973 CHARISMA	UK	CS6
GORDON HUNTLEY	STEEL(A					

MAC KISSOON	V	(AB	MIKE LONDON	V	(A	KATHY KISSOON	V	(AB	ZOOT MONEY	K V (BCD
IAN MATTHEWS	V	(BC	TIMI DONALD	D	(C	BOB RONGA	B V	(C	B J COLE	STEEL(CD
DICK PARRY	SAX	(C	RICHARD THOMPSON	G	(C	NEIL INNES	G	(C	JOHN MEGGINSON	K (C
MIKE KELLIE	D	(C	MARTIN CARTHY	BANJO(C		GILLIAN NOEL	V	(C	PAUL KENT	V (C
KARENE WALLACE	V	(C	GERRY CONWAY	D	(CD	MICK KAMINSKI	VLN	(D	PAT DONALDSON	B (D
OLLIE HALSALL	G	(D	SONNY FRANCIS	K	(D	RAY WEHRSTEIN	SAX	(D		

R107 BRUCE ROBERTS

BRUCE ROBERTS	K V	(A	(A) BRUCE ROBERTS		1978 ELEKTRA	US 7E119 UK	K52061			
DAVID FOSTER	K	(A								
JIM CREGAN	G	(A	BOBBYE HALL	PERC (A	RON CARTER	B	(A	JOHN JARVIS K	(A
STEVE CROPPER	G	(A	IAN UNDERWOOD	K	(A	BROOKS HONNICUTT	V	(A	DONALD DUCK DUNN	B(A
JEFF PORCARO	D	(A	FRED TACKETT	G	(A	TOMMY VIG	PERC (A	MIKE PORCARO	B(A
BOB GLAUB	B	(A	GRADY TATE	D	(A					

R108 HOWARD ROBERTS

HOWARD ROBERTS	G	(ABCD	(A) THE REAL HOWARD ROBERTS		19 CONCORD	US	53
DAVE GRUSIN	ORG	(D	(B) ANTELOPE FREEWAY		19 IMPULSE		AS9207
MIKE WOFFORD	PNO	(D	(C) SOUNDS		1974 CAPITOL		11247
JERRY SCHEFF	B	(D	(D) EQUINOX EXPRESS ELEVATOR		1975 IMPULSE		IMPL 8004
JOHN GUERIN	D	(D					
MAILTO CORREA	PERC (D	DIANA LEE	V	(D	ED MICHAL	SYN (D	

R108A LAVADA JUNE ROBERTS

LAVADA JUNE ROBERTS V PNO(A	(A) LAVADA		1976 PYE			12126
RICHARD CROOKS	D	(A				
WELDON MYRICK	STEEL(A	FRANK OWENS	ORG (A	DON PAYNE	B	(A	PAUL PRESTOPINO G (A
BOB SYLVESTER	CELLO(A					

R109 RICK ROBERTS

RICK ROBERTS	G V	(ABC	(A) WINDMILLS		1972 A&M UK AMLH64372 US	SP 4372				
DON HENLEY	D V	(A	(B) SHE IS A SONG		1973 A&M	US	SP 4404			
BERNIE LEADON	G V	(A	(C) BEST OF		19 A&M	US	SP 4744			
RANDY MEISNER	B	(A								
JACKSON BROWNE	V	(A	AL PERKINS	STEEL(AB	JOE LALA	PERC (AB	CHRIS HILLMAN	B (A
DALLAS TAYLOR	D	(A	DAVID CROSBY	V	(A	JANE GETZ	PNO V(A	BYRON BERLINE	FDL(A
LEE SKLAR	B	(A	MIKE UTLEY	ORG	(A	MARC BENNO	G	(A	PAUL HARRIS	K (B
GEORGE GRANTHAM	D V	(B	KENNY PASSARELLI	B	(A	JOE WALSH	G	(B	JOE VITALE	D (B
RUSTY YOUNG	G	(B	STEVE FROMHOLZ	B V	(B					

R110 B A ROBERTSON

BRIAN ALEXANDER ROBERTSON V(ABC	(A) WRINGING APPLAUSE		1973 ARDENT	US	ADS	2804
GRAHAM JARVIS	D	(B	(B) INITIAL SUCCESS		1980 ASYLUM	UK	K52216
ALAN JONES	B	(B	(C) BULLY FOR YOU		1981 ASYLUM	UK	K52275
BILLY LIVSEY	K	(B					
TERRY BRITTEN	G	(B					

B111 ROBINS

BOBBY NUNN	V	(	(A) ROCK'ROLL WITH ROBINS		1976 WHIPPETT	US	703
TY TERRELL	V	(	(B) THE BEST OF		1976 GNP CRESCENDO	US	9034
ROY RICHARDS	V	(					
BILLY RICHARDS	V	(	GRADY CHAPMAN	V	(	CARL GARDNER	V	(	RICHARD BERRY	V (
PETE LEWIS	G	(	MARIO DELAGARDE	B	(	JOHNNY OTIS	D	(	DEVONIA WILLIAMS	PNO(
LEARD BELL	D	(	DON JOHNSON	TPT	(	LEE GRAVES	TPT	(	LORENCE HOLDEN	SAX(
JAMES VON STREETER SAX (	WALTER HENRY	B	(	GEORGE WASHINGTON	TROM (	GIL BERNAL	SAX(
MIKE STOLLER	G	(	BARNEY KESSEL	G	(	CHARLIE NORRIS	G	(	RALPH HAMILTON	B (
JESSE SAILES	D	(								

R112 FENTON ROBINSON

FENTON ROBINSON	G V	(ALL	(A) SOMEBODY LOAN ME A DIME	197 SONET SNTF686 ALLIGATOR 4705 TRIO6218
STEVE DITZELL	G	(B	(B) I HEAR SOME BLUES DOWNSTAIRS	1978 SONET SNTF712 ALLIGATOR 4710 TRIO6219
BILL HEID	K	(AB	(C) & LARRY DAVIS	19 PYTHON FR PLP 24
LARRY EXUM	B	(B	(D) MONDAY MORNING BOOGIE & BLUES	19 77 US 7200
EARL CROSSLEY	SAX	(A	(E) GETAWAY	19 77 US 77 109
D BALDWIN	SAX	(A					
ASHWARD GATES	D	(B	BILL MACFARLAND	TROM (AB	BILL BRIMFIELD	TPT (B	LARRY DAVIS	(C
MIGHTY JOE YOUNG	G	(A	CORNELIUS BOYSON	B	(A	TONY GOODEN	D	(A	NORVAL D HODGES TPT(A
ELMER BROWN JR	TPT	(A								

FREDDY ROBINSON   R113

```
FREDDY ROBINSON   G V  (AB       (A) AT THE DRIVE IN        19   POLYDOR UK 2325 085 US ENTERPRISE1025
AL VESOVO         G    (A        (B) BLACK FOX              19   CAPITOL                        20162
HARVEY MASON      D    (A
PAUL HUMPHREY     D    (A   JOE SAMPLE      K   (A   WILTON FELDER    B   (A   MONK HIGGINS    ORG (A
BOBBYE HALL       PERC (A   CLYDIE KING  V     (B
```

L C ROBINSON   R114

```
L C ROBINSON G V VLN STEEL(AB    (A) UPS & DOWNS           1972 ARHOOLIE       US        1062
JAMES MADISON     G    (A        (B) HOUSE CLEANING BLUES  1974 BLUESWAY       US    BLS 6082
SAMUEL LAWHORN    G    (A
CALVIN JONES      B    (A   WILLIE SMITH     D   (A   JOE PINETOP PERKINS PNO(A  CHARLIE MUSSELWHITE HCA(A
DAVID ALEXANDER   PNO  (A   WILLIAM HYATT    B   (A   TEDDY WINSTON       D  (A  KEN SWANK        D  (B
ROBERT HOOKER     PNO  (B   LEX BOYD SILVA   B   (B   LUTHER TUCKER       G  (B
```

SMOKEY ROBINSON & THE MIRACLES   R115

```
SMOKEY ROBINSON   V(ALL EXCEPT **   HI WE'RE THE MIRACLES           1961 TAMLA                 US 220
WILLIAM GRIFFIN   V    (**          COOKIN' WITH THE MIRACLES       196  TAMLA                 US 223
WAH WAH WATSON    G    (Z           SHOP AROUND                     1962 TAMLA                 US 224
RICHARD LITTLEFIELD G  (Z           I'LL TRY SOMETHING NEW          196  TAMLA                 US 230
MARLO HENDERSEN   G    (Z           CHRISTMAS WITH THE MIRACLES     196  TAMLA                 US 236
DAVID T WALKER    G    (Z           FABULOUS MIRACLES               1963 TAMLA                 US 238
MARV TARPIN       D    (Z           MIRACLES ON STAGE               196  TAMLA                 US 241
JAMES GADSON      D    (Z           DOIN' MICKEY'S MONKEY           1963 TAMLA                 US 245
ED GREENE         D    (Z           TEARS OF A CLOWN                196  TAMLA                 US 246
SCOTTIE HARRIS    D    (Z           I LIKE IT LIKE THAT             196  TAMLA    UK  TML11003
CHUCK RAINEY      B    (Z           GREATEST HITS                   196  TAMLA    UK STML11072
JAMES JAMESON     B    (Z           THE FABULOUS MIRACLES           1964 STATESIDE UK SL  10099
WAYNE TWEED       B    (Z           GOING TO A GO GO                1964 TAMLA    UK STML11024 US 267
DAVID SHIELDS     B    (Z           MIRACLES FROM THE BEGINNING     1965 TAMLA    UK  TML11031
SCOTT EDWARDS     B    (Z           AWAY WE GO GO                   1965 TAMLA    UK STML11044 US 271
SONNY BURKE       K    (Z           MAKE IT HAPPEN                  196  TAMLA    UK STML11067 US 276
SYLVESTER RIVERS  K    (Z           GREATEST HITS VOL 2             196  TAMLA    UK STML11233 US 280
MICHAEL B SUTTON  K    (Z           LIVE                            196  TAMLA                 US 289
JOHN BARNES       K    (Z           SPECIAL OCCASION                196  TAMLA                 US 290
RONNIE McNEIR     K    (Z           TIME OUT                        196  TAMLA                 US 295
BOB SMITTY        VIBES(Z           FOUR IN BLUE                    196  TAMLA                 US 297
FRED SMITH        WIND (Z           WHAT LOVE HAS JOINED TOGETHER   1970 TAMLA                 US 301
PATRICIA HENLEY   V    (Z           POCKETFUL OF MIRACLES           197  TAMLA                 US 306
CLAUDETTE ROBINSON V   (Z           ONE DOZEN ROSES                 197  TAMLA                 US 312
JESSIE RICHARDSON V    (Z           FLYING HIGH TOGETHER            197  TAMLA                 US 318
JAMES BRADFORD    PNO  (Z           SMOKEY & THE MIRACLES           1971 TAMLA    UK STML11172
JAMES SLEDGE      CONGA(Z           1957/1972                       1973 TAMLA    UK STMA 8008
PAULINHO DA COSTA PERC (Z           (**) RENAISSANCE                1973 TAMLA    UK STMA 8010
IVORY DAVIS       V    (Z           SMOKEY                          1973 TAMLA    UK STMG 8012 US 328
CAROLYN DENNIS    V    (Z           ANTHOLOGY                       1974 TAMLA                    793
MELBA BRADFORD    V    (Z           PURE SMOKEY                     1974 TAMLA    UK STML11265 US 331
FREDRICK ROCHE    K    (Z           (**) DO IT BABY                 1974 TAMLA    UK STML11276 US 334
MICHAEL JACOBSEN  CELLO(Z           QUIET STORM                     1974 TAMLA    UK STML11288 US 337
ROBERT ZIMMITTI   PERC (Z           (++) CITY OF ANGELS             1974 TAMLA    UK STML12010 US 339
CHERYL COOPER     V    (Z           LOVE MACHINE                    1975 TAMLA    UK STML12020
BRENDA SUTTON     V    (Z           SMOKEYS FAMILY ROBINSON         1975 TAMLA    UK STML12021 US 341
RONNIE WHITE      V    (            (**) POWER OF THE MUSIC         1975 TAMLA    UK STML12038
BOBBY ROGERS      V    (            DEEP IN MY SOUL                 1977 TAMLA    UK STML12055 US 350
PETE MOORE        V    (            BIG TIME(SOUNDTRACK)            1977 TAMLA    UK STML12068 US 355
MARV TAMPLIN      G    (            SMOKEY'S WORLD                  1978 TAMLA    UK STML12076
                                    (Z) LOVE BREEZE                 1978 TAMLA    UK STML12081 US 359
                                    SMOKIN'  (LIVE)                 1978 TAMLA                 US 363
                                    WHERE THERES SMOKEY             1979 TAMLA    UK STML12115 US 366
                                    (**) LOVE CRAZY                 19   CBS                   US 34450
                                    (**) MIRACLES                   19   CBS                   US 34910
                                    TEARS OF A CLOWN                19   PICKWICK              US  3389
                                    FROM THE BEGINNING              19   BELL                 US  1063
                                    TEARS OF A CLOWN                1979 MFP      UK    50422
                                    BEING WITH YOU                  1981 MOTOWN   UK STML12151
```

TOM ROBINSON BAND   R116

```
TOM ROBINSON      B V  (ALL         (A) POWER IN THE DARKNESS       1978 EMI EMC 3226 CAPITOL US 11778
DANNY KUSTOW      G V  (AB1         (B) TRB2                        1979 EMI EMC 3296 HARVEST US 11930
DOLPHIN TAYLOR    D V  (A1          (C) SECTOR 27                   1980 FONTANA              6359 039
MARK AMBLER       K    (A           (1) MAY 1978
NICK PLYTAS       K    (1
IAN 'QUINCE' PARKER K V(B   PRESTON HEYMAN    D V  (B   KASIM SULTON    V   (B   CAROL GRIMES    V  (B
BARRY ST JOHN     V    (B   NIAMH CHAMBERS    V    (B   JO BURT         B   (C   STEVE B         G  (C
DEREK QUINTON     PERC (C
```

VICKI SUE ROBINSON   R117

```
VICKI SUE ROBINSON V   (ABC         (A) NEVER GONNA LET YOU GO      1976 RCA  UK RS 1051    APLI 1256
                                    (B) VICKI SUE ROBINSON          1976 RCA  UK RS 1095    APLI 1829
                                    (C) HALF & HALF                 1978 RCA  UK PL12294    APLI 2294
```

MAGGIE & TERRE ROCHE   R117A

```
MAGGIE ROCHE      V G  (A           (A) SEDUCTIVE REASONING         1975 CBS       US       33232
TERRE ROCHE       G V  (A
```

THE ROCHES   R118

```
SUZZY ROCHE       G V  (AB          (A) THE ROCHES                  1979 WB            US  3298
MAGGIE ROCHE      SYN G V (AB        (B) NURDS                      1980 WB  UK K56855 US  3475
TERRE ROCHE       G V  (AB
ROBERT FRIPP      G    (A   TONY LEVIN     B  (A   JIM MAELEN      PERC (A  LARRY FAST  SYN   (A
JAY DEE DAUGHERTY D    (B   FRED SMITH     B  (B   LINCOLN GOINES  B    (B  JON MATHIAS  B    (B
GABRIEL KATONA    SYN  (B   BOB CONTI      PERC(B  BOBBY GORDON         (B
```

```
R118A                                        ROCCO
    RUSSELL DUNLOP     D    (A         (A) ROCCO                    1976 20TH CENTURY    US      T505
    TIM PARTRIDGE      B    (A
    LEO DE CASTRO      V    (A    HARRIS CAMPBELL  G V (A   SUNIL DE SILVA   PERC (A   TONY ANSELL      K (A
    SPOONS BUCHANAN    SAX  (A    MICK KENNY       SYN (A   MARK PUNCH       G  (A    RALPH WHITE      HRNS(A
    TUI RICHARDS       G    (A
R119                              ROCK'N'ROLL ALL STARS
                                  (A) RED CHINA ROCKS            1972 B+C                      BCM 104
R120                              ROCK FOLLIES(TV SHOW)
    JULIE COVINGTON    V    (AB        (A) ROCK FOLLIES          1976 ISLAND ILPS 9362 POLYDOR 2302054
    CHARLOTTE CORNWELL V    (AB        (B) ROCK FOLLIES 77       1977                   POLYDOR 2302072
    RULA LENSKA        V    (AB
    SUE JONES DAVIS    V    (B    RAY RUSSELL      G   (AB  ANDY MACKAY      SAX (AB   TONY STEVENS     B (AB
    CHRIS PARREN       K    (B    PETER VAN HOOKE  D   (AB  BRIAN CHATTON    K  (A     ROBIN WILLIAMS   VLN(A
    SADIE MACKENZIE    V    (A
R121                                  ROCK HOUSE
    MARTIN STONE       G    (         (A) ROCK HOUSE    (EP)         1979          LIMP           KOOL1
    PETE SHELLEY       D    (
    KEITH TILLMAN      B    (    DAVID COXHILL     SAX (    MICK O'NEAL      SAX (
R122                                  ROCK WORKSHOP
    HARRY BECKETT      HRNS (AB        (A) ROCK WORKSHOP         1970    CBS          UK       64075
    BUD PARKES         HRNS (AB        (B) THE VERY LAST TIME    1971    CBS          UK       64394
    TONY ROBERTS       WIND (AB
    BOB DOWNES         WIND (AB   DEREK WADSWORTH  TROM (AB  ROBIN JONES      D  (A     BRIAN MILLER     K (AB
    PHIL WAINMAN       PERC (B    ALAN RUSHTON     D   (AB  DARYL RUNSWICK   B  (AB    RAY RUSSELL      G (AB
    ALAN GREED         K V  (AB   GINGER HARPER    V   (AB  ALEX HARVEY      V  (A     TONY UTER        PERC(B
R122A                                 ROCKET 88
    ALEXIS KORNER      G V  (A         (A) ROCKET 88             1981²   ATLANTIC US SD19293 UK  K50776
    JACK BRUCE         B    (A
    CHARLIE WATTS      D    (A    IAN STEWART   PNO (A   BOB HALL      PNO (A   DON WELLER  SAX (A
R123                                  ROCKETS
    DAVID GILBERT      V    (ABC       (A) LOVE TRANSFUSION      1977 RCA           UK    PL 12572
    JIM McCARTY        G V  (ABC       (B) ROCKETS              1979 RSO    RSS 7   UK    2394 224
    JOHN BADANJEK      D V  (ABC       (C) NO BALLADS           1980 RSO    RSS 20  UK    2394 250
    DENNIS ROBBINS     G V  (ABC
    JOHN FRAGA         B    (AB   DONNIE DACUS PNO V   (BC  DAVID HOOD       B  (B     CHUCK LEAVELL    K (B
    ANITA POINTER      V    (C    RUTH POINTER     V   (C   LEE MICHAELS     ORG (C    DAN KEYLON       B (C
R123A                                 ROCKETS(60s)
    DANNY WHITTEN      G V  (A         (A) ROCKETS              1968 WHITEWHALE        US    WWS7116
    LEON WHITSELL      G V  (A
    GEORGE WHITSELL    G    (A    RALPH MOLINA     D   (A   BILLY TALBOT     B  (A     BOBBY NOTKOFF    VLN (A
R123B                                 ROCKETS (FRANCE)
    CHRISTIAN LEBARTZ  V    (          (A) ROCKETS              19      DORBY              DBR 20005
    ALAIN GROETZINGER  D    (          (B) ON THE ROAD AGAIN    19      DORBY              DBR 20014
    GERARD L'HER       B V  (          (C) PLASTEROID           19      ROCKLAND           RKL 20137
    ALAIN MARATRAT     G K V(          (D) LIVE                 19      ROCKLAND           RKL 20197
    FABRICE EUAGLIOTTI K   (           (E) GALAXY               1980    ROCKLAND           RKL 20208
R124                                  ROCKIN' BERRIES
    ROY AUSTIN              (          IN TOWN                  1964 PICCADILLY        NPL 38013
    TERRY BOND             (          LIFE IS JUST A BOWL OF BERRIES  1965 PICCADILLY  NPL 38022
    CHUCK BOTFIELD         (          EP I DIDN'T MEAN TO HURT YOU    1964 PICCADILLY  NEP 34639
    CLIVE LEA              (          EP NEW FROM THE ROCKIN' BERRIES 1965 PICCADILLY  NEP 34043
    GEOFF TURTON           (          BLACK GOLD               1976 SATRIL           SATL 4002
    KEN RODWAY             (
    BOBBY THOMPSON         (
R124A                        ROCKIN' DOPSIE & THE CAJUN TWISTERS
    ROCKIN' DOPSIE RUBIN V ACC(ALL     (A) DOIN' THE ZYDECO     1976 SONET        UK    SNTF  718
    CHESTER ZENO       PERC (ABCD      (B) ZY DE BLUE           1977 SONET        UK    SNTF  761
    MAJOR HANDY HARRIS G    (ABCD      (C) HOLD ON!             1979 SONET        UK    SNTF  800
    AUGUST CHARLES     SAX  (AB        (D) BIG BAD ZYDECO       1980 SONET        UK    SNTF  851
    JOSEPH EDWARDS     D    (ABC
    MORRIS FRANCES     B V  (ABCD JOHN PARKER HART SAX (CD ALTON RUBIN      D  (D
R124B                                 ROCKIN' HORSE
                                      (A) ROCKIN' HORSE         1977 RCA           US APLI0937
R124C                        ROCKIN' LOUIE & THE MAMMA JAMMERS
                                      (A) IT WILL STAND         19      CHARLY       CR 30185
R125                                  JESS RODEN
    JESS RODEN         V    (ALL       (A) JESS RODEN               1974 ISLAND        UK  ILPS
                                                                                           9286
    ALLEN TOUSSAINT    PNO  (A         (B) YOU CAN KEEP YOUR HAT ON 1976 ISLAND       UK  ILPS 9349
    ART NEVILLE        ORG  (A         (C) PLAY IT DIRTY PLAY IT CLASS 1977 ISLAND    UK  ILPS 9442
    JOESEPH MODELISTE  D    (A         (D) BLOWIN'                  1977 ISLAND       UK  ILPS 9496
    GEORGE PORTER      B    (A         (E) PLAYER NOT THE GAME      1977 ISLAND       UK  ILPS 9506
    LEO NOCENTELLI     G    (A         (F) STONECHASER              1980 ISLAND       UK  ILPS 9531
    NEW ORLEANS HRNS        (A         (EP) LIVE                    1976 ISLAND       UK  IEP    3
    SIMON KIRKE        D    (A
    JOHN BUNDRICK      K    (A    RICHARD BAILEY   D   (A   MICK FEAT        B  (A     ROY DAVIES       K (A
    GEORGE LEE         SAX  (A    ALLAN SHARP CONGA    (A   STEVE GREGORY    FLT (A    RICHARD DIGA SMITH K(A
    REBOP KWAKU BAAH   PERC (A    MICK WEAVER      K   (A   PAT DONALDSON    B  (A     STEVE WEBB       G V(ABCD
    BRUCE ROBERTS      G V  (BCD  CHRIS GOWER TROM     (BCD RONNIE TAYLOR   SAX (BCD   JOHN CARTWRIGHT  B G (BCDF
    PETE HUNT          D    (BCD  BILLY LIVESY     K   (BCD LEON PENDARVIS  K   (EF    ROB MOUNSEY      K (EF
    SHIRLEY SCOTT      K    (E    ANTHONY JACKSON  B   (EF  FRANCISCO CENTENO B (E     MILT HINTON      B (E
    CLIFFORD MORRIS    G    (E    JOHN TROPEA      G   (E   LANCE QUINN      G  (E     JEFF MIRONOV     G (EF
    FRANKLIN MICARE    G    (E    GARY MURE        D   (E   BUDDY WILLIAMS   D  (E     ERROL BENNETT    PERC(E
    RUBENS BASSINI     PERC (E    DAVID CAREY      VIBES(E  HAROLD VICK      SAX (E     SCOTT HAMILTON   SAX (E
    MICHAEL LEE GRAY   V    (E    DELORES HALL     V   (E   BENNY DIGGS      V  (E     ARNOLD McCULLER  V (E
    LOU MARINI         WIND (E    RAYMOND BECKENSTEIN WIND(EF GEORGE MARGE   HRNS (E    ALAN RUBIN       HRNS(E
    JON FADDIS         HRNS (E    VIRGIL JONES     HRNS (EF  BURT COLLINS    HRNS (E    MICHAEL LAWRENCE HRNS(E
    VICTOR PAZ         HRNS (E    ALAN RAPH        TROM (E   TOM MALONE       TROM(E    WAYNE ANDRE      TROM(EF
                                                                                         (CONTINUED)
```

JESS RODEN

(CONTINUED)

HOWARD JOHNSON	WIND (EF	STRING SECTION	(EF	PAT REBILLOT	K (F	GEORGE T CLINTON	K (F		
JEFF LAYTON	G (F	CLIFF MORRIS	G (F	DAVID LANDALL	G (F	JAKI WHITREN	V (F		
JANICE PENDARVIS	V (F	LUTHER VANDROSS	V (F	JOSHIE ARMSTEAD	V (F	PAT RYAN	SAX (F		
DAVE TOFANI	WIND (F	HAROLD VICK	WIND (F	ALEX FOSTER	WIND (F	BILLY SLAPIN	WIND(F		
ROMEO PENQUE	WIND (F	CHRIS PARKER	D (F	RICHARD CROOKS	D (F	PETER BUNETTA	D (F		
NEIL BUNETTA	D (F	RICK CHUDAKOFF	B (F	ERROL BENNETT	PERC (F	ARNO LUCAS	PERC(F		
CHANDRA ARMSTEAD	V (F	ZACHARY SANDERS	V (F	BARBARA MASSEY	V (F	LEE GOODALL	CLAR(F		
LEW SOLOFF	HRNS (F	DAVE TAYLOR	HRNS (F	BARRY ROGERS	HRNS (F				

TOMMY ROE

TOMMY ROE	G V (ALL	SHEILA	1963	ABC	US	ABC432
JACK SARGENT	D (*	SOMETHING FOR EVERYBODY	1963	ABC	US	ABC467
HAL BLAINE	D (*	SWEET PEA	1966	ABC	US	ABC575
JOE OSBORN	B (*	ITS NOW A WINTERS DAY	196	ABC	US	ABC594
KEITH ALLISON	B (*	PHANTASY	1967	ABC	US	ABC610
RICHARD LAWS	G (*	DIZZY	196	ABC	US	ABC683
MAXINE WILLARD	V (*	12 IN A ROE	1970	ABC	US	ABC700
BEN BENAY	G (*	WE CAN MAKE MUSIC	1970	ABC	US	ABC714
LARRY KNECHTEL	K (*	GREATEST HITS	1970	STATESIDE	UK	SSL10296
DON RANDI	PNO (*	(*) BEGINNINGS	1971	ABC		ABC732
DAVE BOONE	FDL (*	16 GREATEST HITS	19	ABC UK ABCL5157	US	ABC762
PLAS JOHNSON	SAX (*	ENERGY	19	MONUMENT	US	MG 7604
GINGER BLAKE	V (*	FULL BLOOM	19	MONUMENT	US	MG 7614
JULIA TILLMAN	V (*					

JOACHIM ROEDELIUS

HANS JOACHIM ROEDELIUS	K SYN V(ALL	(A) DURCH DIE WUSTE	1978 SKY		SKY014
SCHAGZERIG GREENE	CELLO(B	(B) JARDIN AU FOU	1978 BARCLAY		90291
CONRAD PLANK	PERC G(C	(C) SELBSTPORTRAIT	1979 SKY		
JASO CHRISTO	G B (C	(D) SELBSTPORTRAIT II	1980 SKY		SKY040
DIETER MOEBIUS	SYN (C	(E) SELBSTPORTRAIT III	1980 SKY		SKY044
		(F) LUSTWANDEL	1981 SKY		SKY058

JIMMY ROGERS

JIMMY ROGERS	G V (ABCD	(A) THATS ALL RIGHT	1974 BLACK & BLUE		33504
FRED BELOW	D (BC	(B) CHICAGO BOUND	19 CHESS		407
WILLIE MABRON	PNO (A	(C) BLUESMASTERS	1976 CHESS		2ACMB207
DAVE MYERS	B (A	(D) & LEFT HAND FRANK	1979 JSP		1008
LOUIS MYERS	G (A				

LEFT HAND FRANK	G V (D	BIG CRAWFORD	B (D	BOB BRUNNING	B (D	RAY WESTON	D (D		
ERNEST COTTON	SAX (BC	EDDIE WARE	PNO (BC	WALTER HORTON	HCA (B	LITTLE WALTER	HCA(BC		
ELGIN EVANS	D (BC	MUDDY WATERS	G (BC	BOB WOODFORK	G (C	JOHNNY JONES	PNO(C		
WILLIE DIXON	B (BC	A J GLADNEY	D (C	J T BROWN	SAX (BC	HENRY GRAY	PNO(BC		
OTIS SPANN	PNO (BC	JOE YOUNG	G (C	WAYNE BENNETT	G (C	S P LEARY	D (C		
LUTHER TUCKER	G (C	FRED ROBINSON	G (C	GEORGE HUNTER	D (C				

ROGUE

TREVOR SPENCER	D (B	(A) FALLEN ANGEL	1975 EPIC	UK	69235
BARRY MORGAN	D (ABC	(B) LET IT GO	1977 EPIC	UK	81987
ALAN TARNEY	B (B	(C) WOULD YOU LET YOUR DAUGHTER	1979 ARIOLA		ARL 5028
LES HURDLE	B (ABC				

J W HODGKINSON	V (ABC	GUY FLETCHER	K V (ABC	TERRY BRITTEN	G (B	RITCHIE BULL	BANJO(B
AL HODGE	G (AC	FRANK RICOTTI	PERC (A	JIMMY JEWELL	SAX (C	B J COLE	STEEL(AC

CHRIS ROHMANN

CHRIS ROHMANN	(	(A) THE MAN I AM TODAY	1974 RCA	UK	SF 8364

ROKOTTO

CLEVELAND WALKER	V (A	(A) ROKOTTO	1977 STATE		ETAT15			
SISTER B	V (A							
STEWART GARDEN	K (A	OWEN LLOYD WISDON	B (A	DEREK HENDERSON	G (A	HUGH PAUL	V (A	
HOWARD McLEOD	D (A							

ROLL UPS

LEA HART JR	G V (A	(A) LOVE DIVE FOR HIGH BALLS	197 BRIDGEHOUSE		BHLP 004
PAUL AIREY	K V (A				
JEFF PETERS	B V (A	RICKY ANDREOS	D (A		

ROLLERCOASTER

RAY WARLEIGH	SAX (A	(A) WONDERIN'	1981 CALIBRE	UK	CABLP1006		
DICK MORRISSEY	SAX (A						
DEREK WATKINS	TPT (A	CHRIS PYNE	TROM (A	ALAN PARKER	G (A	MIKE PYNE	PNO (A
RON MATTHEWSON	B (A	BARRY MORGAN	D (A	KARL JENKINS	K (A	MIKE RATLEDGE	K (A

ROLLING STONES

MICK JAGGER	G K V(ALL	(A) THE ROLLING STONES	1964 DECCA	UK LK4605	US LONDON	PS375
KEITH RICHARD	G V K(ALL	(B) THE ROLLING STONES 2	1965 DECCA	UK SLK4661		
BRIAN JONES	G V (ABCDEFGHJKLMR	(C) 12X5	1965		US LONDON	PS402
IAN STEWART	PNO (GEPQUZ,JJ	(D) THE ROLLING STONES NOW	1965		US LONDON	PS420
MICK AVORY	D (	(E) OUT OF OUR HEADS	1965 DECCA	UK SKL4733	US LONDON	PS429
DICK TAYLOR	G B (	(F) DECEMBERS CHILDREN	1965		US LONDON	PS451
CHARLIE WATTS	D (ALL	(G) AFTERMATH	1966 DECCA	UK SKL4786	US LONDON	PS476
BILL WYMAN	V B SYN (ALL	(H) HIGHTIDE & GREEN GRASS	1966 DECCA	UK TXA 101	US LONDON	NPS 1
RON WOOD	G B V (I	(I) GOT LIVE IF YOU WANT IT	1967 LONDON			SL226/7
MICK TAYLOR	G V (QUZY	(J) BETWEEN THE BUTTONS	1967 DECCA	UK SKL4852	US LONDON	PS499
TONY CHAPMAN	D (	(K) FLOWERS	1967		SKL16487 US LONDON	PS509
JIM PRICE	HRNS (QU	(L) SATANIC MAJESTIES REQUEST	1967 DECCA	UK TKS 103	US LONDON	NPS 2
BOBBY KEYS	HRNS (QU	(M) BEGGARS BANQUET	1968 DECCA	UK SKL4955	US LONDON	PS539
NICKY HOPKINS	K (LMQUZ,HH,	(N) LET IT BLEED	1969 DECCA	UK SKL5025	US LONDON	NPS 4
BILLY PRESTON	K (QUZ,HH,JJ	(O) THROUGH THE PAST DARKLY	1969 DECCA	UK SKL5019	US LONDON	NPS 3
RY COODER	G (Q	(P) GET YER YA YAS OUT	1970 DECCA	UK SKL5065	US LONDON	NPS 5
OLLIE BROWN	PERC (HH,JJ,	(Q) STICKY FINGERS	1971 ROLLING STONE			COC 59100
WAYNE PERKINS	G (HH,	(R) STONE AGE	1971 DECCA	UK SKL5084		
HARVEY MANDEL	G (HH,	(S) GIMME SHELTER	1971 DECCA	UK SKL5101		
PAUL BUCKMASTER	(Q	(T) MILESTONES	1971 DECCA	UK SKL5098		
JACK NITZSCHE	K (EGQ	(U) EXILE ON MAIN STREET	1972 ROLLING STONE UK	69100 US		2900
J W ALEXANDER	PERC (E	(V) ROCK'N'ROLLIN' STONES	1972 DECCA	UK SKL5149		
JIM DICKINSON	PNO (Q	(W) HOT ROCKS 1964/71	1972		US LONDON	606/7
					(CONTINUED)	

R133 (CONTINUED)

ROLLING STONES

JIMMY MILLER	PERC	(QU	(X) MORE HOT ROCKS	1972		US LONDON	626/7
ROCKY DZIDZORNU	PERC	(Q	(Y) GOATS HEAD SOUP	1973 ROLLING STONE	59101	US	39106
CLYDIE KING	V	(U	(Z) ITS ONLY ROCK'N'ROLL	1974 ROLLING STONE UK	59103	US	RS 79101
VANETTA FIELDS	V	(U	(AA) NO STONE UNTURNED	1973 DECCA		UK SKL5173	
JESSE KIRKLAND	V	(U	(BB) ROLLED GOLD	1975 DECCA		UK ROST 1/2	
TAMMI LYNN	V	(U	(CC) METAMORPHOSIS	1975 DECCA		UK SKL5212 US ABCKO	ANA 1
SHIRLEY GOODMAN	V	(U	(CC) METAMORPHOSIS	1975		CAN LONDON PS 573	
DR JOHN	V	(U	(DD) MADE IN THE SHADE	1975 ROLLING STONE UK	59104	US	79102
JOE GREEN	V	(U	(EE) STONE AGE/GOT LIVE	1975 TELDEC		EURO	SD3024
KATHI McDONALD	V	(U	(FF) AROUND & AROUND	197 DECCA		UK SLK6315	
BILL PLUMMER	B	(U	( ) LIVE	197 LONDON		JAPAN	SL226/7
AL PERKINS	STEEL	(U	(HH) BLACK & BLUE	1976 ROLLING STONE UK	59106	US	79104
RAY COOPER	PERC	(Z	(JJ) LOVE YOU LIVE	1977 ROLLING STONE UK	89101	US	2 9001
BLUE MAGIC	V	(Z	(KK) SOME GIRLS	1978 ROLLING STONE UK CUN39108			
CHARLIE JOLLY	TABLA	(Z	( ) ROLLING STONES SOLID ROCK	19 DECCA		UK TAB1	
ED LEACH	PERC	(Z	( ) ROLLING STONES (PROFILE)	19 TELDEC		GERM	624001
KENNY JONES	D	(Z	( ) DECEMBERS CHILDREN	1981 DECCA			
SUGAR BLUE	HCA	(KK,	( ) SUCKING IN THE SEVENTIES	1981 ROLLING STONES UK			
WILLY WEEKS	B	(Z	(EP) ROLLING STONES	1964 DECCA		UK DFE 8560	
IAN MACLAGAN	K	(KK,	(EP) 5X5	1964 DECCA		UK DFE 8590	
MEL COLLINS	SAX	(KK,	(EP) GOT LIVE IF YOU WANT	1965 DECCA		UK DFE 8620	

R133A

ROMANTICS

MIKE SKILL	G V	(A		(A) ROMANTICS	1980 EPIC	UK	84095
WALLY PALMAR	G V	(A		(B) NATIONAL BREAKOUT	1980 EPIC	UK	84176
RICH COLE	B V	(A	JIMMY MARINOS	D V (A			

R134

MAX ROMEO

MAX ROMEO	V	(ALL		(A) REVELATION TIME		1975 SOUNDTRAC		TSL 1000
BARRY LLEWELLYN	V	(B		(B) WAR IN A BABYLON		1976 ISLAND	UK	ILPS 9392
EARL MORGAN	V	(B		(C) RONDOS		19 KING KONG		KANT1
MARCIA GRIFFITHS	V	(B		(D) OPEN THE IRON GATES		1978 UA	US	LA 803
CYNTHIA SCOLAS	V	(B		(E) RECONSTRUCTION		1978 MANGO	UK	MLPS 9503
BORIS GARDNER	B	(E						
MICKY RICHARDS	D	(E	KEITH STERLING	PNO (E	EARL LINDO	K CLAR(E DAVID MADDEN	TPT (E
BOBBY ELLIS	HRNS	(E	GLEN DA COSTA	SAX (E	VIN GORDON	TROM (E EARL SMITH	G (E
ERNIE RANGLIN	G	(E	SHEENA	V (E	JIMMY RILEY	V (E RICKY STORME	V (E

R135

RONETTES

VERONICA BENNETT(SPECTOR)	V(ALL			(A) TODAYS HITS	1963 PHILLES	US	4004
ESTELLE BENNETT	V	(		(B) CHRISTMAS GIFT	1963 PHILLES	US	4005
NEDRA TALLEY	V	(		(C) FABULOUS RONETTES	1964 PHILLES	US	4006
CAROL KAYE	B	(		(D) THE RONETTES	1965 COLPIX	US	486
HAL BLAINE	D	(		(E) SING THEIR GREATEST HITS	1975 PHIL SPECTOR	UK	2307 003
LEON RUSSELL	K	(					
CHIP FIELDS	V	(	DENISE EDWARDS	V (			

R136

MICK RONSON

MICK RONSON	G V K	(AB		(A) SLAUGHTER ON THE TENTH AVENUE	1974 RCA		APLI0353
IAN HUNTER	G V	(		(B) PLAY DONT WORRY	1975 RCA		APLI0681
TREVOR BOLDER	B HRN	(AB					
DAVID HENTSCHEL	K	(A	AYNSLEY DUNBAR	D (AB MIKE GARSON	K (AB MARGARET RONSON	V (A
BEVERLY BAXTER	V	(B	RITCHIE DHARMA	D (B VICKI BROWN	V (B TONY NEWMAN	D (B
PAUL FRANCIS	D	(B					

R137

LINDA RONSTADT

LINDA RONSTADT	V	(ALL	(A) HAND SOWN HOME GROWN	1969 CAPITOL(RI 1975)		ST208
DAN DUGMORE	G	(GJKOP	(B) SILK PURSE	1970 CAPITOL		ST407
WADDY WACHTEL	G V	(JKOP	(C) LINDA RONSTADT	1972 CAPITOL		ST635
KENNY EDWARDS	B V	(FGJKIOP	(D) DONT CRY NOW	1974 ASYLUM UK SYL9012	US SD5064	
RICK MAROTTA	D	(JOP	(D) DONT CRY NOW	1974 ASYLUM UK K43002 RI		
DON GROLNICK	K	(JKOP	(E) DIFFERENT DRUM	1975 CAPITOL UK VMP1010 RI CAPS 1004		
PETER ASHER G V PERC		(FGJKOP	(F) HEART LIKE A WHEEL	1974 CAPITOL		11358
CHARLES VEAL	VLN	(J	(G) PRISONER IN DISGUISE	1975 ASYLUM UK SYL8761	US 7E1045	
DAVID CAMPBELL	VLA	(FJ	(G) PRISONER IN DISGUISE	1975 ASYLUM UK K53015 RI		
DENNIS KARMAZYN	CELLO	(FJ	(H) HASTEN DOWN THE WIND	1976 ASYLUM UK K53045	US 7E1072	
RICHARD FEVES	B	(FJ	(I) GREATEST HITS	1976 ASYLUM UK K53055	US 6E 106	
MIKE AULDRIDGE	B	(JP	(J) SIMPLE DREAM	1977 ASYLUM UK K53065	US 6E 104	
DOLLY PARTON	V	(J	(K) LIVING IN THE USA	1978 ASYLUM UK K53085	US 6E 155	
STEVE FORMAN	PERC	(JOP	(L) RETROSPECTIVE	1977 CAPITOL UK CAPSP102	US 11629	
DON HENLEY	V D	(CFJO	(M) THE SOUTHERN BELLE	1978 EMI IMP		05085068
LARRY HAGLER	V	(JO	(N) STONE PONEYS FEATURING L.RONSTADT 1975 CAPITOL		11383
JOHN DAVID SOUTHER	V	(CFGIJ	(O) GREATEST HITS	1980 ASYLUM UK K52255	US 5E 516	
HERB PEDERSEN	V	(FCGJI	(P) MAD LOVE	1980 ASYLUM UK K52210		
DAVID SANBORN	SAX	(KO				

ANDREW GOLD	K G V	(FGIKOP	RUSS KUNKEL	D	(GKFOP	DAVID LINDLEY	FDL	(FG	JIM CONNOR	HCA	(G
LOWELL GEORGE	G	(G	NIGEL OLSSON	D	(G	DANNY KORTCHMAR	G	(GOP	DAVID KEMPER	D	(GI
DAN FRANCISCO	V	(G	EMMYLOU HARRIS	V	(FG	GLEN D HARDIN	PNO	(G	DAVID GRISMAN	MAND	(G
JAMES TAYLOR	G	(G	MARIA MULDAUR	V	(FG	EDDIE BLACK	G	(FG	PAT HENDERSON	V	(GKO
JULIA TILLMAN	V	(G	MAXINE WILLARD	V	(G	MIKE MAINIERI	VIBES	(K	SHIRLEY MATTHEWS	V	(FIKO
JIM GILSTRAP	V	(KO	JOHN LEHMAN	V	(KO	DAVID LASLEY	V	(K	ARNOLD McCULLER	V	(K
CLYDIE KING	V	(FI	SNEAKY PETE	STEEL	(FIC	JIMMY FADDEN	HRNS	(CFI	WENDY WALDMAN	V	(FIO
CHRIS ETHRIDGE	B	(FI	BOB WARFORD	G	(F	DENNIS ST JOHN	D	(F	EMORY GORDY	B	(F
CISSY HOUSTON	V	(F	JOYCE NESBITT	V	(F	LLOYD MYERS	D	(F	PAUL CRAFT	G	(F
JOHN STARLING	G	(F	TOM GUIDERA	B	(F	DANNY PENDLETON	STEEL	(F	JOHN BOYLAN	G	(CFI
GLENN FREY	G	(CF	TIM SCHMIT	B	(F	JIM GORDON	D	(I	JIMMY GORDON	HRNS	(I
BERNIE LEADON	G	(I	AL CIOLA	G	(I	MARK GOLDENBERG	G	(OP	BOB GLAUB	B	(OP
BILL PAYNE	K	(OP	ROSEMARY BUTLER	V	(OP	NICOLETTE LARSON	V	(OP	KARLA BONOFF	V	(O
PETER BERNSTEIN	G	(P	MICHAEL BODDICKER	SYN	(P	MIKE BOWDEN	B	(CI	RICHARD BOWDEN	G	(CI
GIB GUILBEAU	FDL V	(CI	TIPPY ARMSTRONG	G	(C	WELDON MYRICK	STEEL	(C	BARRY BECKETT	K	(C
DAVID HOOD	B	(C	DEAN WEBB	MAND	(C	JOHN MARTIN	G V	(C	RANDY MEISNER	B V	(C
ROGER HAWKINS	D	(C	MERRY CLAYTON	V	(C	DIANNE DAVIDSON	V	(C	MISS ONA	V	(C
BERNIE LEADON	G V	(C	WESLEY PRITCHETT	B	(C	BUDDY EMMONS	STEEL	(C	LYLE RITZ	B	(C

(CONTINUED)

LINDA RONSTADT   R137

ANDY JOHNSON	G	(I	PETE WADE	G	(I	SPOONER OLDHAM	PNO(I	NORBERT PUTNAM	B (I
MICKEY McGEE	D	(I	MARTI McCALL	V	(I	MICHAEL BOTTS	D (I	GAIL MARTIN	TROM(I
DON RANDI	K	(I	NINO TEMPO	SAX	(I	MACK JOHNSON	TPT (I	DARRELL LEONARD	TPT(I
BUDDY SPICHER	BAN FDL	(I	GINGER HOLLADAY	V	(I	MARY HOLLADAY	V (I		

ROOGALATOR   R138

DANNY ADLER	G	(A1		(A) PLAY IT BY EAR		1977 DO IT	UK	RIDE 1
NICK PLYTAS	K	(A		(1) 1978				
JUSTIN HILDRETH	D	(A1						
JULIAN SCOTT	B	(A1						

ROOT BOY SLIM & THE SEX CHANGE BAND   R139

ROOT BOY SLIM		(A) ROOT BOY SLIM & THE SEX CHANGE BAND	1978 WB	US 3160	ILLEGAL 79	003
(FOSTER MACKENZIE III)V(AB		(B) ZOOM	1979	ILLEGAL	UK	004
RATTLESNAKE RATTLES	B(AB					
(BOB GREENLEE)						

COSMO GREEK(WALT ANDREWS	G(A	ERNIE E LOCKEROOM	G(A	RON HOLLOWAY	SAX (A	TOMMY RUGER	D (A	
MICKI LEE JONNIE	V (A	CHERIE GRASSO	V (A	FLACO FALCON	PERC (A	KATHE'SPECIAL K'RUSSELL	V(A	
WINSTON 'SPOTS'KELLY	K(A							

BIFF ROSE   R139A

BIFF ROSE	V PNO(A		(A) CHILDREN OF LIGHT	1968 TETRAGRAMMATON	US T 116	
VAN DYKE PARKS	SYN (A					
NICK WOODS	SYN (A	BENNY BARTH	D (A			

TIM ROSE   R140

TOM ROSE	V	(ALL	(A) TIM ROSE	1967	CBS	UK 63168	US 9577
BERNARD PURDIE	D	(A	(B) THROUGH ROSE COLOURED SPECS	1969	CBS	UK 63636	US 9772
FELIX PAPPALARDI	B	(A	(C) LOVE A KIND OF HATE STORY	1970	CAPITOL	US 673	
JAY BERLINER	G	(A	(D) TIM ROSE	1972	PLAYBOY	US 101	
HUGH McCRACKEN	G	(A	(E) TIM ROSE	1974	DAWN	UK DNLS3062	
			(F) THE MUSICIAN	1975	ATLANTIC UK K50183		
			(G) RETROSPECTIVE	1977	CAPITOL		

ROSE GARDEN   R140A

DIANA DI ROSE	G	(A	(A) ROSE GARDEN	1968	ATCO	SD 33225
JOHN NORDEN	G	(A				
JAMES GROSHONG	G	(A	WILLIAM FLEMING B (A	BRUCE BOUDIN	D (A	

ROSE ROYCE   R141

ROSE NORWALT	V	(C	(A) CAR WASH	1976 MCA		UK	MCSP 278	
GWEN 'ROSE' DICKEY	V	(D	(B) BEST OF CARWASH	1977 MCA		UK	MCF 2799	
TERRY SANTIEL	CONGA(CD	(C) IN FULL BLOOM	1977 WHITFIELD US 3074 UK			K56394	
HENRY GARNER	D V	(CD	(D) STRIKES AGAIN	1978 WHITFIELD US 3227 UK			K56527	
LEQUEINT JOBE	B V	(CD	(E) RAINBOW CONNECTION IV	1979 WHITFIELD US 3387 UK			K56714	
MICHAEL MOORE	SAX	(CD	(F) GOLDEN TOUCH	1980 WHITFIELD US 3512 UK			K56881	
KENNY COPELAND	TPT V(CD	(G) GREATEST HITS	1980 WHITFIELD			RRTV1	
KENJI BROWN	G V	(CD						
MICHAEL NASH	K	(CD	FREDDIE DUNN	TPT (CD	MARK DAVIS	K (CD	WAH WAH WATSON	G (CDE
JAMES GADSON	D	(C	JACK ASHFORD	D (CDE	VICTOR NYX	K (D	CORNELIUS GRANT	G (D
JIMMY VALDEZ	D	(D	WALTER DOWNING	K (DE	MARK KENOLY	B (D	LAFAYETTE TREY STONE	G(E
ISY MARTIN	G	(E						

ALAN ROSS   R142

ALAN ROSS	G V	(ABCD	(A) ROSS	1974	RSO	UK	2394 127
STEVE EMERY	V B	(AB	(B) PIT & THE PENDULUM	1975	RSO	UK	2394 144
BOB JACKSON	K V	(AB	(C) ARE YOU FREE ON SATURDAY	1977	EBONY		EBY 1000
TONY FERNANDEZ	D	(AB	(D) RESTLESS NIGHTS	1978	EBONY	UK	EBY 1003
REUBEN WHITE	PERC	(AB					
FRANK WILSON	K V	(C	JOHN COOKE	K V (CD ED SPEVOCK	D (CD PETE DENNIS	B V (CD	
TOM COMPTON	D	(C	CHRIS FLETCHER	PERC V(C CRAIG ANDERS	D V (D STRINGS	(C	

DOCTOR ROSS   R143

DOCTOR ROSS V HCA G PERC(ALL		(A) HIS FIRST RECORDINGS	19	ARHOOLIE	F1065	
BOB HALL	PNO (C	(B) LIVE AT MONTREUX	19	ATLANTIC 2460 169 BIG BEAR 18		
LAFAYETTE LEAKE	PNO (B	(C) THE HARMONICA BOSS	1974	BIG BEAR	BEAR 2	
LOUIS MYERS	G	(B	(D) JIVIN' THE BLUES	197	BIG BEAR	BEAR15	
DAVID MYERS	B	(B	(E) CALL THE DOCTOR	19	TESTAMENT	2206	

ROSSINGTON COLLINS BAND   R143A

	(A) A CONVERSATION WITH	19	MCA	5130
	(B) ANY TIME ANYWHERE	19	MCA	US

ROTARY CONNECTION   R144

MINNIE RIPPERTON	V	(	(A) ROTARY CONNECTION	1968 CHESS CRL 4538 CADET	LPS 312
			(B) ALADDIN	196 CADET	LPS 317
			(C) PEACE AT LAST	1969 CADET	LPS 318
			(D) SONGS	196 CADET	LPS 322
			(E) DINNER MUSIC	19 CADET	LPS 328
			(F) TRIP ONE	1973 CHECKER	6467 300

ARLEN ROTH   R144A

ARLEN ROTH	G V	(A	(A) HOT PICKUPS	1980 SONET	UK	SNTF 845	
MICHAEL BRAUN	D	(A	(B) GUITARIST	19	US		
IVAN ELIAS	B	(A					
DEAN KRAUS	K	(A	STEPHANIE DAVY V (A	THE PERSUASIONS	V (A	KEVIN KELLY V (A	

MICHAEL ROTHER   R145

MICHAEL ROTHER	G B SYN	(ALL	(A) FLAMMENDE HERZEN	1976	SKY	SKY 007
JAKI LEIBEZEIT	D	(ABC	(A) FLAMMENDE HERZEN	197	RADAR (UNRELEASED)	RAD 8
			(B) STERNTALER	1978	SKY	SKY 013
			(C) KATZENMUSIK	1979	SKY	SKY 033

ROUGH DIAMOND   R146

DAVID BYRON	V	(A	(A) ROUGH DIAMOND	1977 ISLAND	ILPS 9490
DAVE CLEMPSON	G	(A			
GEOFF BRITTON	D	(A	DAMON BUTCHER K (A WILLIE BATH	B (A	

ROUNDABOUT   R147

CHRIS CURTIS	V	(A	(A) 1967
DAVE CURTIS	V	(A	
BOBBY CLARK	D	(A	JON LORD K (A RITCHIE BLACKMORE G (A

```
R148                              ROWAN BROTHERS
  PETER ROWAN      V G MAND(C    (A) THE ROWAN BROTHERS        19   CBS              US    31297
  LORIN ROWAN      G V (C        (B) ROWANS                  1976 ASYLUM UK K53023   US   7E1038
  CHRIS ROWAN      G V (C        (C) SIBLING RIVALRY         1976 ASYLUM             US   7E1073
  BILL ELLIOTT     PNO (C        (D) JUBILATION                19 ASYLUM             US   7E1114
  JOE CARROLL      B   (C
  RICHARD GREENE   VLN (C   PETER WALSH     B  (C   WALLY DROGAS    D  (C   JORDAN AMARANTHA CONGA(C
  K DUDLEY GLANZ   D   (C   JIMMY HODDER    D  (C   MARK STEIN      D  (C
R148A                                    ROXY
  BOB SEGARINI     G B V PERC(A  (A) ROXY                    1970  ELEKTRA          US   EKS74063
  RANDY BISHOP     G B K V (A
  JIM DE COCQ      K G (A   JOHN McDONALD   D PERC(A JAMES MORRIS   K  (A
R149                                  ROXY MUSIC
  BRYAN FERRY      V K (ALL      (A) ROXY MUSIC     1972 UK ISLAND ILPS9200 RI POLYDOR 2302 048
  PAUL THOMPSON    D   (ALL      (A) ROXY MUSIC      197 US REPRISE  RS2114 RI ATCO          36133
  ANDY MACKAY      SAX (ALL      (B) STRANDED       1973 UK ISLAND ILPS9252 RI POLYDOR 2302 050
  BRIAN ENO        SYN K(AC12    (B) STRANDED        197     US ATCO                          7045
  ROGER BUNN       G   (1        (C) FOR YOUR PLEASURE 1973 UK ISLAND ILPS9232 RI POLYDOR 2302 049
  DAVY OLIST       G   (         (C) FOR YOUR PLEASURE 197 US WB      BS2629 RI ATCO          36134
  PHIL MANZANERA   G   (ALL      (D) COUNTRY LIFE    1974 UK ISLAND ILPS9303 RI POLYDOR 2302 051
  GRAHAM SIMPSON   B   (A12      (D) COUNTRY LIFE     197 US ATCO                            36106
  RIK KENTON       B   (I        (E) SIREN          1975 UK ISLAND ILPS9344 RI POLYDOR 2302 052
  JOHN GUSTAFSON   B   (BCEF     (E) SIREN          1975 US ATCO                            36127
  JOHN PORTER      B   (C        (F) VIVA           1976 UK ISLAND ILPS9400 RI POLYDOR 2302 053
  JOHN WETTON      B   (F        (F) VIVA           1976 US ATCO                            36139
  EDDIE JOBSON     K VLN(BDEF    (G) MANIFESTO      1979 UK POLYDOR                      POLH 001
  CHRIS LAURENCE   B   (B        (H) FLESH & BLOOD  1980 UK POLYDOR 2302 099            POLH 002
  SAL MAIDA        B   (BF       (I) GREATEST HITS  1977 UK POLYDOR 2302 073 US ATCO         38103
  RICK WILLS       B   (BF       (1) 1970/71   (2) 1971/72
  NEIL HUBBARD     G   (H
  SIRENS           V   (F   GARY TIBBS      B  (GH PAUL CARRACK   K (G  ALLEN SCHWARZBERG  D (H
  ANDY NEWMARK     D   (H   SIMON PHILLIPS  D  (H  ALAN SPENNER   B (H  NEIL JASON         B (H
  DEXTER LLOYD     D   (1
R150                               THE ROYALS
  ROY COUSINS          (ALL      (A) PICK UP THE PIECES    1977 MAGNUM DEAD1004 RI UA   LBR1010
  LEROY WALLACE    D   (B        (B) ISRAEL   BE WISE      1978 BALLISTIC            UAG 30206
  MIKEY            D   (B        (C) TEN YEARS AFTER       1978 UA                   UAS 30189
  WINSTON WRIGHT   K   (B
  ANSEL COLLINS    K   (B   VIN GORDON     HRNS (B  HEADLEY BENNETT HRNS (B LLOYD PARKS B (B
  BAGGA            B   (B   ROBBY SHAKESPEARE B (B RANCHIE McLEAN  G (B   PABLO BLACK G (B
  BUBBLER          G   (B   ROBERT LYN      G  (B  WINSTON         G (B   SKULLY    PERC (B
  STICKY           PERC (B
R151                           RUBBER CITY REBELS
  ROD FIRESTONE    V   (         (A) FROM AKRON          1977  CLONE            US
  BUZZ CLICK       G V (
  DONNIE DAMAGE    B   (    MICHAEL VON HAMMER D  (
R152                          RUBEN & THE JETS
  RUBEN LADRON DE GuEVARA V TAM( (A) FOR REAL            1973 MERCURY          SRM 1 659
  TONY DURAN       G V K(A
  ROBERT CAMARENA  G V (A   JOHNNY MARTINEZ B V ORG(A ROBERT ROBERTS SAX (A BILL WILD B V (A
  BOB ZAMORA       D   (A   JIM SHERWOOD    SAX  (A
R153                                RUBETTES
  ALAN WILLIAMS    G FLT K (      (A) WE CAN DO IT       1975 STATE            ETAT  001
  TONY THORPE      G K D(         (B) RUBETTES           1975 STATE            ETAT  004
  MICK CLARKE      B   (          (C) SIGN OF THE TIMES  1976 STATE            ETAT  006
  BILL HURD        K   (          (D) BEST OF            1976 STATE            ETAT  008
  JOHN RICHARDSON  D   (          (E) WHERE ITS AT       1976 POLYDOR          2383 306
  PETER ARNESEN    K   (          (F) BABY I KNOW        1977 STATE            ETAT  012
                                  (G) SOMETIME IN OLDCHURCH 1978 POLYDOR       2383 480
                                  (H) STILL UNWINDING    1978 POLYDOR          2383 520
R154                                RUBICON
  DENNIS MARCELLINO WIND (A       (A) RUBICON            1978 20TH CENTURY          BT 552
  BRADLEY GILLIS   G   (A
  GREG ECKLER      D   (A   JERRY MARTINI   SAX  (A  MAX HASKETT     TPT (A JIM PUGH     K (A
  JACK BLADES      B   (A
R155                                RUBINOOS
  JOHN RUBIN       G V (A         (A) THE RUBINOOS       1977 BESERKLEY US 34778 UK BSERK10
  TOMMY DUNBAR     G   (A         (B) BACK TO THE DRAWING BOARD 1979 BESERKLEY     UK BSERK18
  ROYSE ADER       B   (A
  DONN SPINDT      D   (A
R156                               RUBY (UK)
  MIKE LENTON      G   (A         (A) RED CRYSTAL FANTASIES 1974 CHRYSALIS       CHR  1061
  JOHN ABBOTT      G V (A
  DAVID KNIGHTS    V G B(A   RAB MUNRO    V PERC   (A GERRY SHURY  STRINGS(A GEOFF SWETTENHAM D (A
  COLIN FAIRLEY    D   (A
R157                               RUBY (US)
  TOM FOGERTY      G V (AB        (A) RUBY              1977 PBR INT            PBRL5001
  RANDY ODA        G K V(AB       (B) ROCK'N'ROLL MADNESS 1978 PBR INT          PBRL5003
  BOBBY COCHRAN    D V (AB
  ANTHONY DAVIS    B V (AB   ED BOGAS     B  (A
R158                                RUEFREX
  JACKIE FORGE     G   (A         (A) ONE BY ONE(EP)    1979 GOOD VIBRATION          GOT 8
  ALAN CLARKE      V   (A
  TOM COULTER      B   (A   PAUL BURGESS    D  (A
R159                              DAVID RUFFIN
  DAVID RUFFIN     V   (ALL       MY WHOLE WORLD ENDED  1969 TAMLA              US   7685
                                  FEELIN' GOOD          1969 TAMLA              US   7695
                                  DAVID RUFFIN          1973 TAMLA UK STML11228  US   7762
                                  ME & ROCK'N'ROLL IS HERE TO STAY 1975 TAMLA UK STML11283 US 7818
                                                                                  (CONTINUED)
                                     [356]
```

DAVID RUFFIN

DAVID RUFFIN		WHO AM I	1975	TAMLA	UK	STML12012	US	7849
		EVERYTHING'S COMING UP LOVE	1976	TAMLA	UK	STML12030	US	7866
		IN MY STRIDE	1977	TAMLA	UK	STML12064	US	7885
		AT HIS BEST	1978	TAMLA	UK	STML12079	US	7895

JIMMY RUFFIN   R160

JIMMY RUFFIN	V	(ALL	JIMMY RUFFIN	1967	POLYDOR	UK	2383 240
			SINGS TOP TEN	1967	SOUL	US	704
			JIMMY RUFFIN WAY	1967	TAMLA	UK	STML11048
			RUFF & READY	1969	TAMLA	UK	STML11106
			RUFF & READY	1969	SOUL	US	708
			FOREVER	1970	TAMLA	UK	STML11161
			GROOVE GOVERNOR	1970	SOUL	US	727
			I AM MY BROTHERS KEEPER	1970	SOUL	US	728
			JIMMY & DAVID RUFFIN	1971	TAMLA	UK	STML11176
			GREATEST HITS	1974	TAMLA	UK	STML11259
			LOVE IS ALL WE NEED	1975	POLYDOR	UK	2383 337

RUFUS   R161

CHAKA KHAN	V	(ABCDEFH	(A) RUFUS	1973	ABC	UK ABCL5114	US	783
RON STOCKERT	K V	(AB	(B) RAGS TO RUFUS	1974	ABC	UK ABCL5952	US	809
KEVIN MURPHY	K V	(ABCDEFGH	(C) RUFUSIZED	1974	ABC	UK ABCL5063	US	837
ANDRE FISCHER	D V	(ABCDE	(D) RUFUS FEATURING CHAKA KHAN	1975	ABC	UK ABCL5151	US	909
AL CINER	G V	(AB	(E) ASK RUFUS	1977	ABC	UK ABCL5203	US	975
DENNIS BELFIELD	B V	(AB	(F) STREET PLAYER	1978	ABC	UK ABCL5239	US	1049
ERIC FISCHER	V	(A	(G) NUMBERS	1979	ABC	UK ABCL5263	US	1098
TONY MAIDEN	G V	(CDEFGH	(H) MASTERJAM	1979	MCA		MCG 4007
BOBBY WATSON	B V	(CDEFGH					

TOWER OF POWER	HRNS (D	RON WOOD	G	(E	MILT HOLLAND	PERC (E	JERRY HEY	TPT (FH
KIM HUTCHCROFT	HRNS (FH	BILL REICHENBACH	TROM (FH	LARRY WILLIAMS	WIND (FH	HELEN LOWE	V (F
EVERETT BRYSON	PERC (FG	JOHN ROBINSON	D	(GH	DAVID WOLINSKI	K V(EFGH	RICHARD CALHOUN D	PERC(F
LEW McCREARY	TROM (H	GARY GRANT	HRNS (H	LARRY HALL	HRNS (H	LOUIS JOHNSON	PERC (H
GEORGE JOHNSON	PERC (H	RICHARD HEATH	PERC (H	FREDDIE HUBBARD	TPT (G	HARVEY MASON	D (G
TRUMAN THOMAS	K (G	CHUCK BROOKE WIND	(G	JOHN ERVIN	TROM (G	RICHARD MIKULS	G (G
BOB GREVE	WIND (G	MAXAYN LEWIS	V (G	LALOMIE WASHBURN	V (G	BILL LAMB	HRNS(G
DAVE GROVER	HRNS (G						

RUMOUR   R162

BRINSLEY SCHWARZ	G	(ABC	(A) MAX	1977	VERTIGO	UK	6360149
BOB ANDREWS	K	(AB	(A) MAX	1977	MERCURY	US	SRM1 1174
STEVE GOULDING	PERC (ABC		(B) FROGS SPROUTS CLOGS & KRAUTS	1979	STIFF	UK	SEEZ 13
ANDY BODNAR	D	(ABC	(C) PURITY OF ESSENCE	1980	STIFF	UK	SEEZ 27
MARTIN BELMONT	G	(ABC					
ALBIE DONNELLY	SAX (A	BOB ROBERTSON	SAX (A	DICK HANSON	TPT (A	DAN ELLIS	TROM (A

INGA RUMPF   R162A

INGA RUMPF	G V	(AB	(A) MY LIFE IS A BOOGIE	1977	RCA		PL28321
ALAN SPENNER	B	(A	(B) I KNOW WHO I AM	1980	RCA		PL13499
GERRY CONWAY	D	(A					
PAUL CARRACK	K	(A	NEIL HUBBARD	G	(A	ROBERT AWHAI	G	(A	VINCE WEBER	PNO (A

RUMPLESTILTSKIN   R162B

		(A) RUMPLESTILTSKIN	1969	BELL	US	6047

RUNAWAYS   R163

LITA FORD	G V	(ABCDEF	(A) THE RUNAWAYS	1976	MERCURY		US SRMI1090
SANDY WEST	D V	(ABCDEF	(B) QUEENS OF NOISE	1977	MERCURY	UK 9100 032	US SRMI1126
JOAN JETT	G V	(ABCDEF	(C) LIVE IN JAPAN	1977	MERCURY	UK 9100 046	
JACKIE FOX	B V	(ABF	(D) WAITIN' FOR THE NIGHT	1977	MERCURY	UK 9100 047	US SRMI3705
CHERIE CURRIE	K V	(DE	(E) AND NOW THE RUNAWAYS	1979	MERCURY	6304 505	
VICKI BLUE	G V	(DE	(E) AND NOW THE RUNAWAYS	1979	CHERRY RED		ARED 3
LAURIE McALLISTER	B	(E	(F) FLAMIN' SCHOOLGIRLS	1980	CHERRY RED		ARED 9
DUANE HITCHINGS	K	(E					

TODD RUNDGREN (& UTOPIA)   R164

TODD RUNDGREN	G V	(ALL	(A) RUNT	1970	BEARSVILLE	UK K45505 US AMPEX	10105
KEVIN ELLIMAN	PERC (		(B) BALLAD OF TODD RUNDGREN	1971	BEARSVILLE	UK K45506 US AMPEX	10116
MOOGY KLINGMAN	K	(C	(C) SOMETHING ANYTHING	1972	BEARSVILLE	UK K65501 US	2BX 2066
FROG LABAT	SYN	(	(D) A WIZARD A TRUE STAR	1973	BEARSVILLE	UK K45513 US	2133
RALPH SHUCKETT	B	(	(D) A WIZARD A TRUE STAR	1980	BEARSVILLE	RI	IR5P10
JOHN SIEGLER	CELLO B (CFJ		(E) TODD	1974	BEARSVILLE	UK K85501 US	6952
ROGER POWELL	K TPT(FJKOP		(F) TODD RUNDGRENS UTOPIA	1974	BEARSVILLE	UK K55501 US	6954
KASIM SULTON	B	(KOP	(G) INITIATION	1975	BEARSVILLE	UK K55504 US	6957
JOHN WILCOX	D	(FJKOP	(H) ANOTHER LIFE	1976	BEARSVILLE	UK K55508 US	6961
HUNT SALES	D	(C	(J) FAITHFUL	1976	BEARSVILLE	UK K55510 US	6981
TONY SALES	B	(C	(K) R A	1977	BEARSVILLE	UK K55514 US	6965
N D SMART	D	(	(L) OOPS WRONG PLANET	1977	BEARSVILLE	UK K55517 US	6970
JOHN SIOMOS	D	(C	(M) HERMIT OF MINK HOLLOW	1978	BEARSVILLE	UK K55521 US	6981
STU WOODS	B	(C	(M) HERMIT OF MINK HOLLOW	1980	BEARSVILLE	RI	IR5P11
RANDY BRECKER	HRNS (C		(N) BACK TO THE BARS	1978	BEARSVILLE	UK K65511 US	6986
MICHAEL BRECKER	HRNS (C		(O) ADVENTURES IN UTOPIA	1980	BEARSVILLE	UK ILP59602	
BARRY ROGERS	TROM (C		(P) DEFACE THE MUSIC	1980	BEARSVILLE	UK ILP59614	
RICK DERRINGER	G	(C	(Q) HEALING	1981	BEARSVILLE	UK ILP59657	
EDWARD OLMOS	C	(C					

AMOS GARRETT	G	(C	BEN KEITH	STEEL	(C	ROBBIE KAGALE	G	(C	BUGSY MAUGH	B	(C
RALPH WASH	G	(C	BILLY MUNDI	D	(C	GENE DINWIDDIE	SAX	(C	SERGE KAKEN CONGA	(C
JIM COLGROVE	B	(C	RICK VITO	G	(C	CHARLIE SCHONING	PNO	(C	JIM HORN	SAX(C
JOHN KELSO	SAX	(C	HOPE RUFF	V	(C	RICHARD COREY	V	(C	VICKI ROBINSON	V	(C
DENNIS COOLEY	V	(C	CECILIA NORFLEET	V	(C	BROOKS BAXES	V	(C	ANTHONY CARRABBA	V	(C
HENRY FANTON	V	(C						

RUNNER   R164A

STEVE GOULD	G V	(A	(A) RUNNER	1979	ACROBAT		ACRO 1
MICKIE FEAT	B V	(A					
DAVE DOWLE	D	(A	ALLAN MEWRILL	G K V(A	RAY COOPER	PERC (A	JON COLE	G (A
IAN LYNN	K	(A	WILLIAM C LYALL	SYN (A			

R165
```
RAY RUSSELL        G B K V (A        (A) RUNNING MAN                          1972 NEON                          NE 11
ALAN GREED         V K B(A
ALAN RUSHTON       D   (A      HARRY BECKETT    HRNS (A  GARY WINDO     SAX (A   ROY CAMERON      V (A
```
R166

RUNNING MAN
RUPHUS
```
SYLVI LILLEGARD    V   (CD       (A) LET YOUR LIGHT SHINE IN            19   BRAIN                         0060 031
JAN SIMONSEN       K   (CD       (B) INNER VOICE                        1977 BRAIN                         0060 060
KJELL LARSON       G   (CD       (C) FLYING COLOURS                     197  BRAIN                         0060 108
THOR BENEDIKSEN    D   (CD       (D) HOT RHYTHMS AND HIGH NOTES         1978 ELECTRIC                      TRIX  8
ASLE NILSEN        B   (CD
TROND VILLA        VLN (C
```
R167

RUSH
```
JOHN RUTSEY        D   (A        (A) RUSH                               197  MERCURY US SRMI1011 UK 9100 011
ALEX LIFESON       G   (ABCDEFH   (B) FLY BY NIGHT                      197  MERCURY US SRMI1023 UK 9100 013
GEDDY LEE          G K B V(ABCDEFH (C) 2112                             1976 MERCURY US SRMI1079 UK 9100 039
NEIL PEART         D   (BCDEFH    (D) CARESS OF STEEL                   1977 MERCURY US SRMI1046 UK 9100 018
                                 (E) ALL THE WORLD'S A STAGE           197  MERCURY US SRM27508    6672 015
                                 (F) FAREWELL TO KINGS                 1977 MERCURY US SRMI1184 UK 9100 042
                                 (G) ARCHIVES (TRIPLE)                 1978 MERCURY US SRM239200  6641 799
                                 (H) HEMISPHERES                       1978 MERCURY US SRM13743 UK 9100 059
                                 (I) CLOSER TO THE HEART (12" EP)      1978 MERCURY              UK RUSH12
                                 (J) PERMANENT WAVES                   1980 ANTHEM US 1021 MERCURY 9100 071
                                 (K) MOVING PICTURES                   1981 MERCURY             UK 6337 160
```
R168

OTIS RUSH
```
OTIS RUSH          G V  (ALL      (A) THIS ONE'S A GOOD UN             1968 BLUE HORIZON           UK 763222
WALTER HORTON      HCA  (AKL      (B) MOURNING IN THE MORNING          1969 COTILLION US 9006 UK ATCOK40495
HAROLD ASHBY       SAX  (AKL      (C) SCREAMING & CRYING               1974 BLACK & BLUE       FR     33516
LITTLE BRO MONTGOMERY PNO(AKL     (D) BLUES LIVE                       1975 TRIO             JAP    PA3086
JESSE GREEN        D    (F        (D) SO MANY ROADS (1 DIFF TRACK)     1978 DELMARK           US    DS 643
LOUIS MILES        G    (AKL      (E) RIGHT PLACE WRONG TIME           1976 BULLFROG          US       301
WILLIE DIXON       B    (AKL      (F) COLD DAY IN HELL                 1976 DELMARK                  DS 638
ODIE PAYNE         D    (AKL      (G) DOOR TO DOOR (1 SIDE)            1976 CHESS            US      1538
RONALD EADES       SAX  (B        (H) CHICAGO BLUES TODAY VOL 2        1966 VANGUARD            VSD 79217
JIMMY JOHNSON      G    (BD       (J) TROUBLES TROUBLES                1978 SONET            UK SNTF 756
AARON VARNELL      SAX  (B        (K) GROANING THE BLUES               1980 FLYRIGHT         UK   LP 560
BARRY BECKETT      K    (B        (L) OTHER TAKES 1956/58 (1 SIDE)     1980 FLYRIGHT         UK   LP 562
GENE MILLER        TOT  (B
DUANE ALLMAN       G    (B   MARK NAFTALIN    K   (B   JOE ARNOLD     SAX (B   ROGER HAWKINS   D  (B
JERRY JEMMOTT      B    (B   RED HOLLOWAY     SAX (KL  LAYFAYETTE LEAKE K   (KL  WAYNE BENNETT   G  (KL
AL DUNCAN          D    (KL  LUCIUS WASHINGTON SAX (KL JODY WILLIAMS  G   (KL  REGGIE BOYD     G  (KL
FRED BELOW         D    (KL  JACKIE BRENSTON  SAX (KL  IKE TURNER     G   (KL  JIMMY DAWKINS   G  (C
JEROME VAN JONES   K    (C   SUNNYLAND SLIM   PNO (C   WILLIE MABON   PNO (C   JAMES GREEN     B  (C
BOB PLUNKETT       D    (C   SYLVESTER BOINES B   (D   TYRONE CENTURY D   (D   DOUG KILMER B   (E
JOHN KAHN          B    (E   BOB JONES        D   (E   FRED BURTON    G   (E   IRA KAMIN       ORG(E
JOHN WILMETH       TPT  (E   RON STALLINGS    SAX (E   HART McNEE     SAX (E   AB LOCKE        SAX(F
CHUCK SMITH        SAX  (F   BIG MOOSE WALKER K   (F   MIGHTY JOE YOUNG G (F   BOB STROGER     B  (F
BOB LEVIS          G    (F
```
R169

TOM RUSH
```
TOM RUSH           V    (ALL     MIND RAMBLIN'                        1963 PRESTIGE          US         14003
HERBIE LOVELLE     D    (*       BLUES SONGS & BALLADS                1965 PRESTIGE          US      7374
TREVOR VEITCH      G    (*       BLUES & FOLK                         1965 TRANSATLANTIC     UK    XTRA5024
WARREN BERNHARDT   K    (*       TOM RUSH                             1965 ELEKTRA                EKS 7288
DUKE BARDWELL      B    (*       TAKE A LITTLE WALK WITH ME           1966 ELEKTRA                EKS 7308
DAVID BROMBERG     G    (*       I GOT A MIND TO RAMBLE               1968 TRANSATLANTIC     UK    XTRA5053
PAUL GRIFFIN       K    (*       TOM RUSH                             19   FANTASY                  24709
RED RHODES         STEEL (*      THE CIRCLE GAME                      1968 ELEKTRA EKS74016 UK RI  K42018
ED FREEMAN         G    (*       CLASSIC RUSH                         196  ELEKTRA EKS74062 UK RI  K42073
RON CARTER         B    (+       (*) TOM RUSH                         1970 CBS    US 9972 UK     63940
                                 WRONG END OF A RAINBOW               1970 CBS    US 30402 UK     64268
                                 MERRIMACK COUNTY                     1972 CBS    US 31306 UK     64887
                                 LADIES LOVE OUTLAWS                  1976 CBS    US 33054 UK     80282
                                 BEST OF                              19   CBS    US 33907
```
R170

JIMMY RUSHING
```
JIMMY RUSHING      (ALL          BLUES I LOVE TO SING                 1977 ACE OF HEARTS     UK    AH 119
RAY CHARLES        (*            LISTEN TO THE BLUES                  176  VANGUARD             SRV73007
IVORY JOE HUNTER   (*            GOIN' TO CHICAGO                     19   VANGUARD             VRS 8518
                                 THE YOU & ME THAT USED TO BE         19   RCA               UK  SF 8234
                                 EVERY DAY I HAVE THE BLUES           1973 BLUESWAY             BLS 6005
                                 SENT FOR YESTERDAY                   1973 BLUESWAY             BLS 6067
                                 IF THIS AIN'T THE BLUES              1974 VANGUARD          UK  VRS 8513
                                 ESSENTIAL JIMMY RUSHING              1978 VANGUARD             VJD  556
                                 (*) THREE OF A KIND                  19   DESIGN            US  DLP 909
```
R171

RICK RUSKIN
```
RICK RUSKIN    G V   (ABC        (A) RICHARD RUSKIN                   1974 TAKOMA            US      1039
DAVID JACKSON      PNO (B        (B) MICROPHONE FEVER                 1975 TAKOMA            US      1044
MIKE BOTTS         D   (B        (C) SIX STRING CONSPIRACY            1976 TAKOMA            US      1057
COLIN CAMERON      B   (B
DICK ROSMINI       K V B(B  MARC CHOVER    B  (B  CASSANDRA THOMAS  V (B  PAULA THOMAS    V (B
CLAUDIA CRUTZINGER V   (B
```
R172

JOHNNY RUSSELL
```
JOHNNY RUSSELL     (ALL          (A) MR & MRS UNTRUE                  1972 RCA               US   LSP4588
                                 (B) CATFISH JOHN                     1973 RCA               US   LSP4851
                                 (C) RED NECKS WHITE SOCKS            1974 RCA               UK   AFLIO345
                                 (D) SHE'S IN LOVE WITH A RODEO MAN   1974 RCA                    AFLIO542
                                 (E) HERE COMES JOHNNY RUSSELL        1975 RCA                    APLI1211
```

LEON RUSSELL

Personnel		Album	Year	Label / Cat.
LEON RUSSELL	V K G B PERC(ALL	(A) LOOKING INSIDE (ASYLUM CHOIR)	1968	SMASH 67107 UK MERCURY 20141
CHRIS STAINTON	K (B	(B) LEON RUSSELL	1970	A&M AMLS 982 RI ISLAND ISA 5005
GEORGE HARRISON	G (B	(B) LEON RUSSELL	1970	SHELTER US 8903 RI 52008
RINGO STARR	D (B	(C) ASYLUM CHOIR II	1971	SHELTER US 8910 RI 52010
CHARLIE WATTS	D (B	(C) ASYLUM CHOIR II	1971	SHELTER UK AMLS 68089
BILL WYMAN	B (B	(D) AND THE SHELTER PEOPLE	1971	SHELTER US 8903 RI 52008
KLAUS VOORMANN	B (B	(D) AND THE SHELTER PEOPLE	1971	A&M AMLS65003 RI ISLAND ISA 5006
B J WILSON	D (B	(E) CARNEY	1972	SHELTER US 8911 RI 52011
ALAN SPENNER	B (B	(E) CARNEY	1972	A&M AMLH68911 RI ISLAND ISA 5007
JIM GORDON	D (B	(F) HANK WILSON'S BACK	1973	A&M AMLS68923 US SHELTER 8923
BUDDY HARMAN	D (B	(G) LEON LIVE	1973	SHELTER US 8917
GREG DEMPSEY	(B	(H) STOP ALL THAT JAZZ	1974	A&M AMLS68262 RI ISLAND ISA 5009
STEVE WINWOOD	K (B	(H) STOP ALL THAT JAZZ	1974	SHELTER US 2108
JIM HORN	SAX (BIJ	(I) WILL O THE WISP	1975	A&M AMLS68309 RI ISLAND ISA 5008
DELANEY BRAMLETT	G (B	(I) WILL O THE WISP	1975	SHELTER US 2138 RI 52200
BONNIE BRAMLETT	V (B	(J) LIVE IN JAPAN	1975	SHELTER RS 5117
BOBBY WHIPLASH	(B	(K) WEDDING ALBUM	1976	PARADISE US 2943 UK K56244
CLYDIE KING	(B	(L) BEST OF LEON RUSSELL	1976	SHELTER US 52004 ISLAND ISA 5013
BOB MOORE	B (F	(M) MAKE LOVE TO THE MUSIC	1977	PARADISE US
MERRY CLAYTON	V (B	(N) AMERICANA	1978	PARADISE UK K56534
JOE COCKER	V (B	(O) WILLIE & LEON	1979	CBS UK 88461
J J CALE	G (FI	(P) LIVE & LOVE	1979	PARADISE US 3341
BILLY SANFORD	G (F	(Q) & NEW GRASS REVIVAL LIVE	1981	WB UK K56891
DIANNE DAVIDSON	G (F			

ERIC CLAPTON G (B	CHUCK BLACKWELL D (EH	CARL RADLE B EFHI	JIM KELTNER B (EHI
DON PRESTON G V (EHI	HAROLD BRADLEY B (EH	JOEY COOPER G V (EH	JOHN GALLIE K (EHO
JOE ZINKAN B (F	RAY EDENTON G (F	PETE DRAKE STEEL(FH	DAVID BRIGGS K (F
PETE WADE G (F	CHARLIE McCOY HCA (F	JOHNNY GIMBLE FDL (F	BOBBY THOMPSON BAN(F
CURLY CHALKER STEEL(F	JIM BUCHANAN FDL (F	BUTCH ROBINS G (F	TUT TAYLOR G (F
JERRY CARRIGAN D (F	PIG ROBBINS K (F	WELDON MYRICK STEEL(F	BONNIE RAITT G (O
BILLY BYRD G (F	CHIP YOUNG G (F	GRADY MARTIN G (F	HAL RUGG SYEEL (F
KARL HIMMEL D (H	HENRY BEST B (H	WILLIAM KENNER MAND (H	LINDA HARGROVE G (H
EDWIN SCRUGGS G (H	JOHN CALE G (H	WILLIE NELSON G (HO	ODELL STOKES G (H
JAMIE OLDAKER D (H	ROBERT WILSON B (HK	CHARLES WILSON K V (H	RONNIE WILSON HRNS(H
TOMMY LOKEY HRNS (H	CHRIS CLAYTON HRNS (H	MARCY LEVY V (H	ANN BELL V (H
PAM THOMPSON V (H	LENA STEPHENS V (H	TEDDY JACK EDDY D (IK	MARY RUSSELL K V(IK
MOON CALHOUN D (I	MASAKO HIRAYAMA BIWA (I	AL JACKSON D (I	STEVE CROPPER G (I
BOBBY MANUEL G (I	DONALD DUCK DUNN B (I	TOMMY ALLSUP G (I	PATRICK HENDERSON K PERC(I
AMBROSE CAMPBELL PERC D(IKO	STEVE DOUGLAS FLT (I	DENNIS MANSFIELD D (K	RICHARD TORRANCE G (K
ROGER LINN G (K	DAVID MINER B (I	TRUMAN THOMAS K (K	JULIUS WECHTER K (K
MARTY GREBB SAX (KNO	GREGG THOMAS D (K	WILLIE WEEKS B (K	NIGEL OLSSON D (K
GARY ROWLES G (K	BOBBY WOMACK G (N	MARC BENNO (AC	BRENT NELSON D (N
JOE CHEMAY B (N	JOHN WOODHEAD G (N	MIKE MEROS K (N	LEE LOUGHNANE TPT(N
JAMES PANKOW TROM (N	WALTER PARAZEIDER SAX (N	WORNELL JONES V (N	PAUL ENGLISH D (O
JIM BOATMAN V (O	REX LUDWICK D (O	JODY PAYNE G V (O	CHRIS ETHRIDGE B (O
BEE SPEARS B (O	MICKEY RAPHAEL HCA (O	MARIA MULDAUR V (O	

RAY RUSSELL

Personnel		Album	Year	Label / Cat.
RAY RUSSELL	G (ALL	(A) TURN CIRCLE	1968	CBS 52586
TONY ROBERTS	SAX (CF	(B) DRAGON HILL	1969	CBS 52663
DARYL RUNSWICK	B (C	(C) RITES & RITUALS	1971	CBS 64271
ALAN RUSHTON	D (C	(D) JUNE 11TH 1971	1971	RCA UK SF8214
HARRY BECKETT	TPT (C	(E) SECRET ASYLUM	1973	BLACK LION BLP12100 2460 207
NICK EVANS	TROM (C	(F) READY OR NOT	1977	DJM DJH20506
SIMON PHILLIPS	D (F			

PETER VAN HOOKE D (F	MO FOSTER B (F	TONY HYMAS K (F	CHRIS PARREN K (F
JOHN PUNTER PERC (F	KAPLAN KAYE PERC (F	MARTIN DROVER TPT (F	MALCOLM GRIFFITHS TROM(F
AL GREED V (F	ANNIE KAVANAGH V (F	MOON WILLIAMS V (F	ANDY MACKAY SAX (F
TIM WHITEHEAD SAX (F	DENNY McCAFFREY V (F	HELEN WRIGHT CELLO(F	LIZ EDWARDS VLN (F
LEVINE ANDRADE VLA (F	GAVIN WRIGHT VLN (F	MIKE RUTHERFORD	

RUSSIA

	Album	Year	Label / Cat.
	(A) RUSSIA	1980	WB US BSK 3414

MIKE RUTHERFORD

Personnel		Album	Year	Label / Cat.
MIKE RUTHERFORD	G B (A	(A) SMALLCREEPS DAY	1980	CHARISMA UK CAS 1149
ANTHONY PHILLIPS	K (A			
NOEL McCALLA	V (A	SIMON PHILLIPS D (A MORRIS PERT PERC (A		

RUTLES

Personnel	Album	Year	Label / Cat.
ERIC IDLE (A	(A) THE RUTLES	1978	WB UK K56459 US 3151
NEIL INNES (A			
RICKI FATAAR (A	JOHN HALSEY (A		

THE RUTS

Personnel		Album	Year	Label / Cat.
MALCOLM OWEN	V (	(A) THE CRACK	1979	VIRGIN UK V2132
PAUL FOX	G (	(B) GRIN & BEAR IT	1980	VIRGIN UK V2188
DAVE RUFFY	D (			
VINCE SEOS	B (			

PAUL RYAN

Personnel		Album	Year	Label / Cat.
PAUL RYAN	K V (A	(A) SCORPIO RISING	1976	CHARISMA UK CAS 1121
RAY ROBERTS	K (A			
DAVE CAKEBREAD	B (A	KEVIN STEPHENSON G (A TONY BEARD D (A		

MAGGIE RYDER

Personnel		Album	Year	Label / Cat.
MAGGIE RYDER	V (A	(A) MAGGIE RYDER	1978	POLYDOR UK 2383 496

MITCH RYDER

Name	Inst	Code	Album	Year	Label		Country	Number
MITCH RYDER	V	(ALL	(A) TAKE A RIDE	1966	NEW VOICE		US	2000
JIM McCARTY	G	(ABCEFI	(A) TAKE A RIDE	1966	STATESIDE		UK	10178
JOE CUBERT	G	(ABCEFI	(B) BREAKOUT	1967	NEWVOICE		US	2002
TONY SUEHY	B	(J	(B) BREAKOUT	1967	STATESIDE		UK	10189
EARL ELIOT		(AEFI	(C) SOCK IT TO ME	1967	NEW VOICE		US	2003
JOHN'BEE' BADANJEK	D	(ABCEFHI	(D) WHAT NOW MY LOVE	1967	DYNAVOICE		US	31901
DAVE OPATIK	G	(J	(D) WHAT NOW MY LOVE	1967	STATESIDE		UK	10229
JIM McCALLISTER	B	(CDEFI	(E) MITCH RYDER SINGS THE HITS	1968	NEW VOICE		US	2005
BOOKER T JONES	K	(G	(F) ALL MITCH RYDERS HITS	196	CREWE		US	1335
DUCK DUNN	B	(G	(G) THE DETROIT MEMPHIS EXPERIENCE	1969	DOT		US	25963
AL JACKSON	D	(G	(H) DETROIT	1971	PARAMOUNT	SPFL277	+	6010
STEVE CROPPER	G	(G	(I) GREATEST HITS	1972	BELLAPHON			15163
STEVE HUNTER	G	(H	(J) HOW GREAT MY VACATION	1979	LINE		GERM	5002
W R COOKE	B	(H	(K) ROCK'N'ROLL LIVE(EP)	1979	LINE		GERM	3004
BRETT TUGGLE	G	(H	(L) NAKED BUT NOT DEAD	1980	LINE		GERM	5046
DIRTY ED	PERC	(H	(M) WE'RE GONNA WIN (EP)	1980	LINE		GERM	3013
HARRY PHILLIPS	K	(H	(N) GOT TO CHANGE FOR A MILLION	1981	LINE		GERM	5100
BOOT HILL	K HCA	(H						

JOHN SAUTER B (H MARK MANKO G (H RICHARD SCHEIN G (JKLMN JOE GUTE G (KLMN
WILSON OWENS D (JKLMN MARK GOUGEON B (JKLMN BILLY CSERNITS K (JKLMN WAYNE GABRIEL G(J
JOHN VASS G (J BILLY LA VERE V (

RYE WHISKEY ROAD BAND

Name	Inst	Code	Album	Year	Label	Number
MIKE WHITE	G V	(A	(A) RUNNING KIND 1979		FOLK HERITAGE	FHR 1017
PETE HANDLEY	V B	(A				

KEN BYNG V G STEEL (A MICK WILLIAMS G (A MAI JONES V (A BERYL WATKINS V (A
KIP GLADWELL D (A

TERJE RYPDAL

Name	Inst	Code	Album	Year	Label		Number
TERJE RYPDAL	G	(ALL	(A) TERJE RYPDAL	1971	ECM		ECM 1016
BOBO STENSON	K	(AX	(B) WHAT COMES AFTER	1974	ECM		ECM 1031
TOM HALVERSEN	K	(A	(C) WHENEVER I SEEM TO BE FAR AWAY	1974	ECM		ECM 1045
ARILD ANDERSEN	B	(A	(D) ODYSSEY (DBL)	1975	ECM		ECM1067/8
BJØRNAR ANDERSEN	B	(A	(E) AFTER THE RAIN	1976	ECM		ECM 1083
JON CHRISTENSEN	B	(ABCFH	(F) WAVES	1978	ECM		ECM 1110
BARRE PHILLIPS	B	(B	(G) RYDAL,VITOUS,DeJOHNETTE	1979	ECM		ECM 1125
ERIK NIORD LARSEN	HRNS	(B	(H) DESCENDRE	1980	ECM		ECM 1144
INGER LISE RYPDAL	V	(AE	(X) SART	1971	ECM		ECM1915
JACK DeJOHNETTE	D	( )	( ) BLEAK HOUSE	19	KARUSSEL	GER	2915 053
MIROSLAV VITOUS	B PNO	(	( ) DREAM	19	KARUSSEL	GER	2915 068
PALLE MIKKELBORG	HRNS	(FH					

ECKEHARD FINTL WIND (A JAN GARBAREK WIND (AX SVEINUNG HOVENSJØ B (BCDF PETE KNUTSEN K (C
ODD ULLEBERG HRN (C SUDFUNK SYMPHONY ORCH (C TORBJØRN SUNDE TROM (D BRYNJOLF BLIX K (D
SVEIN CHRISTIANSEN D (D

S F F

Name	Inst	Code	Album	Year	Label	Number
EDWARD SCHICKE	D	(ABC	(A) SYMPHONIC PICTURES	1976	BRAIN	0060 010
GERHARD FUHRS	K SYN	(ABC	(B) SUNBURST	1977	BRAIN	0060 068
HEINZ FROHLING	G	(ABC	(C) TICKET TO EVERYWHERE	1979	BRAIN	0060 173
EDVARD BRUMUND RUTHER	B	(ABC				

S R C

Name	Inst	Code	Album	Year	Label	Country	Number
SCOTT RICHARDSON	V	(ABC	(A) SRC	1968	CAPITOL	US	2991
GLENN QUACKENBUSH	K V	(ABC	(B) MILESTONES	1969	CAPITOL	US	134
STEVE LYMAN	G V	(AB	(C) TRAVELLER'S TALE	1970	CAPITOL	US	273
E G CLAWSON	D V	(BC					

ROBIN DALE B V (A AL WILMOT B V (C RAY GOODMAN G (C GARY QUACKENBUSH G (A

S V T

Name	Inst	Code
JACK CASADY	B	(A
BILL GIBSON	D	(A
NICK BUCK	K	(A

BRIAN MARNELL G V (A

SABOTAGE

Album	Year	Label	Number
(A) SUBTERFUGE(EP)	19	OPTIMISTIC	OPT004

SABREJETS

Album	Year	Label	Number
(A) RADIOLAND (EP)	1979	BLUEPORT	BLU5

SAD CAFE

Name	Inst	Code	Album	Year	Label		Number
PAUL YOUNG	V	(BCDEF	(A) SAD CAFE (MATERIAL USED ON (B)	1976	CHRYSALIS (NOT RELEASED)		1114
ASHLEY MULFORD	G	(BCDEF	(B) FANX TARA	1977	RCA		PL 25101
TONY CRESSWELL	D	(BCD	(C) HUNGRY EYES	1977	RCA		PB 5062
JOHN STIMPSON	B V	(BCDEF	(D) MISPLACED IDEALS	1978	RCA		PL 25133
VIC EMERSON	G V	(BCDEF	(E) FACADES	1979	RCA		PL 25249
LENNY SACHS	SAX	(D	(F) SAD CAFE	1980	RCA	SAD LP4 +	PL 25319
JOHN PUNTER	PERC	(D	(G) LIVE	1981	RCA UK		SAD LP5
DOREEN CHANTER	V	(D					
IRENE CHANTER	V	(D					

DAVE IRVING D (EF IAN WILSON G V (BDEF LENNI ZAKSEN SAX(F

SADISTIC MIKA BAND

Name	Inst	Code	Album	Year	Label	Country	Number
MIKA KATOH	V	(	(A) SADISTIC MIKA BAND	1974	HARVEST	UK	SHSP 4029
KAZUHIKO KATOH	G V	(	(B) BLACK SHIP	1975	HARVEST	UK	SHSP 4043
REI OHARA	B V	(	(C) HOT MENU	1976	HARVEST	UK	SHSP 4049
YUKIHORO TAKAHASHI	D	(					
MAYAYOSHI TAKANAKA	G	(					

HIROSHI IMAI K SAX(

SAGA

Name	Inst	Code	Album	Year	Label	Number
MICHAEL SADLER	K V	(AB	(A) IMAGES AT TWILIGHT	1980	POLYDOR	2391 437
STEVE NEGUS	D	(AB	(B) SILENT KNIGHT	1980	POLYDOR	2374 166
IAN CRICHTON	G	(AB				
JIM CRICHTON	SYB B	(AB				

JIM GILMOUR K V (B GREG CHADD K V (A

SAGITTARIUS

Name	Code	Album	Year	Label	Country	Number
CURT BOETCHER	(AB	(A) PRESENT TENSE	1968	CBS	US	9644
MIKE FENNELLY	(A	(B) THE BLUE MARBLE	1969	TOGETHER	US	1002
LEE MALLORY	(A					
DOUG RHODES	(A					
KEITH OLSEN	(AB					
GARY USHER	(AB					

DOUG RHODES (A SANDY SALISBURY (A JOE STEC (A RON EDGAR (A
KEITH OLSEN (AB GLEN CAMPBELL (A BRUCE JOHNSTON (A STEVE CLARK (A

SAHARA

```
HENNES HERING      K   (A        (A) SAHARA                          1973 DAWN         UK  DNLS 3068
MICHAEL HOFMANN WIND SYN(A
ALEX PITTWOHN  HCA SAX V(A    HARRY ROSENKIND D PERC(A STEFAN WISSNET    B V (A   NICHOLAS WOODLAND  G(A
```

DOUG SAHM & THE SIR DOUGLAS QUINTET

```
DOUG SAHM         G V FDL(ALL   (A) BEST OF SIR DOUGLAS QUINTET    1965 TRIBE US 37001 UK LONDONHAU8311
MARTIN FIERRO     SAX  (G       (A) BEST OF SIR DOUGLAS QUINTET    1976 CRAZY CAJUN       RI       1003
WAYNE TALBERT     PNO  (G       (B) HONKY BLUES(SIR DOUGLAS)       1968 SMASH         US         67108
TERRY HENRY       HRNS (        (C) MENDOCINO                      1969 SMASH         US         67115
WHITNEY FREEMAN   B    (        (C) MENDOCINO                      1975 OVAL                      5001
FRANK MORIN     V HRNS (CKM      (D) 1+1+1=4                       1970 PHILIPS                600 344
MEL MARTIN        SAX  (G       (E) TOGETHER AFTER FIVE            1970 SMASH         US         67130
BILL ATWOOD       SAX  (        (F) RETURN OF DOUG SALDANA         1971 PHILIPS                600 353
JOHN PEREZ        D    (CM      (G) DOUG SAHM & THE BAND           1973 ATLANTIC US 7254   UK K40466
AUGIE MEYER       K    (CGKM     (H) TEXAS TORNADO                 1974 ATLANTIC US 7287
KEN KOSEK         FDL  (G        (I) ROUGH EDGES                   1973 MERCURY  US SRMi 655
HARVEY KAGAN      B    (CKM      (J) GROOVERS PARADISE             1974 WB                      K56067
JIM STALLINGS     B    (M        (K) TEXAS ROCK FOR COUNTRY ROLLERS 1976 DOT     US 2057 ABC UK   5186
GEORGE RAINS      D    (GK      (L) LIVE LOVE                      1977 TEXAS   US 1007
JACK BARBER     B V    (GO      (N) DOUG SAHM                      1979 HARLEM  US 1005
BOB DYLAN  V G K HCA   (G        (O) HELL OF A SPELL               1980 TAKOMA   US
DR JOHN           K    (G        (O) HELL OF A SPELL               1980 CHRYSALIS             UK CHR1249
DAVID BROMBERG    G    (G
DAVID NEWMAN      SAX  (G   WAYNE JACKSON    TPT (G  WILLIE BRIDGES   SAX (G   JACK WALRATH    TPT (G
CHARLIE OWENS     STEEL(G   ANDY STATMAN     MAND (G  ARIF MARDIN     PNO (G   FLACO JIMINEZ   ACC (G
ATWOOD ALLEN    G V    (G   DOUG CLIFFORD    D   (J  STU COOK        D   (J   LINK DAVIS    K FDL V(J
GARY POTTERTON    STEEL(J   RON STALLINGS    SAX (J  JOE RAE     MARIMBA (J   ROCKY MORALES   SAX (O
LEON BAEBY            (J    JOHN OXENDINE    D   (O  KELLY DUNN      K   (O   LOUIE BUSTOS    SAX (O
CHARLES McBURNEY  TPT (O
```

SAILOR

```
GRANT SERPELL     D V (ABCD      (A) SAILOR                        1974 EPIC US 33248       UK  80337
GEORG KAJANUS   G V K(ABCD       (B) TROUBLE                       1975 EPIC US 34039       UK  69192
HENRY MARSH       K V (ABCF      (C) THIRD STOP                    1976 EPIC                 UK  81637
PHIL PICKETT    G K V(ABCF       (D) CHECK POINT                   1977 EPIC                 UK  82256
VIRGINIA TAYLOR      (F          (E) GREATEST HITS                 1978 EPIC                 UK  82754
GAVIN TAYLOR         (F          (F) DRESSED TO DROWN              1981 CARIBOU              UK  84534
```

ENDLE ST CLOUD

```
ENDLE ST CLOUD       (A          (A) THANK YOU ALL VERY MUCH       19   INT ARTISTS           IALP 12
D F POTTER           (A
PETE BLACK           (A    JAMES HARRELL        (A
```

JOHN ST FIELD

```
JOHN ST FIELD(JACKIE LEVEN) V G K(A  (A) CONTROL                  19   MCA
JOE KUCCER        WIND (A
JOHN HAYNES       D    (A   PHIL RYAN            (A
```

BRIDGET ST JOHN

```
BRIDGET ST JOHN   G V K(ALL      (A) ASK ME NO QUESTIONS          1969 DANDELION US 101     UK  62750
RON GEESIN        G K  (B        (B) SONGS FOR A GENTLE MAN       1971 DANDELION          UK  DAN8007
RICK SANDERS      G    (BC       (B) SONGS FOR A GENTLE MAN       1971 ELEKTRA   US              74104
JOHN MARTYN       G    (C        (C) THANK YOU FOR                1972 DANDELION          UK  2310 193
RICK KEMP         B    (C        (D) JUMBLE QUEEN                 1974 CHRYSALIS          UK  CHR 1062
PIP PYLE         D    (C
GORDON HUNTLEY    STEEL(C   IAN WHITEMAN    K    (C   ANDY ROBERTS    G   (C  DAVE MATTACKS  D (C
TIM RENWICK       G    (C   WILLIE WILSON   D    (C   BRUCE THOMAS    B   (C
```

ROY ST JOHN

```
ROY ST JOHN          (A          (A) ROY ST JOHN(EP)             1977 VIRGIN             UK  VEP 1002
```

ST PARADISE

```
ROB GRANGE        B V (A          (A) ST PARADISE                1979 WB     US BSK 3281   UK K56689
DENNY CARMASSI    D V (A
DEREK ST HOLMES   G V (A   JOHN CORY        K V (A   MARTY CONN     K    (A
```

BUFFY SAINTE MARIE

```
BUFFY ST MARIE    V G (ALL       (A) IT'S MY WAY                 1964 VANGUARD              VSD79142
CHARLIE McCOY     HCA  (J         (A) IT'S MY WAY                 196  FONTANA        UK    TFL 6040
BILLY SANFORD          (J         (B) MANY A MILE                1965 VANGUARD              VSD79171
DAVID BRIGGS      K    (J         (B) MANY A MILE                196  FONTANA        UK    TFL 6047
NORBERT PUTNAM    B    (J         (C) LITTLE WHEEL SPIN          1966 VANGUARD              VSD79211
KENNY BUTTREY     D    (J         (C) LITTLE WHEEL SPIN          196  FONTANA        UK    TFL 6071
SID SHARP         STRINGS(J       (D) FIRE ,FLEET & CANDLE LIGHT 1967 VANGUARD              VSD79250
MEMPHIS HORNS          (J         (E) I'M GONNA BE A COUNTRY GIRL AGAIN 1968 VANGUARD       VSD79280
JACK NITZSCHE     PNO  (G         (F) ILLUMINATIONS              1970 VANGUARD              VSD79300
MERRY CLAYTON     V    (G         (G) SHE USED TO WANNA BE A BALLERINA 1971 VANGUARD        VSD79311
RY COODER         G    (G         (H) MOON SHOT                  1972 VANGUARD              VSD79330
RUSS TITELMAN          (G         (J) QUIET PLACES               1973 VANGUARD              VSD79330
GAYLE LEVANT      HARP (G         (K) BEST OF          (DBL)     1973 VANGUARD              VSD  3/4
JESSE ED DAVIS    G    (G         (L) NATURAL NORTH AMERICAN CHILD 1974 VANGUARD            VSD79340
BOBBY WEST             (G         (M) BEST OF VOL 2   (DBL)      1974 VANGUARD              VSD33/44
DANNY WHITTEN          (G         (N) BUFFY                      1974 MCA         US 405    MCG 3517
RALPH MOLINA           (G         (O) CHANGING WOMAN             1975 MCA         US 451 UK MCF 2594
BILLY TALBOT           (G         (P) GOLDEN HOUR                1976 PYE                UK GH 825
NEIL YOUNG             (G         (Q) SWEET AMERICA              1976 ABC         US 929 UK ABCL5168
CARLOS PARDEIRO        (G
ARIEL GONZALES         (G
BOB BOZINA        G    (F
```

SAINTS

```
CHRIS BAILEY      V    (A         (A) I'M STRANDED               1977 HARVEST         UK  SHSP 4065
ED KUEPPER        G    (A         (A) I'M STRANDED               1977 SIRE            US        6039
IVOR HAY          D    (A         (B) ETERNALLY YOURS            1978 HARVEST         UK  SHSP 4078
KIM BRADSHAW      B    (A         (C) PREHISTORIC SOUNDS         1978 HARVEST         UK  SHSP 4094
ALASTAIR WARD     B    (
```

S12 SALLYANGIE

MIKE OLDFIELD	G V	(A	(A) CHILDREN OF THE SUN	1968 TRANSATLANTIC	UK	TRA176
SALLY OLDFIELD	V	(A				
TERRY COX	D	(A	REY WARLEIGH FLT (A			

S12A SALUKI

KJELL RONNINGEN	K	(A	(A) SALUKI	1976 COMPENDIUM	FIN FIDARO 6
PETER BERG NILSEN	V SAX(A				
SVERRE BEYER	B	(A	BJORN JENSEN D PERC (A	FREDDY DAHL	G V (A

S13 SAM & DAVE

SAM DAVID MOORE	V	(ALL	(A) SAM & DAVE	1966 ROULETTE	US	25323
DAVE PRATER	V	(ALL	(B) HOLD ON I'M COMIN'	1966 STAX	US	708
			(C) DOUBLE DYNAMITE	1966 STAX US 712 ATLANTIC UK588181
			(D) SOUL MEN	1967 STAX US 725 ATLANTIC UK580185
			(E) I THANK YOU	1968 ATLANTIC US 8205 UK588154
			(F) BEST OF	1969 ATLANTIC US 8218 UK588155
			(F) BEST OF	1972 ATLANTIC RI UK K40027
			(G) STAR COLLECTION	1974 WB GERM 20073
			(H) BACK ATCHA	1975 UA US LA 524

S14 SAM APPLE PIE

SAM SAMSON	(	(A) SAM APPLE PIE	1969 DECCA	UK	SKLR5005
SNAKE JACKSON	(	(B) EAST 17	1973 DJM	UK	DJLPS429
MARTIN BELL	D (			
MARK DeMAJO	B (	DAVE CHARLES D (ANDY JOHNSON	G (BOB RENNIE	B (
TINKERBELL SMITH	G (			

S14A SAM THE SHAM & THE PHARAOHS

DOMINGO 'SAM' SAMUDIO	V K(ALL	(A) WOOLY BULLY	1965	MGM	US	4297
DAVID MARTIN	B	(ABCDE	(B) THEIR SECOND ALBUM	1965	MGM	US	4314
RAY STINNET	G	(ABCDE	(C) ON TOUR	1966	MGM	US	4347
JERRY PATTERSON	D	(ABCDE	(D) 'LIL RED RIDING HOOD	1966	MGM	US	4407
BUTCH GIBSON	SAX	(ABCDE	(E) BEST OF	1967	MGM	US	4422
			(F) NEFERTITI(REVUE)	1967	MGM	US	4479
			(G) TEN OF PENTACLES	196	MGM	US	4526
			(H) SAM,HARD & HEAVY	1970	ATLANTIC	US	SD 8271

S14B SAMLA MAMMAS MANNA(SWED)

HANS BRUNIUSSON	D	(ALL	(A) SAMLA MAMMAS MANNA	1971 SILENCE	SRS 4604
LARS HOLLMER	K	(ALL	(B) MALTID	1973 SILENCE	SRS 4621
LARS KRANTZ	B	(ALL	(C) KLOSSA KNAPITATET	1974 SILENCE	SRS 4627
BEBBEN OBERG	CONGA(A1	(D) SNORUNGARNAS SYMFONI	1976 MUSIKNATET WAXHOLM	MNW 70P
COSTE APETREA	G	(BC3D	(E) FOR ALDRE NYBEGYNNARE	1978 SILENCE	SRS 4640
KALLE ERIKSSON	TPT	(D	(1) 1970 (2) 1972		
ULF ARTAN WALLANDER	SAX (D	(3) 1972 (4) 1976		
EINO HAAPALA	G	(E5	(5) 1977		
GREGORY FITZPATRICK	(D			

S14C JOE SAMPLE

JOE SAMPLE	K	(ALL	(A) RAINBOW SEEKER	1978 ABC US AA1050	UK ABCL5245
STIX HOOPER	D	(AC	(B) FANCY DANCE	1979 SONET	UK SNTF 788
ROBERT POPWELL	B	(A	(C) CARMEL	1979 ABC US AA1126	UK ABCL 5366
PAULINHO DA COSTA	PERC (AD	(D) VOICES IN THE RAIN	1981 MCA	UK MCG 4016
GARNETT BROWN	TROM (A			
ERNIE WATTS	WIND (A	FRED JACKSON SAX (A WILLIAM GREEN	WIND (A ROBERT O BRYANT	TPT(A
JAY DAVERSA	TPT (A	STEVE MADAIO TPT (A RAY PARKER	G (A RAY BROWN	B (D
DEAN PARKS	G (AD	BARRY FINNERTY G (A BILLY ROGERS	B (A DAVID T WALKER	G (A
FLORA PURIM	V (D	JOSIE JAMES V (D PAULINE WILSON	V (D ABRAHAM LABORIEL	B (D
NIKA REJTO	FLT (D	JERRY HEY HRNS (D L SUBRAMANIAM	VLN (D JOHN COLLINS	(D

S14D SAMSON

PAUL SAMSON	G V	(AB	(A) SURVIVORS	1979 LASER	LAP 1
CHRIS AYLMER	B	(AB	(B) HEAD ON	1980 GEM	UK	GEMLP108
BRUCE BRUCE	V	(AB	(C) SAMSON	1981 GEM	UK	GEMLP113
THUNDERSTICKS	D	(AB			

S15 FUZZY SAMUELS

CALVIN'FUZZY' SAMUELS	G B V(A	(A) FUZZY SAMUELS	1974 VIRGIN	UK	CA2002

S16 SAMURAI

DAVE LAWSON	K V	(A	(A) SAMURAI	1971 GREENWICH	UK GSLP 1003
TONY EDWARDS	G V	(A			
JOHN EATON	B	(A	LENNIE WRIGHT D PERC (A KENNY BEVERIDGE	D (A TONY ROBERTS	WIND(A
DON FAY	SAX	(A			

S17 DAVID SANBORN

DAVID SANBORN	SAX K (ALL	(A) TAKING OFF	1975 WB	US 2873	UK K56148
HERB BUSHLER	B	(B	(B) SANBORN	1976 WB	US 2957
HIRAM BULLOCK	G V	(BCE	(C) DAVID SANBORN BAND	1977 WB	US 3051
ROSALINDA DELEON	K	(BC	(D) HEART TO HEART	1978 WB	US 3189
PAUL SIMON	V	(B	(E) HIDEAWAY	1980 WB	US 3379
WADDY WACHTEL	G	(E			
VICTOR LEWIS	D V	(B	PATTI AUSTIN V (B PHOEBE SNOW	V (B JUMMA SANTOS	PERC(BC
LANI GROVES	V	(BC	MICHAEL BRECKER SAX (A RANDY BRECKER	TPT (A HOWARD JOHNSON	HRNS(A
TOM MALONE	TROM (A	STEVE KHAN G (A BUZZY FEITEN	G (A JOE BECK	G (A
DON GROLNICK	K	(AE	WILL LEE B (A CHRIS PARKER	D (A RICK MAROTTA	D (AE
RALPH MACDONALD	PERC (AE	PETER GORDON HRNS (A JOHN CLARK	HRNS (A JOSE MADERA	PERC(A
WARREN SMITH	PERC (A	STEVE GADD D (AE MARK EGAN	B (C DALE OEHLER	K (C
KAT McCORD	V	(C	CHRISTINE FAITH V (HAMISH STUART	V (C STRINGS	(AE
DAVID SPINOZZA	G	(E	DANNY KORTCHMAR G (E JAMES TAYLOR	V (E

S18 DAVID SANCIOUS

DAVID SANCIOUS	K G V PERC(ALL	(A) FOREST OF FEELING	1975 EPIC	US	33441
GERALD CARBOY	B	(ABC1	(B) TRANSFORMATION	1976 EPIC	US	33939
ERNEST CARTER	D V	(ABC1	(C) TRUE STORIES	1978 ARISTA	UK	SPART1082
GAIL BOGGS	(C	(1) 1979 MARCH			
ALEX LIGERTWOOD	(C1	(D) DANCE OF THE AGE OF ENLIGHTENMENT	197 ARISTA	US	4130
BRENDA MADISON	(C	(E) BRIDGE	1981 ARISTA	UK	SPART1162

[362]

SAND
S18A

JACK MEUSSDORFFER	G V	(A		(A) SAND	1973 BARNABY	US	BR 15006
DAN ROSS	G V STEEL	(A					
DAN WILSON	V	(A	RICH GOOCH	B V (A STEVE	(A		

SANDALS
S18B

(A) ENDLESS SUMMER (SOUNDTRACK)	19 WORLD PACIFIC US	ST1832

SANTANA
S19

CARLOS SANTANA	G V	(ALL	(A) SANTANA	1968 CBS	US 9781	UK 63815
WITH			(B) ABRAXAS	1970 CBS	US 30130	UK 64087
GREG ROLIE	K V	(ABDE1234	(C) WITH BUDDY MILES	1971 CBS		UK 65142
DAVID BROWN	B	(ABDL235	(D) SANTANA III	1972 CBS	US 30595	UK 69015
MIKE SHRIEVE	D	(ABDEJK34	(E) CARAVANSERAI	1972 CBS	US 31610	UK 65299
MIKE CARABELLO	PERC	(ABD3	(F) LOVE DEVOTION SURRENDER	1973 CBS		UK 69037
NEAL SCHON	G	(DE34	(G) WELCOME	1974 CBS	US 32445	UK 69040
JOSE CHEPITOS AREAS	PERC	(ABDEK345	(H) ILLUMINATIONS	1974 CBS	US 32900	UK 69063
RICO REYES	PERC	(DE34	(I) GREATEST HITS	1974 CBS	US 33080	UK 69081
TOM COSTER	K V	(EJKLH5678	(J) BORBOLETTA	1974 CBS	US 33135	UK 69084
ARMANDO PERAZA	PERC	(EFJKLR56	(K) LOTUS (TRIPLE)	1975 CBS		UK 66325
LEON PATILLO	V PERC	(57J	(L) AMIGOS	1976 CBS	US 33576	UK 86005
TOM FRAZER	G	(1	(M) FESTIVAL	1977 CBS	US 34423	UK 86020
ROD HARPER	D	(1	(N) MOONFLOWER	1977 CBS	US 34914	UK 88272
GUS RODRIGUES	B	(1	(O) ONENESS	1979 CBS		UK 86037
MARCUS MALONE	PERC	(2	(P) INNER SECRETS	1979 CBS		UK 86075
BOB LIVINGSTONE	D	(2	(Q) MARATHON	1979 CBS		UK 86098
TOM RUTLEY	B	(34E	(R) SWING OF DELIGHT (DBL)	1980 CBS		22075
COKE ESCOVEDO	PERC	(34D	(S) ZEBOP	1981 CBS		UK 84946
VICTOR PANTOJA	PERC	(3	(1) 1966/67 (2) 1967/69 (3) 1971 (4) 1971			
WILLIE BOBO	PERC	(3	(5) 1974/74 (6) 1976 (7) 1976 (8) 1976			
PHIL FORD	TABLAS	(H				

PETE ESCOVEDO	PERC	(	LEON THOMAS	V	(K	RICHARD KERMODE	K	(K	MINGO LEWIS	PNO (EF
BYRON MILLER	B	(6	GREG WALKER	V	(56L	LEON CHANCLER	D	(56JL	JULES BROUSSARD	(HJ5
FRANCISCO AQUABELLA	PERC	(R6	TOM CROUCHER	V	(7	RAUL REKOW		(78R	PABLO TELLEZ	B V (78
JOHN SANTOS	PERC	(7	DAVID PRATER	D	(7	GAYLORD BIRCH	D	(7	LUTHER RABBS	V (8
GRAHAM LEAR	D	(8	JOEL		(8	DOUGLAS RAUCH	B G	(EFJ	TOWER OF POWER	HRNS(D
LUIS GASCA	TPT	(D	LINDA TILLEY	V	(D	MARIO OCHOA	K	(D	GREG ERRICO	PERC(D
HADLEY CALIMAN	SAX	(E	WENDY HAAS	K	(D	DAVID RODRIGUES	G	(E	LENNY WHITE	PERC(E
JAMES BOND	B	(H	RHIL BROWNE	PERC	(FGH	DAVID HOLLAND	B	(H	JACK DeJOHNETTE	PERC(H
ALICE COLTRANE	K HARP	(H	JULIA TILLMAN	V	(L	IVORY STONE	B	(L	MAXINE WILLARD	V (L
JOHN McLAUGHLIN	G	(F	BILLY COBHAM	D	(F	JAN HAMMER	K	(F	LARRY YOUNG	ORG (F
DON ALIAS	D	(F	STANLEY CLARKE	B	(F	AIRTO MOREIRA	D	(J	FLORA PURIM	V (J
HERBIE HANCOCK	K	(R	WAYNE SHORTER	SAX	(R	RON CARTER	B	(R	TONY WILLIAMS	D (R
ORESTES VILATO	PERC	(R	HARVEY MASON	D	(R	RUSSELL TUBBS	WIND	(R	DAVID MARGEN	B (R
GRAHAM LEAR	D	(R	ALEX LIGERTWOOD	V	(R	STRINGS		(H		

SANFORD TOWNSEND
S20

JOHN TOWNSEND	V	(AB		(A) SMOKE FROM A DISTANT FIRE	1976 WB	US BS 2966				
ED SANFORD	K V	(AB		(B) DUOGLIDE	1977 WB	US BS 3081	UK K56476			
STEVE CROPPER	G	(B								
OTIS HALE	G SAX	(B	FRED TACKETT	G	(B	PAUL BARRERE	G	(B	DAVID PAICH	K (B
HERB PEDERSEN	V	(B	JERRY McGEE	G	(B	MIKE UTLEY	PNO	(B	JEFF PORCARO	D (B
DAVID HUNGATE	B	(B	MILT HOLLAND	PERC	(B	BILL PAYNE	K	(B	RICHARD TORRANCE	V (B
DICK HALLIGAN	STRINGS	(B								

VERONIQUE SANSON
S21

VERONIQUE SANSON	(AB		(A) AMOUREUSE	1972 ELEKTRA	K42106
			(B) HOLLYWOOD	1978 ELEKTRA	K52063

SANTA BARBARA MACHINEHEAD
S22

JON LORD	K	(AB	(A) BLUES ANTHOLOGY VOL.3	1968 IMMEDIATE	UK IMLPO19
RON WOOD	G	(AB	(B) BEST OF BRITISH BLUES	19 IMMEDIATE	GERM 048 90677
KIM GARDNER	B	(AB			
TWINK	D	(AB	THE THREE TRACKS THEY RECORDED ARE ON THE ABOVE COMPILATION ALBUMS		

BOB SARGEANT
S23

BOB SARGEANT	G V K	(A		(A) FIRST STARRING ROLE	1975 RCA	LPLI 5076			
COZY POWELL	D	(A							
JOHN WOODS		(A	JACK LANCASTER	WIND (A	JERRY SMITH	(A	CLIVE CHAMAN	B	(A
ROBIN LUMLEY		(A	RITCHIE DHARMA	D (A	MIKE GARSON	(A	WALT MONAGHAN	B	(A
HERBIE FLOWERS	B	(A							

SAROFEEN & SMOKE
S24

(A) DO IT	1971 PYE	UK NSPL28153
(B) SAROFEEN & SMOKE	197 GWP	US 2029

SASS
S25

PAUL CARUSO	D V	(A	(A) 1976
DANA WEST	G V	(A	
VERNON WEST	B V	(A	

SASSAFRAS
S26

DAI SHELL	G	(ABC1		(A) EXPECTING COMPANY	1973 POLYDOR	2383 245			
TERRY BENNETT	V	(ABC		(B) WHEELIN' & DEALIN'	1975 CHRYSALIS	CHR 1076			
RALPH EVANS	G V	(ABC1		(C) RIDING HIGH	1976 CHRYSALIS	CHR 1100			
RICKY JOHN HOLT	B V	(ABC1		(1) MAY 1978					
ROBERT JONES	D V	(AC							
STEVE FINN	B	(B	EDDIE WILLIAMS	G V	(1	CHRIS SHARLEY	D	(B	JEFF JONES D (1
ROB REYNOLDS	D	(A	DICK OWEN	D	(B				

SATIN WHALE
S26A

(A) DESERT PLACES	197 BRAIN	GERM 0040 120

SATSFACTION
S27

MIKE COTTON	HRNS	(1		(A) SATISFACTION	1971 DECCA	UK SKL 5075
LEM LUBIN	B	(1		(1) 1970 SEPT		
JOHN BEECHAM	TROM	(1				
DEREK GRIFFITHS	G V	(1	NICK NEWELL	SAX (1	BERNIE HIGGINSON	D V (1

S28

SATURNALIA

ALETTA	V	(A	(A) MAGICAL LOVE		MATRIX	1973		TRIX 1
TOM CROMPTON	D	(A						
ROD ROACH	G	(A	ADRIAN HAWKINS	V	(A	RICHARD HOUGHTON	B	(A

S28A

SAVAGE GRACE

JOHN SEANOR	K	(AB	(A) SAVAGE GRACE	1970	REPRISE	US	RS6399
LARRY ZACK	D	(AB	(B) SAVAGE GRACE 2	1972	REPRISE	US	RS6434
AL JACQUEZ	B V	(AB					
RON ROSS	G V	(AB					

S29

SAVAGE RESURRECTION

BILL HARPER		(A	(A) SAVAGE RESURRECTION	1968 MERCURY US SR61156 UK SMCL20123	
RANDY HAMMON		(A			
JEFF MYER		(A	STEVE LANGE	(A	JOHN PALMER	(A

S30

SAVAGE ROSE

ANNISETTE	V	(ALL	(A) SAVAGE ROSE	1968	POLYDOR	543 031	184	144
ANDERS KOPPEL	K	(ALL	(B) IN THE PLAIN	1968	POLYDOR	543 051	46	292
THOMAS KOPPEL	K V	(ALL	(C) TRAVELLIN'	1969	POLYDOR		184	316
ILSE MARIA KOPPEL	K	(ABCEK	(D) YOUR DAILY GIFT	1971	POLYDOR		2380	004
NILS TUXEN	G	(BCDF	(D) YOUR DAILY GIFT	1971	RCA	UK SF8169 US GREGAR		103
ALEX RIEL	D	(BCDEF	(E) REFUGEE	1972	POLYDOR		2380	014
FLEMMING OSTERMANN	G	(A	(E) REFUGEE	1972	RCA	UK SF8250 US GREGAR		104
JOHN URIBE	G	(E	(F) POP HISTORY	1972	POLYDOR		2675	018
KEN GUDMAND	D	(J	(G) DODENS TRIUMF	1972	POLYDOR		2380	016
RUDOLF HANSEN	B	(J	(H) BABYLON	1973	POLYDOR		2380	019
BEN WEBSTER	SAX	(H	(J) WILD CHILD	1973	POLYDOR		2380	021
JENS RUGSTED	V B	(ABCDF	(K) I'M SATISFIED	197	KARUSSEL		2499	010
PEER FROST	G	(J						

S31

SAVOY BROWN

KIM SIMMONDS	G HCA	(ALL	(A) SHAKE DOWN	1967	DECCA	UK SKL4883	
BRYCE PORTIUS	V	(A	(B) GETTING TO THE POINT	1968	DECCA	UK SKL4925	
MARTIN STONE	G	(A	(C) BLUE MATTER	1968	DECCA	UK SKL4994	US PARROT 71027
RAY CHAPPELL	B	(A	(D) A STEP FURTHER	1969	DECCA	UK SKL5013	US PARROT 71029
LEO MANNINGS	D	(A	(E) RAW SIENNA	1970	DECCA	UK SKL5030	US PARROT 71036
BOB HALL	PNO	(ABCD	(F) LOOKING IN	1970	DECCA	UK SKL5066	US PARROT 71042
CHRIS YOULDEN	V	(BCDE	(G) STREET CORNER TALKING	1970	DECCA	UK TXS 104	US PARROT 71047
LONESOME DAVE PEVERETT	G	(BCDEF	(H) HELLBOUND	1972	DECCA	UK TXS 107	US PARROT 71024
RIVERS JOBE	B	(BC	(J) LIONS SHARE	1973	DECCA	UK SKL5152	US PARROT 71057
ROGER EARL	D	(BCDEF	(K) JACK THE TOAD	1973	DECCA	UK TXS 112	US PARROT 71059
TONE STEVENS	PERC B	(CDEF	(L) BOOGIE BROTHERS	1974	DECCA	UK SKL5186	US LONDON PS638
OWEN FINNEGAN	PERC	(F	(M) WIRE FIRE	1975			US LONDON PS659
DAVE WALKER	V	(GHJ	(N) SKIN'N'BONES	1976			US LONDON PS670
ANDY SYLVESTER	B	(GH	(O) SAVAGE RETURN	1978			US LONDON PS718
DAVE BIDWELL	D	(GHJK	(P) BLUES ROOTS	1978	DECCA	UK ROOTS 7	
PAUL RAYMOND	V K G	(GHJKNM					

JACKIE LYNTON	V	(K	STAN WEBB	G V	(L	MILLER ANDERSON	G V	(L	RON BERG	D PERC	(K
ERIC DILLON	D	(L	JIMMY LEVERTON	B	(L	IAN ELLIS	B V	(NO	TOM FARNELL	D	(NO
MIKE VERNON	PERC	(CD	PHIL REID	VLN	(D	DEREK WADSWORTH	TROM	(C	BRIAN PERRIN	TROM	(C
TERRY FLANNERY	TROM	(C	KEITH MARTIN	TROM	(C	ALAN MOORE	TROM	(C	BUTCH HUDSON	TPT	(D
KENNY WHEELER	TPT	(D	EDDIE BLAIR	TPT	(D	RAY DAVIS	HRNS	(D	BOBBY HAUGHEY	HRNS	(D
DON LUSHER	TROM	(D	JOHN EDWARDS	TROM	(D	BOB EFFORD	SAX	(D	REX MORRIS	SAX	(D
DON HONEYWILL	SAX	(D	STAN SULTZMAN	SAX	(K	SUE GLOVER	V	(K	SUNNY LESLIE	V	(K
FRANK RICOTTI	PERC	(K	ANDY PYLE	B	(JK	BARRY MURRAY	PERC	(K	ANDY RAE	B	(M

S32

RAY SAWYER

RAY SAWYER	G V	(A	(A) RAY SAWYER			1977 CAPITOL				11591
STEVE GIBSON	G	(A								
DOYLE GRISHAM	STEEL	(A	SHANE KEISTER	K	(A	BOBBY OGDIN	PNO	(A	LARRY LONDIN	D	(A
KENNY MALONE	D	(A	TED REYNOLDS	B	(A	LISA SILVER	FDL V	(A	BUDDY SPICHER	FDL	(A
SHERI KRAMER	V	(A	DIANE TIDWELL	V	(A	STRING SECTION		(A			

S32A

SAXON

BIFF	V	(ABC	(A) SAXON	1979	CARRERE		CAL110
PAUL QUINN	G	(ABC	(B) WHEELS OF STEEL	1980	CARRERE		CAL115
GRAHAM OLIVER	G	(ABC	(C) STRONG ARM OF THE LAW	1980	CARRERE	2934 129	CAL120
PETE GILL	D	(ABC					
STEVE DAWSON	B	(ABC					

S33

SKY SAXON BLUES BAND

SKY SAXON		(A	(A) FULL SPOON OF SEEDY BLUES	1967	GNP CRESCENDO US	2040
DARYL HOOPER	K	(A			
JAN SAVAGE	G	(A	RICK ANDRIDGE	D	(A

S34

LEO SAYER

LEO SAYER	V HCA G	(ALL	(A) SILVERBIRD	1973	CHRYSALIS	UK CHR1050 WB US 2738	
MIKE GILES	D	(ABC	(B) JUST A BOY	1974	CHRYSALIS	UK CHR1068 WB US 2836	
HENRY SPINETTI	D	(A	(C) ANOTHER YEAR	1975	CHRYSALIS	UK CHR1087 WB US 2885	
BOB HENRIT	D	(A	(D) ENDLESS FLIGHT	1976	CHRYSALIS	UK CHR1125 WB US 3101	
RUSS BALLARD	K G	(AC	(E) THUNDER IN MY HEART	1977	CHRYSALIS	UK CHR1154 WB US 3089	
DAVE WINTOUR	B	(A	(F) LEO SAYER	1978	CHRYSALIS	UK CHR1198 WB US 3200	
DAVE COURTNEY	PNO	(AB	(G) THE VERY BEST OF	1979	CHRYSALIS	UK CHR1222	
MAX CHETWYN	G	(A	(H) HERE	1979	CHRYSALIS	UK CDL1240	
CLIFF HALL	PNO	(B	(I) SHOW MUST GO ON	1979	PICKWICK	UK SHM3035	
PAUL KEOGH	G	(BC	(J) LIVING IN A FANTASY	1980	CHRYSALIS	UK CDL1297	
DAVE MARKEE	B	(BC					

DAVE ROSE	PNO	(B	JAMES LITHERLAND	G	(B	BILL SMITH	B	(B	JOHN MEALING	ORG (B
LIZA STRIKE	V	(B	THEODORE THUNDER	D	(B	BARRY ST JOHN	V	(B	KEITH NELSON	BANJ(B
FRANK FARRELL	K	(C	TERRY STARR	TPT	(C	NICK NEWELL	FLT	(C	JOHNNY VAN DERRICK	VLN(C
DAVID KATZ ORCHESTRA		(C	JEFF PORCARO	D	(E	ABE LABORIEL	B	(E	LEE RITENOUR	G	(E
FRED TACKETT	G	(E	TOM SNOW	PNO	(E	LENNY CASTRO	CONGA	(E	MICHAEL OMARTIAN	K	(E
LARRY CARLTON	G	(E	JAY GRAYDON	G	(E	CLYDIE KING	V	(E	BEN ADKINS	B	(E
DAVID HUNGATE	B	(E	IRA NEWBORN	G	(E	TOM SCOTT	SAX	(E	SHIRLEY MATTHEWS	V	(E
RAY PARKER	G	(E	JACK ASHFORD	PERC	(E	JAMES NEWTON HOWARD	K	(E	BECKY LEWIS	V	(E
BOBBYE HALL	PERC	(E								

(A) LEAVE ME ALONE (EP)   1980 CLUBLAND
SCAFFOLD   S35

MIKE McGEAR	V	(ABCDE	(A) McGOUGH & McGEAR		1967 PARLOPHONE	UK	PCS	7047
ROGER McGOUGH	V	(ABCDE	(B) AN EVENING WITH SCAFFOLD		1968 PARLOPHONE	UK	PCS	7051
JOHN GORMAN	V	(BCDE	(C) LILY THE PINK		1969 PARLOPHONE	UK	PCS	7077
JOHN MEGGINSON	K	(DE	(D) FRESH LIVER		1973 ISLAND	UK	ILPS	9234
GERRY CONWAY	D	(DE	(E) SOLD OUT		1975 WB	UK	K56097	
LOL CREME	GYSMO(E		(B) THANK YOU VERY MUCH		1968 BELL	US		6018
HELEN COX	V	(E						

ZOOT MONEY	K	(DE	ANDY ROBERTS	G V	(DE	OLLIE HALSALL	G	(DE	BRIAN JONES	SAX	(E
FRANK RICOTTI	PERC	(E	NEIL INNES	K G	(D	RAY WARLEIGH	FLT	(D	ANTHONY WHITE	G	(D
NORMAN YARDLEY	HCA	(D	TIM RICE	V	(D	ROGER BALL	SAX	(D	MALCOLM DUNCAN	SAX	(D
MIKE ROSEN	TPT	(D	HARRY BECKETT	TPT	(D	DORIS TROY	V	(D	PAUL KORDA	V	(D
JIMMY HELMS	V	(D	ALAN GORRIE	V	(D	DAVE RICHARDS	B V	(E	ROB TOWNSEND	D	(E
JIMI HENDRIX	G	(B	DAVE MASON	G	(B	MIKE VICKERS		(B			

BOZ SCAGGS   S36

BOZ SCAGGS	G V	(ALL	(A) BOZ	1965 POLYDOR		LPHM	46253
GEORGE RAINS	D	(CD	(B) BOZ SCAGGS	1969 ATLANTIC	UK	588 205 US	8239
BOB ARTHUR	B	(	(B) BOZ SCAGGS	RI 1971 ATLANTIC	UK	K40419 US	19166
JOHN ANDREWS	G	(	(C) MOMENTS	1971 CBS	UK	64248 US	30454
DAVID BROWN	B	(CD	(D) BOZ SCAGGS & HIS BAND	1971 CBS	UK	64431 US	30796
JYMN YOUNG	K	(CD	(D) BOZ SCAGGS & HIS BAND	197 CBS RI		US	31848
MEL MARTIN	HRNS	(CD	(E) MY TIME	1972 CBS	UK	64975 US	31384
DOUG SIMRIL	G PNO(	(D	(F) SLOW DANCER	1974 CBS	UK	65953 US	33760
TOM POOLE	HRNS	(	(G) SILK DEGREES	1976 CBS	UK	81193 US	33920
ART O'HARA		(	(H) DOWN TWO THEN LEFT	1977 CBS	UK	86028 US	34729
PAT O'HARA	HRNS	(CD	(J) HITS	1980 CBS	UK	84706	
PAUL BECKER	HRNS	(	(K) MIDDLEMAN	1980 CBS	UK	86094	
ROGER HAWKINS	D	(B					

EDDIE HINTON	G	(B	JIM JOHNSON	G	(B	PETER CARR	G	(	DAVE HOOD B		(B
CLAYTON IVEY	K	(	SID SHARP	STRINGS(		JOE PORCARO		(	JEFF PORCARO		(
FRED TACKETT	G	(	LES DUDEK	G	(	DUANE ALLMAN	G DOB(B		JOHN MADRID	HRNS	(
ADRIA TAPIA	SAX	(	LENNY CASTRO	PERC	(	SCOTT EDWARDS	B	(	STEVE LUTHER	G	(
JAY WINDING	K	(	JOHN McFEE	STEEL	(	CURLEY COOKE	G	(C	COKE ESCOVEDO	PERC(C	
PETE ESCOVEDO	PERC	(C	BILL ATWOOD HRNS		(C	RITA COOLIDGE	V	(CD	BEN SIDRAN	VIBES(C	
CHEPITO AREAS	PERC	(D	DOROTHY MORRISON	V	(D	MIKE CARABELLO	PERC	(D	LEE CHARLTON		(D
BARRY BECKETT	K	(B	CHARLES CHALMERS	SAX	(B	FLOYD NEWMAN	SAX	(B	BEN CAULEY	TPT	(B
GENE MILLER	TPT	(B	JOE ARNOLD	SAX	(B	JAMES MITCHELL	SAX	(B	JEANNIE GREENE	V	(B
MARY HOLLADAY	V	(B	DONNA THATCHER	V	(B	TRACY NELSON	V	(B	IRMA ROUTEN	V	(B
JOYCE DUNN	V	(B	AL LESTER	FDL			(B				

SCARECROW   S36A

JOHN STEWART	G V	(A	(A) SCARECROW LIVE	1978 SPILT MILK		SMFM1127(
DAVE RUMSEY	D	(A				
BILL PUPLETT	G	(A	DICK WILLIAMSON	B	(A	

SCARS   S37

PAUL RESEARCH	G	(A	(A) AUTHOR! AUTHOR!	1981 PRE	UK	PREX 5
CALUNN MACKAY	D	(A				
BOBBY KING	V	(A	JOHN MACKIE B	(A		

SCENE STEALER   S37A

(A) FIRST OFFENCE   1978 EMI   066 60275
SCENT ORGAN   S38

STEVE MIKNENAS	G	(A	(A) 1978		
JOHN HODGSON	B	(A	ROGER TAYLOR D	(A	

JANNE SCHAFFER   S39

JANNE SCHAFFER	G V	(ALL	(A) JANNE SCHAFFER	1973 4LEAF	SWED	EFG	7232
BJORN LINDH	K FLT	(ABD	(A) THE CHINESE	1974 VERTIGO	UK	6360	107
STEFAN BROLUND	B	(ABD	(B) ANDRA LP	1974 EUROPA FILM	SWED EFG 501	2106	
OLA BRUNKERT	D	(AB	(B) SECOND ALBUM	1975 VERTIGO	UK	6360	118
JAN TOLF	PERC	(A	(C) KARTHARSIS	1977 CBS	UK	81733	
JAN BANDEL	PERC VIBES(AB		(D) EARMEAL	1979 CBS	UK	83002	
MALANDO GASSAMA	PERC	(ABD					

SLIM NOTINI	V PNO(A		HALAN NYQVIST	TPT	(A	SVEN LARSSON	TROM (A		BENGT KARLSSON	G	(A
LUCAS LINDHOLM	B	(B	PETER OSTLUND	D	(B	PER SAHLBERG	G	(B	PETER ROBINSON	K	(BD
JOHN GUSTAFSON	B	(B	MADS WINDING	B	(B	JEFF PORCARO	D	(D	STEVE PORCARO	K	(D
MIKE PORCARO	B	(D	JOE PORCARO	PERC (D							

ARMAND SCHAUBROECK   S40

ARMAND SCHAUBROECK		(ALL	(A) A LOT OF PEOPLE WOULD LIKE TO SEE US DEAD	19	MIRROR	
			(B) SHAKIN' SHAKIN'	1978	MIRROR	MIRROR 5
			(C) I CAME TO VISIT	19	MIRROR	

MICHAEL SCHENKER GROUP   S41

MICHAEL SCHENKER	G	(A	(A) MICHAEL SCHENKER GROUP	1980 CHRYSALIS	UK	CHR 1302
GARY BARDEN	V	(A				
SIMON PHILLIPS	D	(A	MO FOSTER	B	(A	DON AIREY	K	(A

GUNTER SCHICKERT   S41A

GUNTER SCHICKERT		(AB	(A) UBERFALLIG	1979 SKY	SKY 032
CHARLES M HEUZ		(A	(B) FARNTVOGEL	19 BRAIN	0040 176

CONRAD SCHNITZLER   S42

CONRAD SCHNITZLER ELECTRONICS(ALL			(A) SCHWARZ	1971 BLOCK	KS 1001
			(B) ROT	1971 BLOCK	KS 1002
			(C) BLAU	1972 BLOCK	KS 1003
			(D) CON	1977 BARCLAY	EGG 90184
			(E) WORK IN PROGRESS	1978 BLOCK	

EBERHARD SCHOENER   S42A

EBERHARD SCHOENER	K	(A	(A) VIDEO FLASHBACK	1979 HARVEST	UK	SHSM 2030
STING	B V	(A				
ANDY SUMMERS	G	(A	STEWART COPELAND D	(A	EVERT FRATERMAN	D (A OLAF KUBLER SAX (A
HANSI STROER	G B	(A	NEPPI NOYA	PERC (A	ORCHESTRA	(A

KLAUS SCHULZE

KLAUS SCHULZE	K SYN(ALL		PICTURE MUSIC	1973 BRAIN	GERM	0001 067
			PICTURE MUSIC	1978 ISADORA		9007
			PICTURE MUSIC	1980 BRAIN		0040 146
			IRRLICHT	197 BRAIN		0001 077
			IRRLICHT	1978 ISADORA		9004
			MOONDAWN	197 BRAIN		0001 088
			MOONDAWN	1978 BRAIN		0060 040
			MOONDAWN	1976 VIRGIN		V2064
			BLACK DANCE	1974 CAROLINE		CA 2003
			TIME WIND	1975 CAROLINE		CA 2006
			CYBORG	197 BRAIN		0021 078
			CYBORG	1978 ISADORA		9005/6
			MIRAGE	1977 ISLAND		ILPS9461
			MIRAGE	1978 BRAIN		0060 040
			BODY LOVE	197 BRAIN		0060 047
			BODY LOVE	1977 ISLAND	UK	ILPS9510
			LIVE	19 BRAIN		0080 048
			BLANCHE	1979 LOGO	UK	1011

S44

SCHUNGE

SCHUNGE	G V (A		(A) BALLAD OF A SIMPLE LOVE	1972 REGAL ZONOPHONE		SLRZ 1033
BOB RICARDO	V (A					
CHRIS SPEDDING	G (A	JEFF CLYNE	B (A	HAIM ROMANO	G (A	BARRY DE SOUZA	D (A
ROY BABBINGTON	B (A	DAVE MACRAE	K (A			

S45

SCION

MARK FISHLOCK	G (A		(A) 1978		
ALI DRENNAM	PERC (A				
ANDY REID	B (A	PHIL BARDEN	K (A	MIKE BARDEN	K (A	CLIVE FISHLOCK	V (A

S45A

SCISSOR FITS

(A) SOON AFTER DARK(EP)   19 TORCH   TOR 005

S45B

SCOPE II

RIK	SYN K B (A		(A) SCOPE II	1975 ATLANTIC	GERM	ATL 50078
ROB FRANKEN	K SYN(A					
RENS NIEUWLAND	G (A	HENK ZOMER	D (A		

S46

ERROLL SCORCHER

ERROLL SCORCHER	(A	(A) RASTA FIRE	1978 BALLISTIC/UA	UAS 30198

S47

SCORPIONS

HERMAN RAREBELL	D (H		(A) LONESOME CROW	1972 BRAIN 0040 023+METRONOME 200191
RUDOLF SCHENKER	G (GH		(B) GOLD ROCK	197 BRAIN 00040016
KLAUS MEINE	V (GH		(C) ACTION	197 BRAIN 0040 0150
ULRICH ROTH	G (GH		(D) I'M GOING MAD	1974 BILLINGSGATE		1004
MICHAEL SCHENKER	G (A		(E) FLY TO THE RAINBOW	1976 RCA		APL1 4025
RUDY LENNERS	D PERC(G		(F) IN TRANCE	1976 RCA		APL1 4128
FRANCIS BUCHOLZ	B (GH		(G) VIRGIN KILLER	1977 RCA		APL1 4225
WOLFGANG DZIONY	D (A		(H) TAKEN BY FORCE	1978 RCA	PL 28309	APL1 2628
LOTHAR HEIMBERG	B (A		(J) TOKYO TAPES	1979 RCA	PL 28331	APL2 3039
			(K) LOVE DRIVE	1979 HARVEST		SHSP 4097
			(L) ANIMAL MAGNETISM	1980 HARVEST		SHSP 4113

S48

COLIN SCOT

COLIN SCOT	G V (ALL		(A) COLIN SCOT WITH FRIENDS	1971 UA	EURO 038 60520 UK UAG29154
RAY GLYNN	MAND G (C		(B) JUST ANOTHER CLOWN	1973 WB		K46236
DAVE ETHRIDGE	B (C		(C) OUT OF THE BLUE	1974 WB		K46281
KIRK DUNCAN	K (C		(A) COLIN SCOT	197 VISA	IMP	1010
BARRY DE SOUZA	D (C					
JUANITA FRANKLIN	V (C	SPARKIE	V (C	TARAGON	V (C	MOX	FLT HCA (C
BRIAN ODGERS	B (C	PHILLIP GOODHAND TAIT	K(C	TONY LUKYN	SYN (C	ERIC HASTINGS	VLN(C
JULIA TURNER	VLN (C	KEITH SMITH	VLN (C	GERRY RICH	VLA (C	KEITH THATCHER	CELLO(C
RUTH LOCK	CELLO(C	PETER GABRIEL	(A	PHIL COLLINS	D (A	PETER HAMMILL	(A
ROBERT FRIPP	G (A	JON ANDERSON	V (A	RICK WAKEMAN	K (A		

S49

JACK SCOTT

JACK SCOTT	V (ALL		(A) WHAT IN THE WORLD	1960 TOP RANK UK 12/024	US	626
			(B) I REMEMBER HANK WILLIAMS	1960 TOP RANK UK 12/034	US	619
			(C) THE SPIRIT MOVES ME	1961 TOP RANK UK 35/109	US	648
			(D) JACK SCOTT	19 CARLTON	US	12107
			(E) WHAT AM I LIVING FOR	19 CARLTON	US	12122
			(F) BURNING BRIDGES	19 CAPITOL	US ST2035
			(G) JACK SCOTT GREATEST HITS	197 PONIE	US	563
			(H) SECOND ALBUM	1977 PONIE	US	7055

S50

TOM SCOTT

TOM SCOTT	SYN WIND (ALL		(A) HONEYSUCKLE BREEZE	1968 IMPULSE	US	AS 9163
ERIC GALE	G (FK		(B) RURAL STILL LIFE	196 IMPULSE	US	AS 9171
HUGH McCRACKEN	G HCA(F		(C) GREAT SCOTT	19 A&M	US	AM 4330
BOB JAMES	K (F		(D) TOM SCOTT & L A EXPRESS	1974 ODE		77021
RALPH MACDONALD	PERC (FK		(E) TOM CAT	1975 ODE		77029
GARY KING	B (FK		(F) NEW YORK CONNECTION	1975 ODE		77033
GEORGE HARRISON	G (F		(G) BLOW IT OUT	1977 EPIC	UK 82285	US	34966
RICHARD TEE	K (FK		(H) TOM SCOTT IN L A	1977 RCA	UK SF8429
CHUCK FINDLEY	TPT (FK		(H) TOM SCOTT IN L A	1977 FLYING DUTCHMAN		BXLI 0833
JACO PASTORIUS	B (H		(I) INTIMATE STRANGERS	1979 CBS	UK 83309
STEVE GADD	D (FK		(J) STREET BEAT	1979 CBS		
DICK HYDE	HRNS (FK		(K) BEST OF	1980 CBS	UK 84347
MAX BENNETT	B (K					
JOHN GUERIN	D (K	LARRY CARLTON	G (K	LARRY NASH	K (K	RICK MAROTTA	D (K
ROBBEN FORD	G (K					

GIL SCOTT HERON

GILL SCOTT HERON	G PNO(ALL	(A) SMALL TALK AT 125TH & LENNOX	1972	FLYING DUTCHMAN					
BRIAN JACKSON	FLT K	(GJK	(B) FREE WILL	1972	FLYING DUTCHMAN		10153		
BARNETT WILLIAMS	PERC (K	(C) PIECES OF A MAN	1973	FLYING DUTCHMAN	BXLI0833	10143			
LEON WILLIAMS	SAX (K	(D) WINTER IN AMERICA	1975	STRATA EAST		19742			
HARVEY MASON	D (K	(E) REVOLUTION WILL NOT BE TELEVISED	1975	RCA	UK	SF8428			
GREG PHILLINGANES	K (K	(E) REVOLUTION WILL NOT BE TELEVISED	1975	FLYING DUTCHMAN		BXLI0613			
ALVIN TAYLOR	D (K	(F) FIRST MINUTE OF A NEW DAY	1975	ARISTA UK ARTY 106	US	4030			
RALPH PENLAND	D (K	(G) FROM S AFRICA TO S CAROLINA	1976	ARISTA UK ARTY 121	US	4044			
MAXINE WILLARD	V (K	(H) IT'S YOUR WORLD	1976	ARISTA UK DARTY 1	US	5001			
JULIA TILLMAN	V (K	(J) BRIDGES	1977	ARISTA UK SPARTY1031	US	4147			
MARTI McCALL	V (K	(K) SECRETS	1978	ARISTA UK SPARTY1073	US	4189			

SCOTTSVILLE SQUIRREL

CHRIS HILLMAN MAND B V	(12	(A) BLUEGRASS FAVOURITES	196	CROWN	US	CST 346	
ED DOUGLAS	B (12	(1) 1958 (2) 1962					
GARY CARR	G (12						
LARRY MURRAY	G (12	KENNY WERTZ BANJO(1 BERNIE LEADON BANJO(2					

SCRATCH & UPSETTERS

		(A) CLOAK & DAGGER	1973	RHINO	SRNO 8002
		(B) SUPER APE	1976	ISLAND	ILPS 9417

THE SCRATCH BAND

ROBERT ORSI	V HCA G(A	(A) THE SCRATCH BAND	1978	LONDON	SHY 8529
CHRISTINE OHLMAN	V (A				
G E SMITH	G (A				

SCREEN IDOLS

CHED CHEESMAN	G (A	(A) PREMIERE	1979	COBRA	CBR 1001
TONY SMITH	G (A				
MICHELLE NIEDDU	V (A	GEOFF APPLEBY B (A WOODY WOODMANSEY D (A			

SCRITTI POLITTI

	(A) HEGEMONY(4 A SIDES)(EP)	1979	ROUGH TRADE	RT 027
	(B) PEEL SESSIONS (EP)	1979	ROUGH TRADE	RT 034

SCROUNGER

PAUL LEWIS	V (A	(A) SNAP	1976	ANCHOR	ANCL 2021
IAN CURNOW	K V (A				
PAUL KEOGH	G (A	RAY RUSSELL G (A MO FOSTER B (A FRANK McDONALD B(A			
MIKE NICHOLLS	D (A	PETER VAN HOOKE D (A JOHN CAMERON STRINGS (A			

THE SCRUFFS

DAVE BRANYAN	G V (A	(A) WANNA MEET THE SCRUFFS	1977	POWERPLAY	HLPP 5050
STEPHEN BURNS	G V PNO (A				
RICK BRANYAN	B PNO V (A	ZEPH PAULSON D V (A			

SEA LEVEL

CHUCK LEAVELL	K (ABCDE	(A) SEA LEVEL	1977	CAPRICORN	US 0178 UK 2429 150
LAMAR WILLIAMS	B (ABCDE	(B) CATS ON THE COAST	1978	CAPRICORN	US 0198 UK 2429 158
JAI JOHANSON	D (AB	(C) ON THE EDGE	1978	CAPRICORN	US 0212
ED DOWLING	TPT (A	(D) LONG WALK ON A SHORT PIER	1979	CAPRICORN	US 0227
JIMMY NALLS	G (ABCDE	(E) BALLROOM	1980	ARISTA US 9531 UK SPARTY 1145	
RANDALL BRAMBLETT	SAX (BCD				
GEORGE WEAVER	D (A	DAVIS CAUSEY G (BCDE DON McCLURE HRNS (A LEO LABRANCHE HRNS (A			
EARL FORD	HRNS 'A	CHARLES FAIRLEY HRNS (A RUDOLPH CARTER HRNS (A JOE ENGLISH D (CDE			
MATT GREELEY	PERC V(DE	TOMMY TALTON V (D DAVID EARLE JOHNSON PERC(D CHARLIE BRENT SAX (D			
TONY DAGRADI	SAX (D	RODNEY LAFON TPT (A JON ROBERT SMITH SAX (D JOE WOOLIE TPT (D			
HAROLD WILLIAMS	SAX (D				

SON SEALS

SON SEALS	G V (ALL	(A) THE SON SEALS BLUES BAND	1974	SONET UK SNTF 679 US ALLIGATOR 4703	
JOHNNY WALKER	ORG (A	(B) MIDNIGHT SON	1977	SONET UK SNTF 728 US ALLIGATOR 4708	
JOHN RILEY	B (A	(C) LIVE & BURNING	1978	SONET UK SNTF 782 US ALLIGATOR 4712	
CHARLES CALDWELL	D (A	(D) CHICAGO FIRE	1980	SONET UK SNTF 838 US ALLIGATOR 4712	
A C REED	SAX (C				
LACY GIBSON	G (C	SNAPPER MITCHUM B (BCD TONY GOODEN D (C ALBERTO GIANQUINTO PNO(BC			
BERT ROBINSON	D (B	REG ALLMON SAX (B KEN COOPER TPT (BD BILL McFARLAND TROM (BD			
MARK WEAVER	G (D	PAUL HOWARD TPT (D DAVID D ANDERSON D (D KING SOLOMON K (D			

TROY SEALS

TROY SEALS	V (AB	(A) PRESENTING TROY SEALS	1973	ATLANTIC	US SD7281
		(B) TROY SEALS	1977	CBS	US 34271

SEALS & CROFTS

JIM SEALS G V SAX FDL	(ALL	(A) SEALS & CROFT	1970	TA	US	5001
DASH CROFTS D MAND V K	G(ALL	(B) DOWN HOME	1970	BELL UK SBLL 139	TA US	5004
LOUIE SHELTON	G V (DEFGIJL	(C) YEAR OF SUNDAY	1972	WB	UK K46133	US 2568
BOBBY LICHTIG	WIND B(DEJ	(D) SUMMER BREEZE	1972	WB	UK K46173	US 2629
WILTON FELDER	B (DEGIJ	(CD) YEAR/SUMMER	1974	WB	UK K66033	US 2809
DAVID PAICH	K (EFGI	(E) DIAMOND GIRL	1973	WB	UK K46218	US 2699
JOHN GUERIN	D (DE	(F) UNBORN CHILD	1974	WB	UK K56028	US 2761
JIM GORDON	D (DE	(G) I'LL PLAY FOR YOU	1975	WB	UK K56116	US 2848
JEFF PORCARO	D (EFGI	(H) GREATEST HITS	1975	WB	UK K56176	US 3109
HARVEY MASON	D (E	(I) GET CLOSER	1976	WB	UK K56209	US 2907
BOBBYE HALL	PERC (EF	(J) SUDAN VILLAGE	1976	WB	UK K56307	US 2976
JOHN FORD COLEY	V (DE	(K) ONE ON ONE	1977	WB	UK K56402	
BUDDY EMMONS	STEEL(F	(L) TAKIN' IT EASY	1978	WB	UK K56484	
DAVID HUNGATE	B (FI					
JACK LENZ	FLT K(G	ED GREENE D (GIJ JIM VARLEY D (G ANTOINE DEARBORN PERC (G				
LARRY FORD	TPT (G	RON KING TPT (G PAUL HUBINON TPT (G BOBBY SHEW TPT (G				
BOBBY CROSBY	WIND (G	JIM HORN WIND (DGI STEVE LEEDS WIND (G GENE CIPRIANO WIND (G				
HENRY SIGISMONTI	WIND (G	DICK HYDE TROM (G JOHN LEYS TROM (G LEW McCREARY TROM (G				
MIKE PORCARO	B (G	OVID STEVENS G (G BILL CUOMO K (J RALPH HUMPHREY D (JL				
MARTY WALSH	G (JL	JOE PORCARO PERC (J DONNA GIPSON V (J SHIRLEY MATTHEWS V (IJL				
MARTY McCALL	V (J	BECKY LOUIS V (J CAROLYN WILLIS V (IJ DEAN PARKS G (J				
LEE RITENOUR	G (IJ	JOE SAMPLE K (IJ RON KRASINSKI D (L JIM KELTNER D (DL				
JAMES DIVISEK	D (L	TONY PELUSO V SYN G (L LARRY ROLANDO G (L DENNIS BELFIELD B (L				

(CONTINUED)

SEALS & CROFT

DAVID PARLATO	B	(L	DOMINIC GENOVA	B	(L	TOM HENSLEY	K	(L	DAVID FOSTER	K	(L
STEVEN OLITZKY	K	(L	DAN FERGUSON	DOBRO(L		BRIAN WHITCOMB	K	(L	DANNY DEARDORFF	HCA	(L
DON MENZA	SAX	(L	ALAN ESTES	VIBES(L		MANOUCHEHR SADEGHI	V	(L	SEAN MACLEOD	V	(L
BOB PHILLIPS	V	(L	GARY SIMS	V	(L	DOUG STRAWN	V	(L	TANYA TUCKER	V	(L
JAMES GILSTRAP	V	(L	VANETTA FIELDS	V	(L	LARRY LICHTIG	PNO	(D	CLARENCE MACDONALD	PNO(D	
MIKE LANG	PNO	(L	MICHAEL OMARTIAN	PNO	(D	RUSS KUNKEL	D	(D	HARVEY BROOKS	B	(D
JOE OSBORN	B	(D	MILT HOLLAND	PERC	(DI	KING ERRISSON	CONGA(D		RED RHODES	STEEL(D	
JOHN HARTFORD	BANJO(D		DEE HIGGINS	V	(D	DONNIE SHELTON	V	(DI	LARRY CARLTON	G	(I
RAY PARKER	G	(I	CAROL CARMICHAEL	V	(I	MYRNA MATTHEWS	V	(I	ENGLAND DAN SEALS	V	(CE

PHIL SEAMAN

PHIL SEAMAN		(ABC1	(A) PHIL SEAMAN NOW...LIVE	1968	VERVE		UK	SVLP 9220
WITH			(B) THE PHIL SEAMAN STORY	1974	DECIBEL			BSM 103
ERIC CLAPTON	G	(1	(C) PHIL ON DRUMS	1975	77			77SEV 12/53
GINGER BAKER	D	(1	(1) AT BLUES FESTIVAL 1968					

SEARCHERS

JOHN McNALLY	G V	(ALL	(A) MEET THE SEARCHERS	1963	PYE		UK	NPL18086
MIKE PENDER	G V	(ALL	(A) MEET THE SEARCHERS	1963	KAPP		US	3363
CHRIS CURTIS	D V	(ABCDEFGH	(A) MEET THE SEARCHERS	1966	GOLDEN GUINEA	UK RI	GGL 0349
TONY JACKSON	B V	(ABCDE	(B) SUGAR & SPICE	1963	PYE		UK	NPL18089
FRANK ALLEN	B	(FGHIJKLMNOPQRST	(B) SUGAR & SPICE	1967	MARBLE ARCH	UK RI	MAL 704
BILLY ADAMSON	D PERC(T		(C) THIS IS	196	KAPP		US	3409
BOB JACKSON	K	(T	(D) NEW SEARCHERS LP	196	KAPP		US	3412
			(E) IT'S THE SEARCHERS	1964	PYE		UK	NPL 18092
			(E) IT'S THE SEARCHERS	1968	MARBLE ARCH		US	MAL 798
			(F) SOUNDS LIKE THE SEARCHERS	1964	PYE		UK	NPL 18111
			(G) SEARCHERS No4	196	KAPP		US	3449
			(H) TAKE ME FOR WHAT I'M WORTH	1965	PYE		UK	NPL 18120
			(H) TAKE ME FOR WHAT I'M WORTH	196	KAPP		US	3477
			(I) SMASH HITS	1967	MARBLE ARCH		UK	MALS 640
			(J) SMASH HITS VOL 2	1967	MARBLE ARCH		UK	MALS 673
			(K) NEEDLES & PINS	1971	HALLMARK		UK	HMA 203
			(L) GOLDEN HOUR	1972	PYE		UK	GH 541
			(M) SECOND TAKE	1972	RCA		UK	SF 8298
			(N) GOLDEN HOUR VOL 2	1973	PYE		UK	GH 564
			(O) NEEDLES & PINS	1974	RCA INT		UK	INTS 1480
			(P) ROCK MUSIC FROM BRITAIN	197	MODE		FR	9029
			(Q) ATTENTION	197	PHONOGRAM		EURO	6434 127
			(R) HEAR HEAR	19	MERCURY		US	SR 60916
			(S) THE SEARCHER FILE	1977	PYE		UK	FILD002
			(T) THE SEARCHERS	1980	SIRE		UK	SRK 6086
			(T) THE SEARCHERS (DIFF TRACKS)	1980	SIRE		UK	SRK 6082
			(U) PLAY FOR TODAY	1981	SIRE		UK	SRK 3523
			(EPs)					
			AIN'T GONNA KISS YOU	1963	PYE		UK	NEP24177
			SWEETS FOR MY SWEET	1963	PYE		UK	NEP24183
			HUNGRY FOR LOVE	1964	PYE		UK	NEP24184
			PLAY THE SYSTEM	1964	PYE		UK	NEP24201
			WHEN YOU WALK IN THE ROOM	1964	PYE		UK	NEP24204
			BUMBLE BEE	1965	PYE		UK	NEP24218
			SEARCHERS 65	1965	PYE		UK	NEP24222
			FOUR BY FOUR	1965	PYE		UK	NEP24228
			TAKE ME FOR WHAT I'M WORTH	1966	PYE		UK	NEP24263

SEASTONES

NED LAGIN	K	(A	(A) SEASTONES	1975	ROUND		US	RX 106
PHIL LESH	B	(A						
JERRY GARCIA	G	(A	DAVID FREIBERG	V	(A	DAVID CROSBY	V	(A	MICKEY HART PERC (A
GRACE SLICK	V	(A	SPENCER DRYDEN	PERC (A					

B B SEATON

B B SEATON		(ABC	(A) THIN LINE BETWEEN LOVE & HATE	1973	TROJAN		TRLS 59
			(B) DANCING SHOES	1974	CAROLINE		CA 2002
			(C) COLOUR IS NOT THE ANSWER	1976	JAMA		JALP 002

SEATRAIN

RICHARD GREENE	VLN	(ABC	(A) SEATRAIN	1969	A&M	US 4171	UK AMLS 941
ANDY KULBERG	FLT B(ABCD		(B) SEATRAIN	1971	CAPITOL US SMAS659	UK EAST 659
DON KRETMAR	SAX	(A	(C) MARBLEHEAD MESSENGER	1972	CAPITOL US SMAS829	UK EAST 829
JOHN GREGORY	G V	(A	(D) WATCH	1973	WB	US BS 2692	UK K 46222
ROY BLUMENFELD	D	(A					
PETER ROWAN	G	(BC	LARRY ATAMANUIK	D	(BC	LLOYD BASKIN	K V	(BCD JULIO CORONADO	D	(D
WILLIAM ELLIOTT	K	(D	PETER WALSH	G V	(D	JIM ROBERTS		(ABC ANDY MUSAR	B	(
SANDRA LEE	V	(D	PAUL PRESTOPINO	G	(D	BOB STUART	TUBA	(D BILL KEITH	BAN(D	
SHA NA NA	V	(D	PAUL SHURE	VLN	(D	BONNIE DOUGLAS	VLN	(D MYRA KESTENBAUM	VLA(D	
DOUG DAVIES	CELLO	(D	ALLAN VOGEL	OBOE	(D	BUELL NEIDLINGER	B	(D WAYNE DALEY	V	(D
JILL SHIRES	FLT	(D								

SEAWIND

PAULINE WILSON	V	(AB	(A) SEAWIND	1976	CTI			5002
BOB WILSON	D	(AB	(B) WINDOW OF A CHILD	1977	CTI			75007
BUD NUANEZ	G V	(AB	(B) WINDOW OF A CHILD	1978	PYE			NSPL18561
KEN WILD	B V	(AB	(D) SEAWIND	1980	A&M US SP4824	UK AMLH 64824
BILL REICHENBACH	TROM	(B						
JERRY HEY	HRNS	(AB	KIM HUTCHCROFT	SAX V(AB		LARRY WILLIAMS	K WIND V(AB	PAULINHO DA COSTA	PERC(A
RALPH MACDONALD	PERC	(A	IAN UNDERWOOD	SYN	(AB	HARVEY MASON	PERC V(AB	BILL SUMMERS	PERC(B
CHARLES VEAL	STRINGS	(B						

JOHN SEBASTIAN

JOHN SEBASTIAN	G V PERC HCA(ALL		(A) JOHN B SEBASTIAN	1970	REPRISE	US 6379	UK K44086
MILT HOLLAND	D	(D	(A) JOHN B SEBASTIAN (WITHDRAWN)	1970	MGM	US 4654	
RUSSELL DASHIELL	G	(D	(B) CHEAPO CHEAPO PRODUCTION PRESENTS	1971	REPRISE	US 2036	UK K44127
AMOS GARRETT	G	(D	(B) CHEAPO CHEAPO	1971	MGM	US 4720	
KENNY ALTMAN	B	(CDE	(C) FOUR OF US	1971	REPRISE	US 2041	UK K44149
POINTER SISTERS	V	(D	(D) TARZANA KID	1974	REPRISE	US 2187	UK K54028
RITCHIE OLSON	CLAR	(D	(E) WELCOME BACK	1976	REPRISE	US 2249	UK K54074

(CONTINUED)

KELLY SHANAHAN	D	(D	DAVID LINDLEY	FDL	(D	RON KOSS	G	(D	JIM GORDON	D	(D
JERRY McKUEN	G	(D	LOWELL GEORGE	G V	(D	BOBBYE HALL	PERC	(D	BUDDY EMMONS	STEEL	(D
EMMYLOU HARRIS	V	(D	DAVID GRISMAN	MAND	(D	PHIL EVERLY	V	(D	PAUL HARRIS	K	(ABC
RY COODER	MAND G	(D	RICHARD BELL	K	(E	DAVID HUNGATE	B	(E	JEFF PORCARO	D	(E
MICHAEL OMARTIAN	K	(E	JEFF BAXTER	STEEL	(E	REGGIE KNIGHTON	G	(E	JON LIND	V	(E
MURRAY WEINSTOCK	PNO	(E	DALLAS TAYLOR	D	(C	JOHN BARBATA	D	(C	FELIX PAPPALARDI	B	(C
MAC REBENNACK	PNO	(C	ESSO STEEL BAND		(C						

SECOND LAYER — S65A

(A) FLESH AS A PROPERTY (EP)	197	TORCH	TOR 001
(B) STATE OF EMERGENCY (EP)	197	TORCH	TOR 006

SECOND VISION — S66

RIC SANDERS	VLN	(A	(A) FIRST STEPS	1980 CHRYSALIS	CHR 1289	
DAVE BRISTOW	K	(A				
JONATHAN DAVIE	B	(A	JOHN ETHERIDGE	G	(A	MICKEY BARKER D PERC(A

SECONDHAND — S67

KEN ELLIOT	K V	(AB	(A) REALITY	1968	POLYDOR	
ROB ELLIOT	V	(AB	(B) DEATH MAY BE YOUR SANTA CLAUS	1970	MUSHROOM	MRE 200
KIERAN O'CONNOR	PERC	(B				
GEORGE HART	V VLN	(B	MOGGY MEAD	G	(B	

THE SECRET — S67A

(A) THE SECRET	1979 OVAL	AMLH68504

SECRET AFFAIR — S68

IAN PAGE	V TPT K	(AB	(A) GLORY BOYS	1979 ISPY	ISPY1
DAVID CAIRNS	G V	(A	(B) BEHIND CLOSED DOORS	1980 ISPY	ISPY2
DENNIS SMITH	B V	(A			
SEB SHELTON	D	(A	DAVE WINTHROP	SAX	(A

SECRET OYSTER — S69

BO THRIGE ANDERSEN	D	(A	(A) FURTIVE PEARL	1973 P.I.	US	9003
JESS STAEHR	B	(BE	(A) SECRET OYSTER	1973 CBS	EURO	65769
CLAUS BØHLING	G	(ABE	(B) SEA SON	1974 CBS UK 80489	EURO	19009
MADS VINDING	B	(A	(B) SEA SON	1974 P.I.	US	9009
KENNETH KNUDSEN	K	(ABE	(C) VIDUNDERLIGE	1975 CBS	EURO	81044
FINN ZIEGLER	VLN	(B	(D) ORLAVER	1976 CHRISTIANA		P1
ERLIN CHRISTENSEN	CELLO	(B	(E) STRAIGHT TO THE KRANKENHAUS	1976 CBS	UK	80489
PALLE MIKKELBORG	TPT	(E				
KASPER WINDING	PERC	(BE	KARSTEN VOGEL SAX K (ABE HANS NIELSEN	VLN (B	BJARNE BOIE RASMUSSEN VLA(B
OLE STREENBERG	D	(BE				

SECTION — S70

DANNY KORTCHMAR	G	(ABC	(A) THE SECTION	1972 WB	UK	K46191
LELAND SKLAR	B	(AB	(B) FORWARD MOTION	1973 WB	UK	K46251
CRAIG DOERGE	K	(AB	(C) FORK IT OVER	1977 CAPITOL		11656
RUSS KUNKEL	D	(AB				
LEE PASTORA	PERC	(B	SERGIO	PERC	(B	

THE SEEDS — S71

SKY SAXON K V HCA		(ABCDE	(A) THE SEEDS	1966 GNP		GNP 2023
DARYL HOOPER	G	(BC	(B) WEB OF SOUND	1966 VOCALION 5VAN8062 +GNP	GNP 2033
RICK ANDRIDGE	D	(BC	(C) FUTURE	1967 VOCALION 5VAN8070 +GNP	GNP 2038
JAN SAVAGE	B	(BC	(D) MERLINS MUSIC BOX(RAW & ALIVE)	1967 GNP	GNP 2043
HARVEY SHARPE	B	(B	(E) FALLIN' OFF THE EDGE	196 GNP	GNP 2107
COOKER	G	(B	(F) SEEDS	1978 SONET	UK SNTF 746

BOB SEGARINI — S72

BOB SEGARINI	G V K	(AB	(A) GOTTA HAVE POP	1978 BOMB 7027 UK EPIC	EPC 83806
MIKE ST DENIS	G V	(AB	(B) GOODBYE L A	1979	UK EPIC	EPC 84086
PHIL ANGERS	B	(AB			
MARK BRONSON	D	(AB	DAVID HENMAN G (A DAVID CLAYTON THOMAS V (A GORD PATON PERC (A
GABOR HEGEDUS	G	(A	KIER BROWNSTONE B (A PAUL IRVINE SAX (A DREW WINTERS V K (AB
DAVID NORRIS ELYE	HRNS	(A	GARWOOD WALLACE G V (B WAYNE MILLS HRNS (B PET KASHUR G (B

BOB SEGER — S73

BOB SEGER	V	(ALL	(A) RAMBLIN' GAMBLIN' MAN	1969 CAPITOL US 172 UKRI77 CAPS 1013
DREW ABBOTT	G	(KLGJ	(B) NOAH	1969 CAPITOL US 236
ALTO REED	HRNS	(GKLJ	(C) MONGREL	1970 CAPITOL US 499 UKRI77 CAPS 1010
CHARLIE ALLEN MARTIN D		(GJKL	(D) BRAND NEW MORNING	1971 CAPITOL US 731
ROBYN ROBBINS	K	(GJKL	(E) SMOKIN' OPs	1972 REPRISE US 2109 UK K44214
GLEN FREY	G	(L	(E) SMOKIN' OPs	1977 CAPITOL RI 11746
CHRIS CAMPBELL	B	(GKLJ	(F) BACK IN 72	1973 REPRISE US 2126 UK K44227
DAVID TEEGARDEN	D	(L	(G) SEVEN	1974 REPRISE US 2184 UK K2184
DON FELDER	G	(L	(G) SEVEN	1977 CAPITOL RI 11748
BARRY BECKETT	K	(KL	(H) BEUTIFUL LOSER	1975 CAPITOL 11378
PETE CARR	G	(KL	(J) LIVE BULLET	1976 CAPITOL US 11523 UK ESTSP 16
JIMMY JOHNSON	H	(KL	(K) NIGHT MOVES	1977 CAPITOL US/UK 11557
DAVE HOOD	B	(KL	(L) STRANGER IN TOWN	1978 CAPITOL US/UK 11698
ROGER HAWKINS	D	(KL	(M) AGAINST THE WIND	1980 CAPITOL US/UK 12041
BILL PAYNE	K	(L	(EP) GET OUT OF DENVER	1977 reprise K12476
DOUG RILEY	K	(KL		
BOB SCHULTZ	K SAX V	(B	VANETTA FIELDS V (L	JAMES LAVELL V (L	CLYDIE KING V (L
EASLEY STANLEY CARTER	V	(L	SHIRLEY MATTHEWS V (L	GEORGE JACKSON V (L	LUTHER WATERS V (L
ORRIN WATERS	V	(L	JULIA TILLMAN V (L	MAXINE WILLARD WATERS V (L	BRANDY V (L
DAN HONAKER	B V G	(BC	PEP PERRINE D (BC	DAN WATSON K V (C	JERRY LUCK ACC(K
JOE MIQUELON	G	(K	SHARON DEE WILLIAMS V (K	LAUREL WARD V (K	RICK MANSKA K (GJ
DAVID BRIGGS	PNO	(G	TOMMY COGBILL B (G	KENNY BUTTREY D (G	DAVE DORAN G (G
TOM CARTMELL	SAX	(G	BILL MUELLER G (G	RANDY MEYERS D (G	CHARLIE McCOY G (G
JIM McCARTY	G	(G	JOHN HARRIS ORG (G	TOM NEME V G K(B	

ALAN SEIDLER — S73A

ALAN SEIDLER		(A	(A) THE DUKE OF OOK	19 BLUE GOOSE BG 2015

SELDOM SCENE

MIKE AULDRIDGE	G DOB(		(A) ACT ONE	19	REBEL	US	SLP1511
BEN ELDRIDGE	BAN (		(B) ACT TWO	19	REBEL	US	SLP1520
JOHN DUFFEY	V (		(C) ACT THREE	19	REBEL	US	SLP1536
JOHN STARLING	V (		(D) OLD TRAIN	19	REBEL	US	SLP1538
LINDA RONSTADT	V (F		(E) RECORDED LIVE	19	REBEL	US	SLP1547/48
			(F) THE SELDOM SCENE ALBUM	19	REBEL	US	SLP1561

SELECTOR

S74

NOEL DAVIES	G (A			(A) TOO MUCH PRESSURE		1980 TWO TONE	UK	TT 5002
DESMOND BROWN	K (A			(B) CELEBRATE THE BULLET		1981 CHRYSALIS	UK	CHR 1306
PAULINE BLACK	V (A							
CHARLEY ANDERSON	B (A	RICO RODRIGUEZ	TROM (A	DICK CUTHELL	TPT (A	JOE REYNOLDS		SAX (A
CHARLEY H BEMBRIDGE D (A		COMPTON AMANOR	G (A	ARTHUR HENDRICKSON V	(A	HILLFIELD BOYS CHOIR (A

SENSATION FIX

S74A

FRANCO FALSINI SYN G V (			(A) VISIONS FUGITIVES	197	ALL EARS		SF 11478
RICHARD URSILLO	B (		(B) FLYING TAPES	197	POLYDOR		2448 074
STEVE HEAD	K D (						
MARCO MARCOVECCHIO D (							

SEMUTA

S74B

| | (A)SEMUTA | 1979 LEE LAMBERT | LAM 101 |

JOHN SERRY

S75

JOHN SERRY	K V D (A		(A) EXHIBITION	1979	CHRYSALIS	UK	CHR 1230
BOB SHEPPARD	SAX (A						
BARRY FINNERTY	G (A	GORDON JOHNSON	B (A	FLIM JOHNSON	B (A	NANCY SHANX	V (A
CARLOS VEGA	D (A	GORDON GOTTLIEB	PERC (A				

SEVENTH WAVE

S76

KEN ELLIOT	K V (AB		(A) THINGS TO COME	1974 GULL	UK	GULP 1001
KIERAN O'CONNOR	PERC (AB		(B) PSI FI	1975 GULL	UK	GULP 1010
TONY UTER	PERC (B					
BRIAN GOULD	K (B	PEPI LEMER	V (B	CHRIS ANSON	SYN (B	PETER LEMER	K (B
STEVE COOK	B (B	HUGH BANTON	K (B	TONY ELLIOT	PERC (B

SEX PISTOLS

S77

JOHN ROTTEN LYDON V	(ABCDE12	(A) NEVER MIND THE BOLLOCKS	1977 VIRGIN UK V2086 US WB	3142
STEVE JONES	G	(ABCDE12	(B) GREAT ROCK'N'ROLL SWINDLE(DBL)	1978 VIRGIN	UK	VD2510
PAUL COOK	D	(ABCDE12	(C) SOME PRODUCT	1979 VIRGIN	UK	VR2
SID VICIOUS	B V	(ABC	(D) FLOGGING A DEAD HORSE	1979 VIRGIN	UK	V 2142
GLEN MATLOCK	B	(12	(E) GREAT ROCK'N'ROLL SWINDLE	1980 VIRGIN	UK	V 2168
NICK KENT	G V	(1	(1) 1975 (2) 1976/77
RONNIE BIGGS	V	(B	
MALCOLM McLAREN	V	(B	

SHA NA NA

S78

JOCKO MARCELLINO	D (C	(A) IS HERE TO STAY	1969 KAMA SUTRA	US	2010
LENNIE BAKER	SAX (C	(A) IS HERE TO STAY	1971 KAMA SUTRA	UK	2319 025
SCOTT POWELL	(	(A) IS HERE TO STAY	197 MODE	FR	9023
JOHNNY CONTARDO	K D (C	(A) IS HERE TO STAY	1974 KAMA SUTRA RI	UK	KSLP7003
DENNIS GREENE	(C	(B) SHA NA NA	1971 KAMA SUTRA	UK	2319 007
DON YORK	(C	(B) SHA NA NA	1971 KAMA SUTRA	US	2034
RITCH JOFFE	D (C	(B) SHA NA NA	1974 KAMA SUTRA RI	UK	KSLP7002
ELLIOT CAHN	G (	(C) THE NIGHT IS STILL YOUNG	1972 KAMA SUTRA	US	2050
CHRIS DONALD	G (	(C) THE NIGHT IS STILL YOUNG	1972 KAMA SUTRA	UK	2319 019
BRUCE CLARKE	B (C	(C) THE NIGHT IS STILL YOUNG	1974 KAMA SUTRA RI	UK	KSLP8001
SCOTT SIMON	K B (C	(D) GOLDEN AGE OF ROCK'N'ROLL	1973 KAMA SUTRA	UK	2623 102
ELLIOTT RANDALL	G (	(D) GOLDEN AGE OF ROCK'N'ROLL	197 K TEL	NE	495
TONY SARTINI	(	(E) FROM THE STREETS OF NEW YORK	1974 KAMA SUTRA	UK	2319 038
VINNIE TAYLOR	G (C	(E) FROM THE STREETS OF NEW YORK	1974 KAMA SUTRA	US	2075
GINO	G (C	(E) FROM THE STREETS OF NEW YORK	1974 KAMA SUTRA	UK	KSLP7004
JOHN BOWZER BAUMAN K (		(F) HOT SOX	1974 KAMA SUTRA	US	2600
HENRY GROSS	G (	(F) HOT SOX	1974 KAMA SUTRA	UK	KSLP7001
CHICO RYAN	(	(G) SHA NA NA NOW	1975 KAMA SUTRA	US	2603
		(H) BEST OF	1976 KAMA SUTRA	US	KSLP2609
		(J) ROCK'N'ROLL REVIVAL	1977 PYE	UK	GH 867

SHADES OF JOY

S78A

MARTIN FIERRO	WIND (A		(A) SHADES OF JOY	1969 FONTANA UK STL 5498 NL 887 807
JACKIE KING	G (A			
EDWARD ADAMS	B (A	JYMM YOUNG	K HRNS(A JOSE RODRIGUEZ	D (A	MILLIE FOSTER	V (A
LEE CHARLTON	VLN (A			

SHADOWFAX

S79

CHICK GREENBERG	WIND (A		(A) WATERCOURSE WAY	1976 PASSPORT	PPSD98013
PHIL MAGGINI	B (A			
DOUG MALUCHNIK	K (A	STUART NEVITT	D PERC(A GREG STINSON	G V (A

THE SHADOWS

S80

HANK MARVIN	G V (ALL	THE SHADOWS	1962 COLUMBIA UK (M)33SX1374 (S)SCX3414
BRUCE WELCH	G V (ALL	OUT OF THE SHADOWS	1962 COLUMBIA UK (M)33SX1458 (S)SCX3449
IAN SAMWELL	B (A	GREATEST HITS	1963 COLUMBIA UK (M)33sx1522 (S)SCX1522
TERRY SMART	D (A	DANCE WITH THE SHADOWS	1964 COLUMBIA UK (M)33SX1619 (S)SCX3511
JET HARRIS	B (BC	THE SOUND OF THE SHADOWS	1965 COLUMBIA UK (M)33SX1736 (S)SCX3554
TONY MEEHAN	D (B	MORE HITS	1965 COLUMBIA UK (M)33SX1791 (S)SCX3578
BRIAN BENNETT	D (CDEGIJ	SHADOW MUSIC	1966 COLUMBIA UK (M)33SX6041 (S)SCX6041
BRIAN LOCKING	B (D	JIGSAW	1967 COLUMBIA UK	SCX6148
JOHN ROSTILL	B (E	HANK,BRUCE,BRIAN & JOHN	1967 COLUMBIA UK	SCX6199
JOHN FARRAR	G V B(FGH	ESTABLISHED 1958	1968 COLUMBIA UK	SCX6282
ALAN JONES	B (HIJ	IT'LL BE ME	1969 STARLINE UK	SRS 5011
FRANCIS MONKMAN	K (H	SOMETHING ELSE	1969 STARLINE UK	SRS 5012
CLIFF HALL	K (IJ	SHADES OF ROCK	1970 COLUMBIA UK	SCX6420
DAVE LAWSON	SYN (J	MUSTANG	1972 MFP UK	MFP 5266
		THE BEST OF	1973 EMI IMP EURO	14804859

(CONTINUED)

SHADOWS

(A) 1958		THE BEST OF	197	EMI IMP EURO		05404300
(B) 1959		SHADOOGIE (TRIPLE)	19	EMI IMP EURO		154 061 129
(C) 1961		ROCKIN' WITH CURLY LEADS	1973	EMI		EMA 762
(D) 1962		SPECS APPEAL	1975	EMI		EMC 3066
(E) 1962		LIVE AT PARIS OLYMPIA	1975	EMI		EMC 3095
(F) 1970		RARITIES	1976	EMI		NUT 2
(G) 1973		THE SHADOWS	1975	EMBER		SE 8031
(H) 1977		TASTY	1977	EMI		EMC 3195
(I) 1979		20 GOLDEN GREATS	1977	EMI		EMTV 3
(J) 1980		BEST OF THE SHADOWS	1977	EMI		EMTV 33
		AT THE MOVIES	1978	MFP		50347
		CHANGE OF ADDRESS	1980	POLYDOR UK		2442 179
		STRING OF HITS	1979	EMI		EMC 3310

SHADOWS OF KNIGHT

JIM SOHNS	V	(ABC	(A) GLORIA	1966	DUNWICH	US	666
WARREN ROGERS	G	(ABC	(A) GLORIA (RI)	1979	RADAR UK	RAD 11	
JERRY McGEORGE	G	(ABC	(B) BACK DOOR MEN	1967	DUNWICH	US	667
TOM SCHIFFOUR	D	(ABC	(C) SHADOWS OF KNIGHT	1968	SUPER K	US	6002
JOE KELLEY	B	(ABC					

SHAFTESBURY

ROGER GRIGG	D K V(A	(A) THE LULL BEFORE THE STORM	1980	O K RECORDS		OKA001
DAVE MARTIN	B V (A					
PETER ROFFEY	G (A					

SHAGRAT THE VAGRANT

MICK FARREN	V (								
STEVE TOOK	V PERC(								
PAUL BUCKMASTER	CELLO(	RUSS HUNTER	B (	TWINK	D (	SID BISHOP	G (		
CORD REES	PNO (								

SHAKE

JOHN CALLIS	G	(A	(A) CULTURE SHOCK (EP)	1979	SIRE UK	SIR 4016	
SIMON TEMPLAR	B	(A					
ANGEL PATERSON	D	(A	TROY TATE	G (A			

SHAKERS

JANET SMALL	K V (A	(A) YANKEE REGGAE	1976	ASYLUM US7E1057	UK	K53036	
CHRIS SOLBERG	G V (A						
BILL WALLACE	G V (A	DON FULTON	B (A	RON RHODES	D (A		

SHAKIN' STREET

FABIENNE SHINE	V (A	(A) SHAKIN' STREET	1980	CBS UK	84115	
ELEWY	G (A					
ROSS THE BOSS	G (A	MIKE WINTER	B (A	JEAN LOU KALONOWSKI	D (A	

SHAKTI

JOHN McLAUGHLIN	G	(ABC	(A) SHAKTI	1976	CBS US 34162	UK	81388
L SHANKAR	VLN V(ABC		(B) HANDFUL OF BEAUTY	1977	CBS US 34372	UK	81664
ZAKIR HUSSAIN	PERC (ABC		(C) NATURAL ELEMENTS	1978	CBS US 34980	UK	82329
T H VINYAKRAM	PERC V(ABC						

SHAM 69

JIMMY PURSEY	V	(	(A) TELL US THE TRUTH	1978	POLYDOR UK	2383 491
ALBIE SLIDER	B	(	(A) TELL US THE TRUTH	1978	SIRE US	6060
DAVE TREGANNA	B	(	(B) THATS LIFE	1979	POLYDOR UK POLD5010+2442 158	
MARK CAIN	D	(	(C) HERSHAM BOYS	1979	POLYDOR UK POLD5025+2442 165	
DAVE PARROS	G	(	(D) THE GAME	1979	POLYDOR UK POLD5033+2442 173	
			(E) FIRST, THE BEST & THE LAST	1980	POLYDOR UK	

SHANGHAI

CLIFF BENNETT	V	(B	(A) SHANGHAI	1974	WB UK	K56093
BRIAN ALTERMAN	G	(B	(B) FALLEN HEROES	1976	THUNDERBIRD	THR 2000
MICK GREEN	G	(AB				
SPEEDY KING	B	(AB	PETE KIRCHER	D (AB	CHUCK BEDFORD V HCA(A	MIKE DEMIAN	K B (A
BARBARA BEDFORD	V	(A				

SHANGO

RICHIE HERNANDEZ	G	(A	(A) TRAMPIN'	19	DUNHILL US	D5 50082
JOE BARILE	D	(A				
MALCOLM EVAN	B	(A	TOMMY REYNOLDS	PERC K(A		

SHANGRILAS

MARY WEISS	V	(	LEADER OF THE PACK	1964	RED BIRD	US	RB 20101
MARYANN GANSER	V	(	SHANGRILAS '65	1965	RED BIRD	US	RB 20104
MARGIE GANSER	V	(	I CAN NEVER GO HOME	1966	RED BIRD	US RI	RB 20104
BETTY WEISS	V	(	GOLDEN HITS	1966	MERCURY	US 61099 UK	20096
			GOLDEN HITS	1973	PHILIPS		6336 215
			TEEN ANGUISH VOL 2	197	CHARLY	UK	CRM 2003
			(EP) REMEMBER (WALKING IN THE SAND)	1976	CHARLY	UK	CEP 109

DEL SHANNON

DEL SHANNON	HATS OFF TO LARRY	1963	LONDON UK 8071
	RUNAWAY	1963	LONDON UK 2402 US BIG TOP 1303
	LITTLE TOWN FLIRT	1963	LONDON UK 8091 US BIG TOP 1308
	HANDY MAN	1965	STATESIDE UK 10115 AMY US 8003
	SINGS HANK WILLIAMS	1965	STATESIDE UK 10130 AMY US 8004
	1,661 SECONDS OF	1965	STATESIDE UK 10140 AMY US 8006
	THIS IS MY BAG	196	LIBERTY UK SLBY1320 US LST 7452
	TOTAL COMMITMENT	1966	LIBERTY UK SLBY1335 US LST 7479
	FURTHER ADVENTURES OF C WESTOVER	196	LIBERTY US LST 7539
	BEST OF	1967	DOT US 25824
	VINTAGE YEARS	19	SIRE US 3708/2
	DEL SHANNON SINGS	19	POST US 9000
	10TH ANNIVERSARY	1971	SUNSET US 50211
	LIVE IN ENGLAND	1973	UA UK UAS29474 US LA 151
	BEST OF	1973	POLYDOR EURO 2870 323
	VERY BEST OF	1975	CONTEMPO CRMD1001

(CONTINUED)

DEL SHANNON

	AND THE MUSIC PLAYS ON	1978 SUNSET	UK	SLS50412
	(EP) DELS OWN FAVOURITES	196 LONDON	UK	REX 1383
	(EP) No2	196 LONDON	UK	REX 1346

S91

SHANTI

ASHISH KHAN	SAROD(A	(A) SHANTI	1971 ATLANTIC	US	SD 8302	
ZAKIR HUSSAIN	TABLA(A					
NEIL SEIDEL	G (A	STEVE HAEHL G V (A STEVE LEACH	V D (A FRANK LUPICA D (A			
PRANESH KHAN	TABLA(A					

S92

SHARKS

CHRIS SPEDDING	G (AB	(A) FIRST WATER	1973 ISLAND UK ILPS9233			
ANDY FRASER	B (A	(B) JAB IT IN YOUR EYE	1974 ISLAND UK ILPS9271		US MCA415	
SNIPS	V (AB					
MARTY SIMON	D (AB	NICK JUDD K (B BUSTA CHERRY JONES B (B				

S92A

DEE DEE SHARP

DEE DEE SHARP	V (ALL	(A) ITS MASHED POTATO TIME	196 CAMEO	US	C 1018
		(B) SONGS OF FAITH	196 CAMEO	US	C 1022
		(C) ALL THE HITS	196 CAMEO	US	C 1032
		(D) DO THE BIRD	196 CAMEO	US	C 1050
		(E) BIGGEST HITS	196 CAMEO	US	C 1062
		(F) DOWN MEMORY LANE	196 CAMEO	US	C 1074
		(G) 18 GOLDEN HITS	196 CAMEO	US	C 2002
		(H) THE CAMEO PARKWAY SESSIONS	1979 LONDON	UK	HAU 8514

S92B

BILLY JOE SHAVER

BILLY JOE SHAVER	V (	(A) OLD FIVE & DIMERS LIKE ME	1974 MONUMENT KZ32293		MG 7621
		(B) WHEN I GET MY WINGS	1976 CAPRICORN	US	CPN 0171
		(C) GYPSY BOY	197 CAPRICORN	US	CPN 0192

S92C

ROCKY SHARPE

	(A) RAMA LAMA (REPLAYS)	1979 CHISWICK	UK	CWK 3010
	(B) ROCK IT TO MARS	1980 CHISWICK	UK	CWK 3013
	(C) DRIP DROP (EP) (RAZORS)	19 ACE	UK	SW6

S93

SHEERWATER

GWEN TAYLOR	V (	
VAUGHN PEARCE	G (	
ROY HOVEY	G (	ALAN METCALFE B (TONY ECCLES D (

S94

PETE SHELLEY

PETE SHELLEY	V (	(A) SKY YEN	1980 GROOVY STP2

S94A

SHEPPARDS

(A) SHEPPARDS	1980 SOLID SMOKE US CS4

S95

SHEPSTONE & DIBBENS

MICHAEL SHEPSTONE	V G PERC
PETER DIBBENS	G V

S95A

PLUTO SHERVINGTON

(A) PLUTO	1976 OPAL PL1002

S95B

SHIELDS

FRANKIE ERVIN	V (A
JESSE BELVIN	(A
JOHNNY GUITAR WATSON	G (A CHARLES WRIGHT (A

(A) 1958

S96

JOHNNY SHINES

JOHNNY SHINES	G V (ALL	(A) LAST NIGHTS DREAM	1969 BLUE HORIZON	UK	763212
WALTER HORTON	HCA (A	(B) MASTERS OF MODERN BLUES	1969 TESTAMENT	US	2212
WILLIE DIXON	B (A	(C) JOHNNY SHINES & BIG WALTER HORTON	1969 TESTAMENT	US	2217
CLIFTON JAMES	D (A	(D) STANDING AT THE CROSSROADS	1969 TESTAMENT	US	2221
OTIS SPANN	PNO (AC	(E) CHICAGO BLUES FESTIVAL	1972 BLACK & BLUE		33502
LEE JACKSON	B (C	(F) JOHNNY SHINES & CO	1972 BIOGRAPH	US	12048
PRINCE CANDY	B (C	(G) SITTING ON TOP	1972 BIOGRAPH	US	12044
RICHARD BAKER	G (H	(H) COUNTRY BLUES	1974 XTRA	UK	XTRA1142
ROBERT LOCKWOOD	(L	(J) JOHNNY SHINES	1974 ADVENT		2803
PHILIP WALKER	G (J	(K) HEY BA BA RE BOP	1978 ROUNDER		2020
DAVID II	SAX (J	(L) DUST MY BROOM	1980 FLYRIGHT	UK	FLY 563
NATHANIEL DOVE	PNO (J				
CHARLES JONES	B (J	DOWNY MURL D (J FRED BELOW D (C BILL BROWN B (C			
LUTHER ALLISON	G (C	DON AUDET HCA (H BOB DERKACH B (H			

S96A

THE SHIP

(A) THE SHIP	1972 ELEKTRA	UK	K42122
(A) A CON FOLK MUSIC JOURNEY	1972 ELEKTRA	USEKS	75036

S97

ELLEN SHIPLEY

ELLEN SHIPLEY	V (AB	(A) ELLEN SHIPLEY	1979 RCA US BXL1 3428 UK	FL13428
RALPH SCHUCKETT	K V (B	(B) BREAKING THROUGH THE ICE AGE	1980 RCA	UK PL13626
RICHIE CERNIGLIA	G V (B			
NICHOLAS LYNN	G V (B	STEVE VITALE B V (B DENNY McDERMOTT	D V (B ALFA ANDERSON V (B	
ONY KAYE	V (B	JEAN PAUL GASPAR V (B ROBIN LUMLEY	SYN (B	

S98

SHIRELLES

ADDIE HARRIS	V (	(A) TONIGHTS THE NIGHT	1961 SCEPTER	US	501
SHIRLEY ALSTON	V (	(A) TONIGHTS THE NIGHT	1961 WAND	UK	1001
DORIS KENNER	V (	(B) SHIRELLES SING	1961 SCEPTER	US	502
BEVERLY LEE	V (	(B) SHIRELES SING	1961 TOP RANK	UK	35 115
		(C) BABY IT'S YOU	1962 SCEPTER	US	504
		(C) BABY IT'S YOU	1962 STATESIDE	UK	10006
		(D) & KING CURTIS TWIST PARTY	196 SCEPTER	US	505
		(E) GREATEST HITS	196 SCEPTER	US	507
		(E) GREATEST HITS	1963 STATESIDE	UK	10041
		(F) FOOLISH LITTLE GIRL	196 SCEPTER	US	511
		(G) SING THE GOLDEN OLDIES	196 SCEPTER	US	516
		(H) GREATEST HITS VOL2	196 SCEPTER	US	560
		(J) SPONTANEOUS COMBUSTION	196 SCEPTER	US	562
		(K) REMEMBER WHEN	196 SCEPTER	US	2 599

(CONTINUED)

(CONTINUED)

SHIRELLES — S98

(L) REMEMBER WHEN VOL 1	19	WAND			1009
(M) REMEMBER WHEN VOL 2	19	WAND			1010
(N) ETERNALLY SOUL	1970	WAND	UK		WNS 4
(O) HAPPY IN LOVE	197	RCA US LSP4581	UK		SF8237
(P) SHIRELLES	1972	RCA	UK		SF8279
(Q) SWINGS THE MOST	19	PRICEWISE	US		4001
(R) SING THEIR BEST	19	SPRINGBOARD	US		4006
(S) VERY BEST OF	19	UA	US		LA 340
(T) GOLDEN HOUR	1973	PYE	UK		GH 824

SHIRLEY & CO — S98A

(A) SHAME SHAME SHAME	1975	PHILIPS		6310 604

SHIRLEY & LEE — S99

SHIRLEY GOODMAN	V	(ALL	
LEONARD LEE	V	(ALL	

(A) LET THE GOOD TIMES ROLL	19	JAYBOY		JSX 2005
" " " " "	19	ALADDIN		807
" " " " "	19	SCORE	US	4023
" " " " "	1960	WARWICK	US	2028
" " " " "	19	IMPERIAL		9179
" " " " "	1975	UA	US	UALA 069
LEGENDARY MASTERS	19	UA	US	UALA 026

SHIRTS — S100

ANNIE GOLDEN	V	(ABC	(A) THE SHIRTS	1978	HARVEST	UK	SHSP4089
ART LOMONICA	G V K	(ABC	(A) THE SHIRTS	1978	CAPITOL	US	SW 11791
RONNIE ARDITO	G V K	(ABC	(B) STREET LIGHT SHINE	1979	HARVEST	UK	SHSP4104
JOHN PICCOLO	G V K	(ABC	(C) INNER SLEEVE	1980	CAPITOL	US	SW 12085
ROBERT RACIOPPO	G	(ABC					

LYLE DEDRICK WIND (B URBIE GREEN WIND (B DIANA HALPRIN VLN (B PAUL EISLER WIND(B
HARVEY ESTRIN FLT (B DAVID TOFANI WIND (B JOHN CRISCIONE D V(ABC

SHIVA'S HEAD BAND — S101

SPENCER PERSKIN	V VLN G	(	(A) TAKE ME TO THE MOUNTAINS	19	CAPITOL	US	538
SUZY PERSKIN	V ORG	(	(B) COMING TO A HEAD	19	ARMADILLO	US	NO No
BRIAN'RED' MOORE	B	(	(C) YESTERDAYS	1978	APE	US	1001
JERRY BRAZIL	D	(					
ROBERT FLYNN JR	G	(					

SHOCKING BLUE — S101A

CORNELIUS VAN DER BEEK	G(A	(A) SHOCKING BLUE	1969 PENNY FARTHING UK PELS500 METRONOME 15373		
MARIK A VERES	V (A	(B) SCORPIOS DANCE	1969 PENNY FARTHING UK PELS510		
KASSJE VAN DER WAL	B (A				
ROBBY VAN LEEUWEN	G (A				

SHOES — S102

GARY. KLEBE	G V (ABC	(A) BLACK VINYL SHOES	1978 PVC 7904 + BLACK VINYL 51477		
JEFF MURPHY	G V (ABC	(A) BLACK VINYL SHOES	1979 SIRE	UK	SRK 6075
JOHN MURPHY	V B (ABC	(B) PRESENT TENSE	1979 ELEKTRA US 6E244 UK		K52187
SKIP MEYER	D (ABC	(C) TONGUE TWISTER	1980 ELEKTRA		

SHOES FOR INDUSTRY — S102A

BASSETT DAVIES	V SAX(A	(A) TALK LIKE A WHELK	1980 FRIED EGG		FRY 1
JOHN SCHOFIELD	D (A				
ANDY BOOT	G (A	TIM NORFOLK G (A STEVE LONNEN	B (A LAZLO	K V(A	

SHOOT — S102B

CRAIG COLLINGE	D (A	(A) ON THE FRONTIER	1973 EMI US 11229 UK EMA '%£	
DAVE GREENE	G V (A			
JIM McCARTY	K V (A	BILL RUSSELL B (A		

SHOOTER — S103

DAVE MATTHEWS	G V (A	(A) SHOOTER	1978 EMI UK	INS3026
STEVE ST CLAIR	G V (A			
JOHN TOWE	D PERC(A	SPENCER SHIRES K G V(A SIMON JAMES DUNN B V(A		

SHOOTING STAR — S103A

STEVE THOMAS	D (A	(A) SHOOTING STAR	1979 VIRGIN UK	V 2130
RON VERLIN	K (A			
CHARLES WALTZ V VLN K	(A VAN McCLAIN	G V (A GARY WEST	V K G D(A	

BRIAN SHORT — S103B

BRIAN SHORT	V (A	(A) ANYTHING FOR A LAUGH	1971 TRANSATLANTIC UK	TRA 245
ALAN WHITE	D (A			
MAX MIDDLETON	K (A	KEN CRADDOCK G K V (A RAY COOPER	PERC (A ED SPEVOCK	PERC(A
PETE KIRTLEY	G MAND V (A	COLIN GIBSON B (A LYN DOBSON	WIND (A COLERIDGE GOODE	B (A

WAYNE SHORTER — S104

WAYNE SHORTER	SAX (ALL	(A) NIGHT DREAMER	1964 BLUENOTE		US	BST 84173
MICHELIN PRELL	D (L	(B) JU JU	1964 BLUENOTE		US	BST 84182
MIROSLAV VITOUS	G (HL	(C) SPEAK NO EVIL	1965 BLUENOTE		US	BST 84194
CHICK COREA	K (HL	(D) ALL SEEING EYE	1966 BLUENOTE		US	BST 84219
RON CARTER	B (L	(E) ADAMS APPLE	1966 BLUNOTE		US	BST 84232
DAVE HOLLAND	B G (L	(F) SCHIZOPHRENIA	1968 BLUNOTE UK BN540026		US	BST 84297
JOHN McLAUGHLIN	G (HL	(G) ODYSSEY OF ISKA	1970 BLUENOTE		US	BST 84363
AIRTO MORIERA	PERC (M	(H) SUPER NOVA	1970 BLUENOTE UK BN540028		US	BST 84332
MILTON NASCIMENTO	(M	(I) SHORTER MOMENTS	19 TRIP		US	5009
SONNY SHARROCK	G (H	(J) SECOND GENESIS	19 VEE JAY		US	
JACK DE JOHNETTE	D (H	(K) WAYNE SHORTER	1974 GNP		US	GNP522075
MARIA BOOKER	V (H	(L) MOTO GROSSO FEIO	1975 BLUENOTE		US	BNLA 014
WALTER BOOKER	G (H	(M) NATIVE DANCER	1975 ERIC UK 80721		US	33418
		(N) ETCETERA	1981 LIBERTY UK LBR 1037			

SHOT GUN — S104A

(A) SHOTGUN	1977 ABC	US		ABCD 979
(B) GOOD,BAD & FUNKY	197 ABC	US		1060
(C) SHOTGUN	197 ABC	US		1118

SHOTGUN EXPRESS — S105

PETER BARDENS	K (	(A) SHOTGUN EXPRESS (EP)	196 COLUMBIA FR	ESRF1864
DAVE AMBROSSE	B (			
PETER GREEN	G (	MICK FLEETWOOD D (ROD STEWART	V (PHIL SAWYER	G (
JOHN MOORSHEAD	G (	BERYL MARSDEN V (		

[373]

SHOW OF HANDS

RICK CUTLER	D	(A	(A) FORMERLY ANTHRAX	1970 ELEKTRA		EKS74084
JACK JACOBSEN	K	(A				
JERRY McCANN	FLT G V	(A				

SHOWADDYWADDY

			(A) SHOWADDYWADDY	1974 BELL	UK	BELLS	248
			(B) STEP TWO	1975 BELL	UK	BELLS	256
			(C) TROCADERO	1976 BELL	UK	SYBKL	8003
WITH BJ COLE	STEEL	(E	(D) SHOWADDYWADDY	1977 MFP	UK		50353
JEFF DALY	SAX	(E	(E) RED STAR	1977 ARISTA	UK SPARTY	1023	
JOHN ACOCK	PNO	(E	(F) GREATEST HITS	1978 ARISTA	UK	ARTY	145
MARTYN FORD ORCHESTRA		(E	(G) CREPES & DRAPES	1979 ARISTA	UK	ARTV	3
			(H) BRIGHT LIGHTS	1980 ARISTA	UK SPART	1142	

SHUSHA

SHUSHA	V	(ALL	(A) PERSIAN LOVE SONGS & MYSTIC CHANTS	1973 LYRICORD LLST7235 +TANGENT	108		
G T MOORE	G K	(CDEF	(B) SONG OF LONG TIME LOVERS	1972 TANGENT		TGS114	
MARTIN HAYWARD	G	(CDE	(C) SHUSHA	1974 UA	UK	UAS29575	
CHRIS LAURENCE	B	(DE	(D) THIS IS THE DAY	1974 UA	UK	UAS29684	
TOM WHYTE	B	(CE	(E) BEFORE THE DELUGE	1975 UA	UK	UAS29879	
TERRY WILSON	B	(E	(F) FROM EAST TO WEST	1978 TANGENT		TGS	138
RICHIE BULL	BANJO	(E	(G) HERE I LOVE YOU	1980 RHAPSODY		RHAP	2
B J COLE	STEEL	(E					

TONY BRAUNAGEL	PERC	(E	BRIAN GASCOIGNE	K ACC	(E	RABBIT BUNDRICK	K	(E	GERRY CONWAY	D (E
DUSTER BENNETT	HCA	(E	THUNDERTHIGHS	V	(E	TIM JONES	PERC K	(E	JACK EMBLOW	ACC (E
GEORGE LARNYOH	HRNS	(E	EDDIE QUANSAH	HRNS	(E	PETER VANDER PUIJE	HRNS	(E	BILL POVEY OCCARINA	(E
ROY CARTER	WIND	(E	FRANK CLARKE	B	(B	MARTIN KERSHAW	G	(B	DUNCAN LAMONT	FLT (AB
DAVID SNELL	HARP	(B	JOHNNY DEANE	D	(B	STANLEY MYERS	PNO	(B	GRAHAM MATTHEWS	D(C
PAUL ROBINSON	D	(F	KUMU HARADA	B	(F	JAMES LASCELLES	K	(F	BROTHER JAMES	PERC(F
BAGER AMINI	D	(F	BRIAN SMITH	FLT	(F	CHAKO YAMASHTA	VLN	(F	PAUL BUCKMASTER	SYN(F
MOX	HCA	(D	BEHBOUDI	ZARB	(D	PAT DONALDSON	B	(D	FRANK RICOTTI	PERC(D
JOHN KIRKPATRICK	ACC	(DG	RICHARD BAILEY	D	(G	DARRYL LE QUE	PERC	(G	PATRICK TISON	G (G
LESLEY DUNCAN	V	(G	JOHN McKENZIE	B	(G	J A GARDET	K	(G	DAVID WINTHROP	SAX (G
GAYLE CUNNINGHAM	V	(G								

SIDE EFFECT

	(A) SIDE EFFECT	197 FANTASY	US	9491
	(B) GOIN' BANANAS	1978 FANTASY FTA 3008 US		9537
	(C) WHAT YOU NEED	197 FANTASY	US	9513

SIDE WINDER

STUART SMITH	G	(	(A) ALL WOUND UP	1979 TANK		332
FRED SCARRET	G	(				
NEIL HARVEY	V	(	STEVE McLAUGHLIN B (YATTA YATES	D (		

BEN SIDRAN

BEN SIDRAN	V PNO	(ALL	(A) FEEL YOUR GROOVE	1971 CAPITOL	US	ST 825	
CLYDE STUBBLEFIELD	D	(BCD	(B) I LEAD A LIFE	1972 BLUE THUMB	US	BTS	40
GEORGE BROWN	D	(BC	(C) DONT LET GO	1972 BLUE THUMB	US	BTS 6012	
PHIL UPCHURCH	D G B	(BCDEF	(D) PUTTIN' IN TIME ON PLANET EARTH	1973 BLUE THUMB	US	BTS	55
CURLEY JAMES COOKE	G	(ABCDE	(E) FREE IN AMERICA	1976 ARISTA	US	AL 4081	
JERRY ALEXANDER	HCA	(C	(F) DOCTOR IS IN	1977 ARISTA SPARTY1022 US		AL 4131	
BUNKY GREEN	SAX	(C	(G) A LITTLE KISS IN THE NIGHT	1978 ARISTA SPART 1064 US		AB 4178	
SONNY SEALS	SAX	(CE					

KIP MERKLEIN	B	(C	RANDY FULLERTON	B	(F	JIM PETERMAN	ORG	(CD	TOM PIAZZA	D (C
RICHARD DAVIS	B	(F	CHUCK DOMANICO	B	(F	JOHN GUERIN	D	(F	TONY WILLIAMS	D (DF
BLUE MITCHELL	TPT	(ABFG	LARRY CARLTON	G	(F	RAY ARMONDO	PERC	(F	DAVID WOODFORD	(G
PHIL WOODS	SAX	(G	GARY MALLABER	D PERC	(AF	GAVIN CHRISTOPHER	V	(BE	CHEEBA SWITZER	V (B
JOHNNY ALMOND	FLT	(B	BRUCE BOTNICK	V	(B	CURT ROADS	SYN	(B	DENNIS OLIVER	B (B
TIM DAVIS	CONGA	(BD	CHARLES DAVIS	SAX	(B	BOB FOLKEDAHL	HRNS	(B	HRN(B	
JIM GORDON	SAX	(B	JIM KELTNER	D	(A	SANDY KONIKOFF	PERC	(A	JUDY SIDRAN	V (A
BOZ SCAGGS	G	(A	PETER FRAMPTON	G	(A	GREG RIDLEY	B	(A	CHRIS DRISCOE	SAX(A
DAVID BROWN	B	(A	GEORGE RAINS	D	(A	MIMI FARINA MELVIN	V	(A	CHARLIE WATTS	D (A
BILL PERKINS	SAX	(D	LAUDIR DE OLIVEIRA	PERC	(D	JOSE SOARES	PERC	(D	STEVE MILLER	G (D
JESSE ED DAVIS	G	(AG	ABE LABORIEL	B	(G	ARTHUR ADAMS	G	(G	GERALD JOHNSON	G (G
ROSE BUTLER	V	(G	MAX GRONENTHAL	B	(G	MIKE FINNIGAN	K V	(G	JAY GRAYDON	G (G
GARY COLEMAN	PERC	(G	BOB GLAUB	B	(G	GARY ZAPPA	B	(E	BILL MEEKER	D (E
HENRY GIBSON	PERC	(E	MARY ANN STEWART	V	(E	RICHARD TEE	K	(E	WOODY SHAW	TPT(E
RANDY BRECKER	HRNS	(E	MICHAEL BRECKER	HRNS	(E	KITTY HAYWOOD	V	(E	VIVIAN HAYWOOD	V (E

PAUL SIEBEL

PAUL SIEBEL	G V	(ALL	(A) WOODSMOKE AND ORANGES	1970 ELEKTRA EKS 74064 RI UK K42040		
DAVID BROMBERG	G	(C	(B) JACK KNIFE GYPSY	1971 ELEKTRA EKS 74081 RI UK K42076		
GARY WHITE		(C	(C) LIVE	1981 RAG BABY	UK	1006

DAN SIEGEL

DAN SIEGEL	K V	(A	(A) THE HOT SHOT	1980	INNER CITY US	1C1111
GARRY HAGBERG	G	(A				
ROB THOMAS	B VLN	(A	GARY HOBBS	D (A	JEFF HOMAN	SAX (A MARC SIEGEL V (A
EDWARD McMANUS	HRNS	(A	CINDY McMANUS	HRNS (A	SUE DAVIS	HARP (A

SIEGEL SCHWALL BAND

CORKY SIEGEL	V K HCA	(ALL	(A) SIEGEL SCHWALL BAND	1966 VANGUARD		VSD 79235	
JIM SCHWALL	G V	(ALL	(B) SAY SIEGEL SCHWALL	1967 VANGUARD		VSD 79249	
JOS DAVIDSON	B	(ABCDEFGHIJ	(C) SHAKE	1968 VANGUARD UK SVRL19044+VSD 79289			
RUSS CHADWICK	D	(ABCDJ	(D) SIEGEL SCHWALL 70	1970 VANGUARD		VSD 6562	
JACK DAWSON	B	(BCDJ	(E) THE SIEGEL SCHWALL BAND	1971 WOODEN NICKEL	US	WNS	1002
SHELDON IRA PLOTKIN	D	(EFGHIK	(E) THE SIEGEL SCHWALL BAND	1971 RCA	UK	SF	8246
ROLLOW RADFORD	B	(EFGHIK	(F) SLEEPY HOLLOW	1972 WOODEN NICKEL	US	WNS	1010
SAN FRANCISCO SYM ORCH		(K	(F) SLEEPY HOLLOW	1972 RCA		LSP	10394
			(G) 953 WEST	1973 TELDEC		1 0121	
			(H) LIVE LAST SUMMER	1974 TELDEC		6 24215	
			(H) LIVE LAST SUMMER	197 WOODEN NICKEL	US	WNS 1 288	
			(I) RIP SIEGEL SCHWALL	1974 TELDEC		6 24217	
			(I) RIP SIEGEL SCHWALL	1974 WOODEN NICKEL	US	WNS 1 554	
			(J) BEST OF	1974 VANGUARD		VSD 79336	
			(K) THREE PIECES FOR BLUES BAND & ORCH	1974 POLYDOR 2530 309			
			(K) S S B & SYM ORCH	1980 POLYDOR 2344 157		2261 031	

SIERRA S114

SNEAKY PETE	STEEL (A	(A) SIERRA	1977 MERCURY	US	SRM1 1179
GIB GUILBEAU	FDL (A				

DAVITT SIGERSON S114A

DAVITT SIGERSON	V (A	(A) DAVITT SIGERSON	1980 ISLAND		ILPS 7011
KENWOOD DENNARD	D (A				
RICHARD CROOKS	D (A	JIMMY RIPPETOE G B (A GORDON JOHNSON	B (A NED ALBRIGHT	PNO (A

BUNNY SIGLER S115

BUNNY SIGLER	K (A	(A) LET THE GOOD TIMES ROLL	19 PARKWAY	US	PS 50000
RAYMOND EARL	B (F	(B) THAT'S HOW LONG I'LL BE LOVING	1974 PHILADELPHIA	UK 80253	US 32859
KIM MILLER	G (F	(C) KEEP SMILIN'	197 PHILADELPHIA		US 33249
SCOTTY MILLER	D (F	(D) MY MUSIC	19 PHILADELPHIA	UK 81755	US 34267
DENNIS RICHARDSON	K (F	(E) LET ME PARTY WITH YOU	1978 SALSOUL	UK	SSLP 1502
LARRY DAVIS	PERC V(F	(F) I'VE ALWAYS WANTED TO SING	1979 SALSOUL	UK	SSLP 1512
JIMMY SIGLER	K V (F				
CHARLES COLLINS	PERC (F	CARLA BENSON V (F EVETTE BENTON	V (F BARBARA INGRAM	V (F

SILENT TYPES S115A

	(A) WAR ECONOMY(EP)	1980 DOUBLE DOSE	SHOT 13

SILICON TEENS S115B

DARRYL	V (A	(A) MUSIC FOR PARTIES	19 MUTE	UK	STUMM 2
JACKI	SYN (A				
PAUL	PERC (A	DIANE SYN (A			

JUDEE SILL S116

JUDEE SILL	G V (ABC	(A) JUDEE SILL	1971 ASYLUM	UK	SYLA 8751
CLYDIE KING	V (A	(B) HEART FOOD	1973 ASYLUM	UK	SYL 9006
VANETTA FIELDS	V (A	(C) TULIPS FROM AMSTERDAM	1979		
RITA COOLIDGE	V (A				
DAVID BEARDEN	(B	LYNN BLESSING (B GENE CIPRIANO	(B VINCE DE ROSA	(B
DOUG DILLARD	(B	OMA DRAKE (B ASSA DRORI	(B BUDDY EMMONS	(B
JESSE EHRLICH	(B	CHRIS ETHRIDGE (B RON FULSOM	(B HARRIS GOLDMAN	(B
JIM GORDON	(B	BOBBYE HALL PERC (B GLORIA JONES	V (B RAY KELLY	(B
WILLIAM KURASCH	(B	LEONARD MALARSKY (B SPOONER OLDHAM	(B RICHARD PERISSI	(B
BILL PLUMMER	(B	EMIL RICHARDS (B RALPH SCHAEFFER	(B LOUIE SHELTON	(B
DAVID SCHWARTZ	(B	CAROLYN WILLIS (B TIBOR ZELIG	(B	

SILLY WIZARD S116A

	(A) SILLY WIZARD	1976 XTRA	UK	XTRA 1158
	(B) CALEDONIA'S SONS	1978 HIGHWAY		SHY 7004
	(C) SO MANY PARTINGS	1979 HIGHWAY	UK	SHY 7007

SILVER S117

JOHN BATDORF	G V (A	(A) SILVER	1976 ARISTA US 4076 UK	ARTY 144
BRENT MYDLAND	V K (A			
RICK GILES	(A	GREG COLLIER G V (A HARRY STINSON	V D(A TOM LEADON	B V (A

SILVERADO S118

EARL GOODWIN	G V (A	(A) SILVERADO	1976 RCA	US	APLI 1792
CARL SHILLO	G V (A	(B) TAKING IT ALL IN STRIDE	19 RCA	US	APLI 2421
JAY D MANESS	G (A				
RON TUTT	D (A	VICTOR FELDMAN PERC VIBES(A AL CASEY	G MAND(A ALAN ESTES	PERC(A
JAMES B GORDON	D (A	EMORY GORDY B (A TOM HENSLEY	K (A	

SILVERHEAD S119

MICHAEL DES BARRES	V (AB	(A) SILVERHEAD	1972 PURPLE UK TPSA 7506 US MCA 306
NIGEL HARRISON	B (B	(B) SIXTEEN & SAVAGED	1973 PURPLE UK TPSA 7511 US MCA 391
ROD DAVIES	PERC V G (B		
PETE THOMPSON	D K (B	ROBBIE BLUNT G (B	

SHEL SILVERSTEIN S120

SHEL SILVERSTEIN	(ALL	(A) HAIRY JAZZ	1961 ELEKTRA	US	176
RAY SAWYER	V (G	(B) INSIDE FOLK MUSIC	1962 ATLANTIC	US	SD 8072
DENNIS LOCORRIERE	V (G	(C) IM SO GOOD , I DONT HAVE TO BRAG	196 CADET	US	4052
JAY DAVID	(G	(D) DRAIN MY BRAIN	196 CADET	US	4054
GEORGE CUMMINGS	(G	(E) CROUCHING ON THE OUTSIDE	197 JANUS		2JLS 3052
BILLY FRANCIS	(G	(F) A BOY NAMED SUE	1968 RCA	US	LSP 4192
RIK ELSWIT	(G	(G) FREAKIN' AT THE FREAKERS BALL	1973 CBS UK 65452 US	31119
AMOS GARRETT	G (J	(G) FREAKIN' AT THE FREAKERS BALL	1979 CBS RI UK 31766	
JANCE GARFAT	(G (H	(H) SONGS & STORIES	1978 PARACHUTE	US	RRLP9007
MIKE FINNIGAN	(G	(J) GREAT CONCH TRAIN ROBBERY	1980 FLYING FISH	US	
ART TWAIN	(G				
JELLY ROLL TURNER	(G	TURK MURPHY (G CHARLES H PETERSON	(G CHARLES DAY	(G
DELL DUCKWORTH	(G	CLYDE GRAVES (G PHILLIP HOWE	(G JAMES MAIHACH	(G
LEON OAKLEY	(G	RICHARD SHUBB (G FRED MERGY	(G SAM BUSH	(J
JOHN HARTFORD	(J	D J FONTANA D (J PIG ROBBINS	K (J	

GENE SIMMONS S121

GENE SIMMONS	G V (A	(A) GENE SIMMONS	CASABLANCA	UK	NBLP 7120
ALLEN SCHWARZBERG	D (A				
NEIL JASON	B (A	ELLIOTT RANDALL G (A SEAN DELANEY	PERC V(A BOB SEGER	V (A
JOE PERRY	(A	HELEN REDDY V (A MITCH WEISSMAN	(A RICHIE RANNO	(A
GORDON GRODY	V (A	RICK NIELSEN G (A MICHAEL DES BARRES	V (A DIVA GRAY	V (A
KATE SAPAL	V (A	FRAN EISENBERG V (A CAROLYN RAY	V (A ERIC TROYER	PNO(A
JANIS IAN	(A	STEVE LACEY G (A JOHN SHANE HOWELL	G (A RICHARD GERSTEIN	PERC(A
JEFF BAXTER	G (A	DONNA SUMMER V (A JOE PECORINO	(A CHER	(A

JEFF SIMMONS S122

JEFF SIMMONS	B V K(AB	(A) NAKED ANGELS SOUNDTRACK	1969 STRAIGHT		STS 1056
FRANK ZAPPA	G (B	(B) LUCILLE HAS MESSED UP MY MIND	1969 STRAIGHT		STS 1057
CRAIG TARWATER	G (B				
IAN UNDERWOOD	SAX (B	RON WOODS D PERC(B JOHN KEHLIOR	D (B	

SIMMS BROTHERS BAND S122A

GEORGE SIMMS	V PERC(A	(A) SIMMS BROTHERS BAND	1979 ELEKTRA	US	6E220
FRANK SIMMS	G V (A				
BUDD TUNICK	D (A	DAVID SPINNER V CONG(A ROBERT SABINO	K (A SHIMMY MAKI	B (A
MICKEY LEONARD	G (A				

S123   SIMON & GARFUNKEL

Personnel	Inst.	Albums
PAUL SIMON	G V	(ALL
ART GARFUNKEL	V	(ALL
FRED CARTER	G	(F
HAL BLAINE	D	(F
JOE OSBORN	B	(F
LARRY KNECHTEL	K	(F
JIMMY HASKELL	STRINGS	(F
ERNIE FREEMAN	STRINGS	(F

Album		Year	Label				
(A)	WEDNESDAY MORNING 3 AM	1966	CBS	UK	63370	US	9049
(B)	THE SOUND OF SILENCE	1966	CBS	UK	62690	US	9269
(C)	PARSLEY SAGE ROSEMARY & THYME	1966	CBS	UK	62860	US	9363
(D)	BOOKENDS	1968	CBS	UK	63101	US	9529
(E)	THE GRADUATE (SOUNDTRACK)	1968	CBS	UK	70042	US	3180
(F)	BRIDGE OVER TROUBLED WATERS	1970	CBS	UK	63699	US	9914
(G)	GREATEST HITS	1972	CBS	UK	69003	US	31350
( )	SIMON & GARFUKEL	1967	ALLEGRO			ALL	836
( )	HITS OF S&G	19	PICKWICK			US	3059
( )	SIMON & GARFUNKEL	19	FONTANA			6430	006
(EP)	I AM A ROCK	19	CBS				6034
(EP)	MRS ROBINSON	19	CBS				6400
(EP)	FEELING GROOVY	19	CBS				6360

S124   CARLY SIMON

Personnel	Inst.	Albums
CARLY SIMON	V G PNO	(ALL
JAMES TAYLOR	G V	(EFGHJK
JIM RYAN	G B	(BCF
JOHN RYAN	B	(BF
PAUL KEOGH	G	(C
KLAUS VOORMANN	B	(CEFG
LOWELL GEORGE	G	(CG
ANDREW GOLD	G D	(EFG
WILLIE WEEKS	B	(EF
LEE SKLAR	B	(E
JOE MONDRAGON	B	(E
JEFF BAXTER	G	(EG

Album		Year	Label				
(A)	CARLY SIMON	1971	ELEKTRA	US	74082	UK	K42077
(B)	ANTICIPATION	1971	ELEKTRA	US	75016	UK	K42101
(AB)	CARLY SIMON /ANTICIPATION	1975	ELEKTRA			UK	K62015
(C)	NO SECRETS	1972	ELEKTRA	US	75049	UK	K42127
(D)	HOTCAKES	1974	ELEKTRA	US	7E1002	UK	K52005
(E)	PLAYING POSSUM	1975	ELEKTRA	US	7E1033	UK	K52020
(F)	THE BEST OF CARLY SIMON	1976	ELEKTRA	US	7E1048	UK	K52025
(G)	ANOTHER PASSAGE	1976	ELEKTRA	US	7E1064	UK	K52036
(H)	BOYS IN THE TREES	1978	FLEKTRA	US	6E 128	UK	K52066
(J)	SPY	1979	ELEKTRA	US	5E 506	UK	K52147
(K)	COME UPSTAIRS	1980	WB	US	BSK3443	UK	K56828

Personnel	Inst.	Alb.	Personnel	Inst.	Alb.	Personnel	Inst.	Alb.	Personnel	Inst.	Alb.
PAUL GLANZ	PNO	(BF	ANDY NEWMARK	D PERC	(BCDEFG	ALVIN ROBINSON	G	(E	PETER ROBINSON	PNO	(C
JIM GORDON	D	(CEF	TONY LEVIN	B	(FJK	NICKY HOPKINS	PNO	(CF	JIM KELTNER	D	(BFG
ROBBIE ROBERTSON	G	(F	JAMES NEWTON HOWARD	K	(E	RAY COOPER	PERC	(CF	PAUL BARRERE		G(G
PAUL GRIFFIN	PNO	(F	RINGO STARR	D	(E	GLENN FREY	G	(G	KIRBY JOHNSON	K	(F
RUSS KUNKEL	D	(E	PATRICK SIMMONS	G	(G	BILL PAYNE	ORG	(G	IVY COTTLER	D	(E
LAURINDO ALEMEIDA	G	(G	NICK DE CARO	ACC	(G	FREDDIE STAEHLE	PERC	(E	STEVE BRUTON	G	(G
RICHARD TFE	K	(HJ	ALAN ESTES	PERC	(E	KENNY GRADNEY	G	(G	KEN BISCHEL	K	(HJ
JIMMY JOHNSON	D	(F	BOB GLAUB	B	(G	DON GROLNICK	K	(HJK	EDDIE BONGO CONGA		(F
TIRAN PORTER	B	(G	BILLY MERNIT	PNO	(EJK	RALPH MACDONALD	PERC	(F	ERIC GALE	G	(H
DR JOHN	PNO G	(EFG	RICHARD PERRY	PERC	(F	CORNELL DUPREE	G	(H	DAVE SANBORN	SAX	(HJ
RITCHIE HAYWARD	D V	(G	GORDON EDWARDS	B	(H	HARVEY ESTRIN RECORDER		(H	RICK JAEGER	D V	(G
JOHN HALL	G	(HJ	GEORGE MARGE RECORDFR		(H	ROBERT GREENIDGE	D	(G	JEFF MIRANOV	G	(H
BOBBY KEYS	SAX	(CF	JOHN HARTMAN	D	(G	HUGH McCRACKEEN	G	(H	TREVOR LAWRENCE	SAX	(E
KEITH KNUDSEN	D	(G	WILL LEE	B	(HJ	DERREK VAN EATON	FLT	(E	MILT HOLLAND	PERC	(G
FRED TACKETT	MANDOCELLO	(G	MICHAEL BRECKER	SAX	(FJ	VICTOR FELDMAN	PERC	(G	ANDREW LOVE	SAX	(G
STEVE GADD	D	(HJK	CRUSHER BENNETT	PERC	(HJ	RUBENS BASSINI	PERC	(H	TOMMY MORGAN	HCA	(E
JOE CARO	G	(J	DAVID SPINOZZA	G	(J	IAN McLAUGHLIN	K	(J	WARREN BERNHARDT	K	(J
RANDY BRECKER	TPT	(J	RICK MAROTTA	D	(JK	KEN LANDRUM		(K	MIKE MAINIERI	K V	(JK
HUBERT LAWS	FLT	(J	FRANK CARILLO	G	(G	CLIFF CARTER	SYN	(J	RAPHAEL CRUZ	PERC	(J
PETER BALLIN	SAX	(J	TOM MALONE	TROM	(J	LEW DELGATTO	SAX	(J	PETE HEWLETT	G V	(K
SID McGINNIS	G V	(K	ED WALSH	OBERHEIM	(K	JERRY GROSSMAN	CELLO	(K	NOVI NOVAG	VLA	(G
DAVID CAMPBELL	VLA	(J	BUD SHANK	FLT	(J	PHIL BODNER	OBOE	(J	MARGRET ROSS	HARP	(K
GLORIA AGOSTINI	HARP	(H	RITA COOLIDGF	V	(E	RODNEY RICHMOND	V	(E	LIZA STRIKE	V	(E
VICKI BROWN	V	(CF	BONNIE BRAMLETT	V	(CF	DORIS TROY	V	(CF	PAUL McCARTNEY	V	(CF
LINDA McCARTNEY	V	(CF	CLYDIE KING	V	(E	CAROLYN WILLIS	V	(E	CAROLE KING	V	(EF
VINI PONCIA	V	(E	MAXINE WILLARD	V	(E	JULIA TILLMAN	V	(E	ABIGALE HANESS	V	(EF
KENNY MOORE	V	(EF	CARL HALL	V	(F	TASHA THOMAS	V	(F	LANI GROVES	V	(F
MIKE McDONALD	V	(G	LUCY SIMON	V	(GJ	ALEX TAYLOR	V	(GK	ELLEN KFARNEY	V	(G
LINDA RONSTADT	V	(G	DOOBIE BROTHERS	V	(G	JACKSON BROWNE	V	(G	LIBBY TITUS	V	(G
LEAH KUNKEL	V	(G	TIM CURRY	V	(J	ULLANDA McCULLOUGH	V	(J	LORAINE NFWMAN	V	(K
MARIA AGUIAR	V	(K	CHRISTINE MARTIN	V	(K	GAIL BOGGS	V	(J	HUGH TAYLOR	V	(K
SARAH MARIA TAYLOR	V	(K	LEE RITENOUR	G	(E	LON VAN EATON SIT	SYN	(E			

S125   PAUL SIMON

Personnel	Inst.	Albums
PAUL SIMON	G V	(ALL
HUX BROWN	G	(B
DAVID SPINOZZA	G	(BC
WALLACE WILSON	G	(B
JERRY HAHN	G	(B
STEFAN GROSSMAN	G	(B
NEVILLE HINDS	ORG	(B
JACKIE JACKSON	B	(B

Album		Year	Label				
(A)	THE PAUL SIMON SONGBOOK	1965	CBS			UK	61579
(B)	PAUL SIMON (MOTHER & CHILD REUNION)	1972	CBS	US	30750	UK	69007
(C)	THERE GOES RHYMIN' SIMON	1973	CBS	US	32280	UK	69035
(D)	LIVE RHYMIN'	1974	CBS	US	32855	UK	69059
(E)	STILL CRAZY AFTER ALL THESE YEARS	1975	CBS	US	33540	UK	86001
(F)	GREATEST HITS ETC	197	CBS	US	35032	UK	86047
(G)	ONE TRICK PONY	1980	WEA	US	3472	UK	K56846

Personnel	Inst.	Alb.	Personnel	Inst.	Alb.	Personnel	Inst.	Alb.	Personnel	Inst.	Alb.
RON CARTER	B	(B	RUSSELL GEORGE	B	(B	JOE OSBORN	B	(B	WINSTON GRENNAN	D	(B
HAL BLAINE	D	(B	VICTOR MONTANEZ	D	(B	DENSIL LANG	PERC	(B	LOS INCAS	PERC	(B
AIRTO MOREIRA	PERC	(BC	LARRY KNECHTEL	K HCA	(B	MIKE MAINIERI	VIBES	(B	FRED LIPSIUS	HRNS	(B
JOHN SCHROER	HRNS	(B	STEVEN TURRE	HRNS	(B	CHARLIE McCOY	HCA	(B	CISSY HOUSTON	B	(B
RONELLE STAFFORD	V	(B	DEIRDRE TUCK	V	(B	VON EVA SIMS	V	(B	STEPHANE GRAPPELLI	VLN	(B
PETE CARR	G	(C	CORNELL DUPREE	G	(C	ALEXANDER GAFA	G	(C	JERRY PUCKETT	G	(C
DAVID HOOD	B	(C	GORDON EDWARDS	B	(C	BOB CRANSHAW	B	(C	RICHARD DAVIS	B	(C
VERNIE ROBBINS	B	(C	ROGER HAWKINS	D	(C	RICK MAROTTA	D	(C	GRADY TATE	D	(C
JAMES STRAUD	D	(C	BARRY BECKETT	K	(C	BOB JAMES	K	(C	PAUL GRIFFIN	PNO	(C
BOBBY SCOTT	PNO	(C	ONWARD BRASS BAND		(C	DON ELLIOTT	VIBES	(C	CARSON WHITSETT	ORG	(C
DIXIE HUMMINGBIRDS	V	(C	MAGGIE ROCHE	V	(C	TERRE ROCHE	V	(C	JIMMY JOHNSON	G	(C
JESSY DIXON SINGERS		(D	URUBAMBA		(D	RICHARD TEE	K V	(G	HIRAM BULLOCK	G	(G
RALPH MACDONALD	PERC	(G	ERIC GALE	G	(G	JEFF MIRONOV	G	(G	JOHN TROPEA	G	(G
JOE BECK	G	(G	STEVE GADD	D	(G	TONY LEVIN	B	(G	HUGH McCRACKEN	G	(G
DON GROLNICK	SYN	(G	JON FADDIS	HRNS	(G	PATTI AUSTIN	V	(G			

S126   SIMPLE MINDS

Personnel	Inst.	Albums
JIM KERR	V	(A
CHARLIE BURCHILL	G V	(A
MICHAEL McNEIL	K V	(A
BRIAN McGEE	D V	(A
DEREK FORBES	B V	(A

Album		Year	Label	
(A)	LIFE IN A DAY	1979	ZOOM	ZULP 001
(B)	REAL TO REAL CACOPHONY	1979	ZOOM	SPART1140
(C)	EMPIRES AND DANCE	1980	ARISTA	SPART1109

MARTIN SIMPSON   S127

MARTIN SIMPSON	G V BAN(A	(A) GOLDEN VANITY	1976 TRAILER	LER 2099
AL SCHMIDT	HCA (A			
PETER THOMPSON	B (A			

VALERIE SIMPSON   S128

| VALERIE SIMPSON | V K (AB | (A) VALERIE SIMPSON EXPOSED | 1971 TAMLA | UK | STML11194 |
| | | (B) VALERIE SIMPSON | 1972 TAMLA | UK | STML11219 |

FRANKIE LEE SIMS   S129

| FRANKIE LEE SIMS | (A | (A) LUCY MAE BLUES | 19 SPECIALTY | UK | SNTF 5004 |
| HUBERT WASHINGTON D | (A | | | | |

SINCEROS   S130

DON SNOW	K V (A	(A) SOUND OF SUNBATHING	1979 EPIC	UK	EPC 83632
BOBBI IRWIN	D (A				
MARK KJELDSEN	G V (A	RON FRANCIS	B V (A		

PETE SINFIELD   S131

PETE SINFIELD	G SYN V (A	(A) STILL	1973 MANTICORE ANTI2001	UK K43501
RICHARD BRUNTON	G (A			
B J COLE	STEEL(A	GREG LAKE	G V (A	SNUFFY WALDEN	G (A	MEL COLLINS	WIND(A
DON HONEYWELL	SAX (A	CHRIS PYNE	TROM (A	GREG BOWDEN	TPT (A	STAN RODERICK	TPT (A
ROBIN MILLER	WIND (A	TIM HINKLEY	PNO (A	PHIL JUMP	K (A	KEITH TIPPETT	PNO (A
BOZ BURRELL	B (A	STEVE DOLAN	B (A	JOHN WETTON	B (A	MIN	D PERC (A
IAN WALLACE	D (A						

SIOUXSIE & THE BANSHEES   S132

SIOUXSIE	V (ALL	(A) THE SCREAM	1978 POLYDOR	UK	POLD 5009
SID VICIOUS	D (1	(B) JOIN HANDS	1979 POLYDOR 2442 264 UK	POLD 164
STEVE SEVERIN	B (ABC123	(C) KALEIDOSCOPE	1980 POLYDOR 2442 177	
MARCO PIRRONI	G (1	(1) SEPT 1976	(2) NOV 1976	(3) 1977	
KENNY MORRIS	D (23A			
JOHN McKAY	SAX (3A	JOHN McGEOCH	G (A3 P FENTON	G (2 STEVE JONES	(C

SIREN   S133

KEVIN COYNE	G V (AB	(A) SIREN	1969 DANDELION US D9 104	63755
DAVE CLAGUE	G B (AB	(B) STRANGE LOCOMOTION	1971 ELEKTRA	US 74087
NICK CUDWORTH	K V (AB	(B) STRANGE LOCOMOTION	1971 DANDELION	UKDAN8001
TAT MEAGER	D (AB			
JOHN CHICHESTER	G (A	COLIN WOOD	K FLT(A MICK GRATTON	G (B

SIRKEL & CO   S134

ERIC SIRKEL	G V (A	(A) SIRKEL & CO	1976 CHARLY	CRL5003
MICK TAYLOR	G (A	(A) SIRKEL & CO	1977 AFFINITY	AFF 1
MARC FRENTZEL	D (A			
GORDON RAITT	B (A	CHRIS MERCER	SAX (A	JOY YATES	V (A	RONNIE LEAHY	K (A
MICK EVE	SAX (A	LIZA STRIKE	V (A	COLIN ALLEN	D (A	ROBIN MILLAR	K (A
RON CARTHY	TPT (A	JACKIE SULLIVAN	V (A			

SISTER SLEDGE   S135

KATHIE SLEDGE	V (BCD	(A) CIRCLE OF LOVE	1975 ATLANTIC	UK K50097 US 36105
DEBBIE SLEDGE	V (BCD	(B) WE ARE FAMILY	1979 COTILLION	UK K50587 US 5209
KIM SLEDGE	V (BCD	(C) LOVE SOMEBODY TODAY	1980 COTILLION	UK K50693
JONI SLEDGE	V (BCD	(D) ALL AMERICAN GIRLS	1981 COTILLION	UK K50774 US 16072
NILE RODGERS	G (B			
BERNARD EDWARDS	B (B	TONY THOMPSON	D (B	ROBERT SABINO	K (B	KAREN MILNE STRINGS(B
CHERYL HONG STRINGS	(B	MARIANNE CARROLLSTRINGS(B	ANDY SCHWARTZ	PNO (B	RAYMOND JONES	K (B
SAMMY FIGUEROA	PERC (B	ALEX FOSTER	WIND (B	JEAN FINEBERG	SAX (B	JON FADDIS	TPT(B
ELLEN SEELING	TPT (B	BARRY ROGERS	TROM (B			

64 SPOONS   S136

TAM NEAL	K D V(	(A) LADIES DONT HAVE WILLIES(EP)	19 BUSHBABY
LYNDON CANNACH	D V K(		
ANDY CRAWFORD	FLT B G (	TED EMMET	TPT K(	JACKO	FLT G V(

SIXTY NINE(69)   S137

| ARMIN STOEWE | K G V(A | (A) CIRCLE OF THE CRAYFISH | 19 PHILIPS | 6305 164 |
| ROLAND SCHUPP | PERC (A | | | |

SKAFISH   S137A

| | | (A) SKAFISH | 1979 ILLEGAL | UK | ILP007 |

SKATELITES   S138

| | | (A) AFRICAN ROOTS | 19 UA | US | LA 799 |

SKID ROW   S139

GARY MOORE	G (A	(A) SKID	1970 CBS	UK	63965
ADRIAN FISHER		(B) 34 HOURS	1971 CBS	UK	64411
ED DEAN		(C) ALIVE & KICKING	1976 RELEASE	RRL 8001
KEVIN McALEA				
NOEL BRIDGEMAN	D (A	BRENDAN'BRUSH' SHIELS B (A		

SKIDS   S140

STUART ADAMSON	G (ABC	(A) SCARED TO DANCE	1979 VIRGIN	UK	V2174
RICHARD JOBSON	V (ABC	(B) DAYS IN EUROPA	1979 VIRGIN	UK	V2138
WILLIE SIMPSON	B (A	(C) ABSOLUTE GAME	1980 VIRGIN	UK	V2174
RUSSELL WEBB	B (BC				
MIKE BAILLIE	D (BC	TOM FELLICHAN	D (A		

SKIN ALLEY   S141

KRZYSZTOF HENRYK JUSKIEWICZ K(ABCD	(A) SKIN ALLEY	1969 CBS	UK	63847
BOB JAMES	G SAX(ABCD	(B) TO PAGHAM & BEYOND	1970 CBS	UK	64140
THOMAS CRIMBLE	B K V(AB	(C) TWO QUID DEAL	1972 TRANSATLANTIC	UK	TRA 260
ALVIN POPE	D (AB	(D) SKINTIGHT	1973 TRANSATLANTIC	UK	TRA 273
NICK GRAHAM V K B FLT (BCD	(D) SKINTIGHT	197 STAX	US	STS3022
TONY KNIGHT	D V (DC				
MARTIN DROVER	HRNS (D	GEOFF DRISCOLL	SAX (D	PHIL KENZIE	SAX (D	DAVE COXHILL	SAX (D
BUD PARKES	HRNS (D						

S142
SKIP BIFFERTY

MICK GALLAGHER	K	(A	(A) SKIP BIFFERTY		1967 RCA		UK	SF7941
GRAHAM BELL	V	(A						
JOHN TURNBULL	G	(A	COLIN GIBSON	B (A TOM JACKMAN	(A			

S143
SKREWDRIVER

| (A) ALL SKREWED UP (45 RPM LP) | 1977 CHISWICK | UK | WIK 3 + | CH3 |
| (EP) SKREWDRIVER | 197 TJM | | | TJM4 |

S144
SKY

JOHN WILLIAMS	G	(AB	(A) SKY	1979 ARIOLA	UK ARLH 5022
HERBIE FLOWERS	B	(AB	(B) SKY2	1980 ARIOLA	UK AD SKY 2
KEVIN PEEK	G	(AB	(C) SKY 3	1981 ARIOLA	UK ASKY 3
TRISTAN FRY	D	(AB			
FRANCIS MONKMAN	K	(AB			

S145
PATRICK SKY

PATRICK SKY	(A	(A) PATRICK SKY	1965 VANGUARD	VSD 79179
		(B) HARVEST OF A GENTLE CLANG	1966 VANGUARD SVRL19054	VSD 79207
		(C) REALITY IS BAD ENOUGH	1968 VERVE	US FTS 3052
		(D) PHOTOGRAPHS	1969 VERVE	US FTS 3079
		(E) SONGS THAT MADE AMERICA FAMOUS	1973 ADELPHI	US AR 4101
		(F) TWO STEPS FORWARD ONE STEP BACK	1975 LEVIATHAN	US 2006

S146
SKY BAND

| (A) SKYBAND | 1975 RCA | US APLIO839 | UK SF 8409 |

S147
SKYHOOKS

GRAEME STRACHEN	V	(ABC	(A) EGO IS NOT A DIRTY WORD	1975 MERCURY UK 6306 900 US SRM11066
ROBERT STARKIE	G	(AB	(B) LIVING IN THE SEVENTIES	19 MERCURY	US SRM11124
REDMOND SYMONS	G V	(A	(C) GUILTY UNTIL PROVEN INSANE	1979 UA	UK UAG30241
GREG MACINTOSH	B	(AB		
FREDDIE KABOODLESCHNITZER D(A PETER JONES K (A COL LOUGHNAN	SAX (A IMANTS STRAUKS D V (B
ROBERT SPENCER G V (B WILBUR WILDE SAX (B TONY ANSELL	K (B EDDIE LEONETH K (B

S148
SKYLARK

DOUG EDWARDS	G	(A	(A) SKYLARK	1972 CAPITOL	11048
STEVE PUGSLEY	B	(A			
ROBBIE KING	K	(A	BOBBY TORRES	CONGA(A PAUL BEAVER	SYN (A PATRICE HOLLOWAY V (A
KITTY DITTO	V	(A	DOMENIC TROIANO	G (	

S149
SKYROCKETS

STEVE BONNETT	G V	(A	(A) 1974
ANDREW BODNAR	B	(A	
STEVE GOULDING	D	(A	WILL STALLIBRASS HCA (A NOEL BROWN	G (A

S149A
SKYWHALE

STEVE ROBSHAW	G K	(A	(A) THE WORLD AT MINDS END	1977 FIREBRAND	DM0013
STAN THEWLIS	HRNS	(A			
PAUL TODD	HRNS	(A	DOUGALL AIRMOLE B (A MICK AVORY	D (A GWYO ZEPIX K (A
JOHN SCHOFIELD	D	(A		

S150
SLACK ALICE

| (A) SLACK ALICE | 1974 PHILIPS | UK | 6308 214 |

S151
SLADE

NODDY HOLDER	G V	(ALL	(A) BEGINNINGS(AMBROSE SLADE)	1969 FONTANA UK STL 5494 US	67592
JIM LEA B V K VLN		(ALL	(B) PLAY IT LOUD	1970 POLYDOR UK 2383 026 US COTILLION9035
DAVE HILL	G V	(ALL	(C) SLADE ALIVE	1972 POLYDOR UK 2383 101 US POLYDOR 5508
DON POWELL	D	(ALL	(D) SLAYED	1972 POLYDOR UK 2383 163 US POLYDOR 5524
			(E) SLADEST	1973 POLYDOR UK 2442 119 US REPRISE 2173
			(F) OLD NEW BORROWED BLUE	1974 POLYDOR UK 2383 261
			(G) IN FLAME (SOUNDTRACK)	1975 POLYDOR UK 2442 126 US WB 2865
			(H) THE BEST OF SLADE	1975 POLYDOR UK 2664 124
			(J) NOBODY'S FOOLS	1976 POLYDOR UK 2383 377 US WB 2936
			(K) WHATEVER HAPPENED TO SLADE	1977 POLYDOR UK 2314 103
			(L) ALIVE VOL 2	1978 BARN UK 2314 106
			(M) RETURN TO BASE	1979 BARN UK BARN 10 + NARB 003
			(N) SLADE SMASHES	1980 POLYDOR UK POLTV 13
			(O) WE'LL BRING THE HOUSE DOWN	1981 CHEAPSKATE UK SKATE 1

S152
SLAPP HAPPY

ANTHONY MOORE	K V	(ALL	(A) SORT OF SLAPP HAPPY	1972 POLYDOR UK 2310 204 RI RECOMMENDED
PETER BLEGVAD	G V CLAR	(ALL	(B) SLAPP HAPPY	1974 VIRGIN UK V2114
DAGMAR KRAUSE	PNO V	(ALL	(C) DESPERATE STRAIGHTS(H COW)	1974 VIRGIN UK V2024
			(D) IN PRAISE OF LEARNING	1975 VIRGIN UK V2027
			(E) CASABLANCA MOON	19 RECOMMENDED UK

S152A
NELSON SLATER

| NELSON SLATER | | | (A) WILD ANGEL | 19 RCA | US | APL1 1306 |

S153
SLAUGHTER & THE DOGS

WAYNE BARRETT	V	(ABC	(A) DO IT DOG STYLE	1978 DECCA	UK	SKL 5292
BRIAN CRANFORD	D	(	(B) LIVE	1978 RABID	UK	HAT 23
HOWARD BATES	B	(ABC	(C) BITE BACK	1980 DJM		DJM 20566
MIKE ROSSI	G	(ABC	(EP) BUILD UP NOT DOWN	19 TJM	UK	TJM 3
MAD MUFFET	D	(A			
EDDIE GARRITY	V	(C	PHIL ROWLAND D (C MORGAN FISHER	K (C CHRIS GENT	SAX (C

S154
SLAVE

MARK ADAMS	B	(DE	(A) SLAVE	1977 COTILLION	UK K50358 US 5200
STEVE ARRINGTON	D V	(DE	(B) HARDNESS OF THE WORLD	1978 COTILLION	UK K50435 US 5201
CHARLES CARTER	SAX	(DE	(C) CONCEPT	1978 COTILLION	UK K50512 US 5206
JIMMY DOUGLAS	V	(E	(D) JUST A TOUCH OF LOVE	1979 COTILLION	UK K50684 US 5217
MARK HICKS	G	(DE	(E) STONE JAM	1980 COTILLION	US 5224
CURT JONES	G V	(DE			
T LOCKETT	SAX V	(DE	FLOYD MILLER V TROM (DE RAYE TURNER	K (DE S WASHINGTON V TPT(DE
DANNY WEBSTER	G V	(DE	STARLEANA YOUNG V (DE		

PERCY SLEDGE

PERCY SLEDGE	V	(ALL						
			WHEN A MAN LOVES A WOMAN	1966	ATLANTIC	UK 2464 002	US	8125
			WARM & TENDER SOUL	1966	ATLANTIC	UK 588 048	US	8132
			THE PERCY SLEDGE WAY	1967	ATLANTIC	UK 587 081	US	8146
			TAKE TIME TO KNOW HER	1968	ATLANTIC			
			THE BEST OF	1969	ATLANTIC	UK 588 153	US	8210
			THE BEST OF	1972	ATLANTIC	UK RI K40026		
			GOLDEN VOICE OF SOUL	1974	ATLANTIC	UK K50169		
			I'LL BE YOUR EVERYTHING	197	CAPRICORN		US	0147
			STAR COLLECTION VOL 1	197	MIDI			20019
			STAR COLLECTION VOL 2	197	MIDI			20065

EARL SLICK BAND
S156

EARL SLICK	G	(AB	(A) EARL SLICK BAND	1976	CAPITOL	11493
JIMMIE MACK	G V	(AB	(B) RAZOR SHARP	1976	CAPITOL	11570
GENE LEPPIK	B V	(AB
BRYAN MADEY	D	(AB	JAY FERGUSON K (A MICHAEL KAMEN PNO (A CLAUDE PEPPER PERC (A

GRACE SLICK
S157

GRACE SLICK	V G K(ALL	(A) MANHOLE	1974	GRUNT	BFLI 0347
PETER KAUKONEN	G B (A	(B) THE BEST OF(GREAT SOCIETY	1975	CBS	80172
DAVID FREIBERG	G V (A	(C) DREAMS	1980	RCA	PL 13544
DAVID CROSBY	V (A	(D) WELCOME TO THE WRECKING BALL	1981	RCA	PL 13851
RON CARTER	B (A
JACK CASADY	B (A	CRAIG CHAQUICO G (A JOHN BARBATA D (A DAVID SNELL HARP(A
JACK ELLORY	FLT (A	TIMOTHY WALKER G (A PAUL KANTNER G V (A GARY DUNCAN G (A
SEEDER PEARS	B (A	CHRIS TAYLOR FLT (A ANDREW McGAVIN HRN (A DOUGLAS MOORE HRNS(A
MICHAEL LAIRD	TPT (A	GEORGE WHITING TPT (A RAYMOND PREMRU TPT (A HAROLD NASH TPT (A
PETER HARVEY	TROM (A	TERENCE MACDONAGH OBOE (A PHILIP HILL OBOE (A FRANK REIDY CLAR(A
ALAN HAKIN	PERC (A	TERENCE EMERY PERC (A ERIC ALLEN PERC (A STAN BARRETT PERC(A

SLIK
S158

MIDGE URE	G V (A	(A) SLIK	1976	BELL	UK SYBEL 8004
BILLY McISAAC	D (A
JIM McGINLAY	(A	KENNY HYSLOP (A

SLITS
S159

PALMOLIVE	D (12	(A) CUT	1979	ISLAND	UK ILPS 9573
TESSA POLLITT	B (12	(B) RETROSPECTIVE	1980	ROUGH TRADE	UK Y 3
ARI UP	V (12	(1) 1976 (2) 1977
KATE KORUS	G (12
VIV ALBERTINE	(2	BUDGIE D (A

P F SLOAN
S160

P F SLOAN	G V HCA (ALL	(A) SONGS OF OUR TIME	1965	DUNHILL	US	50004
JOE OSBORN	D (D	(B) 12 MORE TIMES	1966	DUNHILL	US	50007
HAL BLAINE	D (D	(C) MEASURE OF PLEASURE	1968	ATCO	US	33268
MIKE OMARTIAN	K (D	(D) RAISED ON RECORDS	1972	EPIC	UK 65179 MUMS US	31260
WAYNE PERKINS	K G (D
CHRIS ETHRIDGE	B (B	JOHN BARBATA D (D ALAN ESTES CONGA(D BEN BENAY BANJO G (D
LARRY KNECHTEL	PNO (D	BARRY BECKETT ORG (D MIKE MELVOIN B (D JAMES BURTON DOBRO(D
RICHARD BENNETT	STEEL(D	BOBBYE HALL PERC (D TONY TERRAN TPT (D DUANE EDDY G (D
SID SHARP	STRINGS (D	ROBERT KRANTZ VLN (D LOREN FARBER V (D RON HICKLIN V (D
JOHN BAYLOR	V (D	TATA VEGA V (D PHYLLIS BROWN V (D JACKIE KELSO WIND (D
JIM HORN	SAX (D	OLLIE MITCHELL TPT (D CONTE CANDOLI TPT (D DICK HYDE TROM (D
MITCH GORDON	V (D	SALLY STEVENS V (D IDA McCUNE V (D EVANGELINE CARMICHAEL V(D

SLY STONE
S161

SLY STONE	V G K(ALL	(A) DANCE TO THE MUSIC	1968	EPIC	US 26371	US RI 30334
FREDDIE STONE	G (DH	(A) DANCE TO THE MUSIC	1968	DIRECTION	UK B 63412
CYNTHIA ROBINSON	TPT (DH	(B) LIFE	1968	EPIC	US 26397	US RI 30333
LARRY GRAHAM	B (D	(C) M*LADY	1968	DIRECTION	UK B 63461
GREG ERRICO	D (D	(D) STAND	1969	EPIC	US 26456	UK 63655
ROSE STONE	V PNO(DH	(E) WHOLE NEW THING	1970	EPIC	US 26456	US RI 30335
JERRY MARTINI	SAX (DH	(F) THERE'S A RIOT GOING ON	1971	EPIC	US 30986	UK 64613
RUSTY ALLEN	B (H	(G) GREATEST HITS	1971	EPIC	US 30325	UK 69002
ANDY NEWMARK	D (H	(H) FRESH	1973	EPIC	US 32134	UK 69039
PAT RIZZO	SAX (H	(I) SMALL TALK	1974	EPIC	US 32930	UK 69070
LITTLE SISTER VOCAL GROUP (H		(J) HIGH ENERGY	1975	EPIC	US 22004	US RI 33462
		(K) HIGH ON YOU	1975	EPIC	US 33835	UK 69165
		(L) HEARD YOU MISSED ME	1976	EPIC	US 34348	UK 81641
		(M) 10 YEARS TOO SOON (E REMIXED)	1979	EPIC		UK 83640
		(N) BACK ON RIGHT TRACK	1979	WB	US 3303	UK K56640
		( ) RECORDED 1964 67	19	SCULPTURE	US SCP 2001

DRINK SMALL
S161A

| DRINK SMALL | G V (A | (A) I KNOW MY BLUES ARE DIFFERENT | 19 | SOUTHLAND | US SLP 1 |

SMALL FACES
S162

STEVE MARRIOTT	G V (ALL	(A) SMALL FACES	1966	DECCA LK4790 NEW WORLD NW 6000
RONNIE LANE	B V (ALL (NOT ST	(B) FROM THE BEGINNING	1967	DECCA LK 4879
KENNY JONES	D (ALL	(C) OGDENS NUT GONE FLAKE	1967	IMMEDIATE IM5P012 IML 1001
IAN McLAGAN	G ORG V(CDEFLPST	(C) OGDENS NUT GONE FLAKE	1968	IMMEDIATE US Z1252 008
JIMMY WINSTON	ORG (A	(C) OGDENS NUT GONE FLAKE	1978	CHARLY UK CR 300015
RICK WILLS	B (ST	(D) AUTUMN STONE	1969	IMMEDIATE IMA101/2+SMIM2107/8
STAN UNWIN	V (C	(E) IN MEMORIAM	1970	IMMEDIATE IMM 022
JOE BROWN	G V (S	(E) IN MEMORIAM	1975	EMI IMP GERM 048 90201
VICKI BROWN	V (ST	(F) WHAM BAM	1970	EMI IMP GERM 048 50719
P P ARNOLD	V (S	(G) ROCK ROOTS	1972	DECCA UK ROOTS 5
DAVE HYNES	V (S	(H) AMEN CORNER & SMALL FACES	1975	NEW WORLD NW 6001
GREG RIDLEY	V (S	(J) VINTAGE YEARS	1975	SIRE 3709
TONY WILLIAMS	V (S	(K) HISTORY OF SMALL FACES	197	IMMEDIATE 052 05108
MEL COLLINS	HRNS (S	(K) HISTORY OF SMALL FACES	197	PRIDE US PRD0014
SAUL SHECKNER	(S	(L) EARLY FACES	197	PRIDE US PRD0001
HELEN CHAPPPELLE	V (T	(M) FIRST STEPS	19	WB UK 1851
LAVINA ROBERTS	V (T	(N) ARCHETYPES	19	MGM US 4955
MADELINE BELL	V (T	(O) FAMOUS POP GROUPS (WITH A CORNER)	19	EMI 148 51812/3
LIZA STRIKE	V (T			(CONTINUED)
SAM BROWN	(T	JIMMY McCULLOCH (T

SMALL FACES

(P) THERE ARE BUT FOUR SMALL FACES		19	IMMEDIATE	US		Z1252008
(Q) SMALL FACES PROFILE		19	TELDEC	GERM		624002
(R) GREATEST HITS		1977	IMMEDIATE			IML 2008
(S) PLAYMATES		1977	ATLANTIC	US SD19113	UK	K50375
(T) 78 IN THE SHADE		1978	ATLANTIC	US SD19171	UK	K50468
(U) LIVE UK 1969		1978	CHARLY		UK	CR 300025
(V) BIG HITS		1980	VIRGIN		UK	V2166
(W) FOR YOUR DELIGHT		1980	VIRGIN		UK	V2178

S162A

JERRY MORIN	G V	(AB	(A) SMALL WONDER					
JIMMY PHILLIPS	K V	(AB	(B) GROWIN		1976	CBS	US	34100
HENRY SMALL	V VLN	(AB			19	CBS	US	34425

SMALL WONDER

LEROY SMART

S163

LEROY SMART		(ALL	(A) SUPERSTAR		1977	THIRD WORLD	TWS 601
			(B) DREAD HOT IN AFRICA		1978	BURNING SOUNDS	BSLP 1004
			(C) IMPRESSIONS		1978	BURNING SOUNDS	BSLP 1005
			(D) JAH LOVES EVERYONE		1978	BURNING SOUND	BSLP 1008

S164

SMIRKS

SIMON MILNER	G V	(A	(A) AMERICAN PATRIOTS(EP)		1979	SMIRKSOUND	DHSS 01
NEIL FITZPATRICK	G	(A					
IAN MORRIS	B	(A	MIKE DOHERTY	V	(A		

S165

GEORGE SMITH

GEORGE SMITH	HCA	(ALL	(A) NO TIME TO JIVE		1970	BLUE HORIZON	UK 763856	
J D NICHOLSON	PNO	(A	(B) ARKANSAS		1971	DERAM SML 1082	IMP DES28059	
BUDDY REED	G	(A	(C) GEORGE SMITH OF THE BLUES		1973	BLUESWAY	US BLS 6029	
GREGG SCHAEFER	G	(A	(D) TRIBUTE TO LITTLE WALTER		197	WORLD PACIFIC	US	21887
MARSHALL HOOKS	G	(A						
JERRY SMITH	B	(A	DICK INNES	D	(A	PEE WEE CRAYTON	G	(A

S166

GORDON SMITH

GORDON SMITH	V HCA G	(ALL	(A) LONG OVERDUE		1968	BLUE HORIZON	UK 763211
PETER GREEN	HCA	(A	(B) TAKIN' TIME		1979	APPALOOSA	ITALY AP002
DEREK HALL	PNO	(A	(C) DOWN ON MEAN STREETS		1980	APPALOOSA	ITALY AP005
JOHN McVIE	B	(A					
MICK FLEETWOOD	D	(A	PAT GROVER	HCA D(BC	BERNIE PALLO	ACC G(BC CRAIG MACKIE	PNO (C

S167

HUEY SMITH

HUEY SMITH	PNO	(ALL	(A) HAVING FUN		19	ACE	US (EP) 104
			(B) HAVING A GOOD TIME		19	ACE	US 1004
			(C) FOR DANCING		19	ACE	US 1015
DR JOHN	K	(D	(D) NIGHT BEFORE CHRISTMAS		19	ACE	US 1027
			(E) ROCK'N' ROLL REVIVAL		19	ACE	US 2021
			(F) ROCKIN' PNEUMONIA		1978	ACE	US
			(F) ROCKIN' PNEUMONIA		1978	CHISWICK	UK CH9

S168

JIMMY SMITH

JIMMY SMITH	ORG	(ALL	(A) THE INCREDIBLE		1962	HMV	CLP 1595
WITH			(B) HOBO FLATS		1963	VERVE	SVLP 9039
RICHARD DAVIS	B	(F	(C) ANY NUMBER CAN WIN		1963	VERVE	SVLP 9057
MILT HINTON	B	(C	(D) WHO'S AFRAID OF VIRGINIA WOLF		1964	VERVE	VLP 9068
BOB BUSHNELL	B	(C	(E) THE CAT		1964	VERVE VLP 9079 RI	2317 010
ART DAVIS	B	(C	(F) MONSTER		1965	VERVE	SVLP 9093
GEORGE DUVIVIER	B	(AE	(G) ORGAN GRINDER SWING		1965	VERVE	SVLP 9108
VINCE GAMBELLA	G	(A	THE BEST OF		196	VERVE	2304 004
BARCY GALBRAITH	G	(A	I GOT MY MOJO WORKING		1966	VERVE	
JIMMY WARREN	G	(A	PETER & THE WOLF		1967	VERVE	SVLP 9159
KENNY BURRELL	G	(CEFG	RESPECT		1967	VERVE	SVLP 9182
BILLY MURE	G	(C	STAY LOOSE		1968	VERVE	SVLP 9182
GRADY TATE	D	(EFG	CHRISTMAS COOKING		1968	VERVE	SVLP 9218
PHIL KRAUS	PERC	(E	FURTHER ADVENTURE		1969	VERVE	1969 9241
ED SHAUGHNESSY	D	(A	THE BOSS		1969	VERVE	SVLP 9247
DON BAILEY	D	(A	JAZZ SPECTRUM		19	VERVE	2355 005
HERB LOVELLE	D	(C	I'M GONNA GIT MYSELF TOGETHER		19	VERVE	2304 020
GEORGE DEVENS	PERC	(C	THE OTHER SIDE OF JIMMY SMITH		19	VERVE	2304 021
BOBBY DONALDSON	D	(C	THE INCREDIBLE JIMMY SMITH		1967	MFP	MFP 1292
DOUG ALLAN	PERC	(C	THE INCREDIBLE JIMMY SMITH		196	BLUENOTE	1525
ART MAROTTI	PERC	(C	FURTHER		19	VERVE	V 68766
MEL LEWIS	D	(C	WALK ON THE WILD SIDE		19	VERVE	2682 025
WARREN T SMITH	PERC	(F	PORTUGUESE SOUL		1974	VERVE	2304 167
JOE NEWMAN	TPT	(AC	JIMMY SMITH		1975	VERVE	2356 080
DON SEVERINSEN	TPT	(A	BLACK SMITH		1975	DJM	DJLPS 451
JOE WILDER	TPT	(A	A NEW STAR SOUND		19	BLUENOTE	BST 81512
ERNIE ROYAL	TPT	(AE	A NEW STAR SOUND VOL 2		19	BLUENOTE	BST 81514
CHARLIE SHAVERS	TPT	(C	AT THE LOWRY ORGAN		1973	DECCA	SKL 5146
JIMMY MAXWELL	TPT	(CE	AT THE ORGAN		19	BLUENOTE	BST 81525
SNOOKY YOUNG	TPT	(CE	AT THE BABY GRAND		19	BLUENOTE	BST 81528
JAMES SEDLAR	TPT	(C	AT THE BABY GRAND		19	BLUENOTE	BST 81529
BERNIE GLOW	TPT	(E	A DATE WITH		19	BLUENOTE	BST 81547
MARKY MARKOWITZ	TPT	(E	A DATE WITH		19	BLUENOTE	BST 81548
THAD JONES	TPT	(E	AT THE ORGAN VOL 2		19	BLUENOTE	BST 81551
TOMMY MITCHELL	TROM	(A	SOUND OF JIMMY SMITH		19	BLUENOTE	BST 81556
JIMMY CLEVELAND	TROM	(ACE	PLAYS PRETTY FOR YOU		19	BLUENOTE	BST 81563
URBIE GREEN	TROM	(AE	GROOVIN' AT SMALLS PARADISE		19	BLUENOTE	BST 81585
BRITT WOODMAN	TROM	(A	GROOVIN' AT SMALLS PARADISE		19	BLUENOTE	BST 81586
KAI WINDING	TROM	(C	GREATEST HITS VOL 2		19	BLUENOTE	BST 83367
MELBA LISTON	TROM	(C	SERMON		19	BLUENOTE	BST 84011
PAUL FAULISE	TROM	(C	HOME COOKING		19	BLUENOTE	BST 84050
BILLY BYERS	TROM	(E	CRAZY BABY		19	BLUENOTE	BST 84030
TONY STUDD	TROM	(E	MIDNIGHT SPECIAL		19	BLUENOTE	BST 84078
BABE CLARKE	SAX	(A	PLAYS FATS WALLER		19	BLUNOTE	BST 84100
ROBERT ASHTON	SAX	(AF	BACK AT THE CHICKEN SHACK		19	BLUENOTE	BST 84117
GERRY DODGION	SAX	(AG	ROCKIN THE BOAT		19	BLUENOTE	BST 84141

(CONTINUED)

PHIL WOODS	SAX (ACF	PRAYER MEETING		19	BLUENOTE		BST 84164
GEORGE BARROW	SAX (A	BUCKET		19	BLUENOTE		BST 84235
MARVIN HOLLADAY	SAX (C	I'M MOVIN' ON		19	BLUENOTE		BST 84255
BUDD JOHNSON	SAX (CF	OPEN HOUSE		19	BLUENOTE		BST 84269
SELDON POWELL	SAX (C	PLAIN TALK		19	BLUENOTE		BST 84296
JEROME RICHARDSON	SAX (CF	GREATEST HITS		19	BLUENOTE		BST 89901
DANNY BANKS	WIND (F	JIMMY SMITH		19	BLUENOTE		BNLA 400
RAY BECKENSTEIN	WIND (F	TOMORROWS SOUND TODAY		1978	GROSVENOR		GRS 1065
GEORGE DORSEY	WIND (F						
HARVEY ESTRIN	WIND (F	RAY ALONGE	HRNE (E	JIMMY BUFFINGTON	HRNS (E	EARL CHAPIN	HRNS (
BILL CORREA	HRNS (E	DON BUTTERFIELD	HRNS (E				

LONNIE LISTON SMITH
S169

LONNIE LISTON SMITH	G V(ALL	ASTRAL TRAVELLING		1974	FLYING DUTCHMAN		BNLI 0163
MARCUS MILLER	B	(ELS	EXPANSIONS	1975	RCA UK SF 8434		BXLI 0934
DONALD SMITH	V FLT(BEL	AFRO DESIA		1975	GROOVEMASTER		GM 3308
RONALD D MILLER	D	(ESL	REFLECTIONS	1976	RCA UK RS 1053		
LINO REYES	D	(ES	VISIONS OF A NEW WORLD	1976	RCA UK SF 8461		BXLI 1196
STEVE THORNTON	PERC (ES	COSMIC FUNK		197	FLYING DUTCHMAN		BXLI 0591
DAVE HUBBARD	FLT (BESL	THINK		19	BLUENOTE		BST 84290
AURELL RAY	G	(ES	TURNING POINT	19	BLUENOTE		BST 84313
BUTCH CAMPBELL	G	(ES	MOVE YOUR HAND	19	BLUENOTE		BST 84326
JIMMY OWENS	TPT (E	DRIVES		19	BLUENOTE		BST 84351
ROBERT FORTUNATO	TPT (E	RENAISSANCE		1977	RCA		APLI11822
VIRGIL JONES	TROM (E	(L) LOVELAND		1978	CBS		82837
TOM MALONE	TROM (E	GOTCHA		1978	TK		TKR 83356
SAM BURTIS	TROM (E	(S)SONG FOR THE CHILDREN	1979	CBS		83609
STRING SECTION		(E	(E) EXOTIC MYSTERIES	1979	CBS		83331
GWEN GUTHRIE	V	(E	(F) LOVE IS THE ANSWER	1980	CBS		84365
BRENDA WHITE	V	(E	(B) BEST OF	1980	RCA	PL	12897
ULLANDA McCULLOUGH	V	(ES	BEST OF	1980	CBS		84348
RAY SIMPSON	V	(E					
ZACHARY SANDERS	V	(E	JAMES ROBINSON	V (S	PETER BROWN	B (S	KEVIN J PERRY	G (S
YVONNE LEWIS	V	(S	JANET WRIGHT	V (S	CECIL McBEE	B (B	LAWRENCE KILLIAN PERC(B
MICHAEL CARVIN	PERC (B	ART GORE	D (B	LEOPOLDO FLEMING	PERC (B	GREG MAKER	B (B
WILBY FLETCHER	D	(B	RAY ARMANDO	PERC (B	ANGEL ALLENDE	PERC (B	AL ANDERSON	B (BL
KEN BISCHEL	SYN (B	LEON PENDARVIS	K (B	GENE BERTONCINI	G (B	GUILHERME FRANCO PERC(B

PATTI SMITH
S170

PATTI SMITH	V G (ALL	(A) HORSES		1975 ARISTA US 4066 UK		ARTY 122
RICHARD SOHL	PNO (1236A	(B) RADIO ETHIOPIA		1976 ARISTA US 4097 UK		SPARTY 1001
LENNY KAYE	G (A1234567	(C) EASTER		1978 ARISTA US 4171 UK		SPARTY 1043
IVAN KRAL	B G K(A234567	(D) WAVE		1979 ARISTA	UK	SPARTY 1086
J D DAUGHERTY	D (A34567	(EP) SET FREE		1978 ARISTA	UK	ARIST 12197
TOM VERLAINE	G (A	(1) 1974	(4) OCT 1976 TOUR	(7) SEPT 1977		
ANDY PALEY	PNO (4	(2) EARLY 1975(59 LATE 76				
LEIGH FOXX	B (5	(3) 1975/76	(6) 1977			
BRUCE BRODY	K (C7					
ALLEN LANIER	G (A					

WHISPERING SMITH
S171

MOSES SMITH	V HCA(A	(A) OVER EASY		19 EXCELLO EX8020+ CONTEMPO CRM 116		
BOBBY POWELL	K V (A	(A) OVER EASY		19 BLUE HORIZON UK	2431 015	
MELVIN HILL	G (A					
HARVEY LEXING	G (A	ALFRED LUCAS	B (A	GREG 'DOC' JOHNSON PERC (A	NOLAN SMITH	PERC(A
LEROY PERO	HRNS (A	WILLIE SINGLETON	HRNS (A	JOHNNIE CAGE	HRNS (A	NAPOLEON MARTIN	HRNS(A
REGGIE MORRISON	HRNS (A	TROMBONE OBRY	TROM (A			

WARREN SMITH
S171A

WARREN SMITH	V G (ABC	(A) FIRST COUNTRY COLLECTION	1961 LIBERTY	US	LRP 3198
		(B) LEGENDARY SUN PERFORMERS	1977 CHARLY UK CR31132 US LAKE 506		
		(EP) WARREN SMITH	1977 CHARLY UK CEP 113		

SMITH PERKINS SMITH
S172

STEVE SMITH	K G V(A	(A) SMITH PERKINS SMITH	1972 ISLAND		ILPS 9198
WAYNE PERKINS	G V (A					
TIM SMITH	K G V(A	BARRY BECKETT	K (A	JAMIE GRANT	V (A	DAVID HOOD	B (A
EDDIE HINTON	G (A	ROGER HAWKINS	D (A	LARRY NICHOLSON	G (A		

CHRIS SMITHERS
S173

CHRIS SMITHERS	G V (A	(A) DON'T IT DRAG ON	1972 POPPY	US	PYS 5704
ERIC KAZ	PNO (A					
BEN KEITH DOBRO STEEL (A		ROD HICKS	B (A	ROY MARKOWITZ	D (A	MARIA MULDAUR	V (A
BONNIE RAITT	V (A	KATHY ROSE	V (A	STU SCHULMAN	VLN (A	HAPPY TRAUM	BAN(A

SMOKIE
S174

PETER SPENCER	V D SAX(ALL	(A) PASS IT AROUND		1975 RAK	UK	SRAK 510
TERRY UTTLEY	V B (ALL	(B) CHANGING ALL THE TIME	1975 RAK	UK	SRAK 517
ALAN SILSON	G V (ALL	(C) MIDNIGHT CAFE	1976 RAK UK SRAK 520 RSO US	13005
CHRIS NORMAN	V G K(ALL	(D) GREATEST HITS	1977 RAK	UK	SRAK 526
		(E) BRIGHT LIGHTS & BACK ALLEYS	1977 RAK UK SRAK 530 RSO US 13029
		(F) MONTREUX ALBUM	1978 RAK	UK	SRKA 6757
		(G) THE OTHER SIDE OF THE ROAD	1979 RAK	UK	SRAK 539
		(H) VERY BEST OF	1980 RAK	UK	SRAK 540

GILLI SMYTH
S175

GILLI SMYTH	V (A	(A) MOTHER		1978 CHARLY	UK	CRL 5007
ORLANDO ALLEN	V (A	(B) FAIRY TALES	1979 CHARLY	UK	CRL 5018
VERA BLUM	VLN (A					
PIP PYLE	D (A	TONY PASCUAL	K (A	DIDIER MALHERBE	SAX (A	DAEVID ALLEN	B G V(A
CHRISTIAN TRITSCH B (A		RAFEL AGUILO	D (A	TALIESEN ALLEN	V (A	PETER LEWIS	V (A
SAM GOPAL	TABLAS(A	ANNIE TRUXELL	V (A	MARTIN TALLENTS	WHISTLE(A	TOM LIPPS	V (A
MATI KLARWEIN	V (A	PEPE MILAN	G (A	JOAN BIBILON	G (A	PATRICK MEADOWS	V (A
FRANK FEHLING	V (A	PHIL SHEPHERD	V (A	STEPHANIE SHEPHERD V (A	ANDREW PAGE	V (A
OONA LIND	V (A	ORLANDO ALLEN	V (A			

S176 SNAFU

BOBBY HARRISON	V PERC(ABC	(A) SNAFU	1974 W W A	WWA 003
MICK MOODY HCA G V	(ABC	(B) SITUATION NORMAL	1974 W W A	WWA 013
PETE SOLLEY	K VLN V(AB	(C) ALL FUNKED UP	1975 CAPITOL	11473
COLIN GIBSON	B (ABC			
TERRY POPPLE	D B (ABC MEL COLLINS SAX (BC STEVE GREGORY SAX (B BUD BEADLE SAX (B
TIM HINKLEY	K (C BRIAN CHATTON K (C VIOLA WILLS V (C LIZA STRIKE V (C

S176A SNATCH

	(A) SHOPPING FOR CLOTHES(EP)	1980 FETISH	FET 004

S177 SNAIL

BOB O'NEILL	G V (AB	(A) SNAIL	1978 CREAM	IMP 1009
KEN KRAFT	G V (AB	(B) FLOW	1979 CREAM	IMP 6005
BRETT BLOOMFIELD	B V (AB			
DON BALDWIN	D V (AB			

S177A SNAKEFINGER

PHIL 'SNAKEFINGER' LITHMAN	(A) GREENER PASTURES	19 RALPH	US
THE RESIDENTS	(B	(B) CHEWING THE SOUND	1979 RALPH	US SNK 7909
DON JACKOVICH	PERC (B			
PHIL CULP	B (B STEVEN BROWN SAX (B

S178 SNIFF N THE TEARS

PAUL ROBERTS	G V (A	(A) FICKLE HEART	1978 CHISWICK WIK9 UK +UK RI CWD3002
LOZ NETTO	G (A	(B) THE GAMES UP	1980 CHISWICK UK CWK3014
MICK DYCHE	G (A			
CHRIS BIRKIN	B (A RON LAWRENCE B (A KEITH MILLER SYN (A LUIGI SALVONI D (A
NOEL McCALLA	V (A ALAN FELDMAN K (A JIM NELLIS V (A

S179 SNIPS

SNIPS	V (AB	(A) VIDEO KING	1976 JET	UK LP 212
MICK DYCHE	G (A	(B) LA ROCCA	1981 EMI	UK EMC 3359
GRAHAM DEACON	D (A			
JOHN BENTLEY	G (A JACKIE BADGER B (A

S180 PHOEBE SNOW

PHOEBE SNOW	G V (ALL	(A) PHOEBE SNOW	1974 A&M	UK AMLS68283
SONNY BURKE	K (C	(A) PHOEBE SNOW	1974 SHELTER US2109	UK ISA 5010
DAVID POMERANZ	K (C	(C) IT LOOKS LIKE SNOW	1976 CBS US 34387 UK 81794
JAMES GADSON	D (C	(D) SECOND CHILDHOOD	1976 CBS US 33952 UK 81162
REGGIE McBRIDE	B (C	(E) AGAINST THE GRAIN	1978 CBS US 34456 UK 82195
STEVE BURGH	G (BCF	(F) NEVER LETTING GO	1978 CBS US 34875 UK 82224
ED GREENE	D (C	( ) ROCK AWAY	1981 ATLANTIC UK K50780
STEVE KHAN	G (F

CHUCK DOMANICO	B (CB RAY PARKER JR G (C HARVEY MASON D (C DAVID BROMBERG G (BC
GREG POREE	G (C ANDY NARELL PERC (C KURT McGETTRICK HRNS (C MEL MARTIN HRNS(C
HADLEY CALIMAN	HRNS (C BOB YANCE HRNS (C GOLDEN AGE JAZZ BAND (C PHIL KEARNS V (CD
MAXINE WILLARD	V (C JULIA TILLMAN V (C ORRIN WATERS V (C HUGH McDONALD B (B
STEVE MOSLEY	D (B PERSUASIONS V (B TEDDY WILSON PNO (B RALPH McDONALD PERC(BDF
JOHN ZOOT SIMS	SAX (B MARGARET ROSS HARP (B DAVE MASON G (B CHUCK ISRAELS B (B
BOB JAMES	B (BF TONY LEVIN B (DF STEVE GADD D (B KEN ASCHER K (DF
HUGH McCRACKEN	G (DF JOHN TROPEA G (D KEN BISCHEL SYN (D RICHARD TEE K (DF
DAVID SANBORN	SAX (D STUART SCHARF G (D RON CARTER B (D JESSE DIXON SINGERS (D
JIMMY YOUNG	D (D DON GROLNICK K (D GORDON EDWARDS B (D GRADY TATE D (DF
PHIL RAMONE	V (D WILL LEE B (DF JEROME RICHARDSON FLT (D

S180A SOCIAL SECURITY

	(A) I DONT WANT MY HEART TO RULE MY HEAD(EP) 19 HEARTBEAT UK PULSE1

S180B SOCRATES

	(A) ON THE WINGS	19 PETERS INT	PILPS9002
	(B) PHOS	19 PETERS INT	PILPS9013

S180C SODS

	(A) MINUTES TO GO	1979 STEP FORWARD UK SFLP 3

S181 SOFT BOYS

ANDY METCALFE	B (1	(A) CAN OF BEES	1979 TWO CRABS CLAW 101 AURAL AUL705
ROBYN HITCHCOCK	G V (1AB	(B) UNDERWATER MOONLIGHT	1980 ARMAGEDDON UK ARMO02
KIMBERLEY REW	G (AB1	(EP) NEAR THE SOFT BOYS	1980 ARMAGEDDON UK ARMO01
MORRIS WINDSOR	D (B1	(1) APRIL 1978		
MATTHEW SELIGMAN	B (B			
ANDY KING	SITAR(B GERRY HALE VLN (B

S181A SOFT HEAP

	(A) SOFT HEAP	1979 CHARLY UK CRL 5014

S182 SOFT MACHINE

LARRY NOLAN	G (1	(A) THE SOFT MACHINE	1968 PROBE US 4500
MIKE RATLEDGE	K (12345ABCDEJ	(B) VOLUME 2	1969 PROBE US 4505 UK SPB 1002
KEVIN AYERS	B V (A1	(B) VOLUME 2	1974 ABC RI UK ABCL 5004
DAEVID ALLEN	G (1	(AB) 1&2	1973 PROBE US 204 RI UK ABC 602
ROBERT WYATT	D (123ABCD	(C) THIRD	1970 CBS US 30339 UK 66246
HUGH HOPPER	B (BCDE2345	(D) FOURTH	1971 CBS US 30754 UK 64280
ANDY SUMMERS	G (1	(E) FIFTH	1972 CBS UK 64806
ELTON DEAN	SAX (2345CD	(E) FIFTH	1979 EMBASSY RI UK 31748
PHIL HOWARD	D (4	(F) SIXTH	1973 CBS US 32260 UK 68214
JOHN MARSHALL	D (5EJKL	(G) SEVENTH	1974 CBS US 32716 UK 65799
ROY BABBINGTON	B (J	(H) BUNDLES	1975 HARVEST UK SHSP4044
KARL JENKINS	(5EKJL	(J) SOFTS	1976 HARVEST UK SHSP4056
ALLAN HOLDSWORTH	G (	(K) ALIVE & WELL IN PARIS	1978 HARVEST UK SHSP4083
ALAN WAKEMAN	SAX (J	(L) LAND OF COCKAYNE	1981 EMI UK EMC 3348
JOHN ETHERIDGE	G (JK	AT THE BEGINNING	1977 CHARLY UK CR300014
RICK SAUNDERS	VLN (K	TRIPLE ECHO	1977 HARVEST UK SHTW 800
STEVE COOK	B (K	FACES & PLACES VOL 7	1971 BYG FR 529907
NICK EVANS	TROM (C2	ROCK GENERATION 7 (1 SIDE)	197 BYG FR 529707
MARK CHARIG	HRNS (2	ROCK GENERATION 8 (1 SIDE)	197 BYG FR 529708
LYN DOBSON	HRNS (23C			
RAB SPALL	VLN (C	(1) 1967/68 (2) 1969 (3) 1970 (4) 1971/72 (5) 1972
JIMMY HASTINGS	WIND (C			
JACK BRUCE	B (L DICK MORRISEY SAX (L ALAN PARKER G (L

SOFT WHITE UNDERBELLY S183

```
ALBERT BOUCHARD    D    (A        (A) 1969 NO ALBUMS
ANDREW WINTERS     B    (A
DONALD ROESER      G    (A    ALLEN LANIER    K G (A   LES BRAUNSTEIN    V   (A
```

SOFTIES S184

```
KEITH LANE         D    (A        (A) NICE & NASTY              1979 CHARLY        UK    CRL  5012
MIKE SMITH         G V  (A
JACK BOOTHE    B G K V  (A
```

MIKE SOFTLEY S185

```
MICK SOFTLEY     V G K(ABC       (A) SUNRISE                   1970 CBS           UK          64098
JERRY DONAHUE      G   (ABC       (B) STREET SINGER             1971 CBS           UK          64395
PAT DONALDSON      B   (ABC       (C) ANY MOTHER DOESN'T GRUMBLE 1972 CBS          UK          64841
TONY COX           K   (ABC
GERRY CONWAY       D   (ABC SUE GLOVER    V  (A   SUNNY LESLIE   V  (A  LYN DOBSON WIND SITAR(AC
LESLEY DUNCAN      V   (A   NED BALEN    TABLAS (A   BARRY CLARKE   G  (A  MIKE VICKERS    K   (A
GRINGO             V   (A   TONY CARR    PERC   (A   STEVE HAYTON   G HCA(B  DAVID HOROWITZ  K   (B
KARL JENKINS       SAX (B   DUDU PUKWANA   SAX  (B   FRANK RICOTTI  PERC (B  RICHARD THOMPSON G  (B
LIZA STRIKE        V   (B   DORIS TROY     V   (B   JIMMY THOMAS   V  (B  BARRY DE SOUZA  PERC(C
```

SOLAR PLEXUS S186

```
TOMMY KORBERG      V   (        (A) CONCERTO GROSSO(SWEDISH)   1972 ODEON    SWED  154 34 573/4
MONICA GROSSO      ORG          (A) CONCERTO GROSSO(ENGLISH)   1972 ODEON    SWED  154 34 684/5
CARL AXEL DOMINIQUE PNO(        (B) SOLAR PLEXUS 2             1973 ODEON    SWED  062 34  797
BOSSE HAGGSTROM    B   (        (C) SOLAR PLEXUS               1973 POLYDOR  UK          2383 222
TOMMY BORGUDD      D   (        (D) DET ER INTE BATEN          1974 HARVEST        062 34  975
GEORG WADENIUS     G   (A       (E) HELLRRE GYCKLARE AN HYCKLARE 1975 HARVEST      062 35  166
```

SOLID GOLD CADILLAC S186A

```
BRIAN GODDING      G   (A       (A) BRAIN DAMAGE               1973 RCA           UK    SF 8365
MALCOLM GRIFFITHS TROM (A
ALAN JACKSON D PERC (A   PHIL MINTON  V TPT   (A   GEORGE AHMAD KHAN WIND K(A   BUTCH POTTER G B K BAN(A
MIKE WESTBROOK     PNO (A
```

SOLUTION S187

```
TOM BARLAGE       K WIND(ABCD   (A) SOLUTION                  1972 DECCA          UK   SKLR 5124
WILLEM ENNES       K   (ABCD     (B) DIVERGENCE                1973 EMI            UK   EMC  3002
GUUS WILLEMSE      B V  (BCD     (C) CORDON BLEU               1975 ROCKET US 2189 UK        ROLL 1
HANS WATERMAN      D   (ABCD     (D) FULLY INTERLOCKING        1977 ROCKET        UK        ROLL 8
RAY COOPER         PERC (D
STUART EPPS        V   (D   PETER VAN DER SANDE B  (A   FRANKIE FISH    V  (C   MICHIEL POS    G SAX(C
```

ERWIN SOMER GROUP S187A

```
ERWIN SOMER  VIBES PERC(A       (A) ERWIN SOMER GROUP         1973 UNIVERSE             UP 110
RUDY VAN DIJK      SAX (A
HELMIG VAN DER VEGT K(A   HANS LAFAILLE   D   (A   JAAP VAN EIK    B  (A
```

SONICS S187B

```
GEORGE TENCIL WALLACE G V K(A   (A) SINDERELLA                1980 LINE      GERM  LLP5052AP
BILL SHAW          D V  (A       (1) HERE ARE THE SONICS       196 ETIQUETTE  US          024
MICHAEL GONE       G   (A        (2) SONICS BOOM               196 ETIQUETTE  US          027
GEORGE CROWE       B   (A        ( ) INTRODUCING THE SONICS    196 JERDEN     US          7007
GERRY ROSLIE       K V (A12      ( ) EXPLOSIVES                196 BUCKSHOT   US          001
JAMES N BITSCH     D   (A        ( ) SONICS                    1977 SRT                  77079
ANDY PARYPA        B V (12
LARRY PARYPA       G V (12   ROB LIND V SAX   (12  BOB BENNETT       D  (12
```

JOEL SONNIER S187C

```
JOEL SONNIER     G V D HCA(A     (A) CAJUN LIFE                1980 SONET UK SNTF 839 US ROUNDER
MICHAEL DOUCET     G   (A
MERLIN FONTENOT    FDL (A   JAY STUTES    DOBRO(A   ROY HUSKY      B  (A  BUDDY HARMON    D  (A
EARL BALL          PNO (A   HENRY STRZELECKI B (A   KENNY KENNERSON PNO (A  GENE O'NEAL    STEEL(A
PETE DRAKE         STEEL(A  BOB MILSAP     G  (A   JOE ALLEN      B  (A  WILLIE ACKERMAN D  (A
BOB WHITE          FDL (A   PHIL BALL      G  (A   VIC JORDAN     G  (A  BILLY REYNOLDS  D  (A
TOMMY WILLIAMS     FDL (A
```

SONNY & CHER S188

```
SONNY BONO         V   (ALL      LOOK AT US                 1964 ATLANTIC US UK 5036 US 33177
CHER BONO          V   (ALL      WONDROUS WORLD OF           1966 ATLANTIC            US 33183
                                 IN CASE YOUR IN LOVE        1967 ATLANTIC            US 33203
                                 GOOD TIMES                  1967 ATLANTIC            US 33214
                                 BEST OF                     196  ATLANTIC UK 588083  US 33219
                                 BEST OF                     1972 ATLANTIC RI         UK K40012
                                 LIVE                        196  KAPP     US 3654
                                 LIVE                        1972 MCA RI   UKMUP5435  US  2009
                                 BEST OF                     1972 CHARTERLINE      ITALY 20024
                                 BABY DON'T GO               19   REPRISE      US   6177
                                 LIVE IN LAS VEGAS           1974 MCA   UK MCSP 257   US 2/8004
                                 MAMA WAS A ROCK'N' ROLL SINGER 1974 MCA UK MCF 3672
                                 ALL I EVER NEED IS YOU      19   KAPP         US   3660
                                 ALL I EVER NEED IS YOU      1974 MCA   UK MCF 2517   US   3660
                                 GREATEST HITS               1975 MCA   UK MCF 2586   US   2117
                                 THE BEAT GOES ON            1975 ATCO         US  11000
```

SONS OF CHAMPLIN S189

```
BILL CHAMPLIN V G K SAX(ALL      (A) LOOSEN UP NATURALLY        1969 CAPITOL   US      SWBB 200
TERRY HAGGERTY     G V (ABCDEFGH  (B) THE SONS                  1969 CAPITOL   US      SKAO 322
GEOFFREY PALMER K B V SAX(ABCDEFGH (C) MINUS SEEDS & STEMS (LIMITED) 1970
JAMES PRESTON      K   (EFGH      (D) FOLLOW YOUR HEART         1971 CAPITOL   US          ST 675
DAVID SCHALLOCK    B V (EFG       (E) WELCOME TO THE DANCE      1973 CBS    US 32341 UK    65663
ROB MOITOZA   B HCA V (H          (F) THE SONS OF CHAMPLIN      1975 ARIOLA  US 50002 UK AAS 1501
STEVE FREDIANI     WIND (GH       (G) CIRCLE FILLED WITH LOVE   1976 ARIOLA  US 50007
JIM HORN           SAX (H         (H) LOVING IS WHY             1977 ARIOLA  US 50017 UK AAS 1505
CHRIS BOND         SYN (H
DAVID FAREY        HRNS (H  CHUCK FINDLEY   TPT  (H   GARY COLEMAN    PERC (H  DON MENZA      SAX (H
PAUL HUBINON       TPT (H   AL STRONG     B  (ABCD  TIM CAINE       SAX  (ABC PHIL WOODS     HRNS(E
BILL BOWEN         D  (ABCD MARK USHAM    HRNS(EF   MIKE ANDREAS    HRNS (EF ERNIE WATTS    SAX (H
```

S190
```
BUNNY McKENZIE     G  (A        (A) REGGAE HIT SHOWCASE                    1980 PLASTIC FANTASTIC        PFULP 350
NEGUS DAWTAS       V  (A
SANTA DAVIS           (A
RANKING REUBEN        (A        T BOW       G  (A  BROTHER NAT      K  (A  RICO      BRASS       (A
TONY ROBINSON      K  (A        SPEEGO      G  (A  ASTON BARRETT   B  (A  TUNGA OF SABANDIS G (A
WIRE LINDO         K  (A        TAN TAN     HRNS (A  CARLTON BARRETT D  (A  CHINNA SMITH         G  (A
                                TENDA I OF ZABANDIS K (A
```

S191
SOPWITH CAMEL
```
PETER KRAEMER V WIND K (AB      (A) SOPWITH CAMEL                         1967 KAMA SUTRA      US      KLPS 8060
TERRY MACNEIL     K G  (AB      (A) HELLO HELLO                           1973 KAMA SUTRA      US RI KSBS 2063
MARTIN BEARD      B    (AB      (B) THE MIRACULOUS HUMP RETURNS           1973 REPRISE US MS 2108 UK    K44251
NORMAN MAYELL D HCA SITAR(AB
WILLIAM SIEVERS   G    (AB
```

S192
SORE THROAT
```
MATT FLOWERS          (        (A) SOONER THAN YOU THINK                  1979 HURRICANE        UK      FLAK 101
DAN FLOWERS       B   (
JUSTIN WARD       V   (         REID SAVAGE G  (   ROBIN KNAPP    D  (   GREGORY MASON    SAX  (
```
S192A
SORROWS
```
                                (A) TAKE A HEART                          1965 PYE             UK      NPL38023
```
S193
SORRY
```
J P CECCARELLI    D  (A         (A) OH KATHY                              1978 KISWELL         FR      29 33109
CLIVE EDWARDS     D  (A
DON DON WEISS     D  (A         BUNNY BRUNEL   B  (A  STEVE CARMEN    B  (A  RONNIE DEVILLE  B  (A
MAX MESUMECCI     K  (A         PAUL IVES    K V  (A  DOMINIQUE RUIZ  G  (A  MICKY           V  (A
JOYCE             V  (A         FLO            V  (A  JACKY           V  (A  RAY HENDRIKSEN  V  (A
STRING SECTION       (A
```
S193A
MARK SOSKIN
```
MARK SOSKIN       K    (A       (A) RHYTHM VISION                         1980 PRESTIGE                P10109
BENNIE MAUPIN  WIND   (A
OSCAR BRASHEAR   HRNS (A         SNOOKY YOUNG   HRNS (A  GEORGE BOHANON  TROM (A  MEL MARTIN    WIND (A
RAY OBIEDO       G   (A          PAUL SOCOLOW    B  (A  HARVEY MASON    D  (A  SAMMY FIGUEROA CONGA(A
```
S193B
SOUND
```
GRAHAM GREEN      B   (          (A) PHYSICAL WORLD (EP)                  19   TORCH           UK      TOR003
ADRIAN BORLAND  G V  (          (B) THE SOUND                            19   TORCH           UK      TOR008
BENITA MARSHALL   K  (          (C) JEOPARDY                             1980 KOROVA          UK      KODE 2
MICHAEL DUDLEY    D  (
```
S193C
SOUND CEREMONY
```
RON WARREN GANDERTON   G   (AB   (A) GUITAR STAR                          1979 CELESTIAL SOUND         RWG1
                                 (B) SOUND CEREMONY                       1980 CELESTIAL SOUND         RWG2
```
S194
SOUNDS INCORPORATED
```
ALAN HOLMES     SAX  (           (A) SOUNDS LIKE                          196  COLUMBIA        UK      SCX 2531
BARRIE CAMERON  SAX  (           (B) SOUNDS INCORPORATED                  1964 COLUMBIA 33SX1659       SCX 3531
TONY NEWMAN       D  (           (C) TWIST AT THE STAR CLUB HAMBURG       1964 PHILIPS                 P48 036L
JOHN ST JOHN GILLARD (           (D) TOP GEAR (EP)                        1964 COLUMBIA        UK      SEG 8360
TERRY FOGG           (           (E) SOUNDS INCORPORATED                  1966 STUDIO TWO      UK      TWO 1449
GRIFF WEST           (           (F) RINKY DINK                           1973 REGAL          UK      SREG1071
WES HUNTER           (
```
S195
SOUR GRAPES
```
RICHARD THOMPSON  G V  (A        (A) 1974 NO LPS
LINDA THOMPSON      V  (A
SIMON NICOL       G V  (A        WILLIE MURRAY   D  (A  STEVE BORRILL   B  (A
```
S195A
TIM SOUSTER
```
TIM SOUSTER       K    (AB       (A) SWIT DRIMZ                           1977 TRANSATLANTIC   UK      TRA 343
                                 (B) THE FUTURE IS NOW(EP)                1977 TRANSATLANTIC   UK      TBG1
```
S196
J D SOUTHER
```
JOHN DAVID SOUTHER G V (ABC      (A) JOHN DAVID SOUTHER                   1972 ASYLUM US SD 5055  UK SYL  9003
NED DOHENY        G    (AB       (A) JOHN DAVID SOUTHER                   1975 ASYLUM             UK  K53026
BRYAN GAROFALO    B    (A        (B) BLACK ROSE                           1976 ASYLUM US 7E1059   UK  K53037
GARY MALLABER   D K    (A        (C) YOU'RE ONLY LONELY                   1979 CBS                UK     83753
GIB GUILBEAU    FDL    (A
DAVID JACKSON   K B    (A        MIKE BOWDEN      B  (A  MICKEY McGEE     D  (A  JOEL TEPP        B  (A
JOHN BARBATA      D    (A        WAYNE PERKINS    G  (A  DANNY KOOTCH     G  (BC WADDY WACHTEL    G  (BC
PAUL STALLWORTH   B    (B        JIM KELTNER      D  (B  DAVID CROSBY     V  (B  ART GARFUNKEL    V  (B
ANDREW GOLD    V G K(B            GLENN FREY       G  (BC KENNY EDWARDS    B  (B  RUSS KUNKEL      D  (B
LINDA RONSTADT    V    (B        PETER ASHER      V  (B  STANLEY CLARKE   B  (B  DAVID DUKE     HRNS (B
VINCENT DEROSA  HRNS   (B        MIKE BOTTS       D  (BC ROY POPER      HRNS (B  DONALD BYRD    HRNS (B
LOWELL GEORGE     G    (B        CHUCK DOMANICO   B  (B  JOHN GUERIN      D  (B  JAMES BOND       B  (B
DON MENZA       FLT    (B        EARL DUMLER  WIND   (B  JOE WALSH        G  (B  DON HENLEY       V  (BC
DON GROLNICK    PNO    (C        RICK MAROTTA     D  (C  DAVID SANBORN  SAX  (C  DAN DUGMORE      G  (C
TOM SCOTT       SAX    (C        JACKSON BROWNE   V  (C  JORGE CALDERON   V  (C  PHIL EVERLY      V  (C
JAI WINDING     ORG    (C        DON FELDER       G  (C  FRED TACKETT     G  (C  JOHN SEBASTIAN HCA(C
```
S197
SOUTHER HILLMAN FURAY BAND
```
JOHN DAVID SOUTHER G V (AB       (A) SOUTHER HILLMAN FURAY BAND           1974 ASYLUM US 7E1006   UK SYLA 8758
CHRIS HILLMAN     B V  (AB       (B) TROUBLE IN PARADISE                  1975 ASYLUM US 7E1036   UK SYLA 8760
RICHIE FURAY    G V    (AB
PAUL HARRIS       K    (AB       AL PERKINS  G STEEL  (AB  JIM GORDON     D  (A  JAMES GUERCIO    G  (B
RON GRINEL        D    (B        GLENN FREY       V  (B  JOE LALA       PERC (AB DON HENLEY       V  (B
```
S198
SOUTHERN COMFORT
```
GORDON HUNTLEY STEEL V(ABC       (A) FROG CITY                            1971 HARVEST          UK      SHSP 4012
CARL BARNWELL   G V K(ABC        (B) SOUTHERN COMFORT                     1971 HARVEST          UK      SHSP  799
MARK GRIFFITHS  G V K(ABC        (B) SOUTHERN COMFORT                     1971 CBS              US           1011
ANDY LEIGH      B V    (ABC      (C) STIR DON'T SHAKE                     1972 HARVEST          UK      SHSP 4021
RAY DUFFY         D    (ABC      (D) DISTILLED (COMP)                     1976 HARVEST          UK      SHSM 2009
DON HARPER      VLN    (C
KEITH CUMMINGS  VLA    (C        PETER MORRIS     K  (C
```
S198A
SOUTHROAD CONNECTION
```
DELWIN GILLMAN B TROM K V(A      (A) POSITIVE ENERGY                      1980 UA   US LT1047    UK   UAG 30316
STEVEN FIELDS     V   (A
LINDA WATSON  V PERC K (A        ELLSWORTH FORRESTER K (A  HAROLD HUTTON  SAX  (V  LOU BARBARIN   TROM(A
MAERETHA STEWART  V   (A         KRYSTAL DAVIS    V  (A  YVONNE LEWIS     V  (A  JEFF MEDINA    G V (A
MICHAEL JONES     V   (A         ALBERT JONES   TPT  (A  RAY BLUE       SAX  (A
```

SOUTHSIDE JOHNNY & THE ASBURY DUKES S199

JOHNNY LYON G V (ALL	(A) LIVE AT THE BOTTOM LINE	1976 EPIC				AS 275
TONY PALLIGROSI TPT V(BC	(B) I DON'T WANT TO GO HOME	1976 EPIC US 34180			UK	81515
RICKY GAZDA TPT V(BCDF	(B) HAVING A PARTY (RI + 1 TRACK)	1979 EMBASSY			RI UK	31772
CARLO NOVI SAX V(BC	(C) THIS TIME IT'S FOR REAL	1977 EPIC US 34668			UK	81909
RICHIE'LA BAMBA'ROSENBERG TROM(BCDF	(D) HEARTS OF STONE	1978 EPIC US 35488			UK	82994
KENNY PENTIFALLO D V (BC	(E) THE JUKES	1979 MERCURY			UK	9100 067
KEVIN KAVANAUGH K V (BCDE	(F) LOVE IS A SACRIFICE	1980 MERCURY			UK	9111 081
EDDIE MANION SAX V(BCDF						

AL BERGER B V (BCDF   STEVE VAN ZANT   G   (D   STEVE BUSLOWE   B   (F   MAX WEINBERG   D   (D
STEVE BECKER   D   (F   STAN HARRISON   SAX   (D   BOB MUCKLIN   TPT   (D   JOEL GRANOLINO   G   (F
BILLY RUSH   G   (EF

SOUTHWEST S199A

JOHN FORD COLEY V (A	(A) SMELL OF INCENSE	19 HIP	US		HIS 7001
ENGLAND DAN SEALS V (A					

SOUTHWIND S199B

JOHN MOON MARTIN G V (B	(A) SOUTHWIND	19 VENTURE	US		VTS 4002
JIM PULTE B (B	(B) READY TO RIDE	19 BLUE THUMB	US		BTS 13
ERIK DALTON D (B	(C) WHAT A PLACE TO LAND	19 BLUE THUMB	US		BTS 26
FONTAINE BROWN K V G(B					

BOB B SOXX & THE BLUE JEANS S200

DARLENE LOVE V (A	(A) ZIP A DEE DOO DAH	1963 PHILLES			PHLP 4002
BOBBY SHEEN V (A	(B) WALL OF SOUND VOL 2	1976 PHIL SPECTOR			2307 004
FANITA JAMES V (A					
GLEN CAMPBELL G (A BILLY STRANGE G (A AL DELORY		(A LEON RUSSELL	PNO (A		
NINO TEMPO SAX (A					

SPACE ART S201

(S)SPACE ART   1977 ARIOLA   UK   AHAL8001

SPACE OPERA S202

BRETT WILSON D PERC(A	(A) SPACE OPERA	1973 EPIC	UK		65557
PHILIP WHITE B G K V (A					
SCOTT FRASER B K V(A DAVID BULLOCK G FLT HCA V(A					

SPANKY & OUR GANG S203

ELAINE'SPANKY'McFARLANE V PERC(ALL	(A) SPANKY & OUR GANG	1967 MERCURY UK SMCL20114	US SR61124
NIGEL PICKERING G B (ABCDE	(B) LIKE TO GET TO KNOW YOU	1968 MERCURY UK SMCL20121	US SR61161
JOHN SEITER D (ABCDE	(C) WITHOUT RHYME OR REASON	1968 MERCURY	US SR61183
MALCOLM HALE D (ABCDE	(D) SPANKY'S GREATEST HITS	1970 MERCURY	US SR61227
KENNY HODGES B (	(E) LIVE	1970 MERCURY	US SR61326
LEFTY BAKER G V (ABCDE	(F) CHANGE	1975 EPIC	US33580
GEOFFREY MYERS B (			

OTIS SPANN S204

OTIS SPANN PNO V(ALL	(A) OTIS SPANN IS THE BLUES	1960 CANDID 8001 + BARNABY US 30246	
BARRY MELTON G (O	(B) BLUES ARE WHERE ITS AT	1963 HMV UK CSD3609 BLUESWAY BLS6003	
LUTHER JOHNSON G (OBH	(C) PORTRAIT IN BLUES	1963 STORYVILLE	SLP157
LONNIE JOHNSON G (C	(D) PIANO BLUES	196 STORYVILLE	SLP168
JOS DAVIDSON B (O	(E) BLUES OF OTIS SPANN	1964 DECCA	UK LK 4615
LONNIE TAYLOR D (O	(F) BLUES NEVER DIE	1965 PRESTIGE US 7319	
LUCILLE SPANN V (OH	(F) BLUES NEVER DIE	1966 STATESIDE	UK SL 10169
MUDDY WATERS G V (LBHQT	(G) NOBODY KNOWS MY TROUBLES	1967 POLYDOR 545 030 +BOUNTY BY 6037	
SAMMY LAWHORN G (BH	(H) BOTTOM OF THE BLUES	1968 BLUESWAY	BLS 6013
MAC ARNOLD B (B	(H) BOTTOM OF THE BLUES	1968 STATESIDE	UK SL 10255
FRANCIS CLAY D (B	(J) FATHERS & SONS	1969 CHESS	CRLS 4556
GEORGE SMITH HCA (B	(K) BIGGEST THING SINCE COLOSSUS	1969 BLUE HORIZON US4802 UK 763217	
LITTLE WILLIE SMITH D (BC	(L) CRACKED SPANNER HEAD	1969 DERAM UK SML 1036	
RANSOM KNOWLING B (LQ	(M) HEART HEAVY WITH TROUBLE	19 BLUESWAY	BLS 6063
SPIT JAMES G (L	(N) WALKING BLUES	1972 EPIC US 31290 UK 64888	
STEVE GREGORY SAX (L	(O) CRYING TIME	1978 VANGUARD	VSD 6514
BUD BEADLE SAX (L	(P) OTIS SPANN	19 EVEREST	US 216
DANNY KIRWAN G (K	(Q) HALF AIN'T BEEN TOLD	19 BLACK CAT	NL 001
ROD M LEE TPT (L	(R) CHICAGO BLUES	19 TESTAMENT	US 2211
S P LEARY D (K	(S) THE EVERLASTING BLUES	19 SPIVEY	US 1013
PETER GREEN G (K	(T) WITH MUDDY WATERS BAND	19 MUSE	US 5008
JOHN McVIE B (K			
JOHNNY YOUNG G (G			

JAMES COTTON   HCA V(FG   JIMMY LEE MORRIS   B   (G   ROBERT WHITEHEAD   D   (G   GEORGE BUFORD   HCA (H
LAWRENCE WIMBERLEY B   (H   MEMPHIS SLIM   K   (Q

SPARKS S205

RON MAEL K V (ALL	(A) SPARKS	1971 BEARSVILLE US 2048	UK K45511
RUSSELL MAEL V (ALL	(B) WOOFER IN TWEETERS CLOTHING	1972 BEARSVILLE US 2110	UK K45510
ADRIAN FISHER G (C	(AB) SPARKS/WOOFER	1975 BEARSVILLE	UK K85505
HARLEY FEINSTEIN G (B	(C) KIMONO MY HOUSE	1974 ISLAND	UK ILPS 9272
EARL MANKEY G (B	(D) PROPAGANDA	1974 ISLAND	UK ILPS 9312
JIM MANKEY G B (B	(E) INDISCREET	1975 ISLAND	UK ILPS 9345
TREVOR WHITE G (	(F) BIG BEAT	1976 CBS US 34359 ISLANDUK ILPS 9445	
IAN HAMPTON B (	(G) INTRODUCING SPARKS	1977 EPIC 34901	UK 82284
DINKY DIAMOND D (C	(H) No 1 IN HEAVEN	1979 VIRGIN	UK V2115
PETER OXENDALE (	(J) BEST OF	1979 ISLAND	UK ILPS 9493
MARTIN GORDON B (C	(K) TERMINAL JIVE	1980 VIRGIN	UK V2137

ROGER RUSKIN SPEAR S206

ROGER RUSKIN SPEAR V K B SAX(AB	(A) ELECTRIC SHOCKS	1972 UA	UK UAS 29508
CHRIS WELCH D (A	(B) UNUSUAL	1973 UA	UK UAG 29381
PETER BANKS G (A			

ROY HOLLINGWORTH   G   (A   TONY NEWMAN   SAX   (A   DAVE GLASSON   PNO   (A   JERRY GARDINER   G   (A
GRAHAM PRESKETT   VLN   (A   SAM SPOONS   (A   CYRIL JORDAN   G   (A   ROGER C MITCHELL   V   (A
JAMES FERRELL   G   (A   DANNY MIHM   D   (A   CHRIS WILSON   V   (A   STEVE WALLER   G   (A
DAVE CLAGUE   B   (A   B J COLE   STEEL(A   ANDY NEWMAN   K V   (B   DAVE CHARLES   D   (B
RICHARD PERSELL   G   (B   JOE RYAN   G   (B   RICHARD TREECE   G   (B   MAGGIE STREDDER SINGERS(B
ARRAN ROE   D   (AB   KEN WHALEY   B   (B   JOHN SAWYER   B   (B

[385]

S207   SPECIALS

TERRY HALL	V	(AB	(A) THE SPECIALS	197''	TWO TONE	UK	CDLTT5001
LYNVAL GOLDING	G V	(AB	(B) MORE SPECIALS	1980	TWO TONE	UK	CHRTT5003
JERRY DAMMAS	K	(AB					
RODDY RADIATION	G	(AB HORACE GENTLEMAN	B	(AB NEVILLE STAPLES	V PERC(A	JOHN BRADBURY	D (A
RHODA DAKER	V	(B KIX THOMPSON	SAX	(B RICO RODRIGUES	HRNS (AB	DICK CUTHELL	HRNS(A

S207A   SPECKLED RED

RUFUS PERRYMAN	V PNO(ALL	(A) DIRTY DOZENS	19	DELMARK		DL 601
		( ) IN LONDON 1960	19	VJM		LC 11
		( ) PIANO BLUES	19	STORYVILLE		SLP 188
		( ) BLUES IN EUROPE	19	STORYVILLE		SLP 187

S208   RONNIE SPECTOR

RONNIE SPECTOR	V	(A	(A) SIREN	1981	RED SHADOW	UK	RED LP002

S209   CHRIS SPEDDING

CHRIS SPEDDING	G V	(ALL	(A) BACKWOODS PROGRESSION	1970	HARVEST	UK	SHSP 4004
STEVE CURRY	B	(E	(B) ONLY LICK I KNOW	1972	HARVEST	UK	SHSP 4017
MICK OLIVER	G	(E	(C) CHRIS SPEDDING	1976	RAK	UK	SRAK 519
DAVE LUTTON	D	(E	(D) HURT	1977	RAK	UK	SRAK 529
HERBIE FLOWERS	B	(D	(E) GUITAR GRAFFITI	2979	RAK	UK	SRAK 534
CLEM CATTINI	D	(D	(F) I'M NOT LIKE EVERYBODY ELSE	1980	RAK	UK	SRAK 542
RAY COOPER	PERC	(DE					

JACK EMBLOW	MUSETTE	(D	CHAS MILLS	V	(CD	CHRISSIE HYNDE	V	(D	JOHN CARTER	V	(D
NEIL LANCASTER	V	(CD	TONY NEWMAN	D	(E	LINDA LEWIS	V	(B	LAURIE ALLEN	D	(B
HAROLD FISHER	D	(D	ALAN HAWKSHAW	PNO	(B	PAUL FRANCIS	D	(B	PHIL DENNYS	K	(B
LES HURDLE	B	(C	BRIAN BENNETT	D	(C	DAVE COCHRAN	B	(C	TONY CARR	D	(C
TONY BURROWS	V	(C	BARRY MORGAN	D	(C	SUE GLOVER	V	(C	SUNNY LESLIE	V	(C
DAVE MATTACKS	D	(F	RICHARD GOWER	V	(F	PHIL LANZON	PNO	(F	PAUL WESTWOOD	B	(F
PHIL FURSDON	V	(F	CHRIS GREEN	CELLO	(F	CHRIS MERCER	SAX	(F	PETE MILLER	V	(F
PETE WILLIAMSON	CELLO(F		TONI CAMPO	B	(B					

S210   SPEED LIMIT

ACKER APPLEBY	V	(A	(A) FIRST OFFENCE	1978	SATRIL		SATL 4011
TONY BAYLIS	D	(A					
DOUGIE DENNIS	B	(A BRIAN SMITH	G	(A DAVID MORRIS	G (A		

S210A   SPEEDOMETERS

ROBBIE WATSON	B V	(A	(A) DAY IN THE LIGHTS	1979	ACROBAT	UK	ACRO5
IAN TAYLOR	G V	(A					
LEE DALLON	K	(A TOMMY EYRE	K	(A MARTIN FINLEY	G V (A STEVE PARRY D	(A
CHRIS GENT	SAX V(A PAUL SPENCER	D	(A				

S210B   SPEEDWAY BLVD

GREGG HOFFMAN	G V	(A	(A) SPEEDWAY BLVD	1980	EPIC	US	36533
DENNIS FELDMAN	B	(A					
ROY HERRING JR	V K PERC(A GLENN DOVE	D	(A JORDAN RUDES	K (A		

S210C   SKIP SPENCE

ALEXANDER 'SKIP' SPENCE(A		(A) OAR	1968	CBS	US	CS 9831

S211   JEREMY SPENCER

JEREMY SPENCER	G V	(ABC	(A) JEREMY SPENCER	1970	REPRISE US RSLP 9002	UK K44105
MICK FLEETWOOD	D	(A	(B) & THE CHILDREN	1973	CBS	US	31990	UK 65387
JOHN McVIE	B	(A	(C) FLEE	1979	ATLANTIC		UK K50624
DANNY KIRWAN	G V	(A					

PETER GREEN	BAN	(A	STEVE GREGORY	SAX	(A	PHIL HAM	G FLT(B	BOAZ	B V (B
MICHAEL	HCA G V	(B	GINNETHON	D PERC	(B	MICHAEL FOGARTY	K V	(C	JEFF SCHOEN	K (C
NEAL JASON	B	(C	AL IZZO	D	(C	BUZ BUCHANAN	D	(C	VICTOR SALAZAR	PERC(C
RAY GOMEZ	G	(C	STEVE THOMPSON	B	(C	SIMON PHILLIPS	D	(C		

S212   JOHN SPENCER'S LOUTS

JOHN SPENCER	G V K(A	(A) THE LAST LP	1978	BEGGARS BANQUET		BEGA3
JOHNNY G	G D V HCA (A					
DAVE THORNE	B BAN(A CHAS AMBLER	K D	(A			

S213   JIMMY SPHEERIS

JIMMY SPHEERIS	V G K(ALL	(A) ISLE OF VIEW	19	CBS US 30988	UK 64919
GEOFF LEVIN	G	(A	(B) JIMMY SPHEERIS	19	CBS US 32157	
DAVID CAMPBELL	VLN	(A	(C) DRAGON IS DANCING	1975	EPIC US 33565	
LEE CALVIN NICOLI	G FLT B V(A	(D) PORTS OF THE HEART	1976	CBS US 34276	

S214   SPHERICAL OBJECTS

STEVE SOLAMAR	V	(AB	(A) PAST & PARCEL	1978	OBJECT	UK	OBJ001
DUNCAN PRESTBURY	K	(AB	(B) ELIPTICAL OPTIMISM	1979	OBJECT	UK	OBJ004
ROGER HILTON	D	(AB	(C) FURTHER ELLIPSES	1980	OBJECT	UK	OBJ012
FREDERICK BURROWS	B	(AB					
JOHN BISSEL-SMITH	G	(AB					

S214A   SPIDER

AMANDA BLUE	V	(A	(A) SPIDER	1980	RSO		2394 260
KEITH LENTIN	G V	(A					
JIMMY LOWELL	B	(A ANTON FIG	D	(A HOLLY KNIGHT	K (A		

S214B   SPIDERZ

GUUS BOERS	V	(A	(A) PRESSURE	1980	HURRICANE		FLAK 103
BART BROUWER	K V	(A					
KOOS CORNELISSEN	G	(A JOHN SNEP	B	(A HENRI HOEYMANS	D (A APPIR BAARS SAX (A

S214C   SPIDERS FROM MARS

PETE McDONALD	V	(A	(A) SPIDERS FROM MARS	1976	PYE	UK	NSPL18479
WOODY WOODMANSEY	D	(A					
DAVE BLACK	G	(A TREVOR BOLDER	B	(A MIKE GARSON	K (A		

S214D   SPIN

REIN VAN DER BROEK	HRNS	(A	(A) SPIN	1976	ARIOLA	US	ST 50013
JAN VANNIK	WIND	(A					
HANS HOLLESTELLE	G	(A JAN HOLLESTELLE	B SYN(A HANS JANSEN	K (A CEES KRANENBURG	(A

DAVID SPINOZZA

DAVID SPINOZZA	G V (A		(A) SPINOZZA		1978 A&M	US	SP4677
JOE CARO	G (A						
ANTHONY JACKSON	B (A	RICK MAROTTA	D (A	MIKE MAINIERI	SYN (A	LEON PENDARVIS	PNO (A
LUTHER VANDROSS	V (A	DAVID LASLEY	V (A	DIVA GRAY	V (A	STEVE JORDAN	D (A
ROB MOUNSEY	PNO (A	ALAN RUBIN	TPT (A	RANDY BRECKER	TPT (A	JOHN FADDIS	TPT (A
WAYNE ANDRE	TROM (A	BARRY ROGERS	TROM (A	DAVID TAYLOR	TROM (A	TONY PRICE	TUBA(A
JOHN TREVOR CLARK	HRNS (A	SHARON MOE	HRNS (A	GEORGE MARGE	WIND (A	GEORGE YOUNG	WIND(A
DAVID TOFANI	WIND (A	KIM CARLSON	V (A	GORDON GRODY	V (A	WARREN BERNHARDT	K (A
GARY MURE	PERC (A	DAVID CAREY	PERC (A	RUBENS BASSINI	PERC (A	DON GROLNICK	PNO (A
MICHAEL BRECKER	SAX (A	LEW SOLOFF	TPT (A	DAVID SANBORN	SAX (A	RONALD CUBER	SAX (A
STRING SECTION	(A						

SPIRIT

S216

RANDY CALIFORNIA	G V(ABCDFGHJKLMNO	(A) SPIRIT	1968 CBS	UK 63278	US	31457
ED CASSIDY	D (ABCDEFGHJKLMNO	(A) SPIRIT	1968 ODE		US Z1244004
JAY FERGUSON	K V(ABCDF	(A) BEST OF(REPACKAGED)	1979 EMBASSY UK 31693		
MARK ANDES	B (ABCDFJ	(AC) SPIRIT/CLEAR	1973 EPIC		US	31457
MIKE FONDALIER	D (	(B) THE FAMILY THAT PLAYS TOGETHER	1968 CBS	UK 63523	US	31461
ROB ARKIN	B (	(B) THE FAMILY THAT PLAYS TOGETHER	1968 ODE		US Z1244014
JOHN LOCKE	K (ABCDEF	(BE)FAMILY/FEEDBACK	1975 EPIC		US	33761
MATT ANDES	G (J	(C) CLEAR SPIRIT	1969 CBS	UK 63729 ODE	Z1244016
JOHN ARLISS	B (	(D) 12 DREAMS OF Dr SARDONICUS	1970 EPIC	UK 64191	US	30267
AL STAEHELY	B V (E	(E) FEEDBACK	1971 EPIC	UK 64507	US	31175
CHRIS STAEHELY	G V (E	(F) BEST OF SPIRIT	1973 EPIC	UK 65585	US	32271
LARRY KNIGHT	B (LMN	(G) SPIRIT OF 76	1975 MERCURY UK 6672 012	US SRM2 804
COZY POWELL	D (	(H) SON OF SPIRIT	1975 MERCURY UK 9100 019	US SRM11053
STU PERRY	D (	(J) FARTHER ALONG	1976 MERCURY		US SRM11094
BARRY KEENE	B (	(K) FUTURE GAMES	1977 MERCURY UK 9100 036	US SRM11133
JOHN TERLEP	B (	(L) LIVE	1977 ILLEGAL UK ILP 001
ERNIE WATTS	SAX (J	(M) LIVE (MADE IN GERMANY)	1978 POTATO	172200
MICHAEL D TEMPLE	MAND (J	(N) LIVE	1978 POTATO		US PR 2001
IAN UNDERWOOD	(J	(O) POTATOLAND	1981 LINE		GER 6 24641
DAVID BLUMBERG	HRNS (J	(O) POTATOLAND	1981 BEGGARS BANQUET	UK BEGA 23
NICK DE CARO	HRNS (J	(O) POTATOLAND	1981 RHINO	US
LAWRENCE WEISBERG	B (J					
TERRY ANDERSON	V (K ****NOTE (L,M,N, ARE DIFFERENT RECORDS BUT OF THE SAME TOUR ,			

TRACKS & MIX ARE DIFFERENT.)

SPIRIT OF JOHN MORGAN

S217

JOHN MORGAN	K V (AB	(A) SPIRIT OF JOHN MORGAN	1969 CARNABY	UK	CNLS 6002
MICK WALKER	D V (A	(B) AGE MACHINE	1970 CARNABY	UK	CNLS 6007
DON WHITAKER	G V (A				
PHIL SHUTT	B (A				

SPIROGYRA

S218

MARTIN COCKERHAM	G V (B	(A) ST RADIGUNDS	1971 B&C		CAS 1042
STEVE BORRILL	B (B	(B) OLD BOOT WINE	1972 PEGASUS		PEG 13
MARK FRANCIS	G V K(B	(C) BELLS BOOTS & SHAMBLES	1973 POLYDOR		2310 246
BARBARA GASKIN	V (B				
DAVE MATTACKS	D (B	JULIAN CUSACK VLN K (B	ALAN LAING	CELLO (B RICK BIDDULPH	MAND(A

SPITBALLS

S219

	(A) SPITBALLS	1978 BESERKLEY	BSERK15

SPIZZ

S219A

MARK COALFIELD	K (A	(A) DO A RUNNER	1980 A&M	UK	AMLE68514
DAVE SCOTT	G (A				
C P SNARE	D (A	JIM SOLAR B (A			

SPLINTER

S220

BILL ELLIOTT	V (ABC	(A) THE PLACE I LOVE	1974 DARK HORSE		AMLH22001
BOBBY PURVIS	V (ABC	(B) HARDER TO LIVE	1975 DARK HORSE		AMLH22006
BILLY PRESTON	K (B	(C) TWO MAN BAND	1977 DARK HORSE US 3073 UK	K56403
EARL PALMER	D (B				
BILL DICKINSON	B (B	GEORGE HARRISON G (B	CHRIS SPEDDING	G (B	JOHN TAYLOR	K (B
JIM KELTNER	D (B	TOM SCOTT HRNS (B	RALPH MACDONALD	PERC (B	WADDY WACHTEL	G (B
BILL NUTTYCOMBE	(B				

SPLIT ENZ

S221

TIM FINN	V K (ALL	(A) MENTAL NOTES	1976 CHRYSALIS	UK	CHR 1131
NEIL FINN	G V (ALL	(B) DIZRHYTHMIA	1977 CHRYSALIS	UK	CHR 1145
NOEL CROMBIE	(ABC	(C) TRUE COLOURS	1980 A&M	UK	AMLH64822
EDDIE RAYNEY	K (C	(D) BEGINNING OF THE ENZ	1980 CHRYSALIS	UK	CHR 1329
JON CHIN	B (	( ) FRENZY	19		
PHIL JUDD	G (				
EDDIE CROWTHER	PERC (	ROBERT COLES HRNS (	MALCOLM GREEN	PERC (C	NIGEL GRIGGS	B (C

SPLODGENESSABOUNDS

S221A

MAX SPLODGE	V (A	(A) SPLODGENESSABOUNDS	1981 DERAM	UK	5ML 1121

MARK SPOELSTRA

S222

MARK SPOELSTRA	(ALL	(A) 5 & 20 QUESTIONS	1965 ELEKTRA		EKS 7283
		(B) STATE OF MIND	1966 ELEKTRA		EKS 7307
		(C) MARK SPOELSTRA	1969 CBS		9793
		(D) MARK SPOELSTRA	197 FOLKWAYS		3572

SPONTANEOUS COMBUSTION

S223

GARY MARGETTS	G V (A	(A) SPONTANEOUS COMBUSTION	1972 HARVEST	UK	SHVL 801
TRIS MARGETTS	B V (A	(B) TRIAD	1972 HARVEST	UK	SHVL 805
TONY BROCK	D (A				

SPOOKY TOOTH

S224

MIKE HARRISON	K V(ABCDEFG	(A) ITS ALL ABOUT SPOOKY TOOTH	1968 ISLAND UK ILP59080	
GARY WRIGHT	K V(ABCEFG	(B) SPOOKY TOOTH	1969 ISLAND UK ILP59098 US A&M 4194
LUTHER GROSVENOR	G (ABCD	(C) CEREMONY	1969 ISLAND UK ILP59107	A&M 4225
GREG RIDLEY	G B (AB	(D) THE LAST PUFF	1970 ISLAND UK ILP59117 US A&M 4266
MIKE KELLIE	D (ABCDG	(E) YOU BROKE MY HEART.....	1973 ISLAND UK ILP59227 US A&M 4385
ANDY LEIGH	B (C	(F) WITNESS	1973 ISLAND UK ILP59255 US	9255
CHRIS STAINTON	K (D	(G) THE MIRROR	1974 ISLAND	US	9292
HENRY McCULLOUGH	G (D	(G) THE MIRROR	1974 GOODEAR UK	EARL 2001
ALAN SPENNER	(D	(G) THE MIRROR	1979 CHARLy UK	CR 30167

(CONTINUED)

```
S224   (CONTINUED)              SPOOKY TOOTH
  MIKE PATTO      V D K(G      (H) POP CHRONIK                    1975 ISLAND         EURO      VOL10
  CHRIS STEWART   B   (EF      (I) THE BEST OF                    1976 ISLAND UK ILPS9368
  MICK JONES      G   (EFG
  BRYSON GRAHAM   D   (EFG VAL BURKE   B V  (G  PIERRE HENRY   ELECTRONICS  (C
S224A                             SPORTS
                             (A) DONT THROW STONES                1979 SIRE                   SRVK 6001
                             (B) SPORTS                           1979 STIFF                  SEEZ   15
                             (C) SPORTS (EP)                      1979 STIFF                  LAST    5
S225                             SPOTNICKS
  BO LANDER       G   (A       THE SPOTNICKS IN LONDON            1961 KARUSSELL              KALPS1012
  BO WINBERG      G   (        THE SPOTNICKS IN PARIS             1963 KARUSSELL              KALPS1014
  BJORN THELIN    B   (        THE SPOTNICKS IN SPAIN             1963 SWEDISC                SWELP   1
  OVE JOHANSSON   D   (        OUTA SPACE                         1963 ORIOLE                 SPS 40037
                               THE SPOTNICKS IN JAPAN             1966 SWEDISC                SWELPC 38
                               THE SPOTNICKS IN WINTERLAND        1966 SWEDISC                SWELPC 48
                               THE SPOTNICKS                      1975 POLYDOR                2482  051
                               BEST OF                            19   POLYDOR                184   151
                               POP GIANTS No 8                    19   BRUNSWICK              2911  519
                               VERY BEST OF                       1977 AIR                    CHM  1171
S226                             SPREADEAGLE
  ANDY BLACKFIELD  G V (A      (A) A PIECE OF PAPER               1972 CHARISMA               CAS  1055
  SAM LLEWELLYN    B V PERC(A
  JIM COPLEY       D   (A  JOHN FIELD   PERC (A  TIM PHILLIPS   V G K(A   NICK        PERC (A
  SHELL            PERC (A
S227                             SPRIGUNS
  MANDY MORTON     G V (ABC     (A) REVEL WEIRD & WILD            1976 DECCA                  SKL  5262
  TOM LING         VLN V(AB     (B) TIME WILL PASS                1977 DECCA                  SKL  5286
  DICK POWELL      G V K(AB     (C) MAGIC LADY                    1979 BANSHEE                BAN  1101
  MIKE MORTON      B V (AB
  CHRIS WOODCOCK   D   (A  WAYNE MORRISON G MAND V(B  TIM HART            (C   B J COLE     STEEL(A
  LEA NICHOLSON CONCERTINA(B  DENNIS DUNSTAN   PERC D(B   GRAEME TAYLOR    (C
S229                          BRUCE SPRINGSTEEN
  BRUCE SPRINGSTEEN G V (ALL   (A) GREETINGS FROM ASBURY PARK N J 1973 CBS       US 31093   UK 65480
  CLARENCE CLEMONS SAX V(ABCDE (B) WILD, INNOCENT & THE EAST STREET 1973 CBS     US 32432   UK 65780
  GARRY TALLENT    B   (ABCDE  (C) BORN TO RUN                    1975 CBS       US 33795   UK 69170
  MAX WEINBERG     D   (CDE    (D) DARKNESS ON THE EDGE OF TOWN   1978 CBS       US 35318   UK 86061
  ROY BITTAN       K   (CDE    (E) THE RIVER                      1980 CBS                  UK 88510
  VINI LOPEZ    D V HRNS (AB   (ABC)BRUCE SPRINGSTEEN(TRIPLE)     1979 CBS                  UK 66353
  DANNY FEDERICI   K V (BCDE
  DAVID SANCIOUS   K SAX(ABC RICHARD BLACKWELL PERC (B   ALBANY TELLONE    SAX (B    STEVE VAN ZANDT  G (CE
  MIKE APPEL       V   (C  ERNEST CARTER      D  (C   RANDY BRECKER  HRNS (C    MICHAEL BRECKER  HRNS(C
  DAVID SANBORN    SAX (C  WAYNE ANDRE       TROM (C   RICHARD DAVIS  B   (AC   HAROLD WHEELER   PNO (A
  MARK VOLMAN      V   (E  HOWARD KAYLAN      V  (E
S230                             SPUD
  DON KNOX         V FDL(AB     (A) A SILK PURSE                  1975 PHILIPS               9108  002
  MICHAEL SMITH    V B  (AB     (B) THE HAPPY HANDFUL             1975 PHILIPS               9108  003
  AUSTIN KENNY     G V  (AB     (C) SMOKING ON THE BOG            1977 SONET                 SNTF  742
  DERMOT O'CONNOR  G SYN(A
  MALCOLM WRAY     V   (A  DON HARRIS        D   (B  DANNY SMITH    PERC (B   JIMMY FAULKNER  G  (B
  RICK EPPING      CONGA(B  STEVE MOORE      PERC (B  DONAL LUNNY    G SYN(A
S230A                            SPY
  DANNY SEIDENBERG VLN  (A      (A) SPY                           1980 KIRSHNER      US        36378
  DAVID NELSON     G V  (A
  BOB GOLDMAN      D   (A  MICHAEL VISCEGLIA B   (A  DAVE LEBOLT    K  (A   JOHN VISLOCKY    V (A
S231                          SPYRO GYRA
  JAY BECKENSTEIN  SAX (BC      (A) MORNING DANCE                 197  INFINITY               INS  2003
  TOM SCHULMAN     K   (BC      (B) SPYRO GYRA                    1977 INFINITY               INS  2008
  DAVID SAMUELS PERC VIBES(BC   (C) CARNIVAL                      1980 MCA                        3087
  JEREMY WALL      K   (BC
  JIM KURZDORFER   B   (BC TOM WALSH          D   (B  EMILE LATIMER  PERC (B   RICK BELL       TROM(B
  FRED MARSHALL    TROM (B  RUBENS BASSINI   CONGA (B  FREDDY RAPILLO G  (B   GREG MILLAR     G  (B
  TONY GARUSSO     TPT  (B  CHET CATALLO      G   (C  WILL LEE       B  (C   ELI KONIKOFF    D  (C
  CRUSHER BENNETT  PERC (C  ROB MOUNSEY       SYN  (C  MICHAEL BRECKER FLT (C   HIRAM BULLOCK   G  (C
  GERARDO VELEZ    PERC (C  RANDY BRECKER    TPT  (C  DAVID DARLING  CELLO(C   JOHN TROPEA     G  (C
  STEVE JORDAN     D   (C  STEVE KROON       PERC (C
S232                             SQUEEZE
  CHRIS DIFFORD    G V (ABCD    (A) SQUEEZE                       1978 A&M                    AMLH68465
  GLENN TILBROOK   G V (ABCD    (B) COOL FOR CATS                 1979 A&M                    AMLH68003
  JULIAN HOLLAND   K   (ABCD    (C) SQUEEZE (10")                 1979 A&M        US          SP3413
  GILSON LAVIS     D   (ABCD    (D) ARGY BARGY                    1980 A&M                    AMLH64802
  JOHN BENTLEY     B   (CD      (EP) PACKET OF THREE              197  DEPTFORD FUN CITY      DFC 01
  HARRY KAKOULLI   B   (ABC
S232A                            BILLY SQUIER
  BILLY SQUIER     G V (A       (A) A TALE OF THE TAPE            1980 CAPITOL                ST  12062
  BRUCE KULICK     G   (A
  BUCKY BALLARD    B   (A  BOBBY CHOUINARD   D   (A  DAVID SANCIOUS  K  (A   RICHARD T BEAR  K  (A
  ERNEST CARTER    PERC (A
S233                             CHRIS SQUIRE
  CHRIS SQUIRE     B G V(A      (A) FISH OUT OF WATER             1975 ATLANTIC   US 18159   UK K50203
  BILL BRUFORD     D   (A
  MEL COLLINS      SAX (A  JIM HASTINGS      FLT  (A  PATRICK MORAZ  K SYN(A   BARRY ROSE      K  (A
  ANDREW BRYCE JACKMAN K (A  ORCHESTRA             (A
S234                             STAA MARX
  ROBIN PARKER     D   (A       (A) 1979
  BARRY SIMS       G V (A
  PETE MACER       G V (A  MARTIN 'KLUTZ'SIMS    B V (A
```

STACKRIDGE

S235

ANDREW CRESWELL-DAVIS	V G K D(ALL	(A) STACKRIDGE	1971 MCA UK MDKS8002 UK 74RI	MCG3505
JAMES WARREN	V B G(ABCF	(B) FRIENDLINESS	1972 MCA UK MKPS2025 UK 74RI	MCF2504
MICHAEL SLATER	V FLT K(ABCDEF	(C) MAN IN A BOWLER HAT	1973 MCA UK	MCG3501
MICHAEL EVANS	V VLN(ABCF	(D) EXTRAVAGANZA	1974 ROCKET ROLLA1 +	PIGL 11
BILLY BRENT	D (A	(D) EXTRAVAGANZA	1974 SIRE US	7509
JIM CRUN WALTER	G B (BCEF	(E) MR MICK	1976 ROCKET UK	ROLL 3
BILLY SPARKLE	D (BCF	(F) PINAFORE DAYS	1974 SIRE US	7503
REG LEOPOLD	VLN (CF	(G) DO THE STANLEY(COMP)	1976 MCA UK	MCF2747
WILLIAM REID	VLN (CF			
GRAEME SCOTT	VLN (CF VIVIAN JOSEPH CELLO(CF JACK EMBLOW	ACC (CF RAY DAVIES TPT (CF		
DEREK TAYLOR	HRNS (CF R CHAMBERLAIN HRNS (CF ROD BOWKETT	K (DF KEITH GEMMELL WIND(DEF		
PAUL KARAS	B V (DF ROY MORGAN D (DF PETER VAN HOOKE	D (E JOANNA CARLIN V (E		
DAVE LAWSON	K (E RAY RUSSELL G (B LAMB	TROM (DF M FRY TUBA(F		

STACKWADDY

S236

JOHN KNAIL	V HCA(1	(A) STACKWADDY	1971 DANDELION DAN 8003 +	2310 154
MICK SCOTT	G (1	(B) BUGGER OFF	1972 DANDELION	2310 231
STUART BARNHAM	B (12	(1) 1966/71 (2) 1973 /76		
STEVE REVELL	D (1			
MIKE SWEENEY	V (2 WAYNE JACKSON B (2 ROBIN GOODWIN	D (2		

STADIUM DOGS

S237

PETE COUSINS	B V (A	(A) WHAT'S NEXT	1978 MAGNET	MAG 5025
PAUL GRIFFITHS	G V (A			
STAN PEARCE	D (A JONATHAN PERKINS K V (A KIRK THORN	G V (A KEVIN WILKINSON D (A		

STAINLESS STEEL

S238

(A) CAN CAN	1978 EMI UK	EMC 3259

STALLION

S238A

(A) STALLION	1977 CASABLANCA UK CAL2014	US 7040
(B) HEY EVERYBODY	19 CASABLANCA	US 7083

STAMPEDERS

S239

RONNIE KING	(ALL	(A) STAMPEDERS	1972 REGALZONOPHONE UK	SLPZ 1032
RICH DODSON	(ALL	(B) FROM THE FIRE	1974 REGALZONOPHONE UK	SLRZ 1039
KIM BERLY	(ALL	(C) NEWDAY	1975 EMI UK	INS 3003
GIBBY LACASSA	PERC (D	(D) HIT THE ROAD	1976 QUALITY US	QLP 1001
GUY MARCHI	HRNS (D			
RANDY MARCHI	HRNS (D BOB ADDUONO HRNS (D			

STANDELLS

S240

LARRY TAMBLYN	K V (C	(A) DIRTY WATER	196 TOWER US	ST5027
TONY VALENTINO	G (C	(B) WHY PICK ON ME	196 TOWER US	ST5044
GARY LANE	(	(C) HOT ONES	196 TOWER US	ST5049
DICK DODD	D (C	(D) TRY IT	196 TOWER US	ST5098
DAVE BURKE	G B (C	(E) LIVE & OUT OF SIGHT	196 SUNSET US	5136
		(F) IN PERSON AT P Ja	196 LIBERTY US	LST 7384

MICHAEL STANLEY

S241

MICHAEL STANLEY	G V (ALL	(A) ROSEWOOD BITTERS	1973 TUMBLEWEED	TW 3505
JONAH KOSLEN	G V (CDEF	(B) FRIENDS & LEGENDS	1975 MCA	MCA 372
DANNY PECCHIO	B V (CDEF	(C) YOU BREAK IT YOU BOUGHT IT	1975 EPIC US	33492
TOMMY DOBECK	D (CDEFG	(D) LADIES CHOICE	1976 EPIC US	33917
BOB PELANDER	K (EFG	(E) STAGE PASS	1977 EPIC US	34661
GARY MARKASKI	V (FG	(F) CABIN FEVER	1978 ARISTA US 4182 UK SPART	1066
KEVIN RALEIGH	K V (G	(G) HEARTLAND	1980 EMI AMERICA UK	AML 3015
MICHAEL GISMONDI	B (G			

PAUL STANLEY

S242

PAUL STANLEY	V G B(A	(A) PAUL STANLEY	1978 CASABLANCA NBLP7123
BOB KULICK	G (A		
RICHIE FONTANA	D (A CRAIG KRAMPF D (A CARMINE APPICE	D (A MARIA VIDAL V (A	
DIANA GRASSELLI	V (A MIRIAM NAOMI VALLE V (A STEVE BUSLOWE	B (A ERIC NELSON B (A	
DOUG KATSAROS	PNO (A STEVE LACEY G (A PEPPI CASTRO	V (A	

VIV STANSHALL

S243

VIV STANSHALL	V WIND(AB1	(A) MEN OPENING UMBRELLAS AHEAD	1974 WB UK	K56052
BUBS WHITE	G (A1	(B) SIR HENRY AT RAWLINSON END	1978 CHARISMA UK	CAS 1139
STEVE WINWOOD	B ORG(A	(1) BIG GRUNT 1969		
GASPAR LAWAL	PERC V(A			
NEIL INNES	K G (A JIM CAPALDI D (A DEREK QUINN	PERC (A RIC GRECH VLN (A		
REBOP K BAAH	PERC (A DORIS TROY V (A MADELINE BELL	V (A BARRY ST JOHN V (A		
AYUS APE	V (A GANI V (A IAN WALLACE	D (1 DENNIS COWAN B (1		
ROGER RUSKIN SPEAR SAX (1 FRED MUNT 1 ZOOT MONEY	PNO (			

STAR PARK

S244

COLIN MOULDING	B (	(NO RECORDS)	
ANDY PARTRIDGE	G (		
TERRY CHAMBERS	D (DAVE CARTNER G (STEVE HUTCHINS	V (JOHNNY PERKINS K (	

STARBUCK

S245

BRUCE BLACKMAN	K V (C	(A) MOONLIGHT FEELS RIGHT	1976 PRIVATE STOCK	PVLP 1008
JIMMY COBB	B V (C	(B) ROCK'N'ROLL ROCKET	1977 PRIVATE STOCK	PVLP 1023
KEN CRYSLER	D (C	(C) SEARCHING FOR A THRILL	1978 UA US LA918 UK	UAS 30221
SLOAN HAYES	K V (			
DARRYL KUTZ	G V (C DAVID SHAVER G V (C BO WAGNER	PNO (JOHN WALKER G V (C		
JOHN FRISTOE	G (C			

STARCASTLE

S246

STEPHEN HAGLER	G V (ABC	(A) STARCASTLE	1976 EPIC US 33914 UK	81347
GARY STRATER	B V (ABC	(B) FOUNTAINS OF LIGHT	1977 EPIC US 34375 UK	81665
HERB SCHILDT	K (ABC	(C) CITADEL	1977 EPIC US 34935 UK	82232
STEPHEN TASSLER	D V (ABC	(D) REAL TO REEL	1978 EPIC US 35441 UK	82916
MATTHEW STEWART	G V (B			
TERRY LUTTRELL	V (B			

STARDRIVE

S247

ROBERT MASON	SYN (AB	(A) INTERGALATIC TROT	1973 ELEKTRA US EKS75058 UK K42140	
JAIME AUSTRIA	B (AB	(B) STARDRIVE	1974 CBS US 44047	
BRUCE DIMAS	PERC (A			
HARVEY SARCH	G (AB MICHAEL BRECKER SAX (A STEPHEN GADD	D (A HOWARD REGO D (B		

S248   **STARDUST**
     (A) STARDUST   1977 SATRIL   SATL 4008

S249   **ALVIN STARDUST**

ALVIN STARDUST	V	(ALL					
		(A) UNTOUCHABLE	1974	MAGNET	UK	MAG	5001
		(B) ALVIN STARDUST	1974	MAGNET	UK	MAG	5004
		(C) ROCK WITH ALVIN	1975	MAGNET	UK	MAG	5007
		(D) GREATEST HITS	1977	MAGNET	UK	MAG	4002

S250   **STARGARD**

ROCHELLE RUNNELS	V K	(ABC	(A) STARGARD	1978	MCA	UK	MCF	2834
DEBRA ANDERSON	V	(ABC	(B) WHAT YOU WAITING FOR	1978	MCA	UK	MCF	2859
JANICE C WILLIAMS	V	(ABC	(C) CHANGING OF THE GARD	1979	WB	US BSK3386 UK	K56746	
KENI BURKE	B	(C						

VERDINE WHITE	B	(C	BUTCH AZEVEDO	D	(C	LARRY TOLBERT	D	(C	JOSEPH BAKER	G	(C
CHARLES FEARING	G	(C	ROBERT PALMER	G	(C	MARK DAVIS	K	(C	DEAN GANT	K	(C
ROBERT WRIGHT	K	(C	EDDIE BROWN	PERC	(C	PAULINHO DA COSTA	PERC	(C	DON MYRICK	HRNS	(C
LOUIS SATTERFIELD	HRNS	(C	RAHEEM LEE MICHAEL DAVIS	(C		FRED JACKSON	HRNS	(C	OSCAR BRASHAR	HRNS	(C
JEROME RICHARDSON	HRNS	(C	GARNETT BROWN	HRNS	(C	BEVERLEY ASHBY	HARP	(C			

S250A   **STARJETS**

PAUL BOWEN		(A	(A) GOD BLESS THE STARJETS	1979 EPIC	UK	83534
TERRY SHARPE		(A				
SEAN MARTIN		(A	LIAM L'ESTRANGE	(A		

S250B   **STARK NAKED**

PAUL VENIER	V K PERC	(A	(A) STARK NAKED	1971 RCA	US LSP 4592	
LYNE BUNN	V	PERC(A				
JIM MONAHAN	G V	(A	JOHN FRAGOS	D PERC(A TOM RUBINS	B (A RICHARD BELSKIN	G (A

S251   **EDWIN STARR**

EDWIN STARR	V	(ALL	(A) SOUL MASTER	1969	TAMLA UK STML11094	US GORDY 931
L MIDDLETON	G	(L	(B) 25 MILES	197		US GORDY 940
J ROBERTS	B	(L	(C) WAR & PEACE	197		US GORDY 948
SPIKE	K	(L	(D) INVOLVED	1972	TAMLA UK STML11199	US GORDY 956
R REED	D	(L	(E) HITS OF EDWIN STARR	1974	TAMLA UK STML11209	
M SINGER	D	(L	(F) HELL UP IN HARLEM	1974	TAMLA UK STML11210	US TAMLA 802
E FLETCHER	PERC	(L	(G) FREE TO BE MYSELF	19	GRANITE	US 1005
K PEACHY	HRNS	(L	(H) AFTERNOON SUNSHINE	1977	GTO UK	GTLP 019
E HILL	HRNS	(L	(J) EDWIN STARR	197	20TH CENTURY	UK BT 538
A HAMILTON	HRNS	(L	(K) CLEAN	1979	20TH CENTURY	UK BT 559
CURT SLETTEN	HRNS	(L	(L) HAPPY RADIO	1979	20TH CENTURY	UK BT 591
JOEL PESKIN	FLT	(L	(M) STRONGER THAN YOU THINK I AM	1980	20TH CENTURY	UK BT 615
H KIM	FLT	(L				

H PRESTON	FLT	(L	D STOUT	FLT	(L	DAVID SHIELDS	B	(M	JAMES GADSON	D	(M
MELVIN D WEBB	D	(M	DAVID T WALKER	G	(M	HOWARD FEITEN	G	(M	RALPH E HAMMER	G	(M
GLENNIS JONES	G	(M	CLARK E SPANGLER	SYN	(M	JIMMY McAFEE	B	(M	JOHN J BARNES	K	(M
LARRY FARROW	K	(M	RONALD COLEMAN	K	(M	EARL VAN DYKE	K	(M	RICK McAFEE	K	(M
EDDIE BROWN	PERC	(M	LUKE METOYER	PERC	(M	LUTHER WARREN	V	(LM	CLIFTON CURTIS	V	M
ORRIN WATERS	V	(LM	MAXINE WILLARD	V	(LM	JULIA TILLMAN	V	(LM	JERRY PETERSON	SAX	(M
WILLIAM CLARK	V	(M	MONROE WRIGHT	V	(M	MAURICE YOUNG	V	(M			

S252   **RINGO STARR**

RINGO STARR	V PERC D	(ALL	(A) SENTIMENTAL JOURNEY	1970	APPLE	UK PCS 7101	US 3422
JOHN LENNON	V	PNO(CF	(B) BEACOUPS OF BLUES	1970	APPLE	UK PAS 10002	US 3368
GEORGE HARRISON	G	(C	(C) RINGO	1973	APPLE	UK PCTC 252	US 3413
PAUL McCARTNEY K	V SAX	(CF	(D) GOODNIGHT VIENNA	1974	APPLE	UK PLS 7168	US 3417
KLAUS VOORMANN	B	(CF	(E) BLAST FROM YOUR PAST	1975	APPLE	UK PCS 7170	US 3422
BILLY PRESTON	K	(C	(F) ROTOGRAVURE	1976	POLYDOR	UK 2302 040	US ATCO 18193
JIM KELTNER	D	(CF	(G) RINGO THE FOURTH	1977	POLYDOR	UK 2310 556	US ATCO 19108
MILT HOLLAND	PERC	(C	(H) BAD BOY	1978	POLYDOR	UK 2310 599	US PORTRAIT35378
LON VAN EATON	PERC	(CG	(NB) RE ISSUES OF APPLE RECORD ARE ON PARLOPHONE/CAPITOL SAME NUMBERS				
DEREK VAN EATON	PERC	(CF	DIFFERENT PREFIX				
LEVON HELM	MAND	(CF					
HARRY NILSSON	V	(CF					

MARTHA REEVES	V	(C	LINDA McCARTNEY	V	(CF	RICHARD PERRY	V	(C	MELISSA MANCHESTER	V(F
JESSE ED DAVIS	G	(F	VAN DYKE PARKS	V K	(F	JOE ESPOSITO	V	(FG	SNEAKY PETE	STEEL(F
MARC BOLAN	G	(C	TOM SCOTT	HRNS	(C	VINI PONCIA	G V	(CFG	JAMES BOOKER	PNO (C
NICKY HOPKINS	PNO	(C	JIMMY CALVERT	G	(C	BOBBY KEYS	SAX	(C	ROBBIE ROBERTSON	G (C
RICK DANKO	FDL	(C	GARTH HUDSON	ACC	(C	MERRY CLAYTON	V	(C	STEVE CROPPER	G (C
TOM HENSLEY	PNO	(F	CHUCK FINDLEY	HRNS	(C	ROBERT GREENIDGE	PERC	(F	JOHN JARVIS	K (F
COOKER LOPRESTI	B	(F	DUITCH HELMER	V	(FG	ERIC CLAPTON	G V	(F	PAUL STALLWORTH	B (F
DANNY KORTCHMAR		(F	DR JOHN	K V	(F	PETER FRAMPTON		(F	DAVID SPINOZZA	G (G
JEFF MIRANOV	G	(G	JOHN TROPEA	G	(G	DON GROLNICK	K	(G	TONY LEVIN	B (G
HUGH McDONALD	B	(G	STEVE GADD	D	(G	CORNELL DUPREE	G	(G	RICHARD TEE	K (G
NICK MARRERO	PERC	(G	JEFF GUTCHEON	K	(G	MARIETTA WATERS	V	(G	MAXINE ANDERSON	V (G
DAVID LASLEY	V	(G	ROBIN CLARK	V	(G	DEBRA GRAY	V	(G	MELISSA MANCHESTER	V (G
LUTHER VANDROSS	V	(G	JIM GILSTRAP	V	(G	DICK FEGY	G	(G	DAVID BROMBERG	FDL G(CG
CHUCK RAINEY	B	(G	DANNY KORTCHMAR	G	(G	BRIE HOWARD	V	(G	LYNN PITNEY	V (G
ARNOLD McCULLER	V	(G	REBECCA LOUIS	V	(G	BETTE MIDLER	V	(G	RANDY BRECKER	HRNS(G
MICHAEL BRECKER	HRNS	(G	KEN BISCHEL	SYN	(G	DON BROOKS	HCA	(G		

S253   **STARRY EYED & LAUGHING**

TONY POOLE	G V K	(AB	(A) STARRY EYED & LAUGHING	1974	CBS	UK 80405	
IAIN WHITMORE	B V	(AB	(B) THOUGHT TALK	1975	CBS	US 33837	UK 80907
MIKE WACKFORD	D	(AB					

ROY CARR	BONGO(A		ROSS McGEENEY	G V	(AB	PAUL TURNER	D	(	DAVID POMEROY	B V	(
ARTHUR MAY	G V	(	B J COLE	STEEL(A		RAY JACKSON	MAND	(A	PETER WOODS	K	(A
RUSS BALLARD	PNO	(A	DAN LOGGINS	HCA	(A	JEFF BANNISTER	K	(B	MICHAEL GORE	CELLO(B	
COLIN WALKER	CELLO(B		FRANK RICOTTI	VIBES(B		PETE ZORN	SAX	(B			

S253A   **STARS & STIPS**

CESAR ZUIDERWIJK	D	(A	(A) NEVERGREEN	1976 POLYDOR	UK 2925 041
BERTUS BORGERS	SAX V(A				
RINUS GERRITSEN	B	(A	ROBERT JAN STIPS K PERC(A		

S254   **STARZ**

BRENDAN HARKIN	G	(	(A) STARZ	1976 CAPITOL	11539
RICHIE RANNO	G	(	(B) VIOLATION	1977 CAPITOL	11617
MIKE LEE SMITH	V	(	(C) ATTENTION SHOPPERS	1978 CAPITOL	11730
PETE SWEVAL	B	(	(D) COLISEUM ROCK	1979 CAPITOL	11861
JOE X		(			

STATUS QUO

Personnel			Albums	Year/Label	Catalogue
FRANCIS ROSSI	G V	(ALL	(A) PICTURESQUE MATCHSTICKABLE	1968 PYE	NSPL18220
RICK PARFITT	K G V	(ALL	(B) SPARE PARTS	1968 PYE	NSPL18301
JOHN COUGHLAN	D	(ALL	(C) MESSAGES FROM THE STATUS QUO	1968 CADET	LSP 315
ALAN LANCASTER	V B G	(ALL	(D) STATUS QUOTATION	1969 MARBLE ARCH	MAL 1193
			(E) MA KELLYS GREASY SPOON	1970 PYE	NSPL18344
			(F) DOG OF TWO HEAD	1971 PYE	NSPL18371
			(G) BEST OF STATUS QUO	1972 PYE	NSPL18402
ROY LYNES	K	(PQSTXWY	(I) GOLDEN HOUR	1973 PYE	GH 556
ROB YOUNG	HCA	(FIKORZc	(I) PILE DRIVER	1973 VERTIGO 6360 082 US A&M 4381
JIMMY HOROWITZ	PNO	(I	(J) HELLO	1974 VERTIGO 6360 098 US A&M 3615
BRUCE FOSTER	K	(F	(K) QUO	1974 VERTIGO 9102 001 US A&M 3649
STEWART BLANDAMER	SAX	(J	(L) ON THE LEVEL	1975 VERTIGO 9102 002 US CAPITOL 11381
JOHN MEALING	PNO	(J	(M) GOLDEN HOUR	1975 PYE	GH 604
DAVID KATZ	HRNS	(V	(N) STATUS QUO	1975 VERTIGO QUO 13
STEVE FARR	SAX	(V	(O) POP CHRONIK VOL 5	1975 PYE	87099
BUD REVO	V	(V	(P) THE REST OF STATUS QUO	1976 PYE	PKL 5546
FRANK RICOTTI	PERC	(UV	(Q) BLUE FOR YOU	1976 VERTIGO 9102 006
ANDY BOWN	K	(JORUVZc	(R) LIVE	1977 VERTIGO 6641 580 US CAPITOL 11623
BERNIE FROST	V	(c	(S) STATUS QUO FILE	1977 PYE	FLD 005
JOY YATES	V	(V	(T) PICTURES OF MATCHSTICK MEN	1977 HALLMARK	257
GRASS	V	(F	(U) ROCKIN ALL OVER THE WORLD	1977 VERTIGO 9102 014 US CAPITOL 11749
TOM PARKER	K	(K	(V) IF YOU CANT STAND THE HEAT	1978 VERTIGO 9102 027
JAQUIE SULLIVAN	V	(V	(W) COLLECTION	1978 PICKWICK	PDA 046
			(X) STATUS QUO	1978 HALLMARK	HMA 260
			(Y) IN MY CHAIR	1979 MODE	FR 9018
			(Z) WHATEVER YOU WANT	1979 VERTIGO 9102 037
			(a) MEAN GIRL	1979 MODE	FR 9053
			(b) JUST FOR THE RECORD	1979 PYE	NSPL18607
			(c) JUST SUPPOSIN'	1980 VERTIGO 6302 057
			(d) GOLD BARS	1980 VERTIGO QUOTV1
			(e) NEVER TOO LATE	1981 VERTIGO 6302 104

STATIC

CHRIS ANSELL	V	(A	(A) 1978	
DAVE BOWDEN	G	(A		
ANDY AITKEN	D	(A	BARRY PHILPOTT	B (A

S256

STEALERS WHEEL

			Albums	Year/Label		
GERRY RAFFERTY	G V	(ABC	(A) STEALERS WHEEL	1973 A&M	US 4377	UK AMLH68121
JOE EGAN	K V	(ABC	(B) FERGUSLIE PARK	1974 A&M	US 4419	UK AMLH68209
RAB NOAKES		(	(C) RIGHT OR WRONG	1975 A&M	US 4517	UK AMLH68293
ROGER BROWN		(	(D) STUCK IN THE MIDDLE WITH YOU (COMP	197 A&M		UK AMLH64708
IAN CAMPBELL	B	(	(E) BEST OF	1981 MFP		UK 50501
STEVE GREGORY	SAX	(B				

PAUL PILNICK	G	(A	ROD COOMBES	D	(A	TONY WILLIAMS	B	(A	DELISLE HARPER B (
LUTHER GROSVENOR	G	(	ANDY STEELE	D PERC	(C	DAVE WINTOUR	B	(C	CHRIS MERCER SAX(BC
CHRIS NEILL	HCA	(BC	BERNIE HOLLAND	G	(BC	HUGH BURNS	G	(C	DAVID BRIGGS K (C
GERALDINE JOSEPHINE	K G	(C	PETER ROBINSON	K	(B	GARY TAYLOR	B SYN	(B	JOE JAMMER G (B
MIKE STOLLER	K	(B	ANDREW STEELE	D	(B	CORKY HALE	HARP	(B	

STEAMHAMMER

			Albums	Year/Label		
KIERAN WHITE	HCA G V	(ABC	(A) STEAMHAMMER	1968 CBS US 26490	UK 63611
MARTIN PUGH	G V	(ABCD	(A) STEAMHAMMER	1970 REFLECTION	REFL1
STEVE DAVY	B V	(ABC	(B) STEAMHAMMER MARK 2	197 CBS	UK 63694
MICK BRADLEY	D	(CD	(C) MOUNTAINS	1970 METRONOME	15 376
LOUIS CENNAMO	B	(CD	(C) MOUNTAINS	1971 BRAIN	201 006
KEITH NELSON	BAN	(C	(D) SPEECH	1972 BRAIN 1009	0040 054
MIKE RUSHTON		(A	(E) THIS IS	1972 BRAIN 201 042	0021 043
MICKY WALLER		(	(F) ROCK GENERATION VOL 6	1971 BYG	529 706
MARTIN QUITTENTON	G	(A	(G) PLACES & FACES VOL 6	197 BYG	529 906
STEVE JOLLIFFE	WIND V	(B			
HAROLD McNAIR	FLT	(A	PETE SEARS	PNO (A	

S258

STEAMPACKET

			Albums	Year/Label	
BRIAN AUGER	K V	(A	(A) FIRST OF THE SUPERGROUPS	1977 CHARLY	UK CR 30020
JULIE DRISCOLL	V	(A			
VIC BRIGGS	G	(A	RICKY BROWN B (A	MICK WALLER D (A	LONG JOHN BALDRY V (A
ROD STEWART	V	(A	PETER GREEN G (	MICK FLEETWOOD D (	

S259

WALTER STEDDING

WALTER STEDDING		(A	(A) WALTER STEDDING 19 ?
ROBERT FRIPP	G	(A	
CHRIS STEIN		(A	RICHARD LLOYD (A

S259A

STEEL MILL

			Albums	Year/Label	
TERRY WILLIAMS	G	(A	(A) GREEN EYED GOD	1975 PENNYFARTHING	UK PELS 549
JEFF WATTS	B	(A			
CHRIS MARTIN	D	(A	DAVE MORRIS K V (A	JOHN CHALLENGER WIND (A	

S260

STEEL PULSE

			Albums	Year/Label	
DAVID HINDS	G V	(ABC	(A) HANDSWORTH REVOLUTION	1978 ISLAND	UK ILPS 9502
BASIL GABBIDON	G V	(ABC	(B) TRIBUTE TO THE MARTYRS	1979 ISLAND	UK ILPS 9568
RONNIE McQUEEN	B	(ABC	(C) CAUGHT YOU	1980 ISLAND	UK ILPS 9613
SELWYN BROWN	K V	(ABC			
PHONSO MARTIN	V PERC	(ABC	STEVE NESBITT D (ABC	MICHAEL RILEY V PERC(A	RICO RODRIGUES TROM(B
GODFREY MADURA	SAX	(ABC	DICKAGE HRNS (B		

S261

S262
STEELY DAN

WALTER BECKER	B V G(ALL	(A) YOU GOTTA WALK IT(SOUNDTRACK)	1971 VISA	US 7005	UK SPARK 78	124
DONALD FAGEN	K V (ALL	(B) CANT BUY A THRILL	1972 ABC	US 758	UK PROBE SPB1062
DENNY DIAS	G (ABCDEFG	(B) CANT BUY A THRILL	1974 ABC		UK	ABCL 5024
JOE DISCEPOLO	D (A	(C) COUNTDOWN TO ECSTASY	1973 ABC	US 779	UK PROBE SPB1079
JIM HODDER	D (ABCD	(C) COUNTDOWN TO ECSTASY	1974 ABC		UK	ABCL 5034
DAVID PALMER	V K (ABC	(D) PRETZEL LOGIC	1974 ABC	US 808	UK PROBE SPBA6282
JEFF BAXTER	G (BCD	(D) PRETZEL LOGIC	1974 ABC		UK	ABCL 5045
JEFF PORCARO	D (DEJ	(E) KATY LIED	1975 ABC	US 846	UK	ABCL 5094
MIKE McDONALD	V (EFGJ	(F) THE ROYAL SCAM	1976 ABC	US 931	UK	ABCL 5161
RICK DERRINGER	G (CEJ	(G) AJA	1977 ABC	US 1006	UK	ABCL 5225
ELLIOTT RANDALL	G (BEF	(H) GREATEST HITS (DBL)	1978 ABC		UK	ABCD 616
DEAN PARKS	G (DEFG	(I) PLUS FOUR (EP)	1977 ABC		UK	ABE 12003
HUGH McCRACKEN	G (EJ	(J) GAUCHO	1980 MCA		UK	MCF 3090
LARRY CARLTON	G (EFGJ

BEN BENAY	G (CD	LEE RITENOUR	G (G	STEVE KHAN	G (GJ	JAY GRAYDON	G (G
MICHAEL OMARTIAN	K (DEG	DAVID PAICH	K (BDE	VICTOR FELDMAN	PERC K(BCDEFGJ	ROYCE JONES	V (C
CHUCK RAINEY	B (EFGJ	WILTON FELDER	B (DE	HAL BLAINE	D (E	TIM SCHMIT	B V (DFG
PLAS JOHNSON	SAX (DFG	OLLIE MITCHELL	TPT (D	JEROME RICHARDSON	SAX (BD	LEW McCREARY	HRNS (DG
ERNIE WATTS	SAX (CD	RAY BROWN	B (C	TOM SCOTT	SAX (GJ	WAYNE SHORTER	SAX (G
PAUL HUMPHREY	D (G	CLYDIE KING	V (BFG	VANETTA FIELDS	V (BFG	SHIRLEY MATTHEWS	V (BCEFG
REBECCA LOUIS	V (G	JOE SAMPLE	K (GJ	BERNARD PURDIE	D (FGJ	PETE CHRISTIEB	SAX (G
JIM HORN	SAX (FG	BILL PERKINS	HRNS (EG	JACKIE KELSO	HRNS (G	CHUCK FINDLEY	HRNS(FG
SLYDE HYDE	TROM (FG	RICK MAROTTA	D (FGJ	PAUL GRIFFIN	K V (FG	DON GROLNICK	K (FGJ
GARY COLEMAN	PERC (FG	ED GREENE	D (G	JIM KELTNER	D (G	SNOOKY YOUNG	HRNS(B
MYRNA MATTHEWS	V (CE	PATRICIA HALL	V (C	JAMES ROLLESTON	V (C	MICHAEL FENELLY	V (C
LANNY MORGAN	SAX (C	JOHN ROTELLA	SAX (C	BOB FINDLEY	HRNS (F	TUBBY BRUCE	(D
STEVE GADD	D (GJ	JOHN KLEMMER	HRNS (F	JIM GORDON	D (D	CAROLYN WILLIS	V (E
JIMMIE HASKELL	HRNS (E	PHIL WOODS	HRNS (E	ERROL BENNETT	PERC (J	MARK KNOPFLER	G (J
DAVE TOFANI	SAX (J	DAVID SANBORN	SAX (J	RON CUBER	SAX (J	RANDY BRECKER	HRNS (J
PAT REBILLOT	K (J	GEORGE MARGE	CLAR (J	HIRAM BULLOCK	G (J	WALTER KANE	CLAR (J
LESLIE MILLER	V (J	NICHOLAS MARRERO	PERC(J	PATTI AUSTIN	V (J	WAYNE ANDRE	TROM (J
TONI WINE	V (J	LANI GROVES	V (J	DIVA GRAY	V (J	GORDON GRODY	V (J
FRANK FLOYD	V (J	ZACK SANDERS	V (J	ANTHONY JACKSON	B (J	ROB MOUNSEY	PNO (J
RALPH McDONALD	PERC (J	MICHAEL BRECKER	SAX (J	VALERIE SIMPSON	V (J

S263
STEELEYE SPAN

ASHLEY HUTCHINGS	B (ABCE	(A) HARK THE VILLAGE WAIT	1970 RCA	UK	SF8113
TIM HART V G DULCIMER	(ALL	(A) HARK THE VILLAGE WAIT	1971 UA	UAG 29160
MADDY PRIOR	V (ALL	(A) HARK THE VILLAGE WAIT	1974 MOONCREST	UK	CREST 22
GAY WOODS	V CONC(A	(A) HARK THE VILLAGE WAIT	1976 CHRYSALIS	US	1120
TERRY WOODS	G V MAND(A	(B) PLEASE TO SEE THE KING	1971 B&C	UK	CAS 1029
MARTIN CARTHY	G V (BCLO	(B) PLEASE TO SEE THE KING	1974 MOONCREST	UK	CREST 4
PETER KNIGHT K V VLN	(BCDEFGHJKP	(B) PLEASE TO SEE THE KING	1976 CHRYSALIS	US	1119
RICK KEMP	B V (DEFGHJKLOP	(C) TEN MAN MOP	1971 PEGASUS	UK	PEG 9
BOB JOHNSON	G V (DEFGHJKP	(C) TEN MAN MOP	1974 MOONCREST	UK	CREST 9
NIGEL PEGRUM	D FLT(GHJKLP	(C) TEN MAN MOP	1976 CHRYSALIS	US	1121
JOHN KIRKPATRICK	V ACC(LO	(D) BELOW THE SALT	1972 CHRYSALIS		CHR 1008
DAVID BOWIE	SAX (G	(E) INDIVIDUALLY & COLLECTIVELY(COMP)	1972 CHARISMA	UK	CS5
PETER SELLERS	V UKE(H	(F) PARCEL OF ROGUES	1973 CHRYSALIS		CHR 1046
		(G) NOW WE ARE SIX	1974 CHRYSALIS		CHR 1053
		(H) COMMONERS CROWN	1975 CHRYSALIS		CHR 1071
		(I) ALMANACK (COMP)	1973 CHARISMA	UK	CS12
		(J) ALL AROUND MY HAT	1975 CHRYSALIS		CHR 1091
		(K) ROCKET COTTAGE	1976 CHRYSALIS		CHR 1123
		(L) STORM FORCE 10	1977 CHRYSALIS		CHR 1151
		(M) ORIGINAL MASTERS(COMP DBL)	1977 CHRYSALIS US 2 1136 UK CJT 3
		(N) TIME SPAN	1977 MOONCREST	UK	CRD 1
		(O) LIVE AT LAST	1978 CHRYSALIS		CHR 1199
		(P) SAILS OF SILVER	1980 CHRYSALIS		CHR 1304

S263A
STEPASIDE

PAUL ASHFORD	B V (A	(A) SIT DOWN & RELAPSE	1980 STEPASIDE	STEP 001
BRENNY BONASS	G V (A
ROBBIE BRENNAN	D V (A	DAVE KODAK	K V (A

S264
LEIGH STEPHENS

LEIGH STEPHENS	G V K(AB	(A) RED WEATHER	1969 PHILIPS	UK	SBL7897
PETE SEARS	B (B	(B) CAST OF THOUSANDS	1971 CHARISMA	UK	CAS 1040
KEVIN WESTLAKE	D (AB

MICK WALLER	D (AB	NICKY HOPKINS	K (A	IAN STEWART	(A	BOB ANDREWS	PNO (B
DICK MORRISSEY	SAX (B	DAVE CASWELL	TPT (B	CHARLENE COLLINS	V (B	KIM GARDNER	B (B
TONY ASHTON	PNO (B	ROY DYKE	D (B	DAVE QUINCY	SAX (B	NOEL NORRIS	TPT (B
ALIKI ASHMAN	V (B	GLENN CORNICK	B (B	JEFF PEACH	SAX (B	LYLE JENKINS	SAX (B
DAVE JACKSON	SAX (B	PETER ROSS	V (B

S265
STEPPENWOLF

JOHN KAY	G V (123456	(A) STEPPENWOLF	1968 DUNHILL	US 50029	UK STATESIDE	5020
GEORGE BIONDO	B V (456	(A) STEPPENWOLF	1968 RCA		UK	RD 7974
JERRY EDMONTON	D (123456	(B) THE SECOND	1968 DUNHILL	US 50037	UK STATESIDE	5003
BOBBY COCHRAN	G (56	(C) AT YOUR BIRTHDAY PARTY	1969 DUNHILL	US 50053	UK STATESIDE	5011
WAYNE COOK	K (6	(D) EARLY STEPPENWOLF	1969 DUNHILL	US 50060	UK STATESIDE	5015
GOLDY McJOHN	K (12345	(E) MONSTER	1970 DUNHILL	US 50066	UK STATESIDE	5021
JOHN MORGAN	B (2	(F) STEPPENWOLF LIVE	1970 DUNHILL	US 50075	UK STATESIDE	5029
RUSHTON MOREVE	B (1	(F) STEPPENWOLF LIVE	197 ABC RI		UK	ABCL5007
NICK ST NICHOLAS	B (3	(G) STEPPENWOLF 7	1970 DUNHILL	US 50090	UK PROBE	SPBA6254
LARRY BYROM	G (34	(H) FOR LADIES ONLY	1970 DUNHILL	US 50110	UK PROBE	SPBA6260
MICHAEL MONARCH	G (12	(J) STEPPENWOLF GOLD	1971 DUNHILL	US 50099	UK PROBE	SPB 1033
(1) 1967		(J) STEPPENWOLF GOLD	197 ABC		UK	ABCL8613
(2) 1967		(K) REST IN PEACE	1972 DUNHILL	US 50124	UK PROBE	SPB 1059
(3) 1969		(L) 16 GREATEST HITS	1974 DUNHILL	US 50135	UK PROBE	SPB 1071
(4) 1970		(L) 16 GREATEST HITS	197 ABC RI		UK	ABCL5076
(5) 1974		(M) SLOW FLUX	1974 EPIC	US 33093	UK	80358
(6) 1974		(N) HOUR OF THE WOLF	1975 EPIC	US 33583	UK	69151
		(O) SKULLDUGGERY	1976 EPIC	US 34120	UK	81328
					(CONTINUED)

STEPPENWOLF

```
(P) MASTERS OF ROCK              1975 ABC              EURO   054 95147
(Q) THE ABC COLLECTION           197  ABC         US   30008
(R) BORN TO BE WILD              197  EPIC        US   34382
(S) 16 GREAT PERFORMANCES        197  ABC         US    4001
```

CAT STEVENS

```
CAT STEVENS        V G K(ALL    (A) MATTHEW & SON               1967 DERAM          UK   SML  1004
ALUN DAVIES        G V (DEFGJL   (B) NEW MASTERS                 1968 DERAM          UK   SML  1018
GERRY CONWAY       D V (FGHLJ    (AB) MATTHEW /NEW MASTERS       197  DERAM          US        18005
JEAN ROUSSEL       K  (GHJLN     (C) WORLD OF CAT STEVENS        1970 DECCA          UK        SPA 93
BRUCE LYNCH        B  (JLN       (D) MONA BONE JAKON             1970 ISLAND UK ISLP 9118 US A&M 4260
JIM RYAN           G  (J         (E) TEA FOR THE TILLERMAN       1971 ISLAND UK ILPS 9135 US A&M 4280
MARK WARNER        G  (J         (F) TEASER & THE FIRECAT        1971 ISLAND UK ILPS 9154 US A&M 4313
ROLAND HARKER      BANJ (J       (G) CATCH BULL AT FOUR          1972 ISLAND UK ILPS 9206 US A&M 4365
JOHN RYAN          B  (DE        (H) FOREIGNER                   1973 ISLAND UK ILPS 9240 US A&M 4391
HARVEY BURNS       D  (DEF       (I) THE BEST OF                 1973 TELDEC         EURO 17009
PETER GABRIEL      FLT (D        (J) BUDDAH & THE CHOCOLATE BOX  1974 ISLAND UK ILPS 9274 US A&M 3623
JACK ROSTEIN       VLN (E        (K) VIEW FROM THE TOP(A+B)      1974 DERAM    UK DPA3019/20
LARRY STEELE       B PERC (F     (L) NUMBERS                     1975 ISLAND UK ILPS 9379 US A&M 4555
ANDREAS TOUMAZIS   (FG           (M) GREATEST HITS               1975 ISLAND UK ILPS 9310 US A&M 4519
ANGELOS HATZIPAVLI (F            (N) IZITSO                      1977 ISLAND UK ILPS 9451 US A&M 4702
ALAN JAMES         B  (G         (O) BACK TO EARTH               1978 ISLAND UK ILPS 9565
LINDA LEWIS        V  (G         ( ) CATS CRADLE                 19   LONDON         US        50010
BERNARD PURDIE     D  (H         ( ) VERY YOUNG & EARLY SONGS    19   DERAM          US        18061
PHIL UPCHURCH      (H
PAUL MARTINEZ      (H   HERBIE FLOWERS    B    (H  PATTI AUSTIN     V  (H  BARBARA MASSEY  V (H
TASHA THOMAS       V  (N   JIM JOHNSON          (N  ANDY NEWMARK        (N  BILL BERG         (N
CHICK COREA        K  (N   ELKIE BROOKS     V   (N  ROGER HAWKINS   D  (N  DAVID HOOD      B (N
BARRY BECKETT      (N   PETE CARR            (N  TIM HENSON          (N  DAVID CAMPBELL    (N
SUZANNE LUNCH      (N   WELDON MYRICK        (N  REGGIE YOUNG        (N  BARRY MORGAN      (N
BRODERICK SMITH    (N   MARJORIE LAGERWALL   (N  CARLA BENSON        (N  EVETTE BENTON     (N
BARBARA INGRAM     (N   RAY GOMEZ        G   (L  SIMON NICOL     G  (L  CHICO BATERA   PERC(L
GORDIE FLEMING     ACC (L   DAVID SANBORN   SAX (L
```

JOHN STEVENS

```
JOHN STEVENS       D  (ALL    (A) CHALLENGE                      1966 EYEMARK         EMPL 1002
ALLAN HOLDSWORTH   G  (P      (B) KARYOBIN                       1968 ISLAND     UK   ILPS 9097
JEFF YOUNG         K  (P      (C) SPONTANEOUS MUSIC ENSEMBLE(OLIV)1969 MARMALADE 608 008 + 2384 009
RON MATTHEWSON     B  (P      (D) SOURCE FROM & TOWARDS          1971 TANGENT    UK   TNGS 107
NICK STEPHENS      B  (M      (E) BIRDS OF A FEATHER             1972 BYG        FR   529  023
RON HERMAN         B  (M      (F) SO WHAT DO YOU THINK           1973 TANGENT    UK   TGS  118
ROBERT CALVERT     SAX (M     (G) FOR YOU TO SHARE               1974 'A'             001
DAVID COLE         G  (M      (H) BOBBY BRADFORD PLUS SME        1974 FREEDOM         24865
EVAN PARKER        (ST        (J) SMO                            1975 'A'             003
NIGEL COOMBES      VLN (R     (K) JOHN STEVENS AWAY              1976 VERTIGO         6360 131
ROGER SMITH        G  (R      (L) SOMEWHERE INBETWEEN            1977 VERTIGO         6360 135
COLIN WOOD         CELLO(R     (M) 'MAZIN' ENNIT                 1977 VERTIGO         6360 141
TREVOR WATTS       (QU        (N) CHEMISTRY                      1977 VINYL           VS   1978
BARRY GUY          (QU        (O) 'AH                            1978 VINYL           VS   111
HOWARD RILEY       PNO (U      (P) TOUCHING ON                   1978 VINYL           VS   105
BOBBY BRADFORD     (H         (Q) NO FEAR                        1978 SPOTLITE        SPJ  556
                              (R) BIO SYSTEMS                    1978 INCUS           24
                              (S) LONGEST NIGHT VOL 1            1978 OGUN            OG 120
                              (T) LONGEST NIGHT VOL 2            1978 OGUN            OG 420
                              (U) END GAME                       1979 JAPO            600  28
                              (V) APPLICATION                    197  SPOTLITE        SPJ  513
                              (W) & SME VOL 1                    1981 NESSA           N17
```

SHAKIN' STEVENS

```
STEVE PRIOR                   (A) LEGEND                         1970 PARLOPHONE      PCS 7112
MIKE BARRATT                  (B) I'M NO D J                     1971 CBS             52901
BRIAN WILLIAMS                (C) ROCKIN'N' SHAKIN'              1972 CONTOUR         2870 152
BOB PETERSEN                  (D) SHAKIN' STEVENS & THE SUNSETS  1974 EMERALD         GES 1121
TREVOR HAWKINS                (E) SHAKIN' STEVENS & THE SUNSETS  1974 PHILIPS         6478 010
                              (F) SHAKIN STEVENS                 1978 TRACK           2406 011
                              (G) THE LEGEND                     1979 EMI             NUT   25
                              (H) MARIE MARIE  (ONE TRACK DIFF)  198  EPIC
                              (H) THIS OLD HOUSE                 1981 EPIC            84985
                              (I) AT THE ROCKHOUSE               1981 MAGNUM FORCE UK MFLP 004
```

B W STEVENSON

```
B W STEVENSON      G V (ALL    (A) B W STEVENSON                 1972 RCA     US   LSP 4685
SID SIMS           B  (A      (B) LEAD FREE                     1972 RCA     US   LSP 4794
DON SIMMONS        D  (A      (C) MY MARIA                      1973 RCA     US   APLI 0088
PAT FERRARI        G  (A      (D) CALABASAS                     1974 RCA     US   APLI 0410
RONALD STEELE      G  (A      (E) WE BE SAILIN'                 1975 WB      US        2901
MICKEY RAPHAEL     HCA (AB     (F) LOST FEELING                  1977 WB      US        3012
ED SHOOK           PERC V(A     (G) BEST OF                       1977 RCA     US   APLI 2394
RICHARD SILEN      PERC (A      (H) LIFELINE                      1980 MCA     US   MCA  3215
KITTY APPLING      V  (A
RAY TATE           STEEL(A   SHANE APPLING    B   (A  BRIAN CHRISTIAN   TAMB (A  JIM GORDON    D   (BCD
DENNIS ST JOHN     D  (B   LARRY CARLTON    G   (BCD DEAN PARKS    G   (B  EMORY GORDY   B   (B
RED RHODES         STEEL(BD  LARRY MUHOBERAC  K   (BCD GIB GUILBEAU  FDL (B  LARRY MURRAY  V   (B
THAD MAXWELL       V  (B   LINDA DILLARD    V   (B  JOE OSBORN    B   (CDF HERB STEINER STEEL MAND(C
LAYTON DE PENNING  G  (C   RODNEY GARRISON  B   (C  DONNIE DOLAN  D   (C  BOBBY RAMBO   G   (D
JAY PRUITT         K  (D   BOBBYE HALL    PERC (D  JIMMY HASKELL  SYN  (D  LINDA RONSTADT V  (D
DANIEL MOORE       V  (DE  ANDREW GOLD      V   (D  KEN EDWARDS    V   (D  KIM CARNES    V   (D
DAVE ELLINGTON     V  (D   JULIA TILLMAN    V   (D  DARLA GRISER   V   (D  CASSELL WEBB   V   (E
FRED KRC           D  (E   RILEY OSBORNE    PNO G(E  STUART SCHULMAN STEEL G (E  WALLER COLLIE  B  (E
TREVOR LAWRENCE    SAX (E   LARRY BUNKER   PERC (E  JIM HORN       SAX  (E  NICK DE CARO STRINGS(E
REGGIE YOUNG       G  (F   STEVE GIBSON     G   (FGH CASEY KELLY   G   (F  DENNIS LINDE   G  (F
LARRY LONDIN       D  (F   SHANE KEISTER    PNO (FGH BOBBY WOOD    PNO (F  RON OATES     PNO(F
FARRELL MORRIS     PERC (F   BUZZ CASON       V   (F  BERGEN WHITE  V STRINGS(FH CAROL MONTGOMERY V (F
SANDY POSEY        V  (F   DOTTIE DELEONIBUS V   (F  ROGER CLARK   D   (F  TERRY McMILLAN PERC HCA(H
STEVE SCHAFFER     B  (H   CHRIS CHRISTIAN  G   (H  JON GION       G   (H  BOBBY OGDIN   K   (H
DIANE TIDWELL      V  (H   SHERI CRAMER     V   (H  LISA SILVER    V   (H
```

AL STEWART

Personnel:

AL STEWART	G V K(ALL									
MARVIN PRESTWICK	G	(B								
JIMMY PAGE	G	(B								
SIMON BECKENRIDGE	G	(B								
ASHLEY HUTCHINGS	B	(B								
BRIAN ODGERS	B	(BDE								
BRIAN BROCKLEHURST	B	(BDE								
MARTYN FRANCIS	D	(B								
HARVEY BURNS	D	(B								
PHIL PHILLIPS	K	(B								
STEPHEN GRAY	G	(C								
GEORG HULTGREEN		(C	GERRY CONWAY	D	(CF	MIKE WOODS		(C	LARRY STEELE		(C
TIM HINKLEY	K	(CE	DUFFY POWER		(C	LOUIS CENNAMO	B	(C	PETER GAVIN	D	(C
TIM RENWICK	G	(DEFGJ	CAL BATCHELOR	B	(D	TIM WALKER	G	(D	BRINSLEY SCHWARZ	G	(D
RICK WAKEMAN	K	(DE	BOB ANDREWS	K	(DE	BRUCE THOMAS	B	(DE	JOHN WILSON	D	(DE
ROGER POPE	D	(D	GRAHAM HUNT	D	(D	JOHN DONELLY	V	(DE	MICK WELTON	V	(DE
KEVIN POWERS	V	(DE	PETE BERRYMAN	G	(E	ISAAC GUILLORY	G	(EF	B J COLE STEEL		(E
PETER WOOD	K	(EFGJ	BOB SARGEANT	K	(E	ALISTAIR ANDERSON	CONC	(E	DAVE SWARBRICK	MAND	(E
HAIM ROMANO	MAND	(E	LUCIANO BRAVO	PERC	(E	LENNOX JAMES	PERC	(E	MICHAEL OLIVER	PERC	(E
FRANK RICOTTI	PERC	(E	ROGER MEDDOWSTAYLOR	PERC	(E	FRANCIS MONKMAN	SYN	(E	KRYSIA KOCJAN		(E
DAVE ELLIS	G	(F	SIMON NICOL	G	(F	STUART COWELL	G	(F	PETE WINGFIELD	K	(F
GEORGE FORD	B	(FG	PETER MOSS	B	(F	BARRY DE SOUZA	D	(F	TONY CARR	PERC	(F
GRAHAM SMITH	HCA	(FG	CHAS MILLS	V	(F	BRIAN BENNETT	V	(F	NEIL LANCASTER	V	(F
PETER WHITE	G	(G	DON LOBSTER	K	(G	STUART ELLIOTT	D	(GJ	BOBBY BRUCE	VLN	(G
PHIL KENZIE	SAX	(GJ	MARION DRISCOLL	PERC	(G	DAVID PACK	V	(G	TONY RIVERS	V	(G
JOHN PERRY	V	(J	PETER ROBINSON	K	(J	JEFF PORCARO	D	(J	TREVOR LUCAS	G	(C

(A) BEDSITTER IMAGES	1967 CBS	UK 63087	RI		64023
(B) LOVE CHRONICLES	1969 CBS	UK			63460
(C) ZERO SHE FLIES	1970 CBS	UK			63848
(D) ORANGE	1972 CBS	UK			64730
(E) PAST, PRESENT & FUTURE	1974 CBS	UK 65726	US JANUS		3063
(F) MODERN TIMES	1975 CBS	UK 80477	US JANUS		7012
(G) YEAR OF THE CAT	1976 RCA	UK RS1082	US JANUS		7072
(H) THE EARLY YEARS	1978 RCA	UK PL25131	US JANUS 2		7026
(J) TIME PASSAGES	1978 RCA	UK PL25173	US ARISTA		4190
(K) 24 PCARROTS	1980 RCA	UK PL25306			

GARY STEWART

GARY STEWART	G V	(ALL								
HAROLD BRADLEY	G B	(F								
TERRY McMILLAN	HCA	(F								
HAL RUGG	STEEL	(F								
WELDON MYRICK	STEEL	(F								
REGGIE YOUNG	G	(F								
HENRY STRZELECKI	B	(F								
MIKE LEECH	B	(F	JERRY SHOOK	G	(F	BUDDY HARMON	D	(F	JERRY CARRIGAN	D	(F
HAYWARD BISHOP	D	(F	DALE SELLERS	G	(F	BOB EMMONS	K	(F	PIG ROBBINS	PNO	(F
BOBBY WOOD	PNO	(F									

(A) YOU'RE NOT THE WOMAN	19 MCA	US		488
(B) OUT OF HAND	1975 RCA	LSA 3215		APLI 0900
(C) STEPPIN' OUT	1976 RCA	LSA 3266		APLI 1225
(D) YOUR PLACE OR MINE	1977 RCA	PL12199		APLI 2199
(E) LITTLE JUNIOR	197 RCA			APLI 2779
(F) GARY	1979 RCA	PL 13288		APLI 3288

JOHN STEWART

JOHN STEWART	G V	(ALL								
BUFFY FORD	V	(ACDEGIJL	RUSS KUNKEL	D	(CDEHJK	BILL MUNDI	PERC	(CE	PETER ASHER	V PERC	(CD
FRED CARTER	G B	(BCD	CAROLE KING	PNO	(C	MICHAEL STEWART	G V	(CDEGL	DOUG KERSHAW	FDL V	(C
CHARLIE McCOY	HCA	(BCF	RALPH SCHUCKETT	K	(C	ABIGALE HANESS	V	(C	DANNY KOOTCH	G	(C
KENNY BUTTREY	D	(BCI	PETER FULLERTON	V	(D	HENRY DILTZ	V HCA	(DEK	RICK CUNHA	V	(D
LLOYD GREEN	STEEL	(B	KATE TAYLOR	V	(D	JIMMY HASKELL	ACC STRING	(DE	LOREN NEWKIRK	PNO	(DEGL
NORBERT PUTNAM	B	(BC	BUDDY EMMONS	STEEL	(DE	GLEN D HARDIN	PNO	(DE	LEE SKLAR	B	(D
BUDDY HARMON	D	(BF	RON TUTT	D	(EH	DAVID KEMPER	D	(E	JERRY SCHEFF	B	(E
HARGUS ROBBINS	PNO	(BF	JAMES BURTON	G DOB	(E	BILL CUNNINGHAM	FDL	(E	MIKE DEASY	G	(E
JERRY SMITH	K	(B	GARY DAVID	PERC	(E	JIM HORN	HRNS	(E	CHARLES FINDLEY	HRNS	(E
BEEGIE CRUZER	K	(B	JACK CARONE	V	(E	LAURA CREAMER	V	(E	JONATHAN DOUGLASK	PERC	(GHL
BERGEN WHITE	V	(B	DAN DUGMORE	STEEL	(GHL	MIKE SETTLE	V	(GHL	DENNY BROOKS	V	(GHL
JOHN 'BUCK' WILKIN	G	(BF	PETER JAMESON	G	(H	ROBERT WACHTEL	G	(H	TOM KEENE	PNO	(H
MARI JOHN WILKIN	V	(B	DANIEL MOORE	V	(H	MARTI McCALL	V	(H	JACKIE WARD	V	(H
JAMES TAYLOR	G V	(C	JON WOODHEAD	G	(I	TROY SEALS	G	(I	REGGIE YOUNG	G	(I
JOEL BISHOP O'BRIEN	D	(C	DAVE KIRBY	G	(I	SHANE KEISTER	K	(I	DAVID BRIGGS	K	(I
BRYAN GAROFALO	B V	(CDEIJ	MICKEY RAPHAEL	HCA	(I	GARY WEISBERG	D PERC	(IJ	CHRIS WHALEN	V	(IJK
BOBBY THOMPSON	BANJ G	(B	HERB PEDERSEN	V	(I	LINDSEY BUCKINGHAM	G V	(J	JOEY CARBONE	V	(JK
CHRIS DARROW FDL	DOBRO	(CDF	STEVE NICKS	V	(J	MARY TORREY	V	(J	RICHARD SHLOSSER	D	(J
JENNIFER		(D	MARY KAY PLACE	B	(J	DAVID JACKSON	B	(J	CROXLEY GUARD	V	(J
KING ERRISSON	PERC	(DE	CATHERINE GUARD	V	(J	WAYNE HUNT	K	(J	DAVID PLATISHON	D	(K
ARNIE MOORE	B V	(DEFGHL	PHIL EVERLY	V	(K	SYDNEY FOX	V	(K	NICOLETTE LARSON	V	(K
LARRY KNECHTEL	PNO	(E	BLAISE TOSTI	V	(K	WENDY WALDMAN	V	(K			
LARRY CARLTON	G	(E									
PAUL HUBINON	HRNS	(E									
JIM GORDON	D	(GL									
JOE OSBORN	B	(H									
STEPHANIE FORD	V	(H									
LISA FREEMAN ROBERTS	V	(IJ									
JOEY HARRIS	G V	(IJ									
BILL CUOMO	K	(I									
JOHN WILLIAMS	B	(I									
MIKE BOTTS	D	(J									
CHRISTINE DE LISLE	V	(J									
DEBORAH TOMPINS	V	(J									
STEVE ROSS	PERC	(K									
LINDA RONSTADT	V	(K									

(A) SIGNALS THROUGH THE GLASS	1968 CAPITOL	US ST 2975	RI 1975		SM2975
(B) CALIFORNIA BLOODLINES	1969 CAPITOL	US ST 203	UK		EST203
(C) WILLARD	1970 CAPITOL	US ST 540	UK		EST540
(D) LONESOME PICKER RIDES AGAIN	1971 WB	US WS1948	UK		K46135
(E) SUNSTORM	1972 WB	US BS2611			
(F) CANNONS IN THE RAIN	1973 RCA	US LSP 4827	UK		SF 8359
(G) CANNONS IN THE RAIN	197 RCA	US AYLI 3731			
(G) PHOENIX CONCERTS LIVE	1974 RCA	US CPLZ 0265	UK		PL20265
(H) WINGLESS ANGELS	1975 RCA	US APLI 0816	UK		SF 8437
(I) FIRE IN THE WIND	1977 RSO	US RS 13027	UK		2394 194
(J) BOMBS AWAY DREAM BABIES	1979 RSO	US RS 13051	UK		2394 228
(K) DREAM BABIES GO HOLLYWOOD	1980 RSO	US RS 13074	UK		RSD 5007
(L) IN CONCERT	1980 RCA	US AFLI 3513			
(M) FORGOTTEN SONGS...	1980 RCA		UK		PL43155

ROD STEWART

ROD STEWART	V	(ALL
CARMINE APPICE	D V	(JM
PHIL CHEN	B V	(JM
JOHN JARVIS	K	(J
BILLY PEEK	G	(JM
JIM CREGAN	G	(JM
GARY GRAINGER	G	(JM
PETE CARR	G	(G
STEVE CROPPER	G	(G
KEITH EMERSON	K	(A
ESSE ED DAVIS	G	(G
JIMMY JOHNSON	G	(G
FRED TACKETT	G	(GM
DAVID LINDLEY VLN	MAND	(G

(A) AN OLD RAINCOAT ...	1970 VERTIGO	UK VO4	US MERCURY		SR61237
(B) GASOLINE ALLEY	1970 VERTIGO	UK 6360 500	US MERCURY		SR61264
(C) EVERY PICTURE TELLS A STORY	1971 MERCURY	UK 6338 063	US		SRM1 609
(D) NEVER A DULL MOMENT	1972 MERCURY	UK 6499 153	US		SRMI 646
(E) SING IT AGAIN ROD	1973 MERCURY	UK 6499 484	US		SRMI 680
(F) SMILER	1974 MERCURY	UK 9104 001	US		SRM11017
(G) ATLANTIC CROSSING	1975 WB	UK K56151	US WB		2875
(H) A NIGHT ON THE TOWN	1976 RIVA	UK RVLP 1	US WB		3116
(I) SHOT OF RHYTHM & BLUES	1976 CRYSTAL	98198	+PRIVATE STOCK PS		2021
( ) VINTAGE YEARS 1969/70	1976 MERCURY	UK 6672 013			
(J) FOOTLOOSE & FANCY FREE	1977 RIVA	UK RVLP 5	US WB		3092
(K) THE BEST OF	1977 MERCURY	UK 6643 030	US		SRM27507
(L) BEST OF VOL 2	1977 MERCURY		US		SRM27509
(M) BLONDES HAVE MORE FUN	1978 RIVA	UK RVLP 8	US WB		3261

(CONTINUED)

ROD STEWART
S273

DONALD DUNN	B	(G	(N) GREATEST HITS	1979 RIVA	UK RODTV1	US WB		3373
BOB CLAN	B	(G	(O) HOT RODS	1980 MERCURY UK 6463 061				
DAVID HOOD	B	(G	(P) FOOLISH BEHAVIOUR	1980 RIVA	UK RVLP 11			

MEMPHIS HORNS   (G

MICK WALLER	D (ABCD	PETE SEARS	PNO	(BCD RON WOOD	B G	(ABC MARTIN QUITTENTON G (ABCD
IAN McLAGAN	ORG(ABCD	DANNY THOMPSON	B	(C ANDY PYLE	B	(C DICK POWELL VLN(BCD
MADELINE BELL	V (C	KENNY JONES	D	(BD MARTIN PUGH	G	(A TOM VIG P PERC (M
LINDA LEWIS	V (M	MIKE FINNIGAN	V	(M MAX GRONENTHAL	V	(M SPIKE HEATLEY B (D
GORDON HUNTLEY	STEEL(D	RONNIE LANE	B	(BD DUANE HITCHINGS	K	(M ROGER BETHELMY D (M
PAULINHO DA COSTA PERC (M		NICKY HOPKINS	K	(M GARY HERBIG	FLT	(M PHIL KENZIE HRNS(M
STEVE MADAIO	TPT (M	TOM SCOTT	WIND (M	SAM MITCHELL	G	(BC DENNIS O'FLYNN VLN(B
MIKE D'ABO	PNO (M					

STICK UP
S274

GARY HOLTON	V	(						
OLLIE HALSALL	G	(	KEITH ELLIS B	(TONY NEWMAN	D	(		

STIFF LITTLE FINGERS
S275

BRIAN FALOON	D	(	(A) INFLAMMABLE MATERIAL	1979 ROUGH TRADE	UK	ROUGH 1
HENRY CLUNEY	G	(	(B) NOBODYS HERO	1980 CHRYSALIS	UK	CHR 1270
JAKE BURNS	G V	(	(C) HANX	1980 CHRYSALIS	UK	CHR 1300
JIM REILLY	D	(	(D) GO FOR IT	1981 CHRYSALIS	UK CHR 1339
ALI McMORDIE	B	(				

STEPHEN STILLS
S276

STEPHEN STILLS	G V	(ALL	(A) STEPHEN STILLS	1970 ATLANTIC UK 2401 004 US	7202
PAUL HARRIS	K	(B	(A) STEPHEN STILLS	1972 ATLANTIC UK K40341 RI	
DALLAS TAYLOR	D	(ABC	(B) STEPHEN STILLS TWO	1971 ATLANTIC UK 2401 013 US	7206
CALVIN SAMUELS	B V	(ABC	(B) STEPHEN STILLS TWO	1972 ATLANTIC UK K40249 RI	
JERRY AIELLO	K	(CDE	(C) STILLS	1975 CBS UK 69146 US	33575
JOE LALA	PERC (CDE		(D) STILLS LIVE	1975 ATLANTIC UK K50214 US	18156
DONNIE DACUS	G V	(CDE	(E) ILLEGAL STILLS	1976 CBS UK 81330 US	34148
RUSS KUNKEL	D	(CD	(F) THE BEST OF	1976 CBS UK K50327 US	18201
KENNY PASSARELLI	B	(CD	(G) THOROUGHFARE GAP	1978 CBS UK 82859 US	35380
RICK ROBERTS	G V	(C	(AB) TWO ORIGINALS	1975 ATLANTIC GER	60063
NEIL YOUNG	G V	(F			

GEORGE TERRY	G	(C	JOE VITALE	D	(E	DAVID CROSBY	V	(ACD GRAHAM NASH	V	(AC
BETTY WHITE	V	(C	LEE SKLAR	B	(C	TUBBY ZIEGLER	D	(CE GEORGE PERRY	B	(E
HOWARD KAYLAN	V	(E	MARK VOLMAN	V	(E	JEFF WHITTAKER	CONGA(A RITA COOLIDGE	V	(A
PRISCILLA JONES	V	(A	JOHN SEBASTIAN	V	(A	SHIRLEY MATTHEWS	V	(A CONRAD ISADORE	D	(AB
JUDITH POWELL	V	(A	LIZA STRIKE	V	(A	LARRY STEELE	V	(A TONY WILSON	V	(A
JIMI HENDRIX	G	(A	ERIC CLAPTON	G	(A	JOHN BARBATA	D	(A CLAUDIA LENNEAR	V	(A
CASS ELLIOT	V	(A	RICHIE HAYWARD	D	(A	BOOKER T JONES	K	(A SIDNEY GEORGE WIND (AB
GASPAR LAWAL	PERC (B	DR JOHN	K	(B	NILS LOFGREN	G K V(B JAMES MITCHELL	SAX (B
FLOYD NEWMAN	SAX	(B	ED LOGAN	SAX	(B	JACK HALE	TROM (B ANDREW LOVE	SAX (B
ROGER HOPPS	HRNS (B	WAYNE JOHNSON	HRNS (B	ROCKY D	PERC (B HENRY DILTZ	V (B
FEARLESS FREDDY	V	(B								

STILLS YOUNG BAND
S276A

STEPHEN STILLS	G V	(A	(A) LONG MAY YOU RUN	1976 REPRISE	UK K54081 US MS2253
NEIL YOUNG	G V	(A			
JOE LALA	PERC (A	JERRY AIELLO	K (A JOE VITALE	FLT D(A GEORGE PERRY B (A

STILLWATER
S277

MIKE CAUSEY	G	(AB	(A) STILLWATER	1977 CAPRICORN US 0186 UK 2429 155
JIMMY HALL	V PERC(AB	(B) I RESERVE THE RIGHT	1979 CAPRICORN US 0210 UK 2429 176	
BOBBY GOLDEN	G	(AB		
SEBIE LACEY	D V	(AB	ALLISON SCARBOROUGH B V(AB ROB WALKER	G V (AB BOB SPEARMAN K (AB

STINGRAY
S278

DENNIS EAST	V	(A	(A) STINGRAY	1979 CARRERE	CAL 113
ALLAN GOLDSWAIN	K	(A			
MIKE PILOT	G V	(A	EDDIE BOYLE	B (A SHAUN WRIGHT	D (A DANNY ANTHILL ORG (A

STINKY TOYS
S279

ELLI MEDEIROS	V	(A	(A) STINKY TOYS	1977 POLYDOR	UK	2393 174
BRUNO CARONE	G	(A				
JACNO	G	(A	ALBIN DERIAT	B (A HERVE ZENOUDA	D (A	

ALAN STIVELL
S280

ALAN STIVELL V FLT PIPES(ALL	(A) RENAISSANCE OF CELTIC HARP	1972 PHILIPS	6414 406
YANN JAKEZ HASSOLD V	(EG	(B) A L'OLYMPIA	1972 FONTANA	6399 005
DAN AR BRAS	G	(ABEG	(C) ALAN STIVELL REFLECTIONS	1973 FONTANA	6399 008
RENE WERNEER	FDL	(BE	(D) FROM CELTIC ROOTS	1974 FONTANA	6325 304
ALAN KLOATR	FLT BOD(AE	(E) A LANGANNET	1975 FONTANA 9101 500	6325 332
LIAM WELDON	BOD (E	(F) IN DUBLIN	1975 FONTANA	9299 547
YANN–FANCH AR MERDY	D(AE	(G) BEFORE LANDING	1977 FONTANA	9286 999
LOEIZ ROUJON	D	(E	(H) SUZI MACGUIRE	1978 IMPACT	6886 122
JANNLUG FAUCHON	D	(E	(J) SYMPHONIE CELTIQUE (DBL)	1980 CBS	88487
YOVENN SICARD	BOMBA(E			

GABRIEL YACOUB G DULC (B	PASCAL STIVE	K	(B	GERARD LEVASSEUR	B	(AB HENRI DELAGARDE CELLOFLT(AB
MICHEL SANTANGELI	D (B	SERJ PARAYRE	PERC (B	MIKAEL KLEC'H	FLT	(B DANIELE BAROLLETTI V (A
MICHEL DELAPORTE	PERC (A	GUY CASCALES	D	(A	GERARD SALKOWSKY	B	(A GILLES TINAYJRE K (A
MIG AR BIZ	BOMBA(A	JEAN MARC DOLLEZ B	(A	ANNE GERMAIN	V	(A CLAUDE GERMAIN V (A
JEAN CLAUDE BRION V	(G	FRANCOISE WALL	V	(A	JACQUES HENDRIX	V	(A PADRIG KERRE FDL DULC(A
ANDREW HERVE	K	(G	MIKAEL HERVE	B	(G	JEAN LUC DANNA	D	(G DAVE SWARBRICK FDL(G
MARIA POPKIEWICZ	V	(G	CLEMENT BAILLY	D	(G	DOMINIQUE LURO	K	(G PATRICK KIFFER B (G
ALAIN HATOT	SAX	(G	ADAM SKEAPING	CELLO(A	LYN DOBSON FLT SITAR PERC(A	RICHARD HARVEY WIND(G
BAGAD BLEIMOR WIND D	(G	CHRIS HAYWARD	FLT PERC(J	ROBBY FINKEL	K	(J MICHEL PREZMAN K (J
DOMINIQUE WIDIEZ	K	(J	MARC PERRU	G	(J	MIKAEL VALY	B	(J ROGER SECCO D (J
PADRIG KERRE FDL MAND(J	ORCHESTRA & CHOIR		(J			

S280A

ORVILLE STOEBER
S280A

ORVILLE STOEBER	G V	(A	(A) ORVILLE STOEBER	1971 UNI	UNLS 120
HARRY PALMER	G	(A			
RAY BARRETT	K	(A	GEORGE DUVIVIER B	(A	

S281
SIMON STOKES
```
SIMON STOKES       V    (ALL    (A) SIMON STOKES & THE NIGHTHAWKS    1971 MGM              US        MGM S4677
BUTCH SENNEVILLE   G    (AB     (B) & THE BLACK WHIP THRILL BAND     1973 SPINDIZZY        US             32075
RANDALL KEITH      G    (A      (C) BUZZARD OF LOVE                  197  U A
ROBERT LEDGER      B    (A
JOE YUELE          D    (A    JOHN LOCKE      K    (B   HARRY GARFIELD    K    (B   CHRISTIAN PENNICK   G (B
MARTY TRYON        B    (A    BILLY GOODNICK  D    (B
```
S282
STONE PONEYS
```
LINDA RONSTADT     V    (ABCDE  (A) STONE PONEYS                     1967 CAPITOL          US        ST   2666
BOB KIMMEL         G    (ABCDE  (B) EVERGREEN VOL 2                  1967 CAPITOL          US        ST   2763
KEN EDWARDS        G    (ABCDE  (C) STONE PONEYS & FRIENDS VOL 3     1968 CAPITOL          US        ST   2863
BILLY MUNDI        D    (A      (D) STONE PONEYS FEATURING L RONSTADT 1976 CAPITOL         US        ST  11383
JOHN T FORSHA      G    (A      (E) STONEY END                      1972 PICKWICK                   SPC  3298
JAMES E BOND JR    B    (A
CYRUS FARYAR       G    (A    PETE CHILDS        G    (A
```
S283
STONE THE CROWS
```
LES HARVEY         G    (ALL    (A) STONE THE CROWS                  1970 POLYDOR          UK   2425 017
MAGGIE BELL        V    (ALL    (B) ODE TO JOHN LAW                  1970 POLYDOR          UK   2425 042
JOHN McGINNIS      K    (ABE    (C) TEENAGE LICKS                    1971 POLYDOR US PD5020 UK  2425 071
COLIN ALLEN        D    (ALL    (D) 'ONTINUOUS PERFORMANCE           1972 POLYDOR          UK   2391 043
JIM DEWAR          B    (ABE    (E) STONE THE CROWS(COMP)            1976 POLYDOR/FLASHBACK UK 2482 279
RONNIE LEAHY       K    (CDE
STEVE THOMPSON     D    (CDE JIMMY McCULLOCH       G    (DE
```
S283A
STONEBOLT
```
BRIAN LOUSLEY      D V  (A      (A) STONEBOLT                        1978 PARACHUTE                  RRL  2006
JOHN WEBSTER       K    (A      (B) KEEP IT ALIVE                    1980 rca                       PL  10357
DAVID WILLS        V    (A
DANNY AITCHISON    B    (A    RAY ROPER        G V  (A
```
S283B
STONEBRIDGE McGUINNESS
```
LOU STONEBRIDGE HCA G K V(A     (A) CORPORATE MADNESS                1980 RCA              UK   PL 25275
TOM McGUINNESS     G    (A
ROY MORGAN         D    (A    PAUL KARAS      B    (A    MO FOSTER      B    (A    MIKE MORAN      K   (A
NICKY PAYN         SAX  (A    DICK HANSON     TPT  (A    CHRIS GOWER    TROM (A    JOHN 'IRISH' EARLE SAX(A
RAY BEAVIS         SAX  (A    FRANK RICOTTI   PERC (A    CHARLIE FAWN   V    (A    MORRIS PERT PERC(A
```
S284
STONEGROUND
```
SAL VALENTINO      G V  (ABC    (A) STONEGROUND                      1971 WB   US WS 1895    UK K46087
TIM BARNES         G V  (ABCDE  (B) FAMILY ALBUM                     1971 WB   US WS 1956    UK K53999
JOHN BLAKELEY      G B  (ABC    (C) STONEGROUND THREE                1972 WB   US BS 2645
PETE SEARS         K B  (A      (D) FLAT OUT                         1976 FLAT OUT   US        FOR 101
MICHAEL MAU        D    (A      (E) HEARTS OF STONE                  1978 WB   US BSK3187
LUTHER BILDT       G V  (A
LYNNE HUGHES       V    (ABC DEIRDRE LAPORTE   V    (ABC ANNIE SAMPSON  V (ABCD  LYDIA PHILLIPS  V  (A
RON NAGLE          K    (A    BRIAN CRODULA    V    (B   LYDIA MORERO   V  (BC    STEPHEN PRICE      (B
CORY LERIOS        V    (BC   JO BAKER         V    (ED  TERRY DAVIS    B V (ED    LENNY LEE GOLDSMITH V(E
SAMMY PIAZZA       D    (D    FRED WEBB        K    (ED  BOB GAUDIO     K  (E     JERRY PETERSON     SAX(D
STEVE FONTANA      PERC (E    TERRY CLEMENTS   HRNS (C   DAVID McCULLOUGH B (C    STEVE PRICE     D  (C
DANNY ARMSTRONG    TROM (D    JULES BROUSSARD  SAX  (D   CAL LEWISTON   TPT (D
JACK SCHROER       SAX  (D    ARMANDO PERAZA   CONGA     (D
```
S284A
STONEHOUSE
```
PETER SEARING      G V  (A      (A) STONEHOUSE CREEK                 1971 RCA              UK   SF 8197
JAMES SMITH        V    (A
IAN SNOW           D    (A    TERRY PARKER     B    (A
```
S285
MIKE STOREY
```
MIKE STOREY K V HCA PERC(AB     (A) STOREY                           1974 MAM                        MAMAS1011
NEIL HUBBARD       G    (A      (B) WHO ARE YOU PLAYING TO           1975 MAM                   AS    1013
WINSTON DELANDRO   G    (AB
MICK WEAVER        K    (A    MIKE WOODS       G    (A   STEVE CHAPMAN  D    (AB   RICHARD BAILEY     D(A
CHARLIE HARRISON   B V  (A    SMILEY DEJONNES  PERC (A   RAY SINGER     PERC V(A   CHRIS MERCER     HRNS(A
RON CARTHY         HRNS (A    STEVE GREGORY    HRNS (A   MICK EVE       HRNS (A   BUD BEADLE       HRNS(A
FRANK COLLINS      V    (A    DYAN BIRCH       V    (A   PADDIE McHUGH  V    (A   CLIVE SARSTEDT   V  (A
STUART BROOKS      B    (B
```
S286
STORIES
```
IAN LLOYD          B V  (ABC    (A) STORIES                          1972 KAMA SUTRA       US   KSBS 2051
MICHAEL BROWN      K SYN(ABC    (B) ABOUT US                         1973 KAMA SUTRA       US   KSBS 2068
STEVE LOVE         G V B(ABC    (C) TRAVELLING UNDERGROUND           1973 KAMA SUTRA       US   KSBS 2078
BRYAN MADEY        D PERC(ABC
KENNETH BISCHEL    K SYN(C    KENNY AARONSON   B    (C   RICH RANNO     G    (
```
S286A
STORMY SIX
```
FRANCO FABBRI      G    (1      (A) L'UNITA                          1970
UMBERTO FIORI      G    (1      (B) UN BIGLIETTO DEL TRAM            197  L'ORCHESTRA           OLP 10001
TOMMASO LEDDI      G    (1      (C) CLICKE                           197  L'ORCHESTRA           OLP 10010
CARLO DE MARTINI   G    (1      (D) L'APPRENDISTA                    197  L'ORCHESTRA           OLP 10012
                                (1) 1973
```
S287
STORYTELLER
```
CAROLINE ATTARD    V    (AB     (A) STORYTELLER                      1970 TRANSATLANTIC    UK      TRA220
RODNEY CLARK       V B  (A      (B) MORE PAGES                       1971 TRANSATLANTIC    UK      TRA232
ROGER MOON         G V  (AB
MIKE ROGERS        V    (AB  CHRIS BELSHAW     B V  (B   TERRY DURHAM   V    (AB  HARRY BECKETT   HRNS(B
HENRY SPINETTI     D    (B
```
S288
DAVIS STOUGHTON
```
DAVID STOUGHTON         (       (A) TRANSFORMER                      19   ELEKTRA                EKS 74034
```
STRAIGHT EIGHT
S288A
```
RICK CASSMAN       G K V(AB     (A) NO NOISE FROM HERE               1979 EEL PIE          UK      EPRP 001
BOOT KINGSMAN      G V SAX(AB    (B) SHUFFLE & CUT                    1980 LOGO            UK      FLUSH 1
STEVE CHERRY       B V  (AB
PAUL SCHOFIELD     B    (A    TIM BEETON       VLN  (A   RUAN O'LOCHLAINN SAX (A  GARY HOLTON     V  (A
PAUL TURNER        K D  (B    ROD BERRIEDALE JOHNSON D(A  RABBIT        K    (A   ANDY HAAS        SAX(B
```
S289
STRAIGHT SHOOTER
```
GEORG BUSCHMANN    V    (AB     (A) MY TIME HOUR TIME               1974 SKY                     SKY 034
FRIEDHELM MISLEJUK D    (A      (B) GET STRAIGHT                     1978 SKY                     SKY 018
GUNTHER STRIEPLING G    (AB     (C) FLYING STRAIGHT                  1981 SKY                     SKY 054
HANS PLANKERT      K    (AB
ROLAND HAASE       B    (AB  PETER KEGLER D PERC    (B
```

NICK STRAKER BAND

S289A

```
NICK STRAKER        K V  (A      (A) A WALK IN THE PARK           1980 CBS              UK       84608
ANDY MANSFIELD      G    (A
DAVE McSHERA        G    (A   TONY HIBBERT      B   (A   PETER HAMMOND    B   (A   PHIL TOWNER      D (A
FERNANDO BUSTAMENTE D    (A
```

STRAND
S289B

```
RICK CALHOUN        V    (A      (A) THE STRAND                   1980 ISLAND           UK       ILPS 9594
SCOTT SHELLY        G V  (A
PETER REILICH       K V  (A   DEAN COTEZ       B V  (A   KELLY SHANAHAN    D   (A
```

RICHARD STRANGE
S290

```
RICHARD STRANGE          (A      (A) PHENOMENAL RISE OF RICHARD STRANGE 1981 ZE          PVC 7917
```

STRANGE DAYS
S291

```
GRAHAM WARD         G V  (A   (A) NINE PARTS TO THE WIND          1975 RETREAT          UK       RTL6005
PHIL WALMAN         B V  (A
EDDIE McNEIL        D PERC(A   EDDIE SPENCE K    (A
```

STRANGLERS
S292

```
HUGH CORNWELL       G V  (ABCDEF    (A) RATTUS NORVEGICUS         1977 A&M US 4648 UA uk  UAG30045
JET BLACK           D    (ABCDEF    (B) NO MORE HEROES            1978 A&M US 4659 UA UK  UAG30200
DAVE GREENFIELD     K V  (ABCDEF    (C) BLACK & WHITE             1978 A&M US 4706 US UK  UAK30222
JEAN JACQUES BURNEL B V(ABCDEF     (D) LIVE(X CERT)               1979            UA UK  UAG30224
ERIC CLARK          SAX  (A         (E) THE RAVEN                 197            UA UK  UAG30262
ALAN WINSTANLEY          (F         (F) THE MEN IN BLACK          1981 LIBERTY          UK  LBG30313
ALDO BOCCA               (F
LAURENCE DIANA           (F
```

STRAPPS
S293

```
ROSS STAGG          G V  (AB    (A) STRAPPS                       1976 HARVEST          UK       SHSP 4055
JOE READ            B V  (AB    (B) SECRET DAMAGE                 1977 HARVEST          UK       SHSP 4064
NOEL SCOTT          K V  (AB    (C) SHARP CONVERSATION            1978 HARVEST          UK       SHSP 4088
MICK UNDERWOOD      D    (AB
```

STRAWBERRY ALARM CLOCK
S294

```
MARK WEITZ          K    (ABCD    (A) INCENSE & PEPPERMINTS       1968 PYE UK 28106 US UNI  73014
LEE FREEMAN V D WIND B (ABCD     (B) WAKE UP ,ITS TOMORROW        1968 UNI          US     73025
ED KING             G V  (ABCD    (C) WORLD IN A SEA SHELL        1968 UNI          US     73035
GARY LOVETRO        B V  (A       (D) GOOD MORNING STARSHINE      19   UNI          US     73054
GEORGE BUNNELL      B    (ABC      (E) BEST OF                    19   UNI          US     73074
RANDY SEOL          D V  (ABC      (F) PSYCH OUT                  19
JIMMY PITMAN        G V  (D        (G) CHANGES                    19   VOCALION            73915
GENE GUNNELS        D    (D
```

STRAWBS
S295

```
DAVE COUSINS        G V  (ALL    (A) ALL OUR OWN WORK (1968 RECORDING) 1973 HALLMARK       SHM  813
RICHARD HUDSON      PERC (BCDEFG    (B) STRAWBS                   1969 A&M              UK  AMLS  936
JOHN FORD           B V  (BCDEFG    (C) DRAGONFLY                 1970 A&M              UK  AMLS  970
RICK WAKEMAN        K    (BCDE      (D) JUST A COLLECTION OF ANTIQUES 1970 A&M   US 4288 UK  AMLS  994
TONY HOOPER         G V  (ABCDE     (E) FROM THE WITCHWOOD        1971 A&M   US 4304 UK  AMLS64304
DAVE LAMBERT        G V  (FGHJKMN    (F) GRAVE NEW WORLD           1972 A&M   US 4344 UK  AML S68078
ROD COOMBES         D    (HJKM      (G) BURSTING AT THE SEAMS     1973 A&M   US 4383 UK  AMLH68144
CHAS CRONK          B    (HJKMN     (H) HERO & HEROINE            1974 A&M   US 3607 UK  AMLH63607
NICKY HOPKINS       K    (B         (I) STRAWBS BY CHOICE         1974 A&M              UK  AMLH68259
BLUE WEAVER         K    (FG        (J) GHOSTS                    1975 A&M   US 4506 UK  AMLH68277
JOHN HAWKEN         K    (HJ        (K) NOMADNESS                 1976 A&M   US 4544 UK  AMLH68331
CLAIRE DENIZ        CELLO(CJ        (L) DEEP CUTS                 1976 OYSTER US 1 1603 UK  2391  234
RON CHESTERMAN      B    (AC        (M) BURNING FOR YOU           1977 OYSTER US 1 1604 UK  2391  287
SANDY DENNY         V    (A         (N) DEAD LINES                1978 ARISTA US  4172 UK SPART 1036
KEN GUDMAND         D    (A         (O) BEST OF                   1978 A&M   US   6005 UK  AMLM66005
ALAN PARKER         G    (B
ANDY WEIGHELL       B    (B    ANNE COLLINS      V   (F   RON VERRELL      D   (B   TREVOR LUCAS      V(F
JOHN MEALING        K    (MN   ROBERT KIRBY      K   (MN  TONY FERNANDEZ   D   (N
```

STRAWHEAD
S295A

```
GREGG BUTLER        V WIND(A      (A) SONGS FROM THE BOOK OF ENGLAND(DBL)1980  TRADITION   UK  TRS 0356
CHRIS POLLINGTON    G K V SYN(A
MALCOLM GIBBONS     G V  (A    PETE ASHWORTH     VLN  (A  STUART GRILLS    TPT  (A  LAWRENCE YATES   HRNS(A
IAN DUCKWORTH       TUBA (A    EDWARD HOYLE      TROM (A  MICHAEL LORMOR   HRNS (A
```

STRAY
S296

```
DEL BROMHAM         G V K(ABCDEFGH    (A) STRAY                   1970 TRANSATLANTIC    UK   TRA216
STEVE GADD   HCA G V  (ABCDE          (B) SUICIDE                 1971 TRANSATLANTIC    UK   TRA233
RITCHIE COLE        D    (ABCDEFGH    (C) SATURDAY MORNING PICTURES 1972 TRANSATLANTIC  UK   TRA248
GARY G GILES        B    (ABCDEFGH    (C) SATURDAY MORNING PICTURES 1972 MERCURY        US   SRM1  624
JIMMY HELMS         TPT  (E           (D) MUDANZAS                1973 TRANSATLANTIC    UK   TRA268
PETE DYER           G V  (GH          (E) MOVE IT                 1974 TRANSATLANTIC    UK   TRA281
                                      (F) TRACKS                  1975 TRANSATLANTIC    UK TRASAM3066
                                      (G) STAND UP & BE COUNTED   1975 DAWN             UK DNLS  3066
                                      (H) HOUDINI                 1976 PYE              UK NSPL18482
                                      (J) HEARTS OF FIRE          1976 PYE              UK NSPL18512
```

STRAY CATS
S296A

```
BRIAN SETZER        G V  (A      (A) STRAY CATS                   1981 ARISTA           UK       STRAY 1
SLIM JIM PHANTOM          (A
LEE ROCKER                (A   GARY BARNACLE    SAX  (A
```

STRAY DOG
S297

```
SNUFFY WALDEN       G V  (AB    (A) STRAY DOG                     1974 MANTICORE              UK K43506
TIM DULAINE         G V  (B     (B) WHILE YOU'RE DOWN THERE       1974 MANTICORE IMP 50151   UK K53504
ALAN ROBERTS        B V  (AB
LES SAMPSON         D    (AB   LUIS CABAZA      K V  (B
```

STRAY GATOR
S298

```
NEIL YOUNG          G V  (
BEN KEITH           STEEL(
JACK NITZSCHE            (    JOHN BARBATA     D   (   KENNY BUTTREY    D   ( TIM DRUMMOND  B    (
```

STREET CORNER SYMPHONY
S298A

```
JAMES GADSON        D    (      (A) HARMONY GRITS                 1975 BANG US                   406
JAMES JAMERSON      B    (      (B) LITTLE FUNK MACHINE           1977 ABC  US             ABC   974
```

```
S299                                    STREETBAND
  PAUL YOUNG      HCA K V (AB      (A) LONDON                              1979 LOGO                    1012
  ROGER KELLY     G V (AB          (B) DILEMMA                            1979 LOGO                    1017
  JOHN GIFFORD    G V (AB
  MICK PEARL      B V (AB  CHAULKIE      D  (AB  CHAZ JANKEL      V K G(A   JOOLS HOLLAND    K (B
  TREVOR RABIN    K (B
S299A                                   STREETHEART
  DARYL GUTHEIL   K V (AB          (A) MEANWHILE BACK IN PARIS            1978 ATLANTIC              KCA 92002
  MATTHEW FRENETTE D V (AB         (B) UNDER HEAVEN OVER HELL             1979 ATLANTIC              KSD 19228
  KENNY SHIELDS   V (AB
  SPIDER SINNAEVE B V (AB  JOHN HANNAH      G V (B   PAUL DEAN         G V (A
S299B                                   STREETMARK
  DOROTHEA RAUKES K (             (A) NORDLAND                           1975 SKY                   SKY003
  THOMAS SCHREIBER G (            (B) EILEEN                             1978 SKY                   SKY011
  GEORG BUSCHMANN V (             (C) DRY                                1979 SKY                   SKY023
  WOLFGANG WESTPHAL B (
  HANS SCHWEISS   D (
S300                                    STREETWALKERS
  ROGER CHAPMAN   HCA V(ALL        (A) STREETWALKERS                     1974 REPRISE       UK      K54017
  CHARLIE WHITNEY G (ALL           (A) STREETWALKERS                     197  MERCURY       US      SRMI 1060
  BOB TENCH       G V (BCDE        (B) DOWNTOWN FLIER                    1975 VERTIGO       UK      6360  123
  TIM HINKLEY     K V (A           (C) RED CARD                         1976 VERTIGO       UK      9102  010
  MAX MIDDLETON   K (A             (C) RED CARD                         1976 MERCURY       US      SRMI 1083
  JOHN WETTON     B V (A           (D) VICIOUS BUT FAIR                 1977 VERTIGO       UK      9102  012
  RIC GRECH       B (A             (D) VICIOUS BUT FAIR                 197  MERCURY       US      SRMI 1135
  NEIL HUBBARD    G (A             (E) STREETWALKERS LIVE(DBL)          1977 VERTIGO       UK      6641  703
  IAN WALLACE     D (A
  MIKE GILES      D (A   GODFREY McLEAN    PERC (A   POLI PALMER      VIBES(ABD LINDA LEWIS    V (A
  PETE WINGFIELD  K (A   BOZ BURRELL       V  (A     JIM CREGAN       V  (A    NICKO           D (BC
  JON PLOTEL      B (BC  MICKEY FEAT       B  (DE    BRIAN JOHNSTON   K  (DE   DAVID DOWLE     D (DE
  MEL COLLINS     HRNS (D
S301                                    STRETCH
  KIRBY           G (ABCD          (A) ELASTIQUE                        1975 ANCHOR        UK      ANCL 2014
  ELMER GANTRY    G V (ABC         (B) CANT BEAT YOUR BRAIN FOR ENTERTAINMENT 1976 ANCHOR  UK      ANCL 2016
  STEVE EMERY     B (ABCD          (C) LIFE BLOOD                       1977 ANCHOR        UK      ANCL 2023
  JEFF RICH       D (B             (D) FORGET THE PAST                  1978 HOT WAX       UK      WH1
  ROSHI           G (A
  PAUL MARTINEZ   B (A   JIM RUSSELL       D  (A     JOHN COOK        K  (AD   CHRIS MERCER    HRNS(AD
  MICK EVE        HRNS (A RON CARTHY       HRNS (A    MIKE BAILEY      HRNS (A  NICKO McBAIN    D (D
  CHRIS FLETCHER  PERC (D
S302                              WILLIAM R STRICKLAND
  WILLIAM R STRICKLAND  (A        (A) WILLIAM R STRICKLAND IS ONLT THE NAME 1969 DERAM     UK      SML 1041
S302A                           PETE STRIDE & JOHN PLAIN
  PETE STRIDE     G V (A          (A) NEW GUITAR IN TOWN                 1980 BEGGARS BANQUET UK    BEGA  17
  JOHN PLAIN      G V (A
  TONY BATEMAN    V B (A  JACK BLACK        D  (A     PETE EDWARDS     HCA V(A   MICK TALBOT     K (A
S303                                    STRIDER
  JIM HAWKINS     B (A            (A) EXPOSED                           1973 G M                   GML  1002
  IAN KEWLEY      K V (A          (B) MISUNDERSTANDING                  1974 G M          UK      GML  1012
  BOB MURREY      G (
  GARY GRAINGER   G (BA  ROB ELLIOT        V  (B     LEE STRELLEZYK   B  (BA   COSMO           G (
  JAY WILLIAMS    G (    MALCOLM MORTIMER  D  (A     LES OLBINSON     PERC (   TONY MILLS        (
  MARK PINDER     D (    TONY BROCK        D V (B     JENNY HAAN       V  (B
S304                                    STRIFE
  JOHN REID       HCA G V (AB     (A) RUSH                              1975 CHRYSALIS             CHR  1063
  GORDON ROWLEY   B V (AB         (B) BACK TO THUNDER                   1978 GULL          UK      GULL 1029
  PAUL H ELLSON   D (A
  DAVID WILLIAMS  D V (B  DON AIREY        K  (B
S305                                    STRIKER
  SCOTT ROSBURG   V B G(          (A) STRIKER                           1978 ARISTA                SPART1059
  RICK TAYLOR     D V (
  RICK RANDLE     V K G(  RICK RAMIREZ     G  (
S306                              STRING DRIVEN THING
  CHRIS ADAMS     G V (ABE        (A) STRING DRIVEN THING               1972 CHARISMA      UK      CAS 1062
  PAULINE ADAMS   V (ABE          (B) MACHINE THAT CRIED                1973 CHARISMA      UK      CAS 1070
  GRAHAME SMITH   VLN (ABC        (C) PLEASE MIND YOUR HEAD             1974 CHARISMA      UK      CAS 1097
  COLIN WILSON    G B (AB         (D) KEEP YER'AND ON IT                1975 CHARISMA      UK      CAS 1112
  BILLY FAIRLEY   D (AB           (E) STRING DRIVEN THING               19   CONCORD               CON 1001
  CLARE SEALEY    CELLO(B
  BILL HATJE      B (B   JAMES EXELL  B V (C    KENNY ROWE       V  (C    GRAHAME WHITE   V (C
  COLIN FAIRLEY   D V (C  ALUN ROBERTS     G V (C    KIMBERLEY BEACON V  (C    HENRY McDONALD  K (C
  ALAN SKIDMORE   SAX (C
S307                                    STRIPJACK
  BRIAN DAVIDSON  B (
  TONY REECE      V (
  ANTHONY COWELL  G (    MO EVANS         D  (
S308                                 BARRETT STRONG
  BARRETT STRONG  V (A            (A) STRONGHOLD                        1975 CAPITOL               EST 11376
S308A                                   STRONGBOW
  BILL BENDER     V K HRNS(A      (A) STRONGBOW                         1975 SOUTHWIND     UK      SWS  6401
  JOHN STELZER    K WIND V(A
  DAVID SMITH     D V (A  MICHAEL SHORTLAND G V (A   JOHN DURZO       B V (A
S309                                    STUD
  JIM CREGAN      G V (A          (A) STUD                              1971 DERAM AML1084 POLYDOR 2310  097
  RICHARD McCRACKEN G B (A        (B) SEPTEMBER                         1972 BASF          GERM    20 29054
  JOHN WILSON     D (A            (C) GOODBYE -LIVE AT COMMAND          1973 BASF          GERM    20 29117
  JOHN WEIDER     VLN G K V(BC
```

STUFF   S310

CORNELL DUPREE	G	(	(A) STUFF	1977 WB	UK K56305	US BS2968
STEVE GADD	D	(	(B) MORE STUFF	1977 WB		US BS3061
ERIC GALE	G	(	(C) STUFF IT	197 WB		US BS3262
RICHARD TEE	K	(	(D) LIVE IN JAPAN	1979 wea	JAP	10629
GORDON EDWARDS	B	(				
CHRIS PARKER	D	(				

JEFF STURGES & UNIVERSE   S311

(A) JEFF STURGES & UNIVERSE   197 MAM   MAMAS1002

DEAN PARKS	G	(A								
DENNIS KELLY	B	(A								
DON BALDWIN	B	(A	HAL STESCH	K	(A	ROGER RAMPTON	PERC (A	MIKE LEWIS	PERC(A
JIMMY MANONE	D	(A	BOBBY SHAW	TPT	(A	TOM PORRELLO	TPT (A	JON MURAKAMI	TPT (A
RICH COOPER	TPT	(A	DEREK WATKINS	TPT	(A	JIM TRIMBLE	TROM (A	BILL BOOTH	TROM(A
STAN NISHAMURA	TROM	(A	ARCHIE WHEELER	SAX	(A	BURT ESTERMAN	SAX (A	DON MENZA	SAX (A
JOHN PHILLIPS	SAX	(A	GARY FREYMAN	SAX	(A	ART MAEBE	HRNS (A	DICK PERISSI	HRNS(A
AUBREY BOUCK	HRNS	(A	RALPH POLLACK	HRNS	(A	JEFF STURGES	(A		

STYLUS   S312

PETER JONES STRINGS HRNS(A			(A) STYLUS	1978 PRODIGAL	PDL 2011
GRAHAM LYALL	HRNS (A				
MIKE CLARKE	HRNS (A	SAM McNALLY	K	(A	PETER CUPPLES	V K G(A	ASHLEY HENDERSON B V (A
RON PEERS	G V (A	TREVOR COURTNEY	D	(A			

POLY STYRENE   S312A

POLY STYRENE   V   (A   (A) TRANSLUCENCE   1980 UA   UAG 30320

LAURIE STYVERS   S313

LAURIE STYVERS	K V	(AB			(A) SPILT MILK	1972 CHRYSALIS	UK CHR1007 US WB1946
TOM PARKER	K	(AB			(B) COLORADO KID	1973 CHRYSALIS	UK CHR1038
ANDREW STEELE	D	(AB					
HENRY SPINETTI	D	(AB	GARY TAYLOR	B	(AB	BRIAN DALY	G (A	ROD KING	STEEL(A
MIKE RICHARDS	D	(A	ADRIAN LEGG	G	(A	JIM LAWLESS	PERC (A	CLAIRE TORRIE	V (A
SUE LYNN	V	(A	NOELEEN BATLEY	V	(A	ALAN PARKER	G (A	JERRY DONAHUE	G (B
DYAN BIRCH	V	(B	FRANK COLLINS	V	(B	PADDY McHUGH	V (B	RODNEY WYATT	G (B
TOMMY EYRE	K	(B	TRISTRAM FRY	PERC	(B	BILLY BEHNKE	G (B	PETE WILLSHER	STEEL(B
CHRISSIE STEWART	B	(B	MICK COX	G	(B	MAL LUKER	SITAR(B	JERRY HOVELL	V (B
GEORGE LEE	SAX	(B	JON FIELD	CONGA(B				

STYX   S314

JAMES YOUNG	G	(ALL	(A) STYX	1972 WOODEN NICKEL	US	BXLI 1008
DENNIS DE YOUNG	K	(ALL	(B) STYX II	1973 WOODEN NICKEL	US	BXLI 1012
CHUCK PANOZZO	B	(ALL	(C) SERPENT IS RISING	1973 WOODEN NICKEL	US	BXLI 0287
JOHN PANOZZO	D	(ALL	(D) MAN OF MIRACLES	1974 WOODEN NICKEL	US	BWLI 0638
JOHN CURULEWSKI	G	(ABCDE	(E) EQUINOX	1975 A&M US 4559	UK	AMLH64559
TOM NARDIN	G	(	(F) CRYSTAL BALL	1976 A&M US 4604	UK	AMLH64604
TOMMY SHAW	G	(FGHJL	(G) GRAND ILLUSION	1977 A&M US 4637	UK	AMLH64637
BILL THAUT	SAX	(L	(H) PIECES OF EIGHT	1978 A&M US 4724	UK	AMLH64724
STEVE EISEN	SAX	(JL	(J) CORNERSTONE	1979 A&M	UK	AMLK63711
JOHN HAYNOR	HRNS (L		(K) BEST OF	197 WOODEN NICKEL	US	BXLI 2250
BILL SIMPSON	HRNS (L		(K) BEST OF	1979 RCA	UK	PL 13116
MARK OHLSEN	HRNS (L		(L) PARADISE THEATER	1980 A&M	UK	AMLK63719
MIKE HALPIN	HRNS (L					
DAN BARBER	HRNS (L					

SUBURBAN STUDS   S315

(A) SLAM   1978 POGO   UK   POW   001

SUBWAY SECT   S316

VIC GODDARD	V	(123	(1) 1977	(2) 1977	(3) 1978		
PAUL MYERS	B	(123					
ROBERT MILLER	G	(123	PAUL SMITH	D	(1	ROB WARD	D	(3	MARK LAFF	D	(2

SUE & SUNNY   S317

| SUE GLOVER | V | (A | (A) SUE & SUNNY | 1970 CBS | UK | 63740 |
| SUNNY LESLIE | V | (A | | | | |

SUGARLOAF   S318

JERRY CORBETTA	K V	(ABCD	(A) SUGARLOAF	1970 LIBERTY	UK	LBS 83415
BOB WEBBER	G B	(ABCD	(B) I GOT A SONG	1973 BRUT	US	6006
BOB RAYMOND	SAX G B	(ABCD	(C) SPACE SHIP EARTH	1974 UA	UK	UAS 29165
BOB MACVITTIE	D	(AC	(D) DON'T CALL US, WE'LL CALL YOU	1975 POLYDOR	UK	2310 394
ROBERT YEAZEL	G V	(C	(D) DON'T CALL US, WE'LL CALL YOU	197 CLARIDGE	US	1000
BOB PICKETT	G B	(				
MYRON POLLOCK	D	(D	LARRY FERRIS	D	(B			

SUICIDE   S319

ALAN VEGA	(	(A) SUICIDE	1978 BRONZE BRON 508+RED STAR IMP
MARTY REV	(	(B) LIVE(LIMITED EDITION)	1979 FRANKI	1
		(C) SUICIDE	1980 ZE	ILPS 7007

SUICIDE COMMANDOS   S320

(A) MAKE A RECORD   1978 BLANK   IMP   002

SUICIDE ROMEO   S320A

(A) PICTURES   1980 ZE   UK   ILPS 7010

BIG JIM SULLIVAN   S321

BIG JIM SULLIVAN	G	(ABC	(A) SITAR BEAT	1968 MERCURY US SR61137 UK SML30001
CHAS HODGES	K FDL G V	(B	(B) BIG JIMS BACK	1974 RETREAT	RTA 4001
IAN WALLACE	D V	(B	(C) SULLIVAN PLAYS OSULLIVAN	1977 MAM	RAM 3003
DAVE PEACOCK	B BAN V	(B			

ROCKY SULLIVAN   S322

| JOHN CIPOLLINA | G | (| (A) ILLEGAL ENTRY | 1981 RAG BABY | RAG 1010 |
| ROCKY SULLIVAN | V | (A | JOEY COVINGTON | D | (| MARIO CIPOLLINA | G B | (A | JARRETT WASHINGTON K | (|

HUBERT SUMLIN   S323

HUBERT SUMLIN	G V	(ALL	(A) HUBERT'S AMERICAN BLUES	19 SCOUT	SC4
LONNIE BROOKS	G	(B	(B) GROOVE	1976 BLACK & BLUE	33511
FRED BELOW	D	(BC	(C) KINGS OF CHICAGO BLUES VOL 2	19 VOGUE	LDM 30175
SUNNYLAND SLIM	V PNO(AD		(D) BLUES ANYTIME (1964)	1980 L+R	GERM	42004
WILLIE MABON	PNO	(AD	(E) GAMBLIN' WOMAN	1980 L+R	GERM	42008
CLIFTON JAMES	D	(AD				
CAREY BELL	V HCA(B	JIMMY DAWKINS	G	(C	JAMES GREEN	B	(C	BILLY BOY ARNOLD	V HCA(C
EDDIE SHAW	SAX (C	JOE CARTER	G V	(C	DAVE MYERS	B	(B	WILLIE DIXON	B	(D

S324   SAFFRON SUMMERFIELD

SAFFRON SUMMERFIELD	V G K(AB	(A) SALISBURY PLAIN	1974	MOTHER EARTH	MUM 1001
GEORGE NORRIS	G V (A	(B) FANCY MEETING YOU HERE	1976	MOTHER EARTH	MUM 1202
LAURIE RHODES	B (A				
ALISON BAILEY	CELLO(A				

S325   BILL SUMMERS

BILL SUMMERS	V PERC FLT(AB			(A) STRAIGHT TO THE BANK	1978 PRESTIGE		PR 10105	
LEO MILLER	V (A			(B) ON SUNSHINE	1979 PRESTIGE		PR 10107	
VIRGINIA AYERS	V (A							
RAY OBIEDO	G (AB	FRED WASHINGTON	B (A	GEORGE BOHANON	TROM (A	BENNY POWELL	TROM(A
DARRYL JACKSON	D (A	OSCAR BRASHEAR	HRNS (A	JOHN BARNES	K (A	RAY BROWN	HRNS(A
LEON CHANCLER	D (A	JERRY HEY	HRNS (AB	DICK HYDE	TROM (A	BILL GREEN	SAX (A
PATTIE BROOKS	V (A	ERNIE WATTS	SAX (A	MAXINE ANDERSON	V (A	LORI HAM	V (B
JOSIE JAMES	V (A	CALVIN TILLERY	V (B	PETSYE POWELL	V (A	TOM POOLE	TPT (B
LARRY BATISTE	TROM V PNO(B	BO FREEMAN	B (B	CLAYTOVEN	SAX PNO V (B	PAUL VAN WAGENINGEN	D(B
PAUL SMITH	K (B	SCOTT ROBERTS	PERC V(B	TIM GORMAN	SYN (B	MARLON McCLAIN	G (B
GARY GALVIN	B (B	GREG PHILLINGANES	PNO (B	LLOYD ADAMS	D (B	GAYLORD BIRCH	D (B
DWAYNE SWEET	K (B	TONY LEWIS	D (B	PHILLIP RICHARDSON	V (B	WAYNE WALLACE	TROM(B
MARK SOSKIN	PNO (B	COLIN PAYNE	ORG (B	LARRY WILLIAMS	SAX (B	MAXINE WILLARD	V (B
MYYA LARK	V (B	CARLBERG JONES	HRNS (B	JULIA TILLMAN	V (B	PAT HENDERSON	V (B
STRINGS	(B						

S326   SUN

(A) LIVE ON DREAM ON	1976	CAPITOL	11461
(B) SUN POWER	1977	CAPITOL	11609
(C) SUNBURN	1978	CAPITOL	11723
(D) DESTINATION SUN	1979	capitol	11941

S326A   SUN ALSO RISES

GRAHAM HEMINGWAY	G V (A	(A) SUN ALSO RISES	1970	VILLAGE THING	UK VTS 2
ANNE HEMINGWAY	V DULC(A				
JOHN TURNER	B (A	ANDY LEGGETT WIND (A			

S327   SUNDANCE

BOB BOWMAN	(A	(A) RAIN STEAM SPEED	1973	DECCA	UK	TXS 111
JOHN LYNAM	(A	(B) CHUFFER	1974	DECCA	UK	SKL 5183
PHIL SAVAGE	(A					

S327A   SUNDAY FUNNIES

RICHARD KOSINSKI	K V (A	(A) SUNDAY FUNNIES	1971	RARE EARTH	US	RS 526
RICHARD MITCHELL	D (A					
RICHARD FIDGE	V (A	RONALD AITKEN G V (A				

S328   SUNFOREST

(A) SOUND OF SUNFOREST	19	NOVA	UK	SDN17

S329   SUNNYLAND SLIM

SUNNYLAND SLIM	V PNO(ALL	(A) SLIM'S GOT THIS THING GOIN' ON	1968	WORLD PACIFIC	US	WPS 21890
ERNEST DONABLE	D (A	(A) SLIM'S GOT THIS THING GOIN' ON	1969	LIBERTY	UK	LBS 83237
MICKEY BAKER	G (K	(B) MIDNIGHT JUMP	1969	BLUE HORIZON	UK	763213
LAYFAYETTE HUDSON	B (K	(C) PEARL HARBOUR BLUES(1 SIDE)	1970	RCA INT	UK	INT 1176
GEORGE SMITH	HCA (A	(D) SAD & LONESOME	1972	JEWEL	US	LPS 5010
LUTHER ALLISON	G (A	(E) PLAYS RAGTIME BLUES	1973	BLUESWAY		BLS 6068
MICK TAYLOR	G (A	(F) & LITTLE BROTHER MONTGOMERY	19	77		77LA 1221
CURTIS TILLMAN	B (A	(G) SUNNYLAND SLIM	19	STORYVILLE		SLP 169
RANDY FULLERTON	G (A	(H) LEGACY OF THE BLUES	1975	SONET	UK	SNTF 671
BIG MAMA THORNTON	D (A	(I) BLUES MASTERS VOL 8	19	BLUE HORIZON	US	4608
ROBERT ELEM	B (A	(J) DECORATION DAY	1980	L+R	GERM	42015
FRANCIS CLAY	D (A	(K) DEPRESSION BLUES	19	FESTIVAL		FLD
HENRY VESTINE	G (A	( ) PATIENCE LIKE JOB	1979	AIRWAY	US	LP 4746
CAREY BELL	HCA (J					
AL WILSON	G (A	LARRY TAYLOR	B (A	PAUL LAGOS	D (A	GUS WRIGHT	D (A
SHAKEY JAKE	HCA (A	FRED BELOW	D (E	DAVE MYERS	B (E	LOUIS MYERS	D (E
JOHNNY SHINES	G (B	WILLIE DIXON	B (B	WALTER HORTON	HCA (B	CLIFTON JAMES	D (B
BLIND JOHN DAVIS	PNO (C	BIG BILL BROONZY	G (C	RANSOM KNOWLING	B (C	JUDGE RILEY	D (C
HUBERT SUMLIN	G (J	JEFF SWAN	G (J	BOB STROGER	B (J	ODIE PAYNE	D (J

S329A   SUNRISE

HANNO HARDERS	K B G(A	(A) CALL ON ME	1978	POLYDOR	UK	2417 120
JORG FRIES	(A					
HOLGER KOPP	G V (A	MICHAEL REINECKE	PERC (A	ADDI RIETENBACH	D K (A	PETER FRANKEN	D PERC(A
ROLF KOHLER	B (A	WERNER LANG	ACC (A	HOLGER VOSS	SAX (A	BENNY BENDORFF	B (A
DICKY TARRACH	D (A	JURGEN SCHRODER	G (A	BRIGITTE	V (A	RALE	V (A

S329B   SUNSHINE

JACK GREEN	B G V(A	(A) SUNSHINE	1972	WB	UK	K46169
GORDON EDWARDS	G K V(A					
PETER OLIVER	G V (A	TERRY SLADE PERC D(A	JOANNE WHITE PERC V(A	ETHEL COLEY PERC V(A		

S330   SUNSHINE COMPANY

MARY NANCE	V PERC(ABC	(A) HAPPY IS THE SUNSHINE COMPANY	1967	IMPERIAL	US	12359
MAURICE MANSEAU	V K G(ABC	(B) SUNSHINE COMPANY	1968	IMPERIAL	US	12368
LARRY SIMS	G V (ABC	(C) SUNSHINE & SHADOWS	1968	LIBERTY	UK	LBS 83159
MEREL BREGANTE	D V (ABC	(C) SUNSHINE & SHADOWS	1968	IMPERIAL	US	12399
DOUGLAS MARK	G VLN V (ABC					
DAVE HODGKINS	G (C					

S331   SUNTREADER

MORRIS PERT	D (A	(A) ZIN ZIN	1973	ISLAND	UK	HELP13
PETER ROBINSON	K (A					
ALYN ROSS	B (A	ROBIN THOMPSON SAX (A				

S332   SUPERCHARGE

ALBIE DONNELLY	WIND V(AB	(A) LOCAL LADS MAKE GOOD	1976	VIRGIN	UK	V 2053
DALE IRVING	D V (A	(B) HORIZONTAL REFRESHMENT	1977	VIRGIN	UK	V 2067
IAIN BRADSHAW	K (A	(C) BODY RHYTHM	1979	VIRGIN	UK	V 2118
LES KARSKI	G V (A	(D) NOW JUMP	19	CRIMINAL	UK	STEAL 10
OZZIE YUE	G V (A	(EP) 4 BY 6	1976	VIRGIN	UK	VEP 1001
TONY DUNMORE	B V (A					
BOB ROBERTSON	SAX V(A	DICK HANSON TPT (A				

SUPERFINE DANDELION
S332A

MIKE McFADDEN	V G HCA	(A				(A) SUPERFINE DANDELION	196 MAINSTREAM	US	S6102

MIKE McFADDEN V G HCA (A
MIKE COLLINS   D V   (A
ED BLACK   G K V(A   RICK ANDERSON   B G (A

(A) SUPERFINE DANDELION   196 MAINSTREAM   US   S6102

SUPERMAX
S332B

KURT HAVENSTEIN   V B K(A   (A) WORLD OF TODAY   1977 ATLANTIC   K50423
CYNTHIA ARRICH   V   (A
TEBLES REYNOLDS   V   (A   RICHARD SCHOENHERZ SYN K(A RAINER MARZ   G (A   JUANITA SCHULZ   V(A
DANIELE FORD   PERC (A   HARTMUT PFANNMULLER   D(A

SUPERSEPFFT
S332C

DIETER KOLB   SYN (A   (A) ROBOTER WERK   1979 CBS   83712
ROBOTERWERKE   D (A

SUPERSISTER
S332D

ROBERT JAN STIPS K (ALL   (A) PRESENT FOM NANCY   1970 POLYDOR   2419 061
RON VAN ECK   B (ALL   (B) TO THE HIGHEST BIDDER   1971 DANDELION 2310 146 POLY2925002
MARCO VROLIJK   D (ABC   (C) PUDDING AND GISTEREN   1972 POLYDOR   2925 007 +   2419 058
SACHA VAN GEEST WIND (ABCD   (D) ISKANDER   1973 POLYDOR   2925 021
CHARLIE MARIANO WIND (D   (E) SUPER STARSHINE No3   197 POLYDOR   2419 030
HERMAN VAN BOEYEN D (D   ( ) SUPERSISTER   19 DWARF   US   PDLP 2001
PIERRE MOERLEN   PERC (D

SUPERTRAMP
S333

ROGER HODGSON   V G (ABCDEFG   (A) SUPERTRAMP   1970 A&M US 4665 UK AMLS 981
RICHARD DAVIES   K V (ABCDEFG   (B) INDELIBLY STAMPED 1971 A&M US 4311 UK AMLS64306
RICHARD PALMER   G (A   (C) CRIME OF THE CENTURY 1974 A&M US 3647 UK AMLS68258
DAVE WINTHROP   SAX (B   (D) CRISIS? WHAT CRISIS? 1975 A&M US 4560 UK AMLH68347
BOB MILLER   D (A   (E) EVEN IN THE QUIETEST MOMENTS 1977 A&M US 4634 UK AMLK64634
KEVIN CURRIE   D (B   (F) BREAKFAST IN AMERICA 1979 A&M US 3708 UK AMLK63708
FRANK FARRELL   B (B   (G) PARIS   1980 A&M   UK AMLM66702
BOB BENBERG   D (CDEFG   ( ) EXTREMES(SOUNDTRACK) 1973 DERAM   UK AML 1095
JOHN HELLIWELL   SAX (CDEFG
DOUGIE THOMPSON   B (CDEFG DICK HYDE   TROM (F

SUPREMES
S333A

DIANA ROSS   V (MEET THE SUPREMES   1964 TAMLA US 606 UK STATESIDE10109
MARY WILSON   V (LIVE AT THE APOLLO   1964 TAMLA US 609
FLORENCE BALLARD V (A BIT OF LIVERPOOL   1965 TAMLA US 621
BARBARA MARTIN   V (WHERE DID OUR LOVE GO   1965 TAMLA US 623
CINDY BIRDSONG   V (COUNTRY WESTERN & POP   1965 TAMLA US 625
JEAN TERRELL   V (HITS   1965 TAMLA   UK TME 2008
LYNDA LAURENCE   V (MORE HITS   1965 TAMLA US 627
SHARI PAYNE   V (WE REMEMBER SAM COOKE   1965 TAMLA US 629 UK TML 11020
SUSAYE GREEN   V (WITH LOVE   1965 TAMLA   UK TML 11002
KAREN JACKSON   V (AT THE COPA   196 TAMLA US 636
                  MERRY CHRISTMAS   1965 TAMLA US 638
                  I HEAR A SYMPHONY   1966 TAMLA US 643 UK STML11028
                  A GO GO   1966 TAMLA US 649 UK STML11039
                  SING MOTOWN   1967 TAMLA   UK STML11047
                  SING HOLLAND DOZIER HOLLAND 1967 TAMLA US 650
                  SING RODGERS & HART   1967 TAMLA US 659 UK STML11054
                  GREATEST HITS   1968 TAMLA US 663 UK STML11063
                  FUNNY GIRL   1968 TAMLA US 672
                  LIVE AT THE TALK OF THE TOWN 1968 TAMLA US 676 UK STML11070
                  REFLECTIONS   1968 TAMLA US 665 UK STML11073
                  LOVE CHILD   1969 TAMLA   UK STML11095
                  JOIN THE TEMPTATIONS   1969 TAMLA US 679 UK STML11096
                  T C B   1969 TAMLA US 682 UK STML11110
                  LET THE SUN SHINE IN   1969 TAMLA US 689 UK STML11114
                  TOGETHER(TEMPTATIONS)   1969 TAMLA US 692 UK STML11122
                  CREAM OF THE CROP   1970 TAMLA US 694 UK STML11137
                  ON BROADWAY(TEMPTATIONS)   1970 TAMLA US 699
                  GREATEST HITS VOL 2   1970 TAMLA US 702 UK STML11146
                  FAREWELL   1970 TAMLA US 708 UK STML11154
                  RIGHT ON   1970 TAMLA US 705 UK STML11157
                  NEW WAYS BUT LOVE STAYS   1971 TAMLA US 720 UK STML11175
                  MAGNIFICENT SEVEN   1971 TAMLA US 717 UK STML11179
                  SURRENDER   197 TAMLA US 723
                  TOUCH   1971 TAMLA US 737 UK STML11189
                  RETURN OF THE MAGNIFICENT SEVEN 1971 TAMLA US 736 UK STML11192
                  DYNAMITE   1972 TAMLA US 745 UK STML11203
                  FLOY JOY   1972 TAMLA US 751 UK STML11210
                  BABY LOVE   1973 MFP   UK SPR 90001
                  GREATEST HITS   1974 TAMLA   UK STML 11256
                  SUPREMES   1973 TAMLA US 756 UK STML11222
                  ANTHOLOGY   1975 TAMLA US 794 UK TMSP 6001
                  SUPREMES   1975 TAMLA US 879 UK STML11293
                  HIGH ENERGY   1976 TAMLA US 863 UK STML12027
                  MARY,SHARI & SUSAYE   1976 TAMLA US 873 UK STML12047
                  STOP IN THE NAME OF LOVE   1976 MFP   UK MFP 50291
                  AT THEIR BEST   197 TAMLA US 904 UK STML12091
                  DIANA ROSS & THE SUPREMES   1977 TAMLA   UK STMX 6001
                  SUPREMES & TEMPTATIONS   1977 TAMLA   UK STMX 6003
                  20 GOLDEN GREATS   1977 TAMLA   UK EMTV 5
                  IT'S HAPPENING   19 MCA   734727

THE SURF PUNKS
S333B

DENNIS DRAGON   D V (A   (A) MY BEACH   1980 EPIC   UK EPC 84346
DREW STEELE   G V K(A

SURPRISE SISTERS
S334

PATRICIA   V (A   (A) SURPRISE SISTERS   1976 GOOD EARTH   GDS 801
LINDA   V (A
SUSAN   V (A   ELLEN   V (A RAY RUSSELL   G (A   BRUCE LYNCH   G (A
JEAN ROUSSEL   K (A   BRENT FORBES   B (A RAY WARLEIGH   SAX (A   FRANK RICOTTI VIBES(A
BLUE WEAVER   K (A   GERRY CONWAY   D (A PHIL KENZIE   SAX (A

[401]

```
S335                              SURFARIS
   PAT CONNOLLY      B V (       (A) WIPE OUT              1963 DOT    US 3535
   JIM FULLER        G   (       (B) SURFARIS PLAY         1963 DECCA US 4470 UK BRUNSWICK 8561
   BOB BERRYHILL     G   (       (C) HIT CITY '64          1964 DECCA US 4487 UK BRUNSWICK 8567
   RON WILSON        D   (       (D) FUN CITY              1964 DECCA US 4560 UK BRUNSWICK 8582
   JIM PASH    G WIND (           (E) HIT CITY '65          1965 DECCA US 4614 UK BRUNSWICK 8605
                                 (F) WHEELS                19   DIPLOMAT  US           2309
                                 (G) YESTERDAYS POP SCENE  1973 CORAL              COPS 6354
                                 (H) WIPE OUT              1973 POLYDOR            2870 335
                                 (J) SURFERS RULE          1976 MCA      US        MCF 2761
                                 (K) GONE WITH THE WAVE    1977 CORAL              CDL 8050
S336                              SURVIVOR
   FRANKIE SULLIVAN  G V (A      (A) SURVIVOR              1979 SCOTTI BROTHERS    SB50698
   DAVE BICKLER      V K (A
   JIM PETERIK       G   (A  GARY SMITH      D   (A  DENNIS KEITH JOHNSON   B (A
S337                              SUSAN
   TOM DICKIE        G V (A      (A) 11976
   CHARLES LELAND    B V (A
   JOHN KALISHES     G   (A  MICHAEL LELAND  D   (A
S338                          SCREAMING LORD SUTCH
   LORD SUTCH        V   (ABC    (A) LORD SUTCH & HEAVY FRIENDS 1970 ATLANTIC UK 2400 008 US COTILLION 9015
   JIMMY PAGE        G   (A      (B) HANDS OF JACK THE RIPPER  1972 ATLANTIC UK   K40313 US COTILLION 9049
   NICKY HOPKINS     K   (A      (C) ALIVE & WELL              1980 BABYLON       GERM        B 80010
   JOHN BONHAM       D   (A
   NOEL REDDING      B   (A  JEFF BECK        G   (A  DANIEL EDWARDS    G B (A  CARLO LITTLE   D  (A
   KENT HENREY       G   (A  MARTIN KOHL      B   (A  RICK BROWN        B   (A  BOB METKE      D  (A
   SID PHILLIPS      SAX (B  MATTHEW FISHER   K   (B  NICK SIMPER       B   (B  ANNETTE BROX   V  (B
   BRIAN KEITH       V TROM(B RITCHIE BLACKMORE G  (B  KEITH MOON        D   (B  VICTOR BROX    V  (B
   PAT TRAVERS       G   (C  JIM GREEN        G   (C  RICK NIELSEN      G   (C  RICHARD PRUT   SAX (C
   COLIN SOLMAN      D   (C  DETLEV RESHOFT   K   (C  MARS COWLING      B   (C  KLAUS VOORMANN B  (C
   REINHARD STROEMER B   (C
S339                     SUTHERLAND BROTHERS (& QUIVER)
   GAVIN SUTHERLAND  B G V(ALL   (A) THE SUTHERLAND BROTHERS BAND 1972 ISLAND UK ILPS9181 RI CBS 82297
   IAIN SUTHERLAND   V G K(ALL   (B) LIFEBOAT                     1972 ISLAND UK ILPS9212 RI CBS 82298
   TIM RENWICK       G   (CDEFGH (C) dREAM KID                    1973 ISLAND UK ILPS9259 RI CBS 82299
   WILLIE WILSON     D   (2CDEFGH (D) BEAT OF THE STREET          1974 ISLAND UK ILPS9288 RT CBS 82300
   BRUCE THOMAS      K   (C      (E) REACH FOR THE SKY            1975 CBS              UK       69191
   KIM LUDMAN        B   (A      (F) SAILING (COMP)               1976 ISLAND UK ILPS9358 US CBS 33982
   NEIL HOPWOOD      D   (A      (G) SLIPSTREAM                   1976 CBS      UK    81593 US    34376
   PETE WOOD         K   (CD     (H) DOWN TO EARTH                1977 CBS      UK    82255 US    35293
   MICK GRABHAM      G   (H      (J) WHEN THE NIGHT COMES DOWN    1979 CBS      UK    83427
   TEX COMER         B   (D      (1) MARCH 1978   (2) OCT 1977
   ALAN ROSS         G   (2
   MICK WEAVER       K   (2  GLEN SPREEN    K   (J  JIM HORN        HRNS (J  STEVE PORCARO    SYN (J
   STEVE FORMAN      PERC (J  JOHN SHEARER   PERC (2  BILL SMITH           (J1 BOB GLAUB          (J1
   MIKE BAIRD            (J1 RITCHIE ZETO      (J1 ALBHY GALUTEN   K   (B  FLACO PADRON     PERC(G
   JOHN HAWKEN       K   (B  BOB RONGA      B   (B  STEVE WINWOOD   K   (B  DAVE MATTACKS    D   (B
   PAT DONALDSON     B   (B  RABBIT BUNDRICK K  (B  ANDY PYLE       B   (H  RICK WILLS       B   (H
   BRIAN BENNETT     PERC (H  JOHN SHEARER      PERC (H
S339A                            SWALLOW
   GEORGE LEH        V   (A      (A) OUT OF THE NEST       1972 WB              UK          K56174
   PARKER WHEELER    V HCA(A
   VERN MILLER       V G B(A  DAVID WOODFORD  WIND K(A  PHIL GREEN    G   (A  MICK ARANDA       D(A
   BOB CAMACHO       K   (A  JAY DEWALD      TPT   (A  ANDY HARP     TPT (A  KERRY BLOUT       SAX (A
   GEORGE KENNEDY    TROM (A  JEFF BAXTER     STEEL(A
S340                             SWAMP DOGG
   JERRY WILLIAMS    V PNO(ALL   (A) TOTAL DESTRUCTION OF YOUR MIND 1970 CANYON    US    LP 7706
   STACY GOSS        HRNS (BG     (B) SWAMP DOGG                     1971 ELEKTRA   UK    EKS 74089
   SONNY ROYAL       WIND (B      (C) CUFFED COLLARED & TAGGED       1972 CREAM     US        9009
   MIKE STOUGH       HRNS (B      (D) FINALLY CAUGHT UP WITH MYSELF  197  MCA               2504
   ROBERT POPS POPWELL B (B      (E) SWAMP DOGG                     19   WIZARD    US        1122
   JESSE CARR        G V (B      (F) GAG A MAGGOT                   1975 PRESIDENT        PTLS 1059
   JASPER GUARINO    D   (B      (F) GAG A MAGGOT                   1973 STONEDOGG         3001
   JIMMY EVANS       D   (G      (G) HAVE YOU HEARD THIS STORY      1975 ISLAND    UK    ILPS 9299
   HARRISON CALLOWAY TPT  (G      (H) NEVER TOO OLD TO BOOGIE        1976 DJM       UK    DJF 20476
   TRAVIS WAMMACK    G HCA(G
   AUDIE WATKINS     PERC (G  RANDY McCORMICK K   (G  LENNY LEBLANC   B   (G  DAVE'BABY'JOHNSON WIND(G
   HARVEY THOMPSON   WIND (G  RON EADES       SAX  (G  CHARLES ROSE    TROM (G  HARRISON CALLOWAY TPT(G
S341                             SWAMPWATER
   THAD MAXWELL      B V (A      (A) SWAMPWATER            1971 RCA US LSP 4572+ KING US  1122
   STAN PRATT        D V (A
   GIB GUILBEAU      FDL G V (A  HERB PEDERSEN   G V (A  JOHN BELAND   G V (A  GLEN D HARDIN   G  (A
S342                             BILLY SWAN
   BILLY SWAN        V   (ALL    (A) I CAN HELP            1975 MONUMENT UK 80615 US CBS  33279
   KRIS KRISTOFFERSON V  (E      (B) ROCK'N'ROLL MOON      1975 MONUMENT UK 69192 US CBS  33805
   RITA COOLIDGE     V   (E      (C) BILLY SWAN            1976 MONUMENT UK 81387 US CBS  34183
   LEO SAYER         HCA (E      (D) FOUR                  1977 MONUMENT UK 81867 US CBS  34473
   JORDANAIRES       V   (E      (E) YOUR OK I'M OK        1978 A&M   UK  AMLH64886    US     4686
   SCOTTY MOORE      G   (E      (F) BILLY SWAN            1978 EMBASSY  UK 31674
   DONALD DUNN       B   (E      (G) AT HIS BEST           1978 MONUMENT     US     MG7629
   ROGER HAWKINS         (D
   DAVID HOOD           (D   BARRY BECKETT       (D  JIMMY JOHNSON       (D  TIM HENSON    K  (D
   MIKE UTLEY        K   (E  STEVE BRUTON    G   (E  SAMMY CREASON   D   (E  JERRY McGEE   G  (E
   BOOKER T JONES    K   (E  OTIS BLACKWELL  PNO (E  DON ROBERTSON   PNO (E  CLYDIE KING   V  (E
   VANETTA FIELDS    V   (E  PAULETTE BROWN  V   (E  NEAL MATTHEWS   V   (E  LOUIS NUNLEY  V  (E
   GORDON STOKER     V   (E  PETE CARR       D   (
```

[402]

SWAN ARCADE
S343

DAVE BRADY	V	(A	(A) SWAN ARCADE	1973 TRAILER	UK	LER2032		
HEATHER BRADY	V	(A	(B) MATCHLESS	197 SHANACHIE		MU 7428		
FRANK TOWARD	V	(A						
JIM BOYES	G V	(A	DAVE FARRER	V	(A	RAB NOAKES	G	(A DAVE BURLAND G V (A
JIMMY HUTCHISON	V	(A	DIXIE KIDD	B	(A	ALASDAIR CAMERON	V	(A

DAVE SWARBRICK
S344

DAVE SWARBRICK	FDL MAND VLA(ABCD	(A) RAGS,REELS & AIRS	1967 POLYDOR		236 514	
BERYL MARRIOTT	K	(BCD	(B) SWARBRICK	1976 TRANSATLANTIC	UK	TRA 337
MARTIN CARTHY	G	(ABC	(C) SWARBRICK 2	1977 TRANSATLANTIC	UK	TRA 341
SIMON NICOL	G	(BCD	(D) LIFT THE LID & LISTEN	1978 SONET	UK	SNTF 763
DAVE PEGG	B	(BCD	(E) THE CEILIDH ALBUM	1978 SONET	UK	SNTF 764
BRUCE ROWLAND	PERC	(BCD				

SAVOURNA STEVENSON CLAR (BCD KATE GRAHAM   FDL (BC ROGER MARRIOTT MELODIAN(BCD ALAN ROBERTSON   ACC(BCD
DIZ DISLEY   G   (A

SWEATHOG
S345

(A) HALLELUJAH   1972 CBS   UK   64784

SWEENEYS MEN
S346

ANDY IRVINE		(AB12	(A) RATTLIN' & ROARIN' WILLY	1968 TRANSATLANTIC	UK	TRA170
JOE DOLAN		(1	(B) TRACKS OF SWEENEY	1969 TRANSATLANTIC	UK	TRA200
TERRY WOODS		(234AB	(A) SWEENEYS MEN	1976 TRANSATLANTIC	UK	TRASAM 37
AL O'DONNELL		(4	(B) TRACKS OF SWEENEY	1977 TRANSATLANTIC	UK	TRASAM 40
HENRY McCULLOUGH	G	(3				
JOHNNY MOYNIHAN		(1234AB	(1) 1966/7 (2) 1967/8 (3) 1968 (4) 1968/9			

THE SWEET
S347

BRIAN CONNOLLY	V	(*ABCDEF	(*) GIMME DAT DING (ONE SIDE)	1970 MFP	UK	5248
STEVE PRIEST	HCA V B	(ALL	(A) FUNNY HOW SWEET COCO CAN BE	1971 RCA	UK	SF8288
MIKE TUCKER	D V	(ALL	(B) SWEETS BIGGEST HITS	1972 RCA	UK	SF8316
FRANK TORPY	G	(	(C) SWEET	1973 BELL	US	1124
MICK STEWART	G	(	(D) SWEET FANNY ADAMS	1974 RCA		LPL15039
ANDY SCOTT	G SYN V	(ALL	(E) DESOLATION BOULEVARD	1975 RCA UK LPL15080 US CAPITOL11395		
GARY MOBERLEY	K	(M	(F) STRUNG UP	1975 RCA		SPC 0001
			(G) GIVE US A WINK	1976 RCA UK RS 1036 US CAPITOL11496		
			(H) OFF THE RECORD	1977 RCA UK PL25172 US CAPITOL11636		
			(I) GOLDEN GREATS	1977 RCA UK PL25111		
			(J) LEVEL HEADED	1978 POLYDOR POLD 5001		2302 077
			(K) THE SWEET	1978 CAMDEN	UK	CDS 1168
			(L) CUT ABOVE THE REST	1979 POLYDOR POLS 5022		
			(M) WATERS EDGE	1980 POLYDOR POLS 1021		2311 009

RACHEL SWEET
S348

RACHEL SWEET	V	(AB	(A) FOOL AROUND	1978 STIFF	UK	SEEZ 12
			(B) PROTECT THE INNOCENT	1980 STIFF	UK	SEEZ 18

SWEET 'D BUSTER
S348A

BERTUS BORGERS	V WIND(ABCD	(A) SWEET'D BUSTER	1977 ARIOLA		25177 XOT	
PAUL SMEENK	G	(ABCD	(B) FRICTION	1978 ARIOLA		25861 XOT
HERMAN DEINUM	B	(ABCD	(C) GIGS	1979 ARIOLA		200 337
HANS LAFAILLE	D	(ABC	(D) SHOT INTO THE BLUE	1979 ARIOLA		200 651
ROBERT JAN STIPS	K	(ABC				
ARNOLD BOGAARL	PERC	(A				
FRANS MIJTS	TPT	(A	JONS PISTOOR K (D PIERRE VAN DER LINDEN D(D			

SWEET F.A.
S348B

CAROL GRIMES	V	(A	(A) SWEET F.A.	1980 MNW	SWED	103P
PETE KIRTLEY	G V	(A				
GARY TWIGG	B	(A	TONY HICKS D (A OLLIE MALLARD K V (A			

SWEET PAIN (US)
S349

DAVID ROIRDAN		(A	(A) SWEET PAIN	196 UA UK UAS 29161 US	6793	
BOB SPALDING		(				
CARL JOHNSON		(	MARTY FOLTZ (FRANK DEMME (J C PHILLIPS (			

SWEET PAIN (UK)
S349A

JOHN O'LEARY	HCA	(A	(A) SWEET PAIN	1969 MERCURY	UK	SMCL20146
KEITH TILLMAN	B	(A	(A) ENGLANDS HEAVY BLUES SUPER SESS	19 MERCURY	US	SR 61231
STUART COWELL	G	(A				
DICK HECKSTALL SMITH	SAX(A	ANNETTE BROX V (A SAM CROZIER PNO V(A JUNIOR DUNN D(A				
ALAN GREED	V	(A				

SWEET SMOKE
S350

MARVIN KAMINOWITZ	G V	(C	(A) JUST A POKE	197 HARVEST	IMP IC062 28886
MARTIN ROSENBERG	PERC	(C	(A) JUST A POKE	197 HARVEST	5C054 24311
ANDREW DERSHIN	B	(C	(B) DARKNESS TO LIGHT	197 HARVEST	IMP IC062 29471
JAY DORFMAN	D	(C	(C) LIVE	1974 HARVEST	IMP IC062 29513
RICK GREENBERG	G	(C			
JOHN CLASSI	PERC	(C			

SWEET THUNDER
S351

(A) SWEET THUNDER   1978 FANTASY   FT 545

SWEET THURSDAY
S352

NICKY HOPKINS	K	(A	(A) SWEET THURSDAY	1969 TETRAGRAMMATON	US	T 12
JON MARK	G V	(A	(A) SWEET THURSDAY	1969 POLYDOR	UK	2310 051
ALUN DAVIES	G V	(A	( ) SWEET THURSDAY	1973 CBS	UK	65573
HARVEY BURNS	D	(A				
BRIAN ODGERS	B WIND	(A				

SWEET WATER
S353

FRED HERRERA	B V	(C	(A) SWEET WATER	19 REPRISE	US	R56313
ALEX DELZOPPO	K V HCA	(C	(B) JUST FOR YOU	19 REPRISE	US	R56417
ALBERT B MOORE	FLT B(C	(C) MELON	1971 REPRISE	US	R56473	
ELPIDIO COBIAN	PERC	(C				
NANSI NEVINS	G V	(C	ALAN MALAROWITZ D (C AUGUST BURNS CELLO(C RICKY FATAAR D(C			

SWEETBOTTOM
S354

WARREN 'VITO' WIEGRATZ	K WIND V(AB	(A) ANGELS OF THE DEEP	1978 ELEKTRA	UK K52110 US 6E 156		
MARK TORROLL	D	(AB	(B) TURN ME LOOSE	1979 ELEKTRA	US 6E 210	
DUANE STUERMER	B V	(AB				
MARTIN J APPEL	G	(AB				

SWELL MAPS

(A) TRIP TO MARINEVILLE	1979	ROUGH TRADE		ROUGH 2
(B) IN 'JANE FROM OCCUPIED EUROPE'	1980	ROUGH TRADE		ROUGH 15

S355

JONATHAN SWIFT

JONATHAN SWIFT	G V	(AB	(A) INTROVERT	1971	CBS	UK	64412
PETER MORGAN	B	(B	(B) SONGS	1972	CBS	UK	64751
HAROLD FISHER	D	(B					
ALAN SPARKES	G	(B	LAURIE ALLEN D (B LES HARVEY G (B ANN ODELL K (B				

S356

SWINGING BLUE JEANS

RAY ENNIS	G	(ALL	(A) TUTTI FRUTTI	1964	REGAL	UK	SREG 1073
RALPH ENNIS	G	(	(B) BLUE JEANS A SWINGING	1964	HMV UK CLP(M)1802 +CSD(S)		1570
LES BRAID	B	(	(C) HIPPY HIPPY SHAKE	1964	IMPERIAL	US	LPS 12261
NORMAN KUHLKE	D	(	(D) SHAKING TIME	1964	ELECTROLA	EURO	83716
			(E) HEY HEY HEY (LIVE)	1965	ELECTROLA	EURO	83927
			(F) THE SWINGING BLUES JEANS	1966	LIVERPOOL SOUND	UK	PSQ030
			(G) THE SWINGING BLUE JEANS	1967	MFP	UK	MFP1163
			(H) HIPPY HIPPY SHAKE	1973	BELLAPHON	EURO	15100
			(J) BRAND NEW & FADED	1974	DART		BULL1001
			(K) SWINGING BLUE JEANS	1978	EMI	UK	NUT 15
			(EP) SHAKE WITH	196	HMV	UK	7EG 8850
			(EP) YOUR NO GOOD	196	HMV	UK	7EG 8868

S357

SWITCH

(A) SWITCH	1978	TAMLA MOTOWN	UK STML1209
(B) SWITH II	1979	TAMLA MOTOWN	UK STML1211

S358

ROOSEVELT SYKES

ROOSEVELT SYKES	PNO V(ALL	(A) BLUES FROM BAR ROOMS	1967	77	UK	77LEU125
JUSTIN ADAMS	G (I	(B) BLUE BIRD No10	19	RCA	FR	PM 4202
CLARENCE FORD	SAX (I	(C) BLUE & RIBALD	19	SOUTHLAND	US	
GEORGE FRENCH	B (I	(D) BLUES	19	FOLKWAYS		382
ALONZO STEWART	D (I	(E) BARRELHOUSE BLUES & STOMPS	19	EUPHONIC	US	120
DON LAWSON	D (F	(F) BIG MAN OF BLUES	1961	EMI	UK	ENC 18
LITTLE BROTHER MONTGOMERY(R		(G) CHICAGO BLUES FESTIVAL	19	BLACK & BLUE	FR	3351
J T BROWN	SAX (B	(H) COUNTRY BLUES PIANO ACE	1974	YAZOO	L	103
WILLIE JAMES LACEY	G(B	(I) DIRTY DOUBLE MOTHER	1973	BLUESWAY	US	BL 607
ARMAND JACKSON	D (B	(J) FEEL LIKE BLOWING MY HORN	19	DELMARK	DS	63
JOHNNY WALKER	K (B	(K) HARD DRIVING BLUES	19	DELMARK	DL	60
JOHN FRAZIER	B (B	(L) HONEYDRIPPER'S DUKE'S MIXTURE	1971	BARCLAY IMP 920 294	+	8060
CHARLES SAUNDERS	D (B	(M) HONEYDRIPPER	19	FANTASY	US	2471
JOHNNY MORTON	TPT (B	(N) IN EUROPE	19	DELMARK	DS	61
OETT MALLARD	SAX (B	(O) MUSIC IS MY BUSINESS	19	BLUE LABOR	US	BL11
LEON WASHINGTON	SAX (B	(P) ORIGINAL HONEYDRIPPER	19	BLIND PIG	US	00
LEONARD GASTON	G (B	(Q) ROOSEVELT SYKES	19	STORYVILLE		SLP 18
ALFRED ELKINS	B (B	(R) URBAN BLUES	19	FANTASY	US	2471
BILL CASIMIR	SAX (B					
ERNEST CRAWFORD	B (B	W B NELSON D (B ROBERT PETE WILLIAMS G(A HOMESICK JAMES G B (K				

S358A

TERRY SYLVESTER

TERRY SYLVESTER	G V	(AB	(A) TERRY SYLVESTER	19	EPIC	US	3307
			(B) I BELIEVE	1976	POLYDOR	UK	2383 39

S359

SYMPHONIC SLAM

TIMO LAINE	SYN G V(A	(A) SYMPHONIC SLAM	1976	A&M	UK	AMLH6902
JOHN LOWRY	D V (A					
DAVID STONE	K V (A					

S360

SYNDICATE OF SOUND

(A) LITTLE GIRL	19	BELL US 6001 STATESIDE UK		SSL1018

S361

SYNERGY

(A) CORDS				
(B) GAMES	19			PB 600
(C) SEQUENCER	1976	SIRE	UK	9103 32
(D) ELECTRONIC REALIZATIONS	1976	SIRE	UK	9299 75

S362

SYREETA

SYREETA WRIGHT	V	(ALL	(A) STEVIE WONDER PRESENTS	1974	TAMLA	UK	STML1126
STEVIE WONDER		(	(B) SYREETA	1975	TAMLA US 808	M6	8445
			(B) SYREETA	197	MOWEST	MWS	700
G C CAMERON		(D	(C) ONE TO ONE	1977	TAMLA US 349	UK	STML1205
			(D) RICH LOVE POOR LOVE	1978	TAMLA US 891	UK	STML1207
			( ) BEST OF	1981	MOTOWN	UK	STMR 901

T1

STEVE T

STEVE T	(A) WEST COAST CONFIDENTIAL	1978	DREAM	US	DA 3500

T2

T FORD & THE BONE SHAKERS

(A) ROCK RATTLE & ROLL	1978	SPLASH	CPLP1004
(B) JUST KEEP IT UP	1979	SPLASH	CPLP 2001

T3

T.I.M.E. (TRUST IN MEN EVERYWHERE)

LARRY BYROM	G	(B	(A) T.I.M.E.	1968	LIBERTY US LST7558	
BILL RICHARDSON	G	(B	(B) SMOOTH BALL	1969	LIBERTY US LST7605 UK LBS83232	
STEVE RUMPH	D	(				
NICK ST NICHOLAS	B	(	PAT COUCHOIS D (B RICHARD TEPP B (B			

T4

T.K.O.

BRAD SINSEL	V	(A	(A) LET IT ROLL	1979	INFINITY	INS 2002
RICK PIERCE	G	(A				
MARK SEIDENVERG	B	(A	DARRYL SIGUENZA D (A TONY BORTKO K G (A			

T5

T 2

KEITH CROSS	G K V(A	(A) IT'LL ALL WORK OUT IN BOOMLAND	1970	DECCA	UK	SKL 5050
PETER DUNTON	D V (A					
BERNARD JINKS	B V (A					

T5A

T V KIDS

(A) TV KIDS	197	BRAIN BOOSTER	TA 001

JUNE TABOR

JUNE TABOR	V	(ALL	(A) SILLY SISTERS	1976 CHRYSALIS	UK	CHR 1101
MADDY PRIOR	V	(A	(B) AIRS & GRACES	1976 TOPIC	UK	12TS 298
TONY HALL	MEL	(AC	(C) ASHES & DIAMONDS	1977 TOPIC	UK	12TS 360
BOB DAVENPORT		(D	(D) BEES ON HORSEBACK	1977 FREE REED	UK	FRR 016
MARTIN CARTHY	G PERC(A		(1) 1977 TOUR			
NIC JONES	FDL G(A					
ANDY IRVINE	MAND (A	DANNY THOMPSON	B (A	GABRIEL McKEON	PIPES(A	JON GILLASPIE K WIND(ABC1
JOHNNY MOYNIHAN	WIND (A	BRIAN GOLBEY	FDL (A	LUIS JARDIM	PERC (A	RICK KEMP	B (C
NIGEL PEGRUM	D	(C	DOUG MORTER	G (C	MARTIN SIMPSON	G (1

TAGGETT

(A) TAGGETT	1974 EMI	UK	EMC 3015

TALBOT BROTHERS

TERRY TALBOT	HCA G V (A		(A) TALBOT BROTHERS	1974 WB US BS2767	UK	K56039
JOHN TALBOT	BAN G V(A					
RUSS KUNKEL	D	(A	LEE SKLAR	B (A	RANDY SCRUGGS	G (A JOSH GRAVES G DOBRO (A
SNEAKY PETE KLEINOW STEEL(A		CREEPER KURNOW	HCA (A	DON DACUS	G (A JOHN JARVIS PNO(A
DAVID LINDLEY	G	(A				

TALISKER

MARK MEGGIDO	B	(A	(A) DREAMING OF GLENISLA	1975 CAROLINE		CA 1513
LINDSAY COOPER	WIND (A		(B) LAND OF STONE	1977 ECM		JAPO60018
DAVE WEBSTER	SAX (ABC		(C) THE LAST BATTLE	1978 VINYL		VS 107
JOHN RANGECROFT	SAX (ABC					
KEN HYDER	D	(ABC JOHN LAWRENCE	B (BC		

TALKING HEADS

DAVID BYRNE	G V (ABCD	(A) TALKING HEADS	1977 SIRE US SR6306	UK	9103 328
TINA WEYMOUTH	B (ABCD	(B) MORE SONGS OF BUILDING & FOOD	1978 SIRE US SR6058	UK	K56531
CHRIS FRANTZ	D (ABCD	(C) FEAR OF MUSIC	1979 SIRE	UK	K56707
JERRY HARRISON	C V K(ABCD	(D) REMAIN IN LIGHT	1980 SIRE	UK	SRK 6095

JAMES TALLEY

JAMES TALLEY	G V (ALL	(A) GOT NO BREAD,NO MILK NO MONEY	1975 CAPITOL		11416
BYRON BACH	CELLO(C	(B) TRYIN' LIKE THE DEVIL	1976 CAPITOL		11494
RICK DURRETT	PNO (C	(C) BLACKJACK CHOIR	1977 CAPITOL		11605
DAVE GILLON	G (C	(D) AIN'T IT SOMETHIN'	1978 CAPITOL		11695
JOHNNY GIMBLE	G (C					
JOSH GRAVES	FDL (C	DOYLE GRISHAM	STEEL(C	STEVE HOSTAK	G (C IRV KANE TROM(C
B B KING	G (C	PEBBLE DANIEL	V (C	MARCIA ROUTH	V (C MIKE LEECH B (C
ANDY McMAHON	K (C	CLARK PIERSON	D V (C	BILLY PUETT	WIND (C JOHN SAYLES FDL (C
DON SHEFFIELD	TPT (C	JERRY SHOOK	G B HCA (C	TOMMY SMITH	TPT (C KYLE TULLIS B (C
REGGIE YOUNG	G (C	MARY JO TALLEY	V (C		

TALTON,STEWART,SANDLIN

TOMMY TALTON	G V (A	(A) HAPPY TO BE ALIVE	1976 CAPRICORN	US	0617
BILL STEWART	D G PERC(A				
JOHN SANDLIN	G B (A	SCOTT BOYER	(A	BONNIE BRAMLETT	(A JOE ENGLISH (A
CHUCK LEAVELL	(A	DRU LOMBAR	(A	STEVE MILLER	(A JOE WALK (A

TAMPA RED

HUDSON'RED'WHITTAKER G V(ALL		(A) TAMPA RED	19 BLUESVILLE	US	BVLP1030
GEORGIA TOM DORSEY PNO (A		(B) HOW LONG	19 BLUESVILLE	US	BVLP1043
BLACK BOB	PNO (DE	(C) BOTTLENECK GUITAR 1928 1937	19 YAZOO	US	1039
BIG MACEO	PNO (DE	(D) THE GUITAR WIZARD	19 RCA		AMX2 5501
WILLIE WILLIAMSON HCA (DE		(E) THE GUITAR WIZARD 1935 1953	19 BLUES CLASSICS	US	25
WALTER HORTON	HCA (DE				
JOHNNY JONES	PNO (				
WILLIE LACEY	G (	ODIE PAYNE	D (	SUGARMAN PENIGAR	SAX (BILL CASIMIR SAX (
JUDGE RILEY	D (	ARMAND JACKSON	SAX (	ERNEST CRAWFORD	B (OETT MALLARD WIND(
TYRELL DIXON	D (	RANSOM KNOWLING	B (	BLIND JOHN DAVIS	PNO (

NORMA TANEGA

NORMA TANEGA G V AUTOHARP(AB	(A) WALKING MY CAT NAMED DOG	1966 NEW VOICE 2001 UK STATESIDE10182
MIKE MORAN	K B V(B	(B) I DONT THINK I WILL HURT	1977 RCA	UK	SF8217
DON PAUL	V	(B			

TANGERINE DREAM

EDGAR FROESE SYN K G B (ALL		(A) ELECTRONIC MEDITATION	1970 OHR		OMM556004
CHRIS FRANKE SYN K (BCDEFGHJKLMN		(B) ALPHA CENTAURI	1971 OHR		OMM556012
PETER BAUMANN SYN K(CDEFGHJKL		(B) ALPHA CENTAURI	1975 POLYDOR		2383 314
CONRAD SCHNITZLER FLT (A		(C) ZEIT	1972 OHR		OMM256021
KLAUS SCHULZE	K (A	(C) ZEIT	1976 VIRGIN	UK	VD 2503
UDO DENNEBOURG	FLT (B	(D) ATEM	1972 OHR		OMM566031
ROLAND PAULCYK		(D) ATEM	1974 POLYDOR		2383 297
STEVE SCHROYDER	ORG (BC	(BD) ATEM /ALPHA	1976 VIRGIN	UK	VD 2504
MICHAEL HOENIG	K (	(E) PHAEDRA	1974 VIRGIN	UK	V 2010
STEVE JOLLIFFE	FLT (M	(F) RUBYCON	1975 VIRGIN	UK	V 2025
KLAUS KRIEGER	D (MN	(G) LIVE	1975 VIRGIN	UK	V 2044
JOHANNES SCHMOELLING K (P		(H) RICOCHET	1976 VIRGIN	UK	V
VOLKER HOMBACH FLT VLN(		(J) STRATOSFEAR	1976 VIRGIN US 34427	UK	V 2068
LANSE HAPSHASH	D (	(K) SORCERER	1977 MCA	UK	MCF 2806
KIRT HERKENBERG	B (	(L) ENCORE (DBL)	1977 VIRGIN US 34014	UK	VD 2506
SVEN JOHANNSON	D (	(M) CYCLONE	1978 VIRGIN	UK	V 2097
		(N) FORCE MAJEURE	1978 VIRGIN	UK	V 2111
		(O) 70/80 (4 LP SET)	1980 VIRGIN	UK	V BOX2
		(P) TANGRAM	1980 VIRGIN	UK	V 2147
		(Q) THIEF	1981 VIRGIN	UK	V 2189

TANGERINE PEEL

(A) SOFT THOUGHTS	1970 RCA	US	LSA 3002

TANGERINE ZOO

(A) TANGERINE ZOO	19 MAINSTREAM	US	6107
(B) OUTSIDE LOOKING ON	19 MAINSTREAM	US	6116

MARC TANNER

MARC TANNER	(	(A) NO ESCAPE	19 WB

TANZ DER YOUTH

```
BRIAN JAMES       G V  (
ALAN POWELL       D    (    TONY MOOR    K   (    ANDY COLQUHOUN      B   (
T13A                                         TARGET
JIM JAMISON       V   (AB         (A) TARGET                19  A&M              US        4607
DAVID SPAIN       D   (AB         (B) CAPTURED              1977 A&M             US        4652
TOM CATHEY        B   (AB
PAUL CANNON       G   (AB  BUD DAVIS    K    (AB
T13B                                       TARHEEL SLIM
ALLEN 'SLIM' BUNN V G  (A         (A)NUMBER 9 TRAIN(EP)     1980 CHARLY          UK    CTD 125
JIMMY SPRUIL      G    (A
T14                                       TARNEY SPENCER
ALAN TARNEY       G V K(ABC       (A) TARNEY SPENCER        1976 BRADLEYS        UK    BRADL1011
TREVOR SPENCER    D    (ABC       (B) THREE'S A CROWD       1978 A&M             UK    AMLH68466
LYNTON NAIFF      K    (B         (C) RUN FOR YOUR LIFE     1979 A&M             UK    AMLH64757
COLIN COOPER           (B
JOE POLLARD            (B   PETER HAYCOCK     (B   TONY RIVERS         (B  JOHN PERRY      (B
STU CALVER             (B   JOHN CUFFLEY      (B   PETER FILLEUL       (B  DEREK HOLT      (B
T15                                     TASAVALLAN PRESIDENTTI
JUKKA TOLONEN     G PNO(ABC       (A) TASAVALLAN PRESIDENTTI 1969 EMI 062 34264 LOVE SWEDLRLP    7
PEKKA POYRY       WIND (BC        (B) LAMBERTLAND           1972 SONET      SWED      SLP2533
VESA AALTONEN     D   (ABC        (B) LAMBERTLAND           1973 SONET SNTF636 LOVE SWED LRLP 60
MANS GROUNDSTROEM B K  (AB        (C) MILKY WAY MOSES       1974 SONET SNTF658 LOVE SWED LRLP102
JUHANN AALTONEN   WIND (A
HEIKKI VIRTANEN   B   (C    EERO RAITTINEN    V PERC(BC FRANK ROBSON    K V  (A
T16                                          TASTE
RORY GALLAGHER    G V  (ALL       (A) TASTE                 1969 POLYDOR UK 583042 US ATCO 33296
RICHARD McCRACKEN B   (ALL        (B) ON THE BOARDS         1970 POLYDOR UK 583083 US ATCO 33322
JOHN WILSON       D   (ALL        (C) LIVE TASTE            1971 POLYDOR        UK      2310 082
                                  (D) FIRST TASTE(1967)     1971 BASF           GERM20 29084 0
                                  (E) LIVE AT I O W         1972 POLYDOR        UK      2383 120
                                  (F) POP HISTORY           197  POLYDOR                2668 003
                                  (G) POP GIANTS No 5       197  BRUNSWICK      EURO 2911 516
                                  (H) MOVIN' ON             197  KARUSSEL       EURO
                                  (J) TASTE                 1977 POLYDOR                2384 076
                                  (K) TASTE                 19   VIOLENT SYSTEM         PN100001
                                  (L) GREATEST ROCK SENSATION 1977 polydor      GER     2499 115
T17                                          TATTOO
THOM MOONEY       D   (A          (A) TATTOO                1976 PRODIGAL          PDL  2003
JEFF HUTTON       K V (A
WALLY BRYSON      G V (A    DAN KIAWON     B    (A   DAVIS THOMAS     G V  (A
T18                                       BERNIE TAUPIN
BERNIE TAUPIN          (ALL       (A) BERNIE TAUPIN         19   ELEKTRA        US      EKS 75020
                                  (B) TAUPIN                1971 DJM            UK      DJLPS 415
                                  (C) HE WHO RIDES THE TIGER 1980 ASYLUM US 6E263 UK     K52220
T19                                         TAXLOSS
PAUL PHILLIPS     G K V(A         (A) HEY MISTER RECORD MAN 1979 LOGO           UK      LOGO 1015
PETE ZORN B G WIND V  (A
MATT FINISH       G   (A    ALLEN KEYS    K SYN  (A   RICHARD BURGESS    D   (A   NAPOLEON GLOSS   D PERC(A
JETT SEOPARDIE    CONGA(A   BILL ZORN          V  (A   KEN NICOL          V   (A
T20                                        ALEX TAYLOR
ALEX TAYLOR       V   (AB         (A) WITH FRIENDS & NEIGHBOURS 1971 ATCO 2400 177 US CAPRICORN  860
JOHNNY SANDLIN    B   (AB         (B) DINNERTIME            1972 CAPRICORN      US              0101
PAUL HORNSBY      K   (AB
TOMMY TALTON      G   (A    BILL STEWART      D   (AB SCOTT BOYER      G V  (AB JAMES TAYLOR     G   (A
KING CURTIS       SAX (A    FRANK WESS      SAX  (A   WILLIE BRIDGES   SAX  (A  RONNIE CUBER    SAX(A
DANNY MOORE       TPT (A    P KOWALSKE        G   (A   JOE RUDD         G    (A  LOU MULLENIX    PERC(B
CHARLES HAYWARD   B   (B    ROGER HAWKINS   PERC (B   CHUCK LEAVELL    K    (B  WAYNE PERKINS   G B(B
JOHN HUGHEY       STEEL(B   JAI JOHANNY JOHANSON PERC(B EARL SIMS      PERC (B  CHARLES CHALMERS V  (B
SANDY RHODES      V   (B    DONNA RHODES      V   (B   GINGER HOLLADAY  V    (B  MARY HOLLADAY   V   (B
TEMPLE RISER      V   (B    STEVE SMITH           (B
T21                                        ALLAN TAYLOR
ALLAN TAYLOR      G V (ALL        (A) SOMETIMES            1971 LIBERTY                 LBG 83483
DAVE MATTACKS     D   (A          (B) THE LADY             1972 UA                      UAS 29275
DAVE PEGG         B   (A          (C) AMERICAN ALBUM       1973 UA                      UAG 29408
DAVE SWARBRICK    VLN (A          (C) AMERICAN ALBUM       1977 MOONCREST       UK     CREST  28
D KELSO HERSTON       (C          (C) AMERICAN ALBUM       1978 ROCKBURGH       UK      ROC  101
SPANKY McFARLANE  V   (C          (D) TRAVELLER            1978 RUBBER          UK      RUB  026
BILLY SANFORD     G   (C
MIKE LEECH            (C    BILLY RILEY         (C   PETE WADE        G    (B  JOHN BUCK WILKIN G  (C
DAVID BRIGGS      PNO (C    JERRY CARRIGAN      (C   BUDDY SPICHER    FDL  (C  JOHNNY GIMBLE   FDL (C
TOMMY COGBILL     B   (C    LARRY BUTLER    K   (C   REGGIE YOUNG     G    (C  STEVE MILLER    K  (C
JAMES COLVARD     G   (C    KARL HIMMEL     D   (C   DON GRANT             (C  JAMES CASON     B  (C
D BERGEN WHITE        (C    PETER JAMESON   G   (C   MIKE OMARTIAN    K    (C  JOHN GUERIN     D  (C
WADDY WACHTEL     G   (C    BRYAN GAROFALO  B   (C   NICK VAN MAARTH       (C  JAMES E BOND JR    (C
MAX HOCH              (C    MARY McCASLIN       (C
T22                                        CHIP TAYLOR
CHIP TAYLOR       V G FDL  (ALL   (A) GASOLINE            1972 POLYDOR 2318074 US BUDDAH   5118
GEORGE KIRIAKIS   G V (BCDF       (B) LAST CHANCE         1974 WB    UK K56036 US WB      2718
JOHN PLATANIA     G   (BCDF       (C) SOME OF US          1974 WB    UK K56077 US WB      2824
JOE RENDA         K   (BCDF       (D) THIS SIDE OF THE BIG RIVER 1975 WB  UK K56152
TOM REILLY        STEEL(C         (E) ANGEL OF THE MORNING (CASSETTE) 1975 BUDDAH   UK  CBDS 4026
JOHN REGAN        B   (C          (F) SOMEBODY SHOOT OUT THE JUKEBOX 1976 CBS      US       34345
CHUCK FIORE       B   (C          (G) SAINT SEBASTIAN     1979 CAPITOL          US       11909
ERIK'RICK' NELSON D   (BC
CHARLIE POWERS    D   (CD   LEE HARRISON      V   (C   JOHN NAGY        PERC (BC MARGARET McGUINN  V (C
ANN McGUINN       V   (C    ANN HEIMBUCH      V   (C   DAVE KAPELL      B    (BDF PETE DRAKE     STEEL(BD
BUDDY SPICHER     FDL (C    DAVID MANSFIELD   FDL (DF  KEN GARRETSON    WIND (D  SANDY BULL     WIND(D
VIC SERMAN        HRNS (DF  JOE STELLITTI   HRNS (DF  RON CARRAN       HRNS (DF  DAVE GRISMAN    MAND (B
THE JORDANAIRES   V   (B    BEAU SEGAL      D   (F   'THUMBS' TAYLOR   PNO (F
```

DAVE TAYLOR
T22A

| DAVE TAYLOR | | | (A) ROCKIN' IN THE SAME OLD WAY | 1979 CHARLY | UK | CRL 5016 |

EDDIE TAYLOR
T23

EDDIE TAYLOR	G V	(ALL	(A) MASTER OF THE MODERN BLUES	1966 TESTAMENT	US	2214
BIG WALTER HORTON	HCA	(A	(B) READY FOR EDDIE	1975 BIG BEAR		BEAR 6
OTIS SPANN	PNO	(A	(C) FEEL SO BAD	1976 DJM	UK	DJM 22065
FRED BELOW	D	(A	(D) BAD BOY A LONG WAY FROM CHICAGO	1978 P/VINE	JAP	PLP 3501
BOB HALL	PNO	(B	(E) BIG TOWN PLAYBOY	1980 CHARLY	UK	CRB 1015
STEVE BEAL	G	(F	(F) MY HEART IS BLEEDING	1980 L&R	GER	42009
ROGER HILL	G	(B				
BOB BRUNNING	B	(B	GRAHAM GALLERY	B	(B	PETE YORK	D	(B	PHILIP WALKER	G(C
GEORGE SMITH	HCA	(C	JIMMY JONES	PNO	(C	CHUCK JONES	B	(C	JOHNNY TUCKER	D(C
LITTLE H WILLIAMS	TAMB	(C	GEORGE KITTA	B	(F	ODIE PAYNE	D	(F	CAREY BELL HCA	(F
SUNNYLAND SLIM	PNO	(F				

HOUND DOG TAYLOR
T24

HOUND DOG TAYLOR	G V	(ALL	(A) & THE HOUSE ROCKERS	1974 SONET UK SNTF676 ALLIGATOR US 4701
BREWER PHILLIPS	G	(ABC*	(B) NATURAL BOOGIE	197 SONET UK SNTF678 ALLIGATOR US 4704
TED HARVEY	D	(ABC*	(C) BEWARE OF THE DOG	197 SONET UK SNTF701 ALLIGATOR US 4707
			(D) LIVE AT FLORENCES(1969)	1980 JSP		1020
			(*) 1972 ANN ARBOR FESTIVAL			

JAMES TAYLOR
T25

JAMES TAYLOR	G V	(ALL	(A) JAMES TAYLOR	1968 APPLE UK SAPCOR 3	US	3352
DANNY KORTCHMAR	G	(BEKL	(B) SWEET BABY JAMES	1970 WB	UK K46043	US	1843
RUSS KUNKEL	D	(EKL	(C) & THE ORIGINAL FLYING MACHINE	1971 EUPHORIA		EUPH 2
PETER ASHER	V	(E	(C) & THE ORIGINAL FLYING MACHINE	197 SPRINGBOARD	US	4023
ALEX TAYLOR	V	(E	(D) MUD SLIDE SLIM	1971 WB	UK K46085	US	2561
KATE TAYLOR	V	(E	(E) ONE MAN DOG	1972 WB	UK K46185	US	2660
HUGH TAYLOR	V	(E	(F) WALKING MAN	1974 WB	UK K56042	US	2794
CAROLE KING	PNO V(BEK		(G) RAINY DAY MAN	1975 DJM	UK DJSLM2007 TRIP US 9513
ABIGALE HANESS	V	(E	(H) GORILLA	1975 WB	UK K56137	US	2866
CARLY SIMON	V	(EK	(J) IN THE POCKET	1976 WB	UK K56197	US	2912
LELAND SKLAR	B	(EKL	(K) THE BEST OF	1976 WB	UK K56309	US	2979
BOBBYE HALL	PERC	(E	(L) J.T.	1977 CBS	UK 86029	US	34811
GEORGE BOHANON	TROM	(E	(M) GREATEST HITS	1977 WB		US	3113
CHRIS DARROW	FDL	(B	(N) FLAG	1979 CBS	UK 86091	
MICHAEL BRECKER	SAX	(EK				
LINDA RONSTADT	V	(EL	JOHN McLAUGHLIN	G	(E	BARRY ROGERS	TROM (E	ART BARON	TROM(E
RANDY BRECKER	TPT	(E	DAN DUGMORE	G	(K	DAVID SPINOZZA	G	(K	DASH CROFTS	MAND(E
JOHN LONDON	B	(BK	RANDY MEISNER	B	(BK	JOHN HARTFORD	FDL	(E	ANDY MUSON	B	(K
CLARENCE MACDONALD PNO	(K	RED RHODES	STEEL(BEK	RALPH MACDONALD	PERC	(K	MILT HOLLAND	PERC (K
BYRON BERLINE	FDL	(K	KENNY ASCHER	K	(K	ANDREW GOLD	V HCA(K	RICK MAROTTA	D	(K
JIM KELTNER	D	(K	BOBBY WEST	B	(BK	GAYLE LEVANT	HARP	(K	DAVID SANBORN	SAX (KL
NICK DE CARO	ORG	(K	VICTOR FELDMAN	PERC (K	HERB PEDERSEN	V	(K	JONI MITCHELL	V	(K
GRAHAM NASH	V	(K	DAVID CROSBY	V	(K	CRAIG DOERGE	K	(EK

JOHNNIE TAYLOR
T26

JOHNNIE TAYLOR	V	(ALL	WANTED ONE SOUL SINGER	19 STAX	US	715
			WHO'S MAKIN' LOVE	1968 STAX	US	2005
			RAW BLUES	196 STAX	US	2008
			RARE STAMPS	196 STAX	US	2012
			J T PHILOSOPHY CONTINUES	1969 STAX UK 1024	US	2023
			ONE STEP BEYOND	19 STAX	US	2030
			GREATEST HITS	197 STAX	US	2032
			TAYLORED IN SILK	1973 STAX UK STX1012	US	3014
			SUPER TAYLOR	1974 STAX UK STX5022	US	5509
			BEST OF	1976 STAX UK STX1049	US	5522
			EARGASM	1976 CBS UK 81201	US	33951
			RATED EXTRAORDINAIRE	1977 CBS	US	34401
			EVER READY	197 CBS	US	35340
			REFLECTIONS	19 RCA	US	APLI 2527
			CHRONICLE VOL 1	1978 STAX UK 7001	US	88001
			CHRONICLE VOL 2	1978 STAX UK 7002	
			DISCO 9000	197 CBS		38004

KATE TAYLOR
T27

KATE TAYLOR	V	(AB	(A) SISTER KATE	1971 COTILLION	US	SD9045
DANNY KORTCHMAR	G PERC(A		(B) KATE TAYLOR	1978 CBS	US	35089
CHARLES LARKEY	B	(A				
JOEL O'BRIEN	D	(A	SANDRA CROUCH	PERC (A	DONNA PRATER	V	(A	LEE SKLAR	B	(A
JOHN HARTFORD	BAN	(A	LINDA RONSTADT	V	(A	JAMES TAYLOR	G	(A	CAROLE KING	V	(A
MERRY CLAYTON	V	(A	RUSS KUNKEL	D	(A	ANDREW LOVE	HRNS	(A	JOHN BIELAND	G	(A
ABIGAIL HANESS	V	(A	WAYNE JACKSON	HRNS	(A	RALPH SCHUCKETT	K	(A	OMA DRAKE	V	(A
PETER ASHER	V	(A	MEMPHIS HORNS		(A	J D SOUTHER	V	(A	

KOKO TAYLOR
T28

KOKO TAYLOR	V	(ABC	(A) I GOT WHAT IT TAKES	1975 SONET UK SNTF687 US ALLIGATOR 4706
MIGHTY JOE YOUNG	G	(A	(B) SOUTHSIDE BABY	1975 BLACK & BLUE		33505
SAMMY LAWHORN	G	(AC	(C) EARTHSHAKER	1978 SONET UK SNTF775 US ALLIGATOR 4711
ABE LOCKE	SAX	(AC				
VINCE CHAPPELLE	D	(AC	BILL HEID	K	(A	CORNELIUS BOYSON	B	(AC	JOHNNY B MOORE	G	(C
PINETOP PERKINS	K	(C	MERVYN HINDS	HCA	(C			

LITTLE JOHNNY TAYLOR
T29

LITTLE JOHNNY TAYLOR		(ALL	(A) EVERYBODY KNOWS ABOUT MY GOODTHING	197 POLYDOR UK 2916 015 US RONN 7530
			(B) OPEN HOUSE	1973 CONTEMPO 1003	US RONN 7532
			(C) SUPER TAYLORS	1974 CONTEMPO		CLP 502
			(D) PART TIME LOVE	1980 CHARLY	UK	CRB 1012
			(E) I SHOULDA BEEN A PREACHER	1981 RED LIGHTNING	UK	RL 0030
			(EP AS LONG AS I DONT SEE YOU	1980 CHARLY	UK	CTD 118

LIVINGSTON TAYLOR
T30

LIVINGSTON TAYLOR	G K V(ABCD		(A) LIVINGSTON TAYLOR	1970 WB	US	WS 3006
PAUL HORNSBY	K	(AB	(B) LIV	1971 WB	UK	K46131
ROBERT POPWELL	B	(AB	(C) OVER THE RAINBOW	1973 CAPRICORN	US	CP 0114
DAVE WOODFORD	WIND	(B	(D) THREE WAY MIRROR	1979 EPIC	US	35540
BILL STEWART	D	(B	PETE CARR	G	(A			
TOMMY TALTON	G	(B	WALTER ROBINSON	B	(B	JOHNNY SANDLIN	B	(AB	GREG PRESTOPINO	V	(B

T31

MICK TAYLOR

MICK TAYLOR	G V	(A1	(A) MICK TAYLOR		1979 CBS		UK	82600
LOWELL GEORGE	G	(A	(1) 1977 LIVE BAND					
PIERRE MOERLEN	D	(A						
JEAN ROUSSEL	PNO	(A	NORMAN MITCHELL TAMB (A MIKE DRISCOLL	D (A KUMA HARADA	B (A			
RICHARD BAILEY	D	(A	ALAN SPENNER B (A RONNIE LEAHY	K (1 STEVE THOMPSON	B (1			
COLIN ALLEN	D	(1						

T32

R DEAN TAYLOR

R DEAN TAYLOR	V	(ALL	(A) I THINK THEREFORE I AM		1970 RARE EARTH			RS 522
			(A) INDIANA WANTS ME		197 TAMLA		UK	STML11185
			(B) L A SUNSET		1975 POLYDOR		UK	2383 399

T32A

TED TAYLOR

TED TAYLOR		(AB	(A) KEEP ON WALKING		1980 CHARLY			CRB 1011
			(B) IT'S TOO LATE(EP)		1980 CHARLY			CTD 111

T33

VINCE TAYLOR

VINCE TAYLOR	V	(ALL	(A) VINCE TAYLOR		19 BARCLAY			280 149
			(B) 100% ROCK	1977	BARCLAY 80984/5	RI	81088/9	
			(C) VINCE TAYLOR (EP)		1979 SPADE			PFE 1

T34

BRAM TCHAIKOVSKY

BRAM TCHAIKOVSKY	G V	(AB	(A) STRANGE MAN CHANGED MAN		1979 RADAR		UK	RAD 17
KEITH BOYCE	D	(A	(B) RUSSIANS ARE COMING		1980 RADAR		UK	RAD 26
MICKY BROADBENT	V B G K	(AB						
DENIS FORBES	G	(AB	KEITH LINE D (B					

T35

TEA

MARK STORACE	V	(AB	(A) TEA		1975 PHILIPS			6305 238
TURO PASCHAYAN	B V	(AB	(B) THE SHIP		1975 PHILIPS			9118 001
ARMAND VOLKER	G V	(AB						
PHILIPPE KIENHOLZ	K V	(AB	ROLI EGGLI D (A DIETER DIERKS	D (B				

T36

TEA & SYMPHONY

JEFF DAW FLT G V		(A	(A) AN ASYLUM FOR THE MUSICALLY INSANE	1969 HARVEST		UK	SHVL 761
JAMES LANGSTON G V	WIND	(A	(B) JO SAGA		1970 HARVEST		UK	SHVL 785
NIGEL PHILLIPS K V	PERC	(A						
BOB LAMB	D	(A	RON CHESTERMAN B (A MICK HINCKS	B (A GUS DUDGEON	PERC (A			

T36A

TEA SET

NICK HAEFFNER	G	(	(A) CUPS & SAUCERS (EP)		1979 WALDOS RECORDS		BS	003
RON WEST	B	(						
DUNCAN STRINGER	G	(	CALLY D (NICK EGAN	V (				

T37

TEAR GAS

ZAL CLEMINSON	G	(AB	(A) PIGGY GO GETTER		PARAMOUNT US 5029 UK FAMOUS SFMA5751			
CHRIS GLEN	B V	(AB	(B) TEAR GAS		REGAL ZONOPHONE UK			SLRZ1021
HUGH McKENNA	K	(B						
TED McKENNA	D	(B	DAVEY BATCHELOR V (A EDDIE CAMPBELL	K V (A WILLIE MONRO	D V (A			

T37A

TEARDROP EXPLODES

JULIAN COPE	B V	(A	(A) KILIMANJARO		1980 MERCURY ZOO			6359 035
DAVID BALFE	K SYN	(A						
GARY DWYER	D	(A	ALAN GILL G (A MICHAEL FINKLER	G (A RAY MARTINEZ	TPT (A			
HURRICANE SMITH	TPT	(A						

T37B

TEARDROPS

BOK BOK		(A	(A) FINAL VINYL		1980 ILLUMINATED			JAMS 2
TONY FRIEL		(A						
STEVE GARVEY		(A	TREV WAYNE (A HELEN BARBROOK	(A				

T37C

TEAZE

BRIAN DANTER	B V	(A	(A) ON THE LOOSE		1978 AQUARIUS			AQR 516
MIKE KOZAK	D	(A	(B) BODY SHOTS		1980 AQUARIUS			AQR 528
MARK BIADAC	G	(A						
CHUCK PRICE	G	(A						

T37D

TEDDY BEARS

PHIL SPECTOR	V	(A	(A) TEDDY BEARS SING		19 IMPERIAL		US	LP 12010
ANNETTE KLEINBARD	V	(A						
MARSHALL LIEB	V	(A						

T37E

RICHARD TEE

RICHARD TEE	K	(AB	(A) STROKIN'		1979 CBS		UK	83339
STEVE GADD	D	(B	(B) NATURAL INGREDIENTS		1980 CBS		UK	84194
ERIC GALE	G	(B						
MATTHEW BRAGG	B	(B	RALPH MACDONALD PERC (B HUGH McCRACKEN	HCA (B TOM SCOTT SAX (B				
JON FADDIS	HRNS	(B	RANDY BRECKER HRNS (B BARRY ROGERS	HRNS (B SELDON POWELL HRNS(B				
VALERIE SIMPSON	V	(B	ULLANDA McCULLOUGH V (B LANI GROVES	V (B STRING SECTION	(B			

T37F

WILLIE TEE

WILLIE TEE		(A	(A) ANTICIPATION		19 UA		US	UALA 655

T37G

TEE SET

FRANKLIN MADJA	B	(A	(A) MY BELLE AMI		19 QUALITY			BM 597
DILL BENWICK	G	(A						
JOOP BLOM	D	(A	HANS VAN EIJCK K (A					

T37H

TELEPHONE BILL & THE SMOOTH OPERATORS

NICK BARRACLOUGH	V	(A	(A) PRETTY SLICK HUH?		1979 SWAMP			WAM679
GERRY HALE	V	(A	(B) LOUNGE MUSIC		1980 SMOOTH DIAL			100
CHRIS COX	B MAND	(A						
ANNE BAKER	V	(A	RICHARD LEE FDL ACC BAN(B					

T38

TELEVISION

TOM VERLAINE	G V	(AB1	(A) MARQUEE MOON		1977 ELEKTRA US 7E1098		UK	K52046
RICHARD LLOYD	G V	(AB1	(B) ADVENTURE		1978 ELEKTRA US 6E 133		UK	K52072
BILLY FICCA	D	(AB1	(1) 1974/5					
FRED SMITH	B	(AB	RICHARD HELL B (1					

T38A

TELEVISION PERSONALITIES

			(A) WHERE'S BILL GRUNDY		19 KINGS ROAD			001
			(B) AND DONT THE KIDS JUST KNOW IT		198 ROUGH TRADE		UK	ROUGH24

TELEX

T38B

DAN LACKSMAN	(AB	(A) LOOKING FOR ST TROPEZ	1979 SIRE UK SRK 6072
MICHAEL MOERS	(AB	(B) NEUROVISION	1980 SIRE UK SRK 6090
MARC MOULIN	(AB		

JOE TEMAIRE & FLOUZE

T38C

JOE TEMAIRE	(A	(A) JOE TEMAIRE & FLOUZE	1980 ROCKET BEL TRAIN11

JACK TEMPCHIN

T39

JACK TEMPCHIN		(A	(A) JACK TEMPCHIN						1978 ARISTA US 4195 UK SPART 1078		
PETE CARR	G	(A									
ROGER CLARK	D	(A	BOB WRAY	B	(A	BARRY BECKETT	K	(A	ANTHONY PARSONS	FLT	(A
GLENN FREY	G V	(A	HARVEY THOMPSON	SAX	(A	RANDY McCORMICK	K	(A	GAY BAKER	B	(A
EDDIE STRUZICK	V	(A	THOM FLORA	V	(A	JENNIFER WARNES	V	(A	JACKSON BROWNE	V	(A

TEMPEST

T40

JON HISEMAN	D	(AB	(A) TEMPEST	1973 BRONZE ILPS 9220
MARK CLARKE	B	(AB	(B) LIVING IN FEAR	1974 BRONZE ILPS 9267
PAUL WILLIAMS	V	(A		
ALLAN HOLDSWORTH	G	(A	OLLIE HALSALL G (B	

TEMPLE CITY KAZOO BAND

T41

DR JIN ZANE	KAZOO(A	(A) SOME KAZOOS (EP)				1978 RHINO RNEP 501		
RICHIE BALANCE	KAZOO(A							
ZAZOOT SIMS	KAZOO(A	TOM 'CAT'KNAPP	KAZOO(A	DAVID ANDREWS	KAZOO(A	DON BUCHANAN	KAZOO(A	
GLEN COBAR	KAZOO(A	PAUL SANOIAN	KAZOO(A	JEFF GINSBERG	KAZOO(A	GREG GORDON	KAZOO(A	
TED KAZOOSKI	KAZOO(A	ELIJAH GOLDSTEIN	KAZOO(A					

TEMPTATIONS

T42

OTIS MILES	V	(1234567	MEET THE TEMPTATIONS	1964 TAMLA UK STML11009 US GORDY 911
MELVIN FRANKLIN	V	(1234567	SING SMOKEY	1965 TAMLA UK TML11016 US GORDY 912
EDDIE KENDRICKS	V	(1234	TEMPTIN' TEMPTATIONS	1965 TAMLA UK STML11023 US GORDY 914
ELDRIDGE BRYANT	V	(2	GETTIN' READY	1966 TAMLA UK STML11035 US GORDY 918
RICHARD STREET	V	(	GREATEST HITS	1967 TAMLA UK STML11042 US GORDY 919
DAVID RUFFIN	V	(3	LIVE	1967 TAMLA UK STML11053 US GORDY 921
DENNIS EDWARDS	V	(4567	WITH A LOT OF SOUL	1967 TAMLA UK STML11057 US GORDY 922
RICKY OWENS	V	(5	IN A MELLOW MOOD	1967 TAMLA UK STML11068 US GORDY 924
DAMON HARRIS	V	(67	WISH IT WOULD RAIN	1968 TAMLA UK STML11079 US GORDY 927
PAUL WILLIAMS	V	(123456	T V SHOW	1967 TAMLA US GORDY 933
			WITH THE SUPREMES	1969 TAMLA UK STML11096
(1) 1959(DISTANTS)			CLOUD NINE	1969 TAMLA UK STML11109 US GORDY 939
(2) 1960			TCB (SUPREMES)	1969 TAMLA UK STML11109 US TAMLA 682
(3) 1962			TOGETHER(SUPREMES)	1970 TAMLA UK STML11122
(4) 1968			PSYCHEDELIC SHACK	1970 TAMLA UK STML11147 US GORDY 947
(5) 1971			PUZZLE PEOPLE	1970 TAMLA UK STML11133 US GORDY 949
(6) 1971			LIVE AT THE TALK OF THE TOWN	1970 TAMLA UK STML11141 US GORDY 953
(7) 1971			LIVE AT THE TALK OF THE TOWN RI	1979 MFP US 50419
			CHRISTMAS CARD	1970 US GORDY 951
			GREATEST HITS VOL 2	1970 TAMLA UK STML11170 US GORDY 954
			THE SKY'S THE LIMIT	1971 TAMLA UK STML11184 US GORDY 957
			SOLID ROCK	1972 TAMLA UK STML11202 US GORDY 961
			ALL DIRECTIONS	1972 TAMLA UK STML11218 US GORDY 962
			MASTERPIECE	1973 TAMLA UK STML11229 US GORDY 965
			1990	1974 TAMLA UK STMA 8016
			10TH ANNIVERSARY	1974 TAMLA M782
			HOUSE PARTY	1975 TAMLA UK STML12006 US GORDY 973
			A SONG FOR YOU	1975 TAMLA UK STMA 8021 US GORDY 969
			WINGS OF LOVE	1976 TAMLA UK STMA 8025 US GORDY 971
			DO THE TEMPTATIONS	1976 TAMLA UK STML12040 US GORDY 975
			GREATEST HITS VOL 3	1977 TAMLA UK STML12061 US
			ANTHOLOGY 1964/73	1977 TAMLA UK TMSP 6003 US GORDY 974
			TEMPTATIONS	1977 TAMLA UK STMX 6002
			HEAR TO TEMPT YOU	1978 ATLANTIC UK K50413 US 19143
			BARE BACK	1978 ATLANTIC UK K50504 US 19188
			SING SMOKEY	1979 MOTOWN UK STMR 9005

TEN C C

T43

ERIC STEWART	G V	(ALL	(A) TEN CC	1973 UK UK UKAL 1005 US 53105
GRAHAM GOULDMAN	G V	(ALL	(B) SHEET MUSIC	1974 UK UK UKAL 1007 US 53107
KEVIN GODLEY	D V	(ABCDE	(C) 100CC	1975 UK UK UKAL 1012 US 53110
LOL CREME	G V	(ABCDE	(D) ORIGINAL SOUNDTRACK	1975 MERCURY UK 9102 500 US SRM1 1029
PAUL BURGESS	D	(G	(E) HOW DARE YOU	1976 MERCURY UK 9102 501 US SRMI 1061
RICK FENN	G	(G	(F) DECEPTIVE BENDS	1977 MERCURY UK 9102 502 US SRMI 3702
STUART TOSH	D	(G	(G) LIVE & LET LIVE	1977 MERCURY UK 6641 698 US SRM2 8600
TONY O'MALLEY	K	(G	(H) BLOODY TOURISTS	1978 MERCURY UK 9102 503 US SRMI 6160
TONY SPATH	PNO	(	(I) GREATEST HITS	1979 MERCURY UK 9102 504 US
JEAN ROUSSEL	K	(	(J) THINGS WE DO FOR LOVE	1979 MERCURY US SRMI 6186
DUNCAN McKAY	K	(	(K) LOOK HEAR	1980 MERCURY UK 9102 505

TEN WHEEL DRIVE

T44

GENYA RAVAN	V HCA	(ABC	(A) CONSTRUCTION No1						1969 POLYDOR US 4008 UK 583 577		
ARAM SCHEFRIN	G V	(ABC	(B) BRIEF REPLIES						1970 POLYDOR US 4024 UK 2425 022		
MIKE ZAGER	K CLAR	(ABC	(C) PECULIAR FRIENDS						1971 POLYDOR US 4062 UK 2425 065		
BILL TAXAS	B	(A	(D) TEN WHEEL DRIVE						1974 CAPITOL US ST 11199		
LEON RIX	D CELLO	(A									
LOUIS HOFF	WIND	(A	DENNIS PARISI	TROM	(AB	JAY SILVA	WIND	(A	RICHARD MEISTERMAN	TPT	(A
PETER HYDE	HRNS	(A	BOB PIAZZA	B	(B	STEVE SATTEN	HRNS	(A	JOHN GATCHELL	HRNS	(B
DAVE LIEBMAN	WIND	(B	JOHN ECKERT	HRNS	(B	ALLEN HERMAN	D	(B	BLAKE HINES	B	(C
DAVID WILLIAMS	D	(C	ALAN GAUVIN	WIND	(C	DEAN PRATT	TPT	(C	TOM MALONE	TROM	(C
DANNY STILES	TPT	(C	FRANK FRINT	TPT	(C	ANN SUTTON	V	(D			

TEN YEARS AFTER

T45

ALVIN LEE	G V	(ALL	(A) TEN YEARS AFTER	1967 DERAM US 18009 UK SML1015
LEO LYONS	B	(ALL	(B) UNDEAD	1968 DERAM US 18016 UK SML1023
CHICK CHURCHILL	D	(ALL	(C) STONEDHENGE	1969 DERAM US 18021 UK SML1029
RIC LEE	D	(ABCDEFGHIJKLMN	(D) SSSSSSSH	1969 DERAM US 18029 UK SML1052
DAVID POTTS	D	(1	(D) SSSSSSSH	1975 CHRYSALIS RI UK CHR 1083
GUS DUDGEON	PERC	(A	(E) CRICKLEWOOD GREEN	1970 DERAM US 18038 UK SML1065
MIKE VERNON	V	(C	(E) CRICKLEWOOD GREEN	1975 CHRYSALIS RI UK CHR 1084

(CONTINUED)

```
T45  (CONTINUED)                    TEN YEARS AFTER
   SIMON STABLE      PERC (C     (F) WATT                    1970 DERAM       US 18050 UK   SML1078
   HAROLD BURGON     V    (K     (F) WATT                    1975 CHRYSALIS RI     UK CHR  1085
                                 (G) ALVIN LEE & CO          1972 DERAM       US 18064 UK   SML1096
   (1) 1967                      (H) A SPACE IN TIME         1972 CHRYSALIS UK 1001  US CBS 30801
                                 (I) ROCK'N'ROLL TO THE WORLD 1972 CHRYSALIS UK 1009 US CBS 31779
                                 (J) RECORDED LIVE           1973 CHRYSALIS UK 1049  US CBS 32288
                                 (K) POSITIVE VIBRATIONS     1974 CHRYSALIS UK 1060  US CBS 32851
                                 (L) GOIN' HOME              1975 CHRYSALIS UK 1077 US DERAM18072
                                 (M) ANTHOLOGY               1976 CHRYSALIS UK 1107
                                 (N) CLASSIC PERFORMANCES    1977 CHRYSALIS UK 1134  US CBS 34366
                                 (O) PROFILE                 19   TELDEC        GERM    624011
                                 (P) LONDON COLLECTION       19   LONDON        US LC 50013
                                 (Q) HEAR ME CALLING         1981 DECCA        UKTAB24
T46                                  TEN YEARS LATER
   ALVIN LEE         G V  (AB    (A) ROCKET FUEL             1978 POLYDOR 2310 605   +    2344 103
   TOM COMPTON       D    (AB    (B) RIDE ON                 1979 POLYDOR              2310 678
   MICK HAWKSWORTH   B    (AB
   BERNIE CLARKE     K    (A     MICK WEAVER      K    (A
T47                                  TENNENT MORRISON
   DAVID MORRISON            (A) TENNENT MORRISON            1972 POLYDOR          UK   2383 152
   JOHN TENNENT      G V  (AB    (B) KEEP IT CLEAN(AS JOE SOAP) 1973 POLYDOR       UK   2383 233
   RONNIE LEAHY      K    (A
   HERBIE FLOWERS    B    (A     JIMMY McCULLOCH    (A   BRIAN ODGERS      (A   CLEM CATTINI    (A
   ROGER McKEW       G    (A     STEVE THOMPSON     (A   COLIN ALLEN       (A   DENNIS LOPEZ    (A
T47A                                 TENNESSEE FARM BAND
   LINDA HERSHFIELD  V    (A     (A) COMMUNION               1977 FARM                  1013
   DAVID CHALMERS    D    (A
   THOMAS DOTZLER    V K SAX(A    MICHAEL SULLENS   B   (A   WALTER RABIDEAU   G V  (A
T47B                                 TENNIS SHOES
                                 (A) MEDIUM WAVE   (EP)      19   BONAPARTE      UK   BONE 3
T47C                                 TERENCE
                                 (A) AN EYE FOR AN EAR       19   DECCA         IMP  DL75137
T48                                  TERRA COTTA
   TOM ATKINSON      G    (1     (A) HARD TO KNOW   (EP)     197  TERRA COTTA         TC 001
   STEVE LUDLAM      G    (1     (1) 1978
   CHRIS WOODCOCK    D    (1
   TERRY COTTAM      V    (1     KELLY CANTLON     B   (1
T49                                  TERRA NOVA
   CHRIS SLADE       D    (
   COLIN PATTENDEN   B    (
   PETE COX          V    (      ROY SHIPSTONE     K   (    CHRIS WEST        G   (
T50                                  TERRAPLANE
   TONY McPHEE       G V  (      ALAN FISH    B    (    HARRY RICKS     D   (
T51                                  TAMMI TERRELL
   TAMMI TERRELL     V    (ALL   (A) UNITED                  1968 TAMLA         UK   STML11062
   MARVIN GAYE       V    (A     (B) YOU'RE ALL I NEED       1968 TAMLA         UK   STML11084
                                 (C) IRRESISTIBLE            1969 TAMLA         US        652
                                 (D) EARLY SHOW              1969 MARBLE ARCH   UK   MAL  1110
T52                                  DEWEY TERRY
   DEWEY TERRY       V    (A     (A) CHIEF                   1973 TUMBLEWEED         TW  3502
   HARVEY MANDEL     G    (A
T53                                  KARL TERRY & THE CRUISER
   KARL TERRY             (A     (A) CRUISIN'                1978 RAW                 RWLP 105
T53A                                 SONNY TERRY & BROWNIE McGHEE
   SONNY TERRY       V HCA(      AT SUGARHILL                19   AMERICA            AM   6071
   BROWNIE McGHEE    G V  (      BACK COUNTRY BLUES          1978 MUSIDISC      FR   CV    956
   DAVE LEE          PNO  (      BLUES FROM EVERYWHERE       19   TRANSATLANTIC      XTRA 1099
   SVEND ERIK NORREGARD   (      BEST OF                     19   STORYVILLE         SLP   217
   PEPPERMINT HARRIS      (      BROWNIE McHEE & SONNY TERRY 1971 STORYVILLE    FR       21020
                                 BROWNIE & SONNY'S BLUES     1960 ROULETTE      US
                                 BROWNIE & SONNY'S BLUES     197  VOGUE         FR        12505
                                 COULDN'T BELIEVE MY EYES    197  BLUESWAY           BLS  6059
                                 GOING DOWN SLOW             1974 MAINSTREAM         L35784
                                 GOING DOWN SLOW             197  MAINSTREAM    US   MRL   407
                                 HOMETOWN BLUES              1974 MAINSTREAM    US   MRL  1019
                                 HOMETOWN BLUES              1969 ACE OF HEARTS      ZAHT  182
                                 HOOTIN' & HOLLERIN'         1975 VOGUE         FR   LDE   894
                                 KEY TO THE HIGHWAY          19   TRANSATLANTIC      XTRA 1004
                                 LONG WAY FROM HOME          197  BLUESWAY           BLS  6028
                                 MIDNIGHT SPECIAL            1978 FANTASY       US   FAN  5973
                                 ON THE ROAD                 19   TRANSATLANTIC      XTRA 1110
                                 SONNY TERRY & WOODY GUTHRIE 19   EMBER              CW    136
                                 SONNY TERRY                 19   TRANSATLANTIC      XTRA 1064
                                 SHOUTS & BLUES              19   AMERICA            AM   6075
                                 SONNY & BROWNIE             1973 A&M           UK   AMLH64379
                                 TRADITIONAL BLUES           1977 CHANT DUMONDE FR   FL  52421
                                 WALK ON                     1977 BULLDOG            BDL  1018
                                 YOU HEAR ME TALKING         1979 MUSE          FR   MR   5131
T54                                  TERRY & THE PIRATES
   TERRY DOLAN       G V  (AB12  (A) THE DOUBTFUL HANDSHAKE  1980 LINE          GERM LLP 5062
   DAVID HAYES       B    (A23   (B) TOO CLOSE FOR COMFORT   1979 WILD BUNCH    ITALY WB 5001
   DAVE CASTER       B V  (B     (1) 1974    (2) 1975    (3) 1977
   ANDY KIRBY        D    (3
   JEFF MYERS        D    (A3  MICHAEL WHITE     B   (3   ANDY KIRBY     D   82    LONNIE TURNER B  (B£
   JOHN CIPOLLINA    G    (A123 GREG DOUGLAS     G   (A123 DAVID WEBER   D   (1   HUTCH HUTCHINSON B (12
   SID PAGE          VLN  (2   NICKY HOPKINS     K   (B2  JIM McPHERSON  K   (2   BONES JONES   D  (B2
   BILL BARON        D    (B   STEVE DERR        G   (B
```

JOE TEX	V	(ALL	THE BEST OF		19	KING	US	935
HAYWARD BISHOP	D	(S	THE BEST OF		1965	PARROT	US	S71002
KARL HIMMEL	D	(S	HOLD ON TO WHAT YOU'VE GOT		1965	ATLANTIC	US	SD8106
BUDDY KILLEN		(R	HOLD ON		1965	CHECKER		2993
BOBBY WOOD	K	(SR	NEW BOSS		1965	ATLANTIC	US	SD8115
LOUIS JOHNSON		(R	GREATEST HITS		1967	ATLANTIC	UK	588089
BOBBY EMMONS	K	(RS	LOVE YOU SAVE		1966	ATLANTIC	US	SD8124
JOHN CHRISTOPHER	G	(S	I'VE GOT TO DO A LITTLE BETTER		19	ATLANTIC	US	SD8133
REGGIE YOUNG	G	(SR	BEST OF		196	ATLANTIC	US	SD8144
TOMMY COGBILL	B	(S	LIVE & LOVELY		1968	ATLANTIC	US	SD8156
LARRIE LONDIN		(R	SOUL COUNTRY		1968	ATLANTIC	UK	588118	US	SD8187
CHARLES ROSE	HRNS	(R	HAPPY SOUL		1969	ATLANTIC	US	SD8211
JOSEPH THOMAS		(R	YOU BETTER GET IT		1969	ATLANTIC	UK	588130
MIKE LEECH	B	(S	BUYING A BOOK		1969	ATLANTIC	UK	588193	US	SD8231
DALE QUILLEN	HRNS	(R	SINGS WITH STRINGS		19	ATLANTIC	UK	2465001	US	SD8254
LEROY HADLEY		(R	FROM THE ROOTS CAME THE RAPPER		196	ATLANTIC	US	SD8292
BEN CAULEY	HRNS	(S	SHOW ME		19	ATLANTIC	UK	2464004
HARRISON CALLOWAY	HRNS	(SR	I GOTCHA		1972	DIAL	US	6002
HARVEY THOMPSON	HRNS	(SR	I GOTCHA		1972	MERCURY	UK	6338 093
RON EADES	HRNS	(SR	(S) SPILL THE BEANS		197	DIAL	US	6004
JAMES BOOKER	PNO	(R	HE WHO IS WITHOUT FUNK		197	DIAL	US	6100
FARRELL MORRIS	PERC	(R	LONDON COLLECTOR SUPER SOUL		19	LONDON	US	50017
PAULA BEBEFIELD		(R	ANOTHER MANS WOMAN		19	POWERPAK	US	305
BETH HAVIS	V	(R	HISTORY OF		19	PRIDE	US	0020
WAYNE BUTLER	HRNS	(R	BUMPS & BRUISES		1977	EPIC	UK	81931	US	34666
CHARLES CHALMERS	V	(R	(R) RUB DOWN		1978	EPIC	UK	82581	US	35079
SANDRA RHODES	V	(R						
DONNA RHODES	V	(R	WAYNE JACKSON HRNS (R STRING SECTION		(R			

JIM MILNE	G K V	(A	(A) A CANDLE FOR JUDITH		1971	DANDELION	UK	DAN 8004
STEPHEN CLAYTON	D PERC	(A						

VAN MORRISON	HVA V	(	ANGRY YOUNG THEM		1965	DECCA	UK	LK 4700
BILLY HARRISON	G	(1	THEM		1965	PARROT	US	PAS71005
ALAN HENDERSON	B	(1	THEM AGAIN		1966	DECCA LK 4751 US PARROT		71008
RONNIE MILLINGS	D	(1	NOW & THEM		1968	TOWER	US	ST 5104
ERIC WIKSEN	PNO	(	TIME OUT,TIME IN FOR THEM		1968	TOWER	US	ST 5116
JACKIE McAULEY	ORG	(1	WORLD OF THEM		1970	DECCA	UK	SPA 86
PAT McAULEY	D	(	THEM		1970	HAPPY TIGER	US	HT 1004
PETER BARDENS	ORG	(	THEM IN REALITY		197	HAPPY TIGER	US	HT 1012
JIMMY PAGE	G	(	BACKTRACKIN'		19	LONDON	US	PS 639
RAY ELLIOT	K	(	THE BEGINNING		1972	DECCA	GERM	ND 772
DAVID HARVEY	D	(	BAD OR GOOD		1972	TELDEC	GERM	3008 1/2
JIM ARMSTRONG	G	(	STORY OF THEM		19	LONDON	US	50001
KEN McDOWELL	V	(	THEM		1973	PARROT	US	71053
JOHN WILSON	D	(	THEM		1973	DERAM	UK	DPA 3001
KEN McLEOD		(	PROFILE		197	TELDEC	GERM	624 005
MARK SCOTT		(	ITS ALL OVER NOW		1975	TELDEC	GERM	628 339
			HERE COMES GLORIA		1976	TELDEC	GERM	628 361
(1) 1963			ROCK ROOTS		1976	DECCA	UK	ROOTS3
			BELFAST GYPSIES		1977	SONET	UK	NTF 738
			BELFAST GYPSIES		19	GRAND PRIX	SWED	GP 9923

(A) BRINGING THE HOUSE DOWN		19			
(B) ONE NIGHT STAND		19			
(C) ALMANAC		1976	CBS 69017 +DJM DJF 20492		

PHIL LYNOTT	B V	(ALL	(A) THIN LIZZY	1971	DECCA	UK	SKL 5082	
BRIAN DOWNEY	D	(ALL	(B) SHADES OF A BLUE ORPHANAGE	1972	DECCA	UK	TXS 108	
ERIC BELL	G	(ABC	(C) VAGABONDS OF WESTERN WORLD	1973	DECCA	UK SKL 5170 US LONDON		636
GARY MOORE	G	(DK	(D) NIGHT LIFE	1974	VERTIGO	UK 6360 116 US MERCURY	SRM11107	
SCOTT GORHAM	G	(DEFGHJKL	(E) FIGHTING	1975	VERTIGO	UK 6360 121 US MERCURY	SRM11108	
BRIAN ROBERTSON	G	(DEFG	(F) JAILBREAK	1976	VERTIGO	UK 9102 008 US MERCURY	SRM11081	
PHIL COLLINS	PERC	(G	(G) JOHNNY THE FOX	1976	VERTIGO	UK 9102 012 US MERCURY	SRM11119	
KIMBERLEY BEACON	V	(G	(H) BAD REPUTATION	1977	VERTIGO	UK 9102 016 US MERCURY	SRM11186	
ROGER CHAPMAN	V	(E	(I) REMEMBERING	1976	DECCA	UK SKL 5249		
IAN MACLAGAN	PNO	(E	(J) LIVE & DANGEROUS	1978	VERTIGO	UK 6641 807 US WB		2 3213
SNOWY WHITE	G	(L	(K) BLACK ROSE	1979	VERTIGO	UK 9102 032		
JEAN ROUSSEL	K	(D	(L) CHINA TOWN	1980	VERTIGO	UK 6359 030		
FRANKIE MILLER	V	(D	( ) THE ROCKER	19	LONDON	US		50004
DARRON WHARTON	K V	(L	( ) PROFILE	19	TELDEC	GERM		624013
MIDGE URE	V	(L	(M) ADVENTURES OF (COMP)	1981	VERTIGO	LIZ TV 1		
TIM HINKLEY	K	(L						

GLEN SWEENEY	PERC	(A	(A) ALCHEMY		1969	HARVEST	UK	SHVL 756
PAUL MINNS	OBOE	(A	(B) THIRD EAR BAND		1970	HARVEST	UK	SHSP 773
RICHARD COFF	VLN	(A	(C) MACBETH		1972	HARVEST	UK	SHSP 4019
MEL DAVIS	CELLO	(A	(D) EXPERIENCES		1976	HARVEST HERITAGE	UK	SHSM 2007
JOHN PEEL JEWS HARP		(A						
DAVE TOMLIN	VLN	(A	URSULA SMITH (SIMON HOUSE VLN (DENIM BRIDGES G (					
PAUL BUCKMASTER	CELLO	(						

RICHARD NOLAN	V	(1	(A) I D MUSIC		197	EPIC	US	BN 26327
BILLY CLARKE	G	(1	(1) 1976					
LENNY DUPONT	G	(1						
JOHN ROI	B V	(1	RICK MARTIN D (1					

```
T62                          THIRD WORLD
     PRILLY            V     (A
     CAT COORE         G B   (ABCDE    (A) THIRD WORLD                   1976 ISLAND              UK    ILPS 9369
     RICHIE            B G   (ABCDE    (B) 96 DEGREES IN THE SHADE       1977 ISLAND              uk    ILPS 9443
     IBO               K V   (ABCDE    (C) JOURNEY TO ADDIS              1978 ISLAND              UK    ILPS 9554
     CORNEL            D     (A        (D) STORY'S BEEN TOLD             1979 ISLAND              UK    ILPS 9569
     CARROT            PERC  (ABCDE    (E) PRISONER IN THE STREET        1980 ISLAND              UK    ILPS 9616
     RUGS              G V   (BCDE
     WILLIE            D     (BCDE CHRIS WOOD      SAX (D  REBOP        PERC (B
T62A                         THIRD WORLD
     STEVE WINWOOD     K G V (A        (A) AIYE KETA                     1973 ISLAND              UK    HELP  14
     REMI KABAKA       V G D B(A
     ABDUL LASISI AMAO V WIND(A
T63                       THIRD WORLD WAR
     TERRY STAMP       G V   (AB       (A) THIRD WORLD WAR              1971 FLY                UK HIFLY4
     JIM AVERY         B     (AB       (B) THIRD WORLD WAR II           1973 TRACK UK 2406 108 GERM 2310 123
     JOHN KNIGHTSBRIDGE G     (B
     RAY FLACKE        G     (B   JOHN HAWKEN      PNO (B    CRAIG COLLINGE    D    (B    JIM PRICE   HRNS (AB
     WINGY             HCA   (A   SPEEDY           PERC (A   FRED SMITH        D    (A    BOBBY KEYS  SAX (A
     TONY ASHTON       K     (A
T63A                         THIRSTY MOON
                                       (A) YELLOW SUNSHINE               197 BRAIN              GERM 0040 124
T64                   THIRTEENTH FLOOR ELEVATORS
     ROCKY ERICSON           (BC       (A) PSYCHEDELIC SOUNDS OF          19 INTERNATIONAL ARTIST US  LP1
     DAN GALINDO       B     (B        (A) PSYCHEDELIC SOUNDS OF        1978 RADAR RI            UK RAD13
     JOHN IKE WALTON         (         (B) EASTER EVERYWHERE             19 INTERNATIONAL ARTIST US  IA5
     DANNY THOMAS            (B        (B) EASTER EVERYWHERE           1979 RADAR RI            UK RAD15
     STACY SUTHERLAND        (B        (C) 13TH FLOOR ELEVATORS          19 INTERNATIONAL ARTIST US  IA8
     BENNY THURMAN           (         (D) BULL OF THE WOODS             19 INTERNATIONAL ARTIST US  IA9
     TOMMY HALL              (BC       (E) AVALON 66                   1977                     FP  1001
                                       (F) YOU REALLY GOT ME (EP)      1978 AUSTIN              UK  RE1
T65                     THIRTY EIGHT SPECIAL
     DONNIE VAN ZANT   V     (A        (A) THIRTY EIGHT SPECIAL        1977 A&M   US 4638  UK  AMLH64638
     STEVE BROOKINS    D     (A        (B) SPECIAL DELIVERY            1978 A&M   US 4684  UK  AMLH64684
     CARL HALL         V     (A        (C) WILD EYED SOUTHERN BOYS     1981 A&M           UK  AMLH64835
     JACK GRONDIN      D     (A
     KEN LYONS         B     (A   DON BARNES       G V (A   JEFF CARLISI   G STEEL (A   TERRY EMERY   PNO (A
     LARRY JUNSTROM    B     (A   DAN HARTMAN      V   (A   LANI GROVES    V      (A   JOCELYN BROWN V   (A
T66                          THIS HEAT
     GARETH WILLIAMS K G B V  (A       (A) THIS HEAT                   1979 PIANO             UK     THIS 1
     CHARLES HAYWARD  PERC K V (A
     CHARLES BULLEN G VLA V CLAR(A
T67                       JACQUES THOLLOT
     JACQUES THOLLOT  D K    (ABCD     (A) QUAND LE SON DEVIENT TROP AIGU 1971 FUTURA           GER  24
     FRANCOIS JEANNEAU SAX   (BCD      (B) WATCH DEVIL GO                19 PALM                     17
     SIEGFRIED KESSLER PNO   (C        (C) RESURGENCE                 1977 MUSICA              MUS 3021
     BEB GUERIN        B     (C        (D) CINQ HOPS                  1978 FREE BIRD           FLY  03
     NANA VASCONCELOS PERC   (C
     FREDERIQUE GEGENBACH V  (C   ELISE ROSS       V   (D   FRANCOIS COUTURIER PNO (D   JEAN PAUL CELEA B (D
     CHRTS HOWARD     FLT    (D   MICHEL GRAILLIER CLAR (D   JEAN FRANCOIS CLARK B (B   CHARLINE SCOTT  V (B
T68                          CARLA THOMAS
     CARLA THOMAS      V     (ALL      (A) GEE WHIZ                    1961 ATLANTIC           US    SD8057
                                       (B) COMFORT ME                  1966 STAX               US    706
                                       (C) CARLA                       1966 STAX               US    709
                                       (D) KING & QUEEN                1967 STAX               US    716
                                       (E) QUEEN ALONE                 1967 STAX               US    718
                                       (F) LOVE MEANS                  1971 STAX US 2044 UK PLORDOR 2362023
                                       (G) MEMPHIS QUEEN               1975 STAX US 2019 UK STAX  STX 1038
                                       (H) BEST OF                       19 ATLANTIC           US    SD8232
                                       (J) CHRONICLE                   1979 STAX               STX 4124
T69                          IAN THOMAS
     IAN THOMAS              (AB       (A) GOODNIGHT MRS CALABASH       1976 CHRYSALIS          UK    CHR  1126
                                       (B) IAN THOMAS                   1976 DJM                UK    DJM 20440
T70                          IRMA THOMAS
     IRMA THOMAS       V     (A        (A) IN BETWEEN TEARS             1980 CHARLY             UK    CRB 1020
                                       (A) IN BTWEEN THE LINES           19 FUNGUS             US    25150
T71                          JOE THOMAS
     JOE THOMAS        FLT   (AB       (A) JOY OF COOKIN'               1974 PEOPLE                   PLEO 15
     MARVIN STAMM      HRNS  (B        (B) MAKE YOUR MOVE               1979 LRC 9327   +     TK    TKR 83374
     GEORGE YOUNG      SAX   (B
     HIRAM BULLOCK     G     (B   RICHARD TRIFAN    SYN (B
T72                          NICKY THOMAS
     NICKY THOMAS            (ALL      (A) TELL IT LIKE IT IS           1971 TROJAN                   TRLS 25
                                       (B) IMAGES OF YOU                 19 HORSE                     HRLP 701
                                       (C) LOVE OF THE COMMON PEOPLE    1976 TROJAN                   TBL  143
T73                          RAY THOMAS
     RAY THOMAS        V FLT(AB        (A) FROM MIGHTY OAKS             1975 THRESHOLD          UK    THS 16
                                       (B) HOPES WISHES & DREAMS        1976 THRESHOLD          UK    THS 17
T74                          RUFUS THOMAS
     RUFUS THOMAS      V     (ALL      WALKING THE DOG                 1964 STAX               US    704
     BILLY RED LOVE    PNO   ((E)      MAY I HAVE YOUR TICKET PLEASE     19 STAX               US    2022
     JOE HILL LOUIS    G     (E        FUNKY CHICKEN                   1970 STAX               US    2028
     HOUSTON STOKES    D     (E        LIVE AT PJs DOIN' THE PUSH & PULL 1970 STAX              US    2039
                                       DID YOU HEAR ME                  197 STAX US 3004 UK POLYDOR 2362028
                                       CROWN PRINCE OF DANCE            1974 STAX US 3008 UK STAX  STX1002
                                       (E)RUFUS THOMAS(EP)             1977 CHARLY             UK    CEP 101
                                       IF THERE WERE NO MUSIC          1977 PYE UK NSPL28241 US AVI  6015
T75                          TIMMY THOMAS
     TIMMY THOMAS            (         (A) TOUCH TO TOUCH               1978 tk                       TKR 82510
                                       ( ) WHY CANT WE LIVE TOGETHER     19 GLADES US 6501 POLYDOR 2956 002
                                       ( ) YOU'RE THE SONG             1975 POLYDOR                   2310 377
                                       ( ) MAGICIAN                    1977 TK                 UK XL  14044
                                       [412]
```

BARBARA THOMPSON T76

BARBARA THOMPSON	SAX PERC(ALL	(A) PARAPHERNALIA	1978 MCA	UK	MCF 2852
JON HISEMAN	D (D	(B) JUBIABA	1978 MCA	UK	MCF 2867
DILL KATZ	B (D	(C) WILD TALES	1979 MCA	UK	
COLIN DUDMAN	K SYN(D	(D) LIVE IN CONCERT	1980 MCA		MCSP 309

ALI THOMPSON T77

ALI THOMPSON	(A	(A) TAKE A LITTLE RHYTHM	1980 A&M	UK AMLH68512

MAYO THOMPSON T78

MAYO THOMPSON	V (A	(A) CORKY'S DEBT TO HIS FATHER	19 TEXAS REVOLUTION US	CFS 2270

RICHARD & LINDA THOMPSON T79

RICHARD THOMPSON	G V (ALL	(A) HENRY THE HUMAN FLY	1972 ISLAND	UK	ILPS 9197
LINDA THOMPSON(PETERS)V(ALL		(B) I WANT TO SEE THE BRIGHT LIGHTS	1974 ISLAND	UK	ILPS 9266
TIMI DONALD	D (ABCDEG	(C) HOKEY POKEY	1974 ISLAND	UK	ILPS 9305
PAT DONALDSON	B (ABCDEG	(D) POUR DOWN LIKE SILVER	1975 ISLAND	UK	ILPS 9348
SANDY DENNY	K V (AE	(E) GUITAR & VOCAL	1976 ISLAND	UK	ICD8
DAVID SNELL	HARP (A	(E) R T LIVE!(MORE OR LESS)	1977 ISLAND	US	ISLA 9421
JEFF COLE	TROM (A	(F) FIRST LIGHT	1978 CHRYSALIS	UK	CHR 1177
JOHN DEFERERI	SAX (A	(G) SUNNY VISTA	1979 CHRYSALIS	UK	CHR 1247
CLAY TOYANI	TPT (A				

SUE DRAHEIM	FDL (A	BARRY DRANSFIELD FDL (A	JOHN KIRKPATRICK ACC (ALL	ASHLEY HUTCHINGS	V B(AD
SIMON NICOL	G K V (BCEFG	BRIAN GULLAND KRUMM(B	RICHARD HARVEY KRUMM(B	ROYSTON WOOD	V (B
TREVOR LUCAS	V (BF	C W S SILVER BAND (BC	IAN WHITEMAN K FLT(CDE	ALY BAIN	FDL(CD
SIDONIE GOOSSENS	HARP (C	DAVE MATTACKS D (DEFG	NIC JONES FDL (D	HENRY LOWTHER	TPT(D
JUDY DYBLE	V (E	IAN MATTHEWS V (EF	MARTIN LAMBLE D (E	PETE ROSS	HCA(E
DAVE SWARBRICK	FDL (E	DAVID PEGG (EG	ANDY NEWMARK D (F	WILLIE WEEKS	B (F
NEIL LARSEN	K (F	CHRIS KARAN PERC (F	DOLORES KEANE WHISTLE (F	DAVE BRADY	V (F
HEATHER BRADY	V (F	BILL CADDICK V (F	PHILIPPA CLARE V (F	JULIE COVINGTON	V (F
ANDY FAIRWEATHER LOW V (F		MADDY PRIOR V (F	PETA WEBB V (F	ANDY ROBERTS	DULC(A
DAVE BURLAND	V (F	MICHAEL SPENCER ARSCOTT D(G	SUE HARRIS WIND (G	PETE WINGFIELD	K (G
RABBIT BUNDRICK	K (G	LUIS JARDIM PERC (G	KATE McGARRIGLE V (G	ANNA McGARRIGLE	V (G
GLEN TILBROOK	V (G	JULIAN LITTMAN V (G	MARC ELLINGTON V (G	OLIVE SIMPSON	V (G
NICOLE TIBBELS	V (G	LINDSAY BENTON V (G	DAVID BEAVAN V (G	BRUCE LYNCH	B (G
GERRY RAFFERTY	V (G	HAFSA ABDUL JABBAS V (G	ABDU RAHIM V (G		

MARC THOR T79A

MARC THOR	V PNO(A	(A) 1976			
RICK CORACIO	B (A				
JAY JAY RASSLER	G (A	STEVEN SILVA G (A	MONO MANN V (A	C MYRA	D (A

BIG MAMA THORNTON T79B

BIG MAMA THORNTON	V (ALL	(A) STRONGER THAN DIRT	1969 MERCURY UK SMCL 20176 US	61225	
CORNELL DUPREE	G (H	(B) SHES BACK	19 BACKBEAT	US	68
RONNIE MILLER	G (H	(C) IN EUROPE	1966 ARHOOLIE	US	F 1028
PAUL GRIFFIN	K (H	(D) CHICAGO BLUES	1967 ARHOOLIE	US	F 1032
WILBUR BASCOMB	B (H	(E) BALL & CHAIN	1968 ARHOOLIE	US	F 1039
JIMMY JOHNSON	D (H	(F) JAIL	1975 VANGUARD		79351
BUDDY LUCAS	SAX (H	(G) SASSY MAMA	1975 VANGUARD		79354
GEORGE SMITH	HCA (H	(H) MAMA'S PRIDE	1978 VANGUARD		VPC4000
STEVE WACHSMAN	G (H	(I) SAVED	197 PENAGRAM	US	10005
WALTER HORTON	HCA (C				
BEE HOUSTON	G (H	J D NICHOLSON K (H	BRUCE SIEVERSON B (H	TODD NELSON	D (H
BILL POTTER	SAX (H	EDDIE BOYD K (C	BUDDY GUY G (C	JIMMY LEE ROBINSON	B(C
FRED BELOW	D (C	FRED McDOWELL G (C	JAMES COTTON HCA (D	OTIS SPANN PNO	(D
MUDDY WATERS	G (D	FRANCIS CLAY D (D			

GEORGE THOROGOOD & THE DESTROYERS T80

GEORGE THOROGOOD	G V (ALL	(A) GEORGE THOROGOOD & THE DESTROYERS	1973 ROUNDER 3013 US UK	SONET SNTF760
JEFF SIMON	D (ALL	(B) MOVE IT ON OVER	1973 ROUNDER 3024 US UK	SONET SNTF781
BILLY BLOUGH	B (B	(C) BETTER THAN THE REST (19749	1979 MCA 3091 +	3037
RON SMITH	G (B	(D) MORE GEORGE THOROGOOD	1980	UK SONET SNTF850
UNCLE MEAT PENNINGTON PERC(B		(E) IT'S ALL ENTERTAINMENT	19 EXCITABLE	EX4504
HANK CARTER	SAX (C			
MICHAEL LEVINE	B (C			

BILLY THORPE T80A

BILLY THORPE	G V (AB	(A) CHILDREN OF THE SUN	1979 POLYDOR	UK	2391 424
LEE SKLAR	B (AB	(B) 21ST CENTURY MAN	1980 ELEKTRA	US	6E 294
ALVIN TAYLOR	D (A				
GIL MATTHEWS	D (B				

THOSE NAUGHTY LUMPS T80B

(EP) ICE CREAM	19 OPEN EYE	UK OE1002

THREE D T80C

RICK ZWIC	V (A	(A) 3D	1980 POLYDOR	2391 445
KEW GINSBERG	G V (A			
TED WENDER	K V (A	NICK STEVENS B V (A	MIKE FINK D (A	

THREE DOG NIGHT T81

DANNY HUTTON	V (12	(A) THREE DOG NIGHT	1969 UK STATESIDE 5006	US DUNHILL 5004B
CHUCK NEGRON	V (12	(B) SUITABLE FOR FRAMING	1969 UK STATESIDE 5013	US DUNHILL 5005B
CORY WELLS	V (12	(C) LIVE AT THE FORUM	1970 UK STATESIDE 5023	US DUNHILL 5006B
MIKE ALLSUP	G (12	(D) IT AINT EASY	1970 UK PROBE SPBA6251	US DUNHILL 5007B
JIM GREENSPOON	K (12	(E) NATURALLY	1971 UK PROBE SPBA6257	US DUNHILL 5008B
JOE SCHERMIE	B (1	(F) GOLDEN BISCUITS	1971 UK PROBE SPB 1035	US DUNHILL 5009B
FLOYD SNEED	D (12	(F) GOLDEN BISCUITS	1974 UK ABC ABCL5014	
JACK RYLAND	B (2	(G) HARMONY	1971 UK PROBE SPB 1047	US DUNHILL 5010B
SKIP KONTE	K (2	(H) SEVEN SEPARATE FOOLS	1972 UK PROBE SPTC 1	US DUNHILL 5011B
(1) 1968/73 (2) 1973/		(I) AROUND THE WORLD	1973 UK PROBE PBSP 113	US DUNHILL 5013B
		(J) CYAN	1973 UK ABC ABCL5039	US DUNHILL 5015B
		(K) HARD LABOUR	1974 UK ABC ABCL5049	US DUNHILL 5016B
		(L) GREATEST HITS	1974 UK ABC ABCL5064	US DUNHILL 5017B
		(M) DOG STYLE	1974	US DUNHILL 5019B
		(N) COMING DOWN YOUR WAY	1975 UK ABC ABCL5120	US ABC 888
		(O) AMERICAN PASTIME	1976 UK ABC ABCL5159	US ABC 928

```
T82                                 THREE MAN ARMY
  PAUL GURVITZ(CURTIS)B (ALL        (A) A THIRD OF A LIFETIME      1971 PEGASUS UK PEG3 US KAMASUTRA 2044
  ADRIAN GURVITZ(CURTIS)G(ALL       (B) THREE MAN ARMY            1973 REPRISE UK K44254 US        2150
  MIKE KELLIE       D   (A          (C) THREE MAN ARMY 2          1974 REPRISE UK K54015
  BUDDY MILES       D   (A          (D) MAHESHE                   1974 POLYDOR              2310 241
  TONY NEWMAN       D   (BC
  BRIAN PARRISH     G   (A
T83                                 THROBBING GRISTLE
  GENESIS P ORRIDGE B C  (ABCD      (A) 1ST ANNUAL REPORT          197  INDUSTRIAL      UK   IRO001
  COSEY FANNI TUTTI G V(ABCD        (B) 2ND ANNUAL REPORT          1977 INDUSTRIAL      UK   IRO002
  CHRIS CARTER      K    (ABCD      (B) 2ND ANNUAL REPORT(RECUT RI) 1979 FETISH         UK   FR2001
  PETER CHRISTOPHER EFFECTS(ABCD    (C) D O A                      1978 INDUSTRIAL      UK   IRO004
                                    (D) 20 JAZZ PUNK GREATS        1979 INDUSTRIAL      UK   IRO008
T84                                 THUNDERCLAP NEWMAN             (E) HEATHEN EARTH    1980 INDUSTRIAL UK IRO009
  ANDY NEWMAN       K    (A         (A) HOLLYWOOD DREAM            1970 TRACK           UK   2406 003
  JIMMY McCULLOCH   G    (
  SPEEDY KEEN       V G D(   PETE TOWNSHEND (BIJOU DRAINS)B( JIM AVERY  B  ( JACK McCULLOCH D (
  CHRIS MORPHET     HCA  (A
T85                                 THUNDERMUG
  BILL DURST        G    (A         (A) THUNDERMUG STRIKES         1972 AXE                  AXS502
  JOE DE ANGELIS    V    (A         (B) TA DAA                     1975 MERCURY         US   SRM1 1039
  JIM CORBETT       B    (A
  ED PRANSKUS       D    (A
T86                                 JOHNNY THUNDERS
  JOHNNY THUNDERS   G V  (A         (A) SO ALONE                   1978 REAL            UK   RAL1
  STEVE MARRIOTT    K    (A
  PETER PERRETT     G V  (A   STEVE JONES    G   (A  BILLY RATH    B   (A  PAUL GRAY     D (A
  PHIL LYNOTT       B    (A   MIKE KELLIE    D   (A  WALTER LURE   G   (A  PAT PALLADIN    (A
  PAUL COOK         D    (A   JOHN IRISH EARLE   (A  STEVE NICOLS  D   (A  HENRI PAUL      (A
T87                                 THUNDERTHIGHS
  CASEY SYNGE       V    (          VOCAL BACKING GROUP
  KAREN FRIEDMAN    V    (
  DARI LALOU        V    (   JUANITA FRANKLIN  V  (
T88                                 THUNDERTRAIN
  GENE PROVIST      G    (1         (A) TEENAGE SUICIDE            1977 JELLY                JPLP1
  RICK PROVOST      B    (1         (1) 1976
  MACH BELL         V    (1   STEVEN SILVA    G   (1  BOB EDWARDS   D   (1
T89                                 TIGER
  BIG JIM SULLIVAN  G    (AB        (A) TIGER                      1976 RETREAT              RTL  6006
  ALAN PARK         K    (B         (B) GOING DOWN LAUGHING        1976 EMI                  EMC  3153
  DAVID McCRAE      K    (A
  NICKY MOORE  HCA V G   (AB  ANDY BROWN   B V  (B  PHIL CURTIS   B   (A  LES WALKER  G V (AB
  BILL McGIILIVRAY  G K V(B   RAY FLACKE    G   (A  BILLY RANKIN  D   (A
T89A                                TIGERS
  TONY JACKS        G V  (A         (A) SAVAGE MUSIC               1980 A&M            US    AP4817
  NICK COLA         K V  (A
  ROSS McGEENEY     G V  (A   NIC POTTER     B   (A  PETE DOBSON   D   (A
T90                                 TIGHT LIKE THAT
  DAVID H PEABODY G V HCA(A         (A)HOKUM                       1972 VILLAGE THING        VTS 12
  DAVID GRIFFITHS VLN G V(A
  BILL SHORTT       PERC (A   HUGH McNULTY    B V (A  ANDY LEGGETT  JUG (A
T91                                 ROGER TILLISON
  ROGER TILLISON         (A         (A) ROGER TILLISON'S ALBUM     19   ATCO           US    SD 33355
  JESSE ED DAVIS    G    (A
  JIM KELTNER       D    (A   LARRY KNECHTEL   K   (A
T92                                 STEVE TILSTON
  STEVE TILSTON     G V  (A         (A) ACOUSTIC CONFUSION         1977 VILLAGE THING   UK    VTS 5
T93                                 TIMBER
  JUDY ELLIOTT      V    (AB        (A) PART OF WHAT YOU HEAR      19   KAPP           US    KS3633
  WAYNE BERRY       B G V(AB        (B) BRING AMERICA HOME         19   ELEKTRA US 74095     UK K42093
  GEORGE CLINTON K V HRNS(AB
  ROGER JOHNSON G V TPT (AB  WARNER DAVIS    D   (AB
T94                                 TIME BOX
  MIKE PATTO        V    (          (A) ORIGINAL MOOSE ON THE LOOSE 1977 COSMOS COLLECTOR US CCLPS9016
  JOHN HALSEY       D    (
  OLLIE HALSALL     G    (   CHRIS HOLMES    K   (  CLIVE GRIFFITHS  B  (
T95                                 KEITH TIPPETT
  KEITH TIPPETT     PNO  (ALL       (A) YOU ARE HERE I AM THERE    1970 POLYDOR              2384 004
  ELTON DEAN        SAX  (ABG       (B) DEDICATED TO YOU           1971 VERTIGO              6360 024
  MARK CHARIG       HRNS (ABG       (C) BLUE PRINT                 1972 RCA             UK    SF 8290
  NICK EVANS        TROM (ABG       (D) EMANEM     T'N'T           19   ?                    3307
  JEFF CLYNE        B    (A         (E) STEAM      T'N'T           19   ?                    SJ 104
  ALAN JACKSON      D    (A         (F) WARM SPIRITS COOL SPIRITS  1977 VINYL                VS 101
  GIORGIO GOMELSKY  BELLS(A         (G) FRAMES     (ARK)           1978 OGUN                 OGD 003/4
  ROBERT WYATT      D    (B         (H) BOTH SIDES NOW             19   POLYDOR              2359 007
  BRYAN SPRING      D    (B
  PHIL HOWARD       D    (B   TONY UTER      CONGA(B  ROY BABBINGTON   B  (BC NEVILLE WHITEHEAD  B (B
  GARY BOYLE        G    (B   KEITH BAILEY    PERC (C  FRANK PERRY  PERC (C  JULIE TIPPETTS  G V (CFG
  TREVOR WATTS      SAX  (FG  COLIN McKENZIE  B   (F  STAN TRACEY  PNO  (DEG BRIAN SMITH    WIND (G
  LARRY STABBINS    WIND (G   HENRY LOWTHER   TPT (G  PETER KOWALKE HRNS (G  HARRY MILLER    B   (G
  LOUIS MOHOLO      D    (G   DAVE AMIS      TROM (G  MAGGIE NICHOLLS V  (G
T96                                 TIR NA NOG
  SONNY CONDELL G V PERC(ABC        (A) TIR NA NOG                 1971 CHRYSALIS       UK    ILPS 9153
  LEO O'KELLY G V VLN   (ABC        (B) A TEAR & A SMILE           1972 CHRYSALIS       UK    CHR  1006
  BRIAN ODGERS      B    (C         (C) STRONG IN THE SUN          1973 CHRYSALIS       UK    CHR  1047
  DAVE MARKEE       B    (C
  JIM RYAN          B    (C   BARRY DE SOUZA  D   (BC ACE FOLLINGTON  D  (C  JEFF JONES    D (C
  MATTHEW FISHER    K    (C   LARRY STEELE    B   (B
```

TITANIC T97

KJELL'CHAPPY'ASPERUD	D	(ACD	(A) TITANIC	1971 CBS		64104
JANNY LOSETH	G	(ACD	(B) SEA WOLF	1972 CBS		64791
JOHN LORCK	D	(AC	(C) EAGLE ROCK	1973 CBS		65661
ARICA SIGGS	B	(	(D) BALLAD OF A ROCK'N'ROLL LOSER	1975 CBS		80786
HELGE GROSLIE	K	(C	(E) RETURN OF DRAKKAR	1978 EGG		900542
ROY ROBINSON	V	(ACD				
JOHN WILLIAMS	B G V(D	KENNY AAS ORG (A ANDREW RAILSTON D (D				

LIBBY TITUS T98

LIBBY TITUS	V	(A	(A) LIBBY TITUS	1977 CBS	US	PC 34152
GRADY TATE	D	(A				
TONY LEVIN	B	(A	DON GROLNICK K (A HUGH McCRACKEN G (A ALAN RUBIN HRNS(A
DAVID NADIEN	VLN	(A	KATHY KIENKE VLN (A ALFRED BROWN VLA (A JANET HAMILTON CELLO(A
PAUL SIMON	V	(A	RONNY ZITO D (A CHUCK ISRAELS B (A GEORGE YOUNG SAX (A
JOE BECK	G	(A	CHRIS PARKER D (A RUSSELL GEORGE D (A JOHN GUERIN D (A
MAX BENNETT	D	(A	HIRTH MARTINEZ G V (A MICHAEL MELVOIN K (A GARTH HUDSON K (A
RICK MAROTTA	D	(A	JOHN TROPEA G (A PATTI AUSTIN V (A LANI GROVES V (A
WILL LEE	B	(A	GWEN GUTHRIE V (A ROBBIE ROBERTSON G (A LARRY MUHOBERAC PNO (A
MARVIN STAMM	TPT	(A	DAVE TOFANI FLT (A PHIL BODNER FLT (A DON BROOKS HCA (A
CRAIG DOERGE	K	(A	CARLY SIMON V (A JAMES TAYLOR V (A

TITUS GROAN T99

		(A) TITUS GROAN	1971 JANUS US 3024 UK DAWN DNLS3012	

TO BE T100

		(A) TO BE	197 BRAIN	0060 053

TOAD T101

		(A) TOAD	1972 RCA	UK SF8241

TOBY T102

ANDT FRASER	V B	(A	(A) 1971 NO ALBUMS
ADRIAN FISHER	G	(A	
STAN SPEAKE	D	(A	

TOBY BEAU T102A

BALDE SILVA	G V HCA	(AB	(A) TOBY BEAU	1978 RCA	UK	PL 12771
STEVE ZIPPER	B V	(AB	(B) MORE THAN A LOVE SONG	1979 RCA	UK	PL 13119
RON ROSE	G V BAN(AB					
DANNY McKENNA	G V	(AB	ROB YOUNG D PERC (AB

TOEFAT T103

CLIFF BENNETT	V	(AB	(A) TOEFAT	1970 PARLOPHONE	UK	7097
KEN HENSLEY	G V	(AB	(A) TOEFAT	1970 RARE EARTH	US	RS 511
LEE KERSLAKE	D V	(A	(B) TOEFAT II	1971 REGAL ZONOPHONE	UK	SLRZ 1015
JOHN GLASCOCK	B	(	(B) TOEFAT II	1971 RARE EARTH	US	RS 525
JOE KONAS	B	(A				
MOX	HCA FLT	(A				

TOLLHOUSE T103A

IAN CUSSICK	V	(A	(A) TOLLHOUSE	1978 NOVA	623430
DIRK STEFFENS	G	(A			
PETER WEIHE	G	(A	ROLF KOHLER B V (A PETER FRANKEN D PERC(A JEAN JACQUES KRAVETZ K(A
HERB GELLER	SAX	(A	BOB LANESE TPT (A HANS UWE REIMERS SAX (A RALE V (A
JIM HOPKINS	V	(A	HEIKO EFFERTZ V (A

JUKKA TOLONEN T104

JUKKA TOLONEN	G	(AB	(A) TOLONEN	1974 SONET UK SNTF652 SW LOVE LP 47
PEKKA POHJOLA	B	(A	(B) THE SUMMER GAMES	197 SW LOVE LP91
PEKKA POYRY	SAX	(AD	(C) THE HOOK	197 SW LOVE LP113
REINO LAING	D	(A	(D) CROSSECTION	1976 SONET UK SNTF699
HEIKKI VIRTANEN	B	(AD	(E) HYSTERICA	197 SW LOVE LP149
RONNE OSTERBERG	D	(A	(F) A PASSENGER TO PARAMARIBO	1978 SONET UK SNTF768 SW LOVE LP231
JUKKA GUSTAVSON	K	(A	(G) MONTREUX BOOGIE	1979 SONET UK SNTF789 SW LOVE LP278
PARONI PAAKKUNAINEN SAX(D			(H) MOUNTAIN STREAM	19
ESA KOTILAINEN	K SYN(D		(J) J T B	1980
ESKO ROSNELL	D	(D		
SAKARI KUKKO	WIND (D		JOSSI AALTO TROM (D

TOMITA T105

ISAO TOMITA	K SYN(ALL		(A) SNOWFLAKES ARE DANCING	1975 RCA	ARL1 0488
			(B) PICTURES AT AN EXHIBITION	1975 RCA	ARL1 0838
			(C) FIREBIRD SUITE	1976 RCA	ARL1 1312
			(D) THE PLANETS(WITHDRAWN)	1977 RCA	RL 11919
			(E) BERMUDA TRIANGLE	1979 RCA	RL 12885
			(F) KOSMOS	1979 RCA	RL 42652

TOMORROW T106

KEITH WEST	V	(A	(A) TOMORROW	1968 PARLOPHONE	PCS 7042
JOHN WOOD	B	(A	(A) TOMORROW	1976 HARVEST UK	SHSP 2110
STEVE HOWE	G	(A	(A) TOMORROW	1968 SIRE US	97012
TWINK	D	(A	(A) TOMORROW	1978 VISA	1002
KEN LAWRENCE	D	(A			
JOHN BURGESS		(			

TONI & TERRY T107

TONI BROWN	V G K(ABD		(A) CROSS COUNTRY	1973 CAPITOL		11137
TERRY GARTHWAITE	V G	(ABCDE	(B) GOOD FOR YOU TOO	1974 MCA		MCF 2558
BILL AIKENS	K	(A	(C) TERRY	1975 ARISTA	UK	ARTY 124
DENNIS LINDE	V B	(A	(D) THE JOY	1977 FANTASY		FT 537
KENNY MALONE	D	(A	(E) HAND IN GLOVE	1978 FANTASY		FT 554
RUSS HICKS	G V	(A				
JIM COLVARD	G	(A	VASSAR CLEMENTS VLN (A CHARLIE McCOY HCA V(A BOBBY THOMPSON G BAN(A
DAVE DORAN	G	(A	JIM METHENY V (A BILLY PUETT HRNS (B LLOYD GREEN STEEL(B
CHUCK COCHRAN	ACC	(B	MARY HOEPFINGER HARP (B KURT McGETTRICK SAX (B TOMMY COGBILL B (B
JERRY CARRIGAN	D	(A	BOBBY WOOD K (B BILLY SANFORD G (B REGGIE YOUNG G (B
JOHN CHRISTOPHER	G	(A	CHIP YOUNG G (B FARRELL MORRIS PERC (B GEORGE TIDWELL HRNS (B
DENNIS GOODE	HRNS (B		BOBBY EMMONS K (B BUDDY SPICHER FDL (B WILLOW WRAY V (CDE
SONNY BURKE	K	(C	WILLIAM SMITH K (CD PATRICE RUSHEN K (C ROGER KELLAWAY K (C
PEGGY STERN	K	(CE	JAMES GADSON D (CD HARVEY MASON D (C JOHN GUERIN D (CE
VALENTINOS	V	(C	BOBBY WOMACK V (C SCOTT MATTHEWS D (C BILL SUMMERS PERC (C
						(CONTINUED)

[415]

TONI & TERRY

```
WILLIE WEEKS      B   (C   RON CARTER       B   (C   CHUCK DOMANICO    B    (C   DAVID GARTHWAITE  B  (C
WAH WAH WATSON    G   (C   HOWARD ROBERTS   G   (C   JOE CRANE         G    (C   BOB FLURIE        G  (C
REGGIE McBRIDE    B   (D   STEVE MITCHELL   D   (D   JOHN BLAKELY      G    (D   ELVIN BISHOP      G  (D
BOBBYE HALL       PERC (D   TAJ MAHAL        G HCA(D   J D MANESS        STEEL(D   JIM HORN          HRNS (D
STEVE MADAIO      HRNS 'D   JIMMY ROBERTS    WIND (D   BILL NAPIER       CLAR (D   JOHNNY ROTELLA    CLAR (D
MICHELLE HARRIS   DULC MAN(D MARJIE ORTEN    DULC MAND(D KENNETH NASH     PERC (D   JAY GRAYDEN       G  (E
VICTOR FELDMAN    K   (E   CLARK GASSMAN    K   (E   MAC CRIDLIN       B    (E   GEORGE MRAZ       B  (E
SHEILAH GLOVER    V   (E   VICKI RANDLE     V   (E   DEE DEE DICKERSON  V    (E   DON SHEFFIELD     HRNS (B
```

T108
TONTON MACOUTE
```
CHRIS GAVIN       G B  (A        (A) TONTON MACOUTE              1971 NEON        UK            NE 4
PAUL FRENCH       K V  (A
NIGEL REVELER     D   (A   DAVE KNOWLES  WIND V(A
```

T109
TONTOS EXPANDING HEADBAND
```
ROBERT MARGOULEFF SYN K(AB       (A) ZERO TIME                  1971 UK ATLANTIC K40251 US EMBRY0732
MALCOLM CECIL     SYN K(AB       (B) ITS ABOUT TIME             1974 POLYDOR               2383 308
```

T110
TOOTS & THE MAYTALS
```
TOOTS HIBBERT     V   (ALL       (A) FROM THE ROOTS             1973 TROJAN                TRLS  63
HUX BROWN         G   (DFJ        (B) FUNKY KINGSTON             1973 DRAGON DRLS5002 ISLAND ILPS9186
JACKIE JACKSON    B   (DHJ        (C) IN THE DARK               1974 DRAGON DRLS5004 ISLAND ILPS9231
PAUL DOUGLAS      B   (DFHJ       (D) REGGAE GOT SOUL           1976 ISLAND                ILPS9374
RAD BRYAN         G   (DF         (E) THE MAYTALS               1978 STATE                 ETAT  16
RALEIGH GORDON    V   (DFGHJ      (F) PASS THE PIPE             1979 ISLAND     NL 200471  UK ILPS9534
JERRY MATHIAS     V   (DFGHJ      (G) BEST OF                   1979 TROJAN                TRLS 171
WINSTON WRIGHT    K   (DFHJ       (H) JUST LIKE THAT            1980 ISLAND     UK ILPS9590
RANCHY McLEAN     B   (F          (J) LIVE                      1980 ISLAND                ILPS9647
JUNIOR KERR       G   (D
CHINNA LINDO      G   (D   GLADSTONE ANDERSON K (D   SONNY BINNS      K   (D   STEVE WINWOOD   K  (D
EMMANUEL RENTZOS  K   (D   CHICAGO STEVE    HCA (D   BOBBY ELLIS      TPT (D   EDDIE QUANSAH   TPT(D
JEROME FRANCISQUE TROM (D   RICO RODRIGUES   TROM (D   RAY ALLEN        SAX (D   DUDU PUKWANA    SAX(D
TOMMY McCOOK      SAX  (D   GEORGE LEE       SAX (D   DENSIL LANG      PERC(D   BROTHER JAMES   PERC(D
TONY UTER         PERC (D   BRUCE ROWLAND    PERC(D   PABLO BLACK      K   (D   WILLIE LINDO    G  (H
MIKEY CHUNG       G   (H   CARL HARVEY      G   (J   HAROLD BUTLER    K   (HJ
```

T111
TOP TOPHAM
```
TOP TOPHAM        G   (A        (A) ASCENSION HEIGHTS          1970 BLUE HORIZON    UK       763857
RICK HAYWARD      G   (A
JOHN MARSHALL     D   (A   COLIN ALLEN      D   (A   HERBIE FLOWERS   B   (A   EDDIE TRIPP     B  (A
BRIAN ODGERS      B   (A   STRING SECTION       (A   PETE WINGFIELD   K   (A   STEVE GREY      K  (A
DUSTER BENNETT    HCA  (A   MIKE VERNON      PERC (A   TERRY NOONAN     TPT (A   BUTCH HUDSON    TPT(A
GREG BOWEN        TPT  (A   NIGEL CARTER     TPT (A   CHRIS PYNE       TROM(A   DANNY ELWOOD    TROM(A
JACK THIRLWELL    TROM (A   ALAN SKIDMORE    SAX (A   DANNY MOSS       SAX (A   TONY COE        SAX (A
STEVE GREGORY     SAX  (A   DON HONEYWELL    SAX (A
```

T111A
TORNADER
```
SANDY TORANO      G   (A        (A) HIT IT AGAIN              1977 POLYDOR         US      PL 1 6098
LARRY ALEXANDER   V   (A
JOHNNY WINTER     G   (A   JOE BECK      G   (A   STEVE FERRONE    D   (A   RANDY BRECKER   HRNS(S
MICHAEL BRECKER   HRNS (A
```

T112
TORNADOS
```
HEINZ BURT        V B G(        (A) SOUND OF (EP)               1962 DECCA           UK   DFE  8510
ROGER JACKSON     K   (          (B) TELSTAR  (EP)              1963 DECCA           UK   DFE  8511
GEORGE BELLAMY    G   (          (C) MORE SOUNDS FROM (EP)      1963 DECCA           UK   DFE  8521
ALAN CADDY        VLN G(         (D) TORNADO ROCK               1963 DECCA           UK   DFE  8533
CLEM CATTINI      D   (          (E) TELSTAR                    196  LONDON          US        3279
                                 (F) AWAY FROM IT ALL           1963 DECCA           UK   LK 4552
                                 (G) WORLD OF                   1972 DECCA           UK   SPA  253
                                 (H) REMEMBERING                1976 DECCA           UK   ROOTS  4
```

T112A
TORONTO
```
NICKI COSTELLO    B   (A        (A) LOOKING FOR TROUBLE         1980  SOLID GOLD       SGT  1000
JIMMY FOX         D   (A
SHERON ALTON      G   (A   HOLLY WOODS      V   (A   SCOTT KREYER     K   (A   BRIAN ALLEN     G  (A
```

T113
RICHARD TORRANCE
```
RICHARD TORRANCE  V B G K(ALL    (A) EUREKA                    1974 A&M             UK   AMLH68266
GARY ROWLES       G V PERC STEEL(B (B) BELLE OF THE BALL        1975 A&M             UK   AMLH68312
DENNIS MANSFIELD  V D VIBES(BE    (C) BAREBACK                 1977 CAPITOL          SW   11610
RICHARD CANTU     PERC (B         (D) ANYTHINGS POSSIBLE       197  CAPITOL          SW   11660
JON LAMB          G B V PERC(B    (E) DOUBLE TAKE              1978 CAPITOL          SW   11699
DUANE SCOTT       V K PERC   (B
TERRY LEE LICK    G V  (E   DAVID WHITE       B V  (E   MELODY JEAN HORNEY K V  (E   BILLY PAYNE  K  (E
VANDER LOCKETT    PERC (E
```

T114
PETER TOSH
```
PETER TOSH        G V K(ALL       (A) LEGALIZE IT              1976 VIRGIN UK V2061 US CBS   34153
CARLTON BARRETT   D   (A          (B) EQUAL RIGHTS             1978 VIRGIN UK V2081 US CBS   34670
ASTON BARRETT     B   (A          (C) BUSH DOCTOR              1978 ROLLING STONES   CUN 39109
ROBBIE SHAKESPEARE B  (ABD        (D) MYSTIC MAN               1979 ROLLING STONES   CUN 39110
TYRONE DOWNEY     K   (A
RITA MARLEY       V   (A   JUDY MOWATT      V   (A   BUNNY WAILER     V   (AB  AL ANDERSON   G  (AB
DONALD KINSEY     G   (A   ROBBIE LEE       HCA (A   RAS LEE          HCA (A   EARL LINDO       (B
MIKEY CHUNG       K G (D   SLY DUNBAR       D   (BD  ROBBIE LYN       K   (D   YVONNE LEWIS   V  (D
KEITH STERLING    PNO (D   STICKY           PERC (D   ED ELIZALDE      G   (D   SAMMY FIGUEROA CONGA(D
SKULLY            D   (D   ED WALSH         SYN (D   GEORGE YOUNG     WIND(D   LOU MARINI     WIND(D
HOWARD JOHNSON    SAX (D   BARRY ROGERS     TROM (D   MIKE LAWRENCE    TPT (D   TAMLINS        V  (D
GWEN GUTHRIE      V   (D   BRENDA WHITE     V   (D   YVONNE LEWIS     V   (D
```

T115
TOTO
```
DAVID PAICH       K   (AB        (A) TOTO                      1978 CBS    US 35317          UK 83148
DAVID HUNGATE     B   (AB        (B) HYDRA                     1979 CBS                       UK 83900
JEFF PORCARO      D   (AB        (C) TURN BACK                 1980 CBS    US 36813          UK 84609
JOE PORCARO       PERC (C
BOBBY KIMBALL     V   (AB   STEVE PORCARO     K   (AB  STEVE LUKATHER   G   (AB
```

TOUCH

DON TULLUCCI	K V (A	(A) TOUCH	1969 DERAM		UK	SML 1033	
JOHN BORDONARO	PERC V(A						
JOEY NEWMAN	G V (A	BRUCE HAUSER	B V (A	JEFF HAWKES	V (A		

TOUCH

CRAIG BROOKS	G V (A	(A) TOUCH	1980 ATCO	US	SD 38123	
MARK MANGOLD	K V (A					
DOUG HOWARD	B V (A	GLENN KITHCART	D (A			

TOURISTS

ANNIE LENNOX	V K FLT(ABC	(A) TOURISTS	1979 LOGO	UK		1018
PETE COOMBES	G V (ABC	(B) REALITY EFFECT	1979 LOGO	UK		1019
DAVE STEWART	G (ABC	(C) LUMINOUS BASEMENT	1980 RCA	RCALP5001 +	PL	25323
EDDY CHIN	B (ABC					
JIM TOOMEY	D (ABC					

ALLEN TOUSSAINT

ALLEN TOUSSAINT	K G HCA(ALL	(A) WILD SOUNDS OF NEW ORLEANS	1958 RCA VICTOR	US		1767
VINCENT TOUSSAINT	G (C	(B) TOUSSAINT	1971 TIFFANY US014	WAND	WNS 14	
LEO NOCENTELLI	G (C	(B) TOUSSAINT	1977 DJM	UK	DJF 22070	
GEORGE PORTER	B (C	(C) LIFE LOVE & FAITH	1972 REPRISE US 2062	UK	K44202	
GEORGE PLUMMER	G (C	(D) SOUTHERN NIGHTS	1975 REPRISE US 2186	UK	K54021	
WALTER PAYTON	B (C	(E) MOTION	1978 WB	US 3142	UK	K56473
JOSEPH MODELISTE	D (C					

JOE LAMBERT	D (C	ALFRED ROBERTS	CONGA(C	SQUIRREL	CONGA(C	GARY BROWN	SAX (C
ALVIN THOMAS	SAX (C	RED TYLER	SAX (C	CLYDE KERR	TPT (BC	FRANCIS ROUSSELLE	TPT(C
JEFF PORCARO	D (E	POPS POPWELL	B (E	CHUCK RAINEY	B (E	LARRY CARLTON	G (E
VICTOR FELDMAN	PERC (E	RICHARD TEE	K (E	PAULINHO DA COSTA	PERC (E	ETTA JAMES	V (E
BONNIE RAITT	V (E	DR JOHN	G K (B	TERRY KELLMAN	G (B	FRED STAEHLE	D (B
EDDIE HOHNER	B (B	ED GREENE	D (B	EARL TURBINTON	SAX (B	FRED KEMP	SAX(B
MERRY CLAYTON	V (B	VANETTA FIELDS	V (B				

TOWER OF POWER

HUBERT TUBBS	V (EG	(A) EAST BAY GREASE	1970 SAN FRANCISO	US	SD204	
LENNY PICKETT	SAX (QBCDEGHJ	(B) BUMP CITY	1972 WB	UK K46167	US	2616
GREG ADAMS	HRNS (ABCDEGHJ	(C) TOWER OF POWER	1974 WB	UK K46223	US	2681
MIC GILLETTE	HRNS (ABCDEGHJ	(D) BACK IN OAKLAND	1974 WB	UK K46282	US	2749
STEVE KUPKA	SAX (CEGHJ	(E) IN THE SLOT	1975 WB	UK K56155	US	2880
BRUCE CONTE	G V (CEGHJ	(F) URBAN RENEWAL	1975 WB	UK K56093	US	2834
CHESTER THOMPSON	K (CEGHJ	(G) LIVE & LIVING COLOUR	1976 WB	UK K56221	US	2924
FRANCIS PRESTIA	B (ABCCFGH	(H) AINT NOTHIN' STOPPIN' US NOW	1976 CBS	UK 81572	US	34302
DAVID GARIBALDI	D (CFGABD	(J) WE CAME TO PLAY	1978 CBS	UK 82239	US	34906
LENNY WILLIAMS	V (C					

BRENT BYARS	(C	RICK STEVENS	V (A	WILLIE FULTON	G V (A	JAY SPELL	PNO (C
BRUCE STEINBERG	HCA (C	BOOTCHE ANDERSON	V (E	MARILYN SCOTT	V (E	PEPPER WATKINS	V (E
DAVID BARTLETT	V (E	RON BECK	V D (EHJ	FRANK BINER	V (E	ROGER RIFKIND	V (D
EDWARD McGEE	V (H	MICHAEL JEFFRIES	B (J	VICTOR CONTE	B (J	SKIP MESQUITE	V WIND(A

COLIN TOWNS

COLIN TOWNS	(A	(A) FULL CIRCLE	1978 VIRGIN	UK	V 2093

PETE TOWNSHEND

PETE TOWNSHEND	G V (AB	(A) WHO CAME FIRST	1972 TRACK UK 2408 210 US MCA	2026
RONNIE LANE	G V (A	(B) EMPTY GLASS	1980 ATCO UK K 50699	
BILLIE NICHOLLS	G V (A			
CALEB QUAYE	G (A			

TOWNSHEND LANE

PETE TOWNSHEND	G (A	(A) ROUGH MIX	1977 POLYDOR UK 2442 147 US MCA 2295	
RONNIE LANE	B G V(A			

ERIC CLAPTON	G (A	CHARLIE WATTS	D (A	RABBIT BUNDRICK	K (A	HENRY SPINETTI	D (A
PETER HOPE EVANS	HCA (A	GRAHAM LYLE	G (A	BENNY GALLAGHER	ACC (A	CHARLIE HART	VLN (A
DAVE MARKEE	B (A	MEL COLLINS	SAX (A	IAN STEWART	PNO (A	JULIAN DIGGLE	PERC (A
TONY GILBERT	(A	CHARLES VORZANGER	VLN (A	STEVE SHINGLES	VLA (A	CHRIS GREEN	CELLO(A
BOZ BURRELL	B (A	JOHN ENTWISTLE	HRNS V(A	BILLY NICHOLLS	V (A	CHRIS LAURENCE	B (A

TOY

ALBERT WOODS	K K V(A	(A) BAD NIGHT	1980 LOGO	UK	MOGO 4010
THES VAN HOMELRYK	G V (A				
RENATO MARCIANO	B (A	PAUL ILLE	D (A		

TOYAH

TOYAH WILCOX	V (ABCD	(A) SHEEP FARMING IN BARNET	1979 SAFARI		SAP1
PETE BUSH	K (AC	(B) TOYAH TOYAH TOYAH	1980 SAFARI		LIVE2
MARK HENRY	B (A	(C) BLUE MEANING	1980 SAFARI		IEYA666
JOEL BOGEB	G (AC	(D) FOUR FROM TOYAH(EP)	1981 SAFARI		TOY1
STEVE BRAY	D (AC				
CHARLES FRANCIS	B (C				

TRACE

RICK VAN DER LINDEN	K (AB	(A) TRACE	1974 VERTIGO	UK	6360 852
JAAP VAN EIK	G (AB	(B) BIRDS	1975 VERTIGO	UK	6413 080
PIERRE VANDER LINDEN	D (B				
IAN MOSLEY	D (B	DARRYL WAY	VLN (B		

TRACTOR

JIM MILNE	G V B(A	(A) TRACTOR	1972 DANDELION	UK	2310 217
STEVE CLAYTON	B K D FLT(A				
DAVE ADDISON	B (				

TRADER HORNE

JUDY DYBLE	K V (A	(A) MORNING WAY	1970 DAWN	UK	DNLS3004
JACKIE McAULEY	K G V(A1	(1) 1970 SUMMER			
RAY ELLIOT	WIND (A				
SAFFRON SUMMERFIELD	G V(1	ANDY WHITE	D (A	JOHN GODFREY	B (A

TRADITION

	(A) ALTERNATIVE ROUTES	1978 RCA	UK	PL25186
	( ) MOVIN' ON	1978 RCA	UK	PL25156
	( ) TELL YOUR FRIENDS	1978 RCA	UK	PL25169

T127   TRAFFIC

```
STEVE WINWOOD    G K V(ALL    (A) Mr FANTASY                      1967 ISLAND UK ILPS 9061 US UA  6651
JIM CAPALDI      D V K(ALL    (B) TRAFFIC                         1968 ISLANDUK ILPS 9081 US UA  6670
CHRIS WOOD       WIND (ALL    (C) LAST EXIT                       1969 ISLAND UK ILPS 9097 US UA  6702
DAVE MASON       G V  (ABCE   (D) JOHN BARLEYCORN MUST DIE        1970 ISLAND UK ILPS 9116 US UA  5504
RICK GRECH       B    (E      (E) WELCOME TO THE CANTEEN          1971 ISLAND UK ILPS 9166 US UA  5550
REBOP BAAH       CONGA(EGH    (F) LOW SPARK OF HIGH HEELED BOY    1971 ISLAND UK ILPS 9180 US      9306
JIM GORDON       D    (E      (G) SHOOT OUT AT THE FANTASY FACTORY 1973 ISLAND UK ILPS 9224
DAVE HOOD        B    (GH     (H) ON THE ROAD                     1974 ISLAND UK ILSD 2
ROGER HAWKINS    D    (GH     (J) WHEN THE EAGLE FLIES            1974 ISLAND UK ILPS 9273
ROSKO GEE        B    (J      (J) WHEN THE EAGLE FLIES            1974 ASYLUM        US  7E1020
BARRY BECKETT    K    (H

                             ( ) LIVE  (NOT RELEASED)            1970 ISLAND UK ILPS 9142
                             ( ) BEST OF                         1969 ISLAND UK ILPS 9112 US UA  5500
                             ( ) HEAVY TRAFFIC                   1975               US UA  4211
                             ( ) MORE HEAVY TRAFFIC              1975               US UA LA526
                             (EP) HOLE IN MY SHOE                1978 ISLAND UK  I EP 7
```

T128   TRAMLINE

```
JOHN McCOY       V HCA(A      (A) SOMEWHERE DOWN THE LINE         1968 ISLAND        UK   ILPS 9088
TERRY SIDGWICK   B V  (A      (B) MOVES OF VEGETABLE CENTURIES    1969 ISLAND        UK   ILPS 9095
TERRY POPPLE     D    (A
MICK MOODY       G    (A
```

T130   TRAMP

```
MICK FLEETWOOD   D    (B      (A) TRAMP                           1973 SPARK         UK   SRLM 2001
DANNY KIRWAN     G    (B      (B) PUT A RECORD ON                 1974 SPARK         UK   SRLP 112
DAVE BROOKS      SAX  (B
DAVE KELLY       V    (B      JO ANN KELLY   V   (B  BOB BRUNNING  B(B  BOB HALL      K (B
IAN MORTON       PERC (B
```

T131   TRANQUILITY

```
TONY LUKYN       K V  (A      (A) TRANQUILITY                     1972 EPIC  UK 64729      US  7801
KEVIN McCARTHY   G    (A      (B) SILVER                          197  EPIC                US  31989
TERRY SHADDICK   G V  (A
BERNARD HAGLEY   G    (A      BERKELEY WRIGHT   G V  (A  PAUL FRANCIS   D  (A
```

T132   TRANSMITTERS

```
CHRIS GEORGE     LYRIC(A      (A) 24 HOURS                        1978 EBONY         UK   EB1002
MIKEL LEE        G    (A      (B) AND WE CALL THAT LEISURE TIME   1981 HEARTBEAT     UK   HB4
SAM DODSON       B G K(AB
JIM CHASE        D    (AB     VINCE CUTLIFFE   G   (A  JOHN QUINN     V (A  DAVE BABY    SAX (B
SID WEELS        B    (B      JULIAN TREASURE  D   (B  ROB CHAPMAN    V K(B
```

T133   TRAPEZE

```
GLENN HUGHES     B    (BCF    (A) TRAPEZE                         1970 THRESHOLD     UK   THS 2
MEL GALLEY       G    (BCEFG  (B) MEDUSA                          1970 THRESHOLD     UK   THS 4
DAVE HOLLAND     D    (BCEFG  (C) YOU ARE THE MUSIC               1972 THRESHOLD     UK   THS 8
PETE WRIGHT      B    (EFG    (D) FINAL SWING                     1974 THRESHOLD     UK   THS11
ROB KENDRICK     G    (EF     (E) HOT WIRE                        1974 WB   US 2828  UK   K56064
PETE GALBY       G V  (G      (F) TRAPEZE                         1975 WB   US       UK   K56165
B J COLE         STEEL(C      (G) HOLD ON/RUNNING                 1978 AURA              AUL 708
ROD ARGENT       K    (C
TERRY ROWLEY G K FLT  (EG     JOHN JONES   V TPT   (   KIRK DUNCAN   K   (C  JOHN OGDEN  PERC (CE
FRANK RICOTTI    PERC (C      JIMMY HASTINGS  SAX  (C  KENNY COLE    V   (E  MISTY BROWNING  V(E
CHRIS MERCER     SAX  (E
```

T134   HAPPY & ARTIE TRAUM

```
HAPPY TRAUM      G    (ABCDEF (A) HAPPY & ARTIE TRAUM             1969 CAPITOL            ST 586
ARTIE TRAUM      G    (ABCFDG (B) DOUBLEBACK                      1971 CAPITOL            ST 799
PATRICK ALGER    MAND (E      (C) MUD ACRES                       1972 ROUNDER US 3001 UK MATCHBOX 239
RICK DANKO       B    (       (D) HARD TIMES IN THE COUNTRY       1975 ROUNDER US 3007
ERIC KAZ              (       (E) RELAX YOUR MIND                 1976 KICKING MULE US 110 UK SNKF 111
TRACY NELSON         (       (F) AMERICAN STRANGER                1978 KICKING MULE       UK SNKF 142
AMOS GARRETT     G    (       (G) LIFE ON EARTH                   1974 ROUNDER    US 3014
MARIA MULDAUR    V    (
BILL KEITH       STEEL(
```

T135   PAT TRAVERS

```
PAT TRAVERS      G V K(ALL    (A) PAT TRAVERS                     1976 POLYDOR US 1 6079  UK 2383 395
PETER MARS COWLING B(ABCDE    (B) MAKIN' MAGIC                    1977 POLYDOR US 1 6103  UK 2383 436
NICKO McBRAIN    D    (C      (C) PUTTIN' IT STRAIGHT             1977 POLYDOR US 1 6121  UK 2383 471
TONY CAREY       K    (C      (D) HEAT IN THE STREET              1979 POLYDOR US 1 6170  UK POLD5005
SUZIE McKINLEY   V    (C      (E) GO FOR WHAT YOU KNOW(LIVE)      1979 POLYDOR           UK POLS1011
BERT HERMISTON   SAX  (C      (F) CRASH & BURN                   1980 POLYDOR           UK POLS1017
SCOTT GORHAM     G    (C
ROY DYKE         D    (A      TOMMY ALDRIDGE   D   (D  PAT THRALL   G SYN (DF
```

T136   JACK TRAYLOR & STEELWIND

```
JACK TRAYLOR     G V  (A      (A) CHILD OF NATURE                 1973 GRUNT             FTR 0194
CRAIG CHAQUICO   G    (A
DANNY VIRDIER    B V  (A      SKIP MORAIRTY    G V (A  DIANA HARRIS   K V (A  KENT MIDDLETON HCA PERC(A
BILL LAUDNER     V    (A      RICK QUINTENAL   V   (A  DAVID FREIBERG  K  (A
```

T137   TREES

```
CELIA HUMPHRIS   K V  (AB1    (A) THE GARDEN OF JANE DELAWNEY     1970 CBS               63837
BIAS BOSHELL     G V B(AB     (B) ON THE SHORE                    1970 CBS               64168
BARRY CLARKE     G    (AB1    (1) 1972
DAVID COSTA      G    (AB1
UNWIN BROWN      D V  (AB     TONY COX   B   (B  MICHAEL JEFFERIES HARP (B  BARRY LYONS   B  (1
ALUN EDEN        D    (1      CHUCK FLEMING  VLN (1
```

T137A   TREMBLERS

```
PETER NOONE   V G K B (A      (A) TWICE NIGHTLY                   1980 EPIC UK 84448 US JOHNSTON 36532
GREGG INHOFER    K G V(A
ROBERT WILLIAMS  D V  (A      GEO CONNER   G V  (A  MARK BROWNE    B   (A  MIKE CAMPBELL      (A
STAN LYNCH            (A      RON BLAIR         (A  JOHN FARRAR        (A  STEPHEN HAGUE      (A
STEVE ALLEN           (A      NIGEL OLSSON      (A  BILL PITCOCK       (A  DARYL DRAGON       (A
```

BRIAN POOLE	V	(ABCHP	(A) BIG HITS OF 1962	1963 ACE OF CLUBS	UK	ACL 1146
RICK WESTWOOD	G V	(	(B) TWIST & SHOUT	1963 DECCA	UK	LK 4550
ALAN BLAKELY	G V	(	(C) IT'S ABOUT TIME	1965 DECCA	UK	LK 4685
DAVE MUNDEN	D V	(	(D) HERE COME THE TREMELOES	1967 CBS	UK	63017
LEN 'CHIP'HAWKES	B V	(	(E) HERE COMES MY BABY	1967 CBS	US	26310
AARON WOOLLEY		(	(F) EVEN THE BAD TIMES ARE GOOD	1967 CBS	US	26326
BOB BENHAM		(	(G) SUDDENLY YOU LOVE ME	1967 CBS US 26363	UK	63138
			(H) 58/68 WORLD EXPLOSION	1968 CBS US 26388		
			(J) LIVE IN CABARET	1969 CBS	UK	63547
			(K) MASTER	1970 CBS	UK	64242
			(L) GREATEST HITS	1970 CBS	UK	64206
			(M) REACH OUT FOR THE TREMELOES	1973 EMBASSY	UK	31031
			(N) SHINER	1974 DJM UK DJLP 5441 +		DJF 20441
			(O) DON'T LET THE MUSIC DIE	1976 DJM	UK	DJF 20447
			(P) REMEMBERING	1977 DECCA	UK	REM 5

TRETTIORIGA KRUGET   T138A

STEFAN FREDIN		(	(A) KRIGSSANG	1975 CBS	UK	80900
DAG LUNDQUIST		(				
ROBERT ZIMA		(	CHRISTER AKERBERG	(		

TRICKSTER   T138B

PHIL BATES	G V	(AB	(A) FIND THE LADY	1977 JET UAS 30132	RI	JETLP 206
COLIN HEWINSON	K SYN	(AB	(B) BACK TO ZERO	1979 JET		JETLP 221
MIKE SHEPPARD	G B	V(A				
PAUL ELLIOTT	D PERC	(AB MICHAEL GROTH G V (B JOHN FINCHAM B V (B				

TRIGGER   T139

JIMMY DUGGAN		(A	(A) TRIGGER	1978 CASABLANCA	UK	NBLP 7092
RITCHIE HOUSE		(A				
TOM NIGRA		(A	DEREK REMINGTON (A			

TRILLION   T139A

RON ANAMAN	B V	(B	(A) TRILLION	1978 EPIC	US	35460
PAT LEONARD	K	(B	(B) CLEAR APPROACH	1980 CBS	US	36206
FRANK BARBALACE	G V	(B				
THOM GRIFFIN	G V	(B BILL WILKINS D PERC(B				

TRINITY   T139B

			(A) UPTOWN GIRL	1977 MAGNUM	DEAD 1003
			(B) ROCK IN THE GHETTO	1979 TROJAN	TRLS 170

TRINITY RIVER BOYS   T140

MICHAEL MURPHEY	G	(A	(A) TRINITY RIVER BOYS	1964 PROSPECTOR NOT RELEASED
MICHAEL NESMITH	G V	(A		
JOHN RAINES	D	(A JOHN LONDON B (A		

TRIO   T141

JOHN SURMAN	SAX	(ABC	(A) THE TRIO	1970 DAWN	UK	DNLS 3006
BARRE PHILLIPS	B	(ABC	(B) CONFLAGRATION	1971 DAWN	UK	DNLS 3022
STU MARTIN	D	(ABC	(C) LIVE AT WOODSTOCK TOWN HALL	1976 DAWN	UK	DNLS 3072

TRITONUS   T141A

PETER K SEILER	K	(A	(A) TRITONUS	1975 BASF	GERM	17 223841
RONALD J D BRAND	B V	G(A				
CHARLIE JOST	D PERC	(A				

TRIUMPH   T142

RIK EMMET	G	(ABC	(A)ROCK'N'ROLL MACHINE	1979 RCA UK PL 12982		APLI 2982
G L MOORE	D	(ABC	(B)JUST A GAME	1979 RCA UK PL 13224		AFLI 3224
MIKE LEVINE	B	(ABC	(C) PROGRESSIONS OF POWER	1980 RCA UK PL 13524		AFLI 3524

TRIUMVIRAT   T143

HELMUT KOELLEN	B G V(BA		(A) MEDITERRANEAN TALES	1972 HARVEST EURO IC 062 29441		
CURT CRESS	D	(E	(B) ILLUSION ON A DOUBLE DIMPLE	1974 HARVEST US 11311 UK		SHSP 4030
BARRY PALMER	V	(DE	(B) ILLUSION ON A DOUBLE DIMPLE	1977 EMI EURO IC 062 29441		
DIETER PETEREIT	B	(E	(C) SPARTACUS	1975 HARVEST US 11392 UK		SHSP 4048
HANS JUERGEN FRITZ	K V	(ABCDE	(D) OLD LOVES DIE HARD	1976 CAPITOL 062 29622		
HANS PAPE	B V	(AB	(E) POMPEII	1977 CAPITOL US 11697 EURO		LC1305
HANS BATHELT	D	(ABCD	(F) A LA CARTE	1978 CAPITOLUS 11862		
DICK FRANGENBERG	B	(D				
ULLA WIESNER	V	(B HANNA DOHTISCH V (B PETER CADERA V (B BRIGITTE THOMAS V (B				

TROGGS   T144

REG PRESLEY	V	(1	FROM NOWHERE	1966 FONTANA	UK	ST 5355
CHRIS BRITTON	G	(1	TROGGLODYNAMITE	1966 PAGE ONE	UK	POL 001
PETE STAPLES	B	(1	WILD THING	1966 ATCO	US	SD 33193
RONNIE BOND	D	(1	WILD THING	1966 FONTANA		27556
TONY MURRAY	B	(	GIVE IT TO ME	1966 FONTANA		85001
COLIN FLETCHER	G	(	CELLOPHANE	1967 PAGE ONE		PGL 003
			BEST OF VOL 1	1967 PAGE ONE		FPR 001
(1) 1966			BEST OF VOL 2	1967 PAGE ONE		FOR 002
			LOVE IS ALL AROUND	1968 FONTANA		SRF 67576
			MIXED BAG	1968 PAGE ONE		POLS 012
			HIP HIP HOORAY	1968 HANSA	GERM	78595
			THE TOP OF THE TROGGS	1968 HANSA	GERM	77817
			TROGGLOMANIA	1969 PAGE ONE		POS 602
			CONTRAST	1970 SILVERLINE		DJSL 009
			THE TROGGS	1975 PENNYFARTHING	UK	PEN 543
			THE TROGGS	1976 PYE	US	12112
			THE TROGG TAPES	1976 PENNYFARTHING	UK	PELS 551
			A GIRL LIKE YOU	1975 DJM		DJML26047
			THE ORIGINAL TROGG TAPES	1976 DJM		DJM 44314
			THE ORIGINAL TROGG TAPES	1976 PRIVATE STOCK	US	2008
			POP CHRONIK	19 HANSA	GERM	87574
			VINTAGE YEARS	1976 SIRE		3714 2

T145 DOMENIC TROIANO

DOMENIC TROIANO	G V	(ALL	(A) DOMENIC TROIANO					1972 MERCURY US SRM1 639	UK 6338105
PENTI GLEN	D	(A	(B) TRICKY					1973 MERCURY US SRM1 670	
HUGH SULLIVAN	K	(A	(C) BURNING AT THE STAKE					1977 CAPITOL	11665
PRAKASH JOHN	B	(A	(D) JOKES ON ME					197 CAPITOL	11772
WILLIAM SMITH	K V	(AB	(E) FRET FEVER					1979 CAPITOL GERM 064 85893 US	11932
ROY KENNER	PERC V	(ABE							
TESSE CALDERONE	V	(AB	SHAWN JACKSON	V	(AB	BUNK GARDNER	SAX	(A	BUZZ GARDNER	TPT (A
JAY CANTRELLI	SAX	(A	LONNIE SHETTER	CLAR	(A	PAUL DELONG	D	(E	DAVE TYSON	K V (E
BOB WILSON	B V	(E	KEN RICE	D	(B	WILLIE WEEKS	B	(B	MONT STARK	SYN (B
GAYLE LEVANT	HARP	(B	PAT HOLLOWAY	V	(B	JOHN WEIDER	VLN	(B	ERNIE WATTS	SAX (B
MARION CHILDERS	TPT	(B	DOUG RICHARDSON	SAX	(B	TOM SCOTT	TPT	(B	WILLIAM GREEN	WIND(B
JOHN KELSO	SAX	(B	RED RHODES	STEEL	(A					

T146 TROOPER

RAY McGUIRE	V HCA(ABCD	(A) TROOPER			1976 EPIC UK 81618	US MCA	2149
BRIAN SMITH	G V	(ABCD	(B) TWO FOR THE SHOW		1977	US MCA	2214
HARRY KALENSKY	B V	(ABCD	(C) KNOCK 'EM DEAD KID		1977 EPIC UK 82296		
TOMMY STEWART	D V	(ABCD	(D) FLYING COLOURS		1979 MCA UK MCF3039	US MCA	2275
RANDY BACHMAN	G	(A	(E) THICK AS THIEVES		198 MCA	US	2377

T147 JOHN TROPEA

JOHN TROPEA	G V SYN(ALL	(A) JOHN TROPEA			1976 JAYBOY JSL7	MARLIN	2200
WILL LEE	B V	(ABC	(B) SHORT TRIP TO SPACE		1977 TK		14061
RICK MAROTTA	D	(ABC	(C) TO TOUCH YOU AGAIN		1979 MARLIN US 2222 +TK UK		83355
EARL CHAPIN	HRNS (B						
DON GROLNICK	K	(ABC	LEON PENDARVIS	ORG	(BC	RUBENS BASSINI	PERC (ABC DAVE TAYLOR TROM (AB
RALPH MACDONALD	PERC	(B	JEFF KING	SAX	(B	RON CARTALEMI	V (B RANDY BRECKER (ABC
JEFF KAWALEK	V	(B	MICHAEL BRECKER	WIND	(ABC	CHARLES BLACKWELL	V (B DAVID SPINOZZA G (B
DUNCAN CLEARY	V	(B	MARGARET ROSS	HARP	(B	BRIAN DRAKE	V (B RICHARD DAVIS B (B
BRUCE GOLDBERG	V	(B	MIKE MAINIERI	VIBES	(B	BILL GUERRA	V (B ROMEO PENQUE WIND(B
STEVE GADD	D	(AB	RON JANNELLI	WIND	(B	LANI GROVES	V (B GEORGE YOUNG HRNS(ABC
JIM BUFFINGTON	HRNS	(B	LEW DEL GATTO	WIND	(ABC	LOU MARINI	WIND (BC EUMIR DEODATO K (A
ELLEN SEELING	TPT	(B	TONY PRICE	HRNS	(BC	JOHN GATCHELL	HRNS (A ALAN RUBIN HRNS (AC
ALLEN SCHWARZBERG	D	(A	DON PAYNE	B	(A	KENNY ASCHER	K (A RON TROPEA PERC(AC
NICK REMO	PERC	(A	C CONRAD		(A	DAVE SANBORN	SAX (AC BOB MINTZER FLT (A
GEORGE OPALISKY	WIND	(A	KEN BERGER	WIND	(A	JEANNIE FINEBERG	SAX (B SAM BURTIS TROM(ABC
STEVE JORDAN	D	(C	PAUL SCHAEFFER	K	(C	RICHARD TEE	K (C JON FADDIS WIND(C
LUTHER VANDROSS	V	(C	DIVA GRAY	V	(C	JOCELYN SHAW	V (C JIM MAELEN PERC(C
BARRY ROGERS	HRNS	(C	DAVE TAYLOR	TROM	(C	STRING SECTION	(ABC

T148 ROBIN TROWER

ROBIN TROWER	G	(ALL	(A) TWICE REMOVED FROM YESTERDAY	1973 CHRYSALIS	CHR 1039
JIMMY DEWAR	B V	(ABCDEFGH	(B) BRIDGE OF SIGHS	1974 CHRYSALIS	CHR 1057
REG ISADORE	D	(AB	(C) FOR EARTH BELOW	1975 CHRYSALIS	CHR 1073
BILL LORDAN	D	(CDEFGHJ	(D) LIVE	1975 CHRYSALIS	CHR 1089
RUSTY ALLEN	B	(FG	(E) LONG MISTY DAYS	1976 CHRYSALIS	CHR 1107
PAULINHO DA COSTA	PERC	(G	(F) CITY DREAMS	1977 CHRYSALIS	CHR 1148
JACK BRUCE	B	(J	(G) CARAVAN TO MIDNIGHT	1978 CHRYSALIS	CHR 1189
			(H) VICTIM OF FURY	1980 CHRYSALIS	CHR 1215
			(J) BRUCE,LORDAN, TROWER B L·T	1981 CHRYSALIS	

T149 DORIS TROY

DORIS TROY	V	(ALL	(A) DORIS TROY			1970 APPLE US ST3371	UK SAPCOR 13	
WINSTON DELANDRO	G	(B	(B) STRETCHING OUT			1974 POLYDOR	PLEO 12	
KEN ELLIOT	SYN	(B	(C) RAINBOW TESTAMENT			19 POLYDOR	2956 001	
HUX BROWN	G	(B	(D) JUST ONE LOOK			19 ATLANTIC UK 2464 001 US	8088	
JACKIE JACKSON	B	(B						
ROSETTA HIGHTOWER	V	(B	PHIL CHEN	B	(B	ROY DAVIES	SYN (B RAD BRYAN	G (B
WINSTON WRIGHT	K	(B	JOANNE WILLIAMS	V	(B	GLADSTONE ANDERSON	V (B WINSTON GRENNAN	V (B
DORIS PAYNE	V	(B						

T149A ROGER TROY

ROGER TROY		(A	(A) ROGER TROY	1976 RCA US	APLI 1910

T150 WILLIAM TRUCKAWAY

WILLIAM TRUCKAWAY	V G K(A	(A) BREAKAWAY				1976 REPRISE UK			K44165
ED BOGAS	VLN MAND VIBES(A								
BOBBY CASTRO	PERC	(A	RUSSELL DASHIELL	G	(A	TERRY DOLAN	G (A BILL DOUGLAS	B (A
JOHN NONZIATO	CONG V(A		BUDDY EMMONS	STEEL(A		RICHARD GREENE	VLN (A LARRY HANKS	JEWSHARP(A
DAVID HAYES	B	(A	DOUG KILMER	B	(A	WALT KOKEN	BANJO FDL (A FRANK MESTROPASQUA	V (A
DOC STORCH		(A	JOHN WATSON	V	(A	CHARLES LLOYD	FLT (A NORM MAYELL	D V (A
DALLAS WILLIAMS	V PERC(A		STOVALL SISTERS	V	(A	ARCELLO GARCIA	V (A VICTOR QUINONES	V (A
JOHN RODRIGUEZ	V	(A						

T151 TRUK

		(A) TRUK TRACKS	1971 CBS UK	64367

T152 TUBES

FEE WAYBILL	V	(ALL	(A) THE TUBES	1975 A&M US SP 4534 UK	AMLH64534
BILL SPOONER	G	(ALL	(B) YOUNG & RICH	1976 A&M US SP 4580 UK	AMLH64580
VINCE WELNICK	K	(ABCDE	(C) NOW	1977 A&M US SP 4632 UK	AMLH64632
RICK ANDERSON	B	(ABCDE	(D) WHAT DO YOU WANT FROM LIVE	1978 A&M US SP 6003 UK	AMLH68460
MICHAEL COTTEN	SYN	(ABCDE	(E) REMOTE CONTROL	1979 A&M UK	AMLH64751
ROGER STEEN	G	(ABCDE	(F) TUBES	1981 CAPITOL	26285
PRAIRIE PRINCE	D	(ABCDE RE STYLES V DANCE (ACDE MINGO LEWIS	PERC (CDE	

T153 TUBEWAY ARMY

GARY NUMAN	V K G(AB	( ) TUBEWAY ARMY	1979 BEGGARS BANQUET UK	BEGA4
PAUL GARDINER	B	(A	(A) REPLICAS	1979 BEGGARS BANQUET UK	BEGA7
JESS LIDYARD	D	(A	(B) THAT'S TOO BAD(EP)	1979 BEGGARS BANQUET UK	BACK2

T154 TOMMY TUCKER

TOMMY TUCKER	V K D(A	(A) MOTHER TUCKER			1977 RED LIGHTNING UK		RL 022
WELDON DEAN YOUNG	G	(A						
BRENDA JONES	B	(A	JOHNNY WILLIAMS	D	(A	EDDIE WILLIAMS	TPT (A MICKEY BAKER	G (A
SCOTT ALLEN	B	(A	GENE ROBERTS	PNO	(A	DONNY HATHAWAY	K (A PAUL WILLIAMS	SAX (A
BUDDY LEWIS	SAX	(A	DONNIE FITZ	V	(A	ROBERT BANKS	K (A GENE JOHNSON	K (A
GREG FITZ	K	(A	PAZANT BROTHERS	HRNS	(A	LEO GATEWOOD	D (A LARRY HOLLOWAY	D (A

TUCKY BUZZARD
T155

TERRY TAYLOR	G	(ABCD	(A) WARM SLASH		1970 CAPITOL	US	
DAVE BROWN	B	(ABCD	(B) COMING ON AGAIN		1971 CAPITOL	US	
JIM HENDERSON	V	(ABCD	(C) ALRIGHT ON THE NIGHT		1973 PURPLE UK TPSA 7510 BASF 292367		
NICK GRAHAM	K	(AB	(D) BUZZARD		1973 PURPLE UK TPSA 7512		
PAUL FRANCIS	D	(AB					

CHRIS JOHNSON D (CD RON TAYLOR G (C PHIL TALBOT G (D PAUL KENDRICK G V (CD
TONY ASHTON K (D RICKY DODD SAX (D JEFF WORKMAN PNO (C BILL WYMAN PNO (D
NOEL NORRIS TPT (D PHIL CORDELL PNO (C JOHN LEE TROM (D DON WELLER HRNS(C

TONY TUFF
T155A

SANTA	D	(A	(A) TONY TUFF	1980 GROVE MUSIC	UK	ILPS9619
CLINTON FERRON	B	(A				
ALRICK FORBES	G V	(A	ALBERT GRIFFITHS G (A ANSEL COLLINS K (A SKULLY PERC(A			
MICHAEL PROPHET	V	(A	YABBY U V (A			

TUFF DARTS
T156

JEFF SALEN	G	(A	(A) TUFF DARTS	1978 SIRE	SRK 6048	
JOHN DI SALVO	B	(A				
BOB BUTANI	G	(A	JAMES MORRISON D (ROBERT GORDON V (KEVIN COLNEY V (			
TOMMY FRENZY	V	(A	JOHN MORELLI D (A JOHN CRISCIONE V (A RONALD ARDITO V (			
ART LAMONICA	V	(A	GEORGE YOUNG SAX (A LEW DELGATTO SAX (A RALPH SCHUCKETT PNO(A			
LANCE QUINN	G	(A	ERIC WEISSBERG STEEL(A IAN HUNTER K (A BOB CLEARMOUNTAIN B (A			

TUNDRA
T157

CHRIS STAINTON	K	(A	(A) TUNDRA	1976 DECCA	UK	SKLR5259
GLEN TURNER	B	(A				
HENRY SPINETTI	D	(A	CHARLIE HARRISON B V (A			

GORDON TURNER
T157A

GORDON TURNER		(A	(A) MEDITATION	1969 CHARISMA	UK	CAS 1009

IKE & TINA TURNER
T158

IKE TURNER G V
TINA TURNER V

P P ARNOLD	V		ACID QUEEN (TINA)	1975 UA	US LA495 UK UNS29875		
VANETTA FIELDS	V	(R	AND THE RAELETTES	19 TANGERINE US 15611			
MERRY CLAYTON	V		BAD DREAMS	1973 US	UK UAS29549		
BONNIE BRAMLETT	V		BEST OF	19 BLUE THUMB US			
EDWARD BURKS	TROM	(NP	BLACK ANGEL	1976 MUSIDISC	CV1342		
McKINLEY JOHNSON	TPT	(NP	BLUES ROOTS (IKE)	1972 UA	US 5576 UK UAG29326		
MARY REED	SAX	(N	BLACK MAN SOUL	19 POMPEII	6003		
JACKIE CLARK	G	(NP	COME TOGETHER	1970 LIBERTY	US 7637 UK LBS83350		
SOKO RICHARDSON	D	(NP	THE COUNTRY OF TINA TURNER	19 UA	US 200		
WARREN DAWSON	B	(NP	CUSSIN' CRYIN' AND CARRYING ON	19 POMPEII	6004		
J D REED	SAX	(N	DELILAHS POWER	1977 UA	US 707 UK UAS30040		
DAVID GARLAND		(P	DANCE WITH	19 SUE	US 2003		
CLAUDE WILLIAMS		(P	DYNAMITE	19 SUE	US 2004		
JIMMIE SMITH		(P	DONT PLAY ME CHEAP	19 SUE	US 2005		
ANDDRE CECCARELLI	D	(M	FANTASTIC	1971 SUNSET	UK SLS550205		
BERNIE ARCADIO	K	(M	FEEL GOOD	1972 UA	UK UAS29377		
JAYCEE CHANAVAT	G	(M	FUNKY MULE	1975 DJM	DJSLM2010		
TONY BONFILS	B	(M	FESTIVAL OF LIVE PERFORMANCES	19 KENT	US 538		
MANU ROCHE	PERC	(M	(M) LOVEEXPLOSION	1978 UA	UK UAG30267		
GEORGES RODI	SYN	(M	GREATEST HITS	19 WB	UK K36001		
GEORGE MARGE	OBOE	(M	GREATEST HITS	197 UA	US LA592		
TOM MALONE	TROM	(M	GREAT ALBUM	1974 ALBUM	ALB 148		
WAYNE ANDRE	TROM	(M	HER MAN HIS WOMAN	1970 CAPITOL	VMP 1013		
BARRY ROGERS	TROM	(M	HUNTER	1970 BLUE THUMB US BTS11			
DAVE TAYLOR	TROM	(M	HUNTER	1970 HARVEST	UK SHSP4001		
MICHAEL BRECKER	SAX	(M	IKE & TINA	1975 DJM	DJMD 8006		
LAWRENCE FELDMAN	SAX	(M	IKE & TINA SHOW II	19 TOMATO	US		
GEORGE YOUNG	SAX	(M	IKE & TINA SHOW II	19 WB	US 1568		
LEW DELGATTO	SAX	(M	IKE & TINA SHOW	19 LOMA	5112		
RANDY BRECKER	TPT	(M	IKE TURNER ROCKS THE BLUES(IKE)	19 CROWN	US 367		
JON FADDIS	TPT	(M	ITS GONNA WORK OUT FINE	19 SUE	2007		
ALAN RUBIN	TPT	(M	IKE & TINA TURNER	19 CENCO	US 5031		
PETER BUNETTA	D	(R	IN PERSON	19 MINIT	US 24018		
BILL HAYNES	B	(R	LIVE IN PARIS	19 LIBERTY	LBS83468/9		
RONNY STOCKERT	K	(R	(L) LET ME TOUCH YOUR MIND	1973 UA	UK UAS29423		
MICHAEL BODDICKER	SYN	(R	(N) NUFF SAID	1971 UA	US 5530 UK UAG29256		
AIRTO MOREIRA	PERC	(R	NUTBUSH CITY LIMITS	1973 UA	UK UAS29557		
MAXAYN LEWIS	V	(R	OOH POO PAH DOO	19 HARMONY	US 30400		
STEPHANIE SPRUILL	V	(R	OUTTA SEASON	19 SUNSET	UK SLS550314		
DEBORAH LINDSEY	V	(R	OUTTA SEASON	19 BLUE THUMB US BT5			
JULIA TILLMAN	V	(R	ON STAGE	19 VALIANT	UK VS 118		
DENISE ECHOLS	V	(R	PEACHES	19 POLYDOR	UK 2916 020		
AL CINER	G	(R	PLEASE PLEASE PLEASE	19 KENT	US 550		
KEN MOORE	PNO V(R		QUEEN	1975 SPRINGBOARD US 4033			
W D SMITH	ORG	(R	(R) ROUGH (TINA)	1979 UA	UK UAG30211		
TONY WALTHERS	B	(R	REVUE	1975 NEW WORLD	MW 6006		
MICHAEL STEPHENSON	V	(R	RIVER DEEP & MOUNTAIN HIGH	1975 A&M	US 4178 UK AMLPB013		
ED GREENE	D	(R	RIVER DEEP & MOUNTAIN HIGH	197 PHILLES	118 4011		
DENNIS BELFIELD	B	(R	RIVER DEEP & MOUNTAIN HIGH	197 LONDON	UK SHU 8298		
MARY RUSSELL	V	(R	RIVER DEEP & MOUNTAIN HIGH	1970 MAYFAIR	UK AMLB1021		
RICK KELLIS	SAX	(R	SO FAR	19 MUSIDISC	CV 1262		
BILL OZ	HCA	(R	SOUL OF	19 KENT	US 519		
			SOUL OF	19 SUE	2001		
			SOUL SELLERS(COMP)	19 LIBERTY	UK LBR 1002		
			STRANGE FRUIT	1974 UA	UK UAG29316		
			SWEET RHODE ISLAND RED	1974 UA	UK UAS29681		
			SIXTEEN GREAT PERFORMANCES	1975 ABC US 4014	UK ABCL5123		
			SOULED FROM THE VAULTS	1975 DJM	DJLMD8006		
			SUPER ORIGINAL SESSIONS	1975 MUSIDISC	ALB 169		
			SO FINE	196 LONDON	UK SHU 8370		
			SO FINE	196 POMPEII US 6000			
			TOO HOT TO HOLD	19 SPRINGBOARD 4011			
			VERY BEST OF	1976 UA	UK UAS29948		
			WORLD OF	1973 UA	US 064 UK UAD60043		

(CONTINUED)

[421]

IKE & TINA TURNER

WORKING TOGETHER		1971 LIBERTY	US 7650	UK LBS83455
WHAT YOU HEAR		1971 UA	US 995	UAD60005/6
I'M TORE UP (IKE)		1978 RED LIGHTNIN'		RL0016

T159

NIK TURNER

NIK TURNER	V WIND(AB	(A) XITINTODY	1978 CHARISMA	UK	CDS 4011
STEVE HILLAGE	G (A	(B) PASS OUT (INNER CITY)	19		
TIM BLAKE	SYN (A				
ALAN POWELL	PERC (A	MIQUETTE GIRAUDY SYN (A			

T160

TURNING POINT

JEFF CLYNE	B (AB	(A) CREATURES OF THE NIGHT	1977 GULL	UK	GULP 1022
BRIAN MILLER	K (AB	(B) SILENT PROMISES	1978 GULL	UK	GULP 1027
DAVID T D BALL	SAX (AB				
PEPE LEMER	V (AB	PAUL ROBINSON D (AB			

T161

TURTLES

HOWARD KAYLAN	K V (ALL	(A) IT AINT ME BABY	1965 WHITE WHALE US		WWS 7111
MARK VOLMAN	G V (ALL	(B) HAPPY TOGETHER	1966 WHITE WHALE US		WWS 7114
AL NICHOL	K V B G(ALL	(B) HAPPY TOGETHER	1967 LONDON	UK	HAU 8330
DON MURRAY	D (1	(C) GOLDEN HITS	1967 WHITE WHALE US		WWS 7127
JOHN BARBATA	D (3	(D) YOU BABY	1967 WHITE WHALE US		WWS 7117
JIM PONS	G B V(3	(E) BATTLE OF THE BANDS	1968 WHITE WHALE UK 8904 US WWS7118		
CHUCK PORTZ	B (12	(E) BATTLE OF THE BANDS	1968 LONDON	UK	SHU 8376
JIM TUCKER	G (123	(F) TURTLE SOUP	1969 WHITE WHALE US		WWS 7124
JOHN SEITER	PNO V D (D	(G) MORE GOLDEN HITS	1970 WHITE WHALE US		WWS 7127
(1) 1965		(H) WOODEN HEAD	1970 WHITE WHALE US		WWS 7133
(2) 1965		(J) HAPPY TOGETHER AGAIN(DBL)	1975 PHILIPS		9299 425
(3) 1966		(J) HAPPY TOGETHER AGAIN	1975 SIRE	US	3703

T161A

TUXEDO MOON

STEVE BROWN	K V SAX (A	(A) HALF MUTE	1980 RALPH	US	TX 8004
BLAINE REININGER VLN V K G B(A					
PETER PRINCIPLE B G SYN(A					

T162

TWENTIETH CENTURY STEEL BAND

(A) WARM HEART, COLD STEEL	1975 UA	UK	UAK 29878
(B) YELLOW BIRD IS DEAD	1976 UA	UK	UAS 29980

T162A

TWENTY SIXTY SIX

VEIT MARVOS	K V (A	(A) AND THEN	1972 UA	UK	UAS 29314
STEVE ROBINSON	SYN K(A				
GEFF HARRISON	V (A	GAGEY MROZECK G V (A DIETER BAUER B (A KONSTANTIN BOMMARIUS D(A			

T162B

20/20

STEVE ALLEN	G V (A	(A) 20/20	1980 PORTRAIT	UK	PRT 83898
RON FLYNT	B V (A				
MIKE GALLO	D (A	CHRIS SILAGYI G V SYN(A			

T163

TWICE AS MUCH

DAVE SKINNER	(AB	(A) OWN UP	1966 IMMEDIATE	UK	IMSP 007
ANDREW ROSE	(AB	(B) THAT'S ALL	1968 IMMEDIATE	UK	IMSP 013
NICKY HOPKINS	K (				
JOHN McLAUGHLIN	G (	ANDY WHITE D (JIMMY PAGE G (			

T164

DWIGHT TWILLEY

DWIGHT TWILLEY G K V PERC(ALL	(A) SINCERELY	1976 SHELTER UK ISA5012 US 52001
PHIL SEYMOUR	D B V(ABC	(B) TWILLEY DONT MIND	1977 SHELTER UK ISA5015 US ARISTA4140
BILL PITCOCK IV	B G (AC	(C) TWILLEY	1979 ARISTA US 4214
JOHNNY JOHNSON	B (A		
LEON RUSSELL	PNO B(A	ROGER LINN G B (A JERRY NAIFEH D (AC JIM LEWIS B D (C
JIMMY HASKELL	STR (A	NOAH SHARK PERC (A GREG BLOCH VLN (C

T165

TWINK

TWINK	D V (AB	(A) THINK PINK	1970 POLYDOR	UK	2343 032
		(B) DO IT (EP) WITH THE FAIRIES)	197 CHISWICK	UK	SW 26

T166

THE TWINKLE BROTHERS

RALSTON GRANT	G V (CD	(A) DO YOUR OWN THING	1977 CARIB' GEMS		
ERIC BERNARD B V PNO (CD		(B) LOVE (10")	1978 FRONT LINE	UK	FCL 5001
NORMAN GRANT	D V (CD	(C) PRAISE JAH	1979 FRONT LINE	UK	FL 1041
BONGO ASHER	PERC (CD	(D) COUNTRYMEN	1980 VIRGIN	UK	V 2169
KARL HYATT	V PERC(CD				
DERRICK BROWN	B (C	ASHTON GRANT G (C P HURLOCK G (C MICHAEL DAN PNO (C
ARNOLD BRECKENRIDGE SYN(C		TOMMY McCOOK HRNS (C VIN GORDON HRNS (C RANCHIE B (C
DAVIDSON DUBOIS	G B (D	MICHAEL SMITH D (D TERRY BARHAM G (D

T166A

TWIST

STEVE CORDUNER	D (A	(A) THIS IS YOUR LIFE	1979 POLYDOR	UK	2383 552
WIMS	G V (A				
PETE MARSH	G V (A	ANDY PASK B (A STEVE NAIVE K (A ELVIS COSTELLO V (A
JIMMY EDWARDS	V (A				

T167

CONWAY TWITTY

CONWAY TWITTY	G V (ALL	SATURDAY NIGHT WITH CONWAY	1959 MGM	US	C801	3786
LORETTA LYNN	V (GKPRT	HITS	1960 MGM	US		4799
BOBBY WOOD	K (C	GREATEST HITS	19 MGM	US		3849
MIKE LEECH	B (C	TOUCH	1961 MGM	US		3943
HENRY STRZELECKI	B (C	HIT THE ROAD	1964 MGM	US		4217
JERRY CARRIGAN	D (C	CONWAY TWITTY	1965 MGM METRO US			110
REGGIE YOUNG	G (C	ROCK'N'ROLL STORY	19 CONTOUR	UK	2870 151	
JOHNNY CHRISTOPHER G (C		CONWAY TWITTY SINGS	19 DECCA US 74724			
TROY SEALS	G (C	LOOK INTO MY TEARDROPS	19 DECCA US 74828			
JOHN HUGHEY	STEEL(C	COUNTRY	19 DECCA US 74913			
JACK HICKS	BAN (C	HERE'S CONWAY TWITTY	19 DECCA US 74990	UK MCA MUPS342		
DON SANDERS	SAX (C	HERE'S CONWAY TWITTY	1974 MCA	UK	MCF 2622	
TOM BRANNON	SAX V(C	NEVER ENDING SONG OF LOVE	1974 CORAL	UK	CDL 8006	
LISA SILVER	FDL (C	I'M SO USED TO LOVING YOU	197 CORAL US 20000			
FARRELL MORRIS	(C	SHAKE IT UP	19 PICKWICK US 3360			
SHELLEY KURLAND	STR (C	STAR SPANGLED SONGS	19 M F P	UK	SPR90064	
LEA JANE BERINATI	V (C	NEXT IN LINE	1968 DECCA US 75062	MCA UK MUPS363		
GINGER HOLLADAY	V (C	YOU KNOW I WOULDN'T LIE	1969 DECCA US 75105	MCA UK MUPS386		
JANIE FRICKE	V (C	YOU CANT TAKE COUNTRY OUT OF CONWAY	1969 MGM	US		4650

(CONTINUED)

(CONTINUED)

DUANE WEST   V   (C

CONWAY TWITTY

Title	Year	Label	Country	Cat	Extra			
HELLO DARLIN'	1970 DECCA	US 75209	US MCA		19
I LOVE YOU MORE TODAY	1970 MCA				
TO SEE MY ANGEL CRY	1970 MCA	UK MUPS412	UK RI	MCF2639
(G)WE ONLY MAKE BELIEVE	1971 DECCA	US 75251	MCA UK MUPS423
CONWAY TWITTY	1971 MGM		UK	2351 006
15 YEARS AGO	1971 MCA	UK MUPS426	MCA RI MCF2647
I WONDER WHAT SHE'LL THINK	1972 MCA	UK MUPS443	MCA RI MCF2653
HOW MUCH MORE CAN SHE STAND	1971 DECCA	US 75276
I CAN'T SEE ME WITHOUT YOU	1972 DECCA	US 75335
(P) LEAD ME ON	1972 DECCA	US 75326
GREATEST HITS VOL 1	1972 DECCA	US 75352
I CANT STOP LOVING YOU	1972 DECCA	US 75361
SINGS THE BLUES	1972 MGM	US 4837
TWENTY GREAT HITS	1972 MGM	US 4884
SHE NEEDS SOMEONE TO HOLD HER	1973 MCA	US 303
(K) LOUISIANA WOMAN/MISSISSIPPIMMAN	1974 MCA		UK MCF2539
YOU'VE NEVER BEEN THIS FAR BEFORE	1974 MCA	US 359	UK MCF2557
CLINGING TO A SAVING HAND	1973 MCA	US 376
HONKY TONK ANGEL	1974 MCA	US 406
COUNTRY PARTNERS	1974 MCA	US 427
I'M NOT THROUGH LOVING YOU YET	1974 MCA	US 441
LINDA ON MY MIND	1975 MCA	US 469	UK MCF2706
(R) FEELIN'S	1975 MCA		UK MCF2717
HIGH PRIEST OF COUNTRY MUSIC	197 MCA	US 2144
TWITTY	197 MCA	US 2176
BEST OF	1976 MCA		UK MCF2737
NOW & THEN	1976 MCA	US 2206	UK MCF2760
(T) UNITED TALENT	1976 MCA		UK MCF2764
GREATEST HITS	1976 MCA	US 2235
BEST OF VOL 2	1977 MCA		UK MCF2788
PLAY GUITAR PLAY	1977 MCA	US 2262	UK MCF2798
DYNAMIC DUO	1977 mcⓐ	US 2278
I'VE ALREADY LOVED YOU IN MY MIND	1977 MCA	US 2293
GEORGIA KEEPS PULLING MY RING	1978 MCA	US 2328	UK MCF 2845
GREATEST HITS	1977 MCA	US 2345
HONKY TONK HEROES	1978 MCA	US 2372
VERY BEST OF	1978 MCA	US 3043
ROCK'N'ROLL (DBL)	1978 POLYDOR		FR 2624 031
SINGS THE GREAT COUNTRY HITS	1978 TEE VEE US 1010
CONWAY	1978 MCA	US 3063	UK MCF 2878
(C)CROSSWINDS	1979 MCA	US 3086	UK MCF 3038
VERY BEST OF LORETTA & CONWAY	1979 MCA	US 3164
COUNTRY ROCK	1979 MCA	FR 414039

TWO TIMERS

JOHN WARNICK	V	(
GEORGE FURY	B	(

JOHNNY JONES G   ANDIE WILLERT   G   (JIM MORRISON   D   (

TYCOON

MARK KREIDER	B V K(A
NORMAN MERSHON	V (A
MICHAEL FONFARA K SYN (A

(A) TYCOON   1979 ARISTA   UK   ARTY 167

MARK RIVERA SAX V (A   JON GORDON   G SYN(A   RICHARD STEINBERG   D(A

TYGERS OF PAN TANG

ROBB WEIR	G V (A
JESS COX	V (A
BRIAN'BIG' DICK	D (A
ROCKY	B (A

(A) WILD CAT   1980 MCA   UK   MCF 3075
(B) SPELLBOUND   1981 MCA   UK   MCF 3104

SEAN TYLA & THE TYLA GANG

SEAN TYLA	G V (ABC
BRIAN TURRINGTON	B (AB
KEN WHALEY	B (BC
BRUCE IRVINE	G (ABC
PETER O'SULLIVAN	B (A
MARTYN WATSON	G V (C
NICK GARVEY	B V (C
KEVIN KINSON	K (C
PETE THOMAS	D (C
JOAN JETT	V (C

(A) YACHTLESS   1977 BESERKLEY UK BSERK 11 US   0057
(B) MOONPROOF   1978 BESERKLEY UK BSERK 16 US   0059
(C) JUST POPPED OUT   1980 LINE GERM 5068 POLYDOR 2391 463

MIKE DESMARAIS   D   (ABC DEKE LEONARD   G V K(A   BAM KING   G (C
BUZZ CHANTER   G   (C   MALCOLM MORLEY   G   (C   TEX COMER   B (C
MICK GROOM   B V (C   BOB DAISLEY   B   (C   ANDY BENNIE   B (C
KENNY LAGUNA   K V (C   FRAN BYRNE   D   (C   TIM ROPER   D (C
MIKE KELLIE   D (C   JOHN EARLE   SAX (C   CARLENE CARTER   V (C
MARK DODSON   V   (C   STEVE JONES   V   (C

BONNIE TYLER

BONNIE TYLER   V   (ABC

(A) THE WORLD STARTS TONIGHT   1977 CHRYSALIS US 1140 RCA UK PL25063
(B) NATURAL FORCE   1978 RCA   UK PL25152
(B) ITS A HEARTACHE   1978 RCA US AFLI12821
(C) DIAMOND CUT   1979 RCA US AFLI3072   UK PL25194

TYNDALL

RUDOLF LANGER	K (A
JURGEN KREHAN	K (A

(A) SONNENLICHT   1980 SKY   GERM   SKY036

JUDIE TZUKE

JUDIE TZUKE	V (AB
MO FOSTER	B (A
PETER VAN HOOKE	D (A
RAY RUSSELL	G (A
MIKE PAXMAN	G PERC(A

(A) WELCOME TO THE CRUISE   1979 ROCKET   UK   TRAIN7
(B) SPORTSCAR   1980 ROCKET   UK   TRAIN9

CHRIS PARREN   K   (A   JOHN PUNTER   PERC (A   ROY BABBINGTON   B (A
SIMON PHILLIPS   D   (A   PAUL HART   K SYN (A

UB40

(A) SIGNING OFF   1980 GRADUATE   GRADLP 2

U BROWN

U BROWN	V (ALL
SANTA	D (E
ROBERT SHAKESPEARE	B (E
WINSTON WRIGHT	K (E
WIRELINDO	K (E
BO PEE	G (E
CHINNA	G (E
SCULLY	PERC (E

(A) SATTA DREAD   1977 KLIK   KLP 9018
(B) LONDON ROCK   1977 THIRD WORLD   TWS 909
(C) REVELATION TIME   1977 LIVE & LOVE   LALP 002
(D) STARSKY & HUTCH   1978 CANCER   CANSLP   001
(E) MI BROWN SOMETHING   1978 FRONT LINE   UK   FL1003
(F) CAN'T KEEP A GOOD MAN DOWN   1979 FRONT LINE   FL1030

UFO

U2

Personnel			Album	Year	Label	Country	Catalog
PETER WAY	B	(ALL	(A) U F O	1971 BEACON		UK	BEAS12
ANDY PARKER	D	(ALL	(B) FLYING	1972 BEACON UK BES19		GERM	NOVA21438
PHIL MOGG	V	(ALL	(AB) U F O /FLYING	1973 DECCA		UK	SD30311/2
MICK BOLTON	G	(AB	(C) PHENOMENON	1974 CHRYSALIS			CHR 1059
MIKE SCHENKER	G	(CDEGHJ	(D) FORCE IT	1975 CHRYSALIS		UK	CHR 1074
DANNY PEYRONEL	K	(E	(E) NO HEAVY PETTING	1976 CHRYSALIS		UK	CHR 1103
PAUL RAYMOND	K	(GHJ	(F) SPACE METAL	1976 NOVA		GERM	6 28363
PAUL CHAPMAN	G	(HL	(G) LIGHTS OUT	1977 CHRYSALIS		UK	CHR 1127
NEIL CARTER	G K V(L		(H) STRANGERS IN THE NIGHT	1978 CHRYSALIS CJT5			CHR 1209
LARRY WALLIS	G	(	(J) OBSESSIONS	1978 CHRYSALIS			CDL 1182
			(K) NO PLACE TO RUN	1979 CHRYSALIS			CDL 1239
			(L) THE WILD, THE WILLING & INNOCENT	1981 CHRYSALIS			CHR 1307
			( ) PROFILE	19 TELDEC		GERM	624007

U.K.

U3

Personnel			Album	Year	Label	Country	Catalog
JOHN WETTON	B G V(ABC		(A) U K	1978 POLYDOR UK 2302 080		US	1 6146
EDDIE JOBSON	VLN K(ABC		(B) DANGER MONEY	1979 POLYDOR UK 2302 089		US	1 6194
BILL BRUFORD	D	(A	(C) NIGHT AFTER NIGHT	1979 POLYDOR UK 2302 096			
ALLAN HOLDSWORTH	G	(A					
TERRY BOZZIO	D	(BC					

UK SUBS

U4

Personnel			Album	Year	Label	Country	Catalog
CHARLIE HARPER	V HCA(ABC		(A) ANOTHER KIND OF BLUES	1979 GEM		UK	GEMLP 100
NICK GARRATT	G	(ABC	(B) BRAND NEW AGE	1980 GEM		UK	GEMLP 106
PAUL SLACK	B	(ABC	(C) CRASH COURSE	1980 GEM		UK	GEMLP 111
PETE DAVIES	D	(ABC	(D) DIMINISHED RESPONSIBILITY	1981 GEM		UK	GEMLP 112

U ROY

U4A

Personnel			Album	Year	Label	Country	Catalog
U ROY		(ALL	(A) DREAD IN A BABYLON	1976 VIRGIN US 34234		UK	V 2048
			(B) NATTY REBEL	1976 VIRGIN		UK	V 2059
			(C) RASTA AMBASSADOR	1977 VIRGIN		UK	V 2092
			(D) DREADLOCKS IN JAMAICA	1977 LIVE & LOVE			LALP 05
			(E) BEST OF	1977 LIVE & LOVE			LALP 08
			(F) VERSION GALORE	1978 FRONT LINE		UK	FL1018
			(G) JAH SON OF AFRICA	1977 FRONT LINE		UK	FL 1023

US SKY

U5

Personnel			Album	Year	Label	Country	Catalog
BOB GREENFIELD	D	(A	(A) DON'T HOLD BACK	1971 RCA		UK	SF 8168
DOUG FIEGER	B	(A					
JOHN COURY	K G	(A	ROB STAWINSKI D (A PAT ARNOLD V (A BOBBY KEYS SAX (A				
GARY WRIGHT	K	(A	JIMMY MILLER PERC (A JIM PRICE SAX (A DORIS TROY V (A				
ALAN WHITE	D	(A	CHRIS WOOD FLT (A FLO BENDER (A				

U2

U5A

Personnel			Album	Year	Label	Country	Catalog
LARRY MULLIN	D	(A	(A) BOY	1980 ISLAND		UK	ILPS9646
ADAM CLAYTON	B	(A					
THE EDGE	G	(A	BOBO V (A				

UBIQUITY

U5B

Personnel			Album	Year	Label	Country	Catalog
			(A) STARBOOTY	19 ELEKTRA		UK	K52068

JAMES'BLOOD'ULMER

U6

Personnel			Album	Year	Label	Country	Catalog
JAMES BLOOD ULMER		(AB	(A) NO WAVE	1980 MOERS MUSIC			MM01072
			(B) MUSIC REVELATION ENSEMBLE	1980		GERM	

ULTIMATE SPINACH

U7

Personnel			Album	Year	Label	Country	Catalog
BARBARA HUDSON	G V	(ABC	(A) ULTIMATE SPINACH	1968 MGM UK 8071		US	SE4518
IAN BRUCE DOUGLAS	V	(AB	(B) BEHOLD & SEE	1968 MGM UK 8094		US	SE4570
KEITH LAHTEINEN	K	(AB	(C) ULTIMATE SPINACH	1969 MGM		US	SE4600
GEOFFREY WINTHROP	G V	(AB					
RICHARD NESE	B	(AB	JEFF BAXTER G V (C MIKE LEVINE B (C RUSS LEVINE D (C				
TED MYERS	G V	(A	TONY SCHEUREN K (C				

ULTRAVOX

U8

Personnel			Album	Year	Label	Country	Catalog
JOHN FOXX	V	(ABCD	(A) ULTRAVOX	1977 ISLAND		UK	ILPS 9449
STEVE SHEARS	K V	(ABD	(B) HA HA HA	1977 ISLAND		UK	ILPS 9505
BILLY CURRIE	K VLN(ABCDE		(C) SYSTEMS OF ROMANCE	1978 ANTILLES US 7069		UK ISLAND	9555
WARREN CANN	D	(ABCDE	(D) THREE INTO ONE (COMP)	1980 ISLAND		UK	ILPS 9614
CHRIS CROSS	B	(ABCDE	(E) VIENNA	1981 ISLAND		UK	CHR 1296
ROBIN SIMON	G	(C	(EP) MAN WHO DIES	1978 ISLAND		UK	IEP 8
MIDGE URE	G V	(E					
ROBIN SINE	G	(D					

UNCLE DOG

U9

Personnel			Album	Year	Label	Country	Catalog
CAROLE GRIMES	V	(A	(A) OLD HAT	1972 SIGNPOST		UK	SG 4253
DAVID SKINNER	K V	(A					
PHILLIP CROOKS	G	(A	TERRY STANNARD D (A JOHN PORTER G B (A SAMMY MITCHELL G (A				
JOHN PEARSON	D	(A	RABBIT BUNDRICK K (A				

UNDERTAKERS

U10

Personnel			Album	Year	Label	Country	Catalog
JACKIE LOMAX	G V	(A	(A) UNDERTAKERS	1964 PYE NOT RELEASED			
BUGS PEMBERTON	D	(A					
CHRIS HUSTON	G	(A	GEORGE NUGENT G (A BRIAN JONES SAX(A				

UNDERTONES

U11

Personnel			Album	Year	Label	Country	Catalog
FEARGAL SHARKEY	V	(AB	(A) THE UNDERTONES	1979 SIRE		UK	SRK 6071
MICKEY BRADLEY	B	(AB	(A) THE UNDERTONES (1 EXTRA TRACK)	1979 SIRE		UK	SRK 6081
JOHN O'NEILL	G	(AB	(B) HYPNOTISED	1980 SIRE		UK	SRK 6088
BILLY DOHERTY	D	(AB	(EP) TEENAGE KICKS	197 GOOD VIBRATION			GOT 4
DAMIAN O'NEILL	G	(AB					

UNDISPUTED TRUTH

U12

Album	Year	Label	Catalog
(A) UNDISPUTED TRUTH	1971 TAMLA UK STML11197	US GORDY 955	
(B) FACE TO FACE	1972 TAMLA UK STMG 8004	US GORDY 959	
(C) LAW OF THE LAND	1973 TAMLA UK STML11240	US GORDY 963	
(D) HIGHER THAN HIGH	1975 TAMLA UK STML12009		
(E) DOWN TO EARTH	1975 TAMLA UK STML11277	US GORDY 968	
(F) COSMIC TRUTH	1975 TAMLA UK STMA 8023	US GORDY 970	
(G) BEST OF	1977 TAMLA UK STMA 8029		
(H) METHOD TO THE MADNESS	197 WB UK K56289	US	2767
(I) SMOKIN'	1979 WB UK K56497		

UNICORN   U13

```
PETER PERRIER      D V  (ABCD      (A) UPHILL ALL THE WAY        1971 TRANSATLANTIC  UK   TRA238
TREVOR MEE       G V FLT  (A       (B) BLUE PINE TREES           1974 CHARISMA       UK   CAS 1092
KEN BAKER        V K G(ABCD        (C) TOO MANY CROOKS           1976 HARVEST        UK   SHSP 4054
PAT MARTIN        B V  (ABCD       (C) UNICORN II                1976 CAPITOL        US   ST 11453
KEVIN SMITH         G  (BCD        (D) ONE MORE TOMORROW         1977 HARVEST        UK   SHSP 4067
DAVID GILMOUR     STEEL (BC        (D) ONE MORE TOMORROW         1977 CAPITOL        US   ST 11692
CHRIS PIDGEON       K  (CD
HOWIE CASEY        SAX (D   BILLY LIVSEY     K  (D
```

UNIQUES   U13A

```
                                   (A) YOU DONT MISS YOUR WATER  1980 CHARLY        UK   CTD 121
```

UNIT 4+ 2   U14

```
BRIAN PARKER LYRICS  (             (A) FIRST ALBUM               1965 DECCA         UK   LK 4697
DAVE MEIKLE       G V  (1          (B) UNIT 4+2 FEATURING CONCRETE & CLAY196 LONDON US  PS 427
TOMMY MOELLER     K V  (1          (C) REMEMBERING               1977 DECCA         UK   REM 6
PETE MOULES        V  (1           (1) 1962
HOWARD LUBIN     G V  (1
BOB GARWOOD        B  (    HUGH LEM HALLIDAY D  (   RUSS BALLARD   G V  (   ROBERT HENRIT   D  (
```

UNITED   U15

```
ANDY PYLE          B  (
JOHN GOSLING       K  (    RON BERG     D  (   DAVE EDWARDS       G V  ( DENNIS STRATTON  GV(
```

UNITED SONS OF AMERICA   U15A

```
GERRY BLAKE       K V  (A          (A) GREETINGS FROM THE U S OF A  19  MERCURY SR 61312 +   6338 036
STEVE WOODS        V PERC(A
RICHARD FREEMAN     G  (A   JERRY RITCHLEY    B  (A   MIKE HUESTIS   D PERC (
```

UNITED STATES OF AMERICA   U16

```
JOSEPH BYRD       K SYN(A          (A) UNITED STATES OF AMERICA   1968 CBS  US  9619   UK   63340
DOROTHY MOSKOWITZ V   (A
GORDON MARRON   VLN SYN V(A  RAND FORBES      B V  (A  CRAIG WOODSON   D PERC (A ED BOGAS    K  (A
```

UNIVERS ZERO   U17

```
DANIEL DENIS     PERC (AB          (A) UNIVERS ZERO              1978 ATEM                  7001
MICHEL BERCKMANS  WIND (AB          (B) HERESIE                  1979 ATEM 7005  UK RECOMMENDED  RR4
MARCEL DUFRANE    VLN  (A
CHRISTIAN GENET     B  (A   PATRICK HANAPPIER VLN  (AB  EMMANUEL NICAISE     HCA  (A   ROGER TRIGAUX G K(AB
GUY SEGERS         B V  (B
```

UNIVERSAL ENERGY   U17A

```
                                   (A) UNIVERSAL ENERGY          1977 HARVEST        UK   SHSP 4075
```

UNIVERSE   U17B

```
GARY PAUL VAN     K V  (A          (A) UNIVERSE                  1977 PBR INTERNATIONAL      PBR 7002
DENNIS LEE ASKEW  G V  (A
WALFREDO REYES    PERC (A
```

PHIL UPCHURCH   U18

```
PHIL UPCHURCH    G B V(ALL         (A) YOU CANT SIT DOWN         1961 BOYD          US         398
TENNYSON STEVENS     (J            (B) YOU CANT SIT DOWN II      196  UA            US        6162
ERIC GALE          G  (J           (C) TWIST THE BIG HIT DANCES  196  UA            US        6175
ARTHUR ADAMS       G  (H           (D) PHIL UPCHURCH             196  CADET         US         826
HARVEY MASON       D  (H           (E) THE WAY I FEEL           1969 CADET         US         840
BOBBYE HALL      PERC (H           (F) FEELING BLUE              19   MILESTONE     US        9010
DOUG BASCOMB       B  (J           (G) PHIL UPCHURCH             19   MARLIN        US        2209
BOB JAMES          K  (J           (H) DARKNESS DARKNESS         1972 BLUE THUMB US 6005 UK  ILPS9219
STEVE GADD         D  (J           (J) UPCHURCH TENNYSON         1975 KUDU                   KU 22
ANDREW SMITH       D  (J           (K) PHIL UPCHURCH             1978 TK                     TKRB2542
DAVID SANBORN     SAX (J
CHUCK RAINEY       B  (H    JOE SAMPLE       K  (H
```

UPP   U19

```
ANDY CLARK        K V  (AB         (A) UPP                       1975 EPIC US   33439   UK   80625
STEVEN AMAZING     D  (AB          (B) THIS WAY UPP              1976 EPIC US   34177   UK   81322
JAMES COPLEY       D  (AB
DAVID BUNCE        G  (B    JEFF BECK      G  (AB TOM SCOTT   SAX  (B  JEANIE ARNOLD    V  (B
CHRISTY THOMPSON   V  (B    GARY COLEMAN   PERC (B  JIMMY GETZOFF    (B
```

UPSETTERS   U20

```
LEE PERRY            (             (A) RETURN OF DJANGO          19   TROJAN              TRL  19
JOHNNY MOORE         (             (B) THE GOOD THE BAD & THE UPSETTERS 1970 TROJAN       TBL 119
VAL BENNETT          (             (C) EASTWOOD RIDES AGAIN      197  TROJAN              TBL 125
WINSTON WRIGHT       (             (D) PRISONER                  197  TROJAN              TBL 127
JIM JACKSON          (             (E) SUPER APE                 1977 ISLAND         UK   ILPS9417
HUX BROWN            (
EASY BECKFORD        (     BOB AITKENS       (   GLEN ADAMS       ( ALVA LAVIS             (
CARLTON BARRETT      (     ASTON BARRETT     (
```

URBAN VERBS   U20A

```
ROBIN ROSE          (A             (A) URBAN VERBS    1         1980 WB   US BSK3418  UK K56810
RODDY FRANTZ        (A
LINDA FRANCE        (A     ROBERT GOLDSTEIN    (   DANNY FRANKEL    (A
```

MICHEL URBANIAK   U21

```
MICHEL URBANIAK VLN SAX(ALL        (A) FUSION                    1974 CBS   US 32852   UK 65744
URSZULA DUDZIAK  PERC V(BCDF        (B) ATMA                     1974 CBS   US 33184
CZESLAW BARTKOWSKI D  (BD           (C) FUSION III               1975 CBS   US 33582
WOJCIECH KAROLAK   K  (B            (D) INACTIN'                 1975 SPIEGELEI         GERM 287847U
RAY MANTILLA     PERC (B            (E) PARATYPHUS B             1975 SPIEGELEI         GERM  28771
JOHN ABERCROMBIE   G  (C            (F) BODY ENGLISH             1976 ARISTA US AL 4086
WLODEK GULGOWSKI   K  (C            (G) ECSTASY                  1978 MARLIN                 2221
ANTHONY JACKSON    B  (C            (H) SERENADE FOR THE CITY    1980 MOTOWN US         M 7944
BRANISLAV KOVACEK D   (D
GERRY BROWN        D  (C    STEVE GADD      D  (C   LARRY CORYELL   G  (C  JOE CARO      G  (CF
BERNARD KAFKA      V  (CF   HAROLD IVORY WILLIAMS K(F  BASIL FEARRINGTON  B  (F  STEVE JORDAN  D  (F
ERROL CRUSHER BENNETT PERC(FADAM MAKOWICZ   PNO  (D   ROMAN DYLAG     B  (D
```

URIAH HEEP

```
MICK BOX        G(ABCDEFGHJKLMNO  (A) VERY'UMBLE VERY 'EAVY  1970 VERTIGO UK 6360 006  MERCURY US SR61294
KEN HENSLEY     K V(ABCDEFGHJKLMNO (A) VERY'UMBLE VERY 'EAVY 1971 BRONZE  RI ILPS9142  BRONZE 77RI BRNA142
DAVID BYRON     V  (ABCDEFGHJKL    (B) SALISBURY            1971 VERTIGO UK 6360 028  MERCURY US SR61319
PAUL NEWTON     B  (ABCK           (B) SALISBURY            1971 BRONZE  RI ILPS9152  BRONZE 77RI BRNA152
KEITH BAKER     D  (BK             (C) LOOK AT YOURSELF     1971 BRONZE  UK ILPS9160  MERCURY US SRM1614
AL NAPIER       D  (AK             (C) LOOK AT YOURSELF     1977 BRONZE  RI          BRNA169
NIGEL OLSSON    D  (A              (D) DEMONS & WIZARDS     1972 BRONZE  UK ILPS9193  MERCURY US SRM1630
IAN CLARKE      D  (CK             (D) DEMONS & WIZARDS     1977 BRONZE  RI          BRNA193
GARY THAIN      B  (DEFGH          (E) MAGICIANS BIRTHDAY   1971 BRONZE  UK ILPS9213  MERCURY US SRM1652
LEE KERSLAKE    D  (DEFGHJKLMNO    (E) MAGICIANS BIRTHDAY   1977 BRONZE  RI          BRNA213
JOHN WETTON     B  (JL             (F) LIVE                 1973 BRONZE  UK ILSD1     MERCURY US SRM7503
TREVOR BOLDER   B V (MNO           (F) LIVE                 1977 BRONZE  RI          BRSP 1
COLIN WOOD      K  (A              (G) SWEET FREEDOM        1973 BRONZE  UK BRNA245   WB      US 2724
JOHN LAWTON     V  (MNO            (G) SWEET FREEDOM        1977 BRONZE  RI          BRNA245
MEL COLLINS     SAX (J             (H) WONDERWORLD          1974 BRONZE  UK ILPS9280  WB      US 2800
B J COLE        STEEL(J            (H) WONDERWORLD          1975 BRONZE  RI          BRNA280
CHRIS MERCER    SAX (O             (J) RETURN TO FANTASY    1975 BRONZE  UK ILPS9335  WB      US 2869
JOHN SLOMAN     V  (               (J) RETURN TO FANTASY    1977 BRONZE  RI          BRNA335
MARK CLARKE     V  (1              (K) THE BEST OF          1975 BRONZE  UK ILPS9375  MERCURY US SRM11070
                                   (K) THE BEST OF          1977 BRONZE  RI          BRNA375
                                   (L) HIGH & MIGHTY        1976 BRONZE  UK ILPS9384  WB      US 2949
                                   (L) HIGH & MIGHTY        1977 BRONZE  RI          BRNA384
                                   (M) FIRE FLY             1977 BRONZE  UK ILPS9483  WB      US 3013
                                   (M) FIRE FLY             1977 BRONZE  RI          BRNA383
                                   (N) INNOCENT VICTIM      1977 BRONZE  UK BRON504   WB      US 3145
                                   (O) FALLEN ANGEL         1978 BRONZE  UK BRNA 512  CHRYSALIS US S 1204
```

UTOPIA

```
DENNY FISCHELSCHER D  (A   (A) UTOPIA                        1973 UA      UK UAG 29438
JIMMY JACKSON      K  (A
LOTHAR MEID        B  (A   ANDY MARX        G (A   JOE NAY       D   (A   CHRIS KARRER   VLV (A
ROLF ZACHER        V  (A   JOHN WEINZIERL   G (A   GEO GREEN     D   (A   JOE QUICK      G   (A
GEORGE BROWN       D  (A   KRISTIAN SCHULZE K (A   RENATE KNAUP  V   (A   FALK ROGNER    K   (A
OLAF KUBLER        SYN (A  SIEGFRID SCHWAB  G (A   PETER KRAMPER SYN (A   EDGAR HOFFMAN  SAX (A
KEITH FORSEY       D  (A   RALF BASTEN      V (A
```

VHF

```
RITCHIE TEETER   D (A   (A) 1979
BRUCE BRODY      K (A   RITCHIE FLIEGLER G (A   DONNIE NOSSOV  B(A
```

VAGRANTS

```
JAY STORCH       K
PETER SABATINO   V      LARRY WEST B   LESLIE WEST   G   ROGER MANSOUR  D
```

VALDY

```
VALDY          V  (AB  (A) VALDY                         1975 A&M US 4538  UK AMLH64538
JIM KELTNER    D  (A   (B) VALDY & THE HOMETOWN BAND     197  A&M US 4592
JERRY SCHEFF   B  (A
FRED TACKETT   G  (G   DAVID PAICH     K    (A   RICHARD GREENE VLN  (A   DALLAS TAYLOR   D(A
JERRY McGEE    G  (A   ELEANOR SEATKIN CELLO(A   JOHN SEBASTIAN HCA  (A   JIM GORDON      D (A
JIM HORN       FLT (A  ALAN MUNDE      BANJO(A   JESSE ED DAVIS G    (A   JAY DEE MANESS  G (A
WILLIAM SMITH  K  (A   KLAUS VOORMANN  B    (A
```

RITCHIE VALENS

```
RITCHIE VALENS   V (A   RITCHIE VALENS       19    DELFI       US       1201
                        RITCHIE              19    DELFI       US       1206
                        RITCHIE              19    LONDON      US    HA 2390
                        IN CONCERT           19    DELFI       US       1214
                        GREATEST HITS        19    DELFI       US       1225
                        GREATEST HITS II     19    DELFI       US       1247
                        GREATEST HITS        19    LONDON      UK    HA 8196
                        ORIGINAL             19    GUEST STAR  US       1484
                        ORIGINAL LA BAMBA    19    GUEST STAR  US       1469
                        RITCHIE VALENS       19    APEX        US       1201
                        HIS GREATEST HITS    19    PRESIDENT         PTL 1001
                        ROCK LI'L DARLIN'    19    JOY              JOYS 254
                        RITCHIE VALENS       1979  LONDON      UK    HAR 8535
```

DINO VALENTI

```
DINO VALENTI(CHESTER POWERS) V (A   (A) DINO VALENTI   1968 CBS UK 63443   US EPIC 26335
```

GARY VALENTINE & THE KNOW

```
GARY VALENTINE   G V (
JOE TURRISI      D   (   RICHARD DANDREN  B  (
```

VALENTINO BAND

```
SAL VALENTINO    V (
JOHN BLAKELEY    G (
LYDIA PHILLIPS   V (   RALPH WALSH  G (   DOUG KILMER  B ( JOHN CHAMBERS   D (
```

MARTHA REEVES & THE VANDELLAS

```
MARTHA REEVES    V (ALL  (A) COME & GET YOU MEMORIES  1963                     US GORDY 902
ROSALIND ASHFORD V (123  (B) HEAT WAVE                1963 TAMLA UK STML11005  US GORDY 907
LOIS REEVES      V (34   (C) DANCE PARTY              1965 TAMLA UK STML11013  US GORDY 915
BETTY KELLY      V (2    (D) WATCH OUT                1966 TAMLA UK STML11051  US GORDY 920
ANNETTE BEARD    V (1    (E) GREATEST HITS            1966 TAMLA UK STML11040
SANDRA TILLEY    V (4    (F) LIVE                     1967                     US GORDY 925
SYLVESTER RIVERS K (W    (G) RIDIN HIGH               1968                     US GORDY 926
DALE WARREN      K (W    (H) SUGAR & SPICE            196                      US GORDY 944
GEORGE SPENCER   K (W    (J) NATURAL RESOURCES        196                      US GORDY 952
GREG LEVIAS      PNO (W  (K) BLACK MAGIC              1974 TAMLA UK STML11204  US GORDY 958
CHARLES FEARING  G (W    (L) GREATEST HITS VOL 2      1974 TAMLA UK STML11223
CORNELIUS GRANT  G (W    (M) ANTHOLOGY                1974 TAMLA UK STML12060  US TAMLA 778
DAVID PRUITT     G (W    (N) REST OF MY LIFE          1977 ARISTA UK SPART 1030
GREG CROCKETT    G (W    (W) WE MEET AGAIN            1978 FANTASY UK FT 544
ROMEO WILLIAMS   B (W
GARNETT BROWN    TROM (W  PHILLIP RANELIN  TROM (W   GROVER MITCHELL  TROM (W   BENJAMIN POWELL  TROM(W
MAURICE SPEARS   TROM (W  JAMES GADSON     D    (W   ANANIAS CHAMBERS CONG (W   ROBERT ZIMITTI   PERC(W
BUBBA CHAMBERS   PERC (W  ROBERT BRYANT    TPT  (W   ALBERT AARONS    TPT  (W   BENJAMIN KIRK    TPT (W
                                                                               (CONTINUED)
```

MARTHA REEVES & THE VANDELLAS V9

```
WILLIAM PETERSON TPT (W   JOHN ROBERTS    TPT (W   ERNIE FIELDS    FLT (W   FRED JACKSON   FLT (W
DONALD CHRISTLIEB WIND (W  WILLIAM GREEN   WIND (W  STRING SECTION          (W
```

CHRISTIAN VANDER V10

```
CHRISTIAN VANDER        (A        (A) TRISTAN ET ISEULT        1978 EGG              FR      90171
```

VAN DER GRAAF GENERATOR V11

```
PETER HAMMILL    K V G(ABCDEFGJ    (A) AEROSOL GREY MACHINE    1968 FONTANA UK        6430 083
NIC POTTER       B     (BCJKM      (A) AEROSOL GREY MACHINE    1968 MERCURY US        SR 61238
DAVE JACKSON     SAX   (BCDEFGJKM   (A) AEROSOL GREY MACHINE    1968 VERTIGO ITALY     6360  510
GUY EVANS        D     (ABCDEFGLKM  (B) THE LEAST WE CAN DO IS WAVE  1969 CHARISMA     CAS  1007
HUGH BANTON      K     (ABCDEFGKM   (C) H TO HE WHO AM THE ONLY ONE  1970 CHARISMA     CAS  1027
KEITH ELLIS      B     (A          (D) PAWN HEARTS            1971 CHARISMA           CAS  1051
GRAHAM SMITH     V     (J          (E) GODBLUFF              1975 CHARISMA           CAS  1109
CHARLES DICKIE   CELLO(J           (F) STILL LIFE            1976 CHARISMA           CAS  1116
CED CURTIS       G B   (KM         (G) WORLD RECORD          1976 CHARISMA           CAS  1120
PIERO MESSINA    K G   (K          (H) THE QUIET ZONE        1977 CHARISMA           CAS  1132
JERRY SALISBURY  HRNS  (B          (J) VITAL LIVE            1978 CHARISMA           CVLD 101
MIKE HURWITZ     CELLO(B           (K) 1968//1971            1973 CHARISMA           CS 2
PIERO MESINA     G PNO(M           (M) LONG HELLO            1973 CHARISMA
ROBERT FRIPP     G     (CD         (N) REPEAT PERFORMANCE    1980 CHARISMA           BG8
```

VAN DUREN V11A

```
VAN DUREN G K B SYN V  (A          (A) STARING AT THE CEILING   1978 LONDON UK SHY8530+BIG SOUND3816
 HILLY MICHAELS  D     (A
DOUG SNYDER      PERC (A    JON TIVEN    G SAX    (A
```

LON & DERREK VAN EATON V12

```
LON VAN EATON G V K D SAX(AB        (A) BROTHER              1973 APPLE            UK   SAPCOR 25
DERREK VAN EATON V B G D (AB        (B) WHO DO YOU OUT DO    1975 A&M             US   SP  4507
RINGO STARR      D     (A
JIM GORDON       D     (AB  KLAUS VOORMANN   B    (AB  ANDY NEWMARK    D   (A   PAUL GLANZ     ORG (A
T J TINDALL      G     (A   MIKE HUGG        D    (A   ALEX GUEVARA  CONGA(A   RICHARD DAVIS  B   (A
JIM KELTNER      D     (B   RICHARD PERRY    PERC (B   TOM HENSLEY     K   (B   VANETTA FIELDS V   (B
BOBBY HARTNAGLE  G     (B   CYNTHIA WEBB     V    (B   FRITZ POASKETT  V   (B   RUSS TURNER    ORG (B
DAVID BEEBE      D     (B   TOM SEUFERT      G    (B   CHUCK FINDLEY  HRNS (B   LANI GROVES    V   (B
MARTHA REEVES    V     (B   TREVOR LAWRENCE  SAX  (B   LYNDA LAWRENCE  V   (B   JAMES GADSON   D   (B
CLYDIE KING      V     (B   GARY WRIGHT      K    (B
```

VANGELIS V13

```
VANGELIS         K     (ALL        (A) DRAGON              1971 CHARLY        UK    CRL 5013
MICHAEL RIPOCHE  B     (AHK        (B) L'APOCALYPSE DES ANIMAUX  1973 POLYDOR        2489 113
BRIAN ODGERS     B     (AH         (C) EARTH               1974 VERTIGO            6499 693
TONY OXLEY       D     (AH         (D) HEAVEN & HELL       1975 RCA   UK RS 1025  US AFLI5110
MICK WALLER      D     (A          (E) ALBEDO .39          1976 RCA   UK RS 1080  US AFLI5136
ARCHIRIS         G     (A          (F) SPIRAL              1977 RCA   UK PL25116  US AFLI2627
YEUNG HAK FUN    V     (K          (G) BEAUBOURG           1978 RCA   UK PL25155  US AFLI3020
KOON FOOK MAN    V     (K          (H) HYPOTHESIS          1978 AFFINITY           AFF 11
                                   (J) BEST OF             1978 RCA   UK PL25174
                                   (K) CHINA               1979 POLYDOR UK POLD5018 US  1 6199
                                   (L) SEE YOU LATER       1980 POLYDOR UK 2302 101
```

VAN HALEN V14

```
EDWARD VAN HALEN G     (AB         (A) VAN HALEN           1978 WB    US BSK3075   UK K56470
ALEX VAN HALEN   D     (AB         (B) VAN HALEN II        1979 WB    US HS 3312   UK K56616
MIKE ANTHONY     B     (AB         (C) WOMEN & CHILDREN FIRST  1980 WB             UK K56793
DAVE ROTH        V     (AB         (EP) VAN HALEN 12"      197  WB                 PRO 705
```

VANILLA FUDGE V15

```
MARK STEIN       K     (ABCDEFG    (A) VANILLA FUDGE       1967 ATLANTIC UK 587 086  US 33224
VINCE MARTELL    G     (ABCDEFG    (B) THE BEAT GOES ON    1968 ATLANTIC UK 587 100  US 33237
TIM BOGERT       B     (ABCDEFG    (C) RENAISSANCE         1968 ATLANTIC UK 587 110  US 33244
CARMINE APPICE   D     (ABCDEFG    (D) NEAR THE BEGINNING  1969 ATLANTIC UK 228 020  US 33278
                                   (E) ROCK'N'ROLL         1970 ATLANTIC UK 288 029  US 33303
                                   (F) STAR COLLECTION     1974 MIDI               MID 0033
                                   (G) WHILE THE WORLD WAS EATING  1975 METRONOME  GERM  200 108
                                   (BE) TWO ORIGINALS      1976 ATLANTIC     GERM      60116
```

CHERRY VANILLA V16

```
CHERRY VANILLA   V     (AB         (A) BAD GIRL            1978 RCA            UK   PL 25122
LOUIS LE PERE    G K V(AB          (B) VENUS DE VINYL      1979 RCA            UK   PL 25217
ZECCA ESQUIBEL   K     (A
HOWIE FINKEL     B     (A   IAN STUART       V    (B   STUART ELLIOTT  D   (AB  ALUN EDEN     D  (B
DAVE QUINN       B     (A   GEORGE FORD      B    (B   ROY BABBINGTON  B   (B   MORRIS PERT   PERC(B
MICHAEL MANUSCE  D     (
```

THIJS VAN LEER V17

```
THIJS VAN LEER FLT K SYN(ALL       (A) INTROSPECTION       1972 CBS                 65589
LETTY DE JONG    V     (A          (B) INTROSPECTION II    1975 CBS                 65913
PAUL BUCKMASTER  K     (C          (C) O MY LOVE           1975 PHILIPS            6303 143
VICTOR FELDMAN   PERC (C           (D) MUSICA PER LA NOTTE DI NATALE  1976 CBS       69239
WILTON FELDER    B     (C          (E) INTROSPECTION III   1978 CBS                 86034
JAMES GADSON     D     (C          (F) NICE TO HAVE MET YOU  1978 CBS               86059
EUGENE CIPRIANO  OBOE  (C
DAVID KEMPER     D     (C   ROSELIE VAN LEER  V    (C   NORMAN BENNO  OBOE (C   LOUIE SHELTON  G  (C
KING ERRISON     CONGA(C   RALPH MACDONALD  PERC (C   RICHARD TEE     K  (F   ERIC GALE      G  (F
ANTHONY JACKSON  B     (F   HARVEY MASON     D    (F   EEF ALBERS      G  (F   STEVE KHAN     G  (F
JON FADDIS       HRNS  (F   RANDY BRECKER    TPT  (F   BARRY ROGERS  TROM (F   DAVE TAYLOR   TROM(F
JAMES BUFFINGTON HRNS  (F   JOHN CLARK       HRNS (F   FRED GRIFFIN  HRNS (F   ALEX FOSTER   SAX (F
MICHAEL BRECKER  SAX   (F   RONNIE CUBER     SAX  (F   TOM SCOTT      SAX (F   BROOKS TILLOTSON HRNS(F
DON CORRADO      HRNS  (F   LOU MARINI       SAX  (F   VIVIAN CHERRY   V  (F   BRENDA WHITE   V  (F
KEN WILLIAMS     V     (F   GWEN GUTHRIE     V    (F   RAYMOND SIMPSON V  (F   ZACH SANDERS   V  (F
BILL EATON       V     (F   LOUIS VAN DIJK   K    (D   ROGIER VAN OTTERLOO  (D  STRINGS            (DF
```

V18 — TOWNES VAN ZANDT

```
V18                                 TOWNES VAN ZANDT
  TOWNES VAN ZANDT   G V  (ALL    (A) FOR THE SAKE OF A SONG      1968 POPPY PYS40001
  PHILLIP DONNELLY   G V  (H      (B) OUR MOTHER THE MOUNTAIN     1969 POPPY PYS40004  TOMATO TOM 7015
  BILLY EARL McLELLAND     G V(H  (C) TOWNES VAN ZANDT            1970 POPPY PYS40007  TOMATO TOM 7014
  CHIPS MOMAN        G V  (H      (D) DELTA MOMMA BLUES           1971 POPPY PYS40012  TOMATO TOM 7013
  RANDY SCRUGGS      G MAND (H    (E) HIGH,LOW & IN BETWEEN       1971 POPPY PYS5700   TOMATO TOM 7012
  TOMMY COGBILL      B    (H      (F) LATE GREAT                  1973 POPPY LA 004    UA UK UAS29442
  BOBBY EMMONS       K    (H      (F) LATE GREAT                  197  TOMATO              TOM 7011
  EDDY ANDERSON      D    (H      (G) LIVE AT THE OLD QUARTER     1977 TOMATO              TOM27001
  TONI WINE          V    (H      (H) FLYING SHOES                1978 TOMATO              TOM 7017
  JIMMY DAY          STEEL(H
  GARY SCRUGGS       HCA  (H   SPOONER OLDHAM   PNO  (H  BILLY BURNETTE    V  (H
```

VAPORS

```
V18A                                   VAPORS
  DAVID FENTON       G V  (A      (A) NEW CLEAR DAYS              1980 UA              UK  UAG 3030
  HOWARD SMITH       D    (A      (B) MAGNETS                     1981 LIBERTY         UK  LBG 30324
  EDWARD BAZALGETTE  G    (A
  STEVE SMITH        B V  (A
```

VAPOUR TRAILS (VTs)

```
V18B                               VAPOUR TRAILS(VTs)
  JOHN McBURNIE      G V  (AB     (A) VAPOUR TRAILS              1979 WB         US BSK3363 UK K56722
  ANDY DALBY         G    (AB     (B) V T s                      1980 CRIMINAL             UK STEAL1
  PHIL CURTIS        B    (AB
  JOHN FERRARO       D    (AB  STEVE HOLLY    D V  (AB  BRIAN MANN     K  (AB  WILLIAM D SMITH  K  (AB
  MICHAEL OMARTIAN   K    (AB  DAVE ROSE      K    (AB  BRIAN CHATTON  K  (AB  DAVID BENOIT     K  (AB
  BETSY COOKE        K V  (AB  PAULINHO DA COSTA PERC (AB TOM SCOTT   SAX (AB  MEL COLLINS      SAX(AB
  VIVIENNE McAULIFFE V    (AB  BILL CHAMPLIN  V    (AB
```

VARDIS

```
V18C                                   VARDIS
  STEVE ZODIAC       G V  (A      (A) 100MPH                      1980 LOGO        UK  MOGO 4012
  ALAN SELWAY        B V  (A      (B) WORLD'S INSANE              1981 LOGO        UK  LOGO 1026
  GARY PEARSON       D    (A
```

BOBBY VEE

```
V19                                 BOBBY VEE
  BOBBY VEE          V    (ALL    DEVIL OR ANGEL                  196  LIBERTY US LST7165
  SONNY CURTIS       G V  (C      BOBBY VEE                       196  LIBERTY US LST7181
  BOB BOGLE          G    (D      WITH STRINGS & THINGS           196  LIBERTY US LST7186
  NOKIE EDWARDS      B    (D      HITS OF THE 50s                 19   LIBERTY US LST7205
  JERRY ALLISON      D    (C      TAKE GOOD CARE OF MY BABY       196  LIBERTY US LST7211  UK LBY 1004
  JOE MAULDIN        D    (C      (C) MEETS THE CRICKETS          1962 LIBERTY US 7228    UK LBY 1086
  DON WILSON         G    (D      (C) MEETS THE CRICKETS          1974 SUNSET             UK SLS50357
  MEL TAYLOR         D    (D      RECORDING SESSION               196  LIBERTY US LST7232  UK LBY 1084
                                  GOLDEN GREATS                   196  LIBERTY US LST7245
                                  MERRY CHRISTMAS                 196  LIBERTY US LST7267
                                  NIGHT HAS A THOUSAND EYES       196  LIBERTY US LST7285  UK LBY 1139
                                  (D) MEETS THE VENTURES          1963 LIBERTY US LST7289  UK LBY 1147
                                  I REMEMBER BUDDY HOLLY          196  LIBERTY US LST7336  UK SBY 1188
                                  SING NEW SOUND FROM ENGLAND     196  LIBERTY US LST7352
                                  HITS OF THE SIXTIES             196  LIBETRY US LST7385
                                  LIVE ON TOUR                    196  LIBERTY US LST7393
                                  GOLDEN GREATS VOLII             196  LIBERTY US LST7464
                                  LOOK AT ME GIRL                 196  LIBERTY US LST7482  UK SBY 1341
                                  COME BACK WHEN YOU GROW UP      1967 LIBERTY US LST7534
                                  JUST TODAY                      196  LIBERTY US LST7554  UK   83112
                                  DO WHAT YOU GOTTA DO            196  LIBERTY US LST7592  UK   83130
                                  FOREVER KIND OF LOVE            196  LIBERTY US LST7612
                                  VERY BEST OF                    1971 SUNSET              UK SLS50271
                                  LEGENDARY MASTERS               1974 UA      US LA 025   UK UAD60055
                                  VERY BEST OF                    1975 UA      US LA 332
                                  TRIBUTE TO BUDDY HOLLY          1978 SUNSET              UK SLS50417
```

TATA VEGA

```
V20                                   TATA VEGA
  TATA VEGA          V    (AB     (A) FULL SPEED AHEAD            1976 TAMLA           UK  STML12039
                                  (B) TOTALLY TATA                1977 TAMLA           UK  STML12058
```

MARTHA VELEZ

```
V21                                 MARTHA VELEZ
  MARTHA VELEZ       V    (ALL    (A) FIENDS & ANGELS             1969 LONDON UK SHK8395 SIRE US 97008
  ERIC CLAPTON       G    (A      (A) FIENDS & ANGELS             1969 BLUE HORIZON      UK   763867
  JACK BRUCE         B    (A      (B) HYPNOTIZED                  1972 POLYDOR US              PD5034
  MITCH MITCHELL     D    (A      (C) MATINEE WEEPERS             1973 SIRE    US 7409  UK       0598
  RICK HAYWARD       G    (A      (D) ESCAPE FROM BABYLON         1976 SIRE    US 7515  UK 9103 252
  DUSTER BENNETT     HCA  (A      (E) AMERICAN HEARTBEAT          1977 SIRE    US 6040  UK 9103 256
  DAVE BIDWELL       D    (A
  ANDY SYLVESTER     B    (A  STAN WEBB      G    (A  JEFF CONDON      HRNS (A  CHRIS WOOD      SAX (A
  CHRISTINE PERFECT  K    (A  MICK WEAVER    K    (A  BRIAN AUGER      ORG  (A  PETER SHELLEY       (A
  KEEF HARTLEY       D    (A  TERRY NOONAN   HRNS (A  PAUL KOSSOFF     G    (A  GARY THAIN      B   (A
  SPIT JAMES         G    (A  JIM CAPALDI    D    (A  BUD PARKES       HRNS (A  DEREK WADSWORTH HRNS(A
  CHRIS MERCER       SAX  (A  KEITH JOHNSON  HRNS (B  DAHAUD SHAAR     D    (B  JOHNNY ALMOND   SAX (A
  JOHN PLATANIA      G    (B  NANCY WADE     K    (B  DON MOORE        B    (B  MIKE WINFIELD   B   (B
  ALAN HAND          K    (B  JOHN KLINGBERG B    (B  GERARDO VELEZ    CONGA(B  BILLY CURTIS    CONGA(B
  COLLIN TILTON      WIND (B  GEORGE DEVENS  PERC (B  SPIDER BARBOUR   G    (B  CISSY HOUSTON   V   (B
  JOSHIE ARMSTEAD    V    (B  JACKIE VERDELL V    (B  RONNELLE STAFFORD V   (B  ASTON BARRETT   B   (D
  CARLTON BARRETT    D    (D  AL ANDERSON    G    (D  EARL SMITH       G    (D  TYRONE DOWNIE   K   (D
  WINSTON WRIGHT     K    (D  GLADSTONE ANDERSON K (D  BERNARD HARVEY   K    (D  LEE PERRY       PERC(D
  BOB MARLEY         PERC (D  RITA MARLEY    V    (D  JUDY MOWATT      V    (D  MARCIA GRIFFITHS V  (D
  DAVID SCANCE       V G K(E  BRIAN CUOMO    K    (E  JOHN SIEGLER     B    (E  PAUL MARCHETTI   D  (E
  JOEL KRANTZ        V    (E  JOHN DI ROBERTIS V  (E  KEN NEMIROFF     V    (E  FRANK D'AGOSTINO V  (E
  PAT ELLINGTON      V    (E  JOAN ELLINGTON V    (E  JUDY ELLINGTON   V    (E  RON CARTALEMI   V   (E
  JOHN ZANGRANDO     SAX  (E  JOHN PAYNE     WIND (E  STEVE SAVAGE     PERC (E  BOB GERLAND     WIND(E
  GEORGE CONSTANINOU STEEL(E  LARRY FAST     SYN  (E  ERNEST ROYAL     HRNS (E  JOHN CLARK      HRNS(E
  JAMES BUFFINGTON   HRNS (E  WAYNE ANDRE    HRNS (E  JOHN GATCHELL    HRNS (E  JANICE ROBINSON HRNS(E
  BUD MARTIN         SAX  (E  MICHAEL CULLEN SAX  (E  PETER SOBEL      ZITHER(E
```

VELVET FOGG

```
V21A                                  VELVET FOGG
                                  (A) VELVET FOGG                 1969 PYE             UK  NSPL18272
```

VELVET OPERA

COLIN FOSTER	G	(A		(A) RIDE A HUSTLERS DREAM	1969 CBS	UK	
JOHN FORD	B	(A					
RICHARD HUDSON	D	(A	JOHN JOYCE	V (A			

VELVET UNDERGROUND

LOU REED	V G K(ABCDEHJ		(A) VELVET UNDERGROUND WITH NICO	1967 VERVE	UK SVLP 9184	US 5008	
JOHN CALE	B K (ABCDE		(A) VELVET UNDERGROUND WITH NICO	196 VERVE		665114	
STERLING MORRISON	G (ABCDE		(A) VELVET UNDERGROUND WITH NICO	1971 MGM	UK 2315 056		
OSTRICH	G (A		(B) WHITE LIGHT WHITE HEAT	1967 VERVE	UK SVLP9201	US 5046	
BILLY YULE	D (D		(B) WHITE LIGHT WHITE HEAT	1971 MGM	UK 2353 024		
MO TUCKER	B (ABCDE		(C) VELVET UNDERGROUND	1969 MGM	UK CS 8108	US4617	
DOUG YULE G B D V K (D			(C) VELVET UNDERGROUND	1971 MGM	UK 2353 022		
NICO	V (AE		(D) LOADED	1970 ATLANTIC 2400 111 COTILLION US 9034			
			(D) LOADED	1971 ATLANTIC UK K40113 MIDI	20069		
			(E) ANDY WARHOL'S V UNDERGROUND	1971 MGM	UK 2683 006		
			(F) LIVE AT MAX'S KANSAS CITY	1972 ATLANTIC UK K30022 COTILLION 9500			
			(G) SQUEEZE	1972 POLYDOR	UK 2383 180		
			(H) VELVET UNDERGROUND ,LOU REED	1973 VERVE	UK 2315 258 PRIDE US 0022		
			(J) VELVET UNDERGROUND LIVE	1974 MERCURY	UK 6643 900 US SRM27504		
			(J) LIVE	1976 MGM	IMP 6643 017		
			( ) POP HISTORY No12	19 KAMA SUTRA UK 2612 021			
			( ) POP HISTORY No19	19 KAMA SUTRA UK 2625 019			
			( ) VELVET UNDERGROUND	1970 MGM	IMP GAS131		
			( ) VELVET UNDERGROUND	1976 MGM	UK 2354 033		
			( ) ARCHETYPES	19 MGM	IMP M3F4950		
			( ) EVIL MOTHERS	19 SKYDOG	US LP 003		

VENTURES

BOB BOGLE	G	(12345	WALK DONT RUN	196	LIBERTY UK LBY1002	US DOLTON	8003
DON WILSON	G	(12345	THE VENTURES	196		US DOLTON	8004
MEL TAYLOR	D	(2345	ANOTHER SMASH	196		US DOLTON	8006
NOKIE EDWARDS	B	(12	COLORFUL VENTURES	196		US DOLTON	8008
HOWIE JOHNSON	D	(1	TWIST PARTY	1962	LIBERTY UK LBY1072		
JERRY McGEE	G	(345	TWIST WITH THE VENTURES	196		US DOLTON	8010
JOHNNY DURRILL	PNO	(45	TWIST PARTY VOL 2	196		US DOLTON	8014
JOE BARILE	PERC	(5	MASHED POTATOES & GRAVY	196		US DOLTON	8016
RED RHODES	STEEL	(5	DANCE PARTY	196		US DOLTON	8017
			PLAY TELSTAR	196		US DOLTON	8019
			SURFING	196	LIBERTY UK LBY1150	US DOLTON	8022
			COUNTRY CLASSICS	196		US DOLTON	8023
			LETS GO	1963	LIBERTY UK LBY1169	US DOLTON	8024
			IN SPACE	196	LIBERTY UK LBY1189	US DOLTON	8027
			FABULOUS	196		US DOLTON	8019
			WALK DONT RUN VOL 2	196	LIBERTY UK SLBY1228	US DOLTON	8031
			KNOCK ME OUT	196	LIBERTY UK SLBY1252	US DOLTON	8033
			ON STAGE	196	LIBERTY UK SLBY1270	US DOLTON	8035
			A GO GO	196	LIBERTY UK SLBY1274	US DOLTON	8037
			CHRISTMAS ALBUM	196	LIBERTY UK SLBY1285	US DOLTON	8038
			WHERE THE ACTION IS	196	LIBERTY UK SLBY1297	US DOLTON	8040
			BATMAN THEME	19		US DOLTON	8042
			GO WITH	196	LIBERTY UK SLBY1323	US DOLTON	8045
			WILD THING	196		US DOLTON	8047
			GUITAR FREAKOUT	196	LIBERTY UK SLBY1345	US DOLTON	8050
			SUPER PSYCHEDELICS	196	LIBERTY UK SLBY1372	US DOLTON	8052
			BEST OF	196	LIBERTY UK SLBY1375		
			GOLDEN GREATS	1965	LIBERTY UK 83046	US	8053
			MILLION DOLLAR WEEKEND	1965	LIBERTY	US	8054
			FLIGHTS OF FANCY	196	LIBERTY	US	8055
			I LIKE IT LIKE THAT	1965	LIBERTY UK 83116		
			THE HORSE	196	LIBERTY	US	8057
			UNDERGROUND FIRE	1969	LIBERTY UK 83193	US	8059
			MORE GOLDEN GREATS	19	LIBERTY UK 83175	US	8060
			HAWAII FIVE O	196	LIBERTY UK	US	8061
			SWAMP ROCK	1969	LIBERTY U K 83289	US	8062
			10TH ANNIVERSARY ALBUM	1970	LIBERTY	US	35000
			VENTURES	197	UA	US	UAX 80
			JIM CROCE SONGBOOK	197	UA	US	UALA 217
			(S) SHAFT	197	UA	UK UAS29280 US	5547
			LEGENDARY MASTERS	1974	UA	UK UAD 60051	
			JOY	1974	UA	UK UAS29340 US	5575
			BEST OF THE POPS	1974	UA	UK UAS29249	
			VERY BEST OF	1975	US EURO 050 96470	US	UALA 331
			VERY BEST OF	1976	SUNSET UK SL550386		
			RUNNING STRONG	197	SUNSET	US	5116
			ROCKY ROAD	197	UA	US LA	586
			ROCK'N'ROLL FOREVER	197	UA	US	5649

VENUS & THE RAZOR BLADES

(A) SONGS FROM SUNSHINE JUNGLE	1978 SPARK	SRLP 125

JOHN VERITY BAND

JOHN VERITY	G V	(A		(A) JOHN VERITY BAND	1974 PROBE	UK SPB1087
GEOFF LYTH	K G	(A				
GERRY SMITH	B	(A	RON KELLY	D (A THUNDERTHIGHS V (A		

MIKE VERNON

MIKE VERNON	V HCA PERC(AB		(A) BRING IT BACK HOME	1971 BLUE HORIZON	UK	2931 003
COLIN ALLEN	D	(B	(B) MOMENT OF MADNESS	1973 SIRE	US	SAS 7410
LAWRENCE GARMAN	HCA	(B				
LEO LYONS	B	(B	FUZZY SAMUELS	B (B ANDY SYLVESTER	B (B RIC LEE	D (B
JOE JAMMER	G	(B	MITCH MITCHELL	D (B PAUL BUTLER	G (B DEREK GRIFFITHS	G (B
NICK SOUTH	B	(B	PETE WINGFIELD	K (B BRUCE ROWLAND	D (B CECIL MOSS	TPT(B
JOHN DONNELLY	TPT	(B	BILLY GRAHAM	TROM (B HOWIE CASEY	SAX (B	

V26B VERTO

```
JEAN PIERRE GRASSET G SYN(AB    (A) KRIG / VOLUBILIS        19   POLE                         0009
GILLES GOUBIN       B   (A      (B) REEL 19/36              1978 FLEAU                        FL 7004
CHARLES GOUBIN      G   (A
CYRIL LEFEBVRE      G   (B   OCTAVE AGOBERT    (B   BENOIT WIDEMANN   SYN (B  DOMINIQUE GRASSET   G(B
PHILIPPE PERRONET   D   (B   JEAN PIERRE FOUQUET B K(B  FRANCOIS ARTIGE   G   (B
```

V26C EDWARD VESALA

```
EDWARD VESALA       V D (ALL     (A) NANA        1970 BLUE MASTER       BLULP 125
JUHANI AALTONEN     WIND (ABDEF   (B) HOT LOTTA   1973 BLUE MASTER       SPEL  306
ARILD ANDERSON      B   (A        (C) I'M HERE    1973 BLUE MASTER       SPEL  311
PETER KOWALD        B   (B        (D) NAN MADOL   1974 JAPO 60007 +  ECM  1077
PETER BROTZMANN     SAX (B        (E) SATU        1976 ECM              1088
KAJ BACKLUND        TPT (D        (F) RODINA      1976 LOVE             LRLP 189
SAKARI KUKKO        FLT (D
JOHANI POUTANEN     V   (D   TEPPO HAUTOANO  B    (D   ELISABETH LEISTOLA HARP (D  MIRCEA STANKO   HRNS (DF
SEPPO PAAKKUNAINEN  WIND(D   PENTTI LANTI    WIND (DF  CHARLIE MANANO     SAX (D   TOMASZ STANKO   TPT (EF
PALLE MIKKELBERG    HRNS (E  TOMASZ SZUKALSKI SAX (EF  KNUT RIISNAES      FLT (E   ROLF HALM       WIND(E
TORBJØRN SUNDE      HRNS (E  TERJE RYPDAL    G    (E   PALLE DAUIELGSON   B   (E   PEKKA POYRY     SAX (E
ESA HELALSVUO       PNO (F   PEKKA RECHAREIT      (F   PEKKA SARMANTO         (F   IRINA MILAN     V   (F
```

V27 PATRICK VIAN

```
PATRICK VIAN            (A    (A) BRUITS ET TEMPS ANALOGUES  1978 EGG    EURO   900 541
```

V28 VIBRATORS

```
IAN CARNOCHAN       G V (A1    (A) PURE MANIA                1977 EPIC    UK    82097
KNOX                G V (ABC1   (B) V 2                       1978 EPIC    UK    82495
JOHN ELLIS          G V (ABC    (C) BATTERIES INCLUDED (COMP) 1980 CBS     UK    31840
PAT COLLIER         G   (A      (1) 1978
JOHN EDWARDS        D   (ABC1
GARY TIBBS         B   (BC1 DON SNOW   K SAX(1  DAVE BIRCH   G  (1  CHRIS SPEDDING  G  (
GREG VANCOOK       G   (C   BEN BRIERLEY B (C
```

V28A SID VICIOUS

```
SID VICIOUS         V   (A     (A) SID VICIOUS               1979 VIRGIN   UK    V2144
```

V29 MIKE VICKERS

```
MIKE VICKERS            (AB    (A) I WISH I WERE A GROUP AGAIN 1968 COLUMBIA UK   SCX  6180
                                (B) A DAY AT THE RACES         1976 DJM      UK   DJSLM2034
```

V30 VIGRASS & OSBORNE

```
PAUL VIGRASS        V   (AB    (A) QUEUES        1972 UNI US 73129   UK    UDLS  501
GARY OSBORNE        G V (AB    (A) QUEUES        1974 MCA            UK RI MCG 3521
BARRY CLARKE        G MAND(B   (B) STEPPIN' OUT  1974 CBS US 33077   UK    80119
MARK GRIFFITHS      G   (B
PETER MORGAN        B   (B   TETSU YAMAUCHI  B   (B   PETER WATKINS   B    (B   HERBIE FLOWERS  B  (B
BARRY DE SOUZA      D   (B   KENNEY JONES    D   (B   RAY COOPER      PERC (B   PETER WOOD      K  (B
ALAN HAWKSHAW       K   (B   JEFF WAYNE      K   (B   DOREEN CHANTER  V    (B   IRENE CHANTER   V  (B
JUANITA FRANKLIN    V   (B   JUDITH POWELL   V   (B   TIM RENWICK     G    (B
```

V32 GENE VINCENT

```
GENE VINCENT        V   (ALL   BLUEJEAN BOP                  195  CAPITOL         T764
CLIFF GALLUP        G   (1     & THE BLUECAPS                196  CAPITOL         T811
JACK NEAL           B   (1     VINCENT ROCKS,BLUECAPS ROLL   196  CAPITOL         T970
WILLIE WILLIAMS     G   (1     RECORD DATE                   196  CAPITOL         T 1059
DICKIE HARRELL      D   (12    SOUNDS LIKE                   196  CAPITOL         T 1207
PAUL PEEK               (2     CRAZY TIMES                   1960 CAPITOL         T 1342
TOMMY FACENDA           (2     CRAZY BEAT                    196  CAPITOL         T20452
BOBBY LEE JONES         (2     SHAKIN UP A STORM             196  CAPITOL         33SX 1646
JOHN MEEKS          G   (*     GENE VINCENT                  1967 LONDON    UK    HAU 8333
JIM GRANT           K   (*     BEST OF GENE VINCENT          1967 CAPITOL         T20957
RED RHODES          STEEL(*    BEST OF VOL 2                 1969 CAPITOL         ST21144
                               (*) I'M BACK & I'M PROUD      1969 DANDELION       63754
JIM GORDON          D   (*     GENE VINCENT                  1970 KAMA SUTRA UK   2019
MARS BONFIRE        G   (*     THE DAY THE WORLD TURNED BLUE 1971 KAMA SUTRA      2027
SKIP BATTIN         B   (*     PIONEERS OF ROCK              1972 STARLINE   UK   SRS  5117
                               STORY VOL 1  1956/57          1973 PATHE      FR   064 81081
(1) 1956                       STORY VOL 2     1958          1973 PATHE      FR   064 81082
(2) 1957                       STORY VOL 3     1959          1973 PATHE      FR   064 81083
                               STORY VOL 4     1960          1973 PATHE      FR   064 81084
                               MEMORIAL ALBUM                19   PATHE      FR   154 81001
                               KING OF FOOLS                 1974 STARLINE   UK   SRS  5177
                               GREATEST                      19   CAPITOL    IMP  052 80230
                               BOP THAT WONT STOP            1974 CAPITOL         ST  11287
                               GENE VINCENT STORY            1975 CAPITOL    IMP  178 81798
                               GREATEST                      1977 CAPITOL    UK   CAPS 1001
                               ROCK'N'ROLL LEGEND(4LP BOXED SET) 1977 EMI     IMP  85071/4
                               GREATEST                      1979 CAPITOL    UK   CAPS 1028
```

V33 VINEGAR JOE

```
ELKIE BROOKS        V K (ABC   (A) VINEGAR JOE           1972 ISLAND   UK   ILPS 9183
ROBERT PALMER       G V (ABC   (B) ROCK'N'ROLL GYPSIES   1972 ISLAND   UK   ILPS 9214
PETE GAGE           K G V(ABC  (C) SIX STAR GENERAL      1973 ISLAND   UK   ILPS 9262
STEVE YORK          HCA B(ABC
TIM HINKLEY         K   (A   ROB TAIT       D   (A   DAVE THOMPSON   K SAX(A  DAVE BROOKS    SAX (A
CONRAD ISADORE      D   (A   KEEF HARTLEY   D   (AB  GASPAR LAWAL    PERC (A  ROGER BALL     HRNS(A
MALCOLM DUNCAN      HRNS (A  JIM MULLEN     G   (B   MIKE DEACON     K V (BC  JOHN WOODS         (BC
PETE GAVIN         D   (C
```

V34 EDDIE 'CLEANHEAD' VINSON

```
EDDIE VINSON        V SAX(ALL  EDDIE CLEANHEAD VINSON    19   TRIP          US   5590
                               THE ORIGINAL CLEANHEAD    1972 PPHILIPS      UK   6369 406
                               CHERRY RED BLUES          19   KING STARDAY  US   1087
                               JAMMING THE BLUES         1975 BLACK LION         BLP 30168
                               EDDIE VINSON              19   B&B                33021
                               CLEANHEADS BACK IN TOWN   19   BETHLEHEM     US   BCP 5005
                               CLEAN MACHINE             1979 MUSE          FR   MR 5116
```

VIOLINSKI — V35

```
MIK KAMINSKI        VLN  (AB    (A) NO CAUSE FOR ALARM    1979 JET      UK  JETLP 219
JOHN MARCANGELO     K    (AB    (B) STOP CLONING ABOUT    1980 JET      UK  JETLP 232
JOHN HODSON         D    (AB
MIKE DE ALBUQUERQUE G V(AB  BAZ DUNNERY    G V (A  PAUL MANN    V B (A  ANDY BROWN   B V(A
IAN WHITMORE        B V  (B
```

VISAGE — V35A

```
STEVE STRANGE       (          (A) VISAGE              1980 POLYDOR   UK  2490 157
MIDGE URE           G (
BILLY CURRIE        VLN (    JOHN McGEOCH  G (   RUSTY EGAN   D ( DAVE FORMULA   K (
BARRY ADAMSON       B (
```

VISITOR 2035 — V36

```
CRAIG PRUESS        KTPT VIBES(   (A) VISITOR 2035     1978 ARIOLA         AHAL 8003
RAY DEEFHOLTS       G (           (B) CAIN       (D)   19
PETER STROUD        B (
NIGEL ROBINSON      D PERC(
```

VITAL DUB — V37

```
                               (A) WELL CHARGED        1977 VIRGIN    UK  V 2055
```

JOE VITALE — V38

```
JOE VITALE          D V (A      (A) ROLLERCOASTER WEEKEND   1975 ATLANTIC  US SD18114 UK K50121
JOE WALSH           G (A
RICK DERRINGER      G (A   NELSON'FLACO' PADRON PERC(A  PHIL KEAGY   G (A
```

VITESSE — V38A

```
RUDI DE QUELJOU     G (A        (A) VITESSE            1979 UA        UK  UAG 30250
HERMAN VAN BOEYEN   D V (A
JAN VAN DER MEY     G V (A  WILCO TOERRE LEERDAM  B V (A
```

MIROSLAV VITOUS — V39

```
MIROSLAV VITOUS B SYN G(ALL     (A) INFINITE SEARCH      1969 EMBRYO   US            SD 524
JOE HENDERSON      SAX  (AB      (B) MOUNTAIN IN THE CLOUDS  1972 ATLANTIC UK K50406 US SD1622
JOHN McLAUGHLIN    G    (AB      (C) MAGICAL SHEPHERD    1976 WB       UK K56219  US BS2925
HERBIE HANCOCK     K    (ABC     (D) MIROSLAV           1978 FREEDOM  UK 41040   US 1040
JACK DE JOHNETTE   D    (ABC     (E) FIRST MEETING      1980 ECM                 1145
JON CHRISTENSEN    D    (EF      (F) M V GROUP          1981 ECM                 1185
OE CHAMBERS        D    (AB
JAMES GADSON       D    (C   AIRTO MOREIRA   PERC (C  CHERYL GRAINGER  V (C  ONIKE   V (C
JOHN SURMAN        WIND (EF  KENNY KIRKLAND  PNO (EF
```

VOICES OF EAST HARLEM — V40

```
BERNICE COLE       V (          (A) RIGHT TO BE FREE     1970 ELEKTRA US 74080  UK 2469 007
GERRI GRIFFIN      V (          (B) BROTHERS & SISTERS   197  ELEKTRA          UK K42119
CYNTHIA SESSIONS   V (          (C) VOICES OF EAST HARLEM 1973 JUST    US       JUST 7
JAMES MISSOURI     V (          (D) CAN YOU FEEL IT      1974 JUST    US       JUST3504
```

ADELBERT VON DEYEN — V41

```
ADELBERT VON DEYEN ALL INST(AB  (A) STEMGAT            1978 SKY              SKY 019
                                (B) MORDBORG           1979 SKY              SKY 029
```

VOYAGER

```
PAUL FRENCH        K V (AB      (A) HALFWAY HOTEL       1979 MOUNTAIN UK  TOPS 124
PAUL HIRSH         K G V(AB      (B) ACT OF LOVE        1980 MOUNTAIN UK  TOPS 127
CHRIS HOOK         B V (AB
JOHN MARTER        D (AB
```

THE WACKERS — W1

```
BOB SEGARINI       G V (ABCD     (A) WACKERING HEIGHTS   1971 ELEKTRA US  EKS 78098
RANDY BISHOP V G B K   (ABCD     (B) HOT WACKS          1972 ELEKTRA US  EKS 75025
MICHAEL STULL      G V PNO(AB     (C) SHREDDER          1972 ELEKTRA US  EKS 75046
BILL KOOTCH TROCHIM V B G(ABCD   (D) WACK'N' ROLL   (NOT RELEASED)
SPENCER T EARNSHAW  D (ABC
BILL HENDERSON      D (A  JACK SCHAEFFER SAX (AC  KATHIE KODAMA  KOTO (B  J P LAUZON  B G PNO(C
DAN YEN MANTOR  CONGAS(C  FRANKIE HART V PERC (C  JERRY MERCER   D (C  RAY BLAKE   V (C
JANET ABRAMSON      V (C
```

WAGES OF SIN — W2

```
TIM RENWICK        G (A         (A) 1968
COLIN FREEMAN       (A  PETER DINES  K (A  VIC FARRAR    (A  JERRY SHIRLEY  D(A
```

ADRIAN WAGNER — W3

```
ADRIAN WAGNER      K (AB        (A) DISTANCES BETWEEN US  1974 ATLANTIC
JOHN CORNWALL      B (B         (B) THE LAST INCA      1978 CHARISMA  UK  CAS 1135
IVO HATFIELD       G (B  MORRIS PERT  D (B
```

BUNNY WAILER — W4

```
BUNNY WAILER       V (ABC       (A) BLACK HEART MAN     1976 ISLAND   uk  ILPS 9415
CARLTON BARRETT    D (A         (B) PROTEST            1977 ISLAND   UK  ILPS 9512
ASTON BARRETT      G (A         (C) SINGS THE WAILERS   1981 ISLAND   UK  ILPS 9629
ROBBY SHAKESPEAR   B (ABC
TYRONE DOWNIE      K (A  TOMMY McCOOK   FLT (AB  PETER TOSH      G (AB  WINSTON WRIGHT   K (AC
DIRTY HARRY     HRNS (AB  BOBBY ELLIS   HRNS (AB  HERMAN MARQUIS HRNS (AB  WILLY PEP       PERC(A
HAROLD BUTLER      K (A  EARL CHINNA SMITH G (AC  FRATTER         G (A  HORSE MOUTH      D (B
MIKE RICHARDS      D (B  EARL LINDO     K (B  TOUTER          K (B  KEITH STERLING   K (BC
SOLOMONIC ENCHANTERS V (B  STICKY      PERC (C  DEAN FRASER   HRNS (C  NAMBO          HRNS(C
SLY DUNBAR         D (C  HEADLEY BENNETT HRNS (C
```

WAILING SOULS — W4A

```
WINSTON'PIPE'MATTHEWS V(A       (A) WILD SUSPENSE      1979 ISLAND   UK  ILPS 9523
LLOYD McDONALD     V (A
RAD BRYAN          G (A  ANSELL COLLINS   K (A  GEORGE HAYE    V (A  TARZAN NELSON   PNO (A
RUDOLPH DENNIS     V (A  LOWELL SLY DUNBAR D (A  RANCHIE McLEAN B (A  VIN GORDON      TROM(A
STICKY THOMPSON PERC (A  RICO          TROM (A  CEDRIC BROOKS  SAX (A  NOEL SIMMS      PERC(A
ROBBIE SHAKESPEARE G (A  BOPEE BOWEN      G (A  DICKAGE       HRNS (A  HEADLEY BENNETT SAX (A
```

LOUDON WAINWRIGHT III

LOUDON WAINWRIGHT II	G V(ALL					
RICHARD CROOKS	D (CEFG					
JOHN CROWDER	B (G					
STEPHEN TUBIN	K (FG					
RON GETMAN	STEEL G (FG					
JIMMY MAELEN	CONGA(F					
ELLIOTT RANDALL	G (F					
JOANNE VENT	V (F					
GWYNNE MICHAELS	V (F					
ERIN ARNOLD DICKINS	V (F					
JEAN ARNOLD	V (F	CHRISTIE THOMPSON V (F	JON COBERT V (F	GEORGE MARGE REC (F
MARVIN STAMM	HRNS (F	HANK JONES K (F	MARKIE MARKOWITZ HRNS (F	RICHARD DAVIS B (F
JOE COCUZZO	D (F	PETER LA BARBERA VIBES(F	MAGGIE ROCHE V (F	TERRE ROCHE V (F
ERIC WEISSBERG	BANJO(FG	CHARLES BROWN III G (CF	KENNETH KOSEK FDL (CFG	GLEN MITCHELL K V (FG
DAVID SANBORN	SAX (CF	PAUL PRESTOPINO (F	DAVE TAYLOR TROM (F	JOHN LISSAUER CLAR(FG
DON HAMMOND	REF (F	HARVEY ESTRIN REC (F	JOHN HALL G (EG	ARLEN ROTH G (G
HUGH McCRACKEN	G (G	LARRY PACKER FDL (G	ERROL BENNETT PERC (G	TEDDY WENDER PNO (C
GREG THOMAS	D (E	RON COLBERTSON (E	HARVEY BROOKS B (E	KLAUS VOORMANN B (E
LYLE RITZ	B (E	RICHARD GREENE VLN (E	MARTIN FIERRO SAX (E	ANNA McGARRIGLE V (E
THOMAS JEFFERSON KAYE	G(C	DON PAYNE B (E	CALVIN HARDY (	FRANK KLEIGER (E
RANDY WALLACE	(E	MARTY GREBB K (E	CHRIS GUEST (E	GEORGE GERDES (E
JIM KELTNER	D (E	JAY MIGLIORI WIND (E	AUSTIN DELONE (E	KATE McGARRIGLE V (E

Album	Year	Label	Country	Cat	Country	Cat
(A) ALBUM 1	1971	ATLANTIC	US SD8260	UK	2400 103
(A) ALBUM 1	1971	ATLANTIC		UK	K40107
(B) ALBUM 2	1972	ATLANTIC	US SD8291	UK	K40272
(C) ALBUM 3	1972	CBS	US 31462	UK	65238
(D) ATTEMPTED MOUSTACHE	1974	CBS	US 32710	UK	65837
(E) UNREQUITED	1975	CBS	US 33369	UK	80696
(F) T SHIRT	1976	ARISTA	US 4063	UK ARTY 127
(G) FINAL EXAM	1978	ARISTA	US 4173	UK SPART1042
(H) LIVE ONE	1979	RADAR		UK	RAD 24

TOM WAITS

TOM WAITS	G V (ALL					
MIKE MELVOIN	K (C					
PETE CHRISTLIEB	SAX (C					
JIM HUGHART	B (CFG					
SHELLEY MANNE	D (C					
LEW TABACKIN	SAX (C					
DA WILLIE GONGA	K (F					
RICK LAWSON	D (F					
ROLAND BAUTISTA	G (FG					
BYRON MILLER	B (F					
FRANK VICARI	SAX (F					
RAY CRAWFORD	G (F	CHARLES KYNARD B (F	CHIP WHITE D (F	BOBBYE HALL PERC (F
HAROLD BATTISTE	PNO (F	SHINE ROBINSON G (F	SCOTT EDWARDS B (F	EARL PALMER D (F
BIG JOHN THOMASSIE	D (G	PLAS JOHNSON SAX (G	GREG COHEN B (G	RONNIE BARRON K (G
VICTOR FELDMAN	PERC (G	MICHAEL LANG PNO (G	MEL COLLINS SAX (1	TIM HINKLEY K (1
CLEM CLEMPSON	G (G	HERBERT HARDESTY SAX (F	BILL GOODWIN D (C	

Album	Year	Label	Country	Cat	Country	Cat
(A) CLOSING TIME	1973	ELEKTRA	US SD5061	UK	SYL 9007
(A) CLOSING TIME	1976	ELEKTRA		UK	K53030
(B) HEART OF A SATURDAY NIGHT	1974	ASYLUM	US 7E1015	UK	K53035
(C) NIGHTHAWKS AT THE DINER	1975	ASYLUM	US 7E2008	UK	SYSP 903
(C) NIGHTHAWKS AT THE DINER	1976	ASYLUM		UK	K63002
(D) SMALL CHANGE	1976	ASYLUM	US 7E1078	UK	K53050
(E) FOREIGN AFFAIRS	1977	ELEKTRA	US 7E1117	UK	K53068
(F) BLUE VALENTINE	1978	ASYLUM	US 6E 162	UK	K53088
(G) HEART ATTACK & VINE	1980	ASYLUM	US 6E 296	UK	K52252
(1) TV SHOW ENGLAND 1979					

JOHNNY WAKELIN

JOHNNY WAKELIN	V (ALL					

Album	Year	Label	Country	Cat
(A) REGGAE SOUL & ROCK'N'ROLL	1976	PYE	UK	NSPL 18521
(B) AFRICAN MAN	1977	PYE	UK	NSPL 18487
(C) DOUBLE TROUBLE	1978	PYE	UK	NSPL 18561
(D) GOLDEN HOUR	1979	PYE	UK	GH 680

RICK WAKEMAN

RICK WAKEMAN	K (ALL					
DAVE WINTOUR	B (A					
CHRIS SQUIRE	B (AG					
CHAS CRONK	B (A					
LES HURDLE	B (A					
MIKE EGAN	G (AG					
DAVE LAMBERT	G (A					
STEVE HOWE	G (A					
ALAN WHITE	D (AG					
BILL BRUFORD	D (A					
BARRY DE SOUZA	D (A	RAY COOPER PERC (A	FRANK RICOTTI PERC (AG	DAVE COUSINS BANJO (A
LISA STRIKE	V (A	LAURA LEE V (A	BARRY ST JOHN V (A	SYLVIA McNEILL V (A
JUDY POWELL	V (A	ASHLEY HOLT V (BCE	GARY PICKFORD HOPKINS V (BC	JEFF CRAMPTON G (C
ROGER NEWELL	B (BCE	BARNEY JAMES D (BC	JOHN HODGSON PERC (C	JOHN DUNSTERVILLE G V(E
TONY FERNANDEZ	D (E	MARTY SHIELD HRNS V (E	REG BROOKS HRNS V(E	BILL ODDIE V (B
ARS LAETA CHOIR	V (B	ROGER DALTREY V (D	PAUL NICHOLAS V (D	LINDA LEWIS V (D
DAVID WILDE	PNO (D	GEORGE MICHIE (D	JOHN FORSYTHE (D	ENG ROCK ENSEMBLE (D
NAT PHILHARMONIC ORCH	(D	BRUCE LYNCH B (J	FRANK GIBSON D (J	NICO RAMSDEN G (J
TONY VISCONTI	(J					

Album	Year	Label	Country	Cat	Country	Cat
(A) 6 WIVES OF HENRY VIII	1973	A&M	US 4361	UK	AMLH64361
(B) JOURNEY TO THE CENTRE OF EARTH	1974	A&M	US 3621	UK	AMLH63621
(C) KING ARTHUR	1975	A&M	US 4515	UK	AMLH64515
(D) LISZTOMANIA	1975	A&M		UK	AMLK64546
(E) NO EARTHLY CONNECTION	1976	A&M	US 4583	UK	AMLK64583
(F) WHITE ROCK	1976	A&M	US 4614	UK	AMLH64614
(G) CRIMINAL RECORD	1977	A&M	US 4660	UK	AMLK64660
(H) BEST KNOWN WORKS	1978	A&M		UK	AMLH68447
(J) RHAPSODIES	1979	A&M		UK	AMLX68508

NARADA MICHAEL WALDEN

NARADA MICHAEL WALDEN	D V(ALL					
JEFF BECK	G (A					
RAY GOMEZ	G (AB					
CARLOS SANTANA	G (AC					
HIRAM BULLOCK	G (BC					
NEIL JASON	B (BC	CLIFF CARTER K (BC	HERBIE MANN SAX (B	NORMA JEAN BELL SAX (AB
SAMMY FIGUEROA	PERC (AB	RAFAEL CRUZ PERC (B	CHRISTINE FAITH V (B	ELLEN DELESTON V (B
CHERYL ALEXANDER	V (BC	WILL LEE B (A	DAVID SANCIOUS K (A	CISSY HOUSTON B V (A
PATTY SCALFA	V (AC	BOB KNAPP HRNS (A	ICARUS JOHNSON G (A	DON MERO SYN (A
LOIS COLIN	HARP (A	JAY GRAYDON G (C	PAT THRALL G (C	KENNY MAZUR G (C
KENI BURKE	B (C	NATE PHILLIPS B (C	NORBERT SCOLEY B (C	GREG PHILLINGANES K (C
BOBBY LYLE	K (C	MICHAEL BRECKER HRNS (C	RANDY BRECKER HRNS (C	AIRTO MOREIRA PERC (C
POINTER SISTERS	V (C	JIM GILSTRAP V (C	CARLA VAUGHN V (C	ALEX BROWN V (C
ANGELA WINBUSH	V (C	BILL LAMB TPT (C	TAWATHA AGEE V (C	CORRADO RUSTICI G V (D
RANDY JACKSON	B (D	FRANK MARTIN K (D	MARC RUSSO SAX (D	DAVID GROVER TPT (D
WAYNE WALLACE	TROM (D					

Album	Year	Label	Country	Cat	Country	Cat
(A) GARDEN OF LOVE LIGHT	1977	ATLANTIC		UK	K50329
(B) I CRY, I SMILE	1978	ATLANTIC		UK	K50417
(C) AWAKENING	1979	ATLANTIC	US SD19222	UK	K50570
(D) VICTORY	1980	ATLANTIC	US SD19279		

WENDY WALDMAN

WENDY WALDMAN	V PNO G DULC(ALL					
DAVID KEMPER	D (D					
KENNY EDWARDS	B G V(CD					
ANDREW GOLD	G V PNO (CD					
WADDY WACHTEL	G (D					
LINDA RONSTADT	V (D					
MICHAEL BOTTS	D (D	KARLA BONOFF V (CD	NICK DE CARO ACC (D	PETER BERNSTEIN B (DE
DAVID FOSTER	K (CD	STEVE CROPPER G (D	KING ERRISSON PERC (D	TAJ MAHAL V (D

Album	Year	Label	Country	Cat
(A) LOVE HAS GOT ME	1973	WB	US BS 2735
(B) GYPSY SYMPHONY	1974	WB	US BS 2792
(C) WENDY WALDMAN	1975	WB	US BS 2859
(D) THE MAIN REFRAIN	1976	WB	US BS 2974
(E) STRANGE COMPANY	1978	WB	US BS 3178

(CONTINUED)

WENDY WALDMAN W9

JIM HORN	WIND (D	MILT HOLLAND	CONGA(D	VICTOR FELDMAN	PERC (D	STEVE FERGUSON K G V(CD		
JAI WINDING	ORG (D	CHUCK FINDLEY	HRNS (D	DON MENZA	HRNS (D	JAY MIGLIORI	HRNS(D	
STEVE BEERS	D (E	MARK GOLDENBERG G PNO G V(E		CRAIG HULL	G V (E	DEBBIE DOBKIN	V PERC(E	
CAT HENDRIKSE	D (E	PETER ROBINSON	PNO (E	PETER WHITE	K (E	JENNIFER WARREN	V (C	
RON TUTT	D (C	EMIL RICHARDS	PERC (C					

WALES / O' REGAN W10

ERIC WALES	V G MAND K(A		(A) READY TO RUN		1977 MOUNTAIN	UK	TOPC5010		
JERRY O'REGAN	G V (A								
JEFF ALLEN	D (A	BARRY DE SOUZA	D (A	ALLAN MAIR	D (A	PETE ZORN	B (A	
ROGER SUTTON	B (A	DAVE MARKEE	B (A	RICHARD BRUNTON	G (A	DAVE ROSE	K (A	
GEOFF WESTLEY	K (A	B J COLE	STEEL(A	TONY COLE	WIND (A	STAN SULZMANN	HRNS(A	
RON ASPERY	HRNS (A	JACK EMBLOW	ACC (A	VICKY BROWN	V (A	LIZA STRIKE	V (A	
BARRY ST JOHN	V (A	IRENE CHANTER	V (A	ANNE CULLEN	V (A			

DAVID T WALKER W10A

DAVID T WALKER	G (AB		(A) DAVID T WALKER		197 ODE	US	SP 77011	
JOE SAMPLE	K (A		(B) SIDEWALK		19 REVUE	US	RS 7297	
JERRY PETERS	K (A							
BILLY PRESTON	K (A	CLARENCE McDONALD K (A		PAUL HUMPHREY	D (A	WILTON FELDER	B (A	
BOBBYE HALL	PERC (A	CURTIS AMY	SAX (A	MERRY CLAYTON	V (A	PATRICE HOLLOWAY V (A		
STEPHANIE SPRUILL	V (A	ANN ESTHER DAVIS	V (A	JOHN LEHMAN	V (A	JIM GILSTRAP	V (A	

JERRY JEFF WALKER W11

JERRY JEFF WALKER	G V (ALL	(A) MR BOJANGLES	1968 ATCO		US	33259	
DAVID BROMBERG	G (ABE	(B) DRIFTIN' WAY OF LIFE	1969 VANGUARD		US	VSD 6521	
GARY ILLINGSWORTH	K (A	(C) FIVE YEARS GONE	1969 ATCO		US	33297	
DONNY BROOKS	HARP (A	(D) BEIN' FREE	1970 ATCO		US	33336	
DANNY MILTON	DOBRO(A	(E) JERRY JEFF WALKER	1972 MCA	US 510	RI 1976	2358	
JODY STECHER	FDL MAND(A	(E) JERRY JEFF WLAKER	1973 MCA	UK MUPS 488	RI 1974	MCF 2518	
BOBBY CRANSHAW	B (A	(E) JERRY JEFF WALKER	1973 DECCA	US		75384	
JERRY JEMMOTT	V (A	(F) VIVA TERLINGUA	1973 MCA	US 382	RI 76	2350	
RON CARTER	B (A	(F) VIVA TERLINGUA	1973 MCA	UK MAPS7164			
BILL LAVORGNA	D (A	(G) WALKERS COLLECTIBLES	1974 MCA	US 450	RI 76	2355	
KENNETH BUTTREY	D (BIJ	(G) WALKERS COLLECTIBLES	1974 MCA	UK		MCF 2592	
NORBERT PUTNAM	B (BIJ	(H) RIDIN' HIGH	1975 MCA	US		2156	
PETE WADE	DOBRO(B	(I) ITS A GOOD NIGHT FOR SINGING	1976 MCA	US 2202	UK	MCG 3522	
HAROLD RUGG	STEEL(B	(J) A MAN MUST CARRY ON (DBL)	1977 MCA	US 2 8013	UK	MCSP 281	
WAYNE MOSS	G (B	(K) CONTRARY TO ORDINARY	1978 MCA	US 3041	UK	MCF 2851	
DAVID BRIGGS	K (BIJ	(L) JERRY JEFF	1978 ELEKTRA	US 6E163	UK	K52106	
PATTERSON BARRETT	STEEL(EJ	(M) TOO OLD TO CHANGE	1979 ELEKTRA	US 6E239			
BEN CARUSO	B (E						
DAVID COOK	STEEL(E	JEFF DUFINE	PNO (E	MARY EGAN	VLN (EF	CRAIG HILLIS	G (EF
ELLEN KEARNEY	V (E	BOB LIVINGSTON K B V(EFHIJL		RAUN MACKINNON	PNO (E	MICHAEL McGARRY	D (E
MICHAEL MURPHEY	G (E	ANDY NEWMARK	D (E	GARY P NUNN K V	(EFHIJ	LARRY PACKER	G VLN(E
MICKEY RAPHAEL	HARP (EF	JIM RICHMOND	D (E	JONATHAN SIMMONS	MAND (E	HERB STEINER	STEEL(EFJ
JOANNE VENT	V (EF	KELLY DUNN	ORG (FHIJ	JOHN INMON	G V (HIJ	TOMAS RAMIREZ	WIND(HJLM
DONNY DOLAN	D (HIJ	WELDON MYRICK	STEEL(IJ	JOHNNY GIMBLE	FDL (IM	CHIP YOUNG	G V (I
BOBBY THOMPSON	BAN (I	SHANE KEISTER	K (I	DEBORAH ALLEN	V (I	REESE WYNANS	K (I
BOBBY RAMBO	G B V(JLM	RON COBB	SAX (JLM	LEO LEBLANC	STEEL(JLM	FRED KRC	D PERC (JLM
DAVE PERKINS	G (JLM	KEITH SYKES	G (L	PENNY NEY	V (L	STEVE ZIRKEL	HRNS(L
MICHAEL MORDECAI	HRNS (LM	CAROLE KING	V (M	RICHARD PRICE	B (M	MARK HALLMAN	D (M
DAVID AMRAM	HRNS (M	FINGERS TAYLOR	HCA (M	GEORGE M JONES	PERC (M	STEVE KEITH	FDL (J
KAREN BROOKS	V (J	SHARI NEUWELL	V (J	VASSAR CLEMENTS	FDL (J	BEE SPEARS	B (J
DON McCLURE	K (J	SUSAN WALKER	V (J	HONDO CROUCH	V (J	CHARLES JOHN QUATRO V(J	
BILL JOOR	(J	JIMMY BAKER	TROM (J	WILLIE NELSON	G V (J	RAY WYLIE HUBBARD	G V(J

JOHNNY' BIG MOOSE' WALKER W11A

JOHNNY WALKER	K (A	(A) RAMBLIN WOMAN	1969 ABC BLUESWAY	US	6036	

JUNIOR WALKER & THE ALL STARS W12

JUNIOR WALKER	SAX V(	SHOTGUN	1965		US SOUL 701	
WILLIE WOODS	G (	SOUL SESSION	1966 TAMLA	UK STML11029	US SOUL 702	
VIC THOMAS	K (	ROADRUNNER	1966 TAMLA	UK STML11038	US SOUL 703	
		LIVE	196 TAMLA	UK STML11152	US SOUL 705	
JAMES GRAVES	D (	HOME COOKIN'	196 TAMLA	UK STML11097	US SOUL 710	
		GREATEST HITS	196 TAMLA	UK STML11120	US SOUL 718	
		WHAT DOES IT TAKE TO WIN YOUR LOVE	196		US SOUL 721	
		A GASSSS	1970 TAMLA	UK STML11167	US SOUL 726	
		RAINBOW FUNK	1971 TAMLA	UK STML11198	US SOUL 732	
		MOODY JUNIOR	1972 TAMLA	UK STML11211	US SOUL 733	
		PEACE & UNDERSTANDING	1973 TAMLA	UK STML11234	US SOUL 738	
		GREATEST HITS VOL 2	1973 TAMLA	UK STML11224		
		ANTHOLOGY	1974 TAMLA	UK TMSP 1129	US M2 786	
		JR WALKER & THE ALL STARS	1974 TAMLA	UK STML11274		
		HOT SHOT	1976 TAMLA	UK STML12018		
		SAX APPEAL	1976 TAMLA	UK STML12033		
		WHOPPER BOPPER SHOW STOPPER	1976 TAMLA	UK STML12048	US SOUL 748	
		MOTOWN SPECIAL	1977 TAMLA	UK STMX 6005		
		20 SUPER HITS	1978 EMI	EURO 062 60061		
		SMOOTH SOUL	1978 TAMLA	UK STML12089	US SOUL 750	

PHILLIP WALKER W12A

PHILLIP WALKER	G V (AB		(A) SOMEDAY YOU'LL HAVE THESE BLUES		1980 SONET	UK	SNTF 831	
AL BRUNO	G (A		(B) BLUES SHOW LIVE AT PIT INN		1980 YUPITERU	JAP YR 23 4002		
BILL MURRAY	K (A							
DENNIS WALKER	B (AB	FREDDIE LEWIS	D (A	AL DEVILLE	TPT (A	ARCHIE FRANCIS	D (A	
VICTOR HILL	D (A	DAVID II	HRNS (A	JOHNNY BANKS	ORG (A	AARON TUCKER	D (A	
MILTON THOMAS	PERC (A	GEORGE SMITH	HCA (B	JOHNNY TUCKER	D (B	MITSUYOSHI AZUMA G (B		
JUNSHI YAMAGISHI	G (B							

T BONE WALKER

W13								
T BONE WALKER	G V (ALL	T B WALKER		196	CAPITOL			T 1958
MIKE OMARTIAN	K (V	THE TRUTH		1968	BRUNSWICK	US		754126
CHARLES BROWN	K (V	THE TRUTH		1968	MCA	UK	MUPS331	RIMCF2617
JAMES BOOKER	K (V	STORMY MONDAY BLUES		1968	STATESIDE	UK		SSL 10223
MAX BENNETT	B (V	STORMY MONDAY		1973	BLUESWAY			BLS 6008
PAUL HUMPHREY	D (V	STORMY MONDAY		197	WET SOUL	US		1002
BEN BENAY	G HCA(V	STORMY MONDAY BLUES		1978	CHARLY	UK		CR 30144
RICHARD BENNETT	G (V	FUNKY TOWN		1969	STATESIDE	UK		SSL 10265
JERRY LACROIX	HCA (V	FUNKY TOWN		1973	BLUESWAY			BLS 6014
DAVID FATHEAD NEWMAN SAX(V		WELL DONE		19	HOME COOKING US			HCS103
MIKE STOLLER	K (V	DIRTY MISTREATER		1973	BLUESWAY			BLS 6058
JOE OSBORN	B V	(I) I WANT A LITTLE GIRL		1973	DELMARK	US		DS 633
DEAN PARKS	G (V	FEELIN' THE BLUES		197	B & B			33019
SWEET INSPIRATIONS V (V		(V) VERY RARE		1974	WB	UK		K94001
DIZZY GILLESPIE	TPT (V	(T) T BONE BLUES		1975	ATLANTIC	UK K40131	US SD8256
JON FADDIS	TPT (V	SINGING THE BLUES		197				
TONY STUDD	TROM (V	CLASSICS OF MODERN BLUES		1976	BLUENOTE			BLAD 533
ZOOT SIMS	SAX (V	JUMPS AGAIN		1980	CHARLY	UK		CRB 1019
HERBIE MANN	FLT (V							

WARREN BERNHARDT	K (V	LOUIE SHELTON	G (V	KING ERRISSON	CONGA (V	JIM GORDON	D (V
JOHN TROPEA	SITAR(V	WILTON FELDER	B (V	LARRY CARLTON	G (V	AL COHN	SAX(V
DAVID T WALKER	G (V	GERRY MULLIGAN	SAX (V	JERRY DODGION	WIND (V	JOE FARRELL	WIND (V
FRANK VICARI	WIND (V	GARNETT BROWN	TROM (V	PAUL FAULISE	TROM (V	SELDON POWELL	WIND(V
MARVIN STAMM	TPT (V	DANNY STILES	TPT (V	MIKE GIBSON	TROM (V	R SRANKIN	G (T
BARNEY KESSEL	G (T	PLAS JOHNSON	SAX (T	JOE COMFORT	B (T	LLOYD GLENN	PNO (T
OSCAR BRADLEY	D (T	GEORGES ARVANITAS PNO (I			S P LEARY	D (I	RAY JOHNSON	PNO (T
EARL PALMER	D (T	BILLY HADNOTT	B (T	HAL SINGER	SAX (I	JACKIE SAMSON	B (I

WALKER BROTHERS

W13A							
JOHN MAUS WALKER	G V (ALL	(A) THE WALKER BROTHERS		1965	STAR CLUB		158 026 ST
SCOTT ENGEL	V G K(ALL	(B) PORTRAIT		1966	STAR CLUB		158 028 ST
GARY LEEDS	V D (ALL	(B) PORTRAIT		1966	PHILIPS		BL 773
STEVE GREY	K G (FJ	(C) IMAGES		1967	STAR CLUB		158 032 ST
DAVE McRAE	K (FJK	(D) STORY		1967	PHILIPS		6640 00
BARRY MORGAN	D (FJ	(E) MAKE IT EASY ON YOURSELF		19	PHILIPS		6336 21
DOUG WRIGHT	D (F	(F) NO REGRETS		1975	GTO		GTLP 00
CHRIS KARAN	PERC (F	(G) SPOTLIGHT ON		1975	PHILIPS		6640 00
ALAN PARKER	G (FJ	(H) IMMORTAL		197	PHILIPS		6870 56
RITCHIE HITCHCOCK	G (F	(J) LINES		1976	GTO		6321 11
JUDD PROCTOR	G (F	(K) NITE FLIGHTS		1978	GTO		GTLP 03
LEN WALKER	G (F						

B J COLE	STEEL(F	BRIAN ODGERS	B (F	BRIAN BENNETT	D (J	SIMON PHILLIPS	D (J
ALAN JONES	B (J	JOHN MEALING	G (J	PAUL KEOGH	G (J	ROGER CHURCHYARD	VLN (J
ALAN SKIDMORE	WIND (JK	JEFF DALY	WIND (J	DAVE WILUS	WIND (J	TRISTAN FRY	PERC (J
LES DAVIDSON	G (K	JIM SULLIVAN	G (K	PETER VAN HOOKE	D (K	MO FOSTER	B (K
FRANK GIBSON	D (K	DILL KATZ	B (K	MORRIS PERT	PERC (K	RONNIE ROSS	SAX (K
CHRIS MERCER	SAX (K						

WALL

(A) BEACHEAD		19	FRESH	FLP 2
(B) PERSONAL TROUBLES & PUBLIC ISSUES	1980	FRESH		LP 2
(EP) GHETTO		1980	FRESH	FRESH 17

ALWYN WALL BAND

W13C						
ALWYN WALL	G V (A	(A) THE PRIZE		1977	MYRRH	MYR 1057
NORMAN BARRETT	G V (A					
PHIL HOLMES	K V (A	TONY HUDSON	B (A NICK BROTHERWOOD D (A			

WALLENSTEIN

W13D							
BILL BARONE	G V (ABCD	(A) BLITZKRIEG		1971	BASF		20 290646
HARALD GROSSKOPF	D (ABC	(B) MOTHER UNIVERSE		1972	BASF		20 291138
JURGEN DOLLASE	K V (ALL	(C) COSMIC CENTURY		19	OHR		KM 58 006
JERRY BERKERS	B V (AB	(D) STORIES SONGS & SYMPHONIES	19	OHR		KM 58 014
JURGEN PLUTA	B PERC(DE	(E) NO MORE LOVE		1977	RCA		PL 30010
JOACHIM REISER	VLN (CD	(F) CHARLINE		1978	RCA		PL 30045
NICKY GEBHARD	D (E	(G) BLUE EYED BOYS		1979	RCA		PL 30061
GERD KLOCKER	G V (E	(H) FRAULEINS		1980	RCA	EURO	064 45932
DIETER MEIER	B (C						
ROLF DOLLASE	FLT (E KIM MERZ	V (FGH PETE BROUGH	G (FGH MICHAEL DOMMERS	G(FGH
CHARLY TERSTAPPEN D	(FGH TERRY PARK	B (FGH					

WALLY

W14							
PETE COSKER	G B V(AB	(A) WALLY		1974	ATLANTIC	UK	K50051
PAUL GERRETT	K V (A	(B) WALLY GARDENS		1975	ATLANTIC	UK	K50180
PAUL MIDDLETON STEEL B (A							
ROGER NARRAWAY	D (AB NICK GLENNIE SMITH K V(B JAN GLENNIE SMITH V (B MADELINE BELL	V (B
PETE SAGE VLN MAND B (AB ROY WEBBER	G V (AB RAY WEHRSTEIN	SAX(B				

WALRUS

W15							
DON RICHARDS	TPT (A	(A) WALRUS		1971	DERAM	UK	SML 1072
ROY VOCE	SAX (A						
BILL HOAD	WIND(A STEVE HAWTHORN	B (A JOHN SCATES	G (A NICK GABB	D (A
BARRY PARFITT	K (A NOEL GREENAWAY	V (A					

JOE WALSH

W16								
JOE WALSH	G V SYN B(ALL	(A) BARNSTORM		1973	DUNHILL US 50130 PROBE UK	6268
KENNY PASSARELLI	B (ABC	(A) BARNSTORM		1974	ANCHOR RI UK		ABCL 5022
JOE VITALE	D (ABCDF	(B) THE SMOKER YOU DRINK		1973	DUNHILL US 50140 PROBE UK	6275
AL PERKINS	STEEL(A	(B) THE SMOKER YOU DRINK		1974	ANCHOR RI UK		ABCL 5033
PAUL HARRIS	K (A	(C) SO WHAT		1974	DUNHILL US 50171		
ROCKE GRACE	K V (B	(C) SO WHAT		1974	ANCHOR		UK ABCL 5055
TOM STEPHENSON	K (C	(D) YOU CANT ARGUE WITH A SICK MIND	1975	ABC US ABCD 932 ANCHOR UK	5156
CLYDIE KING	V (B	(E) SO FAR SO GOOD		1978	ANCHOR		UK ABCL 5240
VANETTA FIELDS	V (B	(F) BUT SERIOUSLY FOLKS		1978	ASYLUM	US 6E 141 UK	K53081
JOE LALA	PERC (B	(G) BEST OF		19	ABC	US 1083	
RICKY FATAAR	D (	(EP) PLUS FOUR		1977	ANCHOR		UK ABE 1202

(CONTINUED)

BRYAN GAROFALO	B V	(C								
J D SOUTHER	G V	(C	DAN FOGELBERG	G V	(C	DAVID MASON	K	(D	WILLIE WEEKS	B (DF
JAY FERGUSON	K V	(DF	DON FELDER	G V	(D	GLENN FREY	V	(CDF	DON HENLEY	V (CDF
ROCKY DZIDZORNU	PERC	(D	ANDY NEWMARK	D	(D	JOEY MURCIA	G	(F	TIM SCHMIT	V (F
CHUCK RAINEY		(A	RON GRINEL	D	(C	GUILLE GARCIA	PERC	(C	JODY BOYER	V (C
JOHN STRONACH	V	(C	RANDY MEISNER	V	(C					

TRAVIS WAMMACK — W16A

TRAVIS WAMMACK	G V HCA (A	(A) NOT FOR SALE	1975 CAPRICORN	UK	2493 133
LEON SHERRILL	G (A				

PETE CARR	G (A	DON CARTEE	D (A	RANDY McCORMICK	K (A	BARRY BECKETT	K (A
JOE HAMILTON	B (A	LENNY LE BLANC	B (A	JIMMY EVANS	D (A	RONNIE OLDHAM	K (A
STACY GOSS	HRNS (A	ROGER CLARK	D (A	RICK HALL	V (A		

WAR — W17

ERIC BURDON	V (ABK	(A) BLACKMANS BURDON	1970 LIBERTY		LDS 8400	314	
DEACON JONES	V (	(B) ERIC BURDON DECLARES WAR	1970 POLYDOR	UK	2310 041		
HAROLD BROWN	D (ABCDEFGHJKLMNO	(C) WAR	1971 UA	US LA5508	UK	LBG83478	
HOWARD SCOTT G	PERC(ABCDEFGHJKLMNO	(C) WAR	RI 1979 MCA UK MCG4003	ISLAND 76	ILPS 9164		
B B DICKERSON B	PERC(ABCDEFGHJKLMNO	(D) ALL DAY MUSIC	1972 UA US LA5546	UK	UAS29269		
CHARLES MILLER	WIND(ABCDEFGHJKLMNO	(D) ALL DAY MUSIC	RI 1979 MCA UK MCF3020	ISLAND 76	ILPS 9177		
LONNIE JORDAN	K (ABCDEFGHJKLMNO	(E) THE WORLD IS A GHETTO	1973 UA	US LA5652	UK	UAS29400	
PAPA DEE ALLEN	PERC(BCDEFGHJKLKNO	(E) THE WORLD IS A GHETTO	RI 1979 MCA UK MCF3021	ISLAND 76	ILPS 9171		
LEE OSKAR	HCA (ABCDEFGHJKLMNO	(F) DELIVER THE WORD	1973 UA	US LA 128	UK	UAG29521	
		(F) DELIVER THE WORD	RI 1979 MCA UK MCF3022	ISLAND 76	ILPS 9194		
		(G) LIVE	1974 UA	US LA 193	UK	UAD60067/8	
		(G) LIVE	RI 1979 MCA UK MCF3040	ISLAND 76	ILSD 8		
		(H) WHY CANT WE BE FRIENDS	1975 UA	US LA 441	UK	UAG29843	
		(H) WHY CANT WE BE FRIENDS	RI 1979 MCA UK MCF3023	ISLAND 76	ILPS 9378		
		(I) GREATEST HITS	1976 UA	US LA 648	ISLAND	ILPS 9413	
		(J) PLATINUM FUNK	1977		ISLAND UK ILPS 9507		
		(K) LOVE IS ALL AROUND	1976 ABC US ABCD 988	UK	ABCL 5207		
		(K) LOVE IS ALL AROUND	1979 MCA UK MCF3025				
		(L) YOUNGBLOOD(SOUNDTRACK)	1978 UA	US LA904	MCA	UK	MCF 2864
		(M) GALAXY	1978 MCA US MCA 3030		MCA	UK	MCF 2822
		(N) MUSIC BAND	1979 MCA	3085	UK RI 79	MCF	4001
		(O) MUSIC BAND 2	1979 MCA UK 3050				
		(P) PLATINUM JAZZ (DBL)	1979 MCA	305			

CLIFFORD T WARD — W18

CLIFFORD T WARD	V K(ALL	(A) SINGER SONGWRITER	1972 DANDELION	UK	2310 216
DEREK THOMAS	GABCDF	(B) HOME THOUGHTS FROM ABROAD	1973 CHARISMA	UK	CAS 1066
KEN WRIGHT	D (ABCD	(C) MANTLEPIECES	1973 CHARISMA	UK	CAS 1077
BEV PEGG	B (A	(D) NO MORE ROCK'N'ROLL	1975 PHILIPS		8109 500
DAVID SKINNER	K (A	(E) ESCALATOR	1975 CHARISMA	UK	CAS 1098
JOHN SAWYER	VIBES(A	(F) WAVES	1976 PHILIPS		9109 216
WILL ROPER	FLT (A	(G) NEW ENGLAND DAYS	1977 PHILIPS		9109 605
JOHN MEALING	K (F				

PAUL KEOGH	G (F	PETE KING	SAX (F	TERRY EDWARDS	B(BCDF	CHRIS SPEDDING	G (D
ALAN PARKER	G (D	MIKE MORAN	K (D	BRIAN ODGERS	B (D	ANDREW STEELE	D (D
CHRIS KARAN	PERC (D	B J COLE	STEEL(D	PETE WINGFIELD	PNO(D	MARTIE ECHITO	K D(G
GENE HOLMES	G V (G	MARC LEVINE	B (G	MARC SINGER	D (G	SID SHARP	STRINGS (G
KEITH SMART	D (F	MICHAEL EASLEY	G (G				

WARHORSE — W19

NICK SIMPER	(AB	(A) WARHORSE	1970	VERTIGO	UK	6360 015
MAC POOLE	D (B	(B) RED SEA	1972	VERTIGO	UK	6360 066
ASHLEY HOLT	V (B				
FRANK WILSON	K PNO(B	PETER PARKER	G (B		

WARM DUST — W20

PAUL CARRACK	K (ABC	(A) AND IT CAME TO PASS	1970	TREND	UK	TNLS 700
TEX COMER	B (ABC	(B) PEACE FOR OUR TIME	1971	TREND	UK	6480 001
LES WALKER	V (BC	(C) THIRD ALBUM	1972	BASF	
ALAN SOLOMON	SAX K V (BC				
JOHN SURGUY	SAX G V (BC	KEITH BAILEY	D (B	DAVE PEPPER	D (C

JENNIFER WARNES — W21

JENNIFER WARNES	K V (ALL	( ) I CAN REMEMBER	1968 PARROT	US	71020	
KENNY EDWARDS	V G (B	( ) SEE ME	1968 PARROT	US	71034	
MIKE FINNIGAN	V (B	( ) JENNIFER	1972 REPRISE		2065	
BRIAN RUSSELL	V (B	(A) JENNIFER WARNES	1977 ARISTA US 4062	UK SPARTY 1006		
NICKY HOPKINS	K (A	(B) SHOT THROUGH THE HEART	1979 ARISTA	UK SPART 1097		
PEGGY SANDVIG	K (A					

JAY GRAYDON	G (A	JIM HORN	WIND (A	DAVE McDANIEL	B (A	RUSS KUNKEL	D (A
JOE CORRERO	D (A	JIM PRICE	K V TROM (A	DANIEL MOORE	V (A	MATTHEW MOORE	V (A
DAN SAWYER	G (A	STEVE MADAIO	TPT (A	SKIP MESQUITE	SAX (A	MAX HASKETT	TPT(A
LAUDIR DE OLIVEIRA	PERC(A	JIM MOORE	V (A	ALAN LINGREN	PNO (A	JOHN HUG	G (A
DOUG ROAHNE	G (A	REINIE PRESS	B (A	DENNIS ST JOHN	D (A	BETH FICHET	V (A
HERB PEDERSEN	V (A	DOUG G LIVINGSTON	PNO (A	BRIAN WHITCOMB	PNO (A	GAYLE LEVANT	HARP (A
MICHAEL BOWDEN	B (A	MATT BETTON	D (A	DOUG HAYWOOD	V (A	BEN BENAY	G (A
DANNY KOOTCH	G (A	ANDREW GOLD	D B K G (B	BLONDIE CHAPLIN	G V (B	JIM GORDON	D (B
BOB GLAUB	D (B	BROCK WALSH	K V (B	DENNY SEIWELL	D (B	BUZZY FEITEN	G (B
ABRAHAM LABORIEL	B (B	MARK OLSON	K (B	MARTY GREBB	K (B	DOUG LIVINGSTON	K STEEL(B
BILL ELLIOTT	PNO (B	WALT RICHMOND	K (B	RICKY FATAAR	D (B	CHICO GOLDSMITH	PERC(B
ROB FRABONI	V (B	PENNY NICHOLS	V (B				

WARSAW PAKT — W21A

(A) WARSAW PAKT	1977 ISLAND		ILPS 9515

WASA EXPRESS — W22

BO HALLGREN	K (AB	(A) ON WITH THE ACTION	1978 SONET	SNTF 771
CARY SHARRAF EL DIN	G (AB	(B) WASA EXPRESS	1979 SONET	SNTF 810
BO HAGGSTROM	B (AB			
AKE ERIKSSON	D (AB	MALLA RONNANDER	HCA (B	

```
W22A                        WASHBOARD DOC,LUCKY & FLASH
  JOSEPH'WASHBOARD'DOCTOR (A        (A) EARLY MORNING BLUES          1980 L&R                    42010
  CAB LUCKY        G V (A
  JOHN'FLASH'WHITNER B V (A   LOUISIANA RED    G V (A
W23                              DELROY WASHINGTON
  DELROY WASHINGTON B V G PERC(AB   (A) I SUS                        1976 VIRGIN        UK        V2060
  CANDY McKENZIE   V   (B          (B) RASTA                        1977 VIRGIN        UK        V2088
  BUNNY McKENZIE   B G (AB
  JUNIOR MARVIN    G   (B    KARL PITTERSON   PERC (B   ANGUS GAYE        D   (AB  AL ANDERSON    G  (AB
  TREVOR STARR     G   (B    DICK CUTHELL PERC HRNS (B   COURTNEY HEMMINGS K   (AB  GEORGE OBAN    PERC(AB
  TONY ROBINSON    K   (AB   RICO             TROM (AB  EDDIE THORNTON    HRNS (AB KEITH GEMMELL  WIND(AB
  JUNIOR KERR      G   (A    LADBROKE GROVE ST CHOIR(A   DONALD GITS       G   (A   PAT THRALL     G  (A
W24                          GENO WASHINGTON(& THE RAM JAM BAND)
  GENO WASHINGTON  V   (ALL         (A) HAND CLAPPIN' FOOT STOMPIN'  1966 PICCADILLY    UK    NPL38026
  HERB PRESTIDGE       (            (A) HAND CLAPPIN' FOOT STOMPIN'  1980 PYE           UK    NSPL18618
  STEVE GREGORY    WIND (           (B) SHAKE A TAIL FEATHER         1968 PICCADILLY    UK    NSPL38029
  BUD BEADLE       SAX  (           (C) HIPSTERS FLIPSTERS          1968 PICCADILLY    UK    NSPL38032
  JEFF WRIGHT           (           (D) RUNNING WILD                1968 PYE           UK    NSPL18219
  JOHN ROBERTS          (           (E) SIFTERS,SHIFTERS,FINGER CLICK MAMA1969 MARBLE ARCH UK  MAL 816
  CARL PALMER      D    (           (F) UP TIGHT                    1969 MARBLE ARCH    UK    MAL 1162
  PETE GAGE        G    (           (G) GOLDEN HOUR                 19   PYE                 GH 594
  ROD BABY              (           (H) GENO'S BACK                 1976 DJM           UK   DJF 20486
  BILLY DAVEY           (           (J) LIVE                        1976 DJM           UK   DJF 20457
  LIONEL KINGHAM   SAX  (           (L) THAT'S WHY HOLLYWOOD LOVES ME 1979 DJM         UK   DJF 20561
  BARRIE MARTIN    PERC (J
  PETE LAMONT      TROM (J   ROGER CHANTLER   D   (J   DAVID BALLENTINE G V (J CHRIS STAINES   B V(J
  MIKE MEROS       K    (J   JOE CHEMAY       B V (L   MIKE BAIRD       D   (L BRENT NELSON    D  (L
  PAULINHO DA COSTA PERC(L   GEORGE DOERING   G   (L   JOEL PESKIN      SAX (L CURT BOETCHER   V  (L
  MUFFY HENDRIX    V    (L   DONNA FEIN           (L
W25                             GROVER WASHINGTON
  GROVER WASHINGTON SAX (ALL        (A) SOUL BOX                    1973 KUDU                KULD 501
  BOB JAMES        K    (DE         (B) INNER CITY BLUES            197  KUDU     KULD 11   KUL   3
  LOUIS JOHNSON    B    (E          (C) ALL THE KINGS MEN           197  KUDU               KUL   7
  GARY KING        B    (DE         (D) MISTER MAGIC                1975 KUDU               KUL  20
  STEVE GADD       D    (E          (E) FEEL SO GOOD                1975 KUDU               KU   24
  RALPH MACDONALD  PERC(DEFN        (F) SECRET PLACE                1976 KUDU               KU   32
  RANDY BRECKER    TPT  (E          (G) SOUL BOX 1                  1976 KUDU               KU   12
  JON FADDIS       TPT  (DEN        (H) SOUL BOX 2                  1976 KUDU               KU   13
  JOHN FROSK       TPT  (E          (J) LIVE AT THE BIJOU           1978 KUDU              SOUL D02
  BOB MILLIKAN     TPT  (E          (K) REED SEED                   1978 TAMLA            STML12099
  ALAN RAPH        TROM (E          (L) PARADISE                    1979 ELEKTRA US6E182 UK  K52130
  BARRY ROGERS     TROM (E          (M) WINELIGHT                   1980 ELEKTRA US 6E305 UK K52262
  DAVE TAYLOR      TROM (E          (N) SKYLARKIN'                  1980 TAMLA          UK STML12131
  PHIL UPCHURCH    B    (D
  HARVEY MASON     D    (DF   ERIC GALE        G      (DFN KENNETH RICE   D  (E  JIMMY MADISON  D  (E
  DAVID GRUSIN     PNO  (F    TONY JACKSON     B      (F   GEORGE MRAZ    B  (F  STEVE KHAN     G  (F
  GERRY NIEWOOD    SAX  (F    JOHN BLAKE   VLN V K    (K   TYRONE BROWN   B  (K  LEONARD GIBBS V PERC(K
  JAMES SIMMONS    K    (K    RICHARD L STEACKER G V  (K   MILLARD VINSON D  (K  ED WALSH       K  (N
  JORGE DALTO      PNO  (N    ALEXANDER OTEY   TPT    (N   MARCUS MILLER  B  (N  RICHARD TEE    K  (N
  IDRIS MUHAMMAD   D    (N    PAUL GRIFFIN     K      (N   MARVIN STAMM   TPT (D
W26                                   WASPS
  JOHNNY RICH      D    (A          (A) 1977 (B) 1979
  STEVE DOMINIC    B    (A
  GARRY WELMAN     G    (A    DAVID OWEN       B     (B   JESSE LYNN DEAN   V  (AB NEIL FITCH    G  (B
  TIM GRANT        D    (B
W26A                                WASTELAND
                                    (A) WANT NOT (EP)               1979 DISASTER
W27                                SADAO WATANABE
  SADAO WATANABE   SAX FLT(ABC      (A) AUTUMN BLOW                 1977 INNERCITY     US    IC 6064
  LEE RITENOUR     G    (AB         (B) CALIFORNIA SHOWER           1979 MIRACLE            MLP3005
  ERNIE WATTS      SAX  (AB         (C) HOW'S EVERTHING (DBL LIVE)  1980 CBS                 22081
  PATRICE RUSHEN   K    (A
  ANTHONY JACKSON  B    (AC   JON FADDIS       TPT   (C   TOKYO PHILHARMONIC ORCH(C  HARVEY MASON  D  (AB
  STEVE FORMAN     PERC (A    DAVE GRUSIN      K     (BC  CHUCK RAINEY   B   (B  PAULINHO DA COSTA PERC(B
  OSCAR BRASHEAR   TPT  (B    GEORGE BOHANON   TROM  (B   RICHARD TEE    K   (C  ERIC GALE      G  (C
  JEFF MIRONOV     G    (C    STEVE GADD       D     (C   RALPH MACDONALD PERC (C
W28                                 MUDDY WATERS
  MUDDY WATERS              G V(ALL  (A) AT NEWPORT                 1960 CHESS 1448      +    CRL  4513
  (McKINLEY MORGANFIELD)            (A) AT NEWPORT                 1967 MARBLE ARCH     UK MAL  661
  JIMMIE ROGERS    G    (RSYa        (A) AT NEWPORT                 1973 CHECKER        UK 6467 306
  WILLIE DIXON     B    (RSY         (B) MUDDY WATERS               1964 PYE INT UK NPL28040 US CHESS203
  PAUL BUTTERFIELD HCA  (X           (B) MUDDY WATERS               1967 MARBLE ARCH    UK MAL  723
  FRED BELOW       D    (RSY         (C) FOLK SINGER                1964 PYE INT NPL28048 US CHESS 1483
  LEROY FOSTER     G    (S           (D) SINGS BIG BILL BROONZY     1964                US CHESS 1444
  BIG CRAWFORD     B    (RSY         (E) MUDDY BRASS & THE BLUES    1966
  ANDREW STEPHENS  B    (ARSY        (F) REAL FOLK BLUES            1966 CHESS  UK CRL4515 US    1501
  PAT HARE         G    (AS          (G) MORE REAL FOLK BLUES       196  CHESS              US   1511
  FRANCIS CLAY     D    (ARSVY       (H) SUPER BLUES                1966 CHESS  UK CRL4529
  WILLIE SMITH     D    (SZabcd      (I) SUPER SUPER BLUES BAND     1968 CHECKER LPS 3010 CHESS CRL 4537
  ELGIN EVANS      D    (SL          (J) ELECTRIC MUD               1968 CADET              LPS  314
  LITTLE WALTER    HCA  (RSY         (K) SAIL ON                    19   CHESS                  1539
  JERRY PORTNOY    HCA  (ad          (L) DOWN ON STOVALLS PLANTATION 19  TESTAMENT     US T2210
  SAM LAWHORN      G    (STVXd       (M) AFTER THE RAIN             1969 CADET LPS 320  CHESS  50017
  OTIS SPANN       PNO  (PRSVY       (N) THEY CALL ME MUDDY WATERS  19   CHESS                  1553
  LEVON HELM       D B  (X           (O) THE BEST OF MUDDY WATERS   19   CHESS      FR    9124 224
  JAMES MADISON    G    (Sd          (P) AFTER THE RAIN             1969 CHESS              CRL 4553
  PAUL OSCHER      HCA  (PSc         (Q) FATHERS & SONS             1969 CHESS 2 127      CRL 4556
  SONNY WIMBERLEY  B    (S           (Q) FATHERS & SONS             1969 CHESS                 50033
  BO DIDDLEY       G V  (I           (R) McKINLEY MORGANFIELD AKA M WATERS 1972 CHESS          60006
                                                                        (CONTINUED)
                                       [436]
```

MUDDY WATERS

JOE NEWMAN	TPT	(T	(S) VINTAGE MUD	1970 SUNNYLAND		KS 100
MARCUS JOHNSON	SAX	(S	(T) LONDON SESSIONS	1972 CHESS 6310 121		60013
CHARLES CALMESE	B	(Zd	(U) CANT GET NO GRINDING	1973 CHESS 6310 129		50023
RORY GALLAGHER	G	(TW	(V) MUD IN YOUR EAR	1973 MUSE		5008
CAREY BELL HARRINGTON	HCA	(TW	(W) LONDON REVISTED	1974 CHESS		60026
RICK GRECH	B	(TW	(X) WOODSTOCK ALBUM	1975 CHESS		60035
STEVE WINWOOD	K	(TW	(Y) CHESS BLUES MASTERS	1977 CHESS NL 6641 639		2ACBM 203
GEORGE FORTUNE	K	(TW	(Z) HARD AGAIN	1977 BLUE SKY US 34449	UK	81853
MITCH MITCHELL	D	(TW	(a) I'M READY	1977 BLUE SKY US 34928	UK	82235
JOHNNY WINTER	G	(Uad	(b) 'UNK IN FUNK	1977 CHESS		60031
BOB MARGOLIN	G	(xzabd	(c) LIVE	1977 CHESS		50012
HERBIE LOVELL	G	(d'	LIVE	1977 BLUE SKY	UK	83422
CHARLES STEPNEY	ORG	(P				
SELDON POWELL	SAX	(T	GARTH HUDSON ACC K SAX(X	HOWLIN WOLF	V HCA(I	PHIL UPCHURCH	G (P
ROSETTA HIGHTOWER	V	(T	WALTER HORTON	HCA (RYa	FRED CARTER	B G (U	ERNIE ROYAL	TPT(T
PINETOP PERKINS	PNO(XZabcd	HOWARD JOHNSON	SAX (X	JOE DENIM	HCA (c	PETE COSEY	G (P
GARNETT BROWN	TROM	(T	LUTHER JOHNSON	G (Vbd	MORRIS JENNINGS	D (P	JAMES COTTON	HCA(ARSYZd
CALVIN JONES	B	(bcd	LOUIS SATTERFIELD B	(P	LITTLE WILLIE SMITH HCA (	TAT HARRIS	G (ARY
PERCY THOMAS	G V	(L	LOUIS FORD	V MAND(L	HENRY SIMS	G VLN(L	CHARLES CHUCK BERRY G (L
LUTHER TUCKER	G	(RY	LEONARD CHESS	PERC (RY	GEORGE BUFORD	HCA (V	

ROGER WATERS

ROGER WATERS		(A	(A) THE BODY (SOUNDTRACK)	1970 HARVEST	UK	SHSP 4008
RON GEESIN		(A				

GERAINT WATKINS

GERAINT WATKINS	K V	(A	(A) GERAINT WATKINS & THE DOMINATORS	1979 VERTIGO		9102 033
ANDY FAIRWEATHER LOW	G V(A					
MICKY GEE	G PERC V B(A	JOHN DAVID	B V PERC(A	DAVE CHARLES	D V (A	HENRY SPINETTI	D V(A
STEVE GREGORY	SAX V(A	BUD BEADLE	SAX V (A			

JOHNNY GUITAR WATSON

JOHNNY GUITAR WATSON	G V(ALL	(A) JOHNNY GUITAR WATSON	196 KING	US	857
EMRY THOMAS	D	(MNOPHQ	(B) BLUES SOUL	196 CHESS		1490
TOMMY ROBERTSON	TROM	(MNO	(C) LARRY WILLIAMS SHOW WITH J G W	1965 DECCA	UK	LK 4691
KNUD JENSEN	SAX	(N	(D) BAD	1966 OKEH		OKS 14118
WALT FOWLER	TPT	(NOQ	(E) TWO FOR THE PRICE OF ONE	1967 OKEH		OKS 14122
MAXWELL DAVIS	SAX	(J	(F) I CRIED FOR YOU	19 CADET		LPS 4056
JIM WYNN	SAX	(J	(G) IN THE FATS BAG	1968 OKEH		OKS 14124
RENE HALL	G	(J	(H) LISTEN	1973 FANTASY EURO 03861279 US		9437
TED BRUNSON	G	(J	(I) GANSTER OF LOVE	19 POWERPAK		306
BARNEY KESSEL	G	(J	(J) THE GANGSTER IS BACK	1975 RED LIGHTNIN'	UK	RL 0013
RUDY COPELAND	K V	(H	(K) I DONT WANT TO BE ALONE	1976 FANTASY	US	9484
ANDRE LEWIS	K B	(H	(L) CAPTURED LIVE	1976 DJM		
J D REED	SAX	(H	(M) AIN'T THAT A BITCH	1976 DJM US DJM 3	UK	DJF 20485
HENRY REED	G SAX(H		(N) A REAL MOTHER FOR YA	1977 DJM US DJLPA7	UK	DJF 50505
DARCUS	V	(P	(O) FUNK BEYOND THE CALL OF DUTY	1977 DJM US 714	UK	DJF 20525
BILL HALEY	SAX	(OQ	(P) GIANT	1978 DJM US 19	UK	DJF 20551
MAXAYN LEWIS	V	(H	(Q) WHAT THE HELL IS THIS	1979 DJM	UK	DJF 20557
PAUL DUNMALL	SAX	(M	(R) LOVE JONES	1980 DJM	UK	DJF 20568
MARCY THOMAS	V	(P				
PETER MARTIN	TPT	(M	WILMA WILSON	V (Q	DEON ESTUS	B (Q	BOBBY HOWARD	B (Q
TONY COLEMAN	TROM	Q	ALBERT WING	SAX (Q	GREGORY DUVAS	TPT (Q	

ROBERT WATSON

ROBERT WATSON	SAX K(A	(A) ESTIMATED TIME OF ARRIVAL	1978 PYE	UK	NSPL28250
WILBY FLETCHER	D	(A	(B) ALL BECAUSE OF YOU	1979 PYE	UK	NSPL28276
PAT PATRICK	SAX	(A				
CHARLES DAVIS	SAX	(A	SINCLAIR ACEY	TPT (A	FRANK WILLIAMS	TPT (A	DICK GRIFFIN	TROM(A
MICHAEL TRENI	TROM	(A	ARTHUR WHITE	SAX (A	VALERI PONOMAREN	G (A	RICHARD CARUSO	TROM(A
BILL SAXTON	SAX	(A	CURTIS LUNDY	B (A	TERUMASA HINO	TPT (A	DENNIS IRWIN	B (A
JOE CARO	G	(A	ROLAND PRINCE	G (A	MONTI ELLISON	PERC (A	JABALI BILLY HART	D(A
WALTER DAVIS	K	(A	BILLY HIGGINS	D (A	PAMELA WATSON	K V (A	

WAH WAH WATSON

WAH!WAH WATSON	G V	(A	(A) ELEMENTARY	1976 CBS UK 81582	US	34328
JULIA TILLMAN	V	(A				
MAXINE WILLARD	V	(A	ORRIN WATERS	V (A	LUTHER WATERS	V (A	RAY PARKER JR	G (A
OLLIE BROWN	D	(A	LOUIS JOHNSON	B (A	SONNY BURKE	K (A	JOHN BARNES	K (A
JOE SAMPLE	PNO	(A	CLARENCE McDONALD	PNO (A	MARK DAVIS	PNO (A	WILLIE WEEKS	B (A
HERBIE HANCOCK	K	(A	BENNIE MAUPIN	SAX (A	ERNIE WATTS	SAX (A	AARON SMITH	D (A
WILTON FELDER	B	(A	HENRY DAVIS	B (A	JAMES JAMESON	B (A	DAVID T WALKER	G (A
DAVID GRUSIN	K	(A				

WATSONIAN INSTITUTE

JOHNNY GUITAR WATSON	G V(A	(A) MASTER FUNK	1978 DJM		DJF 20529
BOBBY HOWARD	B V	(A				
GIP NOBLE	K	(A	EMRY THOMAS	D V (A	TOMMY ROBERTSON TROM B V(A	

ERNIE WATTS

ERNIE WATTS	SAX FLT PERC V(A	(A) LOOK IN YOUR HEART	1980 ELEKTRA	US	6E 285
PETE ROBINSON	K	(A				
DAN DEAN	B	(A	ALEX ACUNA	D (A	RON COOK	G (A	PAULINHO DA COSTA	PERC(A

WATTS 103RD STREET BAND

CHARLES WRIGHT	V	(	(A) CORNBREAD & GRITS	1967 WB	US	1741
MELVIN DUNLOP	B	(	(B) IN THE JUNGLE BABE	1969 WB	US	1801
AL McKAY	G	(	(C) EXPRESS YOURSELF	1970 WB	US	1864
BERNARD BLACKMAN	G	(				
RAY JACKSON	TROM	(	JOHN RAYFORD	SAX (	GABRIEL FLEMMING	TPT (	BILL CANNON SAX	(
JAMES GADSON	D	(				

WAVEMAKER

JOHN LEWIS	K	(AB	(A) WHERE ARE WE CAPTIAN	1975 POLYDOR	UK	2383 331
BRIAN HODGSON	K	(AB	(B) NEW ATLANTIS	1977 POLYDOR	UK	2383 434
TONY McVEY	PERC	(AB				
JON KEHLIOR	PERC	(A				

W35 DARRYL WAY

```
DARRYL WAY        VLN K(ALL   (A) SATURATION POINT            1973 DERAM UK SML1104  LONDON JAP LAX1037
DEK MESSECAR      B V  (CE    (B) CANIS LUPUS                 1974 DERAM UK SDL  14  LONDON JAP LAX1036
JOHN ETHERIDGE    G    (      (AB) SATURATION/CANIS           19   LONDON            IMP      6 23113
IAN MOSLEY        D    (CDE   (C) NIGHT MUSIC                 1974 DERAM UK SML1116  LONDON JAP LAX1116
JOHN HODKINSON    V    (C     (D) CONCERTO FOR ELEC VLN & SYN 1978 ISLAND            UK       ILPS 9550
FRANCIS MONKMAN   SYN  (D     (E) DARRYL WAY'S WOLF           1974 LONDON            US       PS  644
```

W36 WEATHER REPORT

```
WAYNE SHORTER         SAX  (ALL   (A) WEATHER REPORT          1970 CBS UK 64521  US 30661  JAP 25AP 941
JOE ZAWINUL           K    (ALL   (B) I SING THE BODY ELECTRIC 1972 CBS UK 64943  US 31356  JAP 25AP 944
ALEJANDRO ACUNA       PERC (FH    (C) SWEETNIGHTER            1973 CBS UK 65532  US 32210  JAP 25AP 945
CHESTER THOMPSON      D    (F     (D) MYSTERIOUS TRAVELLER    1974 CBS UK 80027  US 32494  JAP 25AP 946
JACO PASTORIUS        B    (FHJ   (E) TAIL SPINNIN'           1975 CBS UK 80734  US 33417  JAP 25AP 947
NARADA MICHAEL WALDEN D(F         (F) BLACK MARKET            1976 CBS UK 81325  US 34099  JAP 25AP 57
MIROSLAV VITOUS       B    (ABCDG (G) LIVE IN TOKYO           1977 CBS SONY               SOPJ 12/13XR
DON ALIAS             PERC (F     (H) HEAVY WEATHER           1977 CBS UK 81775  US 34418  JAP 25AP 357
MANOLO BADRENA        PERC (HJ    (J) Mr GONE                 1978 CBS UK 82775
DOM UM ROMAO          PERC (BCDG  (K) NIGHT PASSAGE           1980 CBS UK 84597
ISHMAEL WILBURN       D    (D
AIRTO MOREIRA    D    (A   ALPHONZE MOUZON  D    (A   ERIC GRAVATT       D    (BCG ANDREW WHITE      HRNS B(BC
HUBERT LAWS      FLT  (B   WILMER WISE      HRNS (B   YOLANDE BAVAN      V    (B   JOSHIE ARMSTEAD    V    (B
ROBERT CHAPMAN   V    (B   RALPH TOWNER     G    (B   HERSCHEL DWELLINGHAM D  (E   ALYRIO LIMA        PERC (E
NGUDU CHANCLER   D    (E   TONTO            K    (E   MURUGA             PERC (C   STEVE GADD         D    (J
TONY WILLIAMS    D    (J   PETER ERSKINE    D    (J   DENIECE WILLIAMS   V    (J   MAURICE WHITE      V    (J
JON LUCIEN       V    (J   ALPHONSA JOHNSON B    (DEF
```

W37 VIVIAN WEATHERS

```
VIVIAN WEATHERS  V PERC(A   (A) BAD WEATHER                   1978 FRONT LINE             FL1025
WINSTON BENNETT  G    (A
KOJO OSEI        D    (A   WINSTON CURNIFFE  D    (D   TONY OSEI    K    (A   EVER DEE       B  (A
FLOYD LAWSON     B PERC(A   JOHN VARNOM      PERC G(A   JANOS BAJTALA K   (A
```

W38 THE WEB

```
JOHN L WATSON    V    (ABC   (A) FULLY INTERLOCKING           1968 DERAM US 18018  UK  SML 1025
TOM HARRIS       WIND (AB    (B) THERAPHOSA BLONDI            1970 DERAM            UK  SML 1058
JOHN EASTON      G    (AB    (C) I SPIDER                     1970 POLYDOR          UK  2383 024
TONY EDWARDS     G    (AB
DICK LEE SMITH   B    (AB   LENNIE WRIGHT  PERC (AB  KENNY BEVERIDGE  PERC D(AB STRING SECTION  (AB
```

W39 JIMMY WEBB

```
JIMMY WEBB       V K  (ALL   (A) JIM WEBB SINGS JIM WEBB      1968 EPIC                  US  26401
DAVID PAICH      K SYN(F     (B) WORDS & MUSIC                1970 REPRISE               US   6421
GEORGE MARTIN    K SYN(F     (C) & SO ON                      1971 REPRISE               US   6448
FRED TACKETT     G    (F     (D) LETTERS                      1972 REPRISE UK K44173      US   2055
DEAN PARKS       G    (F     (E) LANDS END                    1974 ASYLUM  UK SYL9014     US   5070
DEE MURRAY       B    (F     (F) EL MIRAGE                    1977 ATLANTIC UK K50370     US  18218
HARVEY MASON     PERC (F
DAVID HUNGATE    B    (F   LARRY KNECHTEL  B    (F   NIGEL OLSSON   D    (F   JIM GORDON     D  (F
LOWELL GEORGE    G    (F
```

W40 RANDY WEBSTER

```
RANDY WEBSTER         (A   (A) BLUES TO AFRICA               19   FREEDOM                FLP 41014
```

W40A RITCHIE WEEMS

```
RITCHIE WEEMS         (A   (A) NATURAL BORN MAN              1965 DUNHILL                202
```

W41 JOHN WEIDER

```
JOHN WEIDER      G V  (A   (A) JOHN WEIDER                   1976 ANCHOR                 ANCL 2018
CHARLIE McCRACKEN B   (A
PIERCE KELLY     D    (A
```

W41A WEIDORJE

```
MICHEL ETTORI        G    (A   (A) WEIDORJE                   1978 COBRA                  COB 37014
JEAN PHILIPPE GOUDE K    (A
PATRICK GAUTHIER     K    (A   KIRT RUST     D    (A   ALAIN GAILLARD  SAX (A   YVON GAILLARD   TPT V(A
BERNARD PAGANOTTI    B V  (A
```

W42 BOB WEIR

```
BOB WEIR         G V  (AB   (A) ACE                           1973 WB    US BS2627 UK  K 46165
DAVID PAICH      K    (B    (B) HEAVEN HELP THE FOOL          1978 ARISTA         UK  SPART1044
DAVID FOSTER     K    (B
MIKE BAIRD       D    (B   MIKE PORCARO  B    (B   TOM SCOTT    WIND (B   BILL CHAMPLIN  K V (B
TOM KELLY        V    (B   NIGEL OLSSON  D    (B   DEE MURRAY   B    (B   WADDY WACHTEL  G   (B
PEGGY SANDVIG    K    (B   LYNETTE GLOUD V    (B   BILL KREUTZMANN D (A   PHIL LESH      B V (A
JERRY GARCIA    G STEEL (A KEITH GODCHAUX PNO (A   DONNA GODCHAUX V  (A   ED BOGAS       STRINGS(A
DAVE TORBERT     B    (A   CARMEN TWILLIE V    (B
```

W43 RUSTY WEIR

```
RUSTY WEIR            (ALL  (A) DONT IT MAKE YOU WANNA DANCE  1975 20TH CENTURY   US  T 469
RUSTY YOUNG          (E    (B) RUSTY WEIR                    1976 20TH CENTURY   US  T 495
CHRIS HILLMAN    B V (E    (C) BLACK HAT SALOON              1976 CBS            US  34319
RICHIE FURAY        (E    (D) STACKED DECK                  1977 CBS            US  34775
HERB PEDERSEN       (E    (E) STONED SLOW RUGGED            1977 ABC            US  AB 820
GIB GUILBEAU        (E
```

W44 TIM WEISBERG

```
TIM WEISBERG     FLT V(ALL  (A) TIM WEISBERG                 1971 A&M   US 3039
TODD ROBINSON    G   (DEGH  (B) DREAMSPEAKER                 1972 A&M   US 3045
DOUG ANDERSON    B   (DEGH  (C) HURTWOOD EDGE                1973 A&M   US 4352
TY GRIMES        D   (EG    (D) TIM WEISBERG 4               1974 A&M   US 3658   UK  AMLH63658
TOM DOUGHERTY    PERC (G    (E) LISTEN TO THE CITY           1975 A&M   US 4545   UK  AMLH64545
BILL STEWART     D   (H     (F) LIVE AT LAST                 197  A&M   US 4600
RICK JAEGER      D   (GH    (G) TIM WEISBERG BAND            1977 UA    US LA773  UK  UAG 30113
JOHN HUG         G   (GH    (H) ROTATIONS                    1978 UA    US LA857  UK  UAG 30175
TOWER OF POWER   HRNS (G    (I) TWIN SONS OF DIFFERENT MOTHERS 1978 EPIC US 35339
CHUCK LEAVELL    K   (GH
DAN FOGELBERG    G V (I   BOBBYE HALL  PERC (H   RONNIE EADES  SAX (H   NEIL LARSEN    K  (GH
                                                                              (CONTINUED)
```

TIM WEISBERG

(CONTINUED)

```
MICKEY RAPHAEL    HCA (H    HARRISON CALLOWAY TPT (H   HARVEY THOMPSON  SAX (B   BEN CAULEY    TPT (H
FRED SELDON       SAX (H    ERNIE CARLSON    TROM (H   LYNN BLESSING   K SYN(DE  MARTY FOLTZ    D (D
JUDEE SILL      G V K(D     TOM PELTIER       V   (D   ART JOHNSON      V  (D
```

LARRY WEISS
W44A

```
LARRY WEISS       V   (A    (A) BLACK & BLUE SUITE              1974 20TH CENTURY              T428
TOM HENSLEY       PNO (A
LEE SKLAR         B   (A    RICK MAROTTA     D   (A   HUGH McCRACKEN  G K(A  JIMMIE HASKELL   K  (A
JAMES HENDRIX     G   (A    JIM KELTNER      D   (A   DEAN PARKS      G  (A  DAVID PARLATO    B  (A
STRING SECTION        (A
```

ERIC WEISSBERG
W45

```
ERIC WEISSBERG  G V FDL (ALL   (A) FOLK BANJO STYLES              1966 POLYDOR      UK
STEVE MANDELL   G V BANJ(CD    (B) NEW DIMENSIONS IN BANJO BLUEGRASS 19 ELEKTRA     US   EKS  7238
CHARLIE BROWN   G V HCA (D     (C) DUELLING BANJO'S               1973 WB   US BS2683 UK   K46214
MARSHALL BRICKMAN      (AB     (D) RURAL FREE DELIVERY            1973 WB          UK   K46260
TONY BROOKS     B V (D
RICHARD BROOKS  D   (D
```

BOB WELCH
W46

```
BOB WELCH       G V (A    (A) FRENCH KISS                  1977 CAPITOL      EST 11663
CHRISTINE McVIE K   (B    (B) THREE HEARTS                 1979             EST 11907
MICK FLEETWOOD  D   (B
STEVE NICKS     V   (B
```

JUNIOR WELLS
W47

```
JUNIOR WELLS    V HCA(ALL   (A) ON TAP                      1966 DELMARK    US   DS 635
BUDDY GUY       G   (BCDKF  (B) IT'S MY LIFE BABY           1966 VANGUARD UKSRVL19028 US VSD79231
FRED BELOW      D   (BEJ    (B) IT'S MY LIFE BABY           1966 FONTANA         TFL6084
LEROY STEWART   B   (B      (C) SOUTH SIDE JAM              196  DELMARK    US   DS 612
WALTER BEASLEY  G   (B      (D) HOODOO MAN BLUES            196  DELMARK    US   DS 628
LITTLE AL       D   (B      (E) BLUES HIT BIG TOWN          196  DELMARK    US   DS 640
WALTER WILLIAMS G   (F      (F) COMING AT YOU               1968 VANGUARD UKSRVL19011 US VSD79262
DOUGLAS FAGAN   SAX (F      (G) YOU'RE TUFF ENOUGH          1968 MERCURY    UK   SMCL20130
TOM CRAWFORD    B   (F      (G) YOU'RE TUFF ENOUGH          1968 BLUE ROCK  US   64002
LEVI WARREN     D   (F      (H) SINGS AT THE GOLDEN BEAR    1968 BLUE ROCK  US   64003
CLARK TERRY     TPT (F      (J) IN MY YOUNGER DAYS          1971 RED LIGHTNING  RL  007
WALLACE DAVENPORT TPT (F    (K) PLAY THE BLUES              1972 ATLANTIC US 33364  UK K40240
JIMMY OWEN      TPT (F      (L) PLEADING THE BLUES          19   ISABEL     FR   900501
TOM McINTOSH    TROM (F     (EP) BLUES WITH A BEAT          197  DELMARK         DJB 1
HENRY GRAY      K   (J
LOUIS MYERS     G   (EJ     DAVID MYERS      B    (EJ  SYL JOHNSON     G   (J  WILLIE DIXON     B  (EJ
EUGENE LOUNGE   D   (J      EARL HOOKER      G    (J   LAFAYETTE LEAKE K   (J  DONALD HAWKINS  SAX(J
JARRETT GIBSON  SAX (J      JOHN WALKER      K    (J   JACK MEYERS     B   (DJ MUDDY WATERS     G  (E
ELMORE JAMES    G   (E      ODIE PAYNE       D    (E   OTIS SPANN      G   (E  JOHNNIE JONES   PNO(E
A C REED        SAX (A      ROOSEVELT SHAW   D    (A   CHARLES MILES   SAX (A  JOHNNY WALKER    K  (A
PHILIP GUY      G   (A      HERMAN APPLEWHITE B   (A   SAM LAWHORN     G   (A
(**) SEE BUDDY GUY ENTRY FOR K LINE UP
```

MARY WELLS
W48

```
MARY WELLS      V   (ALL    BYE BYE BABY                    1961 TAMLA US 600 ORIOLE 63 UK 40051
MARVIN GAYE     V   (*      ONE WHO REALLY LOVES YOU        1962 TAMLA         US        605
                            TWO LOVERS                      1962 TAMLA US 607 ORIOLE 63 UK 40045
                            ON STAGE                        1962 TAMLA         US        611
                            GREATEST HITS                   1963 TAMLA US 616 UK   TML 11032
                            TOGETHER *                      1964 STATESIDE     UK        10097
                            TOGETHER *                      1964 TAMLA         US        613
                            MY  GUY                         1964 STATESIDE     UK        10095
                            MY GUY                          1964 TAMLA         US        617
                            MARY WELLS                      1965 STATESIDE     UK        10133
                            MARY WELLS                      196  20TH CENTURY  US        4171
                            LOVE SONGS OF THE BEATLES       196  STATESIDE     UK        10171
                            LOVE SONGS OF THE BEATLES       196  20TH CENTURY  US        4178
                            OOH!                            1966 MOVIETONE     US        71010
                            VINTAGE STOCK                   1967 TAMLA         US        653
                            TWO SIDES OF                    196  ATCO          US        33199
                            SERVIN' UP SOME SOUL            1968 JUBILEE       US        8018
                            SERVIN' UP SOME SOUL            1968 STATESIDE     UK        10266
```

PHILLIP J WELLS
W48A

```
PHILLIP J WELLS  ALL INST(A   (A) THE LAST SURVIVORS            1978 SOLID GOLD         SGRLP 101
```

MICHAEL WENDROFF
W48B

```
MICHAEL WENDROFF G HCA V(A    (A) SOUTHPAW                     1974 BUDDAH            BDS  5609
BOB KULICK       G    (A
MIKE MONTGOMERY  K    (A      JIM GREGORY     B   (A   GREGG DIAMOND  PERC D V (A  JIMMY MAELEN  PERC V(A
P J ROSS         V    (A      RALPH MOSS      V   (A   JOANNE VENT    V   (A  STEVE MORGAN    V  (A
STRING SECTION        (A
```

WEREWOLVES
W48C

```
                              (A) THE WEREWOLVES             1978 RCA  AFLI2746   uk   PL 12746
                              (B) SHIP OF FOOLS              197  RCA  AFLI3079
```

DAVID WERNER
W48D

```
DAVID WERNER    G V K(A    (A) DAVID WERNER                1979 EPIC          UK      83862
MARK DOYLE      G K B V (A
THOM MOONEY     D    (A    ALBRITTON McLAIN B   (A   KEN BISCHEL    SYN  (A  RICHARD HUNTER  HCA (A
TIM CAPELLO     SAX  (A    IAN HUNTER       V   (A   MAXINE DIXON   V   (A
```

HOWARD WERTH & THE MOONBEAMS
W49

```
HOWARD WERTH    G V  (A    (A) KING BRILLIANT              1975 CHARISMA UK CAS11-04 US ROCKET2180
MIKE MORAN      K    (A
FRED GANDY      B    (A    BOB WESTON       G   (A   ROGER POPE     D   (A  PHIL DUNNE      (A
GUS DUDGEON     PERC (A
```

FRANK WESS
W50

```
FRANK WESS           (AB   (A) FLUTE OF THE LOOM            1973 ENTERPRISE        ENS5006
                           (B) COMMODORE YEARS              1973 ATLANTIC          SD 2 306
                           (C) WESS TO MEMPHIS              197  ENTERPRISE        ENS5001
```

W51   LESLIE WEST

LESLIE WEST	G V (ALL		(A) MOUNTAIN				1969 WINDFALL/BELL			4500
N D SMART	D (A		(B) LESLIE WEST BAND				1975 PHANTOM			PHS 701
FELIX PAPPALARDI	K B (A		(C) THE GREAT FATSBY				1875 RCA UK			RS1009
NORMAN LANDSBERG	K (A									
CORKY LAING	D (BC	MICK JONES	G (B	DON KRETMAR	B (BC	SREDNI VOLLNER	HCA (BC
KEN ASCHER	K (B	BILL GELBER	B (B	HILDA HARRIS	V (B	TASHA THOMAS	V (B
SHARON REDD	V (B	CARL HALL	V (B	MICK JAGGER	G (C	JOEL TEPP	G (C
HOWIE WYETH	PNO (C	GARY WRIGHT	PNO (C	MARTY SIMON	PNO (C	NICK FERRANTELLA	D (C
KEN HINKLE	B (C	FRANK VICARI	HRNS (BC	DANA VALERY	V (C	JAY TRAYNOR	V (C

W52   WEST BRUCE & LAING

LESLIE WEST	G V (ABC	(A) WHY DONTCHA	1972 CBS	UK 65314	WINDFALL US 31929
JACK BRUCE	B V (ABC	(B) WHAT EVER TURNS YOU ON	1973 RSO	UK 2394 107	WINDFALL US 32216
CORKY LAING	D (ABC	(C) LIVE & KICKIN'	1974 RSO	UK 2394 128	WINDFALL US 32899

W53   WEST COAST POP ART EXPERIMENTAL BAND

BOB MARKLEY	(ALL	(A) PART ONE	1967 REPRISE		US	6247
DAN HARRIS	G V (ALL	(B) VOL2	1967 REPRISE		US	6270
SHAUN HARRIS	G B V(ALL	(C) A CHILD'S GUIDE TO GOOD & EVIL	1968 REPRISE	5106		6298
		(D) WHERE'S MY DADDY?	19 AMOS		US	AAS 7004
		(A) FIRST ALBUM RI	197 MIDI			K24024

W53A   WEST ROAD BLUES BAND

TAKASHI NAGAI	V (A		(A) WEST ROAD			1975 BOURBON	JAP	BUC3001
SHINJI SHIOTSUGU	G (A							
JUNSHI YAMAGISHI	G (A	TADASHI KOBORI	B (A	TERUO MATSUMOTO	D (A	RYUICHIRO SENOH	HCA(A
HIROSHI SATO	K (A	RYUICHI IDE	K (A	MARI KANEKO	V (A		

W54   WET WILLIE

JIMMY HALL SAX	V HCA(ALL	(A) WET WILLIE	1971 ATLANTIC	UK K40281	US SD 861
JACK HALL	B V (ALL	(A) WET WILLIE	1971 CAPRICORN		US 0138
RICKY HIRSCH	G V (ABCDEFGH	(B) WET WILLIE II	1972 CAPRICORN		US 0109
JOHN ANTHONY	K V (ABCDEFGH	(C) DRIPPIN' WET	1973 CAPRICORN	UK K47512	US 0113
LEWIS ROSS	D (ABCDEFGH	(D) KEEP ON SMILIN'	1974 CAPRICORN	UK 2429 115	US 0128
WICK LARSEN	G (B	(E) DIXIE ROCK	1975 CAPRICORN	UK 2429 124	US 0149
ELLA AVERY	V (BDE	(F) WETTER THE BETTER	1976 CAPRICORN	UK 2429 137	US 0166
SUSIE STORM	V (B	(G) LEFT COAST LIVE	1977 CAPRICORN	UK 2429 151	US 0182
SCOTT BOYER	STEEL(B	(H) GREATEST HITS	1977 CAPRICORN		US 0200
JAI JOHANNY JOHANSON	(BC	(J) MANORISMS	1978 EPIC	UK 82330	US 34983
DONNA HALL	V (DEF	(K) WHICH ONE'S WILLIE	1979 EPIC		US 35794
JOYCE KNIGHT	V (DE				
EARL FORD	TROM (DE	MIKE DUKE	K V(EFGJK	TOM DOWD	PERC (E	MAMA HALL	K V (E
SUSAN HALL	V (E	PAUL HORNSBY	K (F	LEO LABRANCHE	TPT (F	SKIP LANE	SAX (F
DEZSO LAKATOS	SAX (F	JEROME JOSEPH	CONGA(F	LESLIE PHILUS LIVELY D V(J	LESLIE HAWKINS	V (F
LARRY BERWALD	G (JK	MARSHALL SMITH	G V (JK	THEOPHILUS LIVELY D V	(JK	PAULETTE BROWN	B (K
VANETTA FIELDS	V (K	ANGELLE TROSCLAIR V	(K	MIGHTY CLOUDS OF JOY V	(K	STEVE MADAIO	TPT (K
LENNY CASTRO	PERC (K	VICTOR FELDMAN	PERC (K	CHUCK FINDLEY	HRNS(K	GARY HERBIG	SAX (K
DAVID LUELL	SAX (K	BOB PAYNE	TROM (K			

W54A   JOHN WETTON

JOHN WETTON	G V K B (A	(A) CAUGHT IN THE CROSSFIRE	1980 POLYDOR EG	UK	EGLP 107
SIMON KIRKE	D PERC(A				
MALCOLM DUNCAN	SAX (A	MARTIN BARRE	G (A		

W55   WHALEFEATHER

MICHAL JONES	G V (A	(A) WHALEFEATHER	1971 BLUE HORIZON	2431 009
M E BLACKMON	K V (A			
LEONARD LE BLANC	B V (A	STEPHEN BACON	PERC (A	

W56   WHIRLWIND

NIGEL DIXON	V (AB	(A) BLOWING UP A STORM 12"	1978 CHISWICK	WIK 7	CWK 3007
MICHAEL LEWIS	G (AB	(A) BLOWING UP A STORM 10"	1978 CHISWICK		CH 4
CHRIS EMO	B (AB	(B) MIDNIGHT	1980 CHISWICK		CWK 3012
PHIL HARDY	D (A				
GARY HASSETT	(B				

W57   WHIRLY WORLD

	(A) WIN OR LOSE (EP)	19 MISSING LINK

W58   ALAN WHITE

ALAN WHITE	D V (A	(A) RAMSHACKLED	1976 ATLANTIC	US SD18167	UK K50217
PETER KIRTLEY	G V (A				
COLIN GIBSON	B PERC(A	KEN CRADDOCK	K V (A	ALAN MARSHALL	V (A	BUD BEADLE	WIND(A
ANDY PHILLIPS	PERC (A	STEVE GREGORY	WIND (A	HENRY LOWTHER	TPT (A		

W59   BUKKA WHITE

BUKKA WHITE	G V (ALL	(A) BUKKA WHITE	1964 CBS		52627
WASHBOARD SAM	PERC (A	(B) SIC 'EM DOGS	196 HERWIN	US	201
HARMONICA BOY	HCA (C	(C) MEMPHIS HOT SHOTS	196 BLUE HORIZON	UK	7 63229
BILL BARTH	G (C	(D) BLUES MASTERS VOL 4	196 BLUE HORIZON	US	4604
TREVOR KEOHLER	PNO (C	(E) MISSISSIPPI BLUES	1969 TAKOMA US 1001	GNP US	10011
ANCHOR	B (C	(F) LEGACY OF THE BLUES	19 SONET	UK	SNTF 609
JIM CROSTHWAIT	PERC (C	(G) SKY SONGS VOL 1	1975 ARHOOLIE		F1019
BIG WILLIE	PERC (GH	(H) SKY SONGS VOL 2	1975 ARHOOLIE		F1020
JOE GRAY	D (C				

W60   CHRIS WHITE

CHRIS WHITE	V PERC(A	(A) MOUTH MUSIC	1976 CHARISMA		CAS 1118
TOM PARKER	K (A				
CLEM CATTINI	D (A	Z JENKINS	G (A	DAVE OLNEY	B (A	SHEL TALMY	PERC (A

W61   KIERAN WHITE

KIERAN WHITE	V G B HCA (A	(A) OPEN DOOR	1975 GULL	UK	GULP 1011
DAVE SHEEN	B D (A				
CHAS JANKEL	K G V(A	ROGER BUNN	B (A	DONAL LUNNEY	SYN G V(A	GEOFF DRISCOLL	WIND(A
TIM STAFFEL	V (A				

LENNY WHITE   W62

LENNY WHITE	D K B(ALL		(A) VENUSIAN SUMMER				1975 NEMPEROR	US 435	UK K50213
DOUG RAUCH	B (A		(B) BIG CITY				1977 NEMPEROR	US 441	UK K50345
DOUG RODRIGUEZ	G (A		(C) ADVENTURES OF ASTRAL PIRATES				1978 ELEKTRA	US 6E121	UK K52065
RAY GOMEZ	G (AB		(D) STREAMLINE				1978 ELEKTRA		UK K52108
JIMMY SMITH	ORG (A								

DAVID SANCIOUS	K (A	WELDON IRVINE	K (A	ONAJE ALLAN GUMBS	K (AB	PATRICK GLEASON	K (AB
PETER ROBINSON	K (A	HUBERT LAWS	FLT (A	DENNIS MACKAY	PERC (A	LARRY YOUNG	ORG (A
TOM HARREL	(A	LARRY CORYELL	G (A	AL DIMEOLA	G (A	BRIAN AUGER	K (B
HERBIE HANCOCK	K (B	VERDINE WHITE	B (B	TOWER OF POWER	HRNS (B	JAN HAMMER	K (B
JERRY GOODMAN	VLN (B	NEAL SCHON	G (B	LINDA TILLERY	V (B	ALEX LIGERTWOOD	G (B
JACK MILLS	G (B	CLIVE CHAMAN	B (B	BENNIE MAUPIN	SAX (B	LENNOX LAINGTON	CONGA(B
PAUL JACKSON	B (B	MARCUS MILLER	B (B	ALEX BLAKE	B (B	MIROSLAV VITOUS	B (B
MIKE GIBBS	PNO (B	LOIS COLIN	HARP (B	GARY KING	D (B	DAVID JOHNSON	CONGA(B

MICHAEL WHITE   W63

MICHAEL WHITE	(ALL	(A) THE SUN & MOON HAVE COME TOGETHER	1969 CAPITOL	US	SKOA 423
BABATUNDE	(J	(B) WEREWOLF	1970 CAPITOL	US	
JOSEPH BARBOZA	(J	(C) 4TH WAY	1971 CAPITOL	US	
NAPOLEON BROCK	(J	(D) SPIRIT DANCE	1972 IMPULSE	US	AS9215
DAVID DANIEL	(J	(E) PNEUMA	1973 IMPULSE	US	AS9221
BRUCE FOWLER	(J	(F) THE LAND OF SPIRIT & LIGHT	1974 IMPULSE	US	AS9241
WALT FOWLER	(J	(G) FATHER MUSIC MOTHER DANCE	1974 IMPULSE	US	AS9268
DEWILLI GONGA	(J	(H) GO WITH THE FLOW	1975 IMPULSE	US	AS9281
MUFFY JAMES	(J	(J) THE X FACTOR	1978 ELEKTRA	UK	K52095
HUBERT LAWS	(J				

BYRON MILLER	(J	AIRTO MOREIRA	(J	EDWARD MYERS	(J	GREGORY PHILLINGANES	(J
PETSYE POWELL	(J	DUANE ROBERSON	(J	PATRICE RUSHEN	(J	MIKE SEMBELLO	(J
ALBERT WING	(J	ROLAND BAUTISTA	(J	MARVIN BOXLEY	(J	PATTIE BROOKS	(J
LEON CHANCLER	(J	RAUL DE SOUZA	(J	KING ERRISSON	PERC (J	

TONY JOE WHITE   W64

TONY JOE WHITE	G V HCA(ALL	(A) BLACK & WHITE	1968 MONUMENT	US 18114	UK SMO 5027
TOMMY McCLURE	B (BF	(B) CONTINUED	1969 MONUMENT	US 18133	UK SMO 5035
SAMMY CREASON	D (BF	(C) TONY JOE	1970 MONUMENT	US 18142	UK SMO 5043
JAMES MILHART	D (BF	(D) TONY JOE WHITE	1971 WB	US 1900	UK K46068
MIKEE UTLEY	ORG (BF	(E) THE TRAIN I'M ON	1972 WB	US 2580	UK K46147
DAVID BRIGGS	K (AF	(F) BEST OF	1973 WB EURO 054 92274	UK K56149
JERRY CARRIGAN	D (AF	(G) HOME MADE ICE CREAM	1973 WB	US 2708	UK K46229
NORBERT PUTNAM	B (AF	(H) EYES	197 20TH CENTURY	BT523
CHIP YOUNG	G (A	(J) TONY JOE WHITE	1977 20th CENTURY	PS2030
JIMMY ISBELL	D (A				

WHITE CAT   W65

CHRIS MILLAR	D (A	(A) MAY 1978			
STEVE TURNER	B (A	EDDIE COX	G (A	KELVIN BLACKLOCK	G V (A

WHITE HORSE   W65A

JON LIND	G V (A	(A) WHITE HORSE	1977 CAPITOL	US	ST 11687
BILLY NICHOLLS	PNO G V(A				

KENNY ALTMAN	G B (A	JEFF PORCARO	D (A	PAUL BARRERE	G (A	BILL PAYNE	SYN K(A
JOE PORCARO	PERC (A	GARY MALLABER	D (A	BOB GLAUB	B (A	CALEB QUAYE	G (A
RUSS KUNKEL	D (A	FRED TACKETT	G (A	CHUCK DOMANICO	B (A	REGGIE KNIGHTON	G(A
DAVY LIVINGSTONE	STEEL(A	DAVID PAICH	PNO (A			

WHITE LIGHTNIN'   W66

BUSTA CHERRY JONES	B V (A	(A) WHITE LIGHTNIN'	1975 ISLAND	US	ILPS9325
DONALD KINSEY	G V (A				
WOODY KINSEY	D V (A				

WHITE MANSIONS (CONCEPT ALBUM)   W67

JESSI COLTER	V (A	(A) WHITE MANSIONS		1978 A&M	UK	AMLX64691
WAYLON JENNINGS	G V (A				
JOHN DILLON	V G K FDL	(A	STEVE CASH	HCA V(A	ERIC CLAPTON	G (A	BERNIE LEADON	G V (A
HENRY SPINETTI	D (A	DAVE MARKEE	B (A	TIM HINKLEY	K (A	PAUL KENNERLEY	V (A

WHITE NOISE   W68

DAVID VORHAUS	(ABC	(A) AN ELECTRIC STORM	1969 ISLAND		ILPS 9099
DELIA DERBYSHIRE	(A	(B) WHITE NOISE	1975 VIRGIN		V 2032
BRIAN HODGSON	(A	(C) RE ENTRY	1980		
PAUL LYTTON	PERC (A				
ANNIE BIRD	V (A	VAL SHAW	V (A	JOHN WHITMAN	V (A

WHITE WATER   W68A

JOHN VASTANO	G (A	(A) OUT OF THE DARKNESS	1973 RCA	US	APLI 0091
RICHARD DOMANE	K TPT(A				
PAUL PHILLIPS	HRNS (A	JOHN EMMA	SAX (A	BOB FIOCCO	B (A	CONRAD CATALANO	D(A

WHITE WITCH   W69

RON GOEDART	V (AB	(A) WHITE WITCH	1972 CAPRICORN	UK	K47505
BUDDY PENDERGRASS	K (AB	(A) WHITE WITCH	1972 CAPRICORN	US	0107
BUDDY RICHARDSON	G (AB	(B) ASPIRITUAL GREETING	1974 CAPRICORN	US	0129
BOBBY SHEA	PERC (AB				
BILL PETERSON	PERC (B	CHARLIE SOUZA	B (B	BEAU FISHER	D V (A

WHITEFACE   W69A

STEVE HARDWICK	G V (A	(A) WHITEFACE	1979 MERCURY	US	SRM13765
KYLE HENDERSON	B V (A				
DOUG BARE	K V (A	BENNY RAPPA	D V (A

WHITESPIRIT   W69B

MALCOLM PEARSON	K (A	(A) WHITESPIRIT	1980 MCA	UK	MCF 3079
PHIL BRADY	B (A				
BRUCE RUFF	V (A	JANICK GERS	G (A	GRAEME VRALLEN	D (A

BOBBY WHITLOCK   W70

BOBBY WHITLOCK	G V (ABC	(A) BOBBY WHITLOCK	1972 DUNHILL US 50121	UK CBS 65109
RICK VITO	G (B	(B) RAW VELVET	1972 DUNHILL US 50131	UK CBS 65301
KEITH ELLIS	B (B	(C) ROCK YOUR SOX OFF	1976 CAPRICORN US 0160	UK 2429 139
DON PONCHER	D (B			

W71

				JAKI WHITREN					
JAKI WHITREN	G V	BANJO(A		(A) RAW BUT TENDER		1973 EPIC	UK		65465
PAT DONALDSON	B	(A							
GERRY CONWAY	D	(A	LINDSAY COOPER	BASSOON(A	ALBERT LEE	G	(A	MARIE GOOSENS	HARP (A
ROB YOUNG	FLT	(A	HENRY VIII	JUG (A	JOHN VAN DERRICK	VLN	(A	GORDON HUNTLEY	STEEL(A
FRANK RICOTTI	PERC	(A	IVAN CHANDLER	K (A	HARRY BECKETT	HRNS	(A	STAN SULZMANN	SAX (A
BRIAN BROCKLEHURST	B	(A	STUART COWELL	G (A	MIKE LESLIE	G V	(A		

W72

			THE WHO				
PETE TOWNSHEND	G K V(ALL	(A) MY GENERATION	1965 BRUNSWICK	UK	LAT 8616
ROGER DALTREY	V HCA(ALL	(A) " " "	1966 DECCA	US	74664
JOHN ENTWISTLE	B K V(ALL	(A) " " "	1972 MCA	US	2044
KEITH MOON	D V (ALL TO 1978	(A) " " "	19 VIRGIN	UK	V2179
KENNY JONES	D	A QUICK ONE	1966 REACTION	UK	593002
NICKY HOPKINS	PNO (AR	" " "	1970 BACKTRACK	UK	2407 008
DAVE ARBUS	VLN (R	WHO SELL OUT	1967 TRACK	UK	613 002
ROD ARGENT	K (T	" " "	1970 BACKTRACK	UK	2407 009
ANDY FAIRWEATHER LOW	V (T	" " "	1967 DECCA	UK	74950
CHRIS STAINTON	K (N	" " "	1974 POLYDOR	GERM	2675 089
ELTON JOHN	PNO V(G	A QUICK ONE/SELL OUT	19 TRACK		2683 038
ERIC CLAPTON	G (G	" " "	197 MCA	US	2046
RON WOOD	G (G	HAPPY JACK	1967 DECCA	US	74892
FUZZY SAMUELS	B (G	" " "	197 MCA	US	2045
CALEB QUAYE	G (G	MAGIC BUS	1968 DECCA	US	75064
MICK RALPHS	G (G	" " "	1972 MCA	US	2047
GRAHAM DEACON	D (G	MAGIC BUS/MY GENERATION	1975 MCA	US	2 4068
PHIL CHEN	B (G	DIRECT HITS	1969 TRACK	UK	613 006
ALAN ROSS	G (G	TOMMY DBL	1969 TRACK	UK	613 013/4
RICHARD BAILEY	D (G	" " DBL	1972 TRACK		2657 002
DAVE WINTOUR	B (G	" "	196 DECCA	US	7205
TONY MURRAY	B (G	" "	197 MCA	US	2-1005
NIGEL OLSSON	D (G	TOMMY PART ONE	1972 TRACK	UK	2406 007
RAY COOPER	PERC (G	TOMMY PART TWO	1972 TRACK	UK	2406 008
DAVEY JOHNSTONE	G (G	(G) TOMMY SOUNDTRACK	1975 POLYDOR		PD 29502
GERALD SHAW	ORG (G	THE BEST OF TOMMY	197 POLYDOR	NL	2383 130
TONY STEVENS	B (G	LIVE AT LEEDS	1970 TRACK	UK	24-6 001
ANN MARGARET	V (G	" " "	1970 DECCA	US	79175
OLIVER REED	V (G	" " "	1972 MCA	US	2022
JACK NICHOLSON	V (G	" " "	197 MCA	US	3023
ROBERT POWELL	V (G	" " "	19 POLYDOR	NL	65 124
PAUL NICHOLAS	V (G	MEATY BEATY BIG & BOUNCY	1971 TRACK	UK	2406 006
TINA TURNER	V (G	" " " " "	1971 DECCA	US	79184
BARRY WINCH	V (G	" " " " "	1972 MCA	US	2025
ARTHUR BROWN	V (G	" " " " "	19 MCA	US	3025
VICTORIA RUSSELL	V (G	POP HISTORY VOL 4	1971 POLYDOR	GERM	2675 012
BEN ARIS	V (G	(K)WHO'S NEXT	1971 TRACK	UK	2408 102
MARY HOLLAND	(G	(K) " "	1971 DECCA	US	79182
JENNIFER BAKER	(G	" " "	1972 MCA	US	2023
SUSAN BAKER	(G	QUADROPHENIA	1973 TRACK	UK	2657 013
IMOGEN CLAIRE	(G	" " "	1973 MCA	US	10004
JULIET KING	(G	(N) " " " SOUNDTRACK	1979 POLYDOR	UK	2625 037
GILLIAN KING	(G	INSTANT PARTY	19 BRUNSWICK	NL	173 269
SIMON TOWNSHEND	(G	POP HEROES	19 POLYDOR	GERM	2459 410
LIZA STRIKE	V (G	THE WHO & JIMI HENDRIX(DBL)	19 KARUSSELL	GERM	2674 001
MYLON LEFEVRE	V (G	WHO DID IT (WITHDRAWN)	19 TRACK	UK	2856 001
BILLY NICHOLLS	(G	GREATEST ROCK SENSATION	19 KARUSSELL	GERM	2345 104
JESS RODEN	V (G	VERY BEST OF	19 POLYDOR	JAP	MFP 1163
MARGO NEWMAN	(G	THE STORY OF THE WHO	19 POLYDOR	JAP	MPZ81012
SARAH McINTOSH	(G	PERFECT COLLECTION	19 POLYDOR	JAP	MP 94478
VICKI BROWN	V (G	I'M A BOY	19 POLYDOR	JAP	SLPM1354
KIP TREVOR	(G	EXCITING	19 POLYDOR	JAP	MP 1385
HELEN CHAPPELLE	(G	GOLDEN DOUBLE ALBUM	19 POLYDOR	JAP	MP93556
PAUL GURVITZ	(G	ODDS & SODS	1974 TRACK	UK	2406 116
ALISON DOWLING	(G	" " "	1974 MCA	US	2126
		BEST OF 1964 74	1975 POLYDOR	UK	2674 017
		BEST OF	1975 POLYDOR		2482 172
		BEST OF	19 POLYDOR	GERM	185 152
		BEST OF LAST TEN YEARS	197 KARUSSEL	GERM	2662 323
		PORTRAIT OF	1975 POLYDOR		2482 100
		WHO (COMP)	197 IMPACT		6886 551
		WHO (COMP)	197 POLYDOR	FR	6371 450
		(R) WHO BY NUMBERS	1975 POLYDOR	UK	2490 129
		(R) " " "	1975 MCA	US	2161
		(R) " " "	19 MCA	US	3026
		STORY OF THE WHO	1976 POLYDOR	UK	2683 069
		" " " "	19 POLYDOR	GERM	2668 015
		(T) WHO ARE YOU	1978 POLYDOR	UK	WHOD5004
		(T) " " "	1978 MCA	US	3050
		KIDS ARE ALRIGHT	1979 POLYDOR	UK	2675 179
		(F) FACE DANCES	1981 POLYDOR	UK	WHOD 5037

W73

			WICHITA FALL				
LARRY WATSON	B	(A	(A) LIFE IS BUT A DREAM	1969 LIBERTY	UK83208 IMPERIAL US12417
DANNY ROUSH	G V	(A			
LEN FEIGIN	D	(A	PHILIP BLACK G V (A		

W73A

			BENOIT WIDEMANN			
BENOIT WIDEMANN	K	(A	(A) STRESS	1980 BALLON NOW	BAL 13002
CLEMENT BAILLY	D	(A			

W74

			WIDOWMAKER				
ARIEL BENDER	G	(AB	(A) WIDOWMAKER	1976 JET UK 2310 432	UK RI JETLP 15
STEVE ELLIS	V	(A	(A) WIDOWMAKER	1976 UA	US LA 642
PAUL NICHOLS	D	(AB	(B) TOO LATE TO CRY	1977 UA UK UAG30038	US LA 723
LLOYD LANGTON	G	(A	BOB DAISLEY B (AB JOHN BUTLER	V (B ZOOT MONEY K (A

[442]

WIGGY BITS
W74A

(A) WIGGY BITS	19	POLYDOR	US	1 6081	

WIGWAM
W75

JIM PEMBROKE	K V	(CHJKLM	(A) HARD & HORNEY	1969 LOVE	IMP	LRLP 9	
RONNIE OSTERBERG	D	(CHJKLM	(B) TOMBSTONE VALENTINE	1970 LOVE	IMP	LRLP19	
JUKKA GUSTAVSON	K	(CHL	(C) FAIRYPORT	1971 LOVE	IMP	LRLP44/55	
PEKKA POHJOLA	B	(CH	(D) WIGWAM	1972 LOVE	IMP	LRLP 511	
PEKKA RECHARDT	G	(HJKLM	(E) WICKED IVORY	1972 LOVE	IMP	LRLP52	
MANS GROUNDSTROEM	B	(JKLM	(F) BEING	1974 LOVE	IMP	LRLP 92	
ESA KOTITAINEN	K	(JM	(G) PIGWORM	1974 LOVE	IMP	LRLP 103	
PAAVO MAIJANEN	B V	(JKLM	(H) LIVE FROM TWILIGHT ZONE	1975 LOVE	IMP	LXLP517/8	
ILMARI VARILA	OBOE	(C	(J) DEAD AT THE NUCLEAR NIGHTCLUB	1975 LOVE IMP LRLP129 UK VIRGIN 2035			
TAPIO LOUHENSALO		(C	(K) LUCKY GOLDEN STRIPES	1976 VIRGIN	UK	2051	
HANNU SAXELIN	WIND	(C	(L) DARK ALBUM	1978 LOVE	IMP	LRLP 227	
RISTO RENSOLA	WIND	(C	(M) RUMOURS ON THE REBOUND	1979 VIRGIN	UK	VGD 3503	
UNTO HAAPA AHO	WIND	(C					
EERO KOIVISTOINEN	SAX	(CM PEKKA POYRY	SAX (C	HESSU HIETANEN	K	(KLM TIMO KOJO	V (L
COSTA APETREA	G	(M					

DANNY WILD
W76

DANNY WILD	(A	(A) WILD IN THE COUNTRY	1978 RAW	RWLP 102	

WILD ANGELS
W77

DANNY HAWKINS	G	(A	(A) OUT AT LAST	1972 DECCA	UK	SKL 5134
ROD COTTER	B	(	(B) LETS GET BACK TO ROCK	19 PYE	UK	GH 614
ROB O'CONNOR	D	(	(C) LIVE AT THE REVOLUTION	19 B+C		BCM 101
BILL KINGSTON	V	(	(D) RED HOT'N'ROCKIN'	19 B+C		BCM 102
MAL GRAY		(	(E) TOO LATE TO CRY	19 JET	UK	UAG 30038
MITCH MITCHELL	G	(				
GEOFF BRITTON	D	(				

WILD HORSES
W78

BRIAN ROBERTSON	G	(A	(A) THE FIRST ALBUM	1979 EPIC	EPC 3326
JIM BAIN	B	(A			
NEIL CARTER	G	(A CLIVE EDWARDS	D (A		

WILD TURKEY
W79

GLEN CORNICK	B G K(AB	(A) BATTLE HYMN	1971 CHRYSALIS	UK	CHR 1002	
TWEKE LEWIS	G	(AB	(B) TURKEY	1972 CHYSALIS	UK	CHR 1010
MICK DYCHE	G V	(B				
JEFF JONES	D	(AB STEVE GURL	K (B GARY PICKFORD HOPKINS G V(AB JON BLACKMORE	G V(A		

WILD WALLY
W80

WILD WALLY	(	(A) I GO APE	1971 CONSTELLATION	CCS 5001	

MARTY WILDE
W81

MARTY WILDE	V	(ALL	DR DOOLITTLE	1968 MARBLE ARCH	UK	MAL 738
BIG JIM SULLIVAN	G	(AB	ROCK'N'ROLL	1970 PHILIPS		6308 010
BRIAN BENNETT	D	(AB	GOOD ROCKIN' THEN & NOW	1974 PHILIPS		6382 102
LICORICE LOCKING	B	(AB	BAD BOY	19 EPIC	US	EPC 3686
TONY BELCHER	G	(AB	(A)WILDE ABOUT MARTY	19 EPIC US 3711 PHILIPS UK		
			WILDCAT	198 PHILIPS	SWED	
			(B) SHOWCASE	1)&= PHILIPS	UK	

WILDERNESS ROAD
W82

NATE HERMAN	G K V(A	(A) WILDERNESS ROAD	19 CBS	US	31118	
WARREN LEMING	G V BANJ (A	(B) THREE GENUINE TRANSPLANT	19 REPRISE	US	PRO 556
ANDY HABAN	B V	(A	(C) SOLD FOR PREVENTION OF DISEASE	19 REPRISE	US	2125
RAY WARD		(A				
TOM HABAN	D V OBOE	(A J A RICHARDSON	B (A			

WILDING BONUS
W82A

DANNY WILDING	FLT	(A	(A) PLEASURE SIGNALS	1978 DJM UK DJF 20553 US VISA 7003	
PETE BONUS	G	(A			
PHIL COLLINS	D	(A PHIL CHEN	B (A KIKI GYAN	K (A REBOP KWAKU BAAH PERC(A
ASHTON TOOTLE	HRNS	(A PHIL TODD	HRNS (A JOHN GOODSALL	G (A BAYETE	K (A
GREGG SHEEHAN	D	(A JOHN GIBLIN	B G (A PRESTON HEYMAN	D (A ROBIN LUMLEY	K (A
ANDY CLARKE	K	(A KATE ST JOHN	OBOE (A MIKE SHRIEVE	D (A CHRIS PARREN	K (A

WILDLIFE
W82B

STEVE OVERLAND	G V	(A	(A) BURNING	1980 CHRYSALIS	UK CHR 1288
MARK BOOTY	K	(A			
CHRIS OVERLAND	G	(A ROB SKEAT	K B (A PETE JUPP	D (A RUPERT HINE K PERC V(A
TREVOR MORAIS	D	(A JOHN GIBLIN	B (A GEOFFREY RICHARDSON	(A

MIKE WILHELM
W83

MIKE WILHELM	(A	(A) WILHELM	1976 ZIG ZAG	UK	UA ZZ1

BIG JOE WILLIAMS
W84

BIG JOE WILLIAMS	G V	(ALL	BIG JOE WILLIAMS	1975 STORYVILLE	SLP224
MARY WILLIAMS	V	(U	BIG JOE WILLIAMS(LEGACY No6)	197 SONET UK SNTF635 US GNP 10016	
SAM FOWLER	V HCA(M		BIG JOE WILLIAMS	19 EVEREST	US 218
WILLIE EALEY	V PNO(M		BIG JOE WILLIAMS	19 WORLD PACIFIC	US 21897
LEE WILLIAMS	V		BLUES FROM MISSISSIPPI DELTA	19 BLUES ON BLUE	US 10003
CHARLIE MUSSELWHITE	HCA(T		BIG JOE & ROBERT PETE WILLIAMS	1975 STORYVILLE	SLP225
ROGER ALLEN CLARK	D	(I	(B) BLUE ON HIGHWAY 49	196 DELMARK	US DL 604
JERRY BRIDGES	B	(I	BACK TO THE COUNTRY	19 TESTAMENT	US 2205
RANSOM KNOWLING	B	(PB	(F)CLASSIC DELTA BLUES	1964 CBS	UK 63813
J D SHORT	G V HCA(S		COUNTRY BLUES	19 SPECIALTY	UK SNTF5014
			DONT LEAVE ME	19 POLYDOR	616 011
			(I)DONT YOUR PLUMS LOOK MELLOW	19 BLUESWAY	UK BLS 6080
			EARLY RECORDINGS	197 MAMLISH	US 3810
			HAND ME DOWN MY OLD WALKING STICK	19 LIBERTY	LBS83207
			HELL BOUND & HEAVEN SENT	19 FOLKWAYS	US FTS31004
			(M)MALVINA MY SWEET WOMAN	1974 OLDIE BLUES	NL OL 2814
			MISSISSIPPI JOE WILLIAMS	19 FOLKWAYS	US 3820
			MISSISSIPPI DELTA BLUES	19 SPIVEY	US 1005

(CONTINUED)

BIG JOE WILLIAMS

(P)NINE STRING GUITAR BLUES	196	DELMARK	US	627
PINEY WOOD BLUES	196	DELMARK	US	602
RAMBLIN' WANDERIN' BLUES	19	STORYVILLE		SLP 163
(S) STAVIN' CHAIN BLUES	196	DELMARK	US	609
(T)THINKING OF WHAT THEY DID	1969	ARHOOLIE	US	1053
(U)TOUGH TIMES	1960	ARHOOLIE	US	1002

W84A

CLAUDE WILLIAMS

```
CLAUDE WILLIAMS          (A    (A) KANSAS CITY GREATS    197  BIG BEAR    UK    BEAR 25
```
W84B

JERRY WILLIAMS & ROADWORK

```
JERRY WILLIAMS      V   (A    (A) TOO FAST TO LIVE    1977 SONET SWED SLP 2604 UK SNTF791
PEDER SUNSAHL      D   (A
INGEMAR RAGEFEDT   G   (A   CAJ HOGBERG B G PNO V (A   DOUGIE LAWTON   G   (A   LARS AKE JOHANSSON PERC G(A
```
W85

JODY WILLIAMS

```
JODY WILLIAMS      G V  (A    (A) LEADING BRAND  (6 TRACKS)   1977 RED LIGHTNIN       RLOO18
BERNARD BARKSON    SAX  (A
HAROLD ASHBY       SAX  (A   LAFAYETTE LEAKE   PNO (A   RED HOLLOWAY   SAX (A   WILLIE DIXON    B (A
BOB GUTHRIE        D    (A
```
W86

JOHN WILLIAMS

```
JOHN WILLIAMS      G    (ALL   (A) CHANGES              1971 FLY          UK    HIFLY5
HERBIE FLOWERS     G B  (ABH   (B) HEIGHT BELOW         1973 FLY          UK    HIFLY 16
FRANCIS MONKMAN    K    (H     (C) GREATEST HITS        1974 CBS                30051
BARRY MORGAN       D    (AH    (D) RHAPSODY             1974 CBS                73350
ADRIAN BRETT       WIND (H     (E) & FRIENDS            1976 CBS                73487
RICHARD HARVEY     REC  (H     (F) SPANISH GUITAR       1976 WESTMINSTER  UK    WG1001
VIC FLICK          G    (H     (G) BEST FRIENDS         1976 RCA          UK    RS1094
LAWRENCE JUBER     G    (H     (AB) CHANGES /HEIGHT BELOW 1977 CUBE RI     UK    TOOFA12
LES THATCHER       G    (H     (H) TRAVELLING           1978 CUBE         UK    HIFLY27
HAROLD FISHER      D    (H     (J) BRIDGES              1979 LOTUS        UK    WH 5015
STUART ELLIOTT     D    (H
PATRICK GOWERS     K    (H   DANNY THOMPSON    B   (A  JIM LAWLESS       PERC (A  CHRIS LAURENCE  B   (A
JOE MUDELE         B    (A   RAY COOPER        PERC (A  BARRY GUARD       PERC (A  ALAN PARKER     G   (A
CHRIS SPEDDING     G    (A   RICK WAKEMAN      K   (A  DAVID SNELL       HARP (A  CHRIS TAYLOR    WIND(AB
ROY WILLCOX        WIND (A   TONY COE          WIND (A  RONNIE CHAMBERLAIN WIND (A  KENNY WHEELER   TPT (A
STANLEY RODERICK   TPT  (A   RALPH IZEN        TPT (A  DEREK WATKINS     TROM (A  NAT PECK        TROM (A
DON LUSHER         TROM (A   PAT HARLEY        TROM (A  RAY PREMRU        TROM (A  RONNIE VERRALL  PERC (A
TERRY COX          PERC (A   TRISTAN FRY       PERC (AB BRIAN GASCOIGNE   PERC (B  CHARLOTTE NASSIM KOTO (B
VIRAM JASANI       TABLA(B   ROY BABBINGTON    B   (B  JOHN MARSHALL     D   (B  WILLIAM DE MONT CELLO (B
MORRIS LUBAN       VLA  (B   BRIAN MOLLINSON   B   (B  CHRIS BOWERS-BROADBENT K(B  DARRYL RUNSWICK  B  (B
PETE MORGAN        B    (B   BARRY DE SOUZA    D   (B  KENNY CLAIRE      D   (B  TREVOR TOMKINS   D  (B
ALAN BRANSCOMBE    VIBES(B   DAVID CORKHILL    FLT (B  JACK ELLORY       FLT (B  GEORGE CROZIER  FLT (B
DUDLEY MOORE       ORG  (B   ROLAND HARKER     G   (B  DICK ABEL         G   (B
```
W87

LARRY WILLIAMS

```
LARRY WILLIAMS        V   (ALL  (A) LIVE              1965 SUE          UK    ILP 922
JOHNNY GUITAR WATSON G   (ABD  (B) THE LARRY WILLIAMS SHOW 1965 DECCA    UK    LK  4691
PLAS JOHNSON         SAX  (C   (C) HERE'S LARRY WILLIAMS 196 SPECIALITY US 2109 UK SNTF5008
ALVIN'RED'TAYLOR     SAX  (C   (D) TWO FOR THE PRICE OF ONE 19 OKEH         OKS 14122
ERNIE FREEMAN        PNO  (C   (E) MISSING & UNISSUED SIDES 19 SPECIALITY FR 2225
RENEE HALL           G    (C   (F) GREATEST HITS       19  OKEH          OKS 12123
BARNEY KESSEL        G    (C
TED BRINSON         B    (C  RAY BROWN         B   (C  EARL PALMER       D   (C  GERALD WILSON   TPT (C
DAVE SHERIDAN       SAX  (AB  TONY HURLEY       SAX (AB  PHILIP GOODHAND TAIT K (AB  IVOR SHAKLETON  G  (AB
KIRK RIDDLE         B    (AB  DICK FORCEY       D   (AB
```
W88

MASON WILLIAMS

```
MASON WILLIAMS       G V  (ALL  (A) PHONOGRAM RECORD   1969 WB           US    WS1729
BILL CUNNINGHAM      G    (H    (B) MASON WILLIAMS EAR SHOW 1969 WB       US    WS1766
RICK CUNHA           G    (H    (C) MUSIC              1969 WB           US    WS1788
AL CASEY             G    (H    (D) HAND MADE          19  WB            US    WS1838
LARRY KNECHTEL       B    (H    (E) THEM POEMS & THINGS 196 JOY                JOY 118
HAL BLAINE           D    (H    (F) LISTENING MATTER   19  EVEREST       US    3265
TOMMY MORGAN         HCA  (H    (G) FEUDIN BANJOS      19  OLYMPIC             7105
STEVE LA FEVER       B    (H    (H) IMPROVED           1971 WB           UK    K46120
MILT HOLLAND         PERC (H    (I) FRESH FISH         197 FLYING FISH   US    FFO59
DAVE DAWSON          V    (H
SUZETTE GRANT        G V  (H   NANCY AMES        V   (H  ARTIE AZENZOR     PNO (H  JAN HYDE        D   (H
GARY CARLSON         G    (H   RONNIE TUTT       D   (H  PATTER SMITH      B   (H
```
W89

PAUL WILLIAMS

```
PAUL WILLIAMS        V    (ALL  (A) DELTA BLUES SINGER 1973 SONET        UK    SNTF 654
GLENN CAMPBELL       G    (A    (1) PAUL WILLIAMS SET 1967
BOB HALL             K    (A    (2) PAUL WILLIAMS SET 1968
KEITH ELLIS          B    (A
EDDIE YARLETT             (A   PAT DONALDSON     B   (A  ALUN DAVIES       G   (A  SPENCER DAVIS   G  (A
JON MARK             G    (A   ROY MILLS         (1  ROD SLADE         B   (1  TEDDY CHILDS    (1
JOHN ALMOND          WIND (12  JIMMY  CRAWFORD   (12  JEFF CONDON       HRNS (12 ALAN WHITE      D  (2
JOHN  WIGGINS             (2   ROGER SUTTON      B   (2
```
W90

TONY WILLIAMS

```
TONY WILLIAMS        D    (A    (A) JOY OF FLYING     1979 CBS           UK    83338
RONNIE MONTROSE      G    (A
HERBIE HANCOCK       K    (A   BRIAN AUGER  K    (A  JAN HAMMER         K   (A  STANLEY CLARKE  B  (A
GEORGE BENSON        G    (A
```
W91

HOMESICK JAMES WILLIAMSON

```
JAMES WILLIAMSON          (ALL  (A) CHICAGO            19  B&B                FR 33034
DAVE MYERS           B    (B    (B) AIN'T SICK NO MORE 1973 BLUESWAY      BLS  6071
EDDIE TAYLOR         B    (B    (C) & SNOOKY PRYOR     197 CAROLINE UK C1502 BIGBEAR   21
SNOOKY PRYOR         HCA  (BCD  (D) HOME SWEET HOMESICK JAMES 1976 BIG BEAR  BEAR10
WILLIE SMITH         D    (B
BOB HALL             PNO  (CD  BOB BRUNNING     B   (CD  JOHN HUNT         D   (CD PETE YORK   D   (D
JIMMIE LEE ROBINSON  B   (D
```

ROBIN WILLIAMSON
W92

ROBIN WILLIAMSON	(ALL	(A) MYRRH	1972 ISLAND	HELP 2
SYLVIA WOODS K HCA V B (C		(B) JOURNEY EDGE	1977 FLYING FISH US	033
CHRISTOPHER CASWELL WIND V(C		(C) AMERICAN STONEHENGE	1978 FLYING FISH US	062
JERRY McMILLAN VLN V(C		(C) AMERICAN STONEHENGE	1978 CRIMINAL UK	STEAL 4
PETE GRANT BAN G(C		(D) GLINT AT THE KINDLING	1979 CRIMINAL UK	STEAL 6
LOUIS KILLEN CONC (C				
DIRK DALTON B (C STU BROTMAN B (C				

SONNY BOY WILLIAMSON 1
W93

SONNY BOY WILLIAMSON V HCA(A	(A) SONNY BOY WILLIAMSON	19 RCA	FXM1 7215
(JOHN LEE WILLIAMSON)	(B) BLUEBIRD BLUES	1970 RCA INT	INT 1088
JOE WILLIAMS G (B	(C) SONNY BOY VOL 1	1975 BLUES CLASSICS	BC3
YANK RACHELL MAND (B	(D) SONNY BOY VOL 2	1975 BLUES CLASSICS	BC20
SPECKLED RED PNO (B	(E) SONNY BOY VOL 3	1975 BLUES CLASSICS	BC24
WILLIE HATCHER MAND (B			
ROBERT LEE McCOY G (B WALTER DAVIS PNO (B JOSH ALTHEIMER PNO (C FRED WILLIAMS D (C			
WASHBOARD SAM PERC (C ARMAND JACKSON D (C BLIND JOHN DAVIS PNO (C ALFRED ELKINS B (C			
BILL BROONZY G (C MATT MURPHY G (D TED SUMMIT G (C RANSOM KNOWLING B (C			
CHARLIE McCOY G (C WALTER DAVIS PNO (C			

SONNY BOY WILLIAMSON II
W94

SONNY BOY WILLIAMSON V (ALL	(A) SONNY BOY & MEMPHIS SLIM	1963 VOGUE		LD 63930
(RICE MILLER)	(B) DOWN & OUT BLUES	1964 CHESS US 1437 UK PYE	NPL	28036
BRIAN AUGER K (M	(B) DOWN & OUT BLUES	1967 MARBLE ARCH UK RI	MAL	662
JOE HARRIOT SAX (M	(C) HELP ME	1964 CHESS	CRE	6001
ALAN SKIDMORE SAX (M	(D) & THE YARDBIRDS	1964 FONTANA UK		TL5277
JIMMY PAGE G (M	(D) & THE YARDBIRDS	1964 MERCURY US		21071
RICKY BROWN B (M	(D) & THE YARDBIRDS	196 FONTANA	858	025
MICK WALLER D (M	(D) & THE YARDBIRDS	1968 FONTANA	SFJL	960
ERIC CLAPTON G (D	(D) & THE YARDBIRDS	1975 PHILIPS	6435	011
KEITH RELF HCA (D	(E) ONE WAY OUT	196 CHESS US 1417 RI	CHV	417
JIM McCARTY D (D	(F) IN MEMORIUM	1965 CHESS	CRL	4510
CHRIS DREJA G B (D	(G) REAL FOLK BLUES	196 CHESS US		1503
PAUL SAMWELL SMITH B (D	(H) MORE FOLK BLUES	196 CHESS US		1509
ERIC BURDON (Q	(I) SONNY BOY WILLIAMSON	19 STORYVILLE	SLP	158
JOHN STEEL D (Q	(J) BLUES OF	19 STORYVILLE	671	170
HILTON VALENTINE G (Q	(K) PORTRAIT IN BLUES	19 STORYVILLE	671	158
MATT MURPHY G (QJKPVW	(L) DONT SEND ME NO FLOWERS	1968 MARMALADE	608	004
CHAS CHANDLER B (Q	(M) THE ORIGINAL	19 BLUES CLASSICS	BC	9
ALAN PRICE K (Q	(N) BUMMER ROAD	19 CHESS US		1536
MEMPHIS SLIM PNO (AJKX	(O) THIS IS MY STORY	19 CHESS		50027
BILLY STEPNEY D (JKW	(P) DONT MAKE A MISTAKE	19 BLUES BALL US		2004
MUDDY WATERS G (EV	(M) JAM SESSION	1975 CHARLY UK	CR	30011
WILLIE DIXON B (EPVW	(Q) & THE ANIMALS	1975 CHARLY UK	CR	30018
BUDDY GUY G (PVW	(U) KING BISCUIT TIME	1976 ARHOOLIE	R	2020
LAFAYETTE LEAKE PNO (PVW	(V) BLUES MASTERS	19 CHESS	2ACBM	206
OTIS SPAN PNO (EPVW	(V) CHICAGO GOLDEN YEARS VOL 4	1976 VOGUE FR	427	004
WALTER DAVIS PNO (R	(W) BYE BYE BIRD	1979 BLUES NIGHT	073	1668
BIG JOE WILLIAMS G (Y	(Y) & MEMPHIS SLIM IN PARIS	19 GNP		10003
OLIVER HARRIS B (P	(Y) & BIG JOE WILLIAMS (1 SIDE)	1980 P VINE JAP	PLP	9014
CLIFF BIVENS V B (PU JOE WILLIE WILKINS G (PU FRED BELOW D	(EPV ODIE PAYNE D (V			
MILTON RECTOR B (V JARRETT GIBSON SAX (PV CLIFTON JAMES D	(PV DAVE CAMPBELL PNO (PU			
FROCK D (U CLARENCE LONNIE PNO (U JIMMY ROGERS G	(EV ROBERT LOCKWOOD G (EPNV			
LUTHER TUCKER G (ENV AL DUNCAN D (U JACK MYYERS B	(PV S P LEARY D (P			
DUKE HUDDLESTON SAX(P				

WILLIE & THE RED RUBBER BAND
W95

WILLIE REDDEN G V (A	(A) WILLIE & THE RED RUBBER BAND	1968 RCA US	LSP 4074
GLEN BALLARD G B (A			
CHARLES ADDINGTON K (A CONLAY BRADFORD D (A LARRY FIELD G (A			

PETE WILLSHER
W96

PETE WILLSHER STEEL G(AB	(A) GUITAR MAGIC	19 JOY	JOYS 158
STUART COWELL G (B	(B) STEEL SEASONS	1977 PYE	NSPL18539
ROB HENDRY G (B			
TONY KELLY G V (B LUCE LANGRIDGE D (B BOB LOVEDAY FDL (B GRAHAM WAYNE B (B			
TRISTRAM FRY PERC (B RAPH RAVENSCROFT WIND (B KEITH MILLER K (B KEITH NELSON BANJ(B			
MANDI WILSON V (B			

DENNIS WILSON
W97

DENNIS WILSON (A	(A) PACIFIC OCEAN BLUE	1977 CARIBOU US 34354	UK 81672

JACKIE WILSON
W98

HES SO FINE	195 BRUNSWICK US 54042	GOLDEN FAVOURITES	196	BRUNSWICK US 754115
LONELY TEARDROPS	1958 BRUNSWICK US 54045	SOMETHIN' ELSE	1964	BRUNSWICK US 754117
DOGGIN' AROUND	1959 BRUNSWICK	SOUL TIME	196	BRUNSWICK US 754118
NIGHT	1960	SPOTLIGHT ON	1965	BRUNSWICK US 754119
SO MUCH	1960 BRUNSWICK US 754050	SOUL GALORE	1966	BRUNSWICK US 754120
SINGS THE BLUES	1960 BRUNSWICK US 754055	SOUL GALORE	196	CORAL UK LVA9232
MY GOLDEN FAVOURITES	1960 BRUNSWICK US 754058	WHISPERS	1966	BRUNSWICK US 754122
MY GOLDEN FAVOURITES	196 CORAL UK LVA9135	HIGHER & HIGHER	1967	BRUNSWICK US 754130
A WOMAN A LOVER A FRIEND	1960 BRUNSWICK US 754059	HIGHER & HIGHER	1967	MCA UK MUPS304
TRY A LITTLE TENDERNESS	1961	MANUFACTURES OF SOUL	196	BRUNSWICK US 754134
YOU AIN'T HEARD NOTHING YET	1961 BRUNSWICK US 754100	TOO MUCH	196	MCA UK MUPS333
BY SPECIAL REQUEST	1961 BRUNSWICK US 754101	I GET THE SWEETEST FEELING	1968	BRUNSWICK US 754138
BY SPECIAL REQUEST	1961 CORAL UK LVA9151	I GET THE SWEETEST FEELING	1968	MCA UK MUPS361
BY SPECIAL REQUEST	1961 CORAL UK SVL3018	GREATEST HITS	19	BRUNSWICK US 754140
BODY & SOUL	1962 BRUNSWICK US 754105	DO YOUR THING	19	BRUNSWICK US 754154
BODY & SOUL	1962 CORAL UK LVA9202	DO YOUR THING	19	MCA UKMUPS 405
WORLDS GREATEST MELODIES	196 BRUNSWICK US 754106	ITS ALL A PART OF LOVE	1971	BRUNSWICK US 754158
WORLDS GREATEST MELODIES	196 CORAL UK LVA9214	YOU GOT ME WALKING	1973	BRUNSWICK US 754172
AT THE COPA	196 BRUNSWICK US 754108	YOU GOT ME WALKING	1973	BRUNSWICK BRLS3001
AT THE COPA	196 CORAL UK LVA9209	GREATEST HITS	197	BRUNSWICK US 754185
BABY WORK OUT	1962 BRUNSWICK US 754110	GREATEST HITS	1973	BRUNSWICK BRLS3004
MERRY CHRISTMAS	196 BRUNSWICK US 754112	VERY BEST OF	1975	BRUNSWICK BRLS3016
SHAKE A HAND	1962 BRUNSWICK US 754113	BEAUTIFUL DAY	197	BRUNSWICK US 754189

```
W98A                                    LARRY JON WILSON
    LARRY JON WILSON        (ALL       (A) NEW BEGINNINGS           1975 MONUMENT US 33382 RI   MC 6635
                                       (B) LET ME SING MY SONGS     1976 MONUMENT US 34041 RI   MC 6636
                                       (C) LOOSE CHANGE             1977 MONUMENT US            MG 7615
                                       (D) THE SOJOURNER            1979 MONUMENT US            MG 7631
W99                                       LEROY WILSON
    LEROY WILSON           (A          (A) BEST OF                  1978 UA        US           LA 807
W99A                                      WILSON /GALE
    FRANK WILSON      K V  (A          (A) GIFT WRAPPED SET         1980 JET       UK           JETLP223
    MELVYN GALE       K V  (A
    ALAN ROSS         G V  (A   STEVE STROUD     B  (A  ADRIAN SHEPARD    D  (A
W99B                                      WIND CHASE
    MARIO MILLO       K V  (A          (A) SYMPHINITY               1976 FESTIVAL               36216
    TOWO PILT         K V  (A
    DOUG BLIGH        D    (A   DUNCAN MCGUIRE   B  (A
W100                                   WIND IN THE WILLOWS
    DEBORAH HARRY     V PERC(A         (A) WIND IN THE WILLOWS      1968 CAPITOL                2956
    GIL FIELDS        D    (A          (A) WIND IN THE WILLOWS      1979 CAPITOL RI             CAPS 1030
    WAYNE KIRBY       B V K(A
    IDA ANDREWS       WIND (A   PETER BRITTAIN   G V  (A   PAUL KLEIN        G V  (A  ANTON CARYSFORTH   D(A
    STEVE DE PHILLIPS B V  (A   PETER C LEEDS    PERC (A   ARTIE KORNFELD    PERC (A  HARRIS WIENER      K V (A
W101                                      JESSE WINCHESTER
    JESSE WINCHESTER  G V K(ALL         (A) JESSE WINCHESTER        1971 AMPEX                  US A10104
    AMOS GARRETT      G    (BC          (B) 3RD DOWN 110 TO GO      1972 BEARSVILLE US 2102     UK K45512
    MARTY HARRIS      B V  (DE          (AB) JESSE WINCHESTER/3RD DOWN 1976 BEARSVILLE          UK K85507
    CHRIS CASTLE      D    (D           (C) LEARN TO LOVE IT        1974 BEARSVILLE US 6953     UK K55506
    BOB COHEN         G    (DE          (D) LET THE ROUGH SIDE DRAG 1976 BEARSVILLE US 6964     UK K55512
    CHRISTIAN STROCH  D    (D           (E) NOTHIN' BUT A BREEZE    1977 BEARSVILLE US 6968     UK K81853
    MAURICE BEAUCHAMP K    (D           (F) A TOUCH ON THE RAINY SIDE 1978 BEARSVILLE US 6984
    RON DAWN          STEEL(DE
    CARLISLE MILLER   SAX  (D   BRUCE MURCHISON  VLN (D   KEN PEARSON       K    (AD  DON HABIB          B  (D
    BOB LUCIER        STEEL(D   DAVE LEWIS       D   (AE  LORRI ZIMMERMANN  V    (D   SHARON RYAN        V  (D
    MICKEY RAPHAEL    HCA  (D   PAUL BUTTERFIELD HCA (D   RICKY SKAGGS      FDL  (E   TOM SZCZESNIAK     ACC(E
    JON CLARKE        SAX  (E   JAMES BURTON     G   (E   EMMYLOU HARRIS    V    (E   HERB PEDERSEN      V  (E
    ANNE MURRAY       V    (E   DIANNE BROOKS    V   (E   NICOLETTE LARSON  V    (E   ROBBIE ROBERTSON G  (A
    LEVON HELM        D    (A   BOB BOUCHER      B   (AB  DAVID REA         G V  (A   GUY BLACK          D  (A
    AL CHERNEY        VLN  (A   ANDRE BENICHOU   G   (B   DOUG SCHMOLZE     G    (B   CHARLES VIBER      VLN(B
    GORD FLEMING      PNO  (B   JIMMY OLIVER     B   (B   GENE COTTON       B    (B   NORMAN SMART       D  (B
    RON FRANKEL       D    (B   SAM KELLY        CONGA(B  DON ABRAMS        PERC (B
W102                                   WINDS OF CHANGE
    BRIAN ADDISON     WIND (A          (A) ILLUSIONS                1979 EMI       UK           EMA 791
    STAN SULZMANN     WIND (A
    ANTON WEINBERG    WIND (A   DAVID WHITE WIND    (A  TONY HYMAS       K SYN (A  JIM LAWLESS        PERC(A
    STEVE GREY        K    (A   BARRY DE SOUZA   D  (A  RICHARD HARVEY    SYN  (A  RICKY HITCHCOCK    G  (A
    PAUL WESTWOOD     B    (A   SIMON PHILLIPS   D  (A  HERBIE FLOWERS    B    (A  FRANK RICOTTI      PERC(A
    LITTLECHAP STRINGS     (A
W103                                      PETE WINGFIELD
    PETE WINGFIELD    K V  (AB          (A) BREAKFAST SPECIAL        1975 ISLAND    UK           ILPS9333
    DELISLE HARPER    B    (A           (B) LOVE BUMPS & DIZZY SPELLS 1976 ISLAND NOT RELEASED
    NEIL HUBBARD      G    (A
    JOSEPH EDWARD WRIGHT G (A   GLEN LE FLEUR    D  (A  CHRIS MERCER      SAX  (A
W103A                                     WINGS (US)
                                       (A) WINGS                    19   DUNHILL     US          DS50046
W104                                      THE WINKIES
    MICHAEL DESMARAIS D   (A           (A) THE WINKIES              1975 CHRYSALIS   US          CHR 1066
    PHILIP RAMBOW     G V  (A
    GUY HUMPHREYS     G V  (A   BRIAN TURRINGTON B V K(A
W105                                      WINTER
                                       (A) WINTER                   197  EMI        UK          EMC 3266
W106                                      EDGAR WINTER
    EDGAR WINTER V SAX K  (ALL         (A) ENTRANCE                 1970 EPIC      US 26503     UK 64083
    JIMMY GILLEN      D    (A          (B) WHITE TRASH              1971 EPIC      US 30512     UK 64298
    RANDAL DOLANON    G    (A          (AB) ENTRANCE WHITE TRASH    1976 EPIC      US 33770     UK 81191
    GENE KURTZ        B    (A          (C) ROAD WORK                1972 EPIC      US 31249     UK 67244
    JOHNNY WINTER G HCA V (ABCF        (D) THEY ONLY COME OUT AT NIGHT 1973 EPIC   US 32584     UK 65074
    RAY ALONGE        HRNS (A          (E) SHOCK TREATMENT          1974 EPIC      US 32461     UK 65640
    EARL W CHAPIN     HRNS (A          (F) JASMINE NIGHTDREAMS      1975 BLUE SKY  US 33483     UK 80772
    BROOKS TILLOTSON  HRNS (A          (G) WITH RICK DERRINGER      1975 BLUE SKY  US 33798     UK 69181
    JERRY LA CROIX V SAX HCA(BCH       (H) RECYCLED                 1977 BLUE SKY  US 34858     UK 82228
    JON SMITH         V SAX(BCH        (J) EDGAR WINTER ALBUM       1979 BLUE SKY               UK 83648
    MIKE McCLELLAN    V TPT(BC
    BOBBY RAMIREZ     D   (BC  GEORGE SHECK     B  (B  FLOYD RADFORD    G    (BH  RICK DERRINGER   G V(BCDEFG
    TASHA THOMAS      V   (B   JANICE BELL      V  (B  CARL HULL        V    (B   MAERETHA STEWART V  (B
    ALBERTINE ROBINSON V  (B   EILEEN GILBERT   V  (B  RAY BARRETO      CONGA(B   RANDY HOBBS      B  (CD
    MARSHALL CYR      TPT (CH  TILLY LAWRENCE   TPT(C  DAN HARTMAN B V G PERC(EDFGH CHUCK RUFF     D V (EDFG
    PAUL PRESTOPINO   G BAN(G  JOHN SIEGLER     B  (G  ROBERT ARNOLD    B    (H   BOZ SCAGGS       G  (
    JERRY WEEMS       G   (    RONNIE MONTROSE  G  (D  GEORGE RECILE    D    (H   DAN MINATRE      G  (H
    JOHNNY BADANAJEK  D   (D   RICK MAROTTA     D  (F
W107                                      JOHNNY WINTER
    JOHNNY WINTER  G V HCA(ALL         (A) JOHNNY WINTER            1969 CBS       US 9826      UK 63619
    EDGAR WINTER SAX K V  (ADMQS        (B) PROGRESSIVE BLUES EXPERIMENT 1969 LIBERTY US LBR1001 UK 83240
    JOHN TURNER       D    (ABDS        (B) PROGRESSIVE BLUES EXPERIMENT 1969 IMPERIAL US 12431
    TOMMY SHANNON     B    (ABDS        (B) PROGRESSIVE BLUES EXPERIMENT 1973 SUNSET            UK 50264
    DENNIS COLLINS    D    (D           (C) FIRST WINTER            1970 CBS       US 7513 BUDDAH UK 2359 011
    MUDDY WATERS      V G  (PS          (D) SECOND WINTER (3 SIDES) 1970 CBS       US 9947      UK 66231
    RICK DERRINGER    G    (FGLMS       (E) STORY                   1971 GRT       US 101 MARBLE ARCH UK 34
    RANDY JO HOBBS    B    (FLMOSG      (F) JOHNNY WINTER AND...    1971 CBS       US 30221     UK 64117
                                                                               (CONTINUED)

                                          [446]
```

JOHNNY WINTER

(CONTINUED)								
RICHARD HUGHES	D	(LOMS	(G) JOHNNY WINTER AND..LIVE	1971	CBS	US 30425	UK 64289
JAMES COTTON	HCA	(PS	(H) ABOUT BLUES	1971	JANUS	US 3008	
PINETOP PERKINS	PNO	(PS	(I) EARLY TIMES	1971	JANUS	US 3023	
BOB MARGOLIN	G	(PS	(J) BEFORE THE STORM	197	JANUS	US 3056	
CHARLES CALMESE	B	(PS	(K) AUSTIN TEXAS	19	UA	US LA139	
WILLIE SMITH	D	(PS	(L) STILL ALIVE & WELL	1973	CBS	US 32188	UK 65484
DAN HARTMAN	B	(MSR	(M) SAINTS & SINNERS	1974	CBS	US 32715	UK 65842
BOBBY CALDWELL	D	(GMS	(N) JOHN DAWSON WINTER III	1974	BLUE SKY	US 33292	UK 80568
TASHA THOMAS	V	(M	(O) CAPTURED LIVE	1976	BLUE SKY	US 33944	UK 69230
CARL HALL	V	(M	(P) NOTHIN' BUT THE BLUES	1977	BLUE SKY	US 34813	UK 82141
LANI GROVES	V	(M	(Q) WHITE HOT & BLUE	1978	BLUE SKY	US 35475	UK 82963
KANSAS	PERC	(M	(R) RAISIN' CAIN	1980	BLUE SKY		UK 84103
BARBARA MASSEY	V	(M	(S) THE JOHNNY WINTER STORY(DBL)	1980	BLUE SKY		UK 22112
RANDY BRECKER	TPT	(M					

ALAN RUBIN	TPT	(M	LEW DELGATTO	SAX	(M	JO JO GUNNE	PERC	(M	JON SMITH	SAX	(M
I P SWEAT	B	(QS	BOBBY TORELLO	D	(QRS	PAT RAMSEY	HCA	(QS	PAT RUSH	G	(QS
RANDY ZEHRINGER	D	(FS	JEREMY STEIG	FLT	(L	TODD RUNDGREN	K	(L	MARK KLINGMAN	PNO	(LS
FLOYD RADFORD	G	(QS	CHUCK RUFF	D	(S	A WYNN BUTLER	SAX	(AS	KARL GARIN	TPT	(AS
JERRY PORTNOY	HRNS	(S	PAUL PRESTOPINO	PERC	(S	JACKDAW	V	(S	DENNIS FERRANTE	V	(S
WILLIE DIXON	B	(AS	WALTER HORTON	HCA	(AS	NORMAN RAY	SAX	(A	CARRIE HOSSELL	V	(A
PEGGY BOWERS	V	(A	ELSIE SENTER	V	(A	JON PARIS	B V HCA G	(R	SUSAN WARFORD	V	(R
KRISTY GRIGGS	V	(R	ALLAN MARTIN	V	(R	BERNADETTE MAZUR	V	(R	TOM STROHMAN	SAX	(R
DAVE STILL	PERC	(R	CINDY MURRAY	V	(R						

JOHNNY & EDGAR WINTER

JOHNNY WINTER	G V	(A	(A) TOGETHER			1976	BLUE SKY	US 34033	UK 81338		
EDGAR WINTER	SAX V	(A									
RICK DERRINGER	G	(A	FLOYD RADFORD	G	(A	RANDY JO HOBBS	B	(A	DAN HARTMAN	K	(A
RICHARD HUGHES	D	(A	CHUCK RUFF	D	(A						

RUBY WINTERS

RUBY WINTERS	V	(AB	(A) RUBY WINTERS	1978	CREOLE		CRLP 512
			(B) SONGBIRD	1979	K TEL		NE 1045

WINTERS BROTHERS BAND

DONNIE WINTERS	G V	(AB	(A) COAST TO COAST	197	ATLANTIC		US 38106
DENNIS WINTERS	G V	(AB	(B) WINTER BROTHERS BAND	1977	ATLANTIC UK K50343	US 36145
GENE WATSON	B	(B					
KENT HARRIS	D	(B	DAVID DAVIS	K	(B		

STEVE WINWOOD

STEVE WINWOOD	K G V	(AB	(A) STEVE WINWOOD	1977	ISLAND		UK	ILPS 9494		
ALAN SPENNER	B	(A	(B) ARC OF A DIVER	1980	ISLAND		UK	ILPS 9576		
WILLIE WEEKS	B	(A								
ANDY NEWMARK	D	(A	JOHN SUSSWELL	D	(A	JUNIOR MARVIN	G	(B	JIM CAPALDI	D (A
REEBOP	PERC	(A								

WIRE

ROBERT GOTOBED	D	(ABC	(A) PINK FLAG	1977	HARVEST US 11757 UK	SHSP 4076
GRAHAM LEWIS	B V	(ABC	(B) CHAIRS MISSING	1978	HARVEST	UK	SHSP 4093
BRUCE CLIFFORD GILBERT	G (A	(C) 154	1979	HARVEST	UK	SHSP 4105
COLIN NEWMAN	G V	(ABC					
MIKE THORNE	K	(B	KATE LUCAS	FLT	(B		

WIRELESS

MIKE CRAWFORD	G	(AB	(A) POSITIVELY HUMAN ,RELATIVELY SANE	19			
STEVE McMURRAY	G	(AB	(B) NO STATIC	1980	ANTHEM		ANR 11025
ALLAN MARSHALL	B V	(AB					
MARTY MORIN	D	(AB					

WISHBONE ASH

STEVE UPTON	D	(ALL	MARTIN TURNER	B	(ALL	GLEN TURNER	G	(	ANDY POWELL	G	(ALL
TED TURNER	G	(ABCDE	LAURIE WISEFIELD	G	(FJKMN	JOHN TOUT	K	(C	GEORGE NASH	K	(D
GRAHAM MAITLAND	PNO	(D	PHIL KENZIE	HRNS	(D	DAVE COXHILL	HRNS	(D	BUD PARKES	HRNS	(D
FLACO PADRON	CONGAS	(F	ALBY GALUTEN	SYN	(F						

(A) WISHBONE ASH	1970	MCA	UK	MKPS2014	(F) THERES THE RUB	1974	MCA	UK	MCF 2575
" "	1970	DECCA	US	75249	" "	197	MCA	US	464
" "	1974	MCA RI UK	MCG3507	" "	197	BARCLAY FR	410029
" "	197	BARCLAY FR	510002	(G) MILESTONES	1974	EMI	EURO 184 50373
" "	197	MCA	US	2343	(H) MASTERS OF ROCK	1975	EMI	EURO 054 96269
(B) PILGRIMAGE	1971	MCA	UK	MDK58004	(J) LOCKED IN	1976	MCA	UK	MCF2750
" "	1974	MCA RI UK	MCG3504	" "	19	BARCLAY FR	410055
" "	197	DECCA	US	75295	(K) NEW ENGLAND	1976	MCA	UK	MCG 3523
" "	197	BARCLAY FR	510007	" "	1976	ATLANTIC US	18200
" "	197	MCA	US	36	" "	197	BARCLAY FR	414006
(C) ARGUS	1972	MCA	UK	MDK58006	(L) CLASSIC ASH	1977	MCA	UK	MCF 2795
" "	197	DECCA	US	75437	" "	197	BARCLAY FR	414015
" "	197	BARCLAY FR	410003	(M) FRONT PAGE NEWS	1977	MCA	UK	MCG3524
" "	1974	MCA RI UK	MCG3510	" "	197	BARCLAY FR	511001
" "	197	MCA RI US	2344	" "	197	MCA	US	2311
(D) WISHBONE FOUR	1973	MCA	UK	MDK58011	(N) NO SMOKE WITHOUT FIRE	1978	MCA	UK	MCG 3528
" "	197	MCA RI UK	MCG3503	" "	1978	MCA	US	3060
" "	197	MCA	US	327	(O) JUST TESTING	1979	MCA	UK	MCF 3052
" "	197	MCA	US	2348	(P) NUMBER THE BRAVE	1981	MCA	UK	MCF 3103
" "	197	MCA	MAP56673				
" "	197	BARCLAY FR	410008				
(E)LIVE DATES	197	MCA	UK	MCSP 254				
" "	197	MCA	US	2 8006				
" "	197	BARCLAY FR	41012/13				

WISHFUL THINKING

KEVIN SCOTT	V	(B	(A) LIVE	1967	DECCA	UK	SKL 4900
BRIAN ALLEN	D V	(AB	(B) HIROSHIMA	1971	B&C		CAS 1038
TONY COLLIER	B V	(B					
JOHN FRANKLIN	G V	(B	TERRY NEW	G V	(	RAY DANIEL	V	(	ROGER CHARLES	B V	(

W115A   WITCHFYNDE

STEVE BRIDGES	V	(AB	(A) GIVE 'EM HELL	1980 RONDELET		UK	ABOUT 1
PETE SURGEY	B	(AB	(B) STAGEFRIGHT	1980 RONDELET		UK	ABOUT 2
GRA SCORESBY	D	(AB					
MONTALO	G	(AB					

W116   BILL WITHERS

BILL WITHERS	V	(ALL	(A) STILL BILL	1972 SUSSEX LPSX 1	US		7014
BRYAN GAROFALO	G	(J	(B) 'JUSTMENTS	1974 SUSSEX LPSX 2	US		8032
JERRY KNIGHT	B	(GHJ	(C) JUST AS I AM	1971 SUSSEX LPSX 3	US		7006
KEN BURKE	B	(HJ	(D) LIVE AT CARNEGIE HALL	1973 SUSSEX LPDX 101	US		7025/2
RUSS KUNKEL	D	(HJ	(E) BEST OF	1975 SUSSEX LPSX 10	US		8037
RALPH MACDONALD	PERC	(HJ	(F) MAKING MUSIC	1975 CBS US 33704		UK	69183
PAUL SMITH	K	(J	(G) NAKED & WARM	1976 CBS US 34327		UK	81580
MIKE JONES	SYN	(H	(H) MENAGERIE	1978 CBS US 34903		UK	82265
RAY PARKER	G	(H	(J) 'BOUT LOVE	1978 CBS US 35596		UK	83176
DEAN GANT	K	(H	(K) 20 BEST OF	1978 METRONOME	GERM		69 030
CLIFF COULTER	K	(GH	(L) BEST OF	1980 CBS		UK	84710
ALVIN TAYLOR	D	(H					

GEOFFREY LEIB		(G	DON FREEMAN		(G	LARRY NASH	K	(G	LARRY TOLBERT	(G
CLARENCE McDONALD	K	(H	MELVIN DUNLOP	B	(G	DOROTHY ASHBY		(G	ERROL BENNETT	PERC (G
YOUSEFF RAHMAN		(G	BENORCE BLACKMON	G	(G	ROCKY DZIDZORNU	PERC	(G	STEPHEN STILS	(C

W116A   JIMMY WITHERSPOON

JIMMY WITHERSPOON	V G	(ALL	GROOVIN' & SPOONIN'	19	ORIGINAL SOUND		7107
GROOVE HOLMES	ORG	(B	(B) SINGS THE BLUES	1964 SOCIETY	UK	SOC968
TEDDY EDWARDS	SAX	(B	EVENING BLUES	1964 STATESIDE 10088 US PRESTIGE7300		
FRANK BUTLER	D	(B	BLUES AROUND THE CLOCK	1965 STATESIDE 10105 US PRESTIGE7314		
JIMMY BOND	B	(B	SOME OF MY BEST FRIENDS ARE THE BLUES	1965 STATESIDE 10114 US PRESTIGE7356		
DANNY KALB	G	(J	BLUE SPOON	1965 STATESIDE 10139 US PRESTIGE7327		
HARVEY MANDEL	G	(J	IN PERSON	1966 VOGUE	VRL3005	
BARRY GOLDBERG	K	(J	LIVE	1968 STATESIDE 10232		
CHARLIE MUSSELWHITE	HCA	(J	(J) BLUES SINGER	1969 STATESIDE 10289 US BLUESWAY6026		
			SPOON IN LONDON	19	US PRESTIGE7418	
ROBBEN FORD	G	(L	BLUES FOR EASY LIVERS	19	US PRESTIGE7475	
			BEST OF	19	US PRESTIGE7713	
(*) LINE UP SEE ERIC BURDON ENTRY			MEAN OLD FRISCO	19	US PRESTIGE7855	
			GOING TO KANSAS CITY	19	RCA US LPM 1639 RI	ANLI1048
			(*) GUILTY	1971 UA	UK	UAG29251
			SPOONFUL	19	BLUENOTE	US	LA534
			HEY MRS JONES	19	REPRISE	US	6012
			SPOON CONCERTS	19	FANTASY	24701
			AT MONTEREY FESTIVAL	19	HI FI JAZZ	421
			& BEN WEBSTER	19	VERVE	US	V68835
			BEST OF	1973 BLUESWAY	BLS 6051
			LOVE IS A 5 LETTER WORD	1975 CAPITOL	11360
			AINT NOBODYS BUSINESS	197 POLYDOR	UK	2460 206
			LIVE	1979 MCA	UK	MCF 3027

W117   WIZARDS CONVENTION

RAY FENWICK	G B V	(A	(A) WIZARDS CONVENTION	197 RCA	UK	RS 1085
MO FOSTER	B	(A				

RICK VAN DER LINDEN	K	(A	EDDIE HARDIN	SYN V	(A	RIC LEE	D	(A	MARK NAUSEEF	D (A
JOHN CROCKER	SAX	(A	JON LORD	PNO	(A	JOHN SLAUGHTER	G	(A	TONY ASHTON	V K(A
PETE YORK	D	(A	LESLIE BINKS	G	(A	GLEN HUGHES	V	(A	HENRY SPINETTI	D (A
ROGER GLOVER	B	(A	DAVID COVERDALE	V	(A	MIKE D'ABO	V	(A	MIKE SMITH	(A
JIMMY HELMS		(A	CHRIS BARBER BAND		(A					

W117A   JAH WOBBLE

JAH WOBBLE		(AB	(A) LEGEND LIVES ON	1980 VIRGIN		UK	V 2159
MARTIN ATKINS	D	(A	(B) V.I.E.P. (EP)	1980 VIRGIN		UK	V36112

W117B   WOOLY WOLSTENHOLME

WOOLY WOLSTENHOLME	V K B G	(A	(A) MAESTOSO	1980 POLYDOR		UK	2374 165
STEVE BROOMHEAD	V MAND G	(A					
KIM TURNER	D V	(A	BILL NIXON	PERC (A	BRIAN DAY	B	(A

W118   BOBBY WOMACK

BOBBY WOMACK	G V	(ALL	LIVE	19 LIBERTY			LST 7645
BARRY BECKETT	K	(DE	UNDERSTANDING	1972 UA US 5577		UK	UAS 29365
CLAYTON IVEY	K	(DE	COMMUNICATION	1973 UA US 5539		UK	UAS 29306
ROGER HAWKINS	D	(DE	(D) FACTS OF LIFE	1973 UA US LA043		UK	UAS 29456
JIMMY JOHNSON	G	(DE	(E) LOOKING FOR A LOVE AGAIN	1974 UA US LA199		UK	UAS 29574
DAVID HOOD	B	(DE	I CAN UNDERSTAND IT	1975 UA		UK	UAS 29715
DAVE TURNER	G	(D	GREATEST HITS	1975 UA US LA346			
TRUMAN THOMAS	K	(E	I DONT KNOW WHAT THE WORLDs COMING TO	1975 UA US LA353		UK	UAS 29762
TIPPY ARMSTRONG	G	(E	SAFETY ZONE	1976 UA US LA544		UK	UAS 29907
LARRY RHEINHARDT	G	(E	B W GOES C W	1976 UA US LA638		UK	UAS 29979
JERRY MASTERS	B	(D	HOME IS WHERE THE HEART IS	197 CBS US 34384		UK	81693
			PIECES	197 CBS US 35083			
			ROADS OF LIFE	1979 ARISTA		UK	ARTY 165

W119   STEVIE WONDER

					US		UK
STEVIE WONDER	V HCA K	(ALL	TRIBUTE TO UNCLE RAY	1963 TAMLA 232	ORIOLE		40049
SCOTT EDWARDS	B	(T	LITTLE STEVIE WONDER	196 TAMLA			54191
DANIEL BEN ZEBULON	PERC	(T	JAZZ SOUL OF LITTLE STEVE	1963 TAMLA 233	STATESIDE		10078
GLORIA BARLEY	V	(T	12 YEAR OLD GENIUS	1963 TAMLA 240	ORIOLE		40053
LANI GROVES	V	(T	WITH A SONG IN MY HEART	196 TAMLA 250			
JIM GILSTRAP	V	(T	AT THE BEACH(HEY MR HARMONICA MAN)	1965 TAMLA 255	STATESIDE		10108
RAY PARKER	G	(T	UPTIGHT	1966 TAMLA 268			STML11036
SHIRLEY BREWER	V	(T	DOWN TO EARTH	1966 TAMLA 272			STML11045
DENIECE WILLIAMS	V	(T	I WAS MADE TO LOVE HER	1967 TAMLA 279			STML11059
TREVOR LAWRENCE	SAX	(T	GREATEST HITS	1968 TAMLA 282			STML11075
DAVID SANBORN	SAX	(T	SOMEDAY AT CHRISTMAS	1969 TAMLA			STML11085
STEVE MADAIO	TPT	(T					(CONTINUED)
JEFF BECK	G	(T					

STEVIE WONDER

(CONTINUED)

					US			UK
BUZZY FEITEN	G	(T	FOR ONCE IN MY LIFE	1969	TAMLA	291		STML11098
DEBRA WILSON	V	(T	EIVETS REDNOW	1969	GORDY	932		
LORIS HARVIN	V	(T	MY CHERIE AMOUR	1970	TAMLA	296		STML11128
BEN BRIDGES	SITAR G	(Z	LIVE	1970	TAMLA	298		STML11150
MICHAEL SEMBELLO	G	(Z	TALK OF THE TOWN	1970	TAMLA			STML11164
LARRY GITTENS	TPT	(Z	SIGNED SEALED DELIVERED	1970	TAMLA	304		STML11169
JOSIE JAMES	V	(Z	WHERE I'M COMING FROM	1971	TAMLA	308		STML11183
RON KERSEY	K	(Z	GREATEST HITS	1972	TAMLA	313		STML11196
EARL DEROUEN	V	(Z	MUSIC OF MY MIND	1972	TAMLA	314		STMA 8002
NATHAN WATTS	B	(Z	(T)TALKING BOOK	1972	TAMLA	319		STMA 8007
HANK REDD	SAX	(Z	INNERVISIONS	1973	TAMLA	326		STMA 8011
RICK ZUNIGAR	G	(Z	FULFILLINGNESS FIRST FINALE	1974	TAMLA	332		STMA 8019
ABDOULAYE SOUMARE	V	(Z	FULFILLINGNESS FIRST FINALE	197	TAMLA		T633 251	
JOE JOHNSON	V	(Z	SONGS IN THE KEY OF LIFE	1976	TAMLA	340		TMSP 6002
ALEXANDRA BROWN	V	(Z	PORTRAIT	1976	EMI	EURO		064 92636
LAMINE KONTE	PERC	V(Z	ANTHOLOGY	1977	TAMLA	804		M 9 804
IBRAHIM CAMARA	PERC	V(Z	WONDERLAND	197	EMI	EURO 064 95182		
KATHY COLLIER	V	(X	(Z)THE SECRET LIFE OF PLANTS	1979	TAMLA			TMSP 6009
SUSAYE GREENE	V	(Z	LIGHT MY FIRE	1979	M F P			50420
DENNY DAVIS	D	(Z	HOTTER THAN JULY	1980	TAMLA			STMA 8035
ISAIAH WINBUSH	V	(Z						
MARVA HOLCOLM	V	(Z						

RON WOOD

					US		UK	
RON WOOD	G V	(ABC	(A) I'VE GOT MY OWN ALBUM TO DO	1974	WB	US 2819	UK	K56065
WILLIE WEEKS	B	(AB	(B) NOW LOOK	1975	WB	US 2872	UK	K56145
IAN MACLAGAN	K	(ABC	(C) GIMME SOME NECK	1979	CBS		UK	83337
KEITH RICHARD	G	(ABC						
MICK JAGGER	G V	(AC	MICK TAYLOR	G B	(ABC	JEAN ROUSSEL	K	(AB	MICK WALLER	D	(A
PETE SEARS	B	(A	MARTIN QUITTENTON	G	(A	ROD STEWART	V	(A	IRENE CHANTER	V	(A
DOREEN CHANTER	V	(A	ANDY NEWMARK	D	(AB	BOBBY WOMACK	G	(B	KENNY JONES	D	(B
BOBBY KEYS	SAX	(C	JIM KELTNER	D	(C	DAVE MASON	G	(C	CHARLIE WATTS	D	(C
MICK FLEETWOOD	D	(C	ROBERT POPWELL	B	(C						

RON WOOD & RONNIE LANE

RON WOOD	G V	(A	(A) MAHONEYS LAST STAND	1976	ATLANTIC	US SD36126 UK K50308	
RONNIE LANE B BAN	G V	(A					
KENNEY JONES	D	(A	PETE TOWNSHEND G PERC (A	IAN McLAGAN	K	(A	
BOBBY KEYS	HRNS	(A	JIM PRICE HRNS (A	BRUCE ROWLAND	D V	(A	BENNY GALLAGHER B (A
MICK WALLER	PERC	(A	RICK GRECH B D VLN (A	IAN STEWART	K	(A	GLYN JOHNS V (A
BILLY NICHOLLS	V	(A					

ROY WOOD

ROY WOOD G V B K HRNS WIND(ALL			(A) BOULDERS	1973	HARVEST	SHVL803 RI SHSM 2021
PAUL ROBINS	K G	(H	(B) WIZZARD BREW	1973	HARVEST	SHSP4025
PETER MACKIE	B	(H	(C) SEE MY BABY JIVE	1974	HARVEST	SHSP4034
BILLY PAUL	SAX	(H	(D) EDDIE & THE FALCONS	1974	WB	K56629
JOHN KURLANDER	K	(A	(E) MUSTARD	1975	JET	JETLP 12
ANDY FAIRWEATHER LOW	V	(H	(F) THE ROY WOOD STORY	1976	HARVEST	SHOW 408
JOHN BONHAM	D	(H	(G) SUPER ACTIVE WIZZO	1977	WB	K56388
CARL WAYNE	V	(H	(H) ON THE ROAD AGAIN	1979	WB	US BSK3247
ANNIE HASLAM	V	(H				
DAVE DONOVAN	D	(H	DICK PLANT V (H	RICK PRICE B V PERC (B	BILL HUNT K HRNS V (B	
HUGH McDOWELL CELLO SYN(B			NICK PENTELOW WIND V (B	MIKE BURNEY WIND (B	KEITH SMART D (B	
CHARLIE GRIMA	D	(BH	CARBAG CHOIR V (B			

ROYSTON & HEATHER WOOD

ROYSTON WOOD	V CONC(A		(A) NO RELATION	1977	TRANSATLANTIC	UK TRA 342
HEATHER WOOD	V	(A				
PETER BELLAMY	V	(A	SIMON NICOL G (A	PENNIE HARRIS V DULC(A	PETE KIRTLEY G MAND(A
TONY HALL MELODEON		(A	ASHLEY HUTCHINGS B (A			

WOODY WOODMANSEYS U BOAT

WOODY WOODMANSEY	D	(A	(A) U BOAT	1977	BRONZE	BRON 501
PHIL PLANT	B	(A				
MARTIN SMITH	G	(A	FRANK MARSHALL K SYN(A	PHIL MURRAY V (A	

JEZZ WOODROFFE

JEZZ WOODROFFE	K	(A	(A) OPPOSITE DIRECTIONS	1980	GRADUATE	UK GRADLP1

TERRY & GAY WOODS

TERRY WOODS V G B MANS(ALL			(A) WOODS BAND	1971	GREENWICH	UK	GSLP 1004
GAY WOODS V CONC DULC(ALL			(A) WOODS BAND	1977	ROCKBURGH	UK	ROC 102
ED DEANE	B G K(AB		(A) WOODS BAND	197	MOONCREST	UK	CREST 29
PAT NASH	D V	(A	(B) BACKWOODS	197	POLYDOR	UK	2383 322
AUSTIN CORCORAN	B G	(A	(C) THE TIME IS RIGHT	1976	POLYDOR	UK	2383 375
JOHN RYAN	B	(A	(D) RENOWNED	197	POLYDOR	UK	2383 406
TONY REEVES	B	(A	(E) TENDERHOOKS	1978	ROCKBURGH	UK	ROC 104
MIKE GILES	D	(B					
DAVE WINTOUR	B	(B	TONY CARR CONGA (B	DAVE MATTACKS D (C	GEOFF WHITEHORN G (B
PETER ARNESEN	K	(B	JOE O'DONNELL VLN (B	DAVE PEGG B (CE	PAT DONALDSON B (CE
TIMI DONALD	D	(C	B J COLE STEEL(C	BRIAN GOLBEY FDL (C	JON GILLASPIE K (C
DAVID MORRISON	G	(C	TRISTIAN FRY VIBES (C	PHIL PALMER G (E	JIM RUSSELL D (E
KATE McGARRIGLE	V PNO(E		KEITH DONALD SAX (E	MARTIN O'CONNOR ACC (E	NEIL TONER MAND (E
FRAN BREEN	PERC (E		JOLYON JACKSON ORG (E		

HENRY WOOLF

HENRY WOOLF		(A	(A) TIBETAN BELLS	1972	ISLAND	UK HELP3
NANCY HEMMING		(A				
DREW GLADSTONE		(A				

WORLD OF OZ

CHRISTOPHER ROBIN		(A	(A) WORLD OF OZ	1969	DERAM	UK SML 1034
DAVID KUBINEC		(A				
TONY CLARKSON		(A	DAVID REA (A			

W127A
```
ROLY KERRIDGE        D    (A              WORLD SERVICE
KEVIN DUNFORD        B    (A          (A) DEFINITE UNCERTAINTIES        1979    COOPER         WARP001
STEVEN LODDER        K VLN(A   GERRY HUNT   G SAX    (A   ALAN HAYMAN  PERC FLT(A
```
W128
```
SONNY WORTHING       K V  (A              SONNY WORTHING
JIM CUOMO            WIND (A          (A) TEENAGE DREAM                 1977    TRANSATLANTIC UK  TRA 344
ELLIOTT RANDALL      G    (A   PETE WINGFIELD  K V (A   PETER VAN HOOKE  D    (A PETE WILSHER    STEEL(A
ISAAC GUILLORY       G    (A   MO FOSTER       B   (A   RITCHIE          G    (A KEITH NELSON    BANJO(A
BARBARA SEXTON       V    (A   MARTIN DROVER   TPT (A   GEORGE CHISHOLM  TPT  (A TONY ROBERTS    SAX (A
JEFF DALY            SAX  (A   DAVID SNELL     HARP(A
```
W129
```
LINK WRAY            G V  (ALL             LINK WRAY
BILLY HODGES         K V  (CF         (A) LINK WRAY & THE WRAY MEN      1960 EPIC          US   LN3661
MORDICAI JONES K MAND (F ]SAME ?     (B) JACK THE RIPPER               1963 SWAN          US   SLP 510
BOBBY HOWARD   K MAND (C              (C) LINK WRAY                     1971 POLYDOR US 24 4064 UK 2489 029
DOUG WRAY            D V G(CFQ        (D) THERES GOOD ROCKIN TONIGHT    1973 UNION PACIFIC      UP 002
STEVE VERROCA        D V  (CF         (E) BE WHAT YOU WANT             1973 POLYDOR US 5047 UK 2391 063
COMMANDER CODY            (E          (F) BEANS & FATBACK              1973 VIRGIN        UK   V 2006
JERRY GARCIA         G    (E          (G) ROCKIN' & HANDCLAPPIN'       1973 EPIC         UK   63267
DAVID BROMBERG       G    (E          (H) RUMBLE                       1974 POLYDOR      UK   2391 128
BOBBY BLACK          STEEL(E          (J) INTERSTATE 10                1975 CAROLINE     UK   C 1511
RUAN OLOCHLAINN      K SAX(K          (K) STUCK IN GEAR                1976 VIRGIN       UK   V 2050
GORDON SMITH         B    (K          (L) ROCK'N'ROLL RUMBLE           19   CHARLY       UK   CR 30171
ARCHIE LEGGET        B    (K          (M) EARLY RECORDINGS             19   CHISWICK /ACE      CH 6
FREDDIE SMITH        D    (K          (N) GREAT GUITAR HITS            19   VERMILLION   US   1924
DAVE GREAVES             (J          (O) SINGS & PLAYS                19   VERMILLION   US   1925
CHARLIE CHARLES      D    (J          (P) YESTERDAY & TODAY            19   RECORD FACTORY US  1929
JOHN DZERIGAN        G    (H          (Q) BULLSHOT                     1979 CHARISMA     UK   CAS 1143
BOZ SCAGGS           G V  (H   MARK JORDAN   K V  (H   RICK SCHLOSSER   D   (H  TOM RUTLEY  B    (H
JOE CRANE            B V K(H   ANDY NARELL PERC K (H   BERNIE KRAUSE    K   (H  PETE ESCOVEDO CONGA(H
BRUCE STEINBERG      HCA  (H   LENNY PICKETT   SAX (H   EMILIO CASTILLO SAX (H  STEVE KUPKA    SAX(H
MIC GILLETTE         TPT  (H   GREG ADAMS      TPT (H   GLENN WALTERS    V  (H  SKIP DRINKWATER V (H
DOROTHY MORRISON     V    (H   ZELLER HURD     V   (H   BILL COMBS       V  (H  JOE SCOTT      V (H
BILLY CROSS          G    (Q   ANTON FIG     D PERC(Q   RICHARD GOTTEHRER K PERC(Q CHRIS ROBINSON K (Q
ROB STONER          B    (Q   HOWIE WYETH     D   (Q   JOANNA MASSEY    V  (Q  RHONDA WRAY    V (Q
ROBIN WRAY           V    (Q
```
W130
```
WRECKLESS ERIC       G V  (ABC            WRECKLESS ERIC
DAVEY PAYNE          SAX  (A          (A) WRECKLESS ERIC               1978 STIFF        UK   SEEZ 6
DAVID WITTON         D    (A          (B) WONDERFUL WORLD OF W ERIC    1978 STIFF        UK   SEEZ 9
CHARLIE HART         K    (A          (C) BIG SMASH        (DBL)       1980 stiff        UK   SEEZ21
BARRY PAYNE          B    (A   STEVE CURRIE    B   (A   JOHN GLYN       SAX (A  STEVE GOULDING D (A
NICK LOWE            G B  (A   GEIR WAADE      D   (B   JOHN BROWN      B   (BC EUNON BRADY    G (B
PETE SOLLEY          K    (B   MALCOLM MORLEY  G   (BC  JOHN EARLE      HRNS(BC DICK HANSON HRNS (BC
JOE PARTRIDGE        G    (B   GARY TAYLOR     V   (B   PETE GOSLING    G   (C  WALTER HACON   G (C
DAVE OTWAY           D    (A   ROGER RETTIG   STEEL(C   MARTIN ACE      V   (C  PHILIPPA THOMAS V (C
```
W131
```
BIG JOHN WRENCHER V HCA(AB            BIG JOHN WRENCHER
EDDIE TAYLOR         G    (A          (A) BIG JOHNS BOOGIE             1975 BIG BEAR          BEAR 5
BOB HALL             PNO  (A          (B) MAXWELL STREET ALLEY BLUES   1978 BARRELHOUSE       BH 2
BOB BRUNNING         B    (A   PETE YORK     D   (A
```
W132
```
BETTY WRIGHT         V    (ALL            BETTY WRIGHT
GREGORY WILKERSON    D    (G          (A) MY FIRST TIME AROUND        1968 ATCO    US 33260
MICHAEL WILKERSON    B    (G          (B) I LOVE THE WAY YOU LOVE ME  1971 ALSTON US 33388 ATLANTIC UK K40364
WILL BRIDGEFORTH     G    (G          (C) HARD TO STOP                1973 ALSTON US 7026 ATLANTIC UK K40514
ROBERT WEBB          V PERC(G          (D) DANGER HIGH VOLTAGE         1975 ALSTON US 4400 RCA     UK SF8408
GARRY GREENE         SAX  (G          (E) EXPLOSION                   1976 ALSTON US 4402 RCA     UK RS1063
MICHAEL SCOTT        TPT  (G          (F) THIS TIME FOR REAL          1977 ALSTON US 4406 TK      UK XL14053
KEVIN KENDRICKS      K    (G          (G) LIVE                        1978 ALSTON US 4408 TK      UK TKR82541
                                      (H) TRAVELING IN THE CIRCLE     1979              TK      UK TKR83352
```
W133
```
GARY WRIGHT          K V  (ALL            GARY WRIGHT
ANDY NEWMARK         D    (D          (A) EXTRACTION                  1970 A&M  A&M      UK  AMLS2004
JIM KELTNER          D    (DE         (C) FOOT PRINT                  1971 A&M  A&M      UKAMLS64296
DAVID FOSTER         K    (DE         (B) RING OF CHANGES (WONDERWHEEL) 1972 A&M        UKAMLH64362
BOBBY LYLE           K    (D          (D) DREAM WEAVER                1976 WB   US 2868  UK  K56141
LORNA WRIGHT         V    (DE         (E) LIGHT OF SMILES             1876 WB   US 2951  UK  K56278
BETTY SWEET          V    (DE         (F) TOUCH & GONE                1977 WB   US 3137  UK  K56435
DAVID POMERANZ       V    (DE         (G) HEADIN' HOME                1979 WB             UK  K56585
HUGH McCRACKEN       G    (A   ALAN WHITE      D   (A   TREVOR BURTON   B   (A  KLAUS VOORMAN  B (A
MIKE KELLIE          D    (A   MICK ABRAHAMS   G   (A   RONNIE MONTROSE G   (D  DORIS TROY     V (A
MADELINE BELL        V    (A   NANETTE NEWMAN  V   (A   BRYSON GRAHAM   D   (C  MIKE JONES     G (C
TOM DUFFY            B    (C   ART WOOD        D   (E   PETER REILICH   K   (E  STEVE PORCARO  B (E
JUSTIN WRIGHT        V    (E
```
W134
```
RICHARD WRIGHT       K V  (A              RICHARD WRIGHT
MEL COLLINS          SAX  (A          (A) WET DREAM                   1978 HARVEST       UK   SHVL 818
LARRY STEELE         B    (A   REG ISADORE    D   (A   SNOWY WHITE      G   (A
```
W134A
```
WILLY FINLAYSON      K V  (A              WRITING ON THE WALL
BILL SCOTT                (A          (A) POWER OF THE PICTS          19   MIDDLE EARTH       MDLS 303
JAKE SCOTT           V    (A   LINNIE PATERSON      V   JIMMY HUSH     (
```
W135
```
ROBERT WYATT         V K D(ALL            ROBERT WYATT
NEVILLE WHITEHEAD B       (A          (A) THE END OF AN EAR          1970 CBS           UK   64189
MARK CHARIG          CORNET (A         (B) ROCK BOTTOM               1974 VIRGIN US 13112 UK  V2017
BRIAN ENO            K G  (C          (C) RUTH IS STRANGER THAN RICHARD 1975 VIRGIN     UK   V2034
ELTON DEAN           SAX  (A          (BC) ROCK BOTTOM?RUTH          1981 VIRGIN       UK   VGD 3505
DAVE SINCLAIR        ORG  (A   CYRIL AYERS    PERC (A   RICHARD SINCLAIR B  (B  LAURIE ALLEN   D (BC
                                                                                    (CONTINUED)
```

[450]

```
HUGH HOPPER       B   (B   IVOR CUTLER    K V  (B   MONGESI FEZA   TPT (B   GARY WINDO    WIND(BC
ALFREDA BENGE     V   (B   FRED FRITH     VLA PNO (BC MIKE OLDFIELD  G   (B   BILL McCORMICK  B  (C
NISAR AHMAD KHAN  SAX (C   JOHN GREAVES B     (C
```

BILL WYMAN   W136

```
BILL WYMAN V B G K    (AB     (A) MONKEY GRIP          1974 ROLLINGSTONE US COC79100 UK COC59102
DANNY KOOTCH     G   (A        (B) STONE ALONE          1976 ROLLINGSTONE US COC79103 UK COC59105
JOE LALA         PERC (A
MAC REBENNACK    PNO (A    DALLAS TAYLOR   D   (A   JOEY MURCIA    G   (A   DUANE SMITH    PNO (A
GEORGE TERRY     G   (A    BYRON BERLINE   FDL (A   JACKIE GRAVES  TROM (A  JOHN McEUEN    BANJ(A
ABIGALE HANESS   V   (A    LEON RUSSELL    PNO (A   WILLIAM SMITH  PNO (A   HUBIE HEARD    K   (A
BETTY WRIGHT     V   (A    GEORGE McCRAE   V   (A   GWEN McCRAE    V   (A   MARK COLBY     HRNS(A
KEN FAULK        HRNS (A   NEAL BONSANTI   HRNS
```

"X"   X1

```
JOHN DOE         B   (A
BILLY ZOOM       G   (A    CHRISTINE CERVENKA  V(A  DON BONEBRAKE   D   (A
```

X RAY SPECS   X2

```
POLY STYRENE     V   (A        (A) GERM FREE ADOLESCENTS    1978 EMI           INS  3023
LARA LOGIC       SAX (
JACK STAFFORD    G   (     PAUL DEAN       B   (   CHRIS CHRYSLER  D   ( STEVE RUDI  SAX (
GLYN JOHNS       SAX (     B P HARDING     D   (   RICHARD BP TEES D   (
```

"XTC"   X3

```
COLIN MOULDING   B   (ABCD     (A) WHITE MUSIC          1978 VIRGIN      UK  V2095
ANDY PARTRIDGE   G   (ABCD     (B) GO TWO               1978 VIRGIN      UK  V2108
TERRY CHAMBERS   D   (ABCD     (C) DRUMS & WIRES        1979 VIRGIN      UK  V2129
BARRY ANDREWS    K   (AB       (D) BLACK SEA            1980 VIRGIN      UK  V2173
DAVID GREGORY    K G (CD       (EP) GO PLUS             1978 VIRGIN      UK VS23312
```

XIT   X4

```
MICHAEL MARTIN   G V (A        (A) PLIGHT OF REDMAN     1972 RARE EARTH US R536 UK SREA 4002
JOMAC SUAZO      B   (A        (A) PLIGHT OF REDMAN     1972 RARE EARTH NL        058 93622
R C GARISS       G PNO(A
LEEJA HERRERA    D PERC(A
```

YACHTS   Y1

```
J J CAMPBELL     V   (         (A) YACHTS               1979 RADAR            UK RAD19
MARTIN DEMPSEY   B   (A        (B) WITHOUT RADAR        1980 RADAR UK RAD27 US POLYDOR16270
MARTIN J WATSON  G V (AB
BOB BELLIS       D   (AB  HENRY PRIESTMAN  K   (AB MICK SKINNER  B ( GLYN HAVARD  B V (B
```

STOMU YAMASHTA   Y2

```
STOMU YAMASHTA   K PERC(ALL    (A) CONTEMPORARY         1972 L'OISEAU            DSLO1
STEVE WINWOOD    K V (HK        (B) RED BUDDHA           1972 BARCLAY           920 376
MICHAEL SHRIEVE  D   (HJK      (C) COME TO THE EDGE     1973 ISLAND            HELP  12
PAT THRALL       G   (HK       (D) THE MAN FROM THE EAST 1973 ISLAND           ILPS9228
PHIL MANZANERA   G   (H        (E) FREEDOM IS FRIGHTENING 1974 ISLAND          ILPS9242
AL DIMEOLA       G   (HJK      (F) ONE BY ONE           1974 ISLAND            ILPS9269
ROSCO GEE        B   (H        (G) RAINDOG              1975 ISLAND            ILPS9319
KLAUS SCHULZE    K   (HJK      (H) GO                   1976 ISLAND            ILPS9387
HUGH HOPPER      (E            (J) GO TOO               1977 ARISTA US4138  UK SPARTY1011
GARY BOYLE       G   (E        (K) GO LIVE FROM PARIS   1978 ISLAND            ISLD  10
BRIAN GASGOIGNE      (E
HISAKO YAMASHTA      (E   DONI HARVEY       (J PAUL JACKSON  (J  BROTHER JAMES    (JK
JEROME RIMSON    B   (K   LINDA LEWIS    V  (J KAREN FRIEDMAN V (K  PETER ROBINSON   (J
JESS RODEN           (J
```

JIMMY YANCEY   Y3

```
JIMMY YANCEY     V PNO(ALL     (A) PURE BLUES           196  ATLANTIC US SD1283
MAMA YANCEY      V   (AB        (B) CHICAGO PIANO VOL 1  1972 ATLANTIC US SD7229 UK  K40406
MICHAEL CROSBY   B   (B        (C) JIMMY YANCEY   VOL 1  19   OLDIE BLUES US         2802
                              (D) JIMMY YANCEY   VOL 2  19   OLDIE BLUES US         2813
```

YANKEES   Y3A

```
                              (A) HIGH 'N' INSIDE       1979 LONDON             SHY8531
```

ZAL YANOVSKY   Y4

```
ZAL YANOVSKY         (A       (A) ALIVE & WELL IN ARGENTINA  19  KAMA SUTRA  UK  2316  003
```

YARDBIRDS   Y5

```
TONY TOP TOPHAM  G   (1    WITH SONNY BOY WILLIAMSON    1964 FONTANA TL5277  RI  SFJL  960
KEITH RELF       V HCA(12345    "    "     "     "       1967 FONTANA              858  025
JIM McCARTY      D   (12345    "    "     "     "       1966 MERCURY   US  SR  61071
CHRIS DREJA      G   (12345    "    "     "     "       1975 PHILIPS        756435  011
PAUL SAMWELL-SMITH B (123  FIVE LIVE YARDBIRDS          1965 COLUMBIA  UK  335X 1677
ERIC CLAPTON     G   (2    FIVE LIVE YARDBIRDS          197  CHARLY    UK  CR 30173
JEFF BECK        G   (34   FOR YOUR LOVE                1965 EPIC      US      26167
JIMMY PAGE       G   (45   HAVING A RAVE UP             1965 EPIC US 26177 CBS GERM GCXC  28
                          THE YARDBIRDS                1966 COLUMBIA      UK  SCX 6063
(1) 1963    (2) 1964  (3) 1965  OVER UNDER SIDEWAYS DOWN  1966 EPIC US 26210 CAPITOL CAN 6202
(4) 1966    (5) 1967           GREAT HITS               1967 EPIC US 26246    US RI  34491
                          LITTLE GAMES                 1967 EPIC US 26313
                          PERFORMANCES BY CLAPTON BECK PAGE  1970 EPIC US 30135
                          ROCK GENERATION              19   BYG       FR    529701/2
                          LIVE YARDBIRDS WITH J PAGE   1971 EPIC US 30615
                          REMEMBER                     1971 STARLINE  UK  5RS 5069
                          HITS OF THE YARDBIRDS        197  CAPITOL   US  DT 6229
                          MORE GOLDEN EGGS             19   BERKELEY  US        1003
                          ERIC CLAPTON & YARDBIRDS     19   SPRINGBOARD US      4036
                          FAVOURITES                   19   EPIC US 34490
                          WITH ERIC CLAPTON            1975 CHARLY    UK  CR  30012
                          WITH JEFF BECK               1975 CHARLY    UK  CR  30013
                          SHAPES OF THINGS             19   BOMB      US        1045
                          SHAPES OF THINGS             19   SPRINGBOARD US      4039
                          SHAPES OF THINGS             1977 CHARLY    UK  CDX  1
                          ATTENTION                    19   FONTANA   GERM 9294  902
                          YARDBIRDS (EP)               1977 CHARLY    UK  CEP 116
```

```
Y5A                                    YELLOW
                         (A) SOLID PLEASURE              1980 RALPH        US
Y6                                  YELLOW DOG
  HERBIE ARMSTRONG  G V (AB   (A) YELLOW DOG              1977 VIRGIN    UK        V 2083
  KENNY YOUNG       G V (AB   (B) BEWARE OF THE DOG       1978 VIRGIN    UK        V 2103
  ROD DEMICK        B   (B
  GARY TAYLOR       B   (A  GERRY CONWAY  D   (A  ANDY ROBERTS        G (A  PHIL PALMER      G (B
  JIM GANNON        G   (A  MICK FEAT     B   (B  PETER VAN HOOKE     D (A  PATER BARDENS    K (B
  PAUL ATKINSON     D   (B  MO FOSTER     B   (B  JACK HALL           B (B  NEVILLE ROBERTS    (B
  SIMON PHILLIPS    D   (B  JIMMY HALL    SAX (B  THEOPHILUS K LIVELY D (B  JACK SPENCE    PERC(B
  PETE SOLLEY           (B
Y6A                          YELLOW MAGIC ORCHESTRA
  RYUICHI SAKAMOTO  K PERC(A  (A) YELLOW MAGIC ORCHESTRA  1979 A&M    UK   AMLH68506
  KENJI OHUMURA     G   (B   (B) XOO MULTIPLES           1980 A&M    UK   AMLH68516
  YUKIHIRO TAKAHASHI D V (B  (C) B G M                   1981 A&M    UK   AMLH64853
  HARUOMI HOSONO    K B (B
  HIDEKI MATSUTAKE      (A  BSHUNICHI HASHIMOTO V (A  MASAYOSHI TAKANAKA G(A  SANDI   V      (B
Y6B                                YELLOW PAYGES
  BILL HAM          G   (A   (A) VOLUME 1                 1969 UNI        US   73045
  BOB BARNES        B   (A
  DAN HORTTER       V HCA(A  DAN GORMAN  D   (A
Y7                                      YES
  CHRIS SQUIRE      B V (ALL     (A) YES                      1969 ATLANTIC US 8243  UK   588 190
  JON ANDERSON      V   (A>M     (A) YES                      1971 ATLANTIC RI        UK   K40034
  BILL BRUFORD      D   (ABCDEF   (B) TIME & A WORD            1970 ATLANTIC US 8273  UK 2400 006
  TONY KAYE         K   (ABC      (B) TIME & A WORD            1971 ATLANTIC RI        UK   K40085
  PETER BANKS       G   (AB       (C) THE YES ALBUM           1971 ATLANTIC US 8283  UK 2400 101
  STEVE HOWE        G   (C>N      (C) THE YES ALBUM           1971 ATLANTIC RI        UK   K40106
  RICK WAKEMAN      K   (DEFGJKLM (D) FRAGILE                 1971 ATLANTIC US 7211  UK 2401 019
  ALAN WHITE        D   (F>N      (D) FRAGILE                 1971 ATLANTIC RI        UK   K50009
  PATRICK MORAZ     K   (HM       (E) CLOSE TO THE EDGE       1972 ATLANTIC US 7244  UK   K50012
  TREVOR HORN       V B (N        (F) YESSONGS      (TPL)     1973 ATLANTIC US 3 100 UK   K60045
  GEOFF  DOWNES     K   (N        (G) TOPOGRAPHIC OCEANS (DBL)1973 ATLANTIC US 2908  UK   K80001
  COLIN GOLDRING    REC (C        (H) RELAYER                 1974 ATLANTIC US 18122 UK   K50096
                                  (J) YESTERDAYS             1975 ATLANTIC US 10103 UK   K50048
                                  (K) GOING FOR THE ONE      1977 ATLANTIC US 19106 UK   K50379
                                  (L) TORMATO                1978 ATLANTIC US 19202 UK   K50518
                                  (M) YESSHOWS               1980 ATLANTIC        UK   K60142
                                  (N) DRAMA                  1980 ATLANTIC US 16019 UK   K50736
Y8                               YESTERDAY & TODAY
  DAVE MENIKETTI    G V (AB   (A) YESTERDAY & TODAY       1976 LONDON         US   PS 677
  JOEY ALVES        G V (AB   (B) STRUCK DOWN             1978 LONDON         US   PS 711
  PHIL KENNEMORE    B V (AB
  LEONARD HAZE      D V (AB
Y8A                                     YOBS
  NODDY OLDFIELD        (A   (A) CHRISTMAS ALBUM          1980 SAFARI         UK   RUDE 1
  EBENEZER POLAK        (A
  KID VICIOUS          (A  H J BEDWETTER   (A
Y9                                   PETE YORK
  PETE YORK         D   (A   (A) PETE YORK PERCUSSION BAND  19 DECCA          UK   TXS 109
Y10                        STEVE YORK'S CAMELO PARDALIS
  STEVE YORK        B   (A   (A) MANOR LIVE               1973 VIRGIN         UK   V 2003
  ELKIE BROOKS      V   (A
  OLLIE HALSALL     G V (A  GRAHAM BOND  K SAX (A  TIM HINKLEY   K (A  IAN WALLACE      D (A
  MARC CHARIG       HRNS (A  JOHN LEE     TROM  (A  BOZ BURRELL   V (A  DAVE THOMPSON    K (A
  DAVE BROOKS       SAX (A  MIKE PATTO    V     (A  ROB TAIT      D (A  DIANE STEWART CONGA V(A
  MICK MOODY        G   (A  PETE GAVIN    D     (A  LOL COXHILL  SAX (A  BARRY DUGGAN   SAX (A
  JIM MULLEN        G   (A  PETE GAGE
Y11                                CHRIS YOULDEN
  CHRIS YOULDEN     V   (AB   (A) NOWHERE CITY            1973 DERAM UK SML 1099
  DEREK GRIFFITHS   G   (B    (B) CITY CHILD              1974 DERAM UK SML 1112 US LONDON 642
  PETE WINGFIELD    K   (B
  ROSCO GEE         B   (B  JACK MILLS    G    (B  TERRY STANNARD  D (B  NICK NEWELL    SAX (B
  MIKE COTTON       TPT (B  DAVE CASWELL  TPT  (B  JOHN BEECHAM  TROM (B  JOY YATES        V (B
  ANNA PEACOCK      V   (B  SUZANNA LYNCH  V   (B
Y12                              JESSE COLIN YOUNG
  JESSE COLIN YOUNG G V (ALL     (A) YOUNGBLOOD          1964 MERCURY    US      SR 61005
  JEFF MYER         D   (DEFGHJ   (B) THE SOUL OF A CITY BOY 1964 CAPITOL US T2070 RI  11267
  SCOTT LAWRENCE    K   (DEFGHJ   (B) THE SOUL OF A CITY BOY  19 CAPITOL VINE  RI  VMP 1009
  JIM ROTHERMEL     WIND (EFGHJ   (C) SONG FOR JULI      1963 WB        US 2734  UK K46262
  KELLY BRYAN       B   (EF       (D) TOGETHER           1974 WB        US 2588
  OZZIE AHLERS      PNO (E        (E) LIGHT SHINE        1974 WB        US 2790  UK K56037
  MARTY DAVID       B   (E        (F) SONGBIRD           1975 WB        US 2845  UK K56110
  JERRY CORBITT     V   (DEF      (G) ON THE ROAD        1976 WB        US 2913  UK K56223
  SUZI YOUNG        V   (DEFGHJ   (H) LOVE ON A WING     1977 WB        US 3033  UK K56358
  RON STALLINGS     SAX (DF       (J) AMERICAN DREAMS    1978 ELEKTRA   US 6E157 UK K52105
  PETER WELKER      TPT (FH
  REX ALLEN         TROM (G  CHUCK PETERSON  SAX (H  HANK DE VITO   STEEL(FH  FELIX PAPPALARDI V (H
  JEFF NEIGHBOR     B    (H  ZANE WOODWORTH  TPT (JH  CHUCK BENNETT  TROM (H  NICOLETTE LARSON V (H
  JOHN BLAKELEY     G    (H  EVERETT FAREY   HRNS (H  GORDON MESSICK TROM (H  DAVID HAYES    B V(GHJ
  RICHARD ANDERSON  HCA  (D  PETER CHILDS    G   (D  EDDY OFFENSTEIN  G (D  JOHN WILMETH   HRNS(D
  JEFF LABES        K    (J  MICHAEL O'NEILL G   (J  ALVIN TAYLOR     D (J  DAVID LINDLEY  VLN (J
  ANNA RIZZO        V    (J  PAMELA MOORE    V   (J  PAULETTE McWILLIAMS V (J  GREG WRIGHT    V (J
  STEPHANIE SPRUILL V    (J  ROGER KENERLY SAINT V (J  JIM GILSTRAP   V (J  GWEN EVANS       V (J
  JOHN LEHMAN       V    (J  FRITZ HEIBRON   TROM (J  RAYMOND LOECKLIE SAX (J  BENNETT FRIEDMAN SAX (J
```

JOHNNY YOUNG
Y13

JOHNNY YOUNG	G V HCA	(ALL	(A) CHICAGO BLUES BAND	1966 ARHOOLIE	US	1029
LOUIS MYERS	G	(E	(B) CHICAGO BLUES	1968 ARHOOLIE	US	1037
PAUL OSCHER	HCA	(D	(C) BLUES MASTER No9	197 BLUE HORIZON	US	4609
SAMMY LAWHORN	G	(D	(D) FAT MANDOLIN	1970 BLUE HORIZON	UK	763852
S P LEARY	D	(AD	(E) I CANT KEEP MY FOOT FROM JUMPING	1973 BLUESWAY	BLS	6075
RICHARD EVANS	B	(E	(F) & HIS FRIENDS	197 TESTAMENT	US	2226
OTIS SPANN	PNO	(AD				
BILL WARREN	D	(E				
WALTER HORTON	HCA	(B	LAFAYETTE LEAKE PNO (B	JAMES COTTON	HCA (A	JIMMY DAWKINS	G (B
ERNEST GATEWOOD	B	(B	JIMMY LEE MORRIS B (A	LESTER DORSIE	D (B		

KENNY YOUNG
Y14

KENNY YOUNG		(AB	(A) CLEVER DOG CHASE THE SUN	19 WB	US	2579
			(B) LAST STAGE FOR SILVERWOOD	19 WB	US	2676

LARRY YOUNG
Y14A

LARRY YOUNG	K	(ALL	GROOVE STREET	196 PRESTIGE	US	7237
			OF LOVE & PEACE	19 BLUENOTE	BST	84242
			CONTRASTS	19 BLUENOTE	US BST	84266
			HEAVEN ON EARTH	19 BLUENOTE	US BST	84304
			FUEL	1976 ARISTA	US AL	4051
			SPACEBALL	197 ARISTA	US AL	4072

MIGHTY JOE YOUNG
Y15

MIGHTY JOE YOUNG	G V	(ALL	(A) CHICKEN HEADS	19 OVATION	US	1437	
BOB REIDY	PNO	(E	(B) LOVE GONE	19 OVATION	US	1443	
SYLVESTER BOINES	B	(E	(C) MIGHTY JOE YOUNG	19 OVATION	US	1706	
ALVINO BENNETT	D	(E	(D) BLUES WITH A TOUCH OF SOUL	19 DELMARK	US	DS 629	
CHARLES BEECHAM	TPT	(E	(E) LEGACY OF THE BLUES (VOL 4)	1972 SONET UK SNTF633 US GNP		10014	
KEN SAJDAK	K	(F	(F) BLUESY JOSEPHINE	1976 BLACK & BLUE		33521	
WILLIE MABON	PNO	(F					
CORNELIUS BOYSON	B	(F	WILLIE HAYES D (F	WALTER HAMBRICK	SAX (E		

NEIL YOUNG
Y16

NEIL YOUNG	G V HCA	(ALL	(A) NEIL YOUNG	1969 REPRISE US RS6317	UK K44059	
JOHN BARBATA	D	(F	(B) EVERYBODY KNOWS THIS IS NOWHERE	1969 REPRISE US RS6349	UK K44073	
TIM DRUMMOND	B	(DFHLJN	(C) AFTER THE GOLDRUSH	1970 REPRISE US RS6383	UK K44088	
JACK NITZSCHE	K	(DFH	(D) HARVEST	1972 REPRISE US RS2032	UK K54005	
BEN KEITH STEEL	G V	(DFHLN	(E) JOURNEY THROUGH THE PAST	1972 REPRISE US RS2480	UK K54015	
DAVID CROSBY	G V	(DFJ	(F) TIME FADES AWAY	1973 REPRISE US RS2151	UK K54010	
JOE YANKEE	B	(F	(G) ON THE BEACH	1974 REPRISE US RS2180	UK K54014	
NICOLETTE LARSON	V	(LN	(H) TONIGHTS THE NIGHT	1975 REPRISE US RS2221	UK K54040	
KENNY BUTTREY	D	(DH	(J) ZUMA	1975 REPRISE US MS2242	UK K54057	
BILLY TALBOT	B	(BCHJLNO	(K) LONG MAY YOU RUN	1976 REPRISE US	UK K54081	
GREG REEVES	B	(C	(L) AMERICAN STARS & BARS	1977 REPRISE US 2261	UK K54088	
NILS LOFGREN	PNO V	(CH	(M) DECADE (TRIPLE)	1978 REPRISE US 3 2257	UK K64037	
RALPH MOLINA	D V	(BCHJLNO	(N) COMES A TIME	1978 REPRISE US 2266	UK K54099	
DANNY WHITTEN	G V	(BC	(O) HAWKS & DOVES	1979 REPRISE	UK K54109	
STEPHEN STILLS	V	(CDJK	(P) RUST NEVER SLEEPS	1979 REPRISE	UK K54105	
JAMES TAYLOR	V	(DFJ	(Q) LIVE RUST	1980 REPRISE US 2 2296	UK K64041	
GRAHAM NASH	V	(DFJ				
JIM MESSINA	B	(A	LINDA RONSTADT V (D	JOHN HARRIS PNO (D	EMMYLOU HARRIS V (L	
KARL HIMMEL	D	(LN	FRANK SAMPEDRO G STRGS(LJNO	CAROLE MAYEDO VLN (L	SPOONER OLDHAM PNO (N	
STRINGS		(N	RUFUS THIBODEAUX FDL (N	JOE OSBORN B (N	LARRIE LONDIN D (N	
J J CALE	G	(N	FARRELL MORRIS PERC (N	GRANT BOATRIGHT G (N	BUCKY BARRETT G (N	
JOHN CHRISTOPHER	G	(N	JERRY SHOOK G (N	STEVE GIBSON G (N	RUSS KUNKEL CONGA(N	
DALE SELLERS	G	(N	RAY EDENTON G (N	RITA FEY AUTOHARP (N	TIM MULLIGAN SAX(N	
LONDON SYM ORCH		(D				

ROY YOUNG
Y17

ROY YOUNG	K V	(AB	(A) THE ROY YOUNG BAND	1971 RCA	UK 5FB161	
JON LEE	TROM	(AB	(B) MR FUNKY	1972 MCA UK MKPS2022 RI	MCF2690	
ALAN DAVIES	D	(AB				
DAVE WENDELLS	G	(AB	HOWIE CASEY SAX (A	PAUL SIMMONS B (	EDDIE THORNTON TPT (B	
RICKY DODD	SAX	(B	RONNIE MACDONALD SAX (B	OWEN McINTYRE G (B	NICK SOUTH B (B	
ROD COOMBES	D	(B	ROBIN JONES PERC (B	DORIS TROY V (A	BARRY ST JOHN V (A	
SUE GLOVER	V	(A	SUNNY LESLIE V (A	LIZA STRIKE V (A	KATHY KISSOON V (A	
ALAN TOWNSEND	HRNS	(AB				

STEVE YOUNG
Y18

STEVE YOUNG	G V	(ALL	(A) ROCK,SALT & NAILS	1969 A&M	US 4177	
JOE ALLEN	B	(E	(B) SEVEN BRIDGES ROAD	1972 REPRISE	US 2081	
KENNY MALONE	D	(E	(B) SEVEN BRIDGES ROAD	1975 BLUE CANYON	US 505	
CHUCK COCHRAN	K	(E	(B) SEVEN BRIDGES ROAD	1976 SONET	UK SNTF 705	
JIM COLVARD	G	(E	(C) HONKY TONK MAN	1976 MOUNTAIN RAILROAD	US 52776	
DAVE KIRBY	G	(E	(D) RENEGADE PICKER	1976 RCA US APL11759 UK	PL11759	
LLOYD GREEN	STEEL	(E	(E) NO PLACE TO FALL	1978 RCA US AHL12510 UK	PL12510	
KRISTIN WILKINSON	VLA	(E				
KARL HIMMEL	D	(BDE	MIKE LEECH B (DE	JERRY SHOOK G HCA(DE	DALE SELLERS G (BDE	
MAC GAYDEN	G	(DE	BUDDY EMMONS STEEL(DE	TRACY NELSON V (E	KIM YOUNG V (DE	
CHARLIE McCOY	HCA	(BE	BUDDY SPICHER VLN (BE	LARRY BYROM G (E	TERRY McMILLAN HCA(D	
JOHNNY GIMBLE FDL MAND		(D	WELDON MYRICK STEEL(B	JOSH GRAVES DOBRO(B	PETER WADE G (B	
BOBBY THOMPSON	B	(B	HENRY STRZELECKI B (B	JERRY SMITH K (B	PETE DRAKE STEEL(B	
FRED CARTER	B	(B	DAVID BRIGGS K (B	RAY EDENTON G (B	JERRY CARRIGAN D (B	
D J FONTANA	D	(B	WILLIE ACKERMAN D (B	BOB MOORE B (B	J B BROWN (B	
GEORGE BOURQUE		(B	SPOOK JAMES (B	CHARLIE JOBES (B	STEVE KEITH (B	
NASHVILLE EDITION	V	(B	PAUL TANNEN V (B	MARY HOLLADAY V (B	GINGER HOLLADAY V (B	

YOUNG & MOODY
Y19

BOB YOUNG	V HCA	(A	(A) YOUNG & MOODY	1977 MAGNET UK MAG5015 UA US LA 759	
MICK MOODY	G V	(A			
GRAHAM PRESKETT VLN B K		(A	KAY GARNER V (A	TERRY STANNARD D (A	JEAN HAWKER V (A
CLAIRE TORRY	V	(A			

Y20   YOUNG MARBLE GIANTS

ALISON STRATTON	V	(AB	(A) COLOSSAL YOUTH		1980 ROUGH TRADE	UK	ROUGH	8
PHILIP MOXHAM	B	(AB	(B) FINAL DAY(EP)		1980 ROUGH TRADE	UK		
STUART MOXHAM	G K	(AB						

Y21   YOUNG TRADITION

HEATHER WOOD	V	(A	(A) GALLERIES					
ROYSTON WOOD	V TAMB	(A	(B) YOUNG TRADITION SAMPLER		1968 VANGUARD		VSD 79295	
PETE BELLAMY	V G CONC	(A	(C) GALLERIES REVISITED		1977 TRANSATLANTIC		TRANSAM13	
DAVID MUNROW SHAWN		(A			1979 TRANSATLANTIC		TRANSAM30	
ROD SKEAPING	VLN	(A	ADAM SKEAPING VLN (A CHRIS HOGWOOD		PERC (A DOLLY COLLINS		ORG (A	
DAVE SWARBRICK FDL MAND(A								

Y22   YOUNGBLOODS

JESSE COLIN YOUNG	G V B(ALL	(A) YOUNGBLOODS		1967 RCA	US	LSP3724	
JERRY CORBITT	G B	(A	(B) EARTH MUSIC		1967 RCA	US	LSP3865
JOE BAUER	D	(HK	(C) ELEPHANT MOUNTAIN		1969 RCA	US	LSP4150
LOWELL LEVINGER	K G	(HK	(D) ROCK FESTIVAL		1970 WB	US	WS 1878
MICHAEL KANE	B	(L	(E) CRABTUNES NOGGINS		197 WB	US	WS 1944
EARTHQUAKE ANDERSON HCA(K			(F) THE BEST OF		1970 RCA	US	LSP4399
			(G) TWO TRIPS		1970 MERCURY	US	SR 61273
			(H) RIDE THE WIND		1971 WB	UK K46100	US	WS 2563
			(J) SUNLIGHT		1971 RCA	UK SF8218	US	LSP4561
			(K) GOOD & DUSTY		1971 WB		US	BS 2566
			(L) HIGH ON A RIDGETOP		1972 WB		US	BS 2653
			(M) GET TOGETHER		19 RCA INT			INTS1170

Y23   'YS'

RENE WERNEER	VLN V(A	(A) MADAME LA FRONTIERE		1976 PHILIPS	FR	9101 056
PASCAL STIVE	K V	(A					
JACKY THOMAS	B V	(A	JACQUES HIGELIN ACC (A MICHEL SANTANGELI D V (A GABRIEL YACOUB G (A
PIERRE CHERREZ	G	(A	JACQUES WIEDERKER CELLO(A				

Z1   Z Z TOP

BILLY GIBBONS	G V	(ALL	(A) FIRST ALBUM		1970 LONDON		US PS 584	
			(A) FIRST ALBUM	RI	1980 WB	GERM 56601	US	3268
DUSTY HILL	B V	(ALL	(B) RIO GRANDE MUD		1972 LONDON UK SHU8433		US PS 612
			(B) RIO GRANDE MUD		1980 WB	GERM 56602	US	3269
FRANK BEARD	D	(ALL	(C) TRES HOMBRES		1973 LONDON UK SHU8459		US PS 631
			(C) TRES HOMBRES		1980 WB	GERM 56602	US	3270
			(D) FANDANGO		1975 LONDON UK SHU8482		UK PS 656
			(D) FANDANGO		1980 WB	GERM 56603	US	3271
			(E) TEJAS		1976 LONDON UK LDU 1		US PS 680
			(E) TEJAS		1980 WB	GERM 56604	US	3272
			(F) BEST OF		197 LONDON		US PS 706
			(F) BEST OF		197 TELEFUNKEN/NOVA GERM		A0623361
			(F) BEST OF		1980 WB		US	3273
			(G) DEGUELLO		1979 WB	UK K56701	US	3361

Z2   Z.N.R

JOSEPH RACAILLE	K SYN V(AB	(A) BARRICADE 3		1976 RECOMMENDE RR7 ISADORA FR 9002
HECTOR ZAZOU	K SYN B(AB	(B) TRAITE DE MECANIQUE POPULAIRE		1970 SCOPA		1002
ANDRE JAUME	SAX (A						
HARVEY NENEUX	G	(A	PATRICK PORTELLA CLAR (A DAVID RUEFF	WIND (AB GILLY BELL	SYN (A
FERNAND D'ARLES	D	(A	MANFRED LE LALO SAX (B CATHERINE ARMAND	SAX (B LOLA TALOT	SAX (B
HUMPHREY NENEUX	V	(B	REMI DEMILLAC VLN (B				

Z3   Z.O.U.(ZON ORCHESTRA UNLIMITED)

ANDRE HERVE	K G V(A	(A) Z.O.U.		1975 POLYDOR	FR	2393 103
MICHEL HERVE	B V	(A					
JOEL HERVE	G V	(A	STEPHAN HERVE D (A MARIA POPKIEWICZ	V (A

Z4   LENNY ZAKATEK

LENNY ZAKATEK	V	(A	(A) LENNY ZAKATEK		1979 A&M	UK	AMLH64777
JOHN GIBLIN	B V	(A					
STUART ELLIOTT	D PERC(A	MAX MIDDLETON K (A ROBERT AHWAI	G (A IAN BAIRNSON	G V (A
MARILYN BAIRNSON	V	(A	STEVE GREGORY SAX (A GEORGE CHISHOLM	HRNS (A STRINGS	(A

Z5   ZAL BAND

ZAL CLEMINSON	G	(A					
LEROI JONES	G	(A	CHRIS GLEN B (A BILLY RANKIN	(A TED McKENNA	D (A

Z6   ZAP POW

(A) ZAP POW WOW		1976 VULCAN		VULP 004
(B) REVOLUTION		1976 TROJAN		TRLS 130
(C) ZAP POW		1978 ISLAND	UK	ILPS 9547

FRANK ZAPPA	G V (ALL	(A) FREAK OUT	1966 VERVE UK SVLP9154
DON SUGARCANE HARRIS	VLN(HJKLS	(A) " "	1966 VERVE US 5005
DON PRESTON	K B (BCDEFGHLMOPQT	(A) " " (DBL)	197 VERVE UK 2683 004
IAN UNDERWOOD G K WIND(CEFHJKLMOQSRY		(A) " "	196 VERVE GERM 710007
RUTH UNDERWOOD K PERC (NRSTOYZc		(B) ABSOLUTELY FREE	1967 VERVE UK SVLP9174 RI 2317 035
DAVID ANDERLE	(	(B) " "	1967 VERVE US 5013
RONNIE AMBLER	WIND (	(B) " "	1967 VERVE GERM 710006
MIKE ALTSCHUL	WIND (PQ	(C) WE'RE ONLY IN IT FOR THE MONEY	1967 VERVE UK SVLP9199 RI 2317 034
HAROLD AYRES	(	(C) " " " "	1967 VERVE US 5045
JIMMY CARL BLACK	D(ABCEFGHLNfD	(C) " " " "	1967 VERVE GERM 710012
TERRY BOZZIO	D (XYZb1	(D) LUMPY GRAVY	1967 VERVE UK SVLP9223 RI 2317 046
BIANCO	K (	(C) " " "	1967 VERVE US 8741
MAX BENNETT	B (JK	(E) CRUISIN WITH RUBEN & THE JETS	1968 VERVE UK SVLP9237 RI 2317 069
TERRY BOLIN	D (	(E) " "	1969 VERVE US 5055
NAPOLEON MURPHY BROCK SAX(STUYbc		(E) " "	1969 VERVE GERM 710020
JACK BRUCE	B (S	(F) MOTHER MANIA	1969 VERVE UK SVLP9239 RI 2317 047
RANDY BRECKER	HRNS (Z	(F) " "	19 VERVE 2351 017
MICHAEL BRECKER	HRNS (Z	(F) " "	1969 VERVE US 5068
CAPTAIN BEEFHEART	V (KYUX	(F) " "	1969 VERVE GERM 710021
BILL BYERS	TROM (PQ	(G) UNCLE MEAT	1969 BIZARRE UK 52024 US 2024
DALE BOZZIO	(ef	(G) " "	1969 REPRISE GERM 64005
EDWIN BEACH	(A	(H) WEASELS RIPPED MY FLESH	1970 REPRISE UK K44019
BEN BARRETT	(H	(H) " "	1970 BIZARRE US 2028
JOHN BERGAMO	PERC (Z	(J) CHUNGAS REVENGE	1970 REPRISE UK K44020
BLOODSHOT ROLLIN'RED HCA(U		(J) " "	1970 BIZARRE US 2030
ADRIAN BELEW	G (Ab1	(K) HOT RATS	1970 REPRISE UK K44078 RI K59021
ARTHUR BARROW	(ef	(K) " "	1970 BIZARRE US 6356
GARY BARONE	TPT (A	(L) BURNT WEENY SANDWICH	1970 BIZARRE UK K44083
JIMMY BOND	B (D	(L) " "	1970 BIZARRE US 6370
DENNIS BUDIMIR	G (D	(HL) WEASELS/BURNT WEENY(2 ORIGINALS) 19	REPRISE UK K64024
JOHN BALKIN	B (D	(M) LIVE AT FILLMORE EAST	1971 REPRISE UK K44150
CHUCK BERGHOFFER	B (D	(M) " "	1971 BIZARRE US US 2042
DICK BARBER	V (DC	(N) 200 MOTELS	1971 UA UK 50003 US LA9956
RAY COLLINS	(ABEGHS	(N) " "	1971 UA GERM 29218/9
DAVE CORONADO	SAX (	(O) JUST ANOTHER BAND FROM LA	1972 REPRISE UK K44179
ROBERT CAMARENA	V (ST	(O) " "	1972 BIZARRE US 2075
RONNIE CUBER	REEDS(Z	(P) THE GRAND WAZOO	1972 REPRISE UK K44209
LEE CLEMENT	PERC (P	(P) " "	1972 BIZARRE US 2093
HERB COHEN	(B	(Q) WAKA JAWAKA	1972 REPRISE UK K44203
LISA COHEN	(B	(Q) " "	1972 BIZARRE US 2094
VINCE COLAIUTA	(ef	(R) OVERNIGHT SENSATION	1973 DICREET UK K41000 US 2149
GENE CIPRIANO	WIND (D	(S) APOSTROPHE	1974 DISCRETUK K59201 US 2175
ERIC CLAPTON	G (CD	(T) ROXY & ELSEWHERE	1974 DISCREET UK K69201 US 2202
DON CHRISTLIEB	WIND (D	(U) ONE SIZE FITS ALL	1974 DISCREET UK K59207 US 2216
MARGINAL CHAGRIN	SAX (e	(V) MOTHERS DAY	197 VERVE 2626 002
FRANKIE CAPP	D (D	(W) ROCK FLASHBACKS	1975 VERVE 2352 057
CHUNCKY	(P	(X) BONGO FURY	1975 DICREET UK K59209 US 2234
WARREN CUCURULLO	(ef	(Y) ZOOT ALLURES	1976 WB UK K56298 US 2970
AYNSLEY DUNBAR	D (GMLOPQJS	(Z) IN NEW YORK	1978 DISCREET UK K69204 US 2/2290
TONY DURAN	G (PQ	(a) STUDIO TAN	1978 DISCREET UK K59210 US 2291
VINCENT DEROSA	HRNS (D	(b) SHEIK YERBOUTI	1979 CBS UK 88339
EARL DUMLER	WIND (D	(b) " "	1979 ZAPPA US 2/1501
GEORGE DUKE	K V (JNPQRSTUXac	(c) SLEEP DIRT	1979 DISCREET UK K59211 US 2292
EUGENE DINOVI	(A	(d) ORCHESTRAL FAVOURITES	1979 DISCREET UK K59212 US 2294
ALEX DMOCHOWSKI(ERRONEOUS B(PRSQ		(e) JOE'S GARAGE ACT 1	1980 CBS UK 86101
DEBBIE	(ST	(e) " " "	1980 ZAPPA US 1/1603
ROY ESTRADA	B V (ABCDEFGHLY1	(f) JOE'S GARAGE ACTS 2&3	1980 CBS UK 88475
VIRGIL EVANS	(A	(f) " "	1980 ZAPPA US 2/1502
ALAN ESTES	PERC (PD	(g) ZAPPA & THE MOTHERS	19 VERVE 2352 057
GENE ESTES	(AD	(1) JAN 1978 TOUR	
DON ELLIS	(B	(h) TINSELTOWN REBELLION	1981 CBS UK 88516
JIM FIELDER	B (		

KIM FOWLEY	(A	HOWARD KAYLAN	V (JMNO	PAT O'HEARN	WIND (D	RANDY THORNTON V (b
LARRY FANOGA	(D	RAY KELLOFF	(A	DAVID OCKER	CLAR (b	CHESTER THOMPSON D (TUXc
VICTOR FELDMAN	PERC (D	RUTH KOMANOFF	(	JIM PONS	V (OMN	ERNIE TACK HRNS(P
TOM FOWLER	B (RSTUXY	CAROL KAYE	(A	JOEL PESKIN	SAX (PQ	VITO (A
JANET FERGUSON	V (PQ	MICHAEL LICKERT	(N	VAN DYKE PARKS	(	AL VIOLA G (D
BRUCE FOWLER TROM (RSTXY		LYNN	(ST	DAVE PARLATO	B (Y	KEN VASSEY (R
CARL FRANZONI	(A	MIKE LANG	K (bY	GEORGE PRICE	(A	NEIL VANG (A
WALT FOWLER	TPT (SY	ANDRE LEWIS	K (bY	RICHARD PERISSI	HRNS (D	HENRY VESTINE (
LOWELL GEORGE	G (HKL	RICKY LANCELOTTI	(R	SPARKY PARKER	B V (Y	MARK VOLMAN V (JMNO
ROY GATON	(A	BILL MUNDI	(BCG	JEAN LUC PONTY	K (KRS	RAY WHITE G (Z
BUZZ GARDNER	HRNS (HL	DAVID MOIRE	V (Yb	DON PARDO	V (Z	DAVID WELLS (A
BUNK GARDNER WIND (BCEFGHL		SAL MARQUEZ TPT	(PQRS	CHRIS PETERSON	V (Q	KEN WATSON (A
RUBEN DE GUEVARA B V (STY		LOU MARINI	REED (Z	JOHN ROTELLA PERC	(ABDP	ERNIE WATTS SAX(P
JIM GORDON	D (S	KERRY McNABB	V (S	KURT RETAR	(AB	BOB WEST B (D
SUSIE GLOVER	V (S	ARTHUR MAEBE	HRNS (D	EMIL RICHARDS PERC	(D	PETER WOLF K (ef
JOHN GUERIN	(DJKS	ED MANN	PERC(Zbe1f	TONY RIZZI	G (D	RON WILLIAMS (D
JIM HAYNES	G (D	TOM MALONE	HRNS (P	ALICE STUART	(	JOHNNY GUITAR WATSON G V(U
RALPH HUMPHREY	D (KRST	MALCOLM McNABB	HRNS (P	STUMUK	SAX (e	DENNIS WALLEY G (Xef
BOB HARRIS	K V (M	LINCOLN MAYORGA	K (D	CRAIG STEWART	(	NELLY WALKER (G
GEORDIE HORMEL	(f	SHELLEY MANNE	D (D	KEN SHROYER TROM	(DPQ	IKE WILLIS (ef
ELLIOT INGBER	G (A	JOANNE CALDWELL McNABB(P		PAUL SMITH	K (D	JAMES YOUMAN (Uc
JOHN JOHNSON	(A	TOM MARIANO	K (1	JEFF SIMMONS	(JOT	BOB ZIMMITTI PERC(P
DR JOHN	K (	AL MANN	(ef	JIM SHERWOOD WIND (BCEFGHL		PAMELA ZARUBICA (BC
PETE JOLLY	K (D	AL MALKIN	(	EMMET SARGEANT	(A	GAIL ZAPPA V (Y
JULES JACOB	WIND (D	TOMMY MARS	K V (be	JOE SAXON	(A	JIMMY ZITO TPT(D
FRED JACKSON	WIND (P	LOU ANNE NEIL	HARP (ZY	DAVID SAMUELS PERC	(Z	
PLAS JOHNSON	(A	TED NASH	WIND (D	RON SELICO	D (K	
EDDIE JOBSON K VLN V	(Z	SHUGGIE OTIS	G (K	ARTIE TRIPP	(EFGHL	
SNEAKY PETE KLEINOW STEEL(Q		TONY ORTEGA	WIND (P	TOMMY TEDESCO	G (D	

JOE ZAWINUL

```
JOE ZAWINUL        K    (ALL      (A) ZAWINUL                          1971 ATCO US 1579      UK      2400 151
GEORGE DAVIS       FLT  (A        (A) ZAWINUL                          1971 ATLANTIC          UK RI   K40349
EARL TURBINTON     SAX  (A        (B) RISE & FALL                      19   VORTEX            US      2002
WOODIE SHAW        TPT  (A        (C) MONEY IN THE POCKET              19   ATCO              US      3003
MIROSLAV VITOUS    B    (A        (D) CONCERTO RETITLED(COMP)          1976 ATLANTIC          US      1694
JIMMY OWENS        TPT  (A
HUBERT LAWS        FLT  (A   HERBIE HANCOCK    K  (A    WALTER BOOKER   B   (A   JOE CHAMBERS        PERC(A
BILLY HART         PERC (A   DAVID LEE         PERC (A  WAYNE SHORTER   SAX (A   JACK DE JOHNETTE    WIND(A
```

ZEPHYR

```
TOMMY BOLIN        G V  (AB       (A) ZEPHYR                           1970 PROBE UK SPB 1006 US      CP4510
CANDY GIVENS       K V  (ABC      (B) GOING BACK TO COLORADO           1971 WB                US      WS1897
JOHN FARIS         K SAX(AB       (C) SUNSET RIDE                      1972 WB                US      WS2603
ROBBIE CHAMBERLAIN      D(A
BOBBY BERGE        D    (B   DAVID GIVENS B V  (ABC
```

WARREN ZEVON

```
WARREN ZEVON G V K B HCA(ALL      (A) WANTED DEAD OR ALIVE             1969 IMPERIAL          US      LP 12456
DAVID LINDLEY      FDL  (BD       (B) WARReN ZEVON                     1976 ASYLUM US 7E1060 UK       K53039
WADDY WACHTEL      G V  (BCD       (C) EXCITABLE BOY                   1978 ASYLUM US 6E 118 UK       K53973
BOB GLAUB          B    (BC       (D) BAD LUCK STREAK IN DANCING SCHOOL 1980 ASYLUM US 5E 509 UK     K52191
LARRY ZACK         D    (B        (E) STAND IN THE FIRE                1980 ASYLUM US 5E 519 UK      K52265
PHIL EVERLY        V    (B
J D SOUTHER        V    (BD  JACKSON BROWNE    G V  (BD  LINDSEY BUCKINGHAM G V  (B   MARTY DAVID       B  (B
GARY MALLABER      D    (A   SID SHARP      STRINGS (B  BOBBY KEYS      SAX (B   JAI WINDING       K V(B
GLENN FREY         G V  (BD  DON HENLEY        V    (BD  ROY MARINELL    B   (B   JORGE CALDERON    V  (BCD
NED DOHENY         G    (B   BONNIE RAITT      V    (B   ROSEMARY BUTLER V   (B   CARL WILSON       V  (B
JEFF PORCARO       D    (C   GREG LADANYI    PERC  (C   KENNY EDWARDS   B   (C   RICK MAROTTA      D  (CD
ARTHUR GERST       HARP (C   LUIS DAMIAN    JARANA (C   DANNY KORTCHMAR G   (C   MANUEL VASQUEZ       (C
RUSS KUNKEL        D    (C   LEE SKLAR         B    (CD  JIM HORN        SAX (C   LINDA RONSTADT    V  (CD
LINDA WARNES       V    (C   JOHN McVIE        B    (B   MICK FLEETWOOD  D   (C   KARLA BONOFF      V  (C
SKIP BATTIN        B    (A   DRACHEN THEAKER   D    (A   ED CARAEFF     PERC (A   SWEET TRIFLES     V  (A
BRENT SEAWELL      B    (A   TOXEY FRENCH      D    (A   JON CORNEAL     D   (A   GENTLEMEN BOYS    V  (BC
DON FELDER         G    (D   JOE WALSH         G    (D   STEVIE NICKS    V   (B
```

ZIGGYBYFIELD & THE BLACKHEART BAND

```
                                  (A) RUNNING                          1980 PVK               UK      PVK 1
```

ZIOR

```
KEITH BONSOR V K B FLT(A          (A) ZIOR                             1971 NEPENTHA          6437 005
JOHN TRUBA         G V  (A
PETER BREWER D PNO HCA(A     BARRY SKEELS      B V  (A
```

ZIPPERS

```
BOB WILLINGHAM     V    (
BILL WILLETT       D    (    DANIELLE FAYE     B V  (    LOU CAMMARATA   G V  (
```

ZIPS

```
JOHN FONTAINE      V    (
GUS GOAD           B    (    MICK BASS         G V  (    TREVOR WALTERS  D   ( ANDY COLQUHOUN G V  (
```

ZOMBIES

```
COLIN BLUNSTONE    V    (B        (A) BEGINS HERE                      1965 DECCA             UK      LK 4679
ROD ARGENT         K    (B        (B) ODESSEY & ORACLE                 1968 CBS UK 63280 US DATE TES 4013
HUGH GRUNDY        D    (B        (C) WORLD OF THE ZOMBIES             1970 DECCA             UK      SPA 85
PAUL ATKINSON      G    (B        (D) TIME OF THE ZOMBIES              1973 EPIC  UK 65728    RI      68262
CHRIS WHITE        B    (B        (D) TIME OF THE ZOMBIES              1973 EPIC              US      32861
PAUL ARNOLD        B    (         (E) ROCK ROOTS                       1976 DECCA             UK      ROOTS2
                                  (F) EARTHDAYS                        19   LONDON            US      PS 557
                                  (G) ZOMBIES                          19   PARROT            US      PAS71001
                                  (H) SHES NOT THERE (DBL)             1976 NOVA              GERM    6/28378
```

ZON

```
DENTON YOUNG       V    (         (A) ASTRAL PROJECTOR                 1978 EPIC              PEC 90442
HOWARD HELM        K    (
KIM HUNT           D    (    JIM SAMSON        B    (    BRIAN MILLER   G   (
```

ZONES

```
WILLY GARDNER      G V  (A        (A) UNDER INFLUENCE(4 DIFF COVERS)   1979 ARISTA           UK      SPART 1095
BILLY McISAAC      K V  (A
RUSSELL WEBB       B V  (A   KENNY HYSLOP      D    (A
```

ZOO

```
PIERRE FANEN       G    (A        (A) ZOO                              19   BARCLAY 521172    RIVIERA521118
JOEL DAYDE         V    (A        (A) ZOO                              19   MAJOR MINOR       UK      SMLP 74
DANIEL CARLET VLN SAX  (AB        (B) I SHALL BE FREE                  1971 RIVIERA                   521147
MICHEL RIPOCHE VLN SAX (AB
TONY CANAL         TPT  (A   ANDRE HERVE       K     (AB  MICHEL BONNECARRERE G(AB  MICHEL HERVE   B  (AB
CHRISTIAN DEVAUX   D    (AB  IAN BELLAMY       V    (B
```

ZOO

```
KETIL STOKKAN      G V  (A        (A) NOREGS HEITASTE                  1980 SNOWFLAKE         CLP 3017
SVERRI DAHL        K V  (A
RUDI HOYNES        TROM (A   ROYER LARSEN      B    (A   TROND NYRUD    WIND (A
```

ZORRO

```
                                  (A) 'ARRODS DON'T SELL 'EM (EP)      19   BRIDGE HOUSE      BHEP 1
```

TAPPER ZUKIE

```
TAPPER ZUKIE            (ALL  MAN AH WARRIOR                           1977 MER               MER 101
                              IN DUB                                   19   STARS         RI FRONT LINE FL1029
                              M P L A                                  19   KLICK         RI FRONT LINE FL1006
                              MAN FROM BOSRAH                          19   STARS
                              PEACE IN THE GHETTO                      1978 FRONT LINE                FL1009
                              TAPPER ROOTS                             1978 FRONT LINE                FL1032
```

WALTER ZWOL	K V (A	(A) ZWOL		1978 EMI			AMS 2003
WOODY WEST	G (A						
DENNIS PINHAM	B V (A	DANNY SMITH	D (A	MARL GENDLE	G (A	JIM ISBELL	D (A
GHIA	CONGA(A	DONNA RHODES	V (A	ROGER COOK	V (A	PHILIP DONNELLY	G (A
RACHEL SIMPSON	V (A	KATHY JOHNSON	V (A	STACEY HEYDEN	G (A	TONY NEWMAN	B (A
CHARLES CHALMERS	V SAX(A	SANDRA RHODES	V (A	RALPH MURPHY	V (A		

ZYGOAT   Z23

(A) ZYGOAT   1975 POLYDOR   2383 270

ZZEBRA   Z24

TERRY SMITH	G (A	(A) ZZEBRA		1974 POLYDOR			2383 296
GUS YEADON	PNO G V (A	(B) PANIC		1975 POLYDOR			2383 326
LIAM GENOCKEY	D V (AB						
JOHN McCOY	B (AB	STEVE BYRD	G (B	ALAN MARSHALL	V (B	TOMMY EYRE	K (B
LOUGHTY AMAO PERC	SAX V(AB	DAVE QUINCY	SAX (AB	JO NEWMAN	V (B	LESLEY DUNCAN	V (B
KIM MOORE	V (B						

Index

The index lists the main headings of each entry and all the musicians included. The references are to entry codes not page numbers. Main entries are indicated by a line under the code, e.g. ACE A7.

Various cross-references have been provided between maiden, former, stage, real names etc.; all elements of composite group names have been indexed.

BLACK Allan R93A
BLACK Barry M152
BLACK Big B282
BLACK Bill B111 F31 P125
BLACK Bobby C173 H26 L37 W129
BLACK Brent P6
BLACK Brittley C225 R49
BLACK Dave (G) K32A S214C
BLACK David 'Jay' (V) J44
BLACK Eddie M209 R137 S332A
BLACK Guy W101
BLACK Harold C. P53
BLACK Jack B196 S302A
BLACK James (D) G4
BLACK James (G) M114B
BLACK Jay see BLACK David
BLACK Jet S292
BLACK Jimmy Carl B72 G25 Z8
BLACK Joane F1
BLACK Larry H26
BLACK Pablo (DIXON Paul) A6 B111A G39 I1A R35B R150 T110
BLACK Pauline S74
BLACK Pete L121A S8A
BLACK Philip W73
Black Bob T9B
BLACK CAT BONES B112
BLACK HEAT B113
BLACK LION L17
BLACK MER'CA B 13
BLACK OAK ARKANSAS B114
BLACK SABBATH B115
BLACK SLATE B116
BLACK UHURU B117
BLACK VELVET B118
BLACK WIDOW B119
Blackbeard see BOVELL Dennis
BLACKBERRIES P6
BLACKBLOOD B120
BLACKBYRDS B121
BLACKFIELD Andy S226
BLACKFOOT B123
BLACKFOOT J D B123A
BLACKFOOT SUE B124
BLACKHAM Denis M1A
BLACKHEART BAND 211A
BLACKJACK B122
BLACKLEY David K27A
BLACKLOCK Kelvin W65
BLACKMAN Berna d W'3
BL'ACKMAN Bruce S245
BLACKMAN Buddy H78A
BLACKMAN David H78A
BLACKMAN Junior A83 H170
BLACKMAN Phil K45
BLACKMON Benorce P67 W116
BLACKMON Buddy B41
BLACKMON Larry C20
BLACKMON M E W55
BLACKMORE Jon W79
BLACKMORE Ritchie D40 H91 O42 R14 R147 S338 G95
BLACKNELL Eugene M238
Blackspy see JAHSON Everald
BLACKWATER JUNCTION B125
BLACKWELL Charles 'Chuck' C155 C168 D26 K51 M53 R173
BLACKWELL Charlie T147
BLACKWELL Otis S342
BLACKWELL Richard S229
BLADD Stephen Jo G19 G122
BLADE Andy E11
BLADES Jack R154
BLAINE Bobby C226 J70 N34
BLAINE Hal A50 B50 B56 B171 B226 C39 C237 G10 H37A J36 J73A L111 M27 M61 MBAC M125A N25 N43 P125 R76 R101 R126 S123 S125 S160 S262
BLAIR Eddie I12 R40B S31
BLAIR Frank G17
BLAIR John H9 H59
BLAIR Ron (B) P70 T127A
BLAKE Alex C147 W62
BLAKE Christopher 'Skyjuice' G39 L58A R29

BLAKE Eaton 'Jah Blake' M109
BLAKE Gerry U15A
BLAKE Ginger A59 B47A
BLAKE John B127 F92 M203 R87 R101 R126
BLAKE John W25
BLAKE Karl L48A
BLAKE Nancy O46
BLAKE Norman B221 D139 K95
BLAKE Ray W1
BLAKE Tim (also MOONWEED Hi T) B125A C137 G66 H64 H119 T159
BLAKELEY John H5 M18 S284 T107 V7 Y12
BLAKELEY Alan T138
BLAKESLEY Malcolm M20
BLAKIN Richie G77C
BLAKLEY Ronee A132 B126 C173 D139
BLAMIRE Robert P58
BLANC Mark A48A
BLANCA Pene N32
BLANCHARD Edgar L118
BLANCO Frank E74
BLAND Bobby 'Blue' B127 K45
BLAND Dave C152 C165
BLAND Madeline F132
BLANDIN Teddy M151
BLANDMER Stewart Q1C S255
BLANKE Toto C201
BLANTON John C216
BLASQUIZ Klaus H89A M49
BLAST FURNACE AND THE HEATWAVES B129
BLAUVELT Howard Arthur H55A R19
BLAZER BLAZER B130
BLEGVAD Peter C90 H101 N9 S152
BLEIMOR Bagad S280
BLENKHORN Clive H129
BLESSING Lynn F68 O12 S116 W44
BLEY Apache P45
BLEY Carla B131 B248 G90 M79
BLEY Paul P35 P45
BLIFFERT Fred J49
BLIGH Doug W99B
BLIMPS B132
BLIND FAITH B134
Blindboy Grunt see DYLAN Bob
BLIPCROTCH Reality D O24B
BLISS Paul D91
BLITZ Johnny D32
BLITZ Urban D89
BLIX Brynholf R178
BLIZZARD OF OZ O33E
BLOCH Gene M84
BLOCH Greg I31 P1 I164
BLOCK Rory B135 G110 L128 L143
BLODWYN PIG B136
BLOK Edward Ninck C243
BLOM Joop T37G
BLONDE ON BLONDE B137
BLONDEL B138
BLONDIE B139
BLONKER B139A
BLOOD B140
BLOOD Bobby G91A
BLOOD Drew F129
BLOOD SWEAT AND TEARS B141
BLOODGROUP B141A
BLOODROCK B142
Bloodshot Rollin' Red Z8
BLOODSTONE B143
BLOOM Eric B154 H185
BLOOMFIELD Brett S177
BLOOMFIELD Mike B63 B144 B202 C195 D2 D19 E33 F67 G61 H15 K2 K81 M238
BLOOMFIELD Steve B145 M105
BLOSSOM TOES B146
BLOSSOMS K81
BLOUGH Billy T80
BLOUIN Carl'Larry' B17 K53 L4 M111 M149

BLOUNT Tina L44
BLOUT Kerry S339A
BLOW FLY B147
BLUE B148
BLUE Amanda S214A
BLUE Austin R53C
BLUE David (COHEN David) B149
BLUE Peter B83
BLUE Ray S198A
BLUE Vicki R163
BLUE ASH B149A
BLUE CAPS V32
BLUE CHEER B150
BLUE JAYS B151
BLUE MAGIC B151A R133
BLUE MINK B152
BLUE MOUNTAIN EAGLE B152A
BLUE NOTES B153
BLUE OYSTER CULT B154
BLUE RIDGE RANGERS F79
BLUE STEEL B154A
BLUEBELLS L4
BLUECHEL Ted A106
BLUEFIELD David B256
BLUES Elwood (AKROYD Dan) B155
BLUES Joliet Jake (BELUSHI John) B155 N10
BLUES BAND B154B
BLUES BROTHERS B155
BLUES DIMENSION B155A
BLUES INCORPORATED B156
BLUES MAGOOS B157
BLUES PROJECT B158
BLUESBLASTERS M13A
BLUESBREAKERS M11
BLUESOLOGY B159
BLUESTONE Harry A52 F134
BLUM Vera S175
BLUMBERG David S216
BLUMBERG Stuart C155 C186
BLUMENFELD Roy B158 S63
BLUNSDON Ian M164
BLUNSTON David M13A
BLUNSTONE Colin B160 E77A M38 P31 Z15
BLUNT Jo D116
BLUNT Robbie B220 B222 C101 G27 J9 S119
BLYTH Graham R93A
BLYTHE Arthur G4
BO STREET RUNNERS B161
BOARD Johnny B233 K45
BOATMAN Bill C14 M53
BOATMAN Jim R173
BOATMAN Merle M30
BOATRIGHT Grant Y16
Boaz S211
BOAZMAN Bill A60 C183 H109
BOB & EARL (GARRETT Bob and LEE Jackie) B162
BOB & MARCIA B163
BOB B,SOXX AND THE BLUE JEANS S200
BOB PEARCE BLUES BAND P47
BOB RIEDY BLUES BAND R85A
BOBBIDAZZLER B164
Bobby Blue Sky D127A
BOBBY FULLER FOUR F133B
BOBIN John L46
Bobo USA
BOBO James M173
BOBO Willie M78 M151 R62 S19
BOCCA Aldo S292
BOCCHINO Chris E31
BOCCHINO Jerri E31
BOCHNER Rick M46
BOCK Richard K36 R25
BOCQUET Roland C60
BODACIOUS B165
BODDIKER Michael B50 B226 C17 C5B E57 H8A H116 J93C J113 L143 M18 M227 N40 O15 P3 P75 R97 R99 R137 T150
BODEN Tony M178C
BODENHAM Geoff A62
BODINE Bill A82 F138

BODINE Rita Jean C77
BODNAR Andrew B176 C42 P25 R162 S149
BODNER Phil C147 D50 I2 J20 K36 K69 K81 L119 M12 M75 P6 S124 T98
BOERS Guus S214B
BOERS Robin G61 M135
BOETCHER Curt B166 C38 J72 M156 S6 W24
BOGAARL Arnold S348A
BOGAN Ann M98
BOGAS Ed B177 C144 R157 T150 U16 W42
BOGDON Ron L24
BOGEB Joel T122B
BOGERT Tim A27 B64A B191 C5 M84
BOGERTY Patrick C81
BOGEY BOYS B166A
BOGGESS Gary I1
BOGGS Gail C62 H9 S18 S124
BOGGS Tom B190
BOGHOSSIAN Sam F134
BOGIE Douglas R1
BOGIE Frank R12
BOGIE Wendy R1
BOGLE Bob V19 V24
BOGNERMAYR Hubert E21A
BOHANNON Jim P49
BOHANON George A11 B144 C17 C45 C76 C153 C179 C180 D59B D103 E7 G121 H96 H150 J75A K45 K48 K56A M21 M78 M229 P126 Q3A R22 S193A S325 T25 W27
BØHLING Claus C185D S69
BOHN Carsten F130A
BOINES Sylvester R168 Y15
BOISADAN Bob C137
BOITA Peter H167
BOIZE B167
BOJE Claus C185D
Bok Bok T37B
BOL Mels C243
BOLAN Marc B168 J75 S252
BOLDEN Isaac M149
BOLDER Trevor B186 R136 S214C U22
BOLES Lanny N23
BOLES Major F116
BOLIN Terry Z8
BOLIN Tommy B169 C147 D40 J31 M218 Z10
BOLLIET Philippe L17
BOLOGNESI Jacques J72
BOLOTIN Michael B124A B169A
BOLT Mike I17B
BOLTON Mick M214 U2
BOLTON Polly D11
BOLTON Steve A115 G100A H73 H111B O9
BOMBACI Thomas L28A
BOMMARIUS Konstantin K11 T162A
BONAROO B170
BONAS Peter C30
BONASS Brendan C87A S263A
BOND Bob B119
BOND Brian P140
BOND Christopher A59 H9 H59 J75A M160 M229 S189
BOND Di G66
BOND Graham A25 B156 B171 B248 D86 H86 K84 M48 Y10
BOND James E, Jr C241 O15 S19 S196 S282 T21 W116A Z8
BOND Jimmy B256 H152 N40 OBA P129
BOND Ronnie T144
BOND Terry R124
BONDAGE Gabriel B172
BONE Patti M227
BONE Ponti C51
BONEBRAKE Don X1
Bones B193
BONES (UK) L117
BONES (US) B173
BONESHAKERS T2
BONEY M B174
BONFANTI Jim R35

BONFILS Tony P115 T158
BONFIRE Mars F94 R16A V32
BONGO Eddie S124
Bongo Asher see GREEN Albert
Bongo Herman A6 C139 G39 P134 R29
BONHAM John B30 L36 S338 W122
BONHAM Vincent R45
BONHOLD Herbert R38
BONILLA Don Armando D83
BONNECARRERE Michel Z18
BONNER Juke Boy B174A
BONNER Leroy O13
BONNERVILLE Ray M232
BONNET Graham B174B R14 R96
BONNETT Steve B176 C4 M45 S149
BONNIWELL Sean M237
BONO Cher see Cher
BONO Salvatore 'Sonny' S188
BONOFF Karla B175 R137 W9 Z11
BONSANTI Neal W136
BONSOR Keith Z12
BONTEMPS ROULEZ B176
BONUS Jack B177 C217
BONUS Pete W82A
BONZIE Frank I1
BONZO DOG BAND B178
BONZO DOG DOO DAH BAND B178
Boofa B95A
Boogie B183
Boogie Woogie Red M90
BOOKER James B179
BOOKER James Carroll III C195 L4 L63 M11 M227 M229 S252 T55 W13
BOOKER Maria S104
BOOKER Walter S104 Z9
BOOKER T AND THE M.G's B180
BOOKIN Barry R101
BOOKIN Mark R101
BOOM BOOM BAND A32
BOOMTOWN RATS B181
BOONE Daniel B286
BOONE Dave R126
BOONE Skip A129
BOONE Steve L133
BOORER Boz P110A
BOORMAN Dave G112
BOOT Andy S102A
BOOT Pete B258
BOOTH Barry P138
BOOTH Bill S311
BOOTH Connie M188
BOOTH Henry B24
BOOTH Mikey see RICHARDS Mikey
BOOTH Richard P103
BOOTH Tim D88
BOOTHE Jack S184
BOOTHE Ken B182
BOOTS B182A
BOOTSMAN R27B
Bootsy see COLLINS William
BOOTSY'S RUBBER BAND B183
BOOTY Mark W82B
BOOZIER Henry B233 K45
Bopee see BOWEN Winston
BOPP Reinhard K11
BOPPIN' BILLIES F40A
BORCH Michael 16
BORD Richard H112
BORDE Hugh V28
BORDEN B.B. M212
BORDEN Richard H112
BORDONARO John T116
BORDY Bob C213
BORG Arto H157C
BORGEOLLI Bill R50
BORGERS Bertus B224A G64 S253A S348A
BORGUDD Tommy S186
BORJAS Larry Q9
BORLAND Adrian O44 S193B
BORN George A88 H99 N9
BORNHOLDT Herbert L139
BORNSCHLEGEL Dieter A113
BOROMEO Charles R40B
BORRILL Steve S195 S218

[463]

BROOKS Denny A132 P129 S272
BROOKS Derek B112
BROOKS Dianne E20 H35 K53 P151 W101
BROOKS Don C247 F128 J18 J31 J48 J53 M41 M232 O27 S252 T98 W11
BROOKS Dudley P125
BROOKS Elkie B226 D4 F65 H50 Q2 S266 V33 Y10
BROOKS Ernie M233 R83 D103 D139 E33 F3A H59 K10 K81 M94 S58 W5
BROOKS Jack K84
BROOKS Joanne H187
BROOKS John O2
BROOKS Karen W11
BROOKS Lala C242
BROOKS Lonnie S323
BROOKS Mike B109
BROOKS Patty B9 S325 W63
BROOKS Paul B227
BROOKS Reg B83 H132 P9 W7
BROOKS Richard W45
BROOKS Roger L75
BROOKS Stuart (B) B112 D133 P128 S285
BROOKS Stuart (Tpt) O18B
BROOME Tom B91
BROOMHEAD Steve W117B
BROONZY Big Bill S329 W93
BROPHY Mick C92A
BROSIUS Chris B274A
BROTHER Bung B228
Brother James C34 C83 D49 H17 H70 L37 S108 T110 Y2
Brother Jomo R35B
Brother Nat S190
BROTHERHOOD OF BREATH B229
BROTHERS JOHNSON J83
BROTHERWOOD Nick W13C
BROTMAN Stuart C179 K6 W92
BROTZMANN Peter G47 V26C
BROUGH Pete W13D
BROUGHTON Alex B230
BROUGHTON Edgar B230
BROUGHTON Loz B230
BROUGHTON Sally B230
BROUGHTON Steve C118 H29 O18
BROUSSARD Austin H31 L75 L115
BROUSSARD Jules D24 M203 S19 S284
BROUSSARD Sam H120 M232
BROUSSARD Tony H59 M111
BROUWER Bart S214B
BROWDER Bill F128
BROWDER Stony Jr D83
BROWN A1 M151
BROWN Alan D9
BROWN Alexandra E31 F33 H96 K48 L28 L55 L63 L65 L143 W8 W119
BROWN Alfred V. C147 T98 W106
BROWN Andy (D) F87
BROWN Andy (K) L64 P10 T89
BROWN Andy (B) B188 F43A V35
BROWN Arthur B231 C18 I22 P31 P145A W72
BROWN Barry M204
BROWN Bill (B) S96
BROWN Bill (Hrns) M143
BROWN Billy M1A
BROWN Bunter B232
BROWN Charles (G) E49 M78 P6 R22 W5 W45
BROWN Charles (K) W13
BROWN Charlie (Sax) P149
BROWN Cheryl R45
BROWN Chris R104
BROWN Clarence 'Gatemouth' B233
BROWN Clyde D116
BROWN Dan C91 I29
BROWN Danny Joe M178A
BROWN Darryl C129
BROWN Dartanyan C90
BROWN Dave (Perc) L72
BROWN Dave (B) (U.K.) T155

BROWN David (B) (U.S.) C217 D12 M167 S19 S36 S111
BROWN David (G) J20 K59
BROWN David (Sax) B109
BROWN Dennis B234
BROWN Derrick T166
BROWN Desmond S74
BROWN Duncan A133
BROWN Earl F134
BROWN Ed F39
BROWN Eddie C153 J92 K45 P44 S250 S251
BROWN Ella J52 M93
BROWN Elmer E7 R112
BROWN Estelle N23
BROWN Fontaine S199B
BROWN Friday M67
BROWN Garnett C17 C129 C147 D50 E7 H19 J75A K45 L66A M75 P149 R21 S14C S250 V9 W13 W28
BROWN Gary D86 G4 M157 P80 T118
BROWN Geoff G7
BROWN George (D) U23
BROWN George (D/K) K80 S111
BROWN Gerald M67
BROWN Gerry A35A C61 C129 C186 C189 K98 L41 M69 U21
BROWN Greg F14
BROWN Harold B268 O35 W17B
BROWN Hux C139 J48 S125 T110 T149 U20
BROWN J,B, Y18
BROWN J,T, F66 H170 J21
BROWN J.W, L64
BROWN James B235
BROWN James (K) B242A P137
BROWN Jeff F26A
BROWN Jennifer F133
BROWN Jimmy B212 R40B
BROWN Jocelyn Q63 I2 T65
BROWN Joe (G) B236 C149 F140 S162
BROWN Joe (B) M17
BROWN Joe (Banjo) P15
BROWN John (B) F10 W130
BROWN John (V) P6
BROWN John (D) B199A
BROWN Julian B231
BROWN Kenji R141
BROWN Kipps A60
BROWN Larry (D) B110 C127 L12 M190A
BROWN Larry (G) J96
BROWN Laurie H11 K61
BROWN Lorenzo C153 H98
BROWN Louis L42
BROWN Marvin A1
BROWN Maxine T70
BROWN Mel B127 B240 H150 K45
BROWN Michael B68 L45 M182 S286
BROWN Miquel O34
BROWN Morrie E, P49
BROWN Niles C60
BROWN Noel P25 S149 H98 H135A L63 M203 O15 P67 P113 P126 R45 R133 W31
BROWN Pat L57A
BROWN Paulette B261 S342 W54
BROWN Pete (V) B171 B237 D58
BROWN Peter (D) S169
BROWN Phil N18 R52
BROWN Phyllis S160
BROWN Randy B238
BROWN Ray (B) B63 B84 B110 B239 H102 M229 S14C S262 W87
BROWN Ray (Tpt) G17 S325
BROWN Richard (K) B54
BROWN Richard (Sax) E55
BROWN Rick (B) A120 B23 F1A P8 S259 S338 W94
BROWN Rick (V) M168

BROWN Robby L64
BROWN Robert see Washboard Sam
BROWN Roger D128 N57 R11 S257
BROWN Ron K45
BROWN Roy B240
BROWN Ruth B241
BROWN Sam A86 B131 C44 M55A M78 S162
BROWN Sammy K. H31
BROWN Selwyn S261
BROWN Sharon F103
BROWN Shirley B242
BROWN Sonny L67B P125
BROWN Stanley B242A
BROWN Steven S177A T161A
BROWN Stewart C148
BROWN Sue K45
BROWN Toni J100 T107
BROWN Tony C237 D139 W45
BROWN Tyrone W25
BROWN Unwin T137
BROWN Vicky B45A C34 C79 E22 F42 H11 H52 H70 K11 L63 M7A N14 P15 R136 S124 S162 W10 W72
BROWN Wilber L128
BROWN William C, K46 G92B
BROWNE Dalton M221D
BROWNE Douglas I10
BROWNE Duncan B160 B243 M140
BROWNE Ivan L49
BROWNE Jackson A59 B244 C45 C233 N53 P137 R22 R109 S124 S196 T39 Z11
BROWNE Mark T137A
BROWNE Phil S19
BROWNE Severin B245
BROWNING Chuck C14
BROWNING John K45
BROWNING Misty K51 T133
BROWNSTONE Kier S72
BROWNSVILLE STATION B246
BROX Annette B171 B247 D129 K84 R92 S338 S349A
BROX Victor B171 B247 D86 D129 K84 R92 S338 S349A
BROZENA Fran B267
BRUCE Bobby B80 C179 F5 G24 H60 P79 S270
BRUCE Bruce S14D
BRUCE Denny H37
BRUCE Jack B131 B156 B171 B248 C189 C218 D99 D124 K84 L70 L103 M40 M79 M80 M111 P119B P122 R5 R60 R122A S182 T148 V21 W52 Z8
BRUCE Michael B103 C182
BRUCE Tubby S262
BRUCE Wayne H195
BRUCE-DOUGLAS Ian U7
BRUFORD Bill A5A B249 F65 G21 G66 H29 H168 K54 N9 P40 P45 S233 U3 W7 Y7
BRUIZER Clive L23
BRUMLEY Tom N21
BRUNEL Bunny C186 S193
BRUNER Kirk F128
BRUNET Max F133A
BRUNIUSSON Hans S14B
BRUNKERT Ola A4 R3 S39
BRUNNING Bob A50A B250
BRUNNING HALL BLUES BAND B250
BRUNNING SUNFLOWER BLUES BAND B250
BRUNO A1 W12A
BRUNO Bill O44A
BRUNO Steve E39
BRUNSON Ted W30
BRUNTON Richard H42 H154
BRUTON Stephen C123 C180 G24 G72 K95 K96 M227 S124 S342
Brutus E62A
BRYAN Kelly G107 Y12

BRYAN Rad C139 D130 H122 J17B R30 R35B R84 T110 T149 W4A
BRYANS Robert B54
BRYANS Richard A131A
BRYANT A,B, P139
BRYANT Andrew B280
BRYANT Brenda B261 G61
BRYANT David B261
BRYANT Eldridge T42
BRYANT Eugene P126
BRYANT Jimmy L65
BRYANT Joel M2
BRYANT Marilyn B221
BRYANT Robert C153 E7 F103C K45 K48 L66A M229 S14C V9
BRYANT Warren M111
BRYDEN Bob C236
BRYER Paul P47
BRYLOWSKI Ron F137
BRYMEN Bruce D122C
BRYON Dennis A49 F7
BRYSON Bill C179
BRYSON Everett Jnr A41 R161
BRYSON Peabo B251 R93 R97
BRYSON Roger J16
BRYSON Wally F90 R35 T17
BUBBLE PUPPY B252
Bubbler see WAUL Franklin
BUCHANAN Bob I23
BUCHANAN Buzzy N43 S211
BUCHANAN Don F54 T41
BUCHANAN Jim D103 R173
BUCHANAN Malcolm A15
BUCHANAN Neil M91
BUCHANAN Robbie C127 G101B L12
BUCHANAN Roy B253
BUCHANAN Rusty E77 O15
BUCHANAN Spoons R118A
BUCHANAN Tony G26A L92
BUCHHOLZ Francis S47
BUCHTEP Forrest M59
Buck B91
BUCK Dirty Dan B197
BUCK Mike F3B
BUCK Nick C217 G94 H161 K13 S3
BUCK Steve G77B
BUCKACRE B254
BUCKBY Pete C26A
BUCKEYE B254A
BUCKINGHAM Lindsey B255 E23 F66 G101B S272 Z11
BUCKINGHAM Steve B213
BUCKINGHAM NICKS B255
BUCKINS Mickey B213
BUCKLER Nick F114
BUCKLER Rick J19
BUCKLEY Kieran D68A
BUCKLEY Stuart D16
BUCKLEY Tim B256
BUCKMASTER Paul A74 B186 F103D J43 S269
BUNKIEWICZ Richard B242A
BUCKNER Juanita D66
BUCKNER Susan J96
BUCKWHEAT B257
BUCKWICH Ray A59
BUDA Max see EPP Fenrus
BUDAMEYER Dave G101A
BUDD Eric F49
BUDD Harold E59
Buddy see HAYE George
BUDDY MILES EXPRESS B151
BUDGIE B258
Budgie L16C S159
BUDHOS Phil H137
BUDIKAS Randy E55A
BUDIMIR Dennis B50 B240 D59B F103C H8A M170 M229 N40 P129 R99 Z8
BUELL Bruce B245
BUFF Ashley E66A
BUFFALO Mad Mississippi D127A
BUFFALO Norton B259 C173 D101 M159
BUFFALO SPRINGFIELD B260 T43
BUFFETT Jimmy B261
BUFFINGTON James C129 D50 J20 K36 L119 M12 M107 N39 T19 S16B V17 V21

BUFORD George 'Mojo' J79A S204 W28
BUGATTI Dominic B189
BUHLER Craig J41 M108
Bulgie see FARQUHARSON Charles
BULKIN Kelly E57
BULKIN Leslie E57
BULL B262
BULL John I18A
BULL Richie K100 M166 P54 R129 S108
BULL Sandy T22
BULL Steve H125
BULLARD Clyde D63
BULLDOG B262A
BULLDOG BREED B262B
BULLDOZER B262C
BULLEN Charles T66
BULLEN Hugh G67
BULLEN Jim C7
BULLEN Roger D11
BULLENS Cynthia 'Cindy' A41 B135 B263 E73 J72 M227 Q3A
BULLET B264
BULLFROG B262D
BULLMEYER Wolfgang F81B
BULLOCK Annie Mae see TURNER Tina
BULLOCK Dan M1
BULLOCK David S202
BULLOCK Hiram A82 F60 J20 M107 M225 S17 S125 S231 S262 T71 W8
BULLOCK Pete A30 H194
BULLOCK Vernon N28
BULLOCK Wayne M32
BULLY Ron G79B
BULTITUDE Paul A13
BUMBLE B, B1
Bumble Bee Slim (EASTON Amos) B265
Bumper M150A
BUNCE David U19
BUNCH B266
BUNDRICK John 'Rabbit' A82 A133 B25 B138 B243 C13 C30 C214 D49 D99 E59 F7 F108 G32 G51 G102 H11 H65 K20 K75 K87 M45 M58 M94 M157 M195 N64 O26 R3 R5 R125 S108 S288A S339 T79 T122 U9
BUNDY Charles C15A C124
BUNDY Rex G2A
BUNETTA A1 P137
BUNETTA Neil R125
BUNETTA Peter C213 P137 R125 T158
BUNKA Roman E52
BUNKER Clive A131B B136 G35 H119 H168 J58
BUNKER Larry B256 F34 F103D J43 S269
BUNN Alan C115
BUNN Allen see Tatheel Slim
BUNN Dick L126
BUNN Lyne S250B
BUNN Roger B237 R149 W61
BUNNELL Dewey A50
BUNNELL George S294
Bunny see SIMPSON Fitzroy
BUNTING Ted C214 M195
BUOYS B267
BURBECK Charles L118
BURBRIDGE Graham K84
BURCH Curtis H65
BURCH Vernon K46
BURCHARD Christian E52
BURCHILL Charlie S126
BURDEN Gary C232
BURDINE Lawrence K45
BURDON Eric A67 B268 H123 W17 W94
BURGER Gary M181A
BURGESS Dave C71
BURGESS John I106
BURGESS Ken M202A
BURGESS Paul B247 C184 R158 T43
BURGESS Pete B188
BURGESS Richard A74 L16

CHALMERS Charles C76 D26 J11 K95 M28 S36 T20 T55 Z22
CHALMERS David T47A
CHALMERS Sandra (Nee RHODES) C76 J11 K95 M28 T20 T55 Z22
CHAMAN Clive A78 A120 B64 D17 D99 H17 H181 K87 L63 M35 S23 W62
CHAMBERLAIN Gerry D50 L21 M107
CHAMBERLAIN Jesse A87 R53
CHAMBERLAIN Robbie Z10
CHAMBERLAIN Ronnie S235 W86
CHAMBERLAND Link L67B
CHAMBERS Ananias V9
CHAMBERS Bubba V9
CHAMBERS Carl B80
CHAMBERS David K78 P45
CHAMBERS George C69
CHAMBERS Jerry M205A
CHAMBERS Jesse B80
CHAMBERS Jimmy B48 C75 C79 D4 J4 Q1
CHAMBERS Joe (G) C69
CHAMBERS Joe (D) C186 V39 Z9
CHAMBERS Joe (V) C179
CHAMBERS John B109 V7
CHAMBERS Lester C69 C179 R22
CHAMBERS Martin P127
CHAMBERS Niamh R116
CHAMBERS Roland K45 L130 N65 014
CHAMBERS Scott P114
CHAMBERS Willie C69
CHAMBERS BROTHERS C69
CHAMBLEE Ed F134
CHAMPION C70
CHAMPION Beverley K1
CHAMPLIN Bill D72A G101B H26A H45 L66A M102 R99 S189 V18B W42
CHAMPS C71
CHANAVAT Jaycee T158
CHANCE Barry B41 B261 N23
CHANCE Floyd K32 L64
CHANCE Slim G107
CHANCLER Ndugu Leon A131D D127 F33 F87A H19 J75A L65 014 R97 S19 S325 W36 W63
CHANDLER Chas A67 W94
CHANDLER Chuck L25
CHANDLER Gene (DIXON Eugene) C72
CHANDLER George C79 C185B E22 G67 020
CHANDLER Ivan D5 W71
CHANDLER Roderick C153
CHANET Chris (RYNAT Eulalie) E69A
CHANEY Larry N23
CHANEY Roy C199A
CHANG Herbert M221D
CHANNEL Bruce C73
CHANTAYS C74
CHANTER Buzz T170
CHANTER Doreen C13 C34 C75 C185B C204 D39 D132 E60 F7 F42 F65 G51 H1 H85 J27 M80 M81 S4 V30 W120
CHANTER Irene C13 C34 C75 C204 D39 D132 E60 F7 G51 H85 J27 M80 S4 V30 W10 W120
CHANTER SISTERS C75
CHANTEREAU M. C1A
CHANTLER Roger B228 F113 W24
CHANTRY Marvin D139 H62 M11
CHAPIN Earl W. C129 S168 T147 W106
CHAPIN Harry C76
CHAPIN Steve C76
CHAPIN Tom C76
CHAPLIN Blondie B56 C77 D13 W21
CHAPLIN Mark L131
CHAPMAN Andru C78

CHAPMAN Clete L3
CHAPMAN Grady P75 R111
CHAPMAN Graham M188
CHAPMAN John C209
CHAPMAN Michael C78 D68
CHAPMAN Paul L114 U22
CHAPMAN Phil M67
CHAPMAN Rob G51A T132
CHAPMAN Roger B47B C79 E46 F12 H123 S300 T59
CHAPMAN Steve A33 J108 M15 P106 S285
CHAPMAN Tony H106 R133
CHAPMAN Vance M182
CHAPPEL Clive L59
CHAPPELL Gary Lee C212
CHAPPELL Les L131
CHAPPELL Nigel C87
CHAPPELL Ray S31
CHAPPELL Russell 046
CHAPPELLE Helen B45A C141 L63 L101 L142A N27C R84
CHAPPELLE Vince T28
CHAPTER THREE M80
CHAQUICO Craig C173 J46 K10 S157 T136
CHARGE C80
CHARIG Mark B2 B159 C63 CB0A D35 H154 K52 K54 N50 S182 T95 W135 Y10
CHARIOT C80B
CHARLATANS C81
CHARLERY Alain M49
CHARLES August R124A
CHARLES Bobby (GUIDRY Robert) B29 B282 C82 L132 W129
CHARLES Darryl 'Chili' A133 C83 C210 G24 H70 H73 M18 M37 018 P15 P28 R82
CHARLES Dave C84 F7 G79 H93 J71 L53 M63 M126 N27 F22A M75 P41
CHARLES Pee Wee L72
CHARLES Peter R19
CHARLES Ray C84 R170
CHARLES Roger W115
CHARLES Tina D93 K41
CHARLES Tony F42 K41
CHARLES Vince A31 A116 H8A
CHARLES CHALMERS SINGERS D26
CHARLES YOUNG CHOIR L117
CHARLIE C85
CHARLIE AND THE PEP BOYS C86
CHARLIE AND THE WIDE BOYS C87
CHARLIE BOY C87A
CHARLIE DANIELS BAND D12
Charlotte C60
CHARLTON Lee B63 M203 S36 S78A
CHARLTON Manny M7 N14
CHARMAN Ricky F21
CHARMING LEMMINGS H169
CHARNOCK Graham M194
CHARRINGTON Valerie H50
CHARRIROW Charlie A41A
CHARTERS Andy M91
CHARTREUSE C88
CHAS AND DAVE C89
CHASE C90
CHASE Bill C70 F109
CHASE Bob H59
CHASE Chevy B194 N10
CHASE Jim T132
CHASE Peter F29
CHASSIN Pascal K77A
CHATER Kerry D74 P145
CHATFIELD Mark G57
CHATMAN Peter see Memphis Slim
CHATTERTON Simon H52
CHATTERTON-DEW Nicholas B54
CHATTON Brian F62 H177 J14 M34 M152 R120 S176 V18B
CHAUDHURI Ashim D67
CHAULK Vince M164 S299
CHAUNCEY Danny M167
CHAUSSE Francois G66

CHAUTEMPS Jean Louis J72
CHAVANAT Jean Claude C62A
CHEAP FLIGHTS C91
CHEAP TRICK C92
CHEATERS C92A
CHEATHAM Bill G16
CHEATHAM Doc M227
CHECKER Chubby (EVANS Ernest) C93
CHEECH & CHONG C94 M170
CHEESMAN Ched S53B
CHEETHAM Willy J4 Q1
CHELSEA C95
CHEMAY Joe C3B J72 N25 P85 R173 W24
CHEMIN Beau D16
CHEN Bobby R39
CHEN Phil A82 A85 B64 B195 B283 C30 C48 D99 F86 G32 H11 H50 H73 J24 L47
CHENIER John M240
CHENIER Ron M240
CHENEVIER Guigou E69A
Cher (nee LAPIER Cherilyn S. later BONO later ALLMAN) C96 S121 S188
CHEREZE Pierre Y23
Cherry R70A
CHERRY Ava B186
CHERRY Don B131 H19 H119 M79
CHERRY Steve S288A
CHERRY Vivian E49 G4 H99 J20 M17 M100 M107 R100
CHERTHOFF Rick B7
CHESBORO Billy F109
CHESS Leonard W28
CHESTER Gary C146 C229
CHESTERMAN Ron D49 M50 S295 T36
CHESTERTON Phil E41
CHETWOOD Michael B30
CHETWYN Max S34
CHEVAL Pierre S280
CHEVETTE Brian E11
CHEVRON Philip R8
CHEW Ray A96 F60
CHEYNES C97
CHI-LITES C98
CHIASSON Warren F60
CHIATE Lloyd M179
CHIC C99
CHICAGO C100
Chicago Joe see JAMMER Joe
Chicago Steve T110
CHICHESTER John S133
CHICKEN SHACK C101
CHIEFTAINS C102
CHIFFONS C103
CHILDERS Marion 'Buddy' E74 M68 N25 T145
CHILDREN C103A
CHILDREN OF GOD C104
CHILDS Peter S282 Y12
CHILDS Phil A71
CHILDS Teddy W89
CHILLI WILLI AND THE RED HOT PEPPERS C105
CHILLIWACK C106
CHILTON Alex B97 B190
CHIMES Terry (also Tory) C130
CHIN Charlie B260 C56 J18
CHIN Eddy T117
CHIN Jon S221
CHIN Valentine Tony A6 B95A B101 B276 H122 M221D
CHINA C107
Chinna see SMITH Earl
CHINO Shuichi H35A
CHIROWSKI Jozef C182 C236 H187 M66
CHISHOLM George A50A F7 F88 L23 M145 020 P100 R61A W128 Z4
CHLANDA Ryche I22
CHOCOLATE AND CLAY C107A
CHOCOLATE WATCHBAND C107B
CHONG Thomas C94

CHOPIN C108
CHOUARD Yves C137
CHOUINARD Bobby E20 033A S323A
CHOVER Marc R171
CHOWNING Rande 046
CHRISMAN Gene K96 015 P125
CHRISMAN Joseph M41
CHRISMAN Woody L110
CHRISTENSEN Denny M232 N53
CHRISTENSEN Erling S69
CHRISTENSEN Jon E11A R178 V39
CHRISTENSON Stacy G1B
CHRISTIAN Billy P91
CHRISTIAN Bobby B251 K77
CHRISTIAN Brian S269
CHRISTIAN Chris S269
CHRISTIAN David P60B
CHRISTIAN Norman K77
CHRISTIANSEN Nicko L95B
CHRISTIANSEN Roy M32
CHRISTIANSEN Svein B12
CHRISTIANSON Bob H12
CHRISTIE Joel M144
CHRISTIE Keith B5 D2 F14
CHRISTIE Lou K81
CHRISTIF Gabor J10A
CHRISTINA Fran F3B
CHRISTLIEB Donald P115 V9 Z8
CHRISTLIEB Peter B127 C158 C180 S262 W6
CHRISTMAS Gene M78
CHRISTMAS Alan A117
CHRISTMAS Annie D88
CHRISTMAS Keith B186 C109 E66 M19
CHRISTO Jaso R127
CHRISTOPHER Dave F135
CHRISTOPHER John C169
CHRISTOPHER Gavin J7 S111 C194 D99 E57 E73 J53 K30 K77 K95 K96 L77 N37 N57 015 P125 P137 R4 T55 T107 T167 Y16
CHRISTOPHERSON Peter T83
CHROME C110
CHROME Cheetah D32
CHRONCHITE Glen D124
CHRONICLE C110A
CHRYSALIS C111
CHRYSLER Chris X2
CHUDACOFF Rick C213 J85A R125
Chuncky Z8
CHUNG Geoffrey D63 F86 I12 J48 M221D R35B
CHUNG Mickey 'Mao' D63 D130 T110 T114
CHURCH Bill H5 M187 M203
CHURCH Joe E33
CHURCHILL Chick C112 F65 T45
CHURCHILL Tony N28
CHURCHYARD Roger D95A K75 M108 W13A
CHURLS C113
CHUTE LIBRE C113A
CHUTER Vernon P47 R104
CHYCOSKI Amie L74
CIAMBOTTI Johnny C42 C144 C193
CIANFLONE Cyril N65
CIANI Suzanne R25
CICCIONE Don F91
CICHON Raymond L28A
CICMARONS C114
CINDRICH Ron L1A
CINELON Mino G66
CINER A1 A51 B225 J38A C.L111 R161 T158
CINILU Mino C113A
CINILU Patrice C113A
CIPOLA Mark C171
CIPOLLINA John C185 C217 G84A H45 M16 M63 Q12 R40 S322 T54
CIPOLLINA Mario H186 L61A Q12 R40
CIPRIANO Eugene A9 A131D C50 C153 L50 M68 N25 P115 S58 S116 V17 Z8
CIRCUS C115

CIRCUS MAXIMUS C116
CIRILO Don F42
CITY C117
CITY BOY C118
CIVIL Peter P131
CIVILIZATION J4A
CIZARD Ed E51
CLAGUE Dave B178 S133 S206
CLAIRE Bob B109
CLAIRE Imogen W72
CLAIRE Kenny W86
CLAIRE T. Will H186
CLAN Bob S273
CLANCY C119
CLANNAD C120
CLANTON Ike E14
CLAPTON Eric B29 B84 B110 B134 B202 C121 C155 C218 D13 D26 D52 D86 D139 F109 F116 G122 H39 H123 H170 K51 K84 L51 L111 M111 027 P122 R173 S59 S252 S276 Z8
CLARA WARD SINGERS C26
CLARE Kenny A109
CLARE Philippa T79
CLAREY Don F48A
CLARK Alan D75
CLARK Allen B233
CLARK Alvin M181C
CLARK Andrew B54 C126 G100A N20 U19 W82A
CLARK Ann H192
CLARK Bobby (D) R147
CLARK Bobby (Perc) 036
CLARK Brian B118
CLARK Buck M111
CLARK Charles K56A
CLARK Dave C122
CLARK Elaine D24
CLARK Eric S292
CLARK Frank (D) A3
CLARK Frank (K) G13
CLARK Frank (G) J72
CLARK Gene B285 C123 D69
CLARK George C207
CLARK Glen M10
CLARK Guy C124
CLARK Iain C223
CLARK Jackie I10 M233 N53 T158
CLARK Jean Francois T67
CLARK John Trevor R31
CLARK Larry M181A
CLARK Louis F126 H55
CLARK Michael H72
CLARK Mike J75A
CLARK Nick B54
CLARK Peter B16
CLARK Peter N48B
CLARK Rhys B72 J69
CLARK Rick M167
CLARK Robin A131 B186 B208 C99 S252
CLARK Rodney S287
CLARK Roger F83A H146 M235 S269 T39 W16A
CLARK Roger Allen M159 W84
CLARK Roy B233
CLARK Sanford C125
CLARK Steve (U.S.) S6
CLARK Steve (B)F5A K5
CLARK Steve (G) D40B
CLARK Susanna C124
CLARK Terry H106
CLARK William S251
CLARK-HUTCHINSON C126
CLARKE Alan R158
CLARKE Allan C127 H132 P31
CLARKE Arthur L69 P149
CLARKE Babe S168
CLARKE Barry C48 L27 S185 T137 V30
CLARKE Bernie F47 T46
CLARKE Billy T61
CLARKE Brian F116
CLARKE Bruce S78
CLARKE Dave R55
CLARKE Delroy R61C
CLARKE Eddie M213
CLARKE Eric 'Fish' H172
CLARKE Frank F14 S108

CRAZY CAVAN AND THE
RHYTHM ROCKERS C215
CRAZY ELEPHANT C215A
CRAZY HORSE C216
CREACH Papa John B169A
C217 H161 J46 K10 M16
CREAM C218
CREAMER Laura J69 L20 M131A
M203 N23 P75 S272
CREAMER Mark J69 L20 N23
CREASEY Clinton B118
CREASMAN George H162A
CREASON Sammy Lee A132
B180 B202 B261 C123 C180
F123A K95 K96 S342 W64
CREATION C219
CREATION (Jap/U.S.) P20
CREATIVE ROCK C219A
CREATIVE SOURCE C220
CREATURES C220A
CREDIBILITY GAP C220B
CREECH David P81
CREED Helios C110
CREED Mary 018
CREEDENCE CLEARWATER
REVIVAL C221
CREEK Cosmo (ANDREWS Walt)
R139
CREGAN Jim B47B B146 D118
F12 H26A H70 H123 L63
R107 S273 S300 S309
CRELLER Gary B259
CREME Lol B247 C222 H163
J110 M67 R20 S35 T43
CRESCENDOS C222A
CRESPO Jimmy F60A L98
CRESS Curt J4B J10A K98
P34 T143
CRESSIDA C223
CRESSWELL Tony M67 S4
CRESTS C223A
CRESWELL-DAVIS Andy K83
S235
CRETU M. B174
CREWSON Roy F106
CRICHTON Ian 55A
CRICHTON Jim 55A
CRICKETS C224 H134
CRIDLIN Mac B110 M18 T107
CRIEFF Tom B255
CRIGENO Nicky L25
CRIGGER Dave A120 P34
CRILL Chester M111
CRILL Connie see EPP
Fenrus
CRIMBLE Thomas S141
CRIME C225
CRIMES Tory see CHIMES
Terry
CRIMINALS C226
Cripple see NELSON Errol
CRISCIONE John S100 T156
CRISP Roger R96
CRISS Pete C227 K67
CRISSINGER Roger 024B P49
CRISTLIEB Don G121
CRITCHLOW Les H184A
CRITTERS C228
CROCE Ingrid C229
CROCE Jim C229
CROCKER Jean-Paul H26A
CROCKER John W117
CROCKETT Greg V9
CRODULA Brian S284
CROFTS Dash A31 C71 S5B
T25
CROLLY Peter C177A
CROMBEY Noel S221
CROMPTON Andy M67
CROMPTON Tom S2B
CRONIN Dan P137
CRONIN Kevin R1A
CRONK Chas S295 W7
CRONOHITE Glenn B177
CRONLEY T.J. B246
CRONSHAW Andrew C230 M45
CROOK Reni B61B
CROOK Ted J71
CROOKES Allan P104A
CROOKS Phillip U9
CROOKS Richard B105 F108A
F109 I2 L4A 015 R108A
R125 S114A W5
CROPPER Clay C107A
CROPPER David P54

CROPPER Steve B110 B155
B180 B202 B253 C58 C109
C158 C231 D5A D115 E15
E40 F134 F139 G10 H92
H120 J22 K46 M85 P114B
R56 R107 R173 R177 S20
S252 S273 W9
CROSBY Bobby E7B S58
CROSBY David B244 B285
C232 C233 C234 G10 H161
J72 K10 K48 M27 M101 M170
N4 R109 S61 S157 S196
S276 T25 Y16
CROSBY Ethan C232
CROSBY Michael Y3
CROSBY AND NASH C233
CROSBY STILLS NASH AND
YOUNG C234
CROSDALE Clarence
'Brooms' D47
CROSLOSE Glen N53
CROSS Billy D139 G74 I24A
W129
CROSS Chris U8
CROSS David C137 K54
CROSS Ed H111B
CROSS Keith T5
CROSS Robert A126
CROSS Tim 018
CROSS COUNTRY C234A
CROSSAN George T75B
CROSSFIRES C234B
CROSSLEY Charlotte E49
CROSSLEY Earl M5 R112
CROSSLEY Raymond G17
CROSSMAN Fred P131
CROSTHWAIT Jim W59
CROTTY P.J. H70
CROUCH Dick P42A
CROUCH Hondo W11
CROUCH Sandra J95 T27
CROUCHER Tom S19
CROUDACE Gary F130
CROW C235
CROWBAR C236
CROWDER John B105 I2 W5
CROWDER Robert D66 H170
CROWE Ben K65
CROWE George S187A
CROWE Simon B181
CROWELL Rodney C50 C124
C237 E20 H35 L36A
CROWFOOT C238
CROWLEY J.C. P98
CROWNS C39B
CROWTHER Eddie S221
CROWTHER Pete B220A M164
CROWTHER Phil (B) 123A
CROWTHER Phillip (D) F40
CROY Dennis M96
CROY Rick B274A M96
CROZIER George W86
CROZIER Neville F130
CROZIER Sam see BROX
Victor
CROZIER Trevor C165
CRUCIFICTION C238A
CRUDUP Arthur 'Big Boy'
C239
CRUICKSHANK Gordon H69
CRIUCKSHANK Pete F40 G112
CRUISERS I53
CRUMB R. C240
CRUNP Bruce M178A
CRUSADERS C241
CRUSE David M2 014
CRUTZINGER Claudia R171
CRUZ Bobby F17
CRUZ Celia F17
CRUZ Rafael B20B K36 M206
S124 W8
CRUZER Beegie C14 C194
S272
CRYAN SHAMES C241A
CRYPT KICKERS P7B
CRYSLER Ken S245
CRYSTAL MANSION C241B
CRYSTALS C242
CSAPO George 090
CSERNITS Billy R177
CUBER Ronnie A123 A131
B57A B85 G19 K36 K69 L41
L80A L119 M17 M46B M108
M111 M225 P99 S215 S262
T20 V17 Z8

CUBERT Joe R177
CUBY AND THE BLIZZARDS
C243
CUCURULLO Warren Z8
CUDWORTH Nick S133
CUFF Mark H35
CUFFLEY John C141 T14
CULLEN Angus C223
CULLEN Anne W10
CULLEN Michael V21
CULLEN Wayne D125
CULLERS Randy K95 L77
CULLEY John B119 C223
CULP Phil S177A
CULPAN David M80
CULPEPPER Tom F116
CULPIN Graham N42
CULT C244
CULTURE C245
CUMBERBATCH Ken H99
CUMBERBATCH Trevor K41
CUMMING Bryan M21 P114
CUMMINGS Burton B9 C38
C246 G115 N26A
CUMMINGS Diana P41
CUMMINGS Douglas P41
CUMMINGS George D85 P112
CUMMINGS George S120
CUMMINGS Julian P41
CUMMINGS Keith S198
CUMMINGS Kris C298
CUMMINGS Pat L44
CUMMINGS Pete G81B
CUMMINGS Vernon 047
CUMMINS Steve H37
CUMMINS Trevor H145
CUNDALL Steve D120
CUNHA Rick C247 H35 H77
S272 W88
CUNNINGHAM Bill B190
C247 N53 S272 W88
CUNNINGHAM Blair J81 R23
CUNNINGHAM Bob M79
CUNNINGHAM C. G79
CUNNINGHAM Carl B36 R56
CUNNINGHAM Casey B173
CUNNINGHAM Gayle S108
CUNNINGHAM George L42
CUNNINGHAM James M212
CUNNINGHAM Ronnie Lee
L26 P77
CUNNINGHAM Steve M57A
R53
CUNNINGHAM Tom K11
CUOMO Bill B170 C123
H116 M18 M123 015 55B
CUOMO Brian G69 I22 V21
CUOMO Jim A33 B104A C119 R134
G46 H65 I22 P5 W128
CUOMO Richard R101
CUPPLES Peter S312
CURE C247A
CURIEL Juanita C129
CURNIFFE Winston P108
W37
CURNOW Creeper T6B
CURNOW Ian S54
CURRIE Billy N63A U8
V35A
CURRIE Cherie C248 R163
CURRIE George D18
CURRIE John P73
CURRIE Kevin B272 S333
CURRIE Laurie A15
CURRIE Steve B168 S209
W130
CURRY Dave L57A
CURRY Tim C249 S124
CURTIS Adrian see
GURVITZ Adrian
CURTIS Andy R33
CURTIS Billy V21
CURTIS Ced V11
CURTIS Chris R147 S60
CURTIS Clem F90A
CURTIS Clifton S251
CURTIS Dave R147
CURTIS Eddie C67
CURTIS John P119
CURTIS Linda P124
CURTIS Little Joe C250
R56
CURTIS Mac C250A
CURTIS Michael C216

CURTIS Nick D99
CURTIS Paul see GURVITZ
Paul
CURTIS Peter D68
CURTIS Phil (formerly
SHUTT Phil) B231 D39 D92
F101 S217 T89 V18B
CURTIS Rick C216
CURTIS Sonny C121 C224
C250B V19
CURULEWSKI John S314
CURVED AIR C251
CUSACK Julian S218
CUSACK Peter F123
CUSANO Vinnie H51 N65
CUSHNIE Scott A16 C217
H62
CUSSEAUX Zulema B57A F103
M12
CUSSICK Ian T103A
CUTHBERT Doug J15A
CUTHELL Dick D49 J16 M127
Q1 R53 R84 S74 S207 S261
W4A W23
CUTLER Chris A88 B69 H101
CUTLER Chris L95A
CUTLER Ian H194
CUTLER Ivor C252 W135
CUTLER Phil 040
CUTLER Rick S106
CUTLIFFE Vince T132
CXIGANY Laszlo G35A
CYANIDE C253
CYBER Ronnie T20
CYBORG John L. C110 C253A
Cyclops I17B
CYMANDE C254
CYR Marshall N23 W106
CYRCLE Les M50
CYRILLE Andrew B131 G90
M79
CYRKLE C255
CZUKAY Holger C25 C145
C256

D.C. NIGHTHAWKS D1
O.F.K.BAND D1A
D.M.Z. D1B
D.P.'s D51
DABNEY Russell J113 P24B
W117
DABON Robert G4 M149
DA CAMERA SINGERS P140
DA COSTA Glen A6 H105
R134
DA COSTA Paulinho B110
B226 C36 C38 C241 D3 DB3
E7 G40 E55 F33 F87A F103C
H150A L65 L119C L143 M128
P44 R97 R99 R115 S14C S4A
S250 S273 T1B V18B W24
W27 W32A
DA CUICA Zeca A131
DACUS Donnie C100 H120
J69 010 P114B R123 S276
T6B
DADA D4
DADDY COOL D4A
DADDY LONGLEGS D5
DAFFERN Willy C31
DAGLAND Karen S333A
D'AGOSTINO Frank I22 V21
DAGRADI Tony L11B S56
DA GREASE Dewey see DEWEY
Greg
DAHL Anders A4
DAHL Freddy S12A
DAHL Sverri Z19
DAHLSTROM Patti D5A
DAHME Jim E39
DAILEY Don D5B
DAILEY Harry B261
DAISLEY Bob 033E R14 T170
W74
DAKER Rhoda S207
DAKING Geoff B157
DAKOTAS D6 K93
Daku 'Potato' 034
DAKUS Wes D6A
D'ALBUQUERQUE Mike D7 E34
V35

DALBY Andy B231 D39 V18B
DALDIN Herman P60B
DALE Dick M191
DALE Glen F87
DALE Paul M91
DALE Peter K52
DALE Robin S2
DALE Rollice K17 039
D'ALEO Angelo D74
DALEY Dan F108A
DALEY John A9
DALEY Joseph M53
DALEY Patt D26
DALEY Wayne S63
DALL'ENESE Gilbert P9
DALLAS Karl D58
DALLAS COUNTY D7A
DALLON Lee S210A
DALTO Jorge B85 M102 W25
DALTON Dirk W92
DALTON Eric F74
DALTON Erik S199B
DALTON Gary J69
DALTON Jack C168
DALTON John K61
DALTON Kathy D8
DALTON Mitch E77A M203
DALTON W.C. R59
DALTON BROTHERS D8A
DALTREY Peter F5A K5
DALTREY Roger D9 W7 W72
DALY Brian F55 H151 S313
DALY Geoff A23 C159 F42
G11 L11 Q2-S107 W13A W128
DALY George P112
DALZIEL Alan P36
DAMAGE Donnie R151
DAMAIN Derek C251
D'AMATO Maria see MULDAUR
Maria
DAMBRAU Jeff L8
DAMERON Tadd D27
DAMIAN Luis F. B244 G24
Z11
DAMIANI Chip R64
D'AMICO Joey C212
D'AMICO Nick C140A
D'AMICO Tony H187
DAMMAS Jerry S207
DAMNATION D9A
DAMNED D10
DAMRON Mark R68
Dan A66
DAN Michael M133 T166
DAN HICKS AND HIS HOT LICKS
H112
DANAHER Thomas A129
DANCE BAND D10A
DANCIK Mitchell J112
DANDO SHAFT D11
D'ANDREA John H60 R54
DANDREN Richard V6
DANDY Jim (MANGRUM J.D.)
B114 F65
DANE Barbara C69 H152
DANELLI Dino B262A C62 F90
N65 R34
DANGEL Rick F69
D'ANGELO Jean Yves K19
D'ANGELO Renato B28
D'ANGELY J.J. Bouchet E18B
DANGERFIELD Matt B196
DANGLER Jackie B261
DANIALSON Ake M137A
DANIEL David W63
DANIEL Pebble N23 N25 I9
DANIEL Ray W115
DANIELAK Stefan
 'Wildschwein' E63 G106
DANIELS Charlie B109 C217
D12 D139 G104 K81 M93 M232
M26 M227 R99
DANIELS Ed G4 J20 K36 L119
M26 M227 R99
DANIELS Eric G79A
DANIELS Gideon B109
DANIELS Jess K45
DANIELS Kenny K27A
DANIELS Ritchie D42
DANIELS Stephen D50
DANIELS Willie C. P67
DANJUMA Ras M133
DANKO Rick B29 D13 D139
F116 H15 L111 S252 T134
DANKO Terry D13 F116 H62
DANKOWITZ Edith I27

Da/De

DANN Earl D17
D'ANNA Elio N60 O33D
DANNA Jean-Luc S280
DANNEMAN Don C255
DANNY AND THE JUNIORS D14
DANNY WILD AND THE
WILDCATS W76
DANTER Brian T37C
DANZA Dave M179
DARBY Alan C7
Darcus W30
DARENSBOURG Joe B221 F5
DARKS Trevor A126 M211A
D'ARLES Fernand Z2
DARLING D15
DARLING David H62 S231
DARLING Diane C194
DARLING Erik C164
DARLINGTON Wilf A103
DARLOW Eva P136
DARNALL John H52A
DARNELL August D83
DAROU Alex K28 P35
DARREN Jenny D16
DARRINGTON Steve B211
DARROW Chris C188 D17 D60
F109 K6 M113 N53 O10 R28A
S272 T25
DARROW Steven D17
DARTS (U.K.) D18
DARTS (U.S.) D18A
DARVILLS Nigel M119
DARWAY Chris C228
DASH Sarah J70 L4
DASHIELL Russell Al C238
D18B H38 S65 T150
DA SILVA Ana R17
DA SILVA Everton P2
DASKOFF Isabelle B15
DATA Darrell B254
DATIMEN Udo K89
DAUGA Philippe B102
DAUGHERTY J.D. N48A R118
S170
DAUGHERTY Pat B114
DAUGHTERS OF ALBION D19
DAUGHTRY Dean A111 C25A
F102 K81 L44
DAUIELGSON Palle V26C
DAULTREY Dots C165
DAUNER Wolfgang D19A P115
DAVANI Pinky L74
DAVANI Dave P4
DAVE CLARK FIVE C122
DAVE DEE DOZY BEAKY MICK
& TICH D20
DAVENPORT Barry G85
DAVENPORT Billy B282 D139
DAVENPORT Bob T6
DAVENPORT Darius La Noue
A129 B194
DAVENPORT Paul B222
DAVENPORT Wallace W47
DAVERSA Jay D127 S14C
DAVEY Billy W24
DAVEY AND THE BADMEN D20A
DAVID Gary S272
DAVID Jay S120
DAVID John (D) D85
DAVID John (B) A26 F7
M128 W29A
DAVID Kal F3A M135 R22
DAVID Marty H139A L111
M203 Y12 Z11
DAVID Randall M84
DAVID CAMPBELL STRINGS
K48
DAVID KATZ ORCHESTRA S34
DAVID PEEL AND THE LOWER
EAST SIDE P53
DAVID SWAIN SECTION M192A
DAVIDOWSKI Steve D79
DAVIDS James C146
DAVIDSON Brent D21
DAVIDSON Brian S307
DAVIDSON Dianne B200 C14
D21 F7 H52A R137 R173
DAVIDSON George B282
DAVIDSON Greg (Ella Guru)
B72
DAVIDSON Jos S113 S204
DAVIDSON Lenny C122
DAVIDSON Les E8 W13A
DAVIDSON Paul Mitchell
C209

DAVIDSON Steve C56
DAVIE Hutch P49
DAVIE Jon G114 S66
DAVIE Alun D22 H70 L63
S266 S352 W89
DAVIES B.G. P129
DAVIES Bassett S102A
DAVIES Brian P129
DAVIES Cam F18 M191
DAVIES Cliff Y17
DAVIES Cyril B156 D23 K84
DAVIES Dave K61
DAVIES Dennis B186
DAVIES Diana C209
DAVIES Digger P10
DAVIES Doug S63
DAVIES Ed O47
DAVIES Gail A132
DAVIES James A34 Q11
DAVIES John (D) M121
DAVIES John (Tpt/K) H69
DAVIES Megan M180A
DAVIES Noel S74
DAVIES Pete U4
DAVIES Phil Q11
DAVIES R. E20
DAVIES Raymond Douglas
(V/G/K) K61
DAVIES Rhell E59
DAVIES Richard S333
DAVIES Rick C112
DAVIES Rod S119
DAVIES Roger H125
DAVIES Ron D23A
DAVIES Roy B47C B77 B283
D95A G67 K51 R125 T149
DAVIES Russell A109
DAVIES Taffy G1
DAVIES Trevor (Dozy) D20
DAVIES Vicki D23A
DAVIES William P107
DA VINCI Paul H42 R40B
CRESWELL-DAVIES Andy
DAVIS Andy Creswell see
DAVIS Ann Esther W10A
DAVIS Anthony R157
DAVIS Art S168
DAVIS Betty D24
DAVIS Billy B24
DAVIS Blind John C135
S329 T9B W93
DAVIS Bobby M68
DAVIS Bud T13A
DAVIS Buddy D12
DAVIS Butch R96
DAVIS Carlton 'Santa' A6
B95A B101 C139 I1A L58A
T155A U1
DAVIS Carolyn L119B
DAVIS Charles M79 S111
W30A
DAVIS Cliff I8 N63
DAVIS Clifford D66 M20A
DAVIS Costo B41
DAVIS Crystal K47
DAVIS Dai A109
DAVIS Danny (NOWLAN
George) A110
DAVIS David W110
DAVIS Delford N50B
DAVIS Dennis F87A J7 W119
DAVIS Digger B230
DAVIS Donna J11 K56A
DAVIS Douglas D99
DAVIS Fannie M22
DAVIS Frank D25A
DAVIS Frank J. C158
DAVIS George (G) N39
DAVIS George (Flt) Z9
DAVIS Graham B137
DAVIS Harvey D63B
DAVIS Henry J113 K46 K51
L2 M218 P67 W31
DAVIS Howard J84
DAVIS Huey C177C
DAVIS Ivory R115
DAVIS Jeff (B) A45
DAVIS Jeff (D) L64
DAVIS Jeff (Tpt) N39
DAVIS Jesse Edwin A116
B84 B144 B221 B244 C123
D26 D99 D139 G121 H39 K45
K46 L51 M53 M111 M159 M191
M227 N23 O16 P28 R98 S10
S111 S252 S273 T91 V3

DAVIS Jesse F42
DAVIS Jimmie L2
DAVIS Jimmy (B) D96
DAVIS Joe Lane C179 C217
K51
DAVIS John (Horns) A96
DAVIS John (K) J92
DAVIS Kim P109A
DAVIS Krystal S198A
DAVIS L.C. B87
DAVIS Larry R112
DAVIS Larry S115
DAVIS Link A102
DAVIS Lloyd P149
DAVIS Louis John P15
DAVIS Lynn D127
DAVIS Mark R141 S250 W31
DAVIS Marlena O33
DAVIS Martha M210A
DAVIS Maxwell J21 W30
DAVIS Mel (Tpt) A131 L69
M12 M75
DAVIS Mel (Cello) T60
DAVIS Mercedes B17
DAVIS Michael (B) D56
M1
DAVIS Mike (Tpt) A23 B83
F14 H50
DAVIS Mike (G) B19
DAVIS Miles D27 M40
DAVIS Ned B253
DAVIS Orville H195 R73
DAVIS Paul (U.K.) G77A
DAVIS Paul (U.S.) A111
D27A
DAVIS Paul (G) C14
DAVIS Paul (Perc) M82
DAVIS Pluma B233 K45 P26
DAVIS Raheem Lee Michael
L65 S250
DAVIS Ray S31 S235
DAVIS Ray M225
DAVIS Raymond F137 P29
DAVIS Richard C40 C186
P25 S139 W125
F109 I2 J48 L69 M21 M78
M79 M125 M177 M203 M233
N65 O15 R22 S111 S125
S168 S229 T147 V12 W5
DAVIS Rob M223
DAVIS Spencer D28 M101
M191 W89
DAVIS Steve B41
DAVIS Sue S112A
DAVIS Terry S284
DAVIS Theresa E55
DAVIS Tim M159 S111
DAVIS Wade 'Holmes' L69
DAVIS Walter W93
DAVIS Walter D86 W30A
DAVIS Warner T93
DAVIS Willie D38A
DAVISON Brian 'Blinky'
A84 D29 G66 H29 N44 R61
DAVISON Ray A30A
DAVISON Tony A72
DAVY Colin F21 L16A
DAVY Stephanie R144A
DAVY Steve S258
DAW Jef T36
DAWE Michael P119
DAWE Tim D29A
DAWES Biff B274A
DAWES Tom C255
DAWKINS Jimmy 'Fastfin-
gers' D30 E67 R168 S323
Y13
DAWN Ron W101
DAWSON Claire A98
DAWSON Colin F140B
DAWSON David C247 W88
DAWSON Jack S113
DAWSON John G84 N32
DAWSON Mark A132 F128
DAWSON Steve S32A
DAWSON Warren T158
DAWTAS Negus S190
DAX Danielle L48A
DAY Billy H70
DAY Bobby (BYRD Robert)
D30A
DAY Brian W117B
DAY Bruce P3
DAY Charles S120
DAY Chuck M18

DAY Doris M125A
DAY George M141C
DAY James C133 G100 K32
M211 V18
DAY Michael F132
DAY Mike L59 R12
DAY Rusty C5
DAY Terry see MIALL Terry
DAY Wyatt A86
DAY BLUNDERS D30B
DAY OF THE PHOENIX D31
DAYAN Dwytt H79
DAYDE Joel Z18
DAYE Cory D83
DAYE Stuart L107 R39
DAYES Kenneth Lloyd C245
DAYEZ Michel J105B
DAYLIGHT D31A
DAYLIGHTERS B193
DAYS Guy N49
DEACON Graham B151 L60
F65 J16 J27 M157 S179 W72
DEACON John Q8
DEACON Mike D18 D39 F65
G89 N57 Q6 V33
DEAD Fred I19A
DEAD BOYS D32
DEAD FINGERS TALK D33
DEAD KENNEDYS D33A
DEAD SEA FRUIT D33B
Deadley Headley see
HEADLEY Felix
DEAF SCHOOL D34
DE AGUERO Joey 'Cosmo'
A116 L128
DEAL Stuart F34
DEALER D34A
DEAN Barry A120
DEAN Bob (G) J40
DEAN Bobby (Trom) F109
M173
DEAN Dan W32A
DEAN Dickie M29
DEAN Ed B73 M114A M157
P25 S139 W125
DEAN Elton B131 B159 C63
D35 D118 H154 H175 K52
N50 P146 S182 T95 W135
DEAN John M180
DEAN Nora C139
DEAN Paul L130A S299A X2
M94 S285
DEAN Richard M232
DEAN Roger M111
DEAN Snoopy H157
DEAN Stephen H9
DEANE Johnny S108
DEANE Marvin R78
DE ANGELIS Joe T85
DEANS Rob H75
DE ANTHONY August M200
DEARBORN Antoine S58
DEARDORFF Danny S58
DEARMAS Annie Rose K30
DEARMORE Terry B41 K95
L77 M11
DEARTH John P99
DEASY Kathy G15 R101
DEASY Mike C11 D23A G15
H102 J69 M125A P125 R101
S272
DE'ATH Rod G5 M202C
DE BASTION Richard B230
DE BERRY Jimmy H159
DEBIJ Louis F136
DE BOIS Richard A27
DEBRECENI Ferenc O24
DEBRIS D35A
DE BUHR Alice F18
DE BURGH Chris D36
DECAMERON D37
DECAMPS Christian A64
DECAMPS Francis A64
DE CARLO Alan 'Addison
Al' B33 L13
DE CARO Nick B84 C11B D5A
G121 J93C K96 L72 M21 M68
M187 O46 P32 S124 S216
S269 T25 W9
DE CASTRO Leo R118A
DECEMBERS CHILDREN D37A
DECENNIUM D37B
DE CHANCY Francois A23
DE CHANT Charles H9
DECKER Jim N25
DECO Sarah P138

LE COCQ Jimmy F13 R148A
DE CONG Ric B166
DE COTEAUX Bert K46
DE COURSON Hughes M57B
DE CRESPIGNY Camilla M202
DE DANANN D38
DEDRICK Lyle S100
DEE Brian J72
DEE Dave see HARMAN Dave
DEE Ellis M1
DEE Ever W37
DEE Joey C254
DEE Joey (DI NICOLA Joe)
D38A
DEE Kiki D39 E40 H123 J72
DEE Koko D127A
DEE Willie G1A
DEEFHOLTS Ray V36
DEEGAN Martin F43A
DEEP D39A
DEEP FIX M194
DEEP PURPLE D40
DEEP SIX D40A
DEES Bruce L60 N23
DEF LEPPARD D40B
DEFENDERS D40C
DEFERERI John T79
DE FLEUR Zenon (HIEROWSKI
Zenon) C199
DE FONDA Frank M131A
DE FUENTES Ruben H135A
DEGAP Gilmore D50
DE GENERES Tommy F105
DE GRASSE Bloomdido Bad
see MALHERBE Didier
DE GREEF Roland M30A
DE GUEVARA Ruben Ladron
R152 Z8
DEHAYE Baudouin J105B
DEINUM Herman B155A C243
H60 S348A
DEI ROSSI Miki L54A
DE JOHNETTE Jack A4A D40D
M79 M138A R178 S19 S104
V39 Z9
DE JONG Letty V17
DEJONG Sacha L127
DE JONG Ted P118
DEJONG Theo K16
DE JONNES Smiley A105 C80
M94 S285
DEKBAR A. R67
DEKENGA Bob F136
DEKKER Cor E27
DEKKER Desmond D41
DE KLERK Rijn Peter K16
DEL VIKINGS D43
DE LA BEDOYERE Count see
STABLE Simon
DELACY Steve H135A
DELAGALTE Georg B174
DELAGARDE Henri S280
DELAGARDE Mario R111
DE LALO Manfred Z2
DELANDRO Winston A99A B48
B105 C39A F86 L63 Q1 S285
T149
DELANEY Sean S121
DELANEY & BONNIE B202
DE LA PARRA Adolfo
'Fito'C26 F109 H150
DE LA PORTE Michel S280
DE LAURO Joey M232
DEL BARRIO Eddie E7
DEL BARRIO George H96
DEL BELLO Lisa D36
DELCLOO Claude M221B
DE LEEUWE Peter E27
DE LEON Rosalinda S17
DELEONIBUS Al L108
DELEONIBUS Dottie K30 N37
S269
DELESTON Gilles W8
DELEUZE Gilles H89A
DELFONICS D42
DELFT Stefan B23
DELGACHO Vince D67
DELGATTO Lew A35A A131
B208 B225 F109 G19 H92
H185 L4A M26 M75 M107 P123
S124 T156 T158 W107
D'ELIA Joe I2
D'ELIA Roger G73
DE LISLE Christine S272
DELIVERANCE D139 W45
DELL Roger P110

[473]

DODGION Jerry C164 D50 J20 M75 N39 S168 W13
DODSON Brian L95
DODSON Mark T170
DODSON Rich S239
DODSON Sam T132
DOE John X1
DOERGE Craig B25 B110 B244 C38 C123 C233 E40 H52A H102 K17 K22 P76 S70 T25 T98
DOERING George A120 W24
DOG SOLDIER D91
DOGGER Bunk D92
DOGGEREL BANK D93
DOHENY Ned R101 S196 Z11
DOHERTY Billy U11
DOHERTY Denny M61 M224
DOHERTY Mike S164
DOHIISCH Hanna T143
DOLAN Donny F128 L122 S269 W11
DOLAN Joe S346
DOLAN Mick H25
DOLAN Steve M25 S131
DOLANON Randel W106
DOLDINGER Klaus P34
DOLEMAN Ron M21
DOLENZ Micky M181
DOLIN Bob B103
DOLL D94
DOLL BY DOLL D95
DOLLAR Beau M211 N23
DOLLASE Jurgen C192 G3A W13D
DOLLASE Rolf W13D
DOLLEZ Jean-Marc S280
DOLLINS Adolph H170
DOLPHIN D95A
DOLPHY Eric H10
DOMAGALSKI Victor H19
DOMANE Richard W68A
DOMANICO Chuck B84 C179 C180 F34 H8A H60 K77 M125 M170 O15 P114 S111 S180 S196 T107 W65A
DOMINATORS W29A
DOMINIC John B161
DOMINIC Steve W26
DOMINIQUE Carl Axel S186
Domino L63
DOMINO Antoine 'Fats' D96
DOMINO Floyd (HABER Jim) A102
DOMINOES H122
DOMMERS Michael W13D
DON AND DEWEY D97
DON ELLIOTT SINGERS N35
DON HARRISON BAND H38
DONABLE Ernest S329
DONAHUE Jerry A82 D49 E41 F6 F89 G27 G98 H42 H74 K24 K75 M21 M45 M108 P75 P107 R11 S185 S313
DONALD Chris S78
DONALD Keith W125
DONALD Peter M48 M74
DONALD Timi B148 C13 D49 E41 F6 G103 I20 K97 M25 M38 M108 P90 R106 T79 W125
DONALDSON Bobby C146 H15 S168
DONALDSON Lloyd 'Jah Bunny' B120 M109 P80C P108 R61C
DONALDSON Pat A30 A62 A82 B138 B266 C9 C13 C109 C165 D2 D49 E41 F6 F21 F89 G27 G32 G98 H11 H42 H48 H65 H110 J84 K28B K97 L30 L36A L63 M19 M21 M25 M38 M108 M121 M180 N63B P107 P138 R106 R125 S108 S185 S339 T79 W71 W89 W125
DONATO Joao F103D
DONEGAN Anthony James 'Lonnie' D100
DONEGAN Patrick 'Chiki' R61A
DONELLY John S270
DONEN David C35C R23

DONIGHT Will B27
DONLINGER Jim A67D
DONLINGER Tom B144
DONNELLAN Jay L128 M204
DONNELLY Albie A29 M127 P25 R162 S332
DONNELLY Ben I18A
DONNELLY Jim H74
DONNELLY John B83 V26A
DONNELLY Philip C133 D99 K77 V18 Z22
DONNER Ral D98
Donovan (LEITCH Donovan) C182 D99
DONOVAN Bob M79
DONOVAN Dave H55 W122
DONOVAN Sparky B204A
DOOBIE BROTHERS D101 S124
DOOMED D102
DOONAN Michael H87
DOORS D103
DORAN Dave B41 S73 T107
DORE Charlie D104 N57
DORFMAN Jay S350
DORMAN Lee C31 I24
DORN Gary L57
DOROUGH Bob F133 G10 P49 R31
DORSET Ray D105 M230
DORSEY George M75 M227 S168
DORSEY Georgia Tom T9B
DORSEY Jack B177
DORSEY Lee D106
DORSEY Leslie F133
DORSEY Tony M9
DORSIE Lester Y13
DOSS Debi D54
DOS SANTOS Luis A131
DOTSON Rosa D30
DOTT Gerard I16
Dottie B91
DOTZLER Thomas T47A
DOUBLEDAY Marcus B144 E33 M151
DOUCET Michel S187C
DOUCETTE D106A
DOUCETTE Jerry B225
DOUCETTE Thom A38
DOUD Earle D106B F109
DOUGHERTY Tom W44
Dougie see BRYAN Rad
DOUGLAS Bill T150
DOUGLAS Bonnie F134 S63
DOUGLAS Carl H73
DOUGLAS Cleon M163
DOUGLAS Cynthia J11 K56A
DOUGLAS David D96
DOUGLAS Don B261
DOUGLAS Ed S52
DOUGLAS Graeme E13 K100
DOUGLAS Greg G84A M16 M18 M159 M167 M179 R40 T54
DOUGLAS Jimmy S154
DOUGLAS Jonathan S272
DOUGLAS Kevin K47
DOUGLAS Mike D62
DOUGLAS Nat B233
DOUGLAS Pam G94 O34 Q1
DOUGLAS Paul T110
DOUGLAS Steve B56 C146 D74 D106C D139 E14 J36 M96 M163 M191 P75 R173
DOUGLAS Val D63 F86 I12 R35B
DOUIEB Gilles C113A
DOUKAS John E6 K40
DOUMA Danny B100
DOVE Glenn S201B
DOVE Nathaniel M238B S96
DOVELLS D106D
DOVER Dave B268
DOW Gary C20
DOWD Tom J31 W54
DOWE Brenton D107
DOWLE David C204 L11 R164A S300
DOWLER Esther L100
DOWLING Alison W72
DOWLING Ed S56
DOWLING Pete B90
DOWN John Headley see HEADLEY-DOWN John

DOWN Sandra P97
DOWNER Andy D48B
DOWNES Bob D108 D118 R122
DOWNES Geoff Y7
DOWNEY Alan P131
DOWNEY Brian M196 T59
DOWNIE C. P2
DOWNIE Tyrone B276 H122 M88 M221D T114 V21 W4
DOWNING Al M26
DOWNING K.K. J102
DOWNING Tom A5
DOWNING Walter R141
DOWN.LINERS SECT D109
DOWNS Tim M82
DOYLE Bobby B141
DOYLE John M47
DOYLE Mark B263 P123 W48D
DOYLE Peter D110
DOYLE Raphael C9 H11
DOYLE-MURRAY Brian N10
Dozy see DAVIES Trevor
DOZY BEAKY MICK & TICH D20
DRAFFEN Willis B143
DRAGGOTA George M58
DRAGON D110A
DRAGON Darryl K14 M238 T137A
DRAGON Dennis B56 S333B
DRAGONAIRES L39A
DRAHEIM Sue A30 A98 E41 R66 T79
DRAHER Dan R85A
DRAINS Bijou see TOWNSHEND Pete
DRAKE Brian T147
DRAKE Jack M211
DRAKE John N63
DRAKE Nick D111
DRAKE Oma B282 C211 H150 J92 N23 P126 S116 T27
DRAKE Pete B17A D112 D139 F35A F126 H26 H62 K32 L42 M13 M41 M68 M211 N23 P63 P125 R173 S187C T22 Y18
DRAKE Richard A35A
DRANES L.C. P26
DRANSFIELD Barry A98 C165 D49 D113 H180 H194 L84 T79
DRANSFIELD Robin D49 D113 L84
DRANSFIELDS D113
DRAPER Lauren I27
DRAPER Ray D86 R92
DREAM D114
DREAMS D115
DREARES Alfred C146
DREITH Dennis B56 B274A M62 P75
DRIER Bobby H135A
DREJA Chris W94 Y5
DRENNAN Al S45
DRESDEN Martin F77
DRESSLAR Len P137
DREYFUSS Michael M37
DRIFTERS D116 M43
DRIFTWOOD D117
DRIGGINS Tony B246
DRIGGS Karl K90
DRILL Dave R23
DRINKARD Cissy see HOUSTON Emily
DRINKWATER Paul C238A
DRINKWATER Skip H97 W129
DRISCOE Chris S111
DRISCOLL Gary E38 R14
DRISCOLL Geoff M80 S141 W61
DRISCOLL Julie see TIPPETTS Julie
DRISCOLL Ken L114
DRISCOLL Marion S270
DRISCOLL Merlene M1
DRISCOLL Mike H23 P124 T31
DRIVER Laurie A14 D119
DRIVERS D119
DROGAS Wally R148

DRONE M.J. (HOWELLS M.J.) D120
DRONES D120
Droppy D82
DRORI Assa S116
DROS Bob B43A
DROVER Martin A23 B47C C39A C75 C109 F7 F42 F86 G67 H50 H65 H173 M157 R174 S141 W128
DRUICK Dwight D121 L101
DRUICK and LORANGE D121
DRUID D122
DRUIDS OF STONEHENGED122A
DRUMGOLE James K47
DRUMMOND Burleigh A48 P31
DRUMMOND Celia (nee HUMPHRIS) T137
DRUMMOND Don P134
DRUMMOND Keith B116
DRUMMOND Pete T137
DRUMMOND Tim A132 B56 B75 C14 C179 C233 C234 D12 D13 D21 H62 M32 M111 M211 N4 P75 S298 Y16
DRUSS Len H1
DRY CITY SCAT BAND D122B
DRYDEN Spencer J46 K10 N32 S61
DUARTE Ernesto B43
DUBE Joe F108A
DUBIN Michael J65
DUBOIS Davidson T166
DUBOIS John D72B
DU CANN John see CANN John
Duchess (Bo Diddley's sister) D66
DUCK Ian B23 H148 J72
DUCKS D122C
DUCKS DELUXE D123
DUCKWORTH Dell S120
DUCKWORTH Ian S295A
DUCONGE Wendel D96
DUDANSKI Richard O25 R17
DUDECK Gerd G120 K98
DUDEK Les A38 B57A D1A D124 M159 M229 S36
DUDES D125
DUDGEON Gus A118 C78 J72 J86 K78 M50 T36 T45 W49
DUDLEY Cordell D24
DUDLEY Michael S193B
DUDLEY Ron K10
DUDMAN Colin T76
DU DOIT Brigette E66
DUDZIAK Viszula U21
DUFALL Dick B209 F48B
DUFFELL Bee M188
Duffo D125A
Duffy D126
DUFFY John A121 S73B
DUFFY Ray E9 E41 F55 G6 J60 K24 M108 S198
DUFFY Tom A73 B79 H87 L80 W133
DUFINE Jeff W11
DUFORT Dave A133 E8
DUFORT Denise G37
DUFRANE Marcel U17
DUGAN Irv D71
DUGGAN Barry D4 Y10
DUGGAN Colin H125
DUGGAN Noel C120
DUGGAN Padraig C120
Duggie see BRYAN Rad
DUGMORE Danny B175 G60 K17 M232 P114 R137 S196 S272 T25
DUGRENOT Joel C137 M87
DUHAN Johnny G81B
DUHIG David J16 N41
DUHIG Tony A105 J16
DUKE Calvin H81
DUKE David C180 H8A N16A R78 R97 S196
DUKE George B85 B214 C129 C147 D127 O39 P115 Z8
DUKE John (B) C179
DUKE John (Wind) P49
DUKE Mike W54
DUKE Phil G73
DUKE Rashid D127
DUKE Will A30

DUKE AND THE DRIVERS D127A
DUKE JUPITER D127B
DUKES D127C
DUKES Alf C201A
DULAINE Timmy S297
DUMAS Tony M102
DUMLER Earl A9 A52 C39 F78 H8A H96 S196 Z8
DUMLER Eric B256
DUMMER John D18 D128
DUMPTRUCK Humphrey N26A
DUNAWAY Dennis B103 C182
DUNBAR Aynsley (also DUNN Aynsley) B64 B186 C78 D129 F68 H5 H185 J46 J99 L51 L107 M16 M111 O39 R60 R136 S349A Z8
DUNBAR Charlie B231
DUNBAR Kent M174
DUNBAR Nigel J110 L46
DUNBAR Noel 'Sly' A6 B95A B234 C245 D63 D71A D130 G39 H172 I12 J17B M149 P134 P135 R29 R30 R84 T114 W4 W4A
DUNBAR Robbie E6 K40
DUNBAR Sly see DUNBAR Noel
DUNBAR Tommy L70 R155
DUNCAN Al G122 L94 M5 R59 R168 W94
DUNCAN Andy G100A O6A
DUNCAN Cleveland P59
DUNCAN Gary Q12 S157
DUNCAN Kirk B151 C127 F65 J27 S48 T133
DUNCAN Lesley B189 D39 D92 D99 D131 E18 E48 E77A F65 H23 H67 H177 J72 N51 P85 S108 S185 Z24
DUNCAN Malcolm 'Mollie' A131 B266 F42 G32 G102 L27 M23 M176 M206 R82 S35 V33 W54A
DUNCAN Pete B211
DUNCAN Steve N21
DUNCAN Terry L3
DUNCAN Wayne D4A
DUNCAN SISTERS G92B
DUNDAS Lord David Paul Nicholas (2nd son of 5th Earl of Zetland) D132
DUNDEE Harris D133
DUNDEE HORNS R3
DUNFORD Kevin W127A
DUNFORD Mike R65
DUNGEY Charles C14
DUNLAP Bruce J20
DUNLOP David B81
DUNLOP Ian I23
DUNLOP Melvin W33 W116
DUNLOP Russell R118A
DUNMALL Paul D11 W30
DUNMORE Tony S332
DUNN Chris C18
DUNN Donald 'Duck' B17A B155 B180 B202 B253 C58 C109 C180 C231 D26 E55 H92 H120 K46 K51 M3 M78 M85 N55 P137 R107 R173 R177 S273 S342
DUNN Franklyn C114
DUNN Freddie R141
DUNN Joyce S36
DUNN Junior see DUNBAR Aynsley
DUNN Kelly F128 L122 S7 W11
DUNN Kevin R80A
DUNN Larry C45 E7 E55 L28 L65
DUNN Monte M23 I2
DUNN Simon James S103
DUNNE Murphy B155
DUNNE Phil W49
DUNNERY Boz V35
DUNNET Iain K94B
DUNSFORD Martin P62
DUNSTAN Dennis S227
DUNSTERVILLE John W7
DUNTON Peter G118 T5
DUPLANT Sylvain A33A
DUPONT Lenny T61
DUPREE Champion Jack D133 G120 K55

DUPREE Cornell A131 B77
B131 C146 C155 E49 F103
H58 H133 J22 K36 K51 K55
M12 M78 M111 M227 N39 N65
P6 P149 S124 S125 S252
S310 T79B
DUPREE Robert I10
DUPREE Simon see SHULMAN
Derek
DUPREY Peter B48
DUQUETTE Ron R101
DURAM Marc B154A
DURAN Tony R152 Z8
DURANT David M67
DURANT Jake F97A
DURANT Tony F132
DURANTE Jose Ordaz M229
DURE Michael F13
DUREN Van D134A
DURET Michel J105B
DURHAM Eric C20
DURHAM Roger B143
DURHAM Terry D135 S287
DURITY Hollis P28
DURRANT Jane C209
DURRETT Rick T9
DURRILL Johnny V24
DURST Bill T85
DURUTTI COLUMN D136
DURY Ian D137 K41
DURZO John S308A
DUST D138
DU TOUR Pierre M49
DUVAS Gregory W30
DUVERNET Antoine L17
DUVIVIER George C146
S168 S280A
DUWE Micky H126
DVORAK Jim J4
DWELLINGHAM Herschel W36
DWIGHT Reg see JOHN Elton

DWIRE Steve R101A
DWYER Bernie F106
DWYER Gary T37A
DYBLE Judy F6 G29A T79
T125
DYCHE Mick S178 S179 W79
DYCK Ralph J15A
DYER Pete R66 S296
DYER Webster N50B
DYER Benny H5B
DYKE Roy A101 B17 C9 F12
M121 S264 T135
DYLAG Roman U21
DYLAN Bob (ZIMMERMAN
Robert; also Blindboy
Grunt) B29 D139 G61 K81
M27 M100E S7 W84
DYMOND John (Beaky) D20
Dynamite Yan B102
DYSON Bobby J53 K95 M11
DZERIGAN John W129
DZIDZORNU Rocky A25 B39
D111 G27 I28 J9 K17 M53
M94 M101 R133 S276 W16
W116
DZIONY Wolfgang S47

E.L.O. C34
E.L.P. C53
EADES Ronnie A37 A133
B200 B210 C26 D99 E57
F23 F4B G61 H40 J11 K30
K96 L9 L77 L146 M235 N23
P79 R168 S340 T55 W44
EAGAN Ed M240
EAGLE E1
EAGLES E2
EAGLES Steve P77A
EAGLESHAM Bobby E3 F59
EAGLESTONE Hugh C57
EALEY Willie W84
EALING Richard C18
EARHART Billy A45
EARL Colin D105 K50 M230
EARL Diane K13
EARL Raymond H133 S115
EARL Roger F81 S31
Earl Bagga P49
EARLAND Charles G4
EARLE John 'Irish' C45
D10A E77A G1 G49 G52 110A
L59 M41A P25 S203B T86

T170 W130
EARLE Steve C124
EARNSHAW Spencer T. W1
EARS J60
EARTH AND FIRE E4
EARTH BAND M80
EARTH OPERA E5
EARTH QUAKE E6
EARTH WIND AND FIRE E7
EARTHQUAKE E7A
EARTHQUIRE E7B
EARTHSTAR E7C
EASLEY Bill E18
EASLEY Michael W8
EASLEY Paul G16
EAST Chris E7D J110 L46
EAST Dennis S278
EAST Nathan F103C
East Boy Ray D33A
EAST OF EDEN E8
EAST SIDE KIDS E8A
EASTER Larry L81 M68
EASTER Mack G122
EASTMAN Eric G64A
EASTON Amos see Bumble
Bee Slim
EASTON Bob L20
EASTON Elliot C41
EASTON Harold B233
EASTON John W38
EASY STREET E9
EASYBEATS E10
EATER E11
EATON Bill G4 V17
EATON Bobby M130
EATON Dick W3B
EATON Benny B157
EATON Stuart O40
EATON Terry F3A R22
EATON William M17
EAVES Hubert F60 L41
M222A
EBANKS Norman 'Junior'
R61A
EBART Klaus A57
EBERITZSCH Herman R75
EBERSON Jon E11A
EBERSON GRAF HOVENSJO
CHRISTENSEN E11A
EBERT Dennis B192
EBIGWE Patrice Q1
ECCLES Tony S93
ECHITO Martie W18
ECHO AND THE BUNNYMEN
E11B
ECHOLS Denise T15B
ECHOLS John L128
ECHOLS Ron G92
ECKERT John D50 T44
ECKLER Greg R154
ECKLEY Dan N37
ECKLUND Peter B221 B202
G72 H182 M228 O15 R22
ECLECTION E12
ECLIPSE E12A
ECONOMOU Bobby P35
EDDI Charlie C60
EDDIE Clifton H34
EDDIE AND THE HOT RODS
E13
EDDIE BOY BAND B192
EDDIE KENDRICKS SINGERS
K48
EDDIE LESTER CHORALE R20
EDDY Duane E14 E74 S160
EDDY Teddy Jack F116 R173
EDELMAN Randy E15
EDELSTEIN Marc A132 C173
EDEN Alun D92 116 M166
P56 T137 V16
EDEN'S CHILDREN E16
EDENTON Ray C50 J13 K32
K96 M11 M41 N37 P63 R173
Y16 Y1B
EDGAR Ron M156 M237 S6
EDGAR BROUGHTON BAND B230
EDGE E17
EDGE Damon C110
EDGE Graeme E18 M189
EDGE The U5A
Edgemont M135
EDGEWORTH Don K84
EDIN Dolores D139 J13
EDISON Harry 'Sweets'
K48 M229

EDISON ELECTRIC BAND E18A
EDITION SPECIALE E188
EDMED John O68
EDMONDSON Bob L8A
EDMONTON Jerry S265
EDMONTON SYMPHONY ORCHES-
TRA P140
EDMUNDS Dave B274A C42
D3 E19 F81 J110 L135 M63
P25
EDMUNDS Hughes 'T-Zap'
(or Tony Zap) G39
EDMUNDS Michael M205A
EDMUNDS Robert Lu A23
EDMUNDS Terry F41
EDNEY John P54
EDRICK Grey B87
EDWARD BEAR (U.K.) E19A
EDWARD BEAR (U.S.) E19B
EDWARDS Alf L137
EDWARDS Alton O34
EDWARDS Bernard C99 S135
EDWARDS Bill J105A
EDWARDS Bob T88
EDWARDS Cindy D17 R28A
EDWARDS Clive S193 W78
EDWARDS Daniel S338
EDWARDS Danny D68A
EDWARDS Dave U15
EDWARDS Dennis T42
EDWARDS Doug H141 S148
EDWARDS Duke R75
EDWARDS Fred D12
EDWARDS George (Steel)
M75
EDWARDS George (G/B) H1
EDWARDS Gordon (B) B131
C155 D50 E49 F103 H9 H133
K17 L21 L51 M12 M111 M1
M233 O15 O27 P6 P128 S124
S125 S180 S310
EDWARDS Gordon (K) K61
L43
EDWARDS Gordon (G/K/V)
S327
EDWARDS Gwendolyn C158
P137 R39
EDWARDS Honey Boy F66
EDWARDS Jackie D82 E19C
EDWARDS James M104
EDWARDS Jimmy T166A
EDWARDS John (B) G94
EDWARDS John (D) V28
EDWARDS John (Irom) H183
S31
EDWARDS Jonathan E20 H35
EDWARDS Joseph R124A
EDWARDS Juma H99
EDWARDS Kenny B175 C171
G60 M108 R22 R137 S196
S269 S282 W9 W21 Z11
EDWARDS Liz R174
EDWARDS Lyn P136
EDWARDS Lynnie E20
EDWARDS Max P2
EDWARDS Mike E34
EDWARDS Mike L95A
EDWARDS Nokie V19 V24
EDWARDS Pete 'Plug' L142
S302A
EDWARDS Rob C168
EDWARDS Roy A98A C159 G35
M45 P77B
EDWARDS Roy E21 R6
EDWARDS Scott A52 A59
B47A B50 B127 B225 B226
C17 C5B C246 E40 E71 H9
H243 J73A J92 J113 K45
M160 M229 R70 R101 R115
W6 W119
EDWARDS Si B41 M11
EDWARDS Skip F50 R100 M2B
M191 R101
EDWARDS Steve (G) E38
EDWARDS Steve (G) M123
EDWARDS Steve (V) G56A
EDWARDS Teddy J97 W116A
EDWARDS Terry W18
EDWARDS Terry N41
EDWARDS Tony S16 W38
EDWARDS HAND E21
EELA CRAIG E21A
Eelco see GELLING Eelco
EFFERT2 Heiko T103A
EFFORD Bob C2 F42 K84 S31

EGAN Joe C127 E22 F7 N57
R11 S257
EGAN Mark M107 M138A S17
EGAN Mary G100 W11
EGAN Mike L63 W7
EGAN Nick H184A T36A
EGAN Rusty R79 V35A
EGAN Walter E23
EGG E24
EGGERMONT Joap G64
EGGLI Roli T35
EHART Phil H4 K9
EHINGER Jim B233
EHRIG Joachim H. 'Eroc'
E63
EHRLICH Jesse A59 B15
B256 R62 S116
EICHLER Glenn F8A
EICHLER J. G79
801 M81
EIGHTEEN CARAT GOLD E25
EIJAS Andrew A4
EIRE APPARENT E26
EISEN Steve S314
EISENBARGER Tony B225
EISENBERG Fran S121
EISENBERG Naomi Ruth H112
EISLER Paul S100
EKLUND Christer A4 B193
J3A
EKLUND Torbjorn H18
EKMAN Pelle H1B
EKSEPTION E27
EL Edward C239
ELASTIC BAND E28
ELBERT Donnie E29
ELBOL Jens M147
EL CHICANO E30
EL COCO E31
EL DIN Cary Sharraf W22
ELDRIDGE Ben A121 S73B
ELECTRIC BANANA P128
ELECTRIC CHAIRS E32
ELECTRIC FLAG E33
ELECTRIC LIGHT ORCHESTRA
E34
ELECTRIC PRUNES E35
ELECTRIC STRING BAND
E35A
ELECTRIC TOILET E35B
ELECTROPHON E35C
ELEKLAD Mohamed M78
ELEM Robert 'Big Mojo'
E35D H37 S329
Elephant (GLASS Dick) E36
ELEPHANTS MEMORY E37
ELEVENTH HOUSE C189
ELEY Lewis S215
Elewy S84
ELF E38
ELFENWEIN Jay K69
EL HADI Suliaman L22
ELI Bobby B135 J92 L130
ELIAS Ivan K59 R144A
ELIAS Manny 123A
ELIJAH HORN SECTION R54
ELIOT Earl R177
ELISCU Bob P11B
Elizabeth P49
ELIZABETH E39
ELIZALDE Ed T114
ELKINS Alfred B193 C135
M129 P142 S358 W93
Ella Guru see DAVIDSON
Greg
ELLAR Colin D16
ELLEFSON Art F14
Ellen S334
ELLER James L16C
ELLEY Jeannie H49
ELLEY Steve A67B
ELLICOTT Rod B63
ELLIMAN Kevin R164
ELLIMAN Yvonne C35C
C121 E40 L120 M101
ELLINGTON David
H52A S269
ELLINGTON Eric E41
ELLINGTON Joan V21
ELLINGTON Judy V21
ELLINGTON Karen
E41
ELLINGTON Marc E41
F6 M108 T79
ELLINGTON Pat V21

ELLIOT Cass E42 M61 M101
M224 S276
ELLIOT Colonel E43
ELLIOT Ken B21 H172 J94
M221A S67 S76 T149
ELLIOT Ramblin' Jack O6
P137
ELLIOT Ray T57 T125
ELLIOT Rob C88 S67 S303
ELLIOT Tony S76
ELLIOTT Bill S220
ELLIOTT Bill E20 O33A R148
W21
ELLIOTT Bobby H132
ELLIOTT David E44 K87
ELLIOTT Dennis F41 F84 H185
I8 L98
ELLIOTT Don (Vibes) A135
S125
ELLIOTT Don (B) M66 N35
ELLIOTT Joe D40B
ELLIOTT Judy A132 T93
ELLIOTT Kenneth P21
ELLIOTT Lindsay H26A N42
ELLIOTT Marion see STYRENE
Poly
ELLIOTT Mary G8
ELLIOTT Mike F90A
ELLIOTT Paul T138B
ELLIOTT Ron B61 C50 E45
G26C L89 M203 N40
ELLIOTT Stuart A22 B280
B286 D36 D127C E77A H26A
O18B P31 R51 S270 V16 W86
Z4
ELLIOTT William S63
ELLIS E46
ELLIS Alan C101
ELLIS Art R31
ELLIS Bobby A6 B101 B234
B276 C139 C245 D71A G39
H122 I12 L58A P140C R29
R35B R84 R134 T110 W4
ELLIS Chris H84A
ELLIS Danny P25 R162
ELLIS Dave E47 M99 S270
ELLIS Don Z8
ELLIS Glyn see FONTANA
Wayne
ELLIS Herb P129
ELLIS Ian C142 N46D S31
ELLIS Ivan G3B
ELLIS Jimmy E22
ELLIS Jock K94A M101
ELLIS Joe G84
ELLIS John (G) V28
ELLIS John (Oboe) F78
ELLIS Joseph M203
ELLIS Keith B191 J105 K79
S274 V11 W70 W89
ELLIS Ken C209
ELLIS Matthew E48
ELLIS Maurice C114
ELLIS Mundy U18
ELLIS Nancy M203
ELLIS Pee Wee B157 C168A
E49 L67B M203 M238
ELLIS Robin M50
ELLIS Steve B39 E46 W74
R10
ELLISON James L4
ELLISON Lorraine E49A K81
ELLISON Monti W30A
ELLNER Kenn C199A
ELLORY Jack B5 S157 W86
ELLSON Paul S304
ELMER GANTRY'S VELVET
OPERA E50
ELMER James B261
ELMORE Greg G12
EL MOLINA BAND C39B
ELOY E50A
EL SADOON Hadi H186
ELSTAR John H116A
ELSTON Charlie E5B
ELSWIT Rik B63 D85 S120
ELTES Polly E59
ELVIN Chris F40
ELWOOD Danny T111
ELWORTHY Billy B169A
ELY Joe E51
ELY Ken J4
ELY Vince P142C
ELYE David Norris S72
Embamba D127

FATOOL Nick F5
FATT P. Harold B230 C78
FATTORUSO Hugo A24 O27A
FATTORUSO Jorge A24 O27A
FAUCHON Jann-Lug S280
FAUERSO Paul L100
FAULISE Paul D50 J20 K36 L119 M12 M75 S168 W13 K1 W136
FAULK Ken D86 F50 H157
FAULKNER Eric C241B
FAULKNER Jeff C88
FAULKNER Jimmy S230
FAULKNER Roland H170
FAUN F29A
FAUNT Jamie C186
FAURE Duncan R3A
FAUST F30
FAUST Luke H139 I21
FAVELA Liver B108
FAVORS Malachi A89
FAWCETT Yvonne F10
FAWN Charlie S283B
FAY Bill F30A
FAY Don A109 D108 J72 S16
FAY Martin L38 C107 G10
FAY Vince B135
FAYAD Frank L38 L28
FAYE Danielle Z13
FEAN John H158
FEAR ITSELF F30B
FEARING Charles C17 R45 S250 V9
Fearless Freddy S276
FEARON Clinton G39
FEARRINGTON Basil F60 M222A U21
FEARRINGTON Norman P115
FEAT Mick A99A A133 B138 G51 K87 L11 L37 L47 M203 R125 R164A S300 Y6
FEATHER Leonard H15
FEATHERS Bubba F31
FEATHERS Charlie F31
FEDERICI Danny A82 P25 S229
FEDERICO Carlos M59
FEDEROW Gabriel M49
FEE Frank Trevor O24B
FEELGOOD Doctor (PERRYMAN William) F32
FEELIES F32A
FEGY Richard B221 S252
FEHLING Frank S175
FEIERMAN Jack F5
FEIGIN Len W73
FEIN Donna W24
FEINGOLD Alan B213
FEINGOLD Andrew D124
FEINSTEIN David E38
FEINSTEIN Harley S205
FEITEN Buzzy B282 C62 C123 D139 F109 H8A J93C L18 L18A L128 M41 N40 R34 S17 W21 W119
FEITEN Howard S251
FEKARIS Dino M106B
FELDER Allan L130
FELDER Don B194 E2 S73 S196 W16 Z11
FELDER Wilton A11 B15 B127 B194 B269A C241 D99 E57 F33 F92 F103D H8 H8A J43 J69 K45 K56A L28 M170 M177 N40 O39 P6 P115 R113 S58 S262 V17 W10A W13 W31
FELDMAN Alan J27 S178
FELDMAN Dennis S210B
FELDMAN Eric Drew B72
FELDMAN Lawrence C85 M46B T158
FELDMAN Stu M238
FELDMAN Victor A37 A132 B110 B127 B194 B225 C118 C45 C50 C171 C213 D50 D59B D74 D101 E40 E74 F34 F92 F103C H96 J93C K45 L1 L71B M21 M68 M84C M102 M170 M229 M232 N25 N40 O37 P3 P106 R70 R78 R97 R99 S118 S124 S262 T25 T107 T118 V17 W6 W9 W54 Z8
FELDTHOUSE Solomon K6
FELICE John R50 R83

FELICIANO Cheo F17
FELICIANO Jose M170 N25 P44 R97
FELIX Julie F35
FELLER Dick C124 F35A
FELLICHAN Thomas S140
FELTHAM Mark N48B
FELTON John D62
FELTS Narvel F35B
FELTS William Ray L64
FENBY Ian M80
FENDER Billy A131D K46
FENDER Griff D18
FENDER Mike C195
FENDERMEN F35C
FENDRICH Charlotte G52
FENN A1 D37 M50
FENN Rick T43
FENNELL Ray C236
FENNELL Tony C63
FENNELLY Michael C211 F36 M82 M156 S6 S262
FENSELL Skip M12
FENSOME Peter K84
FENT Lance P46
FENTON David V18A
FENTON Graham M105
FENTON P. S132
FENTON Paul C37
FENTON Shane (JEWRY Bernard; later STARDUST Alvin) F37 S249
FENWICK Ray C185B D28 D66 F16 F38 G31 G50 L120 O8 W117
FEOLLER Peter B107
Fergus see JONES Euton
FERGUS F38A
FERGUSON Dan B50 E57 H92 J92 S58
FERGUSON Dave R27
FERGUSON Dave F128
FERGUSON Doug C19 G71
FERGUSON Howard R50
FERGUSON Janet Z8
FERGUSON Jay F5 F39 J64 M191 S156 S216 W16
FERGUSON Jerry Jay L69
FERGUSON Joe B221
FERGUSON Keith F38
FERGUSON Lloyd 'Judge' M149
FERGUSON Michael C81
FERGUSON Robert L86
FERGUSON Stephen N2 P106 W9
FERGUSON Tony C29 D58 K94
FERGUSSON Alex A43
FERNANDEZ Gonzalo 12
FERNANDEZ Tony N56 R142 S295 W7
FERNBACH Andy F40
FERNBACH Dave F40
FERRANTE Dennis M233 R60 W107
FERRANTELLA Nick W51
FERRARI Mario F135
FERRARI Pat L65 S269
FERRARO Gary B169A
FERRARO John V108
FERREIRA Bob A136 C158 I31 M151
FERRELL Flash M65
FERRELL James L115A S206
FERRER Miguel M191
FERRETTI Rick M1
FERREZ Diana F41
FERRIER A1 F40A
FERRIER Renate 127
FERRIO Cheryl C76
FERRIS Dana M96
FERRIS Ed A121
FERRIS Glenn A131 C147 D127 R22
FERRIS Larry S318
FERRIS Roger N56
FERRIS WHEEL F41
FERRON Anthony D139
FERRON Clinton P140C I155A
FERRONE Steve A120 A131 F60 K36 K51 M206 T111A
FERRONNE Tommy D86
FERRY Bryan F42 R149

FETTA John Paul F102 R39
FEVER TREE F43
FEVES Richard R137
FEWINS Mike C187
FEY Don C101
FEY Rita Y16
FEZA Mongezi A105 B229 C63 D37 H101 P15 P146 W135
FIALKA Karel F43A
FICCA Billy T38
FICHET Beth B244 J41 W21
FICIAL Ben E. F129
FICK Ole B275
FIDDLER John B219 M121
FIDGE Richard S327A
FIDLIN Paul A30A
FIEGER Doug K69A U5
FIEL Lanny B261
FIEL Rick B261
FIELD Bobby E52B G122
FIELD Graham F44 P54 R33
FIELD John S226
FIELD Jon A105 I20 J16 K41 M94 N41 O15 S313
FIELD Larry C158 W95
FIELDER Jim B141 B256 B260 C123 H120 K81 O15 Z8
FIELDS F44
FIELDS Ernie J75A V9
FIELDS Frank D96
FIELDS Gerry A35 A133 C183 E41 M80 R92
FIELDS Gil A47 W100
FIELDS Howie C76
FIELDS Jerry (SINGH Guruvir) P73
FIELDS Linda A113 R38
FIELDS Ray P26
FIELDS Steven S198A
FIELDS Vanetta A11 A37 A50 B84 B226 B253 B256 B261 B282 C77 C123 C155 C180 C182 C217 C246 D23A D26 D86 D101 D103 F50 G15 P110 U23 G87 G121 H5 H179 H181 K14 K45 L9 L44 L128 M18 M89A M102 N4 O39 P6 P126 Q3A R22 R101 R133 S58 S73 S116 S262 S342 T118 T158 V12 W16 W54
FIERR Anton L126A
FIERRO Martin C195 G9 G84 M211 Q12 S7 S78A W5
FIFE Fay R70A R74
FIFIELD Bill J110 L46
FIG Anton A82 F111 J48 S214A W129
FIGUEROA Sammy B208 C99 K36 K47 M206 M225 S135 S193A T114 W8
FILANDA Helga A57
FILLEUL Peter C141 O1 T14
FIMBRES Yvonne M53
Fin G1
FINCH F45
FINCH Barnaby L28 P125A
FINCH Barry F81C
FINCH Otis H150
FINCH Richard H157 K1
FINCHAM John T138B
FINCHER Mick A133
FINCLAIR Barry S215
FINDLEY Bob H8A P75 S262
FINDLEY Chuck A11 A37 B201 B225 B244 C45 C153 C158 C171 C180 C213 D5A D72A D74 D99 D127 E40 F92 G15 G120A H39 H181 J75A J93C K45 K48 K95 L18A L19 M18 M74 M102 M125A M170 M229 N16A N40 P137 R78 R87 R99 R101 S50 S189 S252 S262 S272 V12 W9 W54 X84
FINDLEY Mike M50
FINEBERG Jeanie B186 C99 127 N65 S135 T147
FINESILVER Mike H109
FINGER Peter F46
FINGERPRINTZ F47
FINGERS Johnny B181
FINISH Matt I19
FINK Mike T80C

FINKEL Howie V16
FINKEL Robby S280
FINKLE Carl M95A
FINKLER Michael T37A
FINLAYSON Willy B73 M80 M118 W134A
FINLEY John R75
FINLEY Martin S210A
FINN Colin J3
FINN Julio B120 M109
FINN Micky B168 H70 M89A M114A
FINN Neil S221
FINN Steve S26
FINN Tim S221
FINN Tom L45
FINNEGAN Owen S31
FINNEGAN Tim E7C
FINNERTY Barry B208 H150A P24B S14C S75
FINNEY Gene C179
FINNIE Lance F9
FINNIGAN Mike B57A B94 D1A D124 F48 F48A F138 G106A M101 M229 S111 S120 S273 W21
FINNIGAN AND WOOD F48A
FINTL Eckehard R178
FIOCCO Bob W68A
FIORE Chuck T22
FIORI Umberto S286A
FIORINO Bob M178B
FIORY Vito L25
FIRE F48B
FIREBALLS F49
FIRE ESCAPE F48C
FIREFALL F50
FIREFLIES F50A
FIRESIGN THEATRE F51
FIRESTONE Rod R151
FIRMIN John B221
FIRST AID F51A
FIRST CHOICE F52
FIRST CLASS F53
FISCHBACK John K48
FISCHELSCHER Danny A57
FISCHER Andre B225 F103D L111 R161
FISCHER Butze G120
FISCHER Clare C241
FISCHER Eric R161
FISCHER Jerry B141
FISCHER Larry 'Wild Man' F54
FISCHER-Z F54A
FISCHLERS M18
Fish see CLARKE Eric
FISH M18
FISH Alan A83 T50
FISH Bob D18 J110
FISH Frankie S187
FISHBAUGH FISHBAUGH AND ZORN F55
FISHBAUGH Gary F55
FISHBAUGH Paula F55
FISHELSON Stan M68
FISHER Adrian B191 S139 S205 T102
FISHER Beau W69
FISHER Connie O35
FISHER Desmond B231
FISHER Even D62
FISHER Harold B189 G11 P54 S209 S355 W86
FISHER Jerry O35
FISHER Keith B67
FISHER Malcolm P54
FISHER Matthew C155 F8B F56 P140 S338 T96
FISHER Morgan B219 H40 M201 M214 O40 S153
FISHER Ralph E52
FISHER Roger H75
FISHER Tony C2 F14 H103 K84
FISHER Wilson G91A
FISHLOCK Clive S45
FISHLOCK Mark S45
FISHMAN Joan C76
FISHMAN Paul A5A
FIST F56A
FITCH Neil W26
FITOUSSI Robert K59 L57
FITZ Donnie T154

FITZ Greg T154
FITZGERALD Alan G7B H5 M187 F123
FITZGERALD G.F. C209 F57
FITZGERALD Joseph D60
FITZGERALD Mark D12
FITZPATRICK Gregory S14B
FITZPATRICK Jon N6
FITZPATRICK Neil S164
FITZPATRICK Ray M53
FIVE AMERICANS F57A
FIVE DIMENSIONS B87
FIVE DOLLAR SHOES F58
FIVE HAND REEL F59
FIVE MAN ELECTRICAL BAND F59A
FIVE ROYALES F59B
FIX Frankie C225
FIZER Charles O21
Flabba see HOLT Errol
FLACK Roberta F60 H58 R97 F123
FLACKE Ray M118 P138 T63 T89
FLAHERTY Tim P104A
FLAK Jon M103A
FLAME F60A
FLAMIN' GROOVIES F61
FLAMING YOUTH F62
FLAMINGO John H92
FLAMM Carol G10
FLANAGAN Tommy L83
FLANDERS Tommy F31
FLANNERY Terry S31
FLASH F63
FLASH AND THE PAN F65A
FLASH Barry K60
FLASH CADILLAC AND THE CONTINENTAL KIDS F64
FLASH FEARLESS F65
FLASHETT Peter P19
FLEET Gordon E10
FLEETWOOD Mick B83 B161 B193 C97 E23 F66 G108B L37 M111 S166 S211 S259 T130 W46 W120 Z11
FLEETWOOD MAC F66
FLEISHER Paul B221 R25 R60
FLEISHMAN Robert J99
FLEMING Chuck J3 T137
FLEMING Gordie M21 S266 W101
FLEMING Leopoldo S169
FLEMING Ray H22
FLEMING William R140A
FLEMMING Gabriel D8 W33
FLETCHER Charles M101
FLETCHER Chris A99A K63 K66 P42A R142 S301
FLETCHER Colin G99 G102
FLETCHER E. S251
FLETCHER Gary B154B K22A
FLETCHER Guy R48 R129
FLETCHER Lyn O40
FLETCHER Mo J14
FLETCHER Mrs. L68
FLETCHER Nigel L68
FLETCHER Wilby S169 W30A
FLETCHER Yvonne N39
FLETCHLEY Marve M188A
FLETT Dave M80
Flick R84
FLICK Vic H24 M100 W86
FLICKENGER Dan B41
FLICKER Mike H75
FLICKS F67
FLIEGEL Ritchie R39 V1
FLIGHT '56 L93
FLINT Hughie B154B B178 F14 G6 M29 M111 N41 P131
FLO AND EDDIE F68
FLOATING BRIDGE T69
FLOCK F70
FLOEGEL Ron R57
FLOH DE COLOGNE F70A
FLOOD J. C76
FLORA Thom T39
Flour M237A
FLOURIDE Klaus D33A
FLOUZE T38C
FLOWERS Cornelius 'Snooky' B144 H186 J95
FLOWERS Dan S192

FLOWERS Herbie A109 B152
B186 C2 C19 C127 D108 F70B
G65 H24 H29 H67 H183 J72
K81 K84 M100 O18B R12 R60
S23 S144 S209 S266 T47
T111 V30 W86 W102
FLOWERS Matt S192
FLOWERS OF ROMANCE F71
FLOYD Babbi J69 L119
FLOYD Eddie F9 F72
FLOYD Frank D63 G4 I2 J20
J69 L119 M17 M225 P24B
S262
FLOYD Neale P58
FLUR Wolfgang K92
FLURIE Bob M126 T107
FLYE Tom B253 C173 L122A
FLYING ACES F73
FLYING BURRITO BROTHERS
F74
FLYING CIRCUS F74A
FLYING ISLAND F74B
FLYING LIZARDS F74C
FLYING MACHINE T25
FLYING SAUCERS F75
FLYING SAUCERS F75A
FLYING SQUAD F75B
FLYNN Bruce C236
FLYNN George A27
FLYNN Malcolm B231
FLYNN Mick J86
FLYNN Robert Jnr. S101
FLYNT Ron T162B
FLYS F76
FLYWHEEL Wolfe J. see
THOMPSON Richard
FOCUS F77
FOGARTY Kevin O24A
FOGARTY Michael S211
FOGEL Marty R60
FOGELBERG Dan B244 F78
W16
FOGERTY John C221 F79 F80
G64B
FOGERTY Tom C221 F80 G64B
R157
FOGG Terry S194
FOGHAT F81
FOLARON Ayinde D47
FOLEY Derek B237 P11
M120
FOLEY Ellen F81A H185
M120
FOLEY Mike R66C
FOLK WEAVERS M45
FOLKEDAHL Bob S111
FOLLER Bubba D139
FOLLINGTON Ace T96
FOLSOM Ronald B15 S116
FOLTZ Marty S349 W44
FOLWELL Bill A86 G122
FONDALIER Mike S216
FONFARA Michael A9 E33
M108 R60 R75 T169
FONTAINE Eli H98
FONTAINE John L119A Z14
FONTAINE Patrick A48A
FONTAINE Richard J4A
FONTANA D.J. M173 M197A
P125 S120 Y18
FONTANA Richie P87A S242
FONTANA Steve S284
FONTANA Wayne (ELLIS
Glyn) M162
FONTAYNE Shane F83A
FONTENOT Merlin S187C
FOODBAND F81B
FOOL F81C
FOOLS F81D
FOOLS GOLD F82
FOOS Ron I25A
FOOT IN COLD WATER F83
FORBERT Steve F83A
FORBES Alrick T155A
FORBES Brent H173 O24A
P54 S334
FORBES Dennis T34
FORBES Derek S126
FORBES Graham G63 I16
P121
FORBES Rand U16
FORCE Roger M178B
FORCEY Dick W87
FORD Barry C119 K45 M133
S358
FORD Clarence D96 N23
FORD Daniele S332B

FORD Dean M89 P31 R48
FORD Earl 'Bone' C62
FORD Eric H121
FORD Frankie F83B
FORD Fred B233
FORD Geoff C238A
FORD George H26A L63
M121 R51 S270 V16
FORD Henri C162
FORD John E50 H173 M181B
R5 R11 R15 R174 S41 S54
S295 V22
FORD Larry S58
FORD Louis W28
FORD Martyn B280 F86 J72
N6 S107
FORD Mary (SUMMER
Colleen) P38
FORD Neil 'Rusty' N8
FORD Patrick M238
FORD Phil S19
FORD Rick N20 O6A
FORD Robben F128 H39 L1
L89 L109 M170 M238 S50
W116A
FORD Ron F137
FORD Rusty L122A
FORD Stephanie S272
FORD T. T2
FORDE Brinsley A107 B276
FORDHAM John C165
FORDHAM Ken B188
FOREIGNER F84
FOREMAN Al H31 L75
FOREMAN Chris M46A
FOREMAN Harold F103C
FOREMAN Michael 'Sugar
Bear' L69 O14
FORESMAN Ed G92B J17
FOREST F85
FOREVER MORE F85A
FORGE Jackie R158
FORMAN David F85B M163
FORMAN Steve B16 B175
B221 B261 C58 C180 E57
F128 H116 H122A J43 L110
M27 M82 M111 O15 P69
P106 R4 R97 R99 R137
S339 W27
FORMERLY FAT HARRY F85C
FORMOSA Jeff H79
FORMOSA Rick L92
FORMULA Dave M47 V35A
FORREST Everald (or
Erroll) M122 P108 R61A
FORREST Jimmy D77 K45
FORREST Norman O15
FORREST Stephen F26
FORRESTER Ellsworth
S198A
FORRESTER Sharon F86
FORRIEST Sonny C146
FORSAY John H103
FORSEY Keith B174 I2
J10A L78 U23
FORSHA John T. S282
FORSSI Ken L128
FORSTER Colin E50
FORSYTHE John W7
FORSYTHE Julie D99
FORTE Bobby K45 M238
FORTE Fabiano see Fabian
FORTINA Carl D139 J72
FORTMAN Demon D48
FORTUNATO Robert S169
FORTUNE Gary C95
FORTUNE Georgie W28
FORTUNES F87
FOSS John B56
FOSSEN Steve H75
FOSTER Al L67B
FOSTER Alex C99 D27 M69
R125 S135 V17
FOSTER Bill P6
FOSTER Bob G114 K32
FOSTER Bruce B226 K67
S255
FOSTER Colin V22
FOSTER David A116 B25
B110 B169 C58 D99 D124
E7 G24 H116 J75A M18
M89A M191 N23 P3 R99
R107 S58 S252 W9 W42
W133
FOSTER David B17 C50

D72A M102
FOSTER Gary B194 D139
FOSTER Graham F88
FOSTER Ian A60
FOSTER Leroy 'Baby Face'
L52 P142 W28
FOSTER Malcolm F88
FOSTER Millie S78A
FOSTER Mo A17 A62 B64
B189 D2 F16 G50 H22 M34
Y6
FOSTER Norm C35A
FOSTER Ron (V) B253
FOSTER Ronnie (K) B85
C129 F60 F87A J7 L28
M102
FOSTER BROTHERS F88
FOTHERGILL Lee K44A
FOTHERINGAY F89
FOTT Solie J. D139
FOTOMAKER F90
FOUBERT Geoff H75
FOUNDATIONS F90A
FOUQUET Jean Pierre V26B
FOUR DUCHESSES M48
FOURNERAT Louis K32
FOURNIER Vernell R59
FOUR SEASONS F91
FOUR TOPS F92 S337
FOURACRE Mike M95
FOURMOST F93
FOUTS Randy G40
FOUTZ Casey C221 F36
FOWLE Thom B254A
FOWLER Bruce B72 D127 W63
Z8
FOWLER Mick F142 G82
FOWLER Rex A135
FOWLER Sam W84
FOWLER Tom D127 H4 I31
P115 Z8
FOWLER Walt C147 W30 W63
Z8
FOWLES Brad C113
FOWLEY Kim B224A F94 K88
Z8
FOX F95
FOX F95A
FOX Art L128
FOX Cliff see HARRIS
Cliff
FOX English John C105
FOX Erry B35A
FOX Eugene E52B
FOX Freddie M68
FOX Jackie R163
FOX Jim C121 J31 T112A
FOX John C209
FOX Lucas M213
FOX MR. M166
FOX Noosha F95
FOX Paul R175A
FOX Simon B54 B130 H3
FOX Steve G55
FOX Sue C209
FOX Sydney S272
FOXTON Bruce J19
FOXWORTH Margaret G92
FOXX F96
FOXX Charles F97
FOXX Inez F97
FOXX John (LEIGH Denis)
F97A U8
FOXX Leigh P13 S170
FOXY F98
FOYE Martin F131
FRABONI Rob D13 W21
FRADY Garland F99
FRAGA John K46 R123
FRAGOS John S250B
FRAIOLI Faith F74B
FRAMPTON Peter B83 D131
F100 H23 H106 H179 L64
S111 S252
FRANCARD Dominique M87
FRANCE Linda U20A
FRANCES Morris R124A
FRANCIS Archie W12A
FRANCIS Billy D85 S120
FRANCIS Charles T122B
FRANCIS David O8A
FRANCIS Erroll 'Sly
Junior' R61A
FRANCIS Hugh N50B

FRANCIS Kevin B228 F113
FRANCIS Mark S218
FRANCIS Martyn S270
FRANCIS Mike A21
FRANCIS Panama C146
FRANCIS Paul B77 F117
F141 H119B R136 S209 T131
T155
FRANCIS Ritchie B96 E80
F101
FRANCIS Ron S130
FRANCIS Sonny R106
FRANCIS Stewart D9 F85A
G44 H155
FRANCISCO Don B100 C238
G60 M123 R137
FRANCISQUE Jerome T110
FRANCKI Hansi F70A
FRANCO Bismarck M53
FRANCO Guilherme S169
FRANCO Joe G69
FRANCOIS Helene R60
FRANCOUR Chuck K90
FRANGENBERG Dick T143
FRANGIPANE Ron D74 M84A
M125
FRANK Bob F101A
FRANK J.B. I17B
FRANK Jeremie R17
FRANK Jim C23 F56 F65 F95
FRANK Rick B87 E37 L51
FRANK Robert C196
FRANKE Chris T11
FRANKE Helmut L78
FRANKEL Danny U20A
FRANKEL Ron W101
FRANKEN Peter S329A T103A
FRANKEN Rob C61 L41 S45B
FRANKHAUSER Merrel M222B
FRANKIE AND JOHNNY F102
FRANKIE LYMON AND THE
TEENAGERS L144
FRANKLIN Aretha F103
FRANKLIN Audrey F103C
FRANKLIN Bobby H98
FRANKLIN Carolyn F103
F103A
FRANKLIN Doug F133
FRANKLIN Elmeo K45
FRANKLIN Erma F103B
FRANKLIN John W115
FRANKLIN Juanita B186 C48
E60 H73 L27 S48 T87 V30
FRANKLIN Melvin (ENGLISH
David) T42
FRANKLIN Mullin F137
FRANKLIN Paul B210
FRANKLIN Reuben J22
FRANKLIN Rodney F103C
FRANKS Clive D39 J72
FRANKS Jim C9 H11
FRANKS Michael F103D H112
FRANKS Tim C6
FRANSEN Ron B169
FRANSSEN Dick K42
FRANTIC F103E
FRANTZ Chris P15 T8
FRANTZ Roddy U20A
FRANZONI Carl Z8
FRASER Andy E59 F104 F108
K84 K87 M111 P15 S92 T102
FRASER Dean B234 D130 W4
FRASER Don J84
FRASER Fi K65
FRASER Glen L82
FRASER Norman A30A
FRASER Scott S202
FRASER Simon C87
FRASER-BINNIE John D78
FRATANGELO Larry F137 K46
FRATER Ian F6
FRATERMAN Evert S42A
FRATERNITY OF MAN F104A
Fratter W4
FRAYNE George (CODY
Commander) C173 N32 W129
FRAZER Tom S19
FRAZIER David M225 P21
FRAZIER Joe 'Speedo' I13C
FRAZIER John S358
FRAZIER Norman L130
FRECHTER Colin B187
FRED John F105
FREDA Michael R54
FREDERICK Jeffrey H189
FREDDIE AND THE DREAMERS
F106

FREDERICK Nat J24
FREDERICKS Bill F107
FREDERICKS Carole M53
FREDERICKS Fred A105
FREDERICKS Henry see MAHAL
Taj
FREDIANI Steve B25 S189
FREDIN Stefan T138A
FREDRIKSZ John L95B
FREE F108
FREE Jane B199
FREE Phil C213A
FREE Scott P75
FREE BEER F108A
FREE CREEK F109
FREE SPIRIT F109A
Freebo (FRIEDBERG Dan) C59
E18A G122 H65 M21 M229 R22
FREEDOM F110
FREEMAN Allan 'Taff' M136B
N18
FREEMAN Arthur N2A
FREEMAN Barry P47
FREEMAN Bo S325
FREEMAN Bobby F110A
FREEMAN Charlie B202 C180
FREEMAN Colin W2
FREEMAN Dave F51A
FREEMAN Don W116
FREEMAN Doug C21A
FREEMAN Earl G66
FREEMAN Ed (K) A102 B253
FREEMAN Ed (G) R169
FREEMAN Ernie (K) C146 W87
FREEMAN Ernie (Str) S123
FREEMAN George M26
FREEMAN Joe L130
FREEMAN Ken B89 D36 G67
H66
FREEMAN Lee S294
FREEMAN Mark O40
FREEMAN Richard U15A
FREEMAN Robert P89A
FREEMAN Sonny K45 P26
FREEMAN Whitney S7
FREEMAN Wilbert K45
FREEPORT F110B
FREER Tony E58
FREESE Goran H18
FREEWAY F110C
FREHLEY Ace F111 H145 K67
FREIBERG David C232 H45
H186 J46 K10 Q12 S61 S157
T136
FREIBERGER Peter B100
FRENCH Brenda K52
FRENCH George S358
FRENCH Jeanne C76
FRENCH John (Drumbo) B72
FRENCH Mick E41
FRENCH Paul T108 V42
FRENCH Peter A115 B250 R28
FRENCH Peter (G) C5
FRENCH Suzanne M37
FRENCH Toxey D71 Z11
FRENETTE Matthew L130B
S299A
FRENTZEL Marc S134
FRENZEL Bruno B107
FRENZI Gera M87
FRENZY Tommy T156
FRESH (1970's) F112
FRESH (1960's) F113
FRESH Pete B35
FRESH START F113A
FRESHLY LAYED BAND F114
FREY Glenn B175 B244 E2
F78 L116 M123 M170 N40 O15
P137 R137 R57 S124 S196
S197 T39 W167 Z11
FREYMAN Gary S311
FRIBERG Carl H122A
FRICIA Dennis G26B
FRICIA Kenny G26B
FRICKE Florian P118
FRICKE Janie B261 E73 J11
T167
FRICKER Sylvia see TYSON
Sylvia
FRIDE Jan G120 K89
FRIED Marty C255
FRIEDBERG Dan see 'Freebo'
FRIEDLEIN Thom A98
FRIEDMAN Bennett Y12

GAYNOR Dave G36A
GAYNOR Mel L71B
GAZDA Ricky 'The G' S199
GEARE Steve L46
GEARHART Charles G72A
GEARY Bob B255
GEBAUER Benny B174 J10A
GEBAUER Gunther J10A
GERHARD Nicky W13D
GEE Andy (GROBER Andy) B39 E46
GEE Micky E19 F7 M63 M128 W29A
GEE Rosko C25 C30 P71A T127 Y2 Y11
GEERE Steve J110
GEESIN Ron G18 S9 W29
GEFFEN David C232
GEGENBACH Frederique T67
GEILS Jerome G19 G122
GELBA Elek P71A
GELBER Bill W51
GELDARD Bill A109 C2 K84 P131
GELDOF Bob B181
GELFAND Steve B57A
GELFS Ian A33A
GELLER Herb L139 T103A
GELLING Eelco C243 G10A G64
GELLOTE Gunnar F83A
GELLY Dave B211 B277
GELSAND Steve H9
GEMMELL Keith A118 R84 S235 W23
GENCH George P40
GENDLE Mark Z22
GENE LOWERY SINGERS C50
GENERATE Dee E11
GENERATION X G20
GENESIS G21
GENET Christian U17
GENGO Joe J88
GENGO Robert J88
GENNARO Sandy B124A
GENO WASHINGTON AND THE RAM JAM BAND W24
GENOCKEY Liam G31 H42 K94B M94 N57 R11 R40B Z24
GENOVA Dominic S58
GENRICH Ax G120
GENT Chris A125 S153 S210A
GENTILE Ronnie C241B
GENTLE Joe H58
GENTLE GIANT G22
GENTLEMAN Horace S207
GENTLEMAN BOYS Z11
GEOFFROY Alain C60
GEOFFROY Daniel R53C
Geordie K43A
GEORDIE G23
GEORGE Bernie P131
GEORGE Chris T132
GEORGE Dave A43
GEORGE Lowell A121 B244 C45 D8 E40 G24 H8 H10 L63 L89 M21 M229 P15 P50 R22 R137 S65 S124 S196 T31 W39 Z8
GEORGE Russell C40 I2 M37 S125 T98
GEORGE Sydney D86 H179 M64 M135 S276
GEORGE BENSON QUARTET B85
GEORGE THOROGOOD AND THE DESTROYERS T80
GEORGIA Robbie M125
GEORGIADES Michael L31 R101
GEORGIOU Steven see STEVENS Cat
GERACI Sonny C140A 044A
GERALD BROWN SINGERS M67
GERALDO Neil D53
GERBER Alan R75
GERDES George W5
GERMAIN Anne S280
GERMAIN Claude S280
GERONIMO BLACK G25
GEROW Teddy F59A
GERRARD Denny H59 P39
GERRARD Denny G25A
GERRARD Donny A116 C38 C180 D99 E40 G101B

GERRETT Paul W14
GERRI Alan R3
GERRITSEN Rinus G64 S253A
GERRY AND THE PACEMAKERS G26
GERS Janick W69B
GERSHMAN Nathan H10
GERSHMAN Paul S215
GERST Arthur B244 Z11
GERSTEIN Richard S121
GETMAN Bob B105 I2 W5
GETZ David B94 J95 M18
GETZ Jane R109
GETZ James M227
GETZ Stan C129 C186
GETZOFF James B15 F134
GEVING Tom H78
GEWISSLER Dieter G66
GEYER Dennis A1
GEYER Renee G26A G106A
GHETTO The C236
GHETTO FIGHTERS H99
GHEZZI Suzi I27
Ghia Z22
GIACOLONE Paul F50A
GIALLOMBARDO Phil J31
GIANQUINTO Albert B109
C195 S57
GIANT CRAB G26B
GIANTS G26C
GIBB Barry B71
GIBB Maurice B71
GIBB Robin B71
GIBBARD John C236 K53
GIBBINGS Mario K41
GIBBINS Mike B16
GIBBON Frankie H7
GIBBON Mick F73
GIBBONS Al M75 M79
GIBBONS Billy B253
GIBBONS Bob M221A
GIBBONS Frankie B66
GIBBONS Ian K61 L68A R52 W129
GIBBONS Malcolm S295A
GIBBONS Mark B72 H166
GIBBONS Mickey R80A
GIBBONS Steve B26 G27
GIBBS Dave 02
GIBBS Derek C254
GIBBS Doug P126
GIBBS George L137
GIBBS Leonard F103C H58 J20 K69 W25
GIBBS Mike W62
GIBBS Terry F34
GIBLIN John B195 B203 B243 B280 C75 D95A E77A G67 H26A M38 M94 M140 R12 W82A W82B Z4
GIBSON Bill L61A S3
GIBSON Brian G23
GIBSON Butch S14A
GIBSON Colin A25 B174B G101 H168 H177 J110 L37 L46 M86 M220 R7 S103B S142 S176 W58
GIBSON Frank D100 W7 W13A
GIBSON Henry R97 S111
GIBSON Ian E7D
GIBSON Jane N41
GIBSON Jarrett 'Gerry' G122 L94 W47 W94
GIBSON Lacy S57
GIBSON Luke K28
GIBSON Mike W13
GIBSON Pete J16 M99 N41
GIBSON Steve (Mand/B/G) C124 C194 E57 L108 R4 S32 S269 Y16
GIBSON Steve (D) M181D
GIBSON Terry D109
GIBSON Wilf E34 J84
GICHIE Locksley C114
GIDEN Pierre Jean C113A
GIFFORD John S299
GIGLIOTTI Tony M178B
GIGSTAD Craig L130A
GIGUERE Russ A106
GIL George B58
GILBANKS Mark M67
GILBEAU Floyd M21
GILBERT Bruce Clifford L66B W112
GILBERT Charlotte L4A P6
GILBERT David N31 R123

GILBERT Eileen B262 K81 P149 W106
GILBERT Jean D110
GILBERT Jeremy P72
GILBERT John C148
GILBERT Ron B157
GILBERT Tony T122
GILBERT Warwick R9
GILDER Nick G29
GILES Gary G. S296
GILES Mike A133 B40 B174B C161 F36 G29A G50 G103 G111 J14 K54 M20 P72 S34 S300 W125
GILES Pete G29A K54 M20
GILES Rick S117
GILES GILES AND FRIPP G29A
GILGAMESH G30
GILKENSON Jeff C247 D70 D71
GILKYSON Lisa M143
GILL Alan T37A
GILL Andy G7C
GILL Bob P138
GILL Geoff D16
GILL Janis P151
GILL Leonard K45
GILL Pete S32A
GILL Stan H71
GILL Vince P151
GILLAN Ian D40 E61 G31
GILLARD Roy C161
GILLASPIE Jon C10 D49 T6 W125
GILLAUT Karl B12A
GILLEN Jimmy W106
GILLESPIE Cherry P138
GILLESPIE Dana G32 K66
GILLESPIE Dizzy W13
GILLETTE Mic B109 B253 C158 C173 C217 D24 H5 J72 J58 P138 T103 J85A L8 L89 M102 T119 W129
GILLETTE Skip G7B
GILLETTE Sonny D97
GILLETTE Steve G33 M108 N53
GILLIAM Michelle see PHILLIPS Michelle
GILLIAM Terry M188
GILLINGHAM Joe M178
GILLIS Bradley R154
GILLIS Jeannot H131A J105B
GILLMAN Delvin S198A
GILLMAN R. N43
GILMER Dave T9
GILMORE Jimmy F49
GILMORE Billy C25A
GILMORE Gary C14 M53
GILMORE Peter C25
GILMORE Steve M194
GILMOUR David B44 C201A G34 H29 P85 W13
GILMOUR Jim S5A
GILMOUR William E58
GILSTON John H110 I16 M67
GILSTRAP Jim B226 D8 E57 F33 F60 H96 J88A L63 L65 L79 L143 M18 M102 M191 N23 R137 S58 S252 W8 W10A W119 Y12
GILTRAP Gordon A6A E47 G35
GIMBLE Johnny A102 B126 B261 C124 C169 E75 F35A F48 J53 M11 M211 N23 R173
GINA X PERFORMANCE G35A
GINHOUSE G36
Ginnethon S211
Gino S78
GINSBERG Allen F133
GINSBERG Jeff T41
GINSBERG Kew T80C
GINSBERG Nate J7
GION Jon S269
GIORDANO Charlie R39
GIORDANO Henri C62A
GIPSON Donna S58
GIRAUDY Miquette G66 H119 T159
GIRL G36A
GIRL SCHOOL G37 M213
GIRLING Michael M203

GIRLS TOGETHER OUTRAGEOU-SLY G38
GIRO Jimmy P148
GIRTON John L. B269A H112 M229
GIRVAN John H132A
GISMONDI Michael S241
GITE Welton J7 P126
GITRY Willie see HARRIS Hi-Tide
GITS Donald 'Gitsie' H172 W23
GITTENS Larry W119
GITTINS Terry H109
GIUFFIA Gregg A65
GIVENS Candy Z10
GIVENS Cliff C179 P114B
GIVENS David Z10
GIVEZANO Eduardo D133
GLACIER G38A
GLAD G38B
GLADIATORS G39
Gladdie see ANDERSON Gladstone
GLADNEY A.J. R128
GLADNEY Robert B111
GLADSTONE G40
GLADSTONE Drew W126
GLADWELL Kip R177A
GLADWIN John B138
GLADYS KNIGHT AND THE PIPS K72
GLAN Pentti 'Whitey' A52 B279A C182 K14 M66 R60 T145
GLANFIELD Lou C209
GLANFIELD Penny C209
GLANZ K.Dudley R148
GLANZ Paul I24A S124 V12
GLASCOCK Brian M210
GLASCOCK John C37 C101 C56 M101 M159 M179 M232 R22 R107 R137 S111 S124 S339 W21 W65A Z11
GLAXO BABIES G51A
GLEASON Patrick H19 M84C W62
GLEMSER Jojo H93
GLEN Chris H52 T37 Z5
GLENCOE G45
GLENMARK Anders A4
GLENMARK Bruno A4
GLENN Lloyd F134 W13
GLENN Roger L8
GLENNGARD Mats H18 L79
GLENNIE-SMITH Jan W14
GLENNIE-SMITH Nick G1 G65 W14
GLICKSTEIN Fred F70
GLOBAL VILLAGE TRUCKING COMPANY G46
GLOBE UNITY G47
GLORIA MUNDI G48
GLORY G48A
GLOSS Napoleon T19
GLOUD Venette A116 E40 H116 L66A O15 R91 R99 W42
GLOVER David B23 H148 J72 K78
GLOVER John G49
GLOVER Leroy C146
GLOVER Roger C202 C202 C204 D40 W9 E61 G31 G50 G95 H22 H121 L120 M7 M34 R14 W117
GLOVER Sheilah T107
GLOVER Steve B237
GLOVER Sue B14 B138 B189 C30 C155 D2 D46 D49 D105 D131 G51 G73 H23 H110 J63 J72 K78 K87 M80 P4 R20 S31 S185 S209 S317 Y17
GLOVER Susie Z8
GLOVER Tony 'Little Son'

K75B
GLOVER Vic H83
GLOW Bernie I2 K81 M12 S168
GLYNN Ray B77 C127 D36 G32 J27 S48
GNIDROLOG G52
GOAD Gus L119A Z14
GOBLE Graham L92
GOBLIN G52A
GODCHAUX Brian G9 G53
GODCHAUX Candy G9
GODCHAUX Donna Jean B221 G9 G53 G84 H186 N32 W42
GODCHAUX Keith B221 G9 G53 G84 H186 W42
GODDARD Paul A111 K81
GODDARD Stuart see ANT Adam
GODDARD Vic S316
GODDEN Chris P47
GODDING Brian B2 B146 C63 D118 K52 L48 M49 M163A S186A
GODDO G53A
GODFREY John D105 M230 T125
GODFREY Pat C151
GODFREY Robert John E58 G54
GODIEGO G55
GODLEY Kevin C222 H163 J110 L43 M67 R20 T43
GODOVITZ Greg G53A
GODS G56
GODS GIFT G56A
GODWIN Jimmy D24
GODZ (1970's) G57
GODZ (1960's) G58
GOEDERT Ron W69
GOETMAN Steve E77
GOETTSCHING Manuel A99 C192
GOFF Brian H29
GOFF Duke C169 J53
GOFFIN Gerry G58A
GOFFIN Louise K48
GOFFIN Sherry K48
GOGAN Barbara P33B
GOIN John F83A
GOINES John H149
GOINES Lincoln R118
GOINES Glen B183 K46
GOINS Herbie G59 K84
GOLBEY Brian C10 T6 W125
GOLD Andrew B110 B175 C38 E15 G10 G60 M21 M229 O15 P114B R137 S124 S196 S269 T25 W9 W21
GOLD Hyman O39
GOLD Jim G60A
GOLD Ken M45
GOLD Ritchie M38
GOLD Steve M2
GOLDBERG Andrew M210
GOLDBERG Barry B77 C216 E33 G61 K2 K81 M68 M135 W116A
GOLDBERG Bruce T147
GOLDBERG Marsh Lynn C76
GOLDBERG Morris B105
GOLDBERG Nettie 'Mama' G61
GOLDBERG Stu K94A M40
GOLDBRIARS G62
GOLDE Ken F14 H83 R40B
GOLDEN Annie S100
GOLDEN Bobby S277
GOLDEN AGE JAZZ BAND S180
GOLDEN DAWN G62A
GOLDEN EAGLE G63
GOLDEN EARRING G64
GOLDENBERG Mark B192 R137 W9
GOLDFIELD Rafael J48
GOLDFLIES David A38 B91
GOLDING Lynval S207
GOLDMAN Bob S230A
GOLDMAN Harris S116
GOLDNER Andy E77B
GOLDRING Colin G52 K65 Y7
GOLDRING Stewart G52 K65
GOLDRUSHERS M45
GOLDSCHMIDT Tommy G120 K11 K89
GOLDSMITH Chico W21

GOLDSMITH Gloria A122
GOLDSMITH Larry M203
GOLDSMITH Lenny Lee S284
GOLDSTEIN Elijah Jobali T41
GOLDSTEIN Morey R49
GOLDSTEIN Robert U20A
GOLDSTEIN Sam E74 P33
GOLDSWAIN Allan S278
GOLGA Eddie L80A
GOLIA Anne K48
GOLIATH G64A
GOLLIWOGS G64B
GOLLY Paul O34
GOMELSKY Giorgio T95
GOMEZ Christine E59
GOMEZ Eddie S116 F103D H59 J54 M79 S215
GOMEZ George B57A
GOMEZ Leroy J72
GOMEZ Ray B214 B253 C129 D50 G64C J75A L41 M200 S211 S266 W8 W62
GOMEZ Tony F90A
GOMM Ian B218 E19 G65 G79 M157
GONE Michael S187B
GONG G66
GONG MOTHER M211A
GONGA Dawilli C147 J75A R99 W6 W63
GONSALES Pablo C254
GONSKY Larry F108A L119B
GONZALES Ariel S10
GONZALES German L95A
GONZALES Robbie D72
GONZALES Terri K36
GONZALEZ G67
GOOCH Rich S18A
GOOD Bruce L72
GOOD Peter B199
GOOD Larry L72
GOOD MISSIONARIES G67A
GOOD OLD BOYS G68
GOOD RATS G69
GOOD THUNDER G70
GOODALL Lee P47 R101A R125
GOODE Coleridge J16 S103B
GOODE Dennis A37 C14 C50 D139 E57 F83A G72 H65 M211 N23 N37 T107
GOODE Les J66
GOODEN Samuel I15
GOODEN Tony R112 S57
GOODGUYS G70A
GOODHAND-TAIT Philip C115 D9 D36 G71 S48 W87
GOODING Paul B264
GOODISON John G50
GOODMAN Dave P110
GOODMAN Erica H117
GOODMAN Jerry F70 H12 M40 W62
GOODMAN Ray S2
GOODMAN Shirley (nee PIXLEY) D86 R133 S99
GOODMAN Steve B261 G72 K77 P41 P137
GOODMAN Timmy G106A
GOODNICK Billy S281
GOODROE Michael M210A
GOODRUM Sandy B261
GOODSALL John B188 B203 B249 H169 L15 W82A
GOODSON Ronnie F105
GOODWIN Bill W6
GOODWIN Earl S118
GOODWIN Robin S236
GOODWYN Mylen A69
GOODY Kim M80
GOOK Roosevelt B144 L146
GOOSE CREEK SYMPHONY G72A
GOOSSENS Marie W71
GOOSSENS Sidonie I79
GOPAL Sam G73 G116A P92 S175
GORDEN Roger B224A
GORDIAN KNOT G73A
GORDON Barry Bull B262
GORDON Billy C177C
GORDON Bobby R118

GORDON Bob L107
GORDON Brenda C158
GORDON Dervin E62
GORDON Greg T41
GORDON Frank D66
GORDON Horatio R45
GORDON Jim (D) B17A B110 B194 B202 B244 B248 C30 C51 C117 C121 C155 C164 C171 C182 C246 D26 D52 D71 D86 D122C G10 G14 G24 G73B G101A G122 H8A H9 H15 H37A H120 H187 J113 K45 K51 L26B L72 L107 L116 M27 M75 M101 M229 M233 N16A N23 O15 O27 P50 P114B R76 R101 R173 S58 S65 S116 S118 S124 S197 S262 S269 S272 T127 V3 V12 V32 W13 W21 W39 Z8
GORDON Jim (Brass/ K) B29 B144 B202 B244 C169 D13 G121 J41 J53 J105A K51 M229 N53 R22 S111
GORDON John James H83
GORDON Jon T169
GORDON Justin N25
GORDON Lennox B234 C245
GORDON Lincoln E62
GORDON Martin J57 R10 S205
GORDON Mitch P33 S160
GORDON Peter C129 D50 J20 L119 M107 M227 P35 S17
GORDON Ralphus 'Raleigh' T110
GORDON Robert G74 T156
GORDON Ron C39
GORDON Shep C182
GORDON Stuart K83 N27 R66
GORDON Tom C90
GORDON Vincent 'Trommie' B101 B234 B276 C245 D71A D130 H105 H122 P135 R134 R150 T166 W4A
GORDON Vince D68A
GORDY Emory A59 A132 B80 B245 C171 C237 E20 H35 J69 L36A N37 P33 P125 R137 S118 S269
GORE Art S169
GORE Bren G3
GORE Michael S252
GORELICK Kenny L119C
GORFAINE Mike E7B
GORGONI Al C146 C234A I2 K81
GORHAM Scott T59 T135
GORILLAS G75
GORIN Kex M49
GORIN Peter R23
GORKA Kenny C228
GORMAN Bob B228 E62B F113 T155
GORMAN Dan E57 Y6B
GORMAN Frederick O31
GORMAN John G103 S35
GORMAN Mike O10A P71
GORMAN Tim L30 S325
GORODETZKY Carl M11
GORRIE Alan A131 F85A H155 K36 K83 M23 M206 S35
GORTON David M67
GOSDIN BROTHERS C123
GOSFIELD Reuben 'Lucky Oceans' A102
GOSHORN Larry P151
GOSHORN Tim P151
GOSKIN Larry C241
GOSLING John C9 K61 U15
GOSLING Pete W130
GOSPEL OAK G76
GOSS Stacy L75 S340 W16A
GOSSETT Gary H38
GOTHERIDGE Keith P103
GOTLIFFE Dave A104
GOTOBED Robert W112
GOTTEHRER Richard D76 G74 W129
GOTTHOFER Catherine M60
GOTTLIEB Dan M138A
GOTTLIEB Gordon M107 S75
GOUBIN Charles V26B
GOUBIN Gilles V26B

GOUDE Jean Philippe P83B W41A
GOUGEON Mark R177
GOUGH Tommy C223A
GOULD Brian S76
GOULD Larry C80B
GOULD Philip M1A
GOULD Steve A99A G97A H73 L11 L37 M23 R33 R164A
GOULDING Steve B176 C42 E19 P25 R162 S149 W130
GOULDING Tim D88
GOULDMAN Graham G76A H163 M162 R20 T43
GOULDREAU Bobby B184
GOULSTONE Chris O6B
GOURD John M134
GOURDINE Anthony L85
GOUT Alan C251
GOWAN Alan G30 H154 N9
GOWELL Anthony S307
GOWER Chris C42 G1 I11 M41A P25 R125 S283B
GOWER Huw R52
GOWER Richard S209
GOWERS Patrick W86
GOYTISLO Fermin H157 K1
GOZZO Alain A114
GRABHAM Mick B31 B98 C148 D127C F56 F65 G77 G97A J110 O18B P95 P140 S339
GRABLE Steven Alan P49
GRACE Rocke G106A W16
GRACE Steve N6
GRACIOUS! G77A
GRADNEY Ken B202 C77 D8 H10 L89 P15 S124
GRADNIER Dee Dee L115
GRADUATE G77B
GRAF Hakon E11A
GRAFFITI G77C
GRAHAM Billy (B/Fid) C169 J53 M108 N25 P106
GRAHAM Billy (Trom) B83 D30 V26A
GRAHAM Billy (V) B274A
GRAHAM Bobby O42
GRAHAM Bryson L37
GRAHAM David F54A
GRAHAM Davy G78
GRAHAM Douglas A9
GRAHAM Ernie C119 E26 G79 H93
GRAHAM Jamie A9
GRAHAM Johnny E7
GRAHAM Kate S344
GRAHAM Larry D24 G79A G80 S161
GRAHAM Nick A115 S141
GRAHAM Nicky G81
GRAHAM Tina G79A
GRAHAM Tommy G79B
GRAHAM CENTRAL STATION G80
GRAHAM PARKER AND THE RUMOUR P25
GRAHAME David M95B
GRAHAN Kyle F19
GRAILLIER Michel M49 T67
GRAINGE Nigel D66
GRAINGER Cheryl V39
GRAINGER Gary S273 S303
GRAMM Benny H137
GRAMM Lou F84 L98
GRAMMER Billy G80A
GRANAHAN Gerry 'Dicky Doo' D63B
GRANAT Marv O24B
GRAND Francis 'Pichenette' E69A
GRAND FUNK RAILROAD G80B
GRAND HOTEL G81
GRAND PRIX G81A
GRANDE Jacques L57
GRANDE John H6
GRANDA Michael 'Supe' O46
GRANDO Richard B221 Q15A
GRANGE Rob N63 S9B

GRANGER Gary D50
GRANNY'S INTENTIONS G81B
GRANOLINO Joel S199
GRANT Art B230
GRANT Ashton T166
GRANT Cornelius R141 V9
GRANT Don T21
GRANT Eddie E62 G39 H175 N50B
GRANT Enroy M221D
GRANT Gary D127 J75A M93 M102 R99 R101 R161
GRANT Jamie S172
GRANT Jerry D63B
GRANT Jewell C146 J21
GRAVY Jim V32
GRANT Keith D109
GRANT Marshall C50
GRANT Neville C139
GRANT Norman T166
GRANT Pete A132 C124 F128 W92
GRANT Ralston T166
GRANT Suzette W88
GRANT Tim W26
GRANT Tom P60A
GRANTHAM George E20 P106 R109
GRAPEFRUIT G82
GRAPPELLY Stephane P115 S125
Grass S255
GRASS ROOTS G83
GRASSEL Douglas O11
GRASSELLI Diana S242
GRASSET Dominique V26B
GRASSET Jean Pierre E69A V26B
GRASSO Cherie R139
GRATEFUL DEAD G84
GRATTON Mick S133
GRATZER Alan R1A
GRAUMAN Lucy H131A
GRAVATT Eric W36
GRAVEL Jean O10B
GRAVENITES Nick B94 B144 E33 G84A
GRAVES Buck A121 D71
GRAVES Carl G101B
GRAVES Clyde S120
GRAVES Derek H58 M2
GRAVES Jackie W136
GRAVES James W12
GRAVES Josh C14 K95 K96 M11 P50 R26 T6B T9 Y18
GRAVES Lee R111
GRAVES Peter D86 F50 P35
GRAVES Tom F58
GRAVESEND Pat J24
GRAVINE Dominic 'Mickey' M12 M75 P6 R21
GRAVIS Frank A123
GRAVY TRAIN G85
GRAY Andy I15A
GRAY Bruce L130
GRAY Dave F120A
GRAY Debra A131 S252
GRAY Diva B57A B253 C99 D127B L119 S121 S215 S262 T147
GRAY Doug D12 M93
GRAY Eddie J30
GRAY Henry A83 H170 L94 R59 R128 W47
GRAY Joe W59
GRAY John B82
GRAY Kris H20A
GRAY Les M223
GRAY Mal W77
GRAY Michael Lee R125
GRAY Nigel K94B
GRAY Paul E13 T86
GRAY Stephen S270
GRAYBEAL Ron L44
GRAYDON Jay A116 B127 B194 B225 C45 C58 C127 C155 C180 C216 D5A D127 E40 F92 F128 H96 J88A M10 M102 M130 M218 M227 R78 R99 S34 S111 S262 T107 W8 W2
GRAYSON Milt J69
GRAYSON Ron M32
GRAZIANO Lee A51
GRAZIANO Tim I1

GREASE BAND F8 G86
Great G61
GREAT BEAR G86A
GREAT JONES G87
GREAT METROPOLITAN STEAM BAND G87A
GREAT SOCIETY G88
GREAT STAMPEDE R106
GREATEST SHOW ON EARTH G89
GREAVES Dave W129
GREAVES Dennis N48B
GREAVES Donald M221D
GREAVES John G90 H101 N9 W135
GREAVES Tony M136B
GREBB Marty F3A L111 M27 R22 R173 W5 W21
GRECH Rick A25 B134 B171 C30 C121 C224 F12 G91 J9 K2 M42 P33 S243 S300 T127 W28 W121
GRECH Yvonne O40
GRECO Ron F61
GREED Alan H43 R122 R165 R174 S349A
GREELEY Matt S56
GREEN G91A
GREEN Al G92
GREEN Alan A20
GREEN Albert 'Bongo Asher' T166
GREEN Bunky G92A S111
GREEN Burton G66
GREEN Chris C19 S209 T122
GREEN Clarence S293
GREEN Colin F14 K72 M100 P91 P131
GREEN Cornelius see Lonesome Sundown
GREEN Danny G92B
GREEN Dave (Sax) B188
GREEN Dave (B) C209
GREEN Doc D116
GREEN Eli M22
GREEN Emanuel 'Manny' D139 I2 J92 K81 O15
GREEN Eunice M133
GREEN Gary G22
GREEN Geo U23
GREEN Graham O44 S193B
GREEN Guitar Slim see Guitar Slim
GREEN Ian Q1
GREEN Jack P128
GREEN Jack S329B
GREEN James R168 S323
GREEN Jerome A83 B87 D66
GREEN Jesse R168
GREEN Jim S308
GREEN Joe J92 N23 P126 R133
GREEN Joel C14
GREEN John D132
GREEN Karl H108
GREEN Kelly F120
GREEN Larry C236
GREEN Lee L62
GREEN Lloyd B285 C14 G92 G93 L77 M33 N37 S272 T107 Y18
GREEN Lyndon J27
GREEN Malcolm S221
GREEN Maxine D124
GREEN Mick K39 P89 S87 F66 G13 G94 M111 M129 S105 S166 S204 S211 S259
GREEN Phil S339A
GREEN Rob G81
GREEN Steve M2
GREEN Stuart K42
GREEN Susaye S333A W119
GREEN Thurman P115
GREEN Urbie M12 R100 S100 S168
GREEN William A11 D77 G121 K48 L66A R97 S14C S325 T145 V9
GREEN Willie Jnr. C179
GREEN BULLFROG G95
GREENAWAY Noel W15
GREENBAUM Norman D88A G96
GREENBERG Chick S79
GREENBERG Peter D18
GREENBERG Phil F85C

GREENBERG Rick S350
GREENBLATT Alan P61
GREENE Dave S102B
GREENE Debbie A59 R22
GREENE Dennis S78
GREENE Ed A31 B50 B127
B194 B225 B226 C12 C30
C58 C153 E57 E71 F92
G120A H8 H9 H122A J73A
J113 K45 K94A M151 M160
M177 M227 M229 N23 P15
P114 R54 R78 R87 R99 R101
R115 S58 S180 S262 T118
T158
GREENE Garry W132
GREENE Jack H49
GREENE Jeannie A28 H62
K46 N55 P125 S36
GREENE Lorne O42
GREENE Marline A28 L50
N37 N55
GREENE Richard B158 C123
C237 F128 H35 K101 L110
M229 N32 O15 P49 Q15A
R148 S63 T150 V3
W5
GREENE Schagzerig R127
GREENFIELD Bob U5
GREENFIELD Robert P81
GREENHALGH Tom A132
GREENHILL Mitch C179
GREENIDGE Robert B245 J41
M17 M53 M191 M232 P15 P28
S124 S252
GREENLEE Bob see RATTLES
Rattlesnake
GREENMAN Chip F140A
M193
GREENSLADE G97
GREENSLADE Arthur F14
F140
GREENSLADE Dave C166 F21
G97 G97A H86 I8
GREENSPOON Jim B64A F94
F109 G24 T81
GREENWAY Brian A69 D125
GREENWAY Roland C236 K53
GREENWICH Ellie C229 G109
GREENWOOD Al F84
GREENWOOD Chico J27 M114A
M193
GREENWOOD Mick G98
GREENWOOD Nick R35
GREEP G99
GREER Maretta F133
GREER Rob C173
GREER Sonny M185
GREEZY WHEELS G100
GREGG Bobby C255 G61 M37
GREGG Brian K39
GREGG Haden N53
GREGOR Max J10A
GREGORIO Michael J88
GREGORY Bill I31
GREGORY Byron L65
GREGORY David X3
GREGORY James H168
GREGORY Jim F58 M154 W48B
GREGORY John B15B S63
GREGORY Michael A30 C165
F132 H194
GREGORY Steve A25 B5 B25
B47C B79 B171 B209 C80
C101 F7 F16 F46 F88 G6
G49 G67 H65 H177 J5 K51
L63 L80 M145 M223 N38
N63B O20 P10 P124 P131
R61A R86 R125 S176 S204
S211 S257 S285 T111 W24
W29A W58 Z4
GREGSON Clive A67C
GREGSON Milt P24B
GREINER Gottfried L120
GREMY Guy George L87
GRENNAN Winston C139 J48
S125 T149
GRESSETT Charlie B233
GREVE Bob H96 L71B R161
GREY Al B233
GREY Steve T111 W13A W102
GREY Tom A121
GREZES Michael E69A
GRICE Brian D66
GRIDLEY TABERNACLE CHOIR
AND ORCHESTRA M166

GRIEG Duncan M95B
GRIEG Keith P88A
GRIEG Stan M129
GRIERSON Ralph J93C N40
GRIFF Zaine G100A
GRIFFIN G101
GRIFFIN Bob C30
GRIFFIN Dale 'Buffin'
B129 M214
GRIFFIN Dick W30A
GRIFFIN Fred V17
GRIFFIN Gary B56 L129
GRIFFIN Gerri V40
GRIFFIN James B206 F48
G101A
GRIFFIN Johnny D25
GRIFFIN Martin H64
GRIFFIN Paul B262 D139
F60 F103 J48 K55 K59 K81
L4A L69 L111 M26 M75 M177
P149 R22 R25 R100 R169
GRIFFIN Reggie M65
GRIFFIN Thom T139A
GRIFFIN Trevor P139D
GRIFFIN William A132 R115
GRIFFITH Marcia B163 M88
R134 V21
GRIFFITH Richard B183
GRIFFITHS Albert G39
P140C T155A
GRIFFITHS Brian B98
GRIFFITHS Clive P37 T94
T90
GRIFFITHS David (G/Vln)
T90
GRIFFITHS David (B) B209
GRIFFITHS Derek A77 A92
B160 D91 S27 V26A Y11
GRIFFITHS Donald A107
B276
GRIFFITHS Geoff B119
GRIFFITHS Hugh P86
GRIFFITHS Jack H16
GRIFFITHS Jim C212
GRIFFITHS Malcolm A23
C39A C109 C204 F7 F14
F42 F86 F88 G31 G67 H42
H154 K84 L23 M205 N63B
R174 S186A W71
GRIFFITHS Mark E41 H43
K24 M108 S198 V30
GRIFFITHS Martin B74
GRIFFITHS Paul S237
GRIGG Roger S81A
GRIGGS Kristy W107
GRIGGS Nigel S221
GRIGSBY Earl D12
GRILL Rob G83 G102
GRILLO M. J113
GRILLS Stuart S295A
GRIMA Charles D66 M180A
W122
GRIMALDI John A77 C91
GRIMES Carol C105 G102
K4 R116 S348B U9
GRIMES Charlie H150 L50
M64
GRIMES Howard G92 P51
GRIMES Jed H87
GRIMES Tiny M65
GRIMES Ty B72 N21 W44
GRIMETHORPE COLLIERY
BAND H29
GRIMM Joe P6 R169
GRIMMELL Chuck H150
GRIMMS G103
GRIN L107
GRINDERSWITCH G104
GRINEL Ron 'Crunchy' F82
M191 S197 W16
GRINGO G105 S185
GRINSTEAD Dave C34
GRISER Darla S269
GRISHAM Doyle B261 C194
E57 P137 S32 T9
GRISMAN David C211 E5
E20 G84 M21 M229 O15 O17
R22 R137 S65 T22
GRITS Vanilla D8
GROB Jeff L119B
GROBSCHNITT G106
GROCHMAL Jack N23
Groco I12
GRODANIER Lisa B174
GRODY Gordon B57A B105

I2 L119 M160 S121 S215
S262
Grock D59A
GROEBER Andreas see GEE
Andy
GROENINK Jan C243 M237A
GROENKE Randy M113
GROETZINGER Alain R123B
GROGAN Cavan C215
GROGER Fritz M136B
GROLNICK Don A96 B208
C44 C189 D115 F60 F103D
F122 G60 J48 J88 K17 M75
M107 N46 R22 R137 S17
S124 S125 S180 S196 S215
S252 S262 T98 T147
GROMBACHER Myron D53
GROMER Alois P118
GRONCKI Darlene N23
GRONDIN Jack T65
GRONENTHAL Max D1A D124
G106A S111 S273
GROOM Don O42
GROOM Lynn G40
GROOM Mick D123 T170
GROOM Roger N5
GROOMS Sherry N23 R4
GROOTNA G107
GROOVY Winston G108
GROPP Gerry J53
GROSHONG James R140A
GROSLIE Helge T97
GROSS Henry G109 S78
GROSS Jeff C76
GROSS Jill H189
GROSS John B171
GROSS Tim A14
GROSS Zelda G109
GROSSART Andy R1
GROSSKOPF Harald A99
C192 G3A W13D
GROSSMAN Hal M228
GROSSMAN Jerry S124
GROSSMAN Severin A23
GROSSMAN Stefan B18 C183
E70 G110 R66 S125
GROSSMITH Derek D131 M50
GROSSO Monica S186
GROSVENOR Luther A87
G111 H40 J9 M214 S224
S257 W74
GROTH Michael T138B
GROUCUTT Kelly E34
GROUNDHOGS G112 H150 M44
GROUNDSTROEM Mans T15
W75
GROVER Bob P88B
GROVER David B109 G121
H96 R161 W8
GROVER Pat B250 B277 M90
S166
GROVES Lani A123 C155
E49 E73 F60 G4 G64 I2
J20 K46 L119 M46B M157
O35 P6 R100 S17 S124
S262 T37E T65 T98 T147
V12 W107 W119
GROVES Moss B82
GROWL G112A
GRUBER Craig E38 O48 R14
GRUDGE Michael B204
GRUEN Peter P109A
GRUN Wili B182A
GRUNBLATT Georges H89A
GRUND Alfred B92
GRUND Atli B92
GRUND Peter B92
GRUNDY Ed B142
GRUNDY Hugh Z15
GRUNDY Malcolm G64A
GRUPALLO Patrice G123
GRUPPO SPORTIVO G113
GRUSHECKLY Joe I24A
GRUSIN Dave A123 F119A
J43 L79 M102 R99 R108
W25 W27 W31
GRUSKA Jay G101B
GRUSKA Michele R4
GRYPHON G114
GUARD Barry B250 M157
O18B W86
GUARD Catherine S272
GUARD Croxley S272
GUARD Dave B256
GUARDIAN ANGELS F14

GUARINO Jasper S340
GUARINO Massimo O33D
GUARNERI Mario C179
GUCCIO Mario M30A
GUDMAND Ken D49 S30 S295
GUERCIO James William B56
L10 M232 S197
GUERIN Bob T67
GUERIN Jean E62A
GUERIN John A59 A132 B17A
B49 B110 B194 B226 B245
B285 E74 F34 F103D G10
G14 H37A H39 L1 L108 M27
M170 O15 P33 P50 P115
P129 R22 R76 R108 S50 S58
S111 S196 T21 T98 T107
Z8
GUERRA Bill T147
GUERRERO Kiko I13B
GUESS WHO G115
GUEST Christopher N10 W5
GUEST Elenor K72
GUEST Reg F55 H180
GUEST William K72
GUEVARA Alex V12
GUIDERA Tom A121 H35 R137
GUIDO Joey B204A
GUIDOTTI Bobby P114
GUIDRY Robert see CHARLES
Bobby
GUILBEAU Gib C160 C216
F74 G116 G121 P32 R137
S114 S196 S269 S341 W43
GUILINO John D50
GUILLERY Adrian H59 J54
GUILLON Dominique L87
GUILLORY Isaac A33 D99
G116A M38 P5 P124 S270
W28
GUIMUNGIE O'Neil E78
GUINN Marty N53
GUISOTTI Bobby N46A
GUITAR Johnny C199
GUITAR Buddy F66
Guitar Slim (STEPHENSON
James also GREEN Guitar
Slim) G116B
GUITIERREZ Steven H96 L28
GULGOWSKI Wlodek D72 U21
GULLAND Brian G114 T79
GULLEY Dennis J14A
GULLEY Russell J14A
GULLICKSON Grant B164
GULLICKSON Lance B164
GULLIKSEN Eric O33C
GULLIVER G117
GUMBLEY Steve C209
GUMBS F. E78
GUMBS Onaje Allan W62
GUN G118
GUNN Peter I18A
GUNN Ray N31
GUNN Tommy A55
GUNN Tommy (G)
GUNNARSON Rutger A4
GUNNELS Gene S294
GUNNIP Daniel M18
GUNNIP David M18
GUNTER Arthur G119
GUNTER Cornel C146
GUNTHER Michel A19A
GUNTRIP Matt B141A
GURL Steve B5 J93 K22A
W79
GURLAND Bob B57A
GURLEY James B94 J95
GURU GURU G120
GURU RAMDAS SINGERS R101
GURVITZ Adrian (CURTIS
Adrian) B20 E18 G118
G120A M151 T82
GURVITZ Paul (CURTIS
Paul) B20 E18 G118 G120A
M151 T82 W72
GUSS Beau M191
GUSTAFSON John A131E A133
B98 C171 F42 G31 G35 H4
M34 M136 O8 P76 Q4 R149
S39
GUSTAVSON Jukka T104 W75
GUSTAVSON Owe H18
GUTCHEON Jeff B221 G72
G87 M229 S252
GUTE Joe R177
GUTHEIL Daryl S299A

GUTHRIE Arlo D101 G121
GUTHRIE Bob M185 W85
GUTHRIE Gwen A123 C155 D63
F60 J20 M17 M107 M222A P126
S169 T98 T114 V17
GUTHRIE Woody G121 T53A
GUTIERREZ Robert B244 G24
GUTTMAN Jon C140A
GUY Barry S267
GUY Billy C146 P75
GUY Buddy G122 H159 H170
L94 M129 T79B W47 W94
GUY Denny G122A
GUY Philip G122 M129 W47
GUY Thomas G122A
GUYLER Nick B93A
GUZIE Andy P141A
GUZMAN Ed D101 R32
GWENDAL G123
GWIN Marty B47A R101
GYAN Kiki O34 Q1 W82A
GYPSY G124
GYPSY A53A
Gypsy Dave D99
GYTHFELDT Paddy H5B

H.P. LOVECRAFT H1
HAAN Jenny B5 L82 S303
HAAPALA Eino S14B
HAAS Andy M95A S288A
HAAS Daniel A64
HAAS James E C180 D74 E15
E40 K59 M102 P85 Q3A R101
HAAS Steve C189
HAAS Wendy A136 C45 O35 S19
HAASE Roland S289
HAASTRUP Joni M53
HABAN Andy W82
HABAN Tom W82
HABER Jim see DOMINO Floyd
HABERMAN Steve C217
HABIB Don W101
HABIBYYA H2
HACKENSACK H3
HACKETT John H4 P72
HACKETT Steve G21 H4
HACON Walter W130
HADDEN Roger G25A H115
HADEN Charlie B131 M79
M138A
HADEN John P24A
HADJAJE Paul S280
HADLEY Gillian P136
HADLEY Leroy T55
HADNOTT Billy W13
HAEFFNER Nick T36A
HAEHL Steve S91
HAGAN Donnell O48
HAGANS Robert 'Buddy' D96
HAGAR Ernie C173
HAGAR Sammy H5 M187
HAGBERG Garry D112A
HAGEN Dean P69
HAGEN Nina H5A
HAGEN Russell R22
HAGGERTY Terry H45 S189
HAGLER Larry R137
HAGLER Sherry B108
HAGLER Stephen S246
HAGLEY Bernard J94 T131
HAGOPIAN Hovaness M192B
HAGSTROMM Bosse S186 W22
HAGUE Ian F21
HAGUE Steve E23 J105A L20
T137A
HAHN Jerry S125
HAHN Mark L102
HAIGHT Lenny M11
HAINES Chris F120A
HAINES Dennis D94
HAINES Jimmy D49
HAINES Norman C78 L104
HAINES Steve A46
HAIR H5B
HAKANSSON Kenny H18
HAKIM Omar G3B
HAKIN Alan S157
HAKINSSON Kim P10
HALDANE Stan B188
HALE Gerky B226 S257
HALE Gerry S181 T37H
HALE Jack B202 C50 D86 D101
F50 G92 G101A J85A M130 N57
P51 P137 S276

HALE Keith C175
HALE Malcolm S203
HALE Otis A1 S20
HALE Teddy Q5
HALE Willie see Little Beaver
HALES Geoffrey A41 O33G
HALEX Harry N4
HALEY Bill (V/G) H6
HALEY William John Clifton 'Bill' (Sax) W30
HALFBREED H7
HALFORD Paul see MOPED Johnny
HALFORD Rob J102
HALINKOVICH Anatole B197
HALKITIS Arris A67E
HALL Albert A109 F14 R48 A50A B154B B250 B277 D128 G112 K22A M90 M238 P142 R122A S31 T23 T130 W89 W91 W131
HALL Bobbye Porter A11 A37 B8 B25 B180 B282 B283 C11B C123 C158 C171 C180 C220 D99 D101 D103 D139 E71 F78 F134 J46 J95 K48 K95 K96 L63 L107 L146 M16 M75 M101 M170 M227 M229 N40 O15 P126 R101 R107 R113 S34 S58 S65 S116 S160 S269 T25 T107 U18 W6 W10A
HALL Bruce R1
HALL Carl K45 L4A P6 P149 R22 S124 T65 W51 W107
HALL Carol H98
HALL Cathy G116A
HALL Chris M157
HALL Christopher D33B
HALL Cliff Q18B S34 S80
HALL Clinton R35B
HALL Coffi M60 M135
HALL Clarence D96
HALL Daniel Lee B27
HALL Daryl H7A H9 G117
HALL Debbie J16 N41
HALL Derek S166
HALL Dolores A102 K48 P6 R125
HALL Donna M93 W54
HALL Geo P142B
HALL Harry F109
HALL Jack W54 Y6
HALL James (K) D39 H116A L117 M157
HALL Jim (B) E9
HALL Jimmy (V/Harm/Sax) D12 G104 S277 W54 Y6
HALL Joe B122
HALL John (D) E62
HALL John (V/G/K) B244 C45 H8 K8 K81 L89 L111 M53 O32 R22 S124 W5
HALL John (K) P139
HALL Lani (Mrs Lani Alpert) H8A
HALL Larry M225 R161
HALL Lon R1A
HALL Mama W54
HALL Pam M221D
HALL Patricia S262
HALL Patti L55
HALL Rene C146 W30 W87
HALL Richard 'Dirty Harry' B276 H122 I12 P134 R8A W4
HALL Rick W16A
HALL Susan M96 W54
HALL Terry S207
HALL Tommy T64
HALL Tony (Mel) C165 T6 W123
HALL Tony (Sax) G32
HALL Vivian 'Talent' A6 R8A
HALL Willie B180 C5B C55 H92 K46 L90 N23
HALL and OATES H9
HALL-SMITH Vanessa F132
HALLER Val E32
HALLEY Dick B254
HALLGREN Bo W22

HALLIDAY Hugh 'Pigmy' U14
HALLIDAY Stuart A34 N27
HALLIGAN Dick B141 K81 M13 S20
HALLIN Pete P125
HALLING Patrick H16B
HALLING Peter D99 H168
HALLMAN Mark K48 N12A W11
HALLMARK Bill G62A
HALLS Mick B250
HALM Rolf V26C
HALPIN Mike S314
HALPRIN Diana S100
HALSALL Chris D119
HALSALL Ollie A133 B191 C13 E59 G103 F20 K81 K97 O40 P37 R106 S35 S274 T94 Y10
HALSEY John A82 C79 D37 H29 H123 I20 M15 P37 P138 R60 R175 T94
HALVERSEN Tom R178
HAM Bill F116 Y6B
HAM Lori S325
HAM Pete B16
HAM Phil S211
HAM Warren B142
HAMANE Michael A53
HAMANN Ken J31
HAMBERG Hilary B269A
HAMBERG Greg H9A
HAMBLETON Fergus H9A
HAMBLETON Greg H9A
HAMBRICK Walter Y15
HAMILL Claire H11 H16B
HAMILTON A. S251
HAMILTON Alexander J22
HAMILTON Andy M41A
HAMILTON Chico H10
HAMILTON Chuck J21
HAMILTON David P40
HAMILTON Edwin F26
HAMILTON Janet T9B
HAMILTON Joe W16A
HAMILTON John D73
HAMILTON Kirk C234A
HAMILTON Mike L109
HAMILTON Ralph C146 F134 R111
HAMILTON Scott R125
HAMILTON Tom A16
HAMILTON Tom P88A
HAMILTON FACE BAND H11A
HAMLETT Ian C3
HAMMEL Dave P54
HAMMER Chuck B186
HAMMER Ian F14
HAMMER Jan A4A B64 B169 B253 C129 C147 H12 J76 M40 M102 N46 S19 W62 W90
HAMMER Ralph E. C155 S251
HAMMILL Peter F121 H13 S48 V11
HAMMON Randy S29
HAMMOND Albert C78 F13 H14
HAMMOND Berea D130
HAMMOND Don W5
HAMMOND Jeffrey J58
HAMMOND John Paul B144 C203 F19 H15 J46 J78
HAMMOND Laurie M46
HAMMOND Paul A115
HAMMOND Peter S289A
HAMMOND Phil P19
HAMMOND Ronnie A111
HAMMOND Steve A40 F21 F29 H121 P76
HAMMOUDI Basil O30A
HAMPTON Ian S205
HAMPTON John M125A
HAMPTON Michael B183 F137 P29
HAMTONES F43A
HANAPPIER Patrick U17
HANCK Terry B109
HANCOCK Butch E51
HANCOCK David H167
HANCOCK Herbie B85 C186 D27 H19 L66A M170 P35 P114 R45 S19 V39 W31 W62 W90 Z9
HANCOX Paul C101 M162
HAND Alan M203 P137 V21

HAND Cal K88
HAND Roger E21 G35 P77B R6
HANDELSMAN Jonathan C222
HANDLEY Jerry B72
HANDLEY Pete R177A
HANDS Terry
HANDY Chip F123
HANESS Abigale J65 K48 M227 R39 S124 S272 T25 T27 W136
HANEY Dave B261
HANEY J.D. M181C
HANKINS Don H170
HANKS Larry T150
HANLEY Steve F10
HANLON Alan C146
HANLON Chris B267
HANLON David D127B
HANLON Tom F103
HANNA Jeff B91 M232 N53
HANNA Roland E49
HANNAFORD Ross D4A
HANNAFORD Tony M195
HANNAH John S299A
HANNETT Martin C184 M233A
HANNIBAL H16
HANNON Biff A122
HANNS Liz P18
HANSEN Randy H16A M31
HANSEN Rudolf S30
HANSEN V. D83A
HANSON Bob F133
HANSON Chris B116
HANSON David G70
HANSON Dick C42 D10A G1 G49 G89 I18A L59 M41A P25 R162 S283B S332 W130
HANSON Junior (MARVIN J.H.) B276 D49 H17 L11 M8B R84 W23 W11
HANSON Lars R73
HANSON Rolf C86
HANSON Silver L1A
HANSON Simon O40
HANSON Tom P137
HANSSON Bo H18 H18A
HANSSON AND KARLSSON H18A
HAPLIN Tom M203
HAPPY THE MAN H19A
HAPSHASH Lanse T11
HAPSHASH AND THE COLOURED CAT H19B
HARADA Kuma C39A G94 J39 K24 M145 M19A M202C M206 R40B S108 T31
HARADA Yujin F20A G55
HARBACH Stephen A30A
HARBERT Richard F108A
HARCK Ken O10A
HARCOURT Charlie C56 H20 J14 J107 L80
HARCOURT'S HEROES H20
HARD ROAD H20A
HARDAWAY Robert R22
HARDEN Bobby E73
HARDERS Hanno S329A
HARDESTY Herbert D96 K45 W6
HARDIN Ardis G92
HARDIN Eddie A131E D28 D66 G50 H22 H24 W117
HARDIN Glen D. C224 C237 E20 H35 L36A N25 P33 P125 R137 S272 S341
HARDIN Joseph K45
HARDIN Louis M192
HARDIN Steve P109A
HARDIN Tim H23
HARDIN AND YORK H24
HARDING B,P, X2
HARDING Bob A29
HARDING Chris P62
HARDING Rob O10A
HARDMEAT H25
HARDWICK Steve W69A
HARDY Calvin W5
HARDY Cliff H183 P131
HARDY Dave F127
HARDY Eddie B87
HARDY Gerry L25

HARDY Helen B237 C79
HARDY Joe G92B
HARDY Lyndon Lee C56
HARDY Phil W56
HARDY Richard K48 N12A
HARE Colin H143
HARE Pat B127 L94 P26 W28
HARGIS Marlon E77
HARGIS Regi B212
HARGRETT Charlie B123
HARGROVE Linda A102 H26 N25 R173
HARKER Malcolm I17A
HARKER Roland J72 S266 W86
HARKIN Brendan B27 F108A S254
HARKIN Pattie Dandy F108A
HARKLEROAD Bill B72 M58
HARLAND Kelly L30
HARLEY Andy A33
HARLEY Mel A67C
HARLEY Pat W86
HARLEY Sam A22 A33 P19
HARLEY Steve (NICE Steven) H26A M35 P31
HARLEY Wayne P49
HARLING Cyril L137
HARLIS H26B
HARLOS Axel 'Felix' G106 Y16
HARLOW Allen P139
HARLOW Larry A47 F17 I2
HARMAN Buddy L64 M197A
HARMAN Dave (DEE Dave) D20
HARMAN Mark Henry K32 P106
HARMON Buddy C14 F126 H26 H65 J53 N37 P63 P125 R173 S187C S271 S272
HARMON Joan B17 K53
HARMONICA H27
Harmonica Boy W59
Harmonica Fats C217
HARMONIUM H28
HARMS Jesse C179
HARNELL Joe M229
HARNETT Eddi H83
HARP Andy S339A
HARPER Bill S29
HARPER Charlie U4
HARPER Delisle (or Lyle) A9B B77 B209 B268 C204 E77A F117 G13 G67 H17 K51 L47 M202A O20 S257 W103
HARPER Don H132 S198
HARPER Ginger R122
HARPER Joe E67 H159
HARPER Rod S19
HARPER Roy B280 H29 P85
HARPER Teddy P59
HARPERS BIZARRE H30
HARPO Slim (MOORE James H31
HARREL Dale Jnr A53
HARREL Tom A136 P99 W62
HARRELL Cynthia L65
HARRELL Dickie V32
HARRELL James L121A P118A S8A
HARRELL Vern L90
HARRELL Vivian D66
HARRIMAN John Carr P73
HARRINGTON Bob K48
HARRINGTON Carey Bell E67
HARRINGTON John C165
HARRINGTON Terry B256 K48
HARRIOT Joe A120 P8 W94
HARRIOTT Derrick H33
HARRIS Addie S98
HARRIS Alan K45 M45
HARRIS Beaver M79
HARRIS Bill C144A
HARRIS Bob L91 Z0
HARRIS Bunny H133
HARRIS Charles D. R101
HARRIS Cliff (also FOX Cliff) M175
HARRIS Damon T42
HARRIS Dan H37A M8A W53
HARRIS Dennis B135 L69 M2 O14

HARRIS Diane R31
HARRIS Diane R31
HARRIS Don (D) S230
HARRIS Don 'Sugarcane' (Vln) D97 H34 H150 M68 M111 O38 P150 Z8
HARRIS Eddie C17
HARRIS Emmylou B29 B221 C123 C124 C237 D139 E20 H35 L36A L89 P33 P50 R22 R137 S65 W101 Y16
HARRIS Freddie P15 P99
HARRIS Geoff K65
HARRIS Greg M205A
HARRIS Hi-Fi R70A R74
HARRIS Hi-Tide(BOYD or GITRY Willie) H35A M111
HARRIS Hilda A35A B262
HARRIS Ivory Joe H120
HARRIS Jack P31
HARRIS Jerry N53A
HARRIS Jet B64 H36 R80 S80
HARRIS Jo Ann D139 P69
HARRIS Joe A40 D96
HARRIS Joey S272
HARRIS Johanna H37A
HARRIS John (K) B41 D21 H52A K88 K95 L77 N57 S73 Y16
HARRIS Jon F108A
HARRIS Keith J14
HARRIS Kenneth N39
HARRIS Kent W110
HARRIS Major Handy R124A
HARRIS Mark H194A
HARRIS Michael (K) B231
HARRIS Michael (Tpt) C45 E7 E45
HARRIS Michelle T107
HARRIS Norman H133 K45 L130 N65
HARRIS Oliver W94
HARRIS Paul A4 A59 B194 C58 C196 D111 F78 F128 H59 H120 K45 K77 K81 M28 M64 M94 M101 M229 O12 P106 R109 R169 S65 S197 S276 W16
HARRIS Pennie K65 W123
HARRIS Peppermint T53A
HARRIS Pete P47
HARRIS Phil A7 C131
HARRIS Ray B5
HARRIS Richard F103
HARRIS Roger F128
HARRIS Ron L65
HARRIS Scottie R115
HARRIS Shakey Jake H37 M48 S329
HARRIS Shaun H37A M8A W53
HARRIS Steve I25
HARRIS Sue A30 H194 K65 T79
HARRIS Tat W28
HARRIS Ted B282
HARRIS Tim F90A
HARRIS Tom W38
HARRIS Tony E66 O18B
HARRIS Tweed H175
HARRIS Voyle R22
HARRIS Walter L63
HARRISON Al C129
HARRISON Bill (D) M176
HARRISON Billy (G) H37B T57
HARRISON Bobby C23 F56
HARRISON Brian (D) D113 L117
HARRISON Brian (B) J15A
HARRISON Charlie A22 M15 M27 P106 S285 T157
HARRISON Don H38
HARRISON Geff D4B H38A I162A
HARRISON George B59 B202 D139 H39 L37 L111 M100E P126 R173 S50 S220 S252
HARRISON Jerry (K/G) R83 T8
HARRISON John B253
HARRISON Lanny M100B

HARRISON Lee T22
HARRISON Martin E52A
HARRISON Mike (V/K) A87
H40 J109 S224
HARRISON Mike (B) M39
HARRISON Nicky M233
HARRISON Nigel B139 M82
N52 S119
HARRISON Norman M108A
HARRISON Olly P77A
HARRISON Patti H39
HARRISON Phil K83
HARRISON Roger R20
HARRISON Spiderman J11
HARRISON Stan S199
HARRISON Stuart H125
HARRISON Terry M233
HARRISON Timmy F29
HARRISON Wilbert H41
HARRIT Niels G12
HARROLD Melanie (also
CARLIN Joanna) H42 S235
HARROP Graham P4
HARRY Deborah B139 W100
HARRY MUSKEE BAND M237A
HARRYMAN Martyn D4
HARSH REALITY H43
HART Adrian P104A
HART Billy H19 H44 W30A
Z9
HART Bobby M181
HART Charlie B237 L16A
T122 W130
HART Dick A109
HART Frankie W1
HART George S67
HART Ken O2
HART Lea R131
HART Martin M111
HART Mickey B259 C232 G84
H45 H186 K10 N32 R77B S61
HART Mike H46 L95
HART Paul T173
HART Ritchie G72A
HART Tim H47 H48 S227
S263
HART Wilbert D42
HART William D42
HARTFORD John A132 B285
C123 D70 D71 H49 S5B S120
T25 T27
HARTLEY Keef A92 C78 D91
D133 H50 M111 V21
HARTLEY Mathieu C247A
HARTMAN Carl H51
HARTMAN Dan H51 T65 W106
W107 W108
HARTMAN Don F129A
HARTMAN John (D) D101
S124
HARTMAN John (K) C77
HARTMAN Warren B41
HARTMANN Hans G120
HARTMANN John H11
HARTNAGLE Bobby V12
HARTSFIELD J.C. H78
HARTWIG Gerald Luciano
G120 K11
HARTY John N30
HARTZLER Brian B256
HARVEY Alex H52 R122
HARVEY Alexander H52A
HARVEY Barry C65
HARVEY Bernard 'Touter'
B95A B276 D130 H122 I19
M88 P140C R30 R84 V21 W4
HARVEY Bill B233 P26
HARVEY Bob (B) J46
HARVEY Bob (D) F134
HARVEY Carl T110
HARVEY Danny L57A
HARVEY David T57
HARVEY Don A127 B195 Y2
HARVEY Hank C211
HARVEY Les L27 S283 S355
HARVEY Neil S110
HARVEY Paul P54
HARVEY Peter S157
HARVEY Pip D109
HARVEY Richard B209 B280
C201A G35 G114 H53 H194
R11 S280 T79 W86 W102
HARVEY Tam H180
HARVEY Ted H194A T24
HARVEY Touter see HARVEY
Bernard

HARVIN Delores 'Loris'
P6 W119
HARWOOD Charlie M108
HARWOOD Kirk B259
HARWOOD Paul M54
HASBOOM Hans F45
HASELDON Tony N53
HASHIAN Sib B184
HASHIMOTO Shunichi Y6A
HASKELL Gordon H54 H65
J68 K54
HASKELL Jimmy C51 F78
M125A N37 P106 S123 S262
S269 S272 T164 W44A
HASKETT Max C158 R154 W21
HASKINS Clarence 'Fuzzy'
F137 P29
HASLAM Annie (WOOD Mrs.
Roy) H55 I22 R65 W122
HASLIM Mary M131A
HASLIP Jimmy B124A P13
HASOLD Yann Jakez S280
HASSALL Dave A5 M67 P138
HASSALL Norman F133A
HASSE Mick D86A
HASSEL John E59
HASSELBACH Mark P119A
HASSELBRINK Ed G10
HASSLES H55A
HASSON Fred M95
HASSON Leary C3 M95
HASTINGS Doug A9 B260 O15
R75
HASTINGS Eric S48
HASTINGS Jim C34 F42 H57
N9 S182 S233 T133
HASTINGS Pye C34 H154
HATANO Toru H55B
HATCHER George H56
HATCHER Keith M225
HATCHER Willie W93
HATFIELD Bobby R87
HATFIELD Ken K47
HATFIELD Ivo W3
HATFIELD AND THE NORTH
H57
HATHAWAY Donnie F60 H58
M126 O15 T154
HATHAWAY Richard N53
HATJE Bill S306
HATOT Alain J72 M49 S280
HATTERSLEY Cleve G100
HATTERSLEY Lissa G100
HATTLER Hellmut G120 K89
HATTON Billy F93
HATTON Steve D31A
HATZIPAVLI Angelos S266
HAUF Butch O30A
HAUGHEY Bobby F14 H183
S31
HAUKE Peter J56
HAUSER Bruce T116
HAUSER Tim M75
HAUSMANN Kalle A57
HAUTOANO Teppo V26C
HAVARD Glyn A23 A105 E17
J16 Y1
HAVENS Richie A31 E33
H4 H59
HAVENSTEIN Kurt S332B
HAVERMANS Cyril F77 H60
HAVIS Beth T55
HAWES Bruce L130
HAWES Hampton B17A
HAWES Jeanette (nee
HUTCHINSON) E7 E55
HAWKEN John G32 G111 H11
I13 N5 R65 S295 S339 T63
HAWKER Jean Y19
HAWKES Greg C41 M131A
HAWKES Jeff T116
HAWKES Len 'Chip' T138
HAWKINS Adrian H157A
HAWKINS Anthony B113A
HAWKINS Brian C161
HAWKINS Charles B113A
HAWKINS Dale H61
HAWKINS Don G122 W47
HAWKINS Geoff C183
HAWKINS George L109 L110
HAWKINS Ginny H63
HAWKINS Herman L64
HAWKINS Hoyt J98 K30 K95
N37 P63 P125
HAWKINS Ira M191

HAWKINS Jalacy
'Screamin'Jay' H63
HAWKINS Jim S303
HAWKINS John W77
HAWKINS Ken M151
HAWKINS Leslie L146 W54
HAWKINS Lynette B259
HAWKINS Reg O42
HAWKINS Roger B123 B126
B200 C14 C30 C139 C179
D27A F23 F48 F123A F134
G10 G61 H15 H62 H92 J11
J14A K46 K87 L79 M10
M235 N55 N65 O15 P79 R4
R137 R168 S36 S73 S125
S172 S266 S342 T20 T127
W118
HAWKINS Ronnie B29 F116
H62
HAWKINS Screamin' Jay
see HAWKINS Jalacy
HAWKINS Tramaine B259
HAWKINS Trevor S268
HAWKLORDS H64
HAWKS see BAND
HAWKSHAW Alan D99 E7D
H183 M100 S209 V30
HAWKSWORTH Mick A63 F56
F141 T46
HAWKWIND H64
HAWORTH Bryn A82 B17 C13
F7 G6 G32 H65 H111 L48
L111 M108 R11
HAWTHORN Steve W15
HAY Barry G64
HAY Ivor S11
HAYASHIDA Ross B109
HAYCOCK Pete C141 T14
HAYDEN Charlie M40
HAYDEN Stacey B86 I10
Z22
HAYE George 'Buddy' W4A
HAYES Chris L61A L67B
HAYES David M18 M203 T54
T150 Y12
HAYES Ernie B87 E49 K81
P6
HAYES Gordon P49
HAYES Isaac J11 M85
HAYES Jimmy H8 P67
HAYES Lonnie L90
HAYES Martin P110
HAYES Sherman C169 J53
HAYES Sloan S245
HAYES Tubby F14
HAYES Willie Y15
HAYLEY Nick P72
HAYMAN Alan W127A
HAYMER James M191
HAYNES Bill T158
HAYNES Bobby C217 C241
HAYNES Cecil 'Jimmy' E62
HAYNES Jim Z8
HAYNES John S8B
HAYNES Rick L72
HAYNES Roy L83
HAYNES Walter C14
HAYNOR John S314
HAYS Drew J17
HAYS Jon P81
HAYTON Steve D5 F35 K75
S185
HAYWARD Charles (D) G66
M81 Q13
HAYWARD Charles (D/K)
T66
HAYWARD Charlie (B) D12
T20
HAYWARD Chris S280
HAYWARD John B141A
HAYWARD Justin B151 F65
H66 J27 M67 M189
HAYWARD Martin M195 S108
HAYWARD Rick J50 L75 P62
T111 V21
HAYWARD Ritchie A82 B135
C179 C195 D8 D72A D101
E40 F100 F104A G24 G121
L89 L111 N21 P15 S124
S276
HAYWARD Russell M67
HAYWELL Tim A19
HAYWOOD Jon Douglas A37
A59 B244 D71 R101 W21
HAYWOOD Kitty L65 P137
S111

HAYWOOD Leon O39
HAYWOOD Marlyn D66
HAYWOOD Valerie C99
HAYWOOD Vivian L65 S111
HAZE Leonard Y8
HAZEL Eddie F137 H68 P29
P113
HAZELL Cecily O18
HAZELWOOD Mike F13
HAZZARD Tony H67 J72
HAZZARD AND BARNES H67
HEAD H69
HEAD (U.S.) H69A
HEAD Anthony H70
HEAD Bushy J21
HEAD Coleman J7 M68 P150
HEAD Dave L23
HEAD Frank L46
HEAD Murray H70
HEAD Steve S74A
HEAD EAST H71
HEADBOYS H71A
HEADHUNTERS H72
HEADLEY Felix 'Deadly'
C245 P134
HEADLEY-DOWN John F100
HEADON Nicky C130
HEADS HANDS & FEET H74
HEADSTONE H73
HEALEY Dennis M111
HEALEY Derek F14 G31 R40B
HEARD Hubert P126 W136
HEARD John D127 P115
HEART H75
HEART Steve N24A
HEARTBREAKERS (PETTY) P70
HEARTBREAKERS (THUNDERS)
H76
HEARTS AND FLOWERS H77
HEARTSFIELD H78
HEARTSMAN Johnny M238
HEARTWOOD H78A
HEAT H79
HEATERS H80
HEATH Cory H98
HEATH Frederick see KIDD
Johnny
HEATH John N6
HEATH Martin A66
HEATH Richard R161
HEATH Tom M147
HEATH Tootie H19
HEATH-HADFIELD David H175
HEATHMAN Mike M59
HEATLEY Spike C2 D31A K84
L111 M50 S273
HEATLIE Bob H71A R1
HEATON Christopher L16
HEATWAVE H81
HEATWAVES B129
HEAVEN H83
HEAVY JELLY H84
HEAVY METAL KIDS H85
HEAVY METAL KIDS H19B
HEBBERT Michael H194
HEBERT Aussie 'Nogo' B95A
HECHT Peter L139
HECKSTALL-SMITH Dick B156
B171 B237 B248 C101 C166
D58 F125 H86 K84 M111
S349A
HECTOR Jesse G75
HEDAYAT Dashiell A35 H86A
HEDDING Timothy M32
HEDGEHOG PIE H87
HEDLEY John D29
HEDWIG Ula C249 M177
HEGARTY Den D18
HEGEDUS Gabor S72
HEIBL Bob A57
HEIBRON Fritz Y12
HEIBS Danny M81
HEID Bill R112 T28
HEIDEMAN Gail M131A
Heil H5A
HEILBRUN Fred J69
HEILHECKER Axel F81B
HEIMAN Nachum D92
HEIMBERG Lothar S47
HEIMBUCH Ann T22
HEINRICH Stuart R60
HEINTZE Dick B253
HEISS Stu K77
Heinz (BURT Heinz) H88
T112
HELALSVUO Esa V26C

HELD Zeus B. B107 G35A H89
HELDON H89A
HELFER Erwin B277 H89B
HELIUM KIDS S244
HELL Richard H76 H90 T38
HELL PREACHERS INC. H91
HELLABY Andy C175
HELLER Dave M1
HELLERMAN Fred C164
HELLFIELD H91A
HELLFIELD Mitch H91A
HELLIWELL John Anthony
B188 D36 S333
HELLYER Terry H65
HELM Buddy B256
HELM Carl H192
HELM Howard Z16
HELM Levon B29 C58 D13
D139 F116 H15 H62 H92 L111
M94 O16 S252 W28 W101
HELMER Duitch R59 R101
S252
HELMER Jim G117 H9 N65
R101
HELMER Johnny P88B
HELMINGER Maurice M221B
HELMIT Red P148
HELMS Jimmy A62 C185B G98
S35 S296 W117
HELP YOURSELF H93
HEMINGWAY Anne S326A
HEMINGWAY Graham S326A
HEMLOCK H94
HEMMES Roel C243
HEMMINGS Courtney A107
B276 W23
HEMMINGS John B188
HEMMINGS Nancy W126
HEMPHILL Alvin K51
HENDERSEN Marlo see
HENDERSON Marlo
HENDERSON Adam T57
HENDERSON Ashley S312
HENDERSON Bill (G) C106
HENDERSON Bill (Vln) E31
HENDERSON Bill (D) W1
HENDERSON Brian N51
HENDERSON Bugs N53A
HENDERSON Connie H97
HENDERSON Derek R130
HENDERSON Dorris E12 H95
L59 R66
HENDERSON Douglas M89
HENDERSON Eddie H19 H97
HENDERSON Eugene P126
HENDERSON Harvey B36
HENDERSON Jimmy (G) B114
HENDERSON Jim (V) T155
HENDERSON Joe C186 E65 V39
HENDERSON Kyle W69A
HENDERSON Leon M1
HENDERSON Marlo B226 E7
E55 H17 M130 M151 M203 R97
R115
HENDERSON Martin E56A
HENDERSON Michael H98
HENDERSON Mike F134
HENDERSON Mike J105A
HENDERSON Pat (V) A37 B8
J8BA M225 M229 M232 R137
S325
HENDERSON Rev Patrick (K)
B169A C179 K51 L107 R173
HENDERSON Pete B164
HENDERSON Robert A9 H8A
HENDERSON Tim P116
HENDERSON Tommy M53
HENDERSON Wayne A134 C241
D27 H96 L71B L143 P6
HENDERSON William see
WILLIAMSON Homesick James
HENDERSON Willie D66
HENDRA Tony N10
HENDRICKS Bobby D116
HENDRICKS James L14 M224
R101
HENDRICKS Tony K94B
HENDRICKSON Arthur S74
HENDRICKSON Richard S215
HENDRIKSE Kat H75 J15A W9
HENDRIKSEN Ray S193
HENDRIX Jacques S280
HENDRIX James W44A
HENDRIX Jimi D38A E26 H99
K70 L91 S35 S276
HENDRIX Muffy W24

KIENHOLZ Philippe T35
KIENKE Kathryn T98
KIFFER Patrick S280
KIHN Greg K40
KIKOINE Gina G35A
KIKUCHI Masabumi D27
KILBRIDE Pat B51
KILBURN Duncan P142C
KILBURN & THE HIGH ROADS K41
KILLEN Buddy K30 T55
KILLEN Louis W92
KILLERS K42
KILLGO Keith B122
KILLIAN Lawrence M26 S169
KILLING FLOOR K43
KILLING JOKE K43A
KILLJOYS K44
KILMER Doug B144 L8 R168 T150 V7
KILMISTER Ian 'Lemmy' C18 H64 M213
KILPATRICK Spider H152
KIM Harry E31 L55 S251
KIMBALL Ali B230
KIMBALL Bobby H26A M232 M233 T115
KIMBALL Tamara B230
KIMBERLEY Peter B8A
KIMBLE Walter D96
KIMMEL Bob S282
KIMSEY Chris B2
KIMSEY Jerome H146 P114
KINBERG Boris G90
KINCAID Mark E35
KIND HEARTS AND ENGLISH K44A
KINDER Michael G1B
KINDLER George B221
KINDLER Steve B64 H12 M40
KINDS Hans C243
KING Alan 'Bam' A7 C39A C131 H65 K52 M148 I170
KING Albert C231 K46
KING Allan 'Kingpin' R61A
KING Andy S181
KING B.B. (KING Riley 'Blues Boy') B127 K45 T9
KING Ben E. (NELSON Benjamin) A131 D116 I22 K47
KING Ben E.Jnr. K47
KING Benjy D53
KING Betty V9
KING Bobby (V) C179 C246 M229 O15 P114B
KING Bobby (V) S37
KING Bobby (G) K47A K51
KING Carole (KLEIN Carole) C117 C134 C233 J65 K45 K48 S124 S272 T25 T27 W11
KING Clydie A11 A37 A50 A132 B63 B84 B201 B226 B256 B282 C77 C155 C171 C180 C211 D8 D23A D26 D103 D124 F50 G15 G87 G121 H179 J72 K45 K49 K95 L9 L44 L107 L146 M101 M191 M232 N4 N13 N23 O39 P6 R54 R101 R113 R133 R137 R173 S34 S73 S116 S124 S262 S342 V12 W16
KING Dave H175
KING E.L. C246
KING Earl K50 M138
KING Ed L146 M120 S294
KING Eldridge C179
KING Freddie K51
KING Gary F60 G4 J20 L119 H107 S50 W25 W62
KING Gillian W72
KING Harold K57
KING Howard F60 H97 M222A M125
KING Ian D34A
KING Jack M159
KING Jackie B177 S78A
KING Jan O29B
KING Jean P125
KING Jeanie P83
KING Jeff N5 T147
KING Jim (Reeds) F12 J9 R92
KING Jimmy B36 R56
KING John M159

KING John G7C
KING Juliet W72
KING Kim L122A
KING Lenny C195
KING Mark M1A
KING Melvin O21
KING Paget H172
KING Pat H111B M80
KING Paul K56 M230
KING Pete (Wind) C2 C34 F14 K84 W18
KING Pete (D) A19
KING Pete (Steel) R80A
KING Ray (Wind) H83
KING Ray (Perc) C254
KING Reg C131 J9 K52 L48 M148
KING Reid C217
KING Riley see KING B.B.
KING Rob (D) D56
KING Robbie (K) H141 S148
KING Rod K41 R11 S313
KING Ron S58
KING Ronnie S239
KING Simon C18 H64 M194
KING Speedy S87
KING Stu Boy D65
KING Sylvia H74
KING Terry C183A
KING Tom (G) O44A
KING Tom (G) D54
KING Tony G39
KING William C174
King Biscuit Boy (NEWELL Richard) C236 E33 H62 K53
King Cool F109
KING CREOLE AND THE COCONUTS K53A
KING CRIMSON K54
King Curtis (OUSLEY Curtis) B202 C146 D133 H58 K51 K55 S98 T20
KING EARL BOOGIE BAND K56
King Errison (JOHNSON Errisson) B80 B245 B256 C58 C153 F92 K46 K56A M177 N16A O15 P126 S58 S272 V17 W9 W13 W63
King Harry K57
KING HARVEST K58
KING OF HEARTS K59
KINGDOM COME B231
KINGDOM COME P60B
KINGFISH K60
KINGHAM Lionel M15 M227 W24
KINGPINS K55
KINGS SINGERS B160
KINGSFORD Jed M137
KINGSMAN Boot S288A
KINGSMAN Pete R20
KINGSON Bob M18
KINGSTON Bill W77
KINGSTON Melt H167
KINKS K61
KINLERS Craig C233
KINNEY George G62A
KINNEY Norma M144
KINORRA Phil A120
KINSEL Frank R101
KINSEY Donald M88 T114 W66
KINSEY Woody W66
KINSLEY Billy M136
KINSLEY Roots B276
KINSON Kevin T170
Kip B137
KIP John B225
KIPNER Steve C127
KIPPER Stan Quica F39 M125
KIPPINGTON LODGE K62
KIPPS Charlie M12
Kirby (G) C251 G48 J39B K63 K66 S301
Kirby (Pno) C216
KIRBY Andy R40 T54
KIRBY Dave C15 H26 H42 J53 M11 N37 S272 V10
KIRBY Robert C161 C202 S295
KIRCHEN Bill C173

KIRCHER Pete H143 M106A S87
KIRCHIN Basil K64
KIRIAKIS George T22
KIRK Benjamin V9
KIRK Robert N56A
KIRKE Simon B14 B112 B138 D133 F108 H11 K87 R3 R125 W54A
KIRKHAM Bill R53A
KIRKHAM Mildred 'Millie' D139 K95 P125
KIRKLAND Eddie H150
KIRKLAND Frank D66
KIRKLAND James N21
KIRKLAND Jesse J92 P126 R133
KIRKLAND Ken K47 V39
KIRKLAND Leroy H63
KIRKMAN Terry A106
KIRKPATRICK Chuck B124A C76 D26
KIRKPATRICK John A30 B105 C206 H194 J72 K65 R11 R23 S108 S263 T79
KIRKPATRICK Katie P44
KIRKPATRICK Scott M28
KIRKPATRICK Spencer H195
KIRSCH Barry R20
KIRTLEY Pete G46 G101
G102 H177 R7 R86 S103B S348B W58 W123
KIRWAN Danny F66 K66 P62 S204 S211 T130
KISH George F14
KISS K67
KISSELBACH Donnie D53
KISSOON Katie E41 K28B M19 M203 R106 Y17
KISSOON Mac E41 K28B M19 R106
KISWINEY Dave Q5
KITAJIMA Osamu A41 H150 O33G
KITCAT Martin G77A H169
KITCHEN Kevin K66
KITE K67A
KITHCART Glenn A55 T116A
KITRELL Christine B193
KITTA George T23
KITZMILLER John N25
KIZER Brad C39B
KJELDSEN Mark S130
KLAASSE Beer F45
KLAATU K68
KLAIN Gary H23
KLAIN Manny N25
KLARWEINI Marti S175
KLASS Lou C146 F134
KLASSEN Karl E63
KLATKA Tony B141
KLAUS LENZ BAND L52B
KLAVETT Dean L131
KLAWON Dan T17
KLEBE Gary S102
KLEC'H Mikael S280
KLEE Ginny D54
KLEE Lucy D54
KLEEER K68A
KLEENEX K68B
KLEIGER Frank W5
KLEIN Betsy F133
KLEIN Carole see KING Carole
KLEIN Daniel G19 G122
KLEIN Harry C34 F14 K75
KLEIN Manny N25
KLEIN Paul W100
KLEIN Warren F94 F104A
KLEINBARD Annette T37D
KLEINOW 'Sneaky' Pete B202 B244 B245 B285 C59 C155 C160 C180 C216 C236 D8 D20 D49 E41 F66 F74 K17 K22 L51 L89 M30 M125A M159 M160 M170 N21 O15 O27 P33 P76 R137 S114 T6B Z8
KLEIST Ken F72
KLEMM Dieter F70A
KLEMMER John B194 H150 M82 S262
KLEVN Bert F133A
KLIEMES Peter A135
KLIMAK Ken D86
KLING Janne A4 L79

KLINGBERG John M203 V21
KLINGER Gunther M136B
KLINGMAN Mark 'Moogy' C195 F109 K81 O39 R164 W107
KLOATR Alan S280
KLOBER Chris H48A
KLOCKER Gerd W13D
KLOETZE Don B261
KLUCZYNSKI Marek B82
KLUGH Earl J20 K69
KLUSTER C145
KNACK K69A
KNAIL John S236
KNAPP Bob M40 W8
KNAPP John G124
KNAPP Peter I1
KNAPP Robin S192
KNAPP Skip M1
KNAPP Tom 'Cat' T41
KNAUP Renate A57 U23
KNECHTEL Larry B17A B110 B206 B285 C140A C171 D5A D23A D26 E14 G10 G14 G15 G101A H37A J36 J69 K14 L111 L116 M61 M84C M101 M125A N25 O15 P125 P129 R76 R101 R126 S123 S125 S160 S252 T91 W39 W88 KNEIL Manfred M136B
KNEPPER Jimmy K81 M79
KNIEMEYER Claus O7
KNIGHT Billy J66
KNIGHT Brendan K72 M1
KNIGHT Curtis H99 K70
KNIGHT Gladys K72
KNIGHT Graham M89
KNIGHT Holly S214A
KNIGHT Jean K71
KNIGHT Jerry B226 H8A J7 P80 R45 W16
KNIGHT Jesse E52B L90
KNIGHT Joyce W54
KNIGHT K.J. N63
KNIGHT Larry C15A S216
KNIGHT Lonnie K77
KNIGHT Merald K72
KNIGHT Peter A30 H194 J75B S263
KNIGHT Stanley B114
KNIGHT Steve (K) M216
KNIGHT Tony D46 S141
KNIGHTON Joan H50
KNIGHTON Reggie K73 S65 W65A
KNIGHTS Dave P140 R156
KNIGHTSBRIDGE John G32 H174 I13 L76B T63
KNOPFLER Dave D75
KNOPFLER Mark D75 M41A S262
KNOTT Ray B5
KNOW Bobby O36
KNOWLES David T108
KNOWLES Errol A136 E65
KNOWLES Geoff P110
KNOWLES Greg M220 P143
KNOWLES Keith M91
KNOWLES Tom C196 K32A
KNOWLES Willie A80
KNOWLING Ransom C135 C239 E67 S204 S329 T9B W84 W93
Knox V2B
KNOX Buddy K74
KNOX Don S230
KNOX Tom B41
KNUDSEN J.D83A
KNUDSEN Keith D101 J85A M144 S124
KNUDSEN Kenneth C185D D31 L41 S69
KNUDSEN Pete B230 P117A
KNUTSEN Pete R178
KOBAYASHI Shigeyuki C253A
KOBLUN Ken B260
KOBORI Tadashi H35A W53A
KOCH Michael J56
KOCJAN Krysia H110 K61 K75 N11 S270
KOCK Franz O47
KODA Cubby B246
KODAK Dave S263A
KODAMA Kathie W1
KODER Jay L119C

KOEHLER Trevor I2D
KOELLEN Helmut T143
KOEMAN Martin K16
KOENIG Art A86
KOERNER 'Spider' John K75A K75B
KOERNER RAY AND GLOVER K75B
KOERTS Chris E4
KOERTS Gerard E4
KOFFMAN Moe K53
KOFSTEIN Mark E7B
KOGER Marijke F81C
KOHL Martin S338
KOHLER Rolf S329A T103A
KOHLIN Jan L79
KOHN Philip C251
KOHON Harold S215
KOIVISTOINEN Eero W75
KOJO Timo W75
KOKEN Walt T150
KOKOMO A22 K76
KOLB Dieter S332C
KOLDENHOVEN Darlene L65
KOLLARUS Gary G87
KOLLIS Ed A132
KOLOC Bonnie K77 P137
KOMANOFF Ruth Z8
KOMINTERN K77A
KONAS Joe G56 I103
KONCALSKI Michael M238
KONDO Tatsuro H35A
KONDOR Robbie F83A H15
KONDZIELA David A135
KONGO Roy Johnston P134
KONGOS John D2 K78 M45
KONIETZKO Harald L5
KONIKOFF Eli S231
KONIKOFF Sanford B27 C155 D26 K45 K46 M53 S111
KONRAD Robert B15
KONTE Lamine W119
KONTE Skip B166 B225 C158
KONZIELA Dave C76
KOOBAS K79
KOOL AND THE GANG K80
KOONTZ Randy P67
KOOPER Al B141 B144 B158 B194 B282 C180 C182 D139 E15 F102 H99 K81 L24 L37 L107 M53 N53 O39
KOOPMAN Pim K16
KOOTCH Danny see KORTCHMAR Danny
KOOYMANS George C243 G64
KOPLAN Michael C80B
KOPP Holger S329A
KOPPEL Anders S30
KOPPEL Ilse Maria S30
KOPPEL Thomas S30
KOPPENHAUER David C21A
KORBA Tom J112
KORBERG Tommy S1B6
KORDA Paul D4 K82 M23 R33 S35
KOREVEC Loren C234A
KORGIS K83
KORN Barbara E7
KORNER Alexis B156 C2 C243 D23 G78 H179 J75B J91 K45 K84 M129 M185 P34 R122A
KORNER Neil G32 N5
KORNFELD Artie K84A W100
KORPS K85
KORTCHMAR Danny (KOOTCH Danny) A16 B175 B244 C38 C117 C123 C138 C158 C233 E40 F68 F133 G60 J65 K14 K48 K86 M191 N23 P114 Q15A R22 R39 R81 R137 S17 S70 S196 S252 S272 T25 T27 W21 W136 Z11
KORUS Kate R17 S159
KOSAK Wayne J15A
KOSEK Kenneth B135 F83A G72 I2 M21 O15 P41 S7 W5
KOSH Paul C251 F42 G22
KOSHIDA Nisako N65
KOSINS Kathy H98
KOSINSKI Richard 'Koz' B100 S327A
KOSLEN Jonah S241
KOSS Ron S65
KOSSOFF Keith B47

[491]

[492]

Mac

McCRACKEN Chet G29
McCRACKEN Gary M112
McCRACKEN Hugh A96 A123
B77 C40 C44 C234A C236
D86 E40 F60 F103D F108A
G10 G27 G109 H9 I2 I21
J20 J48 J69 K45 K51 L4A
M9 M12 M21 M125 M143 M225
N65 O15 R140 R169 S50
S124 S125 S180 S262 T37E
T98 W5 W44A
McCRACKEN Richard S309
T16
McCRACKLIN Jimmy B233
M13A
McCRAE George R12
McCRAE George (V) L24 W136
McCRAE Gwen L24 W136
McCRAE Shel F87
McCRARY Everett H150
McCREARY Lew A131D B127
C180 D99 F92 F134 H8A L50
M68 M229 N16A N25 R78 R99
R161 S58 S262
McCREARY Macey L7
McCREARY Mary see RUSSELL
Mary
McCRORY Martha D139 G72
J53 M11
McCUE Sammy E74
McCULLER Arnold C249 H8
J48 M177 P119 R125 R137
S252
McCulloch P145A
McCULLOCH Andrew F44 G97
K54 M35 M80
McCULLOCH Danny A67 K52
McCULLOCH Jack T84
McCULLOCH Jimmy D9 D127C
G29 H29 K20 L27 M9 M23
M111 S162 S283 T47 T84
McCULLOUGH David S284
McCULLOUGH Henry C35D C78
C155 D84 F7 F104 G86 H29
H123 L7 L101 M9 M15 M157
S224 S346
McCULLOUGH Ullanda A96
A123 D63 F60 M111 R100
S124 S169 T37E
McCULLUM Paul M178
McCULLUM Robert see
NIGHTHAWK Robert
McCUNE Ida S160
McCUNE Susie L72
McCURDY Ron M111
McCURN George C179
McCUSKER Vince F131
McDADE Butch A45
McDANIEL Elias see
DIDDLEY Bo
McDANIEL Lenny M111
McDANIEL Willard J21
McDANIELS Buddy M111
McDANIELS David A120 C155
H166 W21
McDANIELS Ernie H8A J41
McDANIELS Eugene F60
McDANIELS Pete B106
McDERMOTT Denny S97
McDERMOTT Tom M192A
McDONAGH Terence S157
McDONALD Al M93
McDONALD Barry D139
MACDONALD Bertie L71A
McDONALD Carl N28
McDONALD Carol I27
McDONALD Clarence C153
C220 E55 H8A H9 H112 K56A
L26B L38 M75 M130 M151
N23 P44 P67 R54 S58 T25
W10A W31 W116
McDONALD Country Joe M18
MACDONALD Donald H23 H59
J54 M55A M125
McDONALD Frank B47B E74
K44A S54
MACDONALD Henry K94 S306
McDONALD Hugh B221 F83A
G72 O15 P121 P137 S180
S252
McDONALD Ian (D) B168 F84
P121
MACDONALD Ian (K/Wind)
C63 C109 K54 L63 L98 M20
M81

MACDONALD Ian (V) see
MATTHEWS Ian
McDONALD John R148A
McDONALD Kathi B94 D24
K25 K51 L107 M16 M101
N55 Q12 R133
McDONALD Larry B283 M53
McDONALD Lloyd W4A
McDONALD Maureen D101
McDONALD Mike B110 C180
D101 G106A J85A J93C L19
L89 M198 N53 R22 S124
S262
McDONALD Paul I1
McDONALD Pete S214C
MACDONALD Ralph A35A A96
A123 A131 B77 B85 B186
B208 C44 C241 D86 G4 G10
G61 H9 H58 J20 J43 J48
J69 K48 K69 L4A L18 M17
M41 M75 M78 M86 M102 N65
P137 P149 R22 R25 S17
S50 S64 S124 S125 S180
S220 S262 T25 T37E T147
V17 W25 W27 W116
McDONALD Robin D6 K93
MACDONALD Ronnie Y17
McDONALD Shelagh C109
M19
McDONALD Stewart K43
McDONALD Susan P83
McDONALD Tesfa C139
MACDONALD Val O47
MACDONALD AND GILES M20
McDONNELL M.J. D58
McDONNELL Pat A126
McDONOUGH Ringo O18
McDOUGAL Don G115
McDOUGAL Gary O33F
McDOUGALL Allan G115
McDOUGALL Dave K20
McDOWELL Annie Mae M22
McDOWELL Fred L61 M22
T79B
McDOWELL Hugh D39 E34
W122
McDOWELL Ken T57
MACDOWELL Ted N41
McDUFF Brother Jack B85
M20A
MACDUFFIE Deborah B105
MACE Ralph B186
McELROY Donna N23
McELROY Etan H111A
McELWAINE Jim P99
McENTEE Robert K48 N12A
MACER Pete S234
McEUEN John M93 M232 N53
W136
McEUEN William N53
McEWAN Tom G12
McFADDEN George 'Biggy'
C179 O15
McFADDEN Mike G72A S332A
McFARLAND Bill C162 R112
S57
McFARLAND Lester L119C
McFARLANE Elaine
'Spanky' A135 B49 M27
M125A S203 T21
McFARLANE George G81
McFARLANE Will B194
G106A R22
McFEE Bob B259
McFEE John B259 C42 C144
C193 H56 M58 M159 M167
M203 S36
McGANN Mac M45
McGARRIGLE Anna M21
M229 T79 W5
McGARRIGLE Kate A30 M21
M229 P137 T79 W5
McGARRIGLE-DOW Janie
M21
McGARRY Michael W11
McGARY Danny P87A
McGAVIN Andrew S157
McGEACHY Bill R12
McGEACHY Fiona R12
McGEAR Mike (McCARTNEY
Mike) G103 M23 S35
McGEARY Michael M232
McGEE Brian S126
McGEE Edward T119

McGEE Jerry B84 B202 B261
C123 C180 F123A K95 K96
M111 S20 S342 V3 V24
McGEE John L2
McGEE Micky B154A B194
B244 M191 R137 S196
McGEENEY Ross S253 T89A
McGEOCH John M47 S132
V35A
McGEORGE Jerry H1 S81
McGETTRICK Kurt H78 K45
M138 S180 T107
McGHEE Billy R1
McGHEE Donna M24
McGHEE L.D. H170
McGHEE R.W. L64
McGHEE Walter Brown
'Brownie' T53A
McGILL Mike D44
McGILL Victor F20
McGILLEVRAY Jim J15A
McGILLIVRAY Bill T89
McGINLAY Jim S158
McGINNIS John S283
McGINNIS Michael P129
McGINNIS Sidney G2 M111
S124
McGLADDERY Brian O33F
McGLINT Mags see BELL
Maggie
McGLOHON Joe H78A
McGLOIRY Michael J7 L65
P126
McGOOGAN Wesley C185B
O6A
McGOUGH Roger G103 M25
P36 S35
McGOVERN Tim (D) C15A
M135 P116
McGOVERN Tim (G) M210A
McGRATH Bat M25A
McGRATH Miranda B194
McGRATH Rick C234A
McGREGOR Chris B229 D111
K84
MACGREGOR Craig F81
McGREGOR Freddie M221D
McGREW Jim B201
McGRIFF Deborah N39
McGRIFF Jimmy M26 P26
McGRUDER Jeanette H98
McGUIGAN Tom M136B
McGUINN Andy T22
McGUINN Margaret T22
McGUINN Roger (formerly
Jim) B49 B285 C164 D139
F116 L97 M27 M28
McGUINN HILLMAN AND
CLARK M28
McGUINNESS Tom B154B
H175 M29
M80 S283B
McGUINNESS FLINT M29
McGUINTY Gloves C183A
McGUIRE Duncan W99B
McGUIRE Larry P115
McGUIRE Barry M30
McGUIRE Ray T146
McGUIRE Ron J41
McGUIRE Sam C238
MACHELL Ted C123
MACHIAVEL M30A
MACHIN Alex F83
MACHINE Tony C226 J70
N34
MACHINE GUN M31
MACHINES M30B
MACHO Joe C229 G109 M203
McHUGH Paddy A85 B21 C7
D9 E9 F42 G32 H56 H65
K76 L37 M5 P100 S285
McILVEEN Greg C177A
McILWAINE Ellen M31A
McINERNEY Mac L76B
McINTOSH Billy M32
McINTOSH Danny B31 G81
McINTOSH David D95
MACINTOSH Greg S141
McINTOSH Lonnie see MACK
Lonnie
McINTOSH Rob (K) F8B
McINTOSH Robbie (G) A120
A131 M80 N46A
McINTOSH Sarah W72

McINTOSH Tom W47
MACINTYRE Earl B29 L119
M53 M227 N39
McINTYRE Matt N30
McINTYRE Onnie A131 H155
K36 K83 M206 Y17
MACIOCI Nicholas see
MASSI Nick
McISAAC Billy S158 Z17
MACIVER David H121
McIVERS John L26
McJOHN Goldy S265
McJOWN Dale P26
MACK Bob H122A
MACK Jimmy M31B S156
MACK Joe D74 F22A M125
R169
MACK John see PEPPER
Claude
MACK Leroy K29
MACK Lonnie (McINTOSH
Lonnie) D103 K51 M32 N25
MACK Warner M33
McKAY Al C45 D50 E7 E55
H97 L65 M102 W33
MACKAY Andy C196 C222 E59
J110 M34 M81 M214 P40
R120 R149 R174
MACKAY Calunn S37
MACKAY David (B) N25
MACKAY David (K) O18B
MACKAY Dennis W62
MACKAY Doug O3
MACKAY Duncan B280 C19
H26A L63 M35 P31 R51 T43
McKAY Ian D73
McKAY John (G) B211
McKAY John (G) S132
McKAY Ken K39
MACKAY Melissa D103
MACKAY Richard O39
MACKAY Ray C151
McKECHNIE Andy F23
McKECHNIE Licorice I16
McKEE Sandy C158
MACKELL Joanne M36
McKENDREE Fran M37
McKENDREE SPRING M37
McKENES Jack O33C
McKENNA Alan J93
McKENNA Danny T102A
McKENNA Hugh H52 M7 T37
McKENNA Larry M2
McKENNA Mae C178 M38
McKENNA Mike M39
McKENNA Ted G5 H52 M7 T37
Z5
McKENNA MENDELSON
MAINLINE M40
McKENNER Richard
H55A
McKENZIE Alastair
(K) Q6
McKENZIE Alistair
(V) B106
McKENZIE Billy A105A
McKENZIE Bunny A107 R84
S190 W23
MACKENZIE Calvin'Rashied'
I19
McKENZIE Candy A107 O34
R84 W23
McKENZIE Colin T95
MACKENZIE Foster III see
Root Boy Slim
MACKENZIE Henry A109
MACKENZIE Jan I17B
McKENZIE John G46 G99
G102 H119 M7A M63 R23
S108
MACKENZIE Matthew L98A
MACKENZIE Sadie M34
McKENZIE Scott M39A
McKEON Gabriel T6
McKERNAN Rod 'Pigpen'
G84
McKEVITT Chris S18
McKEW Roger D100 H67 I20
J14 T47
MACKIBBON Al O39
McKIDD Robin N5
MACKIE Craig S166
MACKIE John (B) S37
MACKIE John (D) B129
McKIE Keith K28

MACKIE Peter W122
MACKILLOP Stuart C7
McKINLEY Billy P73
McKINLEY Jeanette P9
McKINLEY L.C. B193
McKINLEY Maurice G61
McKINLEY Sheila P9
McKINLEY Suzie T135
McKINNEY Jerry G92B
McKINNEY Mabron H164
McKINNEY Michael F128 M232
McKINNIE Dee M111
MACKINNON Gordon C140A
MACKINNON Jamie C59
MACKINNON Raun G72 M37 P137
W11
MACKINTOSH Jill D89 F65 G97
McKITTY Donovan P15
McKNIGHT Dwayne'Obsidiktion
Blackbyrd' H72 J75A
McKRIETH Neville L71B
McKUEN Jerry S65
McLACHLAN Roger L92
McLAGAN Ian F4 J105 M39B
N27 R79 R133 S162 S273 T59
W120 W121
McLAIN Albritton W48D
McLAIN Marlon H96
McLAREN Malcolm S77
McLAUGHLIN Ian S124
McLAUGHLIN John A120 B131
B171 B248 C129 D27 F14 L70
M40 S19 S85 S104 T25 T163
V39
McLAUGHLIN Steve S110
MACLEAN Bryan
McLEAN David A32
McLEAN Don M41
MACLEAN Errol Ranchie B231
B276 C245 G13 G39 H122 H172
R30 R35B R150 T166 W4A
MACLEAN Godfrey A120 B171
C80 G13 G67 G94 H17 H181
S300
McLEAN Ian A63 R44
McLEAN Norrie P77B
McLEAN Ranchie see MACLEAN
Errol
McLEEN Ernest D96
McLELLAND Sandy M41A
MACLEOD Alan K97
McLEOD Howard R130
MACLEOD Ian R10
MACLEOD Jeanette M136B
McLEOD Ken T57
MACLEOD Sean P76A S58
McLEVY John K75
MACLOUGHLIN Gerry G3
MACMAHON Andrew (K) B221
B261 C133 J53 L60 M211 N23
T9
McMAHON Andrew 'Blueblood'
M41B
McMAHON Gerard G106A
McMANUS Cindy S112A
McMANUS Declan see COSTELLO
Elvis
McMANUS Edward S112A
McMASTERS Andy D123 M215
McMENEMY Jamie B51
MACMILLAN Allan C182 R60
McMILLAN Jerry W92
McMILLAN Lawrie E18
McMILLAN Terry N37 S269
S271 Y18
McMONAGLE Grainne C120
McMONAGLE Monty F75B
McMORDIE Ali S275
McMULLEN Pat C199
McMULLIN Klyde C108
McMURRAY Steve W113
McNABB Joanne Caldwell Z8
McNABB Kerry Z8
McNABB Malcolm Z8
McNAIR Harold A25 C2 C21
C223 D99 K84 M42 M50 M94
S25B
McNALLY John S60
McNALLY Sam S312
McNALLY Stephen R102A
McNAMARA Janie P137
McNATT Howard O15
McNAUGHT Mike D105 L136 M6
McNEAL Maggie A27 C243 L95B

[496]

emphis Slim (CHATMAN - Peter) C26 H150 M129 S204 W94
MEMPHIS STRINGS G92
MENACE M131
MENARDO Dominic M26
MENDELL Steve N23
MENDELSON Andy M131A P123
MENDELSON Benno A46
MENDELSON Joe M39 M312
MENDELSON Richard M131A
MENDES Warren N11A
MENDOZA Mark D65
MENE James B105 P146
MENIKETTI Dave Y8
MENTAL M132A
MENTAL AS ANYTHING M132B
MENZA Don A31 C158 C180 F134 G60 H150 K77 L50 M229 R87 S58 S189 S196 S311 W9
MENZER Kim B275
MERCER Chris A62 B25 B47C M141B B209 C75 C80 C159 D30 D36 D86 F21 F42 F86 F125 G67 H50 H94 J5 J34 J105 K51 L63 M7 M11 M157 M168 M195 M202A M233 N6 N18 P76 Q1 R12 S134 S209 S257 S285 S301 T133 U22 V21 W13A W103
MERCER Jerry A69 B253 W1
MERCEREAU Bob B268
MERCHANT Jimmy L144
MERCIER Peadar C102
MERCURIO Frank E65
MERCURIUS S.Flavius H29
MERCURY Eric F60 F109
MERCURY Freddy H185 Q8
MERGER M133
MERGY Fred S120
MERICAHTI Harri J3A
MERKLEIN Kip S111
MERLIN G. C169
MERLINO Gene G121
MERLINO John D99
MERNIT Billy B263 S124
MERO Don W8
MEROS Gene P3
MEROS Mike R173 W24
MERRIAM Charlie M96
MERRILL John P46
MERRITT Max M134
MERRITT Randy F103C
MERRIWEATHER Big Maceo T9B
MERRYWEATHER Neil G61 M60 M135
MERSEYBEATS M136
MERSHON Norman T169
MERTON PARKAS M136A
MERZ Kim W130
MESA Omar M72
MESQUITE Skip C158 D24 H146 P114 W4
MESSAGE M136B
MESSECAR Dek C34 W35
MESSENGER Bob C39
MESSENGER Doug M203
MESSENGER Tony J63
MESSER Tim P137
MESSICK Gordon Y12
MESSINA Jay A16 C236
MESSINA Jim A132 B260 K22 L110 M136C P106 Y16
MESSINA Nick M111
MESSINA Phil J48
MESSINA Pierro V11
MESSING Charlie G74
MESSING Paul N65
MESTROPASQUA Frank T150
MESUMECCI Max S193
METABOLIST M137
METCALFE Alan S93
METCALFE Andy S181
METCALFE John D34A
METEORS M137A
METERS D86 H138
METHENY Jim T107
METHENY Pat M138A M170
METHI Terje P117A
METHOD M139
METHUSALEM M139A
METKE Bob S33B

METOYER Luke S251
METRO M140
METZGER Bob M108
METZNER Doug M18
MEUSSDORFFER Jack S18A
MEWBORN John C158
MEWRILL Allan R164A
MEYER Augie M141 S7
MEYER Freddi M141A
MEYER George R28 R38
MEYER George (K) H185
MEYER Jeffrey M18
MEYER Jonathan P115
MEYER Skip S102
MEYER Walter M210
MEYERS Bill M102
MEYERS Craig F140A
MEYERS Mike J11
MEYERS Randy S73
MEYNET Roland E62A
MHLONGO Vicky Busiswe C83 J4
MI SEX M141B
MIALL Terry Lee (also DAY Terry) M175
MIAMI HORNS L26
MIAMIS M141C
MICARE Franklin R125
MICAS Stephan M142
MICELY Joe F105
Michael F43
MICHAEL Gil B111
MICHAEL SCHENKER GROUP S41
MICHAELS Billy R50A
MICHAELS Carson M37
MICHAELS Dave H1
MICHAELS Elliot E32
MICHAELS Gordon M143
MICHAELS Gwynne M5
MICHAELS Hilly F81A H51 V11A
MICHAELS Jay B169A
MICHAELS Lee M144 M159 R123
MICHAELS Lloyd M79
MICHAELS Nick B90
MICHAELS Roy C56
MICHAL Ed R108
MICHALSKI John C199A
Michel C60
MICHEL Ted D139
MICHIE Chris P114
MICHIE George W7
Mick see WILSON Michael
MICKENS Robert K80
MIDDAUGH Chris B56
MIDDEL Willy C243
MIDDLEBROOKS Ralph 013
MIDDLEMIST Kink C235
MIDDLETON Greg H192 117C
MIDDLETON Kent T136
MIDDLETON L. S251
MIDDLETON Max B64 B70 B237 B280 H29 H181 L63 L111 M145 M206 N14 P119B R15 S103B S300 Z4
MIDDLETON Orwin A59
MIDDLETON Paul W14
MIDGLEY C.J.T. see Beau
MIDLER Bette S252
MIDNIGHT HANDCLAP SECTION F81B
MIDNIGHT OIL M146
MIDNIGHT RAGS M146A
MIDNIGHT SUN M147
MIDNIGHTERS B24
MIDNITE Steve C205
MIELKE Gary P151
MIER Harry B5
MIESSNER Brian A15
MIETTE Jean Jacques L17
MIGDEN Steve C165
MIGHTY BABY M148
MIGHTY CLOUDS OF JOY W54
MIGHTY DIAMONDS M149
Mighty Flea see CONNERS Gene
MIGIL 5 M150
MIGLIORE Tony E73
MIGLIORI Jay A131D B56 C76 D8 M75 P75 W5 W9
MIHALY Tamas 024
MIHM Danny F61 L115A S206

MIJTS Frans M237A S348A
Mike R3
MIKE HERON'S REPUTATION H110
MIKE SLOT AND BUMPER M150A
MIKENAS Ed R100
Mikey Boo see RICHARDS Mikey
MIKKELBORG Palle C61 L41 R178 S69 V26C
MIKNENAS Steve S38
MIKSA Florian Pilkington see PILKINGTON-MIKSA Florian
MIKULS Richard R161
MIKUS Heinz F7A
MILAN Irina V26C
MILAN Pepe P92 S175
MILANESE Luciano N60
MILANO Fred D74
MILES Barry D72 L119 M26 M107
MILES Buddy D24 E33 H99 L107 M40 M151 T82
MILES Charles W47
MILES Denise Pantos M151 B109 F80 G104 H147 H150
MILES Helene W. K25 L111 R100
MILES John (K/G) M152
MILES Johnnie (D) H129 K4
MILES Lee R62
MILES Otis (later WILLIAMS Otis) T42
MILES Victoria J10A
MILHART James W64
MILIO Peter L8 M18 M68
MILK Christopher M153
MILK'N'COOKIES M154
MILKWOOD M155
MILLAR Chris W65
MILLAR Greg S231
MILLAR Robin S134
MILLAR Todd A9 C169
MILLAS Larry 16
MILLENNIUM M156
MILLER Abraham L2
MILLER Adam C13 J48 N45
MILLER Al L108
MILLER Ben D56
MILLER Bill E62B
MILLER Bob (D) S333
MILLER Bob (G) M178B
MILLER Brian (K) I29 R122 T160
MILLER Brian (G) Z16
MILLER Byron D127 F87A H19 L65 S19 W6 W63
MILLER Carlisle W101
MILLER Carol Lee B56
MILLER Charles B268 H92 035 W17
MILLER Count J24
MILLER Daniel F4A
MILLER Darcy C62
MILLER David L140
MILLER Eddie K45
MILLER Floyd S154
MILLER Frank R38
MILLER Frankie F65 F104 J75B J103 M15 M157 T58
MILLER Gene 'Bowlegs' R168 S36
MILLER George R35B
MILLER Geri F109
MILLER Glen John A47
MILLER Glenn C106
MILLER Harry B229 C63 C183 D10B K54 N50 045 P146 I95
MILLER Jacob I19 M158
MILLER Jerry M174
MILLER Jimmy G27 L103 M159 R133 U5
MILLER Jimmie (G) L16D
MILLER Joe C107A H170
MILLER John F5 K23
MILLER John (B) B256 K81
MILLER Keith S178 W96
MILLER Kim H133 014 S115
MILLER Larry D56

MILLER Leo S325
MILLER Leslie R25 S262
MILLER Marcus A82 B81 K47 K69 S169 W25 W62
MILLER Merle F122 L4A M84A
MILLER Mike (Wind) E57 G16
MILLER Mike (G/B) P76
MILLER Nelson B276
MILLER Pete S209
MILLER Phil C209 G102 H57
MILLER Rice see WILLIAMSON Sonny Boy II
MILLER Robert S316
MILLER Robin H4 K54 S131
MILLER Ronald D. S169 T79B
MILLER Scotty H133 S115
MILLER Shorty 014
MILLER Stan E6
MILLER Steve (U.K.) C34 C209 D5 D128 F108 G102 H43 H57 K84 M158A
MILLER Steve (U.S.-K) B109 F80 G104 H147 H150 L81 M68 T9A T21
MILLER Steve (U.S.-G) B87 M135 M159 S111
MILLER Tracy A61
MILLER Vern R64 S339A
MILLER FRASER BAND F104
MILLIGAN Sean A133
MILLIKAN Bob C186 D50 L4A W25
MILLIKEN John D77 G122A
MILLINER Ras P134
MILLINER Steve A3 B112
MILLING Ronnie T57
MILLINGTON M160
MILLINGTON Jean B186 F18 M160 M191
MILLINGTON June F18 I27 M160
MILLINS Paul K25
MILLION Jeb B130
MILLIUS Mike F58
MILLMAN David M80
MILLO Mario W99B
MILLS Abe B240 039
MILLS Albert L71A
MILLS Alison M53
MILLS Chas F53 S209 S270
MILLS Eleanore F60
MILLS Fred D24
MILLS Jack A120 K25 W62 Y11
MILLS Jerry M232 046
MILLS John Stuart E79
MILLS Lorenzo A53
MILLS Paul M195
MILLS Richard F30A
MILLS Roy W89
MILLS Tony (B) B83
MILLS Tony S303
MILLS Wayne S72
MILLS-COCKELL John M160A
MILLWARD Mike F93
MILLWARD Simon M137
MILNE Billy F8A
MILNE Ian K94B
MILNE Jim B60 T56 T124
MILNE Karen C99 S135
MILNER Bruce E72A
MILNER Phil D68
MILNER Simon S164
MILSAP Bobby S187C
MILSAP Ronnie P125
MILT MATTHEWS INC. M108A
MILTON Danny W11
MILTON Eddie King B193
MILTON Jake Q16
MILTON Leslie C11
MIMMS Charles H97
MIMMS Garnet M161
MIMMS Ken L126
Min S311
MINATRE Dan W106
MINCE Graham H69
MINCY Wayne R101
MINDBENDERS M162
MINER David A41 R173
MING Leslie B3
MINGAY Roger 042

MINGE Jerry A66
MINGUS Sharon J92
MINHINNIT Ray H116A M157 P77
MINK Ben A52 H117
MINK DEVILLE M163
MINNEAR Kerry G22
MINNS David H169
MINNS Paul I60
MINOR Bull C15
MINOR Carter H78A
MINOR David G88
MINORS M202B
MINSKY Ronald G61
MINSKY Susandra D83
MINTER Iverson see Louisiana Red
MINTER Lindsey N13
MINTER Paul N13
MINTER Vivian L126
MINTON Phil C209 N9 S186A
MINTZER Bob F108A T147
MIQUELON Joe S73
MIRACLES R115
MIRAGE M163A
MIRANDA Ismael F17
MIRANOV Jeffrey A. A96 B155 B263 F60 H99 J20 J48 K47 L63 M21 M26 M111 N2A N65 R22 R25 R125 S124 S125 S252 W27
MIRO Steve M163B
MIRREN Agnes K65
MISENER Bill C182
MISHIRO Kenji C110A
MISLEJUK Friedhelm S289
Miss Ona R137
MISSOURI James V40
Mr.Snips see Snips
Mister T, Being G66
MR.BIG M164
MR.BLOE M165
MR.FOX M166
MISTRESS M167
MISTY M167A
MISUNDERSTOOD M168
MITCH RYDER AND THE DETROIT WHEELS R177
MITCHELL Adam M39 M75 P39
MITCHELL Bernardine B213
MITCHELL Billie H59
MITCHELL Billy (G) J5
MITCHELL Billy (V) C144A
MITCHELL Blue B144 C217 M111 M169 032 R62 S111
MITCHELL Bob J96 039
MITCHELL Bruce A29 B247
MITCHELL Craig C76
MITCHELL Dan M221C
MITCHELL Dave D30B
MITCHELL Glen W5
MITCHELL Grover V9
MITCHELL Ian M169A
MITCHELL James D86 D101 F50 G92 G101A M130 M172 N57 P51 P137 S36 S276
MITCHELL John (D) C209 F14 N9
MITCHELL John (Hrns) M18
MITCHELL Jonah P145A
MITCHELL Joni (nee ANDERSON Roberta Joan) A59 B17A B29 B244 C232 C233 L1 M170 N4 T25
MITCHELL Kim M112
MITCHELL Lindsay L98 P139
MITCHELL Liz B174
MITCHELL Mitch (also MANCHOVITZ Henry) B248 C15A C79 C189 F109 H99 H123 R21 R96 V21 V26A W28
MITCHELL Mitch (G) W77
MITCHELL Norman B20 T31
MITCHELL Oliver 'Ollie' A131D B17A B201 C180 D139 J65 K45 K4B M6B M191 N25 S160 S262
MITCHELL Phil J110
MITCHELL Roger S206
MITCHELL Roscoe A89
MITCHELL Royston A98
MITCHELL Sam A133 B23 C119 G102 G110 M45 M171 M238 S273 U9

[499]

Mi/Mo

MITCHELL Steve D26 T107
MITCHELL Tom J20 S168
MITCHELL Tony H116
MITCHELL Vince J95
MITCHELL Willie M172
MITCHUM Snapper S57
MITTELDORF Tom C18
MITER David D77
Mitteregger H5A
MIYASHTA Fumio F20A
MIZAROLLI John B19
MIZELL Hank M173
MIZEROLLO John O47
MNGQIKANA Bizo A105 P146
Mo R35B
MO Moses M212
MO-DETTES M173A
MOAN Patti C216
MOBBS Nick B5
MOBERLEY Gary M152 M190
S347
MOBY GRAPE M174
MODELISTE Joseph 'Zig' D86
K53 M39B M138 M125 T118
MODELS M175
MODERATES M175A
MODERN LOVERS R83
MODERN MAN M175B
MODERN SHOMYO STUDY GROUP
M78
MODNIL Tommie F25
MOE Rick M168
MOE Sharon S215
MOEBIUS Dieter 'Mobi' C145
E59 G120 H27 M175C R127
MOEBIUS AND PLANK M175C
MOELLER Tommy U14
MOELLING Dee J53
MOERLEN Benoit G66 O18
MOERLEN Pierre G66 H119
O18 S332D T31
MOERS Michael T39
MOFFATT Katy F138 M232
MOFFET Gary A69
MOGG Phil U2
MOGINIE James M146
MOGUL THRASH M176
MOHAMMED Amin A93
MOHAMMED Georgia A9
MOHAWK Essra (nee HURVITZ
Sandy) M177
MOHN David B276
MOHOLO Louis A105 N50 P146
T95
MOIR Fenwick K32A
MOIRE David Z8
MOITOZA Rob S189
MOJO HANNAH M178
MOLAN Bill C165
Mole O25
MOLE John C167 L99 M196
MOLINA Ralph C216 L107 N57
R123A S10 Y16
MOLINAUX John R66
MOLINEAUX Othello B43
MOLL Jose Maria B43
MOLLAND Joey B16 N12
MOLLIN Fred H117
MOLLINGER Max G113
MOLLINSON Brian W86
MOLLOY Matt B185 P93
MOLLOY Mick B73
MOLLY HATCHET M178A
MOLNAR Gyorgy O24
MOLONEY Paddy C102 G10 M23
MOMAN Chips C124 K30 V18
MOMENTS J11
MOMOLUVICH Laza P72
MOMS APPLE PIE M178B
MONACO Randy M70
MONAGHAN Walt A5 I8 S23
MONAHAN Jim S250B
MONARCH Michael D57 S265
MONARDO Meco F109
MONARI Buck B17A P126
MONCRIEFF Tom E23
MONDAY Paul B233
MONDRAGON Joe S124
MONET Kash B208
MONETTE Ray R32
MONEY M178C
MONEY Eddie M179

MONEY George 'Zoot'A40
A67 A133 B268 C210 D100
E41 E46 F117 G94 G103 K84
M23 M25 M180 R106 S35
S243 W74
MONEY P.R. H110
MONGREL M180A
MONICKS Fred O30A
MONK Elaine L126
MONK Meredith M180B
MONKEES M181
MONKMAN Francis A62 B280
C161 C201A C251 M81 R12
S80 S144 S270 W35 W86
MONKS (1960's) M181A
MONKS (1970's) M181B
MONOCHROME SET M181C
MONRO Willie T37
MONROE M181D
MONSTERMAKER Mark M180B
MONTAGE M182
MONTAGU Jeremy H194
Montalo W115A
MONTALTO Bob H15
MONTANA Vincent J92 K45
N65
MONTANEZ Victor S125
MONTE CAZAZZA M182A
Montego Joe N63 O15
MONTEIRO Stan B177 C217
MONTEITH Sandy C132
MONTEZ Chris M183
MONTEZUMA Johnny B261
MONTGOMERY Bob H134
MONTGOMERY Bobby B17
MONTGOMERY Carol D139 M11
S269
MONTGOMERY David A73 P159
MONTGOMERY Gary C168
MONTGOMERY James C59 M184
MONTGOMERY Joe L52
MONTGOMERY John M37
MONTGOMERY Lee A132
MONTGOMERY Little Brother
(Eurreal) M48 M185 R168
S329 S358
MONTGOMERY Mike B12 K87
L9 L57 W48B
MONTGOMERY Monk C241
MONTGOMERY Robbie B144
D86 F42 M203 R22
MONTGOMERY Tammy see
TERRELL Tammi
MONTGOMERY Wynell P126
MONTGOMERY-CAMPBELL Hugh
E24 H57
MONTRELL Roy D96 D106
MONTROSE M187
MONTROSE Ronnie B63 G7B
H19 H51 M187 M203 W90
W106 W133
MONTY PYTHON M188
MONUMENT M188A
MOODY Mick B174B C75 C79
C204 H42 H177 J105 J110
L46 M157 M180 R11 S176
T128 Y10 Y19
MOODY BLUES M189
MOON (RAY OWEN'S) R44
MOON (U.K.) M190
MOON (U.S.A.) M190A
MOON Chuck P73
MOON Doug B72
MOON James G16
MOON Keith C35D F65 H29
H110 L51 M191 S338 W72
MOON Roger S287
MOONBEAMS W49
MOONDOG M192
MOONEY John M192A
MOONEY Malcolm C25
MOONEY Ralph A132 B279
C169 J53
MOONEY Thom H111A N16 O15
P24 T17 W48D
MOONQUAKE M192B
MOONRIDER M193
MOONWEED Hi T see BLAKE
Tim
MOOR Tony T13
MOORCOCK Michael C18 H64
M194
MOORE Alan (D) J102
MOORE Alan (Trom) S31

MOORE Alan (Pno) M173
N37
MOORE Albert B. S353
MOORE Anthony A29 A133
H101 M80 S152
MOORE Arnie F128 H59
S272
MOORE Barry B141A
MOORE Benny E52B
MOORE Bob R31
MOORE Bobby L. D139 H26
M41 M68 M174 M197A N37
P63 P125 R173 Y18
MOORE Brian 'Red' S101
MOORE Charles M1
MOORE Christy P93
MOORE Colin O18
MOORE Daniel (D) B221
C77 C109 C123 C155 S269
S272 W21
MOORE Danny (Tpt) P149
T20
MOORE Darryl J92
MOORE Dave N56
MOORE Derek N18
MOORE Don V21
MOORE Douglas S157
MOORE Dudley W86
MOORE Eddie H133 L130
M222A
MOORE Eric G57
MOORE G.L. T142
MOORE Gary A78 C167 D88
G1A H169 L99 M196 P119B
S139 T59
MOORE Gerry C104
MOORE Glen C189 O30 P45
MOORE J.Alan E73
MOORE James see HARPO
Slim
MOORE Jim L4 L118 W21
MOORE Johnny (V) D116
F59B
MOORE Johnny (V) U20
MOORE Johnny (G) T28
MOORE Kenneth L. P126
T158
MOORE Kenny S124
MOORE Kermit C147 K36
MOORE Kevin C217
MOORE Kim Z24
MOORE Larry M2
MOORE Laverna N37
MOORE Lorraine P99
MOORE Lyndsey K61
MOORE Lynn D66
MOORE Melba B221 C77
C123 C155 E40 M190A
MOORE Melba K81
MOORE Melvin B240 O39
MOORE Merrill M197
MOORE Michael (B) M21
M229 S215
MOORE Michael (Sax) M141
MOORE Nicky H3
T89
MOORE Nigel L142
MOORE Pamela Y12
MOORE Pat G72A
MOORE Pete see MOORE
Warren
MOORE Pete I15A
MOORE Phil M102
MOORE Samuel David P35
P125A S13
MOORE Scotty L64 M197A
M201 P125 S342
MOORE Steve S230
MOORE Susan M227
MOORE Tim C76 G117 K17
M198 R22
MOORE Tiny A102
MOORE Tom M221C
MOORE Warren A132
MOORE Warren 'Pete'
R115
MOORSHEAD John B171
B247 D129 H84 L7 S105
MOPED Johnny (HALFORD
Paul) M199
MORAIRTY Skip T136
MORAIS Trevor B47B C30
Q2 W82B

MORALES Carlos D24
MORALES Enrique B43
MORALES Hernanos
B43
MORALES Miguel B43
MORALES Pancho H9 H181
MORALES Richie M200
MORALES Rocky D13 S7
MORALES Urbano I13B
MORAN Gayle C189 M40
MORAN Mike A62 A109 A133
B280 C201A D2 D36 F13 F86
F120A G31 G32 G50 H111
K78 M233 S283B T10 W18
W49
MORAN Paul B166A
MORAN Pete A60
MORANTE Massimo G52A
MORAZ Patrick H168 J14
M55 M189 M200 R61 S233
Y7
MORAZ Rene M200
MORCOMBE Richard D93 P131
MORDECAI Michael W11
MORDUE Eddie C109 H121
MORE A. M200A
More Ears see FAGAN
Glaister
MOREIRA Airto A24 A131
B214 C129 C186 D50 D127
H181 J20 J75A K36 M40
M170 O15 P45 R77B S19
S104 S125 T158 V39 W8 W36
W63
MORELAND George I28
MORELL John A131D M227
P129
MORELLI John T156
MORERO Lydia S284
MORETTI Joe D131 E74 H121
K39
MOREVE Rushton S265
Morey E69A
MORFORD Gene B226 J72 K14
MORFORD Lewis P33
MORGAN M201
MORGAN Barry A109 B152
C2 C6 C78 C201A D39 E48
E74 F13 F14 F101 G11 G97
H132A J63 J72 J84 K84 L15
M50 M58 P91 P107 P131
P141 R12 R129 R132
S209 S266 W13A W86
MORGAN Charlie B280 O40
MORGAN Chris C26
MORGAN Chuck B202
MORGAN Dave (Perc) M1
MORGAN Dave (B) B242
MORGAN Earl H105 R134
MORGAN Glyn C238A
MORGAN Graham J4 J16 J86
Q1
MORGAN James B231
MORGAN John (K) S217
MORGAN John (V) C165
MORGAN John Russell S265
MORGAN Lanny H8A S262
MORGAN Michael M221
MORGAN Mike (G) M239 P41
MORGAN Peter (B) B21 H66
H121 S355 V30 W86
MORGAN Peter (D) C238A
MORGAN Ron E35
MORGAN Roy S235 S283B
MORGAN Scott M1
MORGAN Steve W48B
MORGAN Tommy C38 M21
S124 W88
MORGAN Warren F65A
MORGANFIELD Mckinley see
WATERS Muddy
MORGANO Doug B230
MORGENHEIM Bruce R21
MORGENSEN Eric C153
MORGENSTEIN Rod D79
MORILLO Barbara C11
MORIN Bob K45
MORIN Frank G84 Q12 S7
MORIN Jerry S162A
MORIN Marty W113
MORIN Ron-Paul M202
MORIZURE Rene K19
MORK Steve D17
MORLEY Malcolm B73 G65
G79 H93 M63 T170 W130

MORLEY Rick C241B
MORMAN Ralph P63A
MORNING M204
MORNING GLORY M205
MORNING STAR M205A
MOROUSE Dennis M101
MORPHET Chris T84
MORREL Tom C15
MORRETTI Joe C127
MORRIS Bobby C71 G121
MORRIS Clifford F60 J92
N2A R125
MORRIS Dave (K) S260
MORRIS David (G) S210
MORRIS Denis K29
MORRIS Farrell B210 B261
C14 C194 E51 E57 F78 H62
H65 H162A J13 K77 K95 K96
L77 L108 M11 N37 O46 R4
R31 S269 T55 T107 T167 Y16
MORRIS George M50
MORRIS Gerry D68
MORRIS Ian S164
MORRIS Jim L57 R148A
MORRIS Jimmy Lee S204 Y13
MORRIS John H125
MORRIS Kenny S132
MORRIS Kerry M123
MORRIS Kevin E7D
MORRIS Mark B. C50 N37
MORRIS Nigel H154 I29
MORRIS Peter B118 S198
MORRIS Rex E48 S31
MORRIS Roger M202A
MORRIS Roger (G) P142C
MORRIS Roy K79
MORRIS Russell A37
MORRIS S. B101
MORRIS Viv H93
MORRIS AND THE MINORS
M202B
MORRISON David T47 W125
MORRISON Dorothy N4 S36
W129
MORRISON George L120
MORRISON James T155
MORRISON Jesse M26
MORRISON Jim (D) T168
MORRISON Jim (V) D103 H99
MORRISON Les D77
MORRISON Monte J79
MORRISON Reggie S171
MORRISON Rex L43
MORRISON Sterling V23
MORRISON Tommy M202C
MORRISON Van B29 H150 M203
T57
MORRISON Walter F137
MORRISON Wayne S227
MORRISSEY Dick B84 B243
F14 I8 K84 L80A M206 N63B
R15 R132 S182 S264
MORRISSEY Joe C90
MORRISSEY Rex H24
MORRISSON Wendell P99
MORRONGIELLO Tommy H185
MORROW Jeff H38
MORSE Peter P129
MORTER Doug D68 H188 T6
MORROW Buddy F48
MORROW Glenn D36
MORROW Jeff H38
MORSE Peter P129
MORSE Steve D79
MORTENSEN Allan M147
MORTER Doug A30 D68 H188
P138 T6
MORTIMER Gareth 'Morty'
R6
MORTIMER Malcolm G22 L59
M195 S303
MORTON Benny M227
MORTON Ian T130
MORTON Johnny S358
MORTON Mandy S227
MORTON Mike S227
MORTON Robin H71A
MORTON Rockette see
BOSTON Mark
MORTON Simon B195 B226
C79 H42 H65 M10B P5
Morty see MORTIMER Gareth
MORWATTS Tom M238A
MOSE Francis G66

PAICH David B17A B25 B47C B194 B226 B244 B245 C38 C155 D13 D124 E40 G101A G120A H8 J85A M102 P114 R87 S20 S58 S262 T115 V3 W39 W42 W65A
PAICH Marty R101
PAIETTA Steve B110 M75
PAIN Ian N30
PAINE Willy P131
PAISLEY David P10
PAISLEY Ronnie P10
PAIVA John F91
PAKULA Lenny B135 M2 N65 O14
PAKVIS Koos F136
PALADIN P11
PALENCIAS Fernando M139A
PALEY Andy M233 P13 S170
PALEY Jonathan P13
PALEY Tom M108
PALEY BROTHERS P13
PALIN Michael M188
PALISELLI Bill A90
PALLEN Joe J53
PALLETT Nick P136
PALLIGROSI Tony 'Muff' S199
PALLO Bernie S166
PALM Barney B199
PALM Roger A4
PALMA Joao F103D
PALMAR Wally R133A
Palmer B102
PALMER Andrew H170
PALMER Barry T143
PALMER Bruce B260 P14
PALMER Carl A115 B231 E53 F21 W24
PALMER Clive C4 F15 I16
PALMER Dave (D) N63
PALMER Dave (V) B100 Q15A S262
PALMER Dave (K) J58 P138
PALMER Del B280
PALMER Earl (B) A40
PALMER Earl (D) A11 A131D B240 B256 C140A D96 E74 H23 H152 K45 L89 L118 M53 M68 M229 M232 N25 N40 P129 R22 S220 W6 W13 W87
PALMER Eugene J96
PALMER Geoffrey S189
PALMER Harry S280A
PALMER John S29
PALMER Jonathan A30A
PALMER N.A. C213A
PALMER Phil A82 B189 C9 E22 H11 M108 W125 Y6
PALMER Poli B146 C79 E12 F12 F100 H123 J9 L63 M108 S300
PALMER Richard S333
PALMER Robert B188 D4 H50 P15 S250 V33
PALMER Robert (Wind) I21
PALMER Ron C76
PALMER Thomas C146
PALMER-JAMES Richard J4B
PALOMAKI Kurt D5 I8
PALSSON Halldor A4
PALUMBO John C212
PAMELA Oliver N64A
PAN P16
PANAMA FRANCIS BLUES BAND P17
PANAMA LIMITED JUG BAND P18
PANDEMONIUM P18A
PANELLI Jack N25
PANG May L51
PANGBORN Ron H98
PANKA Peter J38
PANKOW James C100 R173
PANKRATZ Pat G100
PANTALUK Pete L74
PANTIES P19
PANTOJA Victor A136 B201 D24 H19 M59 M78 M151 S19
PAPALIA Giovanni A86
PAPANIKOLAOU Apostolos C219A

PAPATHANASSIOU Vangelis see Vangelis
PAPE Hans T143
PAPPALARDI Felix B11 B70 B248 C218 F70 J86A M216 N12 P20 R140 S65 W51 Y12
PAPPERT Johannes K89
PARADISE EXPRESS P21
PARAFFIN JACK FLASH LTD P22
PARAMOUNTS P23
PARASZ David G115
PARAYRE Serj S280
PARAZEIDER Walter C100 R173
PARCELY Templeton see EPP Fenrus
PARDEIRO Carlos S10
PARDO Don Z8
PARDUE Gene M179
PARFITT Barry W15
PARFITT Rick I22 S255
PARIS P24
PARIS Jamie H186
PARIS Jon H111A W107
PARISH HALL P24A
PARISI Dennis T44
PARK Alan B74 P10 T89
PARK Ken H166
PARK Ray N32
PARK Terry W13D
PARKER Alan A109 B152 B280 C2 C127 C201A D135 E22 F13 F14 H167 H183 J72 K84 M100 P131 R11 R132 S182 S295 S313 W13A W18 W86
PARKER Andy (D) U2
PARKER Andy (G) B89
PARKER Beaver B254A
PARKER Brian U14
PARKER Christopher B105 B208 B282 E49 F103 F108A H139A L111 M12 M41 M69 M125 M227 M229 N65 P15 R22 R125 S17 S310 T98
PARKER Cliff L3
PARKER David C251
PARKER Dennis (B) B253
PARKER Dennis P18
PARKER Dennis (V) P24B
PARKER Eric H185 J32
PARKER Evan B229 D135 G47 S267
PARKER Fiona M67
PARKER Geoff C76
PARKER Graham C42 P25
PARKER Gregg I17C O48
PARKER Ian 'Quince' R116 I23
PARKER Jim D93
PARKER Jim (Pno) B156
PARKER John 'Knocky' E67
PARKER John (K) C217
PARKER Johnny (B) B233
PARKER Johnny (Sax) M13A
PARKER Judi C76
PARKER Junior B127 M26 P26
PARKER Maceo B183 P29
PARKER Maggie M111
PARKER Mick M220
PARKER Mike H172A
PARKER Paulette M203
PARKER Peter W19
PARKER Phil H37
PARKER Ray Jnr (G) B50 B110 B127 C30 C45 C155 C220 C246 E71 H19 H98 J92 J113 L63 M102 M151 P114 R78 R99 S14C S34 S58 S180 W31 W116 W119
PARKER Ray (K) C35A
PARKER Robert (V) P27
PARKER Robert (Sax) L118 M179
PARKER Robin S234
PARKER Sparky Z8
PARKER Terry S284A
PARKER Tom D93 E41 R11 S255 S313 W60
PARKER-HART John R124A
PARKES Bud C63 D108 D118 D133 F7 G98 R122 S141 V21 W114
PARKES John H16

PARKIN Ian B54
PARKINS Bob M151
PARKINSON Keith F51A
PARKS Bennie F109 K56A
PARKS Chris A67C
PARKS Dawn J96
PARKS Dean A59 B17A B47 B127 B194 B206 C30 C180 C241 D5A D74 E15 E40 E71 E74 F33 F92 G10 G24 G101A H37A H150A J69 K45 K48 L26B M160 M177 M227 N16A N23 O37 P48 R78 R87 R101 S14C S58 S262 S269 S311 W13 W39 W44A
PARKS Douglas J96
PARKS Gregory J96
PARKS Lloyd A6 B95A B231 B234 C245 G39 I12 P135 R84 R150
PARKS Michael J96
PARKS Pete F16A
PARKS Robin J96
PARKS Stu F23
PARKS Van Dyke B61 B256 C164 C179 D8 O6 P28 R22 R139A S252 Z8
PARLATO David O15 S58 W44A Z8
PARLIAMENT P29
PARNABY George C251
PARNELL Rick A115 H157A N60
PARR Elven E52B
PARR James J21
PARR Steve B272
PARRAN J.D. B282 B29
PARREN Chris C30 E77A G65 H173 M34 R120 R174 T173 W82A
PARRIS Bryan M160
PARRIS Wayne B204
PARRISH Brian B17 E18 M121 P30 T82
PARRISH George D50
PARROS Dave S86
PARROT Kevin O33F
PARRY Dick B83 B178 D30 E60 G77 L75 P85 Q17 R106
PARRY Ken B268
PARRY Steve R10 S210A
PARSON Robert M65
PARSONS Alan P31
PARSONS Amanda G30 H57 N9
PARSONS Anthony M235 T39
PARSONS Gene B285 F74
PARSONS Gram B285 D26 F74
PARSONS Jeff D33
PARSONS John F3
PARSONS Steve C171
PARTON Dolly H35 P50 R137
PARTRIDGE Andy S244 X3
PARTRIDGE Don A6A
PARTRIDGE Jo A22 C107 D39 H26A H111 J86 L27 W130
PARTRIDGE Tim R118A
PARTY PIECE F51
PARUDO John B192
PARYPA Andy S187B
PARYPA Larry S187B
Pasadena M238A
PASCHAYAN Turo T35
PASCHAL Tony S175
PASCOAL Hermeto Q71
PASEIRO Arnold A4
PASH Jim S335
PASK Andrew (also WHORLIX Captain) E77A L16 M106A T166A
PASQUA Alan D139 L70
PASS Joe A40 C241
PASSAGE D33
PASSARELLI Kenny F78 H8 J72 K51 M64 R109 S276 W16
PASSIONS P33B
PASSPORT P34
PASTERNAK John B30 B222
PASTORA Lee A41 C147 S70
PASTORA Sergio K51

PASTORIUS Jaco D72 H19 M138A M170 P35 S50 W36
Patato L142A
PATERSON Angel R74 S83
PATERSON Ann M111
PATERSON Jimmy D59A
PATERSON Linnie W134A
PATERSON Robert M41A
PATERSON Tommy J14A
PATILLO Leon F137 S19
PATON David B280 D36
PATON Gord S72
Patricia S334
PATRICK Lee A5 D16
PATRICK Pat W30A
PATT Loni H194
PATTEN Brian G103 P36
PATTEN Edward K72
PATTENDEN Colin M80 O18B T49
PATTERSON Alvin 'Seeco' M88
PATTERSON Bob E39
PATTERSON Bobby P36A
PATTERSON Brenda A28 D139
PATTERSON Jerry S14A
PATTERSON Karen M101
PATTERSON Patrick C254
PATTI LABELLE AND THE BLUEBELLS L4
PATTISON Davey G7B
PATTO P37
PATTO Johnny K39
PATTO Mike (McCARTHY Mike) B161 B191 C63 E46 H123 K84 L37 P37 S224 T94 Y10
PAUL Alan M75
PAUL Barry H85
PAUL Billy G27 W122
PAUL Byron H78A
PAUL David H104 J94 N8
PAUL Don T10
PAUL Henri T86
PAUL Henry O43
PAUL Hugh R130
PAUL Laurie O24B
PAUL Les (POLFUS Lester) A110 D72 P38
PAUL Philip K51
PAUL Terry D139 K95 K96
PAUL REVERE AND THE RAIDERS R70
PAULCYK Roland T11
PAULING Clarence F59B
PAULING Lowman F59B
PAULINO Alan R50
PAULIS George D27
PAULMAN Ray H62
PAULSEN Chris M167
PAULSON Bruce G24
PAULSON Zeph S55
PAUPERS P39
PAVA Enrico G47
PAVEY Lee K61
PAVLI Pete G25A H115 M194 P10
PAVLOV'S DOG P40
PAWLE Ivan D88
PAWLETT Yvonne F11
PAWLIK Ray N13
PAWULSKA Barbara B141A
PAXMAN Mike T173
PAXTON Gary S. C14 H26 H134A L42 M186
PAXTON Jennifer P41
PAXTON Katy P41
PAXTON Tom P41
PAYDOS Paul C11B
PAYN Nicky D54 M7A M190 S283B
PAYNE Barry W130
PAYNE Bill A37 B110 B135 B244 C45 D8 D101 E20 E40 E57 G10 G24 H8 H10 H26A H35 J85A L19 L89 M75 M198 M229 M232 P15 P32 P114 R22 R137 S20 S73 S124 T113 W65A
PAYNE Chris (B) M127
PAYNE Christopher (K) N63A
PAYNE Colin S325

PAYNE Davey D137 K41 W130 H59 I2 M125 R108A T147 W5
PAYNE Don A135 B253 C76
PAYNE Doris T149
PAYNE Fran L89
PAYNE Gordon C14 C169 G53 J53
PAYNE Jim (D) B157
PAYNE Jim (D) J94
PAYNE Jody F128 R173
PAYNE John B221 M203 O15
PAYNE Karla A21
PAYNE Lamorris N66
PAYNE Les M55B
PAYNE Odie B87 E67 G122 J21 L126 M48 R168 S329 T9B T23 W47 W94
PAYNE Rob (Perc) G92
PAYNE Robert (Trom) A122 W54
PAYNE Shari S333A
PAYNE Simon Pico C179
PAYTON Denis C122
PAYTON Larry B204
PAYTON Laurence F92
PAYTON Weller T118
PAZ P42A
PAZ Victor C85 D50 F17 J20 L21 L69 P99 R125
PAZANT BROTHERS T154
PEABODY David H. T90
PEABODY Laurence C30
PEACE P43
PEACE Warren B186
PEACEMAKER Gary D12
PEACEY Geoffrey B12A L10
PEACH Bob K44
PEACH Geoff D29 S264
PEACH Norman E7C
PEACHES and HERB P44
PEACHEY Eric D86A K35
PEACHY K. S251
PEACOCK Annette B249 L63 M203 P45 Y11
PEACOCK Brian P139D
PEACOCK Dave C89 E41 G9B L36A P56 P124 S321
PEACOCK Gary D40D
PEACOCK Roger C97
PEAK Don C76 O10 R76
PEANUT BUTTER CONSPIRACY P46
PEAR Lewis K69
PEARCE Bob B228 P47
PEARCE Jamie F26
PEARCE Stan S237
PEARCE Vaughn S93
PEARL P48
PEARL Debbie P48
PEARL Leslie P48
PEARL Mick Q1B S299
PEARL HARBOUR P48A
PEARLS BEFORE SWINE P49
PEARMAN Francis R45
PEARNELL Zola M161
PEARS Seeder S157
PEARSE Derek K65
PEARSE John M202
PEARSON Colin C175
PEARSON Eugene M5
PEARSON Gary V18C
PEARSON John (D) E76 R92 U9
PEARSON John C236
PEARSON Keith P49A
PEARSON Kenny J95 M21 W101
PEARSON Malcolm W69B
PEART Neil R167
PEARTREE Jonathan K77
PECCHIO Danny S241
PECHANAERT Paul D133
PECK Nat A109 W86
PECORINO Joe S121
PEDERSEN Gerald M238
PEDERSEN Herb A59 B221 C45 C127 C200 D71 E20 G24 H35 H120 K95 L19 L72 P33 P50 P137 R101 R137 S20 S272 S341 T25 W21 W43 W101
PEDERSEN Niels Henning P115
PEDRINI Tom C179
PEEBLES Ann P51

RICHARDSON Del (Wendell) C83 F86 F108 I12 O34 R82 S115
RICHARDSON Dennis H133 O14 S115
RICHARDSON Devon A6
RICHARDSON Doug E31 L55 T145
RICHARDSON Geoffrey C8 C34 G49 Q2 W82B
RICHARDSON J.A. W82
RICHARDSON J.P. see Big Bopper
RICHARDSON Jerome A131D E7 H8A K17 K45 R99 S168 S180 S250 S262
RICHARDSON Jessie R115
RICHARDSON Jim I8
RICHARDSON Joe 'Groundhog' C146 C203
RICHARDSON John L106
RICHARDSON John (D) R153
RICHARDSON John (G) G61 M135
RICHARDSON Larry L130
RICHARDSON Phil (Vln) B259 S329
RICHARDSON Phillip (V) S329
RICHARDSON Ralph B48 C30 F66
RICHARDSON Scott S2
RICHARDSON Soko M111 R62 T158
RICHARDSON Tim C183
RICHARDSON Tracy B57A
RICHARDSON Verna C58 M101
RICHEY Dennis M12
Richie T62
RICHIE Lionel C174
RICHMAN Alex B283
RICHMAN Jonathan R83
RICHMAN Sue E77 O15
RICHMOND Al J20
RICHMOND Dannie M86
RICHMOND Dave J72 M80 M100
RICHMOND Fritz B244 C179 F19 K101 M227
RICHMOND Ham B83
RICHMOND Jim W11
RICHMOND Rodney S124
RICHMOND Walt D13 W21
RICHRATH Gary R1A
RICKERT Ralf C241
RICKFORS Michael H132
RICKS Harry T50
RICKS Jerry H9
Rico see RODRIGUES Rico
Rico the Knife D51
RICOTTI Frank A109 B5 B40 B47B B174B B189 B288 C34 C201A C251 D37 D49 D92 D132 F14 G11 G32 H67 J63 L80 M100 M239 O18A P10 P72 R11 R40B R129 S31 S35 S108 S185 S253 S255 S270 S283B S334 T133 W7 W71 W102
RICOTTI AND ALBUQUERQUE R85
RIDDLE Kirk C115 L145 W87
RIDDLE Paul D12 M93
RIDGUARD Nicky B116
RIDLEY Greg A87 G27 H179 K45 M89A S111 S162 S224
RIDLEY John D56A
RIEDY Bob R85A
RIEL Alex S30
RIETENBACH Addi
RIETENBACK Joachim L139
RIFF Jane M34
RIFF RAFF R86
RIFF RAFF R86A
RIFKIN Joshua C70
RIFKIND Roger T119
RIGDEN Roger C165
RIGGINS Nat L128A
RIGGS Bob F129A
RIGHTEOUS BROTHERS R87
RIGOR MORTIS E60
RIISNAES Knut V26C
Rik S45B
RIKKI AND THE LAST DAYS OF EARTH R88
RILEY Billy F31 L64
RILEY Billy Lee A111 C50 R89 T21

RILEY Doug K53 L72 L107 S73
RILEY Edgar Jnr. A131C
RILEY Herman B240 E7
RILEY Howard S267
RILEY Jake L2
RILEY Jimmy R89A R134
RILEY John S57
RILEY Judge S329
RILEY Lawrence 'Judge' C239 T9B
RILEY Marc F10
RILEY Michael S261
RILEY Paul C105 E19
RILEY Pete C141
RILEY Terry C13 R90
RILEY Tommy J71 L53 M128 L72 M11 M41 M68 M211 P63 R4 R103 R173 S120 S271
RILEY Vinnie D136
RILLERA Butch J38A
RIMBAUD Penny C213A
RIMELL Keith K44
RIMSON Jerome A127 C79 H73 H169 Q1 Y2
RINDER Laurin E31 L55 R91
RING Little Bobby P151
RING OF TRUTH R92
RINGS R93
RINKY DINK AND THE CRYSTAL SET R93A
RIO Chuck C71
RIOT R94
RIOT ROCKERS R95
RIOT SQUAD R96
RIP CHORDS R96A
RIPCORDS L57A
RIPERTON Minnie C17 O33G R97 R144
Ripke B155A
RIPPETOE Jimmy S114A
RIPPLE Max D34
RISBERG Jan A4
RISCH Tony P115
RISER Paul A96
RISER Temple P125 T20
RISING SONS R98
RISNER Angela C54
RISTON Jean M55
RISTORI Jean M200
RITCHIE Billy C142
RITCHIE Ian D34
RITCHIE June K61
RITCHLEY Jerry U15A
RITENOUR Lee A31 A122 B85 B100 B110 B127 B225 C129 C171 D127 E15 E40 E57 F92 F119A H8A H97 H122A J75A J113 K45 L79 M102 M111 M160 M218 N39 P114B R78 R97 R99 S34 S58 S124 S262 W27
RITTER Lee I18
RITTER Preston E35
RITZ Lyle B56 E74 H112 R76 R137 W5
RITZ Richie R169
RIVERA Al O38
RIVERA Eddie C62
RIVERA Fred B201
RIVERA Mark B154 T169
RIVERA Miguel K48 N12A
RIVERA Pete R32
RIVERA Scarlet B214 D139 J70 R100
RIVERS Johnny (RAMISTELLA Johnny) P50 R101
RIVERS Sam C155
RIVERS Sylvester H98 J92 M6 N62 R66 R122 R174 S16 R45 R115 V9
RIVERS Tony D9 H26A H65 H175 K63 K66 L63 M7 M45 R51 S270 T16
RIVETS Rick B204A N34
RIVITS R101A
RIX Harry G27
RIX Jerry J10A
RIX Leon T44
RIZZI Tony Z8
RIZZO Anna B144 G107 M18 Y12
RIZZO Pat A37 C11B C179 S161
ROACH Paul K27A

ROACH Rod H157A S28
ROAD R102
ROADMASTER R102A
ROADS Curt S111
ROADWORK W84B
ROADY Tom F48 G10 H146 J11 J22 L79 M235
ROAHNE Doug W21
ROBB Joe J96
ROBB Tom B213 D27A L44 M157
ROBBI Paul P97
ROBBINS Dennis K46 R123
ROBBINS Hargus 'Pig' B17A C14 D70 D139 E73 E75 H26 H49 H65 J53 L42 L72 M11 M41 M68 M211 P63 R4 R103 R173 S120 S271 S272
ROBBINS Nick K3A
ROBBINS Robyn S73
ROBBINS Ron O39
ROBBINS Steve P15
ROBBINS Vernie S125
ROBERG Tex R104
ROBERSON Bryce H170
ROBERSON Duane W63
ROBERT RENTAL AND THE NORMAL R66B
Robert The Rook J7
ROBERTON Sandy E41
ROBERTS Al Jnr R105
ROBERTS Alan S297
ROBERTS Alfred G100 K53 L118 T118
ROBERTS Alun S306
ROBERTS Andy A133 B178 C18 C78 D92 E41 E76 F117 G97 G103 H29 I20 K28B K83 L95 L117 M19 M23 M25 M108 P36 P90 P138 R106 S9 S35 T79 Y6
ROBERTS Bambi F128
ROBERTS Bruce (G)I11 R104 R125
ROBERTS Bruce (K) R107
ROBERTS Chapman W36
ROBERTS Dave (Trom) A1
ROBERTS Don L110
ROBERTS Donna A132
ROBERTS Elliot C232
ROBERTS Frank H154 I29 J4 P34 P146
ROBERTS Gene T154
ROBERTS Howard A131D B63 M68 M135 R108 T107
ROBERTS J. S251
ROBERTS Jim S63
ROBERTS Jimmy L111 M111 T107
ROBERTS John W24
ROBERTS John V9
ROBERTS Judy M68
ROBERTS Lavada June R108A
ROBERTS Lavina S162
ROBERTS Lenny K59 P24B
ROBERTS Lisa B8 B256 C58 F103C H62 H181 I2 L26B L111 M18 S272
ROBERTS Maz P19
ROBERTS Neville Y6
ROBERTS Paul S178
ROBERTS Ray R175B
ROBERTS Rick E41 F50 F74 H120 R109 S276
ROBERTS Robert R152
ROBERTS Scott S325
ROBERTS Tony G110 L136
ROBERTSON Alan S344
ROBERTSON Albertine D139 K81 P6 W106
ROBERTSON Alvin H79
ROBERTSON Barney C169 J53
ROBERTSON Bob R162 S332
ROBERTSON Brian H123 T59 W78
ROBERTSON Brian Alexander R110 J53
ROBERTSON Carter C169 J53
ROBERTSON Charlie C183A

ROBERTSON Cliff J53
ROBERTSON Curtis Jnr H119
ROBERTSON Dave D56A
ROBERTSON Don C169 J53 S342
ROBERTSON Eric D36 H117
ROBERTSON George J84
ROBERTSON Graham A29
ROBERTSON Jaime 'Robbie' B29 D13 D139 H15 H62 H92 L111 M170 S124 S252 T98 W101
ROBERTSON Jimmy D2
ROBERTSON Richie F3
ROBERTSON Rob B83
ROBERTSON Sandy R93
ROBERTSON Tommy W30 W32
ROBIN Alen D106B
ROBIN Christopher A127
ROBIN WILLIAMSON AND HIS MERRY BAND W92
ROBINS O38 R111
ROBINS Butch R173
ROBINS Paul W122
ROBINSON Albertine J48
ROBINSON Alvin Bishop D86 M229 S124
ROBINSON Andrea E77 M18
ROBINSON Andy A59 M203
ROBINSON Arthur F134
ROBINSON Barry C34
ROBINSON Bert S57
ROBINSON Charles K51
ROBINSON Chris N34 W129
ROBINSON Claudette R115
ROBINSON Cleophus L90
ROBINSON Cynthia S161
ROBINSON David (D) C41 D1B P116 R83
ROBINSON David (G) M46
ROBINSON Felix C102
ROBINSON Fenton R112
ROBINSON Freddy H37 L94 M111 M238B R113 R128
ROBINSON Gale R78
ROBINSON Harry M108
ROBINSON Helen L59
ROBINSON James S169
ROBINSON Janice L69 N39 V21
ROBINSON Jimmy Lee L94 T79B W91
ROBINSON John (D) R161
ROBINSON John (G) R66A
ROBINSON L.C. 'Good Rockin' R114
ROBINSON Lee B231
ROBINSON Leigh C236
ROBINSON Marilyn E7
ROBINSON Melvin P125A
ROBINSON Nigel V36
ROBINSON Olsie C146
ROBINSON P. M96
ROBINSON Paul (V) D73
ROBINSON Paul (D) S108 I160
ROBINSON Paul (D) B167
ROBINSON Perry B131 J18
ROBINSON Pete (D) B222
ROBINSON Peter (K) B98 B203 C129 F42 H121 O8 P46 P76 Q4 S39 S124 S257 S270 S331 W9 W32A W62 Y2
ROBINSON Rex F91
ROBINSON Richard R85A
ROBINSON Robby F91
ROBINSON Roland H99 M151 N29
ROBINSON Ronald 'Nambo' B234 W4
ROBINSON Roy T97
ROBINSON Rudy C153 K46
ROBINSON Sandi P46
ROBINSON Sharon H116 K94A O15
ROBINSON Shine W6
ROBINSON Steve T162A
ROBINSON Terry K65
ROBINSON Todd W4A
ROBINSON Tom C9 H11 M195 R116
ROBINSON Tony B120 R61C S190 W23
ROBINSON Valerie C168A

ROBINSON Vicki Sue M46B
ROBINSON Walter T30
ROBINSON William 'Smokey' R115
ROBINSON Chris E37
ROBOT Ronnie R3A
Roboterwerke S332C
ROBSHAW Steve S149A
ROBSON Frank T15
ROBSON Garry N63A
ROCCO R118A
ROCHE Frederick R115
ROCHE Jim E8 N46D
ROCHE Maggie R117A R118 S125 W5
ROCHE Manu T158
ROCHE Suzzy R118
ROCHE Terre F121 R117A
ROCHES R118 S125 W5
ROCHES R118
ROCK Bobby M151
ROCK The C236
ROCK FOLLIES R120
ROCK HOUSE R121
ROCK'N'ROLL ALL STARS R119
ROCK WORKSHOP R122
Rockaday Johnnie B244
ROCKER Lee S296A
ROCKET Ricky A128
ROCKET 88 R122A
ROCKETS C216
ROCKETS (U.S. 1970's) R123
ROCKETS (U.S. 1960's) R123A
ROCKETS (France) R123B
ROCKIN' BERRIES R124
ROCKIN' DOPSIE AND THE CAJUN TWISTERS R124A
ROCKIN' HORSE R124B
ROCKIN' LOUIE AND THE MAMMA JAMMERS R124C
Rocky H84
Rocky (B) T169A
ROCKY ERICKSON AND THE ALIENS E62B
ROCKY MOUNTAIN ARSENAL CHOIR D33A
ROD Mike M75
RODBY John C179
RODBY Steve P137
RODD John A30 C165 H194
RODDY Rod N53
RODEN Jess B188 B222 B283 C30 O49 G102 H50 K87 M214 R101A R125 W72 Y2
RODEN Shirley D54 G35 K61 M194
RODERICK Stanley S131 W86
RODFORD Jim A77 B160 B243 F36 K61 L76B P77
RODGERS Al K81
RODGERS Nile C99 S135
RODGERS Paul B14 B138 F108 K84 K87 M202C P43
RODI Georges J113 T158
RODMAN Arthur F117
RODMAN Judy G92B
RODNEY Mark B47A
RODNEY Winston B276
RODRIGUES David D24 S19
RODRIGUES Gus S19
RODRIGUES Manuel I13B
RODRIGUES Paul C30 M94 M127 R84 S74 S190 S207 S261 T110 W4A W23
RODRIGUEZ Alex M59
RODRIGUEZ Art L18A P125A
RODRIGUEZ Cecilio E40
RODRIGUEZ Dennis G112A
RODRIGUEZ Dougie F109 W62
RODRIGUEZ Eddie E30
RODRIGUEZ Frank Q9
RODRIGUEZ Joe C195
RODRIGUEZ John M75 T150
RODRIGUEZ Jorge L130A
RODRIGUEZ Jose S78A
RODRIGUEZ Marty C31
RODRIGUEZ Paul D68
RODRIGUEZ Pete F17
RODRIGUEZ Sergio C121
RODS E13
RODWAY Ken R124
RODWELL Dave A20
ROE Arran S206

ROE Jesse J49
ROE Tommy R126
ROEDELIUS Hans Joachim
C145 E59 G120 H27 R127
ROEDER Klaus K92
ROELOFS Annemarie H101
ROELOFS Joop Q1B
ROENA Robert F17
ROESER Donald B154 S183
ROESGER Rob N63
ROESSLER Paul D33A
ROFFEY Peter S81A
ROGER C. REALE AND RUE
MORGUE R50A
ROGERS Alvin D74 D139 F19
I2
ROGERS Arnold H170
ROGERS Barry A131 B225
C44 C99 C168A D39 D63
D115 E49 F3A F17 J20 J72
K36 L21 L41 L80A L119 M17
M26 M46B M69 R125 R164
S135 S215 T25 T37E T114
T147 T158 V17 W25
ROGERS Billy C241 S14C
ROGERS Brian L106
ROGERS Cledwyn B116
ROGERS D.J. L66A
ROGERS Duane P126
ROGERS Gil A21
ROGERS Gwen C168A
ROGERS Harlan R101
ROGERS Janet F132
ROGERS Jimmy B87 H170 L94
M5 R128 W94
ROGERS Kenny H52A
 ROGERS Larry B111
ROGERS Mick A131B G97
H175 M80 P139D
ROGERS Mike S287
ROGERS Nat L85
ROGERS Richard F11
ROGERS Robert A132 R115
ROGERS Rosalind C168A
ROGERS Shorty N25
ROGERS Verlene B226
ROGERS Warren S81
ROGERSON Paul P60B
ROGNER Falk A57 U23
ROGUE R129
ROHL Gilly M67
ROHMANN Chris R129A
ROI John T61
ROINAES Peter H5B
ROIRDAN David S349
ROJAS Carmine L4
ROKER Mickey M75
ROKOTTO R130
Roland B280
ROLAND Duane M178A
ROLAND Paul M146A
ROLANDO Larry S58
ROLFE Gerard D68A
ROLIE Gregg C217 C232 I31
J99 S19
ROLL Del H50 R96
ROLL UPS R131
ROLLARD Ray P6
ROLLE Marian P99
ROLLERCOASTER R132
ROLLESTON James P151 S262
ROLLING STONES R133
ROLLINS Bill R31
ROLLO Zoot Horn see
HARKLEROAD Bill
Rolly K19
ROLT Roger D86A
ROMAN Isadore O39
ROMAN Jacques P147
ROMAN Mimi C146
ROMAN Philippe P147
ROMANO Haim J55 S44 S270
ROMANTICS R133A
ROMAO Dom Um C44 P45 W36
ROME Richie H192 L69
ROMEO Max (SMITH Maxie)
R134
ROMEO Roger D61
ROMERO Jo R20
RON HICKLIN SINGERS C50
L107
Ron the Ripper C225
RONANDER Mats A4
RONDINELLI Bob R14
RONETTES H99 R135
RONGA Bob E41 L117 M108
P90 R106 S339

RONNANDER Malla W22
RONNIE PAISLEY'S BAND
P10
RÖNNINGEN Kjell S12A
RONSON Margaret 'Maggie'
R23 R136
RONSON Mick B186 C78 D139
F81A F116 H185 M27 M84A
M214 P45 R23 R39 R60
R136
RONSON Rick P151
RONSON Susie H185
RONSTADT Linda A52 A121
A132 B131 B175 B221 F109
G60 H35 L19 M229 N23 N53
O15 O32 P33 P50 R137
S73B S124 S196 S269 S272
S282 T25 T27 W9 Y16 Z11
ROOGALATOR R138
ROOKWOOD Anthony
'Benjamin' R61A
ROONEY Herbert E76A
ROONEY Neil P110A
Root Boy Slim (MACKENZIE
Foster I71) R139
ROOT BOY SLIM AND THE
SEX CHANGE BAND R139
Roots see KINSLEY Roots
ROOTS P108
ROPER Billy C87A
ROPER Dennis C87A
ROPER Ray S283A
ROPER Tim D123 M63 T170
ROPER Will W18
ROSA Mike J18 Q15A
ROSA Valerie M37
ROSALES Leo M59
ROSALIA Pat M75
ROSAND Aaron I2
ROSARIO Pablo B186
ROSBOTHAM Joseph
G64A
ROSBURG Scott H16A
S305
ROSCH Art P112
ROSE Andrew T163
ROSE Barry S233
ROSE Biff R139A
ROSE Bob C40 L4A
ROSE Charles A133
B200 B210 C26 D99 F23 F48
G61 H40 J11 K30 K96 L9
L75 M235 N23 P79 S340
V18B W10
ROSE Dave D95A L47 S34
ROSE Diana 'Di' R140A
ROSE Harvey B247
ROSE Kathy S173
ROSE Mike C254 J4
ROSE Norman N10
ROSE Robin U20A
ROSE Ron T102A
ROSE Tim R140
ROSE Tony B32 K65
ROSE William 'Skip' M238
ROSE GARDEN R140A
ROSE ROYCE R141
ROSEBROUGH Richard H160
ROSELINO Frank R99
ROSEN Larry B223
ROSEN Mike B266 E12 H50
M23 M176 S35 V33
ROSENBAUM Enrico A53A
ROSENBERG Al E72
ROSENBERG Martin S350
ROSENBERG Richie 'La
Bamba' S199
ROSENBURG John C186
ROSENFELD Eric P13
ROSENGARDEN Neal H54
ROSENGARTEN Bob C146
ROSENKIND Harry S6A
ROSENTHAL Ann H57
ROSENTHAL Arnold D26
ROSENTHAL Jurgen E50A
Roshi S301
Rosi G3A
ROSKAMS Alan G13
ROSLIE Gerry S187B
ROSMAN Ronnie J30
ROSMINI Dick A132 R171
ROSNELL Esko T104
ROSS Alan E60 E61 R142
S339 W72 W99A
ROSS Alyn S331
ROSS Cameo J96

ROSS Colin C165
ROSS Dan S18A
ROSS Davy H71A
ROSS Debi M194
ROSS Diana G17 S333A
ROSS 'Doctor' Charles
Isiah A50A R143
Ross Elise T67
ROSS Jack M173
ROSS Jimbo E31 R91
ROSS Lewis W54
ROSS Margaret S124 S180
S215 T147
ROSS Merria E31
ROSS Nathan A131D
ROSS P.J. W48B
ROSS Ronnie (Sax) A109
C2 F42 K84 R60 W13A
ROSS Ron (G) S28A
ROSS Steve S272
ROSS Willie O14
Ross The Boss S84
ROSSELSON Leon C47
ROSSET Renato N60
ROSSI Bobby G72
ROSSI Francis (formerly
Mike) E77A I22 S255
ROSSI Mike S153
ROSSI Neil B221
ROSSI Philibert H89A
ROSSI Walter P80
ROSSINGTON Gary L146
ROSSINGTON COLLINS BAND
R143A
ROSSINI Stephane N64A
ROSSUNOLO Wally M151
ROSSY Joe C99
ROSTEIN Jack S266
ROSTILL John F101 R80 S80
ROTA San C241B
ROTARY CONNECTION R144
ROTCHELLE Dave P101
ROTELLA Johnny A132 B256
F5 M18 M229 O15 S262 T107
Z8
ROTELLA Thom B225 M229
ROTH Arlen B105 R144A W5
ROTH Dave V14
ROTH Don N37
ROTH Edward M135
ROTH Mark H59
ROTH Ulrich E7A S47
ROTHENBERG Ned F11
ROTHER Michael C145 H27
N26 R145
ROTHERMEL Jam B221 G72
M203 P114 P137 T107 Y12
ROTHFIELD Ron see Raja
Ram
ROTHSTEIN Bob M41
ROTHSTEIN Jack D131
ROTHWELL Linda G64A
ROTHWELL Ric H106 M162
ROTTEN Johnny (LYDON
John) P144 S77
ROUGH DIAMOND R146
ROUJON Loeiz S280
ROULETTE Fred B177 M68
M238
ROUNDABOUT R147
ROUSH Danny W73
ROUSSEL Coco H89A
ROUSSEL Jean A82 A113
B226 C30 C83 C155 C201A
C210 D22 D49 E73 F21 H11
H17 H50 H177 J4 J34 J105
K87 L63 O34 P15 P80 R82
S266 S334 T31 T43 T58
W120
ROUSSEL Pierrot H89A
ROUSSELET Richard J105B
ROUSSELLE Francis T118
ROUSSOS Dennis A67E
ROUTEN Irma Jean M191
M211 N23 S36
ROUTH Jack C50
ROUTH Marcia N23 N25 T9
ROUTLEDGE Clive B141A
ROW Allan B242A
ROWAN Chris B177 R148
ROWAN Lorin B177 R148
ROWAN Paul A60 G110 P56
ROWAN Peter E5 O17 R148
S63
ROWAN Roger I20

ROWANS P112 R148
ROWBOTHAM Dave D136
ROWE Benny H150
ROWE Bob A60 F40
ROWE Dennis B3
ROWE Edward K45
ROWE Hansford G66 M94
ROWE Keith A56A F123
ROWE Kenny C29 S306
ROWEBERRY Dave A67 H11
ROWELL Tony M80
ROWLAND Bruce C48 C155
D26 F6 F7 F42 F125 G6 G86
H65 H84 L16A L101 M15 M34
M94 M202A O8 P76 S344
T110 V26A W121 Y11
ROWLAND Danny C124 H52A
ROWLAND Kevin D59A K44
ROWLAND Phil S153
ROWLAND Steve F12
ROWLES Gary D72A F68 L128
R173 T113
ROWLEY Gordon S304
ROWLEY Nick A133 L80
ROWLEY Terry H66 H176
T133
ROXY R148A
ROXY MUSIC R149
ROY Badal M40
ROY Brigitte C137
ROY Davy C7
ROY LONEY AND THE PHANTOM
MOVERS L115A
ROY YOUNG BAND D9 Y17
ROYAL Ernie J97 K51 K81
P149 S168 V21 W28
ROYAL Marshal M229
ROYAL Sonny L75 P79 S340
ROYAL Theodore L4 M149
ROYAL PHILHARMONIC
ORCHESTRA D40
ROYAL SPADES see MAR-KEYS
ROYALS R150
ROYER Ray P140
ROYSTER Phillip B261 G16
ROYSTON Bruce M203
ROZELLE Robert L128
ROZZELLE Roland M160
RUBBER CITY REBELS R151
RUBEN AND THE JETS R152
RUBENHOLD Leon O41
RUBETTES R153
RUBICON R154
RUBIN Alan A123 B141 B155
C44 C62 C129 D50 F109 G4
G19 H92 J20 M26 M75 M107
R125 S215 T98 T147 T158
W107
RUBIN Alton R124A
RUBIN Danny J112
RUBIN John R155
RUBIN Marc M2
RUBIN Nathan M18 M203
RUBIN Rockin' Dopsie
B154B R124A
RUBINI Mike N53
RUBINOOS R155
RUBINS Tom S250B
RUBINSTEIN David M174
RUBINSTEIN Jamie B288
RUBY (U.K.) R156
RUBY (U.S.) R157
RUBY Frank F60A F102
RUBY Ron G61
RUBY Roy B144
RUCKER Big Daddy O38
RUCKER Karl B283 G26C
RUCKER Washington K56A
RUDD Clifford M2
RUDD Joe T20
RUDD Michael A79
RUDD Phil A2
RUDD Roswell B131 M79
RUDELBERGER Fritz E21A
RUDES Jordan S210B
RUDI Steve J19 X2
RUDNYTSKY Dorian N4 N36
RUDOLPH Paul C18 D58 E59
H64 K38 P84 R93
RUE MORGUE R50A
RUEDA Sue C21A
RUEFF David Z2
RUEFREX R158
RUFF Bruce W69B
RUFF Chuck W106 W107 W108
RUFF Hope R164

RUFF Willie D103 O39
RUFFIN David R159 R160 T42
RUFFIN Jimmy R160
RUFFINO Bobby
RUFFY Dave R175A
RUFUS R161
RUGER Tommy R139
RUGG Harold 'Hal' B17A C124
E75 M11 R4 R173 S271 W11
RUGINSTEIN Rugy R38
Rugs T62
RUGSTED Jens S30
RUHL Gary G1B
RUITER Bert A27 F77
RUITER Ria B224A
RUIZ Dominique S193
RUIZ Hilton N39
RUIZ Mike M154
RUMMANS Michael H135A
RUMOUR L16C P25 R162
RUMPF Inga A113 F130A R162A
RUMPH Steve T3
RUMPLESTILTSKIN R162B
RUMSEY Dave S36A
RUNAWAYS R163
RUNCIMAN Chris P136
RUNDGREN Todd C195 D53 F81
F109 G80B H9 M120 N16 R164
W107
RUNNELS Rochelle S250
RUNNER R164A
RUNNING MAN R165
RUNSWICK Darryl A98 A109
C109 D108 L136 P31 R122
R174 W86
RUPHUS R166
RUSE Humbert P72
RUSH R167
RUSH Alan K95 L77
RUSH Billy S199
RUSH Joe D105 M230
RUSH Little Willie S199
RUSH Otis G122 K46 R168
RUSH Pat W107
RUSH Tom R169
RUSHEN Patrice H97 J75A L28
M40 P115 R97 R99 T107 W27
W63
RUSHENT Martin G22 G65
RUSHING Jimmy R170
RUSHTON Alan D108 R122 R165
R174
RUSHTON Mick S258
RUSKIN Richard 'Rick' R171
RUSSELL Bill S102B
RUSSELL Brenda C38 P15
RUSSELL Brian C38 C171 H117
K53 P15 W21
RUSSELL Emile B233 C146
RUSSELL Frank C177A
RUSSELL Jeff B250
RUSSELL Jim C251 I18A J68
K66 M108 S301 W125
RUSSELL John (D) D17
RUSSELL John (G) A19
RUSSELL Johnny R172
RUSSELL Joseph H8 P67
RUSSELL Karl C179
RUSSELL Kathe 'Special K'
R139
RUSSELL Leon B202 C121
C123 C155 C180 D23A D26
D139 E74 H39 J36 K45 K51
M101 O16 R173 S200 T164
W136
RUSSELL Martin E58
RUSSELL Mary (nee
McCREARY) M14 R173 T158
RUSSELL Ray B45A B47B B171
B247 C75 C108 D108 E77A
F30A H173 K83 M157 R120
R122 R165 R174
S54 S235 S334 T173
RUSSELL Rick P54
RUSSELL Rufus F134
RUSSELL Tom G40
RUSSELL Victoria W72
RUSSIA R174A
RUSSO Marc W8
RUSSO Mike M22
RUSSOTTO Irv M32
RUST Kurt W41A
RUSTICI Corrado N60 W8
RUSTICI Danielo N60 O33D
RUTH Emily A23
RUTHER Edward Brumund S1

RUTHER Wyatt H10
RUTHERFORD Mike G21 H4
P72 P174B R174
RUTHERFORD Paul M29
RUTLEDGE Jim B142
RUTLES R175
RUTLEY Tom A136 S19 W129
RUTS R175A
RUTSEY John R167
RYAN Chico S78
RYAN Craig C86
RYAN Eddie P53
RYAN James P6
RYAN Jim C228 C229 D39
D131 E60 F56 G32 M156
S124 S266 T96
RYAN Joe S206
RYAN John (B) H48 M19
S124 S266 W125
RYAN John (K) G81B
RYAN Mark B165 K13 Q12
RYAN Pat A102 R125
RYAN Paul R175B
RYAN Paul (Sax) F47
RYAN Phil A58 B96 B237
E80 G6 J71 M63 N27 S8B
RYAN Roz H98
RYAN Sharon W101
RYAN Terry B268
RYAN-CARTER Tosh B247
RYDELL Bobby C93
RYDER Maggie L60 O40
R40B R176
RYDER Mitch (LA VERE
Billy) R177
RYE Steve B250 E41 G112
RYE WHISKEY ROAD BAND
R177A
RYECROFT Frank J84
RYERSON Art C146
RYKIEL Jean Philippe
H119
RYNAT Eulalie see CHANET
Chris
RYNOSKL Michael M222
RYPDAL Inger Lise R178
RYPDAL Terje H34 M79
M205 R178 V26C

S.Michael C86
S.A.H.B. H52
S.F.F. S1
S.R.C. S2
S.V.T. S3
SAATCHI Philip A5A
SABATINO Peter V2
SABEL Peter I22
Saber M75
SABER Andy M139A
SABIN John C111
SABINO Robert C99 S122A
S135
SABOTAGE S3A
SABREJETS S3B
SABY Paul H122A
SACHER Martin B199
SACHS Jon E37
SACHS Lenny S4
SAD CAFE S4
SADEGHI Manouchehr S5B
SADISTIC MIKA BAND S5
SADLER Larry H51
SADLER Michael C164
SADLER Tony H169
SADLOWSKI Dieter R38
SAFKA Melanie see
Melanie
SAGA S5A
SAGE Pete W14
SAGER Gareth P117
SAGITTARIUS S6
SAHARA S6A
SAHL Michael C164
SAHLBERG Per A4 S39
SAHM Doug D13 G84 M141
S7
SAILES Jessie C146 J21
R111
SAILOR S8
SAIN Oliver E52B L90
ST.CLAIR Steve S103
ST.CLAIRE Alex(Snouffer)
B72

ST.CLOUD Endle P118A S8A
ST.DENIS Mike S72
ST.FIELD John (LEVIN
Jackie) D95 S8B
ST.JAMES Phyllis C246
F103C H62
ST.JAMES Sylvia D127 H96
ST.JAMES Tony F103C
ST.JOHN Barry A35 A133
B23 B83 C204 C210 D39 D54
E18 F7 F42 G50 G98 H52
H74 H175 J72 K11 L63 M7
N14 N57 P85 R116 S34 S243
S257 W7 W10 Y17
ST.JOHN Bridget A133 C78
S9
ST.JOHN Dennis A59 B29
B80 H52A N37 R137 S269
W21
ST.JOHN Dick D63A
ST.JOHN John G77C
ST.JOHN Kate W82A
ST.JOHN Phillip A82
ST.JOHN R.Powell Jnr M211
ST.JOHN Roy S9A
ST.JOHN-GILLARD John S194
ST.JULIEN Robert M48
ST.NICHOLAS Jody N2
ST.NICHOLAS Nick S265 T3
ST.PARADISE S9B
ST.ROCH Christian W101
SAINT ROCK Chris H196
SAINTE MARIE Buffy D99
N32 S10
SAINTS S11
SAINTY Ian M121
SAIRMAN Danny B223
SAISSE Phillipe D72
SAJDAK Ken Y15
SAKAMOTO Meguni G55
SAKAMOTO Ryuichi Y6A
SAKS Toby C11A
SALAMONE Ross L13
SALAS Jerry E30
SALAZAR Victor S211
SALBER Gunter L120
SALEEM Kashif B3
SALEM Freddie O43
SALEN Jeff T156
SALES Hunt I10 M82 P24
R164
SALES Tony I10 M82 R164
SALISBURY Jerry B22
B171 V11
SALISBURY Sandy S6
SALISBURY Tom M203
P114
SALKOWSKY Gerard
S280
SALLEY Roley B135
SALLYANGIE S12
SALMINEN Simo O18
SALMON Godfrey E46
SALMON Trevor 'Seal'R61A
SALTER William B77
M17 P49 P137 R31
SALTSBERG Mike B269A
SALUKI S12A
SALVONI Luigi S17B
M190
SALZMAN Buddy C76
C146 C255 H23 I2
M125
Sam see SAMUELS Carlton
SAM Robert G80
SAM AND DAVE S13
SAM APPLE PIE S14
SAM GOPAL G73
SAM THE SHAM AND
THE PHARAHUS S14A
SAMARTINO Leonard
F54
SAMARTINO Sandra
F54
SAMBARATO John M28
SAMLA MAMMAS MANNA
S14B
SAMPEDRO Frank C216
Y16
SAMPINAIO Joe N2
SAMPLE Joe A11 A52 A131D
A132 B17A C153 C241 E71
F33 F103D H8 J43 J92 K45
K46 L28 M170 P76 P129 R99
R101 R113 S14C S5B S262
U18 W10A W31

SAMPSON Annie B109 S284
SAMPSON Charles C20
SAMPSON Leslie R102 S297
SAMPSON Sam F26A S14
SAMS David H110 W102
SAMSON S14D
SAMSON Jackie W13
SAMSON Jim Z16
SAMSON Les R55
SAMSON Paul S14D
SAMUDIO Domingo 'Sam'
S14A
SAMUELS Andrew R57
SAMUELS Bruce B278
SAMUELS Calvin 'Fuzzy'
A133 C83 C180 C234 D86
H120 M64 N4 S15 S276
V26A W72
SAMUELS Carlton 'Sam'
B276
SAMUELS David B105 S231
Z8
SAMUELS Jerry see
Napoleon XIV
SAMUELS Keith 'Doc' B213
SAMURAI S16
SAMWELL Ian R80 S80
SAMWELL-SMITH Paul W94
Y5
SAN FRANCISCO SYMPHONY
ORCHESTRA S113
San Frisco Jeff B233
M13A
SANAELL Robert D77
SANBORN David B169 B169A
B186 B208 B282 C44 C62
C189 C195 C213 C249 D39
F3A F83A F103D G109 H8
H58 H185 J20 J48 J72 K36
L4A L41 L107 L119 M17
M40 M41 M69 M75 M107
M125 M143 N36 P35 P99
P151 R22 R100 R137 S17
S124 S180 S196 S215 S229
S262 S266 T25 T147 U18
W5 W119
SANCHEZ Freddie E30
SANCHEZ Mario C241B
SANCIOUS David L. B248
C129 D124 S18 S229 S232A
W8 W62
SAND S18A
SANDALS S18B
SANDERS Don T167
SANDERS Ed F133
SANDERS Kevin M62
SANDERS Marty J44
SANDERS Neil C2 K84
SANDERS Pharoah M79
SANDERS Ric A30 S9 S66
S182
SANDERS Steve L44
SANDERS Stu C153
SANDERS Zachary F60 G4
J20 J69 L119 M17 M225
R125 S169 S262 V17
SANDERSON Duncan D58 P84
SANDFORD Butch K20
Sandi Y6A
SANDKE Jordan H170
SANDLER Harry O33C
SANDLER Myron A131D
SANDLES Verlin M53
SANDLIN Johnny A38 B91
B109 B200 H164 H195 J52
K30 K60 T9A T20 T30
SANDON Alan H116
SANDS Kenny K45
SANDVIG Peggy B221 B255
C155 G24 P129 W21 W42
SANDY McCLELLAND AND THE
BACKLINE M41A
SANFORD Billy C194 F126
G72 H65 J13 J53 K77 L42
L10B M11 M41 N37 R173
S10 T21 T107
SANFORD Ed S20
SANFORD Gary J10 R35B
SANFORD Laurie K33
SANFORD Rick D61
SANFORD and TOWNSEND S20
SANG Samantha C38
SANO Tatsuya O33G
SANOIAN Paul T41
SANSON Veronique S21
Santa see DAVIS Carlton

SANTA BARBARA MACHINEHEAD
S22
SANTAMARIA Mongo F17 J20
S22
SANTANA S19
SANTANA Carlos B144 C170
C217 K81 M40 M151 S19 W8
SANTANA Francisco R100
SANTANA Jorge M59
SANTANA Jose M59
SANTANGELI Michel S280
Y23
SANTARELLA Tony J88
SANTI Erminia L120
SANTI Richard B144
SANTIAGO Herman L144
SANTIEL Robert L2
SANTIEL Terry N66 R141
SANTINI Gene P114
SANTOS John S19
SANTOS Jumma E49 L67B M53
S17
SANTOS Patti I31 N32
SAPAL Kate S121
SAPSTEAD Bob M201
SARCH Harvey S247
SARGEANT Bob A5 C23 C251
E76 J107 M181C S23 S270
SARGEANT Emmet Z8
SARGENT Jack R126
SARKISSIAN Louis M49
SARMANTO Pekka V26C
SARNEY Joy J110
SAROFEEN AND SMOKE S24
SAROYAN Kathleen M101
SARSTEDT Clive J70A S285
SARSTEDT Peter P41
SARTINI Tony S78
SASAKI Michael C158
SASHATUNES M170
SASS S25
SASS Bobby O24A
SASSAFRAS S26
SASSER Larry L42
SATCHELL Clarence
O13
SATCHFIELD Keith
F56A
SATHIE Kesh F35
L117 M94 R66
SATIN Arnie D106D
SATIN WHALE S26A
SATISFACTION S27
SATO Hiroshi W53A
SATO Masahiko P115
SATTEN Steve T44
SATTERFIELD Louis
C45 E55 H170 L65
S250 W28
SATURNALIA S28
SATYRS J54
SAUBER Tom C179
C237
SAULNIER Michelle
M49
SAULSBY Marion H98
SAUNDERS Charles
S35B
SAUNDERS Fernando
B64 H12 M40
SAUNDERS John C183A
SAUNDERS Martin
R6B
SAUNDERS Merl D24
F80 G9 G53 G84 M53
M227 R22
SAUNDERS Orville
B122
SAUNDERS Roger A133
F110 G49 M121
SAUNDERS Russ C146
SAUNDERS Steve A30
C251 F42
SAUNDERS Tony L67B
N43
SAUTER Ed F48
SAUTER John N63
R177
SAVAGE Bob K33
SAVAGE Boryan N53
SAVAGE Jan S33 S71
SAVAGE Phil S327
SAVAGE Reid S192
SAVAGE Rick D40B
SAVAGE Steve V21

SAVAGE GRACE S28A
SAVAGE RESURRECTION S29
SAVAGE ROSE S30
SAVAKUS Russell A. F19 I3
M41
SAVAL Paco F81B
SAVIANO Tommy C45 N25
SAVICH Bill J74
SAVIGAR Kevin E9 P138
SAVOY BROWN S31
SAWARD Jill F140B
SAWYER Dan (Wind) M74
SAWYER Dan (G) C155 W21
SAWYER John S206 W18
SAWYER Phil C97 D28 K10
S105
SAWYER Ray D85 P112 S32
S120
SAXELIN Hannu W75
SAXON S32A
SAXON Joe Z8
SAXON Sky S33 S71
SAXTON Bill W30A
SAYER Eddy A93
SAYER Gerard 'Leo' D100 K17
S34 S342
SAYLES John T9
SCABIES Rat D10 D102
SCABS S34A
SCAFFOLD S35
SCAGGS Boz D124 M159 S36
S111 W106 W129
SCAIFE Ronnie B111
SCALA Ralph B157
SCALESE Gary I24A
SCALFA Patty W8
SCANCE David I22 V21
SCANLON Craig F10
SCANLON Diane C62
SCARANGELLA Jack C62
SCARBOROUGH Allison S277
SCARBOROUGH Skip C45 C220
E7 E55 M212
SCARBURY Joey Harrison B221
D71 P50
SCARECROW S36A
SCARF Bob C59
SCARLET Will B221 H161
SCARPELL Gino G53A
SCARRET Fred S110
SCARS S37
SCATER Vann F13
SCATES John W15
SCAVONE Myke R19
SCENE STEALER S37A
SCENT ORGANS S38
SCHABB Bruno G120
SCHABER Gerhard M136B
SCHACHER Mel G80B
SCHACKNE Ginger P6
SCHACTER Jules I2
SCHAEFER Gregg B13 S165
SCHAEFER Gunnar J56
SCHAEFER Jack W1
SCHAEFFER K.J133
SCHAEFFER Paul A82 B57A
B155 B208 B263 M46B M111
N2A T147
SCHAEFFER Ralph S116
SCHAEFFER Roland G120
SCHAEFFER Steve H8A O15
SCHAF Manfred F47
SCHAFFER Janne A4 L79 R3
S39
SCHAFFER Steve E75 S269
SCHAFFNER Katherin M98
SCHALLOCK David B94 B221
S189
SCHAMACH Richard E16
SCHAPER Hendrik P34
SCHARF Stu I2 K81 N65 P49
S180
SCHARFER Swain B190
SCHAUB Roger G123
SCHAUBROECK Armand S40
SCHECTER Aaron K81
SCHEFF Jerry A52 A132 B84
B202 B255 D103 D139 G40 M82
P125 R101 R10B S272 V3
SCHEFIN Aram T44
SCHEIN Richard R177
SCHELHAAS Jan C19 C34 N8
SCHELL Andreas L5
SCHELL Johnny Lee B6 M39B
SCHENIMAN Bill F111
SCHENKER Michael S41 S47
U2

SCHENKER Rudolf S47
SCHERMAN Paul E48
SCHERMIE Joe F94 T81
SCHERPENZEEL Ton K16
SCHERRER Rolf H18
SCHEUERELL Casey P115
SCHEUREN Tony U7
SCHICKE Edward S51
SCHICKE FUHRS FROHLING S41
SCHICKERT Gunther S41A
SCHIERBEEK Harry B104A
SCHIFF Steve N50A
SCHIFFOUR Tom S81
SCHILDT Herb S246
SCHILLING Bob F47
SCHINDLER Chris A56
SCHITZLER Conny T11
SCHLINGER Sol K81
SCHLITT John H71
SCHLOSS David Lee H131A
B110 B135 C246 G10 G120A
H62 J22 J85A K59 L19 M75
M187 M203 P112 P123 S272
W129
SCHMALENBACH Dirk E7C
SCHMIDT A1 S127
SCHMIDT Elmar E52A
SCHMIDT Irmin C25 C256
SCHMIDT Markus F70A
SCHMIDT Peter M136B
SCHMIDT Wolfgang P34
SCHMIDTCHEN Detler E58
SCHMIERER Richie G109
SCHMIT Tim A37 B194 C58
C123 E2 F50 H120 M27 M232
N40 P106 R137 S262 W16
SCHMOELLING Johannes T11
SCHMOLZE Doug W101
SCHNAUER Hubert E21A
SCHNEIDER Florian see
SCHNEIDER-ESLEBEN Florian
SCHNEIDER Fred B2A
SCHNEIDER Howard F60
SCHNEIDER Larry C147
SCHNEIDER-ESLEBEN Florian
K92 O30A
SCHNEIER Harold A131D
SCHNIER Stan I16 R55
SCHNITZLER Conrad C145 S42
SCHOEMAKER Tineke B43A
SCHOEN Jeff B208 S211
SCHOENER Eberhard L120
S42A
SCHOENHERZ Richard S332B
SCHOFIELD John S102A S149A
SCHOFIELD Paul S208A
SCHOFIELD Willie F9
SCHOLES Kim C76
SCHOLLE Jon E49 M21
SCHOLZ Tom B184
SCHON Neal A136 D24 J99
M16 S19 W62
SCHON Peter M237A
SCHONING Charlie R164
SCHOOLHOUSE KIDS H51
SCHOTT Karl-Heinz A113
B12A F130A
SCHOUTEN Charles K16
SCHREIBER Thomas S299B
SCHRODER Jurgen S329A
SCHROER Ellen K76
SCHROER John 'Jack' C172
M203 N32 S125 S284
SCHROYDER Steve T11
SCHUCKETT Ralph B7 B149
C138 C195 F108A J65 K48
L4A M26 M160 M233 R164 S97
S272 T27 T156
SCHUELEIN Rainer A98
SCHULMAN Jim F128
SCHULMAN Joy D67
SCHULMAN Rich C50
SCHULMAN Stuart E20 O33A
S173 S269
SCHULMAN Tom S231
SCHULTE Joerg B182A
SCHULTZ Ben K2 M151
SCHULTZ Bob S73
SCHULZ Arndt H26B P117A
SCHULZ Bernd R28
SCHULZ Juanita S332B
SCHULZE Klaus A99 C192 G3A
S43 T11 Y2
SCHULZE Kristian J4B J10A

SCHUNGE S44
SCHUNK Gary C153
SCHUNZEL Heino N61
SCHUPP Roland S137
SCHUSTER Steven G9 G84
H186 H45
SCHUSTER Sylvia C23 N51
SCHUURMAN Jan C243 M237A
SCHWAB Siegfried D19A
E52 U23
SCHWALL Jim S113
SCHWARTZ Andy C99 S135
SCHWARTZ Chuck G7A
SCHWARTZ David S116
SCHWARTZ Gene L102
SCHWARTZ Glenn J31 P6
SCHWARTZ Ron G2A
SCHWARTZ Stan F128 P119
SCHWARTZ Willie C179
SCHWARZ Brinsley B218
C42 D84 D123 E19 G79 K62
M157 P25 R162 S270
SCHWARZ Paul F108A
SCHWARZBERG Allen A135
B57A B208 B263 C76 C182
C234A C249 D115 F60 G2
G109 H99 I2 J20 J88 J92
L21 L107 M26 M46B M203
M216 N6A N65 P6 P15 R25
R149 S121 T147
SCHWEBKE Warner O10
SCHWEID Ellis G72A
SCHWEISS Hans S299B
SCHWENKE Jorg A19A
SCHWENNSON Max Paul K30
SCHWIMMER Robbie P45
SCHWITTERS Kurt E59
Scientist I1A
SCION S45
SCIPIO Steve C254
SCISSOR FITS S45A
SCOFIELD John C147 D127
SCOLAS Cynthia R134
SCOLEY Norbert W8
SCOOT Shazzi B230
SCOPE I1 S45B
SCOPPETTONE Dick H30
SCORCHER Errol S46
SCORESBY Gra W115A
SCORFINA Steve P40
SCORPION S47
SCOT Colin S48
SCOTT Andy (G) S347
SCOTT Andy (K) B8A
SCOTT Bessie Ruth N39
SCOTT Bill W134A
SCOTT Bob (D) H112
SCOTT Bobby (Pno) S125
SCOTT Bon A2
SCOTT Brian L71A
SCOTT Calman D130
SCOTT Charline T67
SCOTT Clifford B240 C180
K51
SCOTT Dave E28
SCOTT Dave (G) S219A
SCOTT Duane T113
SCOTT Eric F68
SCOTT Freddie L24 L86
SCOTT Graeme S235
SCOTT Howard B268 O35
W17
SCOTT J. F14
SCOTT Jack S49
SCOTT Jake W134A
SCOTT Joe (V) A82 W129
SCOTT Joe (Tpt) B127
B233 P26
SCOTT Joe (K) Q1
SCOTT John C184
SCOTT Julian M1A
R138
SCOTT Keith K84
SCOTT Ken (Perc)
K24
SCOTT Ken K81
SCOTT Kenneth N66
SCOTT Kevin W115
SCOTT Laurence I29
SCOTT Lincoln 'Style'
SCOTT Lindsay J3 L47
M45
SCOTT Marilyn N32 T119

SCOTT Mark T57
SCOTT Michael W132
SCOTT Mick S236
SCOTT Nigel Ross G48
SCOTT Noel S293
SCOTT Ozzie H122
SCOTT Ray H186
SCOTT Richard M67
SCOTT Robin M1A
SCOTT Ronnie F14
SCOTT Shirley D25 R125
SCOTT Stuart M180A
SCOTT Terry H83
SCOTT Tim C76
SCOTT Tom A59 A132 B6
B9 B17A B25 B110 B155
B256 C38 C39 C129 C147
D99 D124 F34 F78 H9 H39
H59 J93C K48 M9 M17 M27
M102 M131A M160 M170
M179 N40 O15 P126 R78
R87 R97 R99 R101 S34 S50
S189 S196 S220 S252 S262
S273 T37E T145 U19 V17
V18B W42
SCOTT Virginia B74
SCOTT-HERON Gil S51
SCOTT HILL Joel see HILL
Joel Scott
SCOTTVILLE SQUIRREL S52
SCRATCH AND THE
UPSETTERS S53
SCRATCH BAND S53A
SCREEN IDOLS S53B
SCRIMSHAW Glenn L76A
SCRIMSHAW Mike L76A
SCRITTI POLITTI S53C
SCRIVENOR Gunnar C194
E57
SCROGGIN Ron K77
SCROUNGER S54
SCRUFFS S55
SCRUGGS Earl C50
SCRUGGS Edwin R173
SCRUGGS Gary C247 K96
V18
SCRUGGS Randy B221 C169
C247 J53 K96 M211 T6B
V18
Scully see SIMMS Noel
SEA David P63
SEA LEVEL S56
SEABOLT Lonnie L3
SEABROOK Ronnie F14
SEADMAN William N2A
SEAL Bob C138
SEALEY Clare S306
SEALS England Dan E57
S58 S199A
SEALS Jim A31 C71 S58
SEALS Melvin B109
SEALS Son (G) S57
SEALS Sonny (Sax) S111
SEALS Troy K30 M32 S57A
S272 T167
SEALS AND CROFTS S58
SEAMAN Phil A25 F14 S59
SEANOR John S28A
SEARCHERS S60
SEARING Peter S284A
SEARS Pete C217 D24 F94
G84A H186 J46 M16 Q12
S258 S264 S273 S284 W120
SEASTONES S61
SEATKIN Eleanor V3
SEATON B.B. S62
SEATRAIN S63
SEAWARD Charles B187
SEAWELL Brent Z11
SEAWIND F103C M102 S64
SEAY Harold C12 C107A
Sebastian M18
SEBASTIAN John A135 C45
C164 C180 C234 D103 E70
F128 H23 L133 M91 N65
O12 R22 S65 S196 S276
V3
SECCO Roger S280
SECHAK Steve L22A
SECKLER Curly H49
SECOND LAYER S65A
SECOND VISION S66
SECONDHAND S67
SECRET S67A
SECRET AFFAIR S68

SECRET OYSTER S69
SECTION S70
SEDLAR James S168
Seeco see PATTERSON Alvin
SEEDS S71
SEEGER Pete G121
SEELING Ellen C99 I27 N65
S135 T147
SEFFER Jeff M49
SEGAL Beau T22
SEGAL George M82
SEGARINI Robert C180 D125
F13 R148A S72 W1
SEGEL Jaime M39B
SEGER Bob M1 S73 S121
SEGERS Guy U17
SEICO BROTHERS E77A
SEIDEL Neil S91
SEIDELIN Mogens D133
SEIDENBERG Danny S230A
SEIDENVERG Mark T4
SEIDLER Alan B135 F5 K23
S73A
SEIFERT Zbigniew K98
SEILER Peter T141A
SEITER Jim B274A B285
F110C
SEITER John A135 C180
H102 S203 T161
SEIWELL Denny D2 D13 F7
G10 G53 L7 L12 M9 M23 N43
N57 Q3A W21
Sel R20
SELDIN Ronnie H11A
SELDOM SCENE S73B
SELDON Fred B256 C213 F92
N16A R78 W44
SELECTER S74
SELF Mack F31
SELICO Ron H37 M111 O39
Z8
SELIGMAN Matthew L100A
S181
SELK John B80 C123 E23
R28A
SELLAR Gordon B74 H52 L7
M11 S271 Y16 Y18
SELLERS Peter S263
SELLERS Roger A74 N62
SELLERS Tom (B) G117
SELLERS Tom (K) A59 B47A
M160 R87
SELWAY Alan V18C
SEMANA Paul A33A
SEMBELLO Michael B110
D127 W63 W119
SEMENS Jim 'Antennae'
(COTTON Jeff) B72 M222B
SEMLER Derek H189
SEMUTA S74B
SENNEVILLE Butch S281
SENOO Ryuichiro W53A W53A
SENSATION FIX S74A
SENSATIONAL ALEX HARVEY
BAND H52
SENTER Elsie W107
SEOL Randy S294
SEOPARDIE Jeff B195 C39A
SEOS Vince R175A
SERAFIN Germano L54A
SERAPHINE Daniel C100
SERMAN Vic T22
SERPELL Grant A17 D2 I4
S8
SERRANO Francisco C168A
SERRANO Paul C17
SERRATI Eddie Q9
SERREO Peter C254
SERRI Moreau K19
SERRY John Jnr. A122 S75
SERWA Al C183A
SESSIONS Cynthia V4O
SETTLE Mike S272
SETZER Brian S296A
SEUFERT Tom L20 V12
SEUR Harry C152A
SEVENTH WAVE S76
SEVEREID Carl M238
SEVERIN Steve S132
SEVERINSEN Don S168
SEVILLA Mickey D83
SEX CHANGE BAND R139
SEX PISTOLS S77
S

SEXTON Barbara W128
SEYMOUR Bob N37
SEYMOUR Chris M208
SEYMOUR George J41
SEYMOUR Manny P6
SEYMOUR Phil M96 T164
SHA NA NA S63 S78
SHAAR Dahaud (SHAW David)
C111 M18 M203 V21
SHACK Richard J31
SHACKLOCK Alan B5
SHACKMAN A1 P49
SHADBOURNE Eugene B131
SHADDICK Terry T131
SHADES OF JOY S78A
SHADOWFAX S79
SHADOWS R80 S80
SHADOWS OF THE KNIGHT S81
SHAFFER Nathan G7A
SHAFFER Paul N10
SHAFRAN Stan B282
SHAFTESBURY S81A
SHAGRAT THE VAGRANT S82
SHAKAHACHI Kazu O15
SHAKE S83
SHAKELFORD Earl D17 E23
I10
SHAKERS S83A
SHAKESLINER Wilmer B233
SHAKESPEARE Chris B93A
SHAKESPEARE Robbie A6 B95A
B234 B276 C245 D63 D130
H122 H172 I1A I12 J17B P2
P134 P135 R30 R84 R150
T114 U1 W4 W4A
SHAKIN' STEVENS AND THE
SUNSETS S268
SHAKIN' STREET S84
SHAKLETON Ivor W87
SHAKTI S85
Sham J63
SHAM 69 S86
SHAMBLIN Eldon A102
SHANAHAN Kelly S65 S289B
SHANAHAN Patrick M123 M156
N21
SHANANDA Aumash J22
SHANE James C26
SHANGHAI S87
SHANGO S87A
SHANGRI-LAS S88
SHANK Bud B63 C153 M170
M229 P115 S124
SHANK Clifford H8A
SHANKAR Lakshmirnarayna
M40 M114A S85
SHANKAR Shiva Q16
SHANKLIN Mike R101
SHANNON Del (WESTOVER
Charles) S89
SHANNON Jeffrey L4
SHANNON Peter N5
SHANNON Tommy W107
SHANTI S91
SHANX Nancy S75
SHAPHIN Andy J96
SHAPIRO Brad J11
SHAPIRO Dave B259 M131A
SHAPIRO Harvey F83A
SHAPIRO Lee F91
SHAPIRO Peter L100
SHAPMAN Brian P4
SHARBONO Doni B91
SHARIF Mirza al A120
SHARK Eric D34
SHARK Noah T164
SHARKEY Feargal U11
SHARKEY Geoff G36
SHARKS S92
SHARLAND Roy F141
SHARLEY Chris S26
SHARMAN Dave K75
SHARP Allan B283 F86 G67
L63 R125
SHARP Arthur N5
SHARP Dee Dee (LARUE
Dione)(Mrs.Kenny GAMBLE)
S92A
SHARP Jackie F14
SHARP Jane B221
SHARP Kevin L52A
SHARP Randy B201
SHARP Sid (Str) A37 B15
B127 C58 C155 D74 F92 H14
K45 M18 M227 P75 P106 R78
S10 S36 S160 W18 Z11

Sk/So

SKIN ALLEY S141
SKIN FLESH AND BONES BAND
B101
SKINNER Bunky Rochelle
J18
SKINNER David B138 C119
F42 G32 K4 M81 I163 U9
W18
SKINNER Jack A132 K95
SKINNER Mick Y1
SKINNER Mike A56
SKIP BIFFERTY H84 S142
SKIPPER Buddy B41 C194
M11
SKLAR Leland A52 A132 B25
B110 B175 B194 B244 C38
C58 C123 C147 C180 C200
C233 D74 D99 D103 E40 E57
F68 G10 G60 G121 H9 H120
K14 K17 K22 K48 K59 K95
K96 L12 L108 M27 M198 P50
P76 P114B R81 R109 S70
S124 S272 S276 T6B T25
T27 T80A W44A Z11
SKOGLUND Bo H18
SKOLNIK Steve F54A
SKORNIA Chris B193A
SKREWDRIVER S143
Skully see SIMMS Noel
SKY S144
SKY J.D. I18
SKY Patrick S145
SKY SAXON BLUES BAND S33
SKYBAND S146
SKYBOAT G16
SKYDOG BAND B278
SKYHOOKS S147
Skyjuice see BLAKE
Christopher
SKYLARK S148
SKYROCKETS S149
SKYWHALE S149A
SLACK Paul U4
SLACK ALICE S150
SLADE S151
SLADE Chris M80 M157 O18B
P41 T49
SLADE Kenny C155
SLADE Rod 'Boots' P131
W89
SLADE Terry C210 H56
S329B
SLAGER Johan K16
SLAIS Bill B109
SLAIS Reni B109
SLAMER Mike C118
SLAPIN Billy R125
SLAPP HAPPY S152
SLATER Michael 'Mutter'
S235
SLATER Nelson S152A
SLATER Rodney B178
SLATTERY Jeff H186
SLAUGHTER Henry P125
SLAUGHTER John W117
SLAUGHTER Rick (WERNHAM
Richard) M215
SLAUGHTER AND THE DOGS
S153
SLAVE S154
SLAVEN Ken L16A
SLAVEN Neil L136
SLEATH Wil P72
SLEDGE Debbie S135
SLEDGE James R115
SLEDGE Joni S135
SLEDGE Kathie S135
SLEDGE Kim S135
SLEDGE Percy S155
SLETTEN Curt O39 S251
SLEXIA Dick P88B
SLICK Darby G80
SLICK Earl B186 H185 M160
S156
SLICK Grace C217 C232 G88
H45 J46 S61 S157
SLICK Jerry G88
SLIDER Albie S86
SLIGTING Jan Willem B43A
SLIK S158
SLIM CHANCE L16A
SLITS S159
SLIWIN Joan B47C
SLOAN Allen D79
SLOAN Claudio R97

SLOAN Eleanor C165
SLOAN P.F. S160
SLOAN Phil F18B
SLOANE Tommy J14
SLOMAN Jon L114 U22
SLONE Bobby K29
Slot M150A
SLUDGE Ricky R49
SLUTSKY Martin M37
SLY AND THE FAMILY STONE
S161
SMALL Charles F19 H59
SMALL Drink S161A
SMALL Dag M220 P143
SMALL Henry S162A
SMALL Janet S83A
SMALL Jonathan H55A
SMALL Linda C58 J105A
SMALL Mick G112A
SMALL FACES S162
SMALL WONDER S162A
SMALLEY Dave R35
SMALLMAN Gary P58
SMART Keith B26 D66 M180A
W18 W122
SMART Leroy S163
SMART Norman Dow II C195
K8 M216 P33 R164 W51 W101
SMART Terry R80 S80
SMASH Gary M46A
SMEDGAARD Carsten J70A
M147
SMEDLEY Julian B187 I20
O40
SMEENK Paul S348A
SMIDT Birgit D83A
Smiggy B148 N43
SMIRKS S164
SMIT Frans A27
SMITH Aaron W31
SMITH Adrian I25
SMITH Al P26
SMITH Alexander B180
SMITH Allan B230
SMITH Allen J79
SMITH Ammer D51
SMITH Andrew (D) C153 G4
J20 O27 U18
SMITH Andy (Banjo) G98
SMITH Angela D66
SMITH Anthony Allen M40
SMITH Art P15
SMITH Bas K43
SMITH Bill (K) J41 S339
SMITH Bill (B) A115 B23
J16 O9 S34
SMITH Bill (D) H91A
SMITH Bob C56 C76 F109
J18
SMITH Brian (Wind) A74
C63 F14 K84 N62 P42A S108
T95
SMITH Brian (B) P5
SMITH Brian (G) S210 T146
SMITH Brian B8A
SMITH Broderick C41A D72B
S266
SMITH Bruce L28 L119C
P117
SMITH Catherine A132 H117
L72
SMITH Charlie (D) B148
D113 L117
SMITH Charles (Tpt) E52B
SMITH Chris (G) C200 P50
SMITH Chris (Trom) F14
SMITH Chris (K) B193A
SMITH Chris 'Judge'(Perc)
H13
SMITH Chuck C162 R16B
SMITH Claydes K80
SMITH Colin A50A M5 P100
SMITH Curly H185 J64 M191
SMITH Curt G77B
SMITH Dalton C180 F134
SMITH Danny B50
SMITH Danny (D) D17 L89
Z22
SMITH Dave (B) K94B
SMITH Dave (D) F67
SMITH David (D/V) S308A
SMITH David K96
SMITH Dean B72
SMITH Dennis (B) A13 S68

SMITH Dennis (D) D108
SMITH Derek L63
SMITH Dee M1A
SMITH Dick D36
SMITH Dick Lee W38
SMITH Don M11
SMITH Donald L41 S169
SMITH Duane W136
SMITH Earl 'Chinna' A6
H172 I1A I12 L58A M88
M149 M221D P2 P134 P140C
R134 S190 U1 V21 W4
SMITH Emma O18
SMITH Feddie B259
SMITH Frank C. D139 M209
SMITH Fred (B) B139 L98A
R118 T38
SMITH Fred (Reeds) R115
SMITH Fred (D) A133 T63
W129
SMITH Fred 'Sonic' (G)
I10 M1
SMITH G. B87
SMITH Garth B284
SMITH Gary S336
SMITH George B13 S165
S204 S329 T23 T79B W12A
SMITH Gerry V26
SMITH Gordon C83 C210 D46
F62 S166 W129
SMITH Graham (Perc) B2
SMITH Graham (V) V11
SMITH Graham (Harm) B105
E9 M50 P131 S270
SMITH Grahame (Vln) A93
D54 G97 H4 H13 H42 S306
SMITH Harry A133
SMITH Herb H58
SMITH Herman J79
SMITH Howard V18A
SMITH Huey 'Piano' S167
SMITH Hurricane T37A
SMITH Jack (Pno) K88
SMITH Jack (D) F31
SMITH James (D) A71
SMITH James (G) J69 M27
M111
SMITH James (V) S284A
SMITH James Allen (K) D24
P15
SMITH James Herb M2
SMITH James Quill M111
SMITH James 'Smitty' (G)
D86
SMITH Jerome (G) H157 K1
SMITH Jerome (D) M185
SMITH Jerry (B) B13 S165
SMITH Jerry (B) F70
SMITH Jerry (G) K27A
SMITH Jerry S23
SMITH Jerry (K) C14 H26
J13 L77 S272 Y18
SMITH Jerry Lee (K) M85
SMITH Jessica May A50
D101 D127 G121 J72 L128
M229
SMITH Jimmie T158
SMITH Jimmy (K) K94A S168
W62
SMITH Jimmy L140
SMITH John B98 G7
SMITH Jon Robert M233 S56
W106 W107
SMITH Keith S48
SMITH Ken C76
SMITH Kester E78 M53
SMITH Kevin U13
SMITH Larry C236 L74
SMITH Lawson B24
SMITH 'Legs' Larry B178
J72
SMITH Leslie O. C213 J93C
SMITH Little Phil G122
SMITH Little Willie H32
S204 W28 W91
SMITH Lloyd B36 F1 M15
SMITH Lonnie Liston B85
SMITH Lorenzo L52
SMITH Marilyn E73
SMITH Mark F10

SMITH Marshall W54
SMITH Martha M80
SMITH Martin (D) D134
G22
SMITH Martin (G) C85
W124
SMITH Maxie see ROMEO
Max
SMITH Michael (D) R70
SMITH Michael (D) T166
SMITH Michael (B) S230
SMITH Mick (Wind) S54
SMITH Micky (B) A43
SMITH Mike (K) C122
SMITH Mike (G) F127
SMITH Mike (V) C6 W117
SMITH Mike (V/G) S184
SMITH Mike Lee S254
SMITH Moses 'Whispering' B282 B170
S171
SMITH Moth G124 M126
SMITH Myrna N23 O15
SMITH Neal B103 C182
SMITH Nigel (B) K35
SMITH Nigel (K) M45 M50
SMITH Nolan G17 K48 M111
Q3A S171
SMITH Pat G61 M111
SMITH Patter W88
SMITH Patti B154 S170
SMITH Paul (D) S316
SMITH Paul (K) M225 S325
W116 Z8
SMITH Pete D97
SMITH Potato C30
SMITH Randall H186
SMITH Ray E73 H74 P107
SMITH Ray (G) H3
SMITH Ray (G) F74B
SMITH Reginald see WILDE
Marty
SMITH Rex R73
SMITH Richard Diga R125
SMITH Robert (G) B82
SMITH Robert (V/G) C247A
SMITH Roger (Cello) F86
SMITH Roger (G) S267
SMITH Ron (G) T80
SMITH Ron (Horns) M59
SMITH Ronald (K) N66
SMITH Russ (B) R21
SMITH Russell (G) A45
SMITH Russell (Tpt) G26A
SMITH Sam N42
SMITH Sammi C124
SMITH Scott L130B
SMITH Simon M136A
SMITH Sterling M123
SMITH Steve (K/G) C11
H160 N55 S172 T20
SMITH Steve (Vln) M11
SMITH Steve (D) F77 J99
P115
SMITH Steve (B/V) V18A
SMITH Stuart S110
SMITH T.V. A14
SMITH Terry F14 I8 Z24
N55 S172
SMITH Tinkerbell S14
SMITH Tish C158
SMITH Tom C76
SMITH Tommy R53
SMITH Tommy (Tpt) M211
N23 T9
SMITH Tommy (V) F60
SMITH Tony (G) L114 S53B
SMITH Tony (D) B64 B177
C217 H12 M59
SMITH Tyrone H170
SMITH Ursula C4 T60
SMITH Velma D30
SMITH Vic B165 G107
SMITH Wally R40B
SMITH Warren (G) E5 L70
M21 M203 P49 S168 S170A
SMITH Warren (Perc) R31
S17
SMITH Whispering see
Moses
SMITH William D. (K)
C179 D100 T158 V18B
SMITH William 'Smitty'
(K) B135 C11B C36 C58

C109 E40 H59 J69 L50 L108
L111 M229 P15 P83 P114 R22
R39 T107 T145 V3 W136
SMITH Willie 'Big Eyes'
(D) H159 R114 W28 W107
SMITH-FIELD Roy A133
SMITH-FROST Bartholomew
M144
SMITH-PERKINS-SMITH S172
SMITHER Chris S173
SMITSKAMP Henk L95B
SMITTY Bob R115
SMOCK Ginger O39
SMOKEY ROBINSON AND THE
MIRACLES R115
SMOKIE S174
SMOOTH OPERATORS T37H
SMOTHERMAN Michael B72
SMOTHERS Otis 'Smokey'
B282 B170
SMYLIE Ivory B177
SMYTH Gilli (also YONI
Shakti) A35 G66 H86A H119
M211A P91 S175
SMYTH Jimmy B166A
SMYTH Mike M182
SMYTHE D.K. R70A R74
SMYTHE Danny B190 Z10
SMYTHE Mick L59
SNAFU S176
SNAIL S177
Snakefinger see LITHMAN
Phil
SNAKES J22
SNAPE K84
Snappin' see BECKFORD Theo
SNARE C.P. S219A
SNARE Lester E55
SNATCH S176A
Sneaks see LEE George
Sneaky Pete see KLEINOW
Sneaky Pete
SNEDDON Andy E8
SNEED Floyd G24 T81
SNELL David H66 P15 S108
SNELL Lester K46 L90
SNEP John S214B
SNIDER Les L74
SNIFF'N'THE TEARS S178
Snips B20 I22 S92 S179
SNITKER S. D83A
Snookie B139
SNOW Don S130 V28
SNOW Hank A110
SNOW Ian S284A
SNOW Michael B160 F41
SNOW Phoebe B221 I2 J48
S17 S180
SNOW Sherry H112
SNOW Tom G40 S34
SNOWDEN Elmer J79
SNYDER Craig J92
SNYDER Doug V11A
SNYDER Gil I24A
SNYDER Steve P33
SOAPER Ray K39
SOARES Jose S111
SOBEL Peter V21
SOCIAL DEVIANTS D58
SOCIAL SECURITY S180A
SOCOLOW Paul
SOCRATES S180B
SODEN Derek C159
SODS S180C
SOFT BOYS S181
SOFT HEAP S181A
SOFT MACHINE S182
SOFT WHITE UNDERBELLY S183
SOFTIES S184
SOFTLEY Mick S185
SOHL Richard S170
SOHNS Jim S81
Sojie G39
SOLAMAR Steve M163B S214
SOLAR Jim S219A
SOLAR PLEXUS S186
SOLBERG Chris S83A
SOLBERG Jim A35A
SOLEE Dennis A102
SOLERA Guiseppe Dino B174
I2 J10A
SOLES Steve A41 C123 D139
F116
SOLID GOLD CADILLAC S186A

[514]

St

STEEL Willie H170
STEEL MILL S260
STEEL-PERKINS Crispian
C161 C251
STEEL PULSE S261
STEELE Andrew D93 F13 F23
H106 P76A R11 S257 S313
W18
STEELE Bill H186
STEELE Drew S333B
STEELE Larry A82 B268 D22
D131 G67 J72 K24 L63 M129
S266 S270 S276 T96 W134
STEELE Ronald S269
STEELE Terry J72
STEELE Tommy B35
STEELER Bob H161
STEELEYE SPAN S263
Steelie see NELSON
  Anthony
STEELWIND T136
STEELY DAN S262
STEEN Roger T152
STEER Martin B231
STEFAN Steffi C78
STEFFENS Dirk B107 T103A
STEGMEYER Doug J20 J69
STEIG Jeremy H59 J54
M55A M177 M225 O27 W107
STEIN Andy A102 C173 L37
P151
STEIN Chris B139 S259A
STEIN Mark M101 R148 V15
STEINBERG Bruce I31 T119
W129
STEINBERG Eleana E49
STEINBERG Louis B180
STEINBERG Penny K48
STEINBERG Richard T169
STEINBORN Andy O36
STEINER Dave I15A
STEINER Herb M232 S269
W11
STEINHARDT Robbie K9
STEINHOLTZ Gerry H112
R99
STEINMAN John M120
STEINMAN Roger M75
STEINMONTS Ken A131A
STEINSIEK Heiko C219A
STEKOL Richard F138
Stelley see NELSON
Anthony
STELLITTI Joe T22
STELLMAN Martin P136
STELTZER John S308A
STEMBRIDGE Jerry E73 J53
STENCH Hilary P48A
STENCH John P48A
STENCH Vic P72
STENGARD Johan A4 L79
STENSSON Bobo H18 R178
STEPASIDE S263A
STEPHAN Steffi B12A L78
STEPHENS Andrew W28
STEPHENS Bruce B150
STEPHENS Charlie E78
STEPHENS Leigh B150 S264
STEPHENS Lena R173
STEPHENS Louis K51
STEPHENS Mike F23
STEPHENS Nick S267
STEPHENS Nicky D55
STEPHENS Tennyson D66
F103D R97 U18
STEPHENS Trevor O47
STEPHENSON Andrew L94
STEPHENSON Harry P103
STEPHENSON Ian J63
STEPHENSON James see
Guitar Slim
STEPHENSON Jody B97
STEPHENSON Kevin R175B
STEPHENSON Michael T158
STEPHENSON Tom W16
STEPNEY Billy L94 M48
W94
STEPNEY Charles W28
STEPPENWOLF S265
STEPTON Rick L74
STERG Gil H155A
Sterling see McCLEOD
Ernest
STERLING John B268 L128

STERLING Keith B101 B234
D130 H105 H172 R134 T114
W4
STERLING Randy D17 H52A
STERN Bobby B174 J10A
STERN Michael C86
STERN Peggy T107
STERN Randy B274A
Sternenmadchen Gille
C192 G3A
STESCH Hal S311
STETTENPOHL Dickie M62
STEURER Bob M182
STEVE DOUGLAS AND THE
REBEL ROUSERS D106C
STEVE GIBBONS BAND G27
STEVE MILLER BAND B87
M159
STEVE MIRO AND THE EYES
M163B
STEVE YORK'S CAMELO
PARDALIS Y10
STEVENS Billy F35
STEVENS Cat (GEORGIOU
Steven) D22 S266
STEVENS Clive M80
STEVENS Dave K84
STEVENS Gordon M174
STEVENS Guy M214
STEVENS Jeri D124
STEVENS Jon D11 M45 M94
S267
STEVENS Mark C179 H8A
J93C K36B
STEVENS Nick T80C
STEVENS Ovid E57 S58
STEVENS Rick T119
STEVENS Rob C212
STEVENS Sally M18 S160
STEVENS Sandra H19
STEVENS Shakin' S268
STEVENS T.M. D27
STEVENS Tennyson U18
STEVENS Tony D30 F81 J34
M34 R120 S31 W72
STEVENSON B.W. F128 S269
STEVENSON Bill E5
STEVENSON Don M174
STEVENSON Jack K4
STEVENSON James C95
STEVENSON John (B) G60A
STEVENSON John (K) C140A
STEVENSON Savourna S344
STEVERS Rick F120
Stevie C78
STEWARD Susan J69 N23
STEWART Al S270
STEWART Alan P89A
STEWART Alonzo S358
STEWART Annie C251
STEWART Babbs H192
STEWART Bill A37 A38
B253 H195 K30 N32 T9A
T20 T30 W44
STEWART Bob (Psaltery)
C109 C165
STEWART Bob (Brass) B131
M53
STEWART Buffy Ford S272
STEWART Chris (B) C155
E26 F7 G6 G53 H94 L101
M94 M157 N57 S224 S313
STEWART Chris (D) G21
STEWART Colleen M160
STEWART Colin P89A
STEWART Craig Z8
STEWART Dave (K) B249
E24 H57 H119 H154 K35
N9 N14
STEWART Dave (G/B) C57A
C253 H119 L117 T117
STEWART Diane A25 B171
Y10
STEWART Eric H163 L43
M67 M162 R20 T43
STEWART Gary S271
STEWART Gaynor D99
STEWART Hamish P19
STEWART Ian B154B K84
R122A R133 S264 T122
W121
STEWART Jim P26
STEWART John S272
STEWART John (V/G) S36A
STEWART John 'Maus' D8A

STEWART Kenny D78 R66A
STEWART Leroy G122 W47
STEWART Louis C9
STEWART Maeretha A35A
B105 C44 D39 D53 D139
F109 H99 J48 K81 L21 L80A
L111 M233 P149 S198A W106
STEWART Mark P117
STEWART Mary Ann D66 S111
STEWART Matthew S246
STEWART Mick (G) S347
STEWART Mick (D) C253
STEWART Micky (G) K39
STEWART Mike (G) M178
STEWART Michael J69 S272
STEWART Paul P89A P117
STEWART Rod A120 B23 B64
F4 J12 S105 S259 S273
W120
STEWART Ronnie P63A
STEWART Simon G46
STEWART Stephen E58
STEWART Sylvester see
STONE Sly
STEWART Tommy C61A T146
STEWART Winston B36
STICK UP S274
Stickman H172
Sticky see THOMPSON
Uzziah
STICKLER Dan H38
STIEF Bo M147
STIFF LITTLE FINGERS S275
STIGNAC Bobby G67
STILES Danny T44 W13
STILES Roy M223
STILL Dave W107
STILLS Stephen B109 B144
B260 C164 C180 C234 H45
H59 H179 K81 M64 M101
M170 S276 S276A W116 Y16
STILLS YOUNG BAND S276A
STILLWATER S277
STIMPSON John M67 S4
Sting (SUMNER Gordon)
P111 S42A
STINGERS B1
STINGRAY S278
STINKY TOYS S279
STINNET Ray S14A
STINSON Albert H10
STINSON Greg E. M68 S79
STINSON Harry S117
STIPE Tom F139
STIPS Robert Jan B224A
C243 G64 S253A S332D
S348A
STIRLING Peter Lee H183
STIRLING-WALL Philip F6
STITH John C196
STIVE Pascal S280 Y23
STIVELL-COCHEVELOU Alan
D17 S280
STOCK David Rip E18A G122
STOCKDALE Rev C185B
STOCKER Carol M80
STOCKER Walt B8
STOCKER Wolfgang E50A
STOCKERT Ron B225 J22
K94A L111 R61 T158
Stockholm Slim B193 M48
STOCKFISH John L72
STRACHAN Brian P18
STOCKLIN John H170
STOCKTON Ann Mason F78
STOCKTON Richard P40
STODDARD Joe F54
STOEBER Orville S280A
STOER Hans E52A
STOEWE Armin S137
STOJKA Harry N60A
STOKER Gordon J98 K30 K95
N37 S342
STOKER Hugh P63
STOKES Bill P54
STOKES Houston P26 T74
STOKES Mike (K) C220
STOKES Michael B42
STOKES O'Dell R173
STOKES Otis L10A
STOKES Robbie H45 H186
STOKES Sheridan R97
STOKES Simon S281
STOKES Val D110

STOKEY Jimmy E77
STOKKAN Ketil Z19
STOLLER Alvin C146
STOLLER Mike C146 P125
R111 S257 W13
STONE Anthony Q11
STONE Chris F142
STONE Curtis B274A
STONE David (K) R14 S359
STONE David (G) M177
STONE David (Flt) M225
STONE Freddie G80 S161
STONE Ivory S19
STONE J. C185B D39 J63
STONE John L59
STONE Lafayette Trey N66
STONE Martin C105 F23
K52 M148 P84 R121 S31
STONE Mike F55
STONE R. C185B D39
STONE Ronald C232
STONE Rosie S161
STONE Russell D92
STONE Sly (STEWART
Sylvester) B109 M16 N32
R1A S161
STONE Winstone F42
STONE CITY BAND J28
STONE PONEYS S282
STONE THE CROWS S283
STONEBOLT S283A
STONEBRIDGE Lou B286
D10A G41 M29 P11 S283B
STONEBRIDGE McGUINNESS
S283B
STONEGROUND S284
STONEHOUSE S284A
STONEMAN Ronnie D12
STONEMAN Scott K29
Stoner D89
STONER Rob D139 F116 G74
M27 M41 M96 W129
STONEY AND MEATLOAF M119
STOOGES I10
STORACE Marc K96A T35
STORCH Doc T150
STORCH Jay V2
STOREY David E58
STOREY Mike A22 G77 K83
N41 S285
STOREY Neil D110A
STORFINGER Fritz M192
STORIES S286
STORM Suzi B123 F48 H146
P79 W54
STORM Warren H31 L75
L115
STORME Ricky R134
STORMVILLE SHAKERS C115
STORMY SIX S286A
STORTI Jack M101
STORYTELLER S287
STOTTS Richie P93A
STOUDER Jim A21
STOUGH Mike L75 S340
STOUGHTON David S288
STOUT David E31 L55 S251
STOVALL Gary P114B
STOVALL SISTERS T150
STOVELLS F80
STOVER Evan B221
STRACHAN Brian P18
STRACHEN Graeme S147
STRADLING Geoff B174
STRAIGHT EIGHT S288A
STRAIGHT SHOOTER S289
STRAIN Sam L85
STRAKER Nick see BAILEY
Nick
STRAKEY George D50
STRAM Tony G2A
STRAND S289B
STRANDLUND Robb D17 R28A
STRANGE Adam R91
STRANGE Billy S200
STRANGE Cass see
CASSIDY Ed
STRANGE Gary N56
STRANGE Kid D89
STRANGE Richard A14
S290
STRANGE Steve V35A
STRANGE DAYS S291
STRANGLERS S292

STRAON Tea D124
STRAPPS S293
STRASSBURG Jimmy E49 L67B
STRATER Gary S246
STRATFORD Charles P79
STRATON Stray B91
STRATTON Alison Y20
STRATTON Dennis I25 U15
STRAUKS Imants S147
STRAUSS James J62
STRAUSS Justin M154
STRAWBERRY ALARM CLOCK S294
STRAWBRIDGE Bob M45
STRAWBS S295
STRAWHEAD S295A
STRAWN Douglas C39 S58
STRAY S296
STRAY CATS S296A
STRAY DOG S297
STRAY GATOR S298
STRAZZA Peter E33 G61
STREDDER Maggie S206
STREENBERG Ole S69
STREET Bill M106A
STREET Richard T42
STREET CORNER SYMPHONY
S298A
STREETBAND S299
STREETHEART S299A
STREETMARK S299B
STREETWALKERS S300
STREIFELD Muriel M49
STRELLEZYK Lee S303
STREMMEL Rudiger C219A
Stretch C79 R40B
STRETCH S301
STRICKLAND Keith B2A
STRICKLAND Madeline H133
STRICKLAND William R. S302
STRIDE Pete L142 S302A
STRIDER S303
STRIEPLING Gunther S289
STRIFE S304
STRIKE Johnny C225
STRIKE Liza A61 A98A A115
A133 B23 B25 B45A B83 B230
C13 C78 C141 C185B C204 C210
D36 D39 D131 F7 F13 F42 G32
G50 H22 H23 H52 H67 H70 H110
H172 H175 H176 H177 H181
J72 K20 L27 L63 M7 M80 N14
O8 O40 P85 S34 S124 S134
S162 S176 S185 S276 W7 W10
W72 Y17
STRINGER Duncan T36A
STRIKER S305
STRING DRIVEN THING S306
STRIPJACK S307
STROEMER Reinhard S338
STROER Hansi S42A
STROGER Bob L126 R168 S329
STROHMAN Tom H51 W107
STROLL Jon P6
STRONACH John W16
STRONG A1 S189
STRONG Barrett S308
STRONG Frank P115
STRONG Ollie L72
STRONG Scott O15 P69
STRONGBOW S308A
STROUD James G92B S125
STROUD Peter V36
STROUD Steve W99A
STRUMMER Joe C130 O25
STRUNZ George G77C
STRUTT Howie C177A
STRUTT Nick M166 P54
STRUZICK Eddie I39
STRUZICK Laura B123 P79
STRZELCZYK Lee F67 S303
STRZELECKI Henry C50 D70
D139 H26 H49 J13 J53 K77
N37 P63 S187C S271 T167 Y18
STUART Alice Z8
STUART Bob S63
STUART Chad D23A
STUART Glen M50
STUART Graham M50
STUART Hamish A131 K36 M206
S17
STUART Ian V16
STUART Michael L128
STUART Rolf I31
STUBBLEFIELD Clyde S111
STUBBS Dick R44

THOMS Peter C85 L16 L37
THOMS Tren I19A
THOMSON Marla E7C
THOMSON Mike O28
THONER Erik J10A
THOR Marc T79A
THORN Kirk S237
THORNBERG Lee J105A L89
THORNE Dave S212
THORNE Mike W112
THORNGREN Doug M75
THORNGREN Eric B262A
THORNHILL Alan A132
THORNTON 'Big Mama' Willie Mae S329 T79B
THORNTON Blair B10
THORNTON Buddy M93
THORNTON Eddie F7 F14 R84 W23 Y17
THORNTON Les B166
THORNTON Paul G58
THORNTON Randy C40
THORNTON Steve C40 R99 S169
THORNYCROFT Bill K43
THOROGOOD George T80
THORPE Billy T80A
THORPE Mel H24
THORPE Paul L68A
THORPE Richard L68A
THORPE Tony R153
THORUP Peter C2 K84
THOSE NAUGHTY LUMPS T80B
THRALL Pat A127 T135 W8 W23
THRASHER Andrew D116
THRASHER Gerhard D116
THRASHER Norman B24
THREE D. T80C
THREE DOG NIGHT T81
THREE MAN ARMY T82
THROBBING GRISTLE T83
THUNDER Theodore B31 L47 O9 P131 S34
THUNDERBIRDS F21
THUNDERBOLTS M44 M99
THUNDERBYRD M27
THUNDERCLAP NEWMAN T84
THUNDERMUG T85
THUNDERS Johnny H76 N34 T86
Thundersticks S14D
THUNDERTHIGHS A42 B231 E37 F65 K24 M214 R60 S108 T87 V26
THUNDERTRAIN T88
THURMAN Benny T64
THURMAN Ed P139A
THURSTON Colin R20
THURSTON Scott I10 N31
THYNE Robin M50
TIANA Mayo C155 J65
TIBBELS Nicole T79
TIBBETTS Ken B91 B253
TIBBS Gary J110 O6A R149 V28
TICE Dave C199
Tich see AMEY Ian
TICKNOR George J99
TIDBALL Dave T160
TIDWELL Diane E57 H49 N37 S32 S269
TIDWELL George C14 G72 H65 N37 T107
TIEFENSEE Martin H37B L10
TIERNAN Mark B256
TIERNEY Tony L140
TIGARD Holly C158
TIGER T89
TIGERS T89A
TIGHT LIKE THAT T90
TILBROOK Adrian B11
TILBROOK Glenn C193 S232 T79
TILFORD Brian C217
TILL John J95
TILLER Paul B112
TILLERY Calvin S325
TILLERY Linda L100 S19 W62
TILLEY Chuck B253
TILLEY Sandra V9
TILLI Dennis C61A
TILLISON Roger T91
TILLMAN Bill B141

TILLMAN Curtis S329
TILLMAN Georgeanna M98
TILLMAN Jimmy M159 R59
TILLMAN Julia A59 A120 B43 B47A B47C B127 B226 C58 C129 C141 C180 C182 C235 D99 D127 E40 F134 H181 I24 J7 K45 K46 K48 L89 M68 M101 M102 M179 M191 M225 N23 O35 P44 P83 R87 R97 R101 R126 R137 S19 S51 S73 S124 S180 S251 S269 S325 T158 W31
TILLMAN Keith D128 D129 M111 R121 S349
TILLOTSON Brooks D50 J20 K36 M12 V17 W106
TILSTON Steve T92 V21
TIMBER T93
TIMBRELL H.J. P125
TIMEBOX T94
TIMMS Daniel P76
TIMONEY Mike H163
TIMPERLEY Clive C32 O25 P33B
TINAYJRE Gilles S280
TINDALL T.J. B135 E18A H133 L130 P15 R22 V12
TINI Ray Jnr. K46
TINNER Rene C25
TINSLEY James C129
TIPPELSKIRCH Mathias P118
TIPPENS Stan M214
TIPPET John K44A
TIPPETT Keith B231 C63 C109 D35 D118 H154 K54 M19 M42 M108 N50 O45 P146 S131 T95
TIPPETTS Julie (nee DRISCOLL) A120 B2 B131 C63 D118 E46 J9 O45 S259 T95
TIPTON Glen J102
TIR NA NOG T96
TISBY Dexter P59
Tish B139
TISON Patrick S108
TITANIC T97
TITCOMB Gordon B135
TITELMAN Russ B72 C11B C50 C179 C206 L89 N40 S10
TITLER Paul D109
TITIMUS Jeff D39
Tito B157
TITUS Libby S124 T98
TITUS GROAN T99
TIVEN John V11A
TKAZYAK Jeff A122
TO BE T100
TOAD T101
TOAD Slimey M199
TOAN Danny C189
TOBALY Marc L57
TOBIN George J73A
TOBIN Karen H161
TOBY T102
TOBY BEAU T102A
TODD Alan B209
TODD Graham B89 M202
TODD Jeff F31
TODD Paul S149A W82A
TODD Phillip C85 P138
TODD Tony C6
TOEFAT T103
TOESCA Louis M49
TOFANI David K69 M107
TOFANI Giampaolo A74A
TOKENS R25
TOKYO PHILHARMONIC ORCHESTRA W27
TOLBERT Larry H8A H192 R45 S250 W116
TOLE Perry N11A
TOLER Dan A38 B91
TOLER David B91
TOLES Michael E55 F134 K46 L90 M172
TOLF Jan S39
TOLHURST Kerryn D72B F81A
TOLHURST Laurence C247A
TOLLES Jim G72A

TOLLHOUSE T103A
TOLMIE David G87
TOLONEN Jukka J3A T15 T104
TOLSON Pete B230 P128
TOM PETTY AND THE HEARTBREAKERS P70
TOM ROBINSON BAND R116
TOMICH Mike H110 I16
TOMINAGA Trevor A74 D118 G30 N62 W86
TOMLIN Dave T60
TOMLINSON Dave A29
TOMLINSON Marie F83A
TOMM Tom F129
TOMMY Glen R66
TOMMY AND THE BIJOUX H110
TOMMY JAMES AND THE SHONDELLS J30
TOMORROW T106
TOMPKINS Deborah S272
TOMPKINS Pam E31
TOMPKINS Tim P141A
TOMPKINS Tom B151 P141A
TOMSCO George F49
TONE S18
TONEY James K45
TONEY John G92
TONEY Kevin B122 N39
TONGUE Deo D16
TONI AND TERRY T107
Tonto W36
TONTO Kathy O47
TONTOH Mac D110 O34 Q1
TONTON MACOUTE T108
TONTO'S EXPANDING HEADBAND T109
Tony Brother H172
Tony Zap see EDMUNDS Hughes
TOOBAD Johnny L32A
TOOGOOD Johnny J14
TOOK Steve Peregrine B168 P84 S82
TOOKER John P49
TOOLEY Ron P35
TOOMEY Glenn K83
TOOMEY Jim A62 B160 C57A K24 P10 T117
TOON Cedric K80
TOON Earl K80
TOOTLE Ashton W82A
TOOTS AND THE MAYTALS T110
TOP Jannik C62A H89A M49 N64A
Top Ten D65
TOPHAM Anthony 'Top' B83 P62 T111 Y5
TORAIN Reg T15
TORANO Joe J93C
TORANO Sandy T111A
TORBALY Marc K59
TORBERT David G84 H186 K60 N32 W42
TORBERT Wayne F94
TORELLO Bobby W107
TORFF Brian F83A
TORFS Peter B35A
TORK Peter M181
TORME Bernie G31
TORNADER T111A
TORNADOS T112
TORNQUIST Greg B173
TORO Yomo F17
TORONTO T112A
TORPEDO Henk N27B
TORPS Gary E57
TORPY Frank S347
TORRANCE Dean A9 E23 J36
TORRANCE Richard R173 S20 T113
TORRENCE Toni D115
TORRES Bobby A135 B245 C155 D86 S148
TORRES Harrold C223A
TORRES Joe F94
TORREY Mary S272
TORROLL Mark S354
TORRY Claire D49 D89 D93 F13 K41 P85 S313 Y19

TOSH Peter M88 T114 W4
TOSH Stuart D9 P31 P81B T43
TOSTI Blaise S272
TOTH T. M39
TOTO T115
TOTO Tolim L127
TOTSANT Fred F66
TOUAT Max E62A
TOUCH (U.K.) I116
TOUCH (U.S.) T116A
TOUCHTON Tim J10A
TOUMAZIS Andreas S266
TOUNTAS Nick M68
TOURIST T117
TOURSEL Ralf E52A
TOUSSAINT Allen B17 B29 D86 D106 G4 K53 L4 L44 L50 L63 L65 M9 M111 M157 R125 T118
TOUSSAINT Joe B233
TOUSSAINT Vincent T18
TOUT John R65 W114
Touter see HARVEY Bernard
TOUW Meike G113
TOVEL Clyde L63
TOWARD Frank S343
TOWE John A14 A43 C95 G20 S103
TOWER Rasmussen R54
TOWER OF POWER A116 B94 B29 B226 C237 H45 J85A L63 L66A M16 M102 R161 S19 T119 W44 W62
TOWNER Phil N30A O6B R61C S289A
TOWNER Ralph O30 W36
TOWNS Colin G31 K94B T120
TOWNSEND Alan Y17
TOWNSEND Glen R101
TOWNSEND John (V) S20
TOWNSEND John (Perc) D33B
TOWNSEND Rob A131E A133 D10A F12 M121 S35
TOWNSHEND Paul B209
TOWNSHEND Pete C121 G6 H110 O40 T84 T121 T122 W72 W121
TOWNSHEND Simon W72
TOWNSHEND Lane T122
TOWNSON Chris J75
TOY T122A
Toyah (WILCOX Toyah) T122B
TOYANI Clay T79
TRABANDT Terry M1
TRACE T123
TRACEY Stan T95
TRACHSEL Kirk Q5
TRACIE Stan F14
TRACTOR T124
TRACY Steve L69B
TRADEL John C220
TRADER HORNE T125
TRADITION T126
TRAFFIC D2B T127
TRAJAN Allan N57
TRAMLINE T128
TRAMP T130
TRANQUILTY T131
TRANSMITTERS T132
TRANTER Lyell M50
TRAPEZE T133
TRASK Thomas J70
TRAUB Bill H1
TRAUM Artie B135 N57 T134
TRAUM Happy D139 S173 T134
TRAUT W. Ross B251 C17
TRAVERS Gary C206
TRAVERS Pat H176 S33B T135
TRAVIS Chandler E20
TRAVIS Michael D105 G30 H154 L136 M6
TRAVIS Pamela K61
TRAVIS Paul L67
TRAVNICEK Paeter N60A
TRAYLOR Jack K10 L136
TRAYNOR Jay J44 W51
TREADWAY Greg M16B
TREADWELL Larry R66C
TREASURE Julian T132
TREE K84A

TREECE Richard F73 G79 H93 L53 M63 S206
TREES Alfreeta A122 K94A
TREES T137
TREGANNA Dave S86
TREMBLERS T137A
TREMELOES T138
TREMOLO Theo B47
TRENCH Fiachra C118 C210 I8 L63
TRENGROVE Chris D128
TRENI Michael W30A
TREPEAU Dominique R66
TREPLE Uli G120
TRETTIORIGA KRIGET T138A
TREVERVA MALE VOICE CHOIR G97
TREVISICK Nick D54 D127C K61
TREVOR Kip B119 W72
TREVOR Kirk P72
TREW Gerry B31
TREWER Heinz G35A
TRICKETT Ed M41
TRICKSTER T138B
TRIEBICH Ami J55
TRIFAN Danny P99
TRIFAN Richard C189 J48 P24B T71
TRIGAUX Roger U17
TRIGGER T139
TRILLION T139A
TRIMBLE Jim S311
TRIMMER Ian B272
TRING Wallace D133
TRINITY D71A T139B
TRINITY RIVER BOYS T140
TRIBUNO Diane B144
TRIO T141
TRIPP Art (MARIMBA Ed) B72 M58 P115 Z8
TRIPP Eddie H19B T111
TRITONUS T141A
TRITSCH Christian A35 G66 H86A S175
TRIUMPH T142
TRIUMVIRAT T143
TRIVIERI Daryl E7C
TROCHIM Bill 'Kootch' D125 F13 W1
TROGGS T144
TROIANO Domenic B279A C195 G115 J31 M66 T145
Trommie see GORDON Vincent
TROOPER T146
TROPEA John A135 C76 C147 C182 D50 D86 F62 I22 L4A M12 M46B M86 M107 M111 M203 N2A N65 R22 R125 S125 S180 S231 S252 T98 T147 W13
TROPEA Ron T147
TROPIC ISLES STEEL BAND H70
TROSCLAIR Angelle W54
TROST Vincent B262D
TROST Willie G8AA
TROTMAN Lloyd C146
TROUTMAN Jody O46
TROWER Robin J103 P23 P140 T148
TROXEL Jim E14
TROY Doris A115 A133 B23 B230 D2 D86 D111 D116 F13 G27 G98 H22 H179 K52 K83 OB P85 S35 S124 S185 S243 T149 U5 Y17
TROY John P119
TROY Roger B144 E33 G8AA T149A
TROYER Eric J48 M157 S121
TRUAX Jay F139
TRUBA John Z12
TRUCKAWAY William T150
TRUCKS Butch A38 C123 J52
TRUDELL John C153
TRUK T151
TRUMBO James M203 N25
TRUNKHILL Marlyn F133
TRUONG Jean My H89A
TRUSILLO Tommy M72
TRUSSELL Keith B132 G1 L59 M99
TRUSTY Scott B68
TRUTH Roger K39
TRUVOR Wes M188A

VASSEY Ken H52A Z8
VASTANO John W68A
VAUGHAN Jimmy F3B
VAUGHAN Roland F66
VAUGHN Carla W8
VAUGHN Sharon D12 L42
VAUGHN Tony D24
VAUGHT David A135 H102 M27
VEAL Charles K17 M102 R137 S64
VEASEY L. B113A
VEE Bobby (VELLINE Robert Thomas) C224 V19 V24
VEE Cookie D66
VEE John M137A
VEEN Gerrit B224A
VEGA Alan S319
VEGA Carlos B80 S75
VEGA David G80
VEGA Robert O35
VEGA Tata E7B S160 V20
VEGAS Bobby P125A
VEGAS Lolly R54
VEGAS Pat R54
VEITCH Peter C8
VEITCH Trevor K77 R169
VEL Peter H194
VELARDES Benny B177 G84
VELASQUEZ Richie C12
VELDKAMP Bert K16
VELEZ Gerardo S231 V21
VELEZ Martha E37 M203 V21
VELIKA Dan G121
VELKER J.J. M135
VELLINE Robert see VEE Bobby
VELVET FOGG V21A
VELVET OPERA E50 V22
VELVET UNDERGROUND V23
VENABLE Kim L44
VENABLE Natalie R22
VENET West P129
VENIER Paul S250B
VENN Glaister M109 R61C
VENNER Chris C91
VENT Jo Ann M37 R60 W5 W11 W48B
VENTURA Rick R94
VENTURES V24
VENUS AND THE RAZORBLADES V25
VERBEKE Patrick H196 K19
VERCAMBE Laurent M57B
VERDEAUX Bruno C137
VERDEAUX Cyrille C137
VERDELL Jackie M203 V21
VERDICK Michael P106
VERDUSCO Darrell M179
VERES Marinka S101A
VERHAGEN Anton O37
VERHEES Evert B35A
VERITY John A77 F56 P77 V26
VERLAINE Tom S170 T38
VERLIN Ron S103A
VERMAZZA John B109
VERNACCHIO Michael E57
VERNIERI Larry D38A
VERNO Buz J70
VERNON Edward C104 D115 L75 L95B O20 S31 T45 T111 V26A
VERRALL Ronnie E74 S295 W06
VERRETT Harrison D96
VERROCA Steve C210 W129
VERTO V26B
VERUCCHI Dick B254
VESALA Edward V26C
VESOVO A1 M78 R113
VESTINE Henry C26 H150 S329 Z8
Vi Ann P21
VIAN Patrick R53C V27
VIBER Charles W101
VIBRATORS V28
Vicar P72
VICARAGE Mo M211A
VICARI Frank G19 L9 L51 L80A M75 W9 W13 W51
VICIOUS Kid Y8A
VICIOUS Sid (BEVERLEY John) F71 S77 S132 V28A

VICK Harold G4 M17 M227 P149 R125
VICKERS Carle L2
VICKERS Harold D86A
VICKERS Mike G22 M80 S35 S185 V29
VICKERY Graham J72
Victoria B208 C76
VICTOR PERAINOS KINGDOM COME P60B
VIDACOVICH John L118
VIDAL Joao A. B43
VIDAL Maria S242
VIDICAN John K6
Vie K51
VIERRA John M18
VIERTEL Jack R22
VIG Tommy B110 D86 G10 R107 S273
VIGEANT Victor M238
VIGRASS Paul D39 F117 L27 V30
VIGRASS AND OSBORNE C48 V30
VILATO Orestes P45 S19
VILLA Trond R166
VILLAREAL Frank C179
VINCENT Gene (CRADDOCK Vincent Eugene) C149 V32
VINCENT James L13
VINCENT Pamela J11 K56A
VINCENT Raymond E66
VINCENT Reggie C182
VINCHON Brigit M1A
VINCI Frankie R97
VINCI Gerry R97
VINDING Mads S69
VINEGAR JOE V33
VINK Peter Q1B
VINNEDGE Char C20B
VINNEGAR Leroy C241 D103
VINSON Eddie 'Cleanhead' O38 V34
VINSON Millard W25
VINYAKRAM T.H. S85
VIOLA A1 R62 Z8
VIOLETTI Gary E69B
VIOLINSKI V35
VIRDIER Danny T136
VIRGIN Dingo see ALLEN Daevid
VIRTANEN Heikki T15 T104
VISAGE V35A
VISAGGIO Michael F8A
VISCIGLIA Mike M21 S230A
VISCELLI Johnny F50A
VISCONTI Mary see HOPKIN Mary
VISCONTI Tony B16B B186 C34 C155 G27 G100A H29 H151 M50 O6A O22 P41 W7
VISION Terry D56A
VISITOR 2035 V36
VISLOCKY John S230A
VISSEN Jan A42
VITAL DUB V37
VITALE Joe E2 F39 F78 N63 R109 S276 S276A V38 W16
VITALE Steve S97
VITESSE V38A
Vito Z8
VITO Rick M27 M111 P137 R164 W70
VITOUS Miroslav C189 D40D M7B R17B S104 V39 W36 W62 Z9
VITT Bill B210 F80 G9
VITTEK David H139A
VIYATE Ryan B224A
VIZARD Ed A102
VIZZUTTI Al C186
VOCE Roy W15
VOELKER H.L. G40
VOGEL Allan S63
VOGEL Karsten B275 S69
VOICE Bob B209 F48B
VOICE Steve L113
VOICES OF EAST HARLEM V40
VOTDOIDS H90
VOIGHT Jim P46
VOLASCO Tony M39
VOLK Philip R70

VOLKER Armand T35
VOLLNER Sredni C203 R100 W51
VOLMAN Mark A132 F68 G69 H120 L51 M82 M191 M198 N13 Q5 S229 S276 T161 Z8
VON ARB Fernando K96A
VON BOHR Manfred B107
VON BUTTLAR Manfred F7A
VON COVAY Tony C203
VON DEYEN Adalbert V41
VON HAMMER Michael R151
VON OSTEN Sigune L120
VON ROHR Chris K96A
VON SENGER Dominik P71A
VON SINNEN Karla G120
VON STREETER James R111
VOOGT Peter E27
VOORMAN Klaus B23 B59 C58 C171 D5A D99 D100 D139 G10 H39 H170 K45 L19 L64 L111 M80 M191 M227 M229 N40 N55 O27 P28 P130 R60 R173 S124 S252 S338 V3 V12 W5
VORHAUS David C105 L5A M1A W68
VORZANGER Charles T122
VOSBURGH Denny C182
VOSS Holger 5329A
VOYAGER V42
VRALLEN Graeme W69B
VROLIJK Marco S332D
Vshailendra H110

WAADE Geir W130
WAALKEN Otto L10
WACHSMAN Steve T79B
WACHTEL Robert 'Waddy' A116 B38 B175 B244 B255 C11B D72A F42 G60 H62 K48 M229 N40 P114 R22 R137 S17 S196 S220 S272 T21 W9 W42 Z11
WACKERS W1
WACKFORD Michael S253
WADA Manani C253A
WADDELL Bruce F21
WADDINGTON John P117
WADDY-Frank Kaah B183
WADE Ann F139
WADE Bill M222
WADE Brett E35 J15A L26B
WADE Chris L82
WADE Cliff D16
WADE Joel J15A
WADE Jonathan B187
WADE Larry C17
WADE Nancy V21
WADE Pete B17A C194 E75 G72 H26 K77 N37 P63 R4 R137 R173 T21 W11 Y18
WADE Roger H50
WADENIUS George B141 S186
WADHAM John C120
WADINGTON Pete D26
WADSWORTH Derek D11B F7 F14 G98 H50 M80 P131 R61A R122 S31 V21
WAGENET Hal I31
WAGER Betsy C76
WAGES of SIN W2
WAGNER Adrian C18 W3
WAGNER Bo S245
WAGNER Dave C235
WAGNER Dick C182 C246 C249 F22 F129A M233 R60
WAGNER Gary P24A
WAGNER Josef G2
WAGNER Lawrence F104A
WAGNER Norm M68
WAGNER Richie I13C
WAGNER Ron A122
WAGON Chuck D64
WAILER Bunny (LIVINGSTONE Neville) T114 WA
WAILERS M8B
WAINMAN Phil A99A B83 R122

WAINWRIGHT BOb L86A
WAINWRIGHT Loudon III W5
WAITE Chris C76
WAITE John B8
WAITE Tony D95
WAITS Tom R22 W6
WAITZMAN Daniel A27
WAKEFIELD Frank G68
WAKELIN Johnny W6A
WAKEMAN Alan A109 S182
WAKEMAN Rick B115 B186 C202 G32 J72 M50 R60 S48 S270 S295 W7 W86 Y7
WALCOTT Collin H59 M180B O30
WALD Allen K95
WALDEN Narada Michael B64 B169 B253 C186 F121 J75A M40 N60 P35 W8 W36
WALDEN Snuffy B225 C109 F108 R3 S131 S297
WALDMAN Jack P15
WALDMAN Randy M102 R97
WALDMAN Wendy B175 C109 M123 M229 R137 S272 W9
WALDO Jimmy N29A
WALDORF Marcia B256
WALDRON Mal E52
WALDROP Donald A1 I31
WALES Eric W10
WALES Howard A1 G9 G84
WALES O'REGAN W10
WALK Fred L81
WALK Joe T9A
WALKELEY Brian F23
WALKER Aaron 'T-Bone' W13
WALKER Ade M55B
WALKER Albert 'Ralph' C245
WALKER Billy B274A
WALKER Bob B211
WALKER Brooker K45
WALKER Cato K45
WALKER Chris E48
WALKER Cleveland R130
WALKER Colin E34 S253
WALKER Dave F66 I7 M167 R40 S31
WALKER David I. B180 B214 C241 E71 F92 K17 K48 K56A L143 M102 O10 P114 P126 R101 R115 S14C S251 W10A W13 W31
WALKER David K94B
WALKER Dennis M238B W12A
WALKER Doug (G) C76
WALKER Doug (G) P47
WALKER Earl 'Baga' C139
WALKER Fred C17
WALKER George D127
WALKER Greg (B) B123 C234A D127B J14A L146
WALKER Greg (V) S19
WALKER Jay B43A BB5A
WALKER Jeanine E73
WALKER Jerry L90
WALKER Jerry Jeff C124 F12B W11
WALKER Jim P144 J92 R21
WALKER Jimmy (Perc) H133
WALKER Jimmy (V) R87
WALKER John 'Big Moose' A83 H147 H150 O8A R16B S57 S35B W11A W47
WALKER John (V/G) S245 M229 W12
WALKER Junior (DE WALT Autry) M229 W12
WALKER Len W13A
WALKER Les T89 W20
WALKER Lilian E76A
WALKER Mel O38
WALKER Mick S217
WALKER Percy B193
WALKER Peter M151
WALKER Phillip S96 T23 W12A
WALKER Raymond L. K30 K95 N37 P63
WALKER Richie M123
WALKER Ritchie I7
WALKER Rob S277
WALKER T-Bone see WALKER Aaron

WALKER Tim H95 S157 S270
WALKER BROTHERS W13A
WALKOE Tim B192
WALL W13B
WALL Alwyn W13C
WALL Dennis D99
WALL Francoise S280
WALL Freddie P15
WALL Hasse P81A
WALL Howard L142
WALL Jeremy S231
WALLACE Alfred L52 P142
WALLACE Billy G115 N26A
WALLACE Bill (V/G) S83A
WALLACE Bruce M204
WALLACE Erik H98
WALLACE Garwood S72
WALLACE George Tenail S187B
WALLACE Gib F14
WALLACE Ian B75 B83 C109 D139 I20 J14 K54 K84 L37 M32 M89A S131 S243 S300 S321 Y10
WALLACE John C76
WALLACE Karene R106
WALLACE Leroy 'Horsemouth' B276 G39 H122 I1A M221D R35B R150 W4
WALLACE Martin N27
WALLACE Randy W5
WALLACE Richard K45
WALLACE Sid L128A
WALLACE Wayne S325
WALLANDER Ulf Artan S14B
WALLE Rune O46
WALLENSTEIN W13D
WALLER Charlie A121
WALLER Graham B136
WALLER Harry P137
WALLER Jerry D17
WALLER Mick (D) A120 B23 B64 H175 P8 S259 S264 S273 V13 W94 W120 W121
WALLER Mickey (G) H85
WALLER Steve G67 H111B M80 R40B S206
WALLER Wally L43 M114A P128
WALLEY Dennis G25 Z8
WALLEY Terry C215
WALLIS Larry M213 P84 U2
WALLY W14
WALMAN Phil S291
WALMSLEY Steve L49
WALRATH Jack K56A S7
WALRECHT Peter B224A
WALRUS W15
WALSH Brendan L124
WALSH Brock B175 G60 W21
WALSH Dan B127
WALSH Ed F60 M143 M222A S124 T114 W25
WALSH James A53A
WALSH Joe E2 E53 F39 F78 J31 K45 M64 M82 M191 N40 P126 R109 S196 V38 W16 Z11
WALSH Marty E40 S58
WALSH Perry B109
WALSH Peter M18 R148 S63
WALSH Ralph M203
WALSH Rob H166
WALSH Steve (K) H4 K9
WALSH Steve (G) F71
WALSH Tom A50 S231
WALSHAW David B91 B109
WALTER Jim 'Crun' S235
WALTER Kenny C77 C216 M151
WALTERS Bob C141
WALTERS Danny B234
WALTERS Glenn H146 W129
WALTERS Jeff B247
WALTERS John (Wind) L16
WALTERS John (Horns) P131
WALTERS Trevor L119A Z14
WALTHER Gitta N60A
WALTHERS Tony F91 T158
WALTZ Charles S103A
WALTON John Ike T64
WAMMACK Travis M235 S340 W16A
WAMMES Ad F45
WANCHIC Mike C196
Wandering John H37
WANSEL Dexter B135 M2
WAR W17

WARBURTON Lew D2
Ward P143
WARD Alan H194
WARD Alastair S11
WARD Andy C19 G71
WARD Bill B115 R93A
WARD Bob (G) C210
WARD Bob (D) S316
WARD Carlos B3 B131
WARD Clara C26
WARD Clifford T. B222 W18
WARD Dale C222A
WARD Dave 'Domino' P47 R104
WARD Graham S291
WARD Jackie C50 C76 E71 H60
L72 N13 S272
WARD Jesse B204
WARD Jim A125
WARD John (D) K288
WARD John (B) E37
WARD Justin S192
WARD Kathy A132 P75
WARD Kingsley D128
WARD Laurel C182 S73
WARD Nigel R93A
WARD Paul O40
WARD Pete M111
WARD Pete 'Baldy' P47
WARD Ray W82
WARD Roy C118
WARD Walter O21
WARDAUGH Andy M67
WARDEN Howard P139B
WARE Alan C90
WARE Craig C169
WARE Eddie R128
WARE John C188 C237 D26 E20
F109 H35 L36A M113 N25
WARE Jon M12
WARE Martin H178A
WARE Robert C169
WARFORD Dr.Robert K. K29
M108 N25 R77 R137
WARFORD Susan W107
WARHORSE W19
WARING Linda N53A
WARING Sally M55A
WARLEIGH Ray A23 B209 B247
C75 C109 D111 E41 F14 F86
H11 H29 H50 H194 J41 K28B
K84 M19 M94 M108 M220 P54
R66 R132 S12 S35 S334
WARLOCKS G84
WARM DUST W20
WARMINGTON Keith A60 K83
WARNER Alan F90A
WARNER Byron D99
WARNER Florence C124 D99
F78 R31
WARNER Mark A62 A133 F42
Q2 S266
WARNER Sieb G64
WARNES Chris M230
WARNES Jennifer C156 C171
C180 P114B T39 W21
WARNES Linda Z11
WARNICK John T168
WARNING Gail R74
WARNOCK Fanny H194
WARREN Alan K32B
WARREN Andrew A10 M181C
WARREN Baby Boy M90
WARREN Bill M5
WARREN Brian B5
WARREN Dale V9
WARREN James (B/G) K83 S235
WARREN Jennifer A59 B245
S272 W9
WARREN Jimmy (G) S168
WARREN John F14
WARREN Kathleen O10
WARREN Levi W47
WARREN Paul (D) B272 F6
WARREN Paul (G) B226 M82
N52
WARREN Peter K98 P115
WARREN-GREEN Chris M80
WARREN-GREEN Nigel H4 M80
WARSAVAGE Vince B135
WARSAW PAKT W21A
WARSHAW Jack A82A
WARWICK Chris J39
WARWICK Clint M189
WARWICK Dee Dee D116
WARWICK Dionne D116

WARY Bob L75
WASA EXPRESS W22
WASAMA Jukka P81A
WASH Martha B221 P21
WASH Ralph B282 R164 V7
WASHBOARD DOC, LUCKY AND
FLASH W22A
Washboard Sam (BROWN
Robert) W59 W93
WASHBURN Dede R100
WASHBURN Donna A132 C155
C179 C247 D69
WASHBURN Lalomie L130A
R161
WASHBURN Skitchy A132
WASHINGTON A.D. G40
WASHINGTON Claudette
B223
WASHINGTON Delroy A107
W23
WASHINGTON Eugene L128A
WASHINGTON Fred D127 H19
S325
WASHINGTON Geno W24
WASHINGTON George (B)
H150
WASHINGTON George (Trom)
R111
WASHINGTON Grover Jnr
G4 J20 J75A M17 M107 W25
WASHINGTON Hubert S129
WASHINGTON Jarrett S322
WASHINGTON Jayotis H8
P67
WASHINGTON Jeanette F137
WASHINGTON Larry B135
WASHINGTON Leon S358
WASHINGTON Lucius R168
WASHINGTON Richard D86
WASHINGTON S. S154
WASHINGTON Tony R84
WASPS W26
WASSON Rance C169 J53
WASTELAND W26A
WATANABE Sadao C186 W27
WATCHAM John A30 C165
H194
WATCHMAN John M202C
WATERHOUSE Andrew A67B
WATERHOUSE Peter A67B
WATERMAN Hans S187
WATERS Chris J50
WATERS Gordon M105
WATERS Julia Tillman see
TILLMAN Julia
WATERS Luther B127 C180
C217 D74 J7 K45 L89 P44
R78 R101 S73 S251 W31
WATERS Marietta S252
WATERS Maxine William
see WILLARD Maxine
WATERS Muddy
(MORGANFIELD McKinley)
B29 D66 H170 J79A L94
R128 S204 T79B W28 W47
W94 W107
WATERS Orrin B127 B226
C180 C217 D74 K45 L89
P44 R78 R101 S73 S180
S251 W31
WATERS Patti B43
WATERS Richard M78
WATERS Roger G18 P85 W29
WATERSON Lal C165
WATERSON Mike C165
WATHEN Ronnie M211A
WATKINS Audie S340
WATKINS Ben H124A
WATKINS Beryl R177A
WATKINS Carolyn A28
WATKINS David D46
WATKINS Derek F14 H183
R40B R132 S311 W86
WATKINS Eddie B226 P44
P114
WATKINS Geraint B158B
F7 R6 429A
WATKINS Julius F133 M79
WATKINS Kit C19 H19A
WATKINS Marianne A28
WATKINS Pepper C123 D70
M11 M229 N32 T119
WATKINS Peter M108 V30

WATKINSON Nick J16A
WATKINSON Terry M112
WATRONS Bill C186 D50
K81 M102
WATSON Al F14
WATSON Andy A10
WATSON Bernard M111
WATSON Bobbie C175
WATSON Bobby P126 R161
WATSON Dan S73
WATSON David Lee L118
WATSON Doc M229
WATSON Gavin K28B
WATSON Gene W110
WATSON Helen M222C N33
WATSON Jim (G/Mand) P52A
WATSON Jim (Tpt) C251
WATSON Jimmy (D) K28
WATSON John (B) N49
WATSON John (V) M59 T150
WATSON John L. (V) W38
WATSON Johnny 'Guitar'
C217 D127 S95B W30 W32
W87 Z8
WATSON Kenneth B256 Z8
WATSON Larry W73
WATSON Linda S198A
WATSON Lloyd E59 M34 M81
WATSON Martin J. Y1
WATSON Martyn T170
WATSON Melvin 'Wah Wah'
see WATSON 'Wah Wah'
WATSON Merle J53 M229
WATSON Mike A4
WATSON Murray D66 C122
WATSO Nigel G50 G99
G102 K63
WATSON Pamela W30A
WATSON Pete M148
WATSON Robbie S210A
WATSON Robert W30A
WATSON Robin A46
WATSON Roger M222C U1
WATSON Shelley B230
WATSON Tony L26A
WATSON 'Wah Wah' (RAGIN
Melvin 'Wah Wah') A31
C153 C220 E57 E71 H19
J92 K46 K51 L41 L66A
M102 M151 P44 P114 R115
R141 T107 W31
WATSON W11 C109
WATSON-TAYLOR Susie I16
WATSONIAN INSTITUTE W32
WATT Hamilton Wesley
P129
WATT Jean C139
WATT-ROY Garth F141 G89
L76B M89 Q1C
WATT-ROY Norman D137 G44
G89 L132
WATTMAN Gary A132
WATTS Arthur H70
WATTS Barry Q1C
WATTS Charlie B156 H170
J36 K84 R122A R133 R173
S111 T122 W120
WATTS Dave J14
WATTS Ernie A11 A52 A59
A131D B127 B221 C45 C153
C182 D74 D86 D127 E57
F92 F103C F119A G121
J75A J93C J113 K45 K48
L41 L79 M68 M82 M89A
M101 M111 M123 M131A
M151 M229 P114 P115 Q3A
R4 R22 R78 R87 R99 S14C
S189 S216 S262 S325 T145
W27 W31 W32A Z8
WATTS Jeff S260
WATTS John F54A
WATTS Lennie C185B
WATTS Nathaniel B110
L66A M102 W119
WATTS Noble C146
WATTS Peter 'Overend'
B219 M214
WATTS Ron B211
WATTS Steve E55A
WATTS Trevor S267 T95
WATTS 103RD STREET W33
WAUGH Pete B247
WAUL Franklin 'Bubbler'
A6 B234 C245 P135 R35B
R150

WAUQUAIRE Phil F4A
WAVEMAKER W34
WAY Darryl C251 G66 K94B
T123 W35
WAY Peter U2
WAY WE LIVE see THE WAY
WE LIVE
WAYBILL Fee T152
WAYNE Carl M219 W122
WAYNE Graham W96
WAYNE Hayden M84A
WAYNE Jeff V30
WAYNE Mick B186 J108 O47
WAYNE Trev T37B
WAYNE COCHRAN AND THE
C.C.RIDERS C150
WAYNE FONTANA AND THE
MINDBENDERS M162
WAYS Al D63B
WEATHER REPORT W36
WEATHERILL Winston F95A
WEATHERS John A58 B96
B171 B237 E80 G22 G86
N27
WEATHERS Lila P108
WEATHERS Vivian P108 W37
WEATHERSPOON David L90
WEAVER Archer L24B
WEAVER Blue A49 C196 E18
F7 M214 R60 S295 S334
WEAVER Deany H134A
WEAVER George S56
WEAVER Ken F133
WEAVER Mark S57
WEAVER Mick (also FROG
Wynder K.) A22 A61 B283
D54 E46 F7 F29 F125 G34
G86 H50 H65 H94 J105
L106 M15 M102C M108 M128
M157 R125 S285 S339 T46
V21
WEB W38
WEBB Bob F39 J31
WEBB Cassell F128 S269
WEBB Champ D103
WEBB Cynthia V12
WEBB Dean B245 C127 D71
R137
WEBB Fred I31 M179 S284
WEBB Gary H134A
WEBB George L64
WEBB Harry Rodger see
RICHARD Cliff
WEBB Jimmy C155 G10 R101
W39
WEBB Keith D99 P11 R62
WEBB Marvin B143
WEBB Melvin S251
WEBB Norman P54
WEBB Peta T79
WEBB Ralston C139
WEBB Robert (Perc) W132
WEBB Robert (K/V) E56A
WEBB Roy Dean P50
WEBB Russell S140 Z17
WEBB Spider P15
WEBB Stan B220 C26 C101
D133 P62 S31 V21
WEBB Steve R125
WEBB Steve L121A
WEBB Steve L81A
WEBB Susan M170
WEBB Tom F70
WEBB Wendy M232
WEBBER Aj H66
WEBBER Andrew Lloyd see
LLOYD-WEBBER Andrew
WEBBER Bob S318
WEBBER Julian Lloyd see
LLOYD-WEBBER Julian
WEBBER Roy W14
WEBER David C185 R40 T54
WEBER Eberhard D19A
M138A
WEBER George D13
WEBER Jack E31 M84
WEBER Jon H112
WEBER Steve F133 H139
WEBER Vince R162A
WEBER Virgil G83
WEBSTER Ben S30
WEBSTER Danny S154
WEBSTER Dave T7
WEBSTER John S283A
WEBSTER Katie L75 L115

WEBSTER Morgan M131
WEBSTER Randy W40
WECHTER Julius B56 H8A
H122A R173
WEDGWOOD Mike C34 C251 E60
J27
WEEK Henry B246
WEEKS David P136
WEEKS Willie A37 A53A B47C
B186 C11B C171 C206 F78
H39 H58 J43 J93C L18 L18A
L63 M229 N40 P114 P114B
R133 R173 S124 T79 T107
T145 W16 W31 W111 W120
WEELS Sid T132
WEEMS Jerry B170 W106
WEEMS Ritchie W40A
WEHLER Mathias A99
WEHR Allen M209
WEHRMEYER Eric G113
WEHRSTEIN Ray R106 W14
WEIDER John 'Will' A67
B218 F12 F65 H140 J27 K39
M193 M202A S309 T145 W41
WEIDORJE W41A
WEIGHELL Alan J72 S295
WEIHE Peter T103A
WEIL Terry H151
WEILLER Jean Pierre H154
WEINBERG Anton W102
WEINBERG Max H185 S199
S229
WEINBERG Sid J20
WEINBERG Warren L65
WEINER Mark H15
WEINER Stephane S208
WEINGARTEN Steve E39
WEINSTEIN Leslie see WEST
Leslie
WEINSTOCK Murray M75 S65
WEINZIERL John A57 U23
WEIR Bob G84 H45 K60 W42
WEIR Robb T169A
WEIR Rusty W43
WEIS Danny A9 C246 I24
M108 O12 R60 R75
WEIS Jerry B141
WEISBERG Gary S272
WEISBERG Larry K13 S216
WEISBERG Steve M232
WEISBERG Tim C39 F78 M101
R62 W44
WEISBURG Richard B57
WEISGARD E. D83A
WEISS Betty S88
WEISS Dawn A9
WEISS Donna A132 C155 C179
C180 C247 D139
WEISS Doudon A33A S193
WEISS Herb H1
WEISS Jerry A47 K81 M13
WEISS Larry W44A
WEISS Mary S88
WEISSBERG Eric C164 C234A
D139 F22A F108A F128 G109
H59 J20 J69 M78 M125 P41
T156 W5 W5
WEISSMAN Mitch S121
WEITZ Mark S294
WELBORN Larry C224
WELCH Bob F66 P24 W46
WELCH Bruce M100 R80 S80
WELCH Chris S206
WELDON Liam S28D
WELDON Paul E19B
WELDON Peter M21
WELFARE STATE C209
WELHAM Hadrian F85
WELHAM Martin F85
WELKER Larry M238
WELKER Peter C158 Y12
WELLANDER Lasse A4
WELLBELOVED Dave G112
WELLER Dave E8
WELLER Don H52 L23 M118
R122A T155
WELLER Freddy R70
WELLER Paul J19
WELLINGTON Canute L71B
WELLINGTON Ever M133
WELLS Cory C180 T81
WELLS David Z8
WELLS John L47
WELLS Junior (BLACKMORE
Amos) G122 M129 R22 W47

WITKOWSKI Rick C212
WITTENBERG John D127
WITTICH Roland D19A
WITTON David W130
Wizard Stan H5
WIZARDS CONVENTION W117
Wizzard M212
WIZZARD W122
WIZZO W122
WOBBLE Jah P144 W117A
WOEHRLE Kathy D127
WOEST Craig E7C
WOFFORD Mike R108
WOJCIECHOWSKI Kajtek A4
WOLBRANDT Peter G120 K89
WOLEN H. Lee J73A
WOLF W35
WOLF B111 B177 F133 G53 M228 P46
WOLF Peter G19 Z8
WOLF E.E.III F43
WOLFE Randy K45
WOLFERT David C127 M227
WOLINSKI David 'Hawk' B33 B192 R161
WOLLSCHON Gerd F70A
WOLSTENHOLME Stewart 'Wooly' B37 M67 W117B
WOLTERS John D85
WOLTZ Paul O15
WOMACK Bobby B84 C180 F33 J95 R173 T107 W118 W120
WOMMACK Bobby A102
WONDER Stevie (JUDKINS Stephen) F87A F100 H51 M101 M151 M229 P114 R97 S362 W119
WONG Jimmy F60
WONG Joseph Arthur B204
WOOD Annagh N45
WOOD Art A92 W133
WOOD Arthur C141
WOOD Bill B17A
WOOD Billatt S7
WOOD Bobby C14 E73 H26 H65 K30 K95 K96 M41 M78 N23 N37 O15 P112 P125 P137 R31 S269 S271 T55 T107 T167 Y18
WOOD Chris A25 C30 C214 F29 F109 H17 H84 H99 J9 L104 M94 M102C T62 T127 U5 V21
WOOD Colin C209 S133 S267 U22
WOOD Danny C78
WOOD Heather D88 H110 W123 Y21
WOOD Jerry F48A
WOOD John I106
WOOD Margaret M80
WOOD Mark L10A
WOOD Orville M221D
WOOD Paul H150
WOOD Peter A82 C78 C165 C251 K24 L27 M108 N12 P25 P41 P85 R101A S253 S270 S339 V30
WOOD Phil M151
WOOD Ron B23 B29 B64 B106 C121 D13 D100 F4 F116 H39 L37 M39B N27C R133 R161 S22 S273 W72 W120 W121
WOOD Roy D66 E34 H55 M219 N48 W122
WOOD Royston A30 A98 C165 D49 T79 W123 Y21
WOOD Steve C237 J41 M108
WOOD Vicki N45
WOODARD Nathan B233
WOODCOCK Chris S227 T48
WOODCOCK Ian E11
WOODFORD David M21 S111 S339A T30
WOODFORD Peter O15
WOODFORK Bob R128
WOODGATE Dan M46A
WOODHAMS Danny 'Woody' C39 K32
WOODHEAD John A7 R173 S272
WOODLAND Nicholas B174 56A
WOODLEY Ken A28
WOODMAN Britt F5 M229 S168

WOODMANSEY Mick 'Woody' B186 G63 S53B S214C W124
WOODROFFE Jezz W124A
WOODROW John L118
WOODRUFFE Gerald B115
WOODS Albert T122A
WOODS Danny C67
WOODS David (G) M37
WOODS Dave(Tpt) B57A
WOODS Elvin H189
WOODS Gay S263 W125
WOODS Holly T112A
WOODS John B79 J107 S23 V33
WOODS Mick E12
WOODS Mike C80 J70A S270 S285
WOODS Nicky (Perc) M30
WOODS Nick (Syn) R139A
WOODS Phil C44 S111 S168 S189 S262
WOODS Ron (D) G61 M151 S122
WOODS Ron (Sax) P6
WOODS Sonny B24
WOODS Steve U15A
WOODS Stu B105 C195 C234A D139 E40 F108A F109 G109 I2 K59 K81 L4A O39 P45 R164
WOODS Sylvia W92
WOODS Terry S263 S346 W125
WOODS Thomas C144A
WOODS Willie W12
WOODS-PEARSON Charles C86
WOODSON Craig U16
WOODSON Elbert R56
WOODWARD Dave P119A
WOODWARD Martin A71
WOODWARD Rob L68
WOODWORTH Zane Y12
WOODY Scott F58
WOODY WOODMANSEY'S U-BOAT W124
WOOL Tony D68A
WOOLAM Steve E34
WOOLEY David B39
WOOLF Clive C152
WOOLF Henry W126
WOOLF Peter C210
WOOLF Stephanie M11
WOOLFOLK Andy C45 E7
WOOLFSON Eric P31
WOOLIE Joe S56
WOOLLEY Aaron T138
WOOLOFF John A200
WOOTEN Denise M26
WOOTEN Michael K48 N12A
WOOTEN P.M. Z10
WOOTON Bob C50
WOOTTON Roger C175
WORDSWORTH Ian N33
WORDSWORTH Linda N33
WORDSWORTH Tom D56A
WORKMAN Flap M39B
WORKMAN Geoff K73
WORKMAN Jeff T155
WORKMAN Michael B91
WORKMAN Nanette M54
WORKMAN Reggie M78 M79
WORLD I20
WORLD OF OZ W127
WORLD SERVICE W127A
WORMALD Alan F51A
WORMAN Ray C165
WORMAN Tim P110A
WORRELL Bernie B183 F137 P29
WORSNOP Rick L114
WORTHING Sonny W128
WORTHY Richard A22 C87
WORTLEY Jim A109
WORTMAN Kurt M203
WOTSON-TELLY Susie H110
WOTTON Al F22
WRAFTERS Tony G51A
WRAY Bob A28 B87 F83A H146 L35 M235 T39
WRAY Doug W129
WRAY Link G74 W129
WRAY Malcolm S230
WRAY Rhonda W129
WRAY Robin W129
WRAY Willow T107

Wreckless Eric W130
WREN Steve H56
WRENCHER Big John A50A W131
WRIGHT Art C153
WRIGHT Arthur B240
WRIGHT Berkeley T131
WRIGHT Betty L24 L86 W132 W136
WRIGHT Bobby N46A
WRIGHT Charles (V) W33
WRIGHT Charles S95B
WRIGHT Charles (G) B240
WRIGHT Dave E66A
WRIGHT David F61
WRIGHT Debbie F137
WRIGHT Denny D100
WRIGHT Doug E9 J91 W13A
WRIGHT Edna B226 E71 J73A U35
WRIGHT Elmon C146
WRIGHT Eric D51
WRIGHT Ernest L85
WRIGHT Gary A35 G27 H39 K45 L48 L64 S224 U5 V12 W51 W133
WRIGHT Gavin M34 Q2 P40 R174
WRIGHT Greg Y12
WRIGHT Gregg E51
WRIGHT Gregory M203
WRIGHT Gus S329
WRIGHT Helen R174
WRIGHT Henry P47
WRIGHT Hoshal E33 M53
WRIGHT Ian S54
WRIGHT Janet D127B S169
WRIGHT Jeff W24
WRIGHT John B57
WRIGHT Joseph Edward II see JAMMER Joe
WRIGHT Joy H176
WRIGHT Justin W133
WRIGHT Ken W18
WRIGHT Lamar C146
WRIGHT Lawrie J14
WRIGHT Lennie S16 W38
WRIGHT Lorna W133
WRIGHT Monroe S251
WRIGHT Norman D43
WRIGHT Pat C242
WRIGHT Pete (B) T133
WRIGHT Pete (B) C213A
WRIGHT Philip Adrian H178A
WRIGHT Richard (K) B44 P85 W134
WRIGHT Richard (G) C209
WRIGHT Rick K45
WRIGHT Robert S250
WRIGHT Robert (V) M96
WRIGHT Ronald W46
WRIGHT Shaun S278
WRIGHT Steve K40
WRIGHT Stevie E10
WRIGHT Syreeta H96 P126 S362 W119
WRIGHT Tim P61
WRIGHT William E73
WRIGHT Winston C139 G39 H105 J48 M133 R150 T110 T149 U1 U20 V21 W4
WRIGHTSON Jimmy J5
WRIGLEY Bernard A103
WRIGLEY George P33
WRITING ON THE WALL W134A
WROE Alan H38A
WU Wendy P77A
WURGLER Roby M139A
WUSTHOFF Gunther F30
WYANT Pete A131D
WYATT Frank H19A
WYATT Robert A35 A133 C13 C63 C209 E59 H34 H57 M79 M81 M106 S182 T95 W135
WYATT Rodney S313
WYCHERLEY Ronald see FURY Billy
WYETH Howard D139 F116 G74 M27 M37 M41 M96 M177 W51 W129
WYETH Rona M41
WYKER Johnny J52

WYLE Sam K51
WYLES Chris N56
WYLIE John F56A
WYMAN Bill H15 H170 J35 M64 R133 R173 T155 W136
WYMAN Dan B225
WYNANS Reese B91 C31 K48 W11
WYNBRANDT Jimmy M141C
WYNBRANDT Tommy M141C
WYNN Big Jim D38 W30
WYNN Dony P15
WYNN Toby L2 M151
WYNN Tom C207
WYNVEEN Tim D36
WYRICK Barbara B123 F48 H146

X X1
X Joe S254
X-RAY SPECS X2
X.T.C. X3
Xeno C92
XIQUES Ed N39
XIT X4
XYN Robert B234

YA YA Daddy B157
Yabby U see JACKSON Vivian
YACHTS Y1
YACKNIN Louis L74
YACOUB Gabriel M57B S280 Y23
YACOUB Marie M57B
YAMAGISHI Junshi H35A W12 W53A
YAMANAKA Akisi C253A
YAMASH'TA Chako S108
YAMASH'TA Hisako Y2
YAMASH'TA Stomu Y2
YAMAUCHI Tetsu F4 F108 H11 K87 R3 V30
YANCE Bob S180
YANCEY Jimmy Y3
YANCEY Mama M185 Y3
YANDELL Paul E73 E75
YANKEE Joe N4
YANKEES Y3A
YANKUS Doug H111A
YANOVSKY Zal L133 M224 Y4
YARBOROUGH Rule G61
YARDBIRDS B64 C121 W94
Y5
YARDLEY Norman M23 S35
YARLETT Eddie W89
YARROW Mick P54
YARROW Peter C30
YASIN Khalid (YOUNG Larry) H99 L70 M40 S19 W62 Y14A
YATES B111 A121
YATES Joy B174B C79 C121 D36 D110 E22 G49 O20 P5 S134 S255 Y11
YATES Lawrence S295A
YATES Yatta S110
YAW Bruce R60
YEADON Gus Z24
YEADON Ted E28
YEAGER Roy A111 B213 D27A
YEARLEY David A117
YEAZEL Robert S310
YELLOW Y5A
YELLOW DOG Y6
YELLOW MAGIC ORCHESTRA Y6A
YELLOW PAYGES I6B
YENTIS Wayne B166
YES Y7
YESSE Kathleen D19
YESTER Jerry A135 B256 H102 L133
YESTER Jim A106
YESTERDAY AND TODAY Y8
YIANNI Christopher D94
YOBS YBA

YOCHMAN Greg M178B
YOHN Wally C90
YOHO Monty O43
YONGE Jim P88A
YONI Shakti see SMYTH Gilli
YORK Chris A102
YORK Don H9 S78
YORK John B285
YORK Mayall K45
YORK Paul D71
YORK Peter A50A B21 B277 D28 H24 H50 L120 N5 N14 P100 T23 W91 W117 W131 Y9
YORK Rusty M32
YORK Steve A82 B171 B231 C101 D4 D86 E8 K38 M80 M238 P15 R40B V33 Y10
YORKE Ritchie C236
YOSHIDA Alan D26
YOSHINO Mickie G55
YOST Walter H23
YOUATT Will A34 M63 N27
YOULDEN Chris S31 Y11
YOUMAN James Z8
YOUMANN Derrick H72
YOUNG Alison C101
YOUNG Angus A2
YOUNG Bob B40 Y19
YOUNG Charles L117
YOUNG Chip C124 E51 H26 K95 K96 L71 M11 N37 P63 P125 R31 R173 T107 W11 W64
YOUNG Colin F90A
YOUNG Denton Z16
YOUNG Don Michael R55
YOUNG Earl H133 K45 L130
YOUNG Eldee L65
YOUNG Eugene 'Snooky' A131D B29 C17 M229 S168 S193A S262 YOUNG Gary D4A J64A
YOUNG George (Wind) A96 B57A B263 C62 C99 G4 H51 H85 K36 K81 L80A L119 M21 M26 M46B M69 M75 M143 N65 P6 S215 T71 T98 T114 T147 T156 T158
YOUNG George E10 F65A
YOUNG James S314
YOUNG James Randolf R56
YOUNG Jeff S267
YOUNG Jesse Colin Y12 Y22
YOUNG Jimmy K47 M26 S180
YOUNG Joachim 'Jymm' D124 K56A M159 S36 S78A
YOUNG Joe R128
YOUNG John M188
YOUNG Johnny (Mand) N46C S204 Y13
YOUNG Johnny see TAYLOR Little Johnny
YOUNG Keith H125A
YOUNG Kenny F95 Y6 Y14
YOUNG Kim Y18
YOUNG Larry see YASIN Khalid
YOUNG M. J92
YOUNG Malcolm A2
YOUNG Maurice S251
YOUNG Michael L98A
YOUNG Mighty Joe A83 I22 M5 M48 R112 R168 T28 Y15
YOUNG Monalisa B201
YOUNG Neil B29 B260 C232 C234 M170 S10 S276 S276A S290 Y16
YOUNG Otha N43
YOUNG Paul M67 Q1C 54 S299
YOUNG Red A82 F116
YOUNG Reggie B77 B126 B210 B261 C14 C50 C124 C169 C194 C247 E73 H26 J53 K30 K77 K96 M78 M108 M157 N23 N37 N57 O15 P125 P137 R4 R31 R100 S266 S269 S271 S272 T9 T21 T55 T107 T167
YOUNG Rob (Wind) S255 W71
YOUNG Rob (D) I102A
YOUNG Rob (K) B209
YOUNG Rob (Perc) C175
YOUNG Ron L119C
YOUNG Roy B82 B186 D9 Y17
YOUNG Rusty A7 A52 F116 I6 J31 K77 L110 N43 P6 P106 R109 W43
YOUNG Snooky see YOUNG Eugene